SENIOR HIGH CORE COLLECTION

EIGHTEENTH EDITION

CORE COLLECTION SERIES

Formerly
STANDARD CATALOG SERIES

JOHN GREENFIELDT, GENERAL EDITOR

CHILDREN'S CORE COLLECTION
MIDDLE & JUNIOR HIGH CORE COLLECTION
SENIOR HIGH CORE COLLECTION
PUBLIC LIBRARY CORE COLLECTION: NONFICTION
FICTION CORE COLLECTION

SENIOR HIGH
CORE COLLECTION

EIGHTEENTH EDITION

EDITED BY

RAYMOND W. BARBER

AND

PATRICE BARTELL

IPSWICH, MASSACHUSETTS

H. W. WILSON
A Division of EBSCO Publishing, Inc.

2011

Printed in the United States of America

ISBN 978-0-8242-1114-1

Library of Congress Cataloging-in-Publication Data

Senior high core collection. — 18th ed. / edited by Raymond W. Barber and Patrice Bartell.
    p. cm. — (Core collections series)
  Kept up to date between editions by three annual supplements.
  Includes bibliographical references and indexes.
  ISBN 978-0-8242-1114-1 (alk. paper)
  1. High school libraries—United States—Book lists. I. Barber, Raymond W. II. Bartell, Patrice. III. H.W. Wilson Company.
  Z1037.S435 2011
  011.62—dc23
                                                          2011026270

CONTENTS

CONTENTS

PREFACE

The *Senior High Core Collection* is a selective list of fiction and nonfiction books for young adults, along with bibliographies and other professional aids for librarians. Annual supplements to this volume will be published in 2012, 2013, and 2014.

In this Edition. This eighteenth edition of the Senior High Core Collection includes more than 7,500 book titles. Of these titles more than half are new since the previous edition. Of special note in this edition are new books on science, computers, social networking, Islam, the environment, and library technology.

Recommended graphic novels are included in this Collection. Fictional graphic novels and materials about graphic novels are listed at 741.5 in the Classified Collection, and nonfiction graphic novels are integrated throughout the rest of the classification. They are all listed together in the Index under Graphic novels.

A limited number of the most highly recommended titles are indicated with a rosette (an asterisk *) at the end of the bibliographic data. This short list, as it were, can serve as a guide to the librarian with a limited budget or one who needs only one or two books in a given area. Approximately one third of the titles fall into this category.

History. The first edition of the Collection was published in 1926 as an author-title list, followed by a fuller version in 1928 that also included a subject index and analytical entries. After the appearance of the second edition in 1932 the Collection was published regularly every five years. Initially it was called *Standard Catalog for High School Libraries*, but when *Junior High School Library Catalog* (now *Middle and Junior High Core Collection*) was introduced in 1965, its scope was changed. It became *Senior High School Library Catalog* in the ninth edition, published in 1967. With the seventeenth edition in 2007 the title was changed to *Senior High Core Collection*, and since that time it has been published every four years.

Preparation. In producing this edition the editors have worked closely with an advisory committee of distinguished librarians, who are listed below. Over the past four years they and other librarians have participated in selecting the books that have entered the Collection. In preparation for this new edition the committee also re-evaluated all the material in the previous edition of the Collection and its Supplements and proposed many new titles. Reviews in the professional literature have also been an important source of information in selecting the material for this Core Collection.

Scope and purpose. The Collection lists books for young people in grades nine through twelve. Throughout the Collection special attention has been given to resources for the librarian, including works on the history and development of young adult literature; literary criticism; bibliographies; other resources for the selection and evaluation of print and non-print materials; guides to the operation of libraries; and works on the use of the Internet in libraries.

The three annual Supplements, which will expand the total coverage by several thousand additional titles, are intended for use with this volume. Schools that must accommodate students reading below their grade level may find it helpful to consult the latest edition of *Middle and Junior High Core Collection* and its Supplements. Materials for more advanced and college-bound students can be found in the *Public Library Core Collection: Nonfiction* and its Supplements. To augment the fiction list with adult and genre titles the user is referred to *Fiction Core Collection* and its Supplements.

All books listed are either published in the United States or published in Canada or the United Kingdom and distributed in the United States and were in print at the time this volume went to press. Original paperback editions are included, as well as paperback reprints of essential titles that have become unavailable in hardcover.

If a book was listed in a previous edition of the Collection and has been deleted in this edition, that deletion is not intended as a sign that the book is no longer valuable. A book may be deleted for a number of reasons, such as its no longer being in print.

This Collection does not aim to support any particular high-school-level curriculum but rather to cover a broad spectrum of topics. Material suitable for both college-bound and non-college-bound students is included, as well as material for independent study and recreational reading. In the nonfiction section special importance is given to curriculum support material in the social and physical sciences and to works devoted to current concerns of youth, such as interpersonal relationships, substance abuse, and health and fitness. New reference books are well represented. The fiction section contains a wide range of literary works that are of interest to young people, many of which are frequently included on school reading lists—classics as well as contemporary and genre fiction. In recent years studies in literary criticism for young people have increasingly been published in series, with one volume devoted to each author. Because it is impossible to list, or even to evaluate, every volume in a voluminous series, a few representative samples have been listed from the most highly recommended series, with a note indicating the series title.

This Core Collection excludes the following: non-print materials; non-English-language materials, with the exception of dictionaries and similar items; textbooks; and books about specific vocations, individual computer programs, and other topics that quickly become outdated.

Organization. The Collection consists of two parts:

Part 1, the Classified Collection, is arranged according to the Dewey Decimal Classification for nonfiction, followed by sections for fiction and story collections. The information supplied for each book includes bibliographic description, suggested subject headings, a descriptive annotation, and frequently an evaluation from a quoted source.

Part 2, the Author, Title, and Subject Index, serves as a comprehensive key to the Classified List.

The Directions for Use of the Core Collection, following this Preface, contain more detailed information about the uses and content of the Core Collection.

Acknowledgments

The H. W. Wilson Company is indebted to the publishers who supplied copies of their books and information about editions and prices. This Core Collection could not have been published without the efforts of the advisory committee, who gave so generously of their time and expertise.

Members of the Advisory Committee:

Priscille Dando
Head Librarian
Robert E. Lee High School
Fairfax County, Virginia

Pamela Spencer Holley
Former President of YALSA
Library Consultant
Fairfax County, Virginia

Joquetta L. Johnson
Library Media Specialist
Milford Hill Academy
Baltimore, Maryland

Gregory Lum
Librarian
Jesuit High School
Portland, Oregon

Vanessa Irvin Morris
Assistant-Teaching Professor
The iSchool at Drexel University
Philadelphia, Pennsylvania

Douglas Uhlmann
Head Librarian
John F. Gummere Library
The William Penn Charter School
Philadelphia, Pennsylvania

Acknowledgments

The F. W. Wilson Company is indebted to the following persons who supplied copies of their books and information about editions and prices. This publication could not have been finished without the efforts of individuals and communities who have so generously given their time and expertise.

Members of the Advisory Committee

DIRECTIONS FOR USE OF THE COLLECTION

USES OF THE CORE COLLECTION

Senior High Core Collection is designed to serve these purposes:

As an aid in purchasing. The Collection is designed to assist in the selection and ordering of titles. Information concerning publisher, ISBN, price, and availability is provided for each title. Since Part 1, the Classified Collection, is arranged according to the Dewey Decimal Classification, the Collection may be used to evaluate parts of the library collection and identify areas that should be updated or strengthened. Annotations point out any sensitive or controversial aspects of a work to assist in judging its suitability for a particular school or community.

As an aid in reference. Reference work and user service is furthered by the information about sequels and companion volumes, by the descriptive and critical annotations in the Classified Collection, and by the subject access in the Index.

As an aid in verification of information. For this purpose full bibliographical data are provided in the Classified Collection. Entries also include recommended subject headings based upon *Sears List of Subject Headings* and a suggested classification derived from the most recent information on the *Abridged Web Dewey*, the online version of the *Abridged Dewey Decimal Classification and Relative Index*. Notes describe editions available and publication history.

As an aid in curriculum support. The classified approach, subject indexing, and annotations are helpful in identifying materials appropriate for classroom use.

As an aid in collection maintenance. In addition to recently published works, the Collection includes titles listed in the previous edition and its Supplements that have retained their usefulness and are still the best titles of their kind. This information affects decisions to rebind, replace, or discard older materials.

As an instructional aid. The Collection is useful in courses that deal with literature and book selection for young people.

DESCRIPTION OF THE COLLECTON

Part 1. Classified Collection

The Classified Collection is arranged with the nonfiction books first, classified by the Dewey Decimal Classification in numerical order from 000 to 999. Individual biographies are classed in 92 and follow the 920s (collective biography). Novels and short story collections, with the symbols "Fic" and "S C," follow the nonfiction.

An Outline of Classification is reproduced on page xv. It should be remembered that many subjects are treated in more than one discipline and so are found in various parts of the classification. If a particular title is not found where it might be expected, the Index should be consulted to determine if the work is classified elsewhere.

Within classes, books are arranged alphabetically under the main entry, usually the author. An exception is made for works of individual biography, classed in 92, which are arranged alphabetically under the name of the person written about. The following is an example of a typical entry and a description of its components:

Kaku, Michio
Physics of the future; how science will shape human destiny and our daily lives by the year 2100. Doubleday 2011 389p il $28.95; ebook $12.99
Grades: 11 12 Adult   **303.49**
1. Science 2. Forecasting
ISBN   978-0-385-53080-4;   978-0-385-52081-1 (ebook)   LC 2010-26569

The author "divides his chapters into 'near future' (until 2030), 'mid-century' (2030 to 2070), and 'far future' (2070 to 2100). Each begins with familiar technology and ongoing research. The near future of computers will give us self-driving cars and computers cheap enough to be disposable. Mid-century will see universal translators, and by 2100 thinking will control computers, producing instant, person-to-person communication and the ability to manipulate our environment, including malfunctioning body parts." Kirkus

"The book's lively, user-friendly style should appeal equally to fans of science fiction and popular science."
Includes bibliographical references.

The name of the author, Michio Kaku, is given in conformity with *Anglo-American Cataloguing Rules*, 2nd edition, 1998 revision. It is inverted and printed in dark or bold-face type. The title of the book is *Physics of the future*, and the subtitle is *How science will shape human destiny and our daily lives by the year 2100*. The book was published by Doubleday in 2011. It has 389 pages and sells for $28.95. There is an ebook that sells for $12.99. (Prices, of course, can change.)

Following the last line of the body of the entry is the grade level indicator: "Grades: 11 12 Adult," which lists every grade or age range for which this titles is recommended. At the end of that line is the figure 303.49 in bold-face type. This is the Dewey Decimal Classification number. The number 303.49 is the classification number for "Social forecasts."

The numbered terms "1. Science" and "2. Forecasting" are the recommended topical subject heading for this book, based on the *Sears List of Subject Headings*.

The ISBN (International Standard Book Number) is included to facilitate ordering. The Library of Congress control number (also called the LC card number) is provided when available.

Next are two notes supplying additional information about the book. The first is a description of the book's content taken from a review in *Kirkus*. The second is a critical note from *Booklist*. Such annotations are useful in evaluating books for selection and in determining which of several books on the same subject is best suited for the individual reader. A note indicates that the book has bibliographical references. Further notes may describes other features of a book, such as sequels, companion volumes, other editions available, and publication history.

Part 2. Author, Title, and Subject Index

All the books in the Classified Collection are listed here in a single alphabet under author, title, series title, and subject. The classification number in bold-face type is the key to the location of the main entry of the book in the Classified Collection. Works classed in 92, individual biography, will be found under the name of the person written about.

Cross-references are made in the index from variant forms of names to the established form, from terms not used as subject headings to the term that is used, and from terms used as subject headings to related or more specific headings.

The following are examples of index entries for the book cited above:

Author	**Kaku, Michio** Physics of the future	**303.49**
Title	**Physics** of the future. Kaku, M.	**303.49**
Subject	**Science** Kaku, M. Physics of the future	**303.49**

Examples of other types of entries:

Joint Author	**Chaltain, Sam** (jt. auth) Haynes, C. First Freedoms	**342**
Compiler	**Allenbaugh, Kay** (comp) Chocolate for a teen's heart. See Chocolate for a teen's heart	**S C**
Translator	**Butcher, William, 1951-** (tr) Verne, J. The extraordinary journeys: Twenty thousand leagues under the sea	**S C**
Illustrator	**Azaceta, Paul** (il) Sable, M. Grounded, vol. 1: Powerless	**S C**
Editor	**Bussey, Jennifer A.** (ed) Hate crimes. See hate crimes	**S C**

Outline of Classification

Reproduced below is the Second Summary of the Dewey Decimal Classification. It will serve as a table of contents for the nonfiction section of the Classified Collection. (Fiction and Story Collections follow the nonfiction.) Note that the inclusion of this outline is not intended as a substitute for consulting the Dewey Decimal Classification itself. This outline is reproduced from Edition 14 of the Abridged Dewey Decimal Classification and Relative Index, published in 2004, by permission of OCLC Online Computer Library Center, Inc., owner of copyright.

SENIOR HIGH CORE COLLECTION

EIGHTEENTH EDITION

CLASSIFIED COLLECTION

000 COMPUTER SCIENCE, KNOWLEDGE & SYSTEMS

001.4 Research; statistical methods

Nobel; a century of prize winners; selected and edited by Michael Worek. 2nd ed. Firefly Books 2010 335p il map $39.95; pa $24.95 *
Grades: 11 12 Adult   **001.4**
1. Nobel Prizes
ISBN   978-1-55407-780-9;   1-55407-780-X;
978-1-55407-741-0 (pa); 1-55407-741-9 (pa)
                    LC 2010-293512
Original Portuguese edition, 2007; first published in English 2008
Presents the lives and accomplishments of more than two hundred Noble Prize winners, from the initial 1901 prizes to the 2009 winners, along with a complete listing of the eight hundred individuals and organizations that have won the prize.
Includes bibliographical references

Selverstone, Harriet S.
Encouraging and supporting student inquiry; researching controversial issues. Libraries Unlimited 2007 xlix, 238p (Libraries Unlimited professional guides in school librarianship) pa $40
Grades: Adult Professional   **001.4**
1. Research 2. Bibliographic instruction 3. High school libraries 4. Intellectual freedom
ISBN 978-1-59158-496-4; 1-59158-496-5
                    LC 2007-9266
The author gives "advice for advocating inquiry-based research, especially for hot topics that are most interesting to students. She advises library media specialists on what constitutes controversial topics, how to collaborate with teachers to foster critical thinking, and how to gain administrative support for this kind of program research. . . . The philosophies and ideas presented make this book an ideal purchase to promote and foster collaboration with the school communities in which many of us work." SLJ
Includes bibliographical references

Tufte, Edward R., 1942-
The visual display of quantitative information. 2nd ed. Graphics Press 2001 197p il $40
Grades: 11 12 Adult   **001.4**
1. Statistics—Graphic methods
ISBN 0-9613921-4-2   LC 2001-271866
First published 1983

This book focuses "on statistical graphics, charts, tables. Theory and practice in the design of data graphics, 250 illustrations of the best (and a few of the worst) statistical graphics, with . . . analysis of how to display data for precise, effective, quick analysis." Publisher's note

Valenza, Joyce Kasman
Power research tools; learning activities & posters; illustrated by Emily Valenza. American Library Association 2003 113p il pa $55 *
Grades: Adult Professional   **001.4**
1. Research 2. Internet resources 3. Internet searching 4. Report writing
ISBN 0-8389-0838-1   LC 2002-8972
Contents: Searching; Ethics; Evaluation; Organizing and communicating
A collection of "lessons, rubrics, graphic organizers, and curriculum designed to help students become successful users of information. Beginning with the first steps of research, the development of a thesis, the material progresses logically through the succeeding steps, covering Boolean operators; search tools and strategies; subject and keyword searching; ethics; plagiarism; documenting and citing resources; creating source and note cards; the process of writing the paper; and quoting, paraphrasing, and summarizing. . . . This is an invaluable resource for teaching information skills in any subject area, in middle school or high school." SLJ

Wilson, A. Paula
100 ready-to-use pathfinders for the Web; a guidebook and CD-ROM. Neal-Schuman Publishers 2005 xxiii, 247p il pa $75 *
Grades: Adult Professional   **001.4**
1. Internet research 2. Reference services (Libraries)
ISBN 1-55570-490-5   LC 2004-40292
This "resource offers step-by-step instructions for creating pathfinders to post on your library's Web site. . . . The CD reproduces . . . specific examples in HTML and plain text as well as providing blank templates for immediate use. . . . The pathfinders are for all age ranges and skill levels and include books, online sources, government sources, magazines, and subject headings that could link to the library's catalog." Voice Youth Advocates
This "is an important addition to the literature of practical library guides." Ref & User Services Quarterly
Includes bibliographical references

001.9   Controversial knowledge

Clark, Jerome
Unnatural phenomena; a guide to the bizarre
wonders of North America; illustrations by John
Clark. ABC-CLIO 2005 xxxiv, 369p il $85
Grades: 11 12 Adult   **001.9**
   1. Curiosities and wonders
   ISBN 1-57607-430-7   LC 2005-11206
"Organized geographically, . . . [this book] explores
the history of bizarre natural phenomena in virtually ev-
ery U.S. state." Publisher's note
   Includes bibliographical references

Coleman, Loren
Cryptozoology A-Z; the encyclopedia of loch
monsters, Sasquatch, Chupacabras, and other
authentic mysteries of nature; {by} Loren Coleman
and Jerome Clark. Simon & Schuster 1999 270p
il pa $13 *
Grades: 11 12 Adult   **001.9**
   1. Reference books 2. Monsters—Encyclopedias
   ISBN 0-684-85602-6   LC 99-31023
"A Fireside book"
Cryptozoology is defined as the study of hidden animals. This encyclopedia "contains nearly two hundred
entries, including cryptids (the name given to these unusual beasts), new animal finds, and the explorers and
scientists who search for them." Publisher's note
   Includes bibliographical references

Sagan, Carl, 1934-1996
The demon-haunted world; science as a candle
in the dark. Random House 1996 457p hardcover
o.p. pa $14.95
Grades: 11 12 Adult   **001.9**
   1. Science
   ISBN 0-394-53512-X; 0-345-40946-9 (pa)
         LC 95-34076
"Using basic tools of science—empiricism, rationalism, and experimentation—Sagan debunks . . . common
fallacies of pseudoscience. In doing so, he speculates as
to how such beliefs arise." Libr J
Sagan "links today's aliens with yesterday's demons
in this lithe, well-supported, sometimes quite wry, and
altogether refreshing performance." Booklist
   Includes bibliographical references

Shermer, Michael
Why people believe weird things;
pseudoscience, superstition, and other confusions
of our time; foreword by Stephen Jay Gould. rev
and expanded. Freeman, W.H. 2002 xxvi, 349p il
pa $16 *
Grades: 11 12 Adult   **001.9**
   1. Science 2. Belief and doubt 3. Parapsychology
   ISBN 0-8050-7089-3   LC 2002-68784
"First Owl Books edition"
First published 1997
   Contents: Science and skepticism; Pseudoscience and
superstition; Evolution and creationism; History and
pseudohistory; Hope springs eternal

The author "explores the very human reasons people
find otherworldly phenomena, conspiracy theories, and
cults so appealing. In . . . [the] chapter, 'Why Smart
People Believe in Weird Things' he takes on science
luminaries like physicist Frank Tippler and others, who
hide their spiritual beliefs behind the trappings of science." Publisher's note
   Includes bibliographical references

004   Data processing. Computer science

Barrett, Joanne R., 1960-
Teaching and learning about computers; a
classroom guide for teachers, librarians, media
specialists, and students. Scarecrow Press 2002
255p il $45
Grades: Adult Professional   **004**
   1. Computers 2. Data processing
   ISBN 0-8108-4450-8   LC 2002-8350
"The 14 chapters in increasing complexity include information about word processing, spreadsheets, charts
and graphics, databases, multimedia presentations, the
Internet, the World Wide Web, creating Web pages,
learning programming, and viruses and copyright law.
. . . Every computer teacher should be in possession of
this book, and it would make a terrific textbook for those
who are teaching teachers." SLJ

Ceruzzi, Paul E.
A history of modern computing. 2nd ed. MIT
Press 2003 445p il pa $22.95
Grades: 9 10 11 12   **004**
   1. Computers 2. Data processing
   ISBN 0-262-53203-4   LC 2002-40799
First published 1998
This history "concentrates on five key moments of
transition: the transformation of the computer in the late
1940s from a specialized scientific instrument to a commercial product; the emergence of small systems in the
late 1960s; the beginning of personal computing in the
1970s; the spread of networking after 1985; and . . . the
period 1995-2001 {including} . . . the Microsoft anti-
trust suit, the rise and fall of the dot-coms, and the advent of open source software." Publisher's note
   Includes bibliographical references

Downing, Douglas
Dictionary of computer and Internet terms; [by]
Douglas A. Downing ... [et al.]; with the assistance
of Sharon Covington. 10th ed. Barron's
Educational Series 2009 554p il (Barron's business
guides) pa $14.99 *
Grades: 9 10 11 12 Adult   **004**
   1. Computers—Dictionaries 2. Internet—Dictionaries
   3. Reference books
   ISBN 978-0-7641-4105-8; 0-7641-4105-8
         LC 2008-44365
   First published 1986 with title: Dictionary of computer
terms
   The book presents more than 3,200 computer-related
terms. Emphasis is placed on information for nontechnical home computer users.

The **Facts** on File dictionary of computer science; edited by John Daintith, Edmund Wright. Rev. ed. Facts on File 2006 273p il (Facts on File science library) $49.50

Grades: 11 12 Adult **004**
1. Reference books 2. Computer science—Dictionaries
ISBN 0-8160-5999-3; 978-0-8160-5999-7
LC 2006-42004

First published 2001; based on the Minidictionary of computing, published 1986 by Oxford University Press

This dictionary provides over 2400 "entries that explain such fundamental concepts as hardware, software, and applications." Publisher's note

"The book will prove a handy reference for budding computer scientists." Voice Youth Advocates

Includes bibliographical references

Farmer, Lesley S. Johnson, 1949-
Teen girls and technology; what's the problem, what's the solution? [by] Lesley Farmer. Teachers College, Columbia University 2008 180p $52; pa $21.95 *

Grades: Adult Professional **004**
1. Information technology 2. Girls—Education
ISBN 978-0-8077-4876-3; 978-0-8077-4875-6 (pa)
LC 2007-47698

Provides a framework that teachers, librarians, youth workers, and parents can use to empower girls to succeed in today's technology-rich world.

"Strong emphasis on curriculum and school-related issues makes this most useful for schools, but larger libraries and systems will also want to consider it." SLJ

Includes bibliographical references

Hafner, Katie
Where wizards stay up late; the origins of the Internet; [by] Katie Hafner and Matthew Lyon. Simon & Schuster 1996 304p il hardcover o.p. pa $16 *

Grades: 11 12 Adult **004**
1. Internet
ISBN 0-684-81201-0; 0-684-83267-4 (pa)
LC 96-19533

The authors tell the "story of some extraordinary computer scientists who, with the Department of Defense in the late 1960s, developed the Arpanet. It is based mostly on interviews with those scientists and engineers who designed and built a revolutionary computer network that spawned the global Internet." Libr J

This "book is excellent at enshrining little known but crucial scientist/administrators like Bob Taylor, Larry Roberts and Joseph Licklider, many of whom laid the groundwork for the computer science industry." Publ Wkly

Includes bibliographical references

Henderson, Harry, 1951-
Encyclopedia of computer science and technology. Rev ed. Facts On File 2009 580p il (Facts on File science library) $87.50 *

Grades: 11 12 Adult **004**
1. Reference books 2. Computers—Encyclopedias 3. Computer science—Encyclopedias
ISBN 978-0-8160-6382-6; 0-8160-6382-6
LC 2008-29156

First published 2003

"The A-to-Z entries run from several paragraphs to two pages in length and provide highly accessible, jargon-free explanations of hardware, software, programming language, notable figures, crucial inventions, and hotly debated civil-liberties issues in a field outpacing legislation. One of the most user-friendly and enlightening books for field outsiders, this handy volume promotes clear understanding of a complex subject." Libr J

Includes bibliographical references

High definition; an A to Z guide to personal technology. Houghton Mifflin 2006 361p il pa $14.95 *

Grades: 9 10 11 12 Adult **004**
1. Reference books 2. Electric household appliances—Dictionaries
ISBN 0-618-71489-8; 978-0-618-71489-6
LC 2006-19549

This dictionary "brings together more than 3000 terms used to describe the components, functions, and applications of devices found in today's homes and offices: cell phones, computers, MP3 players, gaming systems, CD and DVD players, and more. . . . This very affordable volume should be part of every reference collection, large and small." Libr J

Pfaffenberger, Bryan, 1949-
Webster's New World computer dictionary. Wiley 2003 422p pa $16.99

Grades: 9 10 11 12 **004**
1. Reference books 2. Computer science—Dictionaries 3. Data processing—Dictionaries
ISBN 0-7645-2478-X
LC 2003-269226

First edition compiled by Laura Darcy and Louise Boston published 1983 by Simon & Schuster with title: Webster's New World dictionary of computer terms

This dictionary defines more than 4,500 of the most frequently used computer terms and demonstrates how they relate to other terms

Reilly, Edwin D.
Milestones in computer science and information technology. Greenwood Press 2003 392p $70

Grades: 9 10 11 12 **004**
1. Computer science 2. Information technology
ISBN 1-573-56521-0
LC 2002-44843

"An Oryx book"

Over 600 alphabetically arranged entries describe the significant developments in computer science and advances in information technology

"The articles are clearly written and accessible, containing essential details without reliance on technical jargon. . . . Extremely useful tools include a listing of the

Reilly, Edwin D.—*Continued*
'Top Ten' milestones, and four separate indexes devoted to personal names, chronology, geography, and general topics." Libr Media Connect
Includes bibliographical references

004.6 Interfacing and communications

Johnson, Doug, 1952-
Learning right from wrong in the digital age; an ethics guide for parents, teachers, librarians, and others who care about computer-using young people. Linworth Pub. 2003 122p pa $44.55 *
Grades: Adult Professional   004.6
1. Internet 2. Computers and children 3. Cheating (Education)
ISBN 1-586-83131-3   LC 2003-43320
"After an overview of the difference between the physical and virtual world in regard to ethical codes, several sections are devoted to scenarios of various behaviors that involve privacy, property, and appropriate use of information. Each scenario provides discussion topics as well as the relationship to National Learning Standards." Libr Media Connect
"Johnson's '3 P's of Technology Ethics,' Privacy, Property, and a(P)propriate use, are effectively and excitingly addressed through both discussion and instructional scenarios." SLJ
Includes bibliographical references

005.8 Data security

Earp, Paul W., 1961-
Securing library technology; a how-to-do-it manual; [by] Paul W. Earp and Adam Wright. Neal-Schuman Publishers 2009 245p il (How-to-do-it manuals for librarians) pa $65
Grades: Adult Professional   005.8
1. Libraries—Security measures 2. Computer security
ISBN 978-1-55570-639-5   LC 2008-46166
"Have you had your identity stolen? Are all firewalls safe from hackers? What is a hop? What is the difference between a virus and a worm? Can someone listen in on your Voice-Over Internet Protocol service? These are just a few questions answered in this manual, which is full of forms, suggestions, and inventories." Libr Media Connect
Includes glossary and bibliographical references

006.3 Artificial intelligence

Henderson, Harry, 1951-
Artificial intelligence; mirrors for the mind. Chelsea House 2007 190p il (Milestones in discovery and invention) $35
Grades: 7 8 9 10 11 12   006.3
1. Artificial intelligence
ISBN 0-8160-5749-4; 978-0-8160-5749-8
                                      LC 2006-16639

This book includes "portraits of the men and women in the vanguard of this innovative field. Subjects include Alan Turing, who made the connection between mathematical reasoning and computer operations; Allen Newell and Herbert Simon, who created a program that could reason like a human being; Pattie Maes, who developed computerized agents to help people with research and shopping; and Ray Kurzweil, who, besides inventing the flatbed scanner and a reading machine for the blind, has explored relationships between people and computers that may exceed human intelligence." Publisher's note
Includes glossary and bibliographical references

006.6 Computer graphics

Hansen, Brad
The dictionary of multimedia; terms & acronyms. 4th ed. Franklin, Beedle & Associates 2005 611p il $50
Grades: 9 10 11 12   006.6
1. Reference books 2. Multimedia—Dictionaries
ISBN 1-88790-273-2
First published 1997
Contains over 5000 technical and multimedia terms from a multidisciplinary perspective including audio, graphics, video, networking, human factors, and general computing. Copyright issues and international standards are addressed. Includes a basic HTML tutorial and an appendix listing books, software, manuals and periodicals, as well as covering digital video, MIDI and Internet development.

006.7 Multimedia systems

Coombs, Karen A.
Library blogging; [by] Karen A. Coombs and Jason Griffey. Linworth Pub. 2008 151p il pa $39.95 *
Grades: Adult Professional   006.7
1. Librarians—Weblogs
ISBN 978-1-58683-331-2; 1-58683-331-6
"This book is an overview of the world of blogs in libraries, including both use and technological discussions. The authors bring you the 'whys' and 'how to' of using a blog in a library context, including the different options available for a library blog, the appropriateness of each option, and the possibilities of each program or service." Publisher's note

Hussey, Tris
Create your own blog; [6 easy projects to start blogging like a pro.] Sams Pub. 2010 273p il pa $21.99 *
Grades: 9 10 11 12 Adult   006.7
1. Weblogs
ISBN 978-0-672-33065-0   LC 2009-51118
Subtitle from cover
This guide to starting your own blog includes advice on planning and setting up blogs, as well as on how to create different kinds of blogs including personal blogs, professional blogs, blogs for podcasting, and video blogs.

Selfridge, Benjamin
A teen's guide to creating Web pages and blogs; [by] Benjamin Selfridge, Peter Selfridge, and Jennifer Osburn. Prufrock Press 2009 148p il pa $16.95
Grades: 5 6 7 8 9 10   **006.7**
1. Web sites—Design 2. Weblogs 3. Internet and teenagers
ISBN 978-1-59363-345-5; 1-59363-345-9
                   LC 2008-40044
First published 2004 by Zephyr Press with title: Kid's guide to creating Web pages for home and school
"This guide begins with basic step-by-step information about HTML, fonts, images, lists, and tables. . . . The book's last half introduces more advanced techniques, such as JavaScript, functions, loops, and applications like Flash and Instant Messenger. . . . Illustrated, with references and a glossary, this attractive paperback has lots of practical content." Voice Youth Advocates
Includes glossary and bibliographical references

011 Bibliographies

American reference books annual 2010 edition, volume 41; edited by Shannon Graff Hysell. Libraries Unlimited 2010 xxiii, 689p $140
Grades: Adult Professional   **011**
1. Reference books—Bibliography 2. Reference books
ISBN 978-1-59884-593-8
Cumulative indexes available 1990-1994; 2000-2004; 2005-2009
Annual. First published 1970
Editor: 1970-2001 Bohdan S. Wynar
"Each issue covers the reference book output (including reprints) of the previous year (i.e., the 1970 volume covers 1969 publications). Offers descriptive and evaluative notes (many of them signed by contributors), with references to selected reviews. Limited to titles in English. Classed arrangement; author-subject-title index." Guide to Ref Books. 11th edition

Magazines for libraries; for the general reader and school, junior college, college, university and public libraries; reviewing the best publications for all serials collections since 1969; edited by Cheryl LaGuardia; created by Bill Katz. 19th ed. ProQuest 2010 995p $520
Grades: Adult Professional   **011**
1. Periodicals—Bibliography 2. Reference books
ISSN 0000-0914
ISBN 978-1-60030-135-3
First published 1969. Frequently revised
First-tenth edition edited by Bill Katz
"Annotated classified guide to recommended periodicals for the general reader and school, college, and public libraries. Provides comparative evaluations and grade and age-level recommendations for all periodicals included." N Y Public Libr Book of How & Where to Look It Up

Recommended reference books for small and medium-sized libraries and media centers, Vol. 30; Shannon Graff Hysell, associate editor. 2010 ed. Libraries Unlimited 2010 344p $75 *
Grades: Adult Professional   **011**
1. Reference books—Bibliography 2. Reference books—Reviews 3. Reference books
ISBN 978-1-59884-592-1
Annual. First published 1981
Each annual volume includes reviews of about 550 titles chosen by the editor as the most valuable reference titles published during the previous year.

011.6 General bibliographies of works for specific kinds of users and libraries

Barr, Catherine
Best books for high school readers; grades 9-12; [by] Catherine Barr and John T. Gillespie. 2nd ed. Libraries Unlimited 2009 1075p $85
Grades: Adult Professional   **011.6**
1. Reference books 2. Young adult literature—Bibliography 3. Teenagers—Books and reading 4. Best books
ISBN 978-1-59158-576-3; 1-59158-576-7
                   LC 2008-50756
First published 1991 by Bowker with title: Best books for senior high readers
"Each title included . . . offers two positive reviews with the exception of some entries in nonfiction series and adult selections suitable for young adults that receive restricted space from journals. All volumes incorporated were in print at the end of October 2008." Voice Youth Advocates

Gillespie, John Thomas, 1928-
Classic teenplots; a booktalk guide to use with readers ages 12-18; [by] John T. Gillespie and Corinne J. Naden. Libraries Unlimited 2006 348p (Children's and young adult literature reference series) $55
Grades: Adult Professional   **011.6**
1. Book talks 2. Young adult literature 3. Teenagers—Books and reading
ISBN 1-59158-312-8   LC 2006017624
"Prefaced by a brief guide to booktalking are one hundred entries for in-print classic titles for teens, taken from the out-of-print Juniorplots and Seniorplots series. Additional titles have been added to round out the eight theme/genre-based sections, which include topics such as Teenage Life and Concerns, Historical Fiction and Other Lands, and Important Nonfiction. . . . This excellent resource offers from sixteen to twenty titles per section." Voice Youth Advocates
Includes bibliographical references

Hubert, Jennifer, 1973-

Reading rants; a guide to books that rock! Neal-Schuman Publishers 2007 265p (Teens @ the library series) pa $49.95

Grades: Adult Professional   **011.6**

1. Reference books 2. Young adult literature—Bibliography

ISBN 978-1-55570-587-9; 1-55570-587-1

                        LC 2006-102711

"Hubert suggests 100 recently published YA titles and arranges them by themes. . . . Each novel includes the following information: the story . . . ; the message . . . ; the most likely audience . . . ; why it rocks; likely titles to 'hook up with,' and citations for reviews. Any library wishing to expand its YA collection or booktalking catalog will want this valuable tool." SLJ

The **official** YALSA awards guidebook; compiled and edited by Tina Frolund for the Young Adult Library Services Association. Neal-Schuman Publishers 2008 171p pa $55

Grades: Adult Professional   **011.6**

1. Reference books 2. Young adult literature—Awards 3. Young adult literature—Bibliography 4. Teenagers—Books and reading 5. Young adults' libraries

ISBN 978-1-55570-629-6; 1-55570-629-0

                        LC 2008-17584

Contents: Using award winners to build better young adult collections; Marketing award-winning books to teens; The Alex award; The Edwards award; The Printz award; Reproducible materials you can use to promote these great reads

This "volume offers one-stop shopping for an overview of the Alex, Printz, and Edwards awards. In addition to annotated bibliographies of winners and honor books, the title includes acceptance speeches for the Printz and Edwards awards and award interviews from YALSA starwarts Mary Arnold, Michael Cart, and Betty Carter." Bull Cent Child Books

Includes bibliographical references

Outstanding books for the college bound; titles and programs for a new generation; edited by Angela Carstensen. American Library Association 2011 164p pa $50 *

Grades: Adult Professional   **011.6**

1. College students 2. Best books

ISBN 978-0-8389-8570-0   LC 2011-11853

"A YALSA publication"

First published 1984

This book lists "over 400 books deemed outstanding for the college bound by the Young Adult Library Services Association (YALSA). . . . [It] includes indexes searchable by topic, year, title, and author." Publisher's note

Includes bibliographical references

Rosow, La Vergne

Accessing the classics; great reads for adults, teens, and English language learners. Libraries Unlimited 2006 301p pa $40

Grades: Adult Professional   **011.6**

1. Best books 2. Reading—Remedial teaching

ISBN 1-56308-891-6; 978-1-56308-891-9

                        LC 2005-30838

"This collection of annotated titles aims at providing resources for anyone who works with inexperienced or low-literacy teenagers or adults." Voice Youth Advocates

"The intended audience is wide-ranging and includes anyone who wishes to foster language and literacy skills. Essential reading." Booklist

Includes bibliographical references

Safford, Barbara Ripp

Guide to reference materials for school library media centers. 6th ed. Libraries Unlimited 2010 236p $60

Grades: Adult Professional   **011.6**

1. Reference books—Bibliography 2. School libraries—Catalogs 3. Instructional materials centers

ISBN 978-1-59158-277-9; 1-59158-277-6

                        LC 2009-51190

First edition by Christine Gehrt Wynar published 1973 with title: Guide to reference books for school media centers

"This volume has been updated to include web-based reference offerings as well as listings of older sources, provided that their content is still valid. . . . This title profiles resources recommended for use by school librarians for collection management, readers' advisory, teaching, general reference materials, the social sciences and humanities, and science and technology. This volume is an excellent starting point for new school librarians, as well as for those who are building a library from scratch." SLJ

Includes bibliographical references

Silver, Linda R., 1940-

Best Jewish books for children and teens; JPS guide. The Jewish Publication Society 2010 325p il pa $20

Grades: Adult Professional   **011.6**

1. Jewish literature—Bibliography 2. Children's literature—Bibliography 3. Young adult literature—Bibliography 4. Best books

ISBN 978-0-8276-0903-7   LC 2010-283705

"Chapters are organized by subject and entries within each include a . . . description of the book and author, and Silver's own insights on what makes it worth reading. There are title, subject, author, and illustrator indexes, title-grouping by reading level, and lists of award winners." Publisher's note

Includes bibliographical references

Welch, Rollie James, 1957-
A core collection for young adults. 2nd ed. Neal-Schuman Publishers 2011 416p (Teens @ the library series) pa $80 *
Grades: Adult Professional   **011.6**
 1. Teenagers—Books and reading 2. Young adults' libraries 3. Young adult literature—Bibliography
ISBN 978-1-55570-692-0; 1-55570-692-4
                              LC 2010-46693
First published 2003 under the authorship of Patrick Jones
Includes CD-ROM
Provides information meant to be a practical manual for developing collections that appeal to teens. Includes a guide to more than 100 "Best" lists, tips for maintaining a core collection, and selection tips for major YA genres.
"The book is a wide-reaching resource that introduces literature with appeal to young adults to an audience new to library work with teens." Voice Youth Advocates
Includes bibliographical references

016.3 Bibliographies of the social sciences

Crew, Hilary S., 1942-
Women engaged in war in literature for youth; a guide to resources for children and young adults. Scarecrow Press 2007 303p (Literature for youth) pa $51
Grades: Adult Professional   **016.3**
 1. Reference books 2. War—Bibliography 3. Women—Bibliography 4. Children's literature—Bibliography 5. Young adult literature—Bibliography
ISBN 978-0-8108-4929-7; 0-8108-4929-1
                              LC 2006-101112
"Crew's guide to print and online sources documents women's roles in wars over the centuries and throughout the world, divided by time periods. . . . This is a great addition for libraries looking for a way to move Women's Studies beyond the month of March." SLJ
Includes bibliographical references

016.3058 Bibliographies of racial, ethnic, national groups

Al-Hazza, Tami Craft
Books about the Middle East; selecting and using them with children and adolescents; [by] Tami Craft Al-Hazza and Katherine T. Bucher. Linworth Pub. 2008 168p pa $39.95
Grades: Adult Professional   **016.3058**
 1. Reference books 2. Middle East—Bibliography 3. Children's literature—Bibliography 4. Young adult literature—Bibliography
ISBN 978-1-58683-285-8; 1-58683-285-9
                              LC 2007-40149
"This book examines the body of literature about the diverse groups of people who inhabit the Middle East, and it also explores a variety of ways in which this literature can be used. . . . It fills a huge gap and should not be overlooked. This powerhouse book will be tremendously helpful to media specialists, educators, and public librarians." Voice Youth Advocates
Includes bibliographical references

Garcha, Rajinder
The world of Islam in literature for youth; a selective annotated bibliography for K-12; [by] Rajinder Garcha, Patricia Yates Russell. Scarecrow Press 2006 xx, 221p (Literature for youth) pa $35
Grades: Adult Professional   **016.3058**
 1. Reference books 2. Islam—Bibliography 3. Children's literature—Bibliography 4. Young adult literature—Bibliography
ISBN 978-0-8108-5488-8; 0-8108-5488-0
                              LC 2005-26645
"This annotated bibliography has more than 700 selected print and electronic resources. Each numbered entry includes complete bibliographic information, a recommended grade level, and a one-paragraph summary and critique." SLJ
"This highly useful bibliography fills a conspicuous gap in a much-needed cultural area." Voice Youth Advocates
Includes bibliographical references

016.7 Bibliographies of the arts

Pawuk, Michael G.
Graphic novels; a genre guide to comic books, manga, and more; foreword by Brian K. Vaughn. Libraries Unlimited 2007 xxxv, 633p il (Genreflecting advisory series) $65 *
Grades: Adult Professional   **016.7**
 1. Reference books 2. Graphic novels—Bibliography
ISBN 1-59158-132-X; 978-1-59158-132-1
                              LC 2006-34156
"This guide is intended to help you start, update, or maintain a graphic novel collection and advise readers about the genre. It covers more than 2,400 titles, including series titles, and organizes them according to genre, subgenre, and theme—from super-heroes and adventure to crime, humor, and nonfiction. Reading levels, awards/recognition, and core titles are identified; and tie-ins with gaming, film, anime, and television are noted." Publisher's note
Includes bibliographical references

016.79143 Bibliographies of motion pictures

Halsall, Jane

Visual media for teens; creating and using a teen-centered film collection; [by] Jane Halsall and R. William Edminster. Libraries Unlimited 2009 xxii, 158p (Libraries Unlimited professional guides for young adult librarians) pa $40

Grades: Adult Professional   **016.79143**

1. Libraries and motion pictures 2. Young adults' libraries 3. Motion pictures—Catalogs

ISBN 978-1-59158-544-2; 1-59158-544-9

LC 2009-20300

"This is an excellent guide for librarians interested in building a popular film collection to satisfy their teen audiences. It offers professionals an organized look at current films that have young adult appeal and provides analysis of the importance of such a collection." SLJ

Includes filmographies and bibliographical references

016.8 Bibliographies of literature

Fichtelberg, Susan

Encountering enchantment; a guide to speculative fiction for teens. Libraries Unlimited 2007 328p (Genreflecting advisory series) $48

Grades: Adult Professional   **016.8**

1. Reference books 2. Fantasy fiction—Bibliography 3. Science fiction—Bibliography 4. Young adult literature—Bibliography

ISBN 1-59158-316-0; 978-1-59158-316-5

LC 2006-33739

"This guide organizes by genre, subgenre, and theme some 1,400 titles of fantasy, science fiction and paranormal titles, most published within the last decade. Chapters cover such subgenres as epic fantasy, wizardry, romance, and mystery, which are further broken down by subgenres and themes. Annotations offer bibliographic information, brief plot summaries, reading levels, alternative media formats (including large print and Braille), and awards information." Publisher's note

"This useful guide should be in every YA collection." SLJ

Includes bibliographical references

Fonseca, Anthony J.

Hooked on horror III; a guide to reading interests; [by] Anthony J. Fonseca and June Michele Pulliam. Libraries Unlimited 2009 xxiii, 515p (Genreflecting advisory series) $62

Grades: Adult Professional   **016.8**

1. Horror fiction—Bibliography 2. Horror films 3. Reference books

ISBN 978-1-59158-540-4   LC 2008-45518

First published 1999 with title: Hooked on horror

This book "provides annotations of horror books published between 2003 and 2008, including collections, anthologies, and series." Voice Youth Advocates

Includes bibliographical references

Frolund, Tina

Genrefied classics; a guide to reading interests in classical literature. Libraries Unlimited 2007 xxiv, 365p (Genreflecting advisory series) $45 *

Grades: Adult Professional   **016.8**

1. Reference books 2. Fiction—Bibliography

ISBN 1-59158-172-9; 978-1-59158-172-7

LC 2006-33740

"By identifying the genre characteristics of more than 400 classic fiction works, and organizing titles according to these features, this guide helps readers find the type of books they enjoy." Publisher's note

Includes bibliographical references

Gannon, Michael B.

Blood, bedlam, bullets, and badguys; a reader's guide to adventure/suspense fiction. Libraries Unlimited 2004 385p (Genreflecting advisory series) $55

Grades: Adult Professional   **016.8**

1. Reference books 2. Adventure fiction—Bibliography 3. Suspense fiction—Bibliography

ISBN 1-563-08732-4   LC 2003-60527

"Fifteen chapters cover subgenres such as espionage, legal and medical thrillers, sea adventures, and novels with elements of the paranormal. Each chapter begins with a definition of the subgenre and brief discussions of its history and appeal. There is also a very useful list of things to keep in mind when advising a reader." Booklist

Includes bibliographical references

Herald, Diana Tixier

Fluent in fantasy; the next generation; [by] Diana Tixier Herald and Bonnie Kunzel. Libraries Unlimited 2008 312p (Genreflecting advisory series) $52

Grades: Adult Professional   **016.8**

1. Reference books 2. Fantasy fiction—Bibliography

ISBN 978-1-59158-198-7; 1-59158-198-2

LC 2007-28840

First published 1999

"More than 2,000 titles are arranged by author in 14 thematic chapters, including 'Epic Fantasy,' 'Arthurian Legend,' and 'Time Travel Romance.' . . . An essential collection development and readers'-advisory tool." Booklist

Includes bibliographical references

Genreflecting; a guide to popular reading interests; edited by Wayne A. Wiegand. 6th ed. Libraries Unlimited 2006 562p (Genreflecting advisory series) $60; pa $45 *

Grades: Adult Professional   **016.8**

1. Reference books 2. Fiction—Bibliography 3. Fiction—History and criticism 4. Books and reading

ISBN 1-59158-224-5; 1-59158-286-5 (pa)

LC 2005-30804

First published 1982 under the authorship of Betty Rosenberg

A listing of recommended titles in such genres as crime, adventure, romance, science fiction, Christian fiction, fantasy, horror, and their subgenres. Besides infor-

Herald, Diana Tixier—*Continued*
mation on authors and titles, the volume provides information on anthologies, bibliographies, critical works, encyclopedias, organizations, and publishers.

Includes bibliographical references

Teen genreflecting 3; a guide to reading interests. Libraries Unlimited 2011 xxiv, 377p (Genreflecting advisory series) $48 *
Grades: Adult Professional   **016.8**
   1. Young adult literature—Bibliography 2. Teenagers—Books and reading 3. Reference books
ISBN 978-1-59158-729-3; 1-59158-729-3
                 LC 2010-40791
First published 1997 with title: Teen genreflecting
"The chapters and subchapters provide a brief overview of the topic and are organized by genre, subgenre, or an overall theme. Each entry is annotated and includes a concise subject list, and some entries include a list of read-alikes. Herald also includes books written for children and those for adults that have teen appeal. . . . Herald suggests using this volume to identify read-alikes, to beef up genre collections, and for library staff to familiarize themselves with the literature. . . . A worthy addition to reference or professional-development collection." SLJ

Includes bibliographical references

Hollands, Neil
Read on . . . fantasy fiction; reading lists for every taste. Libraries Unlimited 2007 210p (Read on series) pa $30
Grades: Adult Professional   **016.8**
   1. Reference books 2. Fantasy fiction—Bibliography
ISBN 978-1-59158-330-1; 1-59158-330-6
                 LC 2007-7841
This book "organizes more than 800 titles into over 100 lists, in such categories as 'The Magic of Threes: Fantasy's Best Trilogies,' 'The Fellowship is the Thing: Companions on a Quest,' 'Fan-to-Sea-Nautical Fantasy,' and 'When Groan Men Scry: Puns as a Fantasy Tradition.'" Publisher's note
"Librarians who do readers advisory for teens or adults will wonder how they ever got along without this funny, opinionated, wide-angle guide." SLJ

Johnson, Sarah L., 1969-
Historical fiction; a guide to the genre. Libraries Unlimited 2005 xxi, 813p (Genreflecting advisory series) $75
Grades: Adult Professional   **016.8**
   1. Reference books 2. Historical fiction—Bibliography
ISBN 1-59158-129-X   LC 2005-47483
"Each category, e.g., 'Traditional Historical Novels,' 'Historical Thrillers,' 'Time-Slip Novels,' is subdivided further by world region and historical era. . . . The annotations also indicate benchmarks of the genre, award winners, and titles recommended for young adults and reading groups. . . . This is an excellent resource." Choice

Includes bibliographical references

Historical fiction II; a guide to the genre. Libraries Unlimited 2009 738p (Genreflecting advisory series) $65
Grades: Adult Professional   **016.8**
   1. Historical fiction—Bibliography 2. Reference books
ISBN 978-1-59158-624-1   LC 2008-45537
Contents: The appeal of the past; Traditional historical novels; Multi-period epics; Romancing the past; Sagas; Western historical novels; Historical mysteries; Adventures in history; Historical thrillers; Literary historical novels; Christian historical fiction; Time-slip novels; Alternate history; Historical fantasy; Resources for librarians and readers
"Johnson has updated her outstanding *Historical Fiction: A Guide to the Genre* (2005) by covering historical fiction from 2004 through mid-2008 and adding such new features as ISBNs for each book and keyword descriptors after each annotation. . . . This volume continues rather than replaces the earlier work, adding more than 2,700 new titles." Booklist

Includes bibliographical references

Latino literature; edited by Sara E. Martínez; foreword by Connie Van Fleet. Libraries Unlimited 2009 xxii, 364p (Genreflecting advisory series) $60
Grades: Adult Professional   **016.8**
   1. American literature—Hispanic American authors—Bibliography 2. Reference books
ISBN 978-1-59158-292-2; 1-59158-292-X
                 LC 2009-26355
"The goal [of this book] is to sample broadly from Latino authors in the U.S., Latin America, Portugal, and Spain. Coverage is limited to works available in English that were first published between the years 1995 and 2008. Approximately 750 entries are divided into 9 chapters: 'General Fiction,' 'Historical Fiction,' 'Women's Fiction,' 'Latina Romance and Love Stories,' 'Mysteries and Suspense,' 'Fantastic Fiction,' 'Young Adult Fiction,' 'Life Stories,' and 'Narrative Nonfiction.' Entries include bibliographic information, a plot summary, an excerpt from the book, awards won, key features, subjects, and similar titles. . . . This well-written book is an essential resource for public and high-school libraries, especially if they serve Latino populations." Booklist

Includes bibliographical references

Leeper, Angela
Poetry in literature for youth. Scarecrow Press 2006 303p (Literature for youth) pa $40
Grades: Adult Professional   **016.8**
   1. Reference books 2. Poetry—Bibliography
ISBN 0-8108-5465-1   LC 2005030719
This "provides annotated listings of titles arranged by subjects. . . . More than 900 entries describe collections, anthologies, performance poetry, poet biographies, and more, for kindergarten through high school." Booklist
"This title is packed with innovative ways to integrate poetry into the K-12 curriculum." SLJ

Includes bibliographical references

Thomas, Rebecca L.

Popular series fiction for middle school and teen readers; a reading and selection guide; [by] Rebecca L. Thomas and Catherine Barr. 2nd ed. Libraries Unlimited 2009 710p (Children's and young adult literature reference series) $65

Grades: Adult Professional　　　　　　**016.8**

1. Reference books 2. Children's literature—Bibliography 3. Young adult literature—Bibliography

ISBN 978-1-59158-660-9　　　　LC 2008-38125

First published 2005

"The authors have identified nearly 2,200 in-print series . . . (including manga, Cine-Manga, and illustrated novels) that will appeal to readers in grades 6-12. Entries are arranged by the series title and contain author, most recent publisher, grade level, notation for availability of accelerated-reader resources, genre, a descriptive three- to five-sentence annotation, and a list of individual titles in the series, arranged by publication date." Booklist

Includes bibliographic references

Wadham, Rachel, 1973-

This is my life; a guide to realistic fiction for teens; [by] Rachel L. Wadham. Libraries Unlimited 2010 431p (Genreflecting advisory series) $55

Grades: Adult Professional　　　　　　**016.8**

1. Young adult literature—Bibliography 2. Teenagers—Books and reading

ISBN 978-1-59158-942-6; 1-59158-942-8

　　　　　　　　　　　　　　LC 2010-24074

This "surveys contemporary realistic fiction for young adults (middle through high school). Wadham . . . annotates some 1,300 titles published for young adults between 1999 and 2009. Arranged by theme, titles represent real-life issues of broad interest (friendship, love, family, work) as well as specific issues faced in 'problem novels' (pregnancy, homelessness, eating disorders, crime and violence, abuse, drugs and alcohol, death, racism). Annotations include plot summaries, availability in audio, awards, grade-level designations, and subject keywords. . . . This is a useful tool for its intended audience of librarians and instructors seeking issue-related fiction." Booklist

Includes bibliographical references

What do I read next? 2011; a reader's guide to current genre fiction. 2011 ed. Gale / Cengage Learning 2011 2v ea $230

Grades: 11 12 Adult　　　　　　**016.8**

1. Reference books 2. Fiction—Bibliography

ISSN 1052-2212

ISBN 978-1-4144-6136-6 (v1); 978-1-4144-8763-2 (v2)

Also available online

Annual. First published 1991 for 1989-1990

A guide to locating new fiction titles in specific genres. Arranged by author within six genre sections, each entry provides publisher and publication date, series name, major characters, time period, geographic setting, review citations, and related books.

016.9　Bibliographies of geography and history

Barancik, Sue, 1944-

Guide to collective biographies for children and young adults. Scarecrow Press 2005 447p pa $44.95

Grades: Adult Professional　　　　　　**016.9**

1. Reference books 2. Biography—Bibliography 3. Children's literature—Bibliography 4. Young adult literature—Bibliography

ISBN 0-8108-5033-8　　　　LC 2004-19560

"This text indexes 721 titles for children and young adults in order to provide access to 5,760 notable individuals from early to modern times. All of the referenced titles were published between 1988 and 2002." Booklist

"A current guide such as this one is essential. . . . A must-have for libraries serving grades 4 through 12." SLJ

Richards, Michael D., 1941-

Term paper resource guide to twentieth-century world history; [by] Michael D. Richards and Philip F. Riley. Greenwood Press 2000 335p $49.95 *

Grades: 9 10 11 12　　　　　　**016.9**

1. Report writing 2. Modern history—Study and teaching

ISBN 0-313-30559-5　　　　LC 99-88458

Companion volume to Term paper resource guide to twentieth-century United States history by Robert Muccigrosso

"The most significant 100 events in world history are arranged chronologically. . . . Each topic is followed by six suggestions for term papers, both traditional and nontraditional in approach, such as interviews, exploring connections between literature and history, group projects, mock trails, and film study." Book Rep

Includes bibliographical references

016.94053　Bibliographies of World War II, 1939-1945

Rosen, Philip, 1928-

Bearing witness; a resource guide to literature, poetry, art, music, and videos by Holocaust victims and survivors; [by] Philip Rosen and Nina Apfelbaum. Greenwood Press 2002 210p $52.95

Grades: Adult Professional　　　　　　**016.94053**

1. Reference books 2. Holocaust, 1933-1945—Bibliography

ISBN 0-313-31076-9　　　　LC 00-69153

This is a resource guide to "over 800 first-person accounts, fiction, poetry, art interpretations, and music by Holocaust victims and survivors, as well as videos relating to the testimony and experiences of Holocaust survivors." Publisher's note

"This volume will be valuable to all who are researching the Holocaust. Its strength lies in the inclusion of materials not often found elsewhere." Booklist

Includes bibliographical references

016.973 Bibliographies of United States history

Craver, Kathleen W.
Term paper resource guide to nineteenth-century U.S. history. Greenwood Press 2008 407p $65 *
Grades: 8 9 10 11 12   **016.973**
1. Reference books 2. Report writing 3. United States—History—19th century—Chronology
ISBN 978-0-313-34810-5; 0-313-34810-3
                              LC 2008-4508
"This comprehensive resource covers important topics such as 'The Sally Hemmings and Thomas Jefferson Connection (1802),' 'Great Chicago Fire (1871),' and 'Plessy v. Ferguson (1899).' Each essay provides a synopsis of the person, event, or place; term-paper suggestions; alternative projects such as making related movies or designing broadsheets; and a listing of accessible primary and secondary print works, and multimedia and Web sources." SLJ
Includes bibliographical references

Hardy, Lyda Mary
Women in U.S. history; a resource guide. Libraries Unlimited 2000 344p pa $45 *
Grades: Adult Professional   **016.973**
1. Reference books 2. Women—United States—Bibliography 3. Women—United States—History
ISBN 1-56308-769-3   LC 00-55849
This overview of historical resources includes primary sources as well as biographies, autobiographies and compilations. Best books, Web sites, and videos are included. Subject and author/title indexes are appended.
Includes bibliographical references

Neumann, Caryn E., 1965-
Term paper resource guide to African American history. Greenwood Press 2009 304p (American mosaic) $65 *
Grades: 9 10 11 12   **016.973**
1. African Americans—History 2. African Americans—Bibliography 3. Report writing 4. Reference books
ISBN 978-0-313-35501-1   LC 2008-51972
"These 100 succinct yet detailed guides for planning research on African-American history cover topics from the early slave trade to North America in 1581 to Hurricane Katrina in 2005. Each approximately four-page section opens with a summary of the time period, followed by lists of term-paper suggestions, alternate topics, and annotated citations to primary and secondary materials. Sources include scholarly print works, authoritative Web sites, and quality movies, supporting a variety of learning styles. . . . While supporting researchers with reliable information, the book clearly puts the direction and depth of research in users' hands." SLJ
Includes bibliographical references

020 Library & information sciences

Core technology competencies for librarians and library staff; a LITA guide; Susan M. Thompson, editor. Neal-Schuman Publishers 2009 248p il pa $65 *
Grades: Adult Professional   **020**
1. Technological innovations 2. Librarians—In-service training 3. Library education 4. Information technology
ISBN 978-1-55570-660-9   LC 2008-46174
In this book, "a coterie of experts identify competencies for technology specialists and describe several competency implementation programs. Useful for everyone from the systems librarian to the 'lone information technology librarian.'" Am Libr
Includes bibliographical references

Kroski, Ellyssa
Web 2.0 for librarians and information professionals. Neal-Schuman Publishers 2008 209p il pa $75
Grades: Adult Professional   **020**
1. Web 2.0
ISBN 978-1-55570-614-2; 1-55570-614-2
                              LC 2007-43249
"Chapters address blogs, RSS feeds and newsreaders, wikis, social bookmarking, photo sharing, social cataloging, video sharing, personalized start pages, social networking software, vertical search engines, social news, productivity tools, podcasting, and mashups. Each chapter includes screen shots . . . explains how libraries are using these tools, and offers some 'Best Practices' (tips for successfully working with Web 2.0 tools)." Libr J
"Whether you are just beginning the journey in the transformation of the Web or want to begin implementing this exciting tool in your library, this outstanding resource will take the mystery out of these concepts and be an excellent addition to your reference section." Libr Media Connect
Includes glossary and bibliographical references

McCain, Mary Maude
Dictionary for school library media specialists; a practical and comprehensive guide; [by] Mary Maude McCain and Martha Merrill. Libraries Unlimited 2001 219p pa $42
Grades: Adult Professional   **020**
1. Reference books 2. School libraries—Dictionaries
ISBN 1-56308-696-4   LC 01-16506
"The book defines more than 375 terms. There are two types of definitions—shorter glossary descriptions (*capital outlay, reboot*) and longer, more detailed treatments (*poetry, proximity operators*). See references (especially from acronyms and abbreviations) and *see also* references facilitate use." Booklist

021.2 Relationships with the community

Gillespie, Kellie M., 1960-
Teen volunteer services in libraries. VOYA Books 2004 133p il (VOYA guides) pa $26.95
Grades: Adult Professional   **021.2**
1. Volunteer work 2. Libraries
ISBN 0-8108-4837-6   LC 2003-17932
This offers "advice about starting and maintaining effective teen volunteer programs in school and public libraries. . . . [The author discusses] recruitment, orientation and training, recognition and retention, and supervision." Publisher's note
"If you are even considering starting a teen volunteer program, you must read this book. If you already have one in your library, this volume still has much to offer." SLJ
Includes bibliographical references

Librarians as community partners; an outreach handbook; edited by Carol Smallwood. American Library Association 2010 204p pa $55
Grades: Adult Professional   **021.2**
1. Libraries and community 2. Libraries—Public relations 3. Cultural programs
ISBN 978-0-8389-1006-1   LC 2009-20359
"Thirty-seven public, school, and academic librarians here share 'how we did outreach good' and produce a joyful collection. . . . Beyond a bounty of ideas are practical suggestions and examples that can be used for the library to approach organizations, groups, and governmental entities for grant applications. While the creative is foremost, the financial and efficient are also addressed with the essential details of who did what, how it was funded, and the nature of follow-up. . . . Even the smallest library with a handful of staff could benefit from this book." Libr J
Includes bibliographical references

Squires, Tasha, 1972-
Library partnerships; making connections between school and public libraries. Information Today, Inc. 2009 203p pa $39.50 *
Grades: Adult Professional   **021.2**
1. Libraries and schools 2. Libraries and students 3. Library cooperation 4. Public libraries 5. School libraries
ISBN 978-1-57387-362-8; 1-57387-362-4
    LC 2008-51647
The author "delves into the many possible avenues for partnership [between school and public libraries], from summer reading programs to book talks to resource sharing and more." Publisher's note
"Squires's confident advice can get beleaguered librarians through . . . difficulties and into mutually productive partnerships." Voice Youth Advocates
Includes bibliographical references

021.7 Promotion of libraries, archives, information centers

Mahood, Kristine
Booktalking with teens. Libraries Unlimited 2010 289p (Libraries Unlimited professional guides for young adult librarians) pa $45 *
Grades: Adult Professional   **021.7**
1. Book talks 2. Teenagers—Books and reading 3. Young adult literature—Bibliography
ISBN 978-1-59158-714-9; 1-59158-714-X
    LC 2009-49893
This "provides advice about preparing, developing, writing, performing and justifying booktalks. . . . Mahood's expertise and enthusiasm are contagious and challenge all of us who work with youth to be as inspiring while sharing books as she is." Booklist
Includes bibliographical references

Phillips, Susan P., 1945-
Great displays for your library step by step. McFarland & Co. 2008 234p il pa $45 *
Grades: Adult Professional   **021.7**
1. Libraries—Exhibitions
ISBN 978-0-7864-3164-9; 0-7864-3164-4
    LC 2007-47450
This volume is a "tool for designing . . . visual statements for library spaces. Each display includes a brief introduction to the subject; an explanation of the genesis of the idea; specifics regarding the information included and its source; step-by-step instructions for assembly; and ideas on how to customize the display to any available space." Publisher's note
"Phillips' enthusiasm, creativity, and breadth of personal interests are evident throughout this book. . . . This text will inspire readers to locate and showcase the treasures in their own collections." SLJ
Includes bibliographical references

Wolfe, Lisa Ann
Library public relations, promotions, and communications; a how-to-do-it manual. 2nd ed. Neal-Schuman Publishers 2005 230p (How-to-do-it manuals for librarians) pa $65 *
Grades: Adult Professional   **021.7**
1. Libraries—Public relations
ISBN 1-55570-471-9   LC 2004-25944
First published 1997
"The book is divided into two parts—'Planning and Evaluation' and 'Strategies and Methodologies'—with many examples of successful communicating and the impact and changes brought by technology. Ideas on putting together a communications plan, creating clear signage and print products, effectively using a library's Web site, and communicating during a crisis will be helpful for all types of libraries and positions." Booklist
Includes bibliographical references

022 Administration of physical plant

Bolan, Kimberly
Teen spaces; the step-by-step library makeover. 2nd ed. American Library Association 2009 225p il pa $40 *
Grades: Adult Professional   **022**
 1. Young adults' libraries
 ISBN 978-0-8389-0969-0   LC 2008-26621
 First published 2003
 "An essential guide for any library planning a teen-space project. . . . After an introductory chapter on teens and their needs within a library, all aspects of teen areas are explained. From the analysis and planning to design and decoration, Bolan outlines the steps to take and the pitfalls to avoid. . . . This book truly is a guide to step-by-step library makeovers." SLJ
 Includes bibliographical references

023 Personnel management (Human resource management)

Giesecke, Joan
Fundamentals of library supervision; [by] Joan Giesecke and Beth McNeil. 2nd ed. American Library Association 2010 189p il (ALA fundamentals series) pa $55
Grades: Adult Professional   **023**
 1. Libraries—Administration 2. Personnel management
 ISBN 978-0-8389-1016-0   LC 2009-28890
 First published 2005
 "The authors give advice on how to build relationships with bosses, peers, and reports; establish good communication skills; create a healthy work climate; motivate others; and build a team. . . . Each chapter includes a succinct bibliography, allowing the new manager to continue his or her education—especially useful for more complex topics like project management." Libr J
 Includes bibliographical references

Zmuda, Allison
Librarians as learning specialists; meeting the learning imperative for the 21st century; [by] Allison Zmuda and Violet H. Harada; foreword by Grant Wiggins. Libraries Unlimited 2008 128p il pa $40
Grades: Adult Professional   **023**
 1. Libraries and schools 2. School libraries 3. Teaching—Aids and devices
 ISBN 978-1-59158-679-1; 1-59158-679-8
          LC 2008-6036
 "The book examines the necessity of a mission-centered mindset and changing the role of a library media specialist to a learning specialist. . . . Written for both school administrators and librarians, the well-documented book gives a workable framework for collaboration. The authors make a good case for opening the doors between classroom and library and provide tools for doing so." SLJ
 Includes bibliographical references

025 Operations of libraries, archives, information centers

Cohn, John M., 1943-
The complete library technology planner; a guidebook with sample technology plans and RFPs on CD-ROM; [by] John M. Cohn and Ann L. Kelsey; with a foreword by Keith Michael Fiels. Neal-Schuman Publishers 2010 xxiv, 163p il pa $99.95
Grades: Adult Professional   **025**
 1. Information technology 2. Libraries—Automation
 ISBN 978-1-55570-681-4; 1-55570-681-9
          LC 2009-41008
 Includes CD-ROM
 "This book provides a comprehensive wealth of information for libraries in need of creating or updating a technology plan. Whether your goal is to introduce an integrated library system (ILS) or transfer from an existing system to a new one, Cohn and Kelsey make clear the strategic planning process involved and provide the tools needed to create a plan, including how to meet funding requirements, implement the plan, and evaluate its success. The accompanying CD-ROM contains 38 sample technology plans and requests for proposals (RFPs) that have been collected from 32 different libraries." Libr J
 Includes bibliographical references

025.04 Information storage and retrieval systems

Berger, Pam
Choosing Web 2.0 tools for learning and teaching in a digital world; [by] Pam Berger and Sally Trexler; foreword by Joyce Valenza. Libraries Unlimited 2010 221p il map pa $40 *
Grades: Adult Professional   **025.04**
 1. Internet in education 2. Web 2.0 3. Information literacy—Study and teaching 4. Internet searching—Study and teaching
 ISBN 978-1-59158-706-4; 1-59158-706-9
          LC 2009-54069
 "The purpose of this book is to provide a framework for navigation within the constant change of learning in the twenty-first century. . . . Chapter topics include social bookmarking, managing and organizing information, blogs and wikis, media sharing, social networking, and digital mapping." Libr Media Connect
 "This guide offers a plethora of ideas for incorporating digital learning into schools in an accessible and reader-friendly manner." Voice Youth Advocates
 Includes glossary and bibliographical references

Diaz, Karen R.
IssueWeb: a guide and sourcebook for researching controversial issues on the Web; [by] Karen R. Diaz, Nancy O'Hanlon. Libraries Unlimited 2004 287p pa $30
Grades: Adult Professional   **025.04**
 1. Internet resources 2. Internet searching—Study and teaching
 ISBN 1-59158-078-1   LC 2003-65946

Diaz, Karen R.—*Continued*

The authors "open with an online research guide that concentrates on finding an appropriate topic, using the right terminology, and evaluating online research, considering bias, balance, and documentation. . . . Recommended Web sites follow, subdivided into reference, legal issues, news, data sources, and advocacy for and against." Choice

"A veritable gold mine of more than 40 well-organized, well-presented issues briefs follows three remarkably clear, concise chapters on finding, evaluating, and incorporating Internet resources." SLJ

Harris, Frances Jacobson

I found it on the Internet; coming of age online. 2nd ed. American Library Association 2010 c2011 234p il pa $45

Grades: Adult Professional   **025.04**
1. Young adults' libraries 2. Internet and teenagers 3. Internet—Social aspects
ISBN 978-0-8389-1066-5   LC 2010-13644
First published 2005

The author offers "advice on how to help young people make good decisions, especially in such thorny areas as music and media sharing; tools for formulating information and communication policies . . . [and] ways of dealing with the problematic issues of hacking, cheating, privacy, harassment, and access to inappropriate content." Publisher's note

Includes bibliographical references

Scheeren, William O.

Technology for the school librarian; theory and practice. Libraries Unlimited 2010 223p il $50

Grades: Adult Professional   **025.04**
1. School libraries 2. Information technology 3. Digital libraries 4. Libraries—Special collections
ISBN 978-1-59158-900-6; 1-59158-900-2
                                    LC 2009-51922

"This title provides information on the practical aspects of technology in the school library as well as the theoretical framework to spark continued learning. Sharing actual case studies as well as practical tips on technology implentation and terminology, this title will be a valuable resource to any school librarian." Libr Media Connect

Includes bibliographical references

Shaw, Maura D.

Mastering online research; a comprehensive guide to effective and efficient search strategies; [by] Maura Shaw. Writers Digest Books 2007 340p il pa $19.99

Grades: 11 12 Adult   **025.04**
1. Internet searching 2. Internet resources 3. Web sites—Directories 4. Internet research
ISBN 978-1-58297-458-3; 1-58297-458-6
                                    LC 2007-11286

Contents: The Internet defined; Conducting basic searches; Conducting advanced searches; Evaluating websites; The world of hyperlinks; The best websites to begin your research; Searching for people and places;

Accessing special search areas; Searching for image, audio, and video files; Research skills for writers; Permissions and copyright issues; Concluding your research

The author describes "the techniques and tools you need to find information ranging from historical data to medical information to images and videos." Publisher's note

The **United** States government internet directory; edited by Peggy Garvin. Bernan Press 2010 627p pa $65 *

Grades: 11 12 Adult   **025.04**
1. Government information—Directories 2. Internet resources—Directories 3. Web sites—Directories 4. Reference books
ISSN 1547-2892
ISBN 978-1-59888-421-0

Annual. First published 2004 with title: The United States government Internet manual. Published in 2009 with title: E-government and web directory

This directory "contains more than 2,000 Web site records, organized into 20 subject-themed chapters; provides descriptions and URLs for each site; . . . includes information about the sponsoring agency; notes the useful or unique aspects of the site; lists some of the major government publications hosted on the site; evaluates the most important and frequently sought sites; provides a roster of congressional members with members' Web sites includes a one-page 'Quick Guide' to the major federal agencies and the leading online library, data source, and finding aid sites; [and] highlights the Freedom of Information Act Web pages to access U.S. federal executive agency records." Publisher's note

Wolfinger, Anne, 1953-

Best career and education web sites; a quick guide to online job search. 6th ed. JIST Works 2009 216p il pa $14.95 *

Grades: 9 10 11 12   **025.04**
1. Job hunting 2. Vocational guidance 3. Labor supply 4. Internet resources 5. Web sites
ISBN 978-1-59357-700-1; 1-59357-700-1
                                    LC 2008-52307

First published 1998 with title: The quick Internet guide to career and college information

This book "contains listing and reviews of . . . [350 recommended] sites on the Internet for learning more about careers, college, training, and job search." Publisher's note

Wolinsky, Art

Internet power research using the Big6 approach. rev ed. Enslow Publishers 2005 64p il (Internet library) lib bdg $22.60; pa $11.93

Grades: Adult Professional   **025.04**
1. Information systems 2. Research
ISBN 0-7660-1563-7 (lib bdg); 0-7660-1564-5 (pa)
                                    LC 2004-22185

First published 2002

Provides instructions for using the "Big6" research method and scenarios for applying the technique to research conducted on the Internet.

The information is presented in "a friendly, informal

Wolinsky, Art—*Continued*

writing style. . . . This is a helpful resource for students who want to hone their research strategies." SLJ

Includes glossary and bibliographical references

025.1 Administration

Casey, Michael E., 1967-

Library 2.0; a guide to participatory library service; [by] Michael E. Casey, Laura C. Savastinuk. Information Today, Inc. 2007 xxv, 172p il pa $29.50

Grades: Adult Professional   025.1

1. Library services 2. Libraries—Public relations

ISBN 978-1-57387-297-3; 1-57387-297-0

LC 2007-5247

"The authors emphasize regular evaluation and retooling of existing services and provide a model for identifying and implementing new services with input from library users, nonusers, and all levels of staff. Topics covered include instituting and managing change, incorporating technology into the Library 2.0 model, and getting buy-in from administrators, staff, and users. The focus is on public libraries, but the concepts could be applied to any type of institution." Libr J

"This title should be required reading for professional library staffs struggling with change and organizational restructure." Libr Media Connect

Includes bibliographical references

Dresang, Eliza T.

Dynamic youth services through outcome-based planning and evaluation; foreword by Virginia Walter. American Library Association 2006 155p il pa $42 *

Grades: Adult Professional   025.1

1. Libraries—Administration 2. School libraries—Activity projects

ISBN 0-8389-0918-3; 978-0-8389-0918-8

LC 2006-7487

In this "guide, three experts who have conducted extensive research and piloted . . . [an] outcome-based program for youth in the St. Louis Public Library, share their findings and proven strategies." Publisher's note

Includes bibliographical references

Farmer, Lesley S. Johnson, 1949-

Neal-Schuman technology management handbook for school library media centers; by Lesley S. Johnson Farmer and Marc E. McPhee. Neal-Schuman Publishers 2010 289p il pa $59.95

Grades: Adult Professional   025.1

1. School libraries 2. Instructional materials centers

ISBN 978-1-55570-659-3; 1-55570-659-2

LC 2010-9301

"This informative, well-researched text is perfect for those in the early stages of integrating technology into their programs. The first chapter begins with an overview of the impact technology has had on society and defines technology and its role in the library, including past, present, and possible future changes, as well as manage-

rial roles of the librarian. Other chapters examine planning for management, assessing, researching, developing a technology plan, acquiring all types of tech resources, and managing the physical space to accommodate equipment and networking." SLJ

Includes bibliographical references

Harvey, Carl A., II

No school library left behind; leadership, school improvement, and the media specialist; [by] Carl A. Harvey II. Linworth Pub. 2008 106p pa $39.95 *

Grades: Adult Professional   025.1

1. School libraries 2. Libraries—Administration 3. Instructional materials centers

ISBN 978-1-58683-233-9; 1-58683-233-6

LC 2007-42178

"The content [of this book] constitutes a crash course in school improvement, covering definitions, history, legislation, research, best practices, assessment, profiles of accreditation associations, and most importantly, a strong rationale for why media specialists should lead the way in school improvement efforts. . . . Of major interest to novice and seasoned practitioners, this guide is timely and relevant." Libr Media Connect

Includes bibliographical references

Independent school libraries; perspectives on excellence; Dorcas Hand, editor. Libraries Unlimited 2010 369p il (Libraries Unlimited professional guides in school librarianship) pa $45 *

Grades: Adult Professional   025.1

1. School libraries 2. Private schools

ISBN 978-1-59158-803-0 (pa); 1-59158-803-0 (pa); 978-1-59158-812-2 (ebook)   LC 2010-14567

"Twenty-one essays by prominent independent school librarians both address the current state of independent school librarianship in the United States and offer suggestions for the future. Pieces cover the library's role in the school, statistical comparisons, staffing, advocacy, assessment, technology, information commons, collaboration, college preparation, programming, traditions, collection development, minors' rights, budgeting, facilities, accreditation, and disaster planning. . . . Librarians from all schools will find a wealth of information here." Voice Youth Advocates

Includes bibliographical references

Leadership and the school librarian; essays from leaders in the field; [compiled by] Mary D. Lankford. Linworth Pub. 2006 132p il pa $44.95

Grades: Adult Professional   025.1

1. School libraries 2. Libraries—Administration

ISBN 1-58683-191-7   LC 2005-34166

"Written by seven Texas library media specialists, the essays examine primary areas of professional responsibility: advocacy, collection development, finances, collaboration, professional development, and information access, focusing on the leadership opportunities that these areas afford." Voice Youth Advocates

"This collection of essays is just what you need to develop your leadership skills." Libr Media Connect

Includes bibliographical references

MacDonell, Colleen

Essential documents for school libraries. 2nd ed. Linworth 2010 xxiv, 156p il $50 *

Grades: Adult Professional   **025.1**

1. Libraries—Administration

ISBN 978-1-58683-400-5   LC 2010-21241

First published 2004

Includes CD-ROM

Contents: Planning documents; Official reports; Publicity; Teaching documents; Programming documents; Procedures; Guidelines

"Each chapter begins with why the documents are needed, followed by practical advice for writing the documents, and examples of how the documents make an effective change in the library media program." Libr Media Connect [review of 2004 edition]

Includes bibliographical references

MacKellar, Pamela H.

Winning grants; a how-to-do-it manual for librarians with multimedia tutorials and grant development tools; [by] Pamela H. MacKellar and Stephanie K. Gerding. Neal-Schuman Publishers 2010 xxi, 242p il (How-to-do-it manuals for librarians) pa $99.95 *

Grades: Adult Professional   **025.1**

1. Grants-in-aid 2. Fund raising

ISBN 978-1-55570-700-2   LC 2010-17965

First published 2006 with title: Grants for libraries

Includes DVD-ROM

This how-to manual is "focused on libraries that are looking for funding for particular projects. Part I details the steps necessary to create a winning grant proposal for public or school libraries. . . . Part II includes real-life stories of projects that won grants. . . . Part III contains templates for planning tools such as checklists and worksheets. These can also be found on a multimedia DVD which includes instructional videos that go along with each chapter." Voice Youth Advocates

"This great all-around resource should be a staple for those just entering the challenging world of grant seeking and for the well-rounded library collection." Libr J

Includes bibliographical references

Martin, Barbara Stein, 1947-

Fundamentals of school library media management; a how-to-do-it manual; [by] Barbara Stein Martin and Marco Zannier. Neal-Schuman Publishers 2009 172p il (How-to-do-it manuals for librarians) pa $59.95 *

Grades: Adult Professional   **025.1**

1. School libraries 2. Instructional materials centers

ISBN 978-1-55570-656-2; 1-55570-656-8

                                         LC 2009-7930

This book "contains useful information to help school librarians manage a myriad of tasks and roles. . . . [The authors] have created a book that is helpful, accessible, and full of down-to-earth, concrete examples." Booklist

Includes bibliographical references

Matthews, Joseph R.

Strategic planning and management for library managers. Libraries Unlimited 2005 150p il pa $40 *

Grades: Adult Professional   **025.1**

1. Libraries—Administration

ISBN 1-59158-231-8   LC 2005-10099

"Part 1 defines a strategy, addresses the need for one, and presents 10 distinct schools of strategic thought. Part 2 differentiates between strategic planning and long-range planning, discusses the benefits of strategic planning, and identifies approaches to preparing and implementing such plans. Part 3 focuses on performance measures, ways to communicate the value of libraries to others, and the 'culture of assessment,' an environment where all library staff are routinely involved in the evaluation process. Information presented throughout the book is clear, practical, readily accessible, well documented, and amply supported by notes, tables, figures, diagrams, and quotes." Booklist

McGhee, Marla W.

The principal's guide to a powerful library media program; a school library for the 21st century; [by] Marla W. McGhee and Barbara A. Jansen. 2nd ed. Linworth 2010 xxviii, 149p pa $45 *

Grades: Adult Professional   **025.1**

1. School libraries 2. Instructional materials centers 3. School superintendents and principals

ISBN 978-1-58683-526-2 (pa); 1-58683-526-2 (pa); 978-1-58683-527-9 (ebook)   LC 2010-21243

First published 2005

Includes CD-ROM. Contact publisher for ebook pricing

"With focused and well-organized topics from understanding the research and standards to supporting and sustaining them through collaborative processes, this . . . offers a great deal of concrete information. . . . This book gives administrators a clear idea of what is required in the media center and the role of the librarian as a specialist. . . . An excellent choice for the professional media specialist's or principal's shelf." SLJ

Includes bibliographical references

School library management; [edited by] Judi Repman and Gail Dickinson. 6th ed. Linworth Pub. 2007 200p il pa $44.95 *

Grades: Adult Professional   **025.1**

1. School libraries 2. Libraries—Administration

ISBN 978-1-58683-296-4; 1-58683-296-4
                                         LC 2006-103468

First published 1987 with title: School library management notebook

"This collection of more than 35 articles written for *Library Media Connection* from 2003 to 2006 is a virtual treasure trove for library media specialists. . . . The book covers the very practical everyday issues such as scheduling and overdues, and also provides invaluable information on data gathering, facilities planning, professional development, the role of the library in the world of standardized testing, the technological future of libraries, and much more." SLJ

Includes bibliographical references

Stueart, Robert D.
Library and information center management. 7th ed. Libraries Unlimited 2007 xxviii, 492p (Library and information science text series) $70; pa $50
Grades: Adult Professional   025.1
1. Libraries—Administration
ISBN 978-1-59158-408-7; 978-1-59158-406-3 (pa)
LC 2007-7922
First published 1977 with title: Library management
This "covers all the essential functions involved in library management. New theories, concepts, and practices currently being developed and used are included. . . . Both novices and veteran managers will find this to be a valuable tool." Booklist
Includes bibliographical references

Tips and other bright ideas for secondary school libraries, volume 3; Sherry York, editor. Linworth Pub. 2006 168p il $36.95
Grades: Adult Professional   025.1
1. High school libraries 2. Libraries—Administration
ISBN 1-58683-210-7; 978-1-58683-210-0
LC 2005-29594
Continues Tips and other bright ideas for school librarians (1991)
"The tips, all from practicing school library media specialists, were collected from Library Media Connection and are categorized into nine sections with a box per section outlining what will be covered. This format is very helpful in locating information quickly and easily. From managing your library and collaborating with teachers to using technology, these tried-and-true tips are well worth the cost of the book." SLJ
Includes bibliographical references

Tips and other bright ideas for secondary school libraries, volume 4; Kate Vande Brake, editor. Linworth 2010 134p pa $35
Grades: Adult Professional   025.1
1. High school libraries 2. Libraries—Administration
ISBN 978-1-58683-418-0   LC 2010-10428
Continues Tips and other bright ideas for school librarians (1991)
The tips included in this book were taken from *Library Media Connection* magazine from 2006-2009. The book "is organized into . . . sections that tackle topics such as managing the library, working with students, collaborating with teachers, teaching research skills, building positive public relations, and using technology." Publisher's note

Toor, Ruth, 1933-
Being indispensable; a school librarian's guide to becoming an invaluable leader; [by] Ruth Toor and Hilda K. Weisburg. American Library Association 2011 170p il pa $42 *
Grades: Adult Professional   025.1
1. School libraries 2. Instructional materials centers 3. Leadership
ISBN 978-0-8389-1065-8; 0-8389-1065-3
LC 2010-14055
This guide helps school librarians understand their roles as leaders in today's school climate and how they

can become invaluable at a time when some librarians are losing their jobs.
"This is a practical, comprehensive guide filled with recommendations and suggestions that are firmly grounded in reality. . . . This is an excellent book to share with a Professional Learning Community of school librarians. It is sure to be a useful resource for personal enrichment and professional development." Voice Youth Advocates
Includes bibliographical references

The **whole** digital library handbook; edited by Diane Kresh for the Council on Library and Information Resources. American Library Association 2007 416p il pa $55
Grades: Adult Professional   025.1
1. Digital libraries
ISBN 978-0-8389-0926-3; 0-8389-0926-4
LC 2006-27498
"Part 1 defines the digital library, e-reference, and the digital library federation. Additional parts cover users, tools, operations, and more. Besides librarians, other experts and commentators on the various technologies present their views on topics ranging from Google's digital book project, to interpretations of NextGen demographic data, to digital preservation. . . . [This] should engender raucous discussions and debates." Booklist
Includes bibliographical references

025.17   Administration of collections of special materials

No shelf required; e-books in libraries; edited by Sue Polanka. American Library Association 2011 182p pa $65 *
Grades: Adult Professional   025.17
1. Electronic books
ISBN 978-0-83891-054-2   LC 2010-14045
"Following a chapter on e-book history are chapters discussing e-books and students' learning; e-books in school, public, and academic libraries; and e-book acquisitions and management. . . . An essential guide to a topic of high importance." Booklist
Includes bibliographical references

025.2   Acquisitions and collection development

Alabaster, Carol
Developing an outstanding core collection; a guide for libraries. 2nd ed. American Library Association 2010 191p il pa $60 *
Grades: Adult Professional   025.2
1. Libraries—Collection development
ISBN 978-0-8389-1040-5   LC 2009-40342
Also available ebook edition $50 and as print/ebook bundle $70
First published 2002
The author suggests "that the general public needs materials beyond current best-sellers and ready-reference works; that those materials should be high-quality, enduring pieces; and that librarians are the best persons to de-

Alabaster, Carol—*Continued*
cide what constitutes appropriate core collections for
their communities. . . . [She also] addresses the technological changes that drastically affect reading habits and
our ability to satisfy the needs of 'the people's university.' . . . [This book is] required reading for all those
charged with the task of adult collection development."
Booklist
Includes bibliographical references

Baumbach, Donna
Less is more; a practical guide to weeding
school library collections. American Library
Association 2006 194p il pa $32 *
Grades: Adult Professional   **025.2**
  1. Libraries—Collection development
  ISBN 978-0-8389-0919-5; 0-8389-0919-1
                      LC 2006-7490
  Contents: The role of weeding in collection develop-
ment (why less is more); General weeding guidelines;
Getting started and keeping on keeping on; Weeding
criteria by topic and Dewey number; What automation
hath wrought; What's next?
  "This outstanding, easy-to-use guide makes weeding
realistic and achievable. . . . This is an indispensable resource for every school library." Booklist
  Includes bibliographical references

Brenner, Robin E., 1977-
Understanding manga and anime. Libraries
Unlimited 2007 335p il pa $40 *
Grades: Adult Professional   **025.2**
  1. Manga—Study and teaching 2. Anime
3. Libraries—Special collections—Graphic novels
4. Libraries—Collection development
  ISBN 978-1-59158-332-5; 1-59158-332-2
                      LC 2007-9773
  Contents: Short history of manga and anime; Manga
and anime vocabulary; Culture clash: East meets West;
Adventures with ninjas and schoolgirls: humor and realism; Samurai and shogun: action, war, and historical fiction; Giant robots and nature spirits: science fiction, fantasy, and legends; Understanding fans and fan culture;
Draw in a crowd: promotion and programs; Collection
development
  The author "provides thorough explanations of manga
and anime vocabulary, potential censorship issues because of cultural disparities, and typical Manga conventions. . . . No professional collection could possibly be
complete without this all-inclusive and exceptional
work." Voice Youth Advocates

Doll, Carol Ann
Managing and analyzing your collection; a
practical guide for small libraries and school
media centers; [by] Carol A. Doll, Pamela Petrick
Barron. American Library Association 2002 93p il
pa $30 *
Grades: Adult Professional   **025.2**
  1. Libraries—Collection development
  ISBN 0-8389-0821-7   LC 2001-53747

This guide to collection development is divided into
chapters covering management objectives, gathering and
analyzing collection data, and weeding
  This is a "book that librarians will actually read from
cover to cover. . . . [It] isn't overwhelming and technical. Instead, it is rather chatty with solid, useful information." Book Rep
  Includes bibliographical references

Gallaway, Beth, 1975-
Game on! gaming at the library. Neal-Schuman
Publishers 2009 306p il pa $55 *
Grades: Adult Professional   **025.2**
  1. Libraries—Special collections 2. Video games
  ISBN 978-1-55570-595-4; 1-55570-595-2
                    LC 2009-14110
  "An essential guide for any librarian who plans on
embracing the video-game phenomenon, or at the very
least, understanding it. . . . [The chapters] are well organized and contain an abundance of practical information.
The sections on selection, collection, and circulation of
video games include relevant advice on policy, cataloging, marketing, storage, and displays. . . . The annotated
list of video games for a core collection is wonderful for
selection purposes." SLJ
  Includes bibliographical references

Goldsmith, Francisca
Graphic novels now; building, managing, and
marketing a dynamic collection. American Library
Association 2005 113p il $35
Grades: Adult Professional   **025.2**
  1. Libraries—Special collections—Graphic novels
  ISBN 0-8389-0904-3   LC 2005-12653
  This book begins with a "theoretical discussion of
graphic novels: an illustrative definition . . . ; a brief but
informative history of the format; and a number of well-
reasoned arguments for bringing the genre into library
collections. The latter half of the book provides many
concrete suggestions for creating, maintaining, promoting, and defending a graphic-novel collection." SLJ
  Includes bibliographical references

The readers' advisory guide to graphic novels.
American Library Association 2010 124p (ALA
readers' advisory series) pa $45
Grades: Adult Professional   **025.2**
  1. Libraries—Special collections—Graphic novels
  2. Graphic novels—Bibliography
  ISBN 978-0-8389-1008-5; 0-8389-1008-4
                    LC 2009-25239
  "After dispelling the two main myths that ghettoize
graphic novels—they are just for adolescents and they
are far less complex than texts without pictures—Goldsmith emphasizes that GNs are a format and not a genre.
She suggests active and passive ways to offer readers'
advisory (RA) from face-to-face encounters with patrons
to book displays and book groups and offers guidance on
helping established GN readers to find new titles they
might enjoy. . . . All in all it is a valuable and quite
readable resource that belongs in every library's professional collection." Voice Youth Advocates
  Includes glossary and bibliographical references

Graphic novels beyond the basics; insights and issues for libraries; Martha Cornog and Timothy Perper, editors. Libraries Unlimited 2009 xxx, 281p il pa $45
Grades: Adult Professional   **025.2**
1. Libraries—Special collections—Graphic novels 2. Graphic novels—History and criticism 3. Comic books, strips, etc.—History and criticism
ISBN 978-1-59158-478-0; 1-59158-478-7
           LC 2009-16189
Editors Cornog and Perper have collected essays by experts Robin Brenner, Francisca Goldsmith, Trina Robbins, Michael R. Lavin, Gilles Poitras, Lorena O'English, Michael Niederhausen, Erin Byrne, and Cornog herself, all about graphic novels in libraries. Topics covered range from the appeal of superheroes to manga, the appeal of comics to women and girls, anime, independent comics, dealing with challenges to the material, and more. Appendices provide resource information on African American-interest graphic novels, Latino-Interest graphic novels, LGBT-interest graphic novels, religious-themed graphic novels, a bibliography of books about graphic novels in libraries, and online resources.
"Whether you are serious about the genre, interested in the history, or looking for ammunition, this book should be on your shelf. The wealth of knowledge and research that went into these essays is impressive, and reading this book will put you on the road to becoming an expert." Libr Media Connect
Includes bibliographical references

Greiner, Tony
Analyzing library collection use with Excel. American Library Association 2007 167p il pa $40 *
Grades: Adult Professional   **025.2**
1. Library circulation 2. Libraries—Collection development 3. Excel (Computer program)
ISBN 978-0-8389-0933-1; 0-8389-0933-7
           LC 2006-101539
The authors "show how to use Excel® to translate circulation and collection data into meaningful reports for making collection management decisions." Publisher's note
Includes bibliographical references

Hughes-Hassell, Sandra
Collection management for youth; responding to the needs of learners; [by] Sandra Hughes-Hassell, Jacqueline C. Mancall. ALA Editions 2005 103p il pa $35
Grades: Adult Professional   **025.2**
1. Libraries—Collection development 2. Instructional materials centers
ISBN 0-8389-0894-2   LC 2004-26911
"The authors present 11 . . . tools for creating a learner-centered collection with suggestions on the best methods for easy implementation of these procedures. . . . Every library media specialist wanting a more practical approach to collection management would find this book an important addition to his or her professional development library." Libr Media Connect
Includes bibliographical references

Intellectual freedom manual; compiled by the Office for Intellectual Freedom of the American Library Association. 8th ed. American Library Association 2010 xxii, 439p pa $65 *
Grades: Adult Professional   **025.2**
1. Intellectual freedom 2. Libraries—Censorship
ISBN 978-0-8389-3590-3; 0-8389-3590-7
           LC 2010-16157
First published 1974
This guide to preserving intellectual freedom includes: ALA interpretations to the Library Bill of Rights; recommendations for special libraries and specific situations; information about legal decisions affecting school and public libraries; and a section on RFID in Libraries.
"All libraries should have a copy of this book to use when writing or revising policies; indispensable." Libr J
Includes bibliographical references

Loertscher, David V., 1940-
Collection development using the collection mapping technique; a guide for librarians; [by] David V. Loertscher, Laura H. Wimberley. Hi Willow Research and Pub. 2009 122p il pa $30 *
Grades: Adult Professional   **025.2**
1. Libraries—Collection development
ISBN 978-1-933170-43-5
This is "a how-to manual for media specialists to formulate and implement a collection development plan based on a collection map. This book is an excellent resource for every novice or veteran media specialist building a collection for 21st century users." Libr Media Connect
Includes bibliographical references

Lukenbill, W. Bernard
Community resources in the school library media center; concepts and methods; [by] W. Bernard Lukenbill. Libraries Unlimited 2004 195p il $45
Grades: Adult Professional   **025.2**
1. School libraries 2. Libraries and community
ISBN 978-1-59158-110-9; 1-59158-110-9
           LC 2004-48926
"This text outlines organizational strategies for managing community resources. . . . Lukenbill includes information such as agency directories, telementoring numbers, historical documents, museum exhibits, photos, and volunteer pools. Expanding the concept of the vertical file, the author presents ideas for developing, managing, marketing, and accessing electronic photo archives, Web site links, school documents, and bulletin boards. One chapter addresses sensitive community information, censorship, privacy, and terrorism concerns. . . . A definitive tool for developing community-resource collections." SLJ

Mayer, Brian
Libraries got game; aligned learning through modern board games; [by] Brian Mayer and Christopher Harris. American Library Association 2010 134p il pa $45
Grades: Adult Professional   025.2
1. Libraries—Special collections 2. Board games
ISBN 978-0-8389-1009-2; 0-8389-1009-2
LC 2009-26839
"This is a valuable resource for K-12 librarians interested in building curriculum-aligned 'designer' game collections. The authors . . . explain how specific games enhance language-arts, social-studies, and math units, and build literacy skills. The two chapters devoted to promoting and justifying the inclusion of games in the library are well documented and a wonderful source to have to convince skeptical administrators. Suggestions for building a core collection, which highlights top recommended games for elementary school, middle school, and high school; a list of game publishers; a list of games discussed; and a glossary of terminology are included." SLJ
Includes bibliographical references

Reichman, Henry, 1947-
Censorship and selection; issues and answers for schools. 3rd ed. American Library Association 2001 223p pa $37 *
Grades: Adult Professional   025.2
1. Censorship 2. School libraries 3. Academic freedom
ISBN 0-8389-0798-9   LC 00-67657
First published 1988
The author "covers the different media (including books, school newspapers, and the Internet), the important court cases (including recent litigations involving Harry Potter, the Internet, and Huck Finn), the issues in dispute (including violence, religion, and profanity), and how the laws on the books can be incorporated into selection policies." Publisher's note
"Reichman's manual provides sound practical advice on how to handle this complex and emotionally charged subject." Voice Youth Advocates
Includes bibliographical references

Scales, Pat R.
Protecting intellectual freedom in your school library; scenarios from the front lines; [by] Pat R. Scales for the Office for Intellectual Freedom. American Library Association 2009 148p (Intellectual freedom front lines) pa $55 *
Grades: Adult Professional   025.2
1. School libraries 2. Intellectual freedom
ISBN 978-0-8389-3581-1; 0-8389-3581-8
LC 2008-39893
"Scales uses court opinions, federal and state laws, and ALA documents to offer solutions for responding to infringements. A broad range of potential scenarios—from challenges to materials in both the library and the classroom, the legality of film rating systems, using computerized reading programs as selection tools and labeling books by reading levels, policies for interlibrary loans and reserves to confidentiality of children's and teens' circulation records—are covered. . . . This resource should be in every school library's professional collection." Voice Youth Advocates
Includes bibliographical references

Symons, Ann K.
Protecting the right to read; a how-to-do-it manual for school and public librarians; [by] Ann K. Symons, Charles Harmon; illustrations by Pat Race. Neal-Schuman 1995 211p il (How-to-do-it manuals for librarians) pa $55
Grades: Adult Professional   025.2
1. Libraries—Censorship 2. Intellectual freedom
ISBN 1-55570-216-3   LC 95-42444
"The authors take readers from discussion of the policies and principles of intellectual freedom to considerations specific to school and public libraries to the protection of freedom on the Internet. . . . Appendixes consist of reprints of documents put out by the ALA and the Minnesota Coalition Against Censorship." Book Rep
"Intellectual freedom issues and guiding principles get a thorough and comprehensive treatment. . . . An essential book." Voice Youth Advocates
Includes bibliographical references

Walker, Barbara J.
The librarian's guide to developing Christian fiction collections for young adults. Neal-Schuman Publishers 2005 200p (The librarian's guides to developing Christian fiction collections) pa $55 *
Grades: Adult Professional   025.2
1. Reference books 2. Libraries—Special collections 3. Christian fiction—Bibliography 4. Teenagers—Books and reading
ISBN 1-55570-545-6   LC 2005-5112
The author discusses issues "such as censorship, the legalities in spending tax dollars on Christian novels, and marketing to an underserved clientele. 'Key Book Titles' offers an extensive, annotated bibliography, organized by topic (Apocalyptic, Bible, Contemporary, Fantasy, Historical, Mystery, Romance, Thrillers, Westerns). . . . A thorough, balanced approach." SLJ
Includes bibliographical references

025.3   Bibliographic analysis and control

Byrne, Deborah J.
MARC manual; understanding and using MARC records. 2nd ed. Libraries Unlimited 1998 xxiii, 263p pa $45
Grades: Adult Professional   025.3
1. MARC formats 2. Cataloging
ISBN 1-56308-176-8   LC 97-35961
First published 1991
This handbook explains the 3 types of MARC records: bibliographic, author, and holdings. MARC database processing and online systems are discussed.
Includes bibliographical references

Intner, Sheila S., 1935-
Standard cataloging for school and public libraries; [by] Sheila S. Intner and Jean Weihs. 4th ed. Libraries Unlimited 2007 286p il pa $50 *
Grades: Adult Professional   **025.3**
1. Cataloging 2. Library classification
ISBN 978-1-59158-378-3; 1-59158-378-0
                                LC 2007-9009
First published 1990
This explains the Anglo-American Cataloging Rules (AACR2), Sears and Library of Congress subject headings, Dewey decimal and Library of Congress classification systems, MARC format, large computer networks, policy manuals, and how to manage a cataloging department.
Includes bibliographical references

Oliver, Chris
Introducing RDA; a guide to the basics. American Library Association 2010 117p il pa $45 *
Grades: Adult Professional   **025.3**
1. Anglo-American cataloguing rules 2. Cataloging
ISBN 978-0-8389-3594-1   LC 2010-21719
"ALA Editions special reports"
Practical advice for catalogers and library administrators on how to make the transition from the Anglo-American cataloging rules (AACR) to Resource description and access (RDA).
This is "a useful guide that provides a clear explanation of what RDA is all about. . . . Highly recommended for novice and experienced catalogers." Libr J
Includes bibliographical references

025.4   Subject analysis and control

Sears list of subject headings; Joseph Miller, editor; Susan McCarthy, associate editor. 20th ed. H.W. Wilson Co. 2010 liii, 847p $150 *
Grades: Adult Professional   **025.4**
1. Subject headings 2. Reference books
ISBN 978-0-8242-1105-9; 0-8242-1105-7
                                LC 2010-5731
Also available Canadian companion. 6th edition published 2001
First published 1923 with title: List of subject headings for small libraries, by Minnie Earl Sears
"The Sears List of Subject Headings delivers a core list of key headings, together with patterns and examples to guide the cataloger in creating additional headings as required. It features: agreement with the Dewey Decimal Classification system to ensure that subject headings conform with library standards; [a] thesaurus-like format; accompanying list of canceled and replacement headings; and legends within the list that identify earlier forms of headings; scope notes accompanying . . . headings where clarification of the specialized use of a term may be required." Publisher's note
Includes bibliographical references

025.5   Services for users

Bell, Suzanne S.
Librarian's guide to online searching. 2nd ed. Libraries Unlimited 2009 287p il pa $45
Grades: Adult Professional   **025.5**
1. Internet searching
ISBN 978-1-59158-763-7; 1-59158-763-8
                                LC 2008-35924
First published 2006
This "online searching guide will be invaluable to anyone starting out or looking for a refresher course on this topic. In clear concise language, the author covers everything from Boolean searching to using specific topic-based databases. . . . This easy-to-use manual, written with just a touch of humor and not a drop of condescension, is sure to be embraced by librarians of all skill levels." Voice Youth Advocates
Includes bibliographical references

Developing an information literacy program, K-12; a how-to-do-it manual and CD-ROM package; developed by the Iowa City Community School District; edited by Mary Jo Langhorne. 2nd ed. Neal-Schuman 2004 432p (How-to-do-it manuals for librarians) pa $89.95
Grades: Adult Professional   **025.5**
1. Bibliographic instruction 2. School libraries 3. Library information networks
ISBN 1-55570-509-X   LC 2004-46046
First published 1998
"Over twenty lessons . . . cover keyword research, library and library materials organization, using nonfiction books, using the library catalog, using online databases, using the Internet, note-taking, creating bibliographies, and more. You will also find planning and assessment forms, checklists, tables, and worksheets for developing, implementing, and instructing your information literacy programs—all reproduced in the book and accompanying CD-ROM." Publisher's note

Ercegovac, Zorana, 1947-
Information literacy; search strategies, tools & resources for high school students and college freshmen. 2nd ed. Linworth Pub. 2008 xxi, 186p pa $44.95
Grades: Adult Professional   **025.5**
1. Information literacy 2. Libraries and students 3. Report writing
ISBN 978-1-58683-332-9; 1-58683-332-4
                                LC 2008-1893
First published 2001
Contents: Introduction to basic research skills; Finding search words; Search strategies; Fact finding: words, concepts, events, places; Fact finding: people, reviews, criticism; Finding works in library collections; Searching & evaluating internet sources; Finding magazine and newspaper articles; Citing in style and summarizing
"This book is a great tool to help . . . [media specialists] build the next generation." Libr Media Connect
Includes bibliographical references

Farkas, Meredith, 1977-

Social software in libraries; building collaboration, communication, and community online. Information Today, Inc. 2007 xxiv, 320p il pa $39.50 *

Grades: Adult Professional **025.5**
1. Libraries and community 2. Telecommunication 3. Information technology
ISBN 978-1-57387-275-1   LC 2007-4515
This "guide provides librarians with the information and skills necessary to implement the most popular and effective social software technologies: blogs, RSS, wikis, social networking software, screencasting, photo-sharing, podcasting, instant messaging, gaming, and more." Publisher's note
Includes bibliographical references

George, Mary W., 1948-

The elements of library research; what every student needs to know. Princeton University Press 2008 201p il pa $14.95 *

Grades: 10 11 12 Adult **025.5**
1. Research 2. Bibliographic instruction
ISBN 978-0-691-13857-2   LC 2008-13733
This guide to library research "covers how to determine a topic, how to figure out what information to look for, and how to put it all together." Univ Press Books for Public and Second Sch Libr, 2009
This "is a very useful tool for students struggling to identify a topic for a term paper, and it effectively frames the subsequent information gathering as a challenging but fun treasure hunt." Ref & User Services Quarterly
Includes bibliographical references

Grassian, Esther Stampfer

Information literacy instruction; theory and practice; [by] Esther S. Grassian and Joan R. Kaplowitz. 2nd ed. Neal-Schuman Publishers 2009 xxvii, 412p pa $75

Grades: Adult Professional **025.5**
1. Information literacy
ISBN 978-155570-666-1; 1-55570-666-5
LC 2009-23647
First published 2001
This "is designed for anyone involved in the creation and management of information literacy programming. Sixteen well-written chapters, organized into five sections, provide both theory and practical applications, with the emphasis on the practical. . . . Several extras appear in the accompanying CD-ROM. . . . A timely, thorough, and endlessly useful must-have title for librarians, teaching librarians, and library schools." Booklist
Includes bibliographical references

Hernon, Peter, 1944-

Assessing service quality; satisfying the expectations of library customers; [by] Peter Hernon + Ellen Altman. 2nd ed. American Library Association 2010 206p il pa $65

Grades: Adult Professional **025.5**
1. Library services 2. Libraries—Public relations
ISBN 978-0-8389-1021-4; 0-8389-1021-1
LC 2009-40332
First published 1998
The authors "concentrate on how to assess service quality and customer satisfaction. Here they suggest . . . ways to think about library services, clarify the distinction between service quality and customer satisfaction, present strategies for developing a customer service plan, identify procedures to measure service quality and satisfaction, and . . . challenge conventional thinking about these powerful principles. . . . Kudos to these authors for providing an essential resource for librarians who understand that folks who walk into their libraries are not patrons but customers." Libr J
Includes bibliographical references

Kern, M. Kathleen

Virtual reference best practices; tailoring services to your library. American Library Association 2009 148p il pa $50 *

Grades: Adult Professional **025.5**
1. Reference services (Libraries)
ISBN 978-0-8389-0975-1   LC 2008-15379
The author "offers advice and assistance for libraries considering VR. . . . Kern's guidebook includes useful forms and exercises for every aspect of the VR process from a market assessment of the library's community served to an evaluation of the service. . . . Even those [libraries] which already offer virtual reference will find assistance and suggestions to improve their services." Voice Youth Advocates
Includes bibliographical references

Lanning, Scott

Essential reference services for today's school media specialists; [by] Scott Lanning and John Bryner. 2nd ed. Libraries Unlimited 2010 141p il pa $45

Grades: Adult Professional **025.5**
1. Reference services (Libraries) 2. School libraries
ISBN 978-1-59158-883-2; 1-59158-883-9
LC 2009-39375
"The content focuses on core reference skills, electronic resources, and leadership. The first few chapters discuss information literacy, evaluation of resources, the role of print resources, and the reference interview. These are followed by chapters on the library catalog, electronic resources, and the Web as a reference tool. Finally, there are several chapters dealing with the teacher-librarians' instructional and leadership roles. The authors use a very accessible tone while providing the basics." Booklist
Includes bibliographical references

Lenburg, Jeff
The Facts on File guide to research. 2nd ed.
Facts on File 2010 xxxvi, 720p (Facts on File
library of language and literature) $50; pa $18.95
Grades: 8 9 10 11 12   **025.5**
 1. Research 2. Information resources
 ISBN   978-0-8160-8121-9;   0-8160-8121-2;
 978-0-8160-8122-6 (pa); 0-8160-8122-0 (pa)
                                  LC 2009-48200
 First published 2005
This guide includes "lists of thousands of resources
and explains general research methods and proper citation of sources. . . . [It features] discussions of Google
and other search engines, subject-specific keyword search
strategies, a cautionary note about Wikipedia, and . . .
more." Publisher's note
 Includes bibliographical references

Saricks, Joyce G.
The readers' advisory guide to genre fiction.
2nd ed. American Library Association 2009 352p
(ALA readers' advisory series) pa $65
Grades: Adult Professional   **025.5**
 1. Reference services (Libraries) 2. Fiction—Bibliogra-
 phy
 ISBN 978-0-8389-0989-8   LC 2008-51029
 First published 2001
 Contents: Understanding the appeal of genre fiction;
 Adventure; Romantic suspense; Suspense; Thrillers; Gentle reads; Horror; Romance; Women's lives and relationships; Literary fiction; Mysteries; Psychological suspense;
 Science fiction; Fantasy; Historical fiction; Westerns
 "Each section includes three or four specific genres
 . . . and features a definition and introduction to the
 genre, the characteristics of the genre's appeal, suggested
 authors and titles, and other practical information. Well-
 crafted back matter add to the ease of navigation. This
 very readable text employs a playful tone that reflects
 Saricks's love of her work and will inspire readers to use
 RA techniques in a variety of ways. [This is] a useful
 tool for both new library employees and established practitioners." Voice Youth Advocates
 Includes bibliographical references

Smith, Susan S.
Web-based instruction; a guide for libraries; [by]
Susan Sharpless Smith. 3rd ed. American Library
Association 2010 236p il pa $65 *
Grades: Adult Professional   **025.5**
 1. Bibliographic instruction 2. Computer-assisted in-
 struction 3. Web sites—Design 4. Library information
 networks
 ISBN 978-0-8389-1056-6; 0-8389-1056-4
                                  LC 2010-6452
 First published 2001
This book covers "tools and trends, including current
browsers, access methods, hardware, and software. [The
author] also supplies tips to secure project funding and
provides strategic guidance for all types of libraries."
Publisher's note
 Includes bibliographical references

Spratford, Becky Siegel
The horror readers' advisory; the librarian's
guide to vampires, killer tomatoes, and haunted
houses; [by] Becky Siegel Spratford [and] Tammy
Hennigh Clausen. American Library Association
2004 161p il (ALA readers' advisory series) pa
$36
Grades: Adult Professional   **025.5**
 1. Horror fiction—History and criticism 2. Reference
 services (Libraries)
 ISBN 0-8389-0871-3   LC 2003-25530
This is a "guide to horror fiction, explaining its appeal
and advising on how librarians unfamiliar with the genre
can broaden their own knowledge and build a viable collection. The text briefly outlines the characteristics of the
main categories, or subgenres, including the usual monsters and occult creatures; extreme suspense of all types;
hauntings and possession; and a section on classic works
of horror, along with tips for interviewing readers of
each subgenre. . . . [This] small, helpful book will be a
boon to readers' advisors needing fresh meat for horror
fans." Libr J
 Includes bibliographical references

Tallman, Julie I., 1944-
Making the writing and research connection
with the I-search process; a how-to-do-it manual;
[by] Julie I. Tallman, Marilyn Z. Joyce. 2nd ed.
Neal-Schuman Publishers 2006 xx, 167p il
(How-to-do-it manuals for librarians) pa $55
Grades: Adult Professional   **025.5**
 1. Bibliographic instruction 2. Young adults' libraries
 3. Research 4. Report writing
 ISBN 1-55570-534-0; 978-1-55570-534-3
                                  LC 2005-32473
 First published 1997
 Joyce's name appears first on the earlier edition
This volume "covers the I-Search process for middle
and high-school students and . . . includes a detailed explanation of I-Search in the context of content units. Although it is useful for the media specialist and teacher
who are familiar with I-Search, novices will also find
valuable information. . . . The accompanying CD-ROM
contains all of the figures found in the book (templates,
handouts, etc.), which can be reproduced and adapted."
Booklist
 Includes bibliographical references

Virtual reference on a budget; case studies;
editors, Teresa Dalston and Michael Pullin.
Linworth Pub. 2008 xx, 191p il pa $39.95
Grades: Adult Professional   **025.5**
 1. Reference services (Libraries)
 ISBN 1-58683-287-5; 978-1-58683-287-2
                                  LC 2007-25987
"Librarians searching for step-by-step guidance on
how to implement virtual reference service will find explicit instructions and many examples in this slim but
dense volume. The overview of the history of digital reference provides an excellent introduction to the topic,
along with definitions of terms, and also offers detailed
case studies from middle school, high school, academic,
and deaf community settings." Voice Youth Advocates
 Includes bibliographical references

Virtual reference service; from competencies to assessment; edited by R. David Lankes . . . [et al.] Neal-Schuman Publishers 2008 206p il (Virtual reference desk series) $75

Grades: Adult Professional   025.5
1. Reference services (Libraries)
ISBN 978-1-55570-528-2   LC 2007-24104

"Featuring essays from the 2005 7th Annual Virtual Reference Desk Conference, this book focuses on the evolving aspects of virtual reference theory, research, and practice. . . . The topics explored include the implementation and expansion of virtual reference programs, and the training and assessment that is necessary to ensure the success of these services. . . . This is a valuable resource for library practitioners involved with reference services." Am Ref Books Annu, 2008

Includes bibliographical references

Volkman, John D.
Collaborative library research projects; inquiry that stimulates the senses. Libraries Unlimited 2008 196p il pa $39 *

Grades: Adult Professional   025.5
1. School libraries 2. Instructional materials centers 3. Bibliographic instruction
ISBN 978-1-59158-623-4; 1-59158-623-2
    LC 2008-640

"This book provides helpful advice in an area central to the mission of school media specialists everywhere—collaboration with teachers. In clear, jargon-free language, Volkman lays out an argument for using his style of collaborative research units. . . . Units on history, literature, science, and other topics are covered. Planning, preparation, and station construction methods are discussed concisely. . . . Volkman's accessible writing provides a well-thought-out, no-nonsense book that will be useful to the novice or experienced school media specialist." Voice Youth Advocates

Includes bibliographical references

Woodward, Jeannette A.
What every librarian should know about electronic privacy. Libraries Unlimited 2007 222p pa $40 *

Grades: Adult Professional   025.5
1. Right of privacy 2. Computer security 3. Internet—Security measures 4. Libraries—Security measures
ISBN 978-1-59158-489-6; 1-59158-489-2
    LC 2007-13566

Contents: Portrait of a library computer user; Protecting library users from identity theft; Privacy threats from the business world; Protecting children and teenagers; Government surveillance, data mining, and just plain carelessness; RFID systems in libraries; The challenge of library records: what to keep and how long to keep it; The Patriot Act quandary: obeying the law and protecting library users; Protecting electronic privacy: a step-by-step plan; Education and advocacy

"Beginning with a breakdown of the types of library clients and their often blasé attitude toward Internet privacy and security, author Jeannette Woodward then proceeds to use those client types as examples for real-world impact of how privacy could be an issue to librarians.

". . . Well written and well researched, this book certainly lives up to its title." Libr Media Connect

Includes bibliographical references

Wyatt, Neal
The readers' advisory guide to nonfiction. American Library Association 2007 318p (ALA reader's advisory series) pa $48

Grades: Adult Professional   025.5
1. Reference services (Libraries) 2. Public libraries
ISBN 978-0-8389-0936-2; 0-8389-0936-1
    LC 2006-102318

Wyatt "focuses on eight popular categories: history, true crime, true adventure, science, memoir, food/cooking, travel, and sports. Within each, she explains the scope, popularity, style, major authors and works, and the subject's position in readers' advisory interviews. Wyatt addresses who is reading nonfiction and why, while providing RAs with the tools and language to incorporate nonfiction into discussions that point readers to what to read next. . . . [This] guide includes nonfiction bibliography, key authors, benchmark books with annotations, and core collections." Publisher's note

Includes bibliographical references

025.7   Physical preparation for storage and use

Schechter, Abraham A.
Basic book repair methods; illustrated by the author. Libraries Unlimited 1999 102p il pa $37 *

Grades: Adult Professional   025.7
1. Books—Conservation and restoration
ISBN 1-56308-700-6   LC 98-50950

Photographs accompany step-by-step instructions for common preservation techniques, from the cleaning of pages and their readhesion, to case reattachment and rebacking.

Includes bibliographical references

025.8   Maintenance and preservation of collections

Halsted, Deborah D.
Disaster planning; a how-to-do-it manual for librarians with planning templates on CD-ROM. Neal-Schuman Publishers 2005 xx, 247p il (How-to-do-it manuals for librarians) pa $85

Grades: Adult Professional   025.8
1. Disaster relief 2. Accidents—Prevention 3. Library resources—Conservation and restoration
ISBN 1-55570-486-7   LC 2003-65152

Includes CD-ROM

"Step-by-step instructions discuss creating a working disaster team, establishing a communications strategy, identifying relief and recovery agencies, developing response plans, and examining issues of cutting-edge library security. . . . This valuable resource is an important addition to most professional collections." Booklist

Includes bibliographical references

027 General libraries, archives, information centers

The **whole** library handbook 4; current data, professional advice, and curiosa about libraries and library services; edited by George M. Eberhart. American Library Association 2006 585p il map $42

Grades: Adult Professional   **027**
1. Library science 2. Libraries—United States 3. Library services
ISBN 0-8389-0915-9; 978-0-8389-0915-7
                              LC 2005-33619
First published 1991
New edition in preparation

This is an "encyclopedic collection of factual data covering all aspects of the library world, together with readable excerpts from recent books and articles on 'librariana.'" Choice
Includes bibliographical references

027.6 Libraries for special groups and organizations

Alire, Camila
Serving Latino communities; a how-to-do-it manual for librarians; [by] Camila Alire, Jacqueline Ayala. 2nd ed. Neal-Schuman Publishers 2007 229p il (How-to-do-it manuals for librarians) pa $59.95 *
Grades: Adult Professional   **027.6**
1. Libraries and Hispanic Americans
ISBN 978-1-55570-606-7; 1-55570-606-1
                              LC 2007-7783
First published 1998

"The information covered helps library staff understand the needs of their library's Latino community; develop successful programs and services; obtain funding for projects and programs; prepare staff to work more effectively with Latinos; establish partnerships with relevant external agencies and organizations; improve collection development; and perform effective outreach and public relations. . . . There are few resources widely available on this topic and none as complete." Libr Media Connect
Includes bibliographical references

Byrd, Susannah Mississippi, 1971-
Bienvenidos! = Welcome! a handy resource guide for marketing your library to Latinos; foreword by Carol Brey-Casiano. American Library Association 2005 110p il pa $20
Grades: Adult Professional   **027.6**
1. Libraries and Hispanic Americans
ISBN 0-8389-0902-7; 978-0-8389-0902-7
                              LC 2005-6315

This "guide covers everything from survey analysis to access and outreach to collection development, and offers practical solutions and suggestions. . . . Byrd includes resources, services, government agencies, projects, professional organizations, etc., making this title a valuable addition to libraries and organizations that are initiating programs directed toward diverse Latino populations." SLJ
Includes bibliographical references

Lerch, Maureen T.
Serving homeschooled teens and their parents. Libraries Unlimited 2004 242p (Libraries Unlimited professional guides for young adult librarians) pa $39
Grades: Adult Professional   **027.6**
1. Home schooling 2. Young adults' libraries
ISBN 0-313-32052-7   LC 2004-46518

"After introductory chapters that dispel many myths about homeschooling and delve into adolescent psychology, the two experts give sound advice and great examples for service plan creation, collection development, programming, and promotion of services." Libr Media Connect
Includes bibliographical references

Library services to youth of Hispanic heritage; Barbara Immroth and Kathleen de la Peña McCook, editors; assisted by Catherine Jasper. McFarland & Co. 2000 197p pa $42.50 *
Grades: Adult Professional   **027.6**
1. Libraries and Hispanic Americans 2. Young adults' libraries
ISBN 0-7864-0790-5   LC 00-37247

In this "collection of essays, more than 20 experts in the field discuss library programs, collections, planning, and evaluation of services for Hispanic youth." Booklist
Includes bibliographical references

027.62 Libraries for specific age groups

Alessio, Amy
A year of programs for teens. American Library Association 2007 159p il pa $35
Grades: Adult Professional   **027.62**
1. Young adults' libraries 2. Teenagers—Books and reading
ISBN 0-8389-0903-5; 978-0-8389-0903-4
                              LC 2006-13758

"Following an overview of the planning component of successful teen programming, this guide is presented as a calendar of ideas for each month of the year. Each month offers three to four programs with the preparation time, the length of the program, the recommended number of teen participants, age range, a shopping list, the setup required, variations or extra activities, and resources. . . . Librarians working with teens will find plenty of fresh ideas here." Booklist
Includes bibliographical references

Anderson, Sheila B.

Extreme teens; library services to nontraditional young adults. Libraries Unlimited 2005 xxiii, 175p (Libraries Unlimited professional guides for young adult librarians) pa $36

Grades: Adult Professional   **027.62**
1. Young adults' libraries 2. Teenagers—Books and reading
ISBN 1-59158-170-2   LC 2005016076

"This accessible manual offers practical advice on working with 'extreme teens,' young adults who, because of their sexuality, educational circumstances, or living situations, tend to be underserved by traditional public library services. Individual sections discuss definitions of various populations, service specifications for subgroups, collection development, and promotional programs. Additional features include statistics, scenarios, cited sources, and lists of recommended print and electronic resources, both fiction and nonfiction." Booklist

Includes bibliographical references

Braun, Linda W.

Risky business; taking and managing risks in library services for teens; [by] Linda W. Braun, Hillias Jack Martin, and Connie Urquhart for the Young Adult Library Services Association. American Library Association 2010 151p pa $55

Grades: Adult Professional   **027.62**
1. Young adults' libraries 2. Teenagers—Books and reading 3. Libraries—Collection development 4. Risk-taking (Psychology)
ISBN 978-0-8389-3596-5; 0-8389-3596-6
                                      LC 2010-5995

"This thought-provoking title will pique awareness and present some 'ah ha!' moments. It involves a degree of risk to provide exemplary library services to young adults in terms of collection building, programming, and technology. This book encourages librarians to take the necessary risks and describes factors to consider in different situations. . . . Of particular interest are chapters devoted to developing a mature, appealing, high-interest YA collection. This section alone makes the book a worthwhile addition." SLJ

Includes bibliographical references

Technically involved; technology-based youth participation activities for your library. American Library Association 2003 138p il pa $34 *

Grades: Adult Professional   **027.62**
1. Young adults' libraries
ISBN 0-8389-0861-6   LC 2003-12021

In this "title, Braun encourages librarians to involve teens in technology-related activities and projects that will benefit them and others. She responds to questions regarding participation, benefits to patrons and libraries, and training. The author provides numerous suggestions for activities. . . . This excellent volume is a must for libraries with teen groups, and a consideration for those that don't have them." SLJ

Includes bibliographical references

Brehm-Heeger, Paula

Serving urban teens. Libraries Unlimited 2008 229p (Libraries Unlimited professional guides for young adult librarians) pa $40

Grades: Adult Professional   **027.62**
1. Young adults' libraries 2. Teenagers—Books and reading
ISBN 978-1-59158-377-6; 1-59158-377-2
                                      LC 2007-45415

This book "begins with definitions and a brief history of library services to urban teens, followed by a description of issues concerning this special group. The remaining chapters detail every aspect of making positive connections with teens, from training staff—the entire library staff—to making space, developing the collection, designing programs, and developing partnerships within the community. . . . It is not only the mission of libraries but also in their self-interest to capture the minds and hearts of youth while they can. This book provides the tools to accomplish the job." Voice Youth Advocates

Includes bibliographical references

Burek Pierce, Jennifer

Sex, brains, and video games; a librarian's guide to teens in the twenty-first century. American Library Association 2008 130p pa $35

Grades: Adult Professional   **027.62**
1. Young adults' libraries 2. Adolescence 3. Teenagers—United States
ISBN 978-0-8389-0951-5; 0-8389-0951-5
                                      LC 2007-21926

"This guide provides new and reevaluated ideas and insights about the sociological, neurological, emotional, and sexual perspectives of adolescence. The author's purpose is to assist librarians as they try to engage teens through relevant and attractive responses to their recreational, informational, and technological needs and interests. . . . It is filled with a great deal of pertinent and thought-provoking advice and information." SLJ

Includes bibliographical references

Doyle, Miranda, 1972-

101+ great ideas for teen library Web sites. Neal-Schuman Publishers 2007 xx, 307p (Teens @ the library series) pa $65 *

Grades: Adult Professional   **027.62**
1. Web sites 2. Young adults' libraries
ISBN 978-1-55570-593-0; 1-55570-593-6
                                      LC 2006-39132

"The theme is that teens are experienced tech users, and libraries need to make their online presence as inviting and informative as their physical space. To make this happen, Doyle provides excellent, inspiring ideas, many of which involve minimal knowledge or expense. . . . Clearly written and well presented, this book provides a variety of ways to provide interaction with young patrons and visibility for library services." Booklist

Includes bibliographical references

Edwards, Margaret A., 1902-1988
The fair garden and the swarm of beasts; the library and the young adult; foreword by Betty Carter for the Young Adult Library Services Association. Centennial ed. American Lib. Assn. 2002 xxxiii, 206p il pa $20 *
Grades: Adult Professional 027.62
1. Young adults' libraries 2. Books and reading
ISBN 0-8389-3533-8 LC 2002-33276
First published 1969 by Hawthorn Bks.
The author "describes methods of working with young adults, the training of young adult librarians and work in the public schools, and provides information on book selection, book talks and displays." Wis Libr Bull [review of 1969 edition]
"This great librarian's blazing devotion to teens and reading makes her book the classic in the field." Voice Youth Advocates
Includes bibliographical references

Excellence in library services to young adults. 5th ed., edited by Amy Alessio for the Young Adult Library Services Association. Young Adult Library Services Association 2008 144p il pa $30
Grades: Adult Professional 027.62
1. Young adults' libraries
ISBN 978-0-8389-8457-4; 0-8389-8457-6
LC 2008-22359
First published 1994
This book "highlights 25 of the best programs across the country, providing ideas for replicating and adapting them in school and public libraries." Publisher's note
Includes bibliographical references

Flowers, Sarah, 1952-
Young adults deserve the best; YALSA's competencies in action; [by] Sarah Flowers for the Young Adult Library Services Association. American Library Association 2011 126p pa $45
Grades: Adult Professional 027.62
1. Librarians 2. Young adults' libraries
ISBN 978-0-8389-3587-3; 0-8389-3587-7
LC 2010-14148
This "guide to the professional competencies developed by the Young Adult Library Services Association of ALA aims to 'outline the skills, the knowledge, and the philosophy that should be a part of the makeup of every librarian who serves teens.' Flowers begins by elaborating on and demonstrating how to execute the YALSA competencies. From there she discusses how to advocate for a teen-services department when none exists. The final section is a compilation of various resources, including the Library Bill of Rights and ALA interpretations of them with regard to labels and rating systems, Internet activity, ethics, and nonprint materials. . . The information is presented in a clear, concise, and conversational manner, making this resource both easy to navigate and a pleasure to read." SLJ
Includes bibliographical references

Gorman, Michele
Connecting young adults and libraries; a how-to-do-it manual; [by] Michele Gorman and Tricia Suellentrop. 4th ed. Neal-Schuman Publishers Inc. 2009 xxxiii, 450p il (How-to-do-it manuals for librarians) pa $85 *
Grades: Adult Professional 027.62
1. Young adults' libraries 2. Young adult literature—Bibliography 3. Teenagers—Books and reading
ISBN 978-1-55570-665-4 LC 2009-17657
First published 1992 under the authorship of Patrick Jones
"This useful, comprehensive handbook on how to best serve young adult library patrons is a must-have for any librarian's professional library. . . . All key topics are covered here—customer service (affirming the fact that young adults are our customers), information literacy, collection development, booktalking, outreach, programming, technology, and more. Each chapter is well organized and includes background on the topic, suggestions to improve services, useful ideas, advice, sources, and works cited. . . . [This] is an excellent professional resource." Voice Youth Advocates
Includes bibliographical references

Hardesty, Constance
The teen-centered writing club; bringing teens and words together. Libraries Unlimited 2008 174p il (Libraries Unlimited professional guides for young adult librarians) pa $40
Grades: Adult Professional 027.62
1. Young adults' libraries 2. Creative writing 3. English language—Composition and exercises
ISBN 978-1-59158-548-0; 1-59158-548-1
LC 2008-11519
"Hardesty encourages librarians to listen to teens and assist them in their search for identity through the written word. . . . From starting a club and the writing activities to share, to grand finales and how to evaluate the program's effectiveness, the author details all the information needed to create such a club. Particularly useful are chapters on the four roles of facilitators, creating a nonfiction writing club, and how to take your efforts online. Many handouts are included, a boon to any busy librarian. An appendix includes resources for publishing. All this information is laid out in a straightforward, positive manner. An essential resource for planning or presenting writing clubs." SLJ
Includes bibliographical references

Helmrich, Erin, 1972-
Create, relate & pop @ the library; services & programs for teens & tweens; [by] Erin Helmrich and Elizabeth Schneider. Neal-Schuman Publishers 2011 218p il pa $60
Grades: Adult Professional 027.62
1. Young adults' libraries 2. Cultural programs
ISBN 978-1-55570-722-4; 1-55570-722-X
LC 2011-4986
The authors show "how to capitalize on the latest trends—from TV, movies, and music to indie and niche interests—by incorporating them into compelling, creative programs. . . . The book encompasses both tradi-

Helmrich, Erin, 1972-—*Continued*
tional and Web 2.0 participatory programming, offering
. . . ideas, program templates, and step-by-step outlines
of methods, supplies, and resources." Publisher's note
"This is a handy guide." SLJ
Includes bibliographical references

Honnold, RoseMary, 1954-
Get connected; tech programs for teens; [by]
RoseMary Honnold for the Young Adult Library
Services Association. Neal-Schuman Publishers
2007 149p il pa $65
Grades: Adult Professional   **027.62**
1. Young adults' libraries 2. Internet and teenagers
3. Information literacy—Study and teaching
ISBN 978-1-55570-613-5; 1-55570-613-4
                                  LC 2007-12847
This book is "divided into three parts: 'Get Connected
for Fun'; 'Get Connected for Education'; and 'Get Connected for Teen Advisory Groups.' Topics within each
chapter include developing recreation and education-
based programs, working with different populations,
working with teens and social-networking sites, developing and working with TAGs, and introducing ideas for
YALSA's Teen Tech Week. . . . This book is a great
resource for starting Library 2.0 to connect with teens,
whether you are working on your own, with a technology integrator, or within the community." Libr J
Includes bibliographical references

More teen programs that work. Neal-Schuman
Publishers 2005 xxi, 245p il (Teens @ the library
series) $49.95
Grades: Adult Professional   **027.62**
1. Young adults' libraries 2. School libraries—Activity
projects 3. Teenagers—Books and reading
ISBN 1-55570-529-4   LC 2004-19032
Follow-up to: 101+ teen programs that work
Contents: Measuring unmeasurable outcomes; Summer
reading and teen read week; More independent programs;
More craft programs; Book themed programs; Food programs; More parties, games, and lock-ins; Programs for
girls; Programs for boys; Programs for tweens; More
programs for teens and adults and teens and children;
Writing programs; Teens in the spotlight; School and life
skills; Teen volunteer and fund raising projects
"Full of practical and excellent information, this is a
definite choice for any library that wants to expand its
programming for teens." SLJ
Includes bibliographical references

Jones, Ella W.
Start-to-finish YA programs; hip-hop
symposiums, summer reading programs, virtual
tours, poetry slams, teen advisory boards, term
paper clinics, and more! Neal-Schuman Publishers
2009 217p il pa $75
Grades: Adult Professional   **027.62**
1. Cultural programs 2. Young adults' libraries
ISBN 978-1-55570-601-2; 1-55570-601-0
                                  LC 2008-50853
Includes CD-ROM

"Each of the 25 programs includes descriptions, goals,
and a how-to-do it section, complete with book display
and program-evaluation suggestions." SLJ
"Jones's creativity, twenty-five years of experience,
and her genuine love for teenagers is obvious in the meticulous and creative programming ideas and materials.
This valuable resource will be appreciated by librarians
in public and school settings." Voice Youth Advocates
Includes bibliographical references

Kan, Katharine
Sizzling summer reading programs for young
adults; [by] Katharine L. Kan for the Young Adult
Library Services Association. 2nd ed. American
Library Association 2006 110p il pa $30 *
Grades: Adult Professional   **027.62**
1. Young adults' libraries 2. Teenagers—Books and
reading
ISBN 0-8389-3563-X
First published 1998
This "presents more than 50 summer reading programs
that have been used successfully with preteens and
teenagers. . . . Submissions represent a cross section of
themes, incentives, activities and budgets. . . . Children
and young adult services librarians will find a wealth of
practical, hands-on information." Booklist

Koelling, Holly
Classic connections; turning teens on to great
literature. Libraries Unlimited 2004 xxi, 405p
(Libraries Unlimited professional guides for young
adult librarians) pa $40
Grades: Adult Professional   **027.62**
1. Teenagers—Books and reading
ISBN 1-59158-072-2   LC 2004-48644
"The book is divided into two sections: Laying the
Groundwork and Making it Happen. The first section
covers the essential elements that define a book as a
classic, reviews adolescent development and reading habits, and discusses what types of classics have teen appeal.
The second section contains a discussion of collection
development, readers' advisory, programming,
booktalking, and promotion of the classics. . . . It is a
valuable book for anyone trying to connect teens to classic literature." Voice Youth Advocates
Includes bibliographical references

Kunzel, Bonnie Lendermon
The teen-centered book club; readers into
leaders; [by] Bonnie Kunzel and Constance
Hardesty. Libraries Unlimited 2006 xxi, 211p
(Libraries Unlimited professional guides for young
adult librarians) pa $40 *
Grades: Adult Professional   **027.62**
1. Young adults' libraries 2. Book clubs (Discussion
groups) 3. Teenagers—Books and reading
ISBN 1-59158-193-1
"Two experienced youth-services librarians introduce
the idea of teen-centered book clubs. . . . In clear prose
supported by research, the authors cover every aspect of
the program, from assessing the needs of the library and
teens to conducting successful meetings to evaluating activities. . . . An excellent reference." SLJ
Includes bibliographical references

Mahood, Kristine

A passion for print; promoting reading and books to teens. Libraries Unlimited 2006 239p il (Libraries Unlimited professional guides for young adult librarians) pa $40

Grades: Adult Professional   **027.62**
  1. Young adults' libraries 2. Teenagers—Books and reading
  ISBN 1-59158-146-X; 978-1-59158-146-8
                  LC 2006-3716
"Beginning with research on reading, Mahood moves on to merchandising principles; developing teen collections, spaces, and Web sites; and finally to booktalking, readers' advisory, and events scheduling. The author's enthusiasm and experience, coupled with citing current studies, other professional books, articles, and Web sites, make her suggestions appealing and attainable. She provides everything from lists of YA genres to easy design principles for displays to suggestions for questions to ask for better readers' advisory." Booklist

Martin, Hillias J., Jr.

Serving lesbian, gay, bisexual, transgender, and questioning teens; a how-to-do-it manual for librarians; [by] Hillias J. Martin, Jr., James R. Murdock. Neal-Schuman Publishers 2007 267p bibl (How-to-do-it manuals for librarians) pa $55 *

Grades: Adult Professional   **027.62**
  1. Young adults' libraries 2. Gay men 3. Lesbians 4. Transsexualism 5. Bisexuality
  ISBN 978-1-55570-566-4; 1-55570-566-9
                LC 2006-39469
"This volume offers abundant useful guidance not only for reaching the target audience, but also for planning and promoting library services to teens in general. . . . The tone is friendly and largely free of jargon. . . . All librarians should turn to this book for pertinent insight on the needs of 5 to 10 percent of the teen population." SLJ
Includes bibliographical references

Miller, Donna P., 1948-

Crash course in teen services. Libraries Unlimited 2008 128p (Crash course) pa $30 *
Grades: Adult Professional   **027.62**
  1. Young adults' libraries
  ISBN 978-1-59158-565-7; 1-59158-565-1
                LC 2007-32758
"Designed for public librarians new to teen service, the book offers advice on relating to teens and creating teen-friendly space as well as tips on teen-centered reference, collection development, readers' advisory, programming, and 'the three Ps': professional resources, professional development, and public relations." Booklist
Includes bibliographical references

More than MySpace; teens, librarians, and social networking; edited by Robyn M. Lupa. Libraries Unlimited 2009 127p (Libraries Unlimited professional guides for young adult librarians) pa $40

Grades: Adult Professional   **027.62**

  1. Young adults' libraries 2. Social networking
  ISBN 978-1-59158-760-6; 1-59158-760-3
"This book discusses aspects of social networking and ways that librarians can leverage it to address teen needs. . . . The topic is certainly timely, and the book's treatment gives librarians handy tools to start connecting with wired teens." Booklist

Ott, Valerie A.

Teen programs with punch; a month-by-month guide. Libraries Unlimited 2006 282p il (Libraries Unlimited professional guides for young adult librarians) pa $40

Grades: Adult Professional   **027.62**
  1. Young adults' libraries 2. Teenagers—Books and reading
  ISBN 1-59158-293-8   LC 2006012775
"Ott has gathered together less-than-conventional program ideas arranged by month. She provides clear instructions, lists of supplemental materials, promotional ideas, reading lists, costs, and suggested grade levels for each one. For librarians with limited budgets, and who may be pressed for time, there are quick and easy ideas that cost little or no money. . . . Many of the programs are designed to draw underserved populations, such as goths, GLBTQ teens, and vegetarians, into the library. . . . This highly informative guide would make a great addition to any YA librarian's professional collection." SLJ
Includes bibliographical references

Teaching Generation M; a handbook for librarians and educators; edited by Vibiana Bowman Cvetkovic and Robert J. Lackie. Neal-Schuman Publishers 2009 368p il pa $85

Grades: Adult Professional   **027.62**
  1. Young adults' libraries 2. Technology 3. Internet and teenagers 4. Information literacy
  ISBN 978-1-55570-667-8; 1-55570-667-3
                LC 2009-17658
"This professional handbook tackles three important topics—who is the millennial generation, what kind of world do millennials live in, and what can we do to teach them? Chapter topics include media literacy, the information search process, Facebook, YouTube, Google, and Wikipedia, gaming, webcomics, mobile technology, cooperative learning, screencasting, and the new generation of research papers. . . . In-text citations make this book more of a resource than a pleasure read, but it is a must-read for non-M-generation librarians new to young adult services and for those new teachers or anyone wanting to understand Web 2.0." Voice Youth Advocates
Includes bibliographical references

Thinking outside the book; alternatives for today's teen library collections; edited by C. Allen Nichols. Libraries Unlimited 2004 xxvi, 189p il (Libraries Unlimited professional guides for young adult librarians) pa $34

Grades: Adult Professional   **027.62**
  1. Young adults' libraries 2. Audiovisual materials 3. Libraries and students
  ISBN 1-59158-059-5   LC 2003-60592

Thinking outside the book—*Continued*

The editor "believes that more 'alternative' materials need to be added to teen collections. These include magazines, graphic novels, comic books, audiobooks, music, videos, Web sites/on-line collections, and game- and CD-ROM-based reference sources. He provides helpful background information for each format as well as sources for reviews, criteria for selection, issues and obstacles to overcome, suggested titles, and purchasing advice. The [editor] also provides a complete chapter on 'shelving and display options' to entice teens into browsing new materials." Libr Media Connect

Includes bibliographical references

Tuccillo, Diane

Library teen advisory groups; [by] Diane P. Tuccillo. Scarecrow Press 2005 165p il (VOYA guides) pa $29.95 *

Grades: Adult Professional   **027.62**

1. Young adults' libraries 2. Volunteer work

ISBN 0-8108-4982-8   LC 2004-13873

Contents: Why teen advisory boards?; Funding options for your teen library advisory program; Ready, set— get started!; Libraries are not boring: activities, events, and projects that make a difference with teens; Teen representation on adult library boards and other community boards; The perks of being a teen library advisory board member; These groups work!; Schools can have advisory groups, too!

"A comprehensive how-to guide that covers all the bases from theory to practice to nitty-gritty detail." SLJ

Includes bibliographical references

Teen-centered library service; putting youth participation into practice; [by] Diane P. Tuccillo. Libraries Unlimited 2010 xxii, 259p il (Libraries Unlimited professional guides for young adult librarians) pa $45

Grades: Adult Professional   **027.62**

1. Young adults' libraries 2. School libraries

ISBN 978-1-59158-765-1; 1-59158-765-4

LC 2009-45692

This offers "guidelines to YA librarians for getting teens to play a part in their libraries. . . . The book begins with a description of this philosophy and places it into context within the history of YA librarianship. Each chapter then deals with specifics: teen advisory groups, writing and performance ideas, ways to meld teens and technology, ideas for community outreach, ways to combine teen and adult library groups, ideas to involve teens who are only around for limited time, and a chapter on assessing your YA participation. . . . This well-organized title is aimed at public librarians and might also be useful to show administrators how important YA services are to the library as a whole." SLJ

Includes bibliographical references

Urban teens in the library; research and practice; edited by Denise E. Agosto and Sandra Hughes-Hassell. American Library Association 2010 208p bibl il pa $60

Grades: Adult Professional   **027.62**

1. Young adults' libraries 2. Teenagers—Books and reading

ISBN 978-0-8389-1015-3; 0-8389-1015-7

LC 2009-25147

"This work does much to explain who urban teens are and what they need from their libraries. The authors examine the existing research—some of which they have performed—that provides a wealth of data for public and school libraries." SLJ

Includes bibliographical references

Welch, Rollie James, 1957-

The guy-friendly YA library; serving male teens. Libraries Unlimited 2007 xxi, 196p (Libraries Unlimited professional guides for young adult librarians) pa $40

Grades: Adult Professional   **027.62**

1. Young adults' libraries 2. Boys—Books and reading
3. Teenagers—Books and reading

ISBN 978-1-59158-270-0; 1-59158-270-9

LC 2006-102882

"The first chapter offers key components for quality service for teen males, while the second chapter explains the characteristics and developmental issues of this population. The book emphasizes reading, with three chapters dedicated to male teen reading habits, topics of interest, and detailed genre coverage. . . . The sixth chapter deals with programming and also explains how the establish an effective teen advisory board. . . . The seventh chapter covers school visits and emphasizes the importance of booktalks. The eighth chapter discusses creating a teen area in the library." Booklist

Includes bibliographical references

027.8   School libraries

Adams, Helen R., 1943-

Ensuring intellectual freedom and access to information in the school library media program. Libraries Unlimited 2008 xxi, 254p il map pa $40 *

Grades: Adult Professional   **027.8**

1. School libraries 2. Censorship 3. Freedom of information

ISBN 978-1-59158-539-8; 1-59158-539-2

LC 2008-16753

This is "an extremely helpful guide for dealing with intellectual-freedom and information-access issues. In chapters geared to school situations and covering topics including selection of resources, the First Amendment, privacy, challenges to resources, the Internet, and access for students with disabilities, Adams offers background on the topic and bulleted lists of strategies for dealing with the issue. . . . This is a book that every school librarian needs to keep handy and share with administrators, colleagues, and parents." Booklist

Includes bibliographical references

American Association of School Librarians

Information power; building partnerships for learning; prepared by the American Association of School Librarians [and] Association for Educational Communications and Technology. American Library Association 1998 205p il pa $42 *

Grades: Adult Professional   **027.8**
1. School libraries 2. Instructional materials centers
ISBN 978-0-8389-3470-8; 0-8389-3470-6
                                        LC 98-23291
First published 1988
This resource "relates the library-media program to the entire educational infrastructure. The authors explicate their themes in terms of standards, indicators, levels of proficiency, goals, principles, and examples of student activities. The appendixes contain essential information on Library Power, AASL's ICON-nect project, the Library Bill of Rights, confidentiality, censorship, access equity, and ethics." SLJ
Includes bibliographical references

Baule, Steven M., 1966-

Facilities planning for school library and technology centers. 2nd ed. Linworth Pub. 2007 134p il pa $39.95
Grades: Adult Professional   **027.8**
1. Instructional materials centers—Design and construction 2. School libraries—Design and construction
ISBN 978-1-58683-294-0; 1-58683-294-8
                                        LC 2006-34179
First published 1992
The author "provides information on how to put together a planning team; how to perform a needs assessment for the library media center or technology lab; how to create bid documents and specification charts; how to develop time lines; and how to plan to move into the new facility once construction is complete. . . . Anyone who is going to build or renovate a facility will want this book." Booklist
Includes bibliographical references

Bishop, Kay, 1942-

The collection program in schools; concepts, practices, and information sources. 4th ed. Libraries Unlimited 2007 xx, 269p il (Library and information science text series) $65; pa $50 *
Grades: Adult Professional   **027.8**
1. School libraries 2. Libraries—Collection development
ISBN   978-1-59158-583-1;   1-59158-583-X; 978-1-59158-360-8 (pa); 1-59158-360-8 (pa)
                                        LC 2007-9005
First published 1988 under the authorship of Phyllis J. Van Orden
Contents: The collection; Collection development; Community analysis and needs assessment; The media center program; Policies and procedures; Selection; General selection criteria; Criteria by format; Acquisitions and processing; Maintenance and preservation; Circulation and promotion of the collection; Evaluation of the collection; Ethical issues and the collection; The curriculum; Special groups of students; Fiscal issues relating to the collection; Opening, moving, or closing the collection

"Media specialists who read this book will be renewed in their quest for excellence in their collections. . . . The book covers A-Z: Acquisitions, Evaluation, Ethical Issues, Inventory, Procedure Manual, Selection, Special Groups of Students, Weeding, etc. . . . This is a must purchase for every school library media center." Libr Media Connect
Includes bibliographical references

Bush, Gail

Tales out of the school library; developing professional dispositions; [by] Gail Bush and Jami Biles Jones; foreword by Theodore R. Sizer. Libraries Unlimited 2010 135p il pa $40
Grades: Adult Professional   **027.8**
1. Librarians 2. School libraries
ISBN 978-1-59158-832-0; 1-59158-832-4
                                        LC 2009-46648
This book "answers the question, how should school librarians conduct themselves in their teaching, communicating, and leading roles in light of the AASL Standards for the 21st-Century Learner? In addition, what factors make an exemplary school librarian who will not only inspire students, but also nurture needed dispositions in them? . . . Readers are introduced to three fictional, yet very realistic school librarians in a series of thought-provoking vignettes that focus on instructional strategies, information literacy, assessment, literacy and reading, diversity, intellectual freedom, communication, advocacy, collaboration, resiliency, leadership, and professional ethics. Each chapter connects to the AASL standards and includes follow-up and discussion questions. All school librarians aiming to become reflective practitioners who model professional dispositions should read this unique book." SLJ
Includes bibliographical references

Church, Audrey P., 1957-

Leverage your library program to help raise test scores; a guide for library media specialists, principals, teachers, and parents. Linworth Pub. 2003 123p il pa $39.95 *
Grades: Adult Professional   **027.8**
1. School libraries 2. Instructional materials centers
ISBN 1-58683-120-8   LC 2003-40080
"In chapter one, recent research on school libraries is provided and briefly explains the results in layman terms. This is followed by a chapter each for the administrators, teachers, and parents that describes what each needs to know about the library and librarian's roles. A chapter is included for the librarian on what they need to do. The final chapter pulls the book together with perspectives from principals and librarians . . . This book can serve as a means to start a dialog with the administration and at the same time as a reference book for the school librarian." Libr Media Connect
Includes bibliographical references

Doll, Carol Ann, 1949-
The resilient school library; [by] Carol A. Doll and Beth Doll. Libraries Unlimited 2010 123p il pa $40
Grades: Adult Professional   **027.8**
  1. School libraries 2. Academic achievement
  ISBN 978-1-59158-639-5; 1-59158-639-9
                LC 2010-21570
"The premise of the research provided in this informative text is that school library media specialists have the opportunity to play a major role in promoting resiliency through library programming and services for at-risk students. . . . The content of this comprehensive and interesting text provides examples; a planning template to follow; and supplementary graphs, charts, and tables." SLJ
  Includes bibliographical references

Downs, Elizabeth, 1953-
The school library media specialist's policy & procedure writer. Neal-Schuman Publishers 2009 195p pa $75 *
Grades: Adult Professional   **027.8**
  1. School libraries
  ISBN 978-1-55570-621-0; 1-55570-621-5
                LC 2009-35177
"School library media specialists who need policies or procedures will surely find what they are looking for in this thorough book. Downs lays the foundation by describing necessary forms and policies for a school library media center, then provides a variety of examples and templates. The book includes mission statements, goals and objectives, budgeting, facilities use, circulation, collection development, disaster management, weeding, copyright, ILL, ethics, and accessibility policies." SLJ

Erikson, Rolf
Designing a school library media center for the future; [by] Rolf Erikson and Carolyn Markuson. 2nd ed. American Library Association 2007 117p il pa $45
Grades: Adult Professional   **027.8**
  1. Instructional materials centers—Design and construction 2. School libraries—Design and construction
  ISBN 978-0-8389-0945-4; 0-8389-0945-0
                LC 2006-37644
First published 2000
"The first chapter offers an overview of the various steps involved in any project. Succeeding chapters cover technology planning, space allocations, furniture and placement, lighting and acoustics, ADA requirements, specifications, and bids." Booklist
  Includes bibliographical references

Farmer, Lesley S. Johnson, 1949-
Collaborating with administrators and educational support staff; [by] Lesley S. J. Farmer. Neal-Schuman Publishers 2007 217p (Best practices for school library media professionals) pa $65 *
Grades: Adult Professional   **027.8**
  1. School libraries 2. Instructional materials centers 3. Schools—Administration
  ISBN 978-1-55570-572-5; 1-55570-572-3
                LC 2006-11171
"Farmer begins by exploring how schools work, the role of the library media specialist, and the background on collaboration. She then discusses, in some depth, how to work with different levels of administrators and key service personnel, such as technology directors, reading specialists, special-education educators, pupil services personnel, and physical health and co-curricular personnel. Farmer concludes with ways of measuring the impact of collaboration and improving literacy, and provides suggestions for becoming a collaborative leader. This book is a must for school districts and a school library media specialists' personal collections." SLJ
  Includes bibliographical references

Hughes-Hassell, Sandra
School reform and the school library media specialist; [by] Sandra Hughes-Hassell and Violet H. Harada. Libraries Unlimited 2007 xxiii, 204p il (Principles and practice series) pa $40 *
Grades: Adult Professional   **027.8**
  1. School libraries
  ISBN 978-1-59158-427-8; 1-59158-427-2
                LC 2007-16437
"This volume covers critical issues impacting school libraries today and offers practical solutions to meet these challenges. Written by leaders in the field such as Pam Berger, Carol Gordon, Barbara Stripling, and Ross Todd, the articles expound on implications of No Child Left Behind legislation, 21st-century literacy requirements, population diversity, and professional growth. . . . This volume will empower current and future school librarians as they embrace its guidelines." SLJ

Johnson, Doug, 1952-
School libraries head for the edge; rants, recommendations, and reflections. Linworth Pub. 2010 196p pa $35
Grades: Adult Professional   **027.8**
  1. School libraries
  ISBN 978-1-58683-392-3; 1-58683-392-8
                LC 2009-22053
"Eighty long-running 'Head for the Edge' columns in Library Media Connection and its predecessor, Technology Connection, are collected here, in topical clusters dealing with professional issues relevant to both veterans and newbies. . . . The columns are reflective, conversational, and characteristically humorous. . . . Chapters end with quotes, questions, and self-evaluative reflection that readers will be inspired to mirror. For all practitioners." SLJ

Jones, Jami Biles

The power of the media specialist to improve academic achievement and strengthen at-risk students; [by] Jami Biles Jones, Alana M. Zambone. Linworth Books 2008 108p il pa $39.95 *

Grades: Adult Professional   **027.8**
   1. Instructional materials centers 2. School libraries 3. Academic achievement
   ISBN 1-58683-229-8; 978-1-58683-229-2
                                   LC 2007-30116
This "volume gives library professionals the information they need to convince the unconvinced of the value of the media center in improving student achievement. Section one provides research results and statistics that identify at-risk students. Section two is devoted to identifying the social and educational approaches that have been proven to help these students. . . . This resource is valuable for media specialists ready to make a change to a student-centered library, thus giving all of their students a chance at higher academic and personal achievement." SLJ
   Includes bibliographical references

Jurkowski, Odin L., 1969-

Technology and the school library; a comprehensive guide for media specialists and other educators. Scarecrow Press 2006 219p pa $45

Grades: Adult Professional   **027.8**
   1. Information technology 2. School libraries—Automation 3. Instructional materials centers—Automation
   ISBN 0-8108-5290-X; 978-0-8108-5290-7
                                   LC 2006-15206
This "manual is a basic primer on school-related technology. The main sections have chapters covering information tools and resources, classroom technologies, technology administration in the school library, and technology training. Each chapter provides a general overview, historical perspective, a detailed set of definitions and explanations, a brief summary of concerns and current research, and a short but carefully chosen list of pertinent Web sites. . . . This accessible guide will be of interest to practicing school librarians, educators and school administrators, and library media students." Booklist
   Includes bibliographical references

Morris, Betty J.

Administering the school library media center. 4th ed, rev and expanded. Libraries Unlimited 2004 683p $70; pa $55 *

Grades: Adult Professional   **027.8**
   1. School libraries 2. Instructional materials centers
   ISBN 0-313-32261-9; 1-59158-183-4 (pa)
                                   LC 2004-41797
First published 1973 under the authorship of John T. Gillespie and Diana L. Spirt with title: Creating a school media program

"This volume covers library media center programming, facilities and technologies, student learning, policies and procedures, and library media specialist roles. . . . Highlights include budget planning and justification, library media job descriptions, and information on the bid process. The chapter on facilities contains infrequently found information on the psychology of color, URLs for Web sites with floor plans, and guidelines for space planning." Booklist

Schuckett, Sandy

Political advocacy for school librarians; you have the power! Linworth Pub. 2004 128p pa $39.95

Grades: Adult Professional   **027.8**
   1. School libraries 2. Libraries and community 3. Lobbying
   ISBN 1-58683-158-5   LC 2004-4869
"Schuckett motivates and explicitly details an exciting 'how-to' of political lobbying at all levels—from the school site and local board all the way to the national level. . . . School librarians need political clout, and Schuckett shows us how to get it." SLJ
   Includes bibliographical references

Stephens, Claire Gatrell

Library 101; a handbook for the school library media specialist; [by] Claire Gatrell Stephens and Patricia Franklin. Libraries Unlimited 2007 233p il pa $35

Grades: Adult Professional   **027.8**
   1. School libraries 2. Instructional materials centers 3. Libraries—Handbooks, manuals, etc.
   ISBN 978-1-59158-324-0; 1-59158-324-1
                                   LC 2007-18420
"This handbook provides information for brand-new and inexperienced librarians preparing for a first job in a school library media center. Articles are divided into four subcategories covering day-to-day operations (library organization, circulation policies, media management, scheduling, staffing, and media center arrangement); collaboration with teachers; collection development and management; and equipment." Booklist
   Includes bibliographical references

Thomas, Margie J. Klink

Re-designing the high school library for the forgotten half; the information needs of the non-college bound student. Libraries Unlimited 2008 78p il $45 *

Grades: Adult Professional   **027.8**
   1. High school libraries 2. Vocational education
   ISBN 978-1-59158-476-6; 1-59158-476-0
                                   LC 2008-14019
"This book explores the informational needs of non-college-bound students and addresses how their high school libraries can be restructured to effectively meet these needs. . . . This book will serve as a valuable resource for those seeking to address the needs of these sometimes-overlooked students." Voice Youth Advocates
   Includes bibliographical references

Valenza, Joyce Kasman

Power tools recharged; 125+ essential forms and presentations for your school library information program; illustrated by Emily Valenza. American Library Association 2004 various paging il pa $55 *

Grades: Adult Professional   **027.8**
1. School libraries 2. Libraries—Public relations
ISBN 0-8389-0880-2   LC 2004-5853

First published 1998 with title: Power tools

This offers a compilation of customizable, reproducible forms and handouts for school library administration and assessment, teaching information literacy, making presentations. Included are such items as templates for a gift book program, letters to parents and faculty members, a checklist of tasks, library equipment sign-out forms, and a reading interest survey.

Includes bibliographical references

Van Deusen, Jean Donham, 1946-

Enhancing teaching and learning; a leadership guide for school library media specialists; [by] Jean Donham. rev. ed. Neal-Schuman Publishers 2008 353p il pa $65

Grades: Adult Professional   **027.8**
1. School libraries 2. Instructional materials centers
ISBN 978-1-55570-647-0; 1-55570-647-9
     LC 2008-23321

First published 1998

This book attempts to show "how to develop and implement an effective library media program by integrating it into the total education environment. Part One covers all aspects of the school environment: students, curriculum and instruction, principals, school district administrators, and the community. Part Two shows you how to use interaction and collaboration to make the school library media program integral to all of these communities." Publisher's note

"This title is well-written, well-researched, and informative. Donham masterfully weaves together current AASL standards and the real world of today's media specialist." Voice Youth Advocates

Includes bibliographical references

The **Whole** school library handbook; edited by Blanche Woolls and David V. Loertscher. American Library Association 2005 448p pa $45 *

Grades: Adult Professional   **027.8**
1. School libraries 2. Instructional materials centers
ISBN 0-8389-0883-7   LC 2004-20198

This reference resource to the school media center includes "facts, . . . articles, checklists, organization contact information, trivia, [and] advice from the field's experts. . . . [It also features] information on fundraising, grant writing, flexible scheduling, promoting the school library, and advocating its value in the school community." Publisher's note

Includes bibliographical references

Woolls, E. Blanche

The school library media manager; [by] Blanche Woolls. 4th ed. Libraries Unlimited 2008 279p il (Library and information science text series) $55; pa $45

Grades: Adult Professional   **027.8**
1. School libraries 2. Instructional materials centers
ISBN 978-1-59158-648-7; 1-59158-648-8; 978-1-59158-643-2 (pa); 1-59158-643-7 (pa)
     LC 2008-18081

First published 1994

Provides information "for teaching the administration of school library media centers. . . . Readers learn how to choose a credential program, how to find the requirements for working in each of the 50 states, what to do when looking for and choosing a job, and how to survive the first week in that new position. . . . Sections also cover: collaborating with teachers, how to write a proposal, and how to accept leadership responsibilities, including the role of a media specialist in the legislative process." Publisher's note

Includes bibliographical references

028.1   Reviews

Adamson, Lynda G.

Literature links to world history, K-12; resources to enhance and entice. Libraries Unlimited 2010 684p (Children's and young adult literature reference series) $65

Grades: Adult Professional   **028.1**
1. World history—Bibliography
ISBN 978-1-59158-470-4   LC 2009-46081

"This annotated bibliography might very well become a school librarian's favorite resource when collaborating with history teachers. . . . Entries include fiction, nonfiction, and multimedia. Sections are divided by world regions and sometimes further by time period, with each section subdivided into fiction, history nonfiction, biography, graphic books, DVDs, and compact discs. . . . Adult books for young adults are included. Entries, arranged alphabetically by author, contain bibliographic information, grade levels, descriptive annotations, and awards, where appropriate." Booklist

Includes bibliographical references

Best books for young adults; edited by Holly Koelling; foreword by Betty Carter. 3rd ed. American Library Association 2007 346p il pa $42 *

Grades: Adult Professional   **028.1**
1. Reference books 2. Teenagers—Books and reading 3. Best books 4. Young adult literature—Bibliography
ISBN 978-0-8389-3569-9; 0-8389-3569-9
     LC 2007-26009

First published 1994 under the editorship of Betty Carter

This "is a classic, standard resource for collection building and on-the-spot readers' advisory. . . . Absolutely indispensable for school and public libraries." Booklist

Includes bibliographical references

The **ultimate** teen book guide; editors, Daniel Hahn & Leonie Flynn; associate editor, Susan Reuben. Distributed to the trade by Holtzbrinck Publishers 2008 432p il $26.95; pa $15.95 *
Grades: Adult Professional   **028.1**
1. Young adult literature—History and criticism 2. Teenagers—Books and reading
ISBN   978-0-8027-9730-8;   0-8027-9730-X; 978-0-8027-9731-5 (pa); 0-8027-9731-8 (pa)
LC 2007-24238
First published 2006 in the United Kingdom
This "volume includes reviews of more than 700 fiction titles, nonfiction, classics, and graphic novels that will be of interest to young adults. The reviewers/contributors are popular authors, librarians, and teens themselves. . . . It's an excellent source for a variety of book reviews spanning time and genre. Useful for students, librarians, and teachers." SLJ

028.5   Reading and use of other information media by young people

Aronson, Marc
Exploding the myths; the truth about teenagers and reading. Scarecrow Press 2000 146p (Scarecrow studies in young adult literature) $29.50 *
Grades: Adult Professional   **028.5**
1. Teenagers—Books and reading
ISBN 0-8108-3904-0   LC 00-61948
Aronson discusses censorship, audience, authenticity, demographics, and YA publishing history. "Whether talking about the graphic novel, poetry, magic realism, or gritty contemporary fiction, he shows that teenagers today are often more open to challenge and diversity in narrative and format than their adult guardians are. What many librarians think is 'popular' is often condescending. Whether you agree with Aronson or not, you'll be caught up in issues that matter. A great starting place for YA literature classes." Booklist

Bartel, Julie
Annotated book lists for every teen reader; the best from the experts at YALSA-BK; [by] Julie Bartel and Pam Spencer Holley for the Young Adult Library Services Association. Neal-Schuman Publishers 2011 270p pa $65
Grades: Adult Professional   **028.5**
1. Teenagers—Books and reading 2. Young adult literature—Bibliography 3. Young adult literature—Stories, plots, etc. 4. Best books
ISBN 978-1-55570-658-6; 1-55570-658-4
LC 2010-33312
"Bartel and Holley have scoured the YALSA-BK archives to find more than 1100 books with broad teen readership. While the book's primary purpose is for readers' advisory, the authors also suggest it will be useful in creating displays as well as igniting creativity. . . . The scope is wide ranging with a good mix of standards, classics, and newer titles. With a highly appropriate title, this volume hits the mark." SLJ
Includes bibliographical references

Bodart, Joni Richards
Radical reads 2; working with the newest edgy titles for teens. Scarecrow Press 2010 479p pa $45
Grades: Adult Professional   **028.5**
1. Teenagers—Books and reading 2. Young adult literature—Bibliography
ISBN 978-0-8108-6908-0; 0-8108-6908-X
LC 2009-25724
Bodart "offers insight into writing book reports and booktalks that secondary school English teachers and library media specialists can share with students. . . . The detailed book entries include citations with suggested reading and interest levels designated by middle school, younger high school, and older high school. Also included are subject areas, character descriptions, a booktalk and booktalk ideas, a list of major themes and ideas, book report ideas, risks, strengths, awards, and full-text reviews. The entries' detail will be an asset in readers' advisory and a quick resource to check the content and reviews for a title that is being questioned." Voice Youth Advocates
Includes bibliographical references

Booth, Heather, 1978-
Serving teens through readers' advisory. American Library Association 2007 159p (ALA readers' advisory series) pa $36 *
Grades: Adult Professional   **028.5**
1. Teenagers—Books and reading 2. Young adult literature—Bibliography 3. Young adults' libraries
ISBN 0-8389-0930-2; 978-0-8389-0930-0
LC 2006-36134
"The first few chapters discuss teen reading habits and why readers' advisory for this group is different and also provide 'tips for the generalist' who may not be an expert in teen fiction. Other chapters cover elements of the readers' advisory interaction . . . and survey the appropriate books. Two unique chapters offer well-thought-out and practical advice on making reading-related homework assignments less painful for staff and students as well as suggestions for providing readers' advisory services to teens through their parents or other adults. . . . [This] is essential reading for all readers' advisors and any library staff who work with teens." Booklist
Includes bibliographical references

Bromann, Jennifer
More booktalking that works. Neal-Schuman 2005 145p (Teens @ the library series) pa $49.95 *
Grades: Adult Professional   **028.5**
1. Book talks 2. Young adults' libraries 3. Teenagers—Books and reading
ISBN 1-55570-525-1   LC 2005-2326
"Bromann has expanded on her previous booktalking title, *Booktalking That Works* (Neal-Schuman, 2001), with additional practical advice based on added years of experience. . . . The first part of this book is arranged in a question-and-answer format covering various aspects of booktalking, from creating and presenting booktalks to choosing books and developing hooks for reluctant readers. This section includes a list of the top-20 types of books to booktalk and 10 very brief quick talks. The sec-

Bromann, Jennifer—*Continued*
ond section offers 200 booktalks of varying length and
covering several fiction and nonfiction genres that she
encourages librarians to adapt for personal use. . . .
School and public librarians will find many helpful hints,
whether they are novice or veteran booktalkers." Booklist

Cart, Michael
Young adult literature: from romance to realism.
rev ed. American Library Association 2010 242p
pa $60 *
Grades: Adult Professional   **028.5**
1. Young adult literature—History and criticism
2. Teenagers—Books and reading
ISBN 978-0-8389-1045-0; 0-8389-1045-9
                                      LC 2010-13674
A revised edition of: From romance to realism: 50
years of growth and change in young adult literature,
published 1996 by HarperCollins Pub.
"This updated and expanded second edition of Cart's
already lively and comprehensive history of young adult
literature (1996) is an essential resource. It is divided
into two sections ('That Was Then' and 'This Is Now'),
and the author once again discusses the history and current moment to offer a broad and loving overview of the
rich literature. . . . Highly accessible and thorough, the
text is a staple for any study of the canon." SLJ
Includes bibliographical references

Dear author; letters of hope; edited by Joan F.
Kaywell; with an introduction by Catherine
Ryan Hyde. Philomel Books 2007 222p $14.99
*
Grades: 8 9 10 11 12   **028.5**
1. Teenagers—Books and reading 2. Authors, American
ISBN 978-0-399-23705-8; 0-399-23705-4
                                      LC 2006-21050
"Chris Lynch, Nancy Garden, and Christopher Paul
Curtis and are just a few of the well-known authors who
respond to real teens' letters in this powerful compilation. Not mere fan mail, the selections speak about teens'
gravest concerns—bullying, derailed friendships, racism,
date rape, incest, illness, divorce, and more—and they
describe how the authors' books helped them face the
heartaches. . . . For some readers, this dialogue between
writers and readers will be inspiring; for those harboring
their own wounding secrets, it may be lifesaving."
Booklist
Includes bibliographical references

Diamant-Cohen, Betsy
Booktalking bonanza; ten ready-to-use
multimedia sessions for the busy librarian.
American Library Association 2009 240p il pa $40
Grades: Adult Professional   **028.5**
1. Book talks 2. Books and reading 3. Children's literature
ISBN 978-0-8389-0965-2; 0-8389-0965-5
                                      LC 2008-15371
"This volume is a collection of scripts for multimedia-
enriched booktalks. After an introductory chapter that explains the reasoning for this approach, 10 scripts are out-

lined. Books, music, video, and Web sites are included
for each one. The programs are geared toward elementa-
ry-aged children, although suggestions for adapting them
for a middle or high school audience are included." SLJ
Includes bibliographical references

Fraser, Elizabeth, 1970-
Reality rules! a guide to teen nonfiction reading
interests. Libraries Unlimited 2008 246p
(Genreflecting advisory series) $48
Grades: Adult Professional   **028.5**
1. Reference books 2. Young adult literature—Bibliography 3. Teenagers—Books and reading
ISBN 978-1-59158-563-3   LC 2007-51063
"This guide focuses on titles created for teens and
those with strong teen appeal. The author covers more
than 500 titles published since 2000, also including
benchmarks and perennial classics." Publisher's note
Includes bibliographical references

Gelman, Judy, 1962-
The kids' book club book; reading ideas,
recipes, activities, and smart tips for organizing
terrific kids' book clubs; [by] Judy Gelman and
Vicki Levy Krupp. Penguin Group 2007 460p pa
$16.95
Grades: Adult Professional   **028.5**
1. Children—Books and reading 2. Teenagers—Books
and reading 3. Children's literature—Bibliography
4. Young adult literature—Bibliography 5. Book clubs
(Discussion groups)
ISBN 978-1-58542-559-4   LC 2006-101469
"Stellar advice on running book clubs is presented in
a friendly format. . . . The first section covers types of
clubs, recruitment, organization, location, and duration.
. . . In the second part, comprising the bulk of the text,
the authors describe the top 50 recommended books arranged by grade level." SLJ
Includes bibliographical references

Gillespie, John Thomas, 1928-
The Newbery/Printz companion; booktalk and
related materials for award winners and honor
books; [by] John T. Gillespie and Corinne J.
Naden. 3rd ed. Libraries Unlimited 2006 503p
(Children's and young adult literature reference
series) $75 *
Grades: Adult Professional   **028.5**
1. Newbery Medal 2. Michael L. Printz award
3. Children's literature—History and criticism
4. Authors 5. Book talks
ISBN 1-59158-313-6   LC 2006-14955
First published 1996 with title: The Newbery companion
This guide to the "Newbery and Printz awards for
children's and young adult literature provides information
on each year's winners and honor books, as well as on
the awards themselves and the librarians for whom they
are named. For each award-winning book, there is a plot
summary, list of characters and themes, background on
the author, incidents for booktalking, related reads, and
. . . ideas for introducing the book to young readers."

Gillespie, John Thomas, 1928——*Continued*
Publisher's note
"This invaluable source should be in every school and public library." Booklist
Includes bibliographical references

Handbook of research on children's and young adult literature; edited by Shelby A. Wolf . . . [et al.] Routledge 2010 555p $295; pa $119.95
Grades: Adult Professional   **028.5**
1. Children's literature—History and criticism 2. Young adult literature—History and criticism
ISBN   978-0-415-96505-7;   0-415-96505-5; 978-0-415-96506-4 (pa); 0-415-96506-3 (pa); 978-0-203-84354-3 (e-book)   LC 2010-16339
"The book examines readers, texts, and cultural contexts of children's literature and across the three intersecting disciplines of Education, English, and Library and Information Science, in an effort to model a multidisciplinary approach to children's literature research. Thirty-seven scholarly articles, by figures such as Eliza Dresang, Rudine Sims Bishop, and Roderick McGillis . . . are counterpointed by responses that often provide more personal perspectives, including insights from noted authors such as Lois Lowry, M. T. Anderson, and Markus Zusak." Bull Cent Child Books

Honnold, RoseMary, 1954-
The teen reader's advisor. Neal-Schuman Publishers 2006 491p (Teens @ the library series) pa $75 *
Grades: Adult Professional   **028.5**
1. Teenagers—Books and reading 2. Young adults' libraries 3. Young adult literature—Bibliography
ISBN 1-55570-551-0   LC 2006-12640
"The first part deals with the challenges of working with teens, from developing a rapport and dealing with the more conservative adults in their lives, to marketing a YA collection to its audience. The author's descriptions of the major awards and lists relating to the literature as well as the list of print and online reader's advisory resources are sure to be helpful. Part two consists of subject and genre lists. Each one has at least 10 titles. The annotations are excellent." SLJ
Includes bibliographical references

Jones, Patrick
Connecting with reluctant teen readers; tips, titles, and tools; [by] Patrick Jones, Maureen L. Hartman, Patricia Taylor. Neal-Schuman Publishers 2006 xxi, 314p $59.95 *
Grades: Adult Professional   **028.5**
1. Teenagers—Books and reading 2. Young adults' libraries 3. Young adult literature—Bibliography
ISBN 1-55570-571-5; 978-1-55570-571-8
LC 2006-12355
"Well written and well researched, this practical hands-on guide to defining and wooing reluctant readers is a must-read for librarians and teachers who work with adolescents. It is divided into three parts: 'Tips That Work,' 'Titles That Work,' and 'Tools That Work.'" SLJ
Includes bibliographical references

Keane, Nancy J.
The big book of teen reading lists; 100 great, ready-to-use book lists for educators, librarians, parents, and teens. Libraries Unlimited 2006 297p pa $35
Grades: Adult Professional   **028.5**
1. Young adult literature—Bibliography 2. Teenagers—Books and reading
ISBN 1-59158-333-0; 978-1-59158-333-2
LC 2006-17627
"Listing fiction and nonfiction published mostly in the last 10 years, this volume is divided into six parts: 'Genres,' 'Characters,' 'Books about Self,' 'Setting,' 'Subjects,' and 'Audience.' . . . Each title entry contains a bibliographic reference and a brief annotation of one or two sentences. Following the six sections, the book provides some sample reproducible bookmarks suggesting further reading on specific topics." Booklist
"Keane has produced another great resource for teachers, librarians, and students, especially reluctant readers." SLJ
Includes bibliographical references

Knowles, Elizabeth, 1946-
Boys and literacy; practical strategies for librarians, teachers, and parents; [by] Elizabeth Knowles and Martha Smith. Libraries Unlimited 2005 xxi, 164p il pa $35 *
Grades: Adult Professional   **028.5**
1. Boys—Books and reading 2. Children's literature—Bibliography 3. Young adult literature—Bibliography
ISBN 1-59158-212-1
"Boys don't seem to like to read. . . . This book briefly explores the research about this situation, outlines strategies to reverse this trend, and lists books within genres that boys enjoy reading. . . . The best part of the book is the author section. . . . For each author covered, there is a complete list of books, contact information, . . . and Web sites. . . . This is a wonderful resource for teachers and parents to begin working on improving literacy with boys." Booklist

Moore, John Noell
Interpreting young adult literature; literary theory in the secondary classroom. Boynton/Cook Pubs. 1997 202p (Young adult literature series) $27.50
Grades: Adult Professional   **028.5**
1. Young adult literature—History and criticism 2. Literature—Philosophy
ISBN 0-86709-414-1   LC 97-5045
Chapters address "formalism, archetypal criticism, structuralism/semiotics, deconstruction, reader-response, feminism, black aesthetics, and cultural studies. Each of these chapters cover key concepts and basic terms of the theory, introduces and interprets a young adult text from that perspective, and invites readers to join the conversation. The concluding section of each chapter discusses other young adult texts that can be approached from that theory and suggests additional critical studies appropriate for teaching these texts." Publisher's note
Includes bibliographical references

Nilsen, Alleen Pace

Literature for today's young adults; [by] Alleen Pace Nilsen, Kenneth L. Donelson. 8th ed. Allyn and Bacon/Pearson 2008 c2009 xx, 491p il $122.20 *

Grades: Adult Professional   028.5

1. Young adult literature—History and criticism 2. Books and reading

ISBN 978-0-205-59323-1; 0-205-59323-2

LC 2008-2625

First published 1980

Authors' names appear in reverse order in 7th ed.

This is an "introduction to young adult literature framed within a literary, historical, and social context. The authors provide teachers with criteria for evaluating books of all genres, from poetry and nonfiction to mysteries, science fiction, and graphic novels. . . . [It also includes coverage of] issues such as pop culture and mass media." Publisher's note

Includes bibliographical references

Pearl, Nancy

Book crush; for kids and teens; recommended reading for every mood, moment, and interest. Sasquatch Books 2007 288p $16.95 *

Grades: Adult Professional   028.5

1. Books and reading 2. Best books

ISBN 1-57061-500-4; 978-1-57061-500-9

LC 2007-13865

Presents lists of recommended book titles for children and teenagers divided into three age groups and then further subdivided into more than 118 categories, including animals, folktales, girl power, autobiographies, comic books, and many others.

"Librarians, parents, and young people will enjoy browsing this resource." Voice Youth Advocates

Quick and popular reads for teens; edited by Pam Spencer Holley for the Young Adult Library Services Association. American Library Association 2009 228p pa $45

Grades: Adult Professional   028.5

1. Young Adult Library Services Association 2. Teenagers—Books and reading 3. Young adult literature—Bibliography

ISBN 978-0-8389-3577-4; 0-8389-3577-X

LC 2008-49691

"This practical guide pulls together the Quick Picks for the Reluctant Young Adult Reader lists and the Popular Paperbacks for Young Adults lists created by the Young Adult Library Services Association (YALSA), a division of the American Library Association (ALA) from 1999 to 2008. . . . [The editor] assembles the lists into separate Nonfiction and Fiction categories, with an additional chapter containing Theme-Oriented Booklists that is useful for putting together displays, bookmarks, or readers' advisory. . . . This essential tool for librarians will help them find that popular book to turn a reluctant reader into a teen who appreciates the enjoyment one comes from reading." Voice Youth Advocates

Includes bibliographical references

Schall, Lucy

Booktalks and beyond; promoting great genre reads to teens. Libraries Unlimited 2007 276p pa $40

Grades: Adult Professional   028.5

1. Teenagers—Books and reading 2. Book talks 3. Young adult literature—Bibliography

ISBN 978-1-59158-466-7; 1-59158-466-3

LC 2006-37492

"A selection of 101 teen-oriented titles published between 2001 and 2006 are organized into 7 genres. . . . Within each genre, titles are arranged into subject groupings. . . . The same information is provided for each book: publication data, reading levels, themes and topics, a description, at least 5 suggested passages for reading aloud, a complete (brief) booktalk, individual or group 'Learning Opportunities' and an annotated list of 5 or 6 related works. This volume will be most useful for librarians new to teen literature, as well as those needing a refresher on more recent titles." Booklist

Includes bibliographical references

Genre talks for teens; booktalks and more for every teen reading interest. Libraries Unlimited 2009 309p pa $40

Grades: Adult Professional   028.5

1. Book talks 2. Teenagers—Books and reading

ISBN 978-1-59158-743-9; 1-59158-743-3

LC 2008-54984

"Schall has chosen about 100 books published since 2003 for inclusion in this volume. . . . Each book includes a summary, a booktalk, a read-aloud/reader response sampling, supporting learning activities, and related works. Books are keyed by theme, reading level, and audience. . . . Because of its varied ways to engage readers and its current coverage, the book is a welcome addition." Booklist

Includes bibliographical references

Silvey, Anita

500 great books for teens. Houghton Mifflin Co. 2006 397p $26 *

Grades: Adult Professional   028.5

1. Teenagers—Books and reading 2. Young adult literature—Bibliography

ISBN 978-0-618-61296-3; 0-618-61296-3

LC 2006-3350

"A Frances Tenenbaum book"

"Silvey selects and annotates five hundred titles for young adults, arranging them loosely in twenty-one chapters by genre and/or area of interest, from 'Adventure and Survival' to 'War and Conflict.' Each book is coded for either younger (12-14) or older (14-18) teens and gets a couple hundred words or so. . . . The selections are both sturdy and wide-ranging." Horn Book

Includes bibliographical references

Sullivan, Michael

Serving boys through readers' advisory. American Library Association 2010 152p (ALA readers' advisory series) pa $48 *

Grades: Adult Professional   **028.5**
  1. Boys—Books and reading 2. Reference services (Libraries)
  ISBN 978-0-8389-1022-1; 0-8389-1022-X
                        LC 2009-26841

"This volume was created to give a general direction when helping most boys select books. . . . Sullivan challenges us to throw out our preconceived notions about how to conduct such an interview. Methods of performing indirect readers' advisory with parents and teachers are included. The excellent booktalks for elementary, middle school, and high school boys alone make this a worthwhile purchase." SLJ

Includes bibliographical references

Zbaracki, Matthew D.

Best books for boys; a resource for educators; foreword by Jon Scieszka. Libraries Unlimited 2008 189p il (Children's and young adult literature reference series) $45

Grades: Adult Professional   **028.5**
  1. Boys—Books and reading 2. Best books 3. Children's literature—Bibliography 4. Young adult literature—Bibliography
  ISBN 978-1-59158-599-2; 1-59158-599-6
                        LC 2007-51065

"This guide offers ideas for educators, librarians, and parents on fiction and nonfiction books that will interest boys in grades three to 10." Publisher's note

"Good source notes guide readers to additional writings on the topic and speak to the author's significant research in his field. Nicely indexed by author, title, and subject, this [is an] easy-to-navigate resource." Voice Youth Advocates

Includes bibliographical references

028.7 Use of books and other information media as sources of information

Behen, Linda D.

Using pop culture to teach information literacy; methods to engage a new generation. Libraries Unlimited 2006 109p il pa $35

Grades: Adult Professional   **028.7**
  1. Information literacy 2. High school libraries 3. Popular culture—United States
  ISBN 1-59158-301-2; 978-1-59158-301-1
                        LC 2006-3710

The author "argues that the best way to effectively teach information literacy skills in the high school library setting is to make instruction relevant and fun by tapping into the interests of teens, particularly through employing pop culture. . . . This short, hands-on guide to information literacy instruction and programming is particularly well suited for those new to the field or experienced librarians looking to infuse some contemporary ideas into their programs." Voice Youth Advocates

Includes bibliographical references

Callison, Daniel, 1948-

The blue book on information age inquiry, instruction and literacy; [by] Daniel Callison and Leslie Preddy. Libraries Unlimited 2006 643p il pa $45 *

Grades: Adult Professional   **028.7**
  1. Information literacy
  ISBN 978-1-59158-325-7; 1-59158-325-X
                        LC 2006-23645

A revised edition of Key Words, Concepts and Methods for Information Age Instruction, published 2003 by LMS Associates

"Part 1 introduces the concepts of information inquiry, providing foundational documents and exploring search and use models, information literacy, standards, the instructional role of library media specialists, online inquiry learning, and resource management. Part 2 offers concrete examples of inquiry applied to the middle-school student research process and supplies reproducible pages for classroom use. Part 3 discusses and defines 51 key terms. Entries here are several pages in length and include citations and references. Indispensable for all school media specialists, this book will also appeal to other readers, who will be impressed by its well-organized design, thoroughness, and practicality." Booklist

Includes bibliographical references

Smith, Jane Bandy

Teaching & testing information literacy skills; [by] Jane Bandy Smith; Lisa Churchill and Lucy Mason, contributors. Linworth Pub. 2005 xx, 138p il pa $44.95

Grades: Adult Professional   **028.7**
  1. Bibliographic instruction 2. School libraries 3. Library information networks
  ISBN 1-58683-078-3   LC 2004-26004

The author "reviews the rise and acceptance of information literacy, traces a continuum from older ideas of isolated library skills to this more inclusive life skill, and presents a frame for curriculum development with five pages of excellent instructional objectives by category and grade level. . . . This powerful book will illuminate the inexperienced and reinvigorate veteran school librarians." SLJ

Includes bibliographical references

Student engagement and information literacy; edited by Craig Gibson. Association of College and Research Libraries 2006 197p pa $27

Grades: Adult Professional   **028.7**
  1. Information literacy 2. Libraries and students
  ISBN 0-8389-8388-X; 978-0-8389-8388-1
                        LC 2006-16956

This book "addresses information literacy in a framework inspired by higher education scholarship and dialogue as it relates to student engagement. Articles are based on what librarians and faculty know about how students learn, how different learning environments affect engagement, and how different groups on campuses can collaborate on student engagement and learning." Publisher's note

Includes bibliographical references

Taylor, Joie

Information literacy and the school library media center. Libraries Unlimited 2006 148p il (Libraries Unlimited professional guides in school librarianship) pa $35

Grades: Adult Professional   **028.7**

1. Information literacy 2. School libraries

ISBN 0-313-32020-9

"Beginning with a description of what it means to be information literate, the author goes on to highlight how the American Association of School Librarians (AASL) and Association for Educational Communications and Technology (AECT) standards can be integrated into the curriculum in ways that complement state and district standards, giving specific examples from several states. She discusses how the library media specialist through flexible scheduling and curriculum mapping can facilitate an environment where students can hone their information literacy skills. . . . Two things make this book exceptional. First the chapter on collaboration is a refreshingly frank discussion of the value of working with classroom teachers that delineates the roles of the teacher and the library media specialist, while being realistic in realizing that barriers do exist to real collaboration. Second the extensive bibliography is filled with books, journal articles, and Web resources that will guide readers to the best practices in information literacy at the current time." Voice Youth Advocates

030 Encyclopedias & books of facts

Olmstead, Larry

Getting into Guinness; one man's longest, fastest, highest journey inside the world's most famous record book. HarperCollins 2008 293p il $24.95

Grades: 9 10 11 12 Adult   **030**

1. Guinness book of world records 2. World records 3. Curiosities and wonders

ISBN 978-0-06-137348-0; 0-06-137348-6

LC 2008-29669

The author holds "two Guinness World Records—playing two rounds of golf on different continents in one day and playing the longest poker session. Here, he interweaves the stories of his successful attempts with a history of the perennially popular record book." Libr J

"The book is endlessly fascinating, an exploration of what makes ordinary people try to do extraordinary things for no other reason than because no one else has ever done them." Booklist

Includes bibliographical references

031 General encyclopedic works in American English

Hirsch, E. D. (Eric Donald), 1928-

The new dictionary of cultural literacy; [by] E.D. Hirsch, Joseph F. Kett, James Trefil. Completely rev and updated, 3rd ed. Houghton Mifflin 2002 647p il maps $29.95

Grades: 8 9 10 11 12 Adult   **031**

1. Reference books 2. English language—Dictionaries

ISBN 0-618-22647-8   LC 2002-27609

First published 1988 with title: The dictionary of cultural literacy

"The text is divided into sections by subject—e.g., fine arts, world politics, life sciences—each with a brief introduction; access is also aided by a thorough index. The entries themselves are complete, concise, and clearly written as well as extensively and effectively cross-referenced." Libr J

The **new** encyclopaedia Britannica. 15th ed. Encyclopædia Britannica 2009 c2010 32v il map apply to publisher for price

Grades: 11 12 Adult   **031**

1. Encyclopedias and dictionaries 2. Reference books

ISBN 978-1-59339-837-8

Also available CD-ROM version and online

First published 1768 in England; in the United States 1902. Now published with the editorial advice of the University of Chicago. First published with current title with the fifteenth edition in 1974. Frequently revised

"In three sections: Propaedia, or outline of knowledge; Macropaedia, with longer in-depth articles covering major topics; and Micropaedia, with shorter A-to-Z ready reference entries. Britannica's reputation as the basic encyclopedia for all libraries and reference collections is based on the writing and knowledge of thousands of expert contributors and consultants. Updated between major editions by the Britannica Book of the Year." NY Public Libr Book of How & Where to Look It Up

Includes bibliographical references

The **World** Book encyclopedia. World Book, Inc. 2010 22v il map set $1,044 *

Grades: 4 5 6 7 8 9 10 11 12 Adult

031

1. Encyclopedias and dictionaries 2. Reference books

ISBN 978-0-7166-0110-4   LC 2009-29267

First published 1917-1918 by Field Enterprises. Frequently revised

Supplemented by: World Book's year in review; another available annual supplement is World Book's science year in review

"A 22-volume, highly illustrated, A-Z general encyclopedia for all ages, featuring sections on how to use World Book, other research aids, pronunciation key, a student guide to better writing, speaking, and research skills, and comprehensive index." Publisher's note

Includes bibliographical references

031.02 American books of miscellaneous facts

Ash, Russell

Top 10 of everything 2010. Hamlyn; Distributed in the US and Canada by Sterling Publishing 2009 256p il $24.95 *

Grades: 8 9 10 11 12 Adult   **031.02**

1. Curiosities and wonders 2. Reference books

ISSN 1541-7697

ISBN 978-0-600-62048-8

Annual. First published 1994 by Dorling Kindersley

Ash, Russell—*Continued*

This "is an entertaining, full-color collection of top ten lists covering an array of topics and disciplines, including, among many others, the universe, music and entertainment, sports, nature, history, and cultures." Libr J

Brahms, William B.

Notable last facts; a compendium of endings, conclusions, terminations and final events throughout history; compiled by William B. Brahms. Reference Desk Press 2005 834p $145

Grades: 11 12 Adult   **031.02**
1. Encyclopedias and dictionaries 2. Reference books
ISBN 0-9765325-0-6   LC 2005-901194

"Notable last facts, as defined by the compiler, are 'any historically significant event, person, place or thing that marks the end of its kind or its era.' These facts [include] the last self-service Horn & Hardart Automat in Manhattan, the last theatrical performance of Sir John Gielgud, the last year hurricanes had no name, the last game played by Red Sox legend Ted Williams, and so forth." Booklist

"This extensive compilation is a groundbreaking core reference work for libraries of all kinds." Choice

Includes bibliographical references

Famous first facts, international edition; a record of first happenings, discoveries, and inventions in world history; {edited by} Steven Anzovin & Janet Podell. Wilson, H.W. 2000 837p $140 *

Grades: 11 12 Adult   **031.02**
1. Encyclopedias and dictionaries 2. Reference books
ISBN 0-8242-0958-3   LC 99-86869

This work "contains more than 5000 firsts from hundreds of countries and ranging in time from 3.5 billion years ago (the age of the oldest continental land discovered) to 2001 (the scheduled date of completion of the first building over 1500 feet tall). . . . {It} groups related entries under broad subject categories (arranged alphabetically) and sub-categories. Within each category or sub-category, entries are arranged chronologically." Publisher's note

Kane, Joseph Nathan, 1899-2002

Famous first facts; a record of first happenings, discoveries, and inventions in American history; [by] Joseph Nathan Kane, Steven Anzovin, & Janet Podell. 6th ed. Wilson, H.W. 2006 1307p il $185 *

Grades: 5 6 7 8 9 10 11 12 Adult

                                                            031.02
1. Encyclopedias and dictionaries 2. United States—History—Dictionaries 3. Reference books
ISBN 978-0-8242-1065-6; 0-8242-1065-4
                                                 LC 2006-3096

Also available CD-ROM version and online

First published 1933

Over 7500 entries cover first occurences in American history, organized into 16 chapters each divided into sections. Sections are alphabetically organized, and individual entries are organized chronologically within each section. Includes five indexes: subject index, index by years, index by days, index to personal names, and geographical index

"Besides serving as an essential ready-reference source, the book is also fun to read out loud to colleagues—when was bubble gum first manufactured in the U.S.? When was the spray can introduced?" Booklist

The **New** York Public Library desk reference. 4th ed. Hyperion 2002 999p il maps $34.95

Grades: 11 12 Adult   **031.02**
1. Encyclopedias and dictionaries 2. Reference books
ISBN 0-7868-6846-5   LC 2002-27480

"A Stonesong Press book"

First published 1989 by Webster's New World

Divided into chapters, this reference features charts, tables, lists, and illustrations providing information in such categories as signs and symbols, mathematics and science basics, the arts, grammar and punctuation, etiquette, personal finance, first aid, and household tips.

Includes bibliographical references

The **New** York Times 2011 almanac; edited by John W. Wright with editors and reporters of the Times. Penguin Reference 2010 1004p map pa $12.95

Grades: 8 9 10 11 12 Adult   **031.02**
1. Almanacs 2. Statistics 3. United States—Statistics 4. Reference books
ISSN 1523-7079
ISBN 978-0-14-311894-7

Annual. First published 1997

This almanac contains a "chronology of the year; major news stories of the year; U.S. history; U.S. presidential biographies; world history; world geography; economic and climate data; major awards in the arts, sciences, and sports; and a wide variety of U.S. demographic information. . . . It is well organized, the table layout is easy to read, and the typeface does not invite eye strain." Am Ref Books Annu, 1998

The **New** York times guide to essential knowledge; a desk reference for the curious mind. Rev. and expanded 2nd ed. St. Martin's Press 2007 1320p il $35

Grades: 11 12 Adult   **031.02**
1. Encyclopedias and dictionaries 2. Reference books
ISBN 978-0-312-37659-8; 0-312-37659-6
                                                 LC 2007-38724

First published 2004

This book "defines nearly every facet of contemporary life—from arts, grammar, mythology, and culture to science, economics, and geopolitical issues. . . . An essential background reference for almost every subject." Libr J

Time almanac 2011. Time Home Entertainment 2010 864p il map $34.95; pa $13.99 *

Grades: 11 12 Adult   **031.02**
1. Almanacs 2. United States—Statistics 3. Reference books
ISBN 978-1-60320-164-3; 978-1-60320-165-0 (pa)

Also available online

"Powered by Encyclopedia Britannica"

Annual. Time almanac began with 1998 edition; absorbed Information please almanac in 1998

Also known as The Time almanac with Information please

Time almanac 2011—*Continued*
Contains statistical and factual material with a general topical arrangement and subject index. Illustrated with news photos and maps.

The **world** almanac and book of facts, 2011. World Almanac Books 2010 c2011 1008p il map $34.95 *
Grades: 6 7 8 9 10 11 12 Adult
                                                      031.02
1. Almanacs 2. Reference books
ISBN 978-1-60057-133-6
Annual. First published 1868. Publisher varies
"This is the most comprehensive and well-known of almanacs. . . . Contains a chronology of the year's events, consumer information, historical anniversaries, annual climatological data, and forecasts. Color section has flags and maps. Includes detailed index." N Y Public Libr Book of How & Where to Look It Up

032.02   English books of miscellaneous facts

Guinness world records. Guinness World Records il * $28.95
Grades: 5 6 7 8 9 10 11 12 Adult
                                                      032.02
1. Curiosities and wonders 2. Reference books
ISSN 1475-7419
Annual. First published 1955 in the United Kingdom; in the United States 1962. Variant titles: Guinness book of records; Guinness book of world records
"Ready reference for current record holders in all fields, some esoteric. Index provides access to information arranged in broad subject categories. Must be replaced annually." N Y Public Libr. Ref Books for Child Collect

060.4   Special topics of general organizations

Robert, Henry Martyn, 1837-1923
Robert's Rules of order newly revised. Perseus Pub. 2000 various paging $37.50 *
Grades: 11 12 Adult   **060.4**
1. Parliamentary practice
ISBN 0-7382-0384-X; 978-0-7382-0384-3
                                      LC 2004-351757
First published 1876 as Pocket manual of rules of order for deliberate assemblies. Title and publisher vary
"A new and enlarged edition by Sarah Corbin Robert, Henry M. Robert III, William J. Evans, Daniel H. Honemann, Thomas J. Balch" New edition in preparation
"Long the standard compendium of parliamentary law, explaining methods of organizing and conducting the business of societies, conventions, and other assemblies. Includes convenient charts and tables." Ref Sources for Small & Medium-sized Libr. 6th edition

Sturgis, Alice
The standard code of parliamentary procedure; original edition by Alice Sturgis. 4th ed, revised by the American Institute of Parliamentarians. McGraw-Hill 2001 xxiv, 285p pa $14.95
Grades: 11 12 Adult   **060.4**
1. Parliamentary practice
ISBN 0-07-136513-3   LC 2001-265929
First published 1950
This guide to the rules of parliamentary procedure includes explanations of their purpose and examples of their use. Also considers ways the Internet and other technologies have rewritten rules of meetings.
Includes bibliographical references

Zimmerman, Doris P., 1931-
Robert's Rules in plain English. Collins 2005 171p pa $7.95
Grades: 9 10 11 12   **060.4**
1. Parliamentary practice
ISBN 0-06-078779-1; 978-0-06-078779-0
First published 1997
Abbreviated essential parliamentary rules condensed from Robert's Rules of order newly revised
Covers methods of organizing and conducting business of societies, organizations, governing bodies, and other types of assemblies.

070.1   Documentary media, educational media, news media

Garner, Joe
We interrupt this broadcast; the events that stopped our lives—from the Hindenburg explosion to the Virginia Tech shooting; [foreword by Walter Cronkite; afterword by Brian Williams; narrated by Bill Kurtis] 10th anniversary ed. Sourcebooks MediaFusion 2008 194p il $49.95
Grades: 7 8 9 10 11 12 Adult   **070.1**
1. Television broadcasting of news 2. Broadcast journalism 3. Disasters
ISBN 978-1-4022-1319-9; 1-4022-1319-0
                                      LC 2008-20015
First published 1998
Includes 3 audio CDs
This book and 3 CD set "documents, in text, audio and black-and-white photographs, the moments when history, for better or for worse (though usually for worse), was made in an instant. . . . In addition to the CDs' reports and sound bites dramatically introduced and explained . . . each event gets about four pages of coverage, with an efficient summary and at least half a dozen photos. . . . These are the kinds of moments that still shock and amaze. This moving book is 'a tribute of sorts' to the events that defined eras, the journalists who reported on them and the media television, radio that made us all witnesses." Publ Wkly

Henderson, Harry, 1951-
Power of the news media. Facts on File 2004
316p il (Library in a book) $45
Grades: 11 12 Adult   **070.1**
1. Broadcast journalism 2. Press
ISBN 0-8160-4768-5   LC 2003-18900
This book "covers the history of news traced through
newspapers, television, radio, and the Internet; issues related to the media; and information on laws related to
the media and how legislation affects our news coverage.
Important cases are reviewed chronologically from 1735
to 2003." Libr Media Connect
The author's "format—breaking topics into quick-hit
subsections—makes it an ideal source for students researching a particular aspect of news media. . . . Every
American should have a working knowledge of the topic,
and this book is a recommended resource." Voice Youth
Advocates
Includes bibliographical references

Seib, Philip M., 1949-
Going live; getting the news right in a real-time,
online world; [by] Philip Seib. Rowman &
Littlefield 2001 197p $24.95
Grades: 9 10 11 12   **070.1**
1. Television broadcasting of news
ISBN 0-7425-0900-1   LC 00-42562
The author "looks at the challenges to news delivery,
profits, and ethics borne of new technology that encourages speed over accuracy. Seib sees a convergence in
news gathering styles of various media that is inspired by
computer-based media. . . . Faced with competitive pressures, many traditional news outlets (with newspapers
leading the way) have developed their own Web sites,
including linkages to other sites and sources, blurring the
line between professional news organizations and others.
. . . This is a compelling look at how news gathering is
changing, for better and worse." Booklist
Includes bibliographical references

070.4   Journalism

Foerstel, Herbert N.
From Watergate to Monicagate; ten
controversies in modern journalism and media.
Greenwood Press 2001 279p il $60.95
Grades: 11 12 Adult   **070.4**
1. Journalism 2. Mass media
ISBN 0-313-31163-3   LC 00-61698
The author discusses "problems facing the media, such
as mergers that drastically reduce the number of independent media, government giveaway of the 'digital spectrum,' PR masquerading as news, the power of lobbyists,
CIA agents in the media, government censorship,
paparazzi, and journalistic plagiarism. . . . Chapters cover radio; TV; newspapers; the Internet; and unlicensed
radio stations, which provide local news coverage that
focus on minorities, community groups, and schools. An
excellent book for journalism and government students
and staff." Book Rep
Includes bibliographical references

Freedman, Samuel G.
Letters to a young journalist. Basic Books 2006
184p (Art of mentoring) $22.95
Grades: 11 12 Adult   **070.4**
1. Journalism 2. Vocational guidance
ISBN 0-465-02455-6; 978-0-465-02455-1
LC 2005-37974
The author takes a "look at the practice of American
journalism. He recalls his own achievements and shortcomings over a long career as well as other great and not
so great moments in American journalism. . . . Freedman speaks very directly and personally, offering encouragement with equal portions of reality about the state of
modern journalism from corporate influences to the blurring of lines between truth and propaganda." Booklist
Includes bibliographical references

Kern, Jonathan, 1953-
Sound reporting; the NPR guide to audio
journalism and production. University of Chicago
Press 2008 382p $55; pa $20
Grades: 11 12 Adult   **070.4**
1. Broadcast journalism 2. Radio—Production and direction
ISBN   978-0-226-43177-2;   0-226-43177-0;
978-0-226-43178-9 (pa); 0-226-43178-9 (pa)
LC 2008-3994
The author "delineates the values and practices that
yield stellar audio journalism. Comprehensive and lucid,
this distinctive handbook explains how sound paints pictures and how narratives are shaped and paced for the
ear instead of the eye." Booklist

Real sports reporting; edited by Abraham
Aamidor. Indiana Univ. Press 2003 260p
$49.95; pa $19.95
Grades: 11 12 Adult   **070.4**
1. Reporters and reporting 2. Sports
ISBN 0-253-34273-2; 0-253-21616-8 (pa)
LC 2003-2448
This book "is divided into two sections. The first,
'Beat Coverage,' features articles on writing about various sports: football, hockey, soccer, golf, tennis, baseball;
there's even a general article on how to write a sports
column. . . . Part two, 'The Rest of the Story,' offers
more general advice, with articles on covering high-
school and college sports, doing freelance sports writing,
and becoming a sports editor. It's a vastly informative
book, a real treat for budding journalists and even a few
sports fans with an interest in writing." Booklist

Reporting America at war; an oral history;
compiled by Michelle Ferrari with commentary
by James Tobin. Hyperion 2003 241p il $23.95
Grades: 11 12 Adult   **070.4**
1. War 2. Reporters and reporting
ISBN 1-401-30072-3   LC 2003-49966
"Beginning with Edward R. Morrow's live reports
during the London blitz and ending with an epilogue on
the second war in Iraq, this oral history contains transcripts of interviews with 11 top correspondents. Murrow
is one of three deceased reporters included (the others
are Martha Gellhorn and Homer Bigart), along with Walter Cronkite, Andy Rooney, Frank Gibney, Malcolm

Reporting America at war—*Continued*
Browne, David Halberstam, Morley Safer, Ward Just, Gloria Emerson, Chris Hedges and Christiane Amanpour. . . . Tobin's introductions and transitional and informational interpolations within the transcripts hold this informative volume together." Publ Wkly

Includes bibliographical references

070.5 Publishing

Todd, Mark
Whatcha mean, what's a zine? the art of making zines and mini comics; [by] Mark Todd + Esther Peal Watson; with contributions by more than 20 creators of Indie-comics and magazines. Houghton Mifflin 2006 110p il pa $12.99
Grades: 7 8 9 10   **070.5**
1. Zines 2. Desktop publishing 3. Comic books, strips, etc.
ISBN 978-0-618-56315-9; 0-618-56315-6
LC 2005-55026
"A zine is a mini-magazine or homemade comic about any topic of the creator's choice, designed for maximum creativity and expression. The authors present a history of self-publishing. . . . Other topics include ideas for zine subjects; copying, binding, and printing tips, including easy-to-understand silk-screening and gocco instruction. . . . Throughout, technical terms are deftly used and advice is dispensed in an accessible, rousing format that includes comics, drawings, and cut-and-paste zine techniques. This well-designed and entertaining resource is sure to find an audience among hip, artistic, and do-it-yourself enthusiasts." SLJ

071 Journalism and newspapers in North America

Burns, Eric
Infamous scribblers; the founding fathers and the rowdy beginnings of American journalism. Public Affairs 2006 467p hardcover o.p. pa $15.95
Grades: 11 12 Adult   **071**
1. Journalism 2. Newspapers—United States
ISBN   978-1-58648-334-0;   1-58648-334-X;
978-1-58648-428-6 (pa); 1-58648-428-1 (pa)
LC 2005-53542
The author "explores the role newspapers played in the founding of the country." Libr J
"From the sniping feuds among Boston's first papers to sex scandals involving Alexander Hamilton and Thomas Jefferson, the snappy patter gives clear indication of how much Burns . . . relishes telling his story." Publ Wkly
Includes bibliographical references

The **New** new journalism; conversations with America's best nonfiction writers on their craft; [edited and with an introduction by] Robert S. Boynton. Vintage Books 2005 xxxiv, 456p pa $13.95
Grades: 11 12 Adult   **071**
1. Journalism
ISBN 1-400-03356-X   LC 2004-57161

The author "offers interviews with 19 writers who detail how and why they produce their work. . . . A fascinating book that makes the reader want to go out and get every book the writers have written as well as those mentioned as sources of inspiration." Booklist

Includes bibliographical references

Written into history; Pulitzer Prize reporting of the twentieth century from the New York times; edited and with an introduction by Anthony Lewis. Times Bks. 2001 xxv, 355p hardcover o.p. pa $17
Grades: 11 12 Adult   **071**
1. Journalism 2. Pulitzer Prizes
ISBN 0-8050-6849-X; 0-8050-7178-4 (pa)
LC 2001-35555
The award-winning articles "are sorted into the following categories: investigative reporting; dangerous stories that put reporters at risk; international news; public advocacy; criticism of the arts; science reporting; and biographical and human-interest stories. Among the topics are Russian slave-labor camps during the 1950s, the Pentagon Papers, the Vietnam War, and exploitation of illegal aliens in the U.S." Booklist
"For anyone interested in recent history or journalism at its best, this book will prove worthwhile." Publ Wkly

080 Quotations

Adler, Mortimer J., 1902-2001
How to think about the great ideas; from the great books of Western civilization; {by} Mortimer J. Adler; edited by Max Weismann. Open Court 2000 xxiv, 530p pa $24.95
Grades: 11 12 Adult   **080**
1. Great books of the Western world
ISBN 0-8126-9412-0   LC 99-45251
This volume contains the transcripts of 52 half-hour segments of Adler's 1953-1954 television program The great ideas
"The book showcases Adler's ideas about all the big categories—truth, beauty, freedom, love, sex, art, justice, rationality, humankind's nature, Darwinism, government." Publ Wkly

100 PHILOSOPHY

Blackburn, Simon
Think: a compelling introduction to philosophy. Oxford Univ. Press 1999 312p $25
Grades: 11 12 Adult   **100**
1. Philosophy
ISBN 0-19-210024-6   LC 00-265266
The author explores such areas as knowledge, mind, free will, identity, God, goodness and justice. "His method is to introduce what other philosophers—primarily Plato, Descartes, Locke, Berkeley, Leibniz, Hume, and Kant—have had to say about these themes. . . . Readers new to the subject could very well be captivated." Libr J

Includes bibliographical references

Bloom, Harold, 1930-
Essayists and prophets. Chelsea House Publishers 2005 221p (Bloom's literary criticism 20th anniversary collection) $38.95; pa $19.95
Grades: 9 10 11 12   **100**
1. Philosophers
ISBN 0-7910-8523-6; 0-7910-8524-4 (pa)
LC 2005-5523
"Bloom muses on some of the greatest philosophical and critical thinkers to have graced the page. Some of the writers covered included Friedrich Nietzsche, William Hazlitt, and Sigmund Freud." Publisher's note
Includes bibliographical references

Phillips, Christopher, 1959-
Socrates café; a fresh taste of philosophy. Norton 2001 232p hardcover o.p. pa $13.95
Grades: 11 12 Adult   **100**
1. Philosophy
ISBN 0-393-04956-6; 0-393-32298-X (pa)
LC 00-62211
"Former journalist Phillips travels around the country to elicit dialogs, questions, and philosophical investigations from nonacademic participants. Elementary schools, senior-citizen facilities, public coffeehouses, and other well-populated venues provide the backdrops for the discussions he reports in this account of what 'doing philosophy' can and does mean in contemporary culture." Libr J
Includes bibliographical references

Van Lente, Fred
Action philosophers! Evil Twin Comics 2006 92p il pa $6.95 *
Grades: 10 11 12   **100**
1. Graphic novels 2. Philosophy—Graphic novels 3. Humorous graphic novels
ISBN 0-9778329-0-2; 978-0-9778329-0-3
This book combines a summary of the basic tenets of philosophers Plato, Bodhidharma, Nietzsche, Thomas Jefferson, St. Augustine, Ayn Rand, Sigmund Freud, Carl Jung, and Joseph Campbell with irreverent artistic portrayals. Imagine Plato as a masked wrestler (shouting "Plato smash!"), or Bodhidharma as a kung fu master. The section on Freud frankly discusses and portrays some of his more controversial psychosexual ideas.

103   Dictionaries, encyclopedias, concordances of philosophy

The **Cambridge** dictionary of philosophy; edited by Robert Audi. 2nd ed. Cambridge Univ. Press 1999 xxxv, 1001p il hardcover o.p. pa $32.99
Grades: 11 12 Adult   **103**
1. Reference books 2. Philosophy—Dictionaries
ISBN 0-521-63136-X; 0-521-63722-8 (pa)
LC 99-12920
First published 1995
This work contains some 4,400 entries including 50 on major contemporary philosophers. Wide coverage of Western philosophy as well as non-Western and non-

European philosophers is included. The rapidly growing fields of philosophy of mind and applied ethics are also covered

The **Oxford** companion to philosophy; edited by Ted Honderich. 2nd ed., new ed. Oxford University Press 2005 1056p il $60 *
Grades: 11 12 Adult   **103**
1. Reference books 2. Philosophy—Encyclopedias
ISBN 0-19-926479-1   LC 2005-275452
First published 1995
"Including more than 2200 alphabetically arranged entries from nearly 300 contributors, . . . [this book] provides an encyclopedic view of philosophy's past and present, its ideas, disputes (the editor himself contributes an article on unlikely philosophical propositions), and key figures, living and dead. . . . This title makes an excellent companion for standard multivolume subject encyclopedias." SLJ
Includes bibliographical references

109   Historical and collected persons treatment of philosophy

Durant, William James, 1885-1981
The story of philosophy; the lives and opinions of the great philosophers; by Will Durant. [2nd ed] Simon & Schuster 1933 412p hardcover o.p. pa $15
Grades: 11 12 Adult   **109**
1. Philosophy—History 2. Philosophers
ISBN 0-671-69500-2; 0-671-20159-X (pa)
First published 1926
A selective account of western thinkers from Socrates and Kant to Schopenhauer and Dewey.
Includes bibliographical references

King, Peter J., 1935-
One hundred philosophers; the life and work of the world's greatest thinkers. Barron's Educ. Ser. 2004 192p il pa $19.95 *
Grades: 11 12 Adult   **109**
1. Philosophers
ISBN 0-7641-2791-8   LC 2003-110643
This is "an overview of 100 important philosophers, from the ancient Greek pre-Socratics to today's analytic philosophers. Each thinker is summarized in an illustrated page . . . with a biographical sketch and summary of major works and ideas." Publisher's note
The author "has done a masterful job in presenting the life and work of what he calls 'the world's greatest thinkers.' . . . The concise and clearly written description of the thinker's life and ideas are just what a student or a layperson needs to gather an overview of the thinker's life and intellectual contributions." Am Ref Books Annu, 2005
Includes bibliographical references

Russell, Bertrand, 1872-1970
A history of Western philosophy; and its
connection with political and social circumstances
from the earliest times to the present day. Simon
& Schuster 1945 xxiii, 895p hardcover o.p. pa $25
Grades: 11 12 Adult   **109**
1. Philosophy—History 2. Philosophers
ISBN 0-671-31400-9; 0-671-20158-1 (pa)
Originally designed and partly delivered as lectures at
the Barnes Foundation in Pennsylvania
Contents: Ancient philosophy; Catholic philosophy;
Modern philosophy.
"My purpose is to exhibit philosophy as an integral
part of social and political life; not as the isolated specu-
lations of remarkable individuals." Preface

Solomon, Robert C., 1942-2007
A short history of philosophy; {by} Robert C.
Solomon, Kathleen M. Higgins. Oxford Univ.
Press 1996 329p hardcover o.p. pa $23.95
Grades: 11 12 Adult   **109**
1. Philosophy—History
ISBN 0-19-508647-3; 0-19-510196-0 (pa)
LC 95-12578
"This general history of philosophy . . . focuses on
Western philosophy, but also discusses non-Western
philosophical traditions. The authors cover major philoso-
phers and movements as well as minor but interesting
figures. They treat serious religious thought as philosoph-
ical, and include information about the Jewish, Christian,
and other religious traditions." Publisher's note
"This is a fine overview of the subject that any interested reader will find rewarding." Libr J
Includes bibliographical references

World philosophers and their works; editor, John
K. Roth; managing editor, Christina J. Moose;
project editor, Rowena Wildin. Salem Press
2000 3v il set $331
Grades: 11 12 Adult   **109**
1. Philosophers
ISBN 0-89356-878-3   LC 99-55143
The editor "presents substantial entries that for 226
philosophers give brief biographies, justify the inclusion
of each thinker, list their most important works, analyze
their lifework, and locate them within the context of philosophy." Choice
Includes bibliographical references

111 Ontology

Adler, Mortimer J., 1902-2001
Six great ideas; truth, goodness, beauty, liberty,
equality, justice: ideas we judge by, ideas we act
on. Simon & Schuster 1997 243p pa $12
Grades: 11 12 Adult   **111**
1. Truth 2. Good and evil 3. Aesthetics 4. Justice
5. Equality 6. Freedom
ISBN 0-684-82681-X
"A Touchstone book"
First published 1981 by Macmillan

"In the first half of this book, Adler discusses the
question whether truth, goodness, and beauty are objective features of the world. . . . The second half of the
book . . . distinguishes different ideals of equality, analyzes several senses of liberty, and argues for the priority
of justice over equality and liberty." Libr J

113   Cosmology (Philosophy of nature)

Lynch, Thomas, 1948-
Bodies in motion and at rest; on metaphor and
mortality. Norton 2000 275p hardcover o.p. pa
$12.95 *
Grades: 11 12 Adult   **113**
1. Life 2. Death
ISBN 0-393-04927-2; 0-393-32164-9 (pa)
LC 00-21355
This collection of essays shows how Americans live
and how they die. It presents attitude toward death and
offers counseling and comforting advice to the bereft.
The author "engages the reader with a mixture of poetic and funerary elements. . . . His voice is rich and
generous." N Y Times

Marshall, Peter H., 1946-
Nature's web; rethinking our place on earth;
[by] Peter Marshall. Paragon House 1994 513p
$29.95
Grades: 11 12 Adult   **113**
1. Philosophy of nature
ISBN 1-55778-652-6   LC 93-17233
In this "search for a new environmental ethic, Mar-
shall . . . traces the development of human attitudes
about nature from ancient times to the present." Publ
Wkly
"This is a wonderful history of 'green' ideas." Choice
Includes bibliographical references

128   Humankind

The **Oxford** companion to the mind; edited by
Richard L. Gregory. 2nd ed. Oxford University
Press 2005 1004p il $75 *
Grades: 11 12 Adult   **128**
1. Reference books 2. Psychology—Dictionaries
ISBN 0-19-866224-6   LC 2004-275127
First published 1987
This book "contains over 1000 alphabetically arranged
entries on all aspects of the mind, including topics in
neurophysiology, communication, psychology, and phi-
losophy, as well as people relevant to the field." Libr J
This "is one of those texts one wishes for enough
hours in the day to read from cover to cover. . . . For
those interested in the mind, this is a wonderful reference
and a resource for learning more about themselves." Sci
Books Films

133.1 Apparitions

Classic American ghost stories; 200 years of ghost lore from the Great Plains, New England, the South, and the Pacific Northwest; edited by Deborah A. Downer. August House 1990 214p $19.95; pa $9.95
Grades: 11 12 Adult   **133.1**
1. Ghosts
ISBN 0-87483-115-6; 0-87483-118-0 (pa)
LC 90-34782
"Editor Deborah Downer brings together stories from newspapers, journals, and magazines, none of which were written as fictitious. An index references story locations by city and state." Publisher's note

Guiley, Rosemary Ellen
The encyclopedia of ghosts and spirits; foreword by Troy Taylor. 3rd ed. Facts on File 2007 564p il $75
Grades: 11 12 Adult   **133.1**
1. Reference books 2. Ghosts—Encyclopedias
ISBN 978-0-8160-6737-4; 0-8160-6737-6
LC 2006-103302
First published 1992
This work examines famous hauntings, historical personages and happenings, and various legends and myths about ghosts and spirits throughout the world. Recent events, new findings about old myths and updated information on major figures in the field are covered.
"Believers and skeptics alike seeking information on various phenomena will find this book useful." Booklist
Includes bibliographical references

133.3 Divinatory arts

Levitt, Susan
Teen feng shui; design your space, design your life. Bindu Books 2003 223p il pa $14.95 *
Grades: 9 10 11 12   **133.3**
1. Feng shui
ISBN 0-89281-916-2   LC 2003-745
"Feng shui, the Chinese art of placement . . . is explored here with a uniquely young adult perspective, focusing almost solely on a teen's bedroom. . . . Teens with an interest in feng shui, eastern philosophies, or self-improvement will find this book accessible and enjoyable." Voice Youth Advocates

Pickover, Clifford A.
Dreaming the future; the fantastic story of prediction. Prometheus Bks. 2001 452p $28 *
Grades: 9 10 11 12   **133.3**
1. Divination 2. Fortune telling 3. Prophecies
ISBN 1-573-92895-X   LC 00-51838
This work examines various methods of fortune-telling, such as tarot cards, the zodiac, astrology and human sacrifice. Major prophecies by famous soothsayers throughout the history of prediction are explored, including the insight of Nostradamus, Edgar Cayce, Jeanne

Dixon and the children of Fatima
"True believers and skeptics alike cannot fail to be won over by Pickover's disarming affection for his subjects . . . this book should delight." Publ Wkly
Includes bibliographical references

133.4 Demonology and witchcraft

Aronson, Marc
Witch-hunt: mysteries of the Salem witch trials. Atheneum Bks. for Young Readers 2003 272p il $18.95 *
Grades: 9 10 11 12   **133.4**
1. Trials 2. Witchcraft 3. Salem (Mass.)—History
ISBN 0-689-84864-1   LC 2002-152768
"An eye-opening exploration of what is known to have taken place in Salem in 1692, and of a variety of interpretations that have been perpetuated about the happenings. A dynamic narrative hooks readers into thinking about the mysteries of the past and their continued influence on modern life." SLJ
Includes bibliographical references

Burns, William E.
Witch hunts in Europe and America; an encyclopedia. Greenwood Press 2003 400p $75
Grades: 9 10 11 12   **133.4**
1. Reference books 2. Witchcraft—Encyclopedias 3. Persecution 4. Trials
ISBN 0-313-32142-6   LC 2003-44074
"After an alphabetical list of entries, there's a chronology from 1307 to 1793, indicating the time span of coverage. Topics include witch hunts in various countries, major individual witch hunts and trials, aspects of the witch-hunting process, demonological writers who were both supporters and opponents of witch-hunting, and subsequent interpretations of the witch hunt by historians and others." Libr Media Connect

Carlson, Laurie M., 1952-
A fever in Salem; a new interpretation of the New England witch trials. Dee, I.R. 1999 197p hardcover o.p. pa $14.95 *
Grades: 11 12 Adult   **133.4**
1. Witchcraft 2. Salem (Mass.)—History
ISBN 1-56663-253-6; 1-56663-309-5 (pa)
LC 99-27520
In this reading of the New England witch trials, Carlson argues that "the 'possessed' of Salem, and perhaps of many other places where witchcraft was suspected, were in thrall not to devilry but to a mysterious disease of the brain, encephalitis lethargica, popularly known as sleeping sickness." New Yorker
"Carlson's compelling narrative begs for assessment by medical experts. A valuable purchase for libraries seeking more than a basic summary of the witch trials." Libr J
Includes bibliographical references

Demos, John, 1937-
Entertaining Satan; witchcraft and the culture of early New England; [by] John Putnam Demos. Updated ed. Oxford University Press 2004 543p il map $74; pa $21.95 *
Grades: 9 10 11 12   **133.4**
  1. Witchcraft 2. New England—History
  ISBN 0-19-517484-4; 0-19-517483-6 (pa)
                         LC 2004-54701
  First published 1982
  "This is not simply a monograph on witchcraft but a major attempt to understand the kind of society and the kind of culture in which witchcraft had a place. To that end Demos employs nearly every conceptual tool available to the historian, including those borrowed from psychology, anthropology, and sociology." N Y Rev Books
  Includes bibliographical references

Goss, K. David, 1952-
The Salem witch trials; a reference guide. Greenwood Press 2007 189p il $55
Grades: 9 10 11 12 Adult   **133.4**
  1. Reference books 2. Trials 3. Witchcraft 4. Salem (Mass.)—History
  ISBN 978-0-313-32095-8   LC 2007-38695
  This reference "examines the origins, the accusations, early interpretations, contemporary interpretations, and the impact of the trials. . . . This book also includes a chronology of events, biographies of key figures involved, fifty primary source documents, a glossary of terms, an annotated bibliography, and a thorough index. . . . This book would be a great addition to any library." Libr Media Connect
  Includes bibliographical references

Guiley, Rosemary Ellen
The encyclopedia of witches, witchcraft, and Wicca. 3rd ed. Facts On File 2008 436p il $85; pa $24.95
Grades: 11 12 Adult   **133.4**
  1. Witchcraft—Encyclopedias 2. Reference books
  ISBN   978-0-8160-7103-6;   0-8160-7103-9; 978-0-8160-7104-3 (pa); 0-8160-7104-7 (pa)
                         LC 2008-8917
  First published 1989 with title: The encyclopedia of witches and witchcraft
  "Spanning centuries and continents, the book defines 480 of witchcraft's and wizardry's major historical events, figures, tools, sites, symbols, and abstract terms. The highly engaging, alphabetically organized entries run several paragraphs in length and deftly clarify a term's etymology as well as its spiritual, historical, or spell-making significance." Libr J
  Includes bibliographical references

Kallen, Stuart A., 1955-
Witches. Lucent Bks. 2000 112p il (Mystery library) lib bdg $27.45
Grades: 9 10 11 12   **133.4**
  1. Witchcraft
  ISBN 1-56006-688-1   LC 00-8062

The first half of this book "covers the history of witchcraft in Europe and America until the mid-eighteenth century. The second half takes a look at modern witchcraft, mainly Wicca, explaining rituals and beliefs with an eye toward demystifying Wicca's practice as religion. The author acknowledges the controversy surrounding witchcraft that still exists today." Booklist
Includes bibliographical references

Satanism; Allen Gaborro, book editor. Greenhaven Press 2007 91p (At issue. Religion) lib bdg $31.80; pa $22.50
Grades: 9 10 11 12   **133.4**
  1. Satanism
  ISBN 978-0-7377-2414-1 (lib bdg); 0-7377-2414-5 (lib bdg); 978-0-7377-2415-8 (pa); 0-7377-2415-3 (pa)
                       LC 2006026964
  "This is a well-constructed collection of essays on Satanism and its role in modern society. The introduction stays neutral, and the essays present a broad range of opinion, from Christian views to secular views and Satanist views." SLJ
  Includes bibliographical references

133.5   Astrology

Lewis, James R., 1949-
The astrology book; the encyclopedia of heavenly influences. 2nd ed. Visible Ink Press 2003 928p il pa $24.95
Grades: 11 12 Adult   **133.5**
  1. Reference books 2. Astrology—Encyclopedias
  ISBN 1-57859-144-9
  Also available in hardcover from Omnigraphics
  First published 1994 by Gale Res. with title: The astrology encyclopedia
  This "defines and explains more than 800 astrological terms and concepts from air signs to Zeus. . . . *The Astrology Book* includes a special section on casting a chart, plus a . . . chapter that explains and interprets every planet in every house and sign. The text also includes a table of astrological glyphs and abbreviations, and a list of organizations, books, periodicals, and Web sites." Publisher's note
  "Although aimed at the believer, Lewis' work may be confidently consulted by the skeptic seeking basic information about astrology." Booklist

Woolfolk, Joanna Martine
The only astrology book you'll ever need. New ed., Taylor Trade Pub. pbk. ed. rev. and updated. Taylor Trade Pub. 2008 534p il pa $19.95 *
Grades: 9 10 11 12   **133.5**
  1. Astrology
  ISBN 978-1-58979-377-4   LC 2001-31798
  First published 1982 by Stein and Day
  Includes CD-ROM
  This book features "planetary tables that allow anyone born between 1900 and 2100 to pinpoint . . . their sun and moon signs, discover their ascendants, and map out the exact positions of the planets at the time of their birth. . . . In addition to revealing the planets' influence

Woolfolk, Joanna Martine—*Continued*
on romance, health, and career, . . . [this book] takes a
closer look at the inner life of each sign." Publisher's
note
Includes bibliographical references

133.9   Spiritualism

Is there life after death? Rebecca K. O'Connor,
book editor. Greenhaven Press 2005 106p (At
issue) hardcover o.p. pa $22.50
Grades: 9 10 11 12   133.9
1. Future life
ISBN 0-7377-2406-4 (lib bdg); 0-7377-2407-2 (pa)
                                                        LC 2004-52399
"Authors in this anthology present both sides of the
argument about the afterlife." Publisher's note
Includes bibliographical references

Roach, Mary
Spook; science tackles the afterlife. Norton 2005
311p il $24.95 *
Grades: 11 12 Adult   133.9
1. Future life 2. Religion and science
ISBN 0-393-05962-6   LC 2005-14450
The author investigates a range of theories and beliefs
about the soul's migration after death.
"Roach perfectly balances her skepticism and her
boundless curiosity with a sincere desire to know. . . .
She is an original who can enliven any subject with wit,
keen reporting and a sly intelligence." Publ Wkly
Includes bibliographical references

141   Idealism and related systems and doctrines

The **essential** transcendentalists; edited and
introduced by Richard G. Geldard. J.P.
Tarcher/Penguin 2005 265p pa $15.95 *
Grades: 11 12 Adult   141
1. Transcendentalism
ISBN 1-58542-434-X   LC 2005-44016
This study "is divided into three main sections. . . .
The first is 'Primary Texts,' with selections from the
writings of Sampson Reed, James Marsh, Amos Alcott
(father of Louisa May), and Ralph Waldo Emerson. The
second, 'Individual Voices,' introduces selections from
Frederic Hedge, Margaret Fuller, and Henry David Thoreau. The last is 'The Transcendental Heritage,' which
features the works of Walt Whitman, Emily Dickinson,
Wallace Stevens, Loren Eiseley, and Annie Dillard. This
is a highly informed, elegantly written, fascinating story
told through commentary, historical overview, and selections from classic works. It belongs in all libraries." Libr
J

Includes bibliographical references

150   Psychology

Cohen, Lisa J.
The handy psychology answer book. Visible Ink
Press 2011 502p il pa $21.95 *
Grades: 11 12 Adult   150
1. Psychology
ISBN 978-1-57859-223-4; 1-57859-2232
                                                        LC 2010-42165
This book covers the fundamentals and history of psy-
chology, plus the practical psychology behind how peo-
ple deal with money, sex, morality, family, children,
aging, addiction, work, and other everyday issues.
"A solid, affordable supplement to introductory psychology texts for readers with a general interest in psychology." Libr J
Includes glossary and bibliographical references

150.19   Systems, schools, viewpoints

Freud, Sigmund, 1856-1939
The basic writings of Sigmund Freud; translated
and edited by A.A. Brill. Modern Lib. 1995 c1938
973p $24.95
Grades: 11 12 Adult   150.19
1. Psychoanalysis
ISBN 0-679-60166-X   LC 95-13411
A reissue of the 1938 edition
Contents: Psychopathology of everyday life; The interpretation of dreams; Three contributions to the theory of
sex; Wit and its relations to the unconscious; Totem and
taboo; The history of the psychoanalytic movement

Jung, C. G. (Carl Gustav), 1875-1961
The basic writings of C. G. Jung; edited with an
introduction by Violet Staub de Laszlo. Modern
Lib. 1993 c1959 xxxiii, 691p $21.95
Grades: 11 12 Adult   150.19
1. Psychoanalysis
ISBN 0-679-60071-X   LC 93-17801
Also available in paperback from Princeton Univ.
Press
This is a reissue of the 1959 edition
This volume contains excerpts from Symbols of trans-
formation, On the nature of the psyche, Relations be-
tween the ego and the unconscious, Psychological types,
Psychology of the transference, and Psychology and reli-
gion. It also includes Archetypes of the collective unconscious, Psychological aspects of the mother archetype,
On the nature of dreams, On the psychogenesis of schizophrenia, Introduction to the religious and psychological
problems of alchemy, and Marriage as a psychological
relationship.
Includes bibliographical references

Rogers, Carl R. (Carl Ransom), 1902-1987
A way of being. Houghton Mifflin 1980 395p
pa $15 hardcover o.p.
Grades: 11 12 Adult   150.19
1. Psychology 2. Humanism
ISBN 0-395-75530-1 (pa)   LC 80-20275

Rogers, Carl R. (Carl Ransom), 1902-1987—
Continued
The author offers a "collection of papers, talks, autobiographical sketches and vignettes of patients' experiences in workshops and therapy." Publ Wkly
"This is a book rich in theoretical insights and experiential sharing, and full of invigorating optimism." Libr J
Includes bibliographical references

Skinner, B. F. (Burrhus Frederic), 1904-1990
About behaviorism. Knopf 1974 256p pa $12 hardcover o.p.
Grades: 11 12 Adult   150.19
1. Behaviorism
ISBN 0-394-71618-3 (pa)
The author defines, analyzes and defends the science of behaviorism with chapters exploring the causes of behavior, operant behavior, verbal behavior, thinking, causes and reasons, knowledge, emotion and self
Includes bibliographical references

Thurschwell, Pamela, 1966-
Sigmund Freud. 2nd ed. Routledge 2009 162p (Routledge critical thinkers) $95; pa $22.95 *
Grades: 11 12 Adult   150.19
1. Freud, Sigmund, 1856-1939 2. Psychoanalysis
ISBN 978-0-415-47368-2; 978-0-415-47369-9 (pa)
First published 2000
"The book contains chapters on early theories, interpretation, sexuality, case histories, maps of the mind, society and religion, and psychoanalysis's aftermath, including feminist criticism and a remarkable summary of Jacques Lacan's role." Booklist [review of 2000 edition]
Includes bibliographical references

150.3 Psychology—Encyclopedias and dictionaries

Cordón, Luis A.
Popular psychology; an encyclopedia. Greenwood Press 2005 274p il $75 *
Grades: 11 12 Adult   150.3
1. Reference books 2. Psychology—Encyclopedias
ISBN 0-313-32457-3   LC 2004-17426
This "encyclopedia explains the accuracies and fallacies of contemporary popular psychology when compared to the discipline practiced by professional psychologists. . . . Entries cover pop psychologists (Noam Chomsky, Deepak Chopra, Dr. Phil McGraw) and historical theoreticians (Erikson, Freud, Jung, Skinner). Other entries treat controversial topics and 'pseudoscience'—e.g., aromatherapy, dianetics/scientology, EMDR, facilitated communication, subliminal perception." Choice
This book "provides a concise guide for anyone seeking to understand the true scientific nature of psychology." Libr Media Connect
Includes bibliographical references

The **Gale** encyclopedia of psychology; Bonnie R. Strickland, executive editor. 2nd ed. Gale Group 2001 701p il $191.50
Grades: 11 12 Adult   150.3
1. Reference books 2. Psychology—Encyclopedias
ISBN 0-7876-4786-1   LC 00-34736
First published 1996
Coverage includes noteworthy people, movements, theories, and important case studies and experiments. The articles, ranging from 25 to 1,500 words examine such diverse topics as abnormal psychology, bipolar disorder, Sigmund Freud and insomnia
Includes bibliographical references

Psychology basics; edited by Frank N. Magill. Salem Press 1998 2v il (Magill's choice) lib bdg set $118.75
Grades: 11 12 Adult   150.3
1. Reference books 2. Psychology—Encyclopedias
ISBN 0-89356-963-1   LC 97-39249
The encyclopedia includes "110 signed articles drawn from Salem's six-volume *Survey of Social Science: Psychology* (1993). Articles represent various areas of psychology, including cognition, developmental psychology, emotion, intelligence, learning, personality, psychopathology, and psychotherapy. . . . Each entry includes labels for type of psychology and field of study . . . a definition of the main entry term; a list of principal terms defined; the article itself divided into overview, applications, and context sections; an annotated bibliography; and a list of related topics in the set." Booklist

Reber, Arthur S.
The Penguin dictionary of psychology; [by] Arthur S. Reber, Rhiannon Allen & Emily S. Reber. 4th ed. Penguin 2009 xxiii, 904p pa $18 *
Grades: 9 10 11 12   150.3
1. Reference books 2. Psychology—Dictionaries
ISBN 978-0-14-103024-1
First published 1985
Contains 17,000 entries on various aspects of psychology, including new developments in neuroscience and social psychology.

152.1 Sensory perception

Herz, Rachel S., 1963-
The scent of desire; discovering our enigmatic sense of smell; [by] Rachel Herz. William Morrow 2007 xxi, 266p $24.95; pa $13.95
Grades: 11 12 Adult   152.1
1. Smell
ISBN 978-0-06-082537-9; 0-06-082537-5; 978-0-06-082538-6 (pa); 0-06-082538-3 (pa)
LC 2007-33563
The author argues that the sense of smell "is vital to our well being—so important to mental and physical health that its loss can drive some people to suicide. Herz explores the relationships between scent, emotion and behavior, emphasizing that scent is an important component of sexual attraction and thus crucial for the survival of our species." Publ Wkly

Herz, Rachel S., 1963-—*Continued*
"This is one of those all-too-rare books that is involving, well written, and solidly grounded in research." Libr J

Includes bibliographical references

152.4 Emotions

Chocolate for a teen's heart; unforgettable stories for young women about love, hope, and happiness; {compiled by} Kay Allenbaugh. Simon & Schuster 2001 219p pa $12
Grades: 9 10 11 12   **152.4**
1. Teenagers 2. Girls
ISBN 0-7432-1380-7   LC 2001-20810
This work presents 55 stories about teen relationships written by teens and women reminiscing about their teen years. It relates the happiness of a first romance, conflicts with parents, and the joys and sorrows of peer relationships.
"This collection of positive stories should prove refreshing and will be popular with fans of inspirational tales." Booklist

Fromm, Erich, 1900-1980
The art of loving. Centennial ed. Continuum 2000 130p $18.95
Grades: 11 12 Adult   **152.4**
1. Love
ISBN 0-8264-1260-2   LC 00-21030
Also available in paperback from HarperCollins Pubs.
A reissue of the title first published 1956
"An astonishingly simple presentation of an abstract subject." Booklist

Goleman, Daniel
Emotional intelligence. 10th anniversary ed. Bantam Books 2006 xxiv, 358p il $29; pa $18
Grades: 11 12 Adult   **152.4**
1. Emotions 2. Intellect
ISBN   978-0-553-80491-1;   0-553-80491-X;
978-0-553-38371-3 (pa); 0-553-38371-X (pa)
                                              LC 2006-283929
First published 1995
The author explains "how to develop our emotional intelligence in ways that can improve our relationships, our parenting, our classrooms, and our workplaces. Goleman assures us that our temperaments may be determined by neurochemistry, but they can be altered." Booklist

Includes bibliographical references

Lorenz, Konrad
On aggression; translated by Marjorie Kerr Wilson. Harcourt Brace Jovanovich 1966 306p pa $13 hardcover o.p.
Grades: 11 12 Adult   **152.4**
1. Aggressiveness (Psychology) 2. Comparative psychology
ISBN 0-15-668741-0 (pa)
"A Helen and Kurt Wolff book"
Original German edition published 1963 in Austria

The author examines aggression in animals and humans, noting both the positive and destructive manifestations of such behavior
Includes bibliographical references

Ottaviani, Jim
Wire mothers; Harry Harlow and the science of love; [by] Jim Ottaviani [and] Dylan Meconis. G. T. Labs 2007 84p il pa $12.95
Grades: 9 10 11 12 Adult   **152.4**
1. Harlow, Harry F., 1905-1981—Graphic novels
2. Graphic novels 3. Love—Graphic novels
ISBN 978-0-9788037-1-1; 0-9788037-1-X
                                              LC 2007-900136
"A General Tektronics Labs book"
In the 1950s, psychologists warned parents about the dangers of too much love; in fact, they denied love was anything more than a base instinct based on the need for food. When scientist Harry Harlow began his experiments on mother love, was more than just an outsider trying to make his name. He was also an unhappy man who knew in his gut the truth about what love, and its absence, meant, and he set about to prove it. His experiments on monkeys and their stark results shocked the world. The emotional intensity of his experiments might be overwhelming for younger readers.
"This nonfiction graphic novel retelling psychologist Harry Harlow's famous experiments is as disturbing as it is excellent." Publ Wkly
Includes bibliographical references

Provine, Robert R.
Laughter; a scientific investigation. Viking 2000 258p il $24.95; pa $14
Grades: 11 12 Adult   **152.4**
1. Laughter
ISBN 0-670-89375-7; 0-14-100225-5 (pa)
                                              LC 00-38227
The author "reviews recent scientific research, philosophical and psychological literature, case studies of abnormal laughter and phenomena like laugh tracks." N Y Times Book Rev
"As soon as Provine . . . introduces his groundbreaking, fun-to-read anthropological study of laughter, . . . the full scope of its strangeness and complexity begins to emerge." Booklist
Includes bibliographical references

153 Conscious mental processes and intelligence

Rose, Steven Peter Russell, 1938-
The future of the brain; the promise and perils of tomorrow's neuroscience; [by] Steven Rose. Oxford University Press 2005 344p il hardcover o.p. pa $16.95
Grades: 11 12 Adult   **153**
1. Brain
ISBN   978-0-19-515420-7;   0-19-515420-7;
978-0-19-530893-8 (pa); 0-19-530893-X (pa)
                                              LC 2004-23578

Rose, Steven Peter Russell, 1938-—*Continued*
The author "discusses the technologies for altering the brain that are apt to appear in the next two decades . . . . The understanding of neuroscience he provides permits his readers to consider the implications of imminent developments." Booklist
Includes bibliographical references

153.1 Memory and learning

Hudmon, Andrew
Learning and memory. Chelsea House Publishers 2005 136p il (Gray matter) $32.95
Grades: 8 9 10 11 12   153.1
1. Psychology of learning 2. Memory 3. Brain
ISBN 0-7910-8638-0   LC 2005-11699
This "volume provides fascinating insights into various processes involved in how we learn different things in different ways. Particularly enlightening is the section differentiating explicit memory (learning facts) and implicit memory (learning processes) . . . The [book features] colorful historical photos and illustrations, process models, and shaded insets." SLJ
Includes bibliographical references

Schacter, Daniel L.
The seven sins of memory; how the mind forgets and remembers. Houghton Mifflin 2001 272p il hardcover o.p. pa $14
Grades: 11 12 Adult   153.1
1. Memory
ISBN 0-618-04019-6; 0-618-21919-6 (pa)
                                      LC 00-53885
The author discusses "the curious processes of memory by classifying its malfunctions into seven categories: transience, absent-mindedness, blocking, misattribution, suggestibility, bias, and persistence. Schacter illustrates each of these 'sins' with examples of routine misfortunes common to all." Libr J
Includes bibliographical references

153.4 Thought, thinking, reasoning, intuition, value, judgment

Gladwell, Malcolm
Blink: the power of thinking without thinking. Little, Brown and Co 2005 277p il $25.95
Grades: 11 12 Adult   153.4
1. Decision making 2. Intuition
ISBN 0-316-17232-4   LC 2004-13916
The author "decodes the science of rapid cognition, those snap judgments made with only the subtlest clues." Christ Sci Monit
Gladwell "has a dazzling ability to find commonality in disparate fields of study. . . . Each case study is satisfying, and Gladwell imparts his own evident pleasure in delving into a wide range of fields and seeking an underlying truth." Publ Wkly
Includes bibliographical references

153.6 Communication

Fast, Julius, 1919-2008
Body language. rev and updated ed. M. Evans 2002 171p pa $15.95
Grades: 11 12 Adult   153.6
1. Nonverbal communication
ISBN 0-87131-982-9
First published 1970
This book discusses the "science of kinesics, the use of nonverbal communication through the means of body movements which may support or contradict our verbal expressions." Best Sellers
Includes bibliographical references

153.7 Perceptual processes

Chabris, Christopher F.
The invisible gorilla; and other ways our intuitions deceive us; [by] Christopher Chabris and Daniel Simons. Crown 2010 306p $27; pa $14
Grades: 11 12 Adult   153.7
1. Perception 2. Memory 3. Thought and thinking
ISBN   978-0-307-45965-7;   0-307-45965-9;
978-0-307-45966-4 (pa); 0-307-45966-7 (pa)
                              LC 2009-45325
The authors "won a 2004 Ig Nobel Prize for their widely reported 'gorilla experiment,' which showed that when people focus on one thing, it's easy to overlook other things—even a woman in a gorilla suit. . . . [In this book,] they explore this habit of 'inattentional blindness' and other common ways in which we distort our perception of reality. Their readable book offers surprising insights into just how clueless we are about how our minds work and how we experience the world." Kirkus
Includes bibliographical references

153.8 Will (Volition)

Bachel, Beverly K., 1957-
What do you really want? how to set a goal and go for it! A guide for teens. Free Spirit 2000 134p il pa $12.95 *
Grades: 7 8 9 10 11 12   153.8
1. Success 2. Motivation (Psychology)
ISBN 1-57542-085-6   LC 00-57286
The book discusses various ways for teenagers to set goals, build support networks, keep themselves motivated in the process and reap the harvest of their successes
Bachel's "helpful advice is well supported by quotations from teens who have tried some of the techniques, and simple, appealing graphics keep things light. . . . Back matter includes goal-setting resources and some helpful organizations and Web sites." Booklist

153.9 Intelligence and aptitudes

Streznewski, Marylou Kelly, 1934-
Gifted grownups; the mixed blessings of extraordinary potential. Wiley 1999 292p $24.95
Grades: 11 12 Adult   **153.9**
  1. Genius
  ISBN 0-471-29580-9   LC 98-29536
Seeking to debunk "the myth that intellectually gifted people are either impractical social misfits or perfect specimens, . . . [the author presents a] study of 100 people aged 18 to 90. . . . [She] explores their experiences with schools, jobs, and in the social world." Libr J
"The book is interesting not only anecdotally, but because it provokes thought about the nature of intelligence and its interactive functioning in our changing society." Readings
Includes bibliographical references

154.6 Sleep phenomena

Lewis, James R., 1949-
The dream encyclopedia; [by] James R. Lewis and Evelyn Dorothy Oliver. 2nd ed. Visible Ink Press 2009 xxi, 410p il pa $24.95
Grades: 11 12 Adult   **154.6**
  1. Dreams—Encyclopedias 2. Reference books
  ISBN 978-1-57859-216-6   LC 2009-5132
  First published 1995 by Gale Res.
This "reference examines more than 250 dream-related topics, from art to history to science, including how factors such as self-healing, ESP, literature, religion, sex, cognition and memory, and medical conditions can all have an effect on dreams. Dream symbolism and interpretation is examined in historical, cultural, and psychological detail." Publisher's note
Includes bibliographical references

154.7 Hypnotism

Rosen, Marvin
Meditation and hypnosis. Chelsea House Publishers 2005 121p il (Gray matter) $32.95
Grades: 9 10 11 12   **154.7**
  1. Hypnotism 2. Meditation
  ISBN 0-7910-8515-5   LC 2005-15848
This book "traces the history of and controversies about manipulating consciousness. Experimentation and medical and psychological applications are discussed in depth, including fascinating subtopics such as brainwashing, dissociation, multiple personalities, and multitasking." SLJ
Includes bibliographical references

155.2 Individual psychology

Steinem, Gloria
Revolution from within; a book of self-esteem. Little, Brown 1992 377p pa $14.95 hardcover o.p.
Grades: 11 12 Adult   **155.2**
  1. Self-esteem 2. Feminism
  ISBN 0-316-81247-1 (pa)   LC 91-11356
The author discusses the importance of self-esteem and offers practical advice on ways of acquiring it.
Steinem's "book unfolds like a flower: it offers literature, art, nature, meditation, and connectedness as ways of finding and exploring the self. . . . Her focus is women, but she is clear that what she has to say is for men, too, and she is neither strident nor dismissive." Libr J
Includes bibliographical references

155.5 Psychology of young people twelve to twenty

Esherick, Joan
Balancing act; a teen's guide to managing stress. Mason Crest Publishers 2005 128p il (Science of health) $24.95 *
Grades: 9 10 11 12   **155.5**
  1. Stress (Psychology)
  ISBN 1-590-84853-5   LC 2004-10693
Contents: Stressed to the max: teens under pressure; The causes of stress; How stress affects your body, mind, and emotions; How stress affects your relationships and responsibilities; Handling stress, pt. 1: flight isn't always bad; Handling stress, pt. 2: facing stress head-on
The author "describes the body's physical reaction to stress, using words and images that young people can easily understand." SLJ
Includes bibliographical references

Espeland, Pamela, 1951-
The gifted kids' survival guide; a teen handbook; [by] Judy Galbraith and Jim Delisle; edited by Pamela Espeland. revised, expanded and updated ed. Free Spirit 1996 295p il pa $15.95
Grades: 9 10 11 12   **155.5**
  1. Gifted children
  ISBN 1-57542-003-1   LC 96-29430
  First published 1983 by Wetherall Publishing Company
Examines issues that are of concern for young people who have been labeled "gifted," discussing what the label means, intelligence testing, educational options, and relationships with parents and friends. Includes first-person essays on being gifted
Includes bibliographical references

Hugel, Bob, 1964-

I did it without thinking; true stories about impulsive decisions that changed lives. Franklin Watts 2008 112p il (Scholastic choices) lib bdg $27; pa $8.95

Grades: 6 7 8 9 10   **155.5**

1. Adolescent psychology 2. Risk-taking (Psychology) 3. Decision making

ISBN 978-0-531-13868-7 (lib bdg); 0-531-13868-2 (lib bdg); 978-0-531-20526-6 (pa); 0-531-20526-6 (pa)

LC 2008-690

Teenagers give their stories of impulsive decisions, their reasons for making them, and the consequences—whether good or bad.

This book is "colorful and compact, with . . . an appealing layout. . . . The stories, while not overly preachy, are brief and generally upbeat. . . . [The] book has excellent black-and-white photographs of a diverse array of teens." SLJ

Includes glossary and bibliographical references

Munroe, Erin A.

The anxiety workbook for girls. Fairview Press 2010 199p pa $14.95

Grades: 7 8 9 10   **155.5**

1. Anxiety 2. Girls—Psychology

ISBN 978-1-57749-232-0   LC 2010-6092

The author "explores everything from family problems and body image to sexuality and depression. The book begins with an overview of anxiety, how it manifests, the difference between helpful and harmful anxiety, and a self-assessment quiz which helps the reader pinpoint what situations cause her to be anxious and what kinds of symptoms she typically experiences. Later sections address topics such as peer pressure, relationships, drugs and alcohol, and strategies and treatments for dealing with all of these in addition to more serious problems such as obsessive compulsive disorder and self-mutilation. . . . This engaging workbook will be a helpful source of information and comfort to those who feel the need for it." Voice Youth Advocates

Palmer, Pat, 1928-

Teen esteem; a self-direction manual for young adults; [by] Pat Palmer, Melissa Alberti Froehner. 3rd ed. Impact Publishers 2010 115p il pa $11.95 *

Grades: 9 10 11 12   **155.5**

1. Self-esteem 2. Conduct of life

ISBN 978-1-88623-087-3   LC 2009-23886

First published 1989

Provides guidance on developing self-esteem and the positive attitude necessary to cope with such adolescent challenges as peer pressure, substance abuse, and sexual expression.

Includes bibliographical references

155.7   Evolutional psychology

Burnham, Terry

Mean genes; from sex to money to food, taming our primal instincts; [by] Terry Burnham and Jay Phelan. Penguin Books 2001 263p pa $15

Grades: 11 12 Adult   **155.7**

1. Genetics 2. Psychology

ISBN 978-0-14-200007-6; 0-14-200007-8

LC 2001-32722

First published 2000 by Perseus Bks.

The authors "explore the genetic evolution of behaviors that sabotage humans' willpower to resist temptation. Debt, fat, drugs, risk, greed, gender, beauty, infidelity, family, and friends and foes are presented as key issues that affect all people." Libr J

"A delightfully readable presentation of the evolutionary, as distinct from the moralized, appreciation of human nature." Booklist

Ridley, Matt

The agile gene; how nature turns on nurture. Perennial 2004 326p pa $13.99 *

Grades: 11 12 Adult   **155.7**

1. Nature and nurture 2. Genetics

ISBN 978-0-06-000679-2; 0-06-000679-X

First published 2003 with title: Nature via nurture

"In February 2001 it was announced that the human genome contains not 100,000 genes, as originally postulated, but only 30,000. This . . . revision led some scientists to conclude that there are simply not enough human genes to account for all the different ways people behave: we must be made by nurture, not nature. . . . [Ridley argues that] nurture depends on genes, too, and genes need nurture. Genes not only predetermine the broad structure of the brain, they also absorb formative experiences, react to social cues, and even run memory. They are consequences as well as causes of the will." Publisher's note

Includes bibliographical references

155.9   Environmental psychology

De la Bédoyère, Camilla

Balancing work and play. Amicus 2010 46p il (Healthy lifestyles) lib bdg $32.80

Grades: 7 8 9 10 11 12   **155.9**

1. Stress (Psychology)

ISBN 978-1-60753-083-1; 1-60753-083-X

"Discusses the importance of and gives tips for managing stress in your teenage years to achieve a balance between studies, jobs, family and friends, hobbies, and other leisure activities." Publisher's note

This book is "well-written and satisfyingly informative. . . . [The] magazine-like format includes numerous sidebars, color photos, and charts." SLJ

Includes glossary

Fitzgerald, Helen

The grieving teen; a guide for teenagers and their friends. Simon & Schuster 2000 222p pa $12

Grades: 11 12 Adult   **155.9**

1. Bereavement 2. Adolescent psychology

ISBN 0-684-86804-0   LC 00-38746

"A Fireside book"

"Chapters consist of typical questions that young adults may have about grief, followed by a 'What You Can Do' section. The topics covered include such contemporary issues as death from AIDS, post-traumatic stress disorder, and Internet support. Fitzgerald provides many real-life experiences and a true sensitivity to differing religious and cultural practices." Libr J

Includes bibliographical references

Gootman, Marilyn E., 1944-

When a friend dies; a book for teens about grieving & healing; edited by Pamela Espeland. Rev. and updated ed. Free Spirit Pub. 2005 118p pa $9.95 *

Grades: 7 8 9 10   **155.9**

1. Death 2. Bereavement

ISBN 1-57542-170-4   LC 2005-447

First published 1994

This offers "information on subjects including: How can I stand the pain? How should I be acting? What is 'normal'? What if I can't handle my grief on my own? and How can I find a counselor or a therapist? Interspersed throughout the book . . . are quotes from teenagers who have experienced grief. . . . Quotes from well-known writers and philosophers give insight into the grieving process and healing." SLJ

Kübler-Ross, Elisabeth

On death and dying. Scribner Classics 1997 286p il $23; pa $13

Grades: 9 10 11 12 Adult   **155.9**

1. Death 2. Terminal care

ISBN 0-684-84223-8; 0-684-83938-5 (pa)

LC 97-177294

A reissue of the title first published 1969 by Macmillan

A look at the psychological, sociological and theological issues faced by the terminally ill and their caregivers

Includes bibliographical references

Myers, Edward, 1950-

When will I stop hurting? teens, loss, and grief; illustrations by Kelly Adams. Scarecrow Press 2004 159p il (It happened to me) $34.50

Grades: 7 8 9 10   **155.9**

1. Bereavement 2. Loss (Psychology)

ISBN 0-8108-4921-6   LC 2003-23698

"Outlining the phases of the grieving process, Myers incorporates . . . personal accounts and quotes from young adults who have experienced the death of a family member into the text. He discusses the range of emotions young people may have from anger and fear to relief and sadness and assures readers that these feelings are normal." SLJ

This book "will be extremely helpful for teens strug-

gling to understand their emotions following the loss of a loved one. Grieving is well explained and the individual nature of grief is stressed." Libr Media Connect

Includes bibliographical references

156 Comparative psychology

Waal, Frans de, 1948-

Our inner ape; a leading primatologist explains why we are who we are; photographs by the author. Riverhead Books 2005 274p il $24.95 *

Grades: 11 12 Adult   **156**

1. Human behavior 2. Primates—Behavior 3. Comparative psychology

ISBN 1-57322-312-3   LC 2005-42768

This book compares human "social behavior with that of two species of apes: chimpanzees and bonobos." N Y Times Book Rev

"Readers might be surprised at how much these apes and their stories resonate with their own lives, and may well be left with an urge to spend a few hours watching primates themselves at the local zoo." Publ Wkly

Includes bibliographical references

158 Applied psychology

Bezdecheck, Bethany

Relationships; 21st-century roles. Rosen Pub. 2010 112p il (A young woman's guide to contemporary issues) lib bdg $31.95

Grades: 7 8 9 10   **158**

1. Interpersonal relations 2. Family 3. Friendship

ISBN 978-1-4358-3540-5; 1-4358-3540-9

LC 2009-12065

"Offers advice on how to build healthy relationships with family members, friends, and boyfriends." Publisher's note

"Facts are shared in a conversational tone, creating the sense of a chat with a big sister. . . . [Though] designed for personal reading and browsing, the data provided are accurate and also lend themselves to use in reports. This . . . will be of great interest." SLJ

Includes glossary and bibliographical references

Canfield, Jack, 1944-

Chicken soup for the teenage soul [I-IV]; [by] Jack Canfield, Mark Victor Hansen, Kimberly Kirberger. Health Communications 1997-2000 4v il hardcover o.p. v1 pa $14.95; v2 pa $9.99; v3 pa $14.95; v4 pa $14.95

Grades: 7 8 9 10 11 12   **158**

1. Interpersonal relations 2. Emotions

ISBN 1-55874-468-1 ([I]); 1-55874-463-0 ([I pa]); 1-55874-615-3 ([II]); 1-55874-616-1 ([II pa]); 1-55874-761-3 ([III]); 0-7573-0233-5 ([IV])

These books cover "teenage subjects running the gamut from love, family ties, and self-esteem to developing values and life crises, such as a death in the family. . . . Teenagers not only helped select the poems, stories, and accounts that have been included but also have written

Canfield, Jack, 1944-—Continued
some of them . . . with a few contributions by well-known people, including Sandra Cisneros, Helen Keller, and Robert Fulghum. . . . This isn't a religious book, but it is an inspirational and motivational one, sometimes funny, sometimes poignant." Booklist [review of 1997 volume]
Includes bibliographical references

Chicken soup for the teenage soul's the real deal; school: cliques, classes, clubs, and more; [compiled by] Jack Canfield, Mark Victor Hansen, Deborah Reber. Health Communications 2005 292p pa $12.95 *
Grades: 7 8 9 10   **158**
1. Interpersonal relations 2. Emotions
ISBN 0-7573-0255-6   LC 2005046051
"The stories included here were submitted by students and are based on their own experiences. Almost every page includes a fun fact, a statistic, or a quiz." SLJ

Fox, Annie, 1950-
Too stressed to think? a teen guide to staying sane when life makes you crazy; by Annie Fox and Ruth Kirschner; edited by Elizabeth Verdick. Free Spirit Pub. 2005 163p il pa $14.95
Grades: 7 8 9 10   **158**
1. Stress (Psychology)
ISBN 1-57542-173-9   LC 2005018484
"This well-organized, upbeat book discusses what stress is and how it affects the body and brain, talks about tools to reduce and control it, and gives suggestions for recognizing the myriad situations that can trigger stress at home and at school and seeking help when necessary. Best of all, each one of these scenarios includes information on how the situation might be addressed." SLJ
Includes bibliographical references

Goleman, Daniel
Social intelligence; the new science of human relationships. Bantam Books 2006 403p il $28; pa $14
Grades: 9 10 11 12 Adult   **158**
1. Emotions 2. Intellect
ISBN   0-553-80352-2;   978-0-553-80352-5; 0-553-38449-X (pa); 978-0-553-38449-9 (pa)
LC 2006-45971
The author "argues for a new social model of intelligence drawn from the emerging field of social neuroscience. . . . Goleman illuminates new theories about attachment, bonding, and the making and remaking of memory as he examines how our brains are wired for altruism, compassion, concern and rapport." Publ Wkly
Includes bibliographical references

Hong, K. L.
Life freaks me out; and then I deal with it. Search Institute 2005 155p il pa $9.95
Grades: 9 10 11 12   **158**
1. Conduct of life
ISBN 1-57482-856-8; 978-1-57482-856-6
LC 2005-9461

The author "takes readers on a . . . journey of her own teen years (and the years since), offering young people guidance on answering life's big questions: Who am I? What's important to me? What am I called to do on this planet? Each chapter focuses on one important 'truth' the author has gleaned from a variety of sources and life experiences." Publisher's note
Includes bibliographical references

Lavinthal, Andrea
Friend or frenemy? a guide to the friends you need and the ones you don't; [by] Andrea Lavinthal and Jessica Rozler. Harper 2008 xxv, 230p il pa $14.95
Grades: 10 11 12 Adult   **158**
1. Friendship
ISBN 978-0-06-156203-7; 0-06-156203-3
This handbook "takes an honest look at the rules and etiquette of friendship in the digital age. . . . [The authors] discuss everything from becoming a better friend to dealing with 'frenemies' (the backstabbers, users, underminers, etc.) and surviving friendship breakups. . . . Lavinthal and Rozler's guide supplies needed information in an engaging, humorous style." Libr J

170 Ethics

Ethics: opposing viewpoints; Roman Espejo, book editor. Greenhaven Press 2010 224p il $39.70; pa $27.50
Grades: 9 10 11 12   **170**
1. Ethics
ISBN 978-0-7377-4767-6; 978-0-7377-4768-3 (pa)
LC 2009-53382

"Opposing viewpoints series"
This book "tackles current subjects such as stem cell research and, even more topically, the recent subprime lending debacle. Each topic opens with a general introduction, followed by articles offering different points of view. The first two sections feature opinion pieces on why people should behave ethically and what motivates ethical behavior, while the latter two sections delve into nitty-gritty issues such as cloning, physician-assisted suicide, and business ethics. The articles present a balance of positions, so debaters and researchers are likely to find support for their own viewpoints." SLJ
Includes bibliographical references

Harper, Hill, 1966-
Letters to a young brother. Gotham Books 2006 176p $20 *
Grades: 9 10 11 12   **170**
1. Boys 2. Conduct of life
ISBN 1-59240-200-3; 978-1-59240-200-7
LC 2006-3699
The author "devotes separate chapters to school and work, sex, and life aspirations, tackling such issues as single parenthood, sexually transmitted diseases, the allure of materialism, and the power of words and faith. . . . Although aimed at young black men, this book, with its contemporary language and approach, should have appeal for youth of both sexes and all races." Booklist

The **history** of Western ethics; edited by Brian Duignan. Britannica Educational Pub. 2011 180p il (The Britannica guide to ethics) lib bdg $35
Grades: 9 10 11 12   **170**
1. Ethics
ISBN 978-1-61530-301-4   LC 2010014726
"This history moves chronologically from ancient legal codes to modem questions pertaining to the environment, human rights, and bioethics. Along the way, readers are effectively introduced to monumental thinkers, including Buddha, Confucius, Socrates, Jesus, Machiavelli, Jeremy Bentham, Karl Marx, and Jean-Paul Sartre. . . . [This book] nicely rounds out most philosophy collections." SLJ
Includes bibliographical references

Weinstein, Bruce D.
Is it still cheating if I don't get caught? [by] Bruce Weinstein; illustrations by Harriet Russell. Roaring Brook 2009 160p il pa $12.95 *
Grades: 8 9 10 11 12   **170**
1. Ethics
ISBN 978-1-59643-306-9; 1-59643-306-X
The author "addresses adolescent ethical dilemmas using a set of five 'Life Principles' (Do No Harm, Make Things Better, Respect Others, Be Fair, Be Loving)." Publ Wkly
"This appealing guide speaks to the ethical dilemmas that all young people experience in their daily lives, and it should prompt considerable conversation and reflection." Kirkus

174 Occupational ethics

Callahan, David, 1965-
The cheating culture; why more Americans are doing wrong to get ahead. Harcourt 2004 353p $26; pa $14 *
Grades: 11 12 Adult   **174**
1. Business ethics 2. Social ethics
ISBN 0-15-101018-8; 0-15-603005-5 (pa)
                                    LC 2003-15529
The author examines "government reports and statistics, studies by social scientists, public opinion polls, and journalistic investigations of scandals and cheating. Callahan also conducted interviews with people who deal with the cheating culture: parents, students, teachers, coaches, athletes, experts in business ethics, stock analysts, lawyers, accountants, doctors, and law enforcement officials." Booklist
"If all business school students could be required to read one book, this should be it." Choice
Includes bibliographical references

Preer, Jean L.
Library ethics; [by] Jean Preer. Libraries Unlimited 2008 255p il pa $45
Grades: Adult Professional   **174**
1. Librarians—Ethics
ISBN 978-1-59158-636-4   LC 2008-21122

"This title takes an inclusive look at why library ethics are needed in the 21st century. This highly practical, substantial, and carefully planned resource is designed to help information professionals figure out their professional values and where they stand when faced with ethical dilemmas. . . . New practitioners entering the field would be wise to use this book as their first professional bible. Those already in the library profession may find this title to be a good refresher." Libr Media Connect
Includes bibliographical references

174.2 Occupational ethics—Medical professions

Biomedical ethics: opposing viewpoints; Viqi Wagner, book editor. Greenhaven Press 2008 256p lib bdg $38.50; pa $26.75 *
Grades: 7 8 9 10   **174.2**
1. Medical ethics 2. Bioethics
ISBN 978-0-7377-3737-0 (lib bdg); 0-7377-3737-9 (lib bdg); 978-0-7377-3738-7 (pa); 0-7377-3738-7 (pa)
                                    LC 2007-34362
"Opposing viewpoints series"
Presents opposing viewpoints on biomedical ethics issues such as stem cell research, human cloning, genetic research and engineering, organ transplants and reproductive technologies.
Includes bibliographical references

Boleyn-Fitzgerald, Miriam
Ending and extending life. Facts On File 2010 222p il (Contemporary issues in science) $35
Grades: 9 10 11 12   **174.2**
1. Medical ethics
ISBN 978-0-8160-6205-8; 0-8160-6205-6
                                    LC 2008-30547
"This title covers the medical innovations that have improved the lives of some and have produced questionable ethical decisions in other cases. . . . This series would be an excellent addition to a science collection and would provide high school students and teachers as well, with information on the recent technical and ethical issues in science and technology." Libr Media Connect
Includes glossary and bibliographical references

Caplan, Arthur L.
Smart mice, not-so-smart people; an interesting and amusing guide to bioethics. Rowman & Littlefield 2006 210p $21.95; pa $14.95
Grades: 11 12 Adult   **174.2**
1. Medical ethics
ISBN   978-0-7425-4171-9;   0-7425-4171-1; 978-0-7425-4172-6 (pa); 0-7425-4172-X (pa)
                                    LC 2006-14275
The author discusses "issues at the center of the new genetics, cloning in the laboratory and in the media, stem cell research, experiments on human subjects, blood donation and organ transplantation, and healthcare delivery." Publisher's note

Genetic engineering: opposing viewpoints; David M. Haugen and Susan Musser, book editors. Greenhaven Press 2009 236p il lib bdg $39.70; pa $27.50 *
Grades: 9 10 11 12   **174.2**
1. Genetic engineering
ISBN 978-0-7377-4368-5 (lib bdg); 0-7377-4368-9 (lib bdg); 978-0-7377-4367-8 (pa); 0-7377-4367-0 (pa)
LC 2008-35440
"Opposing viewpoints series"
A collection of articles explore the social and ethical issues raised by genetic engineering. Governmental and agricultural implications are discussed.
Includes bibliographical references

Lovegrove, Ray
Health; ethical debates in modern medicine. Black Rabbit Books 2008 c2009 46p il map (Dilemmas in modern science) lib bdg $34.25
Grades: 7 8 9 10   **174.2**
1. Medical ethics
ISBN 978-1-59920-095-8; 1-59920-095-3
LC 2007-35690
"Presents both sides of modern medical issues, including drug testing, organ transplants, genetic engineering, and stem cell research." Publisher's note
This title is "easy to navigate as evocative photographs, charts, and sidebars help break down complicated arguments into manageable parts for easy digestion." SLJ
Includes glossary and bibliographical references

Medical ethics; Noel Merino, book editor. Greenhaven Press 2010 c2011 222p (Current controversies) $39.70; pa $27.50 *
Grades: 9 10 11 12   **174.2**
1. Medical ethics
ISBN   978-0-7377-4915-1;   0-7377-4915-6; 978-0-7377-4916-8 (pa); 0-7377-4916-4 (pa)
LC 2010015315
Topics discussed in this anthology include organ transplants, government involvement in health care, reproductive technologies, and assisted suicide.
Includes bibliographical references

Morrison, Adrian R.
An odyssey with animals; a veterinarian's reflections on the animal rights & welfare debate. Oxford University Press 2009 272p $29.95
Grades: 11 12 Adult   **174.2**
1. Medicine—Research 2. Animal experimentation 3. Animal welfare
ISBN 978-0-19-537444-5   LC 2008-53834
The author "argues that humane animal use in biomedical research is an indispensable tool of medical science, and that efforts to halt such use constitute a grave threat to human health and wellbeing." Publisher's note
Includes bibliographical references

Stem cells: opposing viewpoints; Jacqueline Langwith, book editor. Greenhaven Press 2007 262p il lib bdg $36.20; pa $24.95
Grades: 10 11 12   **174.2**
1. Stem cell research
ISBN   978-0-7377-3648-9   (lib   bdg); 978-0-7377-3649-6 (pa)   LC 2007-2991
"Opposing viewpoints series"
"This book presents essays, speeches, and articles that offer different opinions on issues related to stem cells. Twenty-eight entries appear under four broad topics: the promise of stem cells to cure diseases, the ethical questions raised by stem cell research, the role of government in that research, and alternatives to the use of embryonic stem cells. Preceding each viewpoint is an introductory summary and a list of three questions that readers are advised to consider as they read. . . . A useful book for students researching stem cell issues for papers or debates." Booklist
Includes bibliographical references

Uschan, Michael V., 1948-
Forty years of medical racism; the Tuskegee experiments. Lucent Books 2005 112p il map (Lucent library of Black history) lib bdg $28.70
Grades: 8 9 10 11 12   **174.2**
1. Human experimentation in medicine 2. Syphilis 3. African Americans—Health and hygiene
ISBN 1-59018-486-6
This is an account of "the Tuskegee Study of Untreated Syphilis in the Negro Male. . . . Halftone photographs of participants and of the persons who designed, conducted, or criticized the project supplement the text. Informational sidebars provide additional descriptions and photographs of some of the damage done by untreated syphilis." SLJ
Includes bibliographical references

176   Ethics of sex and reproduction

Cloning; Nancy Harris, book editor. Greenhaven Press 2005 192p (Exploring science and medical discoveries) lib bdg $34.95; pa $23.70
Grades: 9 10 11 12   **176**
1. Cloning
ISBN 0-7377-1965-6 (lib bdg); 0-7377-1966-4 (pa)
LC 2003-56829
"Current cloning controversies are discussed in eight essays, which consider everything from the overriding question of whether humans should be cloned, to the pros and cons of regulating cloning technologies, therapeutic and reproductive cloning, and whether animals should be used in research. Six essays delve into the future of cloning. Wide ranging and probing, this compilation . . . is a smart place to introduce the subject." Booklist
Includes bibliographical references

Cloning; Louise I. Gerdes, book editor. Greenhaven Press 2006 141p il (Introducing issues with opposing viewpoints) $32.45
Grades: 7 8 9 10 11 12   **176**
1. Cloning
ISBN 0-7377-3220-2   LC 2005-46292

Cloning—*Continued*

"In this compilation, authors debate some of the controversies surrounding the cloning of people and animals." Publisher's note

Includes bibliographical references

Cloning; William Dudley, book editor. Greenhaven Press 2005 c2006 112p il (Writing the critical essay) $26.20 *

Grades: 7 8 9 10   176

1. Cloning

ISBN 0-7377-3196-6

"An Opposing viewpoints guide"

This presents essays representing various points of view on the ethics of cloning and includes questions designed to aid the reader in analyzing each essay.

Includes bibliographical references

Cloning; Sylvia Engdahl, book editor. Greenhaven Press 2006 198p il (Contemporary issues companion) lib bdg $39.70

Grades: 9 10 11 12   176

1. Cloning

ISBN 0-7377-2771-3; 978-0-7377-2771-5

LC 2005055062

This title discusses public attitudes towards cloning, the cloning of people and animals, and cloning human embryos for research.

Includes bibliographical references

Cloning: opposing viewpoints; Tamara L. Roleff, book editor. Greenhaven Press 2006 176p il lib bdg $34.95; pa $23.70 *

Grades: 9 10 11 12   176

1. Cloning

ISBN 0-7377-3311-X (lib bdg); 0-7377-3312-8 (pa)

LC 2005-46165

"Opposing viewpoints series"

"Scientists, politicians, and seriously ill patients examine the issue of cloning and the issues of whether cloning is ethical, whether cloning research can cure diseases, whether adult or embryonic stem cells should be used in research, and whether cloning should be banned." Publisher's note

Includes bibliographical references

The **ethics** of cloning; David M. Haugen, Susan Musser & Kacy Lovelace, book editors. Greenhaven Press 2009 129p (At issue. Health) $31.80; pa $22.50 *

Grades: 9 10 11 12   176

1. Cloning

ISBN   978-0-7377-4312-8;   0-7377-4312-3; 978-0-7377-4311-1 (pa); 0-7377-4311-5 (pa)

LC 2008054001

An anthology of essays discussing the moral ramifications of human cloning, therapeutic cloning, reproductive cloning, and the cloning of animals.

Includes bibliographical references

Green, Ronald Michael, 1942-

Babies by design; the ethics of genetic choice. Yale University Press 2007 279p il hardcover o.p. pa $19 *

Grades: 11 12 Adult   176

1. Medical genetics 2. Genetic engineering 3. Reproductive technology

ISBN   978-0-300-12546-7;   0-300-12546-1; 978-0-300-14308-9 (pa); 0-300-14308-7 (pa)

LC 2007-19927

"A Caravan book"

The author offers a discussion "of human genetic self-modification and the possibilities it opens up. . . . [He] outlines the new capabilities of genomic science, addresses . . . questions of safety that genetic interventions pose, and explores questions of parenting and justice." Publisher's note

"By providing examples, contextualizing issues within the framework of stories in popular fiction, and presenting a balanced view of the topics, the author allows the reader to fully explore the issues embedded in the scientific transformation created by the genomic revolution." Sci Books Films

Includes bibliographical references

178   Ethics of consumption

Kerr, Jim

Food; ethical debates on what we eat. Smart Apple Media 2009 46p il map (Dilemmas in modern science) lib bdg $34.25

Grades: 7 8 9 10   178

1. Food industry 2. Genetic engineering

ISBN 978-1-59920-094-1; 1-59920-094-5

LC 2007-39651

"Presents both sides of food production issues, including animal welfare, high-tech farming, genetically modified foods, organic farming, food distribution, and world hunger." Publisher's note

This title is "easy to navigate as evocative photographs, charts, and sidebars help break down complicated arguments into manageable parts for easy digestion." SLJ

Includes glossary and bibliographical references

179   Other ethical norms

Animal experimentation: opposing viewpoints; David M. Haugen, book editor. Greenhaven Press 2007 234p il lib bdg $38.50; pa $26.75 *

Grades: 9 10 11 12   179

1. Animal experimentation

ISBN 978-0-7377-3346-4 (lib bdg); 0-7377-3346-2 (lib bdg); 978-0-7377-3347-1 (pa); 0-7377-3347-0 (pa)

LC 2006-31196

"Opposing viewpoints series"

This is an exploration of scientific, religious, and ethical viewpoints on various issues of animal experimentation, including cloning, genetic engineering, and animal donors.

Includes bibliographical references

Animal rights; Nick Treanor, book editor. Greenhaven Press 2005 222p (History of issues) lib bdg $34.95; pa $23.70

Grades: 9 10 11 12   179

1. Animal rights

ISBN 0-7377-1905-2 (lib bdg); 0-7377-1906-0 (pa)

LC 2003-67680

"This anthology includes chapters on the historical roots of the issue, the philosophical debates about animal rights, the controversial tactics used by some animal rights activists, and on the relationship between animal rights and science." Publisher's note

Includes bibliographical references

McCain, John S., 1936-

Why courage matters; the way to a braver life; [by] John McCain with Mark Salter. Random House 2004 209p il $16.95

Grades: 11 12 Adult   179

1. Courage

ISBN 1-400-06030-3   LC 2003-58626

Senator McCain tells his favorite stories of courage. "In offering anecdotes of individuals whose actions embody the rarity of true courage, his well-drawn examples range from Navajo leaders to Colorado River explorers to Jewish freedom fighter Hannah Senesh and Burmese dissident and Nobel Peace Prize-recipient Aung San Suu Kyi. He reflects on the wellsprings of courage, defining it as conscious self-sacrifice 'for the sake of others or to uphold a virtue,' encompassing actions that may be spurred by honor, outrage, a sense of duty, one's conscience, or moral obligation." SLJ

Phillips, Christopher, 1959-

Six questions of Socrates; a modern-day journey of discovery through world philosophy. W. W. Norton 2004 320p hardcover o.p. pa $14.95

Grades: 11 12 Adult   179

1. Philosophy

ISBN 0-393-05157-9; 0-393-32679-9 (pa)

LC 2003-18200

Contents: What is virtue?; What is moderation?; What is justice?; What is good?; What is courage?; What is piety?

"As he travels the world, Phillips challenges ordinary people with the central questions of Socrates' philosophy." Booklist

The author's "smooth, natural style enables readers to feel that they are part of the discussion at hand, making the book engaging and accessible to those who may have been put off by the formality of traditional works." SLJ

Includes bibliographical references

Ravilious, Kate

Power; ethical debates about resources and the environment. Black Rabbit Books 2009 46p il map (Dilemmas in modern science) lib bdg $29.25

Grades: 7 8 9 10   179

1. Natural resources—Management 2. Conservation of natural resources

ISBN 978-1-59920-096-5; 1-59920-096-1

LC 2007-35691

"Presents both sides of environmental issues involving natural resources, including environmental ethics, power and energy, renewable resources, transportation and travel, and wood and water use." Publisher's note

This title is "easy to navigate as evocative photographs, charts, and sidebars help break down complicated arguments into manageable parts for easy digestion." SLJ

Includes glossary and bibliographical references

Shevelow, Kathryn, 1951-

For the love of animals; the rise of the animal protection movement. Henry Holt and Co. 2008 352p il $27.50

Grades: 9 10 11 12 Adult   179

1. Animal rights movement

ISBN 978-0-8050-8090-2; 0-8050-8090-2

LC 2007-47353

The author "documents the history of animal cruelty and the slow, controversial and much maligned rise of the animal protection movement in 17th and 18th-century England. . . . This is a fascinating, often disturbing and frequently funny book, a must read for anyone concerned with the treatment of animals and a call to action for the next generation of animal rights activists." Publ Wkly

Includes bibliographical references

Yount, Lisa

Animal rights. Rev ed. Facts On File 2008 332p il (Library in a book) $45 *

Grades: 9 10 11 12   179

1. Animal rights

ISBN 978-0-8160-7130-2; 0-8160-7130-6

LC 2007-27687

First published 2004

This book "provides an overview of the history of the animal rights movement and reactions to it, as well as the issues of animal experimentation, conditions on factory farms, laboratory animals, animals in entertainment, hunting, and the actions of those involved in the animal rights debate." Publisher's note

Includes glossary and bibliographical references

179.7 Respect and disrespect for human life

Assisted suicide; Sylvia Engdahl, book editor. Greenhaven Press 2009 229p (Current controversies) $39.70; pa $27.50

Grades: 9 10 11 12   179.7

1. Euthanasia

ISBN   978-0-7377-4132-2;   0-7377-4132-5; 978-0-7377-4133-9 (pa); 0-7377-4133-3 (pa)

LC 2008023279

An anthology of essays discussing the ethical issues surrounding assisted suicide.

Includes bibliographical references

The **Ethics** of abortion; Christine Watkins, book editor. Greenhaven Press 2005 112p (At issue. Social issues) hardcover o.p. pa $19.95 *

Grades: 9 10 11 12   179.7

1. Abortion

ISBN 0-7377-2709-8 (lib bdg); 0-7377-2710-1 (pa)

LC 2005-45119

The Ethics of abortion—*Continued*
"Members of the pro-choice and pro-life movements offer conflicting arguments about whether—and in what cases—abortion can be considered ethical." Publisher's note [review of 2000 edition]
Includes bibliographical references

Euthanasia; Loreta M. Medina, book editor. Greenhaven Press 2005 235p (History of issues) lib bdg $34.95; pa $23.70 *
Grades: 9 10 11 12   179.7
1. Euthanasia
ISBN 0-7377-2005-0 (lib bdg); 0-7377-2006-9 (pa)
                                    LC 2004-40501
The essays contained in this book discuss the history of and the legal battles and current ethical debate over euthanasia and assisted suicide. Contributors include Charles Francis Potter, William Rehnquist, and John Shelby Spong.
Includes bibliographical references

Euthanasia; Sylvia Engdahl, book editor. Greenhaven Press 2006 c2007 183p (Contemporary issues companion) $39.70; pa $27.50
Grades: 9 10 11 12   179.7
1. Euthanasia
ISBN 0-7377-3251-2; 978-0-7377-3251-1; 0-7377-3252-0 (pa); 978-0-7377-3252-8 (pa)
                                    LC 2006022933
Areas covered include "new technology; medical ethics . . . the legal changes and implications, primarily in Oregon and the Netherlands; and religion and ethics, including the fine line between active and passive euthanasia." Booklist
Includes bibliographical references

Euthanasia: opposing viewpoints; Carrie L. Snyder, book editor. Greenhaven Press 2006 269p il lib bdg $34.95; pa $23.70
Grades: 7 8 9 10   179.7
1. Euthanasia
ISBN 0-7377-2933-3 (lib bdg); 0-7377-2934-1 (pa)
                                    LC 2005-55110
"Opposing viewpoints series"
"The four chapters explore whether euthanasia is ethical, if it should be legalized, if legalization would lead to involuntary killing, and under what circumstances, if any, doctors should assist in suicide." Booklist [review of 2000 edition]
Includes bibliographical references

Physician-assisted suicide; James H. Ondrey, book editor. Greenhaven Press 2006 101p (At issue. Health) $31.80; pa $22.50
Grades: 9 10 11 12   179.7
1. Euthanasia
ISBN 0-7377-3245-8; 978-0-7377-3245-0; 0-7377-3246-6 (pa); 978-0-7377-3246-7 (pa)
                                    LC 2006016760
An anthology of essays discussing "whether or not to legalize physician-assisted suicide. Proponents argue that competent, terminally ill patients should have the right to end their lives when they choose. Opponents contend

that legalization of this practice would lead to abuses." Publisher's note
Includes bibliographical references

The **right** to die; Jennifer Dorman, book editor. Greenhaven Press 2010 117p (At issue. Civil liberties) $31.80; pa $22.50
Grades: 9 10 11 12   179.7
1. Right to die 2. Euthanasia
ISBN 978-0-7377-4684-6; 0-7377-4684-X; 978-0-7377-4683-9 (pa); 0-7377-4683-1 (pa)
                                    LC 2009048657
A collection of fourteen essays examining both sides of the debate over a person's right to die, addressing topics such as physician-assisted suicide, euthanasia, and legal policies related to the issue.
Includes bibliographical references

Yount, Lisa
Right to die and euthanasia. rev ed. Facts on File 2007 312p il (Library in a book) $45 *
Grades: 11 12 Adult   179.7
1. Right to die 2. Euthanasia
ISBN 978-0-8160-6275-1   LC 2006-33424
First published 2000 with title: Physician-assisted suicide and euthanasia
This reference source contains an overview of the subjects, a chronology of significant events (including the Terri Schiavo case), biographical information on important figures, a glossary of terms, and an annotated bibliography.
Includes glossary and bibliographical references

180 Ancient, medieval & eastern philosophy

Price, Joan A.
Ancient and Hellenistic thought. Chelsea House 2008 118p (Understanding philosophy) $35
Grades: 9 10 11 12   180
1. Ancient philosophy
ISBN 978-0-7910-8739-8   LC 2007-28320
This book "covers pre-Socratic, Classical, and Hellenistic philosophers and their theories, illuminating some of the first and most enduring answers given about the nature of the world and those who live in it." Publisher's note
Includes glossary and bibliographical references

181 Eastern philosophy

Creel, Herrlee Glessner, 1905-1994
Chinese thought from Confucius to Mao Tsê-tung. University of Chicago Press 1953 292p pa $15 hardcover o.p. *
Grades: 9 10 11 12   181
1. Chinese philosophy
ISBN 0-226-12030-9 (pa)
This history of Chinese philosophy and thought features discussions of: Confucius, Mo Tzu, Menacius, Hsün Tzu, Taoism, Buddhism, and Neo-Confucianism.
Includes bibliographical references

Whitfield, Susan
Philosophy and writing. Sharpe Focus 2009 80p
il map (Inside ancient China) $34.95
Grades: 7 8 9 10   **181**
1. Chinese philosophy 2. Chinese literature 3. China—
Civilization
ISBN 978-0-7656-8168-3; 0-7656-8168-4
      LC 2008-31167
"Whitfield covers religion and philosophy [of ancient
China] and how they have been passed down using various precursors to books and printing. . . . [This is illustrated with] fine and frequent color photographs and reproductions. Readers will be rewarded . . . with clear,
accessible writing, peppered liberally with entertaining
stories from history." SLJ
Includes glossary and bibliographical references

184   Platonic philosophy

Hare, R. M. (Richard Mervyn)
Plato. Oxford Univ. Press 1982 82p (Past
masters series) pa $9.95 hardcover o.p. *
Grades: 11 12 Adult   **184**
1. Plato
ISBN 0-19-287585-X (pa)   LC 83-159441
The author examines the chief Platonic concepts in
their political and intellectual contexts
Includes bibliographical references

Plato
The selected dialogues of Plato; the Benjamin
Jowett translation; revised, and with an
introduction by Hayden Pelliccia. Modern Lib.
2000 xxii, 323p hardcover o.p. pa $14
Grades: 9 10 11 12   **184**
1. Philosophy
ISBN 0-679-60228-3; 0-375-75840-2 (pa)
      LC 00-30552
This compilation gathers together Plato's most important writings. The topics addressed include: poetic interpretation; cross-examination to arrive at the truth; the nature of rhetoric, psychology and love; and Socrates' art
of persuasion in attempting to save his own life
"This {work} is a needed and welcome addition to the
translations of the *Dialogues*. Recommended for all libraries with holdings of the major philosophical writers."
Libr J
Includes bibliographical references

185   Aristotelian philosophy

Adler, Mortimer J., 1902-2001
Aristotle for everybody; difficult thought made
easy. Macmillan 1978 206p pa $13 hardcover o.p.
Grades: 11 12 Adult   **185**
1. Aristotle, 384-322 B.C.
ISBN 0-684-83823-0 (pa)   LC 78-853
Adler traces "in the simplest language and with occa-
sional modern analogues, the logic and growth of Aris-
totle's basic doctrines." Publ Wkly
Includes bibliographical references

190   Modern western philosophy

Great thinkers of the Western world; edited by
Ian P. McGreal. HarperCollins Pubs. 1992 572p
$47
Grades: 11 12 Adult   **190**
1. Philosophy 2. Theology 3. Science
ISBN 0-06-270026-X   LC 91-38362
"The major ideas and classic works of more than 100
outstanding Western philosophers, physical and social
scientists, psychologists, religious writers, and theolo-
gians." Title page
"This guide to 116 selected authors . . . spans the ancient Greeks to the first half of the twentieth century.
. . . The guide is arranged chronologically by the
birthdate of the writer. Each entry contains birth and
death dates, a list of the author's major ideas, an essay
of three to five pages, and a short annotated list of secondary sources. . . . Its readable essays . . . are accessible to the layperson." Booklist

Magee, Bryan
The story of philosophy. DK Pub. 1998 240p il
hardcover o.p. pa $20
Grades: 11 12 Adult   **190**
1. Philosophy
ISBN 0-7894-3511-X; 0-7894-7994-X (pa)
      LC 98-3780
This "illustrated volume converts two-and-a-half millennia of Western philosophy into a colorful parade of
provocative figures—from Heraclitus to Heidegger—who
have enlarged the boundaries of thought." Booklist
"Writing with a clear and lively style, Magee provides
an excellent introduction to the topic." SLJ
Includes bibliographical references

Price, Joan A.
Contemporary thought. Chelsea House 2008
160p il (Understanding philosophy) $35
Grades: 9 10 11 12   **190**
1. Modern philosophy
ISBN 978-0-7910-8792-3   LC 2007-28465
"Framing the evolution of post-Enlightenment philosophy, . . . [this book] begins with a discussion of the
British Empiricists and Kant's analysis of the capacity of
reason. Biographies and examinations of the Idealists,
Materialists, Utilitarians, Individualists, Analytics, Phe-
nomenologists, and Existentialists reveal how philosophers from each of these schools of thought sought to
explain the increasingly more secular and industrialized
world of the 18th, 19th, and 20th centuries." Publisher's
note
Includes glossary and bibliographical references

Medieval and modern philosophy. Chelsea
House 2008 136p (Understanding philosophy) $35
Grades: 9 10 11 12   **190**
1. Medieval philosophy 2. Modern philosophy
ISBN 978-0-7910-8740-4   LC 2007-28321
This book "covers the philosophical ideas of the Mid-
dle Ages and the Renaissance as well as those of the
Protestant Reformation and the age of the Continental
Rationalists." Publisher's note
Includes glossary and bibliographical references

Western philosophy; an illustrated guide; general editor, David Papineau. Oxford University Press 2004 224p il $35 *

Grades: 9 10 11 12 **190**

1. Philosophy

ISBN 0-19-522143-5   LC 2004-10215

Contents: World by Tim Crane; Mind and body by Jesse Prinz; Knowledge by Adam Morton; Faith by John Cottingham; Ethics and aesthetics by Brenda Almond; Society by Jonathan Woolf

"The lucid writing, with multiple examples and illuminating analogies, will engage readers and provoke them into thought before they know it. . . . This most attractive volume makes its discipline irresistible." SLJ

Includes bibliographical references

191   United States and Canada

Rand, Ayn, 1905-1982

The Ayn Rand reader; edited by Gary Hull and Leonard Peikoff; introduction by Leonard Peikoff. Plume Bks. 1999 497p pa $16.95

Grades: 9 10 11 12 **191**

1. Capitalists and financiers 2. Objectivism (Philosophy)

ISBN 0-452-28040-0   LC 98-26698

This compilation contains excerpts from all of Rand's novels and serves as an introduction to her basic philosophy expressed in all of her works, fiction as well as nonfiction

193   Germany and Austria

Nietzsche, Friedrich Wilhelm, 1844-1900

The portable Nietzsche; selected and translated, with an introduction, prefaces, and notes, by Walter Kaufmann. Viking 1954 687p pa $17 hardcover o.p.

Grades: 11 12 Adult **193**

ISBN 0-14-015062-5 (pa)

"The Viking portable library"

Includes the complete texts of Thus spake Zarathustra, Twilight of the idols, The antichrist, and Nietzsche contra Wagner. Selections from other works, notes and letters complete the volume

200   RELIGION

Armstrong, Karen

The battle for God; fundamentalism in Judaism, Christianity, and Islam. Knopf 2000 442p $29.95; pa $15.95 *

Grades: 11 12 Adult **200**

1. Religious fundamentalism

ISBN 0-679-43597-2; 0-345-39169-1 (pa)

     LC 99-34022

This is a "study of fundamentalism among Jews (in Israel), Christians (American Protestants), and Muslims (Sunni Egyptians and Shiite Iranians). Armstrong argues that all strains of fundamentalism, despite their differences, are fearful defenses against modernity. . . . The author is sympathetic to the human need for spiritual meaning, but she points out that the intellectual flaws of fundamentalist beliefs are customarily accompanied by paranoia, anger, and aggression—which, in turn, frequently betray the message of the faith." New Yorker

Includes bibliographical references

Bowker, John, 1935-

World religions; contributing consultants: David Bowker [et al.] DK Pub. 1997 200p il maps $35; pa $16.95

Grades: 11 12 Adult **200**

1. Religions 2. Religion

ISBN 0-7894-1439-2; 0-7566-1772-3 (pa)

     LC 96-38277

Each chapter begins with an "introduction and is followed by one-or-two page sections that explain the basic tenets of the faith, symbols, events, people, buildings, works of art, and the differences and similarities to other religions. Hinduism, Buddhism, Judaism, Christianity, and Islam are included as are Jainism, Sikhism, Chinese and Japanese religions, and Native religions." SLJ

Breuilly, Elizabeth

Religions of the world; the illustrated guide to origins, beliefs, traditions & festivals; [by] Elizabeth Breuilly, Joanne O'Brien, Martin Palmer; consultant editor, Martin E. Marty. rev ed. Facts on File 2005 160p il map $29.95 *

Grades: 7 8 9 10 **200**

1. Religions

ISBN 0-8160-6258-7   LC 2005051101

First published 1997

This "looks at the key issues of faith as it exists today. It includes features on beliefs, traditions, festivals and practices of the major faiths and also looks at and discusses the differences within as well as between the faiths." Publisher's note

This "is a valuable resource, covering the beliefs and practices of 10 major religions and lavishly illustrated with color photos, maps, diagrams, and charts." SLJ

Includes bibliographical references

Controversial new religions; edited by James R. Lewis and Jesper Aagaard Petersen. Oxford Univ. Press 2004 496p $74; pa $29.95

Grades: 11 12 Adult **200**

1. Cults

ISBN 0-19-515682-X; 0-19-515683-8 (pa)

     LC 2003-24374

"This volume collects papers on those specific New Religious Movements (NRMS) that have generated the most scholarly attention. With few exceptions, these organizations are also the controversial groups that have attracted the attention of the mass media, often because they have been involved in, or accused of, violent or anti-social activities. Among the movements . . . profiled are such groups as the Branch Davidians, Heaven's

Controversial new religions—*Continued*
Gate, Aum Shinrikyo, Solar Temple, Scientology, and Falun Gong." Publisher's note
Includes bibliographical references

The **Founders** on religion; a book of quotations; James H. Hutson, editor. Princeton University Press 2005 xxx, 244p hardcover o.p. pa $17.95
Grades: 11 12 Adult   **200**
1. Statesmen—United States 2. Quotations 3. United States—Religion
ISBN   978-0-691-12033-1;   0-691-12033-1;
978-0-691-13383-6 (pa); 0-691-13383-2 (pa)
LC 2005-15974
The editor has "gleaned, introduced, and edited quotations from 17 founders of the US. . . . This scholarly compilation, organized under 79 categories, shows the variety and complexity of the founders' thought, and will challenge current political and religious opinions of the Left and Right." Choice
Includes bibliographical references

Guiley, Rosemary Ellen
The encyclopedia of angels; foreword by Lisa Schwebel. 2nd ed. Facts on File 2004 398p il $75; pa $24.95
Grades: 11 12 Adult   **200**
1. Reference books 2. Angels—Dictionaries
ISBN 0-8160-5023-6; 0-8160-5024-4 (pa)
LC 2003-60147
First published 1996
"Guiley's encyclopedia provides researchers with a historical and phenomenological approach to studying angels by examining what folklore, myth, and religion have contributed to research in the field. . . . Brief bibliographies follow most of the alphabetically arranged entries, which cover topics such as encounters with angels and the roles of angels in religion, culture, and art." Choice
Includes bibliographical references

Introduction to the world's major religions; Lee W. Bailey, general editor. Greenwood Press 2006 6v set $325 *
Grades: 11 12 Adult   **200**
1. Religions
ISBN 0-313-33634-2   LC 2005-30883
Contents: v1 Judaism by Emily Taitz; v2 Confucianism and Taoism by Randall L. Nadeau; v3 Buddhism by John M. Thompson; v4 Christianity by Lee W. Bailey; v5 Islam by Zayn R. Kassam; v6 Hinduism by Steven J. Rosen
"Each volume contains an introduction by the author, time line, and narrative chapters on the history, texts and tenets, branches, practice worldwide (including demographics), rituals and holidays, and major figures. The end matter consists of a glossary, bibliography, and index to the set. . . . The volumes are straightforward and well structured to help locate the answers to most questions asked about beliefs, practices, holidays, and definitions of the major religions people encounter." Booklist
Includes glossary and bibliographical references

Milestone documents of world religions; exploring traditions of faith through primary sources; David M. Fahey, editor in chief. Schlager Group 2010 3v il (Milestone documents) set $325
Grades: 11 12 Adult   **200**
1. Religions 2. Christianity and other religions 3. Reference books
ISBN 978-0-9797758-8-8
This set "comprises 94 documents, ranging from the Pyramid Texts, carved on pyramid walls between 2404 BCE and 2193 BCE, to Calling Humanity, a collection of works by Brazilian spiritual writer José Trigueirinho, published in 2002. The focus is on the five major religious traditions (Buddhism, Christianity, Judaism, Hinduism, and Islam), but documents from other religion-based practices, like Baha'i, Gnosticism, and even atheism and witchcraft, are included as well. Entries are arranged chronologically and include both the primary document and discussion." Booklist
Includes bibliographical references

Williams, Juan
This far by faith; stories from the African-American religious experience; [by] Juan Williams and Quinton Dixie. Morrow 2003 326p il hardcover o.p. pa $15.95 *
Grades: 11 12 Adult   **200**
1. African Americans—Religion 2. African Americans—History
ISBN 0-06-018863-4; 0-06-093424-7 (pa)
LC 2002-71884
This study of African American worship "interweaves stories of individual spiritual journeys and accounts of church leaders and religious movements. The authors . . . [aim to] link blacks' faith to their ongoing fight for equality." Christ Sci Monit
"Brief topical articles and captioned illustrations supplement the main text, creating a balanced, readable, and nuanced introduction to the power of faith to sustain the African American community." Libr J

The **Wilson** chronology of the world's religions; edited by David Levinson with contributions from John Bowman [et al.] Wilson, H.W. 2000 688p $110
Grades: 8 9 10 11 12 Adult   **200**
1. Religion—History—Chronology
ISBN 0-8242-0978-8   LC 99-52362
"The entries cover religion in the prehistoric and ancient world; world religions, sects, and cults; religious tolerance and intolerance; state religions; and many other topics. The chronology is supplemented by 250 informational sidebars which provide coverage of religions and sects, religious leaders, texts, and major events." Publisher's note
Includes bibliographical references

World religions; [by] Michael J. O'Neal and J. Sydney Jones; Neil Schlager and Jayne Weisblatt, editors. UXL/Thomson Gale 2007 c2006 6v il map (World religions reference library) set $290

Grades: 7 8 9 10 11 12   **200**
1. Religions
ISBN 1-4144-0226-0; 978-1-4144-0226-0
        LC 2006-12295

Also available as separate sets; contact publisher for more information

Includes bibliographical references

Contents: Almanac, v1; Almanac, v2; Biographies, v1; Biographies, v2; Primary sources; Cumulative index

"This set deals with the development and current practice of religions and philosophies. . . . The Almanac volumes surveys 18 religions and philosophies. Biographies contains 50 biographies, and Primary Sources covers 18 sacred writings." Booklist

200.3   Religion—Encyclopedias and dictionaries

Encyclopedia of religious and spiritual development; editors, Elizabeth M. Dowling, W. George Scarlett. Sage Publications 2006 xxiv, 528p $150

Grades: 11 12 Adult   **200.3**
1. Youth—Religious life—Encyclopedias 2. Reference books
ISBN 0-7619-2883-9   LC 2005-12704

"A SAGE reference publication"

"This work addresses the complexity of factors involved in religious and spiritual development. . . . The work includes over 250 entries written by 125 international scholars on religions and traditions, institutions, and important texts and practices that have had an impact throughout history." Libr J

"This book deserves a place in every library because it is a rich source of insight and information on topics of growing relevance and interest." Choice

Includes bibliographical references

The **encyclopedia** of world religions; Robert S. Ellwood, general editor; Gregory D. Alles, associate editor. Rev. ed. Facts on File 2006 514p il map (Facts on File library of religion and mythology) $50 *

Grades: 7 8 9 10 11 12   **200.3**
1. Religions—Encyclopedias 2. Reference books
ISBN 0-8160-6141-6; 978-0-8160-6141-9
        LC 2005-56750

First published 1998

This encyclopedia "covers all the major and minor religions of the world, including the religions of the ancient world; the major religions practiced around the world today; religions of contemporary indigenous peoples; definitions of religious symbols and ideas; key leaders and thinkers; and terms and definitions." Publisher's note

Includes bibliographical references

The **HarperCollins** dictionary of religion; general editor, Jonathan Z. Smith; associate editor, William Scott Green; area editors, Jorunn Jacobsen Buckley [et al.]; with the American Academy of Religion. HarperSanFrancisco 1995 154p il maps $47.50

Grades: 11 12 Adult   **200.3**
1. Religion 2. Reference books
ISBN 0-06-067515-2   LC 95-37024

Published "in association with the American Academy of Religion."

"The 3200-plus articles are written by a team of 327 religion scholars, experts in their respective fields. . . . In addition to the standard alphabetically arranged articles on persons, holy days, rituals, deities, scriptures, etc., there are ten major articles dealing with ancient and modern religious traditions and one on the study of religion." Libr J

Wilkinson, Philip, 1955-
Illustrated dictionary of religions. DK Pub. 1999 128p hardcover o.p. pa $12.95 *

Grades: 11 12 Adult   **200.3**
1. Religion—Dictionaries 2. Reference books
ISBN 0-7894-4711-8; 0-7566-2018-X (pa)
        LC 99-30403

"Following an introductory section that discusses what religion is and what role it plays in society, content is divided into chapters covering the major religious traditions. There are also sections on ancient and primal religions and on new religions. Occultism, the New Age Movement, and the Moonies are mentioned here. . . . Throughout the text, a wealth of illustrations depicts religious practice and artifacts and representations of religion in art." Booklist

200.9   Historical, geographic, persons treatment

Balmer, Randall Herbert
Religion in twentieth century America; {by} Randall Balmer. Oxford Univ. Press 2001 142p il (Religion in American life) $28

Grades: 7 8 9 10   **200.9**
1. United States—Religion
ISBN 0-19-511295-4   LC 00-60674

The author "traces the evolution of various movements, including the Pentecostal, Fundamentalist, Evangelical, and New Age movements, the emergence of the Religious Right, Promise Keepers, and televangelism." Booklist

"This title is accessible and reliable, brief and lively, and makes a fine addition to most libraries." SLJ

Includes bibliographical references

The **Cambridge** illustrated history of religions; edited by John Bowker. Cambridge Univ. Press 2002 336p il (Cambridge illustrated history) $40 *

Grades: 11 12 Adult   **200.9**
1. Religions
ISBN 0-521-81037-X   LC 2001-37866

The Cambridge illustrated history of religions—
Continued

"The major religions get thoroughgoing treatment, with short introductions also given to the Zoroastrianism; the religions of Greece, Rome, Egypt, and Mesopotamia; aboriginal religions; and new religious movements. . . . Christianity receives a separate chapter as well as substantial treatment in chapters on Chinese, Korean, and Japanese religions. . . . This volume presents a large amount of information in an engaging way, offering much scholarly insight for the lay reader." Libr J

Includes bibliographical references

Eastern religions; origins, beliefs, practices, holy texts, sacred places; general editor, Michael D. Coogan; [contributors] Vasudha Narayanan . . . [et al.] Oxford University Press 2005 552p il $35; pa $19.95 *
Grades: 11 12 Adult   **200.9**
1. South Asia—Religion 2. East Asia—Religion
ISBN   0-19-522190-7;   978-0-19-522190-9;
0-19-522191-5 (pa); 978-0-19-522191-6 (pa)
                              LC 2004-30376

This is an introduction "to major South Asian and East Asian religious traditions. Four expert authors introduce Hinduism, Buddhism, Taoism, Confucianism, and Shinto. To aid comparison, each article has parallel sections on origins and historical development, aspects of the divine, sacred texts, sacred persons, ethical principles, sacred space, sacred time, death and the afterlife, and society and religion. The clear, crisp prose avoids academic jargon without losing the complexity and richness of the traditions being examined." Libr J

Includes bibliographical references

Encyclopedia of religion in America; edited by Charles H. Lippy, Peter W. Williams. CQ Press 2010 4v il set $600
Grades: 10 11 12 Adult   **200.9**
1. North America—Religion—Encyclopedias
2. Reference books
ISBN 978-0-87289-580-5   LC 2010-18656

"The four volumes encompass a wealth of material, covering many of the denominations and religious movements that have originated or grown in North America, including the United States, Canada, Mexico and Caribbean. Significant coverage is given to Roman Catholicism, the myriad Protestant sects, Islam, Judaism, and Asian religions. Other articles cover topics such as architecture, education, gender roles, missions, music, religious thought, and worship." Voice Youth Advocates

Includes bibliographical references

Friedenthal, Lora

Religions of Africa; [by] Lora Friedenthal and Dorothy Kavanaugh; [senior consulting editor, Robert I. Rotberg] Mason Crest Publishers 2007 112p il map (Africa: progress & problems) $24.95 *
Grades: 9 10 11 12   **200.9**
1. Africa—Religion
ISBN 978-1-59084-958-3; 1-59084-958-2
                              LC 2006-31090

This book "covers traditional African beliefs, plus the spread of Christianity and Islam, and how they are practiced today." SLJ

Includes bibliographical references

Gaustad, Edwin Scott

New historical atlas of religion in America; by Edwin Scott Gaustad and Philip L. Barlow; with the special assistance of Richard W. Dishno. Oxford Univ. Press 2001 xxiii, 435p maps $160 *
Grades: 11 12 Adult   **200.9**
1. United States—Church history 2. United States—Religion
ISBN 0-19-509168-X   LC 00-30001

First published 1976 with title: Historical atlas of religion in America

"A completely reorganized, updated, and expanded edition of Gaustad's 1962 original work and the 1976 revision, this beautifully illustrated atlas presents a historical narrative of America's rich and diverse religious past. Lively text along with 260 colorful, detailed maps and 200 other graphics provide the histories, migration, developments, and growths of religious communities in the United States." Am Libr

Queen, Edward L.

Encyclopedia of American religious history; [by] Edward L. Queen II, Stephen R. Prothero, and Gardiner H. Shattuck, Jr.; foreword by Martin E. Marty, editorial adviser; book producer, Marie A. Cantlon. 3rd ed. Facts On File 2009 3v il (Facts on File library of American history) set $250 *
Grades: 11 12 Adult   **200.9**
1.   United   States—Religion—Encyclopedias
2. Reference books
ISBN 978-0-8160-6660-5   LC 2007-52350

First published 1995

This reference source presents over 800 articles examining different religions, religious leaders, events, and other topics that helped shape the history of religion in America. The coverage extends from Puritan America to the moral majority.

Includes bibliographical references

Religion in America: opposing viewpoints; David Haugen and Susan Musser, book editors. Greenhaven Press 2011 237p il $39.70; pa $27.50 *
Grades: 8 9 10 11 12   **200.9**
1. United States—Religion
ISBN   978-0-7377-4988-5;   0-7377-4988-1;
978-0-7377-4989-2 (pa); 0-7377-4989-X (pa)
                              LC 2010016975

"Opposing viewpoints series"

This volume explores the topics relating to religion in the United States by presenting varied expert opinions that examine many of the different aspects that comprise these issues.

Includes bibliographical references

201 Religious mythology, general classes of religion, interreligious relations and attitudes, social theology

Atlas of the world's religions; edited by Ninian Smart and Frederick W. [i.e. M.] Denny; [cartographic editor, Ailsa Heritage; cartography, Advanced Illustration Ltd.] 2nd ed. Oxford University Press 2007 272p il map $110
Grades: 11 12 Adult **201**
1. Religions—Maps 2. Atlases 3. Reference books
ISBN 978-0-19-533401-2; 0-19-533401-9
First published 1999

"Beginning with a geographic examination of Palaeolithic religions, the text and maps chart the growth and development of religions throughout history, including the rise and fall of secular alternatives such as New Age belief systems and Marxism. Most of the ten sections are organized by major religion, i.e., the Hindu world, Buddhism, Judaism, Christianity, Islam, and indigenous religions, while the remainder is given to regional treatments of religion. . . . This is an attractive, informative, and practical reference tool that emphasizes the role geography plays in shaping culture and religion." Libr J
Includes bibliographical references

Campbell, Joseph, 1904-1987

Creative mythology. Arkana 1991 c1968 730p (The masks of God, v4) pa $18
Grades: 11 12 Adult **201**
1. Mythology in literature
ISBN 978-0-14-019440-1; 0-14-019440-1
First published 1968 by Viking

"This volume explores the whole inner story of modern culture since the Dark Ages, treating modern man's unique position as the creator of his own mythology." Publisher's note
Includes bibliographical references

Occidental mythology. Arkana 1991 c1964 564p (The masks of God, v3) pa $18
Grades: 11 12 Adult **201**
1. Mythology
ISBN 978-0-14-019441-8; 0-14-019441-X
First published 1964 by Viking

"A systematic . . . comparison of the themes that underlie the art, worship, and literature of the Western world." Publisher's note
Includes bibliographical references

Oriental mythology. Arkana 1991 c1962 561p (The masks of God, v2) pa $18
Grades: 11 12 Adult **201**
1. Oriental mythology
ISBN 978-0-14-019442-5; 0-14-019442-8
First published 1962 by Viking

"An exploration of Eastern mythology as it developed into the distinctive religions of Egypt, India, China, and Japan." Publisher's note
Includes bibliographical references

The power of myth; [by] Joseph Campbell, with Bill Moyers; Betty Sue Flowers, editor. Doubleday 1988 231p il hardcover o.p. pa $29.95 *
Grades: 11 12 Adult **201**
1. Mythology 2. Religious art 3. Spiritual life
ISBN 0-385-24773-7; 0-385-24774-5   LC 88-4218
Also available in paperback from Anchor Bks. $14.95 (ISBN 0-385-41886-8)

This companion to a public television series records conversations between Campbell and Bill Moyers. Campbell reflects on themes and symbols from world religions and mythologies and explores their relevance for his own spiritual journey.

"Campbell is the hero on his own voyage of discovery. This well-bound book on lovely paper with helpful illustrations from art is highly recommended for all libraries." Choice

Primitive mythology. Arkana 1991 c1959 504p (The masks of God, v1) pa $18
Grades: 11 12 Adult **201**
1. Mythology
ISBN 978-0-14-019443-2; 0-14-019443-6
First published 1959 by Viking

The author "discusses the primitive roots of mythology, examining them in light of . . . discoveries in archaeology, anthropology, and psychology." Publisher's note
Includes bibliographical references

Davis, Kenneth C.

Don't know much about mythology; everything you need to know about the greatest stories in human history but never learned. HarperCollins Publishers 2005 545p $26.95; pa $14.95 *
Grades: 9 10 11 12 Adult **201**
1. Mythology
ISBN   0-06-019460-X;   978-0-06-019460-4; 0-06-093257-0 (pa); 978-0-06-093257-2 (pa)
LC 2005-43341

The author "examines the myths created by societies ranging from Egypt, Greece and Rome to Africa, India and the Americas, proceeding . . . by way of question and answer as he surveys each mythmaking culture. . . . His survey provides a superb starting point for entering the world of mythology." Publ Wkly
Includes bibliographical references

Eliot, Alexander

The universal myths; heros, gods, tricksters, and others; with contributions by Joseph Campbell and Mircea Eliade. New Am. Lib. 1990 310p pa $15 *
Grades: 9 10 11 12 **201**
1. Mythology
ISBN 0-452-01027-6   LC 89-38161
"A Meridian book"
First published 1976 by McGraw Hill with title: Myths

This volume provides a "retelling of so-called universal myths, which Eliot and associates have drawn from various cultures worldwide and organized by commonali-

Eliot, Alexander—*Continued*
ty of theme. . . . It is Eliot's contention that the ubiquity of such myths argues strongly for the essential oneness of humankind. Essays by Joseph Campbell and Mircea Eliade bolster this view." Booklist
Includes bibliographical references

Frazer, Sir James George, 1854-1941
The new golden bough; a new abridgment of the classic work; edited and with notes and foreword by Theodor H. Gaster. Phillips 1959 xxx, 738p $51.95
Grades: 11 12 Adult	**201**
1. Mythology 2. Religions 3. Superstition
ISBN 0-87599-036-3
"A comparative study of world religions, magic, vegetation and fertility beliefs and rites, kingship, taboos, totemism and the like." New Century Handb of Engl Lit
Includes bibliographical references

McIntosh, Kenneth, 1959-
When religion & politics mix; how matters of faith influence political policies; by Kenneth McIntosh, M.Div., and Marsha McIntosh. Mason Crest Publishers 2005 112p il (Religion and modern culture) $22.95 *
Grades: 7 8 9 10	**201**
1. Church and state—United States 2. Religion and politics
ISBN 1-59084-971-X; 978-1-59084-971-2
LC 2005-3057
This is an "overview of where U.S. voters stand on the relevance of religion in their personal and public lives. The book explores topics such as abortion, same-sex marriage, and stem cell research, and it compares religious views in the U.S. with Canada's more secular perspectives. . . . [The book provides] a lucid perspective on different beliefs within and beyond various religions." Booklist
Includes bibliographical references

World mythology; the illustrated guide; Roy Willis, general editor. Oxford University Press 2006 311p il map pa $22.50 *
Grades: 8 9 10 11 12	**201**
1. Mythology
ISBN 0-19-530752-6; 978-0-19-530752-8
LC 2005-30779
First published 1993 by Holt & Co.
This book describes "the myths of Egypt, the Middle East, India, China, Tibet, Mongolia, Japan, Greece, Rome, the Celtic lands, Northern and Eastern Europe, the Arctic, North and South America, Mesoamerica, Africa, Australia, Oceania, and Southeast Asia." Libr J [review of 1993 edition]
Includes bibliographical references

201.03 Religious mythology— Encyclopedias and dictionaries

Leeming, David Adams, 1937-
A dictionary of creation myths; [by] David Adams Leeming with Margaret Adams Leeming. Oxford University Press 1995 330p il pa $23.95
Grades: 11 12 Adult	**201.03**
1. Creation—Encyclopedias 2. Reference books
ISBN 0-19-510275-4	LC 95-39961
First published 1994 by ABC-CLIO with title: Encyclopedia of creation myths
This book "provides access to information on the beliefs (both exotic and ordinary) of ancient civilizations from Sumeria and Babylonia to Egypt, Greece, and ancient Rome, from India and China to Japan and Indonesia, as well as the rich mythological history of Native Americans, the indigenous peoples of Australia, and many other cultures." Publisher's note
Includes bibliographical references

Mercatante, Anthony S.
The Facts on File encyclopedia of world mythology and legend; [by] Anthony S. Mercatante & James R. Dow. 3rd ed. Facts On File 2008 2v il (Facts on File library of religion and mythology) set $150 *
Grades: 11 12 Adult	**201.03**
1. Mythology—Encyclopedias 2. Reference books
ISBN 978-0-8160-7311-5	LC 2007-51965
First published 1988
"Entries include . . . scholarly terms, figures important in folklore and mythology, the historical figures that have inspired myths and folklore, and the authors who wrote down folktales or used folklore and mythology extensively in their work. Many . . . entries focus on the mythology and folklore of Cambodia, Tibet, Ukraine, and other areas." Publisher's note
"Jammed with information and filled with both impressive scholarship and entertaining tidbits . . . it is highly recommended for all libraries." Libr J
Includes bibliographical references

Philip, Neil
Mythology of the world; [by] Neil A. Philip. Kingfisher 2004 159p il map $24.95 *
Grades: 9 10 11 12	**201.03**
1. Mythology
ISBN 0-7534-5779-2	LC 2003-26801
The author combines "analysis about mythology and culture, first in general and then about each region of each continent, with brief versions of particular myths, commentary on their origins, and their connections with history, geography, spirituality, and more. . . . Philip's lengthy discussion on myth and society is as fascinating as the particulars of each story." Booklist

U-X-L encyclopedia of world mythology. UXL 2009 5v il set $314
Grades: 7 8 9 10 11 12	**201.03**
1. Mythology—Encyclopedias 2. Reference books
ISBN 978-1-41443-030-0; 1-41443-030-2
LC 2008-12696

U-X-L encyclopedia of world mythology—*Continued*

"In A-Z format, the set provides more than 300 entries for five content areas: characters, deities, myths, themes, and cultures. . . . The entries generally range from three to four pages. . . . Recommended for middle- and high-school libraries." Booklist

203 Public worship and other practices

Encyclopedia of religious rites, rituals, and festivals; Frank A. Salamone, editor. Routledge 2004 487p il (Routledge encyclopedias of religion and society) $150
Grades: 11 12 Adult   203
1. Religions—Encyclopedias 2. Rites and ceremonies 3. Reference books
ISBN 0-415-94180-6   LC 2003-20389
"A Berkshire Reference work"
"Articles describing types of practices common to many cultures treat such topics as death rituals, hunting rituals, puberty rites, and sport and ritual. Specific occasions that involve ceremonies include Divali, Easter, Ramadan, and Yom Kippur. Some practices like cannibalism, haircutting rituals, and snake handling are described in separate articles." SLJ
"The entries can be understood by readers unfamiliar with the topics covered, but the work is suitable for all levels of scholars." Choice
Includes bibliographical references

How to be a perfect stranger; the essential religious etiquette handbook; edited by Stuart M. Matlins & Arthur J. Magida. 5th ed. SkyLight Paths Pub. 2011 402p ("Perfect stranger" series) pa $19.99 *
Grades: 11 12 Adult   203
1. Etiquette 2. Rites and ceremonies
ISBN 978-1-59473-294-2   LC 2010-31668
First published 1996-1997 in two volumes by Jewish Lights Pub.
This guide "provides brief overviews of many religions: services, life-cycle events, home celebrations. It explains rituals so that those unfamiliar with them will know what to expect, how to dress, whether to bring a gift, and so on. It also has a glossary, explains various religious calendars, and lists religious festivals." Booklist

Leeming, David Adams, 1937-
The Oxford companion to world mythology. Oxford University Press 2006 xxxvii, 469p $65 *
Grades: 11 12 Adult   203
1. Mythology—Dictionaries 2. Reference books
ISBN 0-19-515669-2   LC 2005-14216
"This volume presents approximately 2,000 concise entries in dictionary format. Leeming, . . . in an attempt to be 'inclusive and reasonably comprehensive,' ranges far outside the Western tradition to cover figures and folklore from Africa, Asia, and the Americas, as well as from the sacred narratives of religions. . . . Approximately 100 black-and-white illustrations, along with a few color plates, provide examples of artistic renderings of various myths. . . . This work should find a place in any general reference collection." Choice
Includes bibliographical references

Religious holidays and calendars; edited by Karen Bellenir. 3rd ed. Omnigraphics 2004 424p $84 *
Grades: 11 12 Adult   203
1. Calendars 2. Religious holidays
ISBN 0-7808-0665-4   LC 2004-041500
First published 1993 under the editorship of Aidan A. Kelly, Peter Dresser, and Linda M. Ross
This "handbook provides an overview of the timekeeping and holiday traditions of the world's religions. Part 1 has four chapters that outline the history of calendars. Part 2 covers 24 religious groups in 17 chapters, each surveying the history of the religion, then listing it chronologically and describing the holidays it celebrates. The 28 contributors provide accurate information in readable, double-columned articles, ranging in length from 66 pages on types of Christianity to one on Scientology." Choice

204 Religious experience, life, practice

Chopra, Deepak
Fire in the heart; a spiritual guide for teens. Simon & Schuster Books for Young Readers 2004 199p $14.95 *
Grades: 9 10 11 12   204
1. Spiritual life 2. Teenagers
ISBN 0-689-86216-4   LC 2003-20174
By recounting his own experiences at age fifteen, Deepak Chopra, a noted Hindu author and physician provides a blueprint for teens who are seeking their own spiritual paths

220.3 Bible—Encyclopedias and topical dictionaries

Eerdmans dictionary of the Bible; David Noel Freedman, editor-in-chief; Allen C. Myers, associate editor; Astrid B. Beck, managing editor. Eerdmans 2000 xxxiii, 1425p il maps $45
Grades: 11 12 Adult   220.3
1. Bible (as subject)—Dictionaries 2. Reference books
ISBN 0-8028-2400-5   LC 00-56124
This "dictionary contains nearly 5,000 alphabetically ordered articles by 600 biblical scholars on the books, persons, places and significant terms found in the Bible." America
"Up-to-date, comprehensive, and well written, the *EDB* is highly recommended." Libr J
Includes bibliographical references

The **Oxford** companion to the Bible; edited by Bruce M. Metzger, Michael D. Coogan. Oxford Univ. Press 1993 xxi, 874p il map $70 *

Grades: 8 9 10 11 12 Adult   **220.3**
1. Bible (as subject)—Dictionaries 2. Reference books
ISBN 0-19-504645-5   LC 93-19315

This volume "contains more than 700 signed entries treating the formation, transmission, circulation, sociohistorical situation, interpretation, theology, uses, and influence of the Bible." Libr J

"The many contributors read as a veritable who's who among biblical scholars. Although this companion is not meant to be an exhaustive reference, it is a highly reliable guide." Booklist

Vine, W. E. (William Edwy), 1873-1949
Strong's concise concordance and Vine's concise expository dictionary of the Bible. Nelson, T. 1999 2v in 1 $29.99 *

Grades: 11 12 Adult   **220.3**
1. Bible—Concordance 2. Reference books
ISBN 0-7852-4254-6   LC 99-29685

This omnibus volume includes Strong's concise concordance, a version of the original published in 1894

This reference provides definitions, explanations of text, and concordance entries in one reference source.

220.5   Bible—Modern versions and translations

Bible.
The Bible: Authorized King James Version; with an introduction and notes by Robert Carroll and Stephen Prickett. Oxford University Press 2008 lxxiv, 1039, 248, 445p il map (Oxford world's classics) pa $18.95 *

Grades: 5 6 7 8 9 10 11 12 Adult   **220.5**
ISBN 978-0-19-953594-1   LC 2008-273825

This Oxford World's Classics version first published 1997

The authorized or King James Version originally published 1611.

Includes bibliographical references

The Holy Bible; containing the Old and New Testaments with the Apocryphal/Deuterocanonical books: New Revised Standard Version. Oxford University Press 1989 xxi, 996, 298, 284p map $29.99 *

Grades: 5 6 7 8 9 10 11 12 Adult   **220.5**
ISBN 0-19-528330-9; 978-0-19-528330-3
LC 90-222105

"Intended for public reading, congregational worship, private study, instruction, and meditation, it attempts to be as literal as possible while following standard American English usage, avoids colloquialism, and prefers simple, direct terms and phrases." Sheehy. Guide to Ref Books. 10th edition. suppl

The New American Bible; translated from the original languages with critical use of all the ancient sources including the revised Psalms and the revised New Testament; authorized by the Board of Trustees of the Confraternity of Christian Doctrine and approved by the Administrative Committee Board of the National Conference of Catholic Bishops and the United States Catholic Conference. Oxford University Press 2006 c2005 xxiii, 1514p $39.99

Grades: 8 9 10 11 12 Adult   **220.5**
ISBN 978-0-19-528904-6; 0-19-528904-8
First published 1970 by Kenedy

"Roman Catholic version based on modern English translations; replaces the Douay edition." N Y Public Libr Book of How & Where to Look It Up

The new Jerusalem Bible; [general editor: Henry Wansbrough] Doubleday 1985 2108p map $45; pa $29.95 *

Grades: 7 8 9 10 11 12 Adult   **220.5**
ISBN   0-385-14264-1;   978-0-385-14264-9;
0-385-24833-4 (pa); 978-0-385-24833-4 (pa)
LC 85-16070

First published in this format 1966 with title: The Jerusalem Bible

"Derives from the French version edited at the Dominican Ecole Biblique de Jerusalem and known as 'La Bible de Jerusalem.' The introductions and notes are 'a direct translation from the French, though revised and brought up to date in some places' but translation of the Biblical text goes back to the original languages." Guide to Ref Books. 11th edition

Seek, find; the Bible for all people: Contemporary English Version. G.P. Putnam's Sons/American Bible Society 2006 1725p $24.95; pa $15.95 *
Grades: 11 12 Adult   **220.5**
ISBN   0-399-15385-3;   978-0-399-15385-3;
0-399-15397-7 (pa); 978-0-399-15397-6 (pa)

"The CEV was published by the American Bible Society in response to an urgent need for a translation that would reach those many millions who are not reading the Bible. The goal was a serious translation—not a paraphrase—combining historical and scholarly accuracy with contemporary language that everyone can understand." Publisher's note

220.6   Bible—Interpretation and criticism (Exegesis)

Manser, Martin H.
Critical companion to the Bible; a literary reference; [by] Martin H. Manser; associate editors, David Barratt, Pieter J. Lalleman, Julius Steinberg. Facts On File, Inc. 2009 488p il (Facts on File library of world literature) $75
Grades: 11 12 Adult   **220.6**
1. Bible—Criticism 2. Bible as literature
ISBN 978-0-8160-7065-7   LC 2008-29257

Manser, Martin H.—*Continued*

This book "examines the Bible as a work of literature, focusing on its language and verbal structures and on the imaginative quality of its thought." Publisher's note

"This reference provides an excellent introduction to not only just the literary but also the theological studies of the Bible through the ages." Booklist

Includes bibliographical references

220.9 Bible—Geography, history, chronology, persons of Bible lands in Bible times

Comfort, Philip Wesley

The complete book of who's who in the Bible; [by] Philip Comfort, Walter A. Elwell. Tyndale House Publishers 2004 626p map pa $14.97

Grades: 11 12 Adult   220.9

1. Bible—Biography 2. Reference books

ISBN 0-8423-8369-7   LC 2004-20184

This book "provides readers with a complete listing of people in the Bible with descriptions of their lives and accomplishments." Publisher's note

Includes bibliographical references

Currie, Robin

The letter and the scroll; what archaeology tells us about the Bible; [by] Robin Currie and Stephen Hyslop. National Geographic 2009 335p il map $40

Grades: 11 12 Adult   220.9

1. Bible (as subject)—Antiquities

ISBN 978-1-4262-0514-9   LC 2009-8572

"This gorgeous book . . . covering the people and events of the Bible, placed into their archaeological context, will delight and inform those who are interested in the Bible from a religious, cultural, or historical perspective. . . . [The book] investigates a variety of topics—such as cities, languages, luxury goods, wars, taxes, writings, and ancient art—through artifacts and archaeological evidence to provide an extensive background for the reader." Libr J

Includes bibliographical references

Oxford Bible atlas; edited by Adrian Curtis. 4th ed. Oxford University Press 2007 229p il map $35 *

Grades: 11 12 Adult   220.9

1. Bible—Geography 2. Reference books

ISBN 0-19-100158-9; 978-0-19-100158-1

First published 1962

This atlas includes "81 full-color illustrations as well as 27 maps—e.g., of Jerusalem and the Holy Land, the Middle East and the eastern Mediterranean lands—all with terrain modeling. The text is divided into four main sections: 'The Setting,' 'The Hebrew Bible,' 'The New Testament,' and 'Archaeology in Bible Lands.' . . . [This is] a handsome background resource for Bible study." Libr J

Includes bibliographical references

The **Oxford** guide to people & places of the Bible; edited by Bruce M. Metzger, Michael D. Coogan. Oxford Univ. Press 2001 xxii, 374p maps $35 *

Grades: 11 12 Adult   220.9

1. Bible (as subject) 2. Reference books

ISBN 0-19-514641-7   LC 00-66900

"This dictionary is a spinoff from *The Oxford Companion to the Bible* (1993) from which the compilers have extracted the articles about people and places. Many of the more than 300 articles in *People and Places* are exactly the same as those in the larger *Companion*, except that the frequent parenthetical references to biblical passages have been deleted. Some articles are extracts from longer articles in the *Companion*. Articles range in length from a short paragraph, such as the nine lines devoted to *Gethsemane*, to as many as nine pages (for *Jerusalem*) or thirteen pages (for *Jesus Christ*). Longer articles are divided into sections, each with a topical subheading. . . . The bibliography has been updated to include references as recent as 2000." Booklist

Includes bibliographical references

The **Oxford** history of the biblical world; edited by Michael D. Coogan. Oxford Univ. Press 1998 643p il maps $60; pa $19.95 *

Grades: 11 12 Adult   220.9

1. Bible—History of biblical events 2. Ancient civilization

ISBN 0-19-508707-0; 0-19-513937-2 (pa)

LC 98-16042

"Organized chronologically, the essays explore the many cultures of ancient Canaan, Israel, Judea, and Palestine from 10,000 B.C.E. to the rise of Islam in the seventh century C.E. Illustrations, maps, charts, chronologies, and bibliographies enhance the uniformly well-written essays. But the strengths of the work are its currency and breadth of coverage and perspective." Libr J

Includes bibliographical references

Tischler, Nancy M., 1931-

Men and women of the Bible; a readers guide. Greenwood Press 2002 267p il $59.95

Grades: 11 12 Adult   220.9

1. Bible—Biography

ISBN 0-313-31714-3   LC 2002-75347

This resource provides "information on 100 biblical characters and their cultural significance in Western civilization. . . . Entries are arranged alphabetically from *Aaron* to *Zephaniah*, concisely written, and adhere to a uniform pattern. Subjects are listed by name with the addition of etymological information. A synopsis of the relevant biblical story follows, utilizing the King James version of the Bible. . . . The author also includes information on each person as a character in later works, including Western literature, legend, and painting." Booklist

Includes bibliographical references

221   Bible. Old Testament (Tanakh)

Bible. O.T.

The Dead Sea scrolls Bible; the oldest known Bible; translated for the first time into English [by] Martin Abegg, Jr., Peter Flint, and Eugene Ulrich. HarperSan Francisco 1999 xxii, 649p $39.95; pa $21.95

Grades: 9 10 11 12   221
   ISBN 0-06-060063-2; 0-06-060064-0 (pa)
                                         LC 99-26866

This book "presents all 220 of the Dead Sea biblical scrolls, arranged to be read in canonical order." Publisher's note

Includes bibliographical references

222   Historical books of Old Testament

Bible. O.T. Pentateuch.

The contemporary Torah; a gender-sensitive adaptation of the JPS translation; revising editor, David E.S. Stein; consulting editors, Adele Berlin, Ellen Frankel, and Carol L. Meyers. Jewish Publication Society 2006 xlii, 412p $28

Grades: 8 9 10 11 12 Adult   222
   ISBN 0-8276-0796-2; 978-0-8276-0796-5
                                       LC 2006-40608

A modern adaptation of the Jewish Publication Society's translation of the Torah. "In places where the ancient audience probably would not have construed gender as pertinent to the text's plain sense, the editors changed words into gender-neutral words; where gender was probably understood to be at stake, they left the text as originally translated, or even introduced gendered language where none existed before. They made these changes regardless of whether words referred to God, angels, or human beings." Publisher's note

The Torah: the five books of Moses; a new translation of the Holy Scriptures according to the Masoretic text; first section. Jewish Publication Society 1963 393p $20; pa $15 *

Grades: 8 9 10 11 12 Adult   222
   ISBN 0-8276-0015-1; 0-8276-0680-X (pa)

This "translation of Genesis, Exodus, Leviticus, Numbers, and Deuteronomy was prepared . . . to present a version of the Bible that takes into account modern insights and knowledge of ancient times. . . . Of chief value to persons of the Jewish religion but of interest to Bible scholars of any religion." Booklist

Chittister, Joan

The tent of Abraham; stories of hope and peace for Jews, Christians, and Muslims; [by] Joan Chittister, Saadi Shakur Chishti, Arthur Waskow; foreword by Karen Armstrong. Beacon Press 2006 218p $24.95 *

Grades: 9 10 11 12   222
   1. Abraham (Biblical figure) 2. Christianity
   3. Judaism 4. Islam
   ISBN 0-8070-7728-3; 978-0-8070-7728-3
                                         LC 2006-1274

"The three coauthors, representing the three major Western faiths (Judaism, Christianity and Islam), explain each religion's basis for a monotheistic multifaith movement by delving into ancient stories." Publ Wkly

"Delicate in telling but bold in message, this book encourages every reader to take an inner pilgrimage to understand better others' viewpoints." Libr J

Kirsch, Jonathan

Moses; a life. Ballantine Bks. 1998 415p map hardcover o.p. pa $14.95

Grades: 11 12 Adult   222
   1. Moses (Biblical figure)
   ISBN 0-345-41269-9; 0-345-41270-2 (pa)
                                         LC 98-25299

The author "distills the vast secondary literature that has grown up around the sparse biblical material on Moses. He draws on the myths, legends, and midrashim of Moses to soften ragged edges left by competing images of him as warrior, magician, shepherd, God's favorite, sorcerer's apprentice, and reluctant prophet." Booklist

Includes bibliographical references

225.9   Bible. New Testament— Geography, history, stories

Ehrman, Bart D.

Peter, Paul, and Mary Magdalene; the followers of Jesus in history and legend. Oxford University Press 2006 285p il hardcover o.p. pa $15.95

Grades: 11 12 Adult   225.9
   1. Peter, the Apostle, Saint 2. Paul, the Apostle, Saint
   3. Mary Magdalene, Saint
   ISBN   0-19-530013-0;   978-0-19-530013-0;
   0-19-534350-6 (pa); 978-0-19-534350-2 (pa)
                                       LC 2005-58996

The author "examines discussions of Simon Peter, the apostle Paul, and Mary Magdalene in Scripture and other writings of the first few centuries." Libr J

Ehrman "presents three of the best known and most important of Jesus' followers and does so in a way that is uncompromising in its scholarship yet utterly engaging for general readers." Booklist

Includes bibliographical references

230 Christianity & Christian theology

Guite, Malcolm
What do Christians believe? belonging and belief in modern Christianity. Walker & Co. 2008 125p map pa $9.95
Grades: 9 10 11 12   230
1. Christianity
ISBN 978-0-8027-1640-8; 0-8027-1640-7
First published 2006 in the United Kingdom
Contents: What is a Christian?; Where are the Christians?; The story of Jesus; The followers of Jesus; The teachings of Jesus; What do Christians do?; Christianity in the world; Christianity in the twenty-first century
Includes bibliograpghical references

Hale, Rosemary Drage
Christianity. Rosen Pub. 2010 112p il (Understanding religions) lib bdg $31.95
Grades: 7 8 9 10   230
1. Christianity
ISBN 978-1-4358-5621-9; 1-4358-5621-X
                                        LC 2009-10295
This book about Christianity "discusses origins and historical development; aspects of the divine; sacred texts, persons, space, and time; ethical principles; death and the afterlife; and society and religion." SLJ
Includes glossary and bibliographical references

The **Quotable** saint; [compiled by] Rosemary Ellen Guiley. Facts on File 2002 368p $45; pa $16.95
Grades: 9 10 11 12   230
1. Christian life—Quotations
ISBN 0-8160-4375-2; 0-8160-4376-0 (pa)
                                        LC 2002-23540
This is a "collection of excerpts from the lives, thoughts, writings, and sayings of the saints. More than 3,000 quotes cover [such topics as] . . . daily life, work, family, marriage, relationships, the afterlife, the soul, and more. The quotes are listed under more than 250 categories, such as God; Creation; Natural World; Humanity; Angels." Publisher's note
"This book will allow readers, especially neophytes to the topic, to brush elbows with much grand and glorious wisdom." SLJ
Includes bibliographical references

230.003 Christianity—Encyclopedias and dictionaries

Encyclopedia of Christianity; edited by John Bowden. Oxford University Press 2005 xli, 1364p il $125
Grades: 11 12 Adult   230.003
1. Reference books 2. Christianity—Encyclopedias
ISBN 978-0-19-522393-4; 0-19-522393-4
                                        LC 2005-48801
"This single volume contains 33 gateway entries to pivotal subjects; 300 major articles . . . [166] boxed items on various themes; and a who's who of 400 (mainly male) historically influential Christians." Christ Century
"This is probably the most comprehensive single-volume encyclopedia of Christianity." Choice
Includes bibliographical references

242 Devotional literature

The **African** prayer book; selected and with an introduction by Desmond Tutu. Doubleday 1995 xx, 139p $21; pa $9.95 *
Grades: 11 12 Adult   242
1. Prayers
ISBN 0-385-47730-9; 0-385-51649-5 (pa)
                                        LC 94-43444
Tutu "draws on the breadth and depth of African spirituality to assemble this little treasury of prayer and devotion. He has arranged material from throughout the African continent and the African diaspora into a traditional pattern of adoration, contrition, thanksgiving, and supplication." Booklist

248 Christian experience, practice, life

Lewis, C. S. (Clive Staples), 1898-1963
The Screwtape letters; with, Screwtape proposes a toast. HarperSanFrancisco 2001 209p $22.95; pa $11.95
Grades: 11 12 Adult   248
1. Christian life 2. Satire
ISBN 0-06-065289-6; 0-06-065293-4 (pa)
                                        LC 00-49860
The Screwtape letters first published 1943 by Macmillan; this combined edition first published 1961 by Macmillan
"A popular work on Christian moral and theological problems. . . . It is in the form of a series of letters in which a devil, Screwtape, advises his nephew, Wormwood, on how to deal with his human 'patients.'" Reader's Ency. 4th edition

248.4 Christian life and practice

Campolo, Anthony
Letters to a young evangelical; the art of mentoring; [by] Tony Campolo. BasicBooks 2007 280p (Art of mentoring) $23 *
Grades: 9 10 11 12   248.4
1. Christian life
ISBN 0-465-00831-3; 978-0-465-00831-5
"In letters to two fictional young evangelicals, Campolo endeavors to challenge and encourage young Christians in much the same way Paul did in his epistles. . . . As Campolo covers such topics as the religious right, fundamentalism, dispensationalism, homosexuality, abortion and Christian-Muslim relations, he admirably steers clear of telling his readers what to think. Rather, he explains his position on the issue at hand, explains the positions of his detractors and leaves his readers to decide for themselves." Publ Wkly

252   Texts of sermons

American sermons; the pilgrims to Martin Luther
King, Jr. Library of Am. 1999 939p $40
Grades: 11 12 Adult   **252**
1. Sermons
ISBN 1-88301-165-5   LC 98-34295
This anthology "rounds up in chronological order 58
sermons, from Robert Cushman's address to the colony
of Plimmoth in New England in 1621 to King's 1968
I've been to the mountaintop speech. Also includes biographical notes and notes on the texts." Libr J
"To peruse this work is to become reacquainted with
the literary eloquence of our distant and recent past and
to observe what has happened to rhetoric itself over the
centuries." N Y Times Book Rev
Includes bibliographical references

John Paul II, we love you; World Youth Day
reflections, 1984-2005; edited by Barbara A.
Murray. Saint Mary's Press 2005 141p il pa
$9.95
Grades: 9 10 11 12   **252**
1. John Paul II, Pope, 1920-2005 2. Youth—Religious
life 3. Church work with youth
ISBN 0-88489-820-2   LC 2004-14396
This book features "excerpts from the pope's official
addresses at World Youth Days past, reflections by youth
from around the world, and an 8-page insert full of color
photos." Publisher's note

King, Martin Luther, Jr., 1929-1968
Strength to love; foreword by Coretta Scott
King. Fortress 2010 168p il pa $20
Grades: 11 12 Adult   **252**
1. Sermons
ISBN 978-0-8006-9740-2
First published 1963 by Harper & Row
A collection of sermons addressing social injustice and
racism.
Includes bibliographical references

Tutu, Desmond
The words of Desmond Tutu; selected by
Naomi Tutu. Newmarket Press 2007 111p il
(Newmarket "Words of" series) $15
Grades: 11 12 Adult   **252**
1. Sermons 2. South Africa—Race relations
ISBN 978-1-55704-719-9
First published 1989
"In this collection of more than 100 excerpts from his
most memorable speeches, sermons, and writings, Tutu
discusses issues . . . ranging from faith and social re-
sponsibility to nuclear disarmament, the Third World,
and women in the Church. . . . This volume also con-
tains the full text of the archbishop's acceptance of the
Nobel Peace Prize." Publisher's note
Includes bibliographical references

261.5   Christianity and secular disciplines

Grant, Edward, 1926-
Science and religion, 400 B.C. to A.D. 1550;
from Aristotle to Copernicus. Greenwood Press
2004 xxvi, 307p il (Greenwood guides to science
and religion) $67.95
Grades: 11 12 Adult   **261.5**
1. Religion and science
ISBN 0-313-32858-7   LC 2004-17429
Contents: Introduction; Aristotle and the beginnings of
two thousand years of natural philosophy; Science and
natural philosophy in the Roman empire; The first six
centuries of Christianity: Christian attitudes toward Greek
philosophy and science; The emergence of a New Europe
after the Barbarian invasions; The medieval universities
and the impact of Aristotle's natural philosophy; The in-
terrelations between natural philosophy and theology in
the fourteenth and fifteenth centuries; Relations between
science and religion in the Byzantine empire, the world
of Islam, and the Latin West
Includes bibliographical references

Olson, Richard, 1940-
Science and religion, 1450-1900; from
Copernicus to Darwin; [by] Richard G. Olson.
Greenwood Press 2004 292p il (Greenwood guides
to science and religion) $65
Grades: 11 12 Adult   **261.5**
1. Religion and science
ISBN 0-313-32694-0   LC 2004-47501
This book "explores the many ways in which religion—its ideas, attitudes, practices, and institutions—in-
teracted with science from the beginnings of the Scientific Revolution to the end of the 19th century." Publisher's
note
The issues discussed "should be especially helpful to
those who are interested in the historical background to
current science-religion issues being debated in the United States." Sci Books Films
Includes bibliographical references

270   History of Christianity

Bass, Diana Butler, 1959-
A people's history of Christianity; the other side
of the story. HarperOne 2009 353p $25.99
Grades: 10 11 12 Adult   **270**
1. Church history
ISBN 978-0-06-144870-6; 0-06-144870-2
                                     LC 2008-51764
The author aims "to give contemporary progressive
. . . Christians a sense of their family history, refracted
through little known as well as famous men and women
whose work within and outside the institutional church
fueled sometimes 'alternative' practices as they tried to
follow Jesus the Prophet." Publ Wkly
"What an exciting book. . . . This easily read book
encourages Christian activism, inclusivity, and transformed hope that can be lived." Libr J
Includes bibliographical references

272 Persecutions in general church history

Pérez, Joseph, 1931-
The Spanish Inquisition; a history; trans. by Janet Lloyd. Yale University Press 2005 248p $26; pa $17 *
Grades: 11 12 Adult   272
1. Inquisition 2. Spain—History
ISBN 0-300-10790-0; 0-300-11982-8 (pa)
LC 2004-114614
The author "tells the history of the Spanish Inquisition from its medieval beginnings to its nineteenth-century ending. . . . He explores the inner workings of its councils, and shows how its officers, inquisitors, and leaders lived and worked." Univ Press Books for Public and Second Sch Libr, 2006
Includes bibliographical references

280 Christian denominations

Atwood, Craig D.
Handbook of denominations in the United States; [by] Craig D. Atwood, Frank S. Mead, Samuel S. Hill. 13th ed. Abingdon Press 2010 416p il $24 *
Grades: 11 12 Adult   280
1. Sects 2. United States—Religion
ISBN 978-1-4267-0048-4; 1-4267-0048-2
LC 2010-07092
First published 1951. Periodically revised
"History and present structure of Christian religious bodies in the United States. Reports on doctrines of different churches. Includes bibliography and index." NY Public Libr Book of How & Where to Look It Up
Includes bibliographical references

Brown, Stephen F.
Catholicism & Orthodox Christianity; by Stephen F. Brown and Khaled Anatolios. 3rd ed. Chelsea House 2009 144p il (World religions) $40
Grades: 7 8 9 10 11 12   280
1. Catholic Church 2. Orthodox Eastern Church
ISBN 978-1-60413-106-2; 1-60413-106-3
LC 2008-43046
First published 2002 by Facts and File
This "traces the roots of [Catholicism and Orthodox Christianity] from the early Christian churches to today. The historical passage of the Catholic and Orthodox faiths is recounted, from the original teachings of Jesus Christ to the separation of the Eastern and Western Churches to recent attempts at reconciliation." Publisher's note
Includes glossary and bibliographical references

Protestantism. 3rd ed. Chelsea House 2009 144p il map (World religions) $40
Grades: 7 8 9 10 11 12   280
1. Protestantism
ISBN 978-1-60413-112-3; 1-60413-112-8
LC 2008-29659

First published 1991 by Facts on File
This "explores the origins, customs, and history of Protestantism, from its beginnings in the Middle Ages to its role in today's world. Current issues, such as the development of new religious denominations, its stance on abortion, the ordination of gays and women, and the relationship between religion and politics, are explored within the framework of the fundamental moral tenets of the faith." Publisher's note
Includes glossary and bibliographical references

282 Roman Catholic Church

The **Catholic** Church: opposing viewpoints; Noah Berlatsky, book editor. Greenhaven Press 2010 231p il $39.70; pa $27.50
Grades: 9 10 11 12   282
1. Catholic Church
ISBN 978-0-7377-5104-8; 978-0-7377-5105-5 (pa)
LC 2010012406
"Opposing viewpoints series"
This anthology discusses topics such as who should be allowed to become priests, homosexuality in the Church, reproductive and sexual issues, and reform within the Church.
Includes bibliographical references

Flinn, Frank K.
Encyclopedia of Catholicism. Facts on File 2006 xxxi, 670p (Encyclopedia of world religions) $75 *
Grades: 11 12 Adult   282
1. Reference books 2. Catholic Church—Encyclopedias
ISBN 0-8160-5455-X; 978-0-8160-5455-8
LC 2006-9645
This encyclopedia "covers the key people, movements, institutions, practices, and doctrines of Roman Catholicism from its earliest origins." Publisher's note
Includes bibliographical references

New Catholic encyclopedia; prepared by an editorial staff at the Catholic University of America. 2nd ed. Gale Group 2003 15v il maps set $1,981
Grades: 11 12 Adult   282
1. Reference books 2. Catholic Church—Encyclopedias
ISBN 978-0-7876-4004-0; 0-7876-4004-2
LC 2002-924
First published 1967 as an update to the Catholic encyclopedia. Kept up-to-date by yearly supplements
Published "in association with the Catholic University of America."
This encyclopedia "covers the history of the eastern churches, the churches of the Protestant Reformation, and other ecclesial communities as well as the Christian roots based in ancient Israel and Judaism. No comprehensive resource on Catholicism can be complete without touching on other world religions as well, including Islam, Buddhism, and Hinduism. This resource provides entries not only on the doctrine, organization, and history of the church, but also on the people, institutions, and social

New Catholic encyclopedia—*Continued*

changes that have affected the church over the years. Arranged alphabetically, the entries run in length from half a page to several pages in length. All entries provide the name of the contributor and a bibliography. Cross-references to related articles are located throughout the work. Adding to the usefulness of the set are more than 3,000 black-and-white photographs, maps, and charts that complement the scholarly articles." Am Ref Books Annu, 2003

O'Toole, James M., 1950-

The faithful; a history of Catholics in America. Belknap Press of Harvard University Press 2008 376p hardcover o.p. pa $17.95

Grades: 11 12 Adult   **282**

1. Catholic Church—United States 2. Catholics—United States 3. United States—Church history

ISBN   978-0-674-02818-0;   0-674-02818-X; 978-0-674-03488-4 (pa); 0-674-03488-0 (pa)

                 LC 2007-38343

The author "tells the history of lay Catholics in America. Beginning with the priestless church of the Colonial period, he goes on to explore the church in the democratic republic, the immigrant church, the church of Catholic Action, the church of Vatican II, and the church in the 21st century. Each chapter begins with a short biography of a lay Catholic of his or her time; the last chapter opens with a portrait of 'Maria,' O'Toole's projection of a typical modern-day Catholic." Libr J

"The genial style of writing together with a plentiful amount of fascinating tidbits will keep all but the most jaded expert going." Publ Wkly

Includes bibliographical references

289.3   Latter-Day Saints (Mormons)

Book of Mormon.

The Book of Mormon; another testament of Jesus Christ; [translated by Joseph Smith, Jr.] Doubleday 2004 586p $24.95 *

Grades: 8 9 10 11 12 Adult   **289.3**

1. Mormons 2. Church of Jesus Christ of Latter-day Saints

ISBN 0-385-51316-X   LC 2004-51982

Also available in other bindings and editions

First published 1830

"Based on golden plates which Joseph Smith claimed were revealed to him, and which he unearthed from Cumorah Hill, New York, this book is roughly similar in structure to the Bible. . . . Emphasized are the doctrines of pre-existence, perfection, the afterlife, and Christ's second coming." Haydn. Thesaurus of Book Dig

Bushman, Claudia L.

Mormons in America; [by] Claudia Lauper Bushman and Richard Lyman Bushman. Oxford Univ. Press 1998 142p il (Religion in American life) $28

Grades: 7 8 9 10   **289.3**

1. Mormons 2. Church of Jesus Christ of Latter-day Saints

ISBN 0-19-510677-6   LC 98-18605

Chronicles the history of the Church of Jesus Christ of Latter-Day Saints beginning in America in the early 1800s and continuing to the present day throughout the world

"A solid resource for libraries. Illustrated with historical material and black-and-white photos. Time line and bibliography appended." Booklist

Includes bibliographical references

289.7   Mennonite churches

Hostetler, John A., 1918-

Amish society. 4th ed. Johns Hopkins Univ. Press 1993 435p il maps hardcover o.p. pa $20 *

Grades: 11 12 Adult   **289.7**

1. Amish

ISBN 0-8018-4441-X; 0-8018-4442-8

                 LC 92-19304

First published 1963

This book discusses the sectarian origins of the Amish, immigration history, family and community life, population trends, farming practices, technological innovations, education, medicine and the effects of government regulation.

Includes bibliographical references

292   Classical religion (Greek and Roman religion)

Adkins, Lesley

Dictionary of Roman religion; [by] Lesley Adkins & Roy A. Adkins. Facts on File 1996 288p il $44

Grades: 11 12 Adult   **292**

1. Reference books 2. Rome—Religion—Dictionaries

ISBN 0-8160-3005-7   LC 95-8355

Also available in paperback from Oxford Univ. Press

This dictionary "provides more than 1,400 brief definitions and descriptions of deities, myths, and persons; cult sites and practices, and terminology and technology drawn from the religions of the Roman Republic and Empire. . . . Although the entries decidedly emphasize archaeology and art history . . . they are clearly and concisely written and refreshingly free of the unexplicated jargon or terminology that can intimidate novices." Choice

Beauman, Sally

The genealogy of Greek mythology; an illustrated family tree of Greek myth from the first gods to the founders of Rome; [by] Vanessa James. Gotham Books 2003 107p il map $25

Grades: 9 10 11 12   **292**

1. Classical mythology 2. Reference books

ISBN 1-592-40013-2   LC 2004-272120

This "book/chart begins with the earliest surviving account of the creation of the universe from Chaos and quickly covers the children of Gaia, the rise of the Titans, and the triumph of the Olympians. The origins of each of the Olympians, their symbols, and their charac-

Beauman, Sally—*Continued*

ters are briefly described. . . . Lists of the gods' children are followed by an index of 3000-plus individuals. When the book is turned over, it opens to a large map of the Aegean Sea, showing the places associated with mythic heroes. This begins the genealogical chart of the mortals who participated in the Trojan War, starting with their immortal ancestors and concluding with their descendants. A map of the Mediterranean Sea shows the routes of the Argonauts, Aeneas, and Odysseus. Lists of Helen's suitors, the 12 labors of Hercules, and more conclude the volume. . . . The appeal here is in the beauty of the more than 125 color photographs of Greek and Roman artwork, the concise biographies, and the elegant ordering of a complex topic." SLJ

Daly, Kathleen N.

Greek and Roman mythology, A to Z; [by] Kathleen N. Daly; revised by Marian Rengel. 3rd ed. Chelsea House Publishers 2009 162p il (Mythology A to Z) lib bdg $45

Grades: 8 9 10 11 12   292
  1. Classical mythology
  ISBN 978-1-60413-412-4; 1-60413-412-7
                                            LC 2009-8243
  First published 1992 by Facts on File

Alphabetically listed entries identify and explain the characters, events, important places, and other aspects of Greek and Roman mythology

"The format is accessible, making the book useful for school assignments, as well as enjoyable for general reading. Each entry provides a clear definition, and retells the stories associated with the character or place. The broad coverage, ample cross-references, and extensive index enable readers to recognize the many connections and interrelationships between characters and myths." SLJ [review of 1992 edition]

  Includes bibliographical references

Graves, Robert, 1895-1985

The Greek myths. Combined ed. Penguin Books 1992 782p pa $19.95

Grades: 11 12 Adult   292
  1. Classical mythology
  ISBN 0-14-017199-1
  Also available two-volume paperback edition
  First published 1955
  On cover: Complete edition

A collection of the author's interpretations of Greek myths based on anthropological and archaeological findings

Hamilton, Edith, 1867-1963

Mythology; illustrated by Steele Savage. Little, Brown 1942 497p il $27.95; pa $13.95 *

Grades: 8 9 10 11 12 Adult   292
  1. Classical mythology 2. Norse mythology
  ISBN 0-316-34114-2; 0-316-34151-7 (pa)
  Contents: The gods, the creation and the earliest heroes; Stories of love and adventure; Great heroes before the Trojan War; Heroes of the Trojan War; Great families of mythology; Less important myths; Mythology of the Norsemen; Genealogical tables

A retelling of Greek, Roman and Norse myths

Mitchell, Adrian, 1932-2008

Shapeshifters; tales from Ovid's Metamorphoses; retold by Adrian Mitchell; illustrated by Alan Lee. Frances Lincoln Children's 2010 c2009 143p il $22.95

Grades: 7 8 9 10   292
  1. Classical mythology
  ISBN 978-1-84507-536-1; 1-84507-536-6

This is a "marvelous re-creation of myth from Ovid. . . . The language is simple and contemporary, moving from rhyme to free verse to prose and back again. . . . All of these stories explore mystery: the origins of flowers, mountains, lakes. Pygmalion, Persephone, Midas and Arachne all appear here . . . [Lee] makes men and women, gods and beasts, sea, sky and leaf shimmer." Kirkus

The **Oxford** dictionary of classical myth and religion; edited by Simon Price and Emily Kearns. Oxford University Press 2003 599p maps $39.95; pa $17.95 *

Grades: 11 12 Adult   292
  1. Classical mythology—Dictionaries 2. Reference books
  ISBN 0-19-280288-7; 0-19-280289-5 (pa)
                                            LC 2004-298013
  Spine title: Classical myth & religion

"Instead of separating mythology and Judeo-Christian religion into separate references, this work covers all religious life in the ancient Greco-Roman world. The result is a generally accessible and academically current compendium of information on gods and holy beings, religious practices, festivals, sacred sites, myths, authors, and texts of the period. The reader will find not only Athena and Zeus but also Jesus Christ and St. Augustine, Mani and Zoroaster." Libr J

Roman, Luke

Encyclopedia of Greek and Roman mythology; [by] Luke Roman and Monica Roman. Facts On File, Inc. 2009 548p il (Facts on File library of religion and mythology) $75

Grades: 9 10 11 12 Adult   292
  1. Classical mythology—Encyclopedias 2. Reference books
  ISBN 978-0-8160-7242-2; 0-8160-7242-6
                                            LC 2009-1235

"Although this volume covers some 300 major figures of classical mythology, the focus is on where and how they appeared in the works of Greek and Roman writers. Thus classical writers whose works featured mythological themes are also included. The most notable aspect of the encyclopedia is the extensive treatment of the relevant texts themselves. More than 50 are featured. . . . This is a beneficial resource for anyone wanting to explore the original classical sources of Greek and Roman mythology." Choice

  Includes bibliographical references

293 Germanic religion

Daly, Kathleen N.
Norse mythology A to Z; [by] Kathleen N. Daly; revised by Marian Rengel. 3rd ed. Chelsea House 2009 128p il map (Mythology A to Z) lib bdg $45
Grades: 8 9 10 11 12   **293**
1. Norse mythology—Dictionaries 2. Reference books
ISBN 978-1-60413-411-7; 1-60413-411-9
LC 2009-13338
First published 1991
Alphabetically listed entries identify and explain the characters, events, and important places of Norse mythology
Includes bibliographical references

294 Religions of Indic origin

Mann, Gurinder Singh
Buddhists, Hindus, and Sikhs in America; [by] Gurinder Singh Mann, Paul David Numrich & Raymond B. Williams. Oxford University Press 2001 158p il (Religion in American life) hardcover o.p. pa $12.95 *
Grades: 7 8 9 10   **294**
1. Buddhism 2. Hinduism 3. Sikhism 4. Asian Americans—Religion
ISBN 0-19-512442-1; 0-19-533311-X (pa)
LC 2001-45151
Presents the basic tenets of these three Asian religions and discusses the religious history and experience of their practitioners after immigration to the United States
"Solid information, a large selection of historical and contemporary photographs, interesting readings from primary sources, and accounts from school-age Buddhists, Hindus, and Sikhs combine to make this is a valuable resource." Booklist
Includes bibliographical references

294.3 Buddhism

Dalai Lama XIV, 1935-
Ethics for the new millennium; [by] His Holiness The Dalai Lama. Riverhead Bks. 1999 237p hardcover o.p. pa $13
Grades: 11 12 Adult   **294.3**
1. Ethics 2. Buddhism
ISBN 1-57322-025-6; 1-57322-883-4 (pa)
LC 99-15138
The Tibetan Buddhist spiritual leader presents advice on leading an ethical life. His book is divided into three sections: the foundation of ethics, ethics and the individual, and ethics and society
"An important book for thoughtful teens to muse over now, and return to in the future." SLJ

Eckel, Malcolm David, 1946-
Buddhism. Rosen Pub. 2010 112p il (Understanding religions) lib bdg $31.95
Grades: 7 8 9 10   **294.3**
1. Buddhism
ISBN 978-1-4358-5619-6; 1-4358-5619-8
LC 2009-10083
Subjects covered in this book include "buddhas and boddhisattvas, Zen meditation, Tantric scriptures, pilgrimage, temples, and festivals and rites." Publisher's note
Includes glossary and bibliographical references

Irons, Edward A.
Encyclopedia of Buddhism; J. Gordon Melton, series editor. Facts on File 2007 xxxv, 634p il map (Encyclopedia of world religions) $75 *
Grades: 9 10 11 12 Adult   **294.3**
1. Buddhism—Encyclopedias 2. Reference books
ISBN 978-0-8160-5459-6   LC 2007-4503
This encyclopedia provides "access to the terms, concepts, personalities, historical events, institutions, and movements that helped shape the history of Buddhism and the way it is practiced today. Although the primary focus of the encyclopedia is clearly on Buddhism in all its forms, it also provides introductions to Daoism, Shinto, Confucianism, and other religious practices in East and Southeast Asia." Publisher's note
Includes bibliographical references

Morris, Tony
What do Buddhists believe? meaning and mindfulness in Buddhist philosophy. Walker & Co. 2008 96p map pa $9.95 *
Grades: 9 10 11 12   **294.3**
1. Buddhism
ISBN 978-0-8027-1655-2; 0-8027-1655-5
First published 2006 in the United Kingdom
An introduction to Buddhism discussing its most important beliefs and core practices, its historical role and its growing pervasiveness throughout the modern world.
Includes bibliographical references

Smith, Huston
Buddhism: a concise introduction; [by] Hurston Smith and Philip Novak. HarperSanFrancisco 2003 242p hardcover o.p. pa $12.95
Grades: 11 12 Adult   **294.3**
1. Buddhism
ISBN 0-06-050696-2; 0-06-073067-6 (pa)
LC 2003-544630
This "book grew out of Smith's *The World's Religions*. . . . The first 12 chapters present his outstanding survey of the life and fundamental teachings of the 'Perfectly Enlightened One,' basic Buddhist concepts, and the major divisions of Buddhism (e.g., Mahayana, Theravada, Zen, and Tibetan). . . . Novak . . . is the primary author of the final six chapters, all-new sections on the migration of Buddhism to the West. Impressively, this informative portion with its emphasis on Buddhism in America lives up to the standards of lucidity so evident in earlier chapters." Libr J
Includes bibliographical references

Wangu, Madhu Bazaz
Buddhism. 4th ed. Chelsea House 2009 144p il
(World religions) $40
Grades: 7 8 9 10 11 12   **294.3**
1. Buddhism
ISBN 978-1-60413-105-5; 1-60413-105-5
LC 2008-51265
First published 1993 by Facts on File
This "tells the story of Buddhism's origins and its de-
velopment into three major schools of thought—and
presents the particular beliefs and practices of those
schools of Buddhism. . . . [This] title explores the con-
cept of the 'socially engaged Buddhist,' the growth and
practice of Buddhism in America, and the recent revival
of Buddhism in Asia." Publisher's note
Includes glossary and bibliographical references

Winston, Diana
Wide awake: a Buddhist guide for teens. Perigee
Bk. 2003 290p pa $13.95
Grades: 7 8 9 10 11 12   **294.3**
1. Buddhism
ISBN 0-399-52897-0   LC 2002-192666
"Switching between anecdotes of her own journey in
Buddhism and advice on how teens can apply the Bud-
dha's teachings to their lives, Winston offers a personal
and thoughtful introduction to Buddhist thought and
practice." Booklist

294.5   Hinduism

Ganeri, Anita, 1961-
The Ramayana and Hinduism. Smart Apple
Media 2003 30p il (Sacred texts) $27.10
Grades: 5 6 7 8 9   **294.5**
1. Hinduism
ISBN 1-58340-242-X   LC 2003-42352
Contents: Origins; Texts and teaching; In daily life
Explains the history and practices of the religion of
Hinduism, especially as revealed through its sacred book,
the Ramayana

Jones, Constance, 1961-
Encyclopedia of Hinduism; [by] Constance A.
Jones and James D. Ryan; J. Gordon Melton,
series editor. Facts on File 2006 xxxvii, 552p il
(Facts on File library of religion and mythology)
$75 *
Grades: 9 10 11 12 Adult   **294.5**
1. Reference books 2. Hinduism—Encyclopedias
ISBN 0-8160-5458-4; 978-0-8160-5458-9
LC 2006-44419
This encyclopedia "focuses on the most significant
groups within this religion, noteworthy teachers and their
contributions, the religions and cultural movements that
enriched its history, and the diaspora of Hindu thought
and practice around the world. Two major religious tradi-
tions that sprang from Hindu influence, Jainism and
Sikhism, also have many entries." Publisher's note
Includes bibliographical references

Narayanan, Vasudha
Hinduism. Rosen Pub. 2010 112p il
(Understanding religions) lib bdg $31.95
Grades: 7 8 9 10   **294.5**
1. Hinduism
ISBN 978-1-4358-5620-2; 1-4358-5620-1
LC 2009-11026
This book about Hinduism "discusses origins and his-
torical development; aspects of the divine; sacred texts,
persons, space, and time; ethical principles; death and the
afterlife; and society and religion." SLJ
Includes glossary and bibliographical references

**Sivananda Yoga Vedanta Center (London, En-
    gland)**
Yoga mind & body. DK Pub. 2008 168p il pa
$15 *
Grades: 11 12 Adult   **294.5**
1. Yoga
ISBN 978-0-7566-3674-6   LC 2008-489063
First published 1996
"This guide stresses the five points of exercise, breath-
ing, meditation, diet, and relaxation for improved health
and happiness. In addition to basic yoga poses, *Yoga
Mind & Body* provides meditation tools, stress relief ex-
ercises, and recipes for healthful nutrition." Publisher's
note

Wangu, Madhu Bazaz
Hinduism. 4th ed. Chelsea House 2009 144p il
(World religions) $40
Grades: 7 8 9 10 11 12   **294.5**
1. Hinduism
ISBN 978-1-60413-108-6; 1-60413-108-X
LC 2008-43047
First published 1991 by Facts on File
This describes the history of Hinduism, its customs,
beliefs, and rites of passage, the Hindu nationalist move-
ment in India, Hinduism and the interfaith movement,
and Hinduism and the environmental movement.
Includes glossary and bibliographical references

294.6   Sikhism

Singh, Nikky-Guninder Kaur
Sikhism. 3rd ed. Chelsea House 2009 144p il
(World religions) $40
Grades: 7 8 9 10 11 12   **294.6**
1. Sikhism
ISBN 978-1-60413-114-7; 1-60413-114-4
LC 2008-29662
First published 1993 by Facts on File
This "describes the basic tenets of Sikhism, examines
the recent move toward greater political independence
within the Indian nation, and covers issues of cultural ad-
aptation, persecution, and subsequent education now tak-
ing place in the West." Publisher's note
Includes glossary and bibliographical references

295   Zoroastrianism (Mazdaism, Parseeism)

Hartz, Paula
Zoroastrianism; by Paula R. Hartz. 3rd ed.
Chelsea House 2009 144p il (World religions) $40
Grades: 7 8 9 10 11 12   **295**
1. Zoroastrianism
ISBN 978-1-60413-116-1; 1-60413-116-0
         LC 2008-35811
First published 1999 by Facts on File
This "analyzes how [Zoroastrianism] has a crucial place in religious history and continues to maintain a devoted following today." Publisher's note
Includes glossary and bibliographical references

296   Judaism

Ehrlich, Carl S.
Judaism. Rosen Pub. 2010 112p il (Understanding religions) lib bdg $31.95 *
Grades: 7 8 9 10   **296**
1. Judaism
ISBN 978-1-4358-5622-6; 1-4358-5622-8
         LC 2009-10055
This "book provides students with an overview of the great religious tradition of Judaism. Readers learn about the covenant with God, the Bible, the Mishnah, and the Talmud. They also read about sects, messianic movements, mysticism, and the Kabbalah. Rabbinical systems of law and custom are covered as are various principles and practices, holy days, and contemporary movements in Judaism." Publisher's note
Includes glossary and bibliographical references

Kessler, Edward, 1927-
What do Jews believe? the customs and culture of modern Judaism. Walker & Co. 2007 117p il pa $9.95 *
Grades: 9 10 11 12   **296**
1. Judaism
ISBN 0-8027-1639-3; 978-0-8027-1639-2
First published 2006 in the United Kingdom
The author "explores the variety of ways in which Jews live their lives: religious and secular, Ashkenazi and Sephardi, Jews in Israel and Jews who live in the diaspora. Kessler asks what Judaism means and what it means to be a Jew, and explores the roots of a religion that goes back some four thousand years and was a major influence on the creation and development of both Christianity and Islam." Publisher's note

Morrison, M. A. (Martha A.), 1948-
Judaism; by Martha A. Morrison and Stephen F. Brown. 4th ed. Chelsea House 2009 144p il (World religions) $40
Grades: 7 8 9 10 11 12   **296**
1. Judaism
ISBN 978-1-60413-110-9; 1-60413-110-1
         LC 2008-29657

First published 1991 by Facts on File under the authorship of Fay Carol Gates
This "presents the basic beliefs of the Jewish religious heritage and highlights the different manners in which these traditions can be upheld. Both Orthodox Judaism and the religious practices and movements within Reformed Judaism, including Reform Judaism, Conservative Judaism, and Reconstructionist Judaism, are explored." Publisher's note
Includes glossary and bibliographical references

Robinson, George
Essential Judaism; a complete guide to beliefs, customs and rituals. Pocket Bks. 2000 xxi, 644p hardcover o.p. pa $20
Grades: 11 12 Adult   **296**
1. Judaism
ISBN 0-671-03480-4; 0-671-03481-2 (pa)
         LC 99-55288
This book "attempts to provide the essentials of Judaism for novices, outsiders and those who, like Robinson, rediscovered their heritage as adults. It's an excellent introductory resource, vast but accessibly organized." Publ Wkly
Includes bibliographical references

296.03   Judaism—Encyclopedias and dictionaries

Karesh, Sara E.
Encyclopedia of Judaism; [by] Sara E. Karesh and Mitchell M. Hurvitz. Facts on File 2006 xxxvi, 602p il (Facts on File library of religion and mythology) $75 *
Grades: 11 12 Adult   **296.03**
1. Reference books 2. Judaism—Encyclopedias
ISBN 0-8160-5457-6   LC 2004-26537
This encyclopedia "covers individuals, places, events, theologies, ideologies, organizations, movements, and denominations that span Jewish history. . . . This is a very good one-volume resource that is especially accessible to young adults and non-Jews." Libr J
Includes bibliographical references

The **New** encyclopedia of Judaism; editor-in-chief, Geoffrey Wigoder; coeditors, Fred Skolnik & Shmuel Himelstein. New York Univ. Press 2002 856p il $79.95
Grades: 11 12 Adult   **296.03**
1. Reference books 2. Judaism—Dictionaries
ISBN 0-8147-9388-6   LC 2002-16614
First published 1989 with title: The Encyclopedia of Judaism
This reference "seeks to present a balanced picture, offering current thinking among scholars in Reform, Conservative, and Orthodox movements and a roster of contributors hailing from Israel, England, and the United States. While the scholarship is solid, the material is readily accessible to a popular audience, and the work is magnificently illustrated." Libr J
Includes bibliographical references

The **Oxford** dictionary of the Jewish religion; editors in chief, R.J. Zwi Werblowsky, Geoffrey Wigoder. Oxford University Press 1997 764p $125

Grades: 8 9 10 11 12 Adult   **296.03**
1. Reference books 2. Judaism—Dictionaries
ISBN 0-19-508605-8   LC 96-45517
"The 2400 entries in this dictionary include unsigned but revised articles from the editors' Encyclopedia of the Jewish Religion (1966), as well as . . . new signed articles covering [topics] . . . and biographies related to the Jewish religion and interfaith relations." Libr J

The **student's** encyclopedia of Judaism; editor-in-chief Geoffrey Wigoder; coeditors Fred Skolnik and Shmuel Himelstein; educational editor Barbara Sutnick. New York University Press 2004 390p il map $39.95

Grades: 9 10 11 12   **296.03**
1. Reference books 2. Judaism—Encyclopedias
ISBN 0-8147-4275-0   LC 2003-65125
Revised and condensed edition of The new encyclopedia of Judaism, published 2002
Identifies and defines people, places, and terms important to the Jewish faith
"The approximately 1000 entries in this handsome and comprehensive volume describe virtually all aspects of Jewish life and culture, including significant and lesser-known people. The articles are clearly written and abundantly cross-referenced. . . . There have been a number of recent reference works about Jews and Judaism for this audience, but this encyclopedia stands out. It is a must for any collection supporting the study of religion." SLJ
Includes bibliographical references

297 Islam, Babism, Bahai Faith

Armstrong, Karen
Islam; a short history. Modern Lib. 2000 xxxiv, 222p maps $19.95; pa $11.95 *
Grades: 11 12 Adult   **297**
1. Islam
ISBN 0-679-64040-1; 0-8129-6618-X (pa)
                    LC 00-25285
This history of the Islamic faith focuses on the religion's attitude toward politics
The author "does an admirable job of presenting Islamic history from an objective, unbiased point of view." Libr J
Includes bibliographical references

Aslan, Reza
No god but God; the origins, evolution, and future of Islam. Random House 2005 xxiv, 310p $25.95; pa $14.95
Grades: 11 12 Adult   **297**
1. Islam
ISBN 1-4000-6213-6; 0-8129-7189-2 (pa)
                    LC 2004-54053

"Beginning with an exploration of the religious climate in the years before the Prophet's Revelation, Aslan traces the story of Islam from the Prophet's life and the so-called golden age of the first four caliphs all the way through European colonization and subsequent independence. . . . This is an excellent overview that doubles as an impassioned call to reform." Booklist
Includes bibliographical references

Ben Jelloun, Tahar, 1944-
Islam explained. New Press (NY) 2002 120p hardcover o.p. pa $13.95
Grades: 11 12 Adult   **297**
1. Islam
ISBN 1-56584-781-4; 1-56584-897-7 (pa)
                    LC 2002-30500
Translated from the French by Franklin Philip
"Cast in the form of an extended conversation between Ben Jelloun and his young daughter. . . . Father and child discuss the history of Islam, what it means to be a Muslim today, the challenges facing the Islamic world, and terrorism. . . . Its openness and emotional honesty, particularly when discussing the tragedy of 9/11, make it a valuable addition to a growing public discourse. As an introduction to the religion, it is spotty, but as a liberal Muslim voice of reconciliation, heartbreak, and compassion, it is priceless." Booklist

Bloom, Jonathan
Islam: a thousand years of faith and power; [by] Jonathan Bloom and Sheila Blair. Yale University Press 2002 268p il map (Yale Nota bene) pa $13.95 *
Grades: 9 10 11 12   **297**
1. Islam—History
ISBN 0-300-09422-1   LC 2001-96195
First published 2000 by TV Bks.
This book narrates the rise of Islam from its origins and the prophet Muhammad, through its height during the Abbasid Empire, the Mongol invasions of the 13th century to the growth of the Ottoman, Persian, and Mughal empires.
Includes bibliographical references

Campo, Juan Eduardo, 1950-
Encyclopedia of Islam; [by] Juan E. Campo. Facts On File 2008 750p il map (Encyclopedia of world religions) $85 *
Grades: 9 10 11 12 Adult   **297**
1. Reference books 2. Islam—Encyclopedias
ISBN 978-0-8160-5454-1; 0-8160-5454-1
                    LC 2008-5621
"In about 600 A-to-Z entries, this encyclopedic guide explores the terms, concepts, personalities, historical events, and institutions that helped shape the history of this religion and the way it is practiced today." Publisher's note
Includes bibliographical references

Encyclopedia of Islam in the United States; edited by Jocelyne Cesari. Greenwood Press 2007 2v il set $199.95
Grades: 10 11 12 Adult   **297**
1. Reference books 2. Islam—Encyclopedias 3. Muslims—United States—Encyclopedias
ISBN 978-0-313-33625-6; 0-313-33625-3
                     LC 2007-16142
"The first volume of this . . . work is an A-Z encyclopedia on American Muslim topics. The second volume offers over 400 pages of primary resources about the social, political, religious, and artistic life of American Muslims." Choice
This set "takes a refreshing look at Islam and Muslims from a uniquely Muslim American perspective. Hence, it is a valuable reference to both Muslims and non-Muslims alike." Am Ref Books Annu, 2008
Includes bibliographical references

Farah, Caesar E.
Islam: beliefs and observances. 7th ed. Barron's 2003 500p map pa $14.95 *
Grades: 9 10 11 12   **297**
1. Islam
ISBN 0-7641-2226-6   LC 2002-25354
First published 1968
This book traces the historical development of Islam starting with its founder, the prophet Muhammad in the early seventh century A.D. Its rapid spread as a religious, cultural and political force is detailed along with an examination of the Koran and other Islamic beliefs and moral obligations
Includes bibliographical references

Gordon, Matthew
Islam; by Matthew S. Gordon. 4th ed. Chelsea House 2009 144p il (World religions) $40
Grades: 7 8 9 10 11 12   **297**
1. Islam
ISBN 978-1-60413-109-3; 1-60413-109-8
                     LC 2008-35810
First published 1991 by Facts on File
This describes the founding of Islam and its spread, The Koran, Hadith, and Islamic law, branches of Islam and their basic beliefs, Muslim customs and rituals, the pattern of Islamic life, and the place of Islam in the modern world.
Includes glossary and bibliographical references

Islam; [by] Matthew S. Gordon. Rosen Pub. 2010 112p il (Understanding religions) lib bdg $31.95
Grades: 7 8 9 10   **297**
1. Islam
ISBN 978-1-4358-5618-9; 1-4358-5618-X
                     LC 2009-10043
This book about Islam "discusses origins and historical development; aspects of the divine; sacred texts, persons, space, and time; ethical principles; death and the afterlife; and society and religion. . . . There is enough substance here to make this . . . a key resource for reports." SLJ
Includes glossary and bibliographical references

Understanding Islam; origins, beliefs, practices, holy texts, sacred places; [by] Matthew S. Gordon. Sterling Pub. Co. 2010 112p pa $9.95 *
Grades: 8 9 10 11 12 Adult   **297**
1. Islam
ISBN 978-1-90748-616-6   LC 2010-2376
First published 2001 by Facts on File
This "exploration of Islam's history, beliefs, and practices . . . [addresses] issues such as political Islam, Islam and Israel, and Islamic fundamentalism." Publisher's note
Includes bibliographical references

Hafiz, Dilara
The American Muslim teenager's handbook; by Dilara Hafiz, Imran Hafiz, and Yasmine Hafiz. [new ed.] Atheneum Books for Young Readers 2009 168p il pa $11.99 *
Grades: 7 8 9 10 11 12   **297**
1. Islam 2. Muslims—United States 3. Conduct of life 4. Teenagers—Religious life
ISBN 978-1-4169-8578-5; 1-4169-8578-6
"Ginee Seo books"
A revised edition of the title first published 2007 by Acacia Pub.
"Casual, colloquial, joking, contemporary, and passionate, this interactive handbook by two Arizona teens and their mom talks about their faith, about what it is like to be both proud Americans and proud Muslims, and about misunderstandings and stereotypes. . . . There are also step-by-step guides on how to pray, how to read the Qur'an, and how to fast at Ramadan. Muslim and non-Muslim teens alike will be caught by the candor, the humor, and the call for interfaith dialogue and tolerance." Booklist
Includes bibliographical references

Hasan, Asma Gull
American Muslims; the new generation. 2nd edition, with study guide. Continuum 2002 204p pa $19.95 *
Grades: 9 10 11 12   **297**
1. Islam 2. Muslims—United States
ISBN 0-8264-1416-8   LC 2003-270056
First published 2000
This book provides basic information about Islam in America: its major tenets, its various sects and its ethnic groups, including African Americans. In an effort to help Americans overcome anti-Muslim stereotypes the author focuses on Muslim American family values, religious freedom and adaptation of their faith to American culture
"From her perspective as a youthful American Muslim feminist, Hasan provides a fluent evaluation of the Islamic community in the US." Choice {review of 2000 edition}
Includes bibliographical references

Illustrated dictionary of the Muslim world; [editor, Felicity Crowe and others] Marshall Cavendish Reference 2010 192p il (Muslim world) $85.64

Grades: 7 8 9 10   **297**
1. Islam—Dictionaries 2. Islamic civilization—Dictionaries 3. Reference books
ISBN 978-0-7614-7929-1; 0-7614-7929-5
        LC 2010008613
Contains hundreds of short entries on Islamic concepts, religious practices, historical events and personalities, geographical places, and fact files of nations with large Muslim populations.
"Attractive trim on the pages, colorful fonts, quality illustrations, and framed (often illustrated) sideboxes create a pleasing layout. Excellent for assignments." SLJ
Includes glossary and bibliographical references

Islam: opposing viewpoints; David M. Haugen, Susan Musser, and Kacy Lovelace, book editors. Greenhaven Press 2009 215p il lib bdg $38.50; pa $26.75 *

Grades: 7 8 9 10   **297**
1. Islam
ISBN 978-0-7377-4526-9 (lib bdg); 978-0-7377-4527-6 (pa)   LC 2009-14564
"Opposing viewpoints series"
Contributors to this anthology discuss such topics as the conflict between Islamic and western cultures, Islam's relationship to violence, and the treatment of women in Islamic societies.
Includes bibliographical references

Islamic beliefs, practices, and cultures. Marshall Cavendish Reference 2010 352p il (Muslim world) lib bdg $114.21

Grades: 7 8 9 10   **297**
1. Islam—Customs and practices 2. Islamic civilization
ISBN 978-0-7614-7926-0; 0-7614-7926-0
        LC 2010008611
"In addition to exploring the beliefs, teachings, and practices of Islam and its holy places, calendar, and festivals, this volume covers Muslim contributions to the arts, architecture, science, literature, philosophy, and the role of the media." Booklist
"Attractive trim on the pages, colorful fonts, quality illustrations, and framed (often illustrated) sideboxes create a pleasing layout. Excellent for assignments." SLJ

Islamic fundamentalism; David M. Haugen, book editor. Greenhaven Press 2008 129p (At issue. Religion) lib bdg $29.95; pa $21.20 *

Grades: 7 8 9 10   **297**
1. Islamic fundamentalism 2. Islam—Relations
ISBN 978-0-7377-3689-2 (lib bdg); 978-0-7377-3690-8 (pa)   LC 2007-29302
Previous edition published 2003 under the editorship of Auriana Ojeda
"After a brief introduction that discusses the various terms used to describe Islamic fundamentalists (such as 'Islamists'), 12 articles from different points of view are presented. . . . Each article includes some fact and some opinion, leaving readers to make up their own minds about the perspectives expressed." SLJ
Includes bibliographical references

Living Islam out loud; American Muslim women speak; edited by Saleemah Abdul-Ghafur. Beacon Press 2005 209p pa $15

Grades: 9 10 11 12   **297**
1. Muslim women 2. Women in Islam 3. Muslims—United States
ISBN 0-8070-8383-6 (pa)   LC 2004-28161
"Themes about negotiating culture, romantic relationships, and faith and spiritual journeys often intersect in the 18 short essays that comprise the book. The majority of writers come from families that immigrated to the United States from the Middle East and Asia, but the book also includes two essays by African-American Muslim women." Sojourners

Modern Muslim societies. Marshall Cavendish Reference 2010 416p il (Muslim world) lib bdg $114.21

Grades: 7 8 9 10   **297**
1. Islam—Customs and practices
ISBN 978-0-7614-7927-7; 0-7614-7927-9
        LC 2010008612
This book "covers marriage and family life, education and employment, organizations, law and politics, and civil and human rights in its first half. 'Focus' features treat topics such as 'Wearing the Veil' and 'Al-Qaeda.' Each chapter of the second half, 'Regional and National Surveys,' covers a different part of the world and its Muslim population." Booklist
"Attractive trim on the pages, colorful fonts, quality illustrations, and framed (often illustrated) sideboxes create a pleasing layout. Excellent for assignments." SLJ

The **Oxford** history of Islam; {edited by} John Esposito. Oxford Univ. Press 1999 749p il map $49.95 *

Grades: 11 12 Adult   **297**
1. Islam
ISBN 0-19-510799-3   LC 99-13219
"Contributors treat, among other things, Muslim history, law, and society; art and architecture; and regional differences. Chapters on the 'Globalization of Islam' and 'Contemporary Islam' are particularly relevant to current events. . . . An ideal one-volume source." Libr J
Includes bibliographical references

Sardar, Ziauddin
What do Muslims believe? the roots and realities of modern Islam. Walker & Co. 2007 140p map pa $9.95

Grades: 9 10 11 12   **297**
1. Islam
ISBN 978-0-8027-1642-2; 0-8027-1642-3
The author discusses "what makes a Muslim; where Muslims come from and who they are today; what, exactly, they believe and how they reflect those beliefs; where Islam is headed; and how you can apply Islam in your life." Publisher's note
Includes bibliographical references

297.1   Sources of Islam

Koran.
The meaning of the glorious Koran; an explanatory translation by Marmaduke Pickthall; with an introduction by William Montgomery Watt. A.A. Knopf 1992 xxiv, 693p il $22 *
Grades: 7 8 9 10 11 12 Adult   **297.1**
ISBN 0-679-41736-2; 978-0-679-41736-1
LC 92-52928
"Everyman's library"
This translation first published 1930
"The sacred scripture of Islam, regarded by Muslims as the Word of God, and except in sura I.—which is a prayer to God—and some few passages in which Muhammad or the angels speak in the first person, the speaker throughout is God." Ency Britannica

297.9   Babism and Bahai Faith

Hartz, Paula
Baha'i Faith. 3rd ed. Chelsea House 2009 144p il (World religions) $40
Grades: 7 8 9 10 11 12   **297.9**
1. Bahai Faith
ISBN 978-1-60413-104-8; 1-60413-104-7
LC 2008043045
First published 2002 by Facts and File
This "explores all aspects of the Baha'i faith, from the original teachings of its founder, Baha'u'llah, to the modern-day communities that exist in 236 countries and territories throughout the world." Publisher's note
Includes glossary and bibliographical references

299   Religions not provided for elsewhere

The **Gnostic** Bible; edited by Willis Barnstone and Marvin Meyer. Rev. ed. Shambhala 2009 881p pa $29.95
Grades: 11 12 Adult   **299**
1. Gnosticism
ISBN 978-1-59030-631-4; 1-59030-631-7
LC 2008-36431
First published 2003
"The book provides Gnostic texts from their Jewish origins, into early Christianities, on into the medieval world. Though it concentrates on the early Jewish-Christian matrix of early Gnosticism, the collection . . . manifests the breadth and depth of Gnostic variations in neo-Platonist, Manichean, Mandean, Islam, and Cathar movements." Choice
Includes bibliographical references

Green, Miranda J. (Miranda Jane)
The world of the Druids. Thames & Hudson 1997 192p il maps hardcover o.p. pa $24.95
Grades: 9 10 11 12   **299**
1. Druids and Druidism 2. Celts
ISBN 0-500-05083-X; 0-500-28571-3 (pa)
LC 96-61291

Published in the United Kingdom with title: Exploring the world of the Druids
Green presents a study of the Druids. She "begins by analyzing the classical writings on Druids. She also discusses the role of historical and archaeological analysis. . . . The author examines the archaeological finds and the conclusions drawn from that. She discusses the Druid resurgence in the 19th century and the Druids' role in the 20th-century neopagan movement." Libr J
"The wide-ranging illustrations from ancient objects to modern ceremonies and modern Druids that are linked with an enthralling text make this a remarkable book." Hist Today
Includes bibliographical references

299.5   Religions of East and Southeast Asian origin

Berthrong, John H., 1946-
Confucianism; a short introduction; [by] John H. and Evelyn Nagai Berthrong. Oneworld Publs. 2000 209p il pa $23.95
Grades: 9 10 11 12   **299.5**
1. Confucianism
ISBN 1-85168-236-8
This book defines what Confucianism is, its underlying principles and its history, development and impact on Chinese life, from families to the imperial state
Includes bibliographical references

Birrell, Anne
Chinese myths. University of Tex. Press 2000 80p (Legendary past) pa $14.95
Grades: 9 10 11 12   **299.5**
1. Oriental mythology
ISBN 0-292-70879-3   LC 00-39296
Published in cooperation with British Museum Press
This book explores the tradition of Chinese myths in the context of world mythology. Topics include: origins and creation myths; myths of the flood; the divine cosmos; gender in myth; metamorphoses; mythic heroes and heroines; and fabled plants and animals

Brennan, J. H.
The magical I ching. Llewellyn Publs. 2000 247p pa $14.95
Grades: 9 10 11 12   **299.5**
1. I ching 2. Divination
ISBN 1-567-18087-6   LC 00-24132
This work presents the history of the I Ching and explains the magical spiritual technique behind this ancient oracle. It also shows how to develop the symbols used in I Ching by using several different methods and analyzes each of the possible sixty-four hexagrams that form the basis of the oracle
Includes bibliographical references

Confucianism; Adriane Ruggiero . . . [et al.] Greenhaven Press 2006 239p il map (Religions and religious movements) $36.20 *

Grades: 9 10 11 12   **299.5**
1. Confucianism
ISBN 0-7377-2567-2; 978-0-7377-2567-4
LC 2004-60581

Presents an overview of Confucianism, including its origins in China, an analysis of the major works and ideas of its founder, its influence on Chinese history and society, its spread to other countries, and its status in modern Asia.

"This volume is an excellent comprehensive collection of historical and cultural essays explaining the Confucian beliefs and impact. . . . It is an essential purchase for public and school libraries." Voice Youth Advocates

Includes bibliographical references

Hartz, Paula
Daoism; by Paula R. Hartz. 3rd ed. Chelsea House 2009 144p il (World religions) $40
Grades: 7 8 9 10 11 12   **299.5**
1. Taoism
ISBN 978-1-60413-115-4; 1-60413-115-2
LC 2008-35809

First published 1993 by Facts on File with title: Taoism

This "traces the history of Daoism and explains its basic thoughts, traditions, and practices. It also details the Daoist movement worldwide and how the limitations of consumerism are leading a younger generation to search for their own spiritual harmony." Publisher's note

Includes glossary and bibliographical references

Shinto; by Paula R. Hartz. 3rd ed. Chelsea House 2009 144p il (World religions) $40
Grades: 7 8 9 10 11 12   **299.5**
1. Shinto
ISBN 978-1-60413-113-0; 1-60413-113-6
LC 2008-29661

First published 1997 by Facts on File

This "examines the basic tenets of Shinto, its evolution in response to other religious influences, and how the original Shinto religion—rooted in an agrarian society—survives in contemporary Japan." Publisher's note

Includes glossary and bibliographical references

Hoobler, Dorothy
Confucianism; by Dorothy and Thomas Hoobler. 3rd ed. Chelsea House 2009 144p il (World religions) $40 *
Grades: 7 8 9 10 11 12   **299.5**
1. Confucianism
ISBN 978-1-60413-107-9; 1-60413-107-1
LC 2008-29656

First published 1993 with authors' names in reverse order

Examines Confucianism in conjunction with its resurgence in China and the rest of the world. Presents its history, basic beliefs, and evolution in response to historical events in China.

Includes glossary and bibliographical references

Roberts, Jeremy, 1956-
Chinese mythology A to Z. 2nd ed. Chelsea House 2009 172p il (Mythology A to Z) lib bdg $45
Grades: 8 9 10 11 12   **299.5**
1. Chinese mythology 2. China—Religion
ISBN 978-1-60413-436-0; 1-60413-436-4
LC 2009-10176

First published 2004

"Coverage includes: Buddhist deities and legendary characters; animal stories, such as the fox legends; important locations, such as shrines and sacred places; [and] allegorical figures, such as the Jade Emperor, the Rain Master, and the Lord of the Granary." Publisher's note

Includes bibliographical references

Japanese mythology A to Z. 2nd ed. Chelsea House 2009 138p il (Mythology A to Z) lib bdg $45
Grades: 8 9 10 11 12   **299.5**
1. Japanese mythology 2. Japan—Religion
ISBN 978-1-60413-435-3   LC 2009-8242

First published 2004

This book about Japanese mythology covers "the early Japanese deities who created the world and the later deities who protect it; *Kami*, the spirits of all aspects of the living world; animals and mythological creatures; demons and bogeymen; shrines and other sacred places; stories from *Kojiki* and other historical records of ancient myths; [and] historical emperors, empresses, heroes, and heroines whose deeds live on in legend." Publisher's note

Includes bibliographical references

The **Wisdom** of the Tao; editor, Julian F. Pas. Oneworld Publs. 2000 223p il $15.95
Grades: 9 10 11 12   **299.5**
1. Taoism
ISBN 1-85168-232-5

Partial contents: The Scriptures of Taoism; The mystery of the Tao and its power; Cosmic reality, life and death; The sage-ruler; Mystical sparkles; Taoist moral principles; Language, dreams and utopias

Includes bibliographical references

299.6 Religions originating among Black Africans and people of Black African descent

Galembo, Phyllis
Vodou; visions and voices of Haiti. Ten Speed Press 2005 xxx, 113p il pa $24.95
Grades: 9 10 11 12   **299.6**
1. Voodooism 2. Haiti
ISBN 1-58008-676-4; 978-1-58008-676-9

First published 1998

The book delves into the symbols and spiritual tradition of Voodoo or Vodou. Both the divine and human faces of real Haitian Vodou are presented together with its current practice involving priestesses, zombies, snakes and swamps.

Includes bibliographical references

Lugira, Aloysius Muzzanganda

African traditional religion; by Aloysius M. Lugira. 3rd ed. Chelsea House 2009 144p il map (World religions) $40

Grades: 7 8 9 10 11 12   **299.6**

1. Africa—Religion

ISBN 978-1-60413-103-1; 1-60413-103-9

LC 2008-51188

First published 1999 by Facts on File with title: African religion

"The African continent is home to more than 6,000 different ethnic and cultural groups, each with its own religious traditions. Yet these many traditions have much in common. . . . [This book] offers a . . . perspective on the beliefs that are a permanent part of Africa's history and future." Publisher's note

Includes glossary and bibliographical references

Lynch, Patricia Ann

African mythology, A to Z; revised by Jeremy Roberts. 2nd ed. Chelsea House 2010 xxiv, 149p il map (Mythology A to Z) lib bdg $45

Grades: 8 9 10 11 12   **299.6**

1. African mythology 2. Africa—Religion

ISBN 978-1-60413-415-5; 1-60413-415-1

LC 2009-33612

First published 2004

This is a "reference to the deities, places, events, animals, beliefs, and other subjects that appear in the myths of various African peoples." Publisher's note

Includes bibliographical references

299.7 Religions of North American native origin

Gill, Sam D., 1943-

Native American religions; an introduction. 2nd ed. Wadsworth/Thomson Learning 2005 142p map pa $82.95

Grades: 11 12 Adult   **299.7**

1. Native Americans—Religion

ISBN 0-534-62600-9   LC 2004-111567

First published 1982

This "introduction to the religions of Native Americans provides an overview of the latest research and thought in this area. In writing the book, Gill aims to introduce an academically and humanistically useful way of trying to appreciate and understand the complexity and diversity of Native American religions, as well as establish them as a significant field within religious studies. In addition, aspects of European-American history are examined in a search for sources of widespread misunderstandings about the character of Native American religions." Publisher's note

Includes bibliographical references

Hartz, Paula

Native American religions; [by] Paula R. Hartz. 3rd ed. Chelsea House 2009 144p il (World religions) $40

Grades: 7 8 9 10 11 12   **299.7**

1. Native Americans—Religion

ISBN 978-1-60413-111-6; 1-60413-111-X

LC 2008051197

First published 1997 by Facts on File

This "presents the history of the Native American religions, starting from their roots as tribal religions, and then details the detrimental effects of European colonization, the annihilation of the Native Americans that threatened the religions, and their sudden restoration in the 20th century." Publisher's note

Includes glossary and bibliographical references

300 SOCIAL SCIENCES, SOCIOLOGY & ANTHROPOLOGY

300.3 Social sciences— Encyclopedias and dictionaries

Dictionary of the social sciences; edited by Craig Calhoun. Oxford Univ. Press 2002 563p $75

Grades: 11 12 Adult   **300.3**

1. Reference books 2. Social sciences—Dictionaries

ISBN 0-19-512371-9   LC 00-68151

This dictionary provides "definitions of key terms, offering entries that also discuss the intellectual issues behind the terms' usage. The entries cover all the social sciences except for law, education, and public administration. . . . Some 275 biographies are included." Libr J

Includes bibliographical references

301 Sociology and anthropology

Best, Joel

Stat-spotting; a field guide to identifying dubious data. University of California Press 2008 132p il $19.95 *

Grades: 9 10 11 12 Adult   **301**

1. Statistics

ISBN 978-0-520-25746-7; 0-520-25746-4

LC 2008-17175

This "is an easily digestible guide to understanding how simple miscalculations, botched translations and inappropriate graphics misled the American public. This concise book helps readers understand how politicians and the media twist statistics to match the goals of their agenda. Author Joel Best describes how things like bloating figures by misplacing a decimal point or using enlarged graphics to visually distract readers from analyzing the data objectively. If you want a better understanding of the reality behind those charts and graphs you see in books, on television and in the media then you need to read this book." Univ Press Books for Public and Second Sch Libr, 2009

Includes bibliographical references

302.2 Communication

Biedermann, Hans, 1930-
Dictionary of symbolism; cultural icons and the meanings behind them; translated by James Hulbert. Meridan Book 1994 465p il pa $25 *
Grades: 11 12 Adult   **302.2**
1. Signs and symbols 2. Reference books
ISBN 0-452-01118-3   LC 93-30616
Original German edition, 1989
This dictionary "incorporates symbols that originated in Asia, Africa, Europe and the 'New World'. There are almost 600 entries from mythology, fairy tale, psychology, religion, and sociology, plus historical and legendary figures. With 2000 black-and-white illustrations, the book is highly attractive. The symbols are accompanied by thorough interpretations based on various sources." SLJ
Includes bibliographical references

Liungman, Carl G., 1938-
Dictionary of symbols. W.W. Norton 1994 596p il pa $21.95 *
Grades: 8 9 10 11 12 Adult   **302.2**
1. Signs and symbols 2. Picture writing 3. Reference books
ISBN 0-393-31236-4; 978-0-393-31236-2
Original Swedish edition, 1974
This dictionary groups "icons according to their graphical style rather than their meaning. For example, all symbols based upon the cross are included in one chapter, those based upon the triangle in another, and those based upon the circle in yet another. Each symbol is succinctly defined and a source of origin (if known) is given. To enhance access, both name and form indexes are provided. This work will certainly become one of the key sources for tracing symbols and their meanings." Am Libr
Includes bibliographical references

302.23 Media (Means of communication)

De Abreu, Belinha S.
Media literacy, social networking, and the web 2.0 environment for the K-12 educator. Peter Lang 2011 189p il (Minding the media: critical issues for learning and teaching) $129.95; pa $33.95
Grades: Adult Professional   **302.23**
1. Media literacy—Study and teaching 2. Internet in education 3. Social networking 4. Web 2.0
ISBN 978-1-4331-1009-2; 978-1-4331-1008-5 (pa)
LC 2010-26812
This book "uses the theme of media literacy as a lens through which to view and discuss social networking and Web 2.0 environments. . . . The book serves as a forum for educators and those interested in the field of media literacy, digital, and social technologies, who seek to bridge curriculum connections as well as understand the online culture of students." Publisher's note
Includes bibliographical references

Is media violence a problem? Stefan Kiesbye, book editor. Greenhaven Press 2010 114p (At issue. Mass media) $31.80; pa $22.50
Grades: 7 8 9 10   **302.23**
1. Mass media 2. Violence
ISBN   978-0-7377-4886-4;   0-7377-4886-9;
978-0-7377-4887-1 (pa); 0-7377-4887-7 (pa)
LC 2010-5726
This volume covers such topics as the effects of media violence on children, violent video games, and the role the FCC should play in regulating media violence.
Includes bibliographical references

King, C. Richard
Media images and representations; foreword by Walter Echo-Hawk; introduction by Paul Rosier. Chelsea House Publishers 2006 117p il (Contemporary Native American voices) lib bdg $30
Grades: 9 10 11 12   **302.23**
1. Native Americans in mass media
ISBN 0-7910-7968-6   LC 2005-7546
This book "examines the wide spectrum of information by and/or about American Indian cultures in film, television, journalism, and on the Internet, as well as high school, collegiate, and professional sports mascots." SLJ
Includes bibliographical references

Mass media: opposing viewpoints; Roman Espejo, book editor. Greenhaven Press/Gale Cengage Learning 2010 250p $39.70; pa $27.50 *
Grades: 8 9 10 11 12   **302.23**
1. Mass media
ISBN   978-0-7377-4530-6;   0-7377-4530-4;
978-0-7377-4531-3 (pa); 0-7377-4531-2 (pa)
LC 2009023849
"Opposing viewpoints series"
A compendium of viewpoints—both pro and con—on several issues relating to the role and regulation of media in American society.
Includes bibliographical references

Television: opposing viewpoints; Margaret Haerens, book editor. Greenhaven Press 2011 213p il $39.70; pa $27.50 *
Grades: 9 10 11 12   **302.23**
1. Television broadcasting
ISBN 978-0-7377-5243-4; 978-0-7377-5244-1 (pa)
LC 2010039232
"Opposing viewpoints series"
This anthology of essays discusses reality television, television advertising, television's role in conveying societal values, and government regulations on television broadcasting.
Includes bibliographical references

302.3 Social interaction within groups

Ellis, Deborah, 1960-
We want you to know; kids talk about bullying.
Coteau Books 2010 120p il $19.95 *
Grades: 5 6 7 8 9 10   302.3
1. Bullies
ISBN 978-1-55050-417-0; 1-55050-417-7
"As part of her work with an anti-bullying campaign
in her local Canadian community, Ellis interviewed
young people between the ages of 9 and 19 about their
experiences. In honest, straightforward prose, she shares
their stories, many as targets and some as perpetrators or
bystanders. . . . Each story is written from the first-
person point of view, some with real names and photos,
providing an intimacy and immediacy that are critical
with these kinds of issues. Readers will find at least one
or two stories they can relate to, and educators should be
able to use many of the narratives to jumpstart conversation." SLJ
Includes bibliographical references

303.3 Coordination and control

Best, Joel
Damned lies and statistics; untangling numbers
from the media, politicians, and activists.
University of Calif. Press 2001 190p $19.95 *
Grades: 9 10 11 12   303.3
1. Statistics
ISBN 0-520-21978-3   LC 00-64910
The author aims to "remind us that we need to treat
statistics skeptically. . . . Best explains {what he sees
as} the four basic sources of flawed statistics (bad guess-
es, deceptive definitions, confusing questions, biased
samples). Then he examines mutant statistics and discusses the illogic of statistical comparisons that attempt
to equate differing time periods, places, groups, or social
problems." Christ Sci Monit
"Invaluable counsel for good citizenship." Booklist
Includes bibliographical references

More damned lies and statistics; how numbers
confuse public issues. University of California
Press 2004 200p il $19.95 *
Grades: 9 10 11 12   303.3
1. Statistics
ISBN 0-520-23830-3   LC 2003-28076
Companion volume to Damned lies and statistics
In this volume, the author continues his "account of
how statistics are produced, used, and misused by everyone from researchers to journalists. . . . {He} illustrates
his points with contemporary statistics about such concerns as school shootings, fatal hospital errors, bullying,
teen suicides, deaths at the World Trade Center, college
ratings, risk of divorce, racial profiling, and fatalities
caused by falling coconuts." Publisher's note
"The book is packed with helpful tips for understanding statistics, and it even manages to make a usually dull
topic entertaining." Booklist
Includes bibliographical references

Huxley, Aldous, 1894-1963
Brave new world revisited. Harper & Row 1958
147p pa $11.95 hardcover o.p. *
Grades: 11 12 Adult   303.3
1. Propaganda 2. Totalitarianism 3. Brainwashing
4. Culture
ISBN 0-06-089852-6 (pa)
In response to his 1932 novel Brave new world "Huxley reconsiders his prophecies and fears that some of
these may be coming true much sooner than he thought."
Oxford Companion to Engl Lit. 5th edition

Prejudice in the modern world reference library.
UXL 2007 5v il set $247 *
Grades: 7 8 9 10 11 12   303.3
1. Prejudices
ISBN 978-1-4144-0204-8
Also available as separate volumes; contact publisher
for more information
Contents: Almanac (2 volumes); Biographies; Primary
Sources; Cumulative Index
This is an "examination of the historical and social
ramifications of prejudice in several societies across the
globe. Two *Almanac* volumes highlight the foundations,
causes, and types of prejudices as well as specific case
studies on prejudice in action in the modern world. *Biographies* highlights key activists, politicians, religious
leaders, as well as ordinary citizens that have played important roles in cases of prejudice in the world, from
Heinrich Himmler and Saddam Hussein to Rosa Parks
and Cesar Chavez. *Primary Sources* uses documents,
speeches, letters and other sources to explain events related to prejudice." Publisher's note
"This is an excellent adjunct to American and world
history units and classes on government, intercultural
heritage, the Holocaust, and law." Booklist

303.4 Social change

Anderson, Terry H., 1946-
The movement and the sixties. Oxford Univ.
Press 1995 500p il pa $19.95 hardcover o.p.
Grades: 11 12 Adult   303.4
1. Radicalism 2. Demonstrations 3. United States—Social conditions
ISBN 0-19-510457-9 (pa)   LC 94-16344
This "book is a national study of U.S. social activism
from 1960 to 1973, focusing on how 'the Movement'
was experienced by participants and exploring why this
activism arose when it did, how it developed, and what
it accomplished." Booklist
Anderson's "sweeping study is a valuable, refreshingly
unbiased reassessment of the '60s legacy." Publ Wkly
Includes bibliographical references

Benjamin, Marina
Rocket dreams; how the space age shaped our
vision of a world beyond. Free Press 2003 242p
hardcover o.p. pa $14
Grades: 11 12 Adult   303.4
1. Astronautics
ISBN 0-7432-3343-3; 0-7432-5534-8 (pa)
    LC 2002-45590

Benjamin, Marina—*Continued*

The author "grew up watching NASA spaceflights on television. In six personal chapters, she describes how she and others have sought to find substitutes for space exploration by investigating aliens in Roswell, NM, shopping in enclosed malls that mimic space stations, colonizing cyberspace, and cooperatively searching for extraterrestrial intelligence." Libr J

This is "an elegantly written memoir, as the author tells about her youthful fascination with the space program and her travels to places like Arecibo and Roswell, as well as her virtual travels among various computer groups over the last 20 years. Space buffs will appreciate many aspects of her story." Publ Wkly

Includes bibliographical references

Diamond, Jared M.

Guns, germs, and steel; the fates of human societies; [by] Jared Diamond. Norton 2005 518p il map $24.95

Grades: 11 12 Adult   303.4

1. Technology and civilization 2. Social change 3. Environmental influence on humans

ISBN 0-393-06131-0; 978-0-393-06131-4

LC 2005-284261

First published 1997

"This book poses a simple but profound question about the distribution of wealth and power in the modern world: 'Why weren't Native Americans, Africans, and Aboriginal Australians the ones who decimated, subjugated, or exterminated Europeans and Asians?'. . . To explore the discrepancies in technological and cultural development he looks not at peoples but at places, and at the natural resources available to different indigenous populations since 11,000 B.C. The scope and the explanatory power of this book are astounding." New Yorker [review of 1997 edition]

Includes bibliographical references

Dissent in America; voices that shaped a nation; [edited by] Ralph F. Young. Pearson Education 2006 792p $35 *

Grades: 11 12 Adult   303.4

1. United States—Politics and government—Sources 2. United States—Social conditions—Sources

ISBN 0-321-44297-0   LC 2006-15415

"Divided chronologically, the anthology collects essays, speeches, organizational statements, songs, posters, interviews, broadsides and texts in other media. . . . For readers with something on their minds, 400 years of precedent may be just what they need to stimulate some questions of their own." Publ Wkly

Globalization: opposing viewpoints; David Haugen and Rachael Mach, book editors. Greenhaven Press 2010 260p il lib bdg $39.70; pa $27.50 *

Grades: 9 10 11 12   303.4

1. Globalization

ISBN 978-0-7377-4771-3 (lib bdg); 0-7377-4771-4 (lib bdg); 978-0-7377-4772-0 (pa); 0-7377-4772-2 (pa)

LC 2009-41735

"Opposing viewpoints series"

Articles in this anthology debate the positives and negatives of globalization.

Includes bibliographical references

Hodge, Russ

The future of genetics; beyond the human genome project; foreword by Nadia Rosenthal. Facts on File 2010 204p il map (Genetics & evolution) $39.50

Grades: 9 10 11 12   303.4

1. Molecular biology 2. Genomes 3. Genetics 4. Medical genetics

ISBN 978-0-8160-6684-1; 0-8160-6684-1

LC 2009-18297

"The book is divided into four major chapters, detailing the genesis of 21st-century genetics research, cultural influences, the mechanics of gene manipulation, and both heartening and startling speculation on future applications. . . . Presented with clarity and objective aplomb, this will prove an excellent learning tool for a highly complex and frequently controversial subject." Libr J

Includes glossary and bibliographical references

The **Radical** reader; a documentary history of the American radical tradition; edited by Timothy Patrick McCarthy and John McMillian; foreword by Eric Foner. New Press 2003 688p $65; lib bdg $21.95 *

Grades: 11 12 Adult   303.4

1. Radicalism

ISBN 1-56584-827-6; 1-56584-682-6 (lib bdg)

LC 2002-41051

The editors present "more than 200 declarations, appeals, editorials, and essays by such radical thinkers (each introduced in a brief bio) as Frederick Douglass, Sarah Grimké, Henry David Thoreau, Upton Sinclair, Emma Goldman, Angela Davis, Betty Friedan, Mario Savio, César Chávez, Rachel Carson, Tony Kushner, and Ralph Nader." Booklist

"By bringing many hard-to-find documents under one cover, this anthology will excite readers in discussing why radicals from all walks of life have made progressive ideals meaningful to Americans. Recommended for college, high school, and public libraries." Libr J

Includes bibliographical references

Tenner, Edward

Our own devices; the past and future of body technology. Alfred A. Knopf 2003 336p hardcover o.p. pa $14.95

Grades: 11 12 Adult   303.4

1. Technology and civilization 2. Technological innovations

ISBN 0-375-40722-7; 0-375-70707-7 (pa)

LC 2002-40694

"Tenner examines the reciprocal relationship between technology (in the broad sense of useful created objects) and technique (the methods we use to employ them) as they have developed together culturally. . . . A handful of examples provide insight into the history, ergonomics, and symbolism of some of the tools that are figuratively and literally closest to us: shoes (thong sandals and athletic varieties), chairs, eyeglasses, and headgear. Tenner also explores technologies that have influenced medicine (bottle feeding), arts (musical keyboards), and commerce (typing keyboards)." Libr J

"For a work that covers such a broad topic, this book is a page-turner, largely due to its clear prose and the au-

Tenner, Edward—*Continued*

thor's approach to the material. While not lavishly illustrated, there seems to be a picture every time one is needed to illustrate the technology being discussed." SLJ

Includes bibliographical references

Turney, Jon

Technology; ethical debates about the application of science. Smart Apple Media 2009 46p il (Dilemmas in modern science) $34.25

Grades: 7 8 9 10   **303.4**

1. Technology 2. Science—Ethical aspects

ISBN 978-1-59920-097-2; 1-59920-097-X

LC 2007-35692

"Presents both sides of issues arising from how we use technology, including Internet use, identity theft, technology and the military, nanotechnology, and robots and automation." Publisher's note

This title is "easy to navigate as evocative photographs, charts, and sidebars help break down complicated arguments into manageable parts for easy digestion." SLJ

Includes glossary and bibliographical references

Yount, Lisa

Biotechnology and genetic engineering. 3rd ed. Facts on File 2008 364p (Library in a book) $45

Grades: 8 9 10 11 12   **303.4**

1. Biotechnology 2. Genetic engineering

ISBN 978-0-8160-7217-0; 0-8160-7217-5

LC 2007041313

First published 2000

This "provides an overview of the history of [biotechnology and genetic engineering] and the opinions surrounding it, ranging from the study of fermentation by French chemist Louis Pasteur in the 1850s to the nascent field of synthetic biology. . . . Coverage includes: Whether or not genetically modified food impacts the environment and health; How biotechnology has transformed the pharmaceutical industry; The legal implications of genetic testing and more." Publisher's note

Includes glossary and bibliographical references

303.49   Social forecasts

Kaku, Michio

Physics of the future; how science will shape human destiny and our daily lives by the year 2100. Doubleday 2011 389p il $28.95; ebook $12.99

Grades: 11 12 Adult   **303.49**

1. Science 2. Forecasting

ISBN 978-0-385-53080-4; 978-0-385-53081-1 (ebook)

LC 2010-26569

The author "divides his chapters into 'near future' (until 2030), 'mid-century' (2030 to 2070) and 'far future' (2070 to 2100). Each begins with familiar technology and ongoing research. The near future of computers will give us self-driving cars and computers cheap enough to be disposable. Mid-century will see universal translators, and by 2100 thinking will control computers, producing instant, person-to-person communication and the ability

to manipulate our environment, including malfunctioning body parts." Kirkus

"The book's lively, user-friendly style should appeal equally to fans of science fiction and popular science." Booklist

Includes bibliographical references

The **way** we will be 50 years from today; 60 of the world's greatest minds share their visions of the next half century; [edited by] Mike Wallace. Thomas Nelson 2008 241p $24.99

Grades: 11 12 Adult   **303.49**

1. Forecasting

ISBN 978-0-8499-0370-0; 0-8499-0370-X

LC 2007-45281

"This collection of essays exploring life in the future is the realization of some of our worst nightmares (water shortages, overpopulation, and nuclear war) but also some hopeful developments: longer and healthier lives, clean energy from the sun and wind. . . . A fascinating look at what may be ahead for human life on the planet." Booklist

Includes bibliographical references

303.6   Conflict and conflict resolution

Gottfried, Ted, 1928-

The fight for peace; a history of antiwar movements in America. 21st Century Bks. 2006 136p il (People's history) $26.60 *

Grades: 7 8 9 10   **303.6**

1. Pacifism 2. Peace 3. War

ISBN 0-7613-2932-3

"Gottfried starts out by explaining that a group in Connecticut rallied together in 2003 to peacefully protest the war against Iraq. . . . Then the author discusses the antiwar movement during the Civil War and proceeds through history, beginning with the ancient Greek play *Lysistrata*. . . . The pictures, political cartoons, and quotes are an excellent addition. . . . This is a book that can be read for general interest as well as for reports." SLJ

Includes bibliographical references

Habeeb, William Mark, 1955-

Civil wars in Africa. Mason Crest Publishers 2007 110p il map (Africa: progress & problems) $24.95

Grades: 9 10 11 12   **303.6**

1. Africa—Social conditions 2. Africa—Politics and government

ISBN 978-1-59084-955-2; 1-59084-955-8

LC 2006-10768

"This book analyzes past and current conditions in Africa to shed light on the historical, cultural, governmental, religious, ethnic, and ideological factors that have caused civil wars to occur. Conflicts like the long-running war in Sudan, the unrest in Liberia and Sierra Leone, and the state failure in Somalia and the Democratic Republic of the Congo are explained. The final chapter discusses ways future civil wars might be avoided." Publisher's note

Includes bibliographical references

Judson, Karen, 1941-
Resolving conflicts; how to get along when you don't get along. Enslow Pubs. 2005 112p il (Issues in focus today) $31.93 *
Grades: 7 8 9 10 11 12   **303.6**
1. Conflict management
ISBN 0-7660-2359-1   LC 2004-28119
The author "describes different kinds of conflicts and how they can be resolved, with a special focus on teens and building their conflict-resolution skills and understanding." Publisher's note
Includes bibliographical references

Mara, Wil
Civil unrest in the 1960s; riots and their aftermath. Marshall Cavendish Benchmark 2009 127p il (Perspectives on) lib bdg $27.95
Grades: 8 9 10 11 12   **303.6**
1. Riots 2. United States—Politics and government—1961-1974 3. United States—Social conditions 4. United States—Race relations
ISBN 978-0-7614-4025-3; 0-7614-4025-9
                              LC 2008-24673
This book describes "the turbulent decade that bore witness to the Civil Right[s] Movement, the divisive Vietnam War, and various other movements concerning women, gays, and the environment. . . . The potency of [this title] lies in the excellent arrangement of numerous well-chosen sidebars and photos, and fluent, concise prose." SLJ
Includes bibliographical references

Violence in the media; Jodie Lynn Boduch, book editor. Greenhaven Press 2008 183p (History of issues) lib bdg $37.40
Grades: 9 10 11 12   **303.6**
1. Violence 2. Mass media
ISBN 978-0-7377-2875-0; 0-7377-2875-2
                              LC 2007-939022
An anthology of essays discussing media violence issues throughout history, from ancient Rome to the present.
Includes bibliographical references

Women on war; an international anthology of women's writings from antiquity to the present; edited and with an introduction by Daniela Gioseffi. 2nd ed. Feminist Press 2003 375p $55; pa $19.95 *
Grades: 11 12 Adult   **303.6**
1. Peace 2. War
ISBN 1-55861-408-7; 1-55861-409-5 (pa)
                              LC 2003-42407
First published 1988 by Simon & Schuster
This collection "gathers together writings by more than 150 women, including renowned poets, novelists, essayists, journalists, and activists, as well as ordinary women with first-hand experience of armed conflict as survivors, refugees, rape victims, nurses, and soldiers. . . . [Contributors include] Isabella Allende, Maya Angelou, Margaret Atwood, Simone de Beauvoir, Gwendolyn Brooks, Emily Dickinson, Marguerite Duras, Slavenka Drakulic, Barbara Ehrenreich, Cynthia Enloe,

Martha Gelhorn [and] Nadine Gordimer." Publisher's note
This is a "powerful and important collection." Booklist
Includes bibliographical references

Woodward, John, 1958-
War; John Woodward, book editor. Greenhaven Press 2006 207p (Current controversies) lib bdg $34.95; pa $23.70
Grades: 9 10 11 12   **303.6**
1. War
ISBN 0-7377-3236-9 (lib bdg); 978-0-7377-3236-8 (lib bdg); 0-7377-3237-7 (pa); 978-0-7377-3237-5 (pa)
                              LC 2005-46261
In this anthology the authors "examine the root causes of war and explore ways to prevent it." Publisher's note
Includes bibliographical references

304.2 Human ecology

The **Atlas** of US and Canadian environmental history; edited by Char Miller. Routledge 2003 248p il map $150 *
Grades: 11 12 Adult   **304.2**
1. Human ecology 2. Environmental policy 3. Atlases 4. Reference books
ISBN 0-415-93781-7   LC 2003-46799
"This resource offers essays written by history scholars on ecological issues for young people. Organized chronologically from 1492 to present times, chapters include two-page treatments of the era's hot topics . . . These controversial topics are explained in a simple, nonbiased way that will appeal to young adults. The statistics offered are frequently enlightening." Voice Youth Advocates
Includes bibliographical references

Diamond, Jared M.
Collapse: how societies choose to fail or succeed. Viking 2005 575p il $29.95; pa $17
Grades: 11 12 Adult   **304.2**
1. Social change 2. Environmental policy
ISBN 0-670-03337-5; 0-14-303655-6 (pa)
                              LC 2004-57152
The author "examines storied examples of human economic and social collapse, and even extinction, including Easter Island, classical Mayan civilization and the Greenland Norse. He explores patterns of population growth, overfarming, overgrazing and overhunting, often abetted by drought, cold, rigid social mores and warfare, that lead inexorably to vicious circles of deforestation, erosion and starvation prompted by the disappearance of plant and animal food sources. . . . Readers will find his book an enthralling, and disturbing, reminder of the indissoluble links that bind humans to nature." Publ Wkly
Includes bibliographical references

Gunn, Angus M., 1920-

Unnatural disasters; case studies of human-induced environmental catastrophes. Greenwood Press 2003 143p il map $55

Grades: 9 10 11 12   **304.2**

1. Disasters 2. Human influence on nature

ISBN 0-313-31999-5   LC 2002-44848

This book focuses on human-induced "disasters including coalmine disasters, dam failures, industrial explosions, nuclear energy accidents, oil spills, terrorist acts, and industrial toxicity and government actions . . . Beginning in 1903 and continuing to September 11, 2001 each event is presented as a case study describing the situation, causes, consequences, and cleanup. The focus is on cases that significantly impacted the environment." Libr Media Connect

"The book is well written and well balanced, and the author . . . has a good grasp of the technical background behind each of the disasters he describes. He discusses not only the technical, but also the economic, political, and sociological backgrounds of each disaster. A good starting place for anyone wanting to research human-caused disasters." Choice

Includes bibliographical references

How geography affects the United States. Greenwood Press 2002 5v il map set $199.95

Grades: 9 10 11 12   **304.2**

1. Human geography 2. United States—Geography 3. United States—Local history

ISBN 0-313-32250-3   LC 2002-75304

Contents: v1 Northeast; v2 Southeast; v3 Midwest; v4 Northwest; v5 Southwest

Explores the ways in which geography has affected the lives of the people of the United States

"This helpful series blends physical characteristics, American history, pop culture, and modern travel information to offer a fresh take on geography, making a potentially dull subject interesting." Voice Youth Advocates

Includes bibliographical references

Weisman, Alan

The world without us. Thomas Dunne Books/St. Martin's Press 2007 324p il $24.95

Grades: 11 12 Adult   **304.2**

1. Human influence on nature

ISBN 978-0-312-34729-1; 0-312-34729-4

     LC 2007-11565

"Teasing out the consequences of a simple thought experiment—what would happen if the human species were suddenly extinguished—Weisman has written a sort of pop-science ghost story, in which the whole earth is the haunted house. Among the highlights: with pumps not working, the New York City subways would fill with water within days. . . . Texas's unattended petrochemical complexes might ignite, scattering hydrogen cyanide to the winds—a 'mini chemical nuclear winter.' After thousands of years, the Chunnel, rubber tires, and more than a billion tons of plastic might remain, but eventually a polymer-eating microbe could evolve, and, with the spectacular return of fish and bird populations, the earth might revert to Eden." New Yorker

Includes bibliographical references

304.6   Population

The **American** people; Census 2000; [edited by] Reynolds Farley and John Haaga. Russell Sage 2005 456p il map $35 *

Grades: 11 12 Adult   **304.6**

1. United States—Population 2. United States—Census

ISBN 0-8715-4273-0   LC 2005-50433

This book "is more than just a compilation of tables and charts of raw census data. It is an interpretative guide to understanding the demographic breakdown of American society. Chapters include: 'Gender Inequalities', 'Cohorts and Socioeconomic Progress' and 'The Lives and Times of the Baby Boomers'. Editors Farley and Haaga show trends in American culture that will not be found anywhere else." Univ Press Books for Public and Second Sch Libr, 2006

Includes bibliographical references

Encyclopedia of genocide and crimes against humanity; Dinah L. Shelton, editor in chief. Macmillan Reference 2004 3v il map set $415

Grades: 11 12 Adult   **304.6**

1. Reference books 2. Genocide—Encyclopedias 3. Atrocities

ISBN 0-02-865847-7   LC 2004-6587

The scope of this encyclopedia starts "with the Roman persecution of Christians and . . . [continues] to recent Sudanese Arab massacres of Sudanese Africans. Arranged alphabetically by topic, each entry contains a narrative, a bibliography including books, reports, and Web sites, and . . . cross-references." Choice

"The editorial team has cast its net wide to create an outstanding comprehensive sourcebook that will be the standard resource for many years." Booklist

Includes bibliographical references

Perl, Lila

Genocide; stand by or intervene? Marshall Cavendish Benchmark 2010 127p il (Controversy!) lib bdg $25.95

Grades: 8 9 10 11 12   **304.6**

1. Genocide

ISBN 978-0-7614-4900-3; 0-7614-4900-0

This book is "examines the U.N.'s efforts to define and make the crime of genocide punishable under international law. . . . [It] is suggested for libraries that need updated books covering 21st-century events." SLJ

Population: opposing viewpoints; Karen F. Balkin, book editor. Greenhaven Press 2005 186p il lib bdg $34.95; pa $23.70 *

Grades: 9 10 11 12   **304.6**

1. Population

ISBN 0-7377-2951-1 (lib bdg); 0-7377-2952-X (pa)

     LC 2004-60862

"Opposing viewpoints series"

Considers opposing opinions on various issues concerning world population including problems of rapid growth, the effects of population on the environment, changes in age demographics within developed nations, and ways of decreasing human fertility.

Includes bibliographical references

Springer, Jane

Genocide. Groundwood Books 2006 144p (Groundwork guides) hardcover o.p. pa $9.95

Grades: 8 9 10 11 12   **304.6**

1. Genocide

ISBN   978-0-88899-681-7;   0-88899-681-0; 978-0-88899-682-4 (pa); 0-88899-682-9 (pa)

"This disturbing history of mass ethnic killings across the world examines the why, when, where, and how genocide takes place. . . . In a lucid, informal text, Springer ably documents particular crimes against humanity, including the transatlantic slave trade, the slaughter of America's Native peoples, the Turkish massacre of the Armenians, the Nanking massacre, the Holocaust, and the Khmer Rouge slaughter in Cambodia." Booklist

304.8   Movement of people

Anderson, Stuart

Immigration. Greenwood 2010 228p il (Greenwood guides to business and economics) $55

Grades: 9 10 11 12   **304.8**

1. United States—Immigration and emigration 2. Immigrants—United States

ISBN   978-0-313-38028-0;   0-313-38028-7; 978-0-313-38029-7 (ebook); 0-313-38029-5 (ebook)

LC 2010-7888

Contact publisher for ebook pricing

"This title uses research and economic theory to explain the current situation in the U.S. as well as to posit possible solutions. After a brief overview of the history of immigration in the country, the topics of both legal and illegal immigration are covered in separate . . . chapters." SLJ

"This excellent study adds a dose of reality to a debate driven by ideology and political opportunism." Choice

Includes bibliographical references

Bailey, Rayna

Immigration and migration; foreword by Lorenzo A. Trujillo. Facts On File 2008 325p (Global issues) $45 *

Grades: 9 10 11 12   **304.8**

1. Immigration and emigration

ISBN 978-0-8160-7106-7; 0-8160-7106-3

LC 2007-18396

This "book discusses the many reasons people choose to immigrate or migrate to other countries, such as to escape poverty and seek employment opportunities, as refugees from war, or for political asylum. . . . After presenting a brief look back through the history of migration and its importance to emerging civilizations, the book focuses on immigration and migration in five countries: the United States, Mexico, France, the Philippines, and South Africa." Publisher's note

Includes glossary and bibliographical references

Benson, Sonia

U.S. immigration and migration almanac; [by] Sonia G. Benson; Sarah Hermsen, project editor. UXL 2004 2v il (U. S. immigration and migration reference library) set $115

Grades: 9 10 11 12   **304.8**

1. United States—Immigration and emigration 2. Reference books

ISBN 0-7876-7732-9   LC 2003-27833

This set "opens with an overview of immigration to and migration patterns within the U.S. and current theories about Pre-Columbian migrations to North America. Separate, well-written chronological chapters cover from the early arrival of the Spanish and English to the more recent immigration of Latino and Caribbean groups." SLJ

Includes bibliographical references

Encyclopedia of American immigration; edited by Carl L. Bankston III. Salem Press 2010 3v il map set $395

Grades: 11 12 Adult   **304.8**

1. United States—Immigration and emigration—Encyclopedias 2. Immigrants—United States—Encyclopedias 3. Reference books

ISBN 978-1-58765-599-9   LC 2009-54334

Also available online

Articles in this encyclopedia cover topics "such as child immigrants, deportation, employment, Holocaust, loyalty oaths, name changing, and numerous other topics. In addition, the work features individual entries on every state, several cities, and 65 ethnic and immigrant groups." Libr J

"A solid starting point for projects on any aspect of American immigration." SLJ

Includes bibliographical references

Immigration; Laura K. Egendorf, book editor. Greenhaven Press 2006 240p il map (History of issues) lib bdg $34.95 *

Grades: 9 10 11 12   **304.8**

1. United States—Immigration and emigration

ISBN 0-7377-2871-X   LC 2005-46156

"Primary and secondary sources are used in this anthology to explore the efficacy of immigration policies and how immigrant populations have changed America for better and for worse." Publisher's note

Includes bibliographical references

Powell, John, 1954-

Encyclopedia of North American immigration. Facts on File 2005 464p il map (Facts on File library of American history) $75 *

Grades: 11 12 Adult   **304.8**

1. United States—Immigration and emigration—Encyclopedias 2. Canada—Immigration and emigration—Encyclopedias 3. Reference books

ISBN 0-8160-4658-1   LC 2004-7361

The author "presents an introduction to immigration to English and French-speaking regions over the past 500 years. . . . His intent is to offer 'a convenient one-volume reference full of straightforward and concise information on people, groups, policies, and events that defined the world's greatest migration of peoples to a con-

Powell, John, 1954-—*Continued*
tinent and shaped their reception in North America.'"
Booklist

"This valuable reference work on a hot topic belongs
in all types of libraries—not only in the US and Canada,
which offered shelter to immigrants, but also in libraries
worldwide." Choice

Includes bibliographical references

305   Social groups

Farmer, Paul, 1959-
Pathologies of power; health, human rights, and
the new war on the poor; with a foreword by
Amartya Sen. University of California Press 2003
402p (California series in public anthropology)
$27.50; pa $16.95
Grades: 9 10 11 12   305
1. Poor—Medical care 2. Human rights
ISBN 0-520-23550-9; 0-520-24326-9 (pa)
                    LC 2002-13311
"The author's central argument is simple: Health care
is a human right. Extreme poverty and the social and political conditions that give rise to it . . . deny people that
right and produce 'unnecessary' deaths. 'Unnecessary,'
because given present-day means of prevention and cure,
those able to afford health care do not die in this manner
. . . The argument is buttressed both by vivid accounts
of the author's experience as a physician and of his patients' unbelievable hardships and courage, and by a
thorough documentation of the larger issues." Antioch
Rev

Includes bibliographical references

Muslims in America; Allen Verbrugge, book
editor. Greenhaven Press 2005 159p
(Contemporary issues companion) lib bdg
$33.70; pa $22.45 *
Grades: 9 10 11 12   305
1. Muslims—United States
ISBN 0-7377-2315-7 (lib bdg); 0-7377-2316-5 (pa)
                    LC 2004-50096
This collection of articles is divided in the following
chapters: A history of islam and Muslims in America;
Muslim life in American society; Muslim American
women; American Muslims after the September 11 attacks; Personal accounts of Muslims in America
"The selections present a good variety of viewpoints.
. . . A very good annotated list of organizations to contact is included. This is a solid selection for reports as
well as for students with a special interest in the subject." SLJ

Includes bibliographical references

305.23   Young people

Bradley, Michael J.
The heart & soul of the next generation;
extraordinary stories of ordinary teens. Harbor
Press 2006 232p pa $14.95
Grades: 9 10 11 12   305.23
1. Adolescent psychology
ISBN 978-0-936197-53-1; 0-936197-53-6
                    LC 2005-52704
The author "draws on his 30 years of experience as a
teen psychologist to profile 20 adolescents who dealt
courageously with pain and suffering. In lively, empathetic prose, he relates cases involving difficult issues indeed, such as the serious illness of a parent, suicide, bullying and abortion. . . . This informed and compassionate look at the courage of teenagers highlights the ability
of young people to triumph over adversity." Publ Wkly

Burton, Bonnie
Girls against girls; why we are mean to each
other and how we can change. Zest Books 2009
128p il pa $12.95
Grades: 7 8 9 10   305.23
1. Girls—Psychology 2. Bullies
ISBN 978-0-9790173-6-0; 0-9790173-6-X
This guide for teenage girls explains why girls can
sometimes be mean to each other, what to do if you are
a victim of bullying, and the importance of treating other
girls with respect.
This offers "excellent coping techniques. . . . Burton
never talks down to her readers, nor does she pull her
punches. Readers will respond to the author's clear respect for the painful nature of the problem." Booklist

The **Courage** to be yourself; true stories by teens
about cliques, conflicts, and overcoming peer
pressure; edited by Al Desetta with Educators
for Social Responsibility. Free Spirit Pub. 2005
145p pa $13.95
Grades: 7 8 9 10 11 12   305.23
1. Teenagers 2. Conduct of life
ISBN 1-57542-185-2   LC 2005-5173
"In 26 first-person stories, real teens write about their
lives." Publisher's note
"There is certainly some value in hearing teens of
many ethnicities and orientations speaking plainly about
being fat, or being from India in a school full of blond,
blue-eyed folk, or being Arab after 9/11." Booklist

Includes bibliographical references

Farrell, Courtney
Children's rights. ABDO Pub. 2010 112p il
(Essential issues) lib bdg $22.95
Grades: 7 8 9 10   305.23
1. Child sexual abuse 2. Child labor
ISBN 978-1-60453-952-3; 1-60453-952-6
                    LC 2009-29938
This book "examines the world's critical issues sur-
rounding children's rights. Readers will learn the histori-
cal background of children's rights, leading up to the

Farrell, Courtney—*Continued*
current and future impact on society. Child marriage, child labor, educational rights of children, child trafficking, child pornography, and child soldiers are discussed." Publisher's note

The text is "well-written, providing examples that put a human face to each problem. Quotes and facts are clearly attributed, and their sources are noted in the extensive back matter. . . . . . [This] will be of great assistance to students writing reports." SLJ

Includes glossary and bibliographical references

Feig, Paul
Kick me; adventures in adolescence. Three Rivers Press (NY) 2002 278p pa $12.95
Grades: 11 12 Adult   **305.23**
1. Adolescence 2. Boys
ISBN 0-609-80943-1   LC 2002-18121

"These interlocking essays—on everything from a sadistic gym teacher and geeky after-class pastimes to obsessive romantic tendencies and a prom that wasn't the best night of the author's life—are terrifically entertaining, although undoubtedly imaginatively amped up for maximum readability." Publ Wkly

Johnson, Arne, 1968-
Indie girl; from starting a band to launching a fashion company, nine ways to turn your creative talent into reality; [by] Arne Johnson & Karen Macklin. Zest Books 2008 136p il pa $16.95
Grades: 7 8 9 10   **305.23**
1. Creation (Literary, artistic, etc.) 2. Women—Vocational guidance
ISBN 978-0-9790173-3-9   LC 2007-935189

The authors "walk readers through the basics of publishing a zine, mounting an art exhibit, forming a dance troupe, organizing a parade, filming a TV show, staging a play, and hosting a poetry slam. Each chapter is sprinkled with suggestions from successful professionals and other 'insiders.' . . . A great choice for readers as they think about their futures." SLJ

Males, Mike A.
Framing youth; ten myths about the next generation. Common Courage Press 1998 391p il hardcover o.p. pa $24.95
Grades: 9 10 11 12 Adult   **305.23**
1. Teenagers—United States 2. Youth—United States 3. Conflict of generations 4. Social problems
ISBN 1-567-51149-X; 1-567-51148-1 (pa)
                                          LC 98-49506

In this discussion "of 10 common myths, Mike Males shows . . . the statistics—about drugs, alcohol, sex, crime, and curfews—to reveal what teens are really like, and what they really need." Publisher's note
Includes bibliographical references

My little red book; edited by Rachel Kauder Nalebuff. Twelve Books 2009 225p $14.99
Grades: 8 9 10 11 12 Adult   **305.23**
1. Menstruation
ISBN 978-0-446-54636-2; 0-446-54636-4
                                          LC 2008-40621

"Presents a collection of stories from a variety of women detailing their experiences of their first period." Publisher's note

"A rich, welcome collection for readers of various ages and, perhaps surprisingly, more than one gender." Booklist

Includes bibliographical references

Nazario, Sonia
Enrique's journey. Random House 2006 291p il $26.95; pa $14.95
Grades: 11 12 Adult   **305.23**
1. Illegal aliens 2. United States—Immigration and emigration
ISBN 1-4000-6205-5;   978-1-4000-6205-8;
0-8129-7178-7 (pa); 978-0-8129-7178-1 (pa)
                                          LC 2005-44347

The author "retraces the travel of immigrants from Central America to El Norte and writes . . . about the trials and tribulations that besiege the journey. Specifically, she focuses on a Honduran boy, Enrique, left behind by his mother, Lourdes, who fled to the United States, like many Central American women before her, to make enough money to give her children a better life back home and ultimately return to them." Libr J

"Descriptions of rapes, beatings, and jailing of immigrant children and accounts of those who suffered loss of limbs falling from freight trains are graphic and disturbing. But no one can doubt the authenticity of this reporting." SLJ

Robbins, Alexandra, 1976-
The overachievers; the secret lives of driven kids. Hyperion 2006 439p $24.95; pa $13.95 *
Grades: 11 12 Adult   **305.23**
1. Workaholism 2. High school students
ISBN 1-4013-0201-7;   978-1-4013-0201-6;
1-4013-0902-2 (pa); 978-1-4013-0902-2 (pa)
                                          LC 2006-41244

The author "follows the lives of students from a Bethesda, Md., high school as they navigate the SAT and college application process. These students are obsessed with success, contending with illness, physical deterioration (senior Julie is losing hair over the pressure to get into Stanford), cheating (students sell a physics project to one another), obsessed parents (Frank's mother manages his time to the point of abuse) and emotional breakdowns. The portraits of the teens are compelling and make for an easy read." Publ Wkly
Includes bibliographical references

The **Struggle** to be strong; true stories by teens about overcoming tough times; edited by Al Desetta, Sybil Wolin. Free Spirit 2000 179p il pa $21.95
Grades: 9 10 11 12   **305.23**
1. Teenagers 2. Conduct of life
ISBN 1-57542-079-1   LC 99-56600

"The structure of the book is based on seven resiliencies: insight, independence, relationships, initiative, creativity, humor, and morality. Each chapter defines the resiliency and its importance, adding teen-authored essays to illustrate the topics and to highlight the importance of struggling to stay strong." Voice Youth Advocates

Talking adolescence; perspectives on communication in the teenage years; edited by Angie Williams & Crispin Thurlow. Peter Lang 2005 292p (Language as social action) pa $32.95

Grades: Adult Professional   305.23
1. Adolescence 2. Communication
ISBN 0-8204-7097-X; 978-0-8204-7097-9
                                LC 2005-15695

A collection of essays discussing ways the ways in which communication affects and influences young people.

Includes bibliographical references

Teen life in Europe; edited by Shirley R. Steinberg; foreword by Richard M Lerner. Greenwood Press 2005 281p il (Teen life around the world) $55

Grades: 9 10 11 12   305.23
1. Youth—Europe
ISBN 0-313-32727-0   LC 2005-15183

"Each chapter covers a country in the region, and is written by a native of that country. The 12 countries profiled include Denmark, England, France, Germany, Ireland, Italy, Malta, The Netherlands, Portugal, Spain, Sweden, and Turkey. Each chapter concludes with a resource guide providing print and electronic sources for additional research." Publisher's note

Includes bibliographical references

Teen life in Latin America and the Caribbean; edited by Cynthia Tompkins and Kristen Sternberg; foreword by Richard M. Lerner. Greenwood 2004 325p il (Teen life around the world) $57.95

Grades: 9 10 11 12   305.23
1. Youth—Latin America 2. Youth—Caribbean region
ISBN 0-313-31932-4   LC 2003-59644

This book describes "the unique challenges and opportunities of teens in 15 Latin American or Caribbean countries." Publisher's note

Includes bibliographical references

Williams, Terrie
Stay strong; simple life lessons for teens. Scholastic 2001 218p hardcover o.p. pa $4.99

Grades: 9 10 11 12   305.23
1. Teenagers 2. Conduct of life 3. Life skills
ISBN 0-439-12971-0; 0-439-12972-9 (pa)

"Drawing on her own success in public relations, the author gives straight-from-the-hip advice to teens on a range of topics. Most of her guidance deals with ethical situations, manners, and personal relationships. Anecdotes and success stories illustrate key ideas, while quotations from teenagers and instructive raps emphasize her point of view." Booklist

Yell-oh girls! emerging voices explore culture, identity, and growing up Asian American; {edited by} Vickie Nam. Quill 2001 xxxv, 297p il pa $13 *

Grades: 11 12 Adult   305.23
1. Asian Americans 2. Teenagers 3. Girls
ISBN 0-06-095944-4   LC 2001-18164

This is an "anthology of essays by young Asian American women. The contributors, from China, Hawaii, Laos, Vietnam, and even India, range in age from 13 to nearly 40. . . . Readers . . . who have felt the pain of being outsiders will be swept along by the authors' sincerity and their efforts to use writing to clarify who they are." Booklist

305.24   Adults

Twenge, Jean M., 1971-
Generation me; why today's young Americans are more confident, assertive, entitled—and more miserable than ever before. Free Press 2006 292p il hardcover o.p. pa $14 *

Grades: 11 12 Adult   305.24
1. Youth—United States
ISBN   0-7432-7697-3;   978-0-7432-7697-9;
0-7432-7698-1 (pa); 978-0-7432-7698-6 (pa)
                                LC 2005-58514

"Lumping together Gen-X and Y under the moniker 'GenMe,' Twenge argues that those born after 1970 are more self-centered, more disrespectful of authority and more depressed than ever before." Publ Wkly

"Accessible and a must-read for the generation they address." Booklist

Includes bibliographical references

305.3   Men and women

Male and female roles: opposing viewpoints; Karen Miller, book editor. Greenhaven Press 2010 229p lib bdg $39.70; pa $27.50 *

Grades: 8 9 10 11 12   305.3
1. Sex role
ISBN 978-0-7377-4528-3 (lib bdg); 0-7377-4528-2 (lib bdg); 978-0-7377-4529-0 (pa); 0-7377-4529-0 (pa)
                                LC 2009-19788

"Opposing viewpoints series"

A series of essays that expresses various perspectives on the individual roles of men and women.

Includes bibliographical references

305.4   Women

Collins, Gail
America's women; four hundred years of dolls, drudges, helpmates, and heroines. Morrow 2003 556p il $27.95; pa $15.95

Grades: 11 12 Adult   305.4
1. Women—United States—History
ISBN 0-06-018510-4; 0-06-122722-6 (pa)
                                LC 2003-51011

This is a history of American women from colonial times to the present

"Collins elegantly and eruditely celebrates the hard-won victories, overwhelming obstacles, and selfless contributions of a captivating array of influential women." Booklist

Includes bibliographical references

Collins, Gail—*Continued*

When everything changed; the amazing journey of American women from 1960 to the present. Little, Brown and Co. 2009 471p il $27.99

Grades: 11 12 Adult   **305.4**
    1. Women—United States—History
    ISBN 978-0-316-05954-1; 0-316-05954-4
                     LC 2008-54933

This book recounts the changes "American women have experienced since 1960." Publisher's note

"Collins can be deadly serious and great fun to read at the same time. A revelatory book for readers of both sexes, and sure to become required reading for any American women's-studies course." Kirkus

Includes bibliographical references

The **Columbia** documentary history of American women since 1941; edited by Harriet Sigerman. Columbia University Press 2003 690p $94; pa $34.50 *

Grades: 11 12 Adult   **305.4**
    1. Women—United States—History—Sources
    ISBN 0-231-11698-5; 0-231-11699-3 (pa)
                     LC 2002-41395

This collection of public and private primary sources includes such topics as employment opportunities, "the ideas and changes brought about by the women's movement, the challenges to and defense of reproductive rights, the backlash against feminism in the name of family values, and new visions for women's lives in the twenty-first century." Publisher's note

Includes bibliographical references

Coppens, Linda Miles, 1944-

What American women did, 1789-1920; a year-by-year reference. McFarland & Co. 2001 259p il hardcover o.p. pa $49.95

Grades: 7 8 9 10   **305.4**
    1. Women—United States—History 2. Women—Social conditions
    ISBN 0-7864-0899-5; 0-7864-3245-4 (pa)
                     LC 00-64010

"A chronological account of women's accomplishments in the areas of domesticity, work, education, religion, the arts, law and politics, and reform efforts. . . . This work will prove useful for students wishing to gain a better perspective of history, particularly social history, as it pertained to women." SLJ

Includes bibliographical references

De Pauw, Linda Grant

Founding mothers; women in America in the Revolutionary era; wood engravings by Michael McCurdy. Houghton Mifflin 1975 228p il hardcover o.p. pa $7.95 *

Grades: 9 10 11 12 Adult   **305.4**
    1. Women—United States—History 2. Women—Social conditions 3. United States—Social life and customs—1600-1775, Colonial period
    ISBN 0-395-21896-9; 0-395-70109-0 (pa)
                     LC 75-17031

"Viewing roles of women who lived during the Revolutionary era from a contemporary feminist perspective . . . {the author} examines Black, white and Native American women as well as women of all social classes, including slaves." SLJ

Includes bibliographical references

Esherick, Joan

Women in the Arab world. Mason Crest Publishers 2005 112p il map (Women's issues, global trends) $22.95

Grades: 7 8 9 10   **305.4**
    1. Women—Arab countries
    ISBN 1-59084-861-6   LC 2004-12709

Contents: The modern Arab world: extremes for women; Arab women in ages past; Religion and Arab women; Arab women and the public world; Family life; Changing their world: Arab women who are making a difference; Unfinished business: issues and controversies facing Arab women today

This book examines the roles of women in Arab countries.

This is "physically attractive, browsable, and up-to-date. . . . It is detailed and thorough, includes many charts and facts, and takes great care to differentiate between what most Arabs do or believe and what may occur in specific countries or among specific groups." SLJ

Includes bibliographical references

The **essential** feminist reader; edited and with an introduction by Estelle B. Freedman. Modern Library 2007 472p pa $17.95 *

Grades: 11 12 Adult   **305.4**
    1. Feminism
    ISBN 0-8129-7460-3; 978-0-8129-7460-7

This collection of writings by feminist authors "features primary source material from around the globe, including short works of fiction and drama, political manifestos, and the work of less well-known writers." Publisher's note

Includes bibliographical references

Goodwin, Jan

Price of honor; Muslim women lift the veil of silence on the Islamic world. rev ed. Plume Bks. 2003 351p il pa $16 *

Grades: 11 12 Adult   **305.4**
    1. Muslim women 2. Islamic countries
    ISBN 0-452-28377-9   LC 2002-28257
    First published 1994 by Little, Brown

The author "examines the movement that is aggressively spreading a fundamentalist version of Islam throughout much of the world. Her interviews with Muslim women in ten countries both fascinate and disturb, for their candor reveals the movement's profound and often devastating effects on them. . . . A necessary purchase." Libr J [review of 1994 edition]

Gourley, Catherine, 1950-
Flappers and the new American woman; perceptions of women from 1918 through the 1920s. Twenty-First Century Books 2008 144p il (Images and issues of women in the twentieth century) lib bdg $38.60 *
Grades: 7 8 9 10   **305.4**
1. Women—United States—History 2. United States—History—1919-1933
ISBN 978-0-8225-6060-9; 0-8225-6060-7
                  LC 2006-28983
This describes images of women in the United States from 1918 through the 1920s.
"The sparkling and engaging [text is] generously expanded by numerous, well-placed black-and-white photographs and period reproductions. . . . Great for research or browsing." SLJ
Includes bibliographical references

Gibson girls and suffragists; perceptions of women from the turn of the century through 1918. Twenty-First Century Books 2008 144p il (Images and issues of women in the twentieth century) lib bdg $38.60 *
Grades: 7 8 9 10   **305.4**
1. Women—United States—History 2. United States—History—1898-1919
ISBN 978-0-8225-7150-6; 0-8225-7150-1
                  LC 2007-1689
This describes the images of women in United States at the beginning of the twentienth century.
"The sparkling and engaging [text is] generously expanded by numerous, well-placed black-and-white photographs and period reproductions. . . . Great for research or browsing." SLJ
Includes bibliographical references

Rosie and Mrs. America; perceptions of women in the 1930s and 1940s. Twenty-First Century Books 2008 144p il (Images and issues of women in the twentieth century) lib bdg $38.60 *
Grades: 7 8 9 10   **305.4**
1. Women—United States—History 2. United States—History—20th century
ISBN 978-0-8225-6804-9; 0-8225-6804-7
                  LC 2006-28984
This describes images of women in the United States in the 1930s and 1940's.
"The sparkling and engaging [text is] generously expanded by numerous, well-placed black-and-white photographs and period reproductions. . . . Great for research or browsing." SLJ
Includes bibliographical references

Hemming, Heidi
Women making America; [by] Heidi Hemming, Julie Hemming Savage. Clotho Press 2009 378p il pa $28.95
Grades: 6 7 8 9 10   **305.4**
1. Women—United States—History 2. Women—United States—Biography
ISBN 978-0-9821271-0-0; 0-9821271-0-3
                  LC 2008-908741

"This hefty volume surveys the role of women in American history from 1770 to the present, focusing primarily on health issues, paid work, home, education, beauty, amusements, and the arts. Each chapter includes a brief summary of historical events and then examines the common threads. . . . The book's innovative and direct approach is sure to capture the attention of young women. Classroom teachers can utilize the plethora of facts to liven social studies and history lessons, and the format is appealing enough to attract browsers." SLJ
Includes bibliographical references

Hoogensen, Gunhild, 1966-
Women in power; world leaders since 1960; [by] Gunhild Hoogensen and Bruce O. Solheim; foreword by Kim Campbell. Praeger Publishers 2006 179p $44.95
Grades: 11 12 Adult   **305.4**
1. Women in politics 2. Women—Political activity
ISBN 978-0-275-98190-7; 0-275-98190-8
                  LC 2006-15398
This book "profiles 22 world leaders who have held the top positions of political power since 1960. Each chapter is devoted to a region of the world. In addition to providing an overview of the political careers of the women who emerged as leaders in these regions, the authors examine the political systems of each region in terms of the involvement of women in politics." Publisher's note
Includes bibliographical references

Lawler, Jennifer
Encyclopedia of women in the Middle Ages. McFarland & Co. 2001 279p $45
Grades: 9 10 11 12   **305.4**
1. Reference books 2. Women—History—Encyclopedias 3. Middle Ages—Encyclopedias
ISBN 0-7864-1119-8   LC 2001-126809
"This encyclopedia contains several hundred entries on the culture, history and circumstances of women in the Middle Ages, from the years 500 to 1500 C.E. . . . There are entries on queens, empresses, and other women in positions of leadership as well as entries on topics such as work, marriage and family, households, employment, religion, and various other aspects of women's lives in the Middle Ages. Genealogies of queens and empresses accompany the text." Publisher's note
Includes bibliographical references

Levy, Ariel, 1974-
Female chauvinist pigs; women and the rise of raunch culture. Free Press 2005 224p $25; pa $14
Grades: 11 12 Adult   **305.4**
1. Feminism 2. Sexism
ISBN 0-7432-4989-5; 0-7432-8428-3 (pa)
                  LC 2005-48811
The author argues that "our popular culture . . . has embraced a model of female sexuality that comes straight from pornography and strip clubs, in which the woman's job is to excite and titillate—to perform for men." N Y Times Book Rev
"A piercing look at how women are sabotaging their

Levy, Ariel, 1974-—*Continued*

own attempts to be seen as equals by going about the quest the wrong way, Levy's engrossing book should be required reading for young women." Booklist

Includes bibliographical references

Matthews, Glenna

American women's history; a student companion. Oxford Univ. Press 2000 368p il (Oxford student companions to American history) lib bdg $60 *

Grades: 7 8 9 10 11 12   **305.4**

1. Women—United States—History

ISBN 0-19-511317-9   LC 99-87245

Alphabetical articles on major events, documents, persons, social movements, and political and social concepts connected with the history of women in America

"Articles vary in length and are easy to read. Many articles are accompanied by a photograph. . . . This is a helpful reference tool that will be useful to students needing information about American women and their contributions to U.S. history." Booklist

Includes bibliographical references

Mays, Dorothy A.

Women in early America; struggle, survival, and freedom in a new world. ABC-CLIO 2004 xxi, 495p il $95

Grades: 9 10 11 12   **305.4**

1. Reference books 2. Women—United States—History—Encyclopedias

ISBN 1-85109-429-6   LC 2004-19721

The author offers "overviews of the diversity, as well as the commonalities, of both immigrant and native women's experience between 1607 and the outbreak of the War of 1812. . . . This resource offers large doses of easily accessible, hard-to-find-elsewhere information. Collections of any size serving students of our country's past will find it a popular and worthwhile addition." SLJ

Includes bibliographical references

Mills, J. Elizabeth

Expectations for women; confronting stereotypes. Rosen Pub. 2010 112p il (A young woman's guide to contemporary issues) lib bdg $31.95

Grades: 7 8 9 10   **305.4**

1. Women 2. Self-perception 3. Body image

ISBN 978-1-4358-3543-6; 1-4358-3543-3

LC 2009-14429

"The author addresses such topics such as plastic surgery, body image, growing up too fast, and how to age gracefully." Voice of Youth Advocates

"Facts are shared in a conversational tone, creating the sense of a chat with a big sister. . . . [Though] designed for personal reading and browsing, the data provided are accurate and also lend themselves to use in reports. This . . . will be of great interest." SLJ

Includes glossary and bibliographical references

Peavy, Linda Sellers, 1943-

Pioneer women; the lives of women on the frontier; [by] Linda Peavy & Ursula Smith. Oklahoma paperbacks ed. University of Oklahoma Press 1998 144p il pa $21.95

Grades: 9 10 11 12 Adult   **305.4**

1. Frontier and pioneer life—West (U.S.) 2. Women—West (U.S.)

ISBN 0-8061-3054-7; 978-0-8061-3054-5

LC 97-40684

First published 1996 by Smithmark Pubs.

An illustrated exploration of women's lives on the Western frontier. Marriages between Anglo men and Indian and Hispanic women are examined as are the lives of women who found employment outside the homestead as teachers, physicians and journalists.

"YAs seeking primary source material for women's studies and on the westward movement will find this exceptional collection of journals, letters, oral histories, and rarely seen photographs an outstanding resource." Booklist

Includes bibliographical references

Peril, Lynn

College girls; bluestockings, sex kittens, and coeds, then and now. Norton 2006 408p il pa $16.95

Grades: 11 12 Adult   **305.4**

1. Women—Education 2. College students

ISBN 978-0-393-32715-1; 0-393-32715-9

LC 2006-18896

This is a "history of the American college girl." N Y Times Book Rev

The author's "witty, irreverent style, her generous use of old advertisements and photos and her careful footnotes make this text unusually user-friendly." Publ Wkly

Includes bibliographical references

The **Quotable** woman, revised edition; the first 5,000 years; compiled and edited by Elaine Bernstein Partnow. Facts On File 2010 1038p (Facts on File library of language and literature) $95 *

Grades: 11 12 Adult   **305.4**

1. Women—Quotations 2. Quotations 3. Reference books

ISBN 978-0-8160-7725-0   LC 2009-39139

First published 1992 as a combined edition of The quotable woman, from Eve to 1799 (1986) and The quotable woman, 1800-1981 (1983) with title: The New Quotable woman

"Entries are arranged chronologically then alphabetically by the names of the women quoted. Indexing is by name, career and occupation, ethnicity and nationality, and subject. . . . The quotations section makes up the first 832 pages of the book, and the bulk of the quotations are from the 20th century. The quotations are interesting and thoughtfully chosen; the women quoted are delightfully varied." Libr J

Rodriguez, Deborah

Kabul Beauty School; an American woman goes behind the veil. Random House 2007 275p $24.95; pa $14.95

Grades: 11 12 Adult 305.4

1. Kabul Beauty School (Afghanistan) 2. Women—Afghanistan 3. Beauty shops

ISBN 978-1-4000-6559-2; 1-4000-6559-3; 978-0-8129-7673-1 (pa); 0-8129-7673-8 (pa)

LC 2006-50384

This is an account of the author's "creation of an academy to train Afghan beauticians." N Y Times (Late N Y Ed)

"Rodriguez's experiences will delight readers as she recounts such tales as two friends acting as 'parents' and negotiating a dowry for her marriage to an Afghan man or her students puzzling over a donation of a carton of thongs. Most of all, they will share her admiration for Afghan women's survival and triumph in chaotic times." SLJ

Rosen, Ruth

The world split open; how the modern women's movement changed America. Rev. and updated. Penguin Books 2006 xlii, 482p il pa $19

Grades: 11 12 Adult 305.4

1. Women's movement 2. Feminism

ISBN 978-0-14-009719-1

First published 2000

"Rosen details the rebirth of feminism, from the liberalism of NOW through women's liberation, which grew out of the civil rights movement. Her focus is on the 'hidden injuries of sex' and how what had been construed as 'personal' problems—abortion, compulsory heterosexuality, rape and sexual violence, prostitution and pornography—became political issues." Publ Wkly

Includes bibliographical references

Voices of resistance; Muslim women on war, faith, & sexuality; edited by Sarah Husain. Seal Press 2006 284p il map pa $16.95 *

Grades: 9 10 11 12 305.4

1. Muslim women

ISBN 978-1-58005-181-1; 1-58005-181-2

LC 2006-5459

This "collection of fiction, poetry, interviews, essays, letters, and artwork celebrates diversity across race, nation, sexuality, and gender. Most contributors live in the U.S., and the focus is on post-9/11 America, connecting multiple immigrant histories and memories of 'home' with the personal and political in contemporary daily life. . . . Sure to spark discussion in college classrooms and among feminist and peace activist groups." Booklist

Includes bibliographical references

Waisman, Charlotte S.

Her story; a timeline of the women who changed America; [by] Charlotte S. Waisman & Jill S. Tietjen. HarperCollins 2008 259p il $29.95 *

Grades: 9 10 11 12 305.4

1. Women—United States—History 2. United States—History—Chronology

ISBN 978-0-06-124651-7; 0-06-124651-4

LC 2007-29942

"This time line illuminates the ways in which hundreds of women changed America through their often-unrecognized contributions in science, education, arts, politics, and social activism, from the 1500s to the present." Booklist

Includes bibliographical references

Waking up American; coming of age biculturally; [edited by] Angela Jane Fountas. Seal Press 2005 232p pa $15.95

Grades: 11 12 Adult 305.4

1. Children of immigrants 2. Women—United States

ISBN 1-58005-136-7; 978-1-58005-136-1

LC 2005-11765

"'Where are you from?' In one of the best of the recent anthologies by new immigrants, young women writers answer that question with immediacy and wit, displaying honesty about the pain, anger, and prejudice at home and outside." Booklist

Wolf, Naomi

The beauty myth; how images of beauty are used against women. Perennial 2002 348p pa $14.95

Grades: 11 12 Adult 305.4

1. Women 2. Sex role 3. Personal appearance

ISBN 0-06-051218-0 LC 2002-72516

First published 1991 by Morrow

A "book about the ways women enslave themselves—and their bank accounts—to an industry that promises physical perfection." N Y Times Book Rev

The author "presents a provocative and persuasive account of the pervasiveness of the beauty ideal in all facets of Western culture." Libr J

Includes bibliographical references

Women in Islam; Diane Andrews Henningfeld, book editor. Greenhaven Press 2011 116p (At issue. Religion) $31.80; pa $22.50 *

Grades: 9 10 11 12 305.4

1. Muslim women 2. Women in Islam

ISBN 978-0-7377-4904-5; 978-0-7377-4905-2 (pa)

LC 2010017203

"This book presents viewpoints that address many of the concerns for women in Islam, from dress to property rights to personal rights." Publisher's note

Includes bibliographical references

Women in the Middle Ages; an encyclopedia; edited by Katharina M. Wilson and Nadia Margolis. Greenwood Press 2004 2v il set $199.95

Grades: 11 12 Adult   **305.4**
1. Reference books 2. Middle Ages—Encyclopedias 3. Women—History—Encyclopedias
ISBN 0-313-33016-6   LC 2004-53042
"In addition to entries on renowned women, there is a . . . number of articles covering topics such as footbinding, clothing, medicine, law, literary motifs, and geography-specific information. Terminology is defined in context, making the work readily accessible to high school students and lay readers." Libr J

Includes bibliographical references

Women's letters; America from the Revolutionary War to the present; edited by Lisa Grunwald & Stephen J. Adler. Dial Press 2005 824p il hardcover o.p. pa $18

Grades: 11 12 Adult   **305.4**
1. Women—United States—History—Sources
ISBN 0-385-33553-9; 0-385-33556-3 (pa)
    LC 2005-41446
This "book, with over 400 letters, is arranged chronologically, covering 230 years of American history. Each of its sections is preceded by a . . . timeline of events, and each letter is introduced with an explanatory note." N Y Times Book Rev
"This is a delightful collection of belles letters in the most literal sense of the term." Publ Wkly

Includes bibliographical references

Women's lives in medieval Europe; a sourcebook; edited by Emilie Amt. 2nd ed. Routledge 2009 277p $125; pa $39.95

Grades: 11 12 Adult   **305.4**
1. Women—Europe 2. Europe—History—476-1492
ISBN 978-0-415-46684-4; 978-0-415-46683-7 (pa)
    LC 2009024316
First published 1993
This book "presents the everyday lives and experiences of women in the Middle Ages. . . . [It includes] sections on marriage and sexuality, and on peasant women and townswomen, as well as a . . . section on women and the law. . . . The book focuses not just on the Christian majority, but also present material about women in minority groups in Europe, such as Jews, Muslims, and those considered to be heretics." Publisher's note

Women's rights; people and perspectives; Crista DeLuzio, editor. ABC-CLIO 2010 xxxix, 296p il (Perspectives in American social history) $85 *

Grades: 9 10 11 12   **305.4**
1. Women's rights 2. Feminism
ISBN 978-1-59884-114-5   LC 2009-31359
This is a "collection of essays exploring the history of the struggle for women's rights in the United States from the colonial period to the present." Publisher's note
"This enlightening source is much more than a roll call of persons and events that influenced women's rights and the suffrage movement. . . . This title will be extremely useful for research, and individual sections are interesting to peruse on their own. " SLJ

Includes bibliographical references

305.5   Social classes

Ehrenreich, Barbara
Nickel and dimed; on (not) getting by in boom-time America. Metropolitan Bks. 2001 221p hardcover o.p. pa $15 *

Grades: 11 12 Adult   **305.5**
1. Minimum wage 2. Labor—United States 3. Poverty
ISBN 0-8050-6388-9; 0-8050-8838-5 (pa)
    LC 00-52514
This is an exposé "of such abstractions as 'living wage' and 'affordable housing.' Ehrenreich worked, for a month at a time, at 'unskilled' jobs—as a waitress and chambermaid in Florida, a housecleaner and nursing-home aide in Maine, a Wal-Mart clerk in Minnesota—to report on how people survive on wages of six or seven dollars an hour." New Yorker
"No real answers to the problem but a compelling sketch of its reality and pervasiveness." Libr J

Issitt, Micah L.
Hippies; a guide to an American subculture. Greenwood Press/ABC-CLIO 2009 xxi, 164p il (Guides to subcultures and countercultures) $35

Grades: 11 12 Adult   **305.5**
1. Hippies 2. Counter culture
ISBN 978-0-313-36572-0   LC 2009-29453
This book "explores the psyche and history of the American counterculture's influence on everything from music and fashion to war, peace, and the mainstream establishment. From hippie leaders and icons such as Timothy Leary to how 1960s America was transformed by the movement, HIPPIES is a powerful pick for any American history collection from high school to college levels." Midwest Book Rev

Includes bibliographical references

305.8   Ethnic and national groups

The **African** American almanac; Christopher A. Brooks, editor; foreword by Benjamin Jealous. 11th ed. Gale Cengage Learning 2011 1601p il map $297 *

Grades: 8 9 10 11 12 Adult   **305.8**
1. African Americans 2. Reference books
ISSN 1071-8710
ISBN 978-1-4144-4547-2
First edition under the editorship of Harry A. Ploski published 1967 by Bellwether with title: The Negro almanac. Periodically revised. Editors vary
"Reference covering the cultural and political history of Black Americans. Includes generous amount of statistical information and biographies of Black Americans, both historical and contemporary." N Y Public Libr. Book of How & Where to Look It Up

African American breakthroughs; 500 years of black firsts; Jay P. Pederson and Jessie Carney Smith, editors. U.X.L 1995 280p il (African American reference library) $58 *

Grades: 6 7 8 9   **305.8**
1. African Americans—History
ISBN 0-8103-9496-0   LC 95-122049
Also available adult version entitled Black firsts (1994) published by Visible Ink Press
"Organized by subject, events are then listed chronologically. Subjects include *Business and Labor*; *Justice, Law Enforcement, and Public Safety*; *Religion*; and *Science, Medicine, and Invention.* . . . Each of the 500 entries consists of three or four sentences on the person or event with the original source or sources cited." Booklist

The **African** Americans; Rodney P. Carlisle, general editor. Facts on File 2011 255p il map (Multicultural America, v3) $55

Grades: 9 10 11 12   **305.8**
1. African Americans—History
ISBN 978-0-8160-7813-4
"*The African Americans* explores this particular ethnic group, presenting . . . [information] including entertainment, work, education, and the contributions and conflicts of African Americans to society. This . . . volume details their social history, customs, and traditions." Publisher's note
Includes glossary and bibliographical references

Antisemitism; a historical encyclopedia of prejudice and persecution; Richard S. Levy, editor. ABC-CLIO 2005 2v il set $185 *

Grades: 11 12 Adult   **305.8**
1. Antisemitism—Encyclopedias 2. Reference books
ISBN 1-85109-439-3   LC 2005-9480
This encyclopedia provides an "overview and examination of anti-Semitism, with 650 double-column entries by over 200 contributors from 21 countries. . . . The focus of this work is on modern times, particularly the 19th and 20th centuries, but there are also many entries on anti-Jewish expression and actions through the ages." Libr J
This is "a balanced, well-written, exceedingly useful, and often compelling tool. . . . Levy's encyclopedia is crucial for any library serving a thinking public." Choice
Includes bibliographical references

The **Arab** Americans; Rodney P. Carlisle, general editor. Facts on File 2011 193p il (Multicultural America, v2) $55

Grades: 9 10 11 12   **305.8**
1. Arab Americans—History
ISBN 978-0-8160-7812-7
"*The Arab Americans* explores the history of this ethnic group in the U.S., including their social history, customs, and traditions, as well as their contributions and conflicts in American society." Publisher's note
Includes glossary and bibliographical references

The **Arabs**; Jean Brodsky Schur, book editor. Greenhaven Press 2005 218p il map (Coming to America) lib bdg $34.95 *

Grades: 8 9 10 11 12   **305.8**
1. Arab Americans
ISBN 0-7377-2148-0   LC 2004-52356
"After a short introduction about Arab immigration, subsequent chapters discuss the various reasons Arabs chose to leave their home countries, the ways in which Arab Christians and Muslims adapted to American culture, and the types of discrimination and anti-Arab stereotyping faced by this group. . . . The selections are clearly written and informative." SLJ
Includes bibliographical references

Aronson, Marc
Race: a history beyond black and white. Atheneum Books for Young Readers 2007 322p il $18.99 *

Grades: 8 9 10 11 12   **305.8**
1. Race 2. Racism
ISBN 978-0-689-86554-1; 0-689-86554-6
                        LC 2007-31912
"Ginee Seo Books"
This is a "history of racism and its antecedents, from ancient Sumer to the Rodney King beating and beyond, interspersed with personal vignettes tailored to a young audience. . . . The pictorial implementation increases the impact of the text. . . . Clearly in evidence . . . are the complexity of race and the tenacity of racism." Horn Book

Asante, Molefi K., 1942-
Erasing racism; the survival of the American nation; [by] Molefi Kete Asante. Rev. and expanded 2nd ed. Prometheus Books 2009 370p il pa $19

Grades: 11 12 Adult   **305.8**
1. Racism 2. African Americans—Civil rights 3. African Americans—Social conditions 4. United States—Race relations
ISBN 978-1-591-02765-2; 1-591-02765-9
                        LC 2009020492
First published 2003
In this "analysis of the history of racism in America, Asante divides the nation into two camps: a white majority who perceives America as a land of promise, and a black minority that is relegated to exist in a wilderness on the margins of society. . . . The key to bridging the racial divide, he argues, lies in getting all Americans to understand and confront the history of slavery. . . . Anyone who has struggled to understand race relations in America or to engage others in open debate about it will glean something valuable from this book." Publ Wkly
Includes bibliographical references

Asian American history and culture; an encyclopedia; Huping Ling and Allan Austin, editors. M.E. Sharpe 2010 2v il set $229

Grades: 11 12 Adult   **305.8**
1. Asian Americans—Encyclopedias 2. Reference books
ISBN 978-0-7656-8077-8   LC 2009-11926

Asian American history and culture—*Continued*

"For larger and medium-sized immigrant populations, there is a narrative history followed by thematic essays and short, concise alphabetically arranged entries on important events, organizations, and people. For each immigrant group, there is a single overview essay. . . . Although Chinese and Japanese are the most frequently mentioned immigrant groups, there is ample information about others as well, such as Burmese, Cambodian, Filipino, Korean, Hmong, Tibetan, and Vietnamese. The student gains an important perspective on global studies by perusing these volumes." Libr Media Connect

Includes bibliographical references

The **Asian** Americans; Rodney P. Carlisle, general editor. Facts on File 2011 244p il map (Multicultural America, v4) $55

Grades: 9 10 11 12   **305.8**
1. Asian Americans—History
ISBN 978-0-8160-7814-1

This book "focuses on the social history, customs, and traditions of Asian Americans across U.S. history." Publisher's note

Includes glossary and bibliographical references

Autobiography of a people; three centuries of African American history told by those who lived it; [compiled by] Herb Boyd. Doubleday 2000 549p hardcover o.p. pa $15 *

Grades: 11 12 Adult   **305.8**
1. African Americans—History—Sources 2. African Americans—Biography
ISBN 0-385-49278-2; 0-385-49279-0 (pa)
         LC 99-16576

This volume contains excerpts from slave narratives, diaries, poems, letters, autobiographies, memoirs and speeches.

"Boyd includes the writers one would expect, such as Phyllis Wheatley, Frederick Douglass, W. E. B. Dubois, Reverend King, Malcolm X, and Colin Powell. But his collection may be most valuable to twenty-first century readers for the less familiar voices he gathers: slaves, freedmen and women, and, later, intellectuals, workers, and activists, whose experiences are captured in a protest or letter or memoir." Booklist

Includes bibliographical references

Avakian, Monique

Atlas of Asian-American history. Facts on File 2002 214p il maps (Facts on File library of American history) $85 *

Grades: 11 12 Adult   **305.8**
1. Asian Americans—History
ISBN 0-8160-3699-3   LC 00-49509

This "overview of the political, social, and cultural history of Asian Americans opens with a discussion of the Asian heritage and ends with comments on Asian America today. Personal anecdotes throughout range from the Chinese miners in 19th-century California to modern day health-care workers from India. Sixty full-color maps, 100 historical photos, and 34 line drawings and graphs lead the reader through discussions of the people of China, Japan, Korea, India, the Philippines, and Southeast Asia." Libr J

Includes bibliographical references

Bayoumi, Moustafa

How does it feel to be a problem? being young and Arab in America. Penguin Press 2008 290p $24.95; pa $15

Grades: 11 12 Adult   **305.8**
1. Arab American youth 2. Arab Americans—Social conditions 3. United States—Race relations
ISBN 978-1-59420-176-9; 978-0-14-311541-0 (pa)
         LC 2007-49272

The author "wondered how younger generations of Arab Americans were faring in a post-9/11 U.S. against the backdrop of fear and suspicion. By focusing on the lives of seven young people living in Brooklyn, Bayoumi offers a revealing portrait of life for people who are often scrutinized but seldom heard from." Booklist

Includes bibliographical references

Black firsts: 4,000 ground-breaking and pioneering historical events; [edited by] Jessie Carney Smith. 2nd ed rev and expanded. Visible Ink Press 2003 787p il $58; pa $24.95 *

Grades: 11 12 Adult   **305.8**
1. African Americans—History
ISBN 1-57859-153-8; 1-57859-142-2 (pa)
         LC 2002-154346

First published 1994 by Gale Research with title: Black firsts; 2,000 years of extraordinary achievement

"The chapters survey broad fields such as 'Arts and Entertainment,' 'Government: Local,' and 'Science and Medicine' and are broken down into more specific subject headings. 'Arts and Entertainment,' for example, encompasses 'Architecture,' 'Dance,' 'Music,' and 'Television,' among others. Under each of these headings, firsts are arranged chronologically. Each is described in an entry ranging from a line or two to half a page, and sources are always cited. . . . Many of the sidebars highlight achievements by women. . . . *Black firsts* remains an important part of the reference collection." Booklist

Includes bibliographical references

Chang, Iris, 1968-2004

The Chinese in America; a narrative history. Viking 2003 496p il hardcover o.p. pa $16

Grades: 11 12 Adult   **305.8**
1. Chinese Americans—History
ISBN 0-670-03123-2; 0-14-200417-0 (pa)
         LC 2002-44858

The author recounts "the immigration of Chinese people to the U.S. from the early nineteenth century to the end of the twentieth. . . . Chang threads personal stories of individuals she came across in her research into her book, making it a much more human account. . . . This is history at its most dramatic and relevant." Booklist

Includes bibliographical references

The **Chinese**; C.J. Shane, book editor. Greenhaven Press 2005 206p map (Coming to America) lib bdg $34.95 *

Grades: 8 9 10 11 12   **305.8**
1. Chinese Americans
ISBN 0-7377-2150-2   LC 2003-67533

This book focuses on the experiences of Chinese immigrants, including the prejudices they faced in America. Includes chronologies and profiles of prominent Chinese

The Chinese—*Continued*
Americans.
Includes bibliographical references

Ciment, James
Atlas of African-American history; [principal writer, James Ciment] Rev ed. Facts On File 2007 250p il map (Facts on File library of American history) $95; pa $24.95 *
Grades: 11 12 Adult   305.8
1. African Americans—History
ISBN   978-0-8160-6713-8;   0-8160-6713-9;
978-0-8160-6714-5 (pa); 0-8160-6714-7 (pa)
                        LC 2007-15796
First published 2001
This work provides an overview of the African diaspora, the African heritage, slavery in early America, the Civil War, Reconstruction, the NAACP, the civil rights years and beyond.
Includes bibliographical references

Curtis, Edward E., IV, 1970-
Muslims in America; a short history. Oxford University Press 2009 144p il (Religion in American life) pa $12.95
Grades: 9 10 11 12 Adult   305.8
1. Muslims—United States
ISBN 978-0-19-536756-0   LC 2008-47566
This book documents "the lives of African, Middle Eastern, South Asian, European, black, white, Hispanic and other Americans who have been followers of Islam." Publisher's note
The author "has authored a fine and succinct history that spans centuries. . . . Although geared toward non-Muslims, American Muslims would also learn a great deal from reading about their own history. . . . [Readers] will undoubtedly be intrigued by Curtis's compelling little read." Publ Wkly
Includes bibliographical references

Danalis, John
Riding the black cockatoo. Allen & Unwin 2009 262p pa $10.99
Grades: 9 10 11 12   305.8
1. Aboriginal Australians—Antiquities
ISBN 978-174175-377-6
"A true story" Cover
"While taking a course in Indigenous Writing, 40-year-old Danalis realized that the Aboriginal skull that sat on his family's mantle for years was morally wrong. . . . [This] is his account of first figuring out how and where to return it, and then the bureaucracy involved, the government's horrifying lack of respect for these people, and the appreciation and ceremony on the part of the Native people when it was returned. This memoir strikes the perfect balance between being informative and giving extraordinary insight into Aboriginal culture." SLJ

Davis, Thomas J.
Race relations in America; a reference guide with primary documents. Greenwood Press 2006 xxx, 301p (Major issues in American history) $75 *
Grades: 9 10 11 12   305.8
1. United States—Race relations—Sources
2. Reference books
ISBN 978-0-313-31115-4; 0-313-31115-3
                        LC 2005-25450
In this "study of racism in the United States, over 90 primary documents provide . . . evidence of how race has affected and shaped our country throughout the years. . . . Documents include excerpts from speeches, letters, pamphlets, books, essays, newspaper, magazine, and journal articles, government reports, congressional debates, laws, and court decisions." Publisher's note
"Through clear prose and evocative documents, this book will help readers see more clearly that the plight of American Indians against the expanding frontier, and the developing storm over black slavery, and the war with Mexico were all taking place in the same time frame, and according to a single matrix of reasoning." Law and Hist Rev
Includes bibliographical references

Discrimination: opposing viewpoints; Jacqueline Langwith, book editor. Greenhaven Press 2008 247p il $36.20; pa $24.95
Grades: 8 9 10 11 12   305.8
1. Discrimination 2. Affirmative action programs
3. Minorities
ISBN   978-0-73773-739-4;   0-73773-739-5;
978-0-73773-740-0 (pa); 0-73773-740-9 (pa)
                        LC 2007-933224
"Opposing viewpoints series"
This covers the topic of discrimination "in pro and con articles written by experts in the field or journalists with relevant experience. Clearly written, well researched, and far reaching, *Discrimination* explores the problem in its many forms." SLJ
Includes bibliographical references

Du Bois, W. E. B. (William Edward Burghardt), 1868-1963
The Oxford W. E. B. Du Bois reader; edited by Eric J. Sundquist. Oxford Univ. Press 1996 680p pa $34.95 *
Grades: 11 12 Adult   305.8
1. African Americans 2. United States—Race relations
ISBN 0-19-509178-7   LC 95-21307
This reader covers Du Bois's "writing career, from the 1890s through the early 1960s. The volume selects key essays and longer works that portray the range of Du Bois's thought on such subjects as African American culture, the politics and sociology of American race relations, art and music, black leadership, gender and women's rights, Pan-Africanism and anti-colonialism, and Communism in the U.S. and abroad." Publisher's note
Includes bibliographical references

Du Bois, W. E. B. (William Edward Burghardt), 1868-1963—*Continued*

The souls of Black folk; edited with an introduction and notes by Brent Hayes Edwards. Oxford University Press 2007 xxxvi, 223p il (Oxford world's classics) pa $12.95
Grades: 11 12 Adult   **305.8**
1. African Americans
ISBN 978-0-19-280678-9; 0-19-280678-5
                                        LC 2006-35193
First published 1903 by McClurg
"A collection of fifteen essays and sketches by W.E.B. Du Bois. In it he describes the lives of African American farmers, sketches the role of music in their churches, details the history of the Freedman's Bureau, discusses the career of Booker T. Washington, and advocates a commitment to higher education for the most talented African American youth." Benet's Reader's Ency of Am Lit
Includes bibliographical references

Encyclopedia of African-American culture and history; the Black experience in the Americas; Colin A. Palmer, editor in chief. 2nd ed. Macmillan Reference USA 2006 6v il map set $695
Grades: 11 12 Adult   **305.8**
1. African Americans—Encyclopedias 2. Reference books
ISBN 0-02-865816-7   LC 2005-13029
First published 1996 under the editorship of Jack Salzman, David L. Smith, and Cornel West
"Readers can find comparative analyses of social movements, languages, religions and family structures in the context of an interdisciplinary framework." Publisher's note
Includes bibliographical references

Encyclopedia of African American history; Leslie M. Alexander and Walter C. Rucker, editors. ABC-CLIO 2010 3v il map (American ethnic experience) set $295
Grades: 9 10 11 12 Adult   **305.8**
1. African Americans—History—Encyclopedias
2. African Americans—Biography—Encyclopedias
3. Reference books
ISBN 978-1-85109-769-2; 978-1-85109-774-6 (ebook)
                                        LC 2009-51262
Contact publisher for ebook pricing
"Each volume in this set begins with a list of entries. The first volume contains entries about Atlantic African, American, and European backgrounds, as well as a section on culture, identity, and community from slavery to the present. The second volume contains entries on political activity and resistance to oppression from the American Revolution to the Civil War. The third volume includes political activity, migration and urbanization from reconstruction to civil rights, and modern African Americans. . . . This is a valuable reference set." Libr Media Connect
Includes bibliographical references

Encyclopedia of African American history, 1619-1895; from the colonial period to the age of Frederick Douglass; editor in chief, Paul Finkelman. Oxford University Press 2006 3v il set $395 *
Grades: 11 12 Adult   **305.8**
1. Reference books 2. African Americans—History—Encyclopedias
ISBN 0-19-516777-5; 978-0-19-516777-1
                                        LC 2005-33701
This encyclopedia, the first of two sets focusing on African-American history, documents "blacks' experiences from the first slave ships to Frederick Douglass's death. The set offers depth, reaching most important persons, events, and developments through 1895 but is written for easy access with multiple cross references, chronologies, topical outlines, and a comprehensive index." Libr J
Includes bibliographical references

Encyclopedia of African American history, 1896 to the present; from the age of segregation to the twenty-first century; editor in chief, Paul Finkelman. Oxford University Press 2009 5v il set $595 *
Grades: 11 12 Adult   **305.8**
1. Reference books 2. African Americans—History—Encyclopedias
ISBN 978-0-19-516779-5   LC 2008-34263
Companion volume to Encyclopedia of African American history, 1619-1895 (2006)
"Focusing on the making of African American society from the 1896 'separate but equal' ruling of Plessy v. Ferguson up to the contemporary period, this encyclopedia traces the transition from the Reconstruction Era to the age of Jim Crow, the Harlem Renaissance, the Great Migration, the Brown ruling that overturned Plessy, the Civil Rights Movement, and the ascendant influence of African American culture on the American cultural landscape." Publisher's note
This resource "excels at gathering discussions of similar or related topics by academics under one heading." Libr J
Includes bibliographical references

Encyclopedia of African American society; Gerald D. Jaynes, general editor. Sage Publications 2005 2v il set $295
Grades: 11 12 Adult   **305.8**
1. Reference books 2. African Americans—Social life and customs—Encyclopedias 3. African Americans—Social conditions—Encyclopedias
ISBN 0-7619-2764-6   LC 2004-25515
"A Sage reference publication"
"With particular focus on social issues, the more than 700 alphabetically arranged articles here seek to provide readers with background information on the history and place of African Americans in this country's cultural and economic matrix. . . . [The entries] encompass subjects as huge as the origins of slavery or the course of the Civil Rights movement down to discussions of the 'Cakewalk,' the 'Sambo stereotype,' and hip-hop's 'Zulu Nation.'" SLJ
"This reference source will prove useful to any African American studies collection, especially those serving

Encyclopedia of African American society—
Continued
high school students and undergraduates." Choice
Includes bibliographical references

Encyclopedia of American Jewish history;
Stephen H. Norwood and Eunice G. Pollack,
editors. ABC-CLIO 2008 2v il map (American
ethnic histories) set $195
Grades: 11 12 Adult   **305.8**
1. Reference books 2. Jews—United States—History—
Encyclopedias
ISBN 978-1-85109-638-1; 1-85109-638-8
                                        LC 2007-13889
"In essays and short entries written by 125 of the
world's leading scholars of American Jewish history and
culture, this encyclopedia explores both religious and
secular aspects of American Jewish life." Publisher's
note
"This work emphasizing the Jewish American experience provides a unique perspective for students and
scholars." Booklist
Includes bibliographical references

Encyclopedia of Muslim-American history; edited
by Edward E. Curtis, IV. Facts on File 2010 2v
628p il (Facts on File library of American
history) set $195
Grades: 9 10 11 12 Adult   **305.8**
1. Reference books 2. Muslims—United States—Encyclopedias
ISBN 978-0-8160-7575-1; 978-1-4381-3040-8 (ebook)
                                        LC 2009-24875
Contact publisher for ebook pricing
The editor "has assembled a fascinating and timely resource detailing the history and contributions of Muslim
Americans in the United States. More than 300 articles,
written by scholars, historians, and experts in Islam and
American history, outline the long legacy and impact that
Muslim Americans have had since their earliest arrival
on slave ships in the 18th century. . . . A necessary and
timely resource to remind us of the vital contributions
that Muslim Americans have made to our culture and society since its founding." Libr J
Includes bibliographical references

Encyclopedia of race and racism; John Hartwell
Moore, editor in chief. Macmillan Reference
USA/Thomson Gale 2008 3v il map (Macmillan
social science library) set $400 *
Grades: 9 10 11 12 Adult   **305.8**
1. Reference books 2. Racism—Encyclopedias
3. Minorities—Encyclopedias
ISBN 978-0-02-866020-2; 0-02-866020-X
                                        LC 2007-24359
The articles in this set cover "subjects such as assaults
on homosexuals and women's groups, ethnic cleansing in
Europe and in Africa, and the history of the treatment of
all minorities around the world. People who were involved in the struggle concerning the rights of others are
also subjects for the articles." Libr Media Connect
"Unrivaled in its scope and content . . . this set will
appeal to almost any serious reader that is interested in
a comprehensive one-stop reference source that provides
a wide-range of subjects from the perspective of various

social sciences." Am Ref Books Annu, 2008
Includes filmography and bibliographical references

Encyclopedia of racism in the United States.
Greenwood Press 2005 3v il set $249.95 *
Grades: 11 12 Adult   **305.8**
1. Reference books 2. Racism—Encyclopedias
3. United States—Race relations—Encyclopedias
ISBN 0-313-32688-6   LC 2005-8523
"The majority of the 450 entries run about a paragraph to a page in length, covering sociological terms,
current and historical events, individuals, organizations,
books, court cases, government programs, and legislation.
Twenty-five of the entries deal with such broad concepts
as affirmative action or the Civil Rights Movement."
Libr J
"With nearly a hundred pages of primary documents,
the Encyclopedia will be a valuable supplement to
studies of racism and multiculturalism." Choice
Includes bibliographical references

Encyclopedia of the peoples of Asia and Oceania.
Facts On File 2009 2v il map (Facts on File
library of world history) set $175
Grades: 9 10 11 12 Adult   **305.8**
1. Reference books 2. Ethnology—Asia—Encyclopedias 3. Ethnology—Oceania—Encycopedias
ISBN 978-0-8160-7109-8; 0-8160-7109-8
                                        LC 2008-3055
"This A-to-Z provides a concise yet thorough introduction to the myriad historical and contemporary peoples of Asia and Oceania, excluding the contemporary
Middle East. . . . Entries range in length from 12 pages
. . . to a half page. Longer entries are subdivided into
sections on origins, history, and culture, accompanied by
maps, time lines, and black-and-white photos. All but the
very briefest have bibliographies, and most include a
short sidebar with basic statistics: location, time period,
ancestry, and language." Libr J
Includes bibliographical references

Epstein, Lawrence J. (Lawrence Jeffrey)
At the edge of a dream; the story of Jewish
immigrants on New York's Lower East Side.
Jossey-Bass 2007 299p il $40
Grades: 11 12 Adult   **305.8**
1. Jews—New York (N.Y.) 2. United States—Immigration and emigration
ISBN 978-0-7879-8622-3   LC 2007-4000
"An Arthur Kurzweil Book; A Lower East Side Tenement Museum Book"
The author "explores why the immigrants left Eastern
Europe, how they came here, and what they found when
they arrived. He describes their journey in steerage, their
life in tenements, and their search for jobs. Also under
discussion are Yiddish theater, journalism, and literature,
as well as such famous personalities as Jacob Adler,
George Burns, Fanny Brice, Irving Berlin, George Gershwin, Sholom Aleichem, Eddie Cantor, and Jack Benny.
. . . Words and pictures combine to make this book a
foremost chronicle of Jewish immigration." Booklist
Includes bibliographical references

The **European** Americans; Rodney P. Carlisle, general editor. Facts on File 2011 243p il map (Multicultural America, v6) $55

Grades: 9 10 11 12   **305.8**
1. European Americans—History
ISBN 978-0-8160-7816-5

"The European Americans examines the history of this ethnic group in America, as well as the foods they ate, how they dressed, entertainment, work, education, popular pastimes, political activity, and their contributions and conflicts in American society." Publisher's note

Includes glossary and bibliographical references

Feagin, Joe R.
White men on race; power, privilege, and the shaping of cultural consciousness; {by} Joe Feagin and Eileen O'Brien. Beacon Press 2003 275p hardcover o.p. pa $18 *

Grades: 11 12 Adult   **305.8**
1. United States—Race relations 2. United States—Social conditions
ISBN 0-8070-0980-6; 0-8070-0983-0 (pa)
                                    LC 2003-11632

"Racism in the U.S., the authors argue, is a far more subtle phenomenon than it used to be, but it exists nonetheless—and it still excludes minorities from opportunities afforded white males. Based on hundreds of interviews with . . . elite white men—business managers, corporate execs, and the like—the book covers a wide range of subjects from the respondent's first encounter with an African American to interracial dating, affirmative action, and (of course) crime. . . . This is not a balanced, multisided look at racism; the authors are presenting a thesis . . . not trying to cover every point of view. Still, they make their case powerfully and persuasively." Booklist

Includes bibliographical references

Finkelstein, Norman H., 1941-
Forged   in   freedom;   shaping   the Jewish-American experience. Jewish Publ. Soc. 2002 204p il $24.95

Grades: 9 10 11 12   **305.8**
1. Jews—United States
ISBN 0-8276-0748-2   LC 2002-453

A history in words and photographs of the growth of the Jewish community in the United States and its contributions to American culture, politics, and economics in the twentieth century

This offers "an easy, open style and spacious design with lots of black-and-white photos. . . . Everyone will find something to argue with here, but this close-up view presents diversity and controversy in many forms." Booklist

Includes bibliographical references

Franklin, John Hope, 1915-2009
From slavery to freedom; a history of African Americans; [by] John Hope Franklin, Evelyn Higginbotham. 9th ed. McGraw-Hill [2010] c2011 xxv, 710p il map $100.63 *

Grades: 11 12 Adult   **305.8**
1. African Americans—History 2. Slavery—United States
ISBN 978-0-07-296378-6; 0-07-296378-6
                                    LC 2009-42935

First published 1947

A survey of African-Americans history from slavery to the present.

Includes bibliographical references

Freedom on my mind; the Columbia documentary history of the African American experience; Manning Marable, general editor; Nishani Frazier and John McMillian, assistant editors. Columbia University Press 2003 734p $80 *

Grades: 11 12 Adult   **305.8**
1. African Americans—History—Sources
ISBN 0-231-10890-7   LC 2003-51605

This "anthology features the works of noteworthy figures of African American history and culture . . . and provides a tapestry of personal correspondence, excerpts from slave narratives and autobiographies, leaflets, speeches, oral histories and interviews, political manifestos, song lyrics, and important statements of black institutions and organizations. . . . A necessary text of readings for both introductory and advanced African American studies courses." Choice

Includes bibliographical references

Gibbon, Piers
Tribe; endangered peoples around the world; [by] Piers Gibbon with Jane Houston. Firefly Books 2010 192p il $45

Grades: 11 12 Adult   **305.8**
1. Ethnology 2. Acculturation
ISBN 978-1-55407-742-7; 1-55407-742-7
                                    LC 2011-380573

Presents the cultures, beliefs, and societal patterns of over two hundred indigenous peoples and describes their degrees of integration with other societies and the integrity of their indigenous identities. Contains some images of nudity.

This is "a wonderful compendium of diversity and a useful platform for thought, providing an opportunity to pose questions to ourselves. . . . It reminds us that there is so much that we still don't know, so much more to the world than we see in our homes and high streets; that the world is wondrous and precious and has an innate value that must be both defended and empowered if it is to survive." Geographical

Includes bibliographical references

Gonzalez, Juan
Harvest of empire; a history of Latinos in America. Rev. ed. Penguin Books 2011 xxiv, 392p map pa $18 *

Grades: 11 12 Adult   **305.8**
1. Hispanic Americans
ISBN 978-0-14-311928-9   LC 2011006880

Gonzalez, Juan—*Continued*
First published 2000
The author notes that with rising immigration "Latinos will constitute the largest minority in the nation by 2010. Gonzalez explores why Spanish and British colonization experiences were so different, particularly the divergence in attitudes on slavery and race. . . . This is an important book for understanding a major American ethnic group." Booklist
Includes bibliographical references

The **Greenwood** encyclopedia of African American civil rights; from emancipation to the twenty-first century; Charles D. Lowery and John F. Marszalek, editors; Thomas Adams Upchurch, associate editor; foreword by David J. Garrow. Greenwood Press 2003 2v il set $175 *
Grades: 11 12 Adult   305.8
1. Reference books 2. African Americans—Civil rights—Encyclopedias 3. United States—Race relations—Encyclopedias
ISBN 0-313-32171-X   LC 2003-40837
First published 1992 with title: Encyclopedia of African-American civil rights
"Entries are alphabetically arranged and cross-referenced, and each is followed by a selected bibliography. Many of the entries focus on seminal political issues of the 1950s and 1960s—*Black Power, March on Washington, Voter Education Project*—but also cover important developments both before and after this time. Other entries are biographical, ranging from politicians to writers, artists, actors, musicians, and athletes. Important literary documents are covered, including not only novels, plays, and political treatises but also journals." Booklist

Griffin, John Howard, 1920-1980
Black like me; the definitive Griffin estate edition, corrected from original manuscripts; foreword by Studs Terkel; with historic photographs by Don Rutledge; and an afterword by Robert Bonazzi. 2nd Wings Press ed., with index. Wings Press 2006 243p il $29.95 *
Grades: 11 12 Adult   305.8
1. African Americans—Southern States 2. Prejudices
ISBN 978-0-930324-73-5
Also available in paperback from Signet
First published 1961 by Houghton Mifflin
The author, "who is white, a Catholic, and a Texan, conceived and carried out the unusual notion of blackening his skin with a newly developed pigment drug and traveling through the Deep South as a Negro. This book, part of which appeared in the Negro magazine Sepia, is a journal account of that experience." New Yorker
Includes bibliographical references

Hall, Loretta
Arab American voices. U.X.L 2000 233p il $58 *
Grades: 7 8 9 10 11 12   305.8
1. Arab Americans
ISBN 0-7876-2956-1   LC 99-37500

Twenty primary source documents from speeches, memoirs, poems, novels, and autobiographies present the words of Americans with roots in Lebanon, Syria, Palestine, Iraq, Egypt, and other Arab nations
"The works selected, from Kahlil Gibran's 'Dead Are My People' to the text of the U.S. government's Antiterrorism and Effective Death Penalty Act of 1986, should provide many new openings for discussions with students." Booklist
Includes glossary and bibliographical references

The **Harvard** guide to African-American history; Evelyn Brooks Higginbotham, editor-in-chief; Leon F. Litwack and Darlene Clark Hine, general editors; Randall K. Burkett, associate editor; foreword by Henry Louis Gates, Jr. Harvard Univ. Press 2001 xxxvi, 923p (Harvard University Press reference library) $125 *
Grades: 11 12 Adult   305.8
1. African Americans—History
ISBN 0-674-00276-8   LC 00-53861
"The first section includes 12 essays on historical research aids divided by topics such as films, newspapers, Internet resources, primary sources on microform, government documents, manuscript collections, and oral history archives. The second section contains comprehensive bibliographies . . . further subdivided into specific themes such as race relations, religion, color and class, politics and voting, urban conditions, and science and technology. The third section provides sources related to special subject matters: autobiographies of African Americans, studies identified by geographic region, and studies of African American women." Libr J

The **Hispanic** Americans; Rodney P. Carlisle, general editor. Facts on File 2011 243p il map (Multicultural America, v1) $55
Grades: 9 10 11 12   305.8
1. Hispanic Americans—History
ISBN 978-0-8160-7811-0
This book "focuses on the social history, customs, and traditions of Hispanic Americans in this country." Publisher's note
Includes glossary and bibliographical references

Horst, Heather A.
Jamaican Americans; [by] Heather A. Horst and Andrew Garner; series editor, Robert D. Johnston. Chelsea House 2007 144p il map (The new immigrants) lib bdg $27.95
Grades: 7 8 9 10 11 12   305.8
1. West Indian Americans 2. Immigrants—United States
ISBN 0-7910-8790-5; 978-0-7910-8790-9
LC 2006-25904
"Drawing on personal stories and historical fact, this . . . book focuses on [Jamaican Americans] and assesses their lasting impact." Publisher's note
The "chatty narrative style may engage readers." Horn Book Guide
Includes bibliographical references

IndiVisible; African-Native American lives in the Americas; general editor, Gabrielle Tayac. Smithsonian Institution's National Museum of the American Indian in association with the National Museum of African American History and Culture and the Smithsonian Institution Traveling Exhibition Service 2009 256p il map pa $19.95
Grades: 11 12 Adult   **305.8**
1. Native Americans—History 2. African Americans—History 3. United States—Ethnic relations 4. Racially mixed people
ISBN 978-1-58834-271-3   LC 2009-34290
"This book complements the IndiVisible exhibition at the National Museum of the American Indian (NMAI). . . . [Tayac] brings together 27 scholars who share what being an African-Native means to them. The book is organized thematically, emphasizing racial policy, community identity issues, peaceful and physical resistance, and cultural lifeways. . . . The volume's photographic images and narrative approach speak well to the collaboration necessary for addressing identity politics—a complicated and often contentious subject." Choice
Includes bibliographical references

Interracial America: opposing viewpoints; Eleanor Stanford, book editor. Greenhaven Press 2006 205p il lib bdg $34.95; pa $23.70 *
Grades: 8 9 10 11 12   **305.8**
1. United States—Race relations 2. Ethnic relations
ISBN 0-7377-2943-0 (lib bdg); 0-7377-2944-9 (pa)
LC 2005-54893
"Opposing viewpoints series"
The question of racial and ethnic differences is addressed sociologically and politically. Attention is given to immigration, affirmative action, interracial marriage, biracial children, and transracial adoption.
"For social-studies classes wishing to delve into the matter of race, this volume should prove helpful when used in conjunction with other source materials. It will be a boon to debaters." SLJ
Includes bibliographical references

The **Irish**; Karen Price Hossell, book editor. Greenhaven Press 2005 207p il (Coming to America) lib bdg $34.95 *
Grades: 8 9 10 11 12   **305.8**
1. Irish Americans
ISBN 0-7377-2154-5   LC 2004-47582
"The contributors to this volume explore why the Irish left their homeland, the experiences of the immigrants and their descendants, and the achievements of notable Irish Americans." Publisher's note
Includes bibliographical references

The **Jewish** Americans; Rodney P. Carlisle, general editor. Facts on File 2011 243p il map (Multicultural America, v5) $55
Grades: 9 10 11 12   **305.8**
1. Jews—United States—History
ISBN 978-0-8160-7815-8
This book offers a "glimpse into the history of . . . [Jewish Americans], as well as their contributions and conflicts in American society." Publisher's note
Includes glossary and bibliographical references

Latino history and culture; an encyclopedia; David J. Leonard and Carmen R. Lugo-Lugo, editors. M.E. Sharpe 2009 2v il set $229
Grades: 9 10 11 12 Adult   **305.8**
1. Hispanic Americans—Encyclopedias 2. Reference books
ISBN 978-0-7656-8083-9; 0-7656-8083-1
LC 2008-47796
"This two-volume encyclopedia traces the history of Latinos in the United States from colonial times to the present, focusing on their impact on the nation in its historical development and current culture." Publisher's note
"By presenting germane facts on notable events, people, groups, and movements in a lucid, well-organized arrangement, the editors have provided an impressive resource." SLJ
Includes bibliographical references

Letters from Black America; edited by Pamela Newkirk. Farrar, Straus, and Giroux 2009 372p il $30
Grades: 9 10 11 12 Adult   **305.8**
1. American letters—African American authors 2. African Americans—Social conditions
ISBN 978-0-374-10109-1; 0-374-10109-4
LC 2008-41265
"This anthology features the writings of individuals who range from highly celebrated to barely literate and presents stories that are of vital historical importance and touchingly personal. Newkirk divides the letters by topic—covering family, courtship and romance, politics and social justice, education and scholarship, war, art and culture, and the African diaspora—and offers concise introductions to each. . . . While this unique collection of letters represents a frank depiction of the black experience, the great achievement is that these writings often go far beyond race and class to simply tell the story of the human experience in America." Libr J
Includes bibliographical references

Marsico, Katie, 1980-
The Trail of Tears; the tragedy of the American Indians. Marshall Cavendish Benchmark 2010 128p il (Perspectives on) lib bdg $27.95
Grades: 7 8 9 10   **305.8**
1. Cherokee Indians 2. Native Americans—Relocation
ISBN 978-0-7614-4029-1; 0-7614-4029-1
LC 2008-41217
"Marsico uses primary sources to show 'conflicting vantage points' to provide an objective, reasoned account that places the Cherokee relocation and the Trail of Tears into the context of American history. She opens with well-written background about the 'principal people,' as the Cherokee called themselves, and then discusses how the post-American Revolution expansion created conflict between the Cherokee and white settlers, the divisions that assimilation efforts and resistance to relocation caused within the tribe and its leadership, and the disastrous removal to Oklahoma. . . . Marsico's book will help students better understand the tragic events and their place in history." SLJ
Includes bibliographical references

Meagher, Timothy J.

The Columbia guide to Irish American history. Columbia University Press 2005 398p (Columbia guides to American history and cultures) $47.50 *

Grades: 11 12 Adult   **305.8**

1. Irish Americans

ISBN 0-231-12070-2   LC 2005-43233

The author "examines Irish American history from the first Irish settlements in the seventeenth century through the famine years in the nineteenth century to the unpredictability of 1960s America and beyond to the twentieth century. Teachers and students interested in the history of Irish America will welcome this book." Univ Press Books for Public and Second Sch Libr, 2006

Includes bibliographical references

The **Mexicans**; C.J. Shane, book editor. Greenhaven Press 2005 221p il map (Coming to America) lib bdg $34.95 *

Grades: 8 9 10 11 12   **305.8**

1. Mexican Americans

ISBN 0-7377-2156-1   LC 2004-46078

This book focuses on the experiences of Mexican immigrants, including those who became Americans by default after the Mexican-American War of 1848 and those who are immigrating today. Includes chronologies and profiles of prominent Mexican Americans

Includes bibliographical references

Milestone documents in African American history; exploring the essential primary sources; Paul Finkelman, editor in chief. Schlager 2010 4v il (Milestone documents) set $395

Grades: 9 10 11 12 Adult   **305.8**

1. African Americans—History—Sources
2. Reference books

ISBN 978-1-9353060-5-4

Also available online

"The 125 signed entries, which have been prepared by experts in history and law, include correspondence, essays, reports, tracts, manifestos, petitions, proclamations, legal opinions, legislation, military orders, narratives, presidential and executive documents, speeches and addresses, and testimony. In addition to document text, each entry includes context, a time line, a biographical profile, explanation and analysis, intended audience, impact, quotes, and more." Booklist

Includes bibliographical references

The **Native** Americans; Rodney P. Carlisle, general editor. Facts on File 2011 242p il map (Multicultural America, v7) $55

Grades: 9 10 11 12   **305.8**

1. Native Americans—History

ISBN 978-0-8160-7817-2

This book "explores the history and customs of [Native Americans,] . . . covering everything from the foods they ate and how they dressed to popular pastimes, political activity, and more." Publisher's note

Includes glossary and bibliographical references

Ochoa, George

Atlas of Hispanic-American history; [by] George Ochoa and Carter Smith. Rev ed. Facts on File 2008 c2009 250p il map (Facts on File library of American history) $95; pa $21.95

Grades: 7 8 9 10   **305.8**

1. Hispanic Americans—History 2. Reference books

ISBN 978-0-8160-7092-3; 978-0-8160-7736-6 (pa)

              LC 2008-20664

First published 2001

This reference chronicles the "cultural, historical, political, and social experiences of Hispanic Americans through the years. . . . [It] examines Spanish, Native American, and African influences and how they combine in different ways to form the varied cultures of Hispanic America." Publisher's note

Includes bibliographical references

Race relations: opposing viewpoints; Karen Miller, book editor. Greenhaven Press 2011 204p il lib bdg $39.70; pa $26.50 *

Grades: 8 9 10 11 12   **305.8**

1. United States—Race relations

ISBN 978-0-7377-4986-1 (lib bdg); 0-7377-4986-5 (lib bdg); 978-0-7377-4987-8 (pa); 0-7377-4987-3 (pa)

              LC 2010028939

"Opposing viewpoints series"

Articles in this anthology present opposing views on the nature of race, the impact of society and the government on race relations, and what the future holds.

Includes bibliographical references

Racism; Noel Merino, book editor. Greenhaven Press 2009 223p (Current controversies) lib bdg $39.70; pa $27.50

Grades: 9 10 11 12   **305.8**

1. Racism 2. United States—Race relations

ISBN 978-0-7377-4462-0 (lib bdg); 0-7377-4462-6 (lib bdg); 978-0-7377-4463-7 (pa); 0-7377-4463-4 (pa)

              LC 2009012037

Articles in this anthology discuss whether racism is a serious problem, society and culture's influence on racism, and affirmative action.

Includes bibliographical references

Rangaswamy, Padma, 1945-

Indian Americans; [by] Padma Rangaswamy. Chelsea House 2007 158p il map (The new immigrants) lib bdg $27.95

Grades: 7 8 9 10 11 12   **305.8**

1. East Indian Americans 2. Immigrants—United States

ISBN 0-7910-8786-7   LC 2006-8384

The author traces the history of new immigrants from India "from the early days of the Punjabi pioneers in California to the triumphs of the 'dot-com generation.'" Publisher's note

Includes bibliographical references

Rose, Tricia

The hip hop wars; what we talk about when we talk about hip hop. BasicCivitas 2008 308p pa $15.95

Grades: 11 12 Adult **305.8**
1. Hip-hop 2. Rap music 3. African Americans—Social conditions
ISBN 978-0-465-00897-1; 0-465-00897-6
LC 2008-31637

"A cultural critic goes inside the world of modern music to argue that hip hop has become a primary way to talk about race in America, examining the key issues on both sides of the debate, from the link among hip hop, violence, and sexism, to whether or not hip hop's portrayal of black culture undermines black advancement." Publisher's note

"Rose's convincing arguments and challenges of assumptions . . . make this an important title. . . . This title definitely deserves readers." Libr J

Includes bibliographical references

Sanna, Ellyn, 1957-

We shall all be free; survivors of racism. Mason Crest Publishers 2009 128p il (Survivors: ordinary people, extraordinary circumstances) lib bdg $24.95

Grades: 7 8 9 10 **305.8**
1. Racism 2. Minorities 3. Prejudices
ISBN 978-1-4222-0458-0; 1-4222-0458-8
LC 2008-50326

"Sanna covers racism of all kinds, including genocide in parts of Africa; the deplorable conditions of Native Americans; anti-Semitism; racism against the Roma, better known as Gypsies, and against African Americans; and the conditions faced by some immigrants. . . . [This title exposes] the underbelly of society, explaining terms that might be unfamiliar and providing multiple examples of the issues." SLJ

Includes bibliographical references

Scarpaci, Vincenza

The journey of the Italians in America; foreword by Gary R. Mormino. Pelican Pub. Co. 2008 319p il $40

Grades: 9 10 11 12 Adult **305.8**
1. Italian Americans 2. Immigrants—United States 3. United States—Immigration and emigration
ISBN 978-1-58980-245-2; 1-58980-245-4
LC 2008-18199

"Primarily a photographic record accompanied by extensive captions and short chapter introductions, this fascinating historical account . . . is divided into nine chapters, from embarkation and arrival to assimilation and ethnic resurgence. The book does not dodge contentious issues, like organized crime and the lionization of Columbus. Its many rare illustrations, including period photos, sheet music, advertisements, and document facsimiles, tell individual stories of survival, persistence, ingenuity, and community with more immediacy than any essay." Libr J

Should America pay? slavery and the raging debate over reparations; {edited by} Raymond A. Winbush. Amistad 2003 396p hardcover o.p. pa $13.95

Grades: 11 12 Adult **305.8**
1. African Americans 2. Slavery—United States
ISBN 0-06-008310-7; 0-06-008311-5 (pa)
LC 2002-27927

The author addresses the issue "of paying reparations to black Americans for slavery. . . . He explores numerous voices within the reparations movement and commentary on the various stages and aspects of the movement. He also examines the significance of grassroots organizations in the development of the reparations movement, as well as legal perspectives and dissenting voices. This is a complete and balanced look at a controversial topic." Booklist

Includes bibliographical references

U-X-L Asian American almanac; edited by Irene Natividad and Susan B. Gall. 2nd ed. U-X-L 2004 268p il map $58 *

Grades: 9 10 11 12 **305.8**
1. Asian Americans
ISBN 0-7876-7598-9 LC 2003-110047

First published 1995 with title: Asian American almanac

"Explores the culture and history of the diverse groups of Americans who descend from Asian and Pacific Island countries: Asian Indian, Cambodian, Chinese, Filipino, Native Hawaiian, Hmong, Indonesian, Korean, Japanese, Laotian, Pacific Island, Pakistani, Thai, and Vietnamese Americans. The Almanac is organized into 17 subject chapters on topics including family, health, religion, employment, civil rights and activism, education, law, demographics, literature and theater, and sports." Publisher's note

Includes glossary and bibliographical references

U-X-L Hispanic American almanac; Sonia G. Benson, Nicolás Kanellos, and Bryan Ryan, editors. 2nd ed. U-X-L 2003 247p il, maps $79 *

Grades: 7 8 9 10 **305.8**
1. Hispanic Americans
ISBN 978-0-7876-6598-2; 0-7876-6598-3
LC 2002-7376

First published 1995 with title: Hispanic American almanac

Explores the history and culture of Hispanic Americans, people in the United States whose ancestors—or they themselves—came from Spain or the Spanish-speaking countries of South and Central America

Includes bibliographical references

What are you? voices of mixed-race young people; [edited by] Pearl Fuyo Gaskins. Holt & Co. 1999 273p il $18.95 *

Grades: 7 8 9 10 **305.8**
1. Racially mixed people 2. Teenagers 3. United States—Race relations
ISBN 0-8050-5968-7 LC 98-37381

Many young people of racially mixed backgrounds discuss their feelings about family relationships, preju-

What are you?—*Continued*

dice, dating, personal identity, and other issues

"While underscoring the complexity of the mixed-race experience, these unadorned voices offer a genuine, poignant, enlightening and empowering message to all readers." SLJ

Includes bibliographical references

Wright, Simeon, 1942-

Simeon's story; an eyewitness account of the kidnapping of Emmett Till; [by] Simeon Wright; with Herb Boyd. Lawrence Hill Books 2010 144p il map $19.95

Grades: 6 7 8 9 10   **305.8**

1. Till, Emmett, 1941-1955 2. Mississippi—Race relations 3. Lynching 4. African Americans—Mississippi 5. Racism 6. Trials (Homicide)

ISBN 978-1-55652-783-8; 1-55652-783-7

                  LC 2009-33631

"Simeon Wright was 12 years old when his cousin Emmett 'Bobo' Till came from Chicago to visit relatives in Mississippi. . . . One hot August night in 1955, Till whistled at a white female store clerk, setting off a chain of events that left an indelible mark not only on our nation's history, but also on the cousin who witnessed Till's gaffe and eventual kidnapping. Wright's story is chilling, and his honest account will hook readers from the beginning." SLJ

Zia, Helen

Asian American dreams; the emergence of an American people. Farrar, Straus & Giroux 2000 356p il hardcover o.p. pa $14

Grades: 11 12 Adult   **305.8**

1. Asian Americans

ISBN 0-374-14774-4; 0-374-52736-9 (pa)

                  LC 99-26746

"Zia surveys the history of Asian Americans, the rapid development of their new political force, and the unique issues they face. This well-written book is an important addition to the growing field of Asian American studies." Libr J

Includes bibliographical references

305.9   Occupational and miscellaneous groups

Bergquist, James M.

Daily life in immigrant America, 1820-1870. Greenwood Press 2008 306p il (Greenwood Press "Daily life through history" series) $49.95

Grades: 9 10 11 12   **305.9**

1. United States—Immigration and emigration 2. Immigrants—United States 3. United States—History—19th century

ISBN 978-0-313-33698-0; 0-313-33698-9

                  LC 2007-35360

This is a "guide to the daily life of ordinary immigrants into the United States during the nineteenth century. Berquist . . . demonstrates that this post-colonial wave of immigrants profoundly impacted national developments within the United States, such as westward expansion, urban growth, industrialization, city and national politics, and even the Civil War. Other chapters examine the typical life of these immigrants—where they came from (mainly Germans, Irish, Englishmen, Scandinavians, and Chinese), why they left their home country, where they settled, how their communities adapted, and the difficulties they had being accepted into the greater communities." Am Ref Books Annu, 2009

The author "has written the best history ever of . . . [this] subject. . . . The perfect history for those who want to learn more about the peopling of the US." Publ Wkly

Includes glossary and bibliographical references

Do religious groups in America experience discrimination? Janel Ginn, book editor. Greenhaven Press 2007 131p (At issue. Religion) lib bdg $28.70; pa $21.20

Grades: 7 8 9 10 11 12   **305.9**

1. United States—Religion 2. Discrimination

ISBN 978-0-7377-3399-0 (lib bdg); 0-7377-3399-3 (lib bdg); 978-0-7377-3400-3 (pa); 0-7377-3400-0 (pa)

                  LC 2006-38935

Topics covered in this anthology "include discrimination against Muslims, Jews, Christians, and Hare Krishnas; religious expression in the U.S. military and in schools; homosexuality in the Episcopal Church; and more. . . . Many high-school readers will want this for personal-interest reading as well as classroom debate." Booklist

Includes bibliographical references

Martínez, Rubén

The new Americans; photographs by Joseph Rodríguez. New Press 2004 251p il $25

Grades: 11 12 Adult   **305.9**

1. United States—Immigration and emigration

ISBN 1-565-84792-X   LC 2003-70621

"This book, a companion to a PBS miniseries, details the lives of seven families who have recently arrived in the United States from the West Bank, Nigeria, the Dominican Republic, Mexico, and India." Libr J

"Masterfully evoking such diverse settings as a Palestinian wedding in Chicago, a raucous ball game in Guatemala City and a torpid migrant trailer camp in California, Martínez's writing is clear-eyed and incisive—and sometimes heartbreaking and hilarious." Publ Wkly

Includes bibliographical references

Moorehead, Caroline

Human cargo; a journey among refugees. H. Holt 2005 330p maps $26; pa $16

Grades: 11 12 Adult   **305.9**

1. Refugees

ISBN 0-8050-7443-0; 0-312-42561-9 (pa)

                  LC 2004-54239

The author "tours a number of refugee milieus, visiting, among others, Liberian refugees in Cairo, Mexican migrants waiting to cross into the United States, Mideastern refugees detained in Australian internment camps and Palestinian refugees still nursing hopes of returning to a homeland they have never seen. . . . Moorehead draws

Moorehead, Caroline—*Continued*

sympathetic portraits of individual refugees, replete with horror stories of the travails they fled and their precarious but hopeful efforts to build new lives, but also pulls back to examine what she says are the sometimes counterproductive policies of aid organizations and the indifference and callousness of Western governments." Publ Wkly

Includes bibliographical references

306   Culture and institutions

American values: opposing viewpoints; David M. Haugen, book editor. Greenhaven Press 2009 227p il lib bdg $39.70; pa $27.50 *

Grades: 9 10 11 12   306

1. Social values 2. United States—Moral conditions
ISBN 978-0-7377-4190-2 (lib bdg); 0-7377-4190-2 (lib bdg); 978-0-7377-4191-9 (pa); 0-7377-4191-0 (pa)
                                             LC 2008-31771

"Opposing viewpoints series"

Articles in this anthology discuss what social values America considers important, whether or not they are threatened, the nature of patriotism, and whether American values can be shared with other nations.

Includes bibliographical references

Fischer, Claude S., 1948-

Century of difference; how American changed in the last one hundred years; [by] Claude S. Fischer and Michael Hout. Russell Sage Foundation 2006 411p il map $45

Grades: 11 12 Adult   306

1. American national characteristics 2. Social change 3. United States—History—20th century 4. United States—Social conditions
ISBN 0-8715-4352-4; 978-0-8715-4352-3
                                             LC 2006-21640

"Differences in American family life, work, and worship between the years of 1900 and 2000 are compared and examined in concise details. While the included statistics and graphs are plentiful and easy to use, most value is provided in the extensive commentary that breaths life into the data comparisons." Univ Press Books for Public and Second Sch Libr, 2007

Includes bibliographical references

Hill, Jeff, 1962-

Life events and rites of passage; the customs and symbols of major life-cycle milestones, including cultural, secular, and religious traditions observed in the United States; by Jeff Hill and Peggy Daniels; foreword by Clifton D. Bryant. Omnigraphics 2008 498p il lib bdg $71 *

Grades: 8 9 10 11 12   306

1. Rites and ceremonies 2. United States—Social life and customs
ISBN 978-0-7808-0735-8   LC 2007-35420

"Provides information about the history, symbols, customs, and traditions of important life-cycle events within the broad range of cultural and religious groups in the United States. Entries are arranged in sections on birth and childhood, coming of age, adulthood, and death and mourning." Publisher's note

"This book provides a good starting point for those needing basic information, especially since it approaches topics from a wide variety of cultural viewpoints." Libr J

Includes bibliographical references

Johnson, Steven

Everything bad is good for you; how today's pop culture is actually making us smarter. Riverhead Books 2005 238p il $23.95; pa $14

Grades: 11 12 Adult   306

1. Popular culture 2. Intellect
ISBN 1-57322-307-7; 1-59448-194-6 (pa)
                                             LC 2005-42769

The author "makes the case that popular culture has become more intellectually challenging in the past 30 years. . . . He suggests that increases in IQ scores in the past century could be related to more challenging entertainment." Christ Sci Monit

This "is a brisk, witty read, well versed in the history of literature and bolstered with research." Time

Includes bibliographical references

Popular culture: opposing viewpoints; David Haugen and Susan Musser, book editors. Greenhaven Press 2011 188p $39.70; pa $27.50 *

Grades: 9 10 11 12   306

1. Popular culture
ISBN 978-0-7377-4980-9; 978-0-7377-4981-6 (pa)
                                             LC 2010014754

"Opposing viewpoints series"

"Explores the value of popular culture, asking: Can it make people smarter? Is blogging journalism? Does reality TV have merit? Is Twitter a catalyst for change? Looks at the relationship between the internet and pop culture; the effect on society of the violence prevalent in pop culture; and the impact of America's pop culture on other parts of the world." Publisher's note

Includes bibliographical references

Social history of the United States; [by] Brian Greenberg . . . [et al.] ABC-CLIO 2009 10v il set $995

Grades: 9 10 11 12 Adult   306

1. United States—Social conditions 2. United States—Economic conditions—20th century 3. United States—Politics and government—20th century 4. Reference books
ISBN 978-1-59884-127-5   LC 2008-21619

This "set discusses the social history of the United States from the 1900s to the 1990s through such themes as Work and the Workplace, Radicalism and Reform, Popular Culture, Sex and Gender, and Religion. . . . Each volume discusses the major issues of its decade, such as Race and Jim Crow, World War I, Communism and American Society, and Immigration and American Life." Libr Media Connect

"This compendium provides a fascinating and informative perspective on topics often overlooked in traditional histories, making it an outstanding choice." SLJ

Includes bibliographical references

Underhill, Paco

The call of the mall; a walking tour through the crossroads of our shopping culture. Simon & Schuster 2004 227p hardcover o.p. pa $14

Grades: 11 12 Adult **306**

1. Shopping centers and malls 2. Consumption (Economics) 3. Consumers

ISBN 0-7432-3591-6; 0-7432-3592-4 (pa)

LC 2003-64960

The author takes readers on a "tour of a typical Saturday at a large, regional mall. He examines the routes there, the shopping center itself, the stores, food, entertainment, ambience. and the customers. He shows why the mall is the way it is and how it could be improved. He provides insight into how the stores are arranged, how they display merchandise. and the different ways that men and women respond to this environment." SLJ

Worldmark encyclopedia of cultures and daily life; editors, Timothy L. Gall and Janeen Hobby. 2nd ed. Gale 2009 5v il map set $551

Grades: 11 12 Adult **306**

1. Ethnology—Encyclopedias 2. Manners and customs—Encyclopedias 3. Reference books

ISBN 978-1-4144-4882-4   LC 2009-4744

First published 1997

This encyclopedia "covers more than 500 cultures from around the world. . . . The five volumes covering four geographical areas—Africa, Americas, Asia and Oceania, and Europe—are arranged alphabetically by country with information about the various cultures and communities that exist within their borders. . . . Each article begins with a block containing key country facts: location, population, language, religion, related articles, and pronunciation assistance. . . . A well-organized, easy-to-use research tool." SLJ

Includes bibliographical references

306.4   Specific aspects of culture

Are athletes good role models? Kathy L. Hahn, book editor. Greenhaven Press 2010 122p (At issue. Sports) lib bdg $31.80; pa $22.50 *

Grades: 9 10 11 12 **306.4**

1. Athletes 2. Conduct of life

ISBN 978-0-7377-4646-4 (lib bdg); 0-7377-4646-7 (lib bdg); 978-0-7377-4647-1 (pa); 0-7377-4647-5 (pa)

LC 2009-37394

The articles in this anthology weigh the merits and demerits of using athletes as role models.

Includes bibliographical references

Body image; Heidi Williams, book editor. Greenhaven Press 2009 112p il (Issues that concern you) lib bdg $33.70

Grades: 9 10 11 12 **306.4**

1. Body image

ISBN 978-0-7377-4182-7; 0-7377-4182-1

LC 2008-26756

This book about body image has an "accessible text and a clear layout. . . . Colorful charts and graphs, color photos with informative captions, and a list of sources to contact add to . . . [its] research value." SLJ

Includes bibliographical references

The **culture** of beauty: opposing viewpoints; Roman Espejo, book editor. Greenhaven Press 2009 c2010 220p il lib bdg $38.50; pa $26.75 *

Grades: 8 9 10 11 12 **306.4**

1. Personal appearance 2. Aesthetics

ISBN 978-0-7377-4508-5 (lib bdg); 0-7377-4508-8 (lib bdg); 978-0-7377-4509-2 (pa); 0-7377-4509-6 (pa)

LC 2009-33675

"Opposing viewpoints series"

Examines both sides of the issues surrounding the obsession with image, from beauty standards to societal impact and from individual aspirations of beauty to effects of the beauty and fashion industries.

Includes bibliographical references

Rap music and culture; Kate Burns, book editor. Greenhaven Press 2008 192p (Current controversies) lib bdg $37.40; pa $25.95

Grades: 9 10 11 12 **306.4**

1. Hip-hop 2. Rap music

ISBN 978-0-7377-3964-0 (lib bdg); 0-7377-3964-9 (lib bdg); 978-0-7377-3965-7 (pa); 0-7377-3965-7 (pa)

LC 2008-17919

"Presents articles both supporting and opposing issues involving rap music and culture, including if it is a significant American cultural movement, if it is a positive medium for young people, and if it perpetuates violence." Publisher's note

"This is a well-organized, thoughtful examination of hip-hop culture in its many permutations." SLJ

Includes bibliographical references

306.7   Sexual relations

Age of consent; Olivia Ferguson and Hayley Mitchell Haugen, book editors. Greenhaven Press 2010 93p (At issue. Teen issues) $31.80; pa $22.50

Grades: 9 10 11 12 **306.7**

1. Youth—Law and legislation 2. Youth—Sexual behavior

ISBN 978-0-7377-4669-3; 0-7377-4669-6; 978-0-7377-4670-9 (pa); 0-7377-4670-X (pa)

LC 2009-40551

"These 13 articles, ranging in length from four to seven pages, tackle the murky moral issue of legislating the age of first consensual sexual experiences. The authors address establishing uniform age-of-consent laws, the dilemma of teaching students about safe sex and then prosecuting them for sexual activity, what to do about sexting, applying a lifelong sex-offender label to a teen, and parental notification of a minor seeking an abortion; and examine sources of pressure for reform. . . . These well-written entries provide solid report information, and the book should be considered for purchase where the curriculum requires material on early sexual circumstances in relation to the law." SLJ

Includes bibliographical references

Burningham, Sarah O'Leary
Boyology; a teen girl's crash course in all things boy; illustrations by Keri Smith. Chronicle Books 2009 167p il pa $12.99
Grades: 6 7 8 9 10 **306.7**
1. Boys—Psychology 2. Interpersonal relations 3. Dating (Social customs)
ISBN 978-0-8118-6436-7; 0-8118-6436-7
LC 2008-5277
"Adolescent girls seeking a deeper understanding of the opposite sex will appreciate this appealing, entertaining guide full of useful facts and sound advice. Burningham . . . explores a wide range of subjects, including how to determine which 'breed' of boy you're dealing with, first dates and the rules of the dating game, setting boundaries, peer conflicts and pressures, dealing with parents, the difference between having a boyfriend and boy friends and coping with the inevitable breakup." Kirkus

Feinstein, Stephen
Sexuality and teens; what you should know about sex, abstinence, birth control, pregnancy, and stds. Enslow Publishers 2010 104p il (Issues in focus today) lib bdg $31.93
Grades: 7 8 9 10 **306.7**
1. Youth—Sexual behavior
ISBN 978-0-7660-3312-2; 0-7660-3312-0
LC 2009-1373
"Discusses sexuality and teens, including teen sex, abstinence, birth control, teen pregnancy, sexually transmitted diseases, and sex education in schools." Publisher's note
"This text provides a well-balanced look at sexual attitudes and behaviors as they relate to today's youth. . . . The book could be useful for basic report and debate information or as a jumping-off point for class discussions." SLJ
Includes glossary and bibliographical references

Forssberg, Manne, 1983-
Sex for guys; translated by Maria Lundin. Groundwood Books/House of Anansi 2007 142p il (Groundwork guides) $15.95; pa $9.95 *
Grades: 7 8 9 10 11 12 **306.7**
1. Sex education 2. Men—Sexual behavior
ISBN 978-0-88899-770-8; 978-0-88899-771-5 (pa)
"Originally published in Sweden, this first person approach speaks directly to a primarily male audience. In a straightforward manner, the author tackles a broad range of sensitive topics such as male and female anatomy, masturbation, orgasm, intercourse, oral and gay sex, sexually transmitted diseases, pornography, and relationships. Facts, opinions, and testimonials by the author and other young adults are . . . presented." Libr Media Connect
This "will prove invaluable to guys bombarded with less sensitive and comprehensive media messages. . . . This is a witty, sane treatment of the things that drive guys crazy—a must read for teens with questions." Bull Cent Child Books
Includes bibliographical references

Sex: opposing viewpoints. Greenhaven Press 2006 208p il lib bdg $34.95; pa $23.70
Grades: 7 8 9 10 **306.7**
1. Sexual behavior
ISBN 0-7377-2959-7 (lib bdg); 0-7377-2960-0 (pa)
LC 2005-52578
"Opposing viewpoints series"
"Authors debate several issues such as premarital sex, gay marriage, and virginity pledges in this . . . anthology." Publisher's note
Includes bibliographical references

Teen sex; Olivia Ferguson, book editor. Greenhaven Press 2010 105p (At issue. Teen issues) $31.80; pa $22.50 *
Grades: 9 10 11 12 **306.7**
1. Youth—Sexual behavior 2. Sexual abstinence 3. Sex education
ISBN 978-0-7377-5095-9; 978-0-7377-5096-6 (pa)
LC 2010022997
The articles in this anthology discuss such topics as abstinence-only education, sex education, how teens view oral sex, and abortion among teens.
Includes bibliographical references

The **truth** about sexual behavior and unplanned pregnancy; Robert N. Golden, general editor, Fred Peterson, general editor; Elissa Howard-Barr and Stacey Barrineau, principal authors. 2nd ed. Facts On File 2009 224p (Truth about series) $35
Grades: 9 10 11 12 **306.7**
1. Sexual behavior 2. Teenage pregnancy 3. Sexual hygiene
ISBN 978-0-8160-7634-5; 0-8160-7634-0
LC 2009-8403
First published 2005 under the editorship of Mark J. Kittleson
Provides "information about everything from contraception to the media's portrayal of sex. . . . [This book offers] advice to teenagers and encourages discussion with parents and peers." Publisher's note
Includes glossary and bibliographical references

Turner, Jeffrey S.
Dating and sexuality in America; a reference handbook. ABC-CLIO 2003 300p (Contemporary world issues) $45 *
Grades: 9 10 11 12 **306.7**
1. Dating (Social customs) 2. Sexual behavior
ISBN 1-85109-584-5
This "preliminary overview of dating and sexuality in the United States includes a history, the standard issues (teenage pregnancy, birth control, sexually transmitted diseases) and contemporary concerns such as Internet dating and club drugs. Dating customs and attitudes toward sexuality in other countries are also explored. . . . Turner does a fine job of presenting the issues in an unbiased, concise, and readable style, avoiding the moralistic overtones found in some works on this topic for this age group." Libr Media Connect
Includes bibliographical references

306.76   Sexual orientation

Alsenas, Linas
Gay America; struggle for equality. Amulet
Books 2008 160p il $24.95
Grades: 7 8 9 10   **306.76**
1. Gay men—Civil rights 2. Lesbians—Civil rights
3. Gay liberation movement 4. Homosexuality
ISBN 978-0-8109-9487-4; 0-8109-9487-9
LC 2007-28066
"This eminently readable work highlights the history
of gays and lesbians in the U.S. Beginning with the Victorian period and following with five more chapters covering the 20th and 21st centuries through 2006. . . . A
good index, excellent notes, and a selected bibliography
of resources, into which the author encourages readers to
'dig deeper,' only increase the usefulness of Gay America." SLJ

Encyclopedia of lesbian, gay, bisexual, and
transgender history in America; Marc Stein,
editor in chief. Thomson Learning 2003 3v set
$380
Grades: 11 12 Adult   **306.76**
1. Homosexuality—United States—History—Encyclopedias 2. Reference books
ISBN 0-684-31261-1   LC 2003-17434
This set "includes approximately 545 articles ranging
from short biographical entries to longer essays surveying topics such as the Stonewall riots, federal law and
policy, same-sex institutions and AIDS. . . . Features include a guide to archival sources, a chronology/timeline,
a historical overview essay and a comprehensive index."
Publisher's note
"Stein puts together an impressive set. . . . This information is available elsewhere, but this resource gathers
it in one easy-to-use source." Voice Youth Advocates
Includes bibliographical references

The **Full** spectrum; a new generation of writing
about gay, lesbian, bisexual, transgender,
questioning, and other identities; edited by
David Levithan & Billy Merrell. Knopf 2006
272p il hardcover o.p. pa $9.95 *
Grades: 8 9 10 11 12   **306.76**
1. Gay men 2. Lesbians 3. Sex role 4. Homosexuality
ISBN 0-375-93290-9; 0-375-83290-4 (pa)
LC 2005-23435
"The 40 contributions to this invaluable collection
about personal identity have two things in common: all
are nonfiction and all are by writers under the age of 23.
Beyond that, diversity is the order of the day, and the result is a vivid demonstration of how extraordinarily
broad the spectrum of sexual identity is among today's
gay, lesbian, bisexual, transgender, and questioning
youth. . . . Insightful, extraordinarily well written, and
emotionally mature, the selections offer compelling, dramatic evidence that what is important is not *what* we are
but *who* we are." Booklist

Gay and lesbian rights in the United States; a
documentary history; edited by Walter L.
Williams and Yolanda Retter. Greenwood Press
2003 317p (Primary documents in American
history and contemporary issues) $49.95 *
Grades: 9 10 11 12   **306.76**
1. Gay men—Civil rights 2. Gay liberation movement
3. Homosexuality
ISBN 0-313-30696-6   LC 2002-35218
"This collection of primary documents . . . [provides]
varying viewpoints on the complex issue of gay and lesbian rights. Personal testimonies, laws, opinion pieces,
court cases, and other documents, dating from colonial
times to the present day [are examined]." Publisher's
note
This volume "is fascinating to anyone interested in or
researching GLBT history. The documents clearly show
the evolution of thought on issues of homosexuality."
Voice Youth Advocates
Includes bibliographical references

Hear me out: true stories of Teens Educating and
Confronting Homophobia; a project of Planned
Parenthood of Toronto; [edited by Frances
Rooney] Second Story Press 2004 197p il pa
$9.95 *
Grades: 8 9 10 11 12   **306.76**
1. Homosexuality 2. Transsexualism 3. Bisexuality
ISBN 1-896764-87-8
"A project of Planned Parenthood of Toronto, this collection of personal accounts of sexual self-discovery by
volunteers in the organization's peer-based T.E.A.C.H.
program (Teens Educating and Confronting Homophobia)
is remarkable for the diversity of social, economic, ethnic, and racial backgrounds represented. The 20 stories
included demonstrate the wide spectrum of gay, lesbian,
queer, transgender, transsexual, and questioning young-
adult experiences. . . . An important and emotionally
powerful collection that is sure to encourage thought and
discussion." Booklist

Homosexuality: opposing viewpoints; Cynthia A.
Bily, book editor. Greenhaven Press 2009 242p
il lib bdg $37.40; pa $25.95 *
Grades: 7 8 9 10 11 12   **306.76**
1. Homosexuality
ISBN   978-0-7377-4214-5   (lib   bdg);
978-0-7377-4215-2 (pa)   LC 2008-24132
"Opposing viewpoints series"
This anthology "presents arguments about the causes
of same-sex preference before delving into some of . . .
today's headlining issues." Booklist
Includes bibliographical references

Huegel, Kelly
GLBTQ; the survival guide for gay, lesbian,
bisexual, transgender, and questioning teens. rev &
updated 2nd ed. Free Spirit Pub. 2011 229p il pa
$15.99 *
Grades: 7 8 9 10 11 12   **306.76**
1. Homosexuality 2. Lesbianism 3. Transsexualism
4. Bisexuality
ISBN 978-1-57542-363-0; 1-57542-363-0
LC 2010-48196

Huegel, Kelly—*Continued*
First published 2003
Describes the challenges faced by gay, lesbian, bisexual, and transgendered teens, offers practical advice, real-life experiences, and accessible resources and support groups.
"The information . . . [this] provides for GLBTQ teens makes it a valuable addition to any high school or public library collection." Voice Youth Advcocates
Includes bibliographical references

Kranz, Rachel
Gay rights; [by] Rachel Kranz, Tim Cusick. Rev ed. Facts on File 2005 362p (Library in a book) $45
Grades: 9 10 11 12   **306.76**
1. Gay men—Civil rights 2. Homosexuality
ISBN 0-8160-5810-5   LC 2005-9832
First published 2000
This is an "overview of gay rights in America. In three sections, the text presents a topical overview, further research, and appendixes." Libr J [review of 2000 edition]
Includes bibliographical references

Marcus, Eric
What if someone I know is gay? answers to questions about what it means to be gay and lesbian. Rev. and updated, 1st Simon Pulse ed. Simon & Schuster 2007 183p pa $8.99 *
Grades: 7 8 9 10 11 12   **306.76**
1. Homosexuality
ISBN 1-4169-4970-4; 978-1-4169-4970-1
First published 2000 by Price/Stern/Sloan
Contents: Basic stuff; Friends and family; Dating, marriage, and kids; Sex; God and religion; School; Parades, activism, and discrimination; For parents
"The content . . . stands strong, and readers will appreciate Marcus's gentle tone and the careful candor that he uses to describe the sometimes-rocky LGB experience. Helpful information about gay-straight alliances and marriage and partnership issues are all addressed." SLJ
Includes bibliographical references

Wright, Kai
Drifting toward love; black, brown, gay, and coming of age on the streets of New York. Beacon Press 2008 224p $24.95
Grades: 11 12 Adult   **306.76**
1. African American gay men 2. Hispanic American gay men 3. New York (N.Y.)
ISBN 978-0-8070-7968-3; 0-8070-7968-5
LC 2007-15759
The author "explores the lives of three young gay men of color. He focuses on their experiences, their friends and families, and their activities as he details their journeys in trying to belong. " Libr J
"An important book about an often-marginalized group." Kirkus

306.8 Marriage and family

Andryszewski, Tricia, 1956-
Same-sex marriage; moral wrong or civil right? Twenty-First Century Books 2008 144p il lib bdg $38.60 *
Grades: 7 8 9 10 11 12   **306.8**
1. Same-sex marriage 2. Gay couples—Legal status, laws, etc.
ISBN 978-0-8225-7176-6; 0-8225-7176-5
LC 2007-10397
This examines the legal and moral issues surrounding same-sex marriage.
This is a "very detailed, in depth overview. . . . The book's design is sure to draw curious browsers, as well as passionately engaged researchers." Booklist
Includes bibliographical references

Daycare and diplomas; essays by teen mothers who stayed in school; by the students at South Vista Educational Center. Fairview Press 2000 89p il pa $9.95 *
Grades: 9 10 11 12   **306.8**
1. South Vista Education Center (Richfield, Minn.)
2. Teenage mothers
ISBN 1-57749-098-3   LC 00-37620
In this work 36 teen mothers share their experiences and views on pregnancy, parenting and staying in school

Fakhrid-Deen, Tina, 1973-
Let's get this straight; the ultimate handbook for youth with LGBTQ parents; [by] Tina Fakhrid-Deen with COLAGE. Seal Press 2010 203p il $15.95 *
Grades: 7 8 9 10   **306.8**
1. Children of gay parents 2. Parent-child relationship
ISBN 978-1-58005-333-4; 1-58005-333-5
LC 2010-1775
"This book is written for youth with a parent(s) that is lesbian, gay, bisexual, transgender, or questioning. Its purpose is informational, as well as introspective and affirming. . . . There are seven chapters focusing on a range of topics, from family dynamics, school, and social issues to religion and activism. . . . Quizzes add to the interactive feel. Youth and adults who were interviewed by the author share their experiences in their own words in a section called 'Our Voices.' These quotations, as well as original poetry, add to the feeling of community." Voice Youth Advocates
Includes glossary and bibliographical references

Gay and lesbian families; Roman Espejo, book editor. Greenhaven Press 2009 105p (At issue. Social issues) $31.80; pa $22.50 *
Grades: 9 10 11 12   **306.8**
1. Same-sex marriage 2. Gay couples 3. Gay parents
ISBN   978-0-7377-4302-9;   0-7377-4302-6;
978-0-7377-4301-2 (pa); 0-7377-4301-8 (pa)
LC 2009004708
Articles in this anthology discuss gay marriage, gay adoption and parenting, and their possible effects on society.
Includes bibliographical references

Gay marriage; Lauri S. Friedman, book editor. Greenhaven Press/Gale Cengage Learning 2010 142p il map (Introducing issues with opposing viewpoints) lib bdg $35.75 *

Grades: 9 10 11 12   **306.8**

1. Same-sex marriage

ISBN 978-0-7377-4734-8; 0-7377-4734-X

LC 2009-052339

First published 2006

Articles in this anthology discuss whether gay marriage should be legalized and the possible effects same-sex marriage could have on society.

Includes bibliographical references

Haskins-Bookser, Laura, 1972-

Dreams to reality; help for young moms: education, career, and life choices; illustrated by Jami Moffett. Morning Glory Press 2006 174p il $21.95; pa $14.95

Grades: 7 8 9 10   **306.8**

1. Teenage mothers 2. Single parent family

ISBN 978-1-932538-37-3; 978-1-932538-36-6 (pa)

LC 2005-58090

The author "bases her book on her own experience as a teenage mother who struggled through poverty and the responsibilities of parenting and eventually went to college. In an empathetic voice, she offers practical advice to young mothers regarding how to budget money and set and attain goals, where to get financial assistance, and how to leave an abusive situation." Libr J

"The book reads easily, making it palatable for busy teen mothers struggling to get through the basics of education, but it covers a lot of important ground and it is highly recommended for school and public libraries." Voice Youth Advocates

Includes bibliographical references

Teenage pregnancy and parenting; Lisa Frick, book editor. Greenhaven Press 2007 215p il (Current controversies) lib bdg $34.95; pa $23.70 *

Grades: 10 11 12   **306.8**

1. Teenage pregnancy 2. Teenage parents 3. Sex education

ISBN 0-7377-3295-4 (lib bdg); 978-0-7377-3295-5 (lib bdg); 0-7377-3296-2 (pa); 978-0-7377-3296-2 (pa)

LC 2006-20089

"This book tackles, in familiar pro/con format, such dilemmas as whether teen pregnancy is really a serious problem, what factors contribute to it, the effectiveness of sex-education programs, adoption and abortion, and whether or not society should view teen parenting in a positive light. Researchers will find the differing views invaluable, allowing them to see both sides of an issue." SLJ

Includes bibliographical references

The **truth** about family life; Robert N. Golden, general editor; Fred L. Peterson, general editor; Mark J. Kittleson, William Kane and Richelle Rennegarbe, advisers to the first edition; Amber Barnes and Julia Watkins, principal authors. 2nd ed. Facts On File 2011 240p (Truth about series) $35 *

Grades: 9 10 11 12   **306.8**

1. Family—United States

ISBN 978-0-8160-7641-3; 0-8160-7641-3

LC 2010-49240

First published 2005 under the authorship of Renée Despres

This book provides "information on family types, their history and role in society, and how to cope with the basic issues that confront families of all kinds." Publisher's note

Includes bibliographical references

Winchester, Elizabeth, 1973-

Sisters and brothers; the ultimate guide to understanding your siblings and yourself; [by] Elizabeth Siris Winchester. Franklin Watts 2008 112p il (Scholastic choices) lib bdg $27; pa $8.95

Grades: 6 7 8 9 10   **306.8**

1. Siblings 2. Family

ISBN 978-0-531-13870-0 (lib bdg); 0-531-13870-4 (lib bdg); 978-0-531-20528-0 (pa); 0-531-20528-2 (pa)

LC 2007-51871

Real-life stories from teenagers about interacting with siblings, whether blood, adopted, foster, or step.

"Colorful and compact, with [an] attractive cover [and] . . . excellent black-and-white photographs of a diverse array of teens." SLJ

Includes glossary and bibliographical references

Worth, Richard, 1945-

Frequently asked questions about teen fatherhood. Rosen Pub. 2010 64p il (FAQ: teen life) lib bdg $29.25 *

Grades: 7 8 9 10   **306.8**

1. Teenage fathers

ISBN 978-1-4358-5325-6; 1-4358-5325-3

LC 2008-51938

"While conversational, [this volume is] surprisingly helpful—even emotive. . . . [This book greets] its intended audience with encouragement and aplomb. Dealing with feelings of disbelief and blame quickly segue into preparing for a birth, staying in school, and considering part-time jobs. Adoption and abortion are given only brief mentions." Booklist

Includes glossary and bibliographical references

306.89   Separation and divorce

The **truth** about divorce; Mark J. Kittleson, general editor; William Kane, advisor; Richelle Rennegarbe, advisor; Barry Youngerman, principal author. Facts on File 2005 180p il (Truth about series) $35 *

Grades: 8 9 10 11 12   **306.89**

1. Divorce 2. Marriage

ISBN 0-8160-5304-9   LC 2004-10236

The truth about divorce—*Continued*

Contents: Child support, spousal support; Children, psychological effects of divorce on; Communication and compromise in divorced families; Custody and visitation; Divorce, adjusting to the realities of; Divorce alternatives; Divorce in America; Divorce, the business side of; Divorce, the legal process of; Divorce, the psychological cost for spouses; Families, blended; Finances and divorce; Generational patterns and adult children of divorce; Help for troubled marriages; Love and marriage; Marriage lifestyles, alternative; Media and divorce; Racially and culturally mixed marriages; Relationship after divorce, parents'; Relationship failure; Relationships, types of; Religion and divorce; Stress factors in marriage, external; Hotlines and helpsites

Includes glossary and bibliographical references

306.9   Institutions pertaining to death

Macmillan encyclopedia of death and dying; Robert Kastenbaum, editor in chief. Macmillan Ref. USA 2002 c2003 2v set $250

Grades: 11 12 Adult   **306.9**
1. Reference books 2. Death—Encyclopedias
ISBN 0-02-865689-X   LC 2002-5809

"The 327 signed entries . . . range in length from a few paragraphs to several pages. . . . Types of entries include causes of death . . . practices surrounding death . . . individuals and events that have influenced the way we think about death . . . and entries on the nature or meaning of death from various multidisciplinary and multicultural perspectives. . . . An appendix profiles and gives contact information for 75 organizations active in death-related education, research, advocacy, or other areas." Booklist

Noyes, Deborah, 1965-

Encyclopedia of the end; mysterious death in fact, fancy, folklore, and more. Houghton Mifflin Co. 2008 143p il $25

Grades: 7 8 9 10 11 12   **306.9**
1. Reference books 2. Death 3. Funeral rites and ceremonies
ISBN 978-0-618-82362-8; 0-618-82362-X
                                      LC 2008-1872

"This stylish A-to-Z encounter with all things related to death and dying shows Noyes . . . at her liveliest. . . . The author offers a broad illumination of spiritual, historical and biological aspects of death. Photos, paintings and engravings in homage to 'the end' make the book dynamic visually, too." Publ Wkly

307.7   Specific kinds of communities

Lorinc, John, 1963-

Cities. Groundwood Books/House of Anansi Press 2008 144p (Groundwork guides) $18.95; pa $10

Grades: 7 8 9 10 11 12   **307.7**

1. Cities and towns 2. Urbanization
ISBN   978-0-88899-820-0;   0-88899-820-1;
978-0-88899-819-4 (pa); 0-88899-819-8 (pa)

"This packed, highly readable [title] . . . does an excellent job of tracing urban history worldwide, raising the big social, political, and economic issues of poverty, migration, conservation, public health, crime, transportation, and much more, always rooted in specific examples of the problems and riches of city life." Booklist

Includes bibliographical references

310.5   General statistics—Serial publications

The **statesman's** yearbook 2011; the politics, cultures and economies of the world; edited by Barry Turner. 147th ed. Palgrave Macmillan 2010 xxxi, 1573p il map $285 *

Grades: 8 9 10 11 12 Adult   **310.5**
1. Statistics 2. Political science 3. Reference books
ISBN 978-0-230-20603-8

Also available online

Annual. First published 1864

"Descriptive and statistical information about international organizations and countries of the world-brief history, area, political status, economy, etc." N Y Public Libr. Ref Books for Child Collect. 2d edition

Includes bibliographical references

317.1   General statistics of Canada

Canadian almanac & directory 2011 = répertoire et almanach canadien 2011. 164th ed. Grey House Publishing Canada 2010 various paging il map $350

Grades: 11 12 Adult   **317.1**
1. Canada—Directories 2. Almanacs 3. Reference books
ISSN 0068-8193
ISBN 978-1-59237-589-9

Also available online

Annual. First published 1847. Publisher varies

"Contains reliable legal, commercial, governmental, statistical, astronomical, departmental, ecclesiastical, financial, educational, and general information." Guide to Ref Books. 11th edition

317.3   General statistics of the United States

Historical statistics of the United States; earliest times to the present; [by] Susan B. Carter . . . [et al.] Millennial ed. Cambridge University Press 2006 5v il set $990 *

Grades: 11 12 Adult   **317.3**
1. United States—Statistics 2. Reference books
ISBN 0-521-81791-9; 978-0-521-81791-2
                                      LC 2005-27089

Also available online

First published 1949 by U.S. Govt. Print. Off. with title: Historical statistics of the United States, 1789-1945

Historical statistics of the United States—*Continued*

"Each of the 39 chapters begins with an essay on the 'quantitative history' of the topic and comments on the reliability of the data and possible limits to interpretation. Included are approximately 1900 tables and 170 maps, graphs, and time lines; the text is fully cross-referenced and indexed. . . . A bargain for all libraries supporting research." Libr J

Includes bibliographical references

United States. Bureau of the Census

Statistical abstract of the United States, 2011; [by the] U.S. Dept. of Commerce, Economics and Statistics Administration, U.S. Census Bureau. 130th ed. U.S. Census Bureau 2010 1010p il map $43; pa $39 *

Grades: 8 9 10 11 12 Adult   **317.3**
1. United States—Statistics 2. Reference books
ISBN 978-0-16-086682-1; 978-0-16-086681-4 (pa)
Also available online
Annual. First published for the year 1878
"Compendium of statistics on the social, political and economic organization of the U.S. presented in tables. Lists other sources of such information." N Y Public Libr. Ref Books for Child Collect. 2d edition

320   Political science

Machiavelli, Niccolò, 1469-1527

The prince. Knopf 1992 xxxi, 190p (Everyman's library) $16 *

Grades: 11 12 Adult   **320**
1. Political science 2. Political ethics
ISBN 0-679-41044-9   LC 91-53225
Also available from the University of Chicago Press and in paperback from Penguin Bks.
Written in 1513
"A handbook of advice on the acquisition, use, and maintenance of political power, dedicated to Lorenzo de Medici." Haydn. Thesaurus of Book Dig

Paine, Thomas, 1737-1809

Collected writings. Library of Am. 1995 906p $35

Grades: 11 12 Adult   **320**
1. Political science
ISBN 1-883011-03-5   LC 94-25756
Contents: Common sense; The crisis and other pamphlets, articles and letters; Rights of man; The age of reason
Includes bibliographical references

320.1   The state

Social contract; essays by Locke, Hume, and Rousseau; with an introduction by Sir Ernest Barker. Oxford Univ. Press 1980 xliv, 307p pa $22.95

Grades: 11 12 Adult   **320.1**

1. Political science 2. State, The
ISBN 0-19-500309-8
First published 1947 in the United Kingdom; 1948 in the United States
Contents: An essay concerning the true original, extent and end of civil government, by J. Locke; Of the original contract, by D. Hume; The social contract, by J. Rousseau
This book contains three major essays dealing with the social contract theory of government, first published 1690, 1748 and 1762 respectively. The introduction by Sir Ernest Barker discusses the history and transformations of the theory before focusing on the ideas of the three authors

320.3   Comparative government

Governments of the world; a global guide to citizens' rights and responsibilities; C. Neal Tate, editor-in-chief. Macmillan Reference USA 2006 4v il map set $395 *

Grades: 11 12 Adult   **320.3**
1. Reference books 2. Comparative government—Encyclopedias
ISBN 0-02-865811-6   LC 2005-10436
"In these volumes, 310 alphabetically arranged articles range in length from 500 to 3,500 words and cover 198 regions ('including every independent nation and several territories') as well as international courts, supranational institutions, concepts central to understanding political organization and human rights, and key individuals who have had positive and negative impacts on the evolution of citizens' rights and responsibilities." Booklist
Includes bibliographical references

320.4   Structure and functions of government

Genovese, Michael A.

Encyclopedia of American government and civics; [by] Michael A. Genovese and Lori Cox Han. Facts On File, Inc. 2008 3v il (Facts on File library of American history) set $250

Grades: 11 12 Adult   **320.4**
1. Reference books 2. United States—Politics and government—Encyclopedias 3. Political science—Encyclopedias
ISBN 978-0-8160-6616-2; 0-8160-6616-7
     LC 2007-43813
"This three-volume set contains more than four hundred essay-length articles intended to provide basic information about the United States government and how it operates as well as insight into how its citizens participate within the political, electoral, and policymaking process. . . . The encyclopedia provides an excellent starting point for students who are researching questions about American government." Voice Youth Advocates
Includes bibliographical references

Starks, Glenn L., 1966-

How your government really works; a topical encyclopedia of the federal government; [by] Glenn L. Starks and F. Erik Brooks. Greenwood Press 2008 334p il $75

Grades: 9 10 11 12 Adult **320.4**
   1. United States—Politics and government—Encyclopedias 2. Reference books
   ISBN 978-0-313-34761-0   LC 2008-24134

The authors' aim is to "bridge the gap between the government's ideal, balanced structure, laid out in the Constitution, and its actual institutionalized form today. . . . Coverage of the government's inner workings includes such subjects as executive-branch appointments, domestic and foreign policy development and execution, the federal budget, the legislative process, the Congressional committee system, the drawing of Congressional districts, the levels of the federal judiciary, aides in all three branches, and the various government offices and oversight agencies." Publisher's note

Includes bibliographical references

320.5   Political ideologies

Calvert, John

Islamism: a documentary and reference guide. Greenwood Press 2007 280p il $85

Grades: 10 11 12 **320.5**
   1. Islamic fundamentalism 2. Islam and politics 3. Reference books
   ISBN 978-0-313-33856-4   LC 2007-26092

"Among the key writers represented in . . . [this] work are Sayyid Qutb, Ayatollah Khomeini, Mahmud Ahmadinejad, Usama bin Laden, Ayman al-Zawahiri, and Abu Mu'sab al-Zarqawi. Nine chapters organize the 41 (mostly excerpted) documents by subjects such as 'Islamist Movements and Thinkers'; 'Islamism, Democracy, and the Limits of Freedom'; 'Women and Family in Islamist Discourses'; and 'Global Jihad.' . . . Each document is followed by 'Context and Analysis' and, usually, further-reading citations." SLJ

"This volume provides much-needed primary source material and analysis for those studying the topic." Choice

Includes bibliographical references

Didion, Joan

Fixed ideas: America since 9.11; preface by Frank Rich. New York Review of Bks. 2003 44p pa $7.95

Grades: 11 12 Adult **320.5**
   1. Nationalism 2. September 11 terrorist attacks, 2001 3. United States—Politics and government—2001-
   ISBN 1-590-17073-3   LC 2003-7251

The author contends that "after September 11, those who initiated discussions regarding the causes of the tragedy were instantly branded as traitors as the White House simultaneously launched the war on terrorism and a public relations campaign that blatantly oversimplified the complex realities involved. . . . First published in the *New York Review of Books*, this is an essential work of clarity in a time of obfuscation." Booklist

Fleming, Thomas, 1945-

Socialism. Marshall Cavendish Benchmark 2007 c2008 143p il (Political systems of the world) lib bdg $39.93

Grades: 7 8 9 10 11 12 **320.5**
   1. Socialism
   ISBN 978-0-7614-2632-5; 0-7614-2632-9
                    LC 2006-33048

"Discusses socialism as a political system, and details the history of socialist governments throughout the world." Publisher's note

"There is solid information here." SLJ

Includes bibliographical references

Laqueur, Walter, 1921-

Fascism; past, present, future. Oxford Univ. Press 1996 263p hardcover o.p. pa $17.95 *

Grades: 11 12 Adult **320.5**
   1. Fascism
   ISBN 0-19-509245-7; 0-19-511793-X (pa)
                    LC 95-17612

"Part 1 examines historical fascism's 'ideology, its specific features, the reasons that it received the support of many millions, and how it came to power;' part 2 sketches fascist, right-wing extremist, neofascist, and radical nationalist populist movements that have emerged since World War II, noting their similarities to and differences from Hitler's and Mussolini's regimes; and part 3 considers 'clerical fascism, that is, radical Islam and similar trends in other religions' and extremist groups in formerly communist states. Laqueur analyzes these subjects judiciously." Booklist

Includes bibliographical references

The **Malcolm** X encyclopedia; edited by Robert L. Jenkins, co-edited by Mfanya Donald Tryman. Greenwood Press 2002 643p il $74.95

Grades: 11 12 Adult **320.5**
   1. Malcolm X, 1925-1965—Encyclopedias 2. Black Muslims—Encyclopedias 3. Reference books
   ISBN 0-313-29264-7   LC 2001-23318

"The major section of the volume consists of 500 essays that create a cross-disciplinary, textured description of the man, his life, his times, and events. . . . Topics include *African nationalism, Civil rights movement, Police brutality, Socialism,* and *White liberals,* among others. Also included are a detailed chronology as well as several thematic essays that provide a framework for the entries that follow. . . . All encyclopedia entries have a short bibliography, but there is an extensive bibliography of books, articles, newspapers, electronic resources, and oral interviews included as a separate section in the volume. . . . The encyclopedia would add a first-stop resource for library users seeking information on this important figure of contemporary American history." Booklist

Includes bibliographical references

321 Systems of governments and states

Perl, Lila
Theocracy. Marshall Cavendish Benchmark 2007 c2008 158p il (Political systems of the world) lib bdg $27.95
Grades: 7 8 9 10 11 12   **321**
  1. Theocracy
  ISBN 978-0-7614-2631-8   LC 2006-26055
"Gives an overview of theocracy as a political system, including and historical discussion of theocratic regimes throughout the world." Publisher's note
Includes bibliographical references

Stefoff, Rebecca, 1951-
Monarchy. Marshall Cavendish Benchmark 2007 c2008 143p il (Political systems of the world) lib bdg $27.95
Grades: 7 8 9 10 11 12   **321**
  1. Monarchy
  ISBN 978-0-7614-2630-1   LC 2006-26384
"Discusses monarchies as a political system, and details the history of monarchies throughout the world." Publisher's note
Includes bibliographical references

321.8 Democratic government

Lansford, Tom
Democracy. Marshall Cavendish Benchmark 2007 c2008 143p il (Political systems of the world) lib bdg $27.95
Grades: 7 8 9 10 11 12   **321.8**
  1. Democracy
  ISBN 978-0-7614-2629-5   LC 2006-25351
"Gives an overview of democracy as a political system, including an historical discussion of democracies throughout the world." Publisher's note
Includes bibliographical references

Laxer, James
Democracy. Groundwood Books 2009 143p (Groundwork guides) $18.95; pa $10
Grades: 8 9 10 11 12   **321.8**
  1. Democracy
  ISBN   978-0-88899-912-2;   0-88899-912-7; 978-0-88899-913-9 (pa); 0-88899-913-5 (pa)
"House of Anansi Press"
This is an "overview of democracy from ancient Greece and Rome through the American and French Revolutions and on through modern movements for democracy in the developing world." Kirkus
This title "stands out for its accessible introduction to historical and contemporary democracy across the globe. Laxer skillfully supports his arguments with examples and avoids pat definitions." Booklist
Includes bibliographical references

321.9 Authoritarian government

Fridell, Ron, 1943-
Dictatorship. Marshall Cavendish Benchmark 2007 144p il (Political systems of the world) lib bdg $27.95
Grades: 7 8 9 10 11 12   **321.9**
  1. Dictators
  ISBN 978-0-7614-2627-1   LC 2006-23121
"Discusses dictatorships as a political system, and details the history of dictatorships throughout the world." Publisher's note
Includes bibliographical references

322 Relation of the state to organized groups and their members

Judson, Karen, 1941-
Religion and government; should they mix? Marshall Cavendish Benchmark 2009 127p il (Controversy!) $25.95
Grades: 7 8 9 10   **322**
  1. Church and state—United States
  ISBN 978-0-7614-4235-6; 0-7614-4235-9
                     LC 2008-44483
"For readers fascinated with the ways in which religion and government work, or try not to work, together in America, this introduction will provide much food for thought. . . . Each chapter examines a different sphere of influence, from politics to education and social welfare, including influential court cases that form the backbone of current policy." SLJ
Includes bibliographical references

322.4 Political action groups

Bartoletti, Susan Campbell, 1958-
They called themselves the K.K.K.; the birth of an American terrorist group. Houghton Mifflin 2010 172p il map $19 *
Grades: 7 8 9 10   **322.4**
  1. Ku Klux Klan 2. Racism 3. White supremacy movements 4. Reconstruction (1865-1876) 5. United States—Race relations
  ISBN 978-0-618-44033-7; 0-618-44033-X
                     LC 2009-45247
"In this comprehensive, accessible account, . . . [the author] draws from documentary histories, slave narratives, newspapers, congressional testimony, and other sources to chronicle the origins and proliferation of the Ku Klux Klan against the charged backdrop of Reconstruction politics and legislation. . . . The author lives up to her introductory promise to avoid censoring racist language and images, and includes some horrifying descriptions of lynchings and murders perpetuated during KKK raids. . . . Her account of attending a Klan meeting while researching the book is chilling to the core." Publ Wkly
Includes bibliographical references

The **Britannica** guide to political and social movements that changed the modern world; edited by Heather M. Campbell. Britannica Educational Pub. in association with Rosen Educational Services 2010 389p il (Turning points in history) lib bdg $45

Grades: 9 10 11 12 **322.4**
1. Social movements
ISBN 978-1-61530-016-7   LC 2009-37443
"This book traces an array of important political and social movements from their inception to their apex, with . . . side discussions of notable proponents." Publisher's note
Includes glossary

Chalmers, David Mark
Hooded Americanism: the history of the Ku Klux Klan. 3rd ed. Duke Univ. Press 1987 c1981 477p il pa $24.95 hardcover o.p. *

Grades: 11 12 Adult **322.4**
1. Ku Klux Klan
ISBN 0-8223-0772-3 (pa)   LC 86-29133
First published 1965 by Doubleday; this is a reissue of the 1981 edition published by Watts
This book recounts the history of the Klan. It describes the sociological and psychological forces behind the Klan, and sets forth its dogmas
"The book is written in a breezy, journalistic style. . . . Especially instructive and sobering is Chalmers' account of the role of the Klan in politics." J Am Hist
Includes bibliographical references

Esposito, John L.
Unholy war; terror in the name of Islam. Oxford Univ. Press 2002 196p hardcover o.p. pa $15.95 *

Grades: 11 12 Adult **322.4**
1. Terrorism—Religious aspects 2. Islam and politics 3. United States—Foreign opinion
ISBN 0-19-515435-5; 0-19-516886-0 (pa)
      LC 2001-58009
The author "explains the teachings of Islam—the Qur-an, the example of the Prophet, Islamic law—about jihad or holy war, the use of violence, and terrorism. He chronicles the rise of extremist groups and examines their frightening worldview and tactics." Publisher's note
"Engaging, evenhanded, and highly readable . . . this is essential reading for every concerned citizen and all those who wish to gain a deeper understanding of contemporary Islam and its internal struggles." Libr J
Includes bibliographical references

Extremist groups: opposing viewpoints; Karen F. Balkin, book editor. Greenhaven Press 2005 202p il map lib bdg $34.95; pa $23.70 *

Grades: 7 8 9 10 11 12 **322.4**
1. Radicalism 2. Right and left (Political science)
ISBN 0-7377-3594-5 (lib bdg); 978-0-7377-3594-9 (lib bdg); 0-7377-3595-3 (pa); 978-0-7377-3595-6 (pa)
"Opposing viewpoints series"
This "look at extremist groups focuses on the intense and often violent clashes that occur when these organizations push the limits of the law and societal tolerance.

The anthology includes a . . . chapter on terrorist groups whose activities pose a threat worldwide." Publisher's note
Includes bibliographical references

Gandhi, Mahatma, 1869-1948
Gandhi on non-violence; selected texts from Mohandas K. Gandhi's Non-violence in peace and war; edited with an introduction by Thomas Merton; preface by Mark Kurlansky. New Directions 2007 101p pa $13.95 *

Grades: 11 12 Adult **322.4**
1. Passive resistance 2. India—Politics and government
ISBN 978-0-8112-1686-9   LC 2007-32262
"A New Directions Paperbook"
First published 1965
In an introductory essay Merton "considers Gandhi's ideas, not in relation to their Indian context, but in terms of their applicability to all men's lives. Brief quotations from Gandhi's writings make up most of the book." Asia: a Guide to Paperbacks
Includes bibliographical references

Gerges, Fawaz A.
Journey of the Jihadist; inside Muslim militancy. Harcourt 2006 312p $25; pa $15

Grades: 11 12 Adult **322.4**
1. Terrorism—Religious aspects 2. Jihad 3. Islamic fundamentalism
ISBN 0-15-101213-X;   978-0-15-101213-8; 0-15-603170-1 (pa); 978-0-15-603170-7 (pa)
      LC 2005-37759
In this "account of the development of militant Islamist praxis and ideology in the contemporary Middle East, Gerges . . . explains what the jihadists are about and what they intend to accomplish. . . . The author's ability to explain complex issues in a jargon-free and easy-flowing narrative makes this book one of the best, most useful, and most timely volumes for nonspecialist readers." Libr J
Includes bibliographical references

Hamilton, Neil A., 1949-
Rebels and renegades; a chronology of social and political dissent in the United States. Routledge 2002 361p il $100 *

Grades: 11 12 Adult **322.4**
1. Radicalism 2. Right and left (Political science)
ISBN 0-415-93639-X   LC 2002-8916
The author "examines the historical role that radicals and reactionaries have played in shaping American society and culture. Arranged in nine chapters, the book features a chronological format that begins in 1620 with the Pilgrims and ends with the September 11, 2001 terrorist attacks. Each chapter opens with an overview of the time period, and individual entries consist of one- or two-page descriptions of radicals, their activities, and their impact." Libr J
Includes bibliographical references

Voices of protest; documents of courage and dissent; edited by Frank Lowenstein, Sheryl Lechner, and Erik Bruun. Distributed by Workman Pub. Co. 2007 560p il $24.95

Grades: 10 11 12   **322.4**
1. Dissent 2. History—Sources
ISBN 978-1-57912-585-1   LC 2007-60380

"Collected here are more than 300 documents—essays, letters, newspaper articles, court decisions, song lyrics, poetry, cartoons, and more—that represent seven main categories of protest: Civil Rights; National Self Determination; Economic Justice; Environmental Conservation; Religious Freedom and Morality; Peace and War; and International Political Freedoms. " Publisher's note

"The bold cover of this book shouts out some of the famous dissenters quoted within: Martin Luther King, Jr.; Margaret Sanger; Pablo Picasso; Mohandas Gandhi; and even Ronald Reagan. . . . It is precisely the inclusion of such unexpected voices, manifested in song lyrics, speeches, essays, sermons, or images from around the globe and throughout time, that makes this comprehensive collection so fresh and groundbreaking." SLJ

Includes bibliographical references

323   Civil and political rights

Civil liberties; Lauri S. Friedman, book editor. Greenhaven Press 2010 144p il map (Introducing issues with opposing viewpoints) lib bdg $34.70

Grades: 7 8 9 10 11 12   **323**
1. Civil rights 2. National security 3. Terrorism
ISBN 978-0-7377-4732-4; 0-7377-4732-3
                   LC 2009-51887

This book "of pro/con essays . . . [is] intended to stimulate discussion of critical social issues and to open readers' minds to divergent opinions. *Civil Liberties* includes discussions of the Patriot Act, the rights of Muslims and Arab Americans, and racial profiling. . . . Active-reading questions preface the essays, which are followed by directions for evaluating the arguments presented. Color photos and other graphics throughout enliven the reading experience." SLJ

Includes bibliographical references

Civil liberties and war; edited by Andrea C. Nayaka. Greenhaven Press/Thomson Gale 2006 78p il (Examining issues through political cartoons) lib bdg $27.45

Grades: 7 8 9 10   **323**
1. Civil rights 2. War—Public opinion 3. Military policy—United States
ISBN 0-7377-2517-6

This "spotlights 16 cartoons related to the suspension of civil liberties and human rights during America's wars. The first chapter presents cartoons from the Civil War to the War in Vietnam, while chapter two considers 'America's War on Terrorism' and chapter three, the current war in Iraq. . . . Each political cartoon is accompanied by a paragraph or two of commentary and a brief note on the cartoonist. The book concludes with a bibliography and an excellent, varied list of 16 relevant organizations and government agencies, with descriptions and contact information." Booklist

Includes bibliographical references

Osborne, Linda Barrett, 1949-
Women of the civil rights movement. Library of Congress 2006 61p il (Women who dare) $12.95 *

Grades: 9 10 11 12   **323**
1. African Americans—Civil rights 2. Civil rights demonstrations 3. Women political activists
ISBN 0-7649-3548-8; 978-0-7649-3548-0
                   LC 2005-49546

This history of the civil rights movement discusses the ways in which women participated in it, including Rosa Parks, Ella Baker and Daisy Bates.

Includes bibliographical references

Thompson, Cooper, 1950-
White men challenging racism; 35 personal stories; [by] Cooper Thompson, Emmett Schaefer, and Harry Brod; with a foreword by James W. Loewen. Duke Univ. Press 2003 xxxvi, 353p $64.95; pa $21.95

Grades: 9 10 11 12   **323**
1. Political activists 2. Racism
ISBN 0-8223-3084-9; 0-8223-3096-2 (pa)
                   LC 2002-14628

This book contains interviews with "35 white men with a range of ages and backgrounds and from across the U.S. . . . who have spent their lives combating racism and social injustice via community organizing, teaching, civil rights advocacy, and a variety of other efforts . . . Among the subjects are Herbert Aptheker, radical historian; Stetson Kennedy, a Klan infiltrator in the 1940s; Richard Lapchick, advocate for racial and gender justice in sports. The contributors explore issues from immigrant rights to interracial relations to gay activism. Readers interested in different perspectives on social justice will enjoy this collection." Booklist

Includes bibliographical references

323.1   Civil and political rights of nondominant groups

American civil rights: primary sources; [compiled by] Phillis Engelbert; edited by Betz Des Chenes. U.X.L 1999 xl, 200p il $58 *

Grades: 8 9 10 11 12   **323.1**
1. Civil rights
ISBN 0-7876-3170-1   LC 99-27167

Presents fifteen documents, including speeches, autobiographical texts, and proclamations, related to the civil rights movement and arranged by category under economic rights, desegregation, and human rights

"The uniqueness of this set lies in the range of people covered. Students will find it an excellent resource for reports and interesting reading." Booklist

Includes bibliographical references

Aretha, David

Freedom Summer. Morgan Reynolds Pub. 2007 128p (The civil rights movement) lib bdg $27.95 *

Grades: 7 8 9 10 11 12   323.1
    1. Mississippi Freedom Project 2. African Americans—Civil rights 3. Mississippi—Race relations
    ISBN 978-1-59935-059-2; 1-59935-059-9
                      LC 2007-23815

This "discusses the collaborative strategies black and white Americans . . . devised to dismantle the restrictive, often violent measures used in the South to prevent most African Americans from voting. . . . [This title is] visually appealing with generous white space around the [text]. Throughout, mostly black-and-white historical photos . . . enhance the [narrative]. Also adding impact are numerous dramatic accounts by participants in the struggle." SLJ
Includes bibliographical references

Montgomery bus boycott. Morgan Reynolds Pub. 2009 128p il (The civil rights movement) $28.95 *

Grades: 7 8 9 10   323.1
    1. Montgomery (Ala.)—Race relations 2. African Americans—Civil rights
    ISBN 978-1-59935-020-2; 1-59935-020-3
                      LC 2008-18679

"The wrenching consequences of Rosa Parks's decision that sparked the Civil Rights Movement are depicted in this well-written book. Descriptions of civil rights activism dating back to 1865 . . . provide historical context and a sense of the fervor surrounding discrimination and segregation. The facts of the boycott are documented with supportive news articles, relevant quotations, moving individual stories, and significant court cases. . . . [Photographs] depict significant figures and document incidents such as meetings and carpooling to avoid buses." SLJ

Includes bibliographical references

Boerst, William J., 1939-

Marching in Birmingham. Morgan Reynolds Pub. 2008 112p il map (The civil rights movement) $27.95 *

Grades: 7 8 9 10 11 12   323.1
    1. King, Martin Luther, Jr., 1929-1968 2. African Americans—Civil rights 3. Birmingham (Ala.)—Race relations
    ISBN 978-1-59935-055-4; 1-59935-055-6
                      LC 2007-26640

This "focuses on Alabama and the organized efforts by both black and white Americans to end local-government-sanctioned segregation and inequality. [This title is] visually appealing with generous white space around the [text]. Throughout, mostly black-and-white historical photos . . . enhance the [narrative]. Also adding impact are numerous dramatic accounts by participants in the struggle." SLJ
Includes bibliographical references

Bowers, Rick, 1952-

The spies of Mississippi; the true story of the spy network that tried to destroy the Civil Rights Movement. National Geographic 2010 120p il $16.95; lib bdg $26.90

Grades: 7 8 9 10   323.1
    1. Mississippi State Sovereignty Commission 2. Mississippi—Race relations 3. African Americans—Civil rights
    ISBN 978-1-4263-0595-5; 1-4263-0595-8; 978-1-4263-0596-2 (lib bdg); 1-4263-0596-6 (lib bdg)
                      LC 2009-18944

"Bowers draws upon archival material, supplemented with his own extensive research, to document the activities of the Mississippi State Sovereignty Commission, a Civil Rights-era state agency that disseminated segregationist propaganda and used Soviet-style methods to spy upon, harass, and harm those who challenged white supremacy. . . . This book's unique perspective will help students understand the previously unknown history of the despicable actions of Mississippi leaders who opposed civil rights and the silent citizens who supported their activities." SLJ
Includes bibliographical references

Boyd, Herb, 1938-

We shall overcome; a living history of the civil rights struggle told in words, pictures and the voices of the participants. Sourcebooks 2004 272p il $45 *

Grades: 11 12 Adult   323.1
    1. African Americans—Civil rights
    ISBN 1-402-20213-X   LC 2004-12509
    Accompanied by 2 CDs

"Through text, images, and actual recordings (found on 2 CDs), Boyd . . . presents some of the major events in the Civil Rights Movement, including the murder of Emmett Till, the march on Washington, and the life and death of Martin Luther King Jr." Libr J
Includes bibliographical references

Civil rights; Karen Balkin, book editor. Greenhaven Press 2004 187p (Current controversies) lib bdg $34.95; pa $23.70 *

Grades: 9 10 11 12   323.1
    1. Civil rights
    ISBN 0-7377-1178-7 (lib bdg); 0-7377-1177-9 (pa)
                      LC 2003-60822

The articles in this anthology explore civil rights issues ranging from censorship to segregation to gun control
Includes bibliographical references

The **Eyes** on the prize civil rights reader; documents, speeches, and firsthand accounts from the black freedom struggle, 1954-1990; general editors, Clayborne Carson {et al.}. Penguin Bks. 1991 764p pa $18 *

Grades: 11 12 Adult   323.1
    1. African Americans—Civil rights 2. United States—Race relations
    ISBN 0-14-015403-5   LC 91-9507

First published 1987 with title: Eyes on the prize: America's civil rights years, a reader and guide

The Eyes on the prize civil rights reader—*Continued*

"An anthology of primary material important in the historiography of this country's civil rights movement. . . . Not simply for reference use, this compilation makes provocative cover-to-cover reading and is extremely worthy of consideration by every library." Booklist

Includes bibliographical references

Hampton, Henry

Voices of freedom; an oral history of the civil rights movement from the 1950s through the 1980s; {by} Henry Hampton and Steve Fayer with Sarah Flynn. Bantam Bks. 1990 692p hardcover o.p. pa $24

Grades: 11 12 Adult   323.1
1. African Americans—Civil rights 2. United States—Race relations
ISBN 0-553-05734-0; 0-553-35232-6 (pa)
                                                        LC 89-18297
This companion to the PBS series "'Eyes on the Prize,' composed of interviews done originally for the TV program, is a riveting document of the civil rights movement of the 1960s and 1970s. The text is arranged in a chronological sequence that reconstructs major events from the murder of Emmett Till in Mississippi in 1955 and the Little Rock integration crisis to the affirmative action cases of the 1970s." Booklist
Includes bibliographical references

King, Martin Luther, Jr., 1929-1968

A testament of hope; the essential writings of Martin Luther King, Jr.; edited by James Melvin Washington. Harper & Row 1986 xxvi, 676p hardcover o.p. pa $23.95 *

Grades: 11 12 Adult   323.1
1. African Americans—Civil rights 2. United States—Race relations
ISBN 0-06-250931-4; 0-06-064691-8 (pa)
                                                        LC 85-45370
"King's most important writings are gathered together in one source. The arrangement is topical: philosophy, sermons and public addresses, essays, interviews and excerpts of his books. The material within each of these categories is arranged chronologically. Included are Dr. King's writings on nonviolence, integration and politics." SLJ
Includes bibliographical references

Why we can't wait; [by] Martin Luther King, Jr. Harper & Row 1964 178p il hardcover o.p. pa $6.95 *

Grades: 11 12 Adult   323.1
1. African Americans—Civil rights 2. Birmingham (Ala.)—Race relations
ISBN 0-06-012395-8; 0-451-52753-4 (pa)
The author first reviews the background of the 1963 civil rights demands. He then describes the strategy of the Birmingham campaign and outlines future action

Litwack, Leon F.

How free is free? The long death of Jim Crow. Harvard University Press 2009 187p (Nathan I. Huggins lectures) $18.95

Grades: 11 12 Adult   323.1
1. African Americans—Civil rights 2. African Americans—Segregation 3. African Americans—Southern States 4. Southern States—Race relations
ISBN 978-0-674-03152-4   LC 2008-36468
In this "examination of African-American life after slavery . . . Litwack recounts the physical brutality and crushing legal oppression of Jim Crow America." Publ Wkly
"An interesting analysis of the dynamics of race and class and how they continue to affect progress." Booklist
Includes bibliographical references

Malaspina, Ann, 1957-

The ethnic and group identity movements; earning recognition. Chelsea House 2007 176p il map (Reform movements in American history) lib bdg $30

Grades: 6 7 8 9 10   323.1
1. Minorities 2. Civil rights 3. Social movements 4. United States—Ethnic relations 5. Multiculturalism
ISBN 978-0-7910-9571-3; 0-7910-9571-1
                                                        LC 2007-21721
"Malaspina explains how leaders within the Asian, disability, Chicano, senior, gay, American Indian, and Muslim communities drew on models of the successful civil and women's rights movements to build group identity and improve the political and social treatment of their members. . . . Illustrations include black-and-white and color photos and period art." SLJ
Includes bibliographical references

Mayer, Robert H.

When the children marched; the Birmingham civil rights movement. Enslow Publishers 2008 176p il map (Prime) $34.60 *

Grades: 7 8 9 10   323.1
1. African Americans—Civil rights 2. Birmingham (Ala.)—Race relations 3. African American children
ISBN 978-0-7660-2930-9; 0-7660-2930-1
                                                        LC 2007-25590
"Children played a significant role in Birmingham's crucial civil rights struggle, and this stirring history of the movement, with many photos, news reports, and quotes from all sides, emphasizes the connections between the young people's power and that of the big leaders. . . . From the cover picture of police escorting African American children to jail, the numerous photos of youth in nonviolent confrontation—marching, attacked by dogs and fire hoses, crammed in prisons—will draw readers with their gripping drama." Booklist
Includes glossary and bibliographical references

Nguyen, Tram

We are all suspects now; untold stories from immigrant communities after 9/11. Beacon Press 2005 187p pa $14 *

Grades: 11 12 Adult   **323.1**
1. Immigrants 2. United States—Ethnic relations 3. War on terrorism 4. September 11 terrorist attacks, 2001
ISBN 0-8070-0461-8   LC 2005-11579

The author "reveals the human cost of the domestic war on terror and examines the impact of post-9/11 policies on people targeted because of immigration status, nationality, race, and religion." Publisher's note

"Mesmerizing personal accounts of poor treatment by the US government, as well as everyday trials and tribulations that immigrants face in the aftermath of September 11th, make this book impossible to put down." Univ Press Books for Public and Second Sch Libr, 2006

Includes bibliographical references

Partridge, Elizabeth

Marching for freedom; walk together, children, and don't you grow weary. Viking 2009 72p il $19.99 *

Grades: 6 7 8 9 10 11 12   **323.1**
1. African Americans—Civil rights 2. Selma (Ala.)—Race relations
ISBN 978-0-670-01189-6; 0-670-01189-4
                              LC 2009-9696

An examination of the march from Selma to Montgomery in 1965 led by Dr. Martin Luther King, Jr., this book focuses on the children who faced terrifying violence in order to walk alongside him in their fight for freedom and the right to vote.

This is a "stirring photo-essay. . . . The vivid text is filled with quotes collected from Partridge's personal interviews with adults who remember their youthful experiences. . . . Filled with large black-and-white photos, every spread brings readers up close to the dramatic, often violent action." Booklist

Includes bibliographical references

Reporting civil rights. Library of Am. 2003 2v ea $40 *

Grades: 11 12 Adult   **323.1**
1. African Americans—Civil rights 2. Journalism 3. United States—Race relations
ISBN 1-931082-28-6 (v1); 1-931082-29-4 (v2)
                              LC 2002-27459

Contents: pt1 American journalism, 1941-1963; pt2 American journalism, 1963-1973

These "volumes present newspaper and magazine articles from the popular and African American press. . . . The 151 writers whose works are collected here include Ralph Ellison, Langston Hughes, John Hersey, Robert Penn Warren, David Halberstam, Jimmy Breslin, James Baldwin, Marshall Frady, and Tom Wolfe. . . . Each volume also contains a chronology and biographical sketches of the contributors." Libr J

"An important anthology for readers interested in the history of the civil rights movement." Booklist

Sugarman, Tracy, 1921-

We had sneakers, they had guns; the kids who fought for civil rights in Mississippi. Syracuse University Press 2009 332p il $34.95

Grades: 11 12 Adult   **323.1**
1. African Americans—Civil rights 2. Mississippi—Race relations
ISBN 978-0-8156-0938-4; 0-8156-0938-8
                              LC 2009-4618

The author, "a participant in Freedom Summer in Mississippi in 1964-65, where the Student Nonviolent Coordinating Committee (SNCC) worked for voter registration efforts and community organizing, writes an introspective memoir complete with many of his original illustrations composed that summer. . . . This book is a testament to the courageous civil rights workers whose perseverance and courage will inspire all readers." Libr J

Turck, Mary, 1950-

Freedom song; young voices and the struggle for civil rights; [by] Mary C. Turck. Chicago Review Press 2009 146p il pa $18.95

Grades: 7 8 9 10   **323.1**
1. Chicago Children's Choir 2. Freedom Singers (Musical group) 3. African Americans—Civil rights 4. African American music
ISBN 978-1-55652-773-9; 1-55652-773-X
                              LC 2008-29673

"The book is divided into chapters that represent the history of the Civil Rights Movement. 'Sunday of Song,' 'Singing in the Churches,' and 'South Africa,' for example, contain information about the factual events while including how the evolution of the music captured the mood and sentiment of the time. The importance of music in the lives of African Americans is described in depth. . . . The accompanying CD allows students to internalize the words and their emotional impact as they listen. Overall, this informative and well-written book is an excellent addition to any collection." SLJ

Includes bibliographical references

323.3 Civil and political rights of other social groups

Biddle, Wendy

Immigrants' rights after 9/11; [by] Wendy E. Biddle. Chelsea House 2008 110p il (Point-counterpoint) lib bdg $32.95 *

Grades: 7 8 9 10   **323.3**
1. Immigrants—United States 2. United States—Immigration and emigration 3. Civil rights
ISBN 0-7910-8682-8; 978-0-7910-8682-7
                              LC 2006-17147

"An overview makes the point that the rules governing immigration issues such as indefinite detention and the right to an attorney have been tightened since 9/11. The debate centers around the question of whether these changes are necessary for the safety of U.S. citizens, or whether they infringe on the civil liberties that are afforded to all American residents, legal or not. . . . This solid work thoroughly presents both sides of the argument." SLJ

Includes bibliographical references

Do children have rights? Christine Watkins, book editor. Greenhaven Press 2010 129p (At issue. Civil liberties) $31.80; pa $22.50 *
Grades: 9 10 11 12   **323.3**
1. Youth—Civil rights
ISBN 978-0-7377-4876-5; 978-0-7377-4877-2 (pa)
    LC 2010021987
The articles in this anthology discuss different aspects of children's rights including child labor, sex education, and drug testing in schools.
Includes bibliographical references

323.44 Freedom of action (Liberty)

Are privacy rights being violated? Ronald D. Lankford, Jr., book editor. Greenhaven Press 2010 109p (At issue. Civil liberties) $31.80; pa $22.50
Grades: 9 10 11 12   **323.44**
1. Right of privacy
ISBN 978-0-7377-4868-0; 978-0-7377-4869-7 (pa)
    LC 2010003358
The topics discussed in this anthology include identity theft, employee privacy rights, the use of video cameras in public places, and No Child Left Behind.
Includes bibliographical references

Dougherty, Terri, 1964-
Freedom of expression and the Internet. Lucent Books 2010 112p il map $33.45
Grades: 7 8 9 10   **323.44**
1. Internet—Social aspects 2. Intellectual freedom 3. Freedom of speech 4. Copyright
ISBN 978-1-4205-0227-5; 1-4205-0227-1
    LC 2010-1547
"This book explores the parameters of freedom of speech and the responsibility that accompanies it, explaining as well the difference between the presentation of fact and opinion. The remainder of the volume is devoted to child-protection policies, concerns about anonymity, copyright issues, trademark violations, 'School Speech and Cyberbullies,' and 'International Free Speech.' The text is well organized and clearly written, outlining the issues in such a way as to be understandable to teens. Color photos, sidebars, discussion questions, and a list of organization contacts are included. This is a good source for report writers." SLJ
Includes bibliographical references

Freedom of expression; Alicia Cafferty Lerner and Adrienne Wilmoth Lerner, book editors. Greenhaven Press 2009 205p il map (Global viewpoints) $37.30; pa $25.70
Grades: 9 10 11 12   **323.44**
1. Freedom of the press 2. Censorship 3. Mass media 4. Freedom of speech
ISBN 978-0-7377-4154-4; 978-0-7377-4155-1 (pa)
    LC 2009-8221
The articles in this anthology "focus on the censorship issues that face artists, journalists, and everyday citizens around the globe. Most of the writing concerns how countries restrict freedoms. Yet some of the most inter-

esting essays center on how these very restrictions can be beneficial in other ways." Booklist
Includes bibliographical references

Fromm, Erich, 1900-1980
Escape from freedom 1941 305p pa $14 hardcover o.p. *
Grades: 9 10 11 12   **323.44**
1. Freedom 2. Social psychology 3. Totalitarianism
ISBN 0-8050-3149-9
"A searching inquiry into the meaning of freedom for modern man. . . . The author stresses the role of psychological factors in the social process, interpreting the historical development of freedom in terms of man's awareness of himself as a significant separate being." Libr J
Includes bibliographical references

Kuhn, Betsy
Prying eyes; privacy in the twenty-first century. Twenty-First Century Books 2008 160p lib bdg $38.60
Grades: 6 7 8 9 10   **323.44**
1. Right of privacy
ISBN 978-0-8225-7179-7   LC 2007-21247
"Kuhn examines the technology, the past and present legal and legislative landscapes, the benefits, and . . . the abuses of recent advances in aerial photography, biometrics, DNA testing, consumer data storage, and other challenges to privacy. . . . This cogent, clearly written assignment title is backed up by substantial source notes, annotated rosters of recent legal decisions, and multimedia resources." Booklist
Includes bibliographical references

323.6 Citizenship and related topics

Ellis, Richard
To the flag; the unlikely history of the Pledge of Allegiance; [by] Richard J. Ellis. University Press of Kansas 2005 297p il hardcover o.p. pa $15.95 *
Grades: 11 12 Adult   **323.6**
1. Pledge of Allegiance
ISBN 0-7006-1372-2; 0-7006-1521-0 (pa)
    LC 2004-23110
The author provides an "account not only of the pledge's 19th century beginnings, but also of its recent use as a political tool. A must read for political junkies of any age!" Univ Press Books for Public and Second Sch Libr, 2006

Is it unpatriotic to criticize one's country? Mary E. Williams, book editor. Greenhaven Press 2005 77p (At issue) hardcover o.p. pa $22.50
Grades: 9 10 11 12   **323.6**
1. Patriotism 2. Dissent
ISBN 0-7377-2396-3 (lib bdg); 0-7377-2397-1 (pa)
    LC 2004-59694
The essays in this book discuss whether or not criticism of or protest against the actions of the U.S. government by its own citizens, especially during a time of war, undermines patriotism.
Includes bibliographical references

324   The political process

Historical atlas of U.S. presidential elections 1788-2004; [by] J. Clark Archer . . . [et al.] CQ Press 2006 164p map $150 *
Grades: 11 12 Adult   **324**
1. Reference books 2. Presidents—United States—Election—Maps 3. Presidents—United States—Election—Statistics 4. Elections—United States—Maps 5. Elections—United States—Statistics
ISBN 1-56802-955-1; 978-1-56802-955-9
LC 2006-42406

This "atlas of election data is divided into three sections. Section one is an overview of United States election history and current procedure as well as the methods as sources used in compiling this volume. Next is a series of full-color presidential election maps, while section three contains individual analyses of each election since Washington's first landslide victory." Voice Youth Advocates

"Offering detailed geographic and historical visual evidence of every presidential election held in the US, this book is a required source of reference." Choice

Includes bibliographical references

Student's guide to elections; advisory editor, Bruce J. Schulman. CQ Press 2008 394p il map (Student's guide to the U.S. government series) $85 *
Grades: 9 10 11 12   **324**
1. Reference books 2. Elections—United States
ISBN 978-0-87289-552-2   LC 2008-13032

In this first volume of a projected four-volume series, "Schulman takes a three-part approach to the topic of United States' elections. He opens with three essays on the Electoral College, the role of political parties, and American democracy. His second part covers more than one hundred election-related topics in alphabetical order, including the presidential elections from 1789 to the 2008 campaign. The third part comprises a collection of primary source documents related to topics covered in the book. . . . This book provides a thorough introduction to the political process." Voice Youth Advocates

Includes bibliographical references

Thomas, Evan
"A long time coming"; the inspiring, combative 2008 campaign and the historic election of Barack Obama; with exclusive, behind-the-scenes reporting by the staff of Newsweek. PublicAffairs 2009 220p il $22.95
Grades: 11 12 Adult   **324**
1. Obama, Barack, 1961- 2. Presidents—United States—Election—2008
ISBN 978-1-58648-607-5   LC 2008-51492

This book on the 2008 election is "compiled from the reporting of the political writers of Newsweek. . . . [This is] a perceptive, smoothly written and generally fair-minded account of both presidential campaigns." N Y Times Book Rev

324.025   The political process— Directories

Political handbook of the world 2011; edited by Thomas C. Muller, William R. Overstreet, Judith F. Isacoff, Tom Lansford. CQ Press 2011 1832p $325
Grades: 11 12 Adult   **324.025**
1. Reference books 2. Political science—Handbooks, manuals, etc. 3. Political parties
ISSN 0913-175X
ISBN 978-1-60871-734-7

Annual. First published 1927 with title: A political handbook of Europe

"Provides data for each country on chief officials, government and politics, political parties, and news media. Sections devoted to intergovernmental organizations and to issues concerned with particular regions; e.g., Middle East, Latin America. Index to geographical, organizational, and personal names." Ref Sources for Small & Medium-sized Libr. 6th edition

324.2   Political parties

Cox, Vicki
The history of the third parties; [by] Vicki Cox. Chelsea House 2007 125p (The U.S. government: how it works) lib bdg $30
Grades: 7 8 9 10   **324.2**
1. Third parties (United States politics) 2. United States—Politics and government
ISBN 978-0-7910-9421-1; 0-7910-9421-9
LC 2006-100704

"Beginning with the Tertium Quids in 1806 and continuing to today's Green Party, . . . [this book] chronicles third parties and their increasing visibility in the American political system." Publisher's note

"Black-and-white photos and sidebars about government history and process enhance the neatly presented volume, which will find wide use in this coming election year. A glossary, bibliography, and suggested book and Web resources conclude." Booklist

Includes glossary and bibliographical references

McNeese, Tim
The progressive movement; advocating social change. Chelsea House 2007 144p il (Reform movements in American history) $30
Grades: 8 9 10 11 12   **324.2**
1. Progressivism (United States politics) 2. Social change 3. United States—Politics and government— 1865-1898
ISBN 978-0-7910-9501-0; 0-7910-9501-0
LC 2007-14920

This chronological history of the progressive movement discusses the events, legislation, and people associated with the movements and includes a chronology and timeline.

Includes bibliographical references

Norton, Augustus R.

Hezbollah; a short history; [by] Augustus Richard Norton. Princeton University Press 2007 187p il map (Princeton studies in Muslim politics) $16.95; pa $12.95

Grades: 11 12 Adult   **324.2**

1. Hezbollah (Lebanon) 2. Lebanon—Politics and government

ISBN   978-0-691-13124-5;   0-691-13124-4; 978-0-691-14107-7 (pa); 0-691-14107-X (pa)

LC 2006-100594

Norton "provides an objective account of the genesis and development of Hezbollah, explaining its central role in contemporary Lebanon. . . . The author demonstrates why Hezbollah has solidified its role as a principal player in Lebanese politics and enhanced its regional prestige." Choice

Includes bibliographical references

Tamimi, Azzam

Hamas: a history from within. Olive Branch Press 2007 372p pa $20 *

Grades: 11 12 Adult   **324.2**

1. Hamas 2. Islam and politics

ISBN 978-1-56656-689-6; 1-56656-689-4

LC 2007-6828

This is a "document-based study of the formation, politics, and actions of Hamas, the Islamist party that recently formed a Palestinian government despite the opposition of the United States and the rival Fatah Party. . . . [The author] has written a sound academic work on a key group that libraries need to have." Libr J

Includes bibliographical references

World encyclopedia of political systems and parties; Neil Schlager and Jayne Weisblatt, editors; Orlando J. Pérez, consulting editor. 4th ed. Facts On File 2006 3v il (Facts on File library of world history) lib bdg set $270

Grades: 9 10 11 12   **324.2**

1. Reference books 2. Political parties—Encyclopedias 3. Comparative government—Encyclopedias

ISBN 0-8160-5953-5; 978-0-8160-5953-9

LC 2005-28118

First published 1983 in two volumes

"Alphabetically arranged by country, the set covers the governments and political parties in 196 nations. . . . Each entry begins with an introduction or basic description of the country. Next, the executive, legislative, and judicial branches are discussed as well as the regional and local government structure. A section on the electoral system discusses suffrage, voter registration, balloting procedures, and voter turnout. . . . [This work] is recommended for high-school, academic, and public libraries." Booklist

Includes bibliographical references

324.5   Nominating candidates

National party conventions, 1831-2008. CQ Press 2010 375p il pa $65

Grades: 11 12 Adult   **324.5**

1. Political conventions 2. Political parties

ISBN 978-1-60426-540-8   LC 2009040264

First published 1995 with title: National party conventions, 1831–1992

This volume offers information about Republican and Democratic Party national conventions including sites, delegates, chief officers and keynote speakers, party organization and rules, credential fights, platform fights, ballots, and candidates.

Includes bibliographical references

324.6   Election systems and procedures; suffrage

Aretha, David

Selma and the Voting Rights Act. Morgan Reynolds Pub. 2007 128p il (The civil rights movement) lib bdg $27.95

Grades: 7 8 9 10 11 12   **324.6**

1. Voting Rights Act of 1965 2. African Americans—Civil rights 3. African Americans—Suffrage 4. Selma (Ala.)—Race relations

ISBN 978-1-59935-056-1; 1-59935-056-4

LC 2007-24655

The author discusses "mid-1960s Alabama and the black struggle to exercise the constitutional right to vote. Even those who know the story of the famous protest marches will be interested in the details here. . . . There are quotes from and photos of the famous as well as the unknown, as well as excerpts from speeches and news photos." Booklist

Includes bibliographical references

Benenson, Bob

Elections A to Z. 3rd ed. CQ Press 2008 xxxvi, 704p il (CQ's American government A to Z series) $85

Grades: 11 12 Adult   **324.6**

1. Reference books 2. Elections—United States—Encyclopedias

ISBN 978-0-87289-366-5   LC 2007-41388

Also available online

First published 1999

"Topics include individuals, current and defunct political parties, and significant events in election history. Landmark court cases on this topic are also discussed. . . . Public libraries and media centers will find this a convenient and useful addition to their collections." Am Ref Books Annu, 2008

Includes bibliographical references

Frost-Knappman, Elizabeth

Women's suffrage in America; an eyewitness history; [by] Elizabeth Frost-Knappman and Kathryn Cullen-DuPont. Updated ed. Facts on File 2005 512p (Eyewitness history) $75 *

Grades: 9 10 11 12   **324.6**

1. Women—Suffrage 2. Women—United States—History

ISBN 0-8160-5693-5   LC 2004-43339

First published 1992

Frost-Knappman, Elizabeth—*Continued*

This volume provides "firsthand accounts of the women's movement—diary entries, letters, speeches, and newspaper accounts—that illustrate how historical events appeared to those who lived through them. Among the eyewitness testimonies included are those of Susan B. Anthony, Sojourner Truth, Lucretia Mott, Frederick Douglass, Helen Keller, and John Quincy Adams. . . . Critical documents such as the Declaration of Rights and Sentiments at Seneca Falls, the Emancipation Address of the Women's National League, the Constitution of the National Loyal Woman Suffrage Association, and the 19th Amendment are paired with capsule biographies of more than 80 key figures." Publisher's note

This is "a lively and important sourcebook for students of American political and cultural history." SLJ [review of 1992 edition]

Includes bibliographical references

Guide to U.S. elections. 6th ed. CQ Press 2010 2v il map set $420 *

Grades: 11 12 Adult   **324.6**

1. Reference books 2. Elections—United States—Statistics

ISBN 978-1-60426-536-1   LC 2009-33938

First published 1975 with title: Congressional Quarterly's guide to U.S. elections

This is a compilation of data drawn from different sources on gubernatorial, congressional, and presidential elections.

"The clearly written, analytical essays . . . focus on key issues such as reapportionment and redistricting, campaign finance, political party development, party conventions, politics and war, the electoral process, and the ethnic and gender composition of Congress. . . . It is an important resource for students and researchers needing historical or contemporary election data and analysis." Choice

Includes bibliographical references

Henderson, Harry, 1951-

Campaign and election reform. Facts on File 2004 316p (Library in a book) $45

Grades: 11 12 Adult   **324.6**

1. Elections—United States 2. Campaign funds—United States

ISBN 0-8160-5136-4   LC 2003-6485

Contents: Introduction to campaign and election reform; The law of campaigns and elections; Chronology; Biographical listing; How to research campaign and election reform; Organizations and agencies

"Beginning with the Declaration of Independence and ending with the 2002 Bipartisan Campaign Reform Act, coverage includes the Electoral College and the complicated world of campaign-finance reform as well as the technology used to record individual voter records. Legislation and court cases that have determined the current electoral process in our country are reviewed and explanations of the legal battles waged during the 2000 presidential election between George Bush and Al Gore are included. . . . A solid one-stop resource." SLJ

Includes bibliographical references

Hillstrom, Laurie

The Voting Rights Act of 1965; [by] Laurie Collier Hillstrom. Omnigraphics, Inc. 2009 244p il (Defining moments) $44

Grades: 11 12 Adult   **324.6**

1. Voting Rights Act of 1965 2. African Americans—Suffrage 3. United States—Politics and government—1961-1974

ISBN 978-0-7808-1048-8; 0-7808-1048-1

LC 2008-38392

"Explains the events that led to the Voting Rights Act of 1965. Details both the racial discrimination and violence that pervaded the South and the civil rights protests that changed American voting rights. Features include a narrative overview, biographies, primary source documents, chronology, glossary, bibliography, and index." Publisher's note

Includes glossary and bibliographical references

Marzilli, Alan, 1970-

Election reform. 2nd ed. Chelsea House 2010 119p il map (Point-counterpoint) lib bdg $35

Grades: 7 8 9 10   **324.6**

1. Elections—United States 2. Politics 3. Campaign funds—United States

ISBN 978-1-60413-691-3; 1-60413-691-X

LC 2009-51401

First published 2004

This book "examines ongoing debates over voting rights and election laws and asks how the United States might reach the ideal of 'one person, one vote.'" Publisher's note

Includes bibliographical references

The **presidential** election process: opposing viewpoints; Tom Lansford, book editor. Greenhaven Press 2008 216p lib bdg $36.20; pa $24.95 *

Grades: 9 10 11 12   **324.6**

1. Presidents—United States—Nomination 2. Presidents—United States—Election 3. Politics

ISBN 978-0-7377-3892-6 (lib bdg); 0-7377-3892-8 (lib bdg); 978-0-7377-3893-3 (pa); 0-7377-3893-6 (pa)

LC 2007-35066

"Opposing viewpoints series"

"This collection of essays addresses the American election process. Four chapters feature pro/con articles on the roles of primaries and conventions in the nomination process, campaign financing, media coverage, and the electoral college. Each chapter has four to six selections offering a wide range of opinions on these themes. . . . An excellent resource for students, teachers, and parents." SLJ

Includes bibliographical references

Presidential elections 1789-2008. CQ Press 2010 295p il map pa $65 *

Grades: 11 12 Adult   **324.6**

1. Presidents—United States—Election

ISBN 978-1-60426-541-5   LC 2009-40267

First published 1995 with title: Presidential elections, 1789–1992

This book offers information about the electoral college, electoral votes and popular votes in each presiden-

Presidential elections 1789-2008—*Continued*
tial election, voter turnout, primary returns, and Democratic and Republican Party conventions.

Includes bibliographical references

Ruth, Janice E.
Women of the suffrage movement; by Janice E. Ruth & Evelyn Sinclair. Library of Congress 2006 64p il (Women who dare) $12.95 *
Grades: 9 10 11 12   **324.6**
1. Suffragists 2. Women—Suffrage
ISBN 0-7649-3547-X; 978-0-7649-3547-3
     LC 2005-40190
This history of the women's suffrage movement includes brief profiles of several key women of that movement, including Elizabeth Smith Miller, Lucy Stone, and Adella Hunt Logan.
Includes bibliographical references

Should the voting age be lowered? Ronnie D. Lankford, book editor. Greenhaven Press 2008 114p (At issue. American politics) lib bdg $29.95; pa $21.20
Grades: 7 8 9 10 11 12   **324.6**
1. Voting age
ISBN 978-0-7377-3936-7 (lib bdg); 0-7377-3936-3 (lib bdg); 978-0-7377-3937-4 (pa); 0-7377-3937-1 (pa)
     LC 2007-35370
This is an anthology of essays discussing different perspectives on lowering the voting age.
Includes bibliographical references

Voting rights: opposing viewpoints; Tom Lansford, book editor. Greenhaven Press 2008 225p il lib bdg $25.95; pa $37.40
Grades: 7 8 9 10 11 12   **324.6**
1. Suffrage
ISBN 978-0-7377-4014-1 (lib bdg); 978-0-7377-4015-8 (pa)   LC 2008-12800
"Opposing viewpoints series"
This title "discusses current issues in the U.S. [related to voting] . . . and also looks at politics in many other countries: women's right to vote in the Arab world and parts of Latin America, the rulings of South Africa's post-apartheid Constitutional Court, and more. . . . For each article, a clear introduction discusses the issues raised, and the book includes an extensive bibliography of books, periodicals, and organizations to contact." Booklist
Includes bibliographical references

324.7   Conduct of election campaigns

Guide to political campaigns in America; Paul S. Herrnson, editor-in-chief; Colton Campbell, Marni Ezra, Stephen K. Medvic, associate editors. CQ Press 2005 457p il $125
Grades: 11 12 Adult   **324.7**
1. Politics 2. Elections—United States
ISBN 1-56802-876-8   LC 2005-18123
Also available online

"Organized into seven sections, [this book] contains 27 chapters that discuss every aspect of the American political campaign process—including a historical overview, nomination politics, voter turnout, polling, debates, and campaign reform. The editors examine various political campaigns, e.g., presidential, congressional, gubernatorial, state, and local. They also look at judicial elections and initiatives and referenda. . . . This volume should be found in every reference collection." Choice
Includes bibliographical references

Political campaigns: opposing viewpoints; Louise I. Gerdes, book editor. Greenhaven Press 2010 245p il lib bdg $38.50; pa $26.75
Grades: 8 9 10 11 12   **324.7**
1. Politics 2. Campaign funds—United States 3. United States—Politics and government
ISBN   978-0-7377-4540-5   (lib   bdg); 978-0-7377-4541-2 (pa)   LC 2009-36044
"Opposing viewpoints series"
This collection of article excerpts "presents factors that may promote and hinder fair campaigns, including the perennial issue of redistricting and recent technological developments, such as Internet donations." Booklist
Includes bibliographical references

325.73   Immigration to the United States

Allport, Alan, 1970-
Immigration policy; by Alan Allport; [rev. by John E. Ferguson, Jr.] 2nd ed. Chelsea House 2009 146p il (Point-counterpoint) $35
Grades: 7 8 9 10   **325.73**
1. United States—Immigration and emigration
ISBN 978-1-60413-126-0; 1-60413-126-8
     LC 2008-35049
First published 2005
"Presents . . . viewpoints on immigration and on making English the official language of the United States." Publisher's note
This book is "well organized, clearly written, and [includes] a rich array of bibliographic resources." SLJ [review of 2005 edition]
Includes bibliographical references

Bausum, Ann
Denied, detained, deported; stories from the dark side of American immigration. National Geographic 2009 111p il $21.95; lib bdg $32.90 *
Grades: 6 7 8 9 10 11 12   **325.73**
1. Immigrants—United States 2. United States—Immigration and emigration
ISBN   978-1-4263-0332-6;   1-4263-0332-7; 978-1-4263-0333-3 (lib bdg); 1-4263-0333-5 (lib bdg)
"This volume deals frankly with the more troubling aspects of United States immigration policy. The author chose the stories of three immigrants. . . . Twelve-year-old German-Jew Herb Karliner was denied entry to the United States at the border when he attempted to escape Nazi Germany. Sixteen-year-old Japanese-American Mary Matsuda was detained with the rest of her family

Bausum, Ann—Continued

during World War II. Labor-activist Emma Goldman was deported for her 'un-American' views. . . . The themes of the three stories are unified by the introduction and conclusion, which deal with Chinese immigration during the late 19th century and the history of immigration across the southern border of the United States, respectively. Photographs throughout will help students relate to the narrative. . . . This is an interesting and readable book." SLJ

Includes bibliographical references

Daniels, Roger

Coming to America; a history of immigration and ethnicity in American life. 2nd ed. Perennial 2002 515p il map pa $17.95 *

Grades: 11 12 Adult   **325.73**

1. Minorities 2. United States—Immigration and emigration

ISBN 0-06-050577-X   LC 2002-72436

First published 1990

"After discussing the topic of immigration in general and sociological theories of why people migrate between countries, Daniel discusses each racial or national group that came to the United States during the various eras of the nation's history." SLJ {review of 1990 edition}

Includes bibliographical references

Illegal immigration: opposing viewpoints; Margaret Haerens, book editor. Greenhaven Press 2007 212p il lib bdg $34.95; pa $23.70 *

Grades: 8 9 10 11 12   **325.73**

1. Illegal aliens 2. United States—Immigration and emigration

ISBN 0-7377-3356-X (lib bdg); 0-7377-3357-8 (pa)
                                     LC 2005-55049

"Opposing viewpoints series"

"The writers present opposing perspectives on such topics as border-patrol efforts, immigration policy reform, racism, the development of a guest worker program, and the connection between illegal immigration and terrorism. . . . Even reluctant readers will find many compelling and inflammatory arguments to hold their interest." SLJ

Includes bibliographical references

Immigration; Debra A. Miller, book editor. Greenhaven Press/Gale Cengage Learning 2010 191p (Current controversies) $39.70; pa $27.50

Grades: 9 10 11 12   **325.73**

1. United States—Immigration and emigration

ISBN   978-0-7377-4709-6;   0-7377-4709-9; 978-0-7377-4710-2 (pa); 0-7377-4710-2 (pa)
                                     LC 2009044185

"Explores the extent to which both legal and illegal immigration are a problem in the United States, including the impact of immigration on the economy, natural resources, and security. Examines the current treatment of illegal immigrants, and potential changes to the U.S. response to illegal immigration. Also looks at how U.S. immigration policy could be reformed to mitigate the problem." Publisher's note

Includes bibliographical references

Nakaya, Andrea C.

Immigration. ReferencePoint Press 2010 104p il (Compact research. Current issues) $25.95

Grades: 8 9 10 11 12   **325.73**

1. United States—Immigration and emigration

ISBN 978-1-60152-095-1; 1-60152-095-6
                                     LC 2009-23404

After an overview of immigration, this addresses such questions as "'How Should the United States Address the Issue of Illegal Immigration?' [and offers] thorough and balanced answers incorporating viewpoints from both ends of the pro/con spectrum. The 'Primary Source Quotes' and 'Facts and Illustrations' sections allow readers to zero in on information that would be particularly helpful in supporting arguments." SLJ

Includes bibliographical references

U.S. immigration and migration. Primary sources; [compiled by] James L. Outman; Lawrence W. Baker, editor. UXL 2004 xxxi, 232p il (U.S. immigration and migration reference library) $65 *

Grades: 9 10 11 12   **325.73**

1. United States—Immigration and emigration

ISBN 0-7876-7669-1   LC 2004-3553

"The 17 excerpts begin with Lord Baltimore's 1649 Declaration of Religious Tolerance and end with Pat Buchanan's views on immigration policies. The letters, articles, government documents, Supreme Court rulings, and the reflections of authors such as Willa Cather and Mark Twain offer a wide variety of viewpoints." SLJ

Includes bibliographical references

Wepman, Dennis

Immigration. Facts on File, Inc. 2008 476p il map (American experience) $80 *

Grades: 7 8 9 10   **325.73**

1. United States—Immigration and emigration

ISBN 978-0-8160-6240-9; 0-8160-6240-4
                                     LC 2007-29713

First published 2002 as a volume in the Eyewitness History series

"This volume covers the years between 1607 and June 2007. Each chapter is divided into three sections: an 18 to 25-page main body, a 'Chronicle of Events' by year, and well-documented 'Eyewitness Testimony.' . . . [The author] maintains a high quality of research and a clear writing style, and provides detailed source documentation." SLJ

Includes bibliographical references

326   Slavery and emancipation

Bailey, Anne C.

African voices of the Atlantic slave trade; beyond the silence and the shame. Beacon Press 2005 289p il map $26; pa $16 *

Grades: 11 12 Adult   **326**

1. Slave trade

ISBN 0-8070-5512-3; 0-8070-5513-1 (pa)
                                     LC 2004-15082

Bailey, Anne C.—*Continued*

The author "focuses on the slave trade from the African perspective. As there are few written African records, in contrast to those found in Europe and the Americas, on this topic, she centers her study on the oral tradition, what she refers to as 'African human libraries.' She primarily focuses on a region in Ghana around one particular oral remembrance told from various perspectives. . . . A fascinating perspective on slavery from the African continent." Booklist

Includes bibliographical references

Bales, Kevin

Slavery today; [by] Kevin Bales and Becky Cornell. Groundwood Books 2008 141p il (Groundwork guides) $18.95; pa $10

Grades: 7 8 9 10   **326**

1. Slavery

ISBN   978-0-88899-772-2;   0-88899-772-8; 978-0-88899-773-9 (pa); 0-88899-773-6 (pa)

"Easy to read and extremely engaging, the work traces the existence and occurrence of slavery in modern factories, jungles, and farms around the world, and discusses prostitution and strategies for ending slavery in the global market. . . . Students will find this book of great use for research papers, but it is also highly readable for personal enrichment. The language used is not complicated, the prose is understandable, and the personal narratives are passionate, even when describing awful, inhumane acts." Libr Media Connect

Includes bibliographical references

Douglass, Frederick, 1817?-1895

Frederick Douglass: selected speeches and writings; edited by Philip S. Foner; abridged and adapted by Yuval Taylor. Hill Bks. 1999 789p pa $32.95 hardcover o.p. *

Grades: 11 12 Adult   **326**

ISBN 1-55652-352-1 (pa)   LC 99-23180

Based on Foner's five-volume The life and writings of Frederick Douglass (1950-1975), this volume "covers Douglass' speeches and writings over a 54-year period. The breadth and depth of his focus and concerns reflected in more than 2,000 speeches, editorials, articles, and letters provide a wellspring of knowledge about the man and his intellect." Booklist

Includes bibliographical references

Edwards, Judith

Abolitionists and slave resistance; breaking the chains of slavery; foreword by Henry Louis Gates. Enslow Publishers 2004 128p il map (Slavery in American history) lib bdg $26.60

Grades: 7 8 9 10   **326**

1. Abolitionists 2. Slavery—United States

ISBN 0-7660-2155-6   LC 2003-13457

Contents: Events leading to abolition; Slavery and the Revolution; The anti-slavery movement gathers force; Abolitionists organize; The Amistad and the new decade; The rebels and the runaways; Escape from slavery; John Brown's raid; On the antislavery side; From slave to soldier

"Edwards examines the growth of the abolition movement and provides examples of some of the ways slaves themselves protested, including theft, work slowdowns, and destruction of property. Rebellions, runaways, and the Underground Railroad are also covered. The sensitive and respectful approach leads to an understanding of the social issues that remain as a legacy of slavery in American society today." SLJ

Includes bibliographical references

Encyclopedia of slave resistance and rebellion; edited by Junius P. Rodriguez. Greenwood Press 2006 2v il (Greenwood milestones in African American history) set $199.95

Grades: 11 12 Adult   **326**

1. Reference books 2. Slavery—United States—Encyclopedias

ISBN 0-313-33271-1; 978-0-313-33271-5

LC 2006-31210

This encyclopedia "focuses solely on the history of resistance in slave societies, most notably in the Americas. The 20-page introduction provides a solid examination of the history of resistance to slavery and begins to examine some of the cultural issues that both maintained slavery and downplayed resistance. . . . The text will serve as a good accompaniment to reference materials on slavery, so that readers understand that with slavery went resistance." Booklist

Includes bibliographical references

Feelings, Tom, 1933-2003

The middle passage; white ships/black cargo; introduction by John Henrik Clarke. Dial Bks. 1995 unp il map $75

Grades: 7 8 9 10   **326**

1. Blacks in art 2. Slavery—Pictorial works

ISBN 0-8037-1804-7   LC 95-13866

"Consisting entirely of Feeling's uncaptioned black-and-white illustrations, this . . . picture book chronicles the inhumane conditions endured by enslaved Africans during 'four centuries of the slave trade.'" Booklist

"A book for careful study and discussion, both at home and in the classroom." N Y Times Book Rev

Includes bibliographical references

Fradin, Dennis B.

Bound for the North Star; true stories of fugitive slaves; [by] Dennis Brindell Fradin. Clarion Bks. 2000 206p il $20 *

Grades: 7 8 9 10   **326**

1. Slavery—United States 2. Underground railroad 3. Abolitionists

ISBN 0-395-97017-2   LC 00-29052

"Fradin here draws on more than 16 slaves' personal experiences to show what slavery was like: the unrelenting racism; the physical brutality, including rape and flogging; the anguish of family separation. . . . The narrative is direct, with no rhetoric or cover-up. . . . This is painful reading about legal racist cruelty and those who resisted it." Booklist

Includes bibliographical references

Fradin, Judith Bloom
5,000 miles to freedom; Ellen and William Craft's flight from slavery; [by] Judith Bloom Fradin and Dennis Brindell Fradin. National Geographic 2006 96p il $19.95; lib bdg $29.90

Grades: 5 6 7 8 9 10   **326**
    1. Craft, Ellen, 1826-1891 2. Craft, William, 19th cent. 3. Slavery—United States
    ISBN 0-7922-7885-2; 0-7922-7886-0 (lib bdg)

"In 1848, light-skinned Ellen Craft, dressed in the clothing of a rich, white man, assumed the identity of Mr. William Johnson and, escorted by his black slave, William, traveled by railroad and boat to reach the North. With the passage of a more stringent Fugitive Slave Law in 1850, the couple . . . decided to travel to England. . . . In 1869, they returned to the United States, opening a school and operating a farm in Georgia. . . . This lively, well-written volume presents the events in their lives in an exciting, page-turner style that's sure to hold readers attention. Black-and-white photographs, illustrations, and reproductions enhance the text." SLJ
Includes bibliographical references

Gann, Marjorie
Five thousand years of slavery; [by] Marjorie Gann and Janet Willen. Tundra Books 2011 168p il map $27.95 *

Grades: 7 8 9 10   **326**
    1. Slavery
    ISBN 978-0-88776-914-6; 0-88776-914-4

"This well-researched global survey introduces readers to slavery practices, customs, suffering, uprisings, and revolts as well as antislavery efforts from ancient Greece and Rome to today's world. . . . Informative documentary photos and factually rich sidebars enhance the text. . . . [This is a] groundbreaking title." SLJ
Includes bibliographical references

Grant, Reg, 1954-
Slavery; real people and their stories of enslavement. DK Pub. 2009 191p il $24.99 *

Grades: 7 8 9 10   **326**
    1. Slavery
    ISBN 978-0-7566-5169-5; 0-7566-5169-7

"This encyclopedic guide to the subject of slavery highlights its history from Mesopotamia through the Atlantic slave trade and into the present day. . . . Photographs, time lines, quotations from historical figures and paintings create a diverse panorama of information. . . . As thorough as it is socially pertinent." Publ Wkly

Growing up in slavery; stories of young slaves as told by themselves; edited by Yuval Taylor; illustrations by Kathleen Judge. Lawrence Hill Books 2005 xxv, 230p il $22.95; pa $9.95 *

Grades: 9 10 11 12   **326**
    1. Slavery—United States
    ISBN 1-55652-548-6; 1-55652-635-0 (pa)

"Ten African Americans—among them Frederick Douglass and Harriet Jacobs, as well as less well-known individuals—tell what it was like to be a child and teenager under slavery. . . . Invaluable for students in search of primary-source material, and many selections will make riveting read-alouds." Booklist
Includes bibliographical references

Horton, James Oliver
Slavery and the making of America; [by] James Oliver Horton [and] Lois E. Horton. Oxford University Press 2004 254p il maps $35; pa $18.95 *

Grades: 11 12 Adult   **326**
    1. Slavery—United States 2. African Americans—History
    ISBN 0-19-517903-X; 0-19-530451-9 (pa)
        LC 2004-13617

The authors "explore the economic, social, and cultural implications of the enslavement of Africans in America, from the selection of slaves from certain regions of Africa to harvest the newly introduced rice crops of the Carolinas to the incentive of freedom offered on both sides of the American Revolution and Civil War to induce the assistance of slaves." Booklist

"The oft-told tale is made fresh through up-to-date slavery scholarship, the extensive use of slave narratives and archival photos and, especially, a focus on individual experience." Publ Wkly

Jewett, Clayton E.
Slavery in the South; a state-by-state history; [by] Clayton E. Jewett and John O. Allen; foreword by Jon L. Wakelyn. Greenwood Press 2004 xxxiii, 305p il $59.95

Grades: 11 12 Adult   **326**
    1. Slavery—United States
    ISBN 0-313-32019-5   LC 2003-60004

The authors "profile 15 states and the District of Columbia. . . . All profiles contain a timeline, slave and free black census data, background on the origins of slavery for the state, and the state's Civil War experience. Many of the sketches include sections on subjects such as slave life, emancipation and reconstruction, slave codes, and economics of slavery." Choice

"Although the book is organized by state, the information is valuable for students who are studying the institution of slavery as a whole." Libr Media Connect
Includes bibliographical references

Lester, Julius
To be a slave; paintings by Tom Feelings. 30th anniversary ed. Dial Bks. 1998 160p il hardcover o.p. pa $6.99

Grades: 6 7 8 9   **326**
    1. Slavery—United States
    ISBN 0-8037-2347-4; 0-14-131001-4 (pa)
        LC 98-5213

A reissue of the title first published 1968

"Through the words of the slave, interwoven with strongly sympathetic commentary, the reader learns what it is to be another man's property; how the slave feels about himself; and how he feels about others. Every aspect of slavery, regardless of how grim, has been painfully and unrelentingly described." Read Ladders for Hum Relat. 6th edition
Includes bibliographical references

Postma, Johannes

The Atlantic slave trade. Greenwood Press 2003 xxii, 177p map (Greenwood guides to historic events, 1500-1900) $45

Grades: 11 12 Adult   **326**

1. Slave trade

ISBN 0-313-31862-X   LC 2002-35338

Also available in paperback from University Press of Florida

The author "covers the entire Atlantic slave trade era, from the 1400s to the final abolition of chattel slavery in the New World in 1888. The focus is on Africa and the entire New World. While he describes the many horrors of the Middle Passage, he also examines how the slave trade contributed to the development of the modern international economy. The last chapters discuss the efforts to abolish the slave trade and its legacy." SLJ

Includes bibliographical references

Schneider, Dorothy

Slavery in America; [by] Dorothy Schneider and Carl J. Schneider. Rev ed. Facts on File 2007 554p il map (American experience) $80; pa $21.95 *

Grades: 11 12 Adult   **326**

1. Slavery—United States

ISBN   0-8160-6241-2;   978-0-8160-6241-6; 0-8160-6839-9 (pa); 978-0-8160-6839-5 (pa)

      LC 2006-24798

First published 2000 as part of the Eyewitness history series

This book recounts the history of slavery, "as well as the Reconstruction period that followed, by examining, chapter by chapter, many of its aspects: the slave catchers and their coffles in Africa, the crowded slave ships, slave auctions, life and labor on plantations, escape attempts and insurrections, and the Civil War and eventual emancipation." Publisher's note

Includes bibliographical references

Segal, Ronald, 1932-

Islam's Black slaves; the other Black diaspora. Farrar, Straus & Giroux 2001 273p maps hardcover o.p. pa $14 *

Grades: 11 12 Adult   **326**

1. Slavery 2. Slave trade

ISBN 0-374-22774-8; 0-374-52797-0 (pa)

      LC 00-62256

This book presents "an overview of black slavery in the Islamic world from its beginnings to modern Sudan and Morocco. . . . {It} explores Islamic slavery in China, India, the Middle East, and Africa and focuses on the differences between Islamic and Western slavery." Libr J

"The strength of this account is the meticulous documentation of what is fact and what is surmise. The dramatic narrative is sure to spark discussion and further research." Booklist

Slave narratives. Library of Am. 2000 1,034p $40

Grades: 11 12 Adult   **326**

1. Slavery—United States 2. African Americans—Biography

ISBN 1-88301-176-0   LC 99-40360

"Appearing in this collection are memoirs penned by well-known activists Nat Turner, Frederick Douglass, William Wells Brown, Henry Bibb, and Sojourner Truth. In addition, several powerful, evocative works by less celebrated writers are also featured. . . . Together these 10 narratives paint a vivid portrait of the cruelties of the institution of slavery. . . . A significant contribution to the literature of the African American experience." Booklist

Includes bibliographical references

Slavery; James D. Torr, book editor. Greenhaven Press 2004 240p map (Opposing viewpoints in world history) hardcover o.p. pa $22.45 *

Grades: 8 9 10 11 12   **326**

1. Slavery—United States

ISBN 0-7377-1705-X; 0-7377-1706-8 (pa)

      LC 2003-44812

This book offers "perspectives on American slavery through a selection of primary sources. The excerpts, culled from speeches, pamphlets, and scholarly texts, are divided into four sections that cover moral issues, slave resistance, abolitionists, and events that led to the Civil War. . . . The entries that are included . . . will greatly enhance students' understanding of the issues. . . . An important, useful addition to the high-school history curriculum." Booklist

Includes bibliographical references

Slavery in America; Orville Vernon Burton, editor. Gale 2008 2v il (Gale library of daily life) set $211

Grades: 9 10 11 12   **326**

1. Slavery—United States 2. Reference books

ISBN 978-1-4144-3013-3; 1-4144-3013-2

      LC 2007-38576

This is a "survey of slavery in the United States between 1619 and the Civil War. . . . Chapters are organized into sections covering subjects such as the Middle Passage and Africa; work; family and community; culture and leisure; health; religion; the business of slavery; resistance and rebellion; and historical reactions for and against the institution. . . . This thought-provoking and thorough reference work will appeal to both general and scholarly audiences. American history students will find it useful for reports and background information." SLJ

Includes bibliographical references

Slavery in the United States; a social, political, and historical encyclopedia; Junius P. Rodriguez, editor. ABC-CLIO 2007 2v il map set $185 *

Grades: 9 10 11 12   **326**

1. Slavery—United States—Encyclopedias 2. Reference books

ISBN 978-1-85109-544-5; 1-85109-544-6

      LC 2006-101351

"Three hundred A-to-Z entries by more than 100 contributors span some 575 pages and highlight people, issues, and events dating from the first colonization through Reconstruction. . . . Primary-source documents include 'John Locke Prepares a Constitution for Carolina (1669)' and 'Frederick Douglass Offers Reflections upon Emancipation (1883).'" Libr J

"This set will be an essential addition to any collec-

Slavery in the United States—*Continued*
tion supporting a middle or high school American Studies curriculum." SLJ

Includes bibliographical references

Slavery today; Ronald D. Lankford, Jr., book editor. Greenhaven Press 2010 137p (At issue. Social issues) $31.80; pa $22.50 *
Grades: 9 10 11 12   **326**
1. Slavery 2. Slave trade
ISBN   978-0-7377-4440-8;   0-7377-4440-5;
978-0-7377-4441-5 (pa); 0-7377-4441-3 (pa)
LC 2009020987
The articles in this anthology discuss modern-day slavery and possible ways to end it.

Includes bibliographical references

White, Shane
The sounds of slavery; discovering African American history through songs, sermons, and speech; [by] Shane White and Graham White. Beacon Press 2005 xxii, 241p hardcover o.p. pa $17 *
Grades: 11 12 Adult   **326**
1. Slavery—United States 2. African Americans—History 3. Plantation life
ISBN 0-8070-5026-1; 0-8070-5027-X (pa)
LC 2004-21447
Includes audio CD
"Drawing on WPA interviews with former slaves, slave narratives, and other historical documents from the 1700s through the 1850s, the authors provide the context for the field calls, work songs, sermons, and other sounds and utterances of slaves on American plantations. The authors also focus on recollections of the wails of slaves being whipped, the barking of hounds hunting down runaways, and the keening of women losing their children on the slave block. The combination of the CD and the book brings vibrancy and texture to a complex history that has been long neglected." Booklist

Includes discography and bibliographical references

Worth, Richard, 1945-
Slave life on the plantation; prisons beneath the sun. Enslow Publishers 2004 128p il (Slavery in American history) lib bdg $26.60
Grades: 7 8 9 10   **326**
1. Slavery—United States 2. Plantation life
ISBN 0-7660-2152-1   LC 2003-24291
Contents: A slave's life; Slavery in the 1600s; Plantation life in 1700s; King Cotton; Relationships between owners and slaves; African-American culture on the plantation; Freedom
"Worth frames his account within the sweep of history, but his focus is on daily life—the work, the hardship (especially the breakup of family life), punishment, and resistance—and he discusses the relationship between owners and slaves, the importance of cotton, and African American culture. [This title includes] several stirring page-long slave narratives as well as black-and-white drawings and photos. The documentation is exemplary." Booklist

Includes glossary and bibliographical references

327.12   Espionage and subversion

Espionage and intelligence; Debra A. Miller, book editor. Greenhaven Press 2007 234p (Current controversies) lib bdg $38.50; pa $26.75
Grades: 9 10 11 12   **327.12**
1. American espionage 2. Intelligence service—United States
ISBN 978-0-7377-3719-6 (lib bdg); 0-7377-3719-0 (lib bdg); 978-0-7377-3720-2 (pa); 0-7377-3720-4 (pa)
LC 2007-931891
Topics in this anthology include the use of torture to gather information, civil rights issues regarding intelligence gathering, and U.S. intelligence with regards to the 9/11 terrorist attacks and Iraq's possession of weapons of mass destruction.

Includes bibliographical references

Owen, David, 1939-
Spies: the undercover world of secrets, gadgets and lies; foreword by Antonio J. Mendez. Firefly Bks. 2004 128p il map $19.95; pa $9.95
Grades: 9 10 11 12   **327.12**
1. Spies 2. Espionage
ISBN 1-55297-795-1; 1-55297-794-3 (pa)
LC 2004-303819
This book covers "the history of espionage from its beginnings until the present day." Booklist
"This is a slick, colorful book. . . . Teens will find a great deal of intriguing information, along with wonderful photos. Social studies teachers will find a wealth of material to support their curriculums, as well." SLJ

Smith, W. Thomas
Encyclopedia of the Central Intelligence Agency; [by] W. Thomas Smith Jr. Facts on File 2003 282p il (Facts on File library of American history) $60; pa $19.95 *
Grades: 11 12 Adult   **327.12**
1. United States. Central Intelligence Agency 2. Reference books
ISBN 0-8160-4666-2; 0-8160-4667-0 (pa)
This encyclopedia includes "more than 500 historical, biographical, and general entries about the intelligence-gathering, covert-action agency established in 1947. . . . Current through March 2003, the encyclopedia also covers predecessor organizations such as the World War II-era Office of Strategic Services (OSS). . . . The work covers terrorism extensively." Booklist

Includes bibliographical references

327.73   United States—Foreign relations

The **American** empire; [edited by] John C. Davenport. Chelsea House 2007 152p il (The world in focus) $35
Grades: 7 8 9 10   **327.73**
1. War on terrorism 2. Imperialism 3. United States—Foreign relations
ISBN 978-0-7910-9195-1; 0-7910-9195-3
LC 2007-3656

The American empire—*Continued*

"The first set of essays searches the past for the origins of American imperialism and the roots of American preeminence. The second section looks at how the United States applies—or sometimes misapplies—its unparalleled power and influence overseas, as well as the domestic implications of such actions. Each of the essays in the final section considers a future in which the United States acknowledges its imperial status and asserts itself accordingly, examining the beneficial and deleterious effects of a self-consciously active empire." Publisher's note

Includes bibliographical references

Global perspectives on the United States; a nation by nation survey; David Levinson and Karen Christensen, editors. Berkshire Pub. Group 2007 2vp il map set $275
Grades: 11 12 Adult   327.73
1. United States—Foreign relations 2. United States—Foreign opinion
ISBN 978-1-9337820-6-5; 1-9337820-6-4
                                        LC 2006-39331
This set assembles "statistics about how the world has perceived the United States." Libr J
"Not recommended reading for thin-skinned patriots; however, a great resource for academic, public, and high-school libraries." Booklist
Includes bibliographical references

Hastedt, Glenn P., 1950-
Encyclopedia of American foreign policy; by Glenn Hastedt. Facts on File 2003 562p il map $85
Grades: 11 12 Adult   327.73
1. Reference books 2. United States—Foreign relations—Encyclopedias
ISBN 0-8160-4642-5   LC 2003-49186
In this reference, Hastedt "addresses the four major foreign policy themes: selection of a grand strategy, the role of the public voice, the policymaking process, and the influence of the past. The more than 475 entries, all by Hastedt, are arranged alphabetically and include people, agencies, documents, and events rather than broader issues and ideological constructs of US foreign policy. Entries are quite readable and rarely run longer than a page; most are also cross-referenced and have bibliographies." Choice
Includes bibliographical references

Laxer, James
Empire. Groundwood Books 2006 144p il map (Groundwork Guides) $15.95
Grades: 8 9 10 11 12   327.73
1. Imperialism 2. United States—Foreign relations
ISBN 978-0-88899-706-7; 0-88899-706-X
                                        LC 2006-497080
This book "compares the American Empire to those of the past, finding much can be learned from the fates of the British, Roman, Chinese, Incan, and Aztec empires." Publisher's note
Includes bibliographical references

Margulies, Phillip, 1952-
America's role in the world; foreword by James M. Goldgeier. Facts On File 2009 358p (Global issues) $45
Grades: 9 10 11 12   327.73
1. United States—Foreign relations 2. United States—Foreign opinion
ISBN 978-0-8160-7611-6; 0-8160-7611-1
                                        LC 2008-32102
"This volume begins with a detailed history of American foreign policy and the debate over what direction it should take. Margulies examines America's role in the world from the perspectives of Europe, Latin America, the Islamic world, Asia, and the former Soviet Union. . . . Readers will also find a chapter on how to research America's role in the world, facts and figures, key players, organizations and agencies, chronology, glossary and and an annotated bibliography. The scholarship exhibited should be a model for all . . . books written for high school students." Libr Media Connect
Includes glossary and bibliographical references

U.S. policy toward rogue nations; James D. Torr, book editor. Greenhaven Press 2004 94p (At issue) lib bdg $28.70; pa $19.95
Grades: 9 10 11 12   327.73
1. United States—Foreign relations
ISBN 0-7377-2196-0 (lib bdg); 0-7377-2197-9 (pa)
                                        LC 2003-62480
This book "considers the doctrine of preemptive war; whether the invasion of Iraq was justified; if the U.S. should support regime change in Syria and Iran; alternative approaches to dealing with North Korea; the value of peace efforts in Sudan; and whether the U.S. should lift sanctions in Libya." SLJ
Includes bibliographical references

328.73   Legislative process in the United States

Barone, Michael
The almanac of American politics 2010; the senators, the representatives and the governors: their records and election results, their states and districts; [by] Michael Barone, Richard E. Cohen. National Journal Group 2009 1726p il map $97.95; pa $79.95
Grades: 11 12 Adult   328.73
1. United States. Congress 2. United States—Politics and government 3. Almanacs 4. Reference books
ISSN 0362-076X
ISBN 978-0-89234-119-1; 978-0-89234-120-7 (pa)
Biennial. First published 1972 by Gambit
"Provides essential data for the assessment of each representative and senator in Congress. Specifics include political background on the state or congressional district, biographies, voting records, group ratings (by such groups as Americans for Democratic Action and Americans for Constitutional Action), and recent election results. Provides information on the governor of each state. Arranged by state. Congressional district maps." Ref Sources for Small & Medium-sized Libr. 6th edition

Congress A to Z. 5th ed. CQ Press 2008 xxxiv, 704p il map (CQ's American government A to Z series) $85 *
Grades: 11 12 Adult   **328.73**
1. United States. Congress 2. Reference books
ISBN 978-0-87289-558-4   LC 2008-11284
"CQ Press, a Division of Congressional Quarterly Inc."
First published 1988
This work provides information on the structure and work of Congress in some 340 alphabetical entries.
Includes bibliographical references

CQ's politics in America, 2010; the 111th Congress; by Congressional Quarterly staff; Chuck McCutcheon and Christina L. Lyons, editors. Congressional Quarterly, Inc. 2009 xxvi, 1214p il $125; pa $89 *
Grades: 11 12 Adult   **328.73**
1. United States. Congress 2. Elections—United States 3. Reference books
ISBN 978-1-60426-602-3; 978-1-60426-603-0 (pa)
Biennial. First published 1981
Also available online
Provides an analysis of every lawmaker in the 111th Congress, including biographical data, contact information, election results, and committee assignments.
"An outstanding, highly detailed guide to contemporary politics." Libr J

Dewhirst, Robert E.
Encyclopedia of the United States Congress; [by] Robert E. Dewhirst; John David Rausch, Jr., associate editor. Facts on File 2006 578p il (Facts on File library of American history) $95
Grades: 11 12 Adult   **328.73**
1. United States. Congress 2. Reference books
ISBN 0-8160-5058-9   LC 2005-28124
This encyclopedia covers "the people, events, and terms involved in the legislative branch of government. It also provides explanations of the relationships between the legislative and other branches of government, court cases, elections, political opponents, congressional leaders, scandals, controversial issues, and the inner workings of Congress." Publisher's note
Includes bibliographical references

Freedman, Eric, 1949-
African Americans in Congress; a documentary history; [by] Eric Freedman, Stephen A. Jones. CQ Press 2008 574p il $115
Grades: 9 10 11 12   **328.73**
1. United States. Congress—History 2. African Americans—History—Sources 3. Statesmen—United States 4. Reference books
ISBN 978-0-87289-385-6; 0-87289-385-5
                               LC 2007-40318
The authors "provide more than 160 primary source documents covering events that have affected the daily lives of African Americans, along with documents from individuals who have served in Congress." Choice
"For students of history, American studies, politics, and journalism, this volume is mandatory." SLJ
Includes bibliographical references

Guide to Congress. 6th ed. CQ Press 2008 2v il map set $350 *
Grades: 11 12 Adult   **328.73**
1. United States. Congress
ISBN 978-0-8728-9295-8   LC 2007-33245
First published 1971 with title: Congressional Quarterly's guide to the Congress of the United States
"Covers history and workings of Congress, with biographical data on all members." N Y Public Libr Book of How & Where to Look It Up
"To really understand Congress, there is nothing better than these large volumes." Booklist
Includes bibliographical references

How Congress works. 4th ed. CQ Press 2008 248p il pa $55 *
Grades: 9 10 11 12   **328.73**
1. United States. Congress
ISBN 978-0-87289-955-1; 0-87289-955-1
                               LC 2008-8427
First published 1983
This work explains the procedures, and rules that govern the Senate and the House as well as party leadership, the legislative process, the committee system and congressional staff.
Includes bibliographical references

Official Congressional directory, 2009-2010; 111th Congress convened January 6, 2009; Joint Committee on Printing, United States Congress. U.S. Government Printing Office 2009 xxiv, 1207p map $55; pa $45 *
Grades: 11 12 Adult   **328.73**
1. United States. Congress—Directories 2. Reference books
ISBN 978-0-16-083728-9; 978-0-16-083727-2 (pa)
Also available online
Biennial
"Covers biographical information, committee assignments of members of Congress, and officers of Congress." N Y Public Libr Book of How & Where to Look It Up

Remini, Robert Vincent, 1921-
The House: the history of the House of Representatives; [by] Robert V. Remini. HarperCollins Publishers 2006 614p il hardcover o.p. pa $19.95
Grades: 11 12 Adult   **328.73**
1. United States. Congress. House—History
ISBN   978-0-06-088434-5;   0-06-088434-7; 978-0-06-134111-3 (pa); 0-06-134111-8 (pa)
                               LC 2006-615801
"The Library of Congress"
The author "traces the development of this quintessential American institution from a struggling, nascent body to the venerable powerhouse it has become since America's rise on the world stage." Publisher's note
"Published under the aegis of the House itself, Remini's work is nonpartisan, civic-minded, and deserving of every library's consideration." Booklist
Includes bibliographical references

Stathis, Stephen W.
Landmark debates in Congress; from the Declaration of independence to the war in Iraq. CQ Press 2009 514p il map $145 *
Grades: 11 12 Adult   **328.73**
1. United States. Congress—History 2. Reference books 3. United States—Politics and government—Sources 4. American speeches 5. Parliamentary practice
ISBN 978-0-87289-976-6; 0-87289-976-4
LC 2008-41380
"Presenting excerpts of speeches delivered in the House of Representatives and the Senate, this volume seeks to give readers 'a window into how Congress, seemingly constituting a cross-section of society, has wrestled with some of the most thorny questions facing American democracy.' Such monumental issues as war, slavery, impeachment of the President, amendments to the Constitution, and other bones of contention illuminate the legislative process. . . . A depiction of real people struggling to solve real problems, this book helps to humanize 'the marble men'—and women—of our national legislative body." Libr J
Includes bibliographical references

Student's guide to Congress; advisory editor, Bruce J. Schulman. CQ Press 2009 379p il map (Student's guide to the U.S. government series) $75 *
Grades: 9 10 11 12   **328.73**
1. United States. Congress 2. Reference books
ISBN 978-0-87289-554-6; 0-87289-554-8
LC 2008-28980
"Part 1 consists of essays that help students explain who gets elected, understand how Congress operates, and appreciate how Congress and the president must work together. Part 2 consists of 142 A-Z entries, from Abscam to Zone whips. . . . Part 3, Primary Source Library, includes portions of the Constitution, Henry Clay's explanation of his support of the War of 1812, Joseph McCarthy's 1950 telegram to Harry Truman alleging that the State Department harbors a nest of communists and communist sympathizers, and the War Powers Resolution of 1973. . . . [This] volume provides a lot of information and thought-provoking material that will serve high-school students in addition to any older researchers interested in this topic." Booklist
Includes bibliographical references

330 Economics

Bussing-Burks, Marie, 1958-
Money for minors; a student's guide to economics. Greenwood Press 2008 200p il $55
Grades: 9 10 11 12   **330**
1. Economics 2. Money
ISBN 978-0-313-34757-3   LC 2008-4496
"Opening with a Dictionary of Economics that contains definitions for more than four hundred economics terms (from ability-to-pay principle to zoning law), she follows with six 'lessons' on such topics as the Federal Reserve Bank, gross domestic product, the federal government's budget process, rising national debt, and the

business cycle." Voice Youth Advocates
"A wonderful reference for all monetary matters. . . . It's a great resource for beginners." SLJ
Includes bibliographical references

Economic literacy; a complete guide. Marshall Cavendish 2009 224p il $99.90 *
Grades: 9 10 11 12   **330**
1. Economics
ISBN 978-0-7614-7910-9; 0-7614-7910-4
LC 2009-9462
This book is "comprised of approximately 50 A-to-Z articles ranging in length from two to four pages. *Economic Literacy* provides clearly outlined historical perspectives on international trade, socialism, and tariffs, balanced with newsworthy items. . . . Articles on globalization, service economy, and sustainable development look toward future developments and include links to organizations, reports, inflation calculators, and more." SLJ
Includes glossary and bibliographical references

330.1 Systems, schools, theories

Heilbroner, Robert L., 1919-2005
The worldly philosophers; the lives, times, and ideas of the great economic thinkers. Rev. 7th ed. Simon & Schuster 1999 365p pa $16
Grades: 11 12 Adult   **330.1**
1. Economists 2. Economics
ISBN 0-684-86214-X   LC 99-14050
"A Touchstone book"
First published 1953
The author traces the story of economics and the great economists from Adam Smith, Malthus, Ricardo, the Utopians, Marx, Veblen and Keynes to those working with the problems of our contemporary world
Includes bibliographical references

330.9 Economic situation and conditions

Blumenthal, Karen
Six days in October; the stock market crash of 1929. Atheneum Bks. for Young Readers 2002 156p il $17.95 *
Grades: 7 8 9 10   **330.9**
1. New York Stock Exchange, Inc. 2. Great Depression, 1929-1939 3. United States—Economic conditions—1919-1933
ISBN 0-689-84276-7   LC 2001-46360
"A Wall Street Journal book"
A comprehensive review of the events, personalities, and mistakes behind the Stock Market Crash of 1929, featuring photographs, newspaper articles, and cartoons of the day
"This fast-paced, gripping . . . account of the market crash of October 1929 puts a human face on the crisis." Publ Wkly
Includes bibliographical references

Encyclopedia of the age of the industrial revolution, 1700-1920; edited by Christine Rider. Greenwood Press 2007 2v il set $225
Grades: 11 12 Adult   **330.9**
1. Reference books 2. Industrial revolution—Encyclopedias
ISBN 978-0-313-33503-7; 0-313-33501-X
LC 2007-1830
"The 150 signed essays in this set cover people, events, and inventions of the Industrial Revolution, and discuss how the movement affected not only business and trade, but also society, politics, and even ecology in many countries. The entries provide important facts, yet are often thoughtful and philosophical. . . . Many other volumes expound on inventions and inventors, but this one stands out for its treatment of Japan, Russia, and other countries, as well as its coverage of the sociological, ecological, and aesthetic implications of this period." SLJ
Includes bibliographical references

Industrial revolution; people and perspectives; Jennifer L. Goloboy, editor. ABC-CLIO 2008 224p il (Perspectives in American social history) $85 *
Grades: 11 12 Adult   **330.9**
1. Industrial revolution 2. Industrialization 3. United States—Social conditions 4. Reference books
ISBN 978-1-59884-065-0; 1-59884-065-7
LC 2008-2366
"This clearly written and carefully researched volume documents . . . [the] early steps toward industrialization from roughly 1800 to 1860, calling attention to groups [such as] women, ethnic and cultural minorities, [and] laborers. . . . This work provides a useful timeline from 1748 to 1860, an abundance of photographs, an assortment of primary documents . . . a bibliography at the end of each chapter and a topical bibliography at the end of the study, and an adequate index. While certainly useful to scholars, this is a work for a general audience that would be a worthwhile addition to high school and university libraries." Am Ref Books Annu, 2009
Includes bibliographical references

Industrialization and empire, 1783 to 1914; edited by Louise Spilsbury. Brown Bear Books 2010 112p il map (Curriculum connections. Atlas of world history) lib bdg $39.95
Grades: 9 10 11 12   **330.9**
1. Modern history 2. World history—19th century 3. Industrial revolution 4. Industrialization 5. Imperialism
ISBN 978-1-933834-69-6   LC 2009-27837
Contents: Introduction; The world in 1812; The world in 1880; The world in 1914; World population; World trade; The age of revolution; Napoleonic Europe; Nationalism in Europe; The industrial revolution; European alliances; The decline of the Ottomans; Africa before the scramble; Africa and European empires; Australia and New Zealand; The decline of Manchu China; Japan in the 19th century; Britain and India; Colonialism and Southeast Asia; Latin America; The growth of Canada; The expansion of the United States; The American Civil War; U.S. population and economy

This book "is divided into thematic and regional maps which are followed by short but very comprehensive articles. . . . [It includes] curriculum context sidebars, important terms students should know, and how the topic ties into other areas." Libr Media Connect
Includes bibliographical references

Outman, James L., 1946-
Industrial Revolution: almanac; [by] James L. Outman, Elisabeth M. Outman. U.X.L 2003 242p il (Industrial revolution reference library) $55
Grades: 8 9 10 11 12   **330.9**
1. Industrial revolution 2. Reference books
ISBN 0-7876-6513-4   LC 2002-155422
Contents: Origins of the Industrial Revolution; The revolution begins: steam engines, railroads, steamboats; New machines and the factory system; The social and political impact of the Industrial Revolution, part 1; The age of petroleum and electricity; The new business models; The social and political impact of the Industrial Revolution, part 2; Globalization
"This is an excellent adjunct to American and world history units and classes on economics and labor movements." Booklist
Includes bibliographical references

Industrial Revolution: primary sources; [by] James L. Outman, Elisabeth M. Outman. U.X.L 2003 212p il (Industrial revolution reference library) $55 *
Grades: 8 9 10 11 12   **330.9**
1. Industrial revolution 2. Reference books
ISBN 0-7876-6515-0   LC 2002-155420
Contents: Economic theory; Adam Smith; The Wealth of Nations; Andrew Ure; The philosophy of manufacturers; Karl Marx; The Communist Manifesto; Andrew Carnegie; The gospel of wealth; Technological advances and criticisms; Thomas Savery; Uses of the fire engine; Leeds letters; Luddites; Samuel Morse; On the telegraph; J. Stillman; The last tie; The Industrial Revolution and working conditions; Sadler Report; Samuel Gompers; Germinal Zola and coal miners; Upton Sinclair; Excerpt from The Jungle; Triangle Shirtwaist fire; Jane Addams; Excerpt from Hull House; Carmen Teoli; Congressional testimony; Politics and law in the Industrial Revolution; United States Supreme Court; Northern Securities v. United States; Theodore Roosevelt; Progressive Party platform
"This is an excellent adjunct to American and world history units and classes on economics and labor movements." Booklist
Includes bibliographical references

330.973   United States—Economic conditions

Benson, Sonia

Development of the industrial U.S.: Almanac; [by] Sonia G. Benson; Jennifer York Stock, project editor. UXL 2006 lv, 216p il (Development of the industrial U.S reference library) $63

Grades: 9 10 11 12   **330.973**

1. Industries—United States 2. Industrial revolution 3. Reference books

ISBN 1-4144-0175-2   LC 2005-15915

This book "consists of 14 chapters, each thoroughly examining one aspect of industrialization, such as railroads or early factories. User-friendly features (research and activity ideas, ample glossaries and word boxes, references to Web sites and print resources) further enhance this product's usefulness." Booklist

Includes bibliographical references

Development of the industrial U.S.: Primary sources; [by] Sonia G. Benson; Jennifer York Stock, project editor. UXL 2006 lii, 205p il (Development of the industrial U.S reference library) $63 *

Grades: 9 10 11 12   **330.973**

1. Industries—United States 2. Industrial revolution

ISBN 1-4144-0179-5   LC 2005-16349

This book "provides excerpts and explications of seminal sources, including legislative acts, accounts of daily life from regular citizens, political cartoons and more." Publisher's note

Includes bibliographical references

Lewis, Michael

The big short; inside the doomsday machine. W.W. Norton 2010 266p $27.95; pa $15.95

Grades: 11 12 Adult   **330.973**

1. United States—Economic conditions 2. Global Financial Crisis, 2008-2009 3. Financial crises

ISBN   978-0-393-07223-5;   0-393-07223-1; 978-0-393-33882-9 (pa); 0-393-33882-7 (pa)

LC 2010-4804

This "is a chronicle of four sets of players in the subprime mortgage market who had the foresight and gumption to short the diciest mortgage deals: Steve Eisner of FrontPoint, Greg Lippmann at Deutsche Bank, the three partners at Cornwall Capital, and most indelibly, Michael Burry of Scion Capital. They all walked away from the rubble with pockets full of gold and reputations as geniuses." Business Week

"'The Big Short' manages to give us the truest picture yet of what went wrong on Wall Street—and why. At times, it reads like a morality play, at other times like a modern-day farce. But as with any good play, its value lies in the way it reveals character and motive and explores the cultural context in which the plot unfolds." Washington Post

331   Labor economics

Murray, R. Emmett

The lexicon of labor; more than 500 key terms, biographical sketches, and historical insights concerning labor in America. Rev. and updated ed. New Press 2010 235p pa $16.95

Grades: 11 12 Adult   **331**

1. Labor—United States—Dictionaries 2. Reference books

ISBN 978-1-59558-226-3   LC 2010-8276

First published 1998

This is an "encyclopedia of 500 entries for terms, concepts, people, legislation, places, and events in U.S. labor history." Booklist

Includes bibliographical references

Reef, Catherine

Working in America. Facts On File 2007 xxviii, 484p il map (American experience) $80

Grades: 11 12 Adult   **331**

1. Labor—United States

ISBN 978-0-8160-6239-3; 0-8160-6239-0

LC 2006-31191

First published 2000

"Each chapter begins with a . . . narrative that chronicles the experience of workers in the United States—from factory workers, cowboys, seamstresses, and newsboys to truck drivers, migrant farm workers, computer programmers, and genetic engineers. Chronologies of important events follow, along with eyewitness testimonies on the experience of working in a wide range of professions and trades—from Thomas Jefferson, Malcolm X, Samuel Gompers, Charlotte Perkins Gilman, Jesse Jackson, Cesar Chavez, and Jane Addams, as well as a wide range of American workers." Publisher's note

Includes bibliographical references

U.S. labor in the twentieth century; studies in working-class struggles and insurgency; edited by John Hinshaw and Paul Le Blanc. Humanity Bks. 2000 397p (Revolutionary studies series) pa $25

Grades: 9 10 11 12   **331**

1. Working class 2. Labor—United States

ISBN 1-573-92865-8   LC 00-40723

Topics discussed "include the migration of African Americans to western Pennsylvania's industrial towns, the role of women and radicals in the first sit-down strikes, A. Philip Randolph's contributions to black American socialism, and the role of labor and radicals in the early civil rights movement." Booklist

Includes bibliographical references

331.1   Labor force and market

Affirmative action; Paul G. Connors, book editor. Greenhaven Press 2009 129p (At issue. Civil liberties) $31.80; pa $22.50 *
Grades: 9 10 11 12   **331.1**
1. Affirmative action programs 2. Discrimination in education 3. Colleges and universities—United States
ISBN   978-0-7377-4278-7;   0-7377-4278-X; 978-0-7377-4277-0 (pa); 0-7377-4277-1 (pa)
LC 2008041617
Articles in this anthology present opposing views on affirmative action in education.
Includes bibliographical references

Affirmative action; a documentary history; edited by Jo Ann Ooiman Robinson. Greenwood Press 2001 400p (Primary documents in American history and contemporary issues) $49.95
Grades: 11 12 Adult   **331.1**
1. Affirmative action programs
ISBN 0-313-30169-7   LC 00-49508
"Presents 400 documents, beginning in 1864 . . . and ending in mid-2000. In between are extracts from speeches, proceedings, legislation, court cases, articles, and more. Each document is accompanied by a brief explanation that puts it in context." Booklist
Includes bibliographical references

Ching, Jacqueline
Outsourcing U.S. jobs. Rosen Pub. 2009 64p il (In the news) lib bdg $21.95; pa $12.65
Grades: 7 8 9 10   **331.1**
1. Outsourcing 2. Labor supply
ISBN 978-1-4358-5039-2 (lib bdg); 1-4358-5039-4 (lib bdg); 978-1-4358-5367-6 (pa); 1-4358-5367-9 (pa)
LC 2008-16890
"*Outsourcing U.S. Jobs* uses clear examples to discuss the global marketplace and the practical and ethical considerations that come with free trade. The specific details are geared toward kids' concerns." Booklist
Includes bibliographical references

331.2   Conditions of employment

Paquette, Penny Hutchins
Apprenticeship; the ultimate teen guide. Scarecrow Press 2005 373p il (It happened to me) $42 *
Grades: 9 10 11 12   **331.2**
1. Apprentices 2. Occupational training 3. Vocational education
ISBN 0-8108-4945-3   LC 2005-8301
"After a brief discussion of the history of apprenticing, the text quickly shifts to apprenticeship today, explaining the organizational structure, various programs, and the nuts and bolts of applying for and entering into an apprenticeship position. Subsequent chapters discuss the various industries that accept apprentices and the benefits of these types of positions." Voice Youth Advocates
"An excellent starting point for teens." SLJ
Includes bibliographical references

331.3   Workers by age group

Herumin, Wendy
Child labor today; a human rights issue. Enslow Publishers 2007 112p il (Issues in focus today) $23.95 *
Grades: 7 8 9 10 11 12   **331.3**
1. Child labor 2. Human rights
ISBN 978-0-7660-2682-7; 0-7660-2682-5
LC 2007010625
"An estimated 218 million children world-wide work in terrible conditions, and this powerful title . . . combines up-to-date facts with moving portraits of individual children who toil in mines, factories, the sex trade; on farms; as domestics, soldiers, and more. . . . Many full-color photos of contemporary young people trapped in harsh workplaces are included." Booklist
Includes bibliographical references

331.4   Women workers

America's working women; a documentary history, 1600 to the present; edited by Rosalyn Baxandall and Linda Gordon, with Susan Reverby. rev and updated. Norton 1995 356p il pa $16.95 hardcover o.p. *
Grades: 11 12 Adult   **331.4**
ISBN 0-393-31262-3 (pa)   LC 94-32194
First published 1976 by Random House
"This chronologically arranged anthology presents an . . . overview of the changing roles and contributions of woman at home, in the fields, and in today's workplace." Booklist
Includes bibliographical references

Freedman, Jeri
Women in the workplace; wages, respect, and equal rights. Rosen Pub. 2009 112p il (A young woman's guide to contemporary issues) lib bdg $31.95
Grades: 7 8 9 10   **331.4**
1. Women—Employment 2. Discrimination in employment 3. Sex discrimination
ISBN 978-1-4358-3541-2; 1-4358-3541-7
LC 2009-13720
"Discusses the history of American women in the workforce and issues that they face, including sexual harassment, equal pay, and maternity leave." Publisher's note
"Facts are shared in a conversational tone, creating the sense of a chat with a big sister. . . . [Though] designed for personal reading and browsing, the data provided are accurate and also lend themselves to use in reports. This . . . will be of great interest." SLJ
Includes glossary and bibliographical references

Reber, Deborah

In their shoes; extraordinary women describe their amazing careers. Simon Pulse 2007 411p il pa $12.99

Grades: 8 9 10 11 12　　　　　　　　**331.4**
1. Women—Employment 2. Occupations 3. Vocational guidance

ISBN 978-1-4169-2578-1; 1-4169-2578-3

LC 2006-34801

"Each chapter contains an interview with its subject . . . as well as sidebars and lists on what to do now to prepare, what the person's day is like, and a time line of how her career took shape over the years. Concrete details about the women's current lives and about how they attained their goals are included. . . . A fine addition to any collection." SLJ

331.7　Labor by industry and occupation

150 great tech prep careers. 2nd ed. Ferguson 2009 561p $85; pa $29.95

Grades: 9 10 11 12　　　　　　　　**331.7**
1. Vocational education 2. Technical education 3. Occupations

ISBN　978-0-8160-7733-5;　0-8160-7733-9; 978-0-8160-7734-2 (pa); 0-8160-7734-7 (pa)

LC 2008-34824

First published 1998 with title: From high school to work

This book describes "jobs in a number of fields that are attainable without a four-year degree—requiring only on-the-job training, an apprenticeship, a certificate, or an associate's degree." Publisher's note

Includes bibliographical references

Career discovery encyclopedia. 7th ed. Ferguson 2009 8v il set $235

Grades: 7 8 9 10 11 12　　　　　　　**331.7**
1. Vocational guidance 2. Occupations 3. Reference books

ISBN 978-0-8160-7931-5; 0-8160-7931-5

LC 2009-3162

First published 1990

This set presents articles describing over 700 jobs or career fields, discussing personal, educational, and professional requirements; ways of exploring the career; salary statistics; job outlook; and how to obtain more information about the career

Christen, Carol

What color is your parachute? for teens; discovering yourself, defining your future; [by] Carol Christen and Richard N. Bolles with Jean M. Blomquist. 2nd ed., rev. Ten Speed Press 2010 178p il pa $15.99

Grades: 9 10 11 12　　　　　　　　**331.7**
1. Applications for positions 2. Vocational guidance 3. Job hunting

ISBN 978-1-58008-141-2　　　LC 2010-483344

First published 2006 with Bolles' name appearing first

The authors "begin by prompting readers to consider their interests, the kinds of people they enjoy and their ideal work environment, and round out the text with quizzes, writing exercises and teen testimonials designed to get teens thinking. Then they offer concrete ideas on how to gain experience (internships, Web sites, etc.) and prepare for interviews." Publ Wkly [review of 2006 ed.]

Includes bibliographical references

Encyclopedia of careers and vocational guidance. 15th ed. Ferguson 2010 5v il set $249.95 *

Grades: 8 9 10 11 12 Adult　　　　　**331.7**
1. Occupations—Encyclopedias 2. Vocational guidance—Encyclopedias 3. Reference books

ISBN 978-0-8160-8313-8; 0-8160-8313-4

LC 2010-17724

First published 1967

"These five volumes contain more than 700 . . . [articles] on careers in nearly 100 industries. Each three to five-page entry provides a concise and engaging profile of fields like accounting, animal care, computers, the environment, publishing, sales, and the visual arts. Included in each job entry are an overview, a history, a description, requirements, employers, advancement, earnings, work environment, outlook, and more." Libr J [review of 2008 edition]

Includes bibliographical references

Exploring tech careers. 4th ed. Ferguson Pub. Co. 2006 2v il set $125

Grades: 9 10 11 12　　　　　　　　**331.7**
1. Technology—Vocational guidance 2. Occupations

ISBN 0-8160-6447-4; 978-0-8160-6447-2

LC 2005-19101

First published 1995 under the editorship of Halli R. Cosgrove

This "two-volume set covers more than 110 technician careers and features interviews with professionals already at work in the field." Publisher's note

Includes bibliographical references

Gregory, Michael G.

The career chronicles; an insider's guide to what jobs are really like: the good, the bad, and the ugly from over 750 professionals. New World Library 2008 262p pa $15.95

Grades: 11 12 Adult　　　　　　　**331.7**
1. Vocational guidance 2. Professions 3. Occupations

ISBN 978-1-57731-573-5; 1-57731-573-1

LC 2008-4088

The author "interviewed hundreds of professionals about their jobs, asking the kind of questions that help show what the job is really like. He profiles twenty-four professions across a wide spectrum of employment categories, such as Health Care, Law, Financial Services, and Arts and Media." Voice Youth Advocates

"This book belongs in every high school library and guidance office." SLJ

O*NET; dictionary of occupational titles. 4th ed. JIST Works 2007 672p $49.95; pa $39.95

Grades: 11 12 Adult　　　　　　　**331.7**
1. Occupations—Dictionaries 2. Reference books

ISBN　978-1-59357-415-4;　1-59357-415-0; 978-1-59357-416-1 (pa); 1-59357-416-9 (pa)

LC 2007-652

O*NET—*Continued*

First published 1998 to replace Dictionary of occupational titles published by the government Printing Office. Frequently revised

"Based on information obtained from the U.S. Department of Labor, the U.S. Census Bureau, and other reliable sources"; "Developed under the direction of Michael Farr with database work by Laurence Shatkin"

This book "puts the official job descriptions and other important information from the U.S. Department of Labor's . . . Occupational Information Network (O*NET) database into [print form]. . . . Descriptions and data included for nearly 950 jobs, covering almost 100 percent of the workforce." Publisher's note

Porterfield, Deborah

Construction and trades. Ferguson 2007 126p il (Top careers in two years) $32.95

Grades: 9 10 11 12   **331.7**

1. Vocational guidance 2. Occupations 3. Building 4. Industrial arts education

ISBN 978-0-8160-6897-5; 0-8160-6897-6

LC 2007-14326

Contents: Carpenter; Plumber; Electrician; Aircraft mechanic; Auto service technician; HVACR engineering technician; Surveyor; Civil engineering technician; Construction site engineer; Interior designer; Mason; Marine service technician

This book "explores the various career options in . . . [the construction and trade] field that students have with an associate's degree, comparable certification, or work/life experience." Publisher's note

Reeves, Diane Lindsey, 1959-

Career ideas for teens in education and training; [by] Diane Lindsey Reeves with Gail Karlitz. Ferguson 2005 183p il (Career ideas for teens) $40; pa $16.95

Grades: 7 8 9 10   **331.7**

1. Teaching 2. Education 3. Vocational guidance

ISBN 0-8160-5295-6; 0-8160-6919-0 (pa)

LC 2004024220

This book explorers 35 occupations in education and training. "Information for each job includes education requirements, relevant Web sites, and median salaries. . . . [It] also covers volunteer opportunities; lists entry-level jobs within the field; provides interview tips and sample questions. . . . [It offers a] lively style and variety of engaging activities." SLJ

Seupel, Celia W.

Business, finance, and government administration. Ferguson 2008 109p il (Top careers in two years) $32.95

Grades: 9 10 11 12   **331.7**

1. Vocational guidance 2. Occupations 3. Business education

ISBN 978-0-8160-6899-9; 0-8160-6899-2

LC 2007-19640

Contents: Office manager; Accounts payable administrator; Insurance adjuster; Human resources assistant; Loan officer; Court reporter; Brokerage assistant; Social services assistant; Executive assistant or executive secretary; Sport and fitness manager

This book provides "information on careers in the business, finance, and government administration industries for students with two-year degrees." Publisher's note

Includes bibliographical references

The **top** 100; the fastest-growing careers for the 21st century. 4th ed. Ferguson 2009 394p $75; pa $19.95

Grades: 9 10 11 12 Adult   **331.7**

1. Vocational guidance 2. Occupations

ISBN 978-0-8160-7729-8; 0-8160-7729-0; 978-0-8160-7730-4 (pa); 0-8160-7730-4 (pa)

LC 2008-35415

First published 1998

This book "details the jobs predicted to have the fastest growth, the most opportunity, and the best earnings in the coming years, according to statistics from the U.S. Department of Labor." Publisher's note

Includes bibliographical references

Unger, Harlow G., 1931-

But what if I don't want to go to college? a guide to success through alternative education. 3rd ed. Ferguson 2006 246p $34.95; pa $16.95 *

Grades: 8 9 10 11 12   **331.7**

1. Occupational training 2. Vocational education 3. Vocational guidance

ISBN 0-8160-6557-8; 0-8160-6558-6 (pa)

LC 2005-55521

First published 1992

This "volume examines careers in 16 industry categories and describes the skills and experiences required for each. It also offers guidance for self-assessment and determining what essential employment skills readers already possess." Publisher's note

United States. Bureau of Labor Statistics

Occupational outlook handbook 2010-2011. U.S. Dept. of Labor Bureau of Labor Statistics 2010 877p il $39 *

Grades: 8 9 10 11 12 Adult   **331.7**

1. Occupations 2. Vocational guidance 3. Reference books

ISBN 978-0-16-084318-1

Also available online, in hardcover and paperback from Jist Publishing, and in paperback from Skyhorse Pub.

Biennial. First published 1949. Supplemented by Occupational Outlook Quarterly, subscription $15

"Gives information on employment trends and outlook in more than 800 occupations. Indicates nature of work, qualifications, earnings and working conditions, how to enter, where to go for more information, etc." Guide to Ref Books. 11th edition

Wyckoff, Claire

Communications and the arts. Ferguson 2007 132p il (Top careers in two years) $32.95

Grades: 9 10 11 12   **331.7**

1. Vocational guidance 2. Occupations 3. Arts 4. Mass media

ISBN 978-0-8160-6898-2; 0-8160-6898-4

LC 2007-14328

Wyckoff, Claire—*Continued*

Contents: Animator; Library technician; Fashion designer; Photographer; Dance instructor; Musician; Broadcast engineer; Interior designer/decorator; Audio technician; Lighting technician; Desktop publishing specialist; Video editor; Tools for career success; Financial aid

This book examines "job opportunities in . . . [the field of arts and communications] for students with an associate's degree, comparable certification, or work/life experience." Publisher's note

Includes bibliographical references

331.8 Labor unions, labor-management bargaining and disputes

Bridegam, Martha A.

Unions and labor laws; by Martha Bridegam. Chelsea House 2009 126p il map (Point-counterpoint) lib bdg $32.95

Grades: 7 8 9 10   **331.8**

1. Labor unions—United States

ISBN 978-1-60413-511-4; 1-60413-511-5

LC 2009-15013

"The work of unions in previous generations helped to create benefits . . . such as weekends off, the 40-hour workweek, and medical benefits. . . . The power of unions, however, has also been responsible for the creation of often corrupt and bullying labor leaders and crippling strikes. 'Unions and Labor Laws' examines these complex issues from a variety of viewpoints." Publisher's note

Includes glossary and bibliographical references

Hillstrom, Kevin

Workers unite! the American labor movement. Omnigraphics 2011 236p il (Defining moments) $55

Grades: 8 9 10 11 12   **331.8**

1. Labor movement 2. Industrial relations

ISBN 978-0-7808-1130-0   LC 2010-26548

"Explains the history of the American labor movement from its earliest origins through 19th-century industrialization, the growth of the labor movement, the current declining influence of labor, and efforts to revitalize American unions. Features include a narrative overview, biographies, primary sources, chronology, glossary, bibliography, and index." Publisher's note

"Though basic and brief, this title is highly recommended for middle school and high school students researching the history of the labor movement. It's both a good place to begin research and a useful reference when reading other works." Libr J

Includes bibliographical references

McNeese, Tim

The labor movement; unionizing America. Chelsea House 2007 168p il (Reform movements in American history) lib bdg $30 *

Grades: 8 9 10 11 12   **331.8**

1. Labor movement 2. Working class 3. Industrial relations 4. Labor unions

ISBN 978-0-7910-9503-4; 0-7910-9503-7

LC 2007-14917

This history of the labor movement discusses the events, legislation, and people associated with the movement and includes a chronology and timeline.

Includes bibliographical references

Skurzynski, Gloria, 1930-

Sweat and blood; a history of U.S. labor unions. Twenty-First Century Books 2008 112p il (People's history) lib bdg $31.93

Grades: 7 8 9 10   **331.8**

1. Labor unions 2. Working class

ISBN 978-0-8225-7594-8; 0-8225-7594-9

LC 2007-50270

This "begins with the roots of unionization in colonial America, cruises through the frenzy of industrialization in the twentieth century, and ends in the present day. . . . The period prints and photographs are well chosen to highlight and comment on the text. Classes studying any part of the industrial or social history of this country will be well served by this valuable resource." Booklist

Includes bibliographical references

332.024 Personal finance

Blatt, Jessica

The teen girl's gotta-have-it guide to money; getting smart about making it, saving it, and spending it; by Jessica Blatt with Variny Paladino; illustrated by Cynthia Frenette. Watson-Guptill Publications 2008 96p il pa $8.95

Grades: 7 8 9 10   **332.024**

1. Personal finance 2. Teenagers—Employment

ISBN 978-0-8230-1727-0; 0-8230-1727-3

LC 2007-25948

Explains to teenage girls how to budget their money, save, invest and create business plans.

"This is a great little reference guide for teenage girls to peruse and learn about money matters. . . . This is an important addition to any collection." KLIATT

Cash and credit information for teens; tips for a successful financial life including facts about earning money, paying taxes, budgeting, banking, shopping, using credit, and avoiding financial pitfalls; edited by Karen Bellenir. 2nd ed. Omnigraphics 2009 424p (Teen finance series) $69 *

Grades: 9 10 11 12   **332.024**

1. Personal finance

ISBN 978-0-7808-1065-5; 0-7808-1065-1

LC 2009012105

First published 2005

Cash and credit information for teens—*Continued*

"Provides information for teens about earning and managing money, spending and using credit wisely, and avoiding fraud. Includes index, resource information, and a list of online money management tools." Publisher's note

Includes bibliographical references

Debt information for teens; edited by Karen Bellenir. Omnigraphics 2008 413p (Teen finance series) $58 *

Grades: 9 10 11 12   **332.024**
1. Consumer credit 2. Personal finance
ISBN 978-0-7808-0989-5   LC 2007-31021

"Tips for a successful financial life including facts about money, interest rates, loans, credit cards, finance charges, predatory lending practices, preventing and resolving debt-related problems, and more." Title page

"This is a valuable resource that will give teens a much-needed advantage in an increasingly confusing and competitive economy." SLJ

Debt: opposing viewpoints; Christina Fisanick, book editor. Greenhaven Press 2010 200p il lib bdg $38.50; pa $26.75 *

Grades: 8 9 10 11 12   **332.024**
1. Consumer credit 2. Debt
ISBN   978-0-7377-4202-2   (lib   bdg);
978-0-7377-4203-9 (pa)   LC 2009-27494

"Opposing viewpoints series"

Examines both sides of the issues surrounding consumer debt, from attitudes towards debt and responsible debt management to national debt and resolving debt problems.

Includes bibliographical references

Gray, Farrah

Reallionaire; nine steps to becoming rich from the inside out; [by] Farrah Gray, with Fran Harris. Health Communications 2004 282p il pa $12.95

Grades: 11 12 Adult   **332.024**
1. Personal finance
ISBN 0-7573-0224-6   LC 2004-62555

The author "grew up in the projects in Chicago and formed his first business organization at age 7, inspired by his mother's will and determination. By age 15, he had developed his own food company for kids, Farr-Out Foods, which he sold for $1.5 million. . . . Although the book is punctuated with what he calls 'Real Points' for success and exercises for things like building a great team and seizing opportunities, the real inspiration is his personal story, which speaks strongly of the importance of mentoring to young people and sends the message that you should never underestimate anyone, especially yourself." Booklist

Kiyosaki, Robert T., 1947-

Rich dad, poor dad for teens; the secrets about money, that you don't learn in school! by Robert T. Kiyosaki with Sharon L. Lechter. Warner Books 2004 132p pa $14.99

Grades: 7 8 9 10   **332.024**
1. Personal finance
ISBN 0-446-69321-9   LC 2004-6069
New edition in preparation

Kiyosaki presents "his approach to how he thinks about accumulating wealth and about having money work for the earner. . . . Teens are encouraged to be creative in developing ways to earn cash and to limit spending. . . . Teens will be attracted by the notion of playing games to learn more about acquiring assets and managing money." SLJ

Lawless, Robert E., 1966-

The student's guide to financial literacy. Greenwood 2010 220p il $85

Grades: 9 10 11 12   **332.024**
1. Personal finance
ISBN 978-0-313-37718-1   LC 2009-50449

"This title covers everything young adults just starting out in the world should be thinking about with respect to their future financial decisions. . . . Beginning with savings, then investments, Lawless breaks the material down into small, digestible sections. . . . The chapters on Tax Considerations and Insurance are must-reads. Excellent charts and graphs support the text, and Guess What? and Beware! boxes offer fascinating related facts and cautions against such things as risky mortgage loans." SLJ

Includes bibliographical references

Personal finance; a guide to money and business. Marshall Cavendish 2009 186p il $99.90 *

Grades: 9 10 11 12   **332.024**
1. Personal finance
ISBN 978-0-7614-7909-3; 0-7614-7909-0
                                 LC 2009-9461

This book is "comprised of approximately 50 A-to-Z articles ranging in length from two to four pages. . . . *Personal Finance* focuses on what readers will encounter in their daily lives, such as debit cards, credit history, job search, pricing, consumer protection, and interest rates. An entry on bundling goods and services looks at its pros and cons and includes a diagram of a computer connection and repair service. The numerous graphs, flow charts, maps, political cartoons, and tables help make sense of complicated concepts." SLJ

Includes glossary and bibliographical references

Savings and investment information for teens; tips for a successful financial life; edited by Karen Bellenir. 2nd ed. Omnigraphics 2009 422p (Teen finance series) $69 *

Grades: 9 10 11 12   **332.024**
1. Saving and investment 2. Personal finance
ISBN 978-0-7808-1064-8   LC 2009-3482
First published 2005

"Including facts about economic principles, wealth development, bank accounts, stocks, bonds, mutual funds, and other financial tools" Title page

Savings and investment information for teens—
Continued

"Provides information for teens about strategies for saving money, investment options, and economic factors that affect personal wealth. Includes index, resource information and recommendations for further reading." Publisher's note

Includes bibliographical references

332.03 Financial economics— Encyclopedias and dictionaries

A **dictionary** of finance and banking. 4th ed. Oxford University Press 2008 471p (Oxford paperback reference) pa $18.95 *

Grades: 11 12 Adult   332.03
1. Reference books 2. Finance—Dictionaries 3. Banks and banking—Dictionaries
ISBN 978-0-19-922974-1   LC 2008-276659

Companion volume to A dictionary of business and management (2006) and A dictionary of accounting (2005)

First published 1993 with title: A dictionary of finance

"Contributors, Barry Brindley . . . [et al.]" Credits

This dictionary "defines more than 5000 words, acronyms, and abbreviations used in banking, finance, economics, money markets, and foreign exchanges. . . . Most of the definitions are brief and easy to understand, cutting through financial jargon and providing many cross-references to other terms." Libr J

332.6 Investment

Connolly, Sean, 1956-
The stock market. Amicus 2010 c2011 46p il (World economy explained) lib bdg $34.25
Grades: 7 8 9 10   332.6
1. Stock exchanges 2. Stocks 3. Financial crises
ISBN 978-1-60753-082-4; 1-60753-082-4
                                 LC 2009-29073
"Explains the functions and history of the Stock Market and its involvement with the 2007 credit crunch." Publisher's note

"Complex concepts like lending, earning, and charging interest are presented simply and with clear examples. Lively photos and 'Personal Account' asides bring home the ramifications for individuals of big-bank collapses." SLJ

Includes glossary

333.7 Land, recreational and wilderness areas, energy

Cunningham, Kevin, 1966-
Soil. Morgan Reynolds Pub. 2010 111p il (Diminishing resources) $28.95
Grades: 8 9 10 11 12   333.7
1. Soil conservation 2. Soils
ISBN 978-1-59935-114-8; 1-59935-114-5
                                 LC 2009-10487

"The first chapter of *Soil* discusses how depletion of this resource began as far back as the Neolithic age, and the book continues through time, closing with today's efforts to conserve soil in places such as Iceland. In addition to being great research resources, [this title is] interesting enough for pleasure reading. [It contains] beautiful, full-page photographs, as well as a helpful time line." SLJ

Includes bibliographical references

Encyclopedia of global resources; editor, Craig W. Allin. Salem Press 2010 4v il map set $395
Grades: 11 12 Adult   333.7
1. Natural resources—Encyclopedias 2. Reference books
ISBN 978-1-58765-644-6; 1-58765-644-2
                                 LC 2010-1984
Also available online

First published 1998 with title: Natural resources

"This four-volume set provides a wide variety of perspectives about Earth's natural resources and explains the interrelationships among resource exploitation, environmentalism, geology, and biology. Allin . . . presents 576 articles on resources such as oil and tar sands, nations from Argentina to Zimbabwe, government laws and conventions, and historical events. . . . [This encyclopedia] offers real value and sheds important light on where we derive our mineral and biological resources, how they are processed, what they are used for, and how they fit into the global economy." Libr J

Includes bibliographical references

How should America's wilderness be managed? Stuart A. Kallen, book editor. Greenhaven Press 2005 123p (At issue) lib bdg $28.70; pa $19.95
Grades: 9 10 11 12   333.7
1. Wilderness areas—Management 2. Human influence on nature 3. Natural resources—Management
ISBN 0-7377-2384-X (lib bdg); 0-7377-2385-8 (pa)
                                 LC 2004-42494

This collection of articles "explores land use issues from many points of view including those of loggers, environmentalists, oil geologists, backpackers, snowmobile riders, and others." Publisher's note

Includes bibliographical references

Magoc, Chris J., 1960-
Environmental issues in American history; a reference guide with primary documents. Greenwood Press 2006 xxxv, 328p il map (Major issues in American history) $85 *
Grades: 11 12 Adult   333.7
1. Environmental policy—United States 2. Human ecology 3. Nature conservation 4. Environmental protection
ISBN 0-313-32208-2   LC 2005-34852
In this "study, primary documents support different sides of various questions, such as the use of water as an energy source, deforestation, gold mining in California, and the emergence of wildlife conservation." Publisher's note

Includes bibliographical references

Rockliff, Mara

Get real. Running Press 2010 112p il pa $10.95
*

Grades: 6 7 8 9 10   **333.7**
1. Consumption (Economics) 2. Consumer education
ISBN 978-0-7624-3745-0; 0-7624-3745-6

Subtitle on cover: What kind of world are you buying?

This book "points out plenty of practical ways for kids to impact their world by making different choices about what food to eat, what clothes to wear, how often to replace a cell phone, and more. . . . Nicely designed, the book has colorful graphic elements on many pages, including photographs and eye-catching digital images incorporating photos. . . . A clearly written guide for reader who want to translate social and environmental awareness into action." Booklist

Includes filmography and bibliographical references

Tabak, John

Wind and water. Facts On File 2009 208p il map (Energy and the environment) $40
Grades: 9 10 11 12 Adult   **333.7**
1. Renewable energy resources
ISBN 978-0-8160-7087-9; 0-8160-7087-3
LC 2008-28247

"Describes conventional hydropower, or wind power, and some of the newer technologies (with less certain futures) that are being introduced to harness the power of ocean currents, ocean waves, and the temperature difference between the upper and lower layers of the ocean." Publisher's note

This book "has value both for the explanations it offers and the questions it raises." SLJ

Includes glossary and bibliographical references

333.71 General topics of natural resources and energy

Global resources: opposing viewpoints; Clare Hanrahan, book editor. Greenhaven Press 2008 233p il $37.40; pa $25.95 *
Grades: 8 9 10 11 12   **333.71**
1. Natural resources—Management 2. Conservation of natural resources
ISBN   978-0-7377-3743-1;   0-7377-3743-3;
978-0-7377-3744-8 (pa); 0-7377-3744-1 (pa)
LC 2007-38577

"Opposing viewpoints series"

This is a collection of essays representing various viewpoints about the following topics: the depletion of oil reserves, food, and water; agricultural policies toward organic farming, genetically modified foods, and fish farming; solar energy, wind power, and biofuels; sustainable development, free-trade agreements, and the sharing of resources.

Includes bibliographical references

333.72 Conservation and protection

Encyclopedia of American environmental history; edited by Kathleen A. Brosnan. Facts On File 2010 4v il map (Facts on File library of American history) set $350 *
Grades: 11 12 Adult   **333.72**
1. Environmental policy—United States—Encyclopedias 2. Environmental protection—Encyclopedias 3. Reference books
ISBN 978-0-8160-6793-0; 978-1-4381-3267-9 (ebook)
LC 2010-21963

Contact publisher for ebook pricing

"Approximately 775 entries written by more than 350 expert contributors bring together the natural, social, and political events; people; geography; and ideas that are important in understanding American environmental history. Documents, maps, charts, historic photographs, an extensive bibliography, and an extremely detailed index add depth and value to this work." Booklist

Includes bibliographical references

The **environment**; William Dudley, book editor. Greenhaven Press 2006 224p (History of issues) lib bdg $34.95
Grades: 9 10 11 12   **333.72**
1. Environmental movement 2. Environmental protection
ISBN 0-7377-2865-5; 978-0-7377-2865-1
LC 2005-46391

"This anthology traces the modern history of environmentalist thought in the United States and the rest of the world, from the 19th-century conservationist movement pioneers such as George Perkins Marsh and John Muir to present-day debates about biodiversity and other environmental issues." Publisher's note

This book "leaves the reader with a balanced presentation of both sides." Voice Youth Advocates

Includes bibliographical references

McDaniel, Carl N., 1942-

Wisdom for a livable planet; the visionary work of Terri Swearingen, Dave Foreman, Wes Jackson, Helena Norberg-Hodge, Werner Fornos, Herman Daly, Stephen Schneider, and David Orr. Trinity University Press 2005 277p hardcover o.p. pa $17.95
Grades: 11 12 Adult   **333.72**
1. Environmental sciences
ISBN 1-595-34008-4; 1-595-34009-2 (pa)
LC 2004-19081

The author personalizes "critical environmental issues via profiles of eight 'visionaries' agitating for a more livable planet. . . . His subjects are prominent in the areas of hazardous waste incineration, biodiversity, sustainable agriculture, appropriate technology, population control, rational economic planning, climate concerns and environmental education. . . . The stories of these eight ecological warriors are profoundly appealing in that they show the diverse ways that people can commit to a common cause." Publ Wkly

Includes bibliographical references

Melville, Greg

Greasy rider; two dudes, one fry-oil-powered car, and a cross-country search for a greener future. Algonquin Books of Chapel Hill 2008 257p pa $15.95

Grades: 11 12 Adult   **333.72**

1. Environmental movement 2. Alternative fuel vehicles 3. Voyages and travels—Anecdotes

ISBN 978-1-56512-595-7; 1-56512-595-9

         LC 2008-25991

"From its punny title, to its unique premise (a man decides to drive from coast to coast in a car powered by used french-fry oil), to its serious message (you, too, can be more environmentally conscious), to its easygoing writing style, this is just a splendid book. . . . It's an exciting and occasionally nail-biting adventure, but the author keeps the book from being a simple road trip by delving fairly deeply into the whole ecological, pro-environmental, self-sufficiency theme, taking the reader along on visits to such interesting places as Google headquarters, a wind farm, a renewable energy lab, and a green home. Melville . . . is a lively stylist, and the book is both entertaining and educational." Booklist

Includes bibliographical references

Mongillo, John F.

Teen guides to environmental science; [by] John Mongillo; with assistance from Peter Mongillo. Greenwood Press 2004 5v il map set $249.95 *

Grades: 9 10 11 12   **333.72**

1. Environmental sciences 2. Human ecology 3. Human influence on nature

ISBN 0-313-32183-3   LC 2004-44869

Contents: v1 Earth systems and ecology; v2 Resources and energy; v3 People and their environments; v4 Human impact on the environment; v5 Creating a sustainable society

"This set would be useful for large public and school libraries with a curriculum that includes environmental studies." SLJ

Includes bibliographical references

Nagle, Jeanne M.

Living green; [by] Jeanne Nagle. Rosen Pub. 2009 64p il (In the news) lib bdg $21.95 *

Grades: 7 8 9 10   **333.72**

1. Environmental protection

ISBN 978-1-43585037-8; 1-435-85037-8

"Accessible and up-to-date. . . . Living Green presents theories of climate change and short biographies of green pioneers before examining the role of government and NGOs in environmental protection, as well as basic, earth-friendly lifestyle changes that individuals can make. Throughout, Nagle addresses the controversies that surround issues, encouraging readers to take a wide, nuanced view." Booklist

Power Scott, Jennifer, 1968-

Green careers; you can make money and save the planet. Lobster Press 2010 240p il pa $16.95

Grades: 8 9 10 11 12   **333.72**

1. Environmental protection 2. Vocational guidance

ISBN 978-1-897550-18-2; 1-897550-18-9

"Written in a breezy, conversational style, this book recounts the stories of 30 young people who are working in environmental jobs. . . . They are eco-entrepreneurs, urban activists, green architects, organic gardeners, animal caretakers, artists, and fashion designers. . . . These inspirational stories are sure to spark interest and creative thinking." SLJ

Sonneborn, Liz

The environmental movement; protecting our natural resources. Chelsea House Publishers 2008 128p il (Reform movements in American history) $30

Grades: 8 9 10 11 12   **333.72**

1. Environmental movement

ISBN 978-0-7910-9537-9; 0-7910-9537-1

         LC 2007-14914

This book "introduces readers to . . . [the environmental] movement, which arose in the United States in the late 1800s in response to the nation's dwindling forests and the pollution caused by a greater number of factories. . . . [This] book also details how environmentalism has become a global effort, led by organizations such as Greenpeace and the World Wildlife Fund." Publisher's note

Includes bibliographical references

333.75   Forest lands

Balliett, James Fargo

Forests; environmental issues, global perspectives. M.E. Sharpe 2010 152p il map (Environmental issues, global perspectives) $55

Grades: 9 10 11 12   **333.75**

1. Forests and forestry

ISBN 978-0-7656-8227-7   LC 2010-12120

"Case studies in Forests explore illegal logging in the Amazon rain forest, examine the effect of increased hunting in the Congo forest, and discuss encroachment on old-growth tropical forests on the Southern Pacific island of Borneo, among other issues relevant to the world's forests." Publisher's note

Includes glossary and bibliographical references

Stenstrup, Allen

Forests. Morgan Reynolds Pub. 2009 c2010 112p il (Diminishing resources) lib bdg $28.95

Grades: 8 9 10 11 12   **333.75**

1. Forests and forestry 2. Forest conservation

ISBN 978-1-59935-116-2; 1-59935-116-1

         LC 2009-31025

This "explores the ecology of forests, the social impact of forests, and what our global community is doing to protect this vital resource." Publisher's note

"This highly readable [book] provides a unique viewpoint on the utilization of natural resources, as scientific and environmental concerns are discussed from a historical perspective. . . . [It contains] beautiful, full-page photographs, as well as a helpful time line." SLJ

Includes bibliographical references

333.79 Energy

Alternative energy; Neil Schlager and Jayne Weisblatt, editors. UXL 2006 3v il map set $165
Grades: 6 7 8 9 10   333.79
1. Renewable energy resources
ISBN 0-7876-9440-1; 978-0-7876-9440-1
LC 2006-3763
"This set objectively presents many of the issues and challenges involved in using new and existing energy sources. . . . The set is well-organized and clearly written." Booklist
Includes bibliographical references

Brune, Michael, 1971-
Coming clean; breaking America's addiction to oil and coal. Sierra Club Books 2008 269p pa $14.95
Grades: 11 12 Adult   333.79
1. Coal 2. Petroleum as fuel 3. Biomass energy 4. Renewable energy resources 5. Environmental movement
ISBN 978-1-57805-149-6   LC 2008-26345
The author "looks at the costs of oil dependency, the dirty mechanics of so-called 'clean coal,' the role played by politics and finance, and the possibilities for a post-oil economy. 'Take Action' sections at the end of each chapter suggest further reading and viewing, ways to profile an adversary, how to identify the most important issues to you, and what to do from there. . . . His guide contains enough solid, interesting information . . . to fill in anyone interested in the present state of the energy economy." Publ Wkly
Includes bibliographical references

Energy alternatives: opposing viewpoints; David Haugen, Susan Musser, and Vickey Kalambakal, book editors. Greenhaven Press 2010 218p il $39.70; pa $27.50 *
Grades: 9 10 11 12   333.79
1. Energy resources 2. Renewable energy resources
ISBN 978-0-7377-4962-5; 978-0-7377-4963-2 (pa)
LC 2009-52253
"Opposing viewpoints series"
Articles in this anthology address such topics as whether alternative energy sources are necessary, different types of alternative energy, and the government's role in advocating the use of alternative sources.
Includes bibliographical references

Heinrichs, Ann
Sustaining Earth's energy resources. Marshall Cavendish Benchmark 2010 c2011 128p il (Environment at risk) lib bdg $39.93 *
Grades: 6 7 8 9 10   333.79
1. Renewable energy resources 2. Energy development
ISBN 978-0-7614-4007-9; 0-7614-4007-0
LC 2008-42010
This book provides "information on Earth's sources of renewable and nonrenewable energy, how they are used, their benefits and disadvantages, their interrelationships

with the natural world, and the future of Earth's sources of energy." Publisher's note
Includes bibliographical references

Kallen, Stuart A., 1955-
Renewable energy research. ReferencePoint Press 2010 c2011 96p il (Inside science) lib bdg $26.95
Grades: 7 8 9 10   333.79
1. Renewable energy resources
ISBN 978-1-60152-129-3; 1-60152-129-4
LC 2010-18102
"This title examines the science behind green technology in the following chapters: *What Is Renewable Energy?*; *Heat and Light*; *Wind and Water*; *Biomass*; and *Hydrogen Fuel Cells*." Publisher's note
This "offers the necessary information for stellar reports. Politics, debates, and ethical concerns are briefly and fairly mentioned, but the . . . [book concentrates] on consistent, documented, and well-balanced scientific coverage. The human stories sprinkled throughout will help kids identify with both scientists and patients." SLJ
Includes bibliographical references

Marcovitz, Hal
Can renewable energy replace fossil fuels? ReferencePoint Press 2010 c2011 95p il (In controversy) lib bdg $26.95
Grades: 10 11 12   333.79
1. Renewable energy resources 2. Fuel
ISBN 978-1-60152-113-2   LC 2009-50482
This book "looks at the costs, limitations, and liabilities of using fossil fuels as well as the practicality of various alternatives." Booklist
Includes bibliographical references

Moan, Jaina L.
Energy use worldwide; a reference handbook; [by] Jaina L. Moan and Zachary A. Smith. ABC-CLIO 2007 337p il (Contemporary world issues) $55
Grades: 9 10 11 12   333.79
1. Energy resources 2. Energy consumption
ISBN 978-1-85109-890-3   LC 2007-7414
The authors "delineate energy consumption's influential political figures and principal challenges while clarifying prospective conservation solutions. The book is rich with illustrative tables and offers a glossary of essential terms." Libr J
Includes glossary and bibliographical references

Nakaya, Andrea C.
Energy alternatives. ReferencePoint Press, Inc. 2008 112p il map (Compact research. Current issues) lib bdg $24.95 *
Grades: 8 9 10 11 12   333.79
1. Renewable energy resources
ISBN 978-1-60152-017-3; 1-60152-017-4
LC 2007-18025

Nakaya, Andrea C.—*Continued*

This "provides a variety of possible alternatives to fossil fuels. Wind, solar, nuclear, hydro, ocean, and geothermal power are examined with the possible benefits and problems associated with each. . . . [This book] will be helpful to students looking for a one-stop information source." SLJ

Includes bibliographical references

Yount, Lisa

Energy supply. Facts on File 2005 296p il (Library in a book) $45

Grades: 11 12 Adult   **333.79**

1. Energy resources 2. Energy consumption

ISBN 0-8160-5577-7   LC 2004-21607

"This title summarizes . . . the many aspects of important energy issues, furnishing a concise overview of major points needed for doing research on this topic." Choice

Includes bibliographical references

333.8   Subsurface resources

Foreign oil dependence; Susan C. Hunnicutt, book editor. Greenhaven Press 2008 106p (At issue. International politics) $31.80; pa $22.50 *

Grades: 9 10 11 12   **333.8**

1. Petroleum industry 2. Energy policy

ISBN 978-0-7377-4060-8; 978-0-7377-4061-5 (pa)

     LC 2007-50858

The articles in this anthology cover topics such as government regulation of the energy industry, energy independence, Iraqi oil, and coal and ethanol as possible alternatives to oil.

Includes bibliographical references

Gardner, Timothy, 1966-

Oil. Morgan Reynolds Pub. 2009 c2010 111p il (Diminishing resources) lib bdg $28.95

Grades: 8 9 10 11 12   **333.8**

1. Petroleum 2. Energy conservation 3. Greenhouse effect

ISBN 978-1-59935-117-9; 1-59935-117-X

     LC 2009-10245

This book about oil "will draw activists, but even readers who do not think they care that much will find the facts devastating. Quotes from authoritative sources . . . about both the historic overview and the contemporary crisis accompany full-color double-page photos that show what is happening now. . . . [The book] discusses in detail the role of the Middle East, the effects of America's addiction to cars, and always, the current focus on global warming." Booklist

Includes bibliographical references

Laxer, James

Oil. Groundwood Books/House of Anansi Press 2008 144p il (Groundwork guides) $15.95; pa $11

Grades: 9 10 11 12 Adult   **333.8**

1. Petroleum industry

ISBN   978-0-88899-815-6;   0-88899-815-5; 978-0-88899-816-3 (pa); 0-88899-816-3 (pa)

     LC 2008-411360

Title on cover: Oil: a Groundwork guide

Provides an overview of the petroleum industry, its history, and its key players; examines the relationship between oil, finance, and politics; and explores the future of oil as supplies diminish and global warming threatens.

"This is an excellent choice for high school readers. . . . [The author] makes a complex subject clear with the aid of time lines of oil history, highlighted points of interest, and a solid list of sources for further reading." Libr J

Includes bibliographical references

Tabak, John

Coal and oil. Facts On File 2009 208p il (Energy and the environment) $40 *

Grades: 9 10 11 12   **333.8**

1. Coal 2. Petroleum as fuel

ISBN 978-0-8160-7083-1; 0-8160-7083-0

     LC 2008-24343

"Tabak discusses the historical development of [oil and coal], . . . explains its current utilization, and considers its potential to meet future global demand. He explains scientific principles and technological requirements for converting energy sources to usable power." SLJ

"This terrifically informative volume . . . is a perfect resource for someone struggling to wrap their brain around some of the most complex energy issues of our time." Booklist

Includes glossary and bibliographical references

Natural gas and hydrogen. Facts On File 2009 203p il map (Energy and the environment) $40

Grades: 9 10 11 12 Adult   **333.8**

1. Natural gas 2. Hydrogen as fuel

ISBN 978-0-8160-7084-8; 0-8160-7084-9

     LC 2008-26072

An "overview of the complex relationship the world has with two significant sources of gaseous fuel. The book discusses the business of natural gas production and the energy futures markets that have evolved as vehicles for speculation and risk management. It also focuses on the possible advantages of adopting hydrogen as a viable source of energy, as well as on the inevitable obstacles that hamper large-scale fuel switching." Publisher's note

Includes glossary and bibliographical references

333.9   Other natural resources

Space exploration; Daniel A. Leone, book editor. Greenhaven Press 2005 95p (At issue) lib bdg $28.70; pa $19.95

Grades: 9 10 11 12   **333.9**

1. Outer space—Exploration 2. Astronautics—United States

ISBN 0-7377-2747-0 (lib bdg); 0-7377-2748-9 (pa)

     LC 2004-58028

The essays in this anthology explore NASA's space initiative involving manned missions to Mars and beyond, in addition to such issues as "weapons in space, privatizing space ventures, and protecting Earth from asteroids." Publisher's note

Includes bibliographical references

333.91 Water and lands adjoining bodies of water

Balliett, James Fargo

Oceans; environmental issues, global perspectives. M.E. Sharpe 2010 156p il map (Environmental issues, global perspectives) $55

Grades: 9 10 11 12   **333.91**

1. Ocean

ISBN 978-0-7656-8229-1   LC 2010-19428

"The case studies in *Oceans* include a discussion of the most remote locations along the Mid-Atlantic Ridge, where new ocean floor is being formed underwater; the Maldive Islands, where rising sea levels may force residents to abandon their communities; and the North Sea, where fishing stocks have been dangerously depleted as a result of multiple nations' unrelenting removal of certain species." Publisher's note

Includes glossary and bibliographical references

Wetlands; environmental issues, global perspectives. M.E. Sharpe 2010 155p il map (Environmental issues, global perspectives) $55

Grades: 9 10 11 12   **333.91**

1. Wetlands

ISBN 978-0-7656-8226-0   LC 2010-12119

This book "provides case studies that illuminate our changing perceptions of one of the world's richest and biologically productive biomes, including the Florida Everglades, the Aral Sea in Central Asia, and Lake Poyong in China. It also highlights efforts that have been undertaken to protect many of these areas." Publisher's note

Includes glossary and bibliographical references

Kaye, Cathryn Berger

Going blue; a teen guide to saving our oceans & waterways; by Cathryn Berger Kaye; with Philippe Cousteau and Earth Echo International. Free Spirit Pub. 2010 151p il map pa $14.95 *

Grades: 6 7 8 9 10   **333.91**

1. Marine ecology 2. Marine pollution 3. Environmental protection

ISBN 978-1-57542-348-7; 1-57542-348-0

LC 2010-16589

Teaches young people about the Earth's water crisis and provides practical suggestions on how readers can identify water-related needs in the community and transform their ideas into action.

"This valuable how-to manual is suitable for an individual student, a family, a youth group, or a school wishing to protect our precious resource of water. This upbeat treasure will challenge anyone interested in environmental activism, whether water related or not. It is a must for any library serving youth." Voice Youth Advocates

Includes bibliographical references

Knapp, Bevil, 1949-

America's wetland; Louisiana's vanishing coast; photographs by Bevil Knapp; text by Mike Dunne. Louisiana State University Press 2005 129p il $39.95

Grades: 11 12 Adult   **333.91**

1. Wetlands 2. Coasts

ISBN 0-8071-3115-6; 978-0-8071-3115-2

LC 2005-9329

"In an eerie prophesy of the flooding to come in New Orleans, this book discusses the job of wetlands in keeping storm surges and waves out of the low-lying areas. Superb color photographs detail fishing, the oil industry, and marine life in the wetlands areas of Louisiana." Univ Press Books for Public and Second Sch Libr, 2006

Petersen, Christine

Renewing Earth's waters. Marshall Cavendish Benchmark 2010 c2011 112p il (Environment at risk) lib bdg $39.93

Grades: 6 7 8 9 10   **333.91**

1. Water conservation 2. Water pollution

ISBN 978-0-7614-4004-8; 0-7614-4004-6

LC 2008-20905

This book provides "information on the interrelationships of the natural world, environmental problems both natural and man-made, the relative risks associated with these problems, and solutions for resolving and/or preventing them." Publisher's note

Includes bibliographical references

333.95 Biological resources

The **atlas** of global conservation; changes, challenges and opportunities to make a difference; [by] Jonathan Hoekstra ... [et al.]; edited by Jennifer L. Molnar. University of California Press 2010 234p il map $49.95

Grades: 9 10 11 12   **333.95**

1. Conservation of natural resources 2. Environmental protection 3. Globalization 4. Atlases 5. Reference books

ISBN 978-0-520-26256-0   LC 2009-23617

"Focusing primarily on biomes and ecosystems, this valuable atlas promotes a deeper understanding of the challenges involved in preserving and maintaining these habitats and resources. Basically an analysis of the current state of the globe, the book highlights conservation challenges through chapters on habitats, species distributions, deforestation, global warming, coastal development, and pollution. . . . The book is unique and well done." Voice Youth Advocates

Includes bibliographical references

Corwin, Jeff

100 heartbeats; the race to save earth's most endangered species. Rodale 2009 303p il $24.99

Grades: 11 12 Adult   **333.95**

1. Endangered species 2. Wildlife conservation

ISBN 978-1-60529-847-4; 1-60529-847-6

LC 2009-23449

Corwin, Jeff—*Continued*

The author looks at several "critically endangered [species] and examines what is being done to save them, beginning with a chapter that discusses the broad causes of extinction—global warming and the loss of habitat—and then examines specific threats to endangered species while looking at animals most at risk from these threats. . . . Corwin's conversational, upbeat style makes readers care about the species in peril." Booklist

Includes bibliographical references

Cousteau, Jacques Yves, 1910-1997

The human, the orchid, and the octopus; exploring and conserving our natural world; [by] Jacques Cousteau and Susan Schiefelbein. Bloomsbury 2007 305p hardcover o.p. pa $16

Grades: 11 12 Adult　　　　　　　　**333.95**

1. Oceanography 2. Nature conservation 3. Human influence on nature

ISBN　978-1-59691-417-9;　1-59691-417-3; 978-1-59691-418-6 (pa); 1-59691-418-1 (pa)

LC 2007-18824

Original French edition, 1997

"This is a comprehensive presentation of the conservation and preservation philosophy that inspired Cousteau to become an activist for the oceans and the earth during his lifetime." Libr J

"Cousteau's reverence for life's miracles . . . shines through in this eloquent testimony on the importance of pursuing higher ideals, particularly the preservation of the oceans and the natural world for future generations." Publ Wkly

Includes bibliographical references

Endangered oceans: opposing viewpoints; Louise I. Gerdes, book editor. Greenhaven Press 2009 234p il lib bdg $38.50; pa $26.75 *

Grades: 8 9 10 11 12　　　　　　　　**333.95**

1. Marine ecology 2. Environmental policy 3. Marine pollution

ISBN　978-0-7377-4210-7　(lib　bdg); 978-0-7377-4211-4 (pa)　　LC 2008-36462

"Opposing viewpoints series"

Articles in this anthology cover such topics as overfishing and loss of coral reefs, government policies to protect ocean life, sustainable fishing, and the effects of human activities on marine mammals.

Includes bibliographical references

Endangered species; Cynthia A. Bily, book editor. Greenhaven Press 2008 128p il map (Introducing issues with opposing viewpoints) lib bdg $33.70 *

Grades: 6 7 8 9 10　　　　　　　　**333.95**

1. Endangered species 2. Nature conservation

ISBN 978-0-7377-3849-0; 0-7377-3849-9

LC 2007-31324

"This book exposes readers to diametrically opposed views. . . . The articles were written by various experts and . . . the color photographs, graphs, and maps add substantially to the visual appeal and content. . . . An illuminating presentation that will improve critical-thinking skills." SLJ

Includes glossary and bibliographical references

Kurlansky, Mark

The world without fish; how could we let this happen? illustrations by Frank Stockton. Workman Pub. 2011 183p il $16.95

Grades: 5 6 7 8 9 10　　　　　　　　**333.95**

1. Commercial fishing 2. Water pollution

ISBN 978-0-7611-5607-9; 0-7611-5607-0

LC 2011-15516

"Brief sections in graphic-novel format follow a young girl, Ailat, and her father over a couple of decades as the condition of the ocean grows increasingly dire, eventually an orange, slimy mess mostly occupied by jellyfish and leatherback turtles. At the end, Ailat's young daughter doesn't even know what the word fish means. This is juxtaposed against nonfiction chapters with topics including types of fishing equipment and the damage each causes, a history of the destruction of the cod and its consequences, the international politics of the fishing industry and the effects of pollution and global warming. . . . Depressing and scary yet grimly entertaining." Kirkus

Riley, Laura

Nature's strongholds; the world's great wildlife reserves; [by] Laura and William Riley. Princeton University Press 2005 672p il maps $49.50

Grades: 9 10 11 12　　　　　　　　**333.95**

1. Wildlife refuges 2. National parks and reserves

ISBN 0-691-12219-9　　　　LC 2004-97392

"The authors present summaries of the major reserves on each continent, discuss the backgrounds of those reserves and the flora and fauna found there, and give . . . guidelines for visiting the sites." Sci Books Films

Includes bibliographical references

Wildlife protection; Yael Calhoun, series editor; foreword by David Seideman. Chelsea House Publishers 2005 xxvii, 122p il (Environmental issues) $26.95 *

Grades: 9 10 11 12　　　　　　　　**333.95**

1. Wildlife conservation

ISBN 0-7910-8204-0　　　　LC 2004-29000

This discussion of wildlife protection issues and challenges includes sections on endangered species and reserves for wildlife protection

Includes bibliographical references

335.4　Marxian systems

Lansford, Tom

Communism. Marshall Cavendish Benchmark 2007 143p il map (Political systems of the world) lib bdg $27.95

Grades: 7 8 9 10　　　　　　　　**335.4**

1. Communism

ISBN 978-0-7614-2628-8　　　　LC 2006-25349

"Gives an overview of communism as a political system, including an historical discussion of communist regimes throughout the world." Publisher's note

Includes bibliographical references

Pipes, Richard

Communism: a history. Modern Lib. 2001 175p hardcover o.p. pa $10.95 *

Grades: 11 12 Adult   **335.4**

1. Communism

ISBN 0-679-64050-9; 0-8129-6864-6 (pa)

LC 2001-275458

"This is a short history on the essentials of communism—as an ideal, as a program outlined by Marx, and as a state established by Lenin to implement the program." Booklist

"As a brief, polemical diatribe . . . this short account of communism should provoke and instruct." Libr J

Includes bibliographical references

337   International economics

Steger, Manfred

Globalization: a very short introduction; [by] Manfred B. Steger. Oxford University Press 2009 147p il map (Very short introductions) pa $11.95

Grades: 11 12 Adult   **337**

1. Globalization

ISBN 978-0-19-955226-9   LC 2009-294674

First published 2003

This book covers "the major causes and consequences of globalization as well as the hotly contested question of whether globalization is, ultimately, a good or a bad thing. . . . The book also examines political movements both for and against globalization, from WTO protests to the recent rise in global jihadism; considers such concepts as 'Americanization' and 'McDonaldization'; and explores the role of the media and communication technologies in the process of cultural globalization." Publisher's note

Includes bibliographical references

338.1   Agriculture

Pollan, Michael

The omnivore's dilemma; the secrets behind what you eat; adapted by Richie Chevat. Young readers ed. Dial Books 2009 298p il $17.99 *

Grades: 5 6 7 8 9 10   **338.1**

1. Food supply 2. Food chains (Ecology)

ISBN 978-0-8037-3415-9; 0-8037-3415-8

LC 2009-9283

Adapted from: The omnivore's dilemma: a natural history of four meals, published 2006 by Penguin Press

"Adopting the role of food detective, the author 'peers behind the curtain' of the modern food industry and finds that the industrial approach to the food chain imperils our health and planet. The four sections of the volume describe differing types of meals: industrial; industrial organic; local sustainable; and hunted, gathered and found. Clear organization and lively writing rooted in fascinating examples make this accessible and interesting." Kirkus

Includes bibliographical references

Pyle, George, 1956-

Raising less corn, more hell; the case for the independent farm and against industrial food. PublicAffairs 2005 xxv, 229p $25

Grades: 11 12 Adult   **338.1**

1. Family farms 2. Agricultural industry

ISBN 1-58548-115-0   LC 2005-41902

"Organizing his book into three neatly named sections—'Wealth,' 'Health,' and 'Security'—Pyle . . . addresses in turn the economic aspects of farming and feeding the United States and the much larger world beyond; health and environmental problems attributed to our present large-scale industrial food production methods; and issues of food safety and security, including genetically modified corn, soybeans, and other crops." Libr J

The author's "well-researched, lucid and passionate argument explains not only what is wrong with U.S. agricultural policy but why it matters." Publ Wkly

338.4   Secondary industries and services

Almond, Steve

Candyfreak: a journey through the chocolate underbelly of America. Algonquin Books of Chapel Hill 2004 266p $21.95

Grades: 11 12 Adult   **338.4**

1. Almond, Steve 2. Candy 3. Chocolate

ISBN 1-56512-421-9   LC 2003-70801

Also available in paperback from Mariner Bks.

The author tells how candy "shaped his childhood and continues his life in ways large and small. . . . Once hundreds of American confectioners delivered regional favorites to consumers, but now the big three of candy—Hershey, Mars, and Nestlé—control the market. To find out what happened to those candies of yesteryear, Almond talks to candy collectors and historians and visits a few of the remaining independent candy companies. . . . Flavored with the author's amusingly tart sense of humor, *Candyfreak* is an intriguing chronicle of the passions that candy inspires and the pleasures it offers." Libr J

Includes bibliographical references

Chaplin, Heather, 1971-

Smartbomb; the quest for art, entertainment, and big bucks in the videogame revolution; [by] Heather Chaplin & Aaron Ruby. Algonquin Books of Chapel Hill 2005 287p hardcover o.p. pa $13.95

Grades: 11 12 Adult   **338.4**

1. Video games

ISBN   1-56512-346-8;   978-1-56512-346-5; 1-56512-545-2 (pa); 978-1-56512-545-2 (pa)

LC 2005-47845

"The story goes back in time to MIT in the late '50s and the development of the first video game. Moving onward to the present, readers meet developers at Nintendo, the creators of Doom, the developers of the Sims series, and players of Massively Multiplayer Online games. . . . This immensely readable book will have great appeal with gaming teens, but should also be required reading

Chaplin, Heather, 1971-—_Continued_
for librarians interested in learning more about gaming
and its role in our culture and our teen-focused libraries."
SLJ
   Includes bibliographical references

Pampel, Fred C.
   Tobacco industry and smoking. Rev. ed. Facts
On File 2009 314p map (Library in a book) $45
Grades: 11 12 Adult   **338.4**
   1. Tobacco industry 2. Smoking
   ISBN 978-0-8160-7793-9; 0-8160-7793-2
                                    LC 2009-396
   First published 2004
   This title about the tobacco industry "highlights
emerging and accelerating trends in the worldwide battle
over tobacco use, with . . . legal and historical
overviews, reference resources, statistics, and a research
guide." Publisher's note
   Includes glossary and bibliographical references

338.5   General production economics

Galbraith, John Kenneth, 1908-2006
   The great crash, 1929; with a new introduction
by the author; foreword by James K. Galbraith.
Houghton Mifflin Co. 2009 206p pa $14.95 *
Grades: 11 12 Adult   **338.5**
   1. Great Depression, 1929-1939 2. United States—
Economic conditions—1919-1933
   ISBN 978-0-547-24816-5
   "A Mariner book"
   First published 1955
   Beginning with the bull market of Coolidge and Hoo-
ver and continuing through the stock market crash, the
author analyzes its causes and speculates about the
chances of another crash.
   Includes bibliographical references

Should the federal government bail out private
   industry? David Haugen, book editor.
   Greenhaven Press 2010 114p (At issue.
   Economy) $30.85; pa $21.85
   Grades: 7 8 9 10   **338.5**
   1. Industrial policy—United States 2. Banks and banking 3. Government lending 4. Economic policy—United States
   ISBN   978-0-7377-4656-3;   0-7377-4656-4;
978-0-7377-4657-0 (pa); 0-7377-4657-2 (pa)
                                    LC 2009-37781
   This "work effectively introduces the Trouble Asset
Relief Program, the collapse of the subprime mortgage
industry, and the highly charged issue of governmental
economic regulation. The now-familiar style of the work
couples diametrically opposed opinions drawn from diverse sources such as the _New York Times_, _U.S. News &
World Report_, and SocialistAlternative.org with a focus
on issues spanning executive bonuses, the auto industry,
student loans, and numerous bailout shortcomings." SLJ
   Includes bibliographical references

338.7   Business enterprises

Katz, Jon
   Geeks; how two lost boys rode the Internet out
of Idaho. Villard Bks. 2000 xliii, 207p hardcover
o.p. pa $13.95
Grades: 11 12 Adult   **338.7**
   1. Data processing
   ISBN 0-375-50298-X; 0-7679-0699-3 (pa)
                                    LC 99-43150
   This book focuses on "Jesse Dailey, a working-class
19-year-old trapped in rural Idaho, where he and his
friend Eric Twilegar fixed computers for a living, and
hacked and surfed the Web, convinced that they were
losers and outcasts. Katz . . . traveled to Idaho to meet
the pair, intending to chronicle their lives. He wound up
encouraging and sometimes assisting Jesse and Eric as
they tried to improve their lives by moving to Chicago,
where they sought better jobs and even considered applying to college." Publ Wkly
   "With Dailey and Twilegar. . . Katz has found the
perfect hook to deliver his big theme: the ascension, via
the Internet, of the once lowly nerd to a position of undeniable social primacy." N Y Times Book Rev

339.2   Distribution of income and wealth

Gilbert, Geoffrey, 1948-
   Rich and poor in America; a reference
handbook.   ABC-CLIO   2008   275p   il
(Contemporary world issues) $55
Grades: 9 10 11 12   **339.2**
   1. Wealth 2. Poverty 3. Economic policy—United
States
   ISBN 978-1-59884-056-8; 1-59884-056-8
                                    LC 2008-9350
   "This work provides . . . [an] overview and analysis
of the increasing gap between the Americans at the top
and bottom of the economic scale." Publisher's note
   Includes bibliographical references

339.4   Factors affecting income and wealth

Poverty: opposing viewpoints; Viqi Wagner, book
   editor. Greenhaven Press 2008 279p il lib bdg
   $37.40; pa $25.95
   Grades: 8 9 10 11 12   **339.4**
   1. Poverty
   ISBN 978-0-7377-3747-9 (lib bdg); 0-7377-3747-6 (lib
bdg); 978-0-7377-3748-6 (pa); 0-7377-3748-4 (pa)
   "Opposing viewpoints series"
   "After an introduction that raises the idea of how poverty is portrayed in the media, the book provides previously published material debating the various issues.
While chapters one through three feature articles that debate the causes and possible solutions to U.S. deprivation, chapter four discusses the issue from a global perspective. . . . This title should be in demand in many libraries." SLJ
   Includes bibliographical references

340 Law

341.23 United Nations

Feinman, Jay M.

1001 legal words you need to know; [the ultimate guide to the language of law] Oxford University Press 2005 239p pa $10.95

Grades: 11 12 Adult   **340**

1. Reference books 2. Law—United States—Dictionaries

ISBN 0-19-518133-6; 978-0-19-518133-3

First published 2003

Subtitle from cover

This "guide to the language of the American legal system . . . defines and explains every term with a sample sentence, and many entries have supplementary notes. In addition, the book includes a number of quick miniguides to legal troubleshooting that includes information on understanding wills, trusts, and inheritance, granting someone the power of attorney, understanding contracts, what to do if you're sued, how to choose a lawyer, exploring law school, and enjoying cop and lawyer dramas." Publisher's note

Includes bibliographical references

Law 101. 3rd ed. Oxford University Press 2010 363p $27.95 *

Grades: 11 12 Adult   **340**

1. Law—United States

ISBN 978-0-19-539513-6   LC 2010-487303

First published 2000

Subtitle on cover: Everything you need to know about American law

This book "covers the main subjects taught in the first year of law school. Readers are introduced to every aspect of the legal system, from constitutional law and the litigation process to tort law, contract law, property law, and criminal law." Publisher's note

340.03 Law—Encyclopedias and dictionaries

Black's law dictionary; Bryan A. Garner, editor in chief. 9th ed. West 2009 xxxi, 1920p $80 *

Grades: 11 12 Adult   **340.03**

1. Law—Dictionaries 2. Reference books

ISBN 978-0-314-19949-2   LC 2009-459279

Also available deluxe edition $123 (ISBN-13: 978-0-314-19950-8) and online

First published 1891 with title: A dictionary of law, under the authorship of Henry Campbell Black. Periodically revised to bring terms up to date

This law dictionary contains more than 45,000 terms, including archaic terms and references to statutes and cases.

Includes bibliographical references

Alger, Chadwick F., 1924-

The United Nations system; a reference handbook. ABC-CLIO 2005 375p (Contemporary world issues) $50 *

Grades: 9 10 11 12   **341.23**

1. United Nations

ISBN 1-85109-805-4   LC 2005-25406

"This book is divided into chapters that cover background and history, problems, controversies and solutions, ambivalent participation of the Untied [sic] States in the UN system, chronologically the emergence and development of the UN system, facts and data, alternative futures of the UN system, directors of organizations, associations and agencies, biographical sketches of present heads of the UN system, selective print and nonprint resources of the United Nations, and an index and information about the author. . . . This book should be in all libraries that need up-to-date information on globalization, the United Nations, and the interrelationship between countries." Am Ref Books Annu, 2006

Includes bibliographical references

Fasulo, Linda M.

An insider's guide to the UN; [by] Linda Fasulo. 2nd ed. Yale University Press 2009 262p il pa $17

Grades: 11 12 Adult   **341.23**

1. United Nations

ISBN 978-0-300-14197-9; 0-300-14197-1

     LC 2008-52231

First published 2003

This "guide to the United Nations surveys the world body's programs and activities, and covers key issues including human rights, climate change, counterterrorism, nuclear proliferation, peacekeeping, and UN reform. It also offers guidelines for setting up a Model UN." Publisher's note

Includes bibliographical references

Gorman, Robert F.

Great debates at the United Nations; an encyclopedia of fifty key issues 1945-2000. Greenwood Press 2001 xli, 451p il $65

Grades: 11 12 Adult   **341.23**

1. United Nations

ISBN 0-313-31386-5   LC 00-57652

The introduction "provides some historical background on the United Nations and the nature of its debates since its inception. Next come discussions of specific issues . . . that have appeared on its agenda. Each entry contains four sections: the significance of the issue; its historical, social, and economic background; the history of the UN discussions . . . and the outcome of the debate. . . . Each discussion ends with a list of suggested readings." SLJ

Includes bibliographical references

Moore, John Allphin, 1940-
Encyclopedia of the United Nations; [by] John
Allphin Moore, Jr., Jerry Pubantz. 2nd ed. Facts
On File 2008 2v il (Facts on File library of world
history) set $125 *
Grades: 11 12 Adult   **341.23**
1. United Nations 2. Reference books 3. International
relations—Encyclopedias
ISBN 978-0-8160-6913-2   LC 2007-29559
First published 2002
This set features entries on "the United Nations's in-
stitutions, procedures, policies, specialized agencies, his-
toric personalities, initiatives, and involvement in world
affairs. . . . The appendixes contain important UN documents, such as the Charter of the United Nations, the
Universal Declaration of Human Rights, the Statute of
the International Court of Justice, and the recent Security
Council Resolution." Publisher's note
Includes bibliographical references

341.242 European regional organizations

The **European** Union; edited by Norris Smith;
editorial advisor, Lynn M. Messina. H.W.
Wilson 2005 177p il map (Reference shelf) $50
*
Grades: 11 12 Adult   **341.242**
1. European Union
ISBN 0-8242-1046-8   LC 2004-62511
This book "examines the EU from its formation, with
a discussion of the economic, political, and social impact
of the organization upon its own members and the rest
of the international community." Publisher's note
Includes bibliographical references

341.6 Law of war

Barkan, Elazar
The guilt of nations; restitution and negotiating
historical injustices. Norton 2000 414p $29.95
Grades: 11 12 Adult   **341.6**
1. Political ethics 2. Human rights 3. International relations 4. Minorities 5. History—Philosophy
ISBN 0-393-04886-1   LC 99-88238
Also available in paperback from Johns Hopkins University Press
The author examines "historical injustices within and
between nations over the past 50 years, urging that we
move toward a theory of restitution that allows victims
and perpetrators to negotiate their understandings of history and identity and to establish a basis for a common
future. Most of Barkan's book is devoted to analysis of
specifics: the Holocaust; U.S. internment of Japanese
Americans; Nazi art in Russian museums and Nazi gold
in Swiss banks; Japanese abuse of 'comfort women';
Eastern Europe after decades of Communism; [and] treatment of indigenous groups on the U.S. mainland."
Booklist
Includes bibliographical references

342 Constitutional and administrative law

Amar, Akhil Reed
America's constitution; a biography. Random
House 2005 657p il $29.95; pa $16.95
Grades: 11 12 Adult   **342**
1. Constitutional history—United States
ISBN 1-400-06262-4; 0-8129-7272-4 (pa)
                                       LC 2004-61464
This is a "guide to the goals and meaning intended by
those who drafted and ratified the original 1787 docu-
ment and its 27 amendments." Economist
"Only rarely do you find a book that embodies schol-
arship at its most solid and invigorating; this is such a
book." Publ Wkly
Includes bibliographical references

Amendment XV; race and the right to vote; Jeff
Hay, book editor. Greenhaven Press 2009 154p
il map (Constitutional amendments: beyond the
Bill of Rights) $34.70 *
Grades: 7 8 9 10 11 12   **342**
1. United States. Constitution. 15th Amendment
2. African Americans—Suffrage
ISBN 978-0-7377-4327-2; 0-7377-4327-1
                                       LC 2009-4704
This book "examines the Fifteenth Amendment, which
allowed all American citizens the right to vote, regardless of race. . . . The sources reproduced . . . illuminate
the controversy and philosophical debate that surround
the amendments." Voice Youth Advocates
Includes bibliographical references

The **annotated** U.S. Constitution and Declaration
of Independence; edited by Jack N. Rakove.
Belknap Press 2009 354p il $24.95 *
Grades: 11 12 Adult   **342**
1. United States. Constitution 2. United States. Decla-
ration of Independence 3. Constitutional law—United
States 4. Constitutional history—United States
ISBN 978-0-674-03606-2; 0-674-03606-9
                                       LC 2009-22907
Contents: The Declaration of Independence; The U.S.
Constitution; Amendments to the Constitution
The author "presents both the Declaration and the
Constitution with carefully laid out annotation that's accessible to general readers as well as high school and
college students. His extended introduction provides a
readable and instructive analysis of how the writing of
the Constitution progressed, especially on matters concerning representation, executive power, and creation of
the amendments. His annotations often rely upon contemporary usage and meaning from the time of the Declaration of Independence and Constitution . . . and he compares such usage to other documents of the time." Libr
J
Includes bibliographical references

Bowen, Catherine Drinker, 1897-1973
Miracle at Philadelphia; the story of the Constitutional Convention, May to September, 1787; foreword by Warren E. Burger. Little, Brown 1986 c1966 346p pa $16.95 hardcover o.p. *

Grades: 11 12 Adult   342
1. United States. Constitutional Convention (1787) 2. Constitutional history—United States
ISBN 0-316-10398-5 (pa)   LC 86-205421
"An Atlantic Monthly Press book"
A reissue of the title first published 1966
"Writing from sources—delegates' letters and diaries; contemporary reports; James Madison's faithful minutes—Catherine Drinker Bowen draws [a] . . . picture of the men, issues and background of the Constitutional Convention held at Philadelphia in the hot summer of 1787." Publ Wkly
Includes bibliographical references

Civil liberties and the Constitution; cases and commentaries; Lucius J. Barker ... [et al.] 9th ed. Longman 2011 845p $112.60 *
Grades: 9 10 11 12   342
1. United States. Supreme Court 2. Civil rights 3. Constitutional law—United States
ISBN 978-0-13-092268-7; 0-13-092268-4
                                  LC 2010027105
First published 1970
"This casebook explores civil liberty problems through a study of leading judicial decisions." Publisher's note
Includes bibliographical references

Civil liberties and war; Jamuna Carroll, book editor. Greenhaven Press 2006 173p il (Issues on trial) lib bdg $34.95 *
Grades: 9 10 11 12   342
1. Civil rights 2. War—Public opinion 3. Military policy—United States
ISBN 0-7377-2503-6; 978-0-7377-2503-2
                                  LC 2005-52761
"This volume examines four significant Supreme Court cases: Charles T. Schenck v. United States (1919), involving suppressing speech that poses a clear and present danger; Toyosaburo Korematsu v. United States (1944), which deals with the evacuation of Japanese Americans; New York Times Co. v. United States (1971), which revolves around the publication of the Pentagon Papers and the issue of prior restraint; and Yaser Esam Hamdi et al. v. Donald H. Rumsfeld et al. (2004), which entails due-process rights and enemy combatants. . . . An important, timely addition for most collections." SLJ
Includes bibliographical references

Civil liberties: opposing viewpoints; Roman Espejo, book editor. Greenhaven Press 2009 265p il $39.70; pa $27.50 *
Grades: 8 9 10 11 12   342
1. Civil rights
ISBN   978-0-7377-4356-2;   0-7377-4356-5;
978-0-7377-4355-5 (pa); 0-7377-4355-7 (pa)
                            • LC 2008-54000
"Opposing viewpoints series"

A collection of essays debating personal freedom and expression, the effects of technology on privacy and how war has affected civil liberties.
Includes bibliographical references

The **Civil** Rights Act of 1964. Greenhaven Press 2004 128p il (At issue in history) lib bdg $29.95; pa $21.20
Grades: 9 10 11 12   342
1. Civil Rights Act of 1964 2. Civil rights
ISBN 0-7377-2304-1 (lib bdg); 0-7377-2305-X (pa)
                                  LC 2003-47288
"This book reviews the history of the landmark legislation, the debate that surrounded it, and its legacy through essays and articles written at the time and more recent pieces that examine the progress made and outlook for the future. . . . A useful collection of primary and secondary sources for reports." SLJ
Includes bibliographical references

Encyclopedia of the American Constitution; edited by Leonard W. Levy and Kenneth L. Karst. 2nd ed, Adam Winkler, associate editor for the second ed. Macmillan Ref. USA 2000 6v set $595
Grades: 11 12 Adult   342
1. Constitutional law—United States 2. Reference books
ISBN 0-02-864880-3   LC 00-29203
First published 1986 in 4 volumes
This "reference contains approximately 3000 contributions from academics, lawyers, and judges concerning key constitutional law cases and legislative developments relating to constitutional issues (e.g., abortion, welfare rights, and affirmative action)." Libr J
Includes bibliographical referencess

Encyclopedia of the First Amendment; edited by John R. Vile, David L. Hudson Jr., David Schultz. CQ Press 2009 2v il set $275 *
Grades: 11 12 Adult   342
1. United States. Constitution. 1st-10th amendments—Encyclopedias 2. Reference books
ISBN 978-0-87289-311-5; 0-87289-311-1
                                  LC 2008-36077
"This two-volume work devotes itself solely to the impact of the First Amendment. . . . More than 200 contributors . . . have written over 1400 topical entries, ranging in length from 250 to 1500 words, all addressing one of the five core freedoms of the First Amendment." Libr J
This "is an excellent resource for anyone who wants to learn more about broadcast regulation, the establishment of religion clause, students' rights, or a myriad of other topics involving the First Amendment and its political, cultural, and legal significance." Booklist
Includes bibliographical references

Feinberg, Barbara Silberdick, 1938-
The Articles of Confederation; the first constitution of the United States. 21st Cent. Bks. (Brookfield) 2002 110p il maps lib bdg $24.90
Grades: 7 8 9 10   342
1. United States. Articles of Confederation
2. Constitutional history—United States 3. United States—Politics and government—1775-1783, Revolution
ISBN 0-7613-2114-4   LC 2001-27441
"Feinberg introduces the history and text of 'The Articles of Confederation and Perpetual Union,' the constitution that guided the U.S. government from 1776 to 1787. . . . Attractively laid out, this solid choice includes many black-and-white illustrations, including portrait paintings, engravings, and maps." Booklist
Includes bibliographical references

Freedom of religion; edited by Gary Zacharias. Greenhaven Press 2004 144p il (Bill of Rights) lib bdg $32.45
Grades: 9 10 11 12   342
1. Freedom of religion 2. Church and state
ISBN 0-7377-2647-4   LC 2004-46074
"This volume explains the history of church/state relations, the establishment and free expression clauses contained in the statement, and arguments that have arisen over it." Publisher's note
Includes bibliographical references

Freedom of speech; edited by William Dudley. Greenhaven Press 2005 128p (Bill of Rights) lib bdg $32.45
Grades: 9 10 11 12   342
1. Freedom of speech 2. Censorship
ISBN 0-7377-1929-X   LC 2004-54149
"This interesting anthology examines the historical origins of the free speech clause of the First Amendment, the evolving interpretations of the First Amendment by the Supreme Court, and the changing public attitudes toward free speech. Included are discussions of such issues as wartime dissent, censorship, hate speech, and flag burning." Publisher's note
Includes bibliographical references

Freedom of the press; Rob Edelman, book editor. Greenhaven Press 2007 181p (Issues on trial) lib bdg $34.95
Grades: 9 10 11 12   342
1. Freedom of the press
ISBN 0-7377-3449-3; 978-0-7377-3449-2
                                          LC 2006-41173
"This anthology offers . . . [an] examination of four landmark court cases involving freedom of the press, each of which was heard by the U.S. Supreme Court." Publisher's note
Includes bibliographical references

Friedman, Ian C.
Freedom of speech and the press. Facts on File 2005 128p il map (American rights) $35
Grades: 7 8 9 10   342
1. Freedom of speech 2. Freedom of the press
ISBN 0-8160-5662-5   LC 2004-21003

Contents: Foundations of free speech and press; Defining free speech and press in a new nation; Influencing American society in the 19th century; Evolving roles in the early 20th century; Engaging patriotism, decency, and race; Vietnam and Watergate; Battles over hateful words; The present and future of free speech and press
Includes bibliographical references

Haugen, David, 1969-
Rights of the disabled; [by] David M. Haugen, with Susan Musser and Andrea DeMott. Facts on File 2008 296p (Library in a book) $45
Grades: 9 10 11 12 Adult   342
1. Handicapped—Civil rights 2. Handicapped—Legal status, laws, etc.
ISBN 978-0-8160-7128-9   LC 2007-34803
Contents: Introduction to disability rights in America; The law and disability rights; Chronology; Biographical listing; Glossary; How to research disability rights issues; Annotated bibliography; Organizations and agencies
This book is an "overview of the history of this topic and opinions surrounding it, ranging from the formation of the League of the Physically Handicapped in 1935 to current efforts to enhance and modify the ADA." Publisher's note
Includes glossary and bibliographical references

Haynes, Charles C.
First freedoms; a documentary history of the First Amendment Rights in America; [by] Charles C. Haynes, Sam Chaltain, Susan M. Glisson. Oxford University Press 2005 255p il $40
Grades: 8 9 10 11 12   342
1. United States. Constitution. 1st-10th amendments
2. Constitutional history—United States
ISBN 978-0-19-515750-5; 0-19-515750-8
                                          LC 2005-31880
This book features "information and primary documents concerning the origins and attacks on the First Amendment. The various documents go from the Charter of Rhode Island and Providence Plantations in 1663 through the Patriot Act of 2001." Libr Media Connect
This is "an excellent resource for all libraries, as well as enjoyable reading for history buffs." SLJ

Head, Tom
Freedom of religion. Facts on File 2005 146p il map (American rights) $35
Grades: 7 8 9 10   342
1. Freedom of religion 2. United States—Religion
ISBN 0-8160-5664-1   LC 2004-20547
Contents: Religious freedom in the American colonies; The freedom of conscience; A diverse religious nation; Religious expression and the law; Conscientious objectors and the draft; Religion in public schools; Freedom from religion?; Religious liberty around the world; The future of religious freedom in America
"This solid, readable volume walks readers through the part religion played in the formation of the colonies and looks at how faith informed the people's lives and the tensions among various religions." Booklist
Includes bibliographical references

Hennessey, Jonathan, 1971-
The United States Constitution; a graphic adaptation; written by Jonathan Hennessey; art by Aaron McConnell. Hill and Wang 2008 149p il $35; pa $16.95 *
Grades: 9 10 11 12 Adult   342
1. United States. Constitution—Graphic novels 2. Graphic novels 3. Constitutional history—United States—Graphic novels
ISBN   978-0-8090-9487-5;   0-8090-9487-8; 978-0-8090-9470-7 (pa); 0-8090-9470-3 (pa)
LC 2008-17927
The author and illustrator go "through the entire U. S. Constitution, article by article, amendment by amendment, explaining their meaning and implications—in comics format. Avoiding the didactic, the book succeeds in being both consistently entertaining and illuminating." Publ Wkly
Includes bibliographical references

Hinds, Maurene J.
You have the right to know your rights; what teens should know. Enslow Pubs. 2005 104p il (Issues in focus today) $31.93 *
Grades: 9 10 11 12   342
1. Youth—Civil rights
ISBN 0-7660-2358-3
The author "outlines for readers the ways in which the rights of young people have changed over time in the United States, and she brings them up-to-date on the topic of young people's rights today. Hinds covers such issues as privacy and self-expression and explains what teens can do if their rights are violated." Publisher's note
Includes bibliographical references

Icenoggle, Jodi, 1967-
Schenck v. United States and the freedom of speech debate. Enslow Pubs. 2005 128p il (Debating Supreme Court decisions) lib bdg $26.60
Grades: 7 8 9 10   342
1. Schenck, Charles 2. Freedom of speech
ISBN 0-7660-2392-3
In the "case of *Schenck v. United States,* the Supreme Court held that people who opposed World War I were not allowed to use their free speech rights to interfere with the draft. . . . [In this book the author] explains the different arguments that have been used for and against free speech." Publisher's note
Includes glossary and bibliographical references

Keenan, Kevin M.
Invasion of privacy; a reference handbook. ABC-CLIO 2005 259p (Contemporary world issues) $50 *
Grades: 11 12 Adult   342
1. Right of privacy
ISBN 1-85109-630-2   LC 2005-18577
"This book provides a comprehensive overview of the right to privacy through a series of essays. . . . Keenan achieves balance by presenting the varying points of

view on the topic and manages to convey the essentials of a complex and timely subject." Libr J
Includes bibliographical references

Lewis, Anthony, 1927-
Freedom for the thought that we hate; a biography of the First Amendment. Basic Books 2007 221p (Basic ideas) $25
Grades: 11 12 Adult   342
1. Freedom of speech 2. Freedom of the press
ISBN 978-0-465-03917-3; 0-465-03917-0
LC 2007-40249
This book examines "free speech controversies—from sedition and obscenity to hate speech and secret wiretapping." N Y Times Book Rev
The author "does a remarkable job of presenting the history and scope of freedom of thought. He writes simply without oversimplifying. . . . Mr. Lewis has produced a concise and wise book. His conclusions are well worth pondering." Economist
Includes bibliographical references

Marzilli, Alan, 1970-
Fetal rights. Chelsea House Publishers 2006 150p il map (Point-counterpoint) $32.95 *
Grades: 9 10 11 12   342
1. Fetus
ISBN 0-7910-8643-7   LC 2005-6533
"This book examines whether the law should recognize an unborn child—or fetus—as a person. Other relevant topics include whether or not women should be prosecuted for using drugs during pregnancy and whether or not a pregnant woman should be forced to undergo medical procedures for the benefit of a fetus." Publisher's note
Includes bibliographical references

Native American rights; Uma Kukathas, book editor. Greenhaven Press 2008 199p (Issues on trial) lib bdg $37.40
Grades: 9 10 11 12   342
1. Native Americans—Civil rights
ISBN 978-0-7377-4076-9   LC 2008-10057
"This book discusses and analyzes various Supreme Court rulings, both historical and contemporary, their impact on American society, and the controversies before and after the court's rulings by various experts in the related fields. . . . This would be a great resource for schools wanting more materials on contemporary Native American issues for use in classes such as American History, English, and Current Events." Libr Media Connect

The **Oxford** guide to United States Supreme Court decisions; edited by Kermit L. Hall, James W. Ely, Jr. 2nd ed. Oxford University Press 2009 499p $35 *
Grades: 11 12 Adult   342
1. United States. Supreme Court 2. Reference books 3. Constitutional law—United States
ISBN 978-0-19-537939-6   LC 2008-23763
First published 1999
The editors "assemble the scholarship of 161 field specialists, who summarize the Supreme Court's 440

The Oxford guide to United States Supreme Court decisions—*Continued*

most significant cases. Scholar-signed, multiparagraph entries are alphabetized by case name, include argued and decided dates, and detail vote divisions. The book closes with a glossary, an appendix containing the complete Constitution, a chronology of justices since 1789, and a list of presidential appointments. An outstanding single-volume reference." Libr J

Includes bibliographical references

Patrick, John J., 1935-

The Bill of Rights; a history in documents. Oxford Univ. Press 2003 205p il map (Pages from history) lib bdg $32.95 *

Grades: 7 8 9 10   342

1. United States. Constitution. 1st-10th amendments
2. Civil rights

ISBN 0-19-510354-8   LC 2002-6294

Contents: The roots of American rights; Rights revolution and in America; The birth of the Bill of Rights; The Bill of Rights marginalized; Rights renewed and denied; A resurgence of rights; Nationalization of the Bill of Rights; Political cartoons on the right to bear arms; Consensus and controversy

Uses contemporary documents to explore the history of the first ten amendments to the U.S. Constitution, the British traditions on which they were based, and their impact on American society

"This attractive and informative volume will be a valuable resource for most collections." SLJ

Includes bibliographical references

Pendergast, Tom, 1964-

Constitutional amendments: from freedom of speech to flag burning; [by] Tom Pendergast, Sara Pendergast, and John Sousanis; Elizabeth Shaw Grunow, editor. U.X.L 2001 3v set $165

Grades: 7 8 9 10   342

1. United States. Constitution. 1st-10th amendments
2. Constitutional law—United States 3. Civil rights

ISBN 0-7876-4865-5   LC 00-67236

"Covering each of the 27 amendments, this 3-vol. resource provides the history and social context of the amendment process. Entries range in length from 10 to 15 pages and begin with the full text of the amendment followed by an essay on the social and political climate that gave rise to its proposal." Publisher's note

"Presentation is very clear. . . . This is definitely a set that belongs in school and public libraries." Booklist

Includes glossary and bibliographical references

Phillips, Tracy A.

Hazelwood v. Kuhlmeier and the school newspaper censorship debate; debating Supreme Court decisions. Enslow Publishers 2006 112p il (Debating Supreme Court decisions) lib bdg $26.60

Grades: 7 8 9 10   342

1. Hazelwood School District v. Kuhlmeier
2. Censorship 3. Freedom of the press 4. Students—Law and legislation

ISBN 0-7660-2394-X   LC 2005034655

This discusses the Supreme Court case involving the censorship of a high school newspaper in Hazelwood Missouri.

This is "objectively and clearly written and would be useful for reports." SLJ

Includes bibliographical references

Racial discrimination; Mitchell Young, book editor. Greenhaven Press 2006 183p il (Issues on trial) lib bdg $34.95

Grades: 8 9 10 11 12   342

1. Race discrimination

ISBN 0-7377-2787-X; 978-0-7377-2787-6

LC 2005-55092

This anthology examines four major court cases involving racial discrimination: Plessy v. Ferguson (1896), Brown v. Board of Education (1954), Wisconsin v. Mitchell (1993), and Grutter v. Bollinger (2003).

Includes bibliographical references

Savage, David G., 1950-

The Supreme Court and individual rights. 5th ed. CQ Press 2009 570p il map pa $52 *

Grades: 9 10 11 12   342

1. United States. Supreme Court 2. Civil rights
3. Constitutional law—United States

ISBN 978-0-87289-424-2   LC 2009-19747

First published 1980 under the authorship of Elder Witt

The author "explores the personal impact of Supreme Court decisions made through 2008. He divides his content into six thematic chapters that explore our guaranteed rights, like Freedom of Speech, along with restricted facets, such as flag burning. With each topic, historic cases involving individuals' rights are carefully explained. Half-page sidebars further clarify complex issues, such as the Court's history regarding cases involving slavery's legality and state sedition laws." Libr J

Includes bibliographical references

Schultz, David A., 1958-

Encyclopedia of the United States Constitution; [by] David Schultz. Facts On File 2009 2v il (Facts on File library of American history) set $150

Grades: 9 10 11 12 Adult   342

1. Constitutional law—United States—Encyclopedias
2. Reference books

ISBN 978-0-8160-6763-3; 0-8160-6763-5

LC 2008-23349

"This reference source can help high-school students, the general public, and other interested parties comprehend the fundamental concepts, evolutionary character, and historic people and events that have shaped the [Constitution.] . . . The alphabetically arranged entries cover terms, events, people, landmark cases, and issues that help explain the Constitution's history. The appendix provides the Declaration of Independence, the Articles of Confederation, the Constitution, and the Bill of Rights as well as 'Other Amendments to the Constitution,' a 'U.S. Constitution Time Line,' and instructions on locating court cases." Booklist

Includes bibliographical references

Supreme Court decisions and women's rights; milestones to equality; edited by Clare Cushman; foreword by Ruth Bader Ginsburg; sponsored by the Supreme Court Historical Society. 2nd ed. CQ Press 2010 310p il $67; pa $57

Grades: 9 10 11 12 **342**
1. United States. Supreme Court 2. Women's rights 3. Sex discrimination 4. Reference books
ISBN 978-1-60871-406-3; 978-1-60871-407-0 (pa)
LC 2010-26076

First published 2001

"This book sets out to chronicle those Supreme Court decisions that directly affected women's rights. All aspects of the law and women's rights are covered in chapters titled Jury Duty, Sex Discrimination, Women in the Family, Single-Sex Schools, Discrimination in the Workplace, Reproductive Rights, and more." Voice Youth Advocates

"A great resource for reports and a handy reference tool for students and teachers alike." SLJ

Includes bibliographical references

Treaties with American Indians; an encyclopedia of rights, conflicts, and sovereignty; Donald L. Fixico, editor. ABC-CLIO 2008 3v il set $285

Grades: 9 10 11 12 Adult **342**
1. Reference books 2. Native Americans—Treaties—Encyclopedias
ISBN 978-1-57607-880-8 LC 2007-27797

The editor "and 149 other contributors examine the historical context that led to the negotiation of hundreds of treaties. They then demonstrate how promises made to Native peoples concerning issues such as sovereignty, land, and cultural preservation have come to plague the political and legal systems of . . . [the U.S. and Canada] as Native peoples rightfully have demanded that past agreements be honored. Included are transcriptions of more than 40 treaties negotiated between 1778 and 1923." Choice

"This set is the most comprehensive source of information on Canadian-Indian treaties and U.S.-Indian treaties." Booklist

Includes bibliographical references

Vile, John R.
The Constitutional Convention of 1787; a comprehensive encyclopedia of America's founding. ABC-CLIO 2005 2v il set $185

Grades: 11 12 Adult **342**
1. Constitutional history—United States—Encyclopedias 2. Constitutional law—United States—Encyclopedias 3. Reference books
ISBN 1-85109-669-8 LC 2005-24214

This "resource covers the people, events, committees, ideology, and documents related to the drafting of the Constitution." SLJ

Includes bibliographical references

Essential Supreme Court decisions; summaries of leading cases in U.S. constitutional law. 15th ed. Rowman & Littlefield Publishers 2010 xxxvi, 535p $59.95; pa $24.95

Grades: 9 10 11 12 **342**
1. United States. Supreme Court 2. Constitutional law—United States 3. Reference books
ISBN 978-1-4422-0384-6; 978-1-4422-0385-3 (pa)
LC 2010-8375

First published 1954 with title: Summaries of leading cases on the Constitution

This volume presents summaries of major cases concerning constitutional law that have been decided by the Supreme Court since its establishment. It is written for students and laypersons.

This is "the most comprehensive single collection of the Court's decisions. . . . It is indispensable for the study of the work of the Supreme Court." Choice

Includes glossary

Weiner, Mark Stuart, 1967-
Black trials; citizenship from the beginnings of slavery to the end of caste; [by] Mark S. Weiner. Alfred A. Knopf 2004 421p $26.95; pa $16.95 *

Grades: 11 12 Adult **342**
1. African Americans—Civil rights 2. Trials
ISBN 0-375-40981-5; 0-375-70884-7 (pa)
LC 2004-40860

The author "examines how court proceedings involving black people—and whites trying to assist them—have served as windows onto race relations and the power of whites over blacks in the U.S. from its earliest days. . . . This book is the best of its kind—a serious, deeply felt reflection on the weight of history on contemporary affairs." Publ Wkly

Includes bibliographical references

What rights should illegal immigrants have? Noël Merino, book editor. Greenhaven Press 2010 106p (At issue. Civil liberties) $31.80; pa $22.50

Grades: 9 10 11 12 **342**
1. Illegal aliens 2. United States—Immigration and emigration 3. Civil rights
ISBN 978-0-7377-4902-1; 0-7377-4902-4; 978-0-7377-4903-8 (pa); 0-7377-4903-2 (pa)
LC 2010-4546

This anthology of essays covers topics related to illegal immigration, such as whether immigration raids are justified and whether existing immigration law violates illegal immigrants' rights.

Includes bibliographical references

344 Labor, social service, education, cultural law

Amendments XVIII and XXI; prohibition and repeal; Sylvia Engdahl, book editor. Greenhaven Press 2009 218p il map (Constitutional amendments: beyond the Bill of Rights) $34.70 *

Grades: 7 8 9 10 11 12   **344**
1. United States. Constitution. 18th Amendment
2. United States. Constitution. 21st Amendment
3. Prohibition
ISBN 978-0-7377-4328-9; 0-7377-4328-X
                                        LC 2008-51451
This book "examines the eighteenth and twenty-first amendments. This volume's historical essays examine both sides of the issue; both for and against Prohibition. . . . Other essays examine the impact of these amendments on the Constitution, and the controversies that still surround intoxicating substances in America." Voice Youth Advocates
Includes bibliographical references

American Bar Association
The American Bar Association guide to workplace law; [principle author, Barbara Fick] 2nd ed. Random House Reference 2006 301p pa $16.95
Grades: 11 12 Adult   **344**
1. Labor—Law and legislation
ISBN 0-375-72140-1; 978-0-375-72140-3
                                        LC 2006-45186
First published 1997
This guide covers laws affecting hiring, sexual harassment, leave time, health insurance, ending an employment relationship, retirement, unions, government employment and workplace rights.
Includes bibliographical references

Barbour, Scott, 1963-
Should marijuana be legalized? ReferencePoint Press 2010 c2011 96p il map (In controversy) lib bdg $26.95
Grades: 9 10 11 12   **344**
1. Marijuana 2. Drugs—Law and legislation
ISBN 978-1-60152-106-4; 1-60152-106-5
                                        LC 2009-40002
This book "discusses medical, judicial, economic, and social concerns that come to light in the debate over legalizing marijuana." Booklist
Includes bibliographical references

Dudley, Mark E.
Engel v. Vitale (1962); religion in the schools. 21st Cent. Bks. (NY) 1995 96p il (Supreme Court decisions) $18.90
Grades: 7 8 9 10   **344**
1. Engel, Stephen 2. Vitale, William J. 3. Religion in the public schools 4. Church and state
ISBN 0-8050-3916-3   LC 95-19435

The author points out that although a 1962 Supreme Court case decided that official prayers in public schools are unconstitutional, the issue of separation of church and state remains.
This volume is "clearly written and well organized." SLJ
Includes bibliographical references

The **environment**; Andrea C. Nakaya, book editor. Greenhaven Press 2006 163p il (Issues on trial) lib bdg $34.95
Grades: 9 10 11 12   **344**
1. Environmental policy—United States
ISBN 0-7377-2797-7; 978-0-7377-2797-5
                                        LC 2005-52713
"This anthology examines four court cases that offer insight into some of America's most important environmental conflicts. . . . There is a wealth of information in this title, which serves as a meaningful reference tool and a prelude to the study of law as a force for major social change." SLJ
Includes bibliographical references

Fridell, Ron, 1943-
Cruzan v. Missouri and the right to die debate; debating Supreme Court decisions. Enslow Publishers 2005 128p il (Debating Supreme Court decisions) lib bdg $26.60
Grades: 7 8 9 10   **344**
1. Cruzan, Nancy 2. Cruzan, Joe, d. 1996 3. Right to die—Law and legislation
ISBN 0-7660-2356-7   LC 2004-20028
Contents: Legal questions; The changing face of death; Through supporters' eyes; Through opponents' eyes; Right to die laws; Lower court cases; U.S. Supreme Court cases; The issues today; Debating the issues
This examines both sides of the debate concerning assisted suicide and related Supreme Court decisions.
Includes glossary and bibliographical references

Hillstrom, Laurie
Roe v. Wade; [by] Laurie Collier Hillstrom. Omnigraphics 2008 249p il (Defining moments) $49
Grades: 9 10 11 12 Adult   **344**
1. Abortion—Law and legislation
ISBN 978-0-7808-1026-6   LC 2008-3524
"Explores the history of abortion in America, describing the Roe v. Wade case, explaining the decision and its implications, and examining the continuing debate over abortion rights and its impact on American society and politics. Features include a narrative overview, biographical profiles, primary source documents, detailed chronology, glossary, annotated sources for further study, bibliography, and index." Publisher's note
Includes glossary and bibliographical references

Hull, N. E. H., 1949-

Roe v. Wade; the abortion rights controversy in American history; [by] N.E.H. Hull and Peter Charles Hoffer. 2nd ed., rev. & expanded. University Press of Kansas 2010 370p (Landmark law cases & American society) $39.95; pa $19.95

Grades: 11 12 Adult   **344**
1. McCorvey, Norma 2. Wade, Henry, 1914-2001 3. Roe v. Wade 4. Abortion—Law and legislation
ISBN   978-0-7006-1753-1;   0-7006-1753-1; 978-0-7006-1754-8 (pa); 0-7006-1754-X (pa)
LC 2010-21294
First published 2001

Thsi book "highlights the abortion issue's historical background; highlights *Roe v. Wade*'s core issues, essential personalities, and key precedents; tracks the case's path through the courts; clarifies the jurisprudence behind the court's ruling in Roe; and gauges its impact on American society and subsequent challenges to it in *Webster v. Reproductive Services* (1989) and *Casey v. Planned Parenthood* (1992). . . . [It includes] chapters covering abortion politics and legal battles in the post-9/11 era." Publisher's note

Includes bibliographical references

Is gun ownership a right? Lea Sakora, book editor. Greenhaven Press 2010 107p (At issue. Civil liberties) $31.80; pa $22.50

Grades: 9 10 11 12   **344**
1. United States. Constitution. 1st-10th amendments 2. Gun control
ISBN   978-0-7377-4428-6;   0-7377-4428-6; 978-0-7377-4429-3 (pa); 0-7377-4429-4 (pa)
LC 2009-26389

Articles in this anthology discuss the Second Amendment and issues related to gun ownership and gun regulation.

Includes bibliographical references

Kowalski, Kathiann M., 1955-

The Earls case and the student drug testing debate; debating Supreme Court decisions. Enslow Publishers 2006 128p il (Debating Supreme Court decisions) lib bdg $26.60

Grades: 7 8 9 10   **344**
1. Earls, Lindsay 2. Students—Law and legislation 3. Drug testing
ISBN 0-7660-2478-4   LC 2005034654

This is an account of the Supreme Court case involving Lindsay Earls, a high school student in Oklahoma who was subjected to a random drug test.

This is "objectively and clearly written and would be useful for reports." SLJ

Includes glossary and bibliographical references

McPherson, Stephanie Sammartino

The Bakke case and the affirmative action debate. Enslow Pubs. 2005 128p il (Debating Supreme Court decisions) lib bdg $26.60

Grades: 7 8 9 10   **344**

1. Bakke, Allan Paul 2. Affirmative action programs
ISBN 0-7660-2526-8

"In 1973, [Allan] Bakke applied to medical school. . . . He was not admitted. When he found out that the medical school class reserved some positions for members of minority groups, he took the university to court, charging discrimination. His case went . . . to the Supreme Court. Is affirmative action an effort to 'level the playing field,' or is it unfair preferential treatment to minorities? . . . [This] explores both sides of the argument as well as related court cases and laws." Publisher's note

Mountjoy, Shane, 1967-

Engel v. Vitale; school prayer and the establishment clause. Chelsea House 2007 128p il (Great Supreme Court decisions) lib bdg $30

Grades: 7 8 9 10   **344**
1. Engel, Stephen 2. Vitale, William J. 3. Religion in the public schools 4. Church and state
ISBN 0-7910-9241-0; 978-0-7910-9241-5
LC 2006-7328

This describes the 1962 Supreme Court case which ruled that official prayers in public schools were unconstitutional.

"Excellent period photos, magazine covers, and portraits of historical figures are closely cued to the [text]. . . . Handsomely packaged, accessible." SLJ

Includes glossary and bibliographical references

Perl, Lila

Cruzan v. Missouri; the right to die? Marshall Cavendish Benchmark 2007 143p il (Supreme Court milestones) $27.95

Grades: 7 8 9 10   **344**
1. Cruzan, Nancy 2. Cruzan, Joe, d. 1996 3. Right to die—Law and legislation
ISBN 978-0-7614-2581-6; 0-7614-258-0
LC 2006-25740

"Perl discusses Nancy Cruzan's parents quest for her right to die following an auto accident and her resulting vegetative state. Highlights include the discussion of religious arguments, physician-assisted suicide, and the cases of Karen Ann Quinlan and Terry Schiavo. . . . Additional information is presented in sidebars. Occasional black-and-white photos add interest." SLJ

Includes bibliographical references

Raskin, Jamin B., 1962-

We the students; Supreme Court cases for and about students. 3rd ed. CQ Press 2008 333p il $52; pa $32 *

Grades: 9 10 11 12   **344**
1. Students—Law and legislation 2. Students—Civil rights
ISBN   978-0-87289-760-1;   0-87289-760-5; 978-0-87289-761-8 (pa); 0-87289-761-3 (pa)
LC 2008-23743

"Cosponsored by the Supreme Court Historical Society"

First published 2000

The author focuses on "Supreme Court cases that affect students and schools. The book is organized into 10

Raskin, Jamin B., 1962-—*Continued*
chapters, opening with a brief overview of what the Constitution is and what it does before discussing free speech, censorship, religion, property searches, discipline, discrimination, harassment, and disabilities. . . . This excellent resource should be in all government classrooms." SLJ

Includes bibliographical references

Reproductive rights; William Dudley, book editor. Greenhaven Press 2006 178p il (Issues on trial) lib bdg $34.95 *
Grades: 9 10 11 12   **344**
1. Abortion—Law and legislation 2. Birth control—Law and legislation
ISBN 0-7377-2511-7; 978-0-7377-2511-7
LC 2005-54268
"This book examines various issues related to the topic via a series of writings about famous Supreme Court cases, ranging from Buck v. Bell in 1927 and Griswold v. Connecticut in 1965 to Roe v. Wade in 1973 and A.Z. v. B.Z. in 2000. The essays include court decisions and dissenting opinions as well as contemporary journalism pieces and retrospective commentary. . . . Students of modern science, biology, genetics, and the law will find this volume informative and interesting." SLJ

Includes bibliographical references

Students' rights; Laura K. Egendorf, book editor. Greenhaven Press 2006 189p il (Issues on trial) lib bdg $34.95
Grades: 9 10 11 12   **344**
1. Students—Civil rights 2. Students—Law and legislation 3. Youth—Civil rights
ISBN 0-7377-2509-5; 978-0-7377-2509-4
LC 2005-52690
"In this anthology judges and commentators explore four key students' rights cases." Publisher's note

Includes bibliographical references

Students' rights: opposing viewpoints; Jamuna Carroll, book editor. Greenhaven Press 2005 207p lib bdg $34.95; pa $23.70 *
Grades: 9 10 11 12   **344**
1. Students—Civil rights
ISBN 0-7377-3088-9 (lib bdg); 0-7377-3089-7 (pa)
LC 2004-59761
"Opposing viewpoints series"
"Essays cover . . . topics such as No Child Left Behind, religion in schools, dress codes, The Patriot Act, access to family-planning information, random drug testing, and illegal immigrants' access to federal financial aide, while posing significant questions to help students develop critical-thinking skills." SLJ

Includes bibliographical references

Telgen, Diane
Brown v. Board of Education. Omnigraphics 2005 xxxiv, 246p il (Defining moments) lib bdg $38
Grades: 7 8 9 10   **344**

1. Brown, Oliver, 1919-1961 2. Topeka (Kan.). Board of Education 3. Segregation in education
ISBN 0-7808-0775-8
This "opens with an 'Important People, Places, and Terms' section and a detailed chronology that takes readers from an 1849 school-segregation case to the 2003 University of Michigan rulings on student diversity. The book includes a narrative overview, biographies of individuals involved, and primary sources. This latter, impressive section gives this treatment of Brown v. Board of Education depth and promotes a greater empathy from readers. . . . Telgen has done a fine job of making this topic accessible to and engaging for today's students." SLJ

Includes bibliographical references

345   Criminal law

Aretha, David
The trial of the Scottsboro boys. Morgan Reynolds Pub. 2007 128p il (The civil rights movement) lib bdg $27.95
Grades: 7 8 9 10 11 12   **345**
1. Scottsboro case 2. Trials 3. African Americans—Civil rights
ISBN 978-1-59935-058-5; 1-59935-058-0
LC 2007-23818
This describes the case of nine young black men between the ages of 13 and 20 who were accused of rape in the 1930s in Alabama by two white women and were sentenced to death.
"Aretha writes clearly, with objectivity and compassion." SLJ

Includes bibliographical references

Capital punishment; Paul G. Connors, book editor. Greenhaven Press 2007 220p (Current controversies) $39.70; pa $27.50 *
Grades: 9 10 11 12   **345**
1. Capital punishment—United States
ISBN   978-0-7377-3711-0;   0-7377-3711-5;
978-0-7377-3712-7 (pa); 0-7377-3712-3 (pa)
LC 2007-25898
An anthology of essays discussing the ethical issues surrounding capital punishment, including whether or not it deters crime.

Includes bibliographical references

Cohen, Laura
The Gault case and young people's rights; debating Supreme Court decisions. Enslow Publishers, Inc. 2006 128p il (Debating Supreme Court decisions) lib bdg $26.60
Grades: 7 8 9 10   **345**
1. Gault, Gerald 2. Juvenile courts 3. Children—Law and legislation
ISBN 0-7660-2476-8   LC 2006001741
Examines the 1967 Supreme Court Case in which the court ruled that juvenile courts cannot deprive children of certain rights guaranteed by the Constitution.
This is "objectively and clearly written and would be useful for reports." SLJ

Includes bibliographical references

Crimes and trials of the century; edited by Steven Chermak and Frankie Y. Bailey. Greenwood Press 2007 2v il set $199.95 *
Grades: 9 10 11 12 Adult   345
1. Trials 2. Administration of criminal justice
ISBN 978-0-313-34109-0   LC 2007-30704
"From the Black Sox scandal of 1919 to the investigations of Abu Ghraib through 2006, this set looks closely at 35 particularly newsworthy American crimes. . . . Clear writing, strong organization, and involving subject matter make this a strong resource." SLJ
Includes bibliographical references

The **death** penalty; Samuel Brenner, book editor. Greenhaven Press 2006 190p il map (Issues on trial) lib bdg $34.95 *
Grades: 9 10 11 12   345
1. Capital punishment—United States
ISBN 0-7377-2507-9; 978-0-7377-2507-0
          LC 2005-58851
This book examines four major court cases involving capital punishment.
Includes bibliographical references

Freedom from cruel and unusual punishment; Kristin O'Donnell Tubb, book editor. Greenhaven Press 2005 144p (Bill of Rights) lib bdg $32.45
Grades: 9 10 11 12   345
1. Punishment 2. Capital punishment
ISBN 0-7377-1925-7   LC 2004-54223
"This anthology discusses the Eighth Amendment, including a history dating back to biblical times, its inseparable ties to the death penalty, and recent rulings and debates." Publisher's note
Includes bibliographical references

Gershman, Gary P.
Death penalty on trial; a handbook with cases, laws, and documents. ABC-CLIO 2005 265p (On trial) $55
Grades: 11 12 Adult   345
1. Capital punishment—United States
ISBN 1-85109-606-X; 978-1-85109-606-0
          LC 2005-1438
"The first half of the book describes the history, court cases, and decisions regarding the death penalty, and the impact of the judicial determinations and how they affect the current legal environment. The second half of the volume consists of excerpts from important judicial decisions between 1892 and 2002; a short glossary related to Key People, Laws, and Concepts; a chronology; a table of cases; and an eight-page annotated bibliography." SLJ
This book "is an excellent choice for the library shelf." Libr Media Connect
Includes bibliographical references

Hoffer, Peter Charles
The Salem witchcraft trials; a legal history. University Press of Kan. 1997 165p (Landmark law cases & American society) hardcover o.p. pa $12.95
Grades: 11 12 Adult   345
1. Trials 2. Salem (Mass.)—History
ISBN 0-7006-0858-3; 0-7006-0859-1 (pa)
          LC 97-19986
"Hoffer discusses the legal nature of the charges of witchcraft, the evidential and procedural characteristics of the trials of the accused, and the roles and attitudes of the ministers and magistrates who controlled the proceedings. . . . Hoffer offers little that is new in terms of interpretation, but he presents it well and in a manner easily grasped by the general reader." Choice
Includes bibliographical references

Individual rights and the police; Mark R. Nesbitt, book editor. Greenhaven Press 2006 188p (Issues on trial) lib bdg $34.95
Grades: 9 10 11 12   345
1. Criminal procedure 2. Civil rights
ISBN 0-7377-2505-2; 978-0-7377-2505-6
          LC 2005-54542
This anthology examines four court cases involving the rights of the accused: Mapp v. Ohio (1961), Miranda v. Arizona (1966), Katz v. United States (1967), and Terry v. Ohio (1968).
Includes bibliographical references

Jacobs, Thomas A.
They broke the law, you be the judge; true cases of teen crime; edited by Al Desetta. Free Spirit Pub. 2003 213p il pa $15.95 *
Grades: 7 8 9 10   345
1. Administration of criminal justice 2. Juvenile courts
ISBN 1-57542-134-8   LC 2003-4814
"This book details 21 cases ranging from truancy to auto theft. Following a description of events leading up to and including the crime itself, readers are given background about the individual, sentencing options, and questions to consider before sentencing, and then asked to make a decision about the case." SLJ
"An excellent introduction to how juvenile justice works, this will be a great resource for classroom and group discussions." Booklist
Includes bibliographical references

Kelly-Gangi, Carol
Miranda v. Arizona and the rights of the accused; debating Supreme Court decisions; [by] Carol Kelly-Gangi. Enslow Publishers 2006 128p il (Debating Supreme Court decisions) lib bdg $26.60
Grades: 7 8 9 10   345
1. Miranda, Ernesto 2. Right to counsel
ISBN 0-7660-2477-6   LC 2006011737
This discusses the Supreme Court case involving a suspect's rights while being questioned by police.
Includes bibliographical references

Khan, Lin Shi

Scottsboro, Alabama; a story in linoleum cuts; [by] Lin Shi Khan and Tony Perez; edited by Andrew H. Lee; foreword by Robin D.G. Kelley. New York Univ. Press 2002 147p il hardcover o.p. pa $21

Grades: 11 12 Adult   345

1. Scottsboro case

ISBN 0-8147-5176-8; 0-8147-5177-6 (pa)

LC 2001-59189

This "graphic book from 1935 reproduces 118 linocuts illustrating the history of African Americans up to and including the Scottsboro trials. . . . [This is] a highly charged political indictment and work of art. The reproductions are excellent, and Lee and Robin D.G. Kelley provide background essays on the trials and the provenance of the book." Libr J

Krygier, Leora, 1952-

Juvenile court; a judge's guide for young adults and their parents. Scarecrow Press 2009 181p il $29.95 *

Grades: 9 10 11 12 Adult   345

1. Juvenile courts 2. Juvenile delinquency

ISBN 978-0-8108-6127-5; 0-8108-6127-5

LC 2008-32075

"This book is Krygier's attempt to inform and prepare young people who are facing a court hearing. From minor traffic violations and truancy charges to fighting and drug and alcohol-related offenses, Krygier unpacks some of the most common terms, procedures, facts, and myths of the juvenile court system so that young people—and their parents—might more efficiently navigate the process. . . . Her approach is serious and straightforward, but remains highly readable as a guide or a reference manual." Voice Youth Advocates

Includes bibliographical references

Larson, Edward J.

The Scopes trial; a photographic history; introduction by Edward Caudill; photo captions by Edward Larson; afterword by Jesse Fox Mayshark. University of Tenn. Press 1999 88p il hardcover o.p. pa $18.95

Grades: 11 12 Adult   345

1. Scopes, John Thomas 2. Evolution—Study and teaching

ISBN 1-57233-080-5; 1-57233-081-3 (pa)

LC 99-50735

The photographs are from the W.C. Robinson and Sue K. Hicks collections, Special Collections, University of Tennessee, Knoxville

"Sandwiching a clutch of generously annotated documentary photos, Caudill's introduction explains what led to the trial. . . . Mayshark's afterword presents the trial's larger historical and political context and its long-lived effects on Tennessee, textbook publishing, and plain speech about hot topics. The slim, handsome book is an ideal primer on its notorious subject." Booklist

Includes bibliographical references

Lewis, Anthony, 1927-

Gideon's trumpet. Random House 1964 262p pa $12.95 hardcover o.p.

Grades: 11 12 Adult   345

1. Gideon, Clarence Earl 2. United States. Supreme Court 3. Law—United States

ISBN 0-679-72312-9 (pa)

An account of the case of a Florida man convicted of burglary which brought about a historic decision of the Supreme Court decreeing that in all states a defendant is entitled to counsel.

Includes bibliographical references

Margulies, Phillip, 1952-

The devil on trial; witches, anarchists, atheists, communists, and terrorists in America's courtrooms; by Phillip Marguiles and Maxine Rosaler. Houghton Mifflin Co. 2008 218p il $22 *

Grades: 7 8 9 10 11 12   345

1. Trials 2. Administration of criminal justice

ISBN 978-0-618-71717-0; 0-618-71717-X

LC 2008-1870

The authors "examine five highly emotional court cases, each of which served as a litmus test for the health of America's justice system at the time it occurred. . . . Each chapter gives historical context of the court proceeding, describes its progression in some detail, and comments on the political and intellectual aftermath. . . . [This is] a highly relevant and riveting book." SLJ

Includes glossary and bibliographical references

Marzilli, Alan, 1970-

The Internet and crime. Chelsea House 2010 120p il (Point-counterpoint) lib bdg $32.95

Grades: 7 8 9 10   345

1. Internet—Law and legislation 2. Computer crimes 3. Consumer protection

ISBN 978-1-60413-506-0; 1-60413-506-9

LC 2009-22139

This book covers "crimes directly related to the Internet, such as stealing personal information or engaging in fraudulent schemes." Publisher's note

Includes bibliographical references

The **right** to a trial by jury; edited by Robert Winters. Greenhaven Press 2005 142p (Bill of Rights) $32.45

Grades: 9 10 11 12   345

1. Jury

ISBN 0-7377-1937-0   LC 2004-52282

This book "examines medieval origins and the colonial implementation of English-style trial processes and includes Supreme Court decisions. It then presents the modern arguments for and against the jury system, with a time line of significant decisions." Voice Youth Advocates

Rights of the accused; Michelle Lewis, book editor. Greenhaven Press 2007 198p (Issues on trial) lib bdg $34.95 *

Grades: 9 10 11 12   **345**

1. Criminal procedure

ISBN 978-0-7377-2795-1; 0-7377-2795-0

LC 2006-38192

This anthology examines in detail the following court cases: Coffin v. United States (1895), Gideon v. Wainwright (1963), Duncan v. Louisiana (1968), and Crawford v. Washington (2004).

Includes bibliographical references

Ruschmann, Paul

Legalizing marijuana. 2nd ed. Chelsea House 2010 144p il (Point-counterpoint) $35

Grades: 7 8 9 10   **345**

1. Marijuana 2. Drugs—Law and legislation

ISBN 978-1-60413-690-6; 1-60413-690-1

LC 2009-51404

First published 2004

This presents arguments for and against legalization of marijuana, including whether or not the drug is dangerous, how marijuana laws are enforced, and whether or not relaxing the laws would be good for society.

Includes glossary and bibliographical references

Miranda rights; series consulting editor, Alan Marzilli. Chelsea House Publications 2006 126p il (Point-counterpoint) lib bdg $32.95

Grades: 7 8 9 10   **345**

1. Miranda, Ernesto 2. Right to counsel

ISBN 0-7910-9229-1; 978-0-7910-9229-3

LC 2006-23655

"This book examines both sides of Miranda-related questions: Is the Miranda decision a violation of separation of powers or the concept of federalism? Does making mandatory the reading of the rules free guilty criminals? Do the warnings affect the validity of confessions?" Publisher's note

Includes bibliographical references

Sherrow, Victoria

Gideon v. Wainwright; free legal counsel. Enslow Pubs. 1995 104p il (Landmark Supreme Court cases) lib bdg $18.95

Grades: 7 8 9 10   **345**

1. Gideon, Clarence Earl 2. Wainwright, Louie L. 3. Legal aid

ISBN 0-89490-507-4   LC 93-45981

This "volume details the genesis of the case that established the right to free legal counsel, the Supreme Court decision, and the arguments presented by the lawyers for each side. A fine addition to the thought-provoking series." Horn Book Guide

Includes bibliographical references

Should juveniles be tried as adults? Christine Watkins, book editor. Greenhaven Press 2008 130p (At issue. Crime) $31.80; pa $22.50

Grades: 9 10 11 12   **345**

1. Juvenile delinquency 2. Criminal procedure 3. Administration of criminal justice

ISBN 978-0-7377-4077-6; 0-7377-4077-9; 978-0-7377-4078-3 (pa); 0-7377-4078-7 (pa)

LC 2008-1001

This title provides articles discussing whether youthful offenders should be tried in adult courts.

Includes bibliographical references

Sorensen, Lita

The Scottsboro Boys Trial; a primary source account. Rosen Pub. Group 2004 64p il (Great trials of the 20th century) lib bdg $29.25

Grades: 8 9 10 11 12   **345**

1. Scottsboro case 2. Trials 3. African Americans—Civil rights

ISBN 0-8239-3975-8   LC 2002-153356

• Contents: Background: a journey interrupted; The story of two white girls; A court in the Old South; The role of the NAACP and the ILD; Appeals, outcomes, and a landmark decision; A long road to justice; Impact of the Scottsboro Boys Trial in American history

An account of the 1931 trial in which African American youths were charged with rape.

This is "packed with information. . . . [An] attractive, intelligent offering." SLJ

Includes bibliographical references

Stefoff, Rebecca, 1951-

Furman v. Georgia; debating the death penalty. Marshall Cavendish Benchmark 2007 127p il (Supreme Court milestones) lib bdg $27.95

Grades: 7 8 9 10   **345**

1. Furman, William Henry 2. Capital punishment

ISBN 978-0-7614-2583-0; 0-7614-2583-7

LC 2007-582

"Stefoff shows how Furman's murder case, guilty verdict, and death sentence went through the process of appeals to the final decision. Discussions of the history of the death penalty and the use of the electric chair, gas chamber, and lethal injection contribute insight into the controversy and complexities of the case. . . . Additional information is presented in sidebars. Occasional black-and-white and color photos add interest." SLJ

Includes bibliographical references

VanMeter, Larry A.

Miranda v. Arizona; the rights of the accused. Chelsea House 2007 112p il (Great Supreme Court decisions) lib bdg $30

Grades: 7 8 9 10   **345**

1. Miranda, Ernesto 2. Right to counsel

ISBN 0-7910-9259-3; 978-0-7910-9259-0

LC 2006-7578

This discusses the case in which the Supreme Court ruled that suspects must be informed of their rights to remain silent and the right to counsel when they are being questioned by the police.

VanMeter, Larry A.—*Continued*
"Excellent period photos, magazine covers, and portraits of historical figures are closely cued to the [text]. Reproductions of primary documents, including Ernesto Miranda's signed confession, greatly enhance the presentation of the [case]. . . . Handsomely packaged, accessible." SLJ
Includes glossary and bibliographical references

346   Private law

Fishman, Stephen
The public domain; how to find & use copyright-free writings, music, art & more. 5th ed. Nolo 2010 462p il map pa $39.99 *
Grades: Adult Professional   346
   1. Copyright
   ISBN 978-1-4133-1205-8; 1-4133-1205-5
                      LC 2009-39940
First published 2001. Frequently revised
This book offers "information about finding copyright-free writings, music, art, photography, software, maps, databases, videos, and more." Publisher's note

Jacobs, Thomas A.
What are my rights? 95 questions and answers about teens and the law. rev. ed. Free Spirit Pub. 2006 199p il pa $14.95
Grades: 7 8 9 10 11 12   346
   1. Youth—Law and legislation
   ISBN 1-57542-028-7   LC 97-8599
First published 1997
This "presents answers to questions about laws that affect teens, encouraging youths to understand both their rights and responsibilities in order to make sound decisions. The book is organized into chapters on family, school, work, teens and their bodies, growing up, criminal behavior, and the legal system. . . . An accessible, current resource." SLJ
Includes bibliographical references

Riley, Gail Blasser
Internet piracy; [by] Gail Riley. Marshall Cavendish Benchmark 2010 111p il (Controversy!) lib bdg $25.95
Grades: 8 9 10 11 12   346
   1. Copyright 2. Internet—Law and legislation
   ISBN 978-0-7614-4902-7; 0-7614-4902-7
                    LC 2009-50574
This "discusses copyright protection, theft of intellectual property, and the rise of online piracy of software, movies, and music. The book addresses the debate between those who push for freedom of information and those who want to crack down on violators. With rapid changes in technology and legislation, [this book is] recommended for all libraries seeking quality and current materials on [this topic]." SLJ
Includes bibliographical references

Simpson, Carol
Copyright for schools; a practical guide. 5th ed. Linworth 2010 xxiii, 252p il pa $45 *
Grades: Adult Professional   346
   1. Fair use (Copyright) 2. Copyright
   ISBN 978-1-58683-393-0; 1-58683-393-6
                    LC 2010-31901
First published 1994 with title: Copyright for school libraries
"Starting with an overview of copyright law, the book goes on to cover specific topics medium by medium, including print, software, music, video, multimedia, and more. It addresses . . . technologies in common use in schools and school libraries and also includes . . . cases and interpretations, statutory citations, guidance on best practices, and real life questions and answers to typical copyright dilemmas faced by schools." Publisher's note
Includes bibliographical references

346.04   Property

Butler, Rebecca P.
Smart copyright compliance for schools; a how-to-do-it manual. Neal-Schuman Publishers 2009 154p il (How-to-do-it manuals for librarians) pa $75 *
Grades: Adult Professional   346.04
   1. Copyright 2. Fair use (Copyright) 3. School libraries
   ISBN 978-1-55570-646-3; 1-55570-646-0
                    LC 2009-3621
This provides "step-by-step directions for developing and implementing a copyright policy for school districts and schools. . . . The clean layout with wide margins makes for easy reading. An excellent addition to the professional shelf." Booklist
Includes bibliographical references

Complete copyright; an everyday guide for librarians; Carrie Russell, editor. American Library Association 2004 262p il spiral bdg $50
Grades: Adult Professional   346.04
   1. Copyright
   ISBN 0-8389-3543-5   LC 2004-7681
New edition in preparation
Russell provides "guidance for both common copyright issues and latest trends, including the intricacies of copyright in the digital world. Through real-life examples, she also illustrates how librarians can be advocates for a fair and balanced copyright law." Publisher's note

Crews, Kenneth D.
Copyright law for librarians and educators; creative strategies and practical solutions; with contributions from Dwayne K. Buttler . . . [et al.] 2nd ed. American Library Association 2006 141p il pa $45 *
Grades: Adult Professional   346.04
   1. Copyright
   ISBN 0-8389-0906-X   LC 2005-13804
First published 2000 with title: Copyright essentials for librarians and educators

Crews, Kenneth D.—*Continued*

New edition in preparation

The author "addresses 18 areas of copyright in 5 parts. He begins with the scope of protectable works as well as works without copyright protection. Next, he discusses the rights of ownership, including duration and exceptions. He then explains fair use and its related guidelines. Part 4 focuses on the TEACH Act, Section 108, and responsibilities and liabilities. Lastly, Crews examines special issues such as the Digital Millennium Copyright Act." Booklist

Includes bibliographical references

Fishman, Stephen

Copyright handbook; what every writer needs to know. 10th ed. Nolo 2008 527p il pa $39.99

Grades: Adult Professional   **346.04**

1. Copyright

ISBN 978-1-4133-0893-8; 1-4133-0893-7

LC 2008-7882

First published 1991. Frequently revised

Includes CD-ROM

"Designed as a practical handbook for writers and publishers. Includes a list of legal aid groups and sample forms." Guide to Ref Books. 11th edition

Includes bibliographical references

Gordon, Sherri Mabry

Downloading copyrighted stuff from the Internet; stealing or fair use? Enslow Publishers 2005 104p il (Issues in focus today) lib bdg $31.93

Grades: 7 8 9 10   **346.04**

1. Copyright 2. Internet

ISBN 0-7660-2164-5

LC 2004-9954

Contents: Downloading: a history; Tools of the underground Internet; The underground Internet today; Free speech? The argument for the underground Internet; Copyright infringement? the argument against the underground Internet; Underground Internet lawsuits and their outcomes; What's next? the future of the underground Internet

This presents "two sides of the ongoing controversy surrounding the use of the Internet to download copyrighted material. . . . The author presents specific legal action and instances to support each side of the debate. . . . Clearly written, this is an accessible treatment of a complex topic." SLJ

Includes glossary and bibliographical references

Hoffmann, Gretchen McCord

Copyright in cyberspace 2; questions and answers for librarians. Neal-Schuman Publishers 2005 271p pa $75

Grades: Adult Professional   **346.04**

1. Copyright 2. Internet

ISBN 1-55570-517-0

LC 2004-18238

First published 2001 with title: Copyright in cyberspace

"The book is divided into four sections covering copyright fundamentals, applying them in cyberspace, specific library applications as they relate to the increasing types

of material that can be copyrighted, and resources. . . . The intricacies of file-sharing, browsing and caching, hyperlinks and framing, licensing, and electronic reserves are covered separately, bolstered by court-case examples, notes, and bibliographies. . . . An indispensable reference for all types of libraries." SLJ

Includes bibliographical references

Internet piracy; James D. Torr, book editor. Greenhaven Press 2005 78p (At issue) lib bdg $28.70; pa $19.95

Grades: 9 10 11 12   **346.04**

1. Copyright—Music

ISBN 0-7377-2328-9 (lib bdg); 0-7377-2329-7 (pa)

LC 2004-42524

This book discusses the effects of free online file sharing, particularly music sharing, on artists and the industry as well as how the government should get involved in the issue. Contributors include Janis Ian, Jack Valenti, and Orson Scott Card.

Includes bibliographical references

Simpson, Carol Mann, 1949-

Copyright catechism; practical answers to everyday school dilemmas; [by] Carol Simpson. Linworth Pub. 2005 192p pa $36.95

Grades: Adult Professional   **346.04**

1. Fair use (Copyright) 2. Copyright

ISBN 1-58683-202-6; 979-1-58683-202-4

LC 2005-18524

Companion volume to Copyright for schools: a practical guide

This "volume looks at practical applications for all types of schools, community organizations, daycare facilities, and colleges. . . . Educators will appreciate Simpson's clear and concise answers for almost every imaginable copyright dilemma." SLJ

Wherry, Timothy Lee

Intellectual property; everything the digital-age librarian needs to know. American Library Association 2008 141p il $50 *

Grades: Adult Professional   **346.04**

1. Copyright 2. Patents 3. Trademarks

ISBN 978-0-8389-0948-5; 0-8389-0948-5

LC 2007-13893

The author "explains the difference between patents, copyrights, and trademarks and when one would want to obtain any one or a combination of the three. He goes on to instruct readers on how technology has simplified the process of both searching and acquiring these three types of intellectual property protection. . . . This informative and necessary volume is a must have for any professional reference collection." Voice Youth Advocates

347 Civil procedure and courts

Baum, Lawrence
The Supreme Court. 10th ed. CQ Press 2009
c2010 256p il pa $39.95 *
Grades: 9 10 11 12   347
1. United States. Supreme Court 2. Constitutional
law—United States
ISBN 978-1-60426-462-3; 1-60426-462-4
LC 2009-32495
First published 1981
This book provides an introduction to various aspects
of the Supreme Court, including the selection of justices,
types of cases chosen, and factors influencing the deci-
sions rendered.
Includes glossary and bibliographical references

Finkelman, Paul, 1949-
Landmark decisions of the United States
Supreme Court; [by] Paul Finkelman, Melvin I.
Urofsky. 2nd ed. CQ Press 2008 791p il $250 *
Grades: 11 12 Adult   347
1. United States. Supreme Court 2. Constitutional
law—United States
ISBN 978-0-87289-409-9   LC 2007-42588
First published 2003
This "provides the historical context and constitutional
perspective of more than 1,000 of the most important Su-
preme Court cases." Publisher's note
Includes bibliographical references

Hartman, Gary R.
Landmark Supreme Court cases; the most
influential decisions of the Supreme Court of the
United States; [by] Gary Hartman, Roy M.
Mersky, [and] Cindy Tate Slavinski. Facts on File
2004 594p (Facts on File library of American
history) $70; pa $21.95
Grades: 11 12 Adult   347
1. United States. Supreme Court 2. Law—United
States
ISBN 0-8160-2452-9; 0-8160-6923-9 (pa)
LC 2003-57776
New edition in preparation
"The authors describe some 350 influential US Su-
preme Court decisions. Arranged by subjects such as
abortion and taxation, the . . . entries include an abstract
of the decision, . . . the case's history, summary of the
arguments, the salient issues involved, its significance,
related cases, and recommended readings including law
journal articles." Choice
This is "an excellent source for beginning researchers.
. . . The discussion of the case's significance and its implications will be useful for students." SLJ
Includes bibliographical references

Jost, Kenneth
The Supreme Court A to Z. 4th ed. CQ Press
2007 622p il (CQ's American government A to Z
series) $85 *
Grades: 8 9 10 11 12 Adult   347
1. United States. Supreme Court
ISBN 0-87289-335-9; 978-0-87289-335-1
LC 2006-38701
First published 1993
This book "provides biographies of past and present
justices, the history of important cases, and explanations
of constitutional principles and legal concepts." Publish-
er's note
Includes bibliographical references

Mauro, Tony
Illustrated great decisions of the Supreme Court.
2nd ed. CQ Press 2006 415p il $81
Grades: 9 10 11 12 Adult   347
1. United States. Supreme Court 2. Constitutional
law—United States
ISBN 1-56802-964-0; 978-1-56802-964-1
LC 2005-30474
First published 2000
For each of the nearly 100 cases summarized the au-
thor provides background facts, highlights of the decision
and assesses the impact on American society. Illustrated
with photos, portraits, political cartoons, and drawings.
Includes a bibliography and a case and subject index.
Includes bibliographical references

The **Oxford** companion to the Supreme Court of
the United States; editor in chief, Kermit L.
Hall; editors, James W. Ely, Jr., Joel B.
Grossman. 2nd ed. Oxford University Press
2005 xxv, 1239p il $65
Grades: 11 12 Adult   347
1. United States. Supreme Court 2. Reference books
ISBN 0-19-517661-8   LC 2004-29463
First published 1992
This encyclopedia includes over 1200 articles "on all
aspects of the court's history, justices, operations, and
cases. Over 300 experts contributed the entries, which
vary in length; some have bibliographic references. The
organization . . . [includes] alphabetical entries, portraits
of the justices, cross-references, and indexes by both case
name and topic." Choice

Patrick, John J., 1935-
The Supreme Court of the United States; a
student companion. 3rd ed. Oxford University
Press 2006 415p il (Oxford student companions to
American government) $60 *
Grades: 9 10 11 12   347
1. United States. Supreme Court
ISBN 978-0-19-530925-6; 0-19-530925-1
LC 2006-8473
First published 1994 with title: The young Oxford
companion to the Supreme Court of the United States
"Entries presented alphabetically include biographies
of justices, decisions of the court, core concepts, ideas
and issues, legal terms and phrases, and procedures,

Patrick, John J., 1935-—*Continued*
practices, and personnel. . . . The inclusion of so many illustrations makes this a welcome and necessary addition to every high school library." Libr Media Connect
Includes bibliographical references

Savage, David G., 1950-
Guide to the U.S. Supreme Court. 5th ed. CQ Press 2010 2v il map set $410 *
Grades: 9 10 11 12 Adult   347
1. United States. Supreme Court 2. Reference books
ISBN 978-0-87289-423-5; 0-87289-423-1
                                    LC 2010-17634
First published 1979 with title: Congressional Quarterly's guide to the U.S. Supreme Court
This "reference work incorporates the work of the U.S. Supreme Court through the 2008–2009 term. The body of the work consists of 22 chapters divided into six parts. Volume 1 covers the history of the Court, how the Court has defined the powers of the branches and levels of government, and how the Court has addressed individual rights. In volume 2, part 4 describes congressional, presidential, media, and public pressures on the Court. Part 5 explains court operations, traditions, personnel, courtrooms, and costs. Part 6 provides brief biographies of the 111 justices." Booklist
This set "is not only timely but highly informative and readable. . . . Savage's understanding and experience with the Court have resulted in an insightful, authoritative source to rival all others." Choice
Includes bibliographical references

Schultz, David A., 1958-
The encyclopedia of the Supreme Court; [by] David Schultz. Facts on File 2005 562p il (Facts on File library of American history) $85 *
Grades: 11 12 Adult   347
1. United States. Supreme Court 2. Reference books
ISBN 0-8160-5086-4   LC 2004-13174
"The purpose of this one-volume resource is to provide 'an overview of the major cases, concepts, and issues and of the personalities who have shaped' the Supreme Court, as well as to provide a sense of its history and impact on American politics." Libr J
"The ease with which one can search this volume, as well as the style of writing and depth of explanation make this a truly valuable resource." Libr Media Connect
Includes bibliographical references

348 Laws, regulations, cases

Major acts of Congress; Brian K. Landsberg, editor in chief. Macmillan Reference USA 2004 3v il set $290
Grades: 11 12 Adult   348
1. Law—United States—Encyclopedias 2. Reference books
ISBN 0-02-865749-7   LC 2003-18747
The editor "offers historical overviews of the importance and impact of 262 major congressional acts from 1789 to 2002. The signed, alphabetically arranged entries range from one to five pages in length and conclude with

bibliographies and occasional Internet resources." SLJ
This "will be a top-tier reference work for students and laypersons researching federal legislation." Booklist
Includes bibliographical references

349 Law of specific jurisdictions, areas, socioeconomic regions, regional intergovernmental organizations

Gale encyclopedia of American law. 3rd ed. Gale/Cengage Learning 2011 14v il map set $1604
Grades: 9 10 11 12 Adult   349
1. Law—United States—Encyclopedias 2. Reference books
ISBN 978-1-4144-3684-5; 1-4144-3684-X; 978-1-4144-4302-7 (ebook); 1-4144-4302-1 (ebook)
                                    LC 2010-45527
First published 1983-1985 with title: The Guide to American law. Previous edition published with title: West's encyclopedia of American law
Contact publisher for ebook pricing
Explains legal terms and concepts in everyday language, covering a wide variety of persons, entities, and events that have shaped the U.S. legal system and influenced public perceptions of it.
Includes bibliographical references

352.13 State and provincial administration

The **book** of the states; [compiled by] the Council of State Governments. 2010 ed. Council of State Governments 2010 627p il map $125
Grades: 11 12 Adult   352.13
1. State governments
ISSN 0068-0125
ISBN 978-0-87292-7667
Biennial, 1935-2001, Annual from 2002. Began publication 1935
"In addition to general articles on various aspects of state government, this source provides many statistical and directory data, the principal state officials, and such information as the nickname, motto, flower, bird, song, and tree of each state." Ref Sources for Small & Medium-sized Libr. 6th edition

352.23 Chief executives

Fellow citizens; the Penguin book of U.S. presidential inaugural addresses; edited with an introduction and commentaries by Robert V. Remini and Terry Golway. Penguin Books 2008 476p $16
Grades: 10 11 12 Adult   352.23
1. Presidents—United States—Inaugural addresses 2. American speeches
ISBN 978-0-14-311453-6; 0-14-311453-0
                                    LC 2008-19970

Fellow citizens—*Continued*

"Two distinguished historians round up every presidential inaugural address and preface it with commentary on the rhetoric and historical context of the discourse. . . . Reflecting the major events of American history, as well as a rhetorical evolution from prolixity to brevity, this . . . is a great resource." Booklist

Includes bibliographical references

Guide to the presidency; Michael Nelson, editor. 4th ed. CQ Press 2008 2v il map set $355
Grades: 11 12 Adult   352.23
1. Presidents—United States
ISBN 978-0-8728-9364-1; 0-8728-9364-2
LC 2007-25322
First published 1989 with title: Congressional Quarterly's guide to the presidency
"The history of the presidency; the powers of the office . . . ; the president as a public figure; relations with other branches of government; life in the White House; and many other topics are covered in 37 chapters authored by academic scholars." Booklist

Includes bibliographical references

My fellow citizens; the inaugural addresses of the presidents of the United States, 1789-2009; with an introduction by Arthur M. Schlesinger, Jr. and commentary by Fred L. Israel. Facts On File 2010 428p (Facts on File library of American history) $45
Grades: 9 10 11 12 Adult   352.23
1. Presidents—United States—Inaugural addresses
ISBN 978-0-8160-8253-7; 0-8160-8253-7
LC 2009-32184
First published 2007
"Features the original text of all 56 inaugural speeches, each with an explanatory essay." Publisher's note

The **presidency** A to Z; Gerhard Peters, editor; John T. Woolley, editor; Michael Nelson, advisory editor. 4th ed. CQ Press 2008 675p il map (CQ's American government A to Z series) $85 *
Grades: 8 9 10 11 12 Adult   352.23
1. Presidents—United States—Encyclopedias 2. Reference books
ISBN 978-0-87289-367-2; 0-87289-367-7
LC 2007-31322
First published 1992 with Michael Nelson's name appearing first
"Volume 1 traces the history of the office from the creation of the United States Constitution to present-day duties and responsibilities. . . . Volume 2 examines the interaction between the President and the other branches of government. It also includes biographies of Presidents, Vice Presidents, and First Ladies and concludes with tables listing the popular and electoral votes in presidential elections, party nominees for President, and cabinet members. . . . Students of history, political science, and public policy will find it useful when looking for background information about the office of the President." Libr J

Includes bibliographical references

Student's guide to the presidency; advisory editor, Bruce J. Schulman. CQ Press 2009 398p il (Student's guide to the U.S. government series) $85
Grades: 9 10 11 12   352.23
1. Presidents—United States 2. Executive power—United States 3. Reference books
ISBN 978-0-87289-555-3   LC 2008-50731
This is an "overview of the history and ongoing evolution of the American executive branch." Publisher's note
"The strength of . . . [this book] is not the entries on each president but rather the information regarding the election process and the executive branch. . . . [This is] a welcome addition to high-school media centers and public libraries." Booklist

Includes bibliographical references

353   Specific fields of public administration

The **United** States government manual 2009/2010; Office of the Federal Register, National Archives and Records Administration. For sale by the Supt. of Docs., U.S. G.P.O. 2009 674p pa $35 *
Grades: 8 9 10 11 12 Adult   353
1. United States—Politics and government—Handbooks, manuals, etc. 2. Reference books
ISBN 978-1-59804-516-1
Annual. First published 1935. Variant title: United States government organization manual
"Official handbook of the Federal government describing the purposes and programs of most Government agencies and listing the top personnel." N Y Public Libr. Ref Books for Child Collect. 2d edition

355   Military science

Axelrod, Alan, 1952-
The encyclopedia of the American armed forces. Facts on File 2005 2v il (Facts on File library of American history) set $175 *
Grades: 11 12 Adult   355
1. United States—Armed forces—Encyclopedias 2. Reference books
ISBN 0-8160-4700-6   LC 2004-20549
"The four sections each document a major branch of the United States military: Army, Navy, Marine Corps, and Air Force. Each branch has an initial list of entries, a list of branch-specific abbreviations and acronyms, and a short bibliography." Choice

Includes bibliographical references

Barker, Geoff P., 1963-
War; [by] Geoff Barker. Smart Apple Media 2010 46p il (Voices) lib bdg $34.25
Grades: 7 8 9 10 11 12   355
1. War
ISBN 978-1-59920-2785; 1-59920-278-6
LC 2009-5418

Barker, Geoff P., 1963-—*Continued*
This discusses "today's headline conflicts in Iraq, Afghanistan, and Gaza, as well as a look back at World War I, the bombing of Hiroshima and Nagasaki, and the fighting in Kosovo, Eritrea, and Cambodia. Ongoing issues include the role of child soldiers, WMDs, and the number of civilian deaths. The . . . blend of current political debate with witnesses' close-up experiences told through photos, narratives, and quotes will draw browsers, and many will go on to find out more." Booklist
Includes glossary and bibliographical references

Buckley, Gail Lumet, 1937-
American patriots; the story of Blacks in the military from the Revolution to Desert Storm; [by] Gail Buckley. Random House 2001 xxiv, 534p il hardcover o.p. pa $15.95
Grades: 11 12 Adult   355
1. African American soldiers 2. United States—Military history 3. United States—Race relations
ISBN 0-375-50279-3; 0-375-76009-1 (pa)
LC 00-51825
This is an account "of blacks in the U.S. military, both at home and abroad, from the 1770s to the 1990s. . . . This readable, spirited story deserves a place in every U.S. history collection, as well as in the black or military collections." Libr J
Includes bibliographical references

The **encyclopedia** of Middle East wars; the United States in the Persian Gulf, Afghanistan, and Iraq conflicts; Spencer C. Tucker, editor; Priscilla Mary Roberts, editor, documents volume; foreword by Anthony C. Zinni. ABC-CLIO 2010 5v 1887p il map set $495
Grades: 11 12 Adult   355
1. Persian Gulf War, 1991—Encyclopedias 2. Afghan War, 2001—Encyclopedias 3. Iraq War, 2003—Encyclopedias 4. Reference books
ISBN 978-1-85109-947-4; 978-1-85109-948-1 (ebook)
LC 2010-33812
Contact publisher for ebook pricing
"The encyclopedia traces 20th- and 21st-century U.S. involvement in the Middle East and south-central Asia, concentrating on the last three decades. Beginning with the 1980–1988 Iran-Iraq War, it covers the 1979–1989 Soviet occupation of Afghanistan, the 1991 Persian Gulf War, allied punitive actions against Iraq during the 1990s, the Afghanistan War, the Iraq War, and the Global War on Terror." Publisher's note
"An essential resource for anyone seeking detailed information and in-depth reading on U.S. actions and involvement in the Middle East region during the last 15 years." Libr J
Includes bibliographical references

Friedman, Lauri S.
Nuclear weapons and security. ReferencePoint Press 2008 112p il map (Compact research. Current issues) lib bdg $24.95
Grades: 8 9 10 11 12   355
1. Nuclear weapons 2. Terrorism
ISBN 978-1-60152-021-0; 1-60152-021-2
LC 2007-16581

"Friedman gives a short history of nuclear arms and describes the current proliferation of such weapons. A section on world survival after a nuclear war discusses the devastating consequences of such an event. . . . [This book] will be helpful to students looking for a one-stop information source." SLJ
Includes bibliographical references

Gale encyclopedia of U.S. history: war. Gale 2008 2v il map set $220
Grades: 9 10 11 12   355
1. United States—Military history—Encyclopedias 2. Reference books
ISBN 978-1-4144-3114-7; 1-4144-3114-7
LC 2007-33628
This set "examines the country's military history, beginning with the conflicts with Native Americans in the 1600s and ending with today's war in Iraq. Each chapter provides a brief overview of one major conflict, its causes, biographies of major figures, key battles, impact on the home front and nonmilitary events at home, the war in an international context, and its aftermath." SLJ
Includes bibliographical references

A **global** chronology of conflict; from the ancient world to the modern Middle East; Spencer C. Tucker, editor. ABC-CLIO 2010 6v il map set $395
Grades: 9 10 11 12 Adult   355
1. Military history—Chronology 2. Historical chronology 3. Reference books
ISBN 978-1-85109-667-1; 1-85109-667-1
LC 2009-32434
This set "presents a concise, chronologically organized history of the major military actions and related events from the earliest recorded conflicts to the present day. The work examines the political and diplomatic forces driving world conflicts, revolutions, forced changes of governments, international treaties, and acts of aggression and terrorism. . . . This should be considered an essential resource for students, researchers, history aficionados, and general readers." Libr J
Includes bibliographical references

Grant, R. G. (Reg G.)
Commanders; history's greatest military leaders. DK Pub. 2010 360p il map $40
Grades: 9 10 11 12 Adult   355
1. Generals 2. Leadership 3. Military history
ISBN 978-0-7566-6736-8; 0-7566-6736-4
LC 2010-282653
At head of title: DK
"Thirty-five hundred years of military leadership are covered in this attractive, concise presentation. The text opens with a detailed table of contents covering five major eras, divided by empires, conflicts, and/or type of warrior or soldier. Each era is introduced and followed by individual entries: Ramesses II is the first entry in the volume and Osama Bin Laden is the last. Biographical profiles begin with the subject's name in a tinted bar followed by his or her title, birth and death dates, key conflicts, and key battles." SLJ

Kallen, Stuart A., 1955-
National security. ReferencePoint Press 2008
112p il map (Compact research. Current issues) lib
bdg $24.95
Grades: 7 8 9 10 11 12   355
1. National security 2. Terrorism
ISBN 978-1-60152-020-3; 1-60152-020-4
                                         LC 2007-1567
This "includes information on the effect of security
concerns on privacy, American foreign policy, and the
Iraq War. . . . [The] volume includes people and groups
associated with the issue, a chronology of events, related
organizations, and suggestions for further research. Chapters open and end with an array of quotes that argue for
or against a particular argument or aspect of the issue,
complete with full citation." SLJ
Includes bibliographical references

Murray, Stuart, 1948-
Atlas of American military history. Facts on File
2004 248p il map hardcover o.p. pa $29.95
Grades: 9 10 11 12   355
1. United States—Military history—Maps
ISBN 0-8160-5578-5; 0-8160-6221-8 (pa)
                                         LC 2004-8994
This "resource traces American military history, beginning with a profile and a timeline, from wars of the colonial period up through the war in Iraq. Arranged
chronologically, various aspects of each conflict and military campaign, both domestic and international, are explored. . . . This volume is a very complete treatment of
American military history and would be a helpful addition to a library's collection, attracting both browsers and
researchers." Libr Media Connect
Includes bibliographical references

Sun-tzu, 6th cent. B.C.
The illustrated art of war; [by] Sun Tzu; the
definitive English translation by Samuel B.
Griffith. Oxford University Press 2005 272p il
map $29.95 *
Grades: 11 12 Adult   355
1. Military art and science
ISBN 0-19-518999-X; 978-0-19-518999-5
                                         LC 2005-10651
An illustrated version of The art of war, a military
treatise written in China during the 6th century BC dis-
cussing different military tactics and strategies.
Includes bibliographical references

Voices of war; stories of service from the home
front and the front lines; edited by Tom Wiener.
National Geographic Society 2004 336p il $30;
pa $6.95 *
Grades: 11 12 Adult   355
1. Veterans 2. United States—Military history
3. United States—Armed forces—Military life
ISBN 0-7922-7838-0; 0-7922-4204-1 (pa)
                                         LC 2004-49986
"Library of Congress Veterans History Project"
This book showcases "the oral histories collected by
the Veteran's History Project, the Library of Congress's

nationwide effort to collect and preserve the stories not
only of war veterans, but also of those who served in
support of the frontline troops. . . . The personal accounts cover the major conflicts of the 20th century,
from World War I to the Persian Gulf War, and include
letters, diaries, and journals. The chapters are nicely arranged to show the commonalities of military experience,
e.g., basic training, daily life, combat, the home front,
and returning home." Libr J

War: from ancient Egypt to Iraq; editorial
consultant, Saul David. DK 2009 512p il $50 *
Grades: 9 10 11 12 Adult   355
1. Military history—Encyclopedias 2. War—Encyclopedias 3. Reference books
ISBN 978-0-7566-5572-3   LC 2010-278612
On cover: The definitive visual history, from Bronze
Age battles to 21st century conflict
"From the Punic wars to the Crusades to the wars of
the league of Cognac and modern conflicts like those in
the former Yugoslavia, War is an outstanding catalog of
conflict. Each of the seven chapters . . . opens with a
time line and is peppered with sidebars of military super-
latives such as youngest commanders, famous female
warriors, and even landmark war movies. . . . An essential reference title for all libraries." Libr J

War: opposing viewpoints; Louise Gerdes, book
editor. Greenhaven Press 2005 239p il lib bdg
$34.95; pa $23.70 *
Grades: 8 9 10 11 12   355
1. War
ISBN 0-7377-2591-5 (lib bdg); 0-7377-2592-3 (pa)
                                         LC 2004-54283
"Opposing viewpoints series"
In this anthology the authors "debate controversies
surrounding the causes and conduct of war, including under what circumstances war is justified, how prisoners
and civilians should be treated, and what measures, if
any, will prevent wars." Publisher's note
Includes bibliographical references

Warry, John, 1916-
Warfare in the classical world; an illustrated
encyclopedia of weapons, warriors, and warfare in
the ancient civilisations of Greece and Rome.
University of Okla. Press 1995 224p il maps pa
$29.95 *
Grades: 9 10 11 12   355
1. Military art and science 2. Military history
ISBN 0-8061-2794-5   LC 95-18643
A reissue of the title first published 1980 by St. Martin's Press
"The many and various technologies of war developed
and employed by the Greeks and Romans are shown
along with the political and social arenas of the times.
. . . Famous leaders—Alexander the Great, Julius Caesar, Bulla, Hannibal, and Pompey—are presented in
mini-biographies with synopses of conditions that provoked war. . . . Useful for history and classical studies,
and a terrific read." SLJ

355.2 Military resources

Military draft: opposing viewpoints; Viqi Wagner, book editor. Greenhaven Press 2007 238p lib bdg $36.20; pa $24.95
Grades: 9 10 11 12   355.2
1. Draft 2. Voluntary military service
ISBN   978-0-7377-3824-7   (lib   bdg); 978-0-7377-3825-4 (pa)   LC 2007-38960
"Opposing viewpoints series"
In this collection of essays, "the draft isn't the only issue brought up; related topics, such as gays in the military and the use of military contractors, are also covered." Booklist
Includes bibliographical references

355.4 Military operations

Tucker, Spencer C., 1937-
Battles that changed history; an encyclopedia of world conflict. ABC-CLIO 2010 c2011 655p il map $95
Grades: 9 10 11 12 Adult   355.4
1. Battles—Encyclopedias 2. Military history—Encyclopedias 3. Reference books
ISBN 978-1-59884-429-0; 978-1-59884-430-6 (ebook)
                                                LC 2010-32810
Tucker "has compiled over 200 battles that had a significant impact on history. About half of the battles are drawn from the 19th through 21st centuries. The earliest account is of the Battle of Megiddo that took place in May 1479 B.C.E., and the last entry is the Iraq war's battle for Baghdad, which took place from March 19 to May 1, 2003. Each entry includes the date, opponents (with the winner denoted by an asterisk), commanders, number of troops, and importance of the battle. . . . This clear and concise overview of the major battles from a number of wars and would be a great addition to the collection of any library." Libr J
Includes bibliographical references

355.8 Military equipment and supplies (Matériel)

Diehl, Sarah J.
Nuclear weapons and nonproliferation; a reference handbook; [by] Sarah J. Diehl, James Clay Moltz. 2nd ed. ABC-CLIO 2008 335p (Contemporary world issues) $55
Grades: 9 10 11 12   355.8
1. Nuclear weapons 2. Arms race
ISBN 978-1-59884-071-1   LC 2007-17651
First published 2002
The author provide a "subject history, a record of past U.S. involvement, an overview of ethical debates, a chronological survey of events, relevant biographical sketches, and lucid definitions of nuclear technologies. Two concluding chapters provide an exhaustive list of international, federal, and nongovernmental nonproliferation organizations. An essential one-stop resource on a timely subject." Libr J
Includes bibliographical references

Preston, Diana
Before the fallout; from Marie Curie to Hiroshima. Walker 2005 438p il $27 *
Grades: 11 12 Adult   355.8
1. Atomic bomb
ISBN 0-8027-1445-5   LC 2004-61953
Also available in paperback from Berkley Books
This history of the making of the atomic bomb covers "half a century, beginning with Marie and Pierre Curie's 1898 discovery of radium and continuing through other important scientific findings (e.g., Einstein's relativity theory and Heisenberg's quantum mechanics)." Libr J
"Avidly researched and gracefully constructed, Preston's revelatory history is rich in telling moments, powerful personalities, intense confrontations, and indelible images of the devastation delivered by nuclear weapons, our Damoclean sword." Booklist
Includes bibliographical references

356 Foot forces and warfare

Haney, Eric L.
Inside Delta Force; the story of America's elite counterterrorist unit. Delacorte Press 2006 246p il hardcover o.p. pa $17 *
Grades: 8 9 10 11 12   356
1. United States. Army. Delta Force
ISBN 0-385-73251-1; 0-385-33936-4 (pa)
                                                LC 2004-30945
"In this adaptation of an adult book, Retired Command Sergeant Major Haney relates a . . . story of the 1977 founding of the ultrasecret counterterrorist unit of the U.S. Army known as Delta Force. . . . Better stock up on copies; you won't want to ration this one." Booklist

358 Air and other specialized forces and warfare; engineering and related services

Biological and chemical weapons; Stefan Kiesbye, book editor. Greenhaven Press 2010 98p (At issue. International politics) $31.80; pa $22.50 *
Grades: 9 10 11 12   358
1. Biological warfare 2. Chemical warfare
ISBN 978-0-7377-4870-3; 978-0-7377-4871-0 (pa)
                                                LC 2010-3357
Contributors to this anthology debating the potential threat of biological and chemical warfare include Andy Oppenheimer, Thomas Frank, and Stephen Maurer.
Includes bibliographical references

Marcovitz, Hal
Biological & chemical warfare. ABDO Pub. Co. 2010 112p il (Essential issues) lib bdg $22.95
Grades: 7 8 9 10   358
1. Chemical warfare 2. Biological warfare
ISBN 978-1-60453-951-6; 1-60453-951-8
                                                LC 2009-29947

Marcovitz, Hal—*Continued*

"This title examines one of the world's critical issues, biological and chemical warfare. Readers will learn the historical background of this issue leading up to its current and future impact on society. The Hague Peace Conventions, the Geneva Protocol, and the Chemical Weapons Convention are discussed." Publisher's note

The text is "well-written, providing examples that put a human face to each problem. Quotes and facts are clearly attributed, and their sources are noted in the extensive back matter. . . . Sidebars provide further information, or, more compellingly, offer stories about those touched by the topic. . . . [This] will be of great assistance to students writing reports." SLJ

Includes glossary and bibliographical references

Weapons of mass destruction: opposing viewpoints; James D. Torr, book editor. Greenhaven Press 2005 207p il lib bdg $33.70; pa $22.45

Grades: 8 9 10 11 12   **358**

1. Weapons

ISBN 0-7377-2250-9 (lib bdg); 0-7377-2251-7 (pa)
LC 2004-47587

"Opposing viewpoints series"

"The viewpoints in the volume examine WMD threats from terrorist groups and 'axis of evil' nations in the following chapters: How Likely Is an Attack Involving Weapons of Mass Destruction? How Should the United States Deal with Countries that Threaten to Develop Weapons of Mass Destruction? What Policies Should the United States Adopt Toward Nuclear Weapons? How Can the United States Defend Itself Against Weapons of Mass Destruction?" Publisher's note

Includes bibliographical references

358.4   Air forces and warfare

Boyne, Walter J., 1929-

The influence of air power upon history. Pelican 2003 447p $35

Grades: 11 12 Adult   **358.4**

1. Air power

ISBN 1-58980-034-6   LC 2002-155441

Contents: Fledgling wings; Air power in World War I; Fighters and bombers; Growth of air power theory; Air power between the wars; The search for air power 1939-41; The growth of air power 1941-43; True air superiority, then air supremacy; The cold war; The cold war 1963-73; Post World War II Middle Eastern wars

This is "a comprehensive, balanced overview of war in the air. . . . Boyne's clearly written book brings air power into the military-history mainstream." Booklist

Includes bibliographical references

359.9   Specialized combat forces; engineering and related services

Bartlett, Merrill L.

Leathernecks: an illustrated history of the U.S. Marine Corps; [by] Merrill L. Bartlett and Jack Sweetman. Naval Institute Press 2008 xx, 479p il map $60

Grades: 10 11 12 Adult   **359.9**

1. United States. Marine Corps—History

ISBN 978-1-59114-020-7; 1-59114-020-X
LC 2008-15582

First published 2001 with title: The U.S. Marine Corps: an illustrated history

A history of the U.S. Marines from the Revolutionary War to the War on Terror, with a brief look at the marines of antiquity.

Includes bibliographical references

361.2   Social action

Drake, Jane

Yes you can! your guide to becoming an activist; [by] Jane Drake & Ann Love. Tundra Books 2010 136p pa $12.95

Grades: 7 8 9 10   **361.2**

1. Social action

ISBN 978-0-88776-942-9; 0-88776-942-X (pa)

"Young people who want to effect change are guided by a sequence of nine steps and inspirational examples of grassroots activism. . . . Each step, or chapter, includes a story, strategies, skills, and a time line of milestones and setbacks. . . . The style is conversational and the tone offers realistic encouragement to teens looking to solve problems. . . . This title will primarily serve as a how-to, although the time lines, an accessible index, and factual information about anti-smoking campaigns, recycling, and children's rights make it a useful historical perspective of activism." SLJ

Halpin, Mikki

It's your world—if you don't like it, change it; activism for teenagers. Simon Pulse 2004 305p pa $8.99 *

Grades: 7 8 9 10   **361.2**

1. Social action

ISBN 0-689-87448-0

"Animal rights, racism, war protest, AIDS, school violence and bullying, women's rights, and promoting tolerance are among the topics covered here. Halpin provides basic information about each one and then makes myriad suggestions for action at home, in the community, the 'five-minute activist,' etc. The ideas are easy to implement. . . .This is an important book that will empower any young adult who would like to make a difference." SLJ

Includes bibliographical references

361.3 Social work

Gay, Kathlyn, 1930-
Volunteering; the ultimate teen guide. Scarecrow Press 2004 127p il (It happened to me) $37.50; pa $14.95
Grades: 7 8 9 10   **361.3**
1. Volunteer work
ISBN   0-8108-4922-4;   978-0-8108-4922-8; 0-8108-5833-9 (pa); 978-0-8108-5833-6 (pa)
LC 2004-8174
Contents: Being a volunteer; Building and repairing; Closing the generation gap; Helping with health care; Helping the homeless, feeding the hungry; Protecting the environment and animals; Preserving the past; Counseling, teaching, and tutoring; Reducing bigotry, prejudice, and racism; Campaigning, communicating, and collecting; Getting started, reaping rewards
"This is a useful tool in that it provides a one-stop resource for teens interested in locating volunteer opportunities." SLJ
Includes bibliographical references

Marcovitz, Hal
Teens & volunteerism. Mason Crest 2005 112p il (Gallup Youth Survey) $22.95
Grades: 7 8 9 10   **361.3**
1. Volunteer work
ISBN 1-59084-877-2   LC 2004004827
This is "based on the findings of the Gallup Youth Survey (a 20-year ongoing survey of teens). . . . [It] covers the gamut of issues surrounding [volunteerism and youth], focusing on mandatory vs. optional community service in high school and college, military service, political community service, and activism. [The book is] well documented." SLJ
Includes bibliographical references

Volunteerism; edited by Frank McGuckin. Wilson, H.W. 1998 177p (Reference shelf) pa $45 *
Grades: 11 12 Adult   **361.3**
1. Volunteer work
ISBN 0-8242-0944-3   LC 98-35206
A collection of reprinted articles from various sources divided into four sections: Society's responsibility and commitment; Private volunteering and AmeriCorps; Volunteerism is not enough; and Rewards of volunteerism
Includes bibliographical references

361.6 Governmental action

Banerjee, Dillon
The insider's guide to the Peace Corps; what to know before you go. 2nd ed. Ten Speed Press 2009 182p map pa $14.95 *
Grades: 11 12 Adult   **361.6**
1. Peace Corps (U.S.)
ISBN 978-1-58008-970-8; 1-58008-970-4
LC 2008-43720

First published 2000 with title: So you want to join the Peace Corps
Contents: Pre-application jitters; How to pack for a two-year trip; Peace Corps training: learning the ropes; Managing your money; Living like the locals; Common medical and safety concerns; Staying in touch with home; Peace Corps gadgets and technology; The social scene; The toughest job you'll ever love?; Rules to live by: Peace Corps policy; Traveling like a pro; Post-Peace Corps
"A guide that tells potential Peace Corps volunteers what to expect, through first-hand advice from recent volunteers." Publisher's note
Includes bibliographical references

Streissguth, Thomas
Welfare and welfare reform; [by] Tom Streissguth. Facts on File 2009 282p (Library in a book) $45
Grades: 11 12 Adult   **361.6**
1. Public welfare
ISBN 978-0-8160-7114-2; 0-8160-7114-4
This book provides "information that readers need to understand and research welfare issues. . . . Resources include capsule biographies, summaries of key cases such as Standard Machine Company v. Davis, a research guide, an annotated bibliography, historic documents such as the Personal Responsibility and Work Opportunity Reconciliation Act of 1996, and an overview of the welfare debate in U.S. history beginning with the first public almshouses in the North American British colonies." Publisher's note
Includes glossary and bibliographical references

362.1 Physical illness

The **AIDS** crisis; a documentary history; edited by Douglas A. Feldman and Julia Wang Miller. Greenwood Press 1998 xxxix, 266p (Primary documents in American history and contemporary issues) $49.95 *
Grades: 11 12 Adult   **362.1**
1. AIDS (Disease)
ISBN 0-313-28715-5   LC 97-26891
This book "presents more than 200 documents on AIDS, from the first medical report in 1981. Most documents are full text, and each is accompanied by a short introduction providing context." Booklist
"An excellent glossary provides the reader with explanations of acronyms and medical terms. . . . This unusual volume is highly recommended." Voice Youth Advocates

Banish, Roslyn, 1942-
Focus on living; portraits of Americans with HIV and AIDS; photographs and interviews by Roslyn Banish; introduction by Paul A. Volberding. University of Massachusetts Press 2003 xxiv, 263p il $50; pa $24.95 *
Grades: 9 10 11 12   **362.1**
1. AIDS (Disease)
ISBN 1-558-49394-8; 1-558-49395-6 (pa)
LC 2002-14512

Banish, Roslyn, 1942-—*Continued*

The author "has been interviewing and photographing Americans who are living with HIV or AIDS; this book collects 40 of her portraits along with transcriptions of her subjects' first-person testimony . . . Banish's unadorned portraits, often shot at her subjects' homes, are subtle and dignified, and the narratives have a lucid strength, even in despair . . . The disease crosses all lines of race, class, gender and sexual orientation, and Banish takes care to include people from all walks of life, fostering an expanded sense of community and further breaking the silence and statistics that surround people living with HIV and AIDS." Publ Wkly

Eating disorders; Lorraine Savage, editor. Thomson / Gale 2008 144p il (Perspectives on diseases and disorders) lib bdg $34.95

Grades: 7 8 9 10   **362.1**
1. Eating disorders
ISBN 978-0-7377-3872-8; 0-7377-3872-3
LC 2007-37455

This book "explores the debilitating illness of anorexia, bulimia and binge eating." Publisher's note
Includes glossary and bibliographical references

Farrell, Courtney

Mental disorders. ABDO Pub. Co. 2010 112p il (Essential issues) lib bdg $22.95

Grades: 7 8 9 10   **362.1**
1. Mental illness
ISBN 978-1-60453-956-1; 1-60453-956-9
LC 2009-29942

"This title examines the world's critical issues surrounding mental disorders. Readers will learn the historical background of mental disorders, leading up to the current and future impact on society." Publisher's note

The text is "well-written, providing examples that put a human face to each problem. Quotes and facts are clearly attributed, and their sources are noted in the extensive back matter. . . . Sidebars provide further information, or, more compellingly, offer stories about those touched by the topic. . . . [This] will be of great assistance to students writing reports." SLJ
Includes glossary and bibliographical references

Fast food; Lauri S. Friedman, book editor. Greenhaven Press 2010 122p il map (Introducing issues with opposing viewpoints) $34.70

Grades: 7 8 9 10 11 12   **362.1**
1. Obesity 2. Convenience foods 3. Restaurants
ISBN 978-0-7377-4733-1; 0-7377-4733-1
LC 2009-51963

This is a collection of essays arguing various viewpoints about fast foods and their effects on health, and whether or not fast food restaurants should be banned, taxed, or regulated.

This "contains some fascinating arguments, including the central question of whether or not fast food makes people fat and sick. Active-reading questions preface the essays, which are followed by directions for evaluating the arguments presented. Color photos and other graphics throughout enliven the reading experience." SLJ
Includes bibliographical references

Gelletly, LeeAnne

AIDS and health issues. Mason Crest Publishers 2007 126p il (Africa: progress & problems) $24.95

Grades: 9 10 11 12   **362.1**
1. AIDS (Disease) 2. Africa
ISBN 978-1-59084-954-5; 1-59084-954-X
LC 2005-23101

"This book explores the current health crisis in Africa, explaining the scope of the problems that the continent faces. It also describes efforts by humanitarian organizations and by African governments to train health-care professionals." Publisher's note
Includes bibliographical references

Kaufman, Miriam

Easy for you to say; q & a's for teens living with chronic illness or disability. Rev. ed. Firefly Books 2005 285p pa $19.95 *

Grades: 9 10 11 12   **362.1**
1. Diseases 2. Physically handicapped
ISBN 1-55407-078-3
First published 1995

This work, "aimed exclusively at teens who are disabled or who have a chronic illness, focuses on individual needs. Written by a Canadian physician who works with adolescents, it is filled with very personal, even courageous questions from teens with varied medical conditions—from spina bifida to cystic fibrosis, to kidney disease. There are a few fairly general chapters—on family dynamics, friendship, and recreation. But the best sections concern medical issues and sexuality." Booklist [review of 1995 edition]
Includes bibliographical references

Naden, Corinne J.

Patients' rights; [by] Corinne Naden. Marshall Cavendish Benchmark 2008 144p il (Open for debate) lib bdg $27.95

Grades: 7 8 9 10   **362.1**
1. Medical care
ISBN 978-0-7614-2576-2; 0-7614-2576-4
LC 2006-21786

"Discusses patients' rights, including the issues surrounding physician-assisted suicide, HMOs, the rights of children, abortion, stem cell research, and the difference between public and private rights." Publisher's note

This book maintains a "balanced tone while providing an abundance of examples and factual information. Many captioned color photos enhance the text." SLJ
Includes bibliographical references

Parks, Peggy J., 1951-

HPV. ReferencePoint Press 2009 104p il map (Compact research. Diseases and disorders) $25.95

Grades: 7 8 9 10 11 12   **362.1**
1. Papillomaviruses
ISBN 978-1-60152-070-8; 1-60152-070-0
LC 2008-44026

Presents an overview of the causes, symptoms, and various types of the Human Papillomavirus; and provides information on available vaccines, health risks of genital HPV, and organizations and advocacy groups.

Parks, Peggy J., 1951-—*Continued*
This book "is a timely overview of the most prevalent sexually transmitted disease among female teens today." Booklist
Includes bibliographical references

Shilts, Randy
And the band played on; politics, people, and the AIDS epidemic. 20th anniversary ed. St Martin's Griffin 2007 630p pa $17.95 *
Grades: 11 12 Adult   **362.1**
1. AIDS (Disease)
ISBN 978-0-312-37463-1
First published 1987
The author traces the history of the AIDS epidemic in the United States.
"Shilts successfully weaves comprehensive investigative reporting and commercial page-turner pacing, political intrigue and personal tragedy into a landmark work." Publ Wkly
Includes bibliographical references

Winick, Judd, 1970-
Pedro & me; friendship, loss, & what I learned. Henry Holt and Co. 2009 187p il pa $16.99
Grades: 7 8 9 10 11 12   **362.1**
1. Zamora, Pedro, 1972-1994—Graphic novels 2. Real world (Television program)—Graphic novels 3. Graphic novels 4. AIDS (Disease)—Graphic novels 5. Friendship—Graphic novels 6. Biographical graphic novels
ISBN 978-0-8050-8964-6
First published 2000
In this "volume—part graphic novel, part memoir—professional cartoonist Winick pays tribute to his Real World housemate and friend Pedro Zamora, an AIDS activist who died of the disease in 1994." Publ Wkly

362.2   Mental and emotional illnesses and disturbances

Mental illness: opposing viewpoints; Mary E. Williams, book editor. Greenhaven Press 2007 238p lib bdg $36.20; pa $24.95 *
Grades: 8 9 10 11 12   **362.2**
1. Mental illness
ISBN 0-7377-2947-3 (lib bdg); 978-0-7377-2947-4 (lib bdg); 0-7377-2948-1 (pa); 978-0-7377-2948-1 (pa)
                                               LC 2006-20106
"Opposing viewpoints series"
New edition in preparation
"This collections of articles, written by individuals with differing opinions and from varying backgrounds, analyzes issues relevant to mental health and public policy." SLJ
Includes bibliographical references

362.28   Suicide

Evans, Glen
The encyclopedia of suicide; {by} Glen Evans, Norman L. Farberow; foreword by Alan L. Berman. 2nd ed. Facts on File 2003 xxxiii, 329p $65
Grades: 11 12 Adult   **362.28**
1. Reference books
ISBN 0-8160-4525-9   LC 2002-27166
First published 1988
Arranged in A-Z format, over 500 entries cover such aspects as causes, history and psychology of suicide. Also covered are philosophical and religious issues as well as sociological viewpoints and research and treatment concerns
Includes bibliographical references

Marcovitz, Hal
Suicide. ABDO Pub. Co. 2010 112p il (Essential issues) lib bdg $22.95
Grades: 7 8 9 10   **362.28**
1. Suicide
ISBN 978-1-60453-958-5; 1-60453-958-5
                                               LC 2009-30354
This book about suicide features "historical background of the issue, leading up to its current and future impact on society. Discussed . . . are the causes of suicide, including mental disorders such as depression and bipolar disorder, and the effects of suicide on the victim's family, friends, and society as a whole." Publisher's note
This is "well-written, providing examples that put a human face to each problem. Quotes and facts are clearly attributed, and their sources are noted in the extensive back matter. . . . Sidebars provide further information, or, more compellingly, offer stories about those touched by the topic. . . . [This] will be of great assistance to students writing reports." SLJ
Includes glossary and bibliographical references

Nelson, Richard E.
The power to prevent suicide; a guide for teens helping teens; [by] Richard E. Nelson, Judith C. Galas; foreword by Bev Cobain; edited by Pamela Espeland. Updated ed. Free Spirit 2006 115p pa $13.95
Grades: 7 8 9 10 11 12   **362.28**
1. Suicide
ISBN 1-57542-206-9; 978-1-57542-206-0
First published 1994
"The authors' premise is that, as trusted and caring friends, YAs have a special role in the prevention of suicide among their peers, and discuss what to do if they observe the danger signals. . . . This book provides clear, practical information and advice." SLJ

Suicide; Paul Connors, book editor. Thomson/Gale 2007 236p (Current controversies) lib bdg $36.20; pa $24.95

Grades: 9 10 11 12   **362.28**

1. Suicide

ISBN   978-0-7377-2488-2   (lib   bdg); 978-0-7377-2489-9 (pa)   LC 2007-1989

First published 2000 under the editorship of Leslie A. Miller and Paul A. Rose

"This title compiles essays and articles that highlight the economic, ethical, political, racial, and religious dimensions of suicide. . . . Debaters and researchers will appreciate this title's diverse collection of primary sources, as well as the entries' concise introductions and the appended bibliography and directory of organizations." Booklist

Includes bibliographical references

Suicide information for teens; health tips about suicide causes and prevention: including facts about depression, risk factors, getting help, survivor support, and more; edited by Kim Wohlenhaus. 2nd ed. Omnigraphics, Inc. 2010 380p (Teen health series) $69 *

Grades: 9 10 11 12   **362.28**

1. Suicide

ISBN 978-0-7808-1088-4   LC 2010015720

First published 2005 under the editorship of Joyce Brennfleck Shannon

"Provides basic consumer health information for teens about suicide risk factors, warning signs, intervention and treatment, and prevention strategies. Includes index, directory of crisis hotlines and support groups, and resource information." Publisher's note

Includes bibliographical references

Suicide: opposing viewpoints; Jacqueline Langwith, book editor. Greenhaven Press 2008 268p lib bdg $38.50; pa $26.75

Grades: 8 9 10 11 12   **362.28**

1. Suicide

ISBN 978-0-7377-4012-7 (lib bdg); 0737740124 (lib bdg); 978-0-7377-4013-4 (pa); 0-7377-4013-2 (pa)
LC 2008-1007

"Opposing viewpoints series"

The articles in this anthology cover topics such as suicide among teens and other types of people, what causes suicide, assisted suicide, and how suicide can be prevented.

Includes bibliographical references

Teen suicide; Emily Schusterbauer, book editor. Greenhaven Press 2009 116p (At issue. Teen issues) $31.80; pa $22.50

Grades: 9 10 11 12   **362.28**

1. Suicide 2. Depression (Psychology) 3. Adolescent psychology

ISBN   978-0-7377-4418-7;   0-7377-4418-9; 978-0-7377-4419-4 (pa); 0-7377-4419-7 (pa)
LC 2008-55845

A collection of articles discussing the problem of teen suicide and what parents, friends, teachers and society can do to prevent the tragedy.

Includes bibliographical references

362.29 Substance abuse

Addiction: opposing viewpoints; Christina Fisanick, book editor. Greenhaven Press 2009 228p il lib bdg $39.70; pa $27.50 *

Grades: 8 9 10 11 12   **362.29**

1. Drug abuse 2. Alcoholism

ISBN 978-0-7377-4352-4 (lib bdg); 0-7377-4352-2 (lib bdg); 978-0-7377-4351-7 (pa); 0-7377-4351-4 (pa)
LC 2008-53997

"Opposing viewpoints series"

Articles in this anthology discuss the nature of addiction, including how addictions can be prevented and treated.

Includes bibliographical references

Axelrod-Contrada, Joan

The facts about drugs and society. Marshall Cavendish Benchmark 2008 143p il (Drugs) $27.95

Grades: 7 8 9 10 11 12   **362.29**

1. Drugs

ISBN 978-0-7614-2674-5

This discusses drugs in relation to history, pop culture, risk factors, gender, the brain, the law, treatment and prevention.

This is "well-organized, attractively illustrated, current, and highly informative." Sci Books Films

Bjornlund, Lydia D.

How dangerous are performance-enhancing drugs? [by] Lydia Bjornlund. ReferencePoint Press 2011 96p il (In controversy) lib bdg $26.95

Grades: 10 11 12   **362.29**

1. Steroids 2. Athletes—Drug use 3. Drug abuse

ISBN 978-1-60152-126-2; 1-60152-126-X
LC 2010-17131

This book "considers the effects of drug use on the integrity of sports as well as on athletes' achievements and health." Booklist

Includes bibliographical references

Teen smoking. Reference Point Press 2010 104p il (Compact research. Current issues) $25.95

Grades: 8 9 10 11 12   **362.29**

1. Smoking

ISBN 978-1-60152-098-2; 1-60152-098-0
LC 2009-28008

This addresses the following questions: How serious a problem is teen smoking?; Who is to blame for teen smoking?; How should teen smoking be regulated?; How can we prevent teen smoking?

"The straightforward presentation of serious subject matter, graphics, and easy access to facts . . . [make this book] excellent . . . for reports and debates." SLJ

Chastain, Zachary

Cocaine; the rush to destruction. Mason Crest Publishers 2008 128p il map (Illicit and misused drugs) $24.95 *

Grades: 7 8 9 10   **362.29**

1. Cocaine 2. Drug abuse

ISBN 978-1-4222-0154-1   LC 2006-29212

Chastain, Zachary—*Continued*

This book "tells the story of cocaine, its history and role in medicine, religion, and even soda production . . . [and includes facts] about the biology behind the highs—and lows—of the drug's effects. . . . [It also] provides information on kicking the cocaine habit." Publisher's note

Includes glossary and bibliographical references

Tobacco; through the smoke screen. Mason Crest Publishers 2008 128p il (Illicit and misused drugs) $24.95 *

Grades: 7 8 9 10   **362.29**
1. Tobacco habit 2. Smoking
ISBN 978-1-4222-0165-7; 1-4222-0165-1
                                            LC 2006-22800

Presents the story of tobacco, its history, its role in culture, and its dangers. Also explains the power of tobacco over smokers and chewers, how cigarette makers help increase its hold and make it more difficult to live without it, and offers suggestions on how to kick the tobacco habit and reverse its ill effects.

Includes glossary and bibliographical references

Club drugs; Roman Espejo, book editor. Greenhaven Press 2009 101p (At issue. Drugs) $31.80; pa $22.50

Grades: 9 10 11 12   **362.29**
1. Ecstasy (Drug)
ISBN   978-0-7377-4290-9;   0-7377-4290-9;
978-0-7377-4289-3 (pa); 0-7377-4289-5 (pa)
                                            LC 2008039334

The articles in this anthology discuss the positives and negatives of drugs such as GHB and ecstacy.

Includes bibliographical references

Currie-McGhee, L. K., 1971-

Drug addiction; [by] Leanne Currie-McGhee. ReferencePoint Press 2010 c2011 96p il (Compact research. Diseases and disorders) lib bdg $26.95
Grades: 8 9 10 11 12   **362.29**
1. Drug abuse
ISBN 978-1-60152-109-5; 1-60152-109-X
                                            LC 2009-45174

Through "overviews, primary sources, and full color illustrations this title examines [such topics as] What Is Drug Addiction? What Causes Drug Addiction? What Are the Dangers of Drug Addiction? and Can Drug Addiction Be Overcome?" Publisher's note

Includes bibliographical references

Drug abuse sourcebook; basic consumer health information about the abuse of cocaine, club drugs, hallucinogens, heroin, inhalants, marijuana, and other illicit substances, prescription medications, and over-the-counter medicines. . . .; edited by Joyce Brennfleck Shannon. 3rd ed. Omnigraphics 2010 645p il (Health reference series) $95

Grades: 11 12 Adult   **362.29**
1. Drug abuse 2. Reference books
ISBN 978-0-7808-1079-2   LC 2010-748

First published 2000 under the editorship of Karen Bellenir

"Provides basic consumer health information about the abuse of illegal drugs and misuse of prescription and over-the-counter medications, with facts about addiction, treatment, and recovery. Includes index, glossary of related terms and directory of resources." Publisher's note

"Well organized and readily accessible to lay readers, this is recommended." Libr J

Includes bibliographical references

Drugs, alcohol, and tobacco; learning about addictive behavior; Rosalyn Carson-DeWitt, editor in chief. Macmillan Ref. USA 2003 3v set $295 *

Grades: 7 8 9 10   **362.29**
1. Drug abuse—Encyclopedias 2. Reference books
ISBN 0-02-865756-X   LC 2002-9270

Based on the Encyclopedia of drugs, alcohol & addictive behavior, 2nd edition, published 2001

"The 190 alphabetically arranged articles range from one to six pages in length and yield a comprehensive look at the nature of, treatments for, and social issues surrounding addictive substances and behaviors. Topics include specific drugs, diagnoses, treatments, legal and social implications, drug trafficking, cultural pressures, and related compulsive behaviors." SLJ

Includes bibliographical references

Drugs and controlled substances; information for students; Stacey Blachford, Kristine Krapp, editors. Gale Group 2003 xxvi, 495p il $115
Grades: 11 12 Adult   **362.29**
1. Drugs 2. Drug abuse
ISBN 0-7876-6264-X   LC 2002-10925

Provides detailed information about the composition, history, effects, uses and abuses of common drugs, including illegal drugs and addictive substances, as well as commonly abused classes of prescription drugs.

"In addition to the well-written essays, sidebars discussing legal issues, misconceptions, history, and news stories add depth to each topic. . . . Currency, scope, and authority are the hallmarks of this highly recommended reference work." Booklist

Includes bibliographical references

Encyclopedia of drugs, alcohol & addictive behavior; [edited by] Pamela Korsmeyer and Henry R. Kranzler. 3rd ed. Macmillan Reference USA 2009 4v il set $620
Grades: 11 12 Adult   **362.29**
1. Drug abuse—Encyclopedias 2. Reference books
ISBN 978-0-02-866064-6; 0-02-866064-1
                                            LC 2008-12719

First published 1995 with title: Encyclopedia of drugs and alcohol

This encyclopedia addresses "social, medical, legal, and political issues related to substance use and addictive behavior." Publisher's note

Includes bibliographical references

Etingoff, Kim

Abusing over-the-counter drugs; illicit uses for everyday drugs. Mason Crest Publishers 2008 128p il (Illicit and misused drugs) $24.95 *

Grades: 7 8 9 10   362.29

1. Nonprescription drugs 2. Drug abuse

ISBN 978-1-4222-0150-3   LC 2006-30112

This book discusses "what drugs are most misused, the effects of misused over-the-counter medications, and what the government is doing to stem the problem. Readers will also find suggestions on how to get help to stop abusing over-the-counter medications." Publisher's note

Includes glossary and bibliographical references

Methamphetamines; unsafe speed. Mason Crest Publishers 2008 128p il (Illicit and misused drugs) $24.95 *

Grades: 7 8 9 10   362.29

1. Methamphetamine 2. Drug abuse

ISBN 978-1-4222-0159-6; 1-4222-0159-7

LC 2006-20684

This book discusses "how methamphetamine was developed, how its use has spread, and how it is used for limited medical purposes. Readers will also learn about methamphetamine abuse." Publisher's note

Includes glossary and bibliographical references

Flynn, Noa

Inhalants and solvents; sniffing disaster. Mason Crest Publishers 2008 128p il map (Illicit and misused drugs) $24.95 *

Grades: 7 8 9 10   362.29

1. Solvent abuse

ISBN 978-1-4222-0157-2   LC 2006-32224

This book offers case studies of young people "who have sniffed, bagged, or ingested inhalants. . . . Readers will also learn how inhalants and solvents act on the brain and body, producing the feelings sought by their users. The author also takes readers down the path of long and short-term effects of inhalant and solvent abuse, including the potential for death with just one use." Publisher's note

Includes glossary and bibliographical references

Gateway drugs: opposing viewpoints; Noël Merino, book editor. Greenhaven Press 2008 198p il lib bdg $37.40; pa $25.95

Grades: 9 10 11 12   362.29

1. Drug abuse

ISBN 978-0-7377-4002-8 (lib bdg); 0-7377-4002-7 (lib bdg); 978-0-7377-4003-5 (pa); 0-7377-4003-5 (pa)

LC 2008-8134

"Opposing viewpoints series"

"This title presents different opinions on the gateway theory of drug use in a fair and unbiased manner. . . . Each article is introduced with a paragraph that provides an overview and the qualifications of the author followed by a list of questions for students to consider while reading that specific piece." SLJ

Includes bibliographical references

Klosterman, Lorrie

The facts about drug dependence to treatment. Marshall Cavendish Benchmark 2008 126p il (Drugs) lib bdg $31.94

Grades: 7 8 9 10 11 12   362.29

1. Drug abuse

ISBN 978-0-7614-2676-9   LC 2007-8780

This discusses the beginnings of drug dependence, its costs, first steps to recovery, rehabilitation, and lifetime freedom from drugs.

This is "well-organized, attractively illustrated, current, and highly informative." Sci Books Films

Includes glossary and bibliographical references

Marijuana: opposing viewpoints; Jamuna Carroll, book editor. Greenhaven Press 2006 224p il lib bdg $34.95; pa $23.70

Grades: 9 10 11 12   362.29

1. Marijuana

ISBN 0-7377-3323-3 (lib bdg); 0-7377-3324-1 (pa)

LC 2005-40421

"Opposing viewpoints series"

This book "examines the many controversies plaguing marijuana: whether it harms the body, has potential for addiction, and impairs driving abilities; whether current marijuana legislation is fair and effective; whether the drug should be legalized and under what circumstances; and how its use should be discouraged." Publisher's note

Includes bibliographical references

Nelson, Sheila

Hallucinogens; unreal visions. Mason Crest Publishers 2008 128p il (Illicit and misused drugs) $24.95 *

Grades: 7 8 9 10   362.29

1. Hallucinogens 2. Drug abuse

ISBN 978-1-4222-0155-8   LC 2007-10789

This book details the history and dangers of hallucinogenic drugs.

Includes glossary and bibliographical references

Newton, David E.

Substance abuse; a reference handbook. ABC-CLIO 2010 298p (Contemporary world issues) $55

Grades: 9 10 11 12 Adult   362.29

1. Drug abuse 2. Reference books

ISBN 978-1-59884-509-9; 978-1-59884-510-5 (ebook)

LC 2010-7451

"A comprehensive look at the physical, historical, cultural, and legal aspects of drug use including information regarding drug regulations in foreign countries and the drug culture in the United States. . . . [This is] a valuable resource for those researching or debating drug, alcohol, and tobacco-related topics." SLJ

Includes glossary and bibliographical references

Olive, M. Foster
Ecstasy; consulting editor, David J. Triggle.
Chelsea House Publishers 2010 109p il
(Understanding drugs) lib bdg $34.95
Grades: 8 9 10 11 12 **362.29**
1. Ecstasy (Drug)
ISBN 978-1-60413-538-1; 1-60413-538-7
LC 2010-5458
This book "book delves into the effects of using Ec-
stasy, from the initial pleasure to the dangerous aftaref-
fects." Publisher's note
Includes glossary and bibliographical references

Pampel, Fred C.
Drugs and sports. Facts on File 2007 284p
(Library in a book) $45 *
Grades: 11 12 Adult **362.29**
1. Athletes—Drug use
ISBN 0-8160-6575-6; 978-0-8160-6575-2
LC 2006-20536
This is an overview of the history of drug use among
athletes "from the performance-enhancement methods of
the ancient Greeks to the recent accusations of drug use
among high-profile professional athletes." Publisher's
note
Includes bibliographical references

Performance enhancing drugs; Louise Gerdes,
book editor. Greenhaven Press 2008 105p (At
issue. Drugs) lib bdg $29.95; pa $21.20 *
Grades: 9 10 11 12 **362.29**
1. Athletes—Drug use 2. Steroids
ISBN 978-0-7377-3693-9 (lib bdg); 0-7377-3693-3 (lib
bdg); 978-0-7377-3694-6 (pa); 0-7377-3694-1 (pa)
LC 2007-32384
This book "is made up of articles written by people
of a variety of backgrounds and viewpoints. Each entry
gives a brief background of the author helping the reader
understand the writer's viewpoint. Policy and controversy
surrounding performance enhancing drugs is discussed
from all perspectives. Entries give clear and up-to-date
information about the health risk, regulation, and banning
of performance enhancing drugs, and the effectiveness of
drug testing." Libr Media Connect
Includes bibliographical references

Sanna, E. J.
Heroin and other opioids; poppies' perilous
children. Mason Crest Publishers 2008 128p il
(Illicit and misused drugs) $24.95 *
Grades: 7 8 9 10 **362.29**
1. Heroin 2. Narcotics 3. Drug abuse
ISBN 978-1-4222-0156-5 LC 2006-28515
"The author takes readers on a trip through the history
of opium production and use, and its role in political history. . . . [This book also provides information on] the
opioids' effects on the body and brain, their long and
short-term side effects, and their dangers." Publisher's
note
Includes glossary and bibliographical references

Marijuana: mind-altering weed. Mason Crest
Publishers 2008 128p il (Illicit and misused drugs)
$24.95 *
Grades: 7 8 9 10 **362.29**
1. Marijuana 2. Drug abuse
ISBN 978-1-4222-0158-9 LC 2006-21208
"This book describes the history of marijuana use, the
dangers of its use, and the legal consequences of using
marijuana. Readers will also learn about the controversies
surrounding the drug—including the issues of
decriminalization and the use of medical marijuana.
Treatment options for marijuana addiction are also discussed." Publisher's note
Includes glossary and bibliographical references

Smoking; Noël Merino, book editor. Greenhaven
Press 2010 143p il (Introducing issues with
opposing viewpoints) $35.75
Grades: 8 9 10 11 12 **362.29**
1. Smoking 2. Tobacco habit
ISBN 978-0-7377-5101-7; 0-7377-5101-0
LC 2010-26766
Replaces the edition published 2006 under the
editorship of Laurie S. Friedman
"The articles in this anthology expose multiple sides
of . . . [the smoking] debate." Publisher's note
Includes bibliographical references

Teen drug abuse: opposing viewpoints; David E.
Nelson, book editor. Greenhaven Press 2010
235p il $39.70; pa $27.50
Grades: 8 9 10 11 12 **362.29**
1. Teenagers—Drug use 2. Drug abuse 3. Youth—Al-
cohol use
ISBN 978-0-7377-4992-2; 978-0-7377-4993-9 (pa)
LC 2010-18884
"Opposing viewpoints series"
A collection of articles and speeches, book excerpts
and quotations on various aspects of teen drug abuse.
Includes bibliographical references

Tobacco and smoking: opposing viewpoints;
Susan Hunnicutt, book editor. Greenhaven Press
2009 222p il lib bdg $39.70; pa $27.50
Grades: 8 9 10 11 12 **362.29**
1. Tobacco habit 2. Smoking 3. Tobacco industry
ISBN 978-0-7377-4242-8 (lib bdg); 0-7377-4242-9 (lib
bdg); 978-0-7377-4243-5 (pa); 0-7377-4243-7 (pa)
LC 2008-28546
"Opposing viewpoints series"
Articles in this anthology discuss topics such as
smokeless tobacco, teen smoking, government regulation
of smoking, and tobacco advertising.
Includes bibliographical references

Tobacco information for teens; health tips about the hazards of using cigarettes, smokeless tobacco, and other nicotine products: including facts about nicotine addiction, nicotine delivery systems, secondhand smoke, health consequences of tobacco use, related cancers, smoking cessation, and tobacco use statistics; edited by Karen Bellenir. 2nd ed. Omnigraphics 2010 440p il (Teen health series) $69

Grades: 7 8 9 10 11 12   **362.29**
1. Smoking 2. Tobacco habit
ISBN 978-0-7808-1153-9; 0-7808-1153-4
      LC 2010023716

First published 2007
"Provides basic consumer health information for teens on tobacco use, addiction, and related diseases, along with tips for quitting smoking. Includes index and resource information." Publisher's note

Includes bibliographical references

Walker, Ida
Addiction in America; society, psychology, and heredity. Mason Crest Publishers 2008 128p il (Illicit and misused drugs) $24.95

Grades: 7 8 9 10   **362.29**
1. Drug abuse 2. Alcoholism 3. Teenagers—Drug use 4. Teenagers—Alcohol use
ISBN 978-1-4222-0151-0   LC 2006-100092
This book "takes a look at what leads people to a life of addiction—the social, psychological, and hereditary factors that might make an individual susceptible to addiction." Publisher's note

Includes glossary and bibliographical references

Addiction treatment; escaping the trap. Mason Crest Publishers 2008 128p il (Illicit and misused drugs) $24.95 *

Grades: 7 8 9 10   **362.29**
1. Drug addicts—Rehabilitation 2. Alcoholics—Rehabilitation
ISBN 978-1-4222-0152-7   LC 2007-6739
This book aims to teach "some definitions important in the study of addiction treatment. Readers will also learn about the history of addiction treatment, including the work and continuing influence of the Washingtonians, the Emmanuel Movement, the Oxford Movement, and of course, Alcoholics Anonymous. Treatment philosophies are also presented." Publisher's note

Includes glossary and bibliographical references

Natural and everyday drugs; a false sense of security. Mason Crest Publishers 2008 128p il (Illicit and misused drugs) $24.95

Grades: 7 8 9 10   **362.29**
1. Drug abuse 2. Nonprescription drugs 3. Caffeine
ISBN 978-1-4222-0160-2   LC 2007-10780
This book details the negative health effects of caffeine and other legal drugs.

Includes glossary and bibliographical references

Painkillers; prescription dependency. Mason Crest Publishers 2008 128p il (Illicit and misused drugs) $24.95 *

Grades: 7 8 9 10   **362.29**
1. Drug abuse 2. Analgesics 3. Narcotics
ISBN 978-1-4222-0161-9; 1-4222-0161-9
      LC 2006-23091
This book provides "information about painkillers and how they are abused. Special attention is given to OxyContin, which has expanded addiction to new groups of people. Treatment methods are also covered." Publisher's note

Includes glossary and bibliographical references

Recreational Ritalin; the not-so-smart drug. Mason Crest Publishers 2008 128p il (Illicit and misused drugs) $24.95

Grades: 7 8 9 10   **362.29**
1. Ritalin 2. Attention deficit disorder 3. Teenagers—Drug use
ISBN 978-1-4222-0162-6   LC 2006-23975
This book offers an overview of ADHD and the drugs most often prescribed to treat it, and how those drugs are being abused.

Includes glossary and bibliographical references

Sedatives and hypnotics; deadly downers. Mason Crest Publishers 2008 128p il (Illicit and misused drugs) $24.95 *

Grades: 7 8 9 10   **362.29**
1. Tranquilizing drugs 2. Drug abuse
ISBN 978-1-4222-0163-3   LC 2006-29392
This book "reveals the long history of sedatives and hypnotics. . . . [It includes information on] how these drugs work and their effects—good and bad. Preventative measures are discussed, as well as treatment options for abuse and addiction." Publisher's note

Includes glossary and bibliographical references

Steroids: pumped up and dangerous. Mason Crest Publishers 2008 128p il map (Illicit and misused drugs) $24.95 *

Grades: 7 8 9 10   **362.29**
1. Steroids 2. Athletes—Drug use
ISBN 978-1-4222-0164-0   LC 2006-38606
This book reveals the dangerous side effects of steroids and offers healthy alternatives to getting in improving strength.

Includes glossary and bibliographical references

362.292   Alcohol

Alcohol; Lauri S. Friedman, book editor. Greenhaven Press 2010 136p il (Introducing issues with opposing viewpoints) lib bdg $35.75

Grades: 9 10 11 12   **362.292**
1. Alcoholism 2. Teenagers—Alcohol use 3. Drunk driving
ISBN 978-0-7377-4730-0; 0-7377-4730-7
      LC 2009-50773
"Explores issues surrounding the use of alcohol and whether or not it constitutes a threat to society. Discusses the impact of underage drinking, and the effectiveness of

Alcohol—*Continued*

banning alcohol advertising or lowering the drinking age. Looks at the problem of drunk driving and potential solutions like stricter laws, sobriety checkpoints, and ignition interlock devices." Publisher's note

Includes bibliographical references

Rosengren, John

Big book unplugged; a young person's guide to Alcoholics Anonymous. Hazelden 2003 121p pa $10.95

Grades: 9 10 11 12   **362.292**
1. Alcoholics Anonymous 2. Teenagers—Alcohol use 3. Alcoholism
ISBN 1-592-85038-3; 978-1-592-85038-9
                                        LC 2003-50828

"Alcoholics Anonymous, more familiarly called The Big Book, was published in 1939. . . . The Big Book describes the basic AA 12-step program, including the personal story of Bill W., credited with founding AA. In this clearly written manual, John R. devotes an interpretive chapter that corresponds to each of the 11 chapters in The Big Book. . . . In addition to those in recovery, this guide will also be useful to their family, friends, counselors and teachers." Publ Wkly

Includes bibliographical references

The **truth** about alcohol; Robert N. Golden, general editor; Fred L. Peterson, general editor; Barry Youngerman, principal author; Heath Dingwell, contributing author; Richelle Rennegarbe, adviser. 2nd ed. Facts on File 2010 230p (Truth about series) $35 *

Grades: 8 9 10 11 12   **362.292**
1. Teenagers—Alcohol use 2. Alcoholism
ISBN 978-0-8160-7639-0; 0-8160-7639-1
                                        LC 2009-53476
First published 2004

This discusses such topics as binge drinking, underage drinking, the prevalence of drinking on college campuses, drunken driving, dealing with alcohol abuse in the family, alcohol advertising and counter-advertising, and seeking help for an alcohol problem.

Includes glossary and bibliographical references

Walker, Ida

Alcohol addiction; not worth the buzz. Mason Crest Publishers 2008 128p il (Illicit and misused drugs) $24.95

Grades: 7 8 9 10   **362.292**
1. Alcoholism 2. Alcoholics—Rehabilitation
ISBN 978-1-4222-0153-4   LC 2006-25415

This book "provides readers with . . . information about alcohol addiction (alcoholism) and other drinking problems. Readers will learn about the history of alcohol use and early attempts to curb drinking, how alcohol affects the brain, and the effects it has on the body in the long and short term. The author also provides information on how individuals with alcohol problems can get help." Publisher's note

Includes glossary and bibliographical references

362.3   Mental retardation

Libal, Autumn

My name is not Slow; youth with mental retardation. Mason Crest Publishers, Inc. 2004 127p il (Youth with special needs) $24.95 *

Grades: 7 8 9 10   **362.3**
1. Mental retardation 2. Down syndrome
ISBN 1-59084-731-8   LC 2003-18435

Through the story of Penelope, a girl growing up with Down's syndrome, this book discusses "mental retardation, the special needs of individuals living with this form of disability, and the support systems available to help people with mental retardation acquire independence and success." Publisher's note

Includes glossary and bibliographical references

362.4   Problems of and services to people with physical disabilities

Encyclopedia of American disability history; edited by Susan Burch; foreword by Paul K. Longmore. Facts On File 2009 3v il (Facts on File library of American history) set $295

Grades: 9 10 11 12 Adult   **362.4**
1. Handicapped—Encyclopedias 2. Reference books
ISBN   978-0-8160-7030-5;   0-8160-7030-X; 978-1-4381-2672-2 (ebook); 1-4381-2672-7 (ebook)
                                        LC 2008-30537

Contact publisher for ebook pricing

"The over 750 entries, contributed by over 350 authors nationwide, cover activists, disabled persons, authors, and inventors. Also covered are topics relating to disability in general, such as disorders, organizations, governmental institutes, acts and legal cases, publications, movements, sites of importance, events, major historical experiences, stereotypes, popular culture, autobiographical essays, and literature." Libr J

Includes bibliographical references

Encyclopedia of disability; general editor, Gary L. Albrecht. Sage Publications 2006 5v il set $850

Grades: 11 12 Adult   **362.4**
1. Handicapped—Encyclopedias 2. Reference books
ISBN 0-7619-2565-1   LC 2005-18301

"Almost 200 of the entries are biographical, treating individuals from Homer and Socrates to Helen Keller and Franklin Roosevelt. Others treat history . . . types of disability . . . [and] attitudes and conditions affecting daily life. . . . [This encyclopedia draws] in readers from a wide range of studies and interests . . . helping them to see disability in an entirely new way." Booklist

Includes bibliographical references

McHugh, Mary

Special siblings; growing up with someone with a disability. rev ed. Paul H. Brookes 2003 xxvii, 241p il pa $21.95 *

Grades: 9 10 11 12   **362.4**
1. Handicapped 2. Siblings
ISBN 1-557-66607-5   LC 2002-28179

McHugh, Mary—*Continued*
First published 1999 by Hyperion
"A look at what it is like to be a sibling of someone with a physical, mental, or emotional disability. McHugh's brother has both cerebral palsy and mental retardation, a fact that has shaped every aspect of her life. In the course of writing this book, she spoke to siblings ranging in age from 6 to 76 years of age who expressed feelings that ran the gamut from compassion to resentment. She writes with painful honesty and includes information about research studies, interviews with experts, and the experiences and stories of many siblings." SLJ
Includes bibliographical references

People with disabilities; Dawn Laney, book editor. Greenhaven Press 2008 207p (The history of issues) lib bdg $37.40
Grades: 8 9 10 11   362.4
1. Handicapped
ISBN 978-0-7377-3972-5   LC 2008-20216
"Four general sections, each of which contains six primary-source essays, address rights, treatments, and care; the ADA, institutions, and capital punishment; education, funding, and inclusion; and technology, surgical procedures, and genetic testing. . . . An excellent resource." SLJ
Includes bibliographical references

362.5 Problems of and services to poor people

Encyclopedia of homelessness; David Levinson, editor. Sage Publications 2004 2v il $295
Grades: 11 12 Adult   362.5
1. Reference books 2. Homelessness—Encyclopedias
ISBN 0-7619-2751-4   LC 2004-9279
"Entries cover homelessness in 8 major U.S. cities and 30 cities and nations around the world, as well as causes of homelessness; historical aspects; housing, policy, health and lifestyle issues; and service systems." Booklist
Includes bibliographical references

Gifford, Clive
Poverty. Smart Apple Media 2010 46p il (Voices) lib bdg $34.25
Grades: 7 8 9 10 11 12   362.5
1. Poverty
ISBN 978-1-59920-277-8; 1-59920-277-8
                               LC 2008-50431
This book "focuses on poor countries and also the poor in rich countries, addressing poverty's causes, the role of welfare and foreign aid, and always, the hardships individuals in need face day to day. . . . [The] blend of current political debate with witnesses' close-up experiences told through photos, narratives, and quotes will draw browsers, and many will go on to find out more." Booklist
Includes glossary and bibliographical references

How can the poor be helped? Jennifer Dorman, book editor. Greenhaven Press 2011 107p (At issue. Social issues) $31.80; pa $22.50
Grades: 9 10 11 12   362.5
1. Public welfare 2. Poverty 3. Poor
ISBN 978-0-7377-5155-0; 978-0-7377-5156-7 (pa)
                               LC 2010050614
Articles in this anthology discuss possible ways to help the poor, including welfare reform, education, and marriage.
Includes bibliographical references

Lüsted, Marcia Amidon, 1962-
Poverty. ABDO Pub. Co. 2010 112p il map (Essential issues) lib bdg $22.95
Grades: 7 8 9 10   362.5
1. Poverty
ISBN 978-1-60453-957-8; 1-60453-957-7
                               LC 2009-30333
Among the topics discussed "are the causes of poverty as well as the effects of poverty, including homelessness, poor education, and poor mental and physical health." Publisher's note
The text is "well-written, providing examples that put a human face to each problem. Quotes and facts are clearly attributed, and their sources are noted in the extensive back matter. . . . Sidebars provide further information, or, more compellingly, offer stories about those touched by the topic. . . . [This] will be of great assistance to students writing reports." SLJ
Includes glossary and bibliographical references

Poverty; David M. Haugen and Matthew J. Box, book editors. Greenhaven Press 2006 108p il (Social issues firsthand) lib bdg $28.70 *
Grades: 8 9 10 11 12   362.5
1. Poverty 2. Poor—United States
ISBN 0-7377-2899-X   LC 2005-45120
"Collecting intimate stories of individuals living in poverty and those helping them, this anthology includes personal narratives of poor people struggling to survive on little or no income, and also writings that convey the thoughts and deeds of people trying to alleviate the plight of the impoverished." Publisher's note
These "16 accounts from poverty's gritty trenches evaporate easy assumptions about the poor, and reveal the obstacles faced by stricken individuals and families hampered by catch-22 social policies, entrenched racial inequities, and logistics such as cleaning up for an interview." Booklist
Includes bibliographical references

Poverty and homelessness; Noël Merino, book editor. Greenhaven Press 2009 210p (Current controversies) lib bdg $39.70; pa $27.50 *
Grades: 9 10 11 12   362.5
1. Homeless persons 2. Poverty
ISBN 978-0-7377-4458-3 (lib bdg); 0-7377-4458-8 (lib bdg); 978-0-7377-4459-0 (pa); 0-7377-4459-6 (pa)
                               LC 2009-12041
Articles in this anthology discuss causes and possible solutions to poverty and homelessness.
Includes bibliographical references

362.7 Problems of and services to young people

Adoption; David M. Haugen and Matthew J. Box, book editors. Greenhaven Press 2005 108p (Social issues firsthand) lib bdg $28.70 *
Grades: 8 9 10 11 12   **362.7**
1. Adoption
ISBN 0-7377-2881-7   LC 2005-46075

"The book explores such diverse issues as gay adoptive parents, open and transracial adoptions, the search for and reunion with birthparents, custody battles, and more. The editors have done an excellent job of selecting 16 lively, articulate, and poignant essays by birthparents, adoptive parents, and adoptees, all offering different perspectives on the process." SLJ

Includes bibliographical references

Adoption: opposing viewpoints; Mary E. Williams, book editor. Greenhaven Press 2006 226p il lib bdg $34.95; pa $23.70
Grades: 7 8 9 10   **362.7**
1. Adoption
ISBN 0-7377-3301-2 (lib bdg); 978-0-7377-3301-3 (lib bdg); 0-7377-3302-0 (pa); 978-0-7377-3302-0 (pa)
                                     LC 2006-43350

"Opposing viewpoints series"
This anthology addresses such topics as "whether adoption should be encouraged; conflicting views on transracial, international, and gay parent adoptions; whose rights are most in need of protection—adoptive or birth parents or those of adoptees; as well as what government policies should be implemented." SLJ

Includes bibliographical references

Feuereisen, Patti
Invisible girls; the truth about sexual abuse; with Caroline Pincus. New and rev. ed. Seal Press 2009 334p pa $16.95
Grades: 9 10 11 12   **362.7**
1. Child sexual abuse
ISBN 978-1-58005-301-3   LC 2010-483060
First published 2005
Subtitle on cover: Book for teen girls, young women, and everyone who cares about them

"This book sets personal narratives within a generalized discussion of sexual abuse of girls and young women. Feuereisen addresses myths about female sexuality and abuse, considers contributing family dynamics, and offers advice on preventing, reporting, and recovering from abuse. Individual chapters are given to father-daughter incest, other incest, abuse by teachers and clergy, and different types of rape. The writing is clear and frank, including sufficient details without becoming salacious." SLJ [review of 2005 edition]

Includes bibliographical references

Gordon, Sherri Mabry
Beyond bruises; the truth about teens and abuse. Enslow 2009 128p il (Issues in focus today) lib bdg $31.93 *
Grades: 7 8 9 10   **362.7**
1. Child abuse 2. Domestic violence 3. Date rape 4. Invective
ISBN 978-0-7660-3064-0; 0-7660-3064-4
                                     LC 2008-12273
"Discusses the various types of abuse teenagers face, including both domestic and dating abuse, the impact abuse has on teens, and several ways to help teens who suffer from some form of abuse." Publisher's note

Includes glossary and bibliographical references

Growing up in the care of strangers; the experiences, insights and recommendations of eleven former foster kids; compiled and edited by Waln K. Brown and John R. Seita. William Gladden Foundation Press 2009 175p pa $27.95
Grades: 10 11 12 Adult   **362.7**
1. Foster children 2. Foster home care 3. Adopted children
ISBN 978-0-9824510-0-7; 0-9824510-0-8
                                     LC 2009-927375
Most of "the authors of the stories in this book . . . suffered dangerous and dysfunctional childhoods requiring removal from their families and placement in out-of-home care. They have chosen to reflect on their childhood experiences through the lens of adult professionals, so that their unique knowledge might reach receptive minds looking to improve services to today's youth." Publisher's note

Includes bibliographical references

Lanchon, Anne
All about adoption; how to deal with the questions of your past; illustrated by Monike Czarnecki; edited by Tucker Shaw. Abrams/Amulet 2006 104p il (Sunscreen) pa $9.95 *
Grades: 7 8 9 10   **362.7**
1. Adoption
ISBN 0-8109-9227-2
"This guide covers an adopted child's traditional worries and concerns, such as establishing identity and living with overprotective parents. It also addresses such squirm-worthy issues as the fear of abandonment, racist comments, and discussing birth parents with adoptive parents. . . . Originally published in France, this handsomely designed self-help title . . . provides practical advice and reassurance for adopted teens and their families." Booklist

Includes bibliographical references

Slade, Suzanne, 1964-
    Adopted: the ultimate teen guide; [by] Suzanne Buckingham Slade; illustrations by Christopher Papile, Mary Sandage, and Odelia Witt; photographs by Chris Washburn. Scarecrow Press 2007 246p il (It happened to me) $45 *
    Grades: 9 10 11 12   **362.7**
    1. Adoption
    ISBN 978-0-8108-5774-2; 0-8108-5774-X
                                    LC 2007-13648
    This "guide features interviews with adoptees, essays by adoptive and birth parents, as well as information on famous adoptees, statistics, and other facts about adoption. Slade offers comprehensive coverage on topics such as transracial, international, and open adoptions, and the pros and cons of seeking information about their birth parents." SLJ
    Includes bibliographical references

Strong at the heart; how it feels to heal from sexual abuse; [compiled] by Carolyn Lehman. Farrar, Straus & Giroux 2005 156p il $18 *
    Grades: 8 9 10 11 12   **362.7**
    1. Child sexual abuse 2. Incest 3. Rape
    ISBN 0-374-37282-9   LC 2004-56280
    "Melanie Kroupa Books"
    This "gathers 11 personal stories by young men and women who experienced rape, molestation, or incest and found healing through speaking out about their abuse. . . . Clearly and candidly written, the narratives recounted here include sufficient details of abuse to be authentic, but never titillating. . . . An attractive, accessible format and black-and-white portraits throughout personalize the presentation." SLJ

Tucker, Neely
    Love in the driest season; a family memoir. Crown Publishers 2004 242p il hardcover o.p. pa $14
    Grades: 11 12 Adult   **362.7**
    1. Adoption 2. Zimbabwe
    ISBN 0-609-60976-9; 1-4000-8160-2 (pa)
                                    LC 2002-154095
    This is a "narrative of two Mississippians in Africa—a white reporter and his African-American wife—who struggle against Third World bureaucracy to adopt an abandoned Zimbabwean baby, as the continent is torn by crisis." SLJ
    "This story about the adoption of a tiny, critically ill Zimbabwean orphan appeals to the head as much as the heart." Christ Sci Monit

362.82   Problems of and services to families

Domestic violence: opposing viewpoints; Mike Wilson, book editor. Greenhaven Press 2008 c2009 217p lib bdg $39.70; pa $27.50
    Grades: 8 9 10 11 12   **362.82**
    1. Domestic violence
    ISBN 978-0-7377-4206-0 (lib bdg); 0-7377-4206-2 (lib bdg); 978-0-7377-4207-7 (pa); 0-7377-4207-0 (pa)
                                    LC 2008-28517

"Opposing viewpoints series"
    Articles in this anthology discuss domestic violence, including its causes and possible remedies.
    Includes bibliographical references

Zehr, Howard
    "What will happen to me?"; by Howard Zehr and Lorraine Stutzman Amstutz; portraits by Howard Zehr. Good Books 2010 c2011 94p il pa $14.95
    Grades: 7 8 9 10   **362.82**
    1. Children of prisoners
    ISBN 978-1-56148-689-2   LC 2010-12419
    This discusses issues facing "children of incarcerated parents. . . . In part one, the statements from the children interviewed are accompanied by full-color photo portraits. What comes through is that they all love their parents unequivocally, but here it is tangible and poignant both in their words and faces. . . . Part two offers advice for caregivers and includes 10 questions often asked by children whose parents are in jail." SLJ
    Includes bibliographical references

362.83   Problems of and services to women

Violence against women; Kate Burns, book editor. Greenhaven Press 2008 221p (Current controversies) lib bdg $38.50; pa $26.75 *
    Grades: 9 10 11 12   **362.83**
    1. Abused women 2. Violence
    ISBN 978-0-7377-3729-5 (lib bdg); 0-7377-3729-8 (lib bdg); 978-0-7377-3730-1 (pa); 0-7377-3730-1 (pa)
                                    LC 2007-29806
    Topics covered in this anthology include rape, domestic violence, the influence of pornography, and violence against women worldwide.
    Includes bibliographical references

362.88   Problems of and services to victims of crimes

Bickerstaff, Linda
    Violence against women; public health and human rights. Rosen Pub. 2010 112p il (A young woman's guide to contemporary issues) lib bdg $31.95
    Grades: 7 8 9 10   **362.88**
    1. Abused women 2. Violence
    ISBN 978-1-4358-3539-9; 1-4358-3539-5
                                    LC 2009-12062
    "Discusses different types of violence against women, preventative measures, ways to support others, and advice on how to get help." Publisher's note
    "Facts are shared in a conversational tone, creating the sense of a chat with a big sister. . . . [Though] designed for personal reading and browsing, the data provided are accurate and also lend themselves to use in reports." SLJ
    Includes glossary and bibliographical references

Simons, Rae, 1957-
Gender danger; survivors of rape, human trafficking, and honor killings; by Rae Simons with Joyce Zoldak. Mason Crest Publishers 2009 128p il (Survivors: ordinary people, extraordinary circumstances) lib bdg $24.95
Grades: 7 8 9 10 **362.88**
1. Abused women 2. Sex crimes 3. Women—Social conditions 4. Violence 5. Rape
ISBN 978-1-4222-0451-1; 1-4222-0451-0
LC 2008-50322
The author discusses "the issues faced by women in this and other cultures. The book looks at rape as a weapon of war, honor killings, female circumcision, and the complex and often dangerous world of transgender individuals." SLJ
Includes bibliographical references

362.883 Problems of and services to victims of rape

The **truth** about rape; Robert N. Golden, general editor, Fred Peterson, general editor; Kathryn Hilgenkamp, Judith Harper, Elizabeth Boskey contributing author[s] 2nd ed. Facts On File 2010 191p il (Truth about series) $35
Grades: 9 10 11 12 **362.883**
1. Rape
ISBN 978-0-8160-7642-0; 0-8160-7642-1
LC 2009-18452
First published 2005 under the editorship of Mark J. Kittleson
"The introduction includes a section on how to use the book as well as a brief discussion of 'Society and the Victims of Rape.' The entries, which are generally a few pages in length, are clear and concise. They answer basic questions that students will have through definitions, statistics, an examination of common myths associated with the subject, and a Q & A." SLJ
Includes glossary

Wilkins, Jessica
Date rape. Crabtree Pub. 2011 48p il (Straight talk about . . .) $29.27; pa $9.95
Grades: 7 8 9 10 **362.883**
1. Date rape
ISBN 978-0-7787-2128-4; 0-7787-2128-0; 978-0-7787-2135-2 (pa); 0-7787-2135-3 (pa)
LC 2010-16397
This book about date rape "also spends a good deal of its pages covering dating violence, both verbal and physical, which girls don't always understand to be problematic. . . . The information . . . is strong and far reaching." Booklist

363.1 Public safety programs

Chernobyl; David Erik Nelson, book editor. Greenhaven Press 2010 220p il map (Perspectives on modern world history) $38.50
Grades: 8 9 10 11 12 **363.1**
1. Chernobyl Nuclear Accident, Chernobyl, Ukraine, 1986
ISBN 978-0-7377-4555-9; 0-7377-4555-X
LC 2009-27203
"This volume contains a wealth of relevant information representing many viewpoints of the current discussions surrounding the 1986 disaster at the Chernobyl nuclear power plant in Ukraine, which led to an official death toll of 56 people. Each article, skillfully drawn from multinational secondary sources, provides researchers with an admirable base for reports." SLJ
Includes glossary and bibliographical references

Cummins, Ronnie
Genetically engineered food; a self-defense guide for consumers; [by] Ronnie Cummins and Ben Lilliston; foreword by Frances Moore Lappé. [2nd, rev ed] Marlowe & Co 2004 237p pa $14.95
Grades: 11 12 Adult **363.1**
1. Food—Biotechnology 2. Farm produce
ISBN 1-569-24469-3 LC 2004-45565
First published 2000
The authors "discuss genetically engineered or modified food focusing on the scientific, political, economic, and health issues. . . . [They] include information on what consumers can do, from smart shopping to grassroots lobbying, to reduce the threat of genetically engineered food." Booklist [review of 2000 edition]
Includes bibliographical references

Espejo, Roman, 1977-
Fast food; Roman Espejo, book editor. Greenhaven Press 2009 96p (At issue. Health) $31.80; pa $22.50 *
Grades: 9 10 11 12 **363.1**
1. Convenience foods 2. Food industry 3. Restaurants
ISBN 978-0-7377-4300-5; 0-7377-4300-X; 978-0-7377-4299-2 (pa); 0-7377-4299-2 (pa)
LC 2008-52832
Articles in this book discuss the controversies surrounding fast food, including its possible links to obesity and other health problems.
Includes bibliographical references

Food safety; Judeen Bartos, book editor. Greenhaven Press 2011 99p (At issue. Health) lib bdg $31.80; pa $22.50
Grades: 9 10 11 12 **363.1**
1. Food adulteration and inspection 2. Food contamination
ISBN 978-0-7377-5149-9 (lib bdg); 978-0-7377-5150-5 (pa) LC 2010-43628
Among the topics discussed in these 10 reprinted articles are government regulations on food, genetically engineered crops, and imported foods.
Includes bibliographical references

Genetically modified food; Diane Andrews Henningfeld, book editor. Greenhaven Press 2009 114p (At issue. Environment) lib bdg $31.80; pa $22.50 *

Grades: 9 10 11 12   363.1
1. Genetically modified foods
ISBN 978-0-7377-4098-1 (lib bdg); 0-7377-4098-1 (lib bdg); 978-0-7377-4099-8 (pa); 0-7377-4099-X (pa)
     LC 2008-29477

Presents a series of essays with varying viewpoints on the subject of genetically modified food. Includes a list of organizations to contact.

Includes bibliographical references

Parks, Peggy J., 1951-
Drunk driving. ReferencePoint Press 2009 96p il (Compact research. Current issues) lib bdg $25.95
Grades: 7 8 9 10   363.1
1. Drunk driving
ISBN 978-1-60152-072-2; 1-60152-072-7
     LC 2008-48499

This "title has an overview of [drunk driving] as well as topic-specific chapters such as 'Who Drives Drunk?' and 'How Should Drunk Drivers Be Punished?' It offers differing ideas on questions that have more than one answer. The colorful graphs and charts contain current information." SLJ

Includes bibliographical references

Petersen, Christine
Protecting earth's food supply. Marshall Cavendish Benchmark 2010 c2011 112p il (Environment at risk) lib bdg $39.93 *
Grades: 6 7 8 9 10   363.1
1. Diseases 2. Food adulteration and inspection 3. Food contamination 4. Food poisoning
ISBN 978-0-7614-4008-6; 0-7614-4008-9
     LC 2008-35949

This book provides "information on Earth's food supply and its protection, the interrelationships of the natural world, environmental problems both natural and manmade, the relative risks associated with these problems, and solutions for resolving and/or preventing them." Publisher's note

Includes bibliographical references

Smith, Terry L.
Nutrition and food safety. Chelsea House 2010 c2011 180p il map (Healthy eating: a guide to nutrition) $35
Grades: 9 10 11 12   363.1
1. Food adulteration and inspection 2. Nutrition
ISBN 978-1-60413-776-7   LC 2010-21324

This book "explores the many risks to our food and water supplies, including bacterial contamination, agricultural pesticides, food additives, allergens, and industrial chemicals." Publisher's note

Includes glossary and bibliographical references

363.2   Police services

Ackerman, Thomas H.
FBI careers; the ultimate guide to landing a job as one of America's finest. 3rd ed. JIST Works 2009 c2010 368p il pa $19.95
Grades: 9 10 11 12   363.2
1. United States. Federal Bureau of Investigation 2. Vocational guidance
ISBN 978-1-59357-730-8; 1-59357-730-3
     LC 2009-38881

First published 2002

This is a "guide for acing the FBI's rigorous selection process and landing a job. The author guides readers . . . through the hiring process for special agents and support personnel. Along the way, he shares tips for standing out from other applicants, completing applications, passing the physical fitness test, getting FBI internships, and . . . more." Publisher's note

Includes bibliographical references

Bell, Suzanne
Encyclopedia of forensic science; foreword by Barry A.J. Fisher; preface by Robert C. Shaler. rev ed. Facts on File 2008 402p il (Facts on File science library) $85 *
Grades: 8 9 10 11 12 Adult   363.2
1. Forensic sciences—Encyclopedias 2. Reference books
ISBN 978-0-8160-6799-2; 0-8160-6799-6
     LC 2008-5862

First published 2003

"In addition to explaining the science of forensics, Bell . . . reviews various disciplines related to forensic science, among them entomology, odontology, and psychology. Other entries cover professional organizations, government agencies, famous names in the field of forensics, evidence, and legal issues. . . . With its clear language and brief entries [this] volume will provide readers with a nuts-and-bolts understanding of the real world of forensic science." Booklist [review of 2003 edition]

Includes bibliographical references

Fakes and forgeries. Facts On File 2008 108p il (Essentials of forensic science) $35
Grades: 7 8 9 10 11 12   363.2
1. Forgery 2. Fraud
ISBN 978-0-8160-5514-2; 0-8160-5514-9
     LC 2008-4502

This is a "fascinating introduction to how scientists identify fraudulent copies, from signatures to oil paintings. . . . Bell moves from examples of the crime that date back to ancient Mesopotamian civilizations all the way through to today's high-tech counterfeiting cases." Booklist

Includes glossary and bibliographical references

Helvarg, David, 1951-
Rescue warriors; the U.S. Coast Guard, America's forgotten heroes. Thomas Dunne Books 2009 xxiii, 356p il $25.95
Grades: 9 10 11 12 Adult   **363.2**
   1. United States. Coast Guard 2. Rescue work 3. Lifesaving
   ISBN 978-0-312-36372-7; 0-312-36372-9
                      LC 2008-44633
"An informative history starting with the Coast Guard's beginnings in the 18th century, written in straightforward prose. The emphasis is on the fifth armed service's record during the 20th and 21st centuries, especially its unparalleled effectiveness and heroism during Hurricane Katrina. . . . This is an excellent title for students interested in the Coast Guard, especially as a possible career choice." SLJ
Includes bibliographical references

Houck, Max M.
Trace evidence. Facts on File 2008 126p il (Essentials of forensic science) $35
Grades: 9 10 11 12   **363.2**
   1. Forensic sciences 2. Criminal investigation
   ISBN 978-0-8160-5511-1; 0-8160-5511-4
                      LC 2008-12786
"Explores the microscopic world in which the forensic scientist works by addressing the issues of what constitutes evidence; important methods of trace analysis, including spectroscopy and chromatography; human and animal hairs and what can be determined by examining them; and manufactured and natural fibers and the many ways in which they appear in textiles and are analyzed in the laboratory." Publisher's note
Includes glossary and bibliographical references

Innes, Brian, 1928-
DNA and body evidence. Sharpe Focus 2008 96p il (Forensic evidence) $39.95
Grades: 7 8 9 10 11 12   **363.2**
   1. DNA fingerprinting 2. Forensic sciences 3. Criminal investigation
   ISBN 978-0-7656-8115-7   LC 2007-6749
This "book begins with the history of DNA and fluid analysis, continues with DNA fingerprinting and gathering evidence, and highlights landmark usage of DNA evidence as well as its routine uses in both the judicial and penal systems. . . . The [book is] comprehensive enough for students with prior knowledge of forensics but approachable for beginners. . . . [It weaves] technical terms and anecdotal evidence into a seamless presentation." SLJ
Includes glossary and bibliographical references

Fingerprints and impressions. Sharpe Focus 2008 96p il (Forensic evidence) $39.95
Grades: 7 8 9 10 11 12   **363.2**
   1. Fingerprints 2. Criminal investigation 3. Forensic sciences
   ISBN 978-0-7656-8114-0   LC 2007-6751
This "covers the origins of fingerprinting and the analysis and usage of fingerprinting data and concludes with its use as admissible evidence in court. . . . [The book

is] comprehensive enough for students with prior knowledge of forensics but approachable for beginners. . . . [It weaves] technical terms and anecdotal evidence into a seamless presentation." SLJ
Includes glossary and bibliographical references

McCage, Crystal
U.S. border control; by Crystal M. McCage. ReferencePoint Press, Inc. 2009 104p il (Compact research. Current issues) $25.95
Grades: 9 10 11 12   **363.2**
   1. United States. Border Patrol 2. United States—Boundaries
   ISBN 978-1-60152-052-4; 1-60152-052-2
                      LC 2007-48332
The author "poses questions via the chapter headings ('Does increased border security protect the United States?'), then answers with succinct explanations composed of statistics and quotes from reliable sources. Also covered are impediments to border control, the Minuteman Project and its surrounding controversy, and future border control policies. . . . The well-structured information provides a solid platform for all sides of the argument." SLJ
Includes bibliographical references

Newton, Michael, 1951-
The encyclopedia of crime scene investigation; foreword by John L. French. Facts On File 2008 334p il (Facts on File crime library) $75; pa $21.95 *
Grades: 9 10 11 12 Adult   **363.2**
   1. Reference books 2. Criminal investigation—Encyclopedias
   ISBN   978-0-8160-6814-2;   0-8160-6814-3;
   978-0-8160-6815-9 (pa); 0-8160-6815-1 (pa)
                      LC 2007-4406
This encyclopedia includes "300 alphabetically arranged articles that describe and discuss crime-solving procedures and technologies. The entries provide a broad treatment of historical and scientific breakthroughs that have attempted to keep pace with criminal ingenuity, such as fingerprinting techniques, ballistics, biometrics, and DNA analysis. . . . Newton's conversational tone and writing style are accessible to high school students, who may use the volume for research or to browse the case studies." SLJ
Includes glossary and bibliographical references

Orr, Tamra
Racial profiling. ABDO Pub. Co. 2010 112p il (Essential viewpoints) lib bdg $32.79
Grades: 7 8 9 10   **363.2**
   1. Racial profiling
   ISBN 978-1-60453-535-8; 1-60453-535-0
                      LC 2008-34915
"This timely book covers racial profiling as practiced in the United States since the terrorist attacks of 9/11, when it has come to center on young men of Middle Eastern extraction. . . . Orr presents arguments for and against the practice in focused, clearly written essays that will help students become informed. . . . There are plen-

Orr, Tamra—*Continued*

ty of color photographs. This book will enhance most collections." SLJ

Includes bibliographical references

Owen, David, 1939-

Hidden evidence; the story of forensic science and how it helped to solve 50 of the world's toughest crimes. Rev. 2nd ed. Firefly Books, Ltd. 2009 288p il pa $24.95

Grades: 11 12 Adult   **363.2**
  1. Forensic sciences 2. Criminal investigation
  ISBN 978-1-55407-540-9; 1-55407-540-8
                                   LC 2010285527

First published 2000

Owen "looks at how forensic science has developed and how techniques have evolved from methods of investigation used in ancient China to computerized DNA analysis. . . . This is fascinating reading for a range of readers from forensic scientists to professional and amateur sleuths, but the graphic illustrations are not for the squeamish." Booklist

Police brutality; Louise I. Gerdes, book editor. Greenhaven Press 2004 206p (Current controversies) lib bdg $34.95; pa $23.70 *

Grades: 9 10 11 12   **363.2**
  1. Police brutality
  ISBN 0-7377-1627-4 (lib bdg); 0-7377-1628-2 (pa)
                                    LC 2003-60738

"Authors in this anthology examine the nature and scope of police brutality, possible causes, and potential reforms." Publisher's note

Includes bibliographical references

Racial profiling; Kathy L. Hahn, book editor. Greenhaven Press 2010 90p (At issue. Social issues) $31.80; pa $22.50

Grades: 9 10 11 12   **363.2**
  1. Racial profiling
  ISBN 978-0-7377-5093-5; 978-0-7377-5094-2 (pa)
                                    LC 2010-15895

This is an anthology of essays by writers offering different opinions on the issue of racial profiling.

Includes bibliographical references

Sapse, Danielle S.

Legal aspects of forensics. Chelsea House 2007 114p il (Inside forensic science) $32.95

Grades: 9 10 11 12   **363.2**
  1. Forensic sciences 2. Criminal investigation
  3. Administration of criminal justice
  ISBN 978-0-7910-8925-5; 0-7910-8925-8
                                    LC 2006-12412

This book "is intended for students who would like to become knowledgeable in the basic aspects of law, as a preparation for the understanding of the scientific methods currently used in the elucidation of crimes. Focusing on the aspects of law that make use of forensic science methods, it does not require a previous background in either law or science, but does provide this background as far as law is concerned." Publisher's note

Includes glossary and bibliographical references

Stefoff, Rebecca, 1951-

Crime labs. Marshall Cavendish Benchmark 2010 95p il (Forensic science investigated) $23.95

Grades: 6 7 8 9 10   **363.2**
  1. Locard, Edmond, 1877-1966 2. Forensic sciences
  ISBN 978-0-7614-4140-3; 0-7614-4140-9
                                   LC 2010-10536

The "titles in the Forensic Science Investigated series stand out not only for their thorough overviews of how forensic science is practiced today but also for their fascinating historical perspectives. . . . *Crime labs* introduces nineteenth-century Frenchman Edmond Locard, creator of the world's first forensic lab." Booklist

Includes bibliographical references

Wagner, E. J.

The science of Sherlock Holmes; from Baskerville Hall to the Valley of Fear, the real forensics behind the great detective's greatest cases. Wiley 2006 244p il $24.95; pa $16.95

Grades: 11 12 Adult   **363.2**
  1. Forensic sciences 2. Criminal investigation
  ISBN   0-471-64879-5;   978-0-471-64879-6;
  0-470-12823-2 (pa); 978-0-470-12823-7 (pa)
                                    LC 2005-22236

The author discusses forensic science in Arthur Conan Doyle's stories of the 'consulting detective' Sherlock Holmes. She compares Holmes's investigative techniques to those used in actual cases such as the killing of Lizzie Borden's parents in 1892, the 1902 murder of Joseph Browne Elwell, and the disappearance of Dr. George Parkman in 1849.

This book "will intrigue readers with incredible stories and amazing tales from the early days of forensic science." Christ Sci Monit

Includes bibliographical references

Walker, Pamela, 1958-

Forensic science experiments; [by] Pamela Walker, Elaine Wood. Facts on File 2009 150p il (Facts on File science experiments) $35

Grades: 7 8 9 10   **363.2**
  1. Forensic sciences 2. Science—Experiments
  ISBN 978-0-8160-7804-2; 0-8160-7804-1
                                    LC 2008-39900

This "contains 20 experiments that allow students to actively engage in scientific inquiry. Projects are presented in a uniform format, with an introduction to the topic, time requirements (35 minutes to 2 weeks), a materials list, numbered procedures, and several analysis questions. . . . The experiments themselves are timely and fascinating. . . . In [this book], a banana autopsy, blood-spatter inquiry, and 'Glitter as Trace Evidence' will hook *CSI* fans. Despite detailed instructions, close teacher supervision is a must." SLJ

Includes glossary and bibliographical references

Warner, Judith Ann, 1950-
U.S. border security; a reference handbook; [by] Judith A. Warner. ABC-CLIO 2010 381p il (Contemporary world issues) $55
Grades: 9 10 11 12   **363.2**
1. United States. Border Patrol 2. United States—Boundaries
ISBN 978-1-59884-407-8   LC 2010-9662
"The eight chapters in this . . . work address history, contemporary issues, and the international context of security, and provide a chronology of events, biographies of major figures, selected documents and data, a directory of involved organizations and agencies, and a list of sources. . . . Its comprehensive coverage includes security concerns at land, sea, and air borders, such as unauthorized entry and smuggling of individuals (including human trafficking); drug trafficking and narcoterrorism; and property offensives such as theft, terrorism, and the smuggling of weapons of mass destruction. This useful compendium fills a gap on the reference shelf." Choice
Includes glossary and bibliographical references

Wright, John D., 1938-
Fire and explosives. Sharpe Focus 2008 96p (Forensic evidence) $39.95
Grades: 7 8 9 10 11 12   **363.2**
1. Forensic sciences 2. Criminal investigation 3. Fires 4. Explosives
ISBN 978-0-7656-8117-1   LC 2007-6750
Contents: How fire and explosives work; What can fires tell investigators; Arson cases; A history of explosives; Detecting, identifying, and tracing explosives; Terrorism and explosives
This book focuses on how forensic science plays a role in investigating explosions and fires.
Includes glossary and bibliographical references

Hair and fibers. Sharpe Focus 2008 96p il (Forensic evidence) $39.95
Grades: 7 8 9 10 11 12   **363.2**
1. Forensic sciences 2. Criminal investigation 3. Hair 4. Fibers
ISBN 978-0-7656-8116-4   LC 2007-6752
Contents: What hair and fibers reveal; Collecting and analyzing hair; Criminal cases involving hair; Collecting and analyzing fibers; Criminal cases involving fibers; Advances in trace evidence
"This volume, about the most familiar examples of trace evidence (hair and fibers), provides readers with well-detailed descriptions of how such fibers are handled at the scene, analyzed in the lab, and used in the courtroom, as well as how the science itself has evolved. . . . Make a place for this on the shelf; interest will be high." Booklist
Includes glossary and bibliographical references

Yount, Lisa
Forensic science; from fibers to fingerprints. Facts on File 2007 206p il (Milestones in discovery and invention) $35 *
Grades: 7 8 9 10 11 12   **363.2**
1. Forensic sciences 2. Criminal investigation
ISBN 0-8160-5751-6; 978-0-8160-5751-1
LC 2006-1748

This book "profiles key figures in this newsmaking field, both pioneers and today's top forensics experts." Publisher's note
Includes glossary and bibliographical references

363.3   Other aspects of public safety

Cunningham, Kevin, 1966-
Wildfires. Morgan Reynolds Pub. 2009 112p il (Extreme threats) lib bdg $28.95
Grades: 7 8 9 10   **363.3**
1. Wildfires
ISBN 978-1-59935-120-9; 1-59935-120-X
LC 2009-25709
This book about wildfires has "black-and-white and color photographs on almost every page. . . . Frequent sidebars, covering as much as a spread, discuss peripheral and often unusual information. The conclusion . . . explains what scientists are doing, or what they anticipate doing, to ameliorate the threat." SLJ
Includes glossary and bibliographical references

Media violence: opposing viewpoints; David Haugen and Susan Musser, book editors. Greenhaven Press 2009 232p il lib bdg $37.40; pa $25.95
Grades: 8 9 10 11 12   **363.3**
1. Violence 2. Mass media
ISBN   978-0-7377-4218-3   (lib   bdg); 978-0-7377-4219-0 (pa)   LC 2008-30355
"Opposing viewpoints series"
This anthology "begins with articles that probe the scope and severity of the phenomenon and then moves on to sections about how violence in the media should be regulated, the effects of violence in the news, and cyberbullying." Booklist
Includes bibliographical references

363.31   Censorship

Caso, Frank
Censorship; foreword by Richard B. Collins. Facts On File 2008 342p (Global issues) $45 *
Grades: 9 10 11 12   **363.31**
1. Censorship
ISBN 978-0-8160-7123-4; 0-8160-7123-3
LC 2007-47075
The author "lays out censorship's lengthy history and follows with a thoughtful account of its various religious, political, and social motives." Libr J
Includes bibliographical references

Censorship; Julia Bauder, book editor. Greenhaven Press 2007 275p (Current controversies) lib bdg $34.95; pa $23.70 *
Grades: 9 10 11 12   **363.31**
1. Censorship
ISBN 978-0-7377-3277-1 (lib bdg); 0-7377-3277-6 (lib bdg); 978-0-7377-3278-8 (pa); 0-7377-3278-4 (pa)
LC 2006-38688

Censorship—*Continued*

Contents: Should offensive speech be censored?; Should high schools and universities censor?; Should pornographic and violent material be censored?; Should speech that endangers national security be censored?

Includes bibliographical references

Censorship; Ronnie D. Lankford, book editor. Greenhaven Press 2010 122p il (Issues that concern you) lib bdg $35.75

Grades: 9 10 11 12   **363.31**
1. Censorship
ISBN 978-0-7377-4744-7; 0-7377-4744-7
LC 2009-50038

Explores the issues surrounding censorship. Presents diversity of opinion on the topic, including both conservative and liberal points of view in an even balance.

Includes bibliographical references

Censorship: opposing viewpoints; Scott Barbour, book editor. Greenhaven Press 2010 217p il $39.70; pa $27.50 *

Grades: 9 10 11 12   **363.31**
1. Censorship 2. Freedom of speech
ISBN 978-0-7377-4761-4; 978-0-7377-4762-1 (pa)
LC 2009-40557

"Opposing viewpoints series"

Articles in this anthology discuss issues relating to censorship including whether there should be limits to free speech, censorship of the Internet, and censorship in other nations including China.

Includes bibliographical references

Green, Jonathon

The encyclopedia of censorship; [by] Jonathon Green, Nicholas J. Karolides. rev ed. Facts on File 2005 xxii, 698p (Facts on File library of world history) $85

Grades: 11 12 Adult   **363.31**
1. Reference books 2. Censorship—Encyclopedias
ISBN 0-8160-4464-3   LC 2004-53211
First published 1990

"The crowded roster of those who have been affected by censorship, as well as the books, films, and other works attacked, are found in these . . . pages. Controversies that have arisen over the years are given historical context; highly valuable national wrap-ups treat the culture, law, and predominant trends of diverse lands." Libr J

Includes bibliographical references

Should music lyrics be censored for violence and exploitation? Roman Espejo, book editor. Greenhaven Press 2008 137p (At issue. Mass media) lib bdg $29.95; pa $21.20

Grades: 9 10 11 12   **363.31**
1. Rap music—Censorship 2. Rap music—History and criticism
ISBN   978-0-7377-4064-6   (lib   bdg);
978-0-7377-4065-3 (pa)   LC 2007-50857

This book "explores the isses surrounding the censorship of violent and misogynistic rap and hip-hop lyrics. Contributors address freedom of speech, the impact of

song content on young people's behavior, violence and sexism in our culture, and the rights and responsibilities of both recording artists and record companies." SLJ

Includes bibliographical references

363.32   Control of violence and terrorism

Burns, Vincent

Terrorism; a documentary and reference guide; [by] Vincent Burns and Kate Dempsey Peterson; foreword by James K. Kallstrom. Greenwood Press 2005 xxxvii, 293p il $75 *

Grades: 11 12 Adult   **363.32**
1. Terrorism
ISBN 0-313-33213-4   LC 2005-3390

This is a "volume of 70 documents, some never before in print, pertaining to terrorism and the US. Readings include speeches, policy statements, letters, reports, and laws. . . . An easy-to-use resource that is full of pertinent information, this volume should be read all the way from the introduction . . . to the resources section." Choice

Includes bibliographical references

Combs, Cindy C.

Encyclopedia of terrorism; [by] Cindy C. Combs and Martin Slann. Rev ed. Facts on File 2007 478p il map (Facts on File library of world history) $95 *

Grades: 11 12 Adult   **363.32**
1. Reference books 2. Terrorism—Encyclopedias
ISBN 0-8160-6277-3; 978-0-8160-6277-5
LC 2006-15853
First published 2002

This encyclopedia provides articles on "the events, people, organizations, and places that have played a major role in international terrorism. Each entry is placed within its . . . historical context to help readers understand the wide-ranging motivations behind terrorist actions." Publisher's note

Includes bibliographical references

Evans, Kimberly Masters

National security; [by] Kim Masters Evans. Gale Cengage 2009 158p il map (Information Plus reference series) pa $55

Grades: 9 10 11 12   **363.32**
1. National security—United States
ISBN 978-1-4144-3380-6

Contents: A historical overview; The organization of national security; International terrorism; The War on Terror: Afghanistan and Iraq; The War on Terror: Homeland Security; Countries of concern; Proliferation of weapons; American civil liberties and the War on Terror; Human rights and the War on Terror; U.S. relations with the Islamic world

This book discusses the war on terror and its effect on civil liberties.

Includes bibliographic references

Friedman, Lauri S.
Terrorist attacks. ReferencePoint Press 2008 128p il map (Compact research. Current issues) lib bdg $24.95

Grades: 7 8 9 10 11 12   363.32

1. Terrorism

ISBN 978-1-60152-022-7; 1-60152-022-0

LC 2007-9907

This "introduces theories as to why people carry out terrorist attacks, how they are executed, and how the attacks might be prevented. . . . [The] volume includes people and groups associated with the issue, a chronology of events, related organizations, and suggestions for further research. Chapters open and end with an array of quotes that argue for or against a particular argument or aspect of the issue, complete with full citation." SLJ

Includes glossary and bibliographical references

Gupta, Dipak K.
Who are the terrorists? Chelsea House 2006 116p il map (The roots of terrorism) lib bdg $35

Grades: 7 8 9 10   363.32

1. Terrorism

ISBN 0-7910-8306-3   LC 2005021627

This "volume discusses the world history as well as the groups and individuals behind today's headlines. . . . Gupta emphasizes that equating Islam with the barbaric acts of a few terrorists is like making the burning crosses of the Ku Klux Klan the essence of Christianity. He also points out the role of the American invasion of Iraq and the images from Abu Ghraib. . . . This is sure to spark vehement group discussion." Booklist

Includes bibliographical references

Henderson, Harry, 1951-
Global terrorism. Rev. ed. Facts on File 2004 316p il map (Library in a book) $45

Grades: 9 10 11 12   363.32

1. Terrorism

ISBN 0-8160-5337-5   LC 2003-63126

First published 2001 with title: Terrorism

This book combines a "general perspective on terrorism (including a historical introduction and theoretical discussion) with recent events and publications. . . . This volume addresses issues such as the Israel-Palestine conflict as well as the U.S. military invasion of Iraq. The attitude toward terrorism in nations such as Pakistan, Saudi Arabia, and Egypt and the public involvement of U.S. armed forces as trainers and advisers in the Philippines and Columbia are covered. The book also sheds light on the actions of North Korea and U.S. responses." Publisher's note

Includes bibliographical references

Kronenwetter, Michael
Terrorism: a guide to events and documents. Greenwood Press 2004 298p il $55 *

Grades: 11 12 Adult   363.32

1. Terrorism

ISBN 0-313-32578-2   LC 2004-6619

This "book examines the phenomenon of terrorism, discussing the methods, tactics, and weapons used by terrorists and exploring the attraction that terrorism holds for many individuals, groups, and movements." Publisher's note

"Kronenwetter's book is seminal to an understanding of terrorism. Honest, insightful, and easily understood, his book articulates the core ideals of terrorism and expertly presents its philosophical motivations within a historical context." Choice

Includes bibliographical references

Netzley, Patricia D.
The Greenhaven encyclopedia of terrorism; by Patricia D. Netzley; Moataz A. Fattah, consulting editor. Greenhaven Press 2007 365p il (Greenhaven encyclopedia of) $77.45 *

Grades: 9 10 11 12   363.32

1. Reference books 2. Terrorism—Encyclopedias

ISBN 978-0-7377-3235-1; 0-7377-3235-0

LC 2007-8156

An alphabetical presentation of definitions and descriptions of terms and events associated with terrorism.

Includes bibliographical references

Terrorism; Michelle E. Houle, book editor.
Greenhaven Press 2005 170p il map (History of issues) lib bdg $34.95; pa $23.70

Grades: 9 10 11 12   363.32

1. Terrorism

ISBN 0-7377-1909-5 (lib bdg); 0-7377-1910-9 (pa)

LC 2004-49716

"The book is divided into five chapters, each one focusing on a different aspect of terrorism: religion-based terrorism, state-sponsored terrorism, terrorism committed in the pursuit of national liberation, terrorism and the U.S., and the difficulties of defining terrorism." Booklist

Includes bibliographical references

Terrorism; David M. Haugen and Matthew J. Box, book editors.
Greenhaven Press 2006 110p il (Social issues firsthand) lib bdg $28.70 *

Grades: 9 10 11 12   363.32

1. Terrorism

ISBN 0-7377-2501-X   LC 2005-40218

This book designed to discuss the personal aspects of controversial issues "includes articles written by Osama bin Laden, Timothy McVeigh, Hizbullah, and a member of Aum Shinrikyo. All of these are in a chapter titled, 'What Motivates a Terrorist?' Later chapters include reports by survivors and family members of Sept. 11, 2001, the Oklahoma City bombing, Palestine, and other terrorist tragedies." Libr Media Connect

Includes bibliographical references

Terrorism; Lauri S. Friedman, book editor.
Greenhaven Press 2011 164p il (Introducing issues with opposing viewpoints) $36.80

Grades: 8 9 10 11 12   363.32

1. Terrorism

ISBN 978-0-7377-4944-1   LC 2010023161

Explores the issue of terrorism by placing opinions from a wide range of sources in a pro/con format. Features articles that express various perspectives on this topic.

Includes bibliographical references

Terrorism: opposing viewpoints; Mike Wilson, book editor. Greenhaven Press 2008 c2009 209p il lib bdg $38.50; pa $26.75
 Grades: 8 9 10 11 12   **363.32**
 1. Terrorism
 ISBN 978-0-7377-4234-3 (lib bdg); 0-7377-4234-8 (lib bdg); 978-0-7377-4235-0 (pa); 0-7377-4235-6 (pa)
          LC 2008-29140
"Opposing viewpoints series"
The articles in this anthology cover such topics as whether terrorism is a serious threat, different types of terrorism, terrorism's causes, and ways to combat terrorism.
Includes bibliographical references

What motivates suicide bombers? Roman Espejo, book editor. Greenhaven Press 2009 c2010 118p (At issue. National security) $31.80; pa $22.50
 Grades: 9 10 11 12   **363.32**
 1. Terrorism 2. Suicide bombers
 ISBN   978-0-7377-4448-4;   0-7377-4448-0; 978-0-7377-4449-1 (pa); 0-7377-4449-9 (pa)
          LC 2009028941
Essays in this anthology discuss the religious, social, and political motivations behind suicide bombings.
Includes bibliographical references

363.33   Control of explosives and firearms

Atkin, S. Beth
 Gunstories; life-changing experiences with guns; interviews and photographs by S. Beth Atkin. HarperCollins Publishers 2006 245p il $16.99; lib bdg $17.89 *
 Grades: 7 8 9 10 11 12   **363.33**
 1. Firearms
 ISBN 0-06-052659-9; 0-06-052660-2 (lib bdg)
          LC 2005-2076
The author "gathers testimonials addressing how guns are an integral part of teens' lives. Situated between oral testimonials, and figuratively placing an exclamation mark on the topic, are summaries of thirty-four school shootings occurring between 1995 and 2005." Voice Youth Advocates
"This book should be useful for students involved in the debate about guns in our culture as well as for those with a general interest in the subject." SLJ

Henderson, Harry, 1951-
 Gun control. rev ed. Facts on File 2005 316p il (Library in a book) $45
 Grades: 11 12 Adult   **363.33**
 1. Gun control
 ISBN 0-8160-5660-9   LC 2004-50651
 First published 2000
This examination of the history and issues of gun control "includes an annotated bibliography, chronology, glossary, biographical listing, a chapter on how to research the topic, laws and court cases, and a list of applicable organizations and agencies." Publisher's note

363.34   Disasters

Are natural disasters increasing? Stefan Kiesbye, book editor. Greenhaven Press 2010 135p (At issue. Disasters) $31.80; pa $22.50
 Grades: 7 8 9 10   **363.34**
 1. Natural disasters
 ISBN 978-0-7377-4665-5; 978-0-7377-4666-2 (pa)
          LC 2009-42506
"This book includes a good selection of viewpoints on weather-related natural disasters, their frequency, and whether or not they are primarily caused by global warming or poor human planning. . . . The concepts are clearly laid out by well-respected professionals in the field, and the arguments are all supported with data." SLJ
Includes bibliographical references

Campbell, Ballard C., 1940-
 Disasters, accidents, and crises in American history; a reference guide to the nation's most catastrophic events. Facts On File 2008 461p il map (Facts on File library of American history) $95
 Grades: 11 12 Adult   **363.34**
 1. Reference books 2. Disasters 3. Accidents
 ISBN 978-0-8160-6603-2; 0-8160-6603-5
          LC 2007-27688
"Chronicling approximately 200 of the nation's worst catastrophes, chosen for their 'immense impact on American civilization,' this useful volume ranges chronologically from Columbus's first voyage through Hurricane Katrina. . . . The articles are informative and clear." SLJ
Includes bibliographical references

Hurricane Katrina; Diane Andrews Henningfeld, book editor. Greenhaven Press 2010 146p (At issue. Disasters) $31.80; pa $22.50
 Grades: 9 10 11 12   **363.34**
 1. Hurricane Katrina, 2005 2. Disaster relief 3. Rescue work
 ISBN 978-0-7377-4882-6; 978-0-7377-4883-3 (pa)
          LC 2010-3359
"This title looks at myriad topics related to the catastrophe and its aftermath. It follows the series format of offering reprinted articles that present positive and negative views. Researchers will be interested in some of the discussions, such as the effects of global warming on future storms, the need to restore wetlands, and the response of FEMA (Federal Emergency Management Agency) to help victims." SLJ
Includes bibliographical references

Katrina: state of emergency; introduction by Ivor van Heerden. Andrews McMeel Pub. 2005 176p il pa $19.95
 Grades: 11 12 Adult   **363.34**
 1. Hurricane Katrina, 2005 2. Disaster relief
 ISBN 0-7407-5844-6; 978-0-7407-5844-7
          LC 2005-935404
At head of title: CNN reports

Katrina: state of emergency—*Continued*

This book "provides a chronological account of the hurricane through a selection of CNN transcripts and photos documenting all facets of the disaster starting from past studies predicting such a tragedy to the path of the hurricane to the consequences surrounding the flooding and delayed rescue efforts." Publisher's note

Robson, David, 1966-

Disaster response. ReferencePoint Press 2009 96p il map (Compact research. Current issues) lib bdg $25.95

Grades: 7 8 9 10   **363.34**
1. Disaster relief
ISBN 978-1-60152-081-4; 1-60152-081-6
LC 2009-2283

"Robson covers disasters ranging from manmade to weather-related and bioterrorism. . . . Hurricane Katrina is discussed in the overview and leads into chapters that question the ability of the United States to handle natural disasters and how it can be improved. . . . Colorful graphs and up-to-date statistics are included. [This title] would be [a] great [addition] for students needing print materials to help with research projects, and for those who require some kind of first-person account included in their research." SLJ

Includes bibliographical references

363.4 Controversies related to public morals and customs

Haugen, David, 1969-

Legalized gambling; [by] David M. Haugen. Facts on File 2006 298p (Library in a book) $45

Grades: 11 12 Adult   **363.4**
1. Gambling
ISBN 0-8160-6054-1   LC 2005-8916

Contents: Introduction to legalized gambling; The law and legalized gambling; Chronology; Biographical listing; Glossary; How to research legalized gambling issues; Annotated bibliography; Organizations and agencies

This is "an excellent introduction and overview of legalized gambling in the United States." Choice

Includes bibliographical references

Hill, Jeff, 1962-

Prohibition. Omnigraphics 2004 xxv, 201p il (Defining moments) $38 *

Grades: 7 8 9 10   **363.4**
1. Prohibition
ISBN 0-7808-0768-5   LC 2004-22643

This book provides an "historical analysis of the Prohibition era (1920-33), including the politics of the Eighteenth Amendment; the Mob wars; the roles played by important public figures, from mobster Al Capone to Prohibition activist Carry Nation to President Warren Harding; and much more. . . . With a detailed glossary, a chronology, and an annotated bibliography, this is an important curriculum resource on the social and political history of an era." Booklist

Includes glossary and bibliographical references

Nathan, Debbie

Pornography. Groundwood Books 2007 144p (Groundwork guides) $15.95

Grades: 10 11 12   **363.4**
1. Pornography
ISBN 0-88899-766-3; 978-0-88899-766-1

This "title examines the controversial, multifaceted topic of pornography and its entry into modern culture, including the instantaneous and unrestricted availability of sexually explicit material on the Internet. . . . [This is] a provocative starting point for further research in media studies, censorship, and human sexuality." Booklist

Includes bibliographical references

Online pornography: opposing viewpoints; Emma Carlson Berne, book editor. Greenhaven Press 2007 229p il lib bdg $36.20; pa $24.95 *

Grades: 9 10 11 12   **363.4**
1. Pornography 2. Internet—Law and legislation
ISBN 978-0-7377-3657-1 (lib bdg); 0-7377-3657-7 (lib bdg); 978-0-7377-3658-8 (pa); 0-7377-3658-5 (pa)
LC 2007-10677

"Opposing viewpoints series"

"The articles here are organized to address the questions: 'Is online pornography harmful to society?,' 'Is online pornography a form of free speech?,' 'Should children be protected from online pornography?,' and 'Should limits be placed on online pornography?' Some of the arguments include whether or not pornography is a growing moral problem, whether or not it is addictive, [and] whether or not online laws should be the same as other pornography laws. . . . This is an excellent addition for middle and high school libraries." SLJ

Includes bibliographical references

363.45 Drug traffic

Drug legalization; Noël Merino, book editor. Greenhaven Press 2010 204p (Current controversies) $39.70; pa $27.50

Grades: 8 9 10 11 12   **363.45**
1. Drugs—Law and legislation
ISBN 978-0-7377-5097-3; 978-0-7377-5098-0 (pa)
LC 2010-19299

"Contributors explore the political, social, and medical dilemma of liberalization and legalization of recreational drugs such as marijuana. Domestic and international prohibition, the war on drugs, and mandatory sentencing are all examined." Publisher's note

Includes bibliographical references

Drug trafficking; Julia Bauder, book editor. Thomson/Gale 2008 258p (Current controversies) lib bdg $37.40; pa $25.95

Grades: 7 8 9 10 11 12   **363.45**
1. Drug traffic
ISBN 978-0-7377-3281-8 (lib bdg); 0-7377-3281-4 (lib bdg); 978-0-7377-3282-5 (pa); 0-7377-3282-2 (pa)
LC 2007-937459

An anthology of essays discussing topics such as whether or not drug trafficking can be stopped, if efforts to curb drug trafficking are harming the United States, and the effects of the War on Drugs on Latin America.

Includes bibliographical references

Parks, Peggy J., 1951-
Drug legalization. ReferencePoint Press 2009 112p il (Compact research. Current issues) lib bdg $25.95
Grades: 9 10 11 12   **363.45**
1. Drugs—Law and legislation 2. Drug abuse
ISBN 978-1-60152-012-8; 1-60152-012-3
LC 2007-16582
"This book looks at marijuana [legalization], but also includes information regarding the legalization of a variety of other controlled substances. . . . Chapters begin by posing questions such as, 'Would legalizing drugs decrease crime?' or 'Would legalizing drugs increase drug addiction?' The book provides different opinions, documented facts, and primary-source quotes to guide readers in forming and articulating their own responses. . . . Useful for persuasive writing and speaking assignments." SLJ
Includes bibliographical references

Sherman, Jill, 1982-
Drug trafficking. ABDO Pub. Co. 2010 112p il (Essential issues) lib bdg $22.95
Grades: 7 8 9 10   **363.45**
1. Drug traffic 2. Drug abuse
ISBN 978-1-60453-953-0; 1-60453-953-4
LC 2009-29935
"Drug farmers, producers, smugglers, dealers, and users are discussed . . . as well as law enforcement against the illegal drug trade." Publisher's note
This is "well-written, providing examples that put a human face to each problem. Quotes and facts are clearly attributed, and their sources are noted in the extensive back matter. . . . [This] will be of great assistance to students writing reports." SLJ
Includes glossary and bibliographical references

363.46   Abortion

Abortion: opposing viewpoints; David Haugen, Susan Musser, and Kacy Lovelace, book editors. Greenhaven Press 2010 206p lib bdg $39.70; pa $27.50 *
Grades: 8 9 10 11 12   **363.46**
1. Abortion
ISBN 978-0-7377-4747-8 (lib bdg); 0-7377-4747-1 (lib bdg); 978-0-7377-4748-5 (pa); 0-7377-4748-X (pa)
LC 2009-41649
"Opposing viewpoints series"
Provides opposing viewpoints on the topic of abortion.
Includes bibliographical references

Abortion wars; a half century of struggle, 1950-2000; edited by Rickie Solinger. University of Calif. Press 1998 413p pa $21.95 hardcover o.p.
Grades: 11 12 Adult   **363.46**
1. Abortion
ISBN 0-520-20952-4 (pa)   LC 97-12261
"A collection of 18 essays written by abortion providers, journalists, reproductive-rights activists, legal strategists, and philosophers. In the introduction the editor

makes it clear that the book is 'unabashedly a pro-rights book.' . . . The time line alone is so valuable that it's practically worth the price of the book." SLJ

Herring, Mark Youngblood, 1952-
The pro-life/choice debate; [by] Mark Herring. Greenwood Press 2003 200p il (Historical guides to controversial issues in America) $49.95 *
Grades: 9 10 11 12   **363.46**
1. Abortion
ISBN 0-313-31710-0   LC 2002-32073
"Herring examines the [abortion] issue from the debate's origin to its current state and expected future. Narrative chapters include discussions of the pro and con arguments associated with abortion, featuring quotes from doctors, politicians, religious figures, and ordinary people." Publisher's note
The author's "discussion of the moral, medical, and legal developments leading up to the modern feminist movement is particularly informative in framing the historical context of current debate . . . Herring writes clearly and presents each side of the debate objectively." Libr J
Includes bibliographical references

McBride, Dorothy E.
Abortion in the United States; a reference handbook. ABC-CLIO 2008 303p (Contemporary world issues) $55
Grades: 9 10 11 12   **363.46**
1. Abortion 2. Pro-life movement 3. Pro-choice movement
ISBN 978-1-59884-098-8; 1-59884-098-3
LC 2007-25876
This is "presentation of the pro-life/pro-choice controversy, showing all aspects of the debate and why it is so difficult to resolve." Publisher's note
"This unbiased reference handbook clearly documents the historical background concerning abortion in the 19th century and beyond." Libr Media Connect
Includes bibliographical references

Naden, Corinne J.
Abortion. Marshall Cavendish Benchmark 2008 143p il (Open for debate) lib bdg $27.95
Grades: 7 8 9 10   **363.46**
1. Abortion
ISBN 978-0-7614-2573-1; 0-7614-2573-X
LC 2006-28525
This book about abortion "features chapters on the history of the debate, the politics surrounding the subject, rape and incest, and medical issues. . . . Many captioned color photos enhance the text." SLJ
Includes bibliographical references

Rose, Melody
Abortion; a documentary and reference guide. Greenwood Press 2008 258p il $85 *
Grades: 11 12 Adult   **363.46**
1. Abortion
ISBN 978-0-313-34032-1; 0-313-34032-3
LC 2007-37489

Rose, Melody—*Continued*
This "reference work explores the evolution of America's abortion debate in a . . . selection of over 40 primary documents by doctors, feminists, religious leaders, politicians, extremists, and judges from the 19th century to the present day." Publisher's note
Includes bibliographical references

363.6 Public utilities and related services

Balliett, James Fargo
Freshwater; environmental issues, global perspectives. M.E. Sharpe 2010 155p il map (Environmental issues, global perspectives) $55
Grades: 9 10 11 12   **363.6**
1. Freshwater ecology 2. Water supply
ISBN 978-0-7656-8230-7   LC 2010-12122
This book "tracks the complex history of the steady growth of humankind's water consumption. . . . The case studies in *Freshwater* look at the efforts to protect and transport water within systems such as New York City; examine how growth has affected freshwater quality in the Lake Baikal region of eastern Russia; and study the success story of the privatized freshwater system in Santiago, Chile, among other relevant issues." Publisher's note
Includes glossary and bibliographical references

Farabee, Charles R., Jr.
National park ranger; an American icon; {by} Charles R. "Butch" Farabee Jr. Roberts Rinehart Publishers 2003 180p il pa $18.95
Grades: 11 12 Adult   **363.6**
1. United States. National Park Service 2. National parks and reserves—United States
ISBN 1-570-98392-5   LC 2003-1022
"In this study of the vocation of park ranger since Maryland's park caretakers in 1696 to the present day, former ranger Farabee not only explores a ranger's role but also touches on the establishment of the National Park Service, the introduction of women rangers, and early resource management. Readers will enjoy the abundance of archival photographs, ranger profiles, and numerous other features." Libr J
Includes bibliographical references

Workman, James G.
Water. Morgan Reynolds Pub. 2009 c2010 111p il (Diminishing resources) lib bdg $28.95
Grades: 8 9 10 11 12   **363.6**
1. Water supply 2. Water conservation
ISBN 978-1-59935-115-5; 1-59935-115-3
LC 2009-28708
This discussion of world water supply and conservation "will draw activists, but even readers who do not think they care that much will find the facts devastating. Quotes from authoritative sources—environmentalists, scientists, and survivors—about both the historic overview and the contemporary crisis accompany full-color double-page photos that show what is happening

now. . . . The discussion ranges from the pros and cons of dams to the price of bottled water." Booklist
Includes bibliographical references

363.7 Environmental problems

Black, Brian, 1966-
Global warming; [by] Brian C. Black and Gary J. Weisel. Greenwood 2010 188p (Historical guides to controversial issues in America) $55
Grades: 9 10 11 12   **363.7**
1. Greenhouse effect 2. Environmental policy—United States
ISBN 978-0-313-34522-7; 978-0-313-34523-4 (ebook)
LC 2010-7137
Contact publisher for ebook pricing
"Black and Weisel discuss climate processes, Earth's geology, past climates and how scientists determine if the Earth is warming, modern industry and its impact on the environment, national and international responses to global warming, the Kyoto Protocol, and more. . . . Each of the six chapters begins with an overview and contains many quotes and references." SLJ
Includes bibliographical references

Braasch, Gary
Earth under fire; how global warming is changing the world. Updated ed. University of California Press 2009 xxx, 267p il pa $24.95
Grades: 11 12 Adult   **363.7**
1. Climate—Environmental aspects 2. Greenhouse effect
ISBN 978-0-520-26025-2
First published 2007
The author presents the "environmental changes resulting from the warming of our climate." Publisher's note
"What sets Earth Under Fire apart from other books on the same topic are the inspiring photographs. These images are an effective tool that helps the reader understand what the implications of climate change are—for people, for other organisms, and for entire ecosystems." Sci Books Films
Includes bibliographical references

Carson, Rachel, 1907-1964
Silent spring; introduction by Linda Lear; afterword by Edward O. Wilson. 40th anniversary ed. Houghton Mifflin 2002 378p il $24; pa $14 *
Grades: 11 12 Adult   **363.7**
1. Pesticides—Environmental aspects 2. Pesticides and wildlife
ISBN 0-618-25305-X; 0-618-24906-0 (pa)
"A Mariner book"
First published 1962
In The silent spring, Carson "contended that the indiscriminate use of weed killers and insecticides constituted a hazard to wildlife and to human beings. Her provocative work inspired many subsequent environmental studies." Reader's Ency. 4th edition

Casper, Julie Kerr

Fossil fuels and pollution; the future of air quality. Facts on File 2010 268p il map (Global warming) $40

Grades: 9 10 11 12   **363.7**

1. Pollution 2. Environmental protection

ISBN 978-0-8160-7265-1; 0-8160-7265-5

             LC 2009-12612

"In this valuable resource, detailed maps, charts, graphs, and sidebars offer useful data on subjects ranging from coal use and production to agriculture and from biofuels to green technology. The author includes an interesting history of technology and the concurrent rise of carbon-based fuels, documentation on current legislation, an outline of the future of emissions, and a discussion of recent public awareness of the effect of global dimming and its potential to mask the warming of the Earth." SLJ

Includes glossary and bibliographical references

Greenhouse gases; worldwide impacts. Facts on File 2010 270p il map (Global warming) $40

Grades: 9 10 11 12   **363.7**

1. Greenhouse effect

ISBN 978-0-8160-7264-4; 0-8160-7264-7

             LC 2009-4727

This book explores the "role these gases play and their global impact on populations and ecosystems worldwide. The goal of this book is to provide readers with an understanding of the various sources of these gases, their interaction with the atmosphere, their effect on natural systems, and why controlling them is critical to the Earth's future climate. Other issues discussed . . . include the role of the ozone and a newly discovered concept called 'global dimming' and how it relates to global warming." Publisher's note

Includes glossary and bibliographical references

Climate change; Arthur Gillard, book editor. Greenhaven Press 2011 116p il map (Issues that concern you) $35.75

Grades: 9 10 11 12   **363.7**

1. Climate—Environmental aspects 2. Greenhouse effect 3. Human influence on nature

ISBN 978-0-7377-5205-2   LC 2010-36735

Several articles discuss the issues surrounding climate change.

Includes bibliographical references

Conserving the environment; Debra A. Miller, book editor. Greenhaven Press 2010 211p (Current controversies) $39.70; pa $27.50

Grades: 8 9 10 11 12   **363.7**

1. Environmental protection 2. Greenhouse effect 3. Environmental movement

ISBN   978-0-7377-4661-7;   0-7377-4661-0; 978-0-7377-4662-4 (pa); 0-7377-4662-9 (pa)

             LC 2009-37782

"Explores the gravity of the global environmental problem with respect to climate, air pollution, overpopulation, water supply, and the health of the oceans. Examines the threat of global warming and the long-term impacts of biodiversity loss and extinction. Discusses potential steps to protect the environment, such as reducing emissions and supporting renewable energy sources, and the role of governments and markets in shaping a sus-

tainable global economy." Publisher's note

Includes bibliographical references

The **environment:** opposing viewpoints; Louise I. Gerdes, book editor. Greenhaven Press 2009 224p il $39.70; pa $27.50

Grades: 8 9 10 11 12   **363.7**

1. Environmental sciences

ISBN 978-0-7377-4362-3; 978-0-7377-4361-6 (pa)

             LC 2008-55846

"Opposing viewpoints series"

This collection of essays offers varying viewpoints on environmental pollution and protection.

Includes bibliographical references

Evans, Kate, 1972-

Weird weather; everything you didn't want to know about climate change but probably should find out; [with an introduction by George Monbiot] Groundwood Books 2007 95p il $15.95; pa $9.95

Grades: 8 9 10 11 12   **363.7**

1. Graphic novels 2. Greenhouse effect—Graphic novels 3. Climate—Environmental aspects—Graphic novels 4. Weather—Graphic novels

ISBN 978-0-88899-838-5; 978-0-88899-841-5 (pa)

First published 2006 in the United Kingdom with title: Funny weather

This book, in graphic novel format, presents "the history of global warming, likely outcomes of current pollution patterns, and what can be done if we hope to survive as a species. Cleverly, the narrative unfolds through the voices of three main characters: an outraged young idealist, a scientist fascinated by the challenges of the situation, and a greedy consumer who is only interested in himself. Accessible and entertaining, this book will be adored by science teachers. . . . Important reading for secondary students and adults." SLJ

Includes bibliographical references

Friedman, Thomas L.

Hot, flat, and crowded; why we need a green revolution—and how it can renew America. Farrar, Straus & Giroux 2008 438p il $27.95 *

Grades: 11 12 Adult   **363.7**

1. Environmental movement 2. Climate—Environmental aspects 3. Energy resources 4. Environmental policy—United States

ISBN 978-0-374-16685-4; 0-374-16685-4

             LC 2008-930589

The author calls for "the United States [to] . . . take the lead in a worldwide effort to replace our wasteful, inefficient energy practices with a strategy for clean energy, energy efficiency, and conservation." Publisher's note

"Friedman's big, passionate, and solidly specific ecological primer, social manifesto, and realistic plan for a green revolution aimed at restoring America's greatness and securing a sustainable future should serve as a playbook for innovators and civic leaders." Booklist

Garbage and recycling: opposing viewpoints; Mitchell Young, book editor. Greenhaven Press 2007 256p il map lib bdg $36.20; pa $24.95 *
Grades: 9 10 11 12   363.7
1. Refuse and refuse disposal 2. Recycling
ISBN 978-0-7377-3651-9 (lib bdg); 0-7377-3651-8 (lib bdg); 978-0-7377-3652-6 (pa); 0-7377-3652-6 (pa)
LC 2007-4374

"Opposing viewpoints series"
Contents: How do political and social systems affect garbage disposal; Is recycling environmentally and economically successful?; Do specific types of waste pose a threat?; Can new technologies solve waste problems?
An anthology of essays with opposing arguments on the topic of recycling and garbage disposal.
Includes bibliographical references

Gelletly, LeeAnne
Ecological issues. Mason Crest Publishers 2007 112p il map (Africa: progress & problems) $24.95
Grades: 9 10 11 12   363.7
1. Environmental degradation 2. Environmental policy—Africa
ISBN 978-1-59084-956-9; 1-59084-956-6
LC 2005-16306

"This book discusses the ecological issues facing Africa today, including deforestation and desertification, threats to the continent's biodiversity, pollution, and shortages of safe drinking water. It also explains steps some African leaders are taking to address and resolve these serious problems." Publisher's note
Includes bibliographical references

George, Rose, 1969-
The big necessity; the unmentionable world of human waste and why it matters. Metropolitan Books 2008 288p il $26
Grades: 11 12 Adult   363.7
1. Sanitation 2. Sewage disposal
ISBN 978-0-8050-8271-5; 0-8050-8271-9
LC 2008-29999

The author "breaks the embarrassed silence over the economic, political, social and environmental problems of human waste disposal. . . . From the depths of the world's oldest surviving urban sewers in to Japan's robo-toilet revolution, George leads an intrepid, erudite and entertaining journey through the public consequences of this most private behavior." Publ Wkly
Includes bibliographical references

Global warming: opposing viewpoints; David Haugen, Susan Musser, and Kacy Lovelace, book editors. Greenhaven Press 2010 249p il map $39.70; pa $27.50 *
Grades: 8 9 10 11 12   363.7
1. Greenhouse effect
ISBN 978-0-7377-4631-0; 0-7377-4631-9; 978-0-7377-4632-7 (pa); 0-7377-4632-7 (pa)
LC 2009-38723

"Opposing viewpoints series"
"Explores whether global warming is a real phenomenon or a myth, addressing possible causes like carbon dioxide, deforestation, melting permafrost, and livestock agriculture. Examines the effects of global warming on the polar ice caps, polar bears and human health, and discusses some proposed strategies to mitigate the impact." Publisher's note
Includes bibliographical references

Gore, Al, 1948-
An inconvenient truth; the planetary emergency of global warming and what we can do about it. Rodale 2006 325p il map pa $23.95 *
Grades: 11 12 Adult   363.7
1. Greenhouse effect 2. Environmental policy—United States 3. Environmental protection 4. Human ecology
ISBN 978-1-59486-567-1; 1-59486-567-1
LC 2006-926537

"Produced by Melcher Media" Verso of title page
This book "lays out the probable consequences of rising temperatures: powerful and more destructive hurricanes fueled by warmer ocean waters; . . . increased soil moisture evaporation, which means drier land, less productive agriculture and more fires; and melting ice sheets in Antarctica and Greenland, which would lead to rising ocean levels, which in turn would endanger low-lying regions of the world from southern Florida to large portions of the Netherlands." N Y Times (Late N Y Ed)
"Gore has put together a coherent account of a complex topic that Americans desperately need to understand. . . . By telling the story of climate change with striking clarity . . . Al Gore may have done for global warming what [Rachel Carson's] Silent Spring [1962] did for pesticides." N Y Rev Books

Our choice; how we can solve the climate crisis; [text adapted by Richie Chevat] Young readers ed. Puffin Books 2009 207p il map $24.99; pa $16.99
Grades: 6 7 8 9 10   363.7
1. Greenhouse effect 2. Environmental protection 3. Environmental policy 4. Human ecology
ISBN 978-0-670-01248-0; 0-670-01248-3; 978-0-14-240981-7 (pa); 0-14-240981-2 (pa)
LC 2010-455157

"This colorful, well-designed volume presents the climate crisis in an easy-to-understand format. Covering many aspects of this complex problem, it addresses the effects of pollution on the environment, the search for alternative energy sources, and offers suggestions for conserving power and reducing the impact of human habitation on the planet. . . . Although the urgency of the current global situation is stressed, the chapters are also laced with hope. Suggestions for change offer positive steps that anyone can take to reduce his carbon footprint, and extend a call to unite globally to save the planet for future generations." Voice Youth Advocates

Kallen, Stuart A., 1955-
Toxic waste. Referencepoint Press 2011 96p il map (Compact research. Energy and the environment) lib bdg $26.95
Grades: 9 10 11 12   363.7
1. Hazardous wastes
ISBN 978-1-60152-124-8; 1-60152-124-3
LC 2009-52242

Kallen, Stuart A., 1955-—*Continued*

This "book discusses the seriousness of toxic and electronic waste, the effectiveness of cleanup efforts, and future challenges. . . . Primary-source quotations; short narrative texts, followed by relevant quotations; a section with a bulleted list of one-sentence facts; pertinent illustrations; and annotated lists of key people, organizations, and advocacy groups are included." SLJ

Includes bibliographical references

Kolbert, Elizabeth

Field notes from a catastrophe; man, nature, and climate change. Bloomsbury Pub. 2006 210p il map hardcover o.p. pa $14.95 *

Grades: 11 12 Adult   363.7

1. Greenhouse effect 2. Climate

ISBN   1-59691-125-5;   978-1-59691-125-3; 1-59691-130-1 (pa); 978-1-59691-130-7 (pa)

LC 2005-30972

This investigation of global warming is an outgrowth of a three-part series (The Climate of Man) that appeared in The New Yorker in 2005. "The book is organized around notes Ms. Kolbert took on 'field trips,' not only to places where climate change is affecting the natural world but also to ones—labs, offices, observatories— where humans are trying to understand the phenomenon of human-induced global warming." N Y Times (Late NY Ed)

"On the burgeoning shelf of cautionary but occasionally alarmist books warning about the consequences of dramatic climate change, Kolbert's calmly persuasive reporting stands out for its sobering clarity." Publ Wkly

Includes bibliographical references

Lynas, Mark, 1973-

High tide; the truth about our climate crisis. Picador 2004 xxxiii, 345p il map pa $14

Grades: 11 12 Adult   363.7

1. Greenhouse effect

ISBN 0-312-30365-3   LC 2004-44661

"In a series of . . . travel narratives, Lynas shows the human side of global warming, taking readers to Britain, North and South America, China, and the South Pacific. He introduces them to folks whose houses and roads are falling crazily through melting permafrost, who are going hungry because fishing lakes have disappeared, and who are becoming refugees because their grasslands have turned to desert. . . . The author clearly explains why these are not isolated incidents, but interrelated parts of a worldwide set of phenomena that soon will affect us all." SLJ

Includes bibliographical references

Macgillivray, Alex

Understanding Rachel Carson's Silent Spring. Rosen Pub. 2011 128p il (Words that changed the world) lib bdg $31.95

Grades: 7 8 9 10   363.7

1. Carson, Rachel, 1907-1964 2. Pesticides—Environmental aspects 3. Pesticides and wildlife 4. Insect pests

ISBN 978-1-4488-1670-5; 1-4488-1670-X

LC 2010-9260

"This focused title examines Rachel Carson's *Silent Spring,* zeroing in on the content and enduring impact of the watershed 1962 work. . . . The text begins with a brief introduction to Carson and her times before moving into an analysis of the text and its indictment of pesticide use, . . . the immediate postpublication response, and its hugely influential legacy today. . . . A useful supplement to environmental-science units, this will easily support student research." Booklist

Includes glossary and bibliographical references

McClelland, Carol L., 1960-

Green careers for dummies; [by] Carol McClelland. John Wiley 2010 340p pa $19.99

Grades: 9 10 11 12 Adult   363.7

1. Environmental sciences—Vocational guidance

ISBN 978-0-470-52960-7   LC 2009-941922

The author "has delivered an excellent volume for anyone interested in a career in the green economy. Whether just starting out or looking for a midlife change, readers will find extremely useful McClelland's descriptions of the development of the green economy, her details on different types of careers available, and her technical advice on using the latest methods for finding green jobs, writing résumés, and doing well in the interview process. She also provides plenty of ideas for further information. . . . An essential resource for anyone looking to take advantage of career opportunities in the green economy, at the right price and easy to use." Libr J

McKibben, Bill

Fight global warming now; the handbook for taking action in your community; [by] Bill McKibben and the Step It Up Team, Phil Aroneanu . . . [et al.] Henry Holt 2007 202p il $13 *

Grades: 11 12 Adult   363.7

1. Environmental movement 2. Greenhouse effect 3. Social action

ISBN 978-0-8050-8704-8; 0-8050-8704-4

LC 2007-25492

"A Holt paperback"

The authors tell the "Step It Up creation story and offer a lively, convincing how-to for revitalizing social-change movements. A set of commonsensical and shrewd organizing principles and a realistic list of priorities are supported by detailed advice and examples, and all are wreathed with clearly stated information about global warming." Booklist

Includes bibliographical references

Miller, Debra A.

Garbage and recycling. Lucent Books 2009 112p il map (Hot topics) $32.45 *

Grades: 7 8 9 10   363.7

1. Refuse and refuse disposal 2. Recycling

ISBN 978-1-4205-0147-6; 1-4205-0147-X

LC 2009-18371

This is a "standout survey of what happens to what we throw away and how those decisions affect the globe. . . . This overview offers a balance of viewpoints in its clear comparison of traditional methods of waste man-

Miller, Debra A.—*Continued*
agement with more sustainable technologies, such as recycling and new landfill techniques. . . . [Sidebars] make for compelling reading, while numerous color photos, charts, and maps will further attract readers' attention." Booklist
Includes bibliographical references

Mooney, Chris
Storm world; hurricanes, politics, and the battle over global warming. Harcourt 2007 392p il map $26
Grades: 11 12 Adult   **363.7**
1. Hurricanes 2. Greenhouse effect
ISBN 978-0-15-101287-9; 0-15-101287-3
LC 2007-09742
This book examines "whether the increasing ferocity of hurricanes is connected to global warming." Publisher's note
"This is certainly one of the most thought-provoking and accessible accounts of climate change to appear since Katrina." Booklist
Includes bibliographical references

Parks, Peggy J., 1951-
Coal power. ReferencePoint Press 2010 c2011 96p il (Compact research. Energy and the environment) $26.95
Grades: 8 9 10 11 12   **363.7**
1. Coal 2. Energy resources
ISBN 978-1-60152-107-1; 1-60152-107-3
LC 2009-40878
Contents: How dependent is the world on coal power?; Does coal burning threaten the environment?; What are the environmental effects of coal mining?; What is the future of coal power?
Includes bibliographical references

Petersen, Christine
Controlling Earth's pollutants. Marshall Cavendish Benchmark 2010 c2011 112p il (Environment at risk) lib bdg $39.93 *
Grades: 6 7 8 9 10   **363.7**
1. Pollution
ISBN 978-0-7614-4005-5; 0-7614-4005-4
LC 2008-30816
This book provides "information on pollution, the interrelationships of the natural world, environmental problems both natural and man-made, the relative risks associated with these problems, and solutions for resolving and/or preventing them." Publisher's note
Includes bibliographical references

Pielke, Roger A. 1, 1968-
The climate fix; what scientists and politicians won't tell you about global warming; [by] Roger Pielke, Jr. Basic Books 2010 276p il $26
Grades: 11 12 Adult   **363.7**
1. Greenhouse effect 2. Climate—Environmental aspects
ISBN 978-0-465-02052-2   LC 2010-21776

The author asks "why has the world been unable to address global warming . . . [and contends that it is] not the fault of those who reject the Kyoto Protocol, but those who support it, and the magical thinking that the agreement represents. . . . Pielke offers a way to repair climate policy and shift the debate away from meaningless targets and toward a revolution in how the world's economy is powered." Publisher's note
"An excellent primer for getting past the politically charged debate clouding the issues. Recommended for readers confused by the deluge of conflicting climate information and willing to revisit the quandary and make their own assessments." Libr J
Includes bibliographical references

Pollution: opposing viewpoints; Louise I. Gerdes, book editor. Greenhaven Press 2011 262p il lib bdg $39.70; pa $26.50 *
Grades: 8 9 10 11 12   **363.7**
1. Pollution
ISBN 978-0-7377-5231-1 (lib bdg); 0-7377-5231-9 (lib bdg); 978-0-7377-5232-8 (pa); 978-0-7377-5232-7 (pa)
LC 2010-51681
"Opposing viewpoints series"
"The authors in this . . . anthology debate several controversial questions, including whether various forms of pollution continue to be a serious problem, whether pollution poses a public health threat, and what policies and programs will best reduce pollution." Publisher's note
Includes bibliographical references

Walker, Gabrielle
The hot topic; what we can do about global warming; [by] Gabrielle Walker and Sir David King. Harcourt 2008 276p il map pa $14 *
Grades: 11 12 Adult   **363.7**
1. Greenhouse effect
ISBN 978-0-15-603318-3   LC 2007-45080
"A Harvest original"
The authors "explain how fossil fuels produce carbon dioxide, show how global warming is affecting individual species and changing entire ecosystems, predict how much more climate change we can afford before things become truly catastrophic, and consider economic and political solutions to the problem." Publ Wkly
"This is the best overview of global warming that this reviewer has read. . . . What is most valuable about this book is that the text clearly explains to lay readers a very complex and highly controversial topic." Libr J
Includes bibliographical references

Wyman, Bruce C.
The Facts on File dictionary of environmental science; [by] Bruce Wyman, L. Harold Stevenson. 3rd ed. Facts on File 2007 498p il (Facts on File science library) $49.50
Grades: 11 12 Adult   **363.7**
1. Reference books 2. Environmental sciences—Dictionaries
ISBN 0-8160-6437-7; 978-0-8160-6437-3
LC 2006-45697
First published 1991 with authors names in reverse order

Wyman, Bruce C.—*Continued*

This dictionary contains over 5,000 cross-referenced entries reflecting the diversity of subjects that are relevant to the environmental field.

363.8   Food supply

Food; Jan Grover, book editor. Greenhaven Press 2008 220p (Current controversies) lib bdg $37.40; pa $25.95

Grades: 7 8 9 10 11 12   **363.8**

1. Diet 2. Nutrition

ISBN 978-0-7377-3793-6 (lib bdg); 0-7377-3793-X (lib bdg); 978-0-7377-3794-3 (pa); 0-7377-3794-8 (pa)
LC 2007-39167

An anthology of essays offering different viewpoints on topics including nutrition, the safety of the food supply, childhood obesity's link to fast food and snack foods, and organic foods.

Includes bibliographical references

363.9   Population problems

Birth control: opposing viewpoints; Beth Rosenthal, book editor. Greenhaven Press 2009 221p lib bdg $37.40; pa $25.95

Grades: 7 8 9 10 11 12   **363.9**

1. Birth control

ISBN   978-0-7377-4194-0   (lib   bdg); 978-0-7377-4195-7 (pa)   LC 2008-26069

"Opposing viewpoints series"

An anthology of essays featuring opposing views on the topic of birth control. "The chapters in *Birth Control* . . . move from broad inquiries ('How does birth control affect society?') to specific topics: should the government fund sex education?" Booklist

Includes bibliographical references

364   Criminology

Crime and criminals: opposing viewpoints; Christina Fisanick, book editor. Greenhaven Press 2009 253p il lib bdg $39.70; pa $27.50 *

Grades: 9 10 11 12   **364**

1. Crime 2. Criminals 3. Administration of criminal justice

ISBN   978-0-7377-4360-9   (lib   bdg); 978-0-7377-4359-3 (pa)   LC 2009-21918

"Opposing viewpoints series"

Articles in this anthology cover issues regarding crime and punishment in America, including prisoners' rights, what can be done to deter crime, and rehabilitation of prisoners.

Includes bibliographical references

Famous American crimes and trials; edited by Frankie Y. Bailey and Steven Chermak. Praeger 2004 5v il (Praeger perspectives) set $375

Grades: 11 12 Adult   **364**

1. Administration of criminal justice

ISBN 0-275-98333-1   LC 2004-50548

This set "examines 70 cases, beginning in 1607 with the trial of accused heretic Quaker Mary Dyer and ending with the 2001 execution of convicted Oklahoma City bomber Timothy McVeigh. . . . This work has definite multidisciplinary appeal." Choice

Includes bibliographical references

Hanes, Sharon M.

Crime and punishment in America, Primary sources; Sarah Hermsen, project editor. UXL 2005 232, lxip il (Crime and punishment in America reference library) $60 *

Grades: 9 10 11 12   **364**

1. Crime—United States 2. Administration of criminal justice

ISBN 0-7876-9168-2   LC 2004-17068

This book "has excerpts from 18 interviews and documents. . . . Examples include the Magna Carta, 'The Plea of Clarence Darrow,' the RICO Act, and 'The Al-Qaeda Training Manual.' In addition to the excerpts, entries are supplemented by helpful material such as definitions of words used." Booklist

Includes bibliographical references

Wolcott, David B.

Crime and punishment in America; [by] David B. Wolcott and Tom Head. Facts on File 2010 417p il map (American experience) $85; pa $21.95

Grades: 11 12 Adult   **364**

1. Crime—United States 2. Administration of criminal justice 3. Punishment 4. Reference books

ISBN 978-0-8160-6247-8; 978-0-8160-7897-4 (pa)
LC 2008-13372

This is a "fascinating glimpse into the history and development of the American criminal justice system and the social contexts that contributed to its evolution from 1500 to now. . . . The chronologically arranged chapters include narrative text describing the crimes and punishments of the period followed by a two to three-page chronicle of events and selections from relevant primary documents." Libr J

Includes glossary and bibliographical references

364.1   Criminal offenses

Altschiller, Donald

Hate crimes; a reference handbook. 2nd ed. ABC-CLIO 2005 247p (Contemporary world issues) $50

Grades: 9 10 11 12   **364.1**

1. Hate crimes

ISBN 1-85109-624-8   LC 2005-7151

First published 1999

This book "covers the alarming increase in hate crimes in the United States and abroad, and the legal, political, and educational efforts to combat intolerance and violence against minority group members." Publisher's note

Includes bibliographical references

Bugliosi, Vincent

Helter skelter; the true story of the Manson murders; {by} Vincent Bugliosi with Curt Gentry. 25th anniversary ed. Norton 1994 528p il $25; pa $13.95

Grades: 11 12 Adult   364.1
    1. Manson, Charles, 1934- 2. Homicide
    ISBN 0-393-08700-X; 0-393-32223-8 (pa)
                         LC 94-20957

    A reissue of the title published 1974
    "This book by the prosecutor at the Tate-LaBianca murder trial tells the inside story of the Manson Family murders, the investigations, and the trial." Libr J

Capote, Truman, 1924-1984

In cold blood; a true account of a multiple murder and its consequences. Random House 2002 343p $22; pa $13

Grades: 11 12 Adult   364.1
    1. Hickock, Richard, 1931-1965 2. Smith, Perry, 1928-1965 3. Homicide
    ISBN 0-375-50790-6; 0-679-74558-0 (pa)
                       LC 2002-282920

    A reissue of the title first published 1966
    "This edition is set from the first American edition of 1966 and commemorates the seventy-fifth anniversary of Random House"—Jacket
    "Truman Capote called his account of the 1959 murder of a Kansas farm family a nonfiction novel. Using information he collected through interviews with townspeople and the killers, Capote created a vivid portrait of the criminals and graphically described the crime, the criminals' escape to Mexico, capture, trial, appeals, and hanging." HarperCollins Reader's Ency of Am Lit. 2nd edition

Dolnick, Edward, 1952-

The rescue artist; a true story of art, thieves, and the hunt for a missing masterpiece. HarperCollins Publishers 2005 270p il $25.95; pa $14.95

Grades: 11 12 Adult   364.1
    1. Munch, Edvard, 1863-1944 2. Art thefts
    ISBN 0-06-053117-7; 978-0-06-053117-1; 0-06-053118-5 (pa); 978-0-06053118-8 (pa)
                      LC 2004-62060

    This is an "account of the 1994 theft of one of the world's most famous paintings, The Scream. . . . This is a tightly woven, fast-paced story." SLJ
    Includes bibliographical references

Gangs; Scott Barbour, book editor. Greenhaven Press 2006 128p il map (Introducing issues with opposing viewpoints) $32.45

Grades: 8 9 10 11 12   364.1
    1. Gangs
    ISBN 0-7377-3221-0   LC 2005-40395

    "In such chapters as, How Can Gang Violence Be Reduced? the issue is presented viewpoint by viewpoint, with an introduction and the author's credentials provided for each essay. Thought-provoking queries are given. . . . Fast Facts are also included. The book is heavily illustrated with color photos, cartoons, and tables. This informative book encourages active reading and makes research accessible for less-able students who are learning critical reading and research skills. A top resource for every library." SLJ

Gangs: opposing viewpoints; Adela Soliz, book editor. Greenhaven Press 2009 213p il $39.70; pa $27.50 *

Grades: 8 9 10 11 12   364.1
    1. Gangs
    ISBN   978-0-7377-4366-1;   0-7377-4366-2; 978-0-7377-4365-4 (pa); 0-7377-4365-4 (pa)
                      LC 2009-10705

    "Opposing viewpoints series"
    A compendium of viewpoints—both pro and con—on several issues relating to the prevalence of gangs in American society.
    Includes bibliographical references

Geary, Rick, 1946-

The Lindbergh child; America's hero and the crime of the century; written and illustrated by Rick Geary. NBM/ComicsLit 2008 unp il map (Treasury of XXth century murder) pa $15.95

Grades: 8 9 10 11 12 Adult   364.1
    1. Lindbergh, Charles, 1902-1974—Graphic novels 2. Graphic novels 3. Kidnapping—Graphic novels 4. Mystery graphic novels 5. Homicide—Graphic novels
    ISBN 978-1-56163-529-0

    Charles Lindbergh was an American hero following his solo crossing of the Atlantic in an airplane. He married into a wealthy family, he and his wife had a baby, they were building their dream home. Then, one night, the baby was abducted from the house. Geary's account retraces all the highly publicized events, ransom notes (false and otherwise), as well as the string of colorful characters who all claimed they could help but instead snookered the Lindberghs. While Bruno Hauptmann was arrested, tried, convicted, and executed, there remain many questions about what really happened. Geary brings them up for readers to consider.
    "A good example of the origins of modern forensics, crime-scene investigation, and celebrity hysteria, this work is an excellent choice for most collections." SLJ

Hanel, Rachael

Identity theft. Marshall Cavendish Benchmark 2011 143p il (Controversy!) lib bdg $25.95

Grades: 8 9 10 11 12   364.1
    1. Identity theft
    ISBN 978-0-7614-4901-0; 0-7614-4901-9

    "Hanel explores types of identity theft, common scams, and prevention, which is a contentious point. Many argue that governmental proposals to secure data are invading people's privacy and civil liberties. . . . With rapid changes in technology and legislation, [this book is] recommended for all libraries seeking quality and current materials on [this topic]." SLJ

Hate crimes; Jennifer Bussey, book editor. Greenhaven Press 2007 237p (The history of issues) lib bdg $37.40

Grades: 9 10 11 12　　　　　　　　**364.1**
1. Hate crimes
ISBN 978-0-7377-2869-9; 0-7377-2869-8
　　　　　　　　　　　　　　　LC 2007-40010

An anthology of essays presenting the history of hate crimes. Topics discussed include hate groups and hate crime legislation.

Includes bibliographical references

Jacobs, Thomas A.

Teen cyberbullying investigated; where do your rights end and consequences begin? Free Spirit Pub. 2010 195p il pa $15.99 *

Grades: 7 8 9 10 11 12　　　　　　**364.1**
1. Bullies 2. Computer crimes
ISBN 978-1-57542-339-5; 1-57542-339-1
　　　　　　　　　　　　　　　LC 2009-43293

This title deals with the "topic of online teen harassment, by both teens and by adults. The author, a former judge, focuses on recent landmark court cases, many of them still pending, and in an informal, interactive style, each chapter discusses one case in detail, bringing together the rights of the victim as well as those of the perpetrator." Booklist

Includes glossary and bibliographical references

Marcovitz, Hal

Gangs. ABDO Pub. Co. 2010 112p il (Essential issues) lib bdg $22.95

Grades: 7 8 9 10　　　　　　　　**364.1**
1. Gangs
ISBN 978-1-60453-954-7; 1-60453-954-2
　　　　　　　　　　　　　　　LC 2009-29862

"Early U.S. gangs, such as the Mafia, are discussed, as well as the formation of large gangs throughout the country, in both urban and rural areas." Publisher's note

The text is "well-written, providing examples that put a human face to each problem. . . . [This] will be of great assistance to students writing reports." SLJ

Includes glossary and bibliographical references

Naimark, Norman M.

Fires of hatred; ethnic cleansing in twentieth-century Europe. Harvard Univ. Press 2001 248p hardcover o.p. pa $18.50 *

Grades: 11 12 Adult　　　　　　**364.1**
1. Genocide 2. Atrocities 3. Ethnic relations 4. Europe—History—20th century
ISBN 0-674-00313-6; 0-674-00994-0 (pa)
　　　　　　　　　　　　　　　LC 00-57500

This "comparative work explores five examples of the brutal separation or elimination of people from territory in central Europe since WWI, illuminating common patterns of 'ethnic cleansing' as a modern phenomenon. In these case studies—Armenians and Greeks in Turkey, Nazis and Jews, Soviet deportations of Chechens/Ingush and Crimean Tatars, expulsions of Germans from Czechoslovakia and Poland, and contemporary Balkan warfare." Choice

Includes bibliographical references

President Kennedy has been shot; by the Newseum with Cathy Trost and Susan Bennett. Sourcebooks 2003 300p il $29.95; pa $19.95 *

Grades: 11 12 Adult　　　　　　**364.1**
ISBN 1-4022-0158-3; 1-4022-0317-9 (pa)
　　　　　　　　　　　　　　　LC 2003-15512

Accompanied by Audio CD

This is a "multimedia reliving of Kennedy's assassination, beginning with Air Force One landing at Love Field and ending with the president's internment at Arlington National Cemetery. The commentaries from some of the nation's foremost journalists, including Mike Wallace, Dan Rather, and Walter Cronkite, have a clarity, drama, and intensity that only newsmen of their stature can provide. . . . The book-CD combination is so well done that many readers will feel as if they have experienced that fateful day." SLJ

Includes bibliographical references

Sexual violence: opposing viewpoints; Louise I. Gerdes, book editor. Greenhaven Press 2008 193p il map lib bdg $38.50; pa $26.75

Grades: 9 10 11 12　　　　　　　　**364.1**
1. Sex crimes 2. Rape 3. Violence
ISBN　　978-0-7377-4010-3　　(lib　bdg);
978-0-7377-4011-0 (pa)　　　　LC 2008-8133

"Opposing viewpoints series"

First published 1997

The articles in this anthology address such topics as rape, sexual predators, pornography, and possible ways to reduce sexual violence.

Includes bibliographical references

Swift, Richard

Gangs. Groundwood 2011 144p (Groundwork guides) $18.95; pa $11

Grades: 7 8 9 10 11 12　　　　　　**364.1**
1. Gangs
ISBN　　978-0-88899-979-5;　　0-88899-979-8;
978-0-88899-978-8 (pa); 0-88899-978-X (pa)

"This riveting volume, which is both comprehensive and concise, explores a complex and potentially controversial issue. Swift frames the issue against the gross social inequities that create gangs and discusses the factors that contribute to their existence, such as racism, poverty, drug use and trafficking, lack of jobs, crumbling global economies, etc. . . . Despite its conveniently compact size, the book is packed with information. . . . This interesting and accessible volume is an essential purchase." SLJ

364.152　Homicide

Alphin, Elaine Marie

An unspeakable crime; the prosecution and persecution of Leo Frank. Carolrhoda Books 2010 152p il lib bdg $22.95

Grades: 9 10 11 12　　　　　　**364.152**
1. Phagan, Mary 2. Frank, Leo 3. Trials (Homicide) 4. Lynching 5. Atlanta (Ga.)
ISBN 978-0-8225-8944-0; 0-8225-8944-3
　　　　　　　　　　　　　　　LC 2008-42300

Alphin, Elaine Marie—_Continued_

"A Junior Library Guild selection"

"This detailed, fully documented account tells of the trial and lynching of a Jewish factory superintendent, falsely accused of the 1913 rape and murder of teenager Mary Phagan in Atlanta. Alphin digs into the roots of anti-Semitism that grew from post-Reconstruction hardship and shows that Leo Frank was viewed, and despised, by many in his community as a 'privileged Yankee Jew.' . . . The details are made even more horrific when accompanied by the numerous black-and-white photos, including court scenes and a picture postcard of the lynching." Booklist

Includes glossary and bibliographical references

Aretha, David

The murder of Emmett Till. Morgan Reynolds Pub. 2007 160p il (The civil rights movement) lib bdg $27.95

Grades: 7 8 9 10 11 12   **364.152**

1. Till, Emmett, 1941-1955 2. Lynching 3. African Americans—Civil rights 4. Mississippi—Race relations

ISBN 978-1-59935-057-8; 1-59935-057-2

LC 2007-26250

"The heinous murder of Emmett Till galvanized the civil rights movement and raised the nation's awareness of the extreme racism in the South. . . . This title . . . details the events surrounding Till's murder, the trial and acquittal of his killers, and the nation's racial climate before and after this milestone in civil rights history." Booklist

Includes bibliographical references

Crowe, Chris

Getting away with murder: the true story of the Emmett Till case. Phyllis Fogelman Bks. 2003 128p il map $18.99

Grades: 7 8 9 10   **364.152**

1. Till, Emmett, 1941-1955 2. Lynching 3. Racism 4. Trials (Homicide) 5. Mississippi—Race relations

ISBN 0-8037-2804-2   LC 2002-5736

This is the story of "the black 14-year-old from Chicago who was brutally murdered while visiting relatives in the Mississippi Delta in 1954. . . . The gruesome, racially motivated crime and the court's failure to convict the white murderers was a powerful national catalyst for the civil rights movement. . . . Crowe's powerful, terrifying account does justice to its subject in bold, direct telling, supported by numerous archival photos and quotes from those who remember." Booklist

Includes bibliographical references

Cullen, Dave, 1961-

Columbine. Twelve 2009 417p $26.99 *

Grades: 10 11 12 Adult   **364.152**

1. Columbine High School (Littleton, Colo.) 2. School shootings

ISBN 978-0-446-54693-5; 0-446-54693-3

LC 2008-31441

This is an account of the shootings at Columbine High School in 1999.

This book "is an excellent work of media criticism, showing how legends become truths through continual citation; a sensitive guide to the patterns of public grief . . . and, at the end of the day, a fine example of old-fashioned journalism." N Y Times Book Rev

Includes bibliographical references

Geary, Rick, 1946-

The saga of the bloody Benders; the infamous homicidal family of Labette County, Kansas. NBM/ComicsLit 2007 unp il $15.95

Grades: 9 10 11 12 Adult   **364.152**

1. Graphic novels 2. Mystery graphic novels 3. Homicide—Graphic novels

ISBN 978-1-56163-498-9

Part of the series, A Treasury of Victorian Murders

In Kansas, around the year 1870, the Bender family ran the Bender Inn and grocery store in Labette County, Kansas. Soon after they open their inn to travelers, people start to disappear, usually people with a fair amount of money with them. When the authorities investigate, the family disappears, and the people of Labette County make grisly discoveries in the Bender Inn's cellar. Geary includes just enough gory details for readers to comprehend the Benders' crimes. Earlier volumes in this series focused on famous nineteenth century murders and criminals, but the crimes of this more obscure family are just as dastardly for true crime aficionados.

The terrible Axe-Man of New Orleans; music and lyrics by Rick Geary. NBM Publishing/ComicsLit 2010 unp il map (Treasury of XXth century murder) $15.99

Grades: 9 10 11 12 Adult   **364.152**

1. Graphic novels 2. Mystery graphic novels 3. Homicide—Graphic novels 4. New Orleans (La.)—History—Graphic novels

ISBN 978-1-56163-581-8   LC 2010-926782

"Nights of terror! A city awash in blood!"

Geary tells the story of the Terrible Axe-Man, who murdered grocers in New Orleans right after World War I. In each case, the murderer removed a piece of the door to the house, borrowed an axe found at the property, then aimed straight for the head of his victim. From May 23, 1918 to October 27, 1919, the Axe-Man killed six people and badly wounded six more, then disappeared. Geary lays out the known facts, then shows some of the speculation. The black and white art helps to mitigate the violence and gore, so the book is suitable for teens who enjoy true-life mysteries.

"Geary's exacting, historically accurate approach makes this . . . a natural for true-crime fans as well as comics lovers." Booklist

Includes bibliographical references

364.2   Causes of crime and delinquency

Gun violence: opposing viewpoints; Louise I. Gerdes, book editor. Greenhaven Press 2010 257p il map $39.70; pa $27.50

Grades: 8 9 10 11 12   **364.2**

1. Firearms 2. Gun control 3. Violence

ISBN 978-0-7377-4966-3; 978-0-7377-4967-0 (pa)

LC 2010-26764

Gun violence: opposing viewpoints—*Continued*
"Opposing viewpoints series"
Articles in this anthology cover the issues surrounding gun violence, including gun control.
Includes bibliographical references

364.36   Juvenile delinquents

Juvenile crime; Noel Merino, book editor. Greenhaven Press 2010 146p il map (Introducing issues with opposing viewpoints) lib bdg $35.75
Grades: 7 8 9 10   **364.36**
1. Juvenile delinquency
ISBN 978-0-7377-4735-5; 0-7377-4735-8
LC 2009-48144
"Examines the causes of juvenile crime and school violence, including gang activity, single parenthood, bullying, and mental illness. Explores the treatment of juvenile offenders in the criminal justice system and the relative importance of rehabilitation and punishment in sentencing. Discusses what can and should be done to prevent crime and violence by children." Publisher's note
Includes bibliographical references

364.6   Penology

Banks, Cyndi
Punishment in America; a reference handbook. ABC-CLIO 2005 319p il (Contemporary world issues) $50 *
Grades: 9 10 11 12   **364.6**
1. Punishment 2. Administration of criminal justice
ISBN 1-85109-676-0   LC 2005-659
"From the Salem witch trials to death row, this work is . . . [an] analysis of the evolution of punishment practices, policies, and problems in America." Publisher's note
Includes bibliographical references

364.66   Capital punishment

The **Death** penalty; Jean Alicia Elster, book editor. Greenhaven Press 2005 237p (History of issues) lib bdg $34.95; pa $23.70
Grades: 9 10 11 12   **364.66**
1. Capital punishment—United States
ISBN 0-7377-1911-7 (lib bdg); 0-7377-1912-5 (pa)
LC 2004-43661
"This volume explores the history of capital punishment in America from the 17th century to the present while covering such . . . topics as cruel and unusual punishment, deterrence, race and gender discrimination, the morality of state-sanctioned killing, and protecting the innocent defendant." Publisher's note
Includes bibliographical references

The **death** penalty; Lauri S. Friedman, book editor. Greenhaven Press 2011 143p il map (Introducing issues with opposing viewpoints) $35.75
Grades: 7 8 9 10   **364.66**
1. Capital punishment—United States
ISBN 978-0-7377-4938-0   LC 2010-30748
"This collection of articles helps students hone in on the main arguments that are used to support and to condemn the death penalty." Publisher's note
Includes bibliographical references

The **death** penalty: opposing viewpoints; Diane Andrews Henningfeld, book editor; Bonnie Szumski, publisher; Helen Cothran, managing editor. Greenhaven Press 2006 223p il hardcover o.p. pa $23.70
Grades: 8 9 10 11 12   **364.66**
1. Capital punishment
ISBN 0-7377-2929-5; 0-7377-2930-9 (pa)
LC 2005-52743
"Opposing viewpoints series"
"Powerful people and organizations contribute essays to the death-penalty debate. Supreme Court Justice Antonin Scala argues that the death penalty is just, and his former colleague, Sandra Day O'Connor, debates whether juveniles should be exempt from it. This nonbiased, comprehensive look at one of today's most difficult issues will be helpful for students writing persuasive essays and for debate groups." SLJ
Includes bibliographical references

Essig, Mark Regan, 1969-
Edison & the electric chair; a story of light and death; {by} Mark Essig. Walker & Co. 2003 358p il $26; pa $15
Grades: 11 12 Adult   **364.66**
1. Edison, Thomas A. (Thomas Alva), 1847-1931
2. Capital punishment
ISBN 0-8027-1406-4; 0-8027-7710-4 (pa)
LC 2003-52507
This describes Thomas Edison's part in developing the electric chair for executions in 1889
"Essig relates Edison's furtive hand in the advent of the chair with flair, skill, and gallows humor." Booklist
Includes bibliographical references

The **ethics** of capital punishment; Christine Watkins, book editor. Greenhaven Press 2011 127p (At issue. Social issues) lib bdg $31.80; pa $22.50 *
Grades: 9 10 11 12   **364.66**
1. Capital punishment
ISBN   978-0-7377-5171-0   (lib   bdg);
978-0-7377-5172-7 (pa)   LC 2010-36737
A compendium of opinion on the moral and ethical issues surrounding capital punishment, including whether it deters murder and whether it's too expensive to retain.
Includes bibliographical references

Henderson, Harry, 1951-
Capital punishment. 3rd ed. Facts on File 2006 316p il (Library in a book) $45 *
Grades: 11 12 Adult **364.66**
1. Capital punishment
ISBN 0-8160-5708-7   LC 2005-13671
First published 1991 under the authorship of Stephen A. Flanders
A look at both sides of this controversial issue from social, political, ethical, and religious perspectives. Includes a glossary, bibliographies, and Internet sources.
Includes bibliographical references

Kuklin, Susan
No choirboy; murder, violence, and teenagers on death row. Henry Holt and Co. 2008 212p il $17.95 *
Grades: 8 9 10 11 12 **364.66**
1. Capital punishment 2. Juvenile delinquency
ISBN 978-0-8050-7950-0; 0-8050-7950-5
     LC 2007-46940
"The book opens with candid interviews that introduce three inmates, all of them teenagers when they committed their crimes. . . . This eye-opening account will likely open minds. . . . The book concludes with solid back matter—notes, glossary, bibliography, and index." Horn Book
Includes glossary and bibliographical references

365   Penal and related institutions

America's prisons: opposing viewpoints; Noah Berlatsky, book editor. Greenhaven Press 2010 224p il map $39.70; pa $27.50 *
Grades: 8 9 10 11 12 **365**
1. Prisons—United States
ISBN   978-0-7377-4956-4;   0-7377-4956-3; 978-0-7377-4957-1 (pa); 0-7377-4957-1 (pa)
     LC 2009-50927
"Opposing viewpoints series"
"This collection of opposing viewpoints provides students an opportunity to weigh the merits of arguments that support or oppose the operation of America's prisons." Publisher's note
Includes bibliographical references

Edge, Laura Bufano, 1953-
Locked up; a history of the U.S. prison system; by Laura B. Edge. Twenty-First Century Books 2009 112p il (People's history) lib bdg $31.93
Grades: 6 7 8 9 10 **365**
1. Prisons—United States
ISBN 978-0-8225-8750-7; 0-8225-8750-5
     LC 2008-26883
"Using primary resources, photographs, and solid research, Edge has written a well-organized and engaging history of our prison system. . . . This book can serve as an excellent resource for reports." SLJ
Includes bibliographical references

Ferro, Jeffrey
Prisons. Rev. ed. Facts On File, Inc. 2011 312p (Library in a book) $45 *
Grades: 11 12 Adult **365**
1. Prisons—United States
ISBN 978-0-8160-8236-0; 978-1-4381-3398-0 (ebook)
     LC 2010-49855
First published 2006
Contact publisher for ebook pricing
This book "examines the state of U.S. prisons and related issues. It focuses on the development of prisons in the United States and how the competing goals of punishment and rehabilitation have shaped the evolution of criminal correction. An overview presents statistics on U.S. prisons and explores the issues behind those statistics, including racial disparity among prisoners and the causes of recidivism. The financial costs of running prisons and the mixed record of private prisons are examined, and laws and legislation relating to issues of incarceration are reviewed." Publisher's note
Includes bibliographical references

Fisher, Robin Gaby
The boys of the dark; a story of betrayal and redemption in the deep south; with Michael O'McCarthy and Robert W. Straley. St. Martin's Press 2010 247p $24.99
Grades: 11 12 Adult **365**
1. Reformatories 2. Adult child abuse victims
ISBN 978-0-312-59539-5   LC 2009-45734
"A journalist collaborates with two former juvenile detention-center inmates to expose a scandal. With the assistance of O'McCarthy and Straley, who served time more than 50 years ago, [Fisher] . . . investigates the Florida School for Boys. For decades, misbehaving boys, many of them preteens, were committed by judges or extralegal authorities as punishment for offenses serious and frivolous alike. . . . During the '50s and '60s, when O'McCarthy and Straley were youthful residents, beatings with leather whips might have led to numerous deaths, and certainly led to physical and emotional scars. . . . A worthy exploration of a regrettably long-lasting true-crime nightmare." Kirkus

How should prisons treat inmates? Kristen Bailey, book editor. Greenhaven Press 2005 95p (At issue) $28.70; pa $19.95
Grades: 9 10 11 12 **365**
1. Prisoners—Civil rights
ISBN 0-7377-2719-5; 0-7377-2720-9 (pa)
     LC 2004-54218
"The viewpoints in this volume explore issues such as inmates' right to vote, privatization of prisons, the necessity of super maximum security, and the general question of how prisoners should be treated on a day-to-day basis." Publisher's note
Includes bibliographical references

Hubner, John
Last chance in Texas; the redemption of criminal youth. Random House 2005 xxv, 277p $25.95
Grades: 11 12 Adult   **365**
1. Giddings State School (Tex.) 2. Juvenile delinquency
ISBN 0-375-50809-0   LC 2005-42892
This book is "about the Capital Offenders Group treatment program at Texas's Giddings State School. The institution houses nearly 400 of the most violent juvenile offenders in a program designed to alter the life trajectory of its residents." SLJ
"Readers of this eye-opening account will find themselves reflecting on their own attitudes about juvenile justice as it's administered today." Booklist

Prisons; Sylvia Engdahl, book editor. Greenhaven Press 2010 230p (Current controversies) $39.70; pa $27.50
Grades: 9 10 11 12   **365**
1. Prisons—United States
ISBN   978-0-7377-4460-6;   0-7377-4460-X;
978-0-7377-4461-3 (pa); 0-7377-4461-8 (pa)
LC 2009024277
Articles in this anthology present differing opinions on the state of prisons in the United States.
Includes bibliographical references

368.4   Government-sponsored insurance

DeWitt, Larry, 1949-
Social security; a documentary history; [by] Larry W. DeWitt, Daniel Béland, and Edward D. Berkowitz. CQPress 2008 557p il $115
Grades: 10 11 12 Adult   **368.4**
1. Social security
ISBN 978-0-87289-502-7; 0-87289-502-5
LC 2007-30363
"There are 30 pages of introductory history, covering from 1935 through 2006. The rest of the book is original documents—171 in all—on 9 general topics: creating Social Security, political struggles, extending benefits, indexing benefits to the rate of inflation, benefits in the 1980s, and controversies over financing. . . . Documents include presidential statements, interviews, acts of Congress, Congressional reports, letters, and studies." SLJ
"Anyone who has an interest in the development of the Social Security program will find this to be an interesting and valuable resource." Am Ref Books Annu, 2008
Includes glossary and bibliographical references

370   Education

Unger, Harlow G., 1931-
Encyclopedia of American education. 3rd ed. Facts on File 2007 3v il (Facts on File library of American history) set $250 *
Grades: 11 12 Adult   **370**
1.   Education—United   States—Encyclopedias
2. Reference books
ISBN 0-8160-6887-9; 978-0-8160-6887-6
LC 2006-22174
First published 1996
This encyclopedia "contains more than 2,000 entries spanning the colonial period to the present. This . . . [reference provides information on different aspects] of education, from the evolution of school curriculum, education funding, and church-state controversies to . . . debates on multiculturalism, prayer in school, and sex education." Publisher's note
Includes bibliographical references

370.117   Multicultural and bilingual education

Bilingual education; Janel D. Ginn, book editor. Greenhaven Press 2008 111p (At issue. Education) lib bdg $29.95; pa $21.20 *
Grades: 10 11 12   **370.117**
1. Bilingual education
ISBN 978-0-7377-3912-1 (lib bdg); 0-7377-3912-6 (lib bdg); 978-0-7377-3913-8 (pa); 0-7377-3913-4 (pa)
LC 2007-938125
"This volume presents 12 signed essays from passionate proponents of and opponents to bilingual education. . . . This volume is well suited for debate topics and provides a list of organizations to contact for more information about the controversy." SLJ
Includes bibliographical references

370.9   Education—Historical, geographic, persons treatment

Friedman, Ian C.
Education reform. Rev. ed. Facts on File 2011 264p il (Library in a book) $45
Grades: 9 10 11 12 Adult   **370.9**
1. Education—United States 2. Education—Aims and objectives 3. Reference books
ISBN 978-0-8160-8238-4   LC 2010-43133
First published 2004
"Coverage includes: current developments regarding teacher incentives, curriculum standards, standardized tests, and homeschooling; the goals and requirements of 'Race to the Top,' a $5 billion education grant program rolled out as part of the Obama administration's Recovery and Reinvestment Act of 2009; . . . [a] survey of the events and major debates surrounding education reform in the United States, from earliest influences through the present; . . . [and] statistics on charter school enrollment and operations." Publisher's note
Includes bibliographical references

371 Schools and their activities; special education

Education: opposing viewpoints; David Haugen and Susan Musser, book editor. Greenhaven Press 2009 290p il lib bdg $39.70; pa $27.50 *
Grades: 9 10 11 12   **371**
1. Public schools 2. School choice
ISBN 978-0-7377-4208-4 (lib bdg); 0-7377-4208-9 (lib bdg); 978-0-7377-4209-1 (pa); 0-7377-4209-7 (pa)
LC 2008-31458

"Opposing viewpoints series"
Articles in this anthology discuss the state of education in the United States, including standardized testing, alternatives to public education, the role of religion in public education, and ways to improve schools.
Includes bibliographical references

371.1 Teachers and teaching, and related activities

Kozol, Jonathan
Letters to a young teacher. Crown Publishers 2007 288p hardcover o.p. pa $14
Grades: 11 12 Adult Professional   **371.1**
1. Teaching
ISBN 978-0-307-39371-5; 0-307-39371-2; 978-0-307-39372-2 (pa); 0-307-39372-0 (pa)
LC 2007-2689

"Through the framing device of actual letters to a first-year grade school teacher at a New England inner-city school, Kozol . . . shares his passions about the education of children, including his opinion that vouchers will benefit the wealthy at the expense of the poor, deep concerns about the privatization of public education, and ongoing disdain for the dishonesty he discerns lying behind the rhetoric about equality in education." Libr J

"The book will delight and encourage first-year (or for that matter, 40th-year) teachers who need Kozol's reminders of the ways that their beautiful profession can bring joy and beauty, mystery and mischievous delight into the hearts of little people in their years of greatest curiosity." Publ Wkly
Includes bibliographical references

371.2 School administration; administration of student academic activities

Mueller, Jonathan, 1947-
Assessing critical skills; [by] Jon Mueller. Linworth Pub. 2008 132p pa $44.95 *
Grades: Adult Professional   **371.2**
1. Educational tests and measurements
ISBN 978-1-58683-282-7; 1-58683-282-4
LC 2008-19609

"According to Mueller, educators need training to instruct students on skills such as problem-solving, information literacy, reasoning, collaboration, and critical thinking. In this thoroughly researched, organized, and concise book, Mueller stresses the need to incorporate authentic assessment throughout the curriculum in order to effectively teach and measure these skills. The author provides numerous detailed tasks and rubrics making it easy for the classroom teacher and media specialist to create authentic assessments." Libr Media Connect
Includes bibliographical references

371.3 Methods of instruction and study

Braun, Linda W.
Listen up! podcasting for schools and libraries. Information Today, Inc. 2007 97p il pa $29.50 *
Grades: Adult Professional   **371.3**
1. Podcasting
ISBN 978-1-57387-304-8   LC 2007-23650

"In six conversational chapters, Braun explains podcasting's technical terms, ongoing development, necessary components such as an RSS feed and a feed reader, creating subscriptions, and methods of distribution." SLJ

"This is a valuable resource for those interested in learning more about podcasting and utilizing the technology to improve their programming and outreach." Booklist
Includes bibliographical references

Crane, Beverley E.
Using WEB 2.0 tools in the K-12 classroom. Neal-Schuman Publishers 2009 189p il pa $59.95
Grades: Adult Professional   **371.3**
1. Internet in education 2. Education—Curricula 3. Web 2.0
ISBN 978-1-55570-653-1; 1-55570-653-3
LC 2008-46167

"In this extensive resource, teachers will find a wealth of suggestions, ideas, unit plans, and answers to questions pertaining to how to integrate and use Web 2.0 tools throughout the curriculum." SLJ

"This excellent resource should be widely appealing to teachers, librarians, and school media specialists." Voice Youth Advocates
Includes glossary and bibliographical references

Fontichiaro, Kristin
Podcasting at school; foreword by Diane R. Chen. Libraries Unlimited 2008 170p il pa $30 *
Grades: Adult Professional   **371.3**
1. Podcasting
ISBN 978-1-59158-587-9; 1-59158-587-2
LC 2007-35040

This title presents "incentives for implementing podcasting within the school curriculum. Part I explains the basics of Web 2.0 and dispels popular myths. [It includes] a review of necessary equipment and software; how to develop effective vocal techniques; and the mechanics of recording, publishing, and distributing a podcast. . . . Ideas for utilizing this technology are given in the second section." SLJ

Fontichiaro, Kristin—*Continued*
"The book provides simple, clear explanations of podcasting terms, procedures, and protocols. . . . This book is an essential purchase for professional development collections." Libr Media Connect
Includes bibliographical references

Harada, Violet H.
Collaborating for project-based learning in grades 9-12; [by] Violet H. Harada, Carolyn H. Kirio, Sandra H. Yamamoto. Linworth Pub. 2008 xxii, 226p il pa $44.95
Grades: Adult Professional   371.3
1. Project method in teaching 2. Instructional materials centers
ISBN 978-1-58683-291-9; 1-58683-291-3
LC 2007-42180
"This resource offers school media specialists insight into learning opportunities available through project-based learning (PBL). . . . The text opens with a clear, detailed, and accessible definition of PBL, puts PBL in context with school reform and the issue of school dropout rates, moves toward explaining and illustrating the school media specialist's responsibilities in maintaining standards of information literacy throughout the PBL process, and reviews the necessary steps in planning actual projects. . . . The balance of theory and practical guidance make the book a sure fit for most high school-based professional collections." Voice Youth Advocates
Includes bibliographical references

Huber, Joe
Ask Mr. Technology, get answers; [by] Joe Huber and Christine Weiser. Linworth Pub. 2007 85p pa $29.95
Grades: Adult Professional   371.3
1. Information technology 2. Computer-assisted instruction 3. Computers and children
ISBN 1-58683-289-1; 978-1-58683-289-6
LC 2007-1956
"Joe Huber, aka 'Mr. Technology,' has been writing a column for *Library Media Connection* since 1995, and this book collects . . . many of the letters featured in those columns. Huber hits on a variety of subjects from software questions to podcasting and everything in between, taking what can often be confusing and frustrating topics and addressing them in clear, easy-to-understand language." Voice Youth Advocates

November, Alan C.
Empowering students with technology. 2nd ed. Corwin Press 2010 115p il pa $25.95
Grades: Adult Professional   371.3
1. Computer-assisted instruction 2. Internet in education
ISBN 978-1-4129-7425-7; 1-4129-7425-9
LC 2009-43649
First published 2001 by Skylight Professional Development
A joint publication with National Association of Secondary School Principals.

"Discusses the relationship of technology to today's learning environment and the potential for technology to encourage students to learn collaboratively. This . . . edition emphasizes current topics such as information literacy, global connectivity, and the educational applications of utilities such as digital cameras and cell phones. The book's usefulness is as a reasource for teachers and librarians to consult in creating, planning, and assisting with school projects in all subjects." Libr Media Connect
Includes bibliographical references

Richardson, Will
Blogs, wikis, podcasts, and other powerful Web tools for classrooms. 3rd ed. Corwin 2010 171p il pa $31.95
Grades: Adult Professional   371.3
1. Internet in education 2. Teaching—Aids and devices 3. Weblogs 4. Wikis (Computer science) 5. Podcasting 6. Online social networks
ISBN 978-1-4129-7747-0; 1-4129-7747-9
LC 2009-51376
First published 2006
"Provides K-12 examples of how Web tools such as blogs, wikis, Facebook, and Twitter allow students to learn more, create more, and communicate better." Publisher's note
"The book is well-written and comprehensive. The author's engaging writing style will instill confidence in readers that they will be able to easily integrate the same technologies with the same results in their classrooms. Readers will not want to stop reading this eye-opening and inspirational book. It is jam-packed with proven ideas, and individuals, especially educators, will want to try out these technologies." Libr Media Connect
Includes bibliographical references

371.7 Student welfare

Hunnicutt, Susan
School shootings; Susan Hunnicutt, book editor. Greenhaven Press 2006 102p (At issue. Crime) lib bdg $28.70; pa $19.95
Grades: 9 10 11 12   371.7
1. School violence
ISBN 0-7377-2416-1 (lib bdg); 978-0-7377-2416-5 (lib bdg); 0-7377-2417-X (pa); 978-0-7377-2417-2 (pa)
LC 2005-54525
"This anthology explores various explanations for rampage school shootings, and examines ways communities have responded." Publisher's note
Includes bibliographical references

Parks, Peggy J., 1951-
School violence. ReferencePoint Press 2008 104p il map (Compact research. Current issues) $25.95
Grades: 8 9 10 11 12   371.7
1. School violence
ISBN 978-1-60152-057-9; 1-60152-057-3
LC 2008-18372

Parks, Peggy J., 1951-—*Continued*

The introduction "looks at the prevalence of [school violence]; causes such as bullying and gangs; the influence of the media, including online sources, on behavior; and the roles of alcohol and drugs, etc. The '. . . at a glance' spread and 'Overview' prepare readers for the more detailed information to come and provide facts about safety issues. Each of four chapters then addresses both sides of a question, followed by four pages of quotes and a section of colorful graphs, charts, and illustrations." SLJ

Includes bibliographical references

School violence; Lucinda Almond, book editor. Greenhaven Press 2008 232p (Current controversies) lib bdg $37.40; pa $25.95 *

Grades: 7 8 9 10 11 12   **371.7**
1. School violence
ISBN 978-0-7377-3795-0 (lib bdg); 0-7377-3795-6 (lib bdg); 978-0-7377-3796-7 (pa); 0-7377-3796-4 (pa)
            LC 2007-29879

An anthology of essays presenting differing viewpoints on topics such as school bullying, the factors that contribute to school violence, gun control laws, and alternative juvenile interventions.

Includes bibliographical references

371.82 Specific kinds of students; schools for specific kinds of students

Mortenson, Greg, 1957-

Stones into schools; promoting peace with books, not bombs, in Afghanistan and Pakistan. Viking 2009 420p il map $26.95

Grades: 11 12 Adult   **371.82**
1. Schools—Afghanistan 2. Schools—Pakistan 3. Humanitarian intervention
ISBN 978-0-670-02115-4   LC 2009-30812

In this follow-up to *Three cups of tea* (2009), the author "continues the story of how the Central Asia Institute (CAI) built schools in northern Afghanistan. Descriptions of the harsh geography and more than one near-death experience impress readers as new faces join Mortenson's loyal 'Dirty Dozen' as they carefully plot a course of school-building through the Badakshan province and Wakhan corridor. . . . To blandly call this book inspiring would be dismissive of all the hard work that has gone into the mission in Afghanistan as well as the efforts to fund it. Mortenson writes of nothing less than saving the future, and his adventure is light years beyond most attempts." Booklist

Perez, William, 1974-

We are Americans; undocumented students pursuing the American dream; foreword by Daniel Solorzano. Stylus 2009 xxxiv, 161p $70; pa $22.50

Grades: 9 10 11 12 Adult   **371.82**
1. Discrimination in education 2. Illegal aliens 3. United States—Immigration and emigration
ISBN 978-1-57922-375-5; 978-1-57922-376-2 (pa)
            LC 2009-26206

The author "plumbs the stories of students living with the constant threat of deportation for an answer to the question, 'What does it mean to be an American?' Raised in this country by parents who gained access illegally, the 16 high school, college and postgraduate students profiled here (standing in for 65,000 nationwide) have each embraced our language, culture and collective dream, but are denied pathways to success. . . . No matter what one's position is on legalizing immigrants, this collection of inspiring, heartbreaking stories puts a number of unforgettable faces to the issue, making it impossible to defend any one side in easy terms or generalities." Publ Wkly

Includes bibliographical references

371.9 Special education

Cohen, Leah Hager

Train go sorry; inside a deaf world. Vintage Bks. 1995 296p pa $14.95

Grades: 11 12 Adult   **371.9**
1. Lexington School for the Deaf (New York, N.Y.) 2. Deaf—Means of communication
ISBN 0-679-76165-9   LC 94-23501

First published 1994 by Houghton Mifflin

"Cohen draws upon her experiences as the hearing grandchild of deaf immigrants to combine personal stories of hearing-impaired individuals with related aspects of deaf culture. Using her first home and her father's place of employment, the Lexington School for the Deaf in New York City, to connect characters and experiences, she shares tales of activities familiar to young adults." Libr J

"Well organized and beautifully written." Booklist

Conroy, Pat

The water is wide. Dial Press Trade Paperbacks 2006 294p pa $14

Grades: 11 12 Adult   **371.9**
1. Socially handicapped children 2. African Americans—Education 3. Public schools—South Carolina
ISBN 978-0-553-38157-3; 0-553-38157-1
            LC 2005-285152

Also available in paperback from Bantam Bks.

First published 1972 by Houghton Mifflin

"A young white teacher goes to an island off the coast of South Carolina to teach a group of functionally illiterate black children. Yamacraw Island is backward and primitive, a world for the most part left untouched by the 20th Century. . . . By ignoring the textbooks and concentrating on meaningful situations and dialogue . . . he begins to make headway. He also, unfortunately arouses the ire of the powers that be and, after fierce struggle, is fired." Libr J

A **Guide** to high school success for students with disabilities; edited by Cynthia Ann Bowman and Paul T. Jaeger; foreword by Chris Crutcher. Greenwood Press 2004 181p $45 *

Grades: 9 10 11 12   **371.9**
1. Handicapped students 2. Academic achievement
ISBN 0-313-32832-3   LC 2004-53041

A Guide to high school success for students with disabilities—*Continued*

"The book covers a wide array of issues including handling difficult teachers, advocating for self, setting high expectations for self and others, use of the library and media centers, extracurricular activities, dating and sexuality, and life after high school. . . . This is a good read for students, parents, and teachers alike." Choice

Includes bibliographical references

Kozol, Jonathan

Savage inequalities; children in America's schools. HarperPerennial 1992 261p pa $14.95

Grades: 11 12 Adult   **371.9**
1. Public schools 2. Socially handicapped children 3. Segregation in education
ISBN 0-06-097499-0; 978-0-06-097499-2
First published 1991 by Crown

In 1988, Kozol "visited schools in over 30 neighborhoods, including East St. Louis, Harlem, the Bronx, Chicago, Jersey City, and San Antonio. In this account, he concludes that real integration has seriously declined and education for minorities and the poor has moved backwards by at least several decades." Libr J

"Jonathan Kozol has written an impassioned book, laced with anger and indignation, about how our public education system scorns so many of our children. 'Savage Inequalities' is also an important book, and warrants widespread attention" N Y Times Book Rev

Includes bibliographical references

Paquette, Penny Hutchins

Learning disabilities; the ultimate teen guide; [by] Penny Hutchins Paquette, Cheryl Gerson Tuttle. Scarecrow Press 2003 301p il (It happened to me) lib bdg $32.50; pa $17.95 *

Grades: 7 8 9 10   **371.9**
1. Learning disabilities
ISBN 0-8108-4261-0 (lib bdg); 0-8108-5643-3 (pa)
LC 2002-17588

This provides an "overview of the most common disabilities. . . . The book also teaches students how to advocate for themselves, informing them of their rights under law both during the school years and after high school graduation. . . . Assistive technology that can help students improve their learning abilities such as Optical Character Recognition (OCR) systems, screen reading software, books on tape, electronic notebooks, and other tools that aid student learning are covered." Publisher's note

"Far more detailed than similiar books from other publishers." Voice Youth Advocates

Includes bibliographical references

Parks, Peggy J., 1951-

Learning disabilities. ReferencePoint Press 2009 96p il (Compact research. Diseases and disorders) lib bdg $25.95

Grades: 7 8 9 10   **371.9**
1. Learning disabilities
ISBN 978-1-60152-077-7; 1-60152-077-8
LC 2009-13445

"Parks explains what learning disabilities are and discusses the causes and overcoming them. The book's strength is that it explains how learning disabilities differ from other types of disorders. . . . Teens will find the overall organization of [this] succinct and easy-to-read [book] useful and attractive." SLJ

Includes bibliographical references

372 Elementary education

Lukenbill, W. Bernard

Health information in a changing world; practical approaches for teachers, schools, and school librarians; [by] W. Bernard Lukenbill and Barbara Froling Immroth. Libraries Unlimited 2010 244p il $45

Grades: Adult Professional   **372**
1. Health education 2. Health—Information services 3. Youth—Health and hygiene
ISBN 978-1-59884-398-9; 1-59884-398-2
LC 2010-7505

"In promoting a holistic approach to teaching, Lukenbill and Immroth assert that health information need not be limited to physical-education classes or specific classroom units. Rather, it can be integrated throughout the curriculum, and school librarians are in the unique position to facilitate and advocate for this change. What follows are suggestions for developing health-information literacy throughout the standard subjects, guides for planning health fairs and other outreach activities, and an overview of search strategies for educators to impart to students." SLJ

"This is quite an impressive book and a real treasure for any professional involved with health education, whether for the classroom, public health, or personal counseling." Voice Youth Advocates

Includes bibliographical references

372.4 Reading

Bernadowski, Carianne

Research-based reading strategies in the library for adolescent learners; [by] Carianne Bernadowski and Patricia Liotta Kolencik. Libraries Unlimited 2010 108p il pa $40

Grades: Adult Professional   **372.4**
1. Reading 2. School libraries
ISBN 978-1-58683-347-3; 1-58683-347-2
LC 2009-21198

"A Linworth Publishing book"

"This book explains six proven strategies—question/answer, think-alouds, reciprocal teaching, anticipation guides, questioning the author, and SQR3 (survey, question, read, recite, and review)—for reading comprehension and three strategies (Semantic Feature Analysis, word maps/journals, and Frayer Models/word sorts) for vocabulary building. . . . Although the strategies are standard approaches, weaving in librarian roles makes this book useful for librarians who serve teens." Booklist

Includes bibliographical references

Bernadowski, Carianne—*Continued*

Teaching literacy skills to adolescents using Coretta Scott King Award winners. Libraries Unlimited 2009 136p il pa $35

Grades: Adult Professional 372.4

1. African Americans in literature 2. Teenagers—Books and reading 3. Coretta Scott King Award

ISBN 978-1-58683-337-4; 1-58683-337-5

LC 2009-15279

"A Linworth Publishing book"

"The book includes award-winning book selections and Coretta Scott King Honor Books. It is a showcase for African-American authors' works, and helps educators working with adolescent students and their reading needs. . . . Each chapter covers one title and contains an annotation, grade level discussion starters, writing prompts, pre-reading activities, literary strategies for reading, post-reading activities, additional information about the author, and additional resources. This book would be a great professional resource, and a must have for those educators that teach adolescents." Libr Media Connect

Includes bibliographical references

372.6 Language arts (Communication skills)

Chatton, Barbara

Using poetry across the curriculum; learning to love language. 2nd ed. Libraries Unlimited 2010 241p pa $40

Grades: Adult Professional 372.6

1. Poetry—Study and teaching

ISBN 978-1-59158-697-5; 1-59158-697-6

LC 2009-36711

First published 1993

"With the emphasis in most schools on improving literacy, fluency, and reading and writing test scores, this book is extremely valuable. Sections are divided into various curricula areas. Each section begins with the national standards for that discipline, then a few paragraphs explain how the poetry in the extensive listing can be used. . . . Because all teachers must incorporate writing into their teaching, having relevant poetry for their curriculum and ideas on how to use it, will make this book popular." Libr Media Connect

Includes bibliographical references

De Vos, Gail, 1949-

Storytelling for young adults; a guide to tales for teens. 2nd ed. Libraries Unlimited 2003 208p $35

Grades: Adult Professional 372.6

1. Storytelling 2. School libraries—Activity projects 3. Books and reading

ISBN 1-563-08903-3 LC 2003-51648

First published 1991

This is a "collection of recommended stories for young adults . . . Brief synopses of the stories are arranged in themed chapters about the fantastic, laughter, folktales, tales of life, tales of the spirit, and tales of the arts and sciences. A few samples are given in their entirety. Author, theme, and title indexes are included as well as a list of the story collections in which the tales appear . . . The strength of this text is that the author has been storytelling with teens for fifteen years, so the recommended stories have the force of being 'tried and true' with this age group . . . It will be helpful for the beginning storyteller in choosing material, particularly in the school setting, and for educators who are trying to find popular stories for the teen audience." Voice Youth Advocates

Includes bibliographical references

Mary Elizabeth

Painless spelling; illustrated by Hank Morehouse. 2nd ed. Barron's 2006 256p il pa $8.99

Grades: 7 8 9 10 372.6

1. English language—Spelling

ISBN 0-7641-3435-3; 978-0-7641-3435-7

LC 2006-42736

First published 1998

Provides guidelines for spelling American English words; explains visual and sound patterns, letter combinations, syllables, compound words, and hyphenation; and includes practical exercises.

373.1 Organization and activities in secondary education

Bluestein, Jane

High school's not forever; [by] Jane Bluestein and Eric Katz. HCI Teens 2005 302p il pa $12.95

Grades: 7 8 9 10 11 12 373.1

1. High school students

ISBN 0-7573-0256-4 LC 2005-50232

"Culled from the responses of some 2000 high and post-high school students, this title gives voice to young people who have lived through the experience and who offer both affirming and cautionary tales as they attempted to navigate the uncertain seas of friendship, depression, academic achievement, drugs, and sexuality. . . . There is no question that this book will enhance most YA collections." SLJ

Includes bibliographical references

Braun, Linda W.

Teens, technology, and literacy; or, Why bad grammar isn't always bad. Libraries Unlimited 2007 105p il pa $30 *

Grades: Adult Professional 373.1

1. Literacy 2. Teenagers—Books and reading 3. Bibliographic instruction 4. Computer-assisted instruction 5. Information technology

ISBN 1-59158-368-3; 978-1-59158-368-4

LC 2006-31714

"Braun shows teachers, administrators, and librarians how to incorporate today's technologies into the development of literacy skills. The author backs up the grammar used in IMs and text messaging by explaining how these technologies promote better literacy in the classroom. . . . This book is a must for most collections." SLJ

Includes bibliographical references

Fireside, Bryna J.
Choices for the high school graduate; a survival guide for the information age. 5th ed. Infobase Pub. 2009 261p il $34.95; pa $16.95
Grades: 9 10 11 12   **373.1**
1. Vocational guidance
ISBN 978-0-8160-7617-8; 0-8160-7617-0;
978-0-8160-7618-5 (pa); 0-8160-7618-9 (pa)
         LC 2008-47835
First published 1997
"Presents students with a wide range of options available to them during and after high school—from early college admissions and entering a trade to joining the military and volunteering abroad." Publisher's note
Includes bibliographical references

Nichols, Beverly
Improving student achievement; 50 research-based strategies. Linworth Pub. 2008 110p il pa $44.95 *
Grades: Adult Professional   **373.1**
1. Academic achievement 2. Schools—Administration 3. Instructional materials centers
ISBN 978-1-58683-293-3; 1-58683-293-X
         LC 2008-6918
Includes CD-ROM
"The text considers 50 data-driven interventions that represent a variety of affective and cognitive strategies. Each 'Research Tip' addresses a specific strategy, and is placed in broad categories such as literacy, curriculum alignment, and assessment. . . . Media specialists need to take leadership roles in building school improvement initiatives, and this resource will help them." Libr Media Connect
Includes bibliographical references

Streisel, Jim, 1971-
High school journalism; a practical guide. McFarland & Co. 2007 224p il $35 *
Grades: 9 10 11 12   **373.1**
1. College and school journalism
ISBN 978-0-7864-3060-4; 0-7864-3060-5
         LC 2007-7509
"The book offers chapters on information gathering, writing, alternative coverage, packaging, and . . . information about Web-based journalism and legal rights. Each section is broken into chapters about researching, interviewing, editing, visual design, and hooking non-readers. Teachers and students will all find something to use in this book." Libr Media Connect

375 Curricula

Managing curriculum and assessment; a practitioner's guide; [by] Beverly Nichols . . . [et al.] Linworth Publishing 2006 170p pa $49.95
Grades: Adult Professional   **375**
1. Education—Curricula 2. Evaluation
ISBN 1-58683-216-6   LC 2006003202
"This is a guide by practitioners who give advice on how to respond to the laws and requirements of No

Child Left Behind. It is an invaluable resource that provides new insights. . . . There are three sections to the guide with an accompanying CD that contains everything in the book and more. . . . This guide is loaded with examples and is a must have for your professional library." Libr Media Connect
Includes bibliographical references

378 Higher education

Jell, John R.
From school to a career; a student's guide to success in the real world; [by] John Jell. ScarecrowEducation 2005 77p il pa $10.95 *
Grades: 9 10 11 12   **378**
1. Vocational education 2. Vocational guidance
ISBN 1-57886-213-2   LC 2004-21308
The author "offers practical advice for how to develop good job skills while in college. He discusses . . . time management, the importance of both formal and informal learning, what makes for relevant work experience in a future career field, and networking. . . . The professional language is easy for teens to understand and sets a good example of how a job seeker or serious college student should speak and write." Voice Youth Advocates

378.1 Organization and activities in higher education

Bardin, Matt
Zen in the art of the SAT; how to think, focus, and achieve your highest score; [by] Matt Bardin and Susan Fine. Houghton Mifflin 2005 220p il pa $7.99
Grades: 9 10 11 12   **378.1**
1. Scholastic Assessment Test 2. Colleges and universities—Entrance requirements
ISBN 0-618-57488-3   LC 2005-4326
"Each chapter explores how students can use principles of Zen Buddhism to move beyond anxiety, build their confidence, and focus on solving the SAT's inscrutable, koanlike questions. . . . It's the advice about mindfulness and transforming nervous energy and negative thoughts, which readers can apply to every life experience, that really distinguishes this title." Booklist
Includes bibliographical references

Barron's ACT; [by] George Ehrenhaft ... [et al.] 16th ed. Barrons 2010 688p il pa $18.99
Grades: 11 12 Adult   **378.1**
1. ACT assessment 2. Colleges and universities—Entrance requirements
ISBN 978-0-7641-4482-0
Also available with CD-ROM $29.99 (ISBN: 978-0-7641-9758-1)
First published 1972 with title: Barron's how to prepare for the American College Testing Program (ACT). Continues How to prepare for the ACT, American College Testing Assessment Program, Barron's How to prepare for the ACT assessment, and Barron's ACT assessment. Frequently revised. Editors vary

Barron's ACT—*Continued*

A guide to achieving higher scores on the ACT which includes subject reviews and practice exams with answers.

Berent, Polly

Getting ready for college. Random House 2003 209p il pa $12.95

Grades: 9 10 11 12   **378.1**

1. College students 2. Colleges and universities—United States

ISBN 0-8129-6896-4   LC 2003-41375

This "manual includes day planners, notes on how to take notes, tips on how to make a 'real life' file, and advice from scores of college students in the trenches as well as campus health-care professionals, college counselors, administrators, and financial-aid advisers." Publisher's note

This "will be useful to any young person getting ready to enter the college milieu. It's a quick, easy read, enriched by quotes from teens." Booklist

Burtnett, Frank, 1940-

Bound-for-college guidebook; a step-by-step guide to finding and applying to colleges. Rowman & Littlefield Education 2009 156p $24.95 *

Grades: 9 10 11 12 Adult   **378.1**

1. Colleges and universities—Entrance requirements 2. College choice 3. College applications

ISBN 978-1-57886-992-3; 1-57886-992-7

LC 2008-39425

In this guide to preparing for college, the author "focuses mainly on the admission process, offering checklists, outlines, and user-friendly qualitative exercises to help students get organized, meet deadlines, and determine which colleges fit their individual objectives. . . . This essential guide is highly recommended for all college-bound students and their parents." Libr J

Includes bibliographical references

Cohen, Harlan

The naked roommate; and 107 other issues you might run into in college. 3rd ed.; Rev. and updated. Sourcebooks 2009 465p pa $14.99

Grades: 9 10 11 12   **378.1**

1. College students

ISBN 978-1-4022-1901-6

First published 2004

"Expert and student advice about: roommates, relationships, classes, friends, finances, dorm life, sex, no sex, alcohol, Greek life, laundry, and everything that really matters in college" Cover

This is "a hilarious and truthful book that gives high school students a look at college life. . . . The advice is sound; the tone is light." SLJ

Includes bibliographical references

Cohen, Katherine

The truth about getting in; a top college advisor tells you everything you need to know. Hyperion 2002 252p $21.95; pa $14.95

Grades: 9 10 11 12   **378.1**

1. College applications 2. Colleges and universities—Entrance requirements

ISBN 0-7868-8747-8; 0-7868-8849-0 (pa)

LC 2003-266705

"Chapters cover a wide variety of topics—from gathering information about colleges and preparing for admissions tests to writing an effective essay and securing financial aid. . . . Cohen's approach is pleasant and positive." Booklist

Conley, David T., 1948-

College knowledge; what it really takes for students to succeed and what we can do to get them ready. Jossey-Bass 2005 xxii, 350p il (Jossey-Bass education series) hardcover o.p. pa $19.95 *

Grades: 11 12 Adult   **378.1**

1. College students 2. Academic achievement

ISBN 0-7879-7397-1; 0-7879-9675-0 (pa)

LC 2004-30569

The author "recounts the preparation or lack thereof during the high school years of three college-bound students and makes it clear that there is a difference between college-eligible and college-ready. He lays out chapter by chapter what is wrong and how it can be remedied. . . . This valuable book belongs in every high school library." SLJ

Includes bibliographical references

DaSilva-Gordon, Maria

Your first year of college; from classroom to dorm room. Rosen Pub. 2010 80p il (Thinking about college) lib bdg $30.60; pa $14.15

Grades: 9 10 11 12   **378.1**

1. College students

ISBN 978-1-4358-3600-6 (lib bdg); 1-4358-3600-6 (lib bdg); 978-1-4358-8506-6 (pa); 1-4358-8506-6 (pa)

LC 2009-15473

"This book provides an introduction to college life, highlighting what makes it different from the high school experience. . . . Chapters include tips on designing one's academic program, studying and staying organized, navigating social and extracurricular opportunities, staying physically and mentally healthy, and managing money." Publisher's note

Includes bibliographical references

Ehrenhaft, George

Writing a successful college application essay. 4th ed. Barron's 2008 170p pa $13.99 *

Grades: 9 10 11 12   **378.1**

1. College applications 2. Colleges and universities—Entrance requirements

ISBN 978-0-7641-3637-5; 0-7641-3637-2

LC 2007-43441

First published 1987 with title: Write your way into college

Ehrenhaft, George—*Continued*

The author gives "advice on deciding what to write, composing an essay, and the rewriting process. . . . The practical advice and concrete examples, especially in the section on editing and rewriting, will prove useful to any student facing the dreaded task of writing application essays." Voice Youth Advocates

Feaver, Peter

Getting the best out of college; a professor, a dean, and a student tell you how to maximize your experience; [by] Peter Feaver, Sue Wasiolek, and Anne Crossman. Ten Speed Press 2008 249p il pa $14.95 *

Grades: 9 10 11 12   **378.1**
1. College students
ISBN 978-1-58008-856-5; 1-58008-856-2
LC 2007-39776

"This educational narrative shows how to get the best out of one's college education. Each chapter provides unique insights into freshman survival with the help of a college dean, professor, and a student. The book covers a variety of topics, including how to deal with that not-so-perfect roommate, how to handle college partying, and how to ask a professor for a letter of recommendation." Voice Youth Advocates

Fiske guide to getting into the right college; [by] Edward B. Fiske & Bruce G. Hammond. 4th ed. Sourcebooks 2010 352p pa $16.99 *

Grades: 11 12 Adult   **378.1**
1. College choice 2. Colleges and universities—Entrance requirements 3. Colleges and universities—Finance
ISBN 978-1-4022-4309-7
First published 1997 by Times Bks.

This guide includes advice and information on constructing applications, writing essays, interviews, the application process, using the Internet when applying for college, and finanical aid.

Gardner, John N.

Step by step to college and career success. 4th ed. Bedford/St. Martin's 2010 xx, 179p il pa $35
Grades: 11 12 Adult   **378.1**
1. College students 2. Success
ISBN 978-0-312-68306-1
First published 2006

This book "offers students . . . information and . . . strategies that they can apply toward their success . . . [Topics covered include] money management, emotional intelligence, technology, and diversity." Publisher's note

Gonsher, Debra

The community college guide; the essential reference from application to graduation; [by] Debra Gonsher and Joshua Halberstam. BenBella Books 2009 279p il pa $14.95 *
Grades: 9 10 11 12   **378.1**

1. Junior colleges
ISBN 978-1-933771-73-1

"Navigating the road of community college is not the most intuitive process, but this book serves as a map to making it through, from the application process to securing employment. The authors clearly outline the book in the table of contents, taking the reader from start to finish. Key areas addressed are handling difficult professors, taking ESL and remediation courses, the pitfalls of procrastination, and test-taking tips. . . . There is something for everyone in this essential purchase whether fresh out of high school, a student from abroad, or an adult returning to college. It will be both a handy reference tool and a treasure for circulation." Voice Youth Advocates
Includes bibliographical references

Green, Sharon

Barron's SAT; [by] Sharon Weiner Green, Ira K. Wolf. 25th ed. Barron's Educational Series 2010 920p il pa $18.99 *
Grades: 9 10 11 12 Adult   **378.1**
1. Scholastic Assessment Test 2. Colleges and universities—Entrance requirements
ISSN 1941-6180
ISBN 978-0-7641-4436-3
Also available edition with CD-ROM $29.99 (ISBN: 978-0-7641-9722-2)
Annual. Continues Barron's how to prepare for the SAT
Includes vocabulary flash cards on perforated card stock

"This manual explains all of the important tactics and strategies for taking the SAT and provides a . . . review of all test topics. It also presents a diagnostic test and five full-length SAT practice tests with all questions answered and explained." Publisher's note
Includes bibliographical references

Grossberg, Blythe N.

Applying to college for students with ADD or LD; a guide to keep you (and your parents) sane, satisfied, and organized through the admission process; by Blythe Grossberg. American Psychological Association 2011 143p il pa $14.95
Grades: 9 10 11 12   **378.1**
1. College applications 2. Learning disabilities 3. Attention deficit disorder
ISBN 978-1-4338-0892-0; 1-4338-0892-7
LC 2010-23130

"Beginning with an encouraging introduction, Grossberg then lays out the path to moving through the application process, which she expands upon in subsequent chapters. An early emphasis on figuring out strengths and weaknesses leads to a section on organization: what to do in your junior year, senior year, and the summer before college. Each time-frame is broken down into specific tasks, such as taking standardized tests and writing college essays, which are also explained in detail. . . . There's such good advice in this including wiping your social networking pages clean that teens without ADD or learning disabilities will find this eminently useful, too." Booklist

Gruber, Gary R.

Gruber's complete SAT guide 2011. 14th ed. Sourcebooks 2010 xxx, 1048p il pa $19.99

Grades: 9 10 11 12 **378.1**

1. Scholastic Assessment Test 2. Colleges and universities—Entrance requirements

ISBN 978-1-4022-3777-5

Annual. First published 1985 by Critical Thinking Book Co. with title: Gruber's complete preparation for the SAT

The author explains the principles behind the test, reviews necessary skills and develops test-taking strategies. Sample tests with answers are provided.

Hernandez, Michele A.

Acing the college application; how to maximize your chances for admission to the college of your choice. Updated. Ballantine Books 2007 262p pa $14.95

Grades: 9 10 11 12 **378.1**

1. College applications

ISBN 0-345-49892-5; 978-0-345-49892-2

LC 2007-281254

First published 2002

On cover: Updated to include the latest changes to the Common Application

This guide to applying for college includes "step-by-step instructions on how to maximize a student's chance of getting into top colleges and universities across the country. . . . The author has successfully broken down what would normally be very dry material, making it sound as though she is discussing it face-to-face." Voice Youth Advocates

Jacobs, Lynn F.

The secrets of college success; [by] Lynn F. Jacobs and Jeremy S. Hyman. Jossey-Bass 2010 198p (Professors' guide) pa $15.95 *

Grades: 9 10 11 12 **378.1**

1. College students 2. Conduct of life 3. Time management

ISBN 978-0-470-87466-0

"While covering the basics found in other 'how to be successful in college'-type books (study skills, time management, test-taking tips), this one also has sections on other issues that students will likely face: how to get into a closed class, studying abroad, working with a professor, and getting one's money's worth. . . . [This] would be a great tool to incorporate into an adviser/advisee program for students on a college track. Learning to implement some of the tips will make them more successful in college, and they will likely reap benefits during their high school tenure as well." SLJ

Includes bibliographical references

Light, Richard J.

Making the most of college; students speak their minds. Harvard Univ. Press 2001 242p hardcover o.p. pa $14.95

Grades: 11 12 Adult **378.1**

1. College students

ISBN 0-674-00478-7; 0-674-01359-X (pa)

LC 00-59728

"Light addresses two major areas: the choices students make to get the most out of college and effective ways for faculty members to help students get the best experience. The book is based on research by more than 60 faculty members from 20 colleges and universities and interviews with undergraduates. . . . Parents and students either in college or headed there will find this book a valuable resource." Booklist

Includes bibliographical references

Marcus, David L.

Acceptance; a legendary guidance counselor helps seven kids find the right colleges—and find themselves. Penguin Press 2009 244p $25.95; pa $16

Grades: 11 12 Adult **378.1**

1. Smith, Gwyeth 2. College choice 3. Educational counseling

ISBN 978-1-59420-214-8; 1-59420-214-1; 978-0-14-311764-3 (pa); 0-14-311764-5 (pa)

LC 2009-8328

The author "chronicles the efforts of acclaimed guidance counselor Gweyth (pronounced to rhyme with Faith) 'Smitty' Smith and seven students to find the best colleges for them. . . . Marcus's poignant book will have readers wishing that they too had had Smitty as a guidance counselor and rooting for the students profiled." Libr J

Includes bibliographical references

Metcalf, Linda

How to say it to get into the college of your choice; application, essay, and interview strategies to get you the big envelope. Prentice Hall Press 2007 229p pa $15.95

Grades: 9 10 11 12 **378.1**

1. College applications

ISBN 978-0-7352-0420-1 LC 2007-3058

"This excellent, comprehensive, college application management guide addresses what to do as well as what to say when choosing and being chosen for post-high school education. . . . Using information from public as well as private schools and anticipating the needs of the homeschooler, she meticulously works through the tests, deadlines, common and specific applications, finances, recommendations, personal essay, parental communication, and appropriate interview attire." Voice Youth Advocates

Navigating your freshman year; how to make the leap to college life and land on your feet; [Natavi Guides, Inc.] Prentice Hall Press 2005 155p il (Students helping students) pa $12.95 *

Grades: 9 10 11 12 **378.1**

1. College students

ISBN 0-7352-0392-X LC 2004-56976

This student-authored guide covers topics such as what to bring with you to college, how to deal with roommates, social activites and dating, and study tips

"There's lots of good advice in the pages of this guide. . . . Leaving home, doing laundry, forming good study habits, finding friends, and seeking help are all dealt with efficiently." Booklist

Includes bibliographical references

Nist, Sherrie L. (Sherrie Lee), 1946-
College rules! how to study, survive, and succeed in college; [by] Sherrie Nist-Olenjnik and Jodi Patrick Holschuh. 3rd ed. Ten Speed Press 2011 342p il pa $14.99
Grades: 9 10 11 12   **378.1**
1. College students 2. Study skills
ISBN 978-1-60774-001-8
First published 2002
This college survival primer by two college professors shares advice and strategies on topics ranging from stress management and test preparation to staying motivated and balancing academics with a social life

Pierce, Valerie, 1957-
Countdown to college; 21 "to-do" lists for high school; [by] Valerie Pierce with Cheryl Rilly. 2nd ed. Front Porch Press 2009 167p il pa $11.95
Grades: 9 10 11 12   **378.1**
1. Colleges and universities—Entrance requirements 2. College applications
ISBN 978-0-9656086-8-8
First published 2003
"Step by step strategies for 9th, 10th, 11th, and 12th graders" Cover
The authors offer "academic and financial advice, such as connecting with couselors and teachers, planning an academic schedule, checking admission requirements at certified institutions, and launching a scholarship search. . . . The junior and senior year chapters include sources for getting through testing, campus visits, essays, Advanced Placement choices, application deadlines, 'senioritis,' and hidden costs as well as packing and planning for the big move." Voice Youth Advocates

Pine, Phil
Peterson's master the SAT 2011; Margaret Moran, editor. 11th ed. Peterson's 2010 820p il pa $29.95
Grades: 9 10 11 12   **378.1**
1. Scholastic Assessment Test 2. Colleges and universities—Entrance requirements
ISBN 978-0-7689-2881-5
Annual. First published with title Master the new SAT
Includes CD-ROM
This book provides "test-taking strategies and helps students prepare for the SAT with . . . reviews and 9 full-length practice tests to help sharpen math, writing, and critical reading skills." Publisher's note

Roberts, Andrew Lawrence, 1970-
The thinking student's guide to college; 75 tips for getting a better education; [by] Andrew Roberts. University of Chicago Press 2010 174p (Chicago guides to academic life) $42; pa $14
Grades: 10 11 12 Adult   **378.1**
1. College choice 2. Higher education 3. Colleges and universities—United States 4. Conduct of life
ISBN 978-0-226-72114-9; 978-0-226-72115-6 (pa)
LC 2009-49905
This "easy-to-read, informative book for students and parents on the college-selection process contains commonsense tips as well as helpful information that most would probably not initially consider when selecting a college. . . . This book is highly recommended for students and parents as a first step, before beginning to consider things like which schools to apply to and potential majors. It will give a larger picture of options to explore when making such an important decision and will help save money, sleep, and calm." Libr J
Includes bibliographical references

Robinson, Adam
Cracking the SAT; [by] Adam Robinson, John Katzman, and the staff of the Princeton Review. 2011 ed. Random House 2010 716p il pa $21.99
Grades: 9 10 11 12   **378.1**
1. Scholastic Assessment Test 2. Colleges and universities—Entrance requirements
ISSN 1934-239X
ISBN 978-0-375-42982-8
Also available with DVD for $34.99
Annual. First published 2005 with title Cracking the new SAT to partially replace Cracking the SAT & PSAT by Adam Robinson and John Katzman
At head of title: The Princeton Review
This guide offers practical advice on how to prepare for the SAT college entrance exam. Practice tests are provided with detailed explanations for each answer. Free access to extra tests, lessons, and drills online is also included.

Rooney, John J.
Preparing for college; practical advice for students and their families; [by] John J. Rooney, John F. Reardon; foreword by Katherine Haley Will. Ferguson 2009 196p $34.95; pa $16.95
Grades: 9 10 11 12   **378.1**
1. College students 2. Colleges and universities—United States
ISBN 978-0-8160-7377-1; 0-8160-7377-5; 978-0-8160-7378-8 (pa); 0-8160-7378-3 (pa)
LC 2008-9025
"Ten chapters cover everything from the decision to attend college and making visits to majors of study, acceptance, and covering tuition. Other information includes how to avoid common mistakes made in the selection process, basing a decision on teaching quality and reasonable cost, making an impressive application, and how to succeed both academically and socially." SLJ
"No other book on the market today gathers so much information into such a concise and user-friendly format." Voice Youth Advocates
Includes bibliographical references

Rosen, Louis, Ph. D.
College is not for everyone; [by] Louis Rosen. ScarecrowEducation 2005 87p il pa $20.95 *
Grades: 9 10 11 12   **378.1**
1. Vocational guidance 2. Higher education
ISBN 1-578-86245-0   LC 2004-29878
The author argues "that schools from secondary through community college are not doing enough to prepare students who are not university bound. . . . This

Rosen, Louis, Ph. D.—*Continued*
book will find the most use in the counselors' offices of schools where there are the largest number of students moving straight into the work force after high school." Voice Youth Advocates
Includes bibliographical references

Rubenstein, Jeff
Cracking the PSAT, NMSQT; [by] Jeff Rubenstein and Adam Robinson. 2011 ed. Random House, Inc. 2010 386p il pa $14.99
Grades: 9 10 11 12   **378.1**
    1. Scholastic Assessment Test 2. Colleges and universities—Entrance requirements
    ISSN 1549-6120
    ISBN 978-0-375-42981-1
    Annual. First published 2005 to partially replace Cracking the SAT & PSAT by Adam Robinson and John Katzman
    At head of title: The Princeton Review
    This guide on how to prepare for the PSAT exam includes practice tests, a listing of important vocabulary words, and the strategies and techniques needed to glean the correct answers to test questions.

Crash course for the SAT; the last-minute guide to scoring high. 4th ed. Random House 2011 230p il pa $9.99
Grades: 9 10 11 12   **378.1**
    1. Scholastic Assessment Test 2. Colleges and universities—Entrance requirements
    ISBN 978-0-375-42831-9
    First published 1999
    At head of title: The Princeton Review
    This book provides strategies and practice questions for students who have little time left to study for the SAT.

Schoem, David
College knowledge for the Jewish student; 101 tips. University of Michigan 2010 232p pa $20.95
Grades: 10 11 12 Adult   **378.1**
    1. College students 2. Life skills 3. Jews—Social life and customs
    ISBN 978-0-472-03430-7   LC 2010-21415
    This book "includes tips on the academic aspects of college life, like communicating with faculty, learning what is where on campus, where to go for help with coursework, how to manage one's time for a balanced experience, etc. In addition, it offers advice on dealing with family, finances, health, and safety, as well as the many social and emotional aspects of this . . . rite of passage." Publisher's note

Silivanch, Annalise
Making the right college choice; technical, 2-year, 4-year. Rosen Pub. Group 2010 80p il (Thinking about college) lib bdg $30.60; pa $14.15; ebook $30.60 *
Grades: 9 10 11 12   **378.1**
    1. College choice
    ISBN   978-1-4358-3598-6   (lib   bdg);
    978-1-4358-8508-0 (pa); 978-1-4488-0070-4 (ebook)
                                        LC 2009-21848

"The major question asked by Silivanch is whether to attend college or not. The author concludes . . . that attending a two or four-year college is a must. She makes the case for college as a rite of passage for high school graduates, arguing that they deny themselves monetary gain and economic status when they do not choose to further their education, a position backed up by salary statistics. The book walks readers briefly through the college application process, and in a departure from the other books, outlines the economy's impact on college selection." SLJ
Includes bibliographical references

Steinberg, Jacques
The gatekeepers; inside the admissions process of a premier college. Viking 2002 xxiii, 292p hardcover o.p. pa $15
Grades: 11 12 Adult   **378.1**
    1. Wesleyan University (Middletown, Conn.)
    2. College applications
    ISBN 0-670-03135-6; 0-14-200308-5 (pa)
                                        LC 2002-16884
    The author follows "the procedures at Wesleyan University for a year . . . [to] see how the admissions process really looks, to the admitters as well as the applicants." N Y Times Book Rev
    "This insightful and readable book should be purchased by all academic and large public libraries." Libr J
    Includes bibliographical references

Up your score; the underground guide to the SAT; by Larry Berger ... [et al.]; illustrations by Chris Kalb. 2011-2012 ed. Workman Pub. 2010 328p il pa $12.95
Grades: 9 10 11 12   **378.1**
    1. Scholastic Assessment Test
    ISBN 978-0-7611-5873-8
    First published 1987 by New Chapter Press with title: Up your S.A.T. score. Frequently revised
    Presents a study guide intended to improve the readers score on the SAT test, and includes vocabulary words, concentration and memory activities, and sample test questions.

Yaverbaum, Eric
Life's little college admissions insights; top tips from the country's most acclaimed guidance counselors; [by] Eric and Cole Yaverbaum. Morgan James Pub. 2010 125p il pa $14.95
Grades: 9 10 11 12   **378.1**
    1. College applications 2. College choice
    ISBN 978-1-60037-728-0
    For this book, "experts from around the country were interviewed and have given many . . . opinions on what's important from their own first hand experience advising hundreds of thousands of students in their careers." Publisher's note

378.3   Student aid and related topics

Bissonnette, Zach

Debt-free U; how I paid for an oustanding college education without loans, scholarships, or mooching off my parents. Portfolio 2010 290p pa $16

Grades: 10 11 12 Adult   **378.3**
1. College costs 2. Personal finance 3. Higher education

ISBN 978-1-59184-298-9   LC 2010-18510

Challenges popular beliefs that college finances must impose financial hardships for parents and students, posing strategies for attending non-private schools, avoiding student loans, and maximizing available resources.

"This is a timely guide to a decision that has important financial ramifications." Booklist

Includes bibliographical references

College Entrance Examination Board

2011 scholarship handbook; [by] College Board. 14th ed. College Board 2010 616p pa $28.99

Grades: 9 10 11 12   **378.3**
1. Scholarships—Directories 2. Reference books

ISBN 978-0-87447-906-5

Annual. First published 1997. Alternate title: College Board scholarship handbook 2011

Information on more than 2,100 undergraduate scholarships, internships, and loan programs. Entries are indexed by category, among them gender, minority status, field of study, and career interest. Includes a planning worksheet to help students organize applications.

Getting financial aid 2011; [by the] College Board. 5th ed. College Board 2010 986p il pa $21.99 *

Grades: 11 12 Adult   **378.3**
1. College costs 2. Student loan funds

ISBN 978-0-8744-7905-8

Annual. First published with title: The college cost book. Continues College Board guide to getting financial aid

This guide covers over 3000 two- and four-year institutions. Provides information on what each college really costs, describes aid packages and includes tips on application procedures.

College financing information for teens; tips for a successful financial life; edited by Karen Bellenir. Omnigraphics, Inc. 2008 438p (Teen finance series) $65 *

Grades: 9 10 11 12   **378.3**
1. College costs 2. Student aid 3. Personal finance

ISBN 978-0-7808-0988-8   LC 2007-43689

"Including facts about planning, saving, and paying for post-secondary education, with information about college savings plans, scholarships, grants, loans, military service, and more." Title page

"This guide deserves a spot in every school, public, and community college library. Filled with information on helping students make choices about higher education, including college selection and applications, it will also help them make sense of the myriad ways to pay for it." SLJ

Includes bibliographical references

High school senior's guide to merit and other no-need funding, 2008-2010; [by] Gail Ann Schlachter, R. David Weber. Reference Service Press 2008 410p $29.95

Grades: 11 12 Adult   **378.3**
1. Scholarships—Directories 2. Student aid—Directories 3. Reference books

ISSN 1099-9132

ISBN 978-1-58841-165-5

Biennial. First published 1996

Lists and describes more than 1000 merit scholarships and other no-need funding programs available to high school seniors and recent graduates.

Hollander, Barbara, 1970-

Paying for college; practical, creative strategies; [by] Barbara Gottfried Hollander. Rosen Pub. 2010 80p il (Thinking about college) lib bdg $30.60; pa $14.15; ebook $30.60 *

Grades: 9 10 11 12   **378.3**
1. College costs 2. Student aid

ISBN 978-1-4358-3599-3 (lib bdg); 1-4358-3599-9 (lib bdg); 978-1-4358-8504-2 (pa); 1-4358-8504-X (pa); 978-1-4488-0071-1 (ebook)   LC 2009-18681

This book "discusses in clear detail the various governmental loans, grants, and scholarships that are available to students." SLJ

Includes bibliographical references

How to pay for college; a library how-to handbook; [by] editors of the American Library Association. American Library Association 2011 170p il $20; pa $14.95

Grades: 11 12 Adult   **378.3**
1. College costs 2. Education—Finance 3. Scholarships 4. Student aid

ISBN 978-0-8389-1077-1; 978-1-61608-155-3 (pa)   LC 2010-47768

Readers "can use this guide to: fill out forms for financial aid, loans, and scholarships; find ways to plan and save for the high cost of college tuition; [and] narrow their search to those schools that are the best fit. . . . [This] guide emphasizes the help that the local library can offer in this process, using its reference materials, the Internet, and the advice of experienced researchers." Publisher's note

Includes bibliographical references

Peterson's how to get money for college; financing your future beyond federal aid. 28th ed. Peterson's 2010 863p pa $33.95 *

Grades: 11 12 Adult   **378.3**
1. College costs 2. Student loan funds 3. Scholarships

ISSN 1541-1591

ISBN 978-0-7689-2886-0

Annual. First published 1983. Variant titles: Paying less for college; College money handbook

Peterson's how to get money for college—*Continued*

A resource for anyone looking to supplement his or her federal financial-aid package with funds from colleges and universities, this directory features information on need-based and non-need gifts, loans, and more.

Schlachter, Gail A.

College student's guide to merit and other no-need funding, 2008-2010; [by] Gail Ann Schlachter, R. David Weber. Reference Service Press 2008 490p $32.50

Grades: 11 12 Adult   **378.3**
1. Scholarships—Directories 2. Student aid—Directories 3. Reference books
ISSN 1099-9086
ISBN 978-1-58841-166-2
First published 1998. Frequently revised
Compiles over thirteen hundred scholarships and college funding programs that are based on merit rather than financial need.

Directory of financial aids for women 2009-2011; [by] Gail Ann Schlachter, R. David Weber. Reference Service Press 2009 552p $45 *

Grades: 11 12 Adult   **378.3**
1. Scholarships—Directories 2. Women—Education—Directories 3. Reference books
ISSN 0732-5215
ISBN 978-1-58841-194-5
Biennial. First published 1978
Describes "scholarships, fellowships, loans, grants, awards, and internships designed primarily or exclusively for women. . . . Lists state sources of educational benefits and offers an annotated bibliography of directories that list general financial aid programs. Program title, sponsoring organization, geographic, subject, and filing date indexes." Ref Sources for Small & Medium-sized Libr. 5th edition

Financial aid for the disabled and their families, 2010-2012; [by] Gail Ann Schlachter, R. David Weber. Reference Service Press 2010 480p $40 *

Grades: 11 12 Adult   **378.3**
1. Scholarships 2. Physically handicapped
ISBN 978-1-58841-204-1
Biennial. First published 1988
"Provides information on a wide range of funding needs in such areas as education, career development, research, and travel. Includes multiple indexes; cross-referenced." N Y Public Libr Book of How & Where to Look It Up

378.73   Higher education—United States

Asher, Donald

Cool colleges for the hyper-intelligent, self-directed, late blooming, and just plain different. 2nd ed. Ten Speed Press 2007 287p il pa $21.95

Grades: 9 10 11 12   **378.73**
1. College choice 2. Colleges and universities—United States—Directories 3. Reference books
ISBN 978-1-58008-839-8; 1-58008-839-2
LC 2007-922323
First published 2000
Profiles more than 40 innovative and unusual schools of higher learning.

Barron's profiles of American colleges, 2011; compiled and edited by the College Division of Barron's Educational Series. 29th ed. Barron's Educational Series, Inc. 2010 1652p map pa $28.99

Grades: 11 12 Adult   **378.73**
1. Colleges and universities—United States—Directories 2. Reference books
ISBN 978-0-7641-9768-0
Annual. First published 1964
This college guide contains "information on enrollments, tuition and fees, academic programs, campus environment, available financial aid, and [more.] . . . Every accredited four-year college in the United States is profiled, and readers are directed to a . . . Web site featuring a FREE ACCESS college search engine that presents exclusive online information to help students match their academic plans and aptitudes with the admission requirements and academic programs of each school." Publisher's note

College Entrance Examination Board

Book of majors 2011; [by] the College Board. 5th ed. Henry Holt 2010 1328p pa $26.99

Grades: 11 12 Adult   **378.73**
1. Colleges and universities—United States—Directories 2. Colleges and universities—Curricula 3. Reference books
ISBN 978-0-8744-7904-1
Annual. First published 1977 with title: The college handbook index of majors. Variant titles: The College Board book of majors; The College Board index of majors and graduate degrees; Index of majors and graduate degrees
Provides information on over nine hundred college majors, including related fields, prior high school subjects, possible courses of study, and career options and trends for graduates.

College handbook 2011; [by] the College Board. Henry Holt 2010 2214p pa $29.99

Grades: 11 12 Adult   **378.73**
1. Colleges and universities—United States—Directories 2. Reference books
ISBN 978-0-8744-7903-4
Annual. First published 1941 by Ginn with title: Annual handbook

College Entrance Examination Board—*Continued*

This work offers "detailed information for college-bound students on such subjects as freshman admissions requirements and procedures, enrollment, majors, expenses, financial aid, and many other areas of interest." N Y Public Libr. Book of How & Where to Look It Up

Fiske, Edward B.

Fiske guide to colleges 2011; [by] Edward B. Fiske, with Robert Logue and the Fiske Guide to Colleges staff. 27th ed. Sourcebooks 2010 xxxv, 780p pa $23.99 *

Grades: 11 12 Adult   **378.73**
1. Colleges and universities—United States—Directories 2. College choice 3. Reference books
ISBN 978-1-4022-0961-1
Annual. First published 1982 with title: The New York Times selective guide to colleges

This guide to some 310 of the best colleges and universities nationwide includes information on admissions, costs, financial aid, housing, social life, and academic strengths and weaknesses.

Kravets, Marybeth

The K & W guide to colleges for students with learning disabilities or attention deficit hyperactivity disorder; [by] Marybeth Kravets and Imy F. Wax. 10th ed. Random House 2010 831p pa $29.99 *

Grades: 9 10 11 12 Adult   **378.73**
1. Learning disabilities 2. Colleges and universities—United States—Directories 3. Reference books
ISSN 1934-4775
ISBN 978-0-375-42961-3
"A resource book for students, parents, and professionals"

Biennial. First published 1991 with title: The K & W guide to colleges for the learning disabled
At head of title: Princeton Review

This guide "includes profiles of over 300 schools, advice from specialists in the field of learning disabilities, and strategies to help students find the best match for their needs." Publisher's note

Morkes, Andrew

College exploration on the internet; a student and counselor's guide to more than 1,000 websites and resources; by Andrew Morkes and Amy McKenna. 2nd ed. College & Career Press 2009 xxxviii, 296p il pa $19.95 *

Grades: 9 10 11 12 Adult   **378.73**
1. College choice 2. Web sites—Directories 3. Reference books
ISBN 978-0-9745251-4-3   LC 2008-28982
First published 2004

"The book is organized into two main sections: college resource Web sites and college/career association Web resources. . . . The sites themselves are organized alphabetically by title and offer a concise summary, the best features, and important information about the site,

including whether the site is fee based. . . . This book is an essential addition to college and career collections in school and public libraries." Voice Youth Advocates
Includes bibliographical references

Peterson's four-year colleges 2012. 42nd ed. Peterson's 2011 1987p il pa $32.95 *

Grades: 11 12 Adult   **378.73**
1. Colleges and universities—United States—Directories 2. Reference books
ISBN 978-0-7689-3279-9
Annual. First published 1966 as part of Peterson's annual guide to undergraduate study. Formerly titled Peterson's guide to four-year colleges

This reference compiles profiles of over 2,500 accredited institutions in the United States with four year undergraduate degree programs.

Peterson's two-year colleges, 2011. 41st ed. Peterson's 2010 554p il pa $29.95 *

Grades: 11 12 Adult   **378.73**
1. Colleges and universities—United States—Directories 2. Reference books
ISSN 1541-5066
ISBN 978-0-7689-2835-8
Annual. First published 1966 as part of Peterson's annual guide to undergradute study. Formerly titled Peterson's guide to two-year colleges

This reference compiles profiles of over 1,500 accredited institutions in the United States with two year associate degree programs.

They teach that in college; [managing editor, Andrew Morkes] 2nd ed. College & Career Press 2008 344p il pa $22.95

Grades: 9 10 11 12   **378.73**
1. Colleges and universities—United States—Directories 2. Colleges and universities—Curricula 3. Reference books
ISBN 978-0-9745251-7-4
First published 2006

"A resource guide to more than 95 interesting college majors" Cover

"With 'ripped from the headlines' immediacy for students who are not interested in run-of-the-mill professions, this invaluable resource profiles careers that fill a job market deamnd and pay well; are offered as majors by no more than 25 percent of the nation's colleges; and are fun." Voice Youth Advocates

Ultimate college guide 2011; by the staff of U.S. News & World Report; Anne McGrath, editor. 8th ed. Sourcebooks Inc. 2010 1765p il pa $29.99

Grades: 9 10 11 12 Adult   **378.73**
1. Colleges and universities—United States—Directories 2. Reference books
ISBN 978-1-4022-4306-6
Annual. First published 2004
At head of title: U.S. News & World Report

This guide features "data on more than 1,400 colleges and universities." Publisher's note

381 Commerce (Trade)

Eltis, David, 1940-
Atlas of the transatlantic slave trade; [by] David Eltis and David Richardson; foreword by David Brion Davis; afterword by David W. Blight. Yale University Press 2010 xxvi, 307p il map (The Lewis Walpole series in eighteenth-century culture and history) $50 *
Grades: 11 12 Adult   381
1. Slave trade—Maps 2. Atlases 3. Reference books
ISBN 978-0-300-12460-6
"For nearly 20 years, the Trans-Atlantic Slave Trade Database project has been diligently tabulating all the slave ship crossings of the Atlantic Ocean, from 1500 to 1900. . . . With 189 informative and handsome maps, Eltis and Richardson relay and interpret the information contained in this rich database, mixing in beautiful historical illustrations and key passages from relevant texts. An accessible narrative, meanwhile, expands on the information in the maps. . . . This marvelous book will change how people think of the slave trade." Foreign Affairs

382 International commerce (Foreign trade)

Goldstein, Natalie
Globalization and free trade; foreword by Frank Musgrave. Facts on File 2007 406p il (Global issues) $45
Grades: 9 10 11 12   382
1. Globalization 2. Free trade
ISBN 0-8160-6808-9; 978-0-8160-6808-1
LC 2006-28874
This book "outlines the history of the expansion and globalization of national economies and explains how globalization evolved to its present state. This . . . volume reviews current issues surrounding globalization, and presents case studies on several countries—including the United States, East Asia, Brazil, Russia, and China—to illustrate both the promise and the problems inherent in today's globalized markets." Publisher's note
Includes glossary and bibliographical references

384 Communications Telecommunication

Henderson, Harry, 1951-
Communications and broadcasting; from wired words to wireless Web. rev ed. Facts on File 2006 201p il (Milestones in discovery and invention) $35
Grades: 7 8 9 10 11 12   384
1. Telecommunication
ISBN 0-8160-5748-6; 978-0-8160-5748-1
LC 2006-5577
First published 1997

This is a "look at the development and interconnection of [the following] scientific ideas: electromagnetism, leading to the telegraph and telephone; Maxwell's wave theory, leading to radio and television; and communications and information theory, from Claude Shannon to the World Wide Web and beyond. In addition, there are . . . portraits of the inventors themselves." Publisher's note
Includes glossary and bibliographical references

390 Customs, etiquette & folklore

The **Greenwood** encyclopedia of daily life; a tour through history from ancient times to the present; Joyce E. Salisbury, general editor. Greenwood Press 2004 6v il map set $599.95 *
Grades: 11 12 Adult   390
1. Manners and customs—Encyclopedias 2. Civilization—Encyclopedias 3. Reference books
ISBN 0-313-32541-3   LC 2003-54724
Contents: v1 The ancient world / Gregory S. Aldrete, volume editor; v2 The medieval world / Joyce E. Salisbury, volume editor; v3 15th and 16th centuries / Lawrence Morris, volume editor; v4 17th and 18th centuries / Peter Seelig, volume editor; v5 19th century / Andrew E. Kersten, volume editor; v6 The modern world / Andrew E. Kersten, volume editor
This "work provides an overview of the material, domestic, recreational, religious, political, intellectual, and economic aspects of daily life in a selection of cultures from six broad historical periods. . . . Each of the six volumes gives a survey of the historical period in each culture covered, which is representative rather than exhaustive, then covers aspects of daily life from broad topics to narrower." Libr J
Includes bibliographical references

391 Costume and personal appearance

Ashenburg, Kathy
The dirt on clean; an unsanitized history; [by] Katherine Ashenburg. North Point Press 2007 358p il $24; pa $15
Grades: 11 12 Adult   391
1. Hygiene 2. Personal grooming
ISBN   978-0-86547-690-5;   0-86547-690-X; 978-0-374-53137-9 (pa); 0-374-53137-4 (pa)
LC 2007-32334
This is a study "of attitudes to hygiene through time." Publisher's note
"Brimming with lively anecdotes, this well-researched, smartly paced and endearing history of Western cleanliness holds a welcome mirror up to our intimate selves, revealing deep-seated desires and fears spanning 2000-plus years." Publ Wkly
Includes bibliographical references

Brasser, Ted J.

Native American clothing; an illustrated history; [by] Theodore Brasser. Firefly Books 2009 368p il map $65

Grades: 9 10 11 12 Adult   **391**
  1. Native American costume 2. Clothing and dress 3. Native Americans—Antiquities
  ISBN 978-1-55407-433-4; 1-55407-433-9
             LC 2009-482555

A collection of photographs from museums, collectors and private dealers that documents five centuries of Native American artistry.

"Featuring an amazing breadth of clothing design, motif, and technique, Brasser's volume makes an excellent cross-collection resource for anyone interested in indigenous art or Native American history." Publ Wkly

Includes bibliographical references

Cosgrave, Bronwyn

The complete history of costume and fashion; from ancient Egypt to the present day. Checkmark Bks. 2001 256p il $37.95 *

Grades: 11 12 Adult   **391**
  1. Costume—History
  ISBN 0-8160-4574-7   LC 00-64401

"This book explores the development of fashion from its simple and practical beginnings to the growth of the multibillion dollar global industry that it is today. . . . Trends in clothing style, fabric, accessories, and footwear {are examined}." Publisher's note

Includes bibliographical references

Cumming, Valerie

The dictionary of fashion history; [by] Valerie Cumming, C.W. Cunnington and P.E. Cunnington. Berg 2010 286p il $99.95; pa $29.95 *

Grades: 11 12 Adult   **391**
  1. Clothing and dress—History—Encyclopedias 2. Fashion—Encyclopedias 3. Reference books
  ISBN 978-1-84788-534-0; 978-1-84788-533-3 (pa)

"Based on A dictionary of English costume 900-1900 by C.W. and P.E. Cunnington and Charles Beard, now completely revised, updated and supplemented to the present day by Valerie Cumming." Title page

"Concise yet detailed, academic, and fabulous, . . . [this book] is truly a dictionary—a compendium of fashion and fashion-related terms, defined in alphabetical order—and it covers 900 C.E. to the present day. . . . [This] is an essential purchase (and great value!) for any library serving patrons with an interest in fashion, clothing, art, history, theater, anthropology, or nearly any area of the social sciences." Libr J

Includes glossary and bibliographical references

DeJean, Joan E.

The essence of style; how the French invented high fashion, fine food, chic cafés, style, sophistication, and glamour. Free Press 2005 303p il $25; pa $15

Grades: 11 12 Adult   **391**
  1. Louis XIV, King of France, 1638-1715 2. Fashion—History 3. France—Social life and customs
  ISBN 0-7432-6413-4; 0-7432-6414-2 (pa)
             LC 2005-40019

A historian of seventeenth-century French culture argues that "the French under Louis XIV set the standards of sophistication, style, and glamour that still rule our lives today." Publisher's note

"An unusual and delightfully educational perspective on snob appeal." Booklist

Includes bibliographical references

DeMello, Margo

Encyclopedia of body adornment. Greenwood Press 2007 xx, 326p il $79.95

Grades: 9 10 11 12 Adult   **391**
  1. Reference books 2. Tattooing—Encyclopedias 3. Body piercing—Encyclopedias 4. Manners and customs—Encyclopedias
  ISBN 978-0-313-33695-9   LC 2007-16304

"Over 200 entries address the major adornments and modifications, their historical and cross-cultural locations, and the major cultural groups and places in which body modification has been central to social and cultural practices." Publisher's note

Includes bibliographical references

Encyclopedia of clothing and fashion; Valerie Steele, editor in chief. Scribner 2005 3v (Scribner library of daily life) set $395

Grades: 11 12 Adult   **391**
  1. Reference books 2. Costume—Encyclopedias 3. Fashion—Encyclopedias
  ISBN 0-684-31394-4   LC 2004-10098

Alphabetically arranged entries range "from a half page for some particular items, clothing types, fibers, and techniques . . . to multiple pages for *Cross dressing; Dandyism; Hats, men's* and *Hats, women's; Kimono; Street style* and *Twentieth century fashion*, among others. Articles on designers or people who influenced fashion . . . are a significant part of the content, as are articles with a historical slant. . . . Many of the articles are entertaining as well as enlightening. . . . *Encyclopedia of Clothing and Fashion* is an exciting and unique resource that excels in depth and range of coverage." Booklist

Fashions of a decade [series] Chelsea House Publishers 2006 8v il set $280 *

Grades: 7 8 9 10 11 12   **391**
  1. Costume
  ISBN 0-8160-7059-8; 978-0-8160-7059-6

Volumes also available separately ea $35

First published 1991-1992

Contents: The 1920s by Jacqueline Herald; The 1930s by Maria Constantino; The 1940s by Patricia Baker; The 1950s by Patricia Baker; The 1960s by Yvonne Connikie; The 1970s by Jacqueline Herald; The 1980s by Vicky Carnegy; The 1990s by Anne McEvoy

Fashions of a decade [series]—*Continued*

This set describes clothing styles of the 20th century in the context of world events, social movements, and cultural movements of each decade.

"These titles provide colorful and fascinating information. . . . Attractive black-and-white illustrations, color photos, reproductions, sketches from magazines and newspapers, and fact boxes enhance and bring to life these lively and accessible texts." SLJ

Graydon, Shari

In your face; the culture of beauty and you. Annick 2004 176p il hardcover o.p. pa $14.95 *
Grades: 7 8 9 10   391
1. Personal appearance 2. Body image
ISBN 1-55037-857-0; 1-55037-856-2 (pa)
The author "looks at fashion across time and cultures, and analyzes the underlying messages in today's focus . . . on thinness, long nails, and high heels. Along the way, she warns both young men and women of the very real dangers of eating disorders, plastic surgery, liposuction, and other body-image 'solutions.' . . . Graydon will make readers laugh as well as think about the issues." Booklist
Includes bibliographical references

The **Greenwood** encyclopedia of clothing through American history 1900 to the present; Amy T. Peterson, general editor [v. 1], Ann T. Kellogg, general editor [v. 2] Greenwood Press 2008 2v il set $199.95
Grades: 9 10 11 12 Adult   391
1. Reference books 2. Clothing and dress—History—Encyclopedias
ISBN 978-0-313-35855-5; 0-313-35855-9
                                    LC 2008-24624
This encyclopedia "surveys the impact of American social, cultural, and economic life on mainstream clothing and the fashion industry. . . . The encyclopedia's placement of fashion within its social and historical context will be interesting to many readers, including theater students and others doing costume research." Booklist
Includes glossary and bibliographical references

The **Greenwood** encyclopedia of clothing through world history; edited by Jill Condra. Greenwood Press 2007 3v il set $349.95
Grades: 11 12 Adult   391
1. Reference books 2. Clothing and dress—History—Encyclopedias
ISBN 978-0-313-33662-1   LC 2007-30705
"Volume one (prehistory to 1500 C.E.) includes cultures such as ancient Greece and Persia; volume two (1501-1800) chronicles dress in places such as Europe, North America, India, and Japan; volume three (1801-present) has an international scope and is arranged chronologically. Each chapter targets a specific period and opens with an accurate and selectively detailed time line and an introduction to the era and the milestones in clothing and textiles, laying an appropriate foundation for the discussion that follows. . . . An outstanding purchase with an ambitious scope." SLJ
Includes bibliographical references

Kelly, Clinton, 1969-

Dress your best; the complete guide to finding the style that's right for your body; [by] Clinton Kelly and Stacy London. Three Rivers Press 2005 255p il pa $18.95
Grades: 11 12 Adult   391
1. Clothing and dress 2. Fashion
ISBN 0-307-23671-4   LC 2005-13681
This fashion guide describes specific male and female body types, and the kinds of outfits that match well with them. "Each type's section opens with a photo of an average-looking model sporting a basic swimsuit, along with comments from the model and the authors. . . . Ladies and gentlemen, start your shopping engines—and don't leave home without this book!" Publ Wkly

Nunn, Joan

Fashion in costume, 1200-2000. 2nd ed. New Amsterdam Bks. 2000 280p pa $18.95
Grades: 11 12 Adult   391
1. Costume—History
ISBN 1-56663-279-X   LC 99-47516
First published 1984 by Schocken Bks. with title: Fashion in costume, 1200-1980
This history of American and European costume covers men's, women's, and children's dress, accessories and jewelry, fabrics, and color. Discusses how historical, social, economic, and artistic events influence fashion
Includes bibliographical references

Paterek, Josephine

Encyclopedia of American Indian costume. Norton 1996 516p il pa $24.95
Grades: 11 12 Adult   391
1. Native American costume—Encyclopedias 2. Reference books
ISBN 0-393-31382-4
First published 1994 by ABC-CLIO
Paterek describes "the clothing used for everyday, war, rites, and ceremonies for men, women, and children in hundreds of tribes in diverse climates stretching over centuries. Well-organized text and 400 drawings and authentic photos plus the cultural essays prefacing the 10 regional groupings and each tribe put the costumes in historical, social, and geographic context. Appendixes cover terminology and the materials used in clothing. The excellent bibliographies in this classic work both document and encourage further reading." Am Libr
Includes bibliographical references

What people wore when; a complete illustrated history of costume from ancient times to the nineteenth century for every level of society; consultant editor Melissa Leventon. St. Martin's Griffin 2008 352p il pa $29.95
Grades: 11 12 Adult   391
1. Clothing and dress—History
ISBN 978-0-312-38321-3; 0-312-38321-5
                                    LC 2008-12938
"This attractive book will appeal to teens looking for quick answers for a last-minute assignment, and it will also be of interest to budding fashionistas and social historians. Leventon has combined current research on cos-

What people wore when—*Continued*
tume and dress through the ages with the detailed beauty of the work of two 19th-century illustrators, Auguste Racinet and Friedrich Hottenroth, to provide a historical and thematic examination of fashion and dress that is both comprehensive and readable." SLJ

Includes glossary and bibliographical references

392   Customs of life cycle and domestic life

Alvarez, Julia, 1950-
Once upon a quinceañera; coming of age in the USA. Viking Adult 2007 278p hardcover o.p. pa $15

Grades: 11 12 Adult   **392**
1. Quinceañera (Social custom) 2. Hispanic Americans—Social life and customs
ISBN   978-0-670-03873-2;   0-670-03873-3; 978-0-452-28830-0 (pa); 0-452-28830-4 (pa)
LC 2006-37561
The author "explores the quinceañera, the coming-of-age ceremony for Latinas turning 15." Publ Wkly
This is an "enlightening look at an important event in the lives of Latinas in America." Booklist
Includes bibliographical references

Fifteen candles; 15 tales of taffeta, hairspray, drunk uncles, and other Quinceañera stories: an anthology; edited by Adriana Lopez. Rayo/HarperCollins 2007 332p il pa $14.95
Grades: 11 12 Adult   **392**
1. Quinceañera (Social custom) 2. Hispanic Americans—Social life and customs
ISBN 978-0-06-124192-5; 0-06-124192-X
LC 2007-14489
"Fifteen writers tell personal, often irreverent stories about *quinceañera*, the traditional celebration that marks a Latina's fifteenth birthday." Booklist
"This collection offers a memorable blend of the sweetness and pain that mark life's milestones." SLJ

393   Death customs

Pringle, Heather Anne, 1952-
The mummy congress; science, obsession, and the everlasting dead; {by} Heather Pringle. Hyperion 2001 368p il hardcover o.p. pa $13.95
Grades: 11 12 Adult   **393**
1. Mummies 2. Forensic anthropology
ISBN 0-7868-6551-2; 0-7868-8463-0 (pa)
LC 00-54487
"Besides outstanding members of the scientific association that gathers as the Mummy Congress, Pringle limns the many varieties of mummies, from the world's oldest, preserved by the high-altitude climate of the Andes, to modern Communist dictators, self-mummifying Buddhists, and the subjects of extreme cosmetic surgery. More astounding than all the fright flicks about shambling, gauze-wrapped menaces wound together." Booklist
Includes bibliographical references

394.1   Eating, drinking; using drugs

Schlosser, Eric
Chew on this; everything you don't want to know about fast food; by Eric Schlosser and Charles Wilson. Houghton Mifflin Co. 2006 304p il $16; pa $9.99
Grades: 6 7 8 9 10   **394.1**
1. Eating habits 2. Convenience foods 3. Food industry
ISBN 0-618-71031-0; 0-618-59394-2 (pa)
LC 2005-27527
"An adaptation of Schlosser's *Fast Food Nation* (Houghton, 2001), *Chew on This* covers the history of the fast-food industry and delves into the agribusiness and animal husbandry methods that support it. . . . Equally disturbing is his revelation of the way that the fast-food giants have studied childhood behavior and geared their commercials and free toy inclusions to hook the youngest consumers. The text is written in a lively, layout-the-facts manner. Occasional photographs add bits of visual interest." SLJ

Fast food nation; the dark side of the all-American meal. Houghton Mifflin 2001 356p il $25 *
Grades: 11 12 Adult   **394.1**
1. Food industry 2. Restaurants 3. Convenience foods
ISBN 0-395-97789-4   LC 00-53886
Also available in paperback from HarperPerennial
"Schlosser documents the effects of fast food on America's economy, its youth culture, and allied industries. . . . Starting with a young woman who makes minimum wage working at a Colorado fast-food restaurant, Schlosser relates the oft-told story of Ray Kroc's founding of McDonald's. The author also tells about the development of the franchise method of business ownership and the health and nutrition implications of fast-food consumption." Booklist
Includes bibliographical references

Tobacco in history and culture; an encyclopedia; Jordan Goodman, editor in chief. Thomson Gale 2005 2v il (Scribner turning points library) set $275
Grades: 11 12 Adult   **394.1**
1. Tobacco—Encyclopedias 2. Reference books
ISBN 0-684-31405-3   LC 2004-7109
The author "focuses on the cultural aspects of tobacco as a drug, health hazard, social phenomena, and economic force." Ref & User Services Quarterly
"This makes an excellent starting point for readers looking for quick entrance to the vast body of knowledge of the history and diversity of tobacco uses, tobacco health, addiction, social control issues, advertising, production, and distribution, among other topics." Choice
Includes bibliographical references

394.26 Holidays

The **American** book of days; compiled and edited by Stephen G. Christianson. 4th ed. Wilson, H.W. 2000 xxvi, 945p $140 *
Grades: 8 9 10 11 12 Adult   394.26
1. Holidays 2. Festivals 3. Reference books
ISBN 0-8242-0954-0   LC 99-86611
First published 1937 under the authorship of George William Douglas

This work "consists of essays that are a day-to-day recounting of selective American historic events, including those of festivals and celebrations. . . . The topics of these essays vary, with the editor highlighting notable activities from military, scientific, ethnic, political, and cultural occurrences. Not limited strictly to events, essays are also devoted to individuals who played a significant role in American history. . . . A comprehensive index and table of contents provide excellent means for finding specific topics." Am Ref Books Annu, 2001

Chase's calendar of events 2011; the ultimate go-to guide for special days, weeks and months. McGraw-Hill 2011 752p il pa $75 *
Grades: Adult Professional   394.26
1. Calendars 2. Holidays 3. Almanacs 4. Reference books
ISSN 1083-0588
ISBN 978-0-07-174026-5
Annual. First published 1958 by Contemporary Bks. under the editorship of William D. and Helen M. Chase with title: Chase's calendar of annual events. Variant title: Chase's annual events
Includes CD-ROM

"Day-by-day listing of national and state holidays, religious observances, special events, festivals and fairs, and historical anniversaries and birthdays. Covers U.S. events primarily, but some international occasions and anniversaries are included." N Y Public Libr Book of How & Where to Look It Up

Christianson, Stephen G.
The international book of days; edited by Lynn M. Messina; contributors, Jennifer Peloso, Norris Smith, Laura Ware. H.W. Wilson 2004 xxxi, 889p il map $140
Grades: 11 12 Adult   394.26
1. Holidays 2. Festivals
ISBN 0-8242-0975-3   LC 2004-42285
This "book presents an international tour of holidays and major historical events. Organized by day of the year, the book covers some 1500 key events in world history." Libr J

Encyclopedia of holidays and celebrations; a country-by-country guide; Matthew Dennis, editor. Facts on File 2006 3v il map (Facts on File library of world history) set $275
Grades: 11 12 Adult   394.26
1. Holidays 2. Festivals
ISBN 0-8160-6235-8; 978-0-8160-6235-5
LC 2005-27700

This is "a three-volume guide that explores holidays and festivals in 206 countries. Volumes I and II are organized alphabetically by country, and volume III contains overviews of major internationally observed holidays and religions. . . . This welcome addition to multicultural studies is attractively laid out, easy to use, great for browsing as well as fact finding, and is highly recommended for high school, public, and college libraries." Ref & User Services Quarterly
Includes bibliographical references

Forbes, Bruce David
Christmas; a candid history. University of California Press 2007 179p il $19.95; pa $12.95
Grades: 9 10 11 12 Adult   394.26
1. Christmas
ISBN 978-0-520-25104-5; 978-0-520-25802-0 (pa)
LC 2007-00366
The author "presents a brief social history of Christmas from pre-Christian winter celebrations to the commercialization of the holiday in American popular culture. The growth of the holiday to include Christmas cards, music and movies are included in this easy to read overview." Univ Press Books for Public and Second Sch Libr, 2008
Includes bibliographical references

Gulevich, Tanya
Encyclopedia of Christmas and New Year's celebrations; illustrated by Mary Ann Stavros-Lanning. Omnigraphics 2003 xx, 977p il $68
Grades: 11 12 Adult   394.26
1. Christmas 2. New Year
ISBN 0-7808-0625-5   LC 2003-40580
First published 2000 with title: Encyclopedia of Christmas

"Over 240 alphabetically arranged entries covering Christmas, New Year's, and related days of observance, including folk and religious customs, history, legends, and symbols from around the world; supplemented by a bibliography and lists of Christmas Web sites and associations. . . . " Title page
The author "covers a variety of secular and sacred aspects of Christmas and New Year's celebrations. . . . This encyclopedic work is useful for those schools where folklore is covered, or for those interested in origins of the holidays." Libr Media Connect
Includes bibliographical references

Hillstrom, Laurie
The Thanksgiving book; [by] Laurie C. Hillstrom. Omnigraphics 2008 328p il $65
Grades: 9 10 11 12 Adult   394.26
1. Thanksgiving Day
ISBN 978-0-7808-0403-6   LC 2007-25708
"A companion to the holiday covering its history, lore, traditions, foods, and symbols, including primary sources, poems, prayers, songs, hymns, and recipes: supplemented by a chronology, bibliography with web sites, and index." Title Page
"This book is definitely a wonderful tribute to the holiday of Thanksgiving." Am Ref Books Annu, 2008
Includes bibliographical references

Holiday symbols and customs. 4th ed., edited by Helene Henderson. Omnigraphics 2009 1321p $94 *
Grades: 11 12 Adult   394.26
1. Holidays 2. Festivals
ISBN 978-0-7808-0990-1   LC 2008-28403
First published 1998 with title: Holiday symbols
"A guide to the legend and lore behind the traditions, rituals, foods, games, animals, and other symbols and activities associated with holidays and holy days, feasts and fasts, and other celebrations, covering ancient, calendar, religious, historic, folkloric, national, promotional, and sporting events, as observed in the United States and around the world" Title page
"Describes the origins of 323 holidays around the world. Explains where, when, and how each event is celebrated, with detailed information on the symbols and customs associated with the holiday. Includes contact information and web sites for related organizations." Publisher's note
Includes bibliographical references

Holidays and anniversaries of the world; Beth A. Baker, editor. 3rd ed. Gale Res. 1998 c1999 1184p $130
Grades: 11 12 Adult   394.26
1. Holidays 2. Festivals 3. Historical chronology
ISBN 0-8103-5477-2   LC 98-38866
First published 1985
"A comprehensive catalogue containing detailed information on every month and day of the year, with coverage of more than 26,000 holidays, anniversaries, fasts and feasts, holy days of the saints, the blesseds, and other days of religious significance, birthdays of the famous, important dates in history, and special events and their sponsors." Title page

Holidays, festivals, and celebrations of the world dictionary; detailing more than 3,000 observances from all 50 states and more than 100 nations: a compendious reference guide to popular, ethnic, religious, national, and ancient holidays. . .; edited by Cherie D. Abbey. 4th ed. Omnigraphics 2010 1323p $144 *
Grades: 8 9 10 11 12 Adult   394.26
1. Holidays—Dictionaries 2. Festivals—Dictionaries 3. Reference books
ISBN 978-0-7808-0994-9   LC 2009-41138
First edition published 1994 compiled by Sue Ellen Thompson and Barbara W. Carlson
"A comprehensive dictionary that describes more than 3,000 holidays and festivals celebrated around the world. Features both secular and religious events from many different cultures, countries, and ethnic groups. Includes contact information for events; multiple appendices with background information on world holidays; extensive bibliography; multiple indexes." Publisher's note

Rajtar, Steve, 1951-
United States holidays and observances; by date, jurisdiction, and subject, fully indexed. McFarland & Co. 2003 165p $45 *
Grades: 11 12 Adult   394.26
1. Holidays 2. Festivals
ISBN 0-7864-1446-4   LC 2002-154293
This "concentrates on observances and holidays established by statute in the U.S. and American Samoa, District of Columbia, Guam, the Northern Mariana Islands, Puerto Rico, and the U.S. Virgin Islands. In addition, UN-designated holidays are included. . . . The text is arranged by month, and chapters for each month are divided into 'Observances with Variable Dates' and 'Observances with Fixed Dates.' Each entry identifies the observance as federal or specific to a state and offers a description that ranges in length from three or four lines to a quarter page. . . . [This] would be a good addition to ready-reference desks in public libraries and information centers in schools." Booklist

Roy, Christian, 1963-
Traditional festivals; a multicultural encyclopedia. ABC-CLIO 2005 2v il set $185
Grades: 9 10 11 12   394.26
1. Festivals
ISBN 1-57607-089-1   LC 2005-10444
"The work attempts to cover festivals from all major religions. Moreover, the text also takes into account festival and feast days from ancient or extinct societies. . . . Articles trace the historical development of festivals as well as geographical variations of these holy and feast days in a comparative framework. . . . This will be a very helpful resource for researchers in the field of comparative religion and culture." Choice
Includes bibliographical references

395   Etiquette (Manners)

Baldrige, Letitia
Letitia Baldrige's new manners for new times; a complete guide to etiquette; illustrations by Denise Cavalieri Fike. Scribner 2003 xxvi, 709p il $35
Grades: 11 12 Adult   395
1. Etiquette
ISBN 0-7432-1062-X   LC 2003-65666
First published 1990 with title: Letitia Baldrige's complete guide to the new manners for the 90's
"Combining correctness, consideration, and common sense in equal measure, Baldrige advises readers on proper ways to approach intricate situations. She addresses same-sex unions, pregnant brides, blended and extended families, and sexual harassment with aplomb." Libr J

Isaacs, Florence
What do you say when—; talking to people with confidence on any social or business occasion. Clarkson Potter Publishers 2009 151p $18
Grades: 9 10 11 12 Adult   395
1. Conversation 2. Etiquette
ISBN 978-0-307-40528-9   LC 2008-40535

Isaacs, Florence—*Continued*

"This small book lays out a strategy for successful networking and socializing through a series of simple tips related to a wide array of common business and social situations. The author offers up hundreds of conversation starters designed to elicit thoughtful responses from acquaintances, colleagues, and even complete strangers. . . . Written in a simple and engaging style, this practical guide is filled with real-world scenarios depicting job interviews, family gatherings, dating, and funerals." SLJ

Martin, Judith, 1938-

Miss Manners' guide to excruciatingly correct behavior; illustrated by Gloria Kamen. freshly updated. Norton 2005 858p il $35

Grades: 11 12 Adult   **395**

1. Etiquette

ISBN 0-393-05874-3   LC 2005-00264

First published 1982 by Atheneum Pubs.

This book "covers such modern dilemmas as dealing with intrusive cell phones, handling guests who can't commit, and determining when e-mail is socially correct." Libr J

"Miss Manners is always as entertaining as she is civilized." Booklist

Packer, Alex J., 1951-

How rude! the teenagers' guide to good manners, proper behavior, and not grossing people out. Free Spirit 1997 465p il pa $19.95

Grades: 7 8 9 10   **395**

1. Etiquette

ISBN 1-57542-024-4   LC 97-13015

This guide to etiquette for teenagers covers such areas as sex etiquette, toilet etiquette, net etiquette (cyberspace behavior) as well as the correct way to answer invitations and standard protocols for life in a "proper" society

"This volume not only uses humor to make the subject palatable but also makes good sense in terms of most young people's everyday lives." Booklist

Includes bibliographical references

Post, Peggy, 1945-

Emily Post's Etiquette. 17th ed., [revised by] Peggy Post. HarperCollins Publishers 2004 876p $39.95 *

Grades: 7 8 9 10 11 12 Adult   **395**

1. Etiquette

ISBN 0-06-620957-9   LC 2004-40508

First published 1922 under the authorship of Emily Post. Periodically revised and updated. Title varies. 11th-15th editions revised by Elizabeth Post; 16th-17th editions revised by Peggy Post

New edition in preparation

"The classic reference for which fork to use has been expanded to include such modern situations as dating, living together, second marriages, and co-ed business traveling." N Y Public Libr Book of How & Where to Look It Up

Senning, Cindy Post

Emily Post prom and party etiquette. Collins 2010 134p il $15.99

Grades: 7 8 9 10 11 12   **395**

1. Etiquette 2. Parties

ISBN 978-0-06-111713-8; 0-06-111713-7

     LC 2009-2795

"Covering parties and special occasions like prom, homecoming, quinceañera, and graduation, the authors have developed a modern set of rules for navigating today's more relaxed social customs with finesse and confidence. Myriad issues are tackled, from how to rent a tuxedo and who pays for what on prom night to table settings and crafting the perfect thank-you note, with important points highlighted. The comprehensive guide gives proper respect to religious occasions and thoughtfully explains how to determine from an invitation whether bringing a date is acceptable or not. Witty line drawings complement the text." SLJ

398   Folklore

De Vos, Gail, 1949-

Tales, rumors, and gossip; exploring contemporary folk literature in grades 7-12. Libraries Unlimited 1996 xx, 405p $39

Grades: Adult Professional   **398**

1. Folklore

ISBN 1-56308-190-3   LC 95-19553

"Aimed at the professional, the book is divided into three sections: an introduction to contemporary legends, the role of these legends in the world around us, and a discussion of individual legends. If you are looking for legends on cults, demonology or Satanism, you'll find them here. . . . Librarians and teachers will use this as a resource for contemporary literature classes." Book Rep

Includes bibliographical references

Guiley, Rosemary Ellen

The encyclopedia of vampires & werewolves; foreword by Jeanne Keyes Youngson. 2nd ed. Facts On File 2011 430p il $85; pa $24.95

Grades: 9 10 11 12 Adult   **398**

1. Vampires—Encyclopedias 2. Werewolves—Encyclopedias 3. Monsters—Encyclopedias 4. Reference books

ISBN   978-0-8160-8179-0;   0-8160-8179-4; 978-0-8160-8180-6 (pa); 0-8160-8180-8 (pa); 978-1-4381-3632-5 (ebook); 1-4381-3632-3 (ebook)

     LC 2010034839

First published 2004 with title: The encyclopedia of vampires, werewolves, and other monsters

Contact publisher for ebook pricing

"Entries describe supposed true historical accounts, how vampires and werewolves come into existence, beliefs about vampires and werewolves, and real-life creatures and cases that may have inspired their legends. . . . Fictional vampires from a range of media are discussed, along with the people who helped create them." Publisher's note

Includes bibliographical references

Nigg, Joe

Wonder beasts; tales and lore of the phoenix, the griffin, the unicorn, and the dragon. Libraries Unlimited 1995 160p il $27.50

Grades: 7 8 9 10   **398**

1. Animals—Folklore

ISBN 1-56308-242-X   LC 94-46797

The author "has compiled material ranging from Herodotus, Ovid, Pliny the Elder, to Chinese and Native American folk tales, and fantasies by Edith Nesbit. Each entry is carefully documented and a reference list at the end provides dozens of full citations for those who'd like to delve deeper. Wonder Beasts will be useful to students who are researching myth and folklore, and to librarians and scholars who are looking for a comprehensive source list on the topic." Voice Youth Advocates

Robson, David, 1966-

Encounters with vampires. ReferencePoint Press 2010 c2011 80p il (Vampire library) lib bdg $26.95

Grades: 7 8 9 10   **398**

1. Vampires

ISBN 978-1-6015-2133-0; 1-6015-2133-2

                      LC 2010-10100

The author "lays out both folklore and real-world reports of bloodsucking beings. Expanding beyond familiar Transylvanian tales and stories of vampires in strictly human form, the author's survey is global, from the Malaysian langsuyar, believed to be responsible for many newborn deaths, to the red-eyed, monstrous Latin American chupacabra, notorious for preying on livestock. . . . Young vampire-fiction fans will find much to ponder here, while the accounts of contemporary murders with purported vampire links may emerge as the most chilling and grisly." Booklist

Includes bibliographical references

World folklore for storytellers; tales of wonder, wisdom, fools, and heroes; Josepha Sherman, editor. Sharpe Reference 2010 368p il $95

Grades: 11 12 Adult   **398**

1. Folklore 2. Storytelling

ISBN 978-0-7656-8174-4   LC 2009-10525

This is "a wonderfully wide-ranging collection of nearly 200 ethnically diverse folktales. Particularly vital is that the stories are organized thematically rather than geographically, allowing for broader symbolic and anthropological comparisons. Each narrative runs several pages, includes a brief explanatory introduction, and consistently concludes with at least two bibliographic references. Pockets of multipage color plates offer images from native folktale anthologies and other relevant artistic renderings." Libr J

Includes bibliographical references

398.03   Folklore—Encyclopedias and dictionaries

American folklore; an encyclopedia; edited by Jan Harold Brunvand. Garland 1996 794p il (Garland reference library of the humanities) pa $44.95 hardcover o.p. *

Grades: 11 12 Adult   **398.03**

1. Reference books 2. Folklore—United States—Encyclopedias

ISBN 0-8153-3350-1 (pa)   LC 95-53734

This volume contains "more than 500 articles covering American and Canadian folklore from holidays, festivals, and rituals to crafts, music, dance, and occupations. Well-chosen black-and-white photographs illustrate many aspects of our rich folklife tradition. Twenty-three ethnic groups receive lengthy articles describing their traditional and contemporary folklore—with the exception of Native Americans." Am Libr

Includes bibliographical references

398.2   Folk literature

Sagas, romances, legends, ballads, and fables in prose form, and fairy tales, folk tales, and tall tales are included here, instead of with the literature of the country of origin, to keep the traditional material together and to make it more readily accessible. Modern fairy tales are classified with Fiction, Story collections (SC)

Asian-Pacific folktales and legends; edited by Jeannette L. Faurot. Simon & Schuster 1995 252p pa $12

Grades: 11 12 Adult   **398.2**

1. Folklore—Asia

ISBN 0-684-81197-9   LC 95-31549

"A Touchstone book"

"The 65 myths and folktales in this volume are gathered from the rich heritage of legends in eight East and Southeast Asian countries, with the largest number of stories coming from China (17). The editor herself translates or retells 14 of the Chinese stories for this collection, while the others are reprinted from existing anthologies. . . . The collection gives a quick, multinational overview of some favorite Asian legends." Libr J

Be afraid, be very afraid; the book of scary urban legends; [collected by] Jan Harold Brunvand. Norton 2004 256p pa $13.95 *

Grades: 9 10 11 12   **398.2**

1. Folklore 2. Legends

ISBN 0-393-32613-6   LC 2004-11798

In this collection of urban legends, the author "has compiled the scariest, grisliest ones—some that are unfamiliar but many that have been heard at sleepovers and depicted in horror movies over the past several years. . . . This is a good addition where such titles are popular." SLJ

Includes bibliographical references

Bulfinch, Thomas, 1796-1867
Bulfinch's mythology; foreword by Alberto Manguel. Modern Library pbk. ed. Modern Library 2004 862p pa $17.95
Grades: 11 12 Adult   **398.2**
1. Mythology 2. Folklore—Europe 3. Chivalry
ISBN 0-375-75147-5   LC 2005-271850
First combined edition published 1913 by Crowell. Originally published in three separate volumes 1855, 1858 and 1862 respectively
Contents: The age of fable; The age of chivalry; Legends of Charlemagne
"The classic work on mythology, Bulfinch's gives brief summations of Greek, Roman, Norse, Arthurian, and other miscellaneous myths and includes notes on the 'Iliad,' the 'Odyssey,' and the 'Aeneid.'" N Y Public Libr Book of How & Where to Look It Up
Includes bibliographical references

Favorite folktales from around the world; edited by Jane Yolen. Pantheon Bks. 1986 498p pa $18 hardcover o.p. *
Grades: 11 12 Adult   **398.2**
1. Folklore 2. Fairy tales
ISBN 0-394-75188-4 (pa)   LC 86-42644
"Selections include tales from the American Indians, the brothers Grimm, Italo Calvino's Italian folk-tales, as well as stories from Iceland, Afghanistan, Scotland, and many other countries. Yolen provides each section with a relevant introduction, often including historical and literary factors, thus alerting readers as to what to look for." SLJ

The **Greenwood** encyclopedia of folktales and fairy tales; edited by Donald Haase. Greenwood Press 2008 3v il set $299.95
Grades: 11 12 Adult   **398.2**
1. Reference books 2. Folklore—Encyclopedias 3. Fairy tales—Encyclopedias
ISBN 978-0-313-33441-2   LC 2007-31698
This encyclopedia "has a global scope, and ranges from antiquity to the present in its 670 entries. It covers commercial films, music, and young adult novels, as well as motifs, writers, tale types, and ethnic groups." SLJ
"Meticulously documented and firmly grounded in scholarly research, most articles feature straightforward language and sufficient background material to be accessible to lay readers and novice researchers." Booklist
Includes bibliographical references

The **Greenwood** library of world folktales; stories from the great collections; edited by Thomas A. Green. Greenwood Press 2008 4v set $299.95
Grades: 11 12 Adult   **398.2**
1. Reference books 2. Folklore
ISBN 978-0-313-33783-3   LC 2007-41323
"Each volume in this set represents a general geographic region: African and Middle East, Asia, Europe, and North and South America. . . . Each folktale lists the title, tradition bearer, date gathered, source where the folktale is drawn, original source of the folktale, national origin, and a brief background about the folktale. . . . It is a wonderful multicultural resource for studying this aspect of world cultures." Libr Media Connect
Includes bibliographical references

Hearne, Betsy Gould, 1942-
Beauties and beasts; by Betsy Hearne; illustrated by Joanne Caroselli. Oryx Press 1993 179p il (Oryx multicultural folktale series) pa $33.95
Grades: 8 9 10 11 12 Adult   **398.2**
1. Fairy tales 2. Folklore 3. Mythology
ISBN 0-89774-729-1   LC 93-16
"The theme of a lonely beast who is transformed by the magic of human love is threaded throughout worldwide variations of the 'Beauty and the Beast' folktale. Author Betsy G. Hearne presents 28 versions of the beloved fable with minimal adaptations from around the world." Publisher's note
"Professionals will be very grateful for this sensitively written, thoughtful, and accessible interpretive collection." J Youth Serv Libr
Includes bibliographical references

Holt, David
Spiders in the hairdo; modern urban legends; collected and retold by David Holt & Bill Mooney. August House 1999 111p il pa $7.95
Grades: 11 12 Adult   **398.2**
1. Folklore—United States
ISBN 0-87483-525-9   LC 99-11973
This "collection of urban myths assembles 50 brief stories from modern oral tradition. Commonly attributed to FOAFs (friends of a friend), they are intriguing and often frightening tales passed along in casual conversation. These tales are the substance of modern folklore, an evolving treasury of evanescent narratives." Libr J
Includes bibliographical references

Latin American folktales; stories from Hispanic and Indian traditions; edited and with an introduction by John Bierhorst. Pantheon Bks. 2002 386p (Pantheon fairy tale & folklore library) hardcover o.p. pa $17
Grades: 11 12 Adult   **398.2**
1. Folklore—Latin America
ISBN 0-375-42066-5; 0-375-71439-1 (pa)
                                   LC 2001-34056
Bierhorst "has collected and translated more than 100 folktales from the Spanish oral tradition as practiced in the Americas, from New Mexico to Nicaragua to Chile. . . . {His} introduction provides the context not only for the evolution and telling . . . of the folktales but also for their recording, primarily by early-twentieth-century folklorists and anthropologists. He then sets his readers loose in a vivid world of tricksters, witches, amorous young men, sneaky wives {and} animals with magical powers. . . . A glossary and registry of motifs adds to this volume's value and enjoyment." Booklist
Includes bibliographical references

Lester, Julius
Black folktales; illustrated by Tom Feelings; with an introduction by the author. 1st Evergreen ed. Grove Press 1992 110p il pa $12
Grades: 9 10 11 12   **398.2**
1. Blacks—Folklore 2. Folklore—Africa
ISBN 0-8021-3242-1   LC 91-7619
"An Evergreen book"
First published 1969 by Baron, R.W.

Lester, Julius—*Continued*

"Lester gives 12 African and Afro-American folk tales such twentieth-century touches as the Lord's reading of the 'TV Guide' and the mention of Rap Brown and Aretha Franklin but his sprightly versions retain the spirit and shape of the original story. . . . These stories of creation, love, folk heroes, and everyday people have a direct simplicity and laconic humor that is both effective and appealing." Booklist

Malory, Sir Thomas, 15th cent.

Le morte Darthur, or, The hoole book of Kyng Arthur and of his noble knyghtes of the Rounde Table; authoritative text, sources and backgrounds, criticism; [by] Sir Thomas Malory; edited by Stephen H.A. Shepherd. Norton 2004 lii, 954p (A Norton critical edition) pa $16.95

Grades: 11 12 Adult   **398.2**

1. Arthur, King
ISBN 0-393-97464-2   LC 2002-26534
Originally published 1485

"The work is a skillful selection and blending of materials taken from the mass of Arthurian legends. The central story consists of two main elements: the reign of King Arthur ending in catastrophe and the dissolution of the Round Table; and the quest of the Holy Grail." Oxford Companion to Engl Lit

Includes bibliographical references

Pickering, David, 1958-

A dictionary of folklore. Facts on File 1999 324p $44 *

Grades: 11 12 Adult   **398.2**

1. Reference books 2. Folklore—Dictionaries 3. Mythology—Dictionaries
ISBN 0-8160-4550-0

The author provides entries "on such subjects as herbal remedies, the superstitions connected with various gemstones, the folklore associated with selected trees, plants, birds, and animals. He also covers the ritual tradition of holidays and festivals and the origins of proverbs and sayings. In addition, the dictionary mentions characters and heroes from selkies to Joe Magarac, fantasy beings such as sprites and pixies, and some urban myths." Libr J

Pyle, Howard, 1853-1911

The story of King Arthur and his knights; written and illustrated by Howard Pyle. Scribner 1984 312p il $22.95

Grades: 8 9 10 11 1 2   **398.2**

1. Arthur, King 2. Arthurian romances
ISBN 0-684-14814-5   LC 84-50167
Also available in paperback from Signet Classics
A reissue of the title first published 1903
The first of a four-volume series retelling the Arthurian legends

This is an account of the times "when Arthur, son of Uther-Pendragon, was Overlord of Britain and Merlin was a powerful enchanter, when the sword Excalibur was forged and won, when the Round Table came into being." Publisher's note

The story of Sir Launcelot and his companions. Dover Publications 1991 340p il pa $13.95

Grades: 8 9 10 11 12   **398.2**

1. Lancelot (Legendary character) 2. Arthurian romances
ISBN 0-486-26701-6   LC 90-22326
A reissue of the title first published 1907 by Scribner

This third book of the series follows "Sir Launcelot's adventures as he rescues Queen Guinevere from the clutches of Sir Mellegrans, does battle with the Worm of Corbin, wanders as a madman in the forest and is finally returned to health by the Lady Elaine." Best Sellers

The story of the champions of the Round Table; written and illustrated by Howard Pyle. Dover Publications 1968 328p il pa $11.95

Grades: 8 9 10 11 12   **398.2**

1. Arthurian romances
ISBN 0-486-21883-X
A reissue of the title first published 1905 by Scribner
Contents: The story of Launcelot; The book of Sir Tristram; The book of Sir Percival

"Pyle's second volume of Arthurian legends will be of interest to motivated students of literature and history, as well as useful in professional collections for comparisons and source work. In spite of the archaic language . . . the narrative depth and graphic force . . . will draw in readers." Booklist

The story of the Grail and the passing of Arthur. Dover Publications 1992 258p il pa $12.95

Grades: 8 9 10 11 12   **398.2**

1. Arthur, King 2. Arthurian romances 3. Grail—Fiction
ISBN 0-486-27361-X   LC 92-29058
A reissue of the title first published 1910 by Scribner

This fourth volume of the series follows the adventures of Sir Geraint, Galahad's quest for the holy Grail, the battle between Launcelot and Gawaine, and the slaying of Mordred

Tingle, Tim

Walking the Choctaw road. Cinco Puntos Press 2003 142p il $24.95; pa $10.95

Grades: 7 8 9 10   **398.2**

1. Choctaw Indians—Folklore 2. Folklore—Southern States
ISBN 0-938317-74-1; 0-938317-73-3 (pa)
                    LC 2003-1069

A collection of stories of the Choctaw people, including traditional lore arising from beliefs and myths, historical tales passed down through generations, and personal stories of contemporary life

"Sophisticated narrative devices and some subtle character nuances give these stories a literary cast, but the author's evocative language, expert pacing, and absorbing subject matter will rivet readers and listeners both." Booklist

Yiddish folktales; edited by Beatrice Silverman Weinreich; translated by Leonard Wolf. Pantheon Bks. 1988 xxxii, 413p il (Pantheon fairy tale & folklore library) pa $18 hardcover o.p.

Grades: 11 12 Adult   398.2
1. Jews—Folklore
ISBN 0-8052-1090-3 (pa)   LC 88-42594
Published in cooperation with Yivo Institute for Jewish Research

A "collection of Yiddish folktales divided into various categories, including allegories, children's tales, humor, legends, and the supernatural. The more than 200 selections from the world of Eastern European Jewry are drawn from the archives of the YIVO Institute of Jewish Research. . . . {This work} brings the Yiddish culture of long ago vividly to life." Booklist

Zitkala-Sa, 1876-1938
American Indian stories, legends, and other writings; edited with an introduction and notes by Cathy N. Davidson and Ada Norris. Penguin Bks. 2003 xlvi, 268p il pa $13
Grades: 9 10 11 12   398.2
1. Native Americans—Folklore 2. Native Americans—Social conditions
ISBN 0-14-243709-3   LC 2002-32268
"Penguin classics"

This is a collection of stories and nonfiction writings by the Sioux writer and activist. "Her work, surprisingly, seems undated. . . . This first comprehensive collection . . . reveals Zitkala-Sa as a crusading, spiritually aware woman." Booklist
Includes bibliographical references

398.9 Proverbs

Cordry, Harold V., 1943-
The multicultural dictionary of proverbs; over 20,000 adages from more than 120 languages, nationalities and ethnic groups. McFarland & Co. 1997 406p hardcover o.p. pa $35
Grades: 11 12 Adult   398.9
1. Proverbs
ISBN 0-7864-0251-2; 0-7864-2262-9 (pa)
LC 96-33264
"The proverbs are arranged under 1300 headings (e.g., accidents, divided loyalty, marriage, and shame), and each includes the nationality, group or language in which it originated." Publisher's note

"This well-organized multicultural dictionary of proverbs not only illustrates the common insights that different cultures share but also provides a rich resource of wisdom that the casual reader can glean from perusing the proverbs in an entry." Am Ref Books Annu, 1998

399 Customs of war and diplomacy

Wagner, Eduard, major
Medieval costume, armour, and weapons; selected and illustrated by Eduard Wagner; text by Zoroslava Drobná & Jan Durdik; with a new introduction by Vladimir Dolinek. Dover Publications 2000 72p il pa $39.95
Grades: 9 10 11 12   399
1. Clothing and dress—History 2. Armor 3. Weapons 4. Medieval civilization
ISBN 0-486-41240-7   LC 00-38419
Original Czech edition, 1956
"An unabridged republication of the work translated by Jean Layton. . . . The only alteration consists in printing the color plates from the original edition in black and white, several of which are repeated in color on the front and back covers, inside and out. A new Introduction has been specially prepared for this edition" Verso of title page

"Over 400 royalty-free illustrations trace the evolution of clothing styles, armor, and weapons during the medieval period in Central Europe—from simple tunics and robes of peasants to the battle equipment and armor of warriors and the fur-lined cloaks and brocaded garments of the aristocracy." Publisher's note
Includes bibliographical references

400 LANGUAGE

Crystal, David, 1941-
The Cambridge encyclopedia of language. 3rd ed. Cambridge University Press 2010 516p il map $99; pa $45
Grades: 11 12 Adult   400
1. Language and languages—Encyclopedias 2. Reference books
ISBN 978-0-521-51698-3; 978-0-521-73650-3 (pa)
LC 2010-502889
First published 1987
This encyclopedia "covers all the major themes of language study, including popular ideas about language, language and identity, the structure of language, speaking and listening, writing, reading, and signing, language acquisition, the neurological basis of language, and languages of the world." Univ Press Books for Public and Second Sch Libr, 1997 [review of 1997 edition]

"A valuable and concise . . . handbook for linguistic beginners, linguistic researchers looking for a quick overview and, most of all, the general reader interested in language." Linguist List
Includes bibliographical references

410   Linguistics

Crystal, David, 1941-
Language and the internet. 2nd ed. Cambridge University Press 2006 304p $29.99 *
Grades: 11 12 Adult   **410**
    1. Language and languages 2. Internet
ISBN 978-0-521-86859-4; 0-521-86859-9
                 LC 2006-12916
First published 2001
"Covering a range of Internet genres, including e-mail, chat, and the Web, this is . . . [an] account of how the Internet is radically changing the way we use language." Publisher's note
Includes bibliographical references

Dalby, Andrew
Dictionary of languages; the definitive reference to more than 400 languages. Columbia Univ. Press 1999 734p il maps $73.50; pa $22.95 *
Grades: 11 12 Adult   **410**
    1. Reference books 2. Language and languages—Dictionaries
ISBN 0-231-11568-7; 0-231-11569-5 (pa)
                 LC 98-87178
This dictionary includes alphabetical entries that "cover all languages with official status as well as those with a written literature and 175 minor languages with significant historical and/or anthropological interest. A preface explains the author's pronunciation scheme. . . . The entries themselves are from two to four pages long. Each one discusses a specific language. . . . With coverage of languages from Abkhaz to Zulu, explanations of Egyptian hieroglyphics and Sumerian script, and a discussion of Chinese dialects and characters, [this] . . . is a welcome addition to public and academic library collections." Booklist

411   Writing systems of standard forms of languages

Humez, Alexander
On the dot; the speck that changed the world; [by] Alexander Humez, Nicholas Humez. Oxford University Press 2008 256p $24.95
Grades: 9 10 11 12 Adult   **411**
    1. Dot (Symbol)
ISBN 978-0-19-532499-0   LC 2008-3320
This is a "study of the importance of the dot in written language. . . . The book features chapters on the dot in its various incarnations and meanings, from the origins of the decimal system to the dot-com phenomenon, from musical notation to proofreading annotations." Libr J
"Ideal for etymologists and trivia buffs, this book covers an array of information and innovations on the relevance of this 'speck.'" Publ Wkly
Includes bibliographical references

412   Etymology of standard forms of languages

Hayakawa, S. I.
Language in thought and action; {by} S.I. Hayakawa and Alan R. Hayakawa. 5th ed. Harcourt Brace Jovanovich 1990 287p il $49.95; pa $16
Grades: 11 12 Adult   **412**
    1. Semantics 2. Thought and thinking 3. English language
ISBN 0-15-550120-8; 0-15-648240-1 (pa)
                 LC 89-84371
First published 1939 with title: Language in action
The author analyzes the nature of language, discusses the processes of thinking and writing, and gives advice on thinking and writing clearly
Includes bibliographical references

413   Dictionaries of standard forms of languages

Corbeil, Jean-Claude
The Firefly five language visual dictionary; [by] Jean-Claude Corbeil, Ariane Archambault. [2nd ed.] Firefly Books 2009 1092p il map $59.95
Grades: 9 10 11 12 Adult   **413**
    1. Polyglot dictionaries 2. Picture dictionaries
3. Reference books
ISBN 978-1-55407-492-1; 1-55407-492-4
                 LC 2010-290437
First published 2004
On cover: English, Spanish, French, German, Italian
This general reference visual dictionary features terms in English, Spanish, French, German, and Italian. Includes sections on astronomy, geography, the animal and vegetable kingdoms, human biology, the home, clothing and accessories, art and architecture, communication, transportation, energy, science, society, and sports.

419   Sign languages

Costello, Elaine
Random House Webster's American Sign Language dictionary: unabridged. Random House Reference 2008 xxxii, 1200p $55 *
Grades: 8 9 10 11 12 Adult   **419**
    1. Reference books 2. Sign language—Dictionaries
ISBN 978-0-375-42616-2; 0-375-42616-7
Also available Random House Webster's American Sign Language dictionary: compact edition pa $21.95 (ISBN 978-0-375-72277-6; 0-375-72277-7)
First published 1994 with title: Random House American Sign Language dictionary
This dictionary includes "over 5,600 signs for the novice and experienced user alike. It includes complete descriptions of each sign, plus full-torso illustrations. There is also a subject index for easy reference as well as alternate signs for the same meaning." Publisher's note

The **Gallaudet** dictionary of American Sign Language; Clayton Valli, editor in chief; illustrated by Peggy Swartzel Lott, Daniel Renner, and Rob Hills. Gallaudet University Press 2005 xli, 558p il $49.95 *

Grades: 8 9 10 11 12 Adult   **419**
1. Sign language—Dictionaries 2. Reference books
ISBN 1-56368-282-6; 978-1-56368-282-7
    LC 2005-51129
This "reference work is composed of approximately 3000 illustrated entries, each showing the American Sign Language equivalent for an English word. The entries are arranged alphabetically and include synonyms where appropriate." Libr J
"This is a very valuable language resource for parents, students, and teachers learning ASL as a first language and as a second language." Choice
Includes bibliographical references

Grayson, Gabriel
Talking with your hands, listening with your eyes; a complete photographic guide to American Sign Language. Square One Pubs. 2002 373p il pa $26.95 *

Grades: 11 12 Adult   **419**
1. Sign language
ISBN 0-7570-0007-X   LC 2002-1125
"The book covers more than 900 signs that represent nearly 1,800 words and phrases, with signs grouped by topic. . . . Grayson provides instructions for each word, explaining the hand shape, the position in front of the body where the sign is made and the type of movement involved in expressing the word." Publ Wkly
"An outstanding, user-friendly resource for those interested in learning ASL." SLJ

420 English and Old English (Anglo-Saxon)

Crystal, David, 1941-
The Cambridge encyclopedia of the English language. 2nd ed. Cambridge Univ. Press 2003 499p il hardcover o.p. pa $35 *

Grades: 11 12 Adult   **420**
1. English language
ISBN 0-521-82348-X; 0-521-53033-4 (pa)
    LC 2003-272259
First published 1995
This "volume is divided into six broad topics that cover the English language's history, vocabulary, grammar, writing and speech systems, usage, and acquisition. Within these major topics, the book is divided into logical subtopics and finally into the basic unit of the text—the two-page spread. . . . The clear and spirited text is stunning, enhanced with over 500 illustrations, making this a particularly rich reference work and a browser's dream." Libr J {review of 1995 edition}

McCrum, Robert
The story of English; [by] Robert McCrum, Willam Cran [and] Robert MacNeil. 3rd rev ed. Penguin Bks. 2003 xxi, 468p pa $16

Grades: 11 12 Adult   **420**
1. English language—History
ISBN 0-14-200231-3   LC 2002-29818
First published 1986 by Viking
A "companion to the PBS television series of the same name. . . . The text covers the history of our language from its roots in Latin through its transplanting to other shores and its infusions from other cultures and languages. . . . Good for browsing, this book is a must for word and history buffs." SLJ [review of 1986 edition]
Includes bibliographical references

421 Writing system, phonology, phonetics of standard English

Vos Savant, Marilyn Mach
The art of spelling; the madness and the method; by Marilyn vos Savant; illustrations by Joan Reilly. Norton 2000 204p il hardcover o.p. pa $12.95 *

Grades: 11 12 Adult   **421**
1. English language—Spelling
ISBN 0-393-04903-5; 0-393-32208-4 (pa)
    LC 00-37228
The author "offers some suggestions for spelling improvement, supplying common roots like anim-, arch-, and spec- and a list of 500 commonly misspelled words. She also includes a few quizzes, with answers in the back of the book. This is not a how-to book, however, for more than half of it examines what spelling ability tells us about intelligence and personality. . . . The bibliography and web site list are nice additions as well." Libr J

422 Etymology of standard English

Gorrell, Gena K. (Gena Kinton), 1946-
Say what? the weird and mysterious journey of the English language. Tundra Books 2009 146p il pa $10.95

Grades: 7 8 9 10 11 12   **422**
1. English language—Etymology
ISBN 978-0-88776-878-1; 0-88776-878-4
"Gorrell takes readers on a quick and amusing historical tour of the English language, looking at how it has been influenced by Latin, Old English, French, and German. . . . This clever and funny book also integrates explanations for tricky grammar and spelling problems as part of the historical explanation for our changing language. Readers are not only given examples of malapropisms but also a list of several words that are often confused. . . . Supplementary materials including a time line and a large number of illustrations will make this book a valuable addition to both public and school libraries." Voice Youth Advocates

Hitchings, Henry, 1974-

The secret life of words; how English became English. Farrar, Straus and Giroux 2008 440p $27

Grades: 8 9 10 11 12 Adult　　　　**422**

1. English language—Etymology

ISBN 978-0-374-25410-0; 0-374-25410-9

LC 2008-26055

"Hitchings here provides a colorful, thematic history of the English language. Treating borrowings and coinages as psychological windows to history, the author takes the reader on a tour of the lexicon from Anglo-Saxon to the present day and shows how new words answer linguistic needs. . . . Hitchings treats the reader to some 3,000 word histories. . . . With 90-plus pages of notes, sources, and useful indexes, this is a fine choice for libraries and a 'smorgasbord' for language aficionados." Choice

Includes bibliographical references

422.03　Etymology of standard English—Dictionaries

Adonis to Zorro; Oxford dictionary of reference and allusion; edited by Andrew Delahunty and Sheila Dignen. 3rd ed. Oxford University Press 2010 406p $34.95

Grades: 11 12 Adult　　　　**422.03**

1. Allusions 2. Reference books

ISBN 978-0-19-956745-4; 0-19-956745-X

LC 2010-549367

First published 2001 with title: The Oxford dictionary of allusions

"This guide to allusions and common references is a moderately priced volume well worth adding to a public, school, community college, or college shelf. Neat and user-friendly, the 1,900 entries, their provenance, definitions, models, and starred cross-references identify a range of familiar terms, from 'Terminator' to 'hobbit,' and from 'My Lai' to the 'sword of Damocles' and 'thirty pieces of silver.' The text makes clever use of fonts, dingbats, and point count to identify authors, sources, and dates." Choice

From bonbon to cha-cha; Oxford dictionary of foreign words and phrases; edited by Andrew Delahunty. 2nd ed. Oxford University Press 2008 411p $24.95; pa $18.99 *

Grades: 11 12 Adult　　　　**422.03**

1. English language—Foreign words and phrases—Dictionaries 2. Reference books

ISBN　978-0-19-954369-4;　0-19-954369-0; 978-0-19-954368-7 (pa); 0-19-954368-2 (pa)

LC 2008-482026

First published 1997 with title: The Oxford dictionary of foreign words and phrases. Paperback has title: Oxford dictionary of foreign words and phrases

This reference "offers coverage of more than 6,000 foreign words and phrases that are in regular use in English today." Publisher's note

Hendrickson, Robert, 1933-

The Facts on File encyclopedia of word and phrase origins. 4th ed., [Updated and expanded ed.] Facts On File 2008 948p (Facts on File library of language and literature) $95; pa $27.95 *

Grades: 11 12 Adult　　　　**422.03**

1. Reference books 2. English language—Etymology—Dictionaries 3. English language—Terms and phrases

ISBN 978-0-8160-6966-8; 978-0-8160-6967-5 (pa)

LC 2007-48223

First published 1987

"This encyclopedia features anecdotes and information on the development of a wide range of words, including slang, proverbs, animal and plant names, place names, nicknames, historical expressions, foreign language expressions, and phrases from literature." Publisher's note

"Because the entries have both scholarly value and the capacity to entertain, the book is ideal for both linguists and lay readers." Libr J

More word histories and mysteries; from aardvark to zombie; from the editors of the American Heritage dictionaries. Houghton Mifflin 2006 288p il pa $12.95

Grades: 8 9 10 11 12 Adult　　　　**422.03**

1. English language—Etymology 2. Reference books

ISBN 978-0-618-71681-4; 0-618-71681-5

LC 2006020835

This "emphasizes the huge number of source languages from which English draws its vast vocabulary—from Sanskrit to French and beyond. The introductory pages give the reader a brief overview of the methods and aims of etymology and a potted history of the origins of English. . . . The editors then present an alphabetical listing of words and their etymology. Each of the 300-plus entries is about half a page to a page long and briefly outlines the origins of the word, its use, and the evolution of its meaning. . . . The book's informative yet informal writing style would appeal to the amateur enthusiast, and accessibility is further enhanced by a useful glossary of linguistic terms." Libr J

The **Oxford** dictionary of English etymology; edited by C. T. Onions; with the assistance of G. W. S. Friedrichsen and R. W. Burchfield. Oxford Univ. Press 1966 1024p $65 *

Grades: 11 12 Adult　　　　**422.03**

1. Reference books 2. English language—Etymology—Dictionaries

ISBN 0-19-861112-9

Also available in a concise edition pa $16.95 (ISBN 0-19-283098-8)

"Authoritative work tracing the history of common English words back to their Indo-European roots. The most complete and reliable etymological dictionary ever published, it serves as a complement to the OED." Ref Sources for Small & Medium-sized Libr. 6th edition

Word histories and mysteries; from abracadabra to Zeus; from the editors of the American Heritage dictionaries. Houghton Mifflin Co. 2004 xvi, 348p il pa $12.95
Grades: 8 9 10 11 12 Adult   **422.03**
1. English language—Etymology 2. Reference books
ISBN 978-0-618-45450-1; 0-618-45450-0
LC 2004014798
"The 400 alphabetically arranged entries here illustrate the diversity from which the English language draws its vocabulary, particularly from the prehistoric base that linguists call Proto-Indo-European. As a result, the editors aim to demonstrate links between the ancient base and modern English. . . . An overall quality resource." Libr J

423 Dictionaries of standard English

The **American** Heritage abbreviations dictionary. 3rd ed., [updated] Houghton Mifflin 2007 294p $6.95
Grades: 9 10 11 12 Adult   **423**
1. Acronyms—Dictionaries 2. Abbreviations—Dictionaries 3. Reference books
ISBN 978-0-618-85747-0
Presents commonly used acronyms and abbreviations along with their meanings.

The **American** Heritage dictionary of phrasal verbs. Houghton Mifflin Co. 2005 466p $19.95
Grades: 11 12 Adult   **423**
1. English language—Terms and phrases 2. Reference books
ISBN 0-618-59260-1; 978-0-618-59260-9
LC 2005-12835
"This dictionary focuses on phrasal verbs, specifically those that have meaning beyond the literal definitions of the words involved." Libr J
"This unique resource belongs on the shelves of most libraries as a complement to standard English-language dictionaries. It will be useful to native English speakers as well as to ESL students." Booklist

The **American** Heritage dictionary of the English language. 4th ed., New updated ed. Houghton Mifflin 2006 xxxvii, 2074p il $60 *
Grades: 11 12 Adult   **423**
1. Reference books 2. English language—Dictionaries
ISBN 0-618-70172-9; 978-0-617-70172-8
First published 1969
This dictionary provides over 210,000 main entries with over 4,000 full-color illustrations. Word histories, synonym paragraphs and regionalisms are also explored. The work also examines the influence of social factors such as age and ethnicity on how American English has been shaped by speakers from every social class.
This "eminently useful dictionary features fabulous full-color design that quickly and effectively guides users to the information they seek." Libr J

The **American** Heritage guide to contemporary usage and style. Houghton Mifflin 2005 512p $19.95 *
Grades: 11 12 Adult   **423**
1. English language—Usage
ISBN 978-0-618-60499-9; 0-618-60499-5
LC 2005-16513
"Drawing on the authoritative knowledge of its lexicographers and the considered collective judgment of a panel of noted writers, the book offers guidance on the simple (the pronunciations of bouquet); the perplexingly redundant (free gift); the often imprecisely used (impeach); the no longer distinct (healthful/healthy); the needless but persistent (irregardless); the easily confused (stationary/stationery); the unfortunately conflated (lay/lie); and many more pitfalls. Articles embodying the precision and lucidity of dictionary definitions explain the history of a word's or expression's usage issue, how and why the issue exists, and the preferred usage." Booklist

Ammer, Christine
The Facts on File dictionary of clichés. 3rd ed. Facts On File 2011 556p (Facts on File library of language and literature) $60; pa $19.95
Grades: 9 10 11 12 Adult   **423**
1. English language—Terms and phrases 2. English language—Usage 3. Reference books
ISBN 978-0-8160-8353-4; 978-0-8160-8354-1 (pa); 978-1-4381-3705-6 (ebook)   LC 2010049234
First published 1992 with title: Have a nice day—no problem!: a dictionary of clichés
"Meanings and origins of thousands of terms and expressions" Cover. Contact publisher for ebook pricing
This book "explains the meanings and origins of more than 4,000 clichés and common expressions. Each entry includes the meaning of the cliché or expression, its origin and early uses, its historical development, and its present-day usage." Publisher's note
Includes bibliographical references

Bartlett's Roget's thesaurus. Little, Brown 1996 xxxii, 1415p $21.95; pa $16.95 *
Grades: 8 9 10 11 12 Adult   **423**
1. English language—Synonyms and antonyms 2. Americanisms 3. Reference books
ISBN 0-316-10138-9; 0-316-73587-6 (pa)
LC 96-18343
This thesaurus "reflects the current state of American English, including terminology from the worlds of composers and television, with such sub-categories as 'Living Things,' 'The Arts,' 'Feelings.' But what really makes the book a joy to use is the tremendously useful lists—everything from phobias to styles and periods of furniture." Am Libr

Concise Oxford American thesaurus. Oxford University Press 2006 996p $19.95 *
Grades: 11 12 Adult   **423**
1. English language—Synonyms and antonyms 2. Reference books
ISBN 0-19-530485-3; 978-0-19-530485-5
LC 2005-35868

Concise Oxford American thesaurus—*Continued*

First published 1997 in the United Kingdom with title: The concise Oxford thesaurus; Original American edition published 1999 with title: The Oxford American thesaurus of current English

This "thesaurus contains over 15,000 entries with more than 350,000 synonyms and is . . . arranged with the typical synonyms listed first. . . . This simple arrangement makes this thesaurus particularly user-friendly." Libr J

Concise Oxford English dictionary; edited by Catherine Soanes, Angus Stevenson. 11th ed., rev. Oxford University Press 2008 xx, 1681p $35 *

Grades: 11 12 Adult   423

1. English language—Dictionaries 2. Reference books

ISBN 978-0-19-954841-5   LC 2008-30091

First published 1911 under the editorship of H. W. Fowler and F. G. Fowler with title: The Concise dictionary of current English

This work contains over 240,000 entries, including derivatives, compounds and abbreviations. It includes explanatory notes on pronunciation, grammatical inflection and etymology.

Includes bibliographical references

Corbeil, Jean-Claude

Merriam-Webster's visual dictionary; [by] Jean-Claude Corbeil, Ariane Archambault; [illustrators, Jean-Yves Ahern . . . [et al.] Merriam-Webster 2006 952p il map $39.95 *

Grades: 11 12 Adult   423

1. Reference books 2. English language—Dictionaries 3. Picture dictionaries

ISBN 978-0-8777-9051-8; 0-8777-9051-5

"Logically organized into 17 broad categories (e.g., astronomy, humans, animals, clothing, and society), with numerous subcategories to make finding the needed terms easy, this is the only visual dictionary that includes definitions with the terms. And its price is very reasonable for such a substantial book. Essential." Libr J

Davidson, Mark

Right, wrong, and risky; a dictionary of today's American English usage. Norton 2006 570p $29.95 *

Grades: 11 12 Adult   423

1. Reference books 2. English language—Usage 3. English language—Dictionaries 4. Americanisms

ISBN 0-393-06119-1   LC 2005-17628

The author "offers a dictionary that 'views the real world of today's American English, identifying usage questions that are debatable, citing conflicting answers, and offering risk-free solutions for each conflict.' . . . Browsers will enjoy the colorful, interesting backstories on the origins of terms such as ground zero, on the sudden warming to the phrase girl talk, and on the widely misunderstood use of the word Neanderthal." Booklist

Includes bibliographical references

Dictionary & thesaurus. Barron's Educational 2007 779p pa $14.99

Grades: 11 12 Adult   423

1. Reference books 2. English language—Dictionaries 3. English language—Synonyms and antonyms

ISBN 978-0-7641-3606-1; 0-7641-3606-2

At head of title: Barron's reference guides

This "volume provides dictionary definitions of more than 40,000 words and phrases and more than 100,000 synonyms. Instead of the usual dictionary-followed-by-thesaurus arrangement, dictionary definitions appear in the top half of each page, and the thesaurus, presenting selected dictionary words from the same page, appears underneath." Booklist

Garner, Bryan A.

Garner's modern American usage. 3rd ed. Oxford University Press 2009 lx, 942p $45 *

Grades: 11 12 Adult   423

1. English language—Usage—Dictionaries 2. Americanisms—Dictionaries 3. Reference books

ISBN 978-0-19-538275-4   LC 2009-9539

First published 1998 with title: A dictionary of modern American usage

This is a "guide to the effective use of the English language. . . . [Featuring] essays on troublesome words and phrases, *GMAU* . . . shows how to avoid the countless pitfalls that await unwary writers and speakers whether the issues relate to grammar, punctuation, word choice, or pronunciation." Publisher's note

"One would be tempted to say that this is clearly one of the best works on the topic, but doing so would be using one of Garner's weasel words (intensives such as clearly that 'actually have the effect of weakening a statement'). Suffice it to say that it is highly recommended for most libraries." Booklist

Includes bibliographical references

Historical thesaurus of the Oxford English dictionary; with additional material from "A Thesaurus of Old English"; [edited by] Christian Kay [et al.] Oxford University Press 2009 2v 3952p set $395

Grades: 9 10 11 12 Adult   423

1. English language—Synonyms and antonyms 2. Reference books

ISBN 978-0-19-920899-9   LC 2009-935029

This "historical thesaurus claims to be the first to include 'almost the entire vocabulary of English, from Old English to the present day,' covering more than 920,000 words and meanings and documenting, through data from the *Oxford English Dictionary*, how words with similar meaning have developed over time." Libr J

"The knowledge compiled in this 40-year project is stunning, and promises to revolutionize the study of the language by making wholly new kinds of questions possible." Choice

Includes bibliographical references

The **Merriam-Webster** dictionary of synonyms and antonyms. Merriam-Webster 1992 443p pa $4.99

Grades: 8 9 10 11 12 Adult   423

1. English language—Synonyms and antonyms 2. Reference books

ISBN 0-87779-906-7   LC 93-119503

First published 1942 with title: Webster's dictionary of synonyms

The Merriam-Webster dictionary of synonyms and antonyms—*Continued*

"This synonym dictionary is an outstanding work. . . . Synonyms and similar words, alphabetically arranged, are carefully defined, discriminated, and illustrated with thousands of quotations. The entries also include antonyms and analogous words." Nichols. Guide to Ref Books for Sch Media Cent. 4th edition

Merriam-Webster's collegiate dictionary. Eleventh ed. Merriam-Webster 2003 1623p il $23.95

Grades: 11 12 Adult   **423**
1. Reference books 2. English language—Dictionaries
ISBN 0-87779-808-7   LC 2003-3674
Also available with CD-ROM $26.95 (978-0-87779-809-5) and online
First published 1898

This edition includes over 165,000 entries, 10,000 new words and meanings, 38,000 etymologies, a handbook of style, an essay on the English language, a special section on signs and symbols, and a free one-year subscription to the Collegiate Web site.

Merriam-Webster's collegiate thesaurus. 2nd ed. Merriam-Webster 2010 16a, 1162p $21.95

Grades: 11 12 Adult   **423**
1. English language—Synonyms and antonyms 2. Reference books
ISBN 978-0-8777-9269-7; 0-8777-9269-0
     LC 2009-42161
Also available online
First published 1976 with title: Webster's collegiate thesaurus

"Employs a conventional dictionary arrangement, and gives synonyms, related terms, idiomatic equivalents, antonyms, and contrasted words as applicable. Cross-references in small capitals." Guide to Ref Books. 11th edition

Metaphors dictionary; [edited by] Elyse Sommer, with Dorrie Weiss. Visible Ink Press 2001 xlvi, 612p $24.95 *

Grades: 11 12 Adult   **423**
1. English language—Terms and phrases
ISBN 1-57859-137-6
First published 1995 by Gale Res.

This is a "collection of 6,500 colorful classic and contemporary comparative phrases (with full annotations and a complete bibliography of sources) . . . organized under 500 timeless and timely themes, ranging from Aloneness to Love to Zeal." Publisher's note
"Any library serving patrons involved in creative writing, composition, public speaking, or literary criticism should add this volume." Am Ref Books Annu, 1996 [entry for 1995 edition]

Mitchell, Kevin M.

Hip-hop rhyming dictionary; for rappers, DJs and MCs. Firebrand Music; Distributed by Alfred Pub. 2003 183p pa $10.95

Grades: 9 10 11 12 Adult   **423**
1. English language—Rhyme 2. Rap music—Dictionaries 3. Hip-hop—Dictionaries 4. Reference books
ISBN 0-7390-3333-6   LC 2003-107925

This rhyming dictionary includes "writing tips to inspire creative lyrics as well as a brief history of rap and the artists who sent hip-hop to the top of the charts." Publisher's note

New Oxford American dictionary. 3rd ed., edited by Angus Stevenson, Christine A. Lindberg. Oxford University Press 2010 xxvi, 2018p il map $60 *

Grades: 11 12 Adult   **423**
1. English language—Dictionaries 2. Americanisms—Dictionaries 3. Reference books
ISBN 978-0-19-539288-3   LC 2010-20033
Also available Concise Oxford American dictionary $19.95 (ISBN-10: 0-19-530484-5; ISBN-13: 978-0-19-530484-8)

First published 1980 with title: The Oxford American dictionary. Editors vary

"This dictionary arranges definitions by most current usage and provides additional guidance in usage notes. Although U.S. English is the focus here, regionalisms from other English-speaking areas are also included. More than 1000 illustrations (e.g., photos, drawings, diagrams) clarify definitions. . . . A labor of love and an unparalleled gift to writers and readers worldwide, the *New Oxford American Dictionary* should be on the reference shelves of every library." Libr J

Oxford American writer's thesaurus; compiled by Christine A. Lindberg. 2nd ed. Oxford University Press 2008 xxvi, 1052p $40 *

Grades: 9 10 11 12 Adult   **423**
1. Reference books 2. English language—Synonyms and antonyms
ISBN 978-0-19-534284-0; 0-19-534284-4
     LC 2008-31259
First published 2004

This book "provides more than 300,000 synonyms and 10,000 antonyms. . . . Additional features include notes on American English usage and word spectrums showing the shades of meaning between polar opposites. The text is enhanced with . . . mini-essays on favorite words by ten noted contemporary writers—David Auburn, Michael Dirda, David Lehman, Erin McKean, Stephin Merritt, Francine Prose, Zadie Smith, Jean Strouse, David Foster Wallace, and Simon Winchester." Publisher's note
"This expansive reference . . . is a functional treasure." Libr J

Random House Webster's college dictionary. [Rev and updated ed] Random House Reference 2005 xxvi, 1597p il map $26.95 *

Grades: 11 12 Adult   **423**
1. Reference books 2. English language—Dictionaries
ISBN 0-375-42600-0   LC 2005-280097
First published 1991 as a successor to The Random House college dictionary

"Each entry in the dictionary presents spelling, along with alternatives, syllabication, pronunciation used in conversational speech (with alternatives), and part of speech. Entries also include meanings and definitions, with the most common usage listed first; historical, technical, or other usages of the term; date of first usage, including place of origin; and other related words that use the same root or stem. . . . The dictionary includes over

Random House Webster's college dictionary—
Continued

207,000 definitions, many of them so new they are not yet found in competing products. . . . For libraries seeking a wide variety of dictionaries, this work will prove especially useful for its inclusion of recent terms and idioms." Am Ref Books Annu, 2001 [entry for 2001 edition]

Random House Webster's unabridged dictionary. 2nd ed. Random House 2005 xxvi, 2230p il map $59.95 *
Grades: 8 9 10 11 12 Adult   **423**
1. English language—Dictionaries 2. Reference books
ISBN 0-375-42599-3
First published 1966 with title: The Random House dictionary of the English language
This dictionary contains over 315,000 entries. A new-words section and an essay on the growth of English are included. 2,400 spot maps and illustrations complement the text

Roget's 21st century thesaurus in dictionary form; the essential reference for home, school, or office; edited by the Princeton Language Institute; Barbara Ann Kipfer, head lexicographer. 3rd ed. Bantam Dell 2005 962p $15; pa $5.99 *
Grades: 8 9 10 11 12 Adult   **423**
1. English language—Synonyms and antonyms 2. Reference books
ISBN 0-385-33895-3; 0-440-24269-X (pa)
"A Delta book"
First published 1992
"Produced by the Philip Lief Group, Inc."
This thesaurus, cross referencing each word with the same concept, provides 500,000 synonyms and antonyms in a dictionary format and includes recently coined and common slang terms and commonly used foreign terms.

Roget's II; the new thesaurus; by the editors of The American Heritage Dictionaries. 3rd ed. Houghton Mifflin 2003 1200p $21
Grades: 8 9 10 11 12 Adult   **423**
1. English language—Synonyms and antonyms 2. Reference books
ISBN 0-618-25414-5
Also available online
First published 1980
The work uses a dictionary format, with words and numbered definitions on the left column of a page, and corresponding numbered synonyms, near-synonyms, antonyms and near-antonyms on the right column.

Sheehan, Michael, 1939-
Word parts dictionary; standard and reverse listings of prefixes, suffixes, roots, and combining forms; [by] Michael J. Sheehan. 2nd ed. McFarland & Co. 2008 286p lib bdg $55 *
Grades: 11 12 Adult   **423**
1. English language—Dictionaries 2. Reference books
ISBN 978-0-7864-3564-7; 0-7864-3564-X
LC 2008-41

First published 2000
"The purpose of this dictionary is to provide convenient word parts to those who may be interested in inventing or deciphering words bearing an established and embedded meaning." Publisher's note

Shorter Oxford English dictionary on historical principles; [editor-in-chief, Lesley Brown] 6th ed., [editor, Angus Stevenson] Oxford University Press 2007 2v il map set $175 *
Grades: 11 12 Adult   **423**
1. Reference books 2. English language—Dictionaries
ISBN 978-0-19-923324-3; 0-19-923324-1
LC 2007-37226
Also available deluxe leather-bound edition with one year's access to online version $350 (ISBN: 978-0-19-923325-0)
First published 1933
Includes CD-ROM
This dictionary "has more than half a million definitions drawn from the Oxford English Corpus database of more than 1.5 billion words. . . . It includes 'all words in current English from 1700 to the present day, plus the vocabulary of Shakespeare, the Authorized Version of the Bible and other major works from before 1700.'" Booklist
Includes bibliographical references

Webster's New College Dictionary. 3rd ed. Houghton Mifflin 2008 1518p il $25.95
Grades: 9 10 11 12 Adult   **423**
1. English language—Dictionaries 2. Reference books
ISBN 978-0-618-95315-8
First published 2005 in a slightly different form with title: Webster's II new college dictionary
This dictionary features more than 200,000 definitions, as well as charts and tables, proofreaders' marks, synonym lists, word histories, and context examples.

Young, Sue
The new comprehensive American rhyming dictionary. Morrow 1991 622p pa $14.95 hardcover o.p. *
Grades: 8 9 10 11 12 Adult   **423**
1. English language—Rhyme 2. Americanisms 3. Reference books
ISBN 0-380-71392-6 (pa)   LC 90-19165
This book contains over 65,000 words and phrases categorized by sound, rather than spelling. It includes many colloquialisms and slang expressions.

427 Historical and geographic variations, modern nongeographic variations

Ammer, Christine
The American Heritage dictionary of idioms. Houghton Mifflin 1997 729p $32; pa $14.95 *
Grades: 11 12 Adult   **427**
1. English language—Idioms 2. English language—Terms and phrases 3. Americanisms 4. Reference books
ISBN 0-395-72774-X; 0-618-24953-2 (pa)
LC 97-12390
"In addition to idioms, the dictionary includes common figures of speech, formula phrases such as 'take care,' emphatic redundancies whose word order cannot be reversed such as 'cease and desist,' common proverbs, colloquialisms, and slang phrases. Each expression is defined briefly and then illustrated by a short, simple sentence showing how it is used in context." SLJ
Includes bibliographical references

Dickson, Paul
Slang! the topical dictionary of Americanisms. Walker & Co. 2006 418p $24.95 *
Grades: 11 12 Adult   **427**
1. Reference books 2. English language—Slang—Dictionaries 3. Americanisms—Dictionaries
ISBN 0-8027-1531-1; 978-0-8027-1531-9
First published 1990 by Pocket Bks.
On cover: New and completely updated
This American slang dictionary "includes 30 topics, such as 'Bureaucratese' and 'Real Estate,' and more than 10,000 words." Libr J
"Informative, reliable, entertaining, and modern, this topical slang dictionary complements the more staid slang lexicons and more scholarly general dictionaries." Booklist
Includes bibliographical references

Green, Jonathon
Green's dictionary of slang. Chambers 2011 3v set $625
Grades: 11 12 Adult   **427**
1. English language—Slang—Dictionaries 2. Reference books
ISBN 978-0-550-10440-3; 0-550-10440-2
"This 6000-page compilation of some 110,000 choice unconventional English specimens is a verbivore's delight. Geographically wide-ranging, this work seeks out and samples vulgar English wherever it is spoken, e.g., South Africa, Australia, New Zealand, and parts of the Caribbean, though British and American slang are most prominent. . . . Each entry follows a standard format and includes a headword; word class (noun, adjective, etc.); variant spellings; word history/derivation; usage notes; meaning, broken down by sense; and citations, which comprise the bulk of the entry, listing date, title of literary work, and author." Libr J

Spears, Richard A.
McGraw-Hill's American idioms dictionary. 4th ed. McGraw-Hill 2007 xxiii, 743p il pa $16.95
Grades: 9 10 11 12   **427**
1. English language—Idioms 2. English language—Terms and phrases 3. Americanisms 4. Reference books
ISBN 978-0-07-147893-9; 0-07-147893-0
LC 2006-46933
First published 1987 with title: NTC's American idioms dictionary
This dictionary contains more than 14,000 idiomatic phrases in American parlance. Meaning, usage and appropriate contexts are given for each idiomatic phrase.
Includes bibliographical references

McGraw-Hill's dictionary of American slang and colloquial expressions. 4th ed. McGraw-Hill 2006 xxix, 546p pa $19.95 *
Grades: 11 12 Adult   **427**
1. Reference books 2. English language—Slang—Dictionaries 3. Americanisms
ISBN 0-07-146107-8; 978-0-07-146107-8
LC 2005-52220
First published 1989 with title: NTC's dictionary of American slang and colloquial expressions
This book offers "definitions of more than 12,000 slang and informal expressions from various sources, ranging from golden oldies such as . . . golden oldie, to recent coinages like shizzle (gangsta), jonx (Wall Street), and ping (the Internet). Each entry is followed by examples illustrating how an expression is used in everyday conversation and, where necessary, International Phonetic Alphabet pronunciations are given, as well as cautionary notes for crude, inflammatory, or taboo expressions." Publisher's note
Includes bibliographical references

428 Standard English usage (Prescriptive linguistics) Applied linguistics

Collis, Harry
101 American English proverbs; [enrich your English Conversation with colorful everyday sayings]; illustrated by Mario Risso. McGraw-Hill 2009 105p il (101 proverbs) pa $12.95
Grades: 9 10 11 12   **428**
1. Proverbs 2. English language—Conversation and phrase books
ISBN 978-0-07-161588-4; 0-07-161588-1
LC 2008-935417
Includes audio MP3 CD
This book for English as a second language students presents common American English proverbs and explains how to use them.

Fowler, H. W., 1858-1933.
Fowler's modern English usage; first edition by
H.W. Fowler. Rev. 3rd ed., by R.W. Burchfield.
Oxford University Press 2004 xxi, 873p $35
Grades: 11 12 Adult **428**
    1. English language—Etymology 2. English lan-
guage—Idioms 3. English language—Usage
4. Reference books
    ISBN 0-19-861021-1; 978-0-19-861021-2
                   LC 2005-271630
    First published 1926 with title: A dictionary of mod-
ern English usage; 2000 edition published with title: The
new Fowler's modern English usage
    This alphabetically arranged guide gives "advice on
grammar, syntax, style, and choice of words." Publisher's
note

Langer de Ramirez, Lori
Empower English language learners with tools
from the Web. Corwin 2010 163p il $70.95; pa
$38.95
Grades: Adult Professional **428**
    1. English language—Study and teaching
2. Computer-assisted instruction
    ISBN 978-1-4129-7242-0; 1-4129-7242-6;
978-1-4129-7243-7 (pa); 1-4129-7243-4 (pa)
                   LC 2009-36786
    "With a hands-on approach, the rationale for the use
of Web 2.0 tools is clearly explained and defended. K-12
project ideas for blogging, wikis, podcasts, video, visual
media, social networking, social bookmarking, and virtual worlds in the context of the ELL classroom are explicitly explained. Each concept includes what, why, how,
when, who, steps for doing it yourself, where to locate
further information, suggested readings, and useful
websites. . . . This resource fills a gap in any school
striving to meet the instructional and social needs of English Language Learners." Libr Media Connect
    Includes bibliographical references

Merriam-Webster's dictionary of English usage.
Merriam-Webster 1994 978p $24.95 *
Grades: 9 10 11 12 **428**
    1. English language—Usage 2. Reference books
    ISBN 0-87779-132-5 LC 93-19289
    First published 1989 with title: Webster's dictionary of
English usage
    This guide looks at English usage from both historical
and contemporary perspectives. Over 20,000 quotations
illustrate the discussion of usage issues. Provides explanations of how accomplished writers have dealt with usage problems. Grammar, spelling and punctuation points
are also covered
    Includes bibliographical references

Mulvey, Dan
Barron's E-Z grammar. 2nd ed. Barron's
Educational Series 2009 208p pa $12.99
Grades: 9 10 11 12 Adult **428**
    1. English language—Grammar
    ISBN 978-0-7641-4261-1; 0-7641-4261-5
                   LC 2008-42424
    First published 2002 with title: Grammar the easy way

Reviews basic grammar, including parts of speech,
sentence structure, and subject-verb agreement; provides
a manual of usage, instruction on writing paragraphs and
research papers, and how to develop one's own style;
and includes exercises and a test.

O'Conner, Patricia T.
Woe is I; the grammarphobe's guide to better
English in plain English. Riverhead Bks. 2003
240p $19.95; pa $14
Grades: 11 12 Adult **428**
    1. English language—Grammar 2. English language—
Usage
    ISBN 1-57322-252-6; 1-59448-006-0 (pa)
                   LC 2003-41416
    First published 1996
    This guide to good English offers advice on punctua-
tion, usage, style and grammar as well as e-mail.
    "The author doesn't take herself or the subject matter
too seriously, offering a delightful romp through the intricacies of our language. . . . She knows her subject,
can convey her message with wit and ease, and does it
all in a compact, easy-to-read format. In short, this is an
entertaining and useful grammar reference." Libr J
    Includes bibliographical references

Ostler, Rosemarie
Dewdroppers, waldos, and slackers; a
decade-by-decade guide to the vanishing
vocabulary of the twentieth century. Oxford
University Press 2003 239p il hardcover o.p. pa
$23
Grades: 8 9 10 11 12 **428**
    1. English language—Slang 2. Reference books
    ISBN 978-0-19-516146-5; 0-19-516146-7;
978-0-19-518254-5 (pa); 0-19-518254-5 (pa)
                   LC 2003-8302
    "This reference work is not simply a slang dictionary.
Along with definitions . . . Ostler includes in each decade's chapter both brief discussions of relevant cultural
topics and a few photos. These short, often humorous essays are a way to provide examples for the terms defined. . . . Ostler's work is fun for browsing; it offers a
unique presentation of recent cultural history." Libr J
    Includes bibliographical references

Peters, Pam
The Cambridge guide to English usage.
Cambridge University Press 2004 608p il $35 *
Grades: 11 12 Adult **428**
    1. English language—Usage 2. Reference books
    ISBN 0-521-62181-X LC 2004-301888
    "Covering over 3000 points of word meaning, spell-
ing, punctuation, grammar, and style, the alphabetically
arranged entries often include references to resources
where the information was found." Libr J
    "Considering the abundance of peculiarities and chal-
lenges in English usage, *Cambridge* will strengthen even
a library well stocked with other guides. It is a serious
book for those serious about language." Booklist

Truss, Lynne
Eats, shoots & leaves; the zero tolerance approach to punctuation. Gotham Books 2004 xxvii, 209p $19.95; pa $12
Grades: 8 9 10 11 12 Adult   **428**
  1. Punctuation
  ISBN 1-59240-087-6; 1-59240-203-8 (pa)
                        LC 2004-40646
  First published 2003 in the United Kingdom
  The author "dissects common errors that grammar mavens have long deplored (often, as she readily points out, in isolation) and makes . . . arguments for increased attention to punctuation correctness. . . . Truss serves up delightful, unabashedly strict and sometimes snobby little book, with cheery Britishisms ('Lawks-a-mussy!') dotting pages that express a more international righteous indignation." Publ Wkly
  Includes bibliographical references

433   Dictionaries of standard German

Random House Webster's German-English, English-German dictionary. Rev. ed. Random House Reference 2006 c1998 547p $12.95 *
Grades: 11 12 Adult   **433**
  1. Reference books 2. German language—Dictionaries
  ISBN 0-375-72194-0; 978-0-375-72194-6
  Also available in paperback from Ballantine Bks.
  First published 1997 with title: Random House German-English English-German dictionary
  In addition to more than 60,000 entries this dictionary also includes notes on pronunciation, lists of abbreviations, tables of irregular verbs and lists of geographical names.

440   Romance languages French

Gaden, Monique
Cracking the SAT. French subject test; [by] Monique Gaden and Simone Ingram. 2011-2012 ed. Random House 2011 232p (Princeton Review series) pa $19.99
Grades: 9 10 11 12   **440**
  1. French language—Study and teaching 2. Scholastic Assessment Test 3. Colleges and universities—Entrance requirements
  ISBN 978-0-375-42815-9
  Annual. First published 2005. Continues Cracking the SAT II: French subject tests
  This guide provides test-taking strategies and sample tests on the subject of French.

443   Dictionaries of standard French

The **Oxford-Hachette** French dictionary; French-English, English-French; edited by Marie-Hélène Corréard, Valerie Grundy. 4th ed., edited by Jean-Benoit Ormal-Grenon, Nicholas Rollin. Oxford University Press/Hachette Livre 2007 xxxviii, 1945p $55 *
Grades: 11 12 Adult   **443**
  1. Reference books 2. French language—Dictionaries
  ISBN 978-0-19-861422-7; 0-19-861422-5
                        LC 2007-14213
  First published 1994
  This work provides coverage of French and English vocabulary in general as well as scientific and technical areas with over 350,000 words and phrases and over 530,000 translations. Supplementary material includes information on French society and culture, including famous places, people and much practical information for those planning to reside in France.

Le **petit** Larousse illustré en couleurs. Larousse 2010 xliv, 1811p il map $59.95
Grades: 9 10 11 12   **443**
  1. French language—Dictionaries 2. Reference books
  ISBN 978-2-03-584088-2
  First published 1906. Title varies
  "150000 definitions, 28000 noms propres, 5000 illustrations, 300 cartes, 105 planches illustrees" Cover; "87000 articles, 5000 illustrations, 321 cartes, Chronologie universelle" Title page
  Earlier editions by Pierre Larousse, published with title: Nouveau petit Larousse illustre, and Petit Larousse. Frequently revised to keep up to date with new words and accepted expressions. Text in French.

460   Spanish and Portuguese languages

Pace, George Roberto
Cracking the SAT. Spanish subject test. 2011-2012 ed. Random House 2011 274p (Princeton Review series) pa $19.99
Grades: 9 10 11 12   **460**
  1. Spanish language—Study and teaching 2. Scholastic Assessment Test 3. Colleges and universities—Entrance requirements
  ISBN 978-0-375-42817-3
  Annual. First published 2005. Continues Cracking the S A T II: Spanish subject test
  This guide provides test-taking strategies and sample tests on the subject of Spanish.

463 Dictionaries of standard Spanish

The **American** Heritage Spanish dictionary; Spanish/English, inglés/español. 2nd ed. Houghton Mifflin 2001 xxx, 1103p $26 *

Grades: 11 12 Adult **463**

1. Reference books 2. Spanish language—Dictionaries

ISBN 0-618-12770-4   LC 2001-24524

Also available online; The Concise American Heritage Spanish dictionary, 2nd edition published 2001 is also available

"With an emphasis on American English and Latin American Spanish, . . . this bilingual dictionary includes new technological, scientific, and business terms. Speakers of all the Americas will appreciate the different meanings of more than 120,000 words, presented in an easy-to-understand design. Notes on grammar usage are a plus." Booklist

The **concise** Oxford Spanish dictionary; Spanish-English, English-Spanish / chief editors, Carol Styles Carvajal, Jane Horwood = El diccionario Oxford esencial: Español-Inglés, Inglés-Español; dirección editorial, Carol Styles Carvajal, Jane Horwood. 4th ed., [edited by] Nicholas Rollin. Oxford University Press 2009 xxii, 1479p $29.95 *

Grades: 6 7 8 9 10 11 12 Adult **463**

1. Spanish language—Dictionaries 2. Reference books

ISBN 978-0-19-956094-3   LC 2009-464493

First published 1996

"Focusing on student users, the *Concise Oxford Spanish Dictionary* contains more than 1450 pages, and two appendixes. Included are the familiar verb tables for both regular and irregular forms. Other useful tools include endpapers that offer Spanish/English proprietary names along with examples of personal and business correspondence (letters and emails)." SLJ

Larousse concise dictionary: Spanish-English, English-Spanish; [project management/dirección, Sharon J. Hunter] Larousse 2006 various paging $22.95; pa $12.95

Grades: 9 10 11 12   **463**

1. Reference books 2. Spanish language—Dictionaries

ISBN   2-03-542138-1;   978-2-03-542138-8; 2-03-542137-3 (pa); 978-2-03-542137-1 (pa)

First published 1999

"With more than 90,000 references and 120,000 translations, including English compounds, English phonetics, and a supplement on life and culture in Spain, Latin America, the United Kingdom, and the U.S., this concise bilingual dictionary provides essential, everyday vocabulary for language learners." Booklist [review of 1999 edition]

Larousse standard diccionario, español-inglés, inglés-español. 3. ed. Larousse 2004 575, 62, 664p $36

Grades: 11 12 Adult   **463**

1. Reference books 2. Spanish language—Dictionaries

ISBN 2-03-542076-8   LC 2004-459150

Replaces the edition published 1996 with title: Larousse English-Spanish, Spanish-English dictionary

With over 174,000 references and 257,000 translations this dictionary covers general, professional and literary vocabulary. Abbreviations, acronyms and proper nouns are included. Contains special sections on language usage arranged alphabetically in main dictionary text.

Multicultural Spanish dictionary; how everyday Spanish differs from country to country. Schreiber Pub. 2006 281p pa $24.95 *

Grades: 9 10 11 12   **463**

1. Reference books 2. Spanish language—Dictionaries

ISBN 978-0-884003-17-5; 0-884003-17-5

LC 2006-13957

First published 1999 under the editorship of Agustín Martínez

"Divided into three parts (English-Spanish, Spanish-English and subject areas) this guide includes the most commonly used words throughout Latin America and Spain in the most common areas of everyday life. As stated in the introduction, it 'is not meant to replace the standard Spanish-English dictionary'; rather, it is a useful basic guide to a variety of common Spanish terms." Booklist [review of 1999 edition]

The **Oxford** Spanish dictionary; Spanish-English, English-Spanish; chief editors Beatriz Galimberti Jarman, Roy Russell. 4th ed. Oxford University Press 2008 xlviii, 1943p $49.95

Grades: 11 12 Adult   **463**

1. Spanish language—Dictionaries 2. Reference books

ISBN 978-0-19-920897-5   LC 2008-26099

First published 1994

On cover: 4th ed. edited by Nicholas Rollin, Carol Styles Carvajal

This "resource covers over 24 varieties of Spanish as it is written and spoken throughout the Spanish-speaking world—from Spain to Mexico, from Peru to the River Plate. . . . [It features] over 300,000 words and phrases, and half a million translations." Publisher's note

"No serious Hispanist in the English-speaking world can do without the magnificent Oxford Spanish dictionaries." Times Lit Suppl

473 Dictionaries of classical Latin

Cassell's Latin dictionary; Latin-English, English-Latin; by D. P. Simpson. Macmillan 1977 c1959 883p thumb-indexed $24.95

Grades: 8 9 10 11 12 Adult   **473**

1. Latin language—Dictionaries 2. Reference books

ISBN 0-02-522580-4   LC 77-7670

Also available in a concise paperback edition for $7.99 (ISBN 0-02-013340-5; ISBN-13: 978-0-02-013340-7)

First published 1854. This edition first published 1959. Previous United States editions published by Funk & Wagnalls with title: Cassell's New Latin dictionary

"Cassell's incorporates current English idiom and Latin spelling into the traditional presentation of classical Latin. The 30,000 entries include generic terms, geographical and proper nouns. Etymological notes and illustrative quotations are provided within entries." Wynar. Guide to Ref Books for Sch Media Cent. 3d edition

491.7 East Slavic languages. Russian

Oxford Russian dictionary; Russian-English, edited by Marcus Wheeler and Boris Unbegaun; English-Russian, edited by Paul Falla; revised and updated by Della Thompson. 4th ed. Oxford University Press 2007 xxi, 1322p $65
Grades: 11 12 Adult **491.7**
  1. Reference books 2. Russian language—Dictionaries
ISBN 978-0-19-861420-3; 0-19-861420-9
LC 2007-9399
First published 1972 with title: The Oxford Russian-English dictionary

This dictionary features over 500,000 words, phrases, and translations and includes a correspondence section and cultural notes as well as special boxes to help with tricky words and terms.

492.4 Hebrew

Zilkha, Avraham
Modern English-Hebrew dictionary. Yale Univ. Press 2002 457p (Yale language series) $55; pa $30
Grades: 11 12 Adult **492.4**
  1. Reference books 2. Hebrew language—Dictionaries
ISBN 0-300-09004-8; 0-300-09005-6 (pa)
LC 2001-26830
This dictionary includes 30,000 entries, with listings for translating words with multiple meanings, newly coined and slang words, common idioms, vocalization of Hebrew words, acronyms, and gender identification and plural forms of irregular nouns

493 Non-Semitic Afro-Asiatic languages

McDonald, Angela, 1974-
Write your own Egyptian hieroglyphs. University of California Press 2007 80p il pa $15.95
Grades: 7 8 9 10 11 12 Adult **493**
  1. Egyptian language 2. Hieroglyphics
ISBN 978-0-520-25235-6 LC 2006-51405
This book "covers the history of ancient Egyptian civilization and the context of this fascinating, early form of writing. Readers learn to create hieroglyphs for names, places, phrases and even insults! Kids from upper elementary through high school and adults will enjoy this fun book." Univ Press Books for Public and Second Sch Libr, 2008
Includes bibliographical references

495.1 Chinese

Li, Dong, 1942-
Tuttle English-Chinese dictionary. Tuttle Pub. 2010 368p il pa $29.95
Grades: 9 10 11 12 Adult **495.1**
  1. Chinese language—Dictionaries 2. Reference books
ISBN 978-0-8048-3992-1 LC 2009-936627
"Containing more than 40,000 words, phrases, and idioms, this comprehensive dictionary offers concise, up-to-date definitions, including the latest vocabulary for business, technology, sports, and the media. Approximately 25,000 headwords and 8,000 phrases and idioms are arranged alphabetically (in blue) for easy access. Each entry consists of grammar codes, Pinyin transliteration for pronunciation of Chinese equivalents, simplified Chinese characters, measure words if appropriate, definitions, related words or phrases, and sample sentences to assist users." Choice

495.6 Japanese

Basic Japanese-English dictionary. 2nd ed. Oxford University Press, Bonjinsha 2004 1000p pa $19.95
Grades: 8 9 10 11 12 Adult **495.6**
  1. Japanese language—Dictionaries 2. Reference books
ISBN 0-19-860859-4 LC 2004-54786
First published 1986 in Japan; 1989 by Oxford University Press

This "dictionary contains over 3,000 entries, which, along with providing basic meanings and grammatical information, also distinguish between senses, list compounds, and give sample sentences and idiomatic expressions. . . . It presents all the Japanese words and phrases in roman script with standard Japanese script alongside. . . . Cross-references direct the user to words of contrasting or related meaning, and, where necessary, the dictionary provides notes on special usage. It also includes [an] appendix which gives an introduction to Japanese grammar." Publisher's note

Kardy, Glenn
Manga University Presents . . . Kana de Manga Special Edition: Japanese Sound FX! writer, Glenn Kardy; artist, Chihiro Hattori. Japanime Co. Ltd./Manga University 2007 110p il pa $9.99
Grades: 6 7 8 9 10 11 12 Adult **495.6**
  1. Graphic novels 2. Manga 3. Japanese language
ISBN 978-4-921205-12-6
What does a cat's meow sound like in Japanese? How about the grumble of an empty stomach, the wail of a police car's siren or the crash of an ocean wave? Japanese manga artists rely heavily upon onomatopoeia—sound-effect words—and this entry in the Kana de Manga / Kanji de Manga language-learning series includes illustrated examples of those sounds in action. It features more than 100 Japanese onomatopoeia and their English equivalents in categories such as "Humans," "Animals," "Machines" and "Nature." The text is written in both English and Japanese hiragana.

Lammers, Wayne P., 1951-

Japanese the manga way; an illustrated guide to grammar & structure. Stone Bridge Press 2005 xxviii, 282p il pa $24.95

Grades: 9 10 11 12   **495.6**
  1. Japanese language
  ISBN 1-880656-90-6   LC 2005-296444

The author "intends to teach absolute beginners how to use manga to learn to speak and read conversational Japanese. . . . For someone who has the patience, drive, and desire to learn the language, the book will be an immense help." SLJ

Includes bibliographical references

495.7   Korean

Adelson-Goldstein, Jayme

Oxford picture dictionary; English/Korean; [by] Jayme Adelson-Goldstein, Norma Shapiro. 2nd ed. Oxford Univ Press 2009 305p il pa $19.95

Grades: 8 9 10 11 12 Adult   **495.7**
  1. Korean language—Dictionaries 2. Picture dictionaries 3. Reference books
  ISBN 978-0-19-474016-6; 0-19-474016-1
                                          LC 2009292655
  First published 1998

Over 4,000 words are defined in labeled illustrations grouped into different thematic areas. Exercises and a pronunciation guide are provided.

Includes bibliographical references

500   SCIENCE

Beyer, Rick

The greatest science stories never told; 100 tales of invention and discovery to astonish, bewilder & stupefy. Harper 2009 214p il $19.99

Grades: 9 10 11 12 Adult   **500**
  1. Science 2. Inventions
  ISBN 978-0-06-162696-8   LC 2009-32741
  At head of title: History presents—

This book features miscellaneous stories about inventions and discoveries in science.

Includes bibliographical references

Brooks, M. (Michael), 1970-

13 things that don't make sense; the most baffling scientific mysteries of our time; [by] Michael Brooks. Doubleday 2008 240p $23.95

Grades: 11 12 Adult   **500**
  1. Science
  ISBN 978-0-385-52068-3; 0-385-52068-9
                                          LC 2008-12443

This "book examines such mysteries as dark matter and dark energy, the prospect of life on Mars, sex and death, free will and the placebo effect, among other head-scratchers. . . . This elegantly written, meticulously researched and thought-provoking book provides window into how science actually works, and is sure to spur intense debate." New Sci

Includes bibliographical references

Bryson, Bill

A short history of nearly everything. Broadway Bks. 2003 544p $27.50; pa $15.95 *

Grades: 9 10 11 12 Adult   **500**
  1. Science
  ISBN 0-7679-0817-1; 0-7679-0818-X (pa)
                                          LC 2003-46006

In presenting this history of science, Bryson's "interest is not simply to discover what we know but to find out how we know it. How do we know what is in the center of the earth, thousands of miles beneath the surface? How can we know the extent and the composition of the universe, or what a black hole is? How can we know where the continents were 600 million years ago?" Publisher's note

"Neither oversimplified nor overstuffed, this exceptionally skillful tour of the physical world covers the basic principles and still has room for profiles of some of the more engaging scientists." N Y Times Book Rev

Includes bibliographical references

Etzkowitz, Henry, 1940-

Athena unbound; the advancement of women in science and technology; {by} Henry Etzkowitz, Carol Kemelgor, Brian Uzzi, with Michael Neushatz {et al.}. Cambridge Univ. Press 2000 282p $55; pa $21 *

Grades: 11 12 Adult   **500**
  1. Women scientists
  ISBN 0-521-56380-1; 0-521-78738-6 (pa)
                                          LC 00-20997

This is an "inquiry into why there are so few women scientists. . . . The authors balance their extremely detailed analysis with a humanistic perspective as they compare and contrast the status of women scientists in different countries, characterize both exclusionary and supportive forms of networking, and, ultimately, offer some surprising and hopeful conclusions." Booklist

Includes bibliographical references

Feynman, Richard Phillips, 1918-1988

The meaning of it all; thoughts of a citizen scientist. Basic Books 2005 c1998 133p pa $13.95

Grades: 11 12 Adult   **500**
  1. Science 2. Religion
  ISBN 0-465-02394-0
  First published 1998 by Addison-Wesley

"Originally delivered as a three-part lecture series at the University of Washington in 1963, this collection touches on such far-ranging topics as the existence or nonexistence of God; the Constitution; and UFOs. . . . These memorable lectures confirm that Feynman's gift of insight extended from the subatomic world to the cosmic, and to the very human as well." Publ Wkly

Flatow, Ira

Present at the future; from evolution to nanotechnology, candid and controversial conversations on science and nature. Collins 2007 354p il $24.95 *

Grades: 11 12 Adult   **500**

1. Science

ISBN 978-0-06-073264-6; 0-06-073264-4

LC 2007-14583

This book describes current thinking "on nanotechnology, space travel, global warming, alternative energies, stem cell research, and using the universe as a super-super computer." Publisher's note

This is "an entertaining and thought-provoking read that leaves you feeling more informed and as though you might have a little more to offer during your next dinner-party conversation." Sci Books Films

Grant, John, 1949-

Corrupted science. Facts, Figures & Fun 2007 336p il $12.95

Grades: 11 12 Adult   **500**

1. Fraud in science

ISBN 978-1-904332-73-2

"Fraud, ideology and politics in science" Cover

Contains brief discussions of examples throughout history of science being corrupted for political, ideological, or fraudulent purposes, including Lysenkoism, science under the Nazis, the Piltdown Man hoax, and recent attempts to discredit global warming.

The **handy** science answer book; compiled by the Carnegie Library of Pittsburgh; [edited by] Naomi E. Balaban and James E. Bobick. 4th ed. Visible Ink Press 2011 679p il pa $21.95

Grades: 11 12 Adult   **500**

1. Science 2. Technology

ISBN 978-1-57859-321-7   LC 2011-429

First published 1994

"The text is divided into various subject areas including physics and chemistry, space, earth, climate and weather, minerals and other materials, energy, technology, and environment, gathering answers to reference questions. . . . A comprehensive index . . . makes the material accessible and easy to find. Pages are full of fascinating tidbits, complemented by illustrations, photos, charts, graphs, and maps." Voice Youth Advocates

Includes bibliographical references

Henderson, Mark, 1974-

100 most important science ideas; key concepts in genetics, physics and mathematics; [by] Mark Henderson, Joanne Baker, Tony Crilly. Firefly Books 2009 431p il $19.95

Grades: 11 12 Adult   **500**

1. Genetics 2. Physics 3. Mathematics

ISBN 978-1-55407-527-0

This book aims to encourage the reader to explore "the 100 most important, groundbreaking ideas that have emerged from the scientific disciplines of genetics, physics, and mathematics. Divided into three sections, each written by one of the authors . . . this work presents

complex scientific topics in a simple, understandable way. . . . Text boxes, entertaining quotations, frequent diagrams, and everyday examples hold the reader's attention and make this work engaging to anyone interested in the world of science." Libr J

Oxford dictionary of scientific quotations; edited by W.F. Bynum and Roy Porter; assistant editors, Sharon Messenger, Caroline Overy. Oxford University Press 2005 712p $60; pa $18.95

Grades: 11 12 Adult   **500**

1. Science 2. Quotations

ISBN 0-19-858409-1; 0-19-861443-8 (pa)

LC 2005-277260

"The quotations collected here are not only by scientists but by writers, politicians, and others with something to say about science. . . . Each entry includes the name of the person being quoted, his or her dates, a . . . biographical statement, and several quotes, with their sources." Booklist

"This hefty volume is a great reference but it is also a great read—open it up to any page and expand the mind with a sampling of scientific ideas and philosophy." Choice

Sagan, Carl, 1934-1996

Broca's brain; reflections on the romance of science. Random House 1979 347p pa $7.99 hardcover o.p.

Grades: 11 12 Adult   **500**

1. Science 2. Philosophy

ISBN 0-345-33689-5 (pa)   LC 78-21810

In this volume Sagan considers the following: "the quest for extraterrestrial life, popular science, and religious questions, as well as numerous concerns more immediate to his own specialty, astronomy." Libr J

The author "is a lucid, logical writer with a gift for explaining science to the layman and infecting the reader with his own boundless enthusiasm and curiosity." Natl Rev

Includes bibliographical references

Wiggins, Arthur W.

The five biggest unsolved problems in science; [by] Arthur W. Wiggins [and] Charles M. Wynn; with cartoon commentary by Sidney Harris. J. Wiley & Sons 2003 234p il pa $14.95

Grades: 11 12 Adult   **500**

1. Science

ISBN 0-471-26808-9   LC 2003-284262

"The problems discussed in this volume are the dueling concepts of mass and masslessness (physics), the passage from chemicals to living matter (chemistry), the complete structure of the proteome (biology), long-range weather forecasting (geology), and the expansion of the universe (astronomy)." Sci Books Films

Includes bibliographical references

500.2 Physical sciences

Rosen, Joe

Encyclopedia of physical science; [by] Joe Rosen and Lisa Quinn Gothard. Facts on File 2009 c2010 2v il (Facts on File science library) set $170
Grades: 11 12 Adult   **500.2**
1. Physical sciences—Encyclopedias 2. Reference books
ISBN 978-0-8160-7011-4; 0-8160-7011-3
LC 2008-36444

"The alphabetized entries include biographies of famous scientists who have contributed to our current understanding of physical science topics. The categories include atomic structure; matter; chemical reactions; motions and forces; conservation of energy and increase in disorder; and interaction of energy and matter. In addition, there are unifying topics with life sciences and Earth sciences." Libr Media Connect

"The layout, color illustrations, and numerous tables make this an accessible reference on an important topic." Libr J

Includes bibliographical references

Walker, Pamela, 1958-

Physical science experiments; [by] Pamela Walker, Elaine Wood. Facts on File 2010 149p il (Facts on File science experiments) $35
Grades: 7 8 9 10   **500.2**
1. Physical sciences 2. Science—Experiments
ISBN 978-0-8160-7807-3; 0-8160-7807-6
LC 2009-23673

Presents tested experiments related to the field of physical science. The experiments are designed to promote interest in science in and out of the classroom, and to improve critical-thinking skills.

Includes glossary and bibliographical references

500.5 Space sciences

Krauss, Lawrence Maxwell

The physics of Star Trek; with a foreword by Stephen Hawking. [Rev. and updated ed.] Basic Books 2007 251p il pa $15
Grades: 11 12 Adult   **500.5**
1. Star trek (Television program) 2. Space sciences
ISBN 978-0-465-00204-7; 0-465-00204-8
LC 2007-18981

First published 1995

This book examines various aspects of the television series *Star Trek* from the perspective of a scientist.

"This is interesting and entertaining and can lead to endless discussions on the science used in all the *Star Trek* series." Sci Books Films

Includes bibliographical references

Launius, Roger D.

Smithsonian atlas of space exploration; [by] Roger D. Launius & Andrew K. Johnston. Collins 2009 230p il map $34.99
Grades: 9 10 11 12 Adult   **500.5**
1. Outer space—Exploration—Pictorial works
ISBN 978-0-06-156526-7   LC 2009-649

This book "relates the story of space exploration in text, photographs, illustrations, and maps from the earliest times to the present. Written at a level geared to the general reader, this topically arranged work is divided into seven parts. . . . Each part contains a number of two or four-page subsections covering topics ranging from the earliest observatories of the ancient world to the possibilities for space flight in the future. . . . Distinguished by outstanding color illustrations and photographs, the very reasonably priced atlas should appeal to a broad audience." Booklist

Includes bibliographical references

Parks, Peggy J., 1951-

Space research. ReferencePoint Press 2010 96p il (Inside science) $26.95
Grades: 8 9 10 11 12   **500.5**
1. Astronautics 2. Outer space—Exploration 3. Space sciences
ISBN 978-1-60152-111-8; 1-60152-111-1
LC 2009-48159

"Parks piles on the research, digging deep into interstellar study, programs that reach into space, and what it all means to the common person, never shying away from detail and onerous proper nouns. . . . The color layout features plenty of photos, boxes, and charts, while Parks delivers a surprisingly spry text." Booklist

Includes bibliographical references

501 Philosophy and theory

The **next** fifty years; science in the first half of the twenty-first century; edited by John Brockman. Vintage Books 2002 301p pa $14.95
Grades: 11 12 Adult   **501**
1. Science 2. Forecasting
ISBN 0-375-71342-5   LC 2001-57368

"A Vintage original"

"This collection of essays provides some interesting and provocative possibilities as to achievements in various areas of science over the next 50 years as projected by current leaders (who are also articulate writers) in their fields." Sci Books Films

This will change everything; ideas that will shape the future; edited by John Brockman; [introduction by Daniel C. Dennett] HarperCollins 2010 xxiii, 390p pa $14.99
Grades: 11 12 Adult   **501**
1. Science 2. Forecasting
ISBN 978-0-06-189967-6

"Author and editor Brockman presents 136 answers to the question, 'What game-changing scientific ideas and developments do you expect to live to see?'" Publ Wkly

"With contributions from Ian McEwan, Steven Pinker, Lee Smolin, Craig Venter, Richard Dawkins and 130 others of their ilk, the book is like an intellectual lucky dip." New Sci

502 Miscellany

Echaore-Yoon, Susan, 1953-
Career opportunities in science; [by] Susan Echaore-McDavid. 2nd ed. Ferguson 2008 332p $49.50; pa $18.95
Grades: 9 10 11 12 **502**
1. Science—Vocational guidance
ISBN 978-0-8160-7132-6; 0-8160-7132-2; 978-0-8160-7133-3 (pa); 0-8160-7133-0 (pa)
LC 2007-40659
First published 2003
This "guide includes 93 profiles of scientific and technical careers. . . . Each entry includes a position description, potential salaries, employment and advancement prospects, necessary education and training, recommended experience and personality traits, a list of professional associations in the field, and entry tips." Choice
This book "will be highly useful to a diverse population of readers. . . . This excellent book is easy to read and the information it presents is clear and concise." Sci Books Films
Includes glossary and bibliographical references

Goldberg, Jan
Careers for scientific types & others with inquiring minds. 2nd ed. McGraw-Hill 2007 146p (McGraw-Hill careers for you series) pa $14.95
Grades: 9 10 11 12 **502**
1. Science—Vocational guidance 2. Technology—Vocational guidance
ISBN 978-0-07-147618-8; 0-07-147618-0
LC 2006-28897
First published 2000 by VGM Career Horizons
This guide for readers considering a career in science includes "inside information on everyday routines of selected jobs, working conditions within the field, and alternate sources to enhance your job search." Publisher's note
Includes bibliographical references

Ochoa, George
The Wilson chronology of science and technology; [by] George Ochoa and Melinda Corey. Wilson, H.W. 1997 440p $105
Grades: 8 9 10 11 12 Adult **502**
1. Science—History 2. Technology—History 3. Reference books
ISBN 0-8242-0933-8 LC 97-22060
This chronology begins in 2,500,000 B.C. and continues into 1997. "Within each year, entries are arranged alphabetically according to one of 13 categories: archaeology; astronomy, space science, and space exploration; biology, biochemistry, agriculture, and ecology; chemistry; earth sciences (geology, oceanography, meteorology) and earth exploration; mathematics; medicine; miscellaneous; paleontology; physics; psychology, neuroscience, and artificial intelligence; social sciences (anthropology, sociology, economics, political science) and linguistics; and technology and engineering." Publisher's note
Includes bibliographical references

Sullivan, Megan
All in a day's work; careers using science; by Megan Sullivan for The Science Teacher. 2nd ed. NSTA Press 2008 140p il pa $15.95
Grades: 9 10 11 12 **502**
1. Science—Vocational guidance
ISBN 978-1-93353-145-8; 1-93353-145-2
LC 2008-24672
"An NSTA Press Journals Collection"
First published 2007
This is a compilation of "interviews from the Science Teacher journal. From astronaut to video-game level designer, each entry poses questions that go beyond basic education requirements and job responsibilities. . . . An excellent choice for career collections, Sullivan's book not only encourages students to take as much math and science as possible in high school, but also emphasizes the commitment to lifelong learning critical for most 21st-century jobs." SLJ
Includes bibliographical references

503 Dictionaries, encyclopedias, concordances

The **American** Heritage science dictionary. [rev. ed] Houghton Mifflin Harcourt 2008 695p il $21.95 *
Grades: 8 9 10 11 12 Adult **503**
1. Science—Dictionaries 2. Reference books
ISBN 978-0-618-88274-8; 0-618-88274-X
LC 2008-276195
First published 2005
This science dictionary has 8,500 entries in all areas of science and includes biographical entries, cross-references, photographs, drawings, tables, and charts.

DK science; the definitive visual guide; editor in chief: Adam Hart-Davis. DK Pub. 2009 512p il $50
Grades: 9 10 11 12 Adult **503**
1. Science—Encyclopedias 2. Reference books
ISBN 978-0-7566-5570-9 LC 2010-281802
This is "a beautiful pictorial history of science, ranging from the prehistoric harnessing of fire to the current race to minimize anthropogenic climate change. Each topic presented within the 512 pages of the text is succinctly described in a chronological sequence, together with a multitude of engaging color visuals. This combination makes the overall presentation as accessible and inviting as that of a coffee-table book, while still maintaining the necessary breadth and depth of detail to make the volume useful as an introductory reference." Sci Books Films

Encyclopedia of science, technology, and ethics; edited by Carl Mitcham. Macmillan Reference USA 2005 4v il map set $450
Grades: 11 12 Adult **503**
1. Science—Ethical aspects—Encyclopedias 2. Technology—Encyclopedias 3. Reference books
ISBN 0-02-865831-0 LC 2005-6968
This "set confronts the major ethical issues of our time in a series of 675 articles, 33 of which are

Encyclopedia of science, technology, and ethics—*Continued*

overviews of topics like computer ethics, while the remainder deal with such 'hot-button' issues as abortion and animal rights." Libr J

This "multivolume work on ethics provides a superb introduction to the issues presented." Booklist

Includes bibliographical references

Gale encyclopedia of science; K. Lee Lerner & Brenda Wilmoth Lerner, editors. 4th ed. Thomson Gale 2008 6v il set $685
Grades: 9 10 11 12 Adult   **503**
1. Reference books 2. Science—Encyclopedias
ISBN 978-1-4144-2877-2; 1-4144-2877-4
                LC 2006-37485
First published 1996
"From algae to zooplankton, assembly lines to Y2K, and from Agent Orange to weapons of mass destruction, this encyclopedia covers every aspect of the scientific world. . . . It is designed to 'instruct, challenge, and excite' a wide range of users and is a good starting point to answer any scientific question." Libr Media Connect
Includes bibliographical references

McGraw-Hill concise encyclopedia of science & technology. 6th ed. McGraw-Hill 2009 2v il map set $295 *
Grades: 11 12 Adult   **503**
1. Science—Encyclopedias 2. Technology—Encyclopedias 3. Reference books
ISBN 978-0-07-161366-8   LC 2008-50987
First published 1984
A condensed version of the McGraw-Hill encyclopedia of science & technology
This encyclopedia features over 7100 articles on branches of technology and science ranging from acoustics to zoology.
Includes bibliographical references

McGraw-Hill encyclopedia of science & technology. 10th ed. McGraw-Hill 2007 20v il map set $2,995
Grades: 11 12 Adult   **503**
1. Science—Encyclopedias 2. Technology—Encyclopedias 3. Reference books
ISBN 978-0-07-144143-8; 0-07-144143-3
                LC 2007-6137
"An international reference work in twenty volumes including an index"
First published 1960 in fifteen volumes
This encyclopedia "contains approximately 7,100 articles on major topics in all categories of science and technology, written for the non-specialist. Each entry begins with general information on the topic. Detailed information follows under headings so the reader can focus on specific areas of interest. All but general survey articles have a bibliography at the end. There is extensive cross-referencing between articles that leads to related topics. Scientists who have been major contributors to their field wrote many articles. The index volume contains a list of contributors, a guide to scientific notation, study guides, a topical index, and an analytical index." Sci Books Films [review of 2002 edition]
Includes bibliographical references

The **new** book of popular science. Scholastic Library Pub. 2008 6v il set $399 *
Grades: 7 8 9 10 11 12   **503**
1. Science—Encyclopedias 2. Technology—Encyclopedias 3. Reference books
ISBN 978-0-7172-1226-2   LC 2007-41858
First published 1924 with title: The book of popular science. Frequently revised
Contents: v1 Astronomy, space science, mathematics, past and future; v2 Earth sciences, energy, environmental sciences; v3 Chemistry, physics, biology; v4 Plant life, animal life; v5 Mammals, human sciences; v6 Technology
The information in this set is classified under such broad categories as astronomy and space science, computers and mathematics, earth sciences, energy, environmental sciences, physical sciences, general biology, plant life, animal life, mammals, human sciences and technology.
Includes bibliographical references

The **Penguin** dictionary of science; editor, M. J. Clugston; author team, N. J. Lord ... [et al.] 3rd ed. Penguin 2009 744p il pa $18
Grades: 9 10 11 12   **503**
1. Science—Dictionaries 2. Reference books
ISBN 978-0-14-103796-7
First published 1943 under the editorship of E.B. Uvarov and Alan Isaacs. Previous edition published with title: The new Penguin dictionary of science
This dictionary covers terms used in chemistry, physics, astronomy, human anatomy, mathematics, computing and other scientific fields. An appendix includes a periodic table, a list of chemical properties, diagrams of amino acids, and other information.

Swedin, Eric Gottfrid

Science in the contemporary world; an encyclopedia; [by] Eric G. Swedin. ABC-CLIO 2005 xxv, 382p il (ABC-CLIO's history of science series) $85
Grades: 9 10 11 12   **503**
1. Science—Encyclopedias 2. Reference books
ISBN 1-85109-524-1   LC 2004-26950
This book "covers developments in the scientific disciplines from the end of World War II to the present day. . . . It makes a make good introductory text to the history of science in the late twentieth and early twenty-first centuries." Booklist
Includes bibliographical references

Van Nostrand's scientific encyclopedia. 10th ed., Glenn D. Considine, editor-in-chief; Peter H. Kulik, associate editor. Wiley 2008 3v il map set $450 *
Grades: 11 12 Adult   **503**
1. Science—Encyclopedias 2. Reference books
ISBN 978-0-471-74338-5   LC 2007-46658
Also available online
First published 1938
This encyclopedia contains articles contains over 10,000 entries on topics such as biology, chemistry, earth science, mathematics and engineering, anatomy and phys-

Van Nostrand's scientific encyclopedia—*Continued*

iology, physics, botany, and space science.

Includes bibliographical references

507.8 Use of apparatus and equipment in study and teaching

Bochinski, Julianne Blair, 1966-

More award-winning science fair projects; illustrated by Judy J. Bochinski-DiBiase. J. Wiley 2004 228p il $29.95; pa $14.95 *

Grades: 7 8 9 10   507.8

   1. Science projects 2. Science—Experiments

   ISBN 0-471-27338-4; 0-471-27337-6 (pa)

                   LC 2003-9477

Presents forty award-winning science fair projects, a section on how to do a science fair project, updates to science fair rules and science supply resources, as well as new material on useful web sites.

Downie, N. A., 1956-

Vacuum bazookas, electric rainbow jelly, and 27 other Saturday science projects; {by} Neil Downie. Princeton Univ. Press 2001 253p hardcover o.p. pa $18.95

Grades: 9 10 11 12   507.8

   1. Science—Experiments 2. Science projects

   ISBN 0-691-00985-6; 0-691-00986-4 (pa)

                 LC 2001-36258

Most projects "illustrate the physics of waves or mechanics, and for the hard-core gadgeteer, Downie appends to each project an explanation of the mathematics describing what's going on with, say, a rotating, ribless umbrella. . . . There is an upgrade of the classic cups-and-string telecom technology, which Downie calls the string radio. He illustrates the basic idea of modern smart-bomb warfare in the shape of a (perfectly safe) guided carpet missile, and throughout he sprinkles a number of amusingly useless labor-saving devices." Booklist

"This book is an excellent source of fun, light-hearted projects for young adults." Sci Books Films

Includes bibliographical references

Dutton, Judy

Science fair season; twelve kids, a robot named Scorch— and what it takes to win. Hyperion 2011 271p $24.99

Grades: 11 12 Adult   507.8

   1. International Science and Engineering Fair 2. Science—Exhibitions 3. Science projects

   ISBN 978-1-4013-2379-0

"Following 12 teens to the Super Bowl of science fairs—the Intel International Science & Engineering Fair (Intel ISEF) brings together 1,500 kids from over 50 countries, and offers up to $4 million in prizes and scholarships—[the author] shows that science can be exciting, creative, even glamorous. . . . [This] is an incredibly fun read, and a reminder that scientists can be heroes, too." Maclean's

Includes bibliographical references

Johnson, George, 1952-

The ten most beautiful experiments. Alfred A. Knopf 2008 192p il $22.95

Grades: 11 12 Adult   507.8

   1. Science—Experiments

   ISBN 978-1-4000-4101-5; 1-4000-4101-5

                 LC 2007-27839

The author describes "10 historic experiments whose elegant simplicity revealed key features of our bodies and our world." Publ Wkly

"Writing up Luigi Galvani's study of frog's legs, James Joule's of heat, Albert Michelson's of light's speed, and Robert Millikan's of the electron's charge, Johnson exerts classic appeal to science readers: presenting the lone genius making a great discovery. Good to go in any library." Booklist

Includes bibliographical references

Vecchione, Glen

Blue ribbon science fair projects. Sterling Pub. Co. 2005 224p il $19.95

Grades: 9 10 11 12   507.8

   1. Science projects 2. Science—Experiments

   ISBN 978-1-4027-1073-5; 1-4027-1073-9

                 LC 2005-13557

"After an introduction to the process of creating science-fair projects and a summary of tips from an experienced science-fair judge, Vecchione . . . [presents] project ideas within the following subject areas: animals, the human body, magnetism, botany, equipment, chemistry, astronomy, physics, and math. . . . Students planning science-fair projects will find this a solid resource." Booklist

Vickers, Tanya M.

Teen science fair sourcebook; winning school science fairs and national competitions. Enslow Publishers 2009 160p il lib bdg $34.60

Grades: 7 8 9 10   507.8

   1. Science—Exhibitions 2. Science projects 3. Science—Experiments

   ISBN 978-0-7660-2711-4; 0-7660-2711-2

                 LC 2008-30779

The author provides tips on how to "create a successful high-powered science fair project, such as Siemens-Westinghouse, from getting started to competing at a regional or national competition." Publisher's note

"The book is clearly written, and its page design, which includes the occasional photo, is colorful. . . . A useful resource for highly motivated students." Booklist

Includes glossary and bibliographical references

Walker, Pamela, 1958-

Environmental science experiments; [by] Pamela Walker, Elaine Wood. Facts on File 2010 153p il (Facts on File science experiments) $35

Grades: 7 8 9 10   507.8

   1. Environmental science 2. Science—Experiments

   ISBN 978-0-8160-7805-9; 0-8160-7805-X

                 LC 2008-53715

This "contains 20 experiments that allow students to actively engage in scientific inquiry. Projects are pres-

Walker, Pamela, 1958-——*Continued*
ented in a uniform format, with an introduction to the
topic, time requirements (35 minutes to 2 weeks), a materials list, numbered procedures, and several analysis
questions. . . . Line drawings, colorful images, and data
tables enhance instructions. . . . The experiments themselves are timely and fascinating. [The book] includes
high-interest investigations into what people throw away,
the safety of reusing water bottles, and a 'bottled versus
tap water' taste test." SLJ
Includes glossary and bibliographical references

508   Natural history

Carroll, Sean B.
Remarkable creatures; epic adventures in the
search for the origins of species. Houghton Mifflin
Harcourt 2009 331p il map $26; pa $14.95
Grades: 11 12 Adult   508
1. Evolution 2. Naturalists
ISBN   978-0-15-101485-9;   0-15-101485-X;
978-0-547-24778-6 (pa); 0-547-24778-8 (pa)
LC 2008-25438
"Examines the contributions of pioneering scientists to
the modern understanding of how Earth and the planet's
life evolved, recounting such important events as Darwin's trip around the world, Charles Walcott's discovery
of pre-Cambrian life, and the Leakeys' probe into humankind's remote past." Publisher's note
"A stirring introduction to the wonder of evolutionary
biology." Kirkus
Includes bibliographical references

Daubert, Stephen
The shark and the jellyfish; more stories in
natural history. Vanderbilt University Press 2009
213p il $24.95
Grades: 11 12 Adult   508
1. Natural history
ISBN 978-0-8265-1629-9; 0-8265-1629-7
LC 2008-29024
"This intriguing book is composed of eight short stories on various subjects in natural history, grouped into
five sections: 'Field & Stream,' 'Air,' 'Sea and Shore,'
'Forest,' and 'Earth and Stars.' Each story weaves a narrative about the interconnections between life and the environment, built around findings that have been published
in the scientific literature. . . . The book provides an engaging and interesting discourse on natural history that is
backed by real science on the subject being covered." Sci
Books Films
Includes bibliographical references

Threads from the web of life; stories in natural
history; with illustrations by Chris Daubert.
Vanderbilt University Press 2006 162p il $24.95
Grades: 11 12 Adult   508
1. Natural history
ISBN 0-8265-1509-6; 978-0-8265-1509-4
LC 2005-23117
The author "illustrates 16 ecological processes with
lively narratives in which he envisions how it might feel

to be at the center of the action: for example, traveling
with a green sea turtle from its feeding grounds in Brazil
to its nesting beaches 2,000 kilometers away on Ascension Island in the eastern Atlantic; riding whirling air
currents with migrating American white pelicans; or fleeing from a predator swordfish with a school of neon flying squid. . . . His natural history tales are instructive
and entertaining, and each is followed by an annotation
explaining the science behind it." Publ Wkly
Includes bibliographical references

Fothergill, Alastair
Planet Earth; as you've never seen it before;
[by] Alastair Fothergill [et al.]; foreword by David
Attenborough. University of California Press 2007
309p il map $39.95 *
Grades: 11 12 Adult   508
1. Habitat (Ecology) 2. Earth
ISBN 978-0-520-25054-3; 0-520-25054-0
LC 2006-50073
In this collection of over 400 photographs of natural
landscapes and wildlife, the author "takes readers on a
kaleidoscopic tour of the flora, fauna and natural history
of the Earth's poles, forests, plains, deserts, mountains
and oceans." Publ Wkly

Gould, Stephen Jay, 1941-2002
The richness of life; the essential Stephen Jay
Gould; edited by Paul McGarr and Steven Rose;
with an introduction by Steven Rose and a
foreword by Oliver Sacks. Norton 2007 654p il
$35
Grades: 11 12 Adult   508
1. Natural history 2. Evolution
ISBN 978-0-393-06498-8; 0-393-06498-0
LC 2006-29208
Frist published 2006 in the United Kingdom
"These 44 essays represent . . . [the author's] best-
known pieces from his books and from essays for Natu-
ral History magazine, as well as never before published
speeches." Publ Wkly
"For collections that have room for only one volume
of his writing, this is the essential one." SLJ
Includes bibliographical references

Hamilton, Neil A., 1949-
Scientific exploration and expeditions; from the
age of discovery to the twenty-first century; [by]
Neil Hamilton. M.E. Sharpe 2011 2v il map set
$165
Grades: 7 8 9 10 11 12   508
1. Scientific expeditions 2. Reference books
ISBN 978-0-7656-8076-1; 0-7656-8076-9
LC 2010-12118
"Hamilton's 115 entries in this set describe the
courses and discoveries of significant scientific expeditions from the early 15th century to mid 2009. . . . The
presentations are systematic, carefully detailed, not exclusively Eurocentric, and when appropriate, skeptical. The
currency of information and focus on science will make
this work particularly useful." SLJ
Includes bibliographical references

Natural history; the ultimate visual guide to everything on Earth; [senior project editor, Kathryn Hennessy] DK 2010 648p il map $50
Grades: 10 11 12 Adult   **508**
1. Natural history 2. Reference books
ISBN 978-0-7566-6752-8; 0-7566-6752-6
LC 2010-283659
At head of title: Smithsonian
"This is an international encyclopedia of life-forms—e.g., fossils, fungi, plants, animals, mammals—that includes vital facts and two to three sentences about each as well as more than 5000 color illustrations in all. Each grouping is introduced by an essay that puts it in biological and evolutionary perspective." Libr J

Savage, Candace, 1949-
Prairie: a natural history; principle photography by James R. Page; illustrations by Joan A. Williams. 2nd ed. Greystone Books 2011 305p il map pa $29.95 *
Grades: 9 10 11 12   **508**
1. Prairies
ISBN 978-1-55365-588-6
First published 2004
Co-published by the David Suzuki Foundation
This "guide to the biology and ecology of the prairies, the Great Plains grasslands of North America . . . [includes information on] declining bird species, enhanced protection of bison, the effect of industrialization on the prairies, and the effect of the increase in coyote numbers on red foxes and swift foxes." Publisher's note

Schaller, George B.
A naturalist and other beasts; tales from a life in the field; with photographs by the author. Sierra Club Books 2007 272p il $24.95
Grades: 11 12 Adult   **508**
1. Wildlife
ISBN 978-1-57805-129-8; 1-57805-129-0
LC 2006-51153
The author "presents 19 short pieces culled from the dozens of articles and books he has published during half a century spent observing animals around the world. The selections include studies of the daily lives of such exotic beasts as jaguars in Brazil; tigers in central India; lions, wildebeest and cheetahs in Tanzania's Serengeti Plain; giant pandas in China; snow leopards in Pakistan; and chiru (antelope) in the uplands of the Tibetan Plateau." Publ Wkly
"Schaller presents exciting animal lore that will inspire readers to learn more about these precious creatures." Booklist
Includes bibliographical references

509   Historical, geographic, persons treatment

Concise history of science & invention; an illustrated time line; edited by Jolyon Goddard. National Geographic 2010 352p il map $40
Grades: 9 10 11 12 Adult   **509**
1. Science—History—Chronology 2. Inventions—History—Chronology 3. Reference books
ISBN 978-1-4262-0544-6; 1-4262-0544-9
LC 2009-18460
At head of title: National Geographic
This volume examines "our species' key scientific and innovative achievements, . . . presenting ten distinct eras from the first glimmers of intelligence to the cutting-edge technologies of the modern world." Publisher's note
"The topical essays and wonderful photos and illustrations make this source useful as a circulating book as well as a reference book." Booklist
Includes glossary and bibliographical references

Crease, Robert P.
The great equations; breakthroughs in science from Pythagoras to Heisenberg. W.W. Norton & Co. 2009 315p il $25.95
Grades: 11 12 Adult   **509**
1. Equations 2. Science—Philosophy 3. Science—History
ISBN 978-0-393-06204-5; 0-393-06204-X
LC 2008-42494
The author "explores 10 rather beautiful equations. He begins with the beguiling simplicity of the equation that bears Pythagoras' name . . . and moves on to Newton's second law of motion and law of universal gravitation, the second law of thermodynamics, Maxwell's celebrated equations, discoveries by Einstein and Schrödinger and, finally, Heisenberg's famous uncertainty principle. . . . Any reader who aspires to be scientifically literate will find this a good starting place." Publ Wkly
Includes bibliographical references

The prism and the pendulum; the ten most beautiful experiments in science. Random House 2003 xxii, 244p il hardcover o.p. pa $14.95 *
Grades: 11 12 Adult   **509**
1. Science—History 2. Science—Experiments
ISBN 1-400-06131-8; 0-8129-7062-4 (pa)
LC 2003-54765
Each scientific experiment discussed here "is followed by an 'interlude,' or commentary, on how the experiment qualifies as most beautiful and how art and science both give meaning to the term 'beauty.'" Sci Books Films

Gribbin, John R.
The scientists; a history of science told through the lives of its greatest inventors; [by] John Gribbin. Random House 2003 xxii, 646p il hardcover o.p. pa $16.95 *
Grades: 11 12 Adult   **509**
1. Scientists 2. Science—History
ISBN 1-4000-6013-3; 0-8129-6788-7 (pa)
LC 2003-46607

Gribbin, John R.—_Continued_

First published 2002 in the United Kingdom with title: Science: a history, 1543-2001

"Starting with the Renaissance, Gribbin traces the development of science over the past 500 years through the lives of the people who made it. From Copernicus and Galileo to Albert Einstein and Linus Pauling, Gribbin carefully places the individual in the time in which he or she lived. . . . He also . . . shows the development of science to be the result of the interplay among three factors: the person, the historical time, and the available technology." Libr J

"Replete with scientific clarity, Gribbin's work is the epitome of what a general-interest history of science should be." Booklist

Includes bibliographical references

Hakim, Joy

The story of science: Aristotle leads the way. Smithsonian Books 2004 282p (Story of science) $24.95 *

Grades: 8 9 10 11 12   **509**

1. Science—History 2. Ancient civilization

ISBN 1-58834-160-7

This "invites readers . . . to meet the forebearers of modern science—Thales, Pythagoras, Archimedes, Aristotle, Arab and Chinese thinkers, Thomas Aquinas, Roger Bacon, and many others—and share in their . . . discoveries in astronomy, math, and physics." Publisher's note

"Hakim has interwoven creation myths, history, physics, and mathematics to present a seamless, multifaceted view of the foundation of modern science. . . . The entire volume is beautifully organized." SLJ

Includes bibliographical references

The story of science: Einstein adds a new dimension. Smithsonian Books 2007 468p il (Story of science) $27.95 *

Grades: 8 9 10 11 12   **509**

1. Science—History 2. Cosmology 3. Quantum theory

ISBN 978-1-58834-162-4; 1-58834-162-3

LC 2007-14096

Hakim delivers a "brisk, intellectually challenging account of the development of quantum theory and modern cosmology. . . . She introduces a teeming cast of deep thinkers who . . . delivered a series of brilliant experiments and insights. . . . Supplemented by a digestible resource list and a generous assortment of illustrations." Booklist

Includes bibliographical references

The story of science: Newton at the center. Smithsonian Books 2005 463p (Story of science) $24.95 *

Grades: 8 9 10 11 12   **509**

1. Science—History 2. Astronomy 3. Physics

ISBN 1-58834-161-5   LC 2004-58465

This "is an account of the history of astronomy and physics from c.1500 to 1900."

"Teachers will find anecdotal information to enliven their lessons; browsers will be fascinated by the sidebars and captioned illustrations that enhance the text or show related information." SLJ

Includes bibliographical references

History of modern science and mathematics; Brian S. Baigrie, editor. Scribner 2002 4v il set $605

Grades: 11 12 Adult   **509**

1. Science—History 2. Mathematics—History

ISBN 0-684-80636-3   LC 2002-4042

This "set attempts to synthesize the history of scientific developments in anthropology, astronomy, biology, chemistry, mathematics, physics, psychology, and the earth sciences. . . . This work ranges from the 17th century to the present without trying to include the most recent developments." Libr J

Includes bibliographical references

Horvitz, Leslie Alan

Eureka!: scientific breakthroughs that changed the world. Wiley 2002 246p il $24.95 *

Grades: 11 12 Adult   **509**

1. Science—History

ISBN 0-471-40276-1   LC 2001-46890

This examines twelve scientific discoveries and their discoverers, including Joseph Priestley and oxygen, Friedrich Kekulé and the structure of carbon compounds, Dmitri Mendeleev and the periodic table, Isaac Newton and gravity, Einstein and the theory of relativity, Philo Farnsworth and television, Alexander Fleming and penicillin, Charles Townes and the laser, Alfred Wegener and continental drift, Darwin and the origin of species, Watson and Crick and the double helix, and Benoit Mandelbrot and fractal geometry.

Includes bibliographical references

Langone, John, 1929-

Theories for everything; an illustrated history of science from the invention of numbers to string theory; [by John Langone, Bruce Stutz, and Andrea Gianopoulos] National Geographic 2006 407p il $40

Grades: 11 12 Adult   **509**

1. Science—History

ISBN 0-7922-3912-1; 978-0-7922-3912-3

LC 2006-21419

This book presents six essays on "discoveries of science and the men and women who contributed to them. The essays are grouped under the following headings: 'The Heavens,' 'The Human Body,' 'Matter and Energy,' 'Life Itself,' 'Earth and Moon,' and 'Mind and Behavior.'" Sci Books Films

"With its profusion of illustrations, this is an inviting orientation to the fascinations of science." Booklist

Includes bibliographical references

Lawson, Russell M., 1957-

Science in the ancient world; an encyclopedia. ABC-CLIO 2004 xxv, 291p il (ABC-CLIO's history of science series) $85 *

Grades: 11 12 Adult   **509**

1. Reference books 2. Science—History—Encyclopedias

ISBN 1-85109-534-9   LC 2004-17715

This book "describes scientific concepts in ancient societies, including the Egyptian, Babylonian, Greek, and

Lawson, Russell M., 1957-—*Continued*
Roman worlds until the fall of the Roman Empire. Most of the entries are about people, concepts, and locales of the Greco-Roman world. Arrangement is alphabetical, supported by good cross-references and indexing." Booklist

Includes bibliographical references

Lightman, Alan P., 1948-
The discoveries; great breakthroughs in 20th century science; [by] Alan Lightman. Pantheon Books 2005 553p il $32.50; pa $16.95 *
Grades: 11 12 Adult   509
    1. Science—History
    ISBN 0-375-42168-8; 0-375-71345-X (pa)
                                        LC 2005-40854
This book "chronicles 25 landmark findings in astronomy, physics, chemistry, and biology in the 20th century. Beginning with Max Planck's quantum theory and ending with Paul Berg's recombinant DNA, these breakthroughs are academically and playfully explored via the nature of the unknown, the circumstances and influences of discovery, and, most originally, the actual words of the scientists." Libr J

Includes bibliographical references

The **Oxford** companion to the history of modern science; editor in chief, J.L. Heilbron; editors, James Bartholomew {et al.}. Oxford Univ. Press 2003 xxviii, 941p il $110
Grades: 11 12 Adult   509
    1. Science—History
    ISBN 0-19-511229-6   LC 2002-153783
This reference on the history of science from the Renaissance through the 20th century includes some 600 articles covering "a broad spectrum of topics in all scientific disciplines (e.g., biotechnology, geology) as well as disciplines that influenced science, such as religion and politics. Also included are the biographies of 100 leading figures (e.g., Isaac Newton, Marie Curie) and coverage of scientific instruments (e.g., microscopes, Geiger counters). Organized alphabetically, the well-written articles include plenty of cross references. Over 100 black-and-white illustrations appear within their appropriate articles, but the eight pages of color illustrations in the middle of the volume are not associated with any article." Libr J

Includes bibliographical references

The **Scientific** revolution; Mitchell Young, book editor. Greenhaven Press 2006 240p il (Turning points in world history) lib bdg $34.95
Grades: 9 10 11 12   509
    1. Science—History
    ISBN 0-7377-2987-2   LC 2005-40268
"This volume offers many essays and articles discussing various aspects of a single subject—the scientific revolution. Each themed chapter includes about a half-dozen entries, introduced by the editor and written mainly by academics. . . . Though the book will be challenging for some students, others will find it a well-organized, informative resource." Booklist

Includes bibliographical references

Spangenburg, Ray, 1939-
The birth of science: ancient times to 1699; [by] Ray Spangenburg and Diane Kit Moser. Facts on File 2004 256p (History of science) $35
Grades: 7 8 9 10   509
    1. Science—History
    ISBN 0-8160-4851-7   LC 2003-19470
First published 1993 with title: The history of science from the ancient Greeks to the scientific revolution
Discusses major scientists as well as scientific knowledge and discoveries from ancient times through the seventeenth century
"Very well written and thoroughly understandable, the book succeeds hugely in its objective to introduce the development of science in an interesting fashion to the intended audience without patronizing or oversimplifying." Sci Books Films [review of 1993 edition]

Includes glossary and bibliographical references

Science frontiers, 1946 to the present; [by] Ray Spangenburg and Diane Kit Moser. Facts on File 2004 272p (History of science) $35
Grades: 7 8 9 10   509
    1. Science—History
    ISBN 0-8160-4855-X   LC 2003-24290
First published 1994 with title: The history of science from 1946 to the 1990s
The authors provide "descriptions of complex scientific theories and lines of research in the latter part of the 20th century—but only in the natural sciences: physics (new particles, lasers, and superconductors), astronomy (quasars, black holes, cosmology, dark matter, planetary geology, and SETI), geology (evolution, plate tectonics, and environmental change), and biology (DNA, biotechnology, the human genome, and retroviruses)." Sci Books Films [review of 1994 edition]

Includes glossary and bibliographical references

Webster, Raymond B.
African American firsts in science and technology; foreword by Wesley L. Harris. Gale Group 1999 462p $80 *
Grades: 11 12 Adult   509
    1. Scientists 2. African American inventors
    ISBN 0-7876-3876-5   LC 99-27346
Presents capsule accounts of notable first achievements by African Americans, arranged in the categories "Agriculture and Everyday Life," "Dentistry and Nursing," "Life Science," "Math and Engineering," "Medicine," "Physical Science," and "Transportation."

Includes bibliographical references

Windelspecht, Michael, 1963-
Groundbreaking scientific experiments, inventions, and discoveries of the 19th century; illustrated by Sandra Windelspecht. Greenwood Press 2003 xxvii, 270p il (Groundbreaking scientific experiments, inventions, and discoveries through the ages) $65
Grades: 9 10 11 12   509
    1. Science—History 2. Technology—History
    ISBN 0-313-31969-3   LC 2002-75305

Windelspecht, Michael, 1963-—*Continued*

This volume presents material "alphabetically by topic with information about the specific experiments, inventions, and discoveries of both women and men. . . . Each entry provides a brief historical discussion that allows the reader to understand the climate of the time of discovery and builds a foundation for understanding the methodology by which the scientists and inventors approached their discoveries, experiments, and inventions and for realizing the implications of these on man's future." Lib Media Connect

Includes bibliographical references

510 Mathematics

Acheson, D. J.

1089 and all that; a journey into mathematics; [by] David Acheson. Oxford Univ. Press 2002 178p il hardcover o.p. pa $17.95

Grades: 11 12 Adult   510

1. Mathematics

ISBN 0-19-851623-1; 0-19-959002-8 (pa)

LC 2002-71547

"This book aims to make mathematics accessible to non-experts and the lay reader. Providing an . . . overview of the subject, the text includes several . . . mathematical conundrums. . . . The book contains several cartoons, sketches and photos." Publisher's note

"Not a page passes without at least one intriguing insight. . . . Anyone who is baffled by mathematics should buy it." New Sci

Adam, John A.

A mathematical nature walk. Princeton University Press 2009 248p il $27.95

Grades: 10 11 12 Adult   510

1. Mathematics 2. Mathematical analysis

ISBN 978-0-691-12895-5; 0-691-12895-2

LC 2008-44828

The author "presents ninety-six questions about many common natural phenomena–and a few uncommon ones–and then shows how to answer them using mostly basic mathematics." Publisher's note

"The general reader will find here a remarkably lucid explanation of how mathematicians create a formulaic model that mimics the key features of some natural phenomenon. . . . Ordinary math becomes adventure." Booklist

Includes bibliographical references

Barrow, John D., 1952-

100 essential things you didn't know you didn't know; math explains your world. W.W. Norton & Co. 2009 284p il $25.95; pa $15.95

Grades: 10 11 12 Adult   510

1. Mathematics

ISBN 978-0-393-07007-1; 978-0-393-33867-6 (pa)

LC 2008-55910

First published 2008 in the United Kingdom

The author uses "mathematics to answer one hundred perplexing questions from everyday life." Publisher's

note

"For those who find something mysterious and intriguing in solving an equation, this collection is a fascinating look into the mind of a professional mathematician and the way in which math can be not simply a row of numbers but a way of looking at the world." SLJ

Includes bibliographical references

Blastland, Michael

The numbers game; the commonsense guide to understanding numbers in the news, in politics, and in life; [by] Michael Blastland and Andrew Dilnot. Gotham Books 2009 210p il $22 *

Grades: 10 11 12 Adult   510

1. Number concept 2. Mathematics 3. Statistics

ISBN 978-1-59240-423-0; 1-59240-423-5

LC 2008-30130

First published 2007 in the United Kingdom with title: The tiger that isn't

The authors "embark on a monumental task of interpreting numerical data and showing how its misinterpretation often leads to misinformation. . . . The authors take a close look at statistics that are accepted at face value—many stemming from scientific or medical discoveries." Publ Wkly

Includes bibliographical references

Boyer, Carl B. (Carl Benjamin), 1906-

A history of mathematics; [by] Carl B. Boyer and Uta Merzbach. 3rd ed. Wiley 2010 xx, 668p il pa $39.95 *

Grades: 11 12 Adult   510

1. Mathematics—History

ISBN 978-0-470-52548-7   LC 2010-3424

First published 1969

"This good general history of mathematics is understandable to the student as well as authoritative for the mathematician." Malinowsky. Best Sci & Technol Ref Books for Young People

Includes bibliographical references

Elwes, Richard, 1978-

Mathematics 1001; absolutely everything that matters in mathematics in 1001 bite-sized explanations. Firefly Books 2010 415p il $24.95

Grades: 9 10 11 12 Adult   510

1. Mathematics

ISBN 978-1-55407-719-9

"Concise essays about a variety of mathematical fields—numbers, algebra, geometry, logic—are arranged here by broad topics along with more specific subjects. The accessible text is written without troublesome jargon and terminology. . . . One can rarely call a mathematics book fun, but that's exactly what Elwes's book is." Libr J

Glazer, Evan, 1971-

Real-life math; everyday use of mathematical concepts; [by] Evan M. Glazer and John W. McConnell. Greenwood Press 2002 165p il $49.95

Grades: 11 12 Adult   510

1. Mathematics

ISBN 0-313-31998-7   LC 2001-58635

Glazer, Evan, 1971-—*Continued*
The authors "have written this book as a reply to students' complaints that they'll never use the mathematical concepts they're being taught. They look at dozens of mathematical concepts and . . . show how these math ideas relate to the world in which students live. . . . The book is thorough and accurate." Libr Media Connect
Includes bibliographical references

Henderson, Harry, 1951-
Mathematics: powerful patterns in nature and society. Facts on File 2007 170p il (Milestones in discovery and invention) $35
Grades: 7 8 9 10 11 12   510
1. Mathematics
ISBN 0-8160-5750-8; 978-0-8160-5750-4
                            LC 2006-24680
"Some mathematicians have discovered relatively simple yet exceedingly powerful patterns that yield insight into aspects of natural and human behavior. . . . [This book] presents 10 essays that profile the minds behind such patterns, many of which have surfaced in recent popular culture." Publisher's note
Includes glossary and bibliographical references

Pickover, Clifford A.
The math book; from Pythagoras to the 57th dimension, 250 milestones in the history of mathematics. Sterling Pub. 2009 527p $29.95
Grades: 8 9 10 11 12 Adult   510
1. Mathematics—History
ISBN 978-1-4027-5796-9   LC 2008-43214
"Beginning millions of years ago with ancient 'ant odometers' and moving through time to our modern-day quest for new dimensions, . . . [this book] covers 250 milestones in mathematical history." Publisher's note
"Pickover's love of mathematics shines through the text and images, and it is likely that the reader will catch at least some of his enthusiasm." Choice
Includes bibliographical references

Rudman, Peter Strom, 1929-
The Babylonian theorem; the mathematical journey to Pythagoras and Euclid; [by] Peter S. Rudman. Prometheus Books 2010 248p il $26
Grades: 11 12 Adult   510
1. Pythagoras 2. Euclid 3. Mathematics—History
ISBN 978-1-59102-773-7; 1-59102-773-X
                            LC 2009-39196
Sequel to How mathematics happened (2007)
"Topics covered include Pythagorean triplets, . . . similar triangles, square-root calculations, and calculations of the volume of a pyramid. . . . This is a well-researched volume on what forms of mathematics existed when similar ideas developed again and again in different cultures. The book's numerous mathematical equations would delight any math student." Sci Books Films
Includes bibliographical references

How mathematics happened; the first 50,000 years; [by] Peter S. Rudman. Prometheus Books 2007 314p il $26 *
Grades: 11 12 Adult   510
1. Mathematics—History
ISBN 1-59102-477-3; 978-1-59102-477-4
                            LC 2006-20255
The author presents a "history of how numbers evolved beyond the finger and stone-counting of hunter-gatherer societies. It all started with the Babylonians, who fit very old body-part measurements into a powerful new arithmetic of squares and square roots. Rudman also probes the physiological logic that equipped the Mayans with base-20 numbers for mapping the heavens, and he scrutinizes the brilliance of Egyptian mathematicians who calculated complex volumes without calculus. Readers can deepen their understanding of ancient feats by working out the numerous 'Fun Questions' Rudman has embedded in his text to provide practical experience with key concepts." Booklist
Includes bibliographical references
Followed by The Babylonian theorem (2010)

Seife, Charles
Proofiness; the dark arts of mathematical deception. Viking 2010 295p il map $25.95
Grades: 9 10 11 12 Adult   510
1. Mathematics
ISBN 978-0-670-02216-8   LC 2010-12127
The author "examines the many ways that people fudge with numbers, sometimes just to sell more moisturizer but also to ruin our economy, rig our elections, convict the innocent and undercount the needy. . . . [This book] reveals the truly corrosive effects on a society awash in numerical mendacity. This is more than a math book; it's an eye-opening civics lesson." N Y Times Book Rev
Includes bibliographical references

Spaihts, Jonathan
Cracking the SAT. Math 1 & 2 subject tests; [by] Jonathan Spaihts; revised by Eric Ginsberg. 2011-2012 ed. Random House 2011 526p (Princeton Review series) pa $19.99 *
Grades: 9 10 11 12   510
1. Mathematics—Study and teaching 2. Scholastic Assessment Test 3. Colleges and universities—Entrance requirements
ISBN 978-0-375-42812-8
First published 2005. Continues Cracking the SAT II: math subject tests
This guide provides test-taking strategies and sample tests on the subject of mathematics.

Stewart, Ian
Letters to a young mathematician. Basic Books 2006 210p il (Art of mentoring) $22.95; pa $15 *
Grades: 11 12 Adult   510
1. Mathematics
ISBN   0-465-08231-9;   978-0-465-08231-5; 0-465-08232-7 (pa); 978-0-465-08232-2 (pa)
                            LC 2005-30384

Stewart, Ian—*Continued*

This book "takes the form of letters from a fictitious mathematician to his niece. The letters span a period of 20 years, from the time the niece is thinking about studying mathematics in high school through the early years of her academic career. The format works wonderfully to introduce readers to the basics of the discipline of mathematics while providing a sense of what mathematicians actually do." Publ Wkly

Professor Stewart's hoard of mathematical treasures. Basic Books 2010 339p il pa $16.95 *

Grades: 9 10 11 12 Adult   **510**

1. Mathematics 2. Mathematical recreations

ISBN 978-0-465-01775-1; 0-465-01775-4

             LC 2010-280702

Sequel to Professor Stewart's cabinet of mathematical curiosities (2009)

First published 2009 in the United Kingdom

This book features "puzzles, jokes, word problems, puns, and history and lore about math. . . . One never knows what's next: a proof that two plus two indeed equals four jostles with a spoof of proof itself. . . . The equal sign makes for a go-to topic for amusing vignettes, while stories about math underlying modern technology underscore the serious side of a subject with which Stewart makes such good sport. A great distraction for math mavens at any knowledge level." Booklist

Tabak, John

Mathematics and the laws of nature; developing the language of science. Rev. ed. Facts on File 2011 xx, 244p il (History of mathematics) $45 *

Grades: 9 10 11 12   **510**

1. Mathematics—History 2. Science—History

ISBN 978-0-8160-7943-8   LC 2010021599

First published 2004

This book "describes the evolution of the idea that nature can be described in the language of mathematics. . . . Chapters explore the earliest attempts to apply deductive methods to the study of the natural world . . . [and go] on to examine the development of classical conservation laws, including the conservation of momentum, the conservation of mass, and the conservation of energy." Publisher's note

Includes bibliographical references

Tattersall, Graham

Geekspeak; how life + mathematics = happiness. Collins 2008 239p il pa $19.95

Grades: 10 11 12 Adult   **510**

1. Mathematics

ISBN 978-0-061-62924-2; 0-061-62924-3

             LC 2008-16134

First published 2007 in the United Kingdom

Tattersall has rescued math from the prison of the classroom and put it to use explaining some of the oft-pondered questions of the world.

"Leavened with armchair fun, such as estimating the weight of the moon or how many flies can power a car, Tattersall's amble might revive the fashion for pocket protectors and horn-rimmed spectacles." Booklist

510.3   Encyclopedias and dictionaries

Darling, David J.

The universal book of mathematics; from Abracadabra to Zeno's paradoxes; [by] David Darling. Wiley 2004 383p il $40

Grades: 11 12 Adult   **510.3**

1. Reference books 2. Mathematics—Encyclopedias

ISBN 0-471-27047-4   LC 2003-24670

"The book's entries include numerous mathematical terms, brief biographies of mathematicians from ancient times to the present, and famous mathematical problems (both solved and unsolved), as well as problems and puzzles of a more recreational nature. It is a spirit of whimsy, the fanciful, and the outrageous that makes this book much more than a dry encyclopedia of mathematical terms, however. Darling's writing style and choice of entries make this an easy book to pick up and page through." Choice

Includes bibliographical references

The **Facts** on File dictionary of mathematics; edited by John Daintith, Richard Rennie. 4th ed. Facts on File 2005 262p il (Facts on File science library) $45; pa $17.95 *

Grades: 9 10 11 12   **510.3**

1. Reference books 2. Mathematics—Dictionaries

ISBN 0-8160-5651-X; 0-8160-5652-8 (pa)

             LC 2005-48762

First published 1980

Among the topics covered are: fractals, sets, chaos theory, computer graphics and hypertext.

Includes bibliographical references

Tanton, James S., 1966-

Encyclopedia of mathematics; [by] James Tanton. Facts on File 2005 568p il (Facts on File science library) $75 *

Grades: 11 12 Adult   **510.3**

1. Reference books 2. Mathematics—Encyclopedias

ISBN 0-8160-5124-0   LC 2004-16785

This encyclopedia "offers more than 800 entries from abacus and compound interest to Bertrand Russell and vector along with essays on the history and evolution of equations and algebra, calculus, functions, geometry, probability and statistics, and trigonometry." SLJ

Includes bibliographical references

511   General principles of mathematics

Kaplan, Robert

The nothing that is; a natural history of zero; illustrations by Ellen Kaplan. Oxford Univ. Press 2000 225p $40; pa $11.95

Grades: 11 12 Adult   **511**

1. Zero (The number)

ISBN 0-19-512842-7; 0-19-514237-3 (pa)

             LC 99-29000

Kaplan, Robert—*Continued*

"Kaplan presents cultural, philosophical, historical, and mathematical developments that either encouraged or discouraged the recognition of the role of zero in counting and computation." Sci Books Films

Seife, Charles

Zero; the biography of a dangerous idea. Viking 2000 248p il hardcover o.p. pa $15

Grades: 11 12 Adult   **511**

1. Zero (The number)

ISBN 0-670-88457-X; 0-14-029647-6 (pa)

    LC 99-36693

"The zero emerges as a daunting intellectual riddle in this . . . chronicle of a once controversial concept as Seife deftly traces the gradual acceptance of the zero and its role as catalyst for the evolution of everything from business to physics to moral thought." Booklist

Includes bibliographical references

511.3   Mathematical logic (Symbolic logic)

Edwards, A. W. F. (Anthony William Fairbank), 1935-

Cogwheels of the mind; the story of Venn diagrams; foreword by Ian Stewart. Johns Hopkins University Press 2004 110p il $25

Grades: 11 12 Adult   **511.3**

1. Venn, John, 1834-1923 2. Symbolic logic

ISBN 0-8018-7434-3   LC 2003-10633

This book is about "who John Venn was, why he conceived of the diagram, and the properties that lie secreted beneath such a seemingly simple mathematical object." Booklist

"This title will appeal to readers studying mathematics and logic, to those who would like to know how scientific and mathematical research is carried out, and to those who are involved in graphic design and the study of the history of art as it relates to math." SLJ

512   Algebra

McKellar, Danica

Hot X; algebra exposed. Hudson Street Press 2010 417p il $26.95

Grades: 9 10 11 12   **512**

1. Algebra

ISBN 978-1-59463-070-5   LC 2010-18163

"Facing down a 432-page book devoted to algebra could give even math whizzes pause, but McKellar makes it work, taking the textbook-meets-Seventeen approach by mixing the explanations and equations with boy talk, quizzes, and testimonials from successful women. While a tutor might use this title as a teaching aid, teen girls will want to explore it on their own. Navigation is easy; students are encouraged to hop from chapter to chapter as their homework demands. . . . While McKellar keeps her focus on how to solve math problems, her approach is both readable and even entertaining." Booklist

Miller, Robert, 1943-

Bob Miller's algebra for the clueless; algebra. 2nd ed. McGraw-Hill 2007 276p il (Bob Miller's clueless series) pa $12.95

Grades: 9 10 11 12   **512**

1. Algebra

ISBN 0-07-147366-1; 978-0-07-148846-4

    LC 2006-8455

First published 1999

This guide to algebra explains such concepts as natural numbers, integers, equations, factoring, radicals and exponents and includes anxiety reducing features and tips for solving difficult problems.

Tabak, John

Algebra; sets, symbols, and the language of thought. Rev. ed. Facts On File 2011 236p il (History of mathematics) $45

Grades: 9 10 11 12   **512**

1. Algebra

ISBN 978-0-8160-7944-5   LC 2010021597

First published 2004

This book "describes the history of both strands of algebraic thought. This . . . resource describes some of the earliest progress in algebra as well as some of the mathematicians in Mesopotamia, Egypt, China, and Greece who contributed to this early period. It goes on to explore the many breakthroughs in algebraic techniques as well as how letters were used to represent numbers." Publisher's note

Includes bibliographical references

Wingard-Nelson, Rebecca

Algebra I and algebra II. Enslow Publishers 2004 64p il (Math success) $22.60 *

Grades: 9 10 11 12   **512**

1. Algebra

ISBN 0-7660-2566-7   LC 2003-27620

New edition in preparation

Contents: The coordinate plane; Lines and slope; Linear equations; More linear equations; Direct variation; Inequalities; Graphs of inequalities; Absolute value; Systems and graphing; Solving systems by substitution; Solving systems by elimination; Systems of inequalities; Systems and problem solving; Relations and functions; Operations and functions; Exponents; Special exponents; Exponential functions; Polynomials; Polynomial operations; Binomial multiplication; Factoring polynomials; Special polynomials; Quadratic functions; Complete the square; The quadratic formula; Rationals; Complex rationals

"The book follows a concise algebraic format and is clearly and simply presented." Sci Books Films

Includes bibliographical references

513   Arithmetic

Bellos, Alex

Here's looking at Euclid; a surprising excursion through the astonishing world of math. Free Press hardcover ed. Free Press 2010 319p il $25; ebook $11.99

Grades: 10 11 12 Adult   **513**
1. Number concept
ISBN 978-1-4165-8825-2; 978-1-4165-9634-9 (ebook)
                 LC 2009-36815

The author "offers a lively romp through many different fields of mathematics as he incorporates ancient discoveries and modern developments alike. Topics include geometry, number theory, the development of sudoku, numerous aspects of pi and its calculation, statistics, probability and its application to gambling, and many other historical tidbits." Libr J

Includes bibliographical references

Tabak, John

Numbers; computers, philosophers, and the search for meaning. Rev. ed. Facts On File 2011 243p il (History of mathematics) $45

Grades: 9 10 11 12   **513**
1. Numbers 2. Counting
ISBN 978-0-8160-7940-7   LC 2010-15830
First published 2004

This book "deals with numbers from the point of view of computation, beginning with the earliest number concepts from ancient Mesopotamian, Chinese, and Mayan mathematicians. It describes the origin and diffusion of Arabic numerals, and it concludes with a discussion of the way that the number system is represented within computers. . . . [It also] describes some of the IEEE standards for floating point arithmetic." Publisher's note

Includes bibliographical references

515   Analysis

Berlinski, David, 1942-

A tour of the calculus. Pantheon Bks. 1995 331p il pa $14.95 hardcover o.p.

Grades: 11 12 Adult   **515**
1. Calculus
ISBN 0-679-74788-5 (pa)   LC 95-4042

This is an introduction to "the foundations of calculus. It is in part an informal history of the subject; the author interweaves the historical fragments with expository sections that [seek to] explain the concepts from a modern viewpoint." Libr J

"Berlinski tangibly grounds the abstract notions, so that attentive readers can ease into and grasp the several full-blown proofs he sets forth." Booklist

Kojima, Hiroyuki, 1958-

The manga guide to calculus; [by] Hiroyuki Kojima, Shin Togami, and Becom Co., Ltd. No Starch Press 2009 238p il pa $19.95 *

Grades: 9 10 11 12   **515**
1. Graphic novels 2. Manga 3. Calculus—Graphic novels
ISBN 978-1-59327-194-7; 1-59327-194-8
                 LC 2008-50189

"Noriko is just getting started as a junior reporter for the *Asagake Times*. She wants to cover the hard-hitting issues, like world affairs and politics, but does she have the smarts for it? Thankfully, her overbearing and math-minded boss, Mr. Seki, is here to teach her how to analyze her stories with a mathematical eye. . . . [He teaches her] that calculus is a useful way to understand the patterns in physics, economics, and the world around us, with help from real-world examples like probability, supply and demand curves, the economics of pollution, and the density of Shochu (a Japanese liquor)." Publisher's note

Maor, Eli

The Facts on File calculus handbook. Facts on File 2003 164p il $35; pa $17.95 *

Grades: 9 10 11 12   **515**
1. Calculus
ISBN 0-8160-4581-X; 0-8160-6229-3 (pa)
                 LC 2003-49027

This resource is "a supplement to calculus or trigonometry course work. The *Handbook*'s primary content is the glossary. Here, the author has compiled terms and expressions commonly used in calculus with . . . definitions and examples. . . . The other sections include a historical overview of the development of calculus, a selection of brief biographies of mathematicians, a timeline of calculus, a collection of charts and tables, and a list of recommened readings and Websites. . . . The conciseness of the definitions and examples, in addition to the historical data, make it a good 'study guide' or review resource for those high school students preparing for AP exams or similar college placement exams. For a quick look up of a definition that will be understandable to the non-math individual, this would be a practical ready-reference resource." Am Ref Books Annu, 2004

Includes bibliographical references

516   Geometry

Gorini, Catherine A.

The Facts on File geometry handbook. Rev ed. Facts on File 2009 342p il (Facts on File science library) $40 *

Grades: 11 12 Adult   **516**
1. Geometry
ISBN 978-0-8160-7389-4   LC 2009-5775
First published 2003

This includes a glossary of over 3,000 entries with labeled diagrams, biographies of over 300 scientists and mathematicians from ancient times to the present, a chronology of geometry history, charts, tables, recommended reading and websites.

Includes glossary and bibliographical references

Mlodinow, Leonard
Euclid's window; the story of geometry from parallel lines to hyperspace. Free Press 2001 306p il pa $15 hardcover o.p.
Grades: 11 12 Adult   **516**
1. Geometry
ISBN 0-684-86524-6 (pa)   LC 00-54351
Mlodinow's monograph "takes the form of five biographical stories, each about a key figure in the development of geometry: Euclid, Descartes, Gauss, Einstein and Witten." New Sci
"This engaging history does an excellent job of explaining the importance of the study of geometry without making the reader learn any geometry." Libr J
Includes bibliographical references

Tabak, John
Beyond geometry; a new mathematics of space and form. Facts on File 2011 xx, 217p il (History of mathematics) $45
Grades: 9 10 11 12   **516**
1. Topology 2. Set theory 3. Geometry
ISBN 978-0-8160-7945-2   LC 2010023887
This book "describes how set-theoretic topology developed and why it now occupies a central place in mathematics. Describing axiomatic method as well as providing a definition of what a geometric property is, this . . . resource examines how early analysts incorporated geometric thinking into their development of the calculus. It also looks at the various mathematicians who struggled to develop a new conceptual framework for mathematics and examines one of the sub-disciplines of set-theoretic topology called dimension theory." Publisher's note
Includes glossary and bibliographical references

Geometry; the language of space and form. Rev. ed. Facts on File 2011 248p il (History of mathematics) $45 *
Grades: 9 10 11 12   **516**
1. Geometry
ISBN 978-0-8160-7942-1   LC 2010018627
First published 2004
This book "describes geometry in antiquity. Beginning with a brief description of some of the geometry that preceded the geometry of the Greeks, it takes up the story of geometry during the European Renaissance as well as the significant mathematical progress in other areas of the world. It also discusses the analytic geometry of René Descartes and Pierre Fermat, the alternative coordinate systems invented by Isaac Newton, and the solid geometry of Leonhard Euler." Publisher's note
Includes glossary and bibliographical references

516.2 Euclidean geometry

Blatner, David
The joy of π. Walker & Co. 1997 129p il hardcover o.p. pa $12 *
Grades: 11 12 Adult   **516.2**
1. Pi
ISBN 0-8027-1332-7; 0-8027-7562-4 (pa)
LC 97-23705

The author discusses the history of the number π, as well as the process of "calculating the ratio of a circle's circumference to its diameter, which has advanced from measuring lengths of string and the 'brute force' of measuring polygons to feeding supercomputers sophisticated algorithms. Sidebars . . . abound, containing a factoid, joke, or doggerel inspired by π." Booklist
Includes bibliographical references

Livio, Mario, 1945-
The golden ratio; the story of phi, the world's most astonishing number. Broadway Bks. 2002 294p hardcover o.p. pa $14.95
Grades: 11 12 Adult   **516.2**
1. Geometry
ISBN 0-7679-0815-5; 0-7679-0816-3 (pa)
LC 2002-23084
The author examines the history and myths of phi, the "golden ratio" of 1.6180339887 that has been related to phenomena as diverse as the arrangements of petals on roses and the breeding patterns of rabbits.
"Overall, an enjoyable work, amply supported by index, extensive references, and ten appendixes presenting mathematical elaborations of text material." Choice
Includes bibliographical references

Maor, Eli
The Pythagorean theorem; a 4,000-year history. Princeton University Press 2007 259p il map $24.95
Grades: 9 10 11 12 Adult   **516.2**
1. Mathematics—History
ISBN 978-0-691-12526-8; 0-691-12526-0
LC 2006-50969
The author "presents an account of the Pythagorean Theorem and its approximate 400 proofs, up to its importance in the Theory of Relativity." Univ Press Books for Public and Second Sch Libr, 2008
"This [is an] interesting and well-written book. . . . I recommend the book highly to students, teachers, and the intelligent general reader interested in a very old, beautiful, and useful result." Sci Books Films
Includes bibliographical references

519.2 Probabilities

Rosenthal, Jeffrey, 1967-
Struck by lightning; the curious world of probabilities; [by] Jeffrey S. Rosenthal. HarperCollins Canada 2005 263p il pa $19.95
Grades: 11 12 Adult   **519.2**
1. Probabilities 2. Chance
ISBN 0-309-09734-7; 978-0-309-09734-5
LC 2005-37021
Rosenthal discusses ways in which probability theory affects such areas of everyday life as crime, travel, gambling, politics, and disease.
"The lighthearted presentation ensures that readers will not feel burdened by all the knowledge they are gaining and the concluding summary—disguised as a final exam—is sure to deliver an A to everyone, which is what Rosenthal deserves for this clever book." Publ Wkly

Tabak, John
Probability and statistics; the science of uncertainty. Rev. ed. Facts on File 2011 252p il (History of mathematics) $45 *
Grades: 9 10 11 12   519.2
  1. Probabilities 2. Statistics
  ISBN 978-0-8160-7941-4   LC 2010026448
  First published 2004
This book "deals with the history of probability, describing the modern concept of randomness and examining 'pre-probabilistic' ideas of what most people today would characterize as randomness. . . . [It] documents some historically important early uses of probability to illustrate some very important probabilistic questions." Publisher's note
Includes bibliographical references

519.5   Statistical mathematics

Cohen, I. Bernard, 1914-2003
The triumph of numbers; how counting shaped modern life. W. W. Norton 2005 209p il $24.95; pa $14.95
Grades: 11 12 Adult   519.5
  1. Statistics
  ISBN   0-393-05769-0;   978-0-393-05769-0; 0-393-32870-8 (pa); 978-0-393-32870-7 (pa)
                LC 2004-27322
This is a "history of numbers and the birth of statistics." Publisher's note
"This book presents a persuasive narrative on how numbers have maintained a prominent role not only in science and government throughout time, but in the daily operations of life." Sci Books Films
Includes bibliographical references

Kault, David
Statistics with common sense. Greenwood Press 2003 257p il $49.95
Grades: 9 10 11 12   519.5
  1. Statistics
  ISBN 0-313-32209-0   LC 2002-75322
Aimed primarily at individuals who learned statistics at an earlier time but never fully grasped the concepts behind it, this resource emphasizes "a working knowledge of understanding the processes not merely memorizing the formulas. The book also illustrates common sense decision-making in the application process, and a . . . description of the full mathematical derivation of some statistical tests. . . . Having a clear understanding of when and how to use 'stats' is the driving force of this book. If your students and teachers need a great guide for statistics, add this volume to your library collection." Libr Media Connect
Includes bibliographical references

Paulos, John Allen
Once upon a number; the hidden mathematical logic of stories. Basic Bks. 1998 214p pa $13 hardcover o.p. *
Grades: 11 12 Adult   519.5
  1. Statistics 2. Symbolic logic
  ISBN 0-465-05159-6 (pa)   LC 98-39252

The author contends "that statistics cannot be disconnected from the stories—or narrative contexts—that attach them to the complexities of the world." Publ Wkly
"Paulos fills this book with so many intriguing nuggets of mathematically sound information about the stories we tell that it deserves rereading, which, because Paulos' voice is so enjoyable, seems no daunting task." Booklist
Includes bibliographical references

Weinstein, Lawrence, 1960-
Guesstimation; solving the world's problems on the back of a cocktail napkin; [by] Lawrence Weinstein and John A. Adam. Princeton University Press 2008 301p il pa $19.95
Grades: 11 12 Adult   519.5
  1. Approximate computation 2. Problem solving
  ISBN 978-0-691-12949-5; 0-691-12949-5
                LC 2007-33928
The authors "briefly review good 'guesstimation' techniques involving numbers (i.e., scientific notation, accuracy, unit conversion) and explain why the use of the geometric mean is preferred over the arithmetic mean. The authors then meander through a wide variety of fascinating problems, roughly arranged in 'world-type' categories: animals, people, transportation, energy, work, Earth's chemical elements, environment, atmosphere, and space. Some of the problems are easy, some are hard—and most will grab the reader's interest." Choice
Includes bibliographical references

520   Astronomy

Angelo, Joseph A.
The Facts on File space and astronomy handbook; [by] Joseph A. Angelo, Jr. Rev. ed. Facts on File 2009 342p il map (Facts on File science library) $40 *
Grades: 11 12 Adult   520
  1. Astronomy 2. Space sciences 3. Reference books
  ISBN 978-0-8160-7388-7   LC 2008-51761
  First published 2002
This handbook is divided into four sections: a glossary of nearly 1,300 entries related to science and astronomy, biographies of over 400 scientists, a chronology, and a set of charts and tables.
Includes bibliographical references

Aveni, Anthony F.
Stairways to the stars; skywatching in three great ancient cultures; [by] Anthony Aveni. Wiley 1997 230p il hardcover o.p. pa $15.95 *
Grades: 11 12 Adult   520
  1. Astronomy—History 2. Ancient civilization
  ISBN 0-471-15942-5; 0-471-32976-2 (pa)
                LC 96-36517
This book "examines the astronomy of three ancient societies: Great Britain and Stonehenge; the Mayas and the cult of Venus; and the Incas and the city of Cuzco, built as . . . [an] observatory. Also included is a chapter on 'naked eye' observing that allows readers to see the

Aveni, Anthony F.—*Continued*
night sky as did our ancient ancestors." Libr J
"An insightful and interesting blend of ancient anthropology and ancient astronomy." Choice
Includes bibliographical references

Bartusiak, Marcia, 1950-
The day we found the universe. Pantheon Books
2009 337p il $27.95
Grades: 9 10 11 12 Adult   520
1. Astronomy—History
ISBN 978-0-375-42429-8; 0-375-42429-6
LC 2008-34377
This is a "narrative about a major advance in astronomy—the discovery of what galaxies are." Booklist
"This is a superb book that interweaves the fascinating
story of a major scientific quest with a cast of characters,
situations, painstaking observations, and imaginative
thinking that reminds us all of the human side of scientific endeavors and the ways in which the universe itself
continuously surprises us." Sci Books Films
Includes bibliographical references

Couper, Heather
The history of astronomy; [by] Heather Couper
& Nigel Henbest; foreword by Arthur C. Clarke.
Firefly Books 2007 285p il $59.95; pa $29.95
Grades: 11 12 Adult   520
1. Astronomy—History
ISBN   978-1-55407-325-2;   1-55407-325-1;
978-1-55407-537-9 (pa); 1-55407-537-8 (pa)
LC 2008-272095
This "history is pieced together through astronomer interviews and visits to historically important astronomy
sites around the world. . . . This is a copiously illustrated, straightforwardly written volume that will appeal to
readers with and without an astronomy background. In
addition to covering astronomy through the ages, the authors do an admirable job explaining current astronomical discoveries and personalities." Choice

Dickinson, Terence
The universe and beyond; foreword by Edward
G. Gibson. 5th ed., Revised and expanded. Firefly
Books 2010 204p il $45; pa $29.95 *
Grades: 9 10 11 12   520
1. Astronomy
ISBN 978-1-55407-640-6; 978-1-55407-748-9 (pa)
First published 1986
Illustrated with over 130 color illustrations and photo-
graphs, this describes the universe, comets, planets, black
holes, galaxies, dark matter, quasars, and other topics.
Includes bibliographical references

Dyson, Marianne J.
Space and astronomy; decade by decade. Facts
on File 2007 284p il map (Twentieth-century
science) $49.50
Grades: 9 10 11 12   520
1. Astronomy—History 2. Space flight
ISBN 978-0-8160-5536-4; 0-8160-5536-X
LC 2006-12547

"This chronology includes astronomical discoveries
(the dwarf planet then called Pluto, pulsars), innovations
in rocketry, exploration of space by crewed and
uncrewed missions, the search for extraterrestrial life,
and even some space-related fiction. . . . Chapters cover
one decade each and include a two-page 'Scientist of the
Decade' section that focuses on the career of one significant person and a time line of important events. . . .
[This book] is extremely well detailed, the writing remains readable from start to finish, and an excellent index provides near-encyclopedic access. A fine history."
SLJ
Includes bibliographical references

Ferris, Timothy
Seeing in the dark; how backyard stargazers are
probing deep space and guarding earth from
interplanetary peril. Simon & Schuster 2002 379p
il hardcover o.p. pa $14
Grades: 11 12 Adult   520
1. Astronomy 2. Astronomers
ISBN 0-684-86579-3; 0-684-86580-7 (pa)
LC 2002-20693
Ferris examines "the 20th-century in spectroscopic
analysis of very distant light from celestial bodies
through the personal experiences of . . . astronomers,
mostly amateurs." Christ Sci Monit
"This book should turn many novices on to astronomy
and captivate those already fascinated by the heavens."
Publ Wkly

Gater, Will
The practical astronomer; [by] Will Gater and
Anton Vamplew; consultant Jacqueline Mitton. DK
Pub. 2010 256p il map pa $19.95
Grades: 7 8 9 10 11 12   520
1. Astronomy
ISBN 978-0-7566-6210-3; 0-7566-6210-9
LC 2010-281460
"This beautifully illustrated volume is a valuable and
accurate guide to observing and understanding the wide
variety and essential characteristics of fascinating astronomical objects that are visible from Earth. . . . [It en-
ables] the reader to learn about coordinate systems; solar
system motions; the nature of light; and how to use the
eye, binoculars, telescopes, cameras, and astronomical atlases and catalogues to explore the heavens directly and
efficiently." Sci Books Films

Hetherington, Edith W.
Astronomy and culture; [by] Edith W.
Hetherington and Norriss S. Hetherington.
Greenwood Press/ABC-CLIO 2009 231p il
(Greenwood guides to the universe) $65 *
Grades: 9 10 11 12   520
1. Astronomy 2. Science and civilization
ISBN   978-0-313-34536-4;   0-313-34536-8;
978-0-313-34537-1 (ebook); 0-313-34537-6 (ebook)
LC 2009-7368
Contact publisher for ebook pricing
This "is a book of exceptional breadth. . . . [The au-
thors] cover topics ranging from how ancient cultures in

Hetherington, Edith W.—*Continued*

Mesopotamia, Greece, and the New World created mythology and calendars to make sense of the sky, to connections between astronomy and religion, to the history of the idea of extraterrestrial life. Besides combining diverse perspectives from the history of science, the history of astronomy, and archaeoastronomy, the book represents a unique attempt to present astronomy integrated with culture, broadly defined." Choice

Includes bibliographical references

Kanipe, Jeff, 1953-

The cosmic connection; how astronomical events impact life on Earth. Prometheus Books 2009 296p il $27.95

Grades: 11 12 Adult   520

1. Astronomy

ISBN 978-1-59102-667-9; 1-59102-667-9

LC 2008-31877

Kanipe sets out to trace "the whole natural history of how events in the near and far universe have influenced life on Earth today, and how they might influence life in the future." Publisher's note

"This extremely well written book would be an engaging read for any person with even the slightest interest in astronomy." Sci Books Films

Includes bibliographical references

Kidger, Mark R., 1960-

Astronomical enigmas; life on Mars, the Star of Bethlehem, and other Milky Way mysteries. Johns Hopkins University Press 2005 297p il map $29.95

Grades: 9 10 11 12   520

1. Astronomy

ISBN 0-8018-8026-2   LC 2004-8937

The author "has organized Astronomical Enigmas around the answers to some questions laypersons frequently pose when meeting a professional astronomer." Choice

"This is a beautifully written book packed with narrative answers to major astronomical topics of current interest." Sci Books Films

Includes bibliographical references

NightWatch: a practical guide to viewing the universe; foreword by Timothy Ferris; illustrations by Adolf Schaller, Victor Costanzo, Roberta Cooke, Glenn LeDrew; principal photography by Terence Dickinson. 4th ed. Firefly Books 2006 192p il $35 *

Grades: 8 9 10 11 12   520

1. Astronomy

ISBN 978-1-55407-147-0; 1-55407-147-X

LC 2006-491527

First published 1983

This "handbook for amateur astronomers combines a text both meaty and hard to put down with a great array of charts, boxes, tables, and dazzling full-color photos of the sky." SLJ [review of 1998 edition]

Includes bibliographical references

Petersen, Carolyn Collins

Visions of the cosmos; {by} Carolyn Collins Petersen, John C. Brandt. Cambridge University Press 2003 218p il $40

Grades: 9 10 11 12   520

1. Astronomy

ISBN 0-521-81898-2   LC 2003-43043

This "book is a comprehensive exploration of astronomy through the eyes of the world's observatories and spacecraft missions." Publisher's note

"Almost every page holds stunningly detailed visual images. Full-page color digital photos such as the birth of a star or the Pillars of Creation captivate readers while the descriptive text explains how these visions were recorded and what they may mean. This book takes the scientific who, what, where, when, and why and puts them in terms a neophyte astronomer can comprehend." Libr Media Connect

Includes bibliographical references

Plait, Philip C.

Death from the skies! these are the ways the world will end . . .; [by] Philip Plait. Viking 2008 326p il $25.95 *

Grades: 11 12 Adult   520

1. End of the world

ISBN 978-0-670-01997-7; 0-670-01997-6

LC 2008-22943

The author "describes the myriad ways that astronomical events could end life on Earth. These include comet and asteroid impacts, massive solar flares, supernova explosions, gamma-ray bursts, black holes, diseases of extraterrestrial origin, the eventual death of the sun, and the wobbly orbit of the sun around our galaxy that could expose us to cosmic rays." Libr J

"The book is extremely informative: Plait explains not only what can destroy the planet but also how it would happen. It's a crash course in astronomy as well as a cautionary tale about the (possibly brief) future of our world." Booklist

Schaaf, Fred

The 50 best sights in astronomy and how to see them; observing eclipses, bright comets, meteor showers, and other celestial wonders. John Wiley 2007 280p il pa $19.95

Grades: 11 12 Adult   520

1. Astronomy

ISBN 978-0-471-69657-5; 0-471-69657-9

LC 2006-36221

The author "begins with some basic information and terminology (altazimuth system, for example, or right ascension) and then plunges right in with the most easily accessible astronomical sight, the starry sky above our heads. For each sight, he not only explains what it is and the best conditions under which to observe it, he also tells us about its historical, mythological, or scientific importance and explores how these far-off wonders can have a very real effect on our humble home world. This could so easily have been a dry-as-dust tome, but Schaaf's enthusiasm overflows every page." Booklist

Includes bibliographical references

Universe; general editor, Martin Rees. DK 2008
512p il pa $27.95 *
Grades: 11 12 Adult   **520**
1. Cosmology
ISBN 978-0-7566-3670-8; 0-7566-3670-1
LC 2008-299650
First published 2005
"The definitive visual guide" Cover
"The volume is divided into three sections. The first, called 'Introduction,' presents an overview of basic concepts, organized under the broad topics 'What Is the Universe?' 'The Beginning and End of the Universe,' 'The View from Earth,' and 'Exploring Space.' The next section, 'Guide to the Universe,' focuses on the features of the solar system, the Milky Way, and the regions beyond. Among the topics that are covered here are the planets; asteroids, comets, and meteors; the stars; and galaxy clusters. . . . Finally, the book has a section called 'The Night Sky,' with entries on each of the 88 constellations, including maps." Booklist
This is "a visually stunning reference that makes browsing irresistible. Every page of this oversized volume is full color, with an eye-pleasing balance of text and graphics." Libr J

Walker, Pamela, 1958-
Space and astronomy experiments; [by] Pamela Walker, Elaine Wood. Facts on File 2010 xx, 152p il (Facts on File science experiments) $35
Grades: 7 8 9 10 11 12   **520**
1. Space sciences 2. Astronomy 3. Science—Experiments
ISBN 978-0-8160-7809-7; 0-8160-7809-2
LC 2009-32825
This book "presents experiments designed to foster understanding of space science and astronomy. Geared to middle and high-school students and their teachers, the 20 experiments convey basic astronomy principles, draw from historic experiments, or explore new technologies. . . . Schools and libraries where students and teachers are looking for science experiments on space and astronomy will find this volume a useful addition to the collection." Booklist
Includes glossary and bibliographical references

Yount, Lisa
Modern astronomy; expanding the universe. Facts on File 2006 204p il (Milestones in discovery and invention) $35
Grades: 7 8 9 10 11 12   **520**
1. Astronomy
ISBN 0-8160-5746-X; 978-0-8160-5746-7
LC 2005-25113
This book profiles "12 men and women whose research and work in new technologies brought about a revolution in the understanding of time and space during the 20th century." Publisher's note
Includes glossary and bibliographical references

520.3 Astronomy—Encyclopedias and dictionaries

Angelo, Joseph A.
Encyclopedia of space and astronomy; [by] Joseph A. Angelo, Jr. Facts on File 2006 740p il (Facts on File science library) $75 *
Grades: 11 12 Adult   **520.3**
1. Astronomy—Encyclopedias 2. Space sciences—Encyclopedias 3. Reference books
ISBN 0-8160-5330-8   LC 2004-30800
This encyclopedia presents "the main concepts, terms, facilities, and people in astronomy. . . . Coverage includes terms such as astrophysics, planetary science, and cosmology, as well as both American and international astronomy and space technology." Publisher's note
Includes bibliographical references

Darling, David J.
The universal book of astronomy from the Andromeda Galaxy to the zone of avoidance; [by] David Darling. Wiley 2003 570p il $40
Grades: 11 12 Adult   **520.3**
1. Astronomy—Dictionaries 2. Reference books
ISBN 0-471-26569-1   LC 2003-13941
This book features "over 3000 alphabetically arranged entries covering history, biography, celestial objects, cosmological phenomena, and more." Libr J
"Designed for nonspecialists, Darling's volume fills a niche in astronomy ready reference. . . . The volume is . . . highly readable and provides bonuses in 22 star charts outlining all 88 constellations in both north and south celestial hemispheres, instructional aids throughout the text, and charts that accompany entries for many stars, galaxies, and clusters and show size, position, etc." Choice
Includes bibliographical references

The **Facts** on File dictionary of astronomy; edited by John Daintith, William Gould. 5th ed. Facts on File 2006 550p il (Facts on File science library) $59.50 *
Grades: 7 8 9 10 11 12   **520.3**
1. Astronomy—Dictionaries 2. Reference books
ISBN 0-8160-5998-5; 978-0-8160-5998-0
LC 2006-40860
First published 1979 under the editorship of Valerie Illingworth
This dictionary includes "more than 3,700 entries . . . that reflect all aspects of astronomy, together with associated terms in spectroscopy, photometry, and particle physics." Publisher's note
Includes bibliographical references

Mitton, Jacqueline
Cambridge illustrated dictionary of astronomy. Cambridge University Press 2007 397p il map $35 *
Grades: 11 12 Adult   **520.3**
1. Astronomy—Dictionaries 2. Reference books
ISBN 978-0-521-82364-7; 0-521-82364-1
LC 2008-295878

Mitton, Jacqueline—*Continued*

First published 1993 in the United Kingdom with title: The Penguin dictionary of astronomy

"Coverage encompasses named astronomical objects, terms and abbreviations most frequently encountered in astronomy, constellations, principal observatories, space missions, and biographical sketches for 70 well-known individuals in the history of the field." Booklist

"With this dictionary Mitton . . . offers a welcome addition to the reference collection." Choice

Oxford dictionary of astronomy; edited by Ian Ridpath. 2nd ed. Oxford University Press 2007 561p il (Oxford paperback reference) pa $18.95 *

Grades: 11 12 Adult   **520.3**

1. Astronomy—Dictionaries 2. Reference books
ISBN 978-0-19-921493-8   LC 2007-40707
First published 1997

This dictionary presents "4200 paragraph-sized definitions, along with illuminating technical graphs and charts. Included is an exhaustive, A-to-Z compilation of eminent figures and significant, if sometimes obscure, scientific phenomena, mission names, and project monikers." Libr J

522 Techniques, procedures, apparatus, equipment, materials

Angelo, Joseph A.

Spacecraft for astronomy; [by] Joseph A. Angelo, Jr. Facts on File, Inc. 2006 288p il (Frontiers in space) $39.50

Grades: 9 10 11 12   **522**

1. Space probes 2. Astronomical instruments 3. Astronomical observatories
ISBN 0-8160-5774-5; 978-0-8160-5774-0
           LC 2006-4875

This "volume describes the historic events, scientific principles, and technical breakthroughs that allow complex orbiting astronomical observatories to increase our understanding of the universe, its origin, and its destiny." Publisher's note

Includes glossary and bibliographical references

Harrington, Philip S.

Star ware; the amateur astronomer's guide to choosing, buying, and using telescopes and accessories. 4th ed. Wiley 2007 417p il pa $21.95

Grades: 11 12 Adult   **522**

1. Telescopes
ISBN 978-0-471-75063-5; 0-471-75063-8
           LC 2006-25134
First published 1994

This guidebook on choosing and caring for telescopes and related equipment also features advice on practical issues such as keeping dew off a corrector plate, warding off mosquitoes, and staying warm outside.

Includes bibliographical references

Kerrod, Robin, 1938-

Hubble: the mirror on the universe; [by] Robin Kerrod and Carole Stott. Rev. ed. Firefly Books 2007 192p il $35 *

Grades: 11 12 Adult   **522**

1. Hubble Space Telescope 2. Outer space—Exploration
ISBN 978-1-55407-316-0; 1-55407-316-2
First published 2003
New edition in preparation

This book is an "introduction to the objects found in our solar system and universe and to the techniques used to study them. In addition, there is a brief history of telescopes and the HST Hubble Space Telescope." Sci Books Films [review of 2003 edition]

Taschek, Karen, 1956-

Death stars, weird galaxies, and a quasar-spangled universe; the discoveries of the Very Large Array telescope. University of New Mexico Press 2006 78p il $17.95

Grades: 9 10 11 12   **522**

1. Radio astronomy 2. Telescopes
ISBN 0-8263-3211-0; 978-0-8263-3211-0
           LC 2005-22841

"The Very Large Array (VLA) radio telescope, located on the Plains of San Agustin, NM, is made up of 27 giant dish antennas. This book describes the array itself; the planets Mercury, Jupiter, and Uranus; the life and death of stars like the sun; death stars and black holes; different types of galaxies; and the future of radio astronomy. . . . The current, authoritative, and interesting text contains considerable astronomical data that would be useful in research and gives a good sense of how these telescopes are changing our view of the universe." SLJ

523 Specific celestial bodies and phenomena

Firefly atlas of the universe; foreword by Arnold Wolfendale. 3rd ed. Firefly Books 2005 288p il $49.95 *

Grades: 11 12 Adult   **523**

1. Astronomy
ISBN 1-55407-071-6   LC 2006-275758

First published 1970 by Rand McNally; this edition first published 2003 in Canada. Variant title: Philip's atlas of the universe

This work begins with a "general historical overview, followed by individual sections on the solar system, the sun, the stars, the structure of the universe and our galaxy's place in it, and over 20 useful star maps, all incorporating the newest scientific data." Libr J [review of 2003 edition]

523.1 The universe, galaxies, quasars

Chaisson, Eric
Epic of evolution; seven ages of the cosmos; illustrated by Lola Judith Chaisson. Columbia University Press 2005 478p il $34.50; pa $22.95
Grades: 11 12 Adult   **523.1**
1. Cosmology 2. Life—Origin
ISBN   0-231-13560-2;   978-0-231-13560-3; 0-231-13561-0 (pa); 978-0-231-13561-0 (pa)
LC 2005-45452
This is "a tour of the seven ages of the cosmos, from the formless era of radiation through the origins of human culture." Publisher's note
The author "has crafted a wonderful vehicle for exploring our universe." Sci Books Films
Includes bibliographical references

Gates, Evalyn
Einstein's telescope; the hunt for dark matter and dark energy in the universe. W.W. Norton 2009 305p il $25.95; pa $16.95
Grades: 11 12 Adult   **523.1**
1. Dark matter (Astronomy) 2. Dark energy (Astronomy)
ISBN 978-0-393-06238-0; 978-0-393-33801-0 (pa)
LC 2008-44455
The author "explores the science of . . . [dark matter and dark energy] and the questions they raise about the universe's origins, its present and its future." Publ Wkly
"Gates writes with a freshness and clarity that make complex ideas such as relativity, lensing, black holes, and the cosmic web understandable." Libr J
Includes bibliographical references

Hawking, Stephen W., 1942-
Black holes and baby universes and other essays; [by] Stephen Hawking. Bantam Bks. 1993 182p pa $18 hardcover o.p.
Grades: 11 12 Adult   **523.1**
1. Cosmology 2. Science—Philosophy
ISBN 0-553-37411-7 (pa)   LC 93-8269
A collection of essays and speeches ranging from autobiographical sketches to theoretical discussions of black holes, relativity and quantum mechanics.
The author "sprinkles his explanations with a wry sense of humor and a keen awareness that the sciences today delve not only into the far reaches of the cosmos, but into the inner philosophical world as well." N Y Times Book Rev

A briefer history of time; [by] Stephen Hawking and Leonard Mlodinow. Bantam Dell 2005 162p il $25 *
Grades: 11 12 Adult   **523.1**
1. Cosmology
ISBN 0-553-80436-7   LC 2005-42949
First published 1988 with title: A brief history of time
The authors describe concepts about space and time, black holes, the origin and nature of the universe, the un-

certainty principle, and the unification of physics. It also discusses string theory, dark matter, and dark energy.
"Hawking and Mlodinow provide one of the most lucid discussions of this complex topic ever written for a general audience. Readers will come away with an excellent understanding of the apparent contradictions and conundrums at the forefront of contemporary physics." Publ Wkly
Includes bibliographical references

Hooper, Dan, 1976-
Dark cosmos; in search of our universe's missing mass and energy. HarperCollins Publishers 2006 240p il $24.95; pa $14.95
Grades: 11 12 Adult   **523.1**
1. Dark matter (Astronomy) 2. Dark energy (Astronomy)
ISBN   978-0-06-113032-8;   0-06-113032-X; 978-0-06-113033-5 (pa); 0-06-113033-8 (pa)
LC 2006-44333
This book discusses "dark matter" and "dark energy," invisible substances which scientists speculate may make up over 95% of the universe.
"Hooper's clear presentation in very simple, jargon-free prose should appeal especially to young people just starting to get excited about the mysteries that still await them in science." Publ Wkly

Kaku, Michio
Parallel worlds; a journey through creation, higher dimensions, and the future of the cosmos. Doubleday 2005 428p il hardcover o.p. pa $15.95
Grades: 11 12 Adult   **523.1**
1. Cosmology 2. Big bang theory 3. String theory
ISBN 0-385-50986-3; 1-4000-3372-1 (pa)
LC 2004-56039
The author "begins by describing the extraordinary advances that have transformed cosmology over the last century, and particularly over the last decade, forcing scientists around the world to rethink our understanding of the birth of the universe, and its ultimate fate. . . . As astronomers wade through the avalanche of data from the WMAP satellite, a new cosmological picture is emerging. So far, the leading theory about the birth of the universe is the 'inflationary universe theory,' a major refinement on the big bang theory." Publisher's note
"This is a riveting popular treatment of the string revolution in physics written by a pioneering theorist in the field. Kaku expounds comprehensibly on why astrophysicists love strings and branes and the way they resolve various vexatious cosmological paradoxes." Booklist

Panek, Richard
The 4 percent universe; dark matter, dark energy, and the race to discover the rest of reality. Houghton Mifflin Harcourt 2011 297p $26
Grades: 11 12 Adult   **523.1**
1. Cosmology 2. Physics 3. Dark matter (Astronomy) 4. Dark energy (Astronomy)
ISBN 978-0-618-98244-8; 0-618-98244-2
LC 2010-25838

Panek, Richard—*Continued*

The author offers an insider's view of the quest for what could be the ultimate revelation: the true substance of the unseen dark matter and energy that makes up some 96% of our universe.

"This is a story about not just science, but also scientists, with enough dueling personalities, epic failures, inspirational triumphs, and out-and-out rivalries to carry a Hollywood blockbuster—should Hollywood ever turn its attention to the world of cosmology." Ad Astra

Includes bibliographical references

523.2   Planetary systems

Benson, Michael

Beyond; a solar system voyage. Abrams Books for Young Readers 2009 121p il $19.95

Grades: 5 6 7 8 9 10   523.2

1. Solar system 2. Astronomy

ISBN 978-0-8109-8322-9; 0-8109-8322-2

LC 2008-22297

"The book's focus is the exploration of the solar system by space probes, with many full-page photos. . . . The author skillfully blends lively narrative with the photos to contribute to the excitement of the explorations. . . . It is an inexpensive but valuable addition for any library." Voice Youth Advocates

Includes glossary and bibliographical references

Daniels, Patricia, 1955-

The new solar system; ice worlds, moons, and planets redefined; foreword by Robert Burnham. National Geographic Society 2009 223p il map $35

Grades: 11 12 Adult   523.2

1. Solar system

ISBN 978-1-4262-0462-3; 1-4262-046-20

LC 2009-10117

This is "a sumptuously illustrated book describing the history, composition, and exploration of the solar system. Aimed at a general audience, the text is highly readable and contains numerous side notes providing fascinating anecdotes and facts about the planets, the sun, and astronomers." Choice

Includes bibliographical references

Encyclopedia of the solar system; editors, Lucy-Ann McFadden, Paul R. Weissman and Torrence V. Johnson. 2nd ed. Academic 2007 xx, 966p il map $99.95 *

Grades: 9 10 11 12   523.2

1. Solar system—Encyclopedias 2. Astronomy—Encyclopedias 3. Reference books

ISBN 978-0-12-088589-3; 0-12-088589-1

LC 2006-937972

First published 1999

This encyclopedia covers "the origin and evolution of the solar system, historical discoveries, and details about planetary bodies and how they interact." Publisher's note

Includes bibliographical references

Jayawardhana, Ray

Strange new worlds; the search for alien planets and life beyond our solar system. Princeton University Press 2011 255p il $24.95

Grades: 11 12 Adult   523.2

1. Life on other planets 2. Extrasolar planets 3. Solar system

ISBN 978-0-691-14254-8; 0-691-14254-8

LC 2010940350

An astronomer discusses the search for extrasolar planets and extraterrestrial life.

"Everything you need to know about alien planet discovery is insightfully described in this engaging book, which will appeal to astronomers, general science buffs, and armchair UFOlogists." Libr J

Includes glossary and bibliographical references

Rivkin, Andrew S., 1969-

Asteroids, comets, and dwarf planets. Greenwood Press 2009 206p il (Greenwood guides to the universe) $65 *

Grades: 9 10 11 12   523.2

1. Solar system 2. Asteroids 3. Comets

ISBN 978-0-313-34432-9; 0-313-34432-9; 978-0-313-34433-6 (ebook); 0-313-34433-7 (ebook)

LC 2009-16114

Contact publisher for ebook pricing

"Covering the solar system's non-moon smaller bodies, from comets plunging out of the distant Oort Cloud to NEO (Near Earth Objects) asteroids and hypothetical 'Vulcan Objects' spinning around the Sun inside Mercury's orbit, Rivkin devotes chapters to orbits, compositions, origins, and relevant space probe missions." SLJ

Includes glossary and bibliographical references

Sobel, Dava

The planets. Viking 2005 270p il $24.95; pa $13 *

Grades: 11 12 Adult   523.2

1. Planets 2. Solar system

ISBN 0-670-03446-0; 0-14-200116-3 (pa)

The author turns her attention to "the planets of our solar system. . . . Sobel explores the planets' origins and oddities through the lens of popular culture, from astrology, mythology, and science fiction to art, music, poetry, biography, and history." Publisher's note

"For newcomers to planetary astronomy, 'The Planets' offers a nimble summary of the latest findings on each planet's features and geology. For those who avidly followed the journeys of the Mariners, Voyagers and Vikings through interplanetary space, it lets us fall in love with the heavens all over again." N Y Times Book Rev

Includes bibliographical references

The **solar** system; editors, David G. Fisher, Richard R. Erickson. Salem Press 2009 c2010 3v il set $364

Grades: 9 10 11 12 Adult   523.2

1. Solar system 2. Reference books

ISBN 978-1-58765-530-2   LC 2009-13008

First published 1998 under the editorship of Roger Smith

The solar system—*Continued*

"These 180 articles offer comprehensive views of the solar system's bodies, dynamics, and phenomena, as well as a thorough account of how they are studied via astronomical observation and space exploration. . . . The cross-references, lengthy subject index, continuous pagination throughout the volumes, and a thematic table of contents, in addition to one by volume, make access particularly easy." SLJ

Includes bibliographical references

523.3   Moon

Mackenzie, Dana

The big splat; or, How our moon came to be. Wiley 2003 232p il $24.95

Grades: 11 12 Adult   **523.3**

1. Moon

ISBN 0-471-15057-6   LC 2003-535402

"Mackenzie's account of humanity's long relationship with Earth's only natural satellite, from a probable lunar calendar found in the Lascaux caves to the new 'giant impact' theory of the moon's origin, is magnetically readable, preternaturally clear, and amazingly concise." Booklist

Includes bibliographical references

523.4   Planets

Boyle, Alan, 1954-

The case for Pluto; how a little planet made a big difference. Wiley 2010 258p il $22.95; ebook $14.99

Grades: 11 12 Adult   **523.4**

1. Pluto (Planet) 2. Solar system

ISBN   978-0-470-50544-1;   0-470-50544-3;
978-0-470-54188-3 (ebook)   LC 2009-15961

This volume examines the history of the discovery of planets. Boyle "chronicles the decision by the International Astronomical Union in 2006 to redefine the definition of a planet. . . . [Boyle argues] that Pluto has unjustly been cast out of the 'Planet Family' and recast as a 'dwarf planet.'" Sci Books Films

Includes bibliographical references

Chaikin, Andrew, 1956-

A passion for Mars; intrepid explorers of the Red Planet; foreword by James Cameron. Abrams 2008 279p il $35

Grades: 11 12 Adult   **523.4**

1. Mars (Planet)—Exploration

ISBN 978-0-8109-7274-2; 0-8109-7274-3

LC 2007-49007

The author "describes the quest to understand and travel to Mars through the eyes of the dreamers and scientists who make planetary exploration possible. . . . I cannot recommend this book highly enough. You will come away from reading it not only knowing more about the exploration of Mars, but also with a better understanding of the word 'passion.'" Sci Books Films

Chaple, Glenn F.

Outer planets. Greenwood Press 2009 199p il (Greenwood guides to the universe) $65 *

Grades: 9 10 11 12   **523.4**

1. Jupiter (Planet) 2. Saturn (Planet) 3. Uranus (Planet) 4. Neptune (Planet)

ISBN 978-0-313-36570-6; 0-313-36570-9

LC 2009-19682

"This book focuses on Jupiter, Saturn, Neptune, and Uranus in great detail, comparing the planets and delving into technical information on each planet. . . . The author's writing style takes a very complex, scientific subject and breaks it down into chapters that are understandable and interesting for the amateur enthusiast, with detailed information for the researcher looking for a credible source." Libr Media Connect

Includes glossary and bibliographical references

Grier, Jennifer A.

Inner planets; [by] Jennifer A. Grier and Andrew S. Rivkin. Greenwood Press 2010 212p il map (Greenwood guides to the universe) $65 *

Grades: 9 10 11 12   **523.4**

1. Mercury (Planet) 2. Venus (Planet) 3. Earth 4. Mars (Planet)

ISBN 978-0-313-34430-5; 0-313-34430-2

LC 2009-42491

This book "covers the inner planets—Mercury, Venus, Earth, and Mars. Thematic chapters discuss all of the many areas of astronomical research surrounding each subject." Publisher's note

"This volume eschews the conventional listing of the numerical data associated with astrophysical texts. Instead, the focus is on explaining processes of planetary formation and change. . . . [The authors] break these processes down into 13 thematic chapters, devoting each to a major concept like plate tectonics, magnetospheres, or atmospheres. Made up largely of engaging text arranged logically with subheadings, chapters are occasionally punctuated by monochromatic illustrations or informational sidebars. . . . A suitable subject primer for high schoolers and lay readers." Libr J

Includes bibliographical references

Hartmann, William K.

A traveler's guide to Mars; the mysterious landscapes of the red planet. Workman Pub. 2003 468p map pa $18.95

Grades: 11 12 Adult   **523.4**

1. Mars (Planet)

ISBN 0-7611-2606-6   LC 2003-41149

"Following an opening chapter discussing what humans have believed and have come to verify about the red planet, the author discusses the three major eras of its 4.5 billion year history. He describes various regions, offering a geological tour of the craters, volcanoes, and the face of Mars. . . . Interspersed throughout are boxed inserts highlighting weather, hazards, financial considerations, geology, etc. Also appearing periodically are sections called 'My Martian Chronicles' in which the astronomer describes his own work and experiences in his quest to learn more about this unusual planet. His writing style will make teens want to keep reading. . . . If you

Hartmann, William K.—*Continued*
can have only one title about Mars, this is the one to buy." SLJ
     Includes bibliographical references

Jones, Barrie William
     Pluto; sentinel of the outer solar system; [by] Barrie W. Jones. Cambridge University Press 2010 231p il $35.99
Grades: 11 12 Adult   **523.4**
     1. Pluto (Planet) 2. Solar system
     ISBN 978-0-521-19436-5; 0-521-19436-9
                   LC 2010-15480
This is "a detailed, matter-of-fact, and thoroughly accessible look at Pluto's origins, its history, and what it can tell us about our solar system—especially its outer reaches. . . . The author writes in a clear, matter-of-fact style, including sidebars on related subjects from Kepler's laws of planetary motion to calculating a planet's surface temperature using nothing more complex than high school algebra." Publ Wkly
     Includes glossary and bibliographical references

Jones, Thomas D.
     Planetology; unlocking the secrets of the solar system; [by] Tom Jones and Ellen Stofan. National Geographic 2008 217p il $35
Grades: 7 8 9 10 11 12   **523.4**
     1. Astrogeology 2. Planets
     ISBN 978-1-4262-0121-9; 1-4262-0121-4
                   LC 2008-10726
"This beautifully produced book provides an introduction to comparative planetology for a general audience. The large-format volume focuses on comparing and contrasting different processes that shape and form the primary planets in the solar system. . . . The writing is crisp and clear, and the choice of imagery and examples is very strong." Choice
     Includes bibliographical references

Karam, P. Andrew
     Planetary motion; by P. Andrew Karam and Ben P. Stein. Chelsea House 2009 117p il (Science foundations) lib bdg $35
Grades: 9 10 11 12   **523.4**
     1. Planets 2. Galaxies
     ISBN 978-1-60413-017-1; 1-60413-017-2
                   LC 2009-2040
Learn how scientists have found new planets outside the solar system, and continue their search for planets like Earth.
     The title offers "a wealth of material, including useful further-reading lists. Great for curricular supplementation, report writers, and science buffs." SLJ
     Includes glossary and bibliographical references

Nardo, Don, 1947-
     Asteroids and comets. Morgan Reynolds Pub. 2009 112p il (Extreme threats) lib bdg $28.95
Grades: 7 8 9 10   **523.4**
     1. Asteroids 2. Comets
     ISBN 978-1-59935-121-6; 1-59935-121-8
                   LC 2009-26295

This book covers "evidence of impacts, types of impactors, giant impacts and mass extinctions, recent impacts and near misses, the current and future danger of near-earth-objects (NEOs), and scientific research on how to address the threat. . . . Features high-gloss pages in mottled green, full-color pictures, and informative sidebars. . . . [It is] well written, nicely designed, and interesting." Voice Youth Advocates
     Includes glossary and bibliographical references

Tyson, Neil De Grasse
     The Pluto files; the rise and fall of America's favorite planet. W.W. Norton 2009 194p il $23.95; pa $15.95
Grades: 8 9 10 11 12 Adult   **523.4**
     1. Pluto (Planet)
     ISBN 978-0-393-06520-6; 0-393-06520-0; 978-0-393-33732-7 (pa); 0-393-33732-4 (pa)
                   LC 2008-40436
An exploration of the controversy surrounding Pluto and its planet status from an astrophysicist at the heart of the controversy.
     The author "uses an engaging mix of facts, photographs, cartoons, illustrations, songs, e-mails, and humor to explain what's up (and down) with Pluto." Christ Sci Monit
     Includes bibliographical references

Weintraub, David A., 1958-
     Is Pluto a planet? a historical journey through the solar system. Princeton University Press 2007 254p il $27.95
Grades: 11 12 Adult   **523.4**
     1. Planets 2. Solar system 3. Pluto (Planet)
     ISBN 0-691-12348-9; 978-0-691-12348-6
                   LC 2006-929630
The author "places the Pluto controversy in context in his . . . account of the development of our solar system and the evolution of the meaning of the word planet, from Aristotle's theories to recent decrees by the International Astronomical Union." Publ Wkly
     Weintraub "provides a very interesting and thought-provoking history concerning the whole idea of planets, and I recommend the book highly to anyone interested in the solar system." Sci Books Films
     Includes bibliographical references

523.5   Meteors, solar wind, zodiacal light

Norton, O. Richard
     Field guide to meteors and meteorites; [by] O. Richard Norton, Lawrence A. Chitwood. Springer 2008 287p il (Patrick Moore's practical astronomy series) pa $39.95
Grades: 9 10 11 12 Adult   **523.5**
     1. Meteors 2. Astrogeology
     ISBN 978-1-84800-156-5 (pa); 1-84800-156-8 (pa); 978-1-84800-157-2 (ebook); 1-84800-157-6 (ebook)
                   LC 2008-921357

Norton, O. Richard—*Continued*

This guide "goes beyond the well-illustrated guide to help meteorite hunters identify their prize (with detailed color photos), and includes the astronomical context needed to understand meteorites and their Earth-bound predecessors, meteoroids. The authors cover astronomical origins, beginning with micrometeoroids, or space dust particles, through meteoroids' believed 'parent,' the asteroid. . . . The Guide offers useful advice on tools (e.g., metal detectors, magnets) to help identify objects and a beginner's guide to laboratory equipment, including microscopes and home chemical tests, to help amateur meteoriticists identify key characteristics for meteorite verification." Choice

Includes glossary

Smith, Caroline, 1976-

Meteorites; [by] Caroline Smith, Sara Russell and Gretchen Benedix. Firefly Books 2009 112p il map $24.95

Grades: 9 10 11 12 Adult   **523.5**

1. Meteorites

ISBN 978-1-55407-515-7

This is an "introduction to meteorites and their scientific importance. . . . The authors describe what extraterrestrial rocks look like and the regions in which they are apt to be found and then delve into their significance to scientists such as themselves. . . . Including photos of recent space missions dedicated to meteoritic research, this is a capable title for libraries needing an introductory book on meteorites." Booklist

Includes bibliographical references

523.6 Comets

Burnham, Robert

Great comets; foreword by David H. Levy. Cambridge Univ. Press 2000 228p pa $22 *

Grades: 11 12 Adult   **523.6**

1. Comets

ISBN 0-521-64600-6   LC 98-50546

The author focuses on the comets Hyakutake in 1996 and Hale-Bopp in 1997, placing them in the context of their predecessors, including Halley's comet, profiles spaceprobes to the comets, and assesses the risks to humanity from comets

"The copious illustrations are . . . supported by a good deal of text. . . . The science is accurate and presented in a nontechnical way. . . . Overall, this is a very fine book." Sci Books Films

Includes bibliographical references

Levy, David H., 1948-

David H. Levy's guide to observing and discovering comets. Cambridge University Press 2003 177p il $70; pa $22.99 *

Grades: 11 12 Adult   **523.6**

1. Comets

ISBN 0-521-82656-X; 0-521-52051-7 (pa)

LC 2002-31547

The author "describes the observing techniques that have been developed over the years—from visual observations and searching, to photography, through to electronic charge-coupled devices (CCDs). He combines the history of comet hunting with the latest techniques, showing how our understanding of comets has evolved over time." Publisher's note

Includes bibliographical references

523.7   Sun

Alexander, David, 1963-

The sun. Greenwood Press/ABC-CLIO 2009 228p il (Greenwood guides to the universe) $65 *

Grades: 9 10 11 12   **523.7**

1. Sun 2. Astrophysics 3. Astronomy

ISBN 978-0-313-34077-2; 0-313-34077-3

LC 2009-6640

This "is a guide to the sun and near-solar environment. The book is very wide-ranging in its scope, giving up-to-date information not only on the processes that power the sun, but also on the physical processes within its atmospheric layers (including the corona, photosphere, and chromosphere), as well as space weather and its effects on Earth and spacecraft. . . . The depth and breadth of this title is such that it will satisfy even the most serious amateur astronomers and science enthusiasts, while at the same time providing less serious readers enough practical information about the effects of solar phenomena on everyday life." Choice

Includes glossary and bibliographical references

Clark, Stuart

The sun kings; the unexpected tragedy of Richard Carrington and the tale of how modern astronomy began. Princeton Univ. Press 2007 211p il $24.95

Grades: 11 12 Adult   **523.7**

1. Carrington, Richard Christopher, 1826-1875 2. Sun 3. Astronomy—History

ISBN 978-0-691-12660-9; 0-691-12660-7

LC 2006-940123

This is a "summary of how our understanding of the sun and its impact on the science of astronomy came to pass." Sci Books Films

"Clark's parade of historical characters dramatize the narrative nicely, and Clark conveys the significance of their scientific observations with plenty of context and thorough references, making this a fascinating work for both casual stargazers and serious astronomy buffs." Publ Wkly

Includes bibliographical references

Harrington, Philip S.

Eclipse! the what, where, when, why, and how guide to watching solar and lunar eclipses. Wiley 1997 280p il maps pa $16.95 *

Grades: 9 10 11 12   **523.7**

1. Solar eclipses 2. Lunar eclipses

ISBN 0-471-12795-7   LC 96-29777

Harrington, Philip S.—*Continued*

This describes solar and lunar eclipses and offers advice on observing and photographing them

"This well-organized book . . . does a fine job of detailing the mechanics of solar and lunar eclipses. . . . Numerous black-and-white photographs and many line drawings and tables in the text are followed by seven helpful appendices and a good index." Sci Books Films

Includes bibliographical references

Lang, Kenneth R.

The Cambridge encyclopedia of the sun. Cambridge Univ. Press 2001 256p il $86 *

Grades: 11 12 Adult   **523.7**

1. Sun

ISBN 0-521-78093-4   LC 00-49365

"Each of the nine chapters addresses a different theme. These themes include physical properties, the magnetic solar atmosphere, solar winds and explosions, solar observations, and the Sun-Earth connection. The volume is well illustrated with figures and photographs in both color and black and white. A 35-page glossary provides definitions of terms and acronyms as well as information on telescopes, satellites, and instruments. A short annotated bibliography and an unannotated directory of Web sites are appended." Booklist

Includes bibliographical references

523.8 Stars

Jones, Lauren V.

Stars and galaxies. Greenwood Press 2010 207p il (Greenwood guides to the universe) pa $65 *

Grades: 9 10 11 12   **523.8**

1. Stars 2. Galaxies

ISBN 978-0-313-34075-8; 0-313-34075-7

LC 2009-34909

"Moving from descriptions of star formation to an explanation of galaxy evolutions, ten highly engaging and accessible chapters make humorous references to pop culture and pose pertinent questions to foster reader interest and understanding. . . . Highly complex and specialized information in later chapters is presented clearly and with great attention to logical detail, along with explanatory sidebars and illustrations." Libr J

Includes bibliographical references

Kaler, James B.

The hundred greatest stars. Copernicus 2002 xxvii, 213p il $32.50

Grades: 11 12 Adult   **523.8**

1. Stars

ISBN 0-387-95436-8   LC 2002-19774

The author "picks a representative of the major star types, such as the red giant, and rounds out his group with a smattering of classical naked-eye stars. . . . Geared for popularity, the book's design presents one image of the star under discussion, either a field view of its position in a constellation or an exuberant HST closeup, faced by Kaler's one-page story about the star's characteristics and inferred history. For the astronomy

buff, an alluring gallery of stars mysterious or simply odd awaits, from magnetars to pulsars to distended monsters on the verge of going supernova." Booklist

Includes bibliographical references

Kerrod, Robin, 1938-

The star guide; learn how to read the night sky star by star. 2nd ed. Wiley 2005 160p il $29.95 *

Grades: 8 9 10 11 12 Adult   **523.8**

1. Stars—Atlases 2. Reference books

ISBN 0-471-70617-5   LC 2004-22953

First published 1993

The presentation for this instructional guide to stargazing "is structured around monthly star maps (for midlatitude observers) in two-page spreads, with a follow-up feature on that month's outstanding constellation. . . . Photos featuring Hubble Space Telescope spectaculars, supplemented by tips for viewing the sun, moon, and planets, round out this attractive book on basic astronomy." Booklist

Scagell, Robin, 1946-

Stargazing with binoculars; [by] Robin Scagell, David Frydman. 2nd ed., updated and rev. Firefly Books 2011 208p il pa $19.95

Grades: 9 10 11 12 Adult   **523.8**

1. Stars 2. Astronomy 3. Binoculars

ISBN 978-1-55407-821-9; 1-55407-821-0

LC 2011-288021

"A Firefly book"

First published 2008

At head of title: Firefly

This is a "guide to using binoculars to view the night sky for newcomers to astronomy. The book includes reviews of the wide range of binoculars on the market and provides advice on features to consider before making a purchase. The authors guide the beginner through the first steps of using binoculars to observe the night sky, describe what will be visible and show how to find specific objects." Publisher's note

Tyson, Neil De Grasse

Death by black hole; and other cosmic quandaries. Norton 2007 384p $24.95; pa $15.95

Grades: 11 12 Adult   **523.8**

1. Cosmology 2. Black holes (Astronomy) 3. Space biology 4. Solar system 5. Religion and science

ISBN   978-0-393-06224-3;   0-393-06224-4; 978-0-393-33016-8 (pa); 0-393-33016-8 (pa)

LC 2006-22058

In this collection of essays that were originally published in Natural History magazine, the author takes readers on a "journey from Earth's hot springs, where extremophiles flourish in hellish conditions, to the frozen, desolate stretches of the Oort Cloud and the universe's farthest reaches, in both space and time. Tyson doesn't restrict his musings to astrophysics, but wanders into related fields like relativity and particle physics. . . . He tackles popular myths (is the sun yellow?) and takes movie directors—most notably James Cameron—to task for spectacular goofs. In the last section the author gives his take on the hot subject of intelligent design." Publ

Tyson, Neil De Grasse—*Continued*
Wkly
"A wonderfully informed viewpoint on the slowly expanding boundaries of human knowledge." Boston Globe
Includes bibliographical references

526 Mathematical geography

Danson, Edwin, 1948-
Weighing the world; the quest to measure the Earth. Oxford University Press 2005 289p il $29.95
Grades: 11 12 Adult   526
1. Science—History 2. Surveying 3. Earth
ISBN 978-0-19-518169-2; 0-19-518169-7
                               LC 2004-66284
This is a "behind-the-scenes look at the scientific events leading to modern map making. . . . Danson presents the stories of the scientists and scholars that had to scale the Andes, cut through tropical forests and how they handled the hardships they faced in the attempt to revolutionize our understanding of the planet." Publisher's note
The author "enlivens data about geodetic surveying, transforming them into greatly interesting dramas of science." Booklist
Includes bibliographical references

The **Map** book; edited by Peter Barber. Levenger Press 2006 360p il map $45 *
Grades: 11 12 Adult   526
1. Maps
ISBN 0-8027-1474-9
"More than 165 maps are chronologically arranged in this . . . volume, each with a descriptive and interpretative text by one of 68 international scholars. . . . This handsome collection of antique and modern cartography, brilliantly reproduced in full color, is highly recommended for all libraries, particularly those with cartographical or related collections." Libr J
Includes bibliographical references

Nicastro, Nicholas
Circumference; Eratosthenes and the ancient quest to measure the globe. St. Martin's Press 2008 223p il map $23.95
Grades: 9 10 11 12 Adult   526
1. Eratosthenes, 3rd cent. B.C. 2. Weights and measures 3. Measurement
ISBN 978-0-312-37247-7; 0-312-37247-7
                               LC 2008-25773
This book describes Eratosthenes of Cyrene, "the ancient Alexandria librarian, and the experiment during which he accurately calculated the distance around the earth using elementary tools." Publisher's note
"Nicastro delivers the deeply human story of a multitalented genius whose tenure as the head of Alexandria's famed library occasioned remarkable achievements in literature, history, linguistics, and philosophy despite the political turmoil that periodically rocked the Ptolemaic world." Booklist
Includes bibliographical references

Raymo, Chet
Walking zero; discovering cosmic space and time along the Prime Meridian. Walker & Co. 2006 194p il maps $22.95
Grades: 11 12 Adult   526
1. Longitude 2. Great Britain—Description and travel
ISBN 0-8027-1494-3; 978-0-8027-1494-7
                               LC 2006-282372
This is the author's "expression of his personal exploration of space, time, and scientific history, inspired partly by his walking the footpaths of southeast England in close proximity to the 0 degrees longitude line. . . . . This work is a thought-provoking, highly enlightening discussion of some of the most fascinating concepts in physics, astronomy, and geology, among other subjects." Sci Books Films
Includes bibliographical references

Sobel, Dava
Longitude; the true story of a lone genius who solved the greatest scientific problem of his time; with a new foreword by Neil Armstrong. Hardcover anniversary ed., [10th anniversary ed., 2005 anniversary ed.] Walker & Co. 2005 184p il $19 *
Grades: 11 12 Adult   526
1. Harrison, John, 1693-1776 2. Longitude
ISBN 0-8027-1462-5; 978-0-8027-1462-6
First published 1995
"In 1714, Britain's Parliament offered the modern equivalent of $12 to anybody who could develop a means of determining longitude at sea. While the likes of Isaac Newton and Edmund Halley sought to calculate longitude by celestial measurement, John Harrison, an uneducated clockmaker, solved the problem with his invention of the chronometer. Science writer Sobel tells this story in a way that enables readers 'to see the globe anew.'" Libr J
Includes bibliographical references

528 Ephemerides

Astronomical almanac for the year 2011; and its companion The astronomical almanac online: data for astronomy, space sciences, geodesy, surveying, navigation and other applications. U.S. Govt. Ptg. Office 2010 various pagings $40 *
Grades: 11 12 Adult   528
1. Nautical almanacs 2. Reference books
ISSN 0737-6421
ISBN 9780-70-774103-1
Also available online
Annual. Formed by the union in 1981 of The American ephemeris and nautical almanac and The Astronomical ephemeris published by Her Majesty's Nautical Almanac Office. Spine title: Astronomical almanac
"With basic information contributed by the ephemeris offices of a number of countries, this collection of tables is the authoritative source for annual astronomical data from the movement of heavenly bodies to the calculation of calendars." Ref Sources for Small & Medium-sized Libr. 6th edition

529   Chronology

Aveni, Anthony F.
Empires of time; calendars, clocks, and cultures; [by] Anthony Aveni. rev ed. University Press of Colo. 2002 332p il pa $22.95
Grades: 11 12 Adult   529
1. Time
ISBN 0-87081-672-1   LC 2002-7120
First published 1989 by Basic Bks.
The author "traces the modern calendar's roots back to Greek pastoral poetry and prehistoric African bone markings, then compares Western, Chinese, Maya, Inca and tribal time systems. He also fathoms our division of time into days, weeks, months, seasons and years for clues to our psychology and worldview." Publ Wkly
Includes bibliographical references

Gleick, James
Faster; the acceleration of just about everything. Pantheon Bks. 1999 324p il pa $14 hardcover o.p.
Grades: 11 12 Adult   529
1. Time
ISBN 0-679-77548-X (pa)   LC 99-21640
Gleick focuses on time and argues that the pace of life has grown faster. He discusses technologies such as "the watch, the typewriter, the phone, the TV, and [the computer, and] . . . the ways these 'time-saving' devices have influenced our world." Christ Sci Monit
The author's "shrewd dissection of the 'psychology of hurriedness' leads to many provocative observations." Booklist

Richards, E. G. (Edward Graham)
Mapping time; the calendar and its history. Oxford Univ. Press 1999 xxi, 438p il pa $43.50 hardcover o.p. *
Grades: 11 12 Adult   529
1. Calendars 2. Time
ISBN 0-19-286205-7 (pa)   LC 98-24957
"An overview of astronomy, time, clocks, writing, arithmetic, and other theoretical issues lays the groundwork for a description of calendar systems from prehistory to the present. Illustrations, charts, and diagrams, including algorithms for the conversion of calendar systems, are also provided." Libr J
Includes bibliographical references

530   Physics

Balibar, Sébastien
The atom and the apple; twelve tales from contemporary physics; translated by Nathanael Stein. Princeton University Press 2008 190p il $24.95
Grades: 10 11 12 Adult   530
1. Physics
ISBN 978-0-691-13108-5   LC 2008-18027

"Balibar examines twelve problems spanning the frontiers of physics, and he devotes a chapter to each issue." Publisher's note
This "is a delightful ramble through many areas of science as well as through the experiences, opinions, passions and frustrations of a leading research physicist. . . . It is a very refreshing read that will do much to bring an understanding of scientific culture to the reader." Times Higher Ed
Includes bibliographical references

Bloomfield, Louis
How everything works; making physics out of the ordinary; [by] Louis A. Bloomfield. Wiley 2007 720p il $40
Grades: 9 10 11 12   530
1. Physics
ISBN 978-0-471-74817-5; 0-471-74817-X
     LC 2006-296744
"Examining everything from roller coasters to radio, knuckleballs to nuclear weapons, *How Everything Works* reveals the answers to such questions as why the sky is blue, why metal is a problem in microwave ovens, how MRIs see inside you, and why some clothes require dry cleaning." Publisher's note
"All but the most hard-core technophile should finy many . . . moments of enlightenment in this delightfully informative book." Am Sci

Cole, K. C.
The hole in the universe; how scientists peered over the edge of emptiness and found everything. Harcourt 2001 274p il pa $14 hardcover o.p.
Grades: 11 12 Adult   530
1. Physics
ISBN 0-15-601317-7 (pa)   LC 00-44947
Cole discusses the history of nothing, "combining the history of zero (a mathematical nothing) with that of the vacuum (a physical nothing). . . . Until Einstein showed that light needed no tangible medium through which to travel, theorists filled the vacuum with 'ether'—the 'enfant terrible' of substances, as Einstein put it. It was subsequently banished." Atl Mon
Includes bibliographical references

The **Facts** on File dictionary of physics; edited by John Daintith, Richard Rennie. 4th ed. Facts on File 2005 278p il (Facts on File science library) $45; pa $17.95 *
Grades: 9 10 11 12   530
1. Reference books 2. Physics—Dictionaries
ISBN 0-8160-5653-6; 0-8160-5654-4 (pa)
     LC 2005-40096
First published 1981
This dictionary contains over 2,500 entries. Among topics covered are: particle physics, cosmology, low-temperature physics, quantum theory, nanotechnology, and superconductivity. Tables list symbols for physical quantities and conversion factors.
Includes bibliographical references

The **Facts** on File physics handbook; the Diagram Group. rev ed. Facts on File 2006 272p il (Facts on File science library) $35 *
Grades: 8 9 10 11 12   **530**
1. Physics
ISBN 0-8160-5880-6   LC 2004-59265
First published 2000
Also covering mathematics and computer science, this reference "contains, in separate sections, a dictionary of around 1500 entries; 250-400 thumbnail biographies; a multipage chronology; and an array of field-specific charts, tables, and diagrams." SLJ [review of 2000 edition]

Includes bibliographical references

Feynman, Richard Phillips, 1918-1988
Six easy pieces; essentials of physics explained by its most brilliant teacher; [by] Richard P. Feynman; originally prepared for publication by Robert B. Leighton and Matthew Sands; introduction by Paul Davies. Basic Books 2005 xxix, 144p il pa $13.95
Grades: 11 12 Adult   **530**
1. Physics
ISBN 978-0-465-02392-9
First published 1995 by Helix Bks.
This book reprints six chapters from Feynman's Lectures on Physics. "In these six chapters, Feynman introduces the general reader to the following: atoms, basic physics, the relationship of physics to other topics, energy, gravitation, and quantum force." Publisher's note

Jargodzki, Christopher, 1944-
Mad about physics; braintwisters, paradoxes, and curiosities; [by] Christopher Jargodzki and Franklin Potter. Wiley 2000 304p il pa $16.95
Grades: 11 12 Adult   **530**
1. Physics
ISBN 0-471-56961-5   LC 00-39914
The authors present 397 questions and answers in physics and astronomy such as why the full moon is nine times brighter than the half moon, why backspin is important in basketball, and why race car drivers accelerate when going around a curve
"This entertaining book is sure to appeal to anyone with an interest in what makes the world work the way it does. . . . The authors' explanations of even the most complicated phenomena are always clear and precise." Booklist

Kakalios, James
The physics of superheroes. Gotham 2005 365p il $26; pa $15
Grades: 11 12 Adult   **530**
1. Physics—Study and teaching 2. Comic books, strips, etc. 3. Heroes and heroines
ISBN 1-59240-146-5; 1-59240-242-9 (pa)
LC 2005-46095
The author "looks at momentum, friction, special relativity, properties of matter, light, magnetism, atomic physics, quantum mechanics, and solid-state physics as

demonstrated by his favorite comic book heroes—including Superman, Flash, and the Invisible Woman—and shows that much of the time, comic book physics is accurate (though he exposes the bloopers, too). The book's a treat for anyone interested in physical science and can be enjoyed readily by math phobes and those with little science education, since Kakalios explains it all with clear detail and a good measure of fun." Libr J

Includes bibliographical references

Kaku, Michio
Physics of the impossible; a scientific exploration into the world of phasers, force fields, teleportation, and time travel. Doubleday 2008 xxi, 329p $26.95
Grades: 11 12 Adult   **530**
1. Physics
ISBN 978-0-385-52069-0; 0-385-52069-7
LC 2007-30290
"From teleportation to telekinesis, Kaku uses the world of science fiction to explore the fundamentals—and the limits—of the laws of physics as we know them today." Publisher's note
"There is a surprising amount of heavyweight, cutting-edge science woven into the fabric of the book. String theory, dark energy, metamaterials and quantum theory are just a few topics—*Physics of the Impossible* is, in fact, an easy-to-read physics primer in disguise." New Sci

Includes bibliographical references

Krauss, Lawrence Maxwell
Fear of physics; a guide for the perplexed; [by] Lawrence M. Krauss. Rev ed. Basic Books 2007 257p il pa $29.95 *
Grades: 11 12 Adult   **530**
1. Physics
ISBN 978-0-465-00218-4; 0-465-00218-8
LC 2007-04700
First published 1993
This overview describes what physics is and the work of physicists.
"The writing style genuinely keeps the reader interested. . . . This book is a great resource if you want insight into what physics really is and what physicists do." Sci Books Films

Includes bibliographical references

Leduc, Steven A., 1965-
Cracking the SAT. Physics subject test. 2011-2012 ed. Random House 2011 495p (Princeton Review series) pa $19.99
Grades: 9 10 11 12   **530**
1. Physics—Study and teaching 2. Scholastic Assessment Test 3. Colleges and universities—Entrance requirements
ISBN 978-0-375-42813-5
Annual. First published 2005. Continues Cracking the SAT II: Physics Subject Test
This guide provides test-taking strategies and sample tests on the subject of physics.

Muller, R.

The instant physicist; [an illustrated guide]; [by] Richard A. Muller; illustrations by Joey Manfre. W.W. Norton c2010 2011 138p il $16.95

Grades: 9 10 11 12 Adult   **530**

1. Physics

ISBN 978-0-393-07826-8   LC 2010-25739

Subtitle from cover

"On left-hand pages, there are brief examinations of interesting or little-known [physics] facts; on right-hand pages, there are Joey Manfre's humorous illustrations based on those facts. . . . Readers will learn a lot from the book: you can outrun a tsunami; plutonium is 1,000 times less toxic than Botox; antimatter isn't science fiction; organically grown foods have more carcinogens than foods sprayed with artificial pesticides. . . . Very entertaining and very informative—a winning combination." Booklist

Nitta, Hideo, 1957-

The manga guide to physics; [by] Hideo Nitta, Keita Takatsu; Trend-pro Co., Ltd. No Starch Press 2009 232p il pa $19.95

Grades: 7 8 9 10   **530**

1. Graphic novels 2. Manga 3. Physics—Graphic novels

ISBN 978-1-59327-196-1; 1-59327-196-4

      LC 2009-12720

First published 2006 in Japan

"Megumi is a great tennis player but not so great at physics. Fortunately, Ryota, the stereotypical geek with a crush on Megumi, offers to help her with physics concepts. Using things Megumi already understands, like tennis and rollerblading, Ryota covers the basics of physics, including action and reaction, force and motion, momentum, and energy. Each concept is presented in graphic format and followed by several pages of text summary, with diagrams as needed. This book is unlikely to stand alone as an introduction to physics, but it could be very useful as a review of concepts or as a supplement to a high-school physics course." Voice Youth Advocates

Ohanian, Hans C.

Einstein's mistakes; the human failings of genius. W.W. Norton & Company 2008 394p il $24.95

Grades: 11 12 Adult   **530**

1. Einstein, Albert, 1879-1955 2. Physics

ISBN 978-0-393-06293-9; 0-393-06293-7

      LC 2008-13155

This book examines Einstein's "mistakes and the role they played in the discovery of his theories." Publisher's note

This "clearly written, fascinating, and exciting book is a gem." Sci Books Films

Includes bibliographical references

Potter, Franklin, 1944-

Mad about modern physics; braintwisters, paradoxes and curiosities; [by] Franklin Potter and Christopher Jargodzki. J. Wiley 2004 296p il pa $16.95

Grades: 9 10 11 12   **530**

1. Physics

ISBN 0-471-44855-9   LC 2004-14941

A collection of physics trivia, with diagrams and illustrations.

Includes bibliographical references

Rosen, Joe

Encyclopedia of physics. Facts on File 2004 386p il (Facts on File science library) $75 *

Grades: 11 12 Adult   **530**

1. Reference books 2. Physics—Encyclopedias

ISBN 0-8160-4974-2   LC 2003-14963

The entries "cover physical concepts, prominent physicists (modern and historical), and physics laboratories, societies, and organizations. The alphabetically arranged entries are supplemented with 11 topical essays that aim to shed some light on physics in a philosophical or practical way. These essays cover such topics as beauty, the nature of the relationship between physics and philosophy, and the desire among some physicists to find the unifying laws governing all physical concepts. . . . The entries are well written, accurate, and include equations where appropriate." Booklist

Includes bibliographical references

530.1   Theories and mathematical physics

Bodanis, David

E=mc2; a biography of the world's most famous equation. Walker & Company 2005 337p il $25

Grades: 11 12 Adult   **530.1**

1. Einstein, Albert, 1879-1955 2. Force and energy 3. Space and time

ISBN 0-8027-1463-3

Also available in paperback from Berkley Pub. Group

First published 2000

The author relates the story of "Einstein's formulation of the equation in 1905 and its association ever after with relativity and nuclear energy. Parallel with the science, Bodanis populates his tale with dramatic lives." Booklist [review of 2000 edition]

Ford, Kenneth William

101 quantum questions; what you need to know about the world you can't see; [by] Kenneth W. Ford. Harvard University Press 2011 291p il $24.95

Grades: 11 12 Adult   **530.1**

1. Quantum theory

ISBN 978-0-674-05099-0   LC 2010-34791

"Ford explains the essential concepts of quantum reality, our small-fast world, full of uncertainty and probability, where all matter can exist in more than one state si-

Ford, Kenneth William—*Continued*

multaneously. Ford brings interesting and entertaining anecdotal and historical material into his answers, organizing and shaping his book around 15 subjects. By using humor and straight talk to answer questions that often bedevil the nonscientist who attempts to grasp this knotty subject, Ford has created an entertaining read and an excellent companion piece to more detailed popular treatments of modern physics." Publ Wkly

Includes bibliographical references

Gott, J. Richard, 1947-

Time travel in Einstein's universe; the physical possibilities of travel through time; {by} J. Richard Gott, III. Houghton Mifflin 2001 291p il hardcover o.p. pa $14

Grades: 11 12 Adult 530.1

1. Space and time 2. Fourth dimension
ISBN 0-395-95563-7; 0-618-25735-7 (pa)

LC 00-54243

"Gott tackles the complexities of attempting to turn the fantasy of time travel into a theoretical possibility in a lively and lucid discussion." Booklist

Includes bibliographical references

Guillen, Michael

Five equations that changed the world; the power and poetry of mathematics. Hyperion 1995 277p hardcover o.p. pa $14.95

Grades: 11 12 Adult 530.1

1. Physics 2. Mathematics
ISBN 0-7868-6103-7; 0-7868-8187-9 (pa)

LC 95-15199

The author discusses "five significant equations in physics and the individuals who developed them. The individuals are Isaac Newton (Universal gravitation), Daniel Bernoulli (hydrodynamic pressure), Michael Faraday (thermodynamics), Rudolf Clausius (thermodynamics), and Albert Einstein (special relativity)." Libr J

"A seamless blend of dramatic biography and mathematical documentary that links the personal with the scientific." Publ Wkly

Hawking, Stephen W., 1942-

The grand design; [by] Stephen Hawking and Leonard Mlodinow. Bantam Books 2010 198p il $28; ebook $28

Grades: 11 12 Adult 530.1

1. Universe 2. Life—Origin 3. Quantum theory 4. String theory
ISBN 978-0-553-80537-6; 0-553-80537-1; 978-0-553-90707-0 (ebook); 0-553-90707-7 (ebook)

"The three central questions of philosophy and science: Why is there something rather than nothing? Why do we exist? Why this particular set of laws and not some other? . . . Along with Caltech physicist Mlodinow . . . Hawking deftly mixes cutting-edge physics to answer those key questions. . . . This is an amazingly concise, clear, and intriguing overview of where we stand when it comes to divining the secrets of the universe." Publ Wkly

Includes bibliographical references

The nature of space and time; [by] Stephen Hawking and Roger Penrose. [New ed.], with a new afterword by the authors. Princeton University Press 2010 145p il (Isaac Newton Institute series of lectures) pa $14.95; ebook $14.95

Grades: 11 12 Adult 530.1

1. Space and time 2. Quantum theory 3. Astrophysics
ISBN 978-0-691-14570-9 (pa); 978-1-4008-3474-7 (ebook)

First published 1996

This volume "takes the form of a debate between Hawking and Penrose at Cambridge in 1994. At the center of the discussion is a pair of powerful theories: the quantum theory of fields and the general theory of relativity. The issue is how—if at all—one can merge the two into a quantum theory of gravity. . . . A substantial background in theoretical physics is needed for full comprehension." Libr J

Includes bibliographical references

The universe in a nutshell; [by] Stephen Hawking. Bantam Bks. 2001 216p il $35

Grades: 11 12 Adult 530.1

1. Quantum theory
ISBN 0-553-80202-X LC 2001-35757

Companion volume to A brief history of time

Hawking "explains the basic laws of physics that govern the universe, beginning with a brief history of the concept of relativity, and then he is off and running to explore time, space, the future, and the possibility of time travel, among other fundamental rules of the universe's road. Admirers of Hawking's previous book will continue to appreciate his ability not only to air fresh, provocative ideas but also to say what he means clearly and without watering down his material or condescending to his audience—he even injects humor into his narrative. The profuse, beautifully rendered illustrations contribute greatly to the reader's understanding of his points." Booklist

Kakalios, James

The amazing story of quantum mechanics; a math-free exploration of the science that made our world. Gotham Books 2010 318p il $26

Grades: 9 10 11 12 Adult 530.1

1. Quantum theory
ISBN 978-1-59240-479-7; 1-59240-479-0

LC 2010-29568

"Though the book does not quite live up to the subtitle's promise of a 'math-free' text, readers need no more than basic algebra to accompany comic-book heroes into well-illustrated explanations of quantum packets of light energy, of the wave functions of particles, and even of the angular spin inherent in both energy and matter. These basic principles illuminate the solid-state physics of semiconductors, the atomic magnetism of MRIs, and the nanotechnology of high-capacity storage batteries. And all of this conceptual heavy lifting comes with entertaining episodes from DC Comics and H. G. Wells' fiction. Physics has never been more fun!" Booklist

Includes bibliographical references

Orzel, Chad

How to teach physics to your dog. Scribner 2009 241p il $24

Grades: 11 12 Adult   **530.1**
1. Physics 2. Quantum theory
ISBN 978-1-4165-7228-2; 1-4165-7228-7
                                          LC 2009-21073

"Particle physicist Orzel has a smart and energetic German shepherd-mix, Emmy, who's interested in what he does for a living that keeps her in treats and kibble. So she asks him about it, and he tells her, with plenty of chaseable bunnies and squirrels illustratively standing-in for photons, electrons, and other particles. . . . It's hard to imagine a better way for the mathematically and scientifically challenged, in particular, to grasp basic quantum physics." Booklist

Includes bibliographical references

Rigden, John S.

Einstein 1905; the standard of greatness. Harvard University Press 2005 173p il $21.95; pa $14.95 *

Grades: 11 12 Adult   **530.1**
1. Einstein, Albert, 1879-1955 2. Quantum theory
ISBN 0-674-01544-4; 0-674-02104-5 (pa)
                                          LC 2004-54049

The author "chronicles the . . . theories that Einstein put forth beginning in March 1905: his particle theory of light, rejected for decades but now a staple of physics; his overlooked dissertation on molecular dimensions; his theory of Brownian motion; his theory of special relativity; and the work in which his famous equation, . . . [energy equals mass times the speed of light squared], first appeared." Publisher's note

"The book is a delight to read, with a lot of interesting, useful information." Choice

Includes bibliographical references

Toomey, David M.

The new time travelers; a journey to the frontiers of physics; [by] David Toomey. W. W. Norton 2007 391p il $28

Grades: 11 12 Adult   **530.1**
1. Space and time
ISBN 978-0-393-06013-3; 0-393-06013-6
                                          LC 2007-11307

This book on the physics of time travel "illustrates dimension-bending concepts with space-time diagrams, M. C. Escher drawings, and the plot of H.G. Wells' Time Machine. Toomey gets a grip on bending the fourth dimension by historically chronicling physicists who have theorized about time travel . . . . If you dream of getting outside your personal light cone, Toomey shows how it might be imagined." Booklist

Includes bibliographical references

530.8   Measurement

The **Economist** desk companion; how to measure, convert, calculate, and define practically anything. Wiley 1998 272p il map $27.95 *

Grades: 11 12 Adult   **530.8**
1. Weights and measures
ISBN 0-471-24953-X   LC 98-17615

First published 1992 by Holt & Co.

"This reference manual provides essential information on measurements, formulas, and calculations on a wide variety of scientific, industrial, economic, and applied technological topics. The introductory section describes the three major world measurement systems, followed by sections containing conversion tables, local units of measurements around the world, and abbreviations and country codes. Subjects include agriculture, finance, health, and transport, among many other topics. . . . This ready-reference volume serves as a superb compilation of material scattered in numerous sources." Libr J

Robinson, Andrew, 1957-

The story of measurement. Thames & Hudson 2007 224p il map $34.95

Grades: 11 12 Adult   **530.8**
1. Measurement
ISBN 978-0-500-51367-5; 0-500-51367-8
                                          LC 2007-921450

This is an illustrated guide to the history and practice of measurement. It covers subjects ranging "from the earliest currency to the birth of the meter, from the force of hurricanes to body mass index, from air pressure, earthquakes, and pollen counts to happiness, blood types, and intelligence." Publisher's note

"Robinson has the knack to explain any number of complex concepts lucidly and with simplicity, without being condescending. . . . He has produced a highly readable book." Times Lit Suppl

Includes bibliographical references

531   Classical mechanics. Solid mechanics

Darling, David J.

Gravity's arc; the story of gravity, from Aristotle to Einstein and beyond; [by] David Darling. J. Wiley 2006 278p $24.95

Grades: 11 12 Adult   **531**
1. Gravity
ISBN 0-471-71989-7; 978-0-471-71989-2
                                          LC 2005-30772

This is a "historical review of the human understanding of gravity from the ancient Greeks to the 21st century. Included are examinations of Greek philosophers and their debates, medieval and Arabic developments, Galileo, Tycho, Kepler, Newton, Eotvos, [and] Einstein. . . . The writing style is clear and reader friendly. . . . Read this book to learn about gravity and experience a model scientific exposition for the scientist and general reader alike." Sci Books Films

Includes bibliographical references

Manning, Phillip, 1936-

Gravity. Chelsea House 2010 139p il (Science foundations) lib bdg $35

Grades: 7 8 9 10   **531**
1. Gravitation 2. Gravity
ISBN 978-1-60413-296-0; 1-60413-296-5
                                          LC 2010-15793

Manning, Phillip, 1936-—*Continued*

This book "explains how two of the greatest scientific minds in history—Isaac Newton and Albert Einstein—finally unraveled most of the mystery surrounding this peculiar force, and how scientists today are continuing to search for answers to the remaining questions." Publisher's note

Includes glossary and bibliographical references

533   Pneumatics (Gas mechanics)

Gardner, Robert, 1929-

Air; green science projects for a sustainable planet. Enslow Publishers 2011 128p il (Team Green science projects) lib bdg $31.93

Grades: 6 7 8 9 10   533

1. Air 2. Air pollution 3. Science—Experiments 4. Science projects

ISBN 978-0-7660-3646-8; 0-7660-3646-4

LC 2010-1120

This book offers science experiments that explain the properties of air, how to conserve energy while heating and cooling air, and how to reduce air pollution.

"Gardner provides plenty of information, well-designed experiments, and demonstrations, and then shares brief science-fair ideas. . . . Experiments and demonstrations are presented with clear step-by-step instructions and occasional illustrations and represent a wide range of complexity." SLJ

Includes glossary and bibliographical references

535.6   Color

Finlay, Victoria

Color: a natural history of the palette. Ballantine Bks. 2002 448p il maps hardcover o.p. pa $14.95

Grades: 11 12 Adult   535.6

1. Color

ISBN 0-345-44430-2; 0-8129-7142-6 (pa)

This "book is a blend of travelogue and historical exploration about the myriad ways color takes on meaning for us, whether as a matter of aesthetics, economics, war or culture. . . . Thanks to Finlay's impeccable reportorial skills and a remarkable degree of engagement, this is an utterly unique and fascinating read." Publ Wkly

Includes bibliographical references

536   Heat

Shachtman, Tom, 1942-

Absolute zero and the conquest of cold. Houghton Mifflin 1999 261p hardcover o.p. pa $14 *

Grades: 11 12 Adult   536

1. Low temperatures—Research

ISBN 0-395-93888-0; 0-618-08239-5 (pa)

LC 99-33305

The author "analyzes the social impact of the chill factor, explains the science of cold and tells the curious tales behind inventions like the thermometer, the fridge and the thermos flask." N Y Times Book Rev

Includes bibliographical references

537   Electricity and electronics

Bodanis, David

Electric universe; the shocking true story of electricity. Crown Publishers 2004 308p hardcover o.p. pa $31 *

Grades: 11 12 Adult   537

1. Electricity 2. Force and energy

ISBN 1-4000-4550-9; 0-307-33598-4 (pa)

LC 2004-11275

The author "examines electricity's theoretical development and how 19th- and 20th-century entrepreneurs harnessed it to transform everyday existence. Going from 'Wires' to 'Waves' to computers and even the human body, Bodanis pairs electrical innovations with minibiographies of their developers, among them Thomas Edison, Alexander Graham Bell, Guglielmo Marconi, Heinrich Herz and Alan Turing." Publ Wkly

"As a storyteller, author David Bodanis is wonderful. . . . This book is directed at a general audience, but it should be required reading for all scientific professionals." Sci Books Films

Includes bibliographical references

538   Magnetism

Verschuur, Gerrit L., 1937-

Hidden attraction; the history and mystery of magnetism. Oxford Univ. Press 1993 256p il hardcover o.p. pa $14.95 *

Grades: 11 12 Adult   538

1. Magnetism

ISBN 0-19-506488-7; 0-19-510655-5 (pa)

LC 92-37690

The author "uses the history of magnetism to illustrate the development of scientific theory and method, from natural phenomena rooted in superstition to the accurate simulations of modern science. An informative study, with details about such scientists as Michael Faraday and James Maxwell and their pioneering work." Booklist

Includes bibliographical references

539.2   Radiation (Radiant energy)

Karam, P. Andrew

Radioactivity; [by] P. Andrew Karam and Ben P. Stein. Chelsea House 2009 124p il (Science foundations) lib bdg $35

Grades: 7 8 9 10 11 12   539.2

1. Radioactivity 2. Radiation

ISBN 978-1-60413-016-4; 1-60413-016-4

LC 2008-38067

This book "explains the science behind radiation, from the radiation in the body to the radiation in the environment; how radiation can create energy and cause destruction; and how it saves lives every day." Publisher's note

"Great for curricular supplementation, report writers, and science buffs." SLJ

Includes glossary and bibliographical references

539.7 Atomic and nuclear physics

Manning, Phillip, 1936-
Atoms, molecules, and compounds. Chelsea House 2008 137p il (Essential chemistry) $35
Grades: 7 8 9 10   **539.7**
1. Atoms 2. Molecules 3. Matter 4. Chemical reactions
ISBN 978-0-7910-9534-8; 0-7910-9534-7
                                        LC 2007-11403
This book "explores the reactions between atoms and shows how the characteristics of the reacting atoms determine the type of molecule produced." Publisher's note
"In relatively few pages, and with lots of colorful, clear illustrations, Manning takes us from Thompson's plum-pudding model of the atom to Rutherford's model to the quantum model, and through the discovery of atomic particles and the teasing out of atomic forces, in a very clear, compelling path. . . . The clear linkages he makes between the different types of chemical bonds and the nature of various materials will remain with the reader." Sci Books Films
Includes glossary and bibliographical references

540 Chemistry

Chemical compounds; Neil Schlager, Jayne Weisblatt, and David E. Newton, editors; Charles B. Montney, project editor. UXL 2006 3v il set $181
Grades: 7 8 9 10   **540**
1. Chemicals
ISBN 1-4144-0150-7; 978-1-4144-0150-8
                                        LC 2005-23636
"This set discusses 180 molecules, both organic and inorganic, that have played an important role in human affairs. Each molecule is depicted by a structural formula and . . . [a] color image of a ball-and-stick model. . . . These pictorial representations are accompanied by a listing of physical properties, a description of how the compound is made, a discussion of common uses and hazards, and often a brief review of the compound's history. . . . The result—a unique way to introduce high school students to chemistry." Choice
Includes bibliographical references

Cobb, Cathy
The joy of chemistry; the amazing science of familiar things; [by] Cathy Cobb & Monty L. Fetterolf. Prometheus Books 2005 393p il hardcover o.p. pa $19
Grades: 11 12 Adult   **540**
1. Chemistry
ISBN 1-591-02231-2; 1-591-02771-3 (pa)
                                        LC 2004-20144
The authors cover "the material of a general chemistry course along with organic, inorganic and analytical chemistry and biochemistry; there's even a chapter on forensic chemistry. . . . They explain everything from flatulence (the chemical composition of intestinal gas) to pizza cheese (why mozzarella rather than, say, parmesan?)." Publ Wkly
Includes bibliographical references

CRC handbook of chemistry and physics; a ready-reference book of chemical and physical data; editor-in-chief, W.M. Haynes; associate editor, David R. Lide. CRC 2010 various pagings il $149.95 *
Grades: 11 12 Adult   **540**
1. Chemistry—Tables 2. Physics—Tables
3. Reference books
ISBN 978-1-4398-2077-3
Also available CD-ROM version and online
First published 1913. Periodically revised
A "reference book containing much-used information on mathematics, chemistry, and physics, including tables, physical constants of chemical elements and compounds, definitions, formulae, etc." AAAS Sci Book List for Young Adults
Includes bibliographical references

The **Facts** on File chemistry handbook; the Diagram Group. Rev. ed. Facts on File 2006 272p il (Facts on File science library) $35 *
Grades: 8 9 10 11 12   **540**
1. Chemistry
ISBN 0-8160-5878-4   LC 2005-55496
First published 2000
In addition to a dictionary of around 1500 entries, this source also includes hundreds of thumbnail biographies and an extensive chronology. Charts, tables, and diagrams are included.
Includes bibliographical references

Lange's handbook of chemistry. 16th ed. McGraw-Hill 2005 various paging il $150 *
Grades: 11 12 Adult   **540**
1. Chemistry—Tables
ISBN 0-07-143220-5; 978-0-07-143220-7
First published 1934. Periodically revised
Originally compiled and edited by Norbert Adolph Lange. Editors vary
"A standard reference source for both students and professional chemists. Sections for: organic compounds; general information, conversion tables, and mathematics; inorganic chemistry; properties of atoms, radicals, and bonds; physical properties; thermodynamic properties; spectroscopy; electrolytes, electromotive force, and chemical equilibrium; physiochemical relationships; polymers, rubbers, fats, oils, and waxes; and practical laboratory information." Guide to Ref Books. 11th edition

Le Couteur, Penny, 1943-
Napoleon's buttons; how 17 molecules changed history; [by] Penny Le Couteur, Jay Burreson. Jeremy P. Tarcher/Penguin Books 2003 375p il hardcover o.p. pa $14.95
Grades: 11 12 Adult   **540**
1. Chemistry
ISBN 1-58542-220-7; 1-58542-331-9 (pa)
                                        LC 2002-032247
The authors "explore how chemical properties of compounds have altered history. The impacts run the gamut from medicine (e.g., penicillin, vitamin C) to social change (e.g., the contraceptive pill and slavery perpetuated by the farming of glucose, or sugar cane, and cellu-

Le Couteur, Penny, 1943-—*Continued*

lose, or cotton) to more direct historical incidents such as the Opium Wars or the spice trade spurring New World exploration." Libr J

"Napoleon's Buttons is a fascinating attempt at recognizing the role of chemistry in the wider world. With its many structural diagrams, the book can resemble a course in organic chemistry, but the chemist-authors are good guides. . . . The best chapter is the one on dyes." Quill & Quire

Includes bibliographical references

Myers, Richard, 1951-

The basics of chemistry. Greenwood Press 2003 373p il (Basics of the hard sciences) $75

Grades: 11 12 Adult   540

1. Chemistry

ISBN 0-313-31664-3   LC 2002-28436

This work covers "atoms, molecules, elements, and compounds; states of matter, bonding, and solutions; kinetics and heat; acids/bases; electrochemistry; nuclear, environmental, organic, and biochemistry; and the chemical industry and careers. Reasonable and informative project ideas are included . . . with adequate instructions for completion." SLJ

"Recommended as a basic overview for public, school, or undergraduate libraries, but not for reference collections." Libr J

Includes bibliographical references

Silver, Theodore

Cracking the SAT. Chemistry subject test; [by] Theodore Silver and the staff of the Princeton Review. 2011-2012 ed. Random House 2011 352p (Princeton Review series) pa $19.99 *

Grades: 9 10 11 12   540

1. Chemistry—Study and teaching 2. Scholastic Assessment Test 3. Colleges and universities—Entrance requirements

ISBN 978-0-375-42814-2

Annual. First published 2005. Continues Cracking the SAT II: chemistry subject test

This guide provides test-taking strategies and sample tests on the subject of chemistry.

540.3   Chemistry—Encyclopedias and dictionaries

Chemistry: foundations and applications. Macmillan Ref. USA 2004 4v il set $395

Grades: 9 10 11 12   540.3

1. Chemistry—Encyclopedias 2. Reference books

ISBN 0-02-865721-7   LC 2003-21038

The alphabetically arranged signed articles "range from concise definitions to multiple-page overviews. Broad areas covered include analytical chemistry applications, biochemistry, elements, energy, environmental chemistry, medicine, organic chemistry, physical chemistry, reactions, states of matter, and structure. . . . In addition to explaining scientific principles, this set relates chemistry to everyday life. . . . An 18-page glossary and 67-page subject index are included in each volume. Glos-

sary definitions also appear in the margins next to the text. . . . Bibliographic references and related Internet resources are listed at the end of many articles." Booklist

A **dictionary** of chemistry; edited by John Daintith. 6th ed. Oxford University Press 2008 584p il (Oxford paperback reference) pa $17.95

Grades: 9 10 11 12 Adult   540.3

1. Chemistry—Dictionaries 2. Reference books

ISBN 978-0-19-920463-2; 0-19-920463-2

LC 2008-274475

Title on cover: Oxford dictionary of chemistry

This book covers "biochemistry, chemoinformatics, forensic chemistry, metallurgy, and geology. The dictionary includes chronologies, biographies, illustrations, tables, chemical structures, feature articles, and eight appendixes." Choice

The **Facts** on File dictionary of chemistry; edited by John Daintith. 4th ed. Checkmark Books 2005 310p il (Facts on File science library) $45; pa $17.95 *

Grades: 9 10 11 12   540.3

1. Chemistry—Dictionaries 2. Reference books

ISBN 0-8160-5649-8; 0-8160-5650-1 (pa)

LC 2005-43785

First published 1981

This reference work includes more than 3,000 cross-referenced entries that identify terms, reactions, techniques and applications in chemistry.

Includes bibliographical references

Rittner, Don

Encyclopedia of chemistry; [by] Don Rittner and Ronald A. Bailey. Facts on File 2005 342p il (Facts on File science library) $75 *

Grades: 11 12 Adult   540.3

1. Chemistry—Encyclopedias 2. Reference books

ISBN 0-8160-4894-0   LC 2004-11242

This encyclopedia "offers more than 2000 articles on topics from ABO blood groups to zwitterionic compound." SLJ

Includes bibliographical references

540.7   Chemistry—Education and related topics

Walker, Pamela, 1958-

Chemistry experiments; [by] Pamela Walker, Elaine Wood. Facts on File 2011 xx, 177p il map (Facts on File science experiments) $40

Grades: 7 8 9 10 11 12   540.7

1. Chemistry 2. Science—Experiments

ISBN 978-0-8160-8172-1   LC 2010-33149

A collection of twenty science projects. "Topics covered include ozone depletion, wood alcohol, heat energy, purifying water, and carbonation in beverages." Publisher's note

Includes glossary and bibliographical references

540.9 Chemistry—Historical and geographic treatment

Greenberg, Arthur
From alchemy to chemistry in picture and story. Wiley-Interscience 2007 xxiii, 637p il $69.95 *
Grades: 11 12 Adult   **540.9**
1. Chemistry—History
ISBN 978-0-471-75154-0; 0-471-75154-5
LC 2006-33564

According to the author, this "is a combination of his two previous books, A Chemical History Tour and The Art of Chemistry, with some additions and revisions. . . . One could open the book at almost any page to learn something about the remarkable history of the chemical sciences." Sci Books Films
Includes bibliographical references

541 Physical chemistry

Cobb, Cathy
Magick, mayhem, and mavericks; the spirited history of physical chemistry. Prometheus Books 2002 420p il $29
Grades: 11 12 Adult   **541**
1. Physical chemistry—History
ISBN 1-573-92976-X   LC 2002-70511

"The history moves from ancient astronomy, mathematics and natural philosophy through early modern developments in mathematics, physics, alchemy, medicinal remedies and chemistry, using the assumption that physical chemists could achieve their aims only after the foundations of mathematics, physics and chemistry were well laid. . . . Cobb's style is lively and swashbuckling." American Scientist
Includes bibliographical references

Manning, Phillip, 1936-
Chemical bonds. Chelsea House 2009 134p il (Essential chemistry) lib bdg $35
Grades: 7 8 9 10   **541**
1. Chemistry
ISBN 978-0-7910-9740-3; 0-7910-9740-4
LC 2008-1981

Examines the nature of the chemical bonds, answering questions about how they form, how they are broken, and how they help define life as we know it
Includes glossary and bibliographical references

546 Inorganic chemistry

Gray, Theodore W.
The elements; a visual exploration of every known atom in the universe; photographs by Theodore Gray and Nick Mann. Black Dog & Leventhal Publishers 2009 240p il $29.95
Grades: 11 12 Adult   **546**
1. Chemical elements—Pictorial works
ISBN 978-1-57912-814-2; 1-57912-814-9
LC 2009-34931

This is a collection of "photographic representations of the 118 elements in the periodic table. . . . Organized in order of appearance on the periodic table, each element is represented by a spread that includes a . . . full-page, full-color photograph that most closely represents it in its purest form. . . . [Also included are] facts, figures, and stories of the elements as well as data on the properties of each, including atomic weight, density, melting and boiling point, valence, electronegativity, and the year and location in which it was discovered." Publisher's note

"This gorgeously photographed guide to the elements can be used as a visual reference, but its brief entries are packed with intriguing tidbits that also make it a fascinating read." Libr J
Includes bibliographical references

Halka, Monica
Alkali & alkaline earth metals; [by] Monica Halka, Brian Nordstrom. Facts on File 2010 xxxv, 172p il (Periodic table of the elements) $40
Grades: 9 10 11 12   **546**
1. Chemical elements 2. Periodic law
ISBN 978-0-8160-7369-6   LC 2009-35152

This book "presents the current scientific understanding of the physics, chemistry, geology, and biology of these two families of elements, including how they are synthesized in the universe, when and how they were discovered, and where they are found on Earth. With information pertaining to the discovery and naming of these elements as well as new developments and dilemmas, this . . . book examines how humans use alkalis and alkaline earths and their benefits and challenges to society, health, and the environment." Publisher's note
Includes glossary and bibliographical references

Halogens and noble gases; [by] Monica Halka, Brian Nordstrom. Facts on File 2010 xxxiii, 157p il (Periodic table of the elements) $40
Grades: 9 10 11 12   **546**
1. Gases 2. Chemical elements 3. Periodic law
ISBN 978-0-8160-7368-9   LC 2009-31088

"Beginning with an overview of chemistry and physics, this volume is arranged into two sections: halogens and noble gases. Each one begins with an introduction to its family and is followed by chapters devoted to a single element or pairs of elements. The chapters focused on elements feature a chart highlighting key information: symbol, atomic number, melting and boiling point, etc. . . . The writing and explanations are clear and would be appropriate for generalists as well as chemistry students." SLJ
Includes glossary and bibliographical references

Lanthanides and actinides; [by] Monica Halka and Brian Nordstrom. Facts on File 2011 xxxiv, 190p il (Periodic table of the elements) $40
Grades: 9 10 11 12   **546**
1. Chemical elements 2. Periodic law
ISBN 978-0-8160-7372-6   LC 2010-6296

This book "explains how they were discovered, as well as the practical applications that these elements have in today's scientific, technological, medical, and military communities. Actinium, thorium, protactinium, uranium, and the transuranium elements are just some of the elements covered." Publisher's note
Includes glossary and bibliographical references

Halka, Monica—*Continued*

Metals and metalloids; [by] Monica Halka and Brian Nordstrom. Facts on File 2011 xxxiii, 158p il (Periodic table of the elements) $40

Grades: 9 10 11 12   **546**
  1. Metals 2. Chemical elements 3. Periodic law
  ISBN 978-0-8160-7370-2   LC 2009049369
  This book "presents the current scientific understanding of the physics, chemistry, geology, and biology of these two families of elements, including the post-transition metals and metalloids." Publisher's note
  Includes glossary and bibliographical references

Nonmetals; [by] Monica Halka and Brian Nordstrom. Facts on File 2010 xxxiv, 187p il (Periodic table of the elements) $40

Grades: 9 10 11 12   **546**
  1. Chemical elements 2. Periodic law
  ISBN 978-0-8160-7367-2   LC 2009-18453
  This book discusses "developments in the research of nonmetals, including where they came from, how they fit into our current technological society, and where they may lead us. . . . Nonmetals explored in this volume include hydrogen, carbon, nitrogen, phosphorus, oxygen, sulfur, and selenium." Publisher's note
  Includes glossary and bibliographical references

Transition metals; [by] Monica Halka and Brian Nordstrom. Facts on File 2011 xxxiv, 190p il (Periodic table of the elements) $40

Grades: 9 10 11 12   **546**
  1. Metals 2. Chemical elements 3. Periodic law
  ISBN 978-0-8160-7371-9   LC 2009054139
  This book discusses "the chemical and physical properties of transition metals and how they are useful in everyday life. Some of the transition metals covered include scandium, yttrium, titanium, manganese, cobalt, and zinc." Publisher's note
  Includes glossary and bibliographical references

Kean, Sam

The disappearing spoon; and other true tales of madness, love, and the history of the world from the periodic table of the elements. Little, Brown and Co. 2010 391p $24.99 *

Grades: 11 12 Adult   **546**
  1. Chemical elements
  ISBN 978-0-316-05164-4; 0-316-05164-0
                 LC 2009-40754
  "Kean's traipse among the elements leads him through a warren of subjects, as he examines how these basic building blocks have factored prominently in astronomy, biology, literature, history, politics, and even cryptozoology. With the anecdotal flourishes of Oliver Sacks and the populist accessibility of Malcolm Gladwell, but without the latter's occasional facileness, he makes even the most abstract concepts graspable for armchair scientists. His keen sense of humor is a particular pleasure." Entertainment Wkly
  Includes bibliographical references

Krebs, Robert E., 1922-

The history and use of our earth's chemical elements; a reference guide; illustrations by Rae Déjur. 2nd ed. Greenwood Press 2006 422p il $75 *

Grades: 11 12 Adult   **546**
  1. Chemical elements
  ISBN 0-313-33438-2; 978-0-313-33438-2
                 LC 2006-12032
  First published 1998
  "The elements are examined within their groups, enabling students to make connections between elements of similar structure. In addition, the discovery and history of each element—from those known from ancient times to those created in the modern laboratory—is explained." Publisher's note
  Includes bibliographical references

Lew, Kristi, 1968-

Acids and bases. Chelsea House 2008 124p il (Essential chemistry) $35

Grades: 7 8 9 10   **546**
  1. Acids 2. Bases (Chemistry)
  ISBN 978-0-7910-9783-0; 0-7910-9783-8
                 LC 2008-24015
  "Introduces acids and bases in nature and everyday life and describes their properties and how they react." Publisher's note
  "Annotated, colorful photographs and illustrations appear on most spreads, and boxed areas and sidebars highlight specific subjects and areas. The explanations are clear and detailed." SLJ
  Includes glossary and bibliographical references

Miller, Ron, 1947-

The elements. Twenty-First Century Books 2006 135p il lib bdg $28.90

Grades: 8 9 10 11 12   **546**
  1. Chemical elements
  ISBN 0-7613-2794-0   LC 2003-20874
  Discusses the history of the periodic table of the elements, includes biographies of major figures in the field of chemistry, and provides information on each element.
  "A useful overview." SLJ
  Includes bibliographical references

Scerri, Eric R.

The periodic table; its story and its significance. Oxford University Press 2007 xxii, 346p il $35

Grades: 11 12 Adult   **546**
  1. Chemical elements 2. Periodic law
  ISBN 978-0-19-530573-9; 0-19-530573-6
                 LC 2005-37784
  This is "a scholarly, thought-provoking book about the history and impact of the periodic table of the elements. A central premise is that the creation of the periodic table was not strictly a 'eureka' moment, but rather the evolution of many thoughts and ideas that continues even today. . . . A thorough history is here, beginning with the Greek concepts of 'elements,' discussing six scientists who influenced the creation of the table, and finishing with more modern influences such as radioactivity, quantum mechanics, and astrophysics." Choice
  Includes bibliographical references

Stwertka, Albert
A guide to the elements. 2nd ed. Oxford Univ.
Press 2002 246p il $37.50; pa $18.95 *
Grades: 9 10 11 12   **546**
1. Chemical elements
ISBN 0-19-515026-0; 0-19-515027-9 (pa)
LC 2002-282309
First published 1996
At head of title: Oxford. New edition in preparation
Presents the basic concepts of chemistry and explains
complex theories before offering a separate article on
each of the building blocks that make up the universe
Includes bibliographical references

West, Krista
Carbon chemistry. Chelsea House 2008 117p il
(Essential chemistry) lib bdg $35
Grades: 7 8 9 10   **546**
1. Carbon
ISBN 978-0-7910-9708-3; 0-7910-9708-0
LC 2007-51318
Explains how carbon is integrated into all facets of
life as we know it and discusses the unique properties of
this essential element.
"Annotated, colorful photographs and illustrations ap-
pear on most spreads, and boxed areas and sidebars high-
light specific subjects and areas. The explanations are
clear and detailed." SLJ
Includes glossary and bibliographical references

549   Mineralogy

Pellant, Chris
Rocks and minerals; Helen Pellant, editorial
consultant; photography by Harry Taylor. 2nd
American ed. Dorling Kindersley 2002 256p il
(Smithsonian handbooks) pa $20
Grades: 11 12 Adult   **549**
1. Rocks 2. Minerals
ISBN 0-7894-9106-0; 978-0-7894-9106-0
First published 1992 as part of the Eyewitness hand-
books series
This field guide to identification of rocks and minerals
includes techniques for collection and classification, and
facts about physical and chemical composition and formation.

Pough, Frederick H., 1906-2006
A field guide to rocks and minerals;
photographs by Jeff Scovil. 5th ed. Houghton
Mifflin 1996 396p il hardcover o.p. pa $20 *
Grades: 8 9 10 11 12   **549**
1. Minerals 2. Rocks
ISBN 0-395-72778-2; 0-395-91096-X (pa)
LC 94-49005
"The Peterson field guide series"
First published 1953
"Sponsored by the National Audubon Society, the Na-
tional Wildlife Federation, and the Roger Tory Peterson
Institute"

This illustrated guide utilizes traditional identification
methods and includes discussions of crystallography,
mineralogy and home laboratory techniques.
Includes bibliographical references

550   Earth sciences & geology

Earth; editor-in-chief, James F. Luhr. Compact ed.
DK Pub. 2007 520p il map pa $24.95 *
Grades: 8 9 10 11 12 Adult   **550**
1. Earth
ISBN 978-0-7566-3332-5; 0-7566-3332-X
LC 2007282646
First published 2003
At head of title: Smithsonian Institution
Presents an overview of the Earth, discussing its inter-
nal structure, the major features of its lands, mountains,
and oceans, its climate, weather, and place in the uni-
verse.

The **Facts** on File Earth science handbook; [by]
the Diagram Group. Rev. ed. Facts on File 2006
272p il (Facts on File science library) $35 *
Grades: 8 9 10 11 12   **550**
1. Earth sciences
ISBN 0-8160-5879-2   LC 2005-44692
First published 2000
This guide to earth sciences contains a dictionary with
around 1400 entries, a chronology, thumbnail biographies, an A to Z list of over 150 advances in earth science, and a list of Tyler Prize winners.
Includes bibliographical references

Williams, David B., 1965-
Stories in stone; travels through urban geology.
Walker 2009 260p il $26
Grades: 11 12 Adult   **550**
1. Urban geology
ISBN 978-0-8027-1622-4   LC 2009-5609
The author "describes the mineralogy and history of
some of the world's most common building materials.
. . . Each chapter showcases a different stone. By de-
scribing how the stones formed and how they are used,
this book reveals that natural and cultural history may lie
no farther than the building next door." Sci News
Includes bibliographical references

550.3   Earth sciences—
Encyclopedias and dictionaries

The **Facts** on File dictionary of earth science. Rev.
ed., edited by Jacqueline Smith. Facts on File
2006 388p il map $55 *
Grades: 11 12 Adult   **550.3**
1. Earth sciences—Dictionaries 2. Reference books
ISBN 0-8160-6000-2   LC 2006-42340
First published 1976 in the United Kingdom with title:
A dictionary of earth sciences.
In this reference work more than 3700 "cross-
referenced entries . . . cover all aspects of Earth science:
geomorphology, stratigraphy, mineralogy, petrology, cli-

The Facts on File dictionary of earth science—
Continued
matology, oceanography, paleontology, hydrology, geophysics, cartography, surveying, and soil science. Key concepts in physics, chemistry, biology, and mathematics are also defined." Publisher's note

Includes bibliographical references

Kusky, Timothy M.
Encyclopedia of Earth and space science; [by] Timothy Kusky; Katherine Cullen, managing editor. Facts on File 2010 2v il map (Facts on File science library) set $170
Grades: 9 10 11 12 Adult   **550.3**
1. Earth sciences—Encyclopedias 2. Space sciences—Encyclopedias 3. Reference books
ISBN 978-0-8160-7005-3   LC 2009-15655
"Topics are organized alphabetically and categorized by National Science Education Standards for Content, grades 9 through 12. Categories include Science as Inquiry, Energy in the Earth System, Geochemical Cycles, Origin and Evolution of the Earth System, Origin and Evolution of the Universe, Science and Technology, Science in Personal and Social Perspectives, History and Nature of Science, and Subdisciplines. Entries encompass beaches and shorelines, climate change, Copernicus, global warming, tsunamis, and volcanos. . . . This is an informative resource that displays the Earth's wonder. It will appeal to an audience of high school and college Earth science and astronomy classes." Libr J

Includes glossary and bibliographical references

551   Geology, hydrology, meteorology

Allaby, Michael, 1933-
Encyclopedia of weather and climate; [illustrations by Richard Garratt] Rev ed. Facts on File 2007 2v il (Facts on File science library) set $165 *
Grades: 11 12 Adult   **551**
1. Meteorology—Encyclopedias 2. Reference books
ISBN 0-8160-6350-8; 978-0-8160-6350-5
                                LC 2006-18295
First published 2002
"The main body of the encyclopedia consists of . . . entries describing processes such as cloud formation, atmospheric phenomena such as rainbows, and some of the techniques and instruments used to study the atmosphere, as well as the units of measurement that scientists use. The . . . coverage also includes the classification systems that are used for climate types, winds, and clouds. Ten appendixes contain . . . supplementary material—such as biographical notes on scientists and lists of the most severe tropical cyclones and tropical storms, weather disasters, and milestones in atmospheric research." Publisher's note

Includes bibliographical references

Cobb, Allan B.
Earth chemistry. Chelsea House 2008 130p il map (Essential chemistry) $35
Grades: 7 8 9 10   **551**
1. Environmental sciences 2. Chemistry
ISBN 978-0-7910-9677-2; 0-7910-9677-7
                                LC 2007-51317
This book explains "chemical or physical changes on Earth, exploring how the atmosphere, hydrosphere, lithosphere, and biosphere relate to and interact with one another." Publisher's note
"Annotated, colorful photographs and illustrations appear on most spreads, and boxed areas and sidebars highlight specific subjects and areas. The explanations are clear and detailed." SLJ

Includes glossary and bibliographical references

Lambert, David, 1932-
The field guide to geology; [by] David Lambert and the Diagram Group. New ed. Checkmark Books 2006 304p il map $39.95; pa $16.95 *
Grades: 11 12 Adult   **551**
1. Geology
ISBN   0-8160-6509-8;   978-0-8160-6509-7; 0-8160-6510-1 (pa); 978-0-8160-6510-3 (pa)
                                LC 2006-48533
First published 1988
This is an "overview of the processes that forged the planet and the technologies that have revolutionized the way that scientists investigate Earth's systems." Publisher's note

Includes bibliographical references

Plate tectonics, volcanoes, and earthquakes; edited by John P. Rafferty. Britannica Educational Pub. in association with Rosen Educational Services 2010 312p il map (Dynamic Earth) lib bdg $45 *
Grades: 6 7 8 9 10   **551**
1. Plate tectonics 2. Volcanoes 3. Earthquakes
ISBN 978-1-61530-106-5; 1-61530-106-2
                                LC 2009042303
"The 2010 earthquake in Haiti, threats to aviation from clouds of volcanic ash and aerosols, and recent changes in the Antarctic make . . . [this] a very updated resource. The process of plate tectonics and prior explanations of the dynamic nature of the earth is followed by explanations of volcanism and seismology. Charts and text describe significant volcanoes and earthquakes that have impacted humans throughout history. . . . [Recommended] for younger youth as well as high school youth since they are highly readable, with details concerning activities of interest to all ages." Voice Youth Advocates

Includes bibliographical references

551.1   Gross structure and properties of the earth

Tomecek, Steve
Plate tectonics. Chelsea House 2009 102p il
(Science foundations) lib bdg $35 *
Grades: 9 10 11 12   **551.1**
1. Plate tectonics
ISBN 978-1-60413-014-0; 1-60413-014-8
                       LC 2008-6054
Examines the evolution of plate tectonic theory from
its beginnings as a wild idea of drifting continents to its
acceptance as the main concept that drives geology to-
day.
This title offers "a wealth of material, including useful
further-reading lists. Great for curricular supplementation,
report writers, and science buffs." SLJ
Includes glossary and bibliographical references

551.2   Volcanoes, earthquakes, thermal waters and gases

Bolt, Bruce A., 1930-2005
Earthquakes; [by] Bruce Bolt. 5th ed. W.H.
Freeman and Co. 2005 390p il map pa $45.95 *
Grades: 9 10 11 12   **551.2**
1. Earthquakes
ISBN 0-7167-7548-4; 978-0-7167-7548-5
                      LC 2005-925607
Also available online
First published 1978
On cover: 2006 centennial update: the big one
The author "provides a brief overview of the history
of earthquakes and seismology, including topics such as
geologic faults, intensity patterns, side effects of earth-
quakes (such as tsunamis), and protection of people and
property." Publisher's note
Includes bibliographical references

Clarkson, Peter
Volcanoes. Voyageur Press 2000 39p il (World
life library) pa $16.95 *
Grades: 9 10 11 12   **551.2**
1. Volcanoes
ISBN 0-89658-502-6   LC 00-36465
This describes the physical nature of volcanoes and
explores many of the world's famous volcanoes and
eruptions, illustrated with color photos and diagrams
Includes bibliographical references

Gates, Alexander E.
Encyclopedia of earthquakes and volcanoes; [by]
Alexander E. Gates, PH.D and David Ritchie. 3rd
ed. Facts on File 2007 346p il map (Facts on File
science library) $75 *
Grades: 11 12 Adult   **551.2**
1. Reference books 2. Earthquakes—Encyclopedias
3. Volcanoes—Encyclopedias
ISBN 0-8160-6302-8   LC 2005-46619

First published 1994
"The book's entries cover information on key environmental issues, economic dilemmas, ethical concerns, advances in research and technology, organizations, and individuals who have left their mark on the fields of volcanology and seismology." Publisher's note
Includes bibliographical references

Kusky, Timothy M.
Earthquakes; plate tectonics and earthquake
hazards; [by] Timothy Kusky. Facts on File 2008
169p il map (Hazardous earth) $39.50 *
Grades: 9 10 11 12   **551.2**
1. Earthquakes 2. Plate tectonics
ISBN 978-0-8160-6462-5; 0-8160-6462-8
                      LC 2007-20832
"Presenting the main ideas of plate tectonics, this . . .
reference provides readers with an understanding of how,
why, and where most earthquakes occur. Coverage includes what happens during an earthquake, using many
examples of hazards such as landslides, passage of seis-
mic-earthquake waves through the ground, and other phenomena that people have encountered during real earthquakes." Publisher's note
Includes glossary and bibliographical references

Nardo, Don, 1947-
Volcanoes. Morgan Reynolds Pub. 2009 112p il
map (Extreme threats) lib bdg $28.95
Grades: 7 8 9 10   **551.2**
1. Volcanoes
ISBN 978-1-59935-118-6; 1-59935-118-8
                      LC 2009-25705
This book "begins with a vivid account of the 79 CE
eruption of Vesuvius, the cataclysm that buried Pompeii
and Herculaneum. Later chapters explore the development of volcanology, formation and location of volcanoes, volcanic avalanches, supervolcanoes and mass extinctions, and the bleak future of humanity with regard
to volcanoes. Throughout, Nardo references specific volcanoes and eruptions and brings the disasters to life by
including primary source quotes from witnesses and scientists." Voice Youth Advocates
Includes glossary and bibliographical references

551.3   Surface and exogenous processes and their agents

Fredston, Jill A.
Snowstruck; in the grip of avalanches; [by] Jill
Fredston. Harcourt 2005 342p il $24; pa $14 *
Grades: 11 12 Adult   **551.3**
1. Avalanches 2. Survival skills
ISBN   978-0-15-101249-7;   0-15-101249-0;
978-0-15-603254-4 (pa); 0-15-603254-6 (pa)
                      LC 2005-20454
"As avalanche experts, . . . [the author and her hus-
band] are often called upon to forecast, trigger, and teach
about avalanches as well as rescue survivors—or, sadly,
more often to recover remains. Fredston's decades of experience distilled into this instructive and personal narra-

Fredston, Jill A.—*Continued*

tive will leave readers with a newfound appreciation for the force, the fury, and the cold sorrow of avalanches." Libr J

Glaciers, sea ice, and ice formation; edited by John P. Rafferty. Britannica Educational Pub. in association with Rosen Educational Services 2010 253p il map (Dynamic Earth) lib bdg $45
Grades: 6 7 8 9 10   **551.3**
  1. Glaciers 2. Ice
  ISBN 978-1-61530-119-5; 1-61530-119-4
                 LC 2010000226

This book "examines the dynamic processes of [glaciers, sea ice, and ice formation]. . . . [It] provides the reader with an understanding of basic processes, historical background, and current phenomena. . . . [Recommended] for younger youth as well as high school youth." Voice Youth Advocates
Includes bibliographical references

Pollack, H. N.

A world without ice; [by] Henry Pollack. Avery 2009 287p il map $26; pa $16
Grades: 11 12 Adult   **551.3**
  1. Glaciers 2. Ice 3. Greenhouse effect
  ISBN 978-1-58333-357-0; 978-1-58333-407-2 (pa)
                LC 2009-30326

This is a "review of ice's unique qualities, its role in geological and human history and why it's disappearing from Earth's glaciers and polar regions." Kirkus
"Seldom has a scientist written so well and so clearly for the lay reader. Pollack's explanations of how researchers can tell that the climate is warming faster than normal are free of the usual scientific jargon and understandable. All readers concerned about global warming and students writing papers on the topic will want this excellent and important volume." Libr J
Includes bibliographical references

551.4   Geomorphology and hydrosphere

Aleshire, Peter

Mountains; foreword by Geoffrey H. Nash. Chelsea House Publishers 2008 144p il map (The extreme Earth) $35
Grades: 8 9 10 11 12   **551.4**
  1. Mountains
  ISBN 978-0-8160-5918-8; 0-8160-5918-7
                LC 2007-20692

This describes how mountains were formed, how they have changed over the span of geologic time, and their contributions to the environment, and goes on to describe specific mountains and mountain ranges including Mount Everest, the Appalachians, the Alps, the Mid-Atlantic Ridge of North America, the Sierra Nevadas, the Andes, Mauna Kea in Hawaii, Mount Saint Helens, Mount Kilimanjaro, and Humphreys Peak, in the southwestern United States.
Includes bibliographical references

Balliett, James Fargo

Mountains; environmental issues, global perspectives. M.E. Sharpe 2010 155p il map (Environmental issues, global perspectives) $55
Grades: 9 10 11 12   **551.4**
  1. Mountains
  ISBN 978-0-7656-8228-4   LC 2010-12121

"The case studies in *Mountains* consider how global warming in East Africa is harming Mount Kenya's regional population, examine the fragile ecology of New Zealand's Southern Alps, and discuss the impact of mountain use over time in New Hampshire's White Mountains, among other critical issues." Publisher's note
Includes glossary and bibliographical references

Collier, Michael, 1950-

Over the coasts. Mikaya Press 2009 120p il map (An aerial view of geology) $34.95
Grades: 9 10 11 12   **551.4**
  1. Geology—North America 2. Coasts 3. Aerial photography
  ISBN 1-931414-42-4; 978-1-931414-42-5
                LC 2009-75245

This volume of aerial photography examines "coastal processes: how waves interact with promontories, dunes, sand spits, barrier islands and human constructions." Publ Wkly
Includes glossary and bibliographical references

Hanson, Erik A.

Canyons; [by] Erik Hanson; foreword by Geoffrey H. Nash. Chelsea House 2007 206p il map (The extreme Earth) $35
Grades: 8 9 10 11 12   **551.4**
  1. Canyons 2. Plate tectonics
  ISBN 0-8160-6435-0; 978-0-8160-6435-9
                LC 2006-15810

Profiles canyons around the world including the Grand Canyon, the Columbia River Gorge, Fish River Canyon, and Monterey Canyon; and describes how and when they were formed, how the landscape has changed over time, and the contribution of each to the environment.
"The story in this book may generate a longing within the reader to visit vistas and hike into canyons for an intimate view of earth history." Sci Books Films
Includes glossary and bibliographical references

Hanson, Jeanne K.

Caves; foreword by Geoffrey H. Nash. Chelsea House 2007 142p il map (The extreme Earth) $35
Grades: 8 9 10 11 12   **551.4**
  1. Caves
  ISBN 978-0-8160-5917-1; 0-8160-5917-9
                LC 2006-11718

The describes types of caves and how they are formed, their exploration, and some specific caves including Mammoth Cave of Kentucky; the caves of Yucatan, Mexico; Lascaux Cave of southwestern France; Lubang Nasib Bagus and the Sarawak Chamber of Borneo, Malaysia; Kazumura Cave of Hawaii; Waitomo Cave of New Zealand; and Wind Cave of South Dakota.
Includes bibliographical references

551.46 Hydrosphere and submarine geology. Oceanography

Aleshire, Peter

Ocean ridges and trenches; foreword by Geoffrey H. Nash. Chelsea House 2007 148p il map (The extreme Earth) $35

Grades: 8 9 10 11 12   **551.46**
1. Ocean bottom 2. Marine ecology
ISBN 978-0-8160-5919-5; 0-8160-5919-5
                              LC 2006-32058

Provides information about the formation of ocean ridges and trenches. Includes ten examples of ridges and trenches from around the world.

Includes bibliographical references

Day, Trevor, 1955-

Oceans; illustrations by Richard Garratt. rev ed. Facts on File 2008 318p il map (Ecosystem) $70

Grades: 8 9 10 11 12 Adult   **551.46**
1. Ocean 2. Oceanography
ISBN 0-8160-5932-2; 978-0-8160-5932-4
                              LC 2006-100769
First published 1999

This volume describes the oceans of the world with regard to their geography, geology, history, chemistry, biology, ecology, exploration, relationship to the atmosphere, economic resources, and management.

Includes glossary and bibliographical references

Desonie, Dana

Oceans; how we use the seas. Chelsea House 2007 215p il map (Our fragile planet) $35

Grades: 8 9 10 11 12   **551.46**
1. Ocean 2. Oceanography 3. Marine ecology
ISBN 978-0-8160-6216-4; 0-8160-6216-1
                              LC 2007-13560

An introduction to how life in our oceans works, and how we are threatening it with pollution and depletion of fisheries.

The author "offers a comprehensive, detailed introduction to ocean science and conservation in this amply illustrated volume." Booklist

Includes glossary and bibliographical references

Hohn, Donovan

Moby-duck; the true story of 28,800 bath toys lost at sea and of the beachcombers, oceanographers, environmentalists, and fools, including the author, who went in search of them. Viking 2011 402p il map $27.95

Grades: 11 12 Adult   **551.46**
1. Ocean currents 2. Toys
ISBN 978-0-670-02219-9; 0-670-02219-5
                              LC 2010-33608

"On Jan. 10, 1992, a container ship traveling south of the Aleutians, . . . en route from Hong Kong to Tacoma, Wash., took a steep roll and lost part of its cargo. . . . Among the lost merchandise were 7,200 packs of bathtub toys. . . . This came to be erroneously understood as the story of 29,000 rubber duckies set adrift and washing up all over the globe. . . . [This book is Hohn's exploration of] the Duck Armada fable." N Y Times (Late N Y Ed)

This "book is a thoroughly engaging environmental/travel title that crosses partisan divides with its solid research and apolitical nature." Booklist

Includes bibliographical references

Hutchinson, S., 1959-

Oceans: a visual guide; [by] Stephen Hutchinson [and] Lawrence E. Hawkins. Firefly Books 2005 303p il map $29.95 *

Grades: 11 12 Adult   **551.46**
1. Oceanography 2. Marine biology
ISBN 1-55407-069-4

"Beginning with the birth of the oceans, the 'cradle of life,' the authors explain tides, salinity, currents, waves, and the diverse and complex ecosystems of the polar, equatorial, and temperate oceans with diagrams, photographs, and concise and clear commentary." Booklist

Kusky, Timothy M.

Tsunamis; giant waves from the sea; [by] Timothy Kusky. Facts on File 2008 134p il (The hazardous Earth) $39.50

Grades: 8 9 10 11 12   **551.46**
1. Tsunamis
ISBN 978-0-8160-6464-9; 0-8160-6464-4
                              LC 2007-23477

"This detailed study of the causes and physics of massive waves covers not only the oceanic sort but also similar phenomena, 'seiches,' that occur in closed bodies of water. . . . After analyzing tsunamis' various forms and behaviors, Kusky delivers harrowing accounts of over a dozen disasters, from those centuries past to the devastating Indian Ocean tsunami in 2004. He then closes with a discussion of early-warning systems. Occasional photos capture the devastation of which these waves are capable." Booklist

Includes bibliographical references

Nichols, C. Reid

Encyclopedia of marine science; [by] C. Reid Nichols and Robert G. Williams. Facts on File 2009 626p il map (Facts on File science library) $85 *

Grades: 11 12 Adult   **551.46**
1. Marine sciences—Encyclopedias 2. Reference books
ISBN 978-0-8160-5022-2; 0-8160-5022-8
                              LC 2007-45166

This "book consists of (a) some 600 encyclopedic definitions of applied science, technology, and engineering terms, (b) twenty 'Feature Essays' distributed among the encyclopedic definitions, and (c) a set of appendices." Sci Books Films

"The expert contributors have packed these pages with top-notch information that will be invaluable to students and reference librarians." SLJ

Includes bibliographical references

Prager, Ellen J., 1962-

Chasing science at sea; racing hurricanes, stalking sharks, and living undersea with ocean experts; [by] Ellen Prager. University of Chicago Press 2008 162p il $22.50; pa $13

Grades: 11 12 Adult   **551.46**

1. Oceanography

ISBN   978-0-226-67870-2;   0-226-67870-9; 978-0-226-67874-0 (pa); 0-226-67874-1 (pa)

LC 2007-49486

This book "assembles anecdotes from colleagues such as marine biologists, geologists and engineers. Their tales range from divers chasing parrotfish poo with plastic bags to oceanographers seeing an actual step in the surface of the sea at the edge of the Gulf Stream. In bringing these briny tales together, Prager explores some of their common themes to convey why many of us study the ocean—and why it matters." Times Higher Ed

"Written in a welcoming, conversational tone, the book not only entertains but delivers some important lessons that will prove useful to any student considering a career in field research." Choice

Includes bibliographical references

Stow, Dorrik A. V.

Oceans: an illustrated reference; [by] Dorrik Stow. University of Chicago Press 2006 c2005 256p il map $55 *

Grades: 11 12 Adult   **551.46**

1. Oceanography 2. Ocean 3. Marine biology

ISBN 0-226-77664-6   LC 2004-55333

"An Andromeda book"

This "reference work presents a thorough overview of the physical, geological, chemical, and biological properties of the world's oceans. . . . [The author's] up-to-date and well-organized volume would make a valuable introduction to a huge field of knowledge." Libr J

Includes bibliographical references

Ulanski, Stan L., 1946-

The Gulf Stream; tiny plankton, giant bluefin, and the amazing story of the powerful river in the Atlantic; [by] Stan Ulanski. University of North Carolina Press 2008 212p il map $28; pa $22

Grades: 11 12 Adult   **551.46**

1. Gulf Stream

ISBN   978-0-8078-3217-2;   0-8078-3217-0; 978-0-8078-8709-7 (pa); 0-8078-8709-9 (pa)

LC 2008-4746

"A Caravan book"

This "book provides the layperson a synopsis of the physical origin, general biology, and rich exploration history of the Gulf Stream. Ulanski . . . offers a concise, engaging blend of science and history for anyone interested in learning about the general flow dynamics, the intricate food webs, and the human use and exploitation of this vital western-boundary current of the North Atlantic Ocean." Choice

Includes bibliographical references

Yount, Lisa

Modern marine science; exploring the deep. Chelsea House 2006 204p il map (Milestones in discovery and invention) $35

Grades: 7 8 9 10 11 12   **551.46**

1. Marine sciences

ISBN 0-8160-5747-8   LC 2005-30562

This book "profiles 12 men and women who led the way into the oceans' deepest waters through research and new technologies. From Charles Darwin to Henry Stommel to Robert Ballard, this volume explores the lives and accomplishments of these scientific revolutionaries." Publisher's note

Includes glossary and bibliographical references

551.48   Hydrology

Burnham, Laurie

Rivers; foreword by Geoffrey H. Nash. Chelsea House 2007 176p il map (The extreme Earth) $35

Grades: 8 9 10 11 12   **551.48**

1. Rivers

ISBN 0-8160-5916-0; 978-0-8160-5916-4

LC 2006-31302

This is a "portrait of 10 of the most unusual rivers that examines what was on-site before the river, how it was formed, how and why it has changed over time, and its contributions to the environment." Publisher's note

Includes glossary and bibliographical references

Collier, Michael, 1950-

Over the rivers. Mikaya 2008 128p il (An aerial view of geology) $34.95

Grades: 9 10 11 12   **551.48**

1. Geology—North America 2. Rivers 3. Aerial photography

ISBN 1-931414-21-1; 978-1-931414-21-0

LC 2008-60051

"This book contains stunning photographs illustrating the geological dynamics of many rivers in the continental United States, such as the Colorado, Mississippi, and Green rivers. This would be a great text for an Earth science classroom to enhance the study of weathering, erosion, and deposition in the development of landscapes sculpted by running water." National Science Teachers Association

Includes bibliographical references

Hanson, Jeanne K.

Lakes; foreword, Geoffrey H. Nash. Facts on File 2007 146p il map (The extreme Earth) $35

Grades: 8 9 10 11 12   **551.48**

1. Lakes

ISBN 978-0-8160-5914-0; 0-8160-5914-4

LC 2005-34327

This describes how lakes are formed, the current environmental health of the lakes and their future prognosis, and some specific bodies of water including the Caspian Sea in the Middle East, the Aral Sea in Western Asia, Lake Superior in North America, Lake Baikal in Central Asia, and Lake Titicaca in South America.

Includes bibliographical references

551.5   Meteorology

Allaby, Michael, 1933-

A chronology of weather; illustrations by Richard Garratt. Rev. ed. Facts on File 2004 196p il (Dangerous weather) $35

Grades: 9 10 11 12   **551.5**

1. Weather—Chronology 2. Natural disasters—Chronology 3. Reference books

ISBN 0-8160-4792-8; 978-0-8160-4792-5

LC 2003-4000

First published 1998

The author answers "questions students and non-specialists have about weather and provides a general overview of the . . . information that shapes the way weather is understood and studied. Features include discussion of how the climates of the world have changed over the centuries; a 5,000-year chronology of dangerous weather, from ca. 3200 BCE to the present; and a chronology of discoveries listing important developments in the understanding of weather." Publisher's note

Includes glossary and bibliographical references

Buckley, Bruce

Weather: a visual guide; [by] Bruce Buckley, Edward J. Hopkins [and] Richard Whitaker. Firefly Books 2004 303p il maps $29.95; pa $27.95

Grades: 11 12 Adult   **551.5**

1. Weather 2. Meteorology

ISBN 1-55297-957-1; 978-1-55297-957-0; 1-55407-430-4 (pa); 978-1-55407-430-3 (pa)

LC 2004-303909

The authors "set the local and seasonal conditions that every person experiences within the context of the global forces that generate weather. Each force, such as giant atmospheric convection cells, is illustrated with a combination of a diagram, satellite photographs, ground-level photographs (often depicting the destruction wrought by violent storms), and . . . captions." Booklist

This is "a comprehensive academic resource with information and glorious color photographs on virtually every aspect of weather." SLJ

Casper, Julie Kerr

Climate systems; interactive forces of global warming. Facts on File 2009 219p il map (Global warming) $40

Grades: 9 10 11 12   **551.5**

1. Climate 2. Greenhouse effect

ISBN 978-0-8160-7260-6; 0-8160-7260-4

LC 2008-40921

"This volume concentrates on the science behind the current [global warming] crisis. The many full-color charts, maps, and graphs aid in understanding the large concepts of the global-climate system, the carbon cycle, plate tectonics and its effects on climate change, local and planetary motions in the atmosphere, and ocean currents. . . . This is an intricate and convoluted subject, but Casper does a good job of explaining the basic science behind the controversy." SLJ

Includes glossary and bibliographical references

Desonie, Dana

Atmosphere; air pollution and its effects. Chelsea House 2007 194p il map (Our fragile planet) $35

Grades: 9 10 11 12   **551.5**

1. Atmosphere 2. Weather 3. Meteorology

ISBN 978-0-8160-6213-3; 0-8160-6213-7

LC 2007-8241

"From the basics defining what is atmosphere and its role in supporting and protecting all life to the more complex issues that have become front page news such as the hole in the ozone layer, air pollution, skin cancer, global warming, and . . . Hurricane Katrina, this book helps the reader delve into the background information that is necessary in understanding why things work the way they do." Libr Media Connect

Includes glossary and bibliographical references

The **Facts** on File dictionary of weather and climate; edited by Jacqueline Smith. Rev. ed. Facts on File 2006 262p il map (Facts on File science library) $49.50 *

Grades: 9 10 11 12 Adult   **551.5**

1. Meteorology—Dictionaries 2. Reference books

ISBN 0-8160-6296-X; 978-0-8160-6296-6

LC 2006-42865

First published 2001

This volume includes "definitions for more than 2000 terms and concepts drawn from meteorology, climatology, and related geoscience disciplines. Entries are conveniently cross-referenced and include common acronyms. More than 60 line drawings complement definitions. The book features useful appendices providing a chronology of important events in the atmospheric sciences and unit conversion tables." Sci Books Films [review of 2001 edition]

Includes bibliographical references

Gunn, Angus M., 1920-

A student guide to climate and weather. Greenwood Press 2010 5v il map set $255

Grades: 9 10 11 12   **551.5**

1. Climate 2. Meteorology 3. Reference books

ISBN 978-0-313-35568-4; 978-0-313-35569-1 (ebook)

LC 2009-42256

Contact producer for ebook pricing

"These volumes discuss the scientific processes that pertain to weather and climate, and the specific ways that weather and climate impact human life." Booklist

Includes glossary and bibliographical references

Harper, Kristine

Weather and climate; decade by decade. Facts on File 2007 xxi, 250p il map (Twentieth-century science) $49.50

Grades: 9 10 11 12   **551.5**

1. Meteorology 2. Climate 3. Physical sciences

ISBN 978-0-8160-5535-7; 0-8160-5535-1

LC 2006-12549

This book traces the "transformation of the study of weather phenomena and climatic conditions into the scientific disciplines of meteorology and climatology. This . . . volume discusses how scientists radically changed

Harper, Kristine—*Continued*

their ideas about weather and climate during the course of the 20th century." Publisher's note

Includes bibliographical references

Streissguth, Thomas

Extreme weather; [by] Tom Streissguth; Michael E. Mann, consulting editor. Greenhaven Press/Gale, Cengage Learning 2011 116p il map (Confronting global warming) $37.10

Grades: 10 11 12   **551.5**
    1. Climate—Environmental aspects 2. Weather
    ISBN 978-0-7377-4859-8; 0-7377-4859-1
                                      LC 2010-24973
"Explores the relationship between global climate change and extreme weather, including air and water chemistry; solar radiation; hurricanes and tropical cyclones; heat waves and other potential future warming; drought, from the Dust Bowl of the 1930s to the current water crisis in California; and the impacts of rainfall, flooding, and El Niño." Publisher's note

Includes glossary and bibliographical references

Walker, Gabrielle

An ocean of air; why the wind blows and other mysteries of the atmosphere. Harcourt 2007 272p il map $25

Grades: 11 12 Adult   **551.5**
    1. Atmosphere
    ISBN 978-0-15-101124-7; 0-15-101124-9
                                      LC 2006-32359
Walker sets out "to unite stories of human research into air pressure, the gases that make up air, the movement of the wind, the ozone layer, ionosphere and outer space, in a history of our atmospheric discovery." New Statesman (Engl)

The author "brings a new perspective to centuries-old stories of wonder and discovery and sheds light on the personalities of the 19th and 20th centuries who have also contributed to the world's body of knowledge. Witty and full of fascinating information, this is a captivating book." Libr J

Includes bibliographical references

Williams, Jack, 1936-

The AMS weather book; the ultimate guide to America's weather. University of Chicago Press 2009 316p il map $35 *

Grades: 9 10 11 12 Adult   **551.5**
    1. Weather 2. Climate 3. Meteorology
    ISBN 978-0-226-89898-8; 0-226-89898-9
                                      LC 2008-35916
"Copublished with the American Meteorological Society"

This book "provides a clearly written, profusely illustrated narrative guide to weather that affects the US. . . . Topics in this 12-chapter volume range from how rainbows are formed and what makes the wind blow, to climate change and how weather satellites work. In addition, Williams highlights profiles of meteorologists and other scientists influential in weather prediction and research, including many women and minorities. This

work, with its attractive, easy-to-understand graphics, offers a useful, engaging basic introduction to a wide variety of weather-related topics." Choice

Includes glossary

551.51 Composition, regions, dynamics of atmosphere

Amato, Joseph Anthony

Dust; a history of the small and the invisible; {by} Joseph A. Amato. University of Calif. Press 2000 288p il hardcover o.p. pa $15.95 *

Grades: 11 12 Adult   **551.51**
    1. Dust 2. Science—Philosophy
    ISBN 0-520-21875-2; 0-520-23195-3 (pa)
                                      LC 99-27115
The author "writes only incidentally about dust; rather, he reviews how humanity's view of the unseen world changed throughout the ages as the ability to see it, through magnification, increased. . . . Amato touches on such diverse topics as the role of light in art, germ theory and medical advances, particle physics, and the effect of artificially made dusts on the environment. He concludes with a philosophical view of the future of humanity as medical and scientific advances takes it into uncharted waters." Choice

Includes bibliographical references

Bowen, Mark

Thin ice; unlocking the secrets of climate in the world's highest mountains. Henry Holt 2005 463p il $30; pa $17 *

Grades: 11 12 Adult   **551.51**
    1. Upper atmosphere 2. Climate—Research
    ISBN 0-8050-6443-5; 0-8050-8135-6 (pa)
                                      LC 2005-40426
"A John Macrae book"

The author "documents the specialized techniques that Thompson used to extract and preserve ice cores from the highest mountains around the world's equator while also examining Thompson's research, which is based on the provocative premise that equatorial mountain glaciers, rather than polar ice, provide the clues to understanding global warming." Libr J

"This book will appeal to mountaineering and climatology buffs, but should be read by everyone concerned about the future of our planet." Publ Wkly

Holmes, Hannah, 1963-

The secret life of dust; from the cosmos to the kitchen counter, the big consequences of little things. Wiley 2001 240p hardcover o.p. pa $14.95

Grades: 11 12 Adult   **551.51**
    1. Dust 2. Science—Philosophy
    ISBN 0-471-37743-0; 0-471-42635-0 (pa)
                                      LC 2001-22368
"Holmes explores how dust has been crucial in the birth of planets, how it affects the earth's environment and weather, and how humans create it as well. Out to communicate straight facts and science, she considers technical points in language that is clear and comprehen-

Holmes, Hannah, 1963-—*Continued*
sible even for those lacking a science background. In addition to the bibliography, Holmes provides a listing of web sites for each chapter so that readers may easily obtain current information and graphics." Libr J

Includes bibliographical references

551.55 Atmospheric disturbances and formations

Emanuel, Kerry A., 1955-
Divine wind; the history and science of hurricanes; [by] Kerry Emanuel. Oxford Univ. Press 2005 285p il $45 *

Grades: 11 12 Adult   551.55
1. Hurricanes
ISBN 0-19-514941-6   LC 2004-13078
This is a study of hurricanes.
"A gripping popular treatment of peril, that will have great resonance in light of recent disasters." Booklist

Includes bibliographical references

Leatherman, Stephen P.
Hurricanes; causes, effects, and the future; by Stephen P. Leatherman and Jack Williams. MBI Pub. Company 2008 72p il (World life library) pa $17.99

Grades: 7 8 9 10   551.55
1. Hurricanes
ISBN 978-0-7603-2992-4   LC 2008-9851
This is a guide to "hurricanes past and present, from the historic Galveston storm of 1900 to the devastating Katrina. . . . The authors explain the formidable wind speed, the heavy rains, and the eye of the hurricane." Publisher's note

Levine, Mark
F5; devastation, survival, and the most violent tornado outbreak of the twentieth century. Miramax Books 2007 307p il map $25.95

Grades: Adult   551.55
1. Tornadoes
ISBN 978-1-4013-5220-2; 1-4013-5220-0
"In April 1974, 148 tornadoes swept across 13 states, killing or wounding hundreds of people, destroying thousands of homes, and causing damage in the billions of dollars. Six of the twisters were of the deadliest variety, the rare category F5. Levine tells this often heartbreaking story by focusing not on the destruction . . . but on the people." Booklist

The author "turns the laconic detail, thorough compression and rhythmic nuance of his best verse to sensational use, producing a work of reportage so artfully structured that it looks pretty good next to 'In Cold Blood.'" N Y Times Book Rev

Includes bibliographical references

Longshore, David
Encyclopedia of hurricanes, typhoons, and cyclones. New ed. Facts on File 2008 468p il map (Facts on File science library) $75

Grades: 8 9 10 11 12 Adult   551.55
1. Hurricanes—Encyclopedias 2. Typhoons—Encyclopedias 3. Cyclones—Encyclopedias 4. Reference books
ISBN 978-0-8160-6295-9; 0-8160-6295-1
LC 2007-32336
First published 1998
This encyclopedia describes named hurricanes, typhoons and cyclones, explains meteorological terms and instruments, and includes biographical data, a chronology, and a list of hurricane safety procedures.
"This is an excellent basic reference work that belongs in all school, public, and academic libraries." Sci Books Films

Includes bibliographical references

Storms, violent winds, and earth's atmosphere; edited by John P. Rafferty. Britannica Educational Pub. in association with Rosen Educational Services 2010 249p il (Dynamic Earth) lib bdg $45

Grades: 6 7 8 9 10   551.55
1. Storms 2. Winds 3. Atmosphere
ISBN 978-1-61530-114-0   LC 2009049109
"This book examines the science that gives us a greater understanding of the patterns that produce hurricanes, tornadoes, cyclones, and a host of related conditions." Publisher's note

Includes bibliographical references

551.6 Climatology and weather

Climate change; in context; Brenda Wilmoth Lerner & K. Lee Lerner, editors. Gale, Cengage Learning 2008 2v il map set $257

Grades: 9 10 11 12   551.6
1. Climate—Environmental aspects—Encyclopedias 2. Reference books
ISBN 978-1-4144-3614-2   LC 2007-51762
"Designed to explain 'the complexity of the 2007 Intergovernmental Panel on Climate Change (IPCC) reports to younger students,' the volumes contain 250 articles contributed by various science writers and academics in geology, law, and environmental science." Booklist
"An excellent resource for research papers and opposing-viewpoint debates that will motivate students to consider carefully all aspects of environmental changes while challenging them to discover solutions." Libr J

Includes bibliographical references

Dow, Kirstin, 1963-
The atlas of climate change; mapping the world's greatest challenge; [by] Kirstin Dow and Thomas E. Downing. Rev. and updated. University of California Press 2007 112p il map pa $21.95 *

Grades: 11 12 Adult   551.6
1. Climate—Environmental aspects—Maps 2. Atlases 3. Reference books
ISBN 978-0-520-25558-6   LC 2010-483727

Dow, Kirstin, 1963——*Continued*
First published 2006
"This atlas examines the causes of climate change and considers its possible impact on subsistence, water resources, ecosystems, biodiversity, health, coastal megacities, and cultural treasures. It reviews historical contributions to greenhouse gas levels, progress in meeting international commitments, and local efforts to meet the challenge of climate change." Publisher's note
Includes bibliographical references

The **encyclopedia** of weather and climate change; a complete visual guide. University of California Press 2010 512p il map $39.95 *
Grades: 9 10 11 12 Adult   551.6
  1. Climate—Environmental aspects—Encyclopedias 2. Meteorology—Encyclopedias 3. Reference books
  ISBN 978-0-520-26101-3   LC 2009-943908
"Major sections fall under the following headings: Engine, Action, Extremes, Watching, Climate, and Change. Chapters within the sections begin with a broad overview of a particular topic, then move on to greater detail. The regional climate guide, focusing on 43 specific locations around the world, is particularly noteworthy. . . . The profuse illustrations carry the information; this title could be just the thing for visual learners." Libr J
Includes glossary

Fagan, Brian M., 1936-
The Little Ice Age; how climate made history 1300-1850; [by] Brian Fagan. Basic Bks. 2000 xxi, 246p il maps hardcover o.p. pa $16.95
Grades: 11 12 Adult   551.6
  1. Climate 2. Europe—History
  ISBN 0-465-02271-5; 0-465-02272-3 (pa)
                               LC 00-48627
"During the Little Ice Age—approximately the 14th to the mid-19th centuries—the climate of northern Europe turned volatile and markedly cooler. . . . [The author explains how] it catalyzed significant social, political, and economic changes throughout the region." Libr J
Includes bibliographical references

The long summer: how climate changed civilization. Basic Books 2003 284p il hardcover o.p. pa $16
Grades: 11 12 Adult   551.6
  1. Climate 2. Civilization—History
  ISBN 0-465-02281-2; 0-465-02282-0 (pa)
                            LC 2003-13917
Fagan discusses global climate change and its relation to human society. He "argues that as humans have organized themselves in increasingly complex ways, their susceptibility to large-scale devastation wrought by climate change has also risen. Ice Age hunter-gatherers were vulnerable to the vagaries of their harsh world, but they had a 'flexibility, mobility, and opportunism' that allowed them to move on if their immediate environment became too difficult. As people formed villages, cities, and empires, they became rooted to environments that inevitably changed." Archaeology
"This book is highly recommended for general audiences considering the implications and the challenges posed by human-induced global climate change." Sci Books Films
Includes bibliographical references

Flannery, Tim F. (Tim Fridjof), 1956-
We are the weather makers; the history of climate change; [by] Tim Flannery; adapted by Sally M. Walker. Candlewick Press 2009 303p il map $17.99
Grades: 7 8 9 10   551.6
  1. Climate—Environmental aspects 2. Greenhouse effect
  ISBN 978-0-7636-3656-2; 0-7636-3656-8
                            LC 2008-939840
An adaptation of The weather makers, published 2005 for adults by Atlantic Monthly Press
"Arguing that climate change and global warming affect us all and that we can be part of the solution, this comprehensive look at the issue includes a clear explanation of the mechanism of the carbon cycle, the role of greenhouse gases on Earth, historical instances of climate change and their causes, descriptions of effects on a variety of habitats, future scenarios and suggestions—both personal and global—about what might be done. . . . A copy belongs in every middle and high-school library." Kirkus
Includes bibliographical references

Fleming, James R.
Fixing the sky; the checkered history of weather and climate control; [by] James Rodger Fleming. Columbia University Press 2010 325p il (Columbia studies in international and global history) $27.95
Grades: 9 10 11 12 Adult   551.6
  1. Weather control 2. Human influence on nature
  ISBN 978-0-231-14412-4   LC 2010-15482
This is a "look at the history of weather modification and similar efforts." N Y Times (Late N Y Ed)
This book "should be read by all who want a better understanding of global climate change and the debate over geoengineering our environment." Sci Books Films
Includes bibliographical references

George, Charles, 1949-
Climate change research; [by] Charles George and Linda George. ReferencePoint Press 2010 c2011 96p il (Inside science) lib bdg $26.95
Grades: 7 8 9 10 11 12   551.6
  1. Climate—Environmental aspects
  ISBN 978-1-60152-128-6; 1-60152-128-6
                            LC 2009-53704
"This title examines the science behind climate change research in the following chapters: What is Climate Change?; Reading Climate Change in the Earth; Temperature and Precipitation; Climate Models; and Climate Technology of the Future." Publisher's note
Includes bibliographical references

Kusky, Timothy M.
Climate change; shifting glaciers, deserts, and climate belts; [by] Timothy Kusky. Facts on File 2009 156p il map (The hazardous Earth) $39.50
Grades: 8 9 10 11 12   551.6
  1. Climate—Environmental aspects 2. Greenhouse effect
  ISBN 978-0-8160-6466-3; 0-8160-6466-0
                            LC 2008-5134

Kusky, Timothy M.—*Continued*

"This is a terrific collection of all of the pertinent science about how climate works, how human activity is affecting climate, and how the earth is responding. Not only is climate science well explained, but there are also detailed examples of how various cultures and regions are being affected by changes in climate." Sci Books Films

Includes glossary and bibliographical references

Nardo, Don, 1947-

Climate change. Morgan Reynolds Pub. 2009 112p il (Extreme threats) lib bdg $28.95

Grades: 7 8 9 10   **551.6**

1. Climate—Environmental aspects 2. Greenhouse effect

ISBN 978-1-59935-119-3; 1-59935-119-6

                       LC 2009-25704

This book about climate change has "black-and-white and color photographs on almost every page. . . . Frequent sidebars, covering as much as a spread, discuss peripheral and often unusual information. The conclusion . . . explains what scientists are doing, or what they anticipate doing, to ameliorate the threat." SLJ

Includes glossary and bibliographical references

Philander, S. George, 1942-

Our affair with El Niño; how we transformed an enchanting Peruvian current into a global climate hazard. Princeton University Press 2004 275p il maps hardcover o.p. pa $17.95 *

Grades: 11 12 Adult   **551.6**

1. El Niño Current 2. Climate

ISBN 0-691-11335-1; 0-691-12622-4 (pa)

                       LC 2003-44235

"The book begins by outlining the history of El Niño, an innocuous current that appears off the coast of Peru around Christmastime—its name refers to the Child Jesus—and originally was welcomed as a blessing. It goes on to explore how our perceptions of El Niño were transformed." Publisher's note

"This is an exceptional book, enjoyable to read and educational at several levels. El Niño is the springboard for a book that thoroughly explains the phenomenon and even goes far beyond it." Sci Books Films

Includes bibliographical references

551.63   Weather forecasting and forecasts, reporting and reports

Cullen, Heidi

The weather of the future; heat waves, extreme storms, and other scenes from a climate-changed planet. HarperCollins 2010 329p il map $25.99; pa $15.99

Grades: 11 12 Adult   **551.63**

1. Climate—Environmental aspects 2. Forecasting

ISBN   978-0-06-172688-0;   0-06-172688-5; 978-0-06-172694-1 (pa); 0-06-172694-X (pa)

This "study predicts global warming scenarios for seven hot spots around the world—and evaluates the re-

sponses of communities, governments, and international organizations." Publ Wkly

"A lively and troubling but not entirely doomsday scenario of our warmer future, which will hopefully persuade readers to pay greater attention." Kirkus

Includes bibliographical references

551.7   Historical geology

Alvarez, Walter, 1940-

T. rex and the Crater of Doom. Princeton Univ. Press 1997 185p il $35

Grades: 11 12 Adult   **551.7**

1. Catastrophes (Geology) 2. Dinosaurs

ISBN 0-691-01630-5   LC 96-49208

The author relates the story of how he "along with four other Berkeley scientists, found the geologic evidence that implicated a cosmic collision in the extinction of the dinosaurs. . . . {Their research involved} the evaluation of a thin iridium-rich layer of clay found in Italy and the search for an impact crater." Booklist

This book "gets the facts across in a lighthearted, almost playful manner. But it's also solid science, a clear and efficient exposition." N Y Times Book Rev

Includes bibliographical references

Fortey, Richard A.

Earth; an intimate history; by Richard Fortey. Knopf 2004 429p il hardcover o.p. pa $19

Grades: 11 12 Adult   **551.7**

1. Stratigraphic geology

ISBN 0-375-40626-3; 0-375-70620-8 (pa)

                       LC 2004-46470

The author "relates his walks in places that visually reveal the deep earth (Vesuvius, Hawaii, the Grand Canyon) as well as sites, which, if not so spectacular, contain puzzling elements that provoked great interpretive controversies. . . . The Alps, the Scottish Highlands, Newfoundland, the Deccan Traps of India—these are among Fortey's destinations as he explains the theory of plate tectonics, showing how the theory came to be, as well as the continents and oceans whose skein of connections it explains. This is a marvelously inviting presentation." Booklist

Includes bibliographical references

552   Petrology

Bishop, A. C. (Arthur Clive)

Guide to minerals, rocks & fossils. Firefly Books 2005 336p il pa $19.95 *

Grades: 9 10 11 12   **552**

1. Rocks 2. Fossils 3. Minerals

ISBN 1-55407-054-6   LC 2005-280972

First published 1974 in the United Kingdom with title: The Hamlyn guide to minerals, rocks, and fossils; 1999 edition published by Cambridge Univ. Press with title: Cambridge guide to minerals, rocks, and fossils

"Minerals, rocks, and fossils are described, illustrated, explained, and related to their natural environment in this

Bishop, A. C. (Arthur Clive)—*Continued*
splendid compact volume. . . . As a most useful field guide for explorers or as a straightforward, beautifully illustrated and written general reference, this book is unparalleled." Choice
Includes bibliographical references

Coenraads, Robert Raymond, 1956-
Rocks and fossils; a visual guide; [by] Robert R. Coenraads. Firefly Books 2005 304p il $29.95
Grades: 11 12 Adult   552
1. Rocks 2. Fossils 3. Minerals
ISBN 1-55407-068-6
In this "introduction to geology and paleontology . . . [the author presents the] facts of how fossils are formed, how rocks are formed, and how plate tectonics work. . . . A science work perfectly suited for general use." Booklist

553.2 Carbonaceous materials

Freese, Barbara
Coal: a human history. Penguin Books 2004 304p il pa $15
Grades: 11 12 Adult   553.2
1. Coal
ISBN 978-0-14-200098-4
First published 2003 by Perseus Bks.
This is "an engrossing account of the comparatively cheap, usually dirty fuel that supported the Industrial Revolution, inspired the building of canals and railroads to move it, and once made London and Pittsburgh famous for their air." N Y Times Book Rev
Includes bibliographical references

553.6 Other economic materials

Kurlansky, Mark
Salt: a world history. Penguin Books 2003 484p il map pa $16 *
Grades: 11 12 Adult   553.6
1. Salt
ISBN 0-14-200161-9   LC 2004-270006
First published 2002 by Walker & Co.
The author shows how salt "has influenced and affected wars, cultures, governments, religions, societies, economies, cooking (there are a few recipes), and foods. In addition, he provides information on the chemistry, geology, mining, refining, and production of salt." Libr J
"Throughout his engaging, well-researched history, Kurlansky sprinkles witty asides and amusing anecdotes. A piquant blend of the historic, political, commercial, scientific and culinary, the book is sure to entertain as well as educate." Publ Wkly
Includes bibliographical references

553.7 Water

Kandel, Robert S.
Water from heaven; the story of water from the big bang to the rise of civilization, and beyond; [by] Robert Kandel. Columbia Univ. Press 2003 311p il maps $29.95; pa $24
Grades: 11 12 Adult   553.7
1. Water
ISBN 0-231-12244-6; 0-231-12245-4 (pa)
                                        LC 2002-31229
Original French edition, 1998
The author "explains the earth's elaborate and essential-to-life water cycle . . . beginning cosmologically with the birth of the solar system and an analysis of various theories as to where the earth's water . . . originated." Booklist
"While dense with facts and figures, Kandel's aquatic history is riveting, an exhaustive and complex examination of our most precious chemical compound." Publ Wkly
Includes bibliographical references

Newton, David E.
Encyclopedia of water. Greenwood Press 2002 401p il $75
Grades: 11 12 Adult   553.7
1. Reference books 2. Water—Encyclopedias
ISBN 1-57356-304-8   LC 2002-70031
"The 236 entries in this book comprise an A-Z overview of water's manifold roles in human society and the natural world throughout history." Publisher's note
Includes bibliographical references

U-X-L encyclopedia of water science; K. Lee Lerner and Brenda Wilmoth Lerner, editors; Lawrence W. Baker, project editor. UXL 2005 3v il set $172
Grades: 9 10 11 12   553.7
1. Reference books 2. Water—Encyclopedias
ISBN 0-7876-7617-9   LC 2004-21651
Contents: v1 Water science; v2 Humans and water: economics, technology, and culture; v3 Humans and water: environmental, legal, and political issues
"This set makes a good addition to libraries in which science or social studies students need current useful information for research projects." Libr Media Connect
Includes bibliographical references

Water: science and issues; E. Julius Dasch, editor in chief. Macmillan Ref. USA 2003 4v il maps set $395 *
Grades: 11 12 Adult   553.7
1. Reference books 2. Water—Encyclopedias
ISBN 0-02-865611-3
"This reference contains more than 300 topical entries . . . about a wide array of topics surrounding the nature, sources, use, desecration, and protection of this most valuable resource. . . . At the beginning of each volume are several tables: metric conversions; symbols, abbreviations, and acronyms; and geologic eras, periods and epochs. Entries range in length from 500 to 2,500 words

Water: science and issues—*Continued*
and include short bibliographies of print and electronic sources. Pages have wide margins, which contain picture captions, definitions of key terms, and boxes of important facts and explanations. . . . The scientific and social aspects of water are well introduced in this set, which is recommended for high-school, public, and undergraduate libraries." Booklist

Includes bibliographical references

553.8 Gems

Oldershaw, Cally
Firefly guide to gems. Firefly Bks. 2004 224p il map $14.95 *
Grades: 11 12 Adult   **553.8**
1. Precious stones 2. Gems
ISBN 1-55297-814-1
This book "opens with extensive introductory material including history, various properties, and lore. Then, each gem is presented with text and charts of specific chemical properties. While most gems are discussed on a single page, some that are well known have longer articles." SLJ

Gems of the world. Firefly Books 2008 256p il hardcover o.p. pa $24.95
Grades: 11 12 Adult   **553.8**
1. Gems
ISBN 978-1-55407-367-2; 1-55407-367-7; 978-1-55407-539-3 (pa); 1554075394 (pa)
     LC 2008-274904
Guide to the indentification and use of gemstones. Includes the geology, chemistry and properties of gemstones, what to look for when buying and how to care for them, plus information on the diamond industry.

Schumann, Walter
Gemstones of the world; [translated by Daniel Shea and Nicole Shea] 4th ed., newly rev. & expanded. Sterling 2009 319p il $24.95
Grades: 9 10 11 12   **553.8**
1. Precious stones
ISBN 978-1-4027-6829-3
First English language edition published 1977
"More than 1,500 full-color photos showcase each precious and semiprecious stone in its rough, natural, polished, and cut renditions. Each entry offers . . . information on the gemstone's formation, structure, physical properties, and characteristics, along with the best methods of working, cutting, and polishing it." Publisher's note

Zoellner, Tom
The heartless stone; a journey through the world of diamonds, deceit, and desire. St. Martins Press 2006 293p map hardcover o.p. pa $16
Grades: 11 12 Adult   **553.8**
1. Diamonds
ISBN 0-312-33969-0; 978-0-312-33969-2; 0-312-33970-4 (pa); 978-0-312-33970-8 (pa)
     LC 2005-33037

The author "probes how 'blood diamonds' are used to fund vicious civil wars in Africa; how De Beers, seeing new markets to exploit, linked diamonds to the ancient yuino ceremony in Japan and played on caste obsession in India; and how India is pushing Belgium and Israel out of the gem trade. . . . This is a superior piece of reportage." Publ Wkly

Includes bibliographical references

557 Earth sciences of North America

Collier, Michael, 1950-
Over the mountains; an aerial view of geology; foreword by John S. Shelton. Mikaya Press 2007 unp il map (An aerial view of geology) $29.95 *
Grades: 8 9 10 11 12   **557**
1. Geology—North America 2. Mountains 3. Aerial photography
ISBN 1-931414-18-1; 978-1-931414-18-0
     LC 2006-47151
The author "expresses his passion for geology through awe-inspiring aerial photographs that reveal how mountains were formed and modified across the eons of time. . . . The four sections of this book explore what mountains are, why some are peaked and others rounded, and why they are often strung together in ranges. . . . Collier's love for the land is contagious, and his flying field trips over the mountains are thrilling." Voice Youth Advocates

Includes bibliographical references

560 Fossils & prehistoric life

Encyclopedia of paleontology; editor, Ronald Singer. Fitzroy Dearborn Pubs. 1999 2v il set $295
Grades: 11 12 Adult   **560**
1. Reference books 2. Fossils—Encyclopedias
ISBN 1-88496-496-6   LC 00-271769
This work has "328 articles that cover all areas of paleontology, including 79 biographies for individuals such as Jean Agassiz, Charles Darwin, and Louis Leakey. The articles are extremely well written, with line drawings, photographs, charts, and other illustrative matter, plus a list of works cited and a further reading list." Booklist

Includes bibliographical references

Haines, Tim
The complete guide to prehistoric life; [by] Tim Haines and Paul Chambers. Firefly Books 2006 216p il $35; pa $24.95 *
Grades: 9 10 11 12   **560**
1. Fossils 2. Dinosaurs
ISBN 1-55407-125-9; 978-1-55407-125-8; 1-55407-181-X (pa); 978-1-55407-181-4 (pa)
     LC 2005-9042575
This book covers "112 of the earliest beasts dating from the Cambrian Period to the Pleistocene Period, with . . . profiles on physical characteristics, lifestyle, habitat and behavior." Publisher's note

Ottaviani, Jim
Bone sharps, cowboys, and thunder lizards; a tale of Edwin Drinker Cope, Othniel Charles Marsh, and the gilded age of paleontology; by Jim Ottaviani & Big Time Attic. G.T. Labs 2005 165p il pa $22.95 *
Grades: 9 10 11 12 Adult   560
   1. Cope, E. D. (Edward Drinker), 1840-1897—Graphic novels 2. Marsh, Othniel Charles, 1831-1899—Graphic novels 3. Fossils—Graphic novels 4. Graphic novels 5. Biographical graphic novels
   ISBN 0-9660106-6-3; 978-0-9660106-6-4
                   LC 2005-920326
   Title from cover
   "Ottaviani portrays the heyday of American dinosaur hunting with a ripsnorting Western feel. Rival scientist/dinosaur hunters Marsh and Cope play out their real-life drama in a mostly accurate historical telling. Copious notes at the back of the book point out where Ottaviani departs from the facts; science and history become fun in his hands." Voice Youth Advocates
   Includes bibliographical references

Poinar, George O.
What bugged the dinosaurs? insects, disease, and death in the Cretaceous; [by] George Poinar, Jr. and Roberta Poinar; with photographs and drawings by the authors. Princeton University Press 2008 264p il map $29.95
Grades: 11 12 Adult   560
   1. Fossils 2. Insects as carriers of disease 3. Parasites 4. Dinosaurs
   ISBN 978-0-691-12431-5; 0-691-12431-0
                   LC 2007-61024
   The authors contend that in the Cretaceous period, insects "dominated life on the planet and played a significant role in the life and death of the dinosaurs. . . . [They argue that] insects infected with malaria, leishmania, and other pathogens, together with intestinal parasites, could have devastated dinosaur populations." Publisher's note
   "No sparing the squeamish here: the Poinars graphically detail the probable diseases, debilitations, and deaths of dinosaurs from the lifecycle perspective of insects that infested them. If the ghoulish factor is not draw enough, the Poinars directly encourage younger readers by emphasizing how wide open paleoentomology is to future researchers." Booklist
   Includes bibliographical references

Prehistoric life; [authors, Douglas Palmer ... et al.; consultants, Simon Lamb ... et al.; senior editors, Angeles Gavira Guerrero, Peter Frances; project editors, Cressida Malins ... et al.; editors, Jamie Ambrose ... et al.] DK 2009 512p il map $40 *
Grades: 7 8 9 10 11 12 Adult   560
   1. Fossils
   ISBN 978-0-7566-5573-0   LC 2010-278841
   Subtitle on cover: The definitive visual history of life on earth
   "Condensing millions of years of life on earth into a 512-page single-volume encyclopedia, this ambitious

work presents earth's history from its formation through the Mesolithic period (Middle Stone Age). . . . Geared to adults, this work will find popularity with science enthusiasts and browsers alike." Booklist

Thompson, Ida
The Audubon Society field guide to North American fossils; with photographs by Townsend P. Dickinson; visual key by Carol Nehring. Knopf 1982 846p il maps flexible bdg $19.95 *
Grades: 11 12 Adult   560
   1. Fossils
   ISBN 0-394-52412-8   LC 81-84772
   "A Chanticleer Press edition. The Audubon Society field guide series"
   "This softbound field guide to fossils is divided into a section of color photographs followed by a section of detailed descriptions. It covers 420 fossils of marine and freshwater invertebrates, insects, plants, and vertebrates that are likely to be found by the amateur." Malinowsky. Best Sci & Technol Ref Books for Young People

567 Fossil cold-blooded vertebrates Fossil Pisces (fishes)

Holmes, Thom
The first vertebrates; oceans of the Paleozoic era. Chelsea House 2008 188p il (The prehistoric Earth) lib bdg $35
Grades: 7 8 9 10   567
   1. Fossils 2. Vertebrates
   ISBN 978-0-8160-5958-4; 0-8160-5958-6
                   LC 2007-45329
   Describes the first instances of vertebrate life in the oceans of the Paleozoic Era, tracing the development of early fish from jawless species to sharks and bony fish.
   This "is a comprehensive, well-written, and easily readable text. . . . The chapters are well-organized." Sci Books Films
   Includes glossary and bibliographical references

567.9 Reptilia

Barnes-Svarney, Patricia
The handy dinosaur answer book; [by] Patricia Barnes-Svarney and Thomas E. Svarney. 2nd ed. Visible Ink Press 2010 274p il (Handy answer book series) pa $21.95
Grades: 9 10 11 12 Adult   567.9
   1. Dinosaurs
   ISBN 978-1-57859-218-0; 1-57859-218-6
                   LC 2009-32573
   First published 2000
   "The student who simply cannot find enough information about dinosaurs will be delighted with this book that has an amazing wealth of information about dinosaurs. The place of the dinosaur in geologic time, theories about the origin and extinction of dinosaurs, anatomy and physiology, descriptions of various dinosaurs, and paleontological methods are all a part of this work. It is

Barnes-Svarney, Patricia—*Continued*
really a comprehensive study of dinosaurs, even if the
format is asking simple questions." Voice Youth Advocates
Includes bibliographical references

Everhart, Michael J.
Sea monsters; prehistoric creatures of the deep;
[by] Mike Everhart. National Geographic 2007
191p il map $30
Grades: 7 8 9 10   **567.9**
1. Fossils 2. Marine animals 3. Prehistoric animals
ISBN 978-1-4262-0085-4; 1-4262-0085-4
                              LC 2007-18671
Includes 1 pair 3-D glasses
Featuring "computer-generated images and 3D film
clips—with 3D glasses—field photography by National
Geographic cameramen, and much more, the book interweaves dramatic scenes of the far, far distant past; up-to-
the-minute scientific profiles of nearly two dozen sea
monsters; and a group portrait of the eccentric Sternberg
family, Kansas-bred pioneers of marine paleontology."
Publisher's note

Holmes, Thom
Last of the dinosaurs; the Cretaceous period.
Chelsea House 2009 232p il map (The prehistoric
Earth) $35
Grades: 9 10 11 12   **567.9**
1. Dinosaurs 2. Fossils
ISBN 978-0-8160-5962-1; 0-8160-5962-4
                              LC 2008-38331
This book "discusses how the changing ecological and
geological conditions in the Early and Late Cretaceous
periods created opportunities for the expansion of dinosaurs. It was also these very climatic and geologic shifts
that contributed to the eventual extinction of large and
small dinosaurs. . . . [Holmes] is thorough, clear, and informative in explaining theories relating to the mass extinction of dinosaurs and other creatures of the time. . . .
Appealing in format and design, the text is supported
with abundant color illustrations, charts, and graphs."
Booklist
Includes glossary and bibliographical references

Holtz, Thomas R., 1965-
Dinosaurs; the most complete, up-to-date
encyclopedia for dinosaur lovers of all ages; by
Dr. Thomas R. Holtz, Jr.; illustrated by Luis V.
Rey. Random House 2007 427p il $34.99; lib bdg
$37.99 *
Grades: 7 8 9 10   **567.9**
1. Dinosaurs
ISBN   978-0-375-82419-7;   0-375-82419-7;
978-0-375-92419-4 (lib bdg); 0-375-92419-1 (lib bdg)
                              LC 2006-102491
This "covers everything from dinosaur eggs to taxono-
my and cladistics to the history of paleontology, glued
together with chapters on the dinosaurs themselves. . . .
The illustrations range from small photos to larger sepia-
toned drawings to even larger full-color paintings. . . .
This eye-catching imagination grabber will be enjoyed
(on different levels) by dinophiles of all ages." SLJ
Includes glossary

Naish, Darren
The great dinosaur discoveries. University of
California Press 2009 192p il map $29.95
Grades: 7 8 9 10 11 12   **567.9**
1. Dinosaurs 2. Fossils
ISBN 978-0-520-25975-1; 0-520-25975-0
                              LC 2009-6140
"From the fragmentary remains of giant extinct ani-
mals found in the early 1800s to the dinosaur wars in the
American West to the amazing near-complete skeletons
found around the world today, Darren Naish tells how
these discoveries have led not only to the recognition of
new species and whole new groups, but also to new theories of evolutionary history." Publisher's note
Includes glossary and bibliographical references

Parker, Steve
Dinosaurus; the complete guide to dinosaurs.
Firefly Books 2004 448p il $49.95 *
Grades: 9 10 11 12   **567.9**
1. Dinosaurs
ISBN 1-55297-772-2   LC 2004-299417
"Arrangement is by group, and 500 dinosaurs are de-
scribed. Each entry includes an illustration and brief in-
formation about the dinosaur's discovery and characteris-
tics. Each entry also includes a 'Dino Factfile' containing
data on scientific name with pronunciation and meaning,
location, size, diet, and time period." Booklist
This is "is a must-have source for libraries where dinosaur study is an annual research unit." Voice Youth
Advocates
Includes bibliographical references

Paul, Gregory S.
The Princeton field guide to dinosaurs.
Princeton University Press 2010 320p il map
(Princeton field guides) $35 *
Grades: 9 10 11 12 Adult   **567.9**
1. Dinosaurs
ISBN 978-0-691-13720-9; 0-691-13720-X
                              LC 2010-14916
"Covering 735 species of dinosaurs, this volume . . .
consists of two main sections. The first is an introduction
that includes a discussion on dinosaur evolution, biology,
behavior, and more. The majority of the information is
found in the 'Group and Species Accounts' section and
is further divided into three groups: 'Theropods,'
'Sauropodomorphs,' and 'Ornithischians.' Entries on each
species . . . typically include information related to their
anatomical characteristics, age, distribution, and habitat."
Booklist
"Though not a field guide to stuff in your backpack,
this exciting addition to dinosaur reference is essential
for high school through university libraries and is highly
recommended for all students of dinosaurs." Libr J
Includes bibliographical references

Sampson, Scott D., 1961-

Dinosaur odyssey; fossil threads in the web of life. University of California Press 2009 332p il map $29.95

Grades: 11 12 Adult   **567.9**

1. Dinosaurs 2. Fossils

ISBN 978-0-520-24163-3; 0-520-24163-0

LC 2009-6150

"Sampson reconstructs the odyssey of the dinosaurs from their humble origins on the supercontinent Pangaea, to their reign as the largest animals the planet has ever known, and finally to their abrupt demise." Publisher's note

"This book draws scientifically accurate pictures in a style that is accessible to researchers and general readers alike." Libr J

Includes bibliographical references

569   Fossil mammalia

Holmes, Thom

Primates and human ancestors; the Pliocene epoch. Chelsea House 2009 158p il (The prehistoric Earth) lib bdg $35

Grades: 7 8 9 10   **569**

1. Primates 2. Fossils 3. Fossil hominids 4. Evolution

ISBN 978-0-8160-5965-2; 0-8160-5965-9

LC 2008-38328

"The book traces the evolution of early hominids in three different sections. The first section provides an overview of evolution, tracing the history of evolutionary thought and presenting the mechanism of evolution. . . . The second section focuses on primates. . . . The last section traces the evolution of the early hominids, pinpointing the transition from ape to hominin in a clear-cut fashion. The book concludes with a look at early human ancestors, including *Australopithecus afarensis*." Sci Books Films

Includes glossary and bibliographical references

Lister, Adrian

Mammoths; giants of the ice age; [by] Adrian Lister and Paul Bahn; foreword by Jean M. Auel. Rev ed. University of California Press 2007 192p il $29.95 *

Grades: 11 12 Adult   **569**

1. Mammoths

ISBN 978-0-520-25319-3; 0-520-25319-1

LC 2007-26369

First published 1994 by Macmillan

This book integrates "research to piece together the story of mammoths, mastodons, and their relatives, icons of the Ice Age." Publisher's note

Includes glossary and bibliographical references

569.9   Hominidae

Fagan, Brian M., 1936-

Cro-Magnon; [by] Brian Fagan. Bloomsbury Press 2010 295p il map $28

Grades: 9 10 11 12 Adult   **569.9**

1. Cro-Magnons 2. Evolution 3. Ice Age 4. Neanderthals 5. Prehistoric peoples

ISBN 978-1-59691-582-4; 1-59691-582-X

LC 2009-25242

Fagan examines "the Ice Age, describes subsequent climate change, and characterizes the lifeways of indigenous and diminishing Neanderthal populations and the evolution and expansion of early modern humans. . . . Fagan's vivid imagination and eloquent writing style paint a fascinating picture of the struggle to adapt to a changing climate." Sci Books Films

Includes bibliographical references

Sarmiento, Esteban

The last human; a guide to twenty-two species of extinct humans; created by G.J. Sawyer and Viktor Deak; text by Esteban Sarmiento, G.J. Sawyer, Richard Milner; with contributions by Donald C. Johanson, Meave Leakey, and Ian Tattersall. Yale University Press 2006 256p il map $45

Grades: 11 12 Adult   **569.9**

1. Fossil hominids 2. Evolution 3. Human beings

ISBN 978-0-300-10047-1; 0-300-10047-7

"A Peter N. Nèvraumont book"

This book "covers 22 species of extinct humans, concluding with the only surviving one, Homo sapiens. . . . Provided for each is information on its emergence, chronology, geographic range, classification, physiology, environment, habitat, cultural achievements, coexisting species, and possible reasons for extinction. Summaries of fossil discoveries for each species are also provided, along with historical notes mentioning publications and controversies." Libr J

"This is fascinating stuff, not least because it drives home just how much of our knowledge about the past is based on inference." New Sci

Includes bibliographical references

570   Life sciences; biology

The **Facts** on File biology handbook; [by] The Diagram Group. rev ed. Facts on File 2006 272p il (Facts on File science library) $35 *

Grades: 8 9 10 11 12   **570**

1. Biology

ISBN 0-8160-5877-6   LC 2004-59270

First published 2000

Topics covered include: amniocentesis, synthesis, hormones, glands, embryo, ventricle, and zygote. Francis Bacon, Edwin Hubble, and Linus Pauling are among the 400 scientists profiled. Includes a chronology of significant developments and discoveries from ancient Greece to the present day. Illustrated with tables, charts, and diagrams.

Includes bibliographical references

Stone, Carol Leth

The basics of biology; Carol Leth Stone. Greenwood Press 2004 280p il (Basics of the hard sciences) $75

Grades: 9 10 11 12 **570**

1. Biology

ISBN 0-313-31786-0 LC 2004-8510

This book "offers an overview of the discipline, including its history and key concepts and principles. Chapter coverage includes ecology, evolution, genetics, body systems, and the classes of living organisms. A handful of experiments accompanies each chapter. The final section is devoted to additional open-ended experiments for assignments or personal study. . . . This overview is well suited to novice students." SLJ

Includes bibliographical references

Wright, Judene

Cracking the SAT. Biology E/M subject test. 2011-2012 ed. Random House 2011 462p (Princeton Review series) pa $19.99

Grades: 9 10 11 12 **570**

1. Biology—Study and teaching 2. Scholastic Assessment Test 3. Colleges and universities—Entrance requirements

ISBN 978-0-375-42810-4

Annual. First published 2005. Continues Cracking the SAT II: biology subject test

This guide provides test-taking strategies and sample tests for the subject of biology.

570.1 Philosophy and theory

Lewis, Mark J.

Classification of living organisms. Rosen Pub. 2011 80p il (Understanding genetics) lib bdg $30.60

Grades: 9 10 11 12 **570.1**

1. Biology—Classification

ISBN 978-1-4358-9535-5

Describes the classification system scientists use to identify and name all living organisms, and explains how animals are categorized based on certain characteristics.

570.3 Life sciences—Encyclopedias and dictionaries

The **Facts** on File dictionary of biology; edited by Robert Hine. 4th ed. Facts on File 2005 406p il (Facts on File science library) $45; pa $17.95 *

Grades: 9 10 11 12 **570.3**

1. Reference books 2. Biology—Dictionaries

ISBN 0-8160-5647-1; 0-8160-5648-X (pa)

LC 2005-40698

First published 1981

Over 3,000 entries cover basic terms as well as names of organs, biological processes, genera and species. Global warming, DNA fingerprinting, and the Human Genome Project are among the topics covered

"The volume is worthwhile for consideration by libraries in need of an up-to-date, relatively inexpensive dictionary that covers basic biological terminology." Booklist

Includes bibliographical references

Rittner, Don

Encyclopedia of biology; [by] Don Rittner and Timothy L. McCabe. Facts on File 2004 400p il $75 *

Grades: 9 10 11 12 **570.3**

1. Reference books 2. Biology—Encyclopedias

ISBN 0-8160-4859-2 LC 2003-21279

Contains approximately 800 alphabetical entries, prose essays on important topics, line illustrations, and black-and-white photographs

Includes bibliographical references

571 Physiology and related subjects

Roach, Mary

Packing for Mars; the curious science of life in the void. W.W. Norton 2010 334p il $25.95 *

Grades: 9 10 11 12 Adult **571**

1. Space biology

ISBN 978-0-393-06847-4; 0-393-06847-1

LC 2010-17113

The author "explores the organic aspects of the space program, such as the dangerous bane of space motion sickness and the challenges of space hygiene. . . . She devotes one chapter to space food and another to zero-gravity elimination, which is a serious matter, even with a term like 'fecal popcorning.' An impish and adventurous writer with a gleefully inquisitive mind and a standup comic's timing, Roach celebrates human ingenuity (the odder the better), and calls for us to marshal our resources, unchain our imaginations, and start packing for Mars." Booklist

Includes bibliographical references

571.3 Anatomy and morphology

Animal and plant anatomy. Marshall Cavendish 2006 11v il set $771.36

Grades: 7 8 9 10 **571.3**

1. Comparative anatomy

ISBN 0-7614-7662-8; 978-0-7614-7662-7

LC 2005-53193

"This set offers an introduction to the external and internal anatomies of 84 organisms. Included are many different life-forms, such as animals, plants, viruses, bacteria, and fungi, although the focus is on mammals. . . . This set would be an asset in public and school libraries." Booklist

Includes bibliographical references

571.6 Cell biology

Panno, Joseph

The cell; nature's first life-form. Rev. ed. Facts on File 2010 286p il (The new biology) $40 *
Grades: 9 10 11 12   **571.6**
1. Cells
ISBN 978-0-8160-6849-4   LC 2009-40063
First published 2004

"The book traces the development of the cell from its first appearance in the 'primordial soup' of the oceans of ancient Earth 3 million years ago, through the emergence of simple bacteria, to the rise of multicellular organisms that eventually became today's plants and animals. The author provides . . . information about the structure and function of the cell, will special emphasis on cell division and cell-to-cell communication essential to the development of multicelled creatures." Publisher's note

Includes glossary and bibliographical references

Wolpert, L. (Lewis)

How we live and why we die; the secret lives of cells; [by] Lewis Wolpert. Norton 2009 240p $24.95
Grades: 11 12 Adult   **571.6**
1. Cells
ISBN 978-0-393-07221-1   LC 2009-9718

The author "provides basic biological information about cell structure, genetics and reproduction, and then discusses the roles cells play in disease, aging, death, reproduction, memory, emotion and . . . more." Publ Wkly

"Including discussion of stem cells and embryonic growth, Wolpert's work will absorb anyone fascinated by the universe inside the cell." Booklist

Includes bibliographical references

571.7 Biological control and secretions

Foster, Russell G.

Rhythms of life; the biological clocks that control the daily lives of every living thing. Yale University Press 2004 276p il $30; pa $18
Grades: 11 12 Adult   **571.7**
1. Biological rhythms
ISBN   0-300-10574-6;   978-0-300-10574-2; 0-300-10969-5 (pa); 978-0-300-10969-6 (pa)
LC 2004-105609

The authors "survey the biological clocks that dictate circadian rhythms, the daily cycles that affect creatures from cockroaches to humans. . . . Biology buffs will marvel at the fascinating material." Publ Wkly

Includes bibliographical references

572.8 Biochemical genetics

Carroll, Sean B.

The making of the fittest; DNA and the ultimate forensic record of evolution; with illustrations by Jamie W. Carroll and Leanne M. Olds. W.W. Norton & Co. 2006 301p il map $25.95 *
Grades: 11 12 Adult   **572.8**
1. DNA 2. Evolution
ISBN 978-0-393-06163-5; 0-393-06163-9
LC 2006-17197

The author presents "discoveries gathered from DNA evidence that confirm Charles Darwin's theory of evolution 'beyond any reasonable doubt.' . . . Readers will gain insight into the evolutionary process and expand their knowledge of how the 'fittest' species were made, from fish that live in subfreezing water to birds that communicate via ultraviolet colors." Libr J

Includes bibliographical references

Takemura, Masaharu, 1969-

The manga guide to molecular biology; [by] Masaharu Takemura, Sakura, Becom Co., Ltd. No Starch Press 2009 225p il pa $19.95 *
Grades: 9 10 11 12   **572.8**
1. Graphic novels 2. Manga 3. Molecular biology—Graphic novels
ISBN 978-1-59327-202-9; 1-59327-202-2
LC 2009-25876

"Rin and Ami have been skipping molecular biology class all semester, and Professor Moro has had enough—he's sentencing them to summer school on his private island. But they're in store for a special lesson. Using Dr. Moro's virtual reality machine to travel inside the human body, they'll get a closeup look at the . . . world of molecular biology. . . . [This guide follows them as they learn] all about DNA, RNA, proteins, amino acids, and more." Publisher's note

Watson, James D., 1928-

The double helix; a personal account of the discovery of the structure of DNA. Scribner 1998 226p il $25; pa $14
Grades: 11 12 Adult   **572.8**
1. DNA 2. Biochemistry—Research
ISBN 0-684-85279-9; 0-7432-1630-X (pa)
LC 98-136787

A reissue of the title first published 1968 by Atheneum Pubs.

Portions of this book were first published in The Atlantic Monthly

This book is a "personal, day-by-day account of how Watson, [Francis] Crick and their collaborators in the years between 1951 and 1963 hit upon the famous 'double helix' model of the 'DNA' [deoxyribonucleic acid] molecule, the fundamental genetical material." America

576.5   Genetics

Endersby, Jim
A guinea pig's history of biology. Harvard University Press 2007 499p il $27.95; pa $18.95
Grades: 11 12 Adult   **576.5**
1. Heredity 2. Genetics 3. Biology—History
ISBN   978-0-674-02713-8;   0-674-02713-2;
978-0-674-03227-9 (pa); 0-674-03227-6 (pa)
                     LC 2007-20824
Endersby chronicles "the history of heredity and genetics, tracing the slow, uncertain path . . . that led us from the ancient world's understanding of inheritance to modern genetics." Publisher's note
"This book would be of interest to anyone fascinated or intrigued by genetics or biological research, as well as any professional or lay student of history and science." Sci Books Films
Includes bibliographical references

Genetics & inherited conditions; editor, Jeffrey A. Knight. Salem Press 2010 3v il (Salem health) set $395 *
Grades: 11 12 Adult   **576.5**
1. Genetics—Encyclopedias 2. Medical genetics—Encyclopedias 3. Reference books
ISBN 978-1-587-65650-7; 1-587-65650-7
                     LC 2010-5289
First published 1999 with title: Encyclopedia of genetics
Includes complimentary access to online companion database Salem Health
"The subjects covered include all aspects of genetics, such as diseases, biology, genetic engineering, social issues, and more. . . . Articles covering diseases and syndromes include such information as definition, risk factors, etiology and genetics, symptoms, screening and diagnosis, treatment and therapy, and prevention and outcomes. For other types of articles, essays are preceded by a brief summary of the significance of the topic and definitions of key terms." Booklist
Includes bibliographical references

Hand, Carol
Introduction to genetics. Rosen Pub. 2010 c2011 80p il (Understanding genetics) lib bdg $30.60
Grades: 9 10 11 12   **576.5**
1. Genetics 2. Heredity
ISBN 978-1-4358-9531-7   LC 2009-40364
Provides an introduction to genetics, including information on the Punnett Square, inheritance patterns and alleles, mitosis, and gene mapping.

New thinking about genetics; edited by Kara Rogers. Britannica Educational Pub. in association with Rosen Educational Services 2010 274p il (21st century science) lib bdg $45
Grades: 9 10 11 12   **576.5**
1. Genetics
ISBN 978-1-61530-104-1   LC 2009-44215
This book introduces "the science of genetics as well as detailing the controversies and implications for future studies." Publisher's note
Includes bibliographical references

Schultz, Mark, 1955-
The stuff of life; a graphic guide to genetics and DNA; written by Mark Schultz; art by Zander Cannon and Kevin Cannon. Hill and Wang 2009 150p il $30; pa $14.95 *
Grades: 9 10 11 12 Adult   **576.5**
1. Graphic novels 2. Genetics—Graphic novels
ISBN 978-0-8090-8946-8; 978-0-8090-8947-5 (pa)
Eisner and Harvey Award winning writer Schultz uses the device of an alien writing a report to describe genetics and DNA in five chapters, from molecular structure of Earth organisms to sexual reproduction to genetic inheritance to genetic counseling and the genome Project and beyond. The black and white cartoons add some humor to the sound information, and the book includes a list of suggested reading ranging from magazines and books to websites, along with a glossary of terms.
Includes bibliographical references

Yount, Lisa
Modern genetics; engineering life. rev ed. Facts on File 2006 204p il map (Milestones in discovery and invention) $35
Grades: 7 8 9 10 11 12   **576.5**
1. Genetics 2. Genetic engineering
ISBN 0-8160-5744-3; 978-0-8160-5744-3
                     LC 2005-18152
First published 1997 with title: Genetics and genetic engineering
This book "profiles 14 men and women who were among the leaders in making important genetic discoveries in research and new technologies. Profiles include James Watson, Francis Crick, Herbert Boyer, Stanley N. Cohen, Michael Bishop, and Harold Varmus." Publisher's note
Includes glossary and bibliographical references

576.8   Evolution

Darwin, Charles, 1809-1882
The Darwin reader; edited by Mark Ridley. 2nd ed. Norton 1996 315p il pa $21.30 *
Grades: 11 12 Adult   **576.8**
1. Evolution 2. Natural selection
ISBN 0-393-96967-3   LC 95-50297
First published in the United Kingdom with title: The essential Darwin; first Norton edition published 1987
This collection presents excerpts from Darwin's most important works including Origin of the species, The descent of man and Coral reef. Illustrations are taken from the original editions
Includes bibliographical references

On the origin of species; David Quammen, general editor. Illustrated ed. Sterling Pub. 2008 544p il $35 *
Grades: 10 11 12 Adult   **576.8**
1. Evolution 2. Natural selection 3. Human origins 4. Heredity
ISBN 978-1-4027-5639-9   LC 2008-6902
Illustrated edition of the book first published 1859 with title: The origin of species by means of natural selection

Darwin, Charles, 1809-1882—*Continued*

"As a milestone not only in the history of science but also in cultural history, *On the Origin of Species* belongs in every library, high school and above. . . . [Quammen] offers a gloriously illustrated and richly annotated volume, which testifies to the book's enduring legacy. Throughout the text, relevant sidebars from other of Darwin's writings, including his *Autobiography*, field notes from the HMS Beagle, and his myriad letters, are presented for their insight. Illustrations include historical images, such as sketches, woodcuts, and portraits of people and places, but also included are contemporary photographs of the flora and fauna that Darwin described." Libr J

Includes bibliographical references

Encyclopedia of evolution; Mark Pagel, editor in chief. Oxford Univ. Press 2002 2v il set $325
Grades: 11 12 Adult   **576.8**
1. Reference books 2. Evolution—Encyclopedias
ISBN 0-19-512200-3   LC 2001-21588
This reference covers topics in evolutionary theory "including developmental biology, social behavior, consciousness, evolution of disease, systematics, population biology, complexity theory, and even art in prehistory. Some biographical articles are also included. . . . [Contributors include] Stephen Jay Gould, Jane Goodall, Sarah Blaffer Hrdy, and John Maynard Smith." Libr J

Evolution; Clay Farris Naff, book editor. Greenhaven Press 2005 222p (Exploring science and medical discoveries) lib bdg $34.95 *
Grades: 8 9 10 11 12   **576.8**
1. Evolution
ISBN 0-7377-2823-X   LC 2004-60590
In this anthology, "nineteen selections are arranged in roughly chronological order, beginning with ancient Greek philosophers whose ideas about nature hinted at evolutionary theories to come. . . . This solid survey provides a good overview with manageable amounts of primary-source materials that would be dauntingly difficult to comprehend in their entirety." SLJ
Includes bibliographical references

Evolution; Don Nardo, book editor. Greenhaven Press 2005 240p il (History of issues) lib bdg $34.95; pa $23.70
Grades: 9 10 11 12   **576.8**
1. Evolution
ISBN 0-7377-2098-0 (lib bdg); 0-7377-2099-9 (pa)
LC 2004-47481
"In this volume, scientists, religious leaders, and others square off in pairs of pro and con essays. Topics include: the nineteenth-century controversy over evolution, modern advances in evolutionary theory, and the debate over teaching evolution in schools." Publisher's note
Includes bibliographical references

Hodge, Russ

Evolution; the history of life on earth; [by] Russ Hodge; foreword by Nadia Rosenthal. Facts On File 2009 252p il (Genetics & evolution) $39.50
Grades: 9 10 11 12   **576.8**
1. Evolution
ISBN 978-0-8160-6679-7; 0-8160-6679-5
LC 2008-29741
This book describes the "impact evolution has had on society and on modern medicine—including the birth of genetic science in the early 1900s and the discovery that genes were made of DNA in the 1950s." Publisher's note
Includes glossary and bibliographical references

Hosler, Jay

Evolution; the story of life on Earth; written by Jay Hosler; art by Zander Cannon and Kevin Cannon. Hill and Wang 2011 150p il $18.95
Grades: 9 10 11 12 Adult   **576.8**
1. Graphic novels 2. Evolution—Graphic novels
ISBN 978-0-8090-9476-9; 0-8090-9476-2
LC 2010-05777
Alien scientist Bloort-183 takes King Floorsh-727 and Prince Floorsh-418 on a tour of Earth's history, explaining the theory of evolution. These are the same aliens who explored human genetics in The Stuff of Life. The illustrations by Kevin Cannon and Zander Cannon (no relation to each other) help human readers see how the theory of evolution explains the beginnings of life on Earth, the four conditions needed for natural selection, the Cambrian explosion, the Permian extinction, sexual selection, the evolution of modern humans, and the Earth scientists who studied the life forms and made the scientific discoveries. The book includes an illustrated glossary, a list of further reading, and endpapers filled with all kinds of dinosaurs.
"This delightful book seems ideal for nonscientists who want to entertainingly brush up their knowledge of evolution as well as for students from middle school on up." Booklist

Keller, Michael, 1976-

Charles Darwin's On the Origin of Species; a graphic adaptation; [by] Michael Keller; art by Nicolle Rager Fuller. Rodale 2009 192p il $19.99; pa $14.99 *
Grades: 9 10 11 12 Adult   **576.8**
1. Darwin, Charles, 1809-1882—Adaptations 2. Evolution—Graphic novels 3. Natural selection—Graphic novels 4. Human origins—Graphic novels 5. Heredity—Graphic novels 6. Graphic novels
ISBN   978-1-60529-697-5;   1-60529-697-X; 978-1-60529-948-8 (pa); 1-60529-948-0 (pa)
LC 2009-11387
"The graphic novel follows *Origin*'s original chapters, combining snippets of Darwin's text with quotes from letters, illustrative examples from his time and from the present, and occasional invented dialog. Fuller's images of people seem clumsy, but her full-color plants, animals, charts, maps, and scientific accoutrements are attractive and effective. . . . [This] version well conveys both the science and the wonder of *Origin*." Libr J

Lew, Kristi, 1968-
Evolution; the adaptation and survival of species. Rosen Pub. 2010 c2011 80p il (Understanding genetics) lib bdg $30.60
Grades: 9 10 11 12   **576.8**
 1. Evolution
 ISBN 978-1-4358-9534-8   LC 2009-46684
Discusses early theories of evolution, the work of Darwin, fossil and other evidence, and the effects of evolution on humans and the future.

Milner, Richard
Darwin's universe; evolution from A to Z; with a foreword by Ian Tattersall and a preface by Stephen Jay Gould. University of California Press 2009 487p il $39.95
Grades: 11 12 Adult   **576.8**
 1. Darwin, Charles, 1809-1882—Encyclopedias
 2. Evolution—Encyclopedias 3. Reference books
 ISBN 978-0-520-24376-7   LC 2008-35575
"The present book, Darwin's Universe, has evolved from two ancestral forms titled The Encyclopedia of Evolution, published in 1990 and 1993. It has been updated, revised, and enhanced with many new essays and illustrations" Verso of title page
 This encyclopedia "presents unusual details about Darwin's life and his famous theory. Entries range from the evolution of social behavior to the Creationist Museum, where dinosaurs are the contemporaries of humans. The style of writing is appropriate for a high-school or college audience, and the book is nicely illustrated and well laid out." Booklist
 Includes bibliographical references

New thinking about evolution; edited by John P. Rafferty. Britannica Educational Pub. in association with Rosen Educational Services 2010 c2011 288p il (21st century science) lib bdg $45
Grades: 9 10 11 12   **576.8**
 1. Evolution
 ISBN 978-1-61530-129-4   LC 2010-848
This book details "the evolutionary process and speciation as well as the continuing debates about evolution's inherent validity." Publisher's note
 Includes bibliographical references

Parker, Andrew, 1967-
In the blink of an eye. Perseus Pub 2003 316p il hardcover o.p. pa $15
Grades: 11 12 Adult   **576.8**
 1. Evolution 2. Fossils
 ISBN 0-7382-0607-5; 0-465-05438-2 (pa)
                                    LC 2003-282077
The author "provides a relatively simple explanation for the sudden explosion of life forms that defines the boundary between the pre-Cambrian and Cambrian eras approximately 543 million years ago: 'The Cambrian explosion was triggered by the sudden evolution of vision' in simple organisms. . . . In readable prose, Parker provides detailed information on the fossil record as well as a wealth of interesting material on the role light plays in environments and how vision operates across a host of

species. Although at times his tangents are a bit distracting, Parker's book will bring his controversial ideas to the general public." Publ Wkly

Rice, Stanley Arthur, 1957-
Encyclopedia of evolution; [by] Stanley A. Rice; foreword by Massimo Pigliucci. Facts on File 2007 468p il (Facts on File science library) $75 *
Grades: 11 12 Adult   **576.8**
 1. Evolution—Encyclopedias 2. Reference books
 ISBN 0-8160-5515-7; 978-0-8160-5515-9
                                    LC 2005-31646
This encyclopedia "contains more than 200 entries that span modern evolutionary science and the history of its development. . . . Five essays that explore . . . questions resulting from studies in evolutionary science are included as well. The appendix consists of a summary of Charles Darwin's Origin of Species." Publisher's note
 Includes bibliographical references

Scott, Eugenie Carol, 1945-
Evolution vs. creationism; an introduction; [by] Eugenie C. Scott; foreword by Niles Eldredge; foreword to second edition by Judge John E. Jones, III. 2nd ed. Greenwood Press 2008 xxvi, 351p il $49.95 *
Grades: 9 10 11 12   **576.8**
 1. Evolution 2. Creationism
 ISBN 978-0-313-34427-5   LC 2008-33529
 First published 2004
"Prior to addressing differing sides of the question, the author provides the reader with an introduction to the concepts of science, evolution, religion, and creationism. A history of the controversy and the varying theories and opinions about it follows. The third section contains . . . excerpts from major works dealing with the scientific, legal, educational, and religious arguments. . . . This informative work provides the reader with a clear, insightful summary of the complicated issues and viewpoints surrounding the evolution/creationism debate." Libr Media Connect [review of 2004 edition]
 Includes bibliographical references

Wilson, David Sloan
Evolution for everyone; how Darwin's theory can change the way we think about our lives. Delacorte Press 2007 390p $24
Grades: 11 12 Adult   **576.8**
 1. Evolution
 ISBN 978-0-385-34021-2; 0-385-34021-4
                                    LC 2006-23685
"Building on diverse examples, Wilson demonstrates that evolution is completely relevant to modern human affairs, including how we use language, create culture and define morality." Publ Wkly
 "Rather than catalog its successes, denounce its detractors or in any way present evolutionary theory as the province of expert tacticians like himself, Wilson invites readers inside and shows them how Darwinism is done, and at lesson's end urges us to go ahead, feel free to try it at home. The result is a sprightly, absorbing and charmingly earnest book that manages a minor miracle,

Wilson, David Sloan—*Continued*
the near-complete emulsifying of science and the 'real world,' ingredients too often kept stubbornly, senselessly apart." N Y Times Book Rev
Includes bibliographical references

Young, Christian C., 1968-
Evolution and creationism; a documentary and reference guide; [by] Christian C. Young and Mark A. Largent. Greenwood Press 2007 298p il $85
Grades: 11 12 Adult   **576.8**
1. Evolution 2. Creationism
ISBN 978-0-313-33953-0; 0-313-33953-8
LC 2007-10682
"This reference work provides over 40 of the most important documents to help readers understand the [evolution versus creationism] debate in the eyes of the people of the time. Each document is from a major participant in the debates from the predecessors of Darwin to the judges of the influential court cases of the present day." Publisher's note
Includes bibliographical references

576.839   Extraterrestrial life

Angelo, Joseph A.
Life in the universe. Facts on File 2007 338p il (Frontiers in space) $39.50
Grades: 9 10 11 12   **576.839**
1. Life on other planets 2. Outer space—Exploration 3. Space biology
ISBN 0-8160-5776-1; 978-0-8160-5776-4
LC 2006-34860
"This volume prepares readers for some of the revelations that space technology may yield this century by discussing the historic events, scientific principles, and technical developments that allow sophisticated robot exploring machines to visit faraway worlds in the solar system as they hunt for signs of life—existent or extinct." Publisher's note
Includes glossary and bibliographical references

Bennett, Jeffrey O.
Beyond UFOs; the search for extraterrestrial life and its astonishing implications for our future; [by] Jeffrey Bennett. Princeton University Press 2008 211p il $26.95
Grades: 11 12 Adult   **576.839**
1. Life on other planets 2. Life—Origin 3. Space biology
ISBN 978-0-691-13549-6; 0-691-13549-5
LC 2007-37872
This book describes research in the field of astrobiology. Bennett discusses questions such as "What is life and how does it begin? What makes a planet or moon habitable? Is there life on Mars or elsewhere in the solar system? How can life be recognized on distant worlds? Is it likely to be microbial, more biologically complex—or even intelligent?" Publisher's note
"The writing style is like that of a fireside chat with an expert in the field: an easy read, but thought provoking." Sci Books Films

Davies, P. C. W., 1946-
The eerie silence; renewing our search for alien intelligence; [by] Paul Davies. Houghton Mifflin Harcourt 2010 241p il $27
Grades: 11 12 Adult   **576.839**
1. Life on other planets 2. Extraterrestrial beings 3. Unidentified flying objects
ISBN 978-0-547-13324-9; 0-547-13324-3
LC 2010-3088
"After 50 years of scanning the skies for signs of extraterrestrial intelligence, astronomers have only silence to report — an eerie silence, Davies argues. Part history of the search, part road map for its future and (large) part mind-stretching exercise, the book provides Davies' perspective on profound questions that have implications far beyond alien hunting." Sci News
Includes bibliographical references

Extraterrestrial life; Sylvia Engdahl, book editor. Greenhaven Press/Thomson Gale 2006 171p (Contemporary issues companion) lib bdg $39.70; pa $27.50
Grades: 9 10 11 12   **576.839**
1. Life on other planets
ISBN 978-0-7377-3253-5 (lib bdg); 0-7377-3253-9 (lib bdg); 978-0-7377-3254-2 (pa); 0-7377-3254-7 (pa)
A collection of articles discussing various aspects of extraterrestrial life including UFO sightings, alien abductions, and scientific evidence for life on other planets from NASA's explorations
Includes bibliographical references

Kaufman, Marc
First contact; scientific breakthroughs in the hunt for life beyond Earth. Simon & Schuster 2011 213p il $26; ebook $12.99
Grades: 11 12 Adult   **576.839**
1. Life on other planets
ISBN 978-1-4391-0900-7; 978-1-4391-3030-8 (ebook)
LC 2010-44630
Kaufman "takes us from beneath the surface of our planet, where scientists hunt for and study 'extremophile' microbes that alter our views of what is necessary for life to exist, to observatories and labs searching deep space for extraterrestrial signals or exoplanets, planets outside the solar system. Not only does the book suggest the breadth of the effort, it reveals how each aspect reveals ideas and science never before suspected. . . . [The author] does what excellent science reporters do—he translates at times difficult concepts into language those of us who barely passed 'Bonehead Chemistry' can understand." Seattle Post-Intelligencer
Includes bibliographical references

Koerner, David
Here be dragons; the scientific quest for extraterrestrial life; [by] David Koerner, Simon LeVay. Oxford Univ. Press 2000 264p il pa $24.95 hardcover o.p.
Grades: 11 12 Adult   **576.839**
1. Life on other planets 2. Life—Origin
ISBN 0-19-514600-X (pa)
LC 99-38170

Koerner, David—*Continued*

In this book the authors explore "the origin of life and its occurrence outside Earth. . . . They offer a broad overview of up-to-date research and thought on topics ranging from the chemistry of life's origins to the search for extra-solar planets, the process of evolution, and the nature of life and the cosmos." Booklist

Includes bibliographical references

577 Ecology

Agosta, William C.

Thieves, deceivers, and killers; tales of chemistry in nature; [by] William Agosta. Princeton Univ. Press 2001 241p $26.95; pa $16.95

Grades: 11 12 Adult   577

1. Ecology 2. Animal communication
ISBN 0-691-00488-9; 0-691-09273-7 (pa)
                                        LC 00-32627

The author "discusses chemical substances used for protection or communications in plants and animals and how these substances have found use as bactericides, repellents, and medicinals. This small book contains many detailed and fascinating descriptions of interspecies interactions and how nature uses chemical substances for communications, defense, and offense in the world of microbes, insects, and mammals." Choice

Includes glossary and bibliographical references

Roston, Eric

The carbon age; how life's core element has become civilization's greatest threat. Distributed to the trade by Macmillan 2008 309p il $25.99

Grades: 11 12 Adult   577

1. Carbon 2. Atmosphere
ISBN 978-0-8027-1557-9; 0-8027-1557-5
                                        LC 2008-2754

"The first half traces carbon's history from the beginning of the universe, the Big Bang, and the nucleosynthesis (the formation of the elements) through the life cycle of stars, and then covers the development of life and dynamics of the 'natural' carbon cycle of Earth. The second section spans the last 150 years and delves into the impact of humans on the climate in creating what Roston calls the 'industrial carbon cycle.' Without using a great deal of scientific jargon, Roston leads us patiently and clearly through this complex issue." Libr J

Includes bibliographical references

Slobodkin, Lawrence B.

A citizen's guide to ecology. Oxford University Press 2003 245p hardcover o.p. pa $14.95

Grades: 11 12 Adult   577

1. Ecology 2. Human influence on nature
ISBN 0-19-516286-2; 0-19-516287-0 (pa)
                                        LC 2002-72826

This book attempts to explain "the ecological world, and how individual citizens can participate in practical decisions on ecological issues. It tackles such issues as

global warming, ecology and health, organic farming, species extinction and adaptation, and endangered species." Publisher's note

"Slobodkin's sober examination of [the issues] . . . offers the empowerment that arises from genuine knowledge about problems." Booklist

Includes bibliographical references

Stolzenberg, William

Where the wild things were; life, death, and ecological wreckage in a land of vanishing predators. Bloomsbury 2008 291p $24.99

Grades: 11 12 Adult   577

1. Predatory animals 2. Ecology 3. Endangered species
ISBN 978-1-59691-299-1; 1-59691-299-5
                                        LC 2008-2392

A look at how the disappearance of the world's great predators has upset the delicate balance of the environment, and what their disappearance portends for the future.

This "is one of those rare books that provide not just an enriching story, but a new, clarifying lens through which to understand the world around us." Christ Sci Monit

Includes bibliographical references

577.2   Specific factors affecting ecology

Casper, Julie Kerr

Changing ecosystems; effects of global warming. Facts on File 2010 254p il map (Global warming) $40

Grades: 9 10 11 12   577.2

1. Ecology 2. Greenhouse effect
ISBN 978-0-8160-7263-7; 0-8160-7263-9
                                        LC 2009-1411

In this book on global warming, the author examines "boreal and tropical forests, grasslands, deserts, mountains, and Arctic and marine environments. Within each section, specific problems such as drought, fire, and the extermination of species are considered, as is the resulting economic impact. The concluding chapter addresses the possibility of adaptation by animal species and vegetation and the need for decisions by qualified policy makers working in conjunction with knowledgeable scientists." SLJ

Includes glossary and bibliographical references

Montaigne, Fen

Fraser's penguins; a journey to the future in Antarctica. Henry Holt and Co. 2010 288p il map $26

Grades: 11 12 Adult   577.2

1. Fraser, Bill 2. Penguins 3. Climate—Environmental aspects 4. Human influence on nature 5. Antarctica—Description and travel
ISBN 978-0-8050-7942-5; 0-8050-7942-4
                                        LC 2010-07151

"A John Macrae book"

Montaigne, Fen—*Continued*

The author "spent five months tracking penguins through the breeding season on the northwestern Antarctica peninsula with the scientist Bill Fraser, and his book is a bittersweet account of the stark beauty of the continent and the climate change that threatens its delicate ecosystem. . . . Montaigne poetically portrays the daunting Antarctic landscape and gives readers an intimate perspective on its rugged, audacious, and charming penguin and human inhabitants." Publ Wkly

Includes bibliographical references

Russell, Edmund, 1957-

War and nature; fighting humans and insects with chemicals from World War I to Silent Spring. Cambridge Univ. Press 2001 315p (Studies in environment and history) $55; pa $20

Grades: 9 10 11 12   **577.2**
1. Chemical warfare 2. Pest control 3. Insect pests
ISBN 0-521-79003-4; 0-521-79937-6 (pa)
                                    LC 00-40323

The author "traces military and agricultural use of poison gases, incendiaries, smokes, insecticides and pesticides, while exploring the toll on human life, culture and the environment." Publ Wkly

This is an "innovative and illuminating study." Booklist

Includes bibliographical references

577.3   Forest ecology

Allaby, Michael, 1933-

Temperate forests; illustrations by Richard Garratt. rev ed. Facts on File 2008 336p il map (Ecosystem) $70

Grades: 7 8 9 10   **577.3**
1. Forest ecology 2. Forests and forestry
ISBN 0-8160-5930-6; 978-0-8160-5930-0
                                    LC 2006-28859

First published 1999

This book "explores the evolution and contributions of this unique environment and how society can and must preserve it." Publisher's note

"Those who are curious about or who are studying the environment and ecosystems . . . will find this book both fascinating and enlightening." Sci Books Films

Includes glossary and bibliographical references

Forsyth, Adrian

Nature of the rainforest; Costa Rica and beyond; photographs by Michael Fogden and Patricia Fogden; foreword by E.O. Wilson. Comstock Pub. Associates 2008 183p il pa $29.95

Grades: 11 12 Adult   **577.3**
1. Rain forest ecology
ISBN 978-0-8014-7475-0; 0-8014-7475-2
                                    LC 2008-19291

"A Zona Tropical publication"

First published 1990 by Camden House (Camden East) with title: Portraits of the rainforest

"There are 17 sections, plus a foreword by E. O. Wilson and a preface. Each section explores either a specific theme or a particular tropical place in Costa Rica (Guanacaste, Monteverde, Osa) or 'beyond' (Amazônia). The themes expore such topics as diversity, nutrient cycles in the tropics, and chemical defenses. . . . Although the book is so clearly and cleverly written that a layperson will easily enjoy it . . . an experienced tropical ecologist can read it and gain new insights. . . . This is an excellent book; come for the pictures and stay for the text!" Sci Books Films

Includes bibliographical references

Moore, Peter D. (Peter Dale)

Tropical forests; illustrations by Richard Garratt. Facts On File 2008 xx, 246p il map (Ecosystem) $70

Grades: 7 8 9 10   **577.3**
1. Rain forest ecology 2. Forests and forestry
ISBN 0-8160-5934-9; 978-0-8160-5934-8
                                    LC 2006-37441

This book "explores the great biodiversity of [tropical] forests, from microbes to mammals, as well as the adaptations of organisms to their environment and to the other species surrounding them. The interactions between organisms and their physical surroundings are examined, as are the processes linking the two into an integrated ecosystem." Publisher's note

Includes glossary and bibliographical references

Preston, Richard

The wild trees; a story of passion and daring. Random House 2007 294p il map $25.95; pa $16

Grades: 11 12 Adult   **577.3**
1. Sillett, Steve 2. Redwood
ISBN   978-1-4000-6489-2;   1-4000-6489-9;
978-0-8129-7559-8 (pa); 0-8129-7559-6 (pa)
                                    LC 2006-48646

The author tells the story of Steve Sillett, Marie Antoine and other naturalists and researchers who climb and explore giant redwoods in northern California

"There is something so elementally boyish in searching out the biggest and tallest, poring over maps and measurements, dubbing these trees with names lifted from J.R.R. Tolkein's Middle Earth. . . . Preston knows how to fold the science into the seams of his narrative, and his dry humor crops up, pleasurably, at the edges of his observations." Cleveland Plain Dealer

577.5   Ecology of miscellaneous environments

Allaby, Michael, 1933-

Deserts; illustrations by Richard Garratt. rev ed. Facts on File 2008 320p il map (Ecosystem) $70 *

Grades: 7 8 9 10   **577.5**
1. Desert ecology 2. Deserts
ISBN 0-8160-5929-2; 978-0-8160-5929-4
                                    LC 2007-00477

First published 2001

Allaby, Michael, 1933-—*Continued*

This book provides "information on the climatic conditions that produce deserts and the climate cycles that make them expand and contract. . . . [It] also explores the locations and general types of deserts, and provides detailed accounts of the most important deserts." Publisher's note

"This book is a good mix of text, excellent maps, photographs, and scientific information." Sci Books Films

Includes glossary and bibliographical references

Gritzner, Charles F.

Deserts. Chelsea House 2006 127p il map (Geography of extreme environments) lib bdg $24.95

Grades: 9 10 11 12   577.5

1. Deserts

ISBN 0-7910-9234-8; 978-0-7910-9234-7

LC 2006-25584

This book on deserts discusses desert weather and climate, geography, the ecosystem, the native cultures that live there, and future prospects for the people that live there.

Includes bibliographical references

Polar regions. Chelsea House 2006 126p il map (Geography of extreme environments) lib bdg $24.95

Grades: 9 10 11 12   577.5

1. Polar regions

ISBN 0-7910-9235-6; 978-0-7910-9235-4

LC 2006-19636

"This volume introduces readers to the climatic 'ends of the Earth,' one of the planet's most unique and perhaps most challenging ecosystems. Polar Regions reveals how these stark locations, once believed to be inhospitable, have in fact been home to a number of culture groups." Publisher's note

Includes glossary and bibliographical references

Moore, Peter D. (Peter Dale)

Tundra; [by] Peter D. Moore; illustrations by Richard Garratt. Facts on File 2006 xx, 220p il (Ecosystem) $39.50

Grades: 7 8 9 10   577.5

1. Tundra ecology

ISBN 0-8160-5325-1; 978-0-8160-5933-1

LC 2005-35618

This discusses "the geography, geology, ecology, economic uses, and future of [tundras]. . . . [It] includes both the polar regions and the peaks of the Earth's highest mountains. . . . [The text is] well organized. . . . Numerous sidebars; captioned maps, diagrams, and scattered charts; and high-quality color photographs of plant and animal life are included." SLJ

Includes bibliographical references

Swan, Robert, 1956-

Antarctica 2041; my quest to save the earth's last wilderness; [by] Robert Swan with Gil Reavill. Broadway Books 2009 290p il map $24.99

Grades: 11 12 Adult   577.5

1. Antarctica—Description and travel
2. Environmental protection

ISBN 978-0-7679-3175-5   LC 2009-10963

The author, "the first person to walk to both the North and South Poles, combines adventure and environmentalism in this thoughtful consideration of Antarctica. His lifelong admiration for Robert Scott inspired him to follow in the explorer's footsteps. . . . This is a man with a mission, and his story is the sort to make you get up and do something—maybe even try to save the world." Booklist

Includes bibliographical references

577.7   Marine ecology

Carson, Rachel, 1907-1964

The edge of the sea; with illustrations by Bob Hines. Houghton Mifflin 1955 276p il pa $14 hardcover o.p.

Grades: 7 8 9 10 11 12 Adult   577.7

1. Marine biology 2. Seashore

ISBN 0-395-92496-0 (pa)

"The seashores of the world may be divided into three basic types: the rugged shores of rock, the sand beaches, and the coral reefs and all their associated features. Each has its typical community of plants and animals. The Atlantic coast of the United States [provides] clear examples of each of these types. I have chosen it as the setting for my pictures of shore life." Preface

Ellis, Richard, 1938-

The empty ocean; plundering the world's marine life; written and illustrated by Richard Ellis. Island Press 2003 367p il hardcover o.p. pa $25 *

Grades: 11 12 Adult   577.7

1. Marine ecology 2. Endangered species

ISBN 1-55963-974-1; 1-55963-637-8 (pa)

The author "explains the economic, political, historical, and biological reasons for declining fisheries, the plight of sea turtles, disappearance of marine birds, slaughter of marine mammals, and destruction of coral reefs." Libr J

"Rather than writing the 'Silent Spring' of the oceans, [Ellis] has produced a book that is likely to provide the inspiration and source materials for such a badly needed work . . . It is also a splendid example of history illuminating ecology, with well-chosen facts that enable us to picture a largely invisible catastrophe." N Y Times Book Rev

Includes bibliographical references

Sheppard, Charles, 1962-2005

Coral reefs. Voyageur Press 2002 72p il (World life library) pa $16.95

Grades: 9 10 11 12   577.7

1. Coral reefs and islands 2. Marine ecology

ISBN 0-8965-8220-5   LC 2002-3005

Sheppard, Charles, 1962-2005—*Continued*
Describes the nature, growth, location, and ecology of coral reefs.
Includes bibliographical references

Walker, Pamela, 1958-
The coral reef; [by] Pam Walker and Elaine Wood. Facts on File 2005 140p (Life in the sea) $35 *
Grades: 6 7 8 9 10   **577.7**
    1. Coral reefs and islands
    ISBN 0-8160-5703-6
"An opening chapter gives detailed coverage of how reefs are formed. Later chapters examine the reefs' inhabitants, from essential microbes to the larger, showier fish, reptiles, and other animals. The final chapter . . . mentions environmental hazards and conservation efforts. . . . The range and depth of information . . . make this a fine addition for science collections." Booklist

577.8 Synecology and population biology

Crump, Martha L.
Sexy orchids make lousy lovers & other unusual relationships; with illustrations by Alan Crump. The University of Chicago Press 2009 214p il $25
Grades: 11 12 Adult   **577.8**
    1. Animal behavior
    ISBN 978-0-226-12185-7; 0-226-12185-2
                                LC 2009-11857
This book describes "unusual natural histories, . . . focusing on extraordinary interactions involving animals, plants, fungi, and bacteria." Publisher's note
"Crump maintains a cheeky sense of humor as she dispels all sorts of myths about the animal kingdom and reveals a wealth of biological information. . . . With Alan Crump's drawings on every page, Marty Crump's discussions on animal and human connections are more friendly chat than lecture; as pleasant a sojourn into so many different worlds as any reader could want." Booklist
Includes bibliographical references

578 Natural history of organisms and related subjects

Weidensaul, Scott
Return to wild America; a yearlong journey in search of the continent's natural soul. North Point Press 2005 xx, 394p il map $26; pa $15 *
Grades: 11 12 Adult   **578**
    1. Peterson, Roger Tory, 1908-1996 2. Fisher, James Maxwell McConnell, 1912-1970 3. Natural history—North America
    ISBN 0-8654-7688-8; 0-8654-7731-0 (pa)
                                LC 2005-47720
Fifty years after the publishing of Roger Tory Peterson's and James Fisher's *Wild America*, the author retraces Peterson and Fisher's steps "from Newfoundland's craggy coastline, down the East Coast, into Mexico and up the West Coast to Alaska. . . . This engrossing state-of-nature memoir, making a vibrant case for preserving America's wild past for future Americans, promises to become a classic in its own right." Publ Wkly
Includes bibliographical references

Wolfe, David W.
Tales from the underground; a natural history of subterranean life. Perseus Bks. 2001 221p il pa $18 hardcover o.p.
Grades: 11 12 Adult   **578**
    1. Soil microbiology
    ISBN 0-7382-0679-2 (pa)
The author discusses the ecology of life in the soil and the earth's rocky crust, including Darwin's experiments with earthworms, Lewis and Clark's first encounter with prairie dogs, the use of genetic tools, and the possible role of primitive underground microbes in evolution.
Wolfe "explains in a straightforward, readable style that there is probably as much biodiversity and even as much biomass below ground as above." New Sci
Includes bibliographical references

578.4 Adaptation

Bonner, John Tyler
Why size matters; from bacteria to blue whales. Princeton University Press 2006 161p il $16.95
Grades: 11 12 Adult   **578.4**
    1. Size
    ISBN 978-0-691-12850-4; 0-691-12850-2
                                LC 2006-04945
"The strength, surface area, complexity, rates of living processes such as metabolism and longevity, and abundance of organisms [are related to body size]." Sci Books Films
The author's "tone is warm and engaging, his illustrative examples are simple to grasp, while his prose is precise, clear and highly readable." Times Lit Suppl
Includes bibliographical references

Gross, Michael, 1963-
Life on the edge; amazing creatures thriving in extreme environments. Plenum Trade 1998 200p il pa $15 hardcover o.p.
Grades: 11 12 Adult   **578.4**
    1. Adaptation (Biology) 2. Stress (Physiology) 3. Life—Origin
    ISBN 0-7382-0445-5 (pa)   LC 98-4622
Translated from the German
Gross introduces a variety of extremophiles, or "organisms that survive in the most hostile habitats—extremes of temperature, salinity, acidity, alkalinity—as well as deep below the earth's surface." Choice
"The book constitutes an accessible introduction to an exciting outpost on the scientific frontier." Booklist
Includes glossary and bibliographical references

Life; extraordinary animals, extreme behaviour; [by] Martha Holmes and Mike Gunton; [with] Rupert Barrington ... [et al.] University of California Press 2010 311p il map $39.95
Grades: 11 12 Adult   **578.4**
1. Adaptation (Biology) 2. Animal behavior
ISBN 978-0-520-26537-0; 0-520-26537-8
                                    LC 2009-31158
First published 2009 in the United Kingdom

"In 2009, to commemorate the 200th anniversary of Charles Darwin's birth, the BBC premiered the ten-episode television documentary Life to great acclaim. . . . Written by the documentary's producers, this impressive companion volume showcases species of fish, amphibians, reptiles, insects, birds, mammals, and plants that have developed unique or unusual strategies for solving 'the eternal problems of life': finding food, escaping predators, attracting mates, and raising young. . . . Even the most casual reader will be awed by the beauty, complexity, and ingenuity of nature as celebrated here." Libr J

578.6 Miscellaneous nontaxonomic kinds of organisms

Fleisher, Paul
Parasites; latching on to a free lunch. Twenty-First Century Books 2006 112p il (Discovery!) lib bdg $29.27
Grades: 7 8 9 10   **578.6**
1. Parasites
ISBN 978-0-8225-3415-0; 0-8225-3415-0
                                    LC 2005-10521
This book describes "all sorts of unpleasant creatures that can feed on your body—head lice, fleas, ticks, tapeworms, and fungi—as well as the huge variety of parasites that feed on animals and plants all around you." Publisher's note
This is "well organized and quite up to date. The photos . . . are plentiful, colorful, and excellent. . . . Clear, concise, and interesting." Voice Youth Advocates
Includes bibliographical references

Foster, Steven, 1957-
A field guide to venomous animals and poisonous plants; North America, North of Mexico; [by] Steven Foster and Roger A. Caras. Houghton Mifflin 1994 244p il pa $21 hardcover o.p. *
Grades: 11 12 Adult   **578.6**
1. Poisonous animals 2. Poisonous plants
ISBN 0-395-93608-X (pa)   LC 94-1641
"The Peterson field guide series"
Sponsored by National Audubon Society, National Wildlife Federation, and Roger Tory Peterson Institute
This guide includes "90 animals from the mildly irritating to the deadly venomous: stinging and biting insects, scorpions and spiders, mammals, and reptiles, with an emphasis on snakes. More than 250 plants are described: wildflowers, weeds and exotic aliens, shrubs, trees, ferns, and mushrooms. The list includes plants that

often cause allergies or dermatitis, such as Poison Ivy, as well as those that are toxic to eat." Publisher's note
Includes glossary and bibliographical references

578.68 Rare and endangered species

Endangered species: opposing viewpoints; Viqi Wagner, book editor. Greenhaven Press 2008 230p map lib bdg $38.50; pa $26.75 *
Grades: 8 9 10 11 12   **578.68**
1. Endangered species 2. Nature conservation
ISBN   978-0-7377-2931-3   (lib   bdg); 978-0-7377-2932-0 (pa)   LC 2007-38314
"Opposing viewpoints series"
This collection of articles offers varying viewpoints on extinction, preservation, property rights, and international cooperation.
Includes bibliographical references

McGavin, George
Endangered; wildlife on the brink of extinction. Firefly Books 2006 192p il map $35
Grades: 7 8 9 10 11 12 Adult   **578.68**
1. Endangered species 2. Rare animals
ISBN 1-55407-183-6; 978-1-55407-183-8
                                    LC 2007-271504
"Featuring more than 400 photographs, this book details the plant and animal species that are either endangered or so severely threatened that they soon will be." Publisher's note
"Written in simple, nonscientific prose and fully illustrated with color photographs, maps, and many sidebars, the book is visually appealing as well as intellectually stimulating." Voice Youth Advocates

McLeish, Todd
Basking with humpbacks; tracking threatened marine life in New England waters. University Press of New England 2009 214p il $26.95
Grades: 11 12 Adult   **578.68**
1. Marine animals 2. Endangered species
ISBN 978-1-58465-676-0; 1-58465-676-X
                                    LC 2009-15170
"This book profiles the biology of over a dozen (mostly) threatened or endangered marine organisms found in New England. Not a scientist himself, the author goes out in the field with marine scientists who are studying these animals, and through hands-on experiences and extensive conversations with the researchers gives the reader an understanding of the basic biology of these animals and the human-caused threats they face. . . . The book will be of interest to students, naturalists, and environmentalists, and will be an enjoyable read for professionals as well." Sci Books Films
Includes bibliographical references

578.7 Organisms characteristic of specific kinds of environments

Burt, William, 1948-
Marshes; the disappearing Edens. Yale University Press 2007 179p il $35
Grades: 11 12 Adult   **578.7**
1. Marshes
ISBN 978-0-300-12229-9; 0-300-12229-2
LC 2006-26961
This book combines photographs of marsh life with information about wetland habitat in North America.
"This well-structured, readable book will be valuable for students, teachers, researchers, and sundry readers interested in a unique kind of wetland. Reading this book is an excellent way to understand marshes as wild places." Choice
Includes bibliographical references

Cramer, Deborah
Smithsonian ocean; our water, our world. Smithsonian Books 2008 295p il map $39.95
Grades: 11 12 Adult   **578.7**
1. Marine biology 2. Marine ecology
ISBN 978-0-06-134383-4; 0-06-134383-8
LC 2008-15633
In this study, Cramer contends that "the vital partnership between earth and the life it nourishes has recently been disrupted." Publisher's note
"With its hundreds of beautiful photographs, the volume is visually enchanting. It is also a vividly, accurately, and clearly written survey of the state of our understanding . . . of the history and current condition of the ocean." Sci Books Films
Includes bibliographical references

Crist, Darlene Trew
World ocean census; a global survey of marine life; [by] Darlene Trew Crist, Gail Scowcroft, James M. Harding, Jr. Firefly Books 2009 256p il map $40
Grades: 10 11 12 Adult   **578.7**
1. Census of Marine Life (Project) 2. Marine animals 3. Marine biology 4. Science—Methodology
ISBN 978-1-55407-434-1; 1-55407-434-7
"The Census of Marine Life is a global network of scientists in more than 80 nations involved in a ten-year project to assess and explain the diversity of life in the oceans. . . . [The authors] describe the various aspects of the Census for the educated layperson. Illustrated with examples of creatures found in all parts of the oceans, including many newly discovered and never-before-described species, chapters cover the different project groups, how they are gathering and publishing data, and why this is important." Libr J
The authors "have produced a highly readable text with stunning photos that should fully engage the public imagination." Publ Wkly
Includes bibliographical references

Guide to wetlands; Patrick Dugan, general editor. Firefly Books 2005 304p il maps pa $19.95 *
Grades: 9 10 11 12   **578.7**
1. Wetlands
ISBN 1-55407-111-9   LC 2006-276145
At head of title on cover: Firefly
This handbook provides "information on the major wetlands of the world, with an emphasis on their ecological roles, human impact, and conservation. The diversity of habitats includes estuaries, tidal flats, floodplains, freshwater marshes, and swamps." Choice
"This book would be a great resource for addressing the ecological role, diversity, and human use of wetlands." Sci Books Films

Marent, Thomas, 1966-
Rainforest; [by] Thomas Marent with Ben Morgan. DK Pub. 2006 360p il map hardcover o.p. pa $24.95 *
Grades: 11 12 Adult   **578.7**
1. Rain forests—Pictorial works
ISBN   0-7566-1940-8;   978-0-7566-1940-4; 0-7566-6599-X (pa); 978-0-7566-6599-9 (pa)
LC 2006-6774
Includes audio CD
This "book is the product of Swiss photographer Marent's passion for exploring rainforests on five continents and over 16 years. His spectacularly beautiful photographs show much about the nature of rainforests and their curious inhabitants, and the accompanying text explains what you are seeing and what it can tell you about these ecosystems. . . . An accompanying CD provides rainforest sounds from various locations. This book . . . is not only beautiful but an excellent source of information. It also shows the amazing diversity of species that makes rainforests unique and valuable." Libr J

Moore, Peter D. (Peter Dale)
Wetlands; illustrations by Richard Garratt. rev ed. Facts on File 2008 270p il map (Ecosystem) $70 *
Grades: 7 8 9 10   **578.7**
1. Wetlands
ISBN 0-8160-5931-4; 978-0-8160-5931-7
LC 2006-37399
First published 2000
This book "examines the diversity of wetlands in the past, present, and future, how they work, and how they can be conserved." Publisher's note
Includes glossary and bibliographical references

Oldfield, Sara
Rainforest; photography by Bruce Coleman Collection; foreword by Mark Rose. MIT Press 2003 160p il map $29.95
Grades: 11 12 Adult   **578.7**
1. Rain forests
ISBN 0-262-15106-5   LC 2002-29559
"Each chapter covers a major rainforest region: Africa, Madagascar, India and Southeast Asia, Indonesia and the Philippines, Central America, the Caribbean, the Amazon

Oldfield, Sara—*Continued*
. . . and Brazil, as well as the temperate rainforests in areas such as Tasmania and North America. The book details habitat, plants and animals, and threats to the precarious balance between humans and rainforests. The introduction provides an overview of the world's rainforests and a summary of current conservation issues." Publisher's note

The author "presents a wonderful overview of both tropical and temperate rainforests. . . . An excellent primer on this imperiled ecosystem." Booklist

Weis, Judith S., 1941-
Salt marshes; a natural and unnatural history; [by] Judith S. Weis and Carol A. Butler. Rutgers University Press 2009 254p il $49.95; pa $23.95
Grades: 11 12 Adult   **578.7**
    1. Salt marshes
    ISBN 978-0-8135-4548-6; 978-0-8135-4570-7 (pa)
                       LC 2008-43710
This is "an outstanding study of North American salt marshes, their natural histories, contributions to human wellbeing, and what their destruction means from human life and property. . . . This account should make an informative treat for any armchair conservationist." Publ Wkly
    Includes bibliographical references

579   Microorganisms, fungi, algae

Ben-Barak, Idan
The invisible kingdom; from the tips of our fingers to the tops of our trash, inside the curious world of microbes. Basic Books 2009 204p $24
Grades: 10 11 12 Adult   **579**
    1. Microbiology
    ISBN 978-0-465-01887-1; 0-465-01887-4
                       LC 2009-19655
First published in 2008 in Australia with title: Small wonders: how microbes rule our world
The author "gives an enthusiastic tour of single-celled life. . . . He touches on myriad microbes in a range of environments, from the abyss of the sea to the inside of humans, explaining how they defend themselves, eat, move, and reproduce." Booklist
    Includes bibliographical references

Rainis, Kenneth G.
A guide to microlife; [by] Kenneth G. Rainis and Bruce J. Russell. Watts 1996 287p il lib bdg $40
Grades: 9 10 11 12   **579**
    1. Microorganisms 2. Microbiology
    ISBN 0-531-11266-7   LC 95-44973
Serves as a guide to be used for the identification of microorganisms and provides information about microlife forms and how they affect other life forms, including human
"A good resource for classrooms, this colorful volume is packed with information." SLJ
    Includes bibliographical references

Sankaran, Neeraja
Microbes and people: an A-Z of microorganisms in our lives. Oryx Press 2000 297p il $62.95
Grades: 11 12 Adult   **579**
    1. Microbiology—Dictionaries 2. Reference books
    ISBN 1-57356-217-3   LC 00-10117
"Entries cover environmental, industrial, and food microbiology, in addition to the microbiology of health and disease. Scientific techniques used for studying microorganisms are discussed, and biographies of key individuals are provided. A chronology of infections and disease epidemics from 430 BC to the present is included as an appendix." Publisher's note

"Because it provides very readable coverage of topics so much in the news lately, this dictionary will be much used in high school, undergraduate, and public libraries." Booklist
    Includes bibliographical references

579.6   Mushrooms

Læssøe, Thomas
Mushrooms; editorial consultant, Gary Lincoff; photography by Neil Fletcher. 2nd American ed. DK Pub. 2002 304p il (Smithsonian handbooks) $20
Grades: 9 10 11 12   **579.6**
    1. Mushrooms
    ISBN 0-7894-8986-4
First published 1998 as part of the Eyewitness handbooks series
This is a "guide to more than 500 species of mushroom and other macrofungi found in northern temperate zones worldwide. . . . For each species, there are one to four sharp, detailed color photos with clues about their identity. There is also a small color painting of habitat suitable for the growth of the species. . . . This book should prove invaluable at any level, from casual nature observer to professional mycologist." Sci Books Films [review of 1998 edition]

Lincoff, Gary
The Audubon Society field guide to North American mushrooms; [by] Gary H. Lincoff; visual key by Carol Nehring. Knopf 1981 926p il $19.95 *
Grades: 7 8 9 10 11 12 Adult   **579.6**
    1. Mushrooms
    ISBN 0-394-51992-2   LC 81-80827
"A Chanticleer Press edition. The Audubon Society field guide series"
This guide to 703 species of common mushrooms provides 762 color photographs and descriptions as keys to identifying these plants.
"The author is an expert on mushroom toxins and instills responsible cautions. The photos are uncommonly beautiful." SLJ

McKnight, Kent H.

A field guide to mushrooms, North America; [by] Kent H. McKnight and Vera B. McKnight; illustrations by Vera B. McKnight. Houghton Mifflin 1987 429p il pa $21 hardcover o.p. *

Grades: 11 12 Adult   **579.6**

1. Mushrooms

ISBN 0-395-91090-0 (pa)   LC 86-27799

"The Peterson field guide series"

"Sponsored by the National Audubon Society and the National Wildlife Federation"

"More than 500 species [of mushrooms] are described and depicted. . . . Edibility of each species is noted and signified by marginal pictograms both in the text and on the colorplates. . . . Appended: a genial chapter of recipes by Anne Dow, glossary, selected references, and index." Booklist

580 Plants (Botany)

Huxley, Anthony Julian, 1920-

Green inheritance; the WWF book of plants; [by] Anthony Huxley; foreword by Sir David Attenborough. Rev., by Martin Walters. University of California Press 2005 192p il map pa $29.95

Grades: 9 10 11 12   **580**

1. Plant conservation

ISBN 0-520-24359-5   LC 2005-52876

"A completely revised and expanded edition of the WWF book of plants"

First published 1985

This book "draws attention to the problems facing the planet at large as well as the ways each individual can conserve natural resources. Overall, the educational and wide-ranging text promotes an appreciation for the wondrous properties of plant life, from basic sustenance and curative powers to the ecology of insects and flowers." Booklist

Includes bibliographical references

Magill's encyclopedia of science; plant life; editor, Bryan D. Ness. Salem Press 2002 4v il map set $457

Grades: 11 12 Adult   **580**

1. Reference books 2. Botany—Encyclopedias

ISBN 1-58765-084-3   LC 2002-13319

This encyclopedia provides "information for any study related to plants, archaea, bacteria, algae, or fungi, from molecular-level processes to planet-wide economic or environmental issues. The 379 signed articles, about half of which are published with revisions and updated bibliographies from several of the publisher's earlier reference books, are arranged into a single alphabet." SLJ

Includes bibliographical references

Stuppy, Wolfgang

The bizarre and incredible world of plants; [by] Wolfgang Stuppy, Rob Kesseler, Madeline Harley; edited by Alexandra Papadakis. Firefly Books 2009 135p il $29.95

Grades: 11 12 Adult   **580**

1. Plants—Pictorial works

ISBN 978-1-55407-533-1; 1-55407-533-5

LC 2009-675174

This is a "gorgeous and mind-blowing volume about the marvelous yet secret lives of plants. The astonishing pictures are matched by scientifically exacting explanations of how plants, which produce oxygen and feed either directly or indirectly all life on Earth, have evolved sophisticated survival strategies, including symbiotic relationships with pollinators." Booklist

Includes bibliographical references

580.7 Education, research, related topics

Gardner, Robert, 1929-

Science projects about plants. Enslow Pubs. 1999 112p il (Science projects) lib bdg $26.60

Grades: 7 8 9 10   **580.7**

1. Plants 2. Science projects 3. Science—Experiments

ISBN 0-89490-952-5   LC 98-6821

Provides instructions for over thirty experiments appropriate for science fairs, involving plant physiology, reproduction, and growth

"The book offers solid ideas for projects." Booklist

Includes bibliographical references

581.6 Miscellaneous nontaxonomic kinds of plants

Laws, Bill

Fifty plants that changed the course of history; written by Bill Laws. Firefly Books 2010 223p il $29.95

Grades: 11 12 Adult   **581.6**

1. Economic botany

ISBN 978-1-55407-798-4; 1-55407-798-2

LC 2011-414731

This is a "guide to the plants that have had the greatest impact on human civilization. Entries feature a description of the plant, its botanical name, its native range and its primary functions edible, medicinal, commercial or practical." Publisher's note

Includes bibliographical references

581.7 Plant ecology, plants characteristic of specific environments

Bodden, Valerie

Critical plant life. Creative Education 2010 48p il (Earth issues) $23.95

Grades: 7 8 9 10   **581.7**

Bodden, Valerie—_Continued_
1. Plant ecology
ISBN 978-1-58341-984-7; 1-58341-984-5
"An examination of the endangerment and extinction of certain plant life, exploring how plants in general affect Earth's biodiversity and temperature, as well as how they contribute to a healthier planet." Publisher's note
"The scientific information is up to date, well written for a lay audience, and presented in a highly engaging and visually appealing format." Sci Books Films
Includes glossary and bibliographical references

Rice, Stanley Arthur, 1957-
Green planet; how plants keep the Earth alive; [by] Stanley A. Rice. Rutgers University Press 2009 298p il map $27.95
Grades: 9 10 11 12 Adult   581.7
1. Plant ecology
ISBN 978-0-8135-4453-3; 0-8135-4453-X
                                      LC 2008-13964
"This work is notable for its breadth of coverage of not only how plants directly affect humans (e.g., agriculture and oxygen production), but also of how plants affect the functioning of the ecosystems that humans need for a range of goods and services (e.g., climate, soil renewal, habitat creation). . . . The 37 illustrations and 18 tables help clarify key points and simplify difficult concepts." Choice
Includes bibliographical references

582.13 Plants noted for their flowers

Burger, William C., 1932-
Flowers: how they changed the world. Prometheus Books 2006 337p il $23
Grades: 11 12 Adult   582.13
1. Flowers
ISBN 1-59102-407-2; 978-1-59102-407-1
                                      LC 2006-2739
This book "begins with basic facts about the morphology and physiology of plant growth and concludes by explaining how plants have played a major role in creating the modern world." Sci Books Films
This is "an engaging and beautifully written look at how flowering plants, over more than 100 million years, have 'transformed terrestrial ecosystems, supported the origin of primates, and helped us humans become the masters of our planet.'" Publ Wkly
Includes bibliographical references

Spellenberg, Richard
Familiar flowers of North America: eastern region; Ann H. Whitman, editor. Knopf 1986 192p il pa $9
Grades: 11 12 Adult   582.13
1. Wild flowers
ISBN 0-394-74843-3   LC 86-045587
"Chanticleer Press editions. The Audubon Society pocket guides"

This guide to 80 eastern wildflowers is arranged by color and shape of the flower and includes color photos, drawings, and descriptions of the plants habitat and range, folklore and history

Familiar flowers of North America: western region; Ann H. Whitman, editor. Knopf 1986 192p il pa $4.95
Grades: 11 12 Adult   582.13
1. Wild flowers
ISBN 0-394-74844-1   LC 86-045586
"Chanticleer Press editions. The Audubon Society pocket guides"
Eighty "color plates, arranged by the color and shape of the flower, fill the main section of this truly pocket-size field guide. Each entry also includes a line drawing, a description of the plant's habitat and range, and a paragraph explaining its place among other flowers and its folklore or history. . . . Appendices include a brief glossary and an alphabetic and a family index." BAYA Book Rev

National Audubon Society field guide to North American wildflowers, western region. 2nd ed rev. Knopf 2001 862p il map $19.95 *
Grades: 7 8 9 10 11 12 Adult   582.13
1. Wild flowers
ISBN 0-375-40233-0   LC 2001-269242
"A Chanticleer Press edition"
First published 1979
"More than 940 . . . full-color images show the wildflowers of western North America close-up and in their natural habitats. . . . Images are grouped by flower color and shape and keyed to . . . descriptions that reflect current taxonomy." Publisher's note

Thieret, John W., 1926-2005
National Audubon Society field guide to North American wildflowers: eastern region; revising author, John W. Thieret; original authors, William A. Niering and Nancy C. Olmstead. Knopf 2001 879p il map (National Audubon Society field guide series) $19.95 *
Grades: 7 8 9 10 11 12 Adult   582.13
1. Wild flowers
ISBN 0-375-40232-2   LC 2001-269241
"A Chanticleer Press edition"
First published 1979 under the authorship of William A. Niering and Nancy C. Olmstead
Spine title: Field guide to wildflowers, eastern region
"Covers the area east of the Rockies and east of the Big Bend area of Texas to the Atlantic. Color photographs together with family and species descriptions make this a most useful field guide." Sci News {review of 1979 edition}

582.16 Trees

Familiar trees of North America: eastern region; Ann H. Whitman, editor; Jerry F. Franklin, John Farrand, Jr., consultants. Knopf 1986 192p il pa $9

Grades: 11 12 Adult   582.16
1. Trees—North America
ISBN 0-394-74851-4   LC 86-045585
"Chanticleer Press editions. The Audubon Society pocket guides"

This pocket field guide covers eighty trees commonly found in the eastern United States. Includes color photos and descriptions of characteristics, habitat, range, history, and uses

Familiar trees of North America: western region; Ann H. Whitman, editor; Jerry F. Franklin, John Farrand, Jr., consultants. Knopf 1986 192p il pa $9

Grades: 11 12 Adult   582.16
1. Trees—North America
ISBN 0-394-74852-2   LC 86-045584
"Chanticleer Press editions. The Audubon Society pocket guides"

This pocket field guide covers eighty trees commonly found in the western United States. "Each color plate is accompanied by a black silhouette of the tree and a small photo of its bark as well as a written description of its characteristics, its habitat and range, and its history and uses. . . . Introductory essays and illustrations provide a key to tree identification. Appendices include descriptions of tree families and an index to common and botanical names." BAYA Book Rev

Plotnik, Arthur, 1937-
The urban tree book; an uncommon field guide for city and town; {by} Arthur Plotnik; in consultation with the Morton Arboretum; illustrated by Mary H. Phelan. Three Rivers Press (NY) 2000 432p il pa $18.95 *
Grades: 11 12 Adult   582.16
1. Trees—United States
ISBN 0-8129-3103-3   LC 99-42452
An inquiry into the characteristics and survival strategies of nearly 200 species of trees

The author "expresses his sense of wonder about urban trees found all over the U.S. with warmth and wit as he recounts their history and lore and medicinal and spiritual legacies. . . . Plotnik also celebrates landmark trees, assesses the new urban forestry movement, and provides a wealth of useful resources." Booklist
Includes bibliographical references

Sibley, David
The Sibley guide to trees; written and illustrated by David Allen Sibley. Alfred A. Knopf 2009 xxxviii, 426p il map $39.95 *
Grades: 11 12 Adult   582.16
1. Trees—North America
ISBN 978-0-375-41519-7   LC 2009-927625

"With more than 4,100 . . . paintings, the Guide highlights the . . . similarities and distinctions between more than 600 tree species—native trees as well as many introduced species." Publisher's note

This "is an outstanding book that should be available in all public libraries, schools, colleges, universities, and homes. The text is comprehensive and the illustrations are pertinent, accurate, and clear." Sci Books Films

590 Animals (Zoology)

Conniff, Richard
Swimming with piranhas at feeding time; my life doing dumb stuff with animals. Norton 2009 299p $25.95; pa $15.95
Grades: 11 12 Adult   590
1. Dangerous animals
ISBN 978-0-393-06893-1; 978-0-393-30457-2 (pa)
                            LC 2008-51234
The author "offers a delightful collection of pieces about his encounters with spiders, crabs, leopards and other fauna. With warmth and simplicity, the author spins a beguiling web as he recalls his travels to rainforests, deserts, inner-city neighborhoods and other locales in search of interesting creatures and the often-quirky scientists who study them. . . . Bright entertainment from a great explainer of the lives of animals." Kirkus
Includes bibliographical references

Dinerstein, Eric, 1952-
Tigerland and other unintended destinations. Island Press 2005 279p $25.95; pa $16.95 *
Grades: 9 10 11 12   590
1. Ecology 2. Nature conservation
ISBN 1-55963-578-9; 1-59726-152-1 (pa)
                            LC 2005-13822
This book "takes readers on Dinerstein's unlikely journey to conservation's frontiers, from early research in Nepal to recent expeditions as head of Conservation Science at the World Wildlife Fund." Publisher's note

The author's "compelling tour of wild places and his vivid portraits of intrepid wildlife defenders offer convincing arguments for providing the treasures of nature with the same reverence and protection we accord cherished works of art." Booklist

Noyes, Deborah, 1965-
One kingdom; our lives with animals—the human-animal bond in myth, history, science, and story. Houghton Mifflin Company 2006 128p il $18
Grades: 7 8 9 10   590
1. Animals
ISBN 0-618-49914-8   LC 2005-25446
In this "photo-essay, Noyes examines the ways that human lives have overlapped with animals and how our beliefs, culture, and science have been impacted throught history by the essential but frequently paradoxical human-animal connection. . . . Readers will find the provocative questions Noyes raises compelling and challeng-

Noyes, Deborah, 1965-—*Continued*
ing, and the lyrical, urgent prose, along with beautiful black-and-white photos of the animals up close, will draw serious students and browsers alike." Booklist

Includes bibliographical references

Smith, Lewis
Why the cheetah cheats; and other mysteries of the natural world. Firefly Books 2009 240p il $29.95
Grades: 11 12 Adult   **590**
1. Animals 2. Zoology 3. Natural history
ISBN 978-1-55407-534-8
"In 100 brief and lively dispatches accompanied by striking photographs, science journalist Smith captures telling moments on the nature research beat. . . . Whether the subject is dire (bats, trees, and corals are dying due to global warming) or fascinating (why female cheetahs are intrepidly promiscuous), Smith writes with equanimity, making for an intriguing, instructive, and up-to-date book of discoveries." Booklist

590.3   Encyclopedias and dictionaries

Animal sciences; Allan B. Cobb, editor in chief. Macmillan Ref. USA 2002 4v il (Macmillan science library) set $395 *
Grades: 11 12 Adult   **590.3**
1. Animals—Encyclopedias 2. Reference books
ISBN 0-02-865556-7   LC 2001-26627
This "work contains approximately 300 signed entries on a variety of topics relating to animal science, including animal development, functions, behavior, ecology, and evolution. The connection between animals and humans is also explored. . . . Also included are biographies of noted scientists who have made 'significant contributions' to the field. . . . Articles appear in alphabetical order and range in length from several paragraphs to several pages. . . . Articles are clear and well written, and the appealing layout includes many colorful photographs, diagrams, and sidebars. . . . This set contains sufficient information to serve the needs of a variety of student users and will appeal to the casual browser as well." Booklist

A **dictionary** of zoology; edited by Michael Allaby. 3rd ed. Oxford University Press 2009 689p il (Oxford paperback reference) pa $19.76
Grades: 9 10 11 12 Adult   **590.3**
1. Zoology—Dictionaries 2. Reference books
ISBN 978-0-19-923341-0; 0-19-923341-1
     LC 2009-419052
First published 1999 with title: Concise Oxford dictionary of zoology
"Illustrated with many line drawings, the book defines terms from animal behavior, evolution, earth history, zoogeography, genetics, and physiology, provides full taxonomic coverage of arthropods and other invertebrates, fish, reptiles, amphibians, birds, and mammals, and introduces . . . material on behavioral ecology and conservation biology." Publisher's note

The **encyclopedia** of animals; a complete visual guide; [text, Jenni Bruce . . . et al.] University of California Press 2004 608p il map $39.95 *
Grades: 7 8 9 10 11 12   **590.3**
1. Animals—Encyclopedias 2. Reference books
ISBN 0-520-24406-0   LC 2004-303646
"The book starts with an introduction to animal evolution, biology, behavior, classification, habitats, and current conservation issues. This is followed by a survey of animals, divided into the standard taxonomic classifications of mammals, birds, reptiles, amphibians, fishes, and invertebrates. . . . Icons and symbols indicate habitat, size, weight, and social and reproductive habits of the various species." Libr J
"This lavishly illustrated chronicle of Earth's biodiversity is a visual delight." Booklist

Magill's encyclopedia of science: animal life; editor, Carl W. Hoagstrom. Salem Press 2002 4v il set $435
Grades: 11 12 Adult   **590.3**
1. Zoology—Encyclopedias 2. Reference books
ISBN 1-58765-019-3   LC 2001-49799
This "is a major revision and update of the six-volume *Magill's Survey of Science: Life Science*, published in 1991. . . . There are 385 signed main entries, ranging in length from 1000 to 3000 words each. . . . The entries cover a wide variety of topics related to animal life and include articles on subjects such as biodiversity and defense mechanisms as well as those on specific species or individual animals. Each entry begins with ready-reference information and a list of principal terms with definitions." Libr J

Includes bibliographical references

590.73   Collections and exhibits of living animals

Anthony, Lawrence
Babylon's ark; the incredible wartime rescue of the Baghdad Zoo; [by] Lawrence Anthony with Graham Spence. Thomas Dunne Books 2007 248p il hardcover o.p. pa $14.95
Grades: 11 12 Adult   **590.73**
1. Baghdad Zoo (Iraq) 2. Zoos 3. Wildlife conservation 4. Iraq War, 2003-
ISBN   978-0-312-35832-7;   0-312-35832-6; 978-0-312-38215-5 (pa); 0-312-38215-4 (pa)
     LC 2006-50573
"This remarkable story recounts the recent wartime rescue of the once-world-renowned Baghdad Zoo through the experiences of a South African conservationist and heroic Iraqi zookeepers." Booklist

French, Thomas, 1958-
Zoo story; life in the garden of captives. Hyperion 2010 288p $24.99
Grades: 11 12 Adult   **590.73**
1. Lowry Park Zoo 2. Zoos
ISBN 978-1-4013-2346-2
The author "chronicles the rise of Lowry Park from one of the worst zoos in the country to one of the best.

French, Thomas, 1958—— *Continued*

. . . This behind-the-scenes look will both entertain and enlighten animal lovers. It is a story that needs to be told, and French does it superbly." Libr J

Includes bibliographical references

Robinson, Phillip T.

Life at the zoo: behind the scenes with the animal doctors. Columbia University Press 2004 293p il $27.95; pa $17.95 *

Grades: 11 12 Adult   **590.73**

1. Zoos

ISBN 0-231-13248-4; 0-231-13249-2 (pa)

LC 2004-43893

A "look at how animal exhibits are designed, how the animals are cared for, and how illness is detected in animals that want to hide any weakness." Booklist

"It would be difficult to cover even one aspect, such as animal health, that might affect the overall management of a zoo, but Dr. Philip Robinson manages to provide an excellent coverage of just about everything that might be involved in the operation of a zoo." Sci Books Films

Includes bibliographical references

591.3 Genetics, evolution, young animals

Arthur, Wallace

Creatures of accident; the rise of the animal kingdom. Hill & Wang 2006 255p hardcover o.p. pa $22

Grades: 11 12 Adult   **591.3**

1. Natural selection 2. Evolution

ISBN 0-8090-4321-1; 978-0-8090-4321-7; 0-8090-3701-7 (pa); 978-0-8090-3701-8 (pa)

LC 2005-33540

The author "advances the argument that the process [of the evolution of life] tends toward greater complexity over time. . . . Arthur sketches out the main structural attributes of complexity in animals, from the cell to organs to embryology to body forms, and when they appeared. . . . Championing naturalistic clarity, Arthur's precision about the processes of evolution will benefit serious students of the topic." Booklist

Includes bibliographical references

O'Brien, Stephen J.

Tears of the cheetah; and other tales from the genetic frontier; foreword by Ernst Mayr. St. Martin's Press 2003 287p il hardcover o.p. pa $14.95

Grades: 11 12 Adult   **591.3**

1. Genetics 2. Endangered species

ISBN 0-312-27286-3; 0-312-33900-3 (pa)

LC 2003-53164

The author discusses the genetic "histories of exotic species such as Indonesian orangutans, humpback whales, and the imperiled cheetah. . . . Among these genetic detective stories we also discover how the Serengeti lions have lived with FIV (the feline version of HIV), where

giant pandas really come from, how bold genetic action pulled the Florida panther from the edge of extinction, how the survivors of the medieval Black Death passed on a genetic gift to their descendents, and how mapping the genome of the domestic cat solved a murder case in Canada." Publisher's note

"O'Brien's exploration of the genetic landscape of a particular species is marvelously revelatory of its history. . . . Molecular biology *can* be difficult to absorb, but not when a clear expositor such as O'Brien has such good stories to tell." Booklist

Includes bibliographical references

591.47 Protective and locomotor adaptations, color

McDougall, Len

Tracking and reading sign; a guide to mastering the original forensic science. Skyhorse Pub. 2010 183p il pa $18.95

Grades: 11 12 Adult   **591.47**

1. Animal tracks 2. Tracking and trailing 3. Animal behavior

ISBN 978-1-61608-006-8; 1-61608-006-X

LC 2009-50543

This book "offers an introduction on the principles of tracking and reading sign by looking at tracks, prints, gaits, scats, scents, and animal behaviors. It provides the reader with tracking and stalking techniques such as cold hunting, camouflage, and using the stump method." Publisher's note

591.5 Behavior

Animal life; Charlotte Uhlenbroek, [editor in chief] DK Pub. 2008 512p il map $50

Grades: 9 10 11 12 Adult   **591.5**

1. Animal behavior 2. Animals—Pictorial works

ISBN 978-0-7566-3986-0; 0-7566-3986-7

LC 2008-300010

This book "provides an excellent overview of the animal world written at a level accessible to students and the general public. Introductory sections cover basics of animal life such as evolution, animal history, classification, and anatomy. Animal behavior receives the most extensive treatment, encompassing living space, hunting and feeding, defense mechanisms, sex and reproduction, birth and development, society, communication, and intelligence." Booklist

Balcombe, Jonathan, 1959-

Pleasurable kingdom; animals and the nature of feeling good. Macmillan 2006 274p il $24.95; pa $14.95

Grades: 11 12 Adult   **591.5**

1. Animal behavior 2. Pleasure

ISBN 1-4039-8601-0; 978-1-4039-8601-6; 1-4039-8602-9 (pa); 978-1-4039-8602-3 (pa)

LC 2006-41734

This is an "examination of positive feelings in animals. . . . [The author] first defines what is meant by

Balcombe, Jonathan, 1959-—*Continued*
pleasure and why it is worthy of study, then looks at several potentially pleasure-causing activities: play, eating, sex, touching, and love. Full of examples both anecdotal and from refereed journals . . . this book not only makes a case for animal pleasure but calls for more research on the science of pleasure in animals, allowing humans to view them in a new way." Booklist
   Includes bibliographical references

Boysen, Sarah Till, 1949-
   The smartest animals on the planet; with a contribution from Deborah Custance. Firefly Books 2009 192p il map $35
Grades: 9 10 11 12 Adult   591.5
   1. Animal behavior 2. Animal intelligence
   ISBN 978-1-5540-7456-3; 1-5540-7456-8
   Subtitle on cover: Extraordinary tales of the natural world's cleverest creatures
   In this study on animal intelligence, "each animal is placed into one of seven categories—tool making and use, communication, learned social behaviors, individual self-awareness, numerical ability, language learning and group cooperation/mutual protection . . . showing how animals place on different axes of intelligence." Publ Wkly
   "Succinctly written and sumptuously illustrated with photographs and diagrams, this appealing book is sure to fascinate the general reader and inspire the science student considering a career in animal behavior or cognition." Libr J

Crump, Martha L.
   Headless males make great lovers; & other unusual natural histories; [by] Marty Crump; with illustrations by Alan Crump. University of Chicago Press 2005 199p il $25; pa $14
Grades: 11 12 Adult   591.5
   1. Animal behavior
   ISBN 0-226-12199-2; 0-226-12202-6 (pa)
                 LC 2005-7592
   "The author draws upon her own observations of nature, and on the scientific literature, to reveal how animals mate, parent, feed, defend, and communicate among themselves in unusual ways." Choice
   "Illustrated throughout with line drawings, and bolstered with a chapter-by-chapter list of references, this marvelous introduction to the whys and wherefores of animal behavior will find an audience in all libraries." Booklist
   Includes bibliographical references

Encyclopedia of animal behavior; edited by Marc Bekoff; foreword by Jane Goodall. Greenwood Press 2004 3v il set $349.95
Grades: 11 12 Adult   591.5
   1. Animal behavior
   ISBN 0-313-32745-9   LC 2004-56073
   This encyclopedia describes "what makes animals tick using techniques that range from molecular approaches to analysis of species. The 300 entries, some stretching to 7000 words, discuss topics as diverse as concept learning in pigeons and stress in dolphins." Libr J
   Includes bibliographical references

Grandin, Temple
   Animals in translation; using the mysteries of autism to decode animal behavior; [by] Temple Grandin and Catherine Johnson. Scribner 2010 356p $28; ebook $18.99 *
Grades: 11 12 Adult   591.5
   1. Animal behavior 2. Autism
   ISBN 978-1-4391-8710-4; 978-1-4391-3084-1 (ebook)
   Also available in paperback from Harvest Books
   First published 2005
   The author contends "that her autistic sensory perceptions (in particular, her intense focus on visual details) enable her to take in the world as animals do. In fact, she argues that autistic people and animals are essentially alike—they see, feel and think in remarkably similar ways." N Y Times Book Rev
   "This fascinating book will teach readers to see as animals see, to be a little more visual and a little less verbal, and, as a unique analysis of animal behavior, it belongs in all libraries." Booklist
   Includes bibliographical references

Grice, Gordon, 1944-
   The red hourglass; lives of the predators. Delacorte Press 1998 259p pa $19 hardcover o.p.
Grades: 11 12 Adult   591.5
   1. Predatory animals 2. Poisonous animals
   ISBN 0-385-31890-1 (pa)   LC 97-41544
   "This collection of seven essays examines several smaller predators, including black widows ('the red hourglass'), tarantulas, mantids, brown recluse spiders, and rattlesnakes. . . . Two essays about larger predators, the pig and the 'canid,' are [also included]." Libr J
   "This book will delight those interested in either animals or literature." Booklist

McCarthy, Susan
   Becoming a tiger; how baby animals learn to live in the wild. HarperCollins 2004 418p hardcover o.p. pa $13.95
Grades: 11 12 Adult   591.5
   1. Animal intelligence
   ISBN 0-06-620924-2; 0-06-093484-0 (pa)
                 LC 2003-67553
   The author examines "the ways that animals figure out how to function in their worlds. . . . One of the basic things a baby animal must learn is how to get from one place to another in a manner appropriate to its species. Other basics involve learning to recognize your own species, to communicate, to find food, and *not* to become some other species' food. McCarthy discusses species as various as horses, bonobos, zebra finches, and fruit-fly maggots to illustrate the learning process." Booklist
   "McCarthy writes clearly and her penchant for humor . . . makes the book an easy read, both for students of learning and those who can't get enough of television's *Animal Planet*." Publ Wkly
   Includes bibliographical references

Schutt, Bill

Dark banquet; blood and the curious lives of blood-feeding creatures; illustrated by Patricia J. Wynne. Harmony 2008 325p il $25.95

Grades: 9 10 11 12 Adult   **591.5**

 1. Bloodsucking animals

 ISBN 978-0-307-38112-5   LC 2008-3061

 "The book emphasizes a diverse array of outlandish animals, from leeches and bed bugs to vampire bats and vampire catfish. . . . [The author] indulges his own fascination with creatures that subsist on blood as he explores some of the macabre, humorous, literary, historical, and scientific aspects of hematophagy." Choice

 "Bloodthirsty readers may well find their appetite whetted for more. A natural history of bloodsuckers that shines in gory glory." Kirkus

 Includes bibliographical references

591.56 Behavior relating to life cycle

Kostyal, K. M., 1951-

Great migrations; official companion to the National Geographic channel global television event; [by] K. M. Kostyal; afterword by series producer David Hamlin. National Geographic 2010 303p il $35

Grades: 9 10 11 12 Adult   **591.56**

 1. Animals—Migration

 ISBN 978-1-4262-0644-3   LC 2010-20998

 This book, "the official companion to the National Geographic Channel television film *Great Migrations*, follows the sequence of the film. The book is divided into sections, each of which emphasizes a feature that makes migration essential to the survival of a variety of animal species. Throughout, the author continuously emphasizes the instincts and internal and external forces that drive animals to make risky, yet deliberate, journeys of hundreds to thousands of miles annually. . . . Over one hundred excellent color pictures illustrate various aspects of migration and daily life for dozens of animal species." Sci Books Films

 Includes bibliographical references

591.59 Communication

Friend, Tim

Animal talk; breaking the codes of animal language. Free Press 2004 274p il $25; pa $15 *

Grades: 11 12 Adult   **591.59**

 1. Animal communication

 ISBN 0-7432-0157-4; 0-7432-0158-2 (pa)

          LC 2003-63107

 "The author describes the methods of, and reasons behind, animal communication and demonstrates that human and animal communication are not so widely disparate as once believed. Friend also gives background details on the basics of communication theory, genetics, evolution, and the progression of scientific thought regarding animal communication. . . . His humorous and engaging prose style makes this a captivating read." Libr J

 Includes bibliographical references

591.68 Rare and endangered animals

Goodall, Jane, 1934-

Hope for animals and their world; how endangered species are being rescued from the brink; [by] Jane Goodall, with Thane Maynard and Gail Hudson. Grand Central Pub. 2009 392p il $27.99; pa $15.99

Grades: 11 12 Adult   **591.68**

 1. Endangered species 2. Wildlife conservation 3. Nature conservation

 ISBN 978-0-446-58177-6; 0-446-58177-1; 978-0-446-58178-3 (pa); 0-446-58178-X (pa)

          LC 2009-11215

 "Section one recounts the revival of six mammal and bird species, including Mongolian miniature horses and Australian wallabies, that became extinct in the wild but are being reintroduced to their natural habitat through captive breeding. Section two describes efforts to bring species back from near extinction, among them Brazil's golden lion tamarin and the North American whooping crane. Section three details continuing efforts to preserve 11 species, including the giant pandas of China, whose bamboo diet is disappearing, and the Asian vultures of India." Publ Wkly

 "An upbeat compendium that will energize both hands-on and armchair conservationists." Kirkus

 Includes bibliographical references

Hammond, Paula, 1966-

The atlas of endangered animals; wildlife under threat around the world. Marshall Cavendish 2010 224p il map lib bdg $99.93 *

Grades: 7 8 9 10 11 12   **591.68**

 1. Endangered species 2. Atlases 3. Reference books

 ISBN 978-0-7614-7872-0; 0-7614-7872-8

          LC 2008-44956

 First published 2006 in the United Kingdom

 This book examines "fifty endangered animals from every corner of the Earth, explaining how species go extinct, as well the successes and failures of captive breeding programs and conservation efforts." Publisher's note

 This "beautifully illustrated . . . [book] features an appealing layout; logical organization; and plenty of full-color drawings, maps, and photographs. . . . Ideal for reports, but animal lovers will enjoy perusing them as well." SLJ

591.7 Animal ecology, animals characteristic of specific environments

Couturier, Lisa, 1962-

The hopes of snakes; and other tales from the urban landscape. Beacon Press 2005 159p $23; pa $14

Grades: 9 10 11 12   **591.7**

 1. Urban ecology 2. Wildlife

 ISBN 0-8070-8564-2; 0-8070-8565-0 (pa)

          LC 2004-15081

Couturier, Lisa, 1962-—_Continued_
The essays in this collection, "ranging in time from
. . . [the author's] childhood to that of her young daughter's, are based on a multitude of experiences with wildlife, chiefly in the New York City metropolitan area and
in Washington, D.C. and its suburbs. Teens will be encouraged by these stand-alone essays to study the world
around them." SLJ

Naskrecki, Piotr
The smaller majority; the hidden world of the
animals that dominate the tropics. Belknap Press
of Harvard University Press 2005 278p il $35
Grades: 11 12 Adult   591.7
1. Invertebrates 2. Animals—Pictorial works
3. Tropics
ISBN 0-674-01915-6; 978-0-674-01915-7
                                        LC 2005-46060
In this book the author "includes over 400 . . . full-
color photographs of animals that are generally smaller
than the human finger. The author . . . [has] collected
images of animals from Costa Rica, Guinea, the Domini-
cal Republic, the Solomon Islands, Australia, South Africa, Botswana, and Namibia." Choice
"Naskrecki's exuberant, expert knowledge of this microscopic world has been distilled down to the most arresting details. Crisp, enjoyable prose, clearly explains
complex biological processes." Publ Wkly
Includes bibliographical references

591.9 Treatment of animals by specific continents, countries, localities

The **illustrated** atlas of wildlife; [by] Channa
Bambaradeniya [et al.] University of California
Press 2009 288p il map $39.95
Grades: 9 10 11 12 Adult   591.9
1. Biogeography 2. Atlases 3. Reference books
ISBN 978-0-520-25785-6; 0-520-25785-5
                                        LC 2008-40625
"This gorgeous book, featuring detailed, customized
maps and more than 800 photographs . . . and original
artworks, presents a spectacular visual survey of wild animals across the globe and describes in detail their habitats, physical characteristics, diet, and behavior. . . . [It
also includes] conservation and preservation data, information about human impact upon the world's complex
ecosystems, and chronicles of the evolution and adaptation of animals over the ages." Education Digest
Includes glossary and bibliographical references

The **new** encyclopedia of aquatic life. Facts on
File 2005 2v il map (Facts on File natural
science library) set $150 *
Grades: 9 10 11 12   591.9
1. Marine animals 2. Freshwater animals
ISBN 0-8160-5119-4
First published 1985 under the editorship of Keith
Banister and Andrew Campbell with title: The encyclo-
pedia of aquatic life

This book "examines the behavior, ecology, and evolution of all fish and invertebrate groups living in Earth's
waters." Publisher's note
Includes bibliographical references

592 Invertebrates

Attenborough, David, 1926-
Life in the undergrowth. Princeton University
Press 2006 288p il $29.95
Grades: 11 12 Adult   592
1. Invertebrates
ISBN 0-691-12703-4   LC 2005-934727
The author "explores the lives of the planet's land-
based invertebrates. Concentrating mainly on insects and
spiders, the author investigates all aspects of the animals'
life cycles." Booklist
"This wonderful exploration of invertebrates exceeds
the requirements for a great nature book through the
strength of its photographs and the quality of its prose."
Publ Wkly

Stewart, Amy, 1969-
The earth moved; on the remarkable
achievements of earthworms. Algonquin Bks. 2004
223p $23.95; pa $12.95
Grades: 11 12 Adult   592
1. Worms
ISBN 1-56512-337-9; 1-56512-468-5 (pa)
                                        LC 2003-52379
The author explores "the impact worms have on humans and on our planet. . . . {She} educates on the vital
roles these creatures play in growing crops, how they can
neutralize the effects of nuclear waste on soil, and their
ability to regenerate new body parts. . . . A book that's
as enlightening as it is entertaining." SLJ
Includes bibliographical references

594 Mollusca and Molluscoidea

Williams, Wendy
Kraken; the curious, exciting, and slightly
disturbing science of squid. Abrams Image 2011
223p il $21.95
Grades: 11 12 Adult   594
1. Squids
ISBN 978-0-8109-8465-3   LC 2010032489
This book "traces sightings of the giant squid throughout the centuries. . . . Discussion of the anatomy, physiology, reproduction, evolution, and taxonomy of
Architeuthis is provided, along with accounts of the author's visits to various scientific laboratories and descriptions of research studies being conducted on the animal.
. . . This serves as a good introduction to the subject for
general readers and an inspiration to young people interested in marine biology." Libr J
Includes filmography and bibliographical references

595.4 Chelicerata Arachnida

Dalton, Stephen
Spiders; the ultimate predators. Firefly Books 2008 208p il lib bdg $34.95 *
Grades: 9 10 11 12 Adult   595.4
  1. Spiders
  ISBN 978-1-55407-346-7; 1-55407-346-4
  This guide provides "information on the . . . array of techniques spiders use for catching their prey: trapping in webs, lassoing, jumping, stealing, chasing, ambushing, spitting, fishing, masquerading as other animals and even attracting prey by mimicking the prey's pheromones. . . . Chapters provide information on habitat, hunting techniques, anatomy, general characteristics and location in the world." Publisher's note
  Includes bibliographical references

Kelly, Lynne
Spiders; learning to love them. Jacana Books 2009 264p il pa $19.95
Grades: 9 10 11 12 Adult   595.4
  1. Spiders 2. Phobias
  ISBN 978-1-74175-179-6; 1-74175-179-9
  "Confirmed arachnophobe (she had nightmares of giant spiders attacking her) Kelly trained herself to love spiders, and in a few months of observing and photographing the spiders around her Melbourne home became a confirmed arachnophile. She first discusses arachnophobia in general and traces the theories as to its roots as a genuine phobia. Her method for overcoming her fear was to first locate spiders around her house and name them. . . . In the course of describing her spiders and their ways, Kelly also imparts what she learned from reading and from scientists, weaving an amazing amount of spider biology into her narrative. . . . This book is a triumph." Booklist
  Includes bibliographical references

595.7 Insecta (Insects)

Brock, James P.
Kaufman field guide to butterflies of North America; [by] Jim P. Brock and Kenn Kaufman; with the collaboration of Rick and Nora Bowers and Lynn Hassler. Houghton Mifflin 2006 c2003 391p il map pa $19.95 *
Grades: 11 12 Adult   595.7
  1. Butterflies
  ISBN 0-618-76826-2; 978-0-618-76826-4
            LC 2006-287515
  First published 2003 with title: Butterflies of North America
  "Each species is listed by common name and scientific name and receives a several-sentence description, including flight time and larval food plants. All except very local or accidental species also are shown on range maps. The illustrations are opposite the written description, with most species pictured in multiple images. . . . The illustrations are created by digital enhancement of photographs. . . . An essential purchase for all libraries." Booklist [review of 2003 edition]

Capinera, John L.
Field guide to grasshoppers, crickets, and katydids of the United States; [by] John L. Capinera, Ralph D. Scott, and Thomas J. Walker. Cornell University Press 2004 249p il maps hardcover o.p. pa $29.95 *
Grades: 11 12 Adult   595.7
  1. Grasshoppers 2. Crickets
  ISBN 0-8014-4260-5; 0-8014-8948-2 (pa)
            LC 2004-10727
  This "field guide to U.S. and Canadian orthoptera introduces 206 of the most common species. . . . It explains classification, morphology (illustrated), biology, sound production, and collection and preservation, and presents pictorial keys to families and subfamilies." Libr J
  "The highlight is certainly the 50 pages of Scott's color illustrations. . . . For those who want to know what's plaguing them when locusts descend, this is the book." Publ Wkly
  Includes bibliographical references

Dourlot, Sonia
Insect museum; describing 114 species of insects and other arthropods, including their natural history and environment. Firefly Books 2009 255p il $39.95
Grades: 9 10 11 12 Adult   595.7
  1. Insects 2. Spiders
  ISBN 978-1-55407-483-9
  "Written text with the collaboration of Patrice Leraut" p. [256]
  "Dourlot's galley of arthropods is a visually arresting introduction to insects and spiders. . . . [Each entry features] a full-page color image of the critter, magnified several times life-size to enhance its monsterlike appearance, and depicted as if set on mounting paper. The image is faced by a page of descriptive data, the etymologies of scientific and common names, and a sidebar of a fun fact or folk story associated with the insect, so the layout gives the effect of looking like the lab book of an enthusiastic collector. . . . Durable both physically and in content, Dourlot's striking tome promises active library usage." Booklist
  Includes bibliographical references

Eisner, Thomas
Secret weapons; defenses of insects, spiders, scorpions, and other many-legged creatures; [by] Thomas Eisner, Maria Eisner, Melody V.S. Siegler. Belknap Press of Harvard University Press 2005 372p il $29.95; pa $18.95
Grades: 11 12 Adult   595.7
  1. Animal defenses 2. Insects 3. Spiders
  ISBN 0-674-01882-6; 0-674-02403-6 (pa)
            LC 2005-41042
  "This volume presents 69 case studies of organisms from 4 orders of spiders, 2 of centipedes, 5 of millipedes, and 10 of insects. Most of the studies address defensive chemistry and identify the chemical(s) involved, how each is acquired, stored, and deployed." Sci Books Films
  "This very readable and well-illustrated book will ap-

Eisner, Thomas—*Continued*
peal to all those interested in disciplines like biology, entomology, and ecology." Choice
Includes bibliographical references

Ellis, Hattie, 1967-
Sweetness & light; the mysterious history of the honeybee. Harmony Books 2004 243p il hardcover o.p. pa $13.95
Grades: 11 12 Adult   595.7
  1. Bees 2. Beekeeping
  ISBN 1-4000-5405-2; 1-4000-5406-0 (pa)
                        LC 2004-4116
The author tells the story of the bee in human history, "from Stone Age honey hunters to modern-day hives on the rooftops of New York City." Publisher's note
"What a delightful volume on the honeybee this is: Not only is the reader treated to a wealth of information on the biology, ecology, and economic importance of that insect, but the interrelationship of the honeybee and humanity throughout history is very nicely presented." Sci Books Films
Includes bibliographical references

Hölldobler, Bert, 1936-
The leafcutter ants; civilization by instinct; [by] Bert Hölldobler and Edward O. Wilson. Norton 2010 c2011 160p il pa $19.95
Grades: 9 10 11 12 Adult   595.7
  1. Ants
  ISBN 978-0-393-33868-3   LC 2010-16202
"Parts of this text have previously appeared in Chapter 9 of 'The Superorganism' by Bert Hölldobler and Edward O. Wilson" Verso of title page
The authors "introduce the general reader to earth's most evolved animal society. With the colony's queen as its reproductive organ; the various ages and types of workers as the brain, heart, and other organs; and the communication among the ants similar to the communication of nerves and ganglia, a leafcutter ant colony can be truly considered as a superorganism." Booklist
Includes bibliographical references

Keller, Laurent
The lives of ants; by Laurent Keller and Élisabeth Gordon; translated by James Grieve. Oxford University Press 2009 252p il $27.95; pa $15.95
Grades: 9 10 11 12 Adult   595.7
  1. Ants
  ISBN   978-0-19-954186-7;   0-19-954186-8; 978-0-19-954187-4 (pa); 0-19-954187-6 (pa)
                    LC 2008-943416
"Keller and Gordon present ant life in 32 chapters, covering the vast expanse and variation of ant behavior, social structure, reproduction, genetics and ecology while highlighting their importance to ecosystems worldwide." Publ Wkly
The authors "provide a lucid . . . overview of any evolution, ecology, biology, behavior, and genetics that easily communicates complex research in these areas to a wide audience." Sci Books Films
Includes bibliographical references

Marshall, Stephen A.
Insects: their natural history and diversity; with a photographic guide to insects of eastern North America. Firefly Books 2006 718p il $95 *
Grades: 11 12 Adult   595.7
  1. Insects
  ISBN 978-1-55297-900-6; 1-55297-900-8
                    LC 2006-389462
This "offers more than 4000 excellent color photographs and concise, accurate information about every major insect family worldwide. . . . This book is simply bigger, prettier, and more comprehensive than any previous publication on insects and will be useful to amateur and professional alike." Libr J
Includes bibliographical references

Moffett, Mark W.
Adventures among ants; a global safari with a cast of trillions. University of California Press 2010 280p il $29.95
Grades: 11 12 Adult   595.7
  1. Ants
  ISBN 978-0-520-26199-0; 0-520-26199-2
                    LC 2009-40610
"This superb book by a first-class writer with an unsurpassed feel for ants begins at the ground level as we come face to face with the creatures, move into their minds, and begin to understand what makes them tick. Moffett organizes his text around six ant lifestyles, each represented by an insect that dominates its habitat: Indian Marauder ants, African army ants, African Weaver ants, Amazon slavemaking ants, Neotropical leaf cutter ants, and the Argentine ant, a global invader. . . . This marvelous volume illustrated with the author's closeup photographs will delight biologists, naturalists, and general readers with a natural history bent." Libr J
Includes bibliographical references

Pyle, Robert Michael
The Audubon Society field guide to North American butterflies; visual key by Carol Nehring and Jane Opper. Knopf 1981 916p il $19.95
Grades: 7 8 9 10 11 12 Adult   595.7
  1. Butterflies
  ISBN 0-394-51914-0   LC 80-84240
"A Chanticleer Press edition. The Audubon Society field guide series"
This guide "introduces more than 600 species of North American butterfly, including those native to the Hawaiian Islands. A section of brilliant color plates (more than 1,000 of them) featuring butterflies in their natural habitats, follows a general introduction and notes on text organization and use." Booklist

Savage, Candace, 1949-
Bees; nature's little wonders. Greystone Books 2008 136p il $26; pa $16.95
Grades: 11 12 Adult   595.7
  1. Bees
  ISBN 978-1-55365-321-9; 978-1-55365-531-2 (pa)
  Co-published by: David Suzuki Foundation

Savage, Candace, 1949-—*Continued*

The author "considers the diversity and biology of bees, including their peculiar sociosexual arrangements, their quirky relationships with flowers, and their startling mental abilities." Publisher's note

"This book is a wonderful read for someone who wants to learn about bees but does not have a scientific background. The writing style is casual and pleasant. Historic poems and artwork pertaining to bees are scattered throughout the book." Sci Books Films

Includes bibliographical references

Schappert, Phil, 1956-

The last Monarch butterfly; conserving the Monarch butterfly in a brave new world. Firefly Books 2004 113p il pa $19.95

Grades: 11 12 Adult **595.7**
1. Monarch butterflies 2. Wildlife conservation
ISBN 1-55297-969-5 LC 2005-357220

Overview of both eastern and western monarch butterflies, including their life cycle and migratory patterns. The impact of natural disasters and increasing residential and industrial development on monarch butterfly populations is also discussed.

"The narrative is enhanced by beautiful photographs and backed up by some 180 references to the scientific literature. . . . Let's hear it for the monarch, an amazing insect; if the reader has any doubts about that, this book will put them to rest." Sci Books Films

Waldbauer, Gilbert

A walk around the pond; insects in and over the water. Harvard University Press 2006 286p il hardcover o.p. pa $16.95

Grades: 11 12 Adult **595.7**
1. Insects 2. Freshwater animals
ISBN 0-674-02211-4; 0-674-02765-5 (pa)
LC 2005-44737

The author "introduces us to the aquatic insects that have colonized ponds, lakes, streams, and rivers, especially those in North America." Publisher's note

"Readers will be inspired to take a closer look at their favorite pond or stream." Booklist

Includes bibliographical references

What good are bugs? insects in the web of life. Harvard University Press 2003 384p il hardcover o.p. pa $17.50

Grades: 11 12 Adult **595.7**
1. Insects
ISBN 0-674-01027-2; 0-674-01632-7 (pa)
LC 2002-27335

The author "instructs readers on the major roles insects play. He provides . . . examples for every aspect of insect ecology he discusses, sprinkling reports from the scientific literature with personal anecdotes from his many years of research." Booklist

This "is an excellent work about the beneficial insects, that vast majority of insect species of which we are generally unaware. . . . The author is an excellent writer and provides many interesting examples." Choice

Includes bibliographical references

596   Chordata

Petersen, Christine

Vertebrates. Watts 2002 128p il $24

Grades: 9 10 11 12 **596**
1. Vertebrates
ISBN 0-531-12020-1 LC 2001-3032

A close look at past and present vertebrates, including fish, birds, amphibians, reptiles, and mammals

The text is "concisely written, logically organized, and relatively free of scientific jargon." Booklist

Includes glossary and bibliographical references

597   Cold-blooded vertebrates Pisces (Fishes)

Benchley, Peter, 1940-2006

Shark trouble; true stories about sharks and the sea. Random House 2002 186p il hardcover o.p. pa $12.95

Grades: 11 12 Adult **597**
1. Sharks 2. Marine animals
ISBN 0-375-50824-4; 0-8129-6633-3 (pa)
LC 2002-283533

"Benchley describes the many types of sharks (including the ones that pose a genuine threat to man), what is and isn't known about shark behavior, the odds against an attack and how to reduce them even further—all reinforced with the lessons he has learned, the mistakes he has made, and the personal perils he has encountered." Publisher's note

"Handy with statistics and quick to crack a joke with himself as the target, Benchley offers riveting accounts of his and his family's up close and personal encounters with sharks, a gigantic manta ray, a friendly killer whale, barracuda, and sundry other wild creatures." Booklist

Capuzzo, Mike

Close to shore; a true story of terror in an age of innocence. Broadway Bks. 2001 317p map pa $14.95 hardcover o.p.

Grades: 11 12 Adult **597**
1. Sharks 2. Animal attacks
ISBN 0-7679-0414-1 (pa) LC 2001-25750

This describes a series of shark attacks in 1916 off the coast of New Jersey.

"A book full of adventure, mounting tension, some gore and excitement, and lots of history." SLJ

Includes bibliographical references

Compagno, Leonard J. V.

Sharks of the world; [by] Leonard Compagno, Marc Dando, Sarah Fowler. Princeton University Press 2005 368p il map (Princeton field guides) hardcover o.p. pa $29.95

Grades: 11 12 Adult **597**
1. Sharks
ISBN 0-691-12071-4; 0-691-12072-2 (pa)
LC 2004-111901

First published in the United Kingdom with title: Field guide to the sharks of the world

Compagno, Leonard J. V.—*Continued*

The authors cover "over 450 species, including many as-yet-unnamed species and some that are only known from a single specimen. Each is illustrated with both a line drawing and a beautifully rendered color painting; in most cases a ventral view of the head and illustrations of the teeth are included. . . . Packed with information, this is an invaluable guide for anyone interested in this fascinating group." Choice

Includes bibliographical references

Eilperin, Juliet

Demon fish; travels through the hidden world of sharks. Pantheon Books 2011 xxi, 295p il $26.95

Grades: 11 12 Adult   **597**

1. Sharks

ISBN 978-0-375-42512-7   LC 2010-30264

Eilperin "describes her travels throughout Asia, South Africa, and the United States in search of shark information and folklore. . . . The author provides a well-written overview of current and past attitudes toward sharks and discusses shark species, physiology, genetics, reproduction, evolution, navigation, and attacks on swimmers." Libr J

Includes bibliographical references

Ferrari, Andrea

Sharks; [by] Andrea and Antonella Ferrari; foreword by Doug Perrine. Firefly Bks. 2002 256p il pa $24.95 *

Grades: 11 12 Adult   **597**

1. Sharks

ISBN 1-55209-629-7   LC 2002-511486

Original Italian edition, 2000

Translated from the original Italian 2000 ed., Tutto squali, by Anna Bennett

"A guide to the appearance and behavior of 120 species of sharks and rays. . . . Illustrated with photographs of sharks and rays in their natural environment. Essays on history, biology, and ecology accompany the text." Publisher's note

"Perrine offers a spellbinding shark gallery." Booklist

Includes bibliographical references

Gilbert, Carter Rowell, 1930-

National Audubon Society field guide to fishes, North America; [by] Carter R. Gilbert, James D. Williams. rev ed, 2nd ed, fully rev. Alfred A. Knopf 2002 607p il maps pa $19.95 *

Grades: 7 8 9 10 11 12 Adult   **597**

1. Fishes—North America

ISBN 0-375-41224-7   LC 2002-20773

"A Chanticleer Press edition"

First published 1983 with title: The Audubon Society field guide to North American fishes, whales, and dolphins

This guide covers over 600 freshwater and saltwater species in detail, with notes on 771 more species.

Page, Lawrence M.

Peterson field guide to freshwater fishes of North America north of Mexico; [by] Lawrence M. Page, Brooks M. Burr; illustrations by Eugene C. Beckham III . . . [et al.]; maps by Griffin E. Sheehy. 2nd ed. Houghton Mifflin Harcourt 2011 663p il map pa $21 *

Grades: 7 8 9 10 11 12 Adult   **597**

1. Fishes—North America

ISBN 978-0-547-24206-4; 0-547-24206-9

    LC 2010-49219

First published 1991 with title: A field guide to freshwater fishes: North America north of Mexico

This guide to identifying different species of freshwater fish in North America includes "maps and information showing where to locate each species of fish—whether that species can be found in miles-long stretches of river or small pools that cover only dozens of square feet." Publisher's note

Includes glossary and bibliographical references

Parker, Steve

The encyclopedia of sharks. New ed., completely rev. and updated. Firefly Books 2008 224p il map pa $24.95

Grades: 9 10 11 12   **597**

1. Sharks—Encyclopedias 2. Reference books

ISBN 978-1-55407-409-9   LC 2008279142

First published 1999

This encyclopedia contains "information on: evolution and design of the shark; classifications and orders; understanding the shark; the life of the shark—how it feeds, breeds and migrates; shark 'supersense'—how it survives in the aquatic environment; [and] the need for protection and conservation." Publisher's note

Schweid, Richard, 1946-

Consider the eel. University of North Carolina Press 2002 181p il map $24.95

Grades: 11 12 Adult   **597**

1. Eels

ISBN 0-8078-2693-6   LC 2001-48067

Also available De Capo paperback edition

The author "tries to fill in the gaps in the eel's astonishing natural history and tie that to sketches of fishery traditions, folklore, literary excerpts and reportage. . . . Anyone with a curiosity about the sea will find Schweid's taste of the eel strangely appealing." Publ Wkly

Includes bibliographical references

597.8 Amphibia (Amphibians)

Beltz, Ellin

Frogs: inside their remarkable world. Firefly Books 2005 175p il $34.95

Grades: 11 12 Adult   **597.8**

1. Frogs 2. Toads

ISBN 1-55297-869-9   LC 2006-365517

The author "picture of the history of the frog, its anatomical makeup, its place in the natural world and the

Beltz, Ellin—*Continued*
threats that are seriously reducing its numbers around the world." Publisher's note

"Beltz presents an entertaining and comprehensive introduction to the order Anura (frogs and toads)." Booklist

Includes bibliographical references

Elliott, Lang
The frogs and toads of North America; a comprehensive guide to their identification, behavior, and calls; [by] Lang Elliott, Carl Gerhardt, and Carlos Davidson. Houghton Mifflin 2009 343p il map pa $19.95 *
Grades: 9 10 11 12 Adult   **597.8**
 1. Frogs 2. Toads
 ISBN 978-0-618-66399-6; 0-618-66399-1
          LC 2008-26090
 Includes audio CD

"The title says it all for this beautiful field guide to all 101 species of frogs and toads found in the U.S. and Canada. Elliott has produced a masterpiece of photographs and particulars of all our native and introduced toads and frogs. Each species is covered in a minimum two-page spread, with common and Latin names, a range map, and a short discussion of appearance, range and habitat, behavior, and voice. . . . The major strength of this book, and one that almost demands its purchase, is the accompanying CD featuring recordings of the calls of every species (with the exception of the two that never vocalize)." Booklist

Includes bibliographical references

597.9 Reptilia (Reptiles)

Attenborough, David, 1926-
Life in cold blood. Princeton University Press 2008 288p il $29.95
Grades: 11 12 Adult   **597.9**
 1. Amphibians 2. Reptiles
 ISBN 978-0-691-13718-6; 0-691-13718-8
          LC 2007-938089
This discussion of amphibians and reptiles was first published as a companion volume to the BBC television series of the same name. "Basic life history including diet, locomotion, reproductive habits, and geographic distribution are presented." Choice

"The writing is crisp and lively, the examples are up to date, and the photography is beautiful. . . . This is a very interesting book, which provides many examples of organisms some of us often overlook." Am Biology Teacher

Conant, Roger, 1909-
A field guide to reptiles & amphibians; eastern and central North America; [by] Roger Conant and Joseph T. Collins; illustrated by Isabelle Hunt Conant and Tom R. Johnson. 3rd ed, expanded. Houghton Mifflin 1998 616p il map (Peterson field guide series) $21
Grades: 7 8 9 10 11 12 Adult   **597.9**
 1. Reptiles 2. Amphibians
 ISBN 0-395-90452-8
          LC 98-13622

First published 1958 with title: A field guide to reptiles and amphibians of the United States and Canada east of the 100th meridian

"Sponsored by the National Audubon Society, the National Wildlife Federation, and the Roger Tory Peterson Institute"

This guide describes 595 species and subspecies, featuring color photos, black and white drawings, and color distribution maps of reptiles and amphibians of the region. Also includes information on transporting live reptiles and amphibians

Includes glossary and bibliographical references

Peterson first guide to reptiles and amphibians; [by] Roger Conant, Robert C. Stebbins, Joseph T. Collins. Houghton Mifflin 1999 c1992 128p il pa $5.95 *
Grades: 9 10 11 12   **597.9**
 1. Reptiles 2. Amphibians
 ISBN 0-395-97195-0
 First published 1992
On cover: A simplified field guide to the snakes, turtles, frogs, lizards, and other reptiles, and amphibians of North America

This is a guide to identification of reptile and amphibian species.

This book is "easy to use. The information is accurate and easy to understand. . . . Useful for browsing as well as for identification in the field." Voice Youth Advocates

Means, D. Bruce, 1941-
Stalking the plumed serpent and other adventures in herpetology. Pineapple Press 2008 238p il $19.95
Grades: 11 12 Adult   **597.9**
 1. Reptiles 2. Amphibians
 ISBN 978-1-56164-433-9   LC 2008-15153
The author reveals the biological complexity and beauty of animals that he has studied, including the rattlesnake that might have served as the model for the mythical plumed serpent of Mayan art.

"As one reads these stories, one begins to feel the author's love of nature, even though he is writing of animals that are not most people's favorites. . . . This reviewer had trouble putting the book down once he started. . . . Valuable for anyone interested in natural history, herpetology, adventure, or a combination of these." Choice

Includes bibliographical references

Stebbins, Robert C. (Robert Cyril), 1915-
A field guide to Western reptiles and amphibians; text and illustrations by Robert C. Stebbins. 3rd ed newly rev. Houghton Mifflin 2003 533p il map (Peterson field guide series) pa $22
Grades: 7 8 9 10 11 12 Adult   **597.9**
 1. Reptiles 2. Amphibians
 ISBN 0-395-98272-3   LC 2002-27561
 First published 1966
"Sponsored by The National Wildlife Federation and the Roger Tory Peterson Institute"

Stebbins, Robert C. (Robert Cyril), 1915-—*Continued*

This "covers all the species of reptiles and amphibians found in western North America. More than 650 full-color paintings and photographs show key details for making accurate identifications. . . . Color range maps give species' distributions. . . . [Includes] information on conservation efforts and survival status." Publisher's note
Includes bibliographical references

597.92   Chelonia

Ferri, Vincenzo
Tortoises and turtles. Firefly Bks. 2002 c1999 255p il pa $24.95 *
Grades: 8 9 10 11 12 Adult   **597.92**
1. Turtles
ISBN 978-1-55209-631-4; 1-55209-631-9
Original Italian edition, 1999
An "illustrated guide to 190 land, marine and freshwater turtles and tortoises . . . describing the physical and biological characteristics of the majority of species." Publisher's note
"Turtle enthusiasts and students writing papers will find this guide and the additional resources it cites invaluable." Voice Youth Advocates
Includes glossary and bibliographical references

Safina, Carl, 1955-
Voyage of the turtle; in pursuit of the Earth's last dinosaur. Holt 2006 383p il map $27.50; pa $17
Grades: 11 12 Adult   **597.92**
1. Turtles
ISBN   978-0-8050-7891-6;   0-8050-7891-6; 978-0-8050-8318-7 (pa); 0-8050-8318-9 (pa)
                             LC 2005-55023
"A John Macrae book"
The author's "main subject is the leatherback, Dermochelys coriacea, largest of all living turtles, which grows to 800 pounds as an average adult." N Y Times Book Rev
"This is a well-written natural history/conservation narrative. General readers will enjoy the book and hopefully will become excited to learn more about critical environmental issues." Sci Books Films
Includes bibliographical references

Spotila, James R., 1944-
Sea turtles; a complete guide to their biology, behavior, and conservation. Johns Hopkins University Press 2004 227p il $24.95 *
Grades: 11 12 Adult   **597.92**
1. Sea turtles
ISBN 0-8018-8007-6   LC 2004-8935
"The volume covers various aspects of sea turtle biology, such as their life history, diving physiology, sense organs, and magnetic orientation. Following the general chapters, individual chapters are devoted to each of the seven species of extant sea turtles." Sci Books Films
"The author is eloquent in his appeal for the conserva-

tion of sea turtles. The best single book on the subject." Booklist
Includes bibliographical references

597.96   Serpentes (Snakes)

Ernst, Carl H.
Snakes of the United States and Canada; [by] Carl H. Ernst, Evelyn M. Ernst. Smithsonian Books 2003 668p il map $70 *
Grades: 11 12 Adult   **597.96**
1. Snakes
ISBN 1-58834-019-8   LC 2002-26924
This "reference begins with an introduction to snake biology and evolution, which is followed by an identification guide and key to the North American species. The heart of the book is the species accounts which . . . [provide] information on identifying features, geographic variation, known fossils, current distribution, habitat type, behavior, reproduction, growth, diet, and predators. Completing the book is a glossary of terms and a . . . reference section." Publisher's note
"This current and comprehensive volume contains all the information currently available on the 131 species of snakes living in North America." Libr J
Includes bibliographical references

Mattison, Christopher
The new encyclopedia of snakes. Princeton University Press 2007 272p il map $35
Grades: 9 10 11 12 Adult   **597.96**
1. Reference books 2. Snakes—Encyclopedias
ISBN 0-691-13295-X; 978-0-691-13295-2
                             LC 2007-922951
First published 1995 by Facts on File with title: The encyclopedia of snakes
This encyclopedia "covers all aspects of snake biology and habitat. This is not a field guide aimed at snake identification. . . . But the work contains a wealth of information about our scaled friends, including patterns of distribution and matters relating to evolution and morphology, feeding, reproduction, and defensive strategies. . . . This captivating work will appeal to students and snake lovers everywhere." Libr J
Includes bibliographical references

O'Shea, Mark
Boas and pythons of the world. Princeton University Press 2007 160p il map $29.95
Grades: 11 12 Adult   **597.96**
1. Boa constrictors 2. Pythons
ISBN 978-0-691-13100-9; 0-691-13100-7
                             LC 2006-932790
The author examines boas and pythons "in a geographic format, covering the Americas, Europe and Asia, Africa and Indian Ocean islands, and Australian and Pacific Coast islands. An introductory section discusses general snake biology, including evolution and anatomy, and also examines constriction, the myths and realities of giant snakes, and conservation. . . . This excellent book is highly recommended." Booklist

O'Shea, Mark—*Continued*

Venomous snakes of the world. Princeton University Press 2005 160p il map $29.95 *

Grades: 11 12 Adult **597.96**
1. Snakes 2. Poisonous animals
ISBN 0-691-12436-1   LC 2005-920576

The author "has produced a compendium of more than 170 venomous snakes, along with their markings, geographical distribution, maximum length, venom, prey, and similar species. But instead of opting for the traditional taxonomic arrangement, he lists these snakes geographically by continent (a final chapter on sea snakes is also included)." Libr J

"Fascinating photographs and descriptions will make this title a favorite." Univ Press Books for Public and Second Sch Libr, 2006

Includes bibliographical references

598 Aves (Birds)

Alderfer, Jonathan

National Geographic birding essentials; all the tools, techniques, and tips you need to begin and become a better birder; [by] Jonathan Alderfer and Jon L. Dunn. National Geographic 2007 224p il pa $15.95 *

Grades: 11 12 Adult   **598**
1. Bird watching
ISBN 978-1-4262-0135-6; 1-4262-0135-4
          LC 2007-30960

This "book offers data on how to begin and how to improve your bird-watching skills. Chapters deal with the pleasures of birding, getting started, where and when birds are found, how common or rare they are at different seasons, parts of a bird, how to identify them, and variations in birds. . . . With a helpful glossary, this is an essential volume for all bird-watchers." Booklist

Includes bibliographical references

The **atlas** of bird migration; tracing the great journeys of the world's birds; general editor Jonathan Elphick; foreword by Thomas E. Lovejoy. Firefly Books 2007 176p il map $35 *

Grades: 11 12 Adult   **598**
1. Birds—Migration
ISBN 978-1-55407-248-4; 1-55407-248-4

First published 1995 by Random House

New edition in preparation

"The first section is a primer on bird migration and habitat usage patterns, consisting of short, illustrated essays on topics like the evolution of migration, the mechanics of flight, birds' navigational methods and how human development affects migration patterns. Succeeding sections examine different families of migrating birds according to geographical distribution, and each has carefully designed maps that show birds' seasonal ranges and migratory routes. The use of color to describe, clarify, distinguish and compare migration patterns is exceptional, and clear explanations of complicated topics (e.g., how birds fly) make it an excellent text for middle and high school students as well as adults." Publ Wkly

Backhouse, Frances

Owls of North America. Firefly Books 2008 215p il map $34.95

Grades: 11 12 Adult   **598**
1. Owls
ISBN 978-1-55407-342-9; 1-55407-342-1

This book "takes an intimate look at the 22 species of typical owls and 1 species of barn owl found in North America. Eight preliminary chapters examine general owl anatomy, hunting and feeding behavior, communication, mating and care of young, and daily behaviors and migration. Profiles of the 23 species follow, covering all owls found in Canada, the U.S., and Mexico north of the Tropic of Cancer. Each species range is depicted on a map, with specifics of appearance, voice, time of daily activity, distribution, habitat, feeding, breeding, migration, and conservation discussed. Heavily illustrated with beautiful, clear photographs." Booklist

Includes bibliographical references

Berger, Cynthia

Owls; illustrations by Amelia Hansen. Stackpole Books 2005 131p il (Wild guide) pa $19.95

Grades: 11 12 Adult   **598**
1. Owls
ISBN 0-8117-3213-4   LC 2005-2317

The author "explores the lives of [owls] . . . including their fearsome hunting abilities, their surprisingly tender courtship rituals, and, of course, their haunting vocalizations. Also included is an identification guide covering the full range of North American species." Publisher's note

Berger "has produced a wonderfully complete yet compact introduction to owls." Booklist

Includes bibliographical references

Burger, Joanna

Birds: a visual guide. Firefly Books 2006 304p il map $29.95 *

Grades: 11 12 Adult   **598**
1. Birds
ISBN 978-1-55407-177-7; 1-55407-177-1

"Divided into six sections, the text considers all aspects of birds' lives. Basic anatomy, evolution, physiology, and intelligence are all touched on in the first section, while bird behavior . . . is covered in the second. A large section examines the taxonomy of birds . . . accompanied by a world map showing its distribution. Habitat, migration, and how birds fill their space are discussed in the fourth section, followed by a look at avian adaptations and lifestyles. The final section, on birds and humans, covers such disparate topics as birds in legend, bird-watching, captive birds, and habitat loss. Beautifully illustrated." Booklist

Chandler, Richard J.

Shorebirds of North America, Europe, and Asia; a photographic guide; [by] Richard Chandler. Princeton University Press 2009 448p il map pa $35

Grades: 11 12 Adult   **598**
1. Birds
ISBN 978-0-691-14281-4; 0-691-14281-5
          LC 2009-921111

Chandler, Richard J.—*Continued*

"Opening with a comprehensive primer on shorebird geography, speciation, appearance and behavior, Chandler goes on to describe feed techniques in fascinating detail, with illustrations showing how birds disturb small prey on mud flats and marsh grasses. Each species is accompanied by a seasonal distribution map, and a thorough bibliography and index backs up clearly written text." Publ Wkly

Includes bibliographical references

Choiniere, Joseph

What's that bird? getting to know the birds around you, coast-to-coast; [by] Joseph Choiniere & Claire Mowbray Goldin; photography by Tom Vezo; ill. by James Robins. Storey Pub. 2005 117p il map $24.95; pa $14.95

Grades: 9 10 11 12   598

1. Birds 2. Bird watching

ISBN 1-58017-555-4; 1-58017-554-6 (pa)

                LC 2004-17307

This book features "facts about bird nesting sites, habitat, song, diet, lifestyle, and migration patterns." Publisher's note

Includes bibliographical references

Chu, Miyoko

Songbird journeys; four seasons in the lives of migratory birds. Walker & Co. 2006 312p il map $23

Grades: 11 12 Adult   598

1. Birds—Migration

ISBN 0-8027-1468-4; 978-0-8027-1468-8

                LC 2006-278075

The author describes the "seasonal migrations of American songbirds. . . . In addition to descriptions of the birds' migrations, habits, and life histories for each season, there are details on hotspots for observing the birds, including web sites, addresses, when to go, and special activities. . . . An excellent overview of a compelling subject; highly recommended." Libr J

Includes bibliographical references

Couzens, Dominic

Extreme birds; the world's most extraordinary and bizarre birds. Firefly Books 2008 287p il $45

Grades: 11 12 Adult   598

1. Birds

ISBN 978-1-55407-423-5; 1-55407-423-1

"Each of 150 species of bizarre birds from around the world is portrayed in a short essay and a showcase color photograph. These superlative birds are organized in four categories: extreme form (e.g., heaviest flier, smallest species, biggest eyes); extreme ability (e.g., fastest swimmer, highest migration, sharpest hearing); extreme behavior (e.g., largest roost, oddest incubation); and extreme family life (e.g., strangest courtship, sibling rivalry, bigamy). The text is interesting, accurate, and up to date with recent discoveries." Am Ref Books Annu, 2009

De Roy, Tui

Albatross; their world, their ways; [by] Tui De Roy, Mark Jones, Julian Fitter. Firefly Books 2008 240p il map $49.95

Grades: 11 12 Adult   598

1. Albatrosses

ISBN 978-1-55407-415-0   LC 2008-274293

"In this magnificent book about a magnificent bird—the revered, now endangered albatross—wildlife photographer De Roy and contributing scientists cover all aspects of albatross beauty, biology, and conservation." Booklist

Includes bibliographical references

Ehrlich, Paul R.

The birder's handbook; a field guide to the natural history of North American birds: including all species that regularly breed north of Mexico; [by] Paul R. Ehrlich, David S. Dobkin, Daryl Wheye. Simon & Schuster 1988 xxx, 785p il pa $21.95 hardcover o.p.

Grades: 11 12 Adult   598

1. Birds—North America

ISBN 0-671-65989-8 (pa)   LC 87-32404

This volume contains "basic information on each of the 646 species of birds in North America, enriched by 250 short essays on all aspects of avian behavior and biology. This book is a companion volume to any illustrated field guide." Am Libr

Includes bibliographical references

Erickson, Laura

The bird watching answer book; everything you need to know to enjoy birds in your backyard and beyond. Storey Pub. 2009 388p il pa $14.95

Grades: 9 10 11 12 Adult   598

1. Bird watching

ISBN 978-1-60342-452-3   LC 2009-23708

At head of title: The Cornell Lab of Ornithology

"Dividing the book into three parts—'For the Birds: Feeding, Watching and Protecting Our Feathered Friends'; 'Bird Brains: Avian Behavior and Intelligence'; and 'All about Birds, Inside and Out'—Erikson organizes a vast amount of bird biology and behavior into manageable snippets. Using a familiar question-and-answer format, the author covers such broad topics as feeding birds and bird migration." Booklist

Includes bibliographical references

Gallagher, Tim

The grail bird; hot on the trail of the Ivory-billed woodpecker. Houghton Mifflin 2005 272p il map $25; pa $14.95

Grades: 11 12 Adult   598

1. Woodpeckers

ISBN 0-618-45693-7; 0-618-70941-X (pa)

                LC 2005-42792

The author "was one of the first to rediscover the ivory-billed woodpecker, a fabled bird long believed extinct." Booklist

"An engaging story of the triumph of conservation, this book is highly recommended for most collections." Libr J

Includes bibliographical references

Hoose, Phillip M., 1947-

The race to save the Lord God Bird; [by] Phillip Hoose. Farrar, Straus and Giroux 2004 196p il map $20

Grades: 7 8 9 10   **598**

1. Woodpeckers 2. Endangered species
ISBN 0-374-36173-8

Tells the story of the ivory-billed woodpecker's extinction in the United States, describing the encounters between this species and humans, and discussing what these encounters have taught us about preserving endangered creatures

"Sharp, clear, black-and-white archival photos and reproductions appear throughout. The author's passion for his subject and high standards for excellence result in readable, compelling nonfiction." SLJ

Includes glossary and bibliographical references

Jacquet, Luc

March of the penguins; from the film by Luc Jacquet; narration written by Jordan Roberts; photographs by Jérôme Maison. National Geographic 2006 unp il $30

Grades: 8 9 10 11 12   **598**

1. Penguins
ISBN 0-7922-6182-8; 978-0-7922-6182-7
                                              LC 2006-295371

"The book delves further than the hit movie into the lives of these remarkable penguins and their story of survival, and it also covers the conditions endured by the film crew to get the footage." Publisher's note

"This fine book works as a stand-alone volume, thanks to its charming photographs and revealing text." Publ Wkly

Kaufman, Kenn

Kaufman field guide to birds of North America; with the collaboration of Rick and Nora Bowers and Lynn Hassler Kaufman. Houghton Mifflin 2005 392p il map pa $18.95

Grades: 11 12 Adult   **598**

1. Birds—North America
ISBN 0-618-57423-9; 978-0-618-57423-0

First published 2000 with title: Birds of North America

For this identification guide "Kaufman selected over 2000 digitally edited photographs, enhanced to improve contrast, color, and the like. The excellent result will appeal to beginning birders perhaps intimidated by illustrations. . . . Kaufman's text is simple and uncluttered, a plus for novices." Libr J

Lynch, Wayne

Penguins of the world; text and photographs by Wayne Lynch. 2nd ed. Firefly Books 2007 175p il map $34.95; pa $24.95

Grades: 11 12 Adult   **598**

1. Penguins
ISBN   978-1-55407-334-4;   1-55407-334-0;
978-1-55407-274-3 (pa); 1-55407-274-3 (pa)
                                              LC 2007-299218

First published 1997

This is a "look at Lynch's discoveries about these flightless seabirds in the field and in scientific journals, during day-to-day as well as birth-to-death observations, and from the smallest to the largest type. While Lynch presents detailed descriptions of everything from mating rituals to eating habits, the best parts of his book are the photographs. Lynch's gorgeous and gorgeously printed images . . . display such a refined visual sensibility that even without accompanying text, the images would still achieve Lynch's goal of presenting the scientific and aesthetic appeal of this unique family of birds." Publ Wkly

Includes bibliographical references

National Audubon Society

Bird; the definitive visual guide; Audubon; [senior editor, Peter Frances; contributors, BirdLife International, David Burnie] DK Pub. 2007 512p il map $50

Grades: 9 10 11 12 Adult   **598**

1. Birds
ISBN 978-0-7566-3153-6; 0-7566-3153-X
                                              LC 2007-282186

Includes audio CD

"More than 10 percent of the world's 10,000 bird species are featured here, often in their natural habitat. Introductory sections discuss bird anatomy, physiology, behavior, evolution, flight, migration, classification, conservation, and geographic distribution. The main section of the book, arranged taxonomically, begins with general features and behavior of bird families. This is followed by photographs of each species and brief physical descriptions, habitat and behavior notes, and a distribution map." Choice

"From flyleaf to fore edge, the visuals are astounding. . . . An enclosed CD with bird calls and songs adds yet another dimension to a glorious work." Libr J

National Geographic complete birds of North America; edited by Jonathan Alderfer. National Geographic 2006 664p il map $35 *

Grades: 11 12 Adult   **598**

1. Birds—North America
ISBN 0-7922-4175-4   LC 2005-54495

Companion volume to Field guide to the birds of North America

This guide includes "chapters for the more than 80 avian families, with an overview of plumage, behavior, distribution, taxonomy, and conservation. This is followed by descriptions of all 962 species (covering identification, similar species, voice, status, and distribution) and sidebars that address such topics as difficult identifications." Libr J

"The book pulls together a remarkable amount of information into what can only be described as one of the finest one-volume reference works ever published on North American birds." Booklist

Includes bibliographical references

National Geographic field guide to the birds of North America; edited by Jon L. Dunn and Jonathan Alderfer. 5th ed. National Geographic 2006 503p il map pa $24 *

Grades: 11 12 Adult   **598**

1. Birds—North America
ISBN 0-7922-5314-0; 978-0-7922-5314-3
                                              LC 2006-49420

National Geographic field guide to the birds of North America—*Continued*

First published 1983 with title: Field guide to the birds of North America

An identification guide to more than 800 species of North American birds. Arranged in family groups, the information for each species includes a full-color illustration, a range map, common and scientific names, measurement, and a description of plumage, distinctive songs and calls, behavior, abundance, and habitat.

Includes bibliographical references

Peterson, Roger Tory, 1908-1996

Peterson field guide to birds of Eastern and Central North America; [by] Roger Tory Peterson, with contributions from Michael DiGiorgio [et al.] 6th ed. Houghton Mifflin Harcourt 2010 445p il map (Peterson field guide series) $19.95

Grades: 5 6 7 8 9 10 11 12 Adult   598

1. Birds—North America

ISBN 978-0-547-15246-2; 0-547-15246-9

LC 2009-37681

First published 1934 with title: A field guide to the birds

This guide to birds found east of the Rocky Mountains contains colored illustrations painted by the author, with a description of each species on the facing page. Views of young birds and seasonal variations in plumage are included.

Peterson field guide to birds of North America; with contributions from Michael DiGiorgio . . . [et al.] Houghton Mifflin Co. 2008 527p il map (Peterson field guide series) $26 *

Grades: 5 6 7 8 9 10 11 12 Adult   598

1. Birds—North America

ISBN 978-0-618-96614-1; 0-618-96614-5

LC 2007-39803

First published 1934 with title: A field guide to the birds. Previously published in two separate parts as A field guide to western birds (1990) and A field guide to the birds of eastern and central North America (2002)

This guide to birds found in North America contains colored illustrations painted by the author, with a description of each species on the facing page. Views of young birds and seasonal variations in plumage are included. The book also includes a URL to video podcasts.

"This field guide is of high quality and should be in millions of birders' and other nature lovers' backpacks." Sci Books Films

Peterson field guide to birds of Western North America; with contributions from Michael DiGiorgio [et al.] 4th ed. Houghton Mifflin Harcourt 2010 493p il map (Peterson field guide series) pa $19.95

Grades: 5 6 7 8 9 10 11 12 Adult   598

1. Birds—North America

ISBN 978-0-547-15270-7; 0-547-15270-1

LC 2009-39158

First published 1941 with title: A field guide to western birds

This guide illustrates over 600 species of birds on 176 color plates. In addition, over 588 range maps are included.

The **Princeton** encyclopedia of birds; edited by Christopher Perrins. Princeton University Press 2009 656p il map pa $35

Grades: 9 10 11 12 Adult   598

1. Birds—Encyclopedias 2. Reference books

ISBN 978-0-691-14070-4; 0-691-14070-7

First published 1985 by Facts on File with title: The encyclopedia of birds. Previous edition published 2003 by Firefly Bks. with title: Firefly encyclopedia of birds

The editor "combines the work of 150 contributors and more than 1000 great color photographs, maps, and other illustrations to produce a stunning book that informs both amateurs and experts. Coverage includes form and function, distribution, diet, breeding biology, and conservation and environment." Libr J

Includes bibliographical references

Sibley, David

The Sibley field guide to birds of Eastern North America; written and illustrated by David Allen Sibley. Knopf 2003 431p il pa $19.95 *

Grades: 11 12 Adult   598

1. Birds—North America

ISBN 0-679-45120-X   LC 2002-114931

Companion volume to The Sibley field guide to birds of western North America

This portable "guide features 650 bird species, plus regional populations found east of the Rocky Mountains. Accounts include . . . illustrations . . . with descriptive caption text pointing out the most important field marks. Each entry contains . . . text concerning frequency, nesting, behavior, food and feeding, voice description, and key identification features." Publisher's note

"All the qualities to be expected in a field guide are here. . . . Image reproduction is crisp, colors are distinct, shading shows well, and despite the very small size, range map colors are clear. . . . Sibley has accomplished the difficult task of condensing . . . [The Sibley guide to birds] to practical field size." Libr J

The Sibley field guide to birds of Western North America; written and illustrated by David Allen Sibley. Knopf 2003 473p il pa $19.95 *

Grades: 11 12 Adult   598

1. Birds—North America

ISBN 0-679-45121-8   LC 2002-114930

Companion volume to The Sibley field guide to birds of eastern North America

This portable "guide features 703 bird species, plus regional populations found west of the Rocky Mountains. Accounts include . . . illustrations . . . with descriptive caption text pointing out the most important field marks. Each entry contains . . . text concerning frequency, nesting, behavior, food and feeding, voice description, and key identification features." Publisher's note

"All the qualities to be expected in a field guide are here. . . . Image reproduction is crisp, colors are distinct, shading shows well, and despite the very small size, range map colors are clear. . . . Sibley has accomplished the difficult task of condensing . . . [The Sibley guide to birds] to practical field size." Libr J

Sibley, David—*Continued*

The Sibley guide to bird life & behavior; illustrated by David Allen Sibley; edited by Chris Elphick, John B. Dunning, Jr., David Allen Sibley. Knopf 2001 588p il maps hardcover o.p. pa $39.95 *

Grades: 11 12 Adult   598
  1. Birds—North America
  ISBN 0-679-45123-4; 1-4000-4386-7 (pa)
                             LC 2001-33903

At head of title: National Audubon Society

This companion volume to The Sibley guide to birds provides "information about birds' lives and behavior. . . . Part 1 ('The World of Birds') discusses basic avian biology, including form, distribution, population, and conservation, in about 100 pages. Part 2 ('Bird Families of North America'), to which over 40 ornithologists contributed, uses a standard format to describe taxonomy, foraging, breeding, range, nests, eggs, longevity, conservation, and more." Libr J

The Sibley guide to birds; written and illustrated by David Sibley. Knopf 2000 544p il maps pa $35 *

Grades: 11 12 Adult   598
  1. Birds—North America
  ISBN 0-679-45122-6   LC 00-41239

"A Chanticleer Press edition"

At head of title: National Audubon Society

"The treatments of each of the 810 species have detailed paintings to show the natural variations in plumage (e.g., juveniles, male/female adults, seasonal and geographic changes). In all, there are more than 6,600 full-color illustrations. . . . The text for each species has a short summary of identification key points, description of vocalizations, and an up-to-date range map." Choice

"This stunning volume stands out as a must have for even casual birders." SLJ

Sterry, Paul

Birds of Eastern North America; a photographic guide; [by] Paul Sterry & Brian E. Small. Princeton University Press 2009 336p il map $45; pa $18.95

Grades: 11 12 Adult   598
  1. Birds—North America
  ISBN 978-0-691-13425-3; 978-0-691-13426-0 (pa)
                             LC 2009-1494

The author "offer birders excellent state-of-the art digital photos and comprehensive, up-to-date data on North American birds. Species information includes common and scientific names, field marks, plumage variation, size, vocalization, range maps provided by Cornell Laboratory of Ornithology, and habitat. Conservation status and observation tips for each species are also included." Libr J

Includes bibliographical references

Birds of Western North America; a photographic guide; [by] Paul Sterry and Brian E. Small. Princeton University Press 2009 416p il map $45; pa $18.95

Grades: 11 12 Adult   598
  1. Birds—North America
  ISBN 978-0-691-13427-7; 978-0-691-13428-4 (pa)
                             LC 2009-1416

The authors "cover more than 500 species an variants—including birds that migrate down the Pacific and Rocky Mountain flyways and over the eastern Pacific Ocean, as well as Eastern birds known to visit—assembling photos, geographical data, species descriptions and field observations from the Cornell Laboratory of Ornithology. Experienced guidebook authors, Sterry and Small present their information in an organized, easy-to-use manner." Publ Wkly

Includes bibliographical references

Tennant, Alan, 1943-

On the wing; to the edge of the earth with the peregrine falcon. Alfred A. Knopf 2004 304p il $26.95; pa $14.95

Grades: 11 12 Adult   598
  1. Falcons
  ISBN 0-375-41551-3; 1-4000-3182-6 (pa)
                             LC 2003-69496

The author "describes his efforts to trail peregrine falcons on their epic migratory flights from the Caribbean to the Arctic. . . . After radio-tagging a young peregrine off the coast of Texas, Tennant teams up with George Vose, a former WWII combat flight instructor, to follow the bird on its spring migration north." Publ Wkly

"An exhilarating and illuminating storyteller, Tennant offers exquisitely poetic descriptions of peregrine falcons—magnificently aerodynamic, keen-sighted, and fearless birds of prey—a galvanizing history of falconry, and a sobering accounting of the consequences of rampant chemical pollution and environmental destruction." Booklist

599   Mammalia (Mammals)

Attenborough, David, 1926-

The life of mammals. Princeton University Press 2002 320p il $35

Grades: 11 12 Adult   599
  1. Mammals
  ISBN 0-691-11324-6   LC 2002-106846

The author "treks across every continent and kind of terrain to introduce us to such unusual and evolutionarily successful creatures as the Patagonian opossum, the Canadian pygmy shrew, the Alpine marmot, and the Malaysian sun bear." Publisher's note

"Heavily illustrated with beautiful photographs and enlivened by Attenborough's friendly, informative writing style, this is a terrific introduction to the wonders of our hairy, milk-producing relatives." Booklist

Elbroch, Mark

Mammal tracks & sign; a guide to North American species. Stackpole Bks. 2003 779p il maps $44.95 *

Grades: 11 12 Adult   **599**

1. Animal tracks

ISBN 0-8117-2626-6   LC 2002-10549

This guide provides "track and trail illustrations, range maps, and full-color photographs showing feeding signs, scat, tunnels, burrows, bedding areas, remains, and more. . . . [It explains] how to find, identify, measure, and interpret the clues mammals leave behind. . . . Includes essays that contextualize tracking as a developing science." Publisher's note

The author "brings an ideal combination of practical experience and careful research to this work. . . . A definitive treatment, Elbroch's book will set the standard for years to come and is essential to anyone interested in tracking this continent's mammals." Libr J

Includes bibliographical references

Forsyth, Adrian

Mammals of North America. Firefly Bks. (Buffalo) 1999 352p il maps hardcover o.p. pa $29.95

Grades: 11 12 Adult   **599**

1. Mammals

ISBN 1-55209-409-X; 1-55407-233-6 (pa)

"The author has limited his work to approximately 150 species that inhabit some of the same territory as humans. . . . Each chapter follows the same format: the common name of the species followed by the Latin name; a color photograph; a sidebar consisting of a map with the habitat shaded, a description, and vital statistics, including life span, diet, habitat, predators, and dental formula; and an article of a few paragraphs to several pages describing the mammal's life in the wild. . . . This resource can be used by students for reports because the text is clear and easy to comprehend." Booklist

Kays, Roland, 1971-

Mammals of North America; [by] Roland W. Kays and Don E. Wilson. 2nd ed. Princeton University Press 2009 248p il map (Princeton field guides) $45; pa $19.95

Grades: 11 12 Adult   **599**

1. Mammals

ISBN 978-0-691-14278-4; 978-0-691-14092-6 (pa)

LC 2009-1417

First published 2002

This "is a durable and portable field guide [to mammals] that should hold up to many years of use. Its range maps are clear, easy to interpret, and placed conveniently adjacent to accompanying text. . . . Kays and Wilson's inclusion of print, scat (carnivore and herbivore), and dive sequence illustrations may be particularly valuable to novices and occasional observers who are more likely to see signs of species than the species themselves." Sci Books Films

Includes bibliographical references

Mammals; editorial consultants, Juliet Clutton-Brock, Don E. Wilson. DK 2002 400p il map (Smithsonian handbooks) hardcover o.p. pa $20

Grades: 9 10 11 12   **599**

1. Mammals

ISBN 0-7513-3374-3; 0-7894-8404-8 (pa)

LC 2001-47823

This book features over 500 profiles of mammals including descriptions, color photos, and facts about the animals.

The **Princeton** encyclopedia of mammals; edited by David W. Macdonald. Princeton University Press 2009 936p il map pa $45

Grades: 9 10 11 12 Adult   **599**

1. Mammals—Encyclopedias 2. Reference books

ISBN 978-0-691-14069-8; 0-691-14069-3

This encyclopedia features a "general introduction to mammals followed by . . . accounts of species and groups that . . . describe form, distribution, behavior, status, conservation, and more." Publisher's note

Includes bibliographical references

Whitaker, John O., Jr.

National Audubon Society field guide to North American mammals. rev ed. Knopf 1996 937p il maps pa $19.95 *

Grades: 6 7 8 9 10 11 12 Adult   **599**

1. Mammals

ISBN 0-679-44631-1   LC 95-81456

First published 1980

This field guide describes 390 species of mammals of North America and includes keys for identification, range maps, information on tracks and anatomy, and 375 color photos

599.2   Marsupialia and monotremata

Flannery, Tim F. (Tim Fridjof), 1956-

Chasing kangaroos; a continent, a scientist, and a search for the world's most extraordinary creature. Grove Press 2007 258p il map hardcover o.p. pa $14 *

Grades: 11 12 Adult   **599.2**

1. Kangaroos 2. Australia—Description and travel

ISBN   978-0-8021-1852-3;   0-8021-1852-6; 978-0-8021-4371-6 (pa); 0-8021-4371-7 (pa)

LC 2006-52628

First published 2004 in Australia with title: Country

"There are 70-odd species of kangaroo: some drink salt water; others live in trees. But as a paleontologist, Flannery is obsessed with finding out when and where the first kangaroos lived. Much of the book is about his searches for the fossils of extinct species in remote areas of the Australian outback." Publ Wkly

"In a time where pride in one's country is a rarity, Flannery has written a love letter to his. . . . Just as much as Chasing Kangaroos is about the evolution of a creature, it's also Flannery's acknowledgement of Austra-

Flannery, Tim F. (Tim Fridjof), 1956- —Continued

lia's inherent uniqueness, a uniqueness he begs is not casually lost in the growing conformity of the global landscape." Paste

Moyal, Ann

Platypus; the extraordinary story of how a curious creature baffled the world. Smithsonian Institution Press 2001 226p il maps $21.95

Grades: 11 12 Adult   **599.2**

1. Platypus

ISBN 1-56098-977-7   LC 2001-20892

Also available in paperback from Johns Hopkins Univ. Press

The author offers an "account of this odd Australian mammal as she follows the story of its discovery, the scientific infighting over its place in taxonomy, and modern efforts to understand its biology and keep and breed it in captivity. The author captures the state of nineteenth-century scientific inquiry beautifully. Well illustrated with period engravings of both the animal and the scientists who fought over it, as well as photographs of the living animal." Booklist

Includes glossary and bibliographical references

599.3   Miscellaneous orders of Eutheria (placental mammals)

Sullivan, Robert, 1963-

Rats: observations on the history and habitat of the city's most unwanted inhabitants. Bloomsbury 2003 242p hardcover o.p. pa $14.95

Grades: 11 12 Adult   **599.3**

1. Rats

ISBN 1-582-34385-3; 1-582-34477-9 (pa)

     LC 2003-16293

This book contains observations on and a history of "rats in New York City, from bar fights in the 1840s to the World Trade Center catastrophe." SLJ

The author "has an excellent sense of narrative, blending interesting anecdotes and snippets of history in such an engaging way that it really is hard to put down the book. The result is a fascinating account that is much bigger than the title implies." Voice Youth Advocates

599.4   Chiroptera (Bats)

Richardson, Phil

Bats. Firefly Books 2011 128p il pa $19.95

Grades: 9 10 11 12 Adult   **599.4**

1. Bats

ISBN 978-1-55407-803-5

This book "describes these mammals' complex life cycles and explains how anyone can watch and study bats and help to conserve them." Publisher's note

Includes bibliographical references

599.5   Cetacea and Sirenia

Bortolotti, Dan

Wild blue; a natural history of the world's largest animal. Thomas Dunne Books 2008 315p il map $24.95 *

Grades: 11 12 Adult   **599.5**

1. Whales

ISBN 978-0-312-38387-9; 0-312-38387-8

     LC 2008-24933

The author "provides the most comprehensive title yet on blue whales for the general reader. Encapsulating everything from statistical analysis of geographic populations to the reports of whalers from centuries past, *Wild Blue* is an effective twenty-first-century fusion of marine biology and international politics." Booklist

Includes bibliographical references

Kelsey, Elin

Watching giants; the secret lives of whales; with photographs by Doc White; additional photographs by François Gohier. University of California Press 2009 201p il $24.95 *

Grades: 11 12 Adult   **599.5**

1. Whales

ISBN 978-0-520-24976-9; 0-520-24976-3

     LC 2008-7782

The author "meditates in 20 linked essays on the resident and visiting cetaceans—including whales, dolphins and orcas—of the Gulf of California." Publ Wkly

"An appealing, agitating foray into the world of whales that ignites both protective instincts and a hungry curiosity to know more." Kirkus

Includes bibliographical references

Reep, Roger L.

The Florida manatee; biology and conservation; [by] Roger L. Reep and Robert K. Bonde. University Press of Florida 2006 189p il map $34.95

Grades: 11 12 Adult   **599.5**

1. Manatees

ISBN 978-0-8130-2949-8; 0-8130-2949-X

     LC 2005-58578

"The authors explore Sirenian history . . . and detail the manatee lifestyle. They explain, with expertise, the neuroanatomy, senses, perception, and behavior, revealing (in a comparative framework) how the aquatic environment demanded solutions very different from those found in terrestrial animals. No other source fulfills more admirably the goal of inspiring and recruiting young talent into the fold of Sirenian conservation around the world." Choice

Includes bibliographical references

599.63   Artiodactyla (Even-toed ungulates)

Watson, Lyall, 1939-2008

The whole hog; exploring the extraordinary potential of pigs; Lyall Watson. Smithsonian Books 2004 208p il $24.95

Grades: 11 12 Adult   **599.63**

    1. Pigs

    ISBN 1-588-34216-6   LC 2004-52248

The author "investigates several distinct pig types, including bushpigs, wild boars, forest hogs and peccaries . . . and offers anecdotes about his childhood pet warthog. . . . Anthropology, biology, geography, psychology are all here in a clearly written, amiable text peppered with trivia tidbits . . . and lots of photos. Even those who read but a handful of these pages will find their opinion of pigs much rosier." Publ Wkly

Includes bibliographical references

599.66   Perissodactyla (Odd-toed ungulates)

Hyde, Dayton O., 1925-

All the wild horses; preserving the spirit and beauty of the world's wild horses; photography by Rita Summers and Charles G. Summers, Jr. MBI Pub. Co. 2006 208p il pa $24.99

Grades: 9 10 11 12 Adult   **599.66**

    1. Horses

    ISBN   978-0-7603-2590-2;   0-7603-2590-1; 978-0-7603-3648-9 (pa); 0-7603-3648-2 (pa)

                LC 2006-015586

This is "an illustrated book showing not just the mustangs of the West, but also the horses and ponies in England, France, Africa (including zebras) and islands off Maryland's and North Carolina's shores. . . . [It] includes both personal experiences and information about horses." South Dakota Magazine

"There is no better book for horse lovers or anyone interested in the horse as an icon of the American West." Booklist

599.67   Proboscidea (Elephants)

Anthony, Lawrence

The elephant whisperer; my life with the herd in the African wild; [by] Lawrence Anthony with Graham Spence. Thomas Dunne Books/St. Martin's Press 2009 368p il $24.99

Grades: 11 12 Adult   **599.67**

    1. Elephants 2. Wildlife refuges

    ISBN 978-0-312-56578-7   LC 2009-23815

This is the author's "robust portrait of Thula Thula, the game land he owns, in cooperation with a number of Zulu tribes, in Zululand—5,000 acres of raw landscape that is thought to have been part of the exclusive hunting grounds of the Zulu king. No longer, since Anthony now runs it as a conservationist lodge, but it continues to produce colorful tales of wild discovery. Most prominent are the many fascinating stories that surround his adoption of the elephants, an unruly bunch he endeavors to make at home on the reserve. With a combination of intuition and experience, the author intelligently discusses many aspects of elephant behavior." Kirkus

Poole, Joyce, 1956-

Elephants. Voyageur Press 1997 72p il (World life library) pa $14.95

Grades: 9 10 11 12   **599.67**

    1. Elephants

    ISBN 0-89658-357-0   LC 97-15272

This describes elephants' "society and strong sense of family, their complex infrasonic communication, their feeding and mating habits, and their chances for survival in a rapidly changing world." Publisher's note

Includes bibliographical references

599.7   Carnivora Fissipedia (Land carnivores)

Ross, Mark

Predator; life and death in the African bush; [by] Mark C. Ross and David Reesor. Abrams 2007 207p il $35

Grades: 9 10 11 12   **599.7**

    1. Predatory animals 2. Animals—Africa

    ISBN 978-0-8109-9301-3; 0-8109-9301-5

                LC 2006-36127

This book examines "the behavior of five African predators (hyena, cheetah, leopard, lion, and crocodile)." Sci Books Films

"Ecological depth and plentiful insight make this an excellent addition to middle and high-school classrooms, while vivid photographs provide a fine virtual tour of the African bush and a great advert for conservation efforts." Publ Wkly

Includes bibliographical references

599.75   Felidae (Cat family)

Alderton, David

Wild cats of the world; photographs by Bruce Tanner. Facts on File 2002 192p il map $35 *

Grades: 7 8 9 10   **599.75**

    1. Wild cats

    ISBN 0-8160-5217-4   LC 2002-34736

    First published 1993

This "volume explores the development and behavior of wild cats, with chapters covering form and function, evolution, and distribution. It also examines each species in detail, providing information on distinctive features such as sight, hearing, hunting techniques, and locomotion." Publisher's note

Includes bibliographical references

Caputo, Philip
Ghosts of Tsavo; stalking the mystery lions of East Africa. National Geographic Soc. 2002 275p il $27; pa $15
Grades: 11 12 Adult   **599.75**
1. Lions 2. Tsavo National Park (Kenya)
ISBN 0-7922-6362-6; 0-7922-4100-2 (pa)
LC 2002-22642
This is a study of the Tsavo lions of Kenya. Philip Caputo discusses "why they are bigger than their counterparts of the Serengeti plains, why the males do not normally grow manes, and why Tsavo lions are more prone than Serengeti lions to make humans a part of their diet. The observable differences between Tsavo lions and Serengeti lions have led some behavioral scientists whom Mr. Caputo interviews to believe that the Tsavo lions are actually a different species." N Y Times (Late N Y Ed)

599.77   Canidae (Dog family)

Grambo, Rebecca L., 1963-
Wolf: legend, enemy, icon; photographs by Daniel J. Cox. Firefly Books 2006 176p il $34.95
Grades: 11 12 Adult   **599.77**
1. Wolves
ISBN 1-55407-044-9
Shifting "between science and myth, with sociological, anthropological, and ethological stops along the way, Grambo explores all sides of the wolf, from both lupine and human perspectives. The many illustrations, which include Daniel Cox's images of wolves in the wild, reinforce the premise of the text." Booklist
Includes bibliographical references

McAllister, Ian, 1969-
The last wild wolves; ghosts of the rain forest; with contributions by Chris Darimont; introduction by Paul C. Paquet. University of California Press 2007 191p il map $39.95
Grades: 11 12 Adult   **599.77**
1. Wolves
ISBN 978-0-520-25473-2; 0-520-25473-2
LC 2007-10887
Includes DVD
This is an account of the author's experiences following two packs of wolves on the north coast of British Columbia. In text and photographs, the wolves are depicted "as they fish for salmon in the fall, target seals [are] hauled out on rocks in winter, and [the wolves] give birth to their young." Publisher's note
"The text is particularly well written and engaging. . . . However, it is the dozens of unique photos sprinkled liberally throughout the book that provide the greatest appeal." Sci Books Films

Smith, Douglas W.
Decade of the wolf; returning the wild to Yellowstone; [by] Douglas W. Smith & Gary Ferguson. Lyons Press 2005 212p il maps $23.95; pa $16.95
Grades: 11 12 Adult   **599.77**
1. Wolves 2. Endangered species 3. Yellowstone National Park
ISBN 1-59228-700-X; 1-59228-886-3 (pa)
LC 2005-40767
This is an "inside look at the Yellowstone Wolf Recovery Project, covering the 10 years that have passed since the U.S. Fish and Wildlife Service made the controversial decision to reintroduce wolves into the national park." Publ Wkly
"Well illustrated with black-and-white and color photographs, this intimate history of the return of the top predator to Yellowstone will find an eager audience." Booklist
Includes bibliographical references

Steinhart, Peter
The company of wolves. Knopf 1995 374p il maps hardcover o.p. pa $14.95
Grades: 11 12 Adult   **599.77**
1. Wolves
ISBN 0-679-41881-4; 0-679-74387-1 (pa)
LC 94-26913
This is "an examination of the relationship between humans and wolves in the wolves' last refuges in the Arctic and in places where the two species live together again as wolves move into new areas, either through their own natural movements or through attempts at reintroduction. Steinhart . . . speaks with wolf biologists, wildlife managers, trappers, ranchers, Native Americans, and others. Though it is clear where Steinhart's sympathies lie, the book is balanced between the wolves' advocates and their opponents." Libr J
Includes bibliographical references

599.78   Ursidae (Bears)

Breiter, Matthias
Bears: [a year in the life] Firefly Books 2005 176p il $34.95
Grades: 11 12 Adult   **599.78**
1. Bears
ISBN 1-55407-077-5   LC 2006-295648
The author offers a "look at three species of bears by following their lives through each month of the year. . . . Breiter works a tremendous amount of natural history into this calendar approach, and his photo illustrations are both apt and beautiful." Booklist
Includes bibliographical references

Busch, Robert
The grizzly almanac; [by] Robert H. Busch. Lyons Press 2000 229p il maps hardcover o.p. pa $19.95
Grades: 11 12 Adult   **599.78**
1. Grizzly bear
ISBN 1-58574-143-4; 1-59228-320-9 (pa)
LC 00-58587

Busch, Robert—*Continued*

The author "traces the evolution of the 'big bear' from its earliest days, describes its habitat and behavior, and recounts grizzly folklore and tales of grizzly attacks. Maintaining that the grizzly's reputation as a vicious killer is undeserved, he makes recommendations for a more peaceful coexistence with humans." Libr J

Includes bibliographical references

Croke, Vicki

The lady and the panda; the true adventures of the first American explorer to bring back China's most exotic animal; [by] Vicki Constantine Croke. Random House 2005 372p il $25.95; pa $14.95

Grades: 11 12 Adult   **599.78**
1. Harkness, Ruth 2. Giant panda
ISBN 0-375-50783-3; 0-375-75970-0 (pa)
                                                          LC 2004-51356

The author tells the "story of Ruth Harkness, the Manhattan bohemian socialite who, against all but impossible odds, trekked to Tibet in 1936 to capture the most mysterious animal of the day: a bear that had for countless centuries lived in secret in the labyrinth of lonely cold mountains." Publisher's note

"This well-written, exhaustively researched and documented book should be on every library's shelves." Libr J

Includes bibliographical references

Ellis, Richard, 1938-

On thin ice; the changing world of the polar bear. Alfred A. Knopf 2009 400p il $28.95

Grades: 11 12 Adult   **599.78**
1. Polar bear 2. Greenhouse effect
ISBN 978-0-307-27059-7; 0-307-27059-9
                                                          LC 2009-20017

This profile of the habitat and life cycle of the polar bear covers the species' venerated position in Inuit culture, its reproductive habits, and the environmental factors that are compromising its ability to survive.

"The real strength of the book is its focus on the polar bear as the poster child of global warming, of how tied the bears are to the arctic ice and what will happen if the ice melts, and of the national and international wrangling over the politics of climate change and the listing of the bear as an endangered species. The polar bear could not ask for a better champion than Ellis in this highly recommended work." Booklist

Includes bibliographical references

Rosing, Norbert

The world of the polar bear. Firefly Books 2006 203p il $45

Grades: 11 12 Adult   **599.78**
1. Polar bear
ISBN 978-1-55407-155-5; 1-55407-155-0

This book contains "a season-by-season account of the life of the polar bear, including feeding, mating, rearing of cubs and journeying from the ice; an intimate look at the animals that share the polar bear's environment, including seals, arctic foxes, walruses and muskoxen; a section on such northern sky phenomena as sun dogs and

the northern lights; [and] many anecdotes and insights about the polar bear." Publisher's note

Includes bibliographical references

Turbak, Gary

Grizzly bears. Voyageur Press 1997 71p il maps (World life library) pa $14.95

Grades: 9 10 11 12   **599.78**
1. Grizzly bear
ISBN 0-89658-334-1   LC 96-42373

This describes grizzly bear habits and habitats, hibernation, and what threatens the bear's existence

Includes bibliographical references

599.79   Pinnipedia (Marine carnivores)

Miller, David, 1959-

Seals & sea lions. Voyageur Press 1998 72p il (World life library) pa $16.95

Grades: 9 10 11 12   **599.79**
1. Seals (Animals)
ISBN 0-89658-371-6   LC 97-44771

This describes the habits and habitats of seals and sea lions and threats to their existence

Includes bibliographical references

599.8   Primates

Goodall, Jane, 1934-

In the shadow of man; photographs by Hugo van Lawick; [with a new preface; foreword by Richard Wrangham] Mariner Books 2009 xxx, 302p il map pa $15.95 *

Grades: 11 12 Adult   **599.8**
1. Chimpanzees
ISBN 978-0-547-33416-5   LC 2009044848
First published 1971
"New ed." Preface

The author describes the chimpanzee group she studied during ten years of field observation in the Gombe Stream Chimpanzee Reserve in Tanzania.

Includes bibliographical references

Through a window; my thirty years with the chimpanzees of Gombe; [with a new preface and a new afterword] Houghton Mifflin Harcourt 2010 xx, 337p il map pa $15.95 *

Grades: 11 12 Adult   **599.8**
1. Chimpanzees
ISBN 978-0-547-33695-4; 0-547-33695-0
                                                      LC 2009045230

First published 1990

This continuation of In the shadow of man "tells two stories: first of how the chimps of Gombe in Tanzania have grown, changed and died, and second, how Goodall and her dedicated group of Tanzanian observers have survived the rigours of the past thirty years. It is beautifully written, and evokes both sympathy and understanding of these animals." Times Lit Suppl

Includes bibliographical references

Morris, Desmond

Planet ape; [by] Desmond Morris with Steve Parker. Firefly Books 2009 288p il $49.95

Grades: 9 10 11 12 Adult **599.8**

1. Apes

ISBN 978-1-55407-566-9

Detail of the great apes, including: where they live, how they live and the challenges they face. Illustrations compare apes with human beings, including their anatomy, social life, physical and mental development, diet and communication.

"Published in a large format (approximately 10 by 11 inches) with hundreds of full-color glossy photographs and illustrations, this beautiful volume is a cross between a coffee-table book and a thorough compendium of ape behavior, anatomy, taxonomy, and lore. . . . The book reads well, is packed full of exciting information, and is just plain fun to browse for hours." Sci Books Films

Preston-Mafham, Rod

Primates of the world; [by] Rod and Ken Preston-Mafham. Facts On File 2002 191p il $35

Grades: 9 10 11 12 **599.8**

1. Primates

ISBN 0-8160-5211-5 LC 2002-34733

First published 1992

"The authors discuss the various species of lemurs, monkeys, and apes; their habitats, social systems, breeding habits and rearing of youth, methods of communication, and feeding preferences; and their ambivalent relationship with the human race." Publisher's note

Redmond, Ian

The primate family tree; the amazing diversity of our closest relatives; foreword by Jane Goodall. Firefly Books 2008 176p il map $35

Grades: 11 12 Adult **599.8**

1. Primates

ISBN 978-1-55407-378-8; 1-55407-378-2

"The book is structured according to the four main branches of the primate family tree and contains . . . information on the natural history, characteristics and behavior of . . . [some] 250 species, along with maps showing the ranges of the species." Publisher's note

The Primate Family Tree "is beautifully designed, and the contents are well organized and will be interesting to all. . . . This is a very attractive, interesting, and informative publication." Sci Books Films

Includes bibliographical references

Russon, Anne E.

Orangutans: wizards of the rainforest. rev ed. Firefly Books 2004 240p il map pa $24.95

Grades: 8 9 10 11 12 **599.8**

1. Orangutan

ISBN 1-55297-998-9 LC 2005-357221

First published 1999 in the United Kingdom

A firsthand account of the lives of orangutans including a scientific history of orangutans, a description of orangutans and their natural habitat, their behavior patterns, rehabilitation operations, the politics of orangutan rescue work, and a look at orangutans released back into the forest.

Includes bibliographical references

Swindler, Daris Ray

Introduction to the primates; [by] Daris R. Swindler; illustrated by Linda E. Curtis. University of Wash. Press 1998 284p il pa $22

Grades: 9 10 11 12 **599.8**

1. Primates

ISBN 0-295-97704-3 LC 97-47149

"Swindler begins with a history of primate research and then covers systematics and an overview of the living primates. He covers such systems as genetics, skull, teeth (with diet and guts), brain, skeleton and locomotion, growth and development (one of his specialities), and social behavior. The fossil history of primates is briefly reviewed, and the book closes with prospects for conservation." Choice

Includes bibliographical references

World atlas of great apes and their conservation; edited by Julian Caldecott and Lera Miles; foreword by Kofi A. Annan. University of California Press, in association with UNEP-WCMC 2005 456p il map $45 *

Grades: 11 12 Adult **599.8**

1. Apes 2. Biogeography 3. Atlases 4. Wildlife conservation 5. Reference books

ISBN 0-520-24633-0; 978-0-520-24633-1

LC 2006-272653

Images, maps and 130-page bibliography available electronically via the World Wide Web

"Each great ape specie is given a separate chapter that contains information on behavior and ecology, communication and tool use, threats and conservation, and exceptionally detailed distribution maps. What sets this book apart is the section that details each country in which apes are found and exactly what conservation efforts are underway." Univ Press Books for Public and Second Sch Libr, 2006

Includes bibliographical references

599.93 Genetics, sex and age characteristics, evolution

Ackerman, Jennifer

Chance in the house of fate; a natural history of heredity. Houghton Mifflin 2001 252p hardcover o.p. pa $14

Grades: 11 12 Adult **599.93**

1. Heredity 2. Genetics

ISBN 0-618-08287-5; 0-618-21909-9 (pa)

LC 00-54122

"Ackerman's subject [is] the genetic links between humans and the rest of the natural world. . . . Along with stories about generational change, Ackerman examines the scientific history of heredity, including the work of scientists like Darwin and Anton van Leeuwenhoek." N Y Times Book Rev

"Ackerman proves to be an exciting and eloquent tour guide through the complex realm of heredity. . . . Adept at selecting vivid analogies sure to please nonscientific readers." Booklist

Includes bibliographical references

Encyclopedia of human evolution and prehistory; editors, Eric Delson [et al.] 2nd ed. Garland 2000 xlv, 753p il (Garland reference library of the humanities) lib bdg $175 *

Grades: 9 10 11 12   **599.93**

1. Human origins—Encyclopedias 2. Reference books

ISBN 0-815-31696-8

First published 1988 under the editorships of Ian Tattersall, Eric Delson, and John Van Couvering

This reference "contains nearly 800 articles written by 54 international, but largely U.S., contributors. The articles are divided between shorter specific articles and longer integrative articles, including articles on concepts and methods, localities and sites, fossils, primate taxa, tool types, archaeological industries, and eminent deceased and living anthropologists. There are also long, integrative articles on major regions such as Western Asia." Am Ref Books Annu, 2001

"This is a very readable, thorough reference source covering every aspect of human evolution and prehistory. The scientific facts, theories, and philosophies pertaining to evolution are presented skillfully and understandably." Booklist

Gibbons, Ann

The first human; the race to discover our earliest ancestors. Doubleday 2006 306p il map hardcover o.p. pa $14.95 *

Grades: 11 12 Adult   **599.93**

1. Fossil hominids 2. Evolution

ISBN   0-385-51226-0;   978-0-385-51226-8; 978-1-4000-7696-3 (pa); 1-4000-7696-X (pa)

LC 2005-53780

The author "explains what paleoanthropologists have been doing over the past 15 years: competing, feuding, and making dramatic discoveries. Anchoring her narrative to the anatomy that is the foundation of physical anthropology, Gibbons intentionally emphasizes the personalities involved." Booklist

This "is a near insider's account that still has the critical distance a nonpartisan can offer." Libr J

Includes bibliographical references

Hodge, Russ

Human genetics; race, population, and disease; foreword by Nadia Rosenthal. Facts on File 2010 228p il (Genetics & evolution) $39.50

Grades: 9 10 11 12   **599.93**

1. Genetics

ISBN 978-0-8160-6682-7; 0-8160-6682-5

LC 2009-10706

This book explores the "topic through a variety of perspectives. . . . Coverage also includes studies of human molecules that have been applied in some fascinating ways, for example to solve historical mysteries, and how modern doctors try to identify the factors that make the body healthy or sick. Finally, this . . . resource explores the rich variety of the human species—differences between individuals and groups, including questions like the genetic meaning of human races and how genes influence behavior and society." Publisher's note

Includes glossary and bibliographical references

Holmes, Thom

Early humans; the Pleistocene & Holocene epochs. Chelsea House 2009 151p il map (The prehistoric Earth) lib bdg $35

Grades: 7 8 9 10   **599.93**

1. Fossil hominids 2. Human origins 3. Evolution

ISBN 978-0-8160-5966-9; 0-8160-5966-7

LC 2008-38936

"The book consists of two sections. The first section describes the early hominins in Chapter 1 and the archaic species of Homo in Chapter 2. The second section reviews the origins and evolution of more modern Homo species in Chapters 3 and 4. The concluding chapter briefly discusses some contemporary topics, including the meaning of human races, the evolution of skin color, the human role in the evolution and extinction of other species, and the impact of the evolution of diseases. . . . [This] is an outstanding contribution to teaching junior high and high school students about evolution in general and human evolution in particular." Sci Books Films

Includes glossary and bibliographical references

Johanson, Donald C.

From Lucy to language; [by] Donald Johanson & Blake Edgar; principal photography, David L. Brill. Rev., updated, and expanded. Simon and Schuster 2006 288p il map $65

Grades: 11 12 Adult   **599.93**

1. Human origins 2. Fossil hominids

ISBN 0-7432-8064-4; 978-0-7432-8064-8

LC 2007-270098

"A Peter N. Nèvraumont book"

First published 1996

This is a "photographic showcase of the essential physical evidence of human origins. . . . Permitting a face-to-face encounter with human ancestors, this work furnishes essential information, [and] an incomparable visual experience." Booklist

Includes bibliographical references

Lucy: the beginnings of humankind; [by] Donald C. Johanson and Maitland A. Edey. Simon & Schuster 1981 409p il pa $16 hardcover o.p.

Grades: 11 12 Adult   **599.93**

1. Human origins 2. Fossil mammals

ISBN 0-671-72499-1 (pa)   LC 80-21759

In November 1974 at a place called Hadar in Ethiopia Donald Johanson "discovered the partial skeleton of an extremely primitive female, erect-walking primate or hominid. . . . The skeleton received the name 'Lucy.' Much later, Lucy received the scientific name, Australopithecus afarensis, and it was determined she was some 3.5 million years old. . . . This book is Johanson's own story of the events leading up to and subsequent to Lucy's discovery." Best Sellers

Includes bibliographical references

Jolly, Alison

Lucy's legacy; sex and intelligence in human evolution. Harvard Univ. Press 1999 518p il hardcover o.p. pa $18.95

Grades: 11 12 Adult   **599.93**

1. Evolution 2. Intellect

ISBN 0-674-00069-2; 0-674-00540-6 (pa)

LC 99-32252

Jolly, Alison—*Continued*

"Lucy is the name given to the fossil skeleton of an Australopithecine, a human ancestor, discovered in Ethiopia. The name may be a misnomer, since there's no way yet of telling whether Lucy was female. No matter. Primatologist Jolly's interest is not so much in Lucy as in the crucial role that females in general have played in human evolution. . . . In clear and clever prose, Jolly shows us how we got so smart, what sex had to do with it, and how our brains have become the central force in evolution." Booklist

Includes bibliographical references

Leakey, Richard E., 1944-

The origin of humankind; [by] Richard Leakey. Basic Bks. 1994 171p il maps (Science masters series) pa $14.95 hardcover o.p.

Grades: 11 12 Adult   **599.93**

1. Human origins

ISBN 0-465-05313-0 (pa)   LC 94-3617

"Leakey summarizes the evolution of theories, from Darwin's to his own, in the process demonstrating the scientific method in action. . . . Covering the taxonomy of skeletons and craniums, shapes of tools, and the first sprouts of art and culture, Leakey knowledgeably points the enthralled neophyte to the wide avenues of future discoveries." Booklist

This "is a worthwhile addition to many kinds of libraries—public, general, science, biological, and psychological." Sci Books Films

Includes bibliographical references

Origins reconsidered; in search of what makes us human; [by] Richard Leakey and Roger Lewin. Doubleday 1992 375p il pa $16.95 hardcover o.p.

Grades: 11 12 Adult   **599.93**

1. Human origins

ISBN 0-385-46792-3 (pa)   LC 92-6661

"Leakey and Lewin discuss how conceptions of human anatomical and behavioral development have been radically altered within the last 12 years by new discoveries and research in other fields. They review the developments and assert Leakey's own hypotheses based on these discoveries. . . . This is an engrossing book written for the layperson, fully explaining anthropological terms and theories when necessary. It's a solid introduction to current theory concerning human development." SLJ

Reilly, Philip, 1947-

Is it in your genes? the influence of genes on common disorders and diseases that affect you and your family; [by] Philip R. Reilly. Cold Spring Harbor Laboratory Press 2004 288p hardcover o.p. pa $19.95 *

Grades: 9 10 11 12   **599.93**

1. Medical genetics

ISBN 0-87969-719-9; 0-87969-721-0 (pa)

     LC 2004-2458

"Drawing on the many questions he has been asked (for example, 'My sister has multiple sclerosis. Am I at an increased risk?'), Reilly discusses over 90 common conditions, diseases, and disorders, arranged from conception to old age." Publisher's note

Includes bibliographical references

Stefoff, Rebecca, 1951-

First humans. Marshall Cavendish Benchmark 2009 c2010 112p il map (Humans: an evolutionary history) lib bdg $37.07

Grades: 7 8 9 10   **599.93**

1. Human origins 2. Fossil hominids

ISBN 978-0-7614-4184-7; 0-7614-4184-0

     LC 2008-34330

"Describes the search for early branches of the human family tree, including the first true humans, members of the genus Homo." Publisher's note

"Stefoff provides an enlightening and entertaining history of the evolution of Homo sapiens, their ancestors, and cousins, from primitive origins to today. The clear, insightful [text is] accented by intriguing sidebars and colorful photos, maps, and graphs." SLJ

Includes glossary and bibliographical references

Ice age Neanderthals. Marshall Cavendish Benchmark 2009 c2010 112p il map (Humans: an evolutionary history) lib bdg $37.07

Grades: 7 8 9 10   **599.93**

1. Neanderthals 2. Fossil hominids 3. Human origins

ISBN 978-0-7614-4186-1; 0-7614-4186-7

     LC 2008-54830

"A history of the Neanderthals, a species of human beings who lived in Eurasia for hundreds of thousands of years and who became extinct when our species, Homo Sapiens, came into being." Publisher's note

"Stefoff provides an enlightening and entertaining history of the evolution of Homo sapiens, their ancestors, and cousins, from primitive origins to today. The clear, insightful [text is] accented by intriguing sidebars and colorful photos, maps, and graphs." SLJ

Includes glossary and bibliographical references

Modern humans. Marshall Cavendish Benchmark 2009 c2010 112p il map (Humans: an evolutionary history) lib bdg $37.07

Grades: 7 8 9 10   **599.93**

1. Human origins 2. Evolution 3. Genetics 4. Fossil hominids

ISBN 978-0-7614-4187-8; 0-7614-4187-5

     LC 2009-12364

"Describes the rise of modern humans, Homo sapiens, including the theories about our origins and how we spread throughout the world, with information based on the latest fossil and DNA studies." Publisher's note

"Stefoff provides an enlightening and entertaining history of the evolution of Homo sapiens, their ancestors, and cousins, from primitive origins to today. The clear, insightful [text is] accented by intriguing sidebars and colorful photos, maps, and graphs." SLJ

Includes glossary and bibliographical references

Origins. Marshall Cavendish Benchmark 2009 c2010 112p il map (Humans: an evolutionary history) lib bdg $37.07

Grades: 7 8 9 10   **599.93**

1. Fossil hominids 2. Human origins

ISBN 978-0-7614-4183-0; 0-7614-4183-2

     LC 2008-34335

"Describes the search for the earliest human ancestors, from ancient apes to the australopiths." Publisher's note

"Stefoff enlivens the text with subjects like the giant

Stefoff, Rebecca, 1951-—Continued

ape, who may have been the kernel of Bigfoot tales. With many color photos, the attractive format goes a long way toward easing the reader into the topic." Booklist

Includes glossary and bibliographical references

Tattersall, Ian

Extinct humans; by Ian Tattersall and Jeffrey H. Schwartz. Westview Press 2000 256p il pa $35 hardcover o.p.

Grades: 11 12 Adult   **599.93**

1. Human origins 2. Fossil hominids 3. Evolution

ISBN 0-8133-3918-9 (pa)   LC 00-22088

The authors explain "why the idea of the one-track, lineal descent of human beings is obsolete and the notion of a 'bushy' evolutionary history, like that of other genera, fits the fossil evidence better." Booklist

Includes bibliographical references

Tudge, Colin

The time before history; 5 million years of human impact. Scribner 1996 366p il maps pa $17.95 hardcover o.p.

Grades: 11 12 Adult   **599.93**

1. Human origins 2. Evolution 3. Mammals

ISBN 0-684-83052-3 (pa)   LC 95-42026

Tudge "begins by putting time into perspective so that we can understand how vast is our past; he helps us see that all evolution is part of a bigger whole—an unfolding process affected by shifting continents, climactic changes, and our own impact on the planet and its ecosystems. . . . He defines our origins in a biological, as well as historical context and applies the lessons that we should learn from our mistakes as well as our achievements to provide a blueprint for the future." Libr J

"With majestic sweep and subtle wit, . . . Tudge brings an astonishing perspective to the story of humanity." Publ Wkly

Includes bibliographical references

Wade, Nicholas

Before the dawn; recovering the lost history of our ancestors. Penguin Press 2006 312p il map $24.95

Grades: 11 12 Adult   **599.93**

1. Evolution 2. Social change

ISBN 1-59420-079-3; 978-1-59420-079-3

            LC 2005-55293

This is a "survey of human evolution for lay readers which considers the emergence of man in his entirety: physical, psychological, and social. . . . Wade's book concentrates on the recent evolutionary past: our last 50,000 years. . . . [It] emphasizes genetic over paleontological evidence." N Y Rev Books

"This is highly recommended for readers interested in how DNA analysis is rewriting the history of mankind." Publ Wkly

Includes bibliographical references

Wells, Spencer, 1969-

The journey of man; a genetic odyssey; photographs by Mark Read. Princeton University Press 2003 224p il map $29.95

Grades: 11 12 Adult   **599.93**

1. Evolution 2. Genetics 3. Human origins

ISBN 0-691-11532-X

Also available in paperback from Random House

The author "chronicles the history of genetic population studies, starting with Darwin's puzzlement over the diversity of humanity he saw first-hand from the deck of the Beagle, and ending with the various attempts to classify human variation on the basis of different political and social agendas." Nature

"Fortunately for the lay reader, Wells has a knack for clear descriptions and clever analogies to help explain the intricacies of the science involved." Libr J

Includes bibliographical references

600   TECHNOLOGY

Cool stuff and how it works; written by Chris Woodford [et al.] Dorling Kindersley Pub. 2005 256p il hardcover o.p. pa $19.99 *

Grades: 9 10 11 12 Adult   **600**

1. Inventions

ISBN 0-7566-1465-1; 0-7566-5834-9 (pa)

            LC 2005-13587

This book "uses advanced imaging technology such as X rays, scanning electron micrographs, and infrared thermograms, along with traditional graphics, to reveal the workings of . . . [high-tech gadgets and appliances] from the Internet and computers to advanced textiles, space-age materials, and medical marvels. . . . This will rate high on the 'cool' factor, whether at home, school, or library." Booklist

Forbes, Peter, 1947-

The gecko's foot; bio-inspiration: engineering new materials from nature. Norton 2006 272p il hardcover o.p. pa $21.95

Grades: 11 12 Adult   **600**

1. Technological innovations 2. Nature

ISBN   0-393-06223-6;   978-0-393-06223-6; 0-393-33797-9 (pa); 978-0-393-33797-6 (pa)

            LC 2006-06731

First published 2005 in the United Kingdom

This is an introduction to the "field of bio-inspiration and its use of life's microscopic features to engineer novel technologies. The volume overviews the history and current status of this field's major research areas and includes material on new adhesives based on the little lizard of the title, on self-cleaning paints modeled on the lotus leaf, and on photonic cells fashioned after butterfly wings." Sci Books Films

"Readers interested in how invention imitates nature, and vice versa, will find much to savor." Publ Wkly

Includes bibliographical references

Langone, John, 1929-
The new how things work; everyday technology explained; art by Pete Samek, Andy Christie, and Bryan Christie. National Geographic Society 2004 272p il $35 *
Grades: 9 10 11 12 Adult   **600**
1. Technology 2. Inventions
ISBN 0-7922-6956-X   LC 2004-50438
First published 1999 with title: National Geographic's how things work
"With eleven chapters, including 'At Home,' 'Building and Buildings,' 'Transportation,' 'At Play,' and 'Tools of Medicine,' the book covers . . . familiar items such as refrigerators and washing machines, planes and trains, elevators and escalators, as well as the not-so-familiar, such as laser surgery and DNA manipulation. . . . {Coverage of recent innovations range} from DVDs and MP3s to plasma screen TVs and wireless Internet technology." Publisher's note

Macaulay, David, 1946-
The new way things work; [by] David Macaulay with Neil Ardley. Houghton Mifflin 1998 400p il $35
Grades: 4 5 6 7 8 9 10 11 12 Adult   **600**
1. Technology 2. Machinery 3. Inventions
ISBN 0-395-93847-3   LC 98-14224
First published 1988 with title: The way things work
Arranged in five sections this volume provides information on "the workings of hundreds of machines and devices—holograms, helicopters, airplanes, mobile phones, compact disks, hard disks, bits and bytes, cash machines. . . . Explanations [are also given] of the scientific principles behind each machine—how gears make work easier, why jumbo jets are able to fly, how computers actually compute." Publisher's note

Parker, Barry R.
Death rays, jet packs, stunts, & supercars; the fantastic physics of film's most celebrated secret agent; [by] Barry Parker. Johns Hopkins University Press 2005 231p il $25
Grades: 11 12 Adult   **600**
1. Physics
ISBN 0-8018-8248-6   LC 2005-7782
"A longtime James Bond fan, Parker takes a look at the science behind the movies and explains what works and what doesn't, and the basic physics involved. . . . A book that's sure to appeal to teens with an interest in gadgets, cars, stunts, trick cinematography, and sports (skiing, bungee jumping)." SLJ
Includes bibliographical references

Woodford, Chris, 1943-
Cool Stuff 2.0 and how it works; written by Chris Woodford and Jon Woodcock. DK Pub. 2007 256p il $24.99 *
Grades: 5 6 7 8 9 10   **600**
1. Inventions 2. Technology
ISBN 978-0-7566-3207-6; 0-7566-3207-2
                                LC 2007-299442

"More than 100 entries present a wide variety of topics with high child appeal, from robot cars to high-tech toilets. . . . Full but uncluttered layouts mix photos, text boxes, diagrams, and captions to highlight key elements. . . . Readers should have an easy time understanding the basics of what each item does, how it is used, and how it works. Along with up-to-date scientific information on high-interest topics, this title has very strong browsing appeal and great booktalk potential." SLJ

Cool stuff exploded. Dorling Kindersley 2008 256p il $24.99
Grades: 7 8 9 10   **600**
1. Inventions
ISBN 978-0-7566-4028-6; 0-7566-4028-8
Includes CD-ROM
"Photographs and computer-generated images provide an inside look at the mechanisms that make many transportation vehicles, home appliances, entertainment systems, and personal electronics function. Futuristic applications and environmental impacts of technology are also included." National Science Teachers Association
Includes glossary

609 Historical, geographic, persons treatment

The **Britannica** guide to inventions that changed the modern world; edited by Robert Curley. Britannica Educational Pub. in association with Rosen Educational Services 2010 386p il (Turning points in history) lib bdg $45
Grades: 9 10 11 12   **609**
1. Inventions—History 2. Technology—History
ISBN 978-1-61530-020-4; 1-61530-020-1
                                LC 2009-37539
Each chapter highlights an invention that was influential enough to alter the modern world.
Includes glossary and bibliographical references

Carlisle, Rodney P.
Scientific American inventions and discoveries; all the milestones in ingenuity—from the discovery of fire to the invention of the microwave oven. Wiley 2004 502p il $40 *
Grades: 9 10 11 12   **609**
1. Inventions—History 2. Technology—History 3. Technological innovations
ISBN 0-471-24410-4   LC 2003-23258
The author presents a "guide to some 418 inventions and discoveries. He organizes his presentation in a chronological manner, using six major periods from ancient times to the present." Sci Books Films
"This fact-filled compendium will delight students with a passion for science and technology, no matter what their age." Publ Wkly

Denny, Mark, 1953-
Ingenium; five machines that changed the world.
Johns Hopkins University Press 2007 176p il $27
Grades: 11 12 Adult   **609**
1. Inventions—History 2. Machinery
ISBN 978-0-8018-8586-0; 0-8018-8586-8
                 LC 2006-26085
Denny analyzes "the bow and arrow, waterwheels and
windmills, counterpoise siege engines, the pendulum
clock anchor escapement mechanism, and the centrifugal
governor." Sci Books Films
The author "has authored a well-written, illustrated,
and informative book that is readable to all but the mentally lazy." Choice
Includes bibliographical references

Ferris, Julie, 1973-
Ideas that changed the world; authors, Julie
Ferris [et al.] DK Pub. 2010 256p il map $24.99
Grades: 6 7 8 9 10   **609**
1. Inventions—History 2. Technology—History
ISBN 978-0-7566-6531-9; 0-7566-6531-0
                LC 2010282281
A guide to technological developments that changed
the world describes each invention and explores its place
in history and how it influenced civilization, discussing
inventions from the wheel to computers.
"Brightly colored and packed with information, this
reference volume delivers. . . . This book could be used
in multiple subject areas. English classes might use it for
general research or units on the decades, social studies
for the major changes over time, and science due to the
technological advancements." Libr Media Connect

Harrison, Ian, 1965-
The book of inventions; how'd they come up
with that. National Geographic Society 2004 288p
il $30 *
Grades: 9 10 11 12 Adult   **609**
1. Inventions—History
ISBN 0-7922-8296-5   LC 2004-49922
"This volume provides the dates, details, and . . . stories of how some of our most interesting and useful objects have been invented. . . . Entries include objects
. . . [such] as the disposable diaper, the zipper, the hair
dryer, the photocopier, the artificial heart, and the traffic
light." Publisher's note
"With sliced bread and the lava lamp among his selected inventions, Harrison aims to please more than
teach. . . . Fun and colorful, Harrison's volume will attract would-be Edisons." Booklist
Includes bibliographical references

Inventors and inventions. Marshall Cavendish
2008 5v il set $399.95
Grades: 6 7 8 9 10   **609**
1. Inventions—History 2. Technology—History
3. Inventors 4. Reference books
ISBN 978-0-7614-7761-7   LC 2007-60868
"*Inventions and Inventors* is designed to introduce students to an array of inventors from the past and present
while encouraging 'interest in and knowledge of science'
by exploring the history, development, and utility of a
wide variety of inventions. This set contains 172 alphabetically arranged articles on a range of inventors as well
as 21 overview articles. . . . The choice of inventors, the
inclusion of more than 1,000 full-color illustrations, and
the highly readable and engaging text all create a valuable reference for students and browsers alike." Booklist
Includes bibliographical references

Macdonald, Anne L., 1920-
Feminine ingenuity; women and invention in
America; {by} Anne Macdonald. Ballantine Bks.
1992 xxiv, 514p il pa $25 hardcover o.p. *
Grades: 9 10 11 12 Adult   **609**
1. Women inventors 2. Inventions
ISBN 0-345-38314-1 (pa)   LC 91-55502
This is a "study of American women's contribution to
science, engineering, and technology as represented in
the issuance of U.S. patents. From the first patent issued
to a woman in 1809, Macdonald traces the uphill struggle women have faced in their efforts to obtain equal
rights—in the area of patent awards as well as in the
broader educational, economic, and social arenas." Libr
J
Includes bibliographical references

The **Seventy** great inventions of the ancient world;
edited by Brian M. Fagan. Thames & Hudson
2004 304p il $40 *
Grades: 9 10 11 12 Adult   **609**
1. Inventions—History 2. Technology—History
ISBN 0-500-05130-5   LC 2004-100250
"Fagan organizes into six categories the 70 things his
three dozen scholarly contributors present. The first category describes the basic natural materials—stone, clay,
and wood—with which humanity began to alter the environment. Ensuing categories catalog their uses, such as in
hunting, farming, or artwork. . . . Stuffed with hundreds
of color photographs, Fagan's work is an estimable
spruce-up option for any library." Booklist
Includes bibliographical references

Sluby, Patricia Carter
The inventive spirit of African Americans;
patented ingenuity. Praeger 2004 xxxviii, 313p il
$39.95 *
Grades: 9 10 11 12   **609**
1. African American inventors
ISBN 0-275-96674-7   LC 2003-64767
This "portrait of many black inventors and scientists
is derived from a comprehensive review of all the patents
that have been issued to African Americans from the
days of slavery to the present high-tech era. Sluby also
includes a brief biography of many little-known male and
female African Americans whose ingenuity contributed to
American industry. . . . An important addition to the literature on contributions of African Americans to US history." Choice
Includes bibliographical references

Strapp, James

Science and technology. Sharpe Focus 2009 80p il (Inside ancient China) $31.45

Grades: 7 8 9 10 **609**

1. Science—China 2. Technology—History 3. Science and civilization

ISBN 978-0-7656-8169-0; 0-7656-8169-2

LC 2008-31168

"This colorful book surveys science and technology developed by the ancient Chinese. Strapp discusses early compasses and mapmaking, the building of canals, and the invention of . . . the wheelbarrow, water clocks, gunpowder, and the harness. The last chapter looks at Chinese medicine and feng shui. . . . The writing is clear and the format is inviting, with many sidebars and pictures. Illustrations include photos of artifacts and maps as well as period artwork and line-and-wash pictures." Booklist

Includes bibliographical references

Van Dulken, Stephen, 1952-

Inventing the 20th century; 100 inventions that shaped the world: from the airplane to the zipper; {by} Stephen Van Dulken; with an introduction by Andrew Phillips. New York Univ. Press 2000 246p il hardcover o.p. pa $17.95

Grades: 11 12 Adult **609**

1. Inventions

ISBN 0-8147-8808-4; 0-8147-8812-2 (pa)

LC 00-41141

This briefly describes inventions of the 20th century, arranged by decade, with text and diagrams from the patent applications

"A fascinating compendium for trivia seekers." Publ Wkly

Includes bibliographical references

Wearing, Judy

Edison's concrete piano; flying tanks, six-nippled sheep, walk-on-water shoes, and 12 other flops from great inventors. ECW Press 2009 270p il pa $14.95

Grades: 11 12 Adult **609**

1. Inventors 2. Inventions

ISBN 978-1-55022-863-2   LC 2009-675182

The author "details 16 inventions that never took off and lists the personality traits that typify the inventive mind. They include determination, rebelliousness, financial unrealism, and thinking in redemptive terms, such as the salvation of humanity. . . . She portrays lively personalities and eccentric projects in concrete prose." Booklist

Includes bibliographical references

610   Medicine & health

Bortolotti, Dan

Hope in hell; inside the world of Doctors Without Borders. Firefly Bks. 2004 303p il $29.95; pa $19.95

Grades: 11 12 Adult **610**

1. Médecins Sans Frontières (Organization)

ISBN 1-55297-865-6; 1-55407-142-9 (pa)

LC 2005-357206

This "portrait of Doctors Without Borders/*Médecins Sans Frontières* (aka MSF), the nonprofit that won the Nobel Peace Prize in 1999, emphasizes the inner workings of the organization and is animated by interviews with mid-level staffers and by site visits to MSF projects in Angola, Afghanistan and Pakistan. In between, . . . Bortolotti traces the history of the world's largest independent medical humanitarian organization, whose genesis was the Biafran horrors of the late '60s." Publ Wkly

"Much of what Bortolotti reports is noticeably absent from the daily headlines, so this eye-opening account is all the more chilling, and MSF's efforts achingly more compelling." Booklist

Includes bibliographical references

Kelly, Kate, 1950-

Old world and new; early medical care, 1700-1840. Facts On File 2010 150p il map (The history of medicine) $40

Grades: 9 10 11 12 **610**

1. Medicine—History

ISBN 978-0-8160-7208-8; 0-8160-7208-6

LC 2009-5163

Discusses the concerns and advances in medicine that occurred during the Enlightenment, a time of significant progress in specific scientific fields.

Includes glosary and bibliographical references

610.3   Medical sciences—
Encyclopedias and dictionaries

Black's medical dictionary. 42nd ed., edited by Harvey Marcovitch. A. & C. Black 2010 764p il $55

Grades: 9 10 11 12 **610.3**

1. Medicine—Dictionaries 2. Reference books

ISBN 978-0-7136-8902-0

First published 1906. Frequently revised

"This dictionary, illustrated with line drawings and graphs, has longer entries than most. Many are several paragraphs long, with extensive information on diseases and parts of the body. The language is accessible to educated lay readers." Ref Sources for Small & Medium-sized Libr. 6th edition

Dorland's illustrated medical dictionary. 32nd ed. Elsevier/Saunders 2011 c2012 xxvii, 2147p il $51.95

Grades: 11 12 Adult **610.3**

1. Medicine—Dictionaries 2. Reference books

ISBN 978-1-4160-6257-8   LC 2011-9789

Also available deluxe edition with CD-ROM $99.95 and online

Dorland's illustrated medical dictionary—*Continued*

First published 1900. Periodically revised

This standard reference includes terms used in medicine, surgery, dentistry, pharmacy, chemistry, nursing, veterinary science, biology, and medical biology. Pronunciation, derivation, and definitions are given.

"This is considered one of the most comprehensive medical dictionaries in print." N Y Public Libr Book of How & Where to Look It Up

Includes bibliographical references

Magill's medical guide; medical editors, Brandon P. Brown ... [et al.] 6th ed. Salem Press 2011 6v il set $495 *

Grades: 9 10 11 12 Adult   **610.3**
1. Medicine—Encyclopedias 2. Reference books
ISBN 978-1-58765-677-4   LC 2010-31862
First published 1995

Includes free access to online companion database Salem Health

Covers diseases, disorders, treatments, procedures, specialties, anatomy, biology, and issues in an A-Z format, with sidebars addressing recent developments in medicine and concise information boxes for all diseases and disorders.

Includes bibliographical references

The **Merck** manual of diagnosis and therapy; Robert S. Porter, editor-in-chief; Justin L. Kaplan, senior assistant editor. 19th ed. Merck Sharp & Dohme Corp. 2011 xxxii, 3754p il $79.95 *

Grades: 11 12 Adult   **610.3**
1. Medicine—Handbooks, manuals, etc. 2. Reference books
ISSN 0076-6526
ISBN 978-0-911910-19-3
Also available online
First published 1899

"A one-volume reference that attempts to cover all but the most obscure diseases. Sections are organized by type of disease or medical specialty." N Y Public Libr Book of How & Where to Look It Up

610.7 Education, research, nursing, related topics

Kirkland, Kyle

Biological sciences; notable research and discoveries. Facts on File 2010 224p il (Frontiers of science) $39.50

Grades: 9 10 11 12   **610.7**
1. Biology 2. Medicine—Research
ISBN 978-0-8160-7439-6; 0-8160-7439-9
                              LC 2009-15651

"This book covers diverse topics such as brain imaging, the human genome, proteins, biodiversity, viruses, and regeneration. Each section traces the history of developments in the field, current research and technology, and where such research is concentrated, and concludes with a recap that often includes new information." Libr

Media Connect
Includes bibliographical references

610.9 Medical sciences—Historical and geographic treatment

Adler, Robert E., 1946-

Medical firsts; from Hippocrates to the human genome. Wiley 2004 232p il $24.95

Grades: 11 12 Adult   **610.9**
1. Medicine—History
ISBN 0-471-40175-7   LC 2003-14212

"The contributors to the annals of medical knowledge [the author] cites include the most famous names—Hippocrates, Pasteur, Freud, Alexander Fleming—and some not so commonly known, such as pioneering gynecologist Soranus (first century C.E.); Ibn al-Nafis (ca. 1210-88), credited as the first to understand and describe pulmonary circulation; and John Snow, an important figure in the war on cholera. . . . Adler discusses each figure's personal, social, and political history as it affected his or her contribution." Booklist

"Adler ably combines good storytelling, clear and cogent scientific explanations [and] a respect for science over superstition." Publ Wkly

Includes bibliographical references

Dawson, Ian

Greek and Roman medicine. Enchanted Lion 2005 64p il map (History of medicine) $19.95

Grades: 9 10 11 12   **610.9**
1. Medicine—History 2. Classical civilization
ISBN 1-59270-036-5   LC 2004-56272

This book covers the methods used by Greek and Roman doctors to heal the sick, the influence of the Greek and Roman gods in medicine of the period, and the importance of the physicians Galen and Hippocrates.

Includes bibliographical references

Medicine in the Middle Ages. Enchanted Lion 2005 64p il map (History of medicine) $19.95

Grades: 9 10 11 12   **610.9**
1. Medicine—History 2. Middle Ages
ISBN 1-59270-037-3   LC 2004-61996

This book "focuses on how travel, which brought the Black Death and competing eastern viewpoints, forced practitioners to reevaluate bleeding, pus generation, battlefield surgery, and the importance of cleanliness." Voice Youth Advocates

Includes bibliographical references

Great medical discoveries; C.J. Shane, book editor. Greenhaven Press 2004 251p il (Turning points in world history) lib bdg $33.70

Grades: 9 10 11 12   **610.9**
1. Medicine—History 2. Medicine—Research
ISBN 0-7377-1437-9   LC 2003-54005

"This collection of essays explores everything from the ancient study of human anatomy to genetic research. The chapters look at discoveries with regard to the structure and function of the human body, disease and disease prevention, medical procedures, and pharmaceuticals. The

Great medical discoveries—*Continued*
concluding chapter addresses the social impact of great
medical discoveries. Articles are gathered from diverse
sources. . . . Young adults will find this book useful for
science or history assignments or if they are researching
inventions or the history of disease." SLJ

Includes bibliographical references

Harding, Anne
Milestones in health and medicine; by Anne S.
Harding. Oryx Press 2000 267p il $59.95
Grades: 11 12 Adult   **610.9**
1. Medicine—History
ISBN 1-57356-140-1   LC 00-32660
"Alphabetically arranged entries emphasize discoveries
and contributions related to medical advancements, although synopsized information is provided on symptoms
and treatments where appropriate. The entries are clear
and concise and assume a reading level commensurate
with the subject matter." SLJ

Includes bibliographical references

Hellman, Hal, 1927-
Great feuds in medicine; ten of the liveliest
disputes ever. Wiley 2001 237p $24.95; pa $15.95
Grades: 11 12 Adult   **610.9**
1. Medicine—History 2. Scientists
ISBN 0-471-34757-4; 0-471-20833-7 (pa)
                                      LC 00-63349
This considers disputes involving such medical scientists as William Harvey, Galvani, Volta, Pasteur, Freud,
Sabin, Salk, and Montagnier
"Hellman eschews comprehensiveness for pith and entertainment, neglecting no unusual 'twist,' 'strange coincidence,' 'cloud of suspicion' or 'lucky break' to height-
en the drama of these medical milestones." Publ Wkly

Includes bibliographical references

Kelly, Kate, 1950-
Early civilizations; prehistoric times to 500 C.E.
Facts on File 2010 174p il map (The history of
medicine) $40
Grades: 6 7 8 9 10   **610.9**
1. Medicine—History 2. Ancient civilization
ISBN 978-0-8160-7205-7; 0-8160-7205-1
                                      LC 2008-43441
"This eye-opening and information-rich [volume] . . .
shows that ancient human beings were quite knowledgeable about health and well-being. This book discusses
medical advances from prehistoric times through the Roman Empire. . . . Coverage is global. . . . Readers will
gain a deepened appreciation of and insights into modern
medicine by examining this book. Because of its inclusion of new research, it is recommended as a first purchase for most libraries." SLJ

Includes bibliographical references

Medicine becomes a science; 1840-1999. Facts
on File 2010 168p il map (The history of
medicine) $40
Grades: 9 10 11 12   **610.9**
1. Medicine—History 2. Science—History
ISBN 978-0-8160-7209-5; 0-8160-7209-4
                                      LC 2009-11598

This book "covers the time period when medicine
moved from guesswork to being a real, measurable science. Because of the sheer amount of material to discuss,
the author details the history episodically by profiling
specific people and their contributions, certain advances
and how they were made, who contributed to them, etc.
The text is highly engaging and readable. Students interested in a career in medicine or in history will enjoy this
book." SLJ

Includes glossary and bibliographical references

Medicine today; 2000 to the present. Facts on
File 2010 160p il map (The history of medicine)
$40
Grades: 9 10 11 12   **610.9**
1. Medicine—History 2. Medical ethics
ISBN 978-0-8160-7210-1; 0-8160-7210-8
                                      LC 2009-16629
This book "describes some of the technology and discoveries that are currently being explored in the world of
medicine, providing information on what some of these
new developments might mean and the possibilities for
tomorrow." Publisher's note

Includes glossary and bibliographical references

The Middle Ages; 500-1450. Facts on File 2010
158p il map (The history of medicine) $40
Grades: 9 10 11 12   **610.9**
1. Medicine—History
ISBN 978-0-8160-7206-4; 0-8160-7206-X
                                      LC 2008-48709
This book shows "what occurred during medieval
times that affected future developments in medicine."
Publisher's note

Includes glossary and bibliographical references

The scientific revolution and medicine;
1450-1700. Facts on File 2010 158p il map (The
history of medicine) $40
Grades: 9 10 11 12   **610.9**
1. Medicine—History
ISBN 978-0-8160-7207-1; 0-8160-7207-8
                                      LC 2008-55603
This book "examines the scientific revolution and how
it has affected future developments in medicine." Publisher's note

Includes glossary and bibliographical references

611 Human anatomy, cytology, histology

Abrahams, Peter H.
McMinn's clinical atlas of human anatomy; [by]
Peter H. Abrahams, Johannes M. Boon, Jonathan
D. Spratt; photography by Ralph T. Hutchings. 6th
ed. Mosby / Elsevier 2008 386p il pa $84.95
Grades: 11 12 Adult   **611**
1. Human anatomy—Atlases 2. Reference books
ISBN 978-0-323-03605-4
First published 1977 under the authorship of R. M. H.
McMinn with title: Color atlas of human anatomy
Includes DVD-ROM

Abrahams, Peter H.—*Continued*

This "atlas incorporates . . . [a] collection of cadaveric, osteological, and clinical images with surface anatomy models, interpretive drawings, orientational diagrams, and diagnostic images." Publisher's note

Bainbridge, David, 1968-

Beyond the zonules of Zinn; a fantastic journey through your brain. Harvard University Press 2008 338p il $25.95

Grades: 11 12 Adult   **611**

1. Brain 2. Nervous system

ISBN 978-0-674-02610-0; 0-674-02610-1

           LC 2007-21595

"In this 'geographical tour' of the nervous system, readers will find an entertaining and enlightening history of neuroscience and a look at the anatomy of the brain. . . . The book's relaxed pace, interesting tangents and broad coverage make this book eminently suitable for anyone curious about the brain." Publ Wkly

Includes bibliographical references

Balaban, Naomi E.

The handy anatomy answer book; [by] Naomi E. Balaban and James E. Bobick. Visible Ink Press 2008 362p il pa $21.95 *

Grades: 9 10 11 12 Adult   **611**

1. Human anatomy 2. Physiology

ISBN 978-1-57859-190-9

"Thirteen chapters cover the body's various systems (circulatory, digestive, endocrine, nervous, etc.) and are preceded by a chapter on basic biology and followed by one on human growth and development. Each section consists of a series of questions and answers organized in a logical fashion, one flowing into the next and progressing from basic to more detailed." SLJ

"This book can provide an excellent way to read and self-test for health and human biology classes. Adults wanting to know more about the subjects covered will also find a wealth of useful and accessible information." Voice Youth Advocates

Gray's anatomy; the anatomical basis of clinical practice. 40th ed. Churchill Livingstone 2008 xxiv, 1551p il $209 *

Grades: 11 12 Adult   **611**

1. Human anatomy 2. Reference books

ISBN 978-0-443-06684-9

First published 1858. Periodically revised. Publisher varies

Variant title: Gray's anatomy of the human body

A comprehensive standard reference work with illustrations, descriptions and definitions.

"Holds its place as a major and authoritative text on systematic anatomy. Recommended." Annals of Internal Medicine

Includes bibliographical references

Hall, Linley Erin

DNA and RNA. Rosen Pub. 2010 c2011 80p il (Understanding genetics) lib bdg $30.60

Grades: 9 10 11 12   **611**

1. DNA 2. RNA

ISBN 978-1-4358-9532-4   LC 2009-46612

Introduces DNA and RNA, discussing how heredity works, what can happen when the code goes wrong, replication, and new advances in science and technology.

Heos, Bridget

The human genome. Rosen Pub. 2010 c2011 80p il (Understanding genetics) lib bdg $30.60

Grades: 9 10 11 12   **611**

1. Genomes 2. Genetics

ISBN 978-1-4358-9533-1   LC 2009-47915

Presents an introduction to genetics, discussing genes, chromosomes, probability, DNA, mutation, and the Human Genome Project.

Hodge, Russ

The molecules of life; DNA, RNA, and proteins; foreword by Nadia Rosenthal. Facts On File 2009 222p il (Genetics & evolution) $39.50 *

Grades: 9 10 11 12   **611**

1. Nucleic acids 2. Proteins 3. Biochemistry 4. Molecular biology

ISBN 978-0-8160-6680-3; 0-8160-6680-9

           LC 2008-37094

"This highly readable book about molecular biology explains how organic molecules drive processes between and within the cells. . . . For those schools wanting to develop a strong science collection, this is a needed resource for it can be used in introductory and advanced biology classes." Libr Media Connect

Includes glossary and bibliographical references

Leonardo, da Vinci, 1452-1519

Leonardo on the human body; [by] Leonardo da Vinci. Dover Publs. 1983 506p il pa $26.95

Grades: 9 10 11 12   **611**

1. Human anatomy

ISBN 0-486-24483-0   LC 82-18285

First published 1952 by H. Schuman with title: Leonardo Da Vinci on the human body

This volume includes 215 black-and-white plates containing some 1200 illustrations. Each plate is accompanied by explanatory notes

Photographic atlas of the body; pictures supplied by the Science Photo Library; foreword by Baroness Susan Greenfield. Firefly Books 2004 288p il $49.95 *

Grades: 9 10 11 12   **611**

1. Human anatomy—Atlases 2. Reference books

ISBN 1-55297-973-3; 978-1-55297-973-0

           LC 2005-357208

"Close-up photography of human anatomy is combined with . . . text to explain the human body's functions and inner workings." Publisher's note

Photographic atlas of the body—*Continued*

"Anyone, old or young, fascinated with the inner workings of the body will be delighted by these strangely compelling images, which look more like strange landscapes and life forms than the interior of our own physical selves." Publ Wkly

Roach, Mary

Stiff; the curious lives of human cadavers. Norton 2003 303p il $23.95; pa $13.95

Grades: 11 12 Adult   **611**

1. Human experimentation in medicine 2. Dead 3. Dissection

ISBN 0-393-05093-9; 0-393-32482-6 (pa)

LC 2002-152908

The author "explains how surgeons and doctors use cadavers donated for research purposes to help the living, and also examines potential new variations on how we bury the dead." Libr J

"For those who are interested in the fields of medicine or forensics and are aware of some of the procedures, this book makes excellent reading." SLJ

Includes bibliographical references

Shubin, Neil

Your inner fish; a journey into the 3.5-billion-year history of the human body. Pantheon Books 2008 229p il map $24 *

Grades: 11 12 Adult   **611**

1. Human anatomy 2. Evolution

ISBN 978-0-375-42447-2; 0-375-42447-4

LC 2007-24699

This is a "look at how the human body evolved into its present state. . . . Shubin excels at explaining the science, making each discovery an adventure, whether it's a Pennsylvania roadcut or a stony outcrop beset by polar bears and howling Arctic winds." Publ Wkly

Includes bibliographical references

612   Human physiology

Anatomy and physiology; an illustrated guide. Marshall Cavendish 2010 192p il (Marshall Cavendish reference) $99.80

Grades: 9 10 11 12   **612**

1. Anatomy 2. Physiology

ISBN 978-0-7614-7881-2; 0-7614-7881-7

LC 2009-2177

"This text begins with a study of the animal cell, its structure and function, and continues with detailed explanations of the major life functions such as reproduction, digestion, respiration/circulation, and locomotion. Each chapter provides a detailed overview of the system structures and how they function along with specific information on variations across species. . . . [This is] a well organized, sequential reference tool for individuals who need information on the animal cell, organ systems, or reproduction." Libr Media Connect

Includes bibliographical references

Carroll, Aaron E.

Don't swallow your gum! myths, half-truths, and outright lies about your body and health; [by] Aaron E. Carroll and Rachel C. Vreeman. St. Martin's Griffin 2009 221p pa $13.95

Grades: 11 12 Adult   **612**

1. Medical misconceptions

ISBN 978-0-312-53387-8; 0-312-53387-X

LC 2009-7363

"Divided into six sections, each comprising approximately 10 'myths' in two pages each, the book covers issues about disease, sex and pregnancy, babies and children, what we eat, and 'controversial' topics. . . . It is easy to imagine teens browsing through and sharing fun tidbits with one another. In fact, with its offhand tone, liberal use of expressions like 'sucks' and 'BS,' the occasional gratuitous gross-out story, short chapters, and compact paperback format, the book reads as if it were written with teen appeal in mind. At the same time, the authors demonstrate clear research and documentation, including more than 40 pages of references." SLJ

Includes bibliographical references

The **complete** human body; the definitive visual guide; Alice Roberts [editor-in-chief] DK Publishing 2010 512p il $50 *

Grades: 8 9 10 11 12 Adult   **612**

1. Human body 2. Diseases

ISBN 978-0-7566-6733-7; 0-7566-6733-X

LC 2010-282438

This is a "guide to the development, form, function, and disorders of the body, illustrated . . . by new computer-generated artworks and the latest medical and microscopic imaging. . . . [It] explores all aspects of the human body, features a region by region anatomy atlas allows the reader to explore the body up close and almost life size, and includes . . . summaries of over 200 diseases and disorders. Includes interactive DVD." Publisher's note

This incorporates "hundreds of stunning images and clearly written text. . . . The extraordinary detail of these pictures will give students an excellent understanding of the body's structure and organization." SLJ

Encyclopedia of human body systems; Julie McDowell, editor. Greenwood 2011 2v il set $125

Grades: 11 12 Adult   **612**

1. Physiology—Encyclopedias 2. Reference books

ISBN 978-0-313-39175-0; 978-0-313-39176-7 (ebook)

LC 2010-21682

"This two-volume set offers readers a concise description of the structure and function of 11 body systems. Sections explain each system's anatomy, cellular chemistry, and organization, together with its relationship to the other body systems. Good writing makes it easy for readers to understand the various systems, and ample tables and line drawings supplement the text." Choice

Includes glossary and bibliographical references

Holmes, Hannah, 1963-
The well-dressed ape; a natural history of myself. Random House 2008 351p $25
Grades: 11 12 Adult	612
1. Human beings 2. Comparative physiology 3. Physical anthropology
ISBN 978-1-4000-6541-7	LC 2008-16582
Explores how the human animal—the eponymous well-dressed ape—fits into the natural world, even as we humans change that world in both constructive and destructive ways.
"A pellucid spin through the contours of the human brain and the folds of the human body." Kirkus
Includes bibliographical references

Laberge, Monique
Biochemistry. Chelsea House 2008 112p il (Essential chemistry) lib bdg $35
Grades: 7 8 9 10 11 12	612
1. Biochemistry
ISBN 978-0-7910-9693-2; 0-7910-9693-9
LC 2007-51316
This title discusses various aspects of biochemistry, including the Human Genome Project.
"The writing style is wholly accessible to a reader with only the most basic background in the life sciences and chemistry. . . . This book amiably introduces the field of biochemistry and could easily inspire further reading in a young reader interested in science." Sci Books Films
Includes glossary and bibliographical references

Macaulay, David, 1946-
The way we work; getting to know the amazing human body; [by] David Macaulay, with Richard Walker. Houghton Mifflin 2008 336p il $35 *
Grades: 6 7 8 9 10	612
1. Human body
ISBN 978-0-618-23378-6; 0-618-23378-4
LC 2008-25109
"Walter Lorraine books"
"The opening chapter introduces basic concepts of biology and chemistry at the cellular level while subsequent chapters take us through the various systems of the body. . . . [Humor] occasionally leavens the information, which, though often complex and technical, is clearly and succinctly presented in double-page spreads, accompanied by an illuminating array of illustrations." Horn Book

Mai, Larry L.
The Cambridge Dictionary of human biology and evolution; [by] Larry L. Mai, Marcus Young Owl, M. Patricia Kersting. Cambridge University Press 2005 648p il pa $60 *
Grades: 9 10 11 12 Adult	612
1. Reference books 2. Biology—Dictionaries 3. Evolution—Dictionaries
ISBN 0-521-66486-1; 978-0-521-66486-8
LC 2004-43553
"This dictionary covers many aspects of human biology: anatomy, growth, physiology, genetics, paleontology,

physical anthropology, primatology, and zoology." Am Ref Books Annu, 2006
"This is one of those dictionaries that will keep even casual browsers intrigued." Choice

Margulies, Sheldon
The fascinating body; how it works. ScarecrowEducation 2004 412p il pa $34.95
Grades: 9 10 11 12	612
1. Human body
ISBN 1-57886-076-8	LC 2003-18883
Contents: Organ systems; Skin; Immunologic system; Eyes; Ears; Respiratory system; Cardiac system; Gastrointestinal system; Endocrine system; Vascular system; Urologic system; Genital system; Hematologic system; Bones and joints; Neurologic system; How doctors make a diagnosis; Final thoughts for teenagers
"This title should be made available to every biology classroom or library media center, not only for the wealth of information, but for its concise and useful explanations of the way our bodies function. . . . This resource is an invaluable tool for the high school science curriculum." Libr Media Connect

McMillan, Beverly
Human body; a visual guide. Firefly Books 2006 304p il $29.95 *
Grades: 9 10 11 12 Adult	612
1. Physiology 2. Human anatomy
ISBN 978-1-55407-188-3; 1-55407-188-7
This book provides "scientific information on the human body, using microphotography, advanced medical imaging and annotated illustrations. The book reveals all the intricacy and beauty of the human body and shows the structure and functions of all the systems that make up a human being." Publisher's note
Includes bibliographical references

Redd, Nancy Amanda
Body drama; real girls, real bodies, real issues, real answers. Gotham 2008 271p pa $20
Grades: 6 7 8 9 10	612
1. Human body 2. Physiology 3. Girls—Health and hygiene 4. Puberty
ISBN 978-1-59240-326-4; 1-59240-326-3
Information for teenage girls about various issues pertaining to their changing physiology
"The author covers a myriad of physical as well as mental health issues, including cutting and depression. . . . It is likely to be a read-and-pass-along book not only for the helpful advice and accurate information but also for the gross-out pictures of head lice, warts, and keloid scars." Voice Youth Advocates
Includes bibliographical references

612.2 Respiration

Petechuk, David
The respiratory system. Greenwood Press 2004 202p il (Human body systems) $65 *
Grades: 9 10 11 12 Adult   612.2
 1. Respiratory system
 ISBN 0-313-32434-4   LC 2004-40445
This book "discusses the functions of each organ and how they work together to allow us to breathe. Respiration is discussed both externally (breathing) and internally at the cellular level. The cardiovascular, nervous, and muscular systems are discussed in relation to the respiratory system." Publisher's note
Includes bibliographical references

612.3 Digestion

Allman, Toney, 1947-
Nutrition and disease prevention. Chelsea House 2010 191p il map (Healthy eating: a guide to nutrition) lib bdg $35
Grades: 7 8 9 10 11 12   612.3
 1. Nutrition 2. Preventive medicine
 ISBN 978-1-60413-777-4; 1-60413-777-0
                                        LC 2009-41337
This book "delves into the complex relationship between nutrition and the prevention of disease. From classic deficiency diseases to problems of metabolism and nutrient absorption, and from severe malnutrition to obesity, nutritional status means the difference between health and sickness or even life and death." Publisher's note
This "volume uses boldface type to introduce important and unknown words to the reader and explains them in an easy to understand manner so the reader can grasp the concept being discussed. . . . [For] classes needing information about the importance of good nutrition . . . [this] would be valuable." Libr Media Connect
Includes glossary and bibliographical references

Brynie, Faith Hickman, 1946-
101 questions about food and digestion that have been eating at you . . . until now. 21st Cent. Bks. (Brookfield) 2002 176p il (101 questions) lib bdg $30.60
Grades: 8 9 10 11 12   612.3
 1. Digestion 2. Nutrition
 ISBN 0-7613-2309-0   LC 2001-52250
Questions and answers explain the human digestive system and how it uses food for nutrition
"Presenting solid research with a lively writing style, this book provides a great deal of information and sound advice on the topic." Booklist
Includes glossary and bibliographical references

Smolin, Lori A.
Basic nutrition; [by] Lori A. Smolin and Mary B. Grosvenor. 2nd ed. Chelsea House 2010 224p il map (Healthy eating: a guide to nutrition) lib bdg $35
Grades: 9 10 11 12   612.3
 1. Nutrition
 ISBN 978-1-60413-801-6   LC 2010-5696
 First published 2005
This book provides "information regarding the six classes of nutrients, how each is broken down and used by the body, and how much of each nutrient an individual needs." Publisher's note
Includes glossary and bibliographical references

Windelspecht, Michael, 1963-
The digestive system. Greenwood Press 2004 xx, 191p il (Human body systems) $65 *
Grades: 9 10 11 12 Adult   612.3
 1. Digestion
 ISBN 0-313-32680-0   LC 2004-40446
This book covers "the upper and lower gastrointestinal tract and accessory organs, such as the gall bladder and liver. . . . The endocrine, circulatory, and lymphatic system are discussed in relation to the digestive system. The history of the research on the digestive system is presented and the future of research in this field is considered." Publisher's note
Includes bibliographical references

612.4 Hematopoietic, lymphatic, glandular, urinary systems

McDowell, Julie
The lymphatic system; [by] Julie McDowell and Michael Windelspecht. Greenwood Press 2004 172p il (Human body systems) $65 *
Grades: 9 10 11 12 Adult   612.4
 1. Lymphatic system
 ISBN 0-313-32494-8   LC 2004-44218
In this book "the lymph system, including lymph nodes and lymphatic circulation are explored and lymphatic functions of the spleen, appendix, and tonsils are discussed. The history of the research on the lymphatic system is presented and the future of research in this field is considered." Publisher's note
Includes bibliographical references

Watson, Stephanie, 1969-
The endocrine system; [by] Stephanie Watson, and Kelli Miller. Greenwood Press 2004 210p il (Human body systems) $65 *
Grades: 9 10 11 12 Adult   612.4
 1. Endocrine glands
 ISBN 0-313-32699-1   LC 2004-40447
This book "discusses the anatomy and function of each organ in the endocrine system. . . . Discussions on insulin, metabolism and menopause are included. . . . The history of the research on the endocrine system is presented and the future of research in this field is con-

Watson, Stephanie, 1969-—*Continued*
sidered. Current controversies and dilemmas of scientists performing this research are explored." Publisher's note
Includes bibliographical references

612.6 Reproduction, development, maturation

Brynie, Faith Hickman, 1946-
101 questions about reproduction; or how 1 + 1 = 3 or 4 or more. Twenty-First Century Books 2006 176p il (101 questions) lib bdg $27.90
Grades: 8 9 10 11 1 2　　　　　　　　**612.6**
1. Pregnancy 2. Childbirth 3. Sex education
ISBN 0-7613-2311-2　　　　LC 2003-16350
Uses a question-and-answer format to present information about physical, medical, and social issues surrounding human reproduction, including birth control, pregnancy, and childbirth.
"This is a splendid companion to Brynie's 101 Questions about Sex and Sexuality (21st Century Bks, 2003); together the books present informative, complementary coverage for browsers and researchers." SLJ
Includes bibliographical references

Nilsson, Lennart, 1922-
A child is born; [photography], Lennart Nilsson; text, Lars Hamberger; translated from the Swedish by Linda Schenck. 4th ed, completely rev and updated. Delacorte Press 2003 239p il $35; pa $21
Grades: 11 12 Adult　　　　　　　　**612.6**
1. Pregnancy 2. Embryology 3. Childbirth
ISBN 0-385-33754-X; 0-385-33755-8 (pa)
　　　　　　　　　　　　LC 2003-43854
"A Merloyd Lawrence book"
Original Swedish edition, 1965; first United States edition, 1966
An illustrated look at male and female reproductive anatomy and physiology, the processes of ovulation and fertilization, fetal development, and labor and delivery.

Panno, Joseph
Aging; modern theories and therapies. Rev. ed. Facts on File 2010 c2011 246p il (The new biology) $40 *
Grades: 9 10 11 12　　　　　　　　**612.6**
1. Aging 2. Longevity
ISBN 978-0-8160-6846-3　　　　LC 2009-47717
First published 2005
This book "describes the field of gerontology and the many theories that scientists have developed over the years to explain the age-related changes that occur in nearly all animals. . . . [Coverage includes] insight on the ways in which humans age, how the aging process has changed over the past thousand years, theoretical aspects of rejuvenation, and . . . studies and effective treatments for Alzheimer's, cardiovascular disease, and osteoporosis." Publisher's note
Includes glossary and bibliographical references

612.7 Musculoskeletal system, integument

Adams, Amy
The muscular system. Greenwood Press 2004 209p il (Human body systems) $65 *
Grades: 9 10 11 12 Adult　　　　　　　　**612.7**
1. Muscles
ISBN 0-313-32403-4　　　　LC 2004-47595
This book "discusses the parts of the muscular system and how they work together to help us move from place to place and to maintain many internal processes, such as a heart beat. Muscle contraction, development, and response during exercise are covered. . . . Muscular system diseases and disorders, symptoms and treatments are [also] explored." Publisher's note
Includes bibliographical references

Brynie, Faith Hickman, 1946-
101 questions about muscles to stretch your mind and flex your brain; by Faith Hickman Brynie. Twenty-First Century Books 2008 176p il (101 questions) lib bdg $30.60
Grades: 8 9 10 11 12　　　　　　　　**612.7**
1. Muscles
ISBN 978-0-8225-6380-8; 0-8225-6380-0
　　　　　　　　　　　　LC 2006-37041
This answers such questions as "What do tendons do? What causes muscle cramps? . . . [This book] makes human physiology accessible, with questions everyone has always wondered about and up-to-date, detailed answers that discuss the complex science in chatty but never condescending style. Like the text, the clear diagrams and photographs deal with everything from basic information . . . to the more advanced." Booklist
Includes glossary and bibliographical references

Dickey, Colin
Cranioklepty; grave robbing and the search for genius. Unbridled Books 2009 308p il $25.95
Grades: 11 12 Adult　　　　　　　　**612.7**
1. Skull 2. Grave robbing 3. Phrenology
ISBN 978-1-932961-86-7　　　　LC 2009-18527
The author relates the story of "the plucky grave robbers who stole the craniums of famed composers Haydn and Beethoven, Swedish mystic Emanuel Swedenborg, artist Francisco Goya, the English doctor and philosopher Sir Thomas Browne and others to sell, study or put on public display. The skull obsession was triggered by the infamous Gall system, created in the late 18th century by Franz Joseph Gall, who theorized that the bumps and dents of the skull could provide a measure of intelligence. . . . Blending science with historical drama, Dickey's book illuminates the mystery and controversy of a bizarre tradition throughout the ages." Publ Wkly
Includes bibliographical references

Kelly, Evelyn B.
The skeletal system; [by] Evelyn Kelly. Greenwood Press 2004 231p il (Human body systems) $65 *
Grades: 9 10 11 12 Adult   **612.7**
1. Skeleton 2. Bones
ISBN 0-313-32521-9   LC 2003-67643
In this book, "both the axial bones of the skeleton and the appendicular bones of the limbs are explored. Joints, ligaments, tendons and cartilage are discussed in relation to the bones of the skeletal system. . . . Skeletal system disorders, symptoms and treatments are [also] explored, including sprains, fractures, arthritis, lyme disease, and carpal tunnel syndrome." Publisher's note
Includes bibliographical references

612.8 Nervous system. Sensory functions

Aamodt, Sandra
Welcome to your brain; why you lose your car keys but never forget how to drive and other puzzles of everyday life; [by] Sandra Aamodt and Sam Wang. Bloomsbury USA 2008 220p il $24.95 *
Grades: 11 12 Adult   **612.8**
1. Brain
ISBN 978-1-59691-283-0; 1-59691-283-9
                              LC 2007-26739
This is a "'user's guide' to our brains. . . . The text is divided into six main parts, covering the brain's basic structure and function, the senses, the brain's development, emotions, rational processes, and altered states. . . . Rather than didactically lecturing, the authors very effectively engage the reader in a comfortable, interesting, and informative dialog." Sci Books Films

Bangalore, Lakshmi
Brain development; series editor, Eric H. Chudler. Chelsea House Publishers 2007 103p il (Gray matter) $32.95
Grades: 8 9 10 11 12   **612.8**
1. Brain
ISBN 978-0-7910-8954-5; 0-7910-8954-1
                              LC 2006-32428
This book "introduces basic brain anatomy and brain development to high school students. It discusses the molecular basis of central nervous system specification, starting from neural induction and pattern formation to neural migration, axon guidance, and synapse formation." Publisher's note
Includes glossary and bibliographical references

Brynie, Faith Hickman, 1946-
101 questions about sleep and dreams that kept you awake nights . . . until now. Twenty-First Century Books 2006 176p il (101 questions) lib bdg $27.93 *
Grades: 8 9 10 11 12   **612.8**
1. Sleep 2. Dreams
ISBN 978-0-7613-2312-9; 0-7613-2312-0
                              LC 2005-17276

This book describes the physical and psychological aspects of sleep and dreams.
The author "presents sometimes rather complicated scientific material in a way that is not only easily understood, but also thoroughly enjoyable." Sci Books Films
Includes bibliographical references

Evans-Martin, Fay
The nervous system; [by] F. Fay Evans-Martin. Chelsea House 2009 222p il (The human body: how it works) lib bdg $35
Grades: 7 8 9 10   **612.8**
1. Nervous system
ISBN 978-1-60413-374-5; 1-60413-374-0
                              LC 2009-22141
Examines the parts, organization, and development of the nervous system, including information on diseases and injuries of the nervous system.
Includes glossary and bibliographical references

The **human** brain book; [by] Rita Carter; Susan Aldridge, Martyn Page, Steve Parker; consultants, Chris Frith, Uta Frith, and Melanie Shulman. DK 2009 256p il $40
Grades: 9 10 11 12 Adult   **612.8**
1. Brain 2. Reference books
ISBN 978-0-7566-5441-2
Includes DVD-ROM
Contents: The brain and the body; Brain anatomy; The senses; Movement and control; Emotions and feelings; The social brain; Language and communication; Memory; Thinking; Consciousness; The individual brain; Development and aging; Diseases and disorders
"This outstanding reference is filled with interesting, detailed information about every possible aspect of the human brain. Three-dimension images and other unique computer-generated visuals complement the massive volume, which also includes more than 50 brain-related diseases and disorders." National Science Teachers Association
Includes glossary

May, Mike
Sensation and perception. Chelsea House Publishers 2007 120p il (Gray matter) lib bdg $35
Grades: 8 9 10 11 12   **612.8**
1. Senses and sensation 2. Perception
ISBN 978-0-7910-8958-3; 0-7910-8958-4
                              LC 2006-38552
This book focuses on how sensory "work, from the mechanics of individual cells to the interactions of thousands of cells in the brain. This book also delves into how our sensory capabilities change with age or damage." Publisher's note
Includes glossary and bibliographical references

McDowell, Julie
The nervous system and sense organs. Greenwood Press 2004 201p il (Human body systems) $65 *
Grades: 9 10 11 12 Adult   **612.8**
1. Nervous system 2. Senses and sensation
ISBN 0-313-32456-5   LC 2003-67638

McDowell, Julie—*Continued*

In this book, "major areas of the brain and the autonomic and peripheral nervous systems are covered. The five senses are discussed in relation to the nervous system. The history of the research on the nervous system is presented and the future of research in this field is considered." Publisher's note

Includes bibliographical references

Morgan, Michael, 1960-

The midbrain. Chelsea House 2006 114p il (Gray matter) $32.95

Grades: 8 9 10 11 12   612.8

1. Brain

ISBN 0-7910-8637-2   LC 2005-11988

This "stars the least flashy, less-well-researched part of the brain responsible for various movements (including Parkinson's problems), vision, hearing, sensuality, defense, and complex eye movements. . . . [This book proceeds] from a physiological model of the brain and address structure and behavior in various species while focusing on humans." SLJ

Includes bibliographical references

Phillips, Sherre Florence

The teen brain. Chelsea House 2007 130p il (Gray matter) lib bdg $32.95

Grades: 8 9 10 11 12   612.8

1. Brain 2. Adolescence

ISBN 978-0-7910-9415-0; 0-7910-9415-4

LC 2007-394

This book "defines adolescence in medical and social terms. One chapter on the reward circuit and thrill-seeking addresses decision-making processes that develop during adolescence. The impact of hormones and sleep cycles are expertly explained in chapters of their own." Voice Youth Advocates

Includes glossary and bibliographical references

Rapport, Richard

Nerve endings; the discovery of the synapse. Norton 2005 240p il hardcover o.p. pa $18.95

Grades: 11 12 Adult   612.8

1. Ramón y Cajal, Santiago, 1852-1934 2. Golgi, Camillo, 1843-1926 3. Nervous system

ISBN 0-393-06019-5; 0-393-33752-9 (pa)

LC 2005-942

This book discusses "Santiago Ramon y Cajal and Camillo Golgi, joint recipients of the 1906 Nobel Prize in Medicine and Physiology. . . . Even when Golgi's own groundbreaking advances in histology allowed him to see a gap between nerve cells, he insisted that cells were connected. At the same time, Cajal used Golgi's own histology methods to propose that neurons communicate over a gap—later called the synapse." Sci Books Films

"Teens studying biology and medicine will find that the book provides an accessible introduction to understanding the structure and function of the nervous system." SLJ

Includes bibliographical references

Turkington, Carol

The encyclopedia of the brain and brain disorders; [by] Carol Turkington and Joseph R. Harris. 3rd ed. Facts On File 2009 434p (Facts on File library of health and living) $75

Grades: 11 12 Adult   612.8

1. Brain—Encyclopedias 2. Reference books

ISBN 978-0-8160-6395-6; 0-8160-6395-8

LC 2007-33543

First published 1996 with title: The brain encyclopedia

With a large focus on memory this edition discusses the functions and elements of the brain, how it works, how it breaks down, and various diseases and disorders that affect it.

Includes bibliographical references

613   Personal health and safety

De la Bédoyère, Camilla

Personal hygiene and sexual health. Amicus 2010 c2011 46p il (Healthy lifestyles) lib bdg $32.80 *

Grades: 7 8 9 10   613

1. Teenagers—Health and hygiene 2. Puberty

ISBN 978-1-60753-087-9; 1-60753-087-2

LC 2009-47571

"Discusses the changes that come with puberty in the teenage years for both boys and girls, including personal hygiene issues, body changes, relationships, sexuality, and more." Publisher's note

This book is "well-written and satisfyingly informative. . . . [The] magazine-like format includes numerous sidebars, color photos, and charts." SLJ

Includes glossary

Dicker, Katie

Diet and nutrition. Amicus 2011 45p il (Healthy lifestyles) lib bdg $32.80

Grades: 7 8 9 10   613

1. Nutrition 2. Teenagers—Health and hygiene 3. Diet 4. Physical fitness

ISBN 978-1-60753-085-5; 1-60753-085-6

LC 2009-44219

"Discusses the importance of having a balanced, healthy diet and a healthy body image in your teenage years, gives information on how the body digests various foods, and gives tips for making healthy choices to avoid eating disorders and obesity." Publisher's note

This book is "well-written and satisfyingly informative." SLJ

Includes glossary

Goldstein, Mark A., 1947-

Boys into men; staying healthy through the teen years; by Mark A. Goldstein and Myrna Chandler Goldstein. Greenwood Press 2000 197p il $45

Grades: 9 10 11 12   613

1. Boys—Health and hygiene 2. Teenagers—Health and hygiene

ISBN 0-313-30966-3   LC 00-21045

Goldstein, Mark A., 1947-—*Continued*
"Dividing adolescence into three time frames—twelve to fourteen, fifteen to eighteen, and nineteen to twenty-one years old—the Goldsteins present information on various areas of physical and emotional growth and development." Voice Youth Advocates
Includes bibliographical references

Libal, Autumn
Can I change the way I look? a teen's guide to the health implications of cosmetic surgery, makeovers, and beyond. Mason Crest Publishers 2005 128p il (Science of health) $24.95
Grades: 7 8 9 10   **613**
1. Teenagers—Health and hygiene 2. Personal grooming
ISBN 1-59084-843-8   LC 2004-1883
"Framing her discussion within an examination of the media influence on our culture's definition of beauty, Libal does an excellent job of discussing the risks and benefits of cosmetics, piercing and tattooing, diet, exercise, and cosmetic surgery. . . . The author also considers, in some detail, the dangers of anorexia nervosa, bulimia, and steroid use." SLJ
Includes bibliographical references

Mayo Clinic family health book; Scott Litin, editor-in-chief. 4th ed., completely rev. and updated. Time Inc. Home Entertainment 2009 1423p il $49.95 *
Grades: 11 12 Adult   **613**
1. Medicine 2. Reference books
ISBN 978-1-60320-077-6; 1-60320-077-0
                                       LC 2010-287052
First published 1990 by Morrow
This book covers over 1,000 illnesses and includes information on immunizations, breast health, genetics, sleep disorders, complementary and alternative medicine, pain management, and end-of-life issues.

McCoy, Kathleen, 1945-
The teenage body book; [by] Kathy McCoy and Charles Wibbelsman; illustrations by Bob Stover and Kelly Grady. Rev and updated. Hatherleigh 2008 300p il pa $17.95 *
Grades: 7 8 9 10 11 12   **613**
1. Teenagers—Health and hygiene 2. Adolescence 3. Sex education
ISBN 978-1-57826-277-9   LC 2009-368424
First published 1979 by Pocket Bks. with authors' names in reverse order
A handbook for teenagers discussing nutrition, health, fitness, emotions, and sexuality, including such topics as body image, drugs, STDs, fad diets and hazards and benefits of the Internet.
"This highly informative book . . . is at the same time easily readable, nonpreachy, and comprehensive. . . . This book should be not only in the library of every middle and high school, but also in the hands of every student and in health education classes." Sci Books Films

Our bodies, ourselves; a new edition for a new era; [by] The Boston Women's Health Book Collective. 35th anniversary ed. Simon & Schuster 2005 832p il pa $24.95 *
Grades: 11 12 Adult   **613**
1. Women—Health and hygiene 2. Women—Psychology
ISBN 0-7432-5611-5   LC 2004-65374
"A Touchstone book"
First published 1971
This encyclopedia of women's health covers such topics as body image, food, alcohol and drugs, holistic healing, psychotherapy, occupational health, violence, relationships and sexuality, sexual health and controlling fertility, childbearing, aging and politics of women and health.
This book "is exceedingly readable, strikingly comprehensive, and thoroughly documented." Libr J
Includes bibliographical references

613.2   Dietetics

Burke, Louise
The complete guide to food for sports performance; a guide to peak nutrition for your sport; [by] Louise Burke, Greg Cox. 3rd ed., Updated and expanded. Allen & Unwin 2010 xxii, 522p il pa $24.95
Grades: 11 12 Adult   **613.2**
1. Athletes—Nutrition 2. Physical fitness
ISBN 978-1-7411-4390-4; 1-7411-4390-X
                                       LC 2010-537626
First published 1992
"This book presents nutrition as an integrated part of an athlete's total performance-enhancing package. General nutrition and exercise physiology information are converted into a plan for day-to-day practice for training and competition preparation. It outlines important differences in nutritional needs for different sports, including the timing of food and liquid intake, and the best foods to achieve maximum energy output." Publisher's note

Diet information for teens; edited by Karen Bellenir. 2nd ed. Omnigraphics 2006 432p (Teen health series) $58 *
Grades: 8 9 10 11 12   **613.2**
1. Nutrition 2. Teenagers—Health and hygiene
ISBN 0-7808-0820-7   LC 2006-4413
First published 2000
"Health tips about diet and nutrition including facts about dietary guidelines, food groups, nutrients, healthy meals, snacks, weight control, medical concerns related to diet, and more." Title page
This "is a compilation of articles on all facets of nutrition, drawn mainly from FDA documents. The information is presented in a straightforward, plainspoken manner." SLJ [review of 2000 edition]
Includes bibliographical references

The **Encyclopedia** of vitamins, minerals, and supplements; [compiled by] Tova Navarra; foreword by Wendy Shankin-Cohen. 2nd ed. Facts on File 2004 xxiii, 353p (Facts on File library of health and living) $65

Grades: 11 12 Adult   **613.2**
1. Vitamins 2. Nutrition 3. Dietary supplements—Encyclopedias 4. Reference books
ISBN 0-8160-4998-X   LC 2003-61662
First published 1996

Over 900 entries in A-Z format focus on how to use vitamins, minerals, and food supplements "safely, their effects on nutrition, their uses as treatment for assorted health concerns, and common misconceptions about them. Articles on individual vitamins and minerals are detailed." Booklist

Includes bibliographical references

Favor, Lesli J.
Weighing in; nutrition and weight management. Marshall Cavendish Benchmark 2007 128p il (Food and fitness) lib bdg $25.95

Grades: 7 8 9 10   **613.2**
1. Weight loss 2. Nutrition
ISBN 978-0-7614-2555-7; 0-7614-2555-1
       LC 2006-101930

This "offers an in-depth look at issues related to body weight. Chapters . . . discuss determining one's ideal weight; health risks associated with weight, from diabetes to anorexia; nutrition and wellness; teen dietary requirements and meal planning; and weight-loss strategies, with possible dangers highlighted. . . . Teens will find this a useful, often thought-provoking resource for personal or class research." Booklist

Includes bibliographical references

Gay, Kathlyn, 1930-
The scoop on what to eat; what you should know about diet and nutrition. Enslow Publishers 2009 112p il (Issues in focus today) lib bdg $31.93 *

Grades: 7 8 9 10   **613.2**
1. Nutrition
ISBN 978-0-7660-3066-4; 0-7660-3066-0
       LC 2008-40382

"Discusses diet and nutrition for young people, including ideas for a well-balanced diet, good and bad foods to eat, the importance of exercise, and eating disorders." Publisher's note

"Bolstered with well-integrated quotes and relevant statistics, [this book offers] an excellent starting point for students seeking [a] broad, thoroughly researched [introduction] to [diet and nutrition]. . . . Illuminating case studies, enhanced with multiple viewpoints, personalize the facts and place them in boarder context." Booklist

Includes glossary and bibliographical references

Ingram, Scott, 1948-
Want fries with that? obesity and the supersizing of America. Franklin Watts 2006 128p il $26 *

Grades: 7 8 9 10   **613.2**
1. Obesity 2. Convenience foods 3. Eating customs
ISBN 0-531-16756-9   LC 2005-5619

This is an "exploration of the physical phenomenon of obesity and its emotional and social ramifications. The text is packed with information on specific dangers such as increased risks of diabetes, cancer, and other health problems. The author casts a critical eye on the effect of advertising and the availability of fast food, both in and out of school, and covers recent state legislation seeking to inform parents of diagnoses of obesity in their children." SLJ

Includes glossary and bibliographical references

Nutrition and well-being A to Z; Delores C.S. James, editor in chief. Macmillan Reference USA 2004 2v il set $175 *

Grades: 9 10 11 12 Adult   **613.2**
1. Reference books 2. Nutrition—Encyclopedias
ISBN 0-02-865707-1   LC 2004-6088

Topics covered "include dietary habits, eating diseases and disorders, health risks and food safety, the eating habits of various ethnic groups, weight loss issues as well as professional matters, and health programs and organizations." Libr J

This is "a no-nonsense, comprehensive encyclopedia that will be of use to students researching health and food-science topics." SLJ

Includes bibliographical references

Smolin, Lori A.
Nutrition and weight management; [by] Lori A. Smolin and Mary B. Grosvenor. 2nd ed. Chelsea House 2010 184p il map (Healthy eating: a guide to nutrition) lib bdg $35

Grades: 7 8 9 10 11 12   **613.2**
1. Nutrition 2. Weight loss
ISBN 978-1-60413-803-0; 1-60413-803-3
       LC 2009-41335
First published 2005

This book "discusses the concept of weight management as well as the role that social, cultural, and genetic factors play in determining weight and body size. Coverage includes the importance of a nutritious diet and what constitutes healthy eating, the physical and psychological effects of being overweight and underweight, and the pros and cons of various diets." Publisher's note

This "volume uses boldface type to introduce important and unknown words to the reader and explains them in an easy to understand manner so the reader can grasp the concept being discussed. . . . [For] classes needing information about the importance of good nutrition . . . [this] would be valuable." Libr Media Connect

Includes glossary and bibliographical references

Vegetarian sourcebook; basic consumer health information about vegetarian diets, lifestyle, and philosophy . . .; edited by Chad T. Kimball. Omnigraphics 2002 360p il (Health reference series) $78 *

Grades: 9 10 11 12 Adult   **613.2**
1. Vegetarianism
ISBN 0-7808-0439-2   LC 2002-70236
"This work answers questions that people might have about the healthfulness of a vegetarian diet as well as how to incorporate it into one's everyday life. . . . The articles in this volume are easy to read and come from authoritative sources." Am Ref Books Annu, 2003

Includes bibliographical references

613.6   Personal safety and special topics of health

Bocij, Paul
Cyberstalking; harassment in the Internet age and how to protect your family. Praeger Publishers 2004 268p $39.95
Grades: 9 10 11 12 Adult   **613.6**
1. Computer crimes
ISBN 0-275-98118-5; 978-0-275-98118-1
                                    LC 2003-68988
This book is devoted "to an examination of cyberstalking, providing an overview of the problem, its causes and consequences, and practical advice for protecting yourself and your loved ones." Publisher's note
"This is an extremely alarming book that focuses on the dark side of the Internet and makes it clear that we are all potential victims of cyberstalkers. . . . It's certain to be popular in libraries." Booklist

Includes bibliographical references

Gervasi, Lori Hartman
Fight like a girl— and win; defense decisions for women. St. Martin's Griffin 2007 285p pa $14.99
Grades: 11 12 Adult   **613.6**
1. Self-defense for women 2. Safety education
ISBN 978-0-312-35772-6; 0-312-35772-9
                                    LC 2007-17216
"Although the author has a black belt in karate, she maintains that 90 percent of self-defense is awareness and common sense. She helps readers set up absolute rules and boundaries, sharpen their observation skills, and trust in their intuition. Physical fitness is stressed, and resources are provided for further training." Libr J

Includes bibliographical references

Piven, Joshua
The worst-case scenario survival handbook; by Joshua Piven and David Borgenicht. Chronicle Bks. 1999 176p il pa $14.95
Grades: 9 10 11 12   **613.6**
1. Safety education 2. Survival after airplane accidents, shipwrecks, etc. 3. Wilderness survival
ISBN 0-8118-2555-8   LC 2001-268229

This offers advice on safety and survival in emergencies from such dangers as quicksand, erupting volcanoes, terrorist attacks, sharks, plane crashes, and bombs.

Sherwood, Ben
The survivors club; the secrets and science that could save your life. Grand Central Pub. 2009 383p il $25.99; pa $14.99
Grades: 11 12 Adult   **613.6**
1. Survival skills 2. Accidents
ISBN   978-0-446-58024-3;   0-446-58024-4;
978-0-446-69885-6 (pa); 0-446-69885-7 (pa)
                                    LC 2008-16203
The author "travels worldwide to gain insight from people who have survived a slew of near fatal phenomena ranging from a mountain lion attack to a Holocaust concentration camp, and interviewing an array of experts to understand the psychology, genetics and jumble of other little things that determines whether we live or die." Publ Wkly
"Is the book science? Self-help? It's a weird amalgam of the two, but somehow it works. . . . The true-life stories are satisfying in a popcorny kind of way, but it's the science that fascinates." Entertainment Wkly

Stilwell, Alexander
The encyclopedia of survival techniques. Lyons Press 2007 192p il map pa $19.95 *
Grades: 11 12 Adult   **613.6**
1. Survival skills 2. Wilderness survival
ISBN 978-1-59921-314-9
First published 2000
Contents: Preparation and equipment; Survival in the desert; Survival at sea; Survival in the tropics; Survival in polar regions; Survival in mountains; Surviving natural disasters; First aid; Firemaking, tools and weapons; Trapping, fishing and plant food; Navigation and signalling; Rafts and river crossings; Ropes and knots; Urban survival
This guide covers preparation, basic skills, equipment, various terrains, natural disasters, and first aid.

Stroud, Les, 1962-
Will to live; dispatches from the edge of survival; [by] Les Stroud with Michael Vlessides. Harper 2011 228p il pa $17.99
Grades: 11 12 Adult   **613.6**
1. Survival after airplane accidents, shipwrecks, etc. 2. Survival skills
ISBN 978-0-06-202657-6
First published 2010 in Canada
Analyzes survival stories, recounting the events that occurred, and evaluating the decisions made utilizing four critical survival elements, in a text that includes practical tips.
The author "offers intelligent tips—if you're traveling somewhere remote, tell people where you're going, take a well-stocked survival kit, and keep a cool head if you get lost—and he does an excellent job of putting readers into the situations he's discussing, making us feel the cold or the panic or the sheer desperation." Booklist

Includes bibliographical references

Survival wisdom & know-how; everything you need to know to subsist in the wilderness; from the editors of Stackpole Books; compiled by Amy Rost. Black Dog & Leventhal Publishers 2007 480p il pa $19.95

Grades: 9 10 11 12 Adult   **613.6**

1. Survival skills 2. Wilderness survival

ISBN 978-1-57912-753-4   LC 2007-25379

This oversized guide covers "every aspect of outdoor adventure and survival . . . Topics include Building Outdoor Shelter, Tracking Animals, Winter Camping, Tying Knots, Orienteering, Reading the Weather, Identifying Edible Plants and Berries, Surviving in the Desert, Bird Watching, Fishing and Ice Fishing, Hunting and Trapping, Canoeing, Kayaking, and White Water Rafting, First Aid, Wild Animals, Cookery, and . . . more." Publisher's note

Includes bibliographical references

Wiseman, John, 1940-

SAS survival handbook; for any climate, in any situation; [by] John "Lofty" Wiseman. Rev. ed. Collins 2009 576p il pa $19.99

Grades: 11 12 Adult   **613.6**

1. Survival skills 2. Survival after airplane accidents, shipwrecks, etc. 3. Wilderness survival

ISBN 978-0-06-173319-2; 0-06-173319-9

LC 2009-502549

First published 1986 in the United Kingdom

This book "is the Special Air Service's complete course in being prepared for any type of emergency. John Wiseman presents real strategies for surviving in any type of situation, from accidents and escape procedures, including chemical and nuclear to successfully adapting to various climates (polar, tropical, desert), to identifying edible plants and creating fire." Publisher's note

613.7   Physical fitness

Brignell, Roger

The pilates handbook. Rosen Pub. 2009 256p il (A young woman's guide to health and well-being) lib bdg $39.95

Grades: 9 10 11 12   **613.7**

1. Pilates method 2. Women—Health and hygiene

ISBN 978-1-4358-5361-4   LC 2009-10317

This guide "looks at the origins and development of Pilates, and how it can enhance mental as well as physical well-being. The exercise section begins with some basic warmup movements, then works through a series of beginner, intermediate, and advanced exercises. It also demonstrates exercises using a Swiss ball and other equipment." Publisher's note

Includes bibliographical references

Burke, Ed, 1949-

The complete book of long-distance cycling; build the strength, skills, and confidence to ride as far as you want; by Edmund R. Burke and Ed Pavelka. Rodale 2000 292p il pa $19.95

Grades: 11 12 Adult   **613.7**

1. Cycling

ISBN 1-57954-199-2   LC 00-9615

This overview covers bike gear, proper nutrition, and what type of bike to buy

"The authors give the lowdown on the latest equipment and explain bike technology without oversimplifying." Booklist

Dicker, Katie

Exercise. Amicus 2010 c2011 46p il (Healthy lifestyles) lib bdg $32.80

Grades: 7 8 9 10   **613.7**

1. Exercise 2. Physical fitness

ISBN 978-1-60753-086-2; 1-60753-086-4

LC 2009-47566

"Discusses in-depth the benefits of exercise for teenagers, including how to make exercise fun and safe and develop it into a lifelong habit." Publisher's note

This book is "well-written and satisfyingly informative. . . . [The] magazine-like format includes numerous sidebars, color photos, and charts." SLJ

Includes glossary

Fahey, Thomas D., 1947-

Basic weight training for men and women. 6th ed. McGraw-Hill 2007 248p il pa $30.63

Grades: 11 12 Adult   **613.7**

1. Weight lifting

ISBN 0-07-304688-4; 978-0-07-304688-4

LC 2005-53132

First published 1989 by Mayfield Pub. Co. with title: Basic weight training

This is a "guide to developing a personalized weight-training program with both free weights and machines. Weight training concepts and specific exercises are grouped by body region, and many photographs, illustrations, diagrams, and figures demonstrate proper technique and form." Publisher's note

Includes bibliographical references

Finney, Sumukhi

The yoga handbook. Rosen Pub. 2010 256p il (A young woman's guide to health and well-being) lib bdg $39.95

Grades: 9 10 11 12   **613.7**

1. Yoga 2. Women—Health and hygiene

ISBN 978-1-4358-5359-1   LC 2009-10509

This guide "offers insight into both the physical and spiritual traditions associated with yoga. Clearly organized, the chapters discuss types of yoga; breathing, diet, and meditation suggestions; and, of course, the poses, which are described step by step, illustrated with small color photos, and bolstered with variations on the basic forms. Finney's experience shows in her enthusiastic tone and in the quotes she culls from ancient texts and contemporary teachers alike." Booklist

Includes bibliographical references

Fitness information for teens; edited by Lisa Bakewell. 2nd ed. Omnigraphics 2009 432p (Teen health series) $65

Grades: 7 8 9 10 11 12   **613.7**

1. Physical fitness

ISBN 978-0-7808-1045-7; 0-7808-1045-7

LC 2008-31334

First published 2004

"Health tips about exercise, physical wellbeing, and health maintenance including facts about conditioning, stretching, strength training, body shape and body image, sports nutrition, and specific activities for athletes and non-athletes" Title page

"Provides basic consumer health information for teens on maintaining health through physical activity. Includes index, resource information and recommendations for further reading." Publisher's note

"This no-nonsense guide packs a great deal into its pages. . . . The text is written in a conversational tone that pairs well with the topic." SLJ

Includes bibliographical references

Hesson, James L.

Weight training for life. 9th ed. Wadsworth/Cengage Learning 2010 178p il $59.95

Grades: 11 12 Adult   **613.7**

1. Weight lifting

ISBN 978-0-495-55909-2; 0-495-55909-1

LC 2010291364

First published 1985 by Morton

New edition in preparation

"The text contains hundreds of full-color photos demonstrating exercises and proper techniques. It also contains forms for writing goals, planning a personal weight-training program, and recording circumference, strength, and muscle endurance measurements." Publisher's note

Includes bibliographical references

Hines, Emmett W., 1956-

Fitness swimming; [by] Emmett Hines. 2nd ed. Human Kinetics 2008 224p il pa $18.95

Grades: 9 10 11 12 Adult   **613.7**

1. Swimming 2. Physical fitness

ISBN 978-0-7360-7457-5; 0-7360-7457-0

LC 2008-13353

First published 1999

The author "has created 60 . . . workouts and 16 sample programs, each arranged into suggested training zones to correspond to your fitness level and performance goals. . . . The text covers stretching, warm-up and cool-down methods, heart rate zone targets, expanded instruction for stroke efficacy, progressive drills, conditioning tips, and fitness assessments." Publisher's note

Includes bibliographical references

Pagano, Joan

Strength training for women; tone up, burn calories, stay strong. Dorling Kindersley 2005 160p il pa $15 *

Grades: 9 10 11 12 Adult   **613.7**

1. Weight lifting 2. Physical fitness 3. Women—Health and hygiene

ISBN 0-7566-0595-4; 978-0-7566-0595-7

LC 2005-295208

The author "begins with a three-part fitness test and questionnaire to assess whether the reader should consult a doctor before beginning her program. For true beginners, she provides an anatomy chart that depicts the major muscle groups and the exercises that are best suited to them. She dispels fitness myths like 'lifting weights will bulk you up' and 'you can spot reduce,' and talks about the risk factors, exercise guidelines and restrictions of osteoporosis. . . . This book may be one of the best substitutes for pricey gym memberships and personal trainers." Publ Wkly

Pawlett, Raymond

The tai chi handbook; [by] Ray Pawlet. Rosen Pub. 2009 246p il (A young woman's guide to health and well-being) lib bdg $39.95

Grades: 9 10 11 12   **613.7**

1. Tai chi 2. Women—Health and hygiene

ISBN 978-1-4358-5360-7   LC 2009-10316

"The Tai Chi Handbook teaches readers . . . about the art, including its history, styles, applications, and moves." Publisher's note

Includes bibliographical references

Schwartz, Ellen, 1949-

I love yoga; a guide for kids and teens; illustrated by Ben Hodson. Tundra Books 2003 122p il pa $9.95 *

Grades: 9 10 11 12   **613.7**

1. Yoga

ISBN 0-88776-598-X   LC 2002-117468

The author "presents the history of yoga, different styles, yoga benefits, concerns, cautions, misconceptions, equipment, and basic postures." Publisher's note

"This is less a how-to book than an upbeat introduction to yoga, well designed to spark the interest of kids and teens." Quill & Quire

Includes bibliographical references

Smolin, Lori A.

Nutrition for sports and exercise; [by] Lori A. Smolin and Mary B. Grosvenor. 2nd ed. Chelsea House 2010 192p il (Healthy eating: a guide to nutrition) lib bdg $35 *

Grades: 9 10 11 12   **613.7**

1. Nutrition 2. Athletes—Nutrition 3. Exercise

ISBN 978-1-60413-804-7   LC 2010-5692

First published 2005

"The book explores the dangers that athletes may face when they neglect their nutritional needs and provides valuable information about how athletes can best achieve optimal nutrition." Publisher's note

Includes glossary and bibliographical references

613.9   Birth control, reproductive technology, sex hygiene

Bell, Ruth

Changing bodies, changing lives; a book for teens on sex and relationships; [by] Ruth Bell and other co-authors of Our bodies, ourselves and Ourselves and our children, together with members of the Teen Book Project. expanded 3rd ed. Times Bks. 1998 411p il pa $24.95 *

Grades: 7 8 9 10 11 12   613.9
  1. Sex education
  ISBN 0-8129-2990-X   LC 97-29249
  First published 1980

This is a "book on sex, physical and emotional health, and personal relationships. . . . Readers . . . will find emotional support as well as specific answers to most of their questions in this nonjudgmental resource." Booklist

Bringle, Jennifer

Reproductive rights; making the right choices. Rosen Pub. 2010 112p il (A young woman's guide to contemporary issues) lib bdg $31.95

Grades: 7 8 9 10   613.9
  1. Pregnancy 2. Birth control 3. Teenage mothers
  ISBN 978-1-4358-3542-9; 1-4358-3542-5
                                  LC 2009-13721

"Explains reasons for using birth control to prevent pregnancy and disease, teaches the history of reproductive rights in the United States, and discusses options available to women facing unplanned pregnancies." Publisher's note

"Facts are shared in a conversational tone, creating the sense of a chat with a big sister. . . . [Though] designed for personal reading and browsing, the data provided are accurate and also lend themselves to use in reports." SLJ

Includes glossary and bibliographical references

Brynie, Faith Hickman, 1946-

101 questions about sex and sexuality—; with answers for the curious, cautious, and confused. Twenty-First Century Books 2003 176p il (101 questions) lib bdg $30.60

Grades: 8 9 10 11 12   613.9
  1. Sex education
  ISBN 0-7613-2310-4   LC 2002-11209

Uses a question-and-answer format to present information about the physical, emotional, and social topics surrounding sex and sexuality

"Brynie emphasizes abstinence as the only sure way of avoiding STDs and pregnancies, but also gives detailed information on contraception. . . . The matter-of-fact style is never condescending or alarmist in tone. . . . Explicit black-and-white illustrations lend an almost clinical touch. . . . The glossary; resource list of books, articles, and Web sites; and extensive citations make Brynie's title good for reports, while the directness of the presentation will appeal to general readers." SLJ

Includes bibliographical references

Hyde, Margaret Oldroyd, 1917-

Safe sex 101; an overview for teens; by Margaret O. Hyde and Elizabeth H. Forsyth. Twenty-First Century Books 2006 128p il (Teen overviews) lib bdg $26.60

Grades: 9 10 11 12   613.9
  1. Youth—Sexual behavior 2. Safe sex in AIDS prevention 3. Birth control 4. Sexually transmitted diseases
  ISBN 0-8225-3439-8; 978-0-8225-3439-6
                                  LC 2005-18806

Contents: How do you decide if you are ready for sex?; Do you choose abstinence?; Why learn about safe sex?; Secret lives of teens; Where you can learn about safe sex; How your sex organs work; What you should know about contraception; Working to prevent teen pregnancy and sexually transmitted diseases

"This thoughtfully written, well-organized introduction to safe-sex issues will make an excellent addition to any public or school library collection." Booklist

Includes bibliographical references

Pardes, Bronwen

Doing it right. Simon & Schuster 2007 143p il pa $14.99

Grades: 7 8 9 10 11 12   613.9
  1. Sex education
  ISBN 978-1-4169-1823-X; 1-4169-1823-X
                                  LC 2006-928450

On cover: making smart, safe, and satisfying choices about sex

The author "tackles the tough questions about sexual orientation, size, abuse, orgasm, pregnancy, STDs, and masturbation among others." Voice Youth Advocates

Pardes "strives to give teens the information they need, without judgment, to make their own decisions. She freely discusses sex without love, reproductive anatomy, transitioning as a transsexual, and sexually transmitted diseases. . . . The openness of this book will be a boon to teens looking for frank discussions of sexuality and making choices." SLJ

Includes bibliographical references

Sex education; Kristen Bailey, book editor. Greenhaven Press 2005 110p (At issue) hardcover o.p. pa $18.70

Grades: 9 10 11 12   613.9
  1. Sex education
  ISBN 0-7377-2418-8 (lib bdg); 0-7377-2419-6 (pa)
                                  LC 2004-49293

The articles in this anthology offer a variety of viewpoints on how sexuality should be taught to America's youth with chapters on abstinence and one addressing the needs of gay teens

Includes bibliographical references

Sexual health information for teens; edited by Sandra Augustyn Lawton. 2nd ed. Omnigraphics 2008 430p il (Teen health series) $69 *

Grades: 7 8 9 10 11 12   613.9
  1. Teenagers—Health and hygiene 2. Sex education
  ISBN 978-0-7808-1010-5; 0-7808-1010-4
                                  LC 2007052454

First published 2003

Sexual health information for teens—*Continued*

"Health tips about sexual development, reproduction, contraception, and sexually transmitted infections including facts about puberty, sexuality, birth control, chlamydia, gonorrhea, herpes, human papillomavirus, syphilis, and more." Title page

"This offering represents the most up-to-date information available on an array of topics. . . . The range of coverage . . . is thorough and extensive. Each chapter includes a bibliographic citation, and the three back sections containing additional resources, further reading, and the index are all first-rate. The few illustrations and diagrams range in quality from good to excellent." SLJ

Includes bibliographical references

Teenage sexuality: opposing viewpoints; Ken R. Wells, book editor. Greenhaven Press 2006 224p il lib bdg $34.95; pa $23.70 *

Grades: 9 10 11 12   **613.9**
  1. Youth—Sexual behavior 2. Sex education
  ISBN 0-7377-3362-4 (lib bdg); 0-7377-3363-2 (pa)
          LC 2005-52664

"Opposing viewpoints series"

Issues covered include teenagers' attitudes about sex, teen pregnancy, sex education, and teenage homosexuality.

Includes bibliographical references

614   Forensic medicine; incidence of injuries, wounds, disease; public preventive medicine

Adams, Bradley J.

Forensic anthropology. Chelsea House 2007 103p il (Inside forensic science) $32.95

Grades: 9 10 11 12   **614**
  1. Forensic anthropology
  ISBN 978-0-7910-9198-2; 0-7910-9198-8
          LC 2006-11030

"This book provides specific information on procedures, tools of the trade, and the science behind this fascinating field, as well as the challenges faced by today's practitioners." Publisher's note

Includes glossary and bibliographical references

Adelman, Howard C.

Forensic medicine. Chelsea House 2007 104p il map (Inside forensic science) $32.95

Grades: 9 10 11 12   **614**
  1. Medical jurisprudence 2. Forensic sciences
  ISBN 978-0-7910-8926-2; 0-7910-8926-6
          LC 2006-20617

This book "is intended as an introduction to the topic [of forensic medicine], which is also known as forensic pathology. Many of the medical terms used in this specialty are defined, and basic physiologic processes are explained." Publisher's note

Includes glossary and bibliographical references

Bass, William M., 1928-

Death's acre; inside the legendary forensic lab the Body Farm where the dead do tell tales; [by] Bill Bass and Jon Jefferson; foreword by Patricia Cornwell. Putnam 2003 304p il $24.95; pa $15 *

Grades: 9 10 11 12 Adult   **614**
  1. Forensic anthropology
  ISBN 0-399-15134-6; 0-425-19832-4 (pa)
          LC 2003-46908

"The author explains the process of decomposition and how bones give clues to identify: approximate age, sex, height, and race, all of which are needed to bring the forensic scientist one step closer to putting a name to a corpse. He describes some of the cases he has been involved with and laughs at himself when he shares stories of mistakes and assumptions. Young adults will gain insight into the forensic process and appreciate Bass's dedication to the truth and his work." SLJ

Blum, Deborah

The poisoner's handbook; murder and the birth of forensic medicine in Jazz Age New York. Penguin Press 2010 319p $25.95; pa $16

Grades: 11 12 Adult   **614**
  1. Poisons and poisoning 2. Toxicology 3. Forensic sciences
  ISBN 978-1-59420-243-8; 1-59420-243-5; 978-0-14-311882-4 (pa); 0-14-311882-X (pa)
          LC 2009-26461

Chronicles the story of New York City's first forensic scientists to describe Jazz Age poisoning cases, including a family's inexplicable balding, Barnum and Bailey's Blue Man, and the crumbling bones of factory workers.

"Blum effectively balances the fast-moving detective story with a clear view of the scientific advances that her protagonists brought to the field. Caviar for true-crime fans and science buffs alike." Kirkus

Includes bibliographical references

Kobilinsky, Lawrence F.

Forensic DNA analysis; [by] Lawrence Kobilinsky, Louis Levine, Henrietta Margolis-Nunno. Chelsea House 2007 114p il (Inside forensic science) $32.95

Grades: 9 10 11 12   **614**
  1. DNA 2. Forensic sciences
  ISBN 978-0-7910-8923-1; 0-7910-8923-1
          LC 2006-25586

"DNA can be used for many applications, from figuring out whether someone is the father of a baby to determining whether a particular person was present at a crime scene. *Forensic DNA Analysis* takes readers through the analysis process and explains the possible results." Publisher's note

Includes glossary and bibliographical references

Lee, Henry C.

Blood evidence; how DNA is revolutionizing the way we solve crimes; [by] Henry C. Lee, Frank Tirnady. Perseus Bks. 2003 xxx, 418p $26

Grades: 11 12 Adult   **614**
  1. DNA fingerprinting 2. Forensic sciences
  ISBN 0-7382-0602-4   LC 2002-105970

Lee, Henry C.—*Continued*

This book "explains the principles and science behind DNA testing and shows how it has both helped solve some of the most puzzling criminal cases in recent history and been used to discredit eyewitness accounts and physical evidence found at the crime scene." Publisher's note

"This volume is an excellent introduction to the science and use of DNA analysis." Publ Wkly

Includes bibliographical references

Stripp, Richard A.

The forensic aspects of poisons. Chelsea House 2007 127p il (Inside forensic science) lib bdg $32.95

Grades: 9 10 11 12   **614**

1. Forensic sciences

ISBN 978-0-7910-9197-5   LC 2006-22825

This book "introduces students to the basic principles of forensic toxicology and the role of poisons in forensic science. Emphasis is placed on the common drugs and poisons that are encountered by a practicing forensic toxicologist and the approach to determining their medicolegal role in establishing the cause of death and disease. Topics explored include homicide by chemical means, the role of drugs and chemicals in other types of accidental and intentional deaths, and how the interpretation of such cases is utilized in the criminal court setting." Publisher's note

Includes glossary and bibliographical references

Walker, Sally M.

Written in bone; buried lives of Jamestown and Colonial Maryland. Carolrhoda Books 2009 144p il map $22.95 *

Grades: 6 7 8 9 10   **614**

1. Forensic sciences 2. Maryland—History 3. Jamestown (Va.)—History 4. United States—History—1600-1775, Colonial period 5. Excavations (Archeology)—United States

ISBN 978-0-8225-7135-3; 0-8225-7135-8

      LC 2007-10768

"Walker takes readers on an archaeological investigation of human and material remains from 17th- and 18th-century Jamestown and colonial Maryland, while addressing relevant topics in forensic anthropology, history, and archaeology. . . . The text succinctly explains complex forensic concepts. . . . Captioned, full-color photographs of skeletal, dental, and artifactual remains shed light on colonial life. Historical documents, illustrated maps, and anatomical drawings complement images of various specialists at work in the field. Photographs of reenactors performing period tasks . . . provide insight into the daily life of the recovered individuals." SLJ

Includes bibliographical references

Wecht, Cyril H., 1931-

Tales from the morgue; forensic answers to nine famous cases including the Scott Peterson & Chandra Levy cases; [by] Cyril Wecht and Mark Curriden with Angela Powell. Prometheus Books 2005 314p il $26

Grades: 11 12 Adult   **614**

1. Forensic sciences 2. Criminal investigation

ISBN 1-59102-353-X   LC 2005-17805

Pathologist Wecht "sorts out the evidence, or lack thereof, in the scandalous circumstances of Scott Peterson and Chandra Levy, explains why he thinks the JFK assassination was a conspiracy and agrees with the original Marilyn Monroe autopsy that found no signs of foul play. . . . What makes Wecht's arguments so persuasive is that he lets scientific facts—or at least his expert interpretation of them—do the talking." Publ Wkly

Includes bibliographical references

Zedeck, Beth E.

Forensic pharmacology; [by] Beth E. Zedeck and Morris S. Zedeck; series editor, Lawrence Kobilinsky. Chelsea House Publishers 2006 138p il (Inside forensic science) $30

Grades: 9 10 11 12   **614**

1. Forensic sciences 2. Pharmacology

ISBN 0-7910-8920-7; 978-0-7910-8920-0

      LC 2006-20624

"This book describes one aspect of forensic science: forensic pharmacology and toxicology of drugs and abuse. The reader is introduced to the daily work of the scientists, the principles of pharmacology and toxicology, the technical anaylsis of drugs, and the characteristics of eight major categories of drugs of abuse." Publisher's note

Includes glossary and bibliographical references

Zugibe, Frederick T.

Dissecting death; secrets of a medical examiner; [by] Frederick Zugibe and David L. Carroll. Broadway Books 2005 240p il $24.95; pa $14

Grades: 11 12 Adult   **614**

1. Forensic sciences 2. Medical jurisprudence 3. Criminal investigation

ISBN 0-7679-1879-7; 0-7679-1880-0 (pa)

      LC 2004-62889

Zugibe "presents 10 challenging cases he encountered, as well as his insights as a self-described Monday-morning quarterback on two of the most notorious crimes of the 1990s: the brutal slaying of JonBenét Ramsey and the murders of Nicole Brown Simpson and Ronald Goldman." Publ Wkly

The authors' "straightforward style makes for clear and fascinating reading, and the cases chosen are intriguing." Booklist

614.4 Incidence of and public measures to prevent disease

Do infectious diseases pose a threat? Diane Andrews Henningfeld, book editor. Greenhaven Press 2009 144p (At issue. Health) $31.80; pa $22.50

Grades: 9 10 11 12   **614.4**
1. Communicable diseases 2. Epidemics 3. Public health
ISBN   978-0-7377-4294-7;   0-7377-4294-1; 978-0-7377-4293-0 (pa); 0-7377-4293-3 (pa)
                              LC 2008049414

Discusses the return of epidemics in modern times, possible causes, and how they are tracked and controlled, and debates whether current preventative measures are effective.

Includes bibliographical references

Encyclopedia of plague and pestilence; from ancient times to the present; George Childs Kohn, editor. 3rd ed. Facts On File 2008 529p il map (Facts on File library of world history) $85 *

Grades: 11 12 Adult   **614.4**
1. Reference books 2. Epidemics—Encyclopedias
ISBN 978-0-8160-6935-4; 0-8160-6935-2
                              LC 2006-41296

First published 1995

This encyclopedia provides "descriptions of more than 700 epidemics, listed alphabetically by location of the outbreak. Each . . . entry includes when and where a particular epidemic began, how and why it happened, whom it affected, how it spread and ran its course, and its outcome and significance." Publisher's note

Includes bibliographical references

Epidemics: opposing viewpoints; David Haugen and Susan Musser, book editors. Greenhaven Press 2011 273p lib bdg $39.70; pa $26.50

Grades: 8 9 10 11 12   **614.4**
1. Epidemics
ISBN   978-0-7377-5219-9;   0-7377-5219-X; 978-0-7377-5220-5 (pa); 0-7377-5220-3 (pa)
                              LC 2010052249

Contents: Do epidemics pose a significant health risk?; How serious was the threat of an H1N1 swine flu pandemic?; Are vaccines harmful?; Are America and the world prepared for coming pandemics?

Articles in this anthology present opposing viewpoints on the subject of epidemics.

Includes bibliographical references

Farrell, Jeanette
Invisible enemies; stories of infectious diseases. 2nd ed. Farrar, Straus & Giroux 2005 272p il $18 *

Grades: 7 8 9 10   **614.4**
1. Communicable diseases
ISBN 0-374-33607-5   LC 2004-57668
First published 1998

The author "focuses on seven dreaded human diseases: smallpox, leprosy, plague, tuberculosis, malaria, cholera, and AIDS. Each chapter provides a description of the physical and psychological effects of the disease on its victims, early theories about its causes, and efforts made to avoid or cure it. Then the methods of research that revealed its cause and developed the means to control its spread are explained in fascinating detail. . . . If every science book for nonspecialists were written with such flair and attention to detail, science would soon become every student's favorite subject." SLJ

Includes glossary and bibliographical references

Goldsmith, Connie, 1945-
Invisible invaders; new and dangerous infectious diseases. Twenty-First Century Books 2006 111p il (Discovery!) lib bdg $29.27

Grades: 7 8 9 10   **614.4**
1. Communicable diseases
ISBN 978-0-8225-3416-7; 0-8225-3416-9
                              LC 2005-17271

This book covers "topics associated with current infectious diseases." Sci Books Films

"This title is a thorough, understandable, and accessible source of current information and medical definitions, and a trail to further research." SLJ

Includes bibliographical references

Grady, Denise
Deadly invaders; virus outbreaks around the world, from Marburg fever to avian flu. Kingfisher 2006 128p il map $16.95

Grades: 7 8 9 10   **614.4**
1. Communicable diseases 2. Viruses
ISBN 978-0-7534-5995-9; 0-7534-5995-7
                              LC 2006004441

"A New York Times book"

"In the first half of the book . . . Grady discusses the Marburg virus, the incurable disease it causes, and its effects on individuals and communities, as seen through the lens of her personal experiences in Angola. . . . Next she offers a short . . . chapter on each of seven deadly diseases: Marburg fever, avian flu, HIV/AIDS, Hantavirus pulmonary syndrome, West Nile disease, SARS, and monkeypox." Booklist

The "writing is informative and compelling. . . . The layout is appealing and includes good-quality, full-color, relevant photographs on almost every spread. . . . A fast-paced, timely, and important book." SLJ

Includes bibliographical references

McKenna, Maryn
Beating back the devil; on the front lines with the disease detectives of the Epidemic Intelligence Service. Free Press 2004 303p hardcover o.p. pa $21.95

Grades: 11 12 Adult   **614.4**
1. Centers for Disease Control and Prevention (U.S.). Epidemic Intelligence Service Program
ISBN 0-7432-5132-6; 1-4391-2310-1 (pa)
                              LC 2004-53214

McKenna, Maryn—*Continued*

"This book celebrates a group of unsung heroes, the Epidemic Intelligence Service (EIS) of the U.S. Centers for Disease Control. Since its inception in 1951, the EIS has sent officers around the world to investigate outbreaks of diseases from polio, smallpox, tuberculosis, SARS, and West Nile Virus to the bioterrorist anthrax attacks." Libr J

"This book should serve as an effective antidote for anyone suffering from the misconception that epidemologists must lead boring lives." Sci Books Films

Includes bibliographical references

Walters, Mark Jerome

Six modern plagues and how we are causing them. Island Press 2003 206p $22; pa $14

Grades: 11 12 Adult   **614.4**

1. Epidemiology 2. Communicable diseases 3. Environmental health 4. Human ecology

ISBN   1-55963-992-X;   978-1-55963-992-7; 1-55963-714-5 (pa); 978-1-55963-714-5 (pa)

LC 2003-15137

The author "examines six modern diseases: mad cow disease, HIV/AIDS, salmonella DT104, Lyme disease, hantavirus, and West Nile virus. Highlighting the main features of the history and impact of each of these diseases, he presents them as 'parables of the unintended consequences of the careless human disruption of the natural systems that are our home.'" Choice

"A quick read and a great introduction to the topic." Libr J

Includes bibliographical references

614.5   Incidence of and public measures to prevent specific diseases and kinds of diseases

Barbour, Scott, 1963-

Is the world prepared for a deadly influenza pandemic? ReferencePoint Press 2010 96p il (In controversy) lib bdg $26.95

Grades: 9 10 11 12   **614.5**

1. Influenza

ISBN 978-1-60152-127-9; 1-60152-127-8

LC 2010-5859

In this book "the lessons of past pandemics are brought to bear on current realities, from lapses in internal cooperation to differing views on mandatory vaccination." Booklist

Includes bibliographical references

Byrne, Joseph Patrick

The black death; [by] Joseph P. Byrne. Greenwood Press 2004 xxx, 231p il map (Greenwood guides to historic events of the medieval world) $45 *

Grades: 9 10 11 12   **614.5**

1. Plague

ISBN 0-313-32492-1   LC 2004-43640

This book "describes the bubonic plague that destroyed large European populations in the 14th century. . . . [The author] has compiled an outstanding reference discussing many theories about the possible causes, transmission, societal implications, economic consequences, and impact on modern medicine." SLJ

Includes bibliographical references

Crosby, Molly Caldwell

The American plague; the untold story of yellow fever, the epidemic that shaped our history. Berkley Books 2006 308p il $24.95

Grades: 11 12 Adult   **614.5**

1. Yellow fever

ISBN 0-425-21202-5; 978-0-425-21202-8

LC 2006-50497

This book tells the "story of yellow fever, recounting Memphis Tennessee's near-destruction and resurrection from the epidemic—and the four men who changed medical history with their battle against an invisible foe that remains a threat to this very day." Publisher's note

The author "offers a forceful narrative of a disease's ravages and the quest to find its cause and cure." Publ Wkly

Includes bibliographical references

Cunningham, Kevin, 1966-

Flu. Morgan Reynolds Pub. 2009 176p il (Diseases in history) lib bdg $28.95

Grades: 8 9 10 11 12   **614.5**

1. Influenza

ISBN 978-1-59935-105-6; 1-59935-105-6

LC 2008-51620

"This informative title reveals the continued concerns surrounding this killer disease and the possibility of a future pandemic. The text, though somewhat scientific, will help students to better understand the history of the virus, how it has mutated and jumped from animals to humans, and new concerns regarding more dangerous forms. . . . Color and black-and-white archival photos, as well as reproduction of a three-dimensional rendering of the flu virus, enhance the text." SLJ

Includes glossary and bibliographical references

Malaria. Morgan Reynolds Pub. 2009 144p il (Diseases in history) lib bdg $28.95

Grades: 8 9 10 11 12   **614.5**

1. Malaria

ISBN 978-1-59935-103-2; 1-59935-103-X

LC 2008-51619

This book "begins with an explanation of the development, the cycle, and conditions conducive to spreading the disease through a parasite, which is clarified with an accompanying illustration of the life cycle. The book continues with a chapter on the relationship of farming practices and land characteristics to the spread, and how the disease affected past civilizations." SLJ

"Provides fascinating information about an ongoing scourge. . . . Here readers have an accessible, well presented account of the continuing struggle against a deadly disease." Voice Youth Advocates

Includes glossary and bibliographical references

Cunningham, Kevin, 1966-—*Continued*
Plague. Morgan Reynolds Pub. 2009 144p il (Diseases in history) lib bdg $28.95
Grades: 8 9 10 11 12   **614.5**
1. Plague
ISBN 978-1-59935-102-5; 1-59935-102-1
LC 2008-51618
"Chapters based upon plagues include one on Justinian's Plague, the Black Death, The Dreadful Pestilence, the Great Plague of London, and the current H1N1 swine flu pandemic. This detailed overview . . . will appeal to more advanced students. The research is thorough and the writing is insightful, thought provoking, and accessible." Voice Youth Advocates
Includes glossary and bibliographical references

Goldsmith, Connie, 1945-
Influenza: the next pandemic? Twenty-First Century Books 2007 112p il (Twenty-first century medical library) lib bdg $27.93
Grades: 6 7 8 9 10   **614.5**
1. Influenza
ISBN 978-0-7613-9457-0; 0-7613-9457-5
LC 2005-23588
The author "traces the history of the flu, giving attention to past outbreaks and epidemics. She also describes flu viruses of today, explains treatments, and details health officials' concerns about bird flu. . . . Good for reports, and a worthy source to update collections." SLJ
Includes bibliographical references

Grady, Sean M., 1965-
Biohazards; humanity's battle with infectious disease; [by] Sean M. Grady and John Tabak. Facts on File 2006 194p il map (Science & technology in focus) $35 *
Grades: 7 8 9 10   **614.5**
1. Communicable diseases
ISBN 0-8160-4687-5   LC 2005-5610
This "work . . . examines the bacteria and viruses that make up a significant part of our world. The threat of bioterrorism; the risks of international travel; the spread, control, and treatment of such newly important diseases as anthrax, hantavirus, and HIV/AIDS, as well as historical ones like the Black Plague and smallpox, are clearly discussed." SLJ
Includes bibliographical references

Johnson, Steven
The ghost map; the story of London's most terrifying epidemic—and how it changed science, cities, and the modern world. Riverhead 2006 299p il map $26.95
Grades: 11 12 Adult   **614.5**
1. Snow, John, 1813-1858 2. Cholera
ISBN 1-59448-925-4; 978-1-59448-925-9
LC 2006-23114
This book "takes place in the summer of 1854. A devastating cholera outbreak seizes London just as it is emerging as a modern city. . . . Dr. John Snow—whose ideas about contagion had been dismissed by the scientif-

ic community—is spurred to intense action when the people in his neighborhood begin dying. . . . Johnson chronicles Snow's day-by-day efforts, as he risks his own life to prove how the epidemic is being spread." Publisher's note
"From Snow's discovery of patient zero to Johnson's compelling argument for and celebration of cities, this makes for an illuminating and satisfying read." Publ Wkly
Includes bibliographical references

Jurmain, Suzanne
The secret of the yellow death; a true story of medical sleuthing. Houghton Mifflin Books for Children 2009 104p il $19
Grades: 6 7 8 9 10   **614.5**
1. Reed, Walter, 1851-1902 2. Yellow fever 3. Medicine—Research 4. Epidemics 5. Cuba—History
ISBN 978-0-618-96581-6; 0-618-96581-5
LC 2009-22499
"Jurmain recounts the six months in 1900 when Dr. Walter Reed and his team of doctors in Cuba determined that mosquitoes carry yellow fever." Kirkus
"This medical mystery is extremely interesting, easy to read, and well illustrated with period photos." SLJ
Includes glossary and bibliographical references

Marlink, Richard G., 1954-
Global AIDS crisis; a reference handbook; [by] Richard G. Marlink and Alison G Kotin. ABC-CLIO 2004 283p il map (Contemporary world issues) $50 *
Grades: 9 10 11 12   **614.5**
1. AIDS (Disease)
ISBN 1-85109-655-8   LC 2004-21402
"Focusing on the worldwide scope of the crisis, this handbook examines a variety of aspects of AIDS in historical, contemporary, and future contexts. . . . A useful resource for students doing research on the worldwide impact of AIDS." SLJ
Includes bibliographical references

Oshinsky, David M., 1944-
Polio; an American story. Oxford University Press 2005 342p il $30; pa $16.95
Grades: 11 12 Adult   **614.5**
1. Poliomyelitis vaccine
ISBN 0-19-515294-8; 0-19-530714-3 (pa)
LC 2004-25249
This is an account of the "effort to find a cure [for polio], from the March of Dimes to the discovery of the Salk and Sabin vaccines." Publisher's note
This book "is a rich and illuminating analysis that convincingly grounds the ways and means of modern American research in the response to polio." N Y Times Book Rev
Includes bibliographical references

Pierce, John R.

Yellow jack; how yellow fever ravaged America and Walter Reed discovered its deadly secrets; [by] John R. Pierce, Jim Writer. J. Wiley 2005 278p il $24.95

Grades: 11 12 Adult   **614.5**
1. Reed, Walter, 1851-1902 2. Yellow fever
ISBN 0-471-47261-1   LC 2004-13845

The authors "describe the probable African origins of the disease, its 350-year history in the Caribbean, and the deadly epidemics that terrorized the colonies and early United States." Sci Books Films

"This chronicle of the rise and eventual fall of yellow fever traces a substantial medical history." Booklist

Includes bibliographical references

Preston, Richard

The hot zone. Random House 1994 300p pa $14 hardcover o.p.

Grades: 11 12 Adult   **614.5**
1. Ebola virus 2. Animal experimentation
ISBN 0-385-49522-6 (pa)   LC 94-13415

"Ebola, a lethal virus that slumbers in an unknown host somewhere in the rain forest, sneaked into the United States in 1989 in a shipment of primates that ended up in a monkey house in Reston, Virginia. This virus jumps between species easily, and takes only weeks to kill its victim, with gory hemorrhaging from various orifices. Preston tells the suspenseful tale of its detection, and gives vivid life to the members of the SWAT team that, for eighteen bio-hazardous days, combatted the strain now known as Ebola Reston." New Yorker

Sehgal, Alfica

Leprosy; foreword by David Heymann. Chelsea House 2006 88p il (Deadly diseases and epidemics) $31.95

Grades: 9 10 11 12   **614.5**
1. Leprosy
ISBN 0-7910-8502-3   LC 2005-10391

Contents: An introduction to leprosy; The spread, signs, and types of leprosy; Leprosy around the world; What causes leprosy?; Host-pathogen interactions; Bringing leprosy under control; Bacteria do not like test tubes; Ongoing reforms and the future

Includes glossary and bibliographical references

Smith, Tara C., 1976-

Ebola and Marburg viruses. 2nd ed. Chelsea House Publishers 2011 104p il (Deadly diseases and epidemics) lib bdg $34.95

Grades: 8 9 10 11 12   **614.5**
1. Ebola virus 2. Marburg virus
ISBN 978-1-60413-252-6; 1-60413-252-3
                                            LC 2010032999

First published 2005

This describes the outbreaks of Marburg and Ebola viruses, their characteristics and ecology, detection and treatment, developing a vaccine, and other hemorrhagic fevers.

Includes glossary and bibliographical references

Spurlock, Morgan, 1970-

Don't eat this book; fast food and the supersizing of America. G. P. Putnam's Sons 2005 308p hardcover o.p. pa $14 *

Grades: 9 10 11 12 Adult   **614.5**
1. Convenience foods 2. Food industry 3. Restaurants
ISBN 0-399-15260-1; 0-425-21023-5 (pa)
                                            LC 2005-43196

The author "describes America's obesity epidemic, its relation to the fast food industry, the industry's cozy relations to U.S. government agencies and how the problem is spreading worldwide. . . . His book is a powerful tool in his rip-roaring campaign to turn around America's love-hate relationship with fast food." Publ Wkly

Includes bibliographical references

Zahler, Diane

The Black Death. Twenty-First Century Books 2009 160p il map (Pivotal moments in history) lib bdg $38.60 *

Grades: 7 8 9 10   **614.5**
1. Plague 2. Middle Ages
ISBN 978-0-8225-9076-7; 0-8225-9076-X
                                            LC 2008-26878

This book discusses the pivotal moment in history when one out of three people died and changed the course of world history, the Black Death.

"This is a well-written and well-researched volume. Full-color illustrations, a note explaining the value of primary sources, a who's who, and careful source notes make this book a valuable addition to history collections." SLJ

Includes glossary and bibliographical references

615 Pharmacology and therapeutics

Allman, Toney, 1947-

Vaccine research. ReferencePoint Press 2010 c2011 96p il (Inside science) lib bdg $26.95

Grades: 7 8 9 10   **615**
1. Vaccination 2. Medicine—Research
ISBN 978-1-60152-131-6; 1-60152-131-6
                                            LC 2010-20635

"This title examines the science behind vaccine research." Publisher's note

This book "offers the necessary information for stellar reports. Politics, debates, and ethical concerns are briefly and fairly mentioned, but the . . . [book concentrates] on consistent, documented, and well-balanced scientific coverage. The human stories sprinkled throughout will help kids identify with both scientists and patients." SLJ

Includes bibliographical references

Amphetamines; edited by Nancy Harris. Greenhaven Press 2005 174p (History of drugs) $34.95

Grades: 9 10 11 12   **615**
1. Amphetamines 2. Methamphetamine
ISBN 0-7377-1949-4   LC 2004-40577

This anthology discusses the history of amphetamine use and the different varieties used over the years, including Ecstacy and methamphetamines. It also discusses how some amphetamines have been used as medicine.

Includes bibliographical references

Antidepressants; edited by William Dudley. Greenhaven Press 2005 188p (History of drugs) $34.95

Grades: 9 10 11 12   **615**

1. Antidepressants

ISBN 0-7377-1951-6   LC 2004-52357

This "anthology traces the history of the invention and selling of antidepressants and their impact on American society. It also examines controversies about their safety and effectiveness." Publisher's note

Includes bibliographical references

Facklam, Margery, 1927-

Modern medicines; the discovery and development of healing drugs; Margery Facklam, Howard Facklam, and Sean M. Grady. rev ed. Facts on File 2004 226p il (Science & technology in focus) $35 *

Grades: 7 8 9 10   **615**

1. Pharmacology 2. Drugs

ISBN 0-8160-4706-5   LC 2003-11489

First published 1992 with title: Healing drugs: the history of pharmacology

Contents: Ancient remedies; A garden of simples; Patent cures and medicine shows; Formalizing pharmacology; A world of wonder drugs; Preemptive strikes; Biological systems management; Miracles in the medicine cabinet; From the laboratory to the pharmacy; Producing modern pills and potions; New uses for old drugs; When drugs go wrong; Back to the Garden?; Herbalists and scientists; Warning signs; Drug-resistant germs; The perils of medicine; Distribution woes; Future trends in pharmacology

"Straightforward, sensibly organized, and well researched, this volume . . . is an excellent introduction." Booklist

Foster, Steven, 1957-

National Geographic desk reference to nature's medicine; [by] Steven Foster and Rebecca L. Johnson. National Geographic Society 2006 416p il map $40

Grades: 11 12 Adult   **615**

1. Medical botany 2. Materia medica 3. Reference books

ISBN 978-0-7922-3666-5; 0-7922-3666-1

The authors "offer an engaging, authoritative, and succinct work on traditional and current medicinal uses for a variety of plants, guidelines for cultivation and preparation, recent research, and cautions. Using a two-page format for each plant, the volume is arranged alphabetically. Sidebars feature colored botanical drawings, color photographs, habitat maps, and interesting information that enlivens the understanding of human experience with the plants." Choice

Includes bibliographical references

Goldsmith, Connie, 1945-

Superbugs strike back; when antibiotics fail. Twenty-First Century Books 2007 112p il (Discovery!) lib bdg $29.27

Grades: 7 8 9 10   **615**

1. Drug resistance 2. Bacteria 3. Antibiotics

ISBN 978-0-8225-6607-6; 0-8225-6607-9

LC 2006-10726

"The emergence of 'superbugs'—antibiotic resistant bacteria—and the threat they pose to public health are examined in this detailed introduction. . . . Full-color tables, sidebars, diagrams, and good-quality photos and micrographs are interspersed throughout. The text is meticulous without being tedious." SLJ

Includes glossary and bibliographical references

Hager, Thomas

The demon under the microscope; from battlefield hospitals to Nazi labs, one doctor's heroic search for the world's first miracle drug. Harmony Books 2006 340p $24.95

Grades: 11 12 Adult   **615**

1. Domagk, Gerhard, 1895-1964 2. Sulfonamides

ISBN 1-4000-8213-7; 978-1-4000-8213-1

LC 2006-4510

The author "narrates the story of the race [by doctors such as Gerhard Domagk] to find the 'magic bullet' to eliminate diseases such as pneumonia, childbed fever, and gonorrhea. . . . Hager connects early innovations in medicine to the fortuitous and intuitive leaps that allowed early 20th-century researchers to create sulfa, the first antibiotic. . . . One is left with a sense of gratitude for the relative safety of modern medical practices." Libr J

Includes bibliographical references

Hallucinogens; edited by Mary E. Williams. Greenhaven Press 2005 203p (History of drugs) $34.95

Grades: 9 10 11 12   **615**

1. Hallucinogens

ISBN 0-7377-1959-1   LC 2004-52394

"Authors discuss the development of such drugs as LSD, mescaline, and psilocybin, defining their dangers, describing their influence on the 1960s counterculture, and debating their potential therapeutic uses." Publisher's note

Includes bibliographical references

Kidd, J. S. (Jerry S.)

Potent natural medicines; Mother Nature's pharmacy; [by] J.S. Kidd and Renee A. Kidd. rev ed. Chelsea House 2006 212p il (Science and society) $35 *

Grades: 7 8 9 10   **615**

1. Pharmacology 2. Medical botany

ISBN 0-8160-5607-2   LC 2005041741

First published 1998 with title: Mother Nature's pharmacy

This introduces "plants' medicinal properties, pioneers who hunted for sources of and applications for botanical treatments, and the ways phytochemical nutrients prevent disease. . . . [Also included] are chapters about recent

Kidd, J. S. (Jerry S.)—*Continued*
research, including investigation into animal sources for
medicine; the impact of field research on native peoples;
and the federal regulation of herb and plant supplements.
. . . This [is] a good choice to support research and debate projects." Booklist
Includes bibliographical references

Klosterman, Lorrie
The facts about drugs and the body. Marshall
Cavendish Benchmark 2006 143p il (Drugs) lib
bdg $42.79
Grades: 7 8 9 10 11 12   615
1. Drugs
ISBN 978-0-7614-2675-2; 0-7614-2675-2
      LC 2007-2260
This discusses the effects of various drugs on the nervous, cardiovascular, respiratory, digestive, and reproductive systems of the body.
"Klosterman has done an excellent job of demonstrating how drugs affect the body functions. The illustrations
and captions enhance the information to make it more
understandable." SLJ
Includes glossary and bibliographical references

Lax, Eric
The mold in Dr. Florey's coat; the story of the
penicillin miracle. Henry Holt and Co. 2004 307p
il hardcover o.p. pa $15 *
Grades: 9 10 11 12 Adult   615
1. Penicillin
ISBN 0-8050-6790-6; 0-8050-7778-2 (pa)
      LC 2003-56685
"A John Macrae book"
Penicillin was discovered in 1928. "But it took a team
of Oxford scientists headed by Howard Florey and Ernest
Chain four more years to develop it as the first antibiotic. . . . Lax tells the story behind the discovery and why
it took so long to develop the drug." Publisher's note
"In this fluent, entertaining report on the history of the
arguably most significant medical discovery of the twentieth century, Lax delves into the lives of the colorful
scientists who played significant roles in developing the
antibiotic." Booklist
Includes bibliographical references

The **Merck** index; an encyclopedia of chemicals,
drugs, and biologicals; Maryadele J. O'Neil,
editor; Patricia E. Heckelman, senior associate
editor; Cherie B. Koch, associate editor; Kristin
J. Roman, assistant editor; Catherine M. Kenny,
editorial assistant; Maryann R. D'Arecca,
administrative assistant. 14th ed. Merck 2006
various paging il $125 *
Grades: 11 12 Adult   615
1. Materia medica—Dictionaries 2. Drugs—Dictionaries 3. Reference books
ISBN 0-911910-00-X; 978-0-911910-00-1
Also available CD-ROM version and online
First published 1889. Periodically revised
Includes CD-ROM

"Technical descriptions of the preparation, properties,
uses, commercial names, and toxicity of drugs and medicines." N Y Public Libr Book of How & Where to Look
It Up

Naden, Corinne J.
The facts about the A-Z of drugs; [by] Corinne
Naden. Marshall Cavendish Benchmark 2007
c2008 156p il (Drugs) lib bdg $42.79
Grades: 7 8 9 10 11 12   615
1. Drugs
ISBN 978-0-7614-2673-8; 0-7614-2673-6
      LC 2007-2267
This discusses drug classifications such as depressants,
hallucinogens, inhalants, narcotics, and stimulants, and
includes an alphabetically arranged description of various
drugs.
This is "well-organized, attractively illustrated, current,
and highly informative." Sci Books Films
Includes glossary and bibliographical references

Rooney, Anne
Dealing with drugs. Amicus 2010 c2011 46p il
(Healthy lifestyles) lib bdg $32.80
Grades: 7 8 9 10   615
1. Drugs
ISBN 978-1-60753-084-8; 1-60753-084-8
"Discusses the risks and realities of teenage drug use
and abuse, including alcohol, marijuana, tobacco, pre-
scription drugs, steroids, inhalants, party drugs such as
ecstasy, and more." Publisher's note
This book is "well-written and satisfyingly informa-
tive. . . . [The] magazine-like format includes numerous
sidebars, color photos, and charts." SLJ
Includes glossary

Winner, Cherie
Circulating life; blood transfusion from ancient
superstition to modern medicine. Twenty-First
Century Books 2007 112p il (Discovery!) $30.60
Grades: 7 8 9 10   615
1. Blood—Transfusion
ISBN 978-0-8225-6606-9; 0-8225-6606-0
      LC 2006-29921
Contents: A fine humor: early ideas about blood; A
closer look at blood; The first transfusions; Answers at
last; Taking blood apart; Old fears, new dangers; Twenty-first century blood transfusion; The future of transfusion
This "compendium is both a history of the art of
transfusions and a scientific discourse on the chemistry
of blood. From early 'bleeding treatments' to the discovery of the circulatory system; from the earliest attempts
at transfusions to Charles Drew's heroic work with plasma in World War II, Winner's clear text takes readers on
an epic trip." SLJ
Includes bibliographical references

615.5   Therapeutics

The **Gale** encyclopedia of alternative medicine; edited by Laurie J. Fundukian, editor. 3rd ed. Gale, Cengage Learning 2009 4v il set $540

Grades: 11 12 Adult **615.5**
1. Alternative medicine—Encyclopedias 2. Reference books
ISBN 978-1-4144-4872-5   LC 2008-16097
First published 2001

This encyclopedia "identifies 150 types of alternative medicine being practiced today, including reflexology, acupressure, acupuncture, chelation therapy, kinesiology, yoga, chiropractic, Feldenkrais, polarity therapy, detoxification, naturopathy, Chinese medicine, biofeedback, Ayurveda and osteopathy." Publisher's note
Includes bibliographical references

Navarra, Tova
The encyclopedia of complementary and alternative medicine; foreword by Adam Perelman. Facts on File 2004 xxiii, 276p $75; pa $18.95

Grades: 11 12 Adult **615.5**
1. Alternative medicine—Encyclopedias 2. Reference books
ISBN 0-8160-4997-1; 0-8160-6226-9 (pa)
                        LC 2003-43415
"The topics in this book . . . range from yoga, chiropractic, and homeopathy to herbal remedies, imagery and visualization, massage, medication, and naturopathy. . . . Besides the entries, this important resource offers appendixes that list professional and lay organizations and herbs used in varieties of medical disciplines, and a time line of the various therapies." Choice
Includes bibliographical references

615.8   Specific therapies and kinds of therapies

Marcovitz, Hal
Gene therapy research. ReferencePoint Press 2010 96p il (Inside science) lib bdg $26.95

Grades: 7 8 9 10 11 12 **615.8**
1. Gene therapy 2. Medicine—Research
ISBN 978-1-60152-108-8; 1-60152-108-1
                        LC 2009-41686
"Opening with an account of successful gene therapy for a rare eye disease, this introduction to the research goes on to speculate about future applications for other inherited diseases. Beginning with basic definitions of such terms as *gene, human genome,* and *DNA,* the well-organized narrative explains the impact of viruses, drugs, cloning, and stem cells on gene therapy and describes recent research." Booklist

Panno, Joseph
Gene therapy; treatments and cures for genetic diseases. Rev. ed. Facts On File 2010 c2011 236p il (The new biology) $40 *

Grades: 9 10 11 12 **615.8**
1. Gene therapy
ISBN 978-0-8160-6850-0   LC 2009-45854

First published 2004
Thsi book "discusses the science behind gene therapy, as well as the ethical and legal issues associated with this therapy." Publisher's note
Includes glossary and bibliographical references

West, Krista
Biofeedback. Chelsea House 2007 98p il (Gray matter) lib bdg $32.95

Grades: 8 9 10 11 12 **615.8**
1. Biofeedback training 2. Brain
ISBN 978-0-7910-9436-5; 0-7910-9436-7
                        LC 2006-101019
"Highlights the uses of this treatment for physical and mental conditions. Brain-wave instruments are explored, studies are noted, and careers in the field are identified. . . . Highly recommended for curriculum support for middle school and high school students who will easily absorb the material presented." Voice Youth Advocates
Includes glossary and bibliographical references

615.9   Toxicology

Brands, Danielle A.
Salmonella. Chelsea House 2005 102p il (Deadly diseases and epidemics) $31.95

Grades: 7 8 9 10 **615.9**
1. Salmonellosis
ISBN 0-7910-8500-7   LC 2005-5348
Contents: Salmonella strikes at the senior prom; Salmonella and food-borne illness; Hosts, sources, and carriers; Salmonella in the body; Treating salmonellosis; Salmonella outbreaks and current research; Other bacteria that cause food poisoning; Preventing salmonellosis
Includes glossary and bibliographical references

Grossman, Elizabeth, 1957-
Chasing molecules; poisonous products, human health, and the promise of green chemistry. Island Press/Shearwater Books 2009 249p $26.95

Grades: 11 12 Adult **615.9**
1. Toxicology 2. Environmental chemistry 3. Commercial products
ISBN 978-1-59726-370-2; 1-59726-370-2
                        LC 2009-28279
The author "tracks the migration of synthetic, petroleum-based molecules emitted by pesticides, cosmetics, food containers, and vinyl. . . . She accompanies scientists to China, the Great Lakes, and the Arctic, where these persistent and pernicious chemicals (82,000 and counting) are found in alarming quantities. . . . Green chemistry aims to replace hazardous synthetic chemicals with chemicals that are 'benign by design.' Grossman's clarion exposé should give this lifesaving initiative a big boost." Booklist
Includes bibliographical references

Landau, Elaine

Food poisoning and foodborne diseases. Twenty-First Century Books 2010 128p il (USA Today health reports: diseases and disorders) lib bdg $34.60

Grades: 7 8 9 10 11 12   **615.9**
1. Communicable diseases 2. Food poisoning
ISBN 978-0-8225-7290-9; 0-8225-7290-7
LC 2009-20325

This book "will drawn an audience with its everyday examples of food risks as well as instructions about how to buy, prepare, cook, and store food. . . . Also included are warnings about how to keep hands and kitchen surfaces clean and what to watch out for in cafeteria and fast-food outlets. . . . [The] accessible design extends the impressive educational data." Booklist

Includes bibliographical references

Satin, Morton

Food alert! the ultimate sourcebook for food safety. 2nd ed. Facts On File 2008 350p il $39.95; pa $14.95 *

Grades: 9 10 11 12 Adult   **615.9**
1. Food contamination 2. Diseases 3. Consumer protection
ISBN   978-0-8160-6968-2;   0-8160-6968-9; 978-0-8160-6969-9 (pa); 0-8160-6969-7 (pa)
LC 2008-11038

First published 1999

The author "divides the text into four major segments: the complex history of food poisoning; major food sources and their characteristic pathogens; dangers extant at the consumer product and home-preservation levels; and pathogens' assorted forms. Three appendixes offer charts detailing various fungal, bacterial, and parasitic types; food preservation guidance; and informational web sites. [This is] accessibly written and extremely well-organized." Libr J

Includes bibliographical references

616   Diseases

Bakalar, Nick

Where the germs are; a scientific safari; {by} Nicholas Bakalar. Wiley 2003 262p il $24.95 *

Grades: 9 10 11 12 Adult   **616**
1. Microbiology 2. Germ theory of disease 3. Bacteria
ISBN 0-471-15589-6   LC 2003-271569

This book is "about our everyday interactions with microbes. . . . It reveals some of the extraordinary things scientists now know about these most ordinary companions." Publisher's note

The author's "excellent chapter on childhood diseases and vaccines should be required reading for parents, and teenagers should be plunked down in a chair with the chapter on sexually transmitted diseases. . . . His writing is witty, and he gives all the details of germs and illnesses without medical school jargon." Publ Wkly

Includes glossary and bibliographical references

Diseases; Bryan Bunch and Jenny Tesar, editors. 3rd rev ed. Scholastic Library Pub. 2006 8v il set $349

Grades: 6 7 8 9 10   **616**
1. Diseases—Encyclopedias 2. Reference books
ISBN 0-7172-6205-7   LC 2006-7986

First published 1997

Alphabetically arranged articles presenting medical information on more than 500 diseases, discussing causes, symptoms, stages of the disease, its likelihood of striking, treatments, prevention, and long-term effects.

"Students will find a goldmine of basic reference information in these attractive . . . volumes." SLJ

Includes bibliographical references

Diseases and disorders. Marshall Cavendish 2007 3v il set $399.93

Grades: 9 10 11 12 Adult   **616**
1. Diseases 2. Medicine
ISBN 978-0-7614-7770-9   LC 2007-60867

"This set provides overview articles on 46 health issues (infertility, ear disorders, trauma, etc.) and basic descriptions of 94 infectious diseases, 139 noninfectious diseases and disorders, and 26 mental disorders. . . . A typical entry starts with a summary statement, followed by descriptions and discussions of causes, symptoms, prevention, diagnosis, and treatments. . . . The presentation of concise factual information in accessible language and in appropriate introductory amounts is a strength of this set. It is also a good starting point to further study through use of its resources lists." Booklist

Includes bibliographical references

Diseases, disorders, and injuries. Marshall Cavendish Reference 2010 c2011 320p il $85.64

Grades: 9 10 11 12   **616**
1. Medicine—Encyclopedias 2. Diseases—Encyclopedias 3. Wounds and injuries—Encyclopedias 4. Reference books
ISBN 978-0-7614-7935-2   LC 2010010057

This is "a simplified and much shorter version of Marshall Cavendish's 18-volume Encyclopedia of Health (2010). . . . More than 200 subjects are arranged A–Z. Articles for diseases and conditions include a description, with causes, symptoms, diagnosis, treatment, and prevention. Articles for parts of the body cover their function and location. Q&A sidebars (written as if by young people) are included in every article." Booklist

The **Gale** encyclopedia of genetic disorders; Laurie J. Fundukain, editor. 3rd ed. Gale 2010 c2011 2v il set $445

Grades: 9 10 11 12   **616**
1. Medical genetics—Encyclopedias 2. Reference books
ISBN 978-1-4144-7602-5; 1-4144-7602-7
LC 2010-2222

First published 2001 under the editorship of Stacey L. Blachford

This encyclopedia provides "information on genetic disorders, including conditions, tests, procedures, treatments and therapies. . . . [The disorders covered include] Down Syndrome, Trisomy, Hemophilia and Tourette Syndrome, and rarely seen diseases such as Meckel Syndrome, Neuraminidase Deficiency and

The Gale encyclopedia of genetic disorders—
Continued
Phenylketonuria." Publisher's note
Includes bibliographical references

Hains, Bryan C.
Pain; series editor, Eric H. Chudler. Chelsea House Publishers 2006 121p il (Gray matter) lib bdg $32.95
Grades: 8 9 10 11 12   616
1. Pain 2. Brain
ISBN 0-7910-8951-7; 978-0-7910-8951-4
                                         LC 2006-15133
This book "explores the workings of the somatosensory and pain systems, how disorders can affect how we process information with these systems, and how pain can be treated." Publisher's note
Includes glossary and bibliographical references

Human diseases and conditions; Miranda Herbert Ferrara, project editor. 2nd ed. Charles Scribner's Sons/Gale Cengage Learning 2010 4v il set $340 *
Grades: 9 10 11 12 Adult   616
1. Medicine—Encyclopedias 2. Reference books
ISBN 978-0-684-31238-5; 0-684-31238-7
                                         LC 2009-6533
First published 2000
"The entries include a brief definition and the phonetic spelling of the term and cover what the disease or condition is and its prevalence, etiology, symptoms, and prevention and treatment. Some entries begin with a brief story about someone who has the disease, and each ends with a list of relevant resources of articles, books, web sites, or health organizations, as well as cross-references. The illustrations are in color, as are term definitions in the margins. . . . The entries are accessible to patrons from a high school reading level and above, and the colorful display adds appeal." Libr J
Includes glossary and bibliographical references

Marcovitz, Hal
Stem cell research. ReferencePoint Press 2011 96p il (Inside science) lib bdg $26.95
Grades: 7 8 9 10   616
1. Stem cell research
ISBN 978-1-60152-130-9; 1-60152-130-8
                                         LC 2010-4128
Discusses the science behind stem cell research and the ways in which stem cells can be used in treatment of disease.
This book "offers the necessary information for stellar reports. Politics, debates, and ethical concerns are briefly and fairly mentioned, but the . . . [book concentrates] on consistent, documented, and well-balanced scientific coverage. The human stories sprinkled throughout will help kids identify with both scientists and patients." SLJ
Includes bibliographical references

Panno, Joseph
Stem cell research; medical applications and ethical controversies. Rev. ed. Facts On File 2010 262p il (The new biology) $40; pa $18.95
Grades: 9 10 11 12   616
1. Stem cell research
ISBN 978-0-8160-6851-7; 978-0-8160-8330-5 (pa)
                                         LC 2009-30506
First published 2005
This book "discusses the different types of stem cells, how they are studied in the laboratory, and the diseases that may be treated with these cells. . . . [It includes] chapters that discuss the origin and evolution of ordinary cells, as well as a . . . discussion of human and animal stem cells, therapeutic cloning, and a new form of stem cell that is produced by reprogramming ordinary skin cells." Publisher's note
Includes glossary and bibliographical references

Shnayerson, Michael
The killers within; the deadly rise of drug-resistant bacteria; {by} Michael Shnayerson, Mark Plotkin. Little, Brown 2002 328p hardcover o.p. pa $14.95
Grades: 11 12 Adult   616
1. Bacteria 2. Antibiotics
ISBN 0-316-71331-7; 0-316-73566-3 (pa)
                                         LC 2002-24177
The authors provide a "look at the overuse of antibiotics, the methods bacteria use to develop resistance, the role of antibiotics as animal growth promoters, and the outlook for antibiotics. . . . Shnayerson and Plotkin have managed to demonstrate their concern over the future of antibiotics while keeping the scientific background manageable for lay readers." Libr J
Includes bibliographical references

Tierno, Philip M., Jr.
The secret life of germs; observations and lessons of a microbe hunter; {by} Philip M. Tierno, Jr. Pocket Bks. 2002 c2001 290p hardcover o.p. pa $14
Grades: 11 12 Adult   616
1. Microorganisms
ISBN 0-7434-2187-6; 0-7434-2188-4 (pa)
                                         LC 2001-36937
This is "the story of bacteria, viruses, and prions and their myriad effects on human beings. From toxic shock syndrome to Lyme disease to diarrheal infections of the Third World, Tierno offers a broad overview of the impact of these microbes on the world today. . . . An interesting book for popular science readers as well as for students doing reports on disease." Libr J
Includes bibliographical references

Van Tilburg, Christopher
Mountain rescue doctor; wilderness medicine in the extremes of nature. St. Martin's Press 2007 293p il hardcover o.p. pa $14.95
Grades: 11 12 Adult   616
1. Mountaineering 2. Rescue work
ISBN 978-0-312-35887-7; 0-312-35887-3; 978-0-312-35888-4 (pa); 0-312-35888-1 (pa)
                                         LC 2007-28304

Van Tilburg, Christopher—*Continued*

The author "is a member of the Hood River Crag Rats, the oldest search-and-rescue (S&R) team in the United States. Both adults and teens will relish his vivid recountings of efforts to rescue sports enthusiasts who got lost or injured in the mountains." Libr J

Wynbrandt, James

The encyclopedia of genetic disorders and birth defects; [by] James Wynbrandt and Mark D. Ludman. 3rd ed. Facts On File 2007 682p (Facts on File library of health and living) $75 *

Grades: 9 10 11 12 Adult   **616**

1. Reference books 2. Birth defects—Encyclopedias
ISBN 978-0-8160-6396-3   LC 2006-100640
First published 1991

This book is a "single-volume reference to genetic disorders and birth defects. Topics are arranged in an . . . A-to-Z format covering everything from . . . basic genetic concepts to . . . screening and diagnostic techniques." Publisher's note

This "is an excellent resource for public and consumer-health libraries with limited budgets. It is a good starting point for research, too." Booklist

Includes bibliographical references

616.02   Special topics of diseases

American Medical Association family medical guide. 4th ed., completely rev. and updated. John Wiley & Sons 2004 1184p il $45 *

Grades: 9 10 11 12 Adult   **616.02**

1. Medicine 2. Health self-care
ISBN 0-471-26911-5   LC 2004-5764
First published 1982

Contents: What you should know: information to keep you healthy; Staying healthy; Diet and health; Exercise, fitness, and health; A healthy weight; Reducing stress; Staying safe; Preventing violence; Preventive health care; Complementary and alternative medicine; First aid and caregiving; First aid; Home caregiving; What are your symptoms?; Symptoms charts; Health issues throughout life; Children's health; Adolescent health; Sexuality; Infertility; Pregnancy and childbirth; Dying and death; Diseases, disorders, and other problems; Disorders of the heart and circulation; Blood disorders; Disorders of the respiratory system; Disorders of the brain and nervous system; Behavioral, emotional, and mental disorders; Disorders of the digestive system; Disorders of the urinary tract; Disorders of the male reproductive system; Disorders of the female reproductive system and urinary tract; Hormonal disorders; Disorders of the immune system; Infections and infestations; Genetic disorders; Disorders of the bones, muscles, and joints; Disorders of the ear; Eye disorders; Disorders of the skin, hair, and nails; Cosmetic surgery; Teeth and gums

"This is a well-organized volume, considering the amount of information it covers." Publ Wkly

The **American** Red Cross first aid and safety handbook; [prepared by] American Red Cross and Kathleen A. Handal; foreword by Elizabeth Dole. Little, Brown 1992 321p il hardcover o.p. pa $18.95 *

Grades: 9 10 11 12 Adult   **616.02**

1. First aid
ISBN 0-316-73645-7; 0-316-73646-5 (pa)
     LC 91-24847

This first aid guidebook is based on course materials used by the Red Cross and covers how to handle such emergencies as allergic reactions, bleeding, choking, and heart attacks.

The **Merck** manual home health handbook; Robert S. Porter, editor-in-chief; Justin L. Kaplan, senior assistant editor; Barbara P. Homeier, assistant editor; editorial board, Richard K. Albert ... [et al.] [3rd ed.] Merck Research Laboratories 2009 xlii, 2306p il $39.95 *

Grades: 11 12 Adult   **616.02**

1. Medicine—Handbooks, manuals, etc.
ISBN 978-0-9119-1030-8   LC 2009-923536
Also available online

First published 1997 with title: The Merck manual of medical information, Home ed

"An editorial board of 207 medical experts contributes to this comprehensive overview of medical practice today, with a special focus on geriatric medicine (including a chapter devoted to enhancing the quality of end-of-life care for patient, caregiver, friends and family). . . . Charts and illustrations aid the book's accessibility, making it Merck's most authoritative and easy-to-read home medical guide yet." Publ Wkly

616.07   Pathology

Murray, Elizabeth A.

Death; corpses, cadavers, and other grave matters. Twenty-First Century Books 2010 112p il (Discovery!) lib bdg $31.93

Grades: 7 8 9 10   **616.07**

1. Death 2. Forensic sciences
ISBN 978-0-7613-3851-2; 0-7613-3851-9
     LC 2009-17436

The author "has written a book that deals with the scientific aspect of life and death. Her experience as a teacher of anatomy and physiology comes through as she explains the living body, what happens when systems shut down, and how postmortem remains can give evidence to solve crimes and the mysteries of diseases. . . . First-person accounts of terminally ill patients and those working in the fields of pathology, hospice, and anatomy clarify subjects presented in the chapters. Color photographs are included throughout, some of which are potentially disturbing. The glossary and bibliography are extensive and helpful. This book provides information for those who are curious about a subject that is not easy to discuss." SLJ

Includes glossary and bibliographical references

Segen, J. C.

The patient's guide to medical tests; everything you need to know about the tests your doctor orders; [by] Joseph C. Segen and Josie Wade. 2nd ed. Facts on File 2002 418p (Facts on File library of health and living) $44 *

Grades: 9 10 11 12 Adult   **616.07**

1. Diagnosis

ISBN 0-8160-4651-4   LC 2002-18824

First published 1997 with Joseph Stauffer as joint author

This "guide presents information on more than 1,000 commonly prescribed tests and procedures. Each entry includes a description of the test, patient preparation required, a description of the procedure itself, the reference range, what abnormal values may signify, and the approximate cost of each test." Publisher's note

616.1 Diseases of cardiovascular system

Mertz, Leslie A.

The circulatory system; [by] Leslie Mertz. Greenwood Press 2004 xx, 217p il (Human body systems) $65 *

Grades: 11 12 Adult   **616.1**

1. Cardiovascular system

ISBN 0-313-32401-8   LC 2004-42449

In addition to the parts and functions of the circulatory system, "blood pressure, blood type and fetal circulation are covered. The history of research on the circulatory system is presented and the future of research in this field is considered. Current controversies and dilemmas, such as stem cell research, are explored." Publisher's note

Includes bibliographical references

616.2 Diseases of respiratory system

Apel, Melanie Ann

Cystic fibrosis; the ultimate teen guide. Scarecrow Press 2006 259p il (It happened to me) $42

Grades: 9 10 11 12   **616.2**

1. Cystic fibrosis

ISBN 0-8108-4821-X   LC 2005-22073

"The first four chapters focus on the definition, source, diagnosis, and grueling treatments of cystic fibrosis before moving on to discuss patient and family reactions to the information and challenges. . . . Gripping personal accounts will pull in readers, teenage and adult, who are not familiar with the disease." Voice Youth Advocates

Includes bibliographical references

Asthma information for teens; health tips about managing asthma and related concerns including facts about asthma causes, triggers and symptoms, diagnosis, and treatment; edited by Kim Wohlenhaus. 2nd ed. Omnigraphics 2010 427p il (Teen health series) $69

Grades: 7 8 9 10 11 12   **616.2**

1. Asthma

ISBN 978-0-7808-1086-0; 0-7808-1086-4

LC 2009048694

First published 2005 under the editorship of Karen Bellenir

"Provides basic consumer health information for teens about asthma causes and treatments, controlling triggers, and coping with asthma at home and school. Includes index, resource information and recommendations for further reading." Publisher's note

Includes bibliographical references

Berger, William E.

Living with asthma. Facts on File 2007 183p (Teen's guides) lib bdg $34.95; pa $14.95

Grades: 7 8 9 10 11   **616.2**

1. Asthma

ISBN 978-0-8160-6483-0 (lib bdg); 0-8160-6483-0 (lib bdg); 978-0-8160-7560-7 (pa); 0-8160-7560-3 (pa)

LC 2007003664

Examines asthma and provides teens with the information they need to understand it.

"There is a great directory of referral and online resources in the appendix. Although there are no illustrations, the text is appealing, well-organized, and accessible for the teen reader." Voice Youth Advocates

Includes glossary

Finer, Kim R., 1956-

Tuberculosis; consulting editor I. Edward Alcamo; foreword by David Heymann. Chelsea House 2003 112p il (Deadly diseases and epidemics) lib bdg $25.95

Grades: 9 10 11 12   **616.2**

1. Tuberculosis

ISBN 0-7910-7309-2   LC 2002-155988

New edition in preparation

Contents: Tuberculosis throughout time; Robert Koch, Selman Waksman, and the near defeat of tuberculosis; The tuberculosis bacterium; Consumption: what happens once you become infected; Transmission from organism to organism; The immune response to tuberculosis infection; Screening for and diagnosis of tuberculosis; The BCG vaccine; Treatment of tuberculosis I: sanatoriums and early drug treatments; Treatment of tuberculosis II: modern drug therapy; The human immunodeficiency virus and tuberculosis

This book examines techniques for identifying, treating, and preventing tuberculosis as well as the social impact of the disease.

Includes glossary and bibliographical references

Giddings, Sharon

Cystic fibrosis. Chelsea House 2009 128p il (Genes & disease) lib bdg $35

Grades: 7 8 9 10   **616.2**
1. Cystic fibrosis
ISBN 978-0-7910-9694-9; 0-7910-9694-7
LC 2008-44771

"Cystic fibrosis is one of the most widespread fatal genetic diseases in the United States. . . . [This book] discusses this genetic disease, its history, current treatments, and how scientists are searching for a cure." Publisher's note

Includes glossary and bibliographical references

Goldsmith, Connie, 1945-

Influenza. Twenty-First Century Books 2010 128p il (USA Today health reports: diseases and disorders) lib bdg $34.60

Grades: 7 8 9 10 11 12   **616.2**
1. Influenza
ISBN 978-0-7613-5881-7; 0-7613-5881-1
LC 2010-01030

This book "talks about the science behind the highly contagious disease, how it has spread to millions, and how to prevent and treat it. . . . [The] accessible design extends the impressive educational data." Booklist

Includes bibliographical references

Kelly, Evelyn B.

Investigating influenza and bird flu; real facts for real lives; [by] Evelyn B. Kelly and Claire Wilson. Enslow Publishers 2010 160p il (Investigating diseases) lib bdg $34.60

Grades: 6 7 8 9 10   **616.2**
1. Influenza 2. Avian influenza
ISBN 978-0-7660-3341-2; 0-7660-3341-4
LC 2009-14802

"Provides information about influenza and bird flu, including treatment, diagnosis, history, medical advances, and true stories about people with the diseases." Publisher's note

"The authors have explained the difficult problems in a clear, readable manner with lots of added pictures. . . . [Recommended] . . . for junior and senior high school students and for the general public." Sci Books Films

Includes glossary and bibliographical references

Lung disorders sourcebook; edited by Dawn D. Matthews. Omnigraphics 2002 678p il (Health reference series) $78 *

Grades: 11 12 Adult   **616.2**
1. Lungs—Diseases
ISBN 0-7808-0339-6   LC 2002-16976

"Basic consumer health information about emphysema, pneumonia, tuberculosis, asthma, cystic fibrosis, and other lung disorders. Including facts about diagnostic procedures, treatment strategies, disease prevention efforts, and such risk factors as smoking, air pollution, and exposure to asbestos, radon, and other agents: along with a glossary and resources for additional help and information." Title page

"This title is a great addition for public and school libraries because it provides concise health information on

the lungs. Readers can start with this reference source and get satisfactory answers before proceeding to other medical reference tools for more in-depth information." Am Ref Books Annu, 2003

Paquette, Penny Hutchins

Asthma; the ultimate teen guide. Scarecrow Press 2003 171p il (It happened to me) $32.50; pa $14.95 *

Grades: 9 10 11 12   **616.2**
1. Asthma
ISBN 0-8108-4633-0; 0-8108-5759-6 (pa)
LC 2002-153542

Contents: How long has this been going on? A history of asthma; What is it? Asthma defined; Diagnosing asthma; Asthma triggers and how to avoid them; What to do about it? Asthma treatments; Dealing With asthma at school; When asthma becomes deadly; Coping with asthma; On your own

"The text explains exactly what is happening to the body as a result of an asthma attack, introduces ways to monitor symptoms or situations that may trigger an asthma attack, and provides an overview of medications that can help teens cope. Young readers will find the numerous sidebars and factoids quite interesting and informative." Lib Media Connect

Includes bibliographical references

Parks, Peggy J., 1951-

Influenza. ReferencePoint Press 2011 96p il map (Compact research: diseases and disorders) lib bdg $26.95

Grades: 7 8 9 10 11 12   **616.2**
1. Influenza 2. Swine influenza
ISBN 978-1-60152-118-7; 1-60152-118-9
LC 2010-26063

This book about influenza "begins with a general overview followed by a focus on statistics, causes, symptoms, treatments, and prevention. [The book] discusses the virus that causes the disease; presents information on prevention through proper hygiene as well as vaccination, especially during epidemics; and warns against public apathy. . . . The readable page design features pull quotes and subtitles, with occasional photos throughout." Booklist

Includes bibliographical references

Serradell, Joaquima

SARS; consulting editor, Hilary Babcock; foreword by David Heymann. 2nd ed. Chelsea House 2009 c2010 117p il map (Deadly diseases and epidemics) $34.95

Grades: 9 10 11 12   **616.2**
1. SARS (Disease)
ISBN 978-1-60413-239-7; 1-60413-239-6
LC 2009-31056

First published 2005

This book "traces the history of the 2003 outbreak and its aftermath, describing the life cycle of the SARS virus, how the disease is spread, and the signs and symptoms." Publisher's note

Includes glossary and bibliographical references

616.3 Diseases of digestive system

Chow, James H., 1948-

The encyclopedia of hepatitis and other liver diseases; [by] James H. Chow, Cheryl Chow. Facts on File 2005 372p (Facts on File library of health and living) $75

Grades: 11 12 Adult   616.3
1. Liver—Diseases—Encyclopedias 2. Reference books

ISBN 0-8160-5710-9; 978-0-8160-5710-8

LC 2005-18489

"With more than 150 entries, coverage ranges from symptoms, treatments, and research to tests, social issues, and much more. Appendixes list . . . relevant organizations, transplantation and Internet resources, and support groups for those with liver-related issues." Publisher's note

Includes bibliographical references

Fredericks, Carrie

Obesity. Reference Point Press 2008 104p il map (Compact research. Current issues) lib bdg $24.95

Grades: 8 9 10 11 12   616.3
1. Obesity

ISBN 978-1-60152-040-1; 1-60152-040-9

LC 2007-42183

Examines the topic of obesity in a format with objective overviews, primary source quotes, illustrated facts, and statistics.

"Both general readers and serious researchers will find something useful in this volume. It facilitates research for less-motivated students and supplies excellent information for better researchers." SLJ

Includes bibliographical references

Goldsmith, Connie, 1945-

Hepatitis. Twenty-First Century Books 2010 128p il (USA Today health reports: diseases and disorders) lib bdg $34.60

Grades: 7 8 9 10 11 12   616.3
1. Liver—Diseases

ISBN 978-0-8225-6787-5; 0-8225-6787-3

LC 2009-20720

This "reveals that an estimated five million Americans have viral Hepatitis A, B, and C, making it a major public health problem. . . . The detailed information is combined with photos and diagrams portraying transmission, vaccines, and effective treatment. . . . [The] accessible design extends the impressive educational data." Booklist

Includes bibliographical references

Minocha, Anil, 1957-

The encyclopedia of the digestive system and digestive disorders; [by] Anil Minocha, Christine Adamec. 2nd ed. Facts on File 2010 c2011 xxvii, 353p il (Facts on File library of health and living) $75 *

Grades: 11 12 Adult   616.3
1. Gastrointestinal system—Encyclopedias 2. Digestive organs—Encyclopedias 3. Reference books

ISBN 978-0-8160-7661-1; 0-8160-7661-8

LC 2010-28790

First published 2004

"Entries explain the organs of the digestive system and how they work, the digestive process, disorders and infectious diseases of the digestive system, and how to maintain good digestive health." Publisher's note

Includes bibliographical references

Obesity; Tom and Gena Metcalf, editors. Thomson / Gale 2008 136p il (Perspectives on diseases and disorders) lib bdg $34.95

Grades: 7 8 9 10   616.3
1. Obesity

ISBN 978-0-7377-3873-5; 0-7377-3873-1

LC 2007-37470

"This book explains what obesity is, provides insight into its causes, and takes a serious look at why it's becoming such an epidemic. Accounts by people who have firsthand experience dealing with being overweight add value to the book." SLJ

Includes glossary and bibliographical references

Obesity: opposing viewpoints; Scott Barbour, book editor. Greenhaven Press 2011 194p $39.70; pa $27.50 *

Grades: 9 10 11 12   616.3
1. Obesity

ISBN 978-0-7377-4978-6; 978-0-7377-4979-3 (pa)

LC 2010004515

"Opposing viewpoints series"

Articles in this anthology discuss the causes of obesity and ways it can be reduced.

Includes bibliographical references

Palmer, Melissa

Dr. Melissa Palmer's guide to hepatitis & liver disease. Avery 2004 470p il pa $16.95

Grades: 11 12 Adult   616.3
1. Liver—Diseases

ISBN 1-58333-188-3   LC 2003-63905

First published 1999

The author "discusses all facets of liver disease, from symptoms and tests to treatment options and lifestyle changes." Publisher's note

616.4   Diseases of hematopoietic, lymphatic, glandular systems Diseases of endocrine system

Allman, Toney, 1947-

Diabetes. Chelsea House 2008 136p il (Genes & disease) lib bdg $35

Grades: 7 8 9 10   **616.4**
   1. Diabetes
   ISBN 978-0-7910-9585-0; 0-7910-9585-1
                           LC 2008-1195
This "well-written book . . . [discusses] diabetes, its treatments, genetic variations contributing to the disease, and the prospects for a cure. The narrative starts with the diagnosis of diabetes and follows with seven chapters." Sci Books Films
   Includes glossary and bibliographical references

Ambrose, Marylou

Investigating diabetes; real facts for real lives. Enslow Publishers 2010 160p il (Investigating diseases) lib bdg $34.60

Grades: 6 7 8 9 10   **616.4**
   1. Diabetes
   ISBN 978-0-7660-3338-2; 0-7660-3338-4
                         LC 2008-30778
"Provides information about diabetes, including treatment, diagnosis, history, medical advances, and true stories about people with the disease." Publisher's note
"The book is a comprehensive primer that can well serve patients with newly diagnosed diabetes and their families with its detailed account of diabetes, the causes of the disease, and its potential consequences." Sci Books Films
   Includes glossary and bibliographical references

American Diabetes Association

American Diabetes Association complete guide to diabetes. 5th ed. American Diabetes Association 2011 499p il pa $22.95 *

Grades: 11 12 Adult   **616.4**
   1. Diabetes
   ISBN 978-1-58040-330-6   LC 2010-41272
   First published 1996
This book describes types of insulin and the best ways to use them, insulin pumps and injection-free insulin techniques in research, new oral diabetes medications and therapies, the use of carbohydrate counting techniques as a meal planning tool as well as information on diabetes in the workplace, school, and day care.
   Includes bibliographical references

Betschart, Jean, 1948-

Type 2 diabetes in teens; secrets for success; [by] Jean Betschart-Roemer. Wiley 2002 223p il pa $14.95 *

Grades: 9 10 11 12   **616.4**
   1. Diabetes
   ISBN 0-471-15056-8
                         LC 2002-2967

This book offers teens advice on "how to keep blood sugar in control; what to do when you get cravings; how to manage your diabetes in school; what to say to your friends and your dates; how to balance exercise and food when you take insulin; where to find help when you need it; ways to eat healthier; [and] how to be patient with yourself and enjoy life." Publisher's note
   Includes bibliographical references

Diabetes information for teens; edited by Sandra Augustyn Lawton. Omnigraphics 2006 410p il (Teen health series) $65

Grades: 8 9 10 11 12   **616.4**
   1. Diabetes
   ISBN 0-7808-0811-8   LC 2005036597
"Health tips about managing diabetes and preventing related complications including information about insulin, glucose control, healthy eating, physical activity, and learning to live with diabetes." Title page
"Students dealing with their own diabetes or that of a friend or family member or those writing reports on the topic will find this a valuable resource." SLJ
   Includes bibliographical references

Hood, Korey K.

Type 1 teens; a guide to managing your life with diabetes; illustrated by Bryan Ische. American Psychological Association 2010 150p il pa $14.95 *

Grades: 9 10 11 12   **616.4**
   1. Diabetes 2. Teenagers—Health and hygiene
   ISBN 978-1-4338-0788-6; 1-4338-0788-2
                        LC 2010-11063
A guide for teens on managing Type 1 diabetes offers strategies and tips on making diabetes a high priority, fighting diabetes burnout, getting help from others, and coping with school and relationships.
"With conversational prose, contemporary reference, and scenarios that will resonate with teens, . . . Hood offers an accessible, supportive resource for youth diagnosed with type-1 diabetes." Booklist

Parker, Katrina

Living with diabetes. Facts On File 2007 170p (Teen's guides) $34.95

Grades: 9 10 11 12   **616.4**
   1. Diabetes
   ISBN 978-0-8160-6346-8; 0-8160-6346-X
                        LC 2007-27679
"All issues relevant to diabetic teens are covered, from the natures of Type 1 and Type 2 diabetes and the choices available to regulate blood sugar, to the importance of diet and exercise and the emotional challenges involved. . . . The information is presented clearly and matter-of-factly and its slightly 'scared-straight' approach lets teens know up front what they are facing and how to deal with it." SLJ
   Includes glossary and bibliographical references

Warshaw, Hope S., 1954-

The diabetes food & nutrition bible; a complete guide to planning, shopping, cooking, and eating; with foreword by Graham Kerr. American Diabetes Association 2001 324p il pa $18.95 *

Grades: 11 12 Adult   **616.4**
1. Diabetes—Diet therapy
ISBN 1-58040-037-X   LC 2001-22343
This book features information on counting carbohydrates, planning meals, vitamins, minerals, and methods of meal preparation. It includes more than 100 recipes.

Yuwiler, Janice

Diabetes. ReferencePoint Press 2009 96p il (Compact research. Diseases and disorders) lib bdg $25.95

Grades: 7 8 9 10   **616.4**
1. Diabetes
ISBN 978-1-60152-076-0; 1-60152-076-X
LC 2009-6173
"Yuwiler discusses type 1 diabetes and its management, type 2 diabetes and its prevention, metabolic syndrome, and medical advances. . . . Subtopics are delineated by brightly colored burgundy headings; blocks of orange-colored sidebars with bright-red print and relevant color photos and illustrations appear throughout. Each chapter ends with several pages of primary-source quotes and facts and illustrations that offer greater clarity to the text." SLJ
Includes bibliographical references

616.5   Diseases of integument

Juettner, Bonnie, 1968-

Acne. Lucent Books 2010 104p il (Diseases and disorders series) lib bdg $33.45

Grades: 7 8 9 10   **616.5**
1. Acne
ISBN 978-1-4205-0215-2; 1-4205-0215-8
LC 2009-33484
First published 2004
"Well-organized chapters present clear information on the causes of acne, types of self-treatment, medical and 'alternative' paths to a cure, the future of treatment, and the psychological ramifications for an affected person. . . . This title will be useful for reports and is a solid addition to health and/or disease collections." SLJ
Includes bibliographical references

Skin health information for teens; edited by Kim Wohlenhaus. 2nd ed. Omnigraphics 2009 418p il (Teen health series) $62

Grades: 8 9 10 11 12   **616.5**
1. Skin—Care 2. Teenagers—Health and hygiene
ISBN 978-0-7808-1042-6; 0-7808-1042-2
LC 2009-22833
First published 2003
"Health tips about dermatological concerns and skin cancer risks including facts about acne, warts, allergies, and other conditions and lifestyle choices, such as tanning, tattooing, and piercing, that affect the skin, nails, scalp, and hair" Title page

"A comprehensive, accessible reference guide. Sources for each topic include reputable Web sites, government agencies, and professional associations that are clearly cited on the first page of every chapter. . . . A handful of black-and-white photos and drawings illustrate the content." SLJ
Includes bibliographical references

Turkington, Carol

The encyclopedia of skin and skin disorders; [by] Carol Turkington, Jeffrey S. Dover; medical illustrations, Birck Cox. 3rd ed. Facts on File 2007 459p (Facts on File library of health and living) $75; pa $17.95 *

Grades: 11 12 Adult   **616.5**
1. Reference books 2. Skin—Encyclopedias
ISBN   0-8160-6403-2;   978-0-8160-6403-8;
0-8160-6404-0 (pa); 978-0-8160-6404-5 (pa)
LC 2005-57402
First published 1996 with title: Skin deep
Paperback published with title: Skin deep
"More than 1,100 entries cover everything from the sun, skin, and acne to skin cancer, cosmetics, and skin lotions." Publisher's note
Includes bibliographical references

616.6   Diseases of urogenital system. Diseases of urinary system

Watson, Stephanie, 1969-

The urinary system. Greenwood Press 2004 207p il (Human body systems) $65 *

Grades: 11 12 Adult   **616.6**
1. Urinary organs
ISBN 0-313-32402-6   LC 2003-67648
The author "discusses the role and function of each part of the urinary system. . . . Watson also explores how the urinary system maintains chemical balance and hydration in the body. The history of research related to the urinary system is presented and the future of research in this field is considered." Publisher's note
Includes bibliographical references

616.7   Diseases of musculoskeletal system

Sayler, Mary Harwell

The encyclopedia of the muscle and skeletal systems and disorders; foreword by Lori Siegel. Facts on File 2005 xx, 389p (Facts on File library of health and living) $75 *

Grades: 11 12 Adult   **616.7**
1. Reference books 2. Musculoskeletal system—Encyclopedias
ISBN 0-8160-5447-9   LC 2003-26606
"The encyclopedia explores and explains why, by midlife, the body visibly complains of overuse and abuse through its aches, pains, stiffness, muscle weakness, and other symptoms of aging. Approximately 500 entries re-

Sayler, Mary Harwell—*Continued*
lating to muscle and skeletal disorders, arranged alphabetically, are presented." Booklist

The author "writes each entry with wit and skill—
amazing among health science encyclopedias. It will be
useful to health care consumers and students for years to
come." Choice

Includes bibliographical references

616.8   Diseases of nervous system and mental disorders

B., David, 1959-
Epileptic. Pantheon Books 2005 361p il $25; pa
$18.95
Grades: 11 12 Adult   **616.8**
1. Epilepsy—Graphic novels 2. Graphic novels
3. Autobiographical graphic novels
ISBN 0-375-42318-4; 0-375-71468-5 (pa)
LC 2004-53419
Original French edition, 2002

"Growing up in the 1960s and 1970s in France's
Loire Valley, Jean-Christophe developed grand mal epilepsy around the age of 11. Pierre-Francois, nine, observes his brother's battle with the physical and social
implications of the disease; their parents' efforts to find
management of it through medical, macrobiotic, and even
psychic interventions; and the author's own development
in this milieu as a boy obsessed with history and warfare
and as a dedicated artist." SLJ

The author's "artwork is magnificent—gorgeously
bold, impressionistic representations of the world not as
it is but as he's taught himself to perceive it. . . . B.'s
illustrations constantly underscore his writing's wrenching psychological depth; readers can literally see how the
chaos of his childhood shaped his vision and mind." Publ
Wkly

Bloom, Ona
Encephalitis; [by] Ona Bloom and Jennifer
Morgan; foreword by David Heymann. Chelsea
House 2006 125p il (Deadly diseases and
epidemics) $31.95
Grades: 9 10 11 12   **616.8**
1. Encephalitis
ISBN 0-7910-8503-1   LC 2005-5518
Contents: An introduction to viral encephalitis; An introduction to viruses: the molecular basis for encephalitis; The immune system and viral infections; The nervous
system and viral infections: etiology of encephalitis; Diagnosis and treatment of encephalitis; Viral and nonviral
causes of encephalitis; Treatment and prevention of encephalitis; Scientific research and the future of encephalitis
Includes glossary and bibliographical references

Brill, Marlene Targ, 1945-
Tourette syndrome. 21st Cent. Bks. (Brookfield)
2002 112p il (Twenty-first century medical library)
lib bdg $26.90
Grades: 8 9 10 11 12   **616.8**
1. Tourette syndrome
ISBN 0-7613-2101-2   LC 2001-41747

Examines the tic disorder known as Tourette syndrome, its symptoms and manifestations, how it can be
controlled and treated, and, through case studies, what it
is like to live with Tourette's

The author covers "most of the information report
writers would be seeking and a section about home and
school is especially helpful to anyone trying to understand the problems faced by a person with this disorder."
Book Rep

Includes glossary and bibliographical references

Dougherty, Terri, 1964-
Epilepsy. Lucent Books 2010 104p il (Diseases
and disorders series) lib bdg $33.45
Grades: 7 8 9 10 11 12   **616.8**
1. Epilepsy
ISBN 978-1-4205-0218-3; 1-4205-0218-2
LC 2009-33344
This "offers a thorough explanation of [epilepsy], giving a basic definition; a discussion of the causes, symptoms, and treatments; a description of living with the disease; and ideas of future treatment and diagnoses. The
color photographs and sidebars help to make the information in the dense text more easily understood, and personal stories provide insight into how individuals deal
with their disease. . . . Different types of seizures and
the varied triggers are explained." Voice Youth Advocates

Includes bibliographical references

Esherick, Joan
The journey toward recovery; youth with brain
injury. Mason Crest Publishers 2004 127p il
(Youth with special needs) hardcover o.p. pa
$14.95 *
Grades: 7 8 9 10   **616.8**
1. Brain damaged children
ISBN 1-59084-734-2; 1-4222-0425-1 (pa)
LC 2003-18640
Through the story of Jerome, a teenager who suffers
a traumatic brain injury from a bike accident, this book
discusses different "forms of brain injury; how these injuries affect people's lives; and how schools, doctors,
and lawmakers are helping youth with this form of special need." Publisher's note

Includes glossary and bibliographical references

Freedman, Jeri
Tay-Sachs disease. Chelsea House 2009 128p il
(Genes & disease) lib bdg $35
Grades: 7 8 9 10   **616.8**
1. Tay-Sachs disease
ISBN 978-0-7910-9634-5; 0-7910-9634-3
LC 2008-44770
This book "discusses the nature of the disease, why it
affects certain groups of people more often than others,
how genetic screening can help detect carriers of the
Tay-Sachs gene, and what options genetic testing and
counseling provide for having children." Publisher's note

Includes glossary and bibliographical references

Goldstein, Natalie

Parkinson's disease. Chelsea House 2008 128p il (Genes & disease) lib bdg $35

Grades: 7 8 9 10   616.8

1. Parkinson's disease

ISBN 978-0-7910-9584-3; 0-7910-9584-3

LC 2008-10494

This book opens "with accounts of people who have [Parkinson's] disease . . . followed by information on history, symptoms, variations, diagnosis, treatments, and research. . . . Chapters devoted to current genetic research and therapies can become dense as they introduce complex topics but photos, diagrams and charts help to clarify the details. . . . [Controversial issues] are introduced fairly." SLJ

Includes glossary and bibliographical references

Kelly, Evelyn B.

Alzheimer's disease. Chelsea House 2008 126p il (Genes & disease) lib bdg $35

Grades: 7 8 9 10   616.8

1. Alzheimer's disease

ISBN 978-0-7910-9588-1; 0-7910-9588-6

LC 2007-51319

"Presenting a history of Alzheimer's disease, this title looks at the human genome and explores how the pieces of the Alzheimer's puzzle are beginning to fit together." Publisher's note

"This well-written book . . . provides a compendium of quality information and resources, including both web-based and written reference material. Kelly discusses all the questions a family needs to know." Sci Books Films

Includes glossary and bibliographical references

Landau, Elaine

Alzheimer's disease; a forgotten life. Franklin Watts 2005 112p il (Health and human disease) $26

Grades: 7 8 9 10   616.8

1. Alzheimer's disease

ISBN 0-531-16755-0   LC 2005-01736

"Landau offers a well-researched, clearly written presentation on Alzheimer's and its effects. Topics discussed include diagnostic tools, possible causes, symptoms, stages, medications, research, and the problems faced by caregivers." Booklist

Includes glossary and bibliographical references

Marcovitz, Hal

Sleep disorders. ReferencePoint Press 2009 104p il (Compact research. Diseases and disorders) lib bdg $25.95

Grades: 7 8 9 10 11 12   616.8

1. Sleep disorders

ISBN 978-1-60152-071-5; 1-60152-071-9

LC 2008-46115

"Marcovitz's coverage ranges from insomnia to potential medical conditions that can lead to death, such as sleep apnea and narcolepsy. This book is a comprehensive overview of an often misunderstood subject." SLJ

Includes bibliographical references

Marcus, Mary Brophy

Sleep disorders. Chelsea House 2009 120p il (Psychological disorders) $37.50

Grades: 8 9 10 11 12   616.8

1. Sleep disorders

ISBN 978-1-60413-085-0; 1-60413-085-7

LC 2008-35019

"Explores the nature and importance of sleep; describes the major sleep disorders, including insomnia, sleep apnea and narcolepsy; and discusses treatment options in children and adults." Publisher's note

Includes glossary and bibliographical references

Schwartz, Maxime, 1940-

How the cows turned mad; translated by Edward Schneider. University of Calif. Press 2003 238p hardcover o.p. pa $15.95

Grades: 11 12 Adult   616.8

1. Prion diseases

ISBN 0-520-23531-2; 0-520-24337-4 (pa)

LC 2002-75514

The author discusses the spread of "mad-cow disease and its human counterpart, variant Creutzfeldt-Jakob disease (vCJD). . . . His book maps out . . . the scientific investigation into how scrapie—a disease that has long been known to afflict sheep—came to cross the species barrier to cows, and then from cows to humans." Economist

"Writing with immense concentration and clarity, French molecular biologist Schwartz makes the long hunt for the unexpected culprit gene utterly engrossing." Booklist

Includes bibliographical references

Shmaefsky, Brian

Meningitis; [by] Brian R. Shmaefsky; consulting editor, Hilary Babcock; foreword by David L. Heymann. 2nd ed. Chelsea House 2010 120p il (Deadly diseases and epidemics) $34.95

Grades: 7 8 9 10   616.8

1. Meningitis

ISBN 978-1-60413-241-0; 1-60413-241-8

LC 2010-8044

First published 2005

This book contains "information on the causes, spread, treatment, and prevention of the disease, as well as . . . [information on] recent meningitis outbreaks, which are a persistent problem in schools and on college campuses." Publisher's note

Includes glossary and bibliographical references

616.85 Miscellaneous diseases of nervous system and mental disorders

Ambrose, Marylou

Investigating eating disorders (anorexia, bulimia, and binge eating); real facts for real lives; [by] Marylou Ambrose and Veronica Deisler. Enslow Publishers 2011 160p il (Investigating diseases) lib bdg $34.60

Grades: 6 7 8 9 10   **616.85**
    1. Eating disorders
    ISBN 978-0-7660-3339-9; 0-7660-3339-2
                                LC 2009-6492

"This book is a well-organized, clear, succinct, and attractive presentation on anorexia, bulimia, and binge eating. In it, the authors have gathered helpful definitions, early religious history, international viewpoints, statistics, family issues, medical and psychological assessments, treatments, medications, and legislation to present information on the future outlook of, and research into, these eating disorders." Sci Books Films

Includes glossary and bibliographical references

Anorexia; Stefan Kiesbye, book editor. Greenhaven Press 2010 100p (At issue. Health) $31.80; pa $22.50 *

Grades: 8 9 10 11 12   **616.85**
    1. Anorexia nervosa
    ISBN   978-0-7377-4866-6;   0-7377-4866-4;
    978-0-7377-4867-3 (pa); 0-7377-4867-2 (pa)
                                LC 2010007870

The articles in this anthology discuss possible causes of anorexia and other issues.

Includes bibliographical references

Autism; Carrie Fredericks, book editor. Greenhaven Press 2008 168p il (Perspectives on diseases and disorders) $34.95

Grades: 7 8 9 10   **616.85**
    1. Autism
    ISBN 978-0-7377-3869-8   LC 2007-37472

"Explores the symptoms, causes and treatment of this lifelong disease that profoundly affects social functioning, language and behavior." Publisher's note

Includes glossary and bibliographical references

Cassell, Dana K.

Encyclopedia of obesity and eating disorders; [by] Dana Cassell, David H. Gleaves. 3rd ed. Facts on File 2006 xx, 362p (Facts on File library of health and living) $75 *

Grades: 9 10 11 12   **616.85**
    1. Reference books 2. Obesity—Encyclopedias
    3. Eating disorders—Encyclopedias
    ISBN 0-8160-6197-1; 978-0-8160-6197-6
                                LC 2005-51375

First published 1994

This encyclopedia "includes more than 450 entries . . . [and features] a history of obesity and eating disorders; chronology of key events, research, and break-throughs; tables listing key facts and statistics; and a directory of resources and Web sites." Publisher's note

Includes bibliographical references

Clark, Arda Darakjian, 1956-

Dyslexia. Thomson Gale 2005 112p il (Diseases and disorders series) $28.70 *

Grades: 9 10 11 12   **616.85**
    1. Dyslexia
    ISBN 1-59018-040-2   LC 2004-14704

This book "explores theories of causation, symptoms, assessments, and remediation. The psychosocial impact of dyslexia on dyslexics and their families is discussed, along with strategies for coping and living with dyslexia." Publisher's note

Includes bibliographical references

Cobain, Bev, 1940-

When nothing matters anymore; a survival guide for depressed teens; edited by Elizabeth Verdick. rev and updated ed. Free Spirit Pub. 2007 146p il pa $14.95 *

Grades: 7 8 9 10   **616.85**
    1. Depression (Psychology)
    ISBN 978-1-57542-235-0; 1-57542-235-2
                                LC 2006-36325

First published 1998

This book written for teens defines depression, describes the symptoms, and explains that depression is treatable

"This practical, reassuring book should be made available to all teens." Voice Youth Advocates

Includes bibliographical references

Connolly, Sucheta

Anxiety disorders; [by] Sucheta Connolly, David Simpson, Cynthia Petty. Chelsea House 2006 132p il (Psychological disorders) lib bdg $37.50

Grades: 8 9 10 11 12   **616.85**
    1. Anxiety 2. Panic disorders 3. Phobias
    4. Post-traumatic stress disorder
    ISBN 0-7910-8543-0   LC 2006-4996

This describes the development, evaluation, and treatment of anxiety disorders including generalized anxiety, separation anxiety, social phobia, specific phobias, panic attacks, obsessive-compulsive disorder, and post-traumatic stress disorder.

"This book will be quite useful in helping adolescents deal with their anxieties." Sci Books Films

Includes glossary and bibliographical references

Corman, Catherine A.

Positively ADD; real success stories to inspire your dreams; [by] Catherine A. Corman and Edward M. Hallowell. Walker 2006 172p il $16.95; lib bdg $17.85 *

Grades: 8 9 10 11 12   **616.85**
    1. Attention deficit disorder
    ISBN   978-0-8027-8988-4;   0-8027-8988-9;
    978-0-8027-8071-3 (lib bdg); 0-8027-8071-7 (lib bdg)
                                LC 2005037184

Corman, Catherine A.—*Continued*

This "profiles 17 adults who began dealing with attention deficit disorder in childhood. Along with political strategist [James] Carville, subjects include a Pulitzer Prizewinning photographer, a major league pitcher, and a young Rhodes scholar. . . . [This is] an encouraging, helpful book for teens with ADD as well as for their parents, teachers, and friends." Booklist

Includes bibliographical references

Depression; Emma Carlson Berne, book editor. Greenhaven 2007 184p (Contemporary issues companion) $36.20; pa $24.95

Grades: 8 9 10 11 12   **616.85**

1. Depression (Psychology)

ISBN   978-0-7377-3645-8;   0-7377-3645-3;
978-0-7377-2451-6 (pa); 0-7377-2451-X (pa)

LC 2007-19643

First published 1999 under the editorship of Henny H. Kim

"Eighteen field specialists have each contributed an essay on topics as diverse as deep brain stimulation and alternative therapies. A chapter on antidepressants and their heavily debated effects concludes the book. Thoughtfully composed, this excellent introduction to a widely recognized condition contains an extensive bibliography and support organization contact list." Libr J

Includes bibliographical references

Eating disorders information for teens; edited by Sandra Augustyn Lawton. 2nd ed. Omnigraphics 2009 377p il (Teen health series) $84

Grades: 8 9 10 11 12   **616.85**

1. Eating disorders

ISBN 978-0-7808-1044-0; 0-7808-1044-9

LC 2008-49387

First published 2005

"Health tips about anorexia, bulimia, binge eating, and other eating disorders including information about risk factors, prevention, diagnosis, treatment, health consequences, and other related issues." Title page

"Provides basic consumer health information for teens about causes, prevention, and treatment of eating disorders, along with healthy eating tips. Includes index, resource information and recommendations for further reading." Publisher's note

"This book pulls together reports, articles, and other primary sources from governmental agencies and nonprofit organizations into one comprehensive volume. It provides an accessible starting place for teens who might be new to library research or overwhelmed by the amount of information available." Voice Youth Advocates

Includes bibliographical references

Eating disorders: opposing viewpoints; Viqi Wagner, book editor. Greenhaven 2007 244p il lib bdg $36.20; pa $24.95 *

Grades: 8 9 10 11 12   **616.85**

1. Eating disorders

ISBN   978-0-7377-3348-8   (lib   bdg);
978-0-7377-3349-5 (pa)   LC 2007-7382

"Opposing viewpoints series"

This collection of essays offers various points of view about eating disorders.

Includes bibliographical references

Evans-Martin, Fay

Down syndrome; [by] F. Fay Evans-Martin. Chelsea House 2008 128p il (Genes & disease) lib bdg $35

Grades: 7 8 9 10   **616.85**

1. Down syndrome

ISBN 978-0-7910-9644-4; 0-7910-9644-0

LC 2008-44773

"Down syndrome is a developmental disorder caused by the presence of an extra copy of chromosome 21. . . . [This book] explains this genetic disease, its history and characteristics, and what scientists are doing to study it." Publisher's note

Includes glossary and bibliographical references

Farrar, Amy

ADHD. Twenty-First Century Books 2010 112p il (USA Today health reports: diseases and disorders) lib bdg $34.60

Grades: 7 8 9 10 11 12   **616.85**

1. Attention deficit disorder

ISBN 978-0-7613-5455-0; 0-7613-5455-7

LC 2010-870

This book describes attention deficit-hyperactivity disorder, its causes and treatments.

This is "liberally sprinkled with relevant articles and 'snapshots' (graphs showing statistical breakdowns of the topic at hand) from the newspaper, providing a competent introduction to primary-source material." SLJ

Includes glossary and bibliographical references

Favor, Lesli J.

Food as foe; nutrition and eating disorders. Marshall Cavendish Benchmark 2007 127p (Food and fitness) lib bdg $25.95

Grades: 7 8 9 10   **616.85**

1. Eating disorders 2. Nutrition

ISBN 978-0-7614-2553-3; 0-7614-2553-5

LC 2006-101931

"Provides a basic, comprehensive introduction to eating disorders, including anorexia, bulimia, and binge eating, with a review of where to find help and how to make wise food choices to become healthy." Publisher's note

This "visually appealing and easy-to-read [volume is] definitely worth having. The information is up-to-date and the format is attractive." SLJ

Includes bibliographical references

Hyde, Margaret Oldroyd, 1917-

Depression; what you need to know; [by] Margaret O. Hyde and Elizabeth H. Forsyth. Watts 2002 112p il lib bdg $24

Grades: 9 10 11 12   **616.85**

1. Depression (Psychology)

ISBN 0-531-11892-4   LC 2002-2488

Discusses the causes and symptoms of depression, who suffers from this condition, and how it can be treated

"The compelling information will keep teens reading. . . . Many examples of teens who have recovered from depression personalize the text, and there are useful help checklists." Booklist

Includes glossary and bibliographical references

Hyman, Bruce M.

Obsessive-compulsive disorder; by Bruce M. Hyman and Cherry Pedrick. Twenty-First Century Books 2003 96p (Twenty-first century medical library) $26.90

Grades: 7 8 9 10   **616.85**

1. Obsessive-compulsive disorder

ISBN 0-7613-2758-4   LC 2002-14252

Contents: What is OCD?; The symptoms of OCD; Treatment of OCD; The impact on family and friends; Living with OCD

Examines the anxiety disorder known as OCD, its symptoms and manifestations, how it can be controlled and treated, and, through case studies, what it is like to live with obsessive-compulsive disorder

"With little else written specifically for young adults on this topic—which has risen to prominence recently in the popular media—this will be useful to report writers as well as to those concerned about their own anxieties." Booklist

Includes glossary and bibliographical references

Mackay, Jenny, 1978-

Phobias. Gale Cengage Learning 2009 103p il (Diseases and disorders series) $33.45

Grades: 9 10 11 12   **616.85**

1. Phobias

ISBN 978-1-4205-0103-2; 1-4205-0103-8

      LC 2008033762

"Lucent Books"

Explains what phobias are, how they are caused, how people live with them, and offers the latest information about treatment.

Includes bibliographical references

Miller, Allen R.

Living with anxiety disorders. Facts on File 2007 202p (Teen's guides) $34.95; pa $14.95 *

Grades: 7 8 9 10   **616.85**

1. Anxiety 2. Panic disorders 3. Phobias 4. Post-traumatic stress disorder

ISBN   978-0-8160-6344-4;   0-8160-6344-3; 978-0-8160-7559-1 (pa); 0-8160-7559-X (pa)

      LC 2007-553

This book "delineates the difference between an anxiety disorder and fear, suggests avenues for evaluation, describes therapies, and devotes a chapter each to social phobia, post-traumatic stress, generalized anxiety disorder, panic disorder, and specific phobias." Libr Media Connect

Includes glossary and bibliographical references

Living with depression. Facts on File 2007 202p (Teen's guides) $34.95; pa $14.95

Grades: 7 8 9 10   **616.85**

1. Depression (Psychology)

ISBN   978-0-8160-6345-1;   0-8160-6345-1; 978-0-8160-7562-1 (pa); 0-8160-7562-X (pa)

      LC 2007-554

This "offers young adults concise information about depression and its treatments. . . . Chapters on treatments offer detailed information on psychotherapy, antidepressants, and self-help approaches such as diet, exercise, and stress management. . . . This book is a timely, useful resource." Booklist

Mooney, Carla, 1970-

Mood disorders. ReferencePoint Press 2010 c2011 96p il (Compact research: diseases and disorders) lib bdg $26.95

Grades: 8 9 10 11 12   **616.85**

1. Depression (Psychology) 2. Manic-depressive illness

ISBN 978-1-60152-119-4; 1-60152-119-7

      LC 2010-5868

This book about mood disorders "begins with a general overview followed by focus on statistics, causes, symptoms, treatments, and prevention. . . . [The book] discusses the two main categories [of mood disorders]: unipolar (if untreated the number-one risk for suicide) and bipolar (which swings between depression and mania.) . . . The readable page design features pull quotes and subtitles, with occasional photos throughout." Booklist

Includes bibliographical references

Orr, Tamra

When the mirror lies; anorexia, bulimia, and other eating disorders. Franklin Watts 2007 144p il pa $17.95

Grades: 7 8 9 10   **616.85**

1. Eating disorders

ISBN 0-531-16791-7   LC 2005-25571

This "guide to the symptoms and effects of eating disorders also includes numerous case studies of various individuals who have experienced living with these challenging conditions. . . . Written in a reader-friendly tone, the book does a good job of presenting the psychological aspects of these diseases and of sympathizing with the young people who are wrestling with them." SLJ

Includes bibliographical references

Parks, Peggy J., 1951-

Autism. ReferencePoint Press 2009 104p il (Compact research. Diseases and disorders) $25.95

Grades: 7 8 9 10 11 12   **616.85**

1. Autism

ISBN 978-1-60152-058-6; 1-60152-058-1

      LC 2008-21335

This book "prevents differing opinions about the alarming increase in diagnosed cases [of autism] and discusses controversial theories about causes (such as preservatives used in vaccines) and treatments (a gluten-free diet)." Booklist

Includes bibliographical references

Down syndrome. ReferencePoint Press 2009 104p il (Compact research. Diseases and disorders) $25.95

Grades: 7 8 9 10 11 12   **616.85**

1. Down syndrome

ISBN 978-1-60152-065-4; 1-60152-065-4

      LC 2008-36644

"This up-to-date, excellent overview of Down syndrome addresses controversies and ethical issues associated with this genetic disorder. Parks also reports on current and potential scientific advances that may prevent it in the future and offer a better quality of life and opportunities for those born with it." SLJ

Includes bibliographical references

Parks, Peggy J., 1951-—*Continued*

Obsessive-compulsive disorder. ReferencePoint Press 2010 c2011 96p il (Compact research: diseases and disorders) lib bdg $26.95

Grades: 8 9 10 11 12   **616.85**

    1. Obsessive-compulsive disorder

    ISBN 978-1-60152-120-0; 1-60152-120-0

                           LC 2010-5872

This book about obsessive-compulsive disorder is written "with objectivity and depth. . . . [It] begins with a general overview followed by a focus on statistics, treatments, and prevention. . . . [The book] shows that the irrational fears of OCD affect males and females across race and class. . . . The readable page design features pull quotes and subtitles, with occasional photos throughout." Booklist

Includes bibliographical references

Self-injury disorder. ReferencePoint Press 2011 96p il (Compact research: diseases and disorders) lib bdg $26.95

Grades: 8 9 10 11 12   **616.85**

    1. Self-mutilation

    ISBN 978-1-60152-112-5; 1-60152-112-X

                           LC 2009-50483

This book about self-injury disorder "begins with a general overview followed by a focus on statistics, causes, symptoms, treatments, and prevention. . . . [The book] states that the main cause of self-inflicted injury is to gain relief from unbearable emotional pain, and it also covers methods of treatment and prevention. The readable page design features pull quotes and subtitles, with occasional photos throughout." Booklist

Includes bibliographical references

Price, Janet, 1964-

Take control of Asperger's syndrome; the official strategy guide for teens with Asperger's syndrome and nonverbal learning disorder; [by] Janet Price and Jennifer Engel Fisher. Prufrock Press 2010 168p pa $16.95 *

Grades: 6 7 8 9 10   **616.85**

    1. Asperger's syndrome

    ISBN 978-1-59363-405-6; 1-59363-405-6

                           LC 2009-50852

"Directly addressing teens diagnosed with Asperger's Syndrome or Nonverbal Learning Disorder, two educational consultants experienced in special-needs issues lay out feasible strategies for success in school and in social interactions." Booklist

Includes bibliographical references

Rompella, Natalie

Obsessive-compulsive disorder; the ultimate teen guide. Scarecrow Press 2009 177p il (It happened to me) lib bdg $40

Grades: 7 8 9 10   **616.85**

    1. Obsessive-compulsive disorder

    ISBN 978-0-8108-5778-0; 0-8108-5778-2

                           LC 2008-46242

Guide that helps teenagers understand obsessive-compulsive disorder, and explains different treatment options.

Includes bibliographical references

Self-mutilation: opposing viewpoints; Mary E. Williams, book editor. Greenhaven Press 2008 228p il lib bdg $37.40; pa $25.95

Grades: 9 10 11 12   **616.85**

    1. Self-mutilation

    ISBN 978-0-7377-3828-5 (lib bdg); 0-7377-3828-6 (lib bdg); 978-0-7377-3829-2 (pa); 0-7377-3829-4 (pa)

                           LC 2007-28156

"Opposing viewpoints series"

"Williams looks at a variety of topics within this emotional disorder, including the seriousness of the problem, whether tattoos and piercings count as deliberate self harm, what triggers the behavior, and what can be done to stop it. . . . Researchers will find good, solid information here." SLJ

Includes bibliographical references

Sonenklar, Carol

Anorexia and bulimia. Twenty-First Century Books 2010 128p il (USA Today health reports: diseases and disorders) lib bdg $34.60

Grades: 7 8 9 10 11 12   **616.85**

    1. Anorexia nervosa 2. Bulimia

    ISBN 978-0-8225-6786-8; 0-8225-6786-5

This describes the symptoms and treatment of anorexia and bulimia.

This book "stands out for the substantial amount of information conveyed in a lively writing style. . . . Graphs, sidebars, diagrams, and other illustrations [are] used judiciously." Booklist

The **truth** about anxiety and depression; Heather Denkmire, principal author; John Perritano, contributing author; Robert N. Golden, general editor, Fred L. Peterson, general editor. 2nd ed. Facts on File 2010 199p il (Truth about series) $35 *

Grades: 7 8 9 10   **616.85**

    1. Anxiety 2. Depression (Psychology)

    ISBN 978-0-8160-7643-7; 0-8160-7643-X

                           LC 2010005461

First published 2004 with title: The truth about fear and depression

Presents information on anxiety and depression, including the genetics of mood and anxiety disorders, gender and depression, types of treatments available, related disorders, and more.

Includes glossary and bibliographical references

The **truth** about eating disorders; Robert N. Golden, Fred L. Peterson general editors; Gerri Freid Kramer, principal author. 2nd ed. Facts on File 2009 208p (Truth about series) $35 *

Grades: 7 8 9 10   **616.85**

    1. Eating disorders

    ISBN 978-0-8160-7633-8; 0-8160-7633-2

                           LC 2008-44036

First published 2004

This discusses anorexia, bulimia, fad diets, and laxative abuse, the causes of eating disorders, how to recognize the disorders, the portrayal of eating disorders in the media, and obesity and weight control

This title does "an excellent job of providing accurate

The truth about eating disorders—*Continued*
information for teens. For reports or for self-help, [it be-
longs] in any library serving young adults." SLJ [review
of 2004 edition]

Includes glossary and bibliographical references

Turkington, Carol
The encyclopedia of autism spectrum disorders;
[by] Carol Turkington, Ruth Anan. Facts on File
2007 324p $75 *
Grades: 11 12 Adult   **616.85**
  1. Reference books 2. Autism—Encyclopedias
  ISBN 0-8160-6002-9; 978-0-8160-6002-3
                                        LC 2005-27227
"More than 300 entries address the different types of
autism, causes and treatments, institutions, associations,
leading scientists, research, social impact, and much
more." Publisher's note
Includes bibliographical references

Veague, Heather Barnett
Personality disorders; consulting editor,
Christine Collins; foreword by Pat Levitt. Chelsea
House Publishers 2007 116p il (Psychological
disorders) lib bdg $37.50
Grades: 9 10 11 12   **616.85**
  1. Personality disorders
  ISBN 0-7910-9002-7; 978-0-7910-9002-2
                                        LC 2006-24072
This book "defines and explains the spectrum of per-
sonality disorders, the social and medical issues related
to them, and how they can be recognized and treated."
Publisher's note
Includes glossary and bibliographical references

Zucker, Bonnie, 1974-
Take control of OCD; the ultimate guide for
kids with OCD. Prufrock Press 2010 179p il pa
$16.95
Grades: 6 7 8 9 10   **616.85**
  1. Obsessive-compulsive disorder
  ISBN 978-1-59363-429-2; 1-59363-429-3
                                        LC 2010-34863
The author "addresses affected young readers directly
and offers a structured set of self-help strategies for coping with diagnosed obsessive-compulsive behavior. Suggesting that the chapters be read in order for best results,
she opens with a nontechnical explanation of the disorder's genetic and neurological roots, then goes on to discuss creating written behavioral 'ladders,' using relaxation techniques effectively, building self-awareness, handling uncertainty, and managing stress." Booklist
Includes bibliographical references

616.86   Substance abuse (Drug abuse)

Gwinnell, Esther
The encyclopedia of drug abuse; [by] Esther
Gwinnell and Christine Adamec. Facts on File
2008 xxxiii, 380p (Facts on File library of health
and living) $75
Grades: 11 12 Adult   **616.86**
  1. Reference books 2. Drug abuse—Encyclopedias
  ISBN 978-0-8160-6330-7; 0-8160-6330-3
                                        LC 2007-21439
This encyclopedia discusses "illegal and legal drugs
and how they impact society. . . . [It] looks at the
worldwide drug trade and the effects of drug abuse in
countries and cultures around the world, as well as in the
United States. This . . . reference [also] examines various types of drugs and how they function, risks, causes
and consequences of abuse, social issues, psychiatric issues, means of prevention, law enforcement efforts, and
drugs in special social groups." Publisher's note
Includes bibliographical references

Hyde, Margaret Oldroyd, 1917-
Smoking 101; an overview for teens; [by]
Margaret O. Hyde, John F. Setaro. Twenty-First
Century Books 2006 128p il lib bdg $26.60
Grades: 8 9 10 11 12   **616.86**
  1. Smoking 2. Tobacco
  ISBN 0-7613-2835-1
                                        LC 2004-22757
Contents: The first cigarette won't kill me; Nicotine:
the addiction culprit; I'll get my tobacco elsewhere; My
smoking and my body: the physiology of smoking; My
smoking and your body: second hand smoke; Ads: a reality check; The global view: what's happening with tobacco in the rest of the world?; The corporate view:
what tobacco companies do; Now that I'm informed . . .
some ideas for quitting
"The message is clear, the facts are well-presented,
and the tone is insightful. These authors understand the
teen audience and how to reach it." SLJ
Includes bibliographical references

616.89   Mental disorders

Hicks, James Whitney, 1964-
Fifty signs of mental illness; a guide to
understanding mental health. Yale University Press
2005 389p (Yale University Press health &
wellness) hardcover o.p. pa $17 *
Grades: 11 12 Adult   **616.89**
  1. Mental illness 2. Abnormal psychology
  ISBN 0-300-10657-2; 0-300-11694-2 (pa)
                                        LC 2004-21535
Contents: Anger; Antisocial behavior; Anxiety; Appetite disturbances; Avoidance; Body image problems;
Compulsions; Confusion; Cravings; Deceitfulness; Delusions; Denial; Depression; Dissociation; Euphoria; Fa-
tigue; Fears; Flashbacks; Grandiosity; Grief; Hallucinations; Histrionics; Hyperactivity; Identity confusion; Im-

Hicks, James Whitney, 1964-—*Continued*
pulsiveness; Intoxication; Jealousy; Learning difficulties; Mania; Memory loss; Mood swings; Movement problems; Nonsense; Obsessions; Oddness; Panic; Paranoia; Physical complaints and pain; Psychosis; Religious preoccupations; Self-esteem problems; Self-mutilation; Sexual performance problems; Sexual preoccupations; Sleep problems; Sloppiness; Speech difficulties; Stress; Suicidal thoughts; Trauma

"A reservoir of useful knowledge, this belongs in almost every library serving real people." Libr J

Marcovitz, Hal
Bipolar disorder. ReferencePoint Press 2008 112p il (Compact research. Diseases and disorders) $25.95
Grades: 6 7 8 9 10   **616.89**
1. Manic-depressive illness
ISBN 978-1-60152-066-1; 1-60152-066-2
     LC 2008-37721
Describes the history, causes, symptoms, and treatments of bipolar disorders.
The text is "factual without being dry, easy to read, and colorful." SLJ
Includes bibliographical references

Meisel, Abigail
Investigating depression and bipolar disorder; real facts for real lives. Enslow Publishers 2010 160p il (Investigating diseases) lib bdg $34.60
Grades: 6 7 8 9 10   **616.89**
1. Manic-depressive illness 2. Depression (Psychology)
ISBN 978-0-7660-3340-5; 0-7660-3340-6
     LC 2008-50060
"Meisel discusses the history, science, diagnosis, and treatment of depression and bipolar disorder. In addition, she shows how these illnesses affect not just the patients, but their families, peers, and friends. She explains the science behind the two conditions, their possible causes, and the varying nature of the illnesses themselves. . . . This is an excellent book for persons from high school age to adults to read and become familiar with these important illnesses." Sci Books Films
Includes glossary and bibliographical references

Mental health information for teens; health tips about mental wellness and mental illness: including facts about mental and emotional health, depression and other mood disorders, anxiety disorders, behavior disorders, self-injury, psychosis, schizophrenia, and more; edited by Karen Bellenir. 3rd ed. Omnigraphics 2010 443p (Teen health series) $62
Grades: 7 8 9 10 11 12   **616.89**
1. Mental health 2. Adolescent psychology 3. Teenagers—Health and hygiene 4. Reference books
ISBN 978-0-7808-1087-7   LC 2010-806
First published 2001
"Provides basic consumer health information for teens about mental illness and treatment, along with tips for maintaining mental and emotional health. Includes index, resource information and recommendations for further reading." Publisher's note

"This is an excellent resource for teens, parents, teachers, librarians, and those concerned with the mental health issues facing middle and high-schoolers today." Libr J
Includes bibliographical references

Noll, Richard, 1959-
The encyclopedia of schizophrenia and other psychotic disorders; foreword by Leonard George. 3rd ed. Facts on File 2007 xx, 409p (Facts on File library of health and living) $75 *
Grades: 11 12 Adult   **616.89**
1. Schizophrenia—Encyclopedias 2. Reference books
ISBN 0-8160-6405-9; 978-0-8160-6405-2
     LC 2005-56749
First published 1992
"Biologically related schizophrenic disorders, genetics, antipsychotic drug treatments, and pathophysiology are a few of the topics explored in the more than 600 entries. . . . The language is clear, making this volume equally suitable for use by patients, scholars, and general readers. A solid addition for health collections." Booklist
Includes bibliographical references

616.9   Other diseases

Coleman, William H., 1937-
Cholera; [by] William Coleman; consulting editor, Hilary Babcock; foreword by David Heymann. Chelsea House 2009 142p il (Deadly diseases and epidemics) lib bdg $29.95
Grades: 9 10 11 12   **616.9**
1. Cholera
ISBN 978-1-60413-232-8; 1-60413-232-9
     LC 2008-28627
First published 2004
"This book describes the history of this infectious disease and discusses characteristics that enable this microorganism to cause serious health problems. The book also discusses the basic bacteriology, immunology, treatment, and epidemiology of the disease. Research that seeks both to cure and to understand the cholera bacillus is also highlighted." Publisher's note
Includes glossary and bibliographical references

Decker, Janet M.
Mononucleosis; [by] Janet Decker and Alan Hecht; consulting editor: Hilary Babcock; foreword by David Heymann. 2nd ed. Chelsea House 2009 128p il (Deadly diseases and epidemics) lib bdg $34.95
Grades: 9 10 11 12   **616.9**
1. Mononucleosis 2. Epstein-Barr virus
ISBN 978-1-60413-234-2; 1-60413-234-5
     LC 2008-28628
First published 2004
"Mononucleosis is caused by the Epstein Barr virus. This book explores the microbiology of the virus as well as treatment and prevention options." Publisher's note
Includes glossary and bibliographical references

Edlow, Jonathan A., 1952-
Bull's-eye: unraveling the medical mystery of Lyme disease. Yale University Press 2003 285p il hardcover o.p. pa $17
Grades: 11 12 Adult   **616.9**
  1. Lyme disease
  ISBN 0-300-09867-7; 0-300-10370-0 (pa)
                                    LC 2002-154119
This account of the discovery of Lyme disease relates how connections were "established between symptoms and tick bites, leading to the discovery of the stages of the disease, its specific microbial cause, and its treatment." Publisher's note
"This well-documented book is . . . as important for the light it sheds on the nature of scientific inquiry within the contemporary social and political context as it is for its information about Lyme disease." Booklist
Includes bibliographical references

Emmeluth, Donald
Botulism; consulting editor, Hilary Babcock; foreword by David L. Heymann. 2nd ed. Chelsea House 2010 144p il map (Deadly diseases and epidemics) $34.95
Grades: 7 8 9 10   **616.9**
  1. Botulism
  ISBN 978-1-60413-235-9; 1-60413-235-3
                                      LC 2010-8111
First published 2005
This book contains "information on this disease, exploring its history, causes, statistics, and . . . diagnostic and treatment breakthroughs. It also includes accounts of numerous recent outbreaks." Publisher's note
Includes glossary and bibliographical references

Freeman-Cook, Lisa
Staphylococcus aureus infections; [by] Lisa and Kevin Freeman-Cook. Chelsea House 2006 182p il (Deadly diseases and epidemics) $31.95
Grades: 9 10 11 12   **616.9**
  1. Bacterial infections
  ISBN 0-7910-8508-2   LC 2005-4958
  Contents: The dangers of staphylococcus aureus infection; Introduction to bacteria; Staphylococcus aureus; The immune system and bacterial virulence factors; Fighting S. aureus infections; Mechanisms of resistance; Methicillin- and vancomycin-resistant S. aureus: a modern epidemic; Prevention of antibiotic resistance; The future of staphylococcus aureus treatment
Includes bibliographical references

Glynn, Ian, 1928-
The life and death of smallpox; [by] Ian and Jenifer Glynn. Cambridge Univ. Press 2004 278p il $25
Grades: 11 12 Adult   **616.9**
  1. Smallpox
  ISBN 0-521-84542-4; 978-0-521-84542-7
                                    LC 2005-297126
The authors "describe the history of the disease from the time of the ancient Egyptian pharaohs to the last natural case, which occurred in Somalia in 1977. . . . This

book is thoroughly researched and eminently readable. Although several books have been written on the history of smallpox, this is the definitive work on the subject." Choice
Includes bibliographical references

Goldsmith, Connie, 1945-
Battling malaria; on the front lines against a global killer. Twenty-First Century Books 2010 c2011 128p il map (Twenty-first century medical library) lib bdg $37.27
Grades: 8 9 10 11 12   **616.9**
  1. Malaria
  ISBN 978-0-8225-8580-0; 0-8225-8580-4
                                    LC 2009-20324
"This book examines how public health organizations work to protect people from malaria-carrying mosquitoes, how doctors care for people who do get malaria, and how researchers try to better understand and fight malaria." Publisher's note
"From the trained scientist who simply wants a review of this global disease to the high school student who is just beginning to understand the life-cycle complexities of a single-celled parasitic organism, readers will appreciate this very nice overview of the challenges that malaria poses for mankind." Sci Books Films
Includes bibliographical references

Guilfoile, Patrick
Antibiotic-resistant bacteria; [by] Patrick G. Guilfoile; founding editor, I. Edward Alcamo; foreword by David Heymann. Chelsea House Publishers 2006 128p il (Deadly diseases and epidemics) $31.95
Grades: 9 10 11 12   **616.9**
  1. Microorganisms 2. Drugs
  ISBN 0-7910-9188-0; 978-0-7910-9188-3
                                    LC 2006-17589
This book "describes pathogens that have become particularly adept at evading a wide range of antibiotics, and highlights how scientists continue to strive to develop new treatments and countermeasures to fight this onslaught." Publisher's note
Includes glossary and bibliographical references

Tetanus; consulting editor, Hilary Babcock; foreword by David Heymann. Chelsea House 2008 100p il map (Deadly diseases and epidemics) $31.95
Grades: 9 10 11 12   **616.9**
  1. Tetanus
  ISBN 978-0-7910-9711-3; 0-7910-9711-0
                                    LC 2007-37928
  Contents: What is tetanus?; Tetanus in history; How does clostridium tetani cause disease?; How is tetanus treated?; How is tetanus prevented?; Continuing concerns and current status of tetanus; Future prospects regarding tetanus
Includes glossary and bibliographical references

Kelly, Evelyn B.
Investigating tuberculosis and superbugs; real facts for real lives; [by] Evelyn B. Kelly, Ian Wilker, and Marylou Ambrose. Enslow Publishers 2010 160p il (Investigating diseases) lib bdg $34.60

Grades: 7 8 9 10   616.9
  1. Drug resistance 2. Tuberculosis
  ISBN 978-0-7660-3343-6; 0-7660-3343-0
                      LC 2009-37811
This "methodically presents medical and statistical information about major kinds of tuberculosis, malaria, AIDS/HIV, and other persistent bacterial, viral, and parasitic pandemics worldwide that are becoming ominously resistant to once-effective treatments. . . . [This is] massively documented with endnotes; supplemented by sidebar insertions, accounts of specific cases, and small color photos; and rounded off with digestible lists of relevant further sources." Booklist
  Includes bibliographical references

Kowalski, Kathiann M., 1955-
Attack of the superbugs; the crisis of drug-resistant diseases. Enslow Pubs. 2005 128p il (Issues in focus today) $31.93 *

Grades: 7 8 9 10   616.9
  1. Diseases 2. Microorganisms 3. Drugs
  ISBN 0-7660-2400-8; 978-0-7660-2400-7
The author "supplies evidence that many existing infections and diseases are becoming resistant to current treatments and provides examples of new, lethal outbreaks and epidemics emerging in this era of modern medicine. . . . This title is a good choice for young adults because it explains what they can do to prevent or minimize infection." SLJ
  Includes bibliographical references

Levy, Janey
The world of microbes; bacteria, viruses, and other microorganisms. Rosen Pub. 2010 c2011 80p il (Understanding genetics) lib bdg $30.60

Grades: 9 10 11 12   616.9
  1. Bacteria 2. Microorganisms
  ISBN 978-1-4358-9536-2   LC 2009-48520
Explains the impact of bacteria, viruses, and other microorganisms on human genetics.

Preston, Richard
The demon in the freezer; a true story. Random House 2002 240p hardcover o.p. pa $7.99 *

Grades: 11 12 Adult   616.9
  1. Smallpox 2. Biological warfare
  ISBN 0-375-50856-2; 0-345-46663-2 (pa)
The author explains "the chemical properties of the smallpox virus; how a single infected person . . . can set off an epidemic; and what this horrendous disease can be like. . . . We learn how the disease was eliminated by an international vaccination campaign in the 1970's; why there are reasons to believe that the Soviet Union grew staggering quantities of the virus, allegedly in part to arm intercontinental missiles; and how the virus might now be used by others as a 'strategic weapon.'" N Y Times Book Rev

Sheen, Barbara, 1949-
MRSA. Lucent Books 2010 104p il (Diseases and disorders series) $33.45

Grades: 7 8 9 10   616.9
  1. Methicillin-Resistant Staphylococcus aureus
  ISBN 978-1-4205-0144-5; 1-4205-0144-5
                      LC 2009-32644
This "offers a thorough explanation of [MRSA] giving a basic definition; a discussion of the causes, symptoms, and treatments; a description of living with the disease; and ideas of future treatment and diagnoses. Each volume lists source notes and organizations to contact. A glossary, index, and ideas for further reading are also included. The color photographs and sidebars help to make the information in the dense text more easily understood, and personal stories provide insight into how individuals deal with their disease." Voice Youth Advocates
  Includes glossary and bibliographical references

Shmaefsky, Brian
Toxic shock syndrome; [by] Brian R. Shmaefsky; consulting editor, Hilary Babcock; foreword by David L. Heymann. 2nd ed. Chelsea House 2010 127p il (Deadly diseases and epidemics) $34.95

Grades: 8 9 10 11 12   616.9
  1. Toxic shock syndrome
  ISBN 978-1-60413-243-4; 1-60413-243-4
                      LC 2010029222
  First published 2003
This describes types of toxic shock syndrome, its causes, diagnosis and treatment.
  Includes glossary and bibliographical references

Turkington, Carol
The encyclopedia of infectious diseases; [by] Carol Turkington, Bonnie Lee Ashby. 3rd ed. Facts On File 2007 412p (Facts on File library of health and living) $75 *

Grades: 11 12 Adult   616.9
  1. Reference books 2. Communicable diseases—Encyclopedias
  ISBN 0-8160-6397-4; 978-0-8160-6397-0
                      LC 2006-13795
  First published 1998
"The alphabetically arranged volume covers diseases, treatment options, and relevant organizations. . . . Information is provided for each disease and includes its cause, symptoms, treatment, and prevention. Major diseases that have had an impact on the world's population (tuberculosis, AIDS) are covered . . . and include a history. This feature makes the volume useful to researchers and students." Booklist [review of 2003 edition]
  Includes bibliographical references

616.95   Sexually transmitted diseases

Ambrose, Marylou
Investigating STDs (sexually transmitted diseases); real facts for real lives; [by] Marylou Ambrose and Veronica Deisler. Enslow Publishers 2010 c2011 160p il (Investigating diseases) lib bdg $34.60
Grades: 7 8 9 10   **616.95**
    1. Sexually transmitted diseases
    ISBN 978-0-7660-3342-9; 0-7660-3342-2
                       LC 2008-50061
The authors offer "facts about sexually transmitted diseases. Real-life examples of how teens deal with these issues are mixed with data from scientific studies, tips on how to live with and treat STDs, and the history of STDs." Publisher's note
Includes glossary and bibliographical references

Dougherty, Terri, 1964-
Sexually transmitted diseases. Lucent Books 2010 96p il (Diseases and disorders series) $32.45
Grades: 7 8 9 10   **616.95**
    1. Sexually transmitted diseases
    ISBN 978-1-4205-0220-6   LC 2009-39583
"This book discusses the most common afflictions, diseases that are usually found in combinations, medical advances, and how the outlook for STDs is complicated by new trends such as drug-resistant strains. Information is also supplied about causes, prevention, diagnosis, and treatment. . . . A number of the photos show some of the horrific physical manifestations in individuals, including infants. . . . [This book] should be considered for first purchase." SLJ
Includes bibliographical references

Moore, Elaine A., 1948-
Encyclopedia of sexually transmitted diseases; [by] Elaine A. Moore with Lisa Marie Moore; illustrations by Marvin G. Miller. McFarland 2005 280p il $65 *
Grades: 11 12 Adult   **616.95**
    1. Reference books 2. Sexually transmitted diseases—Encyclopedias
    ISBN 0-7864-1794-3   LC 2004-18309
"This encyclopedia offers entries on such topics as diseases, treatments, statistics, care centers and departments, risk factors, prevention issues, legal issues, associations and organizations, procedures, and relevant historical and political information. Entries on sexually transmitted diseases include history, causes and origins, risk factors, precautions, incidence, symptoms, special problems relating to gender, race, or poverty level, diagnosis, descriptions of diagnostic tests, defining illnesses and related disorders, treatment (drug regimens, therapies, side effects, and alternative medicine), and considerations in pregnancy." Publisher's note
Includes bibliographical references

Sexually transmitted diseases: opposing viewpoints; Margaret Haerens, book editor. Greenhaven Press 2007 213p lib bdg $34.95; pa $23.70 *
Grades: 10 11 12   **616.95**
    1. Sexually transmitted diseases
    ISBN 0-7377-3333-0 (lib bdg); 978-0-7377-3333-4 (lib bdg); 0-7377-3334-9 (pa); 978-0-7377-3334-1 (pa)
                  LC 2006-17067
"Opposing viewpoints series"
Topics discussed in this anthology include "whether sexually transmitted diseases are serious problems, how the government should educate youth about STDs, what individuals should do to reduce their spread, and how the global AIDS crisis should be addressed." SLJ
Includes bibliographical references

616.97   Diseases of immune system

Cunningham, Kevin, 1966-
HIV/AIDS. Morgan Reynolds Pub. 2009 144p il (Diseases in history) lib bdg $28.95
Grades: 8 9 10 11 12   **616.97**
    1. AIDS (Disease)
    ISBN 978-1-59935-104-9; 1-59935-104-8
                  LC 2008-51616
"Explores the origin of the two types of HIV viruses and the reasons why poverty, promiscuity, and the common use of world blood supplies enable its horrible and devastatingly rapid spread. . . . This detailed overview . . . will appeal to more advanced students. The research is thorough and the writing is insightful, thought provoking, and accessible." Voice Youth Advocates
Includes glossary and bibliographical references

Ehrlich, Paul
Living with allergies; [by] Paul M. Ehrlich, with Elizabeth Shimer Bowers. Facts On File 2009 168p (Teen's guides) $34.95; pa $14.95
Grades: 7 8 9 10 11 12   **616.97**
    1. Allergy
    ISBN   978-0-8160-7327-6;   0-8160-7327-9; 978-0-8160-7742-7 (pa); 0-8160-7742-8 (pa)
                  LC 2008-34352
This "book addresses allergy triggers, preventing allergic reactions, what to expect from treatment, paying for care, and how to help yourself, friends, or family members who may have allergies." Publisher's note
Includes glossary and bibliographical references

Gordon, Sherri Mabry
Peanut butter, milk, and other deadly threats; what you should know about food allergies. Enslow Publishers 2006 112p il (Issues in focus today) $31.93 *
Grades: 8 9 10 11 12   **616.97**
    1. Food allergy
    ISBN 0-7660-2529-2   LC 2005-29219
Discusses what it is like to live with food allergies, how teens and their families cope with them, the causes

Gordon, Sherri Mabry—*Continued*
of food allergies, and the research being done to prevent and control them

"The format is open, with plenty of white space, making the book accessible to reluctant readers. Full-color photos, helpful case studies, and a list of reputable organizations to contact for further information are included." SLJ

Includes glossary and bibliographical references

James, Otto
AIDS. Smart Apple Media 2010 46p il (Voices) lib bdg $34.95
Grades: 7 8 9 10 11 12   **616.97**
1. AIDS (Disease)
ISBN 978-1-59920-282-2; 1-59920-282-4
LC 2009-5417

"*AIDS* looks at causes, prevention, treatment, and the chances of a cure and also discusses abstinence, safe sex, the cost of AIDS drugs, and much more. . . . [The] blend of current political debate with witnesses' close-up experiences told through photos, narratives, and quotes will draw browsers, and many will go on to find out more." Booklist

Includes glossary and bibliographical references

Marsico, Katie, 1980-
HIV/AIDS. ABDO Pub. Co. 2010 112p il (Essential issues) lib bdg $22.95
Grades: 7 8 9 10   **616.97**
1. AIDS (Disease)
ISBN 978-1-60453-955-4; 1-60453-955-0
LC 2009-29954

This book discusses "global impacts of HIV/AIDS, medications to help infected persons, and medical research and education to prevent contraction of HIV/AIDS." Publisher's note

This is "well-written, providing examples that put a human face to each problem. Quotes and facts are clearly attributed, and their sources are noted in the extensive back matter. . . . Sidebars provide further information, or, more compellingly, offer stories about those touched by the topic. . . . [This] will be of great assistance to students writing reports." SLJ

Includes glossary and bibliographical references

Quicksand; HIV/AIDS in our world; by Anonymous. Candlewick Press 2009 103p $15.99
Grades: 6 7 8 9 10   **616.97**
1. AIDS (Disease)
ISBN 978-0-7636-1589-5; 0-7636-1589-7
LC 2009-7761

"The anonymous author explains her motivation for writing this book by telling readers that ten years ago, when HIV/AIDS was still considered a taboo subject, her brother-in-law was diagnosed with the disease. She writes in a truthful, open manner, addressing common questions about HIV/AIDS and providing easy-to-understand and honest advice. . . . The author's personal insight is what makes this book an important addition. Topics address everything from the history of HIV/AIDS to how to protect oneself from the disease. She also provides suggestions on how to cope with hearing that a

family or friend has HIV/AIDS. . . . The author's focus on how the disease affects all people, whether they have contracted HIV/AIDS or not, makes this book a must-have for all teen collections." Voice Youth Advocates

Includes glossary and bibliographical references

Watstein, Sarah B.
The encyclopedia of HIV and AIDS; [by] Sarah Barbara Watstein, Stephen E. Stratton; foreword by Evelyn J. Fisher. 2nd ed. Facts on File 2003 660p $71.50 *
Grades: 11 12 Adult   **616.97**
1. Reference books 2. AIDS (Disease)—Dictionaries
ISBN 0-8160-4808-8   LC 2002-35220
"Facts on File library of health and living"
First published 1998 with title: The AIDS dictionary

This volume includes "entries covering the basic biological, medical, financial, legal, political, and social issues and terms associated with HIV and AIDS. Entries explain symptoms and treatments, opportunistic infections, prevention strategies, and much more. Appendixes include HIV/AIDS associations, education centers, clinical trials, hotlines, publications, and additional material." Publisher's note

"The coverage is . . . broad and the language is pitched for the intended audience of nonspecialists . . . vastly expanded and brought up to date. . . . Recommended." Choice

Includes bibliographical references

616.99 Tumors and miscellaneous communicable diseases

Bozzone, Donna M.
Causes of cancer. Chelsea House 2007 136p il (Biology of cancer) lib bdg $35
Grades: 8 9 10 11 12   **616.99**
1. Cancer
ISBN 978-0-7910-8819-7; 0-7910-8819-7
LC 2007-9174

This book "delves into the many factors responsible for causing cancer, from environmental conditions to abnormal in vitro and in vivo developments to viruses and cancers caused by exposure to radiation." Publisher's note

Includes glossary and bibliographical references

Cancer information for teens; edited by Lisa Bakewell and Karen Bellenir. 2nd ed. Omnigraphics 2010 445p il (Teen health series) $69
Grades: 8 9 10 11 12   **616.99**
1. Cancer
ISBN 978-0-7808-1085-3; 0-7808-1085-6
LC 2009-28456

First published 2004

"Health tips about cancer awareness, prevention, diagnosis, and treatment including facts about cancers of most concern to teens and young adults, cancer risk factors, and coping strategies for teens fighting cancer or dealing with cancer in friends or family members." Title page

Cancer information for teens—*Continued*

"Written specifically for teens or their family members who have cancer, this volume will be a helpful, authoritative resource that should lead readers to further information about it. . . . It offers information that is current, accurate, and accessible." SLJ

Includes bibliographical references

Casil, Amy Sterling

Pancreatic cancer; current and emerging trends in detection and treatment. Rosen Pub. 2009 64p il (Cancer and modern science) lib bdg $29.25

Grades: 7 8 9 10 11 12　　　　　　　　**616.99**

1. Pancreas—Cancer

ISBN 978-1-4358-5008-8; 1-4358-5008-4

　　　　　　　　　　　　　　　LC 2008-25132

This book describes pancreatic cancer and its treatment.

"Clearly aimed at teens who have cancer or know someone who does, . . . [this title combines] lots of technical detail about anatomy, physiology, and pathology with a personal, interactive style. . . . With a highly readable design, including crisp color photos and anatomical diagrams, the [book] will also serve the needs of student researchers. Also features excellent, extensive back matter." Booklist

Includes glossary and bibliographical references

Cramer, Scott D.

Prostate cancer; founding editor, the late I. Edward Alcamo; foreword by David Heymann. Chelsea House 2007 136p il map (Deadly diseases and epidemics) $31.95

Grades: 7 8 9 10 11 12　　　　　　　　**616.99**

1. Prostate gland—Cancer

ISBN 0-7910-8935-5; 978-0-7910-8935-4

　　　　　　　　　　　　　　　LC 2006-24074

"This book provides a . . . look at this dangerous disease with insights on prevention, recognition, and treatment." Publisher's note

Includes glossary and bibliographical references

Ferreiro, Carmen, 1958-

Lung cancer; founding editor, the late, I. Edward Alcamo; foreword by David Heymann. Chelsea House 2006 144p il (Deadly diseases and epidemics) $31.95

Grades: 7 8 9 10 11 12　　　　　　　　**616.99**

1. Lung cancer

ISBN 0-7910-8937-1; 978-0-7910-8937-8

　　　　　　　　　　　　　　　LC 2006-10422

This book offers "details on new methods for early detection, improvements in conventional treatment (surgery, chemotherapy, and radiotherapy), and the development of new therapies that specifically target cancer cells." Publisher's note

Includes glossary and bibliographical references

Fies, Brian

Mom's cancer. Abrams ComicArts 2008 115p il $14.95

Grades: 9 10 11 12 Adult　　　　　　　　**616.99**

1. Graphic novels 2. Biographical graphic novels 3. Cancer—Graphic novels

ISBN 978-0-8109-7107-3

First published 2006

When writer/cartoonist Fies learned his mother had cancer and that it had already spread from her lungs, he used webcomics to depict what was happening to his mother and the rest of the family as Mom fought the cancer. All the pain, the heartache, the little battles won, the effects on Fies' relationships with his sisters, the ultimate hope are all on the page. In the end, Mom beat the cancer. In an afterword, Fies tells the reader that some of the medications just wore down his mother's body, and she died shortly before the book was published.

Freedman, Jeri

Brain cancer; current and emerging trends in detection and treatment. Rosen Pub. 2009 63p il (Cancer and modern science) lib bdg $29.25

Grades: 7 8 9 10 11 12　　　　　　　　**616.99**

1. Brain—Cancer

ISBN 978-1-4358-5011-8; 1-4358-5011-4

　　　　　　　　　　　　　　　LC 2008-22086

This book combines "lots of technical detail about anatomy, physiology, and pathology with a personal, interactive style. . . . *Brain Cancer* includes a section on Coping with School and Community that speaks directly to students with the disease and encourages them to stay active and involved. It also looks in detail at different types of brain cancer, detection and diagnosis, and present and future treatments." Booklist

Includes glossary and bibliographical references

Goldsmith, Connie, 1945-

Skin cancer. Twenty-First Century Books 2010 128p il (USA Today health reports: diseases and disorders) lib bdg $34.60

Grades: 7 8 9 10 11 12　　　　　　　　**616.99**

1. Skin—Diseases 2. Cancer

ISBN 978-0-7613-5469-7; 0-7613-5469-7

　　　　　　　　　　　　　　　LC 2010-10003

This describes causes, prevention, and treatments of skin cancer.

This is "liberally sprinkled with relevant articles and 'snapshots' (graphs showing statistical breakdowns of the topic at hand) from the newspaper, providing a competent introduction to primary-source material." SLJ

Includes glossary and bibliographical references

McKinnell, Robert Gilmore

Prevention of cancer; [by] Robert G. McKinnell; consulting editor, Donna M. Bozzone. Chelsea House 2008 144p il (Biology of cancer) lib bdg $31.95

Grades: 8 9 10 11 12　　　　　　　　**616.99**

1. Cancer

ISBN 978-0-7910-8827-2; 0-7910-8827-8

　　　　　　　　　　　　　　　LC 2007-34259

This book is "highly readable with interesting anecdotes as well as key scientific information to enable students to make informed choices in lifestyle to lower their risk of cancer. . . . [It] focuses on cancers of the skin,

McKinnell, Robert Gilmore—*Continued*
uterus, breast, and lung, emphasizing that at least half of cancers are preventable if people avoid risk factors and maintain healthy life styles. . . . The positive and non-preachy tone . . . empowers students to assume responsibility to reduce their risk to cancer rather than to accept cancer as part of our lives." Voice Youth Advocates
Includes glossary and bibliographical references

Panno, Joseph
Cancer; the role of genes, lifestyle, and environment. Facts On File 2010 c2011 246p il (The new biology) $40 *
Grades: 9 10 11 12   **616.99**
1. Cancer
ISBN 978-0-8160-6848-7   LC 2009-50783
First published 2004
This book "explores the many facets of cancer research, from basic genetic and cellular mechanisms to the danger of carcinogens and the influence of lifestyle. . . . Chapters focus on the unique characteristics of normal cells, cancer cells, cancer genes, and cancer progression, as well as the recent shift in the scientific community regarding the root cause of cancer." Publisher's note
Includes bibliographical references

Silverstein, Alvin
Cancer; [by] Alvin & Virginia Silverstein & Laura Silverstein Nunn. Twenty-First Century Books 2006 121p il (Twenty-first century medical library) lib bdg $26.90
Grades: 9 10 11 12   **616.99**
1. Cancer
ISBN 0-7613-2833-5; 978-0-7613-2833-9
                                      LC 2003-12638
Explains different types of cancer, their causes, symptoms and treatment, and, through case studies, what it is like to live with cancer.
This book "will interest readers who want to learn everything they can about the current medical state of cancer research, diagnosis, and treatment." SLJ
Includes bibliographical references

Spencer, Juliet V.
Cervical cancer; founding editor, the late I. Edward Alcamo; foreword by David Heymann. Chelsea House 2006 128p il map (Deadly diseases and epidemics) $31.95
Grades: 7 8 9 10 11 12   **616.99**
1. Cervix—Cancer
ISBN 0-7910-8941-X; 978-0-7910-8941-5
                                      LC 2006-12586
This "volume explains the causes, symptoms, progress, and treatment of cervical cancer." Publisher's note
Includes glossary and bibliographical references

617.1 Injuries and wounds

Everyday sports injuries. DK 2010 272p il pa $21.95 *
Grades: 9 10 11 12   **617.1**

1. Sports medicine 2. Wounds and injuries
ISBN 978-0-7566-5737-6
"Featuring more than 150 step-by step exercise routines for recovery after injury, improving strength and performance, and reducing risk of injury, . . . [this is a] guide to recognizing, treating, and preventing injury, with the goal of getting back in action as soon as possible." Publisher's note

Minigh, Jennifer L., 1971-
Sports medicine. Greenwood Press 2007 251p (Health and medical issues today) $45
Grades: 11 12 Adult   **617.1**
1. Sports medicine
ISBN 978-0-313-33894-6; 0-313-33894-9
                                      LC 2007-21471
This book "provides readers and researchers . . . [an] introduction to the medical, scientific, legal, and cultural issues surrounding sports medicine and its import in today's world of healthcare." Publisher's note
Includes glossary and bibliographical references

Oakes, Elizabeth H., 1951-
The encyclopedia of sports medicine; [by] Elizabeth Oakes; foreword by Connie Lebrun. Facts on File 2005 322p il (Facts on File library of health and living) $75 *
Grades: 11 12 Adult   **617.1**
1. Reference books 2. Sports medicine—Encyclopedias
ISBN 0-8160-5334-0   LC 2003-24720
"More than 150 entries . . . describe causes, diagnosis, prevention, and treatment of sports injuries for amateur and professional athletes." Booklist
"This is an excellent resource for weekend, varsity high school and college, and professional athletes, and for trainers." Choice
Includes bibliographical references

Shryer, Donna
Peak performance; sports nutrition. Marshall Cavendish Benchmark 2007 142p il (Food and fitness) $37.07
Grades: 7 8 9 10   **617.1**
1. Athletes—Nutrition 2. Sports medicine 3. Physical fitness
ISBN 978-0-7614-2554-0; 0-7614-2554-3
                                      LC 2007-2271
"Provides a basic, comprehensive introduction to sports nutrition, including information on how nutrients help the athlete reach peak performance, with a review of the food pyramid and how to read labels to make healthy food choices." Publisher's note
This is "timely, well written, and appealing. . . . Charts and graphs highlight the textual information and enhance the usability of [this book]." Libr Media Connect
Includes glossary and bibliographical references

Sports injuries information for teens; edited by Karen Bellenir. 2nd ed. Omnigraphics 2008 429p il (Teen health series) $62 *

Grades: 7 8 9 10 11 12   **617.1**

1. Sports medicine 2. Wounds and injuries

ISBN 978-0-7808-1011-2; 0-7808-1011-2

                 LC 2008-9793

First published 2004

"Health tips about acute, traumatic, and chronic injuries in adolescent athletes including facts about sprains, fractures, and overuse injuries, treatment, rehabilitation, sport-specific safety guidelines, fitness suggestions, and more." Title page

"Along with physiological information about injuries and treatments, the special needs of teen athletes are considered in this comprehensive overview. . . . The information presented is copious and concise." SLJ [review of 2004 edition]

Includes bibliographical references

617.7   Ophthalmology

Kornmehl, Ernest W., 1959-

LASIK: a guide to laser vision correction; [by] Ernest W. Kornmehl, Robert K. Maloney, Jonathan M. Davidorf. 2nd ed. Addicus Books 2006 121p il pa $14.95 *

Grades: 11 12 Adult   **617.7**

1. Eye—Surgery

ISBN 1-886039-79-8; 978-1-886039-79-7

                 LC 2005-35027

First published 2001

"Among the topics the authors cover: how laser surgery works, who is a good candidate for surgery, finding a qualified surgeon, what to expect from the procedure, and post-procedure care." Publisher's note

"The color illustrations are clear and instructive, and the risks and complications associated with the procedure are well delineated." Libr J

617.9   Operative surgery and special fields of surgery

Cheney, Annie

Body brokers; inside America's underground trade in human remains. Broadway Books 2006 205p $23.95; pa $14 *

Grades: 11 12 Adult   **617.9**

1. Procurement of organs, tissues, etc.

ISBN   0-7679-1733-2;   978-0-7679-1733-9; 0-7679-1734-0 (pa); 978-0-7679-1734-6 (pa)

                 LC 2005-54278

This is an exposé of "the lucrative business of procuring, buying, and selling human cadavers and body parts." Publisher's note

This book "speeds along like a circular saw through a thigh joint. It's a zippy, entertaining read, and more formal, scholarly works on the topic are not." N Y Times Book Rev

Includes bibliographical references

McClellan, Marilyn

Organ and tissue transplants; medical miracles and challenges. Enslow Pubs. 2003 128p il (Issues in focus) lib bdg $20.95

Grades: 7 8 9 10   **617.9**

1. Transplantation of organs, tissues, etc. 2. Artificial organs

ISBN 0-7660-1943-8   LC 2002-8401

Explores the history of organ transplantation, as well as its medical, ethical, financial, and personal aspects, providing insights into the latter through stories of organ donors and recipients

"With its useful black-and-white photos, anatomical diagram, pie chart, and statistics, this book is equally approachable for curious readers and report writers." SLJ

Includes glossary and bibliographical references

Schwartz, Tina P., 1969-

Organ transplants; a survival guide for the entire family: the ultimate teen guide. Scarecrow Press 2005 243p il (It happened to me) $36.50 *

Grades: 7 8 9 10   **617.9**

1. Transplantation of organs, tissues, etc.

ISBN 0-8108-4924-0   LC 2004-21563

"The 13 chapters, written in a question-and-answer format, detail the steps involved from diagnosis and being placed on a waiting list to pre and post-surgery. . . .The well-written text is complemented by a comprehensive section of suggestions for additional information. . . . Texts with this breadth of coverage are rare." SLJ

Includes bibliographical references

618   Other branches of medicine. Gynecology and obstetrics

Hollen, Kathryn H.

The reproductive system. Greenwood Press 2004 xx, 193p il (Human body systems) $65 *

Grades: 11 12 Adult   **618**

1. Reproductive system

ISBN 0-313-32449-2   LC 2004-43638

This book "discusses the reproductive organs, hormones, conception through childbirth and development after birth including puberty. The history of research on the reproductive system is presented and the future of research in this field is considered. Current controversies and dilemmas are also explored." Publisher's note

Includes bibliographical references

Krohmer, Randolph W.

The reproductive system; [by] Randolph Krohmer. Chelsea House 2009 116p il (The human body: how it works) lib bdg $35

Grades: 7 8 9 10   **618**

1. Reproductive system

ISBN 978-1-60413-373-8; 1-60413-373-2

                 LC 2009-22140

Examines the workings of the male and female reproductive systems and the complex process of human reproduction.

Includes glossary and bibliographical references

Zach, Kim K., 1958-
Reproductive technology. Lucent Books 2005
112p il (Great medical discoveries) $27.45 *
Grades: 9 10 11 12   **618**
  1. Reproductive technology
  ISBN 1-59018-344-4   LC 2003-15403
  Contents: Reproductive technology: new hope for in-
fertile couples; Treating male infertility: artificial and donor insemination; Fertility enhancement: drug therapy
and microsurgery; The keystone of assisted reproduction:
in vitro fertilization; Surrogacy, egg donation, and embryo adoption; Preventing inherited disease:
preimplantation genetic diagnosis; Drawing the line: ethical, moral, and social questions
  "For students studying ethics or science, this book will
provide concise, clear information for reports. . . . Teens
will find understandable, complete explanations for their
assignments or clarification if there are fertility issues
within their families" SLJ
  Includes bibliographical references

618.1 Gynecology

Waters, Sophie
Seeing the gynecologist. Rosen Pub. Group
2007 47p il (Girls' health) $19.95
Grades: 7 8 9 10 11 12   **618.1**
  1. Women—Health and hygiene 2. Girls—Health and
hygiene
  ISBN 978-1-4042-1948-9; 1-4042-1948-X
                                          LC 2007-1633
  "Introductory chapters include a brief introduction to
the physiology of women's reproduction and menstruation, but the majority of the book covers the specifics of
a gynecological visit, from choosing a doctor and insurance concerns to what happens during a pelvic exam.
. . . The accessible text is informative and supportive."
Booklist
  Includes bibliographical references

Weiss, Marisa C.
Taking care of your 'girls'; a breast health guide
for girls, teens, and in-betweens; [by] Marisa C.
Weiss and Isabel Friedman. Three Rivers Press
2008 237p il pa $15.95
Grades: 9 10 11 12   **618.1**
  1. Breast 2. Girls—Health and hygiene
  ISBN 978-0-307-40696-5   LC 2008-17457
  The authors "have surveyed 3,000 mothers and their
daughters to produce this chatty but informative book on
breast health for girls and adolescents. The text covers
everything from getting the first bra to risk factors for
breast cancer . . . and is peppered with questions posed
by girls of all ages, ranging from when to start regular
breast exams to why breasts sometimes feel painful or
tender. . . . This empowering book will be an excellent
impetus for honest conversations about breast health and
development." Publ Wkly
  Includes bibliographical references

618.3 Diseases and complications of pregnancy

Tsiaras, Alexander
From conception to birth; a life unfolds; {by}
Alexander Tsiaras; text by Barry Werth.
Doubleday 2002 283p il $35 *
Grades: 9 10 11 12   **618.3**
  1. Prenatal diagnosis 2. Pregnancy
  ISBN 0-385-50318-0   LC 2002-24707
  Using images created with newly developed medical
imaging technology, "the book tracks the development of
a baby from the moment of conception, through the ex-
plosively complex early stages of development and the
amazing stages of growth as the baby is nurtured by the
mother, ending with the joy of birth." Publisher's note

618.92 Pediatrics

Attention deficit/hyperactivity disorder; William
Dudley, book editor. Greenhaven Press 2005
77p (At issue) lib bdg $28.70; pa $19.95 *
Grades: 9 10 11 12   **618.92**
  1. Attention deficit disorder
  ISBN 0-7377-2258-4 (lib bdg); 0-7377-2259-2 (pa)
                                          LC 2004-54303
  "This anthology features . . . opinions on the extent
of ADHD, its causes, and what kinds of treatment are
best." Publisher's note
  Includes bibliographical references

Attention deficit hyperactivity disorder; Heidi
Williams, book editor. Greenhaven Press 2011
133p il map (Issues that concern you) $35.75
Grades: 9 10 11 12   **618.92**
  1. Attention deficit disorder
  ISBN 978-0-7377-4950-2; 0-7377-4950-4
                                          LC 2010-13958
  "Following a brief introduction, this volume contains
14 short articles on ADHD, current treatments, and con-
troversies. . . . A useful resource for students with
ADHD and their parents and teachers is appended." SLJ
  Includes bibliographical references

Nakaya, Andrea C.
ADHD. ReferencePoint Press 2009 108p il map
(Compact research. Diseases and disorders) $25.95
Grades: 7 8 9 10 11 12   **618.92**
  1. Attention deficit disorder
  ISBN 978-1-60152-062-3; 1-60152-062-X
  "ADHD thoroughly examines the disorder and incor-
porates numerous first-person accounts, including some
from adults who find that the condition helps them excel
in the workplace." Booklist
  Includes bibliographical references

Rouba, Kelly, 1980-
Juvenile arthritis; the ultimate teen guide.
Scarecrow Press 2009 289p il (It happened to me)
lib bdg $49
Grades: 7 8 9 10 **618.92**
1. Arthritis
ISBN 978-0-8108-6055-1; 0-8108-6055-4
LC 2008-42317
"Rouba gives advice on living with the disease, including treatment options, diet and exercise tips, and managing mental and physical health." Voice Youth Advocates
Includes bibliographical references

620 Engineering

Berlow, Lawrence H., 1945-
The reference guide to famous engineering landmarks of the world; bridges, tunnels, dams, roads, and other structures. Oryx Press 1997 c1998
250p il $73.95 *
Grades: 11 12 Adult **620**
ISBN 0-89774-966-9 LC 97-36051
"The main section is an alphabetically arranged, double-column compendium of facts and histories of 600 structures. The format of each entry begins with the structure's location and date of construction. Size is often given, including metric, and the basic facts of the construction are provided. . . . A biography section provides background on 52 significant engineers or designers. A chronology section begins with the oldest surviving dam in the world (in Egypt) and continues to 2010, when a monster skyscraper, Millennium Tower, will be completed in Tokyo." Booklist

Hall, J. Storrs
Nanofuture; what's next for nanotechnology; foreword by K. Eric Drexler. Prometheus Books 2005 333p il $29 *
Grades: 11 12 Adult **620**
1. Nanotechnology
ISBN 1-59102-287-8 LC 2005-1789
The author covers "the physical principles of engineering at the atomic scale, possible applications of nanomachines, and their potential alteration of human society." Booklist
"This book fills a niche as a brief, inspirational introduction to nanotechnology for budding nanoscientists as well as the general public." Choice

Molotch, Harvey Luskin
Where stuff comes from; how toasters, toilets, cars, computers, and many other things come to be as they are; [by] Harvey Molotch. Routledge 2003 324p il $35; pa $29.95
Grades: 11 12 Adult **620**
1. Engineering
ISBN 0-415-94400-7; 0-415-95042-2 (pa)
LC 2003-1191

The author examines "the complicated, dynamic relationships between inventor, society, corporation, regulator, shopkeeper, community, family and customer. . . . Myriad links, he argues, ultimately produce and constantly change what we want, buy, keep and throw away; thus, neither consumers nor producers are to be blamed for our numerous possessions. . . . Molotch's description of systemic person-product complexes could work to end blame-the-consumer guilt-mongering in the popular discourse." Publ Wkly
Includes bibliographical references

Petroski, Henry
Success through failure; the paradox of design.
Princeton University Press 2006 235p il hardcover o.p. pa $21.95
Grades: 11 12 Adult **620**
1. Engineering 2. Design
ISBN 978-0-691-12225-0; 0-691-12225-3; 978-0-691-13642-4 (pa); 0-691-13642-4 (pa)
LC 2005-34126
The author explores the "relationship between success and failure in engineering design. Ingenuity is explored as a pendulum that swings between success and failure, driven by design philosophy and practices in a given place and time. Case studies and examples include bridges, spacecrafts, airports, buildings with architectural celebrity, New Coke, U-Locks, and notable structures that have suffered from performance issues." Libr J
An "engaging and readable book. . . . Petroski uses countless interesting case histories to show how failure motivates technological advancement." IEEE Spectrum
Includes bibliographical references

Tobin, James, 1956-
Great projects; the epic story of the building of America: from the taming of the Mississippi to the invention of the Internet. Free Press 2001 322p il maps hardcover o.p. pa $31.95
Grades: 11 12 Adult **620**
ISBN 0-7432-1064-6; 1-4516-1301-6 (pa)
LC 2001-33016
This describes eight construction projects and innovations including "the flood-control works of the lower Mississippi, Hoover Dam, Edison's lighting system, the spread of electricity across the nation, the great Croton Aqueduct, the bridges of New York City, Boston's revamped street system, known as the Big Dig, and the [Internet]." Publisher's note
"The clearly written, nontechnical narratives are lively and comprehensive." Libr J
Includes bibliographical references

620.1 Engineering mechanics and materials

Finkelstein, Norman H., 1941-
Plastics; [by] Norman H. Finkelstein. Marshall Cavendish Benchmark 2007 c2008 144p il (Great inventions) lib bdg $27.95
Grades: 7 8 9 10 **620.1**
1. Plastics
ISBN 978-0-7614-2600-4 LC 2006020909

Finkelstein, Norman H., 1941-—*Continued*
"An examination of the origin, history, development, and societal impact of the development of plastics." Publisher's note
Includes glossary and bibliographical references

Freinkel, Susan, 1957-
Plastic; a toxic love story. Houghton Mifflin Harcourt 2011 324p $27
Grades: 11 12 Adult   **620.1**
   1. Plastics
   ISBN 978-0-547-15240-0   LC 2010-43019
"At first a godsend, [plastic] reduced dependence on shrinking natural resources, such as the shell of the hawksbill turtle (combs) or elephants' ivory (billiard balls and piano keys.) Ultimately it democratized materialism, making everything available to everybody, cheaply. Now, the partner we've found in plastic 'can rightly inspire both our deepest admiration and our strongest disgust.' To describe its history, wonders and dangers, journalist Freinkel reviews eight products: the comb, the chair, the Frisbee, the IV bag, the disposable lighter, the grocery bag, the soda bottle and the credit card. You will not look casually at any of them again." Cleveland Plain Dealer
Includes bibliographical references

621   Applied physics

Alley, Richard B.
Earth; the operators' manual. W.W. Norton 2011 479p il $27.95
Grades: 11 12 Adult   **621**
   1. Energy development 2. Renewable energy resources 3. Greenhouse effect
   ISBN 978-0-393-08109-1   LC 2010-54016
The author "presents a primer on combatting global warming. The book begins with a history of how fuel—from trees, whale oil, and petroleum—has been instrumental to civilization and how we tend to exhaust our sources. He goes on to explain how scientists study climate change and why the evidence is convincing, and ends with a call to action and an overview of possible solutions. . . . This optimistic book ought to convince even the most obstinate climate-change denier." Publ Wkly
Includes bibliographical references

621.3   Electrical, magnetic, optical, communications, computer engineering; electronics, lighting

Jonnes, Jill, 1952-
Empires of light; Edison, Tesla, Westinghouse, and the race to electrify the world. Random House 2003 416p il hardcover o.p. pa $15.95
Grades: 9 10 11 12   **621.3**
   1. Edison, Thomas A. (Thomas Alva), 1847-1931 2. Tesla, Nikola, 1856-1943 3. Westinghouse, George, 1846-1914 4. Electric power
   ISBN 0-375-50739-6; 0-375-75884-4 (pa)
                                      LC 2002-31866

The author "details the rise and fall of the three visionaries who harnessed electricity, while also offering a critique of corporate greed. Her tale emphasizes the 'War of the Electric Currents,' in which Thomas Edison sought to defend the primacy of his direct current electrical system against George Westinghouse's higher-voltage and more broadly applicable alternating current system. Nikola Tesla, the somewhat kooky Serbian genius (and former Edison man), joined the fray on Westinghouse's side with his AC induction motor. Jonnes serves up plenty of color in an engaging and relaxed style." Publ Wkly
Includes bibliographical references

McNichol, Tom
AC/DC; the savage tale of the first standards war. Jossey-Bass 2006 198p $26.95
Grades: 11 12 Adult   **621.3**
   1. Edison, Thomas A. (Thomas Alva), 1847-1931 2. Tesla, Nikola, 1856-1943 3. Westinghouse, George, 1846-1914 4. Electric currents 5. Electricity
   ISBN 978-0-7879-8267-6; 0-7879-8267-9
                                      LC 2006013041
"A little more than 100 years ago, two titans of industry faced off in one of the most vicious battles the marketplace had ever seen. On one side, Thomas Edison, inventor extraordinaire, the creator of the phonograph and the electric light; on the other, George Westinghouse, tycoon and titan, backing the mysterious eastern European inventor Nikola Tesla. They fought over the very nature of the electrical system in America: would it be built on alternating current (as Westinghouse proposed), or direct current la Edison? Though a battle over electrical standards sounds dry, this tale is anything but. McNichol's solid if brief survey of this relatively unknown moment in the history of technology ranges from macabre electrocutions of hapless animals (and eventually prison inmates) as demonstrations of the 'Death Current' to the gleaming 'electrical wonderland' of the 1893 World's Columbian Exhibition in Chicago." Publ Wkly
Includes bibliographical references

Shulman, Seth
The telephone gambit; chasing Alexander Graham Bell's secret. W. W. Norton & Co. 2008 256p il $24.95
Grades: 11 12 Adult   **621.3**
   1. Bell, Alexander Graham, 1847-1922 2. Gray, Elisha, 1835-1901 3. Telephone
   ISBN 978-0-393-06206-9; 0-393-06206-6
                                      LC 2007-30904
The author argues that Alexander Graham Bell is not the true inventor of the telephone.
This book "does a neat job of painting, in rapid brush strokes, a portrait of the thrilling era of innovation in which Bell lived and also of the interesting circumstances of his life. . . . [He] also manages to lace his work with just enough technology to tell his story without losing the interest of any low-tech readers." Christ Sci Monit
Includes bibliographical references

621.31 Generation, modification, storage, transmission of electric power

Ford, R. A.

Homemade lightning; creative experiments in electricity. 3rd ed. McGraw-Hill 2001 257p il $24.95

Grades: 9 10 11 12 **621.31**
1. Electric generators 2. Science—Experiments
ISBN 0-07-137323-3 LC 2001-41014
First published 1991

This offers information about electrostatic generators and instruction for building various types, including experiments with electrohorticulture, gravitation and electricity, cold light, and electric tornadoes

621.381 Electronics

Reid, T. R.

The chip; how two Americans invented the microchip and launched a revolution. rev ed. Random House 2001 309p pa $13.95

Grades: 11 12 Adult **621.381**
1. Kilby, Jack, 1923-2005 2. Noyce, Robert, 1927-1990 3. Microelectronics
ISBN 0-375-75828-3 LC 2001-19694
First published 1984

"Reid explains the technology, traces the history of electronics, and tells the stories of the two young engineers who created the silicon microchip and launched the global information industry." Booklist

"Reid has successfully combined a work in the history of technology with important insights concerning today's world of high technology." Choice

Includes bibliographical references

Schultz, Mitchel E.

Grob's basic electronics. 11th ed. McGraw-Hill 2011 xxvi, 1206p il $155.31 *

Grades: 11 12 Adult **621.381**
1. Electricity 2. Electronics
ISBN 978-0-07-351085-9; 0-07-351085-8
LC 2010-8273
First published 1959 under the authorship of Bernard Grob. Periodically revised

Includes CD-ROM

An introductory text on the fundamentals of electricity and electronics for technicians in radio, television, and industrial electronics.

Includes glossary

621.3841 Specific topics in general radio

The **ARRL** handbook for radio communications 2011. 88th ed. American Radio Relay League 2010 various pagings il $49.95

Grades: 11 12 Adult **621.3841**

1. Radio—Handbooks, manuals, etc.
ISSN 1547-1470
ISBN 978-0-87259-095-3

Annual. Began publication 1926. Editions 1 through 61 published with title: The Radio amateur's handbook. Editions 62 through 79 published with title: The ARRL handbook for radio amateurs

Includes CD-ROM

"Chapters cover fundamentals and changing technology in the field and include many tables, circuit diagrams, photographs, and occasional references." Guide to Ref Books. 11th edition

621.43 Internal-combustion engines

Miller, Ron, 1947-

Rockets. Lerner 2008 112p il (Space innovations) lib bdg $31.93

Grades: 7 8 9 10 **621.43**
1. Rockets (Aeronautics) 2. Rocketry
ISBN 978-0-8225-7153-7; 0-8225-7153-6
LC 2006-21220

The author "describes the history of rocket science, beginning in ancient China, where saltpeter, sulfur, and charcoal were first combined to create gunpowder. . . . The stories of the development of rockets through time are complemented by short biographies of important scientists such as Robert Goddard, stories of young model rocket makers, and sidebars explaining the science that makes rockets work. . . . It is a good choice for high school libraries, as well as for boys who are interested in science and nonfiction." Voice Youth Advocates

Includes bibliographical references

621.46 Electric and related motors

Gabrielson, Curt

Kinetic contraptions; build a hovercraft, airboat, and more with a hobby motor. Chicago Review Press 2010 176p il pa $16.95

Grades: 7 8 9 10 **621.46**
1. Automobiles—Models 2. Motorboats—Models 3. Airplanes—Models
ISBN 978-1-55652-957-3; 1-55652-957-0
LC 2009-25695

The author "describes projects intended to foster in students a passion for electrical experimentation as they construct more than 20 motor-powered devices. With sections dedicated to creating machines that run on land, water, and air, as well as spinning machines (such as a snow globe) and bizarre machines (such as a bubble maker), the book has projects designed to appeal to everyone." Education Digest

621.47 Solar-energy engineering

Tabak, John
Solar and geothermal energy. Facts on File 2009 206p il map (Energy and the environment) $40
Grades: 9 10 11 12 Adult   **621.47**
  1. Renewable energy resources
  ISBN 978-0-8160-7086-2; 0-8160-7086-5
           LC 2008-26741
This book "describes two of the least environmentally disruptive sources of power by which electricity is generated today. In addition to describing the nature of solar and geothermal energy and the processes by which these sources of energy can be harnessed, this . . . book details how they are used in practice to supply electricity to the power markets." Publisher's note
Includes glossary and bibliographical references

621.48 Nuclear engineering

Tabak, John
Nuclear energy. Facts on File 2009 206p il map (Energy and the environment) $40
Grades: 9 10 11 12 Adult   **621.48**
  1. Nuclear energy
  ISBN 978-0-8160-7085-5; 0-8160-7085-7
           LC 2008-26036
This "title discusses the physics and technology of energy production, reactor design, nuclear safety, the relationship between commercial nuclear power and nuclear proliferation, and attempts made by the United States to resolve the problem of nuclear waste disposal." Publisher's note
Includes glossary and bibliographical references

621.8 Machine engineering

Gurstelle, William
Adventures from the technology underground; catapults, pulsejets, rail guns, flamethrowers, tesla coils, air cannons, and the garage warriors who love them. Clarkson Potter 2006 224p $25; pa $13.95
Grades: 11 12 Adult   **621.8**
  1. Machine design
  ISBN 1-4000-5082-0; 0-307-35125-4 (pa)
           LC 2005-20412
The author takes "readers into the hidden communities of people involved in developing hurling machines (catapults and trebuchets), pulse jet engines, flamethrowers, tesla coil-powered electric current theater, air cannons, robots, high-powered rockets, and magnetic linear accelerator guns. . . . Gurstelle balances scientific explanations of the technologies with profiles of the people who built them and descriptions of the events at which they were showcased." Libr J
Includes bibliographical references

622 Mining and related operations

Reece, Erik
Lost mountain; a year in the vanishing wilderness: radical strip mining, and the devastation of Appalachia; foreword by Wendell Berry; photographs by John J. Cox. Riverhead Books 2006 250p il $24.95; pa $14 *
Grades: 11 12 Adult   **622**
  1. Coal mines and mining 2. Human influence on nature 3. Appalachian region
  ISBN 1-59448-908-4; 1-59448-236-5 (pa)
           LC 2005-52921
The author explores the effects of strip mining on the landscape of Eastern Kentucky.
Reece "has written an impassioned account of a business rife with industrial greed, devious corporate ownership and unenforced environmental laws. It's also a heartrending account of the rural residents whose lives are being ruined by strip-mining's relentless, almost unfettered, encroachment." Publ Wkly
Includes bibliographical references

623.4 Ordnance

Conant, Jennet
109 East Palace; Robert Oppenheimer and the secret city of Los Alamos. Simon & Schuster 2005 425p map hardcover o.p. pa $14
Grades: 11 12 Adult   **623.4**
  1. McKibbin, Dorothy Scarritt, 1897-1985 2. Oppenheimer, J. Robert, 1904-1967 3. Los Alamos Scientific Laboratory 4. Manhattan Project 5. Atomic bomb
  ISBN 0-7432-5007-9; 0-7432-5008-7 (pa)
           LC 2005-42497
In this history of the creation of the atomic bomb, the author focuses "on daily life in Los Alamos. She tells the story largely through the eyes of Dorothy McKibben, who was in charge of the project's Santa Fe office, at 109 East Palace Street. This unassuming storefront was the portal to Los Alamos for all the physicists and military personnel who arrived in New Mexico." Booklist
"Anyone interested in the history of atomic weapons will find this book totally engrossing." Sci Books Films
Includes bibliographical references

Reinhardt, Hank, 1934-2007
The book of swords. Baen Pub. Enterprises 2009 235p il $35; pa $20
Grades: 11 12 Adult   **623.4**
  1. Swords—History 2. Weapons—History
  ISBN 978-1-439-13281-4; 978-1-439-13282-1 (pa)
           LC 2009-18226
"Drawing on information from grave excavations, illustrations of battle scenes, and many classical and medieval literary sources, this book discusses how contemporaries showed swords were used." Publisher's note
Includes bibliographical references

623.88   Seamanship

Pawson, Des
The handbook of knots. Expanded ed. DK 2004
176p il pa $17
Grades: 11 12 Adult   **623.88**
1. Knots and splices
ISBN 0-7566-0374-9; 978-0-7566-0374-8
LC 2004-274491
First published 1998
"This is a step-by-step guide to tying and using more
than 100 knots. . . . There's a chapter on rope construction, rope materials, and properties of ropes and their
main uses. It's very informative and put together concisely." BAYA Book Rev [review of 1998 edition]

624   Civil engineering

Macaulay, David, 1946-
Underground. Houghton Mifflin 1976 109p il
hardcover o.p. pa $9.95
Grades: 5 6 7 8 9   **624**
1. Civil engineering
ISBN 0-395-24739-X; 0-395-34065-9 (pa)
In this "examination of the intricate support systems
that lie beneath the street levels of our cities, Macaulay
explains the ways in which foundations for buildings are
laid or reinforced, and how the various utilities or transportation services are constructed." Bull Cent Child
Books
"Introduced by a visual index—a bird's eye view of
a busy, hypothetical intersection with colored indicators
marking the specific locations analyzed in subsequent
pages—detailed illustrations are combined with a clear,
precise narrative to make the subject comprehenssible
and fascinating." Horn Book
Includes glossary

Reeves, Diane Lindsey, 1959-
Career ideas for teens in architecture and
construction; [by] Diane Lindsey Reeves with Gail
Karlitz and Don Rauf. Ferguson 2005 170p il
(Career ideas for teens) $40
Grades: 7 8 9 10   **624**
1. Architecture 2. Building 3. Engineering
4. Vocational guidance
ISBN 0-8160-5289-1   LC 2004-20030
The careers described in this book include architect,
carpenter, electrician, interior designer, and urban planner

625.2   Railroad rolling stock

McDonnell, Greg, 1954-
Locomotives; the modern diesel & electric
reference. Boston Mills Press 2008 240p il $49.95;
pa $29.95
Grades: 11 12 Adult   **625.2**
1. Locomotives
ISBN 978-1-55046-493-1; 978-1-55407-896-7 (pa)
LC 2009417490

First published 2002 by Kalmbach Publishing with ti-
tle: Field guide to modern diesel locomotives
This book "covers all mainline models built for North
American railroads from the mid-1970s to today, from
EMD Dash 2s and GE Dash 7s to the latest 70 Series
and Evolution Series models, as well as Green Goats,
Gensets and mainline passenger electric-powered locomo-
tives." Publisher's note

628   Sanitary and municipal engineering Environmental protection engineering

The **ECO** guide to careers that make a difference.
Island Press 2005 xxi, 400p il hardcover o.p. pa
$30
Grades: 9 10 11 12   **628**
1. Ecology—Vocational guidance
ISBN 1-559-63966-0; 1-559-63967-9 (pa)
LC 2004-24493
"This excellent book is appropriate as reference mate-
rial for anyone seeking information about careers involv-
ing the environment. Students at the high school [level]
. . . will get a clear picture of the scope of these careers
and the job market within each category." Sci Books
Films
Includes bibliographical references

628.4   Waste technology, public toilets, street cleaning

Gardner, Robert, 1929-
Recycle; green science projects for a sustainable
planet. Enslow Publishers 2011 128p il (Team
Green science projects) lib bdg $31.93
Grades: 6 7 8 9 10   **628.4**
1. Recycling 2. Science—Experiments 3. Science projects
ISBN 978-0-7660-3648-2; 0-7660-3648-0
LC 2009-37903
This describes science projects about recycling, including experiments and information about plastics, solid
waste and decomposition, composting, aluminum, and
paper.
"Gardner provides plenty of information, well-
designed experiments, and demonstrations, and then
shares brief science-fair ideas. . . . Experiments and
demonstrations are presented with clear step-by-step instructions and occasional illustrations and represent a
wide range of complexity." SLJ
Includes glossary and bibliographical references

Maczulak, Anne E.
Waste treatment; reducing global waste; [by]
Anne Maczulak. Facts on File 2010 198p il (Green
technology) $40
Grades: 9 10 11 12   **628.4**
1. Refuse and refuse disposal 2. Waste minimization
3. Recycling
ISBN 978-0-8160-7204-0; 0-8160-7204-3
LC 2008-45054

Maczulak, Anne E.—*Continued*

"Divided into eight chapters, this volume explains the various means to treat and eliminate waste. Emphasizing that waste management is a global issue, chapters explore incineration, vitrification, solidification and stabilization, compaction, and wastewater treatment. Each chapter begins with a concise overview introducing the main points and ends with a conclusion summarizing those items. . . . A useful resource and reference book for advanced science students." SLJ

Includes glossary and bibliographical references

628.5 Pollution control technology and industrial sanitation engineering

Maczulak, Anne E.

Cleaning up the environment; hazardous waste technology; [by] Anne Maczulak. Facts on File 2010 226p il (Green technology) $40

Grades: 9 10 11 12   **628.5**
1. Hazardous waste sites 2. Environmental protection
ISBN 978-0-8160-7198-2; 0-8160-7198-5
LC 2008-42367

"This comprehensive and somewhat technical discussion of the various methods used for the cleanup of environmental waste will be a valuable addition to science units. . . . . This is a vitally important subject not often discussed in environmental literature and is a welcome addition for use in classroom studies and for those considering a career in the field." SLJ

Includes glossary and bibliographical references

New thinking about pollution; edited by Robert Curley. Britannica Educational Pub. in association with Rosen Educational Services 2010 c2011 269p il map (21st century science) lib bdg $45

Grades: 9 10 11 12   **628.5**
1. Pollution
ISBN 978-1-61530-135-5   LC 2010-9095

This "volume explores the root causes of pollution, as well as the local and global responses and constantly emerging technologies that allow governments and ordinary citizens to cope with an increasingly toxic environment and landscape." Publisher's note

Includes bibliographical references

628.9 Other branches of sanitary and municipal engineering

Fire fighters; stories of survival from the front lines of firefighting; edited by Clint Willis. Thunder's Mouth Press 2002 351p il pa $17.95 *

Grades: 11 12 Adult   **628.9**
1. Fire fighting
ISBN 1-56025-402-5   LC 2002-18147

This is a collection of 21 accounts of fighting fires in urban, rural, and forest environments, previously published in books and magazines between 1963 and 2001, by such authors as Edward Abbey, Norman Maclean,

Stephen Pyne, and Studs Terkel

"Mere display guarantees this collection's circulation." Booklist

Includes bibliographical references

629.13 Aeronautics

Abrams, Michael

Birdmen, batmen, and skyflyers; wingsuits and the pioneers who flew in them, fell in them and perfected them. Harmony Books 2006 304p il $23.95; pa $13.95 *

Grades: 11 12 Adult   **629.13**
1. Aeronautics—History
ISBN   1-4000-5491-5;   978-1-4000-5491-6; 1-4000-5492-3 (pa); 1-978-1-4000-5492-3 (pa)
LC 2005-32409

"From ancient myths through China 'sometime in the sixth century A.D.' to present-day skydivers, Abrams chronicles the men and their various models of wings that have taken to the air in hope of flying like a bird. The tales of flight range from the silly and mysterious to the inspiring and unbelievable." Publ Wkly

Includes bibliographical references

Dick, Ron, 1931-

The early years; [by] Ron Dick and Dan Patterson. Firefly Books 2003 240p il (Aviation century) $39.95

Grades: 11 12 Adult   **629.13**
1. Aeronautics—History
ISBN 978-1-55046-407-8; 1-55046-407-8

"Dick's text carries the reader from the antics of the wing walkers and aerobatic pilots of the day to the sheer persistence of such distance flyers as Charles Lindbergh and the crew of the Southern Cross. The vying aircraft in these contests are captured in all of their antiquated beauty." Libr J

Includes bibliographical references

The golden age; [by] Ron Dick and Dan Patterson. Boston Mills Press 2004 287p il (Aviation century) $39.95

Grades: 11 12 Adult   **629.13**
1. Aeronautics—History
ISBN 1-55046-409-4; 978-1-55046-409-2
LC 2005-298220

This book "chronicles the history of aviation from 1919 to 1939. . . . Any readers interested in the history of flying will treasure this profusely illustrated book." Booklist

Includes bibliographical references

War & peace in the air; [by] Ron Dick and Dan Patterson. Boston Mills Press 2006 352p il (Aviation century) $49.95

Grades: 11 12 Adult   **629.13**
1. Aeronautics—History
ISBN 978-1-55046-430-6; 1-55046-430-2

This book "explores the influence of aviation in the major wars and minor conflicts since World War II. The

Dick, Ron, 1931-—_Continued_

authors also examine the dangers of flight, including airborne disasters, accident investigations and threats from terrorism, and speculate on the myriad ways in which aviation will change in the near and far future." Publisher's note

Includes bibliographical references

Wings of change. Boston Mills 2005 288p il (Aviation century) $39.95

Grades: 11 12 Adult   **629.13**
    1. Aeronautics—History
    ISBN 978-1-55046-428-3; 1-55046-428-0

"This book takes an eclectic look at several strands of aviation history. Chapter 1 focuses on commercial airlines since 1945, but includes material on the business aviation sector as well as bush flying and the use of aircraft in fighting wildfires. The second chapter considers personal and private flying, but begins coverage in the 1930s and proceeds to the present, and includes the sport of soaring. Chapter 3 treats lighter-than-air subjects, from 18th-century hot-air balloons through current balloon meets, and incorporates a discussion of the dirigible era of the 1920s-30s. In chapter 4, autogiros and helicopters are analyzed through the 20th century, with coverage of both civil and military developments. Chapter 5 looks at high-speed research, primarily as a series of biographical sketches." Choice

Includes bibliographical references

Grant, R. G. (Reg G.)

Flight: 100 years of aviation. DK Pub. 2002 440p il hardcover o.p. pa $24.95 *

Grades: 11 12 Adult   **629.13**
    1. Aeronautics—History
    ISBN 0-7894-8910-4; 0-7566-1902-5 (pa)
                       LC 2002-73935

Grant "divides this book into sections that include a prehistory of flight and the Wright brothers; accounts of air combat in World War I, and a focus on the 'golden age' that recounts the flights of Charles Lindbergh, Amelia Earhart, Jimmy Doolittle, and the great airships and flying boats. He also presents a history of aircraft's role in World War II (the Battle of Britain, the air war at sea, and the Allied bombing raids on Axis cities); the cold war and Vietnam; space travel; and jet passenger travel." Booklist

"The impressive illustrations include over 300 gorgeous, full-color profiles of the world's major military and civilian aircraft and space vehicles." Libr J

Haynsworth, Leslie

Amelia Earhart's daughters; the wild and glorious story of American women aviators from World War II to the dawn of the space age; {by} Leslie Haynsworth and David Toomey. Morrow 1998 322p il pa $14 hardcover o.p. *

Grades: 11 12 Adult   **629.13**
    1. Women air pilots 2. Women astronauts
    ISBN 0-380-72984-9 (pa)   LC 98-8727

This "study of American women aviators concentrates almost exclusively on the WASPs of World War II and the would-be female astronauts of the early 1960s." Booklist

Includes bibliographical references

Marshall, David

Wild about flying! dreamers, doers, and daredevils; [by] David Marshall & Bruce Harris. Firefly Books 2003 232p il $35 *

Grades: 9 10 11 12   **629.13**
    1. Aeronautics—History
    ISBN 1-55297-849-4   LC 2004-297806

This is a "history of aviation told through brief biographies of the most central people in the saga of flight. . . . With its unique focus and accurate, understandable technical data, this volume is a great addition to YA collections." SLJ

Smithsonian atlas of world aviation; charting the history of flight from the first balloons to today's most advanced aircraft; [compiled by] Dana Bell. HarperCollins 2008 230p il map $39.95

Grades: 9 10 11 12 Adult   **629.13**
    1. Aeronautics—History 2. Historical atlases
    3. Reference books
    ISBN 978-0-06-125144-3; 0-06-125144-5
                       LC 2007-47574

This "book offers a . . . textual and visual tour of civilian, military, and commercial aviation from the earliest balloon flights to today's most advanced aircraft." Publisher's note

"Bell's writing . . . adds immeasurably to the value of this atlas: it is articulate, clear, informative, and, above all, accurate." SLJ

Includes bibliographical references

Tobin, James, 1956-

To conquer the air; the Wright Brothers and the great race for flight. Free Press 2003 433p il hardcover o.p. pa $16

Grades: 11 12 Adult   **629.13**
    1. Wright, Orville, 1871-1948 2. Wright, Wilbur, 1867-1912 3. Aeronautics—History
    ISBN 0-684-85688-3; 0-7432-5536-4 (pa)
                       LC 2002-44778

"In this centenary of the airplane, Tobin recreates the course, in its technological and biographical dimensions, of the Wright brothers' claim to its invention." Booklist

"This book represents the most forceful argument to date for the brothers' monumental legacy to the history of flight. . . . This lucidly written and exhaustively researched study is recommended for all aviation collections and all libraries." Libr J

Includes bibliographical references

629.133   Aircraft types

Chiles, James R.

The god machine; from boomerangs to black hawks, the story of the helicopter. Bantam Dell 2007 354p il hardcover o.p. pa $16

Grades: 11 12 Adult   **629.133**
    1. Helicopters
    ISBN 978-0-553-80447-8; 978-0-553-38352-2 (pa)
                       LC 2007-28575

Chiles, James R.—*Continued*

The author "chronicles helicopter development from ancient observations of birds and boomerangs in flight to Leonardo da Vinci's aerodynamic ideas to modern police, fire, and medical response helicopters." Libr J

This "is an engaging blend of pop science and pop culture." Publ Wkly

Includes bibliographical references

629.2   Motor land vehicles, cycles

Sobey, Ed

A field guide to automotive technology. Chicago Review Press 2008 207p il pa $14.95

Grades: 11 12 Adult   **629.2**

1. Automobiles 2. Mechanics

ISBN 978-1-55652-812-5   LC 2008046620

The author "helps readers identify items on, inside, and under the car, as well as under the hood, and explains what they do and why. He also painlessly reviews a few principles of science and mechanics here and there. The 130 entries range from basic to complex, from bumper and windshield to differential and constant velocity joint boot. . . . Most of the material concerns passenger vehicles, but there are also sections on off-road vehicles, motorcycles, buses, and human-powered conveyances." SLJ

629.22   Types of vehicles

Kettlewell, Caroline

Electric dreams; one unlikely team of kids and the race to build the car of their dreams. Carroll & Graf 2004 290p hardcover o.p. pa $14.95 *

Grades: 9 10 11 12   **629.22**

1. Electric automobiles

ISBN 0-7867-1271-6; 0-7867-1485-9 (pa)

This "story tells how a twice-totaled 1985 two-door Ford Escort was transformed by students from the poorest county in North Carolina to win the first Mid-Atlantic High School Electric Vehicle Challenge." SLJ

"The word 'inspirational' is applied to too many books, but it comfortably fits this one, with its genuinely likable cast of unlikely achievers. This is essential reading for any serious environmentalist, as it makes the case that EVs might play even in the conservative South." Publ Wkly

629.222   Passenger automobiles

Edmonston, Louis-Philippe

Car smarts; hot tips for the car crazy; [by] Phil Edmonston and Maureen Sawa; illustrated by Gordon Suavé. Tundra 2004 76p il pa $15.95

Grades: 7 8 9 10   **629.222**

1. Automobiles

ISBN 0-88776-646-3

This offers a "look at the history and design of automobiles. . . . [It] discusses how cars work. . . . A chap-

ter on ownership talks about financial issues, negotiating, and maintenance. The closing section covers the automotive future, with information on ecological issues, alternative fuels, hybrids, and fuel cells." SLJ

"Written in a lively style, the book provides solid information. . . . The many illustrations include colorful paintings, drawings, and photos as well as excellent diagrams of a car's working parts." Booklist

629.227   Cycles

Davidson, Jean, 1937-

Jean Davidson's Harley-Davidson family album; 100 years of the world's greatest motorcycle in rare photos; foreword by Sarah Harley and Arthur Harley. Voyageur Press 2003 128p il $19.95

Grades: 9 10 11 12   **629.227**

1. Davidson family 2. Harley family 3. Harley-Davidson, Inc. 4. Motorcycles

ISBN 0-89658-629-4   LC 2002-151809

The granddaughter of one of the founders of the Harley-Davidson company "shares the history, legends, and many personal photos of the marque that simply defines *motorcycle* for most people. . . . As fun as the book is for motorcycle enthusiasts, it also is important in terms of filling a niche in the overall history of the American vehicle business." Booklist

629.28   Tests, driving, maintenance, repairs

Bicycling magazine's basic maintenance and repair; simple techniques to make your bike ride better and last longer; edited by Ed Pavelka. Rodale Press 1999 135p il pa $9.99

Grades: 11 12 Adult   **629.28**

1. Bicycles—Maintenance and repair

ISBN 1-57954-170-4   LC 99-35338

An illustrated guide to do-it-yourself repairs and maintenance procedures designed to prevent on-road breakdowns

Christensen, Lisa

Clueless about cars; an easy guide to car maintenance and repair; [by] Lisa Christensen, with Dan Laxter. Rev. and updated ed. Firefly Books 2007 174p il pa $16.95

Grades: 11 12 Adult   **629.28**

1. Automobiles—Maintenance and repair

ISBN 978-1-55407-333-7; 1-55407-333-2

First published 2004

On cover: With a new chapter on hybrid cars

This book describes "each major system of the automobile, what can go wrong and how to prevent breakdowns. Step-by-step do-it-yourself instructions are provided for the most important engine maintenance routines and basic automotive repairs." Publisher's note

Downs, Todd

The bicycling guide to complete bicycle maintenance & repair; for road & mountain bikes. Expanded and rev. 6th ed. Rodale 2010 395p il pa $23.99 *

Grades: 11 12 Adult   **629.28**
  1. Bicycles—Maintenance and repair
  ISBN 978-1-60529-487-2; 1-60529-487-X
                    LC 2010-26471

First published 1986 with title: Bicycling magazine's Complete guide to bicycle maintenance and repair

This illustrated guide includes step-by-step instructions for major and minor repairs and maintenance for many types of bicycles.

Gravelle, Karen

The driving book; everything new drivers need to know but don't know to ask; illustrated by Helen Flook. Walker & Co. 2005 170p il $16.95; pa $9.95 *

Grades: 9 10 11 12   **629.28**
  1. Automobile drivers
  ISBN 0-8027-8933-1; 0-8027-7706-6 (pa)
                    LC 2004-58485

This guide covers such topics as "automobile maintenance, getting gasoline, the differences between city and country driving, bad weather, the usefulness of cell phones in emergencies, and road rage. The book is clearly written and well organized, but it is also humorous and appealing, with lighthearted illustrations throughout." SLJ

Ramsey, Dan, 1945-

Teach yourself visually car care & maintenance; by Dan Ramsey and Judy Ramsey. Visual / Wiley 2009 210p il (Visual read less, learn more) pa $24.95

Grades: 11 12 Adult   **629.28**
  1. Automobiles—Maintenance and repair
  ISBN 978-0-470-37727-7   LC 2009-920042

This book covers "how to change oil and other fluids; rotate tires; replace fuel pumps, air filters, and batteries; and . . . more." Publisher's note

Includes glossary

Stalder, Erika

In the driver's seat; a girl's guide to her first car. Zest Books 2009 127p il pa $14.95

Grades: 9 10 11 12   **629.28**
  1. Automobiles—Maintenance and repair
  ISBN 978-0-9800732-4-9   LC 2009-933013

"This nifty hot-pink-and-black guide to buying, understanding, maintaining, and styling a first car will be a real help to new drivers, and it is the size and shape of an owner's manual, so it will store nicely in the glove compartment. The tips range from the very basic (how to release the hood latch and prop it open) to diagrams and descriptions of brake rotors and calipers, as well as directions for checking and replacing air filters. Charts of symptoms indicating possible problems and what to do about them are useful." Booklist

Zinn, Lennard

Zinn & the art of road bike maintenance; illustrated by Todd Telander. 3rd ed. Velo Press 2009 424p il pa $24.95

Grades: 9 10 11 12 Adult   **629.28**
  1. Bicycles—Maintenance and repair
  ISBN 978-1-934030-42-4   LC 2009-15195
First published 2000

This book covers the different components of a road bike, lists the tools bike owners need to tackle simple and advanced projects, and demonstrates with 295 illustrations how to work on each part.

Includes bibliographical references

629.4   Astronautics

Angelo, Joseph A.

The Facts on File dictionary of space technology; [by] Joseph A. Angelo, Jr. rev ed. Facts on File 2004 474p $49.95; pa $19.95 *

Grades: 11 12 Adult   **629.4**
  1. Reference books 2. Astronautics—Dictionaries
  ISBN 0-8160-5222-0; 0-8160-5223-9 (pa)
                  LC 2003-49148

"Facts on File science library"

First published 1982 with title: The dictionary of space technology

This dictionary contains approximately 1,500 cross-referenced entries that present the basic concepts and phrases in the science of space, spaceflight, and space technology. Among the topics covered are: abort modes; ballistic missile defense; launch vehicles; Milstar; ocean remote sensing; robotics and space stations

Space technology. Greenwood Press 2003 394p il (Sourcebooks in modern technology) $65

Grades: 9 10 11 12   **629.4**
  1. Astronautics 2. Space sciences 3. Outer space—Exploration
  ISBN 1-57356-335-8   LC 2002-75310

This book examines "the history, technology, impact, and goals of space flight. Angelo organizes his material into 10 topical chapters, beginning with a historical overview, followed by a chronology encompassing both Ptolemy and the February 2003 loss of the space shuttle Columbia, then discussions of space-related physics and technology, military and civilian applications, current issues, and future plans." SLJ

"This book is a good source of general information, easily read and understood by most high school students, and will provide plenty of good information for reports and papers." Lib Media Connect

Includes bibliographical references

Burrows, William E.

This new ocean; the story of the first space age. Random House 1998 723p il pa $18.95 hardcover o.p.

Grades: 11 12 Adult   **629.4**
  1. Astronautics 2. Outer space—Exploration
  ISBN 0-375-75485-7 (pa)   LC 98-3252

Burrows, William E.—*Continued*

This is a "history of space exploration, from its ancient roots in mythology and literature to the theoreticians and pioneering engineers who made it a reality in this century." Libr J

"'This New Ocean' is most distinguished by the successful integration of three different story lines: manned space flight, the militarization of space and space science." N Y Times Book Rev

Includes bibliographical references

Carlisle, Rodney P.

Exploring space. rev ed. Chelsea House 2010 120p il (Discovery and exploration) lib bdg $35
Grades: 7 8 9 10   **629.4**
1. Astronautics 2. Outer space—Exploration
ISBN 978-1-60413-188-8; 1-60413-188-8
                                    LC 2009-25585
First published 2005 by Facts on File
This describes the history of space exploration, from early astronomers to first steps into space by Germans, Soviets, and Americans, space flight to the Moon, space stations, space shuttles, unmanned space exploration, the Hubble space telescope, radio telescopes, and possible future explorations
Includes glossary and bibliographical references

Evans, Kimberly Masters

Space exploration; triumphs and tragedies; [by] Kim Masters Evans. 2010 ed. Gale, Cengage Learning 2011 184p il map (Information Plus reference series) pa $55
Grades: 9 10 11 12   **629.4**
1. Outer space—Exploration
ISBN 978-1-4144-4122-1
"Formerly published by Information Plus, Wylie, Texas"
This book is a brief history of space exploration, with chapters on NASA, the space shuttle program, and the international space station.

Hardesty, Von, 1939-

Epic rivalry; the inside story of the Soviet and American space race; [by] Von Hardesty and Gene Eisman; foreword by Sergei Khrushchev. National Geographic Society 2007 275p il map $28; pa $16.95
Grades: 11 12 Adult   **629.4**
1. Outer space—Exploration 2. Cold war 3. Astronautics—United States 4. Astronautics—Soviet Union
ISBN 978-1-4262-0119-6; 978-1-4262-0321-3 (pa)
                                    LC 2007-17393
"The authors compare the U.S. and Soviet space exploration programs during the cold war." Libr J
"This is a true saga, full of daring, danger, death, ego conflicts, and triumphs. . . . All readers should love this fabulous and profusely illustrated combined story." Sci Books Films
Includes bibliographical references

National Geographic encyclopedia of space; [compiled by] Linda K. Glover; with Andrew Chaikin . . . [et al.]; foreword by Buzz Aldrin. National Geographic Society 2004 400p il map $40 *
Grades: 11 12 Adult   **629.4**
1. Reference books 2. Astronautics 3. Astronomy—Encyclopedias 4. Outer space—Exploration
ISBN 0-7922-7319-2   LC 2004-55229
The essays in this encyclopedia "discuss deep space, our solar system and space travel. There are also sections on using space to study Earth and on the military and intelligence uses of space. The essays in general are readable and show the implications of astronomy for life on Earth, such as the impact of solar flares on the weather. . . . This volume will suit astronomy enthusiasts better than total novices. Everyone, however, can enjoy the gorgeous photos." Publ Wkly

Zimmerman, Robert, 1953-

The chronological encyclopedia of discoveries in space. Oryx Press 2000 410p il maps $95 *
Grades: 11 12 Adult   **629.4**
1. Outer space—Exploration 2. Astronautics
ISBN 1-57356-196-7
"Over 1,000 entries record the date of launch, name of the spacecraft(s), summary of the mission, names of the crew members, experiments, problems, and discoveries in a clear and concise fashion. Seemingly every single space mission is included, encompassing spaceflight with and without human crews, military and civilian ventures, public and commercial ventures, planetary probes, and communications satellites. . . . An excellent, cross-referencing system within the text, as well as extensive subject indices by satellite, mission, and nation or consortia, helps the reader follow particular interests in detail. . . . There is no comparable source to this volume for its comprehensiveness and conciseness." Sci Books Films
Includes bibliographical references

629.43   Unmanned space flight

Zimmerman, Robert, 1953-

The universe in a mirror; the saga of the Hubble Telescope and the visionaries who built it. Princeton University Press 2008 287p il $29.95
Grades: 11 12 Adult   **629.43**
1. Hubble Space Telescope
ISBN 978-0-691-13297-6; 0-691-13297-6
                                    LC 2007-943159
This book "tells the story of . . . [the Hubble Space Telescope] and the visionaries responsible for its extraordinary accomplishments." Publisher's note
"Must reading for armchair astrophysicists." Booklist
Includes bibliographical references

629.45   Manned space flight

Ackmann, Martha

The Mercury 13: the untold story of thirteen American women and the dream of space flight. Random House 2003 239p il hardcover o.p. pa $13.95 *

Grades: 11 12 Adult   **629.45**

1. Project Mercury 2. Women astronauts

ISBN 0-375-50744-2; 0-375-75893-3 (pa)

LC 2002-37118

Ackmann discusses the 1961 testing of women pilots who were being considered for the Mercury space program, and why the initiative was eventually dropped. "The trials narrowed the field of women to 13—hence Ackmann's title—and . . . the women performed at the same level as the men. {Ackmann also addresses} what happened to them afterward." Time

"Mercury 13 is both an outstanding work of research and an exceptionally readable and well-told story. Readers will gain new perspectives on space, medicine, women, and American culture, and will appreciate the magnitude of what was lost when the women were grounded." SLJ

Includes bibliographical references

Angelo, Joseph A.

Human spaceflight. Facts on File 2007 370p il (Frontiers in space) $39.50

Grades: 11 12 Adult   **629.45**

1. Space flight 2. Outer space—Exploration 3. Astronautics

ISBN 0-8160-5775-3; 978-0-8160-5775-7

LC 2006-29488

This book "follows the evolution of space technology from the dawn of the space age to the present day. Chapters include 'The Dream of Human Spaceflight,' 'Living in Space,' 'Space Walks and the Gemini Project,' 'Moonwalks and the Apollo Project,' and 'Space Shuttle.'" Booklist

Includes glossary and bibliographical references

French, Francis

In the shadow of the moon; a challenging journey to Tranquility, 1965-1969; [by] Francis French and Colin Burgess; with a foreword by Walter Cunningham. University of Nebraska Press 2007 425p il (Outward odyssey) $29.95 *

Grades: 11 12 Adult   **629.45**

1. Space flight to the moon 2. Astronautics—United States 3. Astronautics—Soviet Union 4. Apollo project

ISBN 978-0-8032-1128-5; 0-8032-1128-7

LC 2006-103047

The authors "chronicle the missions on which American astronauts learned how to live in space for more than a few hours; steer a spacecraft around the Earth at almost 20,000 miles an hour; rendezvous with a companion ship; and navigate to another world and return safely." Publ Wkly

"This book will have an important place in the recorded history of space exploration." Sci Books Films

Includes bibliographical references

Kevles, Bettyann

Almost heaven; the story of women in space; [by] Bettyann Holtzmann Kevles. MIT Press 2006 280p il pa $16.95

Grades: 11 12 Adult   **629.45**

1. Women astronauts

ISBN 978-0-262-61213-5; 0-262-61213-5

LC 2006-41945

First published 2003 by Basic Books

This is a "history of the U.S. space program, with special emphasis on, and stories about, the women who have had the courage to venture into space. Each one is special, the book reveals; yet they all share a spirit of adventure and a willingness to put up with hardship in order to fulfill their dream." Sci Books Films

Includes bibliographical references

Pyle, Rod

Destination moon; the Apollo missions in the astronauts' own words. HarperCollins Publishers 2005 192p il $24.95; pa $14.95 *

Grades: 11 12 Adult   **629.45**

1. Project Apollo 2. Space flight to the moon

ISBN 0-06-087349-3; 0-06-087350-7 (pa)

LC 2005-51350

This "survey of the Apollo moon program includes a brief summary of each flight and attempted flight of the great effort, from the fatal fire on Pad 34 in 1967 to the landing of a scientist on the moon in Apollo 17 in 1972. . . . Space collections of all sizes should welcome Pyle's book, and smaller ones will find it invaluable." Booklist

Stone, Tanya Lee

Almost astronauts; 13 women who dared to dream. Candlewick Press 2008 133p il $24.99; pa $17.99 *

Grades: 5 6 7 8 9 10   **629.45**

1. Project Mercury—History 2. Women astronauts 3. Sex discrimination

ISBN   978-0-7636-3611-1;   0-7636-3611-8; 978-0-7636-4502-1 (pa); 0-7636-4502-8 (pa)

LC 2008-17487

"In 1960, thirteen American women passed the physical exams required to become astronauts as surely as any of the men already involved in NASA's early space flight endeavors, but they were disqualified solely because of their gender. This book is their story. . . . Any girl with an interest in space flight or the history of women's rights will enjoy this account and applaud these courageous pioneers." Voice Youth Advocates

Includes bibliographical references

Wolfe, Tom

The right stuff. Picador 2008 352p pa $16

Grades: 11 12 Adult   **629.45**

1. Astronauts 2. Astronautics—United States

ISBN 0-312-42756-5; 978-0-312-42756-6

First published 1979 by Farrar, Straus & Giroux

This volume chronicles "the handful of adrenaline-junkie military test pilots who became the Mercury astronauts. Their story is juxtaposed against that of Chuck Yeager, the ace of aces pilot who broke the sound barrier

Wolfe, Tom—*Continued*

but couldn't apply to the space program because he lacked a college degree. . . . A terrific read from beginning to end." Libr J

629.47 Astronautical engineering

Reynolds, David West

Kennedy Space Center; gateway to space. Firefly Books 2006 248p il $40

Grades: 11 12 Adult 629.47

1. John F. Kennedy Space Center 2. Astronautics—United States

ISBN 1-55407-039-2; 978-1-55407-039-8

Containing an "overview of the space program from the view of the facilities that launched the missions and the people who made it happen, Reynolds's work is full of elegant descriptions and compelling details that highlight the vast technology and the indomitable human spirit." Voice Youth Advocates

Includes bibliographical references

629.8 Automatic control engineering

Brooks, Rodney Allen

Flesh and machines; how robots will change us. Pantheon Bks. 2002 260p il hardcover o.p. pa $14

Grades: 11 12 Adult 629.8

1. Robots 2. Artificial intelligence

ISBN 0-375-42079-7; 0-375-72527-X (pa)

LC 2001-36636

"A scientist at MIT's famous artificial intelligence lab, Brooks here splits his book in two: the first part describes various robots he and his group have built; the second part philosophizes on the nature of artificial intelligence." Booklist

A "stimulating book written by one of the major players in the field . . . about the state of robotics and its short-term future. It also offers surprisingly deep glimpses into what it is to be human. Brooks appears to have gained a boundless appreciation for human beings by attempting to copy them." N Y Times Book Rev

Henderson, Harry, 1951-

Modern robotics; building versatile machines. Chelsea House 2006 xx, 188p il (Milestones in discovery and invention) $35

Grades: 7 8 9 10 11 12 629.8

1. Robots

ISBN 0-8160-5745-1 LC 2005-31805

This book presents "biographies of the men and women who were and are the leaders in bringing about this change through research and new technologies." Publisher's note

Includes glossary and bibliographical references

631.4 Soil science

Gardner, Robert, 1929-

Soil; green science projects for a sustainable planet. Enslow Publishers 2011 128p il (Team Green science projects) lib bdg $31.93

Grades: 6 7 8 9 10 631.4

1. Science—Experiments 2. Science projects 3. Soils

ISBN 978-0-7660-3647-5; 0-7660-3647-2

This book offers science experiments that explain the properties of soil, erosion, and methods to conserve soil.

"Gardner provides plenty of information, well-designed experiments, and demonstrations, and then shares brief science-fair ideas. . . . Experiments and demonstrations are presented with clear step-by-step instructions and occasional illustrations and represent a wide range of complexity." SLJ

Includes glossary and bibliographical references

632 Plant injuries, diseases, pests

Stewart, Amy, 1969-

Wicked bugs; the louse that conquered Napoleon's army & other diabolical insects; etchings and drawings by Briony Morrow-Cribbs. Algonquin Books of Chapel Hill 2011 271p il $18.95

Grades: 11 12 Adult 632

1. Insect pests 2. Spiders 3. Mites 4. Ticks

ISBN 978-1-56512-960-3 LC 2011-3629

"Ranging from verdant South American jungles to Manhattan's cold concrete canyons, Stewart amusingly but analytically profiles the baddest bugs around in quick but attention-grabbing snapshots of little creatures that pack a lot of punch. Bed bugs and bookworms, rat fleas and filth flies all come under Stewart's curious gaze as she exposes their evil habits and lethal charms. No alarmist setting out to stoke preexisting phobias, Stewart shares her natural fascination with the insect world to help readers recognize both the threats and the wonders that could be lurking in corner crevices or come wafting in on the next gentle breeze." Booklist

Includes bibliographical references

Waldbauer, Gilbert

Insights from insects; what bad bugs can teach us. Prometheus Books 2005 311p il $18

Grades: 11 12 Adult 632

1. Insect pests

ISBN 1-59102-277-0 LC 2004-26928

The author "profiles a rogue's gallery of unhealthful, unprofitable, and unsavory creatures from the mosquito and house fly to an array of agricultural scourges. From their ingenious strategies for wreaking havoc and evading retribution from predators, toxic plant chemicals, insecticides and eradication programs, he gleans lessons about the Darwinian struggle for survival and the complex, easily upset balance of ecosystems. Waldbauer's lucid, engaging style, informed by accessible discussions of his and other scientists' research, maintains a lab-coated tone of interested objectivity." Publ Wkly

Includes bibliographical references

634.9   Forestry

Brown, Daniel, 1951-
Under a flaming sky; the great Hinckley
firestorm of 1894; [by] Daniel James Brown.
Lyons Press 2006 256p il map $22.95
Grades: 11 12 Adult   **634.9**
 1. Forest fires 2. Minnesota
 ISBN 1-59228-863-4; 978-1-59228-863-2
"On September 1, 1894, a firestorm consumed timber-
boomtown Hinckley, Minnesota, and three nearby ham-
lets. Brown, grandson of an 11-year-old survivor, makes
riveting, affecting, white-knuckle reading of that horrify-
ing, internationally reported day's lethal passage."
Booklist
 Includes bibliographical references

Raven, Catherine, 1959-
Forestry. Chelsea House Publishers 2006 126p il
(Green world) $37.50
Grades: 7 8 9 10   **634.9**
 1. Forests and forestry 2. Forest ecology
 ISBN 0-7910-8752-2; 978-0-7910-8752-7
                                    LC 2005-21244
Contents: Welcome to the forest planet; Tree talk: the
physiology of how trees grow; The kings: forest gymno-
sperms; Trouble in the forest: angiosperms; The forest
family tree: intra-forest dynamics; Thinking like a forest:
ecology; Forest animals; Fire in the forest
 This book "explores the science of forestry, from the
types of trees and shrubs grown for commercial and medicinal use, to the impact of trees on the environment
and human society. . . . [This] is an excellent book in
its content, instructional value, technical quality, and
photography." Sci Books Films
 Includes bibliographical references

635   Garden crops (Horticulture) Vegetables

Learn to garden; [contributors, Guy Barter ... [et
al.]] 1st American ed. DK Pub. 2008 352p il pa
$22.95
Grades: 11 12 Adult   **635**
 1. Gardening
 ISBN 978-0-7566-3443-8; 0-7566-3443-1
                                    LC 2008-297619
"Based on content first published in Learn to Garden,
Dorling Kindersley, 2005" Verso of title page. Subtitle
on cover: A practical introduction to gardening
 This book covers how to "plant perennials, annuals
and bulbs; prune trees and shrubs; make a new lawn or
a gravel garden; select and grow roses, grasses, and
ferns; grow vegetables and herbs in containers; [and]
keep pests and diseases under control." Publisher's note

Smith, Jeremy N.
Growing a garden city; how farmers, first
graders, counselors, troubled teens, foodies, a
homeless shelter chef, single mothers, and more
are transforming themselves and their
neighborhoods through the intersection of local
agriculture and community—and how you can,
too; [by] Jeremy N. Smith; foreword by Bill
McKibben; photographs by Chad Harder and Sepp
Jannotta. Skyhorse Pub. 2010 225p il $24.95
Grades: 11 12 Adult   **635**
 1. Community gardens
 ISBN 978-1-61608-108-9   LC 2010-12369
"'How It Works' sections are based on and incorporate material originally prepared by Garden City Harvest"
 This book offers "photographs and personal narratives
of community garden members, graduate students and
first graders, a low-income senior and troubled teen, a
foodie, a food bank officer, and . . . more. They describe their setbacks and successes involved with community gardening and show how to build on and emulate
their achievements anywhere across the country and
around the world." Publisher's note
 "Bright, vibrant, and buoyantly accessible, this effer-
vescent celebration of the local food movement thrums
with regional, national, and international implications."
Booklist

Smith, Miranda, 1944-
Your backyard herb garden; a gardener's guide
to growing over 50 herbs plus how to use them in
cooking, crafts, companion planting, and more.
Rodale Press 1997 160p map hardcover o.p. pa
$16.95
Grades: 9 10 11 12   **635**
 1. Herb gardening 2. Herbs
 ISBN 0-87596-767-1; 0-87596-994-1 (pa)
                                    LC 96-23153
This guide offers information about planning and preparing an herb garden, growing and caring for herbs, using them for cooking, health, and beauty, and includes an
illustrated directory of more than 70 herbs
 Includes bibliographical references

635.9   Flowers and ornamental plants

The **American** Horticultural Society A-Z
encyclopedia of garden plants; Christopher
Brickell, H. Marc Cathey, editors-in-chief. Rev.
US ed. DK Pub. 2004 1099p il map $80 *
Grades: 11 12 Adult   **635.9**
 1. Reference books 2. Ornamental plants—Encyclopedias
 ISBN 0-7566-0616-0   LC 2004-559196
 First published 1997
 This volume "covers over 2000 genera with more than
15,000 individual entries of annuals, perennials, trees,
shrubs, climbers, rock plants, biennials, bulbs, orchids,
and much more. . . . Arranged by genus, each entry includes family name, a description of the genus, native
habitat, garden uses, cultivation, propagation, and pests

The American Horticultural Society A-Z ency-clopedia of garden plants—*Continued*
and diseases. The entries contain a description, height, width, USDA hardiness zones, heat zones, and cultivars." Libr J

"Equal parts gem and tool, this book is like a diamond. Clear, concise, and thoroughly useful, it fits the needs of all gardeners." Am Ref Books Annu, 2005

Hewitt, Terry
The complete book of cacti & succulents. Dorling Kindersley 1993 176p il hardcover o.p. pa $20

Grades: 11 12 Adult   **635.9**
1. Cactus 2. Succulent plants
ISBN 1-56458-337-6; 0-7894-1657-3 (pa)
            LC 93-22107
An illustrated look at the history and cultivation of more than 300 plants. Ideas for containers and display are included.

636   Animal husbandry

Halligan, Karen
Doc Halligan's What every pet owner should know; prescriptions for happy, healthy cats and dogs; illustrations by Liz Wells. HarperCollins Publishers 2007 324p il $24.95; pa $15.95 *

Grades: 9 10 11 12 Adult   **636**
1. Cats 2. Dogs 3. Pets—Health and hygiene
ISBN 978-0-06-089859-5; 0-06-089859-3; 978-0-06-089860-1 (pa); 0-06-089860-7 (pa)
            LC 2007-60869
"Emphasizing canine (and feline) wellness, . . . [the author] gives clear advice about preventing illness and injuries through sensible nutrition, regular grooming, dental care, and partnering with your veterinarian." Libr J

Wells, Jeff
All my patients have tales; favorite stories from a vet's practice. St. Martin's Press 2009 226p il $24.95; pa $13.99

Grades: 11 12 Adult   **636**
1. Veterinary medicine
ISBN 978-0-312-53739-5; 0-312-53739-5; 978-0-312-60639-8 (pa); 0-312-60639-7 (pa)
            LC 2008-35868
"Newly minted veterinarian Wells is on one of his first calls—a cow trying to deliver a dead calf—when after two hours of unceasing labor, he decides to try another approach, and one of the on-looking farmers says, 'That's what you should have done to begin with!' So begins the education of a young vet, the on-the-job training that no amount of schooling can provide. . . . A move to Colorado didn't immediately improve his finances but did improve his buffalo-wrangling skills and his ability to remove porcupine quills from overzealous dogs and donkeys. Another winning veterinary memoir deserving of space next to the immortal James Herriot and his heirs." Booklist

636.08   Specific topics in animal husbandry

Farthing, Pen
One dog at a time; saving the strays of Afghanistan. Thomas Dunne Books 2010 308p il $24.99

Grades: 11 12 Adult   **636.08**
1. Dogs 2. Afghan War, 2001-—Personal narratives
ISBN 978-0-312-60774-6; 0-312-60774-1
            LC 2010-20605
"Farthing, a British Royal Marine, describes his struggles to save stray dogs languishing and dying in the streets of wartorn Afghanistan. . . . Farthing's remarkable story will inspire, shock, and move readers, introducing them, perhaps for the first time, to war's most voiceless and unintentional victims." Publ Wkly
Includes bibliographical references

Winegar, Karin
Saved; rescued animals and the lives they transform; text by Karin Winegar; photographs by Judy Olausen; foreword by Jane Goodall; preface by Temple Grandin. Da Capo Lifelong 2008 xxiii, 212p il $25.95; pa $18

Grades: 11 12 Adult   **636.08**
1. Pets 2. Animal welfare
ISBN 978-0-7382-1276-0; 0-7382-1276-8; 978-0-306-81842-4 (pa); 0-306-81842-6 (pa)
            LC 2008-20616
"This book is about people trying to heal the damage done to animals and how animals heal suffering human beings." Publisher's note
Includes bibliographical references

636.089   Veterinary sciences. Veterinary medicine

Nakaya, Shannon Fujimoto
Kindred spirit, kindred care; making health decisions on behalf of our animal companions. New World Library 2005 155p pa $13.95 *

Grades: 9 10 11 12   **636.089**
1. Pets—Health and hygiene
ISBN 1-57731-507-3   LC 2005-880
"Devoting entire chapters to choosing a veterinarian, understanding diagnostic and treatment options, managing care, and coping with death and its aftermath, and providing sidebars filled with pertinent questions to ask at various stages of treatment management, Nakaya arms conscientious caregivers with the information they will need to make the best choices for their animal companions. A necessary and noble guide to easing those stressful situations every animal lover must face." Booklist
Includes bibliographical references

636.1   Equines. Horses

Edwards, Elwyn Hartley
The encyclopedia of the horse; photography by
Bob Langrish, Kit Houghton. [Rev. and updated]
DK 2008 464p il $40 *

Grades: 11 12 Adult   **636.1**
1. Horses—Encyclopedias 2. Reference books
ISBN 978-0-7566-2894-9
"A Dorling Kindersley book"
First published 1994. Previously published with title:
The new encyclopedia of the horse
The author "traces the evolution of the horse, covering
every major breed of horse and pony as well as the con-
tribution the horse has made to civilization. The Visual
Breed Guide portrays more than 150 of the world's ma-
jor breeds of horse and pony. . . . The origin, history,
and uses of each breed are explained." Publisher's note

Faurie, Bernadette
The horse riding & care handbook. Lyons Press
2000 160p il hardcover o.p. pa $19.95
Grades: 11 12 Adult   **636.1**
1. Horses 2. Horsemanship
ISBN 1-58574-058-6; 1-58574-517-0 (pa)
"Each section contains pictures or diagrams to clarify
the explanations, from horse evolution and history with
humans to markings, colors, and breeds. Topics such as
tack, how to mount, a first riding lesson, and techniques
of western riding are all simply described with wonderful
graphics." Libr J

Price, Steven D., 1940-
The horseman's illustrated dictionary. Lyons
Press 2000 214p il hardcover o.p. pa $16.95
Grades: 11 12 Adult   **636.1**
1. Horses 2. Horsemanship
ISBN 1-58574-146-9; 1-59228-098-6 (pa)
    LC 00-62147
This dictionary includes definitions and derivations of
words about horses and horsemanship

636.4   Swine

Montgomery, Sy
The good good pig; the extraordinary life of
Christopher Hogwood. Ballantine Books 2006
228p il $21.95; pa $13.95
Grades: 11 12 Adult   **636.4**
1. Pigs
ISBN   0-345-48137-2;   978-0-345-48137-5;
0-345-49609-4 (pa); 978-0-345-49609-6 (pa)
    LC 2005-57094
This is a "description of the 14-year life of a 750-
pound pet pig who was named after the conductor
[Christopher Hogwood]. Anyone who has ever loved a
pet can enjoy reading about the relationship between
Montgomery and her Christopher." Sci Books Films

636.7   Dogs

American Kennel Club
The complete dog book; American Kennel Club.
20th ed. Ballantine Books 2006 xxi, 858p il $35
*
Grades: 7 8 9 10 11 12 Adult   **636.7**
1. Dogs
ISBN 0-345-47626-3; 978-0-345-47626-5
    LC 2005-48263
"Official publication of the American Kennel Club"
First published 1935. Periodically revised
"The official guide to 124 AKC registered breeds and
their history, appearance, selection, training, care and
feeding, and first aid. Some color plates." N Y Public
Libr. Ref Books for Child Collect. 2d edition

Arden, Andrea
Dog-friendly dog training; illustrations by Tracy
Dockray. 2nd ed. Wiley Pub. 2007 232p il $18.99
*
Grades: 9 10 11 12 Adult   **636.7**
1. Dogs—Training
ISBN 978-0-470-11514-5; 0-470-11514-9
    LC 2007-7079
First published 2000 by Howell Book House
"This straightforward, color-illustrated book by a char-
ter member of the APDT [Association of Pet Dog Train-
ers] focuses on a dog-friendly, positive approach [to
training]. The essential title for libraries with tight bud-
gets." Libr J

Burch, Mary R.
Citizen canine; ten essential skills every
well-mannered dog should know. Kennel Club
Books 2010 256p il pa $14.95 *
Grades: 9 10 11 12 Adult   **636.7**
1. Dogs—Training
ISBN 978-1-593786-44-1   LC 2009-28847
On cover: An official training publication of the
American Kennel Club
"Often a component of therapy dog assessment, the
Canine Good Citizen (CGC) test has become a popular
way to document a dog's manners. . . . [The author]
outlines the ten test items and demonstrates how to teach
your dog these skills. . . . This well-indexed guide is es-
sential reading for dog owners, whether the goal is obe-
dience training, therapy dog work, or simply polite pets."
Libr J

Coile, D. Caroline
The dog breed bible. Barron's Educational
Series 2007 192p il $16.99
Grades: 9 10 11 12 Adult   **636.7**
1. Dogs
ISBN 978-0-7641-6000-4; 0-7641-6000-1
    LC 2006-36904
"Descriptions and photos of every breed recognized by
the AKC" Cover

Coile, D. Caroline—_Continued_

"More than 160 American Kennel Club–recognized breeds in the areas of sporting, hound, working, terrier, toy, nonsporting, herding, and 'miscellaneous'—those not yet placed in an AKC group—are beautifully described here in a condensed version of _Barron's Encyclopedia of Dog Breeds_. . . . Full-page entries contain the breed name; brief descriptions of history, temperament, upkeep, and health concerns; a captioned color photo of the full body and close up of snout area; and highlighted data on the origin, function, coat, color, and height and weight of the breed. . . . This small, spiral-bound book is perfect for circulating or reference collections in school and public libraries." Booklist

Coppinger, Raymond

Dogs; a new understanding of canine origin, behavior, and evolution; [by] Raymond Coppinger and Lorna Coppinger. University of Chicago Press 2002 352p il pa $18

Grades: 11 12 Adult   **636.7**
1. Dogs
ISBN 0-226-11563-1   LC 2002-20404
First published 2001 by Scribner

"Taking a biological approach to the study of canine behavior and intelligence, the authors promulgate a theory of how the dog evolved. They explain in depth how the interplay of nature and nurture and critical periods of development produced an animal that has more shapes and sizes and uses than any other. . . . They define what constitutes a breed and criticize today's purebred breeding programs." Libr J

"This important book belongs in all libraries." Booklist

Includes bibliographical references

Fogle, Bruce

Dog: the definitive guide for dog owners. Firefly Books 2010 384p il $39.95; pa $29.95 *
Grades: 11 12 Adult   **636.7**
1. Dogs
ISBN 978-1-55407-779-3; 978-1-55407-700-7 (pa)

This is a "one-volume compendium on everything canine. He begins with an explanation of the dog's evolution, genetics, and classification. Then he delves into the human-dog relationship, giving . . . information and advice about selecting and training a new puppy, surviving its adolescence, enjoying its adulthood, coping with its declining years, and, finally, coming to grips with its demise. . . . [This is] an easy-to-read, attractive, indispensable guide for the novice and veteran dog owner alike." Libr J

Includes bibliographical references

Foster, Stephen, 1962-

Walking Ollie, or, Winning the love of a difficult dog. Perigee Books 2008 177p il pa $12
Grades: 9 10 11 12 Adult   **636.7**
1. Dogs 2. Pets
ISBN 978-0-3995-3429-4   LC 2008-275298
First published 2006 in the United Kingdom

The author "chronicles the many trials and misadventures of first-time dog ownership as he and his girlfriend consider various breeds, traipse through the woods with an eccentric vizsla breeder, scour animal shelters—and finally meet their match in Ollie, a fearful, stubborn saluki-greyhound mix. . . . Ollie makes for an entertaining and completely unpredictable subject, and this book will delight animal lovers with its warmth and wit." Publ Wkly

Franklin, Jon

The wolf in the parlor; the eternal connection between humans and dogs. Henry Holt 2009 283p $25

Grades: 9 10 11 12 Adult   **636.7**
1. Dogs
ISBN 978-0-8050-9077-2; 0-8050-9077-0
                                          LC 2009-2227

Building on evolutionary science, archaeology, behavioral science, and the firsthand experience of watching his own dog evolve from puppy to family member, Franklin posits that man and dog are more than just inseparable; they are part and parcel of the same creature.

"Among a plethora of books on breeding, disciplining, loving and lamenting the loss of man's best friend, this thoughtful discourse is a best of breed." Publ Wkly

Geeson, Eileen

Ultimate dog grooming; additional material by Barbara Vetter & Lia Whitmore. Firefly Books 2004 288p il $29.95; pa $27.95

Grades: 11 12 Adult   **636.7**
1. Dogs
ISBN 1-55297-873-7; 1-55407-328-6 (pa)

The author "offers a three-part introduction to grooming for both owners and professionals. In Part 1, she briefly addresses what an owner needs to know about grooming as well as how to choose the right groomer. Part 2 is geared toward those who want to become professional groomers. . . . The bulk of the book offers well-done profiles of 170 dog breeds—arranged by coat type—that include worthwhile tips and hints. Supplementing the text are more than 500 color illustrations, ranging from detailed drawings to photographs." Libr J

Katz, Jon

A good dog; the story of Orson, who changed my life. Villard Books 2006 224p il $21.95; pa $13.95

Grades: 11 12 Adult   **636.7**
1. Dogs
ISBN   978-1-4000-6189-1;   1-4000-6189-X;
978-0-8129-7149-1 (pa); 0-8129-7149-3 (pa)
                                          LC 2006-42163

"Orson was Katz's 'lifetime dog,' the one he felt a powerful, life-changing connection with—but Orson was a difficult dog. In a lyrical series of vignettes, the author writes of his working border collie, Rose (the personality opposite of Orson); the rooster, Winston; sheep; donkeys; and the impossible Orson, whom Katz thought was destined to work sheep but whose work became the author. This is a lovely memoir." Booklist

Kihn, Martin
   Bad dog; a love story. Pantheon Books 2011
213p $23.95; ebook $11.99
Grades: 11 12 Adult   **636.7**
   1. Dogs
   ISBN 978-0-307-37915-3; 978-0-307-37987-0 (ebook)
                                          LC 2010-35355
"Meet Hola, a gorgeous purebred Bernese mountain
dog so badly managed by her human that walks were 'a
haphazard dance of death' and greetings 'full-body
slam[s] . . . just this side of actionable.' Now meet the
human: Kihn, a Yale grad with an M.B.A., a deep neurotic streak, and a serious drinking problem. When his
wife leaves, Kihn realizes he must get his life under control, and that includes Hola. Soon man and dog are enrolled in various training programs so that Hola can earn
her Canine Good Citizen certificate from the American
Kennel Club. . . . This sharply written, darkly funny
memoir-cum-dog story-cum-recovery tale is a quick, absorbing read that will serve a wide audience well." Libr
J

Lufkin, Elise
   To the rescue; found dogs with a mission;
photographs by Diana Walker; foreword by Bonnie
Hunt. Skyhorse Pub. 2009 150p il $19.95
Grades: 9 10 11 12 Adult   **636.7**
   1. Animals and the handicapped 2. Dogs
   ISBN 978-1-60239-772-9   LC 2009-12164
This book "presents a collection of essays about rescued dogs, illustrated with black-and-white photos. The
dogs' stories are told in the first person by their owners,
revealing what is known of their backgrounds and what
they are doing today. All of the dogs are workers—some
as therapy dogs for hospice patients, mental patients, or
children in read-to-the-dog programs; others are search-
and-rescue dogs or assistance dogs." Booklist
   "This feel-good book should please animal and dog-
lovers, especially those who live with a working dog."
Publ Wkly
   Includes bibliographical references

The **original** dog bible; the definitive source for
all things dog; edited by Kristin Mehus-Roe.
2nd ed. Bowtie Press 2009 831p il pa $29.95
Grades: 11 12 Adult   **636.7**
   1. Dogs
   ISBN 978-1-933958-82-8   LC 2008-44402
   First published 2005
This book "opens with an astute and wonderfully illustrated survey of dogs' considerable role in history and
popular culture, using both period and artifact photographs. Because it is more a guide to responsible dog
ownership than a breed standards guide, the book is subsequently divided into eight segments and 34 chapters,
which offer indispensable guidance on pet-relevant emergencies, travel, exercise, training, health regimens, and
end-of-life concerns. An informative, extremely enjoyable
read, regardless of pet ownership." Libr J
   Includes bibliographical references

Rogers, Tammie
   4-H guide to dog training and dog tricks.
Voyageur Press 2009 176p il pa $18.99
Grades: 5 6 7 8 9 10   **636.7**
   1. Dogs—Training
   ISBN 978-0-7603-3629-8; 0-7603-3629-6
                                          LC 2009-17040
"This is not simply a how-to-train book; it is also a
guide to cultivating a respectful relationship with your
dog. The excellent information is comprehensive, and it
is presented in a clear and detailed style. The author covers different training methods, discussing the tools needed from food to collar selection. Using this manual, dog
owners can move through the basics (sit, down, etc.) to
obedience competition and fun tricks and activities." SLJ
   Includes bibliographical references

636.8   Cats

Bessant, Claire
   Cat manual; the complete step-by-step guide to
understanding and caring for your cat. Haynes
2009 143p il $32.95 *
Grades: 11 12 Adult   **636.8**
   1. Cats
   ISBN 978-1-84425-675-4; 1-84425-675-8
                                          LC 2009-923208
   At head of title: Haynes
This manual to owning and caring for cats discusses
cat personalities, training, and health issues.

Herriot, James
   James Herriot's cat stories; with illustrations by
Lesley Holmes. St. Martin's Press 1994 161p
$17.95
Grades: 11 12 Adult   **636.8**
   1. Cats
   ISBN 0-312-11342-0   LC 94-20131
A "collection of favorite cat tales from Herriot's veter-
inary practice. Retired after over 50 years in practice,
Herriot continues to entertain young and old alike with
his storytelling ability. His current collection includes
'Alfred, the Sweet-Shop Cat,' 'Boris and Mrs. Bond's
Cat Establishment,' 'Moses Found Among the Rushes,'
and others." Libr J

Page, Jake
   Do cats hear with their feet? where cats come
from, what we know about them, and what they
think about us; illustrations by Jake Page;
photographs by Susanne Page; preface by Michael
W. Fox. Smithsonian Books 2008 204p il $24.95
Grades: 11 12 Adult   **636.8**
   1. Cats 2. Wild cats
   ISBN 978-0-06-145648-0; 0-06-145648-9
                                          LC 2008-6776
   The author "traces cats from the time they first adapted their feline form about 20 million years ago. He gives
readers a cat's-eye view of why cats hunt even when
they are full, why territory is so important, and why no
self-respecting cat would eat vegetables. . . . There is

Page, Jake—*Continued*

solid science content that will help readers recognize we should let cats be cats and what a darn good job they have done of domesticating *us*." Libr J

Includes bibliographical references

636.9   Other mammals

McKimmey, Vickie, 1959-

Ferrets. T.F.H. Publications 2007 111p il (Animal Planet pet care library) $11.95

Grades: 9 10 11 12 Adult   **636.9**

1. Ferrets

ISBN 978-0-7938-3787-8   LC 2007-14332

This book on ferret care features advice "from animal experts on a variety of topics, including feeding, housing, grooming, training, health care, and fun activities." Publisher's note

Includes bibliographical references

Russell, Geoff

Mini encyclopedia of rabbit breeds & care; a color directory of the most popular breeds and their care. Firefly Books 2009 208p il pa $19.95

Grades: 9 10 11 12 Adult   **636.9**

1. Rabbits

ISBN 978-1-55407-474-7; 1-55407-474-6

LC 2010-483165

This "mini encyclopedia features more than 40 of the most popular breeds and varieties of rabbit. . . . [Each breed profile features information on:] character; appearance; typical weight; temperament; suitability as a pet; country of origin; [and] special features of coat types and colors." Publisher's note

Includes bibliographical references

638   Insect culture

Benjamin, Alison

A world without bees; [by] Alison Benjamin, Brian McCallum. Pegasus Books 2009 298p il $26

Grades: 11 12 Adult   **638**

1. Bees 2. Beekeeping

ISBN 978-1-60598-065-2

"In 2007, newspapers began carrying reports of a strange and widespread disease affecting the hives of honeybees. The bees were dying in droves. The potentially catastrophic situation was dubbed colony collapse disorder (CCD), and it touched beekeepers and farmers throughout the world. . . . The authors launch an intelligent, open-minded investigation into possible agents of collapse—first noting that such collapses have been periodic in the bee industry—including parasites, pesticides, global warming, genetically modified transgenic pollens and stress from long shipping times." Kirkus

Includes bibliographical references

Buchmann, Stephen

Honey bees; letters from the hive. Delacorte Press 2010 212p il $16.99; lib bdg $19.99

Grades: 7 8 9 10   **638**

1. Bees 2. Honey

ISBN   978-0-385-73770-8;   0-385-73770-X; 978-0-385-90683-8 (lib bdg); 0-385-90683-8 (lib bdg)

LC 2010-6093

Based on the adult book, Letters from the hive: an intimate history of bees, honey, and humankind published by Delacorte Press in 2005

"This sweeping survey engagingly discusses bee biology and behavior and examines humanity's relationship with bees, from prehistoric times to the present, through their significant roles in art, religion, literature and medicine. Buchmann, a beekeeper and entomologist, also offers a great deal of information about honey. . . . The text is illustrated with black-and-white photographs and documented with source notes." Kirkus

Readicker-Henderson, Ed

A short history of the honey bee; humans, flowers, and bees in the eternal chase for honey; images by Ilona; text by E. Readicker-Henderson. Timber Press 2009 163p il $19.95

Grades: 9 10 11 12 Adult   **638**

1. Beekeeping 2. Bees 3. Honey

ISBN 978-0-88192-942-3; 0-88192-942-5

LC 2008-50286

This book describes "the story of the honey bee—why it is named Apis mellifera, how it has evolved from a solitary creature to one that travels in groups, why it stings, and how pollination really works." Publisher's note

"The author's passion for the subject shines through." Booklist

Includes bibliographical references

639.2   Commercial fishing, whaling, sealing

Kurlansky, Mark

The last fish tale; the fate of the Atlantic and survival in Gloucester, America's oldest fishing port and most original town. Riverhead Books 2009 xxix, 269p il map pa $16

Grades: 11 12 Adult   **639.2**

1. Commercial fishing 2. Gloucester (Mass.)

ISBN 978-1-59448-374-5

First published 2008 by Ballantine Books

The author "provides a delightful, intimate history and contemporary portrait of the quintessential northeastern coastal fishing town: Gloucester, Mass., on Cape Anne. Illustrated with his own beautifully executed drawings, Kurlansky's book vividly depicts the contemporary tension between the traditional fishing trade and modern commerce, which in Gloucester means beach-going tourists." Publ Wkly

Includes bibliographical references

639.3   Culture of cold-blooded vertebrates. Of fishes

Alderton, David
Firefly encyclopedia of the vivarium. Firefly Books 2007 224p il $39.95
Grades: 9 10 11 12 Adult   **639.3**
1. Terrariums 2. Reptiles 3. Amphibians 4. Insects 5. Invertebrates
ISBN 978-1-55407-300-9; 1-55407-300-6
A "reference for those starting out with a terrarium or vivarium, it covers . . . [a range] of suitable animals, from invertebrates to large snakes and lizards. David Alderton explains how to design setups that re-create natural habitats, as well as more clinical environments for closely monitoring difficult or delicate species. A brief account of some of the more suitable vivarium plants and their requirements is also included. The book is divided into three main sections—Reptiles, Amphibians and Invertebrates." Publisher's note
"With its vibrant photographs and easy reading level, this text is suggested for school and public libraries that are in need of a basic guide." Booklist
Includes bibliographical references

Bartlett, Richard D., 1938-
Lizard care from A to Z; [by] R.D. Bartlett & Patricia Bartlett. 2nd ed. Barron's Educational Series 2008 186p il pa $12.99
Grades: 11 12 Adult   **639.3**
1. Lizards
ISBN 978-0-7641-3890-4; 0-7641-3890-1
LC 2008-8533
First published 1997
"The authors describe differing dietary needs for herbivorous, insectivorous and omnivorous lizards. They also give advice on indoor and outdoor caging, and show you how to create terraria to suit different kinds of lizard: cool desert, warm desert, semi-aquatic, cool woodland, tropical woodland, and escarpment." Publisher's note
Includes glossary and bibliographical references

De Vosjoli, Philippe
The art of keeping snakes; from the experts at Advanced Vivarium Systems. Advanced Vivarium Systems 2004 232p il (Herpetocultural library) pa $16.95
Grades: 9 10 11 12 Adult   **639.3**
1. Snakes
ISBN 978-1-882770-63-2; 1-882770-63-3
LC 2005-271302
This book covers "how to setup and maintain a vivaria . . . [as well as] which snakes are the best display snakes and how to handle, feed, and care for them." Publisher's note
Includes bibliographical references

639.34   Fish culture in aquariums

Alderton, David
Encyclopedia of aquarium & pond fish. Dorling Kindersley 2005 400p il hardcover o.p. pa $24.95 *
Grades: 11 12 Adult   **639.34**
1. Reference books 2. Fishes—Encyclopedias
ISBN 0-7566-0941-0; 0-7566-3678-7 (pa)
This reference provides care and identification information on over 800 freshwater, saltwater, coldwater and tropical fish, showing "what each fish looks like, what food they eat, which species they can cohabit with and how big they grow." Publisher's note
The author "has created the definitive work on the subject, with photos to match." Libr J

Boruchowitz, David E.
Mini aquariums. T.F.H. Publications 2008 256p il $34.95
Grades: 9 10 11 12 Adult   **639.34**
1. Aquariums 2. Fishes
ISBN 978-0-7938-0573-0   LC 2007-30146
"The book discusses the important elements concerning setup, equipment, and the wide range of specimens including fish, vegetation, coral, invertebrates, and amphibians. The author dispels myths and misconceptions about goldfish and other types of misunderstood species. Although this volume focuses on small aquariums, it lends itself to responsible and creative larger aquarium systems and will educate and inspire those who enjoy them." Libr J
Includes bibliographical references

Jennings, Greg
The new encyclopedia of the saltwater aquarium. Firefly Books 2007 304p il $49.95
Grades: 11 12 Adult   **639.34**
1. Reference books 2. Marine aquariums 3. Fishes—Encyclopedias
ISBN 978-1-55407-182-1; 1-55407-182-8
LC 2007-296089
First published 2003 under the authorship of Nick Dakin with title: Complete encyclopedia of the saltwater aquarium
"Over 150 species of reef fish, invertebrates and algae are described: their distribution in the wild, size, behavior, diet, aquarium requirements and compatibility. A large, full color photograph appears for each featured species, with personal recommendations on the fish considered best for the beginner." Publisher's note
Includes bibliographical references

Maître-Allain, Thierry
Aquariums; the complete guide to freshwater and saltwater aquariums; [by] Thierry Maitre-Allain and Christian Piednoir; [English translation by Matthew Clarke] Firefly Books 2006 281p il $39.95 *
Grades: 11 12 Adult   **639.34**

Maître-Allain, Thierry—*Continued*

1. Aquariums 2. Marine aquariums
ISBN 1-55407-085-6

The authors "walk the novice through all aspects of setting up and maintaining an underwater habitat. . . . Beautiful photos clearly illustrate this good all-in-one handbook that will fill the needs of beginning aquarists." Booklist

Includes bibliographical references

639.9   Conservation of biological resources

DeNapoli, Dyan

The great penguin rescue; 40,000 penguins, a devastating oil spill, and the inspiring story of the world's largest animal rescue. Free Press 2010 307p il map $26
Grades: 10 11 12 Adult   639.9
1. Penguins 2. Oil spills
ISBN 978-1-4391-4817-4; 1-4391-4817-1
LC 2010-17156

"In June 2000, deNapoli was a New England Aquarium penguin specialist when an oil tanker sinking off the African coast triggered a massive spill threatening the local colony of 75,000 African penguins—representing 40 percent of this vulnerable species' global population. She and other penguin researchers rushed to Cape Town to assist in the rescue and rehabilitation of nearly 20,000 oiled birds and several thousand abandoned penguin chicks. She describes her rehabilitation-supervisor experience." Libr J

This "firsthand account of the rescue of the oiled penguins (all of whom fought against their rescuers), repeated washing of each bird, force-feeding, and guano cleanup plunges the reader into the maelstrom of animal rescue and rehabilitation on such a large scale." Booklist

Includes bibliographical references

Owens, Delia

The eye of the elephant; an epic adventure in the African wilderness; [by] Delia and Mark Owens. Houghton Mifflin 1992 305p il hardcover o.p. pa $16
Grades: 11 12 Adult   639.9
1. Elephants 2. Wildlife conservation
ISBN 0-395-42381-3; 0-395-68090-5 (pa)
LC 92-17691

This is an account of the authors' efforts to save elephants in the Luangwa Valley of Zambia from poachers by involving and educating the local people.

This "is a provocative, disturbing, and eminently readable work." Nat Hist

Includes bibliographic references
Followed by Secrets of the savanna

Owens, Mark

Secrets of the savanna; twenty-three years in the African wilderness unraveling the mysteries of elephants and people; [by] Mark and Delia Owens. Houghton Mifflin 2006 230p il map $26; pa $14.95
Grades: 11 12 Adult   639.9
1. Elephants 2. Wildlife conservation
ISBN   978-0-395-89310-4;   0-395-89310-0;
978-0-618-87250-3 (pa); 0-618-87250-7 (pa)
LC 2005-23842

Sequel to The eye of the elephant

The authors "describe traveling to the 'remote and ruggedly beautiful' Luangwa Valley, in northeastern Zambia, to help save the North Luangwa National Park, where the elephant population had been decimated by poachers." Publ Wkly

"This book, full of adventure and a few hair-raising moments, deserves a wide readership." Libr J

Includes bibliographical references

640   Home & family management

The **experts'** guide to 100 things everyone should know how to do; created by Samantha Ettus. Clarkson Potter Publishers 2004 326p $19.95 *
Grades: 9 10 11 12   640
1. Home economics 2. Life skills
ISBN 1-4000-5256-4; 978-1-4000-5256-1
LC 2004-2546

"These experts and 94 more show you how to read a newspaper (New York Times publisher [Arthur] Sulzberger), tell a joke (comedian [Howie] Mandel), save money (financial guru [Suze] Orman), and, well, pretty much anything else you can think of. . . . The authors call the book 'Cliff Notes to life,' and that about sums it up. It's more fun than Cliff Notes, though." Booklist

Fagerstrom, Derek

Show me how; 500 things you should know, instructions for life from the everyday to the exotic; [by] Derek Fagerstrom, Lauren Smith & the Show Me team. Collins Design 2008 unp il pa $24.99
Grades: 9 10 11 12   640
1. Life skills
ISBN 978-0-06-166257-7

"A show me now book"

"In a series of 500 nearly wordless, . . . step-by-step procedurals, readers learn how to do hundreds of . . . tasks, including: Perform CPR, dance the tango, pack a suitcase, win a bar bet, play the blues, make authentic sushi rolls, fight a shark . . . and 493 more essentials of modern life." Publisher's note

Nakone, Lanna

Organizing for your brain type; finding your own solution to managing time, paper, and stuff. St. Martin's Griffin 2005 xlvii, 222p pa $13.95 *
Grades: 11 12 Adult   640
1. Home economics 2. Time management
ISBN 0-312-33977-1   LC 2004-60159

Nakone, Lanna—*Continued*

"A quiz at the beginning assigns readers to the maintaining, harmonizing, innovating, or prioritizing style. Nakone then describes the strengths and weaknesses of each type and matches a prescription for how that type can best manage time. . . . This book should do well in most libraries." Libr J

Includes bibliographical references

641   Food and drink

Allen, Stewart Lee

In the devil's garden; a sinful history of forbidden food. Ballantine Bks. 2002 315p hardcover o.p. pa $13.95

Grades: 11 12 Adult   641

1. Food 2. Eating customs 3. Cooking 4. Menus

ISBN 0-345-44015-3; 0-345-44016-1 (pa)

LC 2001-43882

"Different cultures and religions have defined certain foods as taboo over the centuries. Allen examines these taboos and looks for possible explanations for forbidding some otherwise edible foodstuffs from human consumption." Booklist

"The historical and cultural links between food, sex and religion make for fascinating reading." Publ Wkly

Includes bibliographical references

641.03   Food and drink—Encyclopedias and dictionaries

Davidson, Alan, 1924-2003

The Oxford companion to food; edited by Tom Jaine; illustrations by Soun Vannithone. 2nd ed. Oxford University Press 2006 907p il map $65 *

Grades: 11 12 Adult   641.03

1. Reference books 2. Food—Encyclopedias

ISBN 0-19-280681-5; 978-0-19-280681-9

LC 2006-48602

First published 1999

"Covering everything from individual ingredients and cooking techniques to food celebrities and national cuisines, the authoritative and engaging The Oxford Companion to Food is one of the best basic culinary reference books available." Libr J

Includes bibliographical references

Rolland, Jacques L., 1945-

The food encyclopedia; over 8,000 ingredients, tools, techniques and people; [by] Jacques L. Rolland and Carol Sherman with other contributors. Robert Rose 2006 701p il $49.95

Grades: 11 12 Adult   641.03

1. Reference books 2. Food—Encyclopedias
3. Cooking—Encyclopedias

ISBN 978-0-7788-0150-4; 0-7788-0150-0

This encyclopedia "has 8,000 entries, with cross-reference on foods, wines, beverages, cooking methods and techniques, and biographies of prominent people." Publisher's note

Includes bibliographical references

641.3   Food

Aaron, Shara, 1975-

Chocolate; a healthy passion; [by] Shara Aaron and Monica Bearden. Prometheus Books 2008 213p il $19.98

Grades: 11 12 Adult   641.3

1. Chocolate

ISBN 978-1-59102-653-2; 1-59102-653-9

LC 2008-26159

"Divided into six chapters, the book covers all facets of the confection. The authors begin by explaining what chocolate is and its origins before moving on to the history of chocolate and how it is grown and harvested. Of particular note are the last two chapters on chocolate and health and the various myths about the food. The authors do an excellent job of explaining the health benefits of chocolate, which is rich in antioxidants and flavonols. They also provide recipes at the end of each chapter, including those for facials, lip balm, and soap." Libr J

Includes bibliographical references

Albala, Ken, 1964-

Food in early modern Europe. Greenwood Press 2003 360p il (Food through history) $49.95

Grades: 9 10 11 12   641.3

1. Food—History 2. Eating customs 3. Europe—Social life and customs

ISBN 0-313-31962-6   LC 2002-28431

The author "explores the complex and interrelated changes that took place in the production and consumption of food in Europe roughly between 1504 and 1800, from first contact with the New World to the beginning of the Industrial Revolution." Choice

"This very scholarly book provides interesting information for both the researcher and browser alike." Libr Media Connect

Includes bibliographical references

The **Cambridge** world history of food; editors, Kenneth F. Kiple, Kriemhild Coneè Ornelas. Cambridge Univ. Press 2000 2v set $190 *

Grades: 11 12 Adult   641.3

1. Food—History

ISBN 0-521-40216-6   LC 00-57181

In slipcase

"The two volumes are arranged in eight parts covering the diet of early man, staple foods, dietary liquids, nutrients and food-related disorders, food and drink around the world, nutrition and health, current food-related issues and concluding with a dictionary of plant foods. . . . *The Cambridge World History of Food* is a thorough study of a topic that is eternally popular. It should become a standard source in reference collections." Booklist

Includes bibliographical references

Foer, Jonathan Safran, 1977-

Eating animals. Little, Brown and Company 2009 341p $25.99; pa $14.99

Grades: 11 12 Adult   **641.3**

1. Vegetarianism

ISBN 978-0-316-06990-8; 978-0-316-06988-5 (pa)

LC 2009-34434

The novelist presents a critique of the food industry and explores arguments in favor of humane agriculture and vegetarianism.

"A blend of solid—and discomforting—reportage with fierce advocacy that will make committed carnivores squeal." Kirkus

Includes bibliographical references

Food and nutrition; editorial advisers, Dayle Hayes, Rachel Laudan. Marshall Cavendish Reference 2009 8v il set $685.84

Grades: 6 7 8 9 10   **641.3**

1. Reference books 2. Food—Encyclopedias 3. Nutrition—Encyclopedias

ISBN 978-0-7614-7817-1   LC 2008-62301

"The 224 alphabetically arranged entries cover a wide range of topics related to food, nutrition, and health, including such subjects as Baking, Bovine growth hormones, Corn, Diabetes, Energy drinks, Liposuction, Macrobiotic eating, and Marketing. Articles that cover cuisines of different cultures and regions of the world and categories of food such as Appetizers and Desserts include sample recipes. Article text is supplemented by boxed facts, tables, charts, maps, and colorful photos. . . . This would be an excellent source for students doing research for science projects or papers on the relationships between food, health, and nutrition." Booklist

Goldstein, Myrna Chandler, 1948-

Controversies in food and nutrition; {by} Myrna Chandler Goldstein and Mark A. Goldstein. Greenwood Press 2002 260p il (Contemporary controversies) $45

Grades: 11 12 Adult   **641.3**

1. Food 2. Nutrition

ISBN 0-313-31787-9   LC 2002-69605

This book explains varying opinions and underlying issues that surround such topics as popular diets, vegetarianism, food irradiation, organic and imported food, vitamin supplementation, food allergies, and genetic modifications

"For anyone confused about the barrage of messages we get every day about nutrition, this is an excellent book. . . . Thoroughly enjoyable to read, the book is designed as a high school or college reference text, but it would also interest the general public." Choice

Includes bibliographical references

Kaufman, Cathy K.

Cooking in ancient civilizations. Greenwood Press 2006 liv, 224p il map (Greenwood Press "Daily life through history" series) $45 *

Grades: 11 12 Adult   **641.3**

1. Food—History 2. Cooking 3. Ancient civilization

ISBN 0-313-33204-5; 978-0-313-33204-3

LC 2006-15692

This cookbook focuses "on the main ancient peoples studied today—the Romans, Mesopotamians, Egyptians, and Greeks. . . . Each group is covered in a chapter that begins with a narrative overview of the environment and resources, cuisine and social class, and a note on sources." Publisher's note

Includes bibliographical references

Menzel, Peter

Hungry planet; what the world eats; photographed by Peter Menzel; written by Faith D'Aluisio. Ten Speed Press 2005 287p il map $40; pa $24.95

Grades: 11 12 Adult   **641.3**

1. Food—Pictorial works

ISBN 978-1-58008-681-3; 978-1-58008-869-5 (pa)

LC 2005-13455

This is "a photographic study of families from around the world, revealing what people eat during the course of one week." Publisher's note

"This is a beautiful, quietly provocative volume." Publ Wkly

Includes bibliographical references

Organic food and farming; Lauri S. Friedman, book editor. Greenhaven Press 2009 138p il (Introducing issues with opposing viewpoints) $34.70

Grades: 6 7 8 9 10   **641.3**

1. Natural foods 2. Organic farming

ISBN 978-0-7377-4483-5; 0-7377-4483-9

LC 2009-36912

"This title first examines the difference between organic and conventional food in terms of human health. The articles have been successfully edited for brevity and clarity. Whether organic farming can improve the world is discussed in the second . . . section of the book. . . . The bulk of the final section discusses the future of organic food and looks at the debate within the organic community on the direction of sustainable agriculture and the label organic. . . . With its colorful graphs and photographs nicely breaking up the text, this . . . book will provide a starting point for assignments." SLJ

Includes bibliographical references

The **Oxford** encyclopedia of food and drink in America; Andrew F. Smith, editor in chief. Oxford University Press 2004 2v il set $250 *

Grades: 11 12 Adult   **641.3**

1. Reference books 2. Food—Encyclopedias 3. Beverages

ISBN 0-19-515437-1; 978-0-19-515437-5

LC 2003-24873

This reference covers "the regions, people, ingredients, foods, drinks, publications, advertising, companies, historical periods, and political and economic aspects pertinent to American cuisine." Publisher's note

"Whether readers make a living studying culinary traditions or just enjoy eating, they'll find this book a marvel. . . . For food lovers of all stripes, this work inspires, enlightens and entertains." Publ Wkly

Rosenblum, Mort

Chocolate: a bittersweet saga of dark and light. North Point Press 2005 290p il $24; pa $14

Grades: 11 12 Adult   **641.3**

1. Chocolate

ISBN 0-86547-635-7; 0-86547-730-2 (pa)

LC 2004-54734

The author "unveils chocolate's history and its various incarnations, including in his fresh and insightful discussions the origins of mole; the differences between, say, Hershey's kisses and Valrhona's products; the invention of Nutella; and the small boutique chocolate artisans found nearly everywhere. . . . A compelling and tasty read." Booklist

Tannahill, Reay

Food in history. new, fully rev and updated ed. Crown 1989 c1988 424p il pa $16 hardcover o.p.

Grades: 9 10 11 12   **641.3**

1. Food—History 2. Dining

ISBN 0-517-88404-6   LC 89-671

First published 1973 by Stein & Day; this edition first published 1988 in the United Kingdom

"A world history of food from prehistoric times . . . this book also traces the way in which food has influenced the entire course of human development." Publisher's note

Includes bibliographical references

641.5 Cooking

American Heart Association

The new American Heart Association cookbook. 8th ed. Clarkson Potter 2010 xxi, 696p il $35 *

Grades: 11 12 Adult   **641.5**

1. Cooking 2. Low-cholesterol diet 3. Heart diseases—Diet therapy

ISBN 978-0-307-40757-3   LC 2009-44692

First published 1973 with title: American Heart Association cookbook

"Each recipe comes with a breakdown of calories, protein content, carbohydrates, cholesterol, fats (broken down by saturated, polyunsaturated and monounsaturated) and sodium content, along with a table of dietary exchange. . . . This book remains a basic in many heart-conscious kitchens." Publ Wkly

Bayless, Rick

Rick & Lanie's excellent kitchen adventures; chef-dad, teenage daughter, recipes and stories; [by] Rick Bayless & Lanie Bayless, with Deann Groen Bayless; photographs by Christopher Hirsheimer. Stewart, Tabori & Chang 2004 231p il $29.95 *

Grades: 7 8 9 10   **641.5**

1. Cooking

ISBN 1-58479-331-7   LC 2004-12627

"The volume is organized by region, with almost every continent covered. Each section begins with a few personal stories from the authors. . . . The recipes range from ultrasimple, such as 'The Simplest Fried Beans' to

elaborate, such as 'Chinese Celebration Hot Pot,' which involves several exotic ingredients and numerous steps. . . . This is a volume filled with delicious recipes that are not necessarily all easy—but are always described in a way that is easy to follow." SLJ

Better homes and gardens new cook book. 15th ed. J. Wiley 2010 660p il $29.95 *

Grades: 11 12 Adult   **641.5**

1. Cooking

ISBN 978-0-470-55686-3   LC 2010-25417

First published 1930 with title: My Better Homes and Gardens cook book. Periodically revised

"A standard cookbook . . . with staple recipes and types of cooking." N Y Public Libr. Book of How & Where to Look It Up

Betty Crocker cookbook; everything you need to know to cook today. 10th ed. Wiley 2005 575p il $29.95; pa $17.95 *

Grades: 11 12 Adult   **641.5**

1. Cooking

ISBN   0-7645-6877-9;   978-0-7645-6877-0; 0-7645-8374-3 (pa); 978-0-7645-8374-2 (pa)

LC 2006-281166

First published with this title 1969 by Golden Press. Periodically revised. Publisher varies. Variant title: Betty Crocker's new cookbook

"This book gives easily readable and understandable recipes. Also has a glossary of cooking terms in back, as well as nutritional guidelines and 'special helps.'" N Y Public Libr. Book of How & Where to Look It Up

Carle, Megan

Teens cook; how to make what you want to eat; [by] Megan and Jill Carle with Judi Carle. Ten Speed Press 2004 146p il pa $19.95

Grades: 7 8 9 10   **641.5**

1. Cooking

ISBN 1-58008-584-9

This cookbook features "recipes for a variety of dishes including chocolate chip scones, potato skins, broccoli cheese soup, steak fajitas, baked macaroni and cheese, and toffee bars. Because Megan is a vegetarian, there are several vegetarian recipes or vegetarian substitutes. . . . Attractive, engaging, and told from a teen perspective, this cookbook will make an excellent addition to any nonfiction collection." Voice Youth Advocates

Cunningham, Marion

The Fannie Farmer cookbook; illustrated by Lauren Jarrett. 13th ed. Knopf 1996 874p il $30 *

Grades: 11 12 Adult   **641.5**

1. Cooking

ISBN 0-679-45081-5   LC 97-162330

First published 1896 under the authorship of Fannie Merritt Farmer. Periodically revised

This standard cookbook focuses on the selection, preparation, and serving of a wide variety of foods

Gold, Rozanne

Eat fresh food; awesome recipes for teen chefs; by Rozanne Gold and her all-star team; photographs by Phil Mansfield. Bloomsbury Children's Books 2009 160p il $21.99; pa $17.99 *

Grades: 6 7 8 9 10   641.5
1. Cooking
ISBN   978-1-59990-282-1;   1-59990-282-6;
978-1-59990-445-0 (pa); 1-59990-445-4 (pa)
                                    LC 2008-42443
"Delicious recipes for aspiring chefs"

"This joyful recipe book features fresh, healthful ingredients and encourages ambitious young chefs to collaborate on such mature dishes as Grape-and-Pignoli Breakfast Cake, Crunchy Wasabi-Lime Salmon with red cabbage and sugar snaps and orange-ginger sweet potato puree. . . . A prime pick for adventurous eaters and a potential catalyst for those in a junk food rut." Publ Wkly

Grant, Mark

Roman cookery; ancient recipes for modern kitchens. Rev. ed. Serif 2008 187p il pa $18
Grades: 9 10 11 12 Adult   641.5
1. Roman cooking
ISBN 978-1-89795-960-2
First published 1999

The author's "theme is everyday Roman food: bread and olive oil form the basic of the simple cuisine that he tells us even emperors ate when not attending extravagant banquets. . . . [He] brings together recipes from the whole span of Roman cookery: . . . sources range from about 400 B.C. to A.D. 500, and from Egypt to northern France." Classical Rev
Includes bibliographical references

Jacob, Jeanne

The world cookbook for students; [by] Jeanne Jacob, Michael Ashkenazi. Greenwood Press 2007 5v il map set $225 *
Grades: 7 8 9 10 11 12   641.5
1. Cooking 2. Eating customs
ISBN 0-313-33454-4; 978-0-313-33454-2
                                    LC 2006-26184
"The volumes are organized alphabetically by country or group name. Each entry includes a brief introduction to the land and people and their cuisine and then an overview of the foodstuffs, typical dishes, and styles of eating in simple bulleted lists. Approximately 5 recipes are provided per country/ethnic group of typical dishes and holiday fare, for a total of 1,198." Publisher's note
Includes bibliographical references

Lee, Jennifer 8., 1976-

The fortune cookie chronicles; adventures in the world of Chinese food. Twelve 2008 307p hardcover o.p. pa $13
Grades: 11 12 Adult   641.5
1. Chinese cooking 2. Restaurants 3. Eating customs
ISBN   978-0-446-58007-6;   0-446-58007-4;
978-0-446-69897-9 (pa); 0-446-69897-0 (pa)
                                    LC 2007-33432

"When a large number of Powerball winners in a 2005 drawing revealed that mass-printed paper fortunes were to blame, the author . . . went in search of the backstory. She tracked the winners down to Chinese restaurants all over America, and the paper slips the fortunes are written on back to a Brooklyn company. This travellike narrative serves as the spine of her cultural history—not a book on Chinese cuisine, but the Chinese food of takeout-and-delivery—and permits her to frequently but safely wander off into various tangents related to the cookie. . . . Like the numbers on those lottery fortunes, the book's a winner." Publ Wkly
Includes bibliographical references

Locricchio, Matthew

Teen cuisine; illustrated by Janet Hamlin; photographs by James Peterson. Marshall Cavendish Children 2010 207p il $22.95
Grades: 6 7 8 9 10   641.5
1. Cooking
ISBN 978-0-7614-5715-2; 0-7614-5715-1
                                    LC 2009-46847
"Presents more than fifty recipes for teenagers who want to cook, with . . . instructions and advice on ingredients, kitchen equipment, and cooking techniques." Publisher's note

"This contemporary collection of recipes will appeal to teen cooks and would make a great gift or an excellent addition to a library's cookbook collection." Voice Youth Advocates

Mackenzie, Jennifer

The complete trail food cookbook; [by] Jennifer MacKenzie, Jay Nutt & Don Mercer. R. Rose 2010 256p il pa $21.95
Grades: 11 12 Adult   641.5
1. Outdoor cooking
ISBN 978-0-778-80236-5
"Over 300 recipes for campers, canoeists and backpackers" Cover

A collection of recipes that can be prepared before or during nature hikes or camping. Contains instructions on how to dehydrate food.

The **manga** cookbook; presented by the Manga University Culinary Institute; illustrations by Chihiro Hattori; [with recipes by Yoko Ishihara] Japanime Co. Ltd. 2007 158p il pa $14.95
Grades: 4 5 6 7 8 9 10 11 12   641.5
1. Manga 2. Graphic novels 3. Japanese cooking—Graphic novels
ISBN 978-4-921205-07-2

Food appears frequently in manga and in anime, but just what are the characters eating? This book is an illustrated step-by-step guide to preparing some Japanese dishes, from onigiri (rice balls) to yakitori (skewered grilled chicken), oshinko (pickled vegetables), udon (Japanese noodles), to traditional sweets and desserts. Definitions of terms and ingredients used, basic cooking guidelines, and instructions on how to properly use chopsticks are all included. The recipes are authentic but have been simplified somewhat so older children and teens with some basic kitchen skills can prepare the foods. Adult

The manga cookbook—*Continued*
supervision is recommended for younger children and for children who aren't very experienced with using knives, measuring spoons, and cooking on the stove.

Manning, Ivy
The adaptable feast; satisfying meals for the vegetarians, vegans, and omnivores at your table; photography by Gregor Torrence. Sasquatch Books 2009 xxii, 249p il pa $23.95
Grades: 11 12 Adult **641.5**
1. Cooking 2. Vegetarian cooking
ISBN 978-1-57061-583-2; 1-57061-583-7
LC 2009-18963
"Each basic recipe has a stopping point in its process where a quantity of the dish is set aside to feed the vegetarians before any meat products go in. In some cases, the meat-free portion is then enriched with the addition of beans or tofu. For the vegan, Manning indicates which ingredients may simply be left out altogether. She turns to meat substitutes, such as seitan, as advice on ensuring that vegans get sufficient complete proteins for sound nutrition." Booklist
Includes bibliographical references

McFeely, Mary Drake
Can she bake a cherry pie? American women and the kitchen in the twentieth century. University of Mass. Press 2000 194p hardcover o.p. pa $16.95
Grades: 9 10 11 12 **641.5**
1. Cooking 2. Women—United States
ISBN 1-55849-250-X; 1-55849-333-6 (pa)
LC 00-23452
"This book shows how cooking developed and evolved during the twentieth century. From Fannie Farmer to Julia Child, new challenges arose to replace the old. Women found themselves still tied to the kitchen, but for different reasons and with the need to acquire new skills." Publisher's note
"This book would be an excellent beginning for in-depth research or for a pleasant introduction to the field. It will have a wide appeal to those interested in women's roles in the 20th century and in home cooking." Choice
Includes bibliographical references

The **new** American plate cookbook; recipes for a healthy weight and a healthy life; American Institute for Cancer Research. University of California Press 2005 306p il $24.95
Grades: 11 12 Adult **641.5**
1. Cooking
ISBN 0-520-24234-3 LC 2004-17993
The recipes in this book are "built around vegetables and whole grains, with an emphasis on brown rice, wheat pasta, and other healthful foods, rather than protein. . . . Recipes are appealing and easy to make and cover every course of a meal. Well-known dishes are reworked, e.g., New England Clam Chowder, to help with the transition to healthier eating." Libr J

Robertson, Robin
Vegan planet; 400 irresistible recipes with fantastic flavors from home and around the world. Harvard Common Press 2003 576p hardcover o.p. pa $21.95
Grades: 11 12 Adult **641.5**
1. Vegetarian cooking
ISBN 1-55832-210-8; 1-55832-211-6 (pa)
LC 2002-7435
The author "offers dozens of imaginative vegan recipes inspired by a wide range of cuisines, from Five-Spiced Portobello Satays and Lebanese Fattoush (bread salad) to Cajun-Style Collards and Moroccan Fava Bean Stew." Libr J

Rombauer, Irma von Starkloff, 1877-1962
Joy of cooking; [by] Irma S. Rombauer, Marion Rombauer Becker, Ethan Becker; illustrated by John Norton. 75th anniversary ed. Scribner 2006 1132p il $30 *
Grades: 11 12 Adult **641.5**
1. Cooking
ISBN 978-0-7432-4626-2; 0-7432-4626-8
LC 2006-51231
First published 1931
"All-purpose cookbook for informal and formal use with American and foreign recipes. Includes menu planning suggestions, nutrition, basic information on foods, basic cooking terminology, and methods of preparation." N Y Public Libr Book of How & Where to Look It Up
This is the "backbone for any library's cookery reference collection, its nearly 4,000 recipes defining essential American home cooking." Booklist

Segan, Francine
Shakespeare's kitchen; Renaissance recipes for the contemporary cook; photographs by Tim Turner. Random House 2003 270p il $35
Grades: 9 10 11 12 **641.5**
1. British cooking
ISBN 0-375-50917-8 LC 2002-36839
"Updating dozens of classic Elizabethan recipes, Segan leads a culinary foray into Shakespeare's time. Each recipe is supplemented with a historical note that places the dish in context. . . . Its playful tone, fascinating side-notes, and apt citations from the Bard's plays make this book as fun to read as it is to cook from." Publ Wkly
Includes bibliographical references

Shimbo, Hiroko
The Japanese kitchen; 250 recipes in a traditional spirit; illustrations by Rodica Prato. Harvard Common Press; distributed by National Bk. Network 2000 512p il hardcover o.p. pa $21.95
Grades: 11 12 Adult **641.5**
1. Japanese cooking
ISBN 1-55832-176-4; 1-55832-177-2 (pa)
LC 00-33505

Shimbo, Hiroko—*Continued*

The author provides a "guide to equipment, techniques, and ingredients, followed by a wide-ranging selection of recipes of all sorts. There are both the homestyle dishes she grew up on and more elaborate ones for special occasions, as well as the traditional Japanese classics, with her own touches, of course, and innovative new recipes. . . . An essential purchase." Libr J

Stern, Sam, 1990-

Cooking up a storm; [by] Sam Stern, with Susan Stern. Candlewick Press 2006 128p il $16.99 *

Grades: 6 7 8 9 10   **641.5**

1. Cooking

ISBN 978-0-7636-2988-5; 0-7636-2988-X

LC 2006-42571

"English teen Sam Stern, with his mother's help, offers this slender, photo-packed cookbook, unusual not only because of its author but also because it focuses on guys. . . . That said, the recipes, presented in a casual but clear voice, will draw both genders. . . . The bright, energetic text and color photos of Sam and his photogenic friends and family will easily pull in aspiring foodies." Booklist

Webb, Lois Sinaiko, 1922-

Holidays of the world cookbook for students; [by] Lois Sinaiko Webb and Lindsay Grace Roten. updated and rev. Greenwood 2011 442p il map $95; pa $32.95

Grades: 5 6 7 8 9 10   **641.5**

1. Cooking 2. Holidays

ISBN   978-0-313-38393-9;   0-313-38393-6; 978-0-313-39790-5 (pa); 0-313-39790-2 (pa); 978-0-313-38394-6 (ebook)   LC 2011-8458

First published 1995 by Oryx Press

"The recipes appear with each country entry, and the countries are arranged in alphabetical order within each region: Africa, Asia and the South Pacific, the Caribbean, Europe, Latin America, the Middle East, and North America." Publisher's note

The multicultural cookbook for students; [by] Lois Sinaiko Webb and Lindsay Grace Roten. Updated & rev. Greenwood Press 2009 354p map $85 *

Grades: 7 8 9 10   **641.5**

1. Cooking

ISBN 978-0-313-37558-3; 0-313-37558-5

LC 2009-26718

First published 1993 under the authorship of Carole Lisa Albyn

"This highly informative cookbook includes not only recipes, but also information on the country, its food staples, and ethnic and cultural divisions. Recipes are divided into seven sections according to geography: Africa, Asia and South Pacific, The Caribbean, Europe, Latin America, The Middle East, and North America. . . . Recipes are then divided by country with a description of the country concentrating on culinary information. A minimum of two recipes per country are also annotated with information about the ingredients or why the dish was important to the area. . . . This book is a great re-source for cultural research even if the actual recipes will not be prepared. There is a comprehensive index by recipe name, country, and ingredients." Libr Media Connect

Includes glossary and bibliographical references

Weinstein, Jay

The ethical gourmet. Broadway 2006 353p il pa $18.95

Grades: 11 12 Adult   **641.5**

1. Cooking—Natural foods

ISBN 0-7679-1834-7; 978-0-7679-1834-3

LC 2005-53630

This "guide to socially responsible eating stresses such sustainable practices as buying locally grown, organic produce." Libr J

"This book may be an eye-opener and mouth-closer for many teens accustomed to fast food." SLJ

Includes bibliographical references

Zanger, Mark H.

The American history cookbook. Greenwood Press 2003 xxiii, 459p il (Cookbooks for students) pa $29.95

Grades: 11 12 Adult   **641.5**

1. Cooking

ISBN 1-57356-376-5   LC 2002-69608

"An Oryx book"

"This book uses historical commentary and recipes to trace the history of American cooking from the first European contact with Native Americans to the 1970s. Each of 50 chronologically arranged topical chapters contain 500-1,000 words of general commentary followed by descriptions and . . . step-by-step instructions for 3-4 recipes. The recipes are drawn from a wide variety of historical cookbooks and other historical sources." Publisher's note

Includes bibliographical references

641.8 Cooking specific kinds of dishes, preparing beverages

Carle, Megan

Teens cook dessert; [by] Megan and Jill Carle, with Judi Carle. Ten Speed Press 2006 158p pa $19.95

Grades: 6 7 8 9 10   **641.8**

1. Desserts 2. Cooking

ISBN 978-1-58008-752-0; 1-58008-752-3

LC 2005-24343

The authors "start out with the all-around favorites, like classic chocolate chip cookies. There are holiday recipes for Halloween dirt pie, complete with cookie tombstones and gummy worms that seem to crawl out of the chocolate 'earth.' The final chapter has fancy foods like vanilla soufflt with chocolate sauce or fresh raspberry napoleons. . . . Not only do the recipes sound delicious, they look delicious in glossy color pictures. . . . The instructions are easy to understand." Voice Youth Advocates

Tack, Karen

Hello, cupcake! [by] Karen Tack and Alan Richardson; text and photographs by Alan Richardson; recipes and food styling by Karen Tack. Houghton Mifflin 2008 230p il pa $15.95

Grades: 9 10 11 12 Adult   **641.8**

1. Cupcakes 2. Cake decorating

ISBN 978-0-618-82925-5   LC 2007-40029

The authors cover "the decorating of cupcakes for almost every conceivable occasion. They choose from a vast array of cupcake accessories, including designables (jelly beans), cuttables (licorice), and rollables (Tootsie Rolls), to name just a few. They also incorporate different techniques for building and dipping as well as 18 cake and frosting recipes. The eye-popping results include Oreo-laden pandas, raspberry-preserve-topped truffles, spaghetti and meatballs, an elegant wedding cake, and Christmas ornaments one could almost hang from a tree. An imaginative, well-illustrated book containing recipes that are so clearly explained and easy to make that kids can also enjoy the fun." Booklist

643 Housing and household equipment

Complete do-it-yourself manual; with the editors of Family handyman. rev and updated. Reader's Digest 2005 528p il $35 *

Grades: 11 12 Adult   **643**

1. Houses—Maintenance and repair

ISBN 0-7621-0579-8   LC 2004-50945

First published 1973 with title: Reader's Digest complete do-it-yourself manual

At head of title: Reader's Digest

This manual for homeowners covers topics such as power tools, plumbing, landscaping, and storage projects with photos, diagrams and illustrations

"Intriguing sidebars on wood refinishers (the fastest drying versus the safest), the financial benefits of renting specialty tools for a large drywall project and other subjects round out this must-have guide." Publ Wkly

646 Sewing, clothing, management of personal and family life

Conrad, Lauren, 1986-

Lauren Conrad style; [by] Lauren Conrad with Elise Loehnen. Harper 2010 230p il $19.99

Grades: 7 8 9 10 11 12   **646**

1. Clothing and dress 2. Dress accessories 3. Personal appearance

ISBN 978-0-06-198914-8   LC 2010-3093

The author "offers a top-to-bottom guide to personal style for readers who don't have stylists. . . . She goes over wardrobe essentials . . . makeup tips, suggestions for working with different types of hair, and advice on how to dress for various occasions. Her voice is consistently entertaining, confident, and accessible, and her advice is practical." Publ Wkly

Jones, Caroline

1001 little fashion miracles. Carlton Books 2008 224p il pa $12.95

Grades: 11 12 Adult   **646**

1. Fashion 2. Women's clothing 3. Clothing and dress

ISBN 978-1-84442-838-0

Author on title page "Esme Floyd"

Offering advice on styles, accessorizing and shopping, this book provides ideas for looking best in different circumstances.

646.2 Sewing and related operations

The **complete** photo guide to sewing; 1200 full-color how-to photos; [created by the editors of Creative Publishing International] Rev. + expanded ed. Creative Pub. International 2009 352p il pa $24.99

Grades: 9 10 11 12 Adult   **646.2**

1. Sewing

ISBN 978-1-58923-434-5; 1-58923-434-0

LC 2008-31264

First published 1999

At head of title: Singer

"Sections include choosing the right tools and notions, using conventional machines and sergers, fashion sewing, tailoring, and home décor projects. Included are step-by-step instructions for basic projects like pillows, tablecloths, and window treatments." Publisher's note

Smith, Alison

Sew step by step. Dorling Kindersley 2011 224p il pa $15.95

Grades: 9 10 11 12 Adult   **646.2**

1. Sewing 2. Dressmaking

ISBN 978-0-7566-7164-8

First published 2009 in the United Kingdom with title: The sewing book

This book covers over 200 sewing techniques using contemporary styles and materials.

646.4 Clothing and accessories construction

Holkeboer, Katherine Strand

Patterns for theatrical costumes; garments, trims, and accessories from ancient Egypt to 1915; [by] Katherine Strand Holkeboer. Drama Book Publishers 1992 342p il pa $35

Grades: 9 10 11 12   **646.4**

1. Costume 2. Sewing

ISBN 0-89676-125-8   LC 92-34985

First published 1984 by Prentice-Hall

Each design "includes black-and-white drawings of the completed garment, pattern pieces for enlarging embellishments to be copied, and, when necessary, illustrations of how to wear the particular costume. A few special costumes—clergy, animals, oriental—are featured as are notes on constructing important accessories." Booklist

Includes bibliographical references

Rannels, Melissa

Sew subversive; down and dirty DIY for the fabulous fashionista; [by] Melissa Rannels, Melissa Alvarado, Hope Meng; illustrated by Hope Meng & 3+Co.; photographs by Matthew Carden. The Taunton Press 2006 186p il pa $14.95

Grades: 11 12 Adult   **646.4**
   1. Women's clothing 2. Sewing
   ISBN 978-1-56158-809-1; 1-56158-809-1
                           LC 2006-1502
The authors "give beginning sewers all the basics, plus 22 tempting projects. Their mission—'subverting' fashion—is all about 'embellishing and customizing clothes—refashioning them to make them uniquely your own.' . . . They start with a solid chapter on hand sewing (mending rips, hemming skirts), then tell you everything you've ever wanted to know about sewing machines but were afraid to ask. T-shirts are torn apart to make mini skirts, shoulder bags and tube tops. . . . With its casual approach and offbeat creations, this is definitely not your mother's sewing book." Publ Wkly

Includes bibliographical references

646.7 Management of personal and family life

Beker, Jeanne

The big night out; Nathalie Dion, illustrator. Tundra Books 2005 80p il pa $15.95 *

Grades: 7 8 9 10   **646.7**
   1. Rites and ceremonies 2. Parties 3. Etiquette
4. Personal grooming
   ISBN 0-88776-719-2
"This book is for young women who are seeking to develop and display their own sense of style as they prepare for a special event. . . . [The author] provides realistic advice on budgeting, planning ahead, and attending to all the details, from accessorizing to practicing hairstyles and makeup application in advance. . . . This book will hold an obvious appeal. Its straightforward style and playful, whimsical illustrations make it easily accessible." Voice Youth Advocates

Bergamotto, Lori

Skin; the bare facts. Zest Books 2009 97p il pa $18.95

Grades: 6 7 8 9 10   **646.7**
   1. Skin—Care 2. Teenagers—Health and hygiene
   ISBN 978-0-9800732-5-6; 0-9800732-5-1
Presents an overview on skin types, methods for treating common problems, and tips for skin care and makeup application.
"There's something for every girl here, whether she's just had her first breakout or needs a refresher on which sunscreen to use and when to reapply." SLJ

Brown, Bobbi

Bobbi Brown teenage beauty; everything you need to look pretty, natural, sexy & awesome; [by] Bobbi Brown & Annemarie Iverson. Cliff St. Bks. 2000 200p il $25; pa $18.95

Grades: 9 10 11 12   **646.7**
   1. Personal grooming 2. Skin—Care
   ISBN 0-06-019636-X; 0-06-095724-7 (pa)
                          LC 00-711795
"Brown and Iverson give teens basic beauty tips and a large boost to their self-esteem. . . . The authors stress the importance of diet and exercise." SLJ

Earle, Liz

Skin care secrets; how to have naturally healthy beautiful skin; special photography by Patrick Drummond and Kate Whitaker; illustrations by Kathy Wyatt. Firefly Books 2010 192p il pa $24.95

Grades: 9 10 11 12 Adult   **646.7**
   1. Skin—Care
   ISBN 978-1-55407-608-6   LC 2010-459161
A guide to naturally beautiful skin at any age.

Espeland, Pamela, 1951-

Life lists for teens; tips, steps, hints, and how-tos for growing up, getting along, learning, and having fun. Free Spirit 2003 264p pa $11.95

Grades: 7 8 9 10 11 12   **646.7**
   1. Conduct of life 2. Life skills
   ISBN 1-57542-125-9   LC 2002-152116
Hundreds of lists provide guidance in areas of young adult life as diverse as selecting a book or a hair color to selecting a mentor
"Espeland's well-organized book has lots of useful information and teen appeal." SLJ

Fornay, Alfred

Born beautiful; the African American teenager's complete beauty guide. John Wiley & Sons 2002 166p il pa $14.95 *

Grades: 8 9 10 11 12   **646.7**
   1. Teenagers—Health and hygiene 2. African American women—Health and hygiene 3. Personal appearance 4. Personal grooming
   ISBN 0-471-40275-3   LC 2002-18131
"An Amber book"
This book on beauty and grooming for African American teenage girls includes information on makeup, hairstyles, nail and skin care, diet, and clothing.

Morgenstern, Julie

Organizing from the inside out for teens; the foolproof system for organizing your room, your time, and your life; [by] Julie Morgenstern and Jessi Morgenstern-Colón; illustrations by Janet Pedersen. Holt & Co. 2002 238p il pa $15 *

Grades: 7 8 9 10   **646.7**
   1. Life skills 2. Time management
   ISBN 0-8050-6470-2   LC 2002-68552

Morgenstern, Julie—*Continued*

The authors "offer practical advice to teenagers who want to get organized. After considering what might be holding them back and the three steps to success (analyze, strategize, attack), the discussion shifts to the two major areas of concern: managing space and managing time. . . . Useful advice in an accessible paperback format." Booklist

The **New** York Times practical guide to practically everything; the essential companion for everyday life; edited by Amy D. Bernstein and Peter W. Bernstein. St. Martin's Press 2006 834p il map $29.95

Grades: 11 12 Adult   **646.7**
1. Life skills
ISBN 0-312-35388-X; 978-0-312-35388-9
                                   LC 2006-45081

This "guide covers a wide range of topics—from 'Getting and Staying Trim' to 'The Braille System'—broken up into broad subject categories such as 'Health,' 'Food & Drink,' 'Money,' 'Careers,' 'House & Garden,' 'Sports & Games,' 'Arts & Entertainment' and 'Everyday Science.' . . . This is a browse-worthy collection of general knowledge that should come in handy next time you're traveling to the Galapagos, building an igloo, or in any of more than 800 other 'everyday' situations." Publ Wkly

Parrish, J. R.

You don't have to learn the hard way; making It in the real world: a guide for graduates. BenBella Books 2009 283p il $19.95

Grades: 11 12 Adult   **646.7**
1. Life skills 2. Success
ISBN 978-1933771-74-8

This book offers advice for teens and college graduates on topics "including: nailing that first big job interview; avoiding dangerous relationship mistakes; mastering the art of managing your finances; circumventing the typical pitfalls of adjusting to the adult world; making friends and forging career alliances; [and] choosing the right mentors." Publisher's note

Shipp, Josh

The teen's guide to world domination; advice on life, liberty, and the pursuit of awesomeness. St. Martin's Griffin 2010 285p il pa $14.99

Grades: 8 9 10 11   **646.7**
1. Conduct of life 2. Interpersonal relations 3. Life skills
ISBN 978-0-312-64154-2; 0-312-64154-0
                                   LC 2010-22069

The author "provides a funny, compassionate, and straight-talking blueprint for teens to achieve fulfillment personally, socially, and professionally. . . . Shipp's fresh and honest approach should make sense to teens seeking guidance and avoids feeling preachy or heavy-handed." Publ Wkly

Spencer, Kit

Pro makeup; salon secrets of the professionals. Firefly Books 2009 255p il $29.95 *

Grades: 8 9 10 11 12 Adult   **646.7**
1. Cosmetics
ISBN 978-1-55407-477-8   LC 2009-279649

This book "provides an organized, attractive overview of makeup application techniques from everyday to costume. The text is enhanced throughout by useful highlights offering tips from professionals on everything from achieving the perfect eyebrow arch to taking the attention away from a wide nose. Bridal and costume party makeup are covered as well. . . . There is a section on developing looks, dealing with skin conditions, choosing equipment, and even applying makeup to men and children." Voice Youth Advocates

Toselli, Leigh

Pro nail care; salon secrets of the professionals. Firefly Books 2009 254p il $29.95 *

Grades: 8 9 10 11 12 Adult   **646.7**
1. Manicuring 2. Personal grooming
ISBN 978-1-55407-478-5   LC 2009-288700

This book "goes well beyond the typical manicure or pedicure. An intriguing history of nail care is provided (who knew they had manicures in ancient Babylon?), as well as a history of nail polish fashion. The anatomy of the hand and foot are examined in detail. Nail diseases and problems are explained with suggested remedies. There are sections on massage, overlay systems, the chemistry of nail products, and a gallery of nail 'looks.' Most interesting is the section on nail art. The looks are explained with step-by-step instructions accompanied by clear photographs." Voice Youth Advocates

Willdorf, Nina

City chic; the modern girl's guide to living large on less. [New ed.] Sourcebooks 2009 271p il pa $14.99

Grades: 9 10 11 12 Adult   **646.7**
1. Young women 2. Life skills 3. Personal finance
ISBN 978-1-4022-1785-2; 1-4022-1785-4
                                   LC 2008-38831

First published 2003

This is a "guide to living well on a dime. Although aimed at women in their twenties and thirties, women in other age brackets will also appreciate the author's hints for saving money in many realms of their lives, including home furnishings, makeup, entertainment, and laundry. Moneysaving ideas range from exercising at home to storing food properly." Libr J

Includes bibliographical references

Yellin, Susan

Life after high school; a guide for students with disabilities and their families; [by] Susan Yellin and Christina Cacioppo Bertsch. Jessica Kingsley Publishers 2010 269p pa $19.95 *

Grades: Adult   **646.7**
1. Handicapped students 2. Handicapped—Employment 3. Vocational guidance
ISBN 978-1-84905-828-5   LC 2010-4298

Yellin, Susan—*Continued*

The authors "provide students with disabilities and their parents an outstanding and highly readable guide to preparing for and transitioning to life after high school. They start by examining the legal landscape and cover defining a disability and creating a paper trail to document the disability and previous accommodations. They move on to college-entrance exams, how to select a college, and the admissions process, and then discuss the transition to full-time work. There is also a chapter devoted to dealing with medical issues without mom." Libr J

Includes bibliographical references

647.9 Specific kinds of public households and institutions

Chalmers, Irena

Food jobs; 150 great jobs for culinary students, career changers and food lovers. Beaufort Books 2008 xxiii, 326p il pa $19.95

Grades: 11 12 Adult   **647.9**

1. Food service 2. Vocational guidance
ISBN 978-0-8253-0592-4; 0-8253-0592-6

LC 2008-26124

The author "offers profiles of food jobs by the dozen—everything from the traditional (maitre d', caterer, dietician) to the behind-the-scenes (restaurant consultant, kitchen designer, hotel promoter) to the holy-cow-I-can-get-paid-for-that? (yacht chef, tea taster, fortune cookie message writer). Chalmers provides . . . information for getting started and succeeding in your chosen culinary role including job descriptions, candid musings on what the job really entails and who it's really for, and testimonials from . . . [people] in the field (Bobby Flay, Todd English, Gordon Hamersly, Francois Payard, Danny Meyer, Anthony Bourdain and more)." Publisher's note

"The book's strength lies in exposing readers to new possibilities and in further illuminating some of the more familiar or traditional jobs and fields. . . . [It] is meant to be both entertaining and helpful as a resource, ideally projecting readers along the paths of their personal and professional aspirations. In short—this book is *useful*." Gastronomica

Includes bibliographical references

649 Child rearing; home care of persons with disabilities and illnesses

Lindsay, Jeanne Warren

Teen dads; rights, responsibilities, and joys. Rev. [3rd] ed. Morning Glory Press 2008 224p il pa $12.95 *

Grades: 9 10 11 12   **649**

1. Teenage fathers 2. Child rearing 3. Parenting
ISBN 978-1-932538-86-1

First published 1993

"This upbeat presentation instructs young men on how to be supportive of their partner and the new baby, assist with the baby's labor and delivery, care for and nurture the child through infancy and the toddler years, and bet-

ter understand their changing relationship with the mother. Short chapters cover, in chronological order, all the issues young parents must face, from the pregnancy test to learning how to properly love, feed, and discipline a curious, growing child." Voice Youth Advocates

Includes bibliographical references

650.1 Personal success in business

Roza, Greg

Great networking skills. Rosen Pub. 2008 64p il (Work readiness) lib bdg $29.25

Grades: 9 10 11 12   **650.1**

1. Interpersonal relations 2. Vocational guidance
ISBN 978-1-4042-1420-0   LC 2007-34841

The author "explains what networking is and what it isn't. Topics include working with friends, family, and academic contacts; staying organized; writing; preparing résumés; making connections; and selling youself." SLJ

Includes glossary and bibliographical references

Sommers, Michael A., 1966-

Great interpersonal skills. Rosen Pub. 2008 64p il (Work readiness) lib bdg $29.25

Grades: 9 10 11 12   **650.1**

1. Interpersonal relations 2. Social skills
ISBN 978-1-4042-1423-1; 1-4042-1423-2

LC 2007-23663

This book "discusses groundwork such as developing conversational skills, creating a good first impression, teamwork, assertiveness, and conflict resolution." SLJ

Includes glossary and bibliographical references

650.14 Success in obtaining jobs and promotions

Enelow, Wendy S.

Best resumes for people without a four-year degree. Impact Publications 2004 185p pa $19.95

Grades: 9 10 11 12   **650.14**

1. Résumés (Employment)
ISBN 1-57023-204-0   LC 2003-100522

This collection of professionally-written résumés "includes four . . . résumé-writing exercises as well as contact information for the professional résumé writers who contributed to this book." Publisher's note

Includes bibliographical references

Hinds, Maurene J.

The Ferguson guide to resumes and job hunting skills; a step-by-step guide to preparing for your job search. Ferguson 2005 248p il $45; pa $16.95 *

Grades: 9 10 11 12   **650.14**

1. Résumés (Employment) 2. Job hunting
ISBN 0-8160-5792-3; 0-8160-5796-6 (pa)

LC 2004-24445

Hinds, Maurene J.—*Continued*

"Included are an annotated roundup of assessment tests, from Myers-Briggs to the Strong Interest Inventory; a litany of common job-hunters' mistakes (for instance, not looking an interviewer directly in the eyes); and, of course, a variety of resumes and cover letters." Booklist

Reeves, Ellen Gordon

Can I wear my nose ring to the interview? the crash course: finding, landing, and keeping your first real job. Workman Pub. 2009 227p pa $13.95

Grades: 10 11 12 Adult   **650.14**
1. Job hunting 2. Interviewing 3. Résumés (Employment)
ISBN 978-0-7611-4145-7; 0-7611-4145-6
LC 2009-279010

This book discusses how to search for a job; create a résumé, cover letter, and list of references; and prepare for job interviews.

Troutman, Kathryn K.

Creating your high school resume; a step-by-step guide to preparing an effective resume for jobs, college, and training programs; [by] Kathryn Kraemer Troutman. 3rd ed. JIST Works 2009 150p il pa $16.95

Grades: 9 10 11 12   **650.14**
1. Résumés (Employment)
ISBN 978-1-59357-662-2
First published 1998

This book "explains why high school students need to work on a resume and keep updating it. In addition to job searching, students will be able to use a resume when applying for college, asking people for recommendations, and applying for scholarships. There are examples from teenagers that demonstrate how to present oneself in the best possible light." Libr Media Connect

Withers, Jennie

Hey, get a job! a teen guide for getting and keeping a job. Jennie Withers 2009 89p il pa $14.99

Grades: 8 9 10 11 12   **650.14**
1. Vocational guidance 2. Occupations
ISBN 978-0-9842354-0-7

This guide "covers all the basics and more for teens about to enter the working world with a style and approach that tells it like it is. . . . Seven chapters cover everything from finding employment opportunities, filling out applications, brainstorming relevant strengths and experience for resumes to interview prep and completing standard employment forms." Voice Youth Advocates

651.7 Communication. Creation and transmission of records

Geffner, Andrea B.

How to write better business letters. 4th ed. Barron's 2007 173p il pa $14.99 *

Grades: 9 10 11 12   **651.7**
1. Business letters
ISBN 0-7641-3539-2; 978-0-7641-3539-2
LC 2006-42953

First published 1982

"This book instructs on how to write effective examples of every kind of business letter. It presents about 75 model letters in categories that include credit applications, letters of inquiry, orders of goods and services, formal business announcements, letters of recommendation, and sales promotional letters of the type used by direct marketers. This book also features examples of different letter formatting styles." Publisher's note

Thomason-Carroll, Kristi L.

Young adult's guide to business communications. Business Books 2004 117p il $14.95 *

Grades: 9 10 11 12   **651.7**
1. Business communication 2. Résumés (Employment) 3. Interviewing
ISBN 0-9723714-4-3   LC 2002-115501

This "guide covers writing a résumé, filling out job applications, interviewing skills, and work etiquette (e.g., the proper form for memos, e-mails, and reports, and interactions with others). Throughout the lively text, the author stresses the importance of making a good impression through careful preparation and presentation." SLJ

Includes bibliographical references

652 Processes of written communication

Butler, William S.

Secret messages; concealment, codes, and other types of ingenious communication; [by] William S. Butler and L. Douglas Keeney. Simon & Schuster 2001 192p il $23

Grades: 11 12 Adult   **652**
1. Cryptography 2. Ciphers
ISBN 0-684-86998-5   LC 00-46368

"Through a series of short stories and anecdotes, this book gives . . . [a] quick tour of codes used by common folk as well as spies. . . . Much of the book is devoted to codes used to convey messages in everyday life. Those used by hospitals, police officers, restaurant staff, and bridge players are addressed. . . . An engaging book that may entice readers to pursue a more in-depth exploration of the topic." SLJ

Includes bibliographical references

658.1   Organization and finance

Bielagus, Peter G.
Quick cash for teens; be your own boss and
make big bucks. Sterling Pub. 2009 249p pa
$12.95
Grades: 7 8 9 10 11 12   **658.1**
1.   Entrepreneurship   2.   Small   business
3. Money-making projects for children
ISBN 978-1-4027-6038-9; 1-4027-6038-8
LC 2008-42793
"Young entrepreneurs wanting to own and operate
their own businesses will find this practical, introductory
guide an excellent source of advice. . . . Bielagus' conversational style and the frequent insertion of anecdotes
from successful teen entrepreneurs make the text accessible." Booklist

658.4   Executive management

Encyclopedia of leadership; editors, George R.
Goethals,   Georgia   J.   Sorenson,   James
MacGregor Burns. Sage Publications 2004 4v il
map set $595
Grades: 11 12 Adult   **658.4**
1. Leadership—Encyclopedias 2. Reference books
ISBN 0-7619-2597-X   LC 2004-1252
"What is leadership? What is a great leader? What is
a great follower? What are the types of leadership? And
how does someone become a leader? This set was designed with the needs of several user communities in
mind, including students, scholars, and professionals who
want to explore such questions." Booklist
Includes bibliographical references

658.8   Management of marketing

Underhill, Paco
Why we buy; the science of shopping. Updated
and rev. Simon & Schuster Pbks. 2009 306p pa
$16; ebook $12.99
Grades: 11 12 Adult   **658.8**
1. Marketing 2. Consumers 3. Shopping
ISBN 978-1-4165-9524-3 (pa); 1-4165-9524-4 (pa);
978-1-4165-6174-3 (ebook); 1-4165-6174-9 (ebook)
LC 2010-483248
First published 1999
"Each chapter delves into a particular aspect of a store
environment and its interface with customers: the importance of signage and why less is more, how men shop,
. . . and clues about waiting time. Throughout, insights
are peppered with one or several examples." Booklist
[review of 1999 edition]

659.1   Advertising

Advertising: opposing viewpoints; Roman Espejo,
book editor. Greenhaven Press 2010 207p il
$39.70; pa $27.50 *
Grades: 9 10 11 12   **659.1**
1. Advertising
ISBN   978-0-7377-4751-5;   0-7377-4751-X;
978-0-7377-4752-2 (pa); 0-7377-4752-8 (pa)
LC 2009050761
"Opposing viewpoints series"
Articles in this anthology discuss whether advertising
is harmful, if it exploits children, and political advertising.
Includes bibliographical references

How does advertising impact teen behavior? David
M. Haugen, book editor. Greenhaven Press 2008
88p (At issue. Teen issues) lib bdg $29.95; pa
$21.20 *
Grades: 9 10 11 12   **659.1**
1. Mass media 2. Advertising 3. Teenagers—Attitudes
ISBN 978-0-7377-3922-0 (lib bdg); 0-7377-3922-3 (lib
bdg); 978-0-7377-3923-7 (pa); 0-7377-3923-1 (pa)
LC 2007-48660
This "is a well-rounded assortment of essays that covers the most salient discussion points in the debate about
what impact advertising has on teen behavior. Authors
address the role it plays in childhood obesity, smoking,
and brand loyalty." SLJ
Includes bibliographical references

660.6   Biotechnology

Biotechnology: changing life through science; [by]
K. Lee Lerner and Brenda Wilmoth Lerner,
editors. Thomson/Gale 2007 3v il set $196
Grades: 8 9 10 11 12   **660.6**
1. Biotechnology 2. Reference books
ISBN 978-1-4144-0151-5
Contents: v1 Medicine; v2 Agriculture; v3 Industry
"This set introduces students to the science of biotechnology, the issues pertaining to biotechnology, and how
the issues impact society. . . . The clean layout features
more than 150 color photographs as well as many diagrams and boxed areas. . . . The articles contain more
than enough information to meet the needs of younger
students as well as general readers." Booklist

Hodge, Russ
Genetic   engineering;   manipulating   the
mechanisms of life; foreword by Nadia Rosenthal.
Facts on File 2009 219p il map (Genetics &
evolution) $39.50
Grades: 9 10 11 12   **660.6**
1. Genetic engineering
ISBN 978-0-8160-6681-0; 0-8160-6681-7
LC 2008-33700
This book "traces the history of genetic science up to
the present day and proposes some thoughts about how
it is likely to affect the future. This . . . resource de-

Hodge, Russ—*Continued*

scribes some of the developments in the first few years of the 21st century and how society is coping with some of the ethical challenges that accompany them." Publisher's note

Includes glossary and bibliographical references

Panno, Joseph

Animal cloning; the science of nuclear transfer. Rev ed. Facts on File 2010 c2011 228p il (The new biology) $40

Grades: 9 10 11 12   **660.6**
  1. Cloning
  ISBN 978-0-8160-6847-0   LC 2009-49945
  First published 2005

"Beginning chapters discuss cloning within the context of a natural process that many animals use as a survival strategy, followed by the historical development of the nuclear transfer procedure, the cloning of Dolly the sheep, the medical applications of cloning technology, and . . . more." Publisher's note

Includes glossary and bibliographical references

Seiple, Samantha

Mutants, clones, and killer corn; unlocking the secrets of biotechnology; [by] Samantha Seiple and Todd Seiple. Lerner 2005 112p il (Discovery!) $27.93

Grades: 7 8 9 10   **660.6**
  1. Biotechnology
  ISBN 0-8225-4860-7

"The Seiples present an overview of biotechnology from its origins in selective breeding to its possible future implications. The writing is clear and a brief outline of genetics is offered. . . . The appealing layout features color photographs, charts, and graphs, as well as informative sidebars. . . . A solid, up-to-date addition for reports and general-interest reading." SLJ

Shannon, Thomas A. (Thomas Anthony), 1940-

Genetic engineering; a documentary history; edited by Thomas A. Shannon. Greenwood Press 1999 xxxi, 282p (Primary documents in American history and contemporary issues) $49.95 *

Grades: 9 10 11 12   **660.6**
  1. Genetic engineering
  ISBN 0-313-30457-2   LC 98-46808

This volume "includes documents on such topics as cloning, diagnostic applications, ethics, genetically altered food, and the Human Genome Project." Booklist

Includes bibliographical references

662   Technology of explosives, fuels, related products

Tabak, John

Biofuels. Facts on File 2009 204p il (Energy and the environment) $40

Grades: 9 10 11 12   **662**
  1. Biomass energy
  ISBN 978-0-8160-7082-4; 0-8160-7082-2
                                           LC 2008-24349

This book identifies "the most common types of biofuels and biofuel technologies and seeks to identify both the advantages and disadvantages associated with their use. . . . [It] describes the ways that biofuels are used and the technical, social, policy, and environmental consequences of large-scale consumption." Publisher's note

This book "has value both for the explanations it offers and the questions it raises." SLJ

Includes glossary and bibliographical references

664   Food technology

Aronson, Marc

Sugar changed the world; a story of magic, spice, slavery, freedom, and science; by Marc Aronson and Marina Budhos. Clarion Books 2010 166p il map $20 *

Grades: 7 8 9 10 11 12   **664**
  1. Sugar—History 2. World history 3. Slavery
  ISBN 978-0-618-57492-6; 0-618-57492-1
                                         LC 2009-33579

"From 1600 to the 1800s, sugar drove the economies of Europe, the Americas, Asia and Africa and did more 'to reshape the world than any ruler, empire, or war had ever done.' Millions of people were taken from Africa and enslaved to work the sugar plantations throughout the Caribbean, worked to death to supply the demand for sugar in Europe. . . . Maps, photographs and archival illustrations, all with captions that are informative in their own right, richly complement the text, and superb documentation and an essay addressed to teachers round out the fascinating volume." Kirkus

Includes bibliographical references

Hayhurst, Chris

Everything you need to know about food additives. Rosen Pub. Group 2002 64p il (Need to know library) lib bdg $27.95

Grades: 9 10 11 12   **664**
  1. Food additives
  ISBN 0-8239-3548-5   LC 2001-1980

This book "introduces common additives and explains reasons for their use, including consumers' finicky preferences; discusses health risks associated with many additives; and offers exciting alternatives to processed foods, such as produce from community-supported agriculture programs." Booklist

Includes bibliographical references

Winter, Ruth, 1930-

A consumer's dictionary of food additives. 7th ed. Three Rivers Press 2009 595p pa $17.95; ebook $17.95 *

Grades: 11 12 Adult   **664**
  1. Food additives—Dictionaries 2. Reference books
  ISBN 978-0-307-40892-1 (pa); 978-0-307-45259-7 (ebook)   LC 2008-40601
  First published 1972. Periodically revised

This guide provides "facts about the safety and side effects of more than 12,000 ingredients—such as preser-

Winter, Ruth, 1930-—*Continued*
vatives, food-tainting pesticides, and animal drugs—that
end up in food as a result of processing and curing."
Publisher's note
Includes bibliographical references

667 Cleaning, color, coating, related technologies

Garfield, Simon
Mauve; how one man invented a color that
changed the world. Norton 2001 222p il pa $13.95
hardcover o.p.
Grades: 11 12 Adult   **667**
1. Perkin, William Henry, 1838-1907 2. Dyes and
dyeing
ISBN 0-393-32313-7 (pa)   LC 00-69533
This volume discusses how a British student, William
Henry Perkin, while trying to synthesize quinine from
coal tar, developed mauve, "the first mass-produced artificial dye. . . . By the turn of the 20th century, because
of Perkin's novel idea, dye makers had 2,000 synthesized
colors at their disposal." N Y Times Book Rev
"The text is understandable by the average layman and
is enjoyable reading for the scientist and non-scientist
alike." Sci Books Films
Includes bibliographical references

674 Lumber processing, wood products, cork

Edlin, Herbert L. (Herbert Leeson), 1913-1976
What wood is that? A manual of wood
identification. Viking 1969 160p il $32.95
Grades: 9 10 11 12 Adult   **674**
1. Wood
ISBN 0-670-75907-4   LC 69-15933
"A Studio book"
The book discusses timber cutting and sawing, wood
identification, including keys for naming timbers, and descriptions of each of the forty trees listed as examples
"The text is of British origin, and does consider some
woods little used in our country; it also omits others very
much used here. The language is universal, however, and
both text and illustrations constitute a notable addition to
the woodworker's library." Libr J

The **Encyclopedia** of wood; a tree-by-tree guide to
the world's most versatile resource; general
editor, Aidan Walker. Facts on File 2005 192p
il map $35 *
Grades: 11 12 Adult   **674**
1. Wood—Encyclopedias 2. Reference books
ISBN 0-8160-6181-5   LC 2004-60849
First published 1989
This book "provides an A-to-Z directory featuring
more than 150 of the world's most popular woods, with
information on growth rate, distribution, key characteristics, working properties, and commercial uses." Publisher's note

"A nice addition to libraries with strong interior design or DIY collections." Libr J
Includes bibliographical references

682 Small forge work (Blacksmithing)

Weitzman, David L., 1936-
Skywalkers; Mohawk ironworkers build the city.
Roaring Brook Press/Flash Point 2010 124p il
$19.99 *
Grades: 8 9 10 11 12 Adult   **682**
1. Building 2. Mohawk Indians 3. Steel construction
4. Skyscrapers 5. Bridges
ISBN 978-1-59643-162-1; 1-59643-162-8
"Stunning photographs complement Weitzman's comprehensive research and clear text in this memorable tribute to Mohawk ironworkers. . . . Weitzman wisely inter-
sperses passages of construction history and technical
technique with numerous personal stories. . . . Plentiful
black and white archival photographs . . . are chilling or
breathtaking. Throughout, Weitzman's admiration and respect for the Mohawk people shine through." Voice
Youth Advocates
Includes glossary and bibliographical references

684 Furnishings and home workshops

Taunton's complete illustrated guide to
woodworking; [by] Lonnie Bird . . . [et al.]
Taunton Press 2005 311p il $29.95
Grades: 11 12 Adult   **684**
1. Woodwork
ISBN 1-56158-769-9   LC 2004-28678
This "guide covers a wide array of woodworking topics. . . . The arrangement is consistent and well thought
out, with illustrated referencing at the beginning of each
chapter." Libr J

Woodwork; a step-by-step photographic guide to
successful woodworking; [writers, Alan
Bridgewater . . . [et al]; illustrator, Simon
Rodway] DK Pub. 2010 400p il $40
Grades: 10 11 12 Adult   **684**
1. Woodwork
ISBN 978-0-7566-4306-5   LC 2010-279214
Thsi book "offers instruction in basic woodworking
techniques and pairs profiles of common and exotic
woods with great photos. The 25 projects, including furnishings and household products, start from simple and
build to complex. While the projects are not particularly
distinctive, the supporting materials make this a key purchase for any woodworking collection. Highly recommended." Libr J

688.7   Recreational equipment

Sobey, Ed
The way toys work; the science behind the
magic 8 ball, etch a sketch, boomerang, and more;
[by] Ed Sobey and Woody Sobey. Chicago
Review Press 2008 178p il pa $14.95
Grades: 11 12 Adult   **688.7**
1. Toys
ISBN 978-1-55652-745-6   LC 2008-1303
This book profiles "50 of the world's most popular
playthings—including their history, trivia, and the technology involved. . . . The guide includes original patent-
application blueprints and photos of the 'guts' of several
devices. Inventors and museum curators also offer their
observations of favorite gizmos while dispelling (or con-
firming) several toy legends." Publisher's note
"This is really quite a nifty book, perfect for collectors, for anyone daring enough to build homemade versions of these classic toys, and even for casual browsers." Booklist
Includes bibliographical references

Stone, Tanya Lee
The good, the bad, and the Barbie; a doll's
history and her impact on us. Viking 2010 130p il
$19.99
Grades: 6 7 8 9 10   **688.7**
1. Handler, Ruth, 1916-2002 2. Mattel Inc. 3. Barbie
dolls
ISBN 978-0-670-01187-2; 0-670-01187-8
LC 2010-7507
"Stone tantalizes with her brief and intriguing survey
of Barbie. She begins with the history of Mattel, started
by self-made businesswoman Ruth Handler in the 1940s,
and moves onto materialism, body image, portrayals of
ethnicity, nudity, taboo and art." Kirkus
Includes bibliographical references

690   Building & construction

Macaulay, David, 1946-
Mill. Houghton Mifflin 1983 128p il $19; pa
$9.95
Grades: 4 5 6 7 8 9 10   **690**
1. Mills 2. Textile industry—History
ISBN 0-395-34830-7; 0-395-52019-3 (pa)
LC 83-10652
This is an "account of the development of four fictional 19th-century Rhode Island cotton mills. In explaining the construction and operation of a simple water-
wheel powered wooden mill, as well as the more complex stone, turbine and steam mills to follow, the author
also describes the rise and decline of New England's textile industry." SLJ
"Well-researched, ambitious, and absorbing, this is another first-rate history lesson from a practiced, perfec-
tionist hand." Booklist

Unbuilding. Houghton Mifflin 1980 78p il $18;
pa $9.95
Grades: 4 5 6 7 8 9   **690**
1. Empire State Building (New York, N.Y.)
2. Building 3. Skyscrapers
ISBN 0-395-29457-6; 0-395-45425-5 (pa)
LC 80-15491
This fictional account of the dismantling and removal
of the Empire State Building describes the structure of a
skyscraper and explains how such an edifice would be
demolished
"Save for the fact that one particularly stunning double-page spread is marred by tight binding, the book is
a joy: accurate, informative, handsome, and eminently
readable." Bull Cent Child Books

700   ARTS

Arts and humanities through the eras. Gale 2004
5v il set $450
Grades: 11 12 Adult   **700**
1. Arts—History 2. Civilization—History
ISBN 0-7876-5695-X   LC 2004-10243
Also available as separate volumes ea $105
Contents: v1 Ancient Egypt (2675 B.C.E.-332 B.C.E.);
v2 Ancient Greece and Rome (1200 B.C.E.-476 C.E.);
v3 Medieval Europe (814-1450); v4 Renaissance Europe
(1300-1600); v5 The age of Baroque and Enlightenment
(1600-1800)
"Each volume consists of nine chapters covering the
major branches of the humanities: architecture and design, dance, fashion, literature, music, philosophy, religion, theater, and visual arts. . . . This outstanding series
offers a wealth of information; the chapters on architecture, dance, and theater alone are worth the price of each
volume." Libr J
Includes bibliographical references

Delacampagne, Ariane, 1959-
Here be dragons; a fantastic bestiary; [by]
Ariane   Delacampagne   and   Christian
Delacampagne. Princeton University Press 2003
199p il $45
Grades: 9 10 11 12   **700**
1. Mythical animals 2. Animals in art
ISBN 0-691-11689-X   LC 2003-51741
After an "assessment of animals in art as dream imagery and religious symbols, the Delacampagnes' five subsequent chapters consider, respectively, the evolution of
the bestiary of nonexistent creatures, portrayals of unicorns and partially human beasts, images of four-footed
flying things and dragons, the issue of influence versus
coincidence in accounting for the similarity of fantastic
animals in disparate cultures, and fantastic animals in
contemporary art . . . The pictures of everything from
the two-horned unicorn . . . on the walls of the Lascaux
caves to a yeti from the pages of *Tintin au Tibet* (1960)
are invariably gorgeous." Booklist
Includes bibliographical references

Encyclopedia of the Harlem Renaissance; Cary D. Wintz, Paul Finkelman, editors. Routledge 2004 2v il map set $325 *

Grades: 11 12 Adult   700
1. Reference books 2. African American arts 3. Harlem Renaissance—Encyclopedias
ISBN 1-57958-389-X   LC 2004-16353

This encyclopedia features "essays on the life and works of major writers, artists, and musicians of the period as well as broader articles on the impact of contemporary political, social, economic, and legal issues on the movement. . . . This thorough and well-organized reference work should appeal to a wide range of users from high school to graduate school students and is recommended for all libraries." Libr J

Includes bibliographical references

Encyclopedia of the romantic era, 1760-1850; Christopher John Murray, general editor. Fitzroy Dearborn 2003 2v il set $325

Grades: 11 12 Adult   700
1. Romanticism
ISBN 1-57958-361-X   LC 2003-42406

"This two-volume cultural encyclopedia contains 770 entries on the arts and sciences of the Romantic Era, including, but not limited to, the Romantic movement. The strengths of this encyclopedia are many, including its geographical coverage (Britain, continental Europe, and the Americas); entries on individuals; discussions of specific works of literature, art, and music; and thematic entries that focus on a broad-range of subjects (e.g. the Dandy, Orientalism, and the Sublime)." Libr Media Connect

Includes bibliographical references

Fallon, Michael, 1966-
How to analyze the works of Andy Warhol. ABDO Pub. Co. 2011 112p il (Essential critiques) $34.22

Grades: 9 10 11 12   700
1. Warhol, Andy, 1928?-1987 2. Art appreciation 3. Art criticism
ISBN 978-1-61613-534-8   LC 2010-15882

This book looks at the works of Andy Warhol "through the lenses of prevalent schools of criticism. The first chapters introduce the concept of critical theory, its purpose, and how to develop and support a thesis statement. In subsequent chapters, an overview of each work is followed by a critique using a particular theory. . . . Critical theories are applied to *32 Campbell's Soup Cans*, *Turquoise Marilyn*, *16 Jackies*, *Brillo Boxes*, and *Mickey Mouse*." SLJ

Includes bibliographical references

Makosz, Rory
Latino arts and their influence on the United States; songs, dreams, and dances. Mason Crest Publishers 2005 112p il (Hispanic heritage) $22.95 *

Grades: 7 8 9 10   700
1. Latin American art 2. Arts—United States
ISBN 1-59084-938-8   LC 2004022968

This "book begins with a general discussion of the ways in which cultures express themselves through their arts. It goes on to discuss the arts of Latin American cultures and their growing prominence in the United States, with emphasis on dance and music. Writing, painting, theater arts, and holidays are also included. . . . [This is] an excellent resource both for students researching Latino arts for reports and for general readers." SLJ

Includes bibligraphical references

Ochoa, George
The Wilson chronology of the arts; [by] George Ochoa and Melinda Corey. Wilson, H.W. 1998 476p $115 *

Grades: 8 9 10 11 12 Adult   700
1. Arts—History
ISBN 0-8242-0934-6   LC 97-23541

First published 1995 by Ballantine Books with title: The timeline book of the arts

"The authors provide a timeline detailing human creativity that progresses from ca. 43,000 B.C.E. to 1997, with 4,000 entries spread over 13 categories of artistic endeavor. . . . The chronology is global in scope and comprehensive in coverage, emphasizing well-established art forms without neglecting the oral traditions and decorative art forms of nonliterate societies and currently emerging art forms. . . . The straightforward organization of this work makes it suitable for many different uses." Recomm Ref Books for Small & Medium-sized Libr & Media Cent, 1999

Smith, Anna Deavere
Letters to a young artist. Anchor Books 2006 227p il pa $13

Grades: 11 12 Adult   700
1. Artists 2. Creation (Literary, artistic, etc.) 3. Conduct of life
ISBN 1-4000-3238-5; 978-1-4000-3238-9
                                       LC 2005-48318

The author "casts her reflections on the creative process, the artist's life and the acting profession as a series of brief letters addressed to a fictitious teenager. . . . With a pithiness that wards away the preachy, Smith succeeds in conveying the pain, the joy and the effort that characterize a life on the stage and in the world." Publ Wkly

Includes bibliographical references

702.8   Techniques, procedures, apparatus, equipment, materials

Colston, Valerie
Aspire: 200 projects to strengthen your art skills. Barron's 2008 128p il pa $21.99

Grades: 10 11 12 Adult   702.8
ISBN 978-0-7641-3811-9   LC 2006-940776
"A Quarto book"

"Written with art students in mind, . . . [this book] includes a section on putting together a portfolio and examples of art-school applicants' sketchbooks and portfolios. The text takes a do-it-yourself approach to learning

Colston, Valerie—*Continued*

a full complement of basic and intermediate techniques. Colston gathers examples and prescribes an assortment of observation exercises and projects that explore such concepts as shadow, distortion, mood, and collage. . . . Colston does a good job of providing an overview of the fundamentals and introducing a wide range of techniques." SLJ

The **Grove** encyclopedia of materials and techniques in art; edited by Gerald W.R. Ward. Oxford University Press 2008 828p il lib bdg $150

Grades: 11 12 Adult   **702.8**

1. Reference books 2. Artists' materials—Encyclopedias 3. Art—Technique—Encyclopedias

ISBN 978-0-19-531391-8; 0-19-531391-7

LC 2008-2486

Ward "has revised and updated approximately 1440 entries and full-length articles . . . from the venerable 34-volume *Grove Dictionary of Art* and added some new entries on topics of 'emerging importance' to produce a comprehensive one-volume resource on all aspects of materials and techniques of the fine arts and crafts, from acrylic painting, alabaster, and aquatint to upholstery, varnish, wood-engraving, and zinc. . . . An essential work for artists, historians, and art students and for the libraries that serve them." Libr J

Includes bibliographical references

Kallen, Stuart A., 1955-

The artist's tools. Lucent Books 2007 104p il (Eye on art) $33.45 *

Grades: 9 10 11 12 Adult   **702.8**

1. Artists' materials

ISBN 1-59018-957-4   LC 2006-17409

"This book describes the origins and characteristics of tools, from charcoal to computers. The focus is on introducing mediums and giving background information rather than on project ideas. An informative overview of paints, ceramics, and technology." SLJ

Includes bibliographical references

Smith, Ray, 1949-

The artist's handbook; [equipment, materials, procedures, techniques] 3rd. ed. DK Pub. 2009 384p il pa $21.95 *

Grades: 11 12 Adult   **702.8**

1. Art—Technique 2. Artists' materials

ISBN 978-0-7566-5722-2; 0-7566-5722-9

LC 2010-502586

First published 1987 by Knopf

Subtitle from cover

An illustrated handbook offers step-by-step projects, reproductions of works by master artists, and instruction in creative techniques, covering everything from drawing and painting to printmaking and digital media.

703 Dictionaries, encyclopedias, concordances of fine and decorative arts

Encyclopedia of art for young people. Chelsea House 2008 8v il set $280 *

Grades: 6 7 8 9 10   **703**

1. Reference books 2. Art—History 3. Art—Encyclopedias

ISBN 978-0-7910-9477-8; 0-7910-9477-4

LC 2007-31020

Contents: v1 Ancient and classical art by Iain Zaczek; v2 Medieval art by Rachel Beckett; v3 The Renaissance by Tony Allan; v4 The Baroque and Neoclassical age by Ian Chilvers; v5 The 19th century by Alice Peebles; v6 The early 20th century by Larry McGinity; v7 Contemporary art by John Glaves-Smith; v8 World art by Rachel Bean and Peter Lewis

This "survey of world art offers . . . illustrated chapters covering the major schools, styles, and specific regions, with sidebars that earmark specific artists, works of art, movements, and techniques, or note 'Connections' (historical and cultural)." SLJ

"This set provides an accessible and engaging introduction to art history, from antiquity to current trends." Booklist

Includes glossary and bibliographical references

704.9 Iconography

Patel, Sanjay

The little book of Hindu deities; from the Goddess of Wealth to the Sacred Cow. Plume 2006 141p il pa $14

Grades: 9 10 11 12   **704.9**

1. Gods and goddesses 2. Hinduism

ISBN 0-452-28775-8; 978-0-452-28775-4

LC 2006-12110

The author describes "the exploits of various deities while drawing us in—literally—with his joyous and unexpected full-color illustrations. . . . Both funny and informative, this is a fresh and breezy introduction to the Hindu gods." Publ Wkly

708 Galleries, museums, private collections of fine and decorative arts

National Gallery of Art; [foreword by Earl A. Powell III] 2nd ed. Thames and Hudson 2006 332p il (World of art) pa $18.95

Grades: 11 12 Adult   **708**

1. National Gallery of Art (U.S.)

ISBN 0-500-20390-3; 978-0-500-20390-3

LC 2005-904459

First published 2004 by National Gallery of Art; Based on John Walker's National Gallery of Art, published 1984

"The collection of the National Gallery of Art in Washington includes works by the greatest masters of

National Gallery of Art—*Continued*
Western art from the twelfth century to the present. . . .
[In this] look at the National Gallery's masterpieces . . .
the works are illustrated in full color, and the curators
have written the texts." Publisher's note

709 Art—Historical, geographic, persons treatment of fine and decorative arts

Atlas of world art; edited by John Onians. Oxford
University Press 2004 352p il maps $150 *
Grades: 11 12 Adult   **709**
1. Art—History—Maps
ISBN 0-19-521583-4   LC 2003-55029
This atlas offers a "framework for coverage of art ac-
tivity around the world from prehistoric times to 2000.
. . . Each of the book's seven parts (each covers a peri-
od in art history) includes a brief illustrated introduction
followed by a standardized sequence of sections on
World, American, European, African, Asian and Pacific
Art." Choice
"Groundbreaking and handsomely produced, this is a
welcome addition to any reference collection." Libr J
Includes bibliographical references

Cole, Bruce, 1938-
Art of the Western world; from ancient Greece
to post-modernism; by Bruce Cole and Adelheid
Gealt; with an introduction by Michael Wood.
Summit Bks. 1989 xx, 345p il pa $22 hardcover
o.p.
Grades: 11 12 Adult   **709**
1. Art—History
ISBN 0-671-74728-2 (pa)   LC 89-4311
"A companion volume to the PBS television series of
the same title, this compact survey of Western art history
is a . . . recapitulation of the conventional high art canon. Written on a level suitable for high school students
and general readers, the volume includes good reproductions of one or two of the best known works by famous
masters of painting, sculpture, and architecture." Libr J

Gardner, Helen, d. 1946
Gardner's art through the ages; a global history;
[revised by] Fred S. Kleiner. Enhanced 13th ed.
Wadsworth, Cengage Learning 2010 c2011 1088p
il map $165.99 *
Grades: 11 12 Adult   **709**
1. Art—History
ISBN 978-0-495-79986-3; 0-495-79986-6
                                  LC 2009-932089
Also available in two separate paperback volumes ea
$138.49 and in a four-volume backpack edition $132.99
First published 1926 by Harcourt Brace & Co.
Includes online art study printed access card
This book surveys world art from prehistoric times to
the present day. Painting, sculpture, architecture and
some decorative arts are considered. Although the focus
is on European art, there are also chapters on ancient
Near Eastern, Asian, pre-Columbian, American Indian,
African and Oceanic art.
Includes bibliographical references

Gombrich, E. H. (Ernst Hans), 1909-2001
The story of art. 16th ed rev and expanded.
Phaidon Press 1995 688p il $49.95; pa $29.95 *
Grades: 11 12 Adult   **709**
1. Art—History
ISBN 0-7148-3355-X; 0-7148-3247-2 (pa)
                                  LC 96-140698
First published 1950
This survey of art examines artistic achievements in
historical context to consider how prevailing social, polit-
ical, and economic factors may have influenced the suc-
cession and popularity of certain artistic styles.
Includes bibliographical references

Hartt, Frederick, 1914-1991
Art: a history of painting, sculpture, architecture.
Prentice Hall 2003 c1993 2v il map pa $122.80 *
Grades: 9 10 11 12   **709**
1. Art—History
ISBN 978-0-13-184155-0; 0-13-184155-6
Each volume is also available separately
A reprint of the volumes first published 1976 by
Abrams. Periodically revised
An illustrated chronological history of art from prehis-
tory to the contemporary period. Timelines link the polit-
ical history, religions, literature, science and technology,
with the painting, sculpture and architecture of each era.

Janson, H. W. (Horst Woldemar), 1913-1982
Janson's history of art; the western tradition;
Penelope J.E. Davies ... [et. al] 8th ed. Prentice
Hall 2011 xxxi, 1152p il map $170.40 *
Grades: 11 12 Adult   **709**
1. Art—History
ISBN 978-0-205-68517-2; 0-205-68517-X
                                  LC 2009-22617
Also available in a two-volume paperback edition
$138
First published 1962 by Abrams with title: History of
art
A history of art from prehistoric cave paintings to vid-
eo art. While the focus is primarily on Western art, brief
discussions of Oriental, Near Eastern, Islamic, African
and Latin American arts are included.
Includes bibliographical references

Kampen O'Riley, Michael
Art beyond the West; the arts of Africa, West
and Central Asia, India and Southeast Asia, China,
Japan and Korea, the Pacific, Africa, and the
Americas. 2nd ed. Pearson Prentice Hall 2006
368p il map pa $121 *
Grades: 11 12 Adult   **709**
1. Art
ISBN 0-13-175152-2   LC 2006-43185
First published 2001 in the United Kingdom by
Abrams
The author "has attempted to encapsulate the entirety
of non-Western art in one volume. . . . [Chapters] range
over Africa, India, Southeast Asia, China, Japan and Ko-
rea, the Americas, and the Pacific and consider such is-

Kampen O'Riley, Michael—*Continued*
sues as post and intercolonialism and postmodernism."
Libr J
   Includes bibliographical references

King, Ross, 1962-
   Art: over 2,500 works from cave to
contemporary; foreword by Ross King. DK Pub.
2008 612p il $50
Grades: 11 12 Adult   **709**
   1. Reference books 2. Art—History 3. Art appreciation
   ISBN 978-0-7566-3972-3; 0-7566-3972-7
                                    LC 2008-301471
   Within each time period, provides examples of significant works in painting, sculpture, drawing and other media. Highlights themes that were important at various
times such as nudes, landscape, still life, and love. Includes brief biographies of some artists and a "closer
look" in depth for the most significant works.
   "Easy to read and use, . . . both newcomers to art
and art connoisseurs will enjoy this picturesque work."
Libr J
   Includes glossary

Little, Stephen, 1954-
   . . . isms: understanding art. Universe 2004
159p il pa $16.95 *
Grades: 11 12 Adult   **709**
   1. Art—History
   ISBN 0-7893-1209-3   LC 2004-94996
   The author "identifies four types of isms: trends specific to the visual arts (perspectivism), broad cultural
trends (romanticism), artist-defined movements (cubism),
and retrospectively named movements (mannerism). He
then moves forward chronologically, deftly defining more
than 50 isms, naming key artists, and showcasing splendid examples." Booklist

Mason, Antony
   A history of Western art; from prehistory to the
20th century; edited by John T. Spike. Abrams
Books for Young Readers 2007 128p il $22.50
Grades: 7 8 9 10   **709**
   1. Art—History
   ISBN 978-0-8109-9421-8; 0-8109-9421-6
                                    LC 2007-10291
   This is a survey of "Western art's 50,000-year history.
. . . With a few exceptions, each spread focuses on a
different time period or movement, spotlighting representative work, from prehistoric cave paintings and ancient
artifacts to contemporary new media. . . . A short narrative paragraph accompanies beautifully reproduced color
images, extensive captions, and text boxes. . . . This
overview gives students a strong visual introduction to
Western art." Booklist

Strickland, Carol
   The annotated Mona Lisa; a crash course in art
history from prehistoric to post-modern; [by] Carol
Strickland and John Boswell. 2nd ed. Andrews
McMeel Pub. 2007 206p il pa $22.99
Grades: 11 12 Adult   **709**
   1. Art—History
   ISBN 978-0-7407-6872-9; 0-7407-6872-7
                                    LC 2009-293905
   "A John Boswell Associates book"
   First published 1992
   Presents the history of art from prehistoric times to
the present day, describes major artists and movements,
and details the influence of art on society through the
ages.

Walden, Sarah
   Whistler and his mother: an unexpected
relationship; secrets of an American masterpiece.
University of Neb. Press 2003 242p il $35
Grades: 9 10 11 12   **709**
   1. Whistler, James McNeill, 1834-1903
   ISBN 0-8032-4811-3   LC 2003-104221
   "Walden, a restorer, was hired by the Louvre to bring
the Portrait of the Artist's Mother: Arrangement in Grey
and Black back from decrepitude. She came to admire
Whistler's formal achievement even as she discovered
the shoddy methods that led to its deterioration. The
book is entrancing. Walden's is a view we seldom get:
the detail of individual brush strokes and choices of paint
and varnish." London Rev Books
   Includes bibliographical references

709.02   Art—6th-15th centuries, 500-1499

Snyder, James
   Art of the Middle Ages; [by] James Snyder,
Henry Luttikhuizen, Dorothy Verkerk. 2nd ed.
Prentice Hall 2006 530p il map hardcover o.p. pa
$134.40 *
Grades: 11 12 Adult   **709.02**
   1. Medieval art 2. Christian art 3. Medieval architec-
ture
   ISBN 0-13-193825-8; 0-13-192970-4 (pa)
                                    LC 2004-60135
   First published 1989 with title Medieval art
   Paperback published with title: Snyder's medieval art
   "Church architecture and decoration receive the bulk
of Snyder's attention, with manuscript illumination and
sumptuary and secular arts presented rather briefly. The
volume is well illustrated, though chiefly in black-and-
white photographs." Libr J [review of 1989 edition]
   Includes bibliographical references

709.04   Art—20th century, 1900-1999

Arnason, H. Harvard

History of modern art; painting, sculpture, architecture, photography; [by] H.H. Arnason, Elizabeth C. Mansfield. 6th ed. Pearson Prentice Hall 2009 830p il $130.67; pa $122.67 *

Grades: 11 12 Adult   709.04

1. Modern art

ISBN   0-205-67367-8;   978-0-205-67367-4; 0-13-606206-7 (pa); 978-0-13-606206-6 (pa)

LC 2009-15436

First published 1969

This covers artists and movements in art from the 19th century to the present, discussing such schools as cubism, surrealism, and abstract impressionism. Video, installation and performance art, sculpture, architecture, and photography are also surveyed.

"An ideal primer on modern art." Libr J

Includes glossary and bibliographical references

Aronson, Marc

Art attack; a short cultural history of the avant-garde. Clarion Bks. 1998 192p il $24

Grades: 7 8 9 10   709.04

1. Modern art 2. Art appreciation 3. Art and society

ISBN 0-395-79729-2   LC 97-22372

"*Art Attack* would make an excellent resource for the secondary level student who might be interested in exploring some creative outlets or as a catalyst for discussions about aesthetics, expression, or contemporary lifestyles." ALAN

Includes bibliographical references

Hodge, Susie, 1960-

How to survive modern art. Tate 2009 127p il pa $19.95

Grades: 6 7 8 9 10   709.04

1. Modern art

ISBN 978-1-85437-749-4; 1-85437-749-3

LC 2009-928894

In this "introduction to modern art, Hodge chronologically surveys significant movements and styles from art nouveau to postmodernism and digital art, while spotlighting artists such as Giacometti, Chagall, Hopper, and Hirst." Publ Wkly

The author "offers a lucid and understandable guide for anyone puzzled or horrified by art that does not exemplify photographic realism. . . . For anyone who has ever struggled with the idea of urinals, soup cans, or monochrome canvasses as art, this book is a thoroughly delightful necessity." Voice Youth Advocates

Moszynska, Anna

Abstract art. Thames & Hudson 1990 240p il (World of art) pa $14.95

Grades: 9 10 11 12   709.04

1. Abstract art

ISBN 0-500-20237-0   LC 88-51347

"The author explains both the general philosophy of abstractionism and the approaches of many individual artists to the form. Paintings and sculptures are featured, as are examples of graphic design and architecture." Booklist

709.1   Art—Treatment by areas, regions, places in general

Khalili, Nasser D., 1945-

Islamic art and culture; a visual history. Overlook Press 2006 186p il $60 *

Grades: 11 12 Adult   709.1

1. Islamic art 2. Islamic civilization

ISBN 1-58567-839-2; 978-1-58567-839-6

This "visual history of Islamic art introduces readers to the diverse peoples, cultures, and styles making up Islam today. Spanning 12 centuries and covering everything from miniature painting to architecture, it shows, e.g., various Qur'ans, coins, armor, and scientific instruments. . . . This is an excellent introduction to the subject that combines aptly chosen and beautifully reproduced photographs with a concise and informative text." Libr J

Includes bibliographical references

709.45   Italian art

Hirst, Michael

Michelangelo and his drawings. Yale Univ. Press 1988 132p il pa $25 hardcover o.p. *

Grades: 11 12 Adult   709.45

1. Michelangelo Buonarroti, 1475-1564

ISBN 0-300-04796-7 (pa)   LC 88-50431

The text of this book "is organized by type of drawing: initial sketches, life studies, compositional drawings, architectural designs, and finished drawings used as gifts. It is followed by a thematically arranged index of drawings and a section of . . . plates." Libr J

"An informative, insightful, and eminently readable book. . . . This is an important contribution to Michelangelo scholarship." Choice

709.5   Asian art

Bingham, Jane

Indian art & culture. Raintree 2004 56p il map (World art & culture) hardcover o.p. pa $9.99

Grades: 6 7 8 9 10   709.5

1. Indic arts 2. India—Civilization

ISBN 978-0-7398-6607-8 (lib bdg); 0-7398-6607-9 (lib bdg); 978-1-4109-2106-2 (pa); 1-4109-2106-9 (pa)

LC 2003-1956

This offers a history of the arts of India, including architecture, wall painting and decoration, stone and wood carving, painting, textiles, ceramics, music, dance, theater and film, and writing, and explains their roles in Indian culture.

"Every page includes interesting and vivid color pho-

Bingham, Jane—*Continued*
tographs of the different art forms and of artists at work.
[This title is] well worth purchasing for the illustrations
alone." SLJ
Includes glossary and bibliographical references

709.51   Chinese art

Tregear, Mary
Chinese art. rev ed. Thames & Hudson 1997
216p il maps (World of art) pa $14.95 *
Grades: 11 12 Adult   **709.51**
1. Chinese art
ISBN 0-500-20299-0
First published 1980 by Oxford Univ. Press
An introduction to major decorative, ceremonial, figurative and narrative aspects of Chinese art. Coverage
ranges from works of Neolithic groups and the bronzes
of the Shang dynasty to Buddhist sculpture, ceramics,
garden design and architecture. Emphasis is also placed
on the interaction of poetry, painting and calligraphy.
Includes bibliographical references

709.52   Japanese art

Khanduri, Kamini
Japanese art & culture. Raintree 2004 56p il
map (World art & culture) lib bdg $33.50
Grades: 6 7 8 9 10   **709.52**
1. Japanese arts 2. Japan—Civilization
ISBN 978-0-7398-6609-2; 0-7398-6609-5
                                        LC 2003-1957
This offers a history of the arts of Japan including
painting, woodblock prints, sculpture, metalwork, pottery,
lacquerware, architecture, gardens, calligraphy, and theater, and explains their places in Japanese culture.
Includes glossary and bibliographical references

709.6   African art

Bingham, Jane
African art & culture. Raintree 2004 56p il map
(World art & culture) hardcover o.p. pa $9.99
Grades: 6 7 8 9 10   **709.6**
1. African art 2. Africa—Civilization
ISBN 978-0-7398-6606-1 (lib bdg); 0-7398-6606-0 (lib
bdg); 978-1-4109-2105-5 (pa); 1-4109-2105-0 (pa)
                                        LC 2003-1955
This describes a variety of art forms of the African
continent and their roles in their respective cultures.
This book is "stunningly illustrated. . . . Every page
includes interesting and vivid color photographs of the
different art forms and of artists at work. [This title is]
well worth purchasing for the illustrations alone." SLJ
Includes glossary and bibliographical references

709.72   Mexican art

Lewis, Elizabeth, 1967-
Mexican art & culture. Raintree 2004 56p il
map (World art & culture) lib bdg $33.50
Grades: 6 7 8 9 10   **709.72**
1. Mexican art 2. Mexico—Civilization
ISBN 978-0-7398-6610-8; 0-7398-6610-9
                                        LC 2003-1958
This offers a history of the arts of Mexico including
architecture, carvings and sculpture, pottery and ceramics, masks, lacquering, textiles and clothing, jewelry,
painting, music and musical instruments, fiestas and festivals, death and burial customs, and toys, and explains
their roles in Mexican culture.
The text is "straightforward and concise, but it's the
excellent selection of high-quality color photos that really
stand out." Booklist
Includes glossary and bibliographical references

709.73   American art

The **American** art book. Phaidon Press 1999 512p
il hardcover o.p. pa $9.95 *
Grades: 11 12 Adult   **709.73**
1. American art
ISBN 0-7148-3845-4; 0-7148-4119-6 (pa)
                                        LC 99-231734
A "survey of American art from colonial days to the
present. By presenting one well-chosen example of the
work of each of 500 painters, photographers, sculptors,
and folk artists in alphabetical order, the editors liberate
their creations from chronology, regionalism, and the cat-
egorization of schools and movements, an approach that
creates some wonderfully unexpected and revealing juxtapositions." Booklist

The **Arts** of the North American Indian; native
traditions in evolution; edited by Edwin L.
Wade; Carol Haralson, coordinating editor.
Hudson Hills Press 1986 324p il hardcover o.p.
pa $35
Grades: 9 10 11 12   **709.73**
1. Native American art
ISBN 0-933920-55-5; 0-933920-56-3 (pa)
                                        LC 85-21932
Published in association with the Philbrook Art Center, Tulsa
"Detailed explanatory captions accompany each illustration and serve as a significant 'subtext' for exhibition
materials, which represent a span of time from the prehistoric to today's avant-garde. . . . A competent glossary as well as bibliography and index enhance the overall
excellence of this volume. Some prior knowledge of the
general topic is advised; this is not a selection for beginners." Choice
Includes bibliographical references

Bearden, Romare, 1914-1988

A history of African-American artists; from 1792 to the present; {by} Romare Bearden & Harry Henderson. Pantheon Bks. 1992 541p il $75 *

Grades: 11 12 Adult   **709.73**
1. African American artists 2. American art
ISBN 0-394-57016-2   LC 89-42782

"Opening in the 18th century with Joshua Johnston, the authors go on to examine the work of Robert S. Duncanson, Henry O. Tanner, Aaron Douglas, Edmonia Lewis, Jacob Lawrence, Auguste Savage, Ellis Wilson, Archibald Motley, Alma Thomas, and others born before 1925. Their lives and careers, which often involved overcoming racial barriers, are portrayed against the backdrop of artistic, social, and political events; black Renaissance and Depression artists receive the most attention." Libr J

"Richly illustrated and written with resounding empathy and pride, this is a major contribution to the literature on African American history and to the annals of American art." Booklist

Bolden, Tonya

Wake up our souls; a celebration of Black American artists; Published in association with Smithsonian American Art Museum. Harry N. Abrams 2004 128p il $24.95 *

Grades: 6 7 8 9 10   **709.73**
1. African American art
ISBN 0-8109-4527-4

Published in association with Smithsonian American Art Museum.

Presents a history of African American visual arts and artists from the days of slavery to the present

"Bolden's writing is rich and lyrical. She smoothly incorporates the historical context, explaining pivotal events and relevant artistic movements clearly and succinctly." SLJ

Creation's journey; Native American identity and belief; edited by Tom Hill and Richard W. Hill, Sr. Smithsonian Institution Press 1994 255p il $45 *

Grades: 11 12 Adult   **709.73**
1. National Museum of the American Indian (U.S.) 2. Native American art
ISBN 1-56098-453-8   LC 94-4757

Published in conjunction with an exhibition held at the National Museum of the American Indian, New York City, October 1994-February 1997

This "volume links stories, anecdotes, descriptions of rituals, and spiritual beliefs to specific art objects, including an Osage cradleboard and a Winnebago bandolier bag. In each essay, the connection between spirituality and the making of art is articulated; each pattern, image, and symbol is shown to be an expression of dreams, visions, and beliefs." Booklist

Includes bibliographical references

Farrington, Lisa E.

Creating their own image; the history of African-American women artists. Oxford University Press 2005 354p il $55 *

Grades: 11 12 Adult   **709.73**
1. African American women 2. African American artists 3. Women artists
ISBN 0-19-516721-X   LC 2003-66171

This is a "study of women of color and their works, starting with slavery, moving through the Harlem Renaissance, and continuing to the new millennium." Libr J

"A richly detailed yet fluent work of trailblazing research, fresh interpretations, and cogent argument, Farrington's treatise discusses vital aesthetic as well as social and cultural issues and creates a vibrant context for such seminal artists as Augusta Savage, Faith Ringgold, Barbara Chase-Riboud, Kara Walker, and many more." Booklist

Roark, Elisabeth Louise

Artists of colonial America; [by] Elisabeth L. Roark. Greenwood Press 2003 207p il (Artists of an era) $59.95 *

Grades: 9 10 11 12   **709.73**
1. American art 2. United States—History—1600-1775, Colonial period
ISBN 0-313-32023-3   LC 2003-47240

"This book presents . . . information and . . . pictures regarding the history and symbolism of colonial art. . . . Important colonial painters such as John Singleton Copely are included. . . . Based on its depth of information, eye-appeal, and value for research, this is a must-buy for every high school art or history collection." Libr Media Connect

Includes bibliographical references

709.8   Latin American art

Scott, John F., 1936-

Latin American art; ancient to modern. University Press of Fla. 1999 xxiv, 240p il $49.95; pa $29.95 *

Grades: 11 12 Adult   **709.8**
1. Latin American art
ISBN 0-8130-1645-2; 0-8130-1826-9 (pa)
     LC 98-46535

A study "of Latin American art from pre-Columbian times to the present, encompassing media ranging from sculpture, pottery, and painting to architecture. Scott . . . addresses the major styles and artists that define each period." Libr J

Includes bibliographical references

711   Area planning (Civic art)

Macaulay, David, 1946-
City: a story of Roman planning and construction. Houghton Mifflin 1974 112p il $18; pa $10.99 *
Grades: 4 5 6 7 8 9 10   **711**
1. City planning—Rome 2. Civil engineering 3. Roman architecture
ISBN 0-395-19492-X; 0-395-34922-2 (pa)
               LC 74-4280
"By following the inception, construction, and development of an imaginary Roman city, the account traces the evolution of Verbonia from the selection of its site under religious auspices in 26 B.C. to its completion in 100 A.D." Horn Book
Includes glossary

720   Architecture

Macaulay, David, 1946-
Building big. Houghton Mifflin 2000 192p il $30; pa $12.95 *
Grades: 5 6 7 8 9 10   **720**
1. Architecture 2. Engineering
ISBN 0-395-96331-1; 0-618-46527-8 (pa)
               LC 00-28116
"Walter Lorraine books"
This companion to the PBS series examines the architecture and engineering of "bridges, tunnels, dams, domes, and skyscrapers. Each section offers an implicitly chronological analysis as it focuses on several significant examples of that particular kind of structure." Bull Cent Child Books
"Macaulay combines his detailed yet vaguely whimsical illustrations with simple, straightforward prose that breaks down complex architectural and engineering accomplishments into easily digestible tidbits that don't insult the intelligence of the reader of any age." N Y Times Book Rev
Includes glossary

720.3   Architecture—Encyclopedias and dictionaries

Burden, Ernest E., 1934-
Illustrated dictionary of architecture; [by] Ernest Burden. 2nd ed. McGraw-Hill 2001 389p il pa $39.95
Grades: 11 12 Adult   **720.3**
1. Reference books 2. Architecture—Dictionaries
ISBN 0-07-137529-5   LC 2001-34558
First published 1998
This volume "is a compilation of more than 5,000 photographs and drawings in nearly 1,500 entries that define the technical and stylistic elements of both current and historical architecture. . . . It is an excellent resource for interested laypeople as well as professionals in the field and is recommended as a ready-reference tool for public, academic, and high-school libraries." Booklist

Ching, Frank, 1943-
A visual dictionary of architecture; {by} Francis D. K. Ching. Van Nostrand Reinhold 1995 319p il $44.95; pa $39.95 *
Grades: 11 12 Adult   **720.3**
1. Reference books 2. Architecture—Dictionaries
ISBN 0-471-28451-3; 0-471-28821-7 (pa)
               LC 95-1476
This volume arranges some "5,000 entries thematically under 68 concepts covering architectural design, history, and technology. The topics, which are treated alphabetically, include building types (church, house, theater), sections (door, roof, stair), features (arch, column, vault), and materials (brick, paint, wood). Terms are logically clustered on oversize pages and defined with both line drawings and text, usually 20 to 100 words." Booklist

Dictionary of architecture & construction; edited by Cyril M. Harris. 4th ed. McGraw-Hill 2005 1089p il $74.95 *
Grades: 11 12 Adult   **720.3**
1. Reference books 2. Architecture—Dictionaries 3. Building—Dictionaries
ISBN 0-07-145237-0   LC 2005-42340
First published 1975
This dictionary features "definitions of more than 27,000 important architecture and construction terms . . . [including] terms in legal areas, technologies, techniques, materials, organizations, historic architectural styles, and architectural trends." Publisher's note
"The handy one-volume format, the reasonable cost, the clarity and accuracy of entries, the legible type and drawings, and the inclusive approach to current developments in the design, building, and scholarly professions related to architecture make this publication a crucial tool." Choice

720.9   Architecture—Historical, geographic, persons treatment

Clements, Gillian
A picture history of great buildings. Frances Lincoln Children's 2007 61p il map $19.95
Grades: 7 8 9 10   **720.9**
1. Buildings 2. Architecture—History
ISBN 978-1-84507-488-3; 1-84507-488-2
An illustrated history of over 9,000 years of great buildings around the world from the tombs of ancient Egypt to the modern skyscrapers of today.
This is "an excellent resource, jam-packed with information for anyone interested in a basic study of architecture throughout the ages." Libr Media Connect
Includes glossary

Glancey, Jonathan
The story of architecture. Dorling Kindersley 2000 240p il hardcover o.p. pa $25 *
Grades: 11 12 Adult   **720.9**
1. Architecture—History
ISBN 0-7894-5965-5; 0-7894-9334-9 (pa)
               LC 00-30434

Glancey, Jonathan—*Continued*

"Devoting nearly half the text to the modern period, Glancey condenses history's panorama into a series of colorful vignettes, each described as having some contemporary relevance. Driven by a contagious enthusiasm, the narrative is enlivened by chatty, sometimes offbeat commentary." Libr J

The **Seventy** wonders of the modern world; 1500 years of extraordinary feats of engineering and construction; edited by Neil Parkyn. Thames & Hudson 2002 304p il $40

Grades: 11 12 Adult   **720.9**
     1. Architecture 2. Curiosities and wonders
     ISBN 0-500-51047-4   LC 2002-100549

Published in the United Kingdom with title: The seventy architectural wonders of our world

"Most of the featured 'wonders' date from the second half of the 20th century. The selections are divided into seven categories: churches, palaces, public buildings, towers and skyscrapers, bridges and railways, canals and dams, and statues. Each entry includes basic information on history, structural and engineering details, innovations, aesthetics, and a sidebar 'fact-file.'" Libr J

Includes bibliographical references

Watkin, David, 1941-

A history of Western architecture. 4th ed. Laurence King 2005 720p il pa $40

Grades: 9 10 11 12 Adult   **720.9**
     1. Architecture—History
     ISBN 978-1-85669-459-9

First published 1986 by Watson-Guptill Publications

This study focuses on the development of architecture in Europe and the United States and includes chapters on Mesopotamian and Egyptian architecture.

"The book is persuasively written, its illustrations are numerous and well chosen, and readers are often introduced to buildings known only to specialists." Choice

Includes bibliographical references

722   Architecture from earliest times to ca. 300

The **Grove** encyclopedia of classical art and architecture; edited by Gordon Campbell. Oxford University Press 2007 2v il map set $250

Grades: 11 12 Adult   **722**
1. Reference books 2. Greek art—Encyclopedias
3. Roman art—Encyclopedias 4. Greek architecture—
Encyclopedias 5. Roman architecture—Encyclopedias
ISBN 978-0-19-530082-6; 0-19-530082-3
                       LC 2007-487

"The two-volume encyclopedia begins with a section on abbreviations, a thematic index, and continues with the A-Z entries, a list of contributors, and an index. . . . Each entry includes the name or term followed by dates and an article ranging from a few hundred words to several pages." Am Ref Books Annu, 2008

"One cannot speak too highly of this publication; it should grace the library of every scholar and library interested in the subject. It is a fundamental resource—

from the most basic entry to the most in-depth reading and research." Choice

Includes bibliographical references

726   Buildings for religious and related purposes

King, Ross, 1962-

Brunelleschi's dome; how a Renaissance genius reinvented architecture. Penguin Books 2001 194p il pa $14

Grades: 11 12 Adult   **726**
     1. Brunelleschi, Filippo, 1377-1446 2. Santa Maria del Fiore (Cathedral: Florence, Italy) 3. Church buildings
     ISBN 0-14-200015-9   LC 2001-280068
     First published 2000 by Walker & Co.

"King illuminates the mysterious sources of inspiration and the secretive methods of architectural genius Filippo Brunelleschi in a fascinating chronicle of the building of his masterwork, the dome of Santa Maria del Fiore in Florence. A remarkable saga of how one incandescent mind performed the one matchless feat that would forever transform architecture from a mechanical craft into a creative art." Booklist

Includes bibliographical references

Macaulay, David, 1946-

Mosque. Houghton Mifflin 2003 96p il $18 *

Grades: 4 5 6 7 8 9 10   **726**
     1. Mosques—Design and construction
     ISBN 0-618-24034-9   LC 2003-177
     "Walter Lorraine books"

Using "a fictional framework to hold his nonfictional material, the author introduces readers to Admiral Suha Mehmet Pasa, a wealthy aristocrat living in Istanbul, who decides in his declining years to fund the building of a mosque and its associated buildings—religious school, soup kitchen, public baths, public fountain, and tomb. Detailing the activities of the architect and workers, Macaulay creates a from-the-ground-up look not only at the actual construction, but also at the uses of the various buildings." SLJ

"Once again Macaulay uses clear words and exemplary drawings to explore a majestic structure's design and construction. . . . In his respectful, straightforward explanation of the mosque's design, Macaulay offers an unusual, inspiring perspective into Islamic society." Booklist

Includes glossary

Pyramid. Houghton Mifflin 1975 80p il $20; pa $9.95 *

Grades: 4 5 6 7 8 9 10   **726**
     1. Pyramids 2. Egypt—Civilization
     ISBN 0-395-21407-6; 0-395-32121-2 (pa)
                       LC 75-9964

The construction of a pyramid in 25th century B.C. Egypt is described. "Information about selection of the site, drawing of the plans, calculating compass directions, clearing and leveling the ground, and quarrying and hauling the tremendous blocks of granite and limestone is conveyed as much by pictures as by text." Horn Book

Includes glossary

727   Buildings for educational and research purposes

Feinberg, Sandra, 1946-
Designing space for children and teens in libraries and public places; [by] Sandra Feinberg and James R. Keller. American Library Association 2010 167p il pa $60
Grades: Adult Professional   **727**
   1. Children's libraries 2. Young adults' libraries 3. Library architecture
   ISBN 978-0-8389-1020-7; 0-8389-1020-3
                  LC 2009-50005
"The librarian new to working with architects and design professionals will find a wealth of information in these pages, as the text begins with the basics of how to choose an architect or design firm and concludes with how to set up a grand opening of the newly designed space or facility. Questions to consider during the process, floor plans, and photographs (color as well as black and white) of children and teen spaces around the world make this a useful how-to guide for librarians and other professionals who work with children, teens, and the facilities that serve them." Voice Youth Advocates
Includes bibliographical references

728.8   Large and elaborate private dwellings

Macaulay, David, 1946-
Castle. Houghton Mifflin 1977 74p il $20; pa $9.95 *
Grades: 4 5 6 7 8 9 10   **728.8**
   1. Castles 2. Fortification
   ISBN 0-395-25784-0; 0-395-32920-5 (pa)
                  LC 77-7159
Macaulay depicts "the history of an imaginary thirteenth-century castle—built to subdue the Welsh hordes—from the age of construction to the age of neglect, when the town of Aberwyfern no longer needs a fortified stronghold." Economist
Includes glossary

729   Design and decoration of structures and accessories

Macaulay, David, 1946-
Built to last. Houghton Mifflin Harcourt 2010 272p il $24.99 *
Grades: 4 5 6 7 8 9 10   **729**
   1. Architecture 2. Castles 3. Mosques—Design and construction 4. Cathedrals
   ISBN 978-0-547-34240-5; 0-547-34240-3
"Significantly updating the Caldecott Honor-winning *Castle* (1977) and *Cathedral* (1973) with new text and full-color illustrations, this hefty volume combines them with a very lightly revised *Mosque* (2003) for a three-in-one architectural spree. No mere colorization of the black-and-white originals of the first two books, . . . the

all-new, often breathtaking images have been drawn by hand and then digitally colored to harmonize, beautifully with the look of *Mosque*. . . . Take a moment to mourn the originals, then celebrate this entirely worthy revision." Kirkus

731.4   Sculpture—Techniques and procedures

Bütz, Richard
How to carve wood; a book of projects and techniques. Taunton Press 1984 215p il pa $19.95
Grades: 11 12 Adult   **731.4**
   1. Wood carving
   ISBN 0-918804-20-5   LC 83-50680
"A Fine Woodworking Book"
The author introduces "the most common types of carving, whittling, chip carving, relief carving, lettering, and architectural carving. The information on tools and their care is very helpful. This is the best book available on the subject." Libr J
Includes bibliographical references

Hessenberg, Karin
Sculpting basics; everything you need to know to create fantastic three-dimensional artwork. Barron's 2005 128p il $23.99 *
Grades: 10 11 12 Adult   **731.4**
   1. Sculpture—Technique
   ISBN 978-0-7641-5843-8; 0-7641-5843-0
"A Quarto book"
The author "presents a fine overview for beginning sculptors. . . . [The book] touches on a wide range of sculptural forms and styles, including the traditional figure, symbolic compositions, and abstract reliefs. . . .For such a slight book, [it] bundles a surprising amount of information." Libr J
Includes bibliographical references

732   Sculpture from earliest times to ca. 500, sculpture of nonliterate peoples

Priwer, Shana
Ancient monuments; [by] Cynthia Phillips and Shana Priwer. Sharpe Focus 2009 112p il (Frameworks) lib bdg $39.95
Grades: 7 8 9 10   **732**
   1. Ancient architecture 2. Megalithic monuments
   ISBN 978-0-7656-8123-2; 0-7656-8123-4
                  LC 2007-40697
This book "presents monuments from ancient civilizations. As well as discussing Egyptian pyramids, Greek temples, Roman buildings, and megalithic monuments in Britain, the book includes interesting chapters on architecture in Mesoamerica, the early Middle East, and ancient China and Japan." Booklist
Includes glossary and bibliographical references

736   Carving and carvings

Engel, Peter, 1959-
10-fold origami; fabulous paperfolds you can make in just 10 steps! Tuttle 2009 96p il $19.95 *

Grades: 8 9 10 11 12 Adult   **736**
1. Origami
ISBN 978-4-8053-1069-4   LC 2009-920075
This craft book features 26 origami models, all of which can be completed with ten major folds. All models are rated in difficulty from Easy to Advanced.

The author's "art subjects range from the wonderfully whimsical to the eminently practical. . . . Who could resist a plateful of sunny-side up eggs and bacon or the stolidly silent black-and-white penguin? Or not be tempted to use a brightly patterned picture frame or decorative party pinwheels?" Booklist

Hayakawa, Hiroshi, 1962-
Kirigami menagerie; 38 paper animals to copy, cut & fold. Sterling Pub. 2009 128p il pa $17.95
Grades: 8 9 10 11 12 Adult   **736**
1. Paper crafts 2. Animals in art
ISBN 978-1-60059-318-5   LC 2008-50622
The author shows how to cut and fold paper shapes to make 38 different types of animals, including sheep, pandas, and dragons.

737.4   Coins

Čuhaj, George S.
2011 standard catalog of world coins, 1901-2000. Krause 2010 2303p il pa $65 *
Grades: 11 12 Adult   **737.4**
1. Coins
ISSN 1556-2263
ISBN 978-1-4402-1158-4
Also available volumes covering the 17th, 18th, 19th and 21st centuries
Annual. First published 1972
This illustrated volume covers coins from throughout the world minted 1901-2000. Prices are provided for each coin in up to four grades of preservation. Includes commemorative issues.

Yeoman, R. S.
A guide book of United States coins; [by] R.S. Yeoman; editor, Kenneth Bressett; research editor, Q. David Bowers; valuations editor, Jeff Garrett. 64th ed. Whitman Pub. 2010 429p il (Official red book series) $16.95 *
Grades: 11 12 Adult   **737.4**
1. Coins 2. Reference books
ISBN 978-0-7948-3148-6
Also available in spiral-binding format
Annual. First published 1946 by Whitman
At head of title: The official red book

This guide "known as the 'Red Book' is an outstanding reference on U.S. coins designed for use in identifying and grading coins. All issues from 1616 to the present are covered. The guide provides historical data, statistics, values, and detailed photographs for each coin. Additional sections deal with specialties such as Civil War and Hard Times tokens, misstruck coins, and uncirculated and proof sets." Nichols. Guide to Ref Books for Sch Media Cent. 4th edition

738.1   Ceramic arts—Techniques, procedures, apparatus, equipment, materials

Müller, Kristin
The potter's studio handbook; a start-to-finish guide to hand-built and wheel-thrown ceramics. Quarry Books 2007 192p il (Back yard series) pa $24.99
Grades: 9 10 11 12 Adult   **738.1**
1. Pottery
ISBN 978-1-59253-373-2; 1-59253-373-6
                                  LC 2007-16693
The author "guides beginners through advanced students in equipping a ceramic studio, handling the design, preparing the clay, constructing slab projects, throwing on a wheel, glazing, and firing. The 16 clay projects featured here include teapots, vases, and dinner plates. Readers can draw inspiration from the creative painting and underglazing examples, as well as the unusual firing techniques for color and texture." Libr J

Nelson, Glenn C.
Ceramics: a potter's handbook; [by] Glenn C. Nelson, Richard Burkett. 6th ed. Wadsworth/Thomson Learning 2002 439p il pa $90.95 *
Grades: 11 12 Adult   **738.1**
1. Ceramics 2. Pottery
ISBN 0-03-028937-8   LC 2001-96329
First published 1960. Periodically revised
This manual for beginner to advanced potters presents forming and decorating techniques, body and glaze recipes, and sources for raw materials and equipment.
Includes bibliographical references

741.2   Drawing and drawings—Techniques, procedures, apparatus, equipment, materials

Edwards, Betty
The new drawing on the right side of the brain. 2nd ed. Jeremy P. Tarcher\Putnam 1999 291p il $27.95; pa $16.95
Grades: 9 10 11 12 Adult   **741.2**
1. Drawing—Technique 2. Creative ability
ISBN   978-0-87477-419-1;   0-87477-419-5; 978-0-87477-424-5 (pa); 0-87477-424-1 (pa)
                                  LC 99-35809

Edwards, Betty—_Continued_

First published 1979 with title: Drawing on the right side of the brain

This book describes the author's technique for teaching people how to draw more accurately and creatively by developing the capabilities of the brain's right side, which, according to "split-brain" research, controls the visual and perceptual functions.

Includes bibliographical references

Hershberger, Carlynne, 1958-

Creative colored pencil workshop; 26 exercises for combining colored pencil with your favorite mediums; [by] Carlynne Hershberger and Kelli Money Huff. North Light Books 2007 144p il $29.99

Grades: 8 9 10 11 12 Adult   **741.2**

1. Colored pencil drawing—Technique 2. Art—Technique

ISBN 1-5818-0818-6; 978-1-5818-0818-6

LC 2006-29402

This "book has a lot to offer teens seeking to hone their drawing and painting skills. Most of the exercises combine colored pencil with other mediums to create scenes from nature. Sometimes several steps are revealed in one image, but the text takes it step-by-step." SLJ

Kutch, Kristy Ann

Drawing and painting with colored pencil; basic techniques for mastering traditional and watersoluble colored pencils. Watson-Guptill Publications 2005 144p il pa $24.95

Grades: 9 10 11 12   **741.2**

1. Colored pencil drawing—Technique 2. Watercolor painting—Technique

ISBN 0-8230-1568-8; 978-0-8230-1568-9

LC 2005-10466

This book "covers traditional colored pencil techniques as well as tips on mastering the new water-soluble colored pencils." Publisher's note

"This excellent book will inspire artists and wannabe artists alike." Voice Youth Advocates

Includes bibliographical references

Micklewright, Keith, 1933-

Drawing: mastering the language of visual expression. Harry N. Abrams 2005 168p il (Abrams studio) pa $29.95

Grades: 11 12 Adult   **741.2**

1. Drawing—Technique

ISBN 0-8109-9238-8   LC 2005-5862

"Using examples of master artists such as Ingres and Michelangelo as well as more contemporary work of Cezanne, Hockney, and others, different aspects of drawing are examined. Each chapter ends with 'Ideas to Explore,' in which the reader is given suggestions for practice. . . . This book is valuable for those learning the theory behind the elements of drawing and for those looking for practical instruction." Voice Youth Advocates

Includes bibliographical references

Scott, Damion

How to draw hip-hop; [by] Damion Scott and Kris Ex. Watson-Guptill 2006 144p il pa $19.95 *

Grades: 7 8 9 10   **741.2**

1. Drawing 2. Hip-hop

ISBN 0-8230-1446-0   LC 2005-29156

"This book combines the bold and energetic lines of graffiti art with the bright colors of cel-shaded video games and an obvious Japanese manga influence. . . . [It discusses] genre-specific concepts like wild style lettering [and] hip-hop clothing. . . . There is no other book of this kind on the market, making it a necessary and relevant purchase." SLJ

Webb, David, 1962-

Drawing handbook; materials, techniques, theory. David and Charles 2008 320p il pa $24.99

Grades: 9 10 11 12 Adult   **741.2**

1. Drawing—Technique 2. Artists' materials

ISBN 978-0-7153-2653-4

"The author encourages readers to keep a daily sketchbook and clearly demonstrates essential aspects of drawing, including paper, pencils, color, shading, and more. The book's English origin is reflected in the writing style. Readers willing to practice stand to benefit greatly." SLJ

741.5   Cartoons, caricatures, comics

Abadzis, Nick

Laika. First Second Books 2007 205p il $17.95 *

Grades: 5 6 7 8 9 10 11 12 Adult   **741.5**

1. Graphic novels 2. Space flight—Graphic novels

ISBN 978-1-59643-101-0; 1-59643-101-6

LC 2006-51907

Laika was the abandoned puppy destined to become Earth's first space traveler. This is her journey. Along with Laika, there is Korolev, once a political prisoner and now a driven engineer at the top of the Soviet space program, and Yelena, the lab technician responsible for Laika's health and life. The book includes a bibliography of books and websites

"Although the tightly packed and vividly inked panels of Abadzis's art tell an impressively complex tale . . . Laika's palpable spirit is what readers will remember." Publ Wkly

Abel, Jessica, 1969-

Drawing words & writing pictures; making comics: from manga, graphic novels, and beyond; [by] Jessica Abel & Matt Madden. First Second Books 2008 282p il pa $29.95

Grades: 9 10 11 12 Adult   **741.5**

1. Graphic novels—Authorship 2. Comic books, strips, etc.—Authorship 3. Drawing—Technique

ISBN 978-1-59643-131-7; 1-59643-131-8

LC 2007-44125

Professional cartoonists Abel and Madden provide a college-level course that takes readers from concept to comic in fifteen lessons. Lessons progress from the ba-

Abel, Jessica, 1969-—*Continued*

sics of defining just what comics are, to single-panel comics, comic strips, panel transitions, pencilling, page composition, lettering, inking, structuring the story, developing characters, panel and title design, world-building, inking with a brush, using scanners and other equipment in reproduction, and creating a 24-hour comic. The first fourteen chapters include homework and extra credit work assignments, and several appendices provide more assignments.

This "book offers step-by-step entry into a complicated series of skills in a nonscary and approachable way." Libr J

Includes bibliographical references

Abouet, Marguerite, 1971-

Aya; [by] Marguerite Abouet & Clément Oubrerie; [translation by Helge Dascher] Drawn & Quarterly 2007 96p il $19.95 *

Grades: 10 11 12 Adult   **741.5**
     1. Graphic novels 2. Friendship—Graphic novels 3. Ivory Coast—Graphic novels
     ISBN 1-894937-90-2; 978-1-894937-90-0

In Ivory Coast of 1978, nineteen-year-old Aya and her friends Adjoua and Bintou live in an oasis of peace and prosperity. Studious Aya wants to become a doctor, but her friends just want to have a good time and enjoy nights with handsome lovers. Soon enough, Adjoua finds out she's pregnant, and she says the father is Moussa, Bintou's boyfriend and the young man Aya's parents were hoping to get for her husband. Moussa's rich parents agree to a wedding, but they show their prejudice against poor townspeople in their arrangements.

Followed by Aya of Yop City (2008)

Allen, Brooke A.

A home for Mr. Easter. NBM Publishing, Inc. 2010 197p il pa $13.99

Grades: 8 9 10 11 12 Adult   **741.5**
     1. Graphic novels 2. Humorous graphic novels 3. Rabbits—Graphic novels
     ISBN 978-1-56163-580-1; 1-56163-580-4

High school student Tesana is large, not too bright, strong, and has always gotten into trouble. A lonely misfit, she tries to fit in better by joining a pep rally planning committee. Once she finds the white rabbits that will be used in the pep rally, she discovers one that is very different: it lays colorful eggs that grant wishes. Tesana believes this is the real Easter Bunny, and she calls him Mr. Easter—and he talks to her. When the football team tries to take Mr. Easter away, Tesana takes them all down and then runs away. Soon they're pursued by cops, an unscrupulous and greedy pet shop owner, laboratory scientists, animal rights protesters, television news crews, a magician/con man, and her mom. Allen was a student at the Savannah School of Art and Design when she wrote this book.

"This is for mature readers who understand the humor, and would be a welcome addition for your multicultural section—female, robust, ethnic." Libr Media Connect

Amberlyn, J. C.

Drawing manga; animals, chibis, and other adorable creatures. Watson-Guptill 2009 160p il $21.99

Grades: 9 10 11 12 Adult   **741.5**
     1. Manga—Drawing 2. Cartooning—Technique
     ISBN 978-0-8230-9533-9   LC 2009-21667

The author "explores traditional pen-and-ink techniques and describes how to create images with computer software. The first part of the volume is devoted to the basic elements of drawing characters, including the anatomical proportions necessary for realistic creatures and ways to manipulate proportions to devise a variety of images. How to convey expression and movement are among other topics discussed. The second section highlights various creatures important to Japanese culture and legend. . . . This is a solid addition to manga-instruction collections." SLJ

An **Anthology** of graphic fiction, cartoons, and true stories; edited by Ivan Brunetti. Yale University Press 2006 400p il $28

Grades: 11 12 Adult   **741.5**
     1. Comic books, strips, etc. 2. American wit and humor
     ISBN 978-0-300-11170-5; 0-300-11170-3
                 LC 2006-14095

Brunetti presents "an overview of the art-comics movement, complete with a handful of the classic newspaper strips that informed today's creators. He finds room for such established veterans as R. Crumb, Lynda Barry, Gilbert and Jaime Hernandez, Daniel Clowes, Gary Panter, and Chester Brown as well as many less-familiar creators. . . . Brunetti admits that his selection criteria are highly personal, but as a cartoonist himself, whose work combines a socially transgressive spirit and impressive formal capability, his idiosyncratic approach is based in professional expertise. If his choices are sometimes arguable, his iconoclasm makes the book livelier and less predictable than such anthologies are wont to be." Booklist

Ashihara, Hinako

Sand chronicles vol. 1; story & art by Hinako Ashihara; [translation, Kinami Watabe; English adaptation, John Werry] Viz Media/Shojo Beat 2008 unp il pa $8.99

Grades: 9 10 11 12   **741.5**
     1. Graphic novels 2. Manga 3. Shojo manga
     ISBN 978-1-4215-1477-2

After her parents divorce, twelve-year-old Ann Uekusa and her mother move from Tokyo to rural Shimane, to stay with Ann's grandparents. Ann finds it difficult to adjust to a small town where everybody knows everybody, and she especially has a hard time with local boy Daigo, whom she finds to be obnoxious. But when Ann's mother deliberately gets lost in the mountains around New Year's Day and dies of exposure, Ann needs the comfort of the people in Shimane, and she finally bonds with her grandmother. The publisher rates this series for older teens, citing "mature themes."

Azuma, Kiyohiko, 1968-

Azumanga Daioh omnibus; translation, Stephen Paul. Yen Press 2009 675p il pa $24.99 *

Grades: 8 9 10 11 12   **741.5**

1. Graphic novels 2. Manga 3. Humorous graphic novels 4. High school students—Graphic novels 5. School stories—Graphic novels

ISBN 978-0-316-07738-5

First published 2001 in Japan

An omnibus edition of a humorous four-volume manga series featuring a Japanese suburban high school class with a ditzy teacher. The adult teachers go drinking occasionally, and there's one male teacher who ogles the girls in their P.E. uniforms.

Baker, Kyle

How to draw stupid and other essentials of cartooning. Watson-Guptill 2008 110p il pa $16.95 *

Grades: 8 9 10 11 12 Adult   **741.5**

1. Cartooning—Technique 2. Graphic novels—Drawing

ISBN 978-0-8230-0143-9   LC 2008-922161

"Baker, an award-winning cartoonist and graphic-novel illustrator, gives aspiring cartoonists irreverent advice about how to succeed in their chosen field. He offers instruction in basic drawing techniques such as choosing the right tools and discusses the importance of learning to draw shapes, exaggerating, and using references. But the author's most inspiring advice focuses on how to succeed as a cartoonist." SLJ

Black, Holly, 1971-

The Good Neighbors; book one: Kin. Graphix 2008 117p (The Good Neighbors) $16.99

Grades: 7 8 9 10 11 12   **741.5**

1. Graphic novels 2. Fantasy graphic novels 3. Fairies—Graphic novels

ISBN 978-0-439-85562-4; 0-439-85562-4

        LC 2007-49008

Sixteen-year-old Rue has grown up in a world much like ours, except that the human world and the world of faerie have co-existed, as good neighbors, for a long time. When Rue's mother disappears and her professor father becomes the main suspect in the murder of a young woman, Rue's life turns strange. As she digs for information to figure out what is happening in her life, Rue discovers that her mother is a faerie and has returned to that realm because of a broken promise.

"This sophisticated tale is well served by Naifeh's stylish, angular illustrations." SLJ

Other titles in this series are:

Kith (2009)

Kind (2010)

Brosgol, Vera, 1984-

Anya's ghost. First Second 2011 221p il $19.99; pa $15.99 *

Grades: 6 7 8 9 10   **741.5**

1. Graphic novels 2. Ghosts—Graphic novels 3. School stories—Graphic novels

ISBN   978-1-59643-713-5;   1-59643-713-8; 978-1-59643-552-0 (pa); 1-59643-552-6 (pa)

        LC 2010036251

Anya, embarrassed by her Russian immigrant family and self-conscious about her body, has given up on fitting in at school but falling down a well and making friends with the ghost there just may be worse.

"A deliciously creepy page-turning gem from first-time writer and illustrator Brosgol. . . . A moodily atmospheric spectrum of grays washes over the clean, tidy panels, setting a distinct stage before the first words appear. . . . In addition to the supernatural elements, Brosgol interweaves some savvy insights about the illusion of perfection and outward appearance. . . . A book sure to haunt its reader long after the last page is turned—exquisitely eerie." Kirkus

Byrne, John, 1963-

Cartooning; the best one-stop guide to drawing cartoons, caricatures, comic strips, and manga; [by] John M. Byrne. Collins 2008 191p il pa $16.95

Grades: 9 10 11 12 Adult   **741.5**

1. Cartooning—Technique

ISBN 978-0-06-147794-2   LC 2008-7587

The author "touches on all aspects of cartooning—history, drawing exercises, types of tools and materials, basic drawing skills, lettering, paneling, storytelling, humor, using computers, marketing, and much more. Various styles are included, with special chapters devoted to caricatures and manga. . . . A solid title with useful information for both beginners and more advanced artists." SLJ

Includes bibliographical references

Campbell, Ross

Shadoweyes; written and illustrated by Ross Campbell. SLG Publishing 2010 unp il pa $14.95

Grades: 8 9 10 11 12   **741.5**

1. Graphic novels 2. Superhero graphic novels 3. Science fiction graphic novels 4. Crime—Graphic novels

ISBN 978-1-59362-189-6; 1-59362-189-2

"In the dystopic future city of Dranac, teen friends Scout and Kyisha help fight crime with their neighborhood watch. Scout, however, is determined to intensify her efforts and becomes obsessed with creating a superhero persona for herself: Shadoweyes." Voice Youth Advocates

"Most convincing is the sharp dialogue, which speaks with such familiar rhythms and sentiment that teens will swear it came out of their own mouths. The art, too, balances a sleek manga technique, credible future looks and grunge fashions, the grotesquerie of zombie flesh, and inventive page composition." Booklist

Cherrywell, Steph

Pepper Penwell and the land creature of Monster Lake; [written and drawn by Steph Cherrywell] SLG Publishing 2011 unp il pa $14.95

Grades: 7 8 9 10 11 12 Adult   **741.5**

Cherrywell, Steph—*Continued*
1. Graphic novels 2. Mystery graphic novels
3. Horror graphic novels 4. Humorous graphic novels
5. Monsters—Graphic novels
ISBN 978-1-59362-205-3

British teenager Pepper Penwell prefers solving mysteries over school work and wants to be a detective like her father. When the latest school boots her out, Pepper takes on the case of a missing drum majorette named Lucy. Accompanied by her brother Alex, who inexplicably (it was some kind of accident) has the body of a bird, Pepper travels to Monster Lake, a town trying to establish itself as a tourist attraction based on its local monster, which is a land creature. In the town, Pepper meets strange people, any of whom could be guilty of kidnapping the wealthy and annoying Lucy. However, after Pepper does find Lucy, there's still the matter of the land monster, which is all too real. British slang (arse, bum) provides the mildly harsh language.

Chiarello, Mark
The DC Comics guide to coloring and lettering comics; [by] Mark Chiarello and Todd Klein; introduction by Jim Steranko. Watson-Guptill Publications 2004 144p il pa $19.95
Grades: 9 10 11 12   741.5
1. Comic books, strips, etc. 2. Cartoons and caricatures 3. Drawing
ISBN 0-8230-1030-9   LC 2004-9753

Contents: Lettering; The lettering profession; Hand lettering; Tools and materials; Getting started with lettering; Lettering text and balloons; Display lettering and sound effects; Elements on the page; Advanced techniques; Logo design; Computer lettering; Hardware and software; Fonts and type; Using Illustrator; Working with Art and Scans; Working with color; The final product

"This is a great resource for YAs seriously interested in graphic storytelling; it will also find an appreciative audience among adults." Booklist

Chmakova, Svetlana, 1979-
Nightschool: the weirn books, volume one; [by] Svetlana Chmakova; toning artist, Dee DuPuy; lettering, JuYoun Lee. Yen Press 2009 190p il pa $12.99
Grades: 7 8 9 10 11 12   741.5
1. Graphic novels 2. Supernatural graphic novels
3. Witches—Graphic novels 4. Mystery graphic novels
ISBN 978-0-7595-2859-8

PS 13W is a regular public high school during the day, but after dark it is the Nightschool attended by werewolves, vampires, and weirns (a particular breed of witch). Sarah has just started her job as the new Night Keeper when she disappears from the school; when her younger sister Alex, a young weirn who's been homeschooled, discovers that Sarah's existence has been wiped out from everyone's memory but hers, she sets out to investigate. Dark forces have caused Sarah's disappearance, and they seem to be watching Alex, too. Meanwhile, Daemon, the teacher of the hunters, must try to figure out what young seer Marina has seen in her visions of a broken seal and what this has to do with his students who were severely injured while they were out on a class trip to the cemetery. This urban fantasy was

first published in Yen Press's manga magazine, Yen Plus.

"Manga fans and teens looking for vampire stories will devour this one and will want to find out more about these characters." SLJ

Cobley, Jason
Frankenstein; the graphic novel; [by] Mary Shelley; script adaptation Jason Cobley; American English adaptation: Joe Sutliff Sanders; linework: Declan Shalvey; coloring: Jason Cardy & Kat Nicholson; lettering: Terry Wiley. Classical Comics 2008 141p il pa $16.95 *
Grades: 6 7 8 9 10 11 12 Adult   741.5
1. Shelley, Mary Wollstonecraft, 1797-1851—Adaptations 2. Graphic novels 3. Horror graphic novels
4. Frankenstein (Fictional character)
ISBN 978-1-906332-49-5

Also available quick text version $16.95 (ISBN: 978-1-906332-50-1)

"Original text version"

Young scientist Victor Frankenstein becomes obsessed with the idea that technology can create life, and works to prove his theories. However, his success doesn't bring him glory, but a living nightmare for himself and everyone around him. This graphic adaptation brings the entire book to the reader, using Shelley's original text for the dialog and narrative. Back matter includes a brief biography of Shelley, her family tree, a description of how she came to write the novel, and information on some of the various adaptations of the story to the stage and to film.

"More than a straightforward retelling, this edition invites readers to explore important social issues such as alienation, the consequences and ethics of scientific studies, as well as the nature of creation and destruction." SLJ

Crilley, Mark, 1966-
Brody's ghost: book 1; story and art by Mark Crilley. Dark Horse Books 2010 88p il pa $6.99
Grades: 8 9 10 11 12 Adult   741.5
1. Graphic novels 2. Adventure graphic novels
3. Mystery graphic novels 4. Fantasy graphic novels
5. Ghosts—Graphic novels
ISBN 978-1-59582-521-6

"The first in a six-volume limited series" Page 4 of cover

In what looks like a near-future city, Brody is down and out, eking out a living by playing guitar on the streets and working part-time as a stock clerk. Then, one day, while playing his guitar, he sees the ghost of a young woman; he thinks he's seeing things, but she won't let him alone until he talks with her. Talia, the ghost, needs to do a great deed before she can get into heaven, and she has decided to solve the mystery of a serial killer called the Penny Murderer, but she needs Brody, who is a ghostseer, to help her. First, though, he needs training to bring out his ghostseer powers, because he doesn't think he has any. Enter Kagemura, the ghost of a samurai, who decides, half-unwillingly, to train Brody. This book is much grittier than Crilley's earlier works, which were more suitable for younger readers; it is aimed more at teen and adult readers and includes some fighting violence but no graphically violent content.

Crilley, Mark, 1966-—*Continued*

"The setting—an unidentified future city partially in ruins—is a masterpiece of drawing, and Brody and the other characters are equally well crafted. . . . The story is more than a match for the art: humor, action, and mystery butt up against the reality of Brody's sad life, giving him the opportunity to change who he is." Booklist

Miki Falls, Book One: Spring. HarperCollins/HarperTeen 2007 176p il pa $7.99

Grades: 7 8 9 10 11 12   **741.5**

1. Graphic novels 2. Friendship—Graphic novels 3. High school students—Graphic novels 4. School stories—Graphic novels

ISBN 978-0-06-084616-9

"This is Miki Yoshida's final year of high school, and she's determined to make this the best year yet. Miki is in control . . . until Hiro Sakurai shows up. The tall, handsome new student is hiding something, and Miki wants to know what." Publisher's note

"Crilley uses mystery to drive the narrative and creates characters that the reader will care about. The black-and-white, manga-style art is beautiful." Voice Youth Advocates

Other titles in this series are:
Miki Falls, Book Two: Summer
Miki Falls, Book Three: Autumn
Miki Falls, Book Four: Winter

The **DC** Comics encyclopedia; the definitive guide to the characters of the DC universe; text by Scott Beatty . . . [et al.]; updated text by Dan Wallace. Updated and expanded. DK Pub. 2008 399p il $40

Grades: 9 10 11 12 Adult   **741.5**

1. DC Comics Group 2. Comic books, strips, etc.—Encyclopedias 3. Reference books

ISBN 978-0-7566-4119-1; 0-7566-4119-5

LC 2008-300609

First published 2004

The authors "meticulously profile 1000 DC heroes and villains created since DC's 1935 founding. The entries are organized alphabetically, by character name, while introductory insets consistently detail first appearance, hero/villain status, physical statistics, and special powers. A genuinely essential DC character reference." Libr J

Dorkin, Evan

Beasts of Burden: animal rites; written by Evan Dorkin; art by Jill Thompson; lettering by Jason Arthur and Jill Thompson. Dark Horse Comics 2010 184p il $19.99 *

Grades: 8 9 10 11 12 Adult   **741.5**

1. Graphic novels 2. Mystery graphic novels 3. Supernatural graphic novels 4. Dogs—Graphic novels 5. Cats—Graphic novels

ISBN 978-1-59582-513-1

Burden Hill is just a nice, quiet suburban town full of houses with yards and white picket fences, demonic frogs, zombie roadkill, ghosts, etc. The humans who live in Burden Hill seem to be totally oblivious to the dangers, but the dogs, and one cat, work together to keep their town safe. Jack the beagle, Pugsley (go figure), Ace the husky, Rex the Doberman, Whitey the terrier, and Orphan the cat deal with a haunted dog house, witches, undead dogs, a werewolf, and other monsters. The book includes some mild bad language ("crap" usually from Pugs) and a fair amount of violence. This book includes the four-issue miniseries plus all of the short stories that originally appeared in The Dark Horse Book of Hauntings, The Dark Horse Book of Witchcraft, The Dark Horse Book of the Dead, and The Dark Horse Book of Monsters. Sarah Dyer co-wrote "A Dog and His Boy" with Evan Dorkin.

"Gorgeous artwork and a smart, witty script elevate this tale of household pets who unite to fight occult menaces in idyllic Burden Hill." Publ Wkly

Drooker, Eric, 1958-

Blood song; a silent ballad; introduction by Joe Sacco. 2nd ed. Dark Horse 2009 unp il pa $19.95

Grades: 11 12 Adult   **741.5**

1. Graphic novels 2. Stories without words

ISBN 978-1-59582-389-2

First published 2002 by Harcourt

"Driven by war from their rural home in Southeast Asia, a young woman and her dog ride the ocean currents to a city in the West. A deeply moving graphic novel, masterfully done." SLJ

Dunning, John Harris

Salem Brownstone; all along the watchtowers; [by] John Harris Dunning and Nikhil Singh. Candlewick Press 2010 unp il lib bdg $18.99

Grades: 9 10 11 12   **741.5**

1. Graphic novels 2. Fantasy graphic novels 3. Supernatural graphic novels 4. Magicians—Graphic novels 5. Circus—Graphic novels

ISBN 978-0-7636-4735-3; 0-7636-4735-7

LC 2009-47413

Upon his father's death, Salem inherits a mansion as well as an unfinished battle with creatures from another world, which requires him to seek the help of his guardian familiar and the colorful performers of Dr. Kinoshita's Circus of Unearthly Delights.

"Salem's world is a haunting one, made only more so by the mysterious and enthralling images that accompany the storyline. The gothic elements, combined with the carnivalesque nature of Dr. Kinoshita's Circus and his performers, mesmerize readers and keep them grounded in the story long after it has ended." Voice Youth Advocates

Eisner, Will, 1917-2005

Comics and sequential art; principles and practices from the legendary cartoonist. W.W. Norton 2008 175p il (The Will Eisner library) pa $22.95 *

Grades: 9 10 11 12 Adult   **741.5**

1. Comic books, strips, etc.—Authorship 2. Graphic novels—Authorship 3. Drawing—Technique

ISBN 978-0-393-33126-4; 0-393-33126-1

LC 2008-20042

First published 1985 by Poorhouse Press

"A Will Eisner instructional book" Cover

Eisner, Will, 1917-2005—*Continued*

This book offers the author's ideas, theories, and advice about graphic storytelling and the uses to which the comic book art form can be applied.

Evanovich, Janet

Troublemaker; a Barnaby and Hooker graphic novel; written by Janet and Alex Evanovich; drawn by Joelle Jones; background pencils, Ben Dewey; inks, Andy Owens; colors, Dan Jackson; letters, Nate Piekos of Blambot. Dark Horse Books 2011 210p il pa $16.99

Grades: 9 10 11 12 Adult   **741.5**
1. Graphic novels 2. Mystery graphic novels 3. Adventure graphic novels 4. Voodooism—Graphic novels
ISBN 978-1-59582-722-7
First published 2010 in two volumes

In book 1, auto mechanic and racecar spotter Alex Barnaby works for racecar driver and general troublemaker Sam Hooker. Alex's friend Felicia needs help when their mutual friend, Rosa the cigar roller, disappears. When Sam and Alex look for the cigar shop owner, Walter Percy, they discover he's also missing, and bad things like explosions happen. They also find a wooden hand that's part of a statue of voodoo Loa Baron Samedi. In book 2, Alex, Sam, Rosa, and Felicia need to find Walter Percy, who stole the statue of Baron Samedi from Nitro, a gangster who practices a nasty form of voodoo. The book includes lots of action but little graphic violence, sexual innuendo but no nudity.

Fairfield, Lesley, 1949-

Tyranny. Tundra Books 2009 114p il pa $10.95
*
Grades: 8 9 10 11 12   **741.5**
1. Graphic novels 2. Eating disorders—Graphic novels
ISBN 978-0-88776-903-0; 0-88776-903-9

"This is one of the most moving and important graphic novels to come along in years. Many stories have been written about teens who try to change what they see in the mirror through anorexia and bulimia, but this one features a girl who is driven by her own personal demon. That demon is called Tyranny, and it is represented by an angry and chaotic swirl of lines that form the shape of a person. . . . Fairfield treats this important subject with intelligence and empathy. . . . The simple yet powerful black-and-white drawings do wonders in bringing the book's message to its readers." SLJ

Flight v2; [editor/art director, Kazu Kibuishi]

Villard 2007 432p il pa $24.95
Grades: 10 11 12 Adult   **741.5**
1. Graphic novels 2. Short stories—Graphic novels 3. Fantasy graphic novels
ISBN 978-0-345-49637-9

Stories are by various authors; previously published by Image Comics; v1 published 2004 by Image Comics; Villard edition published 2007

In this themed story collection, "more than 30 accomplished young artists take off on the theme, sometimes loosely construed, of flight. . . . At more than 400 pages, there is something in this elegantly produced collection for everyone, including readers who usually snub comics." Booklist

Flight v3; [editor/art director, Kazu Kibuishi]

Ballantine Books 2006 351p il pa $24.95
Grades: 9 10 11 12 Adult   **741.5**
1. Graphic novels 2. Short stories—Graphic novels 3. Fantasy graphic novels
ISBN 978-0-345-49039-1; 0-345-49039-8
LC 2006-45883
Sequel to Flight v2 (2005)

This third volume of Flight includes 26 short stories by mostly young writers, many of whom have webcomics. Some, such as Michael Gagne and Becky Cloonan, have published a number of books. The stories range from whimsical interludes to ironic fables to mini-epics of derring-do; ironically, most of the stories have only a tangential connection to the theme of flight.

Giffen, Keith

Blue Beetle: Shellshocked; writers, Keith Giffen & John Rogers; Cully Hamner . . . [et al], pencillers; Phil Balsman, Pat Brosseau, letterers; David Self, Guy Major, colorists; Cully Hamner, Phil Moy, Duncan Rouleau, Jack Purcell, inkers. DC Comics 2006 144p il pa $12.99
Grades: 8 9 10 11 12 Adult   **741.5**
1. Graphic novels 2. Superhero graphic novels 3. Adventure graphic novels 4. Blue Beetle (Fictional character)
ISBN 978-1-4012-0965-0

Ted Kord, the Blue Beetle, is dead; but the Blue Beetle scarab has chosen a new guardian, El Paso teenager Jaime Reyes. Supernatural powers can be a blessing or a curse, and when it comes to the powers of the Scarab, you don't get one without the other. The new hero will now have to deal with increasingly strange and dangerous days ahead, as he learns to handle his new skills while intergalactic trouble comes looking for him.

Gipi, 1963-

Notes for a war story; translated by Spectrum. First Second Books 2007 126p il pa $16.95
Grades: 10 11 12 Adult   **741.5**
1. Graphic novels 2. Crime—Graphic novels 3. War—Graphic novels
ISBN 978-1-59643-261-1   LC 2006-49716
Original Italian edition, 2004

Giuliano, a loner among outsiders, is one of three young drifters caught up in the whirlwind of a war in the Balkans. The three boys are like passing shadows; they live in abandoned houses, dodge the occasional bomb, and steal car parts for money. Meeting Felix—a powerful, fast-talking mercenary—changes everything for them. Felix is an expert manipulator; he speaks to their ambition and to their desires for power, wealth, and purpose. They're instantly hooked, especially the trio's unofficial leader, Stefano, and they soon escalate from petty crime to working on behalf of a mafia-style militia, bullying and extorting money in Felix's name. But as Giuliano comes to realize, they don't know what they're fighting for—if they're even fighting for anything. There's some naturally occurring violence and harsh language.

Graphic Classics volume eight: Mark Twain; edited by Tom Pomplun. 2nd ed. Eureka Productions 2007 144p il pa $11.95
Grades: 9 10 11 12 Adult   **741.5**

Graphic Classics volume eight: Mark Twain—
Continued
1. Twain, Mark, 1835-1910—Adaptations 2. Graphic
novels 3. Adventure graphic novels 4. Humorous
graphic novels 5. Short stories—Graphic novels
ISBN 978-0-9787919-2-6
First published 2004

This book includes an adaptation of "Tom Sawyer
Abroad" by Tom Pomplun and George Sellas, "The
Mysterious Stranger" by Rick Geary, "A Dog's Tale" by
Lance Tooks, "The Celebrated Jumping Frog of
Calaveras County" by Kevin Atkinson, and "The Carni-
val of Crime in Connecticut" by Antonella Caputo and
Nick Miller. Also in this volume are "Is He Living or Is
He Dead?," "A Curious Pleasure Excursion," and eight
women artists interpret Mark Twain's "Advice to Little
Girls."

"With a terrific lineup of artists and unbeatable material, Pomplun has assembled a collection of Mark
Twain's work that should delight graphic novel fans and
anyone seeking to boost their general cultural knowledge." Publ Wkly [review of 2004 edition]

Graphic Classics volume eleven: O. Henry; edited
by Tom Pomplun. Eureka Productions 2005
144p il pa $11.95
Grades: 7 8 9 10 11 12 Adult   **741.5**
1. Henry, O., 1862-1910—Adaptations 2. Graphic
novels 3. Short stories—Graphic novels
ISBN 978-0-9746648-2-0

This volume of Graphics Classics adapts some of the
short stories by O. Henry, the master of the surprise ending. Stories include 'The Ransom of Red Chief,' illustrated by Johnny Ryan, 'The Gift of the Magi,' illustrated
by Lisa Weber, 'The Caballero's Way' (the original story
of the Cisco Kid), illustrated by Mark A. Nelson, and
more.

Graphic Classics volume fifteen: Fantasy classics;
edited by Tom Pomplun. Eureka Productions
2008 144p il pa $11.95
Grades: 8 9 10 11 12 Adult   **741.5**
1. Graphic novels 2. Fantasy graphic novels
3. Horror graphic novels 4. Short stories—Graphic
novels
ISBN 978-0-9787919-3-3

This volume provides graphic novel adaptations of
Mary Shelley's *Frankenstein*, "Rappaccini's Daughter"
by Nathaniel Hawthorne, "The Glass Dog" by L. Frank
Baum, "The Dream Quest of Unknown Kadath" by H. P.
Lovecraft, and poems "After the Fire" by Lord Dunsany
and "The Dream-Bridge" by Clark Ashton Smith. There
are a few instances of mild violence and mild language
in some of the stories. Illustrators include Skot Olsen,
Lance Tooks, Brad Teare, and Leong Wan Kok; adapters
include Rod Lott, Lance Tooks, Antonella Caputo, and
Ben Avery.

Graphic Classics volume four: H. P. Lovecraft;
edited by Tom Pomplun. 2nd ed. Eureka
Productions 2007 144p il pa $11.95
Grades: 7 8 9 10 11 12 Adult   **741.5**
1. Lovecraft, H. P. (Howard Phillips), 1890-1937—
Adaptations 2. Graphic novels 3. Horror graphic nov-
els 4. Short stories—Graphic novels
ISBN 978-0-9746648-9-7
First published 2002

Here are comic book adaptations of stories by
Lovecraft, master of the macabre and creator of the
Cthulhu Mythos. It includes adaptations of "The Shadow
Over Innsmouth," illustrated by Simon Gane and
"Dreams in the Witch House," by Pedro Lopez. Plus:
"Sweet Ermengarde," a rare comedy by Lovecraft. Re-
turning from the previous edition are "Reanimator," "The
Shadow Out of Time," "The Terrible Old Man" and
"The Cats of Ulthar." Illustrations of headless corpses
and monstrous beings might disturb more tender sensibil-
ities.

Graphic Classics volume fourteen: Gothic
classics; edited by Tom Pomplun. Eureka
Productions 2007 144p il pa $11.95
Grades: 7 8 9 10 11 12 Adult   **741.5**
1. Graphic novels 2. Horror graphic novels 3. Short
stories—Graphic novels
ISBN 978-0-9787919-0-2

This volume includes graphic adaptations of classic
novels Carmilla by Joseph Sheridan Le Fanu, The Mysteries of Udolpho by Ann Radcliffe, and Northanger Abbey by Jane Austen, along with shorter works "The Oval
Portrait" by Edgar Allan Poe, "At the Gate" by Myla Jo
Closser, and "I've a Pain in My Head" by Jane Austen.
Radcliffe's novel is one mentioned by Austen in
Northanger Abbey and is a famous gothic novel from the
late eighteenth century, considered to be the world's first
best-seller. Le Fanu's vampire novel was published twenty-five years before Stoker's Dracula. Austen wrote
Northanger Abbey as a satire of the popular gothic
genre.

Graphic Classics volume seven: Bram Stoker;
edited by Tom Pomplun. 2nd ed. Eureka
Productions 2007 144p il pa $11.95
Grades: 7 8 9 10 11 12 Adult   **741.5**
1. Stoker, Bram, 1847-1912—Adaptations 2. Graphic
novels 3. Horror graphic novels 4. Fantasy graphic
novels 5. Short stories—Graphic novels
ISBN 978-0-9787919-1-9
First published 2003

This collection includes a comics adaptation of
Dracula by Rich Rainey and Joe Ollmann, "The Judge's
House" by Gerry Alanguilan, "Torture Tower" by
Onsmith Jeremi, and "The Lair of the White Worm" by
South African artist Rico Schacherl. Also "The Bridal of
Death," an excerpt from "The Jewel of Seven Stars" by
J.B. Bonivert and "The Wondrous Child" illustrated by
Evert Geradts. The book includes some violence, and one
panel of partial nudity.

"A must-read for fans of horror comics, this collection
also works as a good introduction to Stoker's contributions to the traditions of Gothic horror." SLJ

Graphic novels and comic books; edited by Kat
Kan. The H.W. Wilson Co. 2010 195p il
(Reference shelf) pa $35 *
Grades: Adult Professional   **741.5**
1. Graphic novels—History and criticism
ISBN 978-0-8242-1100-4; 0-8242-1100-6
                                LC 2010-34209

"This collection of articles from scholarly journals,
newspapers, and blogs gives a well-rounded overview of
graphic novels, as well as a strong argument for their

Graphic novels and comic books—*Continued*

place in schools and libraries. The first section chronicles the growing mainstream acceptance of graphic novels in the United States. . . . Susequent sections look at these books as complex works of literature, as education and literacy aids, and as significant additions to library collections, with advice for librarians on how to purchase, catalog, file, and promote them. In the final section, readers hear from writers and artists . . . who clearly convey the joy they get from this medium. This is both an entertaining and highly practical read." SLJ

Includes bibliographical references

Gulledge, Laura Lee

Page by Paige. Amulet Books 2011 unp il $18.95; pa $9.95

Grades: 7 8 9 10 11 12   **741.5**

1. New York (N.Y.)—Graphic novels 2. Artists—Graphic novels 3. Graphic novels 4. Humorous graphic novels 5. Friendship—Graphic novels

ISBN 978-0-8109-9721-9; 0-8109-9721-5; 978-0-8109-9722-6 (pa); 0-8109-9722-3 (pa)

Teenage Paige Turner (blame her writer parents) moves to New York City from Virginia, and she finds the big city rather overwhelming. She decides to buy a sketchbook and sort out her thoughts and feelings in drawings. Soon she does make some friends, and she explores more of the city, but as she begins to feel happier, she clashes with her parents. All of this goes into her sketchbook journal, which she starts to show to her new friends—Jules, Longo, and Gabe. The book is organized by Paige's "rules," which she uses to try to change herself, such as "Rule #2: Draw what you know. If you feel it or see it . . . DRAW IT!"

"Gulledge's b&w illustrations are simple but well-suited to their subject matter; the work as a whole is a good-natured, optimistic portrait of a young woman evolving toward adulthood." Publ Wkly

Hambly, Barbara

Anne Steelyard: the garden of emptiness, act I; an honorary man. Penny Farthing Press 2008 unp il pa $14.95 *

Grades: 9 10 11 12 Adult   **741.5**

1. Graphic novels 2. Adventure graphic novels 3. Middle East—Graphic novels 4. Archeology—Graphic novels

ISBN 978-0-9719012-9-2

Written by Barbara Hambly; pencils by Alex Kosakowski and Ron Randall; colors by Mike Garcia

In 1908, the Middle East is a region in turmoil; while Germany and Great Britain posture at each other in a prelude to the First World War, men called the Young Turks challenge the Turkish Sultans for control of the Ottoman Empire. Archeologists excavate relics and treasures from the desert sands, their work beginning to demystify human history and managing to bring wealth and fame (or infamy) to those archeologists. Anne Steelyard is a British archeologist who wants to make that one huge discovery which will make her reputation, free her from her father and force the male-dominated field to recognize her as an equal. However, even as she tries to set up an expedition, the politics of the place and time provide obstacles from the Turkish government, from the British, and from society itself. The book includes some violence.

Hamilton, Tim

Ray Bradbury's Fahrenheit 451; the authorized adaptation; introduction by Ray Bradbury. Hill and Wang 2009 148p il $30; pa $16.95 *

Grades: 10 11 12 Adult   **741.5**

1. Bradbury, Ray, 1920-—Adaptations 2. Graphic novels 3. Science fiction graphic novels

ISBN 978-0-8090-5100-7; 978-0-8090-5101-4 (pa)

LC 2009-4804

"A novel graphic from Hill and Wang"

"It's no wonder Hamilton's comic novelization is authorized by Bradbury himself: this evocative button-pusher will almost certainly entice readers to seek out the original. . . . When Montag, the fireman whose job it is to 'fix' forbidden libraries by reducing them to cinder, becomes enticed by the printed word, his treason unleashes no less than subterfuge, paranoia, thuggery, and even robotic killer dogs. Hamilton renders much of the story in triptych panels and moody, two-tone palettes that blot characters' features into Munch-like skulls." Booklist

Hart, Christopher

Drawing cutting edge anatomy; the ultimate reference guide for comic book artists. Watson-Guptill Publications 2004 144p il pa $19.95

Grades: 9 10 11 12   **741.5**

1. Artistic anatomy 2. Figure drawing 3. Cartoons and caricatures 4. Comic books, strips, etc.

ISBN 0-8230-2398-2   LC 2004-12864

"This drawing tutorial shows artists how to draw the exaggerated musculature of super-sized figures in action poses." Publisher's note

"This book covers the basics in good detail. . . . Attractively presented and educational, this title will be popular with comic-book fans who like to draw." SLJ

Manga for the beginner; everything you need to start drawing right away! Watson-Guptill Publications 2008 192p il $21.95 *

Grades: 5 6 7 8 9 10   **741.5**

1. Graphic novels—Drawing 2. Manga—Drawing

ISBN 978-0-8230-3083-5; 0-8230-3083-0

LC 2007-40490

"Hart's latest drawing book . . . contains detailed and easy-to-follow instructions for drawing types of shojo manga (aimed at girls) and shonen manga (aimed at boys). . . . He describes in concise language and through clear illustrations how to use lettering, lighting effects, and other techniques to achieve a certain mood to advance a plot. . . . Anyone even slightly interested in drawing manga will find it appealing." Voice Youth Advocates

Hartzell, Andy

Fox bunny funny. Top Shelf Productions 2007 102p il pa $10

Grades: 9 10 11 12 Adult   **741.5**

Hartzell, Andy—*Continued*
1. Graphic novels 2. Animals—Graphic novels
3. Stories without words—Graphic novels 4. Fantasy
graphic novels
ISBN 978-1-891830-97-6

The rules are simple: you're either a fox or a bunny.
Foxes oppress and devour, bunnies suffer and die. Everyone knows their place. Everyone's satisfied. So what
happens when a secret desire puts you at odds with your
society? Starting from a simple premise—and without using a single word—this book leads the reader on a zigzag chase in and out of rabbit holes, and through increasingly strange landscapes where funny animals have serious identity problems. The tale swerves from slapstick to
horror and back again before landing at the inevitable
climax, in which all the old rules are shattered. Some
moments of violence and dismemberment might be disturbing for some readers.

"Deftly presented in crisp black-and-white, blockprint-like panels, this is a must for libraries supporting
LGBT collections." Booklist

Harvey, Robert C.
The art of the comic book; an aesthetic history.
University Press of Miss. 1996 288p il (Studies in
popular culture) pa $22 hardcover o.p. *
Grades: 11 12 Adult   **741.5**
1. Comic books, strips, etc. 2. Popular culture—United
States
ISBN 0-87805-758-7   LC 95-377

Harvey "attempts to situate the comic book in terms
of its evolution from the comic strip to the world of publishing as a whole. . . . {He describes the} change
brought upon comics by the institution of the Comics
Code in 1954, which put horror and detective stories out
of business and ushered in the primacy of superheroes.
He also {examines} . . . the art itself, focusing on the
development of the vocabulary of panel, layout, story,
and style, and the relationship between writer and artist
during various stages of comic book history. In addition,
he . . . {discusses Will Eisner}, Gil Kane, Frank Miller,
and Robert Crumb." Libr J

Includes bibliographical references

Heuvel, Eric, 1960-
A family secret; [English translation, Lorraine T.
Miller] Farrar, Straus and Giroux 2009 62p il
$18.99; pa $9.99
Grades: 7 8 9 10 11 12   **741.5**
1. Graphic novels 2. Holocaust, 1933-1945—Graphic
novels 3. Jews—Graphic novels 4. Grandmothers—
Graphic novels
ISBN   978-0-374-32271-7;   0-374-32271-6;
978-0-374-42245-3 (pa); 0-374-42265-6 (pa)
                  LC 2009-13943
"Anne Frank House"
Original Dutch edition, 2003

While searching his Dutch grandmother's attic for
yard sale items, Jeroen finds a scrapbook which leads
Gran to tell of her experiences as a girl living in Amsterdam during the Holocaust, when her father was a Nazi
sympathizer and Esther, her Jewish best friend, disappeared

This is a "moving graphic novel. . . . The art is in
ink and watercolor, with very clear, highly detailed panels. . . . [A] gripping story." Booklist

Hickman, Troy
Common Grounds: Baker's dozen. Image
Comics/Top Cow Productions 2004 144p il pa
$14.99
Grades: 9 10 11 12 Adult   **741.5**
1. Graphic novels 2. Superhero graphic novels
ISBN 978-1-58240-841-5

Superheroes and supervillains need a place where they
can relax, unwind, and not worry about the next battle.
Common Grounds is just such a place—a chain of coffee
shops with bakery counters, totally neutral ground. Here,
hero and villain can relax and take a break in the
restroom ("Head Games"), a teenage superhero who
doubts herself and an older superpowered religious Jew
can encourage each other ("Sanctuary"), a group of overweight heroes can meet ("Fat Chance"), or formerly evil
monsters can get custom takeout and shoot the breeze
("Where Monsters Dine"). The book includes a baker's
dozen (thirteen) stories.

Hicks, Faith Erin
Zombies calling. SLG Publishing 2007 104p il
pa $9.95
Grades: 8 9 10 11 12 Adult   **741.5**
1. Graphic novels 2. Horror graphic novels
3. Humorous graphic novels 4. Zombies—Graphic
novels
ISBN 978-1-59362-079-0

Anglophile/zombie movie fan/college student Joss is
going crazy in the middle of exams week, but when her
college campus is overrun with actual zombies, she
knows what to do. With her roommate Sonnet and their
buddy Robyn, Joss uses the Rules gleaned from years of
watching zombie movies to fight the undead hordes.
When the first rule is that the ordinary person suddenly
becomes a total ass-kicking cool fighter able to beat off
zombies with no fighting lessons, yeah, it's cool. Except
the zombies just keep coming and coming. . . . The
book has some harsh language and lots of black and
white zombie fighting action without gore.

Hill, Joe
Locke & key: welcome to Lovecraft; written by
Joe Hill; art by Gabriel Rodriguez. IDW
Publishing 2008 158p il $24.99; pa $19.99
Grades: 10 11 12 Adult   **741.5**
1. Graphic novels 2. Horror graphic novels
3. Mystery graphic novels
ISBN 978-1-60010-237-0; 978-1-60010-384-1 (pa)

After Rendell Locke is murdered by a former student,
Sam Lesser, who then tried to find and kill the rest of
the family, Nina Locke takes her children, Tyler, Kinsey,
and Bode to Lovecraft, Massachusetts, to live with
Rendell's brother Duncan in Keyhouse. Tyler needs to
deal with the guilt he feels because of a conversation
with Sam Lesser, in which he said Sam should kill his
dad. Kinsey had taken Bode and hidden from Sam, keeping them both safe, but she feels as though she'll never
be safe again. Bode finds a door at Keyhouse, and when

Hill, Joe—*Continued*

he goes through it, he dies and his ghost wanders around. There's definitely something weird at Keyhouse, and something is living at the bottom of the well in the well house—something that uses both Bode and Sam Lesser—and wants revenge. The book includes bloody violence. Joe Hill is the son of Stephen King.

"This first of . . . several volumes delivers on all counts, boasting a solid story bolstered by exceptional work from Chilean artist Rodriguez . . . that resembles a fusion of Rick Geary and Cully Hamner with just a dash of Frank Quitely." Publ Wkly

Hinds, Gareth, 1971-

Beowulf; adapted and illustrated by Gareth Hinds. Candlewick Press 2007 unp il $21.99; pa $9.99 *

Grades: 8 9 10 11 12 Adult   **741.5**
1. Beowulf—Graphic novels 2. Graphic novels 3. Adventure graphic novels 4. Monsters—Graphic novels
ISBN   978-0-7636-3022-5;   0-7636-3022-5; 978-0-7636-3023-2 (pa); 0-7636-3023-3 (pa)
LC 2006-49023
Graphic novel adaptation of the Old English epic poem, Beowulf

"For fantasy fans both young and old, this makes an ideal introduction to a story without which the entire fantasy genre would look very different; many scenes may be too intense for very young readers." Publ Wkly

The Odyssey. Candlewick Press 2010 248p il $24.99; pa $14.99 *

Grades: 7 8 9 10 11 12   **741.5**
1. Homer—Adaptations 2. Graphic novels 3. Greek mythology—Graphic novels
ISBN   978-0-7636-4266-2;   0-7636-4266-5; 978-0-7636-4268-6 (pa); 0-7636-4268-1 (pa)

This is "the most lavish retelling of Homer yet. . . . Hinds lets the epic story take its time, with a slow build and pages that aren't afraid to alternate packed dialogue with titanic action. The sumptuous art, produced with grain, texture, and hue, evokes a time long past while detailing every line and drop of sweat on Odysseus' face and conveying the sheer grandeur of seeing a god rise out of the ocean." Booklist

Hornschemeier, Paul

Mother, come home; with an introduction by Thomas Tennant. Fantagraphics 2004 128p il

Grades: 11 12 Adult   **741.5**
1. Graphic novels 2. Mental illness—Graphic novels
ISBN 978-1-56097-973-9 (pa)

In this "story, a young child struggles with the death of his mother and his father's collapse. Clean-lined artwork leaves plenty of room for strong emotional content linked to themes of euthanasia, suicide, and depression." Booklist

Igarashi, Daisuke

Children of the sea, vol. 1. Viz Media/Viz Signature 2009 320p il pa $14.99

Grades: 7 8 9 10 11 12   **741.5**

1. Graphic novels 2. Ocean—Graphic novels 3. Fantasy graphic novels 4. Mystery graphic novels 5. Manga 6. Adventure graphic novels
ISBN 978-1-4215-2914-1; 1-4215-2914-9

"As a young girl, Ruka sees a fish turn into light and disappear at the aquarium where her father works, but no one believes her. Years later, the mystery of the ghost of the sea unfolds before Ruka and a pair of mysterious young boys, Umi and Sora." Publ Wkly

"Igarashi's storytelling is quiet, thoughtful, and thought provoking, but it is his drawings that make this manga so amazing. Extremely detailed settings turn panels into mini-masterpieces." Booklist

Inada, Shiho

Ghost hunt, Vol. 1; manga by Shiho Inada; story by Fuyumi Ono; translated by Akira Tsubasa; adapted by David Walsh; lettered by Foltz Design. Del Rey Manga 2005 216p il pa $10.95

Grades: 8 9 10 11 12 Adult   **741.5**
1. Graphic novels 2. Manga 3. Shojo manga 4. Horror graphic novels
ISBN 0-345-48624-2

A decrepit old building stands on the campus of Mai's high school; every time the school tries to demolish it, unexplained accidents occur. Finally, the school hires a psychic researcher, and when Mai accidentally injures his assistant and damages an expensive camera, Shibuya (the researcher) insists she work off her debt by helping him. A miko (Shinto priestess), a Buddhist monk, and a Roman Catholic exorcist also come—but none of their methods work to stop the strange occurrences. Despite herself, Mai gets drawn into the investigation. This is the first of an ongoing manga series that provides some ghostly thrills without graphic violence, bad language, or sexual innuendo.

Inoue, Takehiko, 1967-

Real, volume 1; story & art by Takehiko Inoue. Viz Media 2008 222p il pa $12.99 *

Grades: 10 11 12 Adult   **741.5**
1. Graphic novels 2. Sports—Graphic novels 3. Manga 4. Basketball—Graphic novels 5. Wheelchair basketball—Graphic novels
ISBN 978-1-4215-1989-0
Original Japanese edition, 2001

Nomiya was the controlling rider on a motorcycle when he got into an accident that paralyzed the young woman riding with him; now he has dropped out of high school in his senior year and feels guilty. Togawa is stuck in a wheelchair but still plays basketball, which was the only thing Nomiya was good at in school. Togawa has quit the wheelchair basketball team, but he still plays. Nomiya starts playing while in a wheelchair, and they soon start a bit of a scam against regular players. They each have their own goals, but can they work together and find a better life for themselves? The book includes some harsh language, partial nudity, and Nomiya commits a bodily act against his school when he leaves.

"A compelling story of tragedy and struggle, *Real* is sure to appeal to teens—especially to male readers." SLJ

Inoue, Takehiko, 1967-—*Continued*

Slam dunk, volume 1; Sakuragi; story and art by Takehiko Inoue; English adaptation Kelly Sue DeConnick. Viz Media/Shonen Jump 2008 197p il pa $7.99 *

Grades: 8 9 10 11 12   **741.5**
1. Graphic novels 2. Manga 3. Shonen manga 4. Basketball—Graphic novels
ISBN 978-1-4215-0679-1

Original Japanese edition, 1991

Hanamichi Sakuragi is a first year student at Shohoku Prefecture High School; he's got a reputation as a bruising fighter and has suffered 50 rejections from girls who were scared of his fighting. He's looked down on sports all his life, but on this first day of high school, he meets Haruko Akagi; she's not scared of him, and she loves basketball. He falls for her completely, enough to try to play basketball. But, he has competition—Kaeda Rukawa is another first year student; he's a star basketball player, and Haruko has a huge crush on him. Then Sakuragi gets on the bad side of the basketball team captain, who happens to be Haruko's older brother. Sakuragi does everything he can to convince Takenori Akagi to let him join the team. However, he has a long way to go before he can build the fundamental skills to play basketball effectively; will he stick it out? There's some fighting, one male student's buttocks get exposed accidentally, but there's no bad language.

Isabella, Tony 1951-

1,000 comic books you must read. Krause Publications 2009 271p il $29.99

Grades: 9 10 11 12 Adult   **741.5**
1. Comic books, strips, etc.—Bibliography 2. Best books
ISBN 978-0-89689-921-6; 0-89689-921-7

Isabella "has the great fortune of not having to decide the thousand finest but rather the thousand that he finds compelling. This lends his hardcover a kaleidoscopic approach to deconstructing the evolution of the American comic rather than focusing on the creme de la creme alone. With its chapters predominantly broken up by decade ('The Fighting Forties,' 'The Fearful Fifties,' etc.), 1000 Comic Books provides short summaries (under 75 words) for each title as well as clear cover scans and creator/ publishing information. A plethora of obscure information is sprinkled through the book. . . . There is no discrimination of subject matter, and even the most ardent comic book reader is bound to learn something new." Cincinnati City Beat

Iwaoka, Hisae, 1976-

Saturn apartments, volume 1; [translation, Matt Thorn] Viz signature ed. Viz Signature 2010 184p il pa $12.99 *

Grades: 7 8 9 10   **741.5**
1. Graphic novels 2. Manga 3. Science fiction graphic novels
ISBN 978-1-4215-3364-3; 1-4215-3364-2

Reads from right to left

Far in the future, humankind has left Earth to live in a gigantic ringlike structure that circles the planet. In this structure, humans have developed a class structure based on where one lives: the higher the floor on which you live, the greater your status. Mitsu has just graduated from junior high and is now expected to work as a window washer, just like his father before him. The thing is, his father disappeared while washing windows and is presumed dead. Window washing means one must get into a space suit and go out of the structure into outer space, 35 kilometers above the Earth's surface; space winds and other hazards make the work dangerous and expensive. Even as he wonders still, five years after his father's disappearance, what happened to him, Mitsu finds his job gives him a unique perspective on the lives of those who live in the Saturn Apartments. This is science fiction from the viewpoint of the mundane service work rather than heroics of space action.

"This story of a young teen struggling to live alone will appeal to YAs, and the introspective nature of the narrative will have plenty of crossover appeal for adult readers as well." Booklist

Jensen, Van

Pinocchio, vampire slayer; written by Van Jensen; created and drawn by Dusty Higgins. SLG Publishing 2009 unp il pa $10.99

Grades: 9 10 11 12 Adult   **741.5**
1. Graphic novels 2. Horror graphic novels 3. Vampires—Graphic novels 4. Pinocchio (Fictional character)
ISBN 978-1-59362-176-6; 1-59362-176-0

LC 2010-278899

After a brief recap of Collodi's novel, this graphic novel takes place a few years later. Pinocchio, still a wooden puppet, now finds he has a use for lying and growing his nose—he breaks off the growth and uses it as a wooden stake to destroy vampires. The blood suckers have come to the town of Nasolungo, they killed his creator/father Geppetto, and now Pinocchio roams the streets at night, seeking vengeance upon the vampires. The book includes violence but only mild language (Pinocchio says "crap" a few times). Along with the violence, the book includes a lot of sardonic humor.

"Heavy shadows and thick lines dominate the panels and provide a midnight-black atmosphere for all the gory mayhem, but it's the humor that makes this so memorable. . . . There's also surprising heart at the story's center that plays with the core theme of fatherhood. There won't be many teen (or adult) graphic-novel readers who won't want this book for its concept alone, and the execution doesn't disappoint." Booklist

Jones, Gerard

Men of tomorrow; geeks, gangsters and the birth of the comic book. Basic Books 2004 320p il $26; pa $15 *

Grades: 11 12 Adult   **741.5**
1. Comic books, strips, etc. 2. Cartoonists
ISBN 0-465-03656-2; 0-465-03657-0 (pa)

LC 2004-9031

This book tells "the surprising story of the young Jewish misfits, hustlers and nerds who invented the superhero and the comic book industry. . . . Springing unheralded out of working-class Jewish immigrant neighborhoods in the depths of the Depression, these young men transformed an odd mix of geekdom, science fic-

Jones, Gerard—*Continued*

tion, and outsider yearnings into blue-eyed chisel-nosed crime-fighters and adventurers who quickly captured the mainstream imagination. . . . He chronicles how the comics sparked a frightened counterattack that nearly destroyed the industry in the 1950's and how later they surged back at an underground level, to inspire a new generation to transmute those long-ago fantasies into art, literature, blockbuster movies and graphic novels." Publisher's note

Kelso, Megan, 1968-

The squirrel mother; stories. Fantagraphics 2006 147p il pa $16.95

Grades: 10 11 12   **741.5**

1. Graphic novels

ISBN 1-56097-746-9; 978-1-56097-746-9

This is a "collection of graphic short stories, all of which originally appeared in various magazines and anthologies between 2000 and 2005. Kelso's work is characterized by subject matter that fits roughly into two disparate camps: personal and semi-autobiographical stories that draw heavily on the details of her childhood and adolescence and stories about the idea of America and American history, such as a trilogy of short pieces about Alexander Hamilton." Publisher's note

"Beautifully packaged, this is a gem of a collection." Publ Wkly

Kim, Susan

Brain camp; by Susan Kim and Laurence Klavan; illustrated by Faith Erin Hicks. First Second 2010 151p il pa $16.99

Grades: 7 8 9 10   **741.5**

1. Graphic novels 2. Science fiction graphic novels 3. Mystery graphic novels 4. Horror graphic novels 5. Camps—Graphic novels

ISBN 978-1-59643-366-3; 1-59643-366-3

Jenna and Lucas are both under-achieving young teens who suddenly receive invitations to join the Fielding Camp for the summer. Pressed by their respective parents to attend, Jenna and Lucas both notice some strange things at the camp, and neither feels like eating the nasty slop served at every meal. The other campers are either intellectually challenged bullies, misfits, or supersmart zombies. At first Dwayne, a self-described spaz, befriends them, but when his cabin "wins" ice cream treats at dinner, Lucas sees the camp counselors sneaking in that night to "inoculate" all his cabin mates. Lucas and Jenna work against time to escape the camp and develop an antidote. Jenna is shown in one panel sitting on a commode when her period comes, and one short sequence shows Lucas having a wet dream and then washing out his stained undies; both situations are nonverbal and drawn with restraint, but school librarians will need to decide whether these two scenes meet their own schools' standards.

The authors present a "well-rounded adventure here, as the far-out (and kind of gross) climax mixes with genuine insight into dealing with parents, fitting into a new crowd, and handling the pressures of performance. Hicks' line work is cool enough to assuage older readers who might be suspicious of the summer-camp setting." Booklist

Kirkman, Robert

Invincible: ultimate collection, Vol. 1. Image Comics 2005 400p il $34.95

Grades: 9 10 11 12   **741.5**

1. Graphic novels 2. Superhero graphic novels

ISBN 1-58240-500-X

Originally published as Invincible, issues #1-13

High school senior Mark Grayson develops super powers, but it's only logical because his father is superhero Omni-Man. Soon enough Mark gets a costume, a mask, and a name—Invincible. He also joins a team of teenage superheroes as they track down the person who is turning fellow students into walking bombs. Then Mark learns that evil sometimes wears the face of someone familiar, someone respected, and loved. And he'll need all the power he can muster to save himself—and Earth. This edition includes extra features, including a sketchbook section.

"The story is compelling, presenting teenage melodrama without a trace of condescension, and even the inevitable superhero-crush-on-a-girl-he-can-never-have subplot receives a fresh spin." Voice Youth Advocates

Kishimoto, Masashi, 1974-

Naruto. vol. 1, The tests of the Ninja; story and art by Masashi Kishimoto; [English adaptation by Jo Duffy] Viz 2003 186p il (Shonen jump graphic novel) pa $7.95

Grades: 7 8 9 10 11 12   **741.5**

1. Graphic novels 2. Manga 3. Shonen manga 4. Martial arts—Graphic novels

ISBN 1-56931-900-6; 978-1-56931-900-0

First published 1999 in Japan

Volume one of an ongoing series; "This graphic novel contains material that was originally published in English in Shonen jump #6-10" Verso of title page

"Teen orphan Naruto wants to become the greatest ninja of all, despite the fact that most people in his village have despised him from birth because a terrible demon has been imprisoned in his body. . . . Teens love this series." Voice Youth Advocates

Koontz, Dean R., 1945-

In odd we trust; created by Dean Koontz; written by Queenie Chan and Dean Koontz; illustrated by Queenie Chan. Del Rey 2008 224p il pa $10.95

Grades: 9 10 11 12 Adult   **741.5**

1. Graphic novels 2. Mystery graphic novels 3. Horror graphic novels 4. Ghosts—Graphic novels

ISBN 978-0-345-49966-0

Nineteen-year-old Odd Thomas works as a fry cook in small town Pico Mundo, California; people come to the diner for his pancakes (among other foods), he's easygoing and friendly. Odd also sees ghosts; the ghosts never talk, but they tend to come to him when they need something done. The latest one is a little boy. Odd's girlfriend Stormy tells him that the dead boy's babysitter, her friend, is worried about her other charge, a young girl. So psychic Odd and pistol-packing Stormy try to find the murderer before he can strike again. This original graphic novel, co-written by illustrator Queenie Chan and illustrated and formatted like manga, is a prequel to

Koontz, Dean R., 1945-—*Continued*

Koontz's bestselling prose novels about Odd Thomas. While it is a murder mystery, there's little in the way of actual violence portrayed in the book.

"This book is a light, diverting read that has the advantage of being a manga that isn't a part of a multivolume series." Booklist

Krensky, Stephen, 1953-

Comic book century; the history of American comic books. Twenty-First Century Books 2007 112p il lib bdg $30.60

Grades: 5 6 7 8 9 10   **741.5**

1. Cartoons and caricatures 2. Comic books, strips, etc.

ISBN 978-0-8225-6654-0; 0-8225-6654-0

LC 2006-20795

Provides a history of comic books in America during the twentieth century, showing how it has influenced and been influenced by American culture. Includes an epilogue about comics in the early twenty-first century

"Frequent full-color comic-book representations and black-and-white photographs, . . . flashy sidebars, and a striking blue background combine well with the accessible text, making this . . . visually appealing as well as highly entertaining." Bull Cent Child Books

Includes bibliographical references

Kubo, Tite, 1977-

Bleach, Vol. 1; [story and art by Tite Kubo; English adaptation, Lance Caselman; translation, Joe Yamazaki] Viz Shonen Jump 2004 190p il pa $7.95

Grades: 9 10 11 12   **741.5**

1. Graphic novels 2. Manga 3. Shonen manga 4. Supernatural graphic novels 5. Adventure graphic novels

ISBN 1-59116-441-9

Teenage Ichigo Kurasaki has always been able to see ghosts, but that never really affected his life, until the night a Hollow, an evil spirit that preys on humans, attacks him. Soul Reaper Rukia Kuchiki tries to help Ichigo save himself and his family, but somehow he manages to absorb all her powers. Now he's a Soul Reaper, and he must work to protect the innocent from the Hollows. This is the first volume of an ongoing manga series that is full of fighting action and irreverent humor.

Kuper, Peter, 1958-

The jungle; [based on the story by] Upton Sinclair; adapted by Peter Kuper. Papercutz 2010 unp il (Classics Illustrated) pa $9.99

Grades: 9 10 11 12 Adult   **741.5**

1. Sinclair, Upton, 1878-1968—Adaptations 2. Graphic novels 3. Meat industry—Graphic novels 4. Immigrants—Graphic novels 5. Chicago (Ill.)—Graphic novels

ISBN 978-1-59707-192-5

First published 1991 by First Publishing

"Jurgis and his family have immigrated to America from Lithuania, settled in Chicago, and found jobs in the meatpacking plant. The family seems to be living the American dream: having their own home, and a means of support, even if the work is hard and disgusting. Peter Kuper's dark, colored, cartoon-style illustrations, framed in black, bring to life Sinclair's original work and highlight the atrocities perpetuated upon the Rudkus family." Libr Media Connect

Lagos, Alexander

The sons of liberty; created and written by Alexander Lagos and Joseph Lagos; art by Steve Walker; color by Oren Kramek; letters by Chris Dickey. Random House 2010 unp il $18.99; lib bdg $21.99; pa $12.99

Grades: 6 7 8 9 10 11 12   **741.5**

1. Graphic novels 2. United States—History—1600-1775, Colonial period—Graphic novels 3. Adventure graphic novels 4. Superhero graphic novels 5. African Americans—Graphic novels

ISBN 978-0-375-85670-9; 0-375-85670-6; 978-0-375-95667-6 (lib bdg); 0-375-95667-6 (lib bdg); 978-0-375-85667-9 (pa); 0-375-85667-9 (pa)

In the mid-eighteenth century American colonies, Graham and Brody work as slaves on a tobacco plantation not far from Philadelphia. When they run away after injuring the plantation owner's son for threatening another slave, they seek Benjamin Lay, an eccentric abolitionist who might give them shelter. Instead, William Franklin, son of Benjamin Franklin, finds them and conducts unknown experiments on them.

"History offers few villains as vile as slaveholders, but this graphic novel is far from being a simple revenge thriller. The use of historical figures and well-researched (but embellished) history, and a willingness to flesh out characters and set up situations to pay off in future installments, makes for an uncommonly complex, literate, and satisfying adventure." Booklist

Larson, Gary

The far side. Andrews & McMeel 1982 unp il pa $8.95

Grades: 9 10 11 12   **741.5**

1. Comic books, strips, etc.

ISBN 0-8362-1200-2   LC 82-72418

A collection of Larson's Far side cartoons

The prehistory of the Far side; a 10th anniversary exhibit. Andrews & McMeel 1989 288p il pa $14.95 hardcover o.p.

Grades: 9 10 11 12   **741.5**

1. Comic books, strips, etc.

ISBN 0-8362-1851-5   LC 89-84813

Retrospective of Larson's work that includes childhood drawings, and stories that evolved into Far side cartoons

Larson, Hope

Mercury. Atheneum Books for Young Readers 2010 234p il $19.99; pa $9.99

Grades: 8 9 10 11 12   **741.5**
 1. Graphic novels 2. Nova Scotia—Graphic novels 3. Supernatural graphic novels
 ISBN   978-1-4169-3585-8;   1-4169-3585-1; 978-1-4169-3588-9 (pa); 1-4169-3588-6 (pa)
                                  LC 2009-903638

Tara is forced to move in with her cousins after her house burns down. She faces a difficult adjustment while her mother is away trying to earn money. Interwoven with this story is that of Tara's ancestors, who in 1859 were convinced by a mysterious stranger to put all their money into searching their property for gold.

"The storytelling, both in words and pictures, brilliantly offers details from Canadian history and modern life. The dialogue varies from funny to poignant. An excellent graphic novel." SLJ

Lat

Kampung boy. First Second 2006 141p il pa $16.95 *

Grades: 7 8 9 10 11 12 Adult   **741.5**
 1. Malaysia—Graphic novels 2. Family life—Graphic novels 3. Muslims—Graphic novels 4. Graphic novels
 ISBN 1-59643-121-0   LC 2005-34135

First published 1979 in Malaysia with title: Lat, the kampung boy

"Malaysian cartoonist Lat uses the graphic novel format to share the story of his childhood in a small village, or kampung. From his birth and adventures as a toddler to the enlargement of his world as he attends classes in the village, makes friends, and, finally, departs for a prestigious city boarding school, this autobiography is warm, authentic, and wholly engaging." Booklist

Town boy. First Second Books 2007 191p il pa $16.95 *

Grades: 7 8 9 10 11 12 Adult   **741.5**
 1. Graphic novels 2. Bildungsromans—Graphic novels 3. Humorous graphic novels 4. Malaysia—Graphic novels
 ISBN 978-1-59643-331-1; 1-59643-331-0
                                  LC 2006-102857

In this sequel to Kampung Boy, it's the late 1960s and Mat is now a teenager attending a boarding school in the town of Ipoh, far from his kampung. He discovers bustling streets, hip music, heady literature, budding romance, and through it all his growing passion for art.

Lee, Stan

Stan Lee's How to draw comics; from the legendary co-creator of Spider-Man, the Incredible Hulk, Fantastic Four, X-Men, and Iron Man. Watson-Guptill Publication 2010 224p il pa $24.99 *

Grades: 9 10 11 12 Adult   **741.5**
 1. Comic books, strips, etc.—Authorship 2. Drawing—Technique
 ISBN 978-0-8230-0083-8   LC 2010-5781

The author "includes chapters on creating comics with computer programs and online resources and how to get work in the 21st century. The book begins with a brief history of comics, then focuses on action-adventure style, romance, humor, horror, and Japanese manga. This is the one book anyone interested in drawing comics should own." Libr J

Includes bibliographical references

Lee, Tony, 1970-

Outlaw: the legend of Robin Hood; a graphic novel; written by Tony Lee; illustrated by Sam Hart; colored by Artur Fujita. Candlewick Press 2009 unp il $21.99; pa $11.99 *

Grades: 7 8 9 10 11 12   **741.5**
 1. Graphic novels 2. Adventure graphic novels 3. Robin Hood (Fictional character) 4. Great Britain—History—1154-1399, Plantagenets—Graphic novels
 ISBN   978-0-7636-4399-7;   0-7636-4399-8; 978-0-7636-4400-0 (pa); 0-7636-4400-5 (pa)
                                  LC 2008-943331

In this retelling of the Robin Hood legend, it's the year 1192, and Robin of Loxley has returned home from the Crusades after receiving news of his father's death. The Sheriff of Nottingham and Sir Guy of Gisburn govern Nottingham at the pleasure of Prince John. When Gisburn treacherously stabs Robin in a murder attempt, Robin escapes to Sherwood Forest, where the outlaws befriend him. With the help of such men as Little John and Friar Tuck, he organizes the outlaws and they start hurting Prince John where it matters–in his moneybags.

"Lee's excellent rendition of the famed selfless hero goes hand-in-hand with Hart's expressive illustrations, featuring lots of closeups and dramatic lighting and a beautiful jewel-toned palette. Teens will get caught up in this exciting page-turner." SLJ

Lehman, Timothy

Manga: masters of the art. HarperCollins/Collins Design 2005 255p il $24.95

Grades: Adult Professional   **741.5**
 1. Graphic novels—Authorship 2. Manga—Authorship
 ISBN 978-0-06-083331-2   LC 2005-930652

This is a practical reference book, a look at how this artwork makes it from concept to reality, and a commentary on the format. The artists featured are: Kia Asamiya (Silent Möbius, Batman: Child of Dreams), CLAMP (Chobits, Tsubasa), Takehiko Inoue (Vagabond, Slam Dunk), Erica Sakurazawa (Between the Sheets, The Aromatic Bitters), Jiro Taniguchi (Icaro, The Walking Man), Yuko Tsuno (Swing Shell), Tatsuya Egawa (Golden Boy, Tokyo University Story), Suehiro Maruo (Mr. Arashi's Amazing Freak Show), Reiko Okano (Onmyoji, Fancy Dance), Mafuyu Hiroki (Apples), Miou Takaya (Crazy Heaven, Map of Sacred Pain), and Usamaru Furuya (Short Cuts, Palepoli). They discuss how they became interested in manga, their first published work, where they get their ideas, the creative process, tips and techniques, artistic influences, the genre itself, and much more. Illustrations and photographs of each artist's most seminal works are accompanied by extensive, explanatory captions. Some of the art depicts nudity, sexual situations, and violence.

Fans "will be fascinated by the behind-the-scenes details and the generous samples from stories that prompt seeking out more." Booklist

Lemire, Jeff

Essex County. Top Shelf Productions 2009 510p il $49.95; pa $29.95 *

Grades: 10 11 12 Adult   **741.5**

1. Graphic novels 2. Orphans—Graphic novels 3. Farm life—Graphic novels 4. Family life—Graphic novels 5. Ontario—Graphic novels

ISBN 978-1-60309-046-9; 978-1-60309-038-4 (pa)

First published 2007-2008 as three separate volumes

Title on verso of title page: Complete Essex County

Contents: Essex County trilogy: Tales from the farm; Ghost stories; The country nurse

Presents the award-winning trilogy of graphic novels set in an imaginary version of the author's hometown, and reveals the problems and issues the families within the community face.

Lewis, A. David, 1977-

The lone and level sands; artists, Marvin Perry Mann and Jennifer Rodgers. 2nd ed. Archaia Studio 2006 147p il pa $17.95

Grades: 9 10 11 12 Adult   **741.5**

1. Bible. O.T. Exodus—Graphic novels 2. Graphic novels 3. Egypt—History—Graphic novels

ISBN 1-932386-12-2

First published 2005 in black and white by Caption Box

Told mostly from the viewpoint of the Pharaoh, this book recounts the well-known story of the Exodus. Moses is portrayed as an old desert rascal, and Ramses II finds himself buffeted on all sides as he contends with a God who speaks through his family and friends and manipulates him to bring about the freedom of the Hebrews.

"The plot moves with inexorable tragedy toward its conclusion, but the book never reads like a catalogue of vignettes about the miseries the Egyptians and Hebrews inflicted on each other. Instead, it is a powerful, moving reconsideration of an otherwise familiar tale. It is guaranteed to provoke." Voice Youth Advocates

Love, Jeremy

Bayou, volume one; created by Jeremy Love; colors by Patrick Morgan. Zuda Comics/DC Comics 2009 unp il pa $14.99 *

Grades: 9 10 11 12 Adult   **741.5**

1. Graphic novels 2. Fantasy graphic novels 3. African Americans—Graphic novels 4. Monsters—Graphic novels 5. United States—History—1933-1945—Graphic novels

ISBN 978-1-4012-2382-3

In a little southern town called Charon in 1933, Lee Wagstaff lives the kind of precarious life that African Americans under Jim Crow laws had to live. She's friends with white Lily Westmoreland, but that friendship doesn't protect her when Lily's mother accuses Lee of theft. Then Lily disappears, victim of a swamp monster, and the town's white men haul her father off to jail, most likely to face a lynching. Lee has to find Lily to save her father, but when she goes to the swamp where Lily disappeared, she falls into a strange land of monsters. There she meets Bayou, a blues-singing swamp monster who helps her, and Lee faces the evil in the strange land to find and save her friend. This book collects the first four chapters of the webcomic by Love, which was one of the first webcomics from Zuda, run by DC Comics. The book includes disturbing images of hanged people, and a white man hits Lee so hard she flies through the air and lands on her back with her face torn up. The "n" word is represented by "n*****" while other harsh language is plainly written. The book contains enough violence to bother squeamish and sensitive readers.

"Extremely beautiful, scary and wonderful, this . . . comic takes readers to a pair of almost familiar, frequently threatening worlds." Publ Wkly

Mashima, Hiro

Fairy tale vol. 1; translated and adapted by William Flanagan; lettered by North Market Street Graphics. Del Rey Manga 2008 202p il pa $10.95

Grades: 8 9 10 11 12   **741.5**

1. Graphic novels 2. Manga 3. Fantasy graphic novels 4. Humorous graphic novels

ISBN 978-0-345-50133-2

Cute girl wizard Lucy wants to join the Fairy Tail, a club for the most powerful wizards (and the most troublesome — they tend to do stuff such as blow up harbors while fighting the bad guys). However, her ambitions land her in the clutches of a gang of unsavory pirates led by a devious magician, who plan to sell her into slavery. Her only hope is Natsu, a strange boy she has met on her travels. Natsu is not the typical hero: he gets motion sickness, eats like a pig, and his best friend is a talking cat. He is a member of the Fairy Tail, however. The book includes some mild fan service (usually cleavage shots), consumption of alcohol, and lots of magical fighting.

Matsumoto, Nina

Yokaiden, volume 1. Del Rey Manga 2008 unp il pa $10.95

Grades: 6 7 8 9 10 11 12   **741.5**

1. Graphic novels 2. Fantasy graphic novels 3. Folklore—Japan—Graphic novels 4. Monsters—Graphic novels

ISBN 978-0-345-50327-5

In what looks like 18th or 19th-century Japan, young Hamachi Uramaki lives with his crotchety old grandmother (his parents died years before); he's obsessed with yokai, Japan's legendary monsters and other supernatural creatures, and he desperately wants to meet one. He does encounter a kappa who fell into a trap, and Hamachi saves the creature he names Madkap. When Hamachi returns home after selling bamboo in town, he finds his grandmother dead and thinks Madkap did it (grandmother had set the kappa trap). He decides to enter the yokai realm to find Madkap and get revenge; but once Hamachi enters, the trick is to survive, for the yokai realm is not meant for humans. This is a global manga story that uses Western page order (left to right). Matsumoto features lesser-known yokai, such as the chochin obake, the paper lantern ghost, and the namahage, an ogre who disciplines naughty children by crippling them for a while. The book includes some violence and mild bad language.

"Matsumoto's manga is silly fun, anchored by a

Matsumoto, Nina—*Continued*

clueless but plucky hero and a dry sense of humor. Taking place in a fantasy setting close to historical Japan, Hamachi's adventures read like lighthearted folktales centered on the wide variety of yokai and the various means of dealing with them." Booklist

McCloud, Scott

Making comics; storytelling secrets of comics, manga, and graphic novels. HarperCollins 2006 264p il pa $22.95 *

Grades: 11 12 Adult   741.5

1. Comic books, strips, etc.—Authorship 2. Graphic novels—Drawing

ISBN 0-06-078094-0; 978-0-06-078094-4

The author "explores practical matters, including comics devices such as panels, word balloons, and sound effects; facial expressions and body language; the creation of convincing and evocative settings; and the different tools artists can use for the job, from pencils to computers. He also delves into the framing of images in panels, the flow of panels on a page, and the relationships between words and pictures in comics. . . . This is thoughtful, fascinating, stimulating, potentially controversial, and inspiring." Libr J

Includes bibliographical references

Reinventing comics; how imagination and technology are revolutionizing an art form. Paradox Press 2000 237p il pa $22.95 *

Grades: 11 12 Adult   741.5

1. Comic books, strips, etc. 2. Cartoons and caricatures

ISBN 0-06-095350-0   LC 00-710457

The author maps out "'12 revolutions', which, he believes, need to take place for comics to survive and finally be recognized as a legitimate art form. The topics progress from the oldest of comic-related arguments (seeking respect) to the use of computer technology to renew and expand its audience. These brilliantly presented discussions concern comics as literature, comics as art, creators' rights, industry innovation, and public perception, among other topics." Libr J

Understanding comics; the invisible art. HarperPerennial 1994 c1993 215p il pa $22.95 *

Grades: 9 10 11 12   741.5

1. Comic books, strips, etc.

ISBN 0-06-097625-X

First published 1993 by Kitchen Sink Press

The author "traces the 3,000-year history (from Egyptian paintings on) of telling stories through pictures; describes the language of comics—its 'grammar' and 'vocabulary'; explains the use of different types of images ranging from ironic to realistic; depicts how artists convey movement and the passage of time and use various symbols as shorthand; and [seeks to demonstrate] the expressive emotional qualities of different drawing styles." Booklist [review of 1993 edition]

Includes bibliographical references

McCreery, Conor

Kill Shakespeare, vol. 1; a sea of troubles; created and written by Conor McCreery and Anthony Del Col; art by Andy Belanger; colors by Ian Herring; lettering by Chris Mowry, Robbie Robbins, and Neil Uyetake. IDW Publishing 2010 unp il pa $19.99

Grades: 10 11 12 Adult   741.5

1. Shakespeare, William, 1564-1616—Graphic novels 2. Graphic novels 3. Fantasy graphic novels 4. Adventure graphic novels

ISBN 978-1-60010-781-8

A shipwrecked Hamlet finds himself in England with Richard III, who wants his help to find and kill the wizard, Will Shakespeare, so that Richard can rule with impunity. Haunted by his father's ghost, who tells Hamlet that killing Shakespeare will let him live again, Hamlet agrees to help the English king. Then he discovers that the Lady Juliet Capulet leads an army of rebellion, aided by Othello and Falstaff. They fight against the corrupt Richard, who consults the witch Hecate (who has her own agenda). Falstaff says that Hamlet is the prophesied Shadow King, who will aid the rebellion, while Richard and his allies only want to use Hamlet to destroy Shakespeare, but all agree that only Hamlet can lead them to the wizard. The book includes bloody action and sexual situations, making this more suited to older teens.

"McCreery and Del Col spin an engrossing action-adventure tale of satisfying complexity, full of mystery, deceit, and gory violence, starring a hero who once again must marshal his determination and decide his path." Libr J

Mechner, Jordan, 1964-

Solomon's thieves; artwork by LeUyen Pham & Alex Puvilland. First Second 2010 139p il pa $12.99

Grades: 6 7 8 9 10   741.5

1. Knights and knighthood—Graphic novels 2. France—History—0-1328—Graphic novels 3. Middle Ages—Graphic novels 4. Graphic novels

ISBN 978-1-59643-391-5; 1-59643-391-4

LC 2010-282641

Life as a Templar Knight returning from the Crusades is dull— bread, beans, and lots and lots of walking. But after Martin stumbles upon his lost love (now married— to someone else), things begin to get more interesting very quickly. There's a vast conspiracy afoot to destroy the Templar Order and steal their treasure. Soon, Martin finds himself one of the only Templars out of prison— and out for revenge!

"Pham and Puvilland . . . are again in top form, balancing grainy, hatched textures and clean spaces to lend a weighty historical feel as a vibrant sense of kineticism brings the action sequences to life." Booklist

Includes bibliographical references

Medley, Linda

Castle waiting. Fantagraphics 2006 456p il $29.95 *

Grades: 5 6 7 8 9 10 11 12   741.5

Medley, Linda—*Continued*
1. Graphic novels 2. Fairy tales—Graphic novels
3. Fantasy graphic novels
ISBN 1-56097-747-7

All of Medley's previously self-published comics are collected here in one volume for the first time. The titular castle was the home of Sleeping Beauty, whose story is retold from the viewpoint of the flibbertigibbet ladies in waiting. After the flighty princess awakens with the kiss of a handsome but not too bright prince, the castle becomes a sanctuary for various misfits. Readers will find references to many fairy tales, folk tales, and nursery rhymes in Medley's book, and her clean, clear black-and-white art reflects the works of classic illustrators such as Arthur Rackham.

Miller, Frank, 1957-
Batman: the Dark Knight strikes again; [by] Frank Miller, Lynn Varley, Todd Klein, Batman created by Bob Kane. DC Comics 2002 247p il hardcover o.p. pa $19.99
Grades: 10 11 12 Adult   **741.5**
1. Batman (Comic strip) 2. Graphic novels
3. Superhero graphic novels
ISBN 1-56389-844-6; 1-56389-929-9 (pa)
              LC 2003-544916

Sequel to Batman: the Dark Knight returns (1986)
"Originally published in single magazine form as Batman: the Dark Knight strikes again 1-3." p [8]
Based on Batman comic strip
"Batman leads the opposition in a dystopian near-future when security concerns have spurred a repressive crackdown. Other costumed heroes side with either the government or Batman. . . . The book's authoritarian society resonates with the post-9/11 environment, though Miller's cheekiness dispels notions that this is serious commentary." Booklist

Miller, Steve
Scared!: how to draw fantastic horror comic characters; [by] Steve Miller and Bryan Baugh. Watson-Guptill Publications 2004 144p il pa $19.95
Grades: 9 10 11 12   **741.5**
1. Monsters in art 2. Cartoons and caricatures
3. Drawing 4. Comic books, strips, etc.
ISBN 0-8230-1664-1   LC 2004-112245

This book "begins with a brief history of horror comics (mostly in the U.S.), profiles of some popular illustrators, useful tips on drawing for the genre (creating 'creepy characters,' for example), and advice on references and resources. The bulk of the book is dedicated to straightforward how-to, with illustrations for a gallery of ghouls showing each character broken down into basic shapes. The approach is especially suited to YA artists just developing an interest in how comics are drawn." Booklist

Miyuki, Takahashi
Musashi #9, Vol. 1; [translation and adaptation by Tony Ogasawara] CMX Manga 2005 206p il pa $9.95
Grades: 9 10 11 12 Adult   **741.5**

1. Graphic novels 2. Manga 3. Adventure graphic novels 4. Spies—Graphic novels
ISBN 1-4012-0540-2

Musashi #9 is the code name for one of the top operatives of ultimate Blue, a secret organization operating independently of any government, whose goal is to maintain world peace. A teenager who displays incredible martial arts skills, wields weapons with aplomb, moves with stealth, and uses disguises, Musashi #9 protects tough teen girl Yayoi when assassins come after her, helps an ex-FBI agent save his kidnapped sister, protects a Russian scientist and his son from spies, and helps two teen boys who stumble upon terrorists targeting the Russian president. The reader discovers, along with Yayoi, that Musashi #9 is actually a girl who usually disguises herself as a boy. This is the first volume of an ongoing manga series. There's lots of action, but minimal graphic depictions of violence and little in the way of harsh language or adult content.

Modern Masters volume twenty-five: Jeff Smith. Twomorrows Publishing 2011 117p il pa $15.95
Grades: 6 7 8 9 10 11 12 Adult   **741.5**
1. Smith, Jeff 2. Graphic novels—History and criticism 3. Comic books, strips, etc.—History and criticism
ISBN 978-1-60549-024-3

This volume in the Modern Masters series focuses on Jeff Smith, creator of Bone. In an interview that covers his childhood, college career, and early work before becoming a cartoonist, Smith talks about how he created Fone Bone when he was just five years old. The artwork in the book includes young Smith's hand-created comics from his childhood. Only a couple of "crap"s slip out. The book includes mostly black and white art and photographs, with a few color illustrations from the Bone comics.

Moore, Alan
Watchmen; Alan Moore, writer; Dave Gibbons, illustrator/letterer; John Higgins, colorist. DC Comics 2005 various paging il $75; pa $19.99
Grades: 11 12 Adult   **741.5**
1. Graphic novels 2. Superhero graphic novels
ISBN 1-4012-0713-8; 978-0-930289-23-2 (pa)

"Originally published in single magazine form as Watchmen 1-12"—verso of title page; trade paperback edition still available

Issued in slipcase. Awards: 1988 Eisner Award for Best Finite Series, Best Graphic Album, Best Writer, Best Writer/Artist; 1988 Hugo Award for Other Forms; 2005 listed in Time Magazine's 100 Greatest English Language Novels; 2006 Eisner Award to Watchmen Absolute Edition for Best Archival Collection, Comic Books

This graphic novel "begins with the paranoid delusions of a half-insane hero called Rorschach. But is Rorschach really insane or has he in fact uncovered a plot to murder super-heroes and, even worse, millions of innocent civilians? On the run from the law, Rorschach reunites with his former teammates in a desperate attempt to save the world and their lives." Publisher's note

"Nearly 20 years after the original publication, 'Watchmen' shows an eerie prescience: the symmetry between current events and the conclusion of its story, concerning a villain who believes he can stave off real war

Moore, Alan—*Continued*

by distracting the populace with a trumped-up one, and an act of mass murder perpetrated in the heart of New York City, is almost too fearful to bear." N Y Times Book Rev

Morrison, Grant

All-Star Superman, Volume One; written by Grant Morrison; pencilled by Frank Quitely. DC Comics 2007 160p il hardcover o.p. pa $12.99

Grades: 8 9 10 11 12 Adult   **741.5**
   1. Graphic novels 2. Superhero graphic novels 3. Superman (Fictional character)
   ISBN 978-1-4012-0914-8; 978-1-4012-1102-8 (pa)

Originally published as All-Star Superman issues #1-6

Writer Morrison and artist Quitely present several episodes in the life of the iconic superhero, Superman. When he saves a group of scientists from burning up in the sun, what no one realizes is that uber-villain Lex Luthor set up everything in order to kill Superman, who absorbed so much solar radiation that it is now slowly killing him. Once Superman learns that he is dying, he sets out to give Lois Lane a birthday she will never forget, by giving her his powers for one day. Then, when Jimmy Olsen takes charge of the science think tank P.R.O.J.E.C.T. for one day, they discover black kryptonite, which makes Superman turn evil. And, in his guise as Clark Kent, he interviews Lex Luthor in prison, but super-villain Parasite is taken from his shielded cell and begins to absorb Superman's powers, causing chaos.

Morse, Scott

The barefoot serpent. Top Shelf Productions 2003 128p il pa $14.95

Grades: 7 8 9 10 11 12   **741.5**
   1. Kurosawa, Akira, 1910-1998—Graphic novels 2. Graphic novels 3. Bereavement—Graphic novels 4. Hawaii—Graphic novels
   ISBN 1-891830-37-6

"A little girl journeys to Hawaii with her parents after her older brother's death. There she meets a little-boy wheeler-dealer and tags along as he hustles a mask he has carved and plays in sand and surf. Rejoining her father, she infects him with her restored spirits; the family flies home refreshed. Sandwiching that story is a child's-picture-book-like sketch of Japanese filmmaker Akira Kurosawa." Booklist

Morvan, Jean David, 1969-

Classics illustrated deluxe #6: the three Musketeers; [by] Alexandre Dumas; adapted by Jean David Morvan, Michel Dufranne, Rubèn, and Marie Galopin. Papercutz 2011 unp il $21.99; pa $16.99

Grades: 5 6 7 8 9 10 11 12 Adult   **741.5**
   1. Dumas, Alexandre, 1802-1870—Adaptations 2. Graphic novels 3. France—History—1589-1789, Bourbons—Graphic novels 4. Adventure graphic novels
   ISBN 978-1-59707-253-3; 978-1-59707-252-6 (pa)

This book is a 70th Anniversary Edition of Classics Illustrated

In seventeenth-century France, young D'Artagnan initially quarrels with, then befriends, three musketeers and joins them in trying to outwit the enemies of the king and queen. This adaptation is suitable for many readers from age ten and up, but parents, teachers, and librarians might want to consider the visual depictions of sexual tensions and situations that might go over most young readers' heads in prose (there are some heaving bosoms, perspiring men, and a couple of scenes in bed), and the violence (most of it occurs off-panel). The book's endpapers include Dumas' introduction to his novel, an Epilogue, a brief biography of Dumas, and an illustrated character guide.

Nagatomo, Haruno

Draw your own Manga; beyond the basics; translated by Françoise White. Kodansha International 2005 111p il pa $19.95 *

Grades: 7 8 9 10 11 12   **741.5**
   1. Graphic novels—Drawing 2. Manga—Drawing
   ISBN 4-7700-2304-9; 978-4-7700-2304-9

Also available: Draw your own Manga; all the basics (2003)

"This advanced manual looks at how to enhance manga with a range of special effects as well as how to use various types of color ink, markers, and airbrushes to reach more creative levels. Supplemented by an interview with the immensely popular Japanese sports manga artist Shinji Mizushima, this book is recommended for any cartoon or animation library." Libr J

Nakahara, Aya

Love*Com Vol. 1; story and art by Aya Nakahara; [translation & English adaptation, Pookie Rolf] Viz Media/Shojo Beat 2007 unp il pa $8.99

Grades: 8 9 10 11 12   **741.5**
   1. Graphic novels 2. Manga 3. Shojo manga 4. Romance graphic novels 5. Humorous graphic novels
   ISBN 978-1-4215-1343-0

First published 2001 in Japan

Risa Koizumi is the tallest girl in class, and the last thing she wants is the humiliation of standing next to Atsushi Otoni, the shortest guy. Fate and the whole school have other ideas, and the two find themselves cast as the unwilling stars of a bizarre romantic comedy duo. Rather than bow to the inevitable, Risa and Atsushi join forces to pursue their true objects of affection. But in the quest for love, will their budding friendship become something more complex?

Nakazawa, Keiji, 1939-

Barefoot Gen volume five: the never-ending war; translated by Project Gen. Last Gasp of San Francisco 2008 268p il pa $14.95

Grades: 9 10 11 12 Adult   **741.5**
   1. Graphic novels 2. Manga 3. Japan—History—1945-1952, Allied Occupation—Graphic novels
   ISBN 978-0-8671-9596-5

A couple of years after WWII ended, life in Hiroshima is slowly recovering, but things are still terribly diffi-

Nakazawa, Keiji, 1939-—*Continued*

cult for people. Gen is in school, but the classes are overcrowded, there are few supplies and little furniture. People are still going hungry, and young orphans, toughened by their experiences, have banded together into gangs and engage in criminal activity just to stay alive. Gen's friend Ryuta is in one such gang, and Gen joins them. When his mother becomes ill, he learns that the Americans are treating the bomb survivors as experimental specimens and decides to get even. This volume includes some harsh language (including several uses of the s-bomb), and violence as Gen and his friends fight against others, especially bullies and adult criminals who try to use them. Since the book was originally published in Japan during the early 1970s, the black and white art may look dated to teens who read contemporary manga. Teachers and schools may want to read through the book first, but the book should be suitable for older high school grades, especially if classes study WWII.

"Nakazawa was a real-life Hiroshima survivor, and his experiences give this manga classic . . . a powerful kick." Publ Wkly

Barefoot Gen volume six: writing the truth; translated by Project Gen. Last Gasp of San Francisco 2008 266p il pa $14.95

Grades: 9 10 11 12 Adult   **741.5**
1. Graphic novels 2. Manga 3. Japan—History—1945-1952, Allied Occupation—Graphic novels
ISBN 978-0-8671-9597-2

Gen and his friends are still trying to survive in postwar Hiroshima. Black marketeers profit from dealing with crooked Americans, and shifty politicians who actively promoted the war and criticized anyone who dissented are now claiming to want only peace. When Gen's mother gets worse, Ryuta robs a criminal gang for money to put her in the hospital, then he has to find a way to stay safe from the gangsters. And Gen continues to try to help others, even as younger brother Akira resents him for always "being out" and never home to help him. The book includes some harsh language (including very occasional use of the s-bomb) and some violence.

Novgorodoff, Danica

Slow storm. First Second 2008 172p il pa $17.95

Grades: 9 10 11 12   **741.5**
1. Graphic novels 2. Immigrants—Graphic novels
ISBN 978-1-5964-3250-5; 1-5964-3250-0
           LC 2007-46202

"This is the tale of young firefighter Ursa, who weathers family and work trouble until a young Mexican, on the run from the police, winds up in her fire engine." Booklist

"Novgorodoff writes a very literate and rich graphic novel. The illustrations are masterfully done and often wordlessly tell the story as well as convey the mood." Voice Youth Advocates

Nowak, Naomi, 1984-

Unholy kinship. NBM 2006 unp il pa $9.95

Grades: 10 11 12 Adult   **741.5**

1. Graphic novels 2. Sisters—Graphic novels 3. Mental illness—Graphic novels 4. Dreams—Graphic novels
ISBN 1-56163-482-4

Young college student Luca has taken care of her mentally unstable older sister Gae ever since their single mother became a permanent resident of St. Mark's Asylum for the Demented. As the fall term starts, Luca starts having strange dreams as Gae begins to deteriorate emotionally. The doctors and nurses from St. Mark's Asylum claim they want to help Gae, but their drugs make things worse. And the dreams become stranger, until Luca can't be sure what is real. The cool tones of the artwork underscore the building sense of doom as the story progresses.

O, Se-Yong, 1955-

Buja's diary. NBM 2005 280p il pa $19.95

Grades: 11 12 Adult   **741.5**
1. Graphic novels 2. Korea (South)—Graphic novels
ISBN 1-56163-448-4; 978-1-56163-448-4
           LC 2005-50519

The thirteen "stories by this Korean 'manwha' (comic book) author relate poignant tales of distressed humanity struggling with family, history, and culture. . . . Although O's eye is not unsympathetic, the world he depicts is unforgiving, sometimes graphically so. . . . Originally published in 1995, this book is a thoughtful examination of the human condition in the Korea of the recent past as well as universally." Voice Youth Advocates

Obata, Yuki

We were there, vol. 1; story & art by Yuki Obata. Viz Media/Shojo Beat 2008 unp il pa $8.99 *

Grades: 10 11 12   **741.5**
1. Graphic novels 2. Manga 3. Shojo manga 4. Romance graphic novels
ISBN 978-1-4215-2018-6
Original Japanese edition, 2002

Fifteen-year-old Nanami Takahashi has just started high school, with high hopes for making friends and doing well, but things don't go as smoothly as she had hoped. She struggles with math, then she gets sort of railroaded into being the class president. She also falls for Motoharu Yano, an irresponsible boy who somehow is the most popular person in the class. His carefree attitude covers his grief for the death of his girlfriend, an older girl whose younger sister is their classmate, Yuri Yamamoto. Nanami struggles with classwork, with the responsibilities of being class president, and with her conflicting feelings about Motoharu. Some of the black and white art looks airbrushed; these pages occur at the beginning of each chapter. Viz has rated this series for older teens due to sexual themes, but they don't occur in this first volume.

Okabayashi, Kensuke

Manga for dummies. Wiley Publishing, Inc. 2007 416p il (--For dummies) pa $19.99

Grades: 9 10 11 12 Adult   **741.5**
1. Graphic novels—Drawing 2. Manga
ISBN 978-0-470-08025-2   LC 2006-939589

Okabayashi, Kensuke—*Continued*

This guide, written and illustrated by Okabayashi, who teaches art at the Educational Alliance Art School in New York City and who has interned with manga creators in Japan, shows aspiring manga artists how to create characters, how to draw weapons, cars, animals, and more, how to create plotlines and storyboards, how to convey motion and emotion, and more.

O'Neil, Dennis, 1939-

The DC comics guide to writing comics; introduction by Stan Lee. Watson-Guptill 2001 128p il $19.95 *

Grades: 11 12 Adult   741.5

1. Comic books, strips, etc.—Authorship
ISBN 0-8230-1027-9   LC 2001-26101

The author "discusses story structure, characterization, script preparation, and other general writing topics. He also covers those more specific to comics writing such as miniseries, maxiseries, and continuity. O'Neil addresses the visual component of the art, the importance of page layout, and the relationship between the writer and the artist." SLJ

"O'Neil addresses the universals of writing in a way that makes the book useful to all aspiring scripters, regardless of their knowledge of comics." Booklist

Ono, Natsume, 1977-

Gente: the people of Ristorante Paradiso, volume 1; story and art by Natsume Ono; translation Joe Yamazaki. Viz Signature 2010 unp il pa $12.99

Grades: 10 11 12 Adult   741.5

1. Graphic novels 2. Manga 3. Josei manga 4. Restaurants—Graphic novels 5. Family—Graphic novels
ISBN 978-1-4215-3251-6

First volume of an ongoing series

In this companion and prequel to Ono's Ristorante Paradiso, readers meet the various handsome, mature, bespectacled men who staff Casetta dell'Orso, a popular restaurant in Rome. The stories in this volume include how Lorenzo, the owner, decides to choose the type of men that his wife Olga finds attractive; how cranky Luciano tries to hide his kind heart even as he babysits his young grandson; how playboy Vito meets a lonely college student at a health club; and more. Ono's somewhat sketchy art style is vastly different from the typical manga, more European than Japanese. While this is rated for Older Teens by the publisher, there is no content to raise any concerns, but its gentle, quiet stories focused on adults may appeal more to older teens and adults.

Pilcher, Tim

The essential guide to world comics; [by] Tim Pilcher, Brad Brooks. Collins & Brown, Distributed in the U.S. by Sterling 2005 319p il pa $19.95 *

Grades: 11 12 Adult   741.5

1. Comic books, strips, etc.
ISBN 1-84340-300-5

The authors "examine the cultural impact of comics in over 20 countries, from Japan—where popular titles sell 6.5 million copies per week—to France, where comics are considered an art form on par with music and poetry." Publisher's note

"A stunning eye-opener to the comics medium's variety." Booklist

Powell, Nate, 1978-

Swallow me whole. Top Shelf Productions 2008 unp il pa $20.95 *

Grades: 10 11 12 Adult   741.5

1. Graphic novels 2. Mental illness—Graphic novels
ISBN 978-1-60309-033-9

Stepsiblings Ruth and Perry share their secrets with each other; Ruth hears insects talking to her, and Perry has to deal with a tiny wizard who forces him to draw all the time. In high school, Ruth is diagnosed as an obsessive compulsive with schizophrenic tendencies, while Perry manages to hide his wizard. Ruth sees cicadas and other insects always surrounding her, to the point that she thinks she's completely covered with them and she can fly. Her Memaw (grandmother) warns her that what she sees can swallow her whole. This book includes considerable use of foul language, especially the f-bomb, and the story takes a very thoughtful, mature reader to comprehend what is happening.

Pyle, Kevin C.

Katman. Henry Holt and Co. 2009 unp il pa $12.99

Grades: 7 8 9 10 11 12   741.5

1. Graphic novels 2. Cats—Graphic novels 3. Friendship—Graphic novels
ISBN 978-0-8050-8285-2; 0-8050-8285-9
                                    LC 2008-937398

Kit is a bored sixteen-year-old with nothing to do one summer when he starts feeding stray cats. He loves it when cool, artistic Jess helps him out, even though he has to endure constant taunting by her disaffected metalhead friends. They make fun of him for being like the local cat lady, but Kit doesn't care—especially after Jess draws him an anime-style avatar named Katman.

"Beautifully simple and straightforward." Voice Youth Advocates

Raicht, Mike

The stuff of legend, book 1; the dark; by Mike Raicht & Brian Smith; illustrated by Charles Paul Wilson III; design & color by Jon Conkling & Michael DeVito. Villard Books 2010 unp il pa $13

Grades: 8 9 10 11 12 Adult   741.5

1. Graphic novels 2. Adventure graphic novels 3. Toys—Graphic novels 4. Fantasy graphic novels
ISBN 978-0-345-52100-2

In 1944, the Boogeyman snatches a boy from his Brooklyn bedroom and drags him into the Dark. Faithful toys including toy soldier The Colonel, Harmony the dancer, Percy the piggy bank, Jester the jack-in-the-box, Princess the Indian girl, Quackers the wooden duck, and Max the teddy bear, along with the boy's dog Scout, venture into the Dark on a rescue mission. When they cross over, the toys come alive and real, but the mission is fraught with danger; the Dark is filled with the bitter,

Raicht, Mike—*Continued*

lost and forgotten toys of the boy's past, and they serve the Master who wants to destroy the boy. The story includes violence and fighting, and one shocking death that makes this sepia-toned book more suitable for older readers.

"Wilson renders the harrowing closet netherworld with full-fleshed detailing and sepia tones that nail both the 1940s time frame and the classicism of children's stories. But don't mistake this for a kids' comic—the violence is often explicit, and the Boogeyman creepy enough to slither his way right back onto grownups' most-terrifying lists." Booklist

Raven, Nicky

Bram Stoker's Dracula; adapted by Nicky Raven; illustrated by Anne Yvonne Gilbert. Candlewick Press 2010 96p il $19.99

Grades: 7 8 9 10   741.5
1. Stoker, Bram, 1847-1912—Adaptations 2. Graphic novels 3. Vampires—Graphic novels 4. Horror graphic novels
ISBN 978-0-7636-4793-3; 0-7636-4793-4
                                        LC 2009-22116

A modern, illustrated retelling of the Bram Stoker classic, in which young Jonathan Harker first meets and then must destroy the vampire, Count Dracula, in order to save those closest to him.

Raven "successfully abridges a vaunted classic. . . . Raven does a great job fleshing out characters that even in Stoker's original felt bloodless. . . . Gilbert's gothic drawings, the crosshatches of which often conceal layers of spooky elements, are a perfect fit for the somber tone." Booklist

Roman, Dave

Agnes Quill; an anthology of mystery; all transcripts written by Dave Roman; illustrated by Jason Ho, Raina Telgemeier, Jeff Zornow and Dave Roman. SLG Publishing 2006 130p il pa $10.95

Grades: 7 8 9 10 11 12   741.5
1. Graphic novels 2. Mystery graphic novels 3. Horror graphic novels
ISBN 978-1-59362-052-3

Orphaned teen Agnes Quill lives in the city of Legerdemain and carries on a family tradition; she can see and communicate with ghosts, and she works as a detective to help them. Her cases range from recovering the mummified head of a ghost's old body in order to save the valuable necklace hidden there, to helping a little girl ghost find her doll, to helping a man find his legs, and more. Roman works with artists including Raina Telgemeier, and their styles range from childlike cartoons to gloomy, atmospheric art full of shadows.

"The variety of drawing styles and Agnes' story of being a teenage detective who can see the dead among the living combine in an interesting read that will likely keep readers' attention." Voice Youth Advocates

Sable, Mark

Grounded, Vol. 1: Powerless; writer/creator, Mark Sable; artist, Paul Azaceta. Image Comics 2006 160p il pa $14.99

Grades: 10 11 12 Adult   741.5
1. Graphic novels 2. Superhero graphic novels 3. High school students—Graphic novels 4. School stories—Graphic novels
ISBN 978-1-58240-641-1

Originally published as a comics miniseries

Ever since he was a little boy, Jonathan just knew that superheroes are real, and that he would eventually come into his power. Now he's in high school, and he has just discovered that he was right all along superheroes are real. In fact, his parents are two of the most famous heroes in the world. Disillusionment sets in when he catches his father in bed with another woman. He also has to face the fact that he has no powers at all, which doesn't help when his parents put him into a school for the children of heroes; he's the only one who doesn't have any. Even as he deals with bullying and nasty pranks, he learns that there's a dark side to the powers.

Sakai, Stan

Usagi Yojimbo, book one. Fantagraphics Books 1999 144p il pa $15.95

Grades: 7 8 9 10 11 12   741.5
1. Graphic novels 2. Adventure graphic novels 3. Rabbits—Graphic novels 4. Samurai—Graphic novels 5. Japan—Graphic novels 6. Usagi Yojimbo (Fictional character)
ISBN 0-930193-35-0; 978-0-930193-35-5
                                        LC 93-239124

First published 1987

Vol. 1 of an ongoing series; Vols. 1-7 published by Fantagraphics; Vols. 8-25 published by Dark Horse Comics

This series contains the adventures of Miyamoto Usagi, a ronin samurai rabbit in 17th-century Japan.

Usagi Yojimbo: Yokai; created, written, and illustrated by Stan Sakai. Dark Horse Books 2009 62p il pa $14.95

Grades: 6 7 8 9 10 11 12 Adult   741.5
1. Graphic novels 2. Adventure graphic novels 3. Monsters—Graphic novels 4. Japan—Graphic novels 5. Samurai—Graphic novels 6. Usagi Yojimbo (Fictional character)
ISBN 978-1-59582-362-5   LC 2009-20024

As he walks through a spooky forest at night, samurai rabbit Usagi Yojimbo encounters a woman who begs him to find her daughter, who was kidnapped and dragged into the forest. That night, the yokai—monsters, demons, and spirits from Japanese folklore—are amassing for a once-a-century attempt to take over the living world. Armed only with his swords and his wit, Usagi can't hope to win against so many supernatural beings, but luckily Sasuke the Demon Queller has come, knowing about the yokais' plan, and together they fight the gathered monsters. The fighting is not graphic or bloody, and the monsters and demons aren't too scary looking for most younger readers.

"Sakai's art deftly demonstrates that comics can be simultaneously cartoony and scary. . . . Usagi Yojimbo is a genuine pleasure for readers of all ages." Publ Wkly

Sala, Richard

Cat burglar black. First Second 2009 126p il pa $16.99

Grades: 5 6 7 8 9 10 **741.5**
1. Graphic novels 2. Orphans—Graphic novels 3. Mystery graphic novels
ISBN 978-1-59643-144-7; 1-59643-144-X

K.'s aunt, who works at the Bellsong Academy for Girls, has invited K. to attend the school. But as soon as she arrives, K. notices some strange goings-on: her aunt has suddenly taken ill; there are only three other students and no regular classes; and a statue speaks to K. when no one else is around.

"The story is structured like a lighthearted cross between a fable and a horror film, but only ever teetering on the edge of horror without depicting it. This could have resulted in a mishmash, but Sala elegantly dances through the creepy and the sweet." SLJ

Schweizer, Chris, 1980-

Crogan's vengeance; book design by Keith Wood; edited by James Lucas Jones with Jill Beaton. Oni Press 2008 185p il pa $14.95 *

Grades: 8 9 10 11 12 Adult **741.5**
1. Graphic novels 2. Adventure graphic novels 3. Pirates—Graphic novels
ISBN 978-1-934964-06-4
Part of the Crogan Adventures series

Catfoot Crogan serves as an honest and honorable sailor on a ship commanded by an unjust captain when the ship is taken over by pirates. In order to save their lives, the sailors all take the oath to become pirates, but Crogan immediately runs afoul of D'Or, a brutal man who enjoys torturing others. Catfoot is a pirate, but he's determined to remain as honest and honorable as he can be, which continually puts him in danger. This swashbuckling tale shows a less romantic story than Rafael Sabatini's *Captain Blood*, with more violence, but it is more action-oriented than merely violent.

"Filled with mutiny, ferocious storms, shark-infested waters, commandeering of ships, and—of course—swashbuckling sword fights, this book has high teen appeal." SLJ

Secret identities; the Asian American superhero anthology. [edited by] Jeff Yang . . . [et al.] New Press 2009 194p il pa $21.95 *

Grades: 9 10 11 12 Adult **741.5**
1. Graphic novels 2. Asian Americans—Graphic novels 3. Superhero graphic novels
ISBN 978-1-59558-398-7 LC 2009-1536

Yang, Shen, Chow, and coeditor Jerry Ma have put together a collection of twenty-six stories by Asian American creators about Asian American superheroes. The book is divided into sections: War and Remembrance, Many Masks, When Worlds Collide, Girl Power, Ordinary Heroes, and From Headline to Hero. The Preface, the Prologue, all section introductions, and the Epilogue, are all done in comic book format. Creators include Gene Luen Yang, Greg Pak, Dustin Nguyen, Kazu Kibuishi, Cliff Chiang, Christine Norrie, and many more. Some stories deal with the Nisei soldiers of the 100th Battalion/442nd Regimental Combat Team during World War II, others confront the idea that the Asian character

can only be the sidekick, still others explore the stereotypical attitudes of some Americans toward Asian Americans. The book includes some violence and some harsh language.

Sfar, Joann

The professor's daughter; [story by] Joann Sfar & [illustrated by] Emmanuel Guibert; translated by Alexis Siegel. First Second Books 2007 63p il pa $16.95

Grades: 7 8 9 10 11 12 Adult **741.5**
1. Graphic novels 2. Humorous graphic novels 3. Romance graphic novels 4. Mummies—Graphic novels
ISBN 978-1-59643-130-0; 1-59643-130-X
LC 2006-22177

In Victorian London, Lillian, the daughter of a famed archeologist, has fallen in love with the mummy of Imhotep IV; he thinks that Lillian bears a strong resemblance to this long-dead wife. Their love faces many obstacles, from Lillian's father, the police, a pirate who is actually Imhotep III (yes, the father and another mummy), even Queen Victoria herself. Dainty Victorian manners mix with broad farce and black comedy in a beautifully illustrated book with muted colors and sepia tones.

The rabbi's cat. Pantheon Books 2005 142p il $21.95; pa $16.95

Grades: 11 12 Adult **741.5**
1. Graphic novels 2. Jews—Graphic novels 3. Rabbis—Graphic novels 4. France—History—1914-1940—Graphic novels 5. North Africa—Graphic novels
ISBN 0-375-42281-1; 0-375-71464-2 (pa)
LC 2004-61406

"A slinky gray cat lives with a rabbi and his beautiful young daughter. One day, the feline eats their parrot, only to find that he has gained the bird's ability to talk. Witty and highly intelligent, the cat immediately decides that he wants to learn more about Judaism, from the Kabbalah to the Torah. . . . There is plenty for teens to like—humor, romance, and theological questioning combined with a folkloric quality to bring to life a multifaceted work." SLJ

Shanower, Eric

A thousand ships. Image Comics 2001 223p il (Age of bronze) hardcover o.p. pa $19.95

Grades: 10 11 12 **741.5**
1. Trojan War—Graphic novels 2. Graphic novels 3. Greek mythology—Graphic novels
ISBN 1-58240-212-4; 1-58240-200-0 (pa)

This is "the first part of a seven-volume graphic novel about the Trojan War. . . . The book begins with the story of Paris, the milk-white bull and the kidnapping of Helen, and goes up to the start of the war." Publ Wkly

"This series retells the story of the Trojan War, going back to the young Trojan prince Paris and the petty rivalry of several goddesses that set the events into motion. Shanower conducted extensive reasearch of the world of that time—its technology, architecture, clothing, armor, and weapons. His books are more 'real' than any Hollywood movie depiction." Voice Youth Advocates

Shanower includes frank sex scenes and doesn't shy away from the brutal violence of war.

Shanower, Eric—*Continued*
Other books in the Age of Bronze series include:
Betrayal (2008)
Sacrifice (2004)
Includes bibliographical references

Siddell, Thomas
Gunnerkrigg Court: orientation; [by] Tom
Siddell. Archaia Studios Press 2009 296p il $26.95
Grades: 6 7 8 9 10 11 12   **741.5**
1. Graphic novels 2. Fantasy graphic novels
ISBN 978-1-932386-34-9; 1-932386-34-3
"The first 14 chapters of Siddell's popular webcomic
are collected here in an alluring hardcover. The premise,
best described as science-fantasy, involves a young girl
named Antimony plopped into a strange boarding-
school/industrial-complex which . . . she knows nothing
about. Discrete chapters . . . all feature varying levels of
jaw-dropping peculiarity, devilish bursts of humor, and
sublime creativity that lurk at the ends of the school's
corridors. The darkly hued artwork is deceptively simplistic and displays a flair for the crucial details of setting and atmosphere." Booklist

Sizer, Paul
Moped army, Vol. 1. Cafe Digital Comics 2005
136p il pa $12.95
Grades: 10 11 12 Adult   **741.5**
1. Graphic novels 2. Science fiction graphic novels
ISBN 0-9768565-4-9; 978-0-9768565-4-2
This graphic novel is set in the same universe as Little
White Mouse (2005). "Feeling unsatisfied with her cir-
cumscribed life and rich, cruel boyfriend, a privileged
teenaged girl runs away to the lower city where the poor
dwell, finding a home and a new 'family' among the
young rebels who call themselves the Moped Army.
Even readers who don't like science fiction will enjoy
this story that depends on strong characterization." Voice
Youth Advocates

Slate, Barbara
You can do a graphic novel. Alpha Books 2010
187p il pa $19.95
Grades: 7 8 9 10   **741.5**
1. Graphic novels—Authorship
ISBN 978-1-59257-955-6; 1-59257-955-8
                LC 2009-930703
"This is a practical book for those who aspire to
create their own graphic novels. Slate . . . is fair handed
with the advice she gives to writers as well as artists.
. . . The instructions and illustrations are easy to follow,
and the format is colorful and eye-catching." SLJ

Stassen, Jean-Philippe
Deogratias; a tale of Rwanda; [by] Stassen;
translated by Alex Siegel. Roaring Brook 2006
79p il pa $17.95
Grades: 11 12 Adult   **741.5**
1. Graphic novels 2. Rwanda—Graphic novels
3. Genocide—Graphic novels
ISBN 1-59643-103-2; 978-1-59643-103-4
                LC 2005-17576

In this "fictionalized account of the Rwandan genocide, readers meet Deogratias, a teenaged Hutu. His
friends Benina and Apollinaria are Tutsi—a race that is
being ethnically cleansed by Hutu extremists. As the
conflict escalates, Deogratias witnesses murders and is
forced to become involved in brutal acts of violence. He
suffers a mental breakdown. The story is told through a
series of flashbacks while he skates the line between rational and insane. Stassen spares his readers none of the
brutality and visceral cruelties of this atrocity. Scenes of
rape, harsh language, and some sexual content solidly
designate this book for a mature audience. . . . A masterful work with vibrant, confident art, this book will
stay with and haunt its readers." SLJ

Stolarz, Laurie Faria, 1972-
Black is for beginnings; adaptation by Barbara
Randall Kesel; artwork by Janina Gørrissen.
Llewellyn Publications/Flux 2009 160p il pa $9.95
Grades: 8 9 10 11 12   **741.5**
1. Graphic novels 2. Romance graphic novels
3. Supernatural graphic novels 4. Dreams—Graphic
novels
ISBN 978-0-7387-1438-7; 0-7387-1438-0
When Stacey, a college student and hereditary witch,
again begins to have disturbing dreams about her former
boyfriend and a little girl who was murdered years earlier, she knows that the dreams are trying to tell her something important, but she does not know what
"The story's weirdo flashes of humor make the darkness bearable, as do the everyday settings of a pizza parlor and dorm room. A unique and somewhat unhinged
blend of realism and fantasy." Booklist

Sturm, James, 1965-
James Sturm's America; God, gold, and golems.
Drawn & Quarterly 2007 192p il $24.95
Grades: 10 11 12 Adult   **741.5**
1. Graphic novels 2. United States—History—Graphic
novels 3. Gold mines and mining—Graphic novels
4. Baseball—Graphic novels 5. Revivals—Graphic
novels
ISBN 978-1-897299-05-0
This book compiles three of Sturm's stories that are
set in quieter periods of American history, during relatively peaceful non-war and pre-Depression times. "The
Revival," set around 1801, portrays frontier life and early
religious revival movements as a couple makes their way
from Ohio westward and stop off at a camp where people push themselves into religious frenzies. "Hundreds of
Feet Below Daylight" examines the people who continue
gold mining after the euphoria has died down and life
becomes tough. Some readers may be shocked by the
brutality exhibited by some of the miners who so desperately hunt for money. "The Golem's Mighty Swing" features a Jewish professional baseball team traveling the
country just trying to get by in the 1920s. Facing racial
and religious taunts and sometimes violence, they try a
gimmick—disguising their African American player as a
golem—in order to generate ticket sales.
"Social issues, including racial prejudice and intolerance, poverty, and family dynamics, are broached via
both plot and character. . . . This [is] an easy crossover
graphic novel for readers who enjoy American history
made into well-told stories." Booklist

Sturm, James, 1965--—*Continued*

Satchel Paige; striking out Jim Crow; by James Sturm & Rich Tommaso; with an introduction by Gerald Early. Jump at the Sun 2007 89p il $16.99; pa $9.99 *

Grades: 6 7 8 9 10 11 12 **741.5**
1. Paige, Satchel, 1906-1982—Graphic novels 2. Baseball—Graphic novels 3. Graphic novels
ISBN 0-7868-3900-7; 0-7868-3901-5 (pa)
LC 2007-61362

This graphic novel is "about fictional Emmet Wilson, a black farmer whose moment of glory as a player in the Negro Leagues came when he scored a run off the great pitcher, Satchel Paige. . . . This visually powerful, suspenseful, even profound story makes an excellent choice for readers interested in baseball or in the history of race relations." Booklist

The **Superhero** book; the ultimate encyclopedia of comic-book icons and Hollywood heroes; edited by Gina Misiroglu with David A. Roach. Visible Ink Press 2004 xxi, 725p il $29.95

Grades: 7 8 9 10 **741.5**
1. Superheroes 2. Cartoons and caricatures 3. Motion pictures
ISBN 0-7808-0772-3 LC 2004-19059

This is an "encyclopedic reference work that profiles superheroes from all companies and in all media. . . . Its 300 full entries provide information on more than 1,000 mythic overachievers, covering . . . comic book, movie, television, and novel superheroes." Publisher's note

This "is a must-buy for comic readers interested in knowing the early roots and conceptions of comic-book heroes." SLJ

Takahashi, Rumiko, 1957-
One-pound gospel, vol. 1. 2nd ed. Viz Media 2008 242p il pa $9.99 *

Grades: 10 11 12 Adult **741.5**
1. Graphic novels 2. Manga 3. Shonen manga 4. Boxing—Graphic novels 5. Humorous graphic novels
ISBN 978-1-4215-2030-8

Kosaku Hatanaka is a talented boxer, but he suffers from an insatiable appetite that makes it extremely difficult to make weight for his boxing matches (he's a featherweight who should weigh 126 pounds). He drives his poor coach crazy and tends to lose matches because he has to starve himself to lose weight, which saps his strength. Then he meets Sister Angela, a novice nun who tries to help him; she's so cute, Kosaku has a crush on her. Between his coach at Mukaida's Gym and Sister Angela's prayers, Kosaku starts to win his bouts—but usually with such bizarre circumstances and incredible luck that his opponents hate him. The boxing action is pretty well done and fairly graphic; this volume doesn't include much at all in the way of strong language, but Viz has put a warning about strong language and realistic violence on the title page. This series was originally published starting in 1989 and is now released in Viz's now standard unflipped tankobon size book.

Talbot, Bryan, 1952-
The tale of one bad rat. 2nd ed. Dark Horse 2010 unp il $19.99

Grades: 9 10 11 12 Adult **741.5**
1. Graphic novels 2. Child sexual abuse—Graphic novels 3. Runaway teenagers—Graphic novels
ISBN 978-1-59582-493-6
First published 1995

"This volume collects issues one through four of the Dark Horse comic-book series" Verso of title page

This book's "heroine is teenager Helen Potter, who has run away from an abusive father and whose path to recovery takes her from a squat in London to refuge at an inn in the British countryside. Along the way, she meets characters and situations that Talbot derives from the work of Helen's namesake, Beatrix Potter, whose life he symbolically links to Helen's. Talbot's vivid, realistic full-color illustration brilliantly evokes the story's settings, yet even more effective are his compassionate characterizations." Booklist

Tamaki, Mariko
Skim; words by Mariko Tamaki; drawings by Jillian Tamaki. Groundwood Books 2008 144p il $18.95

Grades: 7 8 9 10 11 12 **741.5**
1. Graphic novels 2. Humorous graphic novels 3. School stories—Graphic novels 4. Friendship—Graphic novels
ISBN 978-0-88899-753-1; 0-88899-753-1

Skim is Kimberly Keiko Cameron, a not-slim half-Japanese would-be Wiccan goth who attends a private school. When classmate Katie Matthews' ex-boyfriend commits suicide, concerned guidance counselors descend upon the school because so many of the student body goes into mourning overdrive. The popular clique starts a new club, Girls Celebrate Life, and make Katie their project, especially after she falls off her roof and breaks both arms. Kim and her best friend Lisa observe all this, but counselors target Kim for her goth tendencies and are convinced she'll become suicidal any moment. All she is, is in love with her English teacher, Ms. Archer, who seems to reciprocate and then leaves the school. As Lisa starts to get sucked into the GLC, Kim and Katie tentatively begin a new friendship. There is only one rather chaste kiss between Kim and Ms. Archer. Artist Jillian Tamaki draws Kim to look like a classical Heian period Japanese woman.

Tan, Shaun
The arrival. Arthur A. Levine Books 2007 unp il $19.99 *

Grades: 6 7 8 9 10 **741.5**
1. Graphic novels 2. Immigrants—Graphic novels 3. Stories without words
ISBN 0-439-89529-4 LC 2006-21706

In this wordless graphic novel, a man leaves his homeland and sets off for a new country, where he must build a new life for himself and his family.

"Young readers will be fascinated by the strange new world the artist creates. . . . They will linger over the details in the beautiful sepia pictures and will likely pick up the book to pore over it again and again." SLJ

Tanabe, Yellow
Kekkaishi, Vol. 1. Viz Action 2005 192p il pa $9.99

Grades: 9 10 11 12 Adult   **741.5**
1. Graphic novels 2. Manga 3. Shonen manga 4. Supernatural graphic novels
ISBN 1-59116-968-2

Junior high student Yoshimori Sumimura is a kekkaishi, a demon hunter; it's the family business. The Yukimuras next door are also kekkaishi, rivals of the Sumimuras. Their daughter Tokine is also a demon hunter. Yoshimori would much rather become a pastry chef, but he can't let Tokine always get the demons. This is the first of an ongoing manga series that has lots of demon hunting action but not too much violence, and considerable humor.

TenNapel, Douglas R.
Iron West. Image Comics 2006 160p il pa $14.99

Grades: 8 9 10 11 12 Adult   **741.5**
1. Graphic novels 2. Science fiction graphic novels 3. Western stories—Graphic novels
ISBN 978-1-58240-630-5

Preston Struck has worked as a con artist and crooked gambler, but when he encounters a horde of technological killers while escaping bounty hunters, he discovers an unfortunate streak of responsibility. Awakened by greedy miners, an alien artifact has begun manufacturing humanoid form robots to kill every human, starting with the town of Twain Harte. Aided by a wizened shaman, a Sasquatch, and the not-too-trusting sheriff, Struck reluctantly sets out to stop the killer robots.

TenNapel uses well-worn cliches of American Westerns and turns them on their heads, including Native American stereotypes, the saloon gal with a heart of gold. The level of violence is similar to that seen in any classic Western movie (think John Wayne films). "This finely balanced piece of work is polished with style." Voice Youth Advocates

Tezuka, Osamu, 1928-1989
Black Jack, volume 1. Vertical, Inc. 2008 287p il pa $16.95 *

Grades: 9 10 11 12 Adult   **741.5**
1. Graphic novels 2. Manga 3. Surgeons—Graphic novels 4. Medical practice—Graphic novels
ISBN 978-1-934287-27-9

Black Jack is the only known name for a mysterious, scarred surgeon from Japan who can perform surgical miracles but is considered to be a creepy mercenary. He will perform highly risky surgeries for an exorbitant price, and he's unlicensed. However, most people don't realize that he actually does a lot for more altruistic reasons as well. In this first volume that reprints the original stories by pioneer mangaka (manga creator) Tezuka, stories include one in which Black Jack operates on a crime boss's son using the body of an unjustly convicted man; and one where he removes a teratoid cystoma from a unidentified wealthy and famous woman, but he refuses to kill the cystoma, which contains the body parts of the woman's unborn twin. While there are some surgical scenes that might not be for the squeamish, the stories offer little in the way of graphic violence or bad lan-

guage while providing action and some thought about ethics and morals.

"With genre-spanning stories—horror, sci-fi, romance—and Tezuka's signature blend of drama, bathos and extreme broad comedy jammed together on every page, *Black Jack* is a wild but extravagantly entertaining ride." Publ Wkly

Thompson, Jason, 1974-
Manga: the complete guide. Ballantine Books/Del Rey Manga 2007 592p il pa $19.95 *

Grades: Adult Professional   **741.5**
1. Graphic novels—Bibliography 2. Manga—Bibliography 3. Reference books
ISBN 978-0-345-48590-8

Former manga editor at Viz, Thompson reviews more than 900 manga titles that have been translated and published in the U.S. This book includes only original manga series published in Japan and then translated into English for U.S. publication. Titles include series that are no longer in print. The book also includes sidebar discussions on the many genres included in manga, including the age and genre divisions and such topics as otaku (hard-core fans), underground manga, and more. Separate sections cover yaoi and gay manga, and adult manga (often called hentai). It also includes an artist index. Each review includes a description of the series, how many volumes it has, an age rating, and content indicators.

Toboso, Yana, 1984-
Black butler, vol. 1; [translation: Tomo Kimura; lettering: Tania Biswas] Yen Press 2010 184p il pa $10.99

Grades: 10 11 12 Adult   **741.5**
1. Graphic novels 2. Manga 3. Fantasy graphic novels 4. Mystery graphic novels 5. Household employees—Graphic novels
ISBN 978-0-316-08084-2

First volume in an ongoing series

Contents: In the morning; In the afternoons; At night; At midnight

In an alternate England, the young Earl Phantomhive, Ciel, lives just outside London; he's only twelve years old, but he runs a massive toy manufacturing company, aided by his butler Sebastian. In this world, magic coexists with science and technology, cars from the early twentieth century drive the roads and Ciel tests video games. Sebastian commands the other workers: Finnian the Gardener (who tends to kill plants), Mey-Rin the klutzy housemaid, and Baldroy the chef, who always has a cigarette dangling from the corner of his mouth. The dapper butler always finds a way to save the day, whether it's transforming a destroyed courtyard into a Japanese rock garden, teaching his young charge to dance the waltz, or saving him from gangsters. He is too good to be true; he is, as he says, "a devil of a butler." The book includes some graphic violence and occasional, mildly bad language ("bastard," "damned").

Trudeau, G. B. (Garry B.), 1948-
The long road home. Andrews McMeel Pub.
2005 93p il (A Doonesbury book) pa $9.95
Grades: 11 12 Adult   **741.5**
1. Doonesbury (Comic strip) 2. Comic books, strips,
etc.
ISBN 0-7407-5385-1; 978-0-7407-5385-5
                                          LC 2004-116364
A collection of the Doonesbury strips from a seven
month period that chronicle the wounding of B.D. in Iraq
and his experiences along the road to rehabilitation.
"Trudeau is a great comic writer whose devotion to
politics and capacity for moral outrage are apparently un-
diminished . . . but he is a great comic writer first, with
the intellectual honesty that implies." N Y Times Book
Rev

Unita, Yumi, 1972-
Bunny drop vol. 1; [translation, Kaori Inoue;
lettering, Alexis Eckerman] Yen Press 2010 196p
il pa $12.99
Grades: 8 9 10 11 12 Adult   **741.5**
1. Graphic novels 2. Manga 3. Josei manga
4. Unmarried fathers—Graphic novels
ISBN 978-0-7595-3122-2
First published 2006 in Japan
Book reads from right to left in the traditional Japanese format
Thirty-year-old bachelor Daikichi is a salaryman, a junior executive, living on his own in Tokyo. When he
goes home for his grandfather's funeral, he discovers that
his grandfather had a younger lover who left him with
a little girl, Rin (which makes her his aunt). The lover
is nowhere to be found, and none of Daikichi's relatives
will have anything to do with Rin, who won't talk to
anyone but sticks close to Daikichi, who closely resembles his grandfather. When no one will step forward to
take care of the six-year-old, Daikichi impulsively decides he will. Once he brings Rin home, the reality of
his new situation finally dawns on him; Daikichi is now
a single father and has to provide care for Rin. There's
one scene with Rin and Daikichi together in their furo
bath (a very typical Japanese family scene), and a few
panels with Rin and Daikichi in their underwear. In one
chapter, Daikichi has to deal with Rin's night time
bedwetting, and Rin is shown changing her clothes.
"This sweet-natured manga shows the joys, frustrations, and quirks of family life; and while it is aimed at
teens, it would also be more than welcome in the hands
of adult readers." Booklist

Urasawa, Naoki, 1960-
Pluto: Urasawa x Tezuka, vol. 1. Viz Media
2009 unp il pa $12.99 *
Grades: 10 11 12 Adult   **741.5**
1. Graphic novels 2. Manga 3. Mystery graphic novels
4. Robots—Graphic novels 5. Astro Boy (Fictional
character)
ISBN 978-1-4215-1918-0
Original Japanese edition, 2004
In a future where humans and robots peacefully coex-
ist, someone or something kills the Swiss robot named
Mont Blanc, a well-loved, powerful, and famous robot.
In Dusseldorf, a robot rights leader named Bernard

Lanke has been brutally murdered, and there are some
disturbing links to Mont Blanc's death. A traffic police
bot has also been killed, and Inspector Gesicht of
Interpol is sent to investigate the murders. When he returns the police bot's memory chip to his robot wife, she
shows Gesicht what her husband saw just before he dies.
He realizes that someone is killing the most advanced robots—and he's one of them. This manga series is
Urasawa's take on a classic Astro Boy story by Osamu
Tezuka: "The Greatest Robot On Earth." Tezuka's famous robot creation, Astro Boy, called Atom in this series (his original name), shows up only in the last panel
of this first volume. The book includes violence.

Urrea, Luis Alberto
Mr. Mendoza's paintbrush; artwork by
Christopher Cardinale; color masking and
compositing, Anthony Cardinale; design, Anne M.
Giangiulio. Cinco Puntos Press 2010 unp il pa
$17.95
Grades: 7 8 9 10 11 12 Adult   **741.5**
1. Graphic novels 2. Humorous graphic novels
3. Artists—Graphic novels 4. Mexico—Graphic novels
ISBN 978-1-933693-23-1   LC 2008-11636
Rosario is a small town in the Sinaloa region of Mexico, nestled into a wet, green, mango-sweet subtropical
landscape. There, Mr. Mendoza wields his paintbrush to
write graffiti with a purpose. When Mr. Mendoza catches
the young narrator and his best friend Jaime spying on
the girls who are swimming, he strips them, writes graffiti all over their bodies, and chases the naked boys
down the street through town. He also appoints himself
as the town's conscience and angers the authorities with
his graffiti on the town's whorehouse, bridge, and other
places. Then, one day, he takes his paint and paintbrush
to the center square and paints steps into the sky and
walks up until he disappears. Women and girls are
shown in their underwear, and the naked boys are shown
only from the back. The talk of sex, the way the boys
sneak peeks at the girls and one of the town's women,
make this book suitable for teens even though the format
resembles a picture book.
"Not only does the art perfectly capture the mood of
the piece—from the blocky woodcuts to the muted earth
tones—but it also reinforces the lucid dreamlike quality
of its magical realism, serving as an enticing invitation
to further explore the genre." Horn Book Guide

Urushibara, Yuki
Mu shi shi 1; translated and adapted by William
Flanagan; lettering, North Market Street Graphics.
Random House/Del Rey Manga 2007 240p il pa
$12.95
Grades: 10 11 12 Adult   **741.5**
1. Graphic novels 2. Manga 3. Seinen manga
4. Fantasy graphic novels 5. Supernatural graphic novels
ISBN 978-0-345-49621-8   LC 2007-295790
The mushi are a primitive life-form that has existed
long before humans came to be. Some mushi can coexist peacefully with mankind, but some are deadly to
humans. Ginko is a mushi-shi, a master who has studied
the mushi and knows how to control them, and to destroy them if need be. He travels the countryside of old

Urushibara, Yuki—*Continued*

Japan, ending infestations and helping people when he can. The publisher has rated this for older teens, but there's little in the way of overt violence, harsh language, or any other content issues in this first volume. As a seinen manga, this was published in Japan for adult men.

Vankin, Deborah

Poseurs; [written by Deborah Vankin; illustrated by Rick Mays; lettering by Robert Clark, Jr., Clem Robins and Drew Gill] Image Comics 2011 149p il pa $16.99

Grades: 8 9 10 11 12   **741.5**

1. Graphic novels 2. Mystery graphic novels 3. Friendship—Graphic novels 4. Kidnapping—Graphic novels

ISBN 978-1-60706-358-2

Jenna's friendship with Mac, a busboy, and Pouri, a Taiwanese partygoer, is tested when Pouri suggests that Jenna and Mac help her stage her own kidnapping in order to to avoid flunking out of school and being sent back to Taiwan. This book was originally meant to be part of DC Comics' Minx line; Mays' black and white art looks clear and spare in the larger size pages of this Image Comics publication. One page shows a nude young woman whose naughty parts are covered by sushi, and on another page, Pouri throws a drink into a man's lap; other than these, there's no overt violence, no bad language (just a lot of Mac-isms), and the one time Jenna and Mac are in bed together, they are fully clothed. The cover copy states "Gossip Girl meets Bret Easton Ellis for the comic book crowd," but the book stays teen friendly throughout.

Vollmar, Rob

The castaways; illustrated by Pablo G. Callejo. NBM/ComicsLit 2007 64p il pa $17.95

Grades: 6 7 8 9 10 11 12   **741.5**

1. United States—History—1919-1933—Graphic novels 2. Graphic novels

ISBN 978-1-56163-492-7

An expanded and newly illustrated edition of the title first published 2002 by Absence of Ink Comic Press

"Afraid that he's just a burden on his family, 13-year-old Tucker Freeman lets himself be driven away from home and jumps on a freight train heading west. His inexperience makes him vulnerable to all the angry, desperate people looking for any way they can survive during America's economic collapse, but fortunately he's taken under the wing of Elijah Hopkins, an elderly colored man who introduces him to the cooperative hobo subculture. . . . Vollmar's script, based on family reminiscences, rings true; his dialogue has the vocabulary and the rhythms of real people talking. . . . Callejo's art creates a solid setting in which Tucker's experience can reveal squalor or grace." Publ Wkly

Watsuki, Nobuhiro, 1970-

Rurouni Kenshin; Meiji swordsman romantic story [Vol. 1]; story and art by Nobuhiro Watsuki; [English adaptation, Gerard Jones; translation, Kenichiro Yagi; touch-up art & lettering, Steve Dutro] Vizbig ed. Viz 2008 576p il pa $17.99

Grades: 10 11 12   **741.5**

1. Graphic novels 2. Manga 3. Japan—History—1868-1945—Graphic novels

ISBN 978-1-4215-2073-5

This twenty-eight volume series was completed in late 2006

"The story of a young wandering samurai—who bears a reverse blade sword and strives not to kill after seeing and committing much bloodshed in the battles to bring the Emperor back to power in 1868—becomes much more than mere historical saga. Kenshin's relationships with new and old friends and enemies makes compelling storytelling." Voice Youth Advocates

Weing, Drew

Set to sea. Fantagraphics 2010 unp il $16.99

Grades: 8 9 10 11 12   **741.5**

1. Graphic novels 2. Seafaring life—Graphic novels 3. Poets—Graphic novels 4. Sea stories—Graphic novels

ISBN 978-1-60699-368-2; 1-60699-368-2

"The unnamed hero is a poet who writes overblown verse about the wonders of sea life, while trying to pay his bar bill with promises of book dedications. That attitude quickly changes when he's shanghaied aboard a clipper bound for Hong Kong." Publ Wkly

The author "has produced a beautiful gem here, with minimal dialogue, one jolting battle scene, and each small page owned by a single panel filled with art whose figures have a comfortable roundness dredged up from the cartoon landscapes of our childhood unconscious, even as the intensely crosshatched shadings suggest the darkness that sometimes traces the edges of our lives. . . . [This book] is playful, atmospheric, dark, wistful, and wise." Booklist

Weinstein, Lauren

Girl stories; by Lauren R. Weinstein. Henry Holt 2006 237p il pa $16.95

Grades: 7 8 9 10 11 12 Adult   **741.5**

1. Graphic novels 2. Humorous graphic novels 3. Girls—Graphic novels 4. Friendship—Graphic novels

ISBN 978-0-8050-7863-3; 0-8050-7863-0

                LC 2005-46205

"Smart, creative Lauren sheds her geeky rep in high school in Weinstein's collection of comic strips, which have to intimacy of a teen's diary. The color-washed sketches have an edgy quality." Booklist

White, Tracy

How I made it to eighteen; a mostly true story. Roaring Brook 2010 151p il $16.99

Grades: 8 9 10 11 12   **741.5**

White, Tracy—*Continued*

1. Autobiographical graphic novels 2. Mental illness—Graphic novels 3. Graphic novels

ISBN 978-1-59643-454-7; 1-59643-454-6

"White's story of a 17-year-old girl's ordeals with depression, addiction, and body image issues is all the more powerful because of its basis in truth. The story follows Stacy Black, whose nervous breakdown leads to her decision to check into the Golden Meadows Hospital for mental health. . . . White's very simple hand-drawn, b&w artistic style enhances the personal touch of the work, creating the effect of an illustrated diary. While text-heavy, the narration is clear-eyed and affecting." Publ Wkly

Wilson, G. Willow

Cairo; written by G. Willow Wilson; art by M.K. Perker; lettered by Travis Lanham. DC Comics/Vertigo 2007 160p il $24.99

Grades: 9 10 11 12 Adult   741.5

1. Graphic novels 2. Fantasy graphic novels 3. Adventure graphic novels

ISBN 978-1-4012-1140-0

A stolen hookah, a spiritual underworld, and a genie on the run change the lives of five strangers in Cairo. A drug runner, a down-on-his-luck journalist, an American expatriate, a troubled young student, and a female Israeli soldier end up all working together to help the jinn that Lebanese American Shaheed calls Shams to recover a special box from the evil magic-wielding drug lord Nar. The book includes some violence.

"Scripting and art complement each other well in an adventure with lots of appeal for readers willing to try a literary graphic novel and for those simply looking for the next good one." Booklist

Wolk, Douglas

Reading comics; how graphic novels work and what they mean. Da Capo Press 2007 405p il $22.95 *

Grades: Adult Professional   741.5

1. Graphic novels—History and criticism

ISBN 978-0-306-81509-6   LC 2007-5232

Suddenly, comics are everywhere: a newly matured art form, filling bookshelves with brilliant, innovative work and shaping the ideas and images of the rest of contemporary culture. In Reading Comics, critic Douglas Wolk shows us why this is and how it came to be. Wolk illuminates the most dazzling creators of modern comics—from Alan Moore to Alison Bechdel to Dave Sim to Chris Ware—and introduces a critical theory that explains where each fits into the pantheon of art. The book is accessible to the hardcore fan and the curious newcomer; it is the first book for people who want to know not just what comics are worth reading, but also the ways to think and talk and argue about them.

Includes bibliographical references

Yang, Gene

American born Chinese; color by Lark Pien. First Second 2006 233p il pa $16.95 *

Grades: 7 8 9 10 11 12   741.5

1. Graphic novels 2. Chinese Americans—Graphic novels

ISBN 978-1-59643-152-2; 1-59643-152-0

LC 2005-58105

In three interconnected stories, the reader meets the Monkey King, who wants to be more than he is, Jin Wang, a Chinese American middle school student who desperately wants to fit in at his new school, and Caucasian-looking Danny, who unaccountably has an extremely stereotypically Chinese cousin, Chin-Kee, whose visit causes great embarrassment.

"True to its origin as a Web comic, this story's clear, concise lines and expert coloring are deceptively simple yet expressive. Even when Yang slips in an occasional Chinese ideogram or myth, the sentiments he's depicting need no translation. Yang accomplishes the remarkable feat of practicing what he preaches with this book: accept who you are and you'll already have reached out to others." Publ Wkly

Animal crackers; by Gene Luen Yang. Slave Labor Graphics 2010 unp il pa $14.95

Grades: 7 8 9 10   741.5

1. Graphic novels 2. Chinese Americans—Graphic novels 3. Bullies—Graphic novels 4. Dreams—Graphic novels 5. Science fiction graphic novels 6. Humorous graphic novels

ISBN 978-1-59362-183-4; 1-59362-183-3

"This volume collects Gordon Yamamoto and the king of the geeks and Loyola Chin and the San Peligran order, both previously published by SLG Publishing" Verso of title page. Subtitle on cover: A Gene Luen Yang collection

Contents: Gordon Yamamoto and the king of the geeks; Sammy the baker and the M.A.C.; Loyola Chin and the San Peligran order

"In the first story, a kinda-bully befriends a nerd whose hatred of his awful father has anthropomorphized into huge, murderous animal crackers. In . . . [Loyola Chin], a girl falls for a dream-spirit named Saint Danger, who plans to save humanity from an alien invasion by deciding who is unfit enough for survival. The two stories share a few tangential relationships, cast of characters, and a secret society of microbots who store data up people's nostrils. The power of Yang's work comes from his ability to juggle a lot of ideas while working on several different levels all at once." Booklist

The eternal smile; three stories. First Second 2009 170p il pa $16.95 *

Grades: 9 10 11 12   741.5

1. Graphic novels 2. Fantasy graphic novels 3. Short stories—Graphic novels

ISBN 978-1-59643-156-0; 1-59643-156-3

Contents: Duncan's kingdom; Grandpa Greenbax and the eternal smile; Urgent request

"Three tales evince very different realities and viewpoints. . . . Duncan, the hero of the first, is desperately seeking the approval of the Princess, though something in his kingdom doesn't seem quite right. In the next, an anthropomorphized, avaricious amphibian named Gran'pa

Yang, Gene—*Continued*

Greenbax seeks to be the richest frog in the land, only to discover that his domain isn't quite what he thought it was. In the last, a painfully shy office worker distorts her own perception—and judgment—to create a reality more pleasing. . . . Begging for multiple readings, this exceptionally clever examination of fantasy and perception is one to be pored over and ruminated upon." Kirkus

Level up; [illustrated by Thien Pham] First Second Books 2011 160p il $15.99

Grades: 10 11 12 Adult   **741.5**

1. Graphic novels 2. Bildungsromans—Graphic novels 3. Angels—Graphic novels 4. College students—Graphic novels 5. Chinese Americans—Graphic novels

ISBN 978-1-59643-235-2   LC 2010-36257

Dennis Ouyang doesn't just play videogames, he's a grand master. However, his father wants him to attend college and become a doctor. Dennis' father dies just before his high school graduation, and Dennis slacks off at college in order to play videogames all the time. After he breaks his academic probation and must leave, five weird little angels arrive and tell him he must fulfill his destiny. They manage to get him reinstated at college, force him hard to give up videogames completely and study. His hard work pays off, he gets into medical school, and he meets several good friends who form a study group. Then things start to fall apart, as Dennis prefers to hang out with his friends Kat, Ipsha, and Hector, and the angels become jealous. Dennis gives up on medical school when he decides he's not really cut out to be a gastroenterologist, and he takes up videogames again. But how will he really live out his life?

"Pham's watercolor artwork, mostly in muted pallet, is a perfect match for Yang's story. This gentle tale of loss and redemption, family responsibility, and dreams might not be to all teens' tastes (especially by the end), but the mix of fantasy and realism will please the right crowd." Voice Youth Advocates

Prime baby; [by] Gene Luen Yang, colors by Derek Kirk Kim. First Second Books 2010 56p il pa $6.99

Grades: 6 7 8 9 10 11 12   **741.5**

1. Graphic novels 2. Science fiction graphic novels 3. Humorous graphic novels 4. Siblings—Graphic novels 5. Extraterrestrial beings—Graphic novels

ISBN 978-1-59643-612-1

Thaddeus K. Fong always preferred to be the center of his family's attention, so the birth of his little sister Maddie has really bothered him. When she's eighteen months old, he notices something about the sounds she makes; her "gaga's" come out in prime numbers. Then his math teacher says that if aliens were ever to try to make contact with humans, it would be through prime numbers. Oh no, Maddie is an intergalactic conduit for invading aliens! Except no one believes Thaddeus. Until Maddie starts burping up strange things that turn out to be little ships for sluglike aliens. They're peaceful missionary types, but that doesn't stop Thaddeus from making them seem hostile. When their parents finally believe Thaddeus, Maddie gets locked up in a research facility. Thaddeus should be ecstatic, his dumb little sister has been put away. So why is he feeling sad? This story was originally serialized in the New York Times magazine and has been printed to preserve the original comic strip

format.

"Sf readers who value humor and humanity (not just slam-bang action), Christians, newcomers to graphic novels, and fans of Yang's simultaneously childlike and sophisticated ability to create and maintain tension should all be satisfied by his new book." Booklist

Yolen, Jane

Foiled; written by Jane Yolen; artwork by Mike Cavallaro. First Second 2010 160p il pa $15.99

Grades: 7 8 9 10   **741.5**

1. Fantasy graphic novels 2. Fencing—Graphic novels 3. Graphic novels

ISBN 978-1-59643-279-6; 1-59643-279-9

"Besting competitors twice her age in tournaments, and keeping a strict routine of fencing practice, homework, and role-playing games, Aliera is a loner and likes it that way—until she becomes lab partners with the cutest boy in school. . . . Turns out her new ruby-handled foil is the key to his interest in her, and to the yet-unseen magical dimension she must keep in balance. . . . [Yolen] has created a strong, conflicted, and relatable girl hero. . . . Cavallaro's artwork suits Aliera's monochrome existence, but burst into life when she finally sees (in color!) the faerie beasties cheering her on." Booklist

Yoshizaki, Seimu

Kingyo used books, vol. 1; [translation, Adrienne Weber] Viz Media/Viz Signature 2010 191p il pa $12.99

Grades: 9 10 11 12 Adult   **741.5**

1. Graphic novels 2. Manga 3. Books and reading—Graphic novels

ISBN 978-1-4215-3362-9

This manga collects several stories based in or connected to Kingyo Used Books, a used manga store in Tokyo. An art student finds inspiration in a manga series based on the life of the famous artist Hokusai; a silly gag manga helps an archer regain his focus in time for a match; a young Japanese man raised in the U.S. uses an old detective manga series from the 1950s to model his life; the manga store owner's son tries to get away from manga by living in Europe, where he discovers that comics are everywhere; a busy housewife rekindles the passion in her life when she rediscovers a shojo manga featuring a dreamy male protagonist. While there is no violence or bad language, all the main characters are adults.

Yumi, Kiiro

Library wars, vol. 1: love & war; story and art by Kiiro Yumi; original concept by Hiro Arikawa; [English translation & adaptation, Kinami Watabe] Shojo beat ed. Viz Media/Shojo Beat 2010 166p il (Shojo beat manga) pa $9.99

Grades: 9 10 11 12 Adult   **741.5**

1. Graphic novels 2. Manga 3. Shojo manga 4. Librarians—Graphic novels 5. Censorship—Graphic novels

ISBN 978-1-4215-3488-6

First published 2008 in Japan

Yumi, Kiiro—*Continued*

In Japan of the near future, the federal government passes the Media Betterment Act, and the Media Betterment Committee goes on book hunts to destroy any "unsuitable" book. The libraries strike back with the Library Defense Force, a paramilitary organization dedicated to protecting the freedom to read. Iku Kasahara started to work for libraries and wants more than anything to join the Library Defense Force; she's physically very capable, but drill instructor Sergeant Dojo doesn't seem to like her very much and pushes her very hard. Iku must improve her library skills as well as her physical skills if she's to work effectively as a soldier librarian.

This book "delivers an appealing, determined female lead in the midst of an intriguing war on censorship being waged in bookstores and libraries." SLJ

Zahler, Thomas F.

Love and capes, vol. 1; do you want to know a secret? story and art by Thomas F. Zahler. IDW Publishing 2008 160p il pa $19.99 *
Grades: 8 9 10 11 12 Adult   **741.5**
  1. Graphic novels 2. Superhero graphic novels 3. Humorous graphic novels 4. Romance graphic novels
  ISBN 978-1-60010-275-2

Independent bookseller Abby falls in love with her accountant, Mark; then he confesses to her that he's the superpowered crime-fighter, the Crusader. How does one have a romantic relationship with a superhero? Even without meaning to do it, Abby gives away Mark's secret to her sister Charlotte. Oops. So begins a "heroically super situation comedy" in which Abby feels she's competing against the beautiful Amazonia (Mark's superpowered ex-girlfriend), not to mention Mark's over-protective mother, and Mark has to deal with Abby's obnoxious brother Quincy, who thinks Mark is a wimp.

Zubkavich, Jim

Skullkickers: 1000 Opas and a dead body; writer/creator, Jim Zub; line art, Edwin Huang and Chris Stevens; colors, Misty Coates and Chris Stevens. Image Comics 2011 unp il pa $9.99
Grades: 9 10 11 12 Adult   **741.5**
  1. Graphic novels 2. Fantasy graphic novels 3. Adventure graphic novels 4. Humorous graphic novels
  ISBN 978-1-60706-366-7

First published in magazine form as Skullkickers #1-5

Two mercenaries, a bald hulk and a feisty dwarf, try to make a living in an unnamed medieval-looking land where technology, magic, and monsters make their lives interesting. Neither of them is particularly intelligent, so they tend to get into a lot of trouble, whether they're fighting fat werewolves or dealing with a nasty necromancer who plans to raise an undead army. Has some violence and features adventures full of fighting and sarcastic humor.

741.6 Graphic design, illustration, commercial art

Bancroft, Tom

Creating characters with personality; introduction by Glen Keane. Watson-Guptill 2006 160p il pa $19.95
Grades: 9 10 11 12   **741.6**
  1. Cartoons and caricatures 2. Graphic arts
  ISBN 0-8230-2349-4; 978-0-8230-2349-3
                    LC 2005-28462

This book "shows artists how to create a distinctive character, then place that character in context within a script, establish hierarchy, and maximize the impact of pose and expression." Publisher's note

742 Perspective in drawing

DuBosque, Doug

Draw 3-D; a step-by-step guide to perspective drawing. Peel Productions 1999 63p il pa $8.99
Grades: 6 7 8 9 10   **742**
  1. Perspective 2. Drawing
  ISBN 0-939217-14-7   LC 98-42174

"Using easy-to-follow, step-by-step sketches, DuBosque introduces readers to the techniques of three-dimensional drawing. Beginning with such elementary concepts as depth, he progresses logically through shading, reflections, and multiple vanishing points. The supportive tone encourages novices to keep trying and not become discouraged." SLJ

743 Drawing and drawings by subject

Eggleton, Bob

Dragons' domain; the ultimate dragon painting workshop; foreword by John A. Davis. Impact 2010 127p il pa $22.99
Grades: 7 8 9 10   **743**
  1. Drawing 2. Dragons in art
  ISBN 978-1-60061-457-6; 1-60061-457-4

"Here is a book for those dragon lovers who are bored with beginner drawing books. Eggleton starts with a thorough discussion of materials and some basic drawing and painting techniques. Then he spends an entire page on each of several key dragon body parts, such as feet, wings, frills, and tails. After some insightful discussion of finding inspiration and references from nature and fantasy pop culture, the artist demonstrates how to create a handful of different types of dragons. . . . The book is full of Eggleton's own work in progressive stages of completion, photographed in color and attractively placed on backgrounds with fantasy-themed borders." SLJ

Graves, Douglas R.

Drawing portraits. Watson-Guptill 1974 159p il pa $16.95 hardcover o.p. *
Grades: 9 10 11 12   **743**

Graves, Douglas R.—*Continued*
1. Drawing 2. Artistic anatomy
ISBN 0-8230-1431-2

The author discusses "the art and craft of portraiture from beginning to end—seeing and drawing the anatomy of the head and hands, posing and lighting the sitter, conveying the weight, texture, and drape of the sitter's clothing, composing the portrait (individual as well as group), and dealing with such auxiliary problems as the relationship between the artist and his sitter." Introduction

Includes bibliographical references

Hart, Christopher
Human anatomy made amazingly easy.
Watson-Guptill 2000 114p il pa $19.95 *
Grades: 11 12 Adult   **743**
1. Artistic anatomy 2. Figure drawing
ISBN 0-8230-2497-0   LC 00-43514

In this work for the beginning artist "Hart simplifies the process in an accessible manual that concentrates on line and forgoes the complexity of color." Libr J

Nice, Claudia, 1948-
Painting your favorite animals in pen, ink, and watercolor. North Light Books 2006 142p il $26.99
Grades: 9 10 11 12   **743**
1. Drawing—Technique 2. Watercolor painting—Technique 3. Animals in art
ISBN 1-58180-776-7; 978-1-58180-776-9
     LC 2006-42516

"Exotics and livestock are included alongside more common pets in this artist's sketchbook. The author shares a wealth of tips and examples, and 10 projects are presented with step-by-step instructions." SLJ

745.5   Handicrafts

Arendt, Madeline
Altered art for the first time. Sterling Pub. 2005 112p il $19.95
Grades: 11 12 Adult   **745.5**
1. Handicraft
ISBN 1-4027-1655-9   LC 2005-10344
"A Sterling/Chapelle Book"

"This guide concentrates on altering books. Beginning with complete coverage of needed and suggested materials and supplies, and taking the reader/crafter step-by-step through a series of specific projects, Arendt shows how to take a book and make, among other things, an attractive journal, a display for souvenirs of a special occasion, or, using a book's covers, a box for holding commemorative items. Her encouraging tone will inspire even new crafters to venture into this rewarding activity." Booklist

Includes bibliographical references

Taylor, Terry
Altered art; techniques for creating altered books, boxes, cards & more. Lark Books 2004 144p il $19.95 *
Grades: 11 12 Adult   **745.5**
1. Handicraft
ISBN 1-57990-550-1   LC 2004-5313

Taylor "begins with a brief history of altered art (Joseph Cornell was an early practitioner), discusses copyright issues with regard to borrowed images, then moves straight into techniques, tools, and a . . . gallery of a variety of artists' works. The author includes a few projects with step-by-step instructions. . . . [This book] is without a doubt one of the finest craft books available." SLJ

745.54   Paper handicrafts

Perdana, Julius
Build your own paper robots; 100s of mecha model designs on CD to print out and assemble; [by] Julius Perdana and Josh Buczynski; with Axel Bernal . . . [et al.] St. Martin's Griffin 2009 96p il $18.95
Grades: 8 9 10 11 12 Adult   **745.54**
1. Paper crafts 2. Robots—Models
ISBN 978-0-312-57370-6   LC 2009-517888
Includes CD-ROM

"Cleverly designed miniature robots, some resembling figures from Star Wars, are ready be cut out and glued together following the exploded diagrams. Color templates can be printed from the enclosed CD or color-copied from the book. Figures include high-tech humanoids, dogs, and war machines." Libr J

Reeder, Dan, 1950-
Papier-mache monsters; turn trinkets and trash into magnificent monstrosities; photographs by Julie, Jeff and Dan Reeder. Gibbs Smith 2009 144p il pa $16.99
Grades: 9 10 11 12 Adult   **745.54**
1. Paper crafts 2. Monsters in art
ISBN 978-1-4236-0555-3; 1-4236-0555-1
     LC 2009-3827

"For lovers of the truly grotesque, Reeder . . . provides detailed photo instructions for large figures constructed of clothes hangers, newspaper, and glue. Cloth skin, teeth, and slathered-on paint finish them off. The toothy dragons are particularly effective." Libr J

Sowell, Sharyn
Paper cutting techniques for scrapbooks & cards. Sterling Pub. 2005 128p il hardcover o.p. pa $12.95 *
Grades: 11 12 Adult   **745.54**
1. Paper crafts 2. Scrapbooks 3. Greeting cards
ISBN 1-4027-1921-3; 1-4027-5387-X (pa)
     LC 2005-15043
"A Sterling/Chapelle book"

The author shows how to "fashion delicate borders, alphabets, flowery frames, and 3D embellishments. How to

Sowell, Sharyn—*Continued*
use vintage papers, cut with patterns or freehand, and understand positive and negative space, are also here." Publisher's note

"Both experienced and novice paper users will learn something from this beautifully illustrated book, which is pretty enough to be an art book in and of itself." Booklist

745.58 Handicrafts from beads, found and other objects

Discover beading; compiled by Lesley Weiss. Kalmbach Books 2006 96p il pa $19.95
   Grades: 9 10 11 12 Adult   **745.58**
   1. Beadwork 2. Beads 3. Jewelry
   ISBN 0-8711-6239-3   LC 2007-273183
All projects have appeared previously in BeadStyle magazine, except for Classic Knotted Pearls and Easy Macramé Necklace

"Focuses on using basic, beginner-friendly beading techniques to create . . . bracelets, necklaces, earrings, and more." Publisher's note

"This visually pleasing beading book for crafters is a smart purchase. . . . This book will appeal to crafting teens and adults and would be a nice addition to any size public library." Voice Youth Advocates

745.594 Decorative objects

Fox, Danielle
   Simply modern jewelry; designs from the editor of Stringing magazine. Interweave Press 2008 120p il pa $21.95
   Grades: 9 10 11 12 Adult   **745.594**
   1. Beadwork 2. Jewelry
   ISBN 978-1-59668-048-7   LC 2007-27338
"The first two dozen pages provide a crash course in identifying the different components of jewelry and the terms that apply to them as well as the tools and techniques used in the projects shown. . . . Each project starts with a chart of materials, tools, and techniques necessary to complete the piece, the finished size, and a simplicity scale. . . . The projects are chic and satisfying, and range from a simple tied-leather-thong necklace to complicated chandelier earrings. For the most part they could be made in a day and worn that evening. A great resource." SLJ

745.6 Calligraphy, heraldic design, illumination

Marsh, Don, 1957-
   Calligraphy. North Light Bks. 1996 128p (First steps series) $18.99
   Grades: 11 12 Adult   **745.6**
   1. Calligraphy
   ISBN 0-89134-666-X   LC 96-4014

This guide to calligraphy is aimed at the beginner and includes various projects such as greeting cards and invitations

"Excellent for secondary school age and above." Libr J

Includes bibliographical references

746 Textile arts

Searle, Teresa
   Felt jewelry; 25 pieces to make using a variety of simple felting techniques. St. Martin's Griffin 2008 128p il pa $21.95
   Grades: 11 12 Adult   **746**
   1. Fabrics 2. Jewelry 3. Handicraft
   ISBN 978-0-312-38356-5; 0-312-38356-8
                      LC 2008-40066
"Craft projects that combine felt with decorative stitching, beads, and other embellishments to create an . . . assortment of twenty-five jewelry items." Publisher's note

"The book is filled with detailed, eye-catching color photographs that will aid beginners and inspire the more accomplished felters." SLJ

746.43 Knitting, crocheting, tatting

Eckman, Edie, 1960-
   The crochet answer book. Storey Pub. 2005 320p il pa $12.95
   Grades: 11 12 Adult   **746.43**
   1. Crocheting
   ISBN 1-58017-598-8   LC 2005-16484
This book features "chapters on topics ranging from equipment needs to resources for more information. . . . Appended are standard crochet abbreviations, common crochet terms and phrases, standard body measurements and sizing, suggested sizes for accessories and household items, and yarn care symbols." Booklist
   Includes bibliographical references

Keen, Sarah
   Knitted wild animals; 15 adorable, easy-to-knit toys. Watson-Guptill 2010 127p il pa $19.99
   Grades: 9 10 11 12 Adult   **746.43**
   1. Knitting 2. Toys
   ISBN 978-0-82303-318-8
First published 2009 in the United Kingdom
"Knitted toys are popular, and Keen's creative designs for wild animals will please children and adults alike. The patterns are easy to follow and range from simple to complex, and the finished products are adorable." Libr J

Obaachan, Annie
   Amigurumi animals; 15 patterns and dozens of techniques for creating cute crochet creatures. St. Martin's Griffin 2008 128p il pa $21.95
   Grades: 9 10 11 12 Adult   **746.43**
   1. Knitting 2. Crocheting 3. Toys
   ISBN 978-0-312-37820-2; 0-312-37820-3
                      LC 2008-299792

Obaachan, Annie—*Continued*

Introduces amigurumi, the Japanese art of crocheting or knitting small stuffed animals, and provides tips on how to design one using patterns and step-by-step instructions for fifteen projects.

"This book would be useful not only for beginners, but also for those who could use technique refreshers or who need to be inspired by the great variety of photographs of completed projects." SLJ

Okey, Shannon

Knitgrrl; learn to knit with 15 fun and funky projects; photography by Shannon Fagan, Christine Okey, and Tamas Jakab; illustrations by Kathleen Jacques. Watson-Guptill 2005 96p il pa $9.95 *

Grades: 7 8 9 10   **746.43**

1. Knitting

ISBN 0-8230-2618-3

This offers instructions for basic knitting techniques and for such projects as scarves, hats, leg warmers, mittens, and bags.

"A lively, teen-friendly book with all the basics, plenty of additional information, and appealing color photos and illustrations." SLJ

Radcliffe, Margaret

The knitting answer book. Storey Pub. 2005 400p il pa $14.95

Grades: 11 12 Adult   **746.43**

1. Knitting

ISBN 1-58017-599-6   LC 2005-16466

Framed as a series of questions that might be asked by knitters, this manual covers knitting "materials, techniques, and resources. . . . Radcliffe answers such specific queries as 'What is the best cast-on when you're planning to add fringe to a piece?' and 'Is there a more durable cast-on I can use for children's clothes?'" Libr J

Taylor, Kathleen

Knit one, felt too; discover the magic of knitted felt with 25 easy patterns. Storey Books 2003 176p il pa $18.95

Grades: 11 12 Adult   **746.43**

1. Knitting

ISBN 1-58017-497-3   LC 2003-50558

"If you knit a loose, oversize garment and then shrink it on purpose, you have turned a wool object into felt . . . Taylor offers 25 projects, first showing how to knit the item, then how to get the desired look. The projects are quite inventive, from toddler slippers shaped like bunnies to wine bags decorated with grapes. Taylor's enthusiasm combined with the straightforward and eye-catching color photos will entice knitters." Booklist

746.46   Patchwork and quilting

Beyer, Jinny

Quiltmaking by hand; simple stitches, exquisite quilts. Breckling Press 2003 262p il pa $29.95

Grades: 11 12 Adult   **746.46**

1. Quilting

ISBN 0-9721218-2-X   LC 2003-15827

In this guide to the "traditional methods of quilt assembly—all by hand, the author begins with threading the needle and progresses to perfecting hand quilting stitches." Libr J

Includes bibliographical references

746.9   Textile products and fashion design

Faerm, Steven

Fashion: design course. Barron's 2010 144p il pa $23.99

Grades: 11 12 Adult   **746.9**

1. Fashion design

ISBN 978-0-7641-4423-3   LC 2009-940543

"Principles, practice, and techniques: the practical guide for aspiring fashion designers" Cover

The author "takes readers through a thorough exploration of the fashion industry, from history to inspiration to the design process to landing a job. There are also 14 practical assignments to help budding designers learn more about the industry. Teens exploring careers in fashion will enjoy the practical advice from industry insiders, and fashion-mad readers of all ages will appreciate the information about how fashion design works." Libr J

Iverson, Annemarie

In fashion; from runway to retail, everything you need to know to break into the fashion industry. Clarkson Potter 2010 324p il pa $16.99

Grades: 9 10 11 12   **746.9**

1. Fashion—Vocational guidance 2. Clothing industry

ISBN 978-0-307-46383-8; 0-307-46383-4

         LC 2009-48121

The author "has written a comprehensive guide for budding fashionistas desiring a career in the competitive fashion world. . . . Chapters like 'Fashionista Boot Camp' and 'Fashionista Survival Guide' provide straight talk and professional direction about educational choices, portfolios, résumés, what to wear, internships, character, ethics, and more. . . . This smart, savvy fashion career guide is packed with practical knowledge and expert guidance from an industry insider." Libr J

Stalder, Erika

Fashion 101; a crash course in clothing; illustrations by Ariel Krietzman. Zest Books 2008 128p il pa $17.95

Grades: 9 10 11 12   **746.9**

1. Clothing and dress 2. Fashion

ISBN 978-0-9790173-4-6; 0-9790173-4-3

         LC 2007-939159

Stalder, Erika—*Continued*

On cover: 300+ illustrated wardrobe items: what they look like and how to wear them, the eras that inspired them, the designers who made them, the celebs who made them hot

This book is "divided into apparel categories, from underwear to overcoats, the chapters introduce archetypal styles (e.g., sailor pants and skinny jeans) with clear line drawings, background history about each style ('Who Made It'), the cultural icons who popularized it ('Who Made It Hot'), and tips for making outfits ('How to Rock It'). . . . Any teen interested in clothing will devour this compendium of quick historical facts and practical advice." Booklist

The **teen** vogue handbook; an insider's guide to careers in fashion. Razorbill 2009 276p il pa $24.95

Grades: 7 8 9 10 11 12   **746.9**
1. Fashion—Vocational guidance 2. Clothing industry
ISBN 978-1-59514-261-0; 1-59514-261-4
                                    LC 2009-10626

"Any teen interested in a career in fashion should read this handbook. It is filled with advice from top designers, photographers, models, stylists, makeup artists, writers, and their interns and assistants. They share how they got started and give tips to those interested in a fashion career. This book looks and reads like a magazine on glossy pages filled with photographs and sidebars, but the interviews give pertinent information on every aspect of work in fashion." Voice Youth Advocates

Includes bibliographical references

751 Painting—Techniques, procedures, apparatus, equipment, materials, forms

Ganz, Nicholas

Graffiti world; street art from five continents; edited by Tristan Manco. Updated ed. Abrams 2009 391p il $35 *

Grades: 11 12 Adult   **751**
1. Street art 2. Mural painting and decoration 3. Graffiti
ISBN 978-0-8109-8049-5   LC 2009-922509
First published 2004

Ganz's survey of graffiti art includes "upward of 2,000 full-color photographs. . . . An ephemeral, often despised, yet irrefutably powerful mode of expression, graffiti has always been political, and although many of the street artists Ganz succinctly profiles have moved away from illegal spray painting, they have not compromised the inherent subversiveness of their work. . . . Ganz's global array captures the power and synergy of this vibrant alternative art world in which artists form crews and collectiveness to ensure that their art is seen." Booklist [review of 2004 edition]

Includes bibliographical references

Sanmiguel, David

Complete guide to materials and techniques for drawing and painting; [text, David Sanmiguel; translation, Michael Brunelle and Beatriz Cortabarria] English language ed. Barrons Educational Series 2008 239p il $26.99

Grades: 9 10 11 12 Adult   **751**
1. Artists' materials 2. Drawing—Technique 3. Painting—Technique
ISBN 978-0-7641-6111-7; 0-7641-6111-3
                                    LC 2007-931258

Original Spanish edition, 2007

"From applicators like pencils and spatulas to auxiliary materials such as fillers and cleaners . . . [this book] covers a variety of artistic media including paint, paper, canvas, and cardboard. . . . The second half of the book describes drawing and painting techniques. . . . Basic enough for a beginning art student and complete enough to hold the interest of practicing artists, this book is a good choice for any collection." Voice Youth Advocates

751.4 Painting—Techniques and procedures

All about techniques in acrylics; {an indispensable manual for artists}; {author, Parramón's Editorial Team}. Barron's 2004 143p il (All about techniques) $26.95

Grades: 11 12 Adult   **751.4**
1. Acrylic painting—Technique
ISBN 0-7641-5710-8   LC 2003-68843
Originally published in Spain

"A brief history of the use of acrylics by people such as Jackson Pollack is followed by sections on the varieties of acrylics available, tools for their use, and techniques for skies, vegetation, landscapes, still lifes, interiors, animals, and the nude. The demonstrations of color mixing, sgraffito, texturing, transparent impastos, and layering with glazes are especially well done." Libr J

"The book is a delight for anyone interested in acrylics." Voice Youth Advocates

751.42 Watercolor painting

Craig, Diana

The new encyclopedia of watercolor techniques; [by] Diana Craig & Hazel Harrison. Running Press 2010 144p il pa $19.95

Grades: 9 10 11 12   **751.42**
1. Watercolor painting—Technique
ISBN 978-0-7624-4050-4; 0-7624-4050-3
                                    LC 2009943398

First published 1990 with title: The encyclopedia of watercolor techniques

The authors offer lessons on how to use water-based media.

Crawshaw, Alwyn
Watercolour for the absolute beginner; [by] Alwyn Crawshaw, Sharon Finmark & Trevor Waugh. Collins 2006 224p il pa $16.95
Grades: 9 10 11 12 Adult   **751.42**
   1. Watercolor painting—Technique
   ISBN 978-0-00-723606-0; 0-00-723606-9
                   LC 2008-360702
Chapter one first published 2000 with title: You can paint watercolour. Chapter two first published 2002 with title: You can paint people in watercolour. Chapter three first published 2002 with title: You can paint animals in watercolour. All three chapters first published in one volume 2004
   Contents: Getting started in watercolour by Alwyn Crawshaw; Painting people by Sharon Finmark; Painting animals by Trevor Waugh
   "This is a compilation of three books by three fine British artists. . . . Condensed into a single volume, the three make a good, inexpensive manual for beginners. There are basic techniques for brushstrokes, color mixing, and design, and instruction on tone, texture, pattern, and movement." Libr J

Hammond, Lee
Paint realistic animals in acrylic with Lee Hammond. North Light Books 2007 127p il pa $24.99
Grades: 9 10 11 12   **751.42**
   1. Animals in art 2. Acrylic painting—Technique
   ISBN 1-58180-912-3; 978-1-58180-912-1
                   LC 2006-36386
   "An appealing array of wild and domesticated animals are presented as acrylic painting projects. The basics are covered as well as the usefulness of grids for accuracy. Sidebars list exactly which colors are to be used, and the author gives special attention to tricky elements such as noses and paws." SLJ

751.45   Oil painting

Willenbrink, Mark, 1962-
Oil painting for the absolute beginner; a clear & easy guide to successful oil painting; by Mark and Mary Willenbrink. North Light Books 2010 127p il pa $24.99
Grades: 10 11 12 Adult   **751.45**
   1. Painting—Technique
   ISBN 978-1-60061-784-3   LC 2010-5056
   Includes DVD
   "Focusing on the needs of the first-time oil painter, this book covers . . . [topics ranging] from the basics to key principles on color and composition." Publisher's note
   "Unlike less successful art books for beginners, this one starts simply and takes the rank amateur to a satisfying level of accomplishment. . . . The accompanying DVD offers useful demonstrations of two complete paintings." Libr J

751.7   Paintings—Specific forms

Ganz, Nicholas
Graffiti women; street art from five continents; foreword by Swoon; introduction by Nancy Macdonald. Abrams 2006 223p il $29.95
Grades: 9 10 11 12 Adult   **751.7**
   1. Street art 2. Mural painting and decoration 3. Women artists
   ISBN 0-8109-5747-7; 978-0-8109-5747-3
                   LC 2006-15287
   "More than 1,000 images from prominent female graffiti and street artists show women challenging stereotypes and succeeding in the male-dominated field of tagging." Booklist
   Includes bibliographical references

752   Color in painting

Bartges, Dan, 1948-
Color is everything; master the use of color in oils, acrylics or watercolors. Oaklea Press 2008 96p il pa $14.99
Grades: 9 10 11 12 Adult   **752**
   1. Color in art 2. Painting—Technique
   ISBN 978-1-892538-36-9; 1-892538-36-9
   On cover: Beginners to advanced painters can learn what all great artists know
   "This accessible book offers the equivalent of an introduction to both color theory and art appreciation worthy of a high school or community college course. Bartges provides clear explanations—well illustrated with both color wheels and famous paintings—of how color schemes work and how to achieve color balance in one's own paintings." SLJ
   Includes bibliographical references

753   Symbolism, allegory, mythology, legend

How to read a painting; lessons from the old masters; [edited by] Patrick de Rynck. H.N. Abrams 2004 383p il $35 *
Grades: 11 12 Adult   **753**
   1. Symbolism in art 2. Art appreciation
   ISBN 0-8109-5576-8   LC 2004-9511
   The editor "presents 150 paintings and frescoes that have attained the status of masterpieces. Each work is displayed on a full-color two-page spread that includes detailed closeups and a meticulous decoding of the painting's subject, symbols, and intent. This is a truly felicitious approach, and the selections are supreme." Booklist
   Includes bibliographical references

759.05   Painting—1800-1899

Bingham, Jane
Impressionism. Heinemann Library 2008 48p il
(Art on the wall) lib bdg $32.86
Grades: 5 6 7 8 9 10   **759.05**
1. Impressionism (Art) 2. French painting
ISBN 978-1-4329-1371-7; 1-4329-1371-9
LC 2008020468
This book "discusses how and why the Impressionist
movement began, looks at how the Impressionists captured the changing effects of light and color in nature,
and examines the different subjects Impressionist artists
chose for their paintings." Publisher's note
This title succeeds "in presenting a bird's-eye view of
[Impressionism] without oversimplification. Information
on individual artists is included in the broader context of
the movement. Visually exciting, with plenty of color,
[the layout is] hip and should appeal to the target audience." SLJ
Includes glossary and bibliographical references

Post-Impressionism. Heinemann Library 2009
48p il (Art on the wall) lib bdg $32.86
Grades: 5 6 7 8 9 10   **759.05**
1. Postimpressionism (Art) 2. French painting
ISBN 978-1-4329-1369-4; 1-4329-1369-7
LC 2008020464
This book "discusses how Post-Impresssionism devel-
oped, examines the distinctive styles of individual Post-
Impressionist artists, and looks at how the Post-
Impressionists used colour, shape, and composition."
Publisher's note
Includes glossary and bibliographical references

759.13   American painting

Fallon, Michael, 1966-
How to analyze the works of Georgia O'Keeffe.
ABDO Pub. Co. 2011 112p il (Essential critiques)
$34.22
Grades: 9 10 11 12   **759.13**
1. O'Keeffe, Georgia, 1887-1986 2. Art appreciation
3. Art criticism
ISBN 978-1-61613-535-5   LC 2010-15883
This book looks at the works of Georgia O'Keeffe
"through the lenses of prevalent schools of criticism. The
first chapters introduce the concept of critical theory, its
purpose, and how to develop and support a thesis state-
ment. In subsequent chapters, an overview of each work
is followed by a critique using a particular theory. . . .
Georgia O'Keeffe's *Evening Star No. V*, *The Black Iris*,
Red Hills with White Shell, and *Pelvis Series Red with
Yellow* are addressed." SLJ
Includes bibliographical references

759.4   French painting

Lucie-Smith, Edward, 1933-
Toulouse-Lautrec. rev and enl ed. Phaidon Press
1983 31p il pa $9.95 hardcover o.p.
Grades: 9 10 11 12   **759.4**

1. Toulouse-Lautrec, Henri de, 1864-1901
ISBN 1-7148-2761-4
First published 1977
"The introductory overview of the artist's life is fol-
lowed by 48 chronologically arranged color plates and
concise, paragraph-length analyses of individual works.
. . . An intelligently written and well-illustrated survey."
Choice

Morris, Catherine
The essential Claude Monet. Harry N. Abrams
1999 112p il (Essential series) $12.95
Grades: 9 10 11 12   **759.4**
1. Monet, Claude, 1840-1926
ISBN 0-8109-5802-3; 978-0-8109-5802-9
This book examines the work of Impressionist painter
Claude Monet.

759.5   Italian painting

Hartt, Frederick, 1914-1991
Michelangelo Buonarroti. H.N. Abrams 2004
126p il (Masters of art) pa $19.95 *
Grades: 11 12 Adult   **759.5**
1. Michelangelo Buonarroti, 1475-1564
ISBN 0-8109-9144-6   LC 2003-22522
Concise edition of the author's Michelangelo, original-
ly published 1964
The forty colorplates in this book include broad views
and close details of Michelangelo's frescoes in the Sis-
tine Chapel and of his other paintings.
Includes bibliographical references

Marani, Pietro C.
Leonardo da Vinci—the complete paintings;
appendices edited by Pietro C. Marani and
Edoardo Villata. Abrams 2000 384p il $85 *
Grades: 11 12 Adult   **759.5**
1. Leonardo, da Vinci, 1452-1519
ISBN 0-8109-3581-3   LC 00-27556
Original Italian edition, 1999
This guide covers Leonardo's 31 paintings "intensive-
ly, recording possible precedents for design and technique in the work of other artists, calling attention to significant details, offering preparatory drawings and cartoons for comparison with the finished, which is not to
say completed, works, and presenting X rays to elucidate
the gestation of the *Mona Lisa* and other paintings
Leonardo spent years striving to perfect. Such scrupulous
attention to Leonardo's total creative process boosts the
number of illustrations, mostly colorplates, to 295."
Booklist
Includes bibliographical references

Wasserman, Jack, 1921-
Leonardo da Vinci. Concise, pbk. ed. Harry N.
Abrams 2003 126p il (Masters of art) pa $21.95
Grades: 11 12 Adult   **759.5**
1. Leonardo, da Vinci, 1452-1519
ISBN 978-0-8109-9130-9; 0-8109-9130-6
LC 2003013703

**Wasserman, Jack, 1921- **—*Continued*
First published 1984
This is a collection of 40 colorplates of Leonardo da Vinci's works, including *Last Supper* and *Mona Lisa.*

759.9492   Dutch painting

Schaffner, Ingrid
The essential Vincent van Gogh. Harry N. Abrams 1998 112p il (Essential series) $12.95 *
Grades: 9 10 11 12   **759.9492**
1. Gogh, Vincent van, 1853-1890
ISBN 0-8109-5813-9; 978-0-8109-5813-5
               LC 98-71931
This book examines the art of disturbed Dutch painter Vincent Van Gogh.

Sweet, Christopher
The essential Johannes Vermeer. Harry N. Abrams 1999 112p il (Essential series) $12.95
Grades: 9 10 11 12   **759.9492**
1. Vermeer, Johannes, 1632-1675
ISBN 0-8109-5801-5; 978-0-8109-5801-2
This book examines the art of great Dutch painter Jan Vermeer.

769.5   Forms of prints

Friedberg, Arthur
Paper money of the United States; a complete illustrated guide with valuations: the standard reference work on paper money; by Arthur L. and Ira S. Friedberg; based on the original work by Robert Friedberg. Coin and Currency Institute 2010 304p il $49.50
Grades: 9 10 11 12   **769.5**
1. Paper money 2. Reference books
ISSN 1099-9981
ISBN 978-0-87184-519-1
First published 1953. Periodically revised
A guide to paper money of the United States from 1861 to the present. Contains descriptions, valuations, and illustrations of notes, fractional currency, and certificates.

770   Photography & computer art

Goldberg, Vicki
The power of photography; how photographs changed our lives. Abbeville Press 1991 279p pa $35 hardcover o.p.
Grades: 11 12 Adult   **770**
1. Photography
ISBN 1-55859-467-1   LC 91-3116
This study of photography "traces the medium from its beginnings with the French daguerreotype of the 1840s to the powerful social tool and all-pervasive 'eye' {the author considers} it has become." SLJ
Includes bibliographical references

Kallen, Stuart A., 1955-
Photography. Lucent Books 2007 112p il (Eye on art) $32.45
Grades: 7 8 9 10 11 12   **770**
1. Photography—History
ISBN 978-1-59018-986-3   LC 2007015978
"This volume surveys the history of photography, from the ancient camera obscura to the digital camera. . . . This title offers a clear overview of an art form that many teens both practice and appreciate." Booklist
Includes bibliographical references

Willis, Deborah, 1952-
Reflections in Black; a history of Black photographers, 1840-1999. Norton 2000 348p il $50; pa $35
Grades: 11 12 Adult   **770**
ISBN 0-393-04880-2; 0-393-32280-7 (pa)
            LC 99-55185
Companion volume to A Smithsonian traveling exhibition
"Willis sketches important figures and traces both developments in photographic techniques and the practice of photography by African Americans. . . . A beautiful and informative album." Booklist
Includes bibliographical references

770.9   Photography—Historical, geographic, persons, treatment

Sandler, Martin W.
Photography: an illustrated history. Oxford Univ. Press 2002 156p il (Oxford illustrated histories) $29.95
Grades: 11 12 Adult   **770.9**
1. Photography—History
ISBN 0-19-512608-4   LC 2001-36602
Presents the history of photography from the daguerreotypes of the mid-1800s to its acceptance as an art form and more
"Most exciting are the images . . . which range from famous examples of photojournalism . . . to fine art. . . . [A] well-done, clearly written overview." Booklist
Includes bibliographical references

775   Digital photography

Doble, Rick
Career building through digital photography. Rosen Pub. 2008 64p il (Digital career building) lib bdg $29.25
Grades: 7 8 9 10   **775**
1. Digital photography 2. Vocational guidance
ISBN 978-1-4042-1941-0; 1-4042-1941-2
            LC 2006-102732
"This title explores the continually expanding world of digital photography and its many career opportunities. Chapter one looks at the advantages of the technology and its history, the range of cameras, and the various

Doble, Rick—*Continued*
online photo-sharing sites. Successive chapters discuss the impact of digital photography on the field of journalism, the use of photo software, dealing with deadlines and basic photography rules, freelance work, setting goals, the various Web sites to display photos, building a portfolio, and organizing one's work." SLJ

Includes bibliographical references

Seamon, Mary Ploski, 1943-
Digital cameras in the classroom; [by] Mary Ploski Seamon and Eric J. Levitt. Linworth Pub 2003 66p il pa $29.95 *
Grades: Adult Professional   775
1. Digital cameras 2. Digital photography
3. Photography in education
ISBN 1-58683-095-3   LC 2003-43337
This offers advice on such topics as "selecting the right camera, how digital imagery works, storing and downloading pictures, and incorporating images into PowerPoints, Web sites, and other projects. A chapter on classroom activities shows . . . how to use digital cameras as an idea generator and . . . teaching tool." Publisher's note
"The author's emphasis on the active learning involved in using digital cameras will encourage the most reluctant teachers and media specialists to see the value of this medium while concise chapters make learning to use a digital camera a reality." SLJ

Includes bibliographical references

776   Computer art (Digital art)

Miller, Ron, 1947-
Digital art; painting with pixels. Twenty-First Century Books 2008 120p il lib bdg $31.93
Grades: 6 7 8 9 10   776
1. Digital art 2. Computer art
ISBN 978-0-8225-7516-0; 0-8225-7516-7
                                        LC 2007-27633
"What is digital art? Where did it come from? Is it even art at all? Ron Miller answers these questions and more." Publisher's note
"Web sites to visit, a glossary and discussions of digital art software add significantly to the book's usefulness." Voice Youth Advocates

Includes glossary and bibliographical references

778.9   Photography of specific subjects

Caputo, Robert
National Geographic photography field guide; people & portraits: secrets to making great pictures. National Geographic Soc. 2001 159p il $21.95 *
Grades: 11 12 Adult   778.9
1. Photography
ISBN 0-7922-6499-1   LC 2001-44918

Also available companion volumes: National Geographic photography field guide landscapes (2002); National Geographic photography field guide: secrets to making great pictures (1999)
This guide explains "the best angles, lighting, and lenses to capture candid photos and portraits of family, friends, and everyone else. How to evoke a subject's true character on film {and} how to compose a formal family portrait." Publisher's note

Includes bibliographical references

779   Photographs

In focus; National Geographic greatest portraits. National Geographic Society 2004 504p il $30
Grades: 11 12 Adult   779
1. Portrait photography
ISBN 0-7922-7363-X   LC 2004-44953
"Comprising 280 portraits by 150 of National Geographic's celebrated photographers . . . the book spans over 100 years and covers the entire globe. Organized chronologically as well as thematically and enriched with essays on the development of photographic styles through decades, it is a tasteful celebration of the medium but even more so of human diversity." Libr J

Latana
Barely exposed. ORO Editions 2009 133p il $40
Grades: 7 8 9 10   779
1. Portrait photography
ISBN 978-0-9820607-0-4; 0-9820607-0-X
Texts in English and in the native languages of the subjects of the photographs
"The work is a compilation of black-and-white photographs depicting sixty young adults from all over the world in—literally and figuratively—a barely exposed state. On the opposite side of the page is a quote intended to express how the subject sees him or herself in the context of life, and/or where and how they might ultimately fit into this world. These passages are usually expressed in the teen's own words, which often prove to be not only insightful but are also sometimes in sharp contrast to the outward appearance of the subject. . . . This book is highly recommended for libraries of all types; if a picture is worth a thousand words, then this one is surely worth a million." Voice Youth Advocates

Photos that changed the world; the 20th century; edited by Peter Stepan; with contributions by Claus Biegerd [et al.] Prestel-Verlag 2000 183p il hardcover o.p. pa $19.95 *
Grades: 11 12 Adult   779
1. Photojournalism
ISBN 3-7913-2395-4; 3-7913-3628-2 (pa)
Translated from the German
Stepan provides "105 images that had the lasting visual power to capture a moment that could be the image of an era held in the instant of a shutter's click for distribution to a generation. . . . The photos are well reproduced and gain from the explanations of time, place, and context included in the excellent short essays that accompany each." Libr J

Through the lens; National Geographic greatest photographs. National Geographic Soc. 2003 504p il $30

Grades: 11 12 Adult   **779**

1. Documentary photography

ISBN 0-7922-6164-X   LC 2003-52757

This is a "collection of 250 photos, mostly in color and drawn from the National Geographic Society's archive. . . . The society's signature blend of dramatic, rigorously composed natural shots and 'family of nations'-style culture peeps are backed by broad captions and text. . . . The six sections ('Europe'; 'Asia'; 'Africa & the Middle East'; 'The Americas'; 'Oceans and Isles'; 'The Universe') include the first color underwater photographs, as well as collaborative work with NASA, and prominently credit the 84 photographers whose work is featured." Publ Wkly

780 Music

Marsalis, Wynton

Marsalis on music. Norton 1995 171p il music $29.95

Grades: 9 10 11 12 Adult   **780**

1. Music

ISBN 0-393-03881-5   LC 95-4470

This book "is designed to show how basic elements of music are shared by different musical styles. Chapters are divided into rhythm, form, wind bands and jazz bands, and practice. Musical examples are provided on an accompanying audio CD. . . . Also included are biographical sketches of composers featured in the book." Libr J

"An outstanding companion to a PBS series. . . . A superb resource for students and for other readers." Booklist

Includes glossary

780.3 Music—Encyclopedias and dictionaries

The **Harvard** concise dictionary of music and musicians; edited by Don Michael Randel. Belknap Press 1999 757p il hardcover o.p. pa $18.95 *

Grades: 11 12 Adult   **780.3**

1. Reference books 2. Music—Dictionaries 3. Music—Bio-bibliography

ISBN 0-674-00084-6; 0-674-00978-9 (pa)

        LC 99-40644

"Entries are arranged alphabetically and encompass terms, musical forms and styles, individual works, and instruments, as well as composers, performers, and theorists." Booklist

The **Oxford** companion to music; edited by Alison Latham. Oxford Univ. Press 2002 1434p il $65 *

Grades: 11 12 Adult   **780.3**

1. Reference books 2. Music—Dictionaries 3. Musicians—Dictionaries

ISBN 0-19-866212-2   LC 2002-537302

"New edition of two quite different earlier companions . . . Oxford companion to music . . . The new Oxford companion to music." Preface

"Among the 8000 entries are articles on composers, theorists, and some performers; instruments, forms, and terms; subjects like electronic music, individual countries, and politics and music; and some pieces (and even some famous arias). Each entry is presented in a dictionary format, with a select index of names appended and sometimes with bibliographic references. . . . The bias is still English, but the book provides cross references to American terms and includes plenty of American composers and musical subjects. A solid reference with a grand pedigree, usefully improved for home and general library use, this is highly recommended for all public libraries." Libr J

Includes bibliographical references

780.89 Music with respect to specific ethnic and national groups

Floyd, Samuel A.

The power of black music; interpreting its history from Africa to the United States; {by} Samuel A. Floyd, Jr. Oxford Univ. Press 1995 316p il pa $18.95 hardcover o.p.

Grades: 11 12 Adult   **780.89**

1. African American music

ISBN 978-0-19-510975-7   LC 94-21

The range of genres the author discusses includes "slaves' ring shouts, turn-of-the-century cotillion dances, jazz, R & B, etc. . . . Complementing the discourse are plenty of musical examples. Academics, critics, scholars, and fans alike stand to gain much from carefully reading this impressive work." Booklist

Includes discography, filmography, and bibliographical references

Southern, Eileen

The music of black Americans; a history. 3rd ed. Norton 1997 xxii, 678p il music hardcover o.p. pa $53.65 *

Grades: 11 12 Adult   **780.89**

1. African American musicians

ISBN 978-0-393-03843-9; 0-393-03843-2; 978-0-393-97141-5 (pa); 0-393-97141-4 (pa)

        LC 96-28811

First published 1971

A chronological survey of African American music in the United States tracing black music from its origin in Africa through colonial America and up to the present

Includes discography and bibliographical references

780.9 Music—Historical, geographic, persons, treatment

Grout, Donald Jay, 1902-1987
A history of western music; [by] J. Peter Burkholder, Donald Jay Grout, Claude V. Palisca. 8th ed. W. W. Norton & Company 2010 xxxiv, 986, 129p il $83.12 *
Grades: 11 12 Adult   **780.9**
1. Music—History and criticism
ISBN 978-0-393-93125-9; 0-393-93125-0
LC 2008-44302
First published 1960
The authors survey the course of Western music from the ancient world to modern atonalism and dodecaphony. They cover vocal and instrumental forms, notation, performance, music-printing, the development of instruments, and biographical information on composers.
Includes bibliographical references

Perlis, Vivian
Composer's voices from Ives to Ellington; an oral history of American music; [by] Vivian Perlis and Libby Van Cleve. Yale University Press 2005 477p il $50
Grades: 11 12 Adult   **780.9**
1. Composers—United States 2. Jazz musicians
ISBN 0-300-10673-4; 9780300106732
LC 2005-361
"In the first of four planned volumes, the authors cover the early 20th century, tapping reminiscences from the OH archives by and about such luminaries as Charles Ives, Edgard Varèse, Carl Ruggles, Charles Seeger, Henry Cowell, George Gershwin, Duke Ellington, and three of Nadia Boulanger's most illustrious students: Aaron Copland, Roy Harris, and Virgil Thompson." Libr J
"This volume offers the reader a unique perspective on the composers who created ragtime, 'new' music, and early jazz. A very enjoyable read supplemented by 2 compact discs that contain excerpts of interviews." Univ Press Books for Public and Second Sch Libr, 2006
Includes bibliographical references

Terkel, Studs, 1912-2008
And they all sang; adventures of an eclectic disc jockey. New Press 2005 xxii, 301p $25.95; pa $16.95
Grades: 11 12 Adult   **780.9**
1. Musicians
ISBN 978-1-59558-003-0; 1-59558-003-4; 978-1-59558-118-1 (pa); 1-59558-118-9 (pa)
LC 2005-43866
In this "collection of 40 interviews, . . . Terkel recalls his venerable radio program, The Wax Museum, which premiered shortly after the end of WWII in 1945, profiling composers, entertainers and impresarios of nearly every type of music. . . . Insightful and daring, Terkel always asks the right questions, whether culturally or musically." Publ Wkly

781.6 Traditions of music

Swafford, Jan
The Vintage guide to classical music. Vintage Bks. 1992 xxi, 597p il pa $17 *
Grades: 11 12 Adult   **781.6**
1. Music appreciation 2. Music—History and criticism
ISBN 0-679-72805-8   LC 91-50217
This guide contains "chronologically arranged essays on nearly 100 composers, from Guillaume de Machaut (ca. 1300-1377) to Aaron Copland (1900-1990), that combine biography with detailed analyses of the major works while assessing their role in the social, cultural, and political climate of their times." Publisher's note
Includes glossary and bibliographical references

781.64 Western popular music

Chang, Jeff
Can't stop, won't stop; a history of the hip-hop generation; introduction by D.J. Kool Herc. St. Martin's Press 2005 546p il hardcover o.p. pa $16 *
Grades: 11 12 Adult   **781.64**
1. Rap music
ISBN 0-312-30143-X; 0-312-42579-1 (pa)
LC 2004-56656
This is "a history of hip-hop and the cultural movement the music inspired." N Y Times Book Rev
"A fascinating, far-reaching must for pop-music and pop-culture collections." Booklist
Includes bibliographical references, discography, and filmography

Morales, Ed
The Latin beat; the rhythms and roots of Latin music from bossa nova to salsa and beyond. Da Capo Press 2003 xxviii, 372p pa $18.95 *
Grades: 9 10 11 12   **781.64**
1. Music—Latin America
ISBN 0-306-81018-2   LC 2003-16423
This book "outlines the musical styles of each country, then traces each form as it migrates north. Morales travels from the Latin ballad to bossa nova to Latin jazz, chronicles the development of the samba in Brazil and salsa in New York, explores the connection between the mambo craze of the 1950's with the Cuban craze of today, and uncovers the hidden history of Latinos in rock and hip hop." Publisher's note
"Displaying an incredible depth of historical and musical knowledge and insight, this book will be a joy to read both for those already steeped in the Latin musical tradition as well as for those recently introduced to the music of, for instance, Tito Puente." Publ Wkly
Includes bibliographical references

781.65   Jazz

Gioia, Ted

The history of jazz. 2nd ed. Oxford University Press 2011 444p il pa $19.95

Grades: 11 12 Adult   **781.65**
1. Jazz music—History and criticism
ISBN 978-0-19-539970-7; 0-19-539970-6
                                    LC 2010-23182
First published 1997

The author "relates the story of African American music from its roots in Africa to the international respect it enjoys today. . . . This well-researched, extensively annotated volume covers the major trends and personalities that have shaped jazz. The excellent bibliography and list of recommended listening make this a valuable purchase for libraries building a jazz collection." Libr J

Includes discography and bibliographical references

Marsalis, Wynton

Jazz A-B-Z; [by] Wynton Marsalis and Paul Rogers; with biographical sketches by Phil Schaap. Candlewick Press 2005 unp il $24.99

Grades: 5 6 7 8 9 10   **781.65**
1. Jazz music 2. Jazz musicians
ISBN 978-0-7636-3434-6   LC 2005-48448

This is an illustrated alphabetically arranged introduction to jazz musicians.

This is a "witty, stunningly designed alphabet catalog. . . . The biographical sketches and notes on poetic forms by Phil Schaap are concise and genuinely informative. . . . Rogers's pastiche full-page portraits, his use of expressive typography and the smaller vignettes he sprinkles throughout are bound to heighten any reader's appreciation of both the musicians and the music. . . . [Marsalis offers] clever . . . poems, wordplays, odes and limericks." N Y Times Book Rev

Moving to higher ground; how jazz can change your life; [by] Wynton Marsalis with Geoffrey C. Ward. Random House 2008 181p il $26

Grades: 10 11 12 Adult   **781.65**
1. Jazz music—History and criticism
ISBN 978-1-4000-6078-8; 1-4000-6078-8
                                    LC 2008-16560

The author "explains in lay readers' terms how jazz works as a diverse musical genre and, more important, how an understanding and appreciation of jazz can enrich one's life. . . . This work is highly recommended." Libr J

The **New** Grove dictionary of jazz; edited by Barry Kernfeld. 2nd ed. Grove's Dictionaries Inc. 2002 3v set $295

Grades: 11 12 Adult   **781.65**
1. Jazz music—Dictionaries 2. Reference books
ISBN 1-56159-284-6   LC 2001-40794
First published 1988 in two volumes

This reference to jazz and jazz musicians includes "more than 7750 entries. . . . [It covers] jazz styles, instruments, record labels, nicknames, guilds and associations, jazz language, libraries and archives, false fingering techniques for horns, festivals, titles of films containing jazz scenes, a list of contrafacts . . . and even biographies of a few jazz writers and critics." Libr J

Includes bibliographical references and discographies

Szwed, John F., 1936-

Jazz 101; a complete guide to learning and loving jazz; {by} John Szwed. Hyperion 2000 354p pa $14.95 *

Grades: 11 12 Adult   **781.65**
1. Jazz music
ISBN 0-7868-8496-7   LC 00-35055

Szwed "proceeds chronologically through jazz history, managing to explore the different trends in jazz that often overlapped and the key players who often reinvented themselves over decades. There are even accounts of the famous nightclubs where jazz history was made. Strong, descriptive reviews of key albums are included as sidebars to give the reader good places to start listening. Very worthwhile." Booklist

Includes bibliographical references

Ward, Geoffrey C.

Jazz; a history of America's music; based on a documentary film by Ken Burns written by Geoffrey C. Ward; with a preface by Ken Burns. Knopf 2000 489p il $65; pa $29.95 *

Grades: 11 12 Adult   **781.65**
1. Jazz music
ISBN 0-679-44551-X; 0-679-76539-5 (pa)
                                    LC 00-22604
Companion volume to PBS series of the same title

The authors "have assembled a comprehensive history with a focus on the musicians and the sociology of jazz. . . . The short articles by Wynton Marsalis, Dan Morgenstern, Gerald Early, Stanley Crouch, and Gary Giddins, which are woven into the text, provide a . . . specific focus on a number of jazz's aspects." Libr J

"The illustrations are copious, including about 500 pieces and running from cover to cover; the text, picture captions, and sidebars reflect the research that went into the six-year project. A very competent and lovingly rendered history." Booklist

Includes bibliographical references

781.66   Rock (Rock 'n' roll)

The **Beatles** anthology. Chronicle Bks. 2000 367p il $60; pa $35

Grades: 11 12 Adult   **781.66**
1. Beatles
ISBN 0-8118-2684-8; 0-8118-3636-3 (pa)
                                    LC 00-23685

The story of the Beatles as "told through quotes from John, Paul, George, and Ringo, as well as the group's closest aides: George Martin, Neil Aspinall, and Derek Taylor. . . . The density of the text is daunting, but the book's browsability makes it as appealing to casual readers as it is indispensable to Beatlemaniacs." Libr J

Includes bibliographical references

Beaujon, Andrew

Body piercing saved my life; inside the phenomenon of Christian rock. Da Capo Press 2006 291p il $16.95

Grades: 11 12 Adult **781.66**

1. Christian rock music

ISBN 0-306-81457-9; 978-0-306-81457-0

LC 2006-6254

The author "chronicles the Christian rock subculture, beginning with the 'Jesus People' of the early 1970s to its substantial popularity today. . . . This important, well-written study of the Christian rock phenomenon brings the personalities to life." Libr J

Includes bibliographical references

Hopper, Jessica

The girl's guide to rocking; how to start a band, book gigs, and get rolling to rock stardom. Workman Pub. 2009 229p il pa $13.95

Grades: 9 10 11 12 **781.66**

1. Rock musicians 2. Music industry—Vocational guidance 3. Women—Vocational guidance

ISBN 978-0-7611-5141-8 LC 2008-52803

This guide features "insider information and tips about starting a rock band. . . . [It includes] details about choosing and learning to play the guitar, bass, drum set, and piano, as well as how to work with amps, microphones, and speakers; assembling and naming the band; practicing and learning songs; recording a solid demo; booking and publicizing performances and touring; and playing a killer show." Libr J

"This guide is a necessary handbook for any aspiring Alicia Keys or Joan Jett." Booklist

Marcus, Sara, 1977-

Girls to the front; the true story of the Riot grrrl revolution. HarperPerennial 2010 367p il pa $14.99

Grades: 11 12 Adult **781.66**

1. Riot grrrl movement 2. Feminism

ISBN 978-0-06-180636-0; 0-06-180636-6

This "history covers a specific time period, 1989–1994, and a particular type of music that turned into a larger social movement. The riot grrrl movement was a potent form of female empowerment as well as a postfeminist reaction to sexism and the rising number of sexual assaults against women when expectations for equality were high. . . . [The author] describes some of the major players on the scene, including individuals (Kathleen Hanna, Tobi Vail) and bands (Bikini Kill, Heavens to Betsy)—all set against the backdrop of the so-called postfeminist period." Booklist

This book is "a brash, gutsy chronicle of the empowering music and feminist movement of the early 1990s." Publ Wkly

Nichols, Travis

Punk rock etiquette; the ultimate how-to guide for punk, underground, DIY, and indie bands. Roaring Brook Press 2008 128p il pa $10.95

Grades: 7 8 9 10 11 12 **781.66**

1. Punk rock music 2. Music industry—Vocational guidance

ISBN 978-1-59643-415-8; 1-59643-415-5

LC 2008-11706

Contents: Forming a band; Songs and recording; Stage etiquette; Putting out your music; Merch; Touring: preheating your oven of destruction; Touring: freeeeeeeeeeeeeedom!!!

"Lively, knowledgeable, witty, and wise, this title offers a sound foundation in the social economics of indie rock. . . . From how to put together a band that functions rather than fights, to designing and creating appealing merchandise and running a successful tour, this heavily illustrated guide covers every aspect of how to be a bona fide DIY rock star for the twenty-first century." Voice Youth Advocates

Rock and roll is here to stay; an anthology; edited by William McKeen; introduction by Peter Guralnick. Norton 2000 672p il $35

Grades: 11 12 Adult **781.66**

1. Rock music

ISBN 0-393-04700-8 LC 99-31759

McKeen "presents 94 excerpts from novels, rock criticism, lyrics, interviews, speeches, personal recollections, and other sources to weave together the history of rock'n'roll." Libr J

The **Rolling** Stone illustrated history of rock & roll; the definitive history of the most important artists and their music; edited by Anthony DeCurtis and James Henke with Holly George-Warren; original editor: Jim Miller. {new ed}. Random House 1992 710p il pa $36.95 *

Grades: 7 8 9 10 **781.66**

1. Rock music

ISBN 0-679-73728-6 LC 92-6339

First published 1976

This history of four decades of rock music includes essays and photographs covering individual artists, groups, trends and styles

Talevski, Nick, 1962-

The unofficial encyclopedia of the Rock and Roll Hall of Fame. Greenwood Press 1998 402p il $60

Grades: 11 12 Adult **781.66**

1. Rock & Roll Hall of Fame and Museum 2. Rock musicians 3. Rock music

ISBN 0-313-30032-1 LC 97-41928

"This book covers the first 150 inductees into the Rock and Roll Hall of Fame. . . . Individuals and groups who have been inducted into the Rock and Roll Hall of Fame are listed alphabetically, with the entries providing both personal and professional information. Each description includes not only dry factual annotations about the individual's achievements, records, etc., but also interest-

Talevski, Nick, 1962-—*Continued*
ing personal information, anecdotes, comments, and insights. At the end of each entry is a bibliography for further reading." Voice Youth Advocates

782.25   Sacred songs

We'll understand it better by and by; pioneering African American gospel composers; edited by Bernice Johnson Reagon. Smithsonian Institution Press 1992 384p il music pa $27.95 hardcover o.p.
Grades: 11 12 Adult   782.25
1. Gospel music 2. African American musicians 3. Composers
ISBN 1-56098-167-9   LC 91-37954
"Reagon and her contributors explore every aspect of gospel's history, spiritual significance, and influence on secular music, but the primary focus is on individuals. The lives and achievements of six pioneering gospel music composers are examined in detail. . . . A splendidly comprehensive and invaluable history." Booklist
Includes discography and bibliographical references

782.42   Songs

The **anthology** of rap; edited by Adam Bradley, Andrew DuBois; foreword by Henry Louis Gates, Jr.; afterword by Chuck D and Common. Yale University Press 2010 867p il $35
Grades: 11 12 Adult   782.42
1. Rap music—History and criticism
ISBN 978-0-300-14190-0; 0-300-14190-4
                                    LC 2010-23316
"The anthology is organized around four eras of rap: old-school, the golden age, mainstream, and the new millennium. Within each of these sections, individual artists are identified for both their artistic influence and cultural impact." Libr J
"For fans, this is an obvious treasure. For skeptical listeners and readers, this mega-anthology strips away rap's performance elements and allows the language itself to pulse, break, spin, and strut in poems of audacity, outrage, insight, sweetness, and nastiness. Here is meter and rhyme, distillation, metaphor, misdirection, leaps of imagination, appropriation, improvisation, and a 'vivid vocabulary' that can be explicit, offensive, funny, dumb, and transcendent." Booklist
Includes bibliographical references

Bynoe, Yvonne
Encyclopedia of rap and hip-hop culture. Greenwood Press 2006 449p il $69.95 *
Grades: 11 12 Adult   782.42
1. Reference books 2. Rap music—Encyclopedias 3. Hip-hop—Encyclopedias
ISBN 0-313-33058-1   LC 2005-19215
This encyclopedia describes "the separate elements embraced by rap and hip-hop: the verbal (MCing), and the musical (DJing), break dancing, and aerosol painting. The alphabetical entries cover all these elements and include most of the well-known rap artists and groups,

along with some less-familiar names. The articles also acknowledge some of rap's detractors. . . . This title will be of interest to browsers and report writers." SLJ
Includes bibliographical references

Furia, Philip, 1943-
The poets of Tin Pan Alley; a history of America's great lyricists. Oxford Univ. Press 1990 322p pa $14.95 hardcover o.p.
Grades: 11 12 Adult   782.42
1. Lyricists 2. Popular music 3. American songs
ISBN 0-19-507473-4   LC 90-35937
This work examines "lyrics from stage and movie musicals and the work of ten lyricists: Irving Berlin, Lorenz Hart, Ira Gershwin, Cole Porter, Oscar Hammerstein, Howard Dietz, Yip Harburg, Dorothy Fields, Leo Robin, and Johnny Mercer. . . . Although primarily a record of one aspect of show business, the book is a good history of American popular culture." Choice
Includes bibliographical references

National anthems of the world; edited by Michael Jamieson Bristow. 11th ed. Weidenfeld & Nicolson 2006 629p $90 *
Grades: 5 6 7 8 9 10 11 12 Adult
                                                 782.42
1. National songs
ISBN 0-304-36826-1
First published 1943 in the United Kingdom with title: National anthems of the United Nations and France
This volume contains national anthems of about 198 nations, including melody and accompaniment. Words are presented in the native language with transliteration provided where necessary. English translations follow. Brief historical notes on the adoption of each anthem are included
"An essential reference resource for all libraries." Libr J

Songwriter's market; Greg Hatfield, editor. 34th annual ed. Writer's Digest 2010 362p il pa $29.99
Grades: 11 12 Adult   782.42
1. Popular music—Writing and publishing
ISSN 0161-5971
ISBN 978-1-58297-954-0
Annual. First published 1978
The main section of this guide consists of listings of music publishers, record companies, producers, managers, booking agents, and firms interested in original music. Also included are articles which present an overview of the songwriting field, and listings of resources such as organizations, workshops, and contests.

784.19   Musical instruments

Baines, Anthony
The Oxford companion to musical instruments; written and edited by Anthony Baines. Oxford University Press 1992 404p il $85
Grades: 8 9 10 11 12 Adult   784.19
1. Musical instruments—Dictionaries 2. Reference books
ISBN 0-19-311334-1   LC 92-8635

Baines, Anthony—*Continued*

Based on The New Oxford companion to music (1983)

This volume presents alphabetically arranged entries for musical instruments. "The individual entries cover specific instruments and families thereof (e.g., Wind Instruments) as well as their representation in different countries (e.g., Africa) and time periods (e.g., Baroque). . . . Playing techniques, a brief history, and a list of the major repertory are [discussed]." Booklist

784.2 Full orchestra (Symphony orchestra)

Steinberg, Michael

The symphony; a listener's guide. Oxford Univ. Press 1995 678p music $42.50; pa $25 *

Grades: 11 12 Adult   **784.2**

1. Symphony 2. Music appreciation 3. Composers

ISBN 0-19-506177-2; 0-19-512665-3 (pa)

LC 95-5568

"Steinberg describes 36 composers and, movement by movement, 118 symphonies, including all the standard repertory . . . as well as a few by less well known composers such as Gorecki, Harbison, Martinu, and Sessions. The writing varies from formal and factual to chatty, with candid asides and stories relevant to the composer, the composition, or an important performance." Libr J

Includes bibliographical references

784.8 Wind band

Bailey, Wayne, 1955-

The complete marching band resource manual; techniques and materials for teaching, drill design, and music arranging; [by] Wayne Bailey; percussion chapter by Thomas Caneva. 2nd ed. University of Pennsylvania Press 2003 290p il spiral bdg $34.95

Grades: 9 10 11 12   **784.8**

1. Bands (Music)

ISBN 0-8122-1856-6   LC 2003-50768

First published 1994

This guidebook for band directors features drill charts and instrumental arrangements.

787.87 Guitars

Bacon, Tony

The ultimate guitar book; {by} Tony Bacon & Paul Day. Knopf 1991 192p il pa $27.50 hardcover o.p.

Grades: 11 12 Adult   **787.87**

1. Guitars

ISBN 0-375-70090-0   LC 91-52714

This is a "chronological history of the guitar, beginning with an example from 1552 and continuing through current times. Covering acoustic, electrical, and bass guitars, including all the big-name manufacturers such as Fender, Gibson, Martin, and Stratocaster, this informative and beautifully illustrated work will have wide appeal." SLJ

Chapman, Richard

The new complete guitarist. rev American ed. DK 2003 208p il pa $20

Grades: 11 12 Adult   **787.87**

1. Guitars

ISBN 0-7894-9701-8   LC 2004-271630

First published 1993 with title: The complete guitarist

This work ranges "from fundamentals such as tuning, scales, chords, picking, and strumming, to advanced techniques of various styles such as rock, blues, and jazz. . . . [It also] includes discussions on such topics as sound and amplification, choosing a guitar, studio and home recording, plus care and maintenance of the instrument. An appealing book in the style of the 'Eyewitness' series." SLJ [review of 1993 edition]

Includes bibliographical references

Chappell, Jon

Guitar all-in-one for dummies. Wiley 2009 xxiv, 666p il pa $34.99

Grades: 11 12 Adult   **787.87**

1. Guitars

ISBN 978-0-470-48133-2

On cover: 8 books in 1. Includes CD-ROM

This conglomeration of eight previously published For Dummies books covers topics such as writing songs and how to play rock and blues guitar.

Complete guitar course; the definitive full-color picture guide to playing guitar; [edited by Sorcha Armstrong, music processed by Paul Ewers; text photographs by George Taylor and Geoff Green] Amsco Publications 2008 127p il (iCanPlayMusic) pa $34.99 *

Grades: 9 10 11 12 Adult   **787.87**

1. Guitars

ISBN 978-0-8256-3591-5

At head of title: iCanPlayMusic. Includes 2 audio CDs and 1 DVD

This course covers how the different parts of the guitar work, guitar techniques, how to maintain the instrument, and music theory. Includes foldouts on the cover that can act as an easel for the book. The focus is primarily on how to play rock music.

Denyer, Ralph

The guitar handbook. [rev ed] Knopf 1992 256p il pa $25 *

Grades: 11 12 Adult   **787.87**

1. Guitars

ISBN 0-679-74275-1   LC 92-53164

"A Dorling Kindersley book"

First published 1982

Contains a learning program covering the range of guitar techniques from simple chords to improvised lead solos, profiles of famous and influential guitarists, an il-

Denyer, Ralph—*Continued*

lustrated chord dictionary, chapters on guitar customizing and recording techniques, and sections on a variety of acoustic and electric guitars, amplification, special effects and stage sound systems.

Hodge, David

The complete idiot's guide to playing bass guitar. Alpha Books 2006 xxii, 308p il pa $22.95

Grades: 9 10 11 12 Adult   **787.87**

1. Guitars

ISBN 978-1-59257-311-0; 1-59257-311-8

Includes audio CD

"This book provides a . . . foundation in reading music, purchasing the right equipment, and care and maintenance of the bass guitar. [It includes] a CD of original music." Publisher's note

Includes bibliographical references

790   Sports, games & entertainment

Encyclopedia of recreation and leisure in America; Gary S. Cross, editor in chief. Charles Scribner's Sons 2004 2v il (Scribner American civilization series) set $270 *

Grades: 11 12 Adult   **790**

1. Reference books 2. Recreation—Encyclopedias

ISBN 0-684-31265-4   LC 2004-4617

"This work provides information on all aspects of leisure in America, including historical influences, cultural changes, economic effects, and more. . . . This is a fascinating look at data useful for research papers, sociological studies, and historical evaluations or simply to satisfy curiosity." Libr J

Includes bibliographical references

790.1   General kinds of recreational activities

Unique games and sports around the world; a reference guide; edited by Doris Corbett, John Cheffers, and Eileen Crowley Sullivan. Greenwood Press 2001 407p hardcover o.p. pa $25 *

Grades: 11 12 Adult   **790.1**

1. Games 2. Sports

ISBN 0-313-29778-9; 0-313-36101-0 (pa)

LC 00-33125

A guide to more than 300 games. "Some involve physical action, like France's *Clubs royale;* others, like *Authors,* played in the U.S., are more intellectual. But most combine cognitive and physical activity. Organized by continents and then individual countries, entries for games note the typical players . . . the object of the game; number of players; equipment and apparel; type and amount of space needed; length of time; origin, purpose, or symbolic meaning; and the rules of play and scoring." Booklist

Includes bibliographical references

791.43   Motion pictures

The **Actor's** book of movie monologues; edited by Marisa Smith and Amy Schewel. Penguin Bks. 1986 xxx, 240p pa $14 *

Grades: 11 12 Adult   **791.43**

1. Motion pictures 2. Monologues

ISBN 0-14-009475-X   LC 86-8093

"Although designed as a sourcebook for aspiring thespians who need material for auditions, this collection of famous movie monologues makes great browsing for all film buffs. . . . Featuring memorable speeches from more than 80 films, the text is arranged chronologically." Booklist

Cavelos, Jeanne

The science of Star Wars. St. Martin's Press 1999 255p hardcover o.p. pa $14.95

Grades: 11 12 Adult   **791.43**

1. Space sciences 2. Star Wars films

ISBN 0-312-20958-4; 0-312-26387-2 (pa)

LC 99-22007

An examination of space travel, aliens, planets, and robots as portrayed in the Star Wars films and books

"If you are willing to address this material seriously, you will find the book stimulating and fun. At points, it does get a bit deeper than, for example, a high school student will be ready to go, but a stretch is not a bad thing." Sci Books Films

Includes bibliographical references

Lanier, Troy, 1967-

Filmmaking for teens; pulling off your shorts; [by] Troy Lanier & Clay Nichols. Michael Wiese Productions 2010 197p il pa $20.95

Grades: 9 10 11 12   **791.43**

1. Cinematography 2. Video recording 3. Motion pictures—Production and direction

ISBN 978-1-932907-68-1   LC 2009-29891

First published 2005

A guide to filmmaking for teens that covers picking a subject, writing a script, production, schedules, expenses, directing, equipment, lighting, sound, editing, and distribution. It also provides tips on techniques.

Leonard Maltin's movie guide; edited by Leonard Maltin; managing editor, Darwyn Carson; associate editor, Luke Sader; contributing editors, Mike Clark ... [et al.]; video editor, Casey St. Charnez; contributors, Jerry Beck, Jessie Maltin. 2011 ed. Plume 2010 1643p pa $20

Grades: 11 12 Adult   **791.43**

1. Motion pictures 2. DVDs 3. Videotapes 4. Reference books

ISBN 978-0-452-29626-8

Also available in paperback from Signet Bks.

Annual. First published 1969 with title: TV movies. Title varies

"Maltin offers 17,000 summary movie reviews. . . . Also included are more than 25,000 combined DVD and video listings. . . . Less commercially familiar works,

Leonard Maltin's movie guide—*Continued*

like foreign films, indies, and cult classics, are given equal billing. Rated on a star system, including a category for 'bomb,' paragraph-long reviews contain actor listings and concise narrative synopses, along with incisive critical considerations. A highly useful, quick reference for film studies and general collections." Libr J

Muir, John Kenneth, 1969-

The encyclopedia of superheroes on film and television. 2nd ed. McFarland & Co. 2008 696p il $75

Grades: 11 12 Adult   **791.43**
  1. Superhero films—Encyclopedias 2. Superhero television programs—Encyclopedias 3. Reference books
  ISBN 978-0-7864-3755-9; 0-7864-3755-3
                        LC 2008-19724
  First published 2004
"Entries start with description and background of the hero. Live-action films are presented with reviewer comments and cast and crew. TV series also present reviewer comments and a description of the series. Episode guides include title, writer and director credits, and air dates as well as episode descriptions and guest casts. . . . A good addition to the pop-culture collection." Booklist
  Includes bibliographical references

Patmore, Chris

Movie making course; principles, practice, and techniques: the ultimate guide for the aspiring filmmaker. Barron's Educational Series, Inc. 2005 144p il pa $19.99 *

Grades: 11 12 Adult   **791.43**
  1. Motion pictures—Production and direction
  ISBN 0-7641-3191-5; 978-0-7641-3191-2
                      LC 2004-111722
"All aspects of the moviemaking process are covered in five sections, including preproduction considerations (types of cameras and film, script writing, and storyboarding), the logistics of the actual shoot, postproduction activities (editing, special effects), suggested projects, and how to market the final product via film festivals and the Internet. . . . This volume will give students the tools necessary to produce a first film with little more than an idea, a video camera, and basic word-processing software." SLJ
  Includes bibliographical references

Richmond, Simon

The rough guide to anime. Rough Guides 2009 292p il pa $18.99

Grades: 9 10 11 12 Adult   **791.43**
  1. Anime 2. Animated films
  ISBN 978-18-58282-053
"The author covers a set of canonical films; popular anime television series; creator and director mini-bios; technical terms described accessibly and with reference to the 50 canonical titles; and includes many two-tone stills from adventure, romance, children's interest, suspense, and historical anime productions. . . . Teens who love anime will find this guide validates their interests, and library staff can turn to it as a reliable way to learn

the vocabulary, icons, and plots of a good variety of examples of the popular art." SLJ
  Includes bibliographical references

Sanello, Frank

Reel v. real; how Hollywood turns fact into fiction. Taylor Pub. Co. 2003 303p il pa $19.95

Grades: 11 12 Adult   **791.43**
  1. Motion pictures
  ISBN 0-87833-268-5   LC 2001-27525
This is "Sanello's comparison of the screen to the record for 70 'historical' flicks . . . {including} such Oscar winners as *Braveheart, Dances with Wolves, Shakespeare in Love, Titanic,* and *A Beautiful Mind.*" Booklist
  Includes bibliographical references

Welsch, Janice R.

Multicultural films; a reference guide; [by] Janice R. Welsch and J. Q. Adams. Greenwood Press 2005 231p il $49.95

Grades: 11 12 Adult   **791.43**
  1. Minorities in motion pictures
  ISBN 0-313-31975-8   LC 2004-22529
This book "is a collection of synopses and brief analyses of selected American films. . . . It is divided into six sections, each of which covers a particular racial or ethnic group. The groups covered are African Americans, Arab and Middle Eastern Americans, Asian Americans, European Americans, Latino/a Americans, and Native Americans. . . . Each entry examines the way race or ethnicity functions in the film." Ref & User Services Quarterly
  Includes bibliographical references

791.45   Television

Morris, Holly, 1965-

Adventure divas; searching the globe for a new kind of heroine. Villard 2005 xx, 283p il hardcover o.p. pa $14.95

Grades: 11 12 Adult   **791.45**
  1. Adventure divas (Television program)
  ISBN 0-375-50827-9; 0-375-76063-6 (pa)
                      LC 2005-45171
The author describes the "people and places she's encountered on the road while filming her PBS series Adventure Divas and other programs." Publisher's note
This "is a delightful triangulation of adventure travel, telecommuting and self-reinvention that proves it does not, in fact, take a rocket scientist to achieve personal flight." N Y Times Book Rev
  Includes bibliographical references

791.5   Puppetry and toy theaters

Blumenthal, Eileen, 1948-

Puppetry; a world history. Abrams 2005 272p il $65 *

Grades: 11 12 Adult   **791.5**
  1. Puppets and puppet plays
  ISBN 0-8109-5587-3   LC 2004-29349

Blumenthal, Eileen, 1948-—*Continued*

This is a "history of the puppet world, from prehistoric times to Tony-winning Broadway hit Avenue Q. . . . This would be a welcome addition to the libraries of performing arts buffs who want to learn more about a lesser known form." Publ Wkly

Includes bibliographical references

792   Stage presentations

Brustein, Robert, 1927-

Letters to a young actor; a universal guide to performance. Basic Books 2005 234p (Art of mentoring) $22.50; pa $15

Grades: 11 12 Adult   **792**

1. Acting 2. Vocational guidance
ISBN 0-465-00806-2; 0-465-00814-3 (pa)
                                                  LC 2004-23438

The author "covers all aspects of an emerging actor's life, from the 'actor's calling' to getting a strong liberal education . . . to strategies for finding work and staying employed." Booklist

"This is a sharp, accessible but far from simplistic Cliffs Notes on being an actor." Publ Wkly

Corson, Richard

Stage makeup; [by] Richard Corson, Beverly Gore Norcross, James Glavan. 10th ed. Ally & Bacon/Pearson 2009 xx, 407p il $141.40 *

Grades: 11 12 Adult   **792**

1. Theatrical makeup
ISBN 978-0-205-64454-4   LC 2008-53845

First published 1942 by Appleton. Periodically revised

The authors discuss the art and technique of theatrical makeup, covering such topics as facial anatomy, various methods for applying greasepaint and other makeup, and the use of beards, wigs, and prosthetic pieces.

Ellis, Roger, 1943-

The complete audition book for young actors; a comprehensive guide to winning by enhancing acting skills. Meriwether Pub 2003 295p il pa $17.95

Grades: 9 10 11 12   **792**

1. Acting
ISBN 1-566-08088-6   LC 2003-21120

First published 1986 by Nelson-Hall with title: An audition handbook for student actors

A step-by-step guide for training young actors to audition well by developing acting skills.

This guide features "chapters on training, background skills, how to select and prepare material for an audition, cold readings, musical theater, and supporting materials such as résumé and head shots . . . The writing is so engaging that it is a pleasure to read straight through. Ellis speaks to his readers as a trusted advisor or coach . . . Acting teachers looking for a text and students looking for a useful and inspiring guidebook will welcome this title." SLJ

Includes bibliographical references

Kuritz, Paul

Fundamental acting; a practical guide. Applause Theatre Bk. Pubs. 1998 157p $24.95 *

Grades: 11 12 Adult   **792**

1. Acting
ISBN 1-55783-304-4   LC 97-27053

"Aimed at the beginning acting student, this book takes a commonsense approach to the craft, building on basic techniques in the first part and then going on to cover two distinct types of theater: comedy and Shakespearean verse. . . . Warm-up exercises, comic dialect guidelines, and a general stage terminology contribute to the usefulness of the book." Libr J

Levy, Gavin

112 acting games; a comprehensive workbook of theatre games for developing acting skills. Meriwether Pub. 2005 237p il pa $17.95

Grades: 9 10 11 12   **792**

1. Acting 2. Games
ISBN 1-56608-106-8; 978-1-56608-106-1
                                                  LC 2005-1784

"The games in this workbook for acting students are divided into twenty different categories, including Relaxtion, Memorization, and Improvisation. The author explains the instructions for each game in a clear manner, including tips on student placement, the appropriate number of participants, and modifications for varying ages. . . . This book is a definite asset to any drama teacher." Voice Youth Advocates

Includes bibliographical references

Marasco, Ron

Notes to an actor. Ivan R. Dee 2007 214p $24.95

Grades: 11 12 Adult   **792**

1. Acting
ISBN 978-1-56663-757-2; 1-56663-757-0
                                                  LC 2007-11653

This is "a compendium of suggestions, inspirations, warnings, and musings about the art of acting. Marasco speaks to actors who already possess at least a basic knowledge of their craft, seeking to heighten their abilities, clarify their artistic choices, eliminate blocks, and make their work more exciting and enriching. . . . This book is truly unique among acting resources. Useful both to those seeking to further their development as actors and to those for whom acting has long been a profession, this is an insightful, invaluable, and definitive work." Choice

Includes bibliographical references

Rogers, Barb, 1947-

Costumes, accessories, props, and stage illusions made easy. Meriwether Pub. 2005 205p il pa $19.95 *

Grades: 8 9 10 11 12   **792**

1. Costume 2. Theater—Production and direction
ISBN 978-1-56608-103-0; 1-56608-103-3
                                                  LC 2005-4359

This book details ways to make theater "costumes with simple tools such as scissors, glue guns, and paint.

Rogers, Barb, 1947-—_Continued_
In addition, there are chapters on how to make hats, gloves, armor, and animal heads, as well as other props and accessories from rummage-sale finds and a little imagination. . . . This is a useful volume for schools and community theaters with little or no budgets for costumes and props." SLJ

Includes bibliographical references

Varley, Joy
Places, please! a manual for high-school theater directors. Smith & Kraus 2001 196p (Young actor series) pa $16.95 *
Grades: 9 10 11 12   **792**
1. Theater—Production and direction
ISBN 1-57525-282-1   LC 01-20316
This guide offers guidance on choosing a script, casting, costuming, working with faculty, rehearsing, directing young actors, stage design and lighting

792.03   Stage presentations— Encyclopedias and dictionaries

Bordman, Gerald Martin
The Oxford companion to American theatre; [by] Gerald Bordman, Thomas S. Hischak. 3rd ed. Oxford University Press 2004 681p $75 *
Grades: 11 12 Adult   **792.03**
1. Reference books 2. Theater—United States—Dictionaries 3. American drama—Dictionaries
ISBN 0-19-516986-7   LC 2003-21367
First published 1984
"The volume includes playwrights, plays, actors, directors, producers, songwriters, famous playhouses, {and} dramatic movements. . . . The book covers not only classic works (such as _Death of a Salesman_) but also many commercially successful plays (such as _Getting Gertie's Garter_), plus entries on foreign figures that have influenced our dramatic development (from Shakespeare to Beckett and Pinter)." Publisher's note
"Individual entries are packed with detail. . . . Hischak provides ample material for researchers, and should be a mainstay of any performing arts reference collection." Choice

The **Cambridge** guide to American theatre; edited by Don B. Wilmeth; assistant to the editor, Leonard Jacobs. 2nd hardcover ed. Cambridge University Press 2007 757p il $150
Grades: 11 12 Adult   **792.03**
1. Reference books 2. Theater—United States—Dictionaries
ISBN 978-0-521-83538-1; 0-521-83538-0
                                      LC 2008-270062
First published 1993
This guide covers different "aspects of the American theatre from its earliest history to the present. Entries include people, venues and companies scattered through the USA, plays and musicals, and theatrical phenomena." Publisher's note

Includes bibliographical references

792.09   Theater—Historical, geographic, persons treatment

Brockett, Oscar G., 1923-2010
History of the theatre; [by] Oscar G. Brockett, Franklin J. Hildy. 10th ed. Pearson 2008 688p il map $113 *
Grades: 11 12 Adult   **792.09**
1. Theater—History 2. Drama—History and criticism
ISBN 978-0-205-51186-0   LC 2009-291794
First published 1968
This work traces the development of the theater from primitive times to the present, with an emphasis on European theater.

Includes bibliographical references

The **Oxford** illustrated history of theatre; edited by John Russell Brown. Oxford Univ. Press 1995 582p il pa $27.50 hardcover o.p. *
Grades: 11 12 Adult   **792.09**
1. Theater—History
ISBN 0-19-285442-9   LC 95-231683
Covering theatre history from the ancient Greeks to the 1990s, this "resource provides a wide variety of information from basic theatre chronology to detailed analyses of several well-known and important plays and playwrights. . . . The emphasis is on European and Western theatre, but a chapter provides a concise summary on Southern and Eastern Asian theatre." SLJ

Includes bibliographical references

792.5   Opera

The **Grove** book of operas; edited by Stanley Sadie; revised by Laura Macy. 2nd ed. Oxford University Press 2006 xxiii, 740p il $39.95; pa $27.95 *   **792.5**
1. Opera—Encyclopedias 2. Reference books
ISBN   978-0-19-530907-2;   0-19-530907-3; 978-0-19-538711-7 (pa); 0-19-538711-2 (pa)
                                      LC 2006-15323
First published 1996 by Macmillan with title: The new Grove book of operas
This is an "alphabetical collection of opera synopses enhanced with brief historical details and cast lists." Choice
"A vital reference on the subject." Libr J

Includes bibliographical references

792.6   Musical plays

Bloom, Ken
Broadway musicals; the 101 greatest shows of all time; [by] Ken Bloom & Frank Vlastnik; new preface by Broadway's leading ladies; foreword by Jerry Orbach. Rev. and updated ed. Black Dog & Leventhal 2010 344p il $40
Grades: 11 12 Adult   **792.6**
1. Musicals
ISBN 978-1-57912-849-4
First published 2004

Bloom, Ken—*Continued*

This is a history of Broadway musicals from the past 100 years. Each entry features commentary, photos and brief features on performers and creators.

Boland, Robert, 1925-

Musicals! directing school and community theatre; {by} Robert Boland and Paul Argentini. Scarecrow Press 1997 xxv, 202p il pa $35

Grades: 11 12 Adult   **792.6**
1. Musicals—Production and direction
ISBN 0-8108-3323-9   LC 97-11996

This is "a handbook for novice directors of the musical. This illustrated nuts-and-bolts compendium includes 22 chapters divided among three major sections addressing preparation, production, and performance. Through accessible prose and a you-can-do-it tone, the authors provide an overview of preproduction planning, auditioning and casting, blocking, stage composition, rehearsals, and choreography, as well as the more technical layers of set design, costumes, and lights." Libr J

Includes bibliographical references

Bordman, Gerald Martin

American musical theatre; a chronicle; {by} Gerald Bordman. 3rd ed. Oxford Univ. Press 2001 917p $75

Grades: 11 12 Adult   **792.6**
1. Musicals
ISBN 0-19-513074-X   LC 00-59812
First published 1978

This book offers "show-by-show, season-by-season descriptions—from the first musical to the 1999/2000 Broadway season. . . . {It} encompasses all musical entertainment from plays, revues, opera bouffe and operettas to one-man and one-woman shows. {It} includes mini-biographies and . . . song, show and people indexes." Publisher's note

Kantor, Michael, 1961-

Broadway: the American musical; [by] Michael Kantor; Laurence Maslon. Bulfinch Press 2004 480p il $60 *

Grades: 11 12 Adult   **792.6**
1. Musicals
ISBN 0-8212-2905-2   LC 2003-69715

Contents: A real live nephew of my Uncle Sam (1893-1919); Syncopated city (1920-1929); I got plenty o' nuttin' (1930-1941); Oh, what a beautiful mornin' (1942-1960); Tradition (1960-1980); Lullaby of Broadway (1980-present)

This companion volume to a PBS documentary includes interviews and photographs of Broadway musicals from 1893 to 2004

"With its beguiling blend of entertainment and history, this splendid work is a must-have." Publ Wkly

Includes bibliographical references

Lamb, Andrew

150 years of popular musical theatre. Yale Univ. Press 2000 380p il $39.95

Grades: 11 12 Adult   **792.6**
1. Musicals
ISBN 0-300-07538-3   LC 00-25281

This volume covers "popular music theater from mid-nineteenth-century French operettas to British and American musical comedies to late-twentieth-century rock operas." Booklist

792.7 Variety shows and theatrical dancing

Nevraumont, Edward J., 1975-

The ultimate improv book; a complete guide to comedy improvisation; [by] Edward J. Nevraumont and Nicholas P. Hanson, with additional material from Kurt Smeaton. Meriwether 2001 272p pa $16.95

Grades: 9 10 11 12   **792.7**
1. Comedy 2. Acting
ISBN 1-56608-075-4   LC 2001-51396

"Suggestions for assembling a capable, compatible team of players, setting up performances guidelines, and keeping the action flowing and on target for the audience preface setups for 60 games. The game-exercises . . . are specifically designed to assist players in using language, literature, song, and movement in their skits." Booklist

Includes bibliographical references

792.8 Ballet and modern dance

Reynolds, Nancy, 1938-

No fixed points; dance in the twentieth century; [by] Nancy Reynolds and Malcolm McCormick. Yale Univ. Press 2003 907p il $50

Grades: 11 12 Adult   **792.8**
1. Dance 2. Ballet 3. Modern dance
ISBN 0-300-09366-7   LC 2003-10754

This is a "narrative of the development of ballet, modern dance, and postmodern choreography. Synthesizing a century's worth of observation and opinion, Reynolds and McCormick chart the pendulum swing of styles and isolate individual contributions. . . . They highlight the significance of factors as large as government funding and as small as the depth of Baryshnikov's demi-plié." New Yorker

"Although everyone will be using the book for reference, Reynolds and McCormick have produced a work that is completely unlike a standard reference book; you don't just look things up in it—you read it. Here is a coherent, reasoned and entertaining chronicle of dance performance in the West over the hundred years that are unquestionably the fullest and most complicated in the long history of this fragmented and elusive art." N Y Times

Includes bibliographical references

Warren, Gretchen
Classical ballet technique; {by} Gretchen Ward Warren; photographs by Susan Cook. University of S. Fla. Press 1989 395p il hardcover o.p. pa $39.95
Grades: 11 12 Adult   **792.8**
    1. Ballet
    ISBN 0-8130-0895-6; 0-8130-0945-6 (pa)
                      LC 89-31141
Text and numerous photographs explain the correct execution of ballet steps
"General material on basic concepts, body structure and proportion, and ballet class proceed this extraordinary manual and guide." Booklist
Includes glossary and bibliographical references

792.803   Ballet and modern dance— Encyclopedias and dictionaries

Craine, Debra
The Oxford dictionary of dance; [by] Debra Craine, Judith Mackrell. 2nd ed. Oxford University Press 2010 502p il (Oxford paperback reference) pa $18.95 *
Grades: 11 12 Adult   **792.803**
    1. Dance—Dictionaries 2. Reference books
    ISBN 978-0-19-956344-9; 0-19-956344-6
                    LC 2010-930321
Based on The concise Oxford dictionary of ballet by Horst Kroegler. First published 2000
"The work covers all aspects of the diverse dance world from classical ballet to modern, from flamenco to hip-hop, from tap to South Asian dance forms and includes . . . entries on technical terms, steps, styles, works and countries, in addition to many biographies of dancers, choreographers, and companies." Publisher's note
Includes bibliographical references

792.9   Stage productions

Grove, Elliot
130 projects to get you into filmmaking. Barron's Educational Series 2009 128p il $21.99 *
Grades: 10 11 12 Adult   **792.9**
    1. Motion pictures—Production and direction 2. Cinematography
    ISBN 978-0-7641-4296-3   LC 2009-928377
At head of title: Aspire
"This may be the most engaging and visually demonstrative introduction to filmmaking available in print. Actual filmic examples of diagrammed screenshots, storyboards, script breakdown sheets, business forms, equipment, lighting, makeup, and shot catalogs help to flesh out attractively the author's attainable 130 steps from idea to direction to postproduction to marketing and publicity." Libr J
Includes glossary

793.73   Puzzles and puzzle games

Pulliam, Tom
The New York times crossword puzzle dictionary; by Tom Pulliam and Clare Grundman. 3rd ed. Times Bks. 1995 656p $27.50; pa $18.95 *
Grades: 11 12 Adult   **793.73**
    1. Reference books 2. Crossword puzzles—Dictionaries
    ISBN 0-8129-2373-1; 0-8129-2823-7 (pa)
                    LC 95-11416
"A Hudson Group book"
First published 1977
This dictionary of synonyms for crossword puzzles includes more than 50,000 entries.
"One of the more useful works of its kind." Ref Sources for Small & Medium-sized Libr. 6th edition

793.74   Mathematical games and recreations

Banks, Robert B.
Slicing pizzas, racing turtles, and further adventures in applied mathematics. Princeton Univ. Press 1999 286p il hardcover o.p. pa $26.95
Grades: 9 10 11 12   **793.74**
    1. Mathematical recreations
    ISBN 0-691-05947-0; 0-691-10284-8 (pa)
                    LC 98-53513
This "is a collection of mathematical investigations. . . . Topics range from prime numbers, sequences, and famous numbers (e.g., pi and e) to questions like what rivers run uphill, what would happen if all ice on the planet were to melt, and how many people have ever lived." Choice
"Banks's style is entertaining but never condescending. Some of the math is pretty tough; it helps if you did well in trigonometry as well as introductory calculus and analytic geometry." Christ Sci Monit
Includes bibliographical references

Stewart, Ian
The magical maze; seeing the world through mathematical eyes. Wiley 1998 268p il $24.95; pa $16.95
Grades: 11 12 Adult   **793.74**
    1. Mathematics 2. Mathematical recreations
    ISBN 0-471-19297-X; 0-471-35065-6 (pa)
                    LC 98-13185
Stewart presents various mathematical puzzles and problems through the metaphorical structure of a maze.
Chapters "contain good discussions of such topics as modular arithmetic, Marilyn vos Savant's Monty-Hall problem, depth-first and other search strategies, static and dynamic symmetry, Turing machines, optimization, fractals, and chaos. This is an excellent mix of topics and the material is very much up-to-date." Choice

793.8 Magic and related activities

Gardner, Martin, 1914-2010

The colossal book of short puzzles and problems; combinatorics, probability, algebra, geometry, topology, chess, logic, cryptarithms, wordplay, physics and other topics of recreational mathematics; edited by Dana Richards. Norton 2006 494p il $35

Grades: 11 12 Adult   **793.8**

1. Mathematical recreations 2. Scientific recreations

ISBN 0-393-06114-0; 978-0-393-06114-7

                   LC 2005-24080

This is a compilation of puzzles from Martin Gardner's "column, 'Mathematical Games,' which appeared for over 25 years in Scientific American. . . . [The topics] include combinatorics, probability, algebra, plane and solid geometry, topology, games, chess, logic, wordplay, and physics, among others. . . . Anyone interested in recreational mathematics should like this book. The puzzles are fascinating and the book is easily browsed. It can also serve as a good reference for (high school and college) teachers seeking interesting problems to complement routine ones in mathematics texts." Sci Books Films

Ottaviani, Jim

Levitation: physics and psychology in the service of deception; [by] Jim Ottaviani and Janine Johnston; lettering by Tom Orzechowski. G. T. Labs 2007 71p il pa $12.95

Grades: 6 7 8 9 10 11 12 Adult   **793.8**

1. Graphic novels 2. Magic tricks—Graphic novels

ISBN 978-0-9788037-0-4

"A General Tektronics Labs book"

This book tells the story of how John Neville Maskelyne developed the stage magic trick of levitation, of the American Harry Kellar, who acquired the trick through devious means, of the old school engineer Guy Jarrett, who perfected the magicians' tricks, and of stage performer Howard Thurston, who inherited the levitation trick from Kellar and ruined it. Or did he? The book includes notes and reprints of old posters and other information on the magicians.

Includes bibliographical references

794.1 Chess

King, Daniel, 1963-

Chess; from first moves to checkmate. New ed. Kingfisher 2010 64p il pa $8.99 *

Grades: 5 6 7 8 9 10 11 12   **794.1**

1. Chess

ISBN 978-0-7534-1930-4

First published 2000

Introduces the rules and strategies of chess, as well as its history and some of the great players and matches.

Naroditsky, Daniel

Mastering positional chess; practical lessons of a junior world champion; [by] Daniel A. Naroditsky. New in Chess 2010 239p il pa $23.95

Grades: 7 8 9 10 11 12   **794.1**

1. Chess

ISBN 978-90-5691-310-6

"Every chapter focuses on a different aspect of playing the game. For example, one of the chapters simply deals with defense and how a player can make a comeback. The author uses many pictures to show positions of the pieces and different moves required to win. There is fabulous dialogue in the different scenarios cited. Each chapter also contains various chess exercises that the reader can try to solve. . . . Although this book is very thorough, it is definitely for the more skilled chess player. Experienced chess players will find it a must read." Voice of Youth Advocates

United States Chess Federation

U.S. Chess Federation's official rules of chess; compiled and sanctioned by the U.S. Chess Federation; Tim Just, chief editor; Daniel B. Burg, editor. 5th ed. Random House Puzzles & Games 2003 xxxvii, 370p il (McKay chess library) pa $18.95

Grades: 11 12 Adult   **794.1**

1. Chess

ISBN 0-8129-3559-4   LC 2003-278349

First published 1974

This "edition features the latest rules, including guidelines for the popular game of speed chess, an updated quick rating system, and the latest conventions of governing tournaments. It also contains explanations of every legal move, a guide to calculating lifetime rankings, guidelines for sponsoring and running a tournament, and a lesson on how to read and write chess notation." Publisher's note

794.8 Electronic games. Computer games

Neiburger, Eli

Gamers . . . in the library?! the why, what, and how of videogame tournaments for all ages. American Library Association 2007 178p pa $42 *

Grades: Adult Professional   **794.8**

1. Video games 2. Computer games 3. Young adults' libraries

ISBN 978-0-8389-0944-7; 0-8389-0944-2

                   LC 2007-10512

This is a "guide to setting up video-gaming tournaments in public libraries. The author . . . [shares] advice on every aspect of this crowd-pleasing lure for kids, tweens, and teens: promotion, hardware and software, rules and regulations, scoring, prizes, snacks, feedback, and follow-up activities." Booklist

"With the writing as vibrant as its topic, . . . [this book] is a must-have professional tool." Voice Youth Advocates

Includes bibliographical references

Parks, Peggy J., 1951-
Video games. ReferencePoint Press 2008 104p
il map (Compact research. Current issues) $25.95
Grades: 8 9 10 11 12   **794.8**
    1. Video games
    ISBN 978-1-60152-053-1; 1-60152-053-0
                                    LC 2007-49886
This "book opens with descriptions of the growing
popularity of video games and the regulation and legislation of content and sales; ratings; connections with violent crime; and health effects, including addiction. An
overview provides further background and context to
these issues, and . . . chapters follow addressing related
questions and providing other related material." SLJ
    Includes bibliographical references

Swaine, Meg
Career building through interactive online
games. Rosen Pub. 2008 64p il (Digital career
building) lib bdg $29.95
Grades: 7 8 9 10   **794.8**
    1. Video games 2. Computer games 3. Vocational
guidance
    ISBN 978-1-4042-1946-5; 1-4042-1946-3
                                    LC 2007-1027
"An overview of the industry briefly outlines the development of earlier, simpler games played on arcade
machines through to the transition to home computers,
video consoles like Nintendo, handheld devices, and the
development of new technology like Blu-ray and the
Wii. . . . Remaining chapters address developing digital
skills and assessing interests, how to go about making
your work visible through Web access, making educational choices, gaining experience, networking, etc. . . .
Students who love video games and want to work with
them will be encouraged by this accessible and informative book." SLJ
    Includes glossary and bibliographical references

796   Athletic and outdoor sports and games

Becoming an ironman; first encounters with the
    ultimate endurance event; edited by Kara
    Douglass. Breakaway Bks. 2001 286p il
    hardcover o.p. pa $14
Grades: 11 12 Adult   **796**
    1. Triathlon
    ISBN 1-891369-24-5; 1-891369-31-8 (pa)
This book surveys the history of the Ironman triathlon,
a competition consisting "of a 2.4-mile swim, a 112-mile
bike race, and a full marathon (26.2-mile run), all done
in one day." Libr J

The Best American sports writing of the century;
    edited by David Halberstam. Houghton Mifflin
    1999 776p $30; pa $18 *
Grades: 11 12 Adult   **796**
    1. Sports
    ISBN 0-395-94513-5; 0-395-94514-3 (pa)
"Although there are pieces about mountain climbing,
tennis and chess, fully half of the selections are about

two sports: baseball and boxing. The book begins with
a Best of the Best section led by Gay Talese's 1966 profile of Joe DiMaggio, 'The Silent Season of a Hero.'. . .
The final section is a special six-piece tribute to a man
who himself claimed to be the best of the best—Muhammad Ali." Publ Wkly

Blumenthal, Karen
Let me play; the story of Title IX, the law that
changed the future of girls in America. Atheneum
Books for Young Readers 2005 152p il $19.95
Grades: 6 7 8 9 10   **796**
    1. Women athletes 2. Sex discrimination
    ISBN 0-689-85957-0   LC 2004-1450
"The author looks at American women's evolving
rights by focusing on the history and future of Title IX,
which bans sex discrimination in U.S. education. . . .
The images are . . . gripping, and relevant political cartoons and fact boxes add further interest. Few books cover the last few decades of American women's history
with such clarity and detail." Booklist
    Includes bibliographical references

Craig, Steve, 1961-
Sports and games of the ancients. Greenwood
Press 2002 271p il (Sports and games through
history) $57.95; pa $25 *
Grades: 11 12 Adult   **796**
    1. Sports—History 2. Ancient history
    ISBN 0-313-31600-7; 0-313-36120-7 (pa)
                                    LC 2001-50101
This "book, arranged by geographic regions, focuses
on the development of sports and games and the effect
they had on the lives of people from the first Olympiad
to the fall of Rome. . . . The author provides descriptions of each sport, explains essential equipment (including how to make it), and the rules of play. . . . Mancala,
stick fighting, sumo wrestling (for both men and wom-
en), go, the log run, tejo, boomerangs, buzkashi, kabaddi,
and Chinese football are among the topics covered. The
material provided is not readily available in other single
resources." SLJ
    Includes bibliographical references

Encyclopedia of sports in America; a history from
    foot races to extreme sports; edited by Murry R.
    Nelson. Greenwood Press 2009 2v il set $175
Grades: 7 8 9 10 11 12 Adult   **796**
    1. Sports—Encyclopedias 2. Reference books
    ISBN 978-0-313-34790-0   LC 2008-34749
    Contents: v1 Colonial years to 1939; v2 1940 to pres-
ent
    The editor "presents a work tracing the history of
sports in America from the Colonial era through about
2007. . . . Horse racing, billiards, basketball, football,
cycling, bowling, sports broadcasting, hockey, golf, baseball, and NASCAR count among the diverse topics. . . .
Written for general readers, this set could easily fill a
niche in middle school and high school libraries, as well
as public libraries, particularly where research on sports
history is a popular topic." Libr J
    Includes bibliographical references

Franck, Irene M.

Famous first facts about sports; {by} Irene M. Franck & David M. Brownstone. Wilson, H.W. 2001 903p $160 *

Grades: 7 8 9 10   **796**
1. Sports
ISBN 0-8242-0973-7   LC 00-43883

"Franck and Brownstone have compiled 5,415 'firsts' covering more than 110 sports. . . . Arranged alphabetically by sport, the concisely described events are listed in chronological order, with headers for time periods. Entries are given consecutive four-digit numbers, which are cited in the five indexes (subjects, years, days, personal names, and geographical locations). . . . The indexes provide essential access and are easy to use. . . . The depth of coverage is impressive." Choice

Includes bibliographical references

Game face; what does a woman athlete look like? [created and developed by] Jane Gottesman; edited by Geoffrey Biddle; foreword by Penny Marshall. Random House 2001 223p il hardcover o.p. pa $19.95 *

Grades: 9 10 11 12   **796**
1. Women athletes 2. Sports
ISBN 0-375-50602-0; 0-812-96868-9 (pa)
                                               LC 00-45976

Book will coincide with a 3-month exhibition at the Smithsonian Institution in Washington, D.C. and will continue as a traveling exhbit over the next five years

"This collection of black-and-white photographs features female athletes-amateurs and professional; team and individual standouts; stars of the past and present; portraits and snapshots; and young and old—engaged in various physical endeavors. The theme is variety and progress in women's sports. Each photo is accompanied by an identification of the sport, occasionally with a quote from the player depicted. . . . A welcome and timely addition for sports' collections." SLJ

Gifford, Clive

Sports. Amicus 2010 c2011 46p il (Healthy lifestyles) lib bdg $32.80

Grades: 7 8 9 10   **796**
1. Sports 2. Physical fitness
ISBN 978-1-60753-088-6; 1-60753-088-0
                                               LC 2009-47567

"Discusses . . . the benefits of participating in sports for teenagers, including how to find the sport that is right for you and how to develop a life-long active lifestyle." Publisher's note

This book is "well-written and satisfyingly informative. . . . [The] magazine-like format includes numerous sidebars, color photos, and charts." SLJ

Includes glossary and bibliographical references

Hastings, Penny

Sports for her; a reference guide for teenage girls. Greenwood Press 1999 254p il $45 *

Grades: 11 12 Adult   **796**
1. Sports for women
ISBN 0-313-30551-X   LC 99-21279

Discusses issues related to girls' participation in sports and provides information on the rules, equipment, training, and more for eight sports which high school girls are most likely to play

Includes bibliographical references

Li, WenFang

Extreme sports. Mason Crest Publishers 2010 c2011 96p il (Getting the edge: conditioning, injuries, and legal & illicit drugs) lib bdg $24.95

Grades: 7 8 9 10   **796**
1. Extreme sports
ISBN 978-1-4222-1729-0; 1-4222-1729-9
                                               LC 2010-7229

This book "offers a general introduction to . . . [extreme sports], its rules, and its history before zeroing in on health and safety concerns. . . . Scanning a broad range of activities, from parachuting to rock climbing to snowboarding, . . . [it] provides useful information and advice on topics such as coping with fear and dealing with environmental injuries." Booklist

Includes bibliographical references

Men in sports; great sports stories of all time from the Greek Olympic games to the American World Series; edited and with an introduction by Brandt Aymar. Crown 1994 499p pa $25 hardcover o.p.

Grades: 11 12 Adult   **796**
1. Sports
ISBN 0-517-88395-3   LC 93-19818

A "collection of nearly fifty sporting entries. Arranged alphabetically, the anthology includes fiction, nonfiction, sports reporting, and excerpts from longer works." Voice Youth Advocates

Musiker, Liz Hartman

The smart girl's guide to sports; a hip handbook for women who don't know a slam dunk from a grand slam. Hudson Street Press 2005 301p il hardcover o.p. pa $15

Grades: 9 10 11 12   **796**
1. Sports
ISBN 1-59463-011-9; 0-452-28950-5 (pa)
                                               LC 2005-18858

This book "covers all the major professional sports: football, basketball, baseball, hockey, golf, soccer, boxing, and even car racing. Each chapter includes a 'Here's How It Works' section that explains the basics of the game; [and] profiles of each sport's timeless greats and 'contemporary cool' players." Publisher's note

"Armed with both facts and humor, Musiker has written what could become an invaluable resource for football, baseball, hockey, basketball, golf, boxing, or NASCAR widows. . . . This guidebook will be a welcome helper for millions of sports-shy women (and men)." Booklist

Includes bibliographical references

Nike is a goddess; the history of women in sports; edited by Lissa Smith; introduction by Mariah Burton Nelson. Atlantic Monthly Press 1998 331p il pa $14 hardcover o.p.

Grades: 11 12 Adult   **796**
1. Sports 2. Women athletes
ISBN 0-87113-761-5   LC 98-27049

This "anthology documents the athletic achievements of female athletes during the late-nineteenth and twentieth centuries. Separate chapters written by noted sports journalists (Grace Lichtenstein, Michelle Kaufman, Karen Karbo) cover such disciplines as basketball, soccer, baseball, swimming, horseback riding, tennis, golf, and hockey, among others." Booklist

"The quality of writing in the different sections varies but each writer is well connected with her field and all give a good background history as well as an assessment of current developments in the sport. Controversial issues are not ignored, and lesbianism is addressed." SLJ

Sokolove, Michael Y.
Warrior girls; protecting our daughters against the injury epidemic in women's sports; [by] Michael Sokolove. Simon & Schuster 2008 308p $25; pa $21.95

Grades: 9 10 11 12 Adult   **796**
1. Sports for women 2. Wounds and injuries 3. Sports medicine
ISBN   978-0-7432-9755-4;   0-7432-9755-4; 978-0-7432-9756-1 (pa); 0-7432-9756-3 (pa)
                                              LC 2008-12176

This is an "examination of the prevalence and sometimes life-altering effect of injuries in women's sports. . . . [The author] examines the differences in male and female anatomy, compares the competitiveness in men's and women's sports, and focuses on a handful of specific individuals to explore how an athlete's drive for perfection can lead to disaster. . . . This well-researched, well-reasoned, and forcefully argued book makes an important contribution to the literature of sports." Booklist

Includes bibliographical references

Sports and athletes: opposing viewpoints; Christine Watkins, book editor. Greenhaven Press 2009 227p il lib bdg $39.70; pa $27.50 *

Grades: 9 10 11 12   **796**
1. Sports 2. Athletes
ISBN 978-0-7377-4542-9 (lib bdg); 0-7377-4542-8 (lib bdg); 978-0-7377-4543-6 (pa); 0-7377-4543-6 (pa)
                                              LC 2008-45344

"Opposing viewpoints series"

Topics covers in this anthology include whether sports benefit children, college sports, equality in sports, and drug use among athletes.

Includes bibliographical references

Sports illustrated 2011 almanac; by the editors of Sports illustrated. Time Home Entertainment 2010 559p il pa $14.99 *

Grades: 7 8 9 10 11 12 Adult   **796**
1. Sports 2. Reference books
ISBN 978-1-60320-863-5

Annual. First published 1991 with title: Sports illustrated . . . sports almanac

"Provides team and individual records and highlights for all major sports. . . . A brief essay opens the section on each sport, followed by page upon page of records, both current and retrospective. Interspersed throughout . . . are black-and-white and color photographs and notable quotations by sports figures." Am Ref Books Annu, 1993

Sports: the complete visual reference; François Fortin [general editor] Firefly Bks. 2000 372p il $39.95; pa $24.95 *

Grades: 8 9 10 11 12 Adult   **796**
1. Sports 2. Reference books
ISBN 1-55209-540-1; 1-55297-807-9 (pa)

This is a "reference source on 120 contemporary sports . . . pulling together the history, physical environment for competitions, roles of the players and officials, specific terms and expressions, and dynamics of each. All of this is done with an emphasis on visual presentation, and each entry includes copious illustrations." Booklist

"A sure winner for any sports reference collection." Am Libr

Wheeler, Dion
The sports scholarships insider's guide; getting money for college at any division. 2nd ed. Sourcebooks 2009 377p il pa $16.99 *

Grades: 9 10 11 12   **796**
1. Athletes 2. Scholarships 3. College sports
ISBN 978-1-4022-1884-2
First published 2005

"Topics include the recruiting process, financial-aid opportunities, academic requirements, preparing credentials, school visits, and negotiating for financial assistance from NCAA division I, II, III and NAIA institutions. The second half of the book includes listings of sports for the various divisions, institution names, and Web addresses." SLJ

Includes glossary

Why a curveball curves; the incredible science of sports; edited by Frank Vizard; foreward by Robert Lipsyte. Hearst Books 2008 224p il (Popular mechanics) $19.95

Grades: 11 12 Adult   **796**
1. Sports 2. Science
ISBN 978-1-58816-475-9; 1-58816-475-6
                                              LC 2007-29702

This collection of articles from Popular Mechanics explains the science behind different sports. In addition to baseball, the book "talks about basketball, soccer, hockey, golf, and several other sports, and it answers some very interesting questions, such as why Gretzky really was the greatest (an innate ability to translate physical cues into action) and how you, too, can bend it (a soccer ball, that is), like Beckham. A must-read for sports fans, physics buffs, and general audiences, too." Booklist

796.03 Sports—Encyclopedias and dictionaries

Berkshire encyclopedia of world sport; David Levinson and Karen Christensen, editors. Berkshire Pub. Group 2005 4v il set $475 *
Grades: 11 12 Adult   **796.03**
1. Reference books 2. Sports—Encyclopedias
ISBN 0-9743091-1-7   LC 2005-13050
"This encyclopedia covers a range of topics from professional and amateur sports and sporting events to national sports and issues and influences affecting athletics. . . . A broad, well-written resource." SLJ
Includes bibliographical references

796.21 Roller skating

Werner, Doug, 1950-
In-line skater's start-up; a beginner's guide to in-line skating and roller hockey. Tracks Pub. 1995 159p il (Start-up sports) pa $9.95
Grades: 9 10 11 12   **796.21**
1. In-line skating
ISBN 1-884654-04-5   LC 95-60153
This work discusses the various techniques and equipment required for both skating and hockey. This illustrated guide also provides safety tips

796.22 Skateboarding

Powell, Ben
Skateboarding skills; the rider's guide. Firefly Books 2008 128p il pa $16.95
Grades: 7 8 9 10 11 12 Adult   **796.22**
1. Skateboarding
ISBN 978-1-55407-360-3; 1-55407-360-X
                                            LC 2008-275044
The author "offers a colorful and useful manual for mastering numerous skateboard tricks. Intended for riders of all ages, the book presents step-by-step breakdowns of skills illustrated with photographs of children around age 12; each step of a trick features a picture and a written description." Libr J

796.323 Basketball

Blais, Madeleine, 1949-
In these girls, hope is a muscle. Warner Bks. 1996 266p pa $13.95
Grades: 11 12 Adult   **796.323**
1. Cathedral High School (Springfield, Mass.)
2. Basketball
ISBN 0-446-67210-6; 978-0-446-67210-8
First published 1995 by Atlantic Monthly Press
"Weaving accounts of players' personal histories with reportage on their on-court performances, Madeleine Blais recounts the dramatic 1992-93 season of the Lady Hurricanes of Amherst (Mass.) Regional High School."

N Y Times Book Rev
"Alternately funny, exciting and moving, the book should be enjoyed not only by girls and women who have played sports but also those who wanted to but let themselves be discouraged." Publ Wkly

Colton, Larry, 1942-
Counting coup; a true story of basketball and honor on the Little Big Horn. Warner Bks. 2000 420p hardcover o.p. pa $14.95 *
Grades: 11 12 Adult   **796.323**
1. Hardin High School (Hardin, Mont.)—Basketball
2. Basketball 3. Women athletes 4. Native Americans—Social conditions
ISBN 0-446-52683-5; 0-446-67755-8 (pa)
                                            LC 00-24987
The author discusses the basketball team of Hardin High School on the Crow Indian Reservation in Montana.
"Readers, male and female, interested in a snapshot of modern Native culture, the normal stresses of high school, or the travails and triumphs of an underdog sports team will love this fascinating, beautifully written book." Voice Youth Advocates

Dohrmann, George
Play their hearts out; a coach, his star recruit, and the youth basketball machine. Ballantine Books 2010 422p il $26
Grades: 10 11 12 Adult   **796.323**
1. Keller, Joe 2. Walker, Demetrius 3. Basketball
ISBN 978-0-345-50860-7; 0-345-50860-2
                                            LC 2010-15470
The author "follows California phenom Demetrius Walker through the cycle of Amateur Athletic Union (AAU) summer league hoops, from playing for ambitious hustler and coach Joe Keller to the face of grassroots basketball, longtime coach Pat Barrett. In a constant search for the next Lebron, just as before for the next Michael Jordan, AAU coaches, with support and financing from shoe giants Nike and Adidas, woo youngsters to their summer league basketball teams with gear, shoes, and promises of a college scholarship. . . . [Dohrmann's] insights into the seamy side of youth basketball are investigative journalism at its best." Libr J

D'Orso, Michael
Eagle blue; a team, a tribe, and a high school basketball season in Arctic Alaska. Bloomsbury Pub. 2006 323p il map $23.95 *
Grades: 11 12 Adult   **796.323**
1. Basketball 2. School sports 3. Fort Yukon (Alaska)
ISBN 978-1-58234-623-6; 1-58234-623-2
                                            LC 2005-25430
The author "follows the Fort Yukon Eagles through their 2005 season to the state championship, shifting between a mesmerizing narrative and the thoughts of the players, their coach and their fans. What emerges is more than a sports story; it's a striking portrait of a community consisting of a traditional culture bombarded with modernity, where alcoholism, domestic violence and school dropout rates run wild." Publ Wkly

Feinstein, John

A march to madness; the view from the floor in the Atlantic Coast Conference. Little, Brown 1997 464p il hardcover o.p. pa $14

Grades: 11 12 Adult   **796.323**

1. Atlantic Coast Conference 2. Basketball

ISBN 0-316-27740-1; 0-316-27712-6 (pa)

LC 97-31060

Feinstein "covers one year with all of the teams in the perennially powerful Atlantic Coast Conference. After introducing each of the schools, their teams, their coaches, and their expectations for the 1996/97 basketball season, the book describes their progress week by week, culminating with Dean Smith's run to the NCAA Final Four. Such a detailed accounting of a sports season could seem interminable to readers, but Feinstein has again produced a narrative that is not only interesting but often exciting." Libr J

FreeDarko presents the macrophenomenal pro basketball almanac; styles, stats and stars in today's game. Bloomsbury USA 2008 219p il $23

Grades: 9 10 11 12 Adult   **796.323**

1. National Basketball Association 2. Basketball

ISBN 978-1-59691-561-9; 1-59691-561-7

Provides "coverage of modern trends and sociopolitical factors influencing major league basketball." Publisher's note

"This is a wonderful basketball book that blends a unique perspective, arresting presentation, and superior knowledge of its subject." Booklist

Joravsky, Ben

Hoop dreams; a true story of hardship and triumph; introduction by Charles Barkley. Turner Pub. (Atlanta) 1995 301p il pa $13.50 hardcover o.p.

Grades: 9 10 11 12   **796.323**

1. Basketball 2. Chicago (Ill.)—Social conditions

ISBN 0-06-097689-6 (pa)   LC 94-46398

"Based on the documentary film of the same name, this book . . . looks at the dream of ghetto youths to play in the NBA." Publ Wkly

Lieberman, Nancy, 1958-

Basketball for women; becoming a complete player; [by] Nancy Lieberman-Cline [and] Robin Roberts with Kevin Warneke. Human Kinetics 1996 283p il pa $16.95

Grades: 11 12 Adult   **796.323**

1. Basketball 2. Women athletes

ISBN 0-87322-610-0   LC 95-17945

The author "begins with a history of the game dating back to the first official women's basketball game at Smith College in 1893. From there she discusses not only the dedication it takes to be a true player, but also basketball's position in her, and hopefully the reader's priorities. . . . Next she suggests the building of the plan, mentally and physically, to begin the ascent to the next level of playing. The following seven chapters are devoted to . . . drill techniques." Voice Youth Advocates

Includes bibliographical references

Oliver, Jon A.

Basketball fundamentals; [by] Jon Oliver. Human Kinetics 2004 141p il (Sports fundamentals series) pa $16.95 *

Grades: 9 10 11 12 Adult   **796.323**

1. Basketball

ISBN 0-7360-4910-X   LC 2003-8873

Subtitle on cover: A better way to learn the basics

This book "begins by teaching basic offensive skills. . . . A separate chapter on defense teaches students how to stop the opposition by playing man-to-man, zone, or combination defense. Chapters are devoted to mastering specific skills including lay-ups, perimeter shooting, passing, dribbling, screening, and rebounding." Publisher's note

Rosen, Charles, 1941-

Crazy basketball; a life in and out of bounds; foreword by Phil Jackson. University of Nebraska Press 2011 301p $24.95

Grades: 11 12 Adult   **796.323**

1. Continental Basketball Association 2. Basketball—Biography

ISBN 978-0-8032-1793-5   LC 2010-26921

The author "recalls his years as a coach in the Continental Basketball Association. . . . The shining star here isn't Rosen or any of the players, it's the game itself. The last half-dozen pages will bring a tear to the eye of anyone for whom the game was or is a passion." Booklist

Simmons, Bill, 1969-

The book of basketball; the NBA according to the sports guy. Ballantine/ESPN Books 2009 715p il $30; pa $18 *

Grades: 11 12 Adult   **796.323**

1. National Basketball Association 2. Basketball

ISBN   978-0-345-51176-8;   0-345-51176-X;
978-0-345-52010-4 (pa); 0-345-52010-6 (pa)

LC 2009-36006

The author "summarizes the history of the league, discusses his personal fandom, includes a great 'what if?' chapter (what if Michael Jordan had been drafted second by Portland instead of third by Chicago?), analyzes Most Valuable Player choices through the years, and dissects the careers of the league's all-time best players. The true NBA fan will dive into this hefty volume and won't resurface for about a week, emerging from the man cave unshaven, smelling of beer and pizza, grinning, and armed with NBA history, insight, anecdotes, statistics, and a dozen new examples of Simmons' Unintentional Comedy Scale. This is just plain fun. Expect significant demand from hoops junkies." Booklist

Includes bibliographical references

Swidey, Neil

The assist; hoops, hope, and the game of their lives. PublicAffairs 2008 358p il $26 *

Grades: 11 12 Adult   **796.323**

1. O'Brien, Jack 2. Charlestown High School (Boston, Mass.) 3. Basketball 4. School sports

ISBN 978-1-58648-469-9; 1-58648-469-9

LC 2007-35826

Swidey, Neil—*Continued*

At the center of this book about Boston's Charlestown High School basketball team "are the interwoven lives of [coach Jack] O'Brien and two of his stars, easygoing Ridley Johnson and fierce Jason 'Hood' White. The book follows Ridley and Hood on their hunt for a state title. But it also stays with them, to see how young men who seldom get second chances survive without their coach hovering over them—and how he survives without them." Publisher's note

"This is a prodigiously reported, compulsively readable book that readers (sport fans or not) will savor." Publ Wkly

796.325 Volleyball

Crisfield, Deborah

Winning volleyball for girls; [by] Deborah W. Crisfield, John Monteleone; foreword by Maria Nolan. 3rd ed. Chelsea House 2009 189p il (Winning sports for girls) lib bdg $44.95; pa $11.96

Grades: 7 8 9 10 11 12   **796.325**

1. Volleyball

ISBN 978-0-8160-7720-5 (lib bdg); 0-8160-7720-7 (lib bdg); 978-0-8160-7721-2 (pa); 0-8160-7721-5 (pa)

LC 2009-5733

"A Mountain Lion book"

First published 1995 by Facts on File

This includes a brief history of volleyball followed by descriptions of the rules, court and equipment, training, techniques such as the spike, the serve, the block, and the pass, offensive and defensive play, putting a team together, and game strategies.

Includes glossary and bibliographical references

Dearing, Joel

Volleyball fundamentals. Human Kinetics 2003 135p il (Sports fundamentals series) pa $14.95

Grades: 9 10 11 12   **796.325**

1. Volleyball

ISBN 0-7360-4508-2   LC 2002-15234

Contents: The W formation; Creating topspin; Serving; Receiving serve; Setting; Attacking; Blocking; Digging; Team defense; Team offense; Transition; Modified games; Scoring systems; Off to the endline

796.332 American football

Bissinger, H. G.

Friday night lights; a town, a team, and a dream. Da Capo Press 2000 367p il pa $15.95

Grades: 11 12 Adult   **796.332**

1. Permian High School (Odessa, Tex.) 2. Football

ISBN 0-306-80990-7   LC 00-40510

First published 1990 by Addison-Wesley

In 1988, the author, a "Philadelphia Inquirer editor, left his job to spend a year with a high school sports team. The sport he picked was football, the location, the . . . West Texas oil town of Odessa. . . . Here 20,000

fans turn out regularly to watch their Permian Panthers win." Libr J

"It is a tricky balancing act, but Mr. Bissinger carries it off: 'Friday Night Lights' offers a biting indictment of the sports craziness that grips not only Odessa but most of American society, while at the same time providing a moving evocation of its powerful allure." N Y Times Book Rev

Complete guide to special teams; American Football Coaches Association; edited by Bill Mallory and Don Nehlen. Human Kinetics 2005 254p il pa $21.95 *

Grades: 11 12 Adult   **796.332**

1. Football

ISBN 0-7360-5291-7   LC 2004-20518

Contents: Punts by Robin Ross; Kickoffs by Greg McMahon; Punt returns by John Harbaugh; Kickoff returns by Dave Ungerer; Extra points and field goals by Lester Erb and Ronald Aiken; Two-point conversions by Urban Meyer; Punt and field goal blocks by Bud Foster; Developing special teams units by Mike Sabock; Punting by Jeff Hays; Kicking off by Joe Robinson; Kicking extra points and field goals by Brian Polian; Long snapping by Bill Legg; Holding for kicks by Steve Kidd; Returning punts and kickoffs by Bill Lynch; Developing special teams players by Joe DeForest

MacCambridge, Michael, 1963-

America's game; the epic story of how pro football captured a nation. Random House 2004 552p il hardcover o.p. pa $15

Grades: 11 12 Adult   **796.332**

1. National Football League 2. Football

ISBN 0-375-50454-0; 0-375-72506-7 (pa)

LC 2004-52003

The author traces pro football's history "with particular attention paid to six key franchises—the Rams, Browns, Colts, Cowboys, Chiefs, and Raiders—and how their fortunes reflected the larger growth of the game itself." Publisher's note

"This magisterial history is a fitting acknowledgment of the sport's legacy." Publ Wkly

Includes bibliographical references

McIntosh, J. S.

Football. Mason Crest Publishers 2010 c2011 96p (Getting the edge: conditioning, injuries, and legal & illicit drugs) lib bdg $24.95

Grades: 7 8 9 10   **796.332**

1. Football

ISBN 978-1-4222-1733-7; 1-4222-1733-7

LC 2010-7230

This book covers basic safety training, equipment, preparation, and precautions related to football. It also covers how to recover quickly from football-related injuries.

Includes bibliographical references

Rielly, Edward J.

Football; an encyclopedia of popular culture. University of Nebraska Press 2009 439p pa $26.95

Grades: 9 10 11 12 Adult   **796.332**

1. Football—Encyclopedias 2. Reference books

ISBN 978-0-8032-9012-9; 0-8032-9012-8

LC 2009-5245

"Rielly's interest is not so much in football per se as in football as a force in American culture. . . . [This volume offers] short essays arranged alphabetically on topics which the author feels are significant both to football and to American history and culture. Some of the selected topics are expected (Bowl Games, Forward Pass, Television Broadcasting) while others are more surprising (Jewelry, September 11 Terrorist Attacks, Wine). Rielly has a relaxed and informal writing style which practically invites you to pull up a chair and make yourself comfortable while he discourses on his chosen topics." PopMatters

Includes bibliographical references

796.334 Soccer

Ayub, Awista

However tall the mountain; a dream, eight girls, and a journey home. Hyperion 2009 235p $23.99; pa $14.99

Grades: 11 12 Adult   **796.334**

1. Soccer 2. Women—Afghanistan

ISBN 978-1-4013-2249-6; 978-1-4013-1025-7 (pa)

LC 2009-23225

Paperback published with title: Kabul girls soccer club

"Ayub, an Afghan-born American, founded the Afghan Youth Sports Exchange (AYSE) to draw Afghan girls into soccer as a method of empowerment. She weaves together the personal stories of the eight girls who pioneered the program, including their training trip to the United States and their return to form teams and compete in Afghanistan. . . . The courage of these eight girls will inspire readers of all backgrounds." Libr J

Buxton, Ted

Soccer skills for young players; {by} Ted Buxton, with Alex Leith and Jim Drewitt; foreword by Gordon Jago. Firefly Bks. (Buffalo) 2000 128p il pa $14.95 *

Grades: 9 10 11 12   **796.334**

1. Soccer

ISBN 1-55209-329-8

"Buxton presents more than 70 drills for beginner to advanced players. The book opens with a few warm-up and stretching exercises. Specific types of drills are illustrated by at least one colorful action photograph; many are also accompanied by a diagram of the play on the field and additional tips outlined in a skill box." SLJ

Crisfield, Deborah

Winning soccer for girls; [by] Deborah W. Crisfield; foreword by Bill Hawkey and Patrick Murphy. 3rd ed. Chelsea House 2010 164p il (Winning sports for girls) lib bdg $39.50; pa $14.95 *

Grades: 7 8 9 10   **796.334**

1. Soccer

ISBN 978-0-8160-7714-4 (lib bdg); 0-8160-7714-2 (lib bdg); 978-0-8160-7715-1 (pa); 0-8160-7715-0 (pa)

LC 2008-50595

"A Mountain Lion book"

First published 1996 by Facts on File

This soccer guidebook contains "material on developing agility, power, and strength and improving ball control and handling. The history and rules of the game are also examined, and a glossary lists soccer terms." Publisher's note

Includes glossary and bibliographical references

Longman, Jere

The girls of summer; the U.S. women's soccer team and how it changed the world. HarperCollins Pubs. 2000 318p il hardcover o.p. pa $14 *

Grades: 11 12 Adult   **796.334**

1. Soccer 2. Women athletes

ISBN 0-06-019657-2; 0-06-093468-9 (pa)

This "retelling of the 1999 Women's World Cup championship match between the U.S. and China weaves together gender issues, the influence of Title IX, and biographies and interviews with key players." Booklist

Includes bibliographical references

Luongo, Albert M., 1939-

Soccer drills; skill-builders for field control. McFarland & Co. 2000 182p pa $24.50

Grades: 9 10 11 12   **796.334**

1. Soccer

ISBN 0-7864-0682-8

LC 99-47698

The author "suggests a systematic plan for skill development, from beginning to advanced drills, based on selected techniques of top competitive world-class players and managers. . . . Thirty-eight illustrations—with clear and concise legends—provide an easy-to-follow visual guide for various playing techniques. Diagrams show proper body positions and stages of progression for drills." Voice Youth Advocates

Luxbacher, Joe

Soccer: steps to success; [by] Joseph A. Luxbacher. 3rd ed. Human Kinetics 2005 198p il (Steps to success activity series) pa $17.95

Grades: 9 10 11 12 Adult   **796.334**

1. Soccer

ISBN 0-736-05435-9

LC 2004-18570

First published 1991

This book describes the skills and concepts used in soccer in twelve steps.

McIntosh, J. S.

Soccer. Mason Crest Publishers 2010 c2011 96p il map (Getting the edge: conditioning, injuries, and legal & illicit drugs) lib bdg $24.94

Grades: 7 8 9 10   **796.334**

1. Soccer

ISBN 978-1-4222-1739-9; 1-4222-1739-6

LC 2010-15259

This book covers basic safety training, equipment, preparation, and precautions related to soccer. It also covers how to recover quickly from soccer-related injuries.

Includes bibliographical references

Mielke, Danny

Soccer fundamentals. Human Kinetics 2003 xx, 129p il (Sports fundamentals series) pa $15.95

Grades: 9 10 11 12 Adult   **796.334**

1. Soccer

ISBN 0-7360-4506-6   LC 2002-15231

This book "devotes separate chapters to mastering specific skills like dribbling, juggling, passing, trapping, executing throw-ins, heading, performing tricks and turns, shooting, and volleying. [It includes] sections on offensive and defensive tactics, scoring systems, goalkeeping, dead ball kicks, strategy, and sportsmanship." Publisher's note

St. John, Warren

Outcasts united; a refugee team, an American town. Spiegel & Grau 2008 307p hardcover o.p. pa $15

Grades: 11 12 Adult   **796.334**

1. Mufleh, Luma 2. Soccer 3. Refugees

ISBN 978-0-385-52203-8; 0-385-52203-7; 978-0-385-52204-5 (pa); 0-385-52204-5 (pa)

LC 2008-40697

This is a "book about an unlikely soccer program in the outlying Atlanta burb of Clarkston, Georgia. . . . Clarkston's residents woke up one morning and found that the city's housing projects had become havens of resettlement for refugee families from war-ravaged locales including Liberia, Afghanistan and Bosnia. Soccer is a pastime like sandlot baseball or touch football to the often-traumatized boys on the Fugees, a ramshackle intramural team of nine to 17-year-olds that St. John follows, along with its Jordanian founder Luma Hassan Mufleh, a Smith-educated woman whose role as volunteer coach quickly expands to extended family member and social worker. St. John's aim is to draw a portrait of small-town America in transition, and his eye for detail is compelling from start to finish." Time Out N Y

Includes bibliographical references

796.34   Racket games

Hinkson, Jim

Lacrosse for dummies; by Jim Hinkson and Joe Lombardi. 2nd ed. John Wiley & Sons Canada, Ltd. 2010 xxvi, 330p il (--For dummies) pa $21.99

Grades: 9 10 11 12 Adult   **796.34**

1. Lacrosse

ISBN 978-0-470-73855-9; 0-470-73855-3

LC 2010-282483

First published 2003

"The book offers everything the beginning player needs to know, from the necessary equipment to the basic rules of the game, with explanations of the women's game and the indoor game, too. It also offers . . . information for the experienced player, including winning offensive and defensive strategies, along with skill-building exercises and drills. Finally, there's information on how armchair lacrosse players can get their fix of the sport on television, online, on in print." Publisher's note

Includes bibliographical references

McAfee, Richard, 1950-

Table tennis; steps to success. Human Kinetics 2009 xx, 203p il (Steps to success sports series) pa $18.95

Grades: 9 10 11 12 Adult   **796.34**

1. Table tennis

ISBN 978-0-7360-7731-6; 0-7360-7731-6

LC 2009-4824

First published 1993 under the authorship of Larry Hodges

Contents: Preparing to play; Hitting drive strokes; Understanding spin and footwork; Executing spin strokes; Serving; Returning serve; Using the five-ball training system; Understanding styles of play and tactics; Playing intermediate strokes; Performing intermediate serves; Competing successfully in tournaments

This book describes the skills and concepts used in table tennis.

Pietramala, David G., 1967-

Lacrosse; technique and tradition; [by] David G. Pietramala and Neil A. Grauer. 2nd ed. Johns Hopkins University Press 2006 300p il $59; pa $37

Grades: 9 10 11 12 Adult   **796.34**

1. Lacrosse

ISBN 978-0-8018-8371-2; 0-8018-8371-7; 978-0-8018-8410-8 (pa); 0-8018-8410-1 (pa)

LC 2005-27696

First published 1976 under the authorship of Bob Scott

This book contains "sections on rules, equipment, preparation, and tactics . . . [and cover topics] such as drills and skills for specific positions, game strategy, clearing tactics, and the history of the game itself—including a section on the Johns Hopkins contributions to lacrosse." Publisher's note

Includes bibliographical references

Swissler, Becky
Winning lacrosse for girls; foreword by Katie Bergstrom. 2nd ed. Chelsea House 2010 212p il (Winning sports for girls) lib bdg $44.95; pa $14.95 *
Grades: 7 8 9 10   **796.34**
  1. Lacrosse
  ISBN 978-0-8160-7712-0 (lib bdg); 0-8160-7712-6 (lib bdg); 978-0-8160-7713-7 (pa); 0-8160-7713-4 (pa)
                           LC 2008-51346
"A Mountain Lion Book"
First published 2004 by Facts on File
This lacrosse guidebook "teaches the game's basic skills, strategies, and drills and how to master them. Chapters cover the history of the game, the basics of stick handling, the rules of play, passing and receiving, offense and defense, key strategies, skills and tactics, conditioning, and . . . more." Publisher's note
Includes bibliographical references

Urick, Dave
Sports illustrated lacrosse; fundamentals for winning; [by] David Urick. Taylor Trade Pub. 2008 233p il pa $14.95 *
Grades: 9 10 11 12   **796.34**
  1. Lacrosse
  ISBN 978-1-58979-344-6; 1-58979-344-7
                           LC 2007036290
First published 1988 by Sports Illustrated
An introduction to the game of lacrosse providing information about equipment, rules, skills, strategy, and training.

Vanderhoof, Gabrielle
Lacrosse. Mason Crest Publishers 2010 c2011 96p il (Getting the edge: conditioning, injuries, and legal & illicit drugs) lib bdg $24.95
Grades: 7 8 9 10   **796.34**
  1. Lacrosse
  ISBN 978-1-4222-1737-5; 1-4222-1737-X
                           LC 2010-12754
This book covers basic safety training, equipment, preparation, and precautions related to lacrosse. It also covers how to recover quickly from lacrosse-related injuries.
Includes bibliographical references

796.342   Tennis

Douglas, Paul
Tennis. Dorling Kindersley 1995 72p il (101 essential tips) pa $5
Grades: 7 8 9 10   **796.342**
  1. Tennis
  ISBN 0-7566-0225-4
Aspects covered include strokes, positions, playing surfaces, dress and equipment
"This is a good text for those just picking up the sport, as well as for those seasoned players who want to brush up on their game or improve their strategy." Voice of Youth Advocates

796.352   Golf

Echikson, William
Shooting for Tiger; how golf's obsessed new generation is transforming a country club sport. PublicAffairs 2009 269p il $24.95
Grades: 11 12 Adult   **796.352**
  1. Golf
  ISBN 978-1-58648-578-8; 1-58648-578-4
                           LC 2009-2003
"Who will be the next Tiger Woods? Echikson profiles the lives of many promising teenage golfers. The behind-the-scenes look at these young people, with their dedicated instructors, overzealous parents, and elite golf academies, provides a glimpse into the psyche of each of the players." SLJ
Includes bibliographical references

St. Pierre, Denise
Golf fundamentals. Human Kinetics 2004 133p il (Sports fundamentals series) pa $15.95
Grades: 9 10 11 12 Adult   **796.352**
  1. Golf
  ISBN 0-7360-5431-6   LC 2004-1617
This guide to playing golf covers topics such as putting, full swings, equipment, rules, and scoring.

796.357   Baseball

Adair, Robert Kemp
The physics of baseball. 3rd ed, rev, updated, and expanded. Perennial 2002 169p il pa $12.95
Grades: 11 12 Adult   **796.357**
  1. Physics 2. Baseball 3. Force and energy
  ISBN 0-06-008436-7   LC 2001-39886
First published 1990
A look at how some physical principles are applied to the game of baseball. Pitching, batting and the properties of bats are discussed
Includes bibliographical references

Angell, Roger
Game time: a baseball companion; edited by Steve Kettmann. Harcourt 2003 398p hardcover o.p. pa $15
Grades: 11 12 Adult   **796.357**
  1. Baseball
  ISBN 0-15-100824-8; 0-15-601387-8 (pa)
                           LC 2002-152611
"A Harvest original"
"Half of the essays in this compilation of highlights from Angell's 40 years of covering baseball for the *New Yorker* have not previously appeared in book form, and even those that have are well worth revisiting. Angell . . . remains the dean of baseball writers." Booklist

The **Baseball** anthology; 125 Years of stories, poems, articles, photographs, drawings, interviews, cartoons, and other memorabilia; general editor, Joseph Wallace; foreword by Sparky Anderson. Abrams 2004 296p il pa $19.95   **796.357**
1. Baseball
ISBN 0-8109-9179-9   LC 2005-284304
"Organized chronologically, the book combines a photo history of the game with a running narrative composed largely of excerpts from a wealth of well-known baseball writers. . . . The pictures are delightful, both for their excellent reproduction and for their content." Booklist

Baseball, the perfect game; an all-star anthology celebrating the game's greatest players, teams, and moments; Josh Leventhal, editor. Voyageur Press 2005 223p il $29.95
Grades: 11 12 Adult   **796.357**
1. Baseball
ISBN 0-89658-668-5   LC 2004-23541
Partial contents: The national game; The origins of baseball; Opening day by Jim Brosnan; The collector: J.R. Burdick and the world of baseball cards by Mark Lamster; Dynasties, more than just those damn Yankees by Gary Gillette and Pete Palmer; The Red Stockings, baseball's first professional team; The Black Sox scandal by Eliot Asinof; 1941, an unmatchable summer by Ray Robinson; Next year arrives, the 1955 Brooklyn Dodgers by Doris Kearns Goodwin; The 1975 World Series, an October classic by Bill Lee; The greatest World Series by Josh Leventhal; 1998: the year that baseball came back . . . by Alan Schwarz
"Hardcore fans of 'America's Game' have a gem in this book. . . . The selections, all beautifully written, clearly are intended for older teens comfortable with documentary-style descriptions." Voice Youth Advocates

Biographical dictionary of American sports, Baseball; edited by David L. Porter. rev and expanded ed. Greenwood Press 2000 3v set $295 *
Grades: 11 12 Adult   **796.357**
1. Baseball
ISBN 0-313-29884-X   LC 99-14840
First published 1987
This set "contains 1,450 signed entries. Individuals were chosen because of their 'impressive statistical records' or because they 'made a major impact on professional baseball' and include major league players; prominent minor league, Negro League, and Girls League players; and various executives, coaches, managers, and umpires. . . . Any library that wants to have a serious baseball reference section will need [this work]." Booklist
Includes bibliographical references

Encyclopedia of women and baseball; edited by Leslie A. Heaphy and Mel Anthony May; foreword by Laura Wulf. McFarland & Co. 2006 438p il $49.95
Grades: 11 12 Adult   **796.357**
1. Women athletes—Encyclopedias 2. Baseball—Encyclopedias 3. Reference books
ISBN 0-7864-2100-2; 978-0-7864-2100-8
                                     LC 2006-8719

"This encyclopedia provides information on women players, managers, teams, leagues, and issues since the mid-19th century. Players are listed by maiden name with married name, when known, in parentheses. Information provided includes birth date, death date, team, dates of play, career statistics and brief biographical notes when available." Publisher's note
The editors "have produced a valuable resource on a seldom studied area of baseball." Choice
Includes bibliographical references

Garman, Judi, 1944-
Softball skills & drills; [by] Judi Garman, Michelle Gromacki. 2nd ed. Human Kinetics 2011 314p il pa $21.95
Grades: 9 10 11 12   **796.357**
1. Softball
ISBN 978-0-7360-9074-2; 0-7360-9074-6
                                     LC 2010-48654
First published 2001
Contents: Hitting; Bunting and slap hitting; Baserunning, stealing, and sliding; Team offense; Throwing; Catching; Infield; Outfield; Team defense; Pitching fundamentals; Movement and off-speed pitches; Pitching practice and game management; Pitcher as a defensive player; The catcher
This book provides "coverage on strategies for every area of the game: hitting, fielding, pitching, catching, and baserunning. . . . [It includes] over 230 drills appropriate for players of all abilities." Publisher's note

Gola, Mark
Winning softball for girls; foreword by Gretchen Cammiso. 2nd ed. Chelsea House 2009 220p il (Winning sports for girls) lib bdg $44.95; pa $14.95 *
Grades: 7 8 9 10   **796.357**
1. Softball
ISBN 978-0-8160-7716-8 (lib bdg); 0-8160-7716-9 (lib bdg); 978-0-8160-7717-5 (pa); 0-8160-7717-7 (pa)
                                     LC 2008-54453
First published 2002 by Facts on File
"Gola covers the history, rules of the game, and necessary equipment as well as tips for hitting, pitching, and base running. The fundamentals of defense and offense are covered, along with a number of drills in each area. In addition, the author details the various positions and gives advice on conditioning. . . . This title could prove useful in balancing baseball-laden collections." SLJ
Includes bibliographical references

Hogan, Lawrence D., 1944-
Shades of glory; the Negro Leagues and the story of African-American baseball; with a foreword by Jules Tygiel. National Geographic 2006 422p il $26 *
Grades: 11 12 Adult   **796.357**
1. Negro leagues 2. Baseball 3. African American athletes
ISBN 0-7922-5306-X; 978-0-7922-5306-8
                                     LC 2006-273216
Published in association with the National Baseball Hall of Fame and Museum

Hogan, Lawrence D., 1944-—*Continued*

This book "traces the history of black baseball from the 19th century to the first great teams, such as the Cuban Giants, and on to the era of the vibrant barnstorming teams from the East Coast, Chicago, and Cuba." Publisher's note

"This is an important, informative, and entertaining contribution to sports history." Booklist

Kahn, Roger, 1927-

Beyond the boys of summer; the very best of Roger Kahn; edited by Rob Miraldi. McGraw-Hill 2005 xxxvi, 364p hardcover o.p. pa $16.95

Grades: 11 12 Adult   **796.357**

1. Baseball

ISBN 0-07-144727-X; 0-07-148119-2 (pa)

LC 2004-24851

This book "presents a showcase of 50 years worth of Kahn's . . . work." Publisher's note

"Kahn is a giant among sports journalists, and this is a fine sampling of his most memorable work." Booklist

Includes bibliographical references

Kelley, Brent P.

Voices from the Negro leagues; conversations with 52 baseball standouts of the period 1924-1960. McFarland & Co. 1998 334p il $45 *

Grades: 11 12 Adult   **796.357**

1. Baseball 2. African American athletes

ISBN 0-7864-2279-3   LC 97-37332

This "book is divided into two sections: the first comprises those who played prior to Jackie Robinson's breaking the color barrier; the second section features those who continued to play in the Negro leagues after Robinson's debut. . . . Kelley also provides biographies of each subject for context and whatever statistics are available. A wonderful book that should be exceedingly popular among fans with an interest in the game's history." Booklist

Includes bibliographical references

Light, Jonathan Fraser, 1957-

The cultural encyclopedia of baseball. 2nd ed. McFarland & Co. 2005 1105p il $75 *

Grades: 11 12 Adult   **796.357**

1. Reference books 2. Baseball—Encyclopedias

ISBN 0-7864-2087-1   LC 2005-1718

First published 1997

This encyclopedia "profiles every Hall of Fame player, as well as every National and American League club (and predecessors). . . . Statistics play a large role in this resource, which includes facts and figures on just about every conceivable event in the game. Cultural references to baseball are noted throughout in numerous quotations. Some of the more fascinating sections include 'Nicknames,' 'Presidents,' and 'Salaries.' Other entries that make for offbeat perusal include 'Freak Accidents,' 'Sex,' and 'Injuries and Illnesses.'" Choice

Includes bibliographical references

McGuire, Mark, 1963-

The 100 greatest baseball players of the 20th century ranked; by Mark McGuire and Michael Sean Gormley. McFarland & Co. 2000 207p $30

Grades: 11 12 Adult   **796.357**

1. Baseball

ISBN 0-7864-0914-2   LC 00-20230

"The authors of this work looked at statistics, the different eras, the 'five tools,' and even oral legend in compiling this list. . . . They've ranked the Negro League players and superstars from around the globe alongside the Major League legends." Publisher's note

Owens, Tom, 1960-

Collecting baseball memorabilia; [by] Thomas S. Owens. Millbrook Press 1996 96p il lib bdg $26.90

Grades: 8 9 10 11 12   **796.357**

1. Baseball—Collectibles

ISBN 1-56294-579-3   LC 95-19827

"This introduction delves into a wide array of baseball collectibles including tickets stubs, team schedules, autographs, and other items that can be obtained at little or no cost. . . . This book has a crisp layout with full-color photos or reproductions on nearly every page. While not a price guide, this title will be of interest to young baseball enthusiasts." SLJ

Includes glossary

Posnanski, Joe

The soul of baseball; a road trip through Buck O'Neil's America. Morrow 2007 276p $24.95

Grades: 11 12 Adult   **796.357**

1. O'Neil, Buck, 1911-2006 2. Baseball 3. United States—Description and travel

ISBN 978-0-06-085403-4; 0-06-085403-0

An account of how the author "spent a year on the road with the iconic Negro Leagues player and manager Buck O'Neil (1911-2006), recording the magnanimous 94-year-old's encounters with scores of fans and his vast repertoire of entertaining stories." Publ Wkly

Ripken, Cal, Jr.

Play baseball the Ripken way; the complete illustrated guide to the fundamentals; [by] Cal Ripken, Jr. and Bill Ripken with Larry Burke. Random House 2004 236p il hardcover o.p. pa $15.95

Grades: 11 12 Adult   **796.357**

1. Baseball

ISBN 1-4000-6122-9; 0-8129-7050-0 (pa)

LC 2003-66725

"Chapters written by Cal cover batting, base running, infield play, and catching; Bill's chapters outline pitching and outfield play. The text is interspersed with . . . photographs as well as sidebars on special tips, and each chapter closes with a review checklist." Libr J

"This book is the next best thing to a personal lesson with the man who broke Lou Gehrig's record of playing in 2,632 consecutive games; it's a comprehensive look at all aspects of how to play baseball that will benefit young players and adult weekend warriors." Publ Wkly

Sokolove, Michael Y.

The ticket out: Darryl Strawberry and the boys
of Crenshaw; [by] Michael Sokolove. Simon &
Schuster 2004 291p hardcover o.p. pa $14

Grades: 11 12 Adult   **796.357**

   1. Strawberry, Darryl 2. Crenshaw High School (Los
Angeles, Calif.) 3. Baseball

   ISBN 0-7432-2673-9; 0-7432-7885-2 (pa)

                  LC 2004-41745

"The individual stories of a vastly talented 1979 L.A.
high-school baseball team come to life in this heartbreaking account of the players' last season and the difficulties
they faced in the years that followed." Booklist

Includes bibliographical references

Vecsey, George

Baseball: a history of America's favorite game.
Modern Library 2006 252p il (Modern Library
chronicles) $21.95 *

Grades: 11 12 Adult   **796.357**

   1. Baseball

   ISBN 0-679-64338-9; 978-0-679-64338-8

                  LC 2006-45033

This history of baseball "unfolds much like a highlights tape, with a breezy background narrative of the
game from its pre-Civil War roots to its current drug
scandals, structured around set pieces spotlighting the
outsized deeds of luminaries like Babe Ruth, Jackie Robinson, Branch Rickey and George Steinbrenner. . . .
Vivid, affectionate and clear-eyed, Vecsey's account
makes for an engaging sports history." Publ Wkly

Includes bibliographical references

Wendel, Tim

Far from home; Latino baseball players in
America; [by] Tim Wendel, José Luis Villegas.
National Geographic Society 2008 159p il $28

Grades: 11 12 Adult   **796.357**

   1. Hispanic American athletes 2. Baseball

   ISBN 978-1-4262-0216-2; 1-4262-0216-4

                  LC 2007-61240

This "book offers revealing photographs of both the
star and the lesser-known Latino players, accompanied
by concise, insightful text. . . . The book mainly points
to Cuban, Puerto Rican, Dominican, and Venezuelan
stars. A useful time line is included." Libr J

The new face of baseball; the one-hundred year
rise and triumph of Latinos in America's favorite
sport; foreword by Bob Costas; color photographs
by Victor Baldizon. Rayo 2003 266p il hardcover
o.p. pa $13.95

Grades: 11 12 Adult   **796.357**

   1. Baseball 2. Hispanic Americans

   ISBN 0-06-053631-4; 0-06-053632-2 (pa)

                  LC 2004-300834

"Going as far back as the mid-nineteenth century, to
the early days of Cuban baseball, Wendel traces the
spread of American baseball fever in the Caribbean and
Mexico." Publisher's note

"Fans will recognize names like Minoso, Clemente,
Cepeda, or Sosa, but it is enlightening to see them presented as part of a single accomplished group . . . This

is an excellent overview." Libr J

Includes bibliographical references

Wilson, Nick

Voices from the pastime; oral histories of
surviving major leaguers, Negro leaguers, Cuban
leaguers, and writers, 1920-1934. McFarland &
Co. 2000 208p il pa $29.95 *

Grades: 11 12 Adult   **796.357**

   1. Baseball

   ISBN 0-7864-0824-3   LC 00-26695

The players and sportswriters not only recount their
own careers, they talk of some of the greatest players in
the history of the game, including Babe Ruth, Josh Gibson, Satchel Paige, Walter Johnson and Martin Dihigo

Includes bibliographical references

796.42   Track and field

Burfoot, Amby

Runner's world complete book of beginning
running. Distributed to the trade by Holtzbrinck
Publishers 2005 320p il pa $17.95 *

Grades: 11 12 Adult   **796.42**

   1. Running

   ISBN 1-59486-022-X   LC 2004-17559

This book offers training advice to beginning runners
and covers topics including stretching, cross-training,
strength exercises, nutrition, and special issues for wom-
en runners.

Includes bibliographical references

Carr, Gerald A., 1936-

Fundamentals of track and field; [by] Gerry
Carr. 2nd ed. Human Kinetics 1999 285p il pa
$24.95

Grades: 9 10 11 12   **796.42**

   1. Track athletics

   ISBN 0-7360-0008-9   LC 98-52218

   First published 1991 by Leisure Press

This book provides "information for teaching and
coaching every track and field event, including such frequently excluded events as the 400-meter hurdles, stee-
plechase, triple jump, hammer throw, and race walking."
Publisher's note

Includes bibliographical references

Housewright, Ed

Winning track and field for girls; foreword by
Jason-Lamont Jackson. 2nd ed. Chelsea House
2009 194p il (Winning sports for girls) lib bdg
$44.95; pa $11.96

Grades: 7 8 9 10 11 12   **796.42**

   1. Track athletics

   ISBN 978-0-8160-7718-2 (lib bdg); 0-8160-7718-5 (lib
bdg); 978-0-8160-7719-9 (pa); 0-8160-7719-3 (pa)

                  LC 2009-9019

   First published 2004 by Facts on File

Housewright, Ed—*Continued*

This includes a brief history of women's track, followed by topics including sprints, hurdles, middle and long distances, relays, jumping events, throwing events, the heptathlon, cross-country, and the triathlon, mental preparations and nutrition, stetches and weight lifting.

Includes bibliographical references

Runner's world complete book of running; everything you need to run for weight loss, fitness, and competition; edited by Amby Burfoot. Rev. & updated ed. Rodale; Distributed by Macmillan 2009 312p il $29.95; pa $21.99

Grades: 11 12 Adult **796.42**

1. Running

ISBN 978-1-60529-545-9; 978-1-60529-579-4 (pa)

LC 2009-33150

First published 1997

Topics covered include: nutrition, injury prevention and treatment, shoe selection, mental readiness, and marathon preparation.

Scott, Dagny

Runner's world complete book of women's running; the best advice to get started, stay motivated, lose weight, run injury-free, be safe, and train for any distance; [by] Dagny Scott Barrios. Rev. and updated ed. Distributed to the trade by Holtzbrinck Publishers 2007 324p il pa $16.95

Grades: 11 12 Adult **796.42**

1. Running

ISBN 978-1-59486-758-3; 1-59486-758-5

LC 2007-30645

First published 2000

Topics covered include racing, nutrition, running during pregnancy, weight loss, and proper clothing.

796.44 Sports gymnastics

McIntosh, J. S.

Gymnastics. Mason Crest Publishers 2010 c2011 96p il (Getting the edge: conditioning, injuries, and legal & illicit drugs) lib bdg $24.95

Grades: 7 8 9 10 **796.44**

1. Gymnastics

ISBN 978-1-4222-1734-4; 1-4222-1734-5

LC 2010-10053

This book "offers a general introduction to . . . [gymnastics], its rules, and its history before zeroing in on health and safety concerns. . . . [It] covers mental preparation as well as the dangers of using drugs such as diuretics and amphetamines." Booklist

Includes bibliographical references

796.48 Olympic games

Guttmann, Allen

The Olympics, a history of the modern games. 2nd ed. University of Ill. Press 2002 214p il (Illinois history of sports) hardcover o.p. pa $16.95

Grades: 11 12 Adult **796.48**

1. Olympic games

ISBN 0-252-02725-6; 0-252-07046-1 (pa)

LC 2001-41383

First published 1992

"Guttmann discusses the intended and actual meaning of the modern Olympic Games, from 1896 to 2000. Recounting the memorable and significant athletic events of the Olympics in terms of their social and political impact, Guttmann . . . [attempts to demonstrate] that the modern games were revived to propagate a political message and continue to serve political purposes." Publisher's note

Includes bibliographical references

Mallon, Bill

Historical dictionary of the Olympic movement; [by] Bill Mallon, with Ian Buchanan. 3rd ed. Scarecrow Press 2006 cxvi, 411p il (Historical dictionaries of religions, philosophies, and movements) $90 *

Grades: 9 10 11 12 **796.48**

1. Olympic games

ISBN 0-8108-5574-7 LC 2005-16706

First published 1995

"The volume covers a wide range of persons, places, and events over a long historical period, stretching back more than a millennium. Entries are in dictionary format and include significant events, Olympic bodies, pioneers of the games, organizations, athletes, and the many participating countries, which now number 202." Booklist

Includes bibliographical references

796.5 Outdoor life

Paulsen, Gary

Woodsong. Bradbury Press 1990 132p map hardcover o.p. pa $6.99

Grades: 7 8 9 10 **796.5**

1. Sled dog racing 2. Outdoor life 3. Minnesota

ISBN 0-02-770221-9; 1-4169-3939-3 (pa)

LC 89-70835

For the author and his family, life in northern Minnesota is a wild experience involving wolves, deer, and the sled dogs that make their way of life possible. Includes an account of Paulsen's first Iditarod, a dogsled race across Alaska

"The book is packed with vignettes that range among various shades of terror and lyrical beauty." Voice Youth Advocates

796.51　Walking

Berger, Karen, 1959-
Advanced backpacking; illustrations by Ron
Hildebrand. Norton 1998 224p il maps (Trailside
series guide) flexible bdg $18.95
Grades: 11 12 Adult　　　　　　　　**796.51**
　1. Backpacking
　ISBN 0-393-31769-2　　　　　　LC 97-43849
This book "is comprised of three sections: Part 1 covers the basics of expedition planning, including route selection, food and water supply, and the treatment of
physical ailments that can occur on the trail; Part 2 considers the special gear and skills necessary for different
weather and terrain and for trekking in foreign countries;
and Part 3 offers a sampling of the most spectacular
trails in the United States along with contact information." Publisher's note
Includes bibliographical references

Hart, John, 1948-
Walking softly in the wilderness; the Sierra
Club guide to backpacking. 4th ed, complete rev
and updated. Sierra Club Books 2005 508p il map
(Sierra Club outdoor adventure guide) pa $16.95
*
Grades: 8 9 10 11 12 Adult　　　　　**796.51**
　1. Backpacking 2. Wilderness areas
　ISBN 1-57805-123-1　　　　　　LC 2004-56554
　First published 1977
This guide for both the novice and experienced hiker
reflects the environmental concerns of the Sierra Club.
Among topics covered are: clothing and equipment; mak-
ing and breaking camp; problem animals and plants; hiking and camping with kids. Listings of conservation and
wilderness travel organizations, map and equipment
sources, land management agencies, and Internet contacts
are appended.
Includes bibliographical references

796.522　Mountaineering

Climb: stories of survival from rock, snow, and
ice; edited by Clint Willis. Thunder's Mouth
Press 2000 259p il pa $16.95
Grades: 11 12 Adult　　　　　　　**796.522**
　1. Mountaineering
　ISBN 1-56025-250-2　　　　　　LC 99-26747
　"An Adrenaline book"
This anthology brings together "writings by some of
the world's best climbers, such as American Jim
Wickwire, Scotsman Hamish MacInnes, and literary
icons Evelyn Waugh and H. G. Wells. This collection
will surely appeal to die-hard veterans of the sport and
newcomers intrigued by risk taking. . . . For all readers,
lessons abound—although the writers may have survived
their ordeals presented here, some did not survive others." Booklist

Coburn, Broughton, 1951-
Everest: mountain without mercy; introduction
by Tim Cahill, afterword by David Breashears.
National Geographic Soc. 1997 256p il maps
hardcover o.p. pa $24
Grades: 11 12 Adult　　　　　　　**796.522**
　1. Mount Everest Expedition (1996)
　2. Mountaineering
　ISBN 0-7922-7014-2; 0-7922-6984-5 (pa)
　　　　　　　　　　　　　　　LC 97-10765
"Bringing an understated yet powerful Bud-
dhist/Sherpa ethical perspective to the tragedy on Everest
chronicled in Jon Krakauer's Into Thin Air, Coburn reports on the IMAX film crew who participated in the
rescue effort when the May 1996 expeditions led by
guides Rob Hall and Scott Fischer ended in death and
crippling injury." Publ Wkly

Krakauer, Jon
Into thin air; a personal account of the Mount
Everest disaster. Villard Bks. 1997 xx, 293p il
$25.95; pa $14.95 *
Grades: 11 12 Adult　　　　　　　**796.522**
　1. Mount Everest Expedition (1996)
　2. Mountaineering
　ISBN 0-679-45752-6; 0-385-49478-5 (pa)
　　　　　　　　　　　　　　　LC 96-30031
This is an account of the author's May 1996 Mount
Everest climbing expedition in which twelve fellow
climbers died during a snow storm
"This tense, harrowing story is as mesmerizing and
hard to put down as any well-written adventure novel."
SLJ
Includes bibliographical references

Mellor, Don
Rock climbing; a trailside guide; illustrations by
Ron Hildebrand. Norton 2003 c1997 191p il
(Trailside series guide) pa $18.95
Grades: 11 12 Adult　　　　　　　**796.522**
　1. Mountaineering
　ISBN 0-393-31653-X　　　　　　LC 96-52821
　On cover: The ultimate illustrated guide
"Designed to be carried on the trail, this will ease be-
ginners into the sport of rock climbing, with step-by-step
illustrated tutorials, safety and first-aid tips, and more."
Libr J
Includes bibliographical references

Ralston, Aron
Between a rock and a hard place. Atria Books
2004 354p il map hardcover o.p. pa $15
Grades: 11 12 Adult　　　　　　　**796.522**
　1. Mountaineering 2. Wilderness survival
　ISBN 0-7434-9281-1; 0-7434-9282-X (pa)
　　　　　　　　　　　　　　　LC 2004-303427
"With precious little water or food, his right arm
pinned for nearly five days by a boulder in a narrow
canyon shaft in central-eastern Utah, Ralston amputated
the arm with his pocketknife, then rappelled and hiked
his way to his own rescue. What makes his account of
his ordeal extraordinary, too, is the detail and precision

Ralston, Aron—*Continued*

Ralston, a former mechanical engineer, brings to the telling, from the almost minute-by-minute chronology of his ordeal to topographical descriptions of the ground he's covered in his life as an outdoor adventurer." Booklist

Includes bibliographical references

796.54 Camping

Callan, Kevin, 1958-

The happy camper; an essential guide to life outdoors. Boston Mills Press; distributed by Firefly Books 2005 320p il pa $19.95

Grades: 9 10 11 12 Adult   **796.54**

1. Camping

ISBN 1-55046-450-7; 978-1-55046-450-4

LC 2005-415489

"A great all-around guide by a top camping expert for campers of any skill level. [It includes] lots of color photos and accessible tips (how to pick a camping spot, stake a tent, build a fire, etc.)." Libr J

Includes bibliographical references

796.6 Cycling and related activities

Bicycling magazine's 1,000 all-time best tips; top riders share their secrets to maximize fun, safety, and performance; edited by Ben Hewitt. Fully rev and updated. Rodale 2005 168p il pa $10.95 *

Grades: 11 12 Adult   **796.6**

1. Cycling

ISBN 978-1-59486-051-5; 1-59486-051-3

LC 2005-638

Replaces Bicyling magazine's 900 all-time best tips

A collection of information on such topics as bicycle models, accessories, riding styles, and repair techniques

Carmichael, Chris

The ultimate ride; get fit, get fast, and start winning with the world's top cycling coach; [by] Chris Carmichael with Jim Rutberg. G.P. Putnam's Sons 2003 325p il hardcover o.p. pa $15 *

Grades: 11 12 Adult   **796.6**

1. Cycling 2. Physical fitness

ISBN 0-399-15071-4; 0-425-19601-1 (pa)

LC 2003-43214

The author offers advice to "serious cyclists wanting to improve their abilities, compete more successfully and train without incurring injuries." Publ Wkly

"This is an excellent guide to obtaining peak performance in cycling competition, but the wealth of training tips and intelligent discussion of nutrition will be almost as valuable to noncompetitive cyclists and even to other athletes serious about conditioning." Booklist

796.63 Mountain biking

Bicycling magazine's mountain biking skills; skills and techniques to master any terrain. Rodale 2005 122p pa $9.95

Grades: 9 10 11 12 Adult   **796.63**

1. Mountain biking

ISBN 978-1-59486-299-1; 1-59486-299-0

LC 2005-23045

First published 1990

This guide to mountain biking covers basic and intermediate skills and techniques including "ways to handle tough terrain, steer clear of hazardous obstacles, and even crash properly to avoid injury." Publisher's note

Crowther, Nicky

The ultimate mountain bike book; the definitive illustrated guide to bikes, components, techniques, thrills and trails; maintenance section by Melanie Allwood. rev 3rd ed. Firefly Bks. 2002 191p il pa $24.95 *

Grades: 9 10 11 12 Adult   **796.63**

1. Mountain bikes

ISBN 1-55297-653-X

First published 1996 by Motorbooks International

"Some of the topics covered are as basic as how to choose a bike, required accessories, and nitty-gritty instructions on how to maintain and care for your equipment. Crowther also includes information about racing, downhill, cross-country, and stunt riding. Although certain topics are written with advanced and competitive riders in mind . . . the book is jam-packed with everything beginner and experienced bikers need to know." SLJ

796.72 Automobile racing

Leslie-Pelecky, Diandra L.

The physics of NASCAR; how to make steel + gas + rubber = speed. Dutton 2008 286p il $25.95

Grades: 9 10 11 12   **796.72**

1. National Association for Stock Car Auto Racing 2. Automobile racing 3. Automobiles—Design and construction

ISBN 978-0-525-95053-0; 0-525-95053-2

LC 2007-46081

"The author, a physicist and devoted NASCAR fan, explains in clear, simple terms what goes into making a NASCAR vehicle, from design to development to construction to test-driving. . . . She introduces us to some of the sport's key players and teaches us (painlessly) more about the physics of speed . . . Fans will flock to this book." Booklist

Includes bibliographical references

Menzer, Joe
The wildest ride; a history of NASCAR (or, How a bunch of good ol' boys built a billion-dollar industry out of wrecking cars). Simon & Schuster 2001 311p il hardcover o.p. pa $14 *
Grades: 11 12 Adult   **796.72**
1. National Association for Stock Car Auto Racing 2. Automobile racing
ISBN 0-7432-0507-3; 0-7432-2625-9 (pa)
LC 2001-031088
This history focuses on the "legacy of the founding France family, the evolution of the cars from modified stock cars to purpose-built racers, and the fan-base expansion of the 1980s and 1990s. . . . Highly entertaining and full of facts." Libr J
Includes bibliographical references

O'Malley, J. J.
Daytona 24 hours; the definitive history of America's great endurance race; foreword by Hurley Haywood; design by Tom Morgan; photos edited by Buzz McKim; results and index by János Wimpffen. David Bull Pub. 2009 452p il $99.95 *
Grades: 9 10 11 12   **796.72**
1. Automobile racing
ISBN 978-1-935007-00-5   LC 2008-941266
First published 2003
The author delivers a "chronicle of the race, year by year (1974 was the only year it wasn't run), and the clear, mostly full-color photos, one on nearly every page, show the crew, the cars, the drivers, the track, and the pulsing action." Booklist

Thunder and glory; the 25 most memorable races in NASCAR Winston Cup history; [from the editors of NASCAR scene] Triumph Books 2004 160p il $34.95; pa $19.95
Grades: 9 10 11 12   **796.72**
1. National Association for Stock Car Auto Racing 2. Automobile racing
ISBN 1-57243-677-8; 1-57243-830-4 (pa)
LC 2006-297046
Includes DVD
"The focus is on 25 of the editors' most memorable Winston Cup races, which are analyzed and recounted with utter reverence. . . . Even nonracing fans will find the drama compelling." Booklist

796.8   Combat sports

Beekman, Scott
Ringside; a history of professional wrestling in America; [by] Scott M. Beekman. Praeger 2006 188p il $39.95 *
Grades: 11 12 Adult   **796.8**
1. Wrestling
ISBN 0-275-98401-X; 978-0-275-98401-4
LC 2006-8230

"This chronological work begins with a brief account of wrestling's global history, and then proceeds to investigate the sport's growth as a specifically American institution." Publisher's note
"An eye-opening reappraisal of a much-maligned sport, and (for wrestling fans) perhaps a much-needed vindication." Booklist
Includes bibliographical references

Greenberg, Keith Elliot, 1959-
Pro wrestling; from carnivals to cable TV. Lerner Publs. 2000 128p il (Sports legacy series) lib bdg $26.60; pa $9.95
Grades: 9 10 11 12   **796.8**
1. Wrestling
ISBN 0-8225-3332-4 (lib bdg); 0-8225-9864-7 (pa)
LC 99-50554
A history of professional wrestling from its roots in legitimate sport to its days as a carnival attraction followed by the growth of regional rivalries and culminating as television-centered entertainment
Includes bibliographical references

Kreidler, Mark
Four days to glory; wrestling with the soul of the American heartland. HarperCollins Publishers 2007 262p il hardcover o.p. pa $13.99 *
Grades: 11 12 Adult   **796.8**
1. Wrestling 2. School sports
ISBN   978-0-06-082318-4;   0-06-082318-6; 978-0-06-082319-1 (pa); 0-06-082319-4 (pa)
LC 2007-272997
Jay Borschel and Dan LeClere aspire to be four-time high school wrestling champions in Iowa.
The author's "deftness in 'Four Days' is in turning a niche sport into one as accessible as baseball or basketball." N Y Times Book Rev

Martin, Ashley P.
The Shotokan karate bible; beginner to black belt. Firefly Books 2007 201p pa $24.95
Grades: 6 7 8 9 10   **796.8**
1. Karate 2. Martial arts
ISBN 978-1-55407-322-1; 1-55407-322-7
LC 2008-270630
An "illustrated guide . . . [for] students of Shotokan karate, from beginners to those earning a black belt. The author outlines and explains the lessons for all 10 gradings." Publisher's note
"Each chapter outlines a grading syllabus, listing the techniques and sparring that the student must master to earn a particular belt, followed by extensive step-by-step photographs illustrating the moves involved. . . . This book of fundamentals is comprehensive and worthy." Voice Youth Advocates
Includes bibliographical references

McIntosh, J. S.

Wrestling. Mason Crest Publishers 2010 96p il (Getting the edge: conditioning, injuries, and legal & illicit drugs) lib bdg $24.95

Grades: 7 8 9 10   **796.8**

1. Wrestling

ISBN 978-1-4222-1743-6; 1-4222-1743-4

LC 2010-17923

This book covers basic safety training, equipment, preparation, and precautions related to wrestling and how to recover quickly from wrestling-related injuries.

Includes bibliographical references

Park, Yeon Hwan

Black belt tae kwon do; the ultimate reference guide to the world's most popular martial art; by Y.H. Park & Jon Gerrard. Facts on File 2000 272p il hardcover o.p. pa $16.95 *

Grades: 11 12 Adult   **796.8**

1. Tae kwon do

ISBN 0-8160-4240-3; 0-8160-4241-1 (pa)

LC 99-57876

Coverage includes practice, warm-up, and advanced techniques and forms, sparring strategies, self-defense, and breaking. Over 700 photographs accompany the text. Appendixes cover official competition rules, weight classes, governing bodies, and international organizations and associations. Includes two glossaries, English to Korean and Korean to English

Pawlett, Raymond

The karate handbook; [by] Ray Pawlett. Rosen Pub. Group 2008 256p il (Martial arts) $39.95 *

Grades: 7 8 9 10 11 12   **796.8**

1. Karate

ISBN 978-1-4042-1394-4; 1-4042-1394-5

LC 2007-32795

This "offers a thorough introduction to karate that covers both the underlying philosophy and the physical practice. A thoughtful, sophisticated history opens the book and discusses karate's roots in Zen Buddhism, the styles of karate, and dojo etiquette. Later spreads feature lucid, step-by-step instructions." Booklist

Includes bibliographical references

Pedro, Jimmy, 1970-

Judo techniques & tactics; [by] Jimmy Pedro with William Durbin. Human Kinetics 2001 183p il (Martial arts series) pa $16.95

Grades: 9 10 11 12 Adult   **796.8**

1. Judo

ISBN 0-7360-0343-6   LC 00-54236

This instructional guide describes the fundamentals of judo, including its history, definitions of terms used, and guides on competition and conditioning.

Includes bibliographical references

Polly, Matthew

American Shaolin; flying kicks, Buddhist monks, and the legend of iron crotch: an odyssey in the new China. Gotham Books 2007 366p il $26; pa $15 *

Grades: 11 12 Adult   **796.8**

1. Martial arts 2. China—Description and travel

ISBN 978-1-592-40262-5; 978-1-59240-337-0 (pa)

LC 2006-25384

"Scrawny, bullied since childhood, and sick of living with his 'Things Wrong with Matt' list, . . . [the author] recounts how he rode out pure instinct to leave college, travel to China, and best his inner demons through the art of kung fu fighting. What follows are fun and fascinating stories of his training with the famous monks at the world-renowned Shaolin temple, the birthplace of martial arts and Zen Buddhism." Libr J

796.9   Ice and snow sports

Stark, Peter

Winter adventure; a complete guide to winter sports; by Peter Stark and Steven M. Krauzer. Norton 1995 224p il (Trailside series guide) flexible bdg $17.95 *

Grades: 11 12 Adult   **796.9**

1. Winter sports

ISBN 0-393-31400-6   LC 95-34646

This guide to winter sports covers sledding, snowshoeing, dogsledding and skijoring, snowboarding, games such as cross-country tag and hare and hounds, the nature of snow and ice, ice skating, iceboating, ice climbing, curling and barrel jumping, winter camping, walking on snow and ice, dressing for winter, and winter safety. It lists organizations, mail-order sources, and information sources

796.93   Skiing and snowboarding

Cazeneuve, Brian

Cross-country skiing; a complete guide; illustrations by Ron Hildebrand. Norton 1995 192p il (Trailside series guide) flexible bdg $17.95 *

Grades: 11 12 Adult   **796.93**

1. Skiing

ISBN 0-393-31335-2   LC 95-5529

This illustrated guide to cross-country skiing covers equipment, techniques, backcountry skiing, clothing, safety, and fitness, and lists organizations, mail-order sources, and information sources

Kleh, Cindy

Snowboarding skills; the back-to-basics essentials for all levels; [photographer, Jed Jacobson] Firefly Books 2007 c2002 128p il pa $16.95

Grades: 7 8 9 10 11 12 Adult   **796.93**

1. Snowboarding

ISBN 1-55297-626-2   LC 2003-467271

Kleh, Cindy—*Continued*

This book features "information on taking lessons, proper nutrition before hitting the slopes, safety, clothing, stretching and preseason exercises, maintaining the equipment, basic moves, proper etiquette, and riding in a variety of snow conditions." SLJ

"Kleh's combination of dead-on practical advice, insider lingo, and near-religious enthusiasm makes this guide to snowboarding an invaluable resource for anyone wanting to try the sport or to advance his or her skills." Booklist

Masoff, Joy, 1951-

Snowboard! your guide to freeriding, pipe & park, jibbing, backcountry, alpine, boardercross, and more; illustrations by Jack Dickason. National Geographic Soc. 2002 64p il (Extreme sports) pa $8.95 *

Grades: 4 5 6 7 8 9   **796.93**
1. Snowboarding
ISBN 0-7922-6740-0   LC 2001-44392

Describes different kinds of snowboarding—freeriding, in the pipe, jibbing, backcountry—and the techniques, equipment, and terminology involved

"Sharp, action-packed photos and punchy, magazine-style prose add to the appeal. . . . Relaxed, readable, and filled with helpful information." Booklist

Werner, Doug, 1950-

Snowboarder's start-up; a beginner's guide to snowboarding; by Doug Werner & Jim Waide; photography by. 2nd ed., completely rev. Tracks Pub. 1998 144p il (Start-up sports) pa $11.95

Grades: 11 12 Adult   **796.93**
1. Snowboarding
ISBN 1-884654-11-8

First published 1993 by Pathfinder Publishing of California

This guide provides "snowboarding techniques and guidelines. Information on equipment, clothing, and gear precedes step-by-step instructions for such basic moves as stopping and turning, as well as speed control and ski-lift maneuvering. Sequential photographs demonstrate proper form, and the conversational tone . . . is perfect for teens and young adults, who make up a large segment of snowboarding enthusiasts. . . . Although an instruction manual can never replace trial and error on the slopes, this friendly guidebook is a good place to start." Booklist

796.962   Ice hockey

A **basic** guide to ice hockey; the U.S. Olympic Committee. Griffin Pub, Distributed by G. Stevens Pub 2002 152p il (Olympic guides) lib bdg $23.93

Grades: 9 10 11 12 Adult   **796.962**
1. Hockey
ISBN 0-8368-3103-9   LC 2001-55096

Provides information on such aspects of ice hockey as the history of Olympic competition, game rules and strategies, relevant nutrition, safety and first aid, and more. Describes Olympic and ice hockey organizations.

Coffey, Wayne R.

The boys of winter; the untold story of a coach, a dream, and, the 1980 U.S. olympic hockey team; foreword by Jim Craig. Crown Publishers 2005 272p il hardcover o.p. pa $13.95

Grades: 9 10 11 12 Adult   **796.962**
1. Hockey 2. Olympic games
ISBN 1-4000-4765-X; 1-4000-4766-8 (pa)
                            LC 2004-14163

The author "offers a nuanced portrait of the 1980 Olympics 'miracle on ice' and the gold medal-winning U.S. hockey team." SLJ

McKinley, Michael, 1961-

Hockey: a people's history. McClelland & Stewart 2006 346p il hardcover o.p. pa $37.50

Grades: 11 12 Adult   **796.962**
1. Hockey
ISBN   0-7710-5769-5;   978-0-7710-5769-4;
0-7710-5771-7 (pa); 978-0-7710-5771-7 (pa)

This history "chronicles hockey from its genesis as a winter substitute for lacrosse. A companion to a similarly titled CBC TV series, the lavishly illustrated book combines punchy boxed features celebrating individuals and hockey oddments and a detailed tracing of the game's development. . . . Essential for general sports as well as hockey-intensive collections." Booklist

Includes bibliographical references

Vanderhoof, Gabrielle

Hockey. Mason Crest Publishers 2010 c2011 96p il (Getting the edge: conditioning, injuries, and legal & illicit drugs) lib bdg $24.95

Grades: 7 8 9 10   **796.962**
1. Hockey
ISBN 978-1-422217-35-1; 1-42217-35-3
                            LC 2010-10054

This book "offers a general introduction to . . . [hockey], its rules, and its history before zeroing in on health and safety concerns. . . . [It] comments on typical injuries to hockey players and spells out NCAA and NHL penalties for using drugs such as steroids and human growth hormone." Booklist

Includes bibliographical references

796.98   Winter Olympic games

Macy, Sue, 1954-

Freeze frame; a photographic history of the Winter Olympics. National Geographic 2006 96p il map $18.95

Grades: 5 6 7 8 9 10   **796.98**
1. Olympic games 2. Winter sports
ISBN 0-7922-7887-9; 978-0-7922-7887-0

Highlights in the history of the Winter Olympics from their inception in 1924 to today, including profiles of the Olympic athletes and information on the lesser-known winter sports. Also includes an Olympic almanac with information about each Olympiad.

This book "has spectacular photographs and clear, captivating prose." SLJ

Includes bibliographical references

Wallechinsky, David, 1948-

The complete book of the Winter Olympics; [by] David Wallechinsky and Jaime Loucky. 2010 ed. Aurum 2009 322p il pa $24.95

Grades: 11 12 Adult **796.98**

1. Olympic games

ISBN 978-1-84513-491-4

First published 1984 by Overlook Press

"From speed skating to snowboarding, bobsleigh to ice hockey, this encyclopedia book gives the medals tables, timings, distances, and scores of every event, and provides . . . information on rules and scoring systems. . . . It covers each event, Games by Games, from the four skating events which first featured in the 1908 London Olympics to freestyle skiing and curling—including discontinued events." Publisher's note

"While the statistics will delight sports geeks, everyone can savor the readable prose accounts that draw out the athletes' character and high points." SLJ

797.1 Boating

Canoeing; outdoor adventures; editors, Pamela S. Dillon, Jeremy Oyen. Human Kinetics 2008 253p il (Outdoor adventures) pa $22.95 *

Grades: 9 10 11 12 Adult **797.1**

1. Canoes and canoeing

ISBN 978-0-7360-6715-7; 0-7360-6715-9

LC 2008-4392

Includes DVD-ROM

The authors "discuss fitness basics, food and nutrition needs, and gear and equipment—from the canoe itself to life jackets, paddles, and clothing. They then cover . . . safety and survival guidelines, including weather, river hazards, capsizing, cold-water safety, and rescue protocols. . . [The DVD included contains] an introduction to paddle sports and basic safety and paddling techniques." Publisher's note

Grant, Gordon

Canoeing; illustrations by Ron Hildebrand. Norton 1997 192p il (Trailside series guide) flexible bdg $18.95

Grades: 11 12 Adult **797.1**

1. Canoes and canoeing

ISBN 0-393-31489-8 LC 96-2151

This guide to canoeing covers equipment, safety, paddling techniques, camping, moving water and white water canoeing. Grant provides lists of organizations, schools, tour organizers and guides, information sources, mail-order sources of equipment, and canoe manufacturers.

Kayaking; editors, Pamela S. Dillon, Jeremy Oyen. Human Kinetics 2009 237p il (Outdoor adventures) pa $22.95

Grades: 9 10 11 12 Adult **797.1**

1. Canoes and canoeing

ISBN 978-0-7360-6716-4; 0-7360-6716-7

LC 2008-32111

"American Canoe Association"

Includes DVD-ROM

"Part I of *Kayaking* explains the background knowledge, fitness fundamentals, equipment and gear selection, nutritional needs, and safety and survival skills for a successful adventure. Part II helps build basic techniques, strokes, and maneuvers. . . [It includes] tips and instruction for the three most popular types of kayaking: sea, river, and whitewater. This book also includes the *Quick-Start Your Kayak* DVD to reinforce the paddling strokes and safety information found in the book. It features videos of kayaking maneuvers." Publisher's note

Includes bibliographical references

Krauzer, Steven M.

Kayaking; whitewater and touring basics; introduction by John Viehman; illustrations by Ron Hildebrand. Norton 1995 192p il (Trailside series guide) flexible bdg $18.95 *

Grades: 11 12 Adult **797.1**

1. Canoes and canoeing

ISBN 0-393-31336-0 LC 95-5527

This illustrated guide to kayaking covers equipment, techniques, and safety. Includes lists of organizations, mail-order sources, and information sources

Sleight, Steve

New complete sailing manual. Rev ed., 1st American ed. DK 2005 448p il map $35

Grades: 9 10 11 12 Adult **797.1**

1. Sailing

ISBN 0-7566-0944-5; 978-0-7566-0944-3

LC 2005-277514

First published 1999 with title: DK complete sailing manual

This sailing manual covers such topics as navigation, ropes and knots, boating safety, boat maintenance, and handling emergencies.

Stuhaug, Dennis O.

Kayaking made easy; a manual for beginners with tips for the experienced. 3rd ed. Globe Pequot Press 2006 264p il (Made easy series) pa $17.95

Grades: 9 10 11 12 **797.1**

1. Canoes and canoeing

ISBN 0-7627-3859-6 LC 2006-43437

First published 1995

This guide offers "a step-by-step approach, first familiarizing you with the gear, then proceeding through the various strokes, and finally covering the complexities of long-distance navigation." Publisher's note

797.2   Swimming and diving

Mullen, P. H., Jr.

Gold in the water; the true story of ordinary men and their extraordinary dream of Olympic glory. Thomas Dunne Bks. 2001 326p il hardcover o.p. pa $14.95

Grades: 11 12 Adult   **797.2**

1. Swimming 2. Olympic games, 2000 (Sydney, Australia)

ISBN 0-312-26595-6; 0-312-31116-8 (pa)

                 LC 2001-31955

"Mullen chronicles the U.S. Olympic swimming team on its journey to the 2000 Summer Games in Sydney. The text moves back and forth in time, giving a sense of the athletes as people and showing what motivates someone to structure his or her whole life toward a single goal." Booklist

798.4   Horse racing

Hillenbrand, Laura

Seabiscuit; an American legend. Random House 2001 399p il $25.95; pa $15.95 *

Grades: 11 12 Adult   **798.4**

1. Horse racing 2. Seabiscuit (Race horse)

ISBN 0-375-50291-2; 0-449-00561-5 (pa)

                 LC 2001-267852

Hillenbrand tells the story of the race horse who defeated "Triple Crown Winner War Admiral in what [has been] called the greatest horse race of all time [Pimlico, Nov. 1, 1938]." Newsweek

"This is a remarkable tale well told by a writer who deftly blends history and sport." Economist

Includes bibliographical references

Ours, Dorothy

Man o' War; a legend like lightning. St Martin's Press 2006 342p il $24.95

Grades: 11 12 Adult   **798.4**

1. Horse racing 2. Man o' War (Race horse)

ISBN 0-312-34099-0; 978-0-312-34099-5

                 LC 2006-41631

This is an account of the thoroughbred racehorse Man o' War, also known as Big Red.

This book "is clearly a labor of love, and it certifies Big Red's claim to immortality." N Y Times Book Rev

Includes bibliographical references

798.8   Dog racing

Paulsen, Gary

Winterdance; the fine madness of running the Iditarod. Harcourt Brace & Co. 1994 256p il $26; pa $15

Grades: 6 7 8 9 10   **798.8**

1. Iditarod Trail Sled Dog Race, Alaska 2. Sled dog racing

ISBN 0-15-126227-6; 0-15-600145-4 (pa)

                 LC 93-42096

"This book is primarily an account of Paulsen's first Iditarod and its frequent life-threatening disasters. . . . However, the book is more than a tabulation of tribulations; it is a meditation on the extraordinary attraction this race holds for some men and women." Libr J

799   Fishing, hunting, shooting

Paulsen, Gary

Father water, Mother woods; essays on fishing and hunting in the North Woods; with illustrations by Ruth Wright Paulsen. Delacorte Press 1994 159p il pa $4.99 hardcover o.p.

Grades: 9 10 11 12   **799**

1. Hunting 2. Fishing

ISBN 0-440-21984-1   LC 94-2737

"This collection of autobiographical essays, identifies {Paulsen's} youthful experiences in the woods and rivers of northern Minnesota. . . . Throughout it all, descriptions of light and water, of fish and wildlife, kindle in the reader a measure of the author's own complex respect for nature." Publ Wkly

799.1   Fishing

Mason, Bill, 1929-

Sports illustrated fly fishing; learn from a master. [rev ed] Sports Illustrated 1994 255p il pa $14.95 *

Grades: 9 10 11 12   **799.1**

1. Fishing 2. Fly casting

ISBN 1-56800-033-2

"Sports illustrated winner's circle books"

First published 1988

An illustrated introduction to the sport of fly fishing. Emphasis is placed on equipment and technique.

Merwin, John

Fly fishing; a Trailside guide; illustrations by Ron Hildebrand. Norton 1996 192p il (Trailside series guide) flexible bdg $19.95 *

Grades: 11 12 Adult   **799.1**

1. Fishing 2. Fly casting

ISBN 0-393-31476-6   LC 96-2141

This illustrated guide to fly fishing covers equipment, tying knots, types of flies, fly casting techniques for different types of fish, and lists organizations, schools, mail-order sources, and information sources.

Include bibliographical references

799.3   Shooting other than game

Engh, Douglas

Archery fundamentals. Human Kinetics 2005 125p il (Sports fundamentals series) pa $15.95

Grades: 9 10 11 12 Adult   **799.3**

1. Archery

ISBN 0-7360-5501-0; 978-0-7360-5501-7

                 LC 2004-11221

Engh, Douglas—*Continued*
Contents: Bows; Arrows; Shooting recurve; Shooting compound; Grips, anchors, and releases; Taking aim; Tight groups; Scoring performance; Accessories; Tuning and repair; Competition
This book provides instruction in the basic skills of archery, including shooting techniques, improving aim, and how to keep score as well as information on care and repair of bows, arrows and other equipment.

800 LITERATURE, RHETORIC & CRITICISM

Amend, Allison, 1974-
Cracking the SAT. Literature subject test; [by] Allison Amend and Adam Robinson. 2011-2012 ed. Random House 2011 242p (Princeton Review series) pa $19.99
Grades: 9 10 11 12 **800**
1. Literature—Study and teaching 2. Scholastic Assessment Test 3. Colleges and universities—Entrance requirements
ISBN 978-0-375-42811-1
Annual. First published 2005. Continues Cracking the SAT II: Writing and literature subject tests
This guide provides test-taking strategies and sample tests on the subject of literature.

Baker, Nancy L., 1950-
A research guide for undergraduate students; English and American literature; [by] Nancy L. Baker and Nancy Huling. 6th ed. Modern Language Association of America 2006 96p il pa $12
Grades: 11 12 Adult **800**
1. Literature—Research 2. English literature—Bibliography 3. American literature—Bibliography 4. Reference books
ISBN 978-0-8735-2924-2; 0-8735-2924-3
LC 2006-7360
First published 1982
This book "provides dozens of research samples from the library's online catalog to new databases. Includes a . . . chapter with bibliographic citation managers." Univ Press Books for Public and Second Sch Libr, 2007
Includes bibliographical references

803 Literature—Encyclopedias and dictionaries

Abrams, M. H. (Meyer Howard), 1912-
A glossary of literary terms; with contributions by Geoffrey Galt Harpham. 8th ed. Thomson, Wadsworth 2005 370p pa $34.95 *
Grades: 11 12 Adult **803**
1. Literature—Dictionaries 2. Reference books
ISBN 1-4130-0218-8; 978-1-4130-0218-8
LC 2004-111345
First published 1957

In a series of essays, the author discusses literary terms and definitions ranging from the traditional to the avant-garde. Subsidiary terms are included under major or generic terms.

Ayto, John
Brewer's dictionary of modern phrase & fable; by John Ayto & Ian Crofton. 2nd ed. Chambers Harrap Pub. Ltd. 2010 853p $39.95 *
Grades: 9 10 11 12 Adult **803**
1. Literature—Dictionaries 2. Allusions 3. Reference books
ISBN 978-0-550-105-646
First published 2000 by Cassell
"Focusing on the 20th and 21st centuries, . . . [this book covers a] selection of buzzwords, catchphrases, slang, nicknames, fictional characters and . . . cultural phenomena from pop culture to politics, literature to technology." Publisher's note

Baldick, Chris
The Oxford dictionary of literary terms. 3rd ed. Oxford University Press 2008 361p (Oxford paperback reference) hardcover o.p. pa $16.95 *
Grades: 11 12 Adult **803**
1. Literature—Dictionaries 2. English language—Terms and phrases 3. Reference books
ISBN 978-0-19-923891-0; 0-19-923891-X; 978-0-19-920827-2 (pa); 0-19-920827-1 (pa)
LC 2008-299352
Also available online
First published 1990 with title: The concise Oxford dictionary of literary terms
This work defines more than 1,200 literary terms. Also provides coverage of traditional drama, rhetoric, literary history, and textual criticism. Includes pronunciation guides on over 200 terms.
Includes bibliographical references

Benet's reader's encyclopedia; edited by Bruce F. Murphy. 5th ed. Collins 2008 1210p $60 *
Grades: 8 9 10 11 12 Adult **803**
1. Literature—Dictionaries 2. Reference books
ISBN 978-0-06-089016-2 LC 2008-31430
First published 1948 under the editorship of William Rose Benet
This encyclopedia contains over 10,000 entries and covers world literature from early times to the present. Includes entries on authors, literary movements, principal characters, plot synopses, terms, awards, myths and legends, etc.
This is "an edifying staple for any literary library." Libr J

Brewer's dictionary of phrase & fable; edited by Camilla Rockwood. 18th ed. Brewer's 2009 xxv, 1460p il $49.95 *
Grades: 5 6 7 8 9 10 11 12 Adult **803**
1. English language—Terms and phrases 2. Literature—Dictionaries 3. Mythology—Dictionaries 4. Allusions 5. Reference books
ISBN 978-0-550-10411-3 LC 2009-379960
First published 1870 under the editorship of Ebenezer Cobham Brewer

Brewer's dictionary of phrase & fable—*Continued*

"Over 15,000 brief entries give the meanings and origins of a broad range of terms, expressions, and names of real, fictitious and mythical characters from world history, science, the arts and literature." N Y Public Libr. Ref Books for Child Collect. 2d edition

Carey, Gary

A multicultural dictionary of literary terms; [by] Gary Carey and Mary Ellen Snodgrass. McFarland & Co. 1999 184p hardcover o.p. pa $29.95
Grades: 11 12 Adult　　　　　　　　　　**803**
1. Literature—Dictionaries 2. Reference books
ISBN 0-7864-0552-X; 0-7864-2950-X (pa)
LC 98-35221
"Using the full spectrum of literature, including drama, poetry, and novels, the authors . . . draw from a cross section of works by people of many races and traditions for both literary terms and the examples used to define them." Libr J
Includes bibliographical references

Harmon, William, 1938-

A handbook to literature. Twelfth ed. Longman 2011 c2012 655p il pa $53.33 *
Grades: 11 12 Adult　　　　　　　　　　**803**
1. Literature—Dictionaries 2. Reference books
ISBN 978-0-205-02401-8; 0-205-02401-7
LC 2010-49056
First published 1936 by Doubleday under the authorship of William Flint Thrall and Addison Hibbard; later editions by William Harmon and C. Hugh Holman
This work provides "explanations of terms, concepts, schools, and movements in literature. Alphabetical arrangement with numerous cross-references as well as bibliographic references for some entries." Guide to Ref Books. 11th edition
Includes bibliographical references

Oxford dictionary of phrase and fable; edited by Elizabeth Knowles. 2nd ed. Oxford University Press 2005 805p $40; pa $18.95 *
Grades: 11 12 Adult　　　　　　　　　　**803**
1. Literature—Dictionaries 2. Allusions 3. Reference books
ISBN 978-0-19-860981-0; 978-0-19-920246-1 (pa)
First published 2000
This work seeks to define words and phrases of British cultural history.
This "is a highly useful tool to help understand what phrases mean and where they come from and should definitely be added to all reference collections." Booklist

Quinn, Edward, 1932-

A dictionary of literary and thematic terms. 2nd ed. Facts on File 2006 474p (Facts on File library of language and literature) $55; pa $19.95 *
Grades: 11 12 Adult　　　　　　　　　　**803**
1. Literature—Dictionaries 2. Reference books
ISBN 0-8160-6243-9; 978-0-8160-6243-0; 0-8160-6244-7 (pa); 978-0-8160-6244-7 (pa)
LC 2005-29826

First published 1999
In addition to basic definitions of terms "this general literary dictionary . . . covers common themes in literature such as love, death, alienation, and time. Literary schools are treated with just enough depth to offer a basic understanding of the major tenets." Libr J [review of 1999 edition]
Includes bibliographical references

808　Rhetoric

American Psychological Association

Concise rules of APA style. 6th ed. American Psychological Association 2009 c2010 280p il $28.95
Grades: 11 12 Adult　　　　　　　　　　**808**
1. Authorship—Handbooks, manuals, etc. 2. Reference books
ISBN 978-1-4338-0560-8; 1-4338-0560-X
LC 2009-11709
First published 2005
This book offers "writing and formatting standards for students, teachers, researchers, and clinicians in the social and behavioral sciences. . . . Readers will learn how to avoid the grammatical errors most commonly reported by journal editors; how to choose the appropriate format for statistics, figures, and tables; how to credit sources and avoid charges of plagiarism; and how to construct a reference list." Publisher's note
Includes bibliographical references

The **autobiographer's** handbook; the 826 National guide to writing your memoir; edited by Jennifer Traig; introduction by Dave Eggers. Henry Holt and Co. 2008 242p pa $15
Grades: 9 10 11 12　　　　　　　　　　**808**
1. Autobiography 2. Biography as a literary form
ISBN 978-0-8050-8713-0; 0-8050-8713-3
LC 2007-47355
"Put out by 826 Valencia, the San Francisco-based nonprofit Eggers started to provide creative writing instruction for middle and high school students, this book presents straightforward, practical ideas and advice from a double-handful of contemporary writers. . . . Their guidance, complemented by writing exercises and work plans, should prove useful, informative and motivating for writers at just about any level." Publ Wkly
Includes bibliographical references

The **Chicago** manual of style. 16th ed. The University of Chicago Press 2010 1026p il $65
Grades: 11 12 Adult　　　　　　　　　　**808**
1. Printing—Style manuals 2. Authorship—Handbooks, manuals, etc. 3. Publishers and publishing—Handbooks, manuals, etc. 4. English language—Usage
ISBN 978-0-226-10420-1; 0-226-10420-6
LC 2009-53612
Also available online
First published 1906 with title: A manual of style
This style manual includes journals and electronic publications, descriptive headings on all numbered paragraphs, and chapters on grammar, usage, and documentation, including guidance on citing electronic sources.
Includes glossary and bibliographical references

Dowhan, Adrienne

Essays that will get you into college; [by] Adrienne Dowhan, Chris Dowhan, and Dan Kaufman. 3rd ed. Barron's 2009 178p pa $13.99 *

Grades: 9 10 11 12   **808**
1. College applications 2. Rhetoric
ISBN 978-0-7641-4210-9; 0-7641-4210-0
LC 2009-13487

First published 1998 under the authorship of Amy Burnham, Daniel Kaufman and Chris Dowhan

"The 50 model essays presented in this book were written by successful Ivy League college applicants. Each essay is followed by critical comments that reveal both strong and weak points in its author's style and content. Also presented is . . . essay-writing advice and instruction." Publisher's note

Dunn, Jessica, 1980-

A teen's guide to getting published; publishing for profit, recognition, and academic success; [by] Jessica Dunn & Danielle Dunn. 2nd ed. Prufrock Press 2006 249p pa $14.95 *

Grades: 7 8 9 10 11 12   **808**
1. Authorship 2. Publishers and publishing
ISBN 1-59363-182-0   LC 2006005109

First published 1997

Danielle Dunn's name appears first on the earlier edition

"In addition to standard advice on publishers and agents, the authors give practical suggestions for finding a writing environment that is accessible to teens, such as school publication staffs and local newspaper internships. . . . Annotated appendixes list Web sites, books, journals, and contests. Also provided is information on mentors, writing camps, and courses catering to young authors, and a valuable list of mainstream publishers who have expressed openness to submissions from teens. This compact, sensible book discusses all kinds of writing." SLJ

Fleming, Robert

The African American writer's handbook; how to get in print and stay in print. One World (NY) 2000 339p pa $12

Grades: 11 12 Adult   **808**
1. Authorship—Handbooks, manuals, etc. 2. African American authors
ISBN 0-345-42327-5   LC 00-102059

The author "discusses the basics of manuscript submissions, tools of writing, and the publishing world. He speaks of issues that many African-American writers must deal with in producing and marketing their books. He also reveals the importance of self-promotion. In subsequent chapters, Fleming entertains book lovers of any race with a tour of the African-American literary world." Libr J

Includes bibliographical references

Fox, Tom

Cite it right; the SourceAid guide to citation, research, and avoiding plagiarism; co-authors, Tom Fox, Julia Johns, Sarah Keller. 3rd ed. SourceAid 2007 226p il pa $19.95 *

Grades: 11 12 Adult   **808**
1. Bibliographical citations 2. Report writing 3. Research 4. Plagiarism
ISBN 978-0-9771957-1-8; 0-9771957-1-6

Previous edition published 2006 with Julia Johns as primary author

"The book opens with a chapter on ethics and avoiding plagiarism, followed by one on research, one on writing a research paper, and a chapter on each of the four major styles—MLA, APA, CMS, and CSE. Everything is clearly explained, and the writers didn't shy away from answering 'dumb' questions of the kind that invariably arise in the minds of first timers." Booklist

Gaines, Ann

Don't steal copyrighted stuff! avoiding plagiarism and illegal internet downloading; [by] Ann Graham Gaines. Enslow Publishers 2008 192p il (Prime) $38.60 *

Grades: 7 8 9 10   **808**
1. Plagiarism 2. Bibliographical citations 3. Copyright
ISBN 978-0-7660-2861-6; 0-7660-2861-5
LC 2007-8370

"The first three chapters explain just what plagiarism is, the types of plagiarism, and what copyright and fair use are. Two chapters explain how to find sources, take notes properly, and construct a project or paper using proper citations in MLA format. . . . Every student should be required to read this. . . . Librarians and teachers who are looking for explanations of copyright and plagiarism and illustrative examples will find this book to be a good resource." Libr Media Connect

Includes bibliographical references

Harper, Elizabeth, 1934-

Your name in print; a teen's guide to publishing for fun, profit, and academic success; [by] Elizabeth Harper and Timothy Harper. St. Martin's Griffin 2005 186p pa $13.95

Grades: 7 8 9 10   **808**
1. Authorship 2. Publishers and publishing
ISBN 0-312-33759-0   LC 2004-24675

The authors "offer chapters and features on a variety of subjects: writing outlets (such as local papers and blogs); article topics; workspaces; book publishing and agents; tips from pros; sample columns; [and] 'glances' at current teen writers. . . . This book will be a useful addition for most libraries." Voice Youth Advocates

Includes bibliographical references

Johnson, Sarah Anne

The art of the author interview; and interviewing creative people. University Press of New England 2005 158p pa $19.95

Grades: 11 12 Adult   **808**
1. Interviewing 2. Reporters and reporting
ISBN 1-58465-397-3   LC 2004-23688

Johnson, Sarah Anne—*Continued*

This book "shows readers how to initiate, research, conduct, and publish interviews with authors and other creative people." Publisher's note

Lasch, Christopher

Plain style; a guide to written English; edited and with an introduction by Stewart Weaver. University of Pa. Press 2002 121p hardcover o.p. pa $14.95

Grades: 11 12 Adult   **808**

1. Rhetoric 2. English language—Grammar

ISBN 0-8122-3673-4; 0-8122-1814-0 (pa)

LC 2002-19163

"The guide is divided into six parts, covering the principles of literary construction; conventions governing punctuation, capitalization, typography, and footnotes; characteristics of bad writing; words often misued; words often mispronounced; and a table of proofreaders' marks." Booklist

Includes bibliographical references

MLA handbook for writers of research papers. 7th ed. Modern Language Association of America 2009 xxi, 292p il pa $22 *

Grades: 9 10 11 12 Adult   **808**

1. Report writing

ISBN 978-1-60329-024-1   LC 2008-47484

First published 1977 with title: MLA handbook for writers of research papers, theses, and dissertations

This manual discusses research strategies, formatting, documenting sources, writing basics and utilizing electronic sources.

Includes bibliographical references

MLA style manual and guide to scholarly publishing. 3rd ed. Modern Language Association of America 2008 xxiv, 336p $32.50 *

Grades: 11 12 Adult   **808**

1. Authorship—Handbooks, manuals, etc.

ISBN 978-0-87352-297-7; 0-87352-297-4

LC 2008-2894

First published 1985 under authorship of Walter S. Achtert and Joseph Gibaldi

This book offers "guidance on writing scholarly texts, documenting research sources, submitting manuscripts to publishers, and dealing with legal issues surrounding publication." Publisher's note

Includes bibliographical references

Plotnik, Arthur, 1937-

Spunk & bite; a writer's guide to punchier, more engaging language & style. Random House 2005 263p hardcover o.p. pa $12.95

Grades: 11 12 Adult   **808**

1. Rhetoric

ISBN 0-375-72115-0; 0-375-72227-0 (pa)

LC 2005-44934

The author "demonstrates how . . . unexpected humor, loquaciousness, and apt description can jolt a writer into engaged authorship. This primer is dotted with illus-

trative examples that range from Shakespeare and J.K. Rowling to Dave Barry and Maeve Binchy. . . . This is an entertaining and engaging choice for writers." Libr J

Prose, Francine, 1947-

Reading like a writer; a guide for people who love books and for those who want to write them. HarperCollins Publishers 2006 273p $23.95; pa $13.95

Grades: 11 12 Adult   **808**

1. Rhetoric 2. Creative writing 3. Books and reading

ISBN   978-0-06-077704-3;   0-06-077704-4; 978-0-06-077705-0 (pa); 0-06-077705-2 (pa)

LC 2005-58457

The author "devotes a chapter each to eight elements of writing: words, sentences, paragraphs, narration, character, dialog, details, and gesture. These chapters are framed by an opening piece that urges close reading as most productive for writers; a chapter devoted to Chekhov, particularly his short stories, as translated by Constance Garnett; and a closing chapter, 'Reading for Courage.'" Libr J

This book "should be greatly appreciated in and out of the classroom. Like the great works of fiction, it's a wise and voluble companion." N Y Times Book Rev

Salzman, Mark

True notebooks. Alfred A. Knopf 2003 330p hardcover o.p. pa $13.95

Grades: 11 12 Adult   **808**

1. Creative writing 2. Juvenile delinquency

ISBN 0-375-41308-1; 0-375-72761-2 (pa)

LC 2002-43435

"While teaching writing to 17-year-olds detained in Los Angeles Central Juvenile Hall, Salzman found himself surprised by the boys' talent. The teens' heartwarming, funny voices are included in his irresistible, provocative memoir." Booklist

Stop plagiarism; a guide to understanding and prevention; edited by Vibiana Bowman Cvetkovic, Katie Elson Anderson. Neal-Schuman Publishers 2010 220p il pa $65

Grades: Adult Professional   **808**

1. Plagiarism

ISBN 978-1-55570-716-3   LC 2010-24860

Includes CD-ROM

"The authors organize the book's ten chapters in three sections: 'Understanding the Problem,' which explains the meaning of plagiarism; 'Finding Remedies,' which suggests answers to the problem; and 'A Practitioner's Toolkit,' which provides sensible resources that will aid in changing the ways students address plagiarism. . . . The accompanying CD-ROM offers Web site connections, tutorials, and a video presentation that can be used in the classroom. Though intended primarily for professionals, the essays in this book are written in a conversational and practical style that makes them accessible to anyone confronting or wishing to know more about plagiarism." Choice

Includes bibliographical references

Strunk, William, 1869-1946

The elements of style; with revisions, an introduction, and a chapter on writing by E.B. White. 4th ed. Allyn & Bacon 1999 105p $14.95; pa $7.95 *

Grades: 11 12 Adult   **808**
1. Rhetoric
ISBN 0-205-31342-6; 0-205-30902-X (pa)
                     LC 99-16419
First privately printed in 1918
This work provides guidelines for proper usage and composition. Misused expressions and commonly misspelled words are discussed. Includes examples.

This work is "prescriptive, conservative, and humorous; in sum, it is the best book available on how to write English prose." Nichols. Guide to Ref Books for Sch Media Cent. 4th edition

Turabian, Kate L., 1893-1987

A manual for writers of research papers, theses, and dissertations; Chicago style for students and researchers; revised by Wayne C. Booth, Gregory G. Colomb, Joseph M. Williams, and University of Chicago Press editorial staff. 7th ed. University of Chicago Press 2007 466p il (Chicago guides to writing, editing, and publishing) $35; pa $17 *

Grades: 11 12 Adult   **808**
1. Report writing 2. Dissertations
ISBN 978-0-226-82336-2; 0-226-82336-9; 978-0-226-82337-9 (pa); 0-226-82337-7 (pa)
                     LC 2006-25443
First published 1937 with title: A manual for writers of dissertations
Designed to serve as a guide to suitable style in the presentation of formal papers—term papers, reports, articles, theses, dissertations—both in scientific and in non-scientific fields.

Student's guide to writing college papers. 4th ed, rev. by Gregory G. Colomb, Joseph M. Williams, and the University of Chicago Press editorial staff. The University of Chicago Press 2010 281p il (Chicago guides to writing, editing, and publishing) $39; pa $15; ebook $15 *

Grades: 9 10 11 12 Adult   **808**
1. Report writing 2. Dissertations
ISBN 978-0-226-81630-2; 978-0-226-81631-9 (pa); 978-0-226-81633-3 (ebook)   LC 2009-31583
First published 1963 with title: Student's guide for writing college papers
This guide covers selecting a topic, collecting material, planning and writing the paper, and preparing footnotes and bibliographies.
Includes bibliographical references

Walker, Janice R.

The Columbia guide to online style; [by] Janice R. Walker and Todd Taylor. 2nd ed. Columbia University Press 2006 xxi, 288p il $45; pa $19.50

Grades: 11 12 Adult   **808**
1. Authorship—Data processing—Handbooks, manuals, etc. 2. Bibliographical citations
ISBN 0-231-13210-7; 978-0-231-13210-7; 0-231-13211-5 (pa); 978-0-231-13211-4 (pa)
                     LC 2006-24383
First published 1998
This is a "resource for citing electronic and electronically accessed sources. It is also a . . . style guide for creating documents electronically for submission for print or electronic publication." Publisher's note
Includes bibliographical references

Winkler, Anthony C.

Writing the research paper; a handbook; [by] Anthony C. Winkler, Jo Ray McCuen-Metherell. 2009 MLA updated ed., 7th ed. Heinle & Heinle 2009 356p il $59.95

Grades: 9 10 11 12   **808**
1. Report writing 2. Research
ISBN 978-0-495-79965-8
First published 1979 by Harcourt Brace Jovanovich
Among the topics addressed are: choosing a topic, finding background sources, punctuation, outlining and using the library.

Writing and publishing; the librarian's handbook; edited by Carol Smallwood. American Library Association 2010 189p (ALA guides for the busy librarian) pa $65

Grades: Adult Professional   **808**
1. Library science 2. Authorship
ISBN 978-0-8389-0996-6; 0-8389-0996-5
                     LC 2009-25047
"The book is divided into five parts, beginning with articles on why librarians should write, followed by the education of a writer—getting started, writing with others, revision, and lessons from publishers. The third part focuses on finding your niche in print—books, newsletters and newspapers, reviewing, magazines and professional journals, essays, textbook writing, children's literature, and writing on specific subjects. Next come pieces on finding your niche online, while the fifth part is about maximizing opportunities." Libr J
"This important writer's guide is readable from cover to cover or by bits and pieces and is a helpful and handy read for every librarian." Libr Media Connect
Includes bibliographical references

808.1   Rhetoric of poetry

Deutsch, Babette, 1895-1982

Poetry handbook: a dictionary of terms. 4th ed. HarperResource 2002 203p pa $14 *

Grades: 11 12 Adult   **808.1**
1. Poetics—Dictionaries 2. Poetry—Terminology 3. Reference books
ISBN 0-06-463548-1
First published 1957 by Funk & Wagnalls

Deutsch, Babette, 1895-1982—*Continued*

"The craft of verse described in dictionary form. Terms and techniques are defined and illustrated." N Y Public Libr. Ref Books for Child Collect. 2d edition

Drury, John, 1950-

The poetry dictionary; foreward by Dana Gioia. 2nd ed. Writer's Digest Books 2006 374p pa $14.99 *

Grades: 11 12 Adult   **808.1**
1. Reference books 2. Poetry—Dictionaries 3. Poetics
ISBN 1-58297-329-6; 978-1-58297-329-6
LC 2005-15113
First published 1995 by Story Press (Cincinnati)
"Spanning the centuries from ode to rap, The Poetry Dictionary contains 284 entries that define movements and schools of poetry, forms of verse, rhyme and stress patterns, and poetic devices. Entries range in length from a paragraph for canto to more than seven pages for sonnet." Booklist [review of 1995 edition]

Fooling with words; a celebration of poets and their craft; edited by Bill Moyers. Morrow 1999 230p hardcover o.p. pa $12

Grades: 11 12 Adult   **808.1**
1. Poetics
ISBN 0-688-17346-2; 0-688-17792-1 (pa)
LC 99-34965
"Moyers here interviews 11 American poets (e.g., Robert Pinsky, Mark Doty, Shirley Geok-lin Lim, and Paul Muldoon) whose voices echo the diversity of the United States—a wonderful jumble of genders, ethnic groups, and religions. This book is not a how-to; interviews (accompanied by the interviewee's poetry) focus on the poet as an individual, the creative process, and enjoying poetry and reveling in its sound." Libr J

Higginson, William J., 1938-

The haiku handbook; how to write, teach, and appreciate haiku; [by] William J. Higginson and Penny Harter; foreword by Jane Reichhold. 25th anniversary ed. Kodansha International 2009 331p pa $18 *

Grades: 11 12 Adult   **808.1**
1. Haiku
ISBN 978-4-770-03113-6; 4-770-03113-0
LC 2009-36628
First published 1985 by McGraw-Hill
This book "presents haiku poets writing in English, Spanish, French, German, and five other languages on an equal footing with Japanese poets. Not only are the four great Japanese masters of the haiku represented (Bashō, Buson, Issa, and Shiki) but also several major Western authors not commonly known to have written haiku. The book presents a . . . history of the Japanese haiku, including the dynamic changes throughout the twentieth century as the haiku has been adapted to suburban and industrial settings. Full chapters are offered on form, the seasons in haiku, and haiku craft, plus background on the Japanese poetic tradition, and the effect of translation on our understanding of haiku." Publisher's note
Includes bibliographical references

Hirsch, Edward

How to read a poem; and fall in love with poetry. Harcourt Brace & Co. 1999 352p $23; pa $15

Grades: 11 12 Adult   **808.1**
1. Poetics 2. Poetry—History and criticism
ISBN 0-15-100419-6; 0-15-600566-2 (pa)
LC 98-50065
"A DoubleTake book"
The author "has gathered an eclectic group of poems from many times and places, with selections as varied as postwar Polish poetry, works by Keats and Christopher Smart, and lyrics from African American work songs. A prolific, award-winning poet in his own right, Hirsch suggests helpful strategies for understanding and appreciating each poem. The book is scholarly but very readable and incorporates interesting anecdotes from the lives of the poets." Libr J
Includes bibliographical references

Jerome, Judson

The poet's handbook. Writer's Digest Bks. 1980 224p $15.99 hardcover o.p.

Grades: 9 10 11 12   **808.1**
1. Poetics
ISBN 1-58297-136-6   LC 80-17270
"This is not the usual alphabetized handbook. It gives a brief but scholarly background of the poet's place in early times and later history and moves on to discuss in individual chapters the craft of poetry: syllable-counting, meter, rhyme, free verse, the rhythms of the English language, and so on. It is more personal than one usually finds such a book to be, and it presents almost everything a beginning poet, as well as one who has mastered the craft, should know." Choice

Kooser, Ted

The poetry home repair manual; practical advice for beginning poets. University of Nebraska Press 2005 163p $19.95; pa $13.95 *

Grades: 11 12 Adult   **808.1**
1. Poetics
ISBN 0-8032-2769-8; 0-8032-5978-6 (pa)
LC 2004-24700
The author's advice "includes both broad and specific ideas on revising, and . . . discussion of matters ranging from the often-underestimated power of simile to employing narrative effectively." Booklist
"Among the many books offering advice on writing poetry, . . . [this book] stands out for its usefulness and, at the same time, for its inspiring view of the purposes of poetry." Midwest Quarterly
Includes bibliographical references

Myers, Jack Elliott, 1941-

Dictionary of poetic terms; [by] Jack Myers, Don Charles Wukasch. University of N. Tex. Press 2003 434p pa $22.95 *

Grades: 11 12 Adult   **808.1**
1. Reference books 2. Poetics—Dictionaries
ISBN 1-57441-166-7   LC 2003-11482
First published 1985 by Longman Press with title: Longman dictionary and handbook of poetry

Myers, Jack Elliott, 1941-—*Continued*

This volume "contains over 1,600 entries on the devices, techniques, history, theory, and terminology of poetry from the Classical period to the present." Publisher's note

"Particularly useful is the plethora of samples from the works of such greats as James Joyce, Edna St. Vincent Millay, Ezra Pound, and Ogden Nash. Although some of the vocabulary is lofty, the definitions, fascinating history, and brief essays combine to form a useful handbook." Libr J

Includes bibliographical references

Oliver, Mary, 1935-

A poetry handbook. Harcourt Brace & Co. 1994 130p pa $13

Grades: 11 12 Adult   808.1
1. Poetics
ISBN 0-15-672400-6   LC 93-49676
"A Harvest original"

A "handbook for young poets on the formal aspects and structure of poetry. Oliver excels at explaining the sound and sense of poetry—from scansion to imagery, diction to voice. She stresses the importance of reading poetry, since, in order to write well, 'it is entirely necessary to read widely and deeply.' Sage advice is given in an entire chapter dedicated to revision, wherein Oliver urges poets to consider their first draft 'an unfinished piece of work' that can be polished and improved later. Written in a pleasant and lucid style, this book is a wonderful resource." Libr J

Seeing the blue between; advice and inspiration for young poets; compiled by Paul B. Janeczko. Candlewick Press 2002 132p $18.99; pa $7.99

Grades: 7 8 9 10   808.1
1. Poetics 2. American poetry—Collections
ISBN 0-7636-0881-5; 0-7636-2909-X (pa)
                                                LC 2001-25882

"Here, thirty-two established poets share their writing secrets in short letters addressed directly to the readers. Although each poet has a distinct voice . . . a familiar mantra quickly develops: read, observe, love words, write, rewrite. . . . Accompanying poems may connect directly to a letter's content, give a representative sample of an individual's body of work, or impart advice." Horn Book Guide

"The letters are personal, friendly, and supportive. . . . A valuable addition to public and school libraries, with the potential for much classroom and personal use." SLJ

808.3   Rhetoric of fiction

Henry, Laurie

The fiction dictionary. Story Press (Cincinnati) 1995 324p hardcover o.p. pa $20.99 *

Grades: 11 12 Adult   808.3
1. Reference books 2. Fiction—Technique
ISBN 1-884910-05-X; 1-884910-54-8 (pa)
                                                LC 95-4269

Henry provides "definitions of 345 terms relating to fiction, including genres, narrative devices, elements of fictional works, and critical theories. In addition to citing examples of works that illustrate a term, she frequently supplements her explanations with brief excerpts from novels and short stories." Booklist

Lukeman, Noah

The plot thickens; 8 ways to bring fiction to life. St. Martin's Press 2002 221p $19.95; pa $12.95

Grades: 11 12 Adult   808.3
1. Fiction—Technique
ISBN 0-312-28467-5; 0-312-30928-7 (pa)
                                                LC 2001-58564

"Lukeman focuses on the mechanics of storytelling. He introduces budding writers to the techniques of characterization (ask yourself questions about the people you've created), the various ways of generating suspense (danger, a ticking clock), and the importance of conflict." Booklist

Piercy, Marge

So you want to write; how to master the craft of writing fiction and memoir; [by] Marge Piercy and Ira Wood. 2nd ed. Leapfrog Press 2005 324p pa $16.95

Grades: 11 12 Adult   808.3
1. Fiction—Technique 2. Biography as a literary form
ISBN 0-9728984-5-X
First published 2001

This book "uses talks, exercises, anecdotes and examples proven in the classroom, to address: How to begin a piece by seducing your reader, How to create characters that embody the infinite contradictions of human behavior, How to master the elements of plotting fiction, How to create a strategy for telling the story of your life, How to learn to read critically, like a professional writer, How to write about painful personal material without coming off as a victim, [and] How to proceed if your work is continually rejected by publishers." Publisher's note

Includes bibliographical references

808.4   Rhetoric of essays

Orr, Tamra

Extraordinary essays. Franklin Watts 2005 128p il (F. W. Prep) $31; pa $9.95 *

Grades: 7 8 9 10   808.4
1. Essay 2. Authorship
ISBN 0-531-16761-5; 0-531-17576-6 (pa)

"This concise, appealingly designed writing guide offers practical advice to students on how to successfully complete essay assignments. Topics covered include choosing a topic, brainstorming, researching, crafting and defending a thesis statement, and revising." Booklist

Includes bibliographical references

808.5   Rhetoric of speech

Pinsky, Robert
The sounds of poetry; a brief guide. Farrar,
Straus & Giroux 1998 129p pa $13 hardcover o.p.
*

Grades: 11 12 Adult   **808.5**
1. Poetry
ISBN 0-374-52617-6   LC 98-18873
Pinsky presents "a manual of proposals on how to
read poems—or, more accurately, how to 'hear more of
what is going on in poems.' That distinction, in Pinsky's
view is vital." Atl Mon
"By bringing his passion for the sound of language—
so evident in his own poems—to his expert interpretations of the work of others, Pinsky cracks open the glass
case that seems to separate poetry from everyday language, allowing the song of each poem to ring bright and
clear." Booklist
Includes bibliographical references

Ryan, Margaret, 1950-
Extraordinary oral presentations. Franklin Watts
2005 128p il (F. W. Prep) $31; pa $9.95 *
Grades: 7 8 9 10   **808.5**
1. Public speaking
ISBN 0-531-16758-5; 0-531-17577-4 (pa)
This offers advice on preparing oral presentations
This book provides "good, practical ideas for stu-
dents." SLJ
Includes bibliographical references

808.53   Debating

The **debatabase** book; a must-have guide for
successful debate; [by] the editors of IDEA;
introduction by Robert Trapp. International
Debate Education Association 2011 227p il pa
$27.95 *
Grades: 9 10 11 12   **808.53**
1. Debates and debating
ISBN 978-1-61770-015-6   LC 2010-52964
First published 2003
Presents background, arguments, and resources on approximately 150 debate topics in diverse areas. Includes
the resolution, context, pro and con, sample motions, and
web links and print resources.
Includes bibliographical references

Discovering the world through debate; a practical
guide to educational debate for debaters,
coaches and judges; [by] Robert Trapp . . . [et
al.]; with the assistance of Judith K. Bowker.
3rd ed. International Debate Education
Association 2005 258p il pa $29.95 *
Grades: 9 10 11 12   **808.53**
1. Debates and debating
ISBN 1-932716-06-8   LC 2005-10911
First published 2000 under the authorship of William
Driscoll

This book discusses how to prepare, structure, and
carry out a debate. Includes chapters on judging and the
appendix presents 50 debate exercises.

Miller, Joe, 1968-
Cross-X; a turbulent, triumphant season with an
inner-city debate squad. Farrar, Straus & Giroux
2006 480p hardcover o.p. pa $17
Grades: 11 12 Adult   **808.53**
1. Debates and debating
ISBN   978-0-374-13194-4;   0-374-13194-5;
978-0-312-42697-2 (pa); 0-312-42697-6 (pa)
                   LC 2005-29829
This "book considers in depth the lives and competitions of Kansas City Central High's debate team." Libr
J
"The reporting is both lively and engrossing, and even
at nearly 500 pages, the book encourages most readers to
learn more about these remarkable teens." Publ Wkly

808.8   Literature—Collections

The **best** teen writing of 2010; edited by Jared
Dummitt; foreword by Davy Rothbart. Alliance
for Young Artists & Writers 2010 285p pa $10
Grades: 7 8 9 10 11 12   **808.8**
1. Teenagers' writings 2. American literature—Collec-
tions
ISSN 1937-1837
ISBN 978-0-545-32793-0
Also available online in .pdf format from publisher's
website
Annual. First published 2003
"The Alliance for Young Artists & Writers presents"
Cover
An anthology of students' writings that won the Scho-
lastic Writing Awards. Includes poetry, essays, and short
fiction.

Flake, Sharon G.
You don't even know me; stories and poems
about boys. Hyperion/Jump at the Sun 2010 195p
$16.99
Grades: 7 8 9 10   **808.8**
1. African Americans—Fiction 2. African Americans—Poetry 3. Boys—Fiction 4. Boys—Poetry
5. Short stories
ISBN 978-1-4231-0014-0; 1-4231-0014-X
"This memorable collection of short stories and poems
offers a glimpse into the urban lives of several African
American boys. . . . Flake offers a vivid, unforgettable
collection. . . . The voices ring true. . . . The stories
and poetry are quite thought provoking." Voice Youth
Advocates

Growing up gay; an anthology for young people;
edited by Bennett L. Singer. New Press (NY)
1993 317p pa $14.95 hardcover o.p.
Grades: 11 12 Adult   **808.8**
1. Literature—Collections 2. Homosexuality
ISBN 1-56584-103-4
Paperback edition has title: Growing up gay/growing
up lesbian

Growing up gay—*Continued*

"Culled from the writings of 56 authors, this book offers a message to gay and lesbian youth that they are not alone. The material here ranges from fiction by James Baldwin, Rita Mae Brown, and David Leavitt to autobiographical essays by Audre Lord, Quentin Crisp, and Martina Navratilova. The book is arranged into categories that encompass self-discovery, relationships, family, and 'facing the world.' . . . Essential for all high school/college libraries and highly recommended for all public libraries." Libr J

I can't keep my own secrets; six-word memoirs by teens famous & obscure: from Smith magazine; edited by Rachel Fershleiser and Larry Smith. HarperTeen 2009 184p il pa $8.99 *

Grades: 7 8 9 10   **808.8**
1. Autobiographies 2. Teenagers' writings
ISBN 978-0-06-172684-2; 0-06-172684-2
LC 2009-14584

"This is a book with nearly 800 authors (all aged thirteen to nineteen) and 800 characters (all real, as far as we know) and 800 stories (which can be read in any order). What every story has in common is that each was written about the author's own life, and that each is the exact same length: six words." Publisher's note

"The ruminations span from the haunting . . . to the funny . . . to the inspirational. . . . A razor focus is put on issues that hit youths the hardest. . . . It has just the right proportion of humor and heartbreak." Booklist

Journalistas; 100 years of the best writing and reporting by women journalists; edited by Eleanor Mills with Kira Cochrane. Carroll & Graf 2005 xx, 364p pa $14.95

Grades: 11 12 Adult   **808.8**
1. Women journalists 2. Literature—Collections
ISBN 0-7867-1667-3

Published in the United Kingdom with title: Cupcakes and kalashnikovs

This anthology contains work by such authors as "Martha Gellhorn, Rebecca West, Susan Sontag and Mary McCarthy. . . . The book is divided into subject areas." N Y Times Book Rev

"From Djuna Barnes' 1914 account of being force-fed to end her hunger strike, to Eleanor Roosevelt's 1938 'My Day' column, to Rose George's 2004 article about gang rapes in France, this collection provides a broad and deep look at reporting by women in the past century." Booklist

Leaving home: stories; selected by Hazel Rochman and Darlene Z. McCampbell. HarperCollins Pubs. 1997 231p pa $11.99 hardcover o.p.

Grades: 6 7 8 9 10   **808.8**
1. Youth—Fiction 2. Short stories
ISBN 0-06-440706-3   LC 96-28979

Includes the following stories: The first day, by E. P. Jones; Dancer, by V. Sears; A gift of laughter, by A. Sherman; Rules of the game, by A. Tan; The circuit, by F. Jiménez; Bad influence, by J. Ortiz Cofer; Dawn, by T. Wynne-Jones; Trip in a summer dress, by A. Sanford; On the rainy river, by T. O'Brien; The setting sun and the rolling world, by C. Mungoshi; Zelzah: a tale from long ago, by N. F. Mazer; "Recitatif," by T. Morrison

An international anthology that reflects the thoughts and feelings of young people as they make their way into the world. Authors represented include Amy Tan, Sandra Cisneros, Tim Wynne-Jones, and Toni Morrison

"The editors have varied the tones, the music, the voices, and the meanings of the pieces, which provide both humorous and heartbreaking stories of the meaning of adolescence." ALAN

Nothing makes you free; writings by descendants of Jewish Holocaust survivors; edited by Melvin Jules Bukiet. Norton 2002 394p hardcover o.p. pa $15.95

Grades: 11 12 Adult   **808.8**
1. Holocaust survivors 2. Holocaust, 1933-1945, in literature 3. Literature—Collections
ISBN 0-393-05046-7; 0-393-32425-7 (pa)
LC 2001-55863

"Excerpts from the works of 30 writers whose parents survived the Holocaust make up this anthology of fiction and memoirs. . . . In these remarkable pieces issues such as guilt, anger, faith, and accountability are explored. They capture not only the experience of the concentration camps but also its powerful legacy, passed down to a new generation through the bond of love that ties parent and child." Booklist

Read all about it! great read-aloud stories, poems, and newspaper pieces for preteens and teens; edited by Jim Trelease. Penguin Bks. 1993 489p il pa $13.95

Grades: 8 9 10 11 12   **808.8**
1. Literature—Collections 2. Authors
ISBN 0-14-014655-5   LC 93-21781

This is a collection of 52 selections of fiction, poetry, and nonfiction from newspapers, magazines, and books by such authors as Cynthia Rylant, Jerry Spinelli, Howard Pyle, Rudyard Kipling, Robert W. Service, Maya Angelou, Moss Hart, Pete Hamill, and Leon Garfield. Includes biographical information about the authors

Webber, Carlie

Gay, lesbian, bisexual, transgender, and questioning teen literature; a guide to reading interests; [by] Carlisle K. Webber. Libraries Unlimited 2010 131p (Genreflecting advisory series) $45

Grades: Adult Professional   **808.8**
1. Homosexuality in literature 2. Young adult literature—Bibliography 3. Libraries—Special collections 4. Reference books
ISBN 978-1-59158-506-0   LC 2010-2577

"This slim volume will be a welcome guide for librarians who want to diversify their collections with current materials or who need readers? advisory assistance for their patrons. The titles are divided into six broad categories, and then subdivided into themes. . . . Each entry is annotated, with notations for awards, reading level, and sexual-identity appropriateness. The final chapter includes a discussion of collection development and the author's core list of fiction and nonfiction." SLJ

Includes bibliographical references

Welcome to Bordertown; new stories and poems of the Borderlands; edited by Holly Black and Ellen Kushner; introduction by Terri Windling. Random House 2011 517p $19.99; lib bdg $22.99; e-book $19.99

Grades: 7 8 9 10   **808.8**

1. Supernatural—Fiction 2. Fantasy fiction 3. Short stories 4. Poetry—Collections

ISBN   978-0-375-86705-7;   0-375-86705-8; 978-0-375-96705-4 (lib bdg); 0-375-96705-2 (lib bdg); 978-0-375-89745-0 (e-book)   LC 2010-35558

Contents: Welcome to Bordertown by Terri Windling and Ellen Kushner; Shannon's law by Cory Doctorow; Cruel sister by Patricia A. McKillip; A voice like a hole by Catherynne M. Valente; Stairs in her hair by Amal El-Mohtar; Incunabulum by Emma Bull; Run back across the border by Steven Brust; A prince of thirteen days by Alaya Dawn Johnson; The sages of elsewhere by Will Shetterly; Soulja grrrl by Jane Yolen; Crossings by Janni Lee Simner; Fair trade by Sara Ryan; Night song for a Halfie by Jane Yolen; Our stars, our selves by Tim Pratt; Elf blood by Annette Curtis Klause; Ours is the prettiest by Nalo Hopkinson; The wall by Delia Sherman; We do not come in peace by Christopher Barzak; A Borderland jump-rope rhyme by Jane Yolen; The Rowan gentleman by Holly Black and Cassandra Clare; The song of the song by Neil Gaiman; A tangle of green men by Charles de Lint

Stories and poems set in the urban land of Bordertown, a city on the edge of the faerie and human world, populated by human and elfin runaways.

"This is punk-rock, DIY fantasy, full of harsh reality and incandescent magic . . . Many of the stories echo with loss and discomfort; standouts include 'Crossings' by Janni Lee Simner, a chilling look at the difference between dreams and reality, and 'A Tangle of Green Men,' Charles De Lint's heartbreaking examination of love, loss and life. Poems and songs (from Patricia A. McKillip, Neil Gaiman and Jane Yolen, among others) balance the fiction. . . . A masterful anthology." Kirkus

808.81   Poetry—Collections

Americans' favorite poems; the Favorite Poem Project anthology; edited by Robert Pinsky and Maggie Dietz. Norton 1999 327p $27.50 *

Grades: 11 12 Adult   **808.81**

1. Poetry—Collections

ISBN 0-393-04820-9   LC 99-31979

"People across America, including many teens, share the poetry they love, and talk about what it means in their lives. Their choices—from John Keats to Lucille Clifton—defy stereotypes, and their comments are heartfelt." Booklist

A **Book** of lumininous things; an international anthology of poetry; edited and with an introduction by Czeslaw Milosz. Harcourt Brace & Co. 1996 xx, 320p pa $15 hardcover o.p.

Grades: 11 12 Adult   **808.81**

1. Poetry—Collections

ISBN 0-15-600574-3   LC 95-38060

"Nobel laureate Milosz states in his introduction that the purpose of this personal and eclectic collection is to present poetry that is 'short, clear, readable, and . . . realistic, that is, loyal toward reality and attempting to describe it as concisely as possible.' . . . Most of the selections are from classical Chinese and 20th-century American and European (primarily Eastern European, Scandinavian, and French) poets." Libr J

A **Book** of women poets from antiquity to now; edited by Aliki Barnstone & Willis Barnstone. rev ed. Schocken Bks. 1992 xxiv, 822p pa $22

Grades: 9 10 11 12   **808.81**

1. Poetry—Women authors—Collections

ISBN 0-8052-0997-2   LC 91-52701

First published 1980

An anthology of representative work by women poets of various literary traditions

City lights pocket poets anthology; edited by Lawrence Ferlinghetti. City Lights Bks. 1995 259p $18.95

Grades: 11 12 Adult   **808.81**

1. Poetry—Collections

ISBN 0-87286-311-5   LC 95-31608

"Drawing from the 52 volumes published in the Pocket Poets series since 1956, this selection provides a handy sampler of many of the prominent avant-garde and leftist poets of the post-WW II era. . . . The series' extensive international scope is highlighted in poems culled from German, Russian, Italian, Dutch, Nicaraguan and Spanish poets." Publ Wkly

Crush: love poems. Word of Mouth Books/KA Productions 2007 72p pa $10

Grades: 8 9 10 11 12   **808.81**

1. Love poetry 2. Poetry—Collections

ISBN 978-1-88801-840-0

"Alexander offers a cosmopolitan menu of tanka, haiku, long titles that lead into short first lines, verbal formulas that lead to sung discoveries, French phrases, prose poems, and poems written in Spanglish. The book is divided into three sections with various speakers, and a fourth section that includes poems by Sherman Alexie, Pablo Neruda, Nikki Giovanni, and the title poem, 'Crush' by Naomi Shihab Nye. . . . This well-crafted anthology will capture the interest of teens." SLJ

Faith & doubt; an anthology of poems; edited by Patrice Vecchione. Henry Holt and Co. 2006 138p $16.95

Grades: 9 10 11 12   **808.81**

1. Poetry—Collections

ISBN 978-0-8050-8213-5; 0-8050-8213-1
LC 2006-18228

A collection of poems from around the world that explores the many facets of faith and doubt.

"This book will be read, considered, and discussed. Some who have been lost will find themselves; others will realize that there is direction even on the misguided path. Lucky are those who stumble upon this unassuming but powerful read." Voice Youth Advocates

Includes bibliographical references

Fire in the soul; 100 poems for human rights; edited by Dinyar Godrej. New Internationalist 2009 184p pa $16.95 *

Grades: 9 10 11 12 Adult   **808.81**

Fire in the soul—*Continued*
1. Human rights—Poetry 2. Poetry—Collections
ISBN 978-1-906523-16-9

"The selections come from a wide array of nations and voices. Some were written originally in English, others in Russian, Portuguese, Turkish, Tagalog, Hebrew, Tigrinya, and other languages. All are from the 20th century and are presented here in English. Every one of these poems comes from a place of great pain, of nearly unimaginable suffering, and all offer stubborn rays of hope. The themes range from the ravages of war and genocide to political and gender persecution, from famine to censorship, from child labor to neglect of the elderly." SLJ

Includes bibliographical references

Holocaust poetry; compiled and introduced by Hilda Schiff. St. Martin's Press 1995 xxiv, 234p hardcover o.p. pa $14.95 *
Grades: 11 12 Adult   **808.81**
1. Holocaust, 1933-1945—Poetry 2. Poetry—Collections
ISBN 0-312-13086-4; 0-312-14357-5 (pa)
LC 95-2708

"In English and in translation from many languages, more than 80 poets—including Wiesel, Fink, Brecht, Yevtushenko, Auden, and Sachs—give voice to what seems unspeakable. Schiff points out that compelling historical accounts document the facts and numbers, but a poem, like a story, makes us imagine how it felt for one person. These poems are stark and deceptively simple." Booklist

Includes bibliographical references

I feel a little jumpy around you; a book of her poems & his poems collected in pairs; [by] Naomi Shihab Nye and Paul B. Janeczko. Simon & Schuster Bks. for Young Readers 1996 256p pa $10 hardcover o.p.
Grades: 7 8 9 10   **808.81**
1. Poetry—Collections
ISBN 0-689-81341-4   LC 95-44904

A collection of poems, by male and female authors, presented in pairings that offer insight into how men and women look at the world, both separately and together

"Though the gender counterpoint really plays little part in the juxtaposition, the pairings are piquant and provide a manageable way to start talking about a very large collection of poetry. An engaging marginal dialogue, taken from Nye's and Janeczko's collaborative fax correspondence, appears alongside the appendix and permits a revealing peek behind the scences. Highly readable notes from contributors are included, as is an index of poems and a gender-segregated index of poets." Bull Cent Child Books

I just hope it's lethal; poems of sadness, madness, and joy; collected by Liz Rosenberg and Deena November. Houghton Mifflin 2005 190p pa $7.99
Grades: 9 10 11 12   **808.81**
1. Poetry—Collections
ISBN 0-618-56452-7   LC 2005-4257

The editors "have brought together poems that, as Rosenberg writes, address 'various aspects of sanity and

madness.' . . . There are works by famous writers, such as Shakespeare, Sylvia Plath, Emily Dickinson, and Rumi, as well as contemporary poets, such as Naomi Shihab Nye." SLJ

"This interesting and rich collection of poetry will have special significance for teen readers." Voice Youth Advocates

Love poems. Knopf 1993 256p (Everyman's library pocket poets) $12.50
Grades: 11 12 Adult   **808.81**
1. Love poetry 2. Poetry—Collections
ISBN 0-679-42906-9   LC 93-11427

Among the poets included are Robert Graves, W. B. Yeats, Pablo Neruda, Boris Pasternak, William Carlos Williams, Anna Akhmatova, Robert Browning and Christina Rossetti. An index of first lines is appended

Music of a distant drum; classical Arabic, Persian, Turkish, and Hebrew poems; translated and introduced by Bernard Lewis. Princeton Univ. Press 2001 222p il hardcover o.p. pa $17.95
Grades: 11 12 Adult   **808.81**
1. Arabic poetry—Collections 2. Hebrew poetry—Collections 3. Persian poetry—Collections 4. Turkish poetry—Collections
ISBN 0-691-08928-0; 0-691-15010-9 (pa)
LC 2001-19858

"Lewis, one of the foremost scholars of the Middle East, has devoted much of his career to the history of Islam; this volume collects his translations of poems—nearly all appearing in English for the first time—that span eleven centuries and four major Middle Eastern traditions. Many of the most striking works address, in spare, stirring lines, the twin demands of serving the self and serving God." New Yorker

Includes bibliographical references

The Oxford book of war poetry; chosen and edited by John Stallworthy. Oxford Univ. Press 1984 xxxi, 358p hardcover o.p. pa $19.95
Grades: 8 9 10 11 12 Adult   **808.81**
1. War poetry 2. Poetry—Collections
ISBN 0-19-214125-2; 0-19-955453-6 (pa)
LC 83-19303

"This comprehensive anthology focuses on poetic treatment of warfare ranging from the battlefields of ancient history to the conflicts in Vietnam, Northern Ireland, and El Salvador." Univ Press Books for Second Sch Libr

This collection "reminds one of the large numbers and great variety of war poems from many centuries that are very good poems. Mr. Stallworthy's selections include most of the best, at least the best in English." N Y Times Book Rev

Includes bibliographical references

Poems to read; a new favorite poem project anthology; edited by Robert Pinsky and Maggie Dietz. Norton 2002 xxv, 352p $27.95 *
Grades: 11 12 Adult   **808.81**
1. Poetry—Collections
ISBN 0-393-01074-0   LC 2002-321

This anthology "features works by a wide selection of well-known, mostly American and European writers from

Poems to read—*Continued*

throughout the ages: Henry King, Rabindranath Tagore, Gwendolyn Brooks, J.W. von Goethe, Issa, Jorie Graham, Robert Herrick, Dionisio Martinez and Frank O'Hara are just a few of them." Publ Wkly

"A graceful, sometimes jubilant, sometimes lyrical, sometimes brooding, but always welcoming and stirring collection." Booklist

Includes bibliographical references

The **Poetry** of our world; an international anthology of contemporary poetry; edited by Jeffrey Paine. HarperCollins Pubs. 2000 xxviii, 511p hardcover o.p. pa $18.95

Grades: 11 12 Adult   **808.81**

1. Poetry—Collections

ISBN 0-06-055369-3; 0-06-095193-1 (pa)

LC 99-34921

In this global anthology "each section is preceded by a thoughtful introduction of several pages by the selector in that area. . . . A stunning and highly readable anthology." Libr J

Poetry speaks: who I am; poems of discovery, inspiration, independence, and everything else. Sourcebooks Jabberwocky 2010 136p $19.99 *

Grades: 5 6 7 8 9 10   **808.81**

1. Poetry—Collections

ISBN 978-1-4022-1074-7; 1-4022-1074-4

This collection "aims at middle-grade readers with more than 100 strikingly diverse poems by writers including Poe, Frost, Nikki Giovanni, and Sandra Cisneros. The works are slotted together in mindful thematic order, beside occasional spot art. . . . Pairing a contemporary poem like Toi Derricotte's 'Fears of the Eighth Grade' alongside Keats's 'When I Have Fears That I May Cease to Be,' results in a refreshing lack of literary hierarchy that enables disparate works to build and reflect upon one another. An accompanying CD features recordings of 44 of the poems. . . . A sound and rewarding introduction to the joys of poetry." Publ Wkly

Revenge and forgiveness; an anthology of poems; edited by Patrice Vecchione. Henry Holt 2004 148p $16.95

Grades: 7 8 9 10   **808.81**

1. Poetry—Collections

ISBN 0-8050-7376-0   LC 2003-56631

A collection of nearly sixty poems dealing with revenge and forgiveness, plus suggested readings about each contributing poet

"For students who are of a philosophical bent and for teachers of poetry, this book of poems about love, hate, and war will be a useful resource." Libr Media Connect

Includes bibliographical references

Risking everything; 110 poems of love and revelation; edited by Roger Housden. Harmony Bks. 2003 173p $20

Grades: 11 12 Adult   **808.81**

1. Poetry—Collections

ISBN 1-400-04799-4   LC 2002-14410

The editor "has placed strong emphasis on contemporary voices such as the American poet laureate Billy Collins and the Nobel Prize–winners Czeslaw Milosz and Seamus Heaney, but the collection also includes some . . . echoes of the past in the form of work by masters such as Goethe, Wordsworth, and Emily Dickinson." Publisher's note

This is "an inspirational anthology sans inspirational chestnuts." Booklist

Side by side; new poetry inspired by art from around our world; collected by Jan Greenberg. Abrams Books for Young Readers 2008 il $19.95 *

Grades: 8 9 10 11 12   **808.81**

1. Art—Poetry 2. Poetry—Collections

ISBN 978-0-8109-9471-3; 0-8109-9471-2

LC 2007-11973

This is an "anthology of accomplished poems inspired by artworks. . . . [Greenberg brings] together the work of poets and artists from around the globe. . . . The poems are grouped loosely into categories, defined in Greenberg's inspirational introduction. . . . Each spread features a poem in its original language, the English translation, and an artwork, usually from the same country or culture as the poem. With a few exceptions, the reproductions of the art, which ranges from ancient to contemporary work, are sharp and clear, and the moving, often startling poems invite readers to savor the words and then look closely at each image." Booklist

This same sky; a collection of poems from around the world; selected by Naomi Shihab Nye. Four Winds Press 1992 212p il hardcover o.p. pa $9.99 *

Grades: 9 10 11 12   **808.81**

1. Poetry—Collections

ISBN 0-02-768440-7; 0-689-80630-2 (pa)

LC 92-11617

A poetry anthology in which 129 poets from sixty-eight different countries celebrate the natural world and its human and animal inhabitants

"Notes on the contributors, a map, suggestions for further reading, an index to countries, and an index to poets are appended, adding additional luster to a book which should prove invaluable for intercultural education as well as for pure pleasure." Horn Book

War and the pity of war; edited by Neil Philip; illustrated by Michael McCurdy. Clarion Bks. 1998 96p il $20

Grades: 5 6 7 8 9 10   **808.81**

1. War poetry 2. Poetry—Collections

ISBN 0-395-84982-9   LC 97-32897

"The selections, covering conflicts from ancient Persia to modern-day Bosnia, are by a wide variety of poets, from the well known (Tennyson, Whitman, Sandburg, Auden), to the obscure (Anakreon from ancient Greece and 11th-century Chinese poet Bunno). . . . The stark and simple scratchboard drawings are reminiscent of the Ernie Pyle illustrations from World War II and are as memorable as the best propaganda." SLJ

World poetry; an anthology of verse from antiquity to our time; Katharine Washburn and John S. Major, editors; Clifton Fadiman, general editor. Norton 1998 xxii, 1338p $45 *

Grades: 11 12 Adult   **808.81**
1. Poetry—Collections
ISBN 0-393-04130-1   LC 97-10879

This volume presents poetry "arranged chronologically in eight sections, from the Bronze and Iron Ages to the 20th century, with each time period subdivided by region and language." Christ Sci Monit

The anthology's "stated aim—'to surprise and delight the common reader'—may seem rather quaint; yet it is a worthy one, and is, on the whole, impressively fulfilled." Times Lit Suppl

Includes bibliographical references

808.82 Drama—Collections

24 favorite one-act plays; edited by Bennett Cerf and Van H. Cartmell. Doubleday 1958 455p pa $14.95

Grades: 11 12 Adult   **808.82**
1. Drama—Collections 2. One act plays
ISBN 0-385-06617-1

A wide assortment of one-act plays includes comedies, tragedies, new and old, Irish, American, Russian, English, and Austrian. Includes the work of such playwrights as Eugene O'Neill, Noel Coward, George S. Kaufman, William Inge, and Dorothy Parker

"A good collection showing the variety of form and subject used by modern masters of the short play." Good Read

100 great monologues from the neo-classical theatre; edited by Jocelyn A. Beard. Smith & Kraus 1994 157p (Monologue audition series) pa $9.95

Grades: 9 10 11 12   **808.82**
1. Monologues 2. Acting
ISBN 1-88039-960-1   LC 94-33114

"Among the neoclassical soliloquies chosen for inclusion are excerpts from the works of Congreve, Dryden, and Comielle. Molière is perhaps the most prominently featured of all the assembled playwrights. Dramatic plays such as Racine's *Phedre* are drawn upon to provide some very potent material, while more comic passages are contained in Sheridan's splendid *The Rivals.*" Booklist

2010: the best men's stage monologues and scenes; edited and foreword by Lawrence Harbison. Smith & Kraus 2010 176p (Monologue and scene study series) pa $14.95 *

Grades: 11 12 Adult   **808.82**
1. Monologues 2. Acting
ISBN 978-1-57525-773-0

Annual. First published 1991 for the 1990 theater season under the editorship of Jocelyn Beard

This is a "selection of monologues and scenes from plays that were produced and/or published in the 2009-2010 theatrical season. Most are for younger performers (teens through thirties), but there are also some . . .

pieces for men in their forties and fifties, and even a few for older performers. Some are comic (laughs), some are dramatic (generally, no laughs)." Publisher's note

2010: the best women's stage monologues and scenes; edited and with a foreword by Lawrence Harbison. Smith & Kraus Book 2010 193p (Monologue and scene study series) pa $14.95 *

Grades: 11 12 Adult   **808.82**
1. Monologues 2. Acting
ISBN 978-1-57525-774-7

Annual. First published 1991 for the 1990 theater season under the editorship of Jocelyn Beard

This is a "selection of monologues and scenes from plays that were produced and/or published in the 2009-2010 theatrical season." Publisher's note

Actor's choice; monologues for teens; edited by Erin Detrick. Playscripts 2008 131p pa $14.95

Grades: 6 7 8 9 10   **808.82**
1. Monologues 2. Acting 3. Drama—Collections
ISBN 978-0-9709046-6-9; 0-9709046-6-5
                                      LC 2007-50166

"This volume of highly entertaining monologues is gleaned from one-act and full-length plays published by Playscripts, Inc. . . . This is an excellent volume to help students prepare for competitions as well as to use in drama, speech, or English classes." SLJ

Allen, Laurie, 1962-
Comedy scenes for student actors; short sketches for young performers. Meriwether Pub. 2009 197p pa $17.95 *

Grades: 9 10 11 12   **808.82**
1. Acting 2. Drama—Collections 3. Comedy
ISBN 978-1-56608-159-7; 1-56608-159-9
                                      LC 2008-41734

"This collection of 31 skits has a nice mix of female and male actors and works well in drama or speech classes. Each piece has a range of two to seven actors with options of up to a dozen, as well as suggested props and stage actions. The scenes are written with a superb sense of comic timing and portray authentic teen characters in high school settings." SLJ

The **Book** of monologues for aspiring actors; [edited by] Marsh Cassady. NTC Pub. Group 1995 212p il pa $23.96 *

Grades: 7 8 9 10   **808.82**
1. Monologues 2. Acting 3. Drama—Collections
ISBN 0-8442-5771-0   LC 94-66239

"The selections range from the classical Greeks to Sam Shepard and Oscar Wilde; they give YA's the opportunity to develop characters of like ages in many different settings. Several questions to probe the actors' imaginations appear at the end of each monologue." SLJ

Caruso, Sandra

The young actor's book of improvisation; dramatic situations from Shakespeare to Spielberg: ages 12-16; [by] Sandra Caruso with Susan Kosoff. Heinemann (Portsmouth) 1998 xx, 259p $22.95 *

Grades: 9 10 11 12   **808.82**
1. Acting
ISBN 0-325-00049-2   LC 97-46817

A sourcebook of techniques designed to develop improvisional skills in young actors

Scenes "are divided thematically—confrontation, fantasy, solo moment, relationships, etc.—and according to the number and gender of the actors. Each brief entry includes the source, characters, place, and time period if relevant, an explanation of the situation, and comments, including tips, notes, and supplemental information to 'enhance the actors' understanding of story and character.'" Booklist

Includes bibliographical references

Cassady, Marsh, 1936-

The book of scenes for aspiring actors. NTC Pub. Group 1995 202p il pa $16.95

Grades: 9 10 11 12   **808.82**
1. Acting 2. Drama—Collections
ISBN 0-8442-5769-9   LC 94-66240

"A collection of scripts for characters between the ages of 12-21. An introductory chapter analyzes the scene and the characters and gives information for both directors and actors on diagraming the set and blocking the action. . . . The selections come from Shakespeare, Jean Anouilh, and Maxwell Anderson and range in diversity from William Gillette's *Secret Service* to Brandon Thomas's *Charley's Aunt* and Arthur Laurents's *West Side Story*." Libr J

Great monologues for young actors; Craig Slaight, Jack Sharrar, editors. Smith & Kraus 1992-1999 3v v1 pa $11.95; v2-v3 pa ea $14.95

Grades: 8 9 10 11 12   **808.82**
1. Monologues 2. Acting 3. Drama—Collections
ISBN 1-880399-03-2 (v1); 0-57525-106-X (v2); 1-57525-408-1 (v3)

"The Young Actors series."

These volumes provide an introduction and acting notes for monologues for men and women drawn from contemporary and classic works

International plays for young audiences; contemporary works from leading playwrights; edited by Roger Ellis. Meriwether 2000 419p pa $16.95 *

Grades: 9 10 11 12   **808.82**
1. Drama—Collections
ISBN 1-56608-065-7   LC 00-55921

"The 12 short plays feature young characters in a variety of settings and situations. While some of the selections are straightforward in style (such as Gustavo Ott's *Minor Leagues)*, others require a creative stretch in order to be able to read and produce them (such as Neil Duffield's racial fable *Skin and Bones)*. . . . All, however, have characters that would be intriguing to young

people and all deal with themes of cultural conflict and understanding." SLJ

Includes bibliographical references

Kehret, Peg, 1936-

Tell it like it is; fifty monologs for talented teens. Meriwether Pub. 2007 117p pa $15.95

Grades: 9 10 11 12   **808.82**
1. Monologues 2. Acting
ISBN 978-1-56608-144-3; 1-56608-144-0

                                      LC 2007-83

"The scenes range from funny to sweet to sad. Several entries concern animals, rites of passage, and historical events. Both contemporary and historical characters display a wide range of emotion, and there is enough flow and peak in all of the monologues for both beginners and advanced students. . . . This excellent book would make a smart purchase in preparation for forensics season." SLJ

More scenes and monologs from the best new plays; an anthology of new dramatic writing from professionally produced plays; edited by Roger Ellis. Meriwether Pub. 2007 233p pa $15.95

Grades: 9 10 11 12   **808.82**
1. Monologues 2. Acting
ISBN 978-1-56608-142-9; 1-56608-142-4

                                      LC 2006-35093

Companion volume to Scenes & monologs from the best new plays (1992)

"The selections range from under a minute to approximately 10 minutes long, making them appropriate for competition or in the classroom. . . . Most of the characters range in age from middle teens to middle 20s. Students can choose from scenes for two women, scenes for two men, scenes for a man and woman, or monologs that don't specify gender. There is a good mix of comic, seriocomic, and serious pieces. . . . High school students and teachers will be pleased with the breadth and depth of the character selections and genres represented." SLJ

Includes bibliographical references

Multicultural scenes for young actors; Craig Slaight and Jack Sharrar, editors. Smith & Kraus 1995 237p (Young actor series) pa $11.95 *

Grades: 9 10 11 12   **808.82**
1. Drama—Collections 2. Acting
ISBN 1-880399-48-2   LC 94-44187

This collection "is organized according to cast requirements, and each of the cuttings from over 40 plays is preceded by source notes and a brief plot summary. Information regarding performance rights is appended. Although a few of the plays have been included in standard compilations, the multicultural theme makes this collection unique." SLJ

Play index. Wilson, H.W. 1953-2007 11v *
Grades: 8 9 10 11 12 Adult Professional
                                      808.82
1. Reference books 2. Drama—Indexes
ISSN 0554-3037

Also available on-line version

Play index—*Continued*

1949-1952 edited by Dorothy Herbert West and Dorothy Margaret Peake $90; 1953-1960 $90 edited by Estelle A. Fidell and Dorothy Margaret Peake; 1961-1967 $90 edited by Estelle A. Fidell; 1968-1972 $90 edited by Estelle A. Fidell; 1973-1977 $90 edited by Estelle A. Fidell; 1978-1982 $90 edited by Juliette Yaakov; 1983-1987 $270 edited by Juliette Yaakov and John Greenfieldt; 1988-1992 $270 edited by Juliette Yaakov and John Greenfieldt; 1993-1997 edited by Juliette Yaakov and John Greenfieldt $270; 1998-2002 edited by John Greenfieldt $270; 2003-2007 edited by John Greenfieldt $315

Play index indexes plays in collections and single plays; one-act and full-length plays; radio, television, and Broadway plays; plays for amateur production; plays for children, young adults, and adults. It is divided into four parts. Part I is an author, title, and subject index; the author or main entry includes the title of the play, brief synopsis of the plot, number of acts and scenes, size of cast, number of sets, and bibliographic information. Part II is a list of collections indexed, and Part III, a cast analysis, lists plays by the type of cast and number of players required

"This index is an excellent source for locating published plays." Safford. Guide to Ref Materials for Sch Media Cent. 5th edition

The **Scenebook** for actors; great monologs & dialogs from contemporary & classical theatre; edited by Norman A. Bert. Meriwether 1990 246p pa $15.95

Grades: 9 10 11 12   **808.82**
1. Drama—Collections 2. Acting
ISBN 0-916260-65-8   LC 90-52983

A collection of scenes, monologues and dialogues from scripts produced after 1975. Selections are for characters aged 18 to 30 and several are written for Afro-American and Hispanic actors

Includes bibliographical references

Scenes from classic plays, 468 B.C. to 1970 A.D.; Jocelyn A. Beard, editor. Smith & Kraus 1993 310p pa $11.95 *

Grades: 9 10 11 12   **808.82**
1. Drama—Collections 2. Acting
ISBN 1-880399-36-9   LC 93-33010

"Arranged chronologically, the selected scenes average three pages in length and involve two to three characters. A one-line description of the setting and of each character is given, as well as a one- to two-sentence synopsis of what is occurring at the opening of the scene. This book must be commended for such a well-balanced representation of time-honored classics." Booklist

Stevens, Chambers, 1968-

Sensational scenes for teens; the scene studyguide for teen actors. Sandcastle Pub. 2001 104p il (Hollywood 101) $14.95

Grades: 9 10 11 12   **808.82**
1. Drama—Collections 2. Acting
ISBN 1-883995-10-8   LC 99-76948

"Stevens presents more than 30 short comedy and drama scenes, all written for two actors with an even mix of boy-boy, girl-girl, and boy-girl casts. The contemporary urban and suburban settings coupled with culturally neutral names allow for racial and ethnic diversity." SLJ

Includes bibliographical references

The **Ultimate** audition book; 222 monologues, 2 minutes & under; edited by Jocelyn A. Beard. Smith & Kraus 1997-2005 2v + v4 (Monologue audition series) ea pa $19.95 *

Grades: 11 12 Adult   **808.82**
1. Monologues 2. Acting
ISBN 1-57525-066-7 (v1); 1-57525-270-8 (v2); 1-57525-420-4 (v4)   LC 97-10471

Volume 2 edited by John Capecci, Laurie Walker, and Irene Ziegler; Variant title: 222 monologues, 2 minutes & under from literature. Volume 4 edited by Irene Ziegleraston and John Capecci; variant title for v4: 222 comedy monologues, 2 minutes & under

This collection draws "upon lesser-known works from significant writers and those of contemporary favorites and reflects a wide range of tone, age, time period, and voice. Divided among female, male, and unisex categories, all meet the obligatory two minutes or less time limit imposed by most directors and auditions." Libr J [review of volume 2]

Includes bibliographical references

808.85 Speeches—Collections

Lend me your ears; great speeches in history; selected and introduced by William Safire. rev and expanded ed. Norton 1997 1055p $39.95 *

Grades: 8 9 10 11 12 Adult   **808.85**
1. Speeches
ISBN 0-393-05931-6   LC 96-43423

First published 1992

Pope Urban II, Bob Dole, Cicero, Jesus, Boris Yeltsin, Richard Nixon and Colin Powell are among the orators represented in this anthology of over 200 speeches grouped chronologically into thematic categories

The **Penguin** book of twentieth-century speeches; edited by Brian MacArthur. 2nd rev ed. Penguin Books 1999 xxix, 525p pa $15.95 *

Grades: 9 10 11 12   **808.85**
1. Speeches
ISBN 0-14-028500-8   LC 00-267955

First published 1992 in the United Kingdom

"Nelson Mandela, Winston Churchill, Emmeline Pankhurst, Martin Luther King, Jr., and Adolf Hitler are among the more than 140 famous speakers whose words are collected in this anthology that teens will use for reference and for browsing." Booklist [review of 1992 edition]

Speeches in world history; [compiled by] Suzanne McIntire; with additional contribution by William E. Burns. Facts on File 2008 648p il (Facts on File library of world history) $85

Grades: 9 10 11 12 Adult   **808.85**
1. Speeches
ISBN 978-0-8160-7404-4; 0-8160-7404-6
     LC 2008-5620

Speeches in world history—*Continued*
"From presidents to religious leaders to the common man, this reference of over 200 speeches provides students with a wide-ranging list of discourses that have had an impact on world history. . . . This outstanding resource will provide students with a well-rounded list of resources as well as tools for their own persuasive speech making." Libr Media Connect

Includes bibliographical references

Words that ring through time; from Moses and Pericles to Obama: fifty-one of the most important speeches in history and how they changed our world; [compiled by] Terry Golway; foreword by Lewis Lapham. Overlook Press 2009 416p $30
Grades: 9 10 11 12 Adult   **808.85**
1. Speeches
ISBN 978-1-59020-231-9   LC 2010-275754

"Selected and introduced by historian Golway, the historically significant speeches in this anthology either crystallized a philosophy or addressed war, revolution, or national liberation. Prefacing them with the immediate contexts of their delivery, Golway permits the words to speak for themselves, without much analysis of their rhetorical arrangement. Readers are immediately immersed in scriptural excerpts from the Bible and the Koran and other declamations from the ancient world, such as Pericles' funeral oration. . . . Good browsing material for history collections." Booklist

Includes bibliographical references

808.88   Collections of miscellaneous writings

American Indian quotations; compiled and edited by Howard J. Langer. Greenwood Press 1996 260p il $65.95 *
Grades: 11 12 Adult   **808.88**
1. Native Americans—Quotations
ISBN 0-313-29121-7   LC 95-33151

"This volume offers 800 quotations covering more than four centuries of American life. Arranged chronologically, the quotations include the words of warriors, poets, politicians, doctors, lawyers, athletes, and others. . . . The book provides brief biographical information about those quoted, including both historical and contemporary figures, and cross-references the material through subject, author, and tribal indexes." Publisher's note

Andrews, Robert, 1957-
Famous lines; a Columbia dictionary of familiar quotations. Columbia Univ. Press 1997 xxiii, 625p $38.95
Grades: 11 12 Adult   **808.88**
1. Quotations 2. Reference books
ISBN 0-231-10218-6   LC 96-43879

This work "contains more than 6,000 witticisms, enduring observations, and incendiary statements from all kinds of people from antiquity to yesterday. Besides identifying the source, Andrews . . . provides details of

the first publication, specific chapter and scene, and even the character speaking. Besides quotes from Shakespeare and Oscar Wilde, readers will find fascinating quotes from Monty Python, Gloria Steinem, and maybe your favorite author, for example, Agatha Christie. The more than 500 subject headings include homelessness, AIDS, sexual harassment, murder, and war." Booklist

Includes bibliographical references

Bartlett, John, 1820-1905
Bartlett's familiar quotations; a collection of passages, phrases, and proverbs traced to their sources in ancient and modern literature. Little, Brown 2002 1431p $50 *
Grades: 8 9 10 11 12 Adult   **808.88**
1. Quotations 2. Reference books
ISBN 0-316-08460-3   LC 2003-269668

First published 1855. Periodically revised. Editors vary

"Arranged chronologically by author, with exact references. Includes many interesting footnotes, tracing history or usage of analogous thoughts, the circumstances under which a particular remark was made, etc. Author and keyword indexes. One of the best books of quotations with a long history." Guide to Ref Books. 11th edition

Includes bibliographical references

The **Columbia** Granger's dictionary of poetry quotations; edited by Edith P. Hazen. Columbia Univ. Press 1992 1132p $131
Grades: 11 12 Adult   **808.88**
1. Quotations 2. Reference books
ISBN 0-231-07546-4   LC 91-42240

This work contains the "most memorable lines written by the greatest poets of English. Quotations are organized alphabetically by poet, and coded so one can find full text in hundreds of current anthologies. With keyword and subject indexing." Univ Press Books for Public and Second Sch Libr

Concise Oxford dictionary of quotations; edited by Susan Ratcliffe. 5th ed. Oxford University Press 2006 580p (Oxford paperback reference) pa $17.95 *
Grades: 11 12 Adult   **808.88**
1. Quotations 2. Reference books
ISBN 0-19-861417-9; 978-0-19-861417-3
     LC 2006-48714

First published 1964

Collected here are quotations by over 2,000 authors from around the world ranging in time from the 8th century BC to the present. Arrangement is alphabetical by the names of authors with sections such as Anonymous, Ballads, The Bible, the Mass in Latin, etc. included in the alphabetical order. Foreign quotations are given in the original language followed by the English translation. Indexed by key words.

Contemporary quotations in black; compiled and edited by Anita King. Greenwood Press 1997 298p il $45
Grades: 11 12 Adult   **808.88**
1. Quotations 2. African Americans—Quotations
ISBN 0-313-29122-5   LC 96-47431

Contemporary quotations in black—*Continued*
"This collection features the words of contemporary African Americans and black Africans. . . . Many of the over 1000 quotations are drawn from magazines and newspaper articles published from 1990 to 1996, and most have never before appeared in anthologies. Those quoted range from journalists and musicians to athletes and physicians. . . . Entries are presented alphabetically by author, quotes are numbered sequentially, and indexing is by author and subject/keyword." Libr J

The **Girls'** book of wisdom; empowering, inspirational quotes from 500 fabulous females; selected and edited by Catherine Dee. Little, Brown 1999 192p pa $8.95
Grades: 9 10 11 12 **808.88**
1. Quotations 2. Women—Quotations
ISBN 0-316-17956-6   LC 99-24741
A collection of quotations from 500 famous women, including suffragists, pioneers, politicians, moms, musicians, athletes, and actors, grouped in such categories as "Friendship," "Confidence," and "Creativity."
"While the included quotes are not revolutionary and are occasionally clichèd, attractive fonts, funky small graphics, and the mix of historical and modern powerful women will make this choice popular among teen girls." Voice Youth Advocates

Heart full of grace; a thousand years of black wisdom; edited by Venice Johnson. Simon & Schuster 1995 unp pa $19.95 hardcover o.p.
Grades: 11 12 Adult   **808.88**
1. African Americans—Quotations
ISBN 0-684-82542-2   LC 95-38106
"This is a diverse anthology of quotations, from the sayings of Martin Luther King and Langston Hughes to political speeches and African proverbs." Libr J

Oxford dictionary of humorous quotations; edited by Ned Sherrin; with a foreword by Alistair Beaton. 4th ed. Oxford University Press 2008 536p hardcover o.p. pa $24.95
Grades: 11 12 Adult   **808.88**
1. Quotations 2. Wit and humor 3. Reference books
ISBN   978-0-19-923716-6;   0-19-923716-6;
978-0-19-957006-5 (pa); 0-19-957006-X (pa)
                                    LC 2008-486673
First published 1995 with title: The Oxford book of humorous quotations
This dictionary "features 5,000 quotations organized into more than 200 subject categories. Quips are arranged by broad themes. . . . Coverage spans the centuries, and you are as likely to find lines by Johnny Depp, Ricky Gervais, and Eddie Izzard are you are those by Noel Coward, William Shakespeare, and George Bernard Shaw. . . . An amusing addition to the reference collection." Booklist

Oxford dictionary of modern quotations; edited by Elizabeth Knowles. 3rd ed. Oxford University Press 2007 479p $39.95; pa $18.95
Grades: 9 10 11 12 Adult   **808.88**
1. Quotations 2. Reference books
ISBN   978-0-19-920895-1;   0-19-920895-6;
978-0-19-954746-3 (pa); 0-19-954746-7 (pa)
                                    LC 2007-36871

First published 1991
"Containing more than 5,000 quotations from authors . . . [such] as Bertolt Brecht, George W. Bush, Homer Simpson, Carl Sagan, William Shatner, and Desmond Tutu, the dictionary is organized alphabetically by author, with . . . cross-referencing and keyword and thematic indexes." Publisher's note

Oxford dictionary of phrase, saying, and quotation; edited by Susan Ratcliffe. 3rd ed. Oxford University Press 2006 xxi, 689p $39.95
Grades: 9 10 11 12   **808.88**
1. Quotations 2. Proverbs 3. English language—Terms and phrases 4. Reference books
ISBN 978-0-19-280650-5; 0-19-280650-5
First published 1997
This book "brings together a profusion of proverbs, phrases, and quotations, arranged by subject or themes from Ability to Youth. The design and layout are clear and well organized. More than 12,000 bon mots from around the globe are included, and the origins and links of these treasured sayings in our language are traced through numerous cross-references." Booklist

Oxford dictionary of quotations; edited by Elizabeth Knowles. 7th ed. Oxford University Press 2009 xxvi, 1155p $50 *
Grades: 11 12 Adult   **808.88**
1. Quotations 2. Reference books
ISBN 978-0-19-923717-3; 0-19-923717-4
                                    LC 2009-464901
First published 1941
Collected here are around 20,000 quotations by nearly 3,500 authors from around the world ranging in time from the 8th century BC to the present. Arrangement is alphabetical by the names of authors with sections such as Advertising Slogans, Epitaphs, Film Lines, Prayers, etc. included in the alphabetical order. Indexed by key words.
Includes bibliographical references

Quotations for all occasions; compiled by Catherine Frank. Columbia Univ. Press 2000 260p $55; pa $18.95 *
Grades: 11 12 Adult   **808.88**
1. Quotations
ISBN 0-231-11290-4; 0-231-11291-2 (pa)
                                    LC 00-24048
This title "organizes its 1500-plus quotes into three sections that cover 150 different occasions. 'Every Year' contains quotes for such annual events as holidays, birthdays, days of the week, and seasons, while 'Occasionally' encompasses quotes for less frequent events, like going back to school, breaking up, quitting smoking, and school reunions. The final section is for 'Once in a Lifetime' experiences, such as turning 16, getting a first car, menopause, and retirement." Libr J
Includes bibliographical references

Science fiction quotations; from the inner mind to the outer limits; edited by Gary Westfahl; with a foreword by Arthur C. Clarke. Yale University Press 2005 xxi, 461p $25
Grades: 11 12 Adult   **808.88**
1. Science fiction 2. Quotations
ISBN 0-300-10800-1   LC 2005-3195

Science fiction quotations—*Continued*

The author "defines a science fiction quotation as coming from novels, short stories, films, and TV programs (with some attention given to plays, radio dramas, and comic books) and being about works of science fiction or from science fiction writers. Organized under topical headings, more than 2,900 quotations offer the wisdom and wit of well-known authors like Arthur C. Clarke and Isaac Asimov as well as lesser-known personalities like J. O. Bailey and Stirling Silliphant and from titles as varied as The Strawberry Window, Cat's Cradle, and The Thing (from another World)." Booklist

The **Yale** book of quotations; edited by Fred R. Shapiro; foreword by Joseph Epstein. Yale University Press 2006 1104p $50 *

Grades: 11 12 Adult   **808.88**
1. Quotations
ISBN 978-0-300-10798-2; 0-300-10798-6
       LC 2006-12317

The more than 12,000 "range over literature, history, popular culture, sports, computers, science, politics, law, and the social sciences, and although American quotations are emphasized, the book's scope is global. The authors represented are as diverse as William Shakespeare, John Lennon, Jack Dempsey, both Presidents Bush, J.K. Rowling, Rita Mae Brown, Confucius, Warren Buffet, and Deng Xiaoping. The entries are arranged by author, then chronologically and alphabetically by source title within the same year. A significant effort was made to trace the first published occurrence of a quotation, and whenever possible the wording is taken from the original source. . . . Electronic products such as the Times Digital Archive, JSTOR, Proquest Historical Newspapers and American Periodical Series, LexisNexis, Newspaperarchive.com, Questia, Eighteenth Century Collections Online, and Literature Online were all used." Libr J

809   Literary history and criticism

African literature and its times; [edited by] Joyce Moss & Lorraine Valestuk. Gale Group 2000 xlv, 544p il (World literature and its times) lib bdg $145.25 *

Grades: 11 12 Adult   **809**
1. African literature—History and criticism
ISBN 0-7876-3727-0   LC 00-24488

Contributors discuss "50 literary works in relation to their social and historical contexts. Each article begins with comments on the genre, setting, and the historical period in which the work takes place, along with information about the author. . . . The work of key writers such as Athol Fugard, Camara Laye, Doris Lessing and Wole Soyinka is discussed as is the writing of others who have more recently emerged on the scene." SLJ

Includes bibliographical references

Bloom, Harold, 1930-

The epic. Chelsea House Publishers 2005 265p (Bloom's literary criticism 20th anniversary collection) $38.95; pa $19.95

Grades: 9 10 11 12   **809**
1. Epic literature—History and criticism
ISBN 0-7910-8229-6; 0-7910-8368-3 (pa)
       LC 2005-5379

"In this volume, Bloom writes on the ancient works of Homer through more modern epics such as Hart Crane's 'The Bridge'." Publisher's note

Burt, Daniel S.

The literary 100; a ranking of the most influential novelists, playwrights, and poets of all time. Rev ed. Facts on File 2009 541p (Facts on File library of world literature) $50; pa $19.95

Grades: 11 12 Adult   **809**
1. Authors 2. Literature—History and criticism
ISBN 978-0-8160-6267-6; 978-0-8160-6268-3 (pa)
       LC 2008-10066

First published 2001

Burt profiles not only familiar authors such as Tolstoy, Shakespeare, Dickens, and Jane Austen, but non-western writers such as Murasaki Shikibu, Du Fu, and Cao Xueqin.

"With definitive worth applied to Eastern and Western literary icons, the ranking equals a debate-spurring thesis, while engaging profiles are an essential literary primer." Libr J

Includes bibliographical references

Campbell, Patricia J., 1930-

Campbell's scoop; reflections on young adult literature; [by] Patty Campbell. Scarecrow Press 2010 245p (Scarecrow studies in young adult literature) $40

Grades: Adult Professional   **809**
1. Young adult literature—History and criticism
2. Teenagers—Books and reading
ISBN 978-0-8108-7293-6; 0-8108-7293-5
       LC 2009-45563

"This resource represents the accumulated wisdom of a veteran librarian, author, speaker, critic, and pioneer of young adult services. Selected from several sources over many years, these essays and articles present a broad collection of critical writing. The articles are grouped into categories that include 'How We Got Here,' 'Trends and Tendencies,' 'Defining YA,' and 'Censorship Near and Far.' . . . Campbell's Scoop is a solidly useful professional title that weighs in on a diversity of topics. Unlike professional books that discuss and recommend specific YA titles, Campbell's Scoop is timeless. The information will not become dated and the breadth of the articles makes the collection relevant to a wide audience." Voice Youth Advocates

Includes bibliographical references

Civil disobedience; edited and with an introduction by Harold Bloom; volume editor, Blake Hobby. Bloom's Literary Criticism 2010 274p (Bloom's literary themes) $45

Grades: 10 11 12 **809**

1. Passive resistance 2. Resistance to government 3. Literature—History and criticism

ISBN 978-1-60413-439-1; 1-60413-439-9

LC 2009-38087

The essays in this compilation explore "classical works of literature—novels, plays, short stories, letters, or speeches—with a common thematic thread. Sources analyzed in *Civil Disobedience* include excerpts from George Orwell's *1984*, Herman Melville's 'Bartleby, the Scrivener,' Arthur Miller's *The Crucible*, and speeches by Malcolm X." SLJ

Includes bibliographical references

Enslavement and emancipation; edited and with an introduction by Harold Bloom; volume editor, Blake Hobby. Bloom's Literary Criticism 2010 288p (Bloom's literary themes) $45

Grades: 10 11 12 **809**

1. Slavery in literature 2. Literature—History and criticism

ISBN 978-1-60413-441-4 LC 2009-38089

The essays in this compilation "explore classical works of literature—novels, plays, short stories, letters, or speeches—with a common thematic thread. . . . Excerpts in *Enslavement and Emancipation* discuss Toni Morrison's *Beloved*, the Declaration of Independence, various slave narratives, and some of Elie Wiesel's novels." SLJ

Includes glossary and bibliographical references

Foster, Brett

Rome; [by] Brett Foster and Hal Marcovitz; introduction by Harold Bloom. Chelsea House 2005 197p il map (Bloom's literary places) $40

Grades: 9 10 11 12 **809**

1. Rome (Italy) 2. Literary landmarks

ISBN 0-7910-7839-6; 978-0-7910-7839-6

LC 2005-13294

This guide to the city of Rome focuses on the places within it that have had an impact on literature. "Rome, the eternal city, boasts a long and rich literary history with strong connections to the English Romantic poets Keats and Shelley, as well as Stendhal, Goethe, and Henry James." Publisher's note

Includes bibliographical references

Herz, Sarah K.

From Hinton to Hamlet; building bridges between young adult literature and the classics; [by] Sarah K. Herz and Donald R. Gallo. 2nd ed., rev. and expanded. Greenwood Press 2005 256p $39.95

Grades: Adult Professional **809**

1. Young adult literature—Study and teaching 2. Youth—Books and reading

ISBN 0-313-32452-2 LC 2005-12728

First published 1996

"Aimed at teachers and librarians, the text offers personal experiences, testimonials, data, and theory for incorporating young adult literature into classrooms. . . . This resource is a must-have for all school libraries." Voice Youth Advocates

Includes bibliographical references

Highet, Gilbert, 1906-1978

The classical tradition; Greek and Roman influences on Western literature. Oxford Univ. Press 1949 xxxviii, 764p pa $29.95 hardcover o.p.

Grades: 11 12 Adult **809**

1. Literature—History and criticism 2. Comparative literature 3. Classical literature

ISBN 0-19-500206-7

"The twenty-four chapters fall into four main sections. The first takes in the Dark and Middle Ages—Anglo-Saxon poetry and prose, French epic and romance, Dante, Petrarch, Boccaccio, Chaucer. The second section comprises eight chapters on the Renaissance—drama, epic, pastoral and romance, lyric, the literature of translation, Rabelais, Montaigne. . . . [The] third section [is] 'The Baroque Age.' . . . After baroque, we come to our fourth and last section, the romantic, or . . . the revolutionary period 'and afterwards.'" Spectator

Includes bibliographical references

Holocaust literature; an encyclopedia of writers and their work; S. Lillian Kremer, editor. Routledge 2002 2v set $455

Grades: 11 12 Adult **809**

1. Holocaust, 1933-1945, in literature

ISBN 0-415-92985-7 LC 2002-23694

"This encyclopedia synthesizes a wide range of literary voices and provides a compelling look at more than 300 novelists, poets, memoirists, dramatists, and other writers who experienced the Holocaust or otherwise integrated the subject into their works." Publisher's note

Includes bibliographical references

Kurian, George Thomas

Timetables of world literature. Facts on File 2003 457p $65 *

Grades: 11 12 Adult **809**

1. Literature—Chronology

ISBN 0-8160-4197-0 LC 2002-3891

Chronicles world literature from the Classical Age through the twentieth century, discussing literary developments and the relationship between literature and the political and social climate of each historical period

"This comprehensive reference . . . helps academic researchers place major works of literature from 58 countries in historical and cultural context." Libr J

Includes bibliographical references

Literary movements for students; presenting analysis, context, and criticism on literary movements; David Galens, project editor. Gale Group 2002 2v il set $185

Grades: 11 12 Adult **809**

1. Literature—History and criticism

ISBN 0-7876-6517-7 LC 2002-10928

Literary movements for students—*Continued*

Entries provide "historical background information on each movement as well as modern critical interpretation of each movement's characteristic styles and themes. Approximately 25 movements are covered, including absurdism, Greek drama, modernism, science fiction/fantasy, surrealism and many others." Publisher's note

Includes bibliographical references

Literature and its times; profiles of 300 notable literary works and the historical events that influenced them. Gale Res. 1997 5v set $741 *

Grades: 11 12 Adult   **809**
1. Literature—History and criticism
ISBN 0-7876-0606-5   LC 97-34339
Also available supplement $293 (ISBN 0-7876-6550-9)

Edited by Joyce Moss and George Wilson

"The editors chose the selections (fiction, poetry, short stories, plays, biographies, and speeches) with the input of public libraries and secondary-school teachers. . . . Each volume covers a time range subdivided by dates and a general description . . . and begins with a brief overview of the historical events of the era, with a timeline providing a synopsis of each period." Libr J

Literature of developing nations for students; Michael L. LaBlanc, Elizabeth Bellalouna, and Ira Mark Milne, editors. Gale Group 2000 2v set $160

Grades: 11 12 Adult   **809**
1. Fiction—History and criticism 2. Developing countries in literature
ISBN 0-7876-4928-7   LC 00-56023
"Each entry begins with an introduction of a few paragraphs to the author and specific novel and then . . . provides plot summary and analysis. Excerpts from essays and articles about the novel are provided . . . and short summaries of major characters, an overview of important themes, historical context, a critical overview, and a bibliography are also included." Libr J

Includes bibliographical references

Literature of the Holocaust; edited and with an introduction by Harold Bloom. Chelsea House 2003 325p (Bloom's period studies) lib bdg $37.95

Grades: 9 10 11 12   **809**
1. Holocaust, 1933-1945, in literature
ISBN 0-7910-7677-6   LC 2003-16888
Contents: The Holocaust in the stories of Elie Wiesel, by T. A. Idinopulos; The problematics of Holocaust literature, by A. H. Rosenfeld; Tragedy and the Holocaust, by R. Skloot; Holocaust documentary fiction: novelist as eyewitness, by J. E. Young; Holocaust and autobiography: Wiesel, Friedländer, Pisar, by J. Sungolowsky; The Holocaust, by D. E. Lipstadt; Primo Levi and the language of witness, by M. Tager; The Utopian space of a nightmare: the diary of Anne Frank, by B. Chiarello; The literature of Auschwitz, by L. L. Langer; Comedic distance in Holocaust literature, by M. Cory; Public memory and its discontents, by G. H. Hartman; Two Holocaust voices: Cynthia Ozick and Art Spiegelman, by L. L. Langer; The Holocaust and literary studies, by J. M.

Peck; Rafael Seligmann's Rubinsteins Versteigerung: the German-Jewish family novel before and after the Holocaust, by R. Robertson; Memorizing memory, by A. Hungerford

Includes bibliographical references

Magill's survey of world literature; edited by Steven G. Kellman. Rev ed. Salem Press 2009 6v il set $499

Grades: 11 12 Adult   **809**
1. Literature—History and criticism 2. Literature—Bio-bibliography 3. Reference books
ISBN 978-1-58765-431-2   LC 2008-46042
First published 1992 under the editorship of Frank Northen Magill

This set "profiles 380 writers in fiction, drama, poetry, and nonfiction. . . . [Each essay] presents biographical and critical analysis. An author's most important works usually are highlighted. Volume 6 contains a glossary, categorical list of authors by gender, identity, etc.; geographical index of authors' countries of origin; and author and title indexes. The essay format includes name, birth and death dates, a statement explaining the writer's literary merit, and examination of key works." Choice

"A solid choice for anyone in need of an inexpensive, broad biocritical literary reference title on world literature." Libr J

Includes glossary and bibliographical references

Masterpieces of world literature; edited by Frank N. Magill. Harper & Row 1989 957p $55

Grades: 8 9 10 11 12 Adult   **809**
1. Literature—History and criticism
ISBN 0-06-270050-2   LC 89-45052
"The work, arranged alphabetically by title, contains plot summaries, character portrayals, and critical evaluations of 270 classics of world literature (novels, plays, stories, poems, and essays), all reprints from other Magill guides." Nichols. Guide to Ref Books for Sch Media Cent. 4th edition

Ruud, Jay

Encyclopedia of medieval literature. Facts on File 2005 734p (Facts on File library of world literature) $75

Grades: 11 12 Adult   **809**
1. Medieval literature—Encyclopedias 2. Reference books
ISBN 0-8160-5497-5   LC 2004-31066
"Each article focuses on key authors, characters, titles, and aspects of works that exemplify the importance of the Middle Ages. The selections are from Europe and Asia and represent various cultural backgrounds. . . . Individuals interested in a source of basic information from which to begin a study of the Middle Ages will find this volume to be especially useful." Am Ref Books Annu, 2006

Includes bibliographical references

Snodgrass, Mary Ellen
Encyclopedia of Gothic literature. Facts on File 2005 480p (Facts on File library of world literature) $65
Grades: 11 12 Adult **809**
1. Gothic revival literature
ISBN 0-8160-5528-9 LC 2004-46986
"This encyclopedia examines the literature in alphabetical entries that describe people, places, works, literary and psychological terms, characters, subgenres, and concepts." SLJ
This is a "solid, very readable and essential contribution to the field of literary genre reference materials." Am Ref Books Annu, 2005
Includes bibliographical references

Stripling, Mahala Yates
Bioethics and medical issues in literature. Greenwood Press 2005 xxviii, 224p (Exploring social issues through literature) $49.95
Grades: 9 10 11 12 **809**
1. Fiction—History and criticism 2. Medicine in literature 3. Ethics in literature
ISBN 0-313-32040-3 LC 2005-1493
"Chapters look at such . . . topics as technology's creature, illness and culture, and end of life issues, with each chapter offering a close examination of two major literary works." Publisher's note
Includes bibliographical references

Whitson, Kathy J.
Encyclopedia of feminist literature. Greenwood Press 2004 300p $65 *
Grades: 11 12 Adult **809**
1. Feminism in literature 2. American literature—Women authors—Bio-bibliography 3. English literature—Women authors—Bio-bibliography 4. Reference books
ISBN 0-313-32731-9 LC 2004-42478
"The women authors included in this volume range from the very familiar—Toni Morrison and Virginia Woolf—to the less well-known—Judith Ortiz Cofer and Shirley Geok-Lin Lim. Nearly 70 writers are represented with an additional 22 'topic' entries on subjects ranging from abolition to the 'woman question.' Author entries include biographical information, major works, and an analysis of at least one work." Libr J
Includes bibliographical references

Women in literature; reading through the lens of gender; edited by Jerilyn Fisher and Ellen S. Silber; foreword by David Sadker. Greenwood Press 2003 xxxix, 358p $65
Grades: 9 10 11 12 **809**
1. Women in literature 2. Literature—History and criticism
ISBN 0-313-31346-6 LC 2002-35212
This is a "collection of two- to three-page signed essays looking at 96 works of fiction (both canonical works and newer/less familiar titles) . . . The literary works run the gamut from Homer and William Shakespeare to Alice Walker and Amy Tan. . . . Teachers looking for ways to shake up their traditional reading

lists and students looking for a different approach to some classics will find this book of interest." SLJ
Includes bibliographical references

Yagoda, Ben
Memoir; a history. Riverhead Books 2009 291p $25.95
Grades: 11 12 Adult **809**
1. Autobiography
ISBN 978-1-59448-886-3; 1-59448-886-X
LC 2009-30859
The author "traces the memoir from its birth in early Christian writings and Roman generals' journals . . . [through the] year of 2007." Publisher's note
"With its mixture of literary criticism, cultural history and just enough trivia, Yagoda's survey is sure to appeal to scholars and bibliophiles alike." Publ Wkly
Includes bibliographical references

809.1 Poetry—History and criticism

Arana, R. Victoria
The Facts on File companion to world poetry; 1900 to the present. Facts on File 2008 532p (Facts on File library of world literature) $85
Grades: 11 12 Adult **809.1**
1. Poetry—History and criticism 2. Reference books
ISBN 978-0-8160-6457-1 LC 2007-1831
"Arana classifies world poetry in broad terms, excluding only those poets from Britain, Ireland, and the US. This volume contains signed entries of moderate length that describe recognized and anthologized poets, significant individual poems, and related aesthetic movements (e.g., French rap, colonialism, hip-hop). . . . The volume's ease of use and inclusion of contemporary poets and movements make it a useful addition to most collections." Choice
Includes bibliographical references

Bloom, Harold, 1930-
Poets and poems. Chelsea House Publishers 2005 487p (Bloom's literary criticism 20th anniversary collection) $38.95
Grades: 9 10 11 12 **809.1**
1. Poetry—History and criticism
ISBN 0-7910-8225-3 LC 2005-8636
"In this volume, Bloom considers poets Emily Dickinson, Walt Whitman, Hart Crane, William Shakespeare, Samuel Taylor Coleridge, William Butler Yeats, and many others." Publisher's note

Classic writings on poetry; edited by William Harmon. Columbia University Press 2003 538p $79; pa $27.50
Grades: 11 12 Adult **809.1**
1. Poetry—History and criticism
ISBN 0-231-12370-1; 0-231-12371-X (pa)
LC 2003-40917
This anthology contains "writing on poetry by such philosophical royalty as Plato, Aristotle, Milton, Sir Philip Sidney, Wordsworth, and Emily Dickinson. Readers

Classic writings on poetry—*Continued*
are given a peek through the hole of history's fence into
the lives and worlds of our poetic geniuses and reminded
of the poem's matchless role in conveying reverence, remembering wars, recording history, entertaining, expressing deep emotion, and above all, allowing the finite
mind, for one moment, to contain infinity." Libr J
Includes bibliographical references

Johanson, Paula
World poetry, "evidence of life". Enslow
Publishers 2010 160p il (Poetry rocks!) lib bdg
$34.60
Grades: 9 10 11 12   **809.1**
1. Poetry—History and criticism 2. Poetry—Author-
ship
ISBN 978-0-7660-3280-4; 0-7660-3280-9
                                                    LC 2009-44156
The author discusses "some of the poetry of famed
world poets, including: Sin-leqi-unninni, Vyasa, Homer,
Du Fu, Omar Khayyam, Rumi, Dante, Bashō,
Shevchenko, Tagore, Ahkmatova, Lorca, Neruda,
Walcott, and Cohen." Publisher's note
Includes glossary and bibliographical references

Planet on the table; poets on the reading life;
editors, Sharon Bryan & William Olsen.
Sarabande Bks. 2003 361p il (Writer's studio)
pa $16.95
Grades: 11 12 Adult   **809.1**
1. Poetry—History and criticism 2. Books and reading
ISBN 1-88933-091-4   LC 2002-7234
In this collection of essays, such writers as Maxine
Kumin, Jacqueline Osherow, Edward Hirsch, and Campbell McGrath discuss their personal reading habits as
well as their thoughts on various works of literary criticism
This is a "vital and illuminating collection. . . . In all,
25 poets share their love for and insights into the fine art
of reading in this glowing sphere of an anthology."
Booklist
Includes bibliographical references

Schwedt, Rachel E., 1944-
Young adult poetry; a survey and theme guide;
[by] Rachel Schwedt and Janice DeLong; foreword
by Mel Glenn. Greenwood Press 2002 192p
$49.95
Grades: 9 10 11 12   **809.1**
1. Poetry—History and criticism 2. Teenagers—Books
and reading
ISBN 0-313-31336-9   LC 2001-33719
This resource features an annotated bibliography of
198 poetry volumes and a thematic guide to over 6000
individual poems. Works span the reading levels from
sixth to twelfth grade and range in style
"This book will certainly help with decisions about
adding specific poetry anthologies to classrooms and library shelves, and, most importantly, knowing the grade
levels for which they are intended." SLJ
Includes bibliographical references

809.2   Drama—History and criticism

Bloom, Harold, 1930-
Dramatists and dramas. Chelsea House
Publishers 2005 306p (Bloom's literary criticism
20th anniversary collection) $38.95
Grades: 9 10 11 12   **809.2**
1. Drama—History and criticism
ISBN 0-7910-8226-1   LC 2005-3094
"Bloom's coverage ranges from the Ancient Greeks to
modern day and includes writers like Aristophanes,
Shakespeare, Moliere, Anton Chekhov, Tennessee Wil-
liams, and Arthur Miller." Publisher's note

Critical survey of drama; edited by Carl Rollyson.
2nd rev ed. Salem Press 2003 8v set $499
Grades: 11 12 Adult   **809.2**
1. Reference books 2. Drama—Dictionaries
3. English drama—Dictionaries 4. American drama—
Dictionaries
ISBN 1-58765-102-5   LC 2003-2190
"Combines, updates, and expands two earlier Salem
Press reference sets: Critical survey of drama, revised
edition, English language series, published in 1994, and
Critical survey of drama, foreign language series, published in 1986." Preface
This set contains "about 630 essays, of which 570 discuss individual dramatists and 60 cover overview topics.
. . . Each essay on a dramatist provides . . . material as
birth and death dates, lists of the author's major dramatic
works (with dates of first production and publication).
Each essay opens with a brief survey of the author's
publications in literary forms other than drama, a summary of the writer's professional achievements and
awards, an extended biographical sketch that centers on
the writer's development as a dramatist, and an extensive
critical analysis of the writer's major dramatic works.
Following this discussion is a list of major publications
in fields other than drama and an annotated bibliography
of critical works about the author." Publisher's note
Includes bibliographical references

Griffiths, Trevor R., 1949-
The Ivan R. Dee guide to plays and playwrights.
Ivan R. Dee 2003 424p il pa $28.95
Grades: 11 12 Adult   **809.2**
1. Reference books 2. Theater—Dictionaries
3. Drama—Dictionaries
ISBN 1-566-63566-7   LC 2003-70127
First published 2003 in the United Kingdom with title:
The theatre guide
This guide "contains biographical sketches and critical
commentary about more than 550 playwrights and their
plays. Griffiths emphasizes the writers rather than their
works and includes only those likely to be produced
nowadays." Choice
This book "provides something that similar guides often omit: scribes, however obscure, who are being published and produced today. . . . Readers will find big
names like George Abbott, Aeschylus, and Edward Albee
as well as newcomers like Welsh dramatist Gary Owen
and Briton Amanda Whittington." Libr J

Patterson, Michael
The Oxford dictionary of plays. Oxford University Press 2005 xxxv, 523p $50 *
Grades: 11 12 Adult   **809.2**
1. Reference books 2. Drama—Dictionaries
ISBN 0-19-860417-3   LC 2004-23698
This is a "digest of 1000 works that span the history of theater from Aristophanes to Michael Frayn's Democracy (2003). The entries, which run between 200 and 400 words, include the date and place of first performance, genre (descriptions of which are included in the preface), setting, cast required, and a synopsis of the action with a one-paragraph assessment of the play." Libr J
Includes bibliographical references

809.3   Fiction—History and criticism

Bloom, Harold, 1930-
Novelists and novels. Chelsea House Publishers 2005 588p (Bloom's literary criticism 20th anniversary collection) $38.95
Grades: 9 10 11 12   **809.3**
1. Fiction—History and criticism
ISBN 0-7910-8227-X   LC 2005-3269
The author discusses "the world's great novelists including Miguel de Cervantes, Charles Dickens, Jane Austen, Franz Kafka, Ernest Hemingway, William Faulkner, and more." Publisher's note
Includes bibliographical references

Short story writers and short stories. Chelsea House Publishers 2005 188p (Bloom's literary criticism 20th anniversary collection) $38.95
Grades: 9 10 11 12   **809.3**
1. Short stories—History and criticism
ISBN 0-7910-8228-8   LC 2005-6399
This book contains the author's "considerations on those writers who shaped the art of the short story; [including] Guy de Maupassant, Edgar Allan Poe, and Sherwood Anderson." Publisher's note

Hooper, Brad
The short story readers' advisory; a guide for librarians. American Lib. Assn. 2000 135p pa $32
Grades: 11 12 Adult   **809.3**
1. Short stories—History and criticism
ISBN 0-8389-0782-2   LC 99-85751
This work contains over 200 critical essays covering short story authors past and present. A step-by-step guide on how to interview readers in order to match their tastes with appropriate stories is included.
Includes bibliographical references

Mystery and suspense writers; the literature of crime, detection, and espionage; Robin W. Winks, editor in chief; Maureen Corrigan, associate editor. Scribner 1998 2v set $250
Grades: 11 12 Adult   **809.3**
1. Reference books 2. Spies in literature
ISBN 0-684-80521-9   LC 98-36812

"Articles on 68 mystery writers ranging from Edgar Allen Poe to Sarah Paretsky run from ten to 20 pages and include information on the life and works as well as solid bibliographies for each author." Libr J

Short story writers; edited by Charles E. May. Rev. ed. Salem Press 2008 3v il (Magill's choice) set $217 *
Grades: 9 10 11 12 Adult   **809.3**
1. Short stories—History and criticism
ISBN 978-1-58765-389-6   LC 2007-32789
First published 1997
This set "covers writers from Giovanni Boccaccio and Geoffrey Chaucer to Anton Chekhov and Sandra Cisneros. . . . Readers, whether in need of a brief critical overview or in search of what to read next, will find this set extremely useful. Each entry includes a brief biography, a list of principal works, a note on other literary forms the author explored, and a concise list of achievements as well as brief essays . . . on particular stories." SLJ
Includes bibliographical references

810.3   American literature— Encyclopedias and dictionaries

Encyclopedia of American literature. 2nd ed. Facts on File 2008 4v il (Facts on File library of American literature) set $375 *
Grades: 11 12 Adult   **810.3**
1. Reference books 2. American literature—Encyclopedias
ISBN 978-0-8160-6476-2   LC 2007-25662
First published 2002
Contents: vol. I. Settlement to the New Republic, 1607-1815 / revised and augmented by Susan Clair Imbarrato; vol. II. The age of Romanticism and realism, 1816-1895 / revised and augmented by Brett Barney; vol. III. Into the modern, 1896-1945 / revised and augmented by George Parker Anderson, Judith S. Baughman, Matthew J. Bruccoli; vol. IV. The contemporary world, 1946 to the present / revised and augmented by Marshall Boswell
Entries in this encyclopedia cover works, writers, movements and other American literature-related topics from colonial times to the present. Each volume includes a chronology.
Includes bibliographical references

The **Greenwood** encyclopedia of multiethnic American literature. Greenwood Press 2005 5v il set $499.95 *
Grades: 11 12 Adult   **810.3**
1. Reference books 2. American literature—Encyclopedias 3. Minorities—Encyclopedias
ISBN 0-313-33059-X   LC 2005-18960
This encyclopedia contains "more than 1100 entries, approximately 1000 of them devoted to individual authors. The remaining entries describe relevant literary topics (e.g., The Blues, Tricksters), key literary works (e.g., The Bluest Eye, Tracks), and other relevant topics (e.g., Holocaust narratives)." Libr J
"A comprehensive set unique in its scope, this ency-

The Greenwood encyclopedia of multiethnic American literature—*Continued*

clopedia is an excellent foundational resource that adds much to the growing field of ethnic American literature." Choice

Includes bibliographical references

Hart, James David, 1911-1990

The Oxford companion to American literature; [by] James D. Hart; with revisions and additions by Phillip W. Leininger. 6th ed. Oxford Univ. Press 1995 779p $49.95 *

Grades: 11 12 Adult   **810.3**

1. Reference books 2. American literature—Dictionaries

ISBN 0-19-506548-4   LC 94-45727

First published 1941

In addition to over 2000 entries for individual authors and more than 1,100 for important works this reference includes entries for literary movements, awards, magazines, printers, book collectors and newspapers. A chronological index of literary and social history is appended.

The Oxford encyclopedia of American literature; Jay Parini, editor-in-chief. Oxford University Press 2004 4v il set $495 *

Grades: 11 12 Adult   **810.3**

1. Reference books 2. American literature—Encyclopedias

ISBN 0-19-515653-6   LC 2002-156325

This set "provides a wealth of reliable information on standard bearers of American literature in an easy-on-the-eyes format for students and general readers." SLJ

810.8   American literature— Collections

911: the book of help; edited by Michael Cart; with Marianne Carus and Marc Aronson. Cricket Bks. 2002 178p $17.95; pa $9.95

Grades: 8 9 10 11 12   **810.8**

1. September 11 terrorist attacks, 2001 2. Terrorism 3. American literature—Collections

ISBN 0-8126-2659-1; 0-8126-2676-1 (pa)   LC 2002-4707

"A Marcato book"

A collection of essays, poems, and short fiction, created in response to the terrorist attacks of September 11, 2001. Contributors include Katherine Paterson, Joan Bauer, Walter Dean Myers, Nikki Giovanni, Arnold Adoff, and Russell Freedman

This "stands out for its rich prose, its unusual reporting, its search for context, its reminder of wonders." NY Times Book Rev

The Chronology of American literature; America's literary achievements from the colonial era to modern times; edited by Daniel S. Burt. Houghton Mifflin 2004 805p il $40

Grades: 11 12 Adult   **810.8**

1. American literature—Collections

ISBN 0-618-16821-4   LC 2003-51142

"This chronology includes more than 8,400 literary works by more than 5,000 writers. Sections for each year are grouped in five chapters by period, from 1582 to 1999. Within each year, entries are grouped by genre, such as diaries and other personal writings, fiction, essays, literary criticism and scholarship, nonfiction, poetry, and drama. Within each genre, authors are listed alphabetically, generally with birth and death dates and short descriptions of named works for the year. . . . *The Chronology of American Literature* is easy to browse and, for book lovers, difficult to put down." Booklist

Includes bibliographical references

Crossing into America; the new literature of immigration; edited by Louis Mendoza and S. Shankar. New Press (NY) 2003 xxvi, 365p hardcover o.p. pa $18.95

Grades: 11 12 Adult   **810.8**

1. American literature—Collections 2. Immigrants

ISBN 1-56584-720-2; 1-56584-895-0 (pa)   LC 2002-41055

"This anthology includes a few poems and some fictional works, but most of the selections are memoirs. The political oppression and economic desperation that prompted immigration to the United States as well as the prejudice and discrimination that people often face once they arrive here are addressed in many of the pieces." SLJ

"A beautiful piece by Cuban American Achy Obejas captures the intergenerational conflict without heroics, and there are electrifying selections from Sandra Cisneros, Jamaica Kincaid, and other famous writers as well as some exciting new voices." Booklist

Includes bibliographical references

Crossing the danger water; three hundred years of African-American writing; edited and with an introduction by Deirdre Mullane. Anchor Bks. (NY) 1993 xxii, 769p pa $20

Grades: 11 12 Adult   **810.8**

1. American literature—African American authors—Collections

ISBN 0-385-42243-1   LC 93-17194

This anthology "includes fiction, autobiography, poetry, songs, and letters by such writers as Frederick Douglass, Sojourner Truth, W.E.B. Du Bois, Zora Neale Hurston, and Richard Wright. Many topics are covered, from slavery, education, the Civil War, Reconstruction, and political issues to spirituals, songs of the Civil Rights movement, and rap music." Libr J

Includes bibliographical references

GirlSpoken: from pen, brush & tongue; edited by Jessica Hein, Heather Holland and Carol Kauppi. Second Story Press 2007 202p il pa $18.95

Grades: 9 10 11 12   **810.8**

1. Teenagers' writings 2. Girls—Poetry

ISBN 978-1-897187-30-2; 1-897187-30-0

"This collection of poetry, short prose, and art is the culmination of a Canadian research and action project designed to effect change by giving creative voice to teen girls. The book is divided into sections with four central themes: Voice, Beauty, Strength, and Becoming. . . . This collection is a welcome addition to the teen

GirlSpoken: from pen, brush & tongue—*Continued*
poetry genre and will appeal to teen girls who enjoy expressing themselves through creative writing and art."
Voice Youth Advocates

Includes bibliographical references

Growing up Latino; memoirs and stories; edited with an introduction by Harold Augenbraum and Ilan Stavans; foreword by Ilan Stavans. Houghton Mifflin 1993 xxix, 344p pa $15 hardcover o.p.
Grades: 6 7 8 9 10   **810.8**
1. American literature—Hispanic American authors—Collections
ISBN 0-395-66124-2   LC 92-32624
"A Marc Jaffe book"
A collection of short stories and excerpts from novels and memoirs written by twenty-five Latino authors. Among the contributors are Julia Alvarez, Oscar Hijuelos, Denise Chávez, Rolando Hinojosa, and Sandra Cisneros.

Includes bibliographical references

Guys write for Guys Read; edited by Jon Scieszka. Viking 2005 272p il $16.99; pa $11.99
Grades: 6 7 8 9 10   **810.8**
1. American literature—Collections
ISBN 0-670-06007-0; 0-670-01144-4 (pa)
          LC 2004-28984
This is a collection of short stories, essays, columns, cartoons, anecdotes, and artwork by such writers and illustrators as Brian Jacques, Jerry Spinelli, Chris Crutcher, Mo Willems, Chris Van Allsburg, Matt Groening, and Neil Gaiman, selected by voters at the Guys Read web site.
This is "a diverse and fast-paced anthology . . . that deserves a permanent place in any collection . . . . There's something undeniably grand about this collective celebration of the intellectual life of the common boy." SLJ

I thought my father was God and other true tales from the National Story Project; edited and introduced by Paul Auster; Nelly Reifler, assistant editor. Holt & Co. 2001 xxi, 383p il hardcover o.p. pa $15
Grades: 11 12 Adult   **810.8**
1. American literature—Collections
ISBN 0-8050-6714-0; 0-312-42100-1 (pa)
          LC 00-54397
"In 1999, novelist Paul Auster . . . and the hosts of National Public Radio's All Things Considered asked listeners to send in true stories to be read on-air as part of the National Story Project. Auster received more than 4,000 submissions; the 180 best are published here." Publ Wkly
"These are stop-you-in-your-tracks stories about hair-raising coincidences, miracles, tragedies, redemption, and moments of pure hilarity." Booklist

Jewish American literature; a Norton anthology; [compiled and edited by] Jules Chametzky [et al.] Norton 2000 xxiv, 1221p il $39.95
Grades: 11 12 Adult   **810.8**
1. American literature—Jewish authors 2. American literature—Collections
ISBN 0-393-04809-8   LC 00-55393
The editors have attempted "to encompass Jewish literature from 1654 to the present in this collection of poems, cartoons, sermons, diaries, letters, stories, speeches, plays, prayers, novel excerpts, and critical writings either translated from Hebrew or Yiddish or written in English. Major sections group the literature chronologically to help identify large movements. . . . This great anthology is essential for Jewish studies and American literature collections." Libr J

Includes bibliographical references

The **Norton** anthology of African American literature; Henry Louis Gates, Jr., general editor, Nellie Y. McKay, general editor. 2nd ed. Norton 2003 2800p 2 computer laser optical discs pa $70.30 *
Grades: 11 12 Adult   **810.8**
1. American literature—African American authors—Collections
ISBN 0-393-97778-1   LC 2003-66176
First published 1996
"The anthology is divided into seven sections, each with a separate introduction giving the sociopolitical factors that impacted on the material included therein. Featured are 120 writers, 52 of whom are women, richly representing African American vernacular literature, poetry, drama, short stories, novels, slave narratives, and autobiographies." Libr J [review of 1996 edition]

Includes bibliographical references

The **Norton** anthology of Latino literature; Ilan Stavans, general editor; [editors], Edna Acosta-Belen [et al.] W.W. Norton & Co. 2010 2489p il map $59.95
Grades: 11 12 Adult   **810.8**
1. American literature—Hispanic American authors—Collections
ISBN 978-0-393-08007-0; 0-393-08007-2
          LC 2010-15108
"This anthology encompasses Latino literature in various genres from authors of Chicano, Mexican, Cuban, Dominican, and Puerto Rican heritages, among others. General editor Stavans . . . and other scholars have anthologized 201 authors, who range from José Martí and William Carlos Williams to Isabel Allende, Julia Alvarez, and Junot Díaz." Libr J
"With a great array of writers celebrated and too little known, and invaluable supporting materials, this grand and affecting treasury of culturally rich and aesthetically dynamic poems, fiction, drama, letters, diaries, and essays illuminates every aspect of Latino life." Booklist

Includes bibliographical references

The **Oxford** book of women's writing in the United States; edited by Linda Wagner-Martin, Cathy N. Davidson. Oxford Univ. Press 1995 596p pa $27.50 hardcover o.p. *

Grades: 11 12 Adult   **810.8**
1. American literature—Women authors—Collections
ISBN 0-19-513245-9 (pa)   LC 95-1499

This anthology provides "samples of the public and private work of 99 women of diverse racial and ethnic backgrounds who write in English and were born in or have lived in the United States over the past four centuries. They include short fiction (almost half of the book), poems, essays, plays, and speeches but have also gone beyond traditional genre categories to include performance pieces, erotica, diaries, letters, and recipes." Libr J

A **Patriot's** handbook; songs, poems, stories, and speeches celebrating the land we love; selected and introduced by Caroline Kennedy. Hyperion 2003 xxiii, 663p il $27.95; pa $16.95

Grades: 11 12 Adult   **810.8**
1. Patriotism 2. American literature—Collections
ISBN 0-7868-6918-6; 1-4013-0707-1 (pa)
                                        LC 2003-49983

In this compilation of prose and poetry, "Kennedy arranges her material into chapters based on general themes, including the flag, portraits of Americans, freedom, and equality. The first selection is the lyrics to the national anthem, and the last one is an excerpt from the fiction of highly esteemed contemporary writer Annie Proulx; selections in between include George Washington's 'Farewell Address,' Sojourner Truth's speech 'Ain't I a Woman,' the text of *Brown v. the Board of Education,* and the words to the Grateful Dead's song 'U.S. Blues.' Kennedy provides a general introduction to the book and introduces each chapter. For personal enjoyment and education, but the reference value is obvious, too." Booklist

The **Portable** sixties reader; edited by Ann Charters. Penguin Bks. 2003 xli, 628p il pa $16 *

Grades: 11 12 Adult   **810.8**
1. United States—History—1961-1974 2. American literature—Collections
ISBN 0-14-200194-5   LC 2002-32266

This reader includes "essays, poetry, and fiction under thematic subjects, such as civil rights; women's rights; the sexual revolution; environmental issues; the antiwar, free-speech, and black-arts movements; and the use of drugs in pursuit of enlightenment. . . . [Includes works by] James Baldwin, Thomas Merton, Susan Sontag, Gary Snyder, Allen Ginsburg, Rachel Carson, Kate Millett, Nikki Giovanni, and many more." Booklist

Includes bibliographical references

Rising voices; writings of young Native Americans; selected by Arlene B. Hirschfelder and Beverly R. Singer. Random House 1993 c1992 131p pa $6.99 *

Grades: 5 6 7 8 9 10   **810.8**
1. American literature—Native American authors—Collections 2. Native Americans 3. Children's writings
ISBN 0-8041-1167-7

First published 1992 by Scribner

A collection of poems and essays in which young Native Americans speak of their identity, their families and communities, rituals, and the harsh realities of their lives.

Sidman, Joyce, 1956-
The world according to dog; poems and teen voices; with photographs by Doug Mindell. Houghton Mifflin 2003 71p il hardcover o.p. pa $7.95

Grades: 8 9 10 11 12   **810.8**
1. Dogs 2. Teenagers' writings 3. American literature—Collections
ISBN 0-618-17497-4; 0-618-28381-1 (pa)
                                        LC 2002-476

A collection of poems about dogs is accompanied by essays by young people about the dogs in their lives
"The teen essays are heartfelt and honest. . . . Sidman's poetic form is succinct, evoking images, memories, and even smells. . . . Readers of all ages who appreciate their canine companions will thoroughly enjoy this slim book." Voice Youth Advocates

Sister to sister; women write about the unbreakable bond; edited by Patricia Foster. Doubleday 1995 354p hardcover o.p. pa $12.95

Grades: 11 12 Adult   **810.8**
1. American literature—Women authors—Collections
ISBN 0-385-47128-9; 0-385-47129-7 (pa)
                                        LC 95-10486

"Contributors to this volume include bell hooks, Robin Behn, Letty Cottin Pogrebin, and Joy Williams. The essays, while all centering on the themes of sisterly relationships, run the literary gamut. Fanciful fiction pieces are included, as are straightforward autobiographical anecdotes and a couple of critical essays. Any library with a demand for contemporary women's literature should have this collection." Libr J

Things I have to tell you; poems and writing by teenage girls; edited by Betsy Franco; photographs by Nina Nickles. Candlewick Press 2001 63p il hardcover o.p. pa $8.99

Grades: 7 8 9 10   **810.8**
1. Teenagers' writings 2. Girls 3. American literature—Collections
ISBN 0-7636-0905-6; 0-7636-1035-6 (pa)
                                        LC 99-46884

A collection of poems, stories, and essays written by girls twelve to eighteen years of age and revealing the secrets which enabled them to overcome the challenges they faced

War is--; soldiers, survivors, and storytellers talk about war; edited by Marc Aronson and Patty Campbell. Candlewick Press 2008 200p $17.99; pa $6.99

Grades: 8 9 10 11 12   **810.8**
1. War stories 2. War poetry 3. American literature—Collections
ISBN   978-0-76363-625-8;   0-76363-625-8; 978-0-7636-4231-0 (pa); 0-7636-4231-2 (pa)
                                        LC 2007-52026

An anthology of fiction, speeches, poems, and essays about war.

War is-—*Continued*

"With this collection, Aronson and Campbell have provided an uncommonly valuable source of hard information and perceptive insight." Booklist

Where we are, what we see; the best young artists and writers in America: a Push anthology; edited by David Levithan. PUSH/Scholastic 2005 220p il pa $7.99

Grades: 7 8 9 10 **810.8**

1. Teenagers' writings 2. American literature—Collections

ISBN 0-439-73646-3   LC 2005-296492

The "young writers and artists in this anthology have been selected from the winners of the Scholastic Art & Writing Awards program. The offerings range from an intense recollection, 'What Cancer Meant,' to a whimsical dictionary of words that don't exist but should. . . . This collection is a real boon for budding writers and artists, who will feel the encouragement and see the possibility of publication." Booklist

You hear me? poems and writing by teenage boys; edited by Betsy Franco. Candlewick Press 2000 107p hardcover o.p. pa $6.99

Grades: 7 8 9 10 **810.8**

1. Teenagers' writings 2. Boys 3. American literature—Collections

ISBN 0-7636-1158-1; 0-7636-1159-X (pa)

LC 99-57129

This is an "anthology of poems, essays, and stories written by young men aged twelve through twenty." Harv Educ Rev

"The voices range from painfully honest to playfully ironic, but all are controlled and powerful as they speak to subjects that teen readers will be familiar with." Voice Youth Advocates

810.9   American literature—History and criticism

Amend, Allison, 1974-

Hispanic-American writers. Chelsea House 2010 128p il (Multicultural voices) $35

Grades: 7 8 9 10 11 12 **810.9**

1. American literature—Hispanic American authors—History and criticism 2. Hispanic American authors

ISBN 978-1-60413-312-7; 1-60413-312-0

LC 2009-46535

Profiles notable Hispanic Americans and their work in the field of literature, including Sandra Cisneros, Julia Alvarez, and Junot Diaz.

"This volume opens with a succinct yet thorough introduction to the historical and cultural context of eight authors. The overview explains the origins and uses of the terms Chicano, Hispanic, and Latino and sketches the histories of the nations where most Hispanic-Americans have their roots. Amend also identifies common themes in Hispanic-American literature such as language and family; however, she also notes each community's unique concerns. . . . Amend also suggests books by other Latino writers for further reading." SLJ

Includes bibliographical references

The **American** renaissance; edited and with an introduction by Harold Bloom. Chelsea House 2003 370p (Bloom's period studies) $37.95

Grades: 9 10 11 12 **810.9**

1. American literature—History and criticism 2. United States—Intellectual life

ISBN 0-7910-7676-8   LC 2003-19991

"Ralph Waldo Emerson's transcendental writings influenced Henry David Thoreau and Walt Whitman, whose works are considered cornerstones of the American literary movement. This volume examines the impact of the American Renaissance on the Western canon of literature." Publisher's note

Includes bibliographical references

American women writers, 1900-1945; a bio-bibliographical critical sourcebook; edited by Laurie Champion; Emanuel S. Nelson, advisory editor. Greenwood Press 2000 407p $95

Grades: 11 12 Adult **810.9**

1. Reference books 2. American literature—Women authors—Bio-bibliography

ISBN 0-313-30943-4   LC 00-22336

"This reference book profiles 58 American women writers who published their significant works between 1900 and 1945. . . . The information is arranged in four sections: 'Biography,' 'Major Works and Themes,' 'Critical Reception,' and 'Bibliography.' . . . The biographical information is brief and includes the most basic details, while the overview of the major works and themes is quite substantive and will be very useful for research. 'Critical Reception,' considers reactions both at the time of publication and today. . . . This book will be a valuable tool for research because it balances coverage of the prominent and the lesser known." Booklist

Includes bibliographical references

Beat culture; lifestyles, icons, and impact; edited by William T. Lawlor. ABC-CLIO 2005 liv, 390p il $85

Grades: 9 10 11 12 **810.9**

1. Reference books 2. Beat generation—Encyclopedias

ISBN 1-85109-400-8   LC 2005-2772

"This volume covers the Beat Generation: the musicians, writers, and artists as well as the culture and history." Booklist

This "single-volume work is possibly the best overview of the topic for high school students." SLJ

Includes bibliographical references

The **Beat** generation; a Gale critical companion; Lynn M. Zott, project editor. Gale 2003 3v (Gale critical companion collection) set $350

Grades: 11 12 Adult **810.9**

1. American literature—History and criticism 2. Beat generation

ISBN 0-7876-7569-5   LC 2002-155786

"Volume 1 gathers a variety of sources that place the movement in cultural context. . . . Volumes 2-3 supply entries for 28 Beat authors. . . . Author entries include a brief biography, notes on major works and critical reception, a list of principal works, a selection of primary sources and secondary criticism, and further readings. . . . The selections include contributions by major Beat Generation scholars and provide a well-balanced, repre-

The Beat generation—*Continued*
sentative view of the Beats." Choice

Includes bibliographical references

The Butterfly's way; voices from the Haitian dyaspora [sic] in the United States; edited by Edwidge Danticat. Soho Press 2001 251p pa $15

Grades: 11 12 Adult   **810.9**
1. American literature—Haitian American authors—Collections
ISBN 1-56947-218-1   LC 00-64085

These "essays and poems talk about the pain and pride of young people who don't belong, both in Haiti and in their places of refuge. A landmark anthology." Booklist

Censored books [I]-II; critical viewpoints; edited by Nicholas J. Karolides, Lee Burress, John M. Kean. Scarecrow Press 1993-2001 2v v1 pa $39.50; v2 $45

Grades: 9 10 11 12   **810.9**
1. American literature—History and criticism 2. Censorship
ISBN 0-8108-4038-3 (v1); 0-8108-4147-9 (v2)

Volume two covering 1985-2000 edited by Nicholas J. Karolides

Authors, librarians, and teachers contribute essays in support of books that are frequently challenged. They examine each work as literature and assess its content relative to societal values

Davis, Cynthia J., 1964-
Women writers in the United States; a timeline of literary, cultural, and social history; [by] Cynthia Davis and Kathryn West. Oxford Univ. Press 1996 488p $60 *

Grades: 11 12 Adult   **810.9**
1. American literature—Women authors 2. American literature—Chronology 3. Women—United States
ISBN 0-19-509053-5   LC 95-31815

In a timeline format, the authors "present information on the full spectrum of women's writing—including fiction, poetry, biography, political manifestos, essays, advice columns, and cookbooks, alongside a chronology of developments in social and cultural history that are especially pertinent to women's lives." Publisher's note

Encyclopedia of African American women writers; edited by Yolanda Williams Page. Greenwood 2007 2v set $175

Grades: 11 12 Adult   **810.9**
1. Reference books 2. American literature—African American authors—Encyclopedias 3. American literature—Women authors—Encyclopedias
ISBN 0-313-33429-3; 978-0-313-33429-0
     LC 2006-31193

This "set covers over 150 African American women novelists, poets, essayists, dramatists, and literary critics in over 1,000 pages of text. . . . Each author entry contains subsections titled 'Biographical Narrative,' 'Major Works,' 'Critical Reception,' and 'Bibliography' (which in turn offers 'Works by' and 'Studies of' listings)."

Choice

"Other works treating this same subject are of a lesser status than Page's title, impressive for its critical and scholarly representation of a growing and important group." Libr J

Includes bibliographical references

Encyclopedia of African-American writing; five centuries of contribution: trials & triumphs of writers, poets, publications and organizations; Shari Dorantes Hatch, editor. 2nd ed. Grey House Pub. 2009 xxii, 863p il $165

Grades: 11 12 Adult   **810.9**
1. American literature—African American authors—Encyclopedias 2. American literature—African American authors—Bio-bibliography 3. Reference books
ISBN 978-1-59237-291-1

First published 2000 by ABC-CLIO with title: African-American writers: a dictionary

"This voluminous and inclusive collection consists of 738 entries that cover authors and other topics related to African American writing, such as newspapers, magazines, journals, and publishers and figures such as educators, playwrights, journalists, academics, editors, and librarians from the past 500 years. . . . Although unsigned, the entries are highly accessible, very current, and chock-full of information for a range of audiences." Libr J

Includes bibliographical references

Encyclopedia of American Indian literature; [edited by] Jennifer McClinton-Temple, Alan Velie. Facts on File 2007 466p (Encyclopedia of American ethnic literature) $75

Grades: 11 12 Adult   **810.9**
1. Native American literature—Encyclopedias 2. Native Americans in literature—Encyclopedias 3. Reference books
ISBN 0-8160-5656-0; 978-0-8160-5656-9
     LC 2006-23762

This "reference work presents information about American Indian literature, including authors from the contiguous 48 states, Alaska, and Canada. . . . The body of the text includes A-Z entries on specific native works and authors, as well as important issues such as 'Reservation Life,' 'Alcoholism,' 'Gaming,' and more. . . . Authors of poetry, plays, nonfiction, and novels are featured." Libr Media Connect

"This book brings together solid information from scattered sources, facilitating research on an esoteric subject." Libr J

Includes bibliographical references

Encyclopedia of American war literature; edited by Philip K. Jason and Mark A. Graves. Greenwood Press 2001 424p $95

Grades: 11 12 Adult   **810.9**
1. American literature—Encyclopedias 2. War in literature 3. Reference books
ISBN 0-313-30648-6   LC 00-42225

The "284 entries provide brief biographical and literary information about writers. . . . The editors focus on fiction rather than historical or nonfictional works. Besides biographical entries, arranged in alphabetical order, the editors include topical entries that provide overviews

Encyclopedia of American war literature—*Continued*
of particular wars and literary genres. Entries include all wars in which Americans have participated." Choice

Includes bibliographical references

The **Greenwood** encyclopedia of African American literature; edited by Hans Ostrom and J. David Macey, Jr. Greenwood Press 2005 5v il set $499.95 *

Grades: 11 12 Adult   **810.9**
1. American literature—African American authors—Encyclopedias 2. Reference books

ISBN 0-313-32972-9   LC 2005-13679

This "set provides coverage of the foundations, development, and proliferation of African American literature, from Colonial times to the present. . . . The depth and breadth of the 1,029 entries make this an invaluable resource." Choice

Includes bibliographical references

The **Harlem** Renaissance; edited and with an introduction by Harold Bloom. Chelsea House 2003 336p (Bloom's period studies) $37.95

Grades: 9 10 11 12   **810.9**
1. American literature—African American authors—History and criticism 2. Harlem Renaissance

ISBN 0-7910-7679-2   LC 2003-16873

"This volume examines the defining themes and style of African-American literature during . . . [the Harlem Renaissance] which laid the groundwork for contemporary African-American writers." Publisher's note

Includes bibliographical references

The **Harlem** Renaissance: a Gale critical companion; foreword by Trudier Harris-Lopez; Janet Witalec, project editor. Gale Res. 2003 3v il (Gale critical companion collection) set $325

Grades: 11 12 Adult   **810.9**
1. American literature—African American authors—History and criticism 2. Harlem Renaissance

ISBN 0-7876-6618-1   LC 2002-10076

"Volume 1 focuses on five topic areas, starting with an overview and background information, then moving on to chapters on social, economic, and political factors; publishing and periodicals; performing arts; and the visual arts. . . . Volumes 2 and 3 are devoted to writers. Eleven female and twenty-two male authors are discussed, among them Arna Bontemps, Marcus Garvey, Angelina Weld Grimké, James Weldon Johnson, and Dorothy West. . . . Most author entries include biographical profiles, lists of principal works, some primary source material, critical essays, and further reading lists. . . . The breadth and depth of *Harlem Renaissance* make it a valuable and unique reference source for academic, public, and high-school libraries." Booklist

Includes bibliographical references

Harlem speaks; a living history of the Harlem Renaissance; edited by Cary D. Wintz. Sourcebooks MediaFusion 2007 xxi, 502p il $29.95

Grades: 9 10 11 12   **810.9**
1. American literature—African American authors—History and criticism 2. African Americans—Intellectual life 3. Harlem Renaissance

ISBN 978-1-4022-0436-4; 1-4022-0436-1

Includes audio CD

The editor "and his collaborators combed the collections of the Smithsonian Institute and the Schomburg Center for Research in Black Culture and found rare sound recordings and photographs of important figures of the Harlem Renaissance, among them Langston Hughes, Claude McKay, Zora Neale Hurston, and Bessie Smith. Examining the politics, literature, music, and visual and performing arts of the 'new Negro,' the book contains chapters on individual figures of the period. As they move through the text, readers are guided to specific tracks on the CD, where they may hear the artist's own voice." Choice

"The visual and auditory impact of this title, paired with an in-depth, accessible text, makes it a good choice for browsing or research." SLJ

Includes bibliographical references

Hill, Laban Carrick
Harlem stomp! a cultural history of the Harlem Renaissance. Little, Brown 2004 151p il hardcover o.p. pa $12.99 *

Grades: 7 8 9 10   **810.9**
1. Harlem Renaissance 2. African Americans—Intellectual life 3. African American arts

ISBN 0-316-81411-3; 0-316-03424-X (pa)
     LC 2002-73067

"This is an account of cultural and intellectual life in Harlem during the first half of the 20th century." Bull Cent Child Books

"The vibrancy, energy, and color of the Harlem Renaissance come to life in this gem of a book packed with poetry, prose, song lyrics, art, and photography created by some of the period's most influential figures. . . . Informative and highly entertaining, it deserves to be shelved in any library." Voice Youth Advocates

Includes bibliographical references

Hillstrom, Kevin
The Harlem Renaissance. Omnigraphics 2008 228p il map (Defining moments) $49

Grades: 7 8 9 10   **810.9**
1. Harlem Renaissance 2. African American arts

ISBN 978-0-7808-1027-3; 0-7808-1027-9
     LC 2007-51132

"Provides a detailed, factual account of the emergence and development of the Harlem Renaissance and its ongoing effect on American society. Features include a narrative overview, biographical profiles, primary source documents, detailed chronology, glossary, and annotated sources for further study." Publisher's note

"This an insightful, highly accessible subject primer for general collections." Libr J

Includes glossary and bibliographical references

Johnson, Claudia D.
Labor and workplace issues in literature; [by] Claudia Durst Johnson. Greenwood Press 2006 183p (Exploring social issues through literature) $49.95
Grades: 9 10 11 12   **810.9**
1. Fiction—History and criticism 2. Work in literature
ISBN 0-313-33286-X   LC 2005-25974
"Each chapter examines the historical background and plot of the work, and discusses the labor and workplace issues raised by the author. It then overviews the history of these issues since the publication of the work and relates the literary text to modern concerns. The volume discusses such issues as low wages, long hours, workplace dangers, unemployment, sexual harassment, lack of job security or medical care, and the struggle of immigrants." Publisher's note
Includes bibliographical references

Magill's survey of American literature; edited by Steven G. Kellman. Rev. ed. Salem Press 2007 6v il set $499
Grades: 11 12 Adult   **810.9**
1. Reference books 2. Literature—History and criticism 3. Literature—Bio-bibliography
ISBN 978-1-58765-285-1; 1-58765-285-4
       LC 2006-16503
First published 1992 with two volume supplement published 1996 under the editorship of Frank Northen Magill
"Examining selected works of 339 U.S. and Canadian writers, from Anne Bradstreet and Benjamin Franklin to Edward Bloor and Octavia E. Butler, this clearly written resource provides sturdy support for assignments, and will also be popular with discussion groups and with general readers of literature." SLJ
Includes bibliographical references

Modern American women writers; edited by Elaine Showalter, Lea Baechler, and A. Walton Litz. Collier Bks. 1993 416p pa $15
Grades: 11 12 Adult   **810.9**
1. American literature—History and criticism 2. Women authors
ISBN 0-02-082025-9   LC 93-22193
First published 1991 by Scribner
"This work focuses on 41 representative American women who have published since 1870. Among those included are Anne Tyler, Alice Walker, and Emily Dickinson. The essays, ranging from 8 to 22 pages, emphasize the social and historical environment in which each wrote." Nichols. Guide to Ref Books for Sch Media Cent. 4th edition

Molin, Paulette Fairbanks
American Indian themes in young adult literature; [by] Paulette F. Molin. Scarecrow Press 2005 183p (Scarecrow studies in young adult literature) $40
Grades: Adult Professional   **810.9**
1. Native Americans in literature 2. Young adult literature—History and criticism
ISBN 0-8108-5081-8   LC 2004-26420

"Eight essays survey literature, mostly published in the past 10 years, with American Indian themes, and written for an audience that includes a wide range of Young Adults—approximately 11 to 18-year-olds." SLJ
This "is a useful reference work, especially for the readers she targets—teachers, librarians, and even publishers and editors of young adult literature—and it provides the most complete bibliography of the genre in print." Amer Indian Culture and Research Journal
Includes bibliographical references

Native American writers; edited and with an introduction by Harold Bloom. New ed. Bloom's Literary Criticism 2010 285p (Modern critical views) $45
Grades: 9 10 11 12   **810.9**
1. American literature—Native American authors 2. Native American literature—History and criticism
ISBN 978-1-60413-591-6; 978-1-4381-3439-0 (ebook)
       LC 2010-6006
First published 1998
For ebook pricing and a complete list of series titles contact publisher
"This volume examines some of the finest Native American writers, including Joy Harjo, Louise Erdrich, James Welch, Sherman Alexie, N. Scott Momaday, Samsom Occom, Zitkala-Ša, and Leslie Marmon Silko." Publisher's note
Includes bibliographical references

Nineteenth-century American women writers; a bio-bibliographical critical sourcebook; edited by Denise D. Knight; Emmanuel S. Nelson, advisory editor. Greenwood Press 1997 534p $110
Grades: 11 12 Adult   **810.9**
1. Reference books 2. American literature—Women authors—Bio-bibliography
ISBN 0-313-29713-4   LC 96-35351
This volume "contains entries for 77 writers whose inclusion was determined by the fact that their best-known works were published during the nineteenth century. . . . Designed as a primary reference guide for researchers, the book includes fiction writers, poets, autobiographers, essayists, and abolitionists." Booklist

Oh, Seiwoong
Encyclopedia of Asian-American literature. Facts On File 2007 384p (Facts on File library of American literature) $75 *
Grades: 11 12 Adult   **810.9**
1. Reference books 2. American literature—Asian American authors—Encyclopedias 3. American literature—Asian American authors—Bio-bibliography
ISBN 0-8160-6086-X; 978-0-8160-6086-3
       LC 2006-26181
The author "traces American writers whose roots are in all parts of Asia, including China, Korea, Japan, Southeast Asia, the Philippines, the Indian subcontinent, and the Middle East. Coverage emphasizes works that are important in the high school and college literary canon, as well as the historically significant and the contemporary." Publisher's note
Includes bibliographical references

Otfinoski, Steven, 1949-
Native American writers. Chelsea House 2010
126p il (Multicultural voices) $35
Grades: 8 9 10 11 12 **810.9**
1. American literature—Native American authors
2. Native American literature—History and criticism
ISBN 978-1-60413-314-1; 1-60413-314-7
LC 2009-41334
"This title introduces 10 major Native American poets
and writers, such as N. Scott Momaday, Louise Erdrich,
James Welch, and Sherman Alexie. An overview preceding the author entries explains the impact of white settlers on the culture of Native Americans, as well as the
utilization of Native American storytelling and traditions
in their literature and development of their writings. . . .
The easily accessible information and fascinating details
of the lives and writings of these authors make this a
useful resource for both informative reading and research." SLJ
Includes bibliographical references

Ramirez, Luz Elena
Encyclopedia of Hispanic-American literature.
Facts On File 2008 430p (Encyclopedia of
American ethnic literature) $75 *
Grades: 11 12 Adult **810.9**
1. American literature—Hispanic American authors—
Encyclopedias 2. Reference books
ISBN 978-0-8160-6084-9; 0-8160-6084-3
LC 2007-34805
This encyclopedia provides "information on over 250
important works, writers, and related topics. . . . Orga-
nized in an A-Z format, entries include significant works,
movements, and topics. . . . The appealing writing
makes this a very readable and fascinating source." Libr
Media Connect
Includes bibliographical references

Romanticism and transcendentalism; 1800-1860;
Jerry Phillips, general editor; Michael Anesko,
adviser and contributor; Andrew Ladd, Karen
Meyers, principal authors. 2nd ed. Facts On File
2010 126p il (Backgrounds to American
literature) $40
Grades: 9 10 11 12 **810.9**
1. American literature—History and criticism
2. Romanticism 3. Transcendentalism
ISBN 978-1-60413-486-5 LC 2009-29630
First published 2005
This "guide to the romantic and transcendentalist era
in American literature . . . [provides] information on the
foundations of romantic thought, romanticism and the
new nation, gothic romance and sentimentalism, transcendentalism, Nathaniel Hawthorne and Herman Melville,
and romanticism and poetic voice." Publisher's note
Includes bibliographical references

Student's encyclopedia of American literary
characters; edited by Matthew J. Bruccoli, Judith
S. Baughman. Facts On File 2008 4v (Facts on
File library of American literature) set $340
Grades: 9 10 11 12 **810.9**
1. American literature—Encyclopedias 2. Characters
and characteristics in literature—Encyclopedias
3. Reference books
ISBN 978-0-8160-6498-4; 0-8160-6498-9
LC 2008-1704
"Some 300 contributors to this set provide 1200-word
summaries and analyses of about 900 characters from
American novels, short stories, poems, plays, and musi-
cal theater." Libr J
"This work contains . . . in-depth character analysis
and warrants purchase for use in both ready reference
and more detailed research." SLJ
Includes bibliographical references

U.S. Latino literature; a critical guide for students
and teachers; edited by Harold Augenbraum and
Margarite Fernández Olmos under the auspices
of the Mercantile Library of New York.
Greenwood Press 2000 215p $49.95
Grades: 9 10 11 12 **810.9**
1. American literature—Hispanic American authors—
History and criticism 2. Hispanic Americans in literature
ISBN 0-313-31137-4 LC 99-462065
Among the works discussed in these eighteen essays
are Rudolfo A. Anaya's Bless me, Ultima, Richard Rodriguez's Hunger of memory, Sandra Cisneros' The
house on Mango Street, and Julia Alvarez's How the
Garcia girls lost their accents
"The critical essays begin with a brief biography of
the author and then center on an analysis of the work's
themes and forms. The essays also include ideas for
teaching the work and suggestions for further reading.
. . . An excellent addition to the professional shelf as
well as literary criticism collections." Book Rep

Wilson, Charles E., 1961-
Race and racism in literature; [by] Charles E.
Wilson, Jr. Greenwood Press 2005 154p
(Exploring social issues through literature) $49.95
*
Grades: 9 10 11 12 **810.9**
1. American literature—History and criticism 2. Race
in literature
ISBN 0-313-32820-X; 978-0-313-32820-6
LC 2005-1494
"The novels discussed here were chosen to represent
various racial and ethnic identities (e.g., black, Asian,
Hispanic, Jewish, Italian, Native American). Each novel
. . . is summarized, discussed in terms of its historical
and social significance, and then discussed again as a
work of literature. . . . [The author] is to be commended
for drawing together a dozen novels that focus on race,
and treating these works in a thoughtful and focused
way." Am Ref Books Annu, 2006
Includes bibliographical references

811 American poetry

Alexie, Sherman, 1966-
Face. Hanging Loose Press 2009 159p $28; pa $15
Grades: 11 12 Adult   **811**
1. Poetry—By individual authors
ISBN   978-1-931236-71-3;   1-931236-71-2;
978-1-931236-70-6 (pa); 1-931236-70-4 (pa)
                           LC 2008-46580
The author "has mastered both the metrical dance and fixed forms. A sequence of sonnets finds the Seven Deadly Sins in marriage, for instance; a villanelle begins with Mount Rushmore but eases into a consideration of America's Presidents, complemented by wry and smart footnotes. . . . There are a lot of serious undercurrents in his poetry, and they are always a pleasure to find." Libr J

Alvarez, Julia, 1950-
The woman I kept to myself; poems. Algonquin Books of Chapel Hill 2004 155p hardcover o.p. pa $14.95
Grades: 11 12 Adult   **811**
1. Poetry—By individual authors
ISBN 1-56512-406-5; 1-61620-072-3 (pa)
                           LC 2003-70807
This "collection of 75 poems is divided into three sections, and each poem has three stanzas, exactly . . . The poet, who is from the Dominican Republic, writes about being raised with her sisters in New York. The subjects are personal—love, marriage, rejection, divorce, death, religion—but also universal." SLJ

Angelou, Maya
The complete collected poems of Maya Angelou. Random House 1994 273p $24.95 *
Grades: 11 12 Adult   **811**
1. Poetry—By individual authors
ISBN 0-679-42895-X   LC 94-14501
This volume contains all of Angelou's published poems including her inaugural poem On the pulse of morning

Appelt, Kathi, 1954-
Poems from homeroom; a writer's place to start. Holt & Co. 2002 114p hardcover o.p. pa $14.95
Grades: 7 8 9 10   **811**
1. Poetics 2. Poetry—By individual authors
ISBN 0-8050-6978-X; 0-8050-7596-8 (pa)
                           LC 2002-67886
A collection of poems about the experiences of young people and a section with information about how each poem was written to enable readers to create their own original poems
Appelt's "poems are at times sensual, dramatic, or violent, and always rhythmic. They are fascinating, smooth, and 'with it.'" SLJ
Includes bibliographical references

Atkins, Jeannine, 1953-
Borrowed names; poems about Laura Ingalls Wilder, Madam C. J. Walker, Marie Curie, and their daughters. Henry Holt & Co. 2010 209p il $16.99 *
Grades: 6 7 8 9 10   **811**
1. Wilder, Laura Ingalls, 1867-1957—Poetry
2. Walker, C. J., Madame, 1867-1919—Poetry
3. Curie, Marie, 1867-1934—Poetry 4. Lane, Rose Wilder, 1886-1968—Poetry 5. Walker, A'Lelia, 1885-1931—Poetry 6. Joliot-Curie, Irène, 1897-1956—Poetry 7. Mother-daughter relationship—Poetry 8. Poetry—By individual authors
ISBN 978-0-8050-8934-9; 0-8050-8934-9
                           LC 2009-23446
"In 1867, three women who achieved great success were born: writer Laura Ingalls Wilder, entrepreneur Madam C. J. Walker, and scientist Marie Curie. All three had complicated relationships with their daughters, relationships that Atkins explores in this unusual volume of poetry. . . . In vivid scenes written with keen insight and subtle imagery, the poems offer a strong sense of each daughter's personality as well as the tensions and ties they shared with their notable mothers." Booklist

Bernier-Grand, Carmen T.
Diego; bigger than life; illustrated by David Diaz. Marshall Cavendish Children 2009 64p il $18.99
Grades: 8 9 10 11 12   **811**
1. Rivera, Diego, 1886-1957—Poetry 2. Poetry—By individual authors
ISBN 978-0-7614-5383-3; 0-7614-5383-0
                           LC 2007-13761
"The life and work of the artist Diego Rivera is told through chronological poems that capture salient points in his life." Publisher's note
This is a "well written and beautifully illustrated volume. . . . Almost all written in first-person from the artist's point of view, the poems convey information succinctly within a context of colorful narrative and clearly expressed emotion. . . . Apart from four reproductions of Rivera's paintings and one photo of the artist, the illustrations are mixed-media pictures by Diaz. Depicting Rivera and his world, these iconic images glow with warmth, light, and color." Booklist
Includes bibliographical references

Frida; viva la vida! long live life! Marshall Cavendish Children 2007 64p il $18.99 *
Grades: 8 9 10 11 12   **811**
1. Kahlo, Frida, 1907-1954—Poetry 2. Poetry—By individual authors
ISBN 978-0-7614-5336-9   LC 2006014479
"Bernier-Grand introduces a famous life with lyrical free-verse poems. Nearly every double-page spread pairs a well-reproduced painting by Frida Kahlo with an original poem that defines turning points in the artist's life. Bernier-Grand's words expertly extend the autobiographical imagery so evident in the art." Booklist
Includes glossary and bibliographical references

Block, Francesca Lia

How to (un)cage a girl. Joanna Cotler Books 2008 119p $15.99; lib bdg $16.89

Grades: 8 9 10 11 12   **811**

1. Girls—Poetry 2. Love poetry 3. Poetry—By individual authors

ISBN   978-0-06-135836-4;   0-06-135836-3; 978-0-06-135837-1 (lib bdg); 0-06-135837-1 (lib bdg)

LC 2008-00629

A collection of love poems for girls.

"A stirring exploration of female suffering and empowerment, this will attract Block's adult readers, too." Booklist

Brooks, Gwendolyn

In Montgomery, and other poems. Third World Press 2003 146p $22.95

Grades: 11 12 Adult   **811**

1. Poetry—By individual authors

ISBN 0-88378-232-4   LC 2003-50749

This is a "posthumous collection consisting primarily of dramatic monologues in a stunning variety of voices, from those of urban children to Winnie Mandela's. Reading the title sequence resembles randomly tuning a radio dial to listen to the diverse voices of Montgomery, Alabama, a city of 'leaning and lostness, glazed paralysis.' . . . Especially moving are the children's monologues. . . . Brooks captures the fierce purity of these children's needs and desires. Her loving witness never sounded more clearly than in these late poems." Booklist

Selected poems. Harper & Row 1963 127p pa $12.95 hardcover o.p. *

Grades: 11 12 Adult   **811**

1. Poetry—By individual authors

ISBN 0-06-088296-4   LC 63-16503

"The subject of this poetry is the lives of African American residents of Northern urban ghettos, particularly women, and Brooks has been praised for her depiction of that experience in forms ranging from terza rima to blues meter." Benet's Reader's Ency of Am Lit

Crisler, Curtis L., 1965-

Tough boy sonatas; illustrations by Floyd Cooper. Wordsong 2007 86p il $19.95 *

Grades: 8 9 10 11 12   **811**

1. African Americans—Poetry 2. City and town life—Poetry 3. Indiana—Poetry 4. Poetry—By individual authors

ISBN 978-1-932425-77-2; 1-932425-77-2

LC 2006-11836

"Crisler presents a collection of potent, hard-hitting poems about growing up in Gary, Indiana. Written mostly in voices of young African American males, the poems evoke the grit and ash of crumbling, burned-out streets as well as the realities of hardscrabble life. . . . Written with skillful manipulation of sound, rhythm, and form, the poems are filled with sophisticated imagery and graphic words . . . and Cooper's illustrations extend . . . the poems' impact. Created in sooty black and gray, the powerful drawings are mostly portraits of anguished young men." Booklist

Cummings, E. E. (Edward Estlin), 1894-1962

Complete poems, 1904-1962; containing all the published poetry; edited by George J. Firmage. rev corr & expanded ed. Norton 1994 xxxii, 1102p $50 *

Grades: 9 10 11 12 Adult   **811**

1. Poetry—By individual authors

ISBN 978-0-87140-152-6; 0-87140-152-5

LC 91-29158

Expanded version of Complete poems, 1913-1962 (1972)

"This volume has been prepared directly from the poet's original manuscripts, preserving the original typography and format. It includes all the previously published works, from *Tulips* (1922) to *Etcetera* (1983), as well as 36 uncollected poems that originally appeared in little magazines or anthologies." Libr J

Dickinson, Emily, 1830-1886

The complete poems of Emily Dickinson; edited by Thomas H. Johnson. Little, Brown 1960 770p $35; pa $19.95 *

Grades: 11 12 Adult   **811**

1. Poetry—By individual authors

ISBN 0-316-18414-4; 0-316-18413-6 (pa)

A chronological arrangement of all known Dickinson poems and fragments

Final harvest; Emily Dickinson's poems; selection and introduction by Thomas H. Johnson. Little, Brown 1961 331p pa $14.99 hardcover o.p.

Grades: 11 12 Adult   **811**

1. Poetry—By individual authors

ISBN 0-316-18415-2

A selection of 575 poems from: The complete poems of Emily Dickinson. The editor's aim has been to allow the reader to realize the full scope and diversity of the poet's work

My letter to the world and other poems; with illustrations by Isabelle Arsenault. KCP Poetry 2008 unp il (Visions in poetry) $17.95; pa $9.95

Grades: 7 8 9 10 11 12   **811**

1. Poetry—By individual authors

ISBN   978-1-55453-103-5;   1-55453-103-9; 978-1-55453-339-8 (pa); 1-55453-339-2 (pa)

This is an illustrated compilation of seven Emily Dickinson poems.

"The long final biographical note about the introvert and recluse who gloried in being 'Nobody' will take readers back to the poetry, which speaks as a 'letter to the world,' as will the clear analysis of the mixed-media illustrations, in which Arsenault links the poet's repeated images of isolation with her intense connections to nature. . . . Dickinson's exploration of the difference between loneliness and rich solitude will resonate with teens." Booklist

Dickinson, Emily, 1830-1886—*Continued*

New poems of Emily Dickinson; edited by William H. Shurr with Anna Dunlap & Emily Grey Shurr. University of N.C. Press 1993 125p hardcover o.p. pa $13.95

Grades: 11 12 Adult   **811**
1. Poetry—By individual authors
ISBN 0-8078-2115-2; 0-8078-4416-0 (pa)
LC 93-20353

This volume increases Dickinson's "body of work by 498 selections. Shurr has accomplished this by combining three volumes of the poet's letters and identifying epigrams, riddles, and various longer lyrical pieces within the prose. These will both challenge and delight serious readers, for wit, unusual rhythms, and musical rhymes predominate." SLJ

Includes bibliographical references

The selected poems of Emily Dickinson. Modern Lib. 1996 295p hardcover o.p. pa $9.95 *

Grades: 11 12 Adult   **811**
1. Poetry—By individual authors
ISBN 0-679-60201-1; 0-679-78335-0 (pa)

This "edition presents the more than four hundred poems that were published between Dickinson's death and 1900. They express her concepts of life and death, of love and nature, and of what Henry James called 'the landscape of the soul.'" Publisher's note

Dove, Rita

American smooth; poems. W.W. Norton 2004 143p $22.95; pa $13.95

Grades: 11 12 Adult   **811**
1. Poetry—By individual authors
ISBN 0-393-05987-1; 0-393-32744-2 (pa)
LC 2004-11793

"In these free-verse poems, Dove speaks from her own perspective—as well as from that of biblical characters, black soldiers from World War I, a ten-year-old girl from Harlem, several musicians, and a pair of dancers. The selections work by lists, line breaks where ideas collide, and a juxtaposition of voices. Then using razor-sharp metaphors, Dove goes for the jugular and usually finds it. Although the book's sense of audience seems inconsistent, with some poems suitable for *A Child's Garden of Verses* and others for *The Kama Sutra*, the poems are evocative." Libr J

Mother love; poems. Norton 1995 77p $17.95; pa $11

Grades: 11 12 Adult   **811**
1. Poetry—By individual authors
ISBN 0-393-03808-4; 0-393-31444-8 (pa)
LC 95-5394

"Most poems included here are autobiographical. Dove writes of childhood bullies, rock songs crooned in the driveway, and, in the long poem, 'Persephone in Hell,' a stay in Paris over 20 years ago. Her language is simple and clear." Libr J

On the bus with Rosa Parks; poems. Norton 1999 95p pa $12.95 hardcover o.p.

Grades: 11 12 Adult   **811**
1. Poetry—By individual authors
ISBN 0-393-32026-X
LC 98-45057

Dove's "poems effortlessly suggest grand narratives and American myths, yet ground themselves tersely in localities, characters, practicalities and particulars. This seventh collection leads off with a Dove specialty, the historical sequence: her 'Cameos' lend broad, social relevance to an intermittently abandoned Depression-era wife and her family." Publ Wkly

Selected poems. Vintage Bks. 1993 xxvi, 210p pa $13 *

Grades: 11 12 Adult   **811**
1. Poetry—By individual authors
ISBN 0-679-75080-0
LC 93-26112

"This volume places three previous collections under one cover. . . . The selection begins with *The Yellow House on the Corner*, Dove's first book, most notable for its poems derived from slave narratives. *Museum*, her second book, offers a potpourri of work that ranges over several continents and many millenia; Dove's tirelessly exact language illuminates the lives of saints, contemporary lifestyles, and Greek myths." Booklist

Eliot, T. S. (Thomas Stearns), 1888-1965

Collected poems, 1909-1962. Harcourt Brace Jovanovich 1963 221p $23 *

Grades: 11 12 Adult   **811**
1. Poetry—By individual authors
ISBN 0-15-118978-1

This volume contains the complete text of 'Collected poems, 1909-1935,' the 'Four quartets,' and several other poems accompanied by brief prefatory notes

The complete poems and plays, 1909-1950. Harcourt Brace & Co. 1952 392p $35 *

Grades: 11 12 Adult   **811**
1. Poetry—By individual authors
ISBN 0-15-121185-X

This book is made up of six individual titles formerly published separately: Collected poems (1909-1935); Four quartets; Old Possum's book of practical cats; Murder in the cathedral; Family reunion; Cocktail party

The waste land, and other poems. Harcourt Brace Jovanovich 1955 c1934 88p pa $8 *

Grades: 9 10 11 12   **811**
1. Poetry—By individual authors
ISBN 0-15-694877-X

Also available in paperback from Penguin Bks.
"A Harvest book"

In addition to Eliot's long poem of despair this volume contains a representative selection of his best known shorter works

Emerson, Ralph Waldo, 1803-1882

Collected poems & translations. Library of Am. 1994 637p $35 *

Grades: 11 12 Adult   **811**
1. Poetry—By individual authors
ISBN 0-940450-28-3
LC 93-40245

Contains Emerson's published poetry, plus selections of his unpublished poetry from journals and notebooks, and some of his translations of poetry from other languages, notably Dante's La vita nuova

Fairchild, B. H. (Bertram H.), 1942-

Early occult memory systems of the Lower
Midwest. Norton 2002 125p hardcover o.p. pa
$15.95

Grades: 11 12 Adult   **811**

1. Poetry—By individual authors
ISBN 0-393-05096-3; 0-393-32566-0 (pa)

LC 2002-71886

This poetry "collection journeys through the intersec-
tions of imagination and history across the plains of the
Midwest." Publisher's note

This is a "strong, compelling collection. . . . If strong
emotion courses through Fairchild's work, it never makes
it lachrymose, thanks to concrete vocabulary and images,
direct syntax, and propulsive rhythms." Booklist

Ferlinghetti, Lawrence

How to paint sunlight; lyric poems & others
(1997-2000). New Directions 2001 94p $19.95; pa
$13.95

Grades: 11 12 Adult   **811**

1. Poetry—By individual authors
ISBN 0-8112-1463-X; 0-8112-1463-X (pa)

LC 00-67860

"A late-career miscellany divided into four sections,
this . . . collection draws some of life's great polari-
ties—light and dark, tragedy and comedy, ecstasy and
despair—into the quotidian whorl of this beloved West
Coast-transplant poet." Publ Wkly

These are my rivers; new & selected poems,
1955-1993. New Directions 1993 308p il pa
$13.95 hardcover o.p. *

Grades: 11 12 Adult   **811**

1. Poetry—By individual authors
ISBN 0-8112-1273-4   LC 93-10383

"Reading this hefty selection from 12 previous volumes, plus 50 pages of new poems, we realize how accurately the poet described himself in 1979: a man who
'thinks he's Dylan Thomas and Bob Dylan rolled together with Charlie Chaplin thrown in.' . . . His style is recognizable throughout—phlegmatic poems running several
pages, often lacking stanza breaks, with short lines at the
left margin or moving across the page as hand follows
eye." Libr J

Frost, Robert, 1874-1963

The poetry of Robert Frost; edited by Edward
Connery Lathem. Holt & Co. 1969 607p hardcover
o.p. pa $18 *

Grades: 11 12 Adult   **811**

1. Poetry—By individual authors
ISBN 0-8050-0502-1; 0-8050-6986-0 (pa)

"A one-volume edition of Frost's eleven volumes of
poetry and two short blank-verse plays. The collection
ranges in time from A Boy's Will (1913) to In the Clearing (1962). . . . {There is} an appendix of bibliographical and textual notes for each of the poems." Nation

Gibran, Kahlil, 1883-1931

The Prophet. Knopf 1923 107p il $15 *

Grades: 11 12 Adult   **811**

1. Poetry—By individual authors
ISBN 0-394-40428-9
Also available pocket library editions

A collection of poems by the mystical writer/artist,
who was born in Lebanon and died in the United States,
in which the prophet Almustafa deals with fundamental
aspects of human life such as love, friendship, good and
evil, self-knowledge, passion and reason, joy and sorrow,
freedom, work, marriage and children, prayer and death

Ginsberg, Allen, 1926-1997

Collected poems, 1947-1997. HarperCollins
Publishers 2006 xx, 1189p il hardcover o.p. pa
$25.99

Grades: 11 12 Adult   **811**

1. Poetry—By individual authors
ISBN   978-0-06-113974-1;   0-06-113974-2;
978-0-06-113975-8 (pa); 0-06-113975-0 (pa)

LC 2006-41191

First published 1984 with title: Collected poems,
1947-1980

This books "reprints the complete text of 1984's Collected Poems 1947-1980, along with the collections that
followed: White Shroud, Cosmopolitan Greetings, and
Death and Fame, including the original book attributes of
each collection. A poet of extremes at times too trusting
of his instincts, Ginsberg could be playful, angry, strident, obscene, graceful, and hilarious in the space of a
page, and by now his readers know they are likely to encounter as many embarrassing poems as enlightening
ones. Still, this compendium provides the most complete
edition of Ginsberg available." Libr J

Giovanni, Nikki

Blues; for all the changes: new poems. Morrow
1999 100p $15

Grades: 11 12 Adult   **811**

1. Poetry—By individual authors
ISBN 0-688-15698-3   LC 98-50996

"Giovanni never loses sight of the people in her work.
In poems built with broken lines and paragraphs of
prose, she spars with the ills that confront us, but every
struggle has a human face." Libr J

Quilting the black-eyed pea; poems and not
quite poems. William Morrow 2002 110p $16.95

Grades: 11 12 Adult   **811**

1. Poetry—By individual authors
ISBN 978-0-06-009952-7; 0-06-009952-6

LC 2002-66025

"Arranged in six untitled sections whose themes are
not self-evident, the poems take an artifact from life and
examine its cultural impact." VOYA

Giovanni "entwines the political and the personal and
celebrates womanhood and black society and culture.
Hers is an embracing, uplifting, and sustaining voice, one
given to both anger and humor." Booklist

The selected poems of Nikki Giovanni
(1968-1995). Morrow 1996 224p $22 *

Grades: 11 12 Adult   **811**

1. Poetry—By individual authors
ISBN 0-688-14047-5   LC 95-31646

Giovanni, Nikki—*Continued*
"Writing as an African American and as a woman, Giovanni speaks with powerful music about politics, love, feminism, and family." Booklist

Grandits, John, 1949-
Blue lipstick; concrete poems. Clarion Books 2007 unp il $15; pa $5.95
Grades: 5 6 7 8 9 10   **811**
  1. Poetry—By individual authors
  ISBN   978-0-618-56860-4;   0-618-56860-3;
978-0-618-85132-4 (pa); 0-618-85132-1 (pa)
                           LC 2006-23332
"This selection introduces readers to Jessie, who impulsively purchases blue lipstick, but later, regretfully decides to give it 'the kiss-off.' Jessie is big sister to Robert, who was featured in Grandits's *Technically, It's Not My Fault* (Clarion, 2004). As he did in that terrific collection, the author uses artful arrangements of text on the page, along with 54 different typefaces, to bring his images and ideas to life. . . . This irreverent, witty collection should resonate with a wide audience." SLJ

Haas, Jessie
Hoofprints: horse poems. Greenwillow Books 2004 208p $15.99; lib bdg $16.89
Grades: 9 10 11 12   **811**
  1. Horses—Poetry 2. Poetry—By individual authors
  ISBN 0-06-053406-0; 0-06-053407-9 (lib bdg)
                           LC 2003-49066
A collection of more than one hundred poems celebrating horses, from ancient times to the present
"Haas's poetic talent is apparent in her deft use of rhymes and rhythms, descriptive narrative verse, occasional touches of humor, and subtle inferences. Her poems display cleverness and, often, spare, vividly descriptive, well-turned phrases." SLJ
Includes glossary and bibliographical references

Harjo, Joy, 1951-
The woman who fell from the sky; poems. Norton 1994 69p pa $12.95 hardcover o.p.
Grades: 11 12 Adult   **811**
  1. Poetry—By individual authors
  ISBN 0-393-31362-X (pa)   LC 96-23014
"Harjo sets 25 prayer-like prose poems in a spooky land of myth . . . depicting an ongoing moral 'war' between forces of creation (northern lights, wolves) vs. destruction (alcoholism, Vietnam). Like contemporary Jobs, the people in these pieces search for an intelligible response to 'the wreck of culture,' their efforts symbolizing the impact of alienation on the psyche." Libr J

Hemphill, Stephanie
Your own, Sylvia; a verse portrait of Sylvia Plath. Alfred A. Knopf 2007 261p $15.99; lib bdg $18.99 *
Grades: 8 9 10 11 12   **811**
  1. Plath, Sylvia—Poetry 2. Poetry—By individual authors
  ISBN 978-0-375-83799-9; 978-0-375-93799-6 (lib bdg)   LC 2006-07253

The author interprets the people, events, influences and art that made up the brief life of Sylvia Plath.
"Hemphill's verse, like Plath's, is completely compelling: every word, every line, worth reading." Horn Book
Includes bibliographical references

Holbrook, Sara
More than friends; poems from him and her; [by] Sara Holbrook and Allan Wolf. Wordsong 2008 64p il $16.95
Grades: 6 7 8 9 10   **811**
  1. Love poetry 2. Poetry—By individual authors
  ISBN 978-1-59078-587-4; 1-59078-587-8
                           LC 2007-50282
"In these parallel poems, a boy and a girl describe their progression from friendship to romance. . . . The simple language expresses strong feelings in a variety of poetic forms. . . . Small black-and-white photos never get in the way of the words, which tell the edgy truth of romance in all its joy and confusion." Booklist

Hughes, Langston, 1902-1967
Poems; selected and edited by David Roessel. Knopf 1999 252p $12.50
Grades: 11 12 Adult   **811**
  1. African Americans—Poetry 2. Poetry—By individual authors
  ISBN 0-375-40551-8   LC 98-55136
The editor presents a representative selection of poetry by the prominent African American writer

Jarrell, Randall, 1914-1965
The complete poems. Farrar, Straus & Giroux 1969 507p pa $22 hardcover o.p. *
Grades: 11 12 Adult   **811**
  1. Poetry—By individual authors
  ISBN 0-374-51305-8 (pa)
Collected here are the entire contents of three published volumes Selected poems (1955), The woman at the Washington Zoo (1960), and The Lost World (1965) plus poems published from 1934 to 1964 but never collected and some never before published

Johnson, James Weldon, 1871-1938
Complete poems; edited with an introduction by Sondra Kathryn Wilson. Penguin Bks. 2000 xxxiii, 202p pa $14 *
Grades: 11 12 Adult   **811**
  1. Poetry—By individual authors
  ISBN 0-14-118545-7   LC 00-39969
This volume contains Fifty years and other poems (1917), God's trombones (1927), Saint Peter relates an incident of the resurrection day (1935), and a number of previously unpublished poems. The editor's introduction considers Johnson's achievements and influence
Includes bibliographical references

Kerouac, Jack, 1922-1969
Pomes all sizes; introduction by Allen Ginsberg.
City Lights Bks. 1992 175p pa $13.95 *
Grades: 11 12 Adult   811
1. Poetry—By individual authors
ISBN 0-87286-269-0   LC 92-1204
"This book, which Kerouac prepared for publication
before his death in 1969, collects poems written between
1954 and 1965. Most are playful—comments about
friends, variations on the sounds of words. Yet a few extremely sensitive longer pieces appear, including
'Caritas,' in which the poet runs after a barefoot beggar
boy to give him money for shoes and then begins to
doubt the boy's veracity. Other intriguing poems reflect
the poet's religious concerns of the moment, running the
gamut of Eastern and Western religions." Libr J

Le Guin, Ursula K., 1929-
Sixty odd; new poems. Shambhala Publs. 1999
98p pa $14
Grades: 11 12 Adult   811
1. Poetry—By individual authors
ISBN 1-57062-388-0   LC 98-37084
"A veritable collage of verse, capturing short literary
snapshots of real and imagined people, places, animals,
and events. . . . Writing with passion, wit, and vision,
Le Guin gives readers sharp, vivid imagery stimulating
all the senses." SLJ

Levertov, Denise, 1923-1997
Sands of the well. New Directions 1996 136p pa
$9.95 hardcover o.p.
Grades: 11 12 Adult   811
1. Poetry—By individual authors
ISBN 0-8112-1361-7 (pa)   LC 96-4324
"The outstanding sections in Levertov's eighteenth
collection are 'Sojourns in the Parallel World' and 'Close
to a Lake,' which contain, respectively, poems about nature and religious poems. . . . In other sections are poems about music, spring, memory, and political protest;
all are technically marvelous, for Levertov remains the
best free verse poet writing in English." Booklist

This great unknowing; last poems; with a note
on the text by Paul A. Lacey. New Directions
1999 68p pa $9.95 hardcover o.p.
Grades: 11 12 Adult   811
1. Poetry—By individual authors
ISBN 0-8112-1458-3 (pa)   LC 98-51469
"At once as intimate as Creeley and as visionary as
Duncan—two Black Mountain poets with whom she is
often associated—Levertov has always written a poetry
that ranges from the specifically personal to the search-
ingly mystical. Yet Levertov, from the mid-'60s until her
death in 1997, has been one of the few writers of her
generation to show that one need not mimic the oracular
qualities of the Beats to make a sociopolitical poetry."
Publ Wkly

Lewis, J. Patrick
Black cat bone; [by] J. Patrick Lewis;
illustrations by Gary Kelley. Creative Editions
2006 48p il $19.95
Grades: 6 7 8 9 10   811
1. Johnson, Robert, 1911-1938—Poetry 2. African
American musicians—Poetry 3. Blues music—Poetry
4. Mississippi—Poetry 5. Poetry—By individual authors
ISBN 978-1-56846-194-6   LC 2005-52298
"Robert Johnson, the celebrated blues musician, is said
to have sold his soul to the devil for his skills on the
guitar. . . . Lewis's verse echoes Johnson's music. . . .
A single line of text parades ghostlike across the bottom
of each page, explaining the aspect of the man's life that
the poem sings of, and becoming a cumulative mini-bio
in itself. A couple of Johnson's own lyrics appear with
the sequence of Lewis's poems where they add to the
narrative tension. Kelley's mixed-media illustrations in
blues and browns add to the mood and enliven the layout." SLJ

Longfellow, Henry Wadsworth, 1807-1882
Poems and other writings. Library of Am. 2000
854p $35 *
Grades: 11 12 Adult   811
1. Poetry—By individual authors
ISBN 1-88301-185-X   LC 00-26678
Edited by J. D. McClatchy
This volume includes "*Hiawatha, Evangeline, The
Courtship of Miles Standish* and 'The Midnight Ride of
Paul Revere.' Here, too, are some surprisingly powerful
lyric and meditative poems—well made, deeply felt, and
not much like the schoolhouse favorites." Publ Wkly
Includes bibliographical references

Lowell, Robert, 1917-1977
Selected poems. Expanded ed. Farrar, Straus and
Giroux 2006 420p pa $18 *
Grades: 11 12 Adult   811
1. Poetry—By individual authors
ISBN 0-374-53006-8; 978-0-374-53006-8
                                     LC 2005-54313
A selection of over 200 poems tracing the develop-
ment of one of the premier confessional poets of his gen-
eration.
Includes bibliographical references

MacLeish, Archibald, 1892-1982
Collected poems, 1917-1982; with a prefatory
note to the newly collected poems by Richard B.
McAdoo. Houghton Mifflin 1985 524p pa $19
hardcover o.p.
Grades: 11 12 Adult   811
1. Poetry—By individual authors
ISBN 0-395-39569-0 (pa)   LC 85-14392
Collects all the known poetry of the author/public servant. As an expatriate in Paris his early work was heavily influenced by Pound and Eliot. After returning to the
States his verse concerned itself more with America's
political, social, and cultural heritage

Masters, Edgar Lee, 1868-1950

Spoon River anthology; edited and with an introduction and annotations by John E. Hallwas. University of Ill. Press 1992 436p il map hardcover o.p. pa $19 *

Grades: 9 10 11 12   **811**

1. Poetry—By individual authors

ISBN 0-252-01561-4; 0-252-06363-5 (pa)

       LC 91-16968

First published 1915 by Macmillan

"The men and women of Spoon River narrate their own biographies from the cemetery where they lie buried. Realistic and sometimes cynical, these free-verse monologues often contradict the pious and optimistic epitaphs written on the gravestones." Reader's Ency. 4th edition

Merrell, Billy, 1982-

Talking in the dark; a poetry memoir. PUSH 2003 136p pa $6.99

Grades: 9 10 11 12   **811**

1. Poetry—By individual authors

ISBN 0-439-49036-7

This "memoir told in verse . . . is about sons and brothers, friends and lovers. The individual poems enhance one another yet stand alone." SLJ

Merrell has "packed away a lot of wisdom about life, death, self-acceptance, and the vararies of love and lust. Likewise, he has honed his writing craft, and his free-verse memoir is rich with metaphor, words carefully chosen to say enough but not to much." Booklist

Merrill, James

The collected poems of James Merrill; edited by J.D. McClatchy and Stephen Yenser. Knopf 2001 xx, 885p $40; pa $27.50

Grades: 11 12 Adult   **811**

1. Poetry—By individual authors

ISBN 0-375-41139-9; 0-375-70941-X (pa)

       LC 00-40542

"Excluded are some juvenilia and light verse, as well as Merrill's book-length poem *The Changing Light at Sandover,* in print as a separate volume. Merrill's sonnets, sapphics, longer sequences and sinuous sentences encompass lyric pathos, ebullient comedy, rapt romance and acrid satire. Their formal sophistication can belie their depth of feeling, which is exactly what some readers love best about Merrill's work." Publ Wkly

Millay, Edna St. Vincent, 1892-1950

Collected poems; edited by Norma Millay. Harper & Row 1956 xxi, 738p pa $22.95 hardcover o.p. *

Grades: 11 12 Adult   **811**

1. Poetry—By individual authors

ISBN 0-06-090889-0 (pa)

The poems in this collection "are divided into two separate sections of lyrics and sonnets, arranged chronologically and printed in groups under the titles of the original volumes, ranging from 'Renascence' of 1917 to 'Mine the harvest,' published in 1954, four years after the poet's death." Booklist

Moore, Marianne, 1887-1972

The poems of Marianne Moore; edited by Grace Schulman. Viking 2003 449p pa $18 hardcover o.p. *

Grades: 11 12 Adult   **811**

1. Poetry—By individual authors

ISBN 0-14-303908-3 (pa)   LC 2003-50159

This collection "contains all of Moore's poems, including 120 previously uncollected and unpublished ones. Organized chronologically to allow readers to follow Moore's development as a poet, the volume includes an introduction, all of Moore's original notes to the poems, along with Schulman's notes, attributions, and some variants." Publisher's note

"The great modernist poet finally gets her due with this outstanding compliation." Libr J

Includes bibliographical references

Mora, Pat

Dizzy in your eyes; poems about love. Alfred A. Knopf 2010 165p il $15.99; lib bdg $18.99

Grades: 7 8 9 10   **811**

1. Love poetry 2. Poetry—By individual authors

ISBN   978-0-375-84375-4;   0-375-84375-2; 978-0-375-94565-6 (lib bdg); 0-375-94565-2 (lib bdg)

       LC 2009-04300

"From family and school to dating and being dumped, the subjects in these 50 poems cover teens' experiences of love in many voices and situations. . . . Mora writes in free verse, as well as a variety of classic poetic forms—including haiku, clerihew, sonnet, cinquain, and blank verse—and for each form, there is an unobtrusive explanatory note on the facing page. The tight structures intensify the strong feelings in the poems, which teens will enjoy reading on their own or hearing aloud in the classroom." Booklist

My own true name; new and selected poems for young adults, 1984-1999; [by] Pat Mora with line drawings by Anthony Accardo. Piñata Bks. 2000 81p il $11.95

Grades: 9 10 11 12   **811**

1. Mexican Americans—Poetry 2. Poetry—By individual authors

ISBN 1-55885-292-1   LC 00-23969

"Interlaced with Mexican phrases and cultural symbols, these powerful selections, representing more than 15 years of work, address bicultural life and the meaning of family. Mora speaks very much from an adult perspective, but her poems are about universal experiences." Booklist

Myers, Walter Dean, 1937-

Harlem; a poem; pictures by Christopher Myers. Scholastic 1997 unp il $16.95

Grades: 5 6 7 8 9 10   **811**

1. African Americans—Poetry 2. Harlem (New York, N.Y.)—Poetry 3. Poetry—By individual authors

ISBN 0-590-54340-7   LC 96-8108

A poem celebrating the people, sights, and sounds of Harlem

"Myers's paean to Harlem sings, dances, and swaggers across the pages, conveying the myriad sounds on the

Myers, Walter Dean, 1937-—*Continued*

streets. . . . Christopher Myers's collages add an edge to his father's words, vividly bringing to life the sights and scenes of Lenox Avenue." Horn Book Guide

Here in Harlem; poems in many voices; written by Walter Dean Myers. Holiday House 2004 88p il $16.95

Grades: 7 8 9 10   811
   1. African Americans—Poetry 2. Harlem (New York, N.Y.)—Poetry 3. Poetry—By individual authors
   ISBN 0-8234-1853-7   LC 2003-67605

"In each poem here, a resident of Harlem speaks in a distinctive voice, offering a story, a thought, a reflection, or a memory. The poetic forms are varied and well chosen. . . . Expressive period photos from Myers' collection accompany the text of this handsome book." Booklist

Nelson, Marilyn, 1946-

Carver, a life in poems. Front St. 2001 103p il $16.95

Grades: 7 8 9 10   811
   1. Carver, George Washington, 1864?-1943 2. Poetry—By individual authors
   ISBN 1-88691-053-7   LC 00-63624

"A series of fifty-nine poems portrays George Washington Carver as a private, scholarly man of great personal faith and social purpose. Nelson fills in the trajectory of Carver's life with details of the cultural and political contexts that shaped him even as he shaped history. As individual works, each poem stands as a finely wrought whole of . . . high caliber." Horn Book Guide

Fortune's bones; the manumission requiem. Front Street 2004 32p il $16.95

Grades: 7 8 9 10   811
   1. Slavery—Poetry 2. African Americans—Poetry 3. Poetry—By individual authors
   ISBN 1-932425-12-8   LC 2004-46917

"This requiem honors a slave who died in Connecticut in 1798. His owner, a doctor, dissected his body, boiling down his bones to preserve them for anatomy studies. The skeleton . . . hung in a local museum until 1970. . . . The museum . . . uncovered the skeleton's provenance, created a new exhibit, and led to the commissioning of these six poems. The selections . . . arc from grief to triumph. . . . The facts inform the verse and open up a full appreciation of its rich imagery and rhythmic, lyrical language." SLJ

Includes bibliographical references

The freedom business; including a narrative of the life & adventures of Venture, a native of Africa. Wordsong 2008 72p il $18.95 *

Grades: 8 9 10 11 12   811
   1. Slavery—Poetry 2. African Americans—Poetry 3. Connecticut—Poetry
   ISBN 978-1-932425-57-4; 1-932425-57-8
                                  LC 2008-04437

"Venture Smith, born Broteer Furro in Guinea, was captured and enslaved at the age of six and brought to America in 1738. . . . His narrative, published in 1798, appears continuously on the left-hand page of each

spread; Nelson's luminous poems appear on the right. Both are thrown into relief by Dancy's mixed-media artwork, which includes images of birds, ropes, chains and blood to heighten the visceral emotions of both texts. . . . Tragic, important, breathtaking." Kirkus

A wreath for Emmett Till; illustrated by Philippe Lardy. Houghton Mifflin 2005 unp il $17 *

Grades: 8 9 10 11 12   811
   1. Till, Emmett, 1941-1955—Poetry 2. Lynching—Poetry 3. Mississippi—Poetry 4. African Americans—Poetry 5. Poetry—By individual authors
   ISBN 0-618-39752-3   LC 2004-9205

This is a "poetry collection about Till's brutal, racially motivated murder. The poems form a heroic crown of sonnets—a sequence in which the last line of one poem becomes the first line of the next. . . . The rigid form distills the words' overwhelming emotion into potent, heart-stopping lines that speak from changing perspectives. . . . When matched with Lardy's gripping, spare, symbolic paintings of tree trunks, blood-red roots, and wreaths of thorns, these poems are a powerful achievement that teens and adults will want to discuss together." Booklist

Nye, Naomi Shihab, 1952-

19 varieties of gazelle; poems of the Middle East. Greenwillow Bks. 2002 142p $16.95; pa $6.99 *

Grades: 7 8 9 10   811
   1. Middle East—Poetry 2. Poetry—By individual authors
   ISBN 0-06-009765-5; 0-06-050404-8 (pa)
                                  LC 2002-771

In this "volume, Nye collects her poems about growing up as an Arab American (her ancestry is Palestinian), including previously published poems and newly written pieces. This rich and varied volume offers insights into the experience of childhood in two very different worlds. . . . This volume will fill a need for classroom use, for young people seeking a more personal understanding of the Middle East, and for readers seeking a connection with their own Middle Eastern background." Bull Cent Child Books

Honeybee; poems & short prose. Greenwillow Books 2008 164p $16.99; lib bdg $17.89

Grades: 8 9 10 11 12   811
   1. Poetry—By individual authors
   ISBN   978-0-06-085390-7;   0-06-085390-5;
   978-0-06-085391-4 (lib bdg); 0-06-085391-3 (lib bdg)
                                  LC 2007-36742

This poetry "anthology is a rallying cry, a call for us to rediscover such beelike traits as interconnectedness, strong community, and honest communication. . . . Teens at the very start of their questioning years will recognize their own angst in Nye's sense of irony, their idealistic optimism in her simple wonder." SLJ

Nye, Naomi Shihab, 1952----_Continued_

You & yours: poems. BOA Editions 2005 87p
(American poets continuum series) hardcover o.p.
pa $15.50
Grades: 11 12 Adult   **811**
1. Poetry—By individual authors
ISBN 1-929918-68-2; 1-929918-69-0 (pa)
                                    LC 2005-11360
"Part one covers Nye's personal experience, at home
with her child in San Antonio or as a 'Frequent Frequent
Flyer' enjoying the sights of Scotland. . . . Part two covers the Middle East." Publ Wkly
"Tender yet forceful, funny and commonsensical, reflective and empathic, Nye writes radiant poems of nature and piercing poems of war, always touching base
with homey details and radiant portraits of family and
neighbors." Booklist

Oliver, Mary, 1935-

New and selected poems. Beacon Press 2005
c1992 2v v1 $28.50; v1 pa $16; v2 $24.95; v2 pa
$16
Grades: 11 12 Adult   **811**
1. Poetry—By individual authors
ISBN 0-8070-6878-0 (v1); 0-8070-6877-2 (v1 pa);
0-8070-6886-1 (v2); 0-8070-6887-X (v2 pa)
Vol. 1 first published 1992; redesigned ed. to accompany the publication of vol. 2
Volume one contains poems written from 1965 to
1992. Volume two contains poems written from 1994 to
2005.

Plath, Sylvia

The collected poems; edited by Ted Hughes.
Harper & Row 1981 351p pa $17.95 hardcover
o.p. *
Grades: 11 12 Adult   **811**
1. Poetry—By individual authors
ISBN 0-06-155889-3 (pa)
Also available in hardcover from Buccaneer Bks.
The collection contains "all the poems Plath wrote,
published and unpublished, from 1956 to 1963, as well
as a sample of her early work." Publ Wkly
"Although her best poems deal with suffering and
death, others are exhilarating and affectionate, and her
tone is frequently witty as well as disturbing." Concise
Oxford Companion to Engl Lit

Crossing the water; transitional poems. Harper
& Row 1971 56p pa $10 hardcover o.p.
Grades: 11 12 Adult   **811**
1. Poetry—By individual authors
ISBN 0-06-090789-4 (pa)
This posthumous collection of poems written in 1960
and 1961 evidences "Plath's preoccupation with death
{which} is conveyed in obsessive use of the word black
to connote despair and in other metaphors. . . . Desperate funnels of words, structured in strength and discipline, allude to nature, people, time and painful experiences of living." Booklist

Poe, Edgar Allan, 1809-1849

Complete poems; edited by Thomas Ollive
Mabbott. University of Ill. Press 2000 xxx, 627p
il pa $25 *
Grades: 11 12 Adult   **811**
1. Poetry—By individual authors
ISBN 0-252-06921-8   LC 00-38639
First published 1969 as volume 1 of: Collected works
of Edgar Allan Poe by Belknap Press of Harvard University Press
This book contains 101 poems and their variants. In
addition to classic poems such as The raven, The bells,
and Annabel Lee, this volume contains previously uncollected poems, fragments, verses published in reviews,
and poems attributed to Poe
Includes bibliographical references

Poems and poetics; Richard Wilbur, editor.
Library of Am. 2003 xxv, 179p (American poets
project) $20
Grades: 11 12 Adult   **811**
1. Poetry—By individual authors
ISBN 1-931082-51-0   LC 2003-46637
"Wilbur wants Poe to be appreciated as a transcendental cosmic theorist and 'the most difficult of the symbolist writers of his century,' and he appends selections
from Poe's writings about poetics to help understanding
of his cosmology and discusses some of Poe's most intense stories to exemplify his symbolism. The poems,
presented chronologically, show again what a young
prodigy Poe was, formulating his poetic thought while
still in his teens, and what a sonorous Romantic musician
he became." Booklist
Includes bibliographical references

Pound, Ezra, 1885-1972

Selected poems. new ed. New Directions 1957
184p pa $8.95 *
Grades: 11 12 Adult   **811**
1. Poetry—By individual authors
ISBN 0-8112-0162-7
First published 1949
This "provides a good sampling of the Pound who
wrote 'A Virginal,' the latter-day Renaissance poet, as
well as the reincarnate Li Po and the other 'personae'
that Ezra wore during the years he spent absorbing the
styles (and not the political thinking) of other centuries."
Saturday Rev

Reynolds, Jason

My name is Jason. Mine too; by Jason Reynolds
and Jason Griffin. HarperTeen 2009 unp il pa
$12.99
Grades: 7 8 9 10   **811**
1. Poetry—By individual authors 2. Artists—Poetry
3. New York (N.Y.)—Poetry
ISBN 978-0-06-154788-1; 0-06-154788-3
                                    LC 2008-43824
"Two former college roommates, both named Jason,
set off for New York City to seek their collective fortunes. . . . As money and food quickly become rare
commodities, the cruel realities of life in the City are all-
too evident for the struggling artists. . . . Touching and

Reynolds, Jason—*Continued*
endearing yet gritty and hip, this story should be highly
appealing to older teens and indeed, many adults." Voice
Youth Advocates

Roethke, Theodore, 1908-1963
The collected poems of Theodore Roethke.
Doubleday 1966 279p pa $14.95 hardcover o.p. *
Grades: 11 12 Adult   811
  1. Poetry—By individual authors
  ISBN 0-385-08601-6 (pa)
Roethke's "refreshingly original rhythms are keenly
articulated and often hypnotic. Although his work is un-
even and he sometimes gives way to self-indulgence or
to surprising naiveté, many of his best poems recreate
disconcertingly intense psychic or mystical experience.
He also had a flair for the seductively lyrical and the
brashly irreverent. He ranks as one of the best poets of
the first postmodern generation." Benet's Reader's Ency
of Am Lit

Sandburg, Carl, 1878-1967
The complete poems of Carl Sandburg. rev and
expanded ed. Harcourt Brace Jovanovich 1970
xxxi, 797p $40
Grades: 11 12 Adult   811
  1. Poetry—By individual authors
  ISBN 0-15-100996-1
  First published 1950
  Introduction by Archibald MacLeish
A collection of seven of the author's books: Chicago
poems, 1916; Cornhuskers, 1918; Smoke and steel, 1920;
Slabs of the sunburnt West, 1922; Good morning, America, 1925; The people, yes, 1936; Honey and salt, 1963
"Known for his free verse, written under the influence
of Walt Whitman and celebrating industrial and agricultural America, American geography and landscape, figures in American history, and the American common
people, {Sandburg} frequently makes use of contemporary American slang and colloquialisms." Herzberg.
Reader's Ency of Am Lit

Selected poems; edited by George Hendrick and
Willene Hendrick. Harcourt Brace & Co. 1996
xxix, 285p pa $16 *
Grades: 11 12 Adult   811
  1. Poetry—By individual authors
  ISBN 0-15-600396-1   LC 95-50686
  "A Harvest original"
"With a preface that puts the poet and his work in
perspective, this 'one-volume edition of Sandburg's best
and most characteristic poetry' is ideal for student and
poetry enthusiast alike." Booklist
  Includes bibliographical references

Sexton, Anne
The complete poems; with a foreword by
Maxine Kumin. Houghton Mifflin 1981 xxiv, 622p
pa $19 hardcover o.p. *
Grades: 11 12 Adult   811
  1. Poetry—By individual authors
  ISBN 0-395-95776-1 (pa)   LC 81-2482

"This collection contains all the poems in the eight
volumes published in Sexton's lifetime, the two published after her death, and seven poems never before in
print." Libr J
"Even before her death in 1974, Sexton's work was
the subject of critical controversy, often dismissed as
mere confessionalism. But, as Maxine Kumin observes in
an insightful introductory essay, Sexton 'delineated the
problematic position of women—the neurotic reality of
the time' and in so doing 'earned her place in the canon.'" Choice

Silverstein, Shel
Where the sidewalk ends; the poems &
drawings of Shel Silverstein. 30th anniversary
special ed. HarperCollins 2004 183p il $17.99; lib
bdg $18.89 *
Grades: 3 4 5 6 7 8 9 10   811
  1. Humorous poetry 2. Nonsense verses 3. Poetry—By
  individual authors
  ISBN 0-06-057234-5; 0-06-058653-2 (lib bdg)
             LC 2004-269335
  First published 1974
  This edition contains 12 new poems
"There are skillful, sometimes grotesque line drawings
with each of the 127 poems, which run in length from
a few lines to a couple of pages. The poems are tender,
funny, sentimental, philosophical, and ridiculous in turn,
and they're for all ages." Sat Rev

Soto, Gary
Partly cloudy; poems of love and longing.
Harcourt 2009 100p $16 *
Grades: 7 8 9 10   811
  1. Love poetry 2. Poetry—By individual authors
  ISBN 978-0-15-206301-6; 0-15-206301-3
             LC 2008-22267
Poet Gary Soto captures the voices of young people
as they venture toward their first kiss, brood over bruised
hearts, and feel the thrill of first love.
"Soto's new book of verse about adolescent love is remarkable. . . . The language of the poems is spare and
evocative, with not one word wasted. . . . Teens will
find these poems very engaging and will relate to how
the emotion of love is expressed in everyday moments."
Voice Youth Advocates

Spires, Elizabeth
I heard God talking to me; William Edmondson
and his stone carvings. Farrar, Straus and Giroux
2009 56p il $17.95 *
Grades: 8 9 10 11 12 Adult   811
  1. Edmondson, William, ca. 1870-1951—Poetry
  2. Artists—Poetry 3. African Americans—Poetry
  4. Religious poetry 5. Sculpture—Poetry 6. Poetry—
  By individual authors
  ISBN 978-0-374-33528-1; 0-374-33528-1
             LC 2008-02343
  "Frances Foster books"
"Moved by a religious vision at age 57, Nashville janitor William Edmondson began carving tombstones and
whimsical figures out of stone in 1931 and went on to

Spires, Elizabeth—*Continued*

attract the attention of international collectors, eventually becoming the first African American artist to have a solo show at the Museum of Modern Art in New York. This handsome picture-book-sized poetry collection pairs full-page, black-and-white photos of Edmondson and his works with poems inspired by the images. . . . Supported by an appended prose biography, these playful, thought-provoking poems introduce a fascinating artist." Booklist

Stevens, Wallace, 1879-1955

The collected poems of Wallace Stevens. Knopf 1954 534p $40; pa $16

Grades: 11 12 Adult   811

1. Poetry—By individual authors

ISBN 0-394-40330-4; 0-679-72669-1 (pa)

Steven's "poems range from descriptive and dramatic lyrics to meditative and discursive discourse, but all show a deep engagement in experience and in art. His musical verse, rich in tropic imagery but precise and intense in statement, is marked by concern with means of knowledge, with the contrast between reality and appearance, and the emphasis upon imagination as giving an aesthetic insight and order to life." Oxford Companion to Am Lit. 6th edition

Swenson, May, 1913-1989

Nature; poems old and new. Houghton Mifflin 1994 xxiii, 240p pa $15 hardcover o.p.

Grades: 11 12 Adult   811

1. Poetry—By individual authors

ISBN 0-618-06408-7 (pa)   LC 93-45642

This collection of Swenson's poetry "brings together poems from several earlier books, as well as poems published only in magazines, and introduces us to nine splendid poems published here for the first time. This collection . . . is brought together with special attention to poems describing the environment; poems of tides and the sea, of birds and gardens, of moods and seasons, of self and others. . . . This is a collection to be treasured; it belongs in all libraries with even a modest selection of poetry." Libr J

Walcott, Derek

Collected poems, 1948-1984. Farrar, Straus & Giroux 1986 515p pa $20 hardcover o.p. *

Grades: 11 12 Adult   811

1. Poetry—By individual authors

ISBN 0-374-52025-9 (pa)   LC 85-20688

"It is difficult to think of a poet in our century who—without ever betraying his native sources—has so organically assimilated the evolution of English literature from the Renaissance to the present, who has absorbed the Classical and Judeo-Christian past, and who has mined the history of Western painting as Walcott has. Throughout his entire body of work he has managed to hold in balance his passionate moral concerns with the ideal of art." Poetry

Includes bibliographical references

Omeros. Farrar, Straus & Giroux 1990 325p pa $16 hardcover o.p.

Grades: 11 12 Adult   811

1. Poetry—By individual authors

ISBN 0-374-52350-9 (pa)   LC 90-33592

This epic poem "follows the wanderings of a present-day Odysseus and the inconsolable sufferings of those who are displaced and traveling with trepidation toward their homes. Written in seven circling books and . . . tercets, the poem illuminates the classical past and its motifs through an extraordinary cast of contemporary characters from the island of Santa Lucia." Publ Wkly

"No poet rivals Mr. Walcott in humor, emotional depth, lavish inventiveness in language or in the ability to express the thoughts of his characters and compel the reader to follow the swift mutations of ideas and images in their minds. This wonderful story moves in a spiral, replicating human thought." N Y Times Book Rev

Walker, Alice, 1944-

Hard times require furious dancing; new poems; foreword and illustrations by Shiloh McCloud. New World Library 2010 165p il $18

Grades: 11 12 Adult   811

1. Poetry—By individual authors

ISBN 978-1-57731-930-6   LC 2010-29972

"A Palm of Her Hand project"

In this poetry collection, the author "writes of loss and disappointment, and the strength that rises from meeting them unflinchingly. . . . These are powerful anthems of womanhood and age, although just as likely to be empowering to men and to the not-yet-old." Booklist

Her blue body everything we know; earthling poems, 1965-1990, complete. Harcourt Brace Jovanovich 1991 463p pa $15 hardcover o.p.

Grades: 11 12 Adult   811

1. Poetry—By individual authors

ISBN 0-15-602861-1 (pa)   LC 90-5160

In this volume of Walker's "complete earlier work, joined to new, previously uncollected poems, we see a quarter century of impressive artistic development." Booklist

Warren, Robert Penn, 1905-1989

The collected poems of Robert Penn Warren; edited by John Burt; with a foreword by Harold Bloom. Louisiana State Univ. Press 1998 xxvi, 830p $44.95

Grades: 11 12 Adult   811

1. Poetry—By individual authors

ISBN 0-8071-2333-1   LC 98-26104

"This immense volume gathers 15 books of poetry—as well as uncollected verse from the beginning and end of his writing life—from a formidable American man of letters and our first poet laureate. . . . Scholars will especially cherish the careful, copious textual and explanatory notes provided by Warren's literary executor Burt . . . and fans of American poetry and literary history alike should welcome this opportunity to explore the prodigious oeuvre of one of the New Criticism's most forceful, convincing proponents." Publ Wkly

Whitman, Walt, 1819-1892

Complete poetry and collected prose. Library of Am. 1982 1380p $35; pa $17.95 *

Grades: 11 12 Adult   **811**

1. Poetry—By individual authors

ISBN 0-940450-02-X; 1-883011-35-3 (pa)

LC 81-20768

Edited by Justin Kaplan

Contents: Leaves of grass (1855); Leaves of grass (1891-92); Complete prose works (1892); Supplementary prose

Leaves of grass; edited and with a new afterword by David S. Reynolds. 150th anniversary ed. Oxford University Press 2005 167p $23 *

Grades: 11 12 Adult   **811**

1. Poetry—By individual authors

ISBN 0-19-518342-8   LC 2004-26509

Also available in paperback from Penguin Classics and Bantam Books

First published 1855

"The book, radical in form and content, takes its title from the themes of fertility, universality, and cyclical life. . . . As he revised and added to the original edition, Whitman arranged the poems in a significant autobiographical order." Reader's Ency. 4th edition

Williams, Norman, 1952-

One unblinking eye; poems. Swallow Press; Ohio University Press 2003 48p $24.95; pa $14.95

Grades: 9 10 11 12   **811**

1. Poetry—By individual authors

ISBN 0-8040-1057-9; 0-8040-1058-7 (pa)

LC 2003-42381

This collection contains "poems about tragedy in America's heartland, aging fathers, departed lovers, and surviving children who died in infancy . . . In Williams' work, precise imagery unites with humanity of feeling to become poetry of everlasting refreshment." Booklist

Williams, William Carlos, 1883-1963

The collected poems of William Carlos Williams. New Directions 1986-1988 2v v1 $40; v1 pa $23.95; v2 $38; v2 pa $22.95 *

Grades: 11 12 Adult   **811**

1. Poetry—By individual authors

ISBN 0-8112-0999-7 (v1); 0-8112-1187-8 (v1 pa); 0-8112-1063-4 (v2); 0-8112-1188-6 (v2 pa)

Contents: v1 1909-1939; edited by A. Walton Litz and Christopher MacGowan; v2 1939-1962; edited by Christopher MacGowan

"Williams's poetry is firmly rooted in the commonplace detail of everyday American life. He conceived of the poem as an object: a record of direct experience that deals with the local and the particular. He abandoned conventional rhyme and meter in an effort to reduce the barrier between the reader and his consciousness of his immediate surroundings. . . . Williams's original approach to poetry, his insistence on the importance of the ordinary, and his successful attempts at making his verse as 'tactile' as the spoken word had a far-reaching effect on American poetry." Reader's Ency. 4th edition

811.008   American poetry— Collections

The **100** best African American poems; (*but I cheated); edited by Nikki Giovanni. Sourcebooks MediaFusion 2010 228p $22.99

Grades: 10 11 12 Adult   **811.008**

1. American poetry—African American authors—Collections 2. African Americans—Poetry

ISBN 978-1-4022-2111-8

Includes audio CD. "Featuring performances on CD by Ruby Dee, Novella Nelson, Nikki Giovanni, Elizabeth Alexander, Sonia Sanchez, Robert Hayden, Marilyn Nelson, and many more friends..."

Giovanni's "vivid and affecting selections add up to a complexly pleasurable anthology. The delight is in the musical, inventive, and vivid language; the astute insights and humor, passion and tenderness. But these are poems born of suffering and injustice, even as they reach for truth and wisdom. . . . Poets and other performers read 36 poems on the accompanying CD." Booklist

100 essential American poems; edited by Leslie M. Pockell. Thomas Dunne Books 2009 288p $24.95; pa $14.99

Grades: 9 10 11 12 Adult   **811.008**

1. American poetry—Collections

ISBN 978-0-312-36980-4; 0-312-36980-8; 978-0-312-62397-5 (pa); 0-312-62397-6 (pa)

LC 2008-38641

In this collection, the editor "focuses on poems that have fueled the American identity. Covering 400 years, the poems range from classic, to familiar (and for nostalgics, poems most likely memorized and recited), to those that touch upon the seminal events in America's history. The collection aims to present an evolving American 'voice' while following the country's growth in human rights, feminism and diversity. . . . A work that serves as reference, comfort, and a reminder poetry's significance in the everyday experience of American life, this is a volume worthy of any shelf." Publ Wkly

180 more; extraordinary poems for every day; selected and with an introduction by Billy Collins. Random House 2005 xxiii, 373p pa $14.95

Grades: 11 12 Adult   **811.008**

1. American poetry—Collections

ISBN 0-8129-7296-1   LC 2005-42798

Sequel to: Poetry 180

This is a second collection of 180 poems for each day of the school year, designed to expose high school students to poetry.

American poetry: the nineteenth century; edited by John Hollander. Library of Am. 1993 2v ea $35 *

Grades: 11 12 Adult   **811.008**

1. American poetry—Collections

ISBN 0-940450-60-7 (v1); 0-940450-78-X (v2)

LC 93-10702

Volume 1 also available in paperback $14.95 (ISBN 1-88301-136-1)

American poetry: the nineteenth century—*Continued*

Contents: v1 Freneau to Whitman; v2 Melville to Stickney; American Indian poetry; Folk songs and spirituals

An anthology of more than 1,000 poems by nearly 150 poets. Arrangement is chronological by poet's date of birth. Biographical sketches of the poets, a chronology of significant events from 1800 to 1900, and an essay on textual selection are included

Hollander has compiled "a selection of nineteenth-century American verse so wonderfully catholic that it not just augments but supersedes every other similar collection." Booklist

American poetry: the seventeenth and eighteenth centuries; edited by David Shields. Library of America 2007 xxiii, 952p $40 *

Grades: 11 12 Adult   **811.008**
1. American poetry—Collections
ISBN 978-1-931082-90-7; 1-931082-90-1
      LC 2007-929763

"Besides hefty helpings of the few figures meagerly represented in general American-lit surveys—Anne Bradstreet, Edward Taylor, John Trumbull, Timothy Dwight, Philip Freneau, Phyllis Wheatley—here are poems short and . . . long by dozens of others, most of them obscure to even thoroughgoing, historically minded poetry lovers. . . . The subject matter isn't all religion and politics. Work, family, leisure, and exceptional events and lives (one man recounts escape from the limited slavery that was indenture) are all written up. And, in regular rhymes and meters, it's all quite readable. Early-American history buffs as much as, if not more than, poetry readers may consider the book a gold mine." Booklist

Includes bibliographical references

American poetry, the twentieth century. Library of Am. 2000 2v ea $35 *

Grades: 11 12 Adult   **811.008**
1. American poetry—Collections
ISBN 1-88301-177-9 (v1); 1-88301-178-7 (v2)
      LC 99-43721

The first two volumes of a projected four volume set
Contents: v1 Henry Adams to Dorothy Parker; v2 E.E. Cummings to May Swenson

"Over 200 poets are represented, all born before 1914, and presented in birth-date order." Publ Wkly

These volumes represent a "remarkable feat of assemblage, with excellent capsule biographies and explanatory notes at the end of each volume—the biographies, especially, are well worth reading." N Y Times Book Rev

Includes bibliographical references

American religious poems; an anthology by Harold Bloom; Harold Bloom and Jesse Zuba, editors. Library of America 2006 685p $40

Grades: 11 12 Adult   **811.008**
1. American poetry—Collections 2. Religious poetry
ISBN 1-931082-74-X   LC 2006-41031

An anthology of "verse on Christian, Jewish, Islamic, Buddhist, Native American spiritual, Transcendentalist and even agnostic themes, from 17th-century European colonists (one poet is Roger Williams, who founded Rhode Island) to up-and-comers in contemporary verse.

Pious readers will have no trouble finding high-quality poetry that confirms their beliefs—from the monk Thomas Merton, the Anglican T.S. Eliot, the Jewish liturgical poet Esther Schor and the Louisiana-based Christian poet Martha Serpas. Yet from the 19th century to the present, from the decidedly heterodox Emily Dickinson forwards, the anthology often highlights the ways in which American spirituality has challenged all doctrines about who God is and what God does. . . . More than half of the book is taken up by 20th-century poets, who offer varied takes on what religion has come to mean in America." Publ Wkly

American war poetry; an anthology; edited by Lorrie Goldensohn. Columbia University Press 2006 413p $27.95 *

Grades: 11 12 Adult   **811.008**
1. War poetry 2. American poetry—Collections
ISBN 0-231-13310-3   LC 2005-54762

"Arranged by war, the book begins with the Colonial period and proceeds through Whitman admiring Civil War soldiers crossing a river to end with Brian Turner, who published his first book in 2005, beckoning a bullet in contemporary Iraq. Many voices, by turns elegiac, outraged, rhetorical and ecstatic are represented." Publ Wkly

Includes bibliographical references

Black poets; [a new anthology] Bantam Books 1985 c1971 xxvi, 353p pa $7.99 *

Grades: 11 12 Adult   **811.008**
1. American poetry—African American authors—Collections
ISBN 0-553-27563-1; 978-0-553-27563-6

This anthology covers African American poetry from slave songs to the works of Gwendolyn Brooks and Nikki Giovanni.

The **Columbia** anthology of American poetry; edited by Jay Parini. Columbia Univ. Press 1995 757p $40.95 *

Grades: 11 12 Adult   **811.008**
1. American poetry—Collections
ISBN 0-231-08122-7   LC 94-32423

"Ranging from Anne Bradstreet to Louise Glück, editor Parini aims to represent 'the main schools of poetry that have co-existed in the United States . . . in proportion to their influence,' including more poetry by women and minorities 'than one generally finds' in older anthologies." Libr J

The **Columbia** book of Civil War poetry; Richard Marius, editor; Keith W. Frome, associate editor. Columbia Univ. Press 1994 xxxvi, 543p il $37.95

Grades: 11 12 Adult   **811.008**
1. American poetry—Collections 2. United States—History—1861-1865, Civil War—Poetry
ISBN 0-231-10002-7   LC 94-6481

"Bret Harte, Walt Whitman, and Robert Frost are but three of the many writers whose poems about the Civil War fill this noteworthy collection." Booklist

Cool salsa; bilingual poems on growing up Latino in the United States; edited by Lori M. Carlson; introduction by Oscar Hijuelos. Holt & Co. 1994 xx, 123p il hardcover o.p. pa $6.99 *

Grades: 5 6 7 8 9 10   **811.008**

1. American poetry—Hispanic American authors—Collections 2. Bilingual books—English-Spanish

ISBN 0-8050-3135-9; 978-0-449-70436-3 (pa); 0-449-70436-X (pa)   LC 93-45798

"This collection presents poems by 29 Mexican-American, Cuban-American, Puerto Rican, and other Central and South American poets, including Sandra Cisneros, Luis J. Rodriguez, Pat Mora, Gary Soto, Ana Castillo, Oscar Hijuelos, Ed J. Vega, Judith Ortiz-Cofer, and other Latino writers both contemporary and historical. Brief biographical notes on the authors are provided. All the poems deal with experiences of teenagers." Book Rep

Eight American poets; an anthology: Theodore Roethke, Elizabeth Bishop, Robert Lowell, John Berryman, Anne Sexton, Sylvia Plath, Allen Ginsberg, James Merrill; edited by Joel Conarroe. Random House 1994 xxiv, 306p il pa $14.95 hardcover o.p.

Grades: 11 12 Adult   **811.008**

1. American poetry—Collections

ISBN 0-679-77643-5 (pa)   LC 94-10186

This anthology contains representative work by eight 20th century American confessional poets

Every shut eye ain't asleep; an anthology of poetry by African Americans since 1945; edited by Michael Harper and Anthony Walton. Little, Brown 1994 327p pa $19 hardcover o.p.

Grades: 11 12 Adult   **811.008**

1. American poetry—African American authors—Collections

ISBN 0-316-34710-8 (pa)   LC 93-10788

"Using Robert Hayden and Gwendolyn Brooks's poetry as 'emblematic' successes, this anthology selects 35 African American poets (spanning three generations) who were born between 1913 and 1962 and came of age after 1945. Besides the well-known Imamu Baraka, Lucille Clifton, Rita Dove, and Etheridge Knight, the editors feature little-known or younger poets like Elizabeth Alexander, Gerald Barrax, Jayne Cortex, and Dolores Kendrick." Libr J

Falling hard; 100 love poems by teenagers; edited by Betsy Franco. Candlewick Press 2008 144p $15.99

Grades: 9 10 11 12   **811.008**

1. Love poetry 2. American poetry—Collections 3. Teenagers' writings

ISBN 978-0-7636-3437-7; 0-7636-3437-9   LC 2007-22401

This is a collection of love poems by young writers, ranging in age from twelve to eighteen.

"The quality here is head and shoulders above most young writers' collections, and in fact it's well above many adult anthologies as well. . . . This will inspire creativity, imitation, and perhaps, around Valentine's Day, a spot of appreciative plagiarism." Bull Cent Child Books

From both sides now; the poetry of the Vietnam War and its aftermath; edited by Phillip Mahony. Scribner 1998 314p hardcover o.p. pa $16

Grades: 11 12 Adult   **811.008**

1. American poetry—Collections

ISBN 0-684-84946-1; 0-684-84947-X (pa)   LC 98-16628

The editor "arranges poems by 135 poets in chronological order 'to simulate the progression of the Vietnam War.' Poems of the North and South Vietnamese, 'boat people,' and postwar Vietnamese American second-generation poets appear beside well-known names (e.g., Ehrhart, Komunyakaa, and Weihl)." Libr J

From totems to hip-hop; edited by Ishmael Reed. Thunder's Mouth Press 2003 xxx, 523p $34.95; pa $17.95

Grades: 11 12 Adult   **811.008**

1. American poetry—Collections

ISBN 1-56025-500-5; 1-56025-458-0 (pa)   LC 2002-75691

"Reed's selections range from classic poems like Carl Sandburg's 'Chicago' to contemporary texts like Tupac Shakur's 'Why Must U Be Unfaithful (4 women).' Along the way, readers will encounter familiar names like Marianne Moore, Claude McKay, Robert Frost, and T.S. Eliot but will also find less anthologized writers like Agha Shadid Ali, Bessie Smith, Speckled Red, Lorna Dee Cervantes, Haki Madhubuti, and the rock'n'roll composers Jerry Leiber and Mike Stoller." Libr J

This is "a dynamic and original anthology, an unprecedented amalgam of poets representing many facets of American culture and society." Booklist

Good poems; selected and introduced by Garrison Keillor. Viking 2002 xxvi, 476p $25.95; pa $15

Grades: 11 12 Adult   **811.008**

1. American poetry—Collections 2. English poetry—Collections

ISBN 0-670-03126-7; 0-14-200344-1 (pa)   LC 2002-16881

Keillor "has put together a collection of close to 300 poems he has read during . . . [the] PBS broadcast, The Writer's Almanac. . . . Poems are arranged by 19 general themes, such as 'Snow,' 'Failure,' and 'A Good Life.' Authors range from well-known oldies like Emily Dickinson and Robert Frost to unknowns like C.K. Williams. . . . An outstanding feature of this collection is that the selections are all so accessible—even folks who say they don't like poetry can find something here to enjoy." SLJ

Harper's anthology of 20th century Native American poetry; edited by Duane Niatum. Harper & Row 1988 xxxii, 396p pa $24.95 hardcover o.p.

Grades: 11 12 Adult   **811.008**

1. American poetry—Native American authors

ISBN 0-06-250666-8 (pa)   LC 86-45023

This collection "contains the work of 36 native American poets, with hearty selections from each. Among the 36 are poets near the mainstream (Scott Momaday, James Welch, Louise Erdrich); those in academe (Gerald Vizenor, Linda Hogan, Jim Barnes); those writing in the tribal oral tradition (Barney Bush, Peter Blue Cloud,

Harper's anthology of 20th century Native American poetry—*Continued*

Wendy Rose); and those working in a modernist voice (Gladys Cardiff, Paula Gunn Allen). This book belongs in every collection that claims to represent the multiple voices of American literature today." Booklist

Includes bibliographical references

Heart to heart; new poems inspired by twentieth-century American art; edited by Jan Greenberg. Abrams 2001 80p il map $19.95 *

Grades: 5 6 7 8 9 10   **811.008**

1. American poetry—Collections 2. American art 3. Art—20th century

ISBN 0-8109-4386-7   LC 99-462335

A compilation of poems by Americans writing about American art in the twentieth century, including such writers as Nancy Willard, Jane Yolen, and X. J. Kennedy.

"From a tight diamante and pantoum to lyrical free verse, the range of poetic styles will speak to a wide age group. . . . Concluding with biographical notes on each poet and artist, this rich resource is an obvious choice for teachers, and the exciting interplay between art and the written word will encourage many readers to return again and again to the book." Booklist

I am the darker brother; an anthology of modern poems by African Americans; edited and with an afterword by Arnold Adoff; drawings by Benny Andrews; introduction by Rudine Sims Bishop; foreword by Nikki Giovanni. rev ed. Simon & Schuster Bks. for Young Readers 1997 208p il hardcover o.p. pa $5.99 *

Grades: 6 7 8 9 10   **811.008**

1. American poetry—African American authors—Collections

ISBN 0-689-81241-8; 0-689-80869-0 (pa)

LC 97-144181

First published 1968

This anthology presents "the African-American experience through poetry that speaks for itself. . . . Because of the historical context of many of the poems, the book will be much in demand during Black History Month, but it should be used and treasured as part of the larger canon of literature to be enjoyed by all Americans at all times of the year. An indispensable addition to library collections." SLJ

Is this forever, or what? poems and paintings from Texas; selected by Naomi Shihab Nye. Greenwillow Books 2004 164p il $19.99

Grades: 7 8 9 10   **811.008**

1. Texas—Poetry 2. Texas in art 3. American poetry—Collections

ISBN 0-06-051178-8   LC 2003-4441

"The poems include moving family tributes, furious self-revelations, and quiet, atmospheric vignettes that find grace and beauty in sunbaked neighborhoods, basic work, and everyday faces. . . . The accompanying artworks are arresting without overpowering the words, and they echo the poems' wide range of styles." Booklist

Letters to America; contemporary American poetry on race; edited by Jim Daniels. Wayne State Univ. Press 1995 230p pa $21.95 *

Grades: 9 10 11 12   **811.008**

1. American poetry—Collections

ISBN 0-8143-2542-4   LC 95-19996

This volume collects "the probings of several dozen American poets on their nation's nightmare. . . . If a large proportion of the poets selected are black, Indian, Chicano, or Asian, that is unsurprising, for they are the ones upon whom the subject thrusts itself most insistently." Booklist

The **Oxford** anthology of African-American poetry; edited by Arnold Rampersad; associate editor, Hilary Herbold. Oxford University Press 2006 432p $32.50 *

Grades: 11 12 Adult   **811.008**

1. American poetry—African American authors—Collections

ISBN 0-19-512563-0; 978-0-19-512563-4

LC 2005-15242

"Predicated on the fact that there is a vast body of poetry written by gifted black poets, this . . . anthology tells the story of African American culture and explicates its crucial role within the larger literary tradition. . . . There is much to admire about the artistry of the poems, and even more to discover about the African American experience." Booklist

The **Oxford** book of American poetry; chosen and edited by David Lehman; associate editor, John Brehm. Oxford University Press 2006 lvii, 1132p $35 *

Grades: 8 9 10 11 12 Adult   **811.008**

1. American poetry—Collections

ISBN 0-19-516251-X; 978-0-19-516251-6

LC 2005-36590

First published 1950 with title: The Oxford book of American verse

This is an anthology of "American poetry from its origins in the 17th century right up to the present." Publisher's note

"The book is not only a sound historical survey, but also gives the reader a powerful taste of poetry's impact upon the wider world." Economist

Includes bibliographical references

Paint me like I am; teen poems from WritersCorps. HarperTempest 2003 128p hardcover o.p. pa $6.99

Grades: 7 8 9 10   **811.008**

1. Teenagers' writings 2. American poetry—Collections

ISBN 0-06-029288-1; 0-06-447264-7 (pa)

LC 2002-5942

"The teen voices in these poems, collected from the WritersCorps youth program, are LOUD—raging, defiant, giddy, lusty, and hopeful. Grouped into arbitrary categories, the poems explore identity, creative expressions, family, neighborhood, drugs, and relationships. . . . A foreword from Nikki Giovanni rounds out this moving collection, which also includes a few thoughtful writing exercises." Booklist

Paper dance; 55 Latino poets; edited by Victor Hernández Cruz, Leroy V. Quintana, and Virgil Suarez. Persea Bks. 1995 242p $14

Grades: 11 12 Adult   **811.008**

1. American poetry—Hispanic American authors— Collections

ISBN 0-89255-201-8   LC 94-15586

"This collection of poetry attests to the richness of culture in the Hispanic diaspora in the U.S., and includes well-known writers such as Julia Alvarez, Luis J. Rodriguez, and Lucha Corpi, to name a few. . . . The poets' themes are as varied as they are intriguing. Ranging in scope from contemplations on race and ethnicity to love and death, they demand that readers pay attention to vital threads in the fabric of the American literary tapestry." SLJ

Poetry 180; a turning back to poetry; selected and with an introduction by Billy Collins. Random House Trade Paperbacks 2003 xxiv, 323p pa $13.95

Grades: 11 12 Adult   **811.008**

1. American poetry—Collections

ISBN 0-8129-6887-5   LC 2002-36949

Also available online

The editor "has collected 180 accessible modern poems: one for each day of the school year and together signifying a 180° turning back to poetry. These are poems, he says, you can 'get' the first time around, and he hopes that high schools will expose students to a poem a day via public address system or assemblies. A fine gathering of contemporary poets." Libr J

Includes bibliographical references

The **Poetry** anthology, 1912-2002; ninety years of America's most distinguished verse magazine; edited by Joseph Parisi & Stephen Young; with an introduction by Joseph Parisi. Ivan R. Dee 2002 lv, 509p $29.95; pa $16.95

Grades: 11 12 Adult   **811.008**

1. American poetry—Collections

ISBN 1-56663-468-7; 1-56663-604-3 (pa)

LC 2002-31178

A collection of 600 poems previously published in Poetry magazine, written by such poets as W.H. Auden, Elizabeth Bishop, Sylvia Plath, James Merrill, and Susan Hahn

This is a "comprehensive and thrilling anthology, a veritable history of twentieth-century poetry in English." Booklist

Poetry speaks expanded; hear poets from Tennyson to Plath read their own work; Elise Paschen & Rebekah Presson Mosby, editors; Charles Osgood, narrator. [2nd ed.] Sourcebooks 2007 384p il $49.95 *

Grades: 11 12 Adult   **811.008**

1. American poetry—Collections 2. English poetry— Collections

ISBN 978-1-4022-1062-4; 1-4022-1062-0

LC 2007-37080

First published 2001 with title: Poetry speaks

Includes 3 audio CDs

"Each of the 47 poets, all deceased, is introduced through a biographical sketch, an essay by a contemporary poet, the text of a few representative poems and . . . select recordings." SLJ

"Reluctant poetry readers may find themselves drawn to the printed page by the spoken work, and poetry fans are likely to find much to love here." Publ Wkly

The **poets** laureate anthology; edited and with introductions by Elizabeth Hun Schmidt; foreword by Billy Collins. W.W. Norton & Co. 2010 liii, 762p $39.95

Grades: 11 12 Adult   **811.008**

1. American poetry—Collections

ISBN 978-0-393-06181-9   LC 2010-21692

At head of title: In association with the Library of Congress

Poems by each of the forty-three poets who have been named our nation's Poet Laureate since the post (originally called Consultant in Poetry to the Library of Congress) was established in 1937.

"A hefty and worthy read that everyone will want to savor. Essential for all contemporary poetry collections." Libr J

A **Poke** in the I; [selected by] Paul Janeczko; illustrated by Chris Raschka. Candlewick Press 2001 35p il hardcover o.p. pa $7.99

Grades: 4 5 6 7 8 9 10   **811.008**

1. American poetry—Collections

ISBN 0-7636-0661-8; 0-7636-2376-8 (pa)

LC 00-33675

"Thirty concrete poems of all shapes and sizes are carefully laid on large white spreads, extended by Raschka's quirky watercolor and paper-collage illustrations. . . . Beautiful and playful, this title should find use in storytimes, in the classroom, and just for pleasure anywhere." SLJ

Postmodern American poetry; a Norton anthology; edited by Paul Hoover. Norton 1994 xxxix, 701p pa $26.95

Grades: 11 12 Adult   **811.008**

1. American poetry—Collections

ISBN 0-393-31090-6   LC 93-22753

Hoover "brings together more than 100 writers from the 1950s and since—Olson, Duncan, O'Hara, Ginsberg, Corso, Dorn, Major, Ashbery, Guest—whose adventures with the language renew it for far more than a readymade membership." Publ Wkly

Red hot salsa; bilingual poems on being young and Latino in the United States; edited by Lori Marie Carlson; introduction by Oscar Hijuelos. Henry Holt 2005 140p $14.95 *

Grades: 7 8 9 10   **811.008**

1. American poetry—Hispanic American authors— Collections 2. Hispanic Americans—Poetry 3. Bilingual books—English-Spanish

ISBN 0-8050-7616-6   LC 2004-54005

This is a "bilingual collection of poems that appear in both Spanish and English. Included are many well-known writers, such as Gary Soto and Luis J. Rodriguez . . . as well as emerging poets. . . . The poems often speak about the complex challenges of being bicultural. . . .

Red hot salsa—*Continued*

Most poems are translated by the poets themselves, and many are written in an inventive blend of languages, which English speakers will easily follow with help from the appended glossary. Powerful and immediate." Booklist

Reflections on a gift of watermelon pickle—and other modern verse; [compiled by] Stephen Dunning, Edward Lueders, Hugh Smith. Lothrop, Lee & Shepard Bks. 1967 c1966 139p il $19.99

Grades: 6 7 8 9 10   **811.008**
1. American poetry—Collections
ISBN 0-688-41231-9

First published 1966 by Scott, Foresman in a text edition

"Although some of the [114] selections are by recognized modern writers, many are by minor or unknown poets, and few will be familiar to the reader. Nearly all are fresh in approach and contemporary in expression. . . . Striking photographs complementing or illuminating many of the poems enhance the attractiveness of the volume." Booklist

Shimmy shimmy shimmy like my sister Kate; looking at the Harlem Renaissance through poems; [edited by] Nikki Giovanni. Holt & Co. 1995 186p $17.95

Grades: 8 9 10 11 12   **811.008**
1. American poetry—African American authors—Collections 2. Harlem Renaissance
ISBN 0-8050-3494-3   LC 95-38617

This anthology includes poems by such authors as Paul Laurence Dunbar, Langston Hughes, Countee Cullen, Gwendolyn Brooks, and Amiri Baraka. Commentary and a discussion of the development of African American arts known as the Harlem Renaissance is provided by editor Giovanni

Includes bibliographical references

Six American poets; an anthology; edited by Joel Connaroe. Random House 1991 xxxiv, 281p il pa $14.95 hardcover o.p.

Grades: 11 12 Adult   **811.008**
1. American poetry—Collections
ISBN 0-679-74525-4 (pa)   LC 91-15375

This anthology contains 247 representative poems by Walt Whitman, Emily Dickinson, Wallace Stevens, William Carlos Williams, Robert Frost and Langston Hughes

Songs from this Earth on turtle's back; contemporary American Indian poetry; edited by Joseph Bruchac. Greenfield Review Press 1983 294p il pa $14.95

Grades: 11 12 Adult   **811.008**
1. American poetry—Native American authors
ISBN 0-912678-58-5   LC 82-82420

"A biographical statement accompanies each sampling from 50 poets representing more than 35 different Native American nations." Libr J

"The collection provides a balance to the volumes of compiled chants and translated (or mistranslated) songs already in most libraries. . . . Writing in English, they display a variety of styles and themes and draw from urban, rural, and reservation backgrounds, yet they share a reverence for the earth and the natural world and a keen understanding of the power of language to create and shape that world." Choice

The **Spoken** word revolution; slam, hip-hop, & the poetry of a new generation; edited by Marc Eleveld; advised by Marc Smith; introduction by Billy Collins. Sourcebooks 2003 241p il $24.95; pa $19.95 *

Grades: 11 12 Adult   **811.008**
1. American poetry—Collections
ISBN 1-4022-0037-4; 1-4022-0246-6 (pa)
                                            LC 2003-841

Includes audio CD

The editors "trace the evolution of spoken-word poetry from the Beats to rap, hip-hop, and performance art. The result is a dynamic and clarifying volume chock-full of fresh and informative commentary by the likes of Billy Collins, Marvin Bell, and Jerry Quickley and an exciting array of knock-out poems by Patricia Smith, Tara Betts, Jeff McDaniel, Roger Bonair-Agard . . . and many more. Eleveld and his contributors not only celebrate the verve, artistry, and significance of performance poetry but also anchor it firmly within the splendid, age-old, and life-sustaining universe of poetry. . . . An accompanying CD presents poets performing their work." Booklist

Sweet nothings; an anthology of rock and roll in American poetry; edited, with an introduction, by Jim Elledge. Indiana Univ. Press 1994 283p pa $16.95 hardcover o.p. *

Grades: 11 12 Adult   **811.008**
1. American poetry—Collections
ISBN 0-253-20864-5 (pa)   LC 93-11795

In this anthology the editor "explores the influence that rock 'n' roll has had on American poets who came of age to the sexy and defiant beat of Otis Redding, Buddy Holly, Aretha Franklin, Bob Dylan, and the Rolling Stones. Elledge's introduction provides a peppy . . . overview of the rise of rock 'n' roll and a sensitive assessment of how rock has shaped poetry both overtly and subtly. His theories are well supported by the poems themselves." Booklist

Includes bibliographical references

Tell the world; teen poems from WritersCorps. HarperTeen 2008 116p $16.99; pa $8.99

Grades: 7 8 9 10 11 12   **811.008**
1. Teenagers' writings 2. American poetry—Collections
ISBN   978-0-06-134505-0;   0-06-134505-9;
978-0-06-134504-3 (pa); 0-06-134504-0 (pa)
                                            LC 2007-49577

"This worthy collection of brief poems offers an array of teen voices. . . . An essay by WritersCorps teacher Michelle Matz adds a vivid picture of her students and their lives. This fine collection should inspire creativity and resonate with teens who find their own hopes, fears, and dreams eloquently voiced in the works of these young poets." SLJ

Time you let me in; 25 poets under 25; selected by Naomi Shihab Nye. Greenwillow Books 2010 236p $16.99; lib bdg $17.89 *
Grades: 8 9 10 11 12   **811.008**
1. American poetry—Collections
ISBN   978-0-06-189637-8;   0-06-189637-3;
978-0-06-189638-5 (lib bdg); 0-06-189638-1 (lib bdg)
LC 2009-19387
"This lively collection by young contemporary writers is rooted in the strong, emotional particulars of family, friendship, childhood memories, school, dislocation, war, and more. . . . Teens will connect with the passionate, unmoderated feelings that are given clarity and shape in each poem." Booklist
Includes bibliographical references

Twentieth-century American poetry; edited by Dana Gioia, David Mason, Meg Schoerke. McGraw Hill 2004 xlvi, 1143p il pa $79.69 *
Grades: 11 12 Adult   **811.008**
1. American poetry—Collections
ISBN 0-07-240019-6   LC 2003-61449
"The text is divided into sections like 'Realism and Naturalism' and 'The Harlem Renaissance,' with each section prefaced by a penetrating overview and each poet introduced by a biographical essay. Included are poets as diverse as Sherman Alexie, Ezra Pound, and Lucille Clifton, along with Nuyorican poets, New Formalists, Beats, imagists, and surrealists. Make room for this affordable, remarkable volume." Libr J
Includes bibliographical references

Unsettling America; an anthology of contemporary multicultural poetry; edited by Maria Mazziotti Gillan and Jennifer Gillan. Penguin Bks. 1994 xxv, 406p pa $18 hardcover o.p.
Grades: 11 12 Adult   **811.008**
1. American poetry—Collections
ISBN 0-14-023778-X (pa)   LC 94-722
This "anthology provides exposure to poets, emerging and established—Louis Simpson, Rita Dove, Luis Rodriguez—who write directly from the immigrant, ethnic and/or religious experience. . . . This collection is a must for anyone seeking an inclusive, unwincing catalogue of the American experience." Publ Wkly

The **Vintage** book of African American poetry; edited and with an introduction by Michael S. Harper and Anthony Walton. Vintage Bks. 2000 xxxiii, 403p pa $14.95 *
Grades: 11 12 Adult   **811.008**
1. American poetry—African American authors—Collections
ISBN 0-375-70300-4   LC 99-39428
"A Vintage original"
"Included in chronological order here are over two centuries of poets, from Jupitor Hammon (1720-1800) to Reginald Shepherd (b.1963). . . . The editors' eloquent, outspoken vision provides a springboard for further examination of what constitutes the mainstream of American poetry." Libr J
Includes bibliographical references

The **Vintage** book of contemporary American poetry; edited and with an introduction by J.D. McClatchy. 2nd ed., newly rev. and expanded ed. Vintage Books 2003 xxxiv, 617p pa $17.95 *
Grades: 11 12 Adult   **811.008**
1. American poetry—Collections
ISBN 1-400-03093-5   LC 2003-269652
"A Vintage original"
First published 1990
"With selections from 65 poets writing over the last 40 years, and with brief notes on their lives and work, this anthology will introduce YAs to much of the best modern poetry." Booklist [review of 1990 edition]
Includes bibliographical references

Visions of war, dreams of peace; writings of women in the Vietnam War; edited by Lynda Van Devanter and Joan A. Furey. Warner Bks. 1991 214p pa $9.95
Grades: 11 12 Adult   **811.008**
1. Vietnam War, 1961-1975—Poetry—Collections
ISBN 0-446-39251-0   LC 90-23284
This anthology collects poetry about the Vietnam War as experienced by women who served and those who remained stateside while their husbands, brothers and fathers fought

Word of mouth; poems featured on NPR's All things considered; edited and introduced by Catherine Bowman. Random House 2003 xx, 182p pa $12
Grades: 11 12 Adult   **811.008**
1. American poetry—Collections
ISBN 0-375-71315-8   LC 2002-28077
This collection includes works by 33 poets, such as Lucille Clifton, Kevin Young, C.D. Wright, Naomi Shihab Nye, Lucia Perillo, and Marilyn Chin
"These inspired selections . . . make for a fresh and enjoyable poetry anthology." Booklist

811.009   American poetry—History and criticism

African-American poets; volume 1: 1700s-1940s; edited and with an introduction by Harold Bloom. New ed. Chelsea House 2009 264p (Modern critical views) lib bdg $45 *
Grades: 9 10 11 12   **811.009**
1. American poetry—African American authors—History and criticism 2. African Americans in literature
ISBN 978-1-60413-400-1   LC 2008-54305
First published 2002
"This volume focuses on the principal African-American poets from colonial times to the Harlem Renaissance and the World War II era. . . . Poets covered in this volume include Phillis Wheatley, author of the first volume of verse published by an African American, and the seminal figures Gwendolyn Brooks, Countee Cullen, Paul Lawrence Dunbar, Langston Hughes, Claude McKay, and Jean Toomer." Publisher's note
Includes bibliographical references

Borus, Audrey
A student's guide to Emily Dickinson. Enslow
Publishers 2005 152p il (Understanding literature)
$27.93
Grades: 7 8 9 10 **811.009**
1. Dickinson, Emily, 1830-1886
ISBN 0-7660-2285-4 LC 2004-18098
"A short discussion of Dickinson's life and times is
followed by a chapter on how to read and analyze her
poems, which would be particularly useful for students
reading her work for the first time. Subsequent chapters
focus on particular themes in the poems such as death
and eternity, truth, faith and reality, the natural world,
and the influence of the Civil War." SLJ
Includes bibliographical references

Buckwalter, Stephanie
Early American poetry, "beauty in words".
Enslow Publishers 2010 160p il (Poetry rocks!) lib
bdg $34.60
Grades: 9 10 11 12 **811.009**
1. American poetry—History and criticism 2. Poets,
American 3. Poetry—Authorship
ISBN 978-0-7660-3277-4; 0-7660-3277-9
LC 2008-53658
"Discusses early American poetry from the early 17th
century into the late 19th century, including short biogra-
phies of poets like Phillis Wheatley and Walt Whitman;
also has examples of poems, poetic techniques, and ex-
plication." Publisher's note
Includes glossary and bibliographical references

Burns, Allan
Thematic guide to American poetry. Greenwood
Press 2002 309p $54.95 *
Grades: 9 10 11 12 **811.009**
1. American poetry—History and criticism
ISBN 0-313-31462-4 LC 2001-58646
This "features 21 narrative essays on such broad
themes in American poetry as 'Art and Beauty,' 'Family
Relations,' 'Loss,' and 'War.' The essays are arranged
alphabetically, and each begins with a theme-related quotation followed by a chronologically arranged discussion
of how the theme is treated differently across individual
poems. . . . The narratives for each poem are pithy and
clear, discussing only generally how the poem portrays
the theme under discussion." Booklist
Includes bibliographical references

Encyclopedia of American poetry, the twentieth
century; edited by Eric L. Haralson. Fitzroy
Dearborn Pubs. 2001 846p $125 *
Grades: 11 12 Adult **811.009**
1. Reference books 2. American poetry—Bio-
bibliography 3. Poets, American—Dictionaries
ISBN 1-57958-240-0
"The volume features more than 400 entries written by
academic contributors on individual poets, landmark poems, and major topics. The poet entries are usually 1,000
to 2,000 words long and offer critical treatment of the
poet's career and major achievements along with a capsule biography. . . . Approximately one-third of the poet
entries include subentries for one or more landmark po-

ems. The 'major topics' entries are longer (around 3,000
words) and include periods or movements (*Black Arts
movement, Dada*), verse traditions (often ethnic, such as
Asian American poetry), and styles and themes (*Confessional poetry, War and antiwar poetry*)." Booklist

The **Facts** on File companion to American poetry.
[New ed.] Facts On File 2008 2v (Facts on File
library of American literature) set $140 *
Grades: 11 12 Adult **811.009**
1. American poetry—History and criticism
ISBN 978-0-8160-6950-7 LC 2006-35417
Volume 2 first published 2004 with title: The Facts on
File companion to 20th-century poetry
Contents: v1 Beginnings to 1900 / [edited by] Randall
Huff; v2 1900 to the present / [edited by] Burt
Kimmelman and Temple Cone
"Volume 1 includes members of the literary pantheon
such as Ralph Waldo Emerson, Walt Whitman, and Emi-
ly Dickinson and represents literary schools ranging from
Quaker poetry to poetry in translation. . . . [Volume 2]
includes the pathos of Sylvia Plath's poetry, the Roman
Catholic/Buddhist-influenced Beat works of Jack
Kerouac, plus the imagist school, objectivist poetry, and
the New York school." Libr J
Includes bibliographical references

Fagan, Deirdre
Critical companion to Robert Frost; a literary
reference to his life and work. Facts on File 2007
454p il $75
Grades: 9 10 11 12 Adult **811.009**
1. Frost, Robert, 1874-1963
ISBN 0-8160-6182-3; 978-0-8160-6182-2
LC 2006-13269
"This encyclopedic guide offers critical entries on
each of Frost's published poems, including such classics
as 'The Road Not Taken,' 'Stopping By Woods on a
Snowy Evening,' and 'The Death of the Hired Man.'"
Publisher's note
Includes bibliographical references

The **Greenwood** encyclopedia of American poets
and poetry; Jeffrey Gray, editor; James
McCorkle and Mary McAleer Balkun, associate
editors. Greenwood Press 2006 5v set $599.95
Grades: 11 12 Adult **811.009**
1. Reference books 2. American poetry—Encyclopedias 3. Poets, American—Encyclopedias
ISBN 0-3133-2381-X LC 2005-25445
"Of the more than 900 alphabetically arranged articles
found here, approximately one third deal with writers
and movements prior to the 20th century. The rest cover
20th- and 21st-century poets and poetry movements."
SLJ
This encyclopedia "provides an excellent overview for
students learning about American poetry." Ref & User
Services Quarterly
Includes bibliographical references

A **Historical** guide to Walt Whitman; edited by David S. Reynolds. Oxford Univ. Press 2000 280p il (Historical guides to American authors) $39.95; pa $19.95 *

Grades: 9 10 11 12   **811.009**
1. Whitman, Walt, 1819-1892
ISBN 0-19-512081-7; 0-19-512082-5 (pa)
                              LC 99-12608

Following a brief biography contributors discuss Whitman's poetics, themes and influence. An illustrated chronology and a bibliographical essay are included.

Includes bibliographical references

Kirk, Connie Ann, 1951-
A student's guide to Robert Frost. Enslow Pubs. 2006 160p il (Understanding literature) $27.93 *

Grades: 7 8 9 10   **811.009**
1. Frost, Robert, 1874-1963
ISBN 0-7660-2434-2   LC 2005-13392

In this book, "the career of this literary giant is examined. . . . Poems are put into historical and biographical context, with special emphasis placed on curriculum-related works, including 'Stopping by Woods on a Snowy Evening,' 'The Road Not Taken,' 'The Gift Outright,' and 'Fire and Ice.'" Publisher's note

Leiter, Sharon
Critical companion to Emily Dickinson; a literary reference to her life and work. Facts on File 2006 448p il $75

Grades: 11 12 Adult   **811.009**
1. Dickinson, Emily, 1830-1886
ISBN 0-8160-5448-7; 978-0-8160-5448-0
                              LC 2005-28123

This book "opens with a foreword by poet and Dickinson scholar Gregory Orr and includes an introduction; an approximately 20-page biography of Dickinson; explications of 150 of her best-known poems (e.g., 'Because I Could Not Stop for Death'); an A-to-Z dictionary of relevant persons, places, and ideas illustrated with black-and-white photos; a chronology; bibliographies; and a comprehensive index." Libr J

Includes bibliographical references

Llanas, Sheila Griffin
Contemporary American poetry, "not the end, but the beginning". Enslow Publishers 2010 160p il (Poetry rocks!) lib bdg $34.60

Grades: 9 10 11 12   **811.009**
1. American poetry—History and criticism 2. Poets, American 3. Poetry—Authorship
ISBN 978-0-7660-3279-8; 0-7660-3279-5
                              LC 2009-23802

The author discusses "some of the poetry of leading contemporary American poets, including: Roethke, Bishop, Stafford, Lowell, Brooks, Wilbur, Ginsberg, Merwin, Rich, Plath, Collins, and Gluck." Publisher's note

Includes glossary and bibliographical references

Modern American poetry, "echoes and shadows". Enslow Publishers 2009 160p il (Poetry rocks!) lib bdg $34.60

Grades: 9 10 11 12   **811.009**
1. American poetry—History and criticism 2. Poets, American 3. Poetry—Authorship
ISBN 978-0-7660-3275-0; 0-7660-3275-2
                              LC 2009-11529

"Explores modern American poetry, including biographies of twelve poets such as Robert Frost, Ezra Pound, and Langston Hughes; excerpts of poems, literary criticism, poetic technique, and explication." Publisher's note

Includes glossary and bibliographical references

Murphy, Russell E.
Critical companion to T.S. Eliot; a literary reference to his life and work; [by] Russell Elliott Murphy. Facts on File 2007 614p il (Facts on File library of American literature) $75

Grades: 9 10 11 12 Adult   **811.009**
1. Eliot, T. S. (Thomas Stearns), 1888-1965
ISBN 978-0-8160-6183-9; 0-8160-6183-1
                              LC 2006-34076

This book "explores the life and works of this Nobel Prize-winning writer, with . . . analyses of Eliot's writing, as well as entries on related topics and relevant people, places, and influences." Publisher's note

"This is an excellent and exhaustive resource and a good buy for most libraries." Booklist

Includes bibliographical references

Oliver, Charles M.
Critical companion to Walt Whitman; a literary reference to his life and work. Facts on File 2005 408p il (Facts on File library of American literature) $65

Grades: 11 12 Adult   **811.009**
1. Whitman, Walt, 1819-1892
ISBN 0-8160-5768-0   LC 2005-4172

The author "begins this work with a biographical essay that includes several illustrations. A large portion of this book addresses Whitman's works, with entries for the individual poems and for the complete volumes. Each entry describes when and where the book was published and includes a brief account of the poem and its context. The third section of the volume covers people, places, publications, and topics related to Whitman's life and work." Choice

Includes bibliographical references

Priddy, Anna
Bloom's how to write about Emily Dickinson; introduction by Harold Bloom. Chelsea House 2008 262p (Bloom's how to write about literature) $45

Grades: 9 10 11 12   **811.009**
1. Dickinson, Emily, 1830-1886 2. Report writing
ISBN 978-0-7910-9492-1   LC 2006-100573

This book offers "paper-topic suggestions, . . . strategies on how to write a strong essay, and an . . . introduction by Harold Bloom on writing about Dickinson.

Priddy, Anna—*Continued*

This . . . volume is designed to help students develop their analytical writing skills and critical comprehension of this important poet and her works." Publisher's note
  Includes bibliographical references

Sylvia Plath; edited by Harold Bloom. Chelsea House 2000 96p (Bloom's major poets) lib bdg $21.95
  Grades: 9 10 11 12   **811.009**
  1. Plath, Sylvia
  ISBN 0-7910-5935-9   LC 00-55590
  Other available series titles in this class include: E.E. Cummings; Walt Whitman; Hilda Doolittle. For complete list of titles contact publisher
  Literary scholars analyze The colossus, The arrival of the bee box, Daddy, Ariel, and Lady Lazarus.
  Includes bibliographical references

812 American drama

Albee, Edward, 1928-

Who's afraid of Virginia Woolf? Scribner Classics 2003 243p $24 *
  Grades: 11 12 Adult   **812**
  ISBN 0-7432-5525-9   LC 2003-54206
  Also available in paperback from Dramatists Play Service and Signet Bks.
  A reissue of the title first published 1962 by Atheneum Pubs.
  Characters: 2 men, 2 women. 3 acts. First produced at the Billy Rose Theatre, New York City, October 13, 1962
  "The play is a virulent unveiling of the relationship between George, a history professor, and his wife, Martha, the college president's daughter. Another couple, Nick and Honey, get caught in the crossfire of George and Martha's verbal and emotional lacerations, and it becomes clear that each character is engaged in an isolated struggle through a personal hell." Reader's Ency. 4th edition

Dabrowski, Kristen

Twenty 10-minute plays for teens. Smith & Kraus 2004 129p (Young actor series) pa $14.95
  Grades: 9 10 11 12   **812**
  1. Acting 2. One act plays
  ISBN 1-57525-405-0
  Also available vols. 2 and 3
  On cover: 20 10-minute plays for teens
  "These brief plays deal with typical adolescent concerns, including dating, parties, sports, and school life, as well as some more controversial topics like being gay, drinking, and suicide. There are roles for up to 14 females and 11 males, but the number of characters can easily be reduced or increased. . . . The content and language make the plays teen-friendly but more appropriate for older high school students, who will recognize the lingo and situations and will enjoy performing them." SLJ

Fairbanks, Stephanie S., 1950-

Spotlight; solo scenes for student actors. Meriwether 1996 115p pa $14.95
  Grades: 9 10 11 12   **812**
  1. Acting 2. Monologues
  ISBN 1-56608-020-7   LC 96-6169
  "Fifty five monologues that feature typical teenage concerns. They run an average of 55 lines each; require minimal props and costumes; and have numbered lines for easy directing and practicing." SLJ

Fleischman, Paul

Zap. Candlewick Press 2005 83p $16.99; pa $5.99
  Grades: 9 10 11 12   **812**
  ISBN 0-7636-2774-7; 0-7636-3234-1 (pa)
                                LC 2005-50790
  Characters: 2 men, 8 women. 1 act. First produced at Pacific Grove High School, Pacific Grove, California, November 1, 2002.
  "Framed as a performance for an imaginary audience armed with remote-control 'zappers,' this is actually seven plays mashed into one: a turgid rendition of Shakespeare's Richard III alternating at audience's whim among six spoofs of other dramaturgical biggies, among them, 'The Russian Play,' 'The English Mystery,' and 'The Southern Play.' Playgoers and actors alike . . . will relish the irreverent chaos as the boundaries between the plays gradually erode." Booklist

Garner, Joan

Stagings; short scripts for middle and high school students; written and illustrated by Joan Garner. Teacher Ideas Press 1995 233p il pa $27
  Grades: 9 10 11 12   **812**
  1. Acting 2. One act plays
  ISBN 1-56308-343-4   LC 95-19013
  "This book presents nine science fiction and fantasy one-act plays for young people to perform. . . . Each script begins with a thorough description of characters and costumes, followed by a scene design, set description and a props list. Other notes describe how a teacher could use the play in the classroom and specifically discuss the best staging possibilities for the script." Book Rep

Gibson, William, 1914-2008

The miracle worker. Scribner 2008 112p pa $12.99 *
  Grades: 11 12 Adult   **812**
  1. Keller, Helen, 1880-1968—Drama 2. Sullivan, Anne, 1866-1936—Drama
  ISBN 978-1-4165-9084-2; 1-4165-9084-6
                                LC 2008-275273
  First published 1957
  A text of the television play, intended for reading, of Anne Sullivan Macy's attempts to teach her pupil, Helen Keller, to communicate.
  "The present text is meant for reading, and differs from the telecast version in that I have restored some passages that read better than they play and others omitted in performance for simple lack of time." Author's note

Goodrich, Frances, 1891-1984

The diary of Anne Frank; by Frances Goodrich and Albert Hackett; newly adapted by Wendy Kesselman. Dramatists Play Service 2000 70p il pa $7.50

Grades: 9 10 11 12 Adult   **812**
1. Netherlands—History—1940-1945, German occupation—Drama 2. World War, 1939-1945—Jews—Drama
ISBN 0-8222-1718-X   LC 2006-455205
First published 1956 by Random House
Characters: 5 men, 5 women. 2 acts. First produced at the Cort Theatre, New York City, October 5, 1955.
Dramatization of Anne Frank: diary of a young girl. Portrays ultimately unsuccessful attempt of Jewish family to remain hidden during the German occupation of Holland.

Gurney, A. R., 1930-

Love letters and two other plays: The golden age and What I did last summer; with an introduction by the playwright. Penguin Bks. 1990 209p pa $14

Grades: 11 12 Adult   **812**
ISBN 978-0-452-26501-1; 0-452-16501-0
LC 90-34177
"A Plume book"
Love letters dramatizes the 30-year epistolary "exchange between an upper-class man and an upper-upper-class woman. . . . *The Golden Age* is an updated, romantic-comic variation upon Henry James' *Aspern Papers* in which a young academic locates an old woman who may possess a missing chapter of *The Great Gatsby* and schemes to get it from her. *What I did Last Summer* is about 14-year-old Charlie's bohemian season with Anna, the Pig Woman, who fosters his creativity as she once did his mother's." Booklist

Hansberry, Lorraine, 1930-1965

A raisin in the sun. Modern Lib. 1995 xxvi, 135p $14.95; pa $6.50 *

Grades: 11 12 Adult   **812**
ISBN 0-679-60172-4; 0-679-75533-0 (pa)
LC 95-16074
Also available in paperback from Plume Bks.
First published 1959
Characters: 8 men, 3 women. 6 scenes in 3 acts. First produced at the Ethel Barrymore Theatre, New York City, March 11, 1959
"Hansberry's drama focuses on the Youngers, a 1950s African-American working-class family in Chicago striving to realize their individual dreams of prosperity and education, and their collective dream of a better life. It was the first play by an African-American woman to be produced on Broadway." Reader's Ency. 4th edition

Hughes, Langston, 1902-1967

Five plays; edited with an introduction by Webster Smalley. Indiana Univ. Press 1963 258p hardcover o.p. pa $14.95

Grades: 11 12 Adult   **812**
ISBN 0-253-32230-8; 0-253-20121-7 (pa)
Contents: Mulatto; Soul gone home; Little Ham; Simply heavenly; Tambourines to glory

Inge, William, 1913-1973

4 plays. Grove Press 1979 c1958 304p pa $16

Grades: 11 12 Adult   **812**
ISBN 0-8021-3209-X   LC 78-73032
"A Black cat book"
First published 1958 by Random House
Contents: Come back, Little Sheba; Picnic; Bus stop; The dark at the top of the stairs

Krell-Oishi, Mary, 1953-

Perspectives; relevant scenes for teens. Meriwether 1997 241p pa $14.95

Grades: 9 10 11 12   **812**
1. Acting 2. Teenagers—Drama
ISBN 1-56608-030-4   LC 97-5405
Consists of 23 original scenes in a variety of styles for high school and college acting students
The scripts "vary in length and tone but have an equal number of male and female parts. Several scenes deal with sensitive subjects (premarital sex, abortion, homosexuality), but they are thoughtfully presented, and the occasional use of strong language is never gratuitous." Booklist

Kushner, Tony

Angels in America; a gay fantasia on national themes. 1st combined pbk. ed. Theatre Communications Group 2003 289p pa $15.95

Grades: 11 12 Adult   **812**
1. Cohn, Roy, 1927-1986—Drama
ISBN 1-55936-231-6   LC 2003-17904
Contents: pt. 1. Millennium approaches; pt. 2. Perestroika
Millennium approaches first presented at the Eureka Theatre Company, San Francisco, May 1991. Perestroika first presented at the Mark Taper Forum, Los Angeles, November 1992.
A look at the political, sexual and religious aspects of contemporary American life set against the AIDS epidemic and the life of Roy Cohn.

McCullers, Carson, 1917-1967

The member of the wedding; a play; an introduction by Dorothy Allison. New Directions 2006 118p pa $11.95 *

Grades: 11 12 Adult   **812**
ISBN 0-8112-1655-1; 978-0-8112-1655-5
LC 2005-36493
First published 1951
Characters: 6 men, 7 women. 3 acts with 3 scenes in the last act. First produced at the Empire Theatre, New York City, January 3, 1950
Based on the author's book of the same title, this is "a study of the loneliness of an overimaginative young Georgian girl." Saturday Rev

McNally, Terrence, 1939-

15 short plays. Smith & Kraus 1994 373p (Contemporary playwrights series) pa $16.95 *

Grades: 11 12 Adult   **812**
ISBN 1-880399-34-2   LC 94-10070

McNally, Terrence, 1939-—*Continued*

Contemporary playwrights series; Plays for actors series

Contents: Bringing it all back; Noon; Botticelli; Next; ¡Cuba si!; Sweet Eros; Witness; Whiskey; Bad habits; The Ritz; Prelude & Liebestod; Andre's mother; The wibbly, wobbly, wiggly dance that Cleopatterer did; Street talk; Hidden agendas

"By providing a sampling of McNally's plays from the late 1960s to the early 1990s, the entire span of his career, this volume allows a great deal of insight into the range and depth of his development as he courses his way through some of the social, political, and sexual forces that have shaped the American temperament. . . . This is a splendid collection and these plays cut to the emotional bone." Voice Youth Advocates

Medoff, Mark Howard

Children of a lesser god; by Mark Medoff. Dramatists Play Service 1998 c1980 87p pa $7.50

Grades: 11 12 Adult   **812**

1. Deaf—Drama

ISBN 0-8222-0203-4   LC 81-132181

Characters: 3 men, 4 women. 2 acts. First produced at the Longacre Theatre, New York City, March 30, 1980

"The sensitive drama of the love and growth of James Leeds, a speech teacher at a state school for the deaf, and Sarah Norman, one of his students, may lack some impact in reading since the effect of Sarah's isolation and skilled signing is lost, but Medoff's story remains a powerful, valuable one." Booklist

Includes bibliographical references

Miller, Arthur, 1915-2005

The crucible; a play in four acts. Viking 1953 145p pa $12 hardcover o.p.

Grades: 11 12 Adult   **812**

1. Witchcraft—Drama 2. Salem (Mass.)—Drama

ISBN 0-14-048138-9 (pa)

Also available in paperback from Dramatists Play Service

Characters: 11 men, 10 women. First produced at the Martin Beck Theatre in New York City, January 22, 1953

A play based on the Salem witchcraft trials of 1692. It deals particularly with the hounding to death of the nonconformist John Proctor.

Death of a salesman; certain private conversations in two acts and a requiem; with an introduction by Christopher Bigsby. Penguin 1998 xxvii, 113p (Penguin twentieth-century classics) pa $12 *

Grades: 11 12 Adult   **812**

ISBN 0-14-118097-8   LC 97-37223

First published 1949

Characters: 8 men, 5 women. First produced at the Morosco Theatre, New York City, February 10, 1949.

"The tragedy of a typical Americana salesman who at the age of sixty-three is faced with what he cannot face: defeat and disillusionment. It is a bitter and moving experience of groping for values and for material success." Wis Libr Bull

Includes bibliographical references

The portable Arthur Miller; original introduction by Harold Clurman; revised edition edited with an introduction by Christopher Bigsby. Penguin Books 2003 xli, 575p (Penguin classics) pa $17 *

Grades: 11 12 Adult   **812**

ISBN 0-14-243755-7   LC 2003-276344

First published 1955

This volume contains the complete texts of Death of a salesman, The crucible, After the fall, The American clock, The last Yankee, and Broken glass. An excerpt from a radio play thought lost for years and two very brief selections from the memoir Timebends are also included.

Includes bibliographical references

O'Neill, Eugene, 1888-1953

The iceman cometh; a play. Vintage Bks. 1946 260p pa $12

Grades: 11 12 Adult   **812**

ISBN 0-375-70917-7

Characters: 16 men, 3 women. First produced at the Martin Beck Theatre, New York City, October 9, 1946

Thoughts and actions of a group of derelicts, habitués of a cheap New York saloon. The time is 1912.

Long day's journey into night; a play; with a foreword by Harold Bloom. 2nd ed. Yale Univ. Press 2002 c1989 179p $22.95; pa $12.95

Grades: 11 12 Adult   **812**

ISBN 0-300-09410-8; 0-300-09305-5 (pa)

            LC 2001-97735

Also available in paperback from Dramatists Play Service

First published 1956

Characters: 3 men, 2 women. 4 acts, 5 scenes. First produced in Stockholm, Sweden, February, 1956

"Among the papers Eugene O'Neill left when he died in 1953 was the manuscript of an autobiography. Not an autobiography in the usual sense, however. For 'Long Day's Journey Into Night' is in the form of a play—a true O'Neill tragedy, set in 1912 in the summer home of a theatrical family that is isolated from the community by a kind of ingrown misery and a sense of doom." N Y Times Book Rev

Rose, Reginald, 1920-2002

Twelve angry men; introduction by David Mamet. Penguin Books 2006 73p (Penguin classics) pa $11

Grades: 9 10 11 12 Adult   **812**

ISBN 0-14-310440-3; 978-0-14-310440-7

            LC 2006-46006

First published 1955 by Dramatic Pub.

Characters: 12 men. 3 acts. Original television broadcast on CBS program Studio One, September 20, 1954.

Television play in which one man in a jury tries to convince the other eleven jurors that the defendant in a murder trial is not guilty.

Shange, Ntozake

For colored girls who have considered suicide, when the rainbow is enuf; a choreopoem. 1st Scribner trade pbk. ed. Scribner 2010 96p il $23; pa $12; ebook $15.99 *

Grades: 11 12 Adult   **812**
    1. African American women—Drama
    ISBN   978-1-4516-2420-5;   1-4516-2420-4;
    978-1-4391-8681-7 (pa);   1-4391-8681-2 (pa);
    978-1-4516-2415-1 (ebook)   LC 2011381105
    First published 1977 by Macmillan
Choreopoem performed by seven women exploring the joys and sorrows of being a black woman. Includes two new poems and a reading group guide.

Simon, Neil

Brighton Beach memoirs. Plume 1995 130p pa $12 *

Grades: 11 12 Adult   **812**
    ISBN 0-452-27528-8   LC 95-21788
    First published 1984 by Random House
"Sex and baseball are the primary preoccupations of 15-year-old Eugene Jerome, narrator of a seriocomic slice of lower-middle-class Jewish family life in Depression-era New York City. The several adolescent characters in the extended family add to the teenage appeal of Simon's . . . play." Booklist

The collected plays of Neil Simon; with an introduction by Neil Simon. New Am. Lib. 1986-1998 4v v1-2 pa ea $19.95 *

Grades: 9 10 11 12   **812**
    ISBN 0-452-25870-7 (v1); 0-452-26358-1 (v2)
                                      LC 86-12639
    v4 available from Touchstone Bks. $15
    "A Plume book"
    Volume 1 originally published 1971 by Random House with title: The comedy of Neil Simon
    Contents v1: Come blow your horn; Barefoot in the park; The odd couple; The star-spangled girl; Promises, promises; Plaza suite; Last of the red hot lovers; v2: Little me; The gingerbread lady; The prisoner of Second Avenue; The Sunshine Boys; The good doctor; God's favorite; California suite; Chapter two; v3: Sweet Charity; They're playing our song; I ought to be in pictures; Fools; The odd couple (female version); Brighton Beach memoirs; Biloxi blues; Broadway bound; v4: Rumors; Lost in Yonkers; Jake's women; Laughter on the 23rd floor; London suite

Lost in Yonkers. Plume 1993 120p (Plume drama) pa $12

Grades: 11 12 Adult   **812**
    ISBN 0-452-26883-4   LC 92-29111
    First published 1991 by Random House
    Characters: 4 men, 3 women. 2 acts. First presented at the Stevens Center for the Performing Arts, Winston-Salem, December 31, 1990.
    This play, "set in 1940s New York, is a sad-funny portrait of a dysfunctional family, headed by a woman who provided for her children but never showed them love." Booklist

Soto, Gary

Novio boy; a play. Harcourt 2006 78p pa $5.95 *

Grades: 7 8 9 10   **812**
    1. Dating (Social customs)—Drama 2. Mexican Americans—Drama
    ISBN 978-0-15-205863-0; 0-15-205863-X
                                      LC 2007-271308
    First published 1997
Rudy anxiously prepares for and then goes out on a first date with an attractive girl who is older than he is.

Surface, Mary Hall, 1958-

Most valuable player and four other all-star plays for middle and high school audiences. Smith & Kraus 1999 176p il (Young actor series) pa $16.95

Grades: 9 10 11 12   **812**
    1. Children's plays, American
    ISBN 1-57525-178-7   LC 99-30018
    Contents: Most valuable player; Prodigy; Dancing solo; Broken rainbows; Blessings
    "The title play is a compelling piece about Jackie Robinson's early days in the major leagues. The other selections deal with Mozart's childhood and issues such as high school drug dealing, racial conflict, learning disability, and the need for artistic expression. They all move along at a fast clip, the characters speak simply and directly, and the language is realistic and occasionally rough. In most cases, the staging is fairly simple." SLJ

Ullom, Shirley, 1938-

Tough acts to follow; seventy-five monologs for teens. Meriwether 2000 155p pa $14.95

Grades: 9 10 11 12   **812**
    1. Monologues 2. Acting
    ISBN 1-56608-057-6   LC 00-24678
    This collection of original short character sketches "is overflowing with one-of-a kind monologues of equal length for both guys and girls, each with a clever title that provides quick insight into the subject matter." Voice Youth Advocates

Wasserman, Dale, 1914-2008

Man of La Mancha; a musical play; lyrics by Joe Darion; music by Mitch Leigh. Random House 1966 82p il hardcover o.p. pa $9.95

Grades: 11 12 Adult   **812**
    ISBN 0-394-40621-4; 0-394-40619-2 (pa)
    Characters: 14 men, 5 women, extras. First produced at the ANTA Washington Square Theatre, New York City, November 22, 1965
    This musical play-adaption of Don Quixote is built around Cervantes' defense, when imprisoned and held for inquisition. He arranges a mock trial performance to present his case.

Wasserstein, Wendy, 1950-2006

The Heidi chronicles and other plays. Vintage Bks. 1991 249p pa $13.95

Grades: 11 12 Adult   **812**
    ISBN 0-679-73499-6   LC 90-55681

Wasserstein, Wendy, 1950-2006—*Continued*
First published 1990 by Harcourt Brace Jovanovich
Contents: Uncommon women and others; Isn't it romantic; The Heidi chronicles
This collection traces "three decades of changing styles, mores, life objectives, and intellectual challenges. Wasserstein examines her characters and their times with great good humor, complexity, depth of feeling, and a firm refusal to accept trite and easy images." Libr J

Wilder, Thornton, 1897-1975
Our town; a play in three acts; foreword by Donald Margulies. HarperCollins Pubs. 2003 xx, 181p $19.95; pa $9.95
Grades: 11 12 Adult   812
ISBN 0-06-053525-3; 0-06-051263-6 (pa)
A reissue with a new foreword of the title first published 1938 by Coward-McCann
Large mixed cast. First produced at McCarter's Theatre, Princeton, N.J., January 22, 1938.
"Presented without scenery of any kind, utilizing a narrator and loose episodic form, adventurous and imaginative in style, this unique play . . . is one of the most distinguished in the modern repertoire. It deals with the simplest and most touching aspects of life in a small town." HarperCollins Reader's Ency of Am Lit

Three plays: Our town, The skin of our teeth, The matchmaker; with a preface. Harper & Row 1957 401p pa $15.95 hardcover o.p. *
Grades: 11 12 Adult   812
ISBN 0-06-051264-4 (pa)
A collection of three titles first copyrighted 1938, 1942, and 1955 respectively. An earlier version of: The matchmaker, was first copyrighted 1939 with title: The merchant of Yonkers
Our town is a portrait of family life in small town America. The skin of our teeth is an allegorical fantasy about man's struggle to survive. The matchmaker is a romantic farce set in the 1880's

Williams, Tennessee, 1911-1983
The glass menagerie; introduction by Robert Bray. New Directions 1999 xxii, 105p pa $7.95 *
Grades: 9 10 11 12   812
ISBN 0-8112-1404-4   LC 98-54624
Also available in paperback from Dramatists Play Service
First published 1945 by Random House; this reissue of New Directions 1949 edition contains Williams' essay The catastrophe of success and production notes. A new critical introduction has been added
Characters: 2 men, 2 women. 2 parts. One set of scenery. First produced at the Civic Theatre, Chicago, December 26, 1944
"A poignant and painful family drama set in St. Louis, in which a frigid and frustrated mother's dreams of her glamorous past as a Southern belle conflict with the grimness of her reduced circumstances, as she persuades her rebellious son Tom to provide a 'gentleman caller' for her crippled daughter, Laura." Oxford Companion to Engl Lit. 6th edition

A streetcar named desire; with an introduction by Arthur Miller. New Directions 2004 192p pa $9.95
Grades: 11 12 Adult   812
ISBN 0-8112-1602-0   LC 2004-11654
First published 1947
Characters: 6 women, 7 men. 11 scenes. First produced at the Barrymore Theatre, New York City, December 3, 1947
"A study of sexual frustration, violence, and aberration, set in New Orleans, in which Blanche Dubois' fantasies of refinement and grandeur are brutally destroyed by her brother-in-law, Stanley Kowalski, whose animal nature fascinates and repels her." Oxford Companion to Engl Lit. 5th edition

Wilson, August
Fences; a play; introduction by Lloyd Richards. New Am. Lib. 1986 101p pa $12 *
Grades: 11 12 Adult   812
ISBN 978-0-452-26401-4   LC 86-5264
Also available in hardcover from Theatre Communications Group
"A Plume book"
Characters: 5 men, 1 woman, 1 girl. 2 acts, 9 scenes. First produced at the Yale Repertory Theatre, New Haven, Connecticut, April 30, 1985
Family drama about black experience in America. 1960's spirit of liberation alienates hard-working father from wife and son.

Jitney. Overlook Press 2001 96p hardcover o.p. pa $14.95
Grades: 11 12 Adult   812
ISBN 978-158567-370-4; 1-58567-370-6
LC 2001-33962
Also available in hardcover from Theatre Communications Group
Characters: 8 men, 1 woman. 2 acts, 8 scenes. This is a revised version of a play written 1979
Drama set in 1977 about gypsy cabdrivers who service Pittsburgh's black Hill District.

Joe Turner's come and gone; a play in two acts. New Am. Lib. 1988 94p pa $12
Grades: 11 12 Adult   812
ISBN 978-0-452-26009-2; 0-452-26009-4
LC 88-1660
Also available in hardcover from Theatre Communications Group
"A Plume book"
Characters: 6 men, 5 women. 2 acts, 10 scenes. 1 setting. First produced at the Yale Repertory Theatre, New Haven, Connecticut, April 29, 1986
This drama looks at life in a Pittsburgh boarding house for blacks in 1911.

Ma Rainey's black bottom; a play in two acts. New Am. Lib. 1985 111p pa $12
Grades: 11 12 Adult   812
ISBN 978-0-452-26113-6; 0-452-26113-9
LC 84-27156
Also available in hardcover from Theatre Communications Group

Wilson, August—*Continued*

"A Plume book"

Characters: 8 men, 2 women. 2 acts. First produced at the Yale Repertory Theatre, New Haven, Connecticut, April 6, 1984

Recording session by Black blues great Ma Rainey for white-owned studio, is setting for exploration of racial relations and conflicts.

The piano lesson. New Am. Lib. 1990 108p hardcover o.p. pa $12 *

Grades: 11 12 Adult   **812**

ISBN 978-0-452-26534-9; 0-452-26534-7

LC 90-38734

Also available in hardcover from Theatre Communications Group

Characters: 5 men, 3 women. 2 acts, 7 scenes. First presented at the Yale Repertory Theatre, New Haven, November 26, 1987

Drama set in 1936 Pittsburgh chronicles black experience in America. Family conflict arises over heirloom piano.

Zindel, Paul

The effect of gamma rays on man-in-the-moon marigolds; a drama in two acts; drawings by Dong Kingman. Harper & Row 1971 108p il pa $6.99 hardcover o.p. *

Grades: 11 12 Adult   **812**

ISBN 0-06-075738-8 (pa)

Also available in paperback from Dramatists Play Service

Characters: 5 women. First produced at the Mercer-O'Casey Theatre, New York City, April 7, 1970

"The play, in the naturalistic tradition, deals with a widow and her two daughters, the imagination of one of whom has been captured by the atom and the possibilities it offers of producing mutations." McGraw-Hill Ency of World Drama

812.008   American drama— Collections

Audition monologs for student actors [I]-[II]; selections from contemporary plays; edited by Roger Ellis. Meriwether 1999-2001 2v pa ea $15.95

Grades: 9 10 11 12   **812.008**

1. Monologues 2. Acting

ISBN 1-56608-055-X (v1); 1-56608-073-8 (v2)

LC 99-37962

"An introduction discusses choosing and performing the monologues, including specific sections on characterization and staging. The selections are evenly divided between those for males and females, and many are for minority actors. Each selection is prefaced by thoughtful character insights and performance suggestions. An excellent, up-to-the-minute resource for serious teen actors." Booklist [review of volume 1]

Black theatre USA; plays by African Americans, 1847 to today; edited by James V. Hatch, Ted Shine. rev and expanded ed. Free Press 1996 pa in 2v 916p hardcover o.p. v1 pa $39.95; v2 pa $26 *

Grades: 11 12 Adult   **812.008**

1. American drama—African American authors—Collections

ISBN 0-684-82306-3; 1-45163650-4 (v1 pa); 0-684-82307-1 (v2 pa)   LC 95-40329

First published 1974

Contents: v1 The early period, 1847-1938; v2 The recent period, 1935-today

Among the plays are: Star of Ethiopia, by W. E. B. Du Bois; A soldier's play, by C. Fuller; Sally's rape, by R. McCauley; Contribution, by T. Shine; Fires in the mirror, by A. D. Smith.

Includes bibliographical references

Fierce & true; plays for teen audiences; Peter & Elissa Adams, editors; The Children's Theatre Company. University of Minnesota Press 2010 219p il pa $17.95

Grades: 7 8 9 10 11 12   **812.008**

1. Drama—Collections

ISBN 978-0-8166-7311-7; 0-8166-7311-X

The Children's Theatre Company "located in Minneapolis, wanted to broaden its audience, so it commissioned four playwrights to create works with young people (ages 12-18) specifically in mind. The results are the full-length plays in this anthology. . . . 'Anon(ymous)' is a contemporary retelling of Homer's Odyssey, set in a dirty North American city, and 'Five Fingers of Funk' is a mature musical celebrating the roots of hip-hop while dealing with issues of poverty and drugs. In 'The Lost Boys of Sudan,' three Dinka refugees flee the horrors of war and begin a harrowing yet humorous journey that takes them to Fargo, ND. And 'Prom' is played out as a frenetic battle between students and chaperones. Each of these selections has a distinctive voice, honoring adolescents as both actor and audience capable of understanding and engaging in today's complex issues." SLJ

Great scenes from minority playwrights; seventy-four scenes of cultural diversity; edited by Marsh Cassady. Meriwether 1997 341p pa $16.95 *

Grades: 9 10 11 12   **812.008**

1. American drama—Collections 2. Minorities in literature 3. Acting

ISBN 1-56608-029-0   LC 97-298

A collection of scenes from Hispanic as well as Native-American, African-American, Jewish-American, and Asian-American theater

"Cassady introduces the plays and precedes each scene with questions intended to clarify characters' motivations or the playwright's intentions. Most plays concern the tragic aspects of prejudice, but two playwrights have chosen a satirical approach. A useful collection for drama classes and theater groups." Booklist

Millennium monologs; 95 contemporary characterizations for young actors; edited by Gerald Lee Ratliff. Meriwether 2002 261p pa $15.95

Grades: 8 9 10 11 12   **812.008**
1. Monologues 2. Acting 3. American drama—Collections
ISBN 1-56608-082-7   LC 2002-13009

An anthology of monologues by contemporary writers, divided into four categories: "Hope and Longing," "Spirit and Soul," "Fun and Fantasy," and "Doubt and Despair." Includes audition techniques

"This fine collection of American monologues is notable for its diversity as well as for the high quality of the material." Booklist

Under 30; plays for a new generation; edited by Eric Lane and Nina Shengold. Vintage 2004 639p pa $17

Grades: 9 10 11 12   **812.008**
1. American drama—Collections
ISBN 1-4000-7616-1   LC 2004043041

Contents: As bees in honey drown; Be aggressive; None of the above; Refuge; This is our youth; Cowtown; Fishing; Harriet Tubman visits a therapist; Icarus's mother; On the edge; Photographs from S-21; Shari says; Small world; Sweet hunk O' trash; Time flies; War at home

The editors "have assembled five full-length plays, 11 shorter plays, and excerpts from four plays, all written for actors under 30." Libr J

"This collection offers thespians plenty of characters to portray in situations that crackle with teen appeal." SLJ

With their eyes; September 11th: the view from a high school at ground zero; edited by Annie Thoms; created by Taresh Batra [et. al.]; photos by Ethan Moses. HarperTempest 2002 228p il hardcover o.p. pa $6.99

Grades: 7 8 9 10   **812.008**
1. Stuyvesant High School (New York, N.Y.) 2. September 11 terrorist attacks, 2001—Drama 3. American drama—Collections 4. Teenagers' writings
ISBN 0-06-051806-5; 0-06-051718-2 (pa)
     LC 2002-4552

"The students of Stuyvesant High School watched through their classroom windows as the World Trade Center was attacked on September 11. This book contains the play that they created based on what students, teachers, janitors, and others within their school community experienced." Voice Youth Advocates

"The speakers reveal their emotions with painful honesty. . . . The book is an obvious choice for reader's theater and for use across the curriculum; its deeply affecting contents will also make compelling personal-interest reading." Booklist

812.009   American drama—History and criticism

Abbotson, Susan C. W., 1961-
Critical companion to Arthur Miller; a literary reference to his life and work. Facts on File 2006 518p il (Facts on File library of American literature) $75

Grades: 9 10 11 12 Adult   **812.009**
1. Miller, Arthur, 1915-2005
ISBN 0-8160-6194-7; 978-0-8160-6194-5
     LC 2006-22902

This book "covers Miller's entire canon, including plays, screenplays, fiction, short stories, and poetry, as well as many of his important essays and critical pieces. Also included are . . . entries on literary, theatrical, and personal figures important to Miller; key terms and topics connected to his work; and various theatrical companies and places with which he has been associated." Publisher's note

Includes bibliographical references

Student companion to Arthur Miller. Greenwood Press 2000 169p (Student companions to classic writers) lib bdg $35 *

Grades: 9 10 11 12   **812.009**
1. Miller, Arthur, 1915-2005
ISBN 0-313-30949-3   LC 99-89069

Another available series title in this class is: Student companion to Tennessee Williams. For complete list of titles contact publisher

A biographical section is followed by "discussion of eight of Miller's major plays that incorporates the impact of other literature and historical events on his work and links themes, language, and characters to events and periods in the writer's life. Chapters on each play address the development of setting and plot, characters, and point of view; provide a historical context; and touch on other relevant literary devices. A bibliography of Miller's play and other works, as well as extensive listings of critical studies, reviews, and criticisms complete the text." SLJ

Includes bibliographical references

August Wilson; edited and with an introduction by Harold Bloom. Chelsea House 2002 85p (Bloom's major dramatists) lib bdg $21.95

Grades: 9 10 11 12   **812.009**
1. Wilson, August
ISBN 0-7910-6362-3   LC 2001-42336

For complete list of titles in this series contact publisher

Following a biography of Wilson this volume provides plot summaries, and critical interpretations of the plays and their characters.

Includes bibliographical references

Death of a salesman, by Arthur Miller; editor, Brenda Murphy. Salem Press 2010 285p (Critical insights) lib bdg $85

Grades: 9 10 11 12   **812.009**
1. Miller, Arthur, 1915-2005
ISBN 978-1-58765-610-1; 1-58765-610-8
     LC 2009-26317

Death of a salesman, by Arthur Miller—*Continued*

"Contains an editor's introduction to the author or work, a perspective from the editors of the . . . literary magazine *The Paris Review*, and a biography of the author. Following these ready-reference chapters is a section, 'Critical Contexts,' that presents four original essays by current scholars." Publisher's note

Includes bibliographical references

Dowling, Robert M., 1970-

Critical companion to Eugene O'Neill; a literary reference to his life and work. Facts On File 2009 2v il (Facts on File library of American literature) set $150

Grades: 11 12 Adult   **812.009**

1. O'Neill, Eugene, 1888-1953

ISBN 978-0-8160-6675-9; 0-8160-6675-2

LC 2008-24135

This set "explores the personal, historical, and artistic influences that combined to form such dark and influential American masterpieces as *The Iceman Cometh*, *The Emperor Jones*, *Mourning Becomes Electra*, *Hughie*, and . . . *Long Day's Journey into Night*." Publisher's note

"These volumes are wonderfully organized and very easy to use. . . . Entries are of a length to provide a good background of O'Neill's works and life." Booklist

Includes bibliographical references

Dunkleberger, Amy

A student's guide to Arthur Miller. Enslow Publs. 2005 160p il (Understanding literature) lib bdg $27.93 *

Grades: 7 8 9 10   **812.009**

1. Miller, Arthur, 1915-2005

ISBN 0-7660-2432-6

This discusses the life of Arthur Miller and his works *All My Sons*, *Death of a Salesman*, *The Crucible*, *A View From the Bridge*, *After the Fall*, *Incident at Vichy*, and *The Price*

"Engaging and informative. . . . The very accessible format and the solid information make [this book] useful to students, and the engaging style should interest casual readers." SLJ

Includes glossary and bibliographical references

Heintzelman, Greta

Critical companion to Tennessee Williams; [by] Greta Heintzelman, Alycia Smith Howard. Facts on File 2005 436p il (Facts on File library of American literature) $65; pa $19.95

Grades: 11 12 Adult   **812.009**

1. Williams, Tennessee, 1911-1983

ISBN 0-8160-4888-6; 0-8160-6429-6 (pa)

LC 2004-7362

"The first comprises a 14-page biography with recommendations for further reading. The second and largest section includes entries for each of Williams's plays, stories, and miscellaneous publications. . . . The third section consists of brief entries on subjects relating to Williams and his work, covering, for example, awards, the Dramatists Guild, Truman Capote, and Washington Uni-

versity. The final section includes a chronology of Williams's life, a bibliography of his work, and a bibliography of secondary sources." Libr J

The authors "offer an excellent resource for those studying Williams's life and extensive body of work." Choice

Includes bibliographical references

Hermann, Spring

A student's guide to Tennessee Williams. Enslow Publishers 2007 160p il (Understanding literature) lib bdg $27.93

Grades: 7 8 9 10   **812.009**

1. Williams, Tennessee, 1911-1983

ISBN 978-0-7660-2706-0; 0-7660-2706-6

LC 2006-36458

"The life and work of Williams are examined. . . . Each work is placed in historical and biographical context, with special emphasis placed on curriculum-related works The Glass Menagerie, A Streetcar Named Desire, and Cat On a Hot Tin Roof, in addition to many other lesser-known works." Publisher's note

Includes glossary and bibliographical references

Loos, Pamela

A reader's guide to Lorraine Hansberry's A raisin in the sun. Enslow Publishers 2008 128p il (Multicultural literature) lib bdg $31.93

Grades: 7 8 9 10   **812.009**

1. Hansberry, Lorraine, 1930-1965 2. African Americans in literature 3. American drama—History and criticism

ISBN 978-0-7660-2830-2; 0-7660-2830-5

LC 2006-17900

"*A Raisin in the Sun* has become part of the literary canon and is required reading for many students. This guide is intended to help them better appreciate the social milieu out of which this play emerged . . . making this volume a fine resource." SLJ

Includes bibliographical references

The **Tennessee** Williams encyclopedia; edited by Philip C. Kolin. Greenwood Press 2004 xxx, 350p $89.95

Grades: 11 12 Adult   **812.009**

1. Williams, Tennessee, 1911-1983

ISBN 0-313-32101-9   LC 2003-59583

The contributors "provide approximately 160 entries on individuals, places, works, and concepts of special significance in Williams's life and career. Entries are alphabetical. . . . This reviewer cannot imagine a more engaging or more useful reference resource for students and scholars of Williams." Choice

Includes bibliographical references

813.009   American fiction—History and criticism

Becnel, Kim E.

Bloom's how to write about F. Scott Fitzgerald; [introduction by Harold Bloom] Chelsea House 2008 232p (Bloom's how to write about literature) $45

Grades: 9 10 11 12   **813.009**

1. Fitzgerald, F. Scott (Francis Scott), 1896-1940
2. Report writing

ISBN 978-0-7910-9482-2   LC 2006-101321

This book offers "paper-topic suggestions, . . . strategies on how to write a strong essay, and an . . . introduction by Harold Bloom on writing about Fitzgerald. This . . . volume is designed to help students develop their analytical writing skills and critical comprehension of this modern master and his major works." Publisher's note

Includes bibliographical references

Blasingame, James B., Jr.

Gary Paulsen. Greenwood Press 2007 164p (Teen reads: student companions to young adult literature) $45 *

Grades: 7 8 9 10 11 12   **813.009**

1. Paulsen, Gary

ISBN 978-0-313-33532-7; 0-313-33532-X

                  LC 2007-21446

"This volume examines a sample of . . . books by Paulsen. A biographical chapter demonstrates how Paulsen's life experiences, notably the Iditarod, have influenced his writing. Each book is analyzed for plot, characterization, setting, and themes." Publisher's note

Includes bibliographical references

Brave new words; the Oxford dictionary of science fiction; edited by Jeffrey Prucher; introduction by Gene Wolfe. Oxford University Press 2007 xxxi, 342p $29.95

Grades: 7 8 9 10 11 12 Adult   **813.009**

1. Science fiction—Dictionaries 2. Reference books

ISBN 978-0-19-530567-8; 0-19-530567-1

                  LC 2006-37280

This is a "dictionary of the language of science fiction based on historical principles. . . . Entries include part of speech, etymology, definition with cross references to related terms, usage status (e.g., historical, jocular, derogatory, obsolete), variant forms, and . . . dated citations and quotations illustrating the usage of the word over time." Libr J

"This new science fiction lexicon . . . is an important and entertaining reference source for any science fiction writer, magazine editor, fan, neophyte reader, or librarian." Choice

Includes bibliographical references

Buckwalter, Stephanie

A student's guide to Jack London. Enslow Publishers 2007 160p il (Understanding literature) lib bdg $27.93

Grades: 7 8 9 10   **813.009**

1. London, Jack, 1876-1916

ISBN 978-0-7660-2707-7; 0-7660-2707-4

                  LC 2006-32815

"The career of this literary giant is examined. . . . Each of his works is placed in historical and biographical context, with special emphasis placed on curriculum-related works. These include The Call of the Wild, White Fang, and several other autobiographical works and short stories." Publisher's note

Includes glossary and bibliographical references

Burkhead, Cynthia

Student companion to John Steinbeck. Greenwood Press 2002 180p (Student companions to classic writers) lib bdg $35.95 *

Grades: 9 10 11 12   **813.009**

1. Steinbeck, John, 1902-1968

ISBN 0-313-31457-8   LC 2002-17134

Another available series title in this class is: Student companion to Ernest Hemingway. For complete list of titles contact publisher

"Examines the life, career, and works of John Steinbeck. . . . Each criticism explores plot and character development, major themes, symbolism, and literary devices. An alternative critical theme is also included. . . . Because Steinbeck is required reading in many high school curriculums, this would be a valuable resource for students." Libr Media Connect

Includes bibliographical references

Burton, Zisca

Bloom's how to write about Toni Morrison; [by] Zisca Isabel Burton; [introduction by Harold Bloom] Chelsea House 2008 212p (Bloom's how to write about literature) $45

Grades: 9 10 11 12   **813.009**

1. Morrison, Toni, 1931- 2. Report writing

ISBN 978-0-7910-9548-5   LC 2007-8096

This book offers "paper-topic suggestions, . . . strategies on how to write a strong essay, and an . . . introduction by Harold Bloom on writing about Morrison. This . . . volume is designed to help students develop their analytical writing skills and critical comprehension of this important author and her works." Publisher's note

Includes bibliographical references

Campbell, Patricia J., 1930-

Robert Cormier; daring to disturb the universe. Delacorte Press 2006 287p pa $41.95; lib bdg $17.99

Grades: 9 10 11 12   **813.009**

1. Cormier, Robert

ISBN 0-385-73046-2 (pa); 978-0-385-73046-4 (pa); 0-385-90074-0 (lib bdg); 978-0-385-90074-4 (lib bdg)

                  LC 2005-23595

The author "writes both a tribute to Robert Cormier and . . . [a] literary analysis that examines the common

Campbell, Patricia J., 1930———*Continued*
themes in his work. She emphasizes Cormier's place in the history of young adult literature, the contrast between the man and his work, and the quality of the works he provided the world." Voice Youth Advocates

"Campbell treats . . . [Cormier's] fans to rare glimpses of his process, and, with her wide perspective on YA literature, puts Cormier's work—including such landmark novels as The Chocolate War and I Am the Cheese—and its wide-reaching reverberations in a context for today's readers and writers." Publ Wkly

Includes bibliographical references

Carson McCullers; edited and with an introduction by Harold Bloom. New ed. Chelsea House 2009 192p (Modern critical views) $45 *
Grades: 9 10 11 12   **813.009**
1. McCullers, Carson, 1917-1967
ISBN 978-1-60413-394-3   LC 2008-38918
First published 1986

Some other available series titles in this class are: Ernest Hemingway; John Steinbeck; Richard Wright; William Faulkner; Amy Tan. For complete list of titles contact publisher

Scholars evaluate the author of The ballad of the sad cafe, The heart is a lonely hunter, and The member of the wedding.

Includes bibliographical references

Cart, Michael
The heart has its reasons; young adult literature with gay/lesbian/queer content, 1969-2004; [by] Michael Cart [and] Christine A. Jenkins. Scarecrow Press 2006 207p (Scarecrow studies in young adult literature) $42
Grades: Adult Professional   **813.009**
1. Homosexuality in literature 2. Young adult literature—History and criticism 3. Teenagers—Books and reading
ISBN 0-8108-5071-0   LC 2005-31320
"Both a comprehensive overview and a lively, detailed discussion of individual landmark books, this highly readable title . . . discusses 35 years of YA books with gay, lesbian, bisexual, transgender, and queer/questioning (GLBTQ) content. . . . With fully annotated bibliographies, including a chronological list, this is a valuable YA and adult resource, sure to be in great demand for personal reference and group discussion." Booklist

Includes bibliographical references

The **Columbia** companion to the twentieth-century American short story; Blanche H. Gelfant, editor. Columbia Univ. Press 2000 660p $83.50; pa $24.50 *
Grades: 11 12 Adult   **813.009**
1. Reference books 2. Short stories—History and criticism 3. American fiction—Bio-bibliography
ISBN 0-231-11098-7; 0-231-11099-5 (pa)
                                  LC 00-31610
"The first 100 pages are devoted to thematic essays that focus on the form of the short story, the development of the genre, several distinct subject types (e.g., short stories of the Holocaust or of the working class), and four different ethnic groups (African American,

Asian American, Chicano Latino American, and Native American). . . . The remainder of the book is devoted to over 100 individual author essays that focus on reading for pleasure and understanding rather than critical interpretation. Entries discuss the development of each author and the content and meaning of his or her major short stories." Libr J

Includes bibliographical references

Crayton, Lisa A.
A student's guide to Toni Morrison. Enslow Publs. 2006 160p il (Understanding literature) lib bdg $27.93 *
Grades: 7 8 9 10   **813.009**
1. Morrison, Toni, 1931-
ISBN 0-7660-2436-9   LC 2005-19069
"Each work is placed in historical and biographical context, with special emphasis placed on curriculum-related material, including The Bluest Eye, Song of Solomon, and Beloved, along with several other noteworthy works." Publisher's note

Includes glossary and bibliographical references

Devlin, James E., 1938-
Elmore Leonard. Twayne Pubs. 1999 164p (Twayne's United States authors series) $32 *
Grades: 11 12 Adult   **813.009**
1. Leonard, Elmore, 1925-
ISBN 0-8057-1694-7   LC 99-42756
Some other available series titles in this class are: Beverly Cleary; F. Scott Fitzgerald; James Salter; Russell Banks. For complete list of titles contact publisher

Following a brief biography the author offers critical interpretation and explication of Leonard's major works. A chronology and annotated bibliography are included.

Includes bibliographical references

Diorio, Mary Ann L.
A student's guide to Herman Melville. Enslow Publs. 2006 160p il (Understanding literature) lib bdg $27.93 *
Grades: 7 8 9 10   **813.009**
1. Melville, Herman, 1819-1891
ISBN 0-7660-2435-0   LC 2005-10159
"Each work is placed in historical and biographical context, with special emphasis placed on curriculum-related works, including his masterpiece, Moby Dick, along with Billy Budd, several of his short stories, including 'Bartleby the Scrivener,' and several of his poetic works." Publisher's note

Includes glossary and bibliographical references

The **Facts** on File companion to the American novel; edited by Abby H.P. Werlock; assistant editor, James P. Werlock. Facts on File 2005 3v (Facts on File library of American literature) set $195 *
Grades: 11 12 Adult   **813.009**
1. American fiction—Encyclopedias 2. American fiction—Bio-bibliography 3. Reference books
ISBN 0-8160-4528-3; 978-0-8160-4528-0
                                  LC 2005-12437

The Facts on File companion to the American novel—*Continued*

"This A-to-Z reference contains 450 biographical overviews of American and foreign-born authors living in the United States and 500 signed analytical essays on their novels. . . . Libraries will value this compact set for including classics as well as hard-to-find contemporary authors." SLJ

Includes bibliographical references

The Facts on File companion to the American short story; edited by Abby H.P. Werlock; assistant editor, James P. Werlock. 2nd ed. Facts On File 2009 2v (Facts on File library of American literature) set $150

Grades: 11 12 Adult   **813.009**
1. Short stories—History and criticism 2. Reference books
ISBN 9780-8160-6895-1   LC 2009-4725
First published 2000

The alphabetically arranged entries cover authors, characters, and major short stories. Literary terms, themes, and motifs are covered. Winners of prizes and awards are noted.

Includes bibliographical references

Fargnoli, A. Nicholas

Critical companion to William Faulkner; a literary reference to his life and work; [by] A. Nicholas Fargnoli, Michael Golay, Robert W. Hamblin. Facts On File 2008 562p il (Facts on File library of American literature) $75 *

                               813.009
1. Faulkner, William, 1897-1962
ISBN 978-0-8160-6432-8   LC 2007-32361
First published 2001 with title: William Faulkner A to Z

"Coverage includes: Faulkner's major works, including novels, short stories, poetry, and nonfiction; descriptions of characters in Faulkner's fiction, such as Benjy and Quentin from *The Sound and the Fury*; details about Faulkner's family, friends, colleagues, and critics; real and fictional places important to Faulkner's life and literary development, from Yoknapatawpha County, Mississippi to Hollywood; interviews and speeches given by Faulkner; [and] ideas and events that influenced his life and works, including slavery, the Civil War, World War I, and civil rights." Publisher's note

Includes bibliographical references

Farrell, Susan Elizabeth, 1963-

Critical companion to Kurt Vonnegut; a literary reference to his life and work; [by] Susan Farrell. Facts On File 2008 532p il (Facts on File library of American literature) $75

Grades: 11 12 Adult   **813.009**
1. Vonnegut, Kurt, 1922-2007
ISBN 978-0-8160-6598-1   LC 2007-37900

This "book covers all his works, including his novels, such as the unforgettable *Slaughterhouse-Five*; his short stories, such as 'Harrison Bergeron'; and his lectures and essays. . . . Entries on his life, related people, places, and topics are also included." Publisher's note

Includes bibliographical references

Gale, Robert L.

An F. Scott Fitzgerald encyclopedia. Greenwood Press 1998 526p $90

Grades: 11 12 Adult   **813.009**
1. Fitzgerald, F. Scott (Francis Scott), 1896-1940—Encyclopedias 2. Reference books
ISBN 0-313-30139-5   LC 98-13976

"In entries from Abbot, Hamilton ('Ham') (a character in The Love Boat) to 'Zone of Accident' (a story published in 1935), Gale covers all Fitzgerald's works and named fictional characters; and biographical sketches of his family, friends, and associates are included. Entries range in length from a single sentence to nearly three pages for Fitzgerald, Zelda and The Great Gatsby. Longer entries include bibliographies." Booklist

Includes bibliographical references

Gillespie, Carmen

Critical companion to Alice Walker; a literary reference to her life and work. Facts on File 2011 452p il (Facts on File library of American literature) $75

Grades: 11 12 Adult   **813.009**
1. Walker, Alice, 1944-
ISBN 978-0-8160-7530-0; 978-1-4381-3488-8 (ebook)
                              LC 2010-18639

This book contains "entries on all of Walker's major works, including such novels as *The Color Purple*, *Meridian*, *The Third Life of Grange Copeland*, and *Possessing the Secret of Joy*; essay collections and essays, such as 'Beauty: When the Other Dancer Is the Self'; poetry collections and poems; and short stories. Each entry on a major work of fiction contains subentries on the work's main characters." Publisher's note

Includes bibliographical references

Critical companion to Toni Morrison; a literary reference to her life and work. Facts On File 2008 484p il (Facts on File library of American literature) $75

Grades: 9 10 11 12 Adult   **813.009**
1. Morrison, Toni, 1931-
ISBN 978-0-8160-6276-8   LC 2006-38231

This book "examines Morrison's life and writing, featuring critical analyses of her work and themes, as well as . . . entries on related topics and relevant people, places, and influences." Publisher's note

Includes bibliographical references

Gloria Naylor: critical perspectives past and present; edited by Henry L. Gates, Jr., and K.A. Appiah. Amistad Press 1993 322p (Amistad literary series) pa $14.95 hardcover o.p.

Grades: 11 12 Adult   **813.009**
1. Naylor, Gloria
ISBN 1-56743-030-9 (pa)   LC 92-45758

This volume collects critical responses to Mama Day, The women of Brewster Place, Linden Hills and Bailey's Cafe

Includes bibliographical references

The **great** Gatsby, by F. Scott Fitzgerald; editor, Morris Dickstein. Salem Press 2009 291p (Critical insights) lib bdg $85 *

Grades: 9 10 11 12   **813.009**
1. Fitzgerald, F. Scott (Francis Scott), 1896-1940
ISBN 978-1-58765-608-8; 1-58765-608-6
    LC 2009-26346

"Contains an editor's introduction to the author or work, a perspective from the editors of the . . . literary magazine *The Paris Review*, and a biography of the author. Following these ready-reference chapters is a section, 'Critical Contexts,' that presents four original essays by current scholars." Publisher's note

Purchase of the volume "allows online access to the print content in its entirety. Students can search the easy-to-navigate database and print out and/or email the desired material, along with a prepared citation. Overall, a fresh take . . . and an excellent choice." SLJ

Includes bibliographical references

The **Greenwood** encyclopedia of science fiction and fantasy; themes, works, and wonders; edited by Gary Westfahl; foreword by Neil Gaiman. Greenwood Press 2005 3v set $349.95

Grades: 11 12 Adult   **813.009**
1. Reference books 2. Science fiction—Encyclopedias 3. Fantasy fiction—Encyclopedias
ISBN 0-313-32950-8   LC 2005-13677

This "encyclopedia consists of two parts. The first part (volumes 1 and 2) takes 400 of the most popular themes found in both science fiction and fantasy literature, and puts them into historical and cultural context. The second (volume 3) contains entries for a selected list of classic novels, films, and television series; these include entries for all the different Star Trek series, Dr. Who, Farscape, Buffy the Vampire Slayer, The Twilight Zone, and The X-Files." Choice

"This is an authoritative and extensive survey of themes and classic works of science fiction and fantasy stories, books, and themes." Libr Media Connect

Includes bibliographical references

Haralson, Eric L.
Critical companion to Henry James; a literary reference to his life and work; [by] Eric Haralson and Kendall Johnson. Facts On File 2009 516p il (Facts on File library of American literature) $75
Grades: 11 12 Adult   **813.009**
1. James, Henry, 1843-1916
ISBN 978-0-8160-6886-9   LC 2008-36451

This book "covers the life and works of Henry James as well as the related people, places, and topics that shaped his writing. Other features in this . . . title include a chronology of James's life, bibliographies of his works and of secondary sources, and black-and-white photographs and illustrations." Publisher's note

Includes bibliographical references

Harper Lee's To kill a mockingbird; edited & with an introduction by Harold Bloom. New ed. Bloom's Literary Criticism 2010 107p (Bloom's guides) $30 *

Grades: 9 10 11 12   **813.009**
1. Lee, Harper, 1926-
ISBN 978-1-60413-811-5   LC 2009-49160

Other available series titles include: Aldous Huxley's Brave new world; William Shakespeare's Macbeth; William Golding's Lord of the flies. For complete list of titles contact publisher

First published 2003

Examines different aspects of Harper Lee's novel about race relations in 1930s Alabama, with a biographical sketch of the author and critical essays on this work.

Includes bibliographical references

A **Historical** guide to Ernest Hemingway; edited by Linda Wagner-Martin. Oxford Univ. Press 1999 248p il (Historical guides to American authors) $45; pa $16.95 *

Grades: 11 12 Adult   **813.009**
1. Hemingway, Ernest, 1899-1961
ISBN 0-19-512151-1; 0-19-512152-X (pa)
    LC 99-10910

Following a brief biography contributors discuss nature, machismo, gender, war and wilderness as themes in Hemingway's fiction. An illustrated chronology and a bibliographical essay are included

Includes bibliographical references

A **Historical** guide to Nathaniel Hawthorne; edited by Larry J. Reynolds. Oxford Univ. Press 2001 223p il (Historical guides to American authors) $34.95; pa $15.95 *

Grades: 9 10 11 12   **813.009**
1. Hawthorne, Nathaniel, 1804-1864
ISBN 0-19-512413-8; 0-19-512414-6 (pa)
    LC 00-58917

Contents: Marble and mud: a biographical sketch, by Brenda Wineapple; Mysteries of mesmerism: Hawthorne's haunted house, by Samuel Coale; Hawthorne and children in the nineteenth century: daughters, flowers, stories, by Gillian Brown; Hawthorne and the visual arts, by Rita K. Colin; Nathaniel Hawthorne and the slavery question, by Jean Fagan Yellin; Illustrated chronology; Hawthorne and history: a bibliographical essay, by Leland S. Person

Includes bibliographical references

Hogan, Walter
Humor in young adult literature; a time to laugh. Scarecrow Press 2005 223p (Scarecrow studies in young adult literature) $40
Grades: Adult Professional   **813.009**
1. Wit and humor—History and criticism 2. Teenagers—Books and reading
ISBN 0-8108-5072-9   LC 2004-18903

The author's "study is organized into eight chapters that generally reflect the stages of YA development, looking at books on family, friends, bullies, and authorities; then books dealing with self-image, love, and ironic perception; and, finally, books that are 'coming-of-age' novels." Booklist

"As a reader's advisory tool, this book is invaluable, paving the way for many laughter-filled hours to come." Voice Youth Advocates

Includes bibliographical references

Jones, Sharon L., 1967-
Critical companion to Zora Neale Hurston; a literary reference to her life and work. Facts On File 2008 288p il (Facts on File library of American literature) $75

Grades: 11 12 Adult   **813.009**
1. Hurston, Zora Neale, 1891-1960
ISBN 978-0-8160-6885-2; 0-8160-6885-2
                                LC 2008-10052
This "covers all her writings, including *Their Eyes Were Watching God*; her landmark works of folklore and anthropology, such as *Mules and Men*; and shorter works." Publisher's note
Includes bibliographical references

The **Joy** Luck Club, by Amy Tan; editor, Robert C. Evans. Salem Press 2010 323p (Critical insights) lib bdg $85

Grades: 9 10 11 12   **813.009**
1. Tan, Amy
ISBN 978-1-58765-626-2; 1-58765-626-4
                                LC 2009-26304
This book introduces *The Joy Luck Club*'s narrative in its "historical context, [provides] a short biography of the author, and offer 'The Paris Review Perspective' on the [work], followed by a series of articles by academics under the headings of 'Critical Contexts' or 'Critical Readings.'" SLJ
Includes bibliographical references

Kerr, Christine
Bloom's how to write about J.D. Salinger; introduction by Harold Bloom. Chelsea House 2008 280p (Bloom's how to write about literature) $45

Grades: 9 10 11 12   **813.009**
1. Salinger, J. D., 1919-2010 2. Report writing
ISBN 978-0-7910-9483-9   LC 2006-100570
This "volume is designed to help students develop their analytical writing skills and critical comprehension of . . . [J.D. Salinger] and his works." Publisher's note
"For librarians who want to counter the daily student complaint 'I don't know where to start!' with concrete direction, Kerr's book might be the answer." SLJ
Includes bibliographical references

Kirk, Connie Ann, 1951-
Critical companion to Flannery O'Connor. Facts on File 2008 415p il (Facts on File library of American literature) $75

Grades: 9 10 11 12 Adult   **813.009**
1. O'Connor, Flannery
ISBN 978-0-8160-6417-5   LC 2007-6512
This book examines O'Connor's "life and works, and includes critical analyses of some of the themes in her writing, as well as entries on related topics and relevant people, places, and influences." Publisher's note
Includes bibliographical references

Kordich, Catherine J.
Bloom's how to write about John Steinbeck; [introduction by Harold Bloom] Bloom's Literary Criticism 2008 264p (Bloom's how to write about literature) $45

Grades: 9 10 11 12   **813.009**
1. Steinbeck, John, 1902-1968 2. Report writing
ISBN 0-7910-9486-3; 978-0-7910-9486-0
                                LC 2006-100571
This book offers "paper-topic suggestions, . . . strategies on how to write a strong essay, and an . . . introduction by Harold Bloom on writing about Steinbeck. This . . . volume is designed to help students develop their analytical writing skills and critical comprehension of this legendary author and his works." Publisher's note
Includes bibliographical references

Litwin, Laura Baskes
A reader's guide to Zora Neale Hurston's Their eyes were watching god. Enslow Publishers 2010 128p il (Multicultural literature) lib bdg $31.93

Grades: 8 9 10 11 12   **813.009**
1. Hurston, Zora Neale, 1891-1960 2. African Americans in literature
ISBN 978-0-7660-3164-7; 0-7660-3164-0
                                LC 2008-38524
An introduction to Zora Neale Hurston's novel Their eyes were watching God for high school students, which includes biographical background on the author, explanations of various literary devices and techniques, and literary criticism for the novice reader.
Includes glossary and bibliographical references

Lüsted, Marcia Amidon, 1962-
How to analyze the works of Stephen King. ABDO Pub. Co. 2011 112p il (Essential critiques) $34.22

Grades: 9 10 11 12   **813.009**
1. King, Stephen, 1947- 2. Horror fiction—History and criticism
ISBN 978-1-61613-536-2   LC 2010-15007
This book looks at the works of Stephen King "through the lenses of prevalent schools of criticism. The first chapters introduce the concept of critical theory, its purpose, and how to develop and support a thesis statement. In subsequent chapters, an overview of each work is followed by a critique using a particular theory. . . . Feminist criticism is applied to *Carrie*, archetypal theory to *The Green Mile*, historical criticism to *The Stand*, and structuralist criticism to the 'Dark Tower' series." SLJ
Includes bibliographical references

Mark Twain's The adventures of Huckleberry Finn; edited and with an introduction by Harold Bloom. Updated ed. Chelsea House 2007 248p (Modern critical interpretations) $45 *

Grades: 9 10 11 12 Adult   **813.009**
1. Twain, Mark, 1835-1910
ISBN 0-7910-9426-X; 978-0-7910-9426-6
                                LC 2006-36858
Other available series titles in this class include: Harper Lee's To kill a mockingbird; Edgar Allan Poe's "The Tell-tale Heart" and other stories; Ernest Hemingway's

Mark Twain's The adventures of Huckleberry Finn—*Continued*

The sun also rises. For a complete list of titles contact publisher

First published 1986

A collection of twelve critical essays on Mark Twain's classic novel.

Includes bibliographical references

Newman, Gerald, 1939-

A student's guide to John Steinbeck; [by] Gerald Newman, Eleanor Newman Layfield. Enslow Publs. 2004 176p il (Understanding literature) $27.93 *

Grades: 9 10 11 12   **813.009**
1. Steinbeck, John, 1902-1968
ISBN 0-7660-2259-5   LC 2004-2304

"The authors discuss . . . [Steinbeck's] books in terms of characters, themes, plots, and symbolism. They devote separate chapters to Of Mice and Men, The Grapes of Wrath, and East of Eden but include other writings as well. . . . A good choice for reports and for a general understanding of this much-studied writer's works." SLJ

Includes glossary and bibliographical references

Nilsen, Alleen Pace

Joan Bauer. Greenwood Press 2007 160p il (Teen reads: student companions to young adult literature) $45

Grades: 9 10 11 12   **813.009**
1. Bauer, Joan
ISBN 978-0-313-33550-1; 0-313-33550-8
                                LC 2007-8191

This book on the works of Joan Bauer includes an "interview with Bauer that is broken into topical sections, a discussion of Bauer's writing style, an examination of Bauer's short stories, and a chapter devoted to each of her novels. . . . This book is a most appropriate and welcome addition for high school libraries as well as high school English teachers' classrooms." Voice Youth Advocates

Includes bibliographical references

Names and naming in young adult literature; [by] Alleen Pace Nilsen, Don L. F. Nilsen. Scarecrow Press 2007 173p (Scarecrow studies in young adult literature) $45

Grades: Adult Professional   **813.009**
1. Young adult literature—History and criticism
2. Characters and characteristics in literature
3. Personal names in literature
ISBN 978-0-8108-5808-4; 0-8108-5808-8
                                LC 2007-11281

This "book consists of an introduction about the role of names in young adult literature, eight essay chapters, a bibliography, and an index. . . . The authors do a good job in writing engaging content. . . . School, public, and academic libraries will find this title an asset." Booklist

Includes bibliographical references

Oliver, Charles M.

Critical companion to Ernest Hemingway; a literary reference to his life and work. Facts on File 2006 630p il (Facts on File library of American literature) $75

Grades: 9 10 11 12 Adult   **813.009**
1. Hemingway, Ernest, 1899-1961
ISBN 0-8160-6418-0; 978-0-8160-6418-2
                                LC 2006-7970

First published 1999 with title: Ernest Hemingway A to Z

"This volume features entries on all of Hemingway's major and minor works, places and events related to his works, major figures in his life, and more. Appendixes include a complete list of Hemingway's works; a chronology; a genealogy; a . . . map for readers of Islands in the Stream; a list of film, stage, and radio adaptations; and a bibliography of secondary sources." Publisher's note

Includes filmography and bibliographical references

Peer pressure in Robert Cormier's The chocolate war; Dedria Bryfonski, book editor. Greenhaven Press 2010 178p il (Social issues in literature) $37.30; pa $25.70

Grades: 9 10 11 12   **813.009**
1. Cormier, Robert 2. Peer pressure
ISBN   978-0-7377-4620-4;   0-7377-4620-3;
978-0-7377-4621-1 (pa); 0-7377-4621-1 (pa)
                                LC 2009-18275

The "reprinted articles [in this book] are broken into three groups: those that focus on the author; those that focus on how the headline issue is exercised within the book itself; and those that expand that issue into contemporary settings. One of the first pieces in *Peer Pressure in Robert Cormier's The Chocolate War* is by Cormier himself, explaining how he adores happy endings even as he finds himself unable to write them. After taking on the novel's famous plot twists, the book moves on to such topics as cyberbullying." Booklist

Includes bibliographical references

Pingelton, Timothy J.

A student's guide to Ernest Hemingway. Enslow Publishers 2005 160p il map (Understanding literature) lib bdg $27.93 *

Grades: 7 8 9 10   **813.009**
1. Hemingway, Ernest, 1899-1961
ISBN 0-7660-2431-8

This discusses Hemingway's life and his novels *In Our Time, The Sun Also Rises, A Farewell to Arms*, and *The Old Man and the Sea*

"Engaging and informative. . . . The very accessible format and the solid information make [this book] useful to students, and the engaging style should interest casual readers." SLJ

Includes glossary and bibliographical references

Reed, Arthea J. S.

Norma Fox Mazer; a writer's world. Scarecrow Press 2000 140p (Scarecrow studies in young adult literature) $36

Grades: 7 8 9 10   **813.009**

1. Mazer, Norma Fox, 1931-2009

ISBN 0-8108-3814-1   LC 00-38759

Other available series titles in this class are: What's so scary about R. L. Stine; Caroline Cooney; Ann Rinaldi; Orson Scott Card. For a complete list of titles contact publisher

"Quoting heavily from the author herself and published reviews of her work, the author provides a chronology of major events in Mazer's life and then goes into deeper detail about her subject's childhood and adolescence and how her upbringing played a vital role in her novels and partnership with her husband, Harry Mazer. Several works are comprehensively analyzed." SLJ

Includes bibliographical references

Rehak, Melanie

Girl sleuth; Nancy Drew and the women who created her. Harcourt 2005 364p il $25; pa $14

Grades: 11 12 Adult   **813.009**

1. Wirt, Mildred A. (Mildred Augustine), 1905-
2. Keene, Carolyn 3. Stratemeyer, Edward, 1862-1930

ISBN 0-15-101041-2; 0-15-603056-X (pa)

      LC 2005-9129

This is an account of "the writers and editors who constituted Carolyn Keene, the pseudonymous author of the [Nancy Drew] series." N Y Times Book Rev

"Packed with revealing anecdotes, Rehak's meticulously researched account of the publishing phenomenon that survived the Depression and WWII . . . will delight fans of the beloved gumshoe whose gumption guaranteed that every reprobate got his due." Booklist

Includes bibliographical references

Rollyson, Carl

Critical companion to Herman Melville; a literary reference to his life and work; [by] Carl Rollyson, Lisa Paddock, and April Gentry. Facts on File 2006 394p il (Facts on File library of world literature) $75

Grades: 9 10 11 12 Adult   **813.009**

1. Melville, Herman, 1819-1891

ISBN 0-8160-6461-X; 978-0-8160-6461-8

      LC 2005-36733

First published 2000 with title: Herman Melville A to Z

Entries in this "volume examine the characters and settings of Melville's novels and short stories, the critics and scholars who commented on his work, and his friends and associates, including such prominent literary figures as Oliver Wendell Holmes and Nathaniel Hawthorne." Publisher's note

Includes bibliographical references

Russell, Sharon A.

Revisiting Stephen King; a critical companion. Greenwood Press 2002 171p (Critical companions to popular contemporary writers) $34.95 *

Grades: 9 10 11 12   **813.009**

1. King, Stephen, 1947-

ISBN 0-313-31788-7   LC 2001-58641

This volume discusses the plot review, character development, and theme of eight of King's books from Desperation (1996) through Dreamcatcher (2001)

"Easy to read and understand, this title would be a good choice for secondary researchers. It's also interesting enough for King fans to enjoy." Libr Media Connect

Includes bibliographical references

Stephen King: a critical companion. Greenwood Press 1996 171p (Critical companions to popular contemporary writers) $35 *

Grades: 9 10 11 12   **813.009**

1. King, Stephen, 1947-

ISBN 0-313-29417-8   LC 95-50460

Some other available series titles in this class are: Kurt Vonnegut; Ray Bradbury; Gloria Naylor; Larry McMurtry; Louise Erdrich. For complete list of titles contact publisher

"Biographical information about King and background information on the horror genre in which he writes are contained in the first two chapters. The chapters that follow cover in detail the author's most important, most popular, and most recent works in chronological order, examining plot and character development and theme." Voice Youth Advocates

Includes bibliographical references

Schroeder, Heather Lee

A reader's guide to Marjane Satrapi's Persepolis. Enslow Publishers 2010 152p il map (Multicultural literature) lib bdg $34.60

Grades: 8 9 10 11 12   **813.009**

1. Satrapi, Marjane, 1969-

ISBN 978-0-7660-3166-1; 0-7660-3166-7

      LC 2008-51820

An introduction to Marjane Satrapi's graphic novel Persepolis for high school students, which includes biographical background on the author, explanations of various literary devices and techniques, and literary criticism for the novice reader.

Includes glossary and bibliographical references

Schultz, Jeffrey D., 1966-

Critical companion to John Steinbeck; a literary reference to his life and work; [by] Jeffrey Schultz, Luchen Li. Facts on File 2005 406p il (Facts on File library of American literature) $65; pa $19.99 *

Grades: 11 12 Adult   **813.009**

1. Steinbeck, John, 1902-1968

ISBN 0-8160-4300-0; 0-8160-4301-9 (pa)

      LC 2004-26100

This "resource is divided into three parts: Biography, Works A-Z, and Related People, Places, and Topics. The first and shortest section provides a summary of Stein-

Schultz, Jeffrey D., 1966-—*Continued*

beck's birth, early childhood, education, and career. The bulk of the book offers descriptions of all of his works—published and unpublished." SLJ

"Useful, succinct, and reasonably priced, it packs an abundance of information into one compact resource." Libr J

Includes bibliographical references

Sorrentino, Paul

Student companion to Stephen Crane; [by] Paul M. Sorrentino. Greenwood Press 2006 171p (Student companions to classic writers) $39.95 *

Grades: 9 10 11 12   **813.009**
  1. Crane, Stephen, 1871-1900
  ISBN 0-313-33104-9   LC 2005-26301
The author "includes facts about Crane's family, background on the Civil War, critical commentaries, as well as discussions about his writings, his literary heritage, and his revered place in American literature. . . . This volume includes a wealth of useful material that will help students better understand and interpret the writings of this great 19th-century author." SLJ

Includes bibliographical references

Sterling, Laurie A.

Bloom's how to write about Nathaniel Hawthorne; [introduction by Harold Bloom] Chelsea House 2008 344p (Bloom's how to write about literature) $45

Grades: 9 10 11 12   **813.009**
  1. Hawthorne, Nathaniel, 1804-1864 2. Report writing
  ISBN 978-0-7910-9481-5   LC 2006-101324
This book offers "paper-topic suggestions, . . . strategies on how to write a strong essay, and an . . . introduction by Harold Bloom on writing about Hawthorne. This . . . volume is designed to help students develop their analytical writing skills and critical comprehension of this important writer and his works." Publisher's note

Includes bibliographical references

The **tales** of Edgar Allan Poe; editor, Steven Frye. Salem Press 2010 293p il (Critical insights) lib bdg $85

Grades: 9 10 11 12   **813.009**
  1. Poe, Edgar Allan, 1809-1849
  ISBN 978-1-58765-616-3; 1-58765-616-7
                                          LC 2009-26318
"Contains an editor's introduction to the author or work, a perspective from the editors of the . . . literary magazine *The Paris Review*, and a biography of the author. Following these ready-reference chapters is a section, 'Critical Contexts,' that presents four original essays by current scholars." Publisher's note

Includes bibliographical references

Tate, Mary Jo

Critical companion to F. Scott Fitzgerald; a literary reference to his life and work; foreword by Matthew J. Bruccoli. Facts on File 2006 464p il (Facts on File library of American literature) $75 *

Grades: 9 10 11 12 Adult   **813.009**
  1. Fitzgerald, F. Scott (Francis Scott), 1896-1940
  ISBN 0-8160-6433-4; 978-0-8160-6433-5
                                          LC 2006-11393
First published 1998 with title: F. Scott Fitzgerald A to Z

This book "studies the legacy of this writer, highlighting significant themes and historical references of his various works." Publisher's note

Includes bibliographical references

The **Toni** Morrison encyclopedia; edited by Elizabeth Ann Beaulieu. Greenwood Press 2003 428p $89.95 *

Grades: 11 12 Adult   **813.009**
  1. Morrison, Toni, 1931- 2. Reference books
  ISBN 0-313-31699-6   LC 2002-21617
"This encyclopedia covers Morrison's works, characters, locations, themes (e.g., *Children*), and general topics (e.g., *Oprah's Book Club*). . . . Also included is a 14-page selected bibliography citing Morrison's novels, essays, stories, and interviews, as well as criticism on Morrison's works selected from books and articles. Typically, articles on themes, general topics, and works span several pages, while entries on characters and locations range from one sentence to one paragraph. A list of references concludes many, but not all, entries." Booklist

Includes bibliographical references

Wright, Sarah Bird

Critical companion to Nathaniel Hawthorne; a literary reference to his life and work. Facts on File 2006 392p il (Facts on File library of American literature) $75

Grades: 11 12 Adult   **813.009**
  1. Hawthorne, Nathaniel, 1804-1864
  ISBN 0-8160-5583-1; 978-0-8160-5583-8
                                          LC 2005-34648
This book "offers critical entries on Hawthorne's novels, short stories, travel writing, criticism, and other works, as well as portraits of characters, including Hester Prynne and Roger Chillingworth. This . . . reference also provides entries on Hawthorne's family, friends—ranging from Herman Melville to President Franklin Pierce—publishers, and critics, as well as periodicals that published his work and important places and events in his life." Publisher's note

Includes bibliographical references

814   American essays

Angelou, Maya

Wouldn't take nothing for my journey now. Random House 1993 141p hardcover o.p. pa $6.99

Grades: 11 12 Adult   **814**
  ISBN 0-679-42743-0; 0-553-56907-4 (pa)
                                          LC 93-5904

Angelou, Maya—*Continued*

The author "shares her thoughts about humankind: how to respect others of different cultures, opinions, and values as taught by universal philosophies. . . . Angelou's prose is brisk, fluid, and entrancing. This work will provide a taste of wisdom to all who read it." Libr J

Baldwin, James, 1924-1987

Collected essays. Library of Am. 1998 869p $35

Grades: 11 12 Adult   814

ISBN 1-883011-52-3   LC 97-23496

The essays in this volume were selected by Toni Morrison. "Morrison has reprinted all of the material contained in Baldwin's previous collected essays, The Price of the Ticket (1985). She has added eleven pieces, the earliest of which dates from 1947—Baldwin's first published review, of a biography of Frederick Douglass, in the Nation—and the latest from 1984." Times Lit Suppl

The **beholder's** eye; a collection of America's finest personal journalism; edited and with an introduction by Walt Harrington. Grove Press 2005 xxii, 256p pa $14

Grades: 11 12 Adult   814

ISBN 0-8021-4224-5   LC 2005-46242

"Each writer takes a unique approach to the subject, drawing the reader into the experience of pit-bull fighting or hunting with the Inuit. Among the collection: Harrington, who is married to a black woman, explores his evolving attitudes on race through the lens of his relationship with his in-laws, Pete Earley returns to his hometown in search of the meaning of a sister's death in their youth, Ron Rosenbaum explores his own outlook on life in a philosophical discourse with then-New York governor Mario Cuomo, Davis Miller is unabashedly starstruck in a comfortable and closeup look at Muhammad Ali at the home of Ali's mother, and Stephen S. Hall is personally probing in his exploration, via MRI, of his own brain and its functioning. These stories are amusing, insightful, and touching in a way that only something personal can be." Booklist

The **Best** American essays of the century; Joyce Carol Oates, editor; Robert Atwan, coeditor; with an introduction by Joyce Carol Oates. Houghton Mifflin 2000 596p hardcover o.p. pa $18 *

Grades: 11 12 Adult   814

ISBN 0-618-04370-5; 0-618-15587-2 (pa)

This anthology includes essays "that contemplate diverse worlds, from nature to courtrooms, war and family memories. Race is a pervasive theme, explored with candor and insight by many, including James Baldwin, Zora Neale Hurston, and, in a jolting 1912 condemnation of a Coatesville, Pennsylvania, lynching, John Jay Chapman." Booklist

"Oates has assembled a provocative collection of masterpieces reflecting both the fragmentation and surprising cohesiveness of various American identities." Publ Wkly

Includes bibliographical references

Bradbury, Ray, 1920-

Bradbury speaks; too soon from the cave, too far from the stars. William Morrow 2005 243p hardcover o.p. pa $14.95

Grades: 11 12 Adult   814

ISBN 0-06-058568-4; 0-06-058569-2 (pa)

LC 2005-41489

In this collection of essays, the author "weighs in on a medley of topics, including the allure of Paris, his enthusiasm for trains, the genesis of his most popular novels, and his reasons for remaining a diehard optimist. . . . By turns whimsical, insightful, and unabashedly metaphoric, his prose is immediately accessible as well as thought-provoking. Fans and nonfans alike should enjoy." Booklist

Du Bois, W. E. B. (William Edward Burghardt), 1868-1963

Writings. Library of Am. 1986 1334p $40; pa $15.95 *

Grades: 11 12 Adult   814

ISBN 0-940450-33-X; 1-883011-31-0 (pa)

LC 86-10565

Edited by Nathan Huggins

Contents: The suppression of the African slave-trade; The souls of black folk; Dusk of dawn; Essays; Articles from The crisis

Includes bibliographical references

Everything I needed to know about being a girl I learned from Judy Blume. Pocket Books 2007 275p hardcover o.p. pa $14

Grades: 11 12 Adult   814

1. Blume, Judy

ISBN 978-1-4165-3104-3; 1-4165-3104-1; 978-1-4391-0265-7 (pa); 1-4391-0265-1 (pa)

"This collection of 24 essays . . . pays tribute to the influence of Judy Blume and her work about coming-of-age as a girl in America. In each piece, the writer reveals what O'Connell calls her 'Judy Blume moment,' telling a heartfelt and revealing story that reflects the same social awkwardness and true-to-life experiences Blume conveys in her novels, from menstruation to childhood bullying to masturbation. . . . Readers who similarly found solace and support in Blume's work should relate easily to these writers through the Blumian characters and themes they evoke." Publ Wkly

A **Historical** guide to Ralph Waldo Emerson; edited by Joel Myerson. Oxford Univ. Press 2000 322p il (Historical guides to American authors) $45; pa $17.95

Grades: 11 12 Adult   814

1. Emerson, Ralph Waldo, 1803-1882

ISBN 0-19-512093-0; 0-19-512094-9 (pa)

LC 99-13122

Contributors discuss the prominent transcendentalist's views on religion, slavery, women's rights, natural science and individualism. Includes a biographical essay and a chronology

Includes bibliographical references

In fact; the best of Creative nonfiction; edited by Lee Gutkind; introduction by Annie Dillard. Norton 2005 xxxvi, 440p pa $15.95

Grades: 9 10 11 12 **814**

ISBN 0-393-32665-9 LC 2004-16506

This anthology of 25 essays from the literary journal Creative Nonfiction "covers the creative nonfiction universe from the personal essay to nature writing, literary journalism, and science writing. . . . This stellar volume will stand as an exciting and defining creative nonfiction primer." Booklist

Kingsolver, Barbara

Small wonder; essays; illustrations by Paul Mirocha. HarperCollins Pubs. 2002 267p $23.95; pa $12.95

Grades: 11 12 Adult **814**

ISBN 0-06-050407-2; 0-06-050408-0 (pa)

LC 2002-276255

"This set of 19 penetrating autobiographical musings on humankind and how we treat each other and the rest of nature coalesced in the stunned aftermath of September 11. . . . Food, motherhood, gardening, literature, television, homelessness, globalization, scientific illiteracy, selfishness, and forgiveness all come under sharp and revelatory scrutiny." Booklist

Kirk, Andrew

Understanding Thoreau's "Civil disobedience". Rosen Pub. 2010 128p il (Words that changed the world) lib bdg $31.95

Grades: 7 8 9 10 **814**

1. Thoreau, Henry David, 1817-1862 2. Resistance to government

ISBN 978-1-4488-1671-2; 1-4488-1671-8

LC 2010-10221

First published 2004 by Barrons with title: Civil disobedience

This considers Thoreau's *Civil Disobedience*, including its "'Context and Creator,' 'Immediate Impact,' 'Legacy,' and 'Aftermath.' . . . [Exploring] the historical context of transcendentalism and resistance to big government. . . . [The] author provides a balance of deep context, expressive writing, and pertinent information." SLJ

Includes glossary and bibliographical references

Walker, Alice, 1944-

Anything we love can be saved; a writer's activism: essays, speeches, statements & letters. Random House 1997 xxv, 225p pa $15.95 hardcover o.p.

Grades: 11 12 Adult **814**

ISBN 0-345-40796-2 (pa) LC 96-41159

Walker has assembled a "wide-ranging collection of personal essays, remarks, letters, speeches and statements, many previously published. . . . Constantly testing and stretching her readers' imaginations and boundaries, Walker expresses her warmth, her anger, her optimism in this provocative, lively collection." Publ Wkly

815.008 American speeches— Collections

American Heritage book of great American speeches for young people; edited by Suzanne McIntire. Wiley 2001 292p il pa $14.95 *

Grades: 7 8 9 10 **815.008**

1. American speeches

ISBN 0-471-38942-0 LC 00-43749

This is a "compendium of more than 100 speeches that span nearly 400 years of American history, from Powhatan (1609) to Senator Charles Robb (2000). Prominent orators include Patrick Henry, Thomas Jefferson, John Kennedy, Richard Nixon, Martin Luther King, Jr., and Malcolm X. . . . The speeches inform readers and provide examples of how the spoken word has affected Americans throughout our past." SLJ

American speeches. Library of America 2006 2v ea $35

Grades: 9 10 11 12 Adult **815.008**

1. American speeches

ISBN 1-931082-97-9 (v1); 1-931082-98-7 (v2)

LC 2006-40928

Contents: pt. 1. Political oratory from the Revolution to the Civil War—pt. 2. Political oratory from Abraham Lincoln to Bill Clinton

This is a collection of over 120 historical speeches delivered between 1761 and 1997.

Includes bibliographical references

Historic speeches of African Americans; introduced and selected by Warren J. Halliburton. Watts 1993 192p il (African-American experience) lib bdg $23 *

Grades: 7 8 9 10 11 12 **815.008**

1. African Americans—History 2. American speeches

ISBN 0-531-11034-6 LC 92-39318

Presents speeches by various African American religious and political leaders from the days of slavery to the present, along with biographical information and historical background.

"Kids will dip into this for personal reading, and for curriculum research; they'll also find stirring pieces to read aloud and think about. The detailed sources at the end of the book make it easy to find out more about the individuals and their ideas." Booklist

In our own words; extraordinary speeches of the American century; edited by Robert G. Torricelli and Andrew Carroll. Kodansha Int. 1999 xxx, 450p $28 *

Grades: 11 12 Adult **815.008**

1. American speeches

ISBN 1-56836-291-9 LC 99-29995

Also available in paperback from Washington Sq. Press

"Arranged by decade from the Progressive Era to the '90s Technological Revolution, this book includes eulogies, sermons, fireside chats, public tributes, commencement addresses, and more. . . . Entries are attributed to Jane Addams, Clarence Darrow, Al 'Scarface' Capone, General George S. Patton, Jack Kerouac, Vince Lombardi, Jane Fonda, Ronald Reagan, and others." SLJ

Includes bibliographical references

U-X-L Asian American voices; edited by Deborah Gillan Straub. 2nd ed. U.X.L 2004 xxv, 315p il $58 *

Grades: 7 8 9 10 11 12   **815.008**
1. Asian Americans 2. American speeches
ISBN 0-7876-7600-4   LC 2003-110048
First published 1997 with title: Asian American voices
This "reference presents full or excerpted speeches, sermons, orations, poems, testimony and other notable spoken words of Asian Americans. Each entry is accompanied by an introduction and boxes explaining terms and events to which the speech refers. The volume is illustrated with photographs and drawings." Publisher's note

816   American letters

Letters of the century; America, 1900-1999; edited by Lisa Grunwald and Stephen J. Adler. Dial Press (NY) 1999 741p il hardcover o.p. pa $18 *

Grades: 11 12 Adult   **816**
1. American letters 2. United States—Civilization
ISBN 0-385-31590-2; 0-385-31593-7 (pa)
     LC 99-16808
This anthology "contains four hundred and twelve letters arranged chronologically to demonstrate the effects of war, the Depression, demographic change, scientific innovation, medical discovery, and artistic experimentation on American life." New Yorker
Among the letter writers gathered are "Carl Van Doren, Huey Long, Franklin D. Roosevelt, Lillian Hellman and a Vietnam soldier named Dusty. This is one of the most original literary tributes to the closing century." Publ Wkly
Includes bibliographical references

817   American humor and satire

Macaulay, David, 1946-
Motel of the mysteries. Houghton Mifflin 1979 95p il pa $13 hardcover o.p.
Grades: 9 10 11 12   **817**
ISBN 0-395-28425-2 (pa)   LC 79-14860
In this satire the author pictures an amateur archeologist, who in the year 4022 stumbles upon an American motel which has been buried in 1985 in "a cataclysmic coincidence of previously unknown proportion {which} extinguished virtually all forms of life on the North American continent." The excavation of the motel and the ensuing explanations and interpretations of its human remains and artifacts provide a humorous satire of archeological finds and civilization, circa 1980

817.008   American humor and satire—Collections

Honey, hush! an anthology of African American women's humor; edited by Daryl Cumber Dance; foreword by Nikki Giovanni. Norton 1997 xxxix, 673p il pa $17.95 hardcover o.p.
Grades: 11 12 Adult   **817.008**
1. American wit and humor 2. African American women
ISBN 0-393-31818-4 (pa)   LC 97-6772
The editor "has collected folktales, proverbs, slave narratives, and cartoons reflecting the humor of African American women. Among those included are authors Audre Lorde and Toni Morrison and comedian Whoopi Goldberg." Libr J
Includes bibliographical references

Russell Baker's book of American humor. Norton 1993 598p $30 *
Grades: 11 12 Adult   **817.008**
1. American wit and humor
ISBN 0-393-03592-1   LC 93-22733
"Two hundred years of American humor have gone into the making of this anthology. . . . In the lineup are many of the old pros—Mark Twain, Fred Allen, James Thurber—and several relative newcomers—Fran Lebowitz, Nora Ephron, P.J. O'Rourke, and Dave Barry. The selections are nicely assorted in substance and are arranged by theme rather than chronology." Libr J
Includes bibliographical references

818   American miscellany

Amper, Susan
Bloom's how to write about Edgar Allan Poe; [introduction by Harold Bloom] Chelsea House 2007 232p (Bloom's how to write about literature) $45
Grades: 9 10 11 12   **818**
1. Poe, Edgar Allan, 1809-1849 2. Report writing
ISBN 978-0-7910-9488-4   LC 2007-8120
This book offers "paper-topic suggestions, . . . strategies on how to write a strong essay, and an . . . introduction by Harold Bloom on writing about Poe. This volume is designed to help students develop their analytical writing skills and critical comprehension of this important author's turbulent life and unforgettable works." Publisher's note
Includes bibliographical references

Barry, Lynda
What it is. Drawn & Quarterly 2008 209p il $24.95 *
Grades: 7 8 9 10 11 12 Adult   **818**
1. Authorship—Graphic novels 2. Creative writing—Graphic novels
ISBN 978-1-897299-35-7; 1-897299-35-4
     LC c2007-9047319
Independent cartoonist Lynda Barry presents an unconventional book that encourages its readers to write by

Barry, Lynda—*Continued*

using her colorful art and asking questions such as "How are monsters different? And how are they the same?" "Can/Do images exist without thinking?" "What is the difference between lying and pretending?" Each question appears with illustrated writing prompts and Barry's own ruminations on the topics. It's a workbook of sorts, but it also exists as a book to be read for itself.

"Every so often a book comes along that surpasses expectations, taking readers on an inspirational voyage that they don't want to leave. This is one such book." SLJ

The **Best** of the West; an anthology of classic writing from the American West; edited by Tony Hillerman. HarperCollins Pubs. 1991 528p pa $18 hardcover o.p.

Grades: 11 12 Adult   **818**
1. West (U.S.) in literature
ISBN 0-06-092352-0 (pa)   LC 90-55930

This anthology's "nonfiction sources run from 500 B.C. to the late nineteenth century; fictional selections by Harte, Crane, Scarborough, Davis, Stegner, and Norris are included. . . . Hillerman's subject groupings (e.g., explorers, settlers, Navajos, Hispanics, cowboys, miners, women, travel, and the military) make sense, and his juxtapositions encourage a thoughtful response." Booklist

Capote, Truman, 1924-1984

A Christmas memory, One Christmas, & The Thanksgiving visitor. Modern Lib. 1996 107p $13.95

Grades: 9 10 11 12   **818**
ISBN 0-679-60237-2   LC 96-26022

In addition to two autobiographical stories A Christmas memory (1966) and The Thanksgiving visitor (1968), this volume includes the memoir One Christmas (1983)

One Christmas describes the Christmas Capote spent with his father in New Orleans when he was six years old. A Christmas memory and The Thanksgiving visitor "center on the author's early years with a family of distant relatives in rural Alabama. Both pay loving tribute to an eccentric old-maid cousin, Miss Sook Faulk, who became his best friend." Publisher's note

Cather, Willa, 1873-1947

Stories, poems, and other writings. Library of Am. 1992 1039p $35 *

Grades: 11 12 Adult   **818**
ISBN 0-940450-71-2   LC 91-62294

This volume contains the novels Alexander's bridge (1912) and My mortal enemy (1926); the poetry collection April twilights, and other poems (1923); the essay collection Not under forty (1936); and the following short story collections: Youth and the bright Medusa (1920); Obscure destinies (1932); The old beauty, and others (1948); and uncollected stories from 1892-1929

Crane, Stephen, 1871-1900

Prose and poetry. Library of Am. 1984 1379p $40; pa $15.95 *

Grades: 11 12 Adult   **818**
1. Short stories
ISBN 0-940450-17-8; 1-883011-39-6 (pa)
     LC 83-19908

Contents: Maggie: a girl of the streets; The red badge of courage; George's mother; The third violet; The monster; Stories, sketches, and journalism, by place and time; Poems

"This collection also includes both Crane's collections of epigrammatic free verses—'The Black Riders' and 'War is kind'—and selections from his uncollected poems." Publisher's note

Dillard, Annie

The Annie Dillard reader. HarperCollins Pubs. 1994 455p pa $15.95 hardcover o.p.

Grades: 11 12 Adult   **818**
ISBN 0-06-092660-0 (pa)   LC 94-19482

This reader includes Holy the firm; excerpts from Pilgrim at Tinker Creek, An American childhood, and Teaching a stone to talk; and a reworked version of the 1978 short story The living

"This selection of writings, chosen by Dillard herself, provides a perfect sampling of her incisive, versatile, and impeccable achievements." Booklist

Pilgrim at Tinker Creek. Harper & Row 1974 271p hardcover o.p. pa $14.95

Grades: 9 10 11 12 Adult   **818**
1. Natural history—Virginia
ISBN 0-06-123332-3 (pa); 978-0-06-123332-6 (pa)

Also available in hardcover from Buccaneer Bks.

Starting with January, Dillard "records the seasons as they come and go at Tinker Creek in Virginia." Time

This work is "in an honored tradition of literature, not quite environmentalism and not the philosophy of science, it is rather the refraction of natural philosophy through the prismatic conscience of art. Highly recommended for the general reader—any general reader, anywhere—who wishes to deepen his awareness of his yard of world and to reflect upon it more profoundly." Choice

Edgar Allan Poe; edited and with an introduction by Harold Bloom. Chelsea House Publishers 2001 99p (Bloom's biocritiques) $35 *

Grades: 9 10 11 12   **818**
1. Poe, Edgar Allan, 1809-1849
ISBN 0-7910-6173-6   LC 2001-53901

Other available series titles include: Tennessee Williams; Toni Morrison; Nathaniel Hawthorne; Mark Twain. For complete list of titles contact publisher

"This title offers a . . . biography of Poe, critical essays of his works, and an introduction by Professor Bloom." Publisher's note

Includes bibliographical references

Eliot, T. S. (Thomas Stearns), 1888-1965

Eliot; poems and prose. Knopf 1998 221p (Everyman's library pocket poets) $12.50

Grades: 11 12 Adult   **818**

Eliot, T. S. (Thomas Stearns), 1888-1965—*Continued*

ISBN 0-375-40185-7

A representative selection of work by the influential modernist poet and critic

Emerson, Ralph Waldo, 1803-1882

The portable Emerson. [rev ed], edited by Carl Bode in collaboration with Malcolm Cowley. Penguin Bks. 1981 xxxix, 670p pa $16.95 *

Grades: 11 12 Adult   **818**

ISBN 0-14-015094-3   LC 81-4047

"The Viking portable library"

First published 1946 by Viking

The editors have provided the following selections: essays, including History, Self-reliance, The over-soul, Circles and The poet; The complete texts of Nature and English traits; biographical essays on Plato, Napoleon, Henry David Thoreau, Thomas Carlyle, and others as well as twenty-two poems.

Includes bibliographical references

The **environment** in Henry David Thoreau's Walden; Gary Wiener, book editor. Greenhaven Press 2010 219p il (Social issues in literature) $38.45; pa $26.50

Grades: 9 10 11 12   **818**

1. Thoreau, Henry David, 1817-1862 2. Nature in literature 3. Environmental protection

ISBN   978-0-7377-4654-9;   0-7377-4654-8; 978-0-7377-4655-6 (pa); 0-7377-4655-6 (pa)

LC 2009-40566

This book "is organized in three sections, beginning with background information about the author and providing insight into how the author's experiences influenced his or her work. Another section presents articles that analyze the relationship between the work and the social issue, all from a variety of perspectives. A final chapter brings the highlighted social issue into contemporary times, discussing its status in society today. . . . [This book] highlights issues of concern and shows how the issues that compelled Thoreau to retreat to Walden Pond are just as important to students today." Voice Youth Advocates

Includes bibliographical references

Franklin, Benjamin, 1706-1790

Autobiography, Poor Richard, and later writings; letters from London, 1757-1775, Paris, 1776-1785, Philadelphia, 1785-1790, Poor Richard's almanack, 1733-1758, The autobiography. Library of America 1997 816p $30 *

Grades: 11 12 Adult   **818**

ISBN 1-883011-53-1   LC 97-21611

"J.A. Leo Lemay wrote the notes and selected the texts for this volume" Prelim. paging

"This collection of Franklin's works begins with letters sent from London (1757-1775) describing the events and diplomacy preceding the Revolutionary War. The volume also contains political satires, bagatelles, pamphlets, and letters written in Paris (1776-1785), where he represented the revolutionary United States at the court of Louis XVI, as well as his speeches given in the Constitutional Convention and other works written in Philadelphia (1785-1790), including his last published article, a . . . satire against slavery. Also included are the . . . prefaces to Poor Richard's Almanack (1733-1758). . . . [The] Autobiography, Franklin's last word on his greatest literary creation—his own invented personality—is presented here in a new edition." Publisher's note

Includes bibliographical references

Frost, Robert, 1874-1963

Collected poems, prose, & plays. Library of Am. 1995 1036p $35 *

Grades: 11 12 Adult   **818**

1. Poetry—By individual authors

ISBN 1-883011-06-X   LC 94-43693

This volume contains "all of the plays, a generous selection of prose, all collected poems, and 94 uncollected poems, as well as 17 poems that were previously unpublished." Libr J

Hawthorne, Nathaniel, 1804-1864

The portable Hawthorne; edited with an introduction by William C. Spengemann. Penguin Books 2005 439p (Penguin classics) pa $18

Grades: 11 12 Adult   **818**

ISBN 0-14-303928-8; 978-0-14-303928-0

LC 2004-65791

This collection "includes writings from each major stage in the career of Nathaniel Hawthorne: a number of his . . . early tales, all of The Scarlet Letter, excerpts from his three subsequently published romances—The House of Seven Gables, The Blithedale Romance, and The Marble Faun—as well as passages from his European journals and a sampling of his last, unfinished works." Publisher's note

Includes bibliographical references

A **Historical** guide to Edgar Allan Poe; edited by J. Gerald Kennedy. Oxford Univ. Press 2001 247p il (Historical guides to American authors) $39.95; pa $15.95 *

Grades: 11 12 Adult   **818**

1. Poe, Edgar Allan, 1809-1849

ISBN 0-19-512149-X; 0-19-512150-3 (pa)

LC 00-20192

Following an introduction this volume presents a "capsule biography situating Poe in his historical context. The subsequent essays in this book cover such topics as Poe and the American publishing industry, Poe's sensationalism, his relationships to gender constructions, and Poe and American privacy. The volume also includes a bibliographic essay, a chronology of Poe's life, a bibliography, illustrations, and an index." Publisher's note

Includes bibliographical references

A **Historical** guide to Henry David Thoreau; edited by William E. Cain. Oxford Univ. Press 2000 285p il maps (Historical guides to American authors) $95; pa $50 *

Grades: 9 10 11 12   **818**

1. Thoreau, Henry David, 1817-1862

ISBN 0-19-513862-7; 0-19-513863-5 (pa)

LC 99-55276

A Historical guide to Henry David Thoreau—
Continued

Scholars assess the essays, social criticism, and natural history writing of the influential Transcendentalist. Includes a biographical essay and chronology

Includes bibliographical references

Hughes, Langston, 1902-1967

The return of Simple; edited by Akiba Sullivan Harper; introduction by Arnold Rampersad. Hill & Wang 1994 xxii, 218p pa $11 hardcover o.p.

Grades: 11 12 Adult **818**

ISBN 0-8090-1582-X (pa) LC 93-45373

This collection brings together the "narrations of the fictional Jesse B. Semple, or 'Simple,' which first appeared in 1943 in [Hughes] column in the Chicago Defender and, later, in the New York Post. Here, edited by a teacher at Spelman College, is an enlightening collection of these social commentaries." Publ Wkly

Hurston, Zora Neale, 1891-1960

Folklore, memoirs, and other writings. Library of Am. 1995 1001p il $35 *

Grades: 11 12 Adult **818**

ISBN 0-940450-84-4 LC 94-21384

Companion volume to Novels and stories (1995)

"This is the first time the unexpurgated version of Hurston's 1942 autobiography, *Dust Tracks on the Road*, is being published; sections deemed too provocative (dealing with politics, race, and sex) have been restored. *Mules and Men* (1935) is a collection of African American folklore she gleaned on travels in the South, while *Tell My Horse* (1938) tenders her personal findings on African-based religion in Jamaica and Haiti. Additionally, 22 magazine and book articles with anthropological themes . . . that have never been gathered into book form are corralled here." Booklist

I know why the caged bird sings, by Maya Angelou; editor, Mildred R. Mickle. Salem Press 2009 285p (Critical insights) lib bdg $85 *

Grades: 9 10 11 12 **818**

1. Angelou, Maya

ISBN 978-1-58765-624-8; 1-58765-624-8

LC 2009-26306

This book discusses the historical context of Maya Angelou's book and includes a biography of the author as well as critical essays on the work.

Includes bibliographical references

Jefferson, Thomas, 1743-1826

Writings. Library of Am. 1984 1600p $35 *

Grades: 11 12 Adult **818**

ISBN 0-940450-16-X LC 83-19917

Edited by Merrill D. Peterson

"Autobiography—A summary view of the rights of British America—Notes on the State of Virginia—Public papers—Addresses, messages, and replies—Miscellany—Letters." Title page

This is "the largest and most skillfully edited single-volume Jefferson ever published." N Y Times Book Rev

Includes bibliographical references

Kerouac, Jack, 1922-1969

The portable Jack Kerouac; edited by Ann Charters. Viking 1995 xxv, 625p pa $17 hardcover o.p. *

Grades: 11 12 Adult **818**

ISBN 0-14-310506-X (pa) LC 94-20120

"Charters has chosen selections from each of Kerouac's 14 novels, which comprise a complex and evocative autobiographical series Kerouac called the Legend of Duluoz. . . . Charters has also included poetry from *San Francisco Blues* and *Book of Haikus,* as well as a group of essays that cover Kerouac's main passions and interests: writing, traveling, jazz, and Buddhism." Booklist

Includes bibliographical references

Lines of velocity; [executive editor, Keren Taylor; associate editors, Cindy Collins . . . [et al.]] WriteGirl 2007 236p pa $19.95

Grades: 9 10 11 12 **818**

1. Teenagers' writings

ISBN 978-0-9741251-5-2

On cover: Words that move from WriteGirl

WriteGirl is "a creative writing and mentoring organization for teen girls in the Los Angeles area. Unlike many such anthologies, this collection includes the work of experienced mentors who volunteered their time to the project, as well as the teen participants. . . . This appealing volume is broken into 10 sections: self, writing, Los Angeles, friendship, love, rants, family, place, origins, and writing experiments. The poetry and prose found in each one are sincere and personal, and one gets the feeling of having discovered a dog-eared, doodle-laden journal among the refuse of a high school parking lot. . . . This anthology is sure to be picked up by aspiring young writers as well as educators looking for inspired samples and interactive exercises." SLJ

London, Jack, 1876-1916

The portable Jack London; edited by Earle Labor. Penguin Bks. 1994 xxxvii, 563p pa $15.95 *

Grades: 11 12 Adult **818**

ISBN 0-14-017969-0 LC 93-38740

Short stories included are: To the man on trail; In a far country; The law of life; A relic of the Pliocene; Nam-Bok the unveracious; To build a fire (1902); Moon-face; Bâtard; Love of life; All Gold Canyon; The apostate; To build a fire (1908); The Chinago; Koolau the leper; Good-by, Jack; Mauki; The strength of the strong; Samuel; A piece of steak; The madness of John Harned; The night-born; War; Told in the drooling ward; The Mexican; The red one; The water baby

This volume contains selected short stories, the complete text of The call of the wild, personal letters, and a sampling of journalistic pieces.

Includes bibliographical references

Magistrale, Tony
Student companion to Edgar Allan Poe.
Greenwood Press 2001 139p (Student companions
to classic writers) $35 *
Grades: 9 10 11 12   **818**
1. Poe, Edgar Allan, 1809-1849
ISBN 0-313-30992-2   LC 00-49071
Another available series title in this class is: Student
companion to Mark Twain. For complete list of titles
contact publisher
An introduction to the life, times and major works. In-
cludes contemporary interpretations of The raven and
The purloined letter
Includes bibliographical references

The **Mark** Twain encyclopedia; editors, J.R.
LeMaster, James D. Wilson; editorial and
research assistant, Christie Graves Hamric.
Garland 1993 xxx, 848p (Garland reference
library of the humanities) $155; pa $65
Grades: 11 12 Adult   **818**
1. Twain, Mark, 1835-1910—Encyclopedias
2. Authors, American—Encyclopedias 3. Reference
books
ISBN 0-8240-7212-X; 0-415-89058-6 (pa)
                                             LC 92-45662
Paperback has title: The Routledge encyclopedia of
Mark Twain
This "reference guide consists of approximately 740
signed articles by noted authorities. The articles cover all
aspects of Twain's life. . . . Each article includes a bibliography. There are a detailed chronology of Twain's
life and a lengthy Clemens genealogy." Am Libr

Maya Angelou; edited and with an introduction by
Harold Bloom. New ed. Bloom's Literary
Criticism 2009 178p (Modern critical views)
$45 *
Grades: 9 10 11 12   **818**
1. Angelou, Maya
ISBN 978-1-60413-177-2   LC 2008-44406
First published 1998
Some other available series titles in this class are:
Margaret Atwood; Langston Hughes; James Baldwin;
Henry David Thoreau. For a complete list of titles con-
tact publisher
Scholars explore social, political and religious themes
in Angelou's prose and poetry.
Includes bibliographical references

Poe, Edgar Allan, 1809-1849
The collected tales and poems of Edgar Allan
Poe. Modern Lib. 1992 1026p $20 *
Grades: 11 12 Adult   **818**
ISBN 0-679-60007-8   LC 92-50231
A reissue of The complete tales and poems of Edgar
Allan Poe published 1938
Short stories included are: The unparalleled adventure
of one Hans Pfaal; The gold-bug; The balloon-hoax; Von
Kempelen and his discovery; Mesmeric revelation; The
facts in the case of M. Valdemar; The thousand-and-
second tale of Scheherazade; Ms. found in a bottle; A
descent into the maelström; The murders in the Rue

Morgue; The mystery of Marie Rogêt; The purloined letter; The black cat; The fall of the House of Usher; The
pit and the pendulum; The premature burial; The masque
of the Red Death; The cask of Amontillado; The imp of
the perverse; The island of the fay; The oval portrait;
The assignation; The tell-tale heart; The system of Doctor Tarr and Professor Fether; The literary life of
Thingum Bob, Esq.; How to write a Blackwood article;
A predicament; Mystification; X-ing a paragrab; Did-
dling; The angel of the odd; Mellonta Tauta; Loss of
breath; The man that was used up; The business man;
Maelzel's chess-player; The power of words; The colloquy of Monos and Una; The conversation of Eiros and
Charmion; Shadow—a parable; Silence—a fable; A tale
of Jerusalem; The sphinx; The man of the crowd; Never
bet the Devil your head; "Thou art the man"; Hop-Frog;
Four beasts in one: the homo-camelopard; Why the little
Frenchman wears his hand in a sling; Bon-bon; Some
words with a mummy; Magazine-writing—Peter Snook;
the domain of Arnheim; Landor's cottage; William Wilson; Berenice; Eleonora; Ligeia; Morella; Metzengerstein;
A tale of the ragged mountains; The spectacles; The Duc
De L'Omelette; The oblong box; King Pest; Three Sun-
days in a week; The devil in the belfrey; Lionizing
This volume contains short stories, poems, and a sampling of Poe's essays, criticism and journalistic writings

Porcellino, John
Thoreau at Walden; by John Porcellino, from
the writings of Henry David Thoreau; introduction
by D.B. Johnson. Hyperion 2008 99p il (Center for
Cartoon Studies presents) $16.99; pa $9.99
Grades: 8 9 10 11 12   **818**
1. Thoreau, Henry David, 1817-1862—Graphic novels
2. Graphic novels
ISBN   978-1-4231-0038-6;   1-4231-0038-7;
978-1-4231-0039-3 (pa); 1-4231-0039-5 (pa)
                                             LC 2007-61358
"Presents in graphic novel format an account of the
two years that Thoreau spent at Walden Pond, excerpted
from Thoreau's writings." Publisher's note
"This book is true in spirit to Thoreau's writings and
to underground comics. It is fairly linear, using short
quotes and simple line drawings to tell of the time the
philosopher spent at Walden Pond. Porcellino chose
many well-known sayings and events and placed them
within a spare visual context." SLJ
Includes bibliographical references

Rasmussen, R. Kent
Bloom's how to write about Mark Twain;
introduction by Harold Bloom. Chelsea House
2007 324p (Bloom's how to write about literature)
$45
Grades: 9 10 11 12   **818**
1. Twain, Mark, 1835-1910 2. Report writing
ISBN 978-0-7910-9487-7   LC 2007-7248
This book offers "paper-topic suggestions, . . . outlined strategies on how to write a strong essay, and an
. . . introduction by Harold Bloom on writing about
Twain. This volume is designed to help students develop
their analytical writing skills and critical comprehension
of this important author and his works." Publisher's note
Includes bibliographical references

Rasmussen, R. Kent—*Continued*

Critical companion to Mark Twain; a literary reference to his life and work; with critical commentary by John H. Davis and Alex Feerst. Rev ed. Facts on File 2007 2v il map (Facts on File library of American literature) set $125
Grades: 11 12 Adult   **818**
  1. Twain, Mark, 1835-1910
  ISBN 0-8160-5398-7; 978-0-8160-5398-8
                         LC 2004-46910
  First published 1995 in one volume with title: Mark Twain A to Z
  Contents: v1. Part I: Biography; Part II: Works A-Z v2. Part III: Related people, places, and topics; Part IV: Appendices
  This companion to the life and works of Mark Twain includes a biography, synopses and critical commentaries on each of his works, discussions about major characters and places in his works, and entries on important people, places, and other aspects of his life.
  Includes glossary, filmography and bibliographical references

Social and psychological disorder in the works of Edgar Allan Poe; Claudia Durst Johnson, book editor. Greenhaven Press 2010 163p il (Social issues in literature) $38.45; pa $26.50
Grades: 9 10 11 12   **818**
  1. Poe, Edgar Allan, 1809-1849 2. Social problems in literature
  ISBN   978-0-7377-5016-4;   0-7377-5016-2; 978-0-7377-5017-1 (pa); 0-7377-5017-0 (pa)
                         LC 2010-83
  This book "is organized in three sections, beginning with background information about the author and providing insight into how the author's experiences influenced his or her work. Another section presents articles that analyze the relationship between the work and the social issue, all from a variety of perspectives. A final chapter brings the highlighted social issue into contemporary times, discussing its status in society today. The articles, all signed, and all from individual contributors, are brief and clearly written, with students in mind. . . . They delve into the aspects of madness, murder, and obsession that make Poe's tales so fascinating to students." Voice Youth Advocates
  Includes bibliographical references

Sova, Dawn B.

Critical companion to Edgar Allan Poe; a literary reference to his life and work. Facts on File 2007 458p il (Facts on File library of American literature) $75 *
Grades: 11 12 Adult   **818**
  1. Poe, Edgar Allan, 1809-1849
  ISBN 0-8160-6408-3; 978-0-8160-6408-3
                        LC 2006-29466
  First published 2001 with title: Edgar Allan Poe, A-Z
  "Biographical, historical, and critical material on Poe's life and work is presented in alphabetical order in three sections. The entries on Poe's works each provide a synopsis, a publication history, and character descriptions, while major works such as 'The Cask of Amontillado'

and 'The Purloined Letter' have . . . [a] commentary and . . . further-reading suggestions." SLJ
  Includes bibliographical references

Stein, Gertrude, 1874-1946

Selected writings; edited with an introduction and notes by Carl Van Vechten and with an essay on Gertrude Stein by F. W. Dupee. Modern Lib. 1962 706p pa $18 hardcover o.p.
Grades: 11 12 Adult   **818**
  ISBN 0-679-72464-8 (pa)
  In addition to the autobiography of Alice B. Toklas and the libretto Four saints in three acts, this volume contains representative selections of Stein's poetry, prose, drama, and criticism.

Writings, 1932-1946. Library of Am. 1998 844p $40
Grades: 11 12 Adult   **818**
  ISBN 1-883011-41-8   LC 97-28916
  Contents: Stanzas in meditation; Lectures in America; The geographical history of America; Ida; Brewsie and Willie; Other works
  In addition to theater pieces, fiction, and poetry "memoir, philosophical speculation, literary criticism and theory, all sorts of briefer forms that are hard to account for but easy to marvel at and even to delight in, pack these volumes, and constitute, as the editors surely intended us to discover, the most consistently achieved representation of new ways of responding to life and new possibilities of getting experience into words that American literature has to show." N Y Times Book Rev

Steinbeck, John, 1902-1968

The grapes of wrath and other writings, 1936-1941. Library of Am. 1996 1067p $35 *
Grades: 9 10 11 12   **818**
  ISBN 1-883011-15-9   LC 96-3725
  The long valley contains the following short stories: Chrysanthemums; White quail; Flight; Snake; Breakfast; Raid; Harness; Vigilante; Johnny Bear; Murder; St. Katy the virgin; Leader of the people
  This volume contains the short story collection The long valley (1938) and the novel The grapes of wrath. Also included is The log from the Sea of Cortez (1941) Steinbeck's narrative about marine research in the Gulf of California and The harvest gypsies, a series of newspaper articles on migrant labor that was published with title Their blood is strong (1938)

Stowe, Harriet Beecher, 1811-1896

The Oxford Harriet Beecher Stowe reader; edited with an introduction by Joan D. Hedrick. Oxford Univ. Press 1999 560p pa $34.95 *
Grades: 11 12 Adult   **818**
  ISBN 0-19-509117-5   LC 97-32020
  The editor provides an "introduction that assesses Stowe's vital impact on nineteenth-century American literature, politics, and culture. The readings are divided into three sections: Early Sketches, Antislavery Writings, and Domestic Culture and Politics. Early Sketches presents the finest writing of Stowe's literary apprenticeship.

Stowe, Harriet Beecher, 1811-1896—*Continued*
Antislavery Writings includes *Uncle Tom's Cabin* in its
entirety. . . . Domestic Culture and Politics shows the
scope of Stowe's thinking on the Victorian home, for
which she was a major propagandist." Publisher's note
Includes bibliographical references

Thoreau, Henry David, 1817-1862
Collected essays and poems. Library of Am.
2001 703p $35 *
Grades: 11 12 Adult   **818**
ISBN 1-883011-95-7   LC 00-46234
Edited by Elizabeth Hall Witherell
Among the 27 essays included are Civil disobedience,
Walking, Martyrdom of John Brown, A Yankee in Cana-
da, and Life without principle. Many of the poems were
taken from Thoreau's journals and manuscripts
Includes bibliographical references

Walden, or, Life in the woods; with an
introduction by Verlyn Klinkenborg. Knopf 1992
xxxi, 295p $19 *
Grades: 11 12 Adult   **818**
ISBN 0-679-41896-2   LC 92-54444
Hardcover and paperback editions also available from
other publishers
"Everyman's library"
First published 1854
"Philosophy of life and observations of nature drawn
from the author's solitary sojourn of two years in a cabin
on Walden Pond near Concord, Massachusetts." Pratt Al-
cove
Includes bibliographical references

Thurber, James, 1894-1961
Writings and drawings. Library of Am. 1996
1004p il $40
Grades: 11 12 Adult   **818**
1. American wit and humor
ISBN 978-1-883011-22-2; 1-883011-22-1
                                       LC 96-5853
Edited by Garrison Keillor
Includes the complete texts of The seal in the bedroom (1932), the autobiography My life and hard times
(1933); the anti-war parable The last flower (1939) and
the children's tale The 13 clocks (1950)
"These stories, parodies, reminiscences, cartoons, and
drawings present Thurber's unique and masterful take on
work, psychotherapy, fantasizing, domesticity, and the
battle between the sexes." Booklist

Twain, Mark, 1835-1910
The innocents abroad [and] Roughing it. Library
of Am. 1984 1027p il $35
Grades: 9 10 11 12   **818**
1. Voyages and travels
ISBN 0-940450-25-9   LC 84-11296
Edited by Guy Cardwell
The innocents abroad (1869) is Twain's humorous account of his adventures in the Holy Land, Italy, and Paris. Roughing it (1872) recounts a trip across the plains
to California and then Hawaii in the early 1860s

Life on the Mississippi; with an introduction by
James M. Cox. Penguin Books 1984 450p
(Penguin Classics) pa $9.95 *
Grades: 9 10 11 12   **818**
1. Mississippi River valley
ISBN 0-14-039050-2   LC 84-1194
A reissue of the title first published 1874
"Its historical sketches, its frequent passages of vivid
description, and its humorous episodes combine to make
[this] a masterpiece of the literature of the Middle West."
Eng and Pope's What to Read

Roughing it; edited with an introduction by
Hamlin Hill. Penguin 1981 590p il (The Penguin
American library) pa $14
Grades: 11 12 Adult   **818**
1. Hawaii—Description and travel
ISBN 0-14-039010-3   LC 81-10593
Hardcover and paperback editions also available from
other publishers
First published 1872
A humorous account of a trip across the plains to Cal-
ifornia and then to Hawaii in the early 1860s.
Includes bibliographical references

Wayne, Tiffany K., 1968-
Critical companion to Ralph Waldo Emerson; a
literary reference to his life and work. Facts On
File 2010 444p il (Facts on File library of
American literature) $75
Grades: 11 12 Adult   **818**
1. Emerson, Ralph Waldo, 1803-1882
ISBN 978-0-8160-7358-0; 978-1-4381-3048-4 (ebook)
                                       LC 2009-24809

Contact publisher for ebook pricing
"This reference book examines the life and works of
a central thinker in American history. . . . It begins with
Emerson's biography for context. Part 2 focuses on 140
significant (in the view of scholars) individual works, including 60 poems (most with one to three pages of synopses, critical commentary, and further reading). Part 3
covers related people, places, and topics. . . . The final
appendixes offer a chronology of Emerson's life and
times, bibliographies of both his works and relevant secondary sources." Choice
Includes bibliographical references

Wharton, Edith, 1862-1937
Novellas and other writings. Library of Am.
1990 1137p il $45 *
Grades: 11 12 Adult   **818**
ISBN 0-940450-53-4   LC 89-62930
Contents: Madame de Treymes; Ethan Frome; Summer; Old New York; The mother's recompense; A backward glance
This volume contains the following novelettes: Madame de Troyes (1907); Ethan Frome (1911); Summer
(1917); The mother's recompense (1925). Old New York
(1924) is a collection of four novelettes: False dawn; The
old maid; The spark; New Year's day. Also included is
the autobiographical A backward glance (1934)
Includes bibliographical references

Wright, Richard, 1908-1960
Works. Library of Am. 1991 2v ea $35 *
Grades: 11 12 Adult   **818**
1. African Americans—Fiction 2. African Americans
ISBN 0-940450-66-6 (v1); 0-940450-67-4 (v2)
LC 91-60540
Contents: v1 Early works; v2 Later works
This set contains the complete novels Native son; The
outsider (1953); and Lawd today! (1963); the story col-
lection Uncle Tom's children; and the memoir Black boy

820.3   English literature— Encyclopedias and dictionaries

The **Continuum** encyclopedia of British literature;
Steven R. Serafin and Valerie Grosvenor Myer,
editors. Continuum 2003 1184p $175
Grades: 11 12 Adult   **820.3**
1. Reference books 2. English literature—Encyclopedias
ISBN 0-8264-1456-7   LC 2002-9231
"Most of the encyclopedia's 1,700 entries are devoted
to writers. . . . The 69 topical articles provide . . . historical overviews of specific genres, themes, literary periods, and geographical areas. Among these are *Caribbean
literature in English, Feminism, Old English,* and *War
and literature.* With the exception of brief author entries
of approximately 300 words or less, articles are signed
and include bibliographical references." Booklist
"This reference work provides a fascinating current
take on the canon. . . . The historical/literary time line
and the lists of prize titles alone will keep researchers
happy." SLJ
Includes bibliographical references

The **Oxford** companion to English literature;
edited by Dinah Birch. 7th ed. Oxford
University Press 2009 1164p $150 *
Grades: 11 12 Adult   **820.3**
1. English literature—Dictionaries 2. English literature—Bio-bibliography 3. American literature—Dictionaries 4. American literature—Bio-bibliography
5. Reference books
ISBN 978-0-19-280687-1   LC 2009-455948
First published 1932 under the editorship of Sir Paul
Harvey
"The subjects of the entries include literary works, authors, themes, archetypes, journals, and forms. . . . This
companion is a highly authoritative resource, with clear,
concise, and approachable entries on literary topics of
high interest to students and scholars of English literature. An essential reference for most public, high school,
and academic libraries." Libr J

820.8   English literature— Collections

The **Norton** anthology of literature by women; the
traditions in English; [compiled by] Sandra M.
Gilbert, Susan Gubar. 3rd ed. W.W. Norton &
Co. 2007 2v map set $76.25 *
Grades: 11 12 Adult   **820.8**
1. American literature—Women authors—Collections
2. English literature—Women authors—Collections
ISBN 978-0-393-93015-3; 0-393-93015-7
LC 2006101170
Volumes 1 and 2 also available separately ea $56.25
First published 1985
Contents: v1 The Middle Ages through the turn of the
century; v2 Early twentieth-century through contempo-
rary
The editors provide representative selections of prose
and poetry by women. Period introductions, biographical
headnotes and bibliographies are provided.
Includes bibliographical references

The **Oxford** anthology of English literature;
general editors: Frank Kermode and John
Hollander. Oxford Univ. Press 1973 6v in 2 il
maps v1 2v pa set $65.95; v2 2v pa set $65.95
Grades: 11 12 Adult   **820.8**
1. English literature—Collections
ISBN 0-19-501657-2 (v1 2v pa); 0-19-501658-0 (v2
2v pa)
Each of the six parts collected here were published
separately. Apply to publisher for prices and availability
Contents: v1 The Middle Ages through the eighteenth
century: Medieval English literature, edited by J. B.
Trapp; The literature of Renaissance England, edited by
John Hollander and Frank Kermode; The Restoration and
the eighteenth century, edited by Martin Price; v2 1800
to the present: Romantic poetry and prose, edited by
Harold Bloom and Lionel Trilling; Victorian prose and
poetry, edited by Lionel Trilling and Harold Bloom;
Modern British literature, edited by Frank Kermode and
John Hollander

820.9   English literature—History and criticism

Backgrounds to English literature. Facts on File
2002 5v set $150
Grades: 11 12 Adult   **820.9**
1. English literature—History and criticism 2. Great
Britain—Civilization
ISBN 0-8160-5125-9   LC 2002-71284
Also available separately ea $27
Contents: v1 The Renaissance, by P. Lee-Browne; v2
The romantics, by N. King; v3 The Victorians, by A.
Cruttenden; v4 The modernist period, 1900-1945, by P.
Lee-Browne; v5 Post-war literature 1945 to the present,
by C. Merz and P. Lee-Browne
This set provides "the historical, cultural, and social
background of each major period. Each volume is a basic
introduction to the period: its history, leaders, important
laws, social and religious movements, scientific develop-

Backgrounds to English literature—*Continued*
ments, and details of daily life in different regions and classes within Great Britain. The set summarizes the literary genres of each period and discusses representative writers and works." Publisher's note

"Will be useful for students studying the social, historical, and cultural influences on authors of the post-war period." SLJ

Includes bibliographical references

Burrow, J. A. (John Anthony)
Medieval writers and their work; Middle English literature 1100-1500. 2nd ed. Oxford University Press 2008 156p pa $32.95
Grades: 9 10 11 12   **820.9**
1. Medieval literature—History and criticism
2. English literature—History and criticism
ISBN 978-0-19-953204-9; 0-19-953204-4
                         LC 2007048243
First published 1982
"Burrow's book deals with circumstances of composition and reception, the main genres, 'modes of meaning' (allegory etc.), and medieval literature's afterlife in modern times. . . . By placing medieval writers in their historical context—the four centuries between the Norman Conquest and the Renaissance—Professor Burrow explains not only how they wrote, but why." Publisher's note

Includes bibliographical references

The **Cambridge** guide to literature in English; edited by Dominic Head. 3rd ed. Cambridge University Press 2006 xxiii, 1241p il $50
Grades: 11 12 Adult   **820.9**
1. Reference books 2. English literature—Dictionaries
3. English literature—Bio-bibliography 4. American literature—Dictionaries
ISBN 978-0-521-83179-6; 0-521-83179-2
                         LC 2006-271458
First published 1988 under the editorship of Ian Ousby

"The scope of material covered . . . extends to the literature of the United Kingdom and well beyond: Africa, Asia, Australia, Canada, the Caribbean, India, New Zealand, and the U.S. are all well represented. . . . Literary terms are explained, literary movements are summarized, and literary magazines are sketched in unsigned entries ranging in length from a few lines to a few paragraphs or more. . . . With its broad coverage, clearly written and accessible text, and relatively modest price, this is a must purchase for most reference collections." Booklist

Dailey, Donna
London; [by] Donna Dailey and John Tomedi; introduction by Harold Bloom. Chelsea House 2005 231p il map (Bloom's literary places) $40
Grades: 9 10 11 12   **820.9**
1. London (England) in literature 2. Literary landmarks
ISBN 0-7910-7841-8   LC 2004-18928
Contents: London today; After the conquest; Elizabethan London; London and the restoration; Georgian and Regency London; Victorian times; London at the turn of the twentieth century; London between the wars; The London of Gravity's rainbow; The millennial city

This guide to the city of London focuses on the places within it that have had an impact on literature.

Includes bibliographical references

Encyclopedia of British writers, 16th-18th centuries; [written and developed by Book Builders LLC] Facts on File 2005 2v set $150
Grades: 11 12 Adult   **820.9**
1. Authors, English—Dictionaries 2. English literature—Bio-bibliography 3. English literature—History and criticism 4. Reference books
ISBN 0-8160-5132-1   LC 2004-47070
Also included in a four-volume set along with Encyclopedia of British writers, 19th and 20th centuries

"Writers 'from Christopher Marlowe to John Donne' and of numerous genres are covered: dramatists, novelists, nonfiction authors, poets, historians, publishers, translators, literary critics, and editors. The alphabetical entries are brief. . . . Those on individuals contain biographical information, works, and a short bibliography. . . . Where patrons do extensive research on these periods, these encyclopedias will prove useful." SLJ

Encyclopedia of British writers, 1800 to the present; general editors, George Stade, Karen Karbiener. 2nd ed. Facts On File 2009 2v (Facts on File library of world literature) set $170
Grades: 9 10 11 12 Adult   **820.9**
1. Authors, English—Dictionaries 2. English literature—Bio-bibliography 3. English literature—History and criticism 4. Reference books
ISBN 978-0-8160-7385-6   LC 2008-22264
First published 2003 with title: Encyclopedia of British writers, 19th and 20th centuries

"This set treats more than 900 authors. Coverage encompasses a range of genres. . . . Volume 1 traverses the nineteenth century, and volume 2 presents writers from the twentieth century on. Within each volume, arrangement is alphabetical. In addition to author entries, the editors have provided short essays on important literary movements such as the Irish Literary Renaissance, Romanticism, and Theater of the Absurd. . . . The entries are engaging and provide enough content to give readers a basic understanding of the life and work of each writer. High-school, college, and public libraries will find this a very useful resource." Booklist

Includes bibliographical references

The **Oxford** companion to Irish literature; edited by Robert Welch, assistant editor, Bruce Stewart. Oxford Univ. Press 1996 xxv, 614p maps $55 *
Grades: 11 12 Adult   **820.9**
1. Irish literature—Dictionaries 2. Reference books
ISBN 0-19-866158-4   LC 95-44943
Encompassing "Ireland's literary heritage from the bardic poets and Celtic sagas to twentieth-century authors like Brian Friel, Edna O'Brien, and Nuala Ni Dhomhnaill, the more than 2,000 unsigned entries cover writers, titles of major works, literary genres and motifs, folklore, mythology, periodicals, associations, and historical figures and events." Booklist

Pool, Daniel

What Jane Austen ate and Charles Dickens knew; from fox hunting to whist: the facts of daily life in nineteenth-century England. Simon & Schuster 1993 416p il maps pa $14 hardcover o.p.

Grades: 11 12 Adult **820.9**

1. English literature—History and criticism 2. Great Britain—Social life and customs

ISBN 0-671-88236-8 (pa)　　　　LC 93-16240

"Modern American readers of 19th-century English novels are often brought up short by bizarre references and puzzling words that did not need explaining when the books were written. Now they do, and Daniel Pool does a charming job of clearing things up in a witty, informal survey of daily life in the Hanoverian-Victorian era." N Y Times Book Rev

Includes bibliographical references

Tomedi, John, 1978-

Dublin; introduction by Harold Bloom. Chelsea House 2005 191p il map (Bloom's literary places) $40

Grades: 9 10 11 12 **820.9**

1. Dublin (Ireland) 2. Literary landmarks

ISBN 0-7910-7836-1　　　　LC 2005-13971

This guide to the city of Dublin focuses on the places within it that have had an impact on literature. "Most notably known as the home of James Joyce and the setting for his masterwork, Ulysses, Dublin is also the birthplace of George Bernard Shaw and was the childhood home of Oscar Wilde." Publisher's note

Includes bibliographical references

The **Victorian** novel; edited and with an introduction by Harold Bloom. Chelsea House 2004 412p (Bloom's period studies) $37.95

Grades: 9 10 11 12 **820.9**

1. English literature—History and criticism

ISBN 0-7910-7678-4

This study of the Victorian novel examines the work of major influential authors including "Charles Dickens, The Brontës, Anthony Trollope, George Eliot, Mrs. Elizabeth Gaskell, William Makepeace Thackeray, and Thomas Hardy." Publisher's note

Includes bibliographical references

World writers in English; Jay Parini, editor. Scribner 2003 2v set $250 *

Grades: 9 10 11 12 **820.9**

1. Literature—History and criticism 2. Literature—Bio-bibliography 3. Reference books

ISBN 0-684-31289-1　　　　LC 2003-14873

"A collection of 40 critical and biographical essays on writers from around the postcolonial world, including India and Asia, Australia and New Zealand, Africa, the Caribbean, and Canada, who write primarily in English. Most write fiction, though poets (Derek Walcott) and playwrights (Wole Soyinka) are also represented. Each 18- to 22-page signed essay includes excerpts from major works along with explication, with 'special attention paid to the cultural matrix that figures in the evolution of [the] writer.'" SLJ

"An essential addition to any general or academic reference collection." Booklist

Includes bibliographical references

821　English poetry

Auden, W. H. (Wystan Hugh), 1907-1973

Auden; poems; selected by Edward Mendelson. Knopf 1995 256p (Everyman's library pocket poets) $12.50

Grades: 11 12 Adult **821**

1. Poetry—By individual authors

ISBN 0-679-44367-3

A representative selection of lyrics that span the influential poet's career

Collected poems; edited by Edward Mendelson. Modern Library 2007 928p $40

Grades: 11 12 Adult **821**

1. Poetry—By individual authors

ISBN 978-0-679-64350-0; 0-679-64350-8

LC 2006-47163

Also available in paperback from Vintage Bks.

Originally published in different form by Random House in 1976

A compilation of all the poems Auden wished to preserve, in his final revisions. Previous collected editions and later shorter poems are included. There is also an absurdist play written 1928: Paid on both sides.

Blake, William, 1757-1827

The complete poetry and prose of William Blake; edited by David V. Erdman; with a new foreword and commentary by Harold Bloom. Newly rev. ed., 1st Calif. ed. University of California Press 2008 xxvi, 990p il $70

Grades: Adult **821**

1. Poetry—By individual authors

ISBN 978-0-520-04473-9

First published 1965 with title: Poetry and prose of William Blake

In addition to all of Blake's poetry, this volume also includes miscellaneous prose, marginalia, and letters

"The crucial preliminary problem [in establishing Blake's text] is simply to make out what Blake wrote. . . . Erdman has used modern aids such as infrared photography and microphotography. . . but his real achievement has been to look at Blake's text more closely and intelligently than any previous editor." N Y Rev Books

The essential Blake; selected and with an introduction by Stanley Kunitz. Ecco Press 1987 92p (Essential poets) hardcover o.p. pa $9.95 *

Grades: 11 12 Adult **821**

1. Poetry—By individual authors

ISBN 0-88001-138-6; 0-06-088793-1 (pa)

LC 86-24087

The editor has selected the poems he feels provide the best introduction to Blake's craft.

Poems. Knopf 1994 283p (Everyman's library pocket poets) $12.50 *

Grades: 11 12 Adult **821**

1. Poetry—By individual authors

ISBN 0-679-43633-2

A collection of representative and epic poems by the visionary Romantic poet, painter and engraver

Brontë, Emily, 1818-1848
Brontë: poems. Knopf 1996 255p (Everyman's library pocket poets) $12.50
Grades: 11 12 Adult   821
1. Poetry—By individual authors
ISBN 0-679-44725-3
A representative selection of Brontë's poetical output including many of her mythical works

Browning, Elizabeth Barrett, 1806-1861
Sonnets from the Portuguese; a celebration of love. St. Martin's Press 1986 [63]p il $9.95 *
Grades: 11 12 Adult   821
1. Poetry—By individual authors
ISBN 0-312-74501-X   LC 86-13755
Hardcover and paperback editions also available from other publishers
A series of sonnets which "were written during a period of seven years and are considered by some scholars to have been inspired by her love for her husband poet Robert Browning." New Century Handb of Engl Lit

Browning, Robert, 1812-1889
Robert Browning's poetry; authoritative texts, criticism; selected and edited by James F. Loucks and Andrew M. Stauffer. 2nd ed. W. W. Norton & Co. 2007 689p (A Norton critical edition) pa $14.50 *
Grades: 11 12 Adult   821
1. Poetry—By individual authors
ISBN 978-0-393-92600-2; 0-393-92600-1
LC 2006-47308
First published 1980
This collection of Browning's poetry, which includes Pauline, "reprints the texts of the seventeen-volume 'Fourth and complete edition' (Smith, Elder), of which all but the final volume were approved by Browning before his death. The poems are ordered chronologically according to their first appearance in book form." Publisher's note

Byron, George Gordon Byron, 6th Baron, 1788-1824
Byron; poems; [this selection by Peter Washington] Knopf 1994 288p (Everyman's library pocket poets) $12.50 *
Grades: 11 12 Adult   821
1. Poetry—By individual authors
ISBN 0-679-43630-8
A selection of lyric and dramatic poetry by the English Romantic poet and satirist.

Chaucer, Geoffrey, d. 1400
The Canterbury tales; translated into modern English by Nevill Coghill. Penguin Books 2003 504p (Penguin Classics) pa $10 *
Grades: 11 12 Adult   821
1. Poetry—By individual authors
ISBN 0-14-042438-5   LC 2003-265749

"A collection of twenty-four stories, all but two of which are in verse, written by Geoffrey Chaucer mainly between 1386 and his death in 1400. The stories are supposed to be related by members of a company of thirty-one pilgrims (including the poet himself) who are on their way to the shrine of St. Thomas at Canterbury. The prologue which tells of their assembly at the Tabard Inn in Southwark and their arrangement that each shall tell two stories on the way to Canterbury and two on the return journey, is a remarkable picture of English social life in the fourteenth century, inasmuch as every class is represented from the gentlefolks to the peasantry." Keller. Reader's Dig of Books

The portable Chaucer; selected, translated and edited by Theodore Morrison. rev ed. Viking 1975 611p pa $15.95 hardcover o.p. *
Grades: 11 12 Adult   821
1. Poetry—By individual authors
ISBN 0-14-015081-1 (pa)
"The Viking portable library"
First published 1949
Contains Troilus and Cressida, The Canterbury tales, selections from The book of the duchess and The bird's parliament, and some short verse.
Includes bibliographical references

Donne, John, 1572-1631
The complete poetry and selected prose of John Donne; edited by Charles M. Coffin; introduction by Denis Donoghue; notes by W. T. Chmielewski. Modern Lib. 2001 xxxii, 697p pa $14.95
Grades: 11 12 Adult   821
1. Poetry—By individual authors
ISBN 0-375-75734-1   LC 2001-30077
A reissue of the Modern Library edition published 1994
This volume contains Donne's love poetry, satires, epigrams, verse letters and holy sonnets. Also includes selected prose and a sampling of private letters.

Gawain and the Grene Knight (Middle English poem).
Sir Gawain and the Green Knight; a new verse translation by W. S. Merwin. Knopf 2002 hardcover o.p. pa $14 *
Grades: 9 10 11 12   821
1. Arthurian romances 2. Poetry—By individual authors
ISBN 0-375-41476-2; 0-375-70992-4 (pa)
LC 2002-20815
"Merwin's *Sir Gawain* replicates the propulsive alliteration and the rhymed-quatrain stanza endings of the original, and the translation appears face-to-face with the Middle English original. A major translation of a major English, and a major horror, classic." Booklist

Hardy, Thomas, 1840-1928
Poems. Knopf 1995 254p (Everyman's library pocket poets) $10.95
Grades: 11 12 Adult   821

Hardy, Thomas, 1840-1928—*Continued*
1. Poetry—By individual authors
ISBN 0-679-44368-1
A representative selection of the English author's verse. An index of first lines is included

Heaney, Seamus
Electric light. Farrar, Straus & Giroux 2001 98p hardcover o.p. pa $13
Grades: 11 12 Adult   821
1. Poetry—By individual authors
ISBN 0-374-14683-7; 0-374-52841-1 (pa)
LC 00-67278
Heaney's "book of poems is a compendium of poetic genres set in an array of forms and tuned to many kinds of experience, the work of a mature poet and world citizen, aware of his cultural authority as a public man and of the rights and responsibilities that go with it." N Y Times Book Rev

Opened ground; selected poems, 1966-1996. Farrar, Straus & Giroux 1998 443p pa $16 hardcover o.p.
Grades: 11 12 Adult   821
1. Poetry—By individual authors
ISBN 0-374-52678-8 (pa)   LC 98-4331
"The best of nobel laureate Heaney's poems, gathered from 12 previous collections, create a substantial volume that charts the course of one man's thoroughly examined personal life and reflects a volatile era in the life of his troubled country, Northern Ireland, though the particulars Heaney renders so vibrantly become archetypal and unbounded in their tragedy and bliss." Booklist

Housman, A. E. (Alfred Edward), 1859-1936
The collected poems of A. E. Housman. Holt & Co. 1965 254p pa $16
Grades: 11 12 Adult   821
1. Poetry—By individual authors
ISBN 0-8050-0547-1
This anthology "constitutes the authorized canon of A. E. Housman's verse as established in 1939." Note on the text

Hughes, Ted, 1930-1998
Selected poems, 1957-1994. Farrar, Straus & Giroux 2002 333p hardcover o.p. pa $15
Grades: 11 12 Adult   821
1. Poetry—By individual authors
ISBN 0-374-25875-9; 0-374-52864-0 (pa)
LC 2002-21603
"With poems that are characteristically alert to the processes of creation as well as self-destruction, this selection displays Hughes's mighty, even terrifying, talent." N Y Times Book Rev

Keats, John, 1795-1821
The major works; edited with an introduction and notes by Elizabeth Cook. Oxford Univ. Press 2001 xxxvi, 667p pa $16.95
Grades: 9 10 11 12   821
1. Poetry—By individual authors
ISBN 0-19-284063-0   LC 2001-272404

First published 1990
This volume contains all the poetry published during Keats' lifetime, including Endymion in its entirety, the Odes, Lamia, and both versions of Hyperion. A number of posthumously published poems are presented along with a selection of Keats' letters. Includes a bibliography, chronology, and a glossary of classical names

Poems. Knopf 1994 253p (Everyman's library pocket poets) $12.50 *
Grades: 11 12 Adult   821
1. Poetry—By individual authors
ISBN 0-679-43319-8   LC 94-2495
A representative collection by the influential English romantic.
Includes bibliographical references

Kipling, Rudyard, 1865-1936
Complete verse; definitive edition. Doubleday 1989 c1940 850p pa $20 hardcover o.p. *
Grades: 11 12 Adult   821
1. Poetry—By individual authors
ISBN 0-385-26089-X (pa)   LC 88-7364
Replaces Rudyard Kipling's verse: definitive edition, published 1940
This edition includes all of Kipling's published poetry and, in addition, more than 20 poems which have not previously appeared in the inclusive edition of his verse

Rossetti, Christina Georgina, 1830-1894
Poems. Knopf 1993 256p (Everyman's library pocket poets) $12.50
Grades: 11 12 Adult   821
1. Poetry—By individual authors
ISBN 0-679-42908-5   LC 93-14362
The poems in this collection are grouped under the following headings: Lyric poems, Dramatic and narrative poems, Rhymes and riddles, Sonnet sequences, Prayers and meditations. An index of first lines is included

Shakespeare, William, 1564-1616
Poems. Knopf 1994 252p (Everyman's library pocket poets) $12.50 *
Grades: 11 12 Adult   821
1. Poetry—By individual authors
ISBN 0-679-43320-1   LC 94-2494
Also available CD-ROM version
A representative selection of Shakespeare's verse.

The sonnets; edited by Rex Gibson. Cambridge Univ. Press 1997 204p il pa $12.50 *
Grades: 9 10 11 12   821
1. Poetry—By individual authors
ISBN 0-521-55947-2   LC 97-149257
"Each of Shakespeare's 154 sonnets is given at least one page, which includes the text of the sonnet, its theme and meaning, one possible interpretation, an explanation of difficult phrases and imagery, and a glossary of the unfamiliar words. The information is not thrust on the reader as the final and only 'correct' interpretation." Book Rep

Shakespeare, William, 1564-1616—*Continued*

The sonnets; edited by Stephen Orgel; with an introduction by John Hollander. Penguin Books 2001 xliv, 164p (The Pelican Shakespeare) pa $4.95 *

Grades: 11 12 Adult   **821**

1. Poetry—By individual authors

ISBN 0-14-071453-7   LC 2001-33200

"A series of 154 sonnets by Shakespeare. Probably composed between 1593 and 1601, they are written in the form of three quatrains and a couplet that has come to be known as Shakespearean. Influenced by, and often reacting against, the popular sonnet cycles of the time, notably Sir Philip Sidney's 'Astrophel and Stella', Shakespeare's sonnets are among the finest examples of their kind." Reader's Ency. 4th edition

Thomas, Dylan, 1914-1953

The poems of Dylan Thomas; edited with an introduction and notes by Daniel Jones; with a preface by Dylan Thomas. rev ed. New Directions 2003 xxix, 320p il $34.95 *

Grades: 11 12 Adult   **821**

1. Poetry—By individual authors

ISBN 978-0-8112-1541-1; 0-8112-1541-5

LC 2002-155790

Includes CD of the poet reading his work

First published 1971

"To the 90 poems Thomas published in Collected Poems, 1934-1952 Jones has added 102 and placed the total, as far as he could determine, in the chronological order of their composition. Some of the poems were still in manuscript form when Thomas died; others had been published in periodicals and anthologies. In an appendix, Jones offers Thomas' early poems—including one written when the poet was 12." Libr J [review of 1971 edition]

Includes bibliographical references

Selected poems, 1934-1952. rev ed. New Directions 2003 214p pa $14.95

Grades: 11 12 Adult   **821**

1. Poetry—By individual authors

ISBN 0-8112-1542-3   LC 2002-155792

First published 1953 with title: The collected poems of Dylan Thomas

"The prologue in verse, written for this collected edition of my poems, is intended as an address to my readers, the strangers. This book contains most of the poems I have written, and all, up to the present year, that I wish to preserve. Some of them I have revised a little." Preface {of 1953 edition}

Wordsworth, William, 1770-1850

Poems. Knopf 1995 256p (Everyman's library pocket poets) $12.50 *

Grades: 11 12 Adult   **821**

1. Poetry—By individual authors

ISBN 0-679-44369-X

A selection of work representative of the prominent Romantic's poetic legacy

Yeats, W. B. (William Butler), 1865-1939

The poems; edited by Richard J. Finneran. 2nd ed. Scribner 1997 xxix, 752p il $40; pa $20 *

Grades: 11 12 Adult   **821**

1. Poetry—By individual authors

ISBN 0-684-83935-0; 0-684-80731-9 (pa)

LC 97-23065

First published 1983 by Macmillan

This edition of the Nobel Laureate's verse contains complete texts of all the poems Yeats is known to have written. Yeats' original rhetorical punctuation has been restored. The editor provides textual histories

821.008   English poetry—Collections

100 essential modern poems; selected and introduced by Joseph Parisi. Ivan R. Dee 2005 305p $24.95 *

Grades: 11 12 Adult   **821.008**

1. English poetry—Collections 2. American poetry—Collections

ISBN 1-56663-612-4   LC 2005-9897

"Each of the 70 individuals whose work is represented receives a short, readable introduction that includes pertinent biographical information, a description of the poet's place in modern literary history, and an analysis of the writer's style. One to three representative poems follow each entry." SLJ

"Preceded by wonderfully conversational and expertly appreciative biocritical essays about each poet, his choices are superb as he lingers over Yeats and Stevens and includes often-overlooked witty and satirical poets, among them Dorothy Parker, Ogden Nash, Kay Ryan, Frank O'Hara, and Billy Collins." Booklist

100 great poems of the twentieth century; [edited by] Mark Strand. Norton 2005 320p $24.95

Grades: 11 12 Adult   **821.008**

1. English poetry—Collections 2. American poetry—Collections

ISBN 0-393-05894-8   LC 2005-2150

The editor "has selected works by poets of Europe and North and South America, and because there are so many gifted American poets, he restricted himself to those born before 1927. The result is a marvelously graceful, shimmering cosmos of poems by the likes of Anna Akhmatova, A. R. Ammons, Amy Clampit, Robert Desnos, Robert Frost, Nazim Hikmet, Kenneth Koch, Edna St. Vincent Millay, Gabriela Mistral, Eugenio Montale, Octavio Paz, and Derek Walcott." Booklist

The **Best** poems of the English language; from Chaucer through Robert Frost; selected and with commentary by Harold Bloom. HarperCollins Publishers 2004 xxviii, 972p $34.95; pa $19.95 *

Grades: 11 12 Adult   **821.008**

1. English poetry—Collections 2. American poetry—Collections

ISBN 0-06-054041-9; 0-06-054042-7 (pa)

LC 2003-51104

"Arranged chronologically by author, the poems are preceded by commentaries that extol their specific virtues and place them in historical context. Taken together, they

The Best poems of the English language—*Continued*

provide an overview of Bloom's own theories of writing, such as his notion that the greatest poems manifest an 'inevitability' of phrasing . . . Bloom rarely bores, and at his best he achieves a cogency . . . worthy of the poets he so deeply admires." Libr J

Includes bibliographical references

Chapters into verse; poetry in English inspired by the Bible; assembled and edited by Robert Atwan & Laurance Wieder. Oxford Univ. Press 1993 2v hardcover o.p. set pa $24.95
Grades: 11 12 Adult   **821.008**
1. Religious poetry—Collections
ISBN 0-19-508493-4; 0-19-513676-4 (pa)
                                        LC 92-37206
Volumes 1 and 2 also available separately in hardcover v1 $45; v2 $42
Contents: v1 Genesis to Malachi; v2 Gospels to Revelation
"An anthology of poems from all eras, styles, and degree of reverence, which take as their major inspiration lines, verses, or chapters from the Bible. Arranged in Biblical order in two volumes . . . the poems are preceded by the appropriate chapters and verses (the King James version has been used throughout). Poets as wide-ranging as Emily Dickinson, Sylvia Plath, and Delmore Schwartz are interspersed with D.H. Lawrence and writers from the Harlem Renaissance." Libr J

The Columbia anthology of British poetry; edited by Carl Woodring and James Shapiro. Columbia Univ. Press 1995 xxxi, 891p $41 *
Grades: 11 12 Adult   **821.008**
1. English poetry—Collections
ISBN 0-231-10180-5   LC 94-46333
This anthology "contains major British poetry from Beowulf to the present day. Poets receive a short biographical introduction along with their poetry. . . . It includes more female poets than most comparable anthologies, and is conducive to browsing. Major poems such as Coleridge's 'Rime of the Ancient Mariner,' Britain's best-loved poems, and newly rediscovered poems are part of this collection." SLJ

The New Oxford book of Irish verse; edited, with translations, by Thomas Kinsella. Oxford Univ. Press 2001 xxx, 423p pa $16.95 *
Grades: 11 12 Adult   **821.008**
1. Irish poetry—Collections
ISBN 0-19-280192-9   LC 2001-278442
Replaces The Oxford Book of Irish verse, XVIIth century-XXth century, chosen by Donagh MacDonagh and Lennox Robinson (1958); this is a reissue of the 1986 edition
"This selection is divided into three parts. Book I opens with the earliest pre-Christian poetry in Old Irish and ends in the fourteenth century with the first Irish poetry in the English language. Book II covers the fourteenth to the eighteenth centuries and Book III the nineteenth and twentieth centuries." Publisher's note

The New Oxford book of Victorian verse. Oxford Univ. Press 1987 xxxiv, 654p pa $25.95 hardcover o.p. *
Grades: 11 12 Adult   **821.008**
1. English poetry—Collections
ISBN 978-0-19-955631-1 (pa)   LC 86-23701
Replaces The Oxford book of Victorian verse, edited by Sir Arthur Quiller-Couch (1912)
An anthology of 19th century English poetry. Among the poets prominently featured are: Clough, Morris, Arnold, the Decadents, Emily Brontë, Clare, Barnes, and Christina Rossetti.
"While general collections should all add Ricks, those retaining [the Quiller-Couch edition] should dust him off and keep him available in order to represent fully Victorian verse and changing attitudes toward it." Libr J

The Norton anthology of modern and contemporary poetry; edited by Jahan Ramazani, Richard Ellmann, Robert O'Clair. 3rd ed. Norton 2003 2v pa set $75 *
Grades: 11 12 Adult   **821.008**
1. English poetry—Collections 2. American poetry—Collections
ISBN 0-393-32429-X   LC 2002-37990
Volumes 1 and 2 also available separately in paperback each $55
First published 1973 with title: The Norton anthology of modern poetry
Contents: v1 Modern poetry; v2 Contemporary poetry
This volume includes "1596 poems by 195 poets. . . . The anthology includes the works of such masters as Walt Whitman, Ezra Pound, Dylan Thomas, Langston Hughes, Gertrude Stein, Lucille Clifton, Louise Erdrich, and Allen Ginsberg. . . . Extensive, and beautifully composed introductions provide insight, observations, and historical context for the selections. . . . This ambitious, highly successful work is a veritable tribute to the enduring power of literature and language." SLJ
Includes bibliographical references

The Norton book of light verse; edited by Russell Baker; with the assistance of Kathleen Leland Baker. Norton 1986 447p $29.95
Grades: 11 12 Adult   **821.008**
1. English poetry—Collections 2. American poetry—Collections 3. Humorous poetry
ISBN 0-393-02366-4   LC 86-18172
Arranged by subject, this anthology presents some four hundred British and American light verse selections. The poems date from the sixteenth-century to the present

The Oxford book of English verse; edited by Christopher Ricks. Oxford Univ. Press 1999 xxxii, 690p $39.95 *
Grades: 11 12 Adult   **821.008**
1. English poetry—Collections
ISBN 0-19-214182-1   LC 99-20831
First published 1900 under the editorship of Sir Arthur Quiller-Couch with title: The Oxford book of English verse, 1250-1900. Present edition replaces The New Oxford book of English verse, 1250-1950, edited by Helen Gardner published 1972

The Oxford book of English verse—*Continued*

This collection "starts with anonymous 13th-century lyric and ends with Seamus Heaney; in between are seven centuries' worth of poems in English from Britain and Ireland. . . . Ricks brings in plenty of dialect verse, excerpts from long poems and verse plays, and a few translations into English. . . . Long after reviewers stop debating how Ricks chose each item, readers will keep returning to these pages to find yet another good poem they've not before seen." Publ Wkly

The **Oxford** book of twentieth-century English verse; chosen by Philip Larkin. Oxford University Press 1993 c1973 651p $35 *
Grades: 8 9 10 11 12 Adult   **821.008**
1. English poetry—Collections
ISBN 0-19-812137-7

This anthology of more than 600 poems by more than 200 twentieth-century British writers includes works by John Masefield, T. S. Eliot, W. B. Yeats, W. H. Auden, Dylan Thomas and Alan Sillitoe

"A strong vein of neo-Georgianism runs throughout the book, resulting in a clear partiality for work that is explicitly, even documentarily, English in locale, for poems that are narrative or anecdotal, for neat, well-populated fables and for moralistic ruminations." New Statesman

The **Top** 500 poems; edited by William Harmon. Columbia Univ. Press 1992 xxx, 1132p $36.95
Grades: 11 12 Adult   **821.008**
1. English poetry—Collections 2. American poetry—Collections
ISBN 0-231-08028-X   LC 91-42239

"Harmon devises an interesting method (collecting the 500 most anthologized shorter English and American poems as indexed in the *Columbia Granger's Index to Poetry,* 8th and 9th eds.) to bring together poetry of the last 750 years that he calls the 'greatest successes'. . . . Each of the 500 poems, arranged in chronological order, has a biographical headnote and editorial comments by the editor." Libr J

Understanding poetry; [edited by] Cleanth Brooks, Robert Penn Warren. 4th ed. Holt, Rinehart & Winston; distributed by Harcourt Brace College Pubs. 1976 xxii, 602p pa $55.50
Grades: 9 10 11 12   **821.008**
1. English poetry—Collections 2. American poetry—Collections 3. Poetry—History and criticism
ISBN 0-03-076980-9
First published 1938

This volume explores the meaning and structure of poetry with discussions of the nuances of theme, dramatic structure and metrics. Approximately 350 English and American poems ranging from the 16th century to the present are included in this collection

821.009   English poetry—History and criticism

The **Facts** on File companion to British poetry, 17th and 18th-centuries; [edited by] Virginia Brackett. Facts On File 2008 488p (Facts on File library of world literature) $85
Grades: 10 11 12 Adult   **821.009**
1. English poetry—History and criticism 2. Reference books
ISBN 978-0-8160-6328-4; 0-8160-6328-1
     LC 2007-26937

The second part of a four-volume series covering "British poetry from its beginnings to the present, this guide focuses on almost 80 poets who wrote during the 1600s and 1700s. . . . [In addition to providing] biographical and critical entries on each poet, Brackett . . . includes articles on approximately 275 individual poems. . . . This is a fine work. The large number of entries on individual poems will be especially welcomed by librarians who are assisting students in locating poetry explication." Booklist

Includes glossary and bibliographical references

The **Facts** on File companion to British poetry, 1900 to the present; [edited by] James Persoon, Robert R. Watson. Facts On File 2008 568p (Facts on File library of world literature) $85
Grades: 10 11 12 Adult   **821.009**
1. English poetry—History and criticism 2. Reference books
ISBN 978-0-8160-6406-9; 0-8160-6406-7
     LC 2007-47593

For this final volume of a four-volume series on British poetry, the editors "have compiled 450 entries, including biographical sketches and critical commentaries on major works as well as 40 additional topics, among them The Great War and poetry, Poetry journals, and Symbolism." Booklist

This title "is extremely well written, clear, and scholarly without being self-indulgently erudite. . . . It engages readers, piquing their interest and drawing them back to those dusty shelves of neglected works. . . . This is a deliciously inspiring collection of essays." SLJ

Includes glossary and bibliographical references

The **Facts** on File companion to British poetry before 1600; [edited by] Michelle Sauer. Facts On File 2008 514p (Facts on File library of world literature) $85
Grades: 10 11 12 Adult   **821.009**
1. English poetry—History and criticism 2. Reference books
ISBN 978-0-8160-6360-4; 0-8160-6360-5
     LC 2007-24865

"The first volume in a four-volume set on British poetry includes English, Scottish, Welsh, and Irish poetry before 1600. . . . Students will find analysis of *Beowulf, The Canterbury Tales, The Faerie Queene, Sir Gawain and the Green Knight*, and Shakespeare's sonnets in one place. The 600 A-Z entries cover poets, poems, terms, and historical events. . . . [This is] an outstanding reference work that should be in high-school, academic, and public libraries where students study British litera-

The Facts on File companion to British poetry before 1600—*Continued*
ture." Booklist
Includes glossary and bibliographical references

Flesch, William, 1956-
The Facts on File companion to British poetry, 19th century. Facts On File 2010 468p (Facts on File library of world literature) $85
Grades: 10 11 12 Adult   **821.009**
1. English poetry—History and criticism 2. Reference books
ISBN 978-0-8160-5896-9   LC 2008-32028
"Over 335 entries explore a wide range of poets, poems, poetic movements, influential journals, and significant terms and concepts. Flesch . . . explores both biographical and critical themes, often at surprising length. Entries focused on specific works are especially detailed and useful for students interested in placing poetry within the context of historical events." Choice
Includes glossary and bibliographical references

Glancy, Ruth F., 1948-
Thematic guide to British poetry; [by] Ruth Glancy. Greenwood Press 2002 303p $64.95
Grades: 9 10 11 12   **821.009**
1. English poetry—History and criticism
ISBN 0-313-31379-2   LC 2002-23252
"This thematic guide offers interpretations of 415 poems, representing the work of over 110 poets spanning seven centuries of British poetry." Publisher's note
This is a "well-organized, easy-to-navigate, authoritative volume." SLJ
Includes bibliographical references

Houle, Michelle M.
Modern British poetry, "the world is never the same". Enslow Publishers 2010 160p il (Poetry rocks!) lib bdg $34.60
Grades: 9 10 11 12   **821.009**
1. English poetry—History and criticism 2. Poets, English 3. Poetry—Authorship
ISBN 978-0-7660-3278-1; 0-7660-3278-7
        LC 2009-15880
"This collection introduces readers to eleven British poets born between 1806 and 1914, including Elizabeth Barrett Browning, Lord Alfred Tennyson, W. B. Yeats, W. H. Auden, and Dylan Thomas. Includes biographical information, historical background, poetry analysis, and several poems by each writer." Publisher's note
Includes glossary and bibliographical references

Johanson, Paula
Early British poetry, "words that burn". Enslow Publishers 2010 160p il (Poetry rocks!) lib bdg $34.60
Grades: 9 10 11 12   **821.009**
1. English poetry—History and criticism 2. Poets, English 3. Poetry—Authorship
ISBN 978-0-7660-3276-7; 0-7660-3276-0
        LC 2008-53657

"Examines early British poetry from the 7th century into the 19th century, including short biographies of poets like William Shakespeare and John Donne; also examples of poems, poetic techniques, and explication." Publisher's note
"This is a great resource for many poetry assignments and English teachers themselves. Students will appreciate the organization of the book including the bright colors, clear headings, portraits, and backgrounds of the poems." Libr Media Connect
Includes glossary and bibliographical references

Poets of World War I: Rupert Brooke & Siegfried Sassoon; edited and with an introduction by Harold Bloom. Chelsea House 2003 83p (Bloom's major poets) lib bdg $22.95
Grades: 9 10 11 12   **821.009**
1. Brooke, Rupert, 1887-1915 2. Sassoon, Siegfried, 1886-1967
ISBN 0-7910-7388-2   LC 2003-6927
This volume includes biographies of the two poets and critical analysis of their poems.
Includes bibliographical references

Poets of World War I: Wilfred Owen & Isaac Rosenberg; Harold Bloom, editor. Chelsea House 2002 111p (Bloom's major poets) lib bdg $22.95
Grades: 9 10 11 12   **821.009**
1. Owen, Wilfred 2. Rosenberg, Isaac, 1890-1918
ISBN 0-7910-5932-4   LC 2001-28515
"This volume contains a short biography of each poet and the analysis of eight poems (four from each poet) from thematic and structural foundations. These criticisms are supported by primary source material, such as letters, diaries, and notes." Book Rep

Rossignol, Rosalyn
Critical companion to Chaucer; a literary reference to his life and work. Facts on File 2006 648p il $85
Grades: 11 12 Adult   **821.009**
1. Chaucer, Geoffrey, d. 1400
ISBN 0-8160-6193-9; 978-0-8160-6193-8
        LC 2006-99
First published 1999 with title: Chaucer A to Z
This book on the works of Chaucer includes a biography of Chaucer, synopses and critical commentary on his works (including the Canterbury Tales), and lists of related people, places and topics.
Includes bibliographical references

822   English drama

Armitage, Simon, 1963-
The odyssey; a dramatic retelling of Homer's epic. W.W. Norton & Co. 2008 266p pa $14.95
                822
ISBN 978-0-393-33081-6   LC 2008-1290
First published 2006 in Great Britain with title: Homer's Odyssey

Armitage, Simon, 1963-—*Continued*

"Originally commissioned by the BBC and broadcast in 2004, Armitage's version is a radio play—a play for voices, now published in book form." N Y Times Book Rev

"Armitage's play will entertain . . . anyone interested in the fresh ways that Homer's story can be told." Publ Wkly

Bolt, Robert

A man for all seasons; a play in two acts. Random House 1962 xxv, 163p il pa $9.50 hardcover o.p.

Grades: 11 12 Adult   **822**
1. More, Sir Thomas, Saint, 1478-1535—Drama
2. Great Britain—History—1485-1603, Tudors—Drama

ISBN 0-679-72822-8 (pa)

Characters: 11 men, 2 women. First produced in the United States at the ANTA Theatre, New York City, November 22, 1961

A play set in sixteenth century England about Sir Thomas More, a devout Catholic, and his conflict with Henry VIII.

Christie, Agatha, 1890-1976

The mousetrap and other plays. New American Library 2000 742p hardcover o.p. pa $7.99

Grades: 7 8 9 10 11 12 Adult   **822**
1. English drama—Collections

ISBN 0-451-20118-3; 0-451-20114-0 (pa)
                                            LC 00-64727

First published 1978 by Dodd, Mead

Contents: Ten little Indians; Appointment with death; The hollow; The mousetrap; Witness for the prosecution; Towards zero; Verdict; Go back for murder

"The noted mystery writer composed adaptations of seven novels and stories into arresting plays as well as creating one original theater piece ('Verdict'). . . . All are as delightful to read for pleasure as Christie's mystery novels, especially since some that earlier appeared in the latter form have been intriguingly altered." Booklist

Fugard, Athol

"Master Harold"— and the boys. Vintage Books 2009 60p pa $12.95

Grades: 11 12 Adult   **822**
1. South Africa—Race relations—Drama

ISBN 978-0-307-47520-6; 0-307-47520-4
                                           LC 2010-292381

First published 1982 by Random House

Characters: 3 men. 1 act. First produced at the Yale Repertory theatre, New Haven, Connecticut, 1982.

Drama with racial overtones set in Port Elizabeth tea room focuses on precocious white South African teenager's relationship with two black men who work for his family, both old enough to be his father.

Pinter, Harold, 1930-2008

The birthday party, and The room; two plays. Grove Press 1961 120p il pa $10

Grades: 9 10 11 12   **822**

ISBN 0-8021-5114-0

"An Evergreen original"

The birthday party, first performed in 1958 and published in 1959, portrays the mental destruction of a young pianist living obscurely in an English seaside town. In The room, first produced in 1957, an elderly couple seems about to be evicted from their boarding house

Pomerance, Bernard

The Elephant Man; a play. Grove Press 1979 71p pa $11 hardcover o.p.

Grades: 11 12 Adult   **822**
1. Merrick, Joseph Carey, 1862-1890—Drama
2. Physically handicapped—Drama

ISBN 0-8021-3041-0 (pa)   LC 79-7792

Characters: 5 men, 2 women. 21 scenes. First produced at the Hampstead Theatre, London, 1977

Play based on the life of John [i.e., Joseph Carey] Merrick who from birth was so grotesquely deformed that he became known as the Elephant Man. Merrick was exhibited as a freak until a London surgeon found him permanent residence in a hospital where he became a favorite of aristocracy and literati.

Shaffer, Peter

Peter Shaffer's Amadeus; with an introduction by the director Sir Peter Hall and a wholly new preface by the author. Perennial Bks. 2001 xxxiv, 124p pa $15

Grades: 11 12 Adult   **822**
1. Mozart, Wolfgang Amadeus, 1756-1791—Drama
2. Salieri, Antonio, 1750-1825—Drama

ISBN 0-06-093549-9   LC 2001-278382

First published 1980 in the United Kingdom

Characters: 9 men, 1 woman, extras. 2 acts. First produced at the National Theater of Great Britain, November 1979

Explores relationship between Autrian court composer Antonio Salieri and the divinely gifted young Wolfgang Amadeus Mozart.

Shaw, Bernard, 1856-1950

Pygmalion . . . and My fair lady; [Pygmalion] by George Bernard Shaw; and My fair lady/based on Shaw's Pygmalion; adaptation and lyrics by Alan Jay Lerner; music by Frederick Loewe. 50th anniversary ed. Signet Classic 2006 219p pa $5.95

Grades: 11 12 Adult   **822**

ISBN 0-451-53009-8

"This is an authorized original paperback edition published by New American Library" Verso of title page

This volume includes the complete texts of Shaw's Pygmalion and Lerner's musical adaptation My fair lady.

Sheridan, Richard Brinsley, 1751-1816

The rivals; [by] Sheridan; edited with introduction and notes by C. J. L. Price. Oxford Univ. Press 1968 140p pa $19.95

Grades: 9 10 11 12   **822**

Sheridan, Richard Brinsley, 1751-1816—Continued

ISBN 0-19-831908-8

In this satirical comedy, first presented in 1775, two gentlemen woo Lydia Languish, a young woman with highly romantic ideas concerning love whose fortune will be forfeited if she marries without the consent of her aunt. The aunt, Mrs. Malaprop, has become famous for her eccentric use of the English language

Stoppard, Tom

Rosencrantz and Guildenstern are dead. Grove Press 1967 126p pa $12 hardcover o.p.

Grades: 11 12 Adult **822**

1. Shakespeare, William, 1564-1616—Parodies, imitations, etc.

ISBN 0-8021-3275-8 (pa)

Characters: 13 men, 2 women, extras. First produced in this form April 11, 1967 in London

This play "took the theatre world on both sides of the Atlantic by storm. The originality of the idea which put Hamlet's two insignificant friends centerstage was matched by the brilliance of the dialogue between these bewildered nonentities." Reader's Ency. 4th edition

Thomas, Dylan, 1914-1953

Under milk wood; a play for voices. New Directions 1954 107p music pa $8.95

Grades: 11 12 Adult **822**

ISBN 0-8112-0209-7

"A radio play for voices. Written in poetic, inventive prose, this play is full of humor, a joyful sense of the goodness of life and love, and a strong Welsh flavor. It is an impression of a spring day in the lives of the people of Llareggub, a Welsh village situated under Milk Wood. It has no plot, but a wealth of characters who dream aloud, converse with one another, and speak in choruses of alternating voices." Reader's Ency. 4th edition

Wilde, Oscar, 1854-1900

The importance of being earnest and other plays; introduction by Terrence McNally; notes by Michael F. Davis. Modern Library 2003 257p pa $9.95

Grades: 11 12 Adult **822**

ISBN 0-8129-6714-3 LC 2003-44566

Contents: Lady Windermere's fan; An ideal husband; The importance of being earnest

The title play, written in 1895, is a drawing room comedy exposing quirks and foibles of Victorian society with plot revolving around amorous pursuits of two men who face social obstacles when they woo young ladies of quality. The book also features Lady Windermere's fan (1893), a four act comedy about a woman who has an affair when she suspects her husband of adultery, and An ideal husband (1895), a comedy about a blackmail scheme involving a lord's investment in the Suez Canal days before the British government's purchase of it, and his wife's reaction to her husband's past misdeeds.

822.008 English drama—Collections

100 great monologues from the Renaissance theatre; edited by Jocelyn A. Beard. Smith & Kraus 1994 186p pa $9.95

Grades: 9 10 11 12 **822.008**

1. Monologues 2. Acting

ISBN 1-880399-59-8 LC 94-19393

A collection of monologues for men and women selected to represent the range of English Renaissance stage roles

822.009 English drama—History and criticism

Ben Jonson; edited and with an introduction by Harold Bloom. Chelsea House 2001 104p (Bloom's major dramatists) $21.95

Grades: 9 10 11 12 **822.009**

1. Jonson, Ben, 1573?-1637

ISBN 0-7910-6359-3 LC 2001-53677

For a complete list of series titles contact publisher

Includes a biographical essay, plot summaries, and critical interpretations of the plays and their characters.

Includes bibliographical references

822.3 William Shakespeare

Aliki

William Shakespeare & the Globe; written & illustrated by Aliki. HarperCollins Pubs. 1999 48p il hardcover o.p. pa $6.99 *

Grades: 4 5 6 7 8 9 **822.3**

1. Shakespeare, William, 1564-1616 2. Globe Theatre (London, England) 3. Shakespeare's Globe (London, England)

ISBN 0-06-027820-X; 0-06-443722-1 (pa)

LC 98-7903

The "text describes Shakespeare's life, the Elizabethan world and entertainments, and the ups and downs of the theatrical industry . . . including tidbits such as the Burbage brothers' piece-by-piece theft of the original Globe Theatre. A fast-forward to the twentieth century then treats Sam Wanamaker's dream of making the Globe rise again." Bull Cent Child Books

"A logically organized and engaging text, plenty of detailed illustrations with informative captions, and a clean design provide a fine introduction to both bard and theater." Horn Book Guide

Andersen, Richard, 1946-

Macbeth; introduction by Joseph Sobran. Marshall Cavendish Benchmark 2008 127p il (Shakespeare explained) lib bdg $29.95

Grades: 7 8 9 10 11 12 **822.3**

1. Shakespeare, William, 1564-1616—Criticism

ISBN 978-0-7614-3029-2; 0-7614-3029-6

LC 2008-14408

"A literary analysis of the play Macbeth. Includes information on the history and culture of Elizabethan England." Publisher's note

Includes glossary and bibliographical references

Appignanesi, Richard

Hamlet; [Richard Appignanesi, text adaptor]; illustrated by Emma Vieceli. Harry N. Abrams/Amulet Books 2007 195p (Manga Shakespeare) pa $9.95

Grades: 8 9 10 11 12 Adult   **822.3**
  1. Shakespeare, William, 1564-1616—Adaptations
  2. Graphic novels
  ISBN 978-0-8109-9324-2; 0-8109-9324-4
  First published in the United Kingdom

Shakespeare's classic play of murder and revenge is here adapted into a manga-style graphic novel. It's now set in 2107, after global climate change has devastated the Earth. Appignanesi uses the text of the play and abridges it to fit the pages, while Vieceli's art vigorously carries the story along. The book includes a summary of the plot and a brief biography of Shakespeare.

Julius Caesar; by William Shakespeare; adapted by Richard Appignanesi; illustrated by Mustashrik. Amulet Books 2008 207p (Manga Shakespeare) pa $9.95

Grades: 8 9 10 11 12   **822.3**
  1. Shakespeare, William, 1564-1616—Adaptations
  2. Graphic novels
  ISBN 978-0-8109-7072-4; 0-8109-7072-4
                              LC 2008-18764

Retells, in comic book format, Shakespeare's play about political intrigue, personal betrayal, and the aftermath of a brutal assassination

"Abridged text is spread out to render it less intimidating. . . . What truly shines in this work, though, is the superlative visualization by newcomer Mustashrik. Working in stark white and inky black, he has created a spare but intense landscape that mirrors the emotions of the characters. . . . Especially for the more artistically minded, this is a raw, striking, and powerful introduction to Shakespeare." Booklist

A midsummer night's dream; illustrated by Kate Brown. Abrams 2008 207p (Manga Shakespeare) pa $9.95

Grades: 7 8 9 10   **822.3**
  1. Shakespeare, William, 1564-1616—Adaptations
  2. Graphic novels
  ISBN 978-0-8109-9475-1; 0-8109-9475-5

Shakespeare's comedy of romance, Faerie, and shenanigans in the forest is adapted into a manga-style graphic novel. Hermia is in love with Lysander, while Demetrius is in love with Hermia, and Helen loves Demetrius. When mischievous fairy Puck decides to have some fun with the powerful love potion he has fetched for Fairy King Oberon, chaos reigns. While the human foursome needs to sort itself out, Oberon seeks revenge against his wife, Queen Titania, by having Puck use the love potion on her so she falls in love with the first creature she sees—who happens to be a yokel to whom Puck gave a donkey's head. The text takes dialog from the original play. The book includes a plot summary and a brief biography of Shakespeare.

Romeo and Juliet; by William Shakespeare; adapted by Richard Appignanesi; illustrated by Sonia Leong. Amulet Books 2007 195p (Manga Shakespeare) pa $9.95

Grades: 8 9 10 11 12   **822.3**
  1. Shakespeare, William, 1564-1616—Adaptations
  2. Graphic novels
  ISBN 978-0-8109-9325-9; 0-8109-9325-2
                              LC 2006-100362

First published in the United Kingdom

Shakespeare's classic play of star-crossed young lovers gets the manga treatment. The book is set in modern Tokyo with rival yakuza gangs and uses somewhat abridged text from the play for the dialogue.

"Although the richness of the language may be lost, the script keeps the spirit of the story intact, hitting all the major speeches." Booklist

The tempest; illustrated by Paul Duffield; [adaptor, Richard Appignanesi] Abrams 2008 207p il (Manga Shakespeare) pa $9.95

Grades: 7 8 9 10   **822.3**
  1. Shakespeare, William, 1564-1616—Adaptations
  2. Graphic novels
  ISBN 978-0-8109-9476-8

Prospero and his daughter Miranda have lived on an isolated island for twelve years, after he had been deposed from his rule as Duke of Naples and cast out to sea to die. A powerful magician, Prospero has caused the survivors of a shipwreck to land on his island, in order to get his revenge, for these survivors are his enemies. Problems arise when Miranda falls in love with Ferdinand, the monster Caliban tries to use the survivors to kill Prospero, and Ariel the sprite is trying to set things right while still obeying Prospero. The book includes a plot summary and a brief biography of Shakespeare

"This adaptation would be useful both as an introduction to the play and as a companion piece for classroom study of it, using images to illuminate the Bard's eloquent poetry." SLJ

Bloom, Harold, 1930-

Hamlet: poem unlimited. Riverhead Bks. 2003 154p hardcover o.p. pa $13

Grades: 11 12 Adult   **822.3**
  1. Shakespeare, William, 1564-1616—Criticism
  ISBN 1-57322-233-X; 1-57322-377-8 (pa)
                              LC 2002-31691

This "is Bloom's attempt to uncover the mystery of both Prince Hamlet and the play itself. . . . Bloom takes us through the major soliloquies, scenes, characters, and action of the play, to explore the enigma at the heart of the drama." Publisher's note

"Far superior to existing theories of performance and worth yards of criticism for each well-wrought page." Libr J

Shakespeare: the invention of the human. Riverhead Bks. 1998 xx, 745p pa $18 hardcover o.p.

Grades: 11 12 Adult   **822.3**
  1. Shakespeare, William, 1564-1616—Criticism
  ISBN 1-57322-751-X (pa)   LC 98-21325

Bloom, Harold, 1930- — *Continued*

In this critical study, Bloom argues "that the plays and poems of Shakespeare are not just 'the center of the Western canon'; they are nothing less than 'secular scripture.'. . . Bloom's book proceeds through genre groupings in rough chronological order." Commentary

"The passion and obsessiveness of Bloom's approach are its greatest recommendation." N Y Rev Books

Boyce, Charles

Critical companion to William Shakespeare; a literary reference to his life and work. Rev. ed. Facts on File 2005 2v il (Facts on File library of world literature) set $104.50 *

Grades: 11 12 Adult   **822.3**
1. Shakespeare, William, 1564-1616—Criticism
ISBN 0-8160-5373-1   LC 2004-25769
First published 1990 with title: Shakespeare A to Z

"The first two-thirds [of this set] covers the plays. Arranged alphabetically by title, the 3000 entries generally consist of a scene-by-scene summary, a commentary, sources, theatrical history, and character sketches. The last one-third features entries for actors, composers, musicians, places that figured in the plays, and miscellaneous items." Libr J

Includes bibliographical references

Bryson, Bill

Shakespeare; the world as stage. Atlas Books/HarperCollins 2007 199p (Eminent lives) $19.95

Grades: 9 10 11 12   **822.3**
1. Shakespeare, William, 1564-1616
ISBN 978-0-06-074022-1; 0-06-074022-1
    LC 2007-21647

In this biography, the author marshals "the usual little facts that others might overlook—for example, that in Shakespeare's day perhaps 40% of women were pregnant when they got married—to paint a portrait of the world in which the Bard lived and prospered. . . . Bryson is a pleasant and funny guide to a subject at once overexposed and elusive—as Bryson puts it, he is a kind of literary equivalent of an electron—forever there and not there." Publ Wkly

Includes bibliographical references

Butler, Colin

The practical Shakespeare; the plays in practice and on the page. Ohio University Press 2005 205p $39.95; pa $19.95 *

Grades: 11 12 Adult   **822.3**
1. Shakespeare, William, 1564-1616—Dramatic production
ISBN 0-8214-1621-9; 0-8214-1622-7 (pa)
    LC 2004-30580

"Notes on staging, acting behaviors, scenes not shown, entrances, exits, characterizations, prologues, choruses, and staging are each featured in the text. References to specific scenes in the plays are used to illustrate and support the material. Any group preparing a production of one of the plays should find this a useful reference." Univ Press Books for Public and Second Sch Libr, 2006

Includes bibliographical references

Cahn, Victor L.

The plays of Shakespeare; a thematic guide. Greenwood Press 2001 361p $49.95

Grades: 9 10 11 12   **822.3**
1. Shakespeare, William, 1564-1616—Themes
ISBN 0-313-30981-7   LC 00-22337

The author approaches Shakespeare "through an analysis of his major themes across several plays. The book contains 19 separate thematic essays devoted to such topics as Fate, Honor, Justice, Love, Money, and Power. Each analysis is abundantly supported with quotations from well-known and often-studied plays." Book Rep

Includes bibliographical references

Cover, Arthur Byron

Macbeth; [by] William Shakespeare; Arthur Byron Cover, adapter; Tony Leonard Tamai, illustrator. Puffin Graphics 2005 176p il pa $9.99 *

Grades: 6 7 8 9 10 11 12   **822.3**
1. Shakespeare, William, 1564-1616—Adaptations
2. Graphic novels
ISBN 0-14-240409-8

Ambitious lord Macbeth murders his king to take the throne because of the predictions of some witches, but his position is never secure, and he takes ever more violent measures to stay in power. Shakespeare's classic play is reinvented here with Japanese manga style art and a futuristic setting on a vast ringworld around a sun.

Coye, Dale F.

Pronouncing Shakespeare's words; a guide from A to Zounds; [by] Dale Coye. Routledge 2002 342p pa $27.95

Grades: 11 12 Adult   **822.3**
1. Shakespeare, William, 1564-1616—Dictionaries
2. Reference books
ISBN 0-415-94182-2   LC 2002-9622
First published 1998 by Greenwood Press

This work provides the correct pronunciation of over 300 words from Shakespeare's plays and poems. An "introduction precedes a phonetic pronunciation guide that includes definitions. Organized by play or poem, words are given in the order in which they appear in a linear reading. Lists at the beginning of each work contain pronunciation guides for place and proper names, the most common 'hard' words, and the most common reduced forms." Libr J

Includes bibliographical references

Fallon, Robert Thomas

A theatergoer's guide to Shakespeare. Dee, I.R. 2001 479p $29.95; pa $18.95 *

Grades: 11 12 Adult   **822.3**
1. Shakespeare, William, 1564-1616—Stories, plots, etc.
ISBN 1-56663-342-7; 1-56663-508-X (pa)
    LC 00-57018

Fallon "begins each summary with a brief scholarly introduction that places the particular play in the Shakespearean canon and in some cases provides helpful historical information. Thereafter Fallon maps out, with

Fallon, Robert Thomas—*Continued*
faultless accuracy, the twists and turns of every play from *King Lear* to *The Two Noble Kinsmen*." Booklist
Includes bibliographical references

Garber, Marjorie
Shakespeare after all. Pantheon Books 2004 989p hardcover o.p. pa $20
Grades: 11 12 Adult   **822.3**
1. Shakespeare, William, 1564-1616—Criticism
ISBN 0-375-42190-4; 0-385-72214-1 (pa)
LC 2004-40063
The author "provides a handbook on Shakespeare's plays. After an introduction supplying standard overviews of the Renaissance theater and Shakespeare's life, she offers a critical essay on each play, complete with bibliographies and filmographies. The strength of this work is that Garber shows how the plays are interrelated by recurring language, characters, and themes, how each era has interpreted Shakespeare for itself, and how Shakespeare continues to shape today's culture." Libr J
Includes bibliographical references

Garfield, Leon, 1921-1996
Shakespeare stories [I]-II; illustrated by Michael Foreman. Houghton Mifflin 1991-1995 c1985-c1994 2v il hardcover o.p. v1 pa $19.95; v2 pa $17
Grades: 7 8 9 10 11 12   **822.3**
1. Shakespeare, William, 1564-1616—Adaptations
ISBN 0-395-56397-6 (v1); 0-395-86140-3 (v1 pa); 0-395-70893-1 (v2); 0-395-89109-4 (v2 pa)
Original volume first published 1985 by Schocken Bks.
In these volumes Garfield has rewritten twenty-one of Shakespeare's plays in narrative form, retaining much of the original language

Gleed, Paul
Bloom's how to write about William Shakespeare; [introduction by Harold Bloom] Chelsea House 2008 244p (Bloom's how to write about literature) $45
Grades: 9 10 11 12   **822.3**
1. Shakespeare, William, 1564-1616—Criticism 2. Report writing
ISBN 978-0-7910-9484-6   LC 2006-102770
This book offers "paper-topic suggestions, . . . strategies on how to write a strong essay, and an . . . introduction by Harold Bloom on writing about Shakespeare. This . . . volume is designed to help students develop their analytical writing skills and critical comprehension of the legendary Bard of Avon and his timeless works." Publisher's note
Includes bibliographical references

The **Greenwood** companion to Shakespeare; a comprehensive guide to students; edited by Joseph Rosenblum. Greenwood Press 2005 4v set $299.95 *
Grades: 11 12 Adult   **822.3**
1. Shakespeare, William, 1564-1616—Criticism
ISBN 0-313-32779-3   LC 2004-28690

"Each of the set's four volumes relates to a specific genre—Overviews and the History Plays (Vol. 1), The Comedies (Vol. 2), The Tragedies (Vol. 3), and The Romances and Poetry (Vol. 4)—and is organized in 'Cliff Notes' fashion, devoting each entry to a single play, long poem, sonnet, or sonnet pair. . . . A great introduction to the Bard." Libr J
Includes bibliographical references

Hamlet; edited and with an introduction by Harold Bloom; volume editor, Brett Foster. Bloom's Literary Criticism 2008 443p (Bloom's Shakespeare through the ages) $50
Grades: 9 10 11 12   **822.3**
1. Shakespeare, William, 1564-1616—Criticism
ISBN 978-0-7910-9592-8; 0-7910-9592-4
LC 2007-50853
This "study guide to one of Shakespeare's greatest plays contains a selection of . . . criticism through the centuries on Hamlet. . . . [It also features] an introduction by Harold Bloom, . . . [a] summary, analysis of key passages, a comprehensive list of characters, a biography of Shakespeare, and more." Publisher's note
Includes bibliographical references

Hester, John
Performing Shakespeare. Crowood 2008 160p il pa $34.95
Grades: 9 10 11 12 Adult   **822.3**
1. Shakespeare, William, 1564-1616—Dramatic production 2. Acting
ISBN 978-1-84797-073-2
This is a "sensible introduction to the mechanics of Shakespearean performance. Voice, movement, verse, character study, interpretation, and ensemble bonding are each treated in distinctive chapters, with exercises. The presentation is excellent; color photographs of recent English productions are juxtaposed with shots of young student actors engaged in various rehearsals." Libr J

Hinds, Gareth, 1971-
King Lear; a play by William Shakespeare; adapted and illustrated by Gareth Hinds. Candlewick Press 2009 c2007 123p il $22.99; pa $11.99 *
Grades: 7 8 9 10 11 12   **822.3**
1. Shakespeare, William, 1564-1616—Adaptations 2. Graphic novels
ISBN 978-0-7636-4343-0; 0-7636-4343-2; 978-0-7636-4344-7 (pa); 0-7636-4344-0 (pa)
A reissue of the title first published 2007 by Thecomic.com
This graphic novel adaptation of Shakespeare's King Lear is "an excellent rendition of one the bard's great tragedies. Using splash pages that open up the settings, washes of otherworldly colors, grotesquely expressive faces . . . and figural work . . . Hinds occasionally attains a visual poetry." Booklist

Hinds, Gareth, 1971-—_Continued_

The merchant of Venice; a play; by William Shakespeare; adapted and illustrated by Gareth Hinds. Candlewick Press 2008 68p il $21.99; pa $11.99

Grades: 8 9 10 11 12 Adult 822.3

1. Shakespeare, William, 1564-1616—Adaptations 2. Graphic novels

ISBN 978-0-7636-3024-9; 978-0-7636-3025-6 (pa)

LC 2007-938349

Hinds uses a sketchy art style and blue and gray tones to illustrate his graphic adaptation of Shakespeare's controversial play. He sets the play in modern Venice and uses more modern language, including prose, at the beginning of the play and then gradually returns to Shakespeare's original language for the courtroom scenes. The play tells the story of a debt owed to a Jewish merchant of Venice, of a strong-willed young woman who is determined to choose her own husband, and of the quest to save a young man from the fate of having a pound of flesh cut from him.

"Fans of the play will find this an intriguing adaptation." Publ Wkly

Julius Caesar; edited and with an introduction by Harold Bloom; volume editor, Pamela Loos. Bloom's Literary Criticism 2007 314p (Bloom's Shakespeare through the ages) $50

Grades: 9 10 11 12 822.3

1. Shakespeare, William, 1564-1616—Criticism

ISBN 978-0-7910-9593-5; 0-7910-9593-2

LC 2007-26814

This "study guide to one of Shakespeare's greatest plays contains a selection of . . . criticism through the centuries on Julius Caesar." Publisher's note

Includes bibliographical references

King Lear; edited and with an introduction by Harold Bloom; volume editor, Neil Heims. Bloom's Literary Criticism 2008 356p (Bloom's Shakespeare through the ages) $50

Grades: 10 11 12 822.3

1. Shakespeare, William, 1564-1616—Criticism

ISBN 978-0-7910-9574-4 LC 2007-29708

This "study guide to one of Shakespeare's most renowned works contains a selection of . . . criticism through the centuries on King Lear." Publisher's note

Includes bibliographical references

Krueger, Susan Heidi

The tempest; [by] Susan H. Krueger; introduction by Joseph Sobran. Marshall Cavendish Benchmark 2009 127p il (Shakespeare explained) lib bdg $29.93

Grades: 7 8 9 10 11 12 822.3

1. Shakespeare, William, 1564-1616—Criticism

ISBN 978-0-7614-3423-8; 0-7614-3423-2

LC 2009-2587

"A literary analysis of the play The Tempest. Includes information on the history and culture of Elizabethan England." Publisher's note

This book offers an "engaging [introduction] to the Bard's work. . . . Krueger's lively, opinionated, and

knowledgeable analysis of the complex play . . . will easily draw students into further discussion." Booklist

Includes glossary and bibliographical references

Macbeth; edited and with an introduction by Harold Bloom; volume editor, Janyce Marson. Bloom's Literary Criticism 2008 402p (Bloom's Shakespeare through the ages) $50

Grades: 9 10 11 12 822.3

1. Shakespeare, William, 1564-1616—Criticism

ISBN 978-0-7910-9594-2 LC 2007-32378

This "study guide to one of Shakespeare's greatest tragedies contains a selection of . . . criticism through the centuries on Macbeth, including commentaries by such . . . critics as Elizabeth Montagu, Samuel Taylor Coleridge, Thomas DeQuincey, John Berryman, Cleanth Brooks, and many others." Publisher's note

Includes bibliographical references

McDonald, John

Henry V: the graphic novel; original text version; [by] William Shakespeare; script adaptation, John McDonald; pencils, Neill Cameron ... ; editor in chief, Clive Bryant. Classical Comics 2008 143p il pa $16.95

Grades: 8 9 10 11 12 Adult 822.3

1. Shakespeare, William, 1564-1616—Adaptations 2. Graphic novels

ISBN 978-1-906332-41-9

Also available plain text version (ISBN: 978-1-906332-42-6) and quick text version (ISBN: 978-1-906332-43-3) ea $16.95

First published 2007 in the United Kingdom

This graphic novel adaptation of Shakespeare's play uses a full and unabridged text combined with full color comic book style illustrations. Young King Henry V goes to war against France when he learns he has a legitimate claim to the French throne.

Mussari, Mark

Othello; [by] Mark Mussari; introduction by Joseph Sobran. Marshall Cavendish Benchmark 2009 111p il (Shakespeare explained) lib bdg $29.95

Grades: 7 8 9 10 11 12 822.3

1. Shakespeare, William, 1564-1616—Criticism

ISBN 978-0-7614-3422-1; 0-7614-3422-4

LC 2008-37506

"A literary analysis of the play Othello. Includes information on the history and culture of Elizabethan England." Publisher's note

Includes glossary and bibliographical references

The sonnets. Marshall Cavendish Benchmark 2010 c2011 127p il (Shakespeare explained) lib bdg $42.79

Grades: 9 10 11 12 822.3

1. Shakespeare, William, 1564-1616—Criticism

ISBN 978-1-60870-018-9 LC 2009-41727

"A literary analysis of Shakespeare's sonnets. Includes information on the history and culture of Elizabethan England." Publisher's note

Includes glossary and bibliographical references

Naden, Corinne J.

Romeo and Juliet. Marshall Cavendish Benchmark 2008 127p il (Shakespeare explained) lib bdg $29.95

Grades: 7 8 9 10 11 12   **822.3**

1. Shakespeare, William, 1564-1616—Criticism

ISBN 978-0-7614-3031-5; 0-7614-3031-8

LC 2008-14407

"A literary analysis of the play Romeo and Juliet. Includes information on the history and culture of Elizabethan England." Publisher's note

The "book opens with a discussion of Shakespeare's life, Elizabethan England, and the theatre. A glossary defines literary terms, and another translates Shakespeare's language into modern English. Overviews and analysis of individual scenes will help students follow the action. . . . Easily comprehended writing and an attractive layout make [this an] excellent choice for students." Libr Media Connect

Includes glossary and bibliographical references

Nostbakken, Faith, 1964-

Understanding Macbeth; a student casebook to issues, sources, and historical documents. Greenwood Press 1997 235p (Greenwood Press literature in context series) $39.95

Grades: 9 10 11 12   **822.3**

1. Shakespeare, William, 1564-1616—Criticism

ISBN 0-313-29630-8   LC 96-35013

For complete list of series titles contact publisher

This work "cites primary 17th-century documents showing the political events that may have influenced Shakespeare's decision to write a tragedy based on royal treason and the evils of witchcraft. The casebook also includes a dramatic analysis of *Macbeth*, showing the elements—character and theme—that shape the play and guiding the reader to a critical understanding of the work." Book Rep

Includes bibliographical references

Olsen, Kirstin

All things Shakespeare; an encyclopedia of Shakespeare's world. Greenwood Press 2002 2v il maps set $150 *

Grades: 11 12 Adult   **822.3**

1. Shakespeare, William, 1564-1616—Encyclopedias
2. Reference books

ISBN 0-313-31503-5   LC 2002-69732

This "encyclopedia describes Shakespeare's physical environment, including common objects, daily activities, and popular beliefs and attitudes. Information is grouped into general topic clusters such as 'Behavior,' 'Clothing and Dress,' 'Furniture,' 'Fire,' and 'War and Peace.' . . . Within the 200-plus entries, references are made to the play, act, and scene in which Shakespeare mentions the item or activity being discussed." Libr J

Othello; edited and with an introduction by Harold Bloom; volume editor, Neil Heims. Bloom's Literary Criticism 2008 325p (Bloom's Shakespeare through the ages) $50

Grades: 9 10 11 12   **822.3**

1. Shakespeare, William, 1564-1616—Criticism

ISBN 978-0-7910-9575-1   LC 2007-26815

This "study guide to one of Shakespeare's greatest plays contains a selection of . . . criticism through the centuries on Othello." Publisher's note

Includes bibliographical references

The **Oxford** companion to Shakespeare; general editor, Michael Dobson; associate general editor, Stanley Wells. Oxford Univ. Press 2001 xxix, 541p il maps hardcover o.p. pa $39.95 *

Grades: 11 12 Adult   **822.3**

1. Shakespeare, William, 1564-1616—Encyclopedias
2. Reference books

ISBN 0-19-811735-3; 0-19-280614-9 (pa)

LC 2001-277478

This volume "illuminates not only Shakespeare's life and works but also the many forms that interpretation of Shakespeare has taken in the centuries since his death." Booklist

Includes bibliographical references

Richert, Scott P.

King Lear. Marshall Cavendish Benchmark 2010 c2011 127p il (Shakespeare explained) lib bdg $42.79

Grades: 8 9 10 11 12   **822.3**

1. Shakespeare, William, 1564-1616—Criticism

ISBN 978-1-60870-016-5   LC 2010-7060

"A literary analysis of the play 'King Lear.' Includes information on the history and culture of Elizabethan England." Publisher's note

Includes glossary and bibliographical references

Riley, Dick

The bedside, bathtub & armchair companion to Shakespeare; {by} Dick Riley & Pam McAllister. Continuum 2001 288p il hardcover o.p. pa $19.95

Grades: 11 12 Adult   **822.3**

1. Shakespeare, William, 1564-1616—Criticism

ISBN 0-8264-1249-1; 0-8264-1250-5 (pa)

LC 2001-17332

"Provides synopses of plays, information about the period in which each play is set, possible plot sources, and notable features and productions of 36 of Shakespeare's plays (Pericles and The Two Noble Kinsmen are not included). Interspersed with chapters on each play are short discussions about topics such as Shakespeare's sonnets, authorship problems, women's roles in 15th- and 16th-century society, and Shakespeare's language." Libr J

Includes bibliographical references

Romeo and Juliet; edited and with an introduction by Harold Bloom; volume editor, Janyce Marson. Bloom's Literary Criticism 2008 339p (Bloom's Shakespeare through the ages) $50

Grades: 9 10 11 12   **822.3**

1. Shakespeare, William, 1564-1616—Criticism

ISBN 978-0-7910-9596-6   LC 2007-50854

This study guide contains a selection of criticism through the centuries on the play, plus a summary, analysis of key passages, a list of characters, and a biography of Shakespeare.

Includes bibliographical references

Saccio, Peter

Shakespeare's English kings; history, chronicle, and drama. 2nd ed. Oxford Univ. Press 2000 284p il map hardcover o.p. pa $14.95

Grades: 9 10 11 12   **822.3**
  1. Shakespeare, William, 1564-1616—Histories
  2. Great Britain—History 3. Great Britain—Kings and rulers
  ISBN 0-19-512318-2; 0-19-512319-0 (pa)
                                             LC 99-43297
First published 1977

This book explores the medieval histories and Tudor chronicles that served as source material for Shakespeare's ten history plays. In addition to explicating the plots, the author also discusses where Shakespeare deviated from his sources. Includes genealogical charts and an appendix of names and titles

Includes bibliographical references

Scheeder, Louis, 1946-

All the words on stage; a complete pronunciation dictionary for the plays of William Shakespeare; {by} Louis Scheeder and Shane Ann Younts. Smith & Kraus 2002 292p (Career development series) pa $24.95 *

Grades: 11 12 Adult   **822.3**
  1. Shakespeare, William, 1564-1616—Language
  ISBN 1-57525-214-7   LC 2001-20182

"This reference work is first a pronunciation dictionary, but also can aid in understanding the rhythm and variants of the iambic pentameter and the interweaving of word ahd rhythm produced by Shakespeare's blank verse. . . . Schools that read or perform Shakespeare in their curriculum will want to have this fine dictionary in the reference collection." Book Rep

Includes glossary and bibliographical references

Schupack, Sara

The merchant of Venice. Marshall Cavendish Benchmark 2009 127p il (Shakespeare explained) lib bdg $29.95

Grades: 7 8 9 10 11 12   **822.3**
  1. Shakespeare, William, 1564-1616—Criticism
  ISBN 978-0-7614-3421-4; 0-7614-3421-6
                                             LC 2009-3166

"A literary analysis of Shakespeare's play The Merchant of Venice. Includes information on the history and culture of Elizabethan England." Publisher's note

Includes glossary and bibliographical references

Sexton, Adam

Shakespeare's Hamlet; [by] Adam Sexton, Tintin Pantoja. The manga ed. Wiley 2008 185p il pa $9.99

Grades: 9 10 11 12   **822.3**
  1. Shakespeare, William, 1564-1616—Adaptations
  2. Graphic novels
  ISBN 978-0-470-09757-1; 0-470-09757-4

A manga adaptation of the Shakespearean tragedy about the prince of Denmark who seeks revenge against his uncle for murdering his father.

Shakespeare, William, 1564-1616

The Columbia dictionary of quotations from Shakespeare; [selected by] Mary and Reginald Foakes. Columbia Univ. Press 1998 516p $63

Grades: 11 12 Adult   **822.3**
  1. Shakespeare, William, 1564-1616—Quotations
  2. Quotations
  ISBN 0-231-10434-0   LC 97-44894

"The book is organized by topics ('Age,' 'Duplicity,' 'Fish'), followed by passages of about five or six lines. After each selection, the citation, the character, and usually the context of the lines are given. If a reference is obscure, the explanation is more elaborate. Indexes provide access by play and poem, by character, and by keyword." SLJ

The complete works; general editors, Stanley Wells and Gary Taylor; editors, Stanley Wells . . . [et al.]; with introductions by Stanley Wells. 2nd ed. Clarendon Press; Oxford University Press 2005 lxxv, 1344p il $40 *

Grades: 11 12 Adult   **822.3**
  ISBN 0-19-926717-0   LC 2005-47272
First published 1986
On cover: The Oxford Shakespeare

This anthology "features a brief introduction to each work as well as [a] General Introduction. . . . [The volume includes] essay on language, a list of contemporary allusions to Shakespeare, an index of Shakespearean characters, a glossary, a consolidated bibliography, and an index of first lines of the Sonnets." Publisher's note

The essential Shakespeare; selected and with an introduction by Ted Hughes. Ecco Press 1991 230p (Essential poets) pa $8 hardcover o.p.

Grades: 11 12 Adult   **822.3**
  ISBN 0-06-088795-8 (pa)   LC 91-17522

Ted Hughes has selected a "combination of sonnets, songs, speeches, and poetry that best illustrate the incredible breadth of Shakespeare's genius. In his introduction, Hughes explores the origins of Shakespeare's language." Publisher's note

The first part of King Henry the Fourth; edited by Claire McEachern. Penguin Books 2000 xlii, 117p il (The Pelican Shakespeare) pa $5 *

Grades: 9 10 11 12   **822.3**
  ISBN 0-14-071456-1   LC 00-269943

Drama concerning problems arising from the deposition and murder of Richard II, of which Henry of Bolingbroke has had a part. Now king and faced with rebellion in Scotland and Wales, Henry and his sons Prince Hal (the Prince of Wales) and Prince John defeat the Percys and wage war against the armies of Northumberland and the Archbishop of York

Includes bibliographical references

King Lear; edited by Stephen Orgel. New ed. Penguin Books 1999 142p il (The Pelican Shakespeare) pa $5 *

Grades: 9 10 11 12   **822.3**
  ISBN 0-14-071476-6   LC 00-503596

The King of Britain divides his kingdom between his two scheming elder daughters and estranges himself from his favorite daughter when she speaks out against him

Shakespeare, William, 1564-1616—*Continued*

Macbeth; edited by Stephen Orgel. Penguin Books 2000 xlvi, 98p il (The Pelican Shakespeare) pa $5 *

Grades: 9 10 11 12   **822.3**
   ISBN 0-14-071478-2   LC 00-266703
   Tragedy concerning a general who murders his king after hearing the prophecies of three witches. Spurred on by his wife, Lady Macbeth, they instigate a series of murders, as well as a war, in his quest (and her ambitions) for the throne of Scotland, ultimately leading to their demise
   Includes bibliographical references

The merchant of Venice; edited by A. R. Braunmuller. Penguin Books 2000 lii, 103p (The Pelican Shakespeare) pa $5 *

Grades: 9 10 11 12   **822.3**
   ISBN 0-14-071462-6   LC 00-702935
   In this dark comedy, a young man, Bassiano, squanders his fortune and, in order to woo the wealthy lady he loves, must borrow money from his friend, Antonio, a Venetian merchant. Antonio, whose own money is invested in merchant ships, must borrow the sum from Shylock, the Jewish moneylender, who later demands a pound of Antonio's flesh when the merchant falls into his debt

A midsummer night's dream; edited by Russ McDonald. Penguin Books 2000 liii, 88p (The Pelican Shakespeare) pa $5 *

Grades: 9 10 11 12   **822.3**
   ISBN 0-14-071455-3   LC 00-33635
   Comedy about the strange events that take place in a forest inhabited by fairies who magically transform the romantic fate of two young couples
   Includes bibliographical references

Much ado about nothing; edited by Peter Holland. [New ed.] Penguin Books 1999 xliv, 98p (The Pelican Shakespeare) pa $5 *

Grades: 9 10 11 12   **822.3**
   ISBN 0-14-071480-4   LC 99-462498
   Romantic comedy about two couples, Hero and Claudio, and Beatrice and Benedick, who, despite personal and familial obstacles, finally unite through the forces of local constables Dogberry and Verges
   Includes bibliographical references

The Norton Shakespeare; Stephen Greenblatt, general editor; Walter Cohen, Jean E. Howard, Katharine Eisaman Maus [editors]; with an essay on the Shakespearean stage by Andrew Gurr. 2nd ed. W.W. Norton 2008 3419p il $77.50 *

Grades: 11 12 Adult   **822.3**
   ISBN 978-0-393-92991-1   LC 2007-46599
   Also available as a two volume paperback set (ISBN: 978-0-393-93151-8)
   "Based on the Oxford edition"
   First published 1997
   The editors' "mission is to make Shakespeare accessible to modern readers. With lengthy introductions provid-

ing insight into Shakespeare's life and times as well as textual notes, marginal glosses, footnotes, and bibliographies, they more than achieve their aim . . . [Includes] an illustrated chronology of Shakespeare's life, and over 150 illustrations. The result is a work of immense scope, scholarship, and richness." Libr J [review of 1997 edition]
   Includes bibliographical references

Othello; [by] William Shakespeare; advisory editors, David Bevington, Barbara Gaines, and Peter Holland. Sourcebooks MediaFusion 2005 402p il (Sourcebooks Shakespeare) pa $14.95

Grades: 9 10 11 12   **822.3**
   ISBN 1-4022-0102-8   LC 2005-23285
   Includes CD-ROM
   This book features the full text of Othello with performance annotations and glossary. The audio CD included features a 1944 performance of the play by Paul Robeson.

Romeo and Juliet; edited by Peter Holland. Penguin Books 2000 xlvi, 128p il (The Pelican Shakespeare) pa $5 *

Grades: 9 10 11 12   **822.3**
   ISBN 0-14-071484-7   LC 00-269942
   Young couple defies long-standing feud that divides their families—the Capulets and the Montagues—as their desperate need to be together, secret meetings, and secret marriage propel them toward tragedy
   Includes bibliographical references

Romeo and Juliet; [by] William Shakespeare; advisory editors, David Bevington, Barbara Gaines, and Peter Holland. Sourcebooks MediaFusion 2005 360p il (Sourcebooks Shakespeare) pa $14.95

Grades: 9 10 11 12   **822.3**
   ISBN 1-4022-0101-X   LC 2005-23286
   Includes CD-ROM
   This book features the full text of the play Romeo and Juliet with performance annotations and a glossary. The audio CD included features recordings of both Ellen Terry and Kate Beckinsale in the roles of Juliet.

The tempest; edited by Peter Holland. [New ed.] Penguin Books 1999 xliv, 84p (The Pelican Shakespeare) pa $5 *

Grades: 9 10 11 12   **822.3**
   ISBN 0-14-071485-5   LC 99-462496
   Prospero, the exiled Duke of Milan, living on an island with his daughter Miranda, raises a tempest that brings his shipwrecked enemies ashore. Now, faced with advancing age, he has the opportunity to punish and forgive his enemies as well as relinquish his magic powers
   Includes bibliographical references

The tragedy of Julius Caesar; edited by William Montgomery; with an introduction by Douglas Trevor. Penguin Books 2000 xlvi, 114p (The Pelican Shakespeare) pa $5 *

Grades: 9 10 11 12   **822.3**
   ISBN 0-14-071468-5   LC 2001-266965
   Brutus, best friend of the Roman ruler Caesar, reluctantly joins a successful plot to murder Caesar and subsequently destroys himself

Shakespeare, William, 1564-1616—*Continued*

The tragedy of Othello, the Moor of Venice; edited by Russ McDonald. Penguin Books 2001 xxix, 145p il (The Pelican Shakespeare) pa $5 *

Grades: 9 10 11 12   **822.3**
   ISBN 0-14-071463-4   LC 2001-33135
   A general serving the Venetian state, Othello is duped by a jealous ensign into thinking that his wife, Desdemona, has been unfaithful. Succumbing to jealousy, he murders her and then, upon learning the truth, commits suicide

The tragical history of Hamlet prince of Denmark. Penguin Books 2001 lviii, 148p (The Pelican Shakespeare) pa $5 *

Grades: 9 10 11 12   **822.3**
   ISBN 0-14-071454-5   LC 2001-31340
   Story about the Prince of Denmark who, upon learning of the death of his father at the hands of his uncle, Claudius, seeks revenge.
   Includes bibliographical references

Shakespeare; editor, Joseph Rosenblum; managing editor, Christina J. Moose. Salem Press 1998 xx, 482p il (Magill's choice) $68

Grades: 11 12 Adult   **822.3**
   1. Shakespeare, William, 1564-1616—Criticism
   ISBN 0-89356-966-6   LC 97-43460
   This work "divides the plays into histories, comedies, tragedies, and romances. The plays are indexed alphabetically and a time line also is included. *Shakespeare* begins with background of the man, the dramatist, and the poet. Each play is examined, including a summary, critical analysis, and bibliography. The poetry section explains each poem, analyzes it, and offers theories on theme." Book Rep
   Includes bibliographical references

The **Shakespeare** encyclopedia; the complete guide to the man and his works. Firefly Books 2009 304p il map $35

Grades: 9 10 11 12 Adult   **822.3**
   1. Shakespeare, William, 1564-1616—Encyclopedias
   2. Shakespeare, William, 1564-1616—Criticism
   3. Reference books
   ISBN 978-1-55407-479-2   LC 2010-291927
   This book "begins with a brief history of Shakespeare's time, and a brief biography. The rest of the book is devoted to his works, the plays, and the poetry." Libr Media Connect
   "This text is a must-have for any school library; accessible for students, librarians, and teachers alike, it provides far more than a simple overview of the writer and his work. In fact, it provides detailed histories and summaries of his major works and poems, including lists of characters, depictions of family trees, and analyses of dominant imagery, motifs, themes, and related quotes. . . . The encyclopedia is both intellectually and aesthetically pleasing." Voice Youth Advocates
   Includes glossary and bibliographical references

Shakespeare for students; critical interpretations of Shakespeare's plays and poetry. 2nd ed., Anne Marie Hacht, editor; foreword by Cynthia Burnstein. Thomson Gale 2007 3v il set $308

Grades: 9 10 11 12   **822.3**
   1. Shakespeare, William, 1564-1616—Criticism
   ISBN 978-1-4144-1255-9; 1-4144-1255-X
                                    LC 2007-8901
   First published as three separate volumes 1992-2000
   "Covering 28 works of Shakespeare, including his sonnets, . . . [this set] provides the following information: a brief overview of each work, a plot summary, characters, themes, stylistic and literary devices, the historical context, a critical overview, a collection of criticism by scholars, a list of sources, and an annotated list for further reading. . . . This three-volume set is of great value to a beginning Shakespeare scholar seeking an introduction to a specific work." Libr J
   Includes bibliographical references

Shakespeare's histories; edited and with an introduction by Harold Bloom. Chelsea House 2000 117p (Bloom's major dramatists) $19.95

Grades: 9 10 11 12   **822.3**
   1. Shakespeare, William, 1564-1616—Criticism
   ISBN 0-7910-5241-9   LC 99-36774
   Another available title about Shakespeare in this series is: Shakespeare's comedies. For a complete list of series titles contact publisher
   This "title contains criticism on Richard III, Henry IV, Parts 1 and 2, and Henry V. Discussion of the individual plays is prefaced by an introduction and a three-page biography of Shakespeare. The entry on each play gives a succinct plot summary, brief descriptions of major characters, and six to eight critical excerpts. A list of the bard's works, further reading, and indexes of themes and ideas complete this comprehensive volume." SLJ
   Includes bibliographical references

Shewmaker, Eugene F.
   Shakespeare's language; a glossary of unfamiliar words in his plays and poems. 2nd ed. Facts On File 2008 xxvii, 628p (Facts on File library of world literature) $75; pa $21.95 *

Grades: 9 10 11 12   **822.3**
   1. Shakespeare, William, 1564-1616—Language
   ISBN 978-0-8160-7125-8; 978-0-8160-7557-7 (pa)
                                   LC 2007-16138
   First published 1996
   This book "contains approximately 17,000 definitions . . . from the adjective 'acerb' in Othello to the verb 'zwaggered' in King Lear. It also features . . . [a] chapter, 'Introduction to Shakespeare and His Language,' which provides . . . background on Shakespeare's life and works, as well as . . . [a] discussion of how modern readers can approach his works in order to best understand and enjoy them." Publisher's note
   "This would be a useful addition to any literature reference section." Libr Media Connect
   Includes bibliographical references

Sobran, Joseph

Hamlet. Marshall Cavendish Benchmark 2008
127p il (Shakespeare explained) lib bdg $29.95
Grades: 7 8 9 10 11 12   **822.3**
  1. Shakespeare, William, 1564-1616—Criticism
  ISBN 978-0-7614-3027-8; 0-7614-3027-X
                                    LC 2008-7090
"A literary analysis of the play Hamlet. Includes information on the history and culture of Elizabethan England." Publisher's note
  Includes glossary and bibliographical references

Henry IV, part 1. Marshall Cavendish
Benchmark 2009 111p il (Shakespeare explained)
lib bdg $29.95
Grades: 7 8 9 10 11 12   **822.3**
  1. Shakespeare, William, 1564-1616—Criticism
  ISBN 978-0-7614-3419-1; 0-7614-3419-4
                                    LC 2008-37510
"A literary analysis of the play Henry IV, part 1. In-
cludes information on the history and culture of Elizabe-
than England." Publisher's note
  Includes glossary and bibliographical references

Julius Caesar. Marshall Cavendish Benchmark
2008 127p il (Shakespeare explained) lib bdg
$29.95
Grades: 7 8 9 10 11 12   **822.3**
  1. Shakespeare, William, 1564-1616—Criticism
  ISBN 978-0-7614-3028-5; 0-7614-3028-8
                                    LC 2008-14404
"A literary analysis of the play Julius Caesar. Includes
information on the history and culture of Elizabethan England." Publisher's note
  Includes glossary and bibliographical references

A midsummer night's dream. Marshall
Cavendish Benchmark 2008 111p il (Shakespeare
explained) lib bdg $29.95
Grades: 7 8 9 10 11 12   **822.3**
  1. Shakespeare, William, 1564-1616—Criticism
  ISBN 978-0-7614-3030-8; 0-7614-3030-X
                                    LC 2008-7079
"A literary analysis of the play A Midsummer Night's
Dream. Includes information on the history and culture
of Elizabethan England." Publisher's note
  This book "provides practical information, skillfully
presented, making the complexities of Shakespearean theater accessible to present-day students. . . . [The author's] contagious enthusiasm and attractive presentation
make this . . . imminently useful for high school and
public libraries." Voice Youth Advocates
  Includes glossary and bibliographical references

The **sonnets**; edited and with an introduction by
Harold Bloom; volume editor, Brett Foster.
Bloom's Literary Criticism 2008 388p (Bloom's
Shakespeare through the ages) $50
Grades: 10 11 12   **822.3**
  1. Shakespeare, William, 1564-1616—Criticism
  ISBN 978-0-7910-9597-3   LC 2008-12830
This "study guide contains a selection of . . . criti-
cism through the centuries of Shakespeare's sonnets."
Publisher's note
  Includes bibliographical references

Spurgeon, Caroline F. E., 1869-1942

Shakespeare's imagery and what it tells us; with
charts and illustrations. Cambridge Univ. Press
1935 408p il pa $29.95 hardcover o.p.
Grades: 9 10 11 12   **822.3**
  1. Shakespeare, William, 1564-1616—Technique
  ISBN 0-521-09258-2 (pa)
"A scholarly study of Shakespeare's use of images
and of his personality and thought as they may be de-
duced from his imagery." Booklist
  "A distinctive contribution to Shakespeare's criticism,
bold and original in idea, scrupulous and exhaustive in
method, and of all things, readable as a detective story."
N Y Times Book Rev

The **tempest**; edited and with an introduction by
  Harold Bloom; volume editor, Neil Heims.
  Bloom's Literary Criticism 2008 276p (Bloom's
  Shakespeare through the ages) $50
Grades: 10 11 12   **822.3**
  1. Shakespeare, William, 1564-1616—Criticism
  ISBN 978-0-7910-9577-5   LC 2007-29605
This "study guide to one of Shakespeare's greatest
plays contains a selection of . . . criticism through the
centuries on The Tempest." Publisher's note
  Includes bibliographical references

William Shakespeare's Hamlet; edited and with an
  introduction by Harold Bloom. New ed.
  Bloom's Literary Criticism 2009 211p (Modern
  critical interpretations) $45
Grades: 9 10 11 12   **822.3**
  1. Shakespeare, William, 1564-1616—Criticism
  ISBN 978-1-60413-632-6   LC 2009-18234
  First published 1986
  For a complete list of series titles contact publisher
This "study guide to one of Shakespeare's greatest
plays contains a selection of . . . contemporary criticism
of *Hamlet*." Publisher's note
  Includes bibliographical references

823.009   English fiction—History and criticism

Anelli, Melissa

Harry, a history; the true story of a boy wizard,
his fans, and life inside the Harry Potter
phenomenon. Pocket Books 2008 356p il pa $16
Grades: 9 10 11 12   **823.009**
  1. Rowling, J. K. 2. Harry Potter (Fictional character)
  ISBN 978-1-4165-5495-0; 1-4165-5495-5
                                    LC 2008-21530
"An analysis of the pop-culture phenomenon surrounding the Harry Potter series, written by the founder of
'The Leaky Cauldron' website, evaluates how the books
inspired international camaraderie and a generation of
new readers." Publisher's note
  "With infectious, at times frenetic, excitement, Anelli
presents two narratives in this hip report on how a boy
wizard became a rock star. . . . Fans will recognize
themselves in these pages, and the curious might finally
understand their friends." Publ Wkly
  Includes bibliographical references

Baker, William, 1944-

Critical companion to Jane Austen; a literary reference to her life and work. Facts on File 2008 644p il (Facts on File library of world literature) $75

Grades: 9 10 11 12 Adult   **823.009**
1. Austen, Jane, 1775-1817
ISBN 978-0-8160-6416-8   LC 2006-102848

This book examines Jane Austen's "life and works, and includes critical analyses of the themes within her writing, as well as entries on related topics and relevant people, places, and influences." Publisher's note

"Janeites (and others) will find . . . [this book] a useful and accessible one-stop resource." Booklist

Includes bibliographical references

Davis, Paul B. (Paul Benjamin), 1934-

Critical companion to Charles Dickens; a literary reference to his life and work. Rev ed. Facts on File 2007 676p il (Facts on File library of world literature) $75 *

Grades: 9 10 11 12 Adult   **823.009**
1. Dickens, Charles, 1812-1870
ISBN 0-8160-6407-5; 978-0-8160-6407-6
LC 2006-3026

First published 1998 with title: Charles Dickens A-Z

This "reference contains entries on this writer's works, including the characters in each work, . . . historical and thematic information, and critical discussion. It also includes entries on related people, places, themes, topics, and influences. Additional features include 116 illustrations, a chronology, a bibliography of primary and secondary sources, and much more." Publisher's note

Includes bibliographical references

Dracula, by Bram Stoker; editor, Jack Lynch. Salem Press 2009 339p (Critical insights) lib bdg $85

Grades: 9 10 11 12   **823.009**
1. Stoker, Bram, 1847-1912
ISBN 978-1-58765-612-5; 1-58765-612-4
LC 2009-26314

This book introduces *Dracula*'s narrative in its "historical context, provide a short biography of the author, and offer 'The Paris Review Perspective' on . . . [the book,] followed by a series of articles by academics under the headings of 'Critical Contexts' or 'Critical Readings.'" SLJ

Includes bibliographical references

The **Facts** on File companion to the British novel. Facts on File 2005 2v (Facts on File library of world literature) set $140 *

Grades: 9 10 11 12 Adult   **823.009**
1. English fiction—History and criticism
ISBN 0-8160-6377-X; 978-0-8160-6377-2
LC 2004-20914

Contents: v1 Beginnings through the 19th century by Virginia Brackett; v2 20th century by Victoria Gaydosik

"This two-volume companion to the British novel contains more than 1000 A-to-Z entries (each averaging several pages in length) on English-writing authors hailing from either the British Isles or the Commonwealth as well as on novels, pertinent literary terms, themes, concepts, influential periodicals, and subgenres." Libr J

"With more than one thousand entries, each with a selected bibliography and a set of very usable appendixes, this work accomplishes much in a compact set." Ref & User Services Quarterly

Includes bibliographical references

Fargnoli, A. Nicholas

Critical companion to James Joyce; a literary companion to his life and work; [by] A. Nicholas Fargnoli, Michael Patrick Gillespie. Rev ed. Facts On File 2006 450p il (Facts on File library of world literature) $65; pa $19.95

Grades: 11 12 Adult   **823.009**
1. Joyce, James, 1882-1941
ISBN 0-8160-6232-3; 978-0-8160-6232-4; 0-8160-6689-2 (pa); 978-0-8160-6689-6 (pa)
LC 2005-15721

First published 1995 with title: James Joyce A to Z

The authors "divide this reference to the writer's life and work into four parts. Part 1 is a brief biography. Part 2 focuses on individual works (e.g., Dubliners), including its publication date, a brief history, a synopsis, early critical reception, contemporary perspectives, and one or two recommended titles for further reading. The entries in Part 3 cover people (including friends and relatives), places, and ideas related to Joyce. Part 4 contains an appendix, a bibliography of the writer's work, a bibliography of secondary sources, chronologies, family trees, and more. . . . [This is] a great primer for those needing a detailed introduction into Joyce's world." Libr J

Includes bibliographical references

Fonstad, Karen Wynn

The atlas of Middle-earth. rev ed. Houghton Mifflin 2001 c1991 210p il maps pa $24

Grades: 9 10 11 12   **823.009**
1. Tolkien, J. R. R. (John Ronald Reuel), 1892-1973
ISBN 0-618-12699-6
"A Mariner book"
First published 1981

A guide to the journeys, lands, peoples, and history of Tolkien's imaginary kingdom

Includes bibliographical references

Great expectations, by Charles Dickens; editor, Eugene Goodheart. Salem Press 2009 312p (Critical insights) lib bdg $85

Grades: 9 10 11 12   **823.009**
1. Dickens, Charles, 1812-1870
ISBN 978-1-58765-614-9; 1-58765-614-0
LC 2009-26312

"Contains an editor's introduction to the author or work, a perspective from the editors of the . . . literary magazine *The Paris Review*, and a biography of the author. Following these ready-reference chapters is a section, 'Critical Contexts,' that presents four original essays by current scholars." Publisher's note

Includes bibliographical references

Horror: another 100 best books; edited by Stephen Jones and Kim Newman; with a foreword by Peter Straub. Carroll & Graf Publishers 2005 456p pa $16.95

Grades: 11 12 Adult   **823.009**

1. Horror fiction—History and criticism 2. Best books

ISBN 0-7867-1577-4

First published 1988

This book "features one hundred of the top names in the horror field discussing one hundred of the most spine-chilling novels ever written. Each entry includes a synopsis of the work as well as publication history, biographical information about the author of each title, and recommended reading and biographical notes on the contributor." Publisher's note

"Horror fans seeking what to read next will not only find out here; they'll also have their taste and appreciative capacity refined by the intelligent, passionate commentary of the 100 writers who selected these 100 books." Booklist

Jane Austen; edited and with an introduction by Harold Bloom. New ed. Chelsea House 2009 315p (Modern critical views) $45

Grades: 11 12 Adult   **823.009**

1. Austen, Jane, 1775-1817

ISBN 978-1-60413-397-4   LC 2008-44616

First published 1986

Other series titles in this class include: Charles Dickens; Mary Wollstonecraft Shelley; Joseph Conrad. For a complete list of titles contact publisher.

A collection of critical essays on Austen and her works. Also includes a chronology of events in her life.

Includes bibliographical references

Mary Shelley's Frankenstein; edited & with an introduction by Harold Bloom. Bloom's Literary Criticism 2007 150p (Bloom's guides) $30

Grades: 9 10 11 12   **823.009**

1. Shelley, Mary Wollstonecraft, 1797-1851

ISBN 978-0-7910-9358-0; 0-7910-9358-1

LC 2007-10199

Other series titles in this class include: Charles Dickens's A tale of two cities; Charles Dickens's Great expectations; William Golding's Lord of the flies. For a complete list of titles contact publisher

This study guide on Mary Shelley's classic novel includes a brief biographical sketch of Shelley, a list of characters, a summary and analysis, and selections from critical essays by different scholars about the work.

Includes bibliographical references

Maunder, Andrew

The Facts on File companion to the British short story. Facts on File 2006 528p (Facts on File library of world literature) $75 *

Grades: 11 12 Adult   **823.009**

1. Short stories—History and criticism

ISBN 0-8160-5990-X; 978-0-8160-5990-4

LC 2006-6897

More than 450 alphabetically arranged entries cover authors, characters, and major short stories. Literary terms, themes, and motifs are covered. Winners of prizes and awards are noted.

Includes glossary and bibliographical references

Mellor, Anne Kostelanetz

Mary Shelley, her life, her fiction, her monsters. Methuen 1988 xx, 275p il pa $26.95 hardcover o.p. *

Grades: 11 12 Adult   **823.009**

1. Shelley, Mary Wollstonecraft, 1797-1851

ISBN 0-415-90147-2 (pa)   LC 87-31249

The author "blends biography and informed criticism here to give a feminist reevaluation of Mary Shelley and her fiction, especially *Frankenstein*. . . . Mellor's book is clearly written and forcefully argued." Choice

Includes bibliographical references

Nardo, Don, 1947-

Understanding Frankenstein. Lucent Bks. 2003 128p il (Understanding great literature) lib bdg $27.45 *

Grades: 7 8 9 10   **823.009**

1. Shelley, Mary Wollstonecraft, 1797-1851

ISBN 1-59018-147-6   LC 2002-12560

Discusses Mary Shelley's sources of ideas for the compelling plot, well-developed characters, and universal themes of "Frankenstein" which have led to its enduring popularity.

"The text is easy to understand. A solid introduction for middle school students." SLJ

Includes bibliographical references

Olsen, Kirstin

All things Austen; an encyclopedia of Austen's world. Greenwood Press 2005 2v il maps set $157.95 *

Grades: 11 12 Adult   **823.009**

1. Austen, Jane, 1775-1817—Encyclopedias 2. Reference books

ISBN 0-313-33032-8   LC 2004-28664

Also available one-volume abridged edition pa $29.95 (ISBN: 978-1-84645-052-5)

This Jane Austen encyclopedia contains "more than 150 well-designed and well-written A-to-Z articles on such topics as clothing, education, politics, religion, science, business, society, and the military of 18th- and 19th-century England." Libr J

"This well-written and meticulously researched work provides a convenient means for general readers, students, and scholars to gain a better understanding of the social, cultural, and political climate of Austen's time." Booklist

Pasachoff, Naomi E., 1947-

A student's guide to the Brontë sisters; [by] Naomi Pasachoff. Enslow Publishers 2010 160p il (Understanding literature) lib bdg $27.93

Grades: 7 8 9 10   **823.009**

1. Brontë, Charlotte, 1816-1855 2. Brontë, Emily, 1818-1848 3. Brontë, Anne, 1820-1849

ISBN 978-0-7660-3267-5; 0-7660-3267-1

LC 2008-15165

"An introduction to the work of Charlotte, Emily, and Anne Bronte for high school students, which includes relevant biographical background on the authors, explanations of various literary devices and techniques, and literary criticism for the novice reader." Publisher's note

Includes glossary and bibliographical references

Poplawski, Paul
A Jane Austen encyclopedia. Greenwood Press 1998 411p il $95 *
Grades: 11 12 Adult **823.009**
   1. Austen, Jane, 1775-1817
   ISBN 0-313-30017-8   LC 97-44880
This volume "examines the life, works, characters, and minutiae of Austeniana. The alphabetically arranged entries include extensive plot summaries that end with lists of major and minor characters, brief character descriptions, and short articles on the author's family and friends." SLJ
Includes bibliographical references

Regis, Pamela
A natural history of the romance novel. University of Pennsylvania Press 2003 224p $24.95; pa $19.95
Grades: 9 10 11 12   **823.009**
   1. Love stories—History and criticism
   ISBN 0-8122-3303-4; 0-8122-1522-2 (pa)
                  LC 2002-45412
The author "traces the genre's history from Samuel Richardson's Pamela to the present. Her excellent study adds much-needed research to the slowly but steadily growing body of scholarship on the popular romance novel." Libr J
Includes bibliographical references

Thomas Hardy; edited and with an introduction by Harold Bloom. Chelsea House 2003 160p (Bloom's major novelists) lib bdg $22.95 *
Grades: 9 10 11 12   **823.009**
   1. Hardy, Thomas, 1840-1928
   ISBN 0-7910-6348-8   LC 2002-151007
Another available series title in this class is: George Eliot. For complete list of titles contact publisher
This title includes a biographical essay, plot summaries, and critical interpretations of the novels and their characters.
Includes bibliographical references

Wagner, Hank
Prince of stories; the many worlds of Neil Gaiman; [by] Hank Wagner, Christopher Golden, and Stephen R. Bissette. St. Martin's Press 2008 546p il $29.95
Grades: 11 12 Adult   **823.009**
   1. Gaiman, Neil, 1960-
   ISBN 978-0-312-38765-5; 0-312-38765-2
                  LC 2008-24762
The authors "have conducted extensive research and interviews in their effort to create a compendium of data about one of fantasy's finest writers. . . . Encyclopedic in scope, this book offers reprints of articles by Gaiman, back stories, interviews with illustrators and others who work with Gaiman, photos, illustrations, and sneak peeks at future works. . . . Well written, well organized, and fun to peruse, this book can be enjoyed as a cover-to-cover read or a random browse. Readers will learn a lot about Gaiman, storytelling and the writing process." Voice Youth Advocates
Includes bibliographical references

William Golding's Lord of the flies; edited and with an introduction by Harold Bloom. New ed. Chelsea House 2008 176p (Modern critical interpretations) $45
Grades: 9 10 11 12 Adult   **823.009**
   1. Golding, William, 1911-1993
   ISBN 978-0-7910-9826-4   LC 2008-2451
   First published 1999
Other available series titles in this class include: George Orwell's 1984; Emily Bronte's Wuthering Heights; Jane Austen's Pride and prejudice; Chinua Achebe's Things fall apart. For complete list of titles contact publisher
These "critical essays on *Lord of the Flies* are supplemented by a chronology of the author's life, a bibliography, and notes about the essay contributors." Publisher's note
Includes bibliographical references

828   English miscellaneous writings

Blake, William, 1757-1827
The portable Blake; selected and arranged with an introduction by Alfred Kazin. Viking 1946 713p il pa $15.95 hardcover o.p. *
Grades: 11 12 Adult   **828**
   ISBN 0-14-015026-9 (pa)
   "The Viking portable library"
A "generous selection of verse, prose, letters, and essays. Blake is shown as an artist and poet against all institutions but ever seeking unity (though his was the mystic's quest) while hunting for realism and naturalism." Cincinnati Public Libr
Includes bibliographical references

Brunsdale, Mitzi
Student companion to George Orwell; [by] Mitzi M. Brunsdale. Greenwood Press 2000 173p (Student companions to classic writers) $35 *
Grades: 9 10 11 12   **828**
   1. Orwell, George, 1903-1950
   ISBN 0-313-30637-0   LC 99-49690
   For complete list of series titles contact publisher
The author explores the works of the noted novelist and social critic. Particular emphasis is placed on Animal farm and Nineteen eighty-four.
Includes bibliographical references

Conrad, Joseph, 1857-1924
The portable Conrad; edited with an introduction by Michael Gorra. Penguin Books 2007 xlvi, 702p (Penguin classics) pa $20 *
Grades: 11 12 Adult   **828**
   ISBN 978-0-14-310511-4; 0-14-310511-6
                  LC 2007-60130
   First published 1947
Contains "*The Secret Agent, Heart of Darkness*, and *The Nigger of the 'Narcissus,'* as well as shorter tales like 'Amy Forster' and 'The Secret Sharer,' a selection of letters, and his observations on the sinking of the Titanic." Publisher's note
Includes bibliographical references

DeGategno, Paul J.

Critical companion to Jonathan Swift; a literary reference to his life and works; [by] Paul J. DeGategno, R. Jay Stubblefield. Facts on File 2006 474p il (Facts on File library of world literature) $75

Grades: 11 12 Adult   **828**
  1. Swift, Jonathan, 1667-1745
  ISBN 0-8160-5093-7; 978-0-8160-5093-2
                                                    LC 2005-25470

This "work is divided into five parts. These parts consist of a ten-page biography of satirist Jonathan Swift (1667-1745); a 'Works A-Z' section that includes synopses and commentaries that generally run to several hundred words on virtually all of Swift's poems, essays, and books; a 'Related Entries' section with similar brief articles on persons, topics, and places relevant to Swift studies; appendixes that include a chronology of Swift's life; a . . . bibliography of primary and secondary works; and an index." Libr J

Includes bibliographical references

Hopkins, Gerard Manley, 1844-1889

Poems and prose of Gerard Manley Hopkins; selected with an introduction and notes by W.H. Gardner. Penguin 1984 c1953 xxxvi, 260p (Penguin classics) pa $16

Grades: 11 12 Adult   **828**
  ISBN 0-14-042015-0

"On entering the Society of Jesus at the age of twenty-four, . . . [the author] burnt all his poetry and 'resolved to write no more, as not belonging to my profession, unless by the wishes of my superiors'. The poems, letters and journal entries selected for this edition were written in the following twenty years of his life, and published posthumously in 1918." Publisher's note

Includes bibliographical references

Huxley, Aldous, 1894-1963

Brave new world: and, Brave new world revisited; foreword by Christopher Hitchens. HarperCollins 2004 xxi, 340p $23.95 *

Grades: 11 12 Adult   **828**
  ISBN 0-06-053526-1   LC 2004-40611
  First published 1960; a combined edition of the two titles published 1932 and 1958 respectively

Brave new world is a satirical novel "set in the year 632 AF (After Ford), it is a grim picture of the world which Huxley thinks our scientific and social developments have already begun to create." Reader's Ency. 4th edition

Kipling, Rudyard, 1865-1936

The portable Kipling; edited and with an introduction by Irving Howe. Viking 1982 xlii, 687p pa $18 hardcover o.p.

Grades: 9 10 11 12   **828**
  ISBN 0-14-015097-8 (pa)   LC 81-52466
  "The Viking portable library"
  Includes the following stories: The strange ride of Morrowbie Jukes; The man who would be king; Without

benefit of clergy; Lispeth; The head of the district; The miracle of Purun Bhagat; The story of Muhammad Din; Jews in Shushan; The courting of Dinah Shadd; On Greenhow Hill; Black Jack; Toomai of the Elephants; The King's ankus; How the Rhinoceros got his skin; The cat that walked by himself; The village that voted the Earth was flat; Brugglesmith; Brother Square-Toes; 'A priest in spite of himself'; The church that was at Antioch; The Eye of Allah; As easy as A.B.C.; Mrs. Bathurst; Friendly Brook; The wish house; Mary Postgate; The gardener; Dayspring mishandled

This volume collects short stories and verse. Included are about 50 poems. "The twenty-eight stories included give about equal weight to 'Stories of India' and 'Soldiers' Tales' and analyses of the effects of world war on disappointed idealists and activists." Christ Sci Monit

Means, A. L.

A student's guide to George Orwell. Enslow Pubs. 2005 176p il (Understanding literature) lib bdg $27.93 *

Grades: 7 8 9 10   **828**
  1. Orwell, George, 1903-1950
  ISBN 0-7660-2433-4

An introduction to the life and work of the author of *1984, Animal Farm* and other works

Includes glossary and bibliographical references

Milton, John, 1608-1674

The portable Milton; edited and with an introduction by Douglas Bush. Viking 1949 693p pa $15.95 hardcover o.p. *

Grades: 11 12 Adult   **828**
  ISBN 0-14-015044-7 (pa)
  "The Viking portable library"

A selection of the early poems and sonnets; "Areopagitica" complete; lengthy selections from the other chief prose works; and the three major poems, "Paradise lost," "Paradise regained," and "Samson Agonistes," complete

Includes glossary and bibliographical references

The **New** Oxford book of literary anecdotes. Oxford University Press 2006 385p il hardcover o.p. pa $16.95

Grades: 11 12 Adult   **828**
  1. English literature—Anecdotes 2. Authors, English—Anecdotes 3. Authors, American—Anecdotes
  ISBN   0-19-280468-5;   978-0-19-280468-6;
  0-19-954341-0 (pa); 978-0-19-954341-0 (pa)
                                                    LC 2005-33698

First published 1975 under the editorship of James Sutherland with title: The Oxford book of literary anecdotes

The editor "has compiled more than 700 anecdotes about English-language writers, from Geoffrey Chaucer to J.K. Rowling. The brief, chronologically-arranged (by subject's birth date) entries offer a glimpse into the personalities and times of these authors." Libr J

Includes bibliographical references

Quinn, Edward, 1932-
Critical companion to George Orwell; a literary reference to his life and work. Facts On File 2009 450p il (Facts on File library of world literature) $75
Grades: 11 12 Adult   **828**
1. Orwell, George, 1903-1950
ISBN 978-0-8160-7091-6   LC 2008-26727
This volume provides a "review of Orwell's life and covers all his novels, nonfiction, and other writings. . . . It is a superb resource for those desiring an introduction to George Orwell, the man and the writer." Booklist
Includes bibliographical references

Shippey, T. A. (Tom A.)
J.R.R. Tolkien; author of the century. Houghton Mifflin 2001 xxxv, 347p $26; pa $13 *
Grades: 11 12 Adult   **828**
1. Tolkien, J. R. R. (John Ronald Reuel), 1892-1973
2. Fantasy fiction—History and criticism
ISBN 0-618-12764-X; 0-618-25759-4 (pa)
                                    LC 2001-16973
First published 2000 in the United Kingdom
"Shippey examines Tolkien's published and many unfinished works (such as *The Silmarillion*), as well as the shorter poems and stories. He convincingly argues that Tolkien deserves to be ranked as a major literary figure." Libr J
Includes bibliographical references

Thomas, Dylan, 1914-1953
A child's Christmas in Wales; illustrated by Chris Raschka. Candlewick Press 2004 unp il $17.99 *
Grades: 2 3 4 5 6 7 8 9   **828**
1. Christmas—Wales
ISBN 0-7636-2161-7   LC 2003-65274
The Welsh poet Dylan Thomas recalls the celebration of Christmas with his family and the feelings it evoked in him as a child.
"Applied to torn paper, the ink and watercolors spread through the fibers, freely forming soft outlines and shadows. The result is an intriguing contemporary take on a story that is by now part of the rather staid canon of Christmas classics." N Y Times Book Rev

Wilde, Oscar, 1854-1900
The portable Oscar Wilde; selected and edited by Richard Aldington and Stanley Weintraub. rev ed. Viking 1981 741p pa $15.95 hardcover o.p. *
Grades: 11 12 Adult   **828**
ISBN 0-14-015093-5 (pa)   LC 80-39827
"The Viking portable library"
First published 1946
This volume contains The critic as artist, The picture of Dorian Gray, Salomé, The importance of being Earnest, De profundis, and selected poems, reviews, letters and phrases from other works.

Woolf, Virginia, 1882-1941
The Virginia Woolf reader; edited by Mitchell A. Leaska. Harcourt Brace Jovanovich 1984 371p pa $16 hardcover o.p. *
Grades: 11 12 Adult   **828**
ISBN 0-15-693590-2 (pa)   LC 84-4478
"A Harvest book"
Excerpts from Woolf's "novels form less than 20 percent of a reader whose selections of short stories, essays, letters, and diary entries are excellent. This collection will be useful to those already familiar with Woolf's novels and seeking an introductory selection of her other writings." Libr J

Yeats, W. B. (William Butler), 1865-1939
The Yeats reader; a portable compendium of poetry, drama, and prose; edited by Richard J. Finneran. Rev. ed. Scribner Poetry 2002 xxii, 566p il $35; pa $18 *
Grades: 11 12 Adult   **828**
ISBN 0-7432-3315-8; 0-7432-2798-0
                                    LC 2002-70670
First published 1997
This book "presents more than one hundred and fifty of his best-known poems . . . plus eight plays, a sampling of his prose tales, and excerpts from his published autobiographical and critical writings. In addition, an appendix offers six early texts of poems that Yeats later revised. Also included are selections from the memoirs left unpublished at his death and complete introductions written for a projected collection that never came to fruition." Publisher's note
Includes bibliographical references

829   Old English (Anglo-Saxon) literature

Beowulf.
Beowulf; a new verse translation. W.W. Norton & Company 2001 xxx, 213p pa $13.95 *
Grades: 11 12 Adult   **829**
ISBN 0-393-32097-9
Other verse and prose translations available from various publishers
This translation first published 1999 by Farrar, Straus & Giroux
Text in English and Old English
This epic of a dragon-slaying hero "is the earliest extant written composition of such length in English, and indeed in all Teutonic literature. Its content was based on Norse legends merged with historical events of the early sixth century in Denmark; this oral tradition was carried to England by Danish invaders of the mid-sixth century, fused with the Christianity they absorbed there, and finally written down by a single but unknown poet c700." Reader's Ency. 4th edition

830.3 German literature— Encyclopedias and dictionaries

Garland, Henry B. (Henry Burnand)
The Oxford companion to German literature; by Henry and Mary Garland. 3rd ed, by Mary Garland. Oxford Univ. Press 1997 951p maps $95 *

Grades: 11 12 Adult   830.3
1. Reference books 2. German literature—Dictionaries 3. German literature—Bio-bibliography
ISBN 0-19-815896-3   LC 96-53309
First published 1976
Entries include biographies, synopses of important works, literary terms and movements, historical events and figures, and material relevant to the social and intellectual background of German literature from the earliest records to the present.

830.9 German literature—History and criticism

The **Cambridge** history of German literature; edited by Helen Watanabe-O'Kelly. Cambridge Univ. Press 1997 613p $90; pa $32 *
Grades: 11 12 Adult   830.9
1. German literature—History and criticism
ISBN 0-521-43417-3; 0-521-78573-1 (pa)
                                LC 95-52412
This work provides a history of German literature "up to the Unification of Germany in 1990. It is a history for our times: well-known authors and movements are set in a wider literary, cultural and political context, standard judgments are reexamined where appropriate, and a new prominence is given to writing by women. . . . Titles and quotations are translated, and there is an extensive bibliography." Publisher's note
A "briskly written survey of German literature that grounds literary practice in the social and historical context of each period and yet does not shortchange the aesthetic qualities of the representative works discussed." Choice

831 German poetry

Rilke, Rainer Maria, 1875-1926
Selected poems of Rainer Maria Rilke; a translation from the German and commentary by Robert Bly. Harper & Row 1981 224p pa $15 hardcover o.p. *
Grades: 9 10 11 12   831
1. Poetry—By individual authors
ISBN 0-06-090727-4 (pa)   LC 78-2114
A bilingual edition of the German poet's verse selected from A Book for the Hours of Prayer, The Book of Pictures, New Poems, The Uncollected and Occasional Poems, and Sonnets to Orpheus. The translator also includes five introductory essays
"Bly's comments make us see Rilke's work in relation to events of the poet's life and to creative inner tensions

within certain periods. They also afford an awareness of Rilke's specific inwardness, a sensibility and disposition of soul very different from that of any American poet." Libr J

832 German drama

Brecht, Bertolt, 1898-1956
Galileo; English version by Charles Laughton; edited and with an introduction by Eric Bentley. Grove Weidenfeld 1991 155p pa $6.95
Grades: 9 10 11 12   832
1. Galilei, Galileo, 1564-1642—Drama
ISBN 0-8021-3059-3   LC 91-22966
"An Evergreen book"
Written 1938-39, first performed 1943
"The play concerns Galileo Galilei's conflict with the church over the application of the Copernican system, which the church viewed as anathema. Brecht deliberately portrays Galileo as a self-serving and decidedly unheroic character, willing to compromise his principles in the face of pressure." Reader's Ency. 4th edition

833.009 German fiction—History and criticism

Erich Maria Remarque's All quiet on the western front; edited and with an introduction by Harold Bloom. New ed. Chelsea House 2009 224p (Modern critical interpretations) $45
Grades: 9 10 11 12   833.009
1. Remarque, Erich Maria, 1898-1970
ISBN 978-1-60413-402-5   LC 2008-45705
First published 2001
For a complete list of titles in this series contact publisher
Nine essays explore the literary merit and political impact of the anti-war classic.
Includes bibliographical references

Franz Kafka's The metamorphosis; edited & with an introduction by Harold Bloom. Chelsea House Publishers 2007 87p (Bloom's guides) $30 *
Grades: 9 10 11 12   833.009
1. Kafka, Franz, 1883-1924
ISBN 0-7910-9298-4; 978-0-7910-9298-9
                                LC 2006-25342
For complete list of series titles contact publisher
This book's "critical extracts cover distinct elements of Kafka's novella, offering a variety of viewpoints. Additional features answer questions about the author, characters, and the story's main points, and direct readers to further reading, with comments on the significance of each source." Publisher's note
Includes bibliographical references

838   German miscellaneous writings

Hermann Hesse; edited and with an introduction
by Harold Bloom. Chelsea House 2002 246p
(Modern critical views) $37.95 *
Grades: 9 10 11 12   **838**
1. Hesse, Hermann, 1877-1962
ISBN 0-7910-7398-X   LC 2002-152671
For complete list of series titles contact publisher
"Essays here include discussions of Hesse's personal
life, writing style, themes, characters, philosophy, and influences. His novels *Siddhartha, Narcissus and
Goldmund, The Glass Bead Game, Steppenwolf,* and
Demian are analyzed as is some of his poetry. Similarities of Hesse's writings with those of André Gide, Mar-
cel Proust, and James Joyce are discussed in several essays. Excerpts of his poems are included in both German
and English." SLJ

Includes bibliographical references

839.3   Dutch, Flemish, Afrikaans
literatures

Frank, Anne, 1929-1945
Anne Frank's Tales from the secret annex; with
translations by Ralph Manheim and Michel Mok.
Doubleday 1984 c1983 136p pa $4.95 hardcover
o.p. *
Grades: 11 12 Adult   **839.3**
ISBN 0-553-58638-6 (pa)   LC 82-45871
Original Dutch edition copyrighted 1949. First English
translation published 1960 in the United Kingdom with
title: Tales from the house behind
This volume presents all of Anne Frank's existing stories, sketches and drafts as well as her personal reminiscences and essays
"The themes and plots of her brief fables are not extraordinary. But their very ordinariness reminds readers
that the writer who kept one of the world's most widely
read diaries was an ordinary child." Horn Book

Prose, Francine, 1947-
Anne Frank; the book, the life, the afterlife.
HarperCollins 2009 322p $24.99 *
Grades: Adult   **839.3**
1. Frank,   Anne,   1929-1945—Authorship
2. Holocaust,   1933-1945—Personal   narratives
3. Creative writing
ISBN 978-0-06-143079-4; 0-06-143079-X
                                  LC 2009-17703
"In this definitive, deeply moving inquiry into the life
of the young, imperiled artist, and masterful literary exegesis of *The Diary of a Young Girl*, Prose tells the
crushing story of the Frank family, performs a revelatory
analysis of Anne's exacting revision of her coming-of-
age memoir, and assesses her father's editorial decisions
as he edited his murdered daughter's manuscript for publication. . . . Extraordinary testimony to the power of literature and compassion." Booklist
Includes bibliographical references

839.8   Danish and Norwegian
literatures

Ibsen, Henrik, 1828-1906
Ibsen: four major plays; translated by Rick
Davis and Brian Johnston. Smith & Kraus 1995
286p (Great translations for actors) pa $19.95 *
Grades: 11 12 Adult   **839.8**
ISBN 1-880399-67-9   LC 95-13632
Designated v1 on cover
Contents: A doll house; Ghosts; An enemy of the peo-
ple; Hedda Gabler
"All four of these versions have been 'production-
tested,' which shows in their graceful and believable dia-
logue and their sheer theatricality. Davis and Johnston
have unlocked the power in Ibsen's works and made it
clear why Ibsen was once *the* playwright for firebrands,
Fabians, and other progressives throughout the world."
Booklist

840.3   French literature—
Encyclopedias and dictionaries

The **New** Oxford companion to literature in
French; edited by Peter France. Oxford Univ.
Press 1995 li, 865p maps $80 *
Grades: 11 12 Adult   **840.3**
1. Reference books 2. French literature—Dictionaries
3. French literature—Bio-bibliography
ISBN 0-19-866125-8
First published 1959 with title: The Oxford companion
to French literature
"This work views literature from the perspective of its
greater cultural context. Accordingly, topics discussed go
beyond the poets, novelists, and dramatists of the traditional French canon, and include philosophy, science, art,
history, linguistics, and cinema. Even strip cartoons and
pamphlets are treated. . . . The more than 3,000 entries
are written by approximately 130 international experts. In
addition to brief entries, there are long articles on general
topics, such as Québec, feminism, Occitan literature, and
the history of the French language." Am Ref Books
Annu, 1996

841   French poetry

Baudelaire, Charles, 1821-1867
Poems. Knopf 1993 256p (Everyman's library
pocket poets) $12.50
Grades: 11 12 Adult   **841**
1. Poetry—By individual authors
ISBN 0-679-42910-7   LC 93-14363
A representative selection of poetry by the French
symbolist.

Chanson de Roland.
The song of Roland; translated, with an introduction, by W.S. Merwin. Modern Library 2001 137p pa $11.95 *
Grades: 11 12 Adult   **841**
1. Roland (Legendary character)
ISBN 0-375-75711-2   LC 00-48989
Also available in paperback from Penguin Classics
"This heroic poem celebrates the mighty feats of Roland, the great French hero in the time of Charlemagne. The medieval legend has replaced and transformed the actual facts of history to a great extent but the epic poem has continued in popularity." Bookman's Manual
Includes bibliographical references

Rimbaud, Arthur, 1854-1891
Poems; [selected by Peter Washington] Knopf 1994 288p (Everyman's library pocket poets) $12.50
Grades: 11 12 Adult   **841**
1. Poetry—By individual authors
ISBN 978-0-679-43321-7; 0-679-43321-X
      LC 94-2496
A collection of work by the French Symbolist known for his daring images and pioneering prose poems

842 French drama

Anouilh, Jean, 1910-1987
Antigone; a play; translated by Jeremy Sams. French 2002 48p pa $6.50
Grades: 11 12 Adult   **842**
ISBN 0-573-62819-X
Characters: 7 men, 3 women. 1 act.
This version of Sophocles' tragedy was composed and originally produced in German-occupied Paris in 1942. Antigone's death represents resistance against a totalitarian regime.

Beckett, Samuel, 1906-1989
Waiting for Godot; tragicomedy in 2 acts. Grove Press 1954 60p il pa $13 hardcover o.p.
Grades: 11 12 Adult   **842**
ISBN 0-8021-3034-8 (pa)
Translated from the French by the author
Originally written in French. The play was first produced in Paris during the winter of 1952
"There are strong biblical references throughout, but Beckett's powerful and symbolic portrayal of the human condition as one of ignorance, delusion, paralysis, and intermittent flashes of human sympathy, hope, and wit has been subjected to many varying interpretations. The theatrical vitality and versatility of the play have been demonstrated by performances throughout the world." Oxford Companion to Engl. Lit. 5th edition

Ionesco, Eugène, 1912-1994
Four plays; translated by Donald M. Allen. Grove Press 1958 160p pa $13
Grades: 9 10 11 12   **842**

ISBN 0-8021-3079-8
Original French edition, 1954
Contents: The bald soprano; The lesson; Jack; or, The submission; The chairs
The bald soprano is a comedy satirizing English middle class life, while Jack, concerns a sulky young man who disappoints his family by refusing to marry the girl of their choice. An avant-garde drama, The chairs focuses on an old couple who receives many imaginary guests. The murder of a young student by his elderly teacher ends a bizarre lesson in The lesson

Rhinoceros, and other plays; translated by Derek Prouse. Grove Press 1960 141p pa $10
Grades: 11 12 Adult   **842**
ISBN 0-8021-3098-4
"An Evergreen book"
Contents: Rhinoceros; The future is in eggs; The leader
Three satirical comedies by a leading dramatist of the "theater of the absurd." In Rhinoceros, one man resists the pressure to conform as everyone about him accepts their transformation into rhinoceroses and he finds himself socially isolated. In The future is in eggs, a couple must produce eggs destined to become intellectuals. The leader is a satire on the mass adulation of political figures in which the leader turns out to be a headless figure

Molière, 1622-1673
The misanthrope and other plays. Signet Classics 2005 524p pa $7.95
Grades: 11 12 Adult   **842**
ISBN 0-451-52987-1; 978-0-451-52987-9
      LC 2006-276841
Contents: The misanthrope; The doctor in spite of himself; The miser; The would-be gentleman; The mischievous machinations of Scapin; The learned women; The imaginary invalid

Sartre, Jean Paul, 1905-1980
No exit, and three other plays. Vintage Bks. 1989 275p pa $12 *
Grades: 11 12 Adult   **842**
ISBN 0-679-72516-4   LC 89-40097
Contents: No exit; The flies; Dirty hands; The respectful prostitute
No exit is a modern morality play; The flies is a reworking of the Orestes-Electra story. The third play concerns a young Communist intellectual's attempt to maintain his integrity as party line changes and personal relationships alter perceptions of his murder of a party boss who had fallen out of favor, but whose memory is later rehabilitated. The last play concerns a prostitute's involvement in false charges of rape against a murdered black man and his companion in a town in the American South

842.009   French drama—History and criticism

Molière. Chelsea House 2003 122p (Bloom's major dramatists) lib bdg $22.95 *
Grades: 9 10 11 12   **842.009**
1. Molière, 1622-1673
ISBN 0-7910-7034-4   LC 2002-155108
For a complete list of series titles contact publisher
Includes a biographical essay, plot summaries, and critical interpretations of the plays and their characters.
Includes bibliographical references

844   French essays

Camus, Albert, 1913-1960
The myth of Sisyphus, and other essays; translated from the French by Justin O'Brien. Knopf 1955 212p pa $12.95 hardcover o.p. *
Grades: 11 12 Adult   **844**
ISBN 0-679-73373-6 (pa)
Personal reflections on the meaning of life and the philosophical questions surrounding suicide

848   French miscellaneous writings

Voltaire, 1694-1778
The portable Voltaire; edited, and with an introduction by Ben Ray Redmen. Viking 1949 569p pa $17 hardcover o.p. *
Grades: 11 12 Adult   **848**
ISBN 0-14-015041-2 (pa)
"The Viking portable library"
The selections from Voltaire's works include: Candide, part one; Three stories: Zadig, Micromegas, and Story of a good Brahmin; Letters, and selections from the Philosophical Dictionary and other works. The editor's introduction gives a biographical sketch of Voltaire.

850.9   Italian literature—History and criticism

The **Cambridge** history of Italian literature; edited by Peter Brand and Lino Pertile. Cambridge Univ. Press 1996 xxi, 701p map hardcover o.p. pa $36.99
Grades: 11 12 Adult   **850.9**
1. Italian literature—History and criticism
ISBN 0-521-43492-0; 0-521-66622-8 (pa)
                                        LC 95-50622
"Leading scholars describe and assess the work of a wide range of writers who have contributed to the Italian literary tradition from its earliest origins to the present day. . . . Translations are provided, along with maps, chronological charts, and . . . bibliographies." Publisher's note
"Contemporary readers will no doubt be delighted to learn more about such topics as the evolution of opera, compositions by Italian women writers, and the development of feminism." Choice

Ruud, Jay
Critical companion to Dante; a literary reference to his life and work. Facts on File 2008 566p il (Facts on File library of world literature) $75
Grades: 11 12 Adult   **850.9**
1. Dante Alighieri, 1265-1321
ISBN 978-0-8160-6521-9   LC 2007-33473
This title covers the works of Dante, including The Divine Comedy, La Vita Nuova, and his philosophical works.
"Ruud has written a useful introductory resource that students and lay readers alike can enjoy." Booklist
Includes bibliographical references

851   Italian poetry

Dante Alighieri, 1265-1321
The portable Dante; translated, edited, and with an introduction and notes by Mark Musa. Penguin Bks. 1995 xliii, 654p pa $17 *
Grades: 11 12 Adult   **851**
1. Poetry—By individual authors
ISBN 0-14-243754-9   LC 94-15988
First published 1947
This book "contains complete verse translations of Dante's two masterworks, The Divine Comedy and La Vita Nuova, as well as a bibliography, notes, and an introduction by . . . Mark Musa." Publisher's note
Contains complete verse translations of The Divine comedy and La vita nuova
Includes bibliographical references

Purgatorio; a new verse translation by W.S. Merwin. Knopf 2000 xxix, 359p hardcover o.p. pa $19.95
Grades: 11 12 Adult   **851**
1. Poetry—By individual authors
ISBN 0-375-40921-1; 0-375-70839-1 (pa)
                                        LC 99-40708
A translation of the central section of The divine comedy. "The 'Purgatorio' is the only section to take place on Earth, and it is also the most human and hopeful. In his introduction, Merwin confides that he has been reading Dante since his adolescence, and his reverence for the poet, his erudition, and the incredible elasticity and naturalness of his translation render this masterpiece (presented in its original Italian on facing pages) fresh and radiant." Booklist

860.3   Spanish literature— Encyclopedias and dictionaries

Concise encyclopedia of Latin American literature; editor, Verity Smith. Fitzroy Dearborn Pubs. 2000 xxi, 678p $75 *
Grades: 11 12 Adult   **860.3**
1. Latin American literature—Encyclopedias 2. Latin American literature—Bio-bibliography 3. Reference books
ISBN 1-57958-252-4
Based on the Encyclopedia of Latin American literature (1997)

Concise encyclopedia of Latin American litera-ture—*Continued*

Contains entries on 50 leading writers and 50 important works of Latin American and Caribbean literature. Also includes survey articles on the literature of individual countries and topical essays. Bibliographies of primary and secondary sources are listed

Includes bibliographical references

Dictionary of Mexican literature; edited by Eladio Cortés. Greenwood Press 1992 xliii, 768p $115

Grades: 11 12 Adult   **860.3**

1. Mexican literature—Dictionaries 2. Reference books
ISBN 0-313-26271-3   LC 91-10529

This volume contains "500 entries covering the most important writers, literary schools, and cultural movements in Mexican literary history. The 41 contributors include American, Mexican, and Hispanic scholars with assistance from some of the authors themselves." Libr J

Includes bibliographical references

860.8 Spanish literature— Collections

The **Tree** is older than you are; a bilingual gathering of poems & stories from Mexico with paintings by Mexican artists; selected by Naomi Shihab Nye. Simon & Schuster Bks. for Young Readers 1995 111p il hardcover o.p. pa $13.95 *

Grades: 7 8 9 10   **860.8**

1. Mexican literature—Collections 2. Bilingual books—English-Spanish
ISBN 0-689-82097-8; 0-689-82087-9 (pa)
                                    LC 95-1565

"This bilingual anthology of poems, stories, and paintings by Mexican writers and artists brims over with a sense of wonder and playful exuberance, its themes as varied and inventive as a child's imagination." Voice Youth Advocates

860.9 Spanish literature—History and criticism

Moss, Joyce, 1951-

Latin American literature and its times; [by] Joyce Moss, Lorraine Valestuk. Gale Group 1999 xxxix, 562p il (World literature and its times) $125

Grades: 11 12 Adult   **860.9**

1. Latin American literature—History and criticism
ISBN 0-7876-3726-2   LC 99-29292

"Highlights Latin American literature and Latino works 'produced in the United States.' Arrangement is alphabetical by title. Lengthy, informative essays discuss individual poems and fiction and nonfiction titles with a focus on the political, economical, social contexts in which the pieces were written. . . . Each essay concludes with a list 'For More Information.' Black-and-white photographs, movie stills, and reproductions are sprinkled throughout." SLJ

Includes bibliographical references

861 Spanish poetry

Borges, Jorge Luis, 1899-1986

Selected poems; edited by Alexander Coleman. Viking 1999 477p pa $20 hardcover o.p.

Grades: 11 12 Adult   **861**

1. Poetry—By individual authors
ISBN 0-14-058721-7 (pa)   LC 99-10318

"Poetry is the heart of Borges' metaphysical, mythical, and cosmopolitan oeuvre. . . . Editor Coleman commissioned a wealth of new translations for this unprecedented and invaluable collection, and the roster of translators includes such luminaries as Robert S. Fitzgerald, W.S. Merwin, Mark Strand, and John Updike." Booklist

Cid, ca. 1043-1099

The poem of the Cid; translated by Rita Hamilton and Janet Perry; with an introduction and notes by Ian Michael. Penguin 1984 c1975 242p map pa $14 *

Grades: 11 12 Adult   **861**

1. Poetry—By individual authors
ISBN 0-14-044446-7

Parallel Spanish text and English translation, with English introduction and notes

"The poem is based on the exploits of Rodrigo or Ruy Diaz de Bivar (c.1043-1099), who was known as 'el Cid.' . . . Similar in form to the 'Chanson de Roland,' the poem is notable for its simplicity and directness and for its exact, picturesque detail. Despite the inclusion of much legendary material, the figure of the Cid who is depicted as the model Castilian warrior, is not idealized to an extravagant degree." Reader's Ency. 4th edition

Neruda, Pablo, 1904-1973

The poetry of Pablo Neruda; edited and with an introduction by Ilan Stavans. Farrar, Straus and Giroux 2003 996p hardcover o.p. pa $20

Grades: 11 12 Adult   **861**

1. Poetry—By individual authors
ISBN 0-374-29995-1; 0-374-52960-4 (pa)
                                    LC 2002-32548

This volume contains translations of nearly 600 poems. "Arranged chronologically and often newly translated, the poems are sometimes accompanied by the Spanish original." Libr J

"Stavans has assembled the most complete anthology of Neruda yet available in English, drawing evenhandedly from the various stages of the poet's long and complex career. Neruda was, it seems, at least half a dozen poets, many of them in competition with the others. Needless to say, there are wonders in these pages that will delight readers unfamiliar with the tumultuously varied planet known as Neruda." Nation

Includes bibliographical references

Neruda, Pablo, 1904-1973—*Continued*

Selected odes of Pablo Neruda; translated, with an introduction by Margaret Sayers Peden. University of Calif. Press 1990 375p (Latin American literature and culture) pa $18.95 hardcover o.p.

Grades: 11 12 Adult **861**
1. Poetry—By individual authors
ISBN 978-0-520-26998-9 (pa)   LC 90-10707

"With the Spanish text and the English translation on facing pages, the beautiful odes of the great Chilean poet pay tribute to simple things in simple words, from bicycles and birds to his suit." Booklist

Twenty love poems and a song of despair; translated by W. S. Merwin; introduction by Cristina García; illustrations by Pablo Picasso. Penguin Books 2004 94p il pa $13 *

Grades: 9 10 11 12 **861**
1. Poetry—By individual authors
ISBN 0-14-243770-0   LC 2003-67611

Original Spanish edition 1924; this translation first published 1971 by Grossman Pubs.

This bilingual collection presents a series of poems that contains "sea and nature imagery that associates woman with the productive forces of Mother Earth." Choice

Includes bibliographical references

Paz, Octavio, 1914-1998

Selected poems; edited by Eliot Weinberger; translated from the Spanish by G. Aroul [et al.] New Directions 1984 147p pa $11.95 hardcover o.p.

Grades: 11 12 Adult **861**
1. Poetry—By individual authors
ISBN 0-8112-0899-0 (pa)   LC 84-9856

"The 67 well-chosen selections show Paz in his several phases and guises—in lyrics and prose poems, in long, free-form pieces and short, impressionistic works—a range of styles representing the best modes of East and West as practiced South over the last half-century. Many of the translations are by his peers (Elizabeth Bishop, Mark Strand, W. C. Williams)." Booklist

870.8   Latin literature—Collections

Atchity, Kenneth John

The classical Roman reader; new encounters with Ancient Rome; edited by Kenneth J. Atchity; associate editor, Rosemary McKenna. Oxford University Press 1998 xxxvi, 438p il pa $24.95 *

Grades: 11 12 Adult **870.8**
1. Latin literature—Collections
ISBN 0-19-512740-4   LC 98-29785

Also available The Classical Greek reader (1996)
First published 1996 by Holt & Co.

"Excerpts by well-known authors are here—Virgil, Horace, Ovid, Juvenal—but so too are nonartistic authors who exemplify Rome's characteristic emphasis on the practical over the abstract. . . . For those uninitiated to

Rome's written legacy but eager to meet it, this varied set of readings makes a memorable match." Booklist
Includes bibliographical references

The **Portable** Roman reader; edited, and with an introduction by Basil Davenport. Viking 1951 656p pa $18 hardcover o.p. *

Grades: 11 12 Adult **870.8**
1. Latin literature—Collections
ISBN 0-14-015056-0 (pa)

"The Viking portable library"

This anthology includes selections from Plautus, Terence, Caesar, Virgil, Seneca, Juvenal as well as complete plays by Plautus and Terence and the anonymous poem Vigil of Venus

870.9   Latin literature—History and criticism

Hamilton, Edith, 1867-1963

The Roman way. Norton 1932 281p pa $12.95 hardcover o.p. *

Grades: 11 12 Adult **870.9**
1. Latin literature—History and criticism 2. Rome—Civilization
ISBN 0-393-31078-7 (pa)

Companion volume to The Greek way

An interpretation of Roman life from the descriptions in the works of great writers from Plautus and Terence to Virgil and Juvenal.

871.008   Latin poetry—Collections

The **Roman** poets; selected and edited by Peter Washington. Knopf 1997 253p il (Everyman's library pocket poets) $12.50 *

Grades: 11 12 Adult **871.008**
1. Latin poetry—Collections
ISBN 0-375-40071-0   LC 98-124022

A representative selection of classical Latin verse.

873   Latin epic poetry and fiction

Ovid, 43 B.C.-17 or 18

Metamorphoses; [by] Ovid; translated and with notes by Charles Martin; introduction by Bernard Knox. W.W. Norton & Co 2004 xxvi, 597p $57; pa $17.95

Grades: 11 12 Adult **873**
ISBN 0-393-05810-7; 0-393-32642-X (pa)
     LC 2003-14491

"A series of tales in Latin verse. . . . Dealing with mythological, legendary, and historical figures, they are written in hexameters, in fifteen books, beginning with the creation of the world and ending with the deification of Caesar and the reign of Augustus." Reader's Ency. 4th edition

Includes bibliographical references

Ovid, 43 B.C.-17 or 18—*Continued*
Tales from Ovid; [translated by] Ted Hughes. Farrar, Straus & Giroux 1997 257p pa $14 hardcover o.p. *

Grades: 11 12 Adult   **873**
1. Poetry—By individual authors
ISBN 0-374-52587-0 (pa)   LC 97-36061

Hughes retells 24 Greco-Roman myths from Ovid's Latin epic *Metamorphoses*.

This is "an inspired act of translation that stands as vigorous poetry in its own right." N Y Times Book Rev

Includes bibliographical references

Virgil
The Aeneid; translated by Robert Fagles; introduction by Bernard Knox. Viking 2006 486p map $40 *

Grades: 11 12 Adult   **873**
1. Poetry—By individual authors
ISBN 0-670-03803-2   LC 2006-47220

Also available in paperback from Vintage and Cambridge Univ. Press

"The Aeneid is in twelve books: the first six in imitation of the Odyssey; the last six, of the Iliad. The Trojan hero is led to Italy, where he is to be the father of a race and of an empire supreme among nations. On his way thither he tarries at Carthage, whose queen, Dido, loves him as with the first love of a virgin. To her he tells the story of Troy. For love of him she slays herself when the gods lead him from her shores. Arrived in Italy he seeks the underworld, under the protection of the Sibyl of Cumae. He emerges thence to overcome his enemies." Keller. Reader's Dig of Books

878 Latin miscellaneous writings

Caesar, Julius, 100-44 B.C.
The Gallic War; with an English translation by H. J. Edwards. Harvard Univ. Press 1958 xxii, 616p il maps $21.50 *

Grades: 11 12 Adult   **878**
1. Rome—History
ISBN 0-674-99080-3

"The Loeb classical library"

Caesar's account of his campaign (58-50 B.C.) to bring the province of Gaul (France) under his control.

880.3 Classical Greek literature— Encyclopedias and dictionaries

The **Oxford** companion to classical literature; edited by M. C. Howatson. 2nd ed. Oxford Univ. Press 1989 615p il maps $65; pa $29.95 *

Grades: 11 12 Adult   **880.3**
1. Reference books 2. Classical literature—Dictionaries
ISBN 0-19-866121-5; 0-19-860081-X (pa)
LC 88-27330

First published 1937 under the editorship of Sir Paul Harvey

New edition in preparation

This work "covers classical literature from the appearance of the Greeks, around 2200 B.C., to the close of the Athenian philosophy schools in A.D. 529. It includes articles on authors, major works, historical notables, mythological figures, and topics of literary significance. Short summaries of major works, chronologies, charts, and maps are special features." Nichols. Guide to Ref Books for Sch Media Cent. 4th edition

Thorburn, John E., Jr.
The Facts on File companion to classical drama. Facts on File 2005 680p map (Facts on File library of world literature) $71.50

Grades: 11 12 Adult   **880.3**
1. Reference books 2. Classical drama—Encyclopedias
ISBN 0-8160-5202-6   LC 2004-16803

This "compendium covers ancient Greek and Roman drama from the 500s B.C.E. through 100 C.E. Approximately 400 alphabetical entries, ranging in length from one sentence to several pages, delve into plays, authors, characters, settings, genres, themes, theatrical terms, historical events, etc." SLJ

"It is difficult to think of any other resource quite this thorough that combines all of Greek and Roman drama into a convenient single-volume publication." Libr J

Includes bibliographical references

880.8 Classical Greek literature— Collections

The **Norton** book of classical literature; edited by Bernard Knox. Norton 1993 866p $29.95 *

Grades: 11 12 Adult   **880.8**
1. Greek literature—Collections
ISBN 0-393-03426-7   LC 92-10378

"A comprehensive volume of more than 300 pieces of classical literature, primarily Greek but also some Roman." Booklist

The **Portable** Greek reader; edited, and with an introduction by W. H. Auden. Viking 1948 726p pa $18 hardcover o.p. *

Grades: 11 12 Adult   **880.8**
1. Greek literature—Collections
ISBN 0-14-015039-0 (pa)

"Selections from representative Greek writers, from Homer to Galen, aimed at providing the reader with an introduction to all facets of Greek culture, rather than to its literature alone. Mr. Auden's preface deals chiefly with the various Greek concepts of the hero, in comparison with our own, and points up the immense differences between the two civilizations." New Yorker

880.9 Classical Greek literature— History and criticism

Ancient Greek literature; K.J. Dover, editor [et al.] 2nd ed. Oxford Univ. Press 1997 187p maps pa $21.95

Grades: 9 10 11 12   **880.9**
1. Greek literature—History and criticism
ISBN 0-19-289294-0   LC 98-120951

Ancient Greek literature—*Continued*
First published 1980

A historical survey of Greek poetry, tragedy, comedy, history, science, philosophy, and oratory from 700 BC to 550 AD. Passages from the works of principal authors are provided in translation.

Includes bibliographical references

Hamilton, Edith, 1867-1963
The Greek way. Norton 1943 347p pa $12.95 hardcover o.p. *
Grades: 11 12 Adult   **880.9**
1. Greece—Civilization
ISBN 0-393-31077-9 (pa)

Companion volume to The Roman way

First published 1930. Variant title: The great age of Greek literature

An account of writers and literary forms of the Periclean Age including discussions of Pindar, Aristophanes, Aeschylus, tragedy, Greek religion and philosophy

881.008   Classical Greek poetry— Collections

The **Oxford** book of classical verse in translation; edited by Adrian Poole and Jeremy Maule. Oxford University Press 1995 xlix, 606p $45 *
Grades: 11 12 Adult   **881.008**
1. Classical poetry—Collections
ISBN 0-19-214209-7

A "collection of classical verse from Homer to Boethius. Translations, modern and older, are brought together in a rich blending of Greek and Latin writings. Some of the greatest poets in the English language—Dryden, Pope, Tennyson, Poe, Byron, Yeats, Browning, Houseman, Wilde, Shelley, and Pound are among the translators. They emphasize the debt English poetry owes to the classics." SLJ

882   Classical Greek dramatic poetry and drama

Aristophanes
Lysistrata; translated, with notes and topical commentaries by Sarah Ruden. Hackett Pub. Co 2003 126p $24.95; pa $5.95
Grades: 11 12 Adult   **882**
ISBN 0-87220-604-1; 0-87220-603-3 (pa)
LC 2002-38750

This is a translation of Aristophanes' comedy with notes and commentary. "The 'topical commentaries' are essays on 'Athenian Democracy', 'Ancient Greek Warfare', 'Athenian Women', and 'Greek Comedy'. . . . The volume is topped off with a selected bibliography and an index to the commentaries." Classical Rev

882.008   Classical Greek dramatic poetry and drama—Collections

Seven famous Greek plays; edited, with introductions by Whitney J. Oates and Eugene O'Neill, Jr. Modern Lib. 1950 xxv, 446p pa $10 hardcover o.p. *
Grades: 9 10 11 12   **882.008**
1. Greek drama—Collections
ISBN 0-394-70125-9 (pa)

Contents: Prometheus bound and Agamemnon by Aeschylus; Oedipus the king and Antigone by Sophocles; Alcestis and Medea by Euripides; The frogs by Aristophanes

Includes bibliographical references

882.009   Classical Greek dramatic poetry and drama—History and criticism

Sophocles' Oedipus rex; edited and with an introduction by Harold Bloom. Updated ed. Chelsea House Publishers 2006 245p (Modern critical interpretations) $45 *
Grades: 11 12 Adult   **882.009**
1. Sophocles
ISBN 0-7910-9309-3; 978-0-7910-9309-2
LC 2006-25276

For complete list of series titles contact publisher

First published 1988

"This collection of essays draws upon a . . . history of criticism and commentary to examine the questions of fate, free will, heroism, and humanity that this powerful tragedy continues to provoke." Publisher's note

Includes bibliographical references

883   Classical Greek epic poetry and fiction

Homer
The Iliad; translated by Robert Fagles; introduction and notes by Bernard Knox. Viking 1990 683p $40; pa $15.95 *
Grades: 8 9 10 11 12 Adult   **883**
1. Poetry—By individual authors
ISBN 978-0-670-83510-2; 978-0-14-027536-0 (pa)
LC 89-70695

Homer's epic of the Trojan War.

"Fagles gives us a stark and terrible poem, an Iliad about, as its first word announces, rage. He conveys, far better than either Lattimore or Fitzgerald, the psychological experience of combat and war." Classical World

The Odyssey; translated by Robert Fitzgerald; with an introduction by Seamus Heaney. Knopf 1992 xxvii, 509p (Everyman's library) $21
Grades: 9 10 11 12 Adult   **883**
1. Poetry—By individual authors
ISBN 978-0-679-41047-8; 0-679-41047-3
LC 92-52903

Homer—*Continued*

Also available in paperback from Farrar, Straus and Giroux

This translation first published 1961 by Anchor Press/Doubleday

"An epic poem in Greek hexameters. . . . The 'Odyssey' is a sequel to the 'Iliad' and narrates the ten years' adventures of Ulysses during his return journey from Troy to his own kingdom, the island of Ithaca." Keller. Reader's Dig of Books

"Fitzgerald's new Odyssey . . . deserves to be singled out for what it is—a masterpiece." Nation

Includes bibliographical references

The Odyssey; translated by Robert Fagles; introduction and notes by Bernard Knox. Viking 1996 541p $35; pa $16 *
Grades: 8 9 10 11 12 Adult   **883**
1. Poetry—By individual authors
ISBN 978-0-670-82162-4; 978-0-14-026886-7 (pa)
LC 96-17280

This is a verse translation of Homer's epic poem

"Fagles' *Odyssey* is the one to put into the hands of younger, first-time readers, not least because of its paucity of notes, which, though sometimes frustrating, is a sign that translation has been used to do the work of explanation. Altogether, an outstanding piece of work." Booklist

Includes bibliographical references

Willcock, Malcolm M.

A companion to the Iliad; based on the translation by Richmond Lattimore. University of Chicago Press 1976 293p il maps pa $14 hardcover o.p.
Grades: 9 10 11 12   **883**
1. Homer—Iliad—Concordances
ISBN 0-226-89855-5 (pa)

"The notes here are directed mostly toward the explanation of words, expressions, and allusions in the text; but they also include summaries of books and sections, and assistance toward the appreciation of Homer's broader composition, by drawing attention to the implications of the narrative and the very effective characterization of the major heroes." Preface

Includes bibliographical references

883.009   Classical Greek epic poetry and fiction—History and criticism

Homer; edited and with an introduction by Harold Bloom. Updated ed. Chelsea House 2006 221p (Modern critical views) $45
Grades: 9 10 11 12   **883.009**
1. Homer
ISBN 0-7910-9313-1; 978-0-7910-9313-9
LC 2006-25325

First published 1986

For a complete list of series titles contact publisher

This book "explores Homer's transformative effect on epic and bardic poetry, as well as his narrative technique and use of language and meter." Publisher's note

Includes bibliographical references

888   Classical Greek miscellaneous

Aristotle, 384-322 B.C.

The basic works of Aristotle; edited, and with an introduction by Richard McKeon. Random House 1941 xxxix, 1487p $49.95; pa $19.95
Grades: 11 12 Adult   **888**
ISBN 0-394-41610-4; 0-375-75799-6 (pa)

Follows the Oxford translation of 1931

Contains entire texts of the following: Physica; De generatione et corruptione; De anima; Parva naturalia; Metaphysica; Ethica Nicomachea; Politica; De poetica

Includes bibliographical references

890   Other literatures

Ancient Egyptian literature; an anthology; translated by John L. Foster. University of Tex. Press 2001 272p hardcover o.p. pa $19.95 *
Grades: 11 12 Adult   **890**
ISBN 0-292-72526-4; 0-292-72527-2 (pa)
LC 00-61607

An anthology of ancient Egyptian poetry, stories, hymns, prayers, and wisdom texts. Includes a discussion of translation, as well as brief information about authorship and date of each selection

Includes bibliographical references

The **Literature** of ancient Egypt; an anthology of stories, instructions, and poetry; edited and with an introduction by William Kelly Simpson; with translations by Robert K. Ritner . . . {et al.}. 3rd. ed., rev. and expanded. Yale Univ. Press 2003 544p il pa $20
Grades: 9 10 11 12   **890**
1. Egyptian literature
ISBN 0-300-09920-7

First published 1973

This is a collection of ancient Egyptian literature, including writings from the late Demotic period

Includes bibliographical references

891   East Indo-European and Celtic literatures

Jalāl al-Dīn Rūmī, Maulana, 1207-1273

The essential Rumi; translated by Coleman Barks, with John Moyne, A.A. Arberry, Reynold Nicholson. Harper 1995 302p $23.95; pa $14.95
Grades: 11 12 Adult   **891**
1. Poetry—By individual authors
ISBN   978-0-06-250958-1;   0-06-250958-6;
978-0-06-250959-8 (pa); 0-06-250959-4 (pa)
LC 94-44995

A collection of ecstatic verse by the 13th-century Sufi mystic

Mahabharata.

The Mahābhārata; an English version based on selected verses; [translated by] Chakravarthi V. Narasimhan. rev ed, with a new preface. Columbia University Press 1998 xxix, 254p (Translations from the Asian classics) hardcover o.p. pa $25.50 *

Grades: 11 12 Adult   891
ISBN 0-231-02624-2; 0-231-11055-3 (pa)
Also available in an illustrated paperback edition from the University of California Press

"One of the two great epic poems of ancient India (the other being the 'Ramayana'), about eight times as long as the 'Iliad' and 'Odyssey' together. It is a great compendium, added to as late as AD 600, although it had very nearly acquired its present form by the 4th century. Covering an enormous range of topics, the Mahabharata, with its famous interpolation, the 'Bhagavadgita', has as its central theme the great war between the sons of two royal brothers, in a struggle for succession." Reader's Ency. 4th edition

Mahabharata. Bhagavadgita.

Bhagavad Gita; a new translation; [translated by] Stephen Mitchell. Harmony Bks. 2000 223p hardcover o.p. pa $13.95 *

Grades: 11 12 Adult   891
ISBN 0-609-60550-X; 0-609-81034-0 (pa)
                                        LC 00-28286
Hardcover and paperback editions also available from other publishers

"An eighteen-part discussion between the god Krishna, an avatar of Vishnu appearing as a charioteer, and Arjuna, a warrior about to enter battle, on the nature and meaning of life. Sometimes called the New Testament of Hinduism, it is an interpolation in the great Hindu epic the Mahabharata." Reader's Ency. 4th edition

Narayan, R. K., 1906-2001

The Ramayana; a shortened modern prose version of the Indian epic (suggested by the Tamil version of Kamban); introduction by Pankaj Mishra. Penguin Books 2006 157p (Penguin classics) pa $13 *

Grades: 11 12 Adult   891
ISBN 0-14-303967-9   LC 2006-45201
First published 1972

A retelling of Prince Rama's courtship of the fourteen-year-old Sita, their exile, Sita's abduction, the search, and the great battle with her abductor Ravana, involving a pantheon of gods, heroes, and evil spirits.

Omar Khayyam

Rubáiyát of Omar Khayyám; rendered into English verse by Edward FitzGerald; with illustrations by Edmund J. Sullivan. St. Martin's Press 1983 75p il $9.95

Grades: 11 12 Adult   891
ISBN 0-312-69527-6   LC 83-9767
Hardcover and paperback editions also available from other publishers

"The Rubaiyat' (Quatrains) of Omar the Tentmaker, of Persia, is composed of a series of stanzas forming 'a medley of love and tavern songs, tinged with Sufi mysticism, and with the melancholy of Eastern fatalism.'" Dickinson. Best Books Ser

891.7   East Slavic literatures. Russian

Chekhov, Anton Pavlovich, 1860-1904

The plays of Anton Chekhov; a new translation by Paul Schmidt. HarperCollins Pubs. 1997 387p pa $15.95 hardcover o.p. *

Grades: 11 12 Adult   891.7
ISBN 0-06-092875-1 (pa)   LC 96-42456
Contents: Swan song; The bear; The proposal; Ivanov; The seagull; A reluctant tragic hero; The wedding reception; The festivities; Uncle Vanya; Three sisters; The dangers of tobacco; The cherry orchard

Handbook of Russian literature; edited by Victor Terras. Yale Univ. Press 1985 558p pa $42 hardcover o.p.

Grades: 11 12 Adult   891.7
1. Reference books 2. Russian literature—Dictionaries
ISBN 0-300-04868-8 (pa)   LC 84-11871

"The volume includes entries on authors, genres, literary movements, and period studies, together with reviews of notable journals. The lengthiest entries run to more than 6,000 words, and the shortest have been kept to a single paragraph." Booklist

"A valuable resource for students, scholars, and general readers." Libr J

Includes bibliographical references

Malcolm, Janet

Reading Chekhov; a critical journey. Random House 2001 209p hardcover o.p. pa $13.95

Grades: 11 12 Adult   891.7
1. Chekhov, Anton Pavlovich, 1860-1904
ISBN 0-375-50668-3; 0-375-76106-3 (pa)
                                        LC 2001-19585

"The author's pilgrimage to Chekhov's Russia—Moscow, St. Petersburg, the gardens of his villa in Yalta—is a reunion with this most reticent of literary fathers. Malcolm analyzes the transformations that Chekhov grants his redeemable roués and guileless heroines, and illuminates the hidden surreality and waywardness of his realism." New Yorker

Includes bibliographical references

The **Portable** nineteenth-century Russian reader; edited by George Gibian. Penguin Bks. 1993 xxii, 641p pa $15.95 *

Grades: 11 12 Adult   891.7
1. Russian literature—Collections
ISBN 0-14-015103-6   LC 92-39863

This collection includes Pushkin's poem 'The Bronze Horseman'; Gogol's 'The Overcoat'; Turgenev's 'First Love'; Chekhov's 'Uncle Vanya'; Tolstoy's 'The Death of Ivan Ilych'; and 'The Grand Inquisitor' episode from

The Portable nineteenth-century Russian reader—*Continued*

Dostoyevsky's 'The Brothers Karamazov'; plus poetry, plays, short stories, novel excerpts, and essays by such writers as Griboyedov, Pavlova, Herzen, Goncharov, Saltykov-Shchedrin, and Maksim Gorky

The **Portable** twentieth-century Russian reader; edited with an introduction and notes by Clarence Brown. Rev. and updated ed. Penguin Books 1993 615p (Penguin classics) pa $18 *
Grades: 9 10 11 12   **891.7**
1. Russian literature—Collections
ISBN 0-14-243757-3   LC 2003-283124
First published 1985

This collection "includes stories by Chekhov, Gorky, Bunin, Zamyatin, Babel, Nabokov, Solzhenitsyn, and Voinovich; excerpts from Andrei Bely's Petersburg, Mikhail Bulgakov's The Master and Margarita, Boris Pasternak's Dr. Zhivago, and Sasha Solokov's A School for Fools; the complete text of Yuri Olesha's 1927 masterpiece Envy; and poetry by Alexander Blok, Anna Akhmatova, and Osip Mandelstam." Publisher's note

892 Afro-Asiatic literatures. Semitic literatures

Gilgamesh.
Gilgamesh; a new English version [by] Stephen Mitchell. Free Press 2004 290p $25; pa $14 *
Grades: 11 12 Adult   **892**
ISBN 0-7432-6164-X; 0-7432-6169-0 (pa)
LC 2004-50072
"Relying on existing translations (and in places where there are gaps, on his own imagination), Mitchell seeks language that is as swift and strong as the story itself. . . . This wonderful new version of the story of Gilgamesh shows how the story came to achieve literary immortality—not because it is a rare ancient artifact, but because reading it can make people in the here and now feel more completely alive." Publ Wkly
Includes bibliographical references

892.7 Arabic literature

Anthology of modern Palestinian literature; edited and introduced by Salma Khadra Jayyusi. Columbia Univ. Press 1992 xxxiii, 744p hardcover o.p. pa $30.50 *
Grades: 11 12 Adult   **892.7**
1. Arabic literature—Collections
ISBN 0-231-07508-1; 0-231-07509-X (pa)
LC 92-5189
"Presented here are translations of poems, stories, and excerpts from novels, as well as works by Palestinian poets who write in English. Also included are personal narratives by Palestinian writers depicting the varied aspects of Palestinian life from the turn of the century to the present. . . . Biographical sketches introduce the authors, and a chronology of modern Palestinian history provides background for some of the events and places referred to

in the selections. The introduction by the editor provides a concise but comprehensive political history of Palestinian literature during the twentieth century." Publisher's note
Includes bibliographical references

Night and horses and the desert; an anthology of classical Arabic literature; edited by Robert Irwin. Anchor Books 2001 462p pa $16 *
Grades: 11 12 Adult   **892.7**
1. Arabic literature—Collections 2. Arabic literature—History and criticism
ISBN 0-385-72155-2   LC 2001-53721
First published 2000 by Overlook Press

This "anthology presents a wide range of classical Arabic poetry and prose, covering the fifth to the 16th centuries from Afghanistan to Andalusia, Spain." Libr J
"The chapter on the Qur'an is perhaps the most essential as it examines just how vital the dogma of Islam has been for the Arabic understanding of culture and art. . . . This persuasive work will surely fill in the gap in the study of Arabic literature in this country." Publ Wkly
Includes bibliographical references

895.1 Chinese literature

Anthology of modern Chinese poetry; edited and translated by Michelle Yeh. Yale Univ. Press 1993 245p pa $21 hardcover o.p. *
Grades: 11 12 Adult   **895.1**
1. Chinese poetry—Collections
ISBN 0-300-05947-7 (pa)   LC 92-16322
Published with assistance from Mary Cady Tew Memorial Fund

"Arranged chronologically, this selection of twentieth-century poetry from China and Taiwan offers a few poems by each of 67 poets born between 1891 and 1963. Its scope is enormous, its range impressive. Editor Yeh's translations are accessible and fluid; her introduction and notes are helpful without being overbearingly scholarly." Booklist
Includes bibliographical references

Liu Siyu, 1964-
A thousand peaks; poems from China; [by] Siyu Liu and Orel Protopopescu; illustrated by Siyu Liu. Pacific View Press 2002 52p il $19.95 *
Grades: 5 6 7 8 9 10   **895.1**
1. Chinese poetry 2. Bilingual books—English-Chinese
ISBN 1-88189-624-2   LC 2001-34008
A collection of thirty-five poems spanning nineteen centuries, representing both famous and lesser-known poets, including both the Chinese text and a literal translation.

This "is an anthology of considerable fascination and broad utility. . . . The layout is neat, tidily fitting each poem's material on a single page and adding a line drawing featuring a relevant Chinese character. The wealth of material here provides a more stimulating entree to Chinese history than any dry textbook." Bull Cent Child Books
Includes bibliographical references

One hundred poems from the Chinese; {edited and translated} by Kenneth Rexroth. New Directions 1956 159p pa $11.95 hardcover o.p. *

Grades: 11 12 Adult   **895.1**

1. Chinese poetry—Collections

ISBN 0-8112-0180-5 (pa)

Also available: One hundred more poems from the Chinese pa $10.95 (ISBN 0-8112-0179-1)

"Nine poets, who lived centuries ago, speak with the poignancy of understatement of unchanging things; the brevity of life, the richness of friendship, the beauties of nature, the inevitability of old age and death." Booklist

Includes bibliographical references

The **Shorter** Columbia anthology of traditional Chinese literature; Victor H. Mair, editor. Columbia Univ. Press 2000 xxx, 741p map (Translations from the Asian classics) $65; pa $26

Grades: 11 12 Adult   **895.1**

1. Chinese literature—Collections

ISBN 0-231-11998-4; 0-231-11999-2 (pa)

LC 00-35878

Abridged version of Columbia anthology of traditional Chinese literature, published 1994

Texts translated from the Chinese

This "abridged volume, which, like the original includes selections of Chinese literature from the beginnings to 1919 . . . retains the characteristics of the original in that it is arranged according to genre rather than chronology and interprets 'literature' very broadly to include not just literary fiction, poetry, and drama, but folk and popular literature, lyrics and arias, elegies and rhapsodies, biographies, autobiographies and memoirs, letters, criticism and theory, and travelogues and jokes. It also contains fresh translations by newer voices in the field." Publisher's note

Includes bibliographical references

895.6   Japanese literature

Anthology of Japanese literature from the earliest era to the mid-nineteenth century; edited by Donald Keene. Grove Press 1955 442p il pa $14.50

Grades: 9 10 11 12   **895.6**

1. Japanese literature—Collections

ISBN 0-8021-5058-6

"UNESCO Collection of representative works: Japanese series"

"Covers the period from 712 A.D., when 'Record of Ancient Matters,' the earliest surviving Japanese book, was completed to about 1850. . . . The selections here include self-contained episodes from plays and novels (among them the classic 'The Tale of Genji'), fairy tales, short stories, and personal reminiscences, and numerous . . . poems." New Yorker

The **Classic** Noh theatre of Japan; [edited and translated] by Ezra Pound and Ernest Fenollosa. New Directions 1959 163p pa $10.95

Grades: 9 10 11 12   **895.6**

1. Nō plays

ISBN 0-8112-0152-X

A collection of classical Japanese No verse dramas, dealing with various aspects of social life and incorporating folklore

From the country of eight islands; an anthology of Japanese poetry; edited and translated [from the Japanese] by Hiroaki Sato and Burton Watson; with an introduction by Thomas Rimer; associate editor: Robert Fagan. Columbia Univ. Press 1987 xliv, 652p pa $29.50

Grades: 11 12 Adult   **895.6**

1. Japanese poetry—Collections

ISBN 0-231-06395-4   LC 86-7881

First published 1981 by University of Wash. Press

This anthology ranges "from the Kojiki (Record of Ancient Matters) . . . to a nineteenth-century transcript of a cycle of rice-planting songs, and from Kakinomoto no Hitimaro, [a] writer of elegies, who lived in the sixth century, to such recent poets as Tomioka Taeko. . . . Also included are Fujiwara no Teika's anthology of one hundred three 'tanka,' a no play, six sequences of 'renga' or linked verse, the 'frog matches' in which Basho participated, and some longer modern poems rendered in full." Publisher's note [1981 edition]

Includes bibliographical references

One hundred poems from the Japanese; {edited and translated} by Kenneth Rexroth. New Directions 1956 143p pa $11.95 hardcover o.p. *

Grades: 11 12 Adult   **895.6**

1. Japanese poetry—Collections

ISBN 0-8112-0181-3 (pa)

Also available: One hundred more poems from the Japanese pa $8.95 (ISBN 0-8112-0619-X)

A bilingual collection of poems drawn chiefly from the traditional Manyōshu, Kokinshū, and Hyakunin Isshu collections and also containing examples of haiku and other later forms. The translator's introduction provides background information on the history and nature of Japanese poetry

Includes bibliographical references

896   African literatures

The **Penguin** book of modern African poetry; edited by Gerald Moore and Ulli Beier. 4th ed. Penguin Books 2007 c1998 xxvi, 448p pa $17 *

Grades: 11 12 Adult   **896**

1. African poetry—Collections

ISBN 978-0-14-042472-0; 0-14-042472-5

First published 1963 in the United Kingdom with title: Modern poetry from Africa

This anthology includes over 200 poems by 67 poets from 23 countries.

Includes bibliographical references

Women writing Africa: the eastern region; edited by Amandina Lihamba . . . [et al.] The Feminist Press at the City University of New York 2007 xxv, 478p (Women writing Africa project) $75; pa $29.95
Grades: 11 12 Adult **896**
1. African literature—Collections 2. Literature—Women authors 3. East Africa
ISBN 978-1-55861-535-9; 1-55861-535-0; 978-1-55861-534-2 (pa); 1-55861-534-2 (pa)
        LC 2006-36534
This collection offers a "portrait of women's lives in Kenya, Malawi, Tanzania, Uganda and Zambia. These pieces span the centuries from 1711 to 2003, address topics ranging from religion to HIV and represent prose and poetry, fiction and nonfiction, lullabies and protest songs. . . . General readers who want to be entertained, educated and chastened about women's struggles and triumphs in east Africa will delight in this literary feast." Publ Wkly
Includes bibliographical references

Women writing Africa: the southern region; edited by M.J. Daymond {et al.}. Feminist Press 2002 xxx, 554p (Women writing Africa project) $75; pa $29.95
Grades: 11 12 Adult **896**
1. African literature—Collections 2. Literature—Women authors 3. Southern Africa
ISBN 1-55861-406-0; 1-55861-407-9 (pa)
        LC 2002-29483
This "resource brings together more than 120 selections by women in six countries of southern Africa, in English and in translation from more than 20 different languages, ranging from wedding songs and work songs to letters, prison diaries, poetry, memoirs, and recent testimony before South Africa's Truth and Reconciliation Commission. . . . The first in a projected series of four regional African collections, this is a must for women's studies and African history and literature collections." Booklist
Includes bibliographical references

Women writing Africa: West Africa and the Sahel; edited by Esi Sutherland-Addy and Aminata Diaw. Feminist Press 2005 477p (Women writing Africa project) $75; pa $29.95
Grades: 9 10 11 12 **896**
1. African literature—Collections 2. Literature—Women authors 3. West Africa 4. Sahel
ISBN 1-55861-501-6; 1-55861-500-8 (pa)
        LC 2005-50708
"This second of four volumes representing the literary expression of African women focuses on 12 West African nations, documenting the history of this expression since upward of six centuries before colonialism and 20th-century independence. . . . [The 132 texts compiled] showcase not just the written word—in the form of letters, diaries, historical documents—but the spoken word as well, in lullabies, songs, and other oral traditions. . . . This anthology provides an epic tale of African history while highlighting African women's valuable contributions to their culture and bringing their voices to life for readers everywhere." Libr J
Includes bibliographical references

897 Literatures of North American native languages

Coltelli, Laura, 1941-
Winged words: American Indian writers speak; [reported by] Laura Coltelli. University of Neb. Press 1990 211p il (American Indian lives) pa $9.95 hardcover o.p. *
Grades: 11 12 Adult **897**
1. American literature—Native American authors
ISBN 0-8032-6351-1 (pa) LC 89-39323
A compilation of interviews with Louise Erdrich, N. Scott Momaday, James Welch and eight other Native American writers.
"Coltelli's questions probe the writers' sources of inspiration, methods of composition, and perceptions of their own and their works' relationship to tribal culture, among other broad areas. But it's the questions Coltelli has tailored to each individual that hit pay dirt and result in some illuminating moments." Booklist
Includes bibliographical references

Coming to light; contemporary translations of the native literatures of North America; edited and with an introduction by Brian Swann. Random House 1994 801p pa $22 hardcover o.p.
Grades: 11 12 Adult **897**
1. Native American literature 2. American literature—Native American authors—Collections
ISBN 0-679-74358-8 (pa) LC 94-13457
"Swann has gathered intact texts from storytellers, singers, and orators. Arranged by region and tribe, each set of translations is prefaced by a lengthy introduction by the translator that sets the stories in context. The focus varies, depending on whether the translator is a linguist, anthropologist, or educator and whether he or she is a Native speaker, of which a fair number are. This wide-ranging collection goes far toward achieving Swann's goal of presenting a collection of reliable translations placed in their cultural and historical environments." Libr J
Includes bibliographical references

Returning the gift; poetry and prose from the first North American Native Writers Festival; Joseph Bruchac, editor, with the support of the Association for the Study of American Indian Literatures. University of Ariz. Press 1994 xxix, 369p (Sun tracks) pa $19.95 hardcover o.p.
Grades: 11 12 Adult **897**
1. Native American literature 2. American literature—Native American authors—Collections
ISBN 0-8165-1486-0 (pa) LC 94-4845
An "anthology of poetry and prose from the recent North American Native Writers' Festival, this provides a rich introduction to the diversity of contemporary Native writing in Canada and the U.S." Booklist

900   HISTORY

Freedman, Grace Roegner
Cracking the SAT. U.S. & world history subject tests; [by] Grace Roegner Freedman; revised by Dan Komarek, Casey Paragin, and Christine Parker. 2011-2012 ed. Random House 2011 449p (Princeton Review series) pa $19.99
Grades: 9 10 11 12   **900**
1. History—Study and teaching 2. Scholastic Assessment Test 3. Colleges and universities—Entrance requirements
ISBN 978-0-375-42816-6
Annual. First published 2005. Continues Cracking the S A T II: U.S. and world history subject tests
This guide provides test-taking strategies and sample tests on the subjects of both American and world history.

901   Philosophy and theory of history

The **Britannica** guide to theories and ideas that changed the modern world; edited by Kathleen Kuiper. Britannica Educational Pub. in association with Rosen Educational Services 2010 383p il (Turning points in history) lib bdg $45
Grades: 9 10 11 12   **901**
1. Modern civilization 2. Intellectual life 3. Science—History 4. Modern philosophy
ISBN 978-1-61530-029-7   LC 2009-48166
This book "covers the development of the sciences and arts with such topics as string theory, musical harmony, and contemporary democracy." Libr Media Connect
Includes glossary and bibliographical references

902   Miscellany of history

Grun, Bernard, 1901-1972
The timetables of history; a historical linkage of people and events. 4th ed. Simon & Schuster 2005 835p $25
Grades: 11 12 Adult   **902**
1. Historical chronology
ISBN 0-7432-7003-7; 978-0-7432-7003-8
LC 2005-49766
"A Touchstone book"
Original German edition, 1946; first published in the United States 1975
"Based on Werner Stein's Kulturfahrplan"
This chronology "includes material from 4500 BCE to 2004. . . . The information is listed by year in seven columns labeled 'History, Politics', 'Literature, Theater', 'Religion, Philosophy, Learning', 'Visual Arts', 'Music', 'Science, Technology, Growth', and 'Daily Life.' . . . This work is an excellent chronological tool, and should be found in all libraries." Choice

National Geographic concise history of the world; an illustrated timeline; edited by Neil Kagan. National Geographic Society 2005 416p il map $40 *
Grades: 11 12 Adult   **902**
1. Historical chronology
ISBN 0-792-28364-3   LC 2005-52248
This history is organized in time line format and broken up into eight historical eras. Includes maps, sidebars, and illustrations.
Includes bibliographical references

National Geographic visual history of the world; [authors, Klaus Berndl . . . et al.] National Geographic Society 2005 656p il $35 *
Grades: 11 12 Adult   **902**
1. World history
ISBN 0-7922-3695-5   LC 2005-541553
"Over 4,000 illustrations and photographs cover individuals and events from prehistory (the beginning to ca. 4000 BCE) to the contemporary world (1945 to the present). . . . This educational and entertaining volume of social, cultural, and military history will appeal to a wide readership." Choice

The **timetables** of American history; Laurence Urdang, editor; with an introduction by Henry Steele Commager and a new foreword by Arthur Schlesinger, Jr. Simon & Schuster [2001] c1996 534p il pa $24 *
Grades: 11 12 Adult   **902**
1. Historical chronology
ISBN 0-7432-0261-9
"A Touchstone book"
First published 1982
"A Laurence Urdang reference book" Verso of title page
Presents information chronologically in tabular form. Each double-page spread has columns for history and politics, the arts, science and technology, and miscellaneous.

The **Wilson** calendar of world history; edited by John Paxton and Edward W. Knappman; contributors: Rodney Carlisle [et al.] Wilson, H.W. 1999 460p il $100
Grades: 11 12 Adult   **902**
1. Historical chronology 2. Calendars
ISBN 0-8242-0937-0   LC 98-50998
"A New England Publishing Associates book"
"Based on S.H. Steinberg's Historical table." Title page
This successor to Steinberg's chronology reports on 25,000 historical events and includes expanded coverage of the arts and sciences as well as events in Latin America, Asia, and Africa. Includes index for people, places, events, concepts, inventions, discoveries, and titles of works.
Includes bibliographical references

903   Dictionaries, encyclopedias, concordances of history

Berkshire encyclopedia of world history; William H. McNeill, senior editor; Jerry H. Bentley [et al.] editorial board. Berkshire Pub. Group 2004 5v set $525

Grades: 11 12 Adult   **903**
1. Reference books 2. World history—Encyclopedias
ISBN 0-97430-910-9

This encyclopedia traces "the development of human history—with a focus on area studies, global history, anthropology, geography, science, arts, literature, economics, women's studies, African-American studies, and cultural studies related to all regions of the world." Publisher's note

Dictionary of historic documents; George Childs Kohn, editor; foreword by Leonard Latkovski. rev ed. Facts on File 2003 646p $75 *

Grades: 9 10 11 12   **903**
1. History—Sources—Dictionaries 2. Reference books
ISBN 0-8160-4772-3   LC 2002-73856
First published 1990

This dictionary provides "information about more than 2,400 significant historic documents in world history. Included are key acts, constitutions, proclamations, treaties, bills, laws, agreements, and speeches, among others, from ancient codes, such as Hammurabi's Code, to modern agreements and speeches, such as the Kyoto Protocol or President George W. Bush's 'Freedom and Fear Are at War' speech. . . . Each entry includes a concise summary describing the principal details of the document, its significance and historical context, as well as primary or secondary sources for further reference." Publisher's note

Encyclopedia of world history; edited by Marsha E. Ackermann . . . [et al.] Facts on File 2008 7v il map (Facts on File library of world history) set $650

Grades: 9 10 11 12 Adult   **903**
1. Reference books 2. World history—Encyclopedias
ISBN 978-0-8160-6386-4; 0-8160-6386-9
                 LC 2007-5158

Contents: v1 The ancient world: prehistoric eras to 600 C.E.; v2 The expanding world: 600 C.E. to 1450; v3 The first global age: 1450 to 1750; v4 Age of revolution and empire: 1750 to 1900; v5 Crisis and achievement: 1900 to 1950; v6 The contemporary world: 1950 to the present; v7 Primary documents; master index

"Alphabetically arranged entries explore the significant events, figures, and themes in world history." Publisher's note

"This set deserves a place on the shelves of every high school library." Voice Youth Advocates

Includes bibliographical references

The **modern** world; Sarolta Takács, general editor. M.E. Sharpe 2008 5v il map set $399

Grades: 7 8 9 10 11 12   **903**
1. Reference books 2. Modern civilization—Encyclopedias 3. World history—Encyclopedias
ISBN 978-0-7656-8096-9   LC 2007-44253

Contents: v1 Civilizations of Africa; v2 Civilizations of Europe; v3 Civilizations of the Americas; v4 Civilizations of the Middle East and Southwest Asia; v5 Civilizations of Asia and the Pacific

"This engaging, well-written set masterfully chronicles world history from 500 C.E. to the present, with a particular emphasis on how changes throughout the years helped shape contemporary society." SLJ

Includes bibliographical references

904   Collected accounts of events

Beyer, Rick
The greatest stories never told; 100 tales from history to astonish, bewilder, & stupefy. HarperResource 2003 214p il $17.95

Grades: 7 8 9 10   **904**
1. History—Miscellanea
ISBN 0-06-001401-6   LC 2004-296419
Based on the television program: Timelab 2000

"Beginning with the year 46 B.C. and ending in 1990, Beyer presents a chronological account of one hundred unknown, partially known, and familar tales about an array of people and events that have shaped the world. . . . They range from the mundane to the fantastic. . . . Extensive research went into the production of this charming work. Primary documents in the form of letters, laws, illustrations, and photographs bring to life these unique and incredible anecdotes." Voice Youth Advocates

Includes bibliographical references

Davis, Lee Allyn
Natural disasters; [by] Lee Davis. New ed. Facts On File 2008 464p (Facts on File science library) $75

Grades: 9 10 11 12   **904**
1. Natural disasters
ISBN 978-0-8160-7000-8; 0-8160-7000-8
                 LC 2007-50846
First published 1992

A worldwide survey of natural disasters throughout history. Over 500 alphabetical entries, organized by disaster type, cover a range of events, including: earthquakes, floods, typhoons, snowstorms, hurricanes, and tornadoes.

Includes bibliographical references

Davis, Paul K., 1952-
100 decisive battles; from ancient times to the present. Oxford University Press 2001 462p il map pa $19.95 *

Grades: 11 12 Adult   **904**
1. Battles 2. Military history
ISBN 0-19-514366-3   LC 00-49183
First published 1999 by ABC-CLIO

Surveys the one hundred most decisive battles in world history from the Battle of Megiddo in 1469 B.C. to Desert Storm, 1991. "Entries are approximately two thousand words long, limiting background details and confining the descriptions to the combatants, the histori-

Davis, Paul K., 1952-—*Continued*
cal setting, the battle itself, and the results. Each entry ends with a list of references used by the author in his research." Voice Youth Advocates

Includes bibliographical references

Diacu, Florin, 1959-
Megadisasters; the science of predicting the next catastrophe. Princeton University Press 2010 195p il $24.95
Grades: 9 10 11 12 Adult   **904**
  1. Natural disasters 2. Forecasting
ISBN 978-0-691-13350-8   LC 2009-29193

The author "presents a civilian-friendly guide to methods, like numerical modeling, used to understand, quantify, and possibly predict disasters. Written simply but without being simplistic, Diacu's text is driven by enthusiasm for his field and its potential for solving some of humanity's big problems." Publ Wkly

Includes bibliographical references

909 World history

Africana: the encyclopedia of the African and African American experience; editors, Kwame Anthony Appiah, Henry Louis Gates, Jr. 2nd ed. Oxford University Press 2005 5v set $550
Grades: 11 12 Adult   **909**
  1. Blacks—Encyclopedias 2. African diaspora—Encyclopedias 3. African Americans—Encyclopedias 4. Africa—Encyclopedias 5. Reference books
ISBN 978-0-19-517055-9; 0-19-517055-5
                                   LC 2004-20222
First published 1999 by Basic Civitas Bks.

This encyclopedia covers "prominent individuals, events, trends, places, political movements, art forms, business and trade, religions, ethnic groups, organizations, and countries on both sides of the ocean. . . . There are articles on contemporary nations of sub-Saharan Africa, ethnic groups from various regions of Africa, African American Academy award winners, Caribbean musical styles, African religions in Brazil, and European colonial powers." Booklist [review of 1999 edition]

Includes bibliographical references

Badcott, Nicholas
Pocket timeline of Islamic civilizations. Interlink 2009 32p il $13.95 *
Grades: 7 8 9 10   **909**
  1. Islamic civilization—Chronology 2. Reference books
ISBN 978-1-56656-758-9; 1-56656-758-0

"Badcott takes readers on a colorful and captivating tour of Islamic civilizations from the 7th to the 20th century. He discusses the rise and fall of dynasties, along with their achievements and contributions in art, medicine, architecture, commerce, and science. . . . The writing style is easy to read. . . . Attractive color photographs of buildings, pottery, jewelry, art, and inventions help maintain readers' interest throughout." SLJ

Includes bibliographical references

Boorstin, Daniel J., 1914-2004
The creators. Random House 1992 811p il hardcover o.p. pa $18.95
Grades: 11 12 Adult   **909**
  1. Civilization 2. Arts 3. Creation (Literary, artistic, etc.)
ISBN 0-394-54395-5; 0-679-74375-8 (pa)
                                   LC 91-39948
In this volume "Boorstin undertakes an interpretive history of creativity in Western civilization. Packed with shrewd, entertaining profiles of Dante, Goethe, Benjamin Franklin and dozens of others, this stimulating synthesis sets the achievements of individual geniuses into a coherent narrative of humanity's advance from ignorance." Publ Wkly

Includes bibliographical references

The discoverers. Random House 1983 745p hardcover o.p. pa $18.95
Grades: 11 12 Adult   **909**
  1. Civilization 2. Exploration 3. Science—History
ISBN 0-394-40229-4; 0-394-72625-1 (pa)
                                   LC 83-42766
The author "leads his reader through . . . anecdotal information of the discoveries of timekeeping, mapmaking, observations of nature, both large and small, and of insights into human social organizations, past and present, in this popularized, general history of 'mankind's need to know.'" Choice

Includes bibliographical references

The seekers; the story of man's continuing quest to understand his world. Random House 1998 298p hardcover o.p. pa $15.95
Grades: 11 12 Adult   **909**
  1. Civilization—History
ISBN 0-679-43445-3; 0-375-70475-2 (pa)
                                   LC 98-15430
Concluding volume of author's trilogy begun with The discoverers and The creators

"This is an account, generally chronological, of how the Western world's heritage of ideas of meaning and purpose was shaped by the thinking of the great philosophers and religious leaders from ancient times to the present. Until the rise of scientific thinking in the 17th century, Boorstin observes, answers were sought from history and human events, but in modern times, ideologies and dogmas overcame that way of thinking." Libr J

Includes bibliographical references

Cahill, Thomas, 1940-
The gifts of the Jews; how a tribe of desert nomads changed the way everyone thinks and feels. Talese 1998 291p (Hinges of history) $23.50; pa $14
Grades: 11 12 Adult   **909**
  1. Bible. O.T. —History of Biblical events 2. Judaism—History 3. Jews—History
ISBN 0-385-48248-5; 0-385-48249-3 (pa)
                                   LC 97-45139
In this colloquial look at the influence of the Hebrew Bible on civilization, the author gives "the Jews credit for revolutionizing the concepts of democracy, universal law, monotheism, linear time, personal vocation, destiny,

Cahill, Thomas, 1940-—*Continued*
self-improvement and the belief in the equality of all humans. He stumbles on the odd aside and occasionally is surprisingly insensitive. . . Still, his passion and breadth of knowledge are admirable." N Y Times Book Rev
Includes bibliographical references

Sailing the wine-dark sea; why the Greeks matter. Talese 2003 304p (Hinges of history) $27.50; pa $14.95
Grades: 11 12 Adult   **909**
   1. Greece—Civilization
   ISBN 0-385-49553-6; 0-385-49554-4 (pa)
                           LC 2003-50725
   This author "begins with a discussion of Homer's *Iliad* and *Odyssey* and how these two epic poems relate to the history of Greece. He then focuses on such themes as the Greek alphabet, literature, and political system, and its playwrights, philosophers, and artists. A final chapter examines the effects that Greco-Roman and Judeo-Christian traditions had on each other." Booklist
   Includes bibliographical references

The **Cambridge** illustrated history of the Islamic world; edited by Francis Robinson. Cambridge Univ. Press 1996 xxiii, 328p map (Cambridge illustrated history) hardcover o.p. pa $36.99
Grades: 11 12 Adult   **909**
   1. Islamic countries—History
   ISBN 0-521-43510-2; 0-521-66993-6 (pa)
                           LC 95-37562
   "Facts about Islam's history and practice are presented, along with its economic, societal, and intellectual structures. Excellent graphics support the text. Maps are extensive and exact." SLJ
   Includes bibliographical references

Cocker, Mark
Rivers of blood, rivers of gold; Europe's conquest of indigenous peoples. Grove Press 2000 416p il hardcover o.p. pa $16
Grades: 11 12 Adult   **909**
   1. Imperialism 2. Genocide 3. Colonies
   ISBN 0-8021-1666-3; 0-8021-3801-2 (pa)
                           LC 99-87927
   The author "looks in detail at the Spanish conquest of Mexico, the British near-extermination of the Tasmanian Aborigines, the white settlers' dispossession of the Apaches, and the German subjugation of the Herero and Nama of South-West Africa. Cocker shows that European imperialism involved the deaths of millions and the complete extinction of numerous distinct peoples." Booklist
   Includes bibliographical references

Daily life through world history in primary documents; Lawrence Morris, general editor. Greenwood Press 2009 3v il set $299.95 *
Grades: 9 10 11 12 Adult   **909**
   1. Reference books 2. Civilization—History—Sources
   3. Manners and customs—History—Sources
   ISBN 978-0-313-33898-4   LC 2008-8925

   Contents: v1 The ancient world / David Matz, volume editor; v2 The Middle Ages and Renaissance / Lawrence Morris, volume editor; v3 The modern world / David M. Borgmeyer and Rebecca Ayako Bennette, volume editors
   "Each of the three volumes . . . begins with a chronology of the era covered as well as a clear, concise historical overview that provides readers with core knowledge of the cultures discussed. The more than 530 entries are grouped into seven categories: domestic, economic, intellectual, material, political, recreational, and religious life." Booklist
   Includes bibliographical references

Encyclopedia of the developing world; Thomas M. Leonard, editor. Routledge 2005 3v set $625
Grades: 11 12 Adult   **909**
   1. Reference books 2. Developing countries—Encyclopedias
   ISBN 1-57958-388-1   LC 2005-49976
   The entries "detail developments from 1945 forward. In addition to basic statistical and geographical information, country-focused entries detail history, economy, and political situation. Thematic entries cover people (e.g., Jomo Kenyatta), historical topics (e.g., colonialism), economic and government models (e.g., communism), the environment (e.g., water) and organizations (e.g., WTO)." Libr J
   Includes bibliographical references

Encyclopedia of the Palestinians; edited by Philip Mattar. Rev. ed. Facts on File 2005 684p il map (Facts on File library of world history) $90 *
Grades: 9 10 11 12   **909**
   1. Reference books 2. Palestinian Arabs—Encyclopedias
   ISBN 0-8160-5764-8   LC 2004-57673
   First published 2000
   This book focuses on "Palestinian history, politics, and society from the late Ottoman period to the present. . . . [This is] the most objective reference compendium to treat Palestinian history as a subject in its own right." Choice
   Includes bibliographical references

Evans, Colin, 1948-
Great feuds in history; ten of the liveliest disputes ever. Wiley 2001 242p hardcover o.p. pa $15.95
Grades: 11 12 Adult   **909**
   1. History—Miscellanea
   ISBN 0-471-38038-5; 0-471-22588-6 (pa)
                           LC 00-43919
   This discusses the following feuds: Elizabeth I vs. Mary, Parliament vs. Charles I, Burr vs. Hamilton, Hatfields vs. McCoys, Stalin vs. Trotsky, Amundsen vs. Scott, Duchess of Windsor vs. Queen Mother, Montgomery vs. Patton, Johnson vs. Kennedy, Hoover vs. King.
   This places "emphasis on the global issues often at stake and how, for better or worse, the feuds changed history. Evans . . . captures all the drama and controversy in these streamlined accounts brimming with invigorated, well-paced prose." Publ Wkly
   Includes bibliographical references

Events that changed the world through the sixteenth century; edited by Frank W. Thackeray and John E. Findling. Greenwood Press 2001 223p il (Greenwood Press "Events that changed the world" series) $39.50
Grades: 9 10 11 12 **909**
1. World history—15th century 2. World history—16th century
ISBN 0-313-29079-2   LC 00-52132
This volume focuses "on the fifteenth and sixteenth centuries, with 10 events ranging from the *Reconquista* (circa 711-1492) to the defeat of the Spanish Armada in 1588." Booklist
Includes bibliographical references

Great events from history, The 17th century, 1601-1700; editor, Larissa Juliet Taylor. Salem Press 2005 2v il map set $160
Grades: 11 12 Adult **909**
1. Reference books 2. World history—17th century
ISBN 1-58765-225-0; 978-1-58765-225-7
    LC 2005-17362
Also available online
Companion volume to Great lives from history, The 17th century, 1601-1700
Some of the essays in this work were originally published in Chronology of European history, 15,000 B.C. to 1997 (1997) and Great events from history: North American series. Rev. ed. (1997)
This set "offers two to three-page essays that detail the major milestones of the century as well as social developments that were reflective of daily life during the period. The perspective here is international and spans a variety of categories, including religion and theology, cultural and intellectual history, expansion and land acquisition, and natural disasters. A list of key figures involved in each event is provided." SLJ
Includes bibliographical references

Great events from history, The Renaissance & early modern era, 1454-1600; editor, Christina J. Moose. Salem Press 2005 2v il map set $160
Grades: 11 12 Adult **909**
1. Reference books 2. Renaissance 3. World history—15th century 4. World history—16th century
ISBN 1-58765-214-5; 978-1-58765-214-1
    LC 2004-28878
Also available online
Companion volume to Great lives from history, The Renaissance & early modern era, 1454-1600
Some of the essays were previously published in various works
This collection of essays covers events in the scientific, intellectual, literary, sociological, political and military disciplines that happened worldwide during the Renaissance.
Includes bibliographical references

A **Historical** atlas of the Jewish people; from the time of the patriarchs to the present; general editor, Eli Barnavi; English edition editor, Miriam Eliav-Feldon; cartography, Michel Opatowski; new edition revised by Denis Charbit. new ed. Schocken Bks. 2002 321p il maps $45
Grades: 11 12 Adult **909**
1. Jews—History—Maps
ISBN 0-8052-4226-0   LC 2003-279553
First published 1992 by Knopf
"Covering three millennia of Jewish history and culture through a combination of concise text, accurate and well-drawn maps, and a sumptuous array of photographs, diagrams, and reproductions of paintings, this atlas succeeds in covering all the main themes of the Jewish experience. The material is arranged chronologically and systematically. . . . The result is a reference that will profit both scholars and lay readers." Libr J [review of 1992 edition]

The **Islamic** world; past and present; John L. Esposito, editor in chief . . . {et al.}. Oxford University Press 2004 3v il map set $325 *
Grades: 9 10 11 12 **909**
1. Reference books 2. Islam—Encyclopedias
ISBN 0-19-516520-9   LC 2003-19665
This book "contains more than 300 entries, ranging in length from a few paragraphs to several pages; many black-and-white photos; color inserts; numerous sidebars, including definitions of unfamiliar terms; an extensive bibliography; and (in each volume) a chronology, glossary, and list of 'People and Places.' The material is accessible, browsable, and current; topics treated include religion and history ('Prayer,' 'Prophets,' 'Crusades'), culture and customs, and political and social issues ('Architecture,' 'Clothing,' 'Intifadah,' 'Taliban,' 'Sexuality')." SLJ

James, Lawrence
The rise and fall of the British Empire. St. Martin's Press 1995 704p il hardcover o.p. pa $21.95
Grades: 11 12 Adult **909**
1. Great Britain—Colonies 2. Commonwealth countries—History
ISBN 0-312-14039-8; 0-312-16985-X (pa)
    LC 95-38774
First published 1994 in the United Kingdom
The author "*surveys* the major periods and events in Britain's rise and decline as a global power without attempting to be the definitive study of any one of those periods or events. . . . James' focus rests primarily on individuals—those who built the British Empire, those who maintained it, and those who, when it came time, eased it out of existence." Booklist

Milestone documents in world history; exploring the primary sources that shaped the world; Brian Bonhomme, editor in chief; Cathleen Boivin, consulting editor. Schlager Group 2010 4v il (Milestone documents) set $395 *
Grades: 9 10 11 12 Adult **909**

Milestone documents in world history—*Continued*

1. World history—Sources
ISBN 978-0-9797758-6-4
Also available online

This set "provides and analyzes 125 important primary-source documents and covers a broad range of world history—from the 2350 B.C.E. Reform Edict of Urukagina to 2000's Constitutive Act of the African Union—and targets all geographic regions. It includes influential documents such as Christopher Columbus's letter to Raphael Sanxis on the discovery of America, Martin Luther's 95 theses, Winston Churchill's 'The sinews of peace' speech, and the Northern Ireland peace agreement." Libr J

Includes glossary

Morgan, Michael Hamilton

Lost history; the enduring legacy of Muslim scientists, thinkers, and artists; [foreword by King Abdullah II of Jordan] National Geographic 2007 301p il map $26; pa $15.95

Grades: 11 12 Adult   **909**

1. Islamic civilization
ISBN   978-1-4262-0092-2;   1-4262-0092-7;
978-1-4262-0280-3 (pa); 1-4262-0280-6 (pa)
      LC 2007-7207

This "is an entertaining popular work that traces a vivid picture of the history of Arabo-Islamic scientific thought. Each chapter opens with a brief narrative passage in which present-day fictional characters of Eastern descent realize that something in their knowledge of themselves and of their history is missing. These vignettes are the starting point for Morgan's story of the Arabo-Islamic sciences and their legacy in modern Western societies." Chemical Heritage

Includes bibliographical references

Ochoa, George

The Wilson chronology of ideas; [by] George Ochoa and Melinda Corey. Wilson, H.W. 1998 431p $115 *

Grades: 8 9 10 11 12 Adult   **909**

1. Civilization—History 2. Philosophy 3. Reference books
ISBN 0-8242-0935-4   LC 97-17591

A chronological presentation of influential philosophical, political, theological and social thought from ancient times to the late 20th century. Sidebars feature profiles of celebrated thinkers

Includes bibliographical references

The **Oxford** encyclopedia of the Islamic world; John L. Esposito, editor in chief. Oxford University Press 2009 6v 3110p il map set $750

Grades: 10 11 12 Adult   **909**

1. Islamic countries—Encyclopedias 2. Islam—Encyclopedias 3. Reference books
ISBN 978-0-19-530513-5; 0-19-530513-2
      LC 2008-40486

"The encyclopedia's 1050 A-to-Z entries, written by an international community of 550 scholars, cover such topics as history, geography, law, religious belief, cul-

ture, politics, economics, and mysticism. . . . Written in clear, jargon-free language, this is a balanced, well-rounded, and evenhanded resource for both scholars and general readers interested in understanding Islam and its place in the world." Libr J

Includes bibliographical references

Pagden, Anthony

Peoples and empires; a short history of European migration, exploration, and conquest from Greece to the present. Modern library ed. Modern Lib. 2001 xxv, 206p hardcover o.p. pa $10.95

Grades: 11 12 Adult   **909**

1. World history 2. Colonies 3. Immigration and emigration
ISBN 0-679-64096-7; 0-8129-6761-5 (pa)
      LC 00-66204

"A Modern chronicles book"

This "overview of European empire building and colonization commences with the diffusion of Greek civilization and traces the subsequent evolution of the ensuing Roman, Spanish, French, and British empires. More interesting than how those empires physically expanded is the insightful discussion on what motivated individual men and entire nations to migrate and conquer." Booklist

Includes bibliographical references

Reformation, exploration, and empire. Grolier 2005 10v il map set $389

Grades: 6 7 8 9 10   **909**

1. World history—16th century 2. World history—17th century 3. Renaissance 4. Modern civilization 5. Reference books
ISBN 0-7172-6071-2

"This set describes a key period of Western history from approximately 1500 to 1700. The more than 240 entries provide a sense of the development of international trade, great cultural achievements, and the spirit of learning. . . . The layout is bright and colorful and features hundreds of illustrations, including maps, charts, tables, and more. Sidebars are plentiful and are used to highlight supplemental stories, information, and primary source materials." Booklist

Smith, Bonnie

Imperialism; a history in documents. Oxford Univ. Press 2000 175p il map (Pages from history) $32.95

Grades: 9 10 11 12   **909**

1. Imperialism 2. World history
ISBN 0-19-510801-9   LC 00-28552

The author "examines the 'high tide' of colonial imperialism, an era characterized by the expansion of European empires in Africa and Asia for financial gain and national power. She opens with background about the racial and economic rationales for imperialism, and then provides chapters about the rapid growth of empires, the role of technology and profits in imperialism, and its impact on the environment." SLJ

Includes bibliographical references

Smith, Tom, 1953-
Discovery of the Americas, 1492-1800. rev ed. Chelsea House 2010 134p il map (Discovery and exploration) lib bdg $35 *
Grades: 7 8 9 10 11   **909**
1. Explorers 2. America—Exploration
ISBN 978-1-60413-195-6; 1-60413-195-0
                                         LC 2009-22330
First published 2005
"This book on the initial exploration and discovery of the Americas covers such topics as Vasco Núñez de Balboa's sighting of the Pacific Ocean in 1513, Hernán Cortés's conquest of present-day Mexico, and the establishment of missions in present-day California by Father Junipero Serra during the late 18th century." Publisher's note
"The chapters are well-illustrated with color and black and white historic photos, illustrations and maps. Chapter layout is clearly organized with helpful subtitles; sidebars develop related themes in eye-catching colors." Libr Media Connect
Includes glossary and bibliographical references

Technology in world history; W. Bernard Carlson, editor. Oxford University Press 2005 7v il maps set $299
Grades: 7 8 9 10   **909**
1. Technology and civilization 2. Reference books
ISBN 0-19-521820-5; 978-0-19-521820-6
                                         LC 2003-55300
"Seeking to explore how people have used technology to shape societies, Carlson and 10 other scholars examine the distinctive development and effects of technology in 18 cultures—defined either geographically (Pacific Peoples, Sub-Saharan Africa) or by historical period (Stone Age, The World Since 1970)." SLJ
Includes bibliographical references

The **Third** World: opposing viewpoints; David M. Haugen, book editor. Greenhaven Press 2006 230p il lib bdg $34.95; pa $23.70
Grades: 11 12   **909**
1. Developing countries
ISBN 0-7377-2965-1 (lib bdg); 978-0-7377-2965-8 (lib bdg); 0-7377-2966-X (pa); 978-0-7377-2966-5 (pa)
                                         LC 2005-54544
"Opposing viewpoints series"
This book is a collection of essays on the problems facing Third World countries.
"This volume would be an excellent resource for more advanced students researching the subject or looking for debate topics." SLJ
Includes bibliographical references

909.07   World history—ca. 500-1450/1500

Andrea, Alfred J., 1941-
Encyclopedia of the crusades. Greenwood Press 2003 xxiii, 356p il, maps $75 *
Grades: 11 12 Adult   **909.07**
1. Reference books 2. Crusades—Encyclopedias 3. Europe—Church history—Encyclopedias
ISBN 0-313-31659-7   LC 2003-48544

This encyclopedia includes "more than 200 entries, each one between approximately 10 lines and four pages in length. . . . The introduction gives the entries some historical context and defines the term *crusade* for the reader. The entries are in alphabetical order and include cross-references in bold type to other entries in the book. Many entries also include suggested readings, both primary sources and historical studies. At the end of the work, the author has included a chronology of important dates and events, a 'Basic Crusade Library' of further readings in bibliographic essay style, and a general index. . . . This encyclopedia is recommended for high-school, undergraduate, and public libraries." Booklist
Includes bibliographical references

The **Crusades**; an encyclopedia; Alan V. Murray, editor. ABC-CLIO 2006 4v il map set $385 *
Grades: 11 12 Adult   **909.07**
1. Reference books 2. Crusades—Encyclopedias
ISBN 1-57607-862-0; 978-1-57607-862-4
                                         LC 2006-19410
This encyclopedia "surveys all aspects of the crusading movement from its origins in the 11th century to its decline in the 16th century." Publisher's note
Includes bibliographical references

Encyclopedia of society and culture in the medieval world; Pam J. Crabtree, editor in chief. Facts On File 2008 4v il map (Facts on File library of world history) set $360
Grades: 9 10 11 12 Adult   **909.07**
1. Reference books 2. Medieval civilization—Encyclopedias
ISBN 978-0-8160-6936-1; 0-8160-6936-0
                                         LC 2007-36571
"Covering the period from 476 to 1500, the encyclopedia contains 71 alphabetically arranged entries on a . . . range of topics. Examples include *Adornment, Education, Family, Gender structures and roles, Government organization, Inventions, Numbers and counting, Religion and cosmology,* and *Transportation.*" Booklist
"This well-organized resource covers a wide range of topics relating to medieval society. . . . A useful and important set." SLJ
Includes bibliographical references

Great events from history, The Middle Ages, 477-1453; editor, Brian A. Pavlac; consulting editors, Byron Cannon, . . . [et al.] Salem Press 2005 2v il map set $160
Grades: 11 12 Adult   **909.07**
1. Reference books 2. Middle Ages 3. Medieval civilization
ISBN 1-58765-167-X; 978-1-58765-167-0
                                         LC 2004-16640
Also available online
Companion volume to Great lives from history, The Middle Ages, 477-1453
Some essays were previously published in Great events from history (1972-1980), Chronology of European history: 15,000 B.C. to 1997 (1997), Great events from history: North American series, revised edition (1997), Great events from history: ancient and medieval series (1972), and Great events from history: modern European series (1973)

Great events from history, The Middle Ages, 477-1453—*Continued*

This set "offers 322 essays, beginning with Confucianism arrives in Japan (fifth or sixth century) and ending with Fall of Constantinople (May 29, 1453)." Booklist

Includes bibliographical references

Jones, J. Sydney

The Crusades, Primary sources; written by J. Sydney Jones; edited by Marcia Merryman Means and Neil Schlager. UXL 2005 c2004 xxvii, 179p il (The Crusades reference library) $63 *

Grades: 11 12 Adult   **909.07**

1. Crusades

ISBN 0-7876-9178-X   LC 2004-18001

This book "consists of 24 full or excerpted documents, first-person accounts, treaties, and speeches; the complete Magna Carta; and a section from the epic poem The Song of Roland. . . . All excerpts from the primary sources are followed by text that illuminates the history of the document and poses discussion questions." Booklist

Includes bibliographical references

Knight, Judson

Middle ages: almanac; edited by Judy Galens. U.X.L 2001 lxv, 226p il map (Middle Ages reference library) $60

Grades: 8 9 10 11 12   **909.07**

1. Middle Ages 2. World history 3. Medieval civilization 4. Reference books

ISBN 0-7876-4856-6   LC 00-59442

This reference's 19 chapters review world history from the fall of the Roman Empire in 500 A.D. to the beginning of the Renaissance in 1500 A.D.

"The volume's strength is its broad coverage; it includes material on India, Southeast Asia, China, Japan, the Americas, and Africa as well as Europe and the Middle East, making it unique among other books for this age group." SLJ

Includes bibliographical references

The **Middle** Ages, 600 to 1492; edited by Helen Dwyer. Brown Bear Books 2009 102p map (Curriculum connections. Atlas of world history) lib bdg $39.95

Grades: 9 10 11 12   **909.07**

1. Middle Ages 2. Medieval civilization 3. Europe—History—476-1492

ISBN 978-1-933834-67-2   LC 2009-27835

Contents: The world in 800 CE; The world in 1000; The world in 1279; The world in 1492; World religions; The Carolingian empire; Viking age Europe; Feudal Europe; War, revolt, and plague; Economy of medieval Europe; Renaissance Europe; Arab conquests; The Arab world divided; The Byzantine Empire; Medieval Turkish empires; The crusades; Africa; Medieval India; Sui and Tang China; Song China; The Mongol empire; The breakup of the Mongol empire; Medieval Japan and Korea; Kingdoms of Southeast Asia; Native cultures of North America; Toltecs and Aztecs; Andean civilizations

This book "is divided into thematic and regional maps which are followed by short but very comprehensive arti-

cles. . . . [It includes] curriculum context sidebars, important terms students should know, and how the topic ties into other areas." Libr Media Connect

Includes bibliographical references

Middle ages: primary sources; [compiled by] Judson Knight; Judy Galens, editor. U.X.L 2000 xxxiv, 161p il (Middle Ages reference library) $60 *

Grades: 8 9 10 11 12   **909.07**

1. Middle Ages

ISBN 0-7876-4860-4   LC 00-59441

This volume contains "19 full or excerpted documents written during this period, including the work of celebrated writers such as St. Augustine, Marco Polo, and Dante as well as less familiar individuals such as Anna Comnena and Lo Kuan-chung. Each selection is placed in its historical context and followed by a section entitled 'What happened next'. . . . Unfamiliar words or terms are defined in sidebars. Each entry has a box profiling the author of the documents and at least two illustrations." Booklist

Includes bibliographical references

O'Neal, Michael, 1949-

The Crusades, Almanac; written by Michael J. O'Neal; edited by Marcia Merryman Means and Neil Schlager. UXL 2005 c2004 xxv, 207p il (The Crusades reference library) $63

Grades: 11 12 Adult   **909.07**

1. Crusades

ISBN 0-7876-9176-3   LC 2004-18003

This book "discusses such topics as the conquering of Jerusalem by the caliph Umar, pilgrimages to the Holy Land, the traditions of chivalry, and territorial expansion and colonization as motivations for the Crusades. Its explanation of the difference and divisions between Sunni and Shiite Islam alone is useful reading for a wider audience." Booklist

Includes bibliographical references

The **Oxford** illustrated history of the Crusades; edited by Jonathan Riley-Smith. Oxford Univ. Press 1995 436p il maps hardcover o.p. pa $26.50 *

Grades: 11 12 Adult   **909.07**

1. Crusades

ISBN 0-19-820435-3; 0-19-285428-3 (pa)

LC 94-24229

Also available non-illustrated edition with title: The Oxford history of the Crusades pa $18.95 (ISBN: 0-19-280312-3)

Scholars explore the complex religious, economic, and military aspects of the Crusades.

Includes bibliographical references

909.08   Modern history, 1450/1500-

The **early** modern world, 1492 to 1783; [editor, Helen Dwyer] Brown Bear Books 2009 112p map (Curriculum connections. Atlas of world history) lib bdg $39.95

Grades: 9 10 11 12   **909.08**
1. Modern history 2. World history—16th century 3. World history—17th century 4. World history—18th century

ISBN 978-1-933834-68-9   LC 2009-27836

Contents: The world in 1530; The world in 1600; The world in 1650; The world in 1715; The world in 1783; Reformation Europe Counter-Reformation Europe; Sweden and the Baltic; The Thirty Years' War; Europe and Louis XIV; European economy; Russian expansion; The ancien regime; The rise of the Ottoman Empire; The decline of the Ottoman empire; Asia and the Safavids; Sub-Saharan Africa; The rise of Mughal India; The successors to Mughal India; Ming China; The rise of Manchu China; Japan and the shogunate; Southeast Asia; The Spanish-American empire; Europeans in North America; Colonial North America; The American Revolution

This book "is divided into thematic and regional maps which are followed by short but very comprehensive articles. . . . [It includes] curriculum context sidebars, important terms students should know, and how the topic ties into other areas." Libr Media Connect

Includes bibliographical references

Gonick, Larry

The cartoon history of the modern world; Part 1: from Columbus to the U.S. Constitution. Collins 2007 259p il pa $17.95

Grades: 9 10 11 12 Adult   **909.08**
1. Graphic novels 2. Modern history—Graphic novels
ISBN 978-0-06-076004-5; 0-06-076004-4
                                    LC 2006-49146

The book begins with a "15-page distillation of pre-Columbian America; and while Europe and North America receive most of the attention, Gonick does include at least some highlights from other parts of the world. Covering such topics as the Protestant Reformation, the British defeat of the Spanish Armada, the Copernican model of the universe, and the American Revolution, he writes and draws with considerable wit and authority, and is obviously well versed in his subject." SLJ

The **Oxford** encyclopedia of the modern world; Peter N. Stearns, editor in chief. Oxford University Press 2008 8v il set $1,255

Grades: 9 10 11 12 Adult   **909.08**
1. Reference books 2. Modern history—Encyclopedias 3. Modern civilization—Encyclopedias
ISBN 978-0-19-517632-2; 0-19-517632-4
                                    LC 2007-39891

This "encyclopedia covers world history from the middle of the 18th century (i.e., the Industrial Revolution) to the present (including Benazir Bhutto's 2007 assassination)." Libr J

"This comprehensive and outstanding resource covers much more than Western civilization. It presents a balanced, inclusive perspective on historical, social, political, and economic issues that students will need in order to function in a global society. . . . Ideal for social studies classes that need well-written and researched information with a global perspective." SLJ

Includes bibliographical references

Tuchman, Barbara Wertheim

The march of folly; from Troy to Vietnam; [by] Barbara W. Tuchman. Knopf 1984 447p il pa $16.95 hardcover o.p.

Grades: 11 12 Adult   **909.08**
1. Modern history
ISBN 0-345-30823-9 (pa)   LC 83-22206

The author analyzes examples of governmental bumbling including the Trojan horse, the U.S. involvement in Vietnam, and the British loss of the American colonies.

Includes bibliographical references

909.7   World history—18th century, 1700-1799

Great events from history, The 18th century, 1701-1800; editor John Powell. Salem Press 2006 2v il map set $160

Grades: 11 12 Adult   **909.7**
1. Reference books 2. World history—18th century
ISBN 978-1-58765-279-0; 1-58765-279-X
                                    LC 2006-5406

Also available online

Companion volume to Great lives from history, The 18th century, 1701-1800

Some essays previously published in Great events from history: North American series (1997) and Chronology of European history (1997)

"Topics include geopolitical events, social and intellectual issues, scientific developments, philosophy, and the arts. The global coverage emphasizes turning points that redirected and shaped history and helped create the modem world. Essays have an average length of 1600 words. Each one begins with a short summary of the topic and includes dates, locales, categories, key figures, text, significance, further reading, see-also references, and cross-referencing to other essays in this set and in the rest of the series. . . . An informative resource." SLJ

Includes bibliographical references

909.81   World history—19th century, 1800-1899

Great events from history, The 19th century, 1801-1900; editor, John Powell. Salem Press 2006 4v il map set $360

Grades: 11 12 Adult   **909.81**
1. Reference books 2. World history—19th century
ISBN 978-1-58765-297-4; 1-58765-297-8
                                    LC 2006-19789

Also available online

Companion volume to Great lives from history, The 19th century, 1801-1900

Some of the essays in this work appeared in various other Salem Press sets

Great events from history, The 19th century, 1801-1900—*Continued*

"These volumes cover the world's most important events and developments from 1801 through 1900. . . . Essays address important social and cultural developments in daily life: major literary movements, significant developments in art and music, trends in immigration, and progressive social legislation." Publisher's note

Includes bibliographical references

909.82 World history—20th century, 1900-1999

1900-1920: the twentieth century; Gary Zacharias, book editor. Greenhaven Press 2004 224p il map (Events that changed the world) lib bdg $34.95
Grades: 7 8 9 10 11 12   909.82
1. World history—20th century
ISBN 0-7377-1752-1   LC 2003-48332

"The period from 1900-1920 marked not only the beginning of a new century but also the seed of many trends and movements that would bear fruit throughout the rest of the 20th century. This book covers major events of this time period, including wars, theories, inventions, disasters, and revolutions." Publisher's note

"There's plenty to intrigue history students, who will relish seeing disparate pieces of history slide smoothly together." Booklist

Includes bibliographical references

1920-1940: the twentieth century; Sharon M. Himsl, book editor. Greenhaven Press 2004 204p il (Events that changed the world) lib bdg $34.95
Grades: 7 8 9 10 11 12   909.82
1. World history—20th century
ISBN 0-7377-1754-8   LC 2003-44864

"Ratification of Nineteenth Amendment, first assembly of League of Nations, . . . Mussolini's March on Rome, Lindbergh's transatlantic flight, Jazz Singer debut, Gandhi's 'Salt March,' Hitler's rise, stock market crash, and 'Operation Dynamo' (rescue at Dunkirk) are among the events discussed, describing a . . . period that begins with the aftermath of World War I and ends with the outbreak of World War II." Publisher's note

Includes bibliographical references

1940-1960: the twentieth century; Jennifer Bussey, book editor. Greenhaven Press 2004 188p il (Events that changed the world) lib bdg $34.95
Grades: 7 8 9 10 11 12   909.82
1. World history—20th century
ISBN 0-7377-1756-4   LC 2002-192798

"The world in 1960 was a very different place than it had been in 1940. . . . How did so much change unfold in twenty years' time? This anthology retraces those fateful footsteps, presenting articles about events spanning from the attack on Pearl Harbor to the launch of Sputnik." Publisher's note

"Several articles (e.g., an excerpt describing the killing of unarmed German guards by concentration camp liberators) are vivid enough to disturb some readers. . . .

There's plenty to intrigue history students, who will relish seeing disparate pieces of history slide smoothly together." Booklist

Includes bibliographical references

1960-1980: the twentieth century; Jennifer A. Bussey, book editor. Greenhaven Press 2004 176p il (Events that changed the world) lib bdg $34.95
Grades: 7 8 9 10 11 12   909.82
1. World history—20th century
ISBN 0-7377-1758-0   LC 2003-53929

"This anthology covers the major events that shaped the world during the pivotal decades of the 1960s and 1970s. Topics covered include the Bay of Pigs invasion, the building of the Berlin Wall, U.S. president Kennedy's assassination, the first moon landing, the U.S. legalization of abortion, the Vietnam War, and the Ayatollah Khomeini's deposition of the shah of Iran." Publisher's note

Includes bibliographical references

1980-2000: the twentieth century; Bryan Grapes, book editor. Greenhaven Press 2004 187p il map (Events that changed the world) lib bdg $34.95
Grades: 7 8 9 10 11 12   909.82
1. World history—20th century
ISBN 0-7377-1760-2   LC 2003-53928

"This anthology follows the 1980s and 1990s as the world moved through the rise of the AIDS epidemic, the fall of the Berlin Wall and the demise of communism in Eastern Europe, the death of the Soviet Union, and the rise of the computer age. Also covered in this volume: The birth of MTV, the nuclear disaster at Chernobyl, the Chinese government's bloody crackdown in Tiananmen Square, the death of apartheid, the dissolution of Yugoslavia, and the cloning of Dolly." Publisher's note

Includes bibliographical references

Cold War; a student encyclopedia; Spencer C. Tucker, volume editor; Priscilla Roberts, editor, documents volume; Paul G. Pierpaoli, Jr., associate editor; Timothy C. Dowling, Gordon E. Hogg, Priscilla Roberts, assistant editors; personal perspective foreword by John S.D. Eisenhower. ABC-CLIO 2007 5v il map set $495
Grades: 9 10 11 12   909.82
1. Reference books 2. Cold war—Encyclopedias 3. World politics—1945—Encyclopedias
ISBN 978-1-85109-847-7   LC 2007-19820

Entries in this encyclopedia "focus on the years 1945 through 1995 and will help students understand the conflicts, the arms race, and the tense climate between the superpowers and their allies. . . . Volume five contains 171 primary-source documents, each preceded by an introduction to help readers grasp the situation surrounding the document's creation. Back matter includes the rank structure for selected Cold War militaries, brief country profiles, and essays on how to read primary sources, maps, charts, tables, and graphs. The comprehensiveness and clarity of this work make it a useful resource." SLJ

Includes bibliographical references

Encyclopedia of conflicts since World War II; edited by James Ciment. 2nd ed. M.E. Sharpe 2007 4v set $439
Grades: 11 12 Adult **909.82**
1. Reference books 2. World politics—1945—Encyclopedias
ISBN 978-0-7656-8005-1; 0-7656-8005-X
LC 2006-14011
First published 1999
This "reference presents descriptions and analyses of more than 170 significant post-World War II conflicts around the globe." Publisher's note
"The illustrations are strong and the maps helpful, and the thumbnail biographies and glossary are useful. A valuable resource for most school and public libraries." SLJ
Includes bibliographical references

Gaddis, John Lewis
The Cold War; a new history. Penguin Press 2005 333p il hardcover o.p. pa $16
Grades: 11 12 Adult **909.82**
1. Cold war 2. World politics—1945-1991
ISBN 1-594-20062-9; 0-14-303827-3 (pa)
LC 2005-53406
The authors "account of Soviet-U.S. relations from WWII to the collapse of the U.S.S.R." Publ Wkly
"Energetically written and lucid, . . . [this book] makes an ideal introduction to the subject." N Y Times (Late N Y Ed)
Includes bibliographical references

Great events from history: The 20th century, 1901-1940; editor, Robert F. Gorman. Salem Press 2007 6v il map set $495
Grades: 11 12 Adult **909.82**
1. Reference books 2. World history—20th century
ISBN 978-1-58765-324-7; 1-58765-324-9
LC 2007-1930
Also available online
Some of the essays in this work originally appeared in various Salem Press publications
This work "identifies key events that helped to shape the course of the history of the world from 1901 to 1940. In more than 1,000 essays, a plethora of topics are presented, including Canada claiming the Arctic Islands (1901); the plague killing 1.2 million in India (1907); Gertrude Ederle swimming the English Channel (1926); Stalin beginning the Purge Trials (1934); and Germany hosting the 1936 Olympics." Booklist
"This set provides access to clear, objective information, especially on topics in the sciences and mathematics." Libr J
Includes bibliographical references

Great events from history: The 20th century, 1941-1970; editor, Robert F. Gorman. Salem Press 2008 6v il map set $495
Grades: 11 12 Adult **909.82**
1. Reference books 2. World history—20th century
ISBN 978-1-58765-331-5; 1-58765-331-1
LC 2007-37204
Also available online
Some of the essays in this work originally appeared in various Salem Press publications

The articles in this set "cover everything from the bombing of Pearl Harbor to the celebration of the First Earth Day. Each article lists a locale, key figures, categories, and a summary of events; readers can search for additional information based on categories or key figures. The sixth volume contains a bibliography, personage, subject, category, and geographical indexes and a chronological list of entries. . . . An excellent cross-reference tool." Libr J
Includes bibliographical references

Great events from history: The 20th century, 1971-2000; editor, Robert F. Gorman. Salem Press 2008 6v il map set $495
Grades: 11 12 Adult **909.82**
1. Reference books 2. World history—20th century
ISBN 978-1-58765-338-4; 1-58765-338-9
LC 2007-51351
Also available online
Some of the essays originally appeared in other Salem Press sets
This set "provides extended coverage of 1,083 major events between 1971 and 2000." Publisher's note
Includes bibliographical references

Hillstrom, Kevin
The Cold War; foreward by Christian Ostermann. Omnigraphics 2006 xx, 536p il (Primary sourcebook series) $65
Grades: 11 12 Adult **909.82**
1. Cold war 2. World politics—1945-1991
ISBN 0-7808-0934-3; 978-0-7808-0934-5
LC 2006-15330
"Examines the Cold War and its impact on America, the Soviet Union, and the world. Features include narrative overviews of key events and trends, 100+ primary source documents, chronology, glossary, bibliography, and subject index." Publisher's note
"The wide-ranging scope of documents compiled in this volume will provide AP history and social studies classes with a wealth of information for research and analysis." Libr Media Connect
Includes glossary and bibliographical references

Kallen, Stuart A., 1955-
Primary sources. Lucent Bks. 2003 112p il map (American war library, Cold War) $27.45 *
Grades: 8 9 10 11 12 **909.82**
1. Cold war 2. United States—Foreign relations—Soviet Union 3. Soviet Union—Foreign relations—United States
ISBN 1-59018-243-X
LC 2002-7896
This "contains documents and essays relating to the Cold War written by some of its key players including diplomats, ambassadors, presidents, and premiers." Publisher's note
Includes bibliographical references

Kaufman, Michael T.

1968. Roaring Brook Press 2009 148p il $22.95
*

Grades: 7 8 9 10 11 12   **909.82**
1. World history—20th century
ISBN 978-1-59643-428-8; 1-59643-428-7
           LC 2008-15471

Kaufman "expertly draws young readers into the worldwide events of a single, watershed year: 1968. . . . Each chapter focuses on a different hot spot around the globe, beginning with the Tet Offensive and the Vietnam War and moving through uprisings in New York, Paris, Prague, Chicago, and Mexico City, as well as the assassinations of Martin Luther King Jr. and Robert F. Kennedy. . . . The images, drawn from the *[New York] Times* archives, are riveting and will easily draw young people into the fascinating, often horrifying events." Booklist

Palmowski, Jan

A dictionary of contemporary world history; from 1900 to the present day. 3rd ed. Oxford University Press 2008 767p il map $50; pa $16.95
*

Grades: 9 10 11 12 Adult   **909.82**
1. Modern history—Dictionaries 2. Reference books
ISBN 978-0-19-929567-8; 978-0-19-929566-1 (pa)
           LC 2008-273688

First published 1997 with title: A dictionary of twentieth-century world history

This dictionary's "2500-plus entries are clear and concise and cover everything from world leaders, both past and present, to . . . information on all the world's nations. . . . [This is a] simple and easy-to-use research tool." Libr J

Tuchman, Barbara Wertheim

The proud tower; a portrait of the world before the war, 1890-1914; [by] Barbara W. Tuchman. 1st Ballantine Books ed. Ballantine Books 1996 528p il pa $15.95

Grades: 11 12 Adult   **909.82**
1. World history—20th century 2. World history—19th century 3. Europe—Social conditions 4. United States—Social conditions
ISBN 0-345-40501-3   LC 96-96511

First published 1966 by Macmillan

The author describes prewar social conditions in the U.S., France, England and Germany.

Includes bibliographical references

Winkler, Allan M., 1945-

The Cold War; a history in documents. Oxford Univ. Press 2000 159p il map (Pages from history) $39.95; pa $22.95 *

Grades: 8 9 10 11 12   **909.82**
1. Cold war 2. United States—Foreign relations—Soviet Union 3. Soviet Union—Foreign relations—United States
ISBN 0-19-512356-5; 0-19-516637-X (pa)
           LC 00-27270

New edition in preparation

Uses contemporary documents to explore the Cold War struggle of the 1950s and 1960s and the lasting effects on American social and cultural patterns

Includes bibliographical references

World wars and globalization, 1914 to 2010; edited by Louise Spilsbury. Brown Bear Books 2010 112p map (Curriculum connections. Atlas of world history) lib bdg $39.95

Grades: 9 10 11 12   **909.82**
1. Modern history 2. World history—20th century 3. Globalization
ISBN 978-1-933834-70-2   LC 2009-27838

Contents: Introduction; The world in 1920; The world in 1950; The world in 1974; The world in 2005; World War I; Interwar Europe; World War II in Europe to 1942; World War II in Europe 1942-1945; Europe divided; Europe after the Cold War; The Americas to 1945; Americas since 1945; Central America and the Caribbean; The making of the Soviet Union; The decline of the Soviet Union; China 1911-1949; Japan and Asia; World War II in Asia; East Asia since 1945; Central and South Asia; The rise of the Pacific Rim; The Middle East and North Africa; Arab-Israeli conflict; The Middle East since 1977; Decolonization and nationalism in Africa

This book "is divided into thematic and regional maps which are followed by short but very comprehensive articles. . . . [It includes] curriculum context sidebars, important terms students should know, and how the topic ties into other areas." Libr Media Connect

909.83   World history—21st century, 2000-2099

Snapshot; the visual almanac for our world today; commissioning editors, Jon Asbury, Peter Taylor; produced for Mitchell Beazley by CIRCA and Heritage Editorial. Mitchell Beazley; distributed by Octopus Books USA 2009 224p il $29.99

Grades: 9 10 11 12 Adult   **909.83**
1. World history—21st century—Pictorial works 2. Almanacs 3. Reference books
ISBN 978-1-84533-523-6

"Broad thematic areas—environment, finance, culture—and specific topics within them—e.g., water, voting, music—are addressed on spreads covered with charts and graphs, archival photos, perceptive and concise comments tightly focused on important details, and Web resources. Intended to be bias free, the volume is highly successful and will appeal to nonfiction, fact-addicted browsers, teen researchers, and activists." SLJ

910 Geography & travel

Allaby, Michael, 1933-
The encyclopedia of Earth; a complete visual guide; [authors, Michael Allaby ... [et al.]] University of California Press 2008 608p il map $39.95
Grades: 9 10 11 12 Adult   **910**
1. Earth sciences—Encyclopedias 2. Reference books
ISBN 978-0-520-25471-8; 0-520-25471-6
LC 2008-6956
This "source includes six main sections. 'Birth' is an overview of Earth's history and evolution; 'Fire' covers its inner workings, structure, and landscape; 'Land' covers rocks, minerals, and habitats; 'Air' covers weather; 'Water' includes information on oceans, rivers, and lakes; and 'Humans' is about humankind's relationship with Earth, including management of its resources. . . . This is a stunning, reasonably priced resource, especially useful for those in need of illustrations or a visual representation of a phenomenon or concept." Choice

United States. Central Intelligence Agency
The CIA world factbook 2011. Skyhorse Pub. 2010 xxvi, 837p map pa $14.95 *
Grades: 11 12 Adult   **910**
1. Geography—Handbooks, manuals, etc. 2. World politics—Handbooks, manuals, etc. 3. Political science—Handbooks, manuals, etc.
ISBN 978-1-61608-047-1
Also available online
Annual. First published 1981
Provides information on such topics as politics, military expenditures, and economics, and shares comprehensive, country-by-country statistical and rate information.

910.2 Geography—Miscellany. Travel guides

100 great journeys; consultant editor, Keith Lye. Hammond World Atlas Corp 2008 191p il map $24.95
Grades: 8 9 10 11 12   **910.2**
1. Voyages and travels 2. Reference books
ISBN 978-0-8437-0994-0; 0-8437-0994-4
"The title covers road trips, historical journeys, explorations, voyages, sacred routes, military campaigns and trails, treks, 'natural splendors,' and literary jaunts, with each spread focusing on one. The colorful maps are prominent against the white pages but not always the main focus; quality color photos and reproductions, multiple shaded sidebars (including short lists of relevant titles), and pull quotes compete for attention. . . . It would be a shame to limit copies of this book to the reference shelves." SLJ

Unesco
World heritage sites; a complete guide to 911 UNESCO world heritage sites. Rev. and updated. Firefly Books 2011 856p il map pa $29.95
Grades: 9 10 11 12 Adult   **910.2**
1. Unesco. World Heritage Committee 2. Historic sites 3. Historic buildings 4. Reference books
ISBN 978-1-55407-827-1; 1-55407-827-X
LC 2010-671075
First published 2009
Each site has an entry explaining its historical and cultural significance, with a description and location map.
"UNESCO's World Heritage mission is to encourage the identification, protection, and preservation of cultural and natural heritage around the world considered to be of outstanding value to humanity. This treasure trove of a book reinforces that mission and, through spectacular photographs, shows how remarkable and beautiful our planet truly is. An excellent (and affordable) addition to any library." Libr J

910.3 Geography—Dictionaries, encyclopedias, concordnces, gazetteers

The **Columbia** gazetteer of the world; edited by Saul B. Cohen. 2nd ed. Columbia University Press 2008 3v set $595
Grades: 11 12 Adult   **910.3**
1. Gazetteers 2. Reference books
ISBN 978-0-231-14554-1   LC 2008-9181
Also available online
First published 1952 with title: The Columbia Lippincott gazetteer of the world
"The 170,000-plus entries cover political, physical, and special places, including monuments and historic sites. . . . Historically accurate, this title can be considered a reference standard." Libr J

Merriam-Webster's geographical dictionary. 3rd ed. Merriam-Webster 1997 1361p maps $32.95 *
Grades: 11 12 Adult   **910.3**
1. Reference books 2. Geography—Dictionaries
ISBN 0-87779-546-0   LC 96-52365
First published 1949 with title: Webster's geographical dictionary
This guide contains data about countries, cities, and physical features. More than 48,000 entries and over 250 maps provide population, size, economic data and historical notes. Pronunciations are included and a table of foreign terms used in English is provided.

The **Oxford** companion to world exploration; David Buisseret, editor in chief. Oxford University Press 2007 2v il map set $250
Grades: 9 10 11 12 Adult   **910.3**
1. Exploration
ISBN 0-19-514922-X; 978-0-19-514922-7
LC 2006-27968
"Published in association with the Newberry Library"

The Oxford companion to world exploration— *Continued*

"The entries are presented in alphabetical order and cover not only individual explorers, but also some geographic regions, wars, commercial operations, and religious organizations. . . . This work will become the first stop for students and general readers who seek either basic information or a starting point for further reading." Sci Books Films

Includes bibliographical references

Worldmark encyclopedia of the nations; [Timothy L. Gall and M. Hobby, editors] 12th ed. Thomson Gale 2007 c2006 5v set il map $535 Grades: 11 12 Adult   **910.3**
1. United Nations 2. Reference books 3. Geography—Encyclopedias 4. World history—Encyclopedias 5. World politics—Encyclopedias
ISBN 1-4144-1089-1

First published 1960

"Factual and statistical information on the countries of the world, exhibited in uniform format under such rubrics as topography, population, public finance, language, and ethnic composition. Country articles appear in volumes 2 through 5, arranged geographically by continent. Volume 1 is devoted to the United Nations and its affiliated agencies. Illustrations, maps." Ref Sources for Small & Medium-sized Libr. 6th edition

910.4   Accounts of travel and facilities for travelers

Anderson, Harry S.

Exploring the polar regions. rev ed. Chelsea House 2010 116p il map (Discovery and exploration) lib bdg $35
Grades: 7 8 9 10   **910.4**
1. Polar regions—Exploration
ISBN 978-1-60413-190-1; 1-60413-190-X
LC 2009-22863

First published 2004 by Facts on File

Covers exploration and discovery of the Arctic and Antarctic regions.

"The chapters are well-illustrated with color and black and white historic photos, illustrations and maps. Chapter layout is clearly organized with helpful subtitles; sidebars develop related themes in eye-catching colors. . . . [This book] attractively and effectively surveys an important . . . area in world studies." Libr Media Connect

Includes glossary and bibliographical references

Ballard, Robert D., 1942-

Return to Titanic; a new look at the world's most famous lost ship; [by] Robert D. Ballard with Michael Sweeney. National Geographic Society 2004 192p il map $30
Grades: 11 12 Adult   **910.4**
1. Titanic (Steamship) 2. Shipwrecks 3. Underwater exploration
ISBN 0-7922-7288-9   LC 2004-55930

The author reviews *Titanic's* "history and the catastrophic events that led to her demise. He describes his dream of turning the ship into a museum on the ocean floor, easily explored from above by computer. . . . It's Ballard's passion and expertise that make this book tick." Publ Wkly

Includes bibliographical references

The **Britannica** guide to explorers and explorations that changed the modern world; edited by Kenneth Pletcher. Britannica Educational Pub., in association with Rosen Educational Services 2010 350p il (Turning points in history) lib bdg $45
Grades: 9 10 11 12   **910.4**
1. Exploration 2. Explorers
ISBN 978-1-61530-028-0   LC 2009-37672

Details discovery expeditions and explorers from throughout history, including exploration of North America, the polar regions, and Mount Everest, and describes archaeological finds including Machu Picchu, Pompeii, and Easter Island.

Includes glossary and bibliographical references

Butler, Daniel Allen

Unsinkable: the full story of the RMS Titanic. Stackpole Bks. 1998 292p il $19.95
Grades: 11 12 Adult   **910.4**
1. Titanic (Steamship) 2. Shipwrecks
ISBN 0-8117-1814-X   LC 98-9294

Also available in paperback from Da Capo Press

This is a history "of the disaster and aftermath, drawing on first-person accounts and solid secondary sources." Libr J

Includes bibliographical references

Delaney, Frank, 1942-

Simple courage; a true story of peril on the sea. Random House 2006 300p il hardcover o.p. pa $14.95
Grades: 11 12 Adult   **910.4**
1. Carlsen, Henrik Kurt, 1915-1989 2. Flying Enterprise (Ship) 3. Shipwrecks
ISBN   1-4000-6524-0;   978-1-4000-6524-0; 0-8129-7595-2 (pa); 978-0-8129-7595-6 (pa)
LC 2006-41766

This book tells the story "of Captain Kurt Carlsen and the Flying Enterprise. On Christmas Day 1951, the World War II Liberty ship Flying Enterprise began splitting apart in a North Atlantic gale, and her cargo of pig iron shifted. Captain Carlsen saw to the safe abandonment of passengers and crew, then remained aboard to help with salvage efforts. He remained aboard, accompanied only by a young radioman who leaped aboard from a rescue ship, until the Flying Enterprise was about to sink under him." Booklist

Includes bibliographical references

Fleming, Fergus, 1959-

Off the map; tales of endurance and exploration; as told by Fergus Fleming. Atlantic Monthly Press 2005 518p il maps $24.95; pa $16

Grades: 11 12 Adult 910.4

1. Explorers 2. Exploration
ISBN 0-8711-3899-9; 0-8021-4272-9 (pa)
LC 2005-47849

First published 2004 in the United Kingdom

This book "consists of 45 biographical essays divided into three parts. 'The Age of Reconnaissance' begins in the 13th century with Marco Polo's wanderings in the Mongol Empire. 'The Age of Inquiry' takes the reader through the 18th century and halfway into the 19th, concluding with the . . . search for Sir John Franklin in the high Arctic. 'The Age of Endeavour' proceeds from the crossing of the Australian continent by Robert Burke and William Wills in 1861 to Umberto Nobile's . . . 1928 flight to the North Pole." N Y Times Book Rev

"Almost comprehensive enough to serve as a reference, this densely packed tome supplies a bewildering wealth of information about some of humanity's most compelling adventures." Publ Wkly

Includes bibliographical references

Gilkerson, William

A thousand years of pirates. Tundra Books 2009 96p il map $32.95

Grades: 6 7 8 9 10 910.4

1. Pirates
ISBN 978-0-88776-924-5; 0-88776-924-1

"Pirates are given scholarly scrutiny in this handsome and invigorating overview. Short but dense chapters introduce the major factions, characters, and incidents that connect the scattered history of seagoing bandits. . . . Gilkerson's grasp of the politics surrounding each nation's pirates . . . is most impressive." Booklist

Includes bibliographical references

Heyerdahl, Thor

Kon-Tiki; across the Pacific by raft; translated by F.H. Lyon. Washington Square Press 1984 240p map (Enriched classics series) pa $5.99

Grades: 11 12 Adult 910.4

1. Kon-Tiki Expedition (1947) 2. Pacific Ocean 3. Ethnology—Polynesia
ISBN 0-671-72652-8 LC 84-42785

Original Norwegian edition, 1948

The "story of the six men who crossed the Pacific from Peru to the Polynesians on a primitive balsa-log raft such as Peruvian natives of the fifth century used, to prove that it was possible that the legendary race that came to Easter Island and the Polynesians could have come from Peru." Wis Libr Bull

Jacobson, Mark, 1948-

12,000 miles in the nick of time; a semi-dysfunctional family circumnavigates the globe; with additional commentary by Rae Jacobson. Atlantic Monthly Press 2003 271p il maps pa $13 hardcover o.p.

Grades: 11 12 Adult 910.4

1. Voyages around the world
ISBN 0-8021-4138-2 (pa) LC 2003-41821

"A few years ago, the Jacobsons . . . spent the summer touring Asia, the Middle East, and part of Europe on the cheap. It wasn't easy to take three middle-class American kids, ages 9 to 16, to Cambodia's Killing Fields, India's Burning Gat, or the sex-shop strewn thoroughfares of Thailand. The book recounts the many trials, tribulations, and ironies of the trip as well as its more usual wonders." SLJ

"The book is very funny—the trip doesn't go exactly as the parents plan—but it is also hugely educational, history presented as a grand adventure. The kids learned a lot, and so do we." Booklist

Includes bibliographical references

Junger, Sebastian

The perfect storm; a true story of men against the sea. Norton 1997 226p il map $23.95; pa $14.95

Grades: 11 12 Adult 910.4

1. Storms 2. Shipwrecks
ISBN 0-393-04016-X; 0-393-33701-4 (pa)
LC 96-42412

Also available in paperback from HarperCollins Pubs.

"With waves as high as a hundred feet and winds so strong that anemometers were torn from their moorings, the storm of the title struck unsuspecting mariners off the coast of Nova Scotia in October, 1991. Junger traces the last voyage of the Andrea Gail—a commercial swordfishing boat that was lost, with all six hands, in the storm—and his account is relentlessly suspenseful." New Yorker

Kinder, Gary

Ship of gold in the deep blue sea. Atlantic Monthly Press 1998 507p pa $16.95 hardcover o.p.

Grades: 11 12 Adult 910.4

1. Central America (Steamship) 2. Shipwrecks
ISBN 978-0-8021-4425-6 LC 97-49812

"On September 12, 1857, the steamship *Central America* sank in a great storm off the coast of South Carolina and settled a mile and a half beneath the waves. Most of the 423 souls on board perished. Lost, too, was $2,189,000 (now worth $1 billion) in California gold. . . . In 1989, a group of investors and treasure salvagers equipped with the latest underwater equipment was able to bring back much of the cargo, including the largest treasure ever recorded. The discovery of this vessel and its riches led to protracted litigation between various claimants, and the case is still in the courts. Kinder has followed the story from its beginning." Libr J

Konstam, Angus

The world atlas of pirates; treasures and treachery on the seven seas, in maps, tall tales, and pictures. The Lyons Press 2010 247p il map $29.95 *

Grades: 10 11 12 Adult 910.4

1. Pirates
ISBN 978-1-59921-474-0

The author "explains how piracy grew and flourished from the early buccaneers to the rogues of popular legends, how it has been snuffed out, and how it has reared its head again with the machine-gun-toting pirates operating on today's high seas." Publisher's note

Macleod, Alasdair, 1963-
Explorers; great tales of adventure and endurance; Royal Geographical Society; [written by Alasdair Macleod] DK in association with the Smithsonian Institution 2010 360p il $40
Grades: 11 12 Adult   **910.4**
  1. Exploration 2. Explorers
  ISBN 978-0-7566-6737-5
"Written by Alasdair Macleod" Verso of title page; "Foreword by Sir Ranulph Fiennes" Cover
"The book covers the history of exploration from the discovery of the ancient Egyptians in Nubia to the exploration of space by the Soviet Union and the United States in the 20th century. . . . [It] is a wonderful introduction to the various personalities who, over a period of several thousand years, devoted themselves, to studying the world and revealing its fascinatingly diverse landscapes, conditions, and cultures." Sci Books Films

Netzley, Patricia D.
Encyclopedia of women's travel and exploration.
Oryx Press 2000 259p il $88.95
Grades: 11 12 Adult   **910.4**
  1. Reference books 2. Voyages and travels—Encyclopedias 3. Women—Travel—Encyclopedias
  ISBN 1-573-56238-6; 978-1-57356-238-6
                   LC 00-10720
"The 315 entries, arranged alphabetically, focus on a wide variety of women explorers, adventurers, and travelers throughout history and across continents. Most entries are biographical, but some examine related topics such as accommodations, solo travel, guide books, and mountaineering, occasionally offering perceptive insights into women's travel experiences and motivations." Choice
Includes bibliographical references

Paine, Lincoln P.
Ships of discovery and exploration. Houghton Mifflin 2000 188p il maps pa $17
Grades: 11 12 Adult   **910.4**
  1. Exploration 2. Ships
  ISBN 0-395-98415-7   LC 00-40802
"A Mariner original"
A look at 125 vessels that have played significant roles in voyages of geographical exploration and scientific discovery. The physical characteristics, construction, and history of each ship is described. Chronologies cover underwater archaeology sites, maritime technology, exploration, and disasters at sea. Illustrated with drawings paintings, photographs, and maps
Includes bibliographical references

Philbrick, Nathaniel
In the heart of the sea; the tragedy of the whaleship Essex. Viking 2000 302p il $24.95; pa $15
Grades: 11 12 Adult   **910.4**
  1. Essex (Whaleship) 2. Shipwrecks
  ISBN 0-670-89157-6; 0-14-100182-8 (pa)
                   LC 99-53740

"On November 20, 1820, the Nantucket whaleship Essex was rammed by a large sperm whale and sank in the Pacific, 'just about as far from land as it was possible to be anywhere on earth.' The episode inspired Melville, but this climactic moment proves less interesting than the story of the survivors' voyage in the ship's whaleboats, a months-long ordeal that included madness and cannibalism. Philbrick nicely links the experiences aboard ship with the values of Nantucket society." New Yorker

Read, Piers Paul, 1941-
Alive; sixteen men, seventy-two days, and insurmountable odds—the classic adventure of survival in the Andes. Harper Perennial 2005 398p il pa $13.95
Grades: 11 12 Adult   **910.4**
  1. Survival after airplane accidents, shipwrecks, etc.
  2. Andes
  ISBN 0-06-077866-0
  First published 1974 by Lippincott
The author describes the extraordinary hardships endured by the survivors of a horrific plane crash in the Andes.

Scieszka, Casey
To Timbuktu; words, Casey Scieszka; art, Steven Weinberg. Roaring Brook Press 2011 478p il pa $19.99
Grades: 9 10 11 12   **910.4**
  1. Voyages around the world 2. American travelers
  ISBN 978-1-59643-527-8   LC 2010-27627
"Nine countries, two people, one true story" Cover
This "is a travelogue that will provide great inspiration for teenagers and young adults who are looking for adventure and self-discovery. After college graduation, Scieszka and her boyfriend set off on an almost two-year jaunt to various parts of Asia and Africa where they lived, worked, and learned far from their homes in the States. She journaled with words while Weinberg did so with sketched illustrations, and the result is an appealing and engaging tale of the ups and downs of their journey." SLJ

Vail, Martha
Exploring the Pacific; [by] Martha Vail; John S. Bowman and Maurice Isserman, general editors. rev ed. Chelsea House 2010 120p il map (Discovery and exploration) $35
Grades: 7 8 9 10   **910.4**
  1. Pacific Ocean 2. Explorers
  ISBN 978-1-60413-197-0; 1-60413-197-7
                   LC 2009-22106
First published 2005 by Facts on File
"Explains how explorers of the Pacific region expanded geographical knowledge and contributed to human understanding by generating maps, charts, paintings, and reports. The book covers such explorers as Bartolomeu Dias, Vasco Nunez de Balboa, Ferdinand Magellan, Alvaro de Mendana, and James Cook." Publisher's note
"The chapters are well-illustrated with color and black and white historic photos, illustrations, and maps. Chap-

Vail, Martha—_Continued_

ter layout is clearly organized with helpful subtitles; sidebars develop related themes in catching colors." Libr Media Connect

Includes glossary and bibliographical references

White, Pamela

Exploration in the world of the Middle Ages, 500-1500; Pamela White, John S. Bowman, and Maurice Isserman, general editors. Rev. ed. Chelsea House 2010 132p il map (Discovery and exploration) $35

Grades: 7 8 9 10   910.4

1. Middle Ages 2. Explorers 3. Exploration
ISBN 978-1-60413-193-2; 1-60413-193-4
                                              LC 2009-30202
First published 2005 by Facts On File

This describes world exploration in the Middle Ages by pilgrims and missionaries, the Vikings, Muslim travelers, Europeans seeking Asia, Marco Polo, and Portuguese sailors, and describes Medieval legends of mythical monsters and lands

Includes glossary and bibliographical references

911   Historical geography

Atlas of classical history; edited by Richard J.A. Talbert. Routledge 1988 217p maps pa $37.95

Grades: 9 10 11 12   911

1. Historical atlases 2. Reference books
ISBN 0-415-03463-9   LC 89-162237
First published 1985 by Macmillan

"Covers Greek and Roman history from Troy and Knossos to the Roman Empire in 314 CE. The black-and-white maps, though small, are very clear. Many city maps. The text is brief, in many cases good mainly for identification, a skeletal history, or verification of a few key dates." Guide to Ref Books. 11th edition

Atlas of exploration; cartography by Philip's; foreword by John Hemming. Oxford University Press 2008 256p il map $50 *

Grades: 9 10 11 12 Adult   911

1. Exploration—Atlases 2. Reference books
ISBN 978-0-19-534318-2   LC 2008-626565
First published 1998 with title: Oxford atlas of exploration

"This atlas describes many of the explorations and participants that changed history and enhanced man's knowledge and perception of the world. . . . The volume is a visual delight, festooned with more than 100 specially drawn maps and 300 b&w and color photographs, period paintings, and illustrations on the various explorations." Libr Media Connect

Goetzmann, William H., 1930-2010

The atlas of North American exploration; from the Norse voyages to the race to the Pole; [by] William H. Goetzmann, Glyndwr Williams; [cartographic director, Malcolm Swanston; maps created by Isabelle Lewis and Jacqueline Land] University of Okla. Press 1998 222p il map pa $29.95

Grades: 9 10 11 12   911

1. America—Exploration 2. Explorers 3. Historical atlases 4. Reference books
ISBN 0-8061-3058-X   LC 97-45731
First published 1992

"This survey atlas, emphasizing exploration from the late 1400s to the late 1800s, is firmly directed toward a general audience. It features excellent color maps and illustrations with two-page 'spreads,' each devoted to the analysis of a particular explorer and each with extracts from the explorer's journals (translated to English if necessary). The atlas takes Columbus and his predecessors as a starting point, and covers all of North America. . . . The writers have endeavored to maintain an objective tone, and in the bibliography give full citations for works mentioned in the text." Libr J

Includes bibliographical references

Hayes, Derek, 1947-

Historical atlas of the United States; with original maps. University of California Press 2007 280p il map $45

Grades: 11 12 Adult   911

1. United States—Historical geography—Maps 2. Atlases 3. Reference books
ISBN 978-0-520-25036-9; 0-520-25036-2
                                              LC 2006-42405

"Hayes has produced an excellent visual history of the land that became the US. The work includes 535 maps gathered from a variety of international collections, coupled with more than 60 other illustrations to chronicle the expansion and development of the nation over the last 500 years." Choice

Includes bibliographical references

Magocsi, Paul R.

Historical atlas of Central Europe; [by] Paul Robert Magocsi. rev and expanded ed. University of Wash. Press 2002 274p maps (History of East Central Europe) pa $45 hardcover o.p.

Grades: 11 12 Adult   911

1. Central Europe—Historical geography—Maps 2. Atlases 3. Reference books
ISBN 0-295-98146-6   LC 2001-27907
First published 1993 with title: Historical atlas of East Central Europe

"The volume is arranged chronologically, with coverage beginning about A.D. 400 (roughly the time of the demise of the Roman Empire) and continuing through the end of the 20th century. The maps and tables provide information on military affairs; population and population movements; economy; ethnolinguistic distributions; and religious, cultural, and educational institutions. All are extremely well done." SLJ

McKitterick, Rosamond

Atlas of the medieval world. Oxford University Press 2004 304p il map $45

Grades: 11 12 Adult   **911**

1. Historical atlases 2. Middle Ages 3. Reference books

ISBN 0-19-522158-3   LC 2004-56816

First published 2003 in the United Kingdom with title: The Times medieval world

This atlas explores "through maps and narrative the millennium from the end of the Roman Empire to the colonization of the Americas. . . . The work features more than 90 digitally produced color political and thematic maps as well as hundreds of sumptuous photographs of art and architecture." Libr J

Includes bibliographical references

Nash, Gary B.

Atlas of American history; [by] Gary B. Nash and Carter Smith. Facts on File 2006 346p il map (Facts on File library of American history) $95 *

Grades: 9 10 11 12   **911**

1. United States—Historical geography—Maps 2. Atlases 3. Reference books

ISBN 0-8160-5952-7; 978-0-8160-5952-2

                       LC 2006-15915

This book "uses more than 200 full-color maps to help bring into focus both the dramatic events and enduring developments that have shaped our national heritage." Publisher's note

Includes bibliographical references

The **new** cultural atlas of China; edited by Tim Cooke. Marshall Cavendish Corp. 2010 192p il map lib bdg $99.93

Grades: 7 8 9 10   **911**

1. China—Maps 2. Atlases 3. Reference books

ISBN 978-0-7614-7875-1; 0-7614-7875-2

                       LC 2009-8600

An account of the world's oldest living civilization, exploring Chinese culture and society from the earliest times to the glories of the imperial age.

Includes glossary and bibliographical references

912   Atlases. Maps

Aczel, Amir D.

The riddle of the compass; the invention that changed the world. Harcourt 2001 178p il maps hardcover o.p. pa $13

Grades: 11 12 Adult   **912**

1. Compass

ISBN 0-15-100506-0; 0-15-600753-3 (pa)

                       LC 00-47153

This book tracks "down the roots of the compass and tells the story of navigation through the ages." Publisher's note

Includes bibliographical references

Atlas of North America; H.J. de Blij, editor; [cartography by Philip's] Oxford University Press 2004 320p il map $125 *

Grades: 5 6 7 8 9 10   **912**

1. Atlases 2. Reference books

ISBN 0-19-516993-X   LC 2004-45005

This "atlas of the three largest countries of North America . . . [features a] thematic section covering physical, historic, economic, urban, social, and cultural topics ranging from environmental change to religious practice and from indigenous peoples to migration patterns." Publisher's note

"This exhaustive, authoritative resource presents a dynamic view of Canada, the U.S., and Mexico." SLJ

Firefly atlas of North America; United States, Canada & Mexico. Firefly Books 2006 272p il map $55

Grades: 11 12 Adult   **912**

1. Atlases 2. Reference books

ISBN 978-1-55407-207-1; 1-55407-207-7

This atlas is "divided into three sections covering the United States (including Puerto Rico and the U.S. Pacific Territories), Canada and Mexico. . . . Each country section opens with a map and a color-coded legend to the regional maps that follow. All 50 U.S. states (plus Washington, D.C.), the 13 Canadian provinces and territories (including Nunavut) and Mexico's 32 states are illustrated." Publisher's note

Hammond world atlas. 5th ed. Hammond World Atlas Corporation 2008 346p il map $59.95 *

Grades: 8 9 10 11 12 Adult   **912**

1. Atlases 2. Reference books

ISBN 978-0-8437-0967-4; 0-8437-0967-7

First published 1992 with title: Hammond atlas of the world

This atlas includes an "illustrated 64-page 'Thematic Section,' a 48-page 'Satellite Section' with more than 40 color photos and a commentary, and 228 pages of . . . full-color physical and political maps representing the world, continents, and regions with detailed . . . computer-generated terrain modeling." Libr J

National Geographic Atlas of China. National Geographic Society 2008 128p il map $26

Grades: 11 12 Adult   **912**

1. Atlases 2. Reference books

ISBN 978-1-4262-0136-3   LC 2008-299395

This atlas of China "maps the entire country with sections covering all provinces—including towns, cities, and transportation networks." Publisher's note

National Geographic atlas of the world. 9th ed. National Geographic Society 2010 153p il $175 *

Grades: 5 6 7 8 9 10   **912**

1. Atlases 2. Reference books

ISBN 978-1-4262-0634-4

First published 1963

"The National Geographic Society presents more than 80 large-format color maps grouped by continent portraying the world with detailed, digitally painted terrain modeling. Each continent is introduced by satellite, political, and physical maps. Political maps for regions and specific countries follow." Libr J

National Geographic visual atlas of the world.
National Geographic Society 2009 416p il map
$100 *
Grades: 11 12 Adult   912
1. Atlases 2. Reference books
ISBN 978-1-4262-0332-9   LC 2008-627044
This atlas "has the usual atlas features but emphasizes
the more than 850 UNESCO World Heritage Sites. . . .
Double-page spreads of regional maps are framed with
four to six color photographs of the heritage sites that
are indicated on the map. . . . Beautiful color photography and clear topical material combined with detailed
maps of areas not covered as well in other world atlases
make the *Visual Atlas* a recommended purchase. This is
a first choice for any library needing a new medium-
priced atlas." Booklist

Includes bibliographical references

The **new** atlas of the Arab world. American
University in Cairo Press 2010 144p il map
$39.50 *
Grades: 11 12 Adult   912
1. Arab countries—Maps 2. Atlases 3. Reference
books
ISBN 978-977-416-419-4
This atlas contains maps of the Arab world "showing
physical features, political boundaries, towns, and communication networks. In addition, each of the twenty-two
countries is the subject of an illustrated essay, with notes
and . . . statistics on the geography, population, history
and politics, and economy of the country. The countries
covered are: Algeria, Bahrain, Comoros, Djibouti, Egypt,
Iraq, Jordan, Kuwait, Lebanon, Libya, Mauritania, Morocco, Oman, Palestine, Qatar, Saudi Arabia, Somalia,
Sudan, Syria, Tunisia, United Arab Emirates, Yemen."
Publisher's note

Oxford atlas of the world; [cartography by
Philip's] 17th ed. Oxford University Press 2010
448p il map $80 *
Grades: 7 8 9 10 11 12 Adult   912
1. Atlases 2. Reference books
ISBN 978-0-19-975128-0   LC 2010-594813
First published 1992. Frequently revised. Variant title:
Atlas of the world
"Copyright © 2010 Philip's; Philip's, a Division of
Octopus Publishing Group Ltd." Verso of title page
Provides maps and satellite photography that reflect
the most recent political, economic, and demographic sta-
tistics, and presents articles addressing the environment
and population matters in major cities of the world.

Times comprehensive atlas of the world. 12th ed.
Times Books 2008 various paging il map $285
Grades: 11 12 Adult   912
1. Atlases 2. Reference books
ISBN 978-0-06-146450-8
First published 1967. Periodically revised
"The classic atlas. Very detailed with listings for most
geographic and urban locations. Index gives longitude
and latitude as well as map reference. Contains . . .
[125] plates and . . . [an] index-gazetteer." Ref Sources
for Small & Medium-sized Libr. 6th edition

Includes glossary

913 Geography of and travel in ancient world

Bowman, John Stewart, 1931-
Exploration in the world of the ancients; by
John S. Bowman; John S. Bowman and Maurice
Isserman, general editors. Rev. ed. Chelsea House
2010 109p il map (Discovery and exploration) $35
Grades: 7 8 9 10   913
1. Ancient geography 2. Explorers 3. Exploration
ISBN 978-1-60413-191-8; 1-60413-191-8
                                        LC 2009-18849
First published 2005 by Facts On File
"This book examines some of the earliest accounts of
Egyptian and Mesopotamian explorations, as well as cov-
ering the Romans, Greeks, Phoenicians, and other ancient
peoples. It concludes at the beginning of the Middle
Ages." Publisher's note
Includes glossary and bibliographical references

915 Geography of and travel in Asia

Belliveau, Denis, 1964-
In the footsteps of Marco Polo; [by] Denis
Belliveau and Francis O'Donnell. Rowman &
Littlefield Publishers 2008 280p il map $29.95
Grades: 9 10 11 12 Adult   915
1. Polo, Marco, 1254-1323? 2. Asia—Description and
travel
ISBN 978-0-7425-5683-6; 0-7425-5683-2
                                        LC 2008-23411
A "companion volume to a PBS documentary traces
the authors' two-year expedition to answer the question
about Marco Polo's alleged visit to China, a venture that
was fraught with the perils and turmoil of the Middle
East and natural threats." Publisher's note
"The stunning photographs in this elegant book should
please even the most casual reader, while the authors'
unpretentious observations will satisfy those who want to
know more about a still alien world. A travel/adventure
book rather than a study of Marco Polo the man or a history of his travels, this volume deserves many readers.
Warmly recommended." Libr J
Includes bibliographical references

Polo, Marco, 1254-1323?
The travels of Marco Polo; edited and revised
from William Marsden's translation, by Manuel
Komroff; introduction by Jason Goodwin. Modern
Library pbk. ed. Modern Library 2001 322p map
pa $13.95
Grades: 11 12 Adult   915
1. Asia—Description and travel 2. Voyages and trav-
els
ISBN 0-375-75818-6   LC 2001-45030
Also available in paperback from Penguin Bks.
An autobiographical account of Marco Polo's thir-
teenth century travels in Asia.

916.6 West Africa and offshore islands

Benanav, Michael
Men of salt; across the Sahara with the caravan of white gold. Lyons Press 2006 220p il map $23.95
Grades: 11 12 Adult   **916.6**
1. Sahara Desert—Description and travel 2. Salt
ISBN 1-59228-772-7; 978-1-59228-772-7
LC 2005-23205
The author describes his experiences after he "joined what is known as the Caravan of White Gold—so-called because the salt was once literally worth its weight in gold—on its mission into the deadly heart of the Sahara to haul back gleaming slabs of solid salt for sale at market." Publisher's note
"Even if readers don't find the idea of spending 40 harrowing days with a caravan crossing some of the world's most unforgiving desert as enticing as Benanav does, that doesn't mean they won't quickly devour his thrilling account of that otherworldly journey." Publ Wkly
Includes bibliographical references

917 Geography of and travel in North America

The **Columbia** gazetteer of North America; edited by Saul B. Cohen. Columbia Univ. Press 2000 1157p il $156
Grades: 11 12 Adult   **917**
1. North America—Gazetteers
ISBN 0-231-11990-9   LC 00-27512
"This work includes more than 50,000 entries covering every incorporated place and country in the United States, along with many unincorporated places and physical features throughout North America. Arranged alphabetically, each entry includes a pronunciation guide, location information, and longitude and latitude where appropriate. If the listing is a municipality, brief population figures are provided as well. . . . Color maps of the physical regions of North America, along with political maps of the region, are included as reference points." Am Ref Books Annu, 2001

Cox, Caroline, 1954-
Opening up North America, 1497-1800; [by] Caroline Cox and Ken Albala. Rev. ed. Chelsea House 2009 140p il map (Discovery and exploration) $35 *
Grades: 7 8 9 10   **917**
1. Explorers 2. America—Exploration
ISBN 978-1-60413-196-3; 1-60413-196-9
LC 2009-27794
First published 2005 by Facts On File
"Integrates in a chronological narrative the voyages taken from Florida to Newfoundland, covering the first recorded contact of John Cabot in 1497 through Alexander Mackenzie's journey across the Rocky Mountains to the Pacific in 1793." Publisher's note
Includes glossary and bibliographical references

Hayes, Derek, 1947-
America discovered; a historical atlas of exploration. Douglas & McIntyre 2004 224p il maps hardcover o.p. pa $35
Grades: 9 10 11 12 Adult   **917**
1. America—Exploration—Maps 2. North America—Historical geography—Maps 3. Historical atlases 4. Reference books
ISBN 1-553-65049-2; 1-553-65450-1 (pa)
LC 2004-52704
The author "chronicles the discovery and exploration of North America. The narrative text of this handsome volume provides the historical context for 280 carefully selected maps from North American and European collections, faithfully reproduced in full color and ranging in date from the early 16th century to several computer-generated images from the late 20th century. . . . Hayes has chosen maps that fascinate the intellect as well as please the eye." Libr J
Includes bibliographical references

Isserman, Maurice
Exploring North America, 1800-1900; [by] Maurice Isserman; John S. Bowman and Maurice Isserman, general editors. Rev. ed. Chelsea House 2010 151p il map (Discovery and exploration) $35 *
Grades: 7 8 9 10   **917**
1. Explorers 2. West (U.S.)—Exploration
ISBN 978-1-60413-194-9; 1-60413-194-2
LC 2009-27860
First published 2005 by Facts On File
"Traces the history of the exploration of western North America and the impact it had on the histories of both the United States and Canada." Publisher's note
Includes glossary and bibliographical references

World and its peoples: the Americas. Marshall Cavendish Reference 2008 11v il map set $499.95
Grades: 7 8 9 10 11 12   **917**
1. Human geography—Encyclopedias 2. Reference books
ISBN 978-0-7614-7802-7; 0-7614-7802-7
LC 2008-62303
Contents: v1 Mexico and Central America; v2 Northern Caribbean; v3 Southern Caribbean; v4 Colombia, Ecuador, Panama and Venezuela; v5 Brazil and the Guiana Coast; v6 Argentina, Paraguay, and Uruguay; v7 Bolivia, Chile, and Peru; v8 Canada and Greenland; v9 Part I United States; v10 Part II United States; v11 Indexes
Each volume in this set "begins with a well-defined overview of its region, organized by color-coded pages into sections covering 'Geography and Climate' and 'History and Movement of Peoples.' The country entries that follow include a time line, flag, and map; key facts on population, government, and transportation; and a closer analysis that varies in length. . . . The Americas is an ideal reference to use for social studies and history, and it will even benefit students in music, language, art, literature, family consumer science, and health and economics classes." SLJ
Includes glossary and bibliographical references

917.3 Geography of and travel in the United States

Curtis, Nancy C.

Black heritage sites; an African American odyssey and finder's guide. American Lib. Assn. 1996 677p il $75

Grades: 11 12 Adult   917.3

    1. Historic sites 2. African Americans—History

    ISBN 0-8389-0643-5   LC 95-5788

    Also available in a two volume paperback edition from New Press

This "guide locates significant places in African-American history and supplies . . . recent addresses, phone numbers, and visitors' information. . . . Organized by region, a historical essay introduces each section, presenting the culture and history in that area." Publisher's note

National Geographic guide to the national parks of the United States; [project manger, Caroline Hickey] 6th ed. National Geographic 2009 480p il pa $26 *

Grades: 9 10 11 12 Adult   917.3

    1. National parks and reserves—United States

    ISBN 978-1-4262-0393-0

    First published 1989

This guide provides information on each of the fifty-eight national parks, including things to do, campgrounds and accommodations, and facilities for the disabled.

"You can't do better than this guide. . . . Highly detailed and beautiful, this one is a must for all collections." Libr J

National Geographic guide to the state parks of the United States. 3rd ed. National Geographic 2008 384p il pa $25

Grades: 11 12 Adult   917.3

    1. Parks—United States

    ISBN 978-1-4262-0251-3

    First published 1997

A guide to more than 200 parks in all 50 states. Each entry provides information on: outstanding scenery and nature; historic and cultural sites; recreational activities; wildlife watching; camping and lodging. 32 maps and 250 color photographs accompany the text.

917.9 Geography of and travel in Great Basin and Pacific Coast states

Brower, Kenneth, 1944-

Yosemite: an American treasure; [prepared by the Book Division, National Geographic Society] National Geographic Society c1997 199p il map (National Geographic park profiles) pa $15

Grades: 11 12 Adult   917.9

    1. Yosemite National Park (Calif.)

    ISBN 0-7922-7030-4

    First published 1990

    Title on cover: National Geographic park profiles: Yosemite

The author, through text and photographs, "details the . . . variety of Yosemite's plants and animals. He chronicles how rivers of ice shaped the valley and relates the saga of the park through its first one hundred years." Publisher's note

Includes bibliographical references

920 Biography & genealogy

Books of biography are arranged as follows: 1. Biographical collections (920) 2. Biographies of individuals alphabetically by name of biographee (92)

Abdul-Jabbar, Kareem, 1947-

Black profiles in courage; a legacy of African American achievement; [by] Kareem Abdul-Jabbar and Alan Steinberg; foreword by Henry Louis Gates, Jr. Morrow 1996 xxiv, 232p il hardcover o.p. pa $13

Grades: 11 12 Adult   920

    1. African Americans—Biography

    ISBN 0-688-13097-6; 0-380-81341-6 (pa)

                               LC 96-26245

This book "profiles the historical achievements of 11 historical black figures from Estevanico de Dorantes to Rosa Parks." Libr J

The authors have provided "interesting and nuanced accounts of heroic African Americans whose accomplishments changed U.S. history. . . . Although Abdul-Jabbar is highly critical of past and present racism in the U.S., he gives credit to the abolitionist movement and leaders such as William Lloyd Garrison for their efforts toward ending slavery." Publ Wkly

Includes bibliographical references

African American lives; edited by Henry Louis Gates, Jr. and Evelyn Brooks Higginbotham. Oxford University Press 2004 xxvi, 1025p $55

Grades: 11 12 Adult   920

    1. African Americans—Biography

    ISBN 0-19-516024-X   LC 2003-23640

This compilation offers "biographies of 611 African-Americans over more than four centuries, beginning with Esteban, the first African known to have set foot in North America, up through writers, academics, artists, activists and more of today. A few of these profiles have been written by notable names—Gerald Early on Muhammad Ali, Clayborne Carson on Martin Luther King Jr. and Malcolm X, John Szwed on Miles Davis—though most are by lesser-known contributors." Publ Wkly

"This work opens multiple fresh vistas on proper African American history. . . . Essential for any serious African American collection." Libr J

Includes bibliographical references

Aikman, David, 1944-

Great souls; six who changed the century. Lexington Books 2003 388p pa $17

Grades: 11 12 Adult   920

    ISBN 0-7391-0438-1

    First published 1998 by Word Pub.

Aikman, David, 1944-—*Continued*

The author interviews six people, "Billy Graham, Nelson Mandela, Aleksandr Solzhenitsyn, Mother Teresa, Pope John Paul II, and Elie Wiesel. He explains how each of these luminaries personify specific virtues that are sorely needed today: salvation, forgiveness, truth, compassion, human dignity, and remembrance." Publisher's note

Includes bibliographical references

The **American** presidency; Compton's by Britannica; editor, Anthony L. Green. Encyclopedia Britannica 2009 138p il map (Learn & explore) $27.95 *

Grades: 7 8 9 10 11 12   **920**
1. Presidents—United States 2. United States—Politics and government
ISBN 978-1-59339-843-9

"The focus of the chronologically arranged *American Presidency* is the individual president, each of whom is covered in three to four pages. Each entry provides a profile of the president from his early days through retirement, highlighting key accomplishments. Students will be engaged by the layout and numerous images, and the time lines and world maps in each entry are useful features. In addition, each First Lady has a small entry." Booklist

Includes bibliographical references

Angelo, Bonnie

First families; the impact of the White House on their lives. Morrow 2005 336p il hardcover o.p. pa $15.95

Grades: 11 12 Adult   **920**
1. White House (Washington, D.C.) 2. Presidents—United States—Family
ISBN 0-06-056356-7; 0-06-056358-3 (pa)
LC 2005-41474

The author "takes readers inside the lives of the presidential families." Libr J

"Relying heavily on the recollections and memoirs of presidential family members, White House staff, and D.C. journalists, this chatty slice of Americana is chock-full of fun First Family facts." Booklist

Includes bibliographical references

Bailey, Neal

Female force; Neal Bailey, writer; Ryan Howe & Joshua LaBello, pencilers. Bluewater 2009 unp il pa $15.99

Grades: 7 8 9 10   **920**
1. Clinton, Hillary Rodham, 1947-—Graphic novels 2. Palin, Sarah, 1964-—Graphic novels 3. Obama, Michelle—Graphic novels 4. Kennedy, Caroline—Graphic novels 5. Women in politics—Graphic novels 6. Graphic novels
ISBN 978-1-42763858-8

This graphic novel includes stories on Hillary Clinton, Sarah Palin, Michelle Obama, and Caroline Kennedy.

"Although the art here is cartoony, and the women can appear middle-aged even in sections about their girlhoods, Bailey's analyses are respectful, insightful, and pro-woman." Booklist

Includes bibliographical references

Bascomb, Neal

The perfect mile; three athletes, one goal, and less than four minutes to achieve it. Houghton Mifflin Co 2004 322p il hardcover o.p. pa $14.95

Grades: Adult   **920**
1. Bannister, Roger, 1929- 2. Landy, John, 1930- 3. Santee, Wes, 1932-2010 4. Running
ISBN 0-618-39112-6; 0-618-56209-5 (pa)
LC 2004-40535

This is the story of the attempts of three athletes—Wes Santee, John Landy and Roger Bannister—to run the four-minute mile.

"Neal Bascomb skillfully transforms [the runners'] efforts into a compelling human drama. His crisp, detailed narrative helps readers step into the milers' spikes." Christ Sci Monit

Includes bibliographical references

Benson, Sonia

Development of the industrial U.S.: Biographies; [by] Sonia G. Benson; Carol Brennan, contributing writer; Jennifer York Stock, project editor. UXL 2006 lvi, 252p il (Development of the industrial U.S reference library) $63

Grades: 9 10 11 12   **920**
1. Industries—United States 2. Industrial revolution
ISBN 1-4144-0176-0   LC 2005-16350

"Subjects range from social workers to society divas and from industrialists to labor organizers and political activists. Articles average about 10 pages and include portraits, illustrations, and sidebars." Booklist

Includes bibliographical references

Berry, Bertice

The ties that bind; a memoir of race, memory, and redemption. Broadway Books 2009 205p $26.95

Grades: 11 12 Adult   **920**
1. Hunn, John, 1818-1894 2. Freeman, John Henry 3. African Americans—Biography 4. Slavery—United States 5. United States—Race relations
ISBN 978-0-7679-2414-6; 0-7679-2414-2
LC 2008-25555

The author "writes of getting past the bitterness of poverty and racism to appreciate the complexities of American slavery and the need to present more nuanced and balanced portraits of race relations." Booklist

"Berry continues to demonstrate an uncanny aptitude for weaving African-American history into entertaining, empowering stories both fictional and personal." Kirkus

Black leaders of the nineteenth century; edited by Leon Litwack and August Meier. University of Ill. Press 1988 344p il (Blacks in the new world) pa $22 hardcover o.p. *

Grades: 9 10 11 12   **920**
1. African Americans—Biography
ISBN 0-252-06213-2 (pa)   LC 87-19439

"Including individual essays on the famous, such as Frederick Douglass and Harriet Tubman, as well as a general discussion of black Reconstructionist leaders at the grass roots, this scholarly collection provides in-depth information." Booklist

Includes bibliographical references

Bowman-Kruhm, Mary

The Leakeys; a biography. Greenwood Press
2005 150p il (Greenwood biographies) $29.95
Grades: 9 10 11 12 **920**
1. Leakey family 2. Leakey, Louis Seymour Bazett,
1903-1972 3. Leakey, Mary D., 1913-1996
4. Leakey, Richard E., 1944- 5. Anthropologists
ISBN 0-313-32985-0; 978-0-313-32985-2
LC 2005-16821
This biography describes the Leakey family's "life in
detail, including their discoveries, publications, controversies, and legacy. A timeline, glossary, and bibliography of print and electronic sources supplement the material." Publisher's note
"Accurate, accessible biographies that go beyond facts
to create engaging profiles of exceptional personalities."
SLJ
Includes glossary and bibliographical references

Bradley, Michael J., 1956-

The age of genius; 1300 to 1800. Facts On File
2006 162p il (Pioneers in mathematics) $29.95
Grades: 7 8 9 10 **920**
1. Mathematics—History 2. Mathematicians
ISBN 0-8160-5424-X LC 2005-32354
This volume presents profiles of mathematicians such
as "Viete, Napier, Fermat, Pascal, Newton, Leibniz, Euler, and Agnesi. . . . The last chapter profiles Benjamin
Banneker, an African-American from the colonial period
in America." Sci Books Films
Includes glossary and bibliographical references

The birth of mathematics; ancient times to 1300.
Facts on File 2006 148p il (Pioneers in
mathematics) $29.95
Grades: 7 8 9 10 **920**
1. Mathematics—History 2. Mathematicians
ISBN 0-8160-5423-1 LC 2005-30563
The author "explores in exact detail the mathematical
advances and other discoveries of 10 early mathemati-
cians, from Thales of Miletus to Leonardo Fibonnaci. Il-
lustrated with many mathematical figures and equations."
Booklist
Includes glossary and bibliographical references

The foundations of mathematics; 1800 to 1900.
Facts On File 2006 162p il (Pioneers in
mathematics) $29.95
Grades: 7 8 9 10 **920**
1. Mathematics—History 2. Mathematicians
ISBN 0-8160-5425-8 LC 2005-33736
This volume presents information on mathematicians
such as Augusta Ada Lovelace, Marie-Sophie Germain,
Mary Fairfax Somerville, Evariste Galois, Georg Cantor,
and Henri Poincare.
Includes glossary and bibliographical references

Mathematics frontiers; 1950 to the present. Facts
on File 2006 148p il (Pioneers in mathematics)
$29.95
Grades: 7 8 9 10 **920**
1. Mathematics—History 2. Mathematicians
ISBN 0-8160-5427-4 LC 2005-36154

This volume presents profiles of mathematicians such
as John Nash, Stephen Hawking, Julia Robinson, Ernest
Wilkins, Jr., John Conway, Fan Chung, Andrew Wiles,
and Sarah Flannery.
Includes glossary and bibliographical references

Modern mathematics; 1900 to 1950. Facts on
File 2006 164p il (Pioneers in mathematics)
$29.95
Grades: 7 8 9 10 **920**
1. Mathematics—History 2. Mathematicians
ISBN 0-8160-5426-6 LC 2005-36152
This volume presents profiles of mathematicians such
as Alan Turing, David Hilbert, Norbert Wiener, Grace
Chisholm Young, Amalie Emmy Noether, and Grace
Murray Hopper.
Includes glossary and bibliographical references

Bruns, Roger

Icons of Latino America; Latino contributions to
American culture; foreword by Ilan Stavans.
Greenwood Press 2008 2v il (Greenwood icons)
set $175
Grades: 11 12 Adult **920**
1. Hispanic Americans—Biography
ISBN 978-0-313-34086-4; 0-313-34086-2
LC 2008-13646
"This set employs a broad definition of 'icon' and in-
cludes real personages, cartoon characters, and Mexican
food among the entries. The engaging articles average 20
to 30 pages in length and contain substantive, document-
ed information. Entries are detailed and interesting." SLJ
Includes bibliographical references

Bussing-Burks, Marie, 1958-

Influential economists. Oliver Press 2003 160p
il (Profiles) $19.95
Grades: 7 8 9 10 **920**
1. Economists
ISBN 1-881508-72-2 LC 2001-59310
Presents information on the lives and work of the
economists Thomas Gresham, Adam Smith, Thomas
Robert Malthus, Karl Marx, John Maynard Keynes, Milton Friedman, and Alan Greenspan
"The author discusses sometimes complex theories in
a straightforward, jargon-free text accessible to most sophisticated teen readers. . . . Informative, well-written,
and fairly interesting." Booklist
Includes glossary and bibliographical references

Butts, Edward, 1951-

She dared; true stories of heroines, scoundrels,
and renegades; [by] Ed Butts; illustrated by
Heather Collins. Tundra Bks. 2005 121p il pa
$8.95
Grades: 6 7 8 9 10 **920**
1. Women—Biography 2. Canada—Biography
ISBN 0-88776-718-4
This "details the lives of some of Canada's most famous and infamous women. The stories showcase explorers, spies, criminals, and pioneers in a variety of career
fields. Organized chronologically from the 16th to the
mid-20th century, this 12-chapter offering is historically
sound and well researched." SLJ

Carey, Charles W.

American inventors, entrepreneurs & business
visionaries; [by] Charles W. Carey, Jr. Rev. ed,
rev. by Ian C. Friedman. Facts On File 2010 xxi,
455p il (Facts on File library of American history)
$95 *

Grades: 11 12 Adult   **920**
 1. Inventors 2. Businesspeople 3. United States—Biography 4. Reference books
 ISBN 978-0-8160-8146-2; 978-1-4381-3336-2 (ebook)
          LC 2009-54269
 First published 2002
 "This biographical dictionary includes profiles of more
than 300 individuals who have made significant and lasting contributions to American industry dating from the
Colonial era to the present. Each entry addresses the subject chronologically through his or her life, focusing on
major professional achievements as well as personal triumphs and tragedies. . . . The book paints a fascinating
portrait of American ingenuity. A well-written biographical dictionary that will appeal to anyone interested in the
history of American invention and entrepreneurialism."
Libr J
 Includes bibliographical references

Caroli, Betty Boyd

First ladies; from Martha Washington to
Michelle Obama. Rev. and updated ed. Oxford
University Press 2010 xxii, 437p il pa $17.95

Grades: 11 12 Adult   **920**
 1. Presidents' spouses—United States
 ISBN 978-0-19-539285-2; 0-19-539285-X
          LC 2010-14673
 First published 1987
 In addition to profiling each woman who has served
as First Lady the author examines the ways the role has
evolved over the years.
 Includes bibliographical references

Cropper, William H.

Great physicists; the life and times of leading
physicists from Galileo to Hawking. Oxford Univ.
Press 2001 500p il hardcover o.p. pa $21.95 *

Grades: 11 12 Adult   **920**
 1. Physicists
 ISBN 0-19-513748-5; 0-19-517324-4 (pa)
          LC 2001-21611
 "Among the scientists presented are Galileo, Newton,
Bohr, Einstein, Gibbs, Faraday, Marie Curie, Rutherford,
Chandrasekhar, and Hawking." Sci Books Films
 The author "incorporates nothing beyond the ken of
high-school calculus students. . . . His reworking of the
abundant extant biographical material enhances the ap-
peal of his book for reflective science students." Booklist
 Includes bibliographical references

Cullen, Katherine E.

Science, technology, and society; the people
behind the science; [by] Katherine Cullen. Chelsea
House 2006 xx, 172p il (Pioneers in science)
$29.95

Grades: 9 10 11 12   **920**
 1. Scientists
 ISBN 0-8160-5468-1; 978-0-8160-5468-8
          LC 2004-30605
 This book "looks at 10 pioneers who have changed
the way society views science and technology forever.
Each chapter contains . . . information on the scientist's
childhood, research, discoveries, and lasting contributions
to the field and concludes with a chronology and a list
of print and Internet references specific to that individual." Publisher's note
 "Readers with substantially different levels of scientific knowledge will find the book comprehensible and interesting." Sci Books Films
 Includes bibliographical references

Davis, Sampson

The pact: three young men make a promise and
fulfill a dream; by Samson Davis, George Jenkins,
and Remeck Hunt; with Lisa Frazier Page.
Riverhead Bks. 2002 248p hardcover o.p. pa $14

Grades: 11 12 Adult   **920**
 1. African Americans—Biography 2. Physicians
 ISBN 1-57322-216-X; 1-57322-989-X (pa)
          LC 2001-59647
 "Three young black men in the medical professions (a
dentist, an emergency-room physician, and an internist)
recall an informal pact they made as youths that guided
them out of their inner-city Newark neighborhoods and
into successful careers. . . . In their own voices, these
three young men tell a compelling story that will inspire
other young people to form and value supportive, long-
term friendships." Booklist

Day, Sara

Women for change. Library of Congress 2007
64p il (Women who dare) $12.95 *

Grades: 9 10 11 12   **920**
 1. Women—United States—Biography 2. Political activists
 ISBN 978-0-7649-3876-4   LC 2006-50349
 This book "connects the stories of two dozen women
who defied expectations in many different ways, speaking out, holding high office, leading strikes, challenging
entrenched dogma." Publisher's note
 Includes bibliographical references

Denlinger, Elizabeth Campbell

Before Victoria; extraordinary women of the
British Romantic era; by Elizabeth Campbell
Denlinger; foreword by Lyndall Gordon. Columbia
University Press 2005 188p il $41.50 *

Grades: 11 12 Adult   **920**
 1. Women—Great Britain 2. Great Britain—History—
19th century
 ISBN 0-231-13630-7   LC 2004-59267

Denlinger, Elizabeth Campbell—*Continued*

"Published on the occasion of the exhibition, Before Victoria: extraordinary women of the British Romantic era, presented at the New York Public Library, Humanities and Social Sciences Library, D. Samuel and Jeane H. Gottesman Exhibition Hall, April 8-July 30, 2005" Verso of title page

This book "offers portraits of a group of women who were scientists, artists, writers, poets, philanthropists and reformers during the Romantic Era and details how their accomplishments changed the social and economic landscape for women." Univ Press Books for Public and Second Sch Libr, 2006

Includes bibliographical references

Distinguished African American scientists of the 20th century; [by] James H. Kessler [et .al.]; with Sigrid Berge, portrait artist, and Alyce Neukirk, computer-graphics artist. Oryx Press 1996 382p il $73.95 *

Grades: 7 8 9 10   **920**
1. Scientists 2. African Americans—Biography
ISBN 0-89774-955-3   LC 95-43880

"One hundred famous and not-so-famous African American scientists (both living and dead) are covered in this biographical reference. . . . Men and women accomplished in anthropology, biology, chemistry, engineering, geology, mathematics, medicine, and physics are included. Those profiled include lesser-known scientists such as Christine Darden (an engineer with NASA) as well as the better known, e.g., George Washington Carver." Libr J

Includes bibliographical references

Dunn, Brad, 1973-

When they were 22; 100 famous people at the turning point in their lives. Andrews McMeel Pub. 2006 179p $12.95

Grades: 9 10 11 12   **920**
1. Celebrities
ISBN 978-0-7407-5810-2; 0-7407-5810-1
LC 2005-57170

This book "tells the stories of famous people and the fateful events and choices they faced at the all-important age of 22. . . . [The personalities profiled range from] writers, actors, and musicians to politicians, hip-hop moguls, criminals, and porn stars." Publisher's note

Includes bibliographical references

Earls, Irene

Young musicians in world history. Greenwood Press 2002 139p il $44.95

Grades: 8 9 10 11 12   **920**
1. Musicians
ISBN 0-313-31442-X   LC 2001-40559

Contents: Louis Armstrong; Johann Sebastian Bach; Ludwig van Beethoven; Pablo Casals; Sarah Chang; Ray Charles; Charlotte Church; Bob Dylan; John Lennon; Midori; Wolfgang Mozart; Niccolo Paganini; Isaac Stern

Profiles thirteen musicians who achieved high honors and fame before the age of twenty-five, representing many different time periods and musical styles

"A useful introduction to some of the musical giants of the last four centuries." SLJ

Includes glossary and bibliographical references

Ellsberg, Robert, 1955-

Blessed among all women; women saints, prophets, and witnesses for our time. Crossroad Pub. 2005 316p $19.95; pa $16.95

Grades: 9 10 11 12   **920**
1. Christian saints 2. Religious biography 3. Women—Biography
ISBN 0-8245-2251-6; 0-8245-2439-X (pa)
LC 2005-11363

Companion volume to All saints (1997)

The author presents short biographies of 136 women he considers holy. The "entries are grouped according to the virtues of the Beatitudes, an arrangement that reflects Ellsberg's definition of saints as 'people who made the Gospel concrete'. . . . Although Ellsberg is yet another man narrating tales of women saints, his accounts are far from one-dimensional. The women he depicts are fully human, which makes them useful spiritual guides." America

Includes bibliographical references

Evans, Harold

They made America; [by] Harold Evans, with Gail Buckland and David Lefer. Little, Brown 2004 496p $40; pa $18.95 *

Grades: 11 12 Adult   **920**
1. Inventors 2. Inventions
ISBN 0-316-27766-5; 0-316-01385-4 (pa)
LC 2003-65954

The author "profiles 70 of America's leading inventors, entrepreneurs and innovators, some better known than others. Along with such obvious choices as Henry Ford, Thomas Edison and the Wright brothers, Evans profiles Lewis Tappan (an abolitionist who dreamed up the idea of credit ratings), Gen. Georges Doriot (pioneer of venture capital) and Joan Ganz Cooney, of the Children's Television Workshop." Publ Wkly

Facts about the presidents; a compilation of biographical and historical information; Joseph Nathan Kane, Janet Podell [editors] 8th ed. Wilson, H.W. 2009 720p $125 *

Grades: 8 9 10 11 12 Adult   **920**
1. Presidents—United States 2. Reference books
ISBN 978-0-8242-1087-8; 0-8242-1087-8
LC 2008056016

First published 1959

The main part of this work provides an individual chapter on each President, from Washington through Barack Obama, presenting such information as family, education, election, Vice President, main events and accomplishments of his administration, and First Lady. Part two contains tables and lists presenting comparative data on all the Presidents

Freedman, Russell

Indian chiefs. Holiday House 1987 151p il $24.95; pa $14.95

Grades: 6 7 8 9 10   **920**
1. Native Americans—Biography
ISBN 0-8234-0625-3; 0-8234-0971-6 (pa)
LC 86-46198

Freedman, Russell—*Continued*

This "book chronicles the lives of six renowned Indian chiefs, each of whom served as a leader during a critical period in his tribe's history. . . . The text relates information about the lives of each chief and aspects of Indian/white relationships that illuminate his actions. Interesting vignettes and quotations are well integrated into the narrative as are dramatic accounts of battles. While the tone of the text is nonjudgmental, an underlying sympathy for the Indians' situation is apparent." Horn Book

Includes bibliographical references

Garrison, Mary, 1952-

Slaves who dared; the stories of ten African-American heroes. White Mane Kids 2002 142p il $19.95 *

Grades: 9 10 11 12   920
1. Slavery—United States 2. African Americans—History
ISBN 1-57249-272-4   LC 2002-22666

"Garrison does a great job of weaving into each narrative many actual quotes, illustrations . . . and the drama of how and where the stories were recorded." Booklist

Includes bibliographical references

Gates, Henry Louis

The African-American century; how Black Americans have shaped our country; {by} Henry Louis Gates, Jr. and Cornel West. Free Press 2000 414p il hardcover o.p. pa $16 *

Grades: 11 12 Adult   920
1. African Americans—Biography 2. African Americans—Intellectual life
ISBN 0-684-86414-2; 0-684-86415-0 (pa)
                                      LC 00-63596

"Gates and West have listed and written biographies of their choices of the 100 most important and influential [African Americans] of the . . . twentieth century. In their opinion the subjects that they have selected have made significant impacts and contributions to American society. . . . The entries are arranged by decade and by the person's period of prominence in society, 1900-1909 through 1990-1999. Profiles include Madame C.J. Walker, Langston Hughes, Carter G. Woodson, Paul Robeson, Thurgood Marshall, and Colin Powell." MultiCult Rev

Includes bibliographical references

Grange, Michael

Basketball's greatest stars. Firefly Books 2010 216p il $35

Grades: 11 12 Adult   920
1. Basketball—Biography
ISBN 978-1-55407-637-6   LC 2010-284742

A history of the National Basketball Association, illustrated through the profiles of its top players, past and present. Also includes the histories of 30 franchises and three essays about the game.

"This is a colorful, picture-driven reading experience. Don't expect an exhaustive history of the NBA, but an interesting summary of stars and teams. . . . Recommended for fans of the NBA who seek a quick reference to the best players the game has ever seen and for all libraries collecting accessible and colorful basketball books." Libr J

Haley, Alex, 1921-1992

Roots; the saga of an American family: the 30th anniversary edition. Vanguard Books 2007 899p pa $15.95 *

Grades: 11 12 Adult   920
1. Haley family 2. Kinte family
ISBN 978-1-59315-449-3; 1-59315-449-6
                                      LC 2007-8822

First published 1976 by Doubleday

This book details Haley's "search for the genealogical history of his family. He describes his trip to Gambia, the African homeland of his ancestors, and recounts the lives of his forebears." Benet's Reader's Ency of Am Lit

Hanes, Richard Clay, 1946-

Crime and punishment in America: biographies; [by] Richard C. Hanes and Kelly Rudd; Sarah Hermsen, project editor. UXL 2005 191, lixp il (Crime and punishment in America reference library) $60

Grades: 9 10 11 12   920
1. Criminals 2. Administration of criminal justice
ISBN 0-7876-9167-4   LC 2004-17066

This book "includes entries on important figures, such as Jane Addams, Allan Pinkerton, Clarence Darrow, Senator Estes Kefauver and others." Publisher's note

Includes bibliographical references

Hannon, Sharon M.

Women explorers. Library of Congress 2007 64p il map (Women who dare) $12.95 *

Grades: 9 10 11 12   920
1. Explorers 2. Women—Biography
ISBN 978-0-7649-3892-4   LC 2006-50706

This book profiles "extraordinary women from the past two centuries who have eagerly sought out high adventure in far-flung corners of the world." Publisher's note

Includes bibliographical references

Hardesty, Von, 1939-

Black wings; courageous stories of African Americans in aviation and space history. HarperCollins Publishers 2007 180p il $21.95

Grades: 11 12 Adult   920
1. African American pilots 2. African American astronauts
ISBN 978-0-06-126138-1   LC 2007-21270

"In association with the Smithsonian National Air and Space Museum"

"This book companion to the Smithsonian National Air and Space Museum exhibit of the same name offers a look at the little-known and long-neglected history of black pioneers in aviation. . . . [Along with] the Tuskegee Airmen, Hardesty profiles barnstormers, including the Blackbirds; William J. Powell, founder of an aviation club; military flyers, including Benjamin O. Davis Jr.; and astronauts Guy Bluford, Ronald McNair, and Mae Jemison. This is an inspiring look at the adventurous individuals who pushed against the limits of racial discrimination to realize their passion for flying." Booklist

Includes bibliographical references

Harlem Renaissance lives from the African American national biography; general editors, Henry Louis Gates, Jr., Evelyn Brooks Higginbotham. Oxford University Press 2009 595p il $50

Grades: 11 12 Adult   **920**
1. African Americans—Intellectual life 2. African Americans—Biography 3. Harlem Renaissance
ISBN 978-0-19-538795-7; 0-19-538795-3
                                   LC 2008-51794

"In association with the American Council of Learned Societies"

"A spinoff of the eight-volume *African American National Biography* (Oxford Univ., 2008), this volume reprints profiles of 300 prominent figures of the era. . . . The signed articles begin with an entry on newspaper publisher Robert Sangstache Abbott of the Defender fame, conclude with author Richard Wright, and in between mix biographies of Langston Hughes, Zora Neale Hurston, and other . . . figures with introductions to subjects such as Casper Holstein (philanthropist, activist, and numbers banker) and comedian Moms Mabley." SLJ

"This authoritative reference work will prove a useful acquisition for high school, public, and academic libraries, particularly for smaller institutions that lack the *African American National Biography*." Libr J

Includes bibliographical references

Harris, Cecil, 1960-
Charging the net; a history of blacks in tennis from Althea Gibson and Arthur Ashe to the Williams sisters; [by] Cecil Harris and Larryette Kyle-DeBose with a foreword by James Blake and an afterword by Robert Ryland. Ivan R. Dee 2007 267p il $26.95

Grades: 11 12 Adult   **920**
1. Tennis 2. African American athletes
ISBN 978-1-56663-714-5; 1-56663-714-7
                                   LC 2007-2747

This book is a "history, built on more than 65 interviews, that tells . . . stories about the lives of black tennis stars like Venus and Serena; Arthur Ashe; Althea Gibson, the Wimbledon champ from Harlem who ended up broke, reclusive and bitter; and Zina Garrison, the Wimbledon finalist." N Y Times Book Rev

"This book will appeal to teens interested in black athletes' contributions to sports, in tennis generally, or in sports facts. It is well documented and may be read for pleasure or for assignments. It also portrays new role models for succeeding in sports and in life, while struggling with discrimination." SLJ

Includes bibliographical references

Haskins, James, 1941-2005
African American religious leaders; [by] Jim Haskins and Kathleen Benson. Wiley 2008 162p il (Black stars) lib bdg $24.95

Grades: 6 7 8 9 10 11 12 Adult   **920**
1. African Americans—Biography 2. African Americans—Religion
ISBN 978-0-471-73632-5; 0-471-73632-5
                                   LC 2007-27347

This is a collective biography of "black religious leaders who helped shape the African American experience—from colonial to modern times." Publisher's note

"It's great to have all these figures between two covers, and even a sampling of the entries captures the importance of religion, and its leaders, in African American life." Booklist

Includes bibliographical references

Hatch, Robert
The hero project; 2 teens, 1 notebook, 13 extraordinary interviews; by Robert Hatch and William Hatch. McGraw-Hill 2006 204p pa $14.95
*

Grades: 6 7 8 9 10   **920**
1. Heroes and heroines
ISBN 0-07-144904-3   LC 2005017518
Contents: Introduction; Sample letter; Pete Seeger; Madeleine L'Engle; Florence Griffith-Joyner; Jimmy Carter; Orson Scott Card; Yo Yo Ma; Elouise Cobell; Carroll Spinney; Desmond Tutu; Lance Armstrong and Linda Kelly Armstrong; Steven Wozniak; Dolores Huerta; Jackie Chan

This is a collection of interviews by two teenaged brothers with some of their heroes.

"The selections are candid and thoughtful, with the boys asking questions about political and spiritual beliefs as well as queries about childhood heroes and family pets." SLJ

Hillstrom, Kevin
American Civil War: biographies; [by] Kevin Hillstrom and Laurie Collier Hillstrom; Lawrence W. Baker, editor. U.X.L 2000 2v il (American Civil War reference library) set $110

Grades: 8 9 10 11 12   **920**
1. United States—History—1861-1865, Civil War—Biography
ISBN 0-7876-3820-X   LC 99-46920
This set "chronicles the lives of 60 famous and lesser-known men and women, including abolitionists, spies, commanders, and writers." SLJ

Includes bibliographical references

Vietnam War: biographies; [by] Kevin Hillstrom and Laurie Collier Hillstrom; Diane Sawinski, editor. U.X.L 2001 2v il (Vietnam War reference library) set $110 *

Grades: 8 9 10 11 12   **920**
1. Vietnam War, 1961-1975—Biography 2. United States—Biography
ISBN 0-7876-4884-1   LC 00-56378
This "focuses on 60 important figures, including military and political leaders (Spiro Agnew, Ngo Dinh Diem, Pol Pot), activists (Daniel Berrigan, Jane Fonda), writers (Le Ly Hayslip, Tim O'Brien), and prominent veterans (Ron Kovic, John McCain) on both sides of the conflict. . . . A picture of each personality accompanies the informative text." Booklist

Includes bibliographical references

Howes, Kelly King

World War II: biographies; [by] Kelly K.
Howes; edited by Christine Slovey. U.X.L 1999
xxxiii, 288p il (World War II reference library)
$60

Grades: 8 9 10 11 12   **920**
1. World War, 1939-1945—Biography
ISBN 0-7876-3895-1   LC 99-27166
"In addition to political and military leaders, the 31 alphabetical entries in *Biographies* include conscientious
objector Franz Jaggerstatter, journalists Dorothy Thompson and Ernie Pyle, physicist J. Robert Oppenheimer,
and Holocaust victim Edith Stein. The profiles range in
length from 6 to 13 pages and most contain at least one
black-and-white photo. Sidebars cover myriad topics such
as Shintoism and examples of the Navajo code." SLJ
Includes bibliographical references

Invisible giants; fifty Americans that shaped the
nation but missed the history books; edited by
Mark C. Carnes. Oxford Univ. Press 2002 316p
il hardcover o.p. pa $19.95
Grades: 11 12 Adult   **920**
1. United States—Biography
ISBN 0-19-515417-7; 0-19-516883-6 (pa)
LC 2001-58785
"All American National Biography entries copyright
2000 by the American Council of Learned Societies."
Verso of title page
The publisher of American National Biography recruited "50 well-known contemporary authors to pick
from it a once-significant, now-obscure person, and re-
print the ANB article prefaced by the selector's one-page
justification. . . . As varied as the individal subjects,
some selectors, such as Jacques Barzun (on critic John
Jay Chapman) or Arthur Schlesinger Jr. (on historian
George Bancroft), concisely point to changing tastes.
. . . Each of these ANB subjects left a mark perceptible
in modern America, filling this volume with surprises for
even the most widely read." Booklist
Includes bibliographical references

Kennedy, John F. (John Fitzgerald), 1917-1963

Profiles in courage. HarperCollins Pubs. 2003
xxii, 245p $19.95; pa $13.95 *
Grades: 7 8 9 10 11 12 Adult   **920**
1. Politicians—United States 2. Courage
ISBN 0-06-053062-6; 0-06-085493-6 (pa)
LC 2003-40676
A reissue of the title first published 1956
This series of profiles of Americans who took coura-
geous stands at crucial moments in public life includes
John Quincy Adams, Daniel Webster, Thomas Hart Ben-
ton, Sam Houston, Edmund G. Ross, Lucius Q. C. La-
mar, George Norris, Robert A. Taft and others.
Includes bibliographical references

Kennedy, Kerry

Speak truth to power; human rights defenders
who are changing our world; photographs by
Eddie Adams; edited by Nan Richardson. Crown
2000 256p il hardcover o.p. pa $34.95
Grades: 7 8 9 10   **920**
1. Human rights
ISBN 0-8129-3062-2; 1-88416-733-0 (pa)
LC 00-34557
"An Umbrage editions book"
This book "is composed of fifty three-page interviews
with people who have made strides in the global fight to
ensure basic human rights for everyone. . . . The Dalai
Lama, Desmond Tutu, and Elie Wiesel are included, but
most subjects are everyday people who have survived
imprisonment, death threats, and torture to bring about
change. . . . Their reports are sad but inspiring. . . . The
haunting photographs and stories are gripping." Voice
Youth Advocates

Knight, Judson

Middle ages: biographies; edited by Judy
Galens. U.X.L 2000 2v (Middle Ages reference
library) set $110
Grades: 8 9 10 11 12   **920**
1. Middle ages—Biography 2. Medieval civilization
ISBN 0-7876-4857-4   LC 00-64864
Among the 50 people profiled are Eleanor of Aquitaine, Henry the Navigator, Kublai Khan, Montezuma I,
and St. Patrick
Each "entry contains illustrations, date spans and pronunciations of names for individuals, sidebars, and a bibliography of books, periodicals, and Web sites." Booklist

Koopmans, Andy

Filmmakers. Lucent Books 2005 112p il
(History makers) $28.70
Grades: 7 8 9 10   **920**
1. Motion picture producers and directors
ISBN 1-59018-598-6   LC 2004-12774
"This collective biography . . . focuses on the struggles, successes, and setbacks of five film directors: Alfred Hitchcock, Stanley Kubrick, Francis Ford Coppola,
Spike Lee, and Peter Jackson. The subjects are well chosen. . . . These biographies inform about cinema history
and have the potential to inspire readers interested in
pursuing a career in film." Booklist
Includes bibliographical references

Lifetimes: the Great War to the stock market
crash: American history through biography and
primary documents; edited by Neil A. Hamilton;
writers, Mark LaFlaur, James M. Manheim,
Renée Miller. Greenwood Press 2002 328p il
$74.95 *
Grades: 11 12 Adult   **920**
1. United States—History—20th century 2. United
States—Biography
ISBN 0-313-31799-2   LC 2001-54700
"Each entry includes a one- to two-page biographical
essay, complete with a black-and-white photo. Primary
sources include autobiographical sketches, reviews of the

Lifetimes: the Great War to the stock market crash: American history through biography and primary documents—*Continued*

subjects' works, commentary from contemporaneous journals, political cartoons, and other materials. The essays are accurate, readable, and objective." Libr J

Includes bibliographical references

Martin, James

My life with the saints. Loyola Press 2006 411p $22.95

Grades: 11 12 Adult   920

1. Christian saints

ISBN 0-8294-2001-0   LC 2005-28466

The author "relates how he discovered various 'saints' and how each has affected his life. . . . Despite a theme built on a particular facet of Catholic belief, Martin's animated style and wide-ranging experiences make this a book readers of diverse backgrounds will enjoy." Publ Wkly

Includes bibliographical references

Matuz, Roger

Reconstruction era: biographies; Lawrence W. Baker, project editor. UXL 2004 xxiv, 246p il (Reconstruction Era reference library) $60 *

Grades: 11 12 Adult   920

1. Reconstruction (1865-1876)

ISBN 0-7876-9218-2   LC 2004-17300

This "volume covers political and military leaders as well as activists, artists, writers, and more. Among them are Louisa May Alcott, Frederick Douglass, Ulysses S. Grant, and Zebulon Vance. Within each biographical entry are cross-references to other individuals covered in this volume." Booklist

Includes bibliographical references

McBrien, Richard P.

Lives of the saints; from Mary and Francis of Assisi to John XXIII and Mother Teresa. HarperSanFrancisco 2001 xxiii, 646p il pa $19.95 hardcover o.p.

Grades: 11 12 Adult   920

1. Christian saints

ISBN 0-06-123283-1 (pa)   LC 00-53933

"This work goes beyond the Roman Catholic Church's list of saints to include those of the Orthodox, Anglican, and Lutheran churches. Concise and well-researched biographical sketches are arranged by feast days, with access provided by indexes for saints, personal names, and subjects. Complementing the biographies are thoughtful essays on the history of saints, their place in religious history, and canonization; a series of seven tables on feast days, patron saints, iconography, and papal canonization." Libr J

Includes bibliographical references

Mendoza, Patrick M.

Extraordinary people in extraordinary times; heroes, sheroes, and villains. Libraries Unlimited 1999 142p il pa $21

Grades: 7 8 9 10   920

1. United States—Biography

ISBN 1-56308-611-5   LC 99-14238

Stories of little-known historical characters from American history. Subjects range from that of the first woman to receive the Congressional Medal of Honor to the first woman to be hanged in the United States. Jeanette Rankin, Jose Marti and two survivors of the Sand Creek Massacre are among those profiled

Includes bibliographical references

Morell, Virginia

Ancestral passions; the Leakey family and the quest for humankind's beginnings. Simon & Schuster 1995 638p il pa $28.95 hardcover o.p.

Grades: 11 12 Adult   920

1. Leakey, Louis Seymour Bazett, 1903-1972 2. Leakey, Mary D., 1913-1996 3. Leakey, Richard E., 1944- 4. Anthropologists 5. Human origins

ISBN 0-684-82470-1 (pa)   LC 95-14306

"The Leakey family, now in its third generation of hunting hominid fossils in East Africa, is the subject of this exquisitely written biography about the search for the beginnings of humankind. . . . With access to volumes of personal and professional papers and extensive interviews with Mary, Richard, and Meave Leakey, as well as many others who played a role in the story of human origins, Virginia Morell has allowed the reader to gain unparalleled insight into the oftentimes complex lives of the world's 'first family of human evolution.'" Sci Books Films

Includes bibliographical references

Morgan, Edmund Sears

American heroes; profiles of men and women who shaped early America; [by] Edmund S. Morgan. W.W. Norton & Co. 2009 278p il $27.95 *

Grades: 11 12 Adult   920

1. United States—History—1600-1775, Colonial period 2. United States—History—1775-1783, Revolution 3. United States—History—1783-1809 4. Heroes and heroines

ISBN 978-0-393-07010-1; 0-393-07010-7

LC 2009-714

"From a body of work stretching back seven decades, . . . [the author] selects 17 essays on characters large and small who illuminate early American history." Kirkus

"This book is a perfect gem. . . . Both specialists and general readers will find this book both authoritative and fun to read." Libr J

My folks don't want me to talk about slavery; twenty-one oral histories of former North Carolina slaves; edited by Belinda Hurmence. Blair 1984 103p hardcover o.p. pa $6.95 *
Grades: 9 10 11 12   **920**
1. Slavery—United States 2. African Americans—Biography
ISBN 0-89587-038-X; 0-89587-039-8 (pa)
           LC 84-16891
The narratives presented here were part of a Federal Writers' project during which some 2,000 former slaves were interviewed during the 1930s
A "unique glimpse of slavery viewed from the less well-recorded side, the side of the subjugated." Sci Books Films
Includes bibliographical references

Not quite what I was planning; six-word memoirs by writers famous and obscure: from Smith magazine; edited by Rachel Fershleiser and Larry Smith. HarperPerennial 2008 225p il pa $12
Grades: 9 10 11 12 Adult   **920**
1. Autobiographies
ISBN 978-0-06-137405-0; 0-06-137405-9
"The editors of SMITH magazine invited readers to contribute brief life stories in the vein of Hemingway's bravura tale, 'For sale: baby shoes, never worn.' The hundreds selected for publication include offerings from children and adults, professional writers, bereaved parents, recovering broken hearts, and people with great pride in showing off their wit. . . . A good combination of inspired, inspiring, and entertaining, this title is eminently browsable and shareable." SLJ

Open the unusual door; true life stories of challenge, adventure, and success by black Americans; edited and with an introduction by Barbara Summers. Graphia 2005 206p pa $7.99
Grades: 7 8 9 10   **920**
1. African Americans—Biography
ISBN 0-618-58531-1
"A wonderful cross section of excerpts from published autobiographies. The 16 stories tell of challenges met and opportunities recognized and realized. Colin Powell's recollection of his introduction to the military life at City College in New York City stands alongside Russell Simmons's retelling of the turning point in his life when, at 16 years of age, he shot at and missed a fellow drug dealer. . . . This little gem of a book should be a first purchase for public and school libraries." SLJ

Ottaviani, Jim
Dignifying science; stories about women scientists; written by Jim Ottaviani and illustrated by Donna Barr . . . [et al.] 3rd ed. G.T. Labs 2009 142p il pa $16.95 *
Grades: 6 7 8 9 10 11 12   **920**
1. Graphic novels 2. Women scientists—Graphic novels 3. Biographical graphic novels
ISBN 978-0-9788037-3-5; 0-9788037-3-5
First published 1999

Ottaviani provides biographical sketches of women scientists such as Lise Meitner, Rosalind Franklin, Barbara McClintock, and Hedy Lamarr (yes, the actress was also an inventor); all the stories are illustrated by women comics artists, including Lea Hernandez, Linda Medley, Anne Timmons, and others.

Outman, James L., 1946-
Industrial Revolution: biographies; [by] James L. Outman, Elisabeth M. Outman. U.X.L 2003 218p il (Industrial revolution reference library) $55 *
Grades: 8 9 10 11 12   **920**
1. Industrial revolution
ISBN 0-7876-6514-2   LC 2002-155421
Contents: Henry Bessemer; Andrew Carnegie; Henry Ford; Robert Fulton; Samuel Gompers; Jay Gould; James J. Hill; Mother Jones; Karl Marx; Rockefeller; Theodore Roosevelt; Adam Smith; George Stephenson; Ida Tarbell; James Watt; George Westinghouse; Eli Whitney
"The 25 essays in [this volume] provide biographical information with an emphasis on each person's contribution or impact on the Industrial Revolution. . . . More than 50 black-and-white photographs complement the text. . . . This is an excellent adjunct to American and world history units and classes on economics and labor movements." Booklist
Includes bibliographical references

U.S. immigration and migration. Biographies; James L. Outman, Roger Matuz, Rebecca Valentine; Lawrence W. Baker, editor. UXL 2004 2v il (U.S. immigration and migration reference library) set $115 *
Grades: 9 10 11 12   **920**
1. United States—Immigration and emigration
ISBN 0-7876-7733-7   LC 2004-3552
This set "profiles 50 men and women who either immigrated to this country or influenced the debate on the treatment of immigrants." SLJ
Includes bibliographical references

Pendergast, Tom, 1964-
The Middle East conflict. Biographies; [by] Tom and Sara Pendergast; [project editor] Ralph Zerbonia. UXL 2006 li, 282p il (U-X-L Middle East conflict reference library) $67
Grades: 9 10 11 12   **920**
1. Israel-Arab conflicts 2. Middle East—History
ISBN 0-7876-9457-6; 978-0-7876-9457-9
           LC 2005-12011
This book "examines twenty-six key figures in the Middle East. . . . Most of the entries range from ten to thirteen pages, and include biographical information as well as the role each person has played. . . . Not only do these biographies serve as an introduction to important figures in the conflict, but they could also prove very useful as a key source for research papers." Ref & User Services Quarterly
Includes bibliographical references

Pendergast, Tom, 1964-—*Continued*

The sixties in America. Biographies; [by] Tom Pendergast and Sara Pendergast; Kathleen J. Edgar, project editor. UXL 2005 lvi, 204p il (U-X-L the sixties in America reference library) $63 *

Grades: 9 10 11 12   **920**
    1. United States—History—1961-1974
    ISBN 0-7876-9247-6   LC 2004-16600

"Biographical entries cover counterculture icons (Bob Dylan, Abbie Hoffman), politicians and newsmakers (John F. Kennedy, Ralph Nader), mainstream celebrities (Vince Lombardi, Walter Cronkite), and individuals associated with specific events." Booklist

Includes bibliographical references

Westward expansion: biographies. U.X.L 2001 xxv, 251p il maps (Westward expansion reference library) $60 *

Grades: 8 9 10 11 12   **920**
    1. Frontier and pioneer life 2. West (U.S.)—Biography
    ISBN 0-7876-4863-9   LC 00-109475

This collective biography profiles a number of legendary figures of the Wild West, including Buffalo Bill, George Custer, Wyatt Earp, Kit Carson, Annie Oakley, Andrew Jackson, Sarah Winnemucca, and Belle Starr

Profiles in courage for our time; edited and introduced by Caroline Kennedy. Hyperion 2002 354p $23.95; pa $14.95

    Grades: 11 12 Adult   **920**
    1. Politicians—United States 2. Courage
    ISBN 0-7868-6793-0; 0-7868-8678-1 (pa)
                                LC 2001-51894

This book "compiles 14 essays lauding political courage. Contributors include Michael Beschloss, E. J. Dionne, Bob Woodward, Anna Quindlen, and Pete Hamill, among others. Each of the 14 essay subjects was a recipient of the Profiles in Courage Award, created by the Kennedy family a decade ago." Booklist

"Unabashedly liberal and pro-government, this collection is a stirring look at people who rarely thought about what they could do for themselves, but always about what they could do for their country." Publ Wkly

Renaissance & Reformation: biographies; Peggy Saari & Aaron Saari, editors. U.X.L 2002 2v il (Renaissance & Reformation reference library) set $105

    Grades: 8 9 10 11 12   **920**
    1. Renaissance
    ISBN 0-7876-5470-1   LC 2001-8609

Profiles fifty people who played a significant role during the Renaissance and Reformation periods in Europe, including John Calvin, Peter Paul Rubens, Catherine de Medici, and Johannes Kepler.

Includes bibliographical references

Scandiffio, Laura

Evil masters; the frightening world of tyrants. Annick Press 2005 230p il map $24.95; pa $12.95

Grades: 7 8 9 10   **920**

    1. Dictators
    ISBN 1-55037-895-3; 1-55037-894-5 (pa)

This "title examines the lives and reigns of seven rulers. The profiles range from the frightening ancient world of the first emperor of China and Nero, emperor of Rome during the first century, to Ivan the Terrible and Robespierre. More recent rulers include Hitler, Stalin, and Saddam Hussein. . . . Maps, photos, reproductions, and half-page fact boxes make the events easier to understand. . . . This is an excellent and thought-provoking resource." SLJ

Includes bibliographical references

Schiff, Karenna Gore

Lighting the way; nine women who changed modern America. Miramax Books/Hyperion 2006 528p il $25.95; pa $17.95

Grades: 11 12 Adult   **920**
    1. Women—United States—Biography
    ISBN 1-4013-5218-9; 1-4013-6015-7 (pa)
                               LC 2005-56247

The author "profiles nine women who helped change the course of history by overcoming injustice in their own lives." Libr J

"This is an inspirational collection of biographies of women of various social, ethnic, and racial backgrounds fighting for social justice." Booklist

Includes bibliographical references

Schnakenberg, Robert

Secret lives of the Supreme Court; what your teachers never told you about America's legendary justices. Quirk Books 2009 288p il pa $17.95

Grades: 11 12 Adult   **920**
    1. United States. Supreme Court 2. Judges
    ISBN 978-1-59474-308-5; 1-59474-308-8

Profiles of America's most legendary justices with hundreds of little-known facts.

"This is a fascinating look behind the somber black robes and solemn faces of U.S. Supreme Court justices." Booklist

Includes bibliographical references

See, Lisa

On Gold Mountain; the one-hundred-year odyssey of my Chinese-American family. 1st Vintage Books ed. Vintage Books 1996 xxi, 394p il, maps pa $15.95

Grades: 11 12 Adult   **920**
    1. Seay family 2. Chinese Americans
    ISBN 0-679-76852-1   LC 96-11821
    First published 1995 by St. Martin's Press

"See's chronicle melds together the life stories of her Chinese and American ancestors, beginning with a great-great-grandfather's journey from China to San Francisco. . . . Her tale is most specific in its descriptions of the hardships and discrimination endured for decades by large numbers of Chinese immigrants." Booklist

"Facing the nimble shell game her family plays with its history, Ms. See has done a gallant and fair-minded job of fashioning anecdote, fable and fact into an engaging account." N Y Times Book Rev

Includes bibliographical references

Sickels, Amy

African-American writers. Chelsea House 2010
141p il (Multicultural voices) $35 *

Grades: 9 10 11 12   **920**

1. American literature—African American authors
2. African Americans in literature 3. African Americans—Intellectual life

ISBN 978-1-60413-311-0   LC 2009-37856

"In this clearly written, informative overview, Sickels examines the lives and major works of writers over the last 40 years. Eight authors are showcased, including Toni Morrison, Maya Angelou, Alice Walker, and Walter Dean Myers. Each chapter opens with a black-and-white photo and a brief biography, with the remainder of it dealing with a critical analysis of one or more of the writer's best-known works. . . . This is an outstanding contribution and should be a first purchase for high-school libraries." SLJ

Includes bibliographical references

Sifters: Native American women's lives; edited by Theda Perdue. Oxford Univ. Press 2001 260p (Viewpoints on American culture) $55; pa $19.95 *

Grades: 11 12 Adult   **920**

1. Native American women

ISBN 0-19-513080-4; 0-19-513081-2 (pa)

                   LC 00-39950

"From Pocahontas, a Powhatan woman of the seventeenth century, to Ada Deer, the Menominee woman who headed the Bureau of Indian Affairs in the 1990s, the essays span four centuries. Each one recounts the experiences of women from vastly different cultural traditions. . . . Contributors focus on the ways in which different women have fashioned lives that remain firmly rooted in their identity as Native women." Publisher's note

Includes bibliographical references

Spitz, Bob

Yeah! yeah! yeah! the Beatles, Beatlemania, and the music that changed the world. Little, Brown 2007 234p il $18.99

Grades: 7 8 9 10   **920**

1. Beatles 2. Rock musicians

ISBN 978-0-316-11555-1; 0-316-11555-X

                   LC 2006-39575

Based on the author's title for adults: The Beatles (2005)

This is "packed with all the fun and fabulousness that were the Beatles. The book begins at the church festival where John and Paul met as teens, and ends with Paul's formal declaration to leave the group. . . . [This is] comprehensive, sensitive to its subjects, and told with a flow that carries readers along. Many smartly chosen black-and-white photographs help re-create the times." Booklist

Staeger, Rob

Ancient mathematicians. Morgan Reynolds Pub. 2006 112p il map (Profiles in mathematics) $28.95

Grades: 7 8 9 10   **920**

1. Mathematicians 2. Greece—Biography 3. Mathematics—History

ISBN 978-1-59935-065-3; 1-59935-065-3

                   LC 2008-7533

"After a brief overview of the role of mathematics in ancient Greece, the book profiles Pythagoras, Euclid, Archimedes, and Hypatia. The presentation is greatly enhanced by full-color maps, reproductions, and artifacts, as well as numerous sidebars, diagrams, and time lines." SLJ

Includes bibliographical references

Stark, Steven D.

Meet the Beatles; a cultural history of the band that shook youth, gender, and the world. HarperEntertainment 2005 344p il $26.95; pa $14.95

Grades: 11 12 Adult   **920**

1. Beatles 2. Rock musicians

ISBN 0-06-000892-X; 0-06-000893-8 (pa)

                   LC 2004-59794

In this biography of the Beatles, the author focuses "as much on the cultural trends that produced the Beatles—and the trends they created—as on the Fab Four themselves. . . . Throughout, Stark is sharp and insightful, even when he wades into the psychoanalytic waters of the John/Yoko and Paul/Linda relationships." Publ Wkly

Starkey, David

Six wives: the queens of Henry VIII. HarperCollins Pubs. 2003 xxvii, 852p il hardcover o.p. pa $16.95 *

Grades: 11 12 Adult   **920**

1. Great Britain—History—1485-1603, Tudors 2. Queens

ISBN 0-694-01043-X; 0-06-000550-5 (pa)

The author covers each of Henry's six wives, "their personalities, their place in the family networks and religious currents at court and the overall patterns of the king's infatuations and disillusionments." Publ Wkly

"Solidly researched and delightfully told, this is highly recommended." Libr J

Includes bibliographical references

Stolen voices; young people's war diaries from World War I to Iraq; edited with commentaries by Zlata Filipovic and Melanie Challenger; foreword by Olara A. Otunnu. Penguin 2007 xxiii, 293p il pa $14 *

Grades: 11 12 Adult   **920**

1. Children and war

ISBN 978-0-14-303871-9; 0-14-303871-0

"A Penguin original"

The editors have "compiled 14 diaries that were kept by children during wartime, from World War I to Iraq. Their poignant voices will break your heart." Libr J

Terkel, Studs, 1912-2008

Hope dies last; keeping the faith in difficult times. New Press 2003 xxix, 326p hardcover o.p. pa $16.95

Grades: 11 12 Adult   **920**

1. Hope 2. United States—Social conditions

ISBN 1-56584-837-3; 1-56584-937-X (pa)

                   LC 2003-50989

Terkel, Studs, 1912-2008—*Continued*

"Terkel talks with objectors, dissenters, observers, protestors, and do-gooders to find out what makes these committed and generous souls tick. He speaks with Ohio congressman and Democratic presidential candidate Dennis Kucinich, a doctor who treats the homeless, teachers, labor activists, recent immigrants, Pete Seeger, and John Kenneth Galbraith. . . . As a collector of true stories and a guardian of free speech, Terkel ensures that grass-root alternatives to the 'official word' are heard from sea to shining sea." Booklist

Vare, Ethlie Ann

Patently female; from AZT to TV dinners: stories of women inventors and their breakthrough ideas; [by] Ethlie Ann Vare, Greg Ptacek. Wiley 2002 220p il $27.95 *

Grades: 11 12 Adult   **920**

1. Women inventors

ISBN 0-471-02334-5   LC 2001-26950

Sequel to: Mothers of invention (1988)

The authors "detail how women's ideas like the cotton gin, automatic sewing machine and even the Brooklyn Bridge have often been attributed to men and how history books and museums like the Smithsonian and the National Inventors Hall of Fame have ignored women's achievements." Publ Wkly

Includes bibliographical references

Vowell, Sarah, 1969-

Assassination vacation. Simon & Schuster 2005 258p il hardcover o.p. pa $14

Grades: 11 12 Adult   **920**

1. Presidents—United States—Assassination 2. United States—Description and travel 3. United States—Local history

ISBN 0-7432-6003-1; 0-7432-6004-X (pa)
                                     LC 2004-59134

The author "takes readers on a pilgrimage of sorts to the sites and monuments that pay homage to Lincoln, Garfield and McKinley, visiting everything from grave sites and simple plaques (like the one in Buffalo that marks the place where McKinley was shot) to places like the National Museum of Health and Medicine, where fragments of Lincoln's skull are on display." Publ Wkly

"[Vowell] has done her homework, providing lucid descriptions of the murders and agile summations of the scholarly assessments of each era." America

Walters, Eric, 1957-

When elephants fight; written by Eric Walters and Adrian Bradbury. Orca Book Publishers 2008 89p il $19.95

Grades: 7 8 9 10   **920**

1. Children and war

ISBN 978-1-55143-900-6; 1-55143-900-X

"The authors detail the lives of children growing up in . . . [war torn nations]. They provide rich, detailed histories of each nation, and explain the current conflicts which have led to the destruction of families and normal childhood. . . . This would be an excellent supplemental text for a high school geography or world civilization program." Libr Media Connect

Watad, Mahmoud

Teen voices from the Holy Land; who am I to you? [by] Mahmoud Watad and Leonard Grob. Prometheus Books 2007 221p il pa $19

Grades: 9 10 11 12   **920**

1. Youth—Israel

ISBN 978-1-59102-535-1   LC 2007-1565

"Based on interviews of thirty-four Palestinian and Israeli teenagers, . . . [this book presents] first-person narratives of their day-to-day lives. These young people describe their ordinary lives, including their interests, facts about their families, friendships, and neighborhoods, as well as their spiritual concerns and dreams for the future." Publisher's note

Includes bibliographical references

What my father gave me; daughters speak; edited by Melanie Little. Annick Press 2010 129p $21.95; pa $12.95

Grades: 10 11 12   **920**

1. Father-daughter relationship 2. Women authors

ISBN 978-1-55451-255-3; 978-1-55451-254-6 (pa)

"In this collection of first-person essays, seven women discuss their adolescent relationships with their fathers and how they affected their adult lives. . . . These and the other essays are intensely personal and honest, and the writers do not shy away from discussing some very painful subjects. Teens will appreciate this honesty and openness, making this anthology a good choice for YA collections." SLJ

Windows into my world; Latino youth write their lives; edited by Sarah Cortez; with an introduction by Virgil Suárez. Piñata Books 2007 210p pa $14.95

Grades: 10 11 12   **920**

1. Hispanic Americans—Biography

ISBN 978-1-55885-482-6; 1-55885-482-7
                                     LC 2006-52470

Autobiographies of Latino youth who struggle with issues such as death, anorexia, divorce, sexuality, etc.

"For young adults of all backgrounds, this collection illuminates both the familiar coming-of-age experiences that transcend cultural differences and the moments that are unique to young Latinos in the States." SLJ

920.003 Dictionaries, encyclopedias, concordances of biography as a discipline

Aaseng, Nathan, 1953-

African-American athletes. Rev. ed. Facts On File 2010 280p il (A to Z of African Americans) $49.50 *

Grades: 11 12 Adult   **920.003**

1. African American athletes—Dictionaries 2. Reference books

ISBN 978-0-8160-7869-1   LC 2010-10023

"Facts on File library of American history"

First published 2003

This book "highlights athletes who have competed at the highest levels in one or more sports. Each entry pro-

Aaseng, Nathan, 1953-—*Continued*

vides . . . [a] biographical profile, concentrating on the events in that person's life related to his or her accomplishments in sports, followed by . . . [a] further reading list on that individual." Publisher's note

Includes bibliographical references

African American biographies. Grolier 2006 10v il set $529

Grades: 6 7 8 9 10 11 12   **920.003**
1. African Americans—Biography—Dictionaries 2. Reference books

ISBN 978-0-7172-6090-4   LC 2005-50391

"Entries cover a gamut of achievers: leaders of abolition, slaves, politicians, civil-rights activists, lawyers, educators, physicians, scientists, religious figures, military personnel, journalists, business leaders, artists, astronauts, entertainers, and sports figures. . . . It is nearly impossible to find fault with this important and visually appealing set. From the high quality of the paper to the layout of the pages, the attention given to creating a superior source is evident. For the student researcher, the material is clear, concise, and user-friendly in presentation." Booklist

Includes bibliographical references

The **African** American national biography; editors in chief, Henry Louis Gates, Jr., Evelyn Brooks-Higginbotham. Oxford University Press 2008 8v il set $995 *

Grades: 11 12 Adult   **920.003**
1. African Americans—Biography—Dictionaries 2. Reference books

ISBN 978-0-19-516019-2   LC 2007-44671

Also available online

Companion volume to African American lives (2004)

"A supplement to the 24-volume *American National Biography* . . . [this biographical encyclopedia] records the contributions of more than 4,000 African Americans—slaves, architects, entertainers, dentists, political leaders, artists, poets, and activists. . . . [This] is a major . . . standard reference work that most libraries of any size will want to have." Booklist

Includes bibliographical references

American authors, 1600-1900; a biographical dictionary of American literature; edited by Stanley J. Kunitz and Howard Haycraft. Wilson, H.W. 1938 846p il (Authors series) $120 *

Grades: 8 9 10 11 12 Adult   **920.003**
1. Authors, American—Dictionaries 2. American literature—Bio-bibliography 3. Reference books

ISBN 0-8242-0001-2

"Complete in one volume with 1300 biographies and 400 portraits." Title page

"This volume contains biographies of 1,300 authors who contributed to the development of American literature, from the founding of Jamestown (1607) to the end of the nineteenth century. Each essay describes the author's life, discusses past and present significance, and evaluates principal works." Safford. Guide to Ref Materials for Sch Media Cent. 5th edition

American Indian biographies; edited by Carole Barrett, Harvey Markowitz, project editor, R. Kent Rasmussen. rev ed. Salem Press 2005 623p il map (Magill's choice) $62

Grades: 8 9 10 11 12 Adult   **920.003**
1. Native Americans—Biography 2. Reference books

ISBN 1-58765-233-1; 978-1-58765-233-2
     LC 2004-28872

First published 1999; some essays originally appeared in Dictionary of world biography, Great lives from history: the Renaissance & early modern era, 1454-1600 (2005), and American ethnic writers (2000)

"The book contains essays on religious, social, and political leaders; warriors; and reformers from the past as well as modern activists, writers, artists, entertainers, scientists, and athletes. . . . A great bargain and an asset in any library that supports an American history curriculum." Booklist

Includes bibliographical references

American national biography; general editors, John A. Garraty, Mark C. Carnes. Oxford Univ. Press 1999 24v set $2,095 *

Grades: 11 12 Adult   **920.003**
1. United States—Biography—Dictionaries 2. Reference books

ISBN 0-19-520635-5   LC 98-20826

Also available online; Also available Supplement 1 published 2002 $150 (ISBN 0-19-515063-5) and Supplement 2 published 2005 $150 (0-19-522202-4), the first two in an ongoing series of Supplements

Conceived as the successor to the Dictionary of American biography, first published between 1926 and 1937; Published under the auspices of the American Council of Learned Societies

"ANB defines 'American' broadly as a person whose significance, achievement, fame, or influence occurred during residence within what is now the US, or whose life or career directly influenced the course of US history. Subjects must have died before 1996. . . . Subjects are arranged alphabetically. The typical entry, 750 to 7,500 words in length, proceeds chronologically, following the major personal and professional events of the subject's life, birth to death. The concluding paragraph attempts to assess the subject's contributions from today's perspective. A brief bibliography after each entry, not meant to be comprehensive, lists major sources, including locations of archives and collections of personal papers." Choice

Includes bibliographical references

Bader, Philip

African-American writers; revised by Catherine Reef. Rev. ed. Facts On File 2010 c2011 340p il (A to Z of African Americans) $49.50 *

Grades: 9 10 11 12 Adult   **920.003**
1. American literature—African American authors—Bio-bibliography 2. African American authors—Dictionaries 3. Reference books

ISBN 978-0-8160-8141-7   LC 2010-05463

First published 2004

This book "profiles popular and prominent African-American writers across many genres of literature. Each entry in this . . . resource provides a biographical pro-

Bader, Philip—*Continued*
file, concentrating on the major literary works and accomplishments of each author as well as an outline of his or her contributions to American literature." Publisher's note
Includes bibliographical references

Baker's biographical dictionary of musicians; Nicolas Slonimsky, editor emeritus; Laura Kuhn, Baker's series advisory editor. Centennial ed. Schirmer Bks. 2001 6v set $800 *
Grades: 11 12 Adult   920.003
1. Music—Bio-bibliography 2. Musicians—Dictionaries 3. Reference books
ISBN 0-02-865525-7   LC 00-46375
First published 1900 in one volume under the authorship of Theodore Baker
"Brief articles about composers, performers, critics, conductors, and teachers arranged alphabetically under surname with pronunciation, list of musical works, and a bibliography of print sources. Includes classical, jazz, rock, country, blues, and other popular musicians." Ref Sources for Small & Medium-sized Libr. 6th edition
"This monumental work collocates information from classical, popular, and jazz music on a scale greater than any other source. Essential for all libraries." Choice
Includes bibliographical references and discographies

Barthelmas, Della Gray, 1920-
The signers of the Declaration of Independence; a biographical and genealogical reference; with a foreword by Frank Borman. McFarland & Co. 1997 334p il hardcover o.p. pa $35
Grades: 11 12 Adult   920.003
1. United States. Declaration of Independence 2. United States—History—1775-1783, Revolution—Biography 3. Reference books
ISBN 0-7864-0318-7; 0-7864-1704-8 (pa)
                            LC 97-11663
Entries begin "with a full-page portrait of the signer and a facsimile of his signature as it appears on the document. The biographies range from one to 10 pages, followed by family information on the person (wives and children), then by genealogies of his and his spouse's ancestors for as many generations as possible." Book Rep

The **Biographical** dictionary of women in science; pioneering lives from ancient times to the mid-20th century; Marilyn Ogilvie and Joy Harvey, editors. Routledge 2000 2v set $250
Grades: 11 12 Adult   920.003
1. Reference books 2. Women scientists—Dictionaries
ISBN 0-415-92038-8   LC 99-17668
"This title includes approximately 2,500 women scientists. . . . Science is defined broadly to include related fields like anthroplogy and sociology. . . . Entries begin with a brief biographical description, with birth and death dates, educational background, and area of professional work. The essays, typically 250 to 750 words long, give only brief early life history before focusing on the subjects' principal scientific contributions. . . . Ogilvie and Harvey's work is a must-have reference tool." Am Ref Books Annu, 2001
Includes bibliographical references

Biographical encyclopedia of artists; Sir Lawrence Gowing, general editor. Facts on File 2005 4v il set $260 *
Grades: 11 12 Adult   920.003
1. Reference books 2. Artists—Biography—Encyclopedias
ISBN 0-8160-5803-2   LC 2005-40500
First published 1983 by Prentice-Hall as volume two of Encyclopedia of visual art
At head of title: Facts on File
"The artists covered include Laurie Anderson, Frank Gehry, Anselm Kiefer, Jan Vermeer, and Andy Warhol. . . . A visual chronology of artists by country and era functions as an index to artists, and an alphabetical artist/subject index concludes the work." Libr J
Includes bibliographical references

Black women in America; Darlene Clark Hine, editor in chief. 2nd ed. Oxford University Press 2005 3v il set $325
Grades: 11 12 Adult   920.003
1. Reference books 2. African American women—Dictionaries
ISBN 0-19-515677-3   LC 2005-1532
First published 1993 by Carlson Pub.
This set features over 300 "profiles of women from the 1800s to the present, including writers, activists, entrepreneurs, educators, ambassadors, and many others, interspersed with the roles they played in Islam, the Left, librarianship, journalism, the labor movement, and more." Libr J
"The essays offer fascinating glimpses into black women's economic, social, and political contributions, even at the grassroots level, and explore issues such as spirituality, domestic servitude, and mixed-race identity in terms of how they have shaped history." SLJ
Includes bibliographical references

Blanchard, Mary Loving, 1952-
Poets for young adults; their lives and works; [by] Mary Loving Blanchard and Cara Falcetti. Greenwood Press 2006 287p il $59.95 *
Grades: 9 10 11 12   920.003
1. Reference books 2. American poetry—Bio-bibliography 3. Poets, American—Dictionaries
ISBN 0-313-32884-6; 978-0-313-32884-8
                            LC 2006-29475
This book "examines the lives and works of seventy-five poets that are read and loved by teens. . . . [The poets covered range] from the modern songwriters such as Bob Dylan and Tupac Shakur, to the nineteen sixties icons Jack Kerouac and Sylvia Plath, to such traditional poets as Edgar Allan Poe and William Blake." Publisher's note
Includes bibliographical references

British authors before 1800; a biographical dictionary; edited by Stanley J. Kunitz and Howard Haycraft; complete in one volume with 650 biographies and 220 portraits. Wilson, H.W. 1952 584p il (Authors series) $95 *
Grades: 11 12 Adult   920.003

British authors before 1800—*Continued*
  1. Reference books 2. Authors, English—Dictionaries
  3. English literature—Bio-bibliography
  ISBN 0-8242-0006-3

"Short biographical essays on principal and marginal figures in British literature. Bibliographies appended to essays." N Y Public Libr. Book of How & Where to Look It Up

British authors of the nineteenth century; edited by Stanley J. Kunitz; associate editor: Howard Haycraft; complete in one volume with 1000 biographies and 350 portraits. Wilson, H.W. 1936 677p il (Authors series) $105 *
  Grades: 11 12 Adult   **920.003**
  1. Reference books 2. Authors, English—Dictionaries
  3. English literature—Bio-bibliography
  ISBN 0-8242-0007-1

"More than a thousand authors of the British Empire (including Canada, Australia, South Africa, and New Zealand) are represented by sketches varying in length from approximately 100 to 2500 words, roughly proportionate to the importance of the subjects." Preface

British writers; edited under the auspices of the British Council; Ian Scott-Kilvert, general editor. Scribner 1979-1992 7v + supplement I-IV set $2379
  Grades: 11 12 Adult   **920.003**
  1. Reference books 2. Authors, English—Dictionaries
  3. English literature—Bio-bibliography 4. English literature—History and criticism
  ISBN 0-684-80587-1

Also available Retrospective supplement I published 2002 $218, Retrospective supplement II published 2002 $218, and Retrospective supplement III published 2009 $218; Continued by ongoing supplementary volumes each $218; Volumes 1-7 also available separately ea $218

For subscription options apply to publisher

"This work presents articles by distinguished contributors on major British writers from the fourteenth century to the present. . . . The biographical sketch that opens each entry is followed by a survey of the author's principal works, a critical evaluation, and an updated bibliography." Ref Sources for Small & Medium-sized Libr. 6th edition

Business leader profiles for students; Sheila M. Dow, editor. Gale Group 1999-2002 2v il $130
  Grades: 9 10 11 12   **920.003**
  1. Businesspeople 2. Reference books
  ISBN 0-7876-2935-9 (v1 op); 0-7876-4889-2 (v2)

"This resource provides information on past and present giants of business and industry. Each alphabetical entry includes an overview of the person's life and career, a discussion of his or her social and economic impact, a brief chronology, and a bibliography. For some, a black-and-white photograph and contact information are also included. Among the approximately 250 entrepreneurs profiled are: L. L. Bean, Andrew Carnegie, Berry Gordy, Jr., Steve Jobs, Ralph Lauren, Joseph Pulitzer, Donald Trump, Lillian Vernon, and Oprah Winfrey. . . . This reference tool will be appreciated by business and economics students and others seeking information on these sometimes elusive subjects." SLJ

Butler, Alban, 1711-1773
  Butler's Lives of the saints. Christian Classics 1956 4v set $149.95; pa set $109.95 *
  Grades: 11 12 Adult   **920.003**
  1. Reference books 2. Christian saints—Dictionaries
  ISBN 0-87061-045-7; 0-87061-137-2 (pa)

Also available in concise editions in paperback from HarperSanFrancisco (edited by Michael Walsh) and from Liturgical Press (edited by Paul Burns)

A reprint of the four volume set published 1956 by Kenedy; New edition of a work first published 1756-1759. The calendar arrangement is retained, but the number of entries has almost doubled and many of the entries have been rewritten in whole or part

"The biographies of the saints and beati are arranged by their feast days with each of the four volumes containing three months. . . . Each volume has a table of contents arranged by the days of the month with a list of the feasts for each day." Booklist

Carey, Charles W.
  African Americans in science; an encyclopedia of people and progress; [by] Charles W. Carey, Jr. ABC-CLIO 2008 2v il set $195 *
  Grades: 9 10 11 12 Adult   **920.003**
  1. Reference books 2. African Americans—Biography—Encyclopedias 3. Scientists—Encyclopedias
  ISBN 978-1-85109-998-6   LC 2008-24609

This resource takes "a detailed look at the accomplishments of African American scientists. . . . Part 1 addresses the accomplishments of individual scientists. Part 2 covers the issues that are of critical importance to the African American scientific community, including science education and careers for blacks and a whole range of topics related to health disparities (e.g., cancer, obesity, cardiovascular issues, and diabetes). Part 3 outlines in more general terms the contributions made by the scientists in Part 1. Part 4 focuses on scientific research and training." Libr J

Includes bibliographical references

Concise dictionary of scientific biography. 2nd ed. Scribner 2000 1097p il $135
  Grades: 9 10 11 12   **920.003**
  1. Reference books 2. Scientists—Dictionaries
  ISBN 0-684-80631-2   LC 00-61231

First published 1981

This volume "integrates the 5,100 biographies from the base set with the 400 biographies found in the *Supplement* and includes photos and portraits of the most-studied scientists." Publisher's note

"This book would be useful as a quick introduction and as a starting point for further study." Am Ref Books Annu, 2001

Contemporary novelists; editors, Neil Schlager and Josh Lauer. 7th ed. St. James Press 2001 xxiv, 1166p (Contemporary writers series) $230
  Grades: 9 10 11 12   **920.003**
  1. Reference books 2. Novelists, English—Dictionaries
  3. American fiction—Bio-bibliography
  ISBN 1-55862-408-2

First published 1972 by St. Martin's Press

Contemporary novelists—*Continued*

Contains bio-critical information on English-language novelists from around the world. Each entry lists essential biographical data; publications according to genre; a brief bibliography of secondary sources; the location of the author's manuscript collection; and a short critical essay on the novels

Includes bibliographical references

Contemporary poets; editor, Thomas Riggs; with a preface by Diane Wakoski. 7th ed. St. James Press 2001 xxiii, 1443p (Contemporary writers series) $230

Grades: 11 12 Adult   **920.003**
1. Reference books 2. Poets, English—Dictionaries 3. Poets, American—Dictionaries 4. American poetry—Bio-bibliography
ISBN 1-55862-349-3   LC 00-45882

First published 1970 with title: Contemporary poets of the English language

"A biographical handbook of contemporary poets, arranged alphabetically. Entries consist of a short biography, full bibliography, comments by many of the poets, and a signed critical essay." Ref Sources for Small & Medium-sized Libr. 6th edition

Includes bibliographical references

Current biography yearbook, 2010; editor, Clifford Thompson; senior editors, Miriam Helbok, Mari Rich. Wilson, H.W. 2011 738p il $185 *

Grades: 8 9 10 11 12 Adult   **920.003**
1. Biography—Periodicals
ISBN 978-0-8242-1113-4

Also available online; Current biography: cumulated index, 1940-2005 available $90 (ISBN 0-8242-1054-9)

Annual. First published 1940 with title: Current biography

Also issued monthly except December at a subscription price of $185 per year (ISSN 0011-3344). Yearbooks 1940-2004 available ea $160; yearbooks 2005-2009 available ea $180

"Biographies of prominent people written in lively, popular prose. Emphasis is on entertainers, star athletes, politicians, and other celebrities. Series is cumulative, with biographies revised and updated occasionally. Each volume has seven-year index." N Y Public Libr Book of How & Where to Look It Up

Distinguished Asian Americans; a biographical dictionary; edited by Hyung-chan Kim; contributing editors, Dorothy Cordova [et al.] Greenwood Press 1999 430p il $65 *

Grades: 11 12 Adult   **920.003**
1. Asian Americans—Biography—Dictionaries 2. Reference books
ISBN 0-313-28902-6   LC 98-41423

"This volume features 166 entries, most ranging from two to three pages, arranged alphabetically by person. The Asian Americans included may be native or foreign-born. . . . All were 'chosen for their outstanding accomplishments in professions that range from labor leaders to political leaders, tennis players to football players, scientists to distinguished inventors, Hollywood actors to Wall Street investors, schoolteachers to scholars, and comedians to community activists.' Among those profiled are Michael Chang, Connie Chung, S.I. Hayakawa, Lance Ito, Bruce Lee, Yo-Yo Ma, I.M. Pei, and Kristi Yamaguchi. . . . [There is] a selected bibliography for each entry." Booklist

Duncan, Joyce, 1946-

Shapers of the great debate on women's rights; a biographical dictionary. Greenwood Press 2008 232p (Shapers of the great American debates) $75

Grades: 9 10 11 12 Adult   **920.003**
1. Reference books 2. Women—Biography—Dictionaries 3. Women political activists—Dictionaries
ISBN 978-0-313-33869-4; 0-313-33869-8
                                                    LC 2008-23050

"The three waves of feminism are explored through the lives of the women who made history in bringing women's issues to the forefront of American society. . . . Many notable women, such as Susan B. Anthony, Elizabeth Cady Stanton, Billie Jean King, Betty Friedan, Helen Gurley Brown, Jane Fonda, and Sandra Day O'Connor, are included in this history of the women's movement in America." Publisher's note

Includes bibliographical references

Encyclopedia of women's autobiography; edited by Victoria Boynton and Jo Malin; Emmanuel S. Nelson, advisory editor. Greenwood Press 2005 2v set $249.95 *

Grades: 11 12 Adult   **920.003**
1. Reference books 2. Autobiography 3. Women—Biography—Encyclopedias
ISBN 0-313-32737-8   LC 2005-8526

The contents "range from autobiographies of individuals (e.g., Adrienne Rich, Sojourner Truth, Isak Dinesen) to those of specific ethnicities or nationalities (e.g., African American Women's Autobiography) to important genres and terms (e.g., Captivity/Prison Narrative, Diary, Feminism, and Voice)." Choice

This set's "encyclopedic and culturally diverse nature should appeal to a wide audience and provide a valuable starting point for further research." Libr J

Includes bibliographical references

Encyclopedia of world biography. 2nd ed. Gale Res. 1998 17v il set $1787

Grades: 11 12 Adult   **920.003**
1. Biography—Dictionaries 2. Reference books
ISBN 0-7876-2221-4   LC 97-42327

Kept up-to-date by yearly supplements. Volumes available 1998-2010 designated volumes 18-30 at $195 ea

First published 1973 with title: McGraw-Hill encyclopedia of world biography

Presents brief biographical sketches which provide vital statistics as well as information on the importance of the person listed. Volumes 1-16 are arranged alphabetically; volume 17 is the index

Encyclopedia of world writers; Thierry Boucquey, general editor; Gary Johnson, advisor; Nina Chordas advisor; [written and developed by Book Builders LLC] Facts on File 2005 3v (Facts on File library of world literature) set $225 *

Grades: 9 10 11 12   **920.003**
1. Reference books 2. Authors—Dictionaries
ISBN 0-8160-6143-2   LC 2004-20551

Vol. 3 first published 2003 with title: Encyclopedia of world writers: 19th and 20th centuries

General editor for Vol. 3: Marie Josephine Diamond; advisors, Maria DiBattista and Julian Wolfreys

This set is "an introduction to the world's writers, not only literary authors but also philosophers, religious thinkers, and essayists. The first two volumes (beginnings through the 18th century) also treat anonymous works and oral traditions." Choice

"This reference will stand out for its scope, particularly the accessible entries on the earliest literary activity." SLJ

Includes bibliographical references

European authors, 1000-1900; a biographical dictionary of European literature; edited by Stanley J. Kunitz and Vineta Colby; complete in one volume with 967 biographies and 309 portraits. Wilson, H.W. 1967 1016p il (Authors series) $115 *

Grades: 11 12 Adult   **920.003**
1. Reference books 2. Literature—Bio-bibliography
ISBN 0-8242-0013-6

Includes continental European writers born after the year 1000 and dead before 1925. Nearly a thousand major and minor contributors to thirty-one different literatures are discussed.

"These biographies provide quick, satisfactory introductions to a staggering variety of authors and literatures." Choice

Extraordinary women of the Medieval and Renaissance world; a biographical dictionary; [by] Carole Levin [et al.] Greenwood Press 2000 327p il $65

Grades: 11 12 Adult   **920.003**
1. Women—Biography—Dictionaries 2. Renaissance 3. Middle ages—Biography 4. Reference books
ISBN 0-313-30659-1   LC 99-55218

This volume presents seventy women who "lived between the tenth and seventeenth centuries. . . . The entries are arranged in alphabetical order, with a brief subheading noting country and occupation. As much information as is known about the person is summarized, including education, family, and achievements. Each article ends with a bibliography of additional sources of information. A number of the articles include portraits." Booklist

Includes bibliographical references

Flores, Angel, 1900-1992
Spanish American authors; the twentieth century. Wilson, H.W. 1992 915p $150

Grades: 11 12 Adult   **920.003**
1. Reference books 2. Authors, Latin American—Dictionaries 3. Latin American literature—Bio-bibliography
ISBN 0-8242-0806-4   LC 92-7591

"A monumental and distinguished work covering more than 330 novelists and poets from Central and South America, Puerto Rico, and the Caribbean, some appearing for the first time in a reference source. Essential in any library supporting study of Latin America. . . . For each writer, provides biographical information, critical analysis and summaries of criticism, and a bibliography of primary and secondary works, excluding dissertations." Guide to Ref Books. 11th edition

Friedman, Ian C.
Latino athletes. Facts on File 2007 278p il (A to Z of Latino Americans) $44 *

Grades: 11 12 Adult   **920.003**
1. Reference books 2. Hispanic Americans—Dictionaries 3. Athletes—Dictionaries
ISBN 978-0-8160-6384-0; 0-8160-6384-2
                                        LC 2006-16901

"Gymnast Trent Dimas, mountain biker Juli Furtado, and speed skater Derek Parra are among the 176 athletes profiled in this volume. . . . Following the entries, athletes are listed by sport, year of birth, and ethnicity or country of origin." Booklist

Includes bibliographical references

Genovese, Michael A.
Encyclopedia of the American presidency. Rev. ed. Facts on File 2010 606p il (Facts on File library of American history) $95

Grades: 11 12 Adult   **920.003**
1. Presidents—United States—Encyclopedias 2. Reference books
ISBN 978-0-8160-7366-5   LC 2008-54208
First published 2003 in the United Kingdom

"Birth and death dates, major public acts, family life, and other particulars give a concise but well-rounded view of each Chief Executive as man and as man of the people. . . . An altogether excellent introduction to the study of the presidency of the United States; articles are informative without being pedantic and interesting while remaining pertinent and to the point." Libr J

Includes bibliographical references

Grant, Michael, 1914-2004
Greek and Latin authors, 800 B.C.-A.D. 1000; a biographical dictionary. Wilson, H.W. 1980 490p il (Authors series) $105

Grades: 11 12 Adult   **920.003**
1. Classical literature—Dictionaries 2. Authors, Greek—Dictionaries 3. Authors, Latin—Dictionaries 4. Reference books
ISBN 0-8242-0640-1   LC 79-27446

Covers more than 370 classical authors. Each entry includes "the pronunciation of the author's name, biograph-

Grant, Michael, 1914-2004—*Continued*
ical background, an overview of major works with critical commentary on the nature and quality of those works, and, where relevant, a brief discussion of the influence of the author's works on later literature." Ref Sources for Small & Medium-sized Libr. 5th edition

Great athletes; edited by The Editors of Salem Press; special consultant Rafer Johnson. Salem Press 2010 13v il set $1,020
Grades: 7 8 9 10 11 12   920.003
1. Athletes—Dictionaries 2. Reference books
ISBN 978-1-58765-473-2; 1-58765-473-3
LC 2009-21905
"This massive undertaking totals 1,470 entries covering athletes in baseball, basketball, boxing, football, golf, auto racing, soccer, tennis, and Olympic sports. Additionally, well-known athletes in other, less recognized sports—such as cycling, skateboarding, stunt riding, martial-arts and chess—are included. . . . Overall, this is a well-put-together and wide-ranging set." Booklist
Includes bibliographical references

Great lives from history, The 17th century, 1601-1700; editor, Larissa Juliet Taylor. Salem Press 2005 2v il set $160
Grades: 11 12 Adult   920.003
1. Reference books 2. Biography—Dictionaries
3. World history—17th century
ISBN 1-58765-222-6; 978-1-58765-222-6
LC 2005-17804
Also available online
Companion volume to Great events from history, The 17th century, 1601-1700
First published as part of the Great lives from history series, published 1987-1995 under the editorship of Frank N. Magill; previously published as half of volume 4 of Dictionary of world biography, published 1998-1999
This "is a collection of biographical essays, ranging from three to five pages in length and documenting the lives of those individuals who helped to shape the history of the 17th century. The coverage is also global and includes both well-known and lesser-known figures." SLJ
Includes bibliographical references

Great lives from history, The 18th century, 1701-1800; editor, John Powell; editor, first edition, Frank N. Magill. Salem Press 2006 2v il map set $160
Grades: 11 12 Adult   920.003
1. Reference books 2. Biography—Dictionaries
3. World history—18th century
ISBN 978-1-58765-276-9; 1-58765-276-5
LC 2006-5336
Also available online
Companion volume to Great events from history, The 18th century, 1701-1800
First published as part of the Great lives from history series, published 1987-1995 under the editorship of Frank N. Magill; previously published as half of volume 4 of Dictionary of world biography, published 1998-1999
"The alphabetically listed subjects encompass 36 areas of expertise and include John Newbery, Pontiac, Qianlong, Hannah More, Pius IV, Paul Revere, and Shah Wali Allah, among others. Each article is approximately

three pages long and lists the subject's major accomplishments, important dates, and areas of achievement. . . . A well-written, useful set." SLJ
Includes bibliographical references

Great lives from history, The 19th century, 1801-1900; editor, John Powell. Salem Press 2006 4v il map set $360
Grades: 11 12 Adult   920.003
1. Reference books 2. Biography—Dictionaries
3. World history—19th century
ISBN 978-1-58765-292-9; 1-58765-292-7
LC 2006-20187
Also available online
Companion volume to Great events from history, The 19th century, 1801-1900
First published as part of the Great lives from history series, published 1987-1995 under the editorship of Frank N. Magill; previously published as volumes 5 and 6 of Dictionary of world biography, published 1998-1999
"A total of 737 essays covering 757 major figures including 123 on women make up the set. . . . Major world leaders appear here, as well as the giants of religious faith who dominated the century: monarchs, presidents, popes, philosophers, writers, social reformers, educators, and military leaders who left their imprint on political as well as spiritual institutions." Publisher's note
Includes bibliographical references

Great lives from history: the 20th century, 1901-2000; editor, Robert F. Gorman. Salem Press 2008 10v il set $795
Grades: 11 12 Adult   920.003
1. Reference books 2. Biography—Dictionaries
3. World history—20th century
ISBN 978-1-58765-345-2   LC 2008-17125
Also available online
First published as part of the Great lives from history series, published 1987-1995 under the editorship of Frank N. Magill; previously published as volumes 7-9 of Dictionary of world biography, published 1998-1999
"This ten-volume set offers 1,330 . . . biographies of major personages in world history (many still living) from 1901-2000. . . . The personages covered are identified with one or more of the following regions: Africa, Asia, Australia, Caribbean, Europe, Latin America, Middle East, North America, South America, and Southeast Asia." Publisher's note
Includes bibliographical references

Great lives from history, The ancient world, prehistory-476 C.E; editor, Christina A. Salowey. Salem Press 2004 2v il, maps set $160
Grades: 11 12 Adult   920.003
1. Reference books 2. Biography—Dictionaries
3. Ancient history
ISBN 1-587-65152-1; 978-1-58765-164-9
LC 2004-705
Also available online
Companion volume to Great events from history, The ancient world, prehistory-476 C.E
First published as part of the Great lives from history series, published 1987-1995 under the editorship of Frank N. Magill; previously published as volume 1 of Dictionary of world biography, published 1998-1999

Great lives from history, The ancient world, prehistory-476 C.E—*Continued*

This "set provides three-to-six-page biographies on major personages from the ancient world. Arranged alphabetically, each article gives basic information such as when and where the individual was born and also where and when he or she died, a description of his or her early life and life's work, the significance of the individual, an annotated bibliography, and related entries in both this set and in the . . . [Great events from history] set." Ref & User Services Quarterly

Includes bibliographical references

Great lives from history, the Middle Ages, 477-1453; editor, Shelley Wolbrink. Salem Press 2005 2v il map set $160

    Grades: 11 12 Adult   **920.003**
    1. Reference books 2. Biography—Dictionaries 3. Middle ages—Biography
    ISBN 1-58765-164-5; 978-1-58765-164-9
                           LC 2004-16696

Also available online

Companion volume to Great events from history, the Middle Ages, 477-1453

First published as part of the Great lives from history series, published 1987-1995 under the editorship of Frank N. Magill; previously published as volume 2 of Dictionary of world biography, published 1998-1999

These "volumes focus on the people throughout the world from after the Fall of Rome, in 476 C.E., to 1453. Coverage is worldwide. . . . Each entry begins with ready-reference information, followed by a summary of the person's life, a paragraph or two on 'Significance,' a list of further readings, and cross-references to entries both within the set and within the [Great events in history] companion set." Booklist

Includes bibliographical references

Great lives from history, the Renaissance & early modern era, 1454-1600; editor, Christina J. Moose. Salem Press 2005 2v il map set $160

    Grades: 11 12 Adult   **920.003**
    1. Reference books 2. Biography—Dictionaries 3. Renaissance
    ISBN 1-58765-211-0; 978-1-58765-211-0
                           LC 2004-28875

Also available online

Companion volume to Great events from history, the Renaissance & early modern era, 1454-1600

First published as part of the Great lives from history series, published 1987-1995 under the editorship of Frank N. Magill; previously published as volume 3 of Dictionary of world biography, published 1998-1999

"This two-volume work offers biographies of 338 historical figures in entries that range from two to five pages in length. A publisher's note in volume 1 explains the set's format and use. All the biographies include name, nationality or ethnicity, historical role, dates, and area(s) of achievement; description of early life, work, and significance; an annotated bibliography; and cross-references." Choice

Includes bibliographical references

Grossman, Mark

World military leaders; a biographical dictionary. Facts on File 2007 414p il (Facts on File library of world history) $75

    Grades: 9 10 11 12 Adult   **920.003**
    1. Reference books 2. Military history—Dictionaries 3. Biography—Dictionaries
    ISBN 0-8160-4732-4; 978-0-8160-4732-1
                           LC 2005-8908

"Spanning the centuries from 3500 BCE to the present, this . . . A-to-Z dictionary presents the stories of the military leaders whose actions precipitated enormous change in the world around them." Publisher's note

Includes bibliographical references

Hamilton, Neil A., 1949-

Presidents; a biographical dictionary; Ian C. Friedman, reviser. 3rd ed. Facts on File 2010 496p il (Facts on File library of American history) $85; pa $19.95 *

    Grades: 11 12 Adult   **920.003**
    1. Presidents—United States—Dictionaries 2. Reference books
    ISBN 978-0-8160-7708-3; 978-0-8160-8247-6 (pa)
                         LC 2009-10191

First published 2001

This book "contains biographies and portraits of all presidents, a . . . chronology of the life of each president, and suggested further reading about each president." Publisher's note

Includes bibliographical references

Heaphy, Maura, 1953-

Science fiction authors; a research guide. Libraries Unlimited 2009 xxx, 318p (Author research series) pa $40

    Grades: Adult Professional   **920.003**
    1. Science fiction—Bio-bibliography 2. Authors—Dictionaries 3. Reference books
    ISBN 978-1-59158-515-2   LC 2008-25708

"Each entry offers a brief biographical sketch, including an author quotation, major awards, and subject tags. A list of the author's major works is grouped under categories such as novels and short stories and is followed by a list of relevant research sources: biographies and interviews, criticism and readers' guides, and Web sites." Booklist

"This volume will be invaluable to reader's advisory librarians and as a 'what to read next' guide for fans of the genre." SLJ

Includes bibliographical references

Hispanic American biographies. Grolier 2006 8v il set $429

    Grades: 6 7 8 9 10 11 12   **920.003**
    1. Hispanic Americans—Dictionaries 2. Reference books
    ISBN 0-7172-6124-7   LC 2006-12294

"This comprehensive set features more than 750 clearly written biographical entries of one or two pages each, covering figures who were born in, or immigrated to, the United States. . . . There is enough information to provide a strong sense of the person's place in history, without giving an overwhelming parade of facts." SLJ

Includes bibliographical references

Holy people of the world; a cross-cultural encyclopedia; Phyllis G. Jestice, editor. ABC-CLIO 2004 3v il set $285
Grades: 11 12 Adult   **920.003**
1. Religious biography—Encyclopedias 2. Reference books
ISBN 1-576-07355-6   LC 2004-22606
"More than 1,000 of the 1,183 entries are biographical sketches of men and women from a variety of religious traditions, including African religions, Amerindian religions, Bahaism, Buddhism, Christianity, Hinduism, Islam, Judaism, Shinto, and Sikhism. There are also survey articles that address aspects of holy people across religious traditions." Booklist
"This edition deserves to become well-worn by the time a second appears." Libr J
Includes bibliographical references

Index to the Wilson authors series. rev 1997 [ed] Wilson, H.W. 1997 135p $45 *
Grades: 9 10 11 12   **920.003**
1. Authors—Dictionaries—Indexes 2. Reference books
ISBN 0-8242-0900-1   LC 96-48600
"Biographical dictionaries in the Wilson authors series; Greek and Latin authors, 800 B.C.-A.D. 1000; European authors, 1000-1900; British authors before 1800; British authors of the nineteenth century; American authors, 1600-1900; Twentieth century authors; Twentieth century authors: first supplement; World authors, 1900-1950; World authors, 1950-1970; World authors, 1970-1975; World authors, 1975-1980; World authors, 1980-1985; World authors, 1985-1990; Spanish American authors: the twentieth century; The junior book of authors; More junior authors; Third book of junior authors; Fourth book of junior authors and illustrators; Fifth book of junior authors and illustrators; Sixth book of junior authors and illustrators; Seventh book of junior authors and illustrators." Title page

Jones, J. Sydney
The Crusades, Biographies; written by J. Sydney Jones; edited by Marcia Merryman Means and Neil Schlager. UXL 2005 c2004 xxii, 230p il (The Crusades reference library) $63
Grades: 11 12 Adult   **920.003**
1. Crusades
ISBN 0-7876-9177-1   LC 2004-18000
This book "includes entries on 25 key figures. Both well-known figures, such as the Muslim leader Saladin and Eleanor of Aquitaine, and those who are maybe less familiar, such as Anna Comnena, the twelfth-century author and Byzantine princess, are covered. Each entry has a boxed quotation by its subject, and most include portraits. The entries are readable and well organized." Booklist
Includes bibliographical references

Kort, Carol
A to Z of American women writers. Rev ed. Facts on File 2007 398p il (Facts on File library of American history) $60
Grades: 11 12 Adult   **920.003**
1. Reference books 2. American literature—Women authors—Dictionaries
ISBN 978-0-8160-6693-3   LC 2007-20534

First published 2000
This dictionary "profiles 186 . . . women, among them poets, essayists, journalists, editors, novelists, memoirists, and numerous other types of writers." Publisher's note
Includes bibliographical references

Life sciences before the twentieth century; biographical portraits; Everett Mendelsohn, editor. Scribner 2002 211p il (Scribner science reference series) $80
Grades: 9 10 11 12   **920.003**
1. Reference books 2. Scientists—Dictionaries 3. Life sciences
ISBN 0-684-80661-4   LC 2001-32045
A collection of about 90 biographical profiles of famous anatomists, biologists, bacteriologists, biochemists, and others involved in the life sciences from ancient times through the nineteenth century

Life sciences in the twentieth century; biographical portraits; Everett Mendelsohn, editor; Brian S. Baigrie, consulting editor. Scribner 2001 207p il (Scribner science reference series) $80
Grades: 11 12 Adult   **920.003**
1. Reference books 2. Scientists—Dictionaries 3. Life sciences
ISBN 0-684-80647-9   LC 00-63789
A collection of about 90 biographical profiles of 20th century scientists in such fields as "anthropology, paleontology, bacteriology, immunology, organic chemistry, crystallography [and] biochemistry." Publisher's note

The **Lincoln** library of sports champions. 8th ed. Lincoln Library 2007 14v il set $523 *
Grades: 9 10 11 12   **920.003**
1. Athletes
ISBN 0-912168-25-0; 978-0-912168-25-8
                                      LC 2006-907320
First published 1975
New edition in preparation
Presents brief, alphabetically arranged biographies of nearly 300 great sports personalities, past and present, from around the world. Features a table of contents arranged by sport and a supplementary reading list.
Includes bibliographical references

MacNee, Marie J.
Outlaws, mobsters & crooks; from the Old West to the Internet; edited by Jane Hoehner. U.X.L 1998-2002 5v il v1-3 set $225; v4 & v5 ea $83
Grades: 8 9 10 11 12   **920.003**
1. Reference books 2. Criminals—Dictionaries
ISBN 0-7876-2803-4 (v1-3); 0-7876-6482-0 (v4); 0-7876-6483-9 (v5)   LC 98-14861
Also available complete five-volume set $360
Contents: v1 Mobsters, racketeers & gamblers, robbers; v2 Computer criminals, spies, swindlers, terrorists; v3 Bandits & gunslingers, bootleggers, pirates; v4 From the Old West to the Internet [1]; v5 From the Old West to the Internet [2]
Presents the lives of seventy-five North American criminals including the nature of their crimes, their moti-

MacNee, Marie J.—*Continued*

vations, and information relating to the law officers who challenged them

"Browsers and researchers alike will make good use of this enjoyable reference set due to its fact-filled content and peek into the lives of such a wide variety of outlaws." Voice Youth Advocates

Mandel, David, 1938-

Who's who in the Jewish Bible. Jewish Publication Society 2007 xx, 422p pa $30

Grades: 9 10 11 12 Adult   920.003
1. Bible. O.T. —Biography—Dictionaries 2. Reference books
ISBN 978-0-8276-0863-4; 0-8276-0863-2
    LC 2007-27288

"Using only the Bible as its basis, this encyclopedia catalogues 3,000 characters from A to Z. General readers and students interested in past Jewish life will find this work most useful as a quick reference for information and a starting point for research." Booklist

Includes bibliographical references

Martinez Wood, Jamie

Latino writers and journalists. Facts on File 2007 294p il (A to Z of Latino Americans) $44 *

Grades: 11 12 Adult   920.003
1. Hispanic Americans—Dictionaries 2. American literature—Hispanic American authors—Bio-bibliography 3. Reference books
ISBN 0-8160-6422-9; 978-0-8160-6422-9
    LC 2006-17394

This book "brings together 150 writers identified as Latino Americans. Approximately one-third of the profiles are accompanied by photographs." Booklist

Includes bibliographical references

Musicians & composers of the 20th century; editor Alfred W. Cramer. Salem Press 2009 5v il set $399

Grades: 9 10 11 12 Adult   920.003
1. Music—Bio-bibliography 2. Musicians—Dictionaries 3. Reference books
ISBN 978-1-58765-512-8   LC 2009-2980

Also available online

"The work covers 614 composers, performers, and teachers, chosen for musical influence as well as fame. All major genres are covered, from classical to rap, along with many subgenres, such as rockabilly, atonal, and funk. . . . This work provides valuable, basic information on the topic as well as multiple, easy-access routes to it. Highly recommended." Libr J

Includes bibliographical references

Musicians since 1900; performers in concert and opera; compiled and edited by David Ewen. Wilson, H.W. 1978 974p il $120

Grades: 11 12 Adult   920.003
1. Musicians—Dictionaries 2. Reference books
ISBN 0-8242-0565-0   LC 78-12727

"Replaces 'Living musicians' and its supplement (1940-57). Gives 'detailed biographical, critical and personal information about 432 of the most distinguished

performing musicians in concert and opera since 1900.'—*Introd.*' . . . A few bibliographical references are given at the end of each biography; a classified list of musicians concludes the volume." Sheehy. Guide to Ref Books. 10th edition

New dictionary of scientific biography; Noretta Koertge, editor in chief. Scribner's 2008 8v il set $995

Grades: 11 12 Adult   920.003
1. Scientists—Dictionaries 2. Reference books
ISBN 978-0-684-31320-7   LC 2007-31384

First published 1970-1980 in 16 volumes with title: Dictionary of scientific biography

Published under the auspices of the American Council of Learned Societies

This biographical dictionary "contains thousands of biographies of mathematicians and natural scientists from all countries and from all historical periods." Publisher's note

Includes bibliographical references

Newton, David E.

Latinos in science, math, and professions. Facts on File 2007 274p il (A to Z of Latino Americans) $44 *

Grades: 11 12 Adult   920.003
1. Hispanic Americans—Dictionaries 2. Scientists—Dictionaries 3. Mathematicians—Dictionaries 4. Reference books
ISBN 978-0-8160-6385-7; 0-8160-6385-0
    LC 2006-16769

Among the figures profiled in this biographical dictionary "are sociology expert Maxine Baca Zinn; Ellen Ochoa, the first Latina in space; and research entomologist Fernando E. Vega." Libr J

Includes bibliographical references

Notable American women; a biographical dictionary completing the twentieth century; Susan Ware, editor; Stacy Braukman, assistant editor. Belknap Press 2004 xxx, 729p $45

Grades: 11 12 Adult   920.003
1. Women—United States—Biography 2. United States—Biography—Dictionaries 3. Reference books
ISBN 0-674-01488-X   LC 2004-48859

This volume includes "stars of the golden ages of radio, film, dance, and television; scientists and scholars; politicians and entrepreneurs; authors and aviators; civil rights activists and religious leaders; Native American craftspeople and world-renowned artists. Women from a broad spectrum of ethnic, class, political, religious, and sexual identities are all acknowledged." Publisher's note

Includes bibliographical references

Notable American women, 1607-1950; a biographical dictionary; Edward T. James, editor; Janet Wilson James, associate editor; Paul S. Boyer, assistant editor. Harvard Univ. Press 1971 3v hardcover o.p. pa set $52

Grades: 11 12 Adult   920.003

Notable American women, 1607-1950—*Continued*

1. Women—United States—Biography 2. United States—Biography—Dictionaries 3. Reference books
ISBN 0-674-62731-8; 0-674-62734-2 (pa)

1,359 American "women—art patrons, astronomers, Indian captives, circus performers, entrepreneurs, inventors, philosophers—are treated in well written articles which range from 400 to 7,000 words. . . . Each article is followed by bibliographical references." Choice

Notable poets; [edited by Frank N. Magill and the editors of Salem Press] Salem Press 1998 3v il (Magill's choice) set $175 *
Grades: 11 12 Adult   **920.003**
1. Poets—Dictionaries 2. Reference books
ISBN 0-89356-967-4   LC 98-26164
"This set largely comprises essays on individual poets reprinted from Frank Magill's much larger Critical Survey of Poetry sets, the English Language Series, and the Foreign Language Series. Coverage 'is designed to survey the essential poets' studied most often in US curricula. The poems range from Homer to Seamus Heany, from Anna Akhmatova to Anne Sexton." Choice

Notable women in the life sciences; a biographical dictionary; edited by Benjamin F. Shearer and Barbara S. Shearer. Greenwood Press 1996 440p il $52.50 *
Grades: 11 12 Adult   **920.003**
1. Women scientists—Dictionaries 2. Reference books
ISBN 0-313-29302-3   LC 95-25603
"Biographical entries of 97 women who have made significant contributions to the life sciences from antiquity to the present. Essays vary in length from two pages to seven and include a biographical essay, notes, bibliography, and a photograph if available." SLJ

Oakes, Elizabeth H., 1951-
Encyclopedia of world scientists. Rev. ed. Facts on File 2007 2v il (Facts on File science library) set $170 *
Grades: 9 10 11 12 Adult   **920.003**
1. Scientists—Encyclopedias 2. Reference books
ISBN 978-0-8160-6158-7; 0-8160-6158-0
LC 2007-6076
First published 2001
This work contains "stories of nearly 1,000 scientists—almost half of whom are female—who have contributed significantly to their fields. All scientific disciplines are represented, as well as all periods of history as far back as 600 BCE." Publisher's note
Includes bibliographical references

Otfinoski, Steven, 1949-
African Americans in the performing arts. Rev. ed. Facts On File 2010 280p il (A to Z of African Americans) $49.50
Grades: 11 12 Adult   **920.003**
1. African Americans—Biography—Dictionaries 2. African American actors—Dictionaries 3. African American dancers—Dictionaries 4. African American musicians—Dictionaries 5. Reference books
ISBN 978-0-8160-7838-7   LC 2009-12400

First published 2003
"Profiling actors, dancers, singers, musicians, composers, and choreographers (the latter two categories only when they are performers as well as creators), alphabetically arranged entries were selected based on 'personal preference, historical importance, variety, and level of achievement.' . . . Entries describe each subject's life and discuss how personal experience affected his or her art. . . . A sound and inexpensive addition for high-school and public libraries." Booklist
Includes bibliographical references

Latinos in the arts. Facts on File 2007 277p il (A to Z of Latino Americans) $44 *
Grades: 11 12 Adult   **920.003**
1. Hispanic Americans—Dictionaries 2. Artists—Dictionaries 3. Actors—Dictionaries 4. Musicians—Dictionaries 5. Reference books
ISBN 978-0-8160-6394-9; 0-8160-6394-X
LC 2006-16900
"This volume profiles more than 178 individuals in the performing and visual arts 'who were born in the United States or who settled here permanently,' among them Marc Anthony, Cameron Diaz, Carmen Miranda, Tito Punete, and Shakira. Each entry concludes with a list of 'Further Reading' . . . and, in many cases, 'Further Listening' and 'Further Viewing.'" Booklist
Includes bibliographical references

Pendergast, Tom, 1964-
U-X-L graphic novelists; [by] Tom Pendergast and Sara Pendergast; Sarah Hermsen, project editor. U-X-L/Thomson Gale 2007 3v lxii, 634p il set $181 *
Grades: 9 10 11 12 Adult   **920.003**
1. Graphic novels—Dictionaries 2. Cartoonists—Dictionaries 3. Reference books
ISBN 1-4144-0440-9; 978-1-4144-0440-0
LC 2006-13711
The three volumes include 75 alphabetically-arranged articles that profile authors, illustrators, and author-illustrators, and include European, American, and Japanese creators. The introduction provides some history of graphic novels, and there is a separate essay on manga.
"This accessible and readable survey of a timely topic should generate considerable attention in school library media center and public library collections. Well researched and documented, with subject and language appropriate for its intended audience, this set is highly recommended." Booklist
Includes bibliographical references

Reef, Catherine
African Americans in the military. Rev ed. Facts On File 2010 284p bibl il (A to Z of African Americans) $49.50
Grades: 11 12 Adult   **920.003**
1. African American soldiers—Dictionaries 2. Reference books
ISBN 978-0-8160-7839-4   LC 2009-31298
First published 2004
This book "covers African American contributions to military efforts from the American Revolution to the

Reef, Catherine—*Continued*

present. The more than 130 entries also include selected persons from the British and French armies as well as the Canadian armed forces, although the U.S. military is the main focus." Booklist

Includes bibliographical references

The **Renaissance** and the scientific revolution; biographical portraits; Brian S. Baigrie, editor. Scribner 2001 210p il (Scribner science reference series) $80

Grades: 11 12 Adult   920.003

1. Scientists—Dictionaries 2. Reference books

ISBN 0-684-80646-0   LC 00-63565

A collection of about 90 biographical profiles of scientists from 1500 to 1800.

Includes bibliographical references

Schneider, Dorothy

First ladies; a biographical dictionary; [by] Dorothy Schneider, Carl J. Schneider. 3rd ed. Facts on File 2010 436p il (Facts on File library of American history) $85 *

Grades: 11 12 Adult   920.003

1. Presidents' spouses—United States—Dictionaries 2. Reference books

ISBN 978-0-8160-7724-3   LC 2009-9047

First published 2001

This book "covers all the women who have held this esteemed 'office' since the founding of the United States. . . . Arranged chronologically by term of presidency, each biographical entry includes a . . . biography emphasizing each first lady's life during the presidency, as well as a chronology, appendixes, and suggestions for further reading." Publisher's note

Includes bibliographical references

Scientists, mathematicians, and inventors; lives and legacies: an encyclopedia of people who changed the world; edited by Doris Simonis; writers, Caroline Hertzenberg [et al.] Oryx Press 1999 244p il (Lives and legacies) $69.95

Grades: 11 12 Adult   920.003

1. Scientists—Dictionaries 2. Mathematicians—Dictionaries 3. Inventors—Dictionaries 4. Reference books

ISBN 1-57356-151-7   LC 98-48484

Profiles people "who influenced their discipline or society at large or who overcame some societal barrier in conducting their careers. Each full-page biography has the person's name; dates; a short title or tag line describing the individual's accomplishments . . . a brief biography; a description of the person's work and its importance, ramifications, and intellectual legacy; a time line that puts personal and professional events in context of world political events; and suggestions for further reading." Sci Books Films

The **Scribner** encyclopedia of American lives; Kenneth T. Jackson, editor in chief; Karen Markoe, general editor; Arnold Markoe, executive editor. Scribner 1998-2010 8v il set $768

Grades: 11 12 Adult   920.003

1. United States—Biography—Dictionaries 2. Reference books

ISBN 0-684-31292-1   LC 98-33793

Individual volumes also available ea $208

Contents: v1 1981-1985; v2 1986-1990; v3 1991-1993; v4 1994-1996; v5 1997-1999; v6 2000-2002; v7 2003-2005; v8 2006-2008

"Scribner envisions SEAL as the continuation of the *Dictionary of American Biography* (DAB). . . . Selection criteria are that the biographees made significant contributions to American life and culture. . . . An appreciable number of women and people of color are recognized. All biographies are signed contributions by 332 scholars." Libr J [review of first two volumes]

Snodgrass, Mary Ellen

Who's who in the Middle Ages; illustrations research by Linda Campbell Franklin. McFarland & Co. 2001 312p il $75

Grades: 11 12 Adult   920.003

1. Middle ages—Biography—Dictionaries 2. Medieval civilization—Dictionaries 3. Reference books

ISBN 0-7864-0774-3   LC 00-56243

"Entries are alphabetical; the scope is from the fifth century to the fifteenth. Each entry, giving an array of names and alternate names for the person, includes both personal and historical details. References are included with each entry, and a bibliography accompanies the whole. Appendices cover the colleges and universities that educated many of the people, and the period's noteworthy events, major monasteries, abbeys and convents and their founders and dates, individuals listed by occupation or contribution, and popes, emperors and monarchs." Publisher's note

Includes bibliographical references

Sonneborn, Liz

A to Z of American Indian women. rev ed. Facts on File 2007 320p il map (Facts on File library of American history) $60 *

Grades: 8 9 10 11 12   920.003

1. Native American women—Dictionaries 2. Reference books

ISBN 978-0-8160-6694-0   LC 2007-8162

First published 1998 with title: A to Z of Native American women

This book "profiles 152 American Indian women who have had an impact on American Indian society and the world at large." Publisher's note

"This resource is of exceptionally high quality." SLJ

Includes bibliographical references

Student's encyclopedia of great American writers; Patricia Gantt, general editor. Facts on File 2009 5v (Facts on File library of American literature) set $425

    Grades: 9 10 11 12 Adult   **920.003**
    1. Authors, American—Encyclopedias 2. American literature—Encyclopedias 3. Reference books
    ISBN 978-0-8160-6087-0   LC 2009-30783

Contents: v1 Beginnings to 1830 by Andrea Tinnemeyer; v2 1830 to 1900 by Paul Crumbley; v3 1900 to 1945 by Robert C. Evans; v4 1945 to 1970 by Blake Hobby; v5 1970 to the present by Patricia M. Gantt

"More than 180 writers currently studied are profiled in this set. chronologically, the volumes begin with colonists such as Anne Bradstreet and revolutionary writers such as Thomas Paine and Thomas Jefferson. Subsequent volumes feature both canonical figures identified with America's literary movements and lesser-known writers gaining public and scholarly interest. . . . This title stands out for its recognition and inclusion of a large number of female writers and writers of a variety of ethnicities." SLJ

Includes bibliographical references

Sutherland, Jonathan, 1958-
African Americans at war; an encyclopedia; [by] Jonathan D. Sutherland. ABC-CLIO 2004 2v set $185 *

    Grades: 11 12 Adult   **920.003**
    1. African American soldiers 2. African Americans—Biography—Encyclopedias 3. United States—Armed forces—Encyclopedias 4. Reference books
    ISBN 1-57607-746-2   LC 2003-21501

"There are more than 250 [alphabetically arranged] entries conveying biographical, thematic, and conceptual information. Well-known leaders (Colin Powell), groups (Buffalo Soldiers), specific units [and battles] . . . have their own entries. . . . This is a superb resource for any . . . library looking to enrich its history, military or African American studies collections." Booklist

U-X-L encyclopedia of world biography; Laura B. Tyle, editor. U.X.L 2003 10v il set $475 *
    Grades: 8 9 10 11 12   **920.003**
    1. Biography—Dictionaries 2. Reference books
    ISBN 0-7876-6465-0   LC 2002-4316

A collection of 750 biographies and portraits of notable historic and current figures in American and world history, literature, science and math, arts and entertainment, and the social sciences.

"The biographies are well written and, although brief, provide information that will be interesting to young adults." Am Ref Books Annu, 2003

Vice presidents; a biographical dictionary; edited by L. Edward Purcell. 4th ed. Facts On File 2010 554p il (Facts on File library of American history) $85
    Grades: 9 10 11 12   **920.003**
    1. Vice-Presidents—United States—Dictionaries 2. Reference books
    ISBN 978-0-8160-7707-6   LC 2009-26068
    First published 1998

This is a "compendium that details the lives and careers of America's vice presidents. . . . [It] contains biographies of each vice president . . . portraits of each vice president, a . . . chronology of their lives, and suggested further reading about each vice president." Publisher's note

Includes bibliographical references

Wayne, Tiffany K., 1968-
American women of science since 1900. ABC-CLIO 2011 2v il set $180
    Grades: 9 10 11 12   **920.003**
    1. Women scientists—Dictionaries 2. Reference books
    ISBN 978-1-59884-158-9; 978-1-59884-159-6 (ebook)
    LC 2010-26838

Combined and updated version of *American women in science* (1994) and *American women in science, 1950 to the present* (1998), both written by Martha J. Bailey

Contact publisher for ebook pricing

"Volume 1 begins with a series of essays exploring the issues women scientists had to overcome to succeed in the profession. . . . The bulk of the set is made up of 500 biographies of the most notable American women scientists of the 20th century. The entries are arranged alphabetically and include the education, professional experience, and concurrent positions of each scientist." Libr J

"Along with providing significant support for research in women's studies and the history of science—particularly since much of the information here is not easily found elsewhere—this resource is chock-full of role models for young women contemplating science careers." SLJ

Includes bibliographical references

Who was who in America; with world notables. Marquis Who's Who 1942-2010 23v set $999.95 *
    Grades: 11 12 Adult   **920.003**
    1. United States—Biography—Dictionaries 2. Reference books
    ISBN 978-0-8379-0282-1

Also available online. Volume 21 and Index also available separately (for $99 and $59, respectively) or together as a set for $159

"Includes sketches removed from 'Who's who in America' because of death of the biographee; date of death and, often, interment location is added." Guide to Ref Books. 11th edition

World artists, 1950-1980; an H.W. Wilson biographical dictionary; {edited} by Claude Marks. Wilson, H.W. 1984 912p il $130 *
    Grades: 11 12 Adult   **920.003**
    1. Artists—Dictionaries 2. Reference books
    ISBN 0-8242-0707-6   LC 84-13152

"The 312 painters, sculptors, and graphic artists in this biographical dictionary were selected from the outstanding artistic figures in the US, Europe, and Latin America. . . . The biographical information includes family, working background, and aesthetic beliefs. There are many quotations from the artist and from critics. Also included is a list of significant collections and a bibliography." Choice

World artists, 1980-1990; an H.W. Wilson biographical dictionary; edited by Claude Marks. Wilson, H.W. 1991 413p il $95 *

Grades: 11 12 Adult   **920.003**

1. Artists—Dictionaries 2. Reference books

ISBN 0-8242-0827-7   LC 91-13183

This volume contains brief biographies of 118 artists from around the world who have been influential in the 1980's

World authors, 1950-1970; a companion volume to Twentieth century authors; edited by John Wakeman; editorial consultant: Stanley J. Kunitz. Wilson, H.W. 1975 1594p il (Authors series) $160 *

Grades: 11 12 Adult   **920.003**

1. Authors—Dictionaries 2. Literature—Bio-bibliography 3. Reference books

ISBN 0-8242-0419-0

This volume includes 959 "authors who came into prominence between 1950 and 1970. . . . Authors were chosen for literary importance or outstanding popularity." Wilson Libr Bull

World authors, 1970-1975; editor, John Wakeman; editorial consultant, Stanley J. Kunitz. Wilson, H.W. 1980 894p il (Authors series) $140 *

Grades: 11 12 Adult   **920.003**

1. Authors—Dictionaries 2. Literature—Bio-bibliography 3. Reference books

ISBN 0-8242-0641-X   LC 79-21874

This volume provides biographical or autobiographical sketches for 348 of the most influential and popular men and women of letters who have come into prominence between 1970 and 1975

World authors, 1975-1980; editor, Vineta Colby. Wilson, H.W. 1985 829p il (Authors series) $140 *

Grades: 11 12 Adult   **920.003**

1. Authors—Dictionaries 2. Literature—Bio-bibliography 3. Reference books

ISBN 0-8242-0715-7   LC 85-10045

This work profiles the lives and works of 379 writers

World authors, 1980-1985; editor, Vineta Colby. Wilson, H.W. 1990 938p il (Authors series) $140 *

Grades: 11 12 Adult   **920.003**

1. Authors—Dictionaries 2. Literature—Bio-bibliography 3. Reference books

ISBN 0-8242-0797-1   LC 90-49782

This volume covers 320 contemporary writers

World authors, 1985-1990; a volume in the Wilson authors series; editor, Vineta Colby. Wilson, H.W. 1995 970p il (Authors series) $140 *

Grades: 11 12 Adult   **920.003**

1. Authors—Dictionaries 2. Literature—Bio-bibliography 3. Reference books

ISBN 0-8242-0875-7   LC 95-41656

This volume covers 345 novelists, playwrights, poets, and other authors who have risen to prominence in the late 1980s

World authors, 1990-1995; editor, Clifford Thompson. Wilson, H.W. 1999 863p il (Authors series) $155 *

Grades: 11 12 Adult   **920.003**

1. Authors—Dictionaries 2. Literature—Bio-bibliography 3. Reference books

ISBN 0-8242-0956-7   LC 99-48161

The 317 authors treated in this volume include novelists, playwrights, and poets who have published significant work in the early 1990s. Also covers essayists, historians, biographers, critics, philosophers, and social scientists who have made exceptional contributions to the literature of our time.

Includes bibliographical references

World authors, 1995-2000; editors, Clifford Thompson, Mari Rich [et. al.] Wilson, H.W. 2003 872p il (Authors series) $160 *

Grades: 8 9 10 11 12 Adult   **920.003**

1. Authors—Dictionaries 2. Literature—Bio-bibliography 3. Reference books

ISBN 0-8242-1032-8   LC 2003-45062

This reference includes 320 novelists, poets, dramatists, essayists, social scientists, and biographers who have published significant works from 1995 through 2000. Each profile details the author's life and career, the circumstances under which their works were produced, and their literary significance.

Includes bibliographical references

World authors, 2000-2005; editors, Jennifer Curry, David Ramm, Mari Rich, Albert Rolls. Wilson, H. W. 2007 800p il (Authors series) $170 *

Grades: 11 12 Adult   **920.003**

1. Authors—Dictionaries 2. Literature—Bio-bibliography 3. Reference books

ISBN 978-0-8242-1077-9

This book "covers some 300 novelists, poets, dramatists, essayists, scientists, biographers, and other authors whose books [were] published 2000 through 2005." Publisher's note

World cultural leaders of the twentieth and twenty-first centuries; [by] Jennifer Durham Bass. 2nd ed. Grey House Publishing 2007 2v il set $195

Grades: 11 12 Adult   **920.003**

1. Biography—Dictionaries 2. Arts—Biography 3. Reference books

ISBN 978-1-59237-118-1; 1-59237-118-3

First published 2000 by ABC-CLIO with title: World cultural leaders of the twentieth century

"Covering 550 men and women who have been influential in the areas of art, dance, film, literature, music, and theater, . . . [this set] provides highlights of their lives, careers, and accomplishments." Am Ref Books Annu, 2008

"The presentation, straightforward and accessible writing style, and 225 images make this source easy, appealing, and likely to be used." Libr J

Includes bibliographical references

World musicians; edited by Clifford Thompson; staff contributors: Denise Bonilla [et al.]; consultants: Justin Dello Joio, Lewis Porter. Wilson, H.W. 1999 1181p il $115 *

Grades: 11 12 Adult **920.003**
1. Musicians—Dictionaries 2. Reference books
ISBN 0-8242-0940-0   LC 98-29205

International in coverage, this volume profiles "contemporary musicians whose specialties range from classical to pop, opera to rap, bluegrass to rock. . . . Written in a lively style and ranging in length from 500 to 3,500 words, the articles cover each musician's personal and professional life and are frequently spiced with quotations from published interviews with the subject and excerpts from critical commentary. Many entries include a black-and-white photo of the musician, and all conclude with a selected bibliography of additional publications and recordings." Booklist

Writers of the American Renaissance; an A-to-Z guide; edited by Denise D. Knight. Greenwood Press 2003 458p $99.95

Grades: 9 10 11 12 **920.003**
1. Authors, American—Dictionaries 2. Literature—Bio-bibliography 3. Reference books
ISBN 0-313-32140-X   LC 2003-52846

This "book is intended as a primary reference guide to 74 authors who wrote during the 19th century. Arranged alphabetically by author last name, each entry in the book includes a biography of the author; a discussion of the author's major works and themes; an overview of the critical reception of the author's works; works cited; and a two-part bibliography that includes works by the author and studies about the author. . . . This volume provides a comprehensive reference tool for students doing author studies and will add greatly to any high school library collection." Libr Media Connect

Includes bibliographical references

Yount, Lisa

A to Z of biologists. Facts on File 2003 390p il (Notable scientists) $45

Grades: 11 12 Adult **920.003**
1. Biologists 2. Scientists—Dictionaries 3. Reference books
ISBN 0-8160-4541-0   LC 2002-13816

"Facts on File science library"

"Each profile focuses on a particular biologist's research and contributions to the field and his or her effect on scientists whose work followed. Their lives and personalities are also discussed through incidents, quotations, and photographs. The profiles are culturally inclusive and span a range of biologists from ancient times to the present day." Publisher's note

Includes bibliographical references

A to Z of women in science and math. rev ed. Facts on File 2007 368p il (Facts on File library of world history) $60 *

Grades: 8 9 10 11 12 **920.003**
1. Women scientists—Dictionaries 2. Women mathematicians—Dictionaries 3. Reference books
ISBN 978-0-8160-6695-7; 0-8160-6695-7
    LC 2007-23966

First published 1999

"More than 195 alphabetically arranged articles detail the lives of women from antiquity through modern day, including well-known scientists and mathematicians and less well-documented individuals. . . . The usefulness of this resource lies not only in the balanced group of profiles that have been assembled, providing a valuable tool for teachers and curriculum developers, but also in the readable and engaging entries themselves." Booklist

Includes bibliographical references

92   Individual biography

Lives of individuals are arranged alphabetically under the name of the person written about. Some subject headings have been added to aid in curriculum work.

Aaron, Hank, 1934-

Stanton, Tom. Hank Aaron and the home run that changed America. William Morrow 2004 249p il hardcover o.p. pa $13.95 *

Grades: 7 8 9 10 **92**
1. Baseball—Biography 2. African American athletes 3. United States—Race relations
ISBN 0-06-057976-5; 0-06-072290-8 (pa)
    LC 2004-46092

The author "covers the time from the funeral of Jackie Robinson in 1972 to the spring of 1974, when Hank Aaron hit his 715th home run and passed Babe Ruth's record." Booklist

"Stanton deftly balances the story of Aaron's professional career, his personal life, and the changes in baseball between the years of Jackie Robinson and today's megastars, such as Ken Griffey, Jr. and Barry Bonds. . . . This book is a must for young adult collections." Voice Youth Advocates

Includes bibliographical references

Abbott, Berenice, 1898-1991

Sullivan, George. Berenice Abbott, photographer; an independent vision. Clarion Books 2006 170p il $20

Grades: 7 8 9 10 **92**
1. Women photographers
ISBN 978-0-618-44026-9; 0-618-44026-7
    LC 2005-30736

A biography of Berenice Abbott, who was a pioneer in the field of professional photography and is particularly acclaimed for her photographs of the streets and buildings of New York City before they were replaced by skyscrapers during a building boom in the 1920s and early 1930s.

"Sullivan brings together an enormous amount of information about Abbott and presents it in a clear, thoughtful manner. . . . Large, clear reproductions of Abbott's photos appear throughout the book." Booklist

Includes bibliographical references

Abdul-Jabbar, Kareem, 1947-

Abdul-Jabbar, Kareem. On the shoulders of giants; my journey through the Harlem Renaissance; [by] Kareem Abdul-Jabbar with Raymond Obstfeld. Simon & Schuster 2007 274p il hardcover o.p. pa $18.99

Grades: 11 12 Adult   92
1. Harlem Renaissance 2. African Americans—Biography
ISBN   1-4165-3488-1;   978-1-4165-3488-4; 1-4165-3489-X (pa); 978-1-4165-3489-1 (pa)
LC 2006-51776
The author "shares his life story, beginning with his childhood in Harlem, moving on to show how he was influenced by the Harlem Renaissance, and including contributions from celebrities like Magic Johnson, Quincy Jones, and Spike Lee." Libr J
"By mixing personal anecdotes with traditional research and reporting, . . . [Abdul-Jabbar] acts as a knowledgeable, passionate tour guide through the artistic and social history of one America's most dynamic creative eras." N Y Times Book Rev
Includes bibliographical references

Abeel, Samantha, 1977-

Abeel, Samantha. My thirteenth winter; a memoir. Orchard Bks. 2003 203p $15.95; pa $15.95

Grades: 9 10 11 12   92
1. Learning disabilities
ISBN 0-439-33904-9; 0-439-33905-6 (pa)
LC 2003-40465
"Abeel recounts her life, from kindergarten through college, with a learning disability that compromises her ability to learn skills based on sequential processing—especially math, spelling, and grammar. . . . Her narrative is interjected with first-person remembrances of painful incidents that left a vivid imprint on her self-worth." Booklist
"This introspective book provides a valuable resource for teachers or counselors working with youth with learning disabilities." VOYA

Achebe, Chinua, 1930-

Achebe, Chinua. The education of a British-protected child; essays. A.A. Knopf 2009 172p $24.95

Grades: 11 12 Adult   92
1. Authors, Nigerian 2. Nigeria
ISBN 978-0-3072-7255-3   LC 2009-17480
The author "presents 17 essays about growing up in colonial Nigeria (hence the title) and his country's history and politics from the viewpoint of a native." Libr J
"Humane and carefully argued responses to events of recent years, coupled with a long look back at the African past." Kirkus
Includes bibliographical references

Adams, Samuel, 1722-1803

Irvin, Benjamin. Samuel Adams; son of liberty, father of revolution; [by] Benjamin H. Irvin. Oxford University Press 2002 176p il (Oxford portraits) $28 *

Grades: 7 8 9 10   92
1. United States—History—1775-1783, Revolution
ISBN 0-19-513225-4   LC 2002-4283
Contents: The elusive Samuel Adams; Samuel Adams's Boston; Raised for rebellion; Tis not in mortals to command success; Sam the publican and the Stamp Act Riots; Mobs and massacre; To save the country; The Coercive Acts and the Continental Congress; Is not America already independent; The storm is now over
Examines the life of Samuel Adams, a hero of the American Revolution who is credited by some with having fired the first shot at Lexington Green, the "shot heard 'round the world"
"Irvin's account of events is exciting and written in a compelling narrative style. He presents an unbiased assessment of Adams's actions and character." SLJ
Includes bibliographical references

Addams, Jane, 1860-1935

Fradin, Judith Bloom. Jane Addams; champion of democracy; by Judith Bloom Fradin and Dennis Brindell Fradin. Clarion Books 2006 216p il $21 *

Grades: 7 8 9 10   92
1. Hull House (Chicago, Ill.) 2. Chicago (Ill.)—Social conditions
ISBN 0-618-50436-1
A biography of the social activist, pacifist, author, founder of Hull House in Chicago, and winner of the Nobel Peace Prize.
"A fascinating and rich life is related in strong, unfussy prose." Booklist
Includes bibliographical references

Akeley, Carl Ethan, 1864-1926

Kirk, Jay. Kingdom under glass; a tale of obsession, adventure, and one man's quest to preserve the world's great animals. Henry Holt 2010 387p il $27.50

Grades: 11 12 Adult   92
1. Taxidermy 2. Zoological specimens—Collection and preservation
ISBN 978-0-8050-9282-0   LC 2009-50706
This is "a rollicking biography of Carl Akeley, an American taxidermist who preserved realistic-looking beasts complete with aura of 'will,' for 20th-century natural history museums. . . . The author spends most of the book following Akeley's African safaris, where he hunts big game and touring tycoons who might fund his projects. . . . [This] is a beguiling, novelistic portrait of a man and an era straining to hear the call of the wild." Publ Wkly
Includes bibliographical references

Al Jundi, Sami, 1962-

Al Jundi, Sami. The hour of sunlight; one Palestinian's journey from prisoner to peacemaker; by Sami al Jundi and Jen Marlowe. Nation Books 2010 344p il pa $16.99

Grades: 11 12 Adult   **92**

1. Palestinian Arabs 2. Prisoners 3. Israel-Arab conflicts

ISBN 978-1-56858-448-5   LC 2010-29340

The authors "trace al Jundi's evolution from Palestinian militant to peacemaker. As teenagers, al Jundi and two friends joined the PLO, but when a bomb exploded as they were building it, one boy was killed, and the other two badly injured—and on the receiving end of Israeli interrogations and torture. Sentenced to a decade in prison, al Jundi dedicates himself to an extensive education program maintained by the prisoners themselves, ultimately committing himself to nonviolence and to bridging the Israeli-Palestinian divide." Publ Wkly

Includes bibliographical references

Alcott, Louisa May, 1832-1888

Alcott, Louisa May. The selected letters of Louisa May Alcott; edited by Joel Myerson and Daniel Shealy; with an introduction by Madeleine B. Stern, associate editor. University of Ga. Press 1995 352p il pa $24.95

Grades: 11 12 Adult   **92**

1. Authors, American 2. Women authors

ISBN 0-8203-1740-3   LC 95-8400

First published 1987 by Little, Brown

This volume contains "a wealth of colorful, determined, cranky, humorous, affectionate correspondence, salted with Yankee colloquialisms. The recipients range from eminent people like Lucy Stone, Ralph Waldo Emerson and publisher Thomas Niles to friends of the Alcott and May families. A large part of the correspondence is about her books. . . . The voice of the writer and woman is palpable throughout, insistent and appealing." Publ Wkly

Includes bibliographical references

Alexander, the Great, 356-323 B.C.

Arrian. Alexander the Great; selections from Arrian; [translated by] J. G. Lloyd. Cambridge Univ. Press 1981 104p il maps (Translations from Greek and Roman authors) pa $17.95

Grades: 9 10 11 12   **92**

1. Greece—History 2. Kings and rulers

ISBN 0-521-28195-4   LC 81-9453

Born over four hundred years after the death of Alexander the Great, Arrian served in the Roman army and devoted his life's work to the study of Alexander's empire, a section of which he governed under the auspices of Rome. Here are selections from his history which focus primarily on Alexander's military campaigns

"This book may seem to be a military account, but first and foremost it is the story of a man." Introduction

Includes bibliographical references

Alhazen, 965-1039

Steffens, Bradley. Ibn al-Haytham; first scientist. Morgan Reynolds Pub. 2007 128p il (Profiles in science) lib bdg $27.95

Grades: 7 8 9 10   **92**

1. Scientists 2. Mathematicians

ISBN 978-1-59935-024-0; 1-59935-024-6

LC 2006-23970

The author "has organized what is known of his subject's life and work into a coherent narrative. . . . Like the history of mathematics, the history of science is incomplete without an acknowledgment of early scholars in the Middle East. This clearly written introduction to al-Haytham, his society, and his contributions does that." Booklist

Includes bibliographical references

Ali, Muhammad, 1942-

Ezra, Michael. Muhammad Ali; the making of an icon. Temple University Press 2009 233p (Sporting) $69.50; pa $24.95

Grades: 11 12 Adult   **92**

1. Boxing—Biography

ISBN 978-1-59213-661-2; 978-1-59213-662-9 (pa)

LC 2008-34323

This is a biography of the heavyweight boxing champion.

"This book increases our understanding of how difficult it is to know the real Ali, a simple man paradoxically imbued with great complexity." Libr J

Includes bibliographical references

Micklos, John. Muhammad Ali; "I am the greatest"; [by] John Micklos, Jr. Enslow Publishers 2010 160p il (American rebels) lib bdg $34.60

Grades: 6 7 8 9 10   **92**

1. Boxing—Biography 2. African American athletes

ISBN 978-0-7660-3381-8; 0-7660-3381-3

LC 2009-17593

"This biography of the three-time heavyweight world champion, Vietnam War protester, and Nobel Peace Prize nominee includes useful context-setting background; Micklos's play-by-play descriptions of Ali's bouts provide just enough detail for boxing fans." Horn Book Guide

Includes bibliographical references

Remnick, David. King of the world: Muhammad Ali and the rise of an American hero. Random House 1998 326p il hardcover o.p. pa $14

Grades: 11 12 Adult   **92**

1. African American athletes

ISBN 0-375-50065-0; 0-375-70229-6 (pa)

LC 98-24539

This book focuses on Ali's career "in the early sixties—roughly, late 1962 to late 1965. . . . Five heavyweight title fights are dealt with in depth: the first Patterson-Liston fight on September 25, 1962, and their rematch on July 22, 1963: the first Liston-Ali fight on February 25, 1964, and their rematch on May 25, 1965: and the first Ali-Patterson fight on November 22, 1965." Nation

"This is the best book ever on Muhammad Ali and one of the best on America in the 1960s." Booklist

Includes bibliographical references

Allende, Isabel

Allende, Isabel. Paula; translated from the Spanish by Margaret Sayers Peden. HarperPerennial 2008 330, 23p pa $14.99

Grades: 11 12 Adult   **92**

1. Allende family 2. Authors, Chilean

ISBN 978-0-06-156490-1

First published 1995

Allende "interweaves the story of her own life with the slow dying of her 28-year-old daughter, Paula." Publ Wkly

Axelrod-Contrada, Joan. Isabel Allende. Marshall Cavendish Benchmark 2010 159p il (Today's writers and their works) $42.79

Grades: 8 9 10 11 12   **92**

1. Authors, Chilean 2. Women authors

ISBN 978-0-7614-4116-8; 0-7614-4116-6

This biography of Isabel Allende places the author in the context of her times and discusses her work.

This book provides "excellent information for reports. . . . [The text is] organized well, lending [itself] to be read in [its] entirety or used as needed for research, and [includes] full-color photos and illustrations." SLJ

Includes bibliographical references

Allred, Lance, 1981-

Allred, Lance. Longshot; the adventures of a deaf fundamentalist Mormon kid and his journey to the NBA. HarperOne 2009 250p $25.99

Grades: 11 12 Adult   **92**

1. Athletes 2. Deafness

ISBN 978-0-06-171858-8; 0-06-171858-0

LC 2009-517317

"Allred played basketball with the University of Utah, then Weber State, before eventually joining the Cleveland Cavaliers in 2008, and recounts in folksy, unpretentious prose his long, arduous dream fulfilled to make the NBA. . . . Allred's voice is humorously self-deprecating and youthfully winning. Frank about his shortcomings . . . he delivers an accessible, competent narrative, with highly unusual details about his Mormon roots." Publ Wkly

Anderson, Laurie Halse, 1961-

Glenn, Wendy J. Laurie Halse Anderson; speaking in tongues. Scarecrow Press 2010 169p (Scarecrow studies in young adult literature) $40 *

Grades: 8 9 10 11 12   **92**

1. Authors, American 2. Women authors

ISBN 978-0-8108-7281-3   LC 2009-30545

"This book is a comprehensive look at the life, work, and thoughts of Laurie Halse Anderson. . . . Any teen with a research paper on Laurie Halse Anderson who is lucky enough to have access to this title will walk away with a high mark." Voice Youth Advocates

Includes bibliographical references

Anderson, Marian, 1897-1993

Kaplan, Howard S. Marian Anderson. Pomegranate 2007 63p il (Women who dare) $12.95 *

Grades: 9 10 11 12   **92**

1. African American singers 2. African American women—Biography

ISBN 978-0-7649-3891-7   LC 2006-48651

This is a biography of the African-American opera singer.

Includes bibliographical references

Keiler, Allan. Marian Anderson; a singer's journey. University of Illinois Press 2002 447p hardcover o.p. pa $21.95

Grades: 11 12 Adult   **92**

1. African American singers 2. African American women—Biography

ISBN 0-684-80711-4; 0-252-07067-4 (pa)

LC 99-43319

"A Lisa Drew book"

First published 2000 by Scribner

"Keiler offers an assessment of the great contralto, the first African American soloist at the Metropolitan Opera." Libr J

The author's "clear, succinct prose, initially lacking narrative coherence, gains strength and momentum as his subject matures from a young and struggling artist into one of the enduring voices of our century." Publ Wkly

Includes discography and bibliographical references

Angelou, Maya

Angelou, Maya. I know why the caged bird sings. Random House 2002 281p $21.95 *

Grades: 11 12 Adult   **92**

1. African American authors 2. Women authors

ISBN 0-375-50789-2   LC 2001-41914

Also available in paperback from Ballantine Bks.

First published 1969

The first volume in the author's autobiographical series covers her childhood and adolescence in rural Arkansas, St. Louis, and San Francisco.

"Angelou is a skillful writer; her language ranges from beautifully lyrical prose to earthy metaphor, and her descriptions have power and sensitivity." Libr J

Followed by Gather together in my name (1974); Singin' and swingin' and gettin' merry like Christmas (1976); The heart of a woman (1981); All God's children need traveling shoes (1986); A song flung up to heaven (2002)

Angelou, Maya. Letter to my daughter. Random House 2008 166p $25 *

Grades: 9 10 11 12 Adult   **92**

1. African American authors 2. Women authors

ISBN 978-1-4000-6612-4   LC 2008-28843

"This collection of short essays, most of them two or three pages long, . . . [combine] personal experience with prescriptions for a meaningful life. Dedicating the book to the daughter she never had, Angelou recounts her childhood in Stamps, AR, where she endured the oppression of racism, an experience that has left its indelible mark on her." Libr J

"A slim volume packed with nourishing nuggets of wisdom." Kirkus

Angelou, Maya—*Continued*

Gillespie, Marcia Ann. Maya Angelou; a glorious celebration; [by] Marcia Ann Gillespie, Rosa Johnson Butler and Richard A. Long; foreword by Oprah Winfrey. Doubleday 2008 191p il $30 *
Grades: 11 12 Adult   **92**
   1. African American authors 2. Women authors
   ISBN 978-0-385-51108-7   LC 2007-31301
This look at Maya Angelou's life as well as her myriad interests and accomplishments by the people who know her best (longtime friends Marcia Ann Gillespie and Richard Long and niece Rosa Johnson Butler) features over 150 sepia portraits, family photographs, and letters. Includes a bibliography of her works.
"A loving tribute to one of the most renowned authors today, this work is highly recommended." Libr J

Nardo, Don. Maya Angelou; poet, performer, activist. Compass Point Books 2009 112p il (Signature lives) lib bdg $34.65
Grades: 6 7 8 9 10   **92**
   1. Women authors 2. African American authors
   ISBN 978-0-7565-1889-9; 0-7565-1889-X
                          LC 2008-41488
A biography of Maya Angelou, poet, performer and activist
The "inviting page design features photos and boxed screens on each spread, and . . . includes a detailed bibliography, source notes, time line and glossary." Booklist
Includes glossary and bibliographical references

Annesley, James

Ekirch, A. Roger. Birthright; the true story that inspired Kidnapped. W.W. Norton & Co. 2010 xxiii, 258p il map $24.95
Grades: 11 12 Adult   **92**
   1. Trials (Kidnapping) 2. Kidnapping
   ISBN 978-0-393-06615-9; 0-393-06615-0
                          LC 2009-33194
This is the story of "James 'Jemmy' Annesley, presumptive heir to multiple titles in England, Ireland and Wales, [who] was kidnapped at the age of 12 in 1728 by his uncle and was sent as an indentured servant to America. He didn't return to Ireland until 13 years later, eventually obtaining justice against his treacherous uncle. . . . [This] tale of kidnapping and betrayal captured the hearts of many and reportedly was the inspiration for Robert Louis Stevenson's popular novel *Kidnapped*." Libr J
"Ekirch provides the necessary context for understanding the characters and events in the tale, including changing courtship and child-rearing practices, the deference that tied poverty-stricken Catholic tenants to landlords and, most important, the kidnapping trade that authorities had difficulty eliminating. An engrossing familial and legal tale told with dash and clarity." Kirkus
Includes bibliographical references

Anthony, Susan B., 1820-1906

Colman, Penny. Elizabeth Cady Stanton and Susan B. Anthony. See entry under Stanton, Elizabeth Cady, 1815-1902

Archimedes, ca. 287-212 B.C.

Hasan, Heather. Archimedes: the father of mathematics. Rosen Pub. Group 2006 112p il (The library of Greek philosophers) lib bdg $33.25
Grades: 9 10 11 12   **92**
   1. Mathematicians
   ISBN 1-4042-0774-0   LC 2005-9992
"This biography charts the life of Archimedes while . . . explaining his mathematical postulates." Publisher's note
Includes bibliographical references

Armstrong, Karen

Armstrong, Karen. The spiral staircase; my climb out of darkness. Knopf 2004 xxii, 305p hardcover o.p. pa $14
Grades: 11 12 Adult   **92**
   ISBN 0-375-41318-9; 0-385-72127-7 (pa)
                          LC 2003-47550
This "is the story of Armstrong's personal spiritual quest, which led her at age 17 to join a convent. However, she found that her own skeptical nature and the physical constraints of convent life crippled her intellectually and spiritually. . . . After seven years, Armstrong left the convent." SLJ

Armstrong, Lance

Armstrong, Lance. It's not about the bike; my journey back to life; [by] Lance Armstrong with Sally Jenkins. Putnam 2000 275p il hardcover o.p. pa $14
Grades: 11 12 Adult   **92**
   1. Athletes
   ISBN 0-399-14611-3; 0-425-17961-3 (pa)
                          LC 00-35612
Armstrong describes his early years growing up in Plano, Texas, his rise through the sports world as a champion American cyclist, his diagnosis and recovery from testicular cancer and his triumph in the 1999 Tour de France.
"Readers will respond to the inspirational recovery story, and they will appreciate the behind-the-scenes cycling information." Booklist

Strickland, Bill. Tour de Lance; the extraordinary story of Lance Armstrong's fight to reclaim the Tour De France. Harmony Books 2010 300p il map $25.99
Grades: 11 12 Adult   **92**
   1. Athletes
   ISBN 978-0-307-58984-2   LC 2010-4504
This is "the story of Lance Armstrong's return in 2009, after a three-year absence, to the Tour de France. . . . Strickland, who had access to Armstrong's inner circle, enhances it with an eye for detail and an understanding of its importance in the context of cycling's own physical demands and singular history. He reminds readers, as if they need it, of Armstrong's supremacy and laser dedication in the sport. . . . An irresistible account of a story that needed telling." Booklist

Arnold, Benedict, 1741-1801

Murphy, Jim. The real Benedict Arnold. Clarion Books 2007 264p il map $20 *

Grades: 7 8 9 10   **92**

1. United States—History—1775-1783, Revolution 2. Generals

ISBN 978-0-395-77609-4; 0-395-77609-0

LC 2007-5700

"Using Arnold's surviving military journals and political documents, Murphy carefully contrasts popular myth with historical fact. . . . As far as possible, he meticulously traces Arnold's life, revealing a complex man who was actually as much admired as he was loathed." Booklist

Includes bibliographical references

Sheinkin, Steve. The notorious Benedict Arnold; a true story of adventure, heroism, & treachery. Roaring Brook Press/Flash Point 2010 337p il map $18.99 *

Grades: 7 8 9 10   **92**

1. United States. Continental Army 2. American Loyalists 3. Generals 4. United States—History—1775-1783, Revolution

ISBN 978-1-59643-486-8; 1-59643-486-4

LC 2010-34797

"Sheinkin sees Arnold as America's 'original action hero' and succeeds in writing a brilliant, fast-paced biography that reads like an adventure novel. . . . The author's obvious mastery of his material, lively prose and abundant use of eyewitness accounts make this one of the most exciting biographies young readers will find." Kirkus

Includes bibliographical references

Arthur, King

Ashe, Geoffrey. The discovery of King Arthur. New pbk. ed. Sutton 2005 244p il map pa $14.95

Grades: 11 12 Adult   **92**

1. Great Britain—Kings and rulers 2. Great Britain—History—0-1066

ISBN 0-7509-4211-8; 978-0-7509-4211-9

LC 2008383248

First published 1985 by Anchor Press/Doubleday

The author explores archeological findings that support the theory that Arthur was a real leader in the 5th century. Arthurian themes in literature and art are also examined.

Includes bibliographical references

Asayesh, Gelareh

Asayesh, Gelareh. Saffron sky; a life between Iran and America. Beacon Press 1999 222p hardcover o.p. pa $15

Grades: 11 12 Adult   **92**

1. Women journalists 2. Iranian Americans

ISBN 0-8070-7210-9; 0-8070-7211-7 (pa)

LC 99-27889

The author "chronicles her life as a series of trips to and from Iran—as a child who spoke no English, on the eve of the 1992 Gulf War as a green card-holding adult, and as the parent of a young biracial American citizen—and in doing so, tells the story of both her family's and

Iran's tumultuous recent history. This beautifully written narrative provides a rare, humanizing glimpse into the politics, culture, and geography of {Iran}." Libr J

Aseel, Maryam Qudrat, 1974-

Aseel, Maryam Qudrat. Torn between two cultures; an Afghan-American woman speaks out; {by} Maryam Qudrat. Capital Bks. 2003 191p $22.95; pa $14.95 *

Grades: 11 12 Adult   **92**

1. Afghan Americans 2. Muslims—United States 3. Muslim women 4. Afghanistan

ISBN 1-931868-36-0; 1-931868-70-0 (pa)

LC 2002-41108

"Capital currents book"

"Aseel, a first-generation Afghan American woman, is an activist in the Muslim community in general and the Afghani community in particular. Woven around her commentary on current events is the fascinating story of her life, including a childhood that balanced both modernity and tradition. Throughout the . . . engaging narrative, Aseel manages to clear up numerous misconceptions about her culture and religion." Booklist

Includes bibliographical references

Ashe, Arthur, 1943-1993

Ashe, Arthur. Days of grace; a memoir; by Arthur Ashe and Arnold Rampersad. Knopf 1993 317p il hardcover o.p. pa $6.99

Grades: 11 12 Adult   **92**

1. Tennis—Biography 2. African American athletes

ISBN 0-679-42396-6; 0-345-38681-7 (pa)

LC 92-54919

Ashe discusses "the issues of greatest import to him: family, education, religion, athletics, health, politics, and social injustice. . . . The bulk of the work centers on his life after retirement from tennis . . . and his championing of various causes, including the fight against AIDS. In anticipation of his passing, he closes with an open letter to his daughter, Camera." Libr J

"This is a truly gripping book. It's gripping, it's moving, it's admirable; and what makes it so is Ashe's capacity for evaluating himself and the world with intelligence and honor." N Y Times Book Rev

Asimov, Isaac, 1920-1992

Asimov, Isaac. It's been a good life; edited by Janet Jeppson Asimov. Prometheus Books 2002 309p il $27

Grades: 9 10 11 12 Adult   **92**

1. Authors, American 2. Scientists

ISBN 1-573-92968-9   LC 2002-20570

The author's widow has "condensed his three-volume autobiography into one handy book covering his life from birth in Russia and immigration with his parents and through careers as a scientist, an sf writer, and a science popularizer, and touching on matters of his humanist faith and his numerous works on the way to his final illness. . . . This is a good introduction to one of the most prolific and distinguished careers in twentieth-century American letters, especially for those unready to immerse themselves in the complete Asimov self-life." Booklist

Includes bibliographical references

Atanasoff, John V.

Smiley, Jane. The man who invented the computer; the biography of John Atanasoff, digital pioneer. Doubleday 2010 246p il $25.95

Grades: 11 12 Adult **92**

1. Computer scientists 2. Inventors

ISBN 978-0-385-52713-2; 0-385-52713-6

LC 2010-18887

The author "explores the story of the now mostly forgotten Atanasoff, a brilliant and engaged physicist and engineer who first dreamed of and built a computational machine that was the prototype for the computer." Publ Wkly

"Engrossing. Smiley takes science history and injects it with a touch of noir and an exciting clash of vanities." Kirkus

Includes bibliographical references

Audubon, John James, 1785-1851

Rhodes, Richard. John James Audubon; the making of an American. Knopf 2004 528p il $30; pa $16

Grades: 11 12 Adult **92**

1. Artists—United States 2. Naturalists

ISBN 0-375-41412-6; 0-375-71393-X (pa)

LC 2003-69489

The author "chronicles Audubon's ineluctable sense of mission, phenomenal skills, and triumph over adversity. . . . Rhodes sets Audubon's engrossing tale within the context of the War of 1812, the Louisiana Purchase, the wars against Native Americans (whom Audubon profoundly admired), and the rapid decimation of the American wilderness. . . . Full of passion and discovery, hardship and transcendence, Audubon's story is at once intimate and mythic, and Rhodes' fresh, comprehensive biography will capture the imagination of readers everywhere." Booklist

Includes bibliographical references

Austen, Jane, 1775-1817

Haggerty, Andrew. Jane Austen; Pride and Prejudice and Emma. Marshall Cavendish Benchmark 2007 127p il (Writers and their works) $39.93

Grades: 9 10 11 12 **92**

1. Authors, English

ISBN 978-0-7614-2589-2 LC 2006-39179

This book features a biography of Jane Austen, a description of the times in which she lived, and a critical discussion of her novels *Pride and Prejudice* and *Emma*.

Includes filmography and bibliographical references

Shields, Carol. Jane Austen. Viking 2001 185p (Penguin lives series) hardcover o.p. pa $13

Grades: 11 12 Adult **92**

1. Authors, English 2. Women authors

ISBN 0-670-89488-5; 0-14-303516-9 (pa)

LC 00-43807

"In chronicling her subject's life and personality, Shields emphasizes Austen's keen ability to listen, observe, and capture clearly the social mores of her time and explore human nature in her writing. Shields contends that historical references are behind many of the scenes and characters in Austen's novels, and as a way of more clearly personalizing Austen's experiences or feelings, she interjects commentary regarding writing and publishing that is presumably based on personal experience." Libr J

Ayers, Nathaniel Anthony

Lopez, Steve. The soloist; a lost dream, an unlikely friendship, and the redemptive power of music. G. P. Putnam's Sons 2008 273p hardcover o.p. pa $15 *

Grades: 11 12 Adult **92**

1. Violinists 2. Homeless persons

ISBN 978-0-399-15506-2; 0-399-15506-6; 978-0-425-23836-3 (pa); 0-425-23836-9 (pa)

LC 2007-46314

The true story of Nathaniel Ayers, a musician who becomes schizophrenic and homeless, and his friendship with Steve Lopez, the Los Angeles columnist who discovers and writes about him in the newspaper.

"With self-effacing humor, fast-paced yet elegant prose and unsparing honesty, Lopez tells an inspiring story of heartbreak and hope." Publ Wkly

Baek, Hongyong, 1912-2002

Lee, Helie. Still life with rice; a young American woman discovers the life and legacy of her Korean grandmother. Scribner 1996 320p pa $13 hardcover o.p.

Grades: 11 12 Adult **92**

1. Korean Americans

ISBN 0-684-82711-5 (pa) LC 95-41921

"Lee traveled from California to Korea to recapture the life of her grandmother. Hongyong Baek (b. 1912) grew up in northern Korea, the daughter of wealthy parents, and at 22 entered into an arranged marriage. . . . Drawing on interviews with her grandmother and writing in her voice, Lee . . . describes the aftermath of the Japanese occupation of Korea, which forced Baek, her husband (with whom she ultimately fell in love) and their children to flee to China in 1939, where they supported themselves by selling opium. After they returned to Korea, the 1950s' civil war caused them extreme hardship. . . . Baek emigrated to the U.S. in 1972." Publ Wkly

"Written with great narrative power and attention to detail, a testament to the will to survive." Booklist

Baker, Russell, 1925-

Baker, Russell. Growing up. New American Library 1983 c1982 278p pa $15

Grades: 11 12 Adult **92**

1. Journalists

ISBN 0-452-25550-3

Also available in paperback from Signet Bks.

"A Plume book"

First published 1982 by Congdon & Weed

This book "recounts the first 24 years of [Baker's] life as the son of an independent and deep-rooted Virginian family." Natl Rev

Balanchine, George, 1904-1983

Gottlieb, Robert Adams. George Balanchine: the ballet maker. HarperCollins\Atlas Books 2004 224p (Eminent lives) $19.95

Grades: 11 12 Adult   **92**
  1. Choreographers 2. Ballet
  ISBN 0-06-075070-7   LC 2004-48856

This biography tells Balanchine's life story "from his near-accidental enrollment, at the age of nine, in St. Petersburg's Imperial School of Ballet, through the deprivation and hunger of Bolshevik Russia, to Diaghilev's Ballets Russes, and finally, in 1933, to the United States and eventually to the New York City Ballet, to which his reputation is forever tied." Publisher's note

"This loving tribute captures Balanchine's legacy: his energy, confidence, lack of pretension and, most important, his joy in creation." Publ Wkly

Includes bibliographical references

Baldwin, James, 1924-1987

Baldwin, James. Conversations with James Baldwin; edited by Fred L. Standley and Louis H. Pratt. University Press of Miss. 1989 297p (Literary conversations series) hardcover o.p. pa $17 *

Grades: 11 12 Adult   **92**
  1. Authors, American 2. African American authors
  ISBN 0-87805-388-3; 0-87805-389-1 (pa)
                  LC 88-36560

"During the sixties, seventies, and eighties, Baldwin participated in more than fifty situations having the format of interview, conversation, discussion or dialogue. . . . The twenty-seven pieces selected for this collection range from 1961 after his fourth book, 'Nobody Knows My Name,' to just prior to his death in a last formal conversation with poet Quincy Troupe." Introduction

Bannister, Nonna, 1927-2004

Bannister, Nonna. The secret Holocaust diaries; the untold story of Nonna Bannister; with Carolyn Tomlin and Denise George. Tyndale House Publishers 2009 299p il $19.99

Grades: 10 11 12 Adult   **92**
  1. World War, 1939-1945—Women 2. World War, 1939-1945—Personal narratives 3. Holocaust, 1933-1945—Personal narratives
  ISBN 978-1-4143-2546-0   LC 2008-50099

"The only World War II survivor of her wealthy Russian, devout Christian family, Nonna Lisowskaya came to the U.S. in 1950, married Henry Bannister, and never spoke about her Holocaust-experience—until a few years before her death in 2004, when she revealed her diaries, originally written in six languages on paper scraps that she had kept in a pillow strapped to her body throughout the war. Now those diaries, in her English translation, tell her story of fleeing Stalinist Russia, not knowing what was waiting in Hitler's Germany, where she saw her mother murdered in the camps, escaped a massacre of Jews shot into a pit, was nursed by Catholic nuns, and much more." Booklist

Barakat, Ibtisam

Barakat, Ibtisam. Tasting the sky; a Palestinian childhood. Farrar, Straus & Giroux 2007 176p $16 *

Grades: 6 7 8 9 10   **92**
  1. Israel-Arab conflicts 2. Palestinian Arabs
  ISBN 0-374-35733-1; 978-0-374-35733-7
                  LC 2006-41265

"Melanie Kroupa books."

"In 1981 the author, then in high school, boarded a bus bound for Ramallah. The bus was detained by Israeli soldiers at a checkpoint on the West Bank, and she was taken to a detention center before being released. The episode triggers sometimes heart-wrenching memories of herself as a young child, at the start of the 1967 Six Days' War, as Israeli soldiers conducted raids, their planes bombed her home, and she fled with her family across the border to Jordan. . . . What makes the memoir so compelling is the immediacy of the child's viewpoint, which depicts both conflict and daily life without exploitation or sentimentality." Booklist

Barrowcliffe, Mark

Barrowcliffe, Mark. The elfish gene; dungeons, dragons and growing up strange. Soho Press 2008 277p $25

Grades: 11 12 Adult   **92**
  1. Authors, English 2. Fantasy games 3. Dungeons & dragons (Game)
  ISBN 978-1-56947-522-5; 1-56947-522-9
                  LC 2008-12471

First published 2007 in the United Kingdom

In this attempt to understand the true inner nerd of the adolescent male, Barrowcliffe relates how he and twenty million other boys grew up in the '70s and '80s absorbed in the world of fantasy roleplaying games like Dungeon & Dragons.

"Barrowcliffe, whose own schoolboy nickname was Spaz, wonderfully captures the insensitivity, insecurity and selfishness of the adolescent male. . . . [He] renders all the comedy and sorrow of early manhood, when boys flee the wretchedness of their real status for a taste of power in imaginary domains." Publ Wkly

Barton, Clara, 1821-1912

Oates, Stephen B. A woman of valor: Clara Barton and the Civil War. Free Press 1994 527p il map hardcover o.p. pa $16.95

Grades: 11 12 Adult   **92**
  1. United States—History—1861-1865, Civil War
  ISBN 0-02-923405-0; 0-02-874012-2 (pa)
                  LC 93-38830

The author "uses both primary and secondary sources in addressing the Civil War career of Clara Barton. . . . An 'angel of the battlefield' who succored the wounded while under fire, Barton also raised funds and supplies through a network of women's support groups, while challenging the conventional belief that nursing was inappropriate for respectable women." Publ Wkly

"This is a carefully written and researched work that brings to life both the Civil War and a period of Barton's life that was to affect her forever." Libr J

Includes bibliographical references

Basie, Count, 1904-1984

Basie, Count. Good morning blues: the autobiography of Count Basie; as told to Albert Murray. Da Capo Press 1995 399p il pa $17.95
Grades: 11 12 Adult   92
1. Jazz musicians 2. African American musicians
ISBN 0-306-81107-3   LC 94-44697
First published 1985 by Random House
"Basie pays tribute to his colleagues and managers (and to John Hammond for 'discovering' him), but does not hesitate to discuss their weaknesses and short-comings; his language is direct and earthy. Although some of the book reads more like a catalogue or itinerary than an autobiography, it will have strong appeal for jazz buffs and fans of the late bandleader." Publ Wkly

Bates, Daisy

Fradin, Judith Bloom. The power of one; Daisy Bates and the Little Rock Nine; by Judith Bloom Fradin & Dennis Brindell Fradin. Clarion Books 2004 178p il $19
Grades: 7 8 9 10   92
1. Central High School (Little Rock, Ark.) 2. School integration 3. Arkansas—Race relations
ISBN 0-618-31556-X   LC 2004-4618
This is a biography of Daisy Bates. Born in a small town in rural Arkansas, Bates was a journalist and activist. In 1957 she mentored the nine black students who were integrated into Central High School in Little Rock, Arkansas
"This compelling biography clearly demonstrates that one person can indeed make a difference." SLJ
Includes bibliographical references

Beah, Ishmael

Beah, Ishmael. A long way gone; memoirs of a boy soldier. Farrar, Straus & Giroux 2007 229p map $22; pa $12 *
Grades: 11 12 Adult   92
1. Sierra Leone—History—Civil War, 1991-
ISBN   978-0-374-10523-5;   0-374-95191-8; 978-0-374-53126-3 (pa); 0-374-53126-9 (pa)
LC 2006-17101
"Sarah Crichton Books"
"In 1993, when the author was twelve, rebel forces attacked his home town, in Sierra Leone, and he was separated from his parents. For months, he straggled through the war-torn countryside, starving and terrified, until he was taken under the wing of a Shakespeare-spouting lieutenant in the government army. Soon, he was being fed amphetamines and trained to shoot an AK-47. . . . Beah's memoir documents his transformation from a child into a hardened, brutally efficient soldier who high-fived his fellow-recruits after they slaughtered their enemies—often boys their own age—and who 'felt no pity for anyone.'" New Yorker

Beethoven, Ludwig van, 1770-1827

Morris, Edmund. Beethoven: the universal composer. HarperCollins Publishers 2005 243p (Eminent lives) $21.95 *
Grades: 11 12 Adult   92
1. Composers
ISBN 0-06-075974-7; 978-0-06-075974-2
LC 2006-274925
This is a biography of the German composer.
The author "clearly admires his subject not only for the work but also for his constant fight against the odds, and he has written an ideal biography for the general reader." Publ Wkly
Includes bibliographical references

Bernstein, Leonard, 1918-1990

Bernstein, Burton. Leonard Bernstein; American original; how a modern renaissance man transformed music and the world during his New York Philharmonic years, 1943-1976; [by] Burton Bernstein and Barbara B. Haws. HarperCollins 2008 223p il $29.95
Grades: 11 12 Adult   92
1. New York Philharmonic 2. Musicians 3. Composers—United States
ISBN 978-0-06-153786-8; 0-06-153786-1
LC 2008-13702
"Essays by nine writers look at various aspects of Bernstein's life and career, placing him in the mid-twentieth-century artistic, social and political contexts he helped to define." Opera News
"A flat-out wonderful book." Booklist

Blashfield, Jean F. Leonard Bernstein; conductor and composer. Ferguson, J.G. 2000 127p il (Ferguson's career biographies) lib bdg $21.95
Grades: 7 8 9 10   92
1. Conductors (Music) 2. Composers
ISBN 0-89434-337-8   LC 00-37580
This illustrated biography looks at the life, career, and influence of the prominent composer/conductor
"A comprehensive time line of Bernstein's life and information about becoming a conductor or a composer are appended. There are three lists of further reading that give books, Web sites, and related places to contact or visit." SLJ

Bernstein, Paula

Schein, Elyse. Identical strangers. See entry under Schein, Elyse

Birkeland, Kristian, 1867-1917

Jago, Lucy. The northern lights. Knopf 2001 297p hardcover o.p. pa $14
Grades: 11 12 Adult   92
1. Scientists
ISBN 0-375-40980-7; 0-375-70882-0 (pa)
LC 2001-29895
"The true story of the man who unlocked the secrets of the aurora borealis." Jacket

Birkeland, Kristian, 1867-1917—*Continued*

This is a "biography of Kristian Birkeland, a Norwegian scientist who discovered the origins of the aurora borealis." Economist

"Instead of a stiff, scholarly biography, British journalist Jago has written a poignantly human story filled with minute, extensively researched details." Libr J

Includes bibliographical references

Black Elk, 1863-1950

Black Elk. Black Elk speaks; being the life story of a holy man of the Oglala Sioux; [as told through] John G. Neihardt; foreword by Vine Deloria, Jr.; with illustrations by Standing Bear; essays by Alexis N. Petri and Lori Utecht. University of Nebraska Press 2004 xxix, 270p il map pa $14.95

Grades: 11 12 Adult   92

1. Oglala Indians 2. Native Americans—Biography
ISBN 0-8032-8385-7   LC 2004-12692

A reprint of the title first published 1932 by Morrow

The Indian whose life story this is, was born in 1863. He was a famous warrior and hunter in his youth, and became a practicing medicine man among his people. Of him Neihardt says, "As an indubitable seer, he seemed to represent the consciousness of the Plains Indian more fully than any other I had ever known."

This "is about as near as you can get to seeing life and death, war and religion, through an Indian's eyes." Outlook

Blume, Judy

Tracy, Kathleen. Judy Blume; a biography. Greenwood Press 2008 127p (Greenwood biographies) $35

Grades: 9 10 11 12   92

1. Authors, American 2. Women authors
ISBN 978-0-313-34272-1; 0-313-34272-5
           LC 2007-37491

The author "explores the life and career of Judy Blume, one of the most successful—and most controversial—authors of [the] twentieth century." Publisher's note

"The book was hard to put down, and will appeal to high school students and adults. It is an inspiration to those who want to be authors." Libr Media Connect

Includes bibliographical references

Bohr, Niels Henrik David, 1885-1962

Ottaviani, Jim. Suspended in language; Niels Bohr's life, discoveries, and the century he shaped; written by Jim Ottaviani; illustrated and lettered by Leland Purvis. 2nd ed. G.T. Labs 2009 318p il pa $24.95 *

Grades: 10 11 12 Adult   92

1. Graphic novels 2. Biographical graphic novels 3. Physicists—Graphic novels 4. Quantum theory—Graphic novels
ISBN 978-0-9788037-2-8

First published 2004

"Additional art by Jay Hosler, Roger Langridge, Steve Leialoha, Linda Medley, and Jeff Parker."

"Quantum physics gets an accessible yet substantive introduction through art that mixes fantasy and realism. Great for teens who like science." Booklist

Includes bibliographical references

Bolt, Usain, 1986-

Bolt, Usain. 9.58; my story: being the world's fastest man; [by] Usain Bolt with Shaun Custis. HarperSport 2010 252p il $26.95

Grades: 11 12 Adult   92

1. Running
ISBN 978-0-00-737139-6

This book follows "the world's fastest man through his mercurial path from a small outlying region of Jamaica to being one of the world's best-known sports personalities. . . . [The author] is brutally frank in relating his development as an athlete, circumstances in Jamaica, training methods, love of nightlife and fast cars, and how he will triumph in London in 2012 and in 2016 Brazil. . . . [This is] is a rich and textured outline of a life of present accomplishment and of future promise lived in the fast lane. A delight for readers of all ages and backgrounds." Libr J

Booth, John Wilkes, 1838-1865

Swanson, James L. Chasing Lincoln's killer; the search for John Wilkes Booth. Scholastic Press 2009 194p il map $16.99

Grades: 7 8 9 10   92

1. Lincoln, Abraham, 1809-1865—Assassination 2. Actors 3. United States—History—1861-1865, Civil War
ISBN 978-0-439-90354-7; 0-439-90354-8
           LC 2008-17994

"This volume is an adaptation of Swanson's *Manhunt: The 12-Day Chase for Lincoln's Killer* (HarperCollins, 2006). Divided into 14 chapters and an epilogue, the sentences are shorter and chapters are condensed from the original but the rich details and suspense are ever present. . . . Excellent black-and-white illustrations complement the text. . . . Readers will be engrossed by the almost hour-by-hour search and by the many people who encountered the killer as he tried to escape. It is a tale of intrigue and an engrossing mystery." SLJ

Bosch, Carl

Hager, Thomas. The alchemy of air. See entry under Haber, Fritz, 1868-1934

Bourgeois, Louise, 1911-2010

Greenberg, Jan. Runaway girl: the artist Louise Bourgeois; [by] Jan Greenberg and Sandra Jordan. Abrams 2003 80p il $19.95

Grades: 7 8 9 10   92

1. Artists—United States 2. Women artists
ISBN 0-8109-4237-2   LC 2002-11922

Contents: Family tapestry; Family secrets; A young artist in Paris; Runaway girl; The New York art scene; The great decade; Spider, spider burning bright

Introduces the life of renowned modern artist Louise Bourgeois, who is known primarily for her sculptures

Bourgeois, Louise, 1911-2010—*Continued*

"In clear, elegant prose, bolstered with numerous quotes from the artist, the authors seamlessly juxtapose stories of Bourgeois' life with relevant artworks. . . . Beautifully reproduced photographs, printed on well-designed pages, offer an excellent mix of the artist's personal life and her art." Booklist

Includes bibliographical references

Boyle, Robert, 1627-1691

Baxter, Roberta. Skeptical chemist; the story of Robert Boyle. Morgan Reynolds Pub. 2006 128p il (Profiles in science) lib bdg $27.95

Grades: 7 8 9 10 **92**
1. Scientists
ISBN 978-1-59935-025-7; 1-59935-025-4
LC 2006-23969

The author makes a "case for Boyle's significance as a key figure in the field of scientific experimentation as well as his contributions to modern chemistry and physics. Well organized and clearly written, her book offers a good view of changes in science and society at this pivotal time and presents a well-rounded view of Boyle, whose interests extended beyond scientific inquiry and discussion." Booklist

Includes bibliographical references

Bragg, Rick

Bragg, Rick. All over but the shoutin'. Pantheon Bks. 1997 xxii, 329p hardcover o.p. pa $14

Grades: 11 12 Adult **92**
1. Journalists
ISBN 0-679-44258-8; 0-679-77402-5 (pa)
LC 97-9918

"Honest, unsentimental, and so elegantly spare it nearly hurts to read, this memoir by Pulitzer Prize-winning journalist Bragg recounts a dirt-poor childhood in Alabama and the debt he owes his mother." Libr J

Brave Bird, Mary

Brave Bird, Mary. Lakota woman; by Mary Crow Dog and Richard Erdoes. 1st HarperPerennial ed. HarperPerennial 1991 263p il pa $13.95

Grades: 8 9 10 11 12 Adult **92**
1. American Indian Movement 2. Political activists 3. Dakota Indians 4. Native Americans—Biography
ISBN 0-06-097389-7 LC 90-55980
First published 1990 by Grove Weidenfeld

"Born in 1955 and raised in poverty on the Rosebud Reservation, Mary Crow Dog escaped an oppressive Catholic boarding school but fell into a marginal life of urban shoplifting and barhopping. A 1971 encounter with AIM (the American Indian Movement), participation in the 1972 Trail of Broken Treaties march on Washington, and giving birth to her first child while under fire at the 1973 siege of Wounded Knee radicalized her." Libr J

"The story of Mary Crow Dog's coming of age in the Indian civil rights movement is simply told—and, at times, simply horrifying." N Y Times Book Rev

Breazeal, Cynthia

Brown, Jordan. Robo world; the story of robot designer Cynthia Breazeal; by Jordan D. Brown. Franklin Watts 2005 108p il (Women's adventures in science) $31

Grades: 7 8 9 10 **92**
1. Robots 2. Women scientists
ISBN 0-531-16782-8 LC 2005000826
Also available in paperback from Joseph Henry Press

A biography of Cynthia Breazeal who designs, builds, and experiments with robots at the MIT Media Lab.

Includes bibliographical references

Brokaw, Tom, 1940-

Brokaw, Tom. A long way from home; growing up in the American heartland. Random House 2002 272p $24.95; pa $12.95

Grades: 11 12 Adult **92**
1. Journalists
ISBN 0-375-50763-9; 0-375-75935-2 (pa)
LC 2002-31865

News anchor Brokaw "shares the events, tone, and tenor of his midwestern upbringing." Booklist

"Peppered with photographs . . . this tribute to an idyllic childhood should please Brokaw's loyal fans." Publ Wkly

Brown, Bradford B., 1929-

Brown, Bradford B. While you're here, Doc; farmyard adventures of a Maine veterinarian. Tilbury House 2006 174p il pa $15

Grades: 9 10 11 12 **92**
1. Veterinary medicine
ISBN 978-0-8844-8279-6; 0-8844-8279-0
LC 2005-32418

This veterinary memoir features "tales of animal doctoring in a small coastal town in 1950s Maine. . . . Full of laconic farmers, hysterical owners, and more feisty animal patients than one can imagine, these stories of backwoods veterinary care are sure to be popular among James Herriot lovers." Booklist

Brown, Claude, 1937-2002

Brown, Claude. Manchild in the promised land. Touchstone 1999 415p pa $14.95 *

Grades: 11 12 Adult **92**
1. African Americans—Biography 2. African Americans—Harlem (New York, N.Y.)
ISBN 0-684-86418-5
First published 1965 by Macmillan

This is "the autobiography of a young black man raised in Harlem. It is a realistic description of life in the ghetto. . . . The core of the book concerns the 'plague' of heroin addiction that swept through Harlem in the 1950s taking the lives of many of Brown's contemporaries." Publ Wkly

Brown, John, 1800-1859

Sterngass, Jon. John Brown. Chelsea House 2009 144p il (Leaders of the Civil War era) lib bdg $30

Grades: 7 8 9 10   **92**

1. Abolitionists

ISBN 978-1-60413-305-9; 1-60413-305-8

LC 2008-44622

This is a biography of the abolitionist, John Brown.

This is an "even-keeled and well-written account of the man's life and times. . . . Sterngass displays a sharp awareness that what makes the man so controversial is also what makes him so fascinating. . . . [This book] should add depth to Civil War studies." Booklist

Includes glossary and bibliographical references

Bruchac, Joseph, 1942-

Bruchac, Joseph. Bowman's store; a journey to myself. 1st Lee & Low ed. Lee & Low Books 2001 315p il pa $9.95

Grades: 7 8 9 10   **92**

1. Abnaki Indians 2. Native Americans—Biography 3. Authors, American

ISBN 1-58430-027-2; 978-1-58430-027-4

LC 2001-16435

A reissue of the title first published 1997 by Dial Books

"Combining Native American stories with personal memories and dreams, Bruchac crafts a memoir of his childhood growing up with his grandparents in upstate New York." Horn Book Guide

"Each episode is constructed with a true storyteller's attention to language and plot development. Students of modern Native American cultures will find plenty of food for thought." Booklist

Buergenthal, Thomas

Buergenthal, Thomas. A lucky child; a memoir of surviving Auschwitz as a young boy. Little, Brown 2009 228p il map $24.99

Grades: 10 11 12   **92**

1. Holocaust, 1933-1945—Personal narratives 2. World War, 1939-1945—Prisoners and prisons 3. Holocaust survivors 4. Auschwitz (Poland: Concentration camp)

ISBN 978-0-316-04340-3; 0-316-04340-0

LC 2008-33732

"Buergenthal was elected American judge at the International Court of Justice, The Hague, in 2000. He is a survivor of Auschwitz, one in a succession of several labor, prison, and death camps where he spent his 10th and 11th years. . . . This is a well-constructed, warm, insightful visit with the man. . . . In addition to being an excellent curriculum-support text, the fine writing and insights here make this book a powerful choice for teens looking for a mentor through emotional and political challenges of their own." SLJ

Bunche, Ralph J. (Ralph Johnson), 1904-1971

Urquhart, Brian E. Ralph Bunche; an American life; [by] Brian Urquhart. Norton 1993 496p il maps hardcover o.p. pa $15.95

Grades: 11 12 Adult   **92**

1. African Americans—Biography 2. United States—Race relations

ISBN 0-393-03527-1; 0-393-31859-1 (pa)

LC 92-46564

The author "describes Bunche's itinerant childhood, academic background, teaching and research, OSS service in World War II, significant contributions at the Dumbarton Oaks Conference of Allied leaders, and troubleshooting and mediation on behalf of the UN throughout the Middle East, Africa, and Asia. . . . Urquhart has made a fascinating narrative of the accomplishments of an American-born international diplomat." Booklist

Includes bibliographical references

Burr, Aaron, 1756-1836

St. George, Judith. The duel: the parallel lives of Alexander Hamilton and Aaron Burr. Viking 2009 97p il $16.99 *

Grades: 6 7 8 9 10   **92**

1. Hamilton, Alexander, 1757-1804 2. Politicians—United States

ISBN 978-0-670-01124-7; 0-670-01124-X

LC 2009-5660

"After a prologue following the steps of Alexander Hamilton and Aaron Burr on the morning of their famous duel, St. George backtracks to trace the 'parallel lives' mentioned in the subtitle. . . . Well researched and organized, the book offers insights into the personalities, lives, and times of Burr and Hamilton." Booklist

Bush, George, 1924-

Naftali, Timothy J. George H.W. Bush; [by] Timothy Naftali. Times Books 2007 202p (American presidents series) $22

Grades: 11 12 Adult   **92**

1. Presidents—United States

ISBN 978-0-8050-6966-2; 0-8050-6966-6

LC 2007-26217

In this biography of the 41st president, the author "argues that Bush I handled the implosion of the Soviet empire nearly perfectly; unseated a thuggish, double-crossing Central American strongman with dispatch; and, diplomatically deferring to Gulf War allies and the UN, restrained his own strong desire to roust Saddam Hussein out of Iraq as well as Kuwait." Booklist

Includes bibliographical references

Bush, George W.

Bruni, Frank. Ambling into history: the unlikely odyssey of George W. Bush. HarperCollins Pubs. 2002 278p pa $12.95 hardcover o.p.

Grades: 11 12 Adult   **92**

1. Presidents—United States

ISBN 0-06-093782-3 (pa)

The author, who covered Bush's 2000 presidential campaign for the New York Times, focuses on Bush's

Bush, George W.—*Continued*

personality and mannerisms as well as his basic interactions with family, friends, and the public.

"Given [Bruni's] familiarity with Bush, one would expect his book to contain revealing insights, and this superb, incisive, and surprising account does not disappoint." Booklist

Includes bibliographical references

Calcines, Eduardo F., 1955-

Calcines, Eduardo F. Leaving Glorytown; one boy's struggle under Castro. Farrar, Straus & Giroux 2009 221p il $17.95 *

Grades: 7 8 9 10   92

1. Cuban refugees 2. Cuba—History—1959-
ISBN 978-0-374-34394-1; 0-374-34394-2
                                    LC 2008-7506

"Calcines's spirited memoir captures the political tension, economic hardship, family stress, and personal anxiety of growing up during the early years of the Castro regime in Cuba. . . . The author shares startling, clear memories about his life in the Glorytown barrio of Cienfuegos. . . . Calcines writes about Cuba with immediacy, nostalgia, and passion. This personal account will acquaint readers with the oppressive and ironic effects of communism." SLJ

Capotorto, Carl, 1959-

Capotorto, Carl. Twisted head; an Italian-American memoir. Broadway Books 2008 306p il $23.95

Grades: 11 12 Adult   92

1. Actors 2. Italian Americans
ISBN 978-0-7679-2861-8   LC 2008-16133

"A zany, erratic, painfully poignant memoir of growing up working class and gay in the Bronx during the '60s and '70s." Kirkus

Carson, Kit, 1809-1868

Remley, David A. Kit Carson; the life of an American border man; by David Remley. University of Oklahoma Press 2011 289p il map (Oklahoma western biographies) $24.95

Grades: 11 12 Adult   92

1. Frontier and pioneer life—West (U.S.)
ISBN 978-0-8061-4172-5   LC 2010-37350

The author "separates the myth from the man in this engrossing portrait of frontiersman Carson (1809–1868) . . . Contrasting dangerous days and rip-roaring action with poignant moments of Carson's family life, Remley challenges recent revisionist representations of Carson as a 'trigger-happy' outlaw and scoundrel. Instead, the nomadic Carson emerges as an aggressive, helpful, and caring man, who 'matured intellectually and ethically as he grew older.' Remley's Old West overview permeates this rich and rewarding work of scholarship." Publ Wkly

Includes bibliographical references

Carson, Rachel, 1907-1964

Levine, Ellen. Rachel Carson; a twentieth-century life. Viking 2007 224p il (Up close) $15.99 *

Grades: 6 7 8 9 10   92

1. Women scientists
ISBN 0-670-06220-1

A biography of the environmental scientist.

"Direct, eloquent, and precise. . . . A balanced, thoroughly researched introduction to an original scientist whose work remains of urgent importance today." Booklist

Includes bibliographical references

Carter, Jimmy, 1924-

Carter, Jimmy. An hour before daylight; memories of my rural boyhood. Simon & Schuster 2001 284p il hardcover o.p. pa $15

Grades: 11 12 Adult   92

1. Carter family 2. Georgia—Social life and customs 3. Presidents—United States
ISBN 0-7432-1193-6; 0-7432-1199-5 (pa)
                                    LC 00-48248

In this memoir, the thirty-ninth president of the United States remembers his childhood in rural Georgia.

This "is social and agricultural history as plain and honest as one of the tables the author makes in his workshop—an American classic." New Yorker

Carter, Robert, 1728-1804

Levy, Andrew. The first emancipator; the forgotten story of Robert Carter, the founding father who freed his slaves. Random House 2005 310p hardcover o.p. pa $15.95

Grades: 11 12 Adult   92

ISBN 0-375-50865-1; 0-375-76104-7 (pa)
                                    LC 2004-54054

The author "examines the unique life of Robert Carter III, one of the wealthiest men in 18th-century America, and his monumental 'Deed of Gift.' This legal document, recorded in 1791, allowed for the largest single emancipation of slaves until the Emancipation Proclamation." Libr J

"This well-written and thoroughly engaging book will certainly appeal to readers interested in the history of 18th- and 19th-century Virginia, but also to those interested in the history of slavery and racism in America and in historical biography." Publ Wkly

Includes bibliographical references

Cary, Lorene

Cary, Lorene. Black ice. Knopf 1991 237p hardcover o.p. pa $10

Grades: 11 12 Adult   92

1. St. Paul's School (Concord, N.H.) 2. African American women—Biography
ISBN 0-394-57465-6; 0-679-73745-6 (pa)
                                    LC 90-52988

"In the early 1970's, an Eastern prep school recruiting minority students opened its doors to Cary, then a 15-year-old Philadelphia high school girl. These affecting recollections explore her experiences—interactions with teachers, an affair with another student, friendships, and problems with prejudice—as well as her struggle to determine her own black identity." Booklist

Cash, Johnny

Neimark, Anne E. Johnny Cash; a twentieth-century life. Viking Childrens Books 2007 207p il (Up close) $15.99

Grades: 8 9 10 11 12   92

1. Country musicians

ISBN 978-0-670-06215-7   LC 2006-10198

"The life of the deeply troubled and powerfully influential music legend is brought vividly to life in this richly detailed biography. . . . Cash's genius as a songwriter and musician as well as his incalculable influence upon music are skillfully explored, and Neimark frequently uses excerpts from Cash's own songs to enrich his compelling life story." Booklist

Includes bibliographical references

Castro, Fidel, 1926-

Coltman, Sir Leycester. The real Fidel Castro; with a foreword by Julia E. Sweig. Yale Univ. Press 2003 335p il map $30; pa $20 *

Grades: 11 12 Adult   92

1. Cuba—Politics and government

ISBN 0-300-10188-0; 0-300-10760-9 (pa)

LC 2003-12942

This biography "offers a fresh assessment of the revolutionary leader. . . . It chronicles the events of Castro's extraordinary life and explores the contradiction between the private character and the public reputation." Univ Press Books for Public and Second Sch Libr, 2004

Includes bibliographical references

Cather, Willa, 1873-1947

Meltzer, Milton. Willa Cather; a biography. Twenty-First Century Books 2008 160p il (Literary greats) $33.26 *

Grades: 7 8 9 10 11 12   92

1. Authors, American 2. Women authors

ISBN 978-0-8225-7604-4; 0-8225-7604-X

LC 2007-25629

A biography of the author of such novels as *O Pioneers!* and *My Antonia.*

"With signature clarity, Meltzer's . . . biography . . . sets his detailed discussion of Cather's life and work against the larger backdrop of her times. . . . The book's handsome, inviting design includes photos on almost every spread." Booklist

Includes bibliographical references

Catherine II, the Great, Empress of Russia, 1729-1796

Whitelaw, Nancy. Catherine the Great and the Enlightenment in Russia. Morgan Reynolds Pub. 2005 160p il map (European queens) lib bdg $24.95 *

Grades: 9 10 11 12   92

1. Russia—Kings and rulers

ISBN 1-931798-27-3; 978-1-931798-27-3

LC 2004-14711

The author "follows Catherine from her youth as a struggling German princess to Russia, where at 16 she wed the profoundly unimpressive Grand Duke Peter,

whom she embraced as a means to the throne. . . . In language both straightforward and compelling, Whitelaw describes the formidable czarina's reign, her love affairs, her vast cultural influence, and the political treachery that surrounded her court." Booklist

Includes bibliographical references

Catlin, George, 1796-1872

Reich, Susanna. Painting the wild frontier: the art and adventures of George Catlin. Clarion Books 2008 160p il map $21 *

Grades: 7 8 9 10 11 12   92

1. Artists—United States 2. Native Americans in art 3. West (U.S.) in art

ISBN 978-0-618-71470-4; 0-618-71470-7

LC 2007-38847

This is a "biography of nineteenth-century painter George Catlin, famous for his portraits of Native American life. . . . A great introduction to Catlin's work as well as an excellent title to use in social studies, history, and art classes." Booklist

Includes bibliographical references

Chagall, Marc, 1887-1985

Kagan, Andrew. Marc Chagall. Abbeville Press 1989 128p il (Modern masters series) hardcover o.p. pa $14.95 *

Grades: 11 12 Adult   92

1. Artists

ISBN 0-89659-932-9; 0-89659-935-3 (pa)

LC 89-6693

This illustrated biography of the Russian Jewish artist explores his paintings, graphics, mosaics, tapestries, and stained glass works. A biochronology and a selected exhibitions list are appended

Includes bibliographical references

Charbonneau, Jean-Baptiste, 1805-1866

Nelson, W. Dale. Interpreters with Lewis and Clark: the story of Sacagawea and Toussaint Charbonneau. See entry under Sacagawea, b. 1786

Charbonneau, Toussaint, ca. 1758-ca. 1839

Nelson, W. Dale. Interpreters with Lewis and Clark: the story of Sacagawea and Toussaint Charbonneau. See entry under Sacagawea, b. 1786

Charlemagne, Emperor, 742-814

Wilson, Derek A. Charlemagne. Doubleday 2006 226p il map $26; pa $14.95 *

Grades: 11 12 Adult   92

1. Kings and rulers

ISBN 0-385-51670-3; 0-307-27480-2 (pa)

LC 2005-48483

This biography of the Frankish emperor "demonstrates how the empire he built led to the development of the European identity." SLJ

The author "writes with clarity and passion, and his thesis is food for thought for both general readers and students." Libr J

Includes bibliographical references

Charles, Ray

Duggleby, John. Uh huh!: the story of Ray Charles. Morgan Reynolds Pub. 2005 160p il $26.95 *

Grades: 7 8 9 10   92

1. African American singers

ISBN 1-931798-65-6   LC 2005-1287

The author "traces Charles' long career and displays a sensitivity to the events surrounding his life (including his bitter battles with heroin and alcohol addiction), as well as a genuine understanding of his music and the breadth of his musical influence. Sidebars on 'race' music, Braille, the Grammys, soul, and rock and roll enrich the narrative." Booklist

Includes bibliographical references

Chavez, Cesar, 1927-1993

Cruz, Bárbara. César Chávez; a voice for farmworkers; [by] Bárbara C. Cruz. Enslow Publishers, Inc. 2005 128p il (Latino biography library) lib bdg $31.93

Grades: 7 8 9 10   92

1. Migrant labor 2. Mexican Americans—Biography

ISBN 0-7660-2489-X   LC 2004-27538

"Cruz takes readers from Chavez's first job as a migrant worker in California at age 10 through his decision to help his fellow workers: his fasts, his activism, the founding and continued involvement in the United Farm Workers Union until his death in 1993. Black-and-white and full-color photos appear throughout." SLJ

Griswold del Castillo, Richard. César Chávez; a triumph of spirit; by Richard Griswold del Castillo and Richard A. Garcia. University of Okla. Press 1995 206p il (Oklahoma western biographies) pa $14.95 hardcover o.p.

Grades: 11 12 Adult   92

1. Migrant labor 2. Mexican Americans—Biography

ISBN 0-8061-2957-3 (pa)   LC 95-15230

"In this biography of the embattled farm labor organizer, del Castillo . . . focuses on Chávez's formation, growth, and development as a leader in the movement to unionize farm workers in the Southwest. . . . Del Castillo's account is balanced, highly readable, and engaging." Libr J

Includes bibliographical references

Stavans, Ilan. Cesar Chavez; a photographic essay. Cinco Puntos Press 2010 91p il pa $13.95

Grades: 7 8 9 10   92

1. Migrant agricultural laborers 2. Mexican Americans—Biography

ISBN 978-1-933693-22-4; 1-933693-22-3

LC 2009-44179

"Chavez secured better working conditions for thousands with his 1970 victory for the United Farm Workers Union by bargaining with the table-grape growers. This photo-biography covers the high points of his career, including ample and pointed quotes by him and touching on his global recognition and interactions with activist Fred Ross Jr., Dolores Huerta, Pope Paul VI, and Senator Robert F. Kennedy. The full-page black-and-white photos give a sense of the man at various ages, of the migrant workers' lives, and of being on the road demonstrating

and striking. The book also includes a comprehensive time line. It is an excellent introduction to social activism from the 1950s through the 1980s." SLJ

Chávez Frías, Hugo

Levin, Judith. Hugo Chávez. Chelsea House Publishers 2007 128p il (Modern world leaders) $30 *

Grades: 7 8 9 10   92

1. Venezuela 2. Presidents—Venezuela

ISBN 0-7910-9258-5; 978-0-7910-9258-3

LC 2006-10611

This is a biography of the Venezuelan president.

Includes bibliographical references

Churchill, Sir Winston, 1874-1965

Rubin, Gretchen Craft. Forty ways to look at Winston Churchill; a brief account of a long life; {by} Gretchen Rubin. Ballantine Books 2003 307p il hardcover o.p. pa $14.95 *

Grades: 9 10 11 12   92

1. Prime ministers—Great Britain 2. Great Britain—Politics and government—20th century

ISBN 0-345-45047-7; 0-8129-7144-2 (pa)

LC 2003-271389

This biography is in the form of "40 brief chapters looking at the British prime minister from multiple angles: Churchill as son, father, husband, orator, painter, historian, enemy of Hitler and many other roles." Publ Wkly

"Rubin has much to offer teens, especially those with only vague notions of the great man." SLJ

Includes bibliographical references

Clemente, Roberto, 1934-1972

Maraniss, David. Clemente; the passion and grace of baseball's last hero. Simon & Schuster 2006 401p il maps hardcover o.p. pa $15 *

Grades: 11 12 Adult   92

1. Baseball—Biography

ISBN   0-7432-1781-0;   978-0-7432-1781-1; 0-7432-9999-X; 978-0-7432-9999-2 (pa)

LC 2006-42235

This is a "biography of the first Latin American player named to the Baseball Hall of Fame." Libr J

The author "has produced a baseball-savvy book sensitive to the social context that made Clemente, a black Puerto Rican, a leading indicator of baseball's future." N Y Times Book Rev

Includes bibliographical references

Santiago, Wilfred. "21"; the story of Roberto Clemente: a graphic novel. Fantagraphics 2011 unp il $22.99

Grades: 11 12 Adult   92

1. Graphic novels 2. Autobiographical graphic novels 3. Baseball—Graphic novels

ISBN 978-1-56097-892-3

"Santiago opens his dazzlingly drawn comics biography of the pioneering Puerto Rican ballplayer on the final game of the 1972 season, with Clemente just one hit

Clemente, Roberto, 1934-1972—*Continued*

shy of joining the 3,000-hit club. Fans will know, of course, that 3,000 would also be his final tally, as he would die in a plane crash delivering relief supplies to the earthquake-rocked Nicaragua that winter. Santiago skitters around formative scenes from Clemente's childhood—striking a complex chord of family, homeland, and a driving passion for baseball—before tracing significant moments from his professional career: staring down racism with the same resolute demeanor with which he faced a high heater, snagging batting championships and fans' hearts many times over, and always looking for ways to honor his heritage." Booklist

Cleopatra, Queen of Egypt, d. 30 B.C.

Burstein, Stanley M. The reign of Cleopatra. Greenwood Press 2004 xxiii, 179p il map (Greenwood guides to historic events of the ancient world) $45 *

Grades: 9 10 11 12   92
    1. Queens 2. Egypt—History
ISBN 0-313-32527-8   LC 2004-14672
    Contents: Historical background; Cleopatra's life; Ptolemaic Egypt: how did it work?; Cleopatra's Egypt: a multicultural story; Alexandria: city of culture and conflict; Conclusion: queen and symbol
    Includes bibliographical references

Nardo, Don. Cleopatra. Lucent Books 2005 112p il map (Lucent library of historical eras, Ancient Egypt) $28.70

Grades: 7 8 9 10   92
    1. Queens 2. Egypt—History
ISBN 1-59018-660-5; 978-1-59018-660-2
                   LC 2004-22071
    Subtitle on cover: Egypt's last pharaoh
    This biography of the Egyptian queen "features quotations from ancient authors, along with Nardo's discussion of how many of these authors were biased, for or against one of the most powerful women in history. He includes her romantic liaisons with Julius Caesar and Marc Antony. . . . A final chapter looks at how Cleopatra has been rendered in literature." SLJ
    Includes bibliographical references

Roller, Duane W. Cleopatra; a biography. Oxford University Press 2010 252p il map (Women in antiquity) $24.95 *

Grades: 11 12 Adult   92
    1. Queens 2. Egypt—History
ISBN 978-0-19-536553-5; 0-19-536553-4
                   LC 2009-24061
    "Basing this chronicle exclusively on primary sources culled from classical antiquity, the author painstakingly separates myth from reality, discounting . . . [Cleopatra's] undeserved reputation as a seductress and concentrating on her impressive—but often overlooked or minimized—political, military, and administrative achievements. This revisionist portrait of one of the most powerful women in the ancient world adds substance and heft to her exotic legacy." Booklist
    Includes bibliographical references

Cochise, Apache Chief, d. 1874

Sweeney, Edwin R. (Edwin Russell). Cochise, Chiricahua Apache chief. University of Okla. Press 1991 xxiii, 501p il maps (Civilization of the American Indian series) pa $24.95 hardcover o.p.

Grades: 11 12 Adult   92
    1. Apache Indians 2. Native Americans—Biography
ISBN 0-8061-2606-X (pa)   LC 90-50699
    The author traces Cochise's "rise to leadership of his Apache band, his . . . skirmishes with the military and others in both the United States and Mexico, and his successful negotiations for a reservation in the homeland of his peoples." Libr J
    "An insightful, and exciting work that ranks with the best efforts of ethnohistory. . . . This book is the definitive life story of history's most important Apache chief and restores him to his proper preeminent role in the region's history." Choice
    Includes bibliographical references

Colvin, Claudette

Hoose, Phillip M. Claudette Colvin; twice toward justice; by Phillip Hoose. Melanie Kroupa Books 2009 133p il $19.95 *

Grades: 6 7 8 9 10   92
    1. African American women—Biography 2. African Americans—Civil rights
ISBN 978-0-374-31322-7; 0-374-31322-9
                   LC 2008-05435
    "Teenager Claudette Colvin's significant contribution to the struggle for equal accommodation is presented in this biography that smoothly weaves excerpts from Hoose's extensive interviews with Colvin and his own supplementary commentary. . . . [Readers learn] why her arrest for refusing to give up her bus seat to a white passenger never became the crucial incident to spark the Montgomery Bus Boycott. . . . Plenty of black-and-white photographs and well-deployed sidebars enhance the text." Bull Cent Child Books
    Includes bibliographical references

Conroy, Pat

Conroy, Pat. My losing season. Talese 2002 402p hardcover o.p. pa $14.95

Grades: 11 12 Adult   92
    1. Authors, American
ISBN 0-385-48912-9; 0-553-38190-3 (pa)
                   LC 2002-66212
    "Novelist Conroy ruminates on the profound effect of his final year as a point guard for the Citadel's basketball team, interweaving stories about the years leading up to college, his abusive father, his love-hate relationship with his school, and his growing fondness for books and writing." Booklist
    "A wonderfully rich, informative, and well-researched reminiscence." Libr J

Cornwell, John, 1940-

Cornwell, John. Seminary boy. Doubleday 2006 321p il $24.95

Grades: 11 12 Adult   92
    ISBN 978-0-385-54186-6; 0-385-51486-7
                   LC 2005-56026

Cornwell, John, 1940---*Continued*

The author "tells the story of his life at an all-male school in the 1950s. Son of a struggling working-class family in London, John was sent to Cotton College to become a Catholic priest. Here, during his teen years, he experienced the best and worst of pre-Vatican II seminary life. Some of his teachers were pious and dedicated men; others were sexual predators. . . . Part spiritual odyssey, part boarding school story, Cornwell's well-crafted memoir is filled with vivid descriptions of people and places and a young boy's struggle to find himself." Libr J

Cousteau, Jacques Yves, 1910-1997

Matsen, Bradford. Jacques Cousteau; the sea king; [by] Brad Matsen. Pantheon Books 2009 296p il $27.95

Grades: 11 12 Adult   **92**

1. Oceanography

ISBN 978-0-375-42413-7; 0-375-42413-X

LC 2009-11640

This biography "places Cousteau's films, books, and fame into the context of the rest of his life—ambitions, childhood, family relationships, friendships, and disagreements. . . . Readers who dive, who are interested in ecology or the oceans, or who simply recognize the name Cousteau, will want to read this full, well-rounded portrait of one of the world's greatest explorers and conservationists. Highly recommended." Libr J

Includes bibliographical references

Cox, Lynne

Cox, Lynne. Swimming to Antarctica; tales of a long-distance swimmer. Knopf 2004 323p $24.95

Grades: 11 12 Adult   **92**

1. Women athletes

ISBN 0-375-41507-6   LC 2003-47577

Also available in paperback from Harvest Bks.

The author "has swum the Mediterranean, the three-mile Strait of Messina, under the ancient bridges of Kunning Lake, [and] below the old summer palace of the emperor of China in Beijing. . . . She writes about the ways in which these swims . . . became vehicles for personal goals." Publisher's note

"Cox is a pleasure. . . . Many passages are grip-the-page exciting, whether she's dodging Antarctic icebergs or Nile River sewage." Booklist

Crane, Kathleen, 1951-

Crane, Kathleen. Sea legs; tales of a woman oceanographer. Westview Press 2003 318p il map hardcover o.p. pa $16

Grades: 11 12 Adult   **92**

1. Oceanography 2. Women scientists

ISBN 0-8133-4004-7; 0-8133-4285-6 (pa)

LC 2003-1690

"Crane chronicles the relentless adversity she faced in becoming a world-class oceanographer with a modest matter-of-factness that almost camouflages the high caliber of her achievements. . . . She was the first to postulate the existence of the now famous deep-sea hot springs. . . . Crane's experiences are diverse, dramatic,

and important; her understanding of international affairs and environmental realities laudable and moving; and her triumphs over personal sorrows and illness impressive and inspiring." Booklist

Includes bibliographical references

Crazy Horse, Sioux Chief, ca. 1842-1877

Freedman, Russell. The life and death of Crazy Horse; drawings by Amos Bad Heart Bull. Holiday House 1996 166p il maps $22.95 *

Grades: 5 6 7 8 9 10   **92**

1. Oglala Indians 2. Native Americans—Biography

ISBN 0-8234-1219-9   LC 95-33303

A biography of the Oglala Indian leader who relentlessly resisted the white man's attempt to take over Indian lands.

This is "a compelling biography that is based on primary source documents and illustrated with pictographs by a Sioux band historian." Voice Youth Advocates

Includes bibliographical references

McMurtry, Larry. Crazy Horse. Viking 1999 148p (Penguin lives series) hardcover o.p. pa $14

Grades: 11 12 Adult   **92**

1. Oglala Indians 2. Native Americans—Biography

ISBN 0-670-88234-8; 0-14-303480-4 (pa)

LC 98-26644

"Though essentially a loner and devoid of political ambition, Crazy Horse was a respected military tactician, equally feared and admired for the strength and the intensity of his convictions. Rather than merely attempting to sort out fact from fiction, McMurtry incorporates conjecture and legend into this philosophical portrait of both the man and the myth." Booklist

Crick, Francis, 1916-2004

Ridley, Matt. Francis Crick; discoverer of the genetic code. Atlas Books 2006 213p (Eminent lives) $19.95 *

Grades: 11 12 Adult   **92**

1. Scientists 2. Genetics

ISBN 0-06-082333-X; 978-0-06-082333-7

LC 2005-55878

This "biography examines the paired strands of Crick's life and work." N Y Times Book Rev

"A briskly written essential for the DNA shelf." Booklist

Includes bibliographical references

Cromwell, Oliver, 1599-1658

Aronson, Marc. John Winthrop, Oliver Cromwell, and the Land of Promise. See entry under Winthrop, John, 1588-1649

Crutcher, Chris, 1946-

Crutcher, Chris. King of the mild frontier: an ill-advised autobiography. Greenwillow Bks. 2003 260p il $16.99; pa $6.99 *

Grades: 8 9 10 11 12   **92**

1. Authors, American

ISBN 0-06-050249-5; 0-06-050251-7 (pa)

LC 2002-11224

Crutcher, Chris, 1946-—*Continued*

Chris Crutcher, author of young adult novels such as "Ironman" and "Whale Talk," as well as short stories, tells of growing up in Cascade, Idaho, and becoming a writer

"Like his novels, Crutcher's autobiography is full of heartbreak, poignancy, and hilarity. . . . This honest, insightful, revealing autobiography is a joy to read." Booklist

Cummings, E. E. (Edward Estlin), 1894-1962

Reef, Catherine. E. E. Cummings. Clarion Books 2006 149p il $21 *
Grades: 7 8 9 10 11 12   92
1. Poets, American
ISBN 978-0-618-56849-9; 0-618-56849-2
LC 2006-10453
Subtitle on cover: A poet's life
This "is an engaging look behind the typography at one of the twentieth century's most familiar poets." Bull Cent Child Books
Includes bibliographical references

Curie, Marie, 1867-1934

Borzendowski, Janice. Marie Curie; mother of modern physics. Sterling Pub 2009 124p il map (Sterling biographies) $12.95; pa $5.95
Grades: 7 8 9 10   92
1. Physicists 2. Chemists 3. Women scientists
ISBN   978-1-4027-6543-8;   1-4027-6543-6; 978-1-4027-5318-3 (pa); 1-4027-5318-7 (pa)
LC 2008-30701
"This interesting, informative biography of the scientist and Nobel Prize winner explores both Curie's personal and professional life. It includes numerous archival and modern photos and reproductions. . . . The book is far more thorough and satisfying than most biographies of Curie for teens." SLJ
Includes bibliographical references

McClafferty, Carla Killough. Something out of nothing; Marie Curie and radium. Farrar, Straus & Giroux 2006 134p il $18 *
Grades: 5 6 7 8 9 10   92
1. Chemists 2. Women scientists
ISBN 0-374-38036-8   LC 2004-56414
This "biography examines Curie's life and work as a groundbreaking scientist and as an independent woman. . . . The groundbreaking science is as thrilling as the personal story. . . . The spacious design makes the text easy to read, and occasional photos . . . bring the story closer." Booklist

Yannuzzi, Della A. New elements; the story of Marie Curie; [by] Della Yannuzzi. Morgan Reynolds Pub. 2006 144p il (Profiles in science) lib bdg $27.95
Grades: 7 8 9 10   92
1. Chemists 2. Women scientists
ISBN 978-1-59935-023-3; 1-59935-023-8
LC 2006-18887
This is a biography "of the first woman to win a Nobel Prize in science. . . . Readers will come away with

a strong portrait of the heralded scientist's life and times (the historical context is nicely integrated), and serious researchers will turn to the bibliography's sturdy selection of titles." Booklist
Includes bibliographical references

Dahl, Roald

Gelletly, LeeAnne. Gift of imagination; the story of Roald Dahl. Morgan Reynolds 2007 160p il (World writers) lib bdg $27.95 *
Grades: 7 8 9 10   92
1. Authors, English
ISBN 978-1-59935-026-4; 1-59935-026-2
LC 2006-17078
This biography "draws connections between the events in Dahl's life and the stories he created." SLJ
"A succinct, informative, and quite readable resource." Booklist
Includes bibliographical references

Dalai Lama II, 1476-1542

Mullin, Glenn H. The second Dalai Lama; his life and teachings; translated, edited, introduced, and annotated by Glenn H. Mullin. Snow Lion Publications 2005 270p pa $16.95
Grades: 9 10 11 12   92
ISBN 1-55939-233-9   LC 2005-281580
The author "has divided his book into three parts: a general introduction to Tibetan religious history and the lineage of the Dalai Lamas, a biography of the Second Dalai Lama (1475-1541), particularly noted for his poetry, and a selection in 25 chapters of his mystical poems, translated and commented on by Mullin." Libr J

Dalai Lama XIV, 1935-

Dalai Lama XIV. Freedom in exile; the autobiography of the Dalai Lama. HarperCollins Pubs. 1990 288p il maps pa $15 hardcover o.p. *
Grades: 11 12 Adult   92
ISBN 0-06-098701-4   LC 89-46523
"A Cornelia & Michael Bessie book"
"The Dalai Lama's story is, in part, a chapter in the 2,500-year history of Buddhism as well as a testament to the 'mendacity and barbarity' of Communist China. He shares the details of his amazing life, a glimpse at some of the mysteries of Tibetan Buddhism, and his unshakable belief in the basic good of humanity." Booklist

Iyer, Pico. The open road; the global journey of the fourteenth Dalai Lama. Bloomsbury 2008 288p $24 *
Grades: 11 12 Adult   92
ISBN 978-0-307-26760-3; 0-307-26760-1
LC 2007-43991
In this biography of the 14th Dalai Lama, "Iyer organizes his observations by smart descriptions of aspects of the Dalai Lama's work and character: icon, monk, philosopher, politician." Publ Wkly
"The combination of Iyer's exacting observations, incisive analysis, and frank respect for the unknowable results in a uniquely internalized, even empathic portrait of

Dalai Lama XIV, 1935-—_Continued_
one of the world's most embraced and least understood guiding lights." Booklist
Includes bibliographical references

Dalí, Salvador, 1904-1989
Ross, Michael Elsohn. Salvador Dali and the surrealists; their lives and ideas: 21 activities. Chicago Review Press 2003 132p il pa $17.95 *
Grades: 9 10 11 12   **92**
1. Artists, Spanish 2. Surrealism
ISBN 1-556-52479-X   LC 2002-155628
Examines the lives and creative work of the surrealist artist Salvador Dalí and other artists and friends who shared his new ways of exploring art. Features art activities that engage the subconscious thoughts and spontaneity of the reader
"This visually stunning work enhances the body of material on the artist and his contemporaries. Eminently readable, the crisply written text is detailed and thorough, including pronunciations of many place and personal names. Dalí's life is presented familiarly, drawing in many details of life as an artist during that period in Europe and the relationships among the surrealists. . . . The attractive layout includes numerous excellent-quality reproductions of the work of Dali and many of the other artists mentioned in the text, and period photographs. . . . A valuable addition to any collection." SLJ
Includes bibliographical references

Dang, Thuy Tram, 1943-1970
Dang, Thuy Tram. Last night I dreamed of peace; the diary of Dang Thuy Tram; translated by Andrew X. Pham; introduction by Frances FitzGerald; notes by Jane Barton Griffith, Robert Whitehurst, and Dang Kim Tram. Harmony Books 2007 225p il map $19.95
Grades: 11 12 Adult   **92**
1. Physicians 2. Vietnam War, 1961-1975—Medical care
ISBN 978-0-307-34737-4; 0-307-34737-0
                                         LC 2007-8201
"In 1970, while sifting through war documents in Vietnam, Fred Whitehurst, an American lawyer serving with a military intelligence dispatch, found a diary no bigger than a pack of cigarettes, its pages handsewn together. Written between 1968 and '70 by Tram, a young, passionate doctor who served on the front lines, it chronicled the strife she witnessed until the day she was shot by American soldiers earlier that year at age 27." Publ Wkly
"The volume will generate much discussion. It is an excellent source for nonfiction booktalks, book groups, World History and English classes, and public libraries everywhere." SLJ

Danticat, Edwidge, 1969-
Danticat, Edwidge. Brother, I'm dying. Alfred A. Knopf 2007 272p hardcover o.p. pa $15 *
Grades: 11 12 Adult   **92**
1. Women authors
ISBN   978-1-4000-4115-2;   1-4000-4115-5; 978-1-4000-3430-7 (pa); 1-4000-3430-2 (pa)
                                       LC 2007-06887

This family memoir by the author of The Dew Breaker (2004) centers on the experiences of "her father, Mira, and his older brother, Joseph." Publisher's note
The author "has written a fierce, haunting book about exile and loss and family love, and how that love can survive distance and separation, loss and abandonment and somehow endure, undented and robust." N Y Times (Late NY Ed)

Danton, Georges Jacques, 1759-1794
Lawday, David. The giant of the French Revolution; Danton, a life. Grove Press 2010 c2009 294p il map $27.50
Grades: 11 12 Adult   **92**
1. France—History—1789-1799, Revolution
ISBN 978-0-8021-1933-9
The author chronicles "the rise and fall of Georges-Jacques Danton (1759-1794), whose booming voice and fervid passion animated both the French Revolution that honored him and the Terror that took his head." Kirkus
"This is the best biography of Danton to be written since Hilaire Belloc's over 100 years ago. Both the scholar and the general reader will find this biography an informative and lively read." Libr J
Includes bibliographical references

Darwin, Charles, 1809-1882
Berra, Tim M. Charles Darwin; the concise story of an extraordinary man. Johns Hopkins University Press 2008 114p il map $19.95
Grades: 11 12 Adult   **92**
1. Naturalists
ISBN 978-0-8018-9104-5; 0-8018-9104-3
                                       LC 2008-11320
This "biography reveals the great scientist as husband, father, and friend. . . . Berra discusses Darwin's revolutionary scientific work, its impact on modern-day biological science, and the influence of Darwin's evolutionary theory on Western thought. . . . [The] book includes 20 color plates and 60 black-and-white illustrations, along with an annotated list of Darwin's publications and a chronology of his life." Publisher's note
Includes bibliographical references

Eldredge, Niles. Charles Darwin and the mystery of mysteries; by Niles Eldredge and Susan Pearson. Rb Flash Point 2010 135p il map lib bdg $19.99
Grades: 7 8 9 10   **92**
1. Beagle Expedition (1831-1836) 2. Naturalists
ISBN 978-1-59643-374-8; 1-59643-374-4
"A Neal Porter book"
Follows Charles Darwin on his journey aboard the HMS Beagle and presents the thinking that led him to the theory of evolution and the writing of The origin of the species. Includes historical photographs and passages from Darwin's personal diary.
"Numerous quotations from Darwin's works and correspondence bring his voice to readers. . . . Eldredge and Pearson have done a fine job of summarizing both Darwin's life and work." SLJ

Darwin, Charles, 1809-1882—*Continued*
Eldredge, Niles. Darwin: discovering the tree of life. Norton 2005 256p il map $35
Grades: 11 12 Adult   92
1. Naturalists
ISBN 0-393-05966-9   LC 2005-18636
This is the companion volume to an exhibition on Darwin presented by the American Museum of Natural History in 2005.
"By closely analyzing Darwin's numerous notebooks, letters, and edited manuscripts, Eldredge draws a multidimensional portrait of the man as a humanist, naturalist, and reluctant evolutionist." Choice
Includes bibliographical references

Heiligman, Deborah. Charles and Emma; the Darwins' leap of faith. Henry Holt and Company 2009 268p il $18.95 *
Grades: 7 8 9 10 11 12   92
1. Darwin, Emma Wedgwood, 1808-1896
2. Naturalists
ISBN 978-0-8050-8721-5; 0-8050-8721-4
                                        LC 2008-26091
"This rewarding biography of Charles Darwin investigates his marriage to his cousin Emma Wedgwood. . . . Embracing the paradoxes in her subjects' personalities, the author unfolds a sympathetic and illuminating account, bolstered by quotations from their personal writings as well as significant research into the historical context." Publ Wkly
Includes bibliographical references

Quammen, David. The reluctant Mr. Darwin; an intimate portrait of Charles Darwin and the making of his theory of evolution. Atlas Books/Norton 2006 304p (Great discoveries) hardcover o.p. pa $14.95 *
Grades: 11 12 Adult   92
1. Naturalists
ISBN   0-393-05981-2;   978-0-393-05981-6;
0-393-32995-X (pa); 978-0-393-32995-7 (pa)
                                        LC 2006-9864
The author "concentrates on how Darwin privately developed his theory of evolution and reluctantly made his ideas public when [Alfred] Wallace began to publish similar theories." Libr J
"This often slyly witty book stands out among the flood of books being published for Darwin's bicentenary." Publ Wkly
Includes bibliographical references

Darwin, Emma Wedgwood, 1808-1896
Heiligman, Deborah. Charles and Emma. See entry under Darwin, Charles, 1809-1882

Davis, Jefferson, 1808-1889
Aretha, David. Jefferson Davis; [by] David A. Aretha. Chelsea House Publishers 2009 112p il (Leaders of the Civil War era) lib bdg $30
Grades: 7 8 9 10   92
1. Confederate States of America 2. Presidents 3. United States—History—1861-1865, Civil War
ISBN 978-1-60413-297-7; 1-60413-297-3
                                        LC 2008-44764

Biography of Jefferson Davis, the president of the confederacy during the Civil War.
Includes glossary and bibliographical references

Dawidoff, Nicholas
Dawidoff, Nicholas. The crowd sounds happy; a story of love, madness, and baseball. Pantheon Books 2008 271p $24.95
Grades: 11 12 Adult   92
1. Baseball—Biography
ISBN 978-0-375-40028-5; 0-375-40028-1
                                        LC 2007-30525
In this memoir, the author describes how his love of baseball helped him through rough periods of his youth, including his father descent into mental illness.
"Essential reading for anyone who wishes a balm for heartbreaks in youth, torn family life, love, and seventh-game losses." Libr J

Delany, Bessie
Delany, Sadie. Having our say. See entry under Delany, Sadie

Delany, Sadie
Delany, Sadie. Having our say; the Delany sisters' first 100 years; [by] Sarah and A. Elizabeth Delany; with Amy Hill Hearth. Kodansha Int. 1993 210p il $20
Grades: 11 12 Adult   92
1. Delany, Bessie 2. Delany family 3. United States—Race relations 4. African American women—Biography
ISBN 1-56836-010-X   LC 93-23890
Also available in paperback from Dell
"The Delany sisters' story is a collective meditation on American life since Sadie's birth in 1889 and Bessie's in 1891 in Raleigh, North Carolina. . . . The sisters migrated to New York City's Harlem in the 1910s and in the 1950s to the suburb of Mt. Vernon, New York. The assertive Bessie battled racism and sexism as the only black female member of her Columbia University Dental School class in the 1920s. The more reticent Sadie became the first black domestic science teacher in the New York City high schools." Libr J
"The combination of the two voices, beautifully blended by Ms. Hearth, evokes an epic history, often cruel and brutal, but always deeply humane in their spirited telling of it." N Y Times Book Rev

Delman, Carmit
Delman, Carmit. Burnt bread & chutney; growing up between cultures; a memoir of an Indian Jewish girl. One World/Ballantine Bks. 2002 xxiv, 261p hardcover o.p. pa $13.95
Grades: 9 10 11 12   92
1. Jews—Biography 2. Culture conflict 3. East Indians 4. Racially mixed people
ISBN 0-345-44593-7; 0-345-44594-5 (pa)
                                        LC 2002-22855
The author's "mother is a direct descendant of the Bene Israel, a tiny, ancient community of Jews . . . of

Delman, Carmit—*Continued*
Western India. Her father is American, a Jewish man of Eastern European descent. They met while working the land of a nascent Israeli state. . . . They hardly took notice of the interracial aspect of their union. But their daughter, Carmit, growing up in America, was well aware of her uncommon heritage." Publisher's note

"Delman's troubled, but ultimately inspiring passage leads her to some universal truths." SLJ

Dickens, Charles, 1812-1870
Caravantes, Peggy. Best of times: the story of Charles Dickens. Morgan Reynolds Pub. 2005 160p il (World writers) $26.95
Grades: 7 8 9 10   **92**
1. Authors, English
ISBN 1-931798-68-0   LC 2005-8405
"Beginning with Dickens' childhood trauma (his father was put in debtors' prison, and Charles, 12, had to work in a blacking factory), this highly readable [book] . . . relates the extraordinary writer's stories to his life and times. . . . [It includes] many interesting quotes, color prints, and photos." Booklist
Includes bibliographical references

Smiley, Jane. Charles Dickens. Viking 2002 212p (Penguin lives series) $19.95 *
Grades: 11 12 Adult   **92**
1. Authors, English
ISBN 0-670-03077-5   LC 2001-45607
"A Penguin life; A Lipper\Viking book"
This "biography examines Dickens' life through his work, starting not with his birth but rather the beginnings of his literary career. After writing short essays for a monthly magazine, Dickens began the serialization of his first novel, *The Pickwick Papers*. Dickens quickly became both a best-selling novelist and a famous man, who had to contend with both the envy of other authors and, much later on, the very public dissolution of his marriage. . . . Smiley's superb and thoughtful analysis should appeal to anyone familiar with the great author's work." Booklist

Dickinson, Emily, 1830-1886
Longsworth, Polly. The world of Emily Dickinson. Norton 1990 136p il maps pa $19.95 hardcover o.p.
Grades: 11 12 Adult   **92**
1. Poets, American 2. Women poets
ISBN 0-393-31656-4 (pa)   LC 90-31672
Drawings, maps, and photographs illustrate the home, friends, landscape and influence of the nineteenth-century American poet.

Meltzer, Milton. Emily Dickinson; a biography. Twenty-first Century Books 2006 128p il (American literary greats) lib bdg $31.93 *
Grades: 7 8 9 10   **92**
1. Poets, American 2. Women poets
ISBN 0-7613-2949-8; 978-0-7613-2949-7
     LC 2003-22978
Examines the life of the reclusive nineteenth-century Massachusetts poet whose posthumously published poetry

brought her the public attention she had carefully avoided during her lifetime.
"This introduction to an important American literary figure is notable for its clear and succinct writing. . . . Excerpts from her letters and poems appear throughout. A worthwhile book for students who might have difficulty with more scholarly works." SLJ
Includes bibliographical references

Dinesen, Isak, 1885-1962
Leslie, Roger. Isak Dinesen; Gothic storyteller. M. Reynolds 2004 128p il (World writers) lib bdg $21.95
Grades: 11 12 Adult   **92**
1. Authors, Danish 2. Women authors
ISBN 1-931798-17-6   LC 2003-22484
Contents: A restless childhood; A romantic youth; A new life in a new land; Difficulty and illness; Life in Africa; Making a home; Leaving Africa; Another new life; Swan song
"Danish author Dinesen, born 1885, was a strong-willed spirit who sought independence and adventure. With her long battle with syphilis figuring prominently in this accounting, this traces the path the writer followed, which led her away from her bourgeois upbringing in Denmark to the unfettered life she enjoyed on her coffee farm at the foot of the Ngong Hills of Nairobi." Booklist
Includes bibliographical references

Dornstein, David Scott, 1963-1988
Dornstein, Ken. The boy who fell out of the sky; a true story. Random House 2006 304p il $23.95; pa $13.95
Grades: 11 12 Adult   **92**
1. Pan Am Flight 103 Bombing Incident, 1988
ISBN 0-375-50359-5; 0-375-70769-7 (pa)
     LC 2005-42683
"On December 21, 1988, Dornstein's older brother, David, went down with Pan Am Flight 103 over Lockerbie, Scotland. Shattered, Dornstein returned to college and tried to move on. But eight years later, he started reading the papers left behind by his brother, who was an unpublished but prolific writer. . . . This memoir cobbles together the author's memories, past news accounts and David's . . . journal entries and letters." Publ Wkly
"Dornstein's account of his relationship with his brother and of his own self-examination is a startlingly honest, completely absorbing look at loss and brotherly love." Booklist
Includes bibliographical references

Douglass, Frederick, 1817?-1895
Adler, David A. Frederick Douglass; a noble life. Holiday House 2010 138p il $18.95 *
Grades: 7 8 9 10   **92**
1. Abolitionists 2. African Americans—Biography
ISBN 978-0-8234-2056-8; 0-8234-2056-6
     LC 2009-29970
A biography of Frederick Douglass, who was born into slavery in 1818 and raised on a Maryland plantation

Douglass, Frederick, 1817?-1895—*Continued*
under brutal conditions and who grew up to become a
famous orator, journalist, author, and adviser to U.S.
presidents.

This is "a thoroughly researched, lucidly written biography. . . . Adler does an excellent job of exploring the
atrocities and dehumanizing indignities . . . visited on
those who lived in slavery." Booklist
Includes bibliographical references

Douglass, Frederick. Autobiographies. Library of
Am. 1994 1126p $35; pa $13.95
Grades: 11 12 Adult   92
 1. Abolitionists 2. African Americans—Biography
 ISBN 0-940450-79-8; 1-883011-30-2 (pa)
                                          LC 93-24168
Contents: Narrative of the life of Frederick Douglass,
an American slave; My Bondage and my freedom; Life
and times of Frederick Douglass

"This one volume containing Douglass's seminal
works is highly recommended for black history collections." Libr J
Includes bibliographical references

Esty, Amos. Unbound and unbroken: the story
of Frederick Douglass. Morgan Reynolds Pub.
2010 c2011 143p il map (Civil rights leaders) lib
bdg $28.95
Grades: 7 8 9 10   92
 1. Abolitionists 2. African Americans—Biography
 ISBN 978-1-59935-136-0; 1-59935-136-6
                                          LC 2009-54287
Traces the life and historical impact of the noted abolitionist, detailing his birth into slavery and harsh upbringing, his subsequent escape, and his emergence as a
leader.

"Multiple biographies have been written about Douglass; however, few capture the depth of his intellect as
an orator and writer. Through interwoven quotes from
his autobiography, speeches, and pictures, this story also
serves as prime research material. Douglass's ingenious
case for the Constitution and fifth of July speech make
the biography accessible from cover to cover." Voice
Youth Advocates
Includes bibliographical references

Frederick Douglass; John R. McKivigan, book
editor. Greenhaven Press 2004 202p (People who
made history) hardcover o.p. pa $22.45
 Grades: 9 10 11 12   92
 1. Abolitionists 2. African Americans—Biography
 ISBN 0-7377-1522-7 (lib bdg); 0-7377-1523-5 (pa)
                                          LC 2002-45488
This volume is composed of essays describing "the
seminal moments of Douglass' life, from slave roots,
learning to read, association with free blacks in Baltimore, discovery of the Columbian Oratory, publication of
his narrative, to editing and publishing his own newspaper, and more. . . . A chronology of his life follows the
essays, along with a detailed bibliography and selections
from primary source documents taken from his autobiographies, letters. speeches, and editorials." Libr Media
Connect

"Though the articles are abridged and accompanied by
helpful summaries, the dense prose will still prove too

challenging for many high-schoolers. However, advanced
history students and teachers should find this a convenient all-in-one resource, especially for supplementing
units on Douglass' autobiographies." Booklist
Includes bibliographical references

Sterngass, Jon. Frederick Douglass. Chelsea
House Publishers 2009 158p il (Leaders of the
Civil War era) lib bdg $30
Grades: 7 8 9 10   92
 1. Abolitionists 2. African Americans—Biography
 ISBN 978-1-60413-306-6; 1-60413-306-6
                                          LC 2008-43023
A biography of the abolitionist, Frederick Douglass.
Includes glossary and bibliographical references

Dr. Dre
Ro, Ronin. Dr. Dre; the biography. Thunder's
Mouth Press 2007 308p $24.95
Grades: 11 12 Adult   92
 1. N.W.A. (Musical group) 2. African American musicians 3. Rap music
 ISBN 1-56025-921-3; 978-1-56025-921-3
This is a biography of the rapper and record company
CEO.

This book "presents the most comprehensive treatment
yet of a pivotal figure and founder of the rap industry."
Booklist
Includes discography, filmography and bibliographical
references

Driskell, David C., 1931-
McGee, Julie L. David C. Driskell; artist and
scholar. Pomegranate 2006 216p il $45
Grades: 11 12 Adult   92
 1. African American artists
 ISBN 0-7649-3747-2; 978-0-7649-3747-7
                                          LC 2006-43184
In this "inquiry into Driskell's life and work, . . .
McGee analyzes with great empathy Driskell's philosophical struggles as he sought to both express his feelings about racial strife in America and stay true to his
art. . . . With an abundance of incandescent reproductions of Driskell's searching and vital work, photographs
documenting his life, and multifaceted and involving
commentary, this unprecedented volume extends the
reach of a great artist and tireless arts advocate."
Booklist
Includes bibliographical references

**Du Bois, W. E. B. (William Edward
Burghardt), 1868-1963**
Bolden, Tonya. W.E.B. Du Bois; a
twentieth-century life. Viking Children's Books
2008 224p il (Up close) $16.99
Grades: 7 8 9 10   92
 1. African Americans—Biography 2. African Americans—Civil rights
 ISBN 978-0-670-06302-4; 0-670-06302-9
                                          LC 2007-52380
"The author covers her subject's life, which spanned
95 years, from Reconstruction to the modern Civil Rights

Du Bois, W. E. B. (William Edward Burghardt), 1868-1963—*Continued*

Movement. . . . This balanced, lively account records his many contributions as a teacher, speaker, Civil Rights activist, sociologist, writer, and cofounder of several organizations, including the NAACP, as well as his failings." SLJ

Includes bibliographical references

Hinman, Bonnie. A stranger in my own house; the story of W.E.B. Du Bois. Morgan Reynolds Pub. 2005 176p il map $26.95

Grades: 7 8 9 10   92
1. African Americans—Biography 2. African Americans—Civil rights
    ISBN 1-931798-45-1   LC 2004-26460
"The long, complex life of this scholar and controversial civil rights leader is examined in this . . . biography. Hinman offers insights into the background, beliefs, and conflicts that shaped and defined Du Bois. . . . The engaging, informative, balanced text is enhanced with documentary photographs and illustrations." SLJ

Includes bibliographical references

Dumas, Firoozeh

Dumas, Firoozeh. Funny in Farsi; a memoir of growing up Iranian in America. Villard Bks. 2003 187p il hardcover o.p. pa $12.95

Grades: 9 10 11 12   92
1. Iranian Americans
    ISBN 1-4000-6040-0; 0-8129-6837-9 (pa)
                                        LC 2002-34921
"In 1972, when she was seven, Firoozeh Dumas and her family moved from Iran to Southern California, arriving with no firsthand knowledge of this country beyond her father's glowing memories of his graduate school years here. . . . Funny in Farsi chronicles the American journey of Dumas's . . . family." Publisher's note

"Dumas has a unique perspective on American culture, and she effortlessly balances the comedy of her family's misadventures with the more serious prejudices they face." Booklist

Dylan, Bob, 1941-

Roberts, Jeremy. Bob Dylan: voice of a generation. Lerner Publications Co. 2005 128p il (Lerner biography) $27.93 *

Grades: 9 10 11 12   92
1. Rock musicians
    ISBN 0-8225-1368-4   LC 2004-2460
This is a biography of the folk-rock singer and songwriter.

"The overall spirit of rebellion and uncompromising emotional honesty . . . will appeal as urgently to today's YAs as it did to an earlier generation." Booklist

Includes bibliographical references

Earhart, Amelia, 1898-1937

Reyburn, Susan. Amelia Earhart. Pomegranate 2006 64p il (Women who dare) $12.95 *

Grades: 9 10 11 12   92
1. Air pilots
    ISBN 0-7649-3545-3; 978-0-7649-3545-9
                                        LC 2005-54951
This book "explores the life of a courageous flier who contributed greatly to the aviation industry and to the advancement of opportunities for women before disappearing in the Pacific near the end of her 1937 round-the-world flight." Publisher's note

Includes bibliographical references

Van Pelt, Lori. Amelia Earhart; the sky's no limit. Forge 2005 239p il (American heroes series) hardcover o.p. pa $12.99 *

Grades: 11 12 Adult   92
1. Air pilots
    ISBN 0-7653-1061-9; 0-7653-2483-0 (pa)
                                        LC 2004-56316
"A Tom Doherty Associates book"

This is an "introduction to the best-known of pioneering female airplane pilots. . . . Everybody ought to have basic knowledge of Earhart; this is a good place to acquire it." Booklist

Includes bibliographical references

Winters, Kathleen C. Amelia Earhart; the turbulent life of an American icon. Palgrave Macmillan 2010 242p il map $25

Grades: 11 12 Adult   92
1. Women air pilots
    ISBN 978-0-230-61669-1   LC 2010-20026
"This book reveals a flawed heroine who was frequently reckless and lacked basic navigation skills, but who was also a canny manipulator of mass media. Winters details how Earhart and her husband, publisher George Putnam, worked to establish her as an international icon, even as other spectacular pilots went unnoticed." Publisher's note

"With erudite analysis of everything from Earhart's flying to her marriage and longtime financial support of her parents and sister, Winters proves there is still much to learn about this American icon." Booklist

Includes bibliographical references

Edison, Thomas A. (Thomas Alva), 1847-1931

Tagliaferro, Linda. Thomas Edison; inventor of the age of electricity. Lerner Publs. 2003 128p il (Lerner biography) lib bdg $25.26 *

Grades: 7 8 9 10   92
1. Inventors
    ISBN 0-8225-4689-2   LC 2002-7603
A biography of Thomas Alva Edison, the inventor of the electric lighting system and the phonograph.

"The life of this remarkable inventor and scientific genius is explored in lively and accessible detail. . . . In this clearly written and thoroughly researched volume, the information flows smoothly and logically." SLJ

Includes bibliographical references

Eisner, Will, 1917-2005

Eisner, Will. Eisner/Miller: a one-on-one interview; conducted by Charles Brownstein. Dark Horse Books 2005 347p il pa $19.95

Grades: 9 10 11 12 **92**

1. Miller, Frank, 1957- 2. Comic books, strips, etc.

ISBN 1-56971-755-9

"In 2002, cartoonist Frank Miller visited with Will Eisner for a free-ranging discussion across several days. Brownstein provided shape to their encounters, giving the two artists a medium in which they could use words to explore the history of American graphic-novel expression, the business concerns of comics publishing, the relationship between art forms such as comics and film, and the meanings of success to each individual. . . . Students will find it valuable both for curriculum support and casual reading." SLJ

Includes bibliographical references

Schumacher, Michael. Will Eisner; a dreamer's life in comics. Bloomsbury 2010 359p il $28

Grades: 11 12 Adult **92**

1. Cartoonists

ISBN 978-1-60819-013-3 LC 2010-11283

"Born in 1917, Will Eisner, now known as the father of the graphic novel, grew up in the Bronx poor but resourceful. . . . [The author] zeroes in on the essence of Eisner's success: his rare ability to unite art (he inherited his phenomenal gift for drawing from his immigrant artist father) with practicality (his mother's specialty). . . . Propelled by Eisner's geyserlike energy and output, Schumacher keenly chronicles Eisner's brilliant career within a lively history of American comics and creates an inspiring portrait of a perpetually diligent and innovative artist whose belief in comics as fine art fueled a new and fertile creative universe." Booklist

Includes bibliographical references

Eleanor, of Aquitaine, Queen, consort of Henry II, King of England, 1122?-1204

Sapet, Kerrily. Eleanor of Aquitaine; medieval queen. Morgan Reynolds Pub. 2006 192p il map (European queens) lib bdg $27.95 *

Grades: 7 8 9 10 11 12 **92**

1. Queens 2. France—History—0-1328 3. Great Britain—History—1154-1399, Plantagenets

ISBN 978-1-931798-90-7; 1-931798-90-7

LC 2006-4865

This "biography provides . . . [an] account of Eleanor's eventful life as well as sets her story within the broader context of her times. . . . An attractive resource for library collections, this biography is rich in both narrative and visual details." Booklist

Includes bibliographical references

Elizabeth I, Queen of England, 1533-1603

Elizabeth I, Queen of England. Elizabeth I; her life in letters; {compiled by} Felix Pryor. University of Calif. Press 2003 144p il $34.95 *

Grades: 9 10 11 12 **92**

1. Queens 2. Great Britain—Kings and rulers 3. Great Britain—History—1485-1603, Tudors

ISBN 0-520-24106-1 LC 2003-59636

This "volume has been published to commemorate the 400th anniversary of Elizabeth I's death in 1603. It illustrates in color and, where possible, in actual size, sixty manuscripts—either by Elizabeth or to her. Each one is accompanied by a running commentary, explaining the document and placing it in its historical context, and selected transcriptions or, where necessary, translations from the originals." Publisher's note

Includes bibliographical references

Emerson, Ralph Waldo, 1803-1882

Caravantes, Peggy. Self-reliance: the story of Ralph Waldo Emerson. Morgan Reynolds Pub. 2010 143p il map (World writers) lib bdg $28.95

Grades: 7 8 9 10 **92**

1. Authors, American

ISBN 978-1-59935-124-7; 1-59935-124-2

LC 2010-8143

Presents the life and career of the eighteenth century New England essayist, poet, and lecturer who advocated a philosophy of self-reliance and individualism and was an important figure in the American Transcendental Movement.

This volume treats "young adult readers with respect and . . . [works] to ease them into scholarly research and writing in an engaging manner." Voice Youth Advocates

Includes bibliographical references

Erlbaum, Janice, 1969-

Erlbaum, Janice. Girlbomb; a halfway homeless memoir. Villard 2006 252p $21.95; pa $13.95

Grades: 11 12 Adult **92**

1. Runaway teenagers

ISBN 1-4000-6422-8; 978-1-4000-6422-9; 0-8129-7456-5 (pa); 978-0-8129-7456-0 (pa)

LC 2005-48643

"At 14, Erlbaum . . . became fed up with her mother's latest abusive husband and left their Brooklyn apartment. This memoir chronicles Erlbaum's teenage years, rife with typical issues that were intensified and complicated by her ongoing search for a place to call home. . . . Erlbaum perfectly captures the gritty landscape of the shelters, streets, and social scene of 1980s Manhattan and the gritty thoughts and feelings of a teenager immersing herself in flaky friends, lewd boys, violence, and drugs." Libr J

Euclid

Hayhurst, Chris. Euclid: the great geometer. Rosen Pub. Group 2006 112p il (The library of Greek philosophers) lib bdg $33.25 *

Grades: 9 10 11 12 **92**

1. Mathematicians

ISBN 1-4042-0497-0 LC 2005-6692

"This book takes readers into Euclid's life, and to the ancient Greece in which he was raised." Publisher's note

Includes bibliographical references

Faraday, Michael, 1791-1867

Russell, Colin Archibald. Michael Faraday; physics and faith; [by] Colin A. Russell. Oxford Univ. Press 2000 124p il (Oxford portraits in science) lib bdg $24.95

Grades: 9 10 11 12   92
  1. Physicists
  ISBN 0-19-511763-8   LC 00-27008

A biography of the nineteenth-century English scientist whose religious beliefs guided his exploration of electricity and magnetism

"Give this to good readers who need a fresh biography subject, especially those who want to know about the history of science and technology." Booklist

Includes bibliographical references

Farmer, Paul, 1959-

Kidder, Tracy. Mountains beyond mountains. Random House 2003 336p hardcover o.p. pa $14.95 *

Grades: 11 12 Adult   92
  1. Physicians
  ISBN 0-375-50616-0; 0-8129-7301-1 (pa)
      LC 2003-41253

This is a "portrait of Paul Farmer (MacArthur 'genius' grant, 1993), a driven, dedicated, rigidly idealistic doctor who commutes between Harvard and Haiti, where he works . . . to relieve the suffering of some of the poorest people on earth." N Y Times Book Rev

"This story is remarkable, and Kidder's skill in sequencing both dramatic and understated elements into a reflective commentary is unsurpassed." SLJ

Includes bibliographical references

Fatsis, Stefan

Fatsis, Stefan. A few seconds of panic; a 5-foot-8, 170-pound, 43-year-old sportswriter plays in the NFL. Penguin Press 2008 340p il hardcover o.p. pa $16

Grades: 9 10 11 12 Adult   92
  1. National Football League 2. Football—Biography
  ISBN 978-1-59420-178-3; 978-0-14-311547-2 (pa)
      LC 2008-2919

For this book, the author attended "the Denver Broncos' training camp in hopes of learning 'one very specific athletic skill'—that is, placekicking—and not to become an NFL-caliber kicker, but to become a 'credible one.' . . . It's an incredibly fascinating read for football fans, squashing the notion that the life of an NFL player is always glamorous." Publ Wkly

Includes bibliographical references

Faulkner, William, 1897-1962

Weinstein, Philip M. Becoming Faulkner; the art and life of William Faulkner; [by] Philip Weinstein. Oxford University Press 2009 250p il $29.95

Grades: 11 12 Adult   92
  1. Novelists, American
  ISBN 978-0-19-534153-9; 0-19-534153-8
      LC 2009-13181

"In his prolog, Weinstein . . . explains his concept of a biography as a work that does more than recount the events of a person's life in chronological order. He seeks to convey something of the disturbing stresses of Faulkner's life as he might have experienced them at the time and to explore how those experiences shaped the great works he produced between 1929 and 1942. . . . This rich work will be well received by Faulknerian students and scholars. Highly recommended." Libr J

Includes bibliographical references

Fermi, Enrico, 1901-1954

Cooper, Dan. Enrico Fermi and the revolutions in modern physics. Oxford Univ. Press 1999 117p il (Oxford portraits in science) lib bdg $28 *

Grades: 7 8 9 10   92
  1. Physicists
  ISBN 0-19-511762-X   LC 98-34471

A biography of the Nobel Prize-winning physicist whose work led to the discovery of nuclear fission, the basis of nuclear power and the atom bomb

"This book will be useful for reports. . . . The extensive list for further reading includes biographies of Fermi, books on both scientific and political aspects of the atomic-bomb project, and information on tours of laboratories involved in nuclear research today." SLJ

Feynman, Richard Phillips, 1918-1988

Krauss, Lawrence Maxwell. Quantum man; Richard Feynman's life in science; [by] Lawrence M. Krauss. W.W. Norton 2011 350p il (Great discoveries) $24.95

Grades: 11 12 Adult   92
  1. Physicists
  ISBN 978-0-393-06471-1; 0-393-06471-9
      LC 2010-45512

In this biography, while the author "focuses on Feynman's scientific pursuits in what is not so much a traditional biography as a study of a professional life, Krauss also describes the noted physicist's vast curiosity, his need to find proofs for things other people simply accepted, such as the rules behind the mechanics of quantum physics, and his unique and captivating way of looking at things from an angle slightly different from anyone else's." Booklist

"This book is highly recommended for readers who want to get to know one of the preeminent scientists of the 20th century." Publ Wkly

Includes bibliographical references

Fillmore, Millard, 1800-1874

Finkelman, Paul. Millard Fillmore. Times Books 2011 171p (American presidents series) $23

Grades: 11 12 Adult   92
  1. Presidents—United States 2. United States—Politics and government—1815-1861
  ISBN 978-0-8050-8715-4   LC 2010-47174

The author "describes Millard Fillmore's nearly forgotten presidency by rigidly contrasting him with Abraham Lincoln, another self-made man who wrestled with racial and regional tensions as president. . . . This book is an enlightening view into the often overlooked begin-

Fillmore, Millard, 1800-1874—*Continued*
nings of the Civil War, which history buffs and students
alike will find enjoyable." Publ Wkly
  Includes bibliographical references

Firlik, Katrina
  Firlik, Katrina. Another day in the frontal lobe;
a neurosurgeon exposes life on the inside. Random
House 2006 271p hardcover o.p. pa $14.95
Grades: 11 12 Adult   92
  1. Physicians
  ISBN 1-4000-6320-5; 0-8129-7340-2 (pa)
                           LC 2005-55260
  The author "recounts how her background as a surgeon's daughter with a strong stomach and a keen interest in the brain led her to this rarefied specialty, and she
describes her . . . trek from medical student to fully
qualified surgeon." Publisher's note
  "This witty and lucid . . . book demythologizes a
complex medical specialty for those of us who aren't
brain surgeons." Publ Wkly
  Includes bibliographical references

Fitzgerald, Ella
  Stone, Tanya Lee. Ella Fitzgerald. Viking 2008
203p il (Up close) $16.99 *
Grades: 7 8 9 10   92
  1. African American singers 2. African American
women—Biography
  ISBN 978-0-670-06149-5; 0-670-06149-2
                           LC 2007-23117
  This is a "strong biography [of the African American
singer]. . . . Stone's smooth, straightforward narrative
draws from authoritative sources. . . . The abundant
quotes from Fitzgerald and her musician peers greatly
develop the narrative." Booklist
  Includes bibliographical references

Fitzgerald, F. Scott (Francis Scott), 1896-1940
  Boon, Kevin A. F. Scott Fitzgerald; [by] Kevin
Alexander Boon. Marshall Cavendish Benchmark
2005 c2006 142p (Writers and their works) lib bdg
$25.95 *
Grades: 7 8 9 10   92
  1. Authors, American
  ISBN 0-7614-1947-0
  "A biography of writer F. Scott Fitzgerald, that describes his era, his major works, his life, and the legacy
of his writing." Publisher's note
  This "attractive, well-organized [book fills] a gap in
literary criticism for intermediate readers. Heavily illustrated with color and black-and-white photographs, [it]
will appeal to students who might be intimidated by longer or more scholarly titles." SLJ
  Includes bibliographical references

  Fitzgerald, F. Scott (Francis Scott). A life in
letters; edited by Matthew J. Bruccoli; with the
assistance of Judith S. Baughman. Scribner 1994
xxiii, 503p hardcover o.p. pa $18
Grades: 11 12 Adult   92
  1. Authors, American
  ISBN 0-684-19570-4; 0-684-80153-1 (pa)
                           LC 93-31011

  "Early letters to his editor, Maxwell Perkins, and
friends, Edmund Wilson and Ernest Hemingway, document Fitzgerald's devotion to craft, exemplified by *The
Great Gatsby* (1925), as well as the novelist's ever-
present financial problems. . . . Letters to his wife, Zelda—when she was hospitalized for mental illness—detail
the destruction of their marriage." Publ Wkly
  "Essential reading for a full understanding of Fitzgerald as an artist and a man." Libr J

Fortunate Eagle, Adam, 1929-
  Fortunate Eagle, Adam. Pipestone; my life in an
Indian boarding school; afterword by Laurence M.
Hauptman. University of Oklahoma Press 2010
193p il pa $19.95
Grades: 9 10 11 12   92
  1. Native Americans—Biography 2. Private schools
  ISBN 978-0-8061-4114-5; 0-8061-4114-X
                           LC 2009-41302
  "Adam Fortunate Eagle entered the Pipestone Indian
Training School at the age of six. From that time until
his graduation at age 16, he spent each school year and
many summers under the care of the teachers and war-
dens at Pipestone. Growing up with other children, some
sent by their families and others enrolled as orphans,
Fortunate Eagle experienced the loneliness of separation,
the camaraderie of school life, and the absence of his
culture. . . . [His story] is filled with school pranks, tender memories, and a growing sense of the world at large
between 1935 and 1945. . . . Fortunate Eagle's memories of his time in an Indian boarding school fill a vital
need in the canon of available literature about the American Indian experience." SLJ
  Includes bibliographical references

Fossey, Dian
  De la Bédoyère, Camilla. No one loved gorillas
more; Dian Fossey, letters from the mist; with
photographs by Bob Campbell. National
Geographic Society 2005 191p il $30 *
Grades: 11 12 Adult   92
  1. Women scientists 2. Gorillas
  ISBN 0-7922-9344-4   LC 2004-57944
  This biography featuring an assemblage of Dian
Fossey's letters to family and friends "reveals both the
intense joy and immense suffering Fossey experienced
during her 18-year sojourn among Rwanda's mountain
gorillas." Booklist
  Includes bibliographical references

France, Diane L.
  Hopping, Lorraine Jean. Bone detective; the
story of forensic anthropologist Diane France.
Franklin Watts 2005 118p il (Women's adventures
in science) lib bdg $31.50
Grades: 7 8 9 10   92
  1. Forensic anthropology 2. Women scientists
  ISBN 0-531-16776-3   LC 2005-0784
  Also available in paperback from Joseph Henry Press
  This "introduces the life and work of a contemporary
forensic anthropologist, from her rural childhood to her
work identifying the victims of the 9/11 tragedies. . . ."

France, Diane L.—*Continued*
The extensive detail gives readers a vivid sense of the daily work of a 'bone detective,' and clear explanations of the science will intrigue and inspire readers." Booklist
Includes glossary and bibliographical references

Francis, of Assisi, Saint, 1182-1226

Green, Julien. God's fool: the life and times of Francis of Assisi; translated by Peter Heinegg. Harper & Row 1985 273p pa $14 hardcover o.p.
Grades: 11 12 Adult   **92**
  1. Christian saints
  ISBN 0-06-063464-2   LC 84-48771
Original French edition, 1983
An "account of the life of Francesco Bernardone, the riotous, reveling son of a silk merchant, who underwent a dramatic, God-inspired personal transformation, eventually becoming known to the world as the beloved saint of Assisi. Green has woven a thick fabric of history into his tale. . . . A remarkable and absorbing profile." Booklist

Francis, John

Francis, John. Planetwalker; 22 years of walking, 17 years of silence; text and illustrations by John Francis. National Geographic 2008 288p il map $26
Grades: 11 12 Adult   **92**
  1. Environmental movement 2. Silence 3. Walking
  ISBN 978-1-4262-0275-9; 1-4262-0275-X
First published 2005 by Elephant Mountain Press
"The author recounts his decision, after witnessing the devastation of an oil spill, to renounce the use of motorized vehicles and take a vow of silence, and his subsequent twenty-two years of walking and formal education." Publisher's note
This "is an inspiring story that will make . . . [readers] think and may help them to realize that global change is possible through individual action." SLJ

Frank, Anne, 1929-1945

Frank, Anne. The diary of a young girl: the definitive edition; edited by Otto H. Frank and Mirjam Pressler; translated by Susan Massotty. Doubleday 1995 340p $29.95; pa $6.99 *
Grades: 6 7 8 9   **92**
  1. Jews—Netherlands 2. Holocaust, 1933-1945 3. World War, 1939-1945—Jews 4. Netherlands—History—1940-1945, German occupation
  ISBN 0-385-47378-8; 0-553-57712-3 (pa)
                  LC 94-41379
"This new translation of Frank's famous diary includes material about her emerging sexuality and her relationship with her mother that was originally excised by Frank's father, the only family member to survive the Holocaust." Libr J

Frank, Anne. The diary of Anne Frank: the critical edition. rev Critical ed. Doubleday 2003 851p il $75
Grades: 11 12 Adult   **92**
  1. World War, 1939-1945—Jews 2. Netherlands—History—1940-1945, German occupation 3. Jews—Netherlands 4. Holocaust, 1933-1945
  ISBN 0-385-50847-6   LC 2003-269527
First published 1989
"Prepared by the Netherlands State Institute for War Documentation; introduced by Harry Paape, Gerrold van der Stroom, and David Barnouw; with a summary of the report by the Netherlands Forensic Institute; compiled by H.J.J. Hardy; edited by David Barnouw and Gerrold van der Stroom; translated by Arnold J. Pomerans, B.M. Mooyaart-Doubleday and Susan Massotty." Title page
This volume brings together "the three known versions of Frank's diary—the original, a self-edited version . . . {and} another edited by her father. It also contains . . . handwriting and paper analyses, new documentation regarding the Frank family's arrest, and . . . information about the diary's troubled publication history." Libr J {review of 1989 edition}
Includes bibliographical references

Jacobson, Sidney. Anne Frank; the Anne Frank House authorized graphic biography; [by] Sid Jacobson and Ernie Colón. Hill and Wang 2010 152p il $30; pa $16.95
Grades: 9 10 11 12 Adult   **92**
  1. Holocaust, 1933-1945—Graphic novels 2. Jews—Netherlands—Graphic novels 3. World War, 1939-1945—Jews—Graphic novels 4. Biographical graphic novels 5. Graphic novels
  ISBN 978-0-8090-2684-5; 978-0-8090-2685-2 (pa)
                LC 2010-5776
"A novel graphic from Hill and Wang"
This is a "graphic biography of Anne Frank . . . covering the lives of Anne's parents, Edith and Otto; Anne's first years in Frankfurt; the rise of Nazism; the Franks' immigration to Amsterdam; war and occupation; Anne's years in the Secret Annex; betrayal and arrest; her deportation and tragic death in Bergen-Belsen; the survival of Anne's father; and his recovery and publication of her astounding diary." Publisher's note
"Panel arrangements effectively show simultaneous events happening in the life of the family and in the world, while brief 'snapshots' provide enough historical information to make motives, fears, and expectations sensible to anyone unfamiliar with the Holocaust's machinery. More than simply poignant, this biography elucidates the complex emotional aspects of living a sequestered adolescence as a brilliant, budding writer." Booklist
Includes bibliographical references

Franklin, Benjamin, 1706-1790

Dash, Joan. A dangerous engine; Benjamin Franklin, from scientist to diplomat; pictures by Dusan Petricic. Frances Foster Books 2006 246p il $17
Grades: 7 8 9 10   **92**
  1. Statesmen—United States
  ISBN 0-374-30669-9   LC 2004-63204

Franklin, Benjamin, 1706-1790—*Continued*

"Franklin's long, productive, and interesting life is vividly recounted in a lively manner. Familiar aspects are covered, from his days as a printer in Philadelphia to his diplomatic service and his role in the development of the fledgling United States democracy. What may be new to some readers is Franklin's dedication to, and life-long love of, science and invention. . . . Witty pen-and-ink illustrations appear throughout." SLJ

Franklin, Benjamin. Not your usual founding father; selected readings from Benjamin Franklin; edited by Edmund S. Morgan. Yale University Press 2006 303p il map hardcover o.p. pa $16 *

Grades: 11 12 Adult   92
   1. Statesmen—United States
   ISBN   0-300-11394-3;   978-0-300-11394-5;
   0-300-12688-3 (pa); 978-0-300-126884 (pa)
                    LC 2006-45706

The editor "explains that this anthology differs from the typical selections of writings by founders, which showcase themes of revolution, war, and political philosophy. Here Morgan pursues the man himself, particularly Franklin's fascination with the curiosities of human behavior. . . . Franklin's humane solicitude and observational acuity surface in varied places (on ship, in Parisian salons) and in varied formats (personal letters, published satires) in such a way that readers encounter directly Franklin's seeming simplicity, which actually masked a deep complexity and which continually makes him the most interesting founder." Booklist

Gaustad, Edwin Scott. Benjamin Franklin; [by] Edwin S. Gaustad. Oxford University Press 2005 143p il (Lives and legacies) $17.95

Grades: 11 12 Adult   92
   1. Statesmen—United States
   ISBN 0-19-530535-3   LC 2005-22906

This is a biography of the American statesman and scientist.

"Only diehard detractors of Franklin's Enlightenment rationalism may deny that Gaustad has written an excellent introduction to this foremost founding father." Booklist

Includes bibliographical references

Wood, Gordon S. The Americanization of Benjamin Franklin. Penguin Press 2004 299p il hardcover o.p. pa $16

Grades: 11 12 Adult   92
   1. Statesmen—United States
   ISBN 1-59420-019-X; 0-14-303528-2 (pa)
                    LC 2003-63254

The author argues that "Franklin's conversion to American patriot was an evolutionary process; for most of his public life, he was a staunch supporter of the British empire. Once he committed to the patriot cause, though, he did so with considerable personal pain and loss. This superbly written work provides a fresh perspective on a justly admired but enigmatic figure." Booklist

Includes bibliographical references

Franklin, Rosalind, 1920-1958

Polcovar, Jane. Rosalind Franklin and the structure of life. Morgan Reynolds 2006 144p il lib bdg $26.95 *

Grades: 7 8 9 10   92
   1. Women scientists 2. DNA
   ISBN 978-1-59935-022-6; 1-59935-022-X
                    LC 2006-16864

A biography of the scientist whose unpublished research led to the discovery of the structure of DNA

"Polcovar writes a rattling good story on two fronts: a woman becoming a scientist in an age when that was still unusual and the complex dynamics of personalities in a field sometimes thought of as impersonal." Booklist

Includes bibliographical references

Frey, James, 1969-

Frey, James. A million little pieces. Talese 2003 381p hardcover o.p. pa $14.95

Grades: 11 12 Adult   92
   1. Drug addicts—Rehabilitation
   ISBN 0-385-50775-5; 0-307-27690-2 (pa)
                    LC 2002-44393

"Frey's high school and college years are a blur of alcohol and drugs, culminating in a full-fledged crack addiction at age 23. As the book begins, his fed-up friends have convinced an airline to let him on the plane and shipped him off to his parents, who promptly put him in Hazelden, the rehabilitation clinic with the greatest success rate, 20 percent. Frey doesn't shy away from the gory details of addiction and recovery; all of the bodily fluids make major appearances here. What really separates this title from other rehab memoirs, apart from the author's young age, is his literary prowess. He doesn't rely on traditional indentation, punctuation, or capitalization, which adds to the nearly poetic, impressionistic detail of parts of the story. . . . This book is highly recommended for teens interested in the darker side of human existence." SLJ

Followed by My friend Leonard (2005)

Friedman, Cory

Patterson, James. Against medical advice; a true story; [by] James Patterson and Hal Friedman. Little, Brown 2008 283p il $26.99

Grades: 11 12 Adult   92
   1. Tourette syndrome 2. Obsessive-compulsive disorder
   ISBN 978-0-316-02475-4; 0-316-02475-9
                    LC 2008-9552

The story of Cory Friedman and his family's decades-long struggle to determine the cause of Cory's neurological disease.

Frost, Robert, 1874-1963

Caravantes, Peggy. Deep woods; the story of Robert Frost. Morgan Reynolds 2006 176p il (World writers) lib bdg $27.95 *

Grades: 7 8 9 10   92
   1. Poets, American
   ISBN 978-1-931798-92-1; 1-931798-92-3
                    LC 2005037514

Frost, Robert, 1874-1963—*Continued*

This "introduces poet Robert Frost. . . . Though focused on the man, Caravantes' presentation includes a few short selections from Frost's verse and, in sidebars, a bit of information about poetic forms. . . . Well organized and clearly written, the book offers a very readable account of Frost's often troubled life as an individual, a family man, a poet, and a public figure." Booklist

Includes bibliographical references

Fugard, Athol

Fugard, Athol. Cousins; a memoir. Theatre Communications Group 1997 152p $19.95

Grades: 11 12 Adult   92

1. Dramatists

ISBN 1-55936-132-8   LC 97-6241

In this "memoir, South Africa's best-known contemporary playwright pays homage to two men who strongly influenced him when he was an impressionable young artist—his cousins Johnnie and Garth. . . . In passing, Fugard also tells a little about his family and boyhood in Port Elizabeth and environs, and he reveals, in tantalizing, brief snatches, which moments in his plays are taken from his life." Booklist

Fung, Inez, 1949-

Skelton, Renee. Forecast Earth; the story of climate scientist Inez Fung. Franklin Watts 2005 116p il (Women's adventures in science) lib bdg $31.50

Grades: 7 8 9 10   92

1. Climate 2. Women scientists

ISBN 0-531-16777-1   LC 2005-05618

Also available in paperback from Joseph Henry Press

This is a biography of Inez Fung, "a climate scientist, someone who studies the causes of weather patterns and how they change over time." Publisher's note

This "volume is filled with full-color photographs of the subject and her work. Students will be comfortable with the style [of this book] and the easy reading level makes [it] accessible for even nonscience-oriented students." SLJ

Includes bibliographical references

Gadaryan, Heranus, 1905-2000

Cetin, Fethiye. My grandmother; a memoir; translated by Maureen Freely. Verso 2008 114p il $21.95

Grades: 11 12 Adult   92

1. Armenian massacres, 1915-1923 2. Armenians—Turkey

ISBN 978-1-84467-169-4; 1-84467-169-0

LC 2008-396857

"Cetin recounts the 1915 Armenian genocide, when the Turks sent thousands of Armenian people to their deaths. . . . [Cretin's grandmother] Christian-born Heranus was rescued from death by a Muslim gendarme who brought her up as the Muslim girl Seher. . . . Cetin was an adult when she learned of these horrors and of her grandmother's original family. . . . [This] is a fascinating account of a story that needs to be heard." SLJ

Gaines, Ernest J., 1933-

Gaines, Ernest J. Conversations with Ernest Gaines; edited by John Lowe. University Press of Miss. 1995 335p il (Literary conversations series) hardcover o.p. pa $15.95 *

Grades: 11 12 Adult   92

1. Authors, American 2. African American authors

ISBN 0-87805-782-X; 0-87805-783-8 (pa)

LC 95-13838

This is a collection of interviews given by the African American author between 1969 and 1994.

Gantos, Jack

Gantos, Jack. Hole in my life. Farrar, Straus & Giroux 2002 199p il $16; pa $8 *

Grades: 7 8 9 10   92

1. Authors, American

ISBN 0-374-39988-3; 0-374-43089-6 (pa)

LC 2001-40957

The author relates how, as a young adult, he became a drug user and smuggler, was arrested, did time in prison, and eventually got out and went to college, all the while hoping to become a writer

"Gantos' spare narrative style and straightforward revelation of the truth have, together, a cumulative power that will capture not only a reader's attention but also empathy and imagination." Booklist

Garrison, William Lloyd, 1805-1879

Esty, Amos. The liberator: the story of William Lloyd Garrison. Morgan Reynolds Pub. 2010 144p il (Civil rights leaders) lib bdg $28.95

Grades: 7 8 9 10   92

1. Abolitionists 2. Slavery—United States

ISBN 978-1-59935-137-7; 1-59935-137-4

LC 2009-54290

This biography of abolitionist William Lloyd Garrison "will hook readers with discussions of the larger political issues as well as [Garrison's] personal struggles. . . . The design . . . is readable, with spacious type and many kinds of illustrations, including color and sepia photos, paintings, and reproductions of famous documents." Booklist

Includes bibliographical references

Gates, Bill, 1955-

Aronson, Marc. Bill Gates. Penguin Group 2008 192p il (Up close) $16.99

Grades: 7 8 9 10   92

1. Microsoft Corporation 2. Businesspeople 3. Computer software industry

ISBN 978-0-670-06348-2; 0-670-06348-7

LC 2008-15552

This is a biography of the businessman who co-founded Microsoft.

"Well researched, thought-provoking, and up-to-date, this biography . . . offers insights into Gates' character as well as an engaging account of his life." Booklist

Gautama Buddha

Armstrong, Karen. Buddha. Viking 2001 xxix, 205p map (Penguin lives series) hardcover o.p. pa $13 *

Grades: 11 12 Adult   92
    ISBN 0-670-89193-2; 0-14-303436-7 (pa)
                      LC 00-43808
    "A Penguin life"
    "Armstrong interprets the mythologized story of the Buddha's abandonment of his life of comfort and privilege; commitment to practicing advanced forms of yoga and nearly fatal asceticism; enlightenment beneath a bodhi tree; and 45 years of wandering and teaching until his death in 483. And as she does so, she lucidly explains his revelations and influence." Booklist
    Includes bibliographical references

Herbert, Patricia. The life of the Buddha; [by] Patricia M. Herbert. Pomegranate; In association with British Library 2005 96p il $19.95

Grades: 9 10 11 12   92
    ISBN 0-7649-3155-5   LC 2004-58721
    First published 1993 in the United Kingdom
    "Drawing on manuscript sources from Burma, Patricia Herbert recounts the story of the Buddha's life as it evolved over the centuries, incorporating legends, miracles, and local variations. The episodes are illustrated in full page color reproductions taken from two Burmese manuscripts that are among the British Library's most prized items." Publisher's note

Genghis Khan, 1162-1227

Rice, Earle. Empire in the east: the story of Genghis Khan. Morgan Reynolds Pub. 2005 160p il $26.95 *

Grades: 9 10 11 12   92
    1. Mongolia—Kings and rulers
    ISBN 1-931798-62-1   LC 2004-30743
    "The biography offers background information about social customs of the times as well as details on the personal history of the man originally called Temujin. . . . A good introduction to the leader's life and brutal times." Booklist
    Includes bibliographical references

Geronimo, Apache Chief, 1829-1909

Sullivan, George. Geronimo; Apache renegade. Sterling 2010 124p il map (Sterling biographies) lib bdg $12.95; pa $5.95

Grades: 7 8 9 10   92
    1. Apache Indians 2. Native Americans—Biography
    ISBN 978-1-4027-6843-9 (lib bdg); 1-4027-6843-5 (lib bdg); 978-1-4027-6279-6 (pa); 1-4027-6279-8 (pa)
                      LC 2009-24135
    "*Geronimo* describes how the Apache leader was feared and hated as he led violent clashes with whites, pursuing bloody vengeance for the massacre of his family and all that his people had lost, an identity far from the romanticized image that glorified him. . . . [The] spacious design is highly scannable, with color background screens, photos, maps, and historic prints throughout." Booklist
    Includes glossary and bibliographical references

Ghahramani, Zarah, 1981-

Ghahramani, Zarah. My life as a traitor; [by] Zarah Ghahramani, with Robert Hillman. Farrar, Straus and Giroux 2008 242p $23

Grades: 11 12 Adult   92
    1. Women—Iran 2. Political prisoners
    ISBN 978-0-374-21730-3; 0-374-21730-0
                      LC 2007-17983
    "Zarah Ghahramani wrote 'My Life as a Traitor' soon after fleeing Iran for Australia. Born in 1981, she never knew a prerevolutionary Iran. . . . In 2001, when she was 20, Ghahramani was tortured and imprisoned at Evin for her role in a protest at Tehran University." N Y Times Book Rev
    "This compelling book is a coming-of-age story in which the author examines her beliefs and emotions while she tells of a country in turmoil." SLJ

Gilbreth, Frank Bunker, 1868-1924

Gilbreth, Frank B. Cheaper by the dozen; [by] Frank B. Gilbreth, Jr., Ernestine Gilbreth Carey. HarperCollins 2005 207p $19.95

Grades: 9 10 11 12 Adult   92
    1. Gilbreth family
    ISBN 0-06-076313-2; 978-0-06-076313-8
                      LC 2005-296378
    Also available Perennial Classics paperback edition
    First published 1948 by Crowell
    This biographical portrait of family life highlights the reminiscences of the twelve Gilbreth children and their adventures with their father, whose time and efficiency studies were applied to domestic life.
    Followed by Belles on their toes (1950)

Goldsworthy, Anna, 1974-

Goldsworthy, Anna. Piano lessons; a memoir. St. Martin's Press 2010 243p $24.99

Grades: 11 12 Adult   92
    1. Pianists
    ISBN 978-0-312-64628-8   LC 2010-40105
    "Australian pianist Goldsworthy was nine years old when she began instruction with the renowned Russian pianist Eleonora Sivan, now relocated to Adelaide. Their pupil-master relationship grew and deepened over the next decade, rendered here in serene, clear, elegant prose, as Goldsworthy, the child of two doctors and musicians, blossomed into a stunning stage force and a vessel of Sivan's deeply intuitive music instruction." Publ Wkly

González, Rigoberto, 1970-

González, Rigoberto. Butterfly boy; memories of a Chicano mariposa. University of Wisconsin Press 2006 207p (Writing in Latinidad) $24.95

Grades: 11 12 Adult   92
    1. Gay men 2. Mexican Americans—Biography
    ISBN 0-299-21900-3; 978-0-299-21900-0
                      LC 2006-6990
    "The son and grandson of farmworkers, constantly moving between Mexico and the U.S., then and now, Gonzalez weaves together three narrative threads: his angry present journey across the border with his estranged father; childhood memories of growing up as a fat, book-

González, Rigoberto, 1970——*Continued*
ish 'sissy-boy'; and his urgent longing now for his sexy, abusive older lover." Booklist

"This moving memoir of a young Chicano boy's maturing into a self-accepting gay adult is a beautifully executed portrait of the experience of being gay, Chicano and poor in the United States." Publ Wkly

Goodall, Jane, 1934-
Bardhan-Quallen, Sudipta. Jane Goodall; a twentieth-century life. Penguin Group 2008 218p (Up close) $16.99
Grades: 7 8 9 10   92
1. Women scientists
ISBN 978-0-670-06263-8; 0-670-06263-4
LC 2007-38206
"This profile of the renowned primatologist highlights her independent spirit and deep love of animals as well as the significant roles Goodall's long-lived mother, Vanne, and the scientist Louis B. Leakey . . . played in shaping her character and career. . . . Readers will be inspired by this account." Booklist

Greene, Meg. Jane Goodall; a biography. Greenwood Press 2005 146p il (Greenwood biographies) $29.95 *
Grades: 9 10 11 12   92
1. Women scientists
ISBN 0-313-33139-1; 978-0-313-33139-8
LC 2005-16818
"Goodall's life is revealed from her earlier days growing up in England and the influence of her mother, to her experiences living and observing chimpanzees in Africa, and her undying efforts to promote conservation of wildlife." Publisher's note
Includes bibliographical references

Gorokhova, Elena
Gorokhova, Elena. A mountain of crumbs; a memoir. Simon & Schuster 2010 308p il $26
Grades: 11 12 Adult   92
1. Saint Petersburg (Russia) 2. Soviet Union—History
ISBN 978-1-4391-2567-0; 1-4391-2567-8
LC 2009-474
In this memoir, Elena Gorokhova discusses growing up in Leningrad, her love of languages and her eventual move to the United States.

"Gorokhova vividly evokes the bleak years of the latter half of the 20th century in Russia, when the Great Patriotic War was followed by the Cold War and food shortages were the norm. . . . Articulate, touching and hopeful." Kirkus

Graham, Martha
Freedman, Russell. Martha Graham, a dancer's life. Clarion Bks. 1998 175p il $18 *
Grades: 7 8 9 10   92
1. Dancers 2. Choreographers 3. Modern dance
ISBN 0-395-74655-8   LC 97-15832
A photo-biography of the American dancer, teacher, and choreographer who was born in Pittsburgh in 1895 and who became a leading figure in the world of modern dance

"A showstopping biography that captures its dynamic subject's personality, vision, and artistry." SLJ
Includes bibliographical references

Grahl, Gary A.
Grahl, Gary A. Skinny boy; a young man's battle and triumph over anorexia. American Legacy Media 2007 243p pa $17.95 *
Grades: 9 10 11 12   92
1. Anorexia nervosa
ISBN 978-0-976154-74-7
"Challenging the assumption that anorexia is an exclusively female affliction, . . . [this memoir describes] how a young man overcame this often fatal disorder." Publisher's note

Grant, Ulysses S. (Ulysses Simpson), 1822-1885
Crompton, Samuel. Ulysses S. Grant; by Samuel Willard Crompton. Chelsea House 2009 120p il (Leaders of the Civil War era) lib bdg $30
Grades: 7 8 9 10   92
1. Presidents—United States 2. Generals
ISBN 978-1-60413-301-1; 1-60413-301-5
LC 2008-44613
A biography of Civil War general and former president Ulysses S. Grant.
Includes glossary and bibliographical references

Rice, Earle. Ulysses S. Grant: defender of the Union; [by] Earle Rice, Jr. Morgan Reynolds 2005 176p il map lib bdg $24.95 *
Grades: 9 10 11 12   92
1. Presidents—United States
ISBN 1-931798-48-6   LC 2004-22345
The author "presents Ulysses S. Grant, touching upon his Ohio boyhood, education at West Point, service in the Mexican War, military leadership during the Civil War, and two terms as president. Rice portrays Grant in an evenhanded manner, making good use of source materials for apt quotations." Booklist
Includes bibliographical references

Grealy, Lucy, 1963-2002
Patchett, Ann. Truth & beauty; a friendship. HarperCollins Publishers 2004 257p hardcover o.p. pa $13.95
Grades: 11 12 Adult   92
1. Women authors
ISBN 0-06-057214-0; 0-06-057215-9 (pa)
LC 2003-67586
"As young writers. Patchett and Lucy Grealy began an intense friendship that lasted until Grealy's tragic death. With intimacy, gracy, and humor, Patchett's memoir captures Lucy's exuberance and her roller-coaster struggles with disfigurement and depression." Booklist

Greene, Nathanael, 1742-1786
Carbone, Gerald M. Nathanael Greene; a
biography of the American Revolution. Palgrave
Macmillan 2008 268p il map $27.95
Grades: 11 12 Adult   92
1. United States. Continental Army 2. Generals
3. United States—History—1775-1783, Revolution—
Campaigns
ISBN 978-0-230-60271-7; 0-230-60271-1
           LC 2007-47595
This is a biography of the American Revolutionary
War general.
"A lucid account of the Revolutionary War from the
point of view of its most successful general." Kirkus
Includes bibliographical references

Gregory, Julie
Gregory, Julie. Sickened; the memoir of a
Munchausen by proxy childhood; foreword by
Marc D. Feldman. Bantam Books 2003 244p il
hardcover o.p. pa $13
Grades: 9 10 11 12   92
1. Child abuse
ISBN 0-553-80307-7; 0-553-38197-0 (pa)
           LC 2003-52405
"Gregory's childhood was marred by a particularly in-
sidious form of child abuse. Her mother used a combina-
tion of malnutrition, overwork, and prescription drugs to
keep the girl in a perpetual state of ill health. . . . She
relays her story not as a victim but as a strong survivor.
. . . As well as being a fascinating read, this book could
give others in similar situations a lifeline back to health."
SLJ

Grinnell, George Bird, 1849-1938
Punke, Michael. Last stand; George Bird
Grinnell, the battle to save the buffalo, and the
birth of the new West. Smithsonian Books/Collins
2007 286p il map $25.95
Grades: 11 12 Adult   92
1. Bison 2. Wildlife conservation 3. West (U.S.)—History
ISBN 978-0-06-089782-6; 0-06-089782-1
           LC 2007-60392
The author "ties together the fascinating story of Grinnell and the threatened treasures he loved. The decline of
the buffalo is a very human story, and the author leads
readers through the hunting culture of the Indians and the
even more ferocious killers from the East that superseded
it." SLJ

Grogan, John, 1957-
Grogan, John. The longest trip home; a memoir.
William Morrow 2008 334p il $25.95
Grades: 11 12 Adult   92
1. Journalists
ISBN 978-0-06-171324-8; 0-06-171324-4
           LC 2008-25913
This is the author's "hilarious and touching memoir of
his childhood in suburban Detroit." Publ Wkly

Guevara, Ernesto, 1928-1967
Miller, Calvin Craig. Che Guevara; in search of
revolution. Morgan Reynolds Pub. 2006 192p il
map (World leaders) lib bdg $27.95 *
Grades: 7 8 9 10   92
1. Cuba—History—1959- 2. Guerrillas
ISBN 978-1-931798-93-8; 1-931798-93-1
           LC 2006-5975
This biography of the guerilla leader is "woven into
. . . [an] account of the global politics of his day, including his role in the Cuban revolution and the show-
down with the U.S. The design is appealing, with clear
type, occasional photos, and maps, and teens will be
drawn to the account of the young leader who made a
difference in spite of an inglorious defeat." Booklist
Includes bibliographical references

Gunther, John, 1929-1947
Gunther, John. Death be not proud; a memoir.
Harper & Row 1949 261p il pa $13.95 hardcover
o.p.
Grades: 7 8 9 10   92
1. Brain—Tumors 2. Cancer
ISBN 0-06-123097-9
A memoir of John Gunther's seventeen-year-old son,
who died after a series of operations for a brain tumor.
Not only a tribute to a remarkable boy but an account of
a brave fight against disease

Guthrie, Woody, 1912-1967
Kaufman, Will. Woody Guthrie, American
radical. University of Illinois Press 2011 270p il
(Music in American life) $29.95
Grades: 11 12 Adult   92
1. Folk musicians
ISBN 978-0-252-03602-6; 0-252-03602-6
           LC 2010-40240
"Drawing on previously unseen letters, song lyrics, es-
says, and interviews with family and friends, Kaufman
traces Guthrie's involvement in the workers' movement
and his development of protest songs. He portrays
Guthrie as a committed and flawed human immersed in
political complexity and harrowing personal struggle."
Libr J
Includes bibliographical references

Partridge, Elizabeth. This land was made for
you and me; the life and songs of Woody Guthrie.
Viking 2002 217p il $21.99
Grades: 7 8 9 10   92
1. Singers
ISBN 0-670-03535-1   LC 2001-46770
A biography of Woody Guthrie, a singer who wrote
over 3,000 folk songs and ballads as he traveled around
the United States, including "This Land is Your Land"
and "So Long It's Been Good to Know Yuh"
This "presents an unflinchingly accurate portrait of a
rambling and unpredictable man. . . . In addition to a
panoply of archival photographs, which add realism to
this engrossing story of a life, the book includes carefully selected quotes from songs, acquaintances, and documents to punctuate the story with authenticating detail
without detracting from the momentum of the narrative."
Bull Cent Child Books
Includes bibliographical references

Haber, Fritz, 1868-1934

Hager, Thomas. The alchemy of air; a Jewish genius, a doomed tycoon, and the scientific discovery that fed the world but fueled the rise of Hitler. Harmony Books 2008 316p $24.95; pa $15
Grades: 11 12 Adult **92**
1. Bosch, Carl 2. Chemists 3. Fertilizers
ISBN 978-0-307-35178-4; 0-307-35178-5; 978-0-307-35179-1 (pa); 0-307-35179-3 (pa)
LC 2008-3192
"A fast-paced account of the early-20th-century quest to develop synthetic fertilizer. . . . Science writing of the first order." Kirkus
Includes bibliographical references

Hahn, David

Silverstein, Ken. The radioactive boy scout; the true story of a boy and his backyard nuclear reactor. Random House 2004 209p hardcover o.p. pa $13.95 *
Grades: 9 10 11 12 **92**
ISBN 0-375-50351-X; 0-8129-6660-0 (pa)
LC 2003-54811
"In the summer of 1995, a teenager in a Detroit suburb . . . managed to build a rudimentary nuclear breeder reactor in a shed behind his mother's house, using radioactive elements obtained from items as ordinary as smoke detectors. He got so far along in his efforts that when the Feds finally caught up with him, the EPA used Superfund money (usually spent on the worst hazardous waste sites) to clean up the shed. . . . [The author] fleshes out David Hahn's atomic escapades." Publ Wkly
"Silverstein tells his shocking story in lively detail that personalizes Hahn's world without sensationalizing." Booklist

Hakakian, Roya

Hakakian, Roya. Journey from the land of no; a girlhood caught in revolutionary Iran. Crown Publishers 2004 245p map hardcover o.p. pa $13
Grades: 9 10 11 12 **92**
1. Iran—History—1979-
ISBN 1-4000-4611-4; 0-609-81030-8 (pa)
LC 2003-21662
The author "recounts her past as a girl growing up in the second largest Jewish community in the Middle East—Tehran—during the takeover of the Ayatollah Khomeini." SLJ
"Political upheavals like the fall of the Shah of Iran and the rise of Islamic fundamentalism may be analyzed endlessly by scholars, but eyewitness accounts like Hakakian's help us understand what it was like to experience such a revolution firsthand. . . . Hakakian's story—so reminiscent of the experiences of Jews in Nazi Germany—is haunting." Publ Wkly

Hāladāra, Bebī

Hāladāra, Bebī. A life less ordinary; a memoir; [by] Baby Halder; translated by Urvashi Butalia. HC 2007 175p $21.95
Grades: 9 10 11 12 **92**
1. Household employees 2. India—Social conditions
ISBN 978-0-06-125581-6; 0-06-125581-5
First published 2006 in India

"Living in utter poverty in Northern India with a physically abusive father, Baby Halder was married off at the age of 12 to a man far older than she. During her teens, she continued to face hardships, including near starvation and the death of her sister. Taking her three children with her, she ran off to Delhi, where she eventually found work as a maid for wealthy families. She became a maid for Prabodh Kumar, a retired professor who encouraged her to read anything she could and to write about her experiences, without dwelling on her lack of education. . . . The writing may not be exceptional, but the voice certainly is, as Halder writes simply and honestly about the heartbreaking details of her life. Moreover, her story carries a message of hope that readers will undoubtedly find empowering." SLJ

Hale, Nathan, 1755-1776

Phelps, M. William. Nathan Hale; the life and death of America's first spy. Thomas Dunne Books 2008 306p $25.95
Grades: 11 12 Adult **92**
1. United States—History—1775-1783, Revolution 2. Spies 3. Soldiers—United States
ISBN 978-0-312-37641-3; 0-312-37641-3
LC 2008-21471
This is a biography of the American Revolutionary War hero.
"This is a well-done, balanced account of a short but interesting life." Booklist
Includes bibliographical references

Hall, Meredith

Hall, Meredith. Without a map; a memoir. Beacon Press 2007 221p $24.95
Grades: 11 12 Adult **92**
1. Authors, American
ISBN 978-0-8070-7273-8; 0-8070-7273-7
LC 2006-27507
"The year: 1965. The place: a small, insular New Hampshire community where church and home life are dominant forces. When Hall becomes pregnant at 16, she is shunned by family members and friends she's known throughout her school years. After traveling to the Middle East and suffering the indignities of loneliness and poverty, which include selling her own blood, she returns to the United States and creates a new life out of her still-palpable grief. . . . The message of redemptive compassion makes this a worthwhile and moving read." Libr J

Hamilton, Alexander, 1757-1804

St. George, Judith. The duel: the parallel lives of Alexander Hamilton and Aaron Burr. See entry under Burr, Aaron, 1756-1836

Hammel, Heidi B.

Bortz, Alfred B. Beyond Jupiter; the story of planetary astronomer Heidi Hammel; [by] Fred Bortz. Franklin Watts 2005 110p il (Women's adventures in science) lib bdg $31.50
Grades: 7 8 9 10 **92**
1. Women astronomers
ISBN 0-531-16775-5 LC 2005-0778

Hammel, Heidi B.—*Continued*

Also available in paperback from Joseph Henry Press

This is a biography of the American astronomer Heidi Hammel

The author "has captured some of the engaging qualities of Heidi Hammel's personality through extensive work with her and with the cooperation of her friends and family." Sci Books Films

Includes glossary and bibliographical references

Hansberry, Lorraine, 1930-1965

Hansberry, Lorraine. To be young, gifted, and Black; Lorraine Hansberry in her own words; adapted by Robert Nemiroff; with drawings and art by Lorraine Hansberry; introduction by James Baldwin; and a new preface by Jewell Handy Gresham Nemiroff. 1st Vintage Books ed. Vintage Books 1995 xxx, 261p il pa $13.95 *

Grades: 11 12 Adult   92

1. African American women—Biography
2. Dramatists, American

ISBN 0-679-76415-1   LC 96-119999

First published 1969 by Prentice-Hall

Work on this book and on the script for the play of the same title, which was presented at New York's Cherry Lane Theatre in 1969, "proceeded concurrently, each drawing upon the experiences and creative discoveries of the other, but ultimately diverging quite drastically." Postscript

Hargreaves, Alice Pleasance Liddell, 1852-1934

Rubin, C. M. The real Alice in Wonderland; a role model for the ages; [by] C.M. Rubin with Gabriella Rose Rubin. AuthorHouse 2010 134p il $29.95

Grades: 7 8 9 10   92

1. Carroll, Lewis, 1832-1898 2. Characters and characteristics in literature

ISBN 978-1-4490-8131-7; 1-4490-8131-2

LC 2010-901865

"Readers will follow this title down the rabbit hole to discover the world of the real Alice who inspired Lewis Carroll's *Alice in Wonderland*. The book moves seamlessly through the life of Alice Pleasance Liddell. . . . This offering paints a full picture of Alice, not only as a child who has captivated literature but also as a woman who was truly ahead of her time. This is a purchase that will do well with a range of people and should be offered as a standard accompaniment to *Alice in Wonderland*. The illustrations and pictures will make it quite popular in a public library." Voice Youth Advocates

Includes bibliographical references

Hari, Daoud

Hari, Daoud. The translator; a tribesman's memoir of Darfur. Random House 2008 204p hardcover o.p. pa $13

Grades: 7 8 9 10 11 12 Adult   92

1. Sudan—History—Darfur conflict, 2003-

ISBN 978-1-4000-6744-2; 1-4000-6744-8; 978-0-8129-7917-6 (pa); 0-8129-7917-6 (pa)

LC 2007-42308

In this memoir, the author recounts his life in Darfur, Sudan before and after the conflict in 2003.

"Those with the courage to join Hari's odyssey may find this a life-changing read." Publ Wkly

Harmon, Adam

Harmon, Adam. Lonely soldier; the memoir of an American in the Israeli Army. Ballantine Books 2006 256p il $25.95

Grades: 11 12 Adult   92

1. Soldiers—Israel

ISBN 0-89141-874-1; 978-0-89141-874-0

LC 2005-58656

This is an "account of a sincere New Englander's move to Israel in 1990, where he enlists as a paratrooper just before the beginning of the Gulf War. . . . An illuminating account of a much-covered conflict, this is a memoir for anyone who wants a look behind the daily headlines." Publ Wkly

Harrison, Benjamin, 1833-1901

Calhoun, Charles W. (Charles William). Benjamin Harrison. Times Books 2005 206p il (American presidents series) $20

Grades: 11 12 Adult   92

1. Presidents—United States

ISBN 0-8050-6952-6; 978-0-8050-6952-5

LC 2004-63778

The author "dusts off an almost thoroughly forgotten chief executive, known primarily for serving between Cleveland's two terms, to disclose a harbinger of the modern, activist president. . . . One of the most revelatory entries in the American Presidents series." Booklist

Includes bibliographical references

Hart, Elva Trevino

Hart, Elva Trevino. Barefoot heart; stories of a migrant child. Bilingual Press/Editorial Bilingüe 1999 236p pa $17

Grades: 9 10 11 12   92

1. Migrant labor 2. Mexican Americans—Biography

ISBN 0-927534-81-9   LC 99-11731

The author recounts her life growing up in a family of migrant farm workers and "reveals the harsh toll that poverty and discrimination took on her family." Publ Wkly

This is "a powerful collection of vignettes." Libr J

Hawk, Tony, 1968-

Hawk, Tony. Hawk; occupation, skateboarder; [by] Tony Hawk with Sean Mortimer. ReganBooks 2000 289p il hardcover o.p. pa $15

Grades: 8 9 10 11 12   92

1. Skateboarding

ISBN 0-06-019860-5; 0-06-095831-6 (pa)

LC 00-40279

In this memoir, the author recalls how he diverted the rebellious nature of his childhood into his love for and determination to excel in skateboarding. He also discusses his experiences with such skateboarding figures as Stacy Peralta, Mark Gonzalez, and Bob Burnquist

Hayslip, Le Ly

Hayslip, Le Ly. When heaven and earth changed places; a Vietnamese woman's journey from war to peace; [by] Le Ly Hayslip with Jay Wurts. Plume 1990 368p pa $16
Grades: 11 12 Adult   **92**
    1. Vietnam War, 1961-1975—Personal narratives
    ISBN 0-452-27168-1   LC 89-13711
    First published 1989 by Doubleday
    "Hayslip was born a Vietnamese peasant in 1949; little more than 20 years later she left for the United States with an American husband. Her early years were spent as a Viet Cong courier and lookout; a black marketeer; an unwed mother; a bar girl; a hospital aide. . . . She was tortured by the South Vietnamese army, raped by Viet Cong, and harassed by Americans. This story is juxtaposed with the tale of her . . . return to Vietnam in 1986." Libr J
    "The book is a searing and human account of Vietnam's destruction and self-destruction. Lucidly, sometimes even lyrically, Ms. Hayslip paints an intensely intimate portrait." N Y Times Book Rev

Hemingway, Ernest, 1899-1961

Boon, Kevin A. Ernest Hemingway; The Sun Also Rises and other works; [by] Kevin Alexander Boon. Marshall Cavendish Benchmark 2007 158p il (Writers and their works) $39.93
Grades: 9 10 11 12   **92**
    1. Authors, American
    ISBN 978-0-7614-2590-8   LC 2006-19235
    "A biography of writer Ernest Hemingway that describes his era, his major works—especially The Sun Also Rises and The Old Man and the Sea, his life, and the legacy of his writing." Publisher's note
    Includes filmography and bibliographical references

Reef, Catherine. Ernest Hemingway; a writer's life. Clarion Books 2009 183p il $20 *
Grades: 8 9 10 11 12   **92**
    1. Authors, American
    ISBN 978-0-618-98705-4; 0-618-98705-3
       LC 2008-32885
    "Reef creates a memorable portrait of the writer and his times, and even readers too young for most of Hemingway's oeuvre will enjoy armchair traveling to the bullfights in Spain, fishing expeditions to the Dry Tortugas and the Marquesas Keys, big-game hunting on the Serengeti and covering the Spanish Civil War. Along the way, they will gain a sense of the writer and his times and will even pick up some writing tips." Kirkus
    Includes bibliographical references

Strathern, Paul. Hemingway in 90 minutes. Ivan R. Dee 2005 117p (Great writers in 90 minutes) $16.95; pa $8.95 *
Grades: 9 10 11 12   **92**
    1. Authors, American
    ISBN 1-56663-659-0; 1-56663-658-2 (pa)
       LC 2005-7511
    In this book, the author offers an "account of Hemingway's life and ideas, and explains their influence on literature and on man's struggle to understand his place in the world." Publisher's note
    Includes bibliographical references

Henry, O., 1862-1910

Caravantes, Peggy. Writing is my business; the story of O. Henry. Morgan Reynolds Pub. 2006 160p il map (World writers) lib bdg $27.95 *
Grades: 7 8 9 10   **92**
    1. Authors, American
    ISBN 978-1-59935-031-8; 1-59935-031-9
       LC 2006-16126
    This is a biography of the short story writer
    "This title grabs readers' attention and never lets go." SLJ
    Includes bibliographical references

Hensley, William L., 1941-

Hensley, William L. Fifty miles from tomorrow; a memoir of Alaska and the real people; [by] William L. Iggiagruk Hensley. Farrar, Straus and Giroux 2008 256p il map $24
Grades: 11 12 Adult   **92**
    1. Inupiat
    ISBN 978-0-374-15484-4; 0-374-15484-8
       LC 2008-31409
    This is a memoir by "Alaska's native rights advocate William L. Iggiagruk Hensley." Bookforum
    The author "manages to make fresh an old narrative of people who arise just as their culture is being erased—be they 'Braveheart' Scotsmen or outback Aborigines. His book is also bright and detailed, moving along at a clip most sled dogs would have trouble keeping up with." N Y Times Book Rev

Herriot, James

Herriot, James. All creatures great and small. 20th anniversary ed. St. Martin's Press 1992 442p $21.95; pa $13.95
Grades: 11 12 Adult   **92**
    1. Veterinary medicine
    ISBN 0-312-08498-6; 0-312-33085-5 (pa)
       LC 92-18975
    First published 1972
    The first volume of Herriot's autobiographical account of the practice of veterinary medicine in Yorkshire, England in the 1930s
    Followed by All things bright and beautiful (1974), All things wise and wonderful (1977), and The Lord God made them all (1981)

Herschel, Caroline Lucretia, 1750-1848

Lemonick, Michael D. The Georgian star. See entry under Herschel, Sir William, 1738-1822

Herschel, Sir William, 1738-1822

Lemonick, Michael D. The Georgian star; how William and Caroline Herschel revolutionized our understanding of the cosmos. W.W. Norton 2009 199p il map (Great discoveries) $23.95; pa $14.95
Grades: 11 12 Adult   **92**
    1. Herschel, Caroline Lucretia, 1750-1848
    2. Astronomers
    ISBN 978-0-393-06574-9; 0-393-06574-X; 978-0-393-33709-9 (pa); 0-393-33709-X (pa)
       LC 2008-29820

Herschel, Sir William, 1738-1822—*Continued*

A tribute to the scientific contributions of William Herschel and his pioneering sister, Caroline, describes their establishment of surveying techniques that are still in use, Caroline's cataloging of nebulae, and William's discovery of infrared radiation.

"A rewarding account of two scientists who not only made great discoveries but enjoyed world recognition during their long, eventful lives." Kirkus

Includes bibliographical references

Hickam, Homer H., 1943-

Hickam, Homer H. Rocket boys; a memoir; [by] Homer H. Hickam, Jr. Delacorte Press 1998 368p $25.95; pa $14 *

Grades: 7 8 9 10 11 12 Adult   92

1. Authors, American 2. West Virginia 3. Aerospace engineers

ISBN 0-385-33320-X; 0-385-33321-8 (pa)

LC 98-19304

"Raised in Appalachian coal country, Homer H. Hickam, Jr., might well have followed his father and grandfather into the mine. But when he was 14, his life was changed by a space launch on the other side of the world. Hickam's story of how a teenage boy's handmade rockets lifted the hopes of a hardscrabble town is told in his [memoir]." Smithsonian

"Even if Hickam stretched the strict truth to metamorphose his memories into Stand By Me-like material for Hollywood . . . the embellishing only converts what is a good story into an absorbing, rapidly readable one that is unsentimental but artful about adolescence, high school, and family life." Booklist

Hirsi Ali, Ayaan, 1969-

Hirsi Ali, Ayaan. Infidel. Free Press 2007 353p il $26; pa $15

Grades: 11 12 Adult   92

1. Muslim women 2. Refugees

ISBN   0-7432-8968-4;   978-0-7432-8968-9; 0-7432-8969-2 (pa); 978-0-7432-8969-6 (pa)

LC 2006-49762

"A Somali by birth and a recently elected member of the Dutch Parliament, Ms. Hirsi Ali had waged a personal crusade to improve the lot of Muslim women. Her warnings about the dangers posed to the Netherlands by unassimilated Muslims made her Public Enemy No. 1 for Muslim extremists, a feminist counterpart to Salman Rushdie. The circuitous, violence-filled path that led Ms. Hirsi Ali from Somalia to the Netherlands is the subject of 'Infidel,' her brave, inspiring and beautifully written memoir." N Y Times (Late N Y Ed)

Hitler, Adolf, 1889-1945

Rice, Earle. Adolf Hitler and Nazi Germany. Morgan Reynolds 2005 176p il map lib bdg $28.95 *

Grades: 7 8 9 10   92

1. Dictators 2. National socialism 3. Germany—Politics and government—1933-1945

ISBN 978-1-931798-78-5; 1-931798-78-8

LC 2005-17825

"Rice begins with details about Hitler's childhood, his early years as an artist, and his time as a soldier in World War I. He then focuses on Hitler's rise to power as dictator and leader of the Nazi Party, the causes and course of World War II, and the Fuhrer's obsessive determination to exterminate the Jews and other 'undesirables.'" Booklist

"Clear, concise writing coupled with impressive illustrations that include black-and-white and color photos of cityscapes and individuals make this book a useful resource." SLJ

Hockenberry, John

Hockenberry, John. Moving violations; war zones, wheelchairs, and declarations of independence. Hyperion 1995 367p pa $15.95 hardcover o.p.

Grades: 11 12 Adult   92

1. Journalists 2. Physically handicapped

ISBN 0-7868-8162-3 (pa)   LC 94-37190

"Correspondent Hockenberry covered the war in the Middle East in a wheelchair, but that's only one of the many triumphs in a life steeped in adversity. Hockenberry describes his struggles to live a full life in spite of his paraplegia in this frank and searing memoir." Booklist

Holiday, Billie, 1915-1959

Holiday, Billie. Lady sings the blues; [Billie Holiday with William Dufty] 50th anniversary ed. Harlem Moon 2006 231p il pa $15.95 *

Grades: 11 12 Adult   92

1. African American singers

ISBN 978-0-7679-2386-6; 0-7679-2386-3

LC 2007-271682

First published 1956 by Doubleday

Includes audio CD

"A hard, bitter and unsentimental book, written with brutal honesty and having much to say not only about Billie Holiday, the person, but about what it means to be poor and black in America." N Y Her Trib Books

Includes discography

Holman, James, 1786-1857

Roberts, Jason. A sense of the world; how a blind man became history's greatest traveler. HarperCollins Publishers 2006 382p il $26.95; pa $14.95

Grades: 11 12 Adult   92

1. Blind

ISBN   0-00-716106-9;   978-0-00-716106-5; 0-00-716126-3 (pa); 978-0-00-716126-3 (pa)

LC 2005-58166

The author "narrates the life of a 19th-century British naval officer who was mysteriously blinded at 25, but nevertheless became the greatest traveler of his time. . . . Roberts does Holman justice, evoking with grace and wit the tale of this man once lionized as 'The Blind Traveler.'" Publ Wkly

Includes bibliographical references

Houdini, Harry, 1874-1926

Lutes, Jason. Houdini: the handcuff king. Hyperion Books for Children/Jump at the Sun 2007 90p il (Center for Cartoon Studies presents) $16.99; pa $9.99 *

Grades: 4 5 6 7 8 9 10   **92**

1. Graphic novels 2. Magicians—Graphic novels 3. Biographical graphic novels

ISBN 978-0-7868-3902-5; 978-0-7868-3903-2 (pa)

On May 1, 1908, magician Harry Houdini performed one of his famous handcuff escapes, this time in handcuffs and leg irons, while jumping off the Cambridge Bridge in Massachusetts into the frigid Boston River. This graphic novel takes the reader through Houdini's day, from 5:00 a.m. as he makes his preparations, makes a practice jump, coaches his wife Bess on how she's to help him, and then makes the jump.

This is a "fascinating graphic novel. . . . The format will instantly draw a lot of attention from readers and then hold on to it. Lutes and Bertozzi use grayscale comic panels to share their story about the life of Harry Houdini in a unique way. . . . The book resembles a hybrid between fiction and nonfiction, and the ingenious choice of format will appeal to a broad age range of readers." Voice Youth Advocates

House, Callie, 1861-1928

Berry, Mary Frances. My face is black is true; Callie House and the struggle for ex-slave reparations. Knopf 2006 314p il $26.95; pa $14.95

Grades: 11 12 Adult   **92**

1. African American women—Biography 2. African Americans—Reparations

ISBN 1-4000-4003-5 (Knopf); 0-307-27705-4 (pa, Vintage); 978-0-307-27705-3 (pa, Vintage)

LC 2004-51330

The author "unearths the intriguing story of Callie House (1861–1928), a Tennessee washerwoman and seamstress become activist, and the organization she led, the National Ex-Slave Mutual Relief, Bounty and Pension Association. . . . Students and scholars of African-American history, as well as those engaged in the current reparations debates, will be deeply informed by the rise and fall of the Ex-Slave Association." Publ Wkly

Includes bibliographical references

Houze, David, 1965-

Houze, David. Twilight people; one man's journey to find his roots. University of California Press 2006 329p il $24.95

Grades: 11 12 Adult   **92**

1. African Americans—Civil rights 2. Apartheid

ISBN 0-520-24398-6; 978-0-520-24398-9

LC 2005-35322

"The George Gund Foundation imprint in African American studies"

"The 1960s U.S. civil rights movement, South Africa's antiapartheid struggle, and the ramifications of mixed-race identity resonate personally with South African-born, Mississippi-raised Houze." Booklist

This "graceful memoir is a sensitive look into racial history in Africa and America, as well as a riveting personal narrative." Publ Wkly

Includes bibliographical references

Hughes, Langston, 1902-1967

Leach, Laurie F. Langston Hughes; a biography. Greenwood Press 2004 xx, 176p (Greenwood biographies) $29.95 *

Grades: 9 10 11 12   **92**

1. Poets, American

ISBN 0-313-32497-2   LC 2003-60131

This book covers the poet's life "from his tumultuous relationship with his father, various patrons, and romantic associations to his desire for recognition as an accomplished African-American literary artist. . . . This book would be a welcome addition to a high school library with a collection of in-depth biographies on literary artists." Libr Media Connect

Includes bibliographical references

Wallace, Maurice O. Langston Hughes; the Harlem Renaissance; [by] Maurice Wallace. Marshall Cavendish Benchmark 2007 144p il (Writers and their works) lib bdg $42.79

Grades: 8 9 10 11 12   **92**

1. Poets, American

ISBN 978-0-7614-2591-5; 0-7614-2591-8

LC 2006-38162

"A biography of writer Langston Hughes that describes his era, his major works—especially his most famous and influential prose and poetry, his life, and and the legacy of his writing." Publisher's note

"The language, pictures, and other references are user-friendly for younger researchers. The [book is] illustrated with photos and reproductions. Useful . . . for circulation or for reference collections." SLJ

Includes filmography and bibliographical references

Hurston, Zora Neale, 1891-1960

Hurston, Zora Neale. Dust tracks on a road; an autobiography; with a foreword by Maya Angelou. 1st Harper Perennial Modern Classic ed. Harper Perennial Modern Classics 2006 308p il pa $13.95 *

Grades: 11 12 Adult   **92**

1. African American authors 2. African American women—Biography

ISBN 0-06-085408-1; 978-0-06-085408-9

LC 2005-52616

"The restored text established by The Library of America"

First published 1942 by Lippincott

On cover: P.S. insights, interviews & more

The author describes her wanderings in and out of schools and jobs as a young girl, finishing her course work at Barnard, and beginning her life's work.

Includes bibliographical references

Lyons, Mary E. Sorrow's kitchen; the life and folklore of Zora Neale Hurston. 1st Collier Books ed. Collier Books 1993 144p il (Great achievers) pa $7.99

Grades: 7 8 9 10   **92**

1. African American authors 2. Women authors

ISBN 0-02-044445-1   LC 92-30600

First published 1990 by Scribner

Hurston, Zora Neale, 1891-1960—*Continued*

This biography details "Hurston's migration from Florida to Baltimore, Washington, D.C., and finally Harlem as well as her travels through the West Indies to collect folklore. The text contains eleven excerpts from Hurston's books. . . . Lyons has created a prime example of biography—fascinating, enlightening, stimulating, and satisfying." Horn Book

Includes bibliographical references

Sapet, Kerrily. Rhythm and folklore; the story of Zora Neale Hurston. Morgan Reynolds Pub. 2008 160p il lib bdg $27.95

Grades: 7 8 9 10 11 12   92

1. African American authors 2. Women authors

ISBN 978-1-59935-067-7; 1-59935-067-X

LC 2008-844

A biography of the African American author and folklorist

"With lots of personal quotes, this lively biography stays true to Hurston's defiant, independent spirit. . . . Sapet give a strong sense of the times, including the Harlem Renaissance. . . . With lots of full-page photos, this biography will encourage teens to read and discuss Hurston's work." Booklist

Includes bibliographical references

IraqiGirl

IraqiGirl. IraqiGirl; diary of a teenage girl in Iraq. Haymarket 2009 205p pa $13

Grades: 6 7 8 9 10   92

1. Iraq War, 2003-—Personal narratives 2. Weblogs

ISBN 978-1-931859-73-8; 1-931859-73-6

"In 2004 in Mosul (the third largest city in Iraq), a 15-year-old girl started a blog detailing her life in the midst of the Iraq War. Her journal encompasses the day-to-day trauma the American invasion has caused her city, her family and friends. . . . [The author's] authentically teenage voice, emotional struggles and concerns make her story all the more resonant." Publ Wkly

Irwin, Cait

Irwin, Cait. Monochrome days; a firsthand account of one teenager's experience with depression; [by] Cait Irwin with Dwight L. Evans and Linda Wasmer Andrews. Oxford University Press 2007 160p il $30; pa $9.95

Grades: 9 10 11 12   92

1. Depression (Psychology)

ISBN 978-0-19-531004-7; 978-0-19-531005-4 (pa)

LC 2006-23381

"The book combines the firsthand experiences of the author with medical information and recommendations for teens struggling with depression." Voice Youth Advocates

Includes bibliographical references

Jackson, Andrew, 1767-1845

Marrin, Albert. Old Hickory; Andrew Jackson and the American people. Dutton Children's Books 2004 262p il $35 *

Grades: 7 8 9 10   92

1. Presidents—United States

ISBN 0-525-47293-2   LC 2003-28299

"More than a biography, this fine study of our seventh president is also a history and analysis of the times in which he lived. . . . Marrin discusses the changes to society brought about by the Industrial Revolution, the railroads, and the rise of the market economy. Written in an engaging style and with a wealth of detail, the book is enhanced by numerous black-and-white illustrations." SLJ

Includes bibliographical references

Remini, Robert Vincent. Andrew Jackson; [by] Robert V. Remini; foreword by General Wesley K. Clark. Palgrave Macmillan 2008 204p il map (Great generals series) $21.95

Grades: 9 10 11 12 Adult   92

1. Generals 2. Presidents—United States

ISBN 0-230-60015-8; 978-0-230-60015-7

LC 2008-394

This is a "study of Jackson from a military perspective. Remini maintains a birth-to-death narrative while keeping the focus on Jackson's fundamental existence as a soldier. The result is a fine introduction based on years of advanced knowledge on the subject, distilled by Remini into a very good read." Libr J

Includes bibliographical references

Wilentz, Sean. Andrew Jackson. Times Books 2005 195p (American presidents series) $20

Grades: 11 12 Adult   92

1. Presidents—United States

ISBN 0-8050-6925-9   LC 2005-52857

The author "shows that our complicated seventh president was a central figure in the development of American democracy. . . . It is rare that historians manage both Wilentz's deep interpretation and lively narrative." Publ Wkly

Includes bibliographical references

Jackson, Michael, 1958-2009

O'Keefe, Sherry. Spin; the story of Michael Jackson. Morgan Reynolds 2010 c2011 144p il (Modern music masters) lib bdg $28.95

Grades: 7 8 9 10   92

1. Rock musicians 2. African American singers

ISBN 978-1-59935-134-6   LC 2009-54191

Discusses the singer's rise to stardom, his changing personal appearance, legal battles, family life, and unexpected death at the age of fifty.

Includes bibliographical references

Jackson, Robert Houghwout, 1892-1954

Jarrow, Gail. Robert H. Jackson; New Deal lawyer, Supreme Court Justice, Nuremberg prosecutor. Calkins Creek 2008 128p il $18.95

Grades: 7 8 9 10   92

1. Judges 2. Nuremberg Trial of Major German War Criminals, 1945-1946

ISBN 978-1-59078-511-9   LC 2007-18858

"Framed by Jackson's famous speech as chief American prosecutor at the 1945 international Nuremberg trial of Nazi war criminals, this detailed biography sets his law career within the history and politics of his time and raises essential issues of human rights." Booklist

Includes bibliographical references

Jackson, Stonewall, 1824-1863

Koestler-Grack, Rachel A. Stonewall Jackson; by Rachel Koestler-Grack. Chelsea House 2009 136p il (Leaders of the Civil War era) lib bdg $30
Grades: 7 8 9 10   **92**
1. Generals
ISBN 978-1-60413-299-1; 1-60413-299-X
LC 2008-44611
A biography of Confederate general Stonewall Jackson.
Includes glossary and bibliographical references

James, Kelle

James, Kelle. Smile for the camera. Simon & Schuster 2010 392p $16.99
Grades: 10 11 12   **92**
1. Fashion models
ISBN 978-1-4424-0623-0   LC 2009-53000
"This completely absorbing memoir follows the author from age 16, when she escaped from an abusive home in the late 1970s to become a model in New York City. Although Kelle ultimately succeeds, her path from squalor to security takes her through more abusive relationships, homelessness and a sensational murder trial. . . . James pulls no punches in her descriptions of the sexual and physical abuse she suffered at the hands of predatory men in the city and in flashback memories of her violent father. . . . Stark in its honesty, the book propels readers forward with a sense of suspense worthy of a thriller." Kirkus

Jefferson, Thomas, 1743-1826

Bober, Natalie. Thomas Jefferson; draftsman of a nation; [by] Natalie S. Bober. University of Virginia Press 2007 360p il $22.95
Grades: 9 10 11 12   **92**
1. Presidents—United States
ISBN 978-0-8139-2632-2   LC 2006-32722
First published 1988 by Atheneum Pubs. with title: Thomas Jefferson: man on a mountain
This is a biography of the author of the Declaration of Independence and third president of the United States, who was also an inventor, architect, farmer, and educator.
"Jefferson's story is one every YA needs to know, and this excellent, well-documented edition is a must-have." SLJ
Includes bibliographical references

Jennings, Kevin, 1963-

Jennings, Kevin. Mama's boy, preacher's son; a memoir. Beacon Press 2006 267p $24.95; pa $15
Grades: 11 12 Adult   **92**
1. Gay men 2. Political activists
ISBN   0-8070-7146-3;   978-0-8070-7146-5; 0-8070-7147-1 (pa); 978-0-8070-7147-2 (pa)
LC 2006-1275
The author, the "founder of a national advocacy group that supports safety and equality for students and teachers in public education, grew up in an impoverished Southern home, the son of an itinerant Baptist preacher and an outspoken firebrand of a mother. Self-described

trailer trash, he fought against a sickly childhood, the early death of his father and the resulting feelings of guilt, and his own nascent homosexuality. He overcame these challenges and more to win an undergraduate scholarship to Harvard." Libr J
"Jennings writes of his journey with graciousness and candor." Voice Youth Advocates

Jeter, Derek, 1974-

Jeter, Derek. The life you imagine; ten steps to ultimate achievement. Crown 2000 xxii, 279p il hardcover o.p. pa $12
Grades: 11 12 Adult   **92**
1. Baseball—Biography
ISBN 0-609-60786-3; 0-609-80718-8 (pa)
LC 00-34533
In this autobiography, Jeter outlines the "ten practical steps, . . . {he} used to fulfill his dream of playing baseball in the major leagues. The ten principles, which reflect the author's journey as an athlete, are based on input from family members, whom he credits for his success." Libr J

Joan, of Arc, Saint, 1412-1431

Pernoud, Régine. Joan of Arc: her story; Régine Pernoud, Marie-Véronique Clin; translated and revised by Jeremy duQuesnay Adams; edited by Bonnie Wheeler. St. Martin's Griffin 1999 xxii, 304p il map hardcover o.p. pa $16.95
Grades: 11 12 Adult   **92**
1. Christian saints 2. France—History—1328-1589, House of Valois
ISBN 0-312-21442-1; 0-312-22730-2 (pa)
LC 98-45059
Original French edition, 1986
This work "traces the appearance of Joan as a documented historical character rather than adhering to a standard chronological sequence. Informing the narrative is a novel interpretation of Joan as a political prisoner. Moving beyond the narrative, the American translator . . . has added a series of appendixes containing valuable contextual material. . . . These materials discuss key historical events, provide biographical information on Joan's contemporaries, and discuss Joan's afterlife in history, literature, folklore, art, and iconography." Libr J
Includes bibliographical references

John Paul II, Pope, 1920-2005

Flynn, Raymond. John Paul II; a personal portrait of the pope and the man. St. Martin's Press 2001 204p il pa $14.95 hardcover o.p.
Grades: 11 12 Adult   **92**
1. Popes
ISBN 0-312-28328-8 (pa)   LC 00-45965
Flynn, the "former mayor of Boston and ex-ambassador to the Vatican, tells us . . . what his book is not: It is not a biography, or an analysis. . . . Flynn views it, rather, as a profile based on his own experiences with Pope John Paul II, dating back to a 1969 visit to Boston of then-Cardinal Karol Wojtyla." Natl Rev

John Paul II, Pope, 1920-2005—*Continued*

Renehan, Edward J. Pope John Paul II; [by] Edward J. Renehan, Jr. Chelsea House 2007 109p il (Modern world leaders) lib bdg $30 *

Grades: 7 8 9 10 11 12   **92**
1. Popes
ISBN 978-0-7910-9227-9 (lib bdg); 0-7910-9227-5 (lib bdg)   LC 2006-10612
This "biography follows the arch of the pontiff's life in the context of world politics." Publisher's note
Includes bibliographical references

Johnson, Andrew, 1808-1875

Gordon-Reed, Annette. Andrew Johnson. Times Books/Henry Holt and Company 2011 166p il (American presidents series) $23

Grades: 11 12 Adult   **92**
1. Presidents—United States 2. United States—Politics and government—1865-1898
ISBN 978-0-8050-6948-8   LC 2010-32595
"Andrew Johnson rose from humble beginnings in the South to serve as Lincoln's second vice president, thus becoming President just as the Civil War was ending. He showed none of his predecessor's political finesse and is often viewed as among the worst to hold the office. . . . [The author] argues that the nation went from the best President to the worst during this most crucial period of its history. This slim study does cover Johnson from birth to death (1808–75), but the focus is assuredly on his presidency." Libr J
Includes bibliographical references

Johnson, Lyndon B. (Lyndon Baines), 1908-1973

Peters, Charles. Lyndon B. Johnson. Times Books 2010 199p (American presidents series) $23

Grades: 11 12 Adult   **92**
1. Presidents—United States 2. United States—Politics and government—1945-
ISBN 978-0-8050-8239-5   LC 2009-45612
"Peters describes Johnson's Texas childhood, his years in Congress, his frustrating years as Kennedy's vice president, and the triumphs and failures of his presidency (1963-68). . . . This book is aimed at general readers who want a brief account of this controversial President. . . . Its intended audience will not be disappointed with this fast-moving story." Libr J
Includes bibliographical references

Johnson, Robert, 1911-1938

Wald, Elijah. Escaping the delta; Robert Johnson and the invention of the blues. Amistad 2004 342p $24.95; pa $14.95

Grades: 11 12 Adult   **92**
1. Blues music 2. African American musicians
ISBN 0-06-052423-5; 0-06-052427-8 (pa)
                                         LC 2003-52287
"In this combination history of blues music and biography of Robert Johnson, Wald . . . explores Johnson's rise from a little known guitarist who died in 1938 to one of the most influential artists in rock and roll. From the blues' meager beginning in the early 1900s to its '30s heyday and its 1960s revival, Wald gives a revisionist history of the music, which he feels, in many instances, has been mislabeled and misjudged." Publ Wkly
The author "writes better than anyone else ever has about the blues. If you read only one book about blues—maybe ever—read this one." Booklist
Includes bibliographical references

Jones, John Paul, 1747-1792

Brager, Bruce L. John Paul Jones; America's sailor. Morgan Reynolds Pub. 2006 160p il map lib bdg $26.95

Grades: 7 8 9 10   **92**
1. Admirals
ISBN 978-1-931798-84-6; 1-931798-84-2
                                         LC 2005-30443
The author "begins with Jones's Scottish childhood, where he developed a bitter resentment of the British class system. He then traces the man's career as a commercial seaman, privateer, naval commander, and soldier of fortune. . . . This often-unflattering portrait of Jones will require readers who can place his good and bad traits in perspective and judge his place in history, making it a good choice for mature students." SLJ
Includes bibliographical references

Joplin, Janis, 1943-1970

Angel, Ann. Janis Joplin; rise up singing; introduction by Sam Andrew. Amulet Books 2010 120p il $19.95 *

Grades: 9 10 11 12   **92**
1. Singers 2. Rock musicians
ISBN 978-0-8109-8349-6   LC 2010-5558
"From interviews with her friends and letters that Joplin wrote home, Angel pieces together her subject's short life, contrasting her conservative upbringing in a small Texas town with the wild 1960s, vividly portrayed both in descriptions and in excellent-quality, full-color and black-and-white photos on almost every page." SLJ
Includes bibliographical references

Jordan, Barbara, 1936-1996

Mendelsohn, James. Barbara Jordan; getting things done. 21st Cent. Bks. (Brookfield) 2000 192p il $23.90

Grades: 9 10 11 12   **92**
1. Women politicians 2. African American women—Biography
ISBN 0-7613-1467-9   LC 00-57776
"An introductory chapter addresses the climate of segregation into which Jordan was born. Illustrated with selected photos of Jordan and period political events, the following chapters trace her rise through elected office to become the first black woman from the South ever elected to the U.S. Congress, followed by her abrupt retirement from public office." Booklist
Includes bibliographical references

Jordan, Michael, 1963-

Halberstam, David. Playing for keeps: Michael Jordan and the world he made. Random House 1999 426p pa $16.95 hardcover o.p.

Grades: 11 12 Adult   **92**
1. Chicago Bulls (Basketball team) 2. African American athletes 3. Basketball—Biography
ISBN 0-7679-0444-3 (pa)   LC 98-49964

Halberstam presents a biography of basketball player Michael Jordan.

"What's particularly effective about Halberstam's storytelling is that he follows Jordan's athletic trajectory, not in chronological order but through juxtaposed images of a hot-blooded college player with an as-yet unpolished game and an even-tempered 30-year-old at the height of his career. Jordan was not born a flawless pro, but developed his gifts by working tirelessly and intensely." Natl Rev

Joseph, Nez Percé Chief, 1840-1904

Hopping, Lorraine Jean. Chief Joseph; the voice for peace. Sterling 2010 124p il map (Sterling biographies) lib bdg $12.95

Grades: 7 8 9 10   **92**
1. Nez Percé Indians 2. Native Americans—Biography
ISBN 978-1-4027-6842-2; 1-4027-6842-7
     LC 2009-24132

This biography is "packed with fast action and detailed analysis. . . . Hopping tells of Joseph's painful decision to leave his land to save Nez Percé lives, choosing peace because he knew they could not win against the U.S. . . . [The] spacious design is highly scannable, with color background screens, photos, maps, and historic prints throughout." Booklist

Includes glossary and bibliographical references

Moulton, Candy Vyvey. Chief Joseph; guardian of the people; [by] Candy Moulton. Forge Books 2005 239p map (American heroes series) $19.95; pa $12.95 *

Grades: 11 12 Adult   **92**
1. Nez Percé Indians 2. Native Americans—Biography
ISBN 0-7653-1063-5; 0-7653-1064-3 (pa)
     LC 2004-56318

"A Tom Doherty Associates book"

The author "focuses on Chief Joseph of the Nez Perce tribe, who, after trying for years to accommodate encroaching white men on his tribal lands, gave up and attempted, in the fall of 1877, to lead his people to safety in Canada. . . . Moving and well documented, this is a superb addition to the American Heroes series." Booklist

Includes bibliographical references

Scott, Robert Alan. Chief Joseph and the Nez Percés; [by] Robert A. Scott. Facts on File 1993 134p il map (Makers of America) lib bdg $25

Grades: 8 9 10 11 12   **92**
1. Nez Percé Indians 2. Native Americans—Biography
ISBN 0-8160-2475-8   LC 92-15885

A biography of the nineteenth-century Nez Percé chief, concentrating on his unending struggle to win peace and equality for his people

Includes bibliographical references

Julian, Percy L., 1899-1975

Stille, Darlene R. Percy Lavon Julian; pioneering chemist. Compass Point Books 2009 112p il map (Signature lives) lib bdg $34.65

Grades: 6 7 8 9 10   **92**
1. Chemists
ISBN 978-0-7565-4089-0; 0-7565-4089-5
     LC 2008-38462

Details the life of chemist Percy Lavon Julian and his accomplishments

The "inviting page design features photos and boxed screens on each spread, and . . . includes a detailed bibliography, source notes, time line and glossary." Booklist

Includes glossary and bibliographical references

Kafka, Franz, 1883-1924

Mairowitz, David Zane. Kafka; [by] David Zane Mairowitz and Robert Crumb; edited by Richard Appignanesi. Fantagraphics Books 2007 176p il pa $14.95

Grades: 10 11 12 Adult   **92**
1. Graphic novels 2. Biographical graphic novels
ISBN 978-1-56097-806-0

Authors names reversed on cover

This book combines a biography of Kafka with illustrated plot descriptions of many of his works, including The Metamorphosis. Crumb renders the stories in comic book form, while the biographical information is presented mostly in text.

Kamara, Mariatu, 1987-

Kamara, Mariatu. The bite of the mango; [by] Mariatu Kamara with Susan McClelland. Annick Press 2008 216p $24.95; pa $12.95 *

Grades: 9 10 11 12   **92**
1. Amputees 2. Children and war 3. Sierra Leone—History—Civil War, 1991-
ISBN 978-1-55451-159-4; 1-55451-159-3; 978-1-55451-158-7 (pa); 1-55451-158-5 (pa)

"Relaying her experiences as a child in Sierra Leone during the 1990s, Kamara chillingly evokes the devastating effects of war. Mariatu is 11 when her tiny village is decimated by rebel soldiers, many of them children like her. Forced to watch as peaceful villagers are tortured and murdered, Mariatu is finally allowed to go free—but only after boy soldiers cut off her hands. . . . This book will unsettle readers—and then inspire them with the evidence of Mariatu's courage." Publ Wkly

Kamkwamba, William

Kamkwamba, William. The boy who harnessed the wind; creating currents of electricity and hope; [by] William Kamkwamba and Bryan Mealer. William Morrow 2009 347p $25.99; pa $14.99 *

Grades: 11 12 Adult   **92**
1. Inventors 2. Windmills
ISBN 978-0-06-173032-0; 0-06-173032-7; 978-0-06-173033-7 (pa); 0-06-173033-5 (pa)
     LC 2010-275963

Autobiography of a teenager in Malawi who builds a windmill and brings electricity to his village.

Kamkwamba, William—*Continued*

"This exquisite tale strips life down to its barest essentials, and once there finds reason for hopes and dreams, and is especially resonant for Americans given the economy and increasingly heated debates over health care and energy policy." Publ Wkly

Kantner, Seth, 1965-

Kantner, Seth. Shopping for porcupine; a life in arctic Alaska. Milkweed Editions 2008 240p il $28; pa $18

Grades: 11 12 Adult   92

1. Authors, American 2. Arctic regions 3. Alaska

ISBN 978-1-57131-301-0; 978-1-57131-311-9 (pa)

LC 2007-46477

The author "shares scenes from life in Alaska, from his childhood in the remote tundra, where his parents lived off the land in an isolated, 'semi-Eskimo existence,' to his current home, the small town of Kotzebue, with his wife and daughter." Publ Wkly

"Crafted with the precision and verve acquired by living off the land, this is a powerful and important book of remembrance, protest, and warning." Booklist

Karr, Mary

Karr, Mary. The Liars' Club; a memoir; [with a new introduction by the author] 10th anniversary ed. Penguin Books 2005 320p pa $15

Grades: 11 12 Adult   92

ISBN 0-14-303574-6; 978-0-14-303574-9

LC 2005-276148

First published 2005

Poet "Karr and her older sister grew up in an east Texas oil town where they learned to cope with their mother's psychotic episodes, the ostracism by neighbors and their father's frequent absences. Karr's happiest times were the afternoons she spent at the 'Liars Club,' where her father and a group of men drank and traded boastful stories." Publ Wkly

"This barbed memoir of a close and calamitous family from a Texas oil town moves with the same quickness as its doubledged title. . . . The revelations continue to the final page, with a misleading carelessness as seductive as any world-class liar's." New Yorker

Katin, Miriam

Katin, Miriam. We are on our own; a memoir. Drawn & Quarterly 2006 122p il $19.95

Grades: 9 10 11 12 Adult   92

1. World War, 1939-1945—Graphic novels 2. Holocaust, 1933-1945—Graphic novels 3. Autobiographical graphic novels

ISBN 1-896597-20-3   LC 2005-9063602

In this WWII memoir, the author recounts "how she and her mother faked their deaths and fled Budapest after the Nazis occupied the city. With forged papers obtained from a black marketer, they escaped to the countryside in the guise of a servant girl and her illegitimate child. Katin relates their harrowing lives there and her mother's desperate search for her missing husband after the war. . . . This impressive book belongs in all serious graphic novel collections and is also a natural for Jewish studies." Booklist

Kay, Jackie

Kay, Jackie. Red dust road; an autobiographical journey. Atlas Books 2010 288p $24 *

Grades: 11 12 Adult   92

1. Authors, Scottish 2. Adoption

ISBN 978-1-935633-34-1

"Adopted by Communists, poet Kay was atheist, gay, and mixed raced in 1960s Scotland. Her efforts to track down her biological parents result in a complete revision of the family lore she had so carefully absorbed over the years. A fire-and-brimstone-spouting Nigerian preacher and a mousy Scottish Alzheimer's patient were not what she was looking for, but it was what Kay—and her adoptive family—found. . . . This is a book about what makes a family and what makes a story. The humor and understanding with which Kay talks about all of her parents is poetic in the largest sense of the word." Libr J

Keat, Nawuth, 1964-

Keat, Nawuth. Alive in the killing fields; surviving the Khmer Rouge genocide; by Nawuth Keat with Martha E. Kendall. National Geographic 2009 127p il map $15.95; lib bdg $23.90

Grades: 7 8 9 10 11   92

1. Cambodian refugees 2. Political refugees

ISBN 978-1-4263-0515-3; 1-4263-0515-X; 978-1-4263-0516-0 (lib bdg); 1-4263-0516-8 (lib bdg)

LC 2008-39805

"At age nine, Keat was rousted from his bed by Khmer Rouge soldiers. After savagely murdering most of his family, they shot him three times and left him for dead. Miraculously, he survived, only to spend the next few years fighting for his life and running from the Khmer Rouge along with his remaining family members." SLJ

"Told with stark simplicity, Nawuth's narrative is memorable yet accessible to young readers." Voice Youth Advocates

Includes bibliographical references

Keckley, Elizabeth, ca. 1818-1907

Fleischner, Jennifer. Mrs. Lincoln and Mrs. Keckley. See entry under Lincoln, Mary Todd, 1818-1882

Keegan, Kyle

Keegan, Kyle. Chasing the high; a firsthand account of one young person's experience with substance abuse; [by] Kyle Keegan, with Howard B. Moss. Oxford University Press 2008 170p (The Annenberg Foundation Trust at Sunnylands' adolescent mental health initiative) $30; pa $9.95

Grades: 9 10 11 12   92

1. Drug abuse

ISBN 978-0-19-531471-7; 978-0-19-531472-4 (pa)

LC 2007-35423

"Keegan grew up in a loving, middle-class family in a small town in New York and wound up homeless and hopeless in California. He recounts his life from his teens through the present; now in his early 30s, he has been clean for two years. By detailing his own 'often-

Keegan, Kyle—*Continued*

harrowing' experiences, the depths of his heroin addiction, and his steps to recovery, Keegan hopes to reach at-risk young people who have experimented with drugs or who are using. . . . This heartfelt, powerfully written book is an easy read and a first choice for all collections." SLJ

Includes bibliographical references

Keller, Helen, 1880-1968

Hess, Aimee. Helen Keller. Library of Congress 2006 64p il (Women who dare) $12.95 *
Grades: 9 10 11 12   92
   1. Blind 2. Deaf
   ISBN 0-7649-3544-5; 978-0-7649-3544-2
                     LC 2005-49545

This book examines Keller's "life and accomplishments with . . . text and dozens of historical photographs. A special section of the book is devoted to Anne Sullivan, who became known as 'the Miracle Worker' for the pioneering teaching methods that allowed Keller to blossom into one of the most admired and respected women of her time." Publisher's note

Includes bibliographical references

Keller, Helen. Helen Keller: selected writings; edited by Kim E. Nielsen; consulting editor, Harvey J. Kaye. New York University Press 2005 317p il (History of disability series) $35
Grades: 11 12 Adult   92
   1. Blind 2. Deaf
   ISBN 0-8147-5829-0   LC 2004-28974

"Published in conjunction with the American Foundation for the Blind"

This is a collection "of Keller's personal letters, political writings, speeches, and excerpts of her published materials from 1887 to 1968." Univ Press Books for Public and Second Sch Libr, 2006

Includes bibliographical references

Keller, Helen. The story of my life; edited and with a preface by James Berger. The restored ed. Modern Library 2003 xlvi, 343p il hardcover o.p. pa $9.95 *
Grades: 8 9 10 11 12 Adult   92
   1. Blind 2. Deaf
   ISBN 0-679-64287-0; 0-8129-6886-7 (pa)
                     LC 2002-40971

First published 1903

This biography of the inspirational Keller contains accounts of her home life and her relationship with her devoted teacher Anne Sullivan.

Includes bibliographical references

Kennedy, Edward Moore, 1932-2009

Sapet, Kerrily. Ted Kennedy. Morgan Reynolds Pub. 2009 144p il (Political profiles) lib bdg $28.95
Grades: 6 7 8 9 10   92
   1. Statesmen—United States
   ISBN 978-1-59935-089-9; 1-59935-089-0
                     LC 2008-34943

This offers "a detailed examination of the senator's life and career. . . . This is a meaty offering that is especially good at setting Kennedy's story against the events of his time. . . . Black-and-white and color photos are well chosen." Booklist

Includes bibliographical references

Kennedy, John F. (John Fitzgerald), 1917-1963

Burner, David. John F. Kennedy and a new generation. 3rd ed. Pearson Longman 2008 c2009 210p il (Library of American biography) pa $23.60
Grades: 11 12 Adult   92
   1. Presidents—United States 2. United States—Politics and government—1961-1974
   ISBN 978-0-205-60345-9; 0-205-60345-9
                     LC 2008-34627

First published 1988 by Little, Brown

"Burner discusses John F. Kennedy (1917-1963) as both an individual and a leader, allowing the reader to examine the changes that took place in the American political and social systems as reflected in the hopeful days of Kennedy's 'Camelot.'" Publisher's note

Includes bibliographical references

Dallek, Robert. Let every nation know; John F. Kennedy in his own words; [by] Robert Dallek and Terry Golway. Sourcebooks MediaFusion 2006 289p il $29.95; pa $19.95
Grades: 11 12 Adult   92
   1. Presidents—United States 2. United States—Politics and government—1961-1974
   ISBN   1-4022-0647-X;   978-1-4022-0647-4; 1-4022-0922-3 (pa); 978-1-4022-0922-2 (pa)
                     LC 2005-37973

This book gives "brief analyses of 31 of JFK's speeches and debates, presented in audio selections on the accompanying CD-ROM. The results reveal Kennedy's eloquence, humor, and grace under pressure. . . . This work illuminates the importance of public address to the success and reputation of presidents and shows that Kennedy mastered this art." Libr J

Includes bibliographical references

Kennedy, Robert F., 1925-1968

Aronson, Marc. Robert F. Kennedy; a twentieth-century life. Viking 2007 204p il (Up close) $15.99
Grades: 8 9 10 11 12   92
   1. Politicians—United States
   ISBN 978-0-670-06066-5; 0-670-06066-6
                     LC 2006-102150

Explores Robert F. Kennedy's life from his childhood to his adult years as Attorney General, New York state senator, and candidate for the presidency of the United States.

"Aronson draws on a wide variety of sources and is very honest in examining his subject as a complete human being, warts and all. . . . This text stands as an unbiased and illuminating resource." SLJ

Includes bibliographical references

Khomeini, Ruhollah

Moin, Baqer. Khomeini; life of the Ayatollah. I. B. Tauris 2009 352p pa $29.50

Grades: 11 12 Adult   **92**

1. Iran—Politics and government

ISBN 978-1-84511-790-0   LC 2010293496

First published 1999 in the United Kingdom

The author "describes the harsh side of the cleric who forever changed the course of Iran's history. . . . The most interesting parts of the book deal with the human side of a man who was little known before his ascent to power and widely misunderstood both before and after." N Y Times Book Rev

Includes bibliographical references

Kincaid, Jamaica

Kincaid, Jamaica. My brother. Farrar, Straus & Giroux 1997 197p hardcover o.p. pa $10

Grades: 11 12 Adult   **92**

1. Women authors

ISBN 0-374-21681-9; 0-374-52562-5 (pa)

                        LC 97-16190

This is "Jamaica Kincaid's account of the life and death of her brother Devon Drew in their homeland of Antigua." N Y Times Book Rev

"Honest, unapologetic, and pure, this is an eloquent and searching elegy for the dead and a prayer of thankfulness for the living." Booklist

King, B. B.

King, B. B. Blues all around me; the autobiography of B.B. King; [by] B.B. King with David Ritz. Avon Bks. 1996 336p il hardcover o.p. pa $15.99

Grades: 11 12 Adult   **92**

1. Blues music 2. African American musicians

ISBN 0-380-97318-9; 0-06-206103-8 (pa)

                        LC 96-27773

King recounts his humble beginnings and his career as a prominent blues guitarist.

"This is one of the best recent pop-music bios. King speaks straight from the soul, it seems, just like he plays the guitar." Booklist

King, Martin Luther, Jr., 1929-1968

Anderson, Ho Che. King; a comics biography. Special ed. Fantagraphics 2010 312p il $34.99 *

Grades: 10 11 12 Adult   **92**

1. Graphic novels 2. Biographical graphic novels
3. African Americans—Biography—Graphic novels
4. African Americans—Civil rights—Graphic novels

ISBN 978-1-60699-310-1

First published 2005

"Much of the book (packaged nicely with previously unprinted material, sketches, and a somewhat beside-the-point modern-day 'prelude' titled *Black Dogs*) tracks King from his college days in the 1950s to his death, jamming each page with noirishly drawn frames and tightly packed political debates. Though all the great moments of his civil rights battle are here (from the March on Washington to his less-successful housing campaign in Chicago), Anderson doesn't resort to the cheap cine-matic trick of success and fadeout. There is more disappointment here than celebration, suffused with the sorrowful sense of a long, long battle just barely begun. A crowning achievement, like the man it portrays." Publ Wkly

Flowers, A. R. I see the promised land; a life of Martin Luther King Jr.; [text by] Arthur Flowers, [illustrations by] Manu Chitrakar, [design by] Guglielmo Rossi. Tara Books 2010 138p il $16.95 *

Grades: 8 9 10 11 12 Adult   **92**

1. African Americans—Civil rights—Graphic novels
2. Biographical graphic novels 3. Graphic novels

ISBN 978-93-80340-04-3; 93-80340-04-4

Presents in graphic novel format the life of the Baptist minister and Noble Peace Prize winner who became the leader and orator of the African American civil rights movement before his assassination in 1968.

"A myth-making take on King's life that has both emotional and intellectual impact, the Flowers/Chitrakar collaboration supplies fresh color and richness to the oft-told history of this game-changer. . . . Designed for adults but fine for teens and up; recommended for all libraries." Libr J

King, Melissa

King, Melissa. She's got next; a story of getting in, staying open, and taking a shot. Houghton Mifflin 2005 181p pa $13

Grades: 11 12 Adult   **92**

1. Basketball—Biography

ISBN 0-618-26456-6   LC 2004-62756

"A Mariner original"

"King grew up in Arkansas shooting baskets in the driveway with her brother. At 27, she moved to Chicago and found herself yearning for the court in an effort to erase an inner emptiness. Her tender memoir chronicles her playing pickup basketball, meandering from playground to gym to YMCA." Publ Wkly

"A sports journalist scores a smooth three-pointer with [this memoir]. . . . Her poetic prose, as rhythmic as a dribble, will carry readers wherever she goes." Kirkus

King, Stephen, 1947-

King, Stephen. On writing; a memoir of the craft. Scribner 2000 288p hardcover o.p. pa $14.95

Grades: 11 12 Adult   **92**

1. Authors, American 2. Authorship

ISBN 0-684-85352-3; 0-671-02425-6 (pa)

                        LC 00-30105

The author recounts "his life from early childhood through the aftermath of the 1999 accident that nearly killed him. Along the way, King touts the writing philosophies of William Strunk and Ernest Hemingway, advocates a healthy appetite for reading, expounds upon the subject of grammar, critiques a number of popular writers, and offers the reader a chance to try out his theories. . . . Recommended for anyone who wants to write and everyone who loves to read." Libr J

King, Stephen, 1947-—*Continued*

Rogak, Lisa Angowski. Haunted heart; the life and times of Stephen King; [by] Lisa Rogak. Thomas Dunne Books 2009 310p il $25.95

Grades: 11 12 Adult   **92**

 1. Authors, American 2. Horror fiction—Authorship

 ISBN 978-0-312-37732-8; 0-312-37732-0

          LC 2008-34209

The author "has produced an unauthorized biography of one of America's most popular novelists. Using King's novels and movies, as well as numerous articles and interviews, as well as other books and web sites about the author, Rogak covers all of the major events of King's life and career. . . . For King's many fans, this is a good introduction to the writer and his work." Libr J

Includes bibliographical references

Stefoff, Rebecca. Stephen King. Marshall Cavendish Benchmark 2010 175p il (Today's writers and their works) lib bdg $42.79 *

Grades: 8 9 10 11 12   **92**

 1. Authors, American

 ISBN 978-0-7614-4122-9; 0-7614-4122-0

This biography of Stephen King places the author in the context of his times and discusses his work.

This book provides "excellent information for reports." SLJ

Includes bibliographical references

Whitelaw, Nancy. Dark dreams; the story of Stephen King. Morgan Reynolds 2005 128p il map (World writers) $26.95 *

Grades: 7 8 9 10   **92**

 1. Authors, American 2. Horror fiction—Authorship

 ISBN 1-931798-77-X   LC 2005-20112

"This well-documented look at King's life introduces the man who has become a legend for reinventing and legitimizing horror. Whitelaw has put together a seamless synthesis of interviews, biographies, and King's own writing, pared down for younger readers and illustrated with plenty of full-color photographs." Booklist

Kingsley, Anna, d. 1870

Schafer, Daniel L. Anna Madgigine Jai Kingsley; African princess, Florida slave, plantation slaveowner. University Press of Fla. 2003 177p il map $24.95

Grades: 11 12 Adult   **92**

 1. Slavery—United States 2. African American women—Biography 3. Plantation life

 ISBN 0-8130-2616-4   LC 2002-33372

"Schafer traces the history of Anna Madgigine Jai from her homeland of Senegal, where she was captured at about 13 years of age in 1806 and sold to Zephaniah Kingsley, a maritime merchant, slave trader, and later an abolitionist. Kingsley eventually married Anna, made her manager of his plantation, and fathered four children with her. . . . This is a fascinating look at an extraordinary woman and the complexities of slavery beyond the common image of slavery in the South." Booklist

Includes bibliographical references

Klein, Stephanie, 1975-

Klein, Stephanie. Moose; a memoir of fat camp. William Morrow 2008 310p $24.95

Grades: 11 12 Adult   **92**

 1. Obesity 2. Weight loss 3. Camps

 ISBN 978-0-06-084329-8; 0-06-084329-2

          LC 2008-2728

"Follows the coming-of-age years of the author, whose life profoundly changed in her twelfth year when she spent a summer at a weight-loss camp, a personal journey that shaped her subsequent philosophies about body image and self-acceptance." Publisher's note

"Readers of Klein's wildly popular blog, Greek Tragedy, will recognize her self-deprecating, uproariously funny voice in frank stories that switch between her life at home and school. . . . Klein shows how teen insecurities stretch deeply into adult life, and how resiliency, humor, and love can overpower them." Booklist

Koehl, Mimi, 1948-

Parks, Deborah. Nature's machines; the story of biomechanist Mimi Koehl; by Deborah Amel Parks. Joseph Henry Press 2005 118p il (Women's adventures in science) lib bdg $31; pa $9.95

Grades: 7 8 9 10   **92**

 1. Biologists 2. Human engineering 3. Women scientists

 ISBN 0-531-16780-1 (lib bdg); 0-309-09559-X (pa)

          LC 2005-10201

Mimi Koehl "wanted to know more about sea anemones, particularly how they survive the turbulent surf on rocky beaches. Her inquiries and experiments led to discoveries in a new field, biomechanics, in which scientists examine how form determines movement and function in the animal kingdom. . . . This [book] should spark the curiosity of any reader." Voice Youth Advocates

Includes bibliographical references

Kohler, Dean Ellis

Kohler, Dean Ellis. Rock 'n' roll soldier; with Susan VanHecke. HarperTeen 2009 278p il $16.99

Grades: 9 10 11 12   **92**

 1. Vietnam War, 1961-1975—Personal narratives 2. Rock musicians

 ISBN 978-0-06-124255-7; 0-06-124255-1

          LC 2008-47702

"A memoir about starting a rock band in the middle of a war zone. Drafted into the Vietnam War, Kohler served in a small port town, enforcing the law as part of his military service. Under orders from his commanding officer, the young MP formed 'Electrical Banana' with a few fellow draftees and enjoyed a wildly popular run of gigs, including a performance on the front lines, before returning home to restart his music career." Kirkus

"Kohler's younger self is appealing, and his reconstructed dialogue sounds genuine. . . . Occasional four-letter words, references to sex, and descriptions of maimed and dead bodies make this quick read best suited for older high school students." Voice Youth Advocates

Kopelman, Jay

Kopelman, Jay. From Baghdad, with love; a Marine, the war, and a dog named Lava; [by] Jay Kopelman with Melinda Roth. Globe Pequot 2006 196p il $22.95

Grades: 11 12 Adult   **92**
   1. Iraq War, 2003——Personal narratives 2. Dogs
   ISBN 978-1-59228-980-6; 1-59228-980-0
                       LC 2006-22144

   The author, an Iraq War veteran, describes his "efforts to safely transport Lava, the stray dog his Marine unit found in the wreckage of Fallujah, back to the U.S. . . . The story of Lava's journey out of Iraq is exciting, but it's to Kopelman and Roth's credit that it's not nearly as harrowing as the story of what the dog left behind." Publ Wkly

   Includes bibliographical references

Kor, Eva Mozes, 1935-

Kor, Eva Mozes. Surviving the Angel of Death; the story of a Mengele twin in Auschwitz; [by] Eva Mozes Kor and Lisa Rojany Buccieri. Tanglewood Pub. 2009 141p il map $14.95

Grades: 7 8 9 10   **92**
   1. Mozes, Miriam, 1935-1993 2. Jews—Persecutions 3. Jews—Hungary 4. Twins 5. Holocaust survivors 6. Holocaust, 1933-1945—Personal narratives
   ISBN 978-1-933718-28-6; 1-933718-28-5
                      LC 2009-9494

   "Born in 1934, Eva and her identical twin, Miriam, were loved and doted over. They lived a comfortable and happy life on their family's farm in Transylvania until the summer of 1940, when their family was herded onto a train with the other Jews in their town and transported to Auschwitz supposedly for their 'protection.' . . . They soon joined a large group of other twins who were under the care of Dr. Josef Mengele, otherwise known as the Angel of Death. . . . Eva's story will have the reader hooked until the very end. . . . This book is an essential purchase for libraries with a Holocaust collection, but it would also be a valuable addition to any library with young impressionable readers." Voice Youth Advocates

Kramer, Clara, 1927-

Kramer, Clara. Clara's war; one girl's story of survival; [by] Clara Kramer with Stephen Glantz. Ecco 2009 339p il $25.99 *

Grades: 11 12 Adult   **92**
   1. Jews—Poland 2. Holocaust, 1933-1945—Personal narratives
   ISBN 978-0-06-172860-0; 0-06-172860-8
   First published 2008 in the United Kingdom

   "Based on her wartime diary, which she kept while hiding in a basement in Poland, Kramer's book vividly recalls the tensions within her hidden community after the Nazis overtook the town of Zolkiew in 1942. Of particular interest are revelations about the family who hid the Kramers, particularly how an anti-Semitic Polish householder demonstrated great courage in shielding Jews in his basement." Libr J

Kraus, Caroline

Kraus, Caroline. Borderlines; a memoir. Broadway Bks. 2004 360p hardcover o.p. pa $12.95

Grades: 9 10 11 12   **92**
   ISBN 0-7679-1403-1; 0-7679-1428-7 (pa)
                    LC 2003-69592

   "Caroline, an intelligent but somewhat naive college graduate, finds herself in a severely dysfunctional and dangerous friendship with troubled and manipulative Jane. Her downward spiral and recovery make for a compelling and suspenseful read." SLJ

Kristofic, Jim, 1982-

Kristofic, Jim. Navajos wear Nikes; a reservation life. University of New Mexico Press 2011 211p il map $26.95

Grades: 11 12 Adult   **92**
   1. Navajo Indians 2. Native Americans—Reservations
   ISBN 978-0-8263-4946-0   LC 2010-37428

   The author "shares his story of being transported at age seven from Pittsburgh to Ganado, Arizona, on the Navajo Indian Reservation by his mother, a nurse who had long nurtured her 'Indian Dream.' Jimmy is the only bilagaana, or white person, in his class, and he struggles with racial teasing from day one. By the third grade, he's learning to escape the daily taunting by helping his 'Navajo enemies' with their schoolwork." Booklist

   Includes bibliographical references

Kuffel, Frances

Kuffel, Frances. Passing for thin; losing half my weight and finding myself. Broadway Books 2004 260p hardcover o.p. pa $14

Grades: 9 10 11 12   **92**
   1. Obesity
   ISBN 0-7679-1291-8; 0-7679-1292-6 (pa)
                    LC 2003-52455

   "Kuffel acknowledges that she began overeating because she loves food and because eating can be a mind-blowing sensual experience. (Here food descriptions are divine, but even better is her confession that she loved the 'Little House' books primarily for Laura Ingalls Wilder's great food writing.) At the same time, she doesn't let anyone off the hook for how she was treated after she became fat." SLJ

Lacks, Henrietta

Skloot, Rebecca. The immortal life of Henrietta Lacks. Crown Publishers 2010 369p il $26

Grades: 11 12 Adult   **92**
   1. African American women—Biography 2. Cancer 3. Human experimentation in medicine
   ISBN 978-1-4000-5217-2   LC 2009-31785

   "Henrietta Lacks, an African American mother of five, was undergoing treatment for cancer at Johns Hopkins University in 1951 when tissue samples were removed without her knowledge or permission and used to create HeLa, the first 'immortal' cell line. HeLa has been sold around the world and used in countless medical research applications, including the development of the polio vaccine. . . . [The author] entwines Lacks's biography, the

Lacks, Henrietta—*Continued*

development of the HeLa cell line, and her own story of building a relationship with Lacks's children." Libr J

"A thorny and provocative book about cancer, racism, scientific ethics and crippling poverty, 'The Immortal Life of Henrietta Lacks' also floods over you like a narrative dam break, as if someone had managed to distill and purify the more addictive qualities of 'Erin Brockovich,' 'Midnight in the Garden of Good and Evil' and 'The Andromeda Strain.' More than 10 years in the making, it feels like the book Ms. Skloot was born to write." N Y Times Book Rev

Includes bibliographical references

Lang, Lang, 1982-

Lang, Lang. Journey of a thousand miles; my story; [by] Lang Lang with David Ritz. Spiegel & Grau 2008 239p il $24.95 *

Grades: 11 12 Adult   **92**

1. Pianists

ISBN 978-0-385-52456-8   LC 2008-732

An autobiography of the Chinese classical piano prodigy.

"Lang tells the story of his childhood without self-pity or bitterness, making his success, and the book itself, all the more satisfying." N Y Times Book Rev

Lange, Dorothea, 1895-1965

Partridge, Elizabeth. Restless spirit: the life and work of Dorothea Lange. Viking 1998 122p il hardcover o.p. pa $12.99 *

Grades: 6 7 8 9   **92**

1. Women photographers

ISBN 0-670-87888-X; 0-14-230024-1 (pa)

LC 98-9807

A biography of Dorothea Lange, whose photographs of migrant workers, Japanese American internees, and rural poverty helped bring about important social reforms

"Generously placed throughout this accessibly written biography are the photographic images that make Lange a pre-eminent artist of the century. The book is elegantly designed and the photographic reproductions are excellent." Bull Cent Child Books

Includes bibliographical references

LaNier, Carlotta Walls, 1942-

LaNier, Carlotta Walls. A mighty long way; my journey to justice at Little Rock Central High School; with Lisa Frazier Page. One World Ballantine Books 2009 284p il $26; pa $16 *

Grades: 11 12 Adult   **92**

1. Central High School (Little Rock, Ark.) 2. School integration 3. Arkansas—Race relations 4. African American women—Biography

ISBN 978-0-345-51100-3; 978-0-345-51101-0 (pa)

LC 2009-28429

"At 14, Lanier was the youngest of the 'Little Rock Nine,' who integrated Little Rock Central High School in 1951; she went on to become the first African American young woman to receive a diploma from the school. Her memoir provides a firsthand account of a seismic shift in American history. . . . [This is] a worthy contribution to the history of civil rights in America." Publ Wkly

Includes bibliographical references

Lavender, Bee

Lavender, Bee. Lessons in taxidermy. Punk Planet Books 2005 160p pa $12.95

Grades: 9 10 11 12   **92**

ISBN 978-1-888451-79-5; 1-888451-79-3

LC 2004-115618

The author "recounts her life spent in and out of hospitals and her subsequent dissociation from her own body and emotions. She struggles with health problems from birth, which are compounded by her surroundings, including frequent encounters with street fights, domestic violence and poverty. . . . Witnessing her strength and sheer determination to live makes this striking book completely engrossing." Publ Wkly

Lawrence, Sarahlee

Lawrence, Sarahlee. River house; a memoir. Tin House Books 2010 272p pa $16.95

Grades: 11 12 Adult   **92**

1. Rafting (Sports) 2. Adventure and adventurers

ISBN 978-0-9825691-3-9   LC 2010-7702

This memoir "is the story of a young woman returning home to her family's ranch and building a log house with the help of her father. An avid river rafter, Sarahlee Lawrence grew up in remote central Oregon and, by the age of twenty-one, had rafted some of the most dangerous rivers of the world as an accomplished river guide. But living her dream led her back to the place she least expected—her dusty beginnings and her family's home." Publisher's note

"Handy with tools and rafts, a good neighbor, and a mighty fine horsewoman, Lawrence is also adept with language, writing with arresting lucidity and a driving need to understand her father, her legacy, the land, community, work, and herself. A true adventure story of rare dimension." Booklist

Lee, Bruce, 1940-1973

Lee, Bruce. Bruce Lee; artist of life; compiled and edited by John Little. Tuttle 1999 269p il $24.95; pa $16.95

Grades: 11 12 Adult   **92**

1. Martial arts 2. Actors

ISBN 0-8048-3131-9; 0-8048-3263-3 (pa)

LC 99-33401

This is a "collection of Lee's private letters and writing, offering insight into the many facets of his life—including his poetry, life philosophies, and his thoughts on martial arts, love, fatherhood, friendship." Publisher's note

"Lee's writings are inspired and inspirational, of interest to his fans and to the multitudes seeking the meaning of life." Booklist

Includes bibliographical references

Miller, Davis. The Tao of Bruce Lee; a martial arts memoir. Harmony Bks. 2000 193p hardcover o.p. pa $15 *

Grades: 11 12 Adult   **92**

1. Martial arts 2. Actors

ISBN 0-609-60477-5; 0-609-80538-X (pa)

LC 99-87697

Lee, Bruce, 1940-1973—*Continued*
Miller chronicles the life of film star and martial arts legend Bruce Lee and the impact Lee had on his life
This book "is equally a study of the nature and role of the hero in popular culture, a poignant and unusual coming-of-age story, and an informative biography." Booklist

Lee, Harper, 1926-
Madden, Kerry. Harper Lee; a twentieth-century life. Viking Children's Books 2009 223p il map (Up close) $16.99 *
Grades: 7 8 9 10   92
1. Authors, American 2. Women authors
ISBN 978-0-670-01095-0; 0-670-01095-2
LC 2008-53911
"In a straighforward, easy-to-read biography, Madden limns familiar incidents from the life of Nelle Harper Lee." Horn Book
"A narrative both well paced and richly detailed . . . this biography will appeal to fans of the novel and to newcomers. . . . Extensive source notes and an excellent bibliography round out this superb biography." Kirkus
Includes bibliographical references

Shields, Charles J. I am Scout: the biography of Harper Lee. Henry Holt & Co. 2008 245p il $18.95 *
Grades: 7 8 9 10   92
1. Authors, American 2. Women authors
ISBN 978-0-8050-8334-7; 0-8050-8334-0
LC 2007-27572
A biography of the author of *To Kill a Mockingbird*
Shields "offers a fascinating look at the unconventional Lee, which captures his elusive subject and her lifelong friend, Truman Capote. . . . Shields' formidable research . . . will impress any student who has ever written a term paper." Booklist
Includes bibliographical references

Lee, Robert E. (Robert Edward), 1807-1870
Blount, Roy. Robert E. Lee; a Penguin life; [by] Roy Blount, Jr. Lipper/Viking Bk. 2003 210p (Penguin lives series) $19.95; pa $13 *
Grades: 11 12 Adult   92
1. Generals 2. United States—History—1861-1865, Civil War
ISBN 0-670-03220-4; 0-14-303866-4 (pa)
LC 2002-32423
This is a biography of "the famous Southern general admired for his military leadership but also scorned for defending the Confederacy. Blount's concise writing keeps his biography trim and succinct, and his admiration for the subject allows for enjoyable reading." Booklist
Includes bibliographical references

McNeese, Tim. Robert E. Lee. Chelsea House 2009 152p il (Leaders of the Civil War era) lib bdg $30
Grades: 7 8 9 10   92
1. Generals 2. United States—History—1861-1865, Civil War
ISBN 978-1-60413-304-2; 1-60413-304-X
LC 2008-44623

A biography of Confederate general Robert E. Lee. Includes glossary and bibliographical references

Robertson, James I., Jr. Robert E. Lee; Virginian soldier, American citizen; [by] James I. Robertson, Jr. Atheneum Books for Young Readers 2005 159p il maps $21.95
Grades: 7 8 9 10   92
1. Generals 2. United States—History—1861-1865, Civil War
ISBN 0-689-85731-4   LC 2003-22108
Contents: The making of a soldier; Nation vs. country; Rocky path to army command; Brilliance in the field; The bloodiest day; Loss of an arm; Gettysburg; Forced on the defensive; From siege to defeat; National symbol
This portrait of the Confederate general "puts particular emphasis on his life during the Civil War years but provides plenty of information on his youth, his early military career, and his postwar years. . . . Useful for reports and interesting in its own right, this well-researched biography will be a solid addition to library collections." Booklist
Includes bibliographical references

Lemon, Alex
Lemon, Alex. Happy; a memoir. Scribner 2010 292p $25
Grades: 11 12 Adult   92
1. Poets, American 2. Brain—Diseases
ISBN 978-1-4165-5023-5; 1-4165-5023-2
LC 2009-27293
The author, a poet, "was a carefree, hard partying, baseball-playing college student at Macalester College in Minnesota in 1997 when he suffered a stroke and later two brain bleeds. Readers are swept along on his rough ride during the next two years, through his nasty travails of frenetic drug and alcohol use, terribly misguided attempts to cope with his deteriorating and frightening condition. . . . Lemon offers a raw and honest narration of his college life, his relationships with girlfriends and family members, especially his loving and quirky mother. . . . [This] is a voltaic narrative that is alternately horrifying and touching." Publ Wkly

Lennon, John, 1940-1980
Partridge, Elizabeth. John Lennon; all I want is the truth; a photographic biography by Elizabeth Partridge. Viking 2005 232p il $24.99 *
Grades: 8 9 10 11 12   92
1. Beatles 2. Rock musicians
ISBN 0-670-05954-4   LC 2005-11850
The author presents a "portrait of a legendary musician, tracing Lennon's life from his birth in 1940 during a German air raid on Liverpool to his murder in Manhattan 40 years later." Publ Wkly
"This handsome book will be eagerly received by both Beatles fans, who are legion, and their elders, who will enjoy reliving the glory days of the Fab Four and exploring the inner workings of a creative talent." SLJ
Includes bibliographical references

Lerner, Gerda, 1920-

Lerner, Gerda. Fireweed; a political autobiography. Temple Univ. Press 2002 377p (Critical perspectives on the past) $34.50; pa $22.95

Grades: 11 12 Adult 92

1. Historians 2. Feminism
ISBN 1-56639-889-4; 1-59213-236-7 (pa)
LC 2001-54248

This is an autobiography by the feminist historian. Lerner "has been a privileged child, a resister, a prisoner, a refugee, a governess, an immigrant, an 'enemy alien,' a lover and wife, an X-ray technician, a mother, a grandmother, a novelist, a musical librettist, an organizer, a student and, ultimately, a historian. . . . 'Beginnings,' the first of four parts covers her early life in Vienna. . . . The remaining three parts of the book deal with Lerner's experiences as an immigrant to, then a proud, though critical, citizen of the United States." Women's Rev Books

"A fascinating memoir." Booklist
Includes bibliographical references

Lewin, W. H. G. (Walter H. G.)

Lewin, W. H. G. (Walter H. G.). For the love of physics; from the end of the rainbow to the edge of time—a journey through the wonders of physics; [by] Walter Lewin and Warren Goldstein. Free Press 2011 302p il $26; ebook $12.99

Grades: 11 12 Adult 92

1. Physicists 2. Colleges and universities—Faculty 3. Physics—Study and teaching
ISBN 978-1-4391-0827-7; 978-1-4391-2354-6 (ebook)
LC 2010-47737

"MIT's Lewin is deservedly popular for his memorable physics lectures . . . and this quick-paced autobiography-cum-physics intro fully captures his candor and lively teaching style. . . . [This text] glows with energy and should please a wide range of readers." Publ Wkly

Lewis, C. S. (Clive Staples), 1898-1963

Hamilton, Janet. C. S. Lewis; twentieth century pilgrim. Morgan Reynolds Pub. 2010 128p il (World writers) lib bdg $28.95

Grades: 7 8 9 10 92

1. Authors, English
ISBN 978-1-59935-112-4; 1-59935-112-9
LC 2009-7134

In this biography of the British author, "Lewis' childhood is well-documented, as is his love of literature as an escape from the real world. Hamilton clearly shows the importance religion played in Lewis's life. The impact that war, and the resulting loss of the imaginative worlds he could find in literature, and his struggle with religious belief are tied directly to his writing." Voice Youth Advocates

Includes bibliographical references

Lewis, John, 1940-

Lewis, John. Walking with the wind; a memoir of the movement; [by] John Lewis with Michael D'Orso. Harcourt 1999 526p il pa $16

Grades: 11 12 Adult 92

1. United States. Congress. House 2. Student Nonviolent Coordinating Committee 3. African Americans—Biography 4. African Americans—Civil rights
ISBN 0-15-600708-8 LC 99-28356
First published 1998 by Simon & Schuster

"The memoirs of Lewis, an African American congressman from Georgia, emphasize his participation in the . . . Civil Rights Movement of the 1960s, when the author served as national chair of the Student Nonviolent Coordinating Committee (SNCC) and held leadership positions in other Civil Rights organizations." Libr J

"The strength of Lewis's powerful new book is not only the witness he bears but also the simplicity of his voice." Newsweek

Li, Charles N., 1940-

Li, Charles N. The bitter sea; coming of age in a China before Mao. HarperCollins Publishers 2008 283p il hardcover o.p. pa $14.99

Grades: 11 12 Adult 92

1. China—History—1949-
ISBN 978-0-06-134664-4; 0-06-134664-0; 978-0-06-170954-8 (pa); 0-06-170954-9 (pa)
LC 2007-25697

The author, "who had an extraordinary life growing up in pre-Communist China, shares his story of betrayal, loss, hope, and triumph in this lyrical account. . . . This brilliant memoir is as much about modern Chinese history as it is about familial relationships." Libr J

Li, Moying, 1954-

Li, Moying. Snow falling in spring; coming of age in China during the cultural revolution. Farrar, Straus and Giroux 2008 176p $16 *

Grades: 7 8 9 10 11 12 92

1. China—History—1949-1976—Personal narratives
ISBN 978-0-374-39922-1; 0-374-39922-0
LC 2006-38356

"This memoir . . . offers a highly personal look at China's Cultural Revolution. The author is four years old when Mao initiates the Great Leap Forward in 1958. . . . Li effectively builds the climate of fear that accompanies the rise of the Red Guard, while accounts of her headmaster's suicide and the pulping of her father's book collection give a harrowing, closeup view of the persecution. Sketches about her grandparents root the narrative within a broader context of Chinese traditions as well as her own family's values." Publ Wkly

Lincoln, Abraham, 1809-1865

Fleming, Candace. The Lincolns; a scrapbook look at Abraham and Mary. Schwartz & Wade Books 2008 177p il map $24.99; lib bdg $28.99 *

Grades: 7 8 9 10 11 12   92

1. Lincoln, Mary Todd, 1818-1882 2. Presidents—United States 3. Presidents' spouses—United States 4. United States—History—1861-1865, Civil War

ISBN 978-0-375-83618-3; 0-375-83618-7; 978-0-375-93618-0 (lib bdg); 0-375-93618-1 (lib bdg)

LC 2007-44113

Fleming twines "accounts of two lives—Abraham and Mary Todd Lincoln—into one fascinating whole. On spreads that combine well-chosen visuals with blocks of headlined text, Fleming gives a full, birth-to-death view of the 'inextricably bound' Lincolns." Booklist

Freedman, Russell. Lincoln: a photobiography. Clarion Bks. 1987 149p il $18; pa $7.95 *

Grades: 5 6 7 8 9 10   92

1. Presidents—United States 2. United States—History—1861-1865, Civil War

ISBN 0-89919-380-3; 0-395-51848-2 (pa)

LC 86-33379

The author "begins by contrasting the Lincoln of legend to the Lincoln of fact. His childhood, self-education, early business ventures, and entry into politics comprise the first half of the book, with the rest of the text covering his presidency and assassination." SLJ

This is "a balanced work, elegantly designed and enhanced by dozens of period photographs and drawings, some familiar, some refreshingly unfamiliar." Publ Wkly

Includes bibliographical references

Gienapp, William E. Abraham Lincoln and Civil War America; a biography. Oxford Univ. Press 2001 239p il maps hardcover o.p. pa $24.95

Grades: 11 12 Adult   92

1. Presidents—United States 2. United States—History—1861-1865, Civil War

ISBN 0-19-515099-6; 0-19-515100-3 (pa)

LC 2001-50056

This biography focuses on the American president's leadership during the Civil War.

"In spite of the book's size, its discriminating history of Lincoln's life is surprisingly rich, and the narrative of his presidency and the unfolding of the war is crisp and coherent." Bookmarks

Includes bibliographical references

Keneally, Thomas. Abraham Lincoln. Viking 2003 183p (Penguin lives series) hardcover o.p. pa $14

Grades: 11 12 Adult   92

1. Presidents—United States 2. United States—History—1861-1865, Civil War

ISBN 0-670-03175-5; 0-14-311475-1 (pa)

LC 2003-268078

"Keneally's Lincoln is a self-actuated farm boy made good by self-discipline, savvy instincts, wit, the wisdom acquired from courtrooms, friendships, and political huckstering—and luck . . . [The author] recounts Lincoln's early missteps in romance, business, and politics and his self-doubts and depression as his star dimmed several times, and he concedes Lincoln's erratic course toward emancipation and a successful strategy for Union victory during the Civil War . . . This is an epic compressed into a tightly written biography that all Americans might read with profit. Keneally's occasional tendency to let folklore stand as fact notwithstanding, there is no better brief introduction to Lincoln and his American dream." Libr J

Koestler-Grack, Rachel A. Abraham Lincoln; [by] Rachel Koestler-Grack. Chelsea House Publishers 2009 128p il (Leaders of the Civil War era) lib bdg $30

Grades: 7 8 9 10   92

1. Presidents—United States 2. United States—History—1861-1865, Civil War

ISBN 978-1-60413-298-4; 1-60413-298-1

LC 2008-43030

A biography of the 16th president of the United States.

Includes glossary and bibliographical references

Lincoln, Abraham. Abraham Lincoln the writer; a treasury of his greatest speeches and letters; compiled and edited by Harold Holzer. Boyds Mills Press 2000 106p il lib bdg $15.95 *

Grades: 7 8 9 10   92

1. Presidents—United States 2. United States—History—1861-1865, Civil War

ISBN 1-56397-772-9   LC 99-66551

"Lincoln's writings include personal letters, notes on the law, excerpts from speeches, debates, and inaugural addresses, letters to parents of fallen soldiers, and telegrams to his family. Reproductions of period photos, portraits, and documents illustrate the text effectively. . . . Highly interesting and a fine resource for students seeking quotations or for those wanting to meet Lincoln through his own words." Booklist

McGovern, George S. (George Stanley). Abraham Lincoln; [by] George McGovern. Times Books/Henry Holt and Co. 2009 184p il (American presidents series) $22

Grades: 9 10 11 12 Adult   92

1. Presidents—United States

ISBN 978-0-8050-8345-3; 0-8050-8345-6

LC 2008-29869

In this biography of Abraham Lincoln, former U.S. senator McGovern "assesses Lincoln's greatness in terms of his ability to use his humble origins, empathy, keen sense of justice, uncommon skill in seeing the essence of an issue, faith in American democracy, gifts of language, and personal self-confidence—all to become a masterly lawyer, a party leader, commander in chief, and a heroic figure with both the vision and the practicality to realize his purposes. . . . This biography warrants reading to catch the sense of Lincoln's greatness, both for his own day and ours." Libr J

Includes bibliographical references

McPherson, James M. Abraham Lincoln. Oxford University Press 2009 79p $12.95 *

Grades: 11 12 Adult   92

1. Presidents—United States

ISBN 978-0-19-537452-0; 0-19-537452-5

LC 2008-35623

Lincoln, Abraham, 1809-1865—*Continued*

"McPherson, America's leading authority on Lincoln and his times, demonstrates his complete command of his subject in this concise but remarkably rich and perceptive biography. . . . This little book is bigger than its pages and should be in every library, schoolhouse, and home." Libr J

Includes bibliographical references

McPherson, James M. Tried by war; Abraham Lincoln as commander in chief. Penguin Press 2008 329p il map hardcover o.p. pa $17

Grades: 11 12 Adult   **92**
    1. United States—History—1861-1865, Civil War
2. United States—Politics and government—1861-
1865 3. Presidents—United States
    ISBN 978-1-594-20191-2; 1-594-20191-9;
978-0-14-311614-1 (pa); 0-14-311614-2 (pa)
                             LC 2008-25229

Evaluates Lincoln's talents as a commander in chief in spite of limited military experience, tracing the ways in which he worked with, or against, his senior commanders to defeat the Confederacy and reshape the presidential role.

This book "is a perfect primer, not just for Civil War buffs or fans of Abraham Lincoln, but for anyone who wishes to understand the evolution of the president's role as commander in chief." N Y Times Book Rev

Includes bibliographical references

Sandler, Martin W. Lincoln through the lens; how photography revealed and shaped an extraordinary life. Walker Pub. Co. 2008 97p il $19.99; lib bdg $20.89

Grades: 6 7 8 9 10   **92**
    1. Presidents—United States 2. United States—History—1861-1865, Civil War—Pictorial works 3. Photography—History
    ISBN 978-0-8027-9666-0; 0-8027-9666-4;
978-0-8027-9667-7 (lib bdg); 0-8027-9667-2 (lib bdg)
                             LC 2008-0219

"When Lincoln became president, photography was new and he joined the 'very first generation of human beings ever to be photographed.' . . . This extraordinary book is a tribute to the way contemporary and future generations came to view Lincoln. . . . Part biography, part history of of the Civil War, the book touches on many interesting topics. . . . Every step of the way there are fascinating photographs. . . . Although it's the pictures that provide the 'wow factor,' Sandler's perceptive words have their own elegance." Booklist

Lincoln, Mary Todd, 1818-1882

Fleischner, Jennifer. Mrs. Lincoln and Mrs. Keckley; the remarkable story of the friendship between a first lady and a former slave. Broadway Bks. 2003 372p il map hardcover o.p. pa $15.95

Grades: 11 12 Adult   **92**
    1. Keckley, Elizabeth, ca. 1818-1907 2. Presidents' spouses—United States
    ISBN 0-7679-0258-0; 0-7679-0259-9 (pa)
                             LC 2002-34493

"A dual biography of two women—one white, free, and privileged in all but happiness and the other black,

initially enslaved, and adept in human relationships, sewing, and money matters—whose lives came together in Washington, DC, during the Civil War and remained stitched together thereafter." Libr J

"The book gives an in-depth look at a time, a friendship, and two very different women. The author's almost conversational writing style will keep readers engrossed." SLJ

Includes bibliographical references

Fleming, Candace. The Lincolns. See entry under Lincoln, Abraham, 1809-1865

Lindbergh, Charles, 1902-1974

Giblin, James. Charles A. Lindbergh; a human hero; [by] James Cross Giblin. Clarion Bks. 1997 212p il $22 *

Grades: 6 7 8 9   **92**
    1. Air pilots
    ISBN 0-395-63389-3   LC 96-9501

A biography of the pilot whose life was full of controversy and tragedy, but also fulfilling achievements

"This sympathetic and informed account (beautifully illustrated with contemporary photographs) is an excellent introduction to Lindbergh and also to the early years of the celebrity society in which we live now." N Y Times Book Rev

Includes bibliographical references

Lloyd, Rachel

Lloyd, Rachel. Girls like us; fighting for a world where girls are not for sale, an activist finds her calling and heals herself. Harper 2011 277p $24.99

Grades: 11 12 Adult   **92**
    1. Girls Educational and Mentoring Services (Organization) 2. Juvenile prostitution 3. Women political activists
    ISBN 978-0-06-158205-9   LC 2010-32458

"In 1998 at age 23, Lloyd founded GEMS (Girls Educational and Mentoring Services), a New York City-based nonprofit organization to help commercially sexually exploited young women and girls. Her memoir recounts her journey from a 13-year-old school dropout in England trying to support her unstable mother through years as a commercially exploited worker in the German sex industry before finding stability and safety. Arriving in the United States, she set out to break the system that had abused her, ultimately altering laws and helping to protect victims from criminal prosecution. . . . This consciousness-shifting book shreds stereotypes and perceptions of prostitution." Libr J

Lobel, Anita, 1934-

Lobel, Anita. No pretty pictures; a child of war. Greenwillow Bks. 1998 193p il hardcover o.p. pa $7.99

Grades: 7 8 9 10   **92**
    1. Jews—Poland 2. Holocaust, 1933-1945—Personal narratives 3. Holocaust survivors
    ISBN 0-688-15935-4; 0-06-156589-X (pa)
                             LC 97-48392

Lobel, Anita, 1934-—*Continued*
The author, known as an illustrator of children's books, describes her experiences as a Polish Jew during World War II and for years in Sweden afterwards

"Lobel brings to these dramatic experiences an artist's sensibility for the telling detail, a seemingly unvarnished memory and heartstopping candor." Publ Wkly

London, Jack, 1876-1916
Stefoff, Rebecca. Jack London; an American original. Oxford Univ. Press 2002 127p il maps (Oxford portraits) lib bdg $28
Grades: 7 8 9 10   92
1. Authors, American
ISBN 0-19-512223-2   LC 2001-53087
"This volume does an excellent job of illuminating London's extraordinary life and career. The narrative is exciting and accessible. . . . The text is supplemented by interesting and informative illustrations, and includes excerpts from primary-source material." SLJ
Includes bibliographical references

Long Tack Sam, 1885-1961
Fleming, Ann Marie. The magical life of Long Tack Sam. Riverhead Books 2007 170p il pa $14
Grades: 11 12 Adult   92
1. Graphic novels 2. Biographical graphic novels 3. Magicians—Graphic novels
ISBN 978-1-59448-264-9; 1-59448-264-0
                                             LC 2007-60352
"Born in a Chinese village, Fleming's great-grandfather was a world-class magician who called places on four continents home during his 70 years. Fleming brilliantly illuminates how dramatically international politics affected his life." Booklist
Includes bibliographical references

Lowman, Margaret
Lowman, Margaret. Life in the treetops; adventures of a woman in field biology; [by] Margaret D. Lowman. Yale Univ. Press 1999 219p il maps hardcover o.p. pa $13.95
Grades: 11 12 Adult   92
1. Botanists 2. Women scientists
ISBN 0-300-07818-8;   978-0-300-07818-3; 0-300-08464-1 (pa); 978-0-300-08464-1 (pa)
                                              LC 98-48691
The author is a botanist who studies canopies, the uppermost layers of forests. "Interwoven with her narrative of field work is the story of how she balanced the needs of marriage, housewifery, children, and eventual single parenthood with college teaching and research trips to locales such as Panama, Australia, and Cameroon." Booklist
Lowman "gives a funny, unassuming and deeply idiosyncratic chronicle of her trials and triumphs as a field biologist of tree canopies and other ecosystems in Australia, New England, Belize, Panama and elsewhere." N Y Times Book Rev
Includes bibliographical references
Followed by It's a jungle up there! (2006)

Lyons, Maritcha Rémond, 1848-1929
Bolden, Tonya. Maritcha; a nineteenth-century American girl. Abrams 2005 47p il $17.95
Grades: 4 5 6 7 8 9 10   92
1. African American women—Biography 2. New York (N.Y.)—Race relations 3. African Americans—New York (N.Y.)
ISBN 0-8109-5045-6   LC 2004-05849
This is a "life history of Maritcha Rémond Lyons, born a free black in 1848 in lower Manhattan. The author draws her biographical sketch primarily from Lyons's unpublished memoir, dated one year before her death in 1929. . . . One of the . . . sections of the book documents the Draft Riots . . . of July 1868, and the impact of them on Maritcha and other citizens." Publ Wkly
"The high quality of writing and the excellent documentation make this a first choice for all collections." SLJ

Maathai, Wangari, 1940-
Maathai, Wangari. Unbowed; a memoir; [by] Wangari Muta Maathai. Knopf 2006 314p il hardcover o.p. pa $15
Grades: 11 12 Adult   92
1. Green Belt Movement (Kenya) 2. Environmentalists 3. Kenya
ISBN 0-307-26348-7;   978-0-307-26348-3; 0-307-27520-5 (pa); 978-0-307-27520-2 (pa)
                                             LC 2006-44729
"Nobel Peace Prize winner Maathai tells the unforgettable story of her Kenya girlhood, struggles as a biologist and professor, and founding of the Green Belt Movement to restore Kenya's decimated forests and provide women with work." Booklist

MacArthur, Douglas, 1880-1964
Frank, Richard B. MacArthur; foreword by Wesley K. Clark. Palgrave Macmillan 2007 224p (Great generals series) hardcover o.p. pa $12.95 *
Grades: 9 10 11 12 Adult   92
1. Generals
ISBN 1-4039-7658-9;   978-1-4039-7658-1; 0-230-61397-7 (pa); 978-0-230-61397-3 (pa)
This biography of the World War II general is an "assessment of both the man and the soldier, covering the failures and triumphs in an assured and dispassionate tone. . . . A good starting point for generalists." Libr J

Madison, James, 1751-1836
Wills, Garry. James Madison. Times Bks. 2002 xx, 184p (American presidents series) $20 *
Grades: 11 12 Adult   92
1. Presidents—United States
ISBN 0-8050-6905-4   LC 2002-19692
The author "maintains that Madison possessed qualities that served him well early in his career but proved to be a handicap during his Presidency. . . . Written with flair, this clear and balanced account is based on a sure handling of the material." Libr J
Includes bibliographical references

Malcolm X, 1925-1965

Helfer, Andrew. Malcolm X; a graphic biography; written by Andrew Helfer; art by Randy DuBurke. Hill and Wang 2006 102p il $15.95 *

Grades: 10 11 12 Adult   **92**
  1. African Americans—Biography—Graphic novels
  2. Black Muslims—Graphic novels 3. Graphic novels
  4. Biographical graphic novels
  ISBN 978-0-8090-9504-9; 0-8090-9504-1
                    LC 2006-13743

The authors "tell the story of Malcolm X's short life—his meeting with Dr. Martin Luther King Jr., the two leaders describing the opposite ideological ends of the fight for civil rights; and his eventual assassination by other members of the Nation of Islam (NOI)—in narration and detailed b&white drawings, sharp as photographs in a newspaper. . . . Helfer and DuBurke have created an evocative and studied look at not only Malcolm X but the racial conflict that defined and shaped him." Publ Wkly

Malcolm X. The autobiography of Malcolm X; with the assistance of Alex Haley; introduction by M. S. Handler; epilogue by Alex Haley; afterword by Ossie Davis. Ballantine Bks. 1992 500p $25; pa $15 *

Grades: 11 12 Adult   **92**
  1. African Americans—Biography 2. Black Muslims
  ISBN 0-345-37975-6; 0-345-37671-4 (pa)
                    LC 92-52659

Also available in hardcover from Amereon
First published 1965 by Grove Press
Based on tape-recorded conversations with Alex Haley, this account of the life of the Black Muslim leader was completed shortly before his murder
Alex Haley "did his job with sensitivity and with devotion. . . . {The book} will have a permanent place in the literature of the Afro-American struggle." N Y Rev Books

Mandela, Nelson

Gaines, Ann. Nelson Mandela and apartheid in world history; {by} Ann Graham Gaines. Enslow Pubs. 2001 128p il maps (In world history) $20.95 *

Grades: 9 10 11 12   **92**
  1. South Africa—Race relations 2. South Africa—Politics and government
  ISBN 0-7660-1463-0   LC 00-10369

This biography of the Nobel Peace Prize laureate "does a fine job of integrating Mandela's personal story with an overview of early South African history and the rise and fall of apartheid." Booklist
Includes bibliographical references

Mandela, Nelson. Mandela; an illustrated autobiography. Little, Brown 1996 208p il map $29.95 *

Grades: 11 12 Adult   **92**
  1. South Africa—Race relations 2. South Africa—Politics and government
  ISBN 0-316-55038-8   LC 96-77497

"This is an illustrated and abridged edition of Long walk to freedom: the autobiography of Nelson Mandela." Verso of title page
"The photos, from a variety of archives and journalistic sources, ably illustrate Mandela and, even more so, the South Africa around him." Libr J

Manzano, Juan Francisco, 1797-1854

Engle, Margarita. The poet slave of Cuba: a biography of Juan Francisco Manzano; art by Sean Qualls. Henry Holt 2006 183p il $16.95 *

Grades: 7 8 9 10   **92**
  1. Poets 2. Slavery—Cuba
  ISBN 0-8050-7706-5; 978-0-8050-7706-3
                    LC 2005-46200

In "free verse, Engle dramatizes the boyhood of the nineteenth-century Cuban slave Juan Francisco Manzano, who secretly learned to read and wrote poetry about beauty and courage in his world of unspeakable brutality." Booklist
"This is a book that should be read by young and old, black and white, Anglo and Latino." SLJ

Mao Zedong, 1893-1976

Naden, Corinne J. Mao Zedong and the Chinese Revolution. Morgan Reynolds Pub. 2009 144p il map (World leaders) lib bdg $28.95

Grades: 7 8 9 10 11 12   **92**
  1. Heads of state 2. China—History—1949-1976
  ISBN 978-1-59935-100-1; 1-59935-100-5
                    LC 2008-27829

This "discusses Chariman Mao Zedong's rise to power and his crucial role in national and international history. . . . Naden's analysis of the significant role of young people will draw YA readers for reports and for personal interest. The readable design, with clear type and lots of historic color photos as well as screens and detailed maps, includes spacious back matter." Booklist
Includes bibliographical references

Marie Antoinette, Queen, consort of Louis XVI, King of France, 1755-1793

Lever, Evelyne. Marie Antoinette; the last queen of France; translated from the French by Catherine Temerson. Farrar, Straus & Giroux 2000 357p il pa $16.95 hardcover o.p.

Grades: 11 12 Adult   **92**
  1. Queens 2. France—History—1589-1789, Bourbons
  ISBN 0-312-28333-4 (pa)   LC 00-28763

The author examines "the opulent Versailles subculture and the queen whose royal excesses served as a major catalyst for the revolutionary upheaval of 1789. Through the skillful use of memoirs and other primary documents, Lever creates an empathic picture of Louis XVI's headstrong wife." Libr J
Includes bibliographical references

Marley, Bob

Miller, Calvin Craig. Reggae poet: the story of Bob Marley. Morgan Reynolds Pub. 2007 128p il $27.95 *

Grades: 7 8 9 10　　　　　　　　　　**92**

1. Reggae music 2. Musicians

ISBN 978-1-59935-071-4; 1-59935-071-8

LC 2007-27476

In this biography of the Jamaican musician "Miller does a fine job showing the effect the music and the politics had on each other. He also skillfully weaves in the complicated topic of the Rastaferian religion and the part ganja (marijuana) plays in it, and he doesn't hesitate when explaining Marley's complicated romantic life. The . . . photos are well chosen." Booklist

Includes bibliographical references

Talamon, Bruce. Bob Marley; spirit dancer; {by} Bruce W. Talamon; text by Roger Steffens; foreword by Timothy White. Norton 1994 128p il pa $13 hardcover o.p.

Grades: 11 12 Adult　　　　　　　　　**92**

1. Singers 2. Black musicians

ISBN 0-393-32173-8 (pa)　　　　LC 94-18321

This book consists mainly of Talamon's photographs of the Jamaican reggae musician, with brief text by Steffens

"Tasteful and well done, Talamon's photographic essay stands in stark contrast to some of the raw, slapdash products intended primarily to cash in on Marley's fame. . . . A moving portrait of a great musician." Booklist

Marquart, Debra, 1956-

Marquart, Debra. The horizontal world; growing up wild in the middle of nowhere. Counterpoint 2006 xxiii, 270p $24; pa $15

Grades: 11 12 Adult　　　　　　　　　**92**

1. Authors, American 2. North Dakota

ISBN　　978-1-58243-345-5;　　1-58243-345-3; 978-1-58243-363-9 (pa); 1-58243-363-1 (pa)

LC 2005-28218

This is a memoir of "a North Dakota farm girl, former rock-and-roll band member, college dropout, professor, and Pushcart Prize-winning writer." Booklist

"The author's elegant, understated sentences are as fertile as freshly tilled rows of loam." N Y Times Book Rev

Includes bibliographical references

Marshall, Thurgood, 1908-1993

Crowe, Chris. Thurgood Marshall; a twentieth-century life. Viking 2008 248p il (Up close) $16.99 *

Grades: 6 7 8 9 10　　　　　　　　　　**92**

1. United States. Supreme Court 2. African Americans—Biography 3. Judges

ISBN 978-0-670-06228-7; 0-670-06228-6

LC 2007-042794

"Marshall served 24 years as the first African American judge on the U.S. Supreme Court, but this biography . . . focuses on his pioneer work as a lawyer and civil rights activist and on the landmark cases in which he fought segregation in public education and elsewhere."

Booklist

"This is a captivating portrait of a heroic champion of justice that also offers great insight into the most pivotal moments of the Civil Rights Movement." Kirkus

Marshall, Thurgood. Thurgood Marshall; his speeches, writings, arguments, opinions, and reminiscences; edited by Mark Tushnet; foreword by Randall Kennedy. Hill Bks. 2001 xxvi, 548p (Library of Black America) $40; pa $24.95

Grades: 11 12 Adult　　　　　　　　　**92**

1. United States. Supreme Court 2. African Americans—Biography 3. African Americans—Civil rights

ISBN 1-55652-385-8; 1-55652-386-6 (pa)

LC 2001-16793

"In a career ranging from his trial and appellate work for the NAACP to his tenure as an associate justice of the Court, Marshall wrought revolutionary changes in U.S. law and politics, and this collection of his legal briefs, writings, speeches, and judicial opinions, plus a never-before-published oral interview, gives us a superior analysis of the advocate, the democrat, the dissenter, and the unflagging fighter for equality." Libr J

Includes bibliographical references

Williams, Juan. Thurgood Marshall; American revolutionary. Times Bks. 1998 459p il pa $16 hardcover o.p.

Grades: 11 12 Adult　　　　　　　　　**92**

1. United States. Supreme Court 2. African Americans—Biography 3. African Americans—Civil rights

ISBN 0-8129-3299-4 (pa)　　　　LC 98-9735

"Williams presents Marshall as a revolutionary 'of grand vision,' but this well-rounded portrait of the man also addresses his vanities and warts, from his ascension to his deflation and subsequent redemption. This is a must read for all Americans concerned with the struggle for civil and individual rights." Booklist

Includes bibliographical references

Martí, José, 1853-1895

Sterngass, Jon. José Martí. Chelsea House Publishers 2007 123p il (Great Hispanic heritage) lib bdg $30 *

Grades: 9 10 11 12　　　　　　　　　　**92**

1. Cuba—History

ISBN 0-7910-8841-3; 978-0-7910-8841-8

LC 2006-19601

This book "follows the life of the dynamic Cuban poet, journalist, and patriot." Publisher's note

Includes bibliographical references

Marton, Kati

Marton, Kati. Enemies of the people; my family's journey to America. Simon & Schuster 2009 272p il $26

Grades: 11 12 Adult　　　　　　　　　**92**

1. Marton, Endre, 1910-2005 2. Marton, Ilona, 1912-2004 3. Journalists 4. Political prisoners 5. Hungary—History

ISBN 978-1-4165-8612-8; 1-4165-8612-1

LC 2009-14480

Marton, Kati—*Continued*
"An American journalist trolls the archives of the Hungarian secret police (AVO) to piece together her parents' imprisonment in and flight from Hungary in the mid-1950s. . . . The author's probing work effectively renders an enormously unsettled, painful time of shifting allegiances and political treachery. . . . A dark, compelling narrative of secrecy and betrayal." Kirkus
Includes bibliographical references

Marx, Karl, 1818-1883
Rössig, Wolfgang. Karl Marx. Morgan Reynolds 2009 112p il (Profiles in economics) lib bdg $28.95
Grades: 8 9 10   92
1. Philosophers
ISBN 978-1-59935-132-2; 1-59935-132-3
LC 2009-29563
"This book presents the life of Karl Marx and places his social and economic theories within the useful context of his youth in a prosperous German family. . . . [The author] provides a well-researched account of Marx's life and his work." Booklist
Includes bibliographical references

Maryam Jameelah, 1934-
Baker, Deborah. The convert; a tale of exile and extremism. Graywolf Press 2011 246p il $23
Grades: 11 12 Adult   92
1. Muslim women
ISBN 978-1-55597-582-1; 1-55597-582-8
"In 1962, 28-year-old Margaret Marcus left her parents' secular Jewish home to live in Lahore in the Muslim household of idealogue and Islamic political leader Maulana Mawdudi. In Pakistan, Marcus changed her name to Maryam Jameelah and penned expressive letters to her parents describing, during the next three decades, her newfound identity, community and the motivations behind her conversion and all-consuming embrace of Islam. Jameelah went on to write not only letters . . . but an enormously popular set of books criticizing Western materialism and exalting life lived according to the laws of the Koran. Baker's account unfolds chronologically through Jameelah's letters, included in the book, as well as various articles she published in American magazines." Kirkus
This "is a cogent, thought-provoking look at a radical life and its rippling consequences." Publ Wkly
Includes bibliographical references

Masters, Jarvis
Masters, Jarvis. That bird has my wings; the autobiography of an innocent man on death row; [by] Jarvis Jay Masters. HarperOne 2009 281p $24.99
Grades: 11 12 Adult   92
1. African Americans—Biography 2. Prisoners
ISBN 978-0-06-173045-0; 0-06-173045-9
LC 2009-22124
The author, "who has been imprisoned on San Quentin's death row since 1990 and become a devout Buddhist, recalls the neglect, abuse and cycle of crime and hopelessness that relegated him to prison by age 19." Publ Wkly
"A heartbreaking memoir; the brutal conditions of Masters's boyhood will be difficult for some readers to take, but his ultimate message of hope and reconciliation is moving and inspiring." Libr J

McCall, Nathan
McCall, Nathan. Makes me wanna holler; a young black man in America. Random House 1994 404p pa $14.95 hardcover o.p.
Grades: 11 12 Adult   92
1. African Americans—Biography
ISBN 0-679-74070-8 (pa)   LC 93-30654
The author relates the "story of his rise from poverty to success as a journalist at the *Washington Post*. He uses graphic language, blunt descriptions, honest expression, introspection, and careful observation to describe his early years in Portsmouth, Virginia, as a young black male, the recipient of a 12-year prison sentence for armed robbery, whose life was dangerously out of control. Insensitivity, alienation, racial hatred, drugs (especially crack), guns, rape, robbery, the black American as an endangered species—McCall covers it all in a depressing yet spellbinding documentary." Libr J

McCandless, Christopher, 1968-1992
Krakauer, Jon. Into the wild. Villard Bks. 1996 207p maps hardcover o.p. pa $12.95 *
Grades: 11 12 Adult   92
1. Alaska—Description and travel
ISBN 0-679-42850-X; 0-385-48680-4 (pa)
LC 95-20008
"Christopher McCandless was a disaffected, idealistic young man who trekked into the Alaskan wilderness in search of transcendence and perished there. This narrative, which ponders his journey and inner life with sympathy and imagination, has YA appeal on many levels." Booklist

McCarthy, Joseph, 1908-1957
Giblin, James. The rise and fall of Senator Joe McCarthy; [by] James Cross Giblin. Clarion Books 2009 294p il $22 *
Grades: 8 9 10 11 12   92
1. Anticommunist movements 2. United States—History—1953-1961
ISBN 978-0-618-61058-7; 0-618-61058-8
LC 2009-15005
"YAs will see the contemporary parallels in this biography of the anti-Communist crusader who rose to power over 50 years ago. . . . Giblin's title, formatted with an open, photo-filled design and written in easy, direct style, makes no superficial connections, and the afterword, 'Another McCarthy?' will prompt discussion about the accusations of terrorism in the aftermath of 9/11. Just as memorable is the scathing commentary from famous journalist Edward Murrow about the differences between dissent and disloyalty." Booklist
Includes bibliographical references

McCourt, Frank

McCourt, Frank. Angela's ashes; a memoir. Scribner 1996 364p il $25; pa $14

Grades: 11 12 Adult   **92**

1. Irish Americans

ISBN 0-684-87435-0; 0-684-84267-X (pa)

LC 96-5335

"Frank McCourt, a teacher, grandfather and occasional actor, was born in New York City, but grew up in the Irish town of Limerick during the grim 1930's and 40's before he came back here as a teen-ager. His recollections of childhood are mournful and humorous, angry and forgiving." N Y Times Book Rev

McElwain, Jason

McElwain, Jason. The game of my life; a true story of challenge, triumph, and growing up autistic; [by] Jason "J-Mac" McElwain with Daniel Paisner. New American Library 2008 243p il hardcover o.p. pa $14 *

Grades: 11 12 Adult   **92**

1. Autism 2. Basketball—Biography

ISBN   978-0-451-22301-2;   0-451-22301-2; 978-0-451-22619-8 (pa); 0-451-22619-4 (pa)

LC 2007-32261

This is the autobiography of Jason McElwain, a.k.a. "J-Mac," a severely autistic high school basketball player and manager of the Greece Athena Trojans high school basketball team.

"Teens and adults, especially those touched by the challenges of autism, will welcome this encouraging story." Voice Youth Advocates

McGough, Matthew

McGough, Matthew. Bat boy; my true life adventures coming of age with the New York Yankees. Doubleday 2005 273p il hardcover o.p. pa $12.95

Grades: 11 12 Adult   **92**

1. New York Yankees (Baseball team)

ISBN 0-385-51020-9; 0-307-27864-6 (pa) .

LC 2004-61756

The author "tells the tale of his two years as batboy for the New York Yankees, in 1992-93." Booklist

This "memoir is much more than an all-access pass to Yankee Stadium and baseball—it is an exquisitely written and observed book about growing up and the beauty of the game." SLJ

Mead, Margaret, 1901-1978

Hess, Aimee. Margaret Mead. Pomegranate 2007 63p il (Women who dare) $12.95 *

Grades: 9 10 11 12   **92**

1. Anthropologists

ISBN 978-0-7649-3875-7   LC 2006-50343

This biography "traces Mead's life, exploring her youth, her studies and her research, her pioneering fieldwork techniques, and the controversies that often swirled around her." Publisher's note

Includes bibliographical references

Mark, Joan T. Margaret Mead; coming of age in America; [by] Joan Mark. Oxford Univ. Press 1998 110p il (Oxford portraits in science) $28 *

Grades: 7 8 9 10   **92**

1. Anthropologists

ISBN 0-19-511679-8   LC 98-18604

An "account of the life and works of the influential, pioneering anthropologist. . . . Mark does a fine job of abstracting Mead's research and published works and showing why they were both critically acclaimed and criticized. The reader-friendly prose is peppered with fascinating anecdotes and photos. Mead herself is presented as a complex, intriguing figure, with fascinating, often contradictory, public and private lives." Booklist

Includes bibliographical references

Mee, Benjamin

Mee, Benjamin. We bought a zoo. Weinstein 2008 261p il $24.95; pa $14.95

Grades: 11 12 Adult   **92**

1. Dartmoor Zoological Park (Sparkwell, England) 2. Zoos

ISBN 978-1-60286-048-3; 978-1-60286-095-7 (pa)

Subtitle on cover: The amazing true story of a young family, a broken down zoo, and the 200 wild animals that change their lives

"Following the death of his father, Mee took on the challenge of helping his 76-year-old mother find a new home. This relatively simple task resulted in life-altering, unexpected outcomes, not the least of which was taking on the responsibility of owning and renovating a dilapidated zoo in rural England. . . . Readers will delight in his anecdotes, most notably about escapees Sovereign the jaguar and Parker the wolf, who attracted a fair share of media attention and antizoo feeling from the public. . . . This engaging adventure will appeal to animal lovers." Libr J

Meltzer, Milton, 1915-2009

Meltzer, Milton. Milton Meltzer; writing matters. Franklin Watts 2004 160p il lib bdg $29

Grades: 7 8 9 10   **92**

1. Authors, American

ISBN 0-531-12257-3   LC 2004-2947

Meltzer "writes about his own life through the prism of his craft. He tells about his growing up in Worcester, Massachusetts, the child of immigrants from the Austro-Hungarian empire, and his coming-of-age during the Depression." Booklist

"The author includes clear, interesting explanations about the American historical and economic events that influenced his life. While this book is a pleasure to read for general interest, it would also supplement units on American history." SLJ

Includes bibliographical references

Melville, Herman, 1819-1891

Reiff, Raychel Haugrud. Herman Melville; Moby Dick and other works. Marshall Cavendish Benchmark 2007 156p il (Writers and their works) $39.93 *

Grades: 9 10 11 12   **92**

1. Authors, American

ISBN 978-0-7614-2592-2   LC 2006-32673

Melville, Herman, 1819-1891—*Continued*
This book features a biography, a description of the times in which he lived, and critical discussions of several of his works, including *Typee, Moby Dick,* "Bartleby, The Scrivener," and *Billy Budd.*
Includes filmography and bibliographical references

Menchú, Rigoberta
Menchú, Rigoberta. I, Rigoberta Menchú; an Indian woman in Guatemala; edited and introduced by Elisabeth Burgos-Debray; translated by Ann Wright. 2nd English-language ed. Verso 2009 294p map $95; pa $22.95
Grades: 9 10 11 12   92
  1. Native Americans—Biography 2. Native Americans—Guatemala 3. Political activists
  ISBN 978-1-84467-445-9; 978-1-84467-418-3 (pa)
           LC 2010292478
First published 1984
This is the story of a twenty-three year old Guatemalan Indian woman. "It was recorded in the course of a single week in Paris, during January 1982, by a Venezuelan friend and admirer, Elizabeth Burgos-Debray. She then edited it as Rigoberta's autobiography, excluding her original questions and inserting linking passages." Times Lit Suppl
  Includes bibliographical references

Meyer, Stephenie, 1973-
Krohn, Katherine E. Stephenie Meyer; dreaming of Twilight. Twenty-First Century Books 2010 112p il (USA Today: lifeline biographies) lib bdg $33.26
Grades: 7 8 9 10 11 12   92
  1. Authors, American 2. Women authors
  ISBN 978-0-7613-5220-4; 0-7613-5220-1
           LC 2010-1425
This book, which profiles "the author of the Twilight series, will certainly attract readers. The fascinating story of where Meyer's initial idea came from (a dream) will intrigue, while the twists and turns it took to get the first book published should be edifying. In a nice bit of balance, the book gives Meyer's critics a voice too." Booklist

Michelangelo Buonarroti, 1475-1564
Somervill, Barbara A. Michelangelo; sculptor and painter. Compass Point Books 2005 112p il map (Signature lives) $30.60; pa $9.95
Grades: 6 7 8 9 10   92
  1. Artists, Italian
  ISBN   0-7565-0814-2;   978-0-7565-0814-2; 0-7565-1060-0 (pa); 978-0-7565-1060-2 (pa)
           LC 2004-17116
This is a biography of the Renaissance painter and sculptor.
The author "presents a candid introduction to her famous Renaissance subject. Her text has a casual tone, and her direct, sometimes colloquial language will capture some reluctant readers." Booklist
  Includes bibliographical references

Middleton, Earl M., 1919-2007
Middleton, Earl M. Knowing who I am; a Black entrepreneur's struggle and success in the American South; [by] Earl M. Middleton, with Joy W. Barnes. University of South Carolina Press 2008 183p il map $29.95
Grades: 11 12 Adult   92
  1. African American businesspeople
  ISBN 978-1-57003-715-3; 1-57003-715-9
           LC 2007-43037
The author, "a successful real-estate broker who has been profiled in the Wall Street Journal, looks back on the extraordinary history of his family, three generations of African Americans struggling against racial limitations in a small southern town. . . . An inspirational autobiography by a man who understands the importance of strong racial and personal identity." Booklist
  Includes bibliographical references

Milk, Harvey
Aretha, David. No compromise: the story of Harvey Milk. Morgan Reynolds 2010 128p il (Civil rights leaders) lib bdg $28.95
Grades: 7 8 9 10 11 12   92
  1. Gay men—Civil rights
  ISBN 978-1-59935-129-2; 1-59935-129-3
           LC 2009-25708
This is a biography of the gay-rights activist and San Francisco politician who was killed in 1973.
This is written "with simple and engaging prose. . . . Full-color and black-and-white photos are interspersed thoughout, giving a sense of the time period." SLJ

Miller, Arthur, 1915-2005
Andersen, Richard. Arthur Miller. Marshall Cavendish Benchmark 2005 c2006 144p il (Writers and their works) lib bdg $25.95 *
Grades: 7 8 9 10   92
  1. Authors, American
  ISBN 0-7614-1946-2
"A biography of writer Arthur Miller that describes his era, his major works, his life, and the legacy of his writing." Publisher's note
This "attractive, well-organized [book fills] a gap in literary criticism for intermediate readers. Heavily illustrated with color and black-and-white photographs, [it] will appeal to students who might be intimidated by longer or more scholarly titles." SLJ

Miller, Frank, 1957-
Eisner, Will. Eisner/Miller: a one-on-one interview. See entry under Eisner, Will, 1917-2005

Milton, John, 1608-1674
Forsyth, Neil. John Milton; a biography. Lion 2008 254p pa $14.95
Grades: 11 12 Adult   92
  1. Poets, English
  ISBN 978-0-7459-5310-6; 0-7459-5310-7
           LC 2009-291343

Milton, John, 1608-1674—*Continued*

In this biography of the seventeenth-century English poet, the author "blends into the biographical data Milton's literary achievements, so where he was in his development can be appreciated. In addition, Forsyth offers a good amount of social/political/religious information of 17th-century England, which allows an even fuller understanding of Milton's world. The audience for this work should be familiar with Milton's body of literature as well as some English history. . . . Forsyth's engrossing and informative book is essential for anyone following classic English literature." Libr J

Includes bibliographical references

Miró, Asha, 1967-

Miró, Asha. Daughter of the Ganges; a memoir; translated by Jamal Mahjoub. Atria Books 2006 274p il hardcover o.p. pa $19.95

Grades: 11 12 Adult   92

1. Adoptees

ISBN   0-7432-8672-3;   978-0-7432-8672-5; 0-7432-8673-1 (pa); 978-0-7432-8673-2 (pa)

LC 2006-40791

"English-language compilation of two books, La hija del Ganges and Las dos caras de la luna, originally published as separate editions" Verso of title page

"This memoir is an assemblage of two books chronicling Miró's first trips back to her native land of India since being adopted in Barcelona at the age of six in 1974." Publ Wkly

"A unique memoir with wide appeal." SLJ

Moaveni, Azadeh, 1976-

Moaveni, Azadeh. Lipstick jihad; a memoir of growing up Iranian in America and American in Iran. Public Affairs 2005 249p $25; pa $13

Grades: 11 12 Adult   92

1. Iran

ISBN 1-58648-193-2; 1-58648-378-1 (pa)

LC 2004-43184

"Moaveni, an Iranian-American who grew up in California, decided to embark on a journey in spring 2000 to rediscover her Iranian heritage. In this account, she . . . conveys the tensions she observed between the fundamentalist mullahs and younger Iranians, who are pushing for a more Westernized, modern Iran. . . . A charming and informative memoir." Libr J

Monet, Claude, 1840-1926

Kallen, Stuart A. Claude Monet. Lucent Books 2009 112p il (Eye on art) lib bdg $32.45

Grades: 7 8 9 10   92

1. Artists, French 2. Impressionism (Art)

ISBN 978-1-4205-0074-5; 1-4205-0074-0

LC 2008-20640

An introduction to the life and career of the artist Claude Monet, and how he painted his way into history.

"This biography paints a clear picture of the artist's life, work, and legacy. . . . The accompanying color reproductions of the artworks and black-and-white photographs of Monet contribute to the book's clean and attractive design. . . . This work stands out as a balanced description of the man's legacy and an enjoyable read." SLJ

Includes glossary and bibliographical references

Monroe, James, 1758-1831

Hart, Gary. James Monroe. Times Books 2005 170p il (American presidents series) $20

Grades: 11 12 Adult   92

1. Presidents—United States

ISBN 978-0-8050-6960-0; 0-8050-6960-7

LC 2005-41928

The author "studies James Monroe, the last of the Virginia dynasty, who, although president at an important time in U.S. history (1817-25), is often overlooked. Hart argues that in the years after the disastrous War of 1812, Monroe was 'the first "national security president."' . . . [This] is a satisfying and informative read." Libr J

Includes bibliographical references

Mooney, Jonathan

Mooney, Jonathan. The short bus; a journey beyond normal. H. Holt 2007 272p hardcover o.p. pa $14.99

Grades: 11 12 Adult   92

1. Handicapped students

ISBN   978-0-8050-7427-7;   0-8050-7427-9; 978-0-8050-8804-5 (pa); 0-8050-8804-0 (pa)

LC 2006-52588

"Considered learning disabled as a child, Mooney still managed to graduate with honors from Brown. Here he recounts a four-month cross-country trip to meet children and adults who have similarly triumphed." Libr J

The author's "target audience is not policy makers but his fellow misfits, and his boundless empathy will surely console those who also face the worst that cruel schoolchildren and the educational bureaucracy have to offer." N Y Times Book Rev

Morris, Jim

Morris, Jim. The oldest rookie; big-league dreams from a small-town guy; {by} Jim Morris with Joel Engel. Little, Brown 2001 276p $22.95; pa $13.95

Grades: 11 12 Adult   92

1. Baseball—Biography

ISBN 0-316-59156-4; 0-446-67837-6 (pa)

LC 00-64269

Paperback published with title: The rookie

"Morris, a high-school baseball coach and former minor-league pitcher, makes a deal with the kids on his team: if they make the play-offs, he'll try for the majors one last time. They do, and he does. It's a fabulous baseball story, full of wonderful humor, but it isn't all about dreams coming true; it also shows how much dreams cost, to the dreamers and to their loved ones." Booklist

Morrison, Toni, 1931-

Andersen, Richard. Toni Morrison. Marshall Cavendish Benchmark 2005 c2006 144p il (Writers and their works) lib bdg $25.95 *

Grades: 7 8 9 10   92

Morrison, Toni, 1931-—*Continued*
    1. Authors, American 2. African American authors
    3. Women authors
    ISBN 0-7614-1945-4
A biography of writer Toni Morrison that describes
her era, her major works, her life, and the legacy of her
writing.
This "attractive, well-organized [book fills] a gap in
literary criticism for intermediate readers. Heavily illustrated with color and black-and-white photographs, [it]
will appeal to students who might be intimidated by longer or more scholarly titles." SLJ
Includes bibliographical references

Morrison, Toni. Conversations with Toni
Morrison; edited by Danille Taylor-Guthrie.
University Press of Miss. 1994 293p (Literary
conversations series) pa $20 hardcover o.p.
Grades: 11 12 Adult   92
    1. Authors, American 2. Women authors 3. African
    American authors
    ISBN 0-87805-692-0 (pa)   LC 93-44738
This is a collection of interviews with and essays
about the Nobel prize winning African American novelist
from a variety of sources from 1974 to 1992.

Mozes, Miriam, 1935-1993
    Kor, Eva Mozes. Surviving the Angel of Death.
See entry under Kor, Eva Mozes, 1935-

Muhammad, d. 632
    Armstrong, Karen. Muhammad; a prophet for
our time. Atlas Books/HarperCollins Publishers
2006 249p map (Eminent lives) $21.95; pa $14.95
*
Grades: 11 12 Adult   92
    ISBN   0-06-059897-2;   978-0-06-059897-6;
    0-06-115577-2 (pa); 978-0-06-115577-2 (pa)
                                     LC 2006-45864
First published 1991 in the United Kingdom with sub-
title: A Western attempt to understand Islam; Original
American edition published 1992 with subtitle: A biogra-
phy of the prophet
This is a biography of the founder of Islam.
"Readers of these pages cannot escape the genius of
Muhammad and his aim for peace and compassion
among nations and among Muslims themselves. . . .
Recommended for all libraries." Libr J
Includes bibliographical references

Muir, John, 1838-1914
    Wilkins, Thurman. John Muir; apostle of nature.
University of Okla. Press 1995 xxvii, 302p il maps
(Oklahoma western biographies) pa $21.95
hardcover o.p.
Grades: 11 12 Adult   92
    1. Naturalists
    ISBN 0-8061-2797-X (pa)   LC 95-11426
"Wilkins follows Muir from his Scottish boyhood,
clouded by a harsh, fundamentalist father, to an adoles-
cence of arduous farmwork in Wisconsin to a lifelong

career of exploration and study of wildernesses, particularly those of the western U.S., and vividly relates some
of Muir's more perilous adventures on cliffside and
snowfield. . . . An affectionate, uncluttered tale of an
American folk hero." Booklist
Includes bibliographical references

Muller, Salomé, b. ca. 1809
    Bailey, John. The lost German slave girl; the
extraordinary true story of the slave Sally Miller
and her fight for freedom. Atlantic Monthly Press
2004 268p hardcover o.p. pa $14
Grades: 11 12 Adult   92
    1. Slavery—United States 2. Racially mixed people
    3. German Americans
    ISBN 0-87113-921-9; 0-8021-4229-X (pa)
                                     LC 2004-50264
"A series of highly contentious trials was held in the
mid-1800s to determine whether Sally Miller, a New Orleans woman, was born a multiracial slave or was in fact
a German immigrant trapped in bondage from childhood.
The stuff of television miniseries, this sensational and
emotional cause celebre of its time is revived into a fresh
drama from the vantage point of the present." Libr J
Includes bibliographical references

Murakami, Haruki, 1949-
    Mussari, Mark. Haruki Murakami. Marshall
Cavendish Benchmark 2010 127p il (Today's
writers and their works) lib bdg $42.79
Grades: 8 9 10 11 12   92
    1. Authors, Japanese
    ISBN 978-0-7614-4124-3; 0-7614-4124-7
    This biography of Haruki Murakami places the author
in the context of his times and discusses his work.
    Includes bibliographical references

Murrow, Edward R.
    Edwards, Bob. Edward R. Murrow and the birth
of broadcast journalism; [by] Robert A. Edwards.
Wiley 2004 174p (Turning points) $19.95
Grades: 11 12 Adult   92
    1. Journalists
    ISBN 0-471-47753-2   LC 2003-21223
    "The author chronicles Murrow's innovations in radio
and television broadcasting, including live radio reports
of the war in progress in Europe in 1940; exposure of
the despotism of Senator Joseph McCarthy on CBS in
1953; the powerful television documentary *Harvest of
Shame* on the deplorable conditions of migrant workers
in the U.S.; and the first in-depth television news program, *See It Now*. . . . Edwards brings to life the early
days of radio and television and the innovations that
Murrow sparked. . . . Readers interested in journalism
will enjoy this slim book." Booklist
    Includes bibliographical references

Myers, Walter Dean, 1937-

Myers, Walter Dean. Bad boy; a memoir. HarperCollins Pubs. 2001 214p $15.95; pa $6.99 *

Grades: 7 8 9 10   92

1. Authors, American 2. African American authors

ISBN 0-06-029523-6; 0-06-447288-4 (pa)

         LC 00-52978

In this memoir "young adult author Walter Dean Myers recalls the life path that lead him to a career in writing. . . . His personal account allows the reader to get a glimpse of Myers, the man, touching on the issues of racism, adoption, self-identity, alcoholism, gang violence, and a speech impediment that almost altered Myers's path to the written word." Voice Youth Advocates

This "is a story full of funny anecdotes, lofty ideals, and tender moments." SLJ

Nader, Ralph

Bowen, Nancy. Ralph Nader; man with a mission. 21st Cent. Bks. (Brookfield) 2002 144p $24.99

Grades: 9 10 11 12   92

1. Consumer protection

ISBN 0-7613-2365-1   LC 2001-41464

A biography of the consumer advocate who has devoted his life to crusading for citizens' rights, and who ran as the Green Party's presidential candidate in 2000

"Young people researching third-party movements, activism, consumer rights, or the role of Lebanese Americans will find this clearly written, well-documented biography an informative resource." Booklist

Includes bibliographical references

Napoleon I, Emperor of the French, 1769-1821

Johnson, Paul. Napoleon. Viking 2002 190p (Penguin lives series) hardcover o.p. pa $13 *

Grades: 11 12 Adult   92

1. France—Kings and rulers

ISBN 0-670-03078-3; 0-14-303745-5 (pa)

         LC 2001-45605

"A Lipper\Viking book"

Johnson "presents a concise appraisal of Napoleon's career and a precise understanding of his enigmatic character. The author views Napoleon, not as an 'idea man' whose ideology was the ladder by which he propelled himself to heights of power, but as an opportunist who took advantage of a series of events and situations he could manipulate into achieving supreme control." Booklist

Includes bibliographical references

Nelson, Horatio Nelson, Viscount, 1758-1805

Czisnik, Marianne. Horatio Nelson; a controversial hero. Hodder Arnold 2005 192p il pa $35 *

Grades: 11 12 Adult   92

1. Great Britain. Royal Navy 2. Admirals

ISBN 0-340-90021-0 (pa); 978-0-340-90021-5 (pa)

         LC 2006-298161

This work on the British admiral "is a collection of essays, offering reflections on aspects of his career, and

on his contemporary and posthumous reputation." Engl Hist Rev

Includes bibliographical references

Nemat, Marina

Nemat, Marina. Prisoner of Tehran; a memoir. Free Press 2007 306p $26 *

Grades: 11 12 Adult   92

1. Political prisoners 2. Iran—History—1979-

ISBN 1-4165-3742-2; 978-1-4165-3742-7

         LC 2006-50191

Nemat was sixteen when she was arrested in Iran in early 1982 for political protests against the new fundamentalist regime. This is an account of her prison experiences.

The author's "story is not so much a political history lesson than it is a memoir of faith and love, a protest against violence that cannot be silenced. . . . Her persistence in standing for goodness is a lesson for us all." Christ Sci Monit

Newton, Sir Isaac, 1642-1727

Ackroyd, Peter. Newton. Nan A. Talese/Doubleday 2006 176p il (Ackroyd's brief lives) $21.95

Grades: 11 12 Adult   92

1. Scientists

ISBN 978-0-385-50799-8; 0-385-50799-2

         LC 2006-45619

This is a biography of the physicist and mathematician.

"Readers will . . . marvel at how many logic-defying complexities fill the life of the genius famous for recognizing in the fall of an apple the force unifying the universe." Booklist

Includes bibliographical references

Boerst, William J. Isaac Newton; organizing the universe. Morgan Reynolds Pub. 2004 144p il (Renaissance scientists) lib bdg $23.95

Grades: 7 8 9 10   92

1. Scientists

ISBN 1-931798-01-X   LC 2003-14571

"Boerst describes Newton's life from his premature birth through an isolated adulthood dominated by study and experimentation to his death at the age of 84. The author deftly explores his subject's accomplishments in relation to the scientific community and notable historical events of the time and includes information concerning his religious views. . . . This well-written book makes an excellent choice for teens exploring scientists or just looking for a good biography." SLJ

Includes bibliographical references

Christianson, Gale E. Isaac Newton. Oxford University Press 2005 144p il (Lives and legacies) $18.95

Grades: 11 12 Adult   92

1. Scientists

ISBN 978-0-19-530070-3; 0-19-530070-X

         LC 2005-9600

This is a biography of the English mathematician and physicist.

Newton, Sir Isaac, 1642-1727—*Continued*
"This enjoyable book gives a more in-depth view of Newton than one can get from any of the brief presentations one finds in science texts. . . . There are minor misstatements of both physics and chemistry in the book, but they should not detract from the excellent job author Gale Christianson does of bringing to light the many facets of the man and his great contributions to all of science." Sci Books Films
Includes bibliographical references

Christianson, Gale E. Isaac Newton and the scientific revolution. Oxford Univ. Press 1996 155p il (Oxford portraits in science) lib bdg $28 *
Grades: 7 8 9 10   92
1. Scientists
ISBN 0-19-509224-4   LC 96-13179
Explores the life and scientific contributions of the famed English mathematician and natural philosopher
This book "reads easily and with a pleasant and comfortable flow. Structured around pivotal moments in Newton's life, the book is an excellent reference for biographical data on the great English scientist; in addition, it affords a fine historical perspective of the scientific revolution." Sci Books Films
Includes bibliographical references

Ng'ugĩ wa Thiongo, 1938-
Ng'ugĩ wa Thiongo. Dreams in a time of war; a childhood memoir. Pantheon Books 2010 256p il $24.95
Grades: 11 12 Adult   92
1. Kikuyu (African people) 2. Kenya
ISBN 978-0-307-37883-5; 0-307-37883-7
                              LC 2009-34107
"When Ngugi is accepted into an elite high school in Kenya, worried about where to get a pair of shoes, his brother is a Mau Mau guerrilla in the mountains. The world-renowned Kenyan writer looks back at his growing up in the 1950s in this crisp, clearly told memoir, which evokes the rising African nationalism of the era in all its conflict and complexity." Booklist

Nostradamus, 1503-1566
Randi, James. The mask of Nostradamus. Scribner 1990 256p il pa $26
Grades: 11 12 Adult   92
1. Prophecies
ISBN 0-87975-830-9   LC 89-70189
A biographical study of "Michel de Notredame, better known as Nostradamus, the famous 16th-century French physician, astrologer and seer. Commentators claim that Nostradamus's cryptic verses accurately prophesied such events and personalities as Napoleon, Hitler, the French Revolution, the Great Fire of London and the invention of the Montgolfier balloon. Nonsense, argues Randi, and his meticulous readings of key quatrains make a potent case for his contention." Publ Wkly
Includes bibliographical references

Nuñez Cabeza de Vaca, Alvar, 16th cent.
Childress, Diana. Barefoot conquistador; Cabeza de Vaca and the struggle for Native American rights. Twenty-First Century Books 2008 160p il map lib bdg $30.60
Grades: 7 8 9 10   92
1. Explorers 2. America—Exploration
ISBN 978-0-8225-7517-7; 0-8225-7517-5
                              LC 2007-22059
"This clearly written biography introduces a 16th-century Spanish explorer who made two expeditions to North and South America and eventually became a champion for Native Americans. . . . Childress's well-researched, lively text will fascinate readers. . . . The pages are sprinkled with period illustrations and maps." SLJ
Includes bibliographical references

Nye, Naomi Shihab, 1952-
Nye, Naomi Shihab. I'll ask you three times, are you ok? tales of driving and being driven. Greenwillow Books 2007 242p $15.99; lib bdg $16.89
Grades: 7 8 9 10 11 12   92
1. Voyages and travels
ISBN 978-0-06-085392-1; 978-0-06-085393-8 (lib bdg)   LC 2006-36548
The author "writes about sudden intimate connections with strangers, especially taxi drivers, who often yield glimpses of family and exile that can sometimes change us. . . . The prose is chatty, fast, and unpretentious, and teens will enjoy the driving stuff and the idea of her kissing in the backseat, and they'll feel her sense of control when she is behind the wheel herself." Booklist

Obama, Barack, 1961-
Abramson, Jill. Obama; the historic journey. Callaway 2009 237p il map $40
Grades: 10 11 12 Adult   92
1. Presidents—United States 2. Presidents—United States—Election—2008 3. African Americans—Biography 4. Racially mixed people
ISBN 978-1-59448-893-1; 1-59448-893-2
                              LC 2009-5050
This title "showcases both the Obama campaign and the Times's own staff expertise on the subject. The photographs, from both documentary and color reproduction perspectives, are the best you'll find. Contributions by Times writers and editors includes both new pieces and reprints from the paper, with new biographical text by Jill Abramson going back to Obama's beginnings." Libr J

Davis, William. Barack Obama; the politics of hope. OTTN Pub. 2008 168p il (Shapers of America) $25.95; pa $16.99
Grades: 6 7 8 9 10   92
1. Presidents—United States 2. African Americans—Biography 3. Racially mixed people
ISBN   1-59556-024-6;   978-1-59556-024-7; 1-59556-032-7 (pa); 978-1-59556-032-2 (pa)
This biography of the president "will give readers a real feel for the man and the forces that shaped him.

Obama, Barack, 1961-—_Continued_
. . . It thoroughly and sensitively dissects Obama's complicated ethnic background and what it meant to him. . . . Davis also does a good job of explaining the realities associated with Obama's losses and wins in the political arena." Booklist
Includes bibliographical references

Obama, Barack. Dreams from my father; a story of race and inheritance. Crown Publishers 2007 c2004 442p $25.95
Grades: 7 8 9 10 11 12 Adult   92
   1. Presidents—United States 2. African Americans—Biography 3. Racially mixed people
   ISBN 978-0-307-38341-9   LC 2007-271892
Also available in paperback from Three Rivers Press
First published 1995 by Times Books
This is the autobiography of the Illinois senator who would later become the 44th president of the United States.
The author "offers an account of his life's journey that reflects brilliantly on the power of race consciousness in America. . . . Obama writes well; his account is sensitive, probing, and compelling." Choice [review of 1995 edition]

Obama, Michelle
Mundy, Liza. Michelle; a biography. Simon & Schuster 2008 217p il $25
Grades: 11 12 Adult   92
   1. Obama, Barack, 1961- 2. African American women—Biography 3. Women lawyers 4. Presidents' spouses—United States
   ISBN 1-4165-9943-6; 978-1-4165-9943-2
      LC 2008-33595
This is a "comprehensive look at Michelle Obama and her relationship with Barack Obama." Libr J
Includes bibliographical references

Ochoa, Ellen, 1958-
Hasday, Judy L. Ellen Ochoa. Chelsea House Publishers 2007 106p il (Great Hispanic heritage) lib bdg $30
Grades: 9 10 11 12   92
   1. Women astronauts
   ISBN 0-7910-8842-1; 978-0-7910-8842-5
      LC 2006-19632
This book "follows the life of the first Hispanic female astronaut who traveled in space." Publisher's note
Includes bibliographical references

Ohno, Apolo, 1982-
Aldridge, Rebecca. Apolo Anton Ohno. Chelsea House 2009 120p il (Asian Americans of achievement) lib bdg $30
Grades: 7 8 9 10   92
   1. Ice skating—Biography
   ISBN 978-1-60413-565-7; 1-60413-565-4
      LC 2009-9918
A biography of Olympic champion speed skater Apolo Anton Ohno.

"Nineteen color photos show Ohno's competitions. . . . The quality of research and in-depth coverage broadens [the book's] usefulness." SLJ
Includes glossary and bibliographical references

O'Neal, Shaquille, 1972-
O'Neal, Shaquille. Shaq talks back; [by] Shaquille O'Neal with Mike Wise. St. Martin's Press 2001 259p il hardcover o.p. pa $7.99
Grades: 11 12 Adult   92
   1. African American athletes 2. Basketball—Biography
   ISBN 0-312-27845-4; 0-312-98259-3 (pa)
      LC 2001-19021
O'Neal "recounts his life story, from his childhood in Newark through winning the 2000 NBA Championship. . . . He speaks frankly about his current and former teammates and coaches, as well as the state of the NBA and of the world in general. . . . Though Shaq devotes a lot of the book to his life off the court (his movies, rap albums, celebrity life), there's enough basketball here to satisfy hardcore hoops junkies." Publ Wkly

Ormes, Jackie, 1911-1985
Goldstein, Nancy. Jackie Ormes; the first African American woman cartoonist. University of Michigan Press 2008 225p il $35
Grades: 10 11 12 Adult   92
   1. Cartoonists 2. African American women—Biography
   ISBN 978-0-472-11624-9; 0-472-11624-X
      LC 2007-35395
This book covers the life and career of Jackie Ormes, who was the first African American woman cartoonist. She wrote and drew comic strips that ran in Black newspapers such as the Pittsburgh Courier and the Chicago Defender. She was part of the Black elite in Chicago and knew other luminaries such as singer Eartha Kitt and musician/composer/conductor Duke Ellington. She was also investigated by the FBI because of her Leftist political ideas and activities. While she did such things as create Torchy paper dolls, based on her beautiful and sexy cartoon character, and cute Patty-Jo dolls, Ormes also used her comic strips to put forth her political views. This book reproduces some of her cartoons and comic strips, in both black and white and in color.
Includes bibliographical references

Orwell, George, 1903-1950
Boon, Kevin A. George Orwell; Animal farm and Nineteen eighty-four; by Kevin Alexander Boon. Marshall Cavendish Benchmark 2009 143p il (Writers and their works) lib bdg $42.79
Grades: 9 10 11 12   92
   1. Authors, English
   ISBN 978-0-7614-2960-9; 0-7614-2960-3
      LC 2007-33743
"A biography of writer George Orwell that describes his era, his major works—the novels _Animal Farm_ and _Nineteen Eighty-Four_—his life, and the legacy of his writing." Publisher's note
Includes filmography and bibliographical references

Oufkir, Malika

Oufkir, Malika. Freedom: the story of my second life; translated by Linda Coverdale. Hyperion 2006 241p $23.95

Grades: 9 10 11 12   **92**
ISBN 1-4013-5206-5; 978-1-4013-5206-6
"Miramax books"

The author, "whose first book, Stolen Lives, recounted her family's 20 years in Moroccan prisons, now continues her story up to the present, revealing what it was like to be thrust into the free world after years of confinement. . . . Ever charming and gracious, Oufkir is a delight to spend time with." Libr J

Oufkir, Malika. Stolen lives; twenty years in a desert jail; {by} Malika Oufkir and Michele Fitoussi; translated by Ros Schwartz. Miramax Bks. 2001 293p il map hardcover o.p. pa $14

Grades: 11 12 Adult   **92**
ISBN 0-7868-6732-9; 0-7868-8630-7 (pa)
LC 00-53220
Original French edition, 1999

This memoir recounts the experiences of Oufkir and her family after she was adopted by King Muhammad V of Morocco as a companion for his daughter. She and her family were imprisoned by Muhammad's son King Hassan II for almost 20 years after her father, General Muhammad Oufkir, was executed for leading an unsuccessful plot to assassinate the king in 1972

This book "will fascinate readers with its singular tale of two kindly fathers, political struggles in a strict monarchy and a family's survival of cruel, prolonged deprivation." Publ Wkly

Owens, Jesse, 1913-1980

Schaap, Jeremy. Triumph; the untold story of Jesse Owens and Hitler's Olympics. Houghton Mifflin 2007 272p il $24; pa $14.95

Grades: 11 12 Adult   **92**
1. African American athletes 2. Olympic games, 1936 (Berlin, Ger.)
ISBN   978-0-618-68822-7;   0-618-68822-6;
978-0-618-91910-9 (pa); 0-618-91910-4 (pa)
LC 2006-26926

"Schaap's chronicle of Jesse Owens's journey to and glorious triumph at the 1936 Berlin Olympics is snappy and dramatic, with an eye for the rousing climax." Publ Wkly

Includes bibliographical references

Paine, Thomas, 1737-1809

Collins, Paul. The trouble with Tom: the strange afterlife and times of Thomas Paine. Bloomsbury 2005 278p map hardcover o.p. pa $15 *

Grades: 11 12 Adult   **92**
ISBN 1-58234-502-3; 1-58234-613-5 (pa)
LC 2005-45240

The author "traces the bizarre story of Thomas Paine's remains through nearly two centuries of American and English history. . . . Part travelogue, part memoir and part historical mystery, this book reads like a wry, witty novel and offers a delicious twist at the end." Publ Wkly

Includes bibliographical references

Palden Gyatso

Palden Gyatso. The autobiography of a Tibetan monk; [by] Palden Gyatso, with Tsering Shakya; foreword by the Dalai Lama; translated from the Tibetan by Tsering Shakya. Grove Press 1997 232p il maps $24; pa $13

Grades: 9 10 11 12   **92**
1. Tibet (China)
ISBN 0-8021-1621-3; 0-8021-3574-9 (pa)
LC 97-39679

Published in the United Kingdom with title: Fire under the snow

Palden Gyatso offers an "account of his life in Tibet—first as a Buddhist monk, then as a prisoner of the Chinese for more than 30 years." Booklist

This is a "wrenching memoir of extraordinary suffering, resistance and endurance." N Y Times Book Rev

Parker, Quanah, Comanche Chief, 1845?-1911

Neeley, Bill. The last Comanche chief: the life and times of Quanah Parker. Wiley 1995 276p il maps hardcover o.p. pa $16.95

Grades: 11 12 Adult   **92**
1. Comanche Indians 2. Native Americans—Biography
ISBN 0-471-11722-6; 0-471-16076-8 (pa)
LC 94-38101

The author traces Parker's "life from youth to warrior chief to respected cattleman. He describes the last wars between the Comanches and settlers, the peyote ritual and pressures on Native Americans to conform to white society. . . . This is a fine portrait of the legendary chief and an illuminating glimpse into the history of the American West." Publ Wkly

Includes bibliographical references

Parks, Rosa, 1913-2005

Brinkley, Douglas. Rosa Parks. Viking 2000 246p (Penguin lives series) hardcover o.p. pa $13 *

Grades: 11 12 Adult   **92**
1. African American women—Biography 2. African Americans—Civil rights
ISBN 0-670-89160-6; 0-14-303600-9 (pa)
LC 00-35916

"A Lipper/Viking book"

"Rosa Parks' story takes readers from rural Alabama to the Montgomery Industrial School for Girls, marriage to barber Raymond Parks, quiet activism in the '30s and '40s, a first experience of integration at the Highlander Folk School, arrest in 1955 and the bus boycott, a move to Detroit, and more than 20 years on the staff of Rep. John Conyers (D-Mich.)." Booklist

Includes bibliographical references

Pasteur, Louis, 1822-1895

Ackerman, Jane. Louis Pasteur and the founding of microbiology. Morgan Reynolds Pub. 2003 144p il (Renaissance scientists) lib bdg $23.95 *

Grades: 7 8 9 10   **92**
1. Scientists
ISBN 1-931798-13-3   LC 2003-17655

Pasteur, Louis, 1822-1895—*Continued*

Follows the life and career of the French scientist who proved the existence of germs and their connection with diseases

"Students interested in science, biography, or medicine will find this an interesting account." SLJ

Includes bibliographical references

Patel, Eboo, 1975-

Patel, Eboo. Acts of faith; the story of an American Muslim, the struggle for the soul of a generation. Beacon Press 2010 195p pa $14

Grades: 11 12 Adult   92

  1. Muslims—United States 2. Multiculturalism

  ISBN 978-0-8070-0622-1; 0-8070-0622-X

                   LC 2010-537438

First published 2007

The author, "a founder of the Interfaith Youth Core, traces the personal journey that led to the group's formation and introduces readers to its philosophy." Kirkus

"Eboo Patel's story as an American Muslim is a powerful account of one hopeful man's struggle against biases in America and how young people can bring together a purpose of common humanity and advance peace in the world." Univ Press Books for Public and Second Sch Libr, 2008

Includes bibliographical references

Paterno, Joe

Pittman, Charles Vernon. Playing for Paterno; one coach, two eras: a father's and son's personal recollections of playing for JoePa; [by] Charlie Pittman and Tony Pittman, as told to Jae Bryson. Triumph Books 2007 194p il $24.95

Grades: 11 12 Adult   92

  1. Penn State Nittany Lions (Football team) 2. Football—Biography

  ISBN 978-1-60078-000-4; 1-60078-000-8

                   LC 2007-8355

The Pittmans "both played for Joe Paterno at Penn State, one in the late 1960s and the other in the early 1990s. . . . Not only do the Pittmans chronicle their own careers on and off the field but they also pepper the book with exciting anecdotes about the Nittany Lions and about the amazing coaching career—more than 40 years and counting—of the man they call JoPa. An inspiring story of loyalty, attitude, and integrity." Booklist

Patrick, Saint, 373?-463?

Bury, John Bagnell. Ireland's saint; the essential biography of St. Patrick; [by] J.B. Bury; edited with introduction and annotations by Jon M. Sweeney. Rev ed. Paraclete Press 2008 205p il map $21.95

Grades: 9 10 11 12 Adult   92

  1. Christian saints

  ISBN 978-1-55725-557-0; 1-55725-557-1

                   LC 2008-17071

First published 1905 with title: The life of St. Patrick and his place in history

"Explores the life of Saint Patrick, his place in history, and the spread of Christianity beyond the Roman Em-

pire." Publisher's note

Sweeney "takes Bury's original text and fashions a contemporary English rendering from it, . . . adding sidebars that highlight recent scholarship and provide new insights into Patrick's life and thought. . . . This edition will . . . appeal to a popular audience." Libr J

Includes bibliographical references

Patrick, Danica, 1982-

Sirvaitis, Karen. Danica Patrick; racing's trailblazer. Twenty-First Century Books 2010 112p il (USA Today: lifeline biographies) lib bdg $33.26

Grades: 7 8 9 10 11 12   92

  1. Automobile racing 2. Women athletes

  ISBN 978-0-7613-5222-8; 0-7613-5222-8

                   LC 2009-45846

This biography is "both informative and eye-catching. . . . Even young readers with little interest in car racing will be caught up in the story behind *Danica Patrick*. . . . This involving story does more than recount the high times. Teammates are killed, loyalties switch, and personal criticism is a fact of life in the limelight." Booklist

Patterson, Floyd

Levy, Alan Howard. Floyd Patterson; a boxer and a gentleman; [by] Alan H. Levy. McFarland & Co. 2008 289p il pa $35 *

Grades: 11 12 Adult   92

  1. Boxing—Biography 2. African American athletes

  ISBN 978-0-7864-3950-8; 0-7864-3950-5

                   LC 2008-32250

This is a "biography of the man who was the youngest world heavyweight champion in boxing history as well as the first boxer to regain the championship after losing it. . . . This book is not only an excellent study of Patterson but a superior source on professional boxing from the mid-1950s through the mid-1970s." Libr J

Includes bibliographical references

Paulsen, Gary

Paulsen, Gary. The beet fields; memories of a sixteenth summer. Delacorte Press 2000 160p hardcover o.p. pa $5.99

Grades: 11 12 Adult   92

  1. Authors, American

  ISBN 0-385-32647-5; 0-440-41557-8 (pa)

                   LC 00-23184

The author recalls his experiences as a migrant laborer and carnival worker after he ran away from home at age sixteen.

"Paulsen's coming-of-age memoir is nearly Steinbeckian in its unadorned but effective prose, and the events of the author's young life have a universality that will draw in readers heading for their own rites of passage." Bull Cent Child Books

Paulsen, Gary—*Continued*

Paulsen, Gary. Eastern sun, winter moon; an autobiographical odyssey. Harcourt Brace Jovanovich 1993 244p il hardcover o.p. pa $16 *
Grades: 11 12 Adult   92
1. Authors, American
ISBN 0-15-127260-3; 0-15-600203-5 (pa)
LC 91-47127

This is an account of the writer's childhood. Paulsen describes his journey to the Philippines at the end of World War II. He and his mother traveled there to join his father, a soldier whom Paulsen had never met.

This "memoir is wonderfully readable. The book is also an interesting portrait of adults as viewed by a child from whom little of the adult world is hidden." Libr J

Peery, Nelson, 1925-

Peery, Nelson. Black radical; the education of an American revolutionary. New Press 2007 242p $24.95
Grades: 11 12 Adult   92
1. African Americans—Biography 2. African Americans—Civil rights 3. Communism—United States
ISBN 978-1-59558-145-7; 1-59558-145-6
LC 2007-9181

Sequel to Black fire (1995)

This is the memoir of an African-American World War II veteran who became a member of the Communist Party in 1946.

"Some readers may chafe at Peery's avowedly Marxist terminology, but the development of [his] revolutionary consciousness is absorbing." Publ Wkly

Peterson, Brenda

Peterson, Brenda. I want to be left behind; finding rapture here on Earth. Da Capo Press 2010 277p $25
Grades: 11 12 Adult   92
1. Nature—Religious aspects 2. End of the world
ISBN 978-0-306-81804-2   LC 2009-22803
"A Merloyd Lawrence book"

This is a "memoir about growing up among Southern Baptists and not quite fitting in. Peterson's story is told through . . . a series of vignettes, tied together by two themes, faith and the environment. She looks back at her childhood, college, and then adulthood, stopping here and there, selecting scenes from her life that show why she finds God outdoors, and why the rapture-obsessed family and community of her youth quickly loses its appeal. . . . Readers interested in a story about leaving behind theologically conservative Christianity and other types of extremism will find Peterson's collection of anecdotes and remembered conversations engaging." Publ Wkly

Picasso, Pablo, 1881-1973

Kallen, Stuart A. Pablo Picasso. Lucent Books 2009 104p il (Eye on art) lib bdg $32.45
Grades: 7 8 9 10   92
1. Artists, French 2. Cubism
ISBN 978-1-4205-0045-5; 1-4205-0045-7
LC 2008-13338

"Kallen tackles the complicated man that was Pablo Picasso and gives readers a look at both his genius and his eccentricities. . . . Visually, this is supported by the many photos of Picasso's art that appear throughout. Excellent sidebars offer solid information on such topics as communism or the influence of the Impressionists. This is just the kind of book that engages enough to become a gateway." Booklist
Includes bibliographical references

Pierce, Franklin, 1804-1869

Holt, Michael F. (Michael Fitzgibbon). Franklin Pierce. Times Books/Henry Holt and Co. 2010 154p (American presidents series) $23
Grades: 11 12 Adult   92
1. Presidents—United States 2. United States—Politics and government—1815-1861
ISBN 978-0-8050-8719-2   LC 2009-36425

The author "creates a solid portrait of both man and President. Pierce, a New Englander known for his charm and good looks, traditionally ranks as one of our nation's worst leaders. Holt does not dispel or challenge any previous assessments but rather tries to explain the pre-Civil War President's actions." Libr J
Includes bibliographical references

Pirsig, Robert M., 1928-

Pirsig, Robert M. Zen and the art of motorcycle maintenance; an inquiry into values. Morrow 1974 412p $26; pa $13.95
Grades: 11 12 Adult   92
ISBN 0-688-00230-7; 0-06-083987-2 (pa)

A collection of the author's philosophical musings inspired by a motorcycle trip with his son

Plath, Sylvia

Reiff, Raychel Haugrud. Sylvia Plath. Marshall Cavendish Benchmark 2008 144p il (Writers and their works) lib bdg $39.93
Grades: 9 10 11 12   92
1. Poets, American
ISBN 978-0-7614-2962-3; 0-7614-2962-X
LC 2007-23799

"A biography of writer Sylvia Plath that describes her era, her major works—the novel *The Bell Jar* and her poetry—her life, and the legacy of her writing." Publisher's note
Includes filmography and bibliographical references

Pocahontas, d. 1617

Jones, Victoria Garrett. Pocahontas; a life in two worlds. Sterling 2010 124p il map (Sterling biographies) lib bdg $12.95; pa $9.95
Grades: 7 8 9 10   92
1. Jamestown (Va.)—History 2. Powhatan Indians 3. Native Americans—Biography
ISBN 978-1-4027-6844-6 (lib bdg); 1-4027-6844-3 (lib bdg); 978-1-4027-5158-5 (pa); 1-4027-5158-3 (pa)
LC 2009-24136

A biography of the daughter of Chief Powhatan and her friendship with the colonists of the Jamestown settlement.

Includes glossary and bibliographical references

Pocahontas, d. 1617—*Continued*

Woodward, Grace Steele. Pocahontas. University of Okla. Press 1969 227p il (Civilization of the American Indian series) pa $17.95 hardcover o.p.
Grades: 9 10 11 12 **92**
1. Powhatan Indians 2. Native Americans—Biography 3. United States—History—1600-1775, Colonial period
ISBN 0-8061-1642-0 (pa)
This is the "story of the appealing daughter of Chief Powhatan and her friendship with the colonists of the Jamestown settlement. . . . Her marriage and brief life in England are vividly re-created." Booklist
Includes bibliographical references

Poe, Edgar Allan, 1809-1849
Ackroyd, Peter. Poe; a life cut short. Nan A. Talese/Doubleday 2008 205p il (Ackroyd's brief lives) $21.95
Grades: 9 10 11 12 Adult **92**
1. Authors, American
ISBN 978-0-385-50800-1; 0-385-50800-X
LC 2008-18244
Explores Poe's literary accomplishments and legacy against the background of his erratic, dramatic, and sometimes sordid life, including his marriage to his thirteen-year-old cousin and his much-written-about problems with gambling and alcohol.
This "readable account should appeal to Poe devotees and newcomers alike." Publ Wkly
Includes bibliographical references

Meltzer, Milton. Edgar Allan Poe; a biography. Twenty-First Century Books 2003 144p $31.90 *
Grades: 7 8 9 10 **92**
1. Authors, American
ISBN 0-7613-2910-2 LC 2002-155802
Contents: Theater in the blood; A quick and clever boy; The teenager; Soldier and poet; In West Point, and out; Satire and science fiction; Editor, novelist, husband; Hoaxes and horrors; The first ever detective story; A popular lecturer; New York: the rich and the poor; "The raven" and fame; Death of the beloved; The last years; Chronology of Poe's life
"More than most other biographers for young people, Meltzer places his subject within the framework of his society. Readers will come away not only with greater knowledge of Poe's life and accomplishments but also a clearer picture of American life in the first half of the nineteenth century." Booklist
Includes bibliographical references

Reiff, Raychel Haugrud. Edgar Allan Poe; tales and poems. Marshall Cavendish Benchmark 2008 157p il (Writers and their works) lib bdg $39.93
Grades: 9 10 11 12 **92**
1. Authors, American
ISBN 978-0-7614-2963-0; 0-7614-2963-8
"A biography of writer Edgar Allan Poe that describes his era, his major works, and the legacy of his writing." Publisher's note
Includes filmography and bibliographical references

Strathern, Paul. Poe in 90 minutes. Ivan R. Dee 2006 111p (Great writers in 90 minutes) $16.95; pa $8.95
Grades: 9 10 11 12 **92**
1. Authors, American
ISBN 978-1-56663-691-9; 1-56663-691-4; 978-1-56663-690-2 (pa); 1-56663-690-6 (pa)
LC 2006-19763
This biographical study of Edgar Allan Poe examines his life and appraises his works, discussing their overall influence on literature. It includes a chronology of his life.
Includes bibliographical references

Polk, James K. (James Knox), 1795-1849
Seigenthaler, John. James K. Polk. Times Books 2004 188p (American presidents series) $20
Grades: 11 12 Adult **92**
1. Presidents—United States
ISBN 0-8050-6942-9 LC 2003-56368
This biography of the often forgotten eleventh president focuses on his accomplishments while in office.
Includes bibliographical references

Prado, Edgar, 1967-
Prado, Edgar. My guy Barbaro; a jockey's journey through love, triumph, and heartbreak with America's favorite horse. Harper 2008 202p il $25.95
Grades: 11 12 Adult **92**
1. Barbaro (Race horse) 2. Horse racing
ISBN 978-0-06-146418-8; 0-06-146418-X
The author relates the "story of Barbaro's rise and fall. One of the most successful jockeys in history, Prado sensed Barbaro's special qualities during a race in Maryland. After going undefeated in their first three races together, Prado and Barbaro shared an easy 2006 Kentucky Derby victory that positioned Barbaro to win the Triple Crown. Disaster struck at the Preakness, however, when Barbaro shattered a leg into more than two dozen pieces just out of the gate. . . . [The author's] journey from a one-room house in Lima, Peru—which he shared with his parents and 10 brothers and sisters—to a place at the top of his profession is fascinating in its own right." Publ Wkly

Presley, Elvis, 1935-1977
Mason, Bobbie Ann. Elvis Presley. Viking 2002 178p (Penguin lives series) hardcover o.p. pa $13 *
Grades: 11 12 Adult **92**
1. Rock musicians
ISBN 0-670-03174-7; 0-14-303889-3 (pa)
LC 2002-28873
"A Lipper/Viking book"
The author "chronicles Elvis' sad story: humble origins, 1954 breakthrough, adoption by 'the Colonel' (manager Tom Parker), early TV appearances, army hitch, the death of his mother, marriage to Priscilla, Hollywood, 1968 'comeback', Las Vegas headliner, prescription drug abuse, meeting with Nixon, and death at 42 in 1977." Booklist
Includes discography, filmography and bibliographical references

Proulx, Annie

Proulx, Annie. Bird cloud; a memoir. Scribner 2011 234p il map $26; ebook $12.99

Grades: 11 12 Adult   **92**

1. Women authors 2. Wyoming—Description and travel

ISBN 978-0-7432-8880-4; 978-1-4391-7171-4 (ebook)

"Proulx bought a 640-acre nature preserve by the North Platte River in Wyoming and started building her dream house, a project that took years and went hundreds of thousands of dollars over budget. In her bustling account, Proulx salivates over the prospect of a Japanese soak tub, polished concrete floor, solar panels, and luxe furnishings that often turn into pricey engineering fiascoes. . . . [This] is a fine evocation of place that becomes a meditation on the importance of a home, however harsh and evanescent." Publ Wkly

Includes bibliographical references

Pullman, Philip, 1946-

Speaker-Yuan, Margaret. Philip Pullman. Chelsea House 2006 118p il (Who wrote that?) lib bdg $30

Grades: 6 7 8 9   **92**

1. Authors, English

ISBN 0-7910-8658-5   LC 2005-8184

This "draws upon an impressive array of sources—particularly Pullman's own writings—to present the groundbreaking author's life and work. . . . What may thrill readers most . . . are the insights into the writing process." Booklist

Includes bibliographical references

Pung, Alice, 1981-

Pung, Alice. Unpolished gem; my mother, my grandmother, and me. Penguin Group 2009 282p pa $15

Grades: 11 12 Adult   **92**

1. Children of immigrants 2. Cambodian refugees 3. Australia

ISBN 978-0-452-29000-6   LC 2008-30365

"A Plume book"

First published 2006 in Australia

The author "recounts the journey her family made over the decades—from China, her grandparents' birthplace, to Cambodia, where her parents are born, through Vietnam and Thailand to Australia where, one month after their arrival, Pung is born. . . . The non-European-immigrant-girl-grows-up story is a familiar one to American readers. What's new about Pung's book is the Australian setting. That twist of focus reveals how more alike than different the experience is." Publ Wkly

Pythagoras

Karamanides, Dimitra. Pythagoras: pioneering mathematician and musical theorist of Ancient Greece. Rosen Pub. Group 2006 112p il map (The library of Greek philosophers) lib bdg $33.25 *

Grades: 9 10 11 12   **92**

1. Mathematicians

ISBN 1-4042-0500-4   LC 2005-11968

Contents: The early years; The traveling student; Egypt and Babylon; A return to Greece; The Pythagorean school; Pythagorean thought; Pythagoras' legacy

This is a biography of Greek mathematician and philosopher.

Includes bibliographical references

Ragusa, Kym

Ragusa, Kym. The skin between us; a memoir of race, beauty, and belonging. W.W. Norton 2006 238p $23.95

Grades: 11 12 Adult   **92**

1. Racially mixed people

ISBN 978-0-393-05890-1; 0-393-05890-5

LC 2005-33673

The author "discusses her 'complex heritage'—her mother is African-American, Native American, Chinese and German; her father is Italian-American." Publ Wkly

"The particulars of Ragusa's story reveal the universal anxiety about belonging and about finding a home in America." Booklist

Raleigh, Sir Walter, 1552?-1618

Aronson, Marc. Sir Walter Ralegh and the quest for El Dorado. Clarion Bks. 2000 222p il map $20

Grades: 7 8 9 10   **92**

1. Explorers

ISBN 0-395-84827-X   LC 99-43096

In this biographical portrait "Ralegh—warrior, champion of North American colonialism, court favorite of Queen Elizabeth I, adventurer and writer—is placed in the center of a broad canvas depicting life in sixteenth-century England and beyond." Horn Book

"Incorporating critical examinations of period art and poetry as well as standard historical documentary evidence and pausing frequently to review and explicitly support its thesis, this title is at once lively, accessible, and challenging. Period illustrations, an index, and fastidiously annotated endnotes and bibliography are included." Bull Cent Child Books

Includes bibliographical references

Ramirez, Manny, 1972-

Rhodes, Jean E. Becoming Manny; inside the life of baseball's most enigmatic slugger; [by] Jean Rhodes and Shawn Boburg. Scribner 2009 304p il $25

Grades: 11 12 Adult   **92**

1. Baseball—Biography

ISBN 978-1-4165-7706-5; 1-4165-7706-8

LC 2009-2348

Authorized biography of Manny Ramirez.

"The authors don't dwell on Ramirez's shortcomings, but neither do they ignore them. On balance, an interesting biography of a baseball lightning rod." Booklist

Randolph, Asa Philip, 1889-1979

Miller, Calvin Craig. A. Philip Randolph and the African American labor movement. Morgan Reynolds 2005 160p il (Portraits of Black Americans) $24.95

Grades: 8 9 10 11 12   **92**

1. African Americans—Biography 2. African Americans—Civil rights 3. Labor unions

ISBN 1-931798-50-8   LC 2004-23706

Randolph, Asa Philip, 1889-1979—*Continued*

A biography of the African American leader

"Miller lucidly traces Randolph's spectacular career while presenting a case study in the effective use of hard-nosed rhetoric and nonviolent tactics to achieve breakthroughs in the fight against segregation. Profusely illustrated with photographs, sometimes in color, and capped by resource lists." Booklist

Includes bibliographical references

Rapp, Emily

Rapp, Emily. Poster child; a memoir. Bloomsbury 2007 229p $23.95; pa $14.95

Grades: 11 12 Adult   **92**

1. Handicapped

ISBN   978-1-59691-256-4;   1-59691-256-1; 978-1-59691-505-3 (pa); 1-59691-505-6 (pa)

LC 2006-12555

"Rapp was an extraordinary child. Born with a congenital defect, she had her left ankle amputated at the age of four. Four years later, after dozens of surgeries, her entire leg below the knee was gone. . . . She became the March of Dimes poster child, an amputee skier, and eventually won a Fulbright Scholarship to Korea. But this is not the story of her achievements. Instead, the book chronicles her poignant journey to make peace with her flaws. . . . Young adults, often obsessed with defects both real and imagined, will identify with the author's need at first to be extraordinary, and then her final acceptance of the imperfect, but valued person she really is." SLJ

Reagan, Ronald, 1911-2004

Helfer, Andrew. Ronald Reagan; a graphic biography; written by Andrew Helfer; art by Steve Buccellato and Joe Staton. Hill and Wang 2007 102p il $16.95

Grades: 9 10 11 12 Adult   **92**

1. Graphic novels 2. Biographical graphic novels 3. Presidents—United States—Graphic novels

ISBN 978-0-8090-9507-0   LC 2006-16437

"A novel graphic from Hill and Wang"

This graphic novel biography covers the life of Ronald Reagan, who began as an actor and ended his career as the fortieth president of the U.S. The book discusses Reagan's work as a union president (Screen Actor's Guild), a General Motors pitchman on television, Governor of California, and his terms as President. It also covers some of the scandals that occurred during his gubernatorial and presidential terms, including the Iran/Contra arms-for-hostages deal, and the assassination attempt by John Hinkley.

Includes bibliographical references

Schaller, Michael. Ronald Reagan. Oxford University Press 2011 105p $12.95

Grades: 11 12 Adult   **92**

1. Presidents—United States

ISBN 978-0-19-975174-7   LC 2010-15726

"Published in Association with the American Council of Learned Societies"

The author "offers a short biography of the 40th President, concentrating mostly on Reagan's two presidential

terms." Libr J

"A fine steppingstone to the vast literature on Reagan, pro and con, Schaller's summary belongs in virtually all U.S. libraries." Booklist

Includes bibliographical references

Sutherland, James. Ronald Reagan; a twentieth century life. Penguin Group 2008 252p il (Up close) $16.99

Grades: 6 7 8 9 10   **92**

1. Presidents—United States

ISBN 978-0-670-06345-1; 0-670-06345-2

LC 2008-21328

"Both a character portrait and an account of Ronald Reagan's life and career(s), this profile sheds as much light on his goals and outlook as it does on his accomplishments. . . . This entry in the valuable Up Close series is a thought-provoking alternative to the plethora of routine assignment titles." Booklist

Reiss, Johanna

Reiss, Johanna. The upstairs room. Crowell 1972 273p hardcover o.p. pa $5.99

Grades: 5 6 7 8 9 10   **92**

1. World War, 1939-1945—Jews 2. Netherlands—History—1940-1945, German occupation 3. Jews—Netherlands 4. Holocaust, 1933-1945—Personal narratives

ISBN 0-690-85127-8; 0-06-440370-X (pa)

"In a vital, moving account the author recalls her experiences as a Jewish child hiding from the Germans occupying her native Holland during World War II. . . . Ten-year-old Annie and her twenty-year-old sister Sini, . . . are taken in by a Dutch farmer, his wife, and mother who hide the girls in an upstairs room of the farm house. Written from the perspective of a child the story affords a child's-eye-view of the war." Booklist

Followed by The journey back

Reyes, Guillermo, 1962-

Reyes, Guillermo. Madre and I; a memoir of our immigrant lives. University of Wisconsin Press 2010 278p il (Writing in Latinidad) pa $18.95

Grades: 11 12 Adult   **92**

1. Hispanic American gay men 2. Immigrants—United States

ISBN 978-0-299-23624-3   LC 2009-41310

The author "had an atypical Latino immigrant experience that provides ample material for this entertaining and stirring memoir. He bares his soul . . . as he tells his story of growing up in Chile, fatherless but with his father's name, and of his journey to Los Angeles, all the while coping with sexuality and body issues. But more than his own coming-of-age, this is the story of his mother, Maria, and her struggles, at times unconventionally approached, to provide a better life for her son. Reyes's recountings of his mother's and her family's adventures are the glue that holds this story together while he writes of shaping his own identity and finding his voice as a writer." Libr J

Rhodes-Courter, Ashley Marie

Rhodes-Courter, Ashley Marie. Three little words; a memoir. Atheneum Books for Young Readers 2008 304p il $17.99; pa $9.99

Grades: 8 9 10 11 12 Adult **92**
1. Adopted children 2. Foster children 3. Foster home care

ISBN 978-1-4169-4806-3; 1-4169-4806-6; 978-1-4169-4807-0 (pa); 1-4169-4807-4 (pa)

LC 2007-21629

The author "chronicles her hardscrabble childhood in foster care, detailing glitches in the system and infringements of laws that led to a string of unsuitable—and sometimes nightmarish—placements for her and her younger half-brother, Luke. Using a matter-of-fact tone at times laced with bitterness, the author recounts how she was wrenched away from her teenage mother at age three and was later removed from her unstable grandfather's home to live in cramped quarters with strangers." Publ Wkly

"This memoir lends a powerful voice to thousands of 'boomerang kids' who repeatedly wind up back in foster care." SLJ

Rice, Condoleezza, 1954-

Felix, Antonia. Condi; the Condoleezza Rice story. New updated ed. Newmarket Press 2005 288p il $19.95

Grades: 11 12 Adult **92**
1. Women politicians 2. African American women—Biography

ISBN 1-55704-675-1 LC 2005-284121

Also available in hardcover from Zondervan and in paperback from Pocket Bks.

First published 2002

"In this portrait of President Bush's national security advisor, Felix . . . presents Rice as perhaps the most influential woman in the history of the U.S. government." Libr J [review of 2002 edition]

Includes bibliographical references

Rice, Condoleezza. Condoleezza Rice; a memoir of my extraordinary, ordinary family and me. Delacorte Press 2010 319p il $16.99; lib bdg $19.99; e-book $9.99

Grades: 7 8 9 10 11 12 **92**
1. Women politicians 2. African American women—Biography

ISBN 978-0-385-73879-8; 0-385-73879-X; 978-0-385-90747-7 (lib bdg); 0-385-90747-8 (lib bdg); 978-0-375-89613-2 (e-book) LC 2010-29878

"The former Secretary of State recounts her life, beginning with her family history and childhood in Birmingham, AL, during the 1950s and '60s. . . . A 16-page insert of black-and-white and color photos adds detail, and the glossary has more information on the many political leaders whom Rice refers to in the book. This valuable memoir about breaking glass ceilings may inspire readers to test their own potential." SLJ

Richardson, Kevin

Richardson, Kevin. Part of the pride; my life among the big cats of Africa; with Tony Park. St. Martin's Press 2009 243p il $25.99

Grades: 11 12 Adult **92**
1. Zookeepers 2. Lions 3. Wild cats

ISBN 978-0-312-55674-7; 0-312-55674-8

LC 2009-16258

"Lion keeper and animal behaviorist Richardson . . . chronicles his life and career while explaining his unique ability to gain the trust of predators like lions and hyenas. . . . An engrossing account of a young life in Africa, this adventurous tale also provides amazing insight into the minds of Africa's most beautiful and dangerous creatures." Publ Wkly

Rickey, Branch, 1881-1965

Breslin, Jimmy. Branch Rickey. Viking 2010 147p (Penguin lives series) $19.95

Grades: 11 12 Adult **92**
1. Brooklyn Dodgers (Baseball team) 2. Baseball—Biography

ISBN 978-0-670-02249-6; 0-670-02249-7

LC 2010-35008

"A Lipper/Viking book"

"Breslin reveals much about the development of baseball, the Dodgers' last years in Brooklyn, and the struggle to overcome the national pastime's racism while tracing the life, deeds, and some (but not all) of Branch Rickey's warts. A breezy read, this 'Penguin Life' is nonetheless insightful, humorous, and biting at times as it traces how the man dubbed 'the Mahatma' by sportswriters emerged from obscurity as an Idaho lawyer to develop the baseball farm system, multiple MLB winners, Vero Beach spring training, the scientific teaching of skills, and the MLB expansion that brought New York the Mets." Libr J

Includes bibliographical references

Riis, Jacob A. (Jacob August), 1849-1914

Pascal, Janet B. Jacob Riis. Oxford University Press 2006 175p il $28

Grades: 9 10 11 12 **92**
1. Reformers

ISBN 978-0-19-514527-4; 0-19-514527-5

LC 2005-7757

Subtitle on cover: Reporter and reformer

"This biography traces Riis's life and evolution into a progressive social reformer. . . . [This is] an insightful work that is sure to hold readers' interest." SLJ

Includes bibliographical references

Ripken, Cal, Jr.

Ripken, Cal, Jr. The only way I know; [by] Cal Ripken, Jr., and Mike Bryan. Viking; distributed by Penguin Putnam 1997 326p il hardcover o.p. pa $12.95

Grades: 11 12 Adult **92**
1. Baseball—Biography

ISBN 0-670-87193-1; 0-14-026626-7 (pa)

LC 97-9159

Ripken, Cal, Jr.—*Continued*

"Cal Junior chronicles his moves through the minor leagues and into the majors in great detail, always pointing out what he learned at each step of the journey and who taught it to him. There are some great baseball anecdotes—especially involving fiery Oriole skipper Earl Weaver—and plenty of the behind-the-scenes detail." Booklist

Robinson, Jackie, 1919-1972

Fussman, Cal. After Jackie; pride, prejudice, and baseball's forgotten heroes: an oral history. ESPN Books 2007 243p il $24.95

Grades: 11 12 Adult   92

1. Baseball—Biography 2. African American athletes
ISBN 1-93306-018-2; 978-1-93306-018-7

The author "traces Robinson's enormous legacy in sports, politics, and the civil rights movement through the men and women who came after him." Publisher's note

Robinson, Jackie. I never had it made; an autobiography; by Jackie Robinson as told to Alfred Duckett; foreword by Cornel West; introduction by Hank Aaron. Ecco Press 1995 xxii, 275p il pa $13.95 hardcover o.p. *

Grades: 11 12 Adult   92

1. Baseball—Biography 2. African American athletes
ISBN 0-06-055597-1   LC 94-45279

A reissue of the title first published 1972 by Putnam

This book "focuses on Robinson's political involvements after his career ended in 1956 and his friendships with such diverse characters as Martin Luther King, Malcolm X, William Buckley and Nelson Rockefeller." Publ Wkly

"Included are introductions by Hank Aaron and Cornel West that provide fresh perspectives on the significance of the legendary star's breaking of major league baseball's color barrier. With each retelling, it is clear that Robinson's story has become less a baseball story than a major cultural milestone in the nation's history." Libr J

Robison, John Elder, 1957-

Robison, John Elder. Look me in the eye; my life with Asperger's. Crown Publishers 2007 288p $25.95 *

Grades: 11 12 Adult   92

1. Asperger's syndrome
ISBN 978-0-307-39598-6; 0-307-39598-7
LC 2007-13139

In this memoir, the author describes growing up with Asperger's syndrome (which went undiagnosed until he was 40 years old), dealing with an alcoholic father and a mentally unstable mother, and developing an affinity for machines that would eventually lead him to a career restoring classic cars.

"Robison's memoir is must reading for its unblinking (as only an Aspergian can) glimpse into the life of a person who had to wait decades for the medical community to catch up with him." Booklist

Includes bibliographical references

Rodriguez, Richard, 1944-

Rodriguez, Richard. Hunger of memory; the education of Richard Rodriguez: an autobiography. Bantam trade pbk. ed. Bantam Books 2004 212p pa $15

Grades: 11 12 Adult   92

1. Mexican Americans—Biography
ISBN 0-553-38251-9   LC 2004-269979

First published 1982 by Godine

An account "of the coming of age of a person of Mexican descent and culture in American society and the inevitable transition in the private life of his family. Rodriguez focuses on his educational experiences, from his parochial elementary school . . . to his university years and subsequent experience as an educator." Libr J

Rogers, Will, 1879-1935

Yagoda, Ben. Will Rogers; a biography. Knopf 1993 409p il pa $24.95

Grades: 11 12 Adult   92

1. Entertainers
ISBN 0-8061-3238-8   LC 92-40177

This is a biography of "the rope-twirling vaudeville monologist, salty political commentator, silent film actor and *New York Times* columnist. . . . [This is] a resonant portrait imbued with Rogers's irreverent spirit, yet attuned to both the strengths and limitations of his commonsense, crackerbarrel world view." Publ Wkly

Includes bibliographical references

Roosevelt, Eleanor, 1884-1962

The Eleanor Roosevelt encyclopedia; edited by Maurine H. Beasley, Holly C. Shulman, and Henry R. Beasley; foreword by Blanche Wiesen Cook; introduction by James McGregor Burns. Greenwood Press 2000 xxvi, 628p il $73.95

Grades: 11 12 Adult   92

1. United States—Politics and government—1933-1945
ISBN 0-313-30181-6   LC 00-23530

This reference work "examines the many roles of our foremost First Lady. Given Roosevelt's significance and appeal, this volume is an exception to the rule that encyclopedic treatments of single individuals belong only in larger collections." Booklist

Includes bibliographical references

Freedman, Russell. Eleanor Roosevelt; a life of discovery. Clarion Bks. 1993 198p il hardcover o.p. pa $11.95 *

Grades: 5 6 7 8 9 10   92

1. Presidents' spouses—United States
ISBN 0-89919-862-7; 0-395-84520-3 (pa)
LC 92-25024

This "traces the life of the former First Lady from her early childhood through the tumultuous years in the White House to her active role in the founding of the United Nations after World War II." Publisher's note

"This impeccably researched, highly readable study of one of this country's greatest First Ladies is nonfiction at its best. . . . Approximately 140 well-chosen black-and-white photos amplify the text." Publ Wkly

Includes bibliographical references

Roosevelt, Eleanor, 1884-1962—*Continued*

Keating, Anjelina Michelle. Eleanor Roosevelt. Library of Congress 2006 64p il (Women who dare) $12.95 *
Grades: 9 10 11 12   **92**
1. Presidents' spouses—United States
ISBN 0-7649-3543-7; 978-0-7649-3543-5
    LC 2005-49544
This autobiography "traces Eleanor's life story, exploring the childhood that left her lonely and insecure, and surveying the challenges and opportunities that spurred her transformation into one of the twentieth century's most admired and respected public citizens." Publisher's note
Includes bibliographical references

Roosevelt, Franklin D. (Franklin Delano), 1882-1945
Freedman, Russell. Franklin Delano Roosevelt. Clarion Bks. 1990 200p il hardcover o.p. pa $9.95 *
Grades: 5 6 7 8 9 10   **92**
1. Presidents—United States 2. United States—Politics and government—1933-1945
ISBN 0-89919-379-X; 0-395-62978-0 (pa)
    LC 89-34986
The author "traces the personal and public events in a life that led to the formation of one of the most influential and magnetic leaders of the twentieth century." Horn Book
"The carefully researched, highly readable text and extremely effective coordination of black-and-white photographs chronicle Roosevelt's priviledged youth, his early influences, and his maturation. . . . Even students with little or no background in American history will find this an intriguing and inspirational human portrait." SLJ
Includes bibliographical references

Roosevelt, Theodore, 1858-1919
Cooper, Michael L. Theodore Roosevelt; a twentieth-century life. Viking 2009 208p il (Up close) $16.99 *
Grades: 7 8 9 10   **92**
1. Presidents—United States
ISBN 978-0-670-01134-6; 0-670-01134-7
    LC 2010-279534
Title on jacket: Theodore Roosevelt adventurer; a twentieth-century life
"This biography presents an evenhanded account of the life and presidency of Theodore Roosevelt. . . . This clearly written biography includes many anecdotes and well-chosen quotes that help bring Roosevelt to life. . . . Cooper offers a solid portrayal of this noteworthy American president." Booklist
Includes bibliographical references

DiSilvestro, Roger L. Theodore Roosevelt in the Badlands; a young politician's quest for recovery in the American West. Walker & Co. 2011 352p il map $27
Grades: 11 12 Adult   **92**
1. Presidents—United States 2. Frontier and pioneer life—North Dakota 3. Ranch life
ISBN 978-0-8027-1721-4   LC 2010-44297
"Focused on TR in his twenties, DiSilvestro's work elaborates on the future president's days devoted to hunting and ranching in the Dakota Territory. . . . With its sources fully researched and capably integrated, DiSilvestro's account definitively fills in this part of TR's story." Booklist
Includes bibliographical references

Donald, Aida D. Lion in the White House; a life of Theodore Roosevelt. Basic Books 2007 287p il hardcover o.p. pa $15.95
Grades: 11 12 Adult   **92**
1. Presidents—United States
ISBN 978-0-465-00213-9; 0-465-00213-7; 978-0-465-01024-0 (pa); 0-465-01024-5 (pa)
    LC 2007-34122
This is a "biography of Theodore Roosevelt. . . . [The author] not only shows how he propelled the United States from provincial status into a world power but also sheds light on how much he identified with his chief political hero, Abraham Lincoln. . . . [This account] will appeal to a broad array of readers, both those already admiring the man and those new to him." Libr J
Includes bibliographical references

Marrin, Albert. The great adventure: Theodore Roosevelt and the rise of modern America. Dutton Children's Books 2007 248p il $30 *
Grades: 8 9 10 11   **92**
1. Presidents—United States
ISBN 978-0-525-47659-7; 0-525-47659-8
    LC 2006-35912
"Marrin offers a twin portrait of American society in a time of profound change and the life of a figure so dominant in the politics and self-image of the time that he has become an enduring symbol. . . . Marrin gives him 'a place in the front rank of our country's heroes,' particularly for his achievements in environmental conservation, but also shows him acting badly. . . . Numerous endnotes and contemporary photos and prints add to this scholarly profile, which . . . will give serious history students a solid grounding in the man's times, career, and forceful character." Booklist
Includes bibliographical references

Renehan, Edward J. The lion's pride: Theodore Roosevelt and his family in peace and war; [by] Edward J. Renehan, Jr. Oxford Univ. Press 1998 289p il $55; pa $44.99 *
Grades: 11 12 Adult   **92**
1. Roosevelt family 2. Presidents—United States
ISBN 0-19-512719-6; 0-19-513424-9 (pa)
    LC 98-23998
Although this work explores Roosevelt's influential role as a former president, it primarily explores his relationship with his four sons and daughter.

Roosevelt, Theodore, 1858-1919—*Continued*
"Renehan's portraits of the children further enrich a superb, real-life family saga." Booklist
Includes bibliographical references

Rosenberg, Ethel, 1915-1953
Philipson, Ilene J. Ethel Rosenberg; beyond the myths; by Ilene Philipson. Rutgers University Press 1993 390p pa $22
Grades: 11 12 Adult   **92**
  1. Spies 2. Trials (Espionage)
  ISBN 0-8135-1917-9; 978-0-8135-1917-3
         LC 92-23750
First published 1988 by Watts
"Without attempting a definitive judgment on whether Ethel Rosenberg was a Communist spy or a martyr to political paranoia, Philipson aims for a deeper understanding of her subject's personality, beliefs, and actions. The book covers the many complex conflicts that made up Rosenberg's life and career." Booklist
This is "a fine psycho-historical study of a complex figure." BAYA Book Rev
Includes bibliographical references

Rowling, J. K.
Kirk, Connie Ann. J.K. Rowling: a biography. Greenwood Press 2003 141p il (Greenwood biographies) $29.95
Grades: 9 10 11 12   **92**
  1. Authors, English 2. Women authors
  ISBN 0-313-32205-8   LC 2002-75330
"Rowling's biography opens with a brief chapter defining her current status in the celebrity world. Subsequent chapters cover her early life and family, her school years, and her early career as a teacher. A long chapter is devoted to Harry Potter, and the volume concludes with controversies and criticisms surrounding the author's life and work." Voice Youth Advocates
"Although there is information about the author herself, the majority of the content is devoted to analyzing her writing. . . . The scholarly writing style and evaluative content make this volume useful to high school students studying Rowling and her work." SLJ
Includes bibliographical references

Runyon, Brent
Runyon, Brent. The burn journals. Alfred A. Knopf 2004 373p hardcover o.p. pa $13.95 *
Grades: 7 8 9 10   **92**
  1. Burns and scalds 2. Suicide
  ISBN 0-375-82621-1; 1-4000-9642-1 (pa)
         LC 2004-5643
"One February day in 1991, Runyon came home from eighth grade . . . and set himself on fire. . . . The dialogue between Runyon and his nurses, parents, and especially his hapless psychotherapists is natural and believable, and his inner dialogue is flip, often funny, and sometimes raw. . . . The authentically adolescent voice of the journals will engage even those reluctant to read such a dark story." SLJ

Rusesabagina, Paul
Rusesabagina, Paul. An ordinary man; an autobiography; [by] Paul Rusesabagina with Tom Zoellner. Viking 2006 207p map $23.95; pa $14
Grades: 11 12 Adult   **92**
  1. Rwanda
  ISBN 0-670-03752-4; 978-0-670-03752-0; 0-14-303860-5 (pa); 978-0-14-303860-3 (pa)
         LC 2005-43488
Paul Rusesabagina, whose story inspired the film *Hotel Rwanda*, discusses "his life before, during, and after the genocide. In early April 1994, hotel manager Rusesabagina filled his rooms with 1,268 people and helped them survive by drinking swimming pool water and eating scavenged food." Christ Today

Russell, Charles M. (Charles Marion), 1864-1926
Hassrick, Peter H. Charles M. Russell. University of Okla. Press 1999 155p il pa $34.95
Grades: 11 12 Adult   **92**
  1. Artists—United States
  ISBN 0-8061-3142-X   LC 98-44419
First published 1989 by Abrams as part of the Library of American art series
A biographical and critical "study of the quintessential cowboy artist. . . . Hassrick describes Russell's career ably and verifies his reputation as a most appealing workingman artist via 52 resplendent colorplates and nearly as many black-and-white figures." Booklist
Includes bibliographical references

Rustin, Bayard, 1910-1987
Miller, Calvin Craig. No easy answers; Bayard Rustin and the civil rights movement. Morgan Reynolds Pub. 2005 160p il lib bdg $24.95
Grades: 7 8 9 10   **92**
  1. African Americans—Civil rights 2. African Americans—Biography
  ISBN 1-931798-43-5   LC 2004-18518
"Miller combines the life story of a great social activist with the history of the struggle for civil rights in the U.S. The politics are exciting, with details of the radical campaigns in the 1940s and 1950s, Rustin's impassioned call for nonviolent protest, and his role in organizing both the Montgomery Bus Boycott and the 1963 March on Washington." Booklist
Includes bibliographical references

Ruth, Babe, 1895-1948
Hampton, Wilborn. Babe Ruth; a twentieth-century life. Viking 2009 203p il (Up close) $16.99
Grades: 6 7 8 9 10   **92**
  1. Baseball—Biography
  ISBN 978-0-670-06305-5; 0-670-06305-3
         LC 2008-21550
"Hampton announces early in this biography of Babe Ruth that his emphasis is on separating fact from legend, and he is not afraid to dig up some of the more tawdry aspects of the slugger's life. . . . The focus here is on Ruth's sad early life and his career as a pitcher with the

Ruth, Babe, 1895-1948—*Continued*
Boston Red Sox. Throughout, an attempt is made to give some sense of the grace, power, and skill of Ruth on the field. . . . [This title,] illustrated with a nice selection of photos, has the advantage of telling the complete, unvarnished story in a snappy, concise style." Booklist
Includes bibliographical references

Rutherford, Ernest, 1871-1937
Reeves, Richard. A force of nature; the frontier genius of Ernest Rutherford. W. W. Norton & Co. 2008 207p il (Great discoveries) $23.95
Grades: 11 12 Adult **92**
   1. Physicists
   ISBN 978-0-393-05750-8; 0-393-05750-X
                   LC 2007-33184
"Atlas books"
The author "re-introduces Ernest Rutherford, one of the founding geniuses of nuclear physics. . . . This biography does an outstanding job of capturing the excitement and almost breathless pace of physics research in the 20th century's first four decades." Publ Wkly
Includes bibliographical references

Sacagawea, b. 1786
Berne, Emma Carlson. Sacagawea; crossing the continent with Lewis & Clark. Sterling 2010 124p il map (Sterling biographies) lib bdg $12.95; pa $5.95
Grades: 7 8 9 10 **92**
   1. Lewis and Clark Expedition (1804-1806)
   2. Shoshone Indians 3. Native Americans—Biography
   4. West (U.S.)—Exploration
   ISBN 978-1-4027-6845-3 (lib bdg); 1-4027-6845-1 (lib bdg); 978-1-4027-5738-9 (pa); 1-4027-5738-7 (pa)
                   LC 2009-24139
"Contrary to myth, *Sacagawea* explains that the Shoshone teen was not a princess, her relationship with Clark was platonic, and she was a peace symbol rather than a guide until they finally reached the Shoshone tribe. . . . [The] spacious design is highly scannable, with color background screens, photos, maps, and historic prints throughout." Booklist
Includes glossary and bibliographical references

Nelson, W. Dale. Interpreters with Lewis and Clark: the story of Sacagawea and Toussaint Charbonneau. University of North Texas Press 2003 174p il, maps $24.95; pa $14.95 *
Grades: 9 10 11 12 **92**
   1. Charbonneau, Toussaint, ca. 1758-ca. 1839
   2. Charbonneau, Jean-Baptiste, 1805-1866 3. Lewis and Clark Expedition (1804-1806)
   ISBN 1-57441-165-9; 1-57441-181-0 (pa)
                   LC 2003-4343
This is a biography of the husband and wife team of interpreters that were a part of the Lewis and Clark Expedition, as well as their son, Jean Baptiste
Includes bibliographical references

Sacks, Oliver W.
Sacks, Oliver W. Uncle Tungsten; memories of a chemical boyhood; [by] Oliver Sacks. Knopf 2001 337p il hardcover o.p. pa $14
Grades: 11 12 Adult **92**
   1. Physicians
   ISBN 0-375-40448-1; 0-375-70404-3 (pa)
                   LC 2001-33738
"Sacks' first scientific love was chemistry, and he presents an avid history of the field within a memoir that pays tribute to his uncle, who welcomed Sacks into his lab, thus encouraging his passion for chemistry and learning." Booklist

Salbi, Zainab
Salbi, Zainab. Between two worlds; escape from tyranny: growing up in the shadow of Saddam; [by] Zainab Salbi and Laurie Becklund. Gotham Books 2005 295p $26; pa $14
Grades: 11 12 Adult **92**
   1. Hussein, Ṣaddām 2. Women—Iraq
   ISBN   1-59240-156-2;   978-1-59240-156-7; 1-59240-244-5 (pa); 978-1-59240-244-1 (pa)
                   LC 2006-276819
The author discusses her childhood in Iraq, how life was changed by the accession to power of Saddam Hussein, her arranged marriage in America to an abusive husband, and her founding of an organization called Women for Women International.
"Through a journey colored with loss and hope, readers encounter a story of self-awakening and of realizing the will to live and survive." Libr J

Salinger, J. D., 1919-2010
Reiff, Raychel Haugrud. J.D. Salinger; The Catcher in the Rye and other works. Marshall Cavendish Benchmark 2007 158p il (Writers and their works) $39.93 *
Grades: 9 10 11 12 **92**
   1. Authors, American
   ISBN 978-0-7614-2594-6   LC 2006-19236
This book contains a biography of J.D. Salinger, a description of the times in which he wrote his most famous works, and critical discussions of his works including *The Catcher in the Rye*.
Includes filmography and bibliographical references

Salk, Jonas, 1914-1995
Kluger, Jeffrey. Splendid solution: Jonas Salk and the conquest of polio. G.P. Putnam's Sons 2004 373p il hardcover o.p. pa $15 *
Grades: 11 12 Adult **92**
   1. Poliomyelitis
   ISBN 0-399-15216-4; 0-425-20570-3 (pa)
                   LC 2004-50527
The author "tells how polio was beaten 50 years ago in one of the triumphs of modern medicine. The narrative naturally centers on Jonas Salk, whose lab developed the first polio vaccine." Publ Wkly
"Can't-put-it-down medical-science history." Booklist
Includes bibliographical references

Salk, Jonas, 1914-1995—*Continued*

Sherrow, Victoria. Jonas Salk; beyond the microscope. 2nd rev ed. Chelsea House 2008 146p il (Makers of modern science) $35

Grades: 7 8 9 10   **92**
1. Scientists 2. Poliomyelitis vaccine
ISBN 978-0-8160-6180-8; 0-8160-6180-7
                              LC 2006-33429
First published 1993 by Facts on File

This biography of Jonas Salk "describes this respected immunologist's medical research and his lifelong efforts to promote scientific and human progress on a global scale." Publisher's note

Includes glossary and bibliographical references

Sandifer, Robert, d. 1994

Neri, Greg. Yummy; the last days of a Southside Shorty; by G. Neri; illustrated by Randy DuBurke. Lee & Low Books 2010 94p il pa $16.95 *

Grades: 8 9 10 11 12   **92**
1. Biographical graphic novels 2. African Americans—Graphic novels 3. Gangs—Graphic novels 4. Violence—Graphic novels 5. Chicago (Ill.)—Graphic novels 6. Graphic novels
ISBN 978-1-58430-267-4 (pa); 1-58430-267-4 (pa)
                              LC 2006-17771
"A graphic novel based on the true story of Robert 'Yummy' Sandifer, an eleven-year old African American gang member from Chicago who shot a young girl and was then shot by his own gang members." Publisher's note

"Neri's straightforward, unadorned prose is the perfect complement to DuBurke's stark black-and-white inks; great slabs of shadow and masterfully rendered faces breathe real, tragic life into the players." Publ Wkly

Santiago, Esmeralda

Santiago, Esmeralda. When I was Puerto Rican; [a memoir] Da Capo Press 2006 c1993 278p pa $13.95

Grades: 11 12 Adult   **92**
1. Puerto Ricans—United States
ISBN 0-306-81452-8; 978-0-306-81452-5
First published 1993 by Addison-Wesley

The author "tells of her childhood in Puerto Rico in the 1950s and of her family's move to New York when she was 13." Libr J

"At once heart-wrenching and remarkably inspirational, this lyrical account depicts rural life in Puerto Rico amid the hardships and tensions of everyday life and Santiago's awakening as a young woman, who, although startled by culture shock, valiantly confronted New York head-on. When in the epilogue Santiago refers to her studies at Harvard, it is both a stirring and poignant reminder of the capacities of the human spirit." Booklist

Other autobiographical titles by the author are:
Almost a woman (1998)
The Turkish lover (2004)

Satrapi, Marjane, 1969-

Satrapi, Marjane. The complete Persepolis. Pantheon Books 2007 341p il pa $24.95 *

Grades: 11 12 Adult   **92**
1. Graphic novels 2. Autobiographical graphic novels 3. Iran—Graphic novels
ISBN 978-0-375-71483-2   LC 2007-60106
Originally published in two separate volumes 2003-2004

This "is the story of Satrapi's . . . childhood and coming of age within a large and loving family in Tehran during the Islamic Revolution; of the contradictions between private life and public life in a country plagued by political upheaval; of her high school years in Vienna facing the trials of adolescence far from her family; of her homecoming—both sweet and terrible; and, finally, of her self-imposed exile from her beloved homeland." Publisher's note

Sayrafiezadeh, Saïd

Sayrafiezadeh, Saïd. When skateboards will be free; a memoir of a political childhood. Dial Press 2009 287p $22; pa $15

Grades: 11 12 Adult   **92**
1. Socialist Workers' Party (U.S.) 2. Socialism
ISBN   978-0-385-34068-7;   0-385-34068-0; 978-0-385-34069-4 (pa); 0-385-34069-9 (pa)
                              LC 2008-51096
"A Dial Press book"

The author presents a memoir "of growing up with (and without) his parents, ardent members of the Socialist Workers Party." N Y Times (Late N Y Ed)

"An enormously talented writer, Sayrafiezadeh ably conveys a complex blend of affection and anger toward his deeply flawed parents in deftly controlled prose. An excellent memoir." Kirkus

Scdoris, Rachael

Scdoris, Rachael. No end in sight; my life as a blind Iditarod racer; [by] Rachael Scdoris and Rick Steber. St. Martin's Press 2006 278p il $22.95; pa $13.95

Grades: 8 9 10 11 12   **92**
1. Women athletes 2. Blind 3. Sled dog racing
ISBN   0-312-35273-5;   978-0-312-35273-8; 0-312-36437-7 (pa); 978-0-312-36437-3 (pa)
                              LC 2005-20897
"Revised and fully updated"
First published 2005 by Two Star

"Twenty-year-old Scdoris, afflicted with a rare eye disorder that makes her 20-200 vision impervious to correction, recounts her journey to Alaska's famous sled dog race in this . . . memoir." Publ Wkly

"Readers will feel every twist and turn in the course, and will eagerly follow the progress of this inspiring athlete." SLJ

Scheeres, Julia, 1967-

Scheeres, Julia. Jesus land; a memoir. Counterpoint 2005 356p $23; pa $14

Grades: 11 12 Adult   **92**

1. Adoption 2. Siblings 3. Child abuse 4. Christian life 5. United States—Race relations

ISBN 1-58243-338-0; 1-58243-354-2 (pa)

    LC 2005-14816

The author writes about her "bond with the boy her fundamentalist family adopted and abused." N Y Times Book Rev

"Tinged with sadness yet pervaded by a sense of triumph, Scheeres's book is a crisply written and earnest examination of the meaning of family and Christian values." Publ Wkly

Schein, Elyse

Schein, Elyse. Identical strangers; a memoir of twins separated and reunited; [by] Elyse Schein, Paula Bernstein. Random House 2007 270p il $25.95

Grades: 11 12 Adult   **92**

1. Bernstein, Paula 2. Twins

ISBN 978-1-4000-6496-0; 1-4000-6496-1

    LC 2007-14488

"Reunited at the age of 35, . . . [the authors, who are identical twins,] embarked on a journey to uncover the story of their separation. Research into their genealogical background revealed an ethically questionable study on identical twins performed by the doctors associated with the agency that facilitated their adoptions. In alternating voices, the women detail their emotional struggles as they navigated their developing relationship and the realities of the circumstances surrounding their birth and separation. . . . Teens will be pulled in by the mystery surrounding the study and the identity of the authors' birth mother." SLJ

Schutz, Samantha, 1978-

Schutz, Samantha. I don't want to be crazy; a memoir of anxiety disorder. PUSH Books 2006 280p $16.99

Grades: 8 9 10 11 12   **92**

1. Anxiety 2. Panic disorders

ISBN 0-439-80518-X   LC 2005028964

"In this moving memoir, Schutz details her struggle with anxiety disorder. . . . Written in verse, this memoir successfully conveys what it is like to suffer from panic attacks." Voice Youth Advocates

Scott, Wendell, 1921-1990

Donovan, Brian. Hard driving: the Wendell Scott story; the odyssey of NASCAR'S first Black driver. Steerfort Press 2008 311p il hardcover o.p. pa $16.99

Grades: 11 12 Adult   **92**

1. Automobile racing 2. African American athletes

ISBN 978-1-58642-144-1; 978-1-58642-160-1 (pa)

    LC 2008-24287

For this biography, the author "interviewed Scott extensively over the last 14 months of his life. He also interviewed more than 200 other individuals, including

Scott's widow and children. The result is the gripping story of a fascinating, brave man who deserves serious recognition for his solitary accomplishment. . . . A must-read for NASCAR fans." Booklist

Includes bibliographical references

Sediqi, Kamela, 1977-

Tzemach Lemmon, Gayle. The dressmaker of Khair Khana; five sisters, one remarkable family, and the woman who risked everything to keep them safe. Harper 2011 256p $24.99

Grades: 11 12 Adult   **92**

1. Taliban 2. Afghanistan 3. Dressmaking 4. Businesswomen

ISBN 978-0-06-173237-9   LC 2010-20774

The author "tells the moving story of Kamila Sidiqi, a young woman in Kabul, Afghanistan, who, out of desperation, started a successful dressmaking business to support her family and other destitute women during the repressive Taliban regime." Libr J

This book "is a fascinating window on Afghan life under the Taliban and a celebration ofwomen the world over who support their loved ones with tenacity, inventiveness and sheer guts." People

Includes bibliographical references

Seeger, Pete

Wilkinson, Alec. The protest singer; an intimate portrait of Pete Seeger. Alfred A. Knopf 2009 151p il $22.95; pa $14

Grades: 11 12 Adult   **92**

1. Singers

ISBN 978-0-307-26995-9; 978-0-307-39098-1 (pa)

    LC 2008-54387

The author "draws on interviews with Seeger and others to present a seamless chronicle of his life and music, vivifying his passion for humanity, love of the environment, and deep curiosity about music." Libr J

Seuss, Dr.

Pease, Donald E. Theodor Seuss Geisel. Oxford University Press 2010 178p il $19.95

Grades: 11 12 Adult   **92**

1. Authors, American 2. Illustrators

ISBN 9780195323023   LC 2009-36478

The author presents a "look into the life of the artist and author best known as Dr. Seuss." Publ Wkly

This "biography offers a succinct, thoroughly researched, and engaging introduction to one of children's literature's most influential creators." Booklist

Includes bibliographical references

Shakur, Tupac

Dyson, Michael Eric. Holler if you hear me: searching for Tupac Shakur. Basic Bks. 2001 292p il hardcover o.p. pa $15

Grades: 11 12 Adult   **92**

1. African American musicians 2. Rap music 3. Hip-hop

ISBN 0-465-01755-X; 0-465-01728-2 (pa)

    LC 2001-36564

Shakur, Tupac—_Continued_

In this biography of the late rapper, Dyson "examines Tupac both culturally and spiritually through a loosely organized series of meditations that begin in Tupac's childhood . . . and move through his manhood." New Yorker

"Dyson's discussion goes beyond slogans and poses to the actualities of 'thug life' and the consequences of Shakur's passions and allegiances. Piquant and analytical." Booklist

Includes bibliographical references

Golus, Carrie. Tupac Shakur; hip-hop idol. Twenty-First Century Books 2010 112p il (USA Today: lifeline biographies) lib bdg $33.26
Grades: 7 8 9 10 11 12   92
1. African American musicians 2. Rap music
ISBN 978-0-7613-5473-4; 0-7613-5473-5
LC 2009-38127

"The story told in _Tupac Shakur_ will be inspirational for some and a cautionary tale for others. Born into poverty, Shakur became one of hip-hop's biggest stars. But even as he climbed up the ladder of success, drugs and violence were always there to pull him back down." Booklist

Includes bibliographical references

White, Armond. Rebel for the hell of it; the life of Tupac Shakur; [new foreword by S.H. Fernando] New ed. Thunder's Mouth Press 2002 xxii, 230p il pa $14.95
Grades: 11 12 Adult   92
1. African American musicians 2. Rap music 3. Hip-hop
ISBN 1-56025-461-0
First published 1997

In this biography of the rap musician and actor, "White outlines his stint as a dancer with the Digital Underground, his breakthrough second album, his three subsequent multiplatinum efforts, and his various roles in such movies as Juice and Poetic Justice. He also details the rapper's trouble with the law, his incarceration at Riker's Island prison, and his untimely death. . . . This will appeal mostly to fans of standard rock biography." Libr J

Includes discography and filmography

Shen, Fan, 1955-

Shen, Fan. Gang of one; memoirs of a Red Guard. University of Nebraska Press 2004 279p (American lives) $24.95; pa $15.95
Grades: 9 10 11 12   92
1. China—History—1949-1976—Personal narratives
ISBN 0-8032-4308-1; 0-8032-9336-4 (pa)
LC 2003-17901

"Shen, age 12 at the start of the Cultural Revolution in 1966, recounts being complicit in arduous Red Guard activities that directly or indirectly led to several gruesome deaths of political 'enemies'—and later falling in love with and marrying the daughter of a man brutally tortured and killed by one of his fellow Red Guards." Publ Wkly

"Teens will strongly identify with Shen's maneuverings around repressive regulations." Booklist

Shepard, Sadia

Shepard, Sadia. The girl from foreign; a search for shipwrecked ancestors, forgotten histories, and a sense of home. Penguin Press 2008 364p il map $25.95; pa $16
Grades: 11 12 Adult   92
1. Jews—India
ISBN 978-1-59420-151-6; 978-0-14-311577-9 (pa)
LC 2008-3912

A young Muslim-Christian woman travels to an insular Jewish community in India to unlock her family's secret history.

"A readable account that gives a vivid taste of life in present-day India as well as a poignant glimpse of complicated family relations." Kirkus

Includes bibliographical references

Sherman, William T. (William Tecumseh), 1820-1891

Koestler-Grack, Rachel A. William Tecumseh Sherman; [by] Rachel Koestler-Grack. Chelsea House Publishers 2009 149p il (Leaders of the Civil War era) lib bdg $30
Grades: 7 8 9 10   92
1. Generals 2. United States—History—1861-1865, Civil War
ISBN 978-1-60413-300-4; 1-60413-300-7
LC 2008-45707

A biography of Union general William Tecumseh Sherman.

Includes glossary and bibliographical references

Woodworth, Steven E. Sherman; [foreword by Wesley K. Clark] Palgrave Macmillan 2009 198p il map (Great generals series) $21.95
Grades: 9 10 11 12 Adult   92
1. Generals 2. United States—History—1861-1865, Civil War
ISBN 0-230-61024-2; 978-0-230-61024-8
LC 2008-22060

This is a biography of the Civil War general.

"An excellent brief life of a major and controversial figure." Booklist

Includes bibliographical references

Siana, Jolene

Siana, Jolene. Go ask Ogre; letters from a deathrock cutter. Process 2005 188p il pa $18.95
Grades: 11 12 Adult   92
1. Self-mutilation
ISBN 0-9760822-1-7; 978-0-9760822-1-7

"When she was 17, Siana wrote a series of letters to punk rocker Ogre, the front man of the '80s band Skinny Puppy. The letters speak of depression and cutting, drug abuse and sex, music and poetry. At one concert, Ogre told her that he saved all her letters and one day would return them. True to his word, two boxes arrived at her door nine years later; inside were illustrated letters and journals filled with her most intimate thoughts and fears. . . . Almost every page of the book is filled with heartbreaking artwork and photos, which brilliantly link the journal entries and letters together, allowing readers to get a look inside the mind of a very creative but disturbed young woman." SLJ

Simon, Beth

Simon, Rachel. Riding the bus with my sister. See entry under Simon, Rachel, 1959-

Simon, Lizzie

Simon, Lizzie. Detour; my bipolar road trip in 4-D. Pocket Books 2001 211p hardcover o.p. pa $13

Grades: 11 12 Adult   92
    1. Mental illness
    ISBN 0-7434-4659-3; 0-7434-4660-7 (pa)
                                            LC 2001-60261

"In fall 1999, twentysomething Simon, who had suffered one full-blown manic episode in her late teens and who controlled her symptoms with lithium, decided to put aside her career as a theatrical producer to seek out other highly successful young manic-depressives. Instead, she encounters a differing array of bipolars, from a multimillionaire who can't control his drug and alcohol use to people who have been institutionalized. . . . This book will resonate with younger readers." Libr J

Simon, Rachel, 1959-

Simon, Rachel. Riding the bus with my sister; a true life journey. Plume 2003 296p pa $15

Grades: 11 12 Adult   92
    1. Simon, Beth 2. Mentally handicapped
    ISBN 0-452-28455-4

First published 2002 by Houghton Mifflin

"Simon's memoir . . . tells the story of her relationship with her sister, Beth, who is mentally retarded. . . . [Rachel] is perplexed by how Beth spends all of her time: riding buses. . . . Rachel's story begins when a newspaper editor suggests that she write a column about riding the bus with her sister. Beth is so pleased to spend time with her that she asks her to continue riding with her for a year. Reluctantly, Rachel agrees." Women's Rev Books

"Clear writing and repeated conversations allow readers to hear the voices of both sisters. There is much to mull over, to enjoy, and to savor in this book." SLJ

Simpson, Colton

Simpson, Colton. Inside the Crips; life inside L.A.'s most notorious gang; [by] Colton Simpson with Ann Pearlman. St. Martin's Press 2005 xxiii, 323p $24.95; pa $14.95

Grades: 11 12 Adult   92
    1. Crips (Gang)
    ISBN 0-312-32929-6; 0-312-30930-X (pa)
                                            LC 2005-42704

The author "provides an insider's perspective on day-to-day life in the Crips, the gang's history (including quite a bit about its rival, the Bloods), and the plight of growing up in the 'hood while wanting a better life. . . . This unvarnished portrayal of gang life is enlightening and even inspiring about a subject badly in need of illumination." Booklist

Sís, Peter, 1949-

Sís, Peter. The wall; growing up behind the Iron Curtain. Farrar, Straus and Giroux 2007 unp il $18 *

Grades: 4 5 6 7 8 9 10   92
    1. Cold war 2. Prague (Czech Republic)
    ISBN 978-0-374-34701-7; 0-374-34701-8
                                            LC 2006-49149

"Frances Foster books"

"The author pairs his remarkable artistry with journal entries, historical context and period photography to create a powerful account of his childhood in Cold War-era Prague." Publ Wkly

Sitting Bull, Dakota Chief, 1831-1890

Stanley, George Edward. Sitting Bull; great Sioux hero. Sterling 2010 124p il map (Sterling biographies) lib bdg $12.95

Grades: 7 8 9 10   92
    1. Dakota Indians 2. Native Americans—Biography
    ISBN 978-1-4027-6846-0 (lib bdg); 1-4027-6846-X (lib bdg)   LC 2009-24141
    This is a biography of the Sioux Indian chief.
    Includes glossary and bibliographical references

Small, David, 1945-

Small, David. Stitches; a memoir. W.W. Norton 2009 329p il $23.95 *

Grades: 10 11 12 Adult   92
    1. Graphic novels 2. Autobiographical graphic novels 3. Family life—Graphic novels 4. Cancer—Graphic novels
    ISBN 978-0-393-06857-3; 0-393-06857-9
                                            LC 2009-22526

David Small grew up in a dysfunctional family, with a radiologist father who was distant, an angry mother who expressed her anger in eloquent silences, and an older brother who played drums a lot to express his frustrations. When he was eleven, he had a lump, a growth, on the side of his neck. Nothing was done until he was fourteen. He thought he was going in for a minor surgery to remove the cyst from his neck; instead, there were two surgeries, and when he woke up, he had no voice— a vocal cord was removed. He later learned he had cancer, something his parents refused to discuss. After he finds his mother in bed with another woman and his father confesses that he exposed him to x-rays when he was very young, Small leaves home at age sixteen, with little except his dreams that his art could be his life. In one early scene, Small shows the indignities wrought upon his body by his father, including an enema. In another scene, young Small and his older brother look at their father's medical books and see a woman's breast and a man's penis; towards the end of the book, Small draws his grandmother stripping all her clothes off and dancing wildly after setting her house on fire. Other than these few images, Small's depictions of his horrible childhood and teen years are quiet and low-key.

"Emotionally raw, artistically compelling and psychologically devastating graphic memoir of childhood trauma." Kirkus

Smith, Alison, 1968-

Smith, Alison. Name all the animals; a memoir. Scribner 2004 319p hardcover o.p. pa $13

Grades: 9 10 11 12   92

ISBN 0-7432-5522-4; 0-7432-5523-2 (pa)

LC 2003-60432

"When Smith was 15, her beloved older brother died suddenly. In a poignant, ultimately hopeful memoir that reads like fiction, Smith describes her own and her parents' journeys through grief and the thrill of a first love that was taboo in her religious community." Booklist

Smith, Joseph, 1805-1844

Remini, Robert Vincent. Joseph Smith. Viking 2002 190p (Penguin lives series) $19.95 *

Grades: 11 12 Adult   92

1. Mormons

ISBN 0-670-03083-X   LC 2001-56762

In this biography of the founder of the Mormon Church, the author "places Smith in the context of his time in terms of the broader social, political, and economic events that influenced him and his church." Libr J

"A masterful evenhanded précis that will engross history and religion readers alike." Booklist

Includes bibliographical references

Snicket, Lemony, 1970-

Abrams, Dennis. Lemony Snicket (Daniel Handler); foreword by Kyle Zimmer. Chelsea House Publishers 2010 117p il (Who wrote that?) lib bdg $35

Grades: 6 7 8 9 10   92

1. Authors, American

ISBN 978-1-60413-726-2; 1-60413-726-6

LC 2010006599

A biography of the author of the *A Series of Unfortunate Events* series.

"Abrams delivers a witty account of his subject. . . . He presents a substantive look at Snicket/Handler, including synopses of and reactions to his adult books, his major influences, and musical interests. Abundant secondary-source quotes, full-color photos and film stills, and a chapter devoted to the series that made him famous will appeal to many readers. This lively biography will not disappoint." SLJ

Includes bibliographical references

Snyder, Kurt

Snyder, Kurt. Me, myself, and them; a firsthand account of one young person's experience with schizophrenia; with Raquel E. Gur, and Linda Wasmer Andrews. Oxford University Press 2007 164p il $30; pa $9.95

Grades: 9 10 11 12 Adult   92

1. Schizophrenia

ISBN   978-0-19-531123-5;   0-19-531123-X; 978-0-19-531122-8 (pa); 0-19-531122-1 (pa)

LC 2007-16619

"The Annenberg Foundation Trust at Sunnylands, the Annenberg Public Policy Center"

"Each chapter begins with Snyder's recollection of his difficulties, starting when he was eighteen, followed by detailed but extremely readable medical information. Many gray-scale sidebars share voices of other schizophrenics as well as history. . . . [Gur and Andrews] review medications, side effects, hospitalization, insurance issues, legal issues, diagnoses, symptoms, treatments, and related problems (substance abuse, depression, anxiety, etc.). Besides compelling thoroughness and readability, Snyder's story provides honesty and not a magic wand." Voice Youth Advocates

Includes bibliographical references

Stalin, Joseph, 1879-1953

Cunningham, Kevin. Joseph Stalin and the Soviet Union. M. Reynolds 2006 208p il map (World leaders) lib bdg $27.95 *

Grades: 9 10 11 12   92

1. Dictators 2. Soviet Union—History

ISBN 978-1-93179-894-5; 1-93179-894-X

LC 2005-32540

"This biography reviews the life of Soviet leader Joseph Stalin and the changes within the country during his long tenure. Although not ignoring his youth and his personal life, the discussion centers on his political leadership and its far-reaching effects. . . . This attractive volume offers a solid biography of Stalin." Booklist

Includes bibliographical references

Stanton, Elizabeth Cady, 1815-1902

Banner, Lois W. Elizabeth Cady Stanton; a radical for woman's rights. Addison Wesley Longman 1997 c1980 189p (Library of American biography) pa $20

Grades: 9 10 11 12   92

1. Feminism 2. Suffragists 3. Women—Suffrage

ISBN 0-673-39319-4

This biography of the nineteenth-century American feminist describes her upbringing, marriage, motherhood, and development as a leader.

Includes bibliographical references

Colman, Penny. Elizabeth Cady Stanton and Susan B. Anthony; a friendship that changed the world. Henry Holt and Company 2011 256p il $18.99

Grades: 7 8 9 10   92

1. Anthony, Susan B., 1820-1906 2. Feminism 3. Suffragists 4. Women—Suffrage

ISBN 978-0-8050-8293-7; 0-8050-8293-X

LC 2010-39762

"Christy Ottaviano books"

"Elizabeth Cady Stanton, a married mother of four boys at the time they met, and Susan B. Anthony, an unmarried schoolteacher, formed a friendship that lasted until Elizabeth's death more than 50 years later. Their tireless work, including advocacy, speeches, organizing and writing, placed them at the center of tumultuous events in the middle of the 19th century. . . . This [is a] lively, very readable narrative. . . . This thoughtful portrayal to two complex women is . . . enhanced by comprehensive backmatter, making this an invaluable addition to the literature of suffrage." Kirkus

Includes bibliographical references

Stanton, Elizabeth Cady, 1815-1902—*Continued*

Ginzberg, Lori D. Elizabeth Cady Stanton; an American life. Hill and Wang 2009 254p il $25 *
Grades: 11 12 Adult   92
  1. Feminism 2. Suffragists 3. Women—Suffrage
  ISBN 978-0-8090-9493-6; 0-8090-9493-2
                                       LC 2008-54395
The author "makes a convincing case for Stanton as the founding philosopher of the American women's rights movement in a lively voice that enhances her eccentric subject. . . . Ginzberg has created a vibrant portrait of a key, often misrepresented figure in American history." Am Hist

Includes bibliographical references

Steinbeck, John, 1902-1968

Meltzer, Milton. John Steinbeck; a twentieth-century life. Viking 2008 237p il (Up close) $16.99
Grades: 7 8 9 10   92
  1. Authors, American
  ISBN 978-0-670-06139-6; 0-670-06139-5
                                       LC 2007-36424
"This compact biography makes excellent connections between the themes of social and economic justice found in Steinbeck's work and the changes that were occurring in America around the time of the Depression. . . . Meltzer's language is concise and easy to understand, and powerful excerpts from Steinbeck's work are integrated throughout. A dozen or so small, black-and-white photographs of Steinbeck at different stages of his life are included." SLJ

Includes bibliographical references

Reef, Catherine. John Steinbeck. Clarion Bks. 1996 163p il $17.95; pa $8.95
Grades: 7 8 9 10   92
  1. Authors, American
  ISBN 0-395-71278-5; 0-618-43244-2 (pa)
                                       LC 95-11500
"The book traces Steinbeck's life from his childhood in California, to his burgeoning writing career and his passion for social justice, to his worldwide recognition. Reef does an excellent job of synthesizing Steinbeck's work, his private life, and his politics and philosophy." Bull Cent Child Books

Includes bibliographical references

Steinbeck, John. Conversations with John Steinbeck; edited by Thomas Fensch. University Press of Miss. 1988 xxi, 116p (Literary conversations series) pa $18 hardcover o.p.
Grades: 11 12 Adult   92
  1. Authors, American
  ISBN 0-87805-360-3 (pa)   LC 88-17538
"This collection of Steinbeck's interviews allows him to speak on his own behalf in an illuminating expression of his intentions, goals, and achievements. From the beginning of his career through his last years the interviews reveal a fascinating, controversial, and captivating personality." Univ Press Books for Second Sch Libr

Includes bibliographical references

Steiner, Matt

Warren, Andrea. Escape from Saigon; how a Vietnam War orphan became an American boy. Farrar, Straus and Giroux 2004 110p il map hardcover o.p. pa $9.95
Grades: 6 7 8 9 10   92
  1. Vietnamese Americans 2. Vietnam War, 1961-1975
  3. Racially mixed people 4. Interracial adoption
  ISBN   978-0-374-32224-3;   0-374-32224-4;
  978-0-374-40023-1 (pa); 0-374-40023-7 (pa)
                                        LC 2003-60672
"Melanie Kroupa books"
Chronicles the experiences of Matt Steiner, an orphaned Amerasian boy, from his birth and early childhood in Saigon through his departure from Vietnam in the 1975 Operation Babylift and his subsequent life as the adopted son of an American family in Ohio.
"The child-at-war story and the facts about the Operation Babylift rescue are tense and exciting. Just as gripping is the boy's personal conflict." Booklist

Stone, Toni, 1921-1996

Ackmann, Martha. Curveball; the remarkable story of Toni Stone, the first woman to play professional baseball in the Negro League. Lawrence Hill Books 2010 274p il $24.95
Grades: 11 12 Adult   92
  1. Baseball—Biography 2. African American athletes
  3. Negro leagues
  ISBN 978-1-55652-796-8   LC 2010-7019
This "book vividly details the trials and triumphs of this sports pioneer, a lifelong 'tomboy' who went on to play with the Indianapolis Clowns and the Kansas City Monarchs. . . . Ackmann has done a commendable job of celebrating the accomplishments of this forgotten gem. It's a grand slam." Jet

Includes bibliographical references

Stowe, Harriet Beecher, 1811-1896

Sonneborn, Liz. Harriet Beecher Stowe. Chelsea House Publishers 2009 120p il (Leaders of the Civil War era) lib bdg $30
Grades: 7 8 9 10   92
  1. Authors, American 2. Abolitionists
  ISBN 978-1-60413-302-8; 1-60413-302-3
                                       LC 2008-44608
Biography of abolitionist and author, Harriet Beecher Stowe.
Includes glossary and bibliographical references

Stringer, Caverly

Stringer, Caverly. Sleepaway school; stories from a boy's life; [by] Lee Stringer. A Seven Stories Press 1st ed. Seven Stories Press 2004 227p $21.95; pa $13.95
Grades: 11 12 Adult   92
  1. African Americans—Biography
  ISBN 1-58322-478-5; 1-58322-701-6 (pa)
                                      LC 2004-3610
"In more than 30 connected true stories, Stringer portrays his boyhood as a poor, black foster child coinciden-

Stringer, Caverly—*Continued*

tally growing up in a wealthy white neighborhood after he was sent to a school for troubled boys—mostly white, middle-class boys." Booklist

The author "deftly tells a believable, candid and vivid tale of a person scarred by his past." Publ Wkly

Sui, Anna

Darraj, Susan Muaddi. Anna Sui. Chelsea House Publishers 2009 120p il (Asian Americans of achievement) $30

Grades: 7 8 9 10   92

1. Fashion designers

ISBN 978-1-60413-570-1; 1-60413-570-0

LC 2009-14608

"Anna Sui is known for her youthful 'baby doll' designs and extravagant combinations inspired by the hippie and rock-'n'-roll fashions of the '60s and early '70s. Readers learn about the setbacks and hard work required to become successful. . . . The quality of research and in-depth coverage broadens [the book's] usefulness. . . . [This book is] inspiring." SLJ

Includes glossary and bibliographical references

Swift, Jonathan, 1667-1745

Aykroyd, Clarissa. Savage satire; the story of Jonathan Swift. Morgan Reynolds Pub. 2006 160p il (World writers) lib bdg $27.95 *

Grades: 7 8 9 10   92

1. Authors, Irish

ISBN 1-59935-027-0; 978-1-59935-027-1

LC 2006-18142

A biography of the Anglo-Irish writer who enjoyed shocking his readers.

"High-school students will find this a useful, informative introduction to the man's life, politics, and writings." Booklist

Includes bibliographical references

Tamm, Jayanti, 1970-

Tamm, Jayanti. Cartwheels in a sari; a memoir of growing up cult. Harmony Books 2009 288p $22.99

Grades: 11 12 Adult   92

1. Chinmoy, Sri

ISBN 978-0-307-39392-0; 0-307-39392-5

LC 2008-36450

The author "recounts her youth as the chosen disciple of Sri Chinmoy, the wildly charismatic leader of a New York-based spiritual sect that counts celebrities and heads of nations among its millions of followers. . . . Witty, compassionate, and often heartbreaking, Tamm's story offers crucial insight into a cult's inner workings and methods of indoctrination. All readers, though, will recognize universal coming-of-age themes as Tamm discards unwanted childhood lessons and begins to shape an independent adult life." Booklist

Tammet, Daniel, 1979-

Tammet, Daniel. Born on a blue day; inside the extraordinary mind of an autistic savant: a memoir. Free Press 2007 226p il $24; pa $14 *

Grades: 11 12 Adult   92

1. Autism 2. Asperger's syndrome 3. Savants (Savant syndrome)

ISBN   1-4165-3507-1;   978-1-4165-3507-2; 1-4165-4901-3 (pa); 978-1-4165-4901-7 (pa)

LC 2006-41331

First published 2006 in the United Kingdom

This "first-person account offers a window into the mind of a high-functioning, 27-year-old British autistic savant with Asperger's syndrome." Publ Wkly

This "autobiography is as fascinating as Benjamin Franklin's and John Stuart Mill's, both of which are, like his, about the growth of a mind." Booklist

Tan, Amy

Mussari, Mark. Amy Tan. Marshall Cavendish Benchmark 2010 125p il (Today's writers and their works) lib bdg $42.79

Grades: 8 9 10 11 12   92

1. Authors, American 2. Chinese Americans—Biography 3. Women authors

ISBN 978-0-7614-4127-4; 0-7614-4127-1

This biography of Amy Tan places the author in the context of her times and discusses her work.

Includes bibliographical references

O'Keefe, Sherry. From China to America; the story of Amy Tan. Morgan Reynolds Pub. 2011 112p il lib bdg $28.95

Grades: 7 8 9 10   92

1. Authors, American 2. Chinese Americans—Biography 3. Women authors

ISBN 978-1-59935-138-4; 1-59935-138-2

LC 2010-7594

"Born in California, the daughter of Chinese immigrants, Tan grew up as an American on the outside and Chinese on the inside. . . . Growing up, Tan faced the loss of her brother and father and the morbid outlook of her mother. Their tumultuous relationship led her to write stories about mother-and-daughter conflict, which later became the basis for *The Joy Luck Club*. This book gives readers a brief overview of the novelist's life and a greater understanding of the inspiration behind her novels." SLJ

Includes bibliographical references

Taylor, Major, 1878-1932

Balf, Todd. Major; a Black athlete, a White era, and the fight to be the world's fastest human being. Crown Publishers 2008 306p il $24; pa $13.95

Grades: Adult   92

1. African American athletes 2. Bicycle racing

ISBN   978-0-307-23658-6;   0-307-23658-7; 978-0-307-23659-3 (pa); 0-307-23659-5 (pa)

LC 2007-20747

The author "chronicles the life of the unlikeliest of stars in the early years of cycling: Marshall 'Major' Taylor. Taylor was an incomparable athlete, poet and celeb-

Taylor, Major, 1878-1932—*Continued*

rity, but he was also a black man living during a time when the scars of the Civil War and slavery were still fresh in the minds of Americans. Balf . . . does great work presenting the complex nature of Taylor's life, including his upbringing in poverty in Indianapolis, the years he was treated as a son by a rich white family, the fans who both worshipped and vilified him and his close relationships with his white trainer and promoter." Publ Wkly

Includes bibliographical references

Tecumseh, Shawnee Chief, 1768-1813

Zimmerman, Dwight Jon. Tecumseh; shooting star of the Shawnee. Sterling 2010 124p il map (Sterling biographies) lib bdg $12.95

Grades: 7 8 9 10   92
    1. Shawnee Indians 2. Native Americans—Biography
    ISBN 978-1-4027-6847-7; 1-4027-6847-8
                      LC 2009-24142
"Lots of detailed physical battles dominate *Tecumseh*, with a strong focus on the Shawnee's brutal displacement by white settlers and the Indians caught up in the tensions between the U.S. and Great Britain. . . . [The] spacious design is highly scannable, with color background screens, photos, maps, and historic prints throughout." Booklist

Includes glossary and bibliographical references

Telfair, Sebastian, 1985-

O'Connor, Ian. The jump; Sebastian Telfair and the high stakes business of high school ball. Rodale 2005 307p il $23.95; pa $13.95

Grades: 11 12 Adult   92
    1. Basketball—Biography
    ISBN 1-59486-107-2; 1-59486-447-0 (pa)
                      LC 2004-26366
In this biography of the up-and-coming basketball player, the author "chronicles Telfair's senior year at Brooklyn's Lincoln High. . . . This will be the most discussed book of the NBA season." Booklist

Teresa, Mother, 1910-1997

Spink, Kathryn. Mother Teresa; a complete authorized biography. HarperSanFrancisco 1997 306p il pa $15.95 hardcover o.p.

Grades: 11 12 Adult   92
    1. Missionaries of Charity 2. Missions—India
    ISBN 0-06-251553-5 (pa)   LC 97-41349
"Spink's biography benefits from her own 18-year involvement with the work of the Missionaries of Charity Order as well as from the intimate relationship she developed over the years with Mother Teresa. . . . A final chapter in the book provides glimpses of Mother Teresa's affection for Princess Diana, a brief description of Mother Teresa's funeral and a short account of the election of Sister Nirmal as her successor." Publ Wkly

Tesla, Nikola, 1856-1943

Aldrich, Lisa J. Nikola Tesla and the taming of electricity. Morgan Reynolds Pub. 2005 160p il $26.95 *

Grades: 9 10 11 12   92
    1. Inventors
    ISBN 1-931798-46-X   LC 2004-18786
The author writes "of Tesla's life, while using sidebars to carry information on related topics such as alternating and direct current, the patent system, and Tesla's dream of wireless power." Booklist

Includes bibliographical references

Burgan, Michael. Nikola Tesla; physicist, inventor, electrical engineer. Compass Point Books 2009 112p il map (Signature lives) lib bdg $34.65

Grades: 6 7 8 9 10   92
    1. Inventors
    ISBN 978-0-7565-4086-9; 0-7565-4086-0
                      LC 2008-35725
A biography of Nikola Tesla, physicist, inventor, and electrical engineer

The "inviting page design features photos and boxed screens on each spread, and . . . includes a detailed bibliography, source notes, time line and glossary." Booklist

Includes glossary and bibliographical references

Thomas, Aquinas, Saint, 1225?-1274

Strathern, Paul. Thomas Aquinas in 90 minutes. Ivan R. Dee 1998 90p (Philosophers in 90 Minutes) $14.95; pa $7.95

Grades: 9 10 11 12   92
    1. Philosophers
    ISBN 1-56663-193-9; 1-56663-194-7 (pa)
                      LC 98-13264
The author offers an "account of Aquinas' life and ideas, and explains their influence on man's struggle to understand his existence in the world. The book also includes selections from Aquinas' writings; a brief list of suggested reading for those who wish to push further; and chronologies that place Aquinas within his own age and in the broader scheme of philosophy." Publisher's note

Includes bibliographical references

Thompson, Craig, 1975-

Thompson, Craig. Blankets; an illustrated novel. Top Shelf 2003 582p il pa $29.95

Grades: 10 11 12 Adult   92
    1. Graphic novels 2. Family life—Graphic novels 3. Autobiographical graphic novels
    ISBN 1-891830-43-0   LC 2004-297892
This "memoir recreates the confusion, emotional pain and isolation of the author's rigidly fundamentalist Christian upbringing, along with the trepidation of growing into maturity. Skinny, naive and spiritually vulnerable, Thompson and his younger brother manage to survive their parents' overbearing discipline (the brothers are sometimes forced to sleep in 'the cubbyhole,' a forbidding and claustrophobic storage chamber) through flights of childhood fancy and a mutual love of drawing . . . Thompson manages to explore adolescent social yearnings, the power of young love and the complexities of

Thompson, Craig, 1975- —*Continued*
sexual attraction with a rare combination of sincerity,
pictorial lyricism and taste. His exceptional b&w drawings balance representational precision with a bold and
wonderfully expressive line for pages of ingenious, in-
ventively composed and poignant imagery." Publ Wkly

Thoreau, Henry David, 1817-1862
Sullivan, Robert. The Thoreau you don't know;
what the prophet of environmentalism really
meant. Collins 2009 354p $25.99 *
Grades: 11 12 Adult   **92**
  1. Authors, American 2. Naturalists
  ISBN 978-0-06-171031-5; 0-06-171031-8
                      LC 2008-34495
  The author "endeavors to free Henry David Thoreau
from his calcified reputation as a cantankerous hermit
and nature worshipper. Sounding like your favorite teacher who manages to make history fun and relevant, Sullivan vibrantly portrays the sage of Walden as a geeky,
curious, compassionate fellow of high intelligence and
deep feelings who loved company, music, and long
walks." Booklist

Thorpe, Jim, 1888-1953
Crawford, Bill. All American; the rise and fall
of Jim Thorpe. John Wiley & Sons, Inc 2004 284p
il $24.95
Grades: 11 12 Adult   **92**
  1. Athletes 2. Native Americans—Biography
  ISBN 0-471-55732-3   LC 2004-14376
  This "terse, punchy biography of sports legend Thorpe
(1888–1953) illuminates the current debate over the exploitation of unpaid college athletes by moneymaking,
headline-grabbing educational institutions." Publ Wkly
  Includes bibliographical references

Tienda, Marta
O'Connell, Diane. People person; the story of
sociologist Marta Tienda. Franklin Watts 2005
108p il map (Women's adventures in science) lib
bdg $31
Grades: 7 8 9 10   **92**
  1. Sociology 2. Mexican Americans—Biography
  ISBN 0-531-16781-X   LC 2005000825
  Also available in paperback from Joseph Henry Press
  A biography of Mexican American sociologist Marta
Tienda.
  This is "interesting, substantive, and eminently read-
able." SLJ
  Includes bibliographical references

Tillage, Leon, 1936-
Tillage, Leon. Leon's story; [by] Leon Walter
Tillage; collage art by Susan L. Roth. Farrar,
Straus & Giroux 1997 107p il hardcover o.p. pa
$6.95
Grades: 4 5 6 7 8 9 10   **92**
  1. African Americans—Biography 2. North Carolina—
  Race relations
  ISBN 0-374-34379-9; 0-374-44330-0 (pa)
                      LC 96-43544

The son of a North Carolina sharecropper recalls the
hard times faced by his family and other African Americans in the first half of the twentieth century and the
changes that the civil rights movement helped bring
about
  The author's "voice is direct, the words are simple.
There is no rhetoric, no commentary, no bitterness. . . .
This quiet drama will move readers of all ages . . . and
may encourage them to record their own family stories."
Booklist

Traig, Jennifer
Traig, Jennifer. Devil in the details; scenes from
an obsessive girlhood. Little, Brown 2004 246p il
hardcover o.p. pa $14.99
Grades: 9 10 11 12   **92**
  1. Obsessive-compulsive disorder
  ISBN 0-316-15877-1; 0-316-01074-X (pa)
                      LC 2004-1417
  "When she was an adolescent, Traig's loose collection
of neuroses coalesced into a hyperreligious form of obsessive-compulsive disorder known as scrupulosity. The
condition finds the once spiritually indifferent teenager
purifying her school binders, using separate bathrooms
for milk and meat, and perplexing and vexing her mixed-
faith family." Booklist
  The author's "efforts to adhere, in a vacuum, to Jewish law, are particularly amusing. She also writes affec-
tionately about her long-suffering family members, who
are funny enough to stage their own sitcom. In the end,
she succeeds in overcoming her illness, providing a provocative yet entertaining memoir in the process." Libr J

Transue, Emily R.
Transue, Emily R. On call; a doctor's days and
nights in residency. St. Martin's Press 2004 242p
hardcover o.p. pa $13.95
Grades: 9 10 11 12   **92**
  1. Physicians
  ISBN 0-312-32483-9; 0-312-32484-7 (pa)
                    LC 2004-46893
  "During her three years as a resident in internal medicine at the University of Washington in Seattle, Transue
wrote about her patients as a way to guard against burnout and share her experiences with friends and family.
This [is a] moving collection of her stories. . . . Her descriptions of medical procedures can be graphic, but she
presents an intriguing picture of a side of medicine many
people never see." Publ Wkly

Truman, Harry S., 1884-1972
Dallek, Robert. Harry S. Truman. Times Books
2008 183p (American presidents series) $22 *
Grades: 11 12 Adult   **92**
  1. Presidents—United States 2. United States—Politics
  and government—1945-1953
  ISBN 978-0-8050-6938-9; 0-8050-6938-0
                    LC 2008-10193
  This is a biography of the 33rd president.
  "Dallek's little book is . . . the best starting point for
knowledge of Truman's life and for an astute assessment
of his career." Publ Wkly
  Includes bibliographical references

Truth, Sojourner, d. 1883

Painter, Nell Irvin. Sojourner Truth; a life, a symbol. Norton 1996 370p il hardcover o.p. pa $15.95 *

Grades: 11 12 Adult   **92**
1. Abolitionists 2. Feminism 3. African American women—Biography
ISBN 0-393-02739-2; 0-393-31708-0 (pa)
                                    LC 95-47595
"Sojourner Truth's remarkable career as a powerful, impassioned speaker and advocate of abolitionism and women's rights spanned more than 30 years. Painter . . . traces Truth's life and legacy using a variety of sources, including her many photographs." Libr J
"Painter persuasively offers us the real woman behind the myth." Publ Wkly
Includes bibliographical references

Tubman, Harriet, 1820?-1913

Clinton, Catherine. Harriet Tubman: the road to freedom. Little, Brown 2004 272p hardcover o.p. pa $14.95 *

Grades: 11 12 Adult   **92**
1. Abolitionists 2. African American women—Biography 3. Underground railroad
ISBN 0-316-14492-4; 0-316-15594-2 (pa)
                                    LC 2003-56185
The author "places Tubman's life within its times, describing, among other things, the history of the abolitionist movement and the impact of the Fugitive Slave Law of 1850." N Y Times Book Rev
"Clinton turns sobriquets into meaningful descriptors of a unique person. In her hands, a familiar legend acquires human dimension with no diminution of its majesty and power." Publ Wkly
Includes bibliographical references

Malaspina, Ann. Harriet Tubman. Chelsea House 2009 120p il (Leaders of the Civil War era) lib bdg $30

Grades: 7 8 9 10   **92**
1. Abolitionists 2. African American women—Biography 3. Underground railroad
ISBN 978-1-60413-303-5; 1-60413-303-1
                                    LC 2008-42412
Biography of Harriet Tubman, former slave and a "conductor" on the Underground Railroad.
Includes glossary and bibliographical references

Turing, Alan Mathison, 1912-1954

Corrigan, Jim. Alan Turing. Morgan Reynolds Pub. 2008 112p il (Profiles in mathematics) lib bdg $27.95

Grades: 7 8 9 10   **92**
1. Mathematicians
ISBN 978-1-59935-064-6; 1-59935-064-5
                                    LC 2007-11704
"Corrigan's descriptions of English mathematician Turing as sporting 'ragged, wrinkled clothes' and few social graces will fit many readers' mental image of a numbers genius. But other aspects of this portrait push against stereotypes. . . . Throughout, candid mentions of Turing's homosexuality help readers contextualize the

scandal he endured after running afoul of the era's discriminatory legislation. Equal sensitivity distinguishes Corrigan's handling of Turing's death, officially (but not decisively) a suicide." Booklist
Includes bibliographical references

Turner, Nat, 1800?-1831

Baker, Kyle. Nat Turner. Abrams 2008 207p il pa $14.95

Grades: 10 11 12 Adult   **92**
1. Graphic novels 2. Biographical graphic novels 3. Slavery—Graphic novels
ISBN 978-0-8109-9535-2; 0-8109-9535-2
                                    LC 2008-6911
Originally published 2006 in four volumes
This book "follows the dark legacy of the Virginia slave rebellion and subsequent murders of at least 55 white slave owners and their families in 1831. . . . Turner is presented as a fiercely intelligent, angry, yet steadfast individual whose potential was dashed in an era of hate and inhumanity. Those characteristics are mirrored in the actions of the slaves' rebellion, in illustrations that are not for the faint of heart or the weak of stomach. The ideas brought forth here are sure to ignite debate and discussion." SLJ
Includes bibliographical references

Twain, Mark, 1835-1910

Caravantes, Peggy. A great and sublime fool; the story of Mark Twain. Morgan Reynolds Pub. 2009 176p il map (World writers) lib bdg $28.95

Grades: 7 8 9 10   **92**
1. Authors, American
ISBN 978-1-599-35088-2; 1-599-35088-2
                                    LC 2008-34139
This "offers a workmanlike but readable account of one of America's first great writers. . . . A nice selection of photographs and artwork complement the narrative. . . . Detailed source notes and an in-depth time line round out this even and reliable . . . biography." Booklist
Includes bibliographical references

Sonneborn, Liz. Mark Twain; foreword by Kyle Zimmer. Chelsea House Publishers 2010 125p il (Who wrote that?) lib bdg $35

Grades: 6 7 8 9 10   **92**
1. Authors, American
ISBN 978-1-60413-728-6; 1-60413-728-2
                                    LC 2010006601
This biography of Mark Twain "begins with the writer's memorable visit to his Missouri hometown in 1902, then tracks back to his early days and his well-known transformation from Sam Clemens to Mark Twain. Sonneborn deals with her material well, hitting all the highlights and keeping the narrative moving along. Good use of details adds interest. . . . A solid purchase." SLJ
Includes bibliographical references

Twain, Mark, 1835-1910—*Continued*

Ward, Geoffrey C. Mark Twain; by Geoffrey C. Ward and Dayton Duncan; based on a documentary film directed by Ken Burns; written by Dayton Duncan and Geoffrey C. Ward; with a preface by Ken Burns; picture research by Susanna Steisel and Pam Tubridy Baucom, and contributions by Russell Banks [et al.] Knopf 2001 269p il map $40

Grades: 11 12 Adult   92

1. Authors, American

ISBN 0-375-40561-5   LC 2001-33820

Companion volume to the PBS television series

"This fascinating biography of Twain contains a treasure trove of photographs and pictures." Booklist

Includes bibliographical references

Umrigar, Thrity N.

Umrigar, Thrity N. First darling of the morning; selected memories of an Indian childhood. Harper Perennial 2008 294, 18p pa $14.95

Grades: 11 12 Adult   92

1. Authors, American 2. Bombay (India)

ISBN 978-0-06-145161-4; 0-06-145161-4

First published 2004 in India

In this memoir, the author "alternates between sweet and biting accounts of her middle-class Parsi upbringing in 1960s and 1970s Bombay. With a mixture of rawness and warmth, she recalls moments from her tumultuous childhood through her teenage years, and finally into her early 20s when she leaves India for the U.S. . . . Umrigar's memoir is colorful and moving." Publ Wkly

Underwood, Rosamond

Wickenden, Dorothy. Nothing daunted. See entry under Woodruff, Dorothy, 1887-1979

Ung, Loung, 1970-

Ung, Loung. Lucky child; a daughter of Cambodia reunites with the sister she left behind. HarperCollins Publishers 2005 268p il $24.95; pa $13.95

Grades: 11 12 Adult   92

1. Ung, Chou 2. Cambodian Americans 3. Cambodia—History—1975-

ISBN 0-06-073394-2; 0-06-073395-0 (pa)

LC 2004-54346

Sequel to First they killed my father

In this "memoir, Ung picks up where her first . . . left off, with the author escaping a devastated Cambodia in 1980 at age 10 and flying to her new home in Vermont. . . . She and her eldest brother, with whom she escaped, left behind their three other siblings. This book is alternately heart-wrenching and heartwarming, as it follows the parallel lives of Loung Ung and her closest sister, Chou, during the 15 years it took for them to reunite." Publ Wkly

Includes bibliographical references

Unger, Zac

Unger, Zac. Working fire; the making of an accidental fireman. Penguin Press 2004 262p hardcover o.p. pa $15

Grades: 11 12 Adult   92

1. Fire fighters—Biography

ISBN 1-59420-001-7; 0-14-303495-2 (pa)

LC 2003-50676

"A young rookie provides a look behind the firehouse doors, bringing close the danger, excitement, and challenge of fighting fire in a big city." Booklist

Van Buren, Martin, 1782-1862

Widmer, Edward L. Martin Van Buren; [by] Ted Widmer. Times Bks. 2005 189p (American presidents series) $20

Grades: 11 12 Adult   92

1. Presidents—United States

ISBN 0-8050-6922-4   LC 2004-53652

This is a "portrait of our eighth president, who, Widmer says, created the modern political party system." Publ Wkly

The author "keenly evokes the environment that enabled Van Buren to thrive. . . . Widmer also lends a certain dignity to Van Buren's post-presidential attempts to resolve the sectional crisis." N Y Times Book Rev

Includes bibliographical references

Vasishta, Madan, 1941-

Vasishta, Madan. Deaf in Delhi; a memoir. Gallaudet University Press 2006 220p il (Deaf lives) pa $29.95

Grades: 11 12 Adult   92

1. Deaf 2. Delhi (India)

ISBN 1-56368-284-2; 978-1-56368-284-1

LC 2005-55214

"A bout with mumps and typhoid left 11-year-old Vasishta deaf. In an India where the word for deaf in at least three languages means someone less than human, there was not much hope for his future. . . . The author weaves stories, set in the India of the 1950s and early '60s, of the holy men to whom his family turned for a cure for him, of his arranged marriage, and of the class system. . . . This book is a must for collections accessed by deaf teens, and it will appeal to young adults interested in Indian culture, multicultural studies, or disabilities." SLJ

Includes bibliographical references

Von Braun, Wernher, 1912-1977

Spangenburg, Ray. Wernher von Braun; rocket visionary; [by] Ray Spangenburg and Diane Kit Moser. Rev ed. Chelsea House 2008 164p il (Makers of modern science) $29.95 *

Grades: 9 10 11 12   92

1. Rocketry 2. Scientists

ISBN 978-0-8160-6179-2; 0-8160-6179-3

LC 2007-52220

First published 1995

This book "examines the life and career of the famed rocket scientist who supervised the development of the powerful rockets used by Apollo astronauts to reach the moon." Publisher's note

Includes glossary and bibliographical references

Vonnegut, Kurt, 1922-2007

Vonnegut, Kurt. Conversations with Kurt Vonnegut; edited by William Rodney Allen. University Press of Miss. 1988 305p (Literary conversations series) pa $15.95 hardcover o.p.

Grades: 11 12 Adult   **92**

1. Authors, American

ISBN 0-87805-358-1 (pa)   LC 88-13968

"In the twenty years of interviews collected here . . . the reader can hear Vonnegut working through his various personae of science fiction writer, black humorist, pop culture guru, and elder statesman toward a truer definition of himself and his art." Univ Press Books for Second Sch Libr

Walker, Rebecca, 1969-

Walker, Rebecca. Black, white and Jewish; autobiography of a shifting self. Riverhead Bks. 2001 320p hardcover o.p. pa $14

Grades: 11 12 Adult   **92**

1. Racially mixed people

ISBN 1-57322-169-4; 1-57322-907-5 (pa)
    LC 00-35292

This is an autobiography by "the daughter of the black writer Alice Walker and a white Jewish lawyer, Mel Leventhal. Rebecca Walker writes that her confusion about being biracial began when her parents divorced when she was 8 years old. From then on, every two years, Walker alternated coast-to-coast between them." NY Times Book Rev

This is an "involving, honest, poignant memoir." Booklist

Walls, Jeannette

Walls, Jeannette. The glass castle; a memoir. Scribner 2005 288p $25; pa $14 *

Grades: 11 12 Adult   **92**

ISBN 0-7432-4753-1; 0-7432-4754-X (pa)
    LC 2004-58907

The author "describes a childhood spent careering across the country, from California to West Virginia, in a succession of ever more rattletrap cars, in pursuit of increasingly implausible get-rich-quick schemes." Time

"Shocking, sad, and occasionally bitter, this gracefully written account speaks candidly, yet with surprising affection, about parents and about the strength of family ties—for both good and ill." Booklist

Warhol, Andy, 1928?-1987

Greenberg, Jan. Andy Warhol; prince of pop; [by] Jan Greenberg & Sandra Jordan. Delacorte Press 2004 193p il hardcover o.p. pa $6.99 *

Grades: 7 8 9 10   **92**

1. Artists—United States 2. Pop art

ISBN 0-385-73056-X; 0-385-73275-9 (pa)
    LC 2003-24102

A biography of the 20th century American artist famous for his Pop art images of Campbell's soup cans and Marilyn Monroe.

"Greenberg and Jordan offer a riveting biography that humanizes their controversial subject without making judgments or sensationalizing." Booklist

Includes glossary and bibliographical references

Washington, Booker T., 1856-1915

Smock, Raymond. Booker T. Washington; black leadership in the age of Jim Crow; [by] Raymond W. Smock. Ivan R. Dee 2009 223p il (Library of African-American biography) $26

Grades: 11 12 Adult   **92**

1. Tuskegee Institute 2. African Americans—Biography 3. African American educators

ISBN 978-1-56663-725-1; 1-56663-725-2
    LC 2009-3277

The author "examines Washington's legacy and how he came to be alternately lauded and lambasted for his practical approach to racism following Reconstruction: to build a school to prepare blacks to occupy the unchallenged place set aside for them in the Jim Crow South. . . . This is a nuanced portrait of an enigmatic man of enduring contribution to black leadership." Booklist

Includes bibliographical references

Washington, Booker T. Up from slavery; edited with an introduction and notes by William L. Andrews. Oxford University Press 2008 xxvii, 196p (Oxford world's classics) pa $9.95 *

Grades: 7 8 9 10 11 12 Adult   **92**

1. Tuskegee Institute 2. African Americans—Biography 3. African American educators

ISBN 978-0-19-955239-9   LC 2008-279129

First published 1901

"The classic autobiography of the man who, though born in slavery, educated himself and went on to found Tuskegee Institute." N Y Public Libr

Includes bibliographical references

Washington, George, 1732-1799

Ellis, Joseph J. His Excellency; George Washington. Knopf 2004 320p il hardcover o.p. pa $15 *

Grades: 11 12 Adult   **92**

1. Presidents—United States

ISBN 1-4000-4031-0; 1-4000-3253-9 (pa)
    LC 2004-46576

This is a "look at America's premier Founding Father, revealing a man with incredible energy, stamina, integrity, and vision as well as one who could be quite insecure, controlling, and shortsighted. Ellis examines the evolution of Washington's personality and challenges conventional scholarship. . . . He also determines that Washington's decisions on slavery were driven more by economics and posterity than purely by morality." Libr J

The author "offers a magisterial account of the life and times of George Washington, celebrating the heroic image of the president whom peers like Jefferson and Madison recognized as 'their unquestioned superior' while acknowledging his all-too-human qualities." Publ Wkly

Includes bibliographical references

Johnson, Paul. George Washington: the Founding Father. HarperCollins Publishers 2005 126p (Eminent lives) $19.95

Grades: 11 12 Adult   **92**

1. Presidents—United States

ISBN 0-06-075365-X   LC 2004-52907

Washington, George, 1732-1799—*Continued*

This is a biography of the first president of the United States.

The author "submits a beautifully cogent, enthrallingly perceptive, and . . . startlingly fresh take on the ultimate American icon." Booklist

Includes bibliographical references

Washington, Martha, 1731-1802

Brady, Patricia. Martha Washington; an American life. Viking 2005 276p il $24.95; pa $15

Grades: 11 12 Adult   92

1. Presidents' spouses—United States
   ISBN 0-670-03430-4; 0-14-303713-7 (pa)
                                            LC 2004-61242

In this book, the original first lady "is depicted as a very human but true heroine who remained steadfast through personal adversity and the uncertainties of war and revolution." Libr J

"Brady's splendid biography offers a compelling new portrait of this passionate, committed founding mother who has unjustly been obscured by others, such as Abigail Adams." Publ Wkly

Includes bibliographical references

Wells-Barnett, Ida B., 1862-1931

Hinman, Bonnie. Eternal vigilance: the story of Ida B. Wells-Barnett. Morgan Reynolds Pub. 2010 128p il (Civil rights leaders) $28.95

Grades: 7 8 9 10   92

1. African American women—Biography 2. African Americans—Civil rights 3. African American educators 4. Women journalists 5. United States—Race relations 6. African Americans—Social conditions 7. Lynching
   ISBN 978-1-59935-111-7; 1-59935-111-0
                                            LC 2010-8144

"Hinman tells of Wells-Barnett's tireless efforts as an antilynching crusader and civil rights advocate. . . . Hinman paints an engaging portrait of the activist who was instrumental in the formation of the NAACP. Each stage of Wells-Barnett's life is placed in historical context, providing students with a better understanding of the world in which she lived. Well-chosen black-and-white photographs and other period materials are included throughout the text." SLJ

Includes bibliographical references

Welty, Eudora, 1909-2001

Welty, Eudora. One writer's beginnings. Harvard Univ. Press 1984 104p il (William E. Massey, Sr. lectures in the history of American civilization) hardcover o.p. pa $12 *

Grades: 11 12 Adult   92

1. Authors, American
   ISBN 0-674-63925-1; 0-674-63927-8 (pa)
                                            LC 83-18638

A series of lectures in which the author reflects on her Southern heritage and her early artistic influences.

Wexler, Nancy S.

Glimm, Adele. Gene hunter; the story of neuropsychologist Nancy Wexler. Franklin Watts 2005 118p il (Women's adventures in science) lib bdg $31.50

Grades: 7 8 9 10   92

1. Huntington's chorea 2. Women scientists
   ISBN 978-0-531-16778-6; 0-531-16778-X
                                            LC 2005-06645

Also available in paperback from Joseph Henry Press

Contents: The dancing disease; Family secrets; Taking on the world; We won't give up; Risk and death; We are all one family; Testing the future; We found it!; In quest of cure

This is a biography of neuropsychologist Nancy Wexler who is searching for the gene responsible for a fatal, inherited sickness called Huntington's disease

This "volume is filled with full-color photographs of the subject and her work. Students will be comfortable with the style of [this book], and the easy reading level makes [it] accessible for even nonscience-oriented students." SLJ

Includes bibliographical references

Wharton, Edith, 1862-1937

Wooldridge, Connie Nordhielm. The brave escape of Edith Wharton; a biography. Clarion Books 2010 184p il $20

Grades: 7 8 9 10   92

1. Authors, American 2. Women authors
   ISBN 978-0-547-23630-8; 0-547-23630-1
                                            LC 2009-33574

"In this thoroughly researched, humanizing biography, Wooldridge writes with lively specifics about both the author and her time. . . . Frequent, well-woven quotes from Wharton's family and friends contribute to a strong sense of an energetic, groundbreaking, and ferociously intelligent writer, but it's the many quotes in Wharton's own voice that leave the most indelible impact." Booklist

White, Ryan

White, Ryan. Ryan White: my own story; by Ryan White and Ann Marie Cunningham. Dial Bks. 1991 277p il hardcover o.p. pa $7.99

Grades: 11 12 Adult   92

1. AIDS (Disease)—Personal narratives
   ISBN 0-8037-0977-3; 0-451-17322-8 (pa)
                                            LC 90-21038

Ryan White describes how he got AIDS, engaged in a legal battle to return to school, and became a celebrity and spokesman for issues concerning the deadly disease

The book contains "surprising snatches of humor and insight that lend dimension to the vulnerable young man whose positive outlook shines through so clearly. Not saccharine, not angry, not bitter, this unusual book, delivered without an ounce of self-pity, seems as honest as it is inspiring. It will touch both adults and teens." Booklist

Whitman, Walt, 1819-1892

Meltzer, Milton. Walt Whitman; a biography. 21st Cent. Bks. (Brookfield) 2002 160p il lib bdg $31.90

Grades: 7 8 9 10   92

1. Poets, American

ISBN 0-7613-2272-8   LC 2001-27798

"The book honestly explores Whitman's character and actions, including his racial prejudice and his tendency to write anonymous (and effective) praises of his own writing. Ultimately, this has a definite edge and relevance that gives it more resonance than blander overviews of the poet. . . . Photographs of Whitman and his family, images of his work, and reproductions of period illustrations . . . liven up the formatting." Bull Cent Child Books

Includes bibliographical references

Reef, Catherine. Walt Whitman. Clarion Bks. 1995 148p il hardcover o.p. pa $7.95

Grades: 7 8 9 10   92

1. Poets, American

ISBN 0-395-68705-5; 0-618-24616-9 (pa)

LC 94-7405

"Here is a biography of Whitman that presents the life of the subject, the world in which he lived, and representative passages from his writings." Voice Youth Advocates

"This is not a biography for pleasure reading, but it could be a source for those interested in historical events of 19th century America. It also would be a good resource for students doing a critique of Whitman's work for an American literature course." Book Rep

Includes bibliographical references

Wiesel, Elie, 1928-

Wiesel, Elie. Night; translated from the French by Marion Wiesel; [with a new preface by the author; foreword by FranSoise Mauriac] Hill and Wang 2006 xxi, 120p $19.95; pa $9 *

Grades: 9 10 11 12   92

1. Holocaust, 1933-1945—Personal narratives 2. Holocaust survivors

ISBN   0-374-39997-2;   978-0-374-39997-9; 0-374-50001-0 (pa); 978-0-374-50001-6 (pa)

LC 2005-936797

Original French edition, 1958

This is "the autobiographical account of an adolescent boy and his father in Auschwitz. Wiesel writes of their battle for survival, and of his battle with God for a way to understand the wanton cruelty he witnesses each day." Publisher's note

Wilder, Laura Ingalls, 1867-1957

Zochert, Donald. Laura: the life of Laura Ingalls Wilder. Avon 1977 c1976 241p pa $5.99

Grades: 11 12 Adult   92

1. Authors, American 2. Women authors 3. Frontier and pioneer life

ISBN 0-380-01636-2

First published 1976 by Regnery

This biography of the author of the "Little House" books describes her early life and offers insight into her works.

Williams, Roger, 1604?-1683

Gaustad, Edwin Scott. Roger Williams; [by] Edwin S. Gaustad. Oxford University Press 2005 150p il (Lives and legacies) $17.95

Grades: 11 12 Adult   92

1. Puritans 2. United States—History—1600-1775, Colonial period

ISBN 0-19-518369-X   LC 2004-25246

This is a biography of "the founder of Rhode Island and of the first Baptist Church in America." Publisher's note

The author "provides not just an excellent introduction to the man but a deep analysis of his largely unacknowledged influence on our political and cultural life." Reason

Wilson, Woodrow, 1856-1924

Lukes, Bonnie L. Woodrow Wilson and the Progressive Era. Morgan Reynolds 2005 192p il lib bdg $26.95

Grades: 7 8 9 10   92

1. Presidents—United States 2. United States—Politics and government—1898-1919

ISBN 978-1-93179-879-2; 1-93179-879-6

LC 2005-15999

"This well-documented, chronological account begins with Wilson's birth in 1856, describes his varied careers, and continues through his death in 1924. . . . The author describes the intense political conflicts of the time, mostly concerning Americas involvement in World War I and then in the League of Nations. Lukes's approach is balanced. . . . Good-quality, full-color and black-and-white photos and reproductions appear throughout." SLJ

Includes bibliographical references

Winthrop, John, 1588-1649

Aronson, Marc. John Winthrop, Oliver Cromwell, and the Land of Promise. Clarion Books 2004 205p il map $20

Grades: 7 8 9 10   92

1. Cromwell, Oliver, 1599-1658 2. Puritans 3. Massachusetts—History—1600-1775, Colonial period 4. Great Britain—History—1603-1714, Stuarts

ISBN 0-618-18177-6   LC 2003-16418

"The accessible text is accompanied by excerpts from primary source documents and vivid illustrations. The author's passion for the period comes across in his writing. Aronson provides an excellent source for historical and biographical data." Voice Youth Advocates

Includes bibliographical references

Wolff, Tobias, 1945-

Wolff, Tobias. This boy's life: a memoir. Atlantic Monthly Press 1989 288p hardcover o.p. pa $14

Grades: 11 12 Adult   92

1. Authors, American

ISBN 0-871-13248-6; 0-8021-3668-0 (pa)

LC 88-17600

The novelist and short story writer "offers an engrossing and candid look into his childhood and adolescence in his first book of nonfiction. In unaffected prose he

Wolff, Tobias, 1945-—_Continued_

recreates scenes from his life that sparkle with the imme-diacy of narrative fiction. The result is an intriguingly guileless book, distinct from the usual reflective com-mentary of autobiography." Libr J

Woodruff, Dorothy, 1887-1979

Wickenden, Dorothy. Nothing daunted; the unexpected education of two society girls in the West. Scribner 2011 286p il $26; ebook $12.99

Grades: 11 12 Adult   92
1. Underwood, Rosamond 2. Women teachers 3. Colorado
ISBN 978-1-4391-7658-0; 978-1-4391-7660-3 (ebook)
LC 2011-08949

"On July 24, 1916, the Syracuse Daily Journal printed the headline: 'Society Girls Go to Wilds of Colorado.' The two young women were Dorothy Woodruff and Ros-amond Underwood, recent graduates of Smith College who, in order to defy their family's expectation of mar-riage, sought work in the small town of Hayden, Colo. Woodruff was the grandmother of . . . [the author], who herself becomes a central character in an informative and engaging narrative. Using letters from her grandmother, newspaper articles, and interviews with descendants, Wickenden retells how Woodruff and Underwood trav-eled to the newly settled state of Colorado to teach at a ramshackle grade school." Publ Wkly
Includes bibliographical references

Woolf, Virginia, 1882-1941

Brackett, Virginia. Restless genius; the story of Virginia Woolf. Morgan Reynolds Pub 2004 144p il (World writers) lib bdg $24.95 *

Grades: 9 10 11 12   92
1. Authors, English 2. Women authors
ISBN 1-931798-37-0   LC 2003-25043

This biography "begins with the people, events, and dynamics of Woolf's childhood, then quickly progresses to her adult life. Throughout, Brackett discusses in some detail the writer's relationships with her father, sister, husband, and, to a lesser extent, other relatives and mem-bers of the Bloomsbury group while focusing increasing-ly on her writings and her mental health." Booklist
Includes bibliographical references

Mills, Cliff. Virginia Woolf; introduction by Betty McCollum. Chelsea House Publishers 2004 130p il (Women in the arts) $22.95; pa $13.25

Grades: 9 10 11 12   92
1. Authors, English 2. Women authors
ISBN 0-7910-7459-5; 0-7910-7953-8 (pa)
LC 2003-9505

Discusses the life and work of the twentieth-century English author, Virginia Woolf.

Woolf's "history is presented in an interesting manner as are the controversies that swirled around her. There are many color illustrations and pictures including insets giving more insight." Libr Media Connect
Includes bibliographical references

Wright, Orville, 1871-1948

Freedman, Russell. The Wright brothers: how they invented the airplane; with original photographs by Wilbur and Orville Wright. Holiday House 1991 129p il hardcover o.p. pa $14.95 *

Grades: 5 6 7 8 9 10   92
1. Wright, Wilbur, 1867-1912 2. Aeronautics—History
ISBN 0-8234-0875-2; 0-8234-1082-X (pa)
LC 90-48440

In this "combination of photography and text, Freed-man reveals the frustrating, exciting, and ultimately suc-cessful journey of these two brothers from their bicycle shop in Dayton, Ohio, to their Kitty Hawk flights and beyond. . . . An essential purchase for younger YAs." Voice Youth Advocates
Includes bibliographical references

Wright, Orville. How we invented the airplane; an illustrated history; edited with an introduction and commentary by Fred C. Kelly; additional text by Alan Weissman. Dover Publs. 1988 c1953 87p il pa $9.95 *

Grades: 11 12 Adult   92
1. Wright, Wilbur, 1867-1912 2. Aeronautics—History
ISBN 0-486-25662-6   LC 87-33037
First published 1953 by D. McKay

This "account by the two inventors . . . covers exper-iments, discovery of aeronautical principles, construction of planes and motors, first flights, and much more. Also included is a later account written by both brothers." Publisher's note
Includes bibliographical references

Wright, Richard, 1908-1960

Wright, Richard. Black boy; (American hunger): a record of childhood and youth; foreword by Edward P. Jones. 60th anniversary ed., 1st ed. HarperCollinsPublishers 2005 419p $24.95; pa $14.95

Grades: 11 12 Adult   92
1. African American authors 2. African Americans—Social conditions
ISBN   0-06-083400-5;   978-0-06-083400-5; 0-06-113024-9 (pa); 978-0-06-113024-3 (pa)
LC 2005-52698
First published 1945 by World Publishing Company
"The restored text established by the Library of Amer-ica"

This autobiographical work concludes with Wright "newly arrived in Chicago in 1927 as a fugitive from the white South that never knew him. [It] relates his nomad-ic life in Tennessee, Arkansas, and Mississippi, aban-doned by his father and with his mother working at me-nial jobs or incapacitated by illness." Benet's Reader's Ency of Am Lit
Includes bibliographical references

Wright, Wilbur, 1867-1912

Freedman, Russell. The Wright brothers: how they invented the airplane. See entry under Wright, Orville, 1871-1948

Wright, Wilbur, 1867-1912—Continued
  Wright, Orville. How we invented the airplane.
See entry under Wright, Orville, 1871-1948

Yamazaki, James N., 1916-
  Yamazaki, James N. Children of the atomic
bomb; an American physician's memoir of
Nagasaki, Hiroshima, and the Marshall Islands;
{by} James N. Yamazaki with Louis B. Fleming.
Duke Univ. Press 1995 182p il maps
(Asia-Pacific) $21.95 *
Grades: 11 12 Adult   92
  1. Physicians 2. Atomic bomb victims 3. Japanese
Americans
  ISBN 0-8223-1658-7   LC 95-6683
  "An army surgeon who was captured at the Battle of
the Bulge, Yamazaki practiced pediatrics after the war.
In this . . . memoir, he recalls his enlistment in the official commission investigating the casualties inflicted by
the Nagasaki explosion." Booklist
  The author "describes the incredible destruction of
lives and buildings, cooperation from Japanese officials
and health care personnel (doctors, nurses, midwives),
firsthand reports from survivors, and the medical studies
of pregnancies and short- and long-term effects on children. . . . This autobiography is unique in the history of
this genre." Choice
  Includes bibliographical references

Zaharias, Babe Didrikson, 1911-1956
  Cayleff, Susan E. Babe: the life and legend of
Babe Didrikson Zaharias. University of Ill. Press
1995 327p il (Women in American history)
$29.95; pa $15.95
Grades: 11 12 Adult   92
  1. Women athletes
  ISBN 0-252-01793-5; 0-252-06593-X (pa)
                                     LC 94-35584
  The author "presents a feminist analysis of the life,
sports career, and legacy of Mildred Ella 'Babe'
Didrikson Zaharias. . . . Cayleff examines Babe's amateur athletic career from high school through the 1932
Olympics, as well as her professional and amateur golf
accomplishments. . . . Although it will undoubtedly be
controversial, *Babe* is a very important book about a
unique and significant figure in US sports." Choice
  Includes bibliographical references

Zellner, Robert, 1939-
  Zellner, Robert. The wrong side of Murder
Creek; a White southerner in the freedom
movement; [by] Bob Zellner, with Constance
Curry; foreword by Julian Bond. NewSouth Books
2008 351p il $27.95
Grades: 11 12 Adult   92
  1. Student Nonviolent Coordinating Committee
  2. Civil rights demonstrations 3. Southern States—
Race relations
  ISBN 978-1-58838-222-1; 1-58838-222-2
                                     LC 2008-25962

  "Zellner's memoir focuses on his experiences as a civil rights activist from 1960 to 1967. He tells a story that
is sometimes horrific, always interesting, and ultimately
inspirational about a white Southerner's commitment to
racial justice. . . . This powerful portrait of a courageous
man is highly recommended." Libr J

Zenatti, Valérie, 1970-
  Zenatti, Valérie. When I was a soldier; a
memoir; translated by Adriana Hunter. Bloomsbury
Children's Books 2005 235p $16.95
Grades: 7 8 9 10   92
  1. Women soldiers 2. Israel
  ISBN 1-58234-978-9
  In this "memoir, Zenatti, first among her group of
friends to be called for compulsory military service,
chronicles two years of growing up in the Israeli army
between 1988 and 1990." SLJ
  A "fast, wry, present-tense memoir. . . . Readers on
all sides of the war-peace continuum, here and there, will
find much to talk about." Booklist

929 Genealogy, names, insignia

Ball, Edward, 1959-
  The genetic strand; exploring a family history
through DNA. Simon & Schuster 2007 265p il $25
Grades: 11 12 Adult   929
  1. Ball family 2. Genetics 3. DNA fingerprinting
  ISBN 0-7432-6658-7; 978-0-7432-6658-1
                                     LC 2007-11513
  "Using locks of hair collected as family keepsakes,
[the author] . . . analyzed DNA samples to trace his
family history. He learned that, probably like most people, his lineage is a diverse racial mixture." Libr J
  "Ball's tale will intrigue America's many amateur
genealogists and also serve as a cautionary tale." Publ
Wkly

Shepherdson, Nancy
  Ancestor hunt; finding your family online.
Franklin Watts 2003 144p il, maps $29.50 *
Grades: 9 10 11 12   929
  1. Genealogy
  ISBN 0-531-15454-8   LC 2002-11646
  This "volume shows you how to search your family
history by using the Internet. Although you usually start
by interviewing your older relatives, Shepherdson shows
you how to take these clues and use them in various
Internet sites and links. She also gives you things to
avoid and tips for doing the interviews. . . . This book
is so chock full of information that you will be returning
to it constantly as you search for your family ancestry."
Libr Media Connect
  Includes bibliographical references

929.4   Personal names

Dictionary of American family names; Patrick Hanks, editor. Oxford Univ. Press 2003 3v set $295 *
  Grades: 11 12 Adult   **929.4**
  1. Personal names—United States
  ISBN 0-19-508137-4   LC 2003-3844

This is a "guide to 70,000 of the most frequently found surnames in the United States. Based on an 88.7 million-name sample culled from a commercial telephone database, the entries indicate the frequency of the name within the sample, plus an explanation of the name." Libr J

"This set will be useful for genealogists, historians, and others curious about their family roots." SLJ

Includes bibliographical references

Hanks, Patrick
  A concise dictionary of first names; [by] Patrick Hanks and Flavia Hodges. 3rd ed. Oxford Univ. Press 2001 314p pa $12.95
  Grades: 9 10 11 12   **929.4**
  1. Personal names
  ISBN 0-19-866259-9
  First published 1992 in the United Kingdom

This volume includes "answers to . . . the meanings and histories of names, how they have risen or fallen in popularity, and who the famous bearers of the names are from history, fiction, and the screen. Detailed appendix material includes European, Arabic, and Indian names." Publisher's note

  A dictionary of first names; [by] Patrick Hanks, Kate Hardcastle, and Flavia Hodges. 2nd ed. Oxford University Press 2006 xxvii, 434p (Oxford paperback reference) pa $16.99
  Grades: 11 12 Adult   **929.4**
  1. Personal names—Dictionaries 2. Reference books
  ISBN 978-0-19-861060-1; 0-19-861060-2
                  LC 2006-49845
  First published 1990

This book "covers over 6,000 names in common use in English, including newly created names and traditional names that have been newly discovered. . . . [Entries list] the age, origin, and meaning of the name, as well as how it has fared in terms of popularity, and notes famous bearers (both historical and fictional). . . . [The book] covers alternative spellings, short forms and pet forms, and masculine and feminine forms, as well as help with pronunciation." Publisher's note

  Includes bibliographical references

929.9   Flags. Forms of insignia and identification

Leepson, Marc, 1945-
  Flag: an American biography. Thomas Dunne Books/St. Martin's Press 2005 334p il $24.95; pa $14.95
  Grades: 11 12 Adult   **929.9**
  1. Flags—United States
  ISBN   978-0-312-32308-0;   0-312-32308-5; 978-0-312-32309-7 (pa); 0-312-32309-3 (pa)
                  LC 2004-65920

"Chronicling the two-centuries-plus history of the U.S. flag, Leepson considers the abundant stories that purport to be the truth about Old Glory." Booklist

"From reverence to kitsch, Americans' attitudes to their flag and its mythology have changed over the years, and Leepson does a creditable job of recounting those changes." Publ Wkly

  Includes bibliographical references

Minahan, James
  The complete guide to national symbols and emblems. Greenwood Press 2010 2v il set $180
  Grades: 8 9 10 11 12 Adult   **929.9**
  1. National emblems—Encyclopedias 2. National characteristics—Encyclopedias 3. Signs and symbols 4. Reference books
  ISBN 978-0-313-34496-1; 978-0-313-34497-8 (ebook)
                  LC 2009-36963
  Contact publisher for ebook pricing

"This set is an impressive compilation of material that should be quite useful for anyone looking for current information about flags, anthems, athletic teams, cuisines, and such. The 200-plus entries cover independent nations of the world and some dependent states and territories that seek greater visibility, such as Wallonia (an autonomous region within Belgium) and Puerto Rico. Volume 1 covers Asia and Oceania, Central and South America, and Europe. Volume 2 covers the Middle East and North Africa, North America and the Caribbean, and sub-Saharan Africa. National flags and coats of arms are shown in color." Booklist

  Includes bibliographical references

Shearer, Benjamin F.
  State names, seals, flags, and symbols; a historical guide; [by] Benjamin F. Shearer and Barbara S. Shearer. 3rd ed, rev and expanded. Greenwood Press 2001 495p il $73.95
  Grades: 8 9 10 11 12 Adult   **929.9**
  1. Geographic names—United States 2. Seals (Numismatics) 3. Flags—United States 4. Reference books
  ISBN 0-313-31534-5   LC 2001-23525
  First published 1987

"Chapters on mottoes, flowers, trees, birds, songs, holidays, and license plates are just a sampling of what is covered, and the format is such that the concisely written material can be found as expeditiously as possible. Even though the book is touted predominantly as a reference tool, the information provided makes fascinating and enlightening reading." Libr J [review of 1994 edition]

  Includes bibliographical references

930 History of ancient world (to ca.499)

The **ancient** world; general editor, Eric Cline; consulting editor, Sarolta Takács. Sharpe Reference 2007 5v il map set $399
Grades: 7 8 9 10   930
1. Ancient civilization—Encyclopedias 2. Reference books
ISBN 978-0-7656-8082-2   LC 2006-101384
Takács is listed as general editor and Cline as consulting editor in volumes 2, 3, and 5.

Contents: v1 Civilizations of Africa; v2 Civilizations of Europe; v3 Civilizations of the Americas; v4 Civilizations of the Near East and Southwest Asia; v5 Civilizations of Asia and The Pacific

This encyclopedia "presents a cultural and societal investigation of ancient Africa, Europe, the Americas, the Near East, Southwest Asia, and Asia and the Pacific. Lucid, fact-packed entries are arranged alphabetically and cover topics such as civilizations and peoples, culture, agriculture, key places, and war and military affairs." SLJ

Includes bibliographical references

The **classical** world, 500 BCE to AD 600 CE; [edited by Clare Collinson] Brown Bear Books 2009 112p il map (Curriculum connections. Atlas of world history) lib bdg $39.95
Grades: 9 10 11 12   930
1. Ancient civilization 2. Classical civilization
ISBN 978-1-933834-66-5   LC 2009-27834
Contents: Introduction; The world in 323 BCE; The world in 200 BCE; The world in 1 BCE; The world in 400 CE; The world in 600 CE; World religions; The Persian wars and Greece; The Peloponnesian war and Macedon; Alexander the great; The Hellenistic world; Parthian and Sasanian Persia; Early Rome and the Punic wars; Growth of the Roman empire; Crisis and recovery of Rome; Fall of the Roman empire; Justinian and the Byzantine empire; The Celts; The Steppe Nomads; The early states of Africa; Mauryan and Gupta India; China; China and the rise of Japan; The Pacific and Southeast Asia; South America and Mexico; The ancient Maya

This book "is divided into thematic and regional maps which are followed by short but very comprehensive articles. . . . [It includes] curriculum context sidebars, important terms students should know, and how the topic ties into other areas." Libr Media Connect

Includes bibliographical references

Encyclopedia of the ancient world; editor, Thomas J. Sienkewicz. Salem Press 2002 3v il maps set $341
Grades: 11 12 Adult   930
1. Ancient civilization—Encyclopedias 2. Reference books
ISBN 0-89356-038-3   LC 2001-49896
This reference work encompasses "not only Greece and Rome but also 'the civilizations, cultures, traditions, monuments and artifacts, significant wars and battles, and important personages of the rest of the world: Europe (outside Greece and Rome), Africa, the Americas, Asia, and Oceania.' The time span is from prehistory to

approximately 700 C.E." Booklist
Includes bibliographical references

The **first** civilizations to 500 BC; edited by Clare Collinson. Brown Bear Books 2010 112p map (Curriculum connections. Atlas of world history) lib bdg $39.95
Grades: 9 10 11 12   930
1. Ancient civilization 2. Ancient history
ISBN 978-1-933834-65-8   LC 2009-27833
Contents: Introduction; The world in 2000 BCE; The world in 1000 BCE; The world in 500 BCE; Peopling the earth; The rise of agriculture; Farmers of the Middle East; Advanced farmers of the Middle East; Cities of Mesopotamia; The first empires; Hittites and Assyrians; Assyria and Babylon; The bible lands; Achemenid Persia; Ancient Egypt: middle and new kingdoms; Neolithic Europe; Bronze age Europe; First civilizations of the Mediterranean; Phoenicia and Greece; Greek city-states; Etruscans, Greeks, and Carthaginians; South Asia; East Asia; The Americas

This book "is divided into thematic and regional maps which are followed by short but very comprehensive articles. . . . [It includes] curriculum context sidebars, important terms students should know, and how the topic ties into other areas." Libr Media Connect

Great events from history, The ancient world, prehistory-476 C.E.; editor, Mark W. Chavalas; consulting editors, Mark S. Aldenderfer . . . [et al.] Salem Press 2004 2v il map set $160
Grades: 11 12 Adult   930
1. Reference books 2. Ancient history
ISBN 1-58765-155-6; 978-1-58765-155-7
                              LC 2004-1360
Also available online
Companion volume to Great lives from history, The ancient world, prehistory-476 C.E.

Some essays previously published in Great events from history (1972-1980), Chronology of European history, 15,000 B.C. to 1997 (1997), and Great events from history, North American series (1997)

"Articles are arranged chronologically, beginning around 25,000 B.C.E. with the San Peoples, who created the first discernible art in Africa, and ends on September 4, 476 C.E. with the fall of Rome, when the last Roman emperor, Romulus Augustulus, was deposed. Articles cover the entire world, with special attention paid to non-European areas. . . . All articles maintain the same structure and give the locale of the event, its category, a summary of the event, its significance, an annotated list of further readings, and cross references to related events." Ref & User Services Quarterly

Includes bibliographical references

Howitt, Carolyn
500 things to know about the ancient world. Barrons Educational Series, Inc. 2007 152p il pa $9.99
Grades: 7 8 9 10   930
1. Ancient civilization
ISBN 978-0-7641-3863-8; 0-7641-3863-4
                              LC 2007-21750

Howitt, Carolyn—*Continued*

This collection of facts about the ancient world includes "facts about marriage and divorce in ancient cultures, the different kinds of clothes the ancients wore and how they fastened them in a time before zippers and Velcro, the magical ways in which ancient Egyptians interpreted dreams, the plants that were used as medicines in ancient civilizations, and . . . more." Publisher's note

Includes bibliographical references

Obregón, Mauricio

Beyond the edge of the sea; sailing with Jason and the Argonauts, Ulysses, the Vikings, and other explorers of the Ancient World. Random House 2001 132p il maps hardcover o.p. pa $11.95

Grades: 11 12 Adult   930

1. Explorers 2. Ancient geography

ISBN 0-679-46326-7; 0-679-78344-X (pa)

LC 00-27173

Obregón "writes of Jason, Ulysses, Far Eastern peoples, and the Vikings. He gives . . . maps of sites possibly visited by these travelers and discusses the difficulties and challenges facing the explorers. . . . He writes about the way such sailors must have navigated and describes the ships they sailed in." Sci Books Films

"Sweeping in scope . . . this book offers several surprisingly provocative and plausible conclusions. . . . The fascinating history of the sea, its mythic and historical figures, and the boats that changed the world are brought into a fresh and interesting perspective." Booklist

Includes bibliographical references

Starr, Chester G., 1914-

A history of the ancient world. 4th ed. Oxford Univ. Press 1991 742p il maps $49.95 *

Grades: 11 12 Adult   930

1. Ancient history

ISBN 0-19-506629-4   LC 90-34970

First published 1965

Incorporating recent archaeological and anthropological discoveries, the author surveys the changing economic and social structures of societies, from prehistory to the fifth century A.D. Egyptian, Assyrian, Chinese and Greek are among the civilizations discussed

Includes bibliographical references

930.1   Archaeology

Ceram, C. W., 1915-1972

Gods, graves, and scholars; the story of archaeology; translated from the German by E. B. Garside and Sophie Wilkins. 2nd rev and substantially enl ed. Knopf 1967 441p il maps pa $11.16 hardcover o.p.

Grades: 11 12 Adult   930.1

1. Archeology

ISBN 0-394-74319-9 (pa)

Original German edition, 1949; first English language edition, 1951

"The story of Champollion and the reading of the Rosetta Stone, the decipherment of the inscriptions on the monument of Darius the Great, Leonard Woolley's famous excavations at Ur, and John Lloyd Stephens' discovery of the ruins of a great Mayan city are . . . told in this book." Doors to More Mature Read

Includes bibliographical references

Hunt, Patrick

Ten discoveries that rewrote history. Plume 2007 226p pa $27.95

Grades: 11 12 Adult   930.1

1. Archeology—History 2. Antiquities 3. Ancient civilization

ISBN 978-0-452-28877-5; 0-452-28877-0

LC 2007-19808

"This book allots one chapter to each of ten key discoveries: the Rosetta stone, Troy, the Assyrian Library at Nineveh, Tutankhamen's Tomb, Machu Picchu, Pompeii, the Dead Sea Scrolls, Akrotiri on Thera, the Olduvai Gorge, and the Tomb of 10,000 Warriors. These discoveries are examined 'in the context of the evolving discipline of archaeology since the eighteenth century.'" Libr J

The author "has produced a wonderful volume of of archaeological history. In doing so, he has provided a seldom seen look at some of the most important scientific developments in the field." Sci Books Films

Includes bibliographical references

McIntosh, Jane

Handbook to life in prehistoric Europe. Facts on File 2006 404p il map (Facts on File library of world history) $70

Grades: 11 12 Adult   930.1

1. Ancient history 2. Ancient civilization 3. Europe—History—To 476

ISBN 978-0-8160-5779-5; 0-8160-5779-6

LC 2005-19775

Also available in paperback from Oxford University Press

This book "focuses primarily on the period from 7000 B.C.E., when agricultural communities first began appearing in southeastern Europe, to the first century C.E., when western Europe was progressively incorporated into the Roman imperium." Publisher's note

Includes bibliographical references

The **Oxford** companion to archaeology; editor in chief, Brian M. Fagan; editors, Charlotte Beck [et al.] Oxford Univ. Press 1996 xx, 844p il maps $75 *

Grades: 11 12 Adult   930.1

1. Archeology—Dictionaries 2. Reference books

ISBN 0-19-507618-4   LC 96-30792

"In addition to broad discussions of specific civilizations such as Islamic, Olmec, and African, there are entries on theories (post processual), ethics, processes (lithics), dating techniques, pop culture (archaeology in film and television), specific sites and site management, plantation archaeology, and human evolution." Booklist

Rubalcaba, Jill

Every bone tells a story; hominid discoveries, deductions, and debates; [by] Jill Rubalcaba and Peter Robertshaw. Charlesbridge 2010 185p il map lib bdg $18.95

Grades: 8 9 10 11 12 **930.1**
1. Fossil hominids 2. Prehistoric peoples 3. Excavations (Archeology) 4. Archeology
ISBN 978-1-58089-164-6; 1-58089-164-0
LC 2008-26961

"Archaeology and paleontology are the exciting focus in this accessible account of four hominins who lived long before recorded history. . . . The informal style never oversimplifies the engaging science and technology, and the authors raise as many questions as they answer in the detailed chapters." Booklist

931 China to 420 A.D.

Hardy, Grant

The establishment of the Han empire and imperial China; [by] Grant Hardy and Anne Behnke Kinney. Greenwood Press 2005 xxx, 170p il (Greenwood guides to historic events of the ancient world) $45

Grades: 9 10 11 12 **931**
1. China—History
ISBN 0-313-32588-X LC 2004-22475

Contents: The establishment of the Han empire: an overview; The center and the periphery; Technological innovation and empire; Social change in Han times; Imperial China in world history; Biographies; Primary documents

This "is a promising eastward expansion of this series on the ancient world." SLJ

Includes bibliographical references

Kleeman, Terry F., 1955-

The ancient Chinese world; [by] Terry Kleeman & Tracy Barrett. Oxford University Press 2005 174p il map (World in ancient times) $32.95

Grades: 7 8 9 10 **931**
1. China—History
ISBN 0-19-517102-0 LC 2004-14408

This book "uses primary sources to describe the history of ancient China and how it still influences the lives of billions of people today." Publisher's note

"Readers seriously interested in history, in archaeology—or in China—will be well served by this engrossing book." SLJ

Includes bibliographical references

Shaughnessy, Edward L., 1952-

Exploring the life, myth, and art of ancient China. Rosen 2009 c2010 144p il map (Civilizations of the world) lib bdg $29.95

Grades: 7 8 9 10 11 12 **931**
1. China—Civilization 2. Chinese mythology 3. Arts—China
ISBN 978-1-4358-5617-2; 1-4358-5617-1
LC 2009-10290

This is an introduction to ancient Chinese civilization

"This beautifully illustrated and well-written [title] . . . is perfect for those assignments where students must look at the culture of a civilization. Artwork and pictures blend seamlessly with the information and the reader is taken on a journey of discovery. Myths are used as the story of how the people view themselves, blended with the discussion of the reality of life. Everyday life is tied to the belief systems and is explained in light of those beliefs. The pictures are beautifully done and there is almost as much information in the captions as there is in the text." Libr Media Connect

Includes glossary and bibliographical references

932 Egypt to 640 A.D.

Ancient Egypt; general editor, David P. Silverman. Oxford Univ. Press 1997 256p il maps hardcover o.p. pa $21.50

Grades: 11 12 Adult **932**
1. Egypt—Civilization
ISBN 0-19-521270-3; 0-19-521952-X (pa)
LC 96-37171

"Twelve contributing scholars have joined Silverman in writing this . . . book that contains 200 color photographs, maps, and charts. Their essays cover such . . . subjects as history, geography, legends, archaeology, religion, economy, art, architecture, and language. There are pieces on international trade and travel, farming, hunting, fishing, mining, capital cities, palaces, fortresses, gender and society, mathematics, medicine, magic, the pharaohs, the cosmos, the cult of the dead, ritual games, the pyramids, tombs, temples, the solar cycle, and hieroglyphs." Booklist

Includes glossary and bibliographical references

Baker, Rosalie F.

Ancient Egyptians; people of the pyramids; [by] Rosalie F. and Charles F. Baker. Oxford Univ. Press 2001 189p il maps (Oxford profiles) $50

Grades: 7 8 9 10 **932**
1. Egypt—Civilization 2. Egypt—Biography
ISBN 0-19-512221-6 LC 2001-21209

"Divided into five periods from the Old Kingdom, about 2686 B.C., to the declining New Kingdom, about 245 B.C., this book profiles some 30 Egyptian leaders, devoting a three- to seven-page chapter to each one. . . . The entries are well written and researched. . . . A useful addition for report writers and subject enthusiasts." SLJ

Includes glossary and bibliographical references

Brier, Bob

The murder of Tutankhamen; a true story. Berkley Books 2005 xx, 264p il pa $14

Grades: 11 12 Adult **932**
1. Tutankhamen, King of Egypt 2. Egypt—History
ISBN 0-425-20690-4; 978-0-425-20690-4
LC 2005-41085

First published 1998 by Putnam

By "combining known historical events with evidence gathered by advanced technologies, Brier has recreated

Brier, Bob—*Continued*
the suspenseful story of religious upheaval and political intrigue that likely resulted in the murder of the teenage King Tutankhamen." Booklist

"Brier obviously knows his subject and is impassioned by it. Readers who enjoy history or true-crime stories will be intrigued by this work." SLJ

Includes bibliographical references

Bunson, Margaret R.
Encyclopedia of ancient Egypt. rev ed. Facts on File 2002 462p il maps $70 *
Grades: 11 12 Adult   932
1. Egypt—Civilization—Encyclopedias 2. Reference books
ISBN 0-8160-4563-1   LC 2002-3550
First published 1991
new edition in preparation
This work consists of "alphabetically arranged entries covering Egypt from around 3200 B.C. to the fall of the New Kingdom in 1070 B.C. There are several broad entries such as *Egypt, Agriculture, and Religion*. The bulk of the book, however, consists of specific entries for kings and queens, gods and goddesses, cities, important documents, etc." Booklist [review of 1991 edition]

Casson, Lionel, 1914-2009
Everyday life in ancient Egypt. rev and expanded ed. Johns Hopkins Univ. Press 2001 163p il hardcover o.p. pa $15.95
Grades: 9 10 11 12   932
1. Egypt—Civilization
ISBN 0-8018-6600-6; 0-8018-6601-4 (pa)
                                       LC 00-59091
First published 1975 by American Heritage Pub. with title: The Horizon book of daily life in ancient Egypt
The author describes the structure of ancient Egyptian society including social classes, family, the role of women, farm life, leisure, the professions and craftsmen, religion, and travel.
Includes bibliographical references

David, A. Rosalie (Ann Rosalie)
Handbook to life in ancient Egypt; [by] Rosalie David. rev ed. Facts on File 2003 417p il map (Facts on File library of world history) $50 *
Grades: 11 12 Adult   932
1. Egypt—Civilization
ISBN 0-8160-5034-1   LC 2002-35229
Also available in paperback from Oxford University Press
First published 1998
This covers such topics as the geography of Ancient Egypt, society and government, religion, funerary beliefs and customs, architecture, trade and transport, the army and navy, economy and industry, and everyday life.
Includes bibliographical references

Fletcher, Joann, 1966-
Exploring the life, myth, and art of ancient Egypt. Rosen Pub. 2009 c2010 144p il map (Civilizations of the world) $29.95
Grades: 7 8 9 10 11 12   932
1. Egypt—Civilization 2. Egypt—Antiquities
ISBN 978-1-4358-5616-5; 1-4358-5616-3
                                        LC 2009-8792
"This attractively designed and handsomely illustrated book offers a rich and informative introduction to ancient Egyptian culture. Abundantly illustrated with beautifully rendered color representations of architecture, works of art, and other artifacts, the book offers insight into the beliefs and rituals, economy, and social organization of ancient Egyptian civilization." Booklist
Includes glossary and bibliographical references

Hawass, Zahi A.
Tutankhamun and the golden age of the pharaohs; [by] Zahi Hawass; photographs by Kenneth Garrett. National Geographic Books 2005 285p il map $35
Grades: 11 12 Adult   932
1. Tutankhamen, King of Egypt 2. Egypt—Antiquities
ISBN 0-7922-3873-7   LC 2005-41678
This companion to an exhibition displaying about 130 items found in the tombs of Tutankhamun and other kings from the same dynasty "describes the physical and symbolic attributes of each object and explains its purpose in the afterlife. . . . An arrestingly visual album destined for high demand." Booklist
Includes bibliographical references

Mertz, Barbara, 1927-
Temples, tombs, & hieroglyphs; a popular history of ancient Egypt. 2nd ed., 1st William Morrow ed. William Morrow 2007 xxvi, 324p il map $26.95 *
Grades: 9 10 11 12 Adult   932
1. Egypt—Antiquities 2. Egypt—Civilization
ISBN 978-0-06-125276-1; 0-06-125276-X
                                        LC 2007-29118
First published 1964 by Coward-McCann
This is an "introduction to the history of ancient Egypt and Egyptology. . . . Mertz gives special attention to such topics as the kingship (yes) of Queen Hatshepsut, the exploits of Thutmose III, and the Amarna Period with its intriguing players Akhenaten, Nefertiti, and Tutankhamen. Presenting both pros and cons of current theories, Mertz also explains in simple language archaeological techniques such as carbon 14 dating and historical chronology. . . . [This is] an excellent introduction for patrons interested in the land of the pharaohs." Libr J

Nardo, Don, 1947-
Arts, leisure, and sport in ancient Egypt. Lucent Books 2005 112p il map (Lucent library of historical eras, Ancient Egypt) $28.70
Grades: 7 8 9 10   932
1. Egypt—Civilization 2. Egyptian art
ISBN 1-59018-706-7   LC 2004030542

Nardo, Don, 1947-—*Continued*
Contents: Artistry in stone; Production of pottery and glass; Clothmaking and leatherworking; Working with metal and wood; Jewelry-making and painting; Writing and literature; Leisure games and sports; Hunting and fishing; Music, singing, and dancing

"Quoting extensively from 19th- and 20th-century Egyptologists, as well as from available ancient sources, Nardo presents a great deal of information in a smooth narrative, accompanied by archival photographs and reproductions of artifacts, illustrations from the past century or so, and even scenes taken from films and documentaries." SLJ

Includes bibliographical references

Netzley, Patricia D.
The Greenhaven encyclopedia of ancient Egypt. Greenhaven Press 2003 336p (Greenhaven encyclopedia of) $74.95
Grades: 8 9 10 11 12　　　　　　　　**932**
　1. Egypt—Antiquities—Encyclopedias 2. Reference books
　ISBN 0-7377-1150-7　　　　　LC 2002-6965
"Alphabetical entries range from prehistory to the time of Greco-Roman domination and are generally between a paragraph and a page in length. Coverage includes individual pharaohs, places, practices, trades, beliefs, artwork, and aspects of daily and family life with entries such as 'furniture,' 'children,' and 'entertaining guests.' Important individuals such as archaeologist Howard Carter are also included." SLJ

Includes bibliographical references

The **Oxford** encyclopedia of ancient Egypt; Donald B. Redford, editor in chief. Oxford Univ. Press 2001 3v set $450 *
Grades: 11 12 Adult　　　　　　　　**932**
　1. Egypt—Civilization—Encyclopedias 2. Egypt—Antiquities—Encyclopedias 3. Reference books
　ISBN 0-19-510234-7　　　　　LC 99-54801
This reference work covers "archaeology, biography, history, language, social history, and more. . . . [It features] essays from more than 250 contributors from various countries and scholarly pursuits, all with solid academic credentials. . . . One is not likely to encounter another work of this magnitude on a subject of such universal interest for some time." Booklist

Includes bibliographical references

Taylor, John H.
Unwrapping a mummy; the life, death and embalming of Horemkenesi. University of Tex. Press 1996 111p il (Egyptian bookshelf) pa $18.95
Grades: 9 10 11 12　　　　　　　　**932**
　1. Horemkenesi 2. Mummies 3. Egypt—Civilization
　ISBN 0-292-78141-5　　　　　LC 95-61446
An exploration of ancient Egyptian civilization based on the study of the mummy of Horemkenesi. Customs surrounding death and the process of mummification are discussed in detail

Includes bibliographical references

933　Palestine to 70 A.D.

Burleigh, Nina
Unholy business; a true tale of faith, greed, and forgery in the holy land. Smithsonian Books 2008 271p $27.50
Grades: 11 12 Adult　　　　　　　　**933**
　1. Golan, Oded 2. Forgery 3. Israel—Antiquities
　ISBN 978-0-06-145845-3　　　　LC 2008-23425
"In 2002, the James Ossuary, an ancient limestone box for bones with an inscription on it that said 'James, son of Joseph, brother of Jesus' was publicized as the first real physical evidence of Jesus Christ's existence. The plot thickened when the ossuary went on tour, creating lots of publicity, a book by advocate Hershel Shanks, and a Discovery Channel documentary. Then the ossuary's owner, Oded Golan, and his antique-dealer associates were charged with forgery. . . . Whether or not readers believe the ossuary is authentic, they will thoroughly enjoy this book." Libr J

935　Mesopotamia and Iranian Plateau to 637 A.D.

Bertman, Stephen
Handbook to life in ancient Mesopotamia. Facts on File 2002 396p il map (Facts on File library of world history) $70
Grades: 11 12 Adult　　　　　　　　**935**
　1. Iraq—Civilization
　ISBN 0-8160-4346-9　　　　　LC 2002-3516
Also available in paperback from Oxford University Press
"*The Handbook to Life in Ancient Mesopotamia* describes the culture, history, and people of this land, as well as their struggle for survival and happiness, from about 3500 to 500 BCE." Publisher's note

Includes bibliographical references

936　Europe north and west of Italian peninsula to ca. 499 A.D.

Cunliffe, Barry, 1939-
The ancient Celts. Penguin Books 1999 324p il map pa $21.95
Grades: 11 12 Adult　　　　　　　　**936**
　1. Celts
　ISBN 0-14-025422-6
First published 1997 by Oxford Univ. Press
This is a "survey of the origins of the Celts and their expansion during the Iron Age through their largely successful subjection by the Romans. . . . [Cunliffe] has written a readable and informative book with many attractive illustrations." Libr J

Includes bibliographical references

936.1 British Isles to 410 A.D. Northern Britain and Ireland

Burl, Aubrey
The stone circles of Britain, Ireland and Brittany. Yale Univ. Press 2000 462p il $60; pa $30
Grades: 9 10 11 12   **936.1**
1. Great Britain—Antiquities 2. Ireland—Antiquities
ISBN 0-300-08347-5; 0-300-11406-0 (pa)
LC 99-87909
First published 1976 with title: The stone circles of the British Isles
This describes the prehistoric stone circles built some 6000 years ago, such as Stonehenge in England, Callanish in Scotland and the cromlechs in Brittany, how and why they were constructed, and how they have been excavated and studied.
"Burl's authoritative book is indispensable for anyone pursuing this tantalizing enigma." Publ Wkly
Includes bibliographical references

937 Roman Empire

Adkins, Lesley
Handbook to life in ancient Rome; [by] Lesley Adkins and Roy A. Adkins. Updated ed. Facts on File 2004 450p il, maps (Facts on File library of world history) $85 *
Grades: 9 10 11 12   **937**
1. Rome—Civilization 2. Rome—Social life and customs
ISBN 0-8160-5026-0   LC 2003-49255
First published 1994
This work covers politics, military affairs, literature, religion, architecture, geography, and social life in ancient Rome from the 8th century B.C. to the 5th century A.D. Illustrated with site-specific photographs and line drawings.
Includes bibliographical references

Aldrete, Gregory S.
Daily life in the Roman city; Rome, Pompeii and Ostia. Greenwood Press 2004 278p il map (The Greenwood Press "Daily life through history" series) $55
Grades: 11 12 Adult   **937**
1. Rome—Social life and customs
ISBN 0-313-33174-X   LC 2004-20943
Also available in paperback from University of Oklahoma Press
This "study of life in the ancient Roman city explains how the city functioned, who lived there, and what the inhabitants' lives were like. . . . Included are accounts of Rome's history, infrastructure, government, and inhabitants, as well as chapters on life and death, the dangers and pleasures of urban living, entertainment, religion, the emperors, and the economy." Publisher's note
Includes bibliographical references

Allan, Tony, 1946-
Life, myth, and art in Ancient Rome. J. Paul Getty Museum 2005 144p il pa $19.95 *
Grades: 11 12 Adult   **937**
1. Roman art 2. Roman mythology 3. Rome—Civilization 4. Rome—Antiquities
ISBN 0-89236-821-7   LC 2004-114326
This is an "illustrated guide to the cultural and political heritage of ancient Rome, including the enduring legacy of its art and architecture, the engineering innovations of its vast system of roads and aqueducts, the . . . myths of its gods and goddesses, and the power of its emperors and legions." Publisher's note
Includes bibliographical references

Baker, Rosalie F.
Ancient Romans; expanding the classical tradition; [by] Rosalie F. and Charles F. Baker III. Oxford Univ. Press 1998 267p il (Oxford profiles) $40
Grades: 9 10 11 12   **937**
1. Rome—History 2. Rome—Biography
ISBN 0-19-510884-1   LC 97-21531
"Drawing on the work of Plutarch, Livy, Tacitus, and Suetonius, the authors recount the history of Rome's rise to power through brief biographies of 39 notable Romans. The five periods covered span the years 400 B.C.E. to A.D. 350." SLJ
"Challenging reading, the book will best serve college-bound students with a basic knowledge of ancient Roman culture and history." Booklist
Includes glossary and bibliographical references

Berry, Joanne, 1971-
The complete Pompeii. Thames & Hudson 2007 256p il map $40
Grades: 11 12 Adult   **937**
1. Pompeii (Extinct city)
ISBN 978-0-500-05150-4; 0-500-05150-X
LC 2007-922095
This book "covers the origins and evolution of the city, the daily life of its residents, the geography of the region, and the eruption of Mt. Vesuvius, as well as a history of the excavation of the site. Easy to read and with full color pictures of the excavation, along with maps, time lines, diagrams, and vivid art reproductions, this book gives a broad and comprehensive introduction to the Pompeian world. . . . High school libraries should be advised that there is a section on eroticism that contains visually and verbally explicit sexual material." Libr J
Includes bibliographical references

Bunson, Matthew
Encyclopedia of the Roman Empire. rev ed. Facts on File 2002 636p il maps $75 *
Grades: 11 12 Adult   **937**
1. Rome—History—Encyclopedias 2. Reference books
ISBN 0-8160-4562-3   LC 2001-53253
First published 1994
This reference work provides information on the key places, people, events, and culture of Roman history,

Bunson, Matthew—*Continued*
from the reign of Julius Caesar to the fall of the last Roman emperor in 476 A.D.

"An excellent ready-reference source." Booklist [review of 1994 edition]

Includes bibliographical references

The **Cambridge** illustrated history of the Roman world; edited by Greg Woolf. Cambridge University Press 2003 384p il map (Cambridge illustrated history) $45

Grades: 11 12 Adult   **937**
1. Rome—History
ISBN 0-521-82775-2   LC 2004-298480

This book explores such topics as "religion, Rome's relationship with Greece, warfare and Empire, and science and culture." Publisher's note

Includes bibliographical references

Ermatinger, James William, 1959-
The decline and fall of the Roman Empire; [by] James W. Ermatinger. Greenwood Press 2004 xxxi, 187p il map (Greenwood guides to historic events of the ancient world) $45

Grades: 9 10 11 12   **937**
1. Rome—History
ISBN 0-313-32692-4   LC 2004-14674

"An overview of the period is presented in the introduction, and is followed by chapters on late Roman culture, society, and economics in late antiquity; religious conflicts in Christian Rome; enemies of Rome; and why and when Rome fell. The narrative chapters conclude with a section placing Rome's fall in modern perspective." Publisher's note

Includes bibliographical references

Hinds, Kathryn, 1962-
Everyday life in the Roman Empire. Marshall Cavendish Benchmark 2010 320p il lib bdg $42.79
Grades: 7 8 9 10   **937**
1. Holy Roman Empire 2. Rome—History
ISBN 978-0-7614-4484-8; 0-7614-4484-X
LC 2009-5913

A compilation of four titles in the Everyday Life in the Roman Empire series, published 2004: The city; The countryside; The Patricians; Religion

"Provides a social history of life in the Roman Empire at its most powerful, from 27 B.C.E. to 200 C.E., and includes descriptions of the ruling classes, the peasantry, and the urban dwellers." Publisher's note

This book combines "clear, bold text with vivid reproductions of period paintings, frescoes, and sculptures, making for [a] stunning [presentation]." SLJ

Includes glossary and bibliographical references

938   Greece to 323 A.D.

Adkins, Lesley
Handbook to life in ancient Greece; [by] Lesley Adkins and Roy A. Adkins. Updated ed. Facts on File 2005 514p il map (Facts on File library of world history) $70 *
Grades: 11 12 Adult   **938**
1. Greece—Civilization
ISBN 0-8160-5659-5   LC 2004-47105
First published 1997

This book covers "all aspects of ancient Greek life—from the beginnings of the Minoan civilization in Crete to the final defeat by the Roman world in 30 BCE." Publisher's note

Includes bibliographical references

Baker, Rosalie F.
Ancient Greeks; creating the classical tradition; [by] Rosalie F. Baker and Charles F. Baker. Oxford Univ. Press 1997 254p il maps (Oxford profiles) $50
Grades: 7 8 9 10   **938**
1. Greece—Biography 2. Greece—Civilization
ISBN 0-19-509940-0   LC 95-26637

"The influence of ancient Greek civilization is chronicled in concise biographies of over 37 Greek statesmen, playwrights, artists, mathematicians, philosophers, and military leaders." Book Rep

"Students looking for biographical or historical information on ancient Greece will find it valuable, as will teachers seeking to integrate the classics into other disciplines." Booklist

Includes glossary and bibliographical references

Cartledge, Paul
Ancient Greece; a history in eleven cities. Oxford University Press 2009 261p il map $19.95
Grades: 10 11 12 Adult   **938**
1. Greece—Civilization 2. Greece—History—0-323
ISBN 978-0-19-923338-0   LC 2009-26999

This is an "overview of Greek history . . . . [as depicted through] synopses of 11 key city-states, each representing a different facet of Greek life and culture, such as politics, gender, and philosophy." Publ Wkly

"Aiming for a general audience, Cartledge achieves a fast-paced, highly engaging romp through ancient Greece. An excellent choice for anyone seeking an introduction to the topic; for all its readability, this book doesn't skimp on the research." Libr J

Includes bibliographical references

Classical Greek civilization, 800-323 B.C.E; edited by John T. Kirby. Gale Group 2001 xxxi, 395p il maps (World eras) $99
Grades: 11 12 Adult   **938**
1. Greece—Civilization
ISBN 0-7876-1707-5   LC 00-47648

"A Manly, Inc. book"

"The volume is divided into 10 topical chapters, among them 'The Arts,' 'Social Class System and the

Classical Greek civilization, 800-323 B.C.E—
Continued
Economy,' 'The Family and Social Trends,' and 'Religion and Philosophy.' . . . Except for chapter one, 'World Events,' which provides context with a list of events outside Greece, each chapter follows the same general plan. A chronology and an overview precede a series of articles on various topics. . . . These articles generally range in length from two to four pages and are followed by biographical profiles." Booklist

This book's "comprehensive coverage of the entire classical Greek period makes it a valuable addition for your library's ancient history collection." Book Rep

Includes glossary and bibliographical references

Skelton, Debra
Empire of Alexander the Great; [by] Debra Skelton & Pamela Dell. Rev. ed. Chelsea House 2009 152p il (Great empires of the past) $35
Grades: 7 8 9 10   **938**
1. Alexander, the Great, 356-323 B.C. 2. Greece—History
ISBN 978-1-60413-162-8   LC 2009-5723
First published 2005
This book "looks at what made Alexander a brilliant military tactician and a charismatic leader. It also explores what the Eastern world learned through contact with Alexander, and what Alexander brought to the West from the Persian Empire." Publisher's note

Includes glossary and bibliographical references

Tritle, Lawrence A., 1946-
The Peloponnesian War; [by] Lawrence Tritle. Greenwood Press 2005 xxiv, 206p il map (Greenwood guides to historic events of the ancient world) $45
Grades: 9 10 11 12   **938**
1. Greece—History—431-404 B.C., Peloponnesian War
ISBN 0-313-32499-9   LC 2004-47506
This book features "biographical sketches, and annotated primary documents. An overview of the war is presented, followed by a presentation of Thucydides' account of the war's causes. A look at the intertwined . . . relation of democracy and empire is offered, as are chapters on how the war was represented in plays, statuary, and pottery." Publisher's note

Includes bibliographical references

Wood, Michael, 1948-
In the footsteps of Alexander the Great; a journey from Greece to Asia. University of Calif. Press 1997 256p il maps hardcover o.p. pa $18.95 *
Grades: 11 12 Adult   **938**
1. Alexander, the Great, 356-323 B.C. 2. Historic sites 3. Asia—Description and travel
ISBN 0-520-21307-6; 0-520-23192-9 (pa)
                                        LC 97-19188
Based on the PBS series, this "book recreates Alexander's 22,000 mile, ten-year expedition from Greece to India, following as much as possible the actual route of his

journey." Publisher's note
This book is "illustrated with a mixture of Alexandrine art from a variety of cultures, landscapes that capture the wide range of geographies through which Alexander and his imperial armies passed, and portraits of cultures . . . in which the influence of that long-ago juggernaut is still visible." Booklist

Includes bibliographical references

938.003   Classical dictionaries

Ancient Greece; edited by Thomas J. Sienkewicz. Salem Press 2007 3v il map (Magill's choice) set $207
Grades: 11 12 Adult   **938.003**
1. Reference books 2. Greece—History—Encyclopedias
ISBN 1-58765-281-1; 978-1-58765-281-3
                                        LC 2006-16525
Some of the essays in this work appeared in various other Salem Press sets

This book is a "comprehensive examination of Greek civilization and its impact on Western history, 'from its earliest archaeological remains until the Battle of Actium in 31 B.C.E.' . . . [The essays included] cover art, daily life and customs, government, literature, medicine and science, war, the role of women, and mythology. Biographical entries profile statesmen, artists, writers, scientists, and philosophers, and relevant entries probe battles, philosophical movements, and types of literature." SLJ

Includes bibliographical references

The **Cambridge** dictionary of classical civilization; edited by Graham Shipley . . . [et al.] Cambridge University Press 2006 xliv, 966p il map $180 *
Grades: 11 12 Adult   **938.003**
1. Reference books 2. Classical civilization—Dictionaries
ISBN 0-521-48313-1; 978-0-521-48313-1
                                        LC 2006-299203
The "entries and more than 500 illustrations focus on social, economic, and cultural aspects of these civilizations from the mid-eighth century BCE to the end of the fifth century." Booklist

Includes bibliographical references

The **Oxford** classical dictionary; edited by Simon Hornblower and Antony Spawforth. 3rd rev ed. Oxford Univ. Press 2003 lv, 1640p $110 *
Grades: 11 12 Adult   **938.003**
1. Reference books 2. Classical dictionaries
ISBN 0-19-860641-9
First published 1949 under the editorship of M. Cary and others
This reference includes over 6,000 entries about the ancient Greco-Roman world, covering such topics as politics, government and economy, religion and mythology, law and philosophy, science and geography, languages, literature, art and architecture, archeology, historical writing, military history, social history, sex, and gender

"This is a work that makes a fascinating world of learning accessible to a broad audience." Booklist

Includes bibliographical references

Sacks, David
Encyclopedia of the ancient Greek world; editorial consultant, Oswyn Murray; revised by Lisa R. Brody. Rev ed. Facts on File 2005 xx, 412p il map (Facts on File library of world history) $75
Grades: 11 12 Adult   **938.003**
1. Reference books 2. Greece—History—Encyclopedias
ISBN 0-8160-5722-2   LC 2004-56429
First published 1995
This encyclopedia covers "ancient Greece, from the dawning of Minoan civilization to the conquest of Rome—2000 years of a remarkable civilization that left an indelible imprint on human history. . . . This is a first-rate purchase for libraries on a topic of endless inquiry and fascination." SLJ
Includes bibliographical references

939   Other parts of ancient world to ca. 640

Civilizations of the Ancient Near East; Jack M. Sasson, editor in chief; John Baines, Gary Beckman, Karen S. Rubinson, associate editors. Hendrickson Publishers 2000 4v in 2 il map set $169.95 *
Grades: 11 12 Adult   **939**
1. Middle East—Civilization
ISBN 1-56563-607-4   LC 00-63144
First published 1995 by Scribner
This "work concentrates on the Near East, broadly defined to include a region from Northeast Africa to India, Pakistan, and Burma, with principal focus on the core areas of Egypt, Syro-Palestine, Mesopotamia, and Anatolia. The time span ranges from the third millennium B.C.E., when writing was invented, to 330 B.C.E., when Alexander triumphed over the Persian Empire. The 189 contributors from five continents and 16 countries include some of the world's finest scholars." Libr J [review of 1995 edition]
Includes bibliographical references

Dictionary of the ancient Near East; edited by Piotr Bienkowski and Alan Millard. University of Pa. Press 2000 342p il maps hardcover o.p. pa $34.95
Grades: 11 12 Adult   **939**
1. Middle East—Antiquities—Dictionaries
2. Reference books
ISBN 0-8122-3557-6; 0-8122-2115-X (pa)
                                        LC 00-21715
"The time period covered is from the Lower Paleolithic (around 1.5 million years ago) to the fall of Babylon to Cyrus the Great in 539 B.C. The geographic scope encompasses Mesopotamia, Iran, Anatolia, the Caucasus, the Levant, and Arabia. There are some entries on major archaeologists and explorers from modern times as well as on ancient cultures, historic and legendary figures, concepts, aspects of daily life, and individual archaeological sites. The 500 articles range from brief paragraphs to a few columns on double-columned pages." Booklist
"The volume's easy-to-follow format, very readable

content and affordable price assure its use by general readers, students and scholars." Choice
Includes bibliographical references

Thomas, Carol G., 1938-
The Trojan War; [by] Carol G. Thomas and Craig Conant. Greenwood Press 2005 209p il map (Greenwood guides to historic events of the ancient world) $45 *
Grades: 9 10 11 12   **939**
1. Trojan War
ISBN 0-313-32526-X   LC 2004-17660
"An overview of Troy and the world of the late Bronze Age is presented in the first chapter, followed by sections on: finding Troy and the Trojan War, Homer and the epic tradition, the force of legend, and Troy in the 21st century." Publisher's note
Includes bibliographical references

940   History of Europe

Davies, Norman
Europe: a history. HarperCollins Publishers 1998 1365p il map pa $25.95
Grades: 9 10 11 12   **940**
1. Europe—History
ISBN 0-06-097468-0   LC 97-32889
First published 1996 by Oxford Univ. Press
This book covers "the rise and fall of Rome, the sweeping invasions of Alaric and Atilla, the Norman Conquests, the Papal struggles for power, the Renaissance and the Reformation, the French Revolution and the Napoleonic Wars, Europe's rise to become the powerhouse of the world, and its eclipse in our own century, following two devastating World Wars." Publisher's note
Includes bibliographical references

World and its peoples: Europe. Marshall Cavendish Reference 2010 13v il map set $714.21
Grades: 8 9 10 11 12   **940**
1. Human geography—Encyclopedias 2. Europe—Civilization—Encyclopedias 3. Europe—History—Encyclopedias 4. Reference books
ISBN 978-0-7614-7883-6   LC 2009-4321
Contents: v1 Ireland and the United Kingdom; v2 France, Andorra, and Monaco; v3 Germany and Switzerland; v4 Belgium, Luxembourg, and Netherlands; v5 Portugal and Spain; v6 Italy, Malta, and San Marino; v7 Central Europe; v8 Estonia, Latvia, Lithuania, and Poland; v9 Scandinavia and Finland; v10 Belarus, Russian Federation, and Ukraine; v11 Greece and the Eastern Balkans; v12 Western Balkans; v13 Indexes
"Each book details the geographical features and climate of the entire region, along with an overview of the history and movement of people in the area. This overview is followed by in-depth coverage of each country (dependencies and the Russian Federation are included), focusing on particulars such as statistics, culture, government, economics, symbols, and national history. . . . With copious resources offered for further research and a meticulous index, this set is an ideal resource for geography, history, and social-studies assignments." SLJ
Includes bibliographical references

940.1   Europe—Early history to 1453

Bishop, Morris, 1893-1973

The Middle Ages. 1st Mariner Books ed. Houghton Mifflin Co. 2001 350p il pa $17 *
Grades: 9 10 11 12   **940.1**
1. Middle Ages 2. Medieval civilization
ISBN 0-618-05703-X   LC 2001-271448
"A Mariner book"
First published 1968 by American Heritage with title: The Horizon book of the Middle Ages
This volume covers the period from the conversion of Constantine in 312 A.D. through the conclusion of the Hundred Years War in 1461.

English, Edward D.

Encyclopedia of the medieval world. Facts on File 2004 2v il map (Facts on File library of world history) set $150 *
Grades: 11 12 Adult   **940.1**
1. Middle Ages—Encyclopedias 2. Reference books
ISBN 0-8160-4690-5   LC 2003-27825
This encyclopedia "covers the time period from the late antique world to about 1500 C.E and includes events, people, institutions, and culture in western and eastern Europe, Scandinavia, North Africa, Byzantium, and the Near East. The 2,000 entries discuss significant people, art, politics, literature, religion, economics, law, science, and warfare in an A-Z format." Booklist
Includes bibliographical references

Gies, Frances

The knight in history. Harper & Row 1984 255p il maps hardcover o.p. pa $14.99
Grades: 11 12 Adult   **940.1**
1. Knights and knighthood 2. Middle Ages
ISBN 0-06-015399-3; 0-06-091413-0 (pa)
     LC 84-47571
This book describes the rise and fall of the institution of knighthood and the influence of the medieval knight throughout history.
Includes bibliographical references

Life in a medieval village; [by] Frances and Joseph Gies. Harper & Row 1990 257p il maps hardcover o.p. pa $14.95
Grades: 11 12 Adult   **940.1**
1. Medieval civilization 2. Middle Ages
ISBN 0-06-016215-5; 0-06-092046-7 (pa)
     LC 89-33759
"Elton, England, is the focal point of the authors' efforts to portray the everyday life and social structure of the High Middle Ages. After giving a brief summary of Elton's origins and development in the Roman and Anglo-Saxon periods, the book examines just how the residents lived and worked within the feudal structure at the beginning of the fourteenth century." Booklist
Includes bibliographical references

Gies, Joseph

Life in a medieval city; [by] Joseph and Frances Gies. HarperPerennial 1981 c1969 274p il map pa $13.95
Grades: 11 12 Adult   **940.1**
1. Middle Ages 2. Medieval civilization
ISBN 0-06-090880-7
First published 1969 by Crowell
"A portrait of a medieval city [Troyes], a flourishing settlement of a type not known in Europe before the Middle Ages." Cincinnati Public Libr
Includes bibliographical references

The **Greenwood** encyclopedia of global medieval life and culture; Joyce E. Salisbury, general editor. Greenwood Press 2009 3v il map set $349.95
Grades: 7 8 9 10 11 12 Adult   **940.1**
1. Medieval civilization—Encyclopedias 2. Reference books
ISBN 978-0-313-33801-4; 0-313-33801-9
     LC 2008-36709
"This set is a much-expanded version of the *Greenwood Encyclopedia of Daily Life, Volume II* (2004). . . . As its title suggests, the new set extends the coverage of medieval life around the globe. . . . The global nature of this encyclopedia sets it apart from other works on the medieval period. Because of its depth and breadth of coverage, it is recommended for high-school, college, and public libraries that need reference works on medieval history." Booklist
Includes bibliographical references

Hamm, Jean S.

Term paper resource guide to medieval history; [by] Jean Shepherd Hamm. Greenwood Press 2010 371p $65 *
Grades: 10 11 12   **940.1**
1. Middle Ages—Bibliography 2. Medieval civilization—Bibliography 3. Report writing 4. Reference books
ISBN 978-0-313-35967-5; 0-313-35967-9
     LC 2009-36249
This book "provides coverage of an extensive time period (410-1485), condensed into 100 significant historical events from the Middle Ages. Organized chronologically, the guide reliably represents cultures from Asia, Africa, and the Americas, but largely focuses on European history. Although not intended to be a comprehensive history, this volume will be an exceedingly useful tool for advanced high school students and beginning undergraduates charged with writing papers on the medieval period. For each entry, the author gives a broad overview of a historical event; recommends related term paper topics and alternative projects; and provides excellent suggestions for primary, secondary, Web, and multimedia sources." Choice
Includes bibliographical references

History of the ancient and medieval world. 2nd ed. Marshall Cavendish Reference 2009 11v il map set $714.21 *
Grades: 7 8 9 10 11 12   **940.1**
1. Ancient history 2. Medieval civilization 3. Middle Ages 4. Reference books
ISBN 978-0-7614-7789-1   LC 2008-60052
First published 1996

Contents: v1 The first civilizations; v2 Western Asia and the Mediterranean; v3 Ancient Greece; v4 The Roman Empire; v5 The changing shape of Europe; v6 The early Middle Ages in western Asia and Europe; v7 Southern and eastern Asia; v8 Europe in the Middle Ages; v9 Western Asia, northern Europe, and Africa in the Middle Ages; v10 The passing of the medieval world; v11 Index

This "set traces the history of humans, beginning with the first primitive civilizations and continuing through the waning days of the Middle Ages." Booklist

This "will become the resource for students seeking information on this time period." SLJ

Includes bibliographical references

Knights; in history and in legend; chief consultant Constance Brittain Bouchard. Firefly Books 2009 304p il map $40
Grades: 11 12 Adult   **940.1**
1. Knights and knighthood 2. Military art and science—History
ISBN 978-1-55407-480-8

The history of knights, from their everyday lives to their clothing, training, heraldry and orders, as well as their role in literature and film, and the decline of traditional knighthood.

"Aimed at history and art history lovers, this work would be excellent reading for medieval history enthusiasts and should be welcomed as a library reference resource." Libr J

Includes bibliographical references

The **Oxford** dictionary of the Middle Ages; edited by Robert E. Bjork. Oxford University Press 2010 4v il map set $595
Grades: 11 12 Adult   **940.1**
1. Middle Ages—Encyclopedias 2. Medieval civilization—Encyclopedias 3. Reference books
ISBN 9780198662624 (set)   LC 2010-923327

"The ODMA's 5,000 entries range in length from one or two sentences (Gargoyle, Drollery) to 10,000 or more words and are consistently well written. . . . The ODMA encompasses areas of Asia, Africa, and the Middle East as well as topics of current scholarship, such as gender studies and Islam. Entries include individuals (Attila, Hildegard of Bingen); technical terms (Hammer beam, squinch); and places (Sutton Hoo)." Booklist

Includes bibliographical references

The **Oxford** history of medieval Europe; edited by George Holmes. Oxford Univ. Press 2001 395p il maps pa $16.95 *
Grades: 11 12 Adult   **940.1**
1. Europe—History—476-1492
ISBN 0-19-280133-3   LC 2002-281715

This is an abridged edition of The Oxford illustrated history of medieval Europe, published 1988

This compact edition covers such subjects as the chivalric code of knights, popular festivals, new art forms, the Black Death, the fall of Rome, and the emergence of the Reformation

Includes bibliographical references

Singman, Jeffrey L.
Daily life in medieval Europe. Greenwood Press 1999 268p il $57.95; pa $25 *
Grades: 9 10 11 12   **940.1**
1. Europe—Social life and customs 2. Europe—History—476-1492 3. Medieval civilization
ISBN 0-313-30273-1; 0-313-36076-6 (pa)
                                        LC 98-46816
Also available online

The author "focuses on details that help readers picture rural and urban medieval life among peasants, monks, and the aristocracy—medieval heating and lighting, bedchambers in cottages and castles, clothing, money and prices, even sanitation. Singman narrows his focus to the years 1100-1300, portraying life in Northern France, England, the Low Countries, and some of Germany." Voice Youth Advocates

Includes bibliographical references

940.2   Europe—1453-

The **eighteenth** century; Europe, 1688-1815; edited by T.C.W. Blanning. Oxford University Press 2000 301p il map (Short Oxford history of Europe) hardcover o.p. pa $43.95
Grades: 10 11 12 Adult   **940.2**
1. Europe—History—18th century 2. Europe—Civilization 3. Europe—Social conditions 4. Europe—Economic conditions
ISBN 0-19-873181-7; 0-19-873120-5 (pa)
                                        LC 00711763

"In this book, six experts analyse . . . the major developments [that occured in eighteenth-century Europe] in politics, society, the economy, religion and culture, warfare and international relations, and in Europe's relations with the world overseas." Publisher's note

Includes bibliographical references

Encyclopedia of the Enlightenment; Alan Charles Kors, editor in chief. Oxford Univ. Press 2003 4v il set $685
Grades: 11 12 Adult   **940.2**
1. Enlightenment—Encyclopedias 2. Philosophy—Encyclopedias 3. Reference books
ISBN 0-19-510430-7   LC 2002-3766

Contents: v1 Abbadie-Enlightenment studies; v2 Enthusiasm-Lyceums and museums; v3 Mably-Ruysch; v4 Sade-Zoology

This reference includes over 700 articles about "philosophic and social changes engendered by the Enlightenment. It {covers} . . . not only France, England, Scotland, the Low Countries, Italy, English-speaking North America, the German states, and Hapsburg Austria but also Iberian, Ibero-American, Jewish, Russian, and Eastern European cultures." Publisher's note

Includes bibliographical references

Europe 1789 to 1914; encyclopedia of the age of industry and empire; Merriman and Jay Winter, editors in chief. Charles Scribner's Sons 2006 5v il map (Scribner library of modern Europe) set $595

Grades: 11 12 Adult   **940.2**
1. Europe—History—1789-1900—Encyclopedias
2. Europe—History—1871-1918—Encyclopedias
3. Europe—Civilization—Encyclopedias 4. Reference books
ISBN 0-684-31359-6; 978-0-684-31359-7
                     LC 2006-7335

This encyclopedia covers "the time period between the onset of the French Revolution to the outbreak of World War I." Publisher's note

Includes bibliographical references

The **European** Renaissance and Reformation, 1350-1600; edited by Norman J. Wilson. Gale Group 2001 xxix, 522p il maps (World eras) $130.75 *

Grades: 11 12 Adult   **940.2**
1. Renaissance 2. Reformation
ISBN 0-7876-1706-7   LC 00-52802

This resource "is comprised of 10 chapters. The first two, focusing on world events and geography, respectively, provide users a global perspective and context for the culture and time period in question. Remaining chapters treat other cultural elements. . . . Each chapter is subdivided into five types of material: chronological, overview, topical, biographical, and documentary. . . . This volume, in addition to its fine organization, structure, and arrangement, is equally impressive for its inclusive, well-written content." Booklist

Includes bibliographical references

Gies, Joseph
Life in a medieval castle; [by] Joseph and Frances Gies. Harper & Row 1979 c1974 272p il pa $14.95

Grades: 11 12 Adult   **940.2**
1. Castles 2. Middle Ages
ISBN 0-06-090674-X   LC 79-103901

First published 1974 by Crowell

Using Chepstow Castle on the Welsh border as a model, the authors provide "descriptions of the medieval world where the castle was household, feudal center, and military target, and by concentrating on Anglo-Norman examples illustrate what existence was like as the dark ages began to brighten." Booklist

Includes glossary and bibliographical references

Hinds, Kathryn, 1962-
Everyday life in the Renaissance. Marshall Cavendish Benchmark 2010 327p il lib bdg $42.79

Grades: 7 8 9 10   **940.2**
1. Renaissance 2. Europe—Civilization
ISBN 978-0-7614-4483-1; 0-7614-4483-1
                    LC 2008-54829

A compilation of four titles in the Everyday Life in the Renaissance series, published 2004: The church; The city; The countryside; The court

"Describes the social and economic structure of life in the Renaissance (from roughly 1400-1600), including the ruling classes, the peasantry, the urban dwellers, and members of the Church and the role each group played in shaping European civilization." Publisher's note

This book combines "clear, bold text with vivid reproductions of period paintings, frescoes, and sculptures, making for [a] stunning [presentation]." SLJ

Includes glossary and bibliographical references

The **nineteenth** century; Europe, 1789-1914; edited by T.C.W. Blanning. Oxford University Press 2000 304p il map (Short Oxford history of Europe) hardcover o.p. pa $43.95

Grades: 10 11 12 Adult   **940.2**
1. Europe—History—1789-1900 2. Europe—Civilization 3. Europe—Social conditions 4. Europe—Economic conditions
ISBN 0-19-873136-1; 0-19-873135-3 (pa)
                     LC 00703223

"In six chapters, experts tackle the big questions relating to the political, international, social, economic, cultural, and imperial history of [nineteenth-century Europe]." Publisher's note

Includes bibliographical references

The **Oxford** illustrated history of modern Europe; edited by T. C. W. Blanning. Oxford Univ. Press 1996 362p il maps hardcover o.p. pa $24.95 *

Grades: 11 12 Adult   **940.2**
1. Europe—History—1789-1900 2. Europe—History—20th century
ISBN 0-19-820374-8; 0-19-285426-7 (pa)

This volume covers "politics, economics, warfare, class structure, art, and culture from the time of the revolution through 1995. Central themes include the idea that revolution against established order was possible, successful, and, once underway, perhaps unstoppable." Libr J

Includes bibliographical references

The **Renaissance**; Raymond Obstfeld and Loretta Obstfeld, book editors. Greenhaven Press 2002 220p il (History firsthand) hardcover o.p. pa $21.20 *

Grades: 9 10 11 12   **940.2**
1. Renaissance
ISBN 0-7377-1080-2 (lib bdg); 0-7377-1079-9 (pa)
                    LC 2001-51296

This anthology gathers primary accounts from religious, artistic, scientific and secular leaders dealing with social and political topics of the day

Includes bibliographical references

The **Renaissance**; an encyclopedia for students; [edited by] Paul F. Grendler. Charles Scribner's Sons 2003 4v set $395 *

Grades: 11 12 Adult   **940.2**
1. Reference books 2. Renaissance—Encyclopedias
ISBN 0-684-31281-6   LC 2003-15672

Adaptation of Encyclopedia of the Renaissance, published 1999

The Renaissance—*Continued*
This encyclopedia includes articles on various aspects of social, cultural, and political history such as literature, government, warfare, and technology, plus maps, charts, definitions, and chronology
"Researchers should find their needs more than satisfied by this appealing and student-friendly resource." SLJ

Renaissance & Reformation: almanac; [by] Peggy Saari & Aaron Saari, editors; Julie Carnagie, project editor. U.X.L 2002 2v il (Renaissance & Reformation reference library) set $105 *
Grades: 8 9 10 11 12   **940.2**
1. Renaissance 2. Reformation
ISBN 0-7876-5467-1   LC 2002-6152
This "is organized into topical chapters that include sidebars with additional information and more than 100 black-and-white illustrations. Volume 1 begins with a time line of important events. Following the time line are a 17-page vocabulary list and a research and activity guide. Chapters . . . deal with topics such as the rise of European monarchies, the Protestant and Catholic Reformations, the scientific revolution, the status of women, and daily life. A concluding bibliography lists books, Web sites, and video recordings and DVDs." Booklist
Includes bibliographical references

Renaissance & Reformation: primary sources; [by] Peggy Saari & Aaron Saari, editors; Julie Carnagie, project editor. U.X.L 2002 201p il (Renaissance & Reformation reference library) $58 *
Grades: 8 9 10 11 12   **940.2**
1. Renaissance 2. Reformation
ISBN 0-7876-5473-6   LC 2002-3928
Contents: On the equal or unequal sin of Eve and Adam, by I. Nogarola; The Prince, by N. Machiavelli; The Muqaddimah, by I. Khaldûn; Notebooks, by L. da Vinci; The Starry messenger, "A grand revolution" (box) by G. Galilie; Merchant of Venice, William Shakespeare (box) by W. Shakespeare; Heptaméron, by Margaret of Navarre; Don Quixote, by M. Cervantes; "Of cannibals," by M. de Montaigne; The description of the new world called the blazing world, by M. Cavendish; "The ninety-five theses or disputation on the power and efficacy of indulgences," by M. Luther; "The sixty-seven articles of Ulrich Zwingli," by H. Zwingli; Ecclesiastical ordinances, Institutes of the Christian religion, by J. Calvin; "Elizabeth, a dutch anabaptist martyr: a letter," by Elizabeth; Spiritual exercises, by Ignatius of Loyola; Centuries, by Nostradamus; The life of Teresa of Jesus, by Teresa de Avila; "Profession of the Tridentine faith," by The Roman Catholic Church; Malleus maleficarum, by H. Kramer and J. Sprenger
This "provides selected specific writings of the time. Introductory information about the original author begins each section, and sidebars list definitions of obscure or antiquated words. Following each document piece is a discussion of the historical effects of the piece along with additional readings." Booklist
Includes bibliographical references

Renaissance and Reformation; editor, James A. Patrick. Marshall Cavendish 2007 6v il set $671.36
Grades: 9 10 11 12 Adult   **940.2**
1. Reference books 2. Renaissance—Encyclopedias 3. Reformation—Encyclopedias
ISBN 978-0-7614-7650-4; 0-7614-7650-4
LC 2006-42600
This encyclopedia provides a "background on the historical period that bridged the medieval and modern worlds, roughly 1300-1700, with emphasis on 1350-1650. . . . This is an extremely impressive publication, lavishly presented, informative, and remarkably enjoyable to read. . . . A must-have for all high-school collections and for public libraries patronized by young adults. Adults will find it appealing as well." Booklist
Includes bibliographical references

Sider, Sandra
Handbook to life in Renaissance Europe. Facts on File 2005 382p il map (Facts on File library of world history) $70
Grades: 11 12 Adult   **940.2**
1. Renaissance 2. Europe—Civilization
ISBN 0-8160-5618-8   LC 2004-20088
This "volume concentrates on Italy's impact on the Renaissance in both northern and southern Europe 1400-c.1600, covering the major movements in government, religion, art and architecture, literature, music, science, education, warfare, commerce, exploration, and daily life." SLJ
This book "furnishes a good, general introduction to the Renaissance, and does so succinctly and with some of the breadth usually found in longer works." Choice
Includes bibliographical references

Streissguth, Thomas
The Napoleonic wars; defeat of the Grand Army. Lucent Books 2003 112p il map (History's great defeats) $27.45
Grades: 9 10 11 12   **940.2**
1. Napoleon I, Emperor of the French, 1769-1821 2. France. Armée. Grande Armeé 3. France—History—1799-1815
ISBN 1-590-18065-8   LC 2002-151712
Contents: The rise and fall of the First Empire; The failed Egyptian Campaign; Failed economics; The Peninsular War; Underestimating the enemy; Choosing the sword; A failure of deception
Provides a look at how Napoleon Bonaparte's egotism, unrealistic dreams, and tendency to underestimate enemies led to the downfall of his Grand Armée during the Napoleonic Wars.
Includes bibliographical references

The Renaissance; by Tom Streissguth; Konrad Eisenbichler, consulting editor. Greenhaven Press 2008 353p il map (Greenhaven encyclopedia of) $77.45 *
Grades: 9 10 11 12   **940.2**
1. Reference books 2. Renaissance—Encyclopedias
ISBN 978-0-7377-3216-0   LC 2007-938127
Title on cover: The Greenhaven encyclopedia of the Renaissance

Streissguth, Thomas—*Continued*

Alphabetically arranged essays provide information about the Renaissance, discussing artistic, social, philosophical, theological, political, and scientific topics, and featuring biographical sketches of significant individuals as well as photographs, illustrations, maps, cross-references, and time lines.

"Entries are well written and concise and provide an excellent introduction to each subject for high-school students. Advanced middle-school social-studies classes could also utilize this resource." Booklist

Wilson, Ellen Judy

Encyclopedia of the Enlightenment; Peter Hanns Reill, consulting editor; Ellen Judy Wilson, principal author. rev ed. Facts on File 2004 670p $75 *

Grades: 11 12 Adult   **940.2**
1. Reference books 2. Enlightenment—Encyclopedias 3. Philosophy—Encyclopedias 4. Europe—Intellectual life
ISBN 0-8160-5335-9   LC 2003-22973
First published 1996

This reference provides a "review of the important ideas, people, and events that shaped the world during the Enlightenment. [It] covers the major changes in science, education, philosophy, art and architecture, and politics which took place during the 17th and 18th centuries and led to the birth of the modern era. . . . The biographical entries cover such notables as Robespierre, Schiller, Fielding, Kant, and Voltaire. . . . Larger public, school, and academic libraries looking for a comprehensive overview of the subject for the student or interested reader will find this a valuable and accessible resource." Libr J

Includes bibliographical references

940.3   World War I, 1914-1918

Bausum, Ann

Unraveling freedom; the battle for democracy on the home front during World War I. National Geographic 2010 88p il $19.95; lib bdg $28.90

Grades: 7 8 9 10   **940.3**
1. United States—Politics and government—1898-1919 2. World War, 1914-1918—United States 3. German Americans 4. Civil rights
ISBN   978-1-4263-0702-7;   1-4263-0702-0;
978-1-4263-0703-4 (lib bdg); 1-4263-0703-9 (lib bdg)
LC 2010-10631

"Bausum describes the events that would eventually lead the U.S. into the European conflict that ultimately led to World War I. She then turns her attention to describing the destruction of civil liberties by President Wilson, Congress, and those in control of political power during the country's campaign to 'make the world safe for democracy.' . . . Black-and-white archival photos and political cartoons are arranged in an artistic manner with informative captions. Appropriate quotations by various people of the time are displayed in elegant fonts. Make this unique and timely offering a definite first purchase." SLJ

Includes bibliographical references

Bosco, Peter I.

World War I. Rev. ed. Chelsea House 2010 182p il map (America at war) $45

Grades: 9 10 11 12   **940.3**
1. World War, 1914-1918—United States
ISBN 978-0-8160-8188-2   LC 2009-28627
First published 1991

This book provides a "portrait of this great conflict, with an emphasis on the critical role played by the United States. . . . [It includes a chapter on] the military innovations in tactics and weaponry." Publisher's note

Burg, David F.

Almanac of World War I; [by] David F. Burg and L. Edward Purcell; introduction by William Manchester. University Press of Ky. 1998 320p il maps hardcover o.p. pa $22

Grades: 11 12 Adult   **940.3**
1. World War, 1914-1918
ISBN 0-8131-2072-1; 0-8131-9087-8 (pa)
LC 98-26625

"The bulk of the text is arranged chronologically by year and date, listing almost daily occurrences from 1914 through 1918. . . . The work is international in scope, covering political and military happenings from around the world. . . . There is really nothing comparable to this volume." Booklist

Includes bibliographical references

Carlisle, Rodney P.

World War I. Facts on File 2006 454p il map (Eyewitness history) $75

Grades: 8 9 10 11 12   **940.3**
1. World War, 1914-1918—Personal narratives
ISBN 0-8160-6061-4; 978-0-8160-6061-0
LC 2005-27236

First published 1992 under the authorship of Joe H. Kirchberger with title: The First World War

This book "provides hundreds of firsthand accounts—from diary entries, letters, speeches, and newspaper accounts—that focus on different warfare issues and on the social and cultural impacts of the war on Europe and the United States. . . . This volume also includes critical documents related to this topic, as well as capsule biographies of key figures, narrative sections, eyewitness testimonies, 102 black-and-white photographs, maps and graphs, a bibliography, notes, a glossary, chronologies, appendixes, and an index." Publisher's note

Includes bibliographical references

Coetzee, Marilyn Shevin, 1955-

World War I; a history in documents; [by] Marilyn Shevin-Coetzee and Frans Coetzee. 2nd ed. Oxford University Press 2011 182p il (Pages from history) $39.95; pa $24.95 *

Grades: 7 8 9 10   **940.3**
1. World War, 1914-1918—Sources
ISBN 978-0-19-973151-0; 978-0-19-973152-7 (pa)
LC 2009049519

First published 2002 with authors' names in reverse order

Coetzee, Marilyn Shevin, 1955-—*Continued*

Offering an "account of the war as more than a purely military phenomenon, . . . [this book] also addresses its profound social, cultural, and economic implications. Authors Marilyn Shevin-Coetzee and Frans Coetzee use editorials, memoirs, newspaper articles, poems, and letters to recreate the many facets of the war." Publisher's note

Includes bibliographical references

Freedman, Russell

The war to end all wars; World War I. Clarion Books 2010 176p il map $22 *

Grades: 6 7 8 9 10   940.3
1. World War, 1914-1918
ISBN 978-0-547-02686-2; 0-547-02686-2
                                         LC 2009-28971

"In his signature lucid style, Freedman offers a photo-essay that examines World War I, the first global war in which modern weapons inflicted mass slaughter and an estimated 20 million people were killed. Interwoven into the big picture of the war's causes and consequences are unforgettable vignettes of German and Allied soldiers, drawn from reports, letters, and diaries, and the personal details are heartbreaking." Booklist

Gilbert, Martin, 1936-

The First World War; a complete history. Holt & Co. 1994 xxiv, 615p il maps hardcover o.p. pa $25

Grades: 11 12 Adult   940.3
1. World War, 1914-1918
ISBN 0-8050-1540-X; 0-8050-7617-4 (pa)
                                           LC 94-27268

This work "covers WW I on all major fronts—domestic, diplomatic, military—as well as such bloody preludes as the Armenian massacre of 1915." Publ Wkly

"What Mr. Gilbert seeks to do, and frequently succeeds in doing, is to humanize, indeed to personalize, World War I. His effort and accomplishment make this a rewarding and significant book." N Y Times Book Rev

Includes bibliographical references

Heyman, Neil M.

World War I. Greenwood Press 1997 xxiii, 257p il maps (Greenwood Press guides to historic events of the twentieth century) $45

Grades: 11 12 Adult   940.3
1. World War, 1914-1918
ISBN 0-313-29880-7   LC 97-1686

This work is "divided into three sections. The first gives an overview of the causes, issues, and ultimately the consequences of a world at war. . . . The second section of the book is a series of biographies of the major political and military participants in the war. . . . The third section of the book is devoted to primary documents from the period." Book Rep

Includes bibliographical references

Pendergast, Tom, 1964-

World War I almanac; [by] Tom Pendergast, Sara Pendergast; edited by Christine Slovey. U.X.L 2001 xl, 210p $60

Grades: 8 9 10 11 12   940.3
1. World War, 1914-1918
ISBN 0-7876-5476-0   LC 2001-53012

This "contains 12 chapters covering major topics related to the period, including the roots of the war; causes of U.S. involvement; the Espionage Act and Sedition Act; weapons of mass destruction; and more. Other features include maps, a detailed chronology of events, sidebars featuring related information, a glossary of 'Words to Know,' research and activity ideas, and a list of further reading sources." Publisher's note

Includes bibliographical references

Stokesbury, James L.

A short history of World War I. Morrow 1981 348p maps hardcover o.p. pa $14.95

Grades: 11 12 Adult   940.3
1. World War, 1914-1918
ISBN 0-688-00128-9; 0-688-00129-7 (pa)
                                           LC 80-22206

This chronologically arranged history of World War I presents both the political and military perspectives.

Includes bibliographical references

Stone, Norman, 1941-

World War One. Basic Books 2009 226p il map $25 *

Grades: 9 10 11 12 Adult   940.3
1. World War, 1914-1918
ISBN 978-0-465-01368-5; 0-465-01368-6
First published 2007 in the United Kingdom
Subtitle on jacket: A short history

The author presents a narrative history of the First World War.

"Stone is as unconventional as he is brilliant, and this provocative interpretation of the Great War combines impressive command of the literature with a telling eye for relevant facts and a sensitive ear for telling epigrams." Publ Wkly

Includes bibliographical references

Strachan, Hew

The First World War. Viking 2004 364p il maps hardcover o.p. pa $16

Grades: 11 12 Adult   940.3
1. World War, 1914-1918
ISBN 0-670-03295-6; 0-14-303518-5 (pa)
                                           LC 2003-62191

The author details the "factors behind World War I, covers the major ground and naval campaigns and battles, and assesses the roles of leading officers and statesmen while simultaneously highlighting the home fronts and the non-European aspects of this cataclysmic event." Libr J

"Readers already familiar with the sequence of events in strict order will benefit most. But all readers will eventually be gripped, and even the most seasoned ones will praise the insights and the original choice of illustrations." Publ Wkly

Includes bibliographical references

The **Treaty** of Versailles; Jeff Hay, book editor. Greenhaven Press 2002 124p il (At issue in history) hardcover o.p. pa $18.70 *

Grades: 9 10 11 12   **940.3**
1. Treaty of Versailles (1919) 2. World War, 1914-1918—Peace
ISBN 0-7377-0827-1 (lib bdg); 0-7377-0826-3 (pa)
                                         LC 2001-40609
This collection of articles examines "the expectations of those who negotiated the treaty, the responses to the treaty by those who were close observers or participants in the negotiations, and more recent assessments of the treaty." Publisher's note
Includes bibliographical references

Tuchman, Barbara Wertheim
The guns of August; [by] Barbara W. Tuchman; [with a new foreword by Robert K. Massie] 1st Ballantine Books ed. Ballantine 1994 xxiv, 511p il, maps pa $14

Grades: 11 12 Adult   **940.3**
1. World War, 1914-1918
ISBN 0-345-38623-X   LC 93-90461
First published 1962 by Macmillan
A history of the negotiations that preceded World War I and the course of the war's first month.
Includes bibliographical references

The Zimmermann telegram. Ballantine Books [1985] c1966 244p il pa $14

Grades: 11 12 Adult   **940.3**
1. World War, 1914-1918—Causes
ISBN 0-345-32425-0   LC 84-91737
First published 1958 by Macmillan
The author discusses the German plan to induce Mexico to attack the U.S. during World War I.
Includes bibliographical references

The **United** States in the First World War; an encyclopedia; editor, Anne Cipriano Venzon; consulting editor, Paul L. Miles. Garland 1995 xx, 830p maps (Garland reference library of the humanities) $155; pa $45 *

Grades: 11 12 Adult   **940.3**
1. World War, 1914-1918—Encyclopedias
2. Reference books
ISBN 0-8240-7055-0; 0-8153-3353-6 (pa)
                                          LC 95-1782
"Biography, economics, civil rights, women's issues, foreign relations, battles, armaments, and conferences are among the topics included. Arrangement is alphabetical, and most articles are brief—between one column and a page. . . . Most articles include brief bibliographies. There are six maps, but no other illustrations." Libr J

Woodward, David R., 1939-
World War I almanac. Facts On File 2009 554p il map (Almanacs of American wars) $95

Grades: 9 10 11 12 Adult   **940.3**
1. World War, 1914-1918 2. Almanacs 3. Reference books
ISBN 978-0-8160-7134-0; 978-1-4381-1896-3 (ebook)
                                         LC 2008-41575

Contact producer for ebook pricing
This almanac covers "all geographic areas affected by the conflict and all belligerents. The day-by-day chronicle, with topical headings within each date, forms the main section of the Almanac. The chronology spans 1871-1923. It includes the main events of the war and its aftermath, including major battles, domestic politics, the Russian Revolution, the periods of American neutrality (1914-17), belligerency on the side of the Allies (1917-18), the Paris Peace Conference, and President Wilson's battle for the League of Nations." Choice
This book "would be a welcome addition to public, school, and academic libraries where a student needs to find basic information quickly." Booklist
Includes glossary and bibliographical references

World War I: a student encyclopedia; Spencer C. Tucker, editor; Priscilla Mary Roberts, editor, documents volume. ABC-CLIO 2005 5v il map set $485

Grades: 9 10 11 12   **940.3**
1. World War, 1914-1918—Encyclopedias
2. Reference books
ISBN 1-85109-879-8   LC 2005-25638
"More than 900 A-to-Z entries that range in length from one to 20 pages cover major campaigns, individual battles, countries, biographies, weapons, diplomatic efforts, and the social and cultural impacts of the war. . . . This well-written and accessible resource is highly recommended for school and public libraries." Libr J
Includes bibliographical references

940.4 Military history of World War I

Eisenhower, John S. D., 1922-
Yanks: the epic story of the American Army in World War I; {by} John S. D. Eisenhower with Joanne Thompson Eisenhower. Free Press 2001 353p il maps hardcover o.p. pa $16

Grades: 11 12 Adult   **940.4**
1. United States. Army 2. World War, 1914-1918—Campaigns
ISBN 0-684-86304-9; 0-7432-2385-3 (pa)
                                         LC 2001-23124
"This history focuses entirely on the challenges, victories, sacrifices . . . and long-term consequences of the American Expeditionary Force (AEF) in Europe during World War I." Libr J
"This is an important work that should help alter the historical picture of the American role in the conflict." Booklist
Includes bibliographical references

Farwell, Byron
Over there; the United States in the Great War, 1917-1918. Norton 1999 336p $27.95; pa $15.95 *

Grades: 11 12 Adult   **940.4**
1. World War, 1914-1918—United States
ISBN 0-393-04698-2; 0-393-32028-6 (pa)
                                         LC 98-35705

Farwell, Byron—*Continued*

This history of American intervention in World War I focuses primarily on the military aspects of the war but also discusses its social and economic impact

"This title does provide good coverage on the intervention in Russia and the role of women in the war, notably the 'Hello Girls.' " Libr J

Includes bibliographical references

Mosier, John, 1944-

The myth of the Great War; a new military history of World War I. HarperCollins Pubs. 2001 381p il hardcover o.p. pa $14.95

Grades: 11 12 Adult   **940.4**
1. World War, 1914-1918—Campaigns
ISBN 0-06-019676-9; 0-06-008433-2 (pa)
LC 00-46103

"After dissecting the major campaigns on the western front, Mosier concludes that Germany's ultimate defeat was the direct result of the influx of American soldiers into France in 1917 and 1918. . . . This is revisionist history that convincingly smashes the myths that Allied governments, leaders, and propagandists worked so hard to promulgate. Mosier's masterful account is a welcome addition." Booklist

Includes bibliographical references

940.5   Europe—1918-

Europe since 1914; encyclopedia of the age of war and reconstruction; John Merriman and Jay Winter, editors in chief. Charles Scribner's Sons/Thomson Gale 2006 5v il map (Scribner library of modern Europe) set $595

Grades: 11 12 Adult   **940.5**
1. Reference books 2. Europe—History—20th century—Encyclopedias 3. Europe—Civilization—Encyclopedias
ISBN 0-684-31365-0; 978-0-684-31365-8
LC 2006-14427

This encyclopedia "details European history from the Bolshevik Revolution to the European Union, linking it to the history of the rest of the world." Publisher's note

Includes bibliographical references

940.53   World War II, 1939-1945

Ackerman, Diane

The zookeeper's wife. W.W. Norton 2007 368p il $24.95 *

Grades: 11 12 Adult   **940.53**
1. Jews—Poland 2. Holocaust, 1933-1945 3. World War, 1939-1945—Jews—Rescue 4. Zoos
ISBN 978-0-393-06172-7; 0-393-06172-8
LC 2007-12635

This is an account of how the director of the Warsaw Zoo and his wife, Jan and Antonina Zabinski, respectively, saved 300 Jews during World War II.

"An exemplary work of scholarship and an 'ecstasy of imagining,' Ackerman's affecting telling of the heroic Zabinskis' dramatic story illuminates the profound connection between humankind and nature, and celebrates life's beauty, mystery, and tenacity." Booklist

Includes bibliographical references

Altman, Linda Jacobs, 1943-

Hidden teens, hidden lives; primary sources from the Holocaust. Enslow Publishers 2010 128p il (True stories of teens in the Holocaust) lib bdg $31.93

Grades: 8 9 10 11 12   **940.53**
1. Holocaust, 1933-1945 2. Holocaust survivors 3. World War, 1939-1945—Children 4. World War, 1939-1945—Personal narratives
ISBN 978-0-7660-3271-2; 0-7660-3271-X
LC 2009-6504

"Explores the lives of children and teens who went into hiding during the Holocaust; looks at various places used as hiding spots, such as barns and attics, and different ways to hide, like assuming false identities, and how these were used as a tool to survive." Publisher's note

"Altman does a great job of providing historical context and realistic commentary for the individual experiences. Photos of teens and news pictures . . . add further dimensions to the text." Booklist

Includes bibliographical references

And justice for all; an oral history of the Japanese American detention camps; [compiled by] John Tateishi; foreword by Roger Daniels. University of Washington Press 1999 xxvii, 262p il, map pa $19.95 *

Grades: 9 10 11 12   **940.53**
1. Japanese Americans—Evacuation and relocation, 1942-1945 2. World War, 1939-1945—United States
ISBN 0-295-97785-X   LC 98-49105

First published 1984 by Random House

"Recollections from 30 Japanese Americans who were placed in government detention camps following Japan's attack on Pearl Harbor lend valuable insight into this tragic event in U.S. history." Booklist

Art from the ashes; a Holocaust anthology; edited by Lawrence L. Langer. Oxford Univ. Press 1995 689p il hardcover o.p. pa $47.95 *

Grades: 11 12 Adult   **940.53**
1. Holocaust, 1933-1945—Personal narratives 2. Holocaust, 1933-1945, in literature
ISBN 0-19-507559-5; 0-19-507732-6 (pa)
LC 94-11446

This collection "includes both fiction and nonfiction, as well as drama and poetry. Among the nonfiction pieces are excerpts from the ghetto diaries of Abraham Lewin (Warsaw) and Avraham Tory (Kovno), an essay from Primo Levi's *The Drowned and the Saved,* and an essay from Elie Wiesel's *Legends of Our Time.*" Booklist

A "remarkable volume, perfectly suited for anyone studying the Holocaust. . . . Compared with [the] first-hand accounts, fiction could be, one would think, only a pallid version of reality. Yet the fiction Mr. Langer collects . . . highlights the reality of the Holocaust with stunning intensity." N Y Times Book Rev

Axelrod, Alan, 1952-
Encyclopedia of World War II; consulting
editor, Jack A. Kingston. Facts on File 2007 2v il
(Facts on File library of world history) set $150
Grades: 11 12 Adult   **940.53**
1. Reference books 2. World War, 1939-1945—Encyclopedias
ISBN 0-8160-6022-3; 978-0-8160-6022-1
       LC 2006-26155
This encyclopedia "provides entries on the people,
groups, events, equipment, and concepts on both sides
that were integral to the war. . . . [This] is an outstanding resource that makes it appropriate for any library
serving patrons with questions about World War II." Am
Ref Books Annu, 2008
Includes bibliographical references

Ayer, Eleanor H.
In the ghettos; teens who survived the ghettos of
the Holocaust. Rosen Pub. Group 1998 64p il map
(Teen witnesses to the Holocaust) $26.50 *
Grades: 7 8 9 10   **940.53**
1. Holocaust, 1933-1945—Personal narratives
ISBN 0-8239-2845-4   LC 98-43859
Chronicles the deportation of Jews into ghettos during
Hitler's Third Reich and presents the narratives of three
individuals who, as teenagers, lived in the ghettos of
Lodz, Theresienstadt, and Warsaw and survived physical
deprivations, abuse, and deportation to the death camps
Includes bibliographical references

Parallel journeys; [by] Eleanor H. Ayer with
Helen Waterford and Alfons Heck. Atheneum Bks.
for Young Readers 1995 244p il hardcover o.p. pa
$5.99
Grades: 7 8 9 10   **940.53**
1. Holocaust, 1933-1945 2. Germany—History—1933-
1945 3. Jews—Germany
ISBN 0-689-31830-8; 0-689-83236-2 (pa)
       LC 94-23277
"Alternating chapters contrast the wartime experiences
of two young Germans—Waterford, who was interned in
a Nazi concentration camp, and Heck, a member of the
Hitler Youth. The volume is composed mainly of excerpts from their published autobiographies, connected by
Ayer's overall account of the era. A powerful and painful picture emerges, vividly describing life before, during, and, most impressively, after the Holocaust." Horn
Book Guide
Includes bibliographical references

Berenbaum, Michael, 1945-
The world must know; the history of the
Holocaust as told in the United States Holocaust
Memorial Museum; Arnold Kramer, editor of
photographs. 2nd ed. United States Holocaust
Memorial Museum 2006 xxi, 250p il pa $29.95 *
Grades: 11 12 Adult   **940.53**
1. United States Holocaust Memorial Museum
2. Holocaust, 1933-1945
ISBN 0-8018-8358-X
First published 1993 by Little, Brown

This book documents the "stories of the Holocaust as
told in the renowned permanent exhibition of the United
States Holocaust Memorial Museum in Washington,
D.C." Publisher's note
"Visually evocative and unsettling, the book, supplemented with a useful bibliography, is an excellent choice
for those with little acquaintance of the subject or those
needing a concise synopsis." Libr J [review of 1993 edi-
tion]
Includes bibliographical references

Bitton-Jackson, Livia
I have lived a thousand years; growing up in the
Holocaust; by Livia E. Bitton-Jackson. Simon &
Schuster Bks. for Young Readers 1997 224p
hardcover o.p. pa $5.99
Grades: 7 8 9 10   **940.53**
1. Holocaust, 1933-1945—Personal narratives
2. Jews—Hungary
ISBN 0-689-81022-9; 0-689-82395-9 (pa)
       LC 96-19971
Based on the author's book for adults, Elli: coming of
age in the Holocaust (1980)
"This memoir covers the last fourteen months of
World War II, during which thirteen-year-old Elli
Friedmann (as the author was then named) and members
of her family are deported from their home . . . to two
ghettos and several camps, including Auschwitz." Bull
Cent Child Books
"This is a memorable addition to the searing accounts
of Holocaust survivors." Horn Book
Includes glossary

Chesnoff, Richard Z., 1937-
Pack of thieves; how Hitler and Europe
plundered the Jews and committed the greatest
theft in history. Doubleday 1999 325p il hardcover
o.p. pa $14
Grades: 11 12 Adult   **940.53**
1. Holocaust, 1933-1945 2. Jews—Persecutions
ISBN 0-385-48763-0; 0-385-72064-5 (pa)
       LC 99-33257
The author outlines the "Nazi plot to segregate Jews
from the economic mainstream by expropriating their
businesses, savings accounts, jewelry, art collections, and
other personal belongings. What is startling, though, is
not the fact that many Germans supported and profited
from this plan, but that large numbers of government officials and private citizens in conquered and neutral European nations enthusiastically jumped on the bandwag-
on." Booklist

Children in the Holocaust and World War II; their
secret diaries; [compiled by] Laurel Holliday.
Pocket Bks. 1995 xxi, 409p il map hardcover
o.p. pa $15 *
Grades: 11 12 Adult   **940.53**
1. Holocaust, 1933-1945—Personal narratives
2. World War, 1939-1945—Children
ISBN 0-671-52054-7; 0-671-52055-5 (pa)
       LC 95-3211
"Diary entries written by young people in ghettos,
concentration camps, cities, and a Copenhagen prison

Children in the Holocaust and World War II—
Continued

camp offer . . . glimpses of life during World War II. Each selection is introduced by a brief biography that includes the author's name, country, age, family circumstances before and during the war, and concludes with circumstances of death or postwar life. Nine girls and 14 boys, Jews and gentiles, aged 10 to 18, are featured." SLJ

"This anthology is a haunting reminder of the impact of war on children. The powerful images will long be remembered." Voice Youth Advocates

Includes bibliographical references

Competing voices from World War II in Europe; edited by Harold J. Goldberg. Greenwood 2010 xxxi, 319p map (Fighting words) $65
Grades: 10 11 12 Adult   **940.53**
1. World War, 1939-1945—Sources 2. World War, 1939-1945—Personal narratives 3. Reference books
ISBN 978-1-84645-033-4; 1-84645-033-0
LC 2009-50073

This collection "presents relatively short primary documents, newspaper headlines, and accounts from participants themselves—soldiers, civilians, victims, and survivors. The materials are organized chronologically into eight chapters, each dealing with a single year from 1938 through 1945. The chapters contain introductions, background, and context as deemed necessary by the editor to guide the reader through the materials." Booklist

This book "amplifies the voices best equipped to communicate the complicated viewpoints and raw emotion of World War II. These texts tell the story more vividly than any neatly linear, retrospectively composed narrative could." Libr J

Includes bibliographical references

Daniels, Roger

Prisoners without trial; Japanese Americans in World War II. Rev. ed. Hill and Wang 2004 162p il (Critical issue series) pa $12
Grades: 11 12 Adult   **940.53**
1. Japanese Americans—Evacuation and relocation, 1942-1945 2. World War, 1939-1945—United States
ISBN 0-8090-7896-1   LC 2004-47328
First published 1993

An account of "the relocation of Japanese Americans during World War II, an injustice prompted not by military necessity but by political and racial motivations. The purpose of this volume is to tell the story in light of the redress legislation enacted in 1988." Libr J [review of 1993 edition]

Includes bibliographical references

Davenport, John, 1960-

The internment of Japanese Americans during World War II; detention of American citizens; [by] John C. Davenport. Chelsea House Publishers 2010 122p il (Milestones in American history) lib bdg $35 *
Grades: 6 7 8 9 10   **940.53**
1. Japanese Americans—Evacuation and relocation, 1942-1945
ISBN 978-1-60413-681-4; 1-60413-681-2
LC 2009-29613

The "chapters outline the impact of the bombing [of Pearl Harbor], the history of Japanese immigrants and citizens in the United States, Executive Order 9066 (permitting evacuation and internment of Japanese citizens on the West coast), Japanese American participation in the armed forces, reparations, and the legacy left by the internment. . . . A sound reference and research work." SLJ

Includes bibliographical references

Dawidowicz, Lucy S.

The war against the Jews, 1933-1945. 10th anniversary ed. Bantam Books 1986 xxxx, 466p il pa $19
Grades: 11 12 Adult   **940.53**
1. Holocaust, 1933-1945 2. Jews—Europe
ISBN 978-0-553-34532-2; 0-553-34532-X
LC 85-48051

A reissue with new introduction and supplementary bibliography of the title first published 1975 by Holt, Rinehart & Winston

"One of the best histories of the mass murder of Jews in World War II. Argues for the centrality of anti-Semitism in Hitler's program." Reader's Adviser

Includes bibliographical references

Drez, Ronald J.

Twenty-five yards of war; the extraordinary courage of ordinary men in World War II. Hyperion 2001 xxii, 296p il hardcover o.p. pa $16
Grades: 11 12 Adult   **940.53**
1. World War, 1939-1945 2. United States—Armed forces
ISBN 0-7868-6783-3; 0-7868-8668-4 (pa)
LC 2001-39077

Based on interviews with World War II veterans, Drez describes the experiences of ten soldiers in such battles as Midway, Tarawa, and Iwo Jima.

"To be sure, some of these veterans' stories have been previously published . . . but Drez manages to present them with freshness and adequate context." Booklist

Includes bibliographical references

Drucker, Olga Levy, 1927-

Kindertransport. Holt & Co. 1992 146p hardcover o.p. pa $9.95
Grades: 9 10 11 12   **940.53**
1. Holocaust, 1933-1945—Personal narratives 2. Jewish refugees
ISBN 0-8050-1711-9; 0-8050-4251-2 (pa)
LC 92-14121

The author describes the circumstances in Germany after Hitler came to power that led to the evacuation of many Jewish children to England and her experiences as a young girl in England during World War II.

This is a "quiet, candid account. . . . Drucker writes with spare truth about how a refugee adjusts and what's both lost and gained." Booklist

Encyclopedia of the Holocaust; Schmuel Spector, Robert Rozett, editors. Facts on File 2000 528p il $93.50 *

Grades: 11 12 Adult   **940.53**
1. Reference books 2. Holocaust, 1933-1945—Encyclopedias
ISBN 0-8160-4333-7   LC 00-30917

Following several introductory essays are "alphabetical entries on people, places, events, organizations, laws, and concepts. The language is clear, but more important is the authenticity of the information and the refusal to surrender to a simplification of issues. There are ample good-quality, black-and-white photographs, some unfamiliar, and also maps and tables. A detailed chronology and a thematic bibliography conclude the volume." SLJ
Includes bibliographical references

Epstein, Eric Joseph, 1959-
Dictionary of the Holocaust; biography, geography, and terminology; [by] Eric Joseph Epstein and Philip Rosen; foreword by Henry R. Huttenbach. Greenwood Press 1997 416p $67.95

Grades: 11 12 Adult   **940.53**
1. Holocaust, 1933-1945—Dictionaries 2. Reference books
ISBN 0-313-30355-X   LC 97-8779

The nearly 2,000 alphabetically arranged entries cover people, places and events related to the Holocaust. "Among the personalities profiled here are Dietrich Bonhoeffer, Anne Frank, Primo Levi, Oskar Schindler, Harry S. Truman, and Elie Wiesel. Place entries include references to well-known locations, the number of prewar Jewish inhabitants, the date of liberation, and the number of Jews left after liberation. Entries dealing with concentration camps are generally the longest and identify camps by location, type, when opened and liberated, nationalities incarcerated, numbers murdered, other victimization, and camp commandants. Among the terms that are defined are many foreign expressions." Booklist

Epstein, Helen, 1947-
Children of the Holocaust; conversations with sons and daughters of survivors. Penguin Books 1988 c1979 355p pa $16

Grades: 9 10 11 12   **940.53**
1. Holocaust, 1933-1945
ISBN 0-14-011284-7   LC 88-9606
First published 1979 by Putnam

A series of interviews with the children of Holocaust survivors living in the U.S., Canada, South America, and Israel.
Includes bibliographical references

Feldman, George
Understanding the Holocaust. U.X.L 1998 2v il maps set $110

Grades: 8 9 10 11 12   **940.53**
1. Holocaust, 1933-1945 2. Germany—Politics and government—1933-1945 3. Germany—History—1933-1945
ISBN 0-7876-1740-7   LC 97-26864

"This overview describes the Holocaust, the events that led up to it, and how the Nazis attempted to eradicate an entire people while fighting a war on two fronts. Sidebars provide information on related individuals, events, and policies. Black-and-white photographs help clarify the text." SLJ
Includes bibliographical references

Gies, Miep, 1909-2010
Anne Frank remembered; the story of the woman who helped to hide the Frank family; [by] Miep Gies and Alison Leslie Gold. Simon & Schuster trade pbk. ed. Simon and Schuster Paperbacks 2009 264p il pa $15 *

Grades: 11 12 Adult   **940.53**
1. Frank family 2. Netherlands—History—1940-1945, German occupation 3. Holocaust, 1933-1945 4. Amsterdam (Netherlands)
ISBN 978-1-4165-9885-5; 1-4165-9885-5
     LC 2009294295

First published 1987
"With a new afterword by the authors" Cover
"A memoir by the courageous Dutch woman who helped hide the Frank family, this book augments the Anne Frank story. Perceptive characterizations, with insight into life in Amsterdam during the Nazi occupation." SLJ

Gilbert, Martin, 1936-
The Holocaust; a history of the Jews of Europe during the Second World War. Holt & Co. 1986 c1985 959p il maps hardcover o.p. pa $17.95

Grades: 11 12 Adult   **940.53**
1. Holocaust, 1933-1945
ISBN 0-03-062416-9; 0-8050-0348-7 (pa)
     LC 85-5523

"Proceeding chronologically from Hitler's rise to power in 1933 to Germany's surrender and the liberation of the concentration camps, [the author] documents the countless horrors of this 'unprecedented explosion of evil over good,' drawing extensively on records and testimonies of those who survived (as well as some who eventually perished)." Booklist
Includes bibliographical references

The Routledge atlas of the Holocaust. 4th ed. Routledge 2009 286p map $120; pa $30.95 *

Grades: 11 12 Adult   **940.53**
1. Holocaust, 1933-1945—Maps 2. Atlases 3. Reference books
ISBN 978-0-415-48481-7; 0-415-48481-2; 978-0-415-48486-2 (pa); 0-415-48486-3 (pa)
     LC 2008-43844

First published 1982 in the United Kingdom with title: The Dent atlas of the Holocaust
The author uses "maps, text, and photographs to document Hitler's attempt to destroy Europe's Jews. . . . Commentary offers statistical information, historical background, and something about the people of the area. Archival photographs bring the events to life. . . . This small but effective work demonstrates the magnitude of the Nazi terror by bringing it down to a personal level." Am Ref Books Annu, 2003 [review of 2002 edition]
Includes bibliographical references

Goldhagen, Daniel

Hitler's willing executioners; ordinary Germans and the Holocaust; [by] Daniel Jonah Goldhagen. Knopf 1996 622p il maps hardcover o.p. pa $16 *

Grades: 11 12 Adult   **940.53**
1. Holocaust, 1933-1945 2. Germany—History—1933-1945 3. Antisemitism 4. National socialism
ISBN 0-679-44695-8; 0-679-77268-5 (pa)
LC 95-38591
The author "endeavors to show that the common apologia for the Germans—that Hitler 'brainwashed' them—is nonsense and that most Germans gave their active assent to genocide. An ordinary German commander, for example, might feel himself bound by a strict code of conduct yet not be at all averse to murdering Jews. The book ends with a detailed notes section and an appendix that explains the correct methodology for studying the Nazi period." Libr J

Gottfried, Ted, 1928-

Displaced persons; the liberation and abuse of Holocaust survivors. 21st Cent. Bks. (Brookfield) 2001 127p il maps (Holocaust) lib bdg $29.90
Grades: 7 8 9 10   **940.53**
1. Jewish refugees 2. Holocaust survivors
ISBN 0-7613-1924-7   LC 00-51225
This book "looks at the suffering of survivors immediately following [World War II] when many people returned 'home' to face racism, displacement, even massacre, and when countries, including the U.S., denied shelter to most refugees. . . . [This volume is] rich with topics for discussion, and the documentation is meticulous." Booklist
Includes glossary and bibliographical references

Heinrichs, Ann

The Japanese American internment; innocence, guilt, and wartime justice. Marshall Cavendish Benchmark 2010 112p il (Perspectives on) $39.93
Grades: 7 8 9 10   **940.53**
1. Japanese Americans—Evacuation and relocation, 1942-1945
ISBN 978-0-7614-4983-6; 0-7614-4983-3
"A solid resource for school reports, this straightforward account includes an overview of the events that led up to the signing of Executive Order 9066, which authorized the relocation of Japanese Americans; details about life in the internment camps; and an examination of the long-term ramifications for the Japanese-American community. Information is accompanied by photographs and illustrations in color and black-and-white. A balanced view of the internment is presented." SLJ

The **Holocaust** encyclopedia; Walter Laqueur, editor; Judith Tydor Baumel, associate editor. Yale Univ. Press 2001 xxxix, 765p il maps $60
Grades: 11 12 Adult   **940.53**
1. Reference books 2. Holocaust, 1933-1945—Encyclopedias
ISBN 0-300-08432-3   LC 00-106567
This "encyclopedia provides fresh and lengthy articles on such topics as antisemitism, historiography, Jewish women, memorials, and resistance, just to brush the surface." Choice
Includes bibliographical references

Houston, Jeanne Wakatsuki, 1934-

Farewell to Manzanar; a true story of Japanese American experience during and after the World War II internment; [by] Jeanne Wakatsuki Houston and James D. Houston. Houghton Mifflin 2002 c1973 188p $15
Grades: 7 8 9 10   **940.53**
1. Manzanar War Relocation Center 2. Japanese Americans—Evacuation and relocation, 1942-1945 3. World War, 1939-1945—United States
ISBN 0-618-21620-0   LC 2002-727748
Also available in paperback from Bantam Bks.
A reissue with a new afterword of the title first published 1973
"The author tells of the three years she and her family spent at Manzanar, a Japanese internment camp. . . . The last part of the book deals with her postwar adolescence and reentry into American life." Libr J
"A spare, powerful memoir." Rochman. Against borders

Isserman, Maurice

World War II; John S. Bowman, general editor. rev ed. Chelsea House 2010 c2011 256p il map (America at war) lib bdg $45
Grades: 8 9 10 11 12   **940.53**
1. World War, 1939-1945—United States 2. United States—History—1933-1945
ISBN 978-0-8160-8185-1; 0-8160-8185-9
LC 2009-52541
First published 1991
This book describes and interprets the role of the United States in World War II.
Includes glossary and bibliographical references

Kopf, Hedda Rosner, 1946-

Understanding Anne Frank's The diary of a young girl; a student casebook to issues, sources, and historical documents. Greenwood Press 1997 272p il maps (Greenwood Press literature in context series) $39.95 *
Grades: 9 10 11 12   **940.53**
1. Frank, Anne, 1929-1945 2. Holocaust, 1933-1945
ISBN 0-313-29607-3   LC 96-50294
This work explores "the diary as literature, the history of the Frank family, Anne's childhood, the plight of Holland's Jewish population, rescuers of Holocaust children, and anti-Semitism in modern Germany. Primary texts, such as diaries and letters of other Holocaust children; excerpts from the Nuremberg Laws; minutes of the Wannsee Conference; and articles from the *New York Times*, are used extensively throughout the book. The author writes compassionately yet objectively." SLJ
Includes glossary and bibliographical references

Lewy, Guenter, 1923-
   The Nazi persecution of the gypsies. Oxford
Univ. Press 2000 306p il hardcover o.p. pa $24.95
Grades: 11 12 Adult   **940.53**
   1. Gypsies 2. World War, 1939-1945—Atrocities
3. National socialism
   ISBN 0-19-512556-8; 0-19-514240-3 (pa)
                              LC 98-52545
   The author "begins with a brief history of the mal-
treatment of Gypsies all over Europe, from the fifteenth
century onward; then, by dint of exhaustive research,
Lewy documents the horrors of their expulsions, deten-
tions, deportations, and deaths during the systematic
madness of the Holocaust." Booklist
   Includes bibliographical references

Life: World War 2; history's greatest conflict in
   pictures; edited by Richard B. Stolley. Little,
   Brown 2001 351p il hardcover o.p. pa $29.95 *
Grades: 11 12 Adult   **940.53**
   1. World War, 1939-1945—Pictorial works 2. World
history—20th century—Pictorial works
   ISBN 0-8212-2771-8; 0-8212-5713-7 (pa)
                           LC 2001-93633
   "A Bulfinch Press book"
   This "album of 665 photographs taken from the ar-
chives of *Life* magazine and other collections begins with
the years 1919 to 1939, the two decades leading up to
World War II. Editor Stolley then proceeds to chronicle
the war, year by year through 1945, and ends with what
he calls 'the war's aftermath,' 1946 to 2001. . . . For
World War II buffs, the book is a natural treasure."
Booklist

Madison, James H.
   World War II; a history in documents. Oxford
University Press 2010 163p il map (Pages from
history) pa $24.95 *
Grades: 8 9 10 11 12   **940.53**
   1. World War, 1939-1945—Sources
   ISBN 978-0-19-533812-6; 0-19-533812-X
                          LC 2009-576
   "Arranged in eight chapters of broad topics, the text
is a collection of excerpts from primary sources. . . . A
variety of sources has been used to convey the thoughts
of people of many nationalities and walks of life. There
are quotes from official documents and laws, personal
letters, books, and music lyrics. . . . [It also] contains
primary sources from China, Japan, Germany, and Russia, in addition to the U.S. It belongs in most secondary
collections." SLJ
   Includes bibliographical references

Mara, Wil
   Kristallnacht; Nazi persecution of the Jews in
Europe. Marshall Cavendish Benchmark 2009
112p il (Perspectives on) lib bdg $39.93
Grades: 7 8 9 10   **940.53**
   1. Jews—Germany   2. Kristallnacht, 1938
3. Holocaust, 1933-1945
   ISBN 978-0-7614-4026-0; 0-7614-4026-7
                          LC 2008-42971

   "Provides comprehensive information on the persecution of Jews in Europe commencing in 1938 and its legacy." Publisher's note
   "The text is supplemented with sidebars and photos
and illustrations, and . . . has source notes, lists of resources for further information, a timeline, and a comprehensive bibliography. . . . [This will be] useful to researchers and report writers." Libr Media Connect
   Includes bibliographical references

Meltzer, Milton, 1915-2009
   Never to forget: the Jews of the Holocaust.
Harper & Row 1976 217p maps pa $9.99
hardcover o.p. *
Grades: 6 7 8 9   **940.53**
   1. Holocaust, 1933-1945
   ISBN 0-06-446118-1 (pa)
   "The mass murder of six million Jews by the Nazis
during World War II is the subject of this compelling
history. Interweaving background information, chilling
statistics, individual accounts and newspaper reports, it
provides an excellent introduction to its subject." Interracial Books Child Bull
   Includes bibliographical references

Mothers, sisters, resisters; oral histories of women
   who survived the Holocaust; edited by Brana
   Gurewitsch. University of Ala. Press 1998 xxi,
   396p (Judaic studies series) hardcover o.p. pa
   $22.95 *
Grades: 9 10 11 12   **940.53**
   1. Holocaust, 1933-1945—Personal narratives
2. Holocaust survivors 3. World War, 1939-1945—
Underground movements 4. Jewish women
   ISBN 0-8173-0931-4; 0-8173-0952-7 (pa)
                          LC 98-19753
   This is a collection of 25 personal narratives of Jewish
women survivors of the Holocaust and their attempts to
save themselves, their families and others
   Includes bibliographical references

Ng, Wendy L.
   Japanese American internment during World
War II; a history and reference guide; [by] Wendy
Ng. Greenwood Press 2002 xxvi, 204p $45
Grades: 8 9 10 11 12 Adult   **940.53**
   1. Japanese Americans—Evacuation and relocation,
1942-1945
   ISBN 0-313-31375-X   LC 00-69128
   Contents: Chronology of events in Japanese American
history: The Japanese in America before World War II;
Evacuation; Life within barbed wire; The question of
loyalty: Japanese Americans in the military and draft resisters; Legal challenges to the evacuation and internment; After the war: Resettlement and redress; Photographic essay
   "The combination of historical facts as presented in
the essays and the ideas and sentiments expressed in the
primary documents gives readers a vivid sense of this period in history. This readable book would be a solid addition to high school, public, and academic libraries."
Voice Youth Advocates
   Includes bibliographical references

Nicholas, Lynn H.

Cruel world; the children of Europe in the Nazi web. A.A. Knopf 2005 632p il maps $35; pa $17.95

Grades: 11 12 Adult   **940.53**
1. World War, 1939-1945—Children 2. Children and war 3. Holocaust, 1933-1945
ISBN 0-679-45464-0; 0-679-77663-X (pa)
     LC 2004-57745

This is an account of the lives of children in Europe during the Holocaust and World War II.

The author "has put together a well-written, compelling history that makes us look at the war era anew." Publ Wkly

Includes bibliographical references

Only what we could carry; the Japanese American internment experience; edited with introduction by Lawson Fusao Inada; preface by Patricia Wakida; afterword by William Hohri. Heyday Bks. 2000 xxiii, 439p il maps pa $18.95 *

Grades: 11 12 Adult   **940.53**
1. Japanese Americans—Evacuation and relocation, 1942-1945
ISBN 1-89077-130-9   LC 00-9182

This anthology includes "poetry, prose, biography, news accounts, formal government declarations, letters, and autobiography along with photographs, sketches, and cartoons. . . . Readers will come away from this book with a deep understanding of the times, the sense of betrayal, and the conflicting feelings among the three major groups of Japanese who went through the ordeal." SLJ

Includes bibliographical references

Oppenheim, Joanne

Dear Miss Breed; true stories of the Japanese American incarceration during World War II and a librarian who made a difference; foreword by Elizabeth Kikuchi Yamada; afterword by Snowden Becker. Scholastic 2006 287p il $22.99 *

Grades: 7 8 9 10   **940.53**
1. Breed, Clara E., 1906-1994 2. Japanese Americans—Evacuation and relocation, 1942-1945 3. World War, 1939-1945—United States 4. Librarians
ISBN 0-439-56992-3; 978-0-439-56992-7
     LC 2004-59009

This "account focuses on Clara Breed, a children's librarian at the San Diego Public Library, and the Japanese-American children she served prior to World War II and whom she continued to serve after their families were sent to an Arizona internment camp. . . . Illustrated with numerous photographs . . . and incorporating copious letters and documents, the book is . . . compelling." Horn Book

Includes bibliographical references

Regis, Margaret, 1937-

When our mothers went to war; an illustrated history of women in World War II. NavPublishing 2008 175p il map pa $29.95

Grades: 11 12 Adult   **940.53**
1. World War, 1939-1945—Women
ISBN 978-1-879932-05-0; 1-879932-05-9
     LC 2008-2833

"This important story tells of the myriad roles women played during the massive U.S. mobilization for World War II. Brilliantly illustrated with black-and-white photos, maps, and posters, and including a well-paced, articulate text based on careful research. . . . This marvelous history tells it all, including the entertainers who raised morale and the war correspondents who were as likely as male journalists to get as close to the fighting as permitted." SLJ

Includes bibliographical references

Reporting World War II. Library of Am. 1995 2v ea $35 *

Grades: 11 12 Adult   **940.53**
1. World War, 1939-1945 2. Reporters and reporting
ISBN 1-883011-04-3 (v1); 1-883011-05-1 (v2)
     LC 94-45463

Contents: v1 American journalism, 1938-1944; v2 American journalism, 1944-1946

This "collection of some 200 entries by nearly 90 writers, drawn from newspapers, magazine articles, broadcast transcripts and book excerpts, recalls WW II campaigns and battles in all theaters but pays attention to the home front as well. It begins with an excerpt from William L. Shirer's *Berlin Diary* and ends with one from John Hersey's *Hiroshima*. . . . This is a treasure trove of war reporting, featuring writing of the highest order." Publ Wkly

Robinson, Greg, 1966-

By order of the president; FDR and the internment of Japanese Americans. Harvard Univ. Press 2001 322p $27.95; pa $19.95 *

Grades: 11 12 Adult   **940.53**
1. Roosevelt, Franklin D. (Franklin Delano), 1882-1945 2. Japanese Americans—Evacuation and relocation, 1942-1945 3. World War, 1939-1945—United States
ISBN 0-674-00639-9; 0-674-01118-X (pa)
     LC 2001-24609

"Using memos, reports, diary entries, letters, and other documents written by FDR and his staff, this book offers [a] look at the role of Roosevelt and his advisers in making the decision to intern." Libr J

This is a "lucid, comprehensive and balanced examination." Publ Wkly

Includes bibliographical references

Robson, David, 1966-

Auschwitz. Lucent Books 2009 104p il (World history series) $33.45

Grades: 7 8 9 10   **940.53**
1. Jews—Persecutions 2. Holocaust, 1933-1945 3. Auschwitz (Poland: Concentration camp)
ISBN 978-1-4205-0131-5; 1-4205-0131-3
     LC 2008-52817

Robson, David, 1966-—_Continued_

"This is a thought provoking book about the horrors of Auschwitz and its role in the Nazis' plan for the 'Final Solution'. . . . The book has photographs and sidebars to expand the text. The author weaves first person narratives about experiences in the concentration camp and chilling quotes from the Nazis' implementation of state-sponsored genocide. . . . This is a needed book in the middle or high school for an introduction to the Holocaust." Libr Media Connect

Includes glossary and bibliographical references

Samuel, Wolfgang W. E.

The war of our childhood; memories of World War II; {reported by} Wolfgang W.E. Samuel. University Press of Miss. 2002 356p il $30

Grades: 11 12 Adult   **940.53**

1. World War, 1939-1945—Children 2. World War, 1939-1945—Personal narratives

ISBN 1-57806-482-1   LC 2002-6172

These "memories by 27 German survivors of World War II relate how as children—ages 3 to 12—they endured air raids, hunger, terror, invading armies, and deprivation. Samuel tells of their resilience under the most trying circumstances and the critical role their mothers played in their lives." Booklist

Schneider, Carl J.

World War II; [by] Carl J. Schneider and Dorothy Schneider. Facts on File 2003 472p il map (Eyewitness history) $75; pa $21.95

Grades: 9 10 11 12   **940.53**

1. World War, 1939-1945—United States 2. United States—History—1933-1945

ISBN 0-8160-4484-8; 0-8160-4485-6 (pa)

                          LC 2002-15268

This volume includes letters, speeches and newspaper articles as well as excerpts from documents and from capsule biographies of key figures.

"This useful volume offers a good blend of historical fact and primary-source material." SLJ

Includes bibliographical references

Shermer, Michael

Denying history; who says the Holocaust never happened and why do they say it? [by] Michael Shermer & Alex Grobman; foreword by Arthur Hertzberg. Updated and expanded ed. University of California Press 2009 334p il (S. Mark Taper Foundation imprint in Jewish studies) pa $19.95 *

Grades: 11 12 Adult   **940.53**

1. Holocaust, 1933-1945—Historiography

ISBN 978-0-520-26098-6

First published 2000

The authors "respond to specific attacks that have been made over the years against the veracity of the accepted 'facts' of the Holocaust;. . . [they also] discuss historical truth, how we know it, and what motivates some people to become deniers." New Leader

"Using the deniers' own words to tear down their arguments, Shermer and Grobman provide a clear method for determining the reality of past events and supply a

powerful weapon for anyone who cares about learning from the credible historical record." Publ Wkly

Includes bibliographical references

Spiegelman, Art

Maus; a survivor's tale. Pantheon Bks. 1996 2v in 1 il $35 *

Grades: 7 8 9 10 11 12 Adult   **940.53**

1. Spiegelman, Vladek—Graphic novels 2. Holocaust, 1933-1945—Graphic novels 3. Graphic novels 4. Biographical graphic novels

ISBN 0-679-40641-7   LC 96-32796

Also available paperback boxed set edition $28 (ISBN 0-679-74840-7)

A combined edition of Maus (1986) and Maus II (1991)

Contents: My father bleeds history; And here my troubles began

In this work "Spiegelman takes the comic book to a new level of seriousness, portraying Jews as mice and Nazis as cats. Depicting himself being told about the Holocaust by his Polish survivor father, Spiegelman not only explores the concentration-camp experience, but also the guilt, love, and anger between father and son." Rochman. Against borders

Stargardt, Nicholas

Witnesses of war; children's lives under the Nazis. Distributed by Random House 2006 493p il map $30; pa $16.95

Grades: 11 12 Adult   **940.53**

1. World War, 1939-1945—Children

ISBN   1-4000-4088-4;   978-1-4000-4088-9; 1-4000-3379-9 (pa); 978-1-4000-3379-9 (pa)

                        LC 2005-50409

First published 2005 in the United Kingdom

The author "divides this work into chapters following the rise, escalation, and defeat of Nazism, concentrating on how children (Jews, patients at mental hospitals, inmates in juvenile homes, 'regular' Germans, and conquered nationalities) coped with this existence." Libr J

This is "a sharp and taut account of misery." Publ Wkly

Includes bibliographical references

Takaki, Ronald T., 1939-2009

Double victory; a multicultural history of America in World War II; [by] Ronald Takaki. Little, Brown 2000 282p il hardcover o.p. pa $19.99 *

Grades: 11 12 Adult   **940.53**

1. World War, 1939-1945—United States 2. United States—Race relations

ISBN 0-316-83155-7; 0-316-83156-5 (pa)

                        LC 99-40374

"Takaki discusses the experiences of African Americans, Indians, Chicanos, Asian Americans from several nations, German and Italian Americans, and Jewish Americans. . . . Despite Jim Crow, internment camps, neglected slums, barrios, reservations, and rejection of Jewish refugees, the nation's not-quite-Americans fought bravely in World War II." Booklist

Includes bibliographical references

Voices of the Holocaust; Lorie Jenkins McElroy, editor. U.X.L 1997 2v set $120

Grades: 9 10 11 12   **940.53**
1. Holocaust, 1933-1945 2. World War, 1939-1945—Jews

ISBN 0-7876-1746-6   LC 97-33195

Contents: v1 Antisemitism, escalation, victims; v2 Resistors, liberation, understanding

"A collection of 34 excerpted or full-text poems, memoirs, articles, essays, speeches, and newspaper accounts written by people who were either victims of the Holocaust or commentators on it at the time. . . . Each document is introduced and followed by information about its impact, what happened to its author, and a list for further reading." SLJ

Includes bibliographical references

Witness; voices from the Holocaust; edited by Joshua M. Greene and Shiva Kumar in consultation with Joanne Weiner Rudof; foreword by Lawrence L. Langer; in association with the Fortunoff Video Archive for Holocaust Testimonies, Yale University. Free Press 2000 xxx, 270p il $26; pa $15 *

Grades: 11 12 Adult   **940.53**
1. Holocaust, 1933-1945—Personal narratives

ISBN 0-684-86525-4; 0-684-86526-2 (pa)
     LC 99-58401

In this companion to the PBS series the editors "have woven together the testimonies of 27 individuals into an unforgettable narrative of the Holocaust: starting with pre-WWII Jewish life, they go on to describe the war's out-break, ghettos, resistance and hiding, death camps, death marches, liberation and life after the Holocaust." Publ Wkly

Includes bibliographical references

Women in the Holocaust; [edited by] Dalia Ofer and Lenore J. Weitzman. Yale Univ. Press 1998 402p hardcover o.p. pa $16.95

Grades: 11 12 Adult   **940.53**
1. Holocaust, 1933-1945 2. Jewish women

ISBN 0-300-07354-2; 0-300-08080-8 (pa)
     LC 97-46011

This is a collection of 21 articles by historians, sociologists, writers, literary scholars and survivors. "The book is divided into four parts: before the war, life in the ghettos, resistance and rescue, and labor camps and concentration camps." Booklist

Includes bibliographical references

Wood, Angela
Holocaust; the events and their impact on real people; written by Angela Gluck Wood; [forward by Steven Spielberg] DK 2007 191p il map $29.99 *

Grades: 7 8 9 10   **940.53**
1. Holocaust, 1933-1945

ISBN 978-0-7566-2535-1; 0-7566-2535-1
     LC 2007-298461

"In association with USC Shoah Foundation, Institute for Visual History and Education"

Includes DVD

"DK's signature editorial aesthetic, combined with the searing testimony of Holocaust survivors collected by the USC Shoah Foundation Institute of Visual History and Education, makes for a sobering and visually compelling work of history. An extraordinary array of materials—Nazi propaganda, documentary photos, artwork, artifacts—are employed in the service of a broadly sweeping chronicle. . . . Each chapter includes a two-page spread entitled Voices, devoted largely to excerpts from 23 interviews in the Foundation's video archives (an accompanying 40-minute DVD contains the actual interviews)." Publ Wkly

World War II: a student encyclopedia; Spencer C. Tucker, editor; Priscilla Mary Roberts, editor, Documents volume; Jack Greene . . . [et al.], assistant editors. ABC-CLIO 2005 5v il map set $485 *

Grades: 9 10 11 12   **940.53**
1. Reference books 2. World War, 1939-1945—Encyclopedias

ISBN 1-85109-857-7; 978-1-85109-857-6
     LC 2004-29951

This "encyclopedia covers the entire scope of the Second World War, from its earliest roots to its continuing impact on global politics and human society." Publisher's note

Includes bibliographical references

WWII: the people's story; Nigel Fountain, general editor. Reader's Digest 2003 315p il map $39.95

Grades: 9 10 11 12   **940.53**
1. World War, 1939-1945

ISBN 0-7621-0376-0   LC 2003-43172

Accompanied by computer disc

"Through letters, speeches, diaries, and interviews, this title provides insight into the thoughts and feelings of presidents and prime ministers during this period as well as soldiers, journalists, and children. Between excerpted comments, the text fills in the background information. . . . Pages are peppered with black-and-white and color photographs and reproductions depicting numerous aspects of the war. . . . An accompanying CD will allow students to hear the firsthand accounts included in the book." SLJ

Includes bibliographical references

Yellin, Emily, 1961-
Our mothers' war; American women at home and at the Front during World War II. Free Press 2004 447p il hardcover o.p. pa $14 *

Grades: 11 12 Adult   **940.53**
1. World War, 1939-1945—Women

ISBN 0-7432-4514-8; 0-7432-4516-4 (pa)
     LC 2004-40496

"Yellin reveals all of the responsibilities held by women, including helping to manufacture aircraft, ships, and other munitions; and, in the process, outproducing all of America's allies and enemies, by far. Readers see war brides who worked hard to maintain the morale of their husbands while surviving long separation, fear, and shortages of virtually everything necessary to support a family. . . . [This book] is an important book because

Yellin, Emily, 1961-—*Continued*
the role played by women in World War II has been regularly ignored." SLJ
Includes bibliographical references

940.54   Military history of World War II

Atwood, Kathryn
Women heroes of World War II; 26 stories of espionage, sabotage, resistance, and rescue; [by] Kathryn J. Atwood. Chicago Review Press 2011 266p il map $19.95
Grades: 7 8 9 10   **940.54**
   1. World War, 1939-1945—Women 2. World War, 1939-1945—Underground movements
ISBN 978-1-55652-961-0; 1-55652-961-9
                     LC 2010-41830
"The 26 women profiled in this collective biography served on the front lines and behind enemy lines in Europe as correspondents, couriers, propagandists, Resistance fighters, saboteurs and spies. . . . Atwood's admiration and enthusiasm for her subjects is apparent in these engaging profiles, and readers will likely be inspired to investigate these fascinating women further." Kirkus
Includes glossary and bibliographical references

Ballard, Robert D., 1942-
Graveyards of the Pacific; from Pearl Harbor to Bikini Atoll; [by] Robert D. Ballard with Michael Hamilton Morgan. National Geographic Soc. 2001 255p il maps $45
Grades: 11 12 Adult   **940.54**
   1. World War, 1939-1945—Naval operations 2. Shipwrecks
ISBN 0-7922-6366-9
This "overview of the Pacific war begins with [an] . . . account of Ballard's search for an elusive midget sub sunk just prior to the attack on Pearl Harbor, and ends with the American nuclear tests on Bikini Island, where captured German and Japanese craft were scuttled." Publisher's note
Includes bibliographical references

Bradley, James
Flags of our fathers; [by] James Bradley with Ron Powers. Bantam Bks. 2000 376p $24.95; pa $14 *
Grades: 11 12 Adult   **940.54**
   1. Rosenthal, Joe, 1911-2006 2. United States. Marine Corps 3. Iwo Jima, Battle of, 1945
ISBN 0-553-11133-7; 0-553-38415-5 (pa)
                     LC 00-25803
This is the "story of the most famous photograph to come out of World War II, the flag-raising on Mount Suribachi during the Battle of Iwo Jima in February 1945. Bradley is the son of one of the six men immortalized in that remarkable photo, and his gripping narrative, vivid descriptions, and heartfelt style make this a powerful story of courage, humility, and tragedy." Libr J
Includes bibliographical references

Brokaw, Tom, 1940-
An album of memories; personal histories from the greatest generation. Random House 2001 314p il maps $29.95; pa $14.95 *
Grades: 11 12 Adult   **940.54**
   1. World War, 1939-1945—Personal narratives
ISBN 0-375-50581-4; 0-375-76041-5 (pa)
                     LC 2001-273436
This volume "gathers letters written to Brokaw by Americans who lived through the Depression and World War II and, in some cases, letters written by their children. Brokaw provides a brief introduction and a time line for each chapter; these cover the Depression, the war in Europe and in the Pacific, and the wartime 'home front,' closing with 'Reflections.' The book is lavishly illustrated with reproductions of photographs, drawings, documents, and other memorabilia of the era." Booklist

Burgan, Michael
Hiroshima; birth of the nuclear age. Marshall Cavendish Benchmark 2009 128p il (Perspectives on) lib bdg $27.95 *
Grades: 8 9 10 11 12   **940.54**
   1. Hiroshima (Japan)—Bombardment, 1945 2. Atomic bomb
ISBN 978-0-7614-4023-9; 0-7614-4023-2
                     LC 2008-29249
This provides information on the Manhattan Project, the bombing of Hiroshima, and its legacy.
"Utilizing an unbiased and chronological narrative, [the author delves] deeply into the [topic], providing an overall representation as well as a substantial degree of insight. . . . The potency of [this title] lies in the excellent arrangement of numerous well-chosen sidebars and photos, and fluent, concise prose." SLJ
Includes bibliographical references

Dick, Ron, 1931-
World War II; [by] Ron Dick and Dan Patterson. Firefly Bks. 2004 352p il (Aviation century) $49.95
Grades: 11 12 Adult   **940.54**
   1. Aeronautics—History 2. World War, 1939-1945—Aerial operations
ISBN 978-1-55046-426-9; 1-55046-426-4
                     LC 2005-278795
This "volume begins with the Battle of Britain and concludes with the Japanese surrender following the destruction of Hiroshima and Nagasaki. Patterson's . . . color photography combines with works of contemporary aviation artists to depict aircraft vividly from all major theaters of war." Libr J
Includes bibliographical references

Dickson, Keith D.
World War II almanac. Facts on File 2008 2v il map (Almanacs of American wars) $150
Grades: 10 11 12 Adult   **940.54**
   1. Reference books 2. World War, 1939-1945 3. Almanacs
ISBN 978-0-8160-6297-3; 0-8160-6297-8
                     LC 2007-11207

Dickson, Keith D.—*Continued*

"Offering more than 1300 pages of day-by-day accounts of political decision making, troop deployments, and military operations, this is an incredibly ambitious work." SLJ

Includes glossary and bibliographical references

Frank, Richard B.

Downfall; the end of the Imperial Japanese Empire. Penguin 2001 484p il map pa $18

Grades: 11 12 Adult   **940.54**

1. World War, 1939-1945—Japan 2. World War, 1939-1945—Aerial operations 3. Japan—History—1868-1945

ISBN 0-14-100146-1

First published 1999 by Random House

"Weaving together the strands of military and diplomatic events, Frank contends that absent the bombings of Hiroshima and Nagasaki the war would have continued for at least several more months, at a cost in Japanese and Allied civilian and combatant lives far in excess of the admittedly awful toll that the atomic bombs exacted. A powerful work of history." Libr J

Includes bibliographical references

Fussell, Paul, 1924-

The boys' crusade; the American infantry in Northwestern Europe, 1944-1945. Modern Lib. 2003 184p hardcover o.p. pa $12.95

Grades: 11 12 Adult   **940.54**

1. World War, 1939-1945—Campaigns 2. World War, 1939-1945—Europe

ISBN 0-679-64088-6; 0-8129-7488-3 (pa)

LC 2003-44556

"A Modern Library chronicles book"

This memoir of World War II includes "a series of essays dealing with strategy, tactics, and leadership from the landings at Normandy to the fall of Berlin. . . . Fussell describes the typical GI as 18 to 20 years old, from all types of social and educational backgrounds, taken from minimal training and thrown into ground combat of the fiercest kind. . . . This work is aimed at correcting the sanitized works of 'sentimental' history the war has inspired. Highly recommended." Libr J

Includes bibliographical references

Goldstein, Donald M.

The way it was; Pearl Harbor, the original photographs; [by] Donald M. Goldstein, Katherine V. Dillon and J. Michael Wenger. Pergamon-Brassey's 1991 181p il maps hardcover o.p. pa $19.95

Grades: 11 12 Adult   **940.54**

1. Pearl Harbor (Oahu, Hawaii), Attack on, 1941—Pictorial works

ISBN 0-08-040573-8; 1-57488-359-3 (pa)

LC 90-49572

This is a collection of photographs of the Japanese attack on Pearl Harbor in 1941.

"The 430 prints in this . . . collection were gathered from various Japanese and U.S. sources, and most have never been seen by the general public. The majority were taken during the height of the air raid itself, many from Japanese cockpits. . . . The overall effect is to give the reader an uncanny sense of being present at the battle." Libr J

The **good** war; an oral history of World War Two; [edited by] Studs Terkel. New Press 1997 589p pa $16.95 *

Grades: 11 12 Adult   **940.54**

1. World War, 1939-1945—Personal narratives

ISBN 1-56584-343-6   LC 2003-389322

First published 1984 by Pantheon Bks.

In a series of interviews Terkel depicts how WWII affected the lives of average Americans.

Hastings, Max

Overlord: D-Day and the battle for Normandy. Simon & Schuster 1984 368p il maps hardcover o.p. pa $22.95

Grades: 11 12 Adult   **940.54**

1. Operation Overlord 2. Normandy (France), Attack on, 1944

ISBN 0-671-46029-3; 0-671-55435-2 (pa)

LC 83-20439

Also available in paperback from Vintage Books

Hastings presents an "analysis of the Normandy campaign. He . . . [considers] the limits of the Allied armies' fighting power compared to the Wehrmacht." Libr J

"Hastings' reportage of the battle is not unworthy to stand with that of the best journalists and writers who witnessed it. . . . He has managed to recreate what it was like for almost everyone who was there." N Y Times Book Rev

Includes bibliographical references

Hersey, John, 1914-1993

Hiroshima; a new edition with a final chapter written forty years after the explosion. Knopf 1985 196p il $26; pa $6.50 *

Grades: 11 12 Adult   **940.54**

1. Hiroshima (Japan)—Bombardment, 1945 2. Atomic bomb 3. World War, 1939-1945—Japan

ISBN 0-394-54844-2; 0-679-72103-7 (pa)

LC 85-40346

First published 1946

An account of the aftermath of the first atomic bomb as reflected in the lives of six survivors

Hillstrom, Laurie

The attack on Pearl Harbor; [by] Laurie Collier Hillstrom. Omnigraphics 2009 237p il (Defining moments) $49

Grades: 7 8 9 10 11 12   **940.54**

1. Reference books 2. Pearl Harbor (Oahu, Hawaii), Attack on, 1941

ISBN 978-0-7808-1069-3; 0-7808-1069-4

LC 2009-4236

"This book is divided into three well-organized sections. Part one provides a narrative overview detailing the events leading up to the attack, the attack itself, and

Hillstrom, Laurie—*Continued*

the aftermath, including the U.S. victory in the Pacific as well as the occupation and reconstruction of Japan after World War II. Part two is composed of eight two to three-page biographies of the important figures such as Yamamoto, Roosevelt, and Doris Miller, the first African-American to receive the Navy Cross. A final section of primary documents from the Japanese attack plan to Truman's announcement of the end of the war provides insight into the war in the Pacific. . . . This work is a must-have for reports and assignments." SLJ

Includes glossary and bibliographical references

Holm, Tom, 1946-

Code talkers and warriors; Native Americans and World War II. Chelsea House 2007 168p il map (Landmark events in Native American history) $35

Grades: 7 8 9 10   **940.54**

1. World War, 1939-1945—Native Americans
ISBN 978-0-7910-9340-5; 0-7910-9340-9
                                                    LC 2006102263

"In this title about Native Americans in World War II, Holm . . . expands considerably on his specific topic to highlight significant miliary roles played by Native Americans in conflicts dating back to the sixteenth century. . . . [This is] outstanding. . . . [A] valuable resource." Booklist

Includes bibliographical references

Kurson, Robert, 1963-

Shadow divers; the true adventure of two Americans who risked everything to solve one of the last mysteries of World War II. Random House 2004 375p il $26.95; pa $14.95

Grades: 9 10 11 12   **940.54**

1. U-869 (Submarine) 2. Excavations (Archeology) 3. Shipwrecks 4. Underwater exploration
ISBN 0-375-50858-9; 0-375-76098-9 (pa)
                                                    LC 2003-60362

"A journalist recounts the adventures of two deep-sea divers who discover a World War II German U-boat off the coast of New Jersey." Booklist

This book "features undersea thrills, a gripping mystery, incredible discoveries, true-blue friendship, life-or-death crises and history unfolding before the reader's eyes." N Y Times (Late N Y Ed)

Includes bibliographical references

Leckie, Robert

Okinawa; the last battle of World War II. Viking 1995 220p il hardcover o.p. pa $13.95

Grades: 11 12 Adult   **940.54**

1. World War, 1939-1945—Campaigns—Okinawa Island
ISBN 0-670-84716-X; 0-14-017389-7 (pa)
                                                    LC 94-39145

In this history of the Battle of Okinawa "Leckie supplies an accessible historical overview of a perplexing war tactic, the kamikaze attack." Booklist

Lord, Walter, 1917-2002

Day of infamy. [60th anniversary ed] Holt & Co. 2001 241p il hardcover o.p. pa $14 *

Grades: 9 10 11 12   **940.54**

1. Pearl Harbor (Oahu, Hawaii), Attack on, 1941
ISBN 0-8050-6809-0; 0-8050-6803-1 (pa)
                                                    LC 00-54247

A reissue of the title first published 1957

Based on over 500 eyewitness reports, this book provides a minute-by-minute account of the Japanese attack on Pearl Harbor.

Megellas, James

All the way to Berlin; a paratrooper at war in Europe. Presidio Press 2003 xxi, 309p il maps $25.95

Grades: 11 12 Adult   **940.54**

1. World War, 1939-1945—Personal narratives 2. World War, 1939-1945—Campaigns 3. World War, 1939-1945—Europe
ISBN 0-89141-784-2   LC 2002-192563

This is the author's account of "the September 1944 assault across the Waal River. . . . The attrition Megellas witnessed over months on the front line, at Anzio and in the Battle of the Bulge, shapes his narrative, but his observations about the craft of killing lend it a distinctive tone. . . . Strongly put and unsentimental, this memoir is a must for the World War II collection." Booklist

Moore, Kate

The Battle of Britain. Osprey 2010 200p il map $29.95

Grades: 7 8 9 10   **940.54**

1. Britain, Battle of, 1940 2. World War, 1939-1945—Great Britain
ISBN 978-1-84603-474-9; 1-84603-474-4

Published in association with the Imperial War Museum

"In the summer and autumn of 1940, Britain faced an unparalleled challenge. Forced to beat a quick retreat from Dunkirk with the German Luftwaffe in hot pursuit, the British dug in for what was to be one of the most remarkable feats in the history of human endurance. In this spectacular oversize volume, Moore recounts with notable lucidity and depth the events and characters from both the British and German home fronts during this critical moment in world history and offers an excellent analysis of prewar preparations by both sides. The most outstanding feature of the work is without a doubt the stunning visuals. The book is packed with a fantastic range of archival photos, maps, and war posters." SLJ

Nelson, Pete

Left for dead; a young man's search for justice for the USS Indianapolis; [by] Peter Nelson; with a preface by Hunter Scott. Delacorte Press 2002 xx, 201p il hardcover o.p. pa $8.95 *

Grades: 7 8 9 10   **940.54**

1. McVay, Charles Butler, III 2. Scott, Hunter 3. Indianapolis (Cruiser) 4. World War, 1939-1945—Naval operations
ISBN 0-385-72959-6; 0-385-73091-8 (pa)
                                                    LC 2001-53774

Nelson, Pete—*Continued*

Recalls the sinking of the U.S.S. Indianapolis at the end of World War II, the navy cover-up and unfair court martial of the ship's captain, and how a young boy helped the survivors set the record straight fifty-five years later.

"Written in simple chronological order, it tells a powerful story." Book Rep

Includes bibliographical references

Overy, R. J. (Richard James), 1947-

The Battle of Britain; the myth and the reality; by Richard Overy. Norton 2001 177p maps hardcover o.p. pa $13.95 *

Grades: 11 12 Adult   **940.54**
1. Britain, Battle of, 1940 2. World War, 1939-1945—Great Britain
ISBN 0-393-02008-8; 0-393-32297-1 (pa)
LC 00-69249

First published 2000 in the United Kingdom with title: The Battle

This is an "account of the battle, its effects on the civilian population and its current place in history." N Y Times Book Rev

Includes bibliographical references

The **Pacific** War; from Pearl Harbor to Hiroshima; editor, Daniel Marston. Pbk. ed. Osprey Pub. 2010 272p il map pa $19.95

Grades: 11 12 Adult   **940.54**
1. World War, 1939-1945—Campaigns—Pacific Ocean
ISBN 978-1-84908-382-9   LC 2010-292672

First published 2005 with title: The Pacific war companion

"These essays on the Pacific theater of WW II, written by a group of international scholars representing Australia, Great Britain, Japan, and the US, cover the wellknown events at Pearl Harbor, the Coral Sea, and Midway; MacArthur's push to the Philippines; Nimitz's island campaign in the central Pacific; Okinawa; and the dropping of the atomic bomb on Hiroshima and Nagasaki. . . . A chronology, detailed maps, and photographs greatly enhance this excellent volume on the Pacific phase of WW II." Choice

Includes bibliographical references

Stanton, Doug

In harm's way; the sinking of the USS Indianapolis and the extraordinary story of its survivors. Holt & Co. 2001 333p il hardcover o.p. pa $14

Grades: 11 12 Adult   **940.54**
1. Indianapolis (Cruiser) 2. World War, 1939-1945—Naval operations 3. Shipwrecks
ISBN 0-8050-6632-2; 0-8050-7366-3 (pa)
LC 00-68254

Stanton discusses the loss of the USS Indianapolis, which was given the "job of carrying components of the Hiroshima bomb from San Francisco to Tinian. . . . The Indianapolis (then) headed for Leyte in the Philippines. . . . On July 30, 1945, the Indianapolis was cruising, unescorted, west of Guam when two torpedoes struck it,

sinking the ship in a few minutes. An estimated 300 men were killed by the blast or entombed below. About 900 went into the Pacific. . . . Only 321 survived; of these, some died later in the hospital." Natl Rev

"Illuminating and emotional without being maudlin, Stanton's book helps explain what many have long considered an inexplicable catastrophe." Publ Wkly

Takaki, Ronald T., 1939-2009

Hiroshima; why America dropped the atomic bomb; [by] Ronald Takaki. Little, Brown 1995 193p il $28; pa $14.95 *

Grades: 11 12 Adult   **940.54**
1. World War, 1939-1945—United States 2. Atomic bomb 3. Hiroshima (Japan)—Bombardment, 1945
ISBN 0-316-83122-0; 0-316-83124-7 (pa)
LC 95-13546

This study of the bombings of Hiroshima and Nagasaki focuses on the psychological motivations of the American decision-makers, especially Harry Truman.

"Right or wrong, the study is a provocative addition to the unresolved debate over the dropping of the atomic bombs." Publ Wkly

Includes bibliographical references

Tomblin, Barbara

G.I. nightingales; the Army Nurse Corps in World War II; [by] Barbara Brooks Tomblin. University Press of Ky. 1996 254p il hardcover o.p. pa $22 *

Grades: 11 12 Adult   **940.54**
1. United States. Army Nurse Corps
ISBN 0-8131-1951-0; 0-8131-9079-7 (pa)
LC 96-1018

This is "an account of the 80,000 army nurses who served during World War II. These nurses participated in every theater of the war; some died while on duty, and many were decorated for their bravery. Along with their deserving stories, the reader learns the history of women nurses in the military." Libr J

Includes bibliographical references

World War II; Don Nardo, book editor. Greenhaven Press 2005 203p il (Opposing viewpoints in world history) hardcover o.p. pa $23.70

Grades: 9 10 11 12   **940.54**
1. World War, 1939-1945
ISBN 0-7377-2587-7 (lib bdg); 0-7377-2588-5 (pa)
LC 2004-52277

"Four chapters discuss the assessment of blame for the attack on Pearl Harbor, the justification for the internment of Japanese Americans, the necessity and morality of using the atomic bomb, and whether the war deserves its nostalgic 'good war' image." SLJ

Includes bibliographical references

940.55 Europe—1945-

Living through the end of the Cold War; edited by
Jeff Hay. Greenhaven Press 2005 141p il
(Living through the Cold War) lib bdg $32.45
Grades: 9 10 11 12   **940.55**
1. Cold war 2. World politics—1945-1991
ISBN 0-7377-2132-4   LC 2004-42437
This book "captures the drama and historical signifi-
cance of declining hostilities between the United States
and Russia. The text offers speeches by Reagan,
Gorbachev, Yelstin, and Havel, plus commentary on
change in Russian lives and the collapse of the Iron Cur-
tain." Libr Media Connect
Includes bibliographical references

941 British Isles

Burns, William E.
A brief history of Great Britain. Facts On File
2010 xxiv, 296p il map (Brief history) $49.50; pa
$19.95 *
Grades: 9 10 11 12 Adult   **941**
1. Great Britain—History
ISBN 978-0-8160-7728-1; 978-0-8160-8124-0 (pa)
                                     LC 2009-8217
This book "narrates the history of Great Britain from
the earliest times to the 21st century, covering the entire
island—England, Wales, and Scotland—as well as associated archipelagos such as the Channel Islands, the Ork-
neys, and Ireland as they have influenced British history.
The central story of this volume is the development of
the British kingdom, including its rise and decline on the
world stage." Publisher's note
Includes bibliographical references

Events that changed Great Britain, from 1066 to
1714; edited by Frank W. Thackeray and John
E. Findling. Greenwood Press 2003 201p il
$46.95
Grades: 9 10 11 12   **941**
1. Great Britain—History
ISBN 0-313-31666-X   LC 2003-45527
This "resource describes and evaluates ten of the most
important events in British history between the Norman
Conquest of 1066 and the Glorious Revolution of 1689
and its aftermath." Publisher's note
Includes bibliographical references

Events that changed Great Britain since 1689;
edited by Frank W. Thackeray & John E.
Findling. Greenwood Press 2002 217p il $44.95
Grades: 9 10 11 12   **941**
1. Great Britain—History
ISBN 0-313-31686-4   LC 2002-16103
Contents: The Industrial Revolution, c.1750-c.1850, by
D. Mitch; The Seven Years' War, 1756-1763, by F. M.
Stowell; The Napoleonic Wars, 1789-1815, by S. J.
Stearns; Pax Britannica, 1815-1914, by L. J. Satre; The
Reform Act of 1832, by T. C. Mackey; The Great Exhi-
bition of 1851, by D. J. Reynolds; Sinn Fein and the
Suffragettes, by K. L. Campbell; World War I, 1914-

1919, by L. P. Thornton; World War II, 1939-1945, by
G. P. Blum; The Thatcher era, 1979-1990, by R. A.
Leiby
"Each chapter deals with a different event and contains an overview, an interpretive essay by an expert on
the topic, an illustration or photograph, and a selected
annotated bibliography. . . . With its concentrated view
on British historic events, this book will be a valuable
resource for high school history collections." Libr Media
Connect

The **Lives** of the kings & queens of England;
edited by Antonia Fraser. rev and updated.
University of Calif. Press 1998 384p il maps
hardcover o.p. pa $27.50 *
Grades: 9 10 11 12   **941**
1. Great Britain—Kings and rulers
ISBN 0-520-21938-4; 0-520-22460-4 (pa)
                                   LC 99-169506
First published 1975 in the United Kingdom; first
United States edition 1995
"A collection of biographical sketches that encompasses the period from the establishment of monarchical
power by the early Norman kings through the reign of
Elizabeth II. . . . Accompanying the text are 175 contemporary illustrations and drawings of the royal coats of
arms." Publisher's note

The **Oxford** illustrated history of Britain; edited
by Kenneth O. Morgan. New ed., Updated ed.
for the 21st century. Oxford University Press
2009 683p il map pa $34.95
Grades: 11 12 Adult   **941**
1. Great Britain—History
ISBN 978-0-19-954475-2   LC 2009293870
First published 1984
Contents: Roman Britain (c. 55 BC-c. AD 440) by Pe-
ter Salway; The Anglo-Saxon period (c. 440-1066) by
John Blair; The early Middle Ages (1066-1290) by John
Gillingham; The later Middle Ages (1290-1485) by
Ralph A. Griffiths; The Tudor Age (1485-1603) by John
Guy; The Stuarts (1603-1688) by John Morrill; The eigh-
teenth century (1688-1789) by Paul Langford; Revolution
and the rule of law (1789-1851) by Christopher Harvie;
The Liberal Age (1851-1914) by H.C.G. Matthew; The
twentieth century (1914-2000) by Kenneth O. Morgan
This work, the product of ten British historians, is a
study of the last two thousand years of British history.
Includes bibliographical references

941.081 British Isles—Reign of
Victoria, 1837-1901

Mitchell, Sally, 1937-
Daily life in Victorian England. 2nd edition.
Greenwood Press 2009 336p il (Greenwood Press
"Daily life through history" series) $49.95 *
Grades: 11 12 Adult   **941.081**
1. Great Britain—History—19th century 2. Great Brit-
ain—Civilization
ISBN 978-0-313-35034-4   LC 2008-31363
Also available online
First published 1996

Mitchell, Sally, 1937-—*Continued*

This volume offers a "glimpse into Victorian daily living, including women's roles; 'Victorian Morality'; leisure; health and medicine; and life in all settings, from workhouses to country estates." Publisher's note

Includes glossary and bibliographical references

941.5 Ireland

Bartoletti, Susan Campbell, 1958-

Black potatoes; the story of the great Irish famine, 1845-1850. Houghton Mifflin 2001 184p il hardcover o.p. pa $9.95 *

Grades: 7 8 9 10   **941.5**
1. Famines 2. Ireland—History
ISBN 0-618-00271-5; 0-618-54883-1 (pa)
                                          LC 2001-24156

The author "examines the causes of the famine, considering the roles of both the potato blight and of social conditions in mid-nineteenth century Ireland." Voice Youth Advocates

"The bibliography (also narrative) provides some of the most fascinating historical reading in the book. Overall, a useful addition to collections, for both personal and research uses." SLJ

Includes bibliographical references

The **Encyclopedia** of Ireland; edited by Brian Lalor; foreword by Frank McCourt. Yale University Press 2003 xxxvii, 1218p il map $65 *

Grades: 11 12 Adult   **941.5**
1. Ireland—Encyclopedias 2. Reference books
ISBN 0-300-09442-6   LC 2003-103834

This encyclopedia contains alphabetically arranged entries from Abbey Theatre to Zozimus, a nineteenth-century balladeer. Coverage includes art, cinema, current events, fashion, food, history, Irish language, literature, music, politics, religion, sports, and biographies of a wide range of famous people of Irish descent, including St. Brigid, Éamon de Valera, John F. Kennedy, Bono, Eugene O'Neill, Mary Robinson, and William Butler Yeats

"This wonderful reference work will delight researchers and lovers of Ireland and the Irish." Choice

State, Paul F., 1950-

A brief history of Ireland. Facts On File 2009 xxiv, 408p il map (Brief history) $49.50; pa $19.95

Grades: 9 10 11 12 Adult   **941.5**
1. Ireland—History
ISBN   978-0-8160-7516-4;   0-8160-7516-6;
978-0-8160-7517-1 (pa); 0-8160-7517-4 (pa)
                                          LC 2008-29243

The author "opens this vibrant reference with an introduction to Ireland's landscape, people, economics, natural resources, and current government. Following this essay-style overview are 11 chronologically organized chapters. Each is devoted to a significant historical watershed, tracing events from Ireland's prehistory to its contemporary prosperity. Appendixes provide at-a-glance portraits

of Northern Ireland and the Irish Republic, including a list of presidents, prime ministers, and a time line of notable dates." Libr J

Includes bibliographical references

941.6 Ulster. Northern Ireland

Cottrell, Robert C., 1950-

Northern Ireland and England; the troubles; foreword by George J. Mitchell; introduction by James I. Matray. Chelsea House 2005 c2004 139p il map (Arbitrary borders) $31.50

Grades: 9 10 11 12   **941.6**
1. Northern Ireland
ISBN 0-7910-8020-X   LC 2004-14440

This book deals with the conflicts involved in the establishment of Northern Ireland and the Peace Line.

Includes bibliographical references

942.01 England—Early history to 1066

Lacey, Robert

The year 1000; what life was like at the turn of the first millennium: an Englishman's world; {by} Robert Lacey, Danny Danziger. Little, Brown 1999 230p hardcover o.p. pa $13.99

Grades: 11 12 Adult   **942.01**
1. Great Britain—History—0-1066
ISBN 0-316-55840-0; 0-316-51157-9 (pa)
                                          LC 98-31254

Lacey and Danziger "have set out to capture what life was like in Anglo-Saxon England at the end of the first millennium. The framework for their story was provided by a priceless written work from that period, 'The Julius Work Calendar.'" Libr J

"This is a superb time capsule, and the authors distill a wealth of historical information into brightly entertaining reading." Publ Wkly

Includes bibliographical references

942.02 England—Norman period, 1066-1154

Howarth, David Armine, 1912-

1066: the year of the conquest; [by] David Howarth; illustrations to chapter headings by Gareth Floyd. Viking 1978 c1977 207p il hardcover o.p. pa $14 *

Grades: 11 12 Adult   **942.02**
1. Great Britain—History—1066-1154, Norman period
2. Hastings (East Sussex, England), Battle of, 1066
ISBN 0-670-69601-3; 0-14-005850-8 (pa)
                                          LC 77-21694

First published 1977 in the United Kingdom

A history of the invasion of England by the Normans and William the Conqueror's victory at the Battle of Hastings.

Includes bibliographical references

942.03   England—Period of House of Plantagenet, 1154-1399

Forgeng, Jeffrey L., 1963-
Daily life in Chaucer's England; [by] Jeffrey L.
Forgeng and Will McLean. 2nd ed. Greenwood
Press 2009 302p il (Greenwood Press "Daily life
through history" series) $49.95 *
Grades: 11 12 Adult   942.03
1. Chaucer, Geoffrey, d. 1400 2. Great Britain—History—1154-1399, Plantagenets
ISBN 978-0-313-35951-4   LC 2008-37469
First published 1995
"This volume examines . . . [different] aspects of life
in medieval England, . . . [including] basic fundamentals
like nutrition, waste management, and table manners.
Readers will explore, seasons, holidays and holy days,
the prevalence and normalcy of death, the average workday, crafts and trade, decorating practices, and recreational activities like archery and falconry." Publisher's note
Includes glossary and bibliographical references

942.04   England—Period of Houses of Lancaster and York, 1399-1485

Weir, Alison
The Wars of the Roses. Ballantine Bks. 1995
462p il hardcover o.p. pa $15.95
Grades: 11 12 Adult   942.04
1. Great Britain—History—1455-1485, War of the
Roses
ISBN 0-345-39117-9; 0-345-40433-5 (pa)
This is an account "of the first phase of the War of
the Roses. Accepting the Tudor view that the conflict
originated with Richard II's deposition, [the author] devotes half of the book to relations between Lancaster and
York from 1399 to 1455. The second half deals with the
period from the first Battle of St. Albans (1455) to the
Battle of Tewkesbury (1471)." Libr J
"No history collection should do without this perfectly
focused and beautifully unfolded account." Booklist

942.05   England—Tudor period, 1485-1603

Elizabethan world reference library. Gale 2007 4v
set $181
Grades: 8 9 10 11 12   942.05
1. Elizabeth I, Queen of England, 1533-1603 2. Great
Britain—History—1485-1603, Tudors
ISBN 978-1-4144-0188-1
Also available as separate volumes; contact publisher
for more information
Contents: Almanac; Biographies; Primary Sources; Cumulative Index
"This accessible set consists of three volumes: *Almanac*, which offers chapter-length essays on political, social, and cultural events and movements that shaped each
era; *Biographies*, in-depth treatments of luminaries who
represent various levels of society and diverse experiences and viewpoints; and *Primary Sources*, collections
of facsimiles and excerpted documents that attempt to
provide insights into the past for the series' intended audience. The new topic will support both social studies
and literature research assignments and will be welcomed
by secondary library media collections." Booklist

Forgeng, Jeffrey L., 1963-
Daily life in Elizabethan England. 2nd ed.
Greenwood Press 2010 xx, 276p il (Greenwood
Press "Daily life through history" series) $49.95 *
Grades: 11 12 Adult   942.05
1. Great Britain—History—1485-1603, Tudors
ISBN 978-0-313-36560-7   LC 2009-27600
First published 1995
This "book easily could be used as a supplemental
text in an advanced history course or sections could be
used by English teachers to give broader meaning to students studying Shakespeare's plays. The well-written material is divided by headings, sub-headings, graphs, pictures, and illustrations. Chapters include a history of Tudor England; society and the course of life; clothing,
food and drink; and the Elizabethan world." Libr Media
Connect
Includes glossary and bibliographical references

942.06   England—Stuart and Commonwealth periods, 1603-1714

Trevelyan, George Macaulay, 1876-1962
The English Revolution, 1688-1689; [by] G. M.
Trevelyan. Oxford University Press 1965 136p pa
$30
Grades: 11 12 Adult   942.06
1. Great Britain—History—1688, Revolution
ISBN 978-0-19-500263-8; 0-19-500263-6
First published 1938 in the United Kingdom
This study covers not only the revolution itself but
also the events of the reign of James II, which led up to
it and the political changes which followed.
Includes bibliographical references

943   Central Europe. Germany

Coy, Jason Philip, 1970-
A brief history of Germany; [by] Jason P. Coy.
Facts on File 2011 288p il map (Brief history)
$49.50; pa $19.95
Grades: 9 10 11 12 Adult   943
1. Germany—History
ISBN 978-0-8160-8142-4; 978-0-8160-8329-9 (pa)
                                   LC 2010-23139
This book provides an "account of the events, people,
and special customs and traditions that have shaped Germany from ancient times to the present." Publisher's note
Includes bibliographical references

Fulbrook, Mary, 1951-
A concise history of Germany. 2nd ed. Cambridge University Press 2004 277p il, maps (Cambridge concise histories) hardcover o.p. pa $22

Grades: 11 12 Adult   **943**
1. Germany—History
ISBN 0-521-83320-5; 0-521-54071-2 (pa)
    LC 2004-271599
First published 1990 in the United Kingdom
This history of Germany "spans the early Middle Ages to the present day. . . . Mary Fulbrook explores the interrelationships between social, political and cultural factors in the light of the latest scholarly controversies." Publ Wkly
Includes bibliographical references

Kort, Michael
The handbook of the new Eastern Europe; [by] Michael G. Kort. 21st Cent. Bks. (Brookfield) 2001 256p il maps lib bdg $39.90

Grades: 7 8 9 10   **943**
1. Eastern Europe 2. Central Europe
ISBN 0-7613-1362-1   LC 00-57708
This handbook begins with a "overview of the region. Economic and historical profiles are given for seven nations plus those in the former Yugoslavia, with an emphasis on post-1989 events after the fall of Communism. . . . Other reference material includes flags of each nation, a chronology of events since 1989, and an encyclopedia. The latter emphasizes names and places, with a few general topics such as environmental pollution." Voice Youth Advocates
"The book will be useful for serious students needing research materials." Horn Book Guide
Includes bibliographical references

Schmemann, Serge
When the wall came down; the Berlin Wall and the fall of Soviet Communism. Kingfisher 2006 127p il map $15.95

Grades: 7 8 9 10   **943**
1. Berlin Wall (1961-1989) 2. Germany (East)—Politics and government 3. Germany—History—1945-1990 4. Cold war
ISBN 0-7534-5994-9; 978-0-7534-5994-2
    LC 2005-23892
"A New York Times book"
The author "describes the rise and defeat of the Nazis and the events that made Berlin and Germany a focal point for the Cold War. He then describes life in divided Germany and the events that led to the fall of the Berlin Wall and the reunification of Germany. A writer with a unique perspective, Schmemann creates an informative and quite readable account. The volume is well illustrated with black-and-white photos." Voice Youth Advocates
Includes bibliographical references

943.086   Germany—Period of Third Reich, 1933-1945

Bartoletti, Susan Campbell, 1958-
Hitler Youth; growing up in Hitler's shadow. Scholastic Nonfiction 2005 176p il map $19.95 *
Grades: 7 8 9 10   **943.086**
1. National socialism 2. Germany—History—1933-1945 3. Holocaust, 1933-1945
ISBN 0-439-35379-3   LC 2004-51040
The author "explores how Hitler gained the loyalty, trust, and passion of so many of Germany's young people." Publisher's note
"Bartoletti draws on oral histories, diaries, letters, and her own extensive interviews with Holocaust survivors, Hitler Youth, resisters, and bystanders to tell the history from the viewpoints of people who were there. . . . The stirring photos tell more of the story. . . . The extensive back matter is a part of the gripping narrative." Booklist
Includes bibliographical references

Dumbach, Annette E. (Annette Eberly)
Sophie Scholl and the white rose; [by] Annette Dumbach, Jud Newborn. New ed. Oneworld 2007 238p il pa $14.95
Grades: 11 12 Adult   **943.086**
1. Scholl, Sophie, 1921-1943 2. Weisse Rose (Resistance group) 3. National socialism
ISBN 978-1-85168-536-3; 1-85168-536-7
First published 1986 with title: Shattering the German night
This book tells "the story of five German university students and their professor, who formed a Nazi-resistance group dubbed the White Rose." Libr J
Includes bibliographical references

943.087   Germany—1945-1990

Bernstein, Eckhard
Culture and customs of Germany. Greenwood 2004 xvi 217p il map (Culture and customs of Europe) $45
Grades: 9 10 11 12   **943.087**
1. Germany—Civilization
ISBN 0-313-32203-1   LC 2003-55491
"The author introduces readers and researchers to post Cold War and post Berlin Wall Germany. . . . Holidays, leisure activities, the German work ethic, eating and drinking, the arts and performing arts, and other aspects of the life of the Germans are portrayed. In light of the many changes in Europe in the past century, this title offers a new, modern update of Germany and its people, culture, and customs. Social studies classes and students in German studies classes will find uses for this title." Libr Media Connect
Includes bibliographical references

944   France and Monaco

Haine, W. Scott

Culture and customs of France. Greenwood Press 2006 315p il map (Culture and customs of Europe) $49.95

Grades: 9 10 11 12   **944**

1. France—Civilization

ISBN 0-313-32892-7; 978-0-313-32892-3

       LC 2006-17935

Contents: The land, people, and history; Religion and thought; Gender, marriage, family and education; Social customs: leisure, holidays, sports, and festivals; Cuisine and fashion; Literature; Media; Cinema; Performing arts; Art, architecture, and housing

Includes bibliographical references

944.04   France—Revolutionary period, 1789-1804

Anderson, James Maxwell, 1933-

Daily life during the French Revolution; [by] James M. Anderson. Greenwood Press 2007 268p il map (Greenwood Press "Daily life through history" series) $49.95

Grades: 9 10 11 12   **944.04**

1. France—History—1789-1799, Revolution

ISBN 0-313-33683-0; 978-0-313-33683-6

       LC 2006-34084

"Chapters include the physical makeup of France; the social and political background of the revolution; the First Republic; religion, church and state; urban life; rural life; family life; the fringe society; clothes and fashion; food and drink; the role of women; military life; education; health and medicine; and writers, artists, musicians and entertainment." Publisher's note

Includes bibliographical references

Doyle, William, 1942-

The Oxford history of the French Revolution. 2nd ed. Oxford University Press 2003 481p maps pa $19.95

Grades: 9 10 11 12   **944.04**

1. France—History—1789-1799, Revolution 2. Europe—History—1789-1900

ISBN 0-19-925298-X   LC 2002-29004

First published 1989

"Beginning with the accession of Louis XVI in 1774, . . . William Doyle traces the history of France through revolution, terror, and counterterror, to the triumph of Napoleon in 1802, along the way analyzing the impact of these events in France upon the rest of Europe." Publisher's note

Includes bibliographical references

The **encyclopedia** of the French revolutionary and Napoleonic Wars; a political, social, and military history; Gregory Fremont-Barnes, editor. ABC-CLIO 2006 3v il map set $285

Grades: 11 12 Adult   **944.04**

1. Reference books 2. France—History—1789-1799, Revolution—Encyclopedias 3. France—History—1799-1815—Encyclopedias

ISBN 1-85109-646-9; 978-1-85109-646-6

       LC 2006-19409

This encyclopedia "provides information on a variety of issues from military topics to cultural, social, and political aspects of this period. Entries include significant battles, weaponry, and important individuals who made a mark, e.g., generals, politicians, writers, composers, and members of the clergy. . . . The last volume has full-text primary source documents, including firsthand accounts of battles, texts of treaties, speeches, and dispatches." Choice

"This is a fantastic resource for anyone researching the period. It is straightforward and user-friendly enough to be helpful to the beginner, but the detail and extensive references will appeal to the more advanced and experienced researcher as well." Booklist

Includes bibliographical references

945   Italian Peninsula and adjacent islands. Italy

Cohen, Elizabeth Storr, 1946-

Daily life in Renaissance Italy; [by] Elizabeth S. Cohen and Thomas V. Cohen. Greenwood Press 2001 316p il maps (Greenwood Press "Daily life through history" series) $57.95; pa $25 *

Grades: 7 8 9 10   **945**

1. Renaissance 2. Italy—Civilization

ISBN   978-0-313-30426-2;   0-313-30426-2; 978-0-313-6114-2 (pa); 0-313-6114-2 (pa)

       LC 00-69150

Also available online

"A brief historical background precedes chapters covering society, families, morality, schooling, marriage, disease, and death, as well as many aspects of rural and city life. . . . The documented information is ideal for student reports and reference questions." Voice Youth Advocates

Includes bibliographical references

The **Oxford** history of Italy; edited by George Holmes. Oxford Univ. Press 1997 386p il maps hardcover o.p. pa $29.95

Grades: 11 12 Adult   **945**

1. Italy—History

ISBN 0-19-820527-9; 0-19-285444-5 (pa)

       LC 98-100006

Paperback published with title: The Oxford illustrated history of Italy

Twelve scholars survey Italian social, political and cultural history from the time of the Roman Empire to the present.

"An excellent choice for readers wanting either a refresher course on Italian history or those who have no background whatsoever in the subject but have a desire to learn the basics." Booklist

946 Iberian Peninsula and adjacent islands. Spain

Fuentes, Carlos, 1928-
The buried mirror; reflections on Spain and the New World. Houghton Mifflin 1992 399p il hardcover o.p. pa $29.95
Grades: 11 12 Adult   **946**
1. Spain—Civilization 2. Latin America—Civilization
ISBN 0-395-47978-9; 0-395-92499-5 (pa)
     LC 91-34312
The author "believes that a common cultural heritage can help the countries of Latin America transcend disunity and fragmentation. . . . [He] explores Spanish America's love-hate relationship with Spain and its search for an identity in its multicultural roots." Publ Wkly
"Every page in this lapidary essay offers profound insight into the Spanish American psyche." Libr J
Includes bibliographical references

947 Eastern Europe. Russia

Gottfried, Ted, 1928-
The road to Communism; illustrated by Melanie Reim. 21st Cent. Bks. (Brookfield) 2002 144p il lib bdg $28.90
Grades: 8 9 10 11 12   **947**
1. Soviet Union—History—1917-1921, Revolution
ISBN 0-7613-2557-3   LC 2001-52252
Chronicles the Czarist Russian Empire in the 1800s, the birth of Bolshevism, events leading to the Russian Revolution of 1917, and the development of new political structures in its aftermath
"Gottfried writes with clarity and distance even as he narrates the dramatic details of the political conflict and the emotion of the 'dream that failed.'" Booklist
Includes glossary and bibliographical references

Kort, Michael
A brief history of Russia. Facts On File 2007 xxiii, 310p il map (Brief history) $45; lib bdg $19.95 *
Grades: 9 10 11 12 Adult   **947**
1. Russia—History
ISBN   978-0-8160-7112-8;   0-8160-7112-8; 978-0-8160-7113-5 (lib bdg); 0-8160-7113-6 (lib bdg)
     LC 2007-32723
"Detailing the social, economic, and political changes and crises that the people of Russia have had to endure, . . . [this book provides an] account of this vast country's history." Publisher's note
Includes bibliographical references

Riasanovsky, Nicholas V., 1923-2011
A history of Russia. 8th ed. Oxford University Press 2011 various paging il map pa $64.95
Grades: 11 12 Adult   **947**
1. Russia—History 2. Soviet Union—History
ISBN 978-0-19-534197-3   LC 2010-23174
First published 1963

This narrative history includes discussions of economics, social organization, religion, and culture.
Includes bibliographical references

Stokes, Gale
The walls came tumbling down; the collapse of communism in Eastern Europe. Oxford Univ. Press 1993 319p hardcover o.p. pa $31.95
Grades: 11 12 Adult   **947**
1. Communism 2. Eastern Europe—Politics and government
ISBN 0-19-506644-8; 0-19-506645-6 (pa)
     LC 92-44862
The author "deals with all the formerly Communist countries in Eastern Europe except Albania, and he traces the history of the collapse of the Soviet-type regimes rather than concentrating . . . on their evolution since the collapse." N Y Times Book Rev
This book "can be recommended as a coherent, well-written history that defines its time frame well, provides sound coverage, makes prudent judgments, and wears its analysis lightly. . . . Stokes's overview traces the ebb and flow of personalities and events in a manner that is both accessible to lay readers and informative to scholars." Libr J

947.08 Russia—1855-

Massie, Robert K., 1929-
The Romanovs; the final chapter. Random House 1995 308p il hardcover o.p. pa $14.95
Grades: 11 12 Adult   **947.08**
1. Nicholas II, Emperor of Russia, 1868-1918 2. House of Romanov 3. Russia—Kings and rulers
ISBN 0-394-58048-6; 0-345-40640-0 (pa)
     LC 95-4718
This book "is divided into three major parts. The first segment—by far the most fascinating and original—focuses on the complex scientific process used in identifying the Romanovs' remains. . . . The second part concerns the various impostors who have claimed to be members of the Russian imperial family. . . . [The] third segment [is] a report on those Romanov émigrés—close relatives of the Czar's—who survived the Bolsheviks' persecution." N Y Times Book Rev
Includes bibliographical references

947.084 Russia (Soviet Union)— 1917-1991

Eaton, Katherine Bliss
Daily life in the Soviet Union; [by] Katherine B. Eaton. Greenwood Press 2004 320p il map (Greenwood Press "Daily life through history" series) $49.95
Grades: 9 10 11 12   **947.084**
1. Soviet Union—History
ISBN 0-313-31628-7   LC 2004-12486
Contents: Ethnic groups and nationalities; Government and law; The military; Economy, class structure, food,

Eaton, Katherine Bliss—*Continued*
clothing, and shopping; Rural life; Housing; Health care
and health problems; Education; The arts; Mass media,
leisure, and popular culture; Religion
"This would be an ideal addition to libraries in high
schools offering a course on Russian and Soviet history."
SLJ

Gay, Kathlyn, 1930-
The aftermath of the Russian Revolution.
Twenty-First Century Books 2009 160p il
(Aftermath of history) lib bdg $38.60
Grades: 8 9 10 11 12   **947.084**
1. Soviet Union—History
ISBN 978-0-8225-9092-7; 0-8225-9092-1
LC 2008-25276
This book "begins with an overview of the Czar's
Russia and the political machinations that brought about
revolution. The disputes between different revolutionary
groups led to the eventual triumph of the Bolsheviks and
the reigns of Lenin and Stalin. Stalin's brutality in partic-
ular receives a lot of attention. The final chapters cover
the transition to a more open society, the fall of the Soviet Union, and the age of Putin." SLJ
Includes glossary and bibliographical references

Wade, Rex A.
The Bolshevik revolution and Russian Civil
War. Greenwood Press 2001 xxiii, 220p il maps
(Greenwood Press guides to historic events of the
twentieth century) $45 *
Grades: 11 12 Adult   **947.084**
1. Soviet Union—History—1917-1921, Revolution
ISBN 0-313-29974-9   LC 00-35322
"A narrative history of the political, economic, and so-
cial background; causes and events of the revolution and
civil war. . . . This book is a product of solid scholar-
ship and an excellent choice for libraries." SLJ
Includes glossary and bibliographical references

Weinberg, Robert
Revolutionary Russia; a history in documents;
[by] Robert Weinberg, Laurie Bernstein. Oxford
University Press 2010 c2011 239p il map (Pages
from history) $39.95; pa $24.95
Grades: 9 10 11 12   **947.084**
1. Soviet Union—History—1917-1921, Revolution—
Sources
ISBN   978-0-19-512225-1;   0-19-512225-9;
978-0-19-533794-5 (pa); 0-19-533794-8 (pa)
LC 2009-38666
This "is a solid historical overview of the October
Revolution and rick Bolshevik culture as well as the terror of the purges and the horrendous conditions of the
gulags. The authors show how forced collectivization led
to famine and the deaths of millions, as well as how the
country's successful transformation from an oppressed
agricultural society to a highly industrialized nation made
it able to withstand a German invasion during the Second
World War." Booklist
Includes bibliographical references

947.085 Russia (Soviet Union)— 1953-1991

Langley, Andrew
The collapse of the Soviet Union; the end of an
empire. Compass Point Books 2006 96p il map
(Snapshots in history) lib bdg $31.93
Grades: 7 8 9 10   **947.085**
1. Soviet Union—History
ISBN 978-0-7565-2009-0; 0-7565-2009-6
LC 2006003003
This "describes leaders, their plans, and their ultimate
downfalls, from the removal of Tsar Nicholas II to the
problems of present-day Russia. [This book is] great for
research . . . brief but comprehensive." SLJ
Includes glossary and bibliographical references

947.7 Ukraine

Otfinoski, Steven, 1949-
Ukraine. Second ed. Facts on File 2004 139p il
map (Nations in transition) $40
Grades: 7 8 9 10   **947.7**
1. Ukraine
ISBN 0-8160-5115-1   LC 2004-43241
First published 1999
Gives a historical and cultural overview of the country
of Ukraine with particular emphasis on changes that have
occurred since the collapse of the Soviet Union
Includes bibliographical references

948 Scandinavia

The **Oxford** illustrated history of the Vikings;
edited by Peter Sawyer. Oxford Univ. Press
1997 298p il maps hardcover o.p. pa $27.50 *
Grades: 11 12 Adult   **948**
1. Vikings
ISBN 0-19-820526-0; 0-19-285434-8 (pa)
LC 97-16649
This illustrated collection of articles includes discussion of the Vikings' impact on England, Iceland, Greenland, Russia, and the Frankish and Danish Empires; Viking ships and ship-building; Viking religion; and the
ways in which Vikings have been portrayed throughout
history. Significant archaeological finds are featured.
Includes bibliographical references

Wolf, Kirsten, 1959-
Daily life of the Vikings. Greenwood Press
2004 187p il map (Greenwood Press "Daily life
through history" series) $55
Grades: 11 12 Adult   **948**
1. Vikings
ISBN 0-313-32269-4   LC 2004-15184
"The work is organized into chapters covering all aspects [of Viking] life: domestic, economic, intellectual,
material, political, recreational, and religious. It includes
a historical timeline of Viking history, complementary
pictures, illustrations, and maps, and a bibliography."
Publisher's note

949.6 Balkan Peninsula

Mazower, Mark
The Balkans: a short history. Modern Lib. 2000
xliii, 188p maps (Modern Library chronicles)
hardcover o.p. pa $11.95
Grades: 11 12 Adult   **949.6**
1. Balkan Peninsula—History
ISBN 0-679-64087-8; 0-8129-6621-X (pa)
LC 00-56244
Mazower "has written a concise history of Europe's
troubled southeastern corner that is both sympathetic to
the region's never-ending struggle for identity and freedom from invaders and critical of its inhabitants' recurring failure to reconcile the religious and cultural differences imposed on them by the powers of the West and
the East." Publ Wkly
This "is an excellent primer on the region's history,
especially the growth of the nation-state in the 19th century." Economist
Includes bibliographical references

949.7 Serbia and Montenegro, Croatia, Slovenia, Bosnia and Hercegovina, Macedonia

Daalder, Ivo H.
Winning ugly; NATO's war to save Kosovo;
[by] Ivo H. Daalder, Michael E. O'Hanlon.
Brookings Institution Press 2000 343p il maps
$26.95; pa $19.95
Grades: 9 10 11 12   **949.7**
1. North Atlantic Treaty Organization 2. Kosovo (Ser-
bia)
ISBN 0-8157-1696-6; 0-8157-1697-4 (pa)
LC 00-9198
This is an "examination of Western, and especially
American, policy [in the Kosovo conflict]." N Y Rev
Books
Includes bibliographical references

Judah, Tim, 1962-
The Serbs; history, myth and the destruction of
Yugoslavia. 3rd ed. Yale University Press 2009
414p il map pa $19
Grades: 11 12 Adult   **949.7**
1. Serbia 2. Yugoslavia—History 3. Yugoslav War,
1991-1995
ISBN 978-0-300-15826-7; 0-300-15826-2
LC 2009039429
First published 1997
Judah explores the role of the Serbs in the Yugoslav
conflict. "The early part is devoted to a summary of Ser-
bian history since the Middle Ages, and the remaining
two-thirds to recent events." London Rev Books
Includes bibliographical references

Sacco, Joe
Safe area Goražde. Fantagraphics Bks. 2000
227p il $28.95; pa $19.95
Grades: 10 11 12 Adult   **949.7**
1. Graphic novels 2. Yugoslav War, 1991-1995—
Graphic novels 3. Bosnia and Hercegovina—Graphic
novels
ISBN 1-56097-392-7; 1-56097-470-2 (pa)
"The war in eastern Bosnia, 1992-1995" Jacket
The author "spent four months in Bosnia, focusing on
the Muslim enclave of Gorazde, where he interviewed
survivors of the city's siege by the Serbs. . . . Most of
the book is devoted to townspeople's accounts of how
they endured shelling and starvation, and to portrayals of
their efforts at resuming their lives while grappling with
the question of how their neighbors could have turned on
them so cruelly. Sacco's precise, expressive drawings tell
the victims' stories more compellingly than the text does
and in more sustained fashion than broadcast journalism
does. As keen as is his eye, his ear for eliciting these
devastating, heartfelt stories gives the book its undeniable
power." Booklist
Includes bibliographical references

950 History of Asia

Columbia chronologies of Asian history and
culture; edited by John S. Bowman. Columbia
University Press 2000 751p map $93
Grades: 9 10 11 12   **950**
1. Asia—History—Chronology 2. Reference books
ISBN 0-231-11004-9   LC 99-47017
"This volume offers chronologies for the countries of
Asia from the Paleolithic era through 1998. . . . The
Middle East and Asiatic Russia are excluded. Chapters
for each of the 26 individual countries that are treated
range from four or five pages . . . to more than 100
pages. Chronologies for most countries are subdivided by
time periods representing major developments in their
history." Booklist
"This reference work breaks new ground in the scope
of its coverage." Libr J

Lane, George, 1952-
Genghis Khan and Mongol rule. Greenwood
Press 2004 xlv, 224p il map (Greenwood guides to
historic events of the medieval world) $45 *
Grades: 9 10 11 12   **950**
1. Genghis Khan, 1162-1227 2. Mongols
ISBN 0-313-32528-6   LC 2004-43639
The author argues "that the Mongols were not neces-
sarily the destructive barbarians of popular history, but
rather an empire that encouraged cultural achievement,
international trade, and even religious tolerance." SLJ
"The book tells a grand story in the brief compass of
seven chapters." Hist Teach
Includes bibliographical references

Wood, Frances
The Silk Road; two thousand years in the heart
of Asia. University of Calif. Press 2002 270p il
maps $29.95; pa $19.95
Grades: 9 10 11 12   **950**
1. Central Asia—History
ISBN 0-520-23786-2; 0-520-24340-4 (pa)
LC 2003-273631

Wood, Frances—*Continued*

"Covering more than 5,000 years, this book . . . illustrated with photographs, manuscripts, and paintings from the collections of the British Library and other museums worldwide, presents an overall picture of the history and cultures of the Silk Road. It also contains many previously unpublished photographs by the great explorers Stein, Hedin, and Mannerheim." Publisher's note

"This historical journey through the byways of the old Silk Road is a beautifully rendered tribute to the thousands of years in which these routes served as the center of trade." Publ Wkly

Includes bibliographical references

951   China and adjacent areas

Berkshire encyclopedia of China; modern and historic views of the world's newest and oldest global power = [Zhonghua quan shu: kua yue li shi he xian dai, shen shi zui xin he zui gu lao de quan qiu da guo] Berkshire Pub. Group 2009 5v il map set $675

Grades: 10 11 12 Adult   951

1. China—Civilization—Encyclopedias 2. China—Social life and customs—Encyclopedias 3. Reference books

ISBN 978-0-9770159-4-8; 0-9770159-4-7

LC 2009-7589

Also available online

"Editorial board and staff: Linsun Cheng ... [et al.]; senior editor, Mary Bagg"—P. [vi]; Parallel title in Chinese characters

"Arranged alphabetically, the nearly 1000 articles cover an . . . array of subjects as they relate to China. Among those explored are the country's history (both ancient and modern), politicians, architecture, food, international relations, and medicine." Libr J

Includes bibliographical references

China: opposing viewpoints; Noah Berlatsky, book editor. Greenhaven Press 2010 214p il $41.70; pa $28.90 *

Grades: 9 10 11 12   951

1. China

ISBN   978-0-7377-4765-2;   0-7377-4765-X; 978-0-7377-4766-9 (pa); 0-7377-4766-8 (pa)

LC 2009045725

"Explores the status of human rights and democracy in China, as well as China's economy and its potential as a military threat. Issues discussed include the global recession, trade imbalances, intellectual property piracy, nuclear nonproliferation, Taiwan and North Korea. Also looks at how China is addressing environmental concerns in the region." Publisher's note

Includes bibliographical references

Ebrey, Patricia Buckley, 1947-

The Cambridge illustrated history of China. 2nd ed. Cambridge University Press 2010 384p il map (Cambridge illustrated history) $90; pa $45

Grades: 11 12 Adult   951

1. China—History

ISBN 978-0-521-19620-8; 978-0-521-12433-1 (pa)

LC 2010-292643

First published 1996

"Ebrey traces the origins of Chinese culture from prehistoric times to the present. She follows its development from the rise of Confucianism, Buddhism, and the great imperial dynasties to the Mongol, Manchu, and Western intrusions and the modern communist state." Publisher's note

Includes bibliographical references

Encyclopedia of modern China; David Pong, editor in chief. Charles Scribner's Sons/Gale, Cengage Learning 2009 4v il map set $520 *

Grades: 10 11 12 Adult   951

1. China—Civilization—Encyclopedias 2. Reference books

ISBN 978-0-684-31566-9; 978-0-684-31571-3 (ebook)

LC 2009-3279

Contact publisher for ebook pricing

"Covering the period 1800 to the present, this attractive and authoritative set includes 936 entries and sidebars by nearly 500 authors. . . . There are main entries for each province (including a map and a box containing key data), major cities, important people, Chinese relations with countries from Australia to Vietnam, and hundreds of miscellaneous subjects." Booklist

Includes bibliographical references

Mah, Adeline Yen, 1937-

China; land of dragons and emperors. Delacorte Press 2009 240p il $17.99; lib bdg $29.99

Grades: 8 9 10 11 12 Adult   951

1. China—History

ISBN   978-0-385-73748-7;   0-385-73748-3; 978-0-385-90669-2 (lib bdg); 0-385-90669-2 (lib bdg)

LC 2008-35331

Mah "brings East to West in this concise, reader-friendly history of China that contains more than 80 photographs of famous figures and artifacts. Spanning 2,000 years of strife and victories, the book mainly focuses on China's six dynasties, which are introduced in chronological order and are followed by brief portraits of post-dynasty leaders. . . . This accessible work will be an invaluable resource for students and young history buffs." Publ Wkly

Includes bibliographical references

Slavicek, Louise Chipley, 1956-

The Great Wall of China; foreword by George J. Mitchell; intro. by James I. Matray. Chelsea House 2004 118p il map (Arbitrary borders) $31.50 *

Grades: 9 10 11 12   951

1. Great Wall of China 2. China—History

ISBN 0-7910-8019-6   LC 2004-10127

Contents: China's legendary wall; Before the great walls; China's first Great Wall: the wall of Qin Shi Huang Di; The Great Wall of the Han dynasty; From the period of disunity through the Mongol conquest: the great wall in war and peace; The Ming wall; The Great Wall in Western and Chinese eyes

Includes bibliographical references

951.04 China—Period of Republic, 1912-1949

Gay, Kathlyn, 1930-
The aftermath of the Chinese nationalist revolution. Twenty-First Century Books 2008 c2009 160p il (Aftermath of history) lib bdg $38.60
Grades: 7 8 9 10 **951.04**
    1. China—History—1912-1949
    ISBN 978-0-8225-7601-3; 0-8225-7601-5
                   LC 2007-15082
This book "offers a lucid account of the civil turmoil that began in China with the successful revolution led by Dr. Sun Yat-sen in 1911, and culminated in the establishment of the People's Republic in 1949." Booklist
Includes bibliographical references

951.05 China—Period of People's Republic, 1949-

Gay, Kathlyn, 1930-
Mao Zedong's China. Twenty-First Century Books 2008 160p il map (Dictatorships) lib bdg $38.60
Grades: 7 8 9 10 **951.05**
    1. Mao Zedong, 1893-1976 2. China—History—1949-1976
    ISBN 978-0-8225-7285-5   LC 2007-5083
The author "places Mao in context with other rulers of China and paints an extraordinary picture of how this young peasant rose nearly to the level of a deity in the eyes of the Chinese people." Voice Youth Advocates

Jiang, Ji-li
Red scarf girl; a memoir of the Cultural Revolution; foreword by David Henry Hwang. HarperCollins Pubs. 1997 285p $16.99; pa $6.99
Grades: 6 7 8 9 10 **951.05**
    1. China—History—1949-1976—Personal narratives
    ISBN 0-06-027585-5; 0-06-446208-0 (pa)
                   LC 97-5089
"This is an autobiographical account of growing up during Mao's Cultural Revolution in China in 1966. . . . Jiang describes in terrifying detail the ordeals of her family and those like them, including unauthorized search and seizure, persecution, arrest and torture, hunger, and public humiliation. . . . Her voice is that of an intelligent, confused adolescent, and her focus on the effects of the revolution on herself, her family, and her friends provides an emotional focal point for the book, and will allow even those with limited knowledge of Chinese history to access the text." Bull Cent Child Books

Schoppa, R. Keith, 1943-
Twentieth century China; a history in documents. 2nd ed. Oxford University Press 2011 214p il map (Pages from history) $39.95; pa $24.95 *
Grades: 9 10 11 12 **951.05**
    1. China—History—20th century—Sources
    ISBN 978-0-19-973201-2; 978-0-19-973200-5 (pa)
                   LC 2010010474
First published 2004
Using primary sources "including official reports and public statements, articles, political posters, cartoons, poetry, songs, and advertisements, R. Keith Schoppa paints a picture of a society undergoing drastic changes, both social and political." Publisher's note
Includes bibliographical references

Slavicek, Louise Chipley, 1956-
The Chinese Cultural Revolution. Chelsea House Publishers 2010 128p il (Milestones in modern world history) lib bdg $35
Grades: 8 9 10 11 12 **951.05**
    1. China—History—1949-1976
    ISBN 978-1-60413-278-6; 1-60413-278-7
                   LC 2008-54885
"From the cover photo onward, young people are front and center in [this book,] . . . which focuses on the Red Guards who heard the anti-establishment call of their leader, Mao Zedong, in 1966. This political upheaval led to the deaths of up to four million Chinese over 10 years." Booklist
Includes bibliographical references

951.9 Korea

Edwards, Paul M., 1933-
Korean War almanac. Facts on File 2006 592p il map (Almanacs of American wars) $85
Grades: 11 12 Adult **951.9**
    1. Korean War, 1950-1953
    ISBN 0-8160-6037-1   LC 2005-9374
    First published 1990 under the authorship of Harry G. Summers
This book "contains a day-by-day chronology of the events and the people involved in this important war." Publisher's note
Includes bibliographical references

The **encyclopedia** of the Korean War; a political, social, and military history; Spencer C. Tucker, volume editor; Paul G. Pierpaoli, Jr., associate editor and editor, documents volume; Jinwung Kim, Xiaobing Li, James I. Matray, assistant editors. 2nd ed. ABC-CLIO 2010 3v il map set $295
Grades: 11 12 Adult **951.9**
    1. Korean War, 1950-1953—Encyclopedias 2. Reference books
    ISBN   978-1-85109-849-1;   1-85109-849-6; 978-1-85109-850-7 (ebook); 1-85109-850-X (ebook)
                   LC 2010-681
First published 2000

The encyclopedia of the Korean War—*Continued*

Contact publisher for ebook pricing

A resource on the confrontation that became the first shooting war of the Cold War, the first limited conflict of the Atomic Age, and the war that led to a dramatic escalation of the national security state while foreshadowing U.S. involvement in Vietnam.

"This is an excellent source for high-school, academic, and public libraries." Booklist

Includes glossary and bibliographical references

Hastings, Max

The Korean War. Simon & Schuster 1987 391p il maps hardcover o.p. pa $16

Grades: 11 12 Adult   **951.9**

1. Korean War, 1950-1953

ISBN 0-671-52823-8; 0-671-66834-X (pa)

         LC 87-16547

The author covers the political and military background of the Korean War, and also discusses how it served as a prelude to the American involvement in the Vietnam War, 15 years later.

This is a "readable, informative and sensible study." Booklist

Includes bibliographical references

Isserman, Maurice

Korean War; John S. Bowman, general editor. Rev. ed. Chelsea House 2010 162p il map (America at war) $45 *

Grades: 9 10 11 12   **951.9**

1. Korean War, 1950-1953

ISBN 978-0-8160-8186-8   LC 2009-36873

First published 1992

Examines the political climate and military situation that led to the Korean War and discusses the key people and events involved in the conflict itself.

Includes glossary and bibliographical references

The Korean War; Dennis Nishi, book editor. Greenhaven Press 2003 240p (Interpreting primary documents) hardcover o.p. pa $23.70

Grades: 7 8 9 10   **951.9**

1. Korean War, 1950-1953

ISBN 0-7377-1202-3 (lib bdg); 0-7377-1201-5 (pa)

         LC 2002-40890

"This anthology contains documents by influential Washington policy makers as well as popular editorialists of the day." Publisher's note

Includes bibliographical references

Peterson, Mark, 1946-

A brief history of Korea; [by] Mark Peterson with Phillip Margulies. Facts On File 2010 328p il map (Brief history) $49.50 *

Grades: 9 10 11 12 Adult   **951.9**

1. Korea—History

ISBN 978-0-8160-5085-7   LC 2009-18889

This book "covers the history of Korea from the origins of the Korean people in prehistoric times to the economic and political situation in North and South Korea today." Publisher's note

Includes bibliographical references

Stokesbury, James L.

A short history of the Korean War. Morrow 1988 276p maps hardcover o.p. pa $13.95

Grades: 11 12 Adult   **951.9**

1. Korean War, 1950-1953

ISBN 0-688-06377-2; 0-688-09513-5 (pa)

         LC 88-5229

Stokesbury seeks to "trace the background of the Korean situation during the . . . years prior to July and August 1950. . . . [There is a discussion] of the first year of maneuvers and battles before and after the Chinese Communists intervened, and also of the . . . fighting from time to time during the two years of peace negotiations." Publisher's note

"Stokesbury's combination of scholarship, clear writing, balanced judgments, and wit has reached a new high. It would be hard to imagine better personality portraits or better coverage of the prisoner-of-war issue." Booklist

Includes bibliographical references

951.93   North Korea (People's Democratic Republic of Korea)

Delisle, Guy, 1966-

Pyongyang: a journey in North Korea; translated by Helge Dascher. Drawn & Quarterly 2005 176p il map hardcover o.p. pa $14.95 *

Grades: 11 12 Adult   **951.93**

1. Korea (North)—Graphic novels 2. Graphic novels

ISBN 1-896597-89-0; 1-897299-21-4 (pa)

This book "documents the two months French animator Delisle spent overseeing cartoon production in North Korea. . . . He records everything from the omnipresent statues and portraits of dictators Kim Il-Sung and Kim Jong-Il to the brainwashed obedience of the citizens." Booklist

"Pyongyang will appeal to multiple audiences: current events buffs, Persepolis fans and those who just love a good yarn." Publ Wkly

952   Japan

Dunn, Charles James

Everyday life in traditional Japan. C.E. Tuttle Co. 1972 c1969 197p il map (TUT books) pa $16.95

Grades: 9 10 11 12   **952**

1. Japan—Civilization 2. Japan—Social life and customs

ISBN 4-8053-1005-7   LC 72-186748

First published 1969 by Putnam

"A description of Japanese life during the stable . . . reign of the Tokugawa shoguns [1600-1850]." Cincinnati Public Libr

Includes bibliographical references

952.03   Japan—1868-1945

Buruma, Ian
Inventing Japan, 1853-1964. Modern Lib. 2003
194p hardcover o.p. pa $12.95
Grades: 11 12 Adult   **952.03**
1. Japan—History
ISBN 0-679-64085-1; 0-8129-7286-4 (pa)
                                  LC 2002-26346
"A Modern Library chronicles book"
"Buruma traces the remarkable metamorphosis that transformed an isolated island shogunate into an expansive military empire and then into a pacified and prosperous democracy. . . . An excellent introductory study." Booklist
Includes bibliographical references

953.8   Saudi Arabia

Wynbrandt, James
A brief history of Saudi Arabia; foreword by Fawaz A. Gerges. 2nd ed. Facts On File 2010 364p il map (Brief history) $49.50; pa $19.95
Grades: 9 10 11 12 Adult   **953.8**
1. Saudi Arabia—History
ISBN 978-0-8160-7876-9; 978-0-8160-8250-6 (pa)
                                  LC 2010-5466
First published 2004
This history of Saudi Arabia covers "pre-Islamic Arabia; Bedouin society and culture; the birth and spread of Islam; the development of and philosophy behind Wahhabism; the origins of House Saud; Saudi Arabia's role in the Middle East; Saudi Arabia's relationship to the United States; the battle between conservative and progressive elements in the monarchy today; [and] the reign of King Abdullah." Publisher's note
Includes glossary and bibliographical references

954   South Asia. India

McLeod, John, 1963-
The history of India. Greenwood Press 2002 xx, 223p (Greenwood histories of the modern nations) $39.95 *
Grades: 11 12 Adult   **954**
1. Mogul Empire 2. India—History—1526-1765
ISBN 0-313-31459-4   LC 2002-276829
The author presents "in broad outlines some of the major events and episodes that make up India's history. . . . This is a useful compilation of important facts relating to Indian history. Its strength lies primarily in the last six chapters in which brief narratives of the struggle for independence and post-independence India down to the close of the twentieth century are nicely presented. All in all, this is a book that all libraries should have." Recomm Ref Books for Small & Medium-sized Libr & Media Cent, 2003
Includes bibliographical references

Ram-Prasad, Chakravarthi
Exploring the life, myth, and art of India. Rosen 2009 c2010 144p il map (Civilizations of the world) lib bdg $29.95
Grades: 7 8 9 10 11 12   **954**
1. India—Civilization 2. Indic mythology 3. Indic art
ISBN 978-1-4358-5615-8; 1-4358-5615-5
                                  LC 2009-9274
This describes the civilization, mythology and art of ancient India
"This beautifully illustrated and well-written [title] . . . is perfect for those assignments where students must look at the culture of a civilization. Artwork and pictures blend seamlessly with the information and the reader is taken on a journey of discovery. Myths are used as the story of how the people view themselves, blended with the discussion of the reality of life. Everyday life is tied to the belief systems and is explained in light of those beliefs. The pictures are beautifully done and there is almost as much information in the captions as there is in the text." Libr Media Connect
Includes glossary and bibliographical references

Singh, Patwant, 1925-
The Sikhs. Knopf 2000 276p il hardcover o.p. pa $14 *
Grades: 11 12 Adult   **954**
1. Sikhs
ISBN 0-375-40728-6; 0-385-50206-0 (pa)
                                  LC 99-31807
The author "traces Sikh history from its origins in the 15th century through Indira Gandhi's 1984 storming of the Golden Temple. . . . Sikhs, he argues, have for centuries been an embattled people because their culture and religion defy the predominant religions in the region, as well as the Indian caste system with its ruling elite." Publ Wkly
Includes bibliographical references

Walsh, Judith E.
A brief history of India. 2nd ed. Facts On File, Inc. 2010 414p il map (Brief history) $49.50; pa $19.95
Grades: 9 10 11 12 Adult   **954**
1. India—History
ISBN 978-0-8160-8143-1; 978-0-8160-8362-6 (pa)
                                  LC 2010-26316
First published 2006
Contents: Land, climate, and prehistory; Caste, kings, and the Hindu world order (1000 B.C.E.-700 C.E.); Turks, Afghans, and Mughals (600-1800); The jewel in the crown (1757-1885); Becoming modern—the colonial way (1800-1900); Toward freedom (1885-1920); Gandhi and the nationalist movement (1920-1948); Constructing the nation (1950-1996); Bollywood and beyond (1947-2009); India in the 21st century (1996-2009)
Includes bibliographical references

954.91   Pakistan

Sinkler, Adrian
Pakistan. Greenhaven Press 2005 127p il map
(Nations in transition) lib bdg $28.70
Grades: 9 10 11 12   **954.91**
1. Pakistan
ISBN 0-7377-1208-2   LC 2004-47598
"This volume opens with the area's history from 15th-
century Mogul times up to Pakistan's creation in 1947.
It then focuses on three major issues: disputed Kashmir
and the costs of the resultant military competition and
conflict with India; the role of Islam in the country's
politics, especially as played out under the leadership of
the various regimes; and demands for ethnic separatism.
. . . This title is a solid offering for report writers." SLJ
Includes bibliographical references

Wynbrandt, James
A brief history of Pakistan; foreword by Fawaz
A. Gerges. Facts On File 2008 324p il map (Brief
history) $49.50 *
Grades: 11 12 Adult   **954.91**
1. Pakistan—History
ISBN 978-0-8160-6184-6; 0-8160-6184-X
    LC 2008-8921
This book about the history of Pakistan includes "dra-
matic events, notable people, and special customs and
traditions that have shaped this country." Publisher's note
Includes glossary and bibliographical references

955   Iran

Iran: opposing viewpoints; Laura K. Egendorf,
book editor. Greenhaven Press 2007 208p il lib
bdg $34.95; pa $23.70 *
Grades: 9 10 11 12   **955**
1. Iran
ISBN 978-0-7377-3417-1 (lib bdg); 0-7377-3417-5 (lib
bdg); 978-0-7377-3418-8 (pa); 0-7377-3418-3 (pa)
    LC 2006-16934
"Opposing viewpoints series"
"These 23 essays represent differing points of view on
whether Iran is a threat to global security, the state of
human rights there, how the United States should respond to the country and its future. . . . This would be
a valuable source of current information for students researching argumentative essays or preparing for debates."
SLJ
Includes bibliographical references

My sister, guard your veil; my brother guard, your
eyes; uncensored Iranian voices; Lila Azam
Zanganeh, editor. Beacon Press 2006 132p il pa
$12
Grades: 11 12 Adult   **955**
1. Iran—Social conditions 2. Women—Iran
ISBN 0-8070-0463-4; 978-0-8070-0463-0
    LC 2005-27496
This "volume features frank interviews with an array
of reputable Iranians—intellectuals, artists, and writers,

some of whom live in exile. Their compelling personal
experiences, views, and opinions answer some persistent
questions about the lives of ordinary people in Iran and
challenge established myths and stereotypes. . . . This
volume opens a window on the irrepressible talents, aspirations, and energy of Iranians both at home and abroad,
despite their adverse conditions" MultiCult Rev

Ramen, Fred
A historical atlas of Iran. Rosen Pub. Group
2003 64p il map (Historical atlases of South Asia,
Central Asia, and the Middle East) lib bdg $30.60
*
Grades: 8 9 10 11 12   **955**
1. Iran—History 2. Atlases 3. Reference books
ISBN 0-8239-3864-6   LC 2002-31031
This focuses on the political history of Iran "as determined by geography and religion. . . . Brief descriptions
of the art and architecture of [the] country testify to the
richness of [this culture]. . . . [This] well-organized and
ambitious [book provides] needed information." SLJ

Wagner, Heather Lehr
The Iranian Revolution. Chelsea House 2010
111p il (Milestones in modern world history) lib
bdg $35
Grades: 7 8 9 10 11 12   **955**
1. Iran—History—1941-1979
ISBN 978-1-60413-490-2; 1-60413-490-9
    LC 2009-22336
"Chapters cover the origin of the Pahlavi dynasty,
[Ayatollah] Khomeini's early life and how he came to
symbolize opposition to the shah's regime, and the
shah's aggressive campaigns of reform and Westernization. . . . A solid addition to the series." SLJ
Includes bibliographical references

Wright, Robin
The last great revolution; turmoil and
transformation in Iran. Knopf 2000 xxiv, 339p il
hardcover o.p. pa $14
Grades: 11 12 Adult   **955**
1. Iran—Politics and government
ISBN 0-375-40639-5; 0-375-70630-5 (pa)
    LC 99-27798
The author "talks to journalists, educators, politicians,
entertainers, and others to present a picture of the cultural and political changes in Iran: the softening of cultural
restrictions, the empowerment of women, and the mod-
ernization of industry and the economy." Booklist
Includes bibliographical references

956   Middle East

The **Continuum** political encyclopedia of the
Middle East; Avraham Sela, editor. rev and
updated ed. Continuum 2002 944p maps $175
Grades: 11 12 Adult   **956**
1. Middle East—Politics and government 2. Middle
East—History
ISBN 0-8264-1413-3   LC 2001-8542
First published 1999 with title: The political encyclo-
pedia of the Middle East

The Continuum political encyclopedia of the Middle East—*Continued*

This "contains entries on countries ranging from Afghanistan to Yemen; political movements and leaders; major foreign nations that impact this area, such as the United States and Russia; religions and religious movements; and regional topics of concern including 'Oil,' 'Terrorism,' 'Water Politics,' and 'Women, Gender and Politics.'. . . Alphabetical entries range from a few paragraphs to lengthy commentaries. . . . Large libraries serving older students will find this a useful . . . source of objective information on the history and issues affecting the contemporary Middle East." SLJ

Includes bibliographical references

Encyclopedia of the modern Middle East & North Africa; Philip Mattar, editor in chief. 2nd ed. Macmillan Reference USA 2004 4v il map set $475

Grades: 11 12 Adult   956
1. Middle East—Encyclopedias 2. North Africa—Encyclopedias 3. Reference books
ISBN 0-02-865769-1   LC 2004-5650
First published 1996

"The set covers the modern history of the Middle East and North Africa, with major sections on Colonialism and Imperialism, the World Wars, the Israeli-Palestinian conflict and the United Nations involvement in the region. Each country in the region is reviewed, detailing its population, economy and government." Publisher's note

"For current, accurate, and non-partisan information on the Middle East and North Africa, this excellent reference set . . . will answer basic questions and serve as a starting point for research on the region." Libr Media Connect

Includes bibliographical references

Encyclopedia of the Ottoman Empire; [edited by] Gábor Ágoston and Bruce Masters. Facts On File 2009 xxxvi, 650p il map (Facts on File library of world history) $85

Grades: 11 12 Adult   956
1. Turkey—History—Ottoman Empire, 1288-1918—Encyclopedias 2. Reference books
ISBN 978-0-8160-6259-1; 0-8160-6259-5
                                   LC 2008-20716

This encyclopedia provides an "overview of the history and civilization of the Ottomans, with more than 400 A-to-Z entries focusing on major events, personalities, institutions, and terms." Publisher's note

Includes bibliographical references

Halliday, Fred

100 myths about the Middle East. University of California Press 2005 269p hardcover o.p. pa $12.95

Grades: 11 12 Adult   956
1. Middle East—Politics and government
ISBN   0-520-24720-5;   978-0-520-24720-8;
0-520-24721-3 (pa); 978-0-520-24721-5 (pa)
                                   LC 2005-53824

The author "debunks one hundred of the most commonly misconstrued 'facts' concerning the Middle East—in the political, cultural, social, and historical spheres."

Publisher's note

"The book is a valuable addition to post-9/11 political literature (it also contains a fascinating glossary of terms that have entered the language since the September 2001 terrorist attacks)." Booklist

Kort, Michael

The handbook of the Middle East; by Michael G. Kort. rev ed. Twenty-First Century Books 2008 320p il map lib bdg $39.95

Grades: 8 9 10 11 12   956
1. Middle East
ISBN 978-0-8225-7143-8; 0-8225-7143-9
                                   LC 2006-34917
First published 2002

Examines the past, present, and future of all the countries in the Middle East, discussing their history and culture

Includes bibliographical references

Lewis, Bernard

The Middle East; a brief history of the last 2,000 years. Scribner 1995 433p il hardcover o.p. pa $16

Grades: 11 12 Adult   956
1. Middle East—History
ISBN 0-684-80712-2; 0-684-83280-1 (pa)
                                   LC 96-4384

"Lewis has chosen to accentuate the social, economic, and cultural changes that have occurred over 20 centuries. He ranges from seemingly trivial concerns (changes in dress and manners in an Arab coffeehouse) to earth-shaking events (the Mongol conquest of Mesopotamia) in painting a rich, varied, and fascinating portrait of a region that is steeped in traditionalism while often forced by geography and politics to accept change." Booklist

Includes bibliographical references

What went wrong? Western impact and Middle Eastern response. Oxford Univ. Press 2002 180p il $23

Grades: 11 12 Adult   956
1. Middle East—History
ISBN 0-19-514420-1   LC 2001-36214
Also available in paperback from HarperCollins Pubs.

Subtitle of paperback edition varies: The clash between Islam and modernity

The author's "fundamental argument is that Muslims became accustomed in the early centuries of their history to perceiving themselves as the bearers of the final and true faith, and so never came to understand or accept the Christian civilization of Western Europe that he maintains has surpassed and humbled them." N Y Times (Late N Y Ed)

"Like many of Lewis's previous writings on this subject . . . this book will undoubtedly generate significant debate and disagreement among scholars regarding the author's analysis of Islamic responses to modernity and Westernization." Libr J

Includes bibliographical references

The **Middle** East. Greenwood Press 2004 5v il map (Discovering world cultures) set $200 *
Grades: 8 9 10 11 12   956

The Middle East—*Continued*

1. Middle East
ISBN 0-313-32922-2

"A Creative Media Applications, Inc. production"

Contents: v1 Bahrain, Cyprus, Egypt; v2 Iran, Iraq, Israel; v3 Jordan, Kuwait, Lebanon, Oman; v4 Qatar, Saudi-Arabia, Syria; v5 Turkey, United Arab Emirates, Yemen

This "set profiles the 16 countries that lie in the geographic region between the Mediterranean Sea and India. . . . Each country . . . is covered in a multipage chapter providing detailed information on ethnic groups, land and resources, history, economy, religion, everyday life, holidays, and the arts. . . . Readers in need of a source of solid, unbiased information will be well served by this resource." Booklist

The **Middle** East; Debra A. Miller, book editor. Greenhaven Press 2008 224p (Current controversies) lib bdg $37.40; pa $25.95

Grades: 7 8 9 10 11 12   **956**

1. Middle East—Foreign relations—United States 2. United States—Foreign relations—Middle East 3. War on terrorism 4. Iraq War, 2003- 5. Israel-Arab conflicts
ISBN   978-0-7377-3960-2   (lib   bdg);
978-0-7377-3961-9 (pa)   LC 2007-37428

An anthology of essays presenting differing opinions on topics such as why the Middle East an area of conflict, whether or not the United States should withdraw its troops from Iraq, if the Israel-Palestinian conflict can be resolved, and if the United States should be involved in the Middle East's problems.

Includes bibliographical references

The **Middle** East: opposing viewpoints; David M. Haugen, Susan Musser and Kacy Lovelace, book editors. Greenhaven Press 2009 261p il map lib bdg $38.50; pa $26.75

Grades: 8 9 10 11 12   **956**

1. Middle East—Politics and government 2. Middle East—Foreign relations—United States 3. United States—Foreign relations—Middle East
ISBN 978-0-7377-4532-0 (lib bdg); 0-7377-4532-0 (lib bdg); 978-0-7377-4533-7 (pa); 0-7377-4533-9 (pa)
LC 2008-55848

"Opposing viewpoints series"

The articles in this anthology cover such topics as U.S. relations with Middle Eastern nations, the Israeli/Palestinian conflict, whether Iran is a threat to the United States, and counterterrorism efforts in Middle Eastern nations.

Includes bibliographical references

Pendergast, Tom, 1964-

The Middle East conflict. Almanac; [by] Tom and Sara Pendergast; [project editor] Ralph Zerbonia. UXL 2006 lxvii, 267p il map (U-X-L Middle East conflict reference library) $67

Grades: 9 10 11 12   **956**

1. Israel-Arab conflicts 2. Middle East—History
ISBN 0-7876-9456-8; 978-0-7876-9456-2
LC 2005-12009

This "is a generalized examination of Middle-Eastern conflict, with a decidedly modern slant. The first two chapters cover the period from ancient times until the mandate system of the 1940s, while the remaining twelve chapters cover the last sixty years." Ref & User Services Quarterly

Includes bibliographical references

The Middle East conflict. Primary sources; [by] Tom and Sara Pendergast; [project editor] Ralph Zerbonia. UXL 2006 xlii, 238p il map (U-X-L Middle East conflict reference library) $67

Grades: 9 10 11 12   **956**

1. Israel-Arab conflicts 2. Middle East—History
ISBN 0-7876-9458-4; 978-0-7876-9458-6
LC 2005-12551

This book "includes numerous declarations, personal accounts, United Nations resolutions, and other primary documents relating to the conflict. Divided into seven chapters arranged by theme, this volume provides a good perspective of the regions troubled history, particularly through the first-person accounts." Ref & User Services Quarterly

Includes bibliographical references

Pouwels, Randall L.

The African and Middle Eastern world, 600-1500. Oxford University Press 2006 175p il map (Medieval and early modern world) $32.95 *

Grades: 9 10 11 12   **956**

1. Islamic civilization 2. Middle East—History 3. Africa—History
ISBN 0-19-517673-1; 978-0-19-517673-5
LC 2004-21476

"The author places readers in the midst of the action, allowing them to witness what it might have been like to live as a young caravan guide in A.D. 600. Thereafter, chapters are enlivened by the lives and exploits of Muhammad and his various successors, an in-depth discussion of the appeal of Islam, and a review of the leadership of men such as Mansa Musa and Sundiata. . . . This accessible and attractive volume is a wonderful introduction to the medieval Islamic world." SLJ

Includes bibliographical references

956.7 Iraq

Atkinson, Rick

In the company of soldiers; a chronicle of combat. H. Holt 2004 319p il maps $25; pa $14 *

Grades: 11 12 Adult   **956.7**

1. United States. Army. Airborne Division, 101st 2. Iraq War, 2003-
ISBN 0-8050-7561-5; 0-8050-7773-1 (pa)
LC 2003-67607

This is an eyewitness account of the war in Iraq. "In the spring of 2003, the author accompanied combat units to Iraq. He spent two months embedded with the 101st Airborne Division's headquarters staff, sharing their daily experiences from initial deployment out of Fort Campbell, KY, to overseas staging areas in Kuwait, and ulti-

Atkinson, Rick—*Continued*

mately bearing witness to the unit's march on Baghdad. His view of the war was from a vantage point that permitted scrutiny of strategy, planning, and decision making at the senior command level." SLJ

Bogdanos, Matthew

Thieves of Baghdad; one marine's passion for ancient civilizations and the journey to recover the world's greatest stolen treasures; [by] Matthew Bogdanos with William Patrick. Bloomsbury 2005 302p il map $25.95; pa $15.95 *

Grades: 11 12 Adult   **956.7**
1. Iraq War, 2003—Destruction and pillage 2. Iraq—Antiquities
ISBN 1-58234-645-3; 1-59691-146-8 (pa)
                                        LC 2005-27652
The author describes the events that took place after he "and several colleagues volunteered to investigate the theft of treasures from Baghdad's Iraq Museum in 2003." Booklist
Bogdanos "cuts through politics and hyperbole to tell an engrossing story abundant with history, colored by stories of brave Iraqis and Americans, and shaded with hope for the future." Publ Wkly
Includes bibliographical references

Campbell, Donovan

Joker one; a Marine platoon's story of courage, sacrifice, and brotherhood. Random House 2009 313p map hardcover o.p. pa $16

Grades: 11 12 Adult   **956.7**
1. Iraq War, 2003—Personal narratives
ISBN 978-1-4000-6773-2; 1-4000-6773-1; 978-0-8129-7956-5 (pa); 0-8129-7956-7 (pa)
                                        LC 2008-23896
This is "a harrowing narrative of [the author's] time as an infantry officer in Ramadi from March to September of 2004. . . . Campbell is a gifted writer who describes his own marines with deep care and attention." Washington Post

Carlisle, Rodney P.

Iraq War; John S. Bowman, general editor. Rev. ed. Chelsea House 2010 208p il map (America at war) $45 *

Grades: 9 10 11 12   **956.7**
1. Iraq War, 2003- 2. Iraq—History
ISBN 978-0-8160-8191-2   LC 2009-34823
First published 2004
This history of the Iraq War "explores the history of the region as well as the recent events leading up to and culminating in this war." Publisher's note
Includes glossary and bibliographical references

Persian Gulf War; John S. Bowman, general editor. Rev. ed. Chelsea House 2010 160p il map (America at war) $45

Grades: 9 10 11 12   **956.7**
1. Persian Gulf War, 1991
ISBN 978-0-8160-8192-9   LC 2009-30844
First published 2003

Contents: In the thick of it; The United States as peacekeeper and policeman; The Middle East situation; Hussein and modern weapons; Kuwait invaded Opertion Desert Shield: a line in the sand; The air war and preliminary ground activities; On the home front; Desert Storm begins; Americans at war: February 26-28; Immediate aftermath; Long-term aftermath; Weapons and tactics; Peacekeeping in the 1990s and Persian Gulf War legacies

Chronicles events leading up to, during, and after the Persian Gulf War.
Includes glossary and bibliographical references

Ellis, Deborah, 1960-

Children of war; voices of Iraqi refugees. Groundwood Books 2009 128p il $15.95; pa $9.95

Grades: 7 8 9 10 11 12   **956.7**
1. Children and war 2. Iraq War, 2003- 3. Refugees
ISBN 978-0-88899-907-8; 0-88899-907-0; 978-0-88899-908-5 (pa); 0-88899-908-9 (pa)
Ellis "interviews child refugees from Iraq, now living in Jordan, and a few who have made it to Canada. . . . Accompanying each of the . . . interviews with young people is a brief introduction and a photo. . . . What is haunting are their graphic recent memories of what they witnessed. . . . An important, current title that will have lasting significance." Booklist
Includes glossary

Fattah, Hala Mundhir, 1950-

A brief history of Iraq; [by] Hala Fattah with Frank Caso. Facts On File 2008 318p il map (Brief history) $49.50 *

Grades: 11 12 Adult   **956.7**
1. Iraq—History
ISBN 978-0-8160-5767-2; 0-8160-5767-2
                                        LC 2008-8451
This book about the history of Iraq "focuses primarily on the societies, peoples, and cultures of Iraq, as well as the regional influences that helped shape the destiny of the ethnicities, religions, sects, and national groups in this country." Publisher's note
Includes glossary and bibliographical references

Feuer, Alan

Over there; from the Bronx to Baghdad. Counterpoint 2005 283p $24

Grades: 11 12 Adult   **956.7**
1. Iraq War, 2003—Personal narratives
ISBN 1-58243-327-5; 978-1-58243-327-1
                                        LC 2004-27149
The author describes the events that occured after he "was bustled off to the Middle East to cover the invasion of Iraq. . . . This is one war memoir that demands to be read." Booklist

Iraq: opposing viewpoints; David M. Haugen, Susan Musser, and Kacy Lovelace, book editors. Greenhaven Press 2009 186p il map lib bdg $38.50; pa $26.75 *

Grades: 8 9 10 11 12   **956.7**
1. Iraq War, 2003-
ISBN 978-0-7377-4524-5 (lib bdg); 978-0-7377-4525-2 (pa)   LC 2008-51446

Iraq: opposing viewpoints—*Continued*

"Opposing viewpoints series"

The articles in this anthology cover such topics as whether or not Iraq is becoming stable after the overthrow of Saddam Hussein and how much the United States should be involved in the rebuilding of Iraq.

Includes bibliographical references

Iraq uncensored; perspectives; edited by James M. Ludes [for the] American Security Project; foreword by John Kerry. Fulcrum 2009 xxiv, 162p il (Speaker's corner) $22.95

Grades: 10 11 12 Adult   956.7

1. Iraq War, 2003- 2. National security—United States 3. Military policy—United States

ISBN 978-1-55591-703-6; 1-55591-703-8

LC 2009-11509

"Although this is not strictly a book for young adults, the length of the essays (most are under 10 pages) and the well-balanced viewpoints make it a good choice for teens looking to learn about the Iraq war beyond the headlines. Sections cover planning for the war, its conduct, the Department of Defense, and the use of national power. Contributors include senators, military leaders, academics, and foreign-policy experts." SLJ

Includes bibliographical references

Koopman, John

McCoy's marines; Darkside to Baghdad. Zenith Press 2004 304p il map $25.95

Grades: 11 12 Adult   956.7

1. United States. Marine Corps 2. Iraq War, 2003—Personal narratives

ISBN 0-760-32088-8; 978-0-760-32088-4

LC 2005-274038

The author "was embedded in the Third Battalion, Fourth Marines, during the most recent war in Iraq. He enjoyed a close working relationship with the CO, the battalion sergeant major, and several other members of the battalion. . . . . [He offers] a rare perspective on the gritty (literally, when a sandstorm blew up) details of ground combat in Iraq and how the modern American marine relates to his buddies, his enemies, and his family back home." Booklist

La Guardia, Anton

War without end; Israelis, Palestinians, and the struggle for a promised land. St. Martin's Griffin 2003 xxii, 436p il map pa $16.95

Grades: 11 12 Adult   956.7

1. Israel-Arab conflicts 2. Israeli national characteristics 3. Palestinian Arabs 4. Zionism

ISBN 0-312-31633-X   LC 2003-41288

First published 2001 in the United Kingdom with title: Holy Land, unholy war: Israelis and Palestinians

"This is fundamentally an examination of two wounded peoples, neither of whom seems capable of surmounting national myths and past hatreds to forge a new future. La Guardia is evenhanded in his criticism of both Israeli and Palestinian leaders, but he does not spare ordinary people. . . . This is an absorbing but heartbreaking examination of a seemingly endless tragedy that continues to unfold before our eyes." Booklist [review of 2002 edition]

Includes bibliographical references

Munier, Gilles

Iraq; an illustrated history. Interlink Books 2003 230p il $18

Grades: 11 12 Adult   956.7

1. Iraq—History

ISBN 1-566-56513-8   LC 2003-13372

This work "betrays the French view of recent events on the Middle East. Its usefulness, however, lies in its offering an excellent introduction to Iraq's 4000-year history and culture. . . . Features like a glossary, sidebars with statistics, schematic maps, a list of relevant web sites, and the book's compact size make this a timely, useful choice for anyone interested in learning more about Iraq." SLJ

Includes bibliographical references

Schwartz, Richard Alan, 1951-

Encyclopedia of the Persian Gulf War. McFarland & Co. 1998 216p il maps hardcover o.p. pa $45

Grades: 11 12 Adult   956.7

1. Persian Gulf War, 1991—Encyclopedias 2. Reference books

ISBN 0-7864-0451-5; 0-7864-4103-8 (pa)

LC 97-51886

"Beginning with a seven-page overview, this encyclopedia presents alphabetically arranged entries that describe the conflict, including key figures, places, battles, diplomacy, and more." SLJ

Includes bibliographical references

Skiba, Katherine M.

Sister in the Band of Brothers; embedded with the 101st Airborne in Iraq. University Press of Kansas 2005 257p il (Modern war studies) $29.95

Grades: 11 12 Adult   956.7

1. United States. Army. Airborne Division, 101st 2. Iraq War, 2003—Personal narratives

ISBN 0-7006-1382-X   LC 2004-26475

The author "was the only woman embedded with the 101st Airborne when the United States invaded Iraq in 2003. She has written a fascinating memoir of her time within the training with other reporters, waiting to invade Iraq and spending the first few months of the war with soldiers in Iraq." Univ Press Books for Public and Second Sch Libr, 2006

Smithson, Ryan

Ghosts of war; my tour of duty. HarperTeen 2009 321p il $16.99; lib bdg $17.89

Grades: 8 9 10 11 12   956.7

1. Iraq War, 2003—Personal narratives 2. Soldiers—United States

ISBN 978-0-06-166468-7; 0-06-166468-5; 978-0-06-166470-0 (lib bdg); 0-06-166470-7 (lib bdg)

LC 2008-35420

"Ryan Smithson was a typical 16-year-old high-school student until 9/11. . . . Smithson enlisted in the Army Reserve the following year and, a year into the Iraq war, was deployed to an Army engineer unit as a heavy-equipment operator. His poignant, often harrowing account, especially vivid in sensory details, chronicles his

Smithson, Ryan—*Continued*
experiences in basic training and in Iraq. . . . This memoir is a remarkable, deeply penetrating read that will compel teens to reflect on their own thoughts about duty, patriotism and sacrifice." Kirkus
Includes glossary and bibliographical references

Stiglitz, Joseph E.
The three trillion dollar war; the true cost of the Iraq Conflict; [by] Joseph E. Stiglitz [and] Linda J. Bilmes. W. W. Norton 2008 xxiii, 311p $22.95
Grades: 11 12 Adult   **956.7**
1. Iraq War, 2003-—Finance 2. War—Economic aspects
ISBN 978-0-393-06701-9; 0-393-06701-7
                                         LC 2007-51400
The authors discuss the cost of the Iraq War.
"This shocking expose, capped with 18 proposals for reform, is a must-read for anyone who wants to understand how the war was financed, as well as what it means for troops on the ground and the nation's future." Publ Wkly
Includes bibliographical references

Stout, Jay A., 1959-
Hammer from above; marine air combat over Iraq. Presidio Press 2006 xxi, 392p il map $25.95; pa $15.95
Grades: 11 12 Adult   **956.7**
1. Iraq War, 2003-—Aerial operations
ISBN 0-89141-865-2; 978-0-89141-865-8; 0-89141-871-7 (pa); 978-0-89141-871-9 (pa)
                                         LC 2005-49175
This is an "account of the role that Marine aircraft played in the launching of Operation Iraqi Freedom in 2003. Stout relies primarily on first-person testimony from dozens of Marines whom he interviewed shortly after they returned from the war." Publ Wkly
"This solid study of marine aviation in the current Iraq war will interest a wide range of aviation buffs and students of the Marine Corps." Booklist
Includes bibliographical references

Swofford, Anthony
Jarhead: a Marine's chronicle of the Gulf War and other battles. Scribner 2003 260p hardcover o.p. pa $15 *
Grades: 11 12 Adult   **956.7**
1. United States. Marine Corps
ISBN 0-7432-3535-5; 0-7432-8721-5 (pa)
                                         LC 2002-30866
The author, "who served in a United States Marine Corps Surveillance and Target Acquisition/Scout-Sniper platoon during the [1991 Gulf War] operation known as Desert Storm [presents an account of his experiences]." N Y Times (Late NY Ed)
This book offers "an unflinching portrayal of the loneliness and brutality of modern warfare and sophisticated analyses of—and visceral reactions to—its politics." Publ Wkly

The **war** in Iraq; Tom Lansford, book editor. Greenhaven Press 2009 241p il map (Global viewpoints) $37.30; pa $25.70
Grades: 9 10 11 12   **956.7**
1. Iraq War, 2003-
ISBN 978-0-7377-4162-9; 0-7377-4162-7; 978-0-7377-4163-6 (pa); 0-7377-4163-5 (pa)
                                         LC 2008-53992
"This collection of 21 essays reprinted from a variety of magazines and newspapers aims to provide a broad, international overview of the complex issues surrounding the conflict. The four chapters cover the war as it relates to United States foreign relations, the Arab-Israeli conflict, international terrorism, and democracy. . . . This work will be a useful tool in current-events classes, and its evenhanded approach offers plenty of substance for classroom discussions." SLJ
Includes bibliographical references

What was asked of us; an oral history of the Iraq War by the soldiers who fought it; [compiled by] Trish Wood. Little, Brown and Co. 2006 309p il map pa $14.99 *
Grades: 11 12 Adult   **956.7**
1. Iraq War, 2003-—Personal narratives
ISBN 978-0-316-01670-4; 0-316-01670-5; 978-0-316-01671-1 (pa); 0-316-01671-3 (pa)
                                         LC 2006-930963
This is "a collection of 41 interviews conducted by Canadian investigative journalist Wood with veterans of the current war in Iraq." Libr J
"Colloquial, coarse and compelling, these narratives flash with humor, horror, nihilism and poesy." Publ Wkly

Yetiv, Steve
The Persian Gulf crisis; [by] Steve A. Yetiv. Greenwood Press 1997 xxi, 197p il maps (Greenwood Press guides to historic events of the twentieth century) $45
Grades: 11 12 Adult   **956.7**
1. Persian Gulf War, 1991
ISBN 0-313-29943-9   LC 96-6554
This work "opens with a chronology, followed by an overview of the crisis, a history of diplomatic initiatives leading to the war, and an account of operations Desert Shield and Desert Storm and their impact on the combatants." Choice
"The author incorporates only that which is pertinent in a style that is interesting and, at times, exciting to read. The inclusion of primary documents from the war, such as UN resolutions and speeches . . . make this title unique." SLJ
Includes bibliographical references

Zeinert, Karen, 1942-2002
The brave women of the Gulf Wars; Operation Desert Storm and Operation Iraqi Freedom; [by] Karen Zeinert & Mary Miller. 21st Century Bks. 2006 112p il $30.60
Grades: 7 8 9 10   **956.7**

Zeinert, Karen, 1942-2002—*Continued*
1. Women in the armed forces 2. Persian Gulf War, 1991—Women
ISBN 0-7613-2705-3
"Zeinert and Miller reinforce the argument that women do, indeed, belong in the U.S. military by highlighting their contributions in Operations Desert Storm (Kuwait) and Iraqi Freedom. . . . The narrative paints a picture of consistent courage under fire and, one terse mention of the abuses at Abu Ghraib Prison aside, of professional conduct. The authors extend their purview with a chapter on women journalists in the campaigns, and while thoroughly villainizing Saddam Hussein, they also indicate that the official justifications for the war in Iraq turned out to be weak at best. A utilitarian but cogent assessment of the topic, well supported by notes and sources." Booklist
Includes bibliographical references

956.94   Palestine. Israel

Armstrong, Karen
Jerusalem; one city, three faiths. Knopf 1996 xxi, 471p il maps hardcover o.p. pa $17.95
Grades: 11 12 Adult   956.94
ISBN 0-679-43596-4; 0-345-39168-3 (pa)
                LC 96-75888
Armstrong's "overarching theme, that Jerusalem has been central to the experience and 'sacred geography' of Jews, Muslims and Christians and thus has led to deadly struggles for dominance, is a familiar one, yet she brings to her sweeping, profusely illustrated narrative a grasp of sociopolitical conditions seldom found in other books." Publ Wkly

Aronson, Marc
Unsettled; the problem of loving Israel. Ginee Seo Books/Athaeneum Books for Young Readers 2008 184p il map $18.99 *
Grades: 9 10 11 12   956.94
1. Israel—History
ISBN 978-1-4169-1261-3; 1-4169-1261-4
             LC 2008-300316
"Ginee Seo books"
An exploration of the history of Israel, its relationships with its neighboring countries, and questions about what Israel should be.
"This title gives a lot of information and forces readers to think deeply about morality, bigotry, politics, and religion. It is a fascinating look at a complicated country." SLJ
Includes bibliographical refererences

Blumberg, Arnold, 1925-
The history of Israel. Greenwood Press 1998 218p (Greenwood histories of the modern nations) $45 *
Grades: 8 9 10 11 12   956.94
1. Israel—History 2. Zionism
ISBN 0-313-30224-3   LC 97-45659

"Starting with a description of life in modern Israel, Blumberg . . . quickly covers Israel's early history, from 3,500 years ago to World War I. . . . The battles leading to independence, the isolation of Israel, conflicts within Israel, the Suez Crisis and subsequent wars, the Intifada, the development of the PLO, and the Peace Process are described in a manner that enables readers to have a much better understanding of the events happening in Israel now." Voice Youth Advocates
Includes bibliographical references

Children of Israel, children of Palestine; our own true stories; [edited by] Laurel Holliday. Pocket Bks. 1998 xxi, 358p il map hardcover o.p. pa $21.95
Grades: 9 10 11 12   956.94
1. Israel-Arab conflicts 2. Israelis 3. Palestinian Arabs
ISBN 0-671-00802-1; 0-671-00804-8 (pa)
             LC 97-42545
This is "a collection of autobiographical tales of growing up in Israel written by both Jews and Palestinians." Libr J
"Holliday says in her eloquent introduction that there is no sweet upbeat solution of easy neutrality, . . . but there is hope in their agreeing to tell their stories in a book together. They are listening to each other, and they make us hear all sides." Booklist
Includes bibliographical references

The **encyclopedia** of the Arab-Israeli conflict; a political, social, and military history; Spencer C. Tucker, volume editor; Priscilla Mary Roberts, editor Documents volume; Paul G. Pierpaoli, Jr, associate editor; David Zabecki, Sherifa Zuhur, assistant editors; foreword by Anthony C. Zinni. ABC-CLIO 2008 4v il map set $395
Grades: 11 12 Adult   956.94
1. Reference books 2. Israel-Arab conflicts—Encyclopedias
ISBN 978-1-85109-841-5; 1-85109-841-0
             LC 2008-9358
"This encyclopedia presents a comprehensive look at the myriad aspects of the continuing clash between Arabs and Israelis. . . . Although the focus is on the Arab-Israeli wars from 1947, many entries, such the one for the Ottoman Empire, help achieve a balance between historical and contemporary context. The work is strengthened by references at the end of each entry, see also and cross-references, birth and death dates in biographical entries, line-drawn maps, and black-and-white photos." Booklist
Includes bibliographical references

Frank, Mitch
Understanding the Holy Land; answering questions about the Israeli-Palestinian Conflict. Viking 2005 152p il map $17.99; pa $8.99 *
Grades: 6 7 8 9 10   956.94
1. Israel-Arab conflicts
ISBN 0-670-06032-1; 0-670-06043-7 (pa)
             LC 2004-14973
The author "tackles the complex subject of the Israeli-Palestinian conflict, making it comprehensible, if not any less horrific. . . . He uses a simple yet wonderfully ef-

Frank, Mitch—*Continued*
fective technique to present the information: questions and answers. . . . Evenhanded and honest." Booklist
Includes bibliographical references

Israel: opposing viewpoints; Myra Immell, book editor. Greenhaven Press 2011 193p map $41.70; pa $28.90 *
Grades: 8 9 10 11 12   **956.94**
1. Israel-Arab conflicts
ISBN   978-0-7377-4974-8;   0-7377-4974-1; 978-0-7377-4975-5 (pa); 0-7377-4975-X (pa)
LC 2010022999
"Opposing viewpoints series"
Articles in this anthology discuss Israel's right to exist, key issues in the conflict between Israel and Palestine, and what U.S. policy should be regarding Israel.
Includes bibliographical references

Miller, Jennifer, 1980-
Inheriting the Holy Land; an American's search for hope in the Middle East. Ballantine Books 2005 xxxiii, 261p map $24.95; pa $14.95 *
Grades: 11 12 Adult   **956.94**
1. Israel-Arab conflicts
ISBN   0-345-46924-0;   978-0-345-46924-3; 0-345-46925-9 (pa); 978-0-345-46925-0 (pa)
LC 2004-66349
The author "is the daughter of one of the chief American negotiators in the Israeli-Palestinian conflict and a longtime participant in the Seeds of Peace program, bringing together Israeli and Palestinian children. Using the many contacts that she has made, from the highest leaders to the children on the street, Miller explores . . . the many different viewpoints and preconceptions of the people involved in the conflict, not excluding her own. . . . This is a superb book on a crucial issue of our time." SLJ
Includes bibliographical references

Reich, Bernard
A brief history of Israel. 2nd ed. Facts On File 2008 382p il map (Brief history) $45; pa $19.95 *
Grades: 9 10 11 12 Adult   **956.94**
1. Israel—History
ISBN 978-0-8160-7126-5; 978-0-8160-7127-2 (pa)
LC 2008-3838
First published 2005
This book "explores Israel's history with an emphasis on the period since its independence in 1948. The chronological narration begins with the time of Abraham and the period of the Israelite kingdoms and continues to World War II and the United Nations Partition Plan. This . . . reference then examines the independent country of Israel, including the Arab–Israeli conflict, domestic politics, Knesset election results, the economy, and international relations." Publisher's note
Includes bibliographical references

958   Central Asia

Hanks, Reuel R.
Central Asia; a global studies handbook. ABC-CLIO 2005 xvii, 467p il map (Global studies) $55 *
Grades: 11 12 Adult   **958**
1. Central Asia
ISBN 1-85109-656-6   LC 2005-14716
This book covers Uzbekistan, Kazakhstan, and Kyrgyzstan. "Each part of the book is divided into a narrative and a reference section. The narrative portion covers the geography and history of each country, along with essays on current economic, social, and cultural trends. The reference section contains a historical chronology; encyclopedic entries on significant people, places, and events in each country; an overview of typical food and drink consumption; basic etiquette; a directory of country-related organizations; and a short, annotated bibliography." Choice
"The superb text makes accessible, whether for reports or general reading, former Silk Road lands that may play increasingly important roles—think of oil-rich Kazakhstan—in the world's economy." SLJ
Includes bibliographical references

Rall, Ted, 1963-
Silk road to ruin; is Central Asia the new Middle East? NBM 2006 303p il map $22.95
Grades: 11 12 Adult   **958**
1. Graphic novels 2. Central Asia—Graphic novels
ISBN 1-56163-454-9; 978-1-56163-454-5
LC 2006-42041
"Moving between narrative and graphic novella interludes, . . . [the author] recounts several trips that he has made in the past decade to the five 'Stans,' those Central Asian nations that were so recently part of the USSR. . . . Rall takes readers on scary bus trips where armed guards threaten Westerners. . . . Diarrhea is a constant and bloody companion. Sports include a deadly horseback event in which opponents whip one another in the eyes." Voice Youth Advocates
Rall's "awestruck descriptions of the region's natural beauty, crowded bazaars, and chaotic sporting tournaments will make adventurous readers want to see it all firsthand." SLJ
Includes bibliographical references

958.1   Afghanistan

Afghanistan; Debra A. Miller, book editor. Greenhaven Press 2010 251p (Current controversies) $40.90; pa $28.35 *
Grades: 9 10 11 12   **958.1**
1. Afghanistan
ISBN 978-0-7377-4642-6; 978-0-7377-4643-3 (pa)
LC 2009037783
"Explores key questions about U.S.-led military involvement in Afghanistan. Have the operations benefited or hurt the region? Should they continue? Is it possible for Afghans to have a democratic government, with free and fair elections, that would prevent warlords and reli-

Afghanistan—*Continued*

gious leaders from dominating the country? And how—with the Taliban, terror cells, the drug trade, and a fledgling government and military—can Afghanistan be stabilized for the long term?" Publisher's note

Includes bibliographical references

Ansary, Mir Tamim

West of Kabul, East of New York; an Afghan American story. Farrar, Straus & Giroux 2002 292p hardcover o.p. pa $13

Grades: 11 12 Adult   **958.1**

1. Afghanistan—Social conditions 2. Islamic civilization

ISBN 0-374-28757-0; 0-312-42151-6 (pa)

The author, an Afghan American, reflects on his dual heritage. In light of the events of September 11, he focuses particular attention on the relationship between Islam and the West.

"While Ansary's political insights can be detached or perhaps purposefully aloof his descriptions of having lived in and identified alternately with the West and the Islamic world are utterly compelling." Publ Wkly

MacPherson, Malcolm C., 1943-2009

Roberts ridge; a story of courage and sacrifice on Takur Ghar Mountain, Afghanistan; [by] Malcolm MacPherson. Delacorte Press 2005 338p il map $25

Grades: 11 12 Adult   **958.1**

1. Afghan War, 2001-

ISBN 0-553-80363-8; 978-0-553-80363-1

         LC 2005-45494

"In March 2002 a team of U.S. Navy SEALS attempted the capture of Takur Ghar, a 10,000-foot-high mountain whose seizure would give the American forces in Afghanistan a key observation post. But the mountain was defended, and when the special forces helicopter reached the peak, it was shredded by enemy fire, and Petty Officer First Class Neil Roberts was thrown from the aircraft. His fellow SEALs were determined to bring him out. This is the story of that attempt. Well told and frightening as well as true, this is a book that bridges the breach between the increasingly professional American military and a civilian culture possessing little knowledge or experience of the military." Booklist

Includes bibliographical references

Rashid, Ahmed

Taliban; militant Islam, oil and fundamentalism in Central Asia. 2nd ed. Yale University Press 2010 319p map pa $17.95 *

Grades: 11 12 Adult   **958.1**

1. Taliban 2. Islamic fundamentalism 3. Islam and politics 4. Afghanistan—Politics and government

ISBN 978-0-300-16368-1; 0-300-16368-1

         LC 2009-938249

First published 2000

The author explains "the Taliban's rise to power, its impact on Afghanistan and the region, its role in oil and gas company decisions, and the effects of changing American attitudes toward the Taliban. He also describes

the new face of Islamic fundamentalism and explains why Afghanistan has become the world center for international terrorism." Publisher's note

Includes bibliographical references

Romano, Amy, 1978-

A historical atlas of Afghanistan. Rosen Pub. Group 2003 64p il map (Historical atlases of South Asia, Central Asia, and the Middle East) lib bdg $30.60

Grades: 8 9 10 11 12   **958.1**

1. Afghanistan 2. Atlases 3. Reference books

ISBN 0-8239-3863-8   LC 2002-31034

Maps and text chronicle the history of Afghanistan, from the Aryan invasion in 1500 B.C. to the rise of the Taliban

This "well-organized and ambitious [book provides] needed information." SLJ

Includes glossary and bibliographical references

The **Taliban:** opposing viewpoints; Noah Berlatsky, book editor. Greenhaven Press 2011 226p il $41.70; pa $28.90

Grades: 8 9 10 11 12   **958.1**

1. Taliban 2. Afghanistan

ISBN 978-0-7377-5239-7; 978-0-7377-5240-3 (pa)

         LC 2010030907

"Opposing viewpoints series"

Articles in this compilation discuss who the Taliban are, how the U.S. should deal with them, and the Taliban's relationships with Pakistan and other nations.

Includes bibliographical references

Wahab, Shaista

A brief history of Afghanistan; [by] Shaista Wahab and Barry Youngerman. 2nd ed. Facts on File 2010 354p il map (Brief history) $49.50; pa $19.95 *

Grades: 11 12 Adult   **958.1**

1. Afghanistan—History

ISBN 978-0-8160-8218-6; 978-0-8160-8219-3 (pa); 978-1-4381-0819-3 (ebook)   LC 2010-19656

First published 2006

Contact publisher for ebook pricing

This history of Afghanistan "examines this country's isolation and how it found itself involved in 30 years of war and anarchy. . . . [It] explores the culture and politics of the Pashtun tribes whose homeland extends across much of Afghanistan and northern Pakistan, as well as the Taliban insurgency and the relationship between local leaders and the central government in Kabul." Publisher's note

Includes bibliographical references

959   Southeast Asia

Phillips, Douglas A.

Southeast Asia; series consulting editor Charles F. Gritzner. Chelsea House Publishers 2006 129p (Modern world cultures) lib bdg $30

Grades: 7 8 9 10   **959**

Phillips, Douglas A.—*Continued*
1. Southeast Asia
ISBN 0-7910-8149-4

This describes the geography, history, people and cultures, politics, economics, and possible future of Southeast Asia.

This "accessible [title is] generously illustrated with colorful photos, maps, and clear charts, graphs, and other statistical data. . . . Phillips does an excellent job of organizing each topic by providing clear and outlined information. The research is well done, and information and statistics are up to date." SLJ

Southeast Asia; a historical encyclopedia from Angkor Wat to East Timor; edited by Ooi Keat Gin. ABC-CLIO 2004 3v il map set $285
Grades: 11 12 Adult   **959**
1. Southeast Asia
ISBN 1-576-07770-5   LC 2004-4813

The countries covered in this book include "Myanmar (Burma), Thailand (Siam), Laos, Cambodia, Vietnam, Malaysia, Singapore, Brunei, the Philippines, Indonesia, and East Timor. This A-Z aims to help students and researchers grasp the fragmented region through 800 detailed articles on archaeology, politics, culture, economic transformation, and more." Libr J

Includes bibliographical references

959.1   Myanmar

Zahler, Diane
Than Shwe's Burma. Twenty-First Century Books 2009 c2010 160p il map (Dictatorships) lib bdg $38.60
Grades: 10 11 12   **959.1**
1. Than Shwe 2. Myanmar—Politics and government
ISBN 978-0-8225-9097-2; 0-8225-9097-2
     LC 2008-50097

The harsh dictatorship that Burma has endured for many years is explored, and Than Shwe's human rights abuses are highlighted.

Includes glossary and bibliographical references

959.6   Cambodia

Ung, Loung, 1970-
First they killed my father; a daughter of Cambodia remembers. HarperCollins Pubs. 2000 240p il hardcover o.p. pa $13.95
Grades: 11 12 Adult   **959.6**
1. Cambodia—History—1975-
ISBN 0-06-019332-8; 0-06-085626-2 (pa)
     LC 99-34707

The author's father was a "high-ranking government official in Phnom Penh. She was only five when the Khmer Rouge stormed the city and her family was forced to flee. They sought refuge in various camps, hiding their wealth and education, always on the move and ever fearful of being betrayed. After 20 months, Ung's father was taken away, never to be seen again. Her story of starvation, forced labor, beatings, attempted rape, separations, and the deaths of her family members is one of horror and brutality." SLJ

959.704   Vietnam—1949-

America in Vietnam; a documentary history; edited with commentaries by William Appleman Williams ... [et al.] Norton 1989 345p map pa $17.95 *
Grades: 11 12 Adult   **959.704**
1. Vietnam War, 1961-1975
ISBN 0-393-30555-4

First published 1985 by Anchor Press/Doubleday

In this collection of original essays and documentary sources, historians try to explain the U.S.-Vietnamese War of 1963-75 within the greater context of two centuries of American involvement in Asia.

Includes bibliographical references

Bloods: an oral history of the Vietnam War by black veterans; [edited by] Wallace Terry. Random House 1984 311p il hardcover o.p. pa $6.99 *
Grades: 11 12 Adult   **959.704**
1. Vietnam War, 1961-1975—Personal narratives
2. African American soldiers
ISBN 0-394-53028-4; 0-345-31197-3 (pa)
     LC 83-42775

Black Vietnam War veterans discuss their experiences in battle and stateside.

This is "an intimate overview that often makes the reader stop, sit back, and think about this war that tore at America. . . . The accounts are moving, powerful and offer several views." Voice Youth Advocates

Includes bibliographical references

Caputo, Philip
A rumor of war; with a twentieth anniversary postscript by the author. Henry Holt and Co. 1996 xxi, 356p pa $15
Grades: 11 12 Adult   **959.704**
1. Vietnam War, 1961-1975—Personal narratives
ISBN 0-8050-4695-X   LC 96-19314

"An Owl book"

First published 1977 by Holt, Rinehart & Winston

These are "the combat recollections of a very young Marine officer in Vietnam in 1965-1966. Caputo later became a newspaperman. . . . He remembers himself as a patriotic youngster, eager to prove his manhood, and then . . . he takes us through his step-by-step discovery that war and manhood and their interrelation are more complicated than he had dreamed." New Yorker

Dear America: letters home from Vietnam; edited by Bernard Edelman for the New York Vietnam Veterans Memorial Commission. Norton 1985 316p il maps hardcover o.p. pa $13.95 *
Grades: 9 10 11 12   **959.704**
1. Vietnam War, 1961-1975—Personal narratives
ISBN 0-393-01998-5; 0-393-32304-8 (pa)
     LC 85-273

"The letters have been intelligently organized to follow a typical tour of duty in Vietnam. . . . Readers will be struck by the variations in attitudes reflected in these letters of the combatants. . . . This is a wonderful book of raw data for the reader to sift through and interpret." Readings

The **encyclopedia** of the Vietnam War; a political, social, and military history; Spencer C. Tucker, editor. 2nd ed. ABC-CLIO 2011 4v il map set $395

Grades: 11 12 Adult   **959.704**
1. Vietnam War, 1961-1975—Encyclopedias
2. Reference books
ISBN 978-1-85109-960-3; 978-1-85109-961-0 (ebook)
                                          LC 2011007604
First published 1998
Contact publisher for ebook pricing
"Written to provide multidimensional perspectives into the conflict, . . . [this encyclopedia] covers not only the American experience in Vietnam, but also the entire scope of Vietnamese history, including the French experience and the Indochina War, as well as the origins of the conflict, how the United States became involved, and the extensive aftermath of this prolonged war." Publisher's note
Includes bibliographical references

Everything we had; an oral history of the Vietnam War; by thirty-three American soldiers who fought it; [edited by] Al Santoli. Random House 1981 265p il hardcover o.p. pa $6.99
Grades: 9 10 11 12   **959.704**
1. Vietnam War, 1961-1975—Personal narratives
2. Veterans
ISBN 0-394-51269-3; 0-345-32279-7 (pa)
                                          LC 80-5309
Interviews with 33 veterans assess the impact the Vietnam War has had on their lives.
Includes glossary

FitzGerald, Frances, 1940-
Fire in the lake; the Vietnamese and the Americans in Vietnam. Little, Brown 1972 491p maps pa $16.95 hardcover o.p. *
Grades: 11 12 Adult   **959.704**
1. Vietnam War, 1961-1975 2. Vietnam—Politics and government
ISBN 0-316-15919-0 (pa)
"An Atlantic Monthly Press book"
This book looks at the effects American intervention had on the Vietnamese social and intellectual landscape.
Includes bibliographical references

Hillstrom, Kevin
Vietnam War: almanac; [by] Kevin Hillstrom and Laurie Collier Hillstrom; Diane Sawinski, editor. U.X.L 2001 293p il (Vietnam War reference library) $60
Grades: 7 8 9 10   **959.704**
1. Vietnam War, 1961-1975
ISBN 0-7876-4883-3   LC 00-56379
This "combines early history from the colonial period, U.S. involvement, and the war years and continues through the reestablishment of diplomacy and trade in recent years. Arranged chronologically, each of the 17 chapters includes 'Words to Know' and 'People to Know.' . . . Highly recommended for the junior- and senior-high-school libraries and public libraries." Booklist
Includes bibliographical references

Vietnam War: primary sources; [by] Kevin Hillstrom and Laurie Collier Hillstrom; Diane Sawinski, editor. U.X.L 2001 various paging (Vietnam War reference library) $60 *
Grades: 7 8 9 10   **959.704**
1. Vietnam War, 1961-1975
ISBN 0-7876-4887-6   LC 00-56377
This "presents 13 full or excerpted speeches and writings 'that reflect the painfully diversified points of view on the war.' . . . Each excerpt includes background material to provide context. Unfamiliar terms and their definitions fill sidebars, along with other relevant information and photographs. The numerous sidebars, photographs, and maps enhance the text." Booklist
Includes bibliographical references

Isserman, Maurice
Vietnam War; John S. Bowman, general editor. Rev. ed. Chelsea House 2010 210p il map (America at war) $45
Grades: 9 10 11 12   **959.704**
1. Vietnam War, 1961-1975
ISBN 978-0-8160-8187-5   LC 2009-39184
First published 1992
This history of the Vietnam War includes a "discussion of the roots of U.S. involvement in Indochina in the days just after World War II and goes on to explore the varied and complex motives behind America's effort to halt the spread of communism in Asia. . . . [It] also features a chapter focusing on the innovative military tactics and weaponry involved throughout the conflict." Publisher's note
Includes glossary and bibliographical references

Karnow, Stanley
Vietnam; a history. 2nd rev & updated ed. Penguin Bks. 1997 768p il maps pa $17.95 *
Grades: 11 12 Adult   **959.704**
1. Vietnam War, 1961-1975 2. Vietnam—History
ISBN 0-14-026547-3
First published 1983
A summation "of over two centuries of conflict in Indochina. Chronicling a tragic history, Karnow presents a balanced and sympathetic view of Vietnamese aspirations and the mishaps that led to American involvement in a 'war nobody won.'" Voice Youth Advocates [review of 1983 edition]
Includes bibliographical references

Kovic, Ron
Born on the Fourth of July. Akashic Books 2005 216p pa $14.95
Grades: 9 10 11 12   **959.704**
1. Vietnam War, 1961-1975—Personal narratives
ISBN 978-1-88845-178-8; 1-88845-178-5
                                          LC 2004-115734
First published 1976 by McGraw-Hill
The autobiography of a young marine who was physically and emotionally scarred by his experience in Vietnam.

Living through the Vietnam War; edited by Samuel Brenner. Greenhaven Press 2005 142p map (Living through the Cold War) lib bdg $32.45
Grades: 9 10 11 12   **959.704**
 1. Vietnam War, 1961-1975 2. United States—History—1961-1974
 ISBN 0-7377-2308-4   LC 2003-62477
"This volume discusses how American life was changed and shaped by the longest war in American history. In separate chapters the volume presents the words of the U.S. government, the views of those against the war, the experiences of soldiers and veterans, and the ways in which Vietnam was portrayed in media and popular culture." Publisher's note
Includes bibliographical references

Maraniss, David
They marched into sunlight; war and peace in Vietnam and America, October 1967. Simon & Schuster 2003 592p il map hardcover o.p. pa $16
Grades: 11 12 Adult   **959.704**
 1. Vietnam War, 1961-1975
 ISBN 0-7432-1780-2; 0-7432-6104-6 (pa)
                                LC 2003-52885
This is a "narrative by a reporter who juxtaposes a ghastly little battle in Vietnam with an antiwar and anti-Dow demonstration at the University of Wisconsin, Madison, on the same day; it captures moral ambiguity everywhere, without stereotyping or condescension." N Y Times Book Rev
Includes bibliographical references

Murray, Stuart, 1948-
Vietnam War; written by Stuart Murray. DK Pub. 2005 71p il (DK eyewitness books) $15.99; lib bdg $19.99
Grades: 7 8 9 10   **959.704**
 1. Vietnam War, 1961-1975
 ISBN   0-7566-1166-0;   978-0-7566-1166-8;
 0-7566-1165-2 (lib bdg); 978-0-7566-1165-1 (lib bdg)
                                LC 2004-24516
"Besides identifying major political and military figures from both sides of the conflict, photos and text also document supporters and protesters, as well as the medical workers and civilians caught in the crossfire. Pictures and descriptions of weaponry and machinery will please military buffs, while troubling descriptions of Napalm and Agent Orange expose the grim realities of warfare." Booklist

Palmer, Laura, 1950-
Shrapnel in the heart; letters and remembrances from the Vietnam Veterans Memorial. Random House 1987 xx, 243p il hardcover o.p. pa $13 *
Grades: 9 10 11 12   **959.704**
 1. Vietnam Veterans Memorial (Washington, D.C.)
 2. Vietnam War, 1961-1975—Personal narratives
 ISBN 0-394-56027-2; 0-394-75988-5 (pa)
                                LC 87-42652
"A collection of letters and poems that have been left at the Vietnam Veterans Memorial, with background information on the deceased and the bereaved writers." Booklist

Reporting Vietnam. Library of Am. 1998 2v il maps v1-v2 ea $35; v2 pa $17.95 *
Grades: 11 12 Adult   **959.704**
 1. Vietnam War, 1961-1975 2. Reporters and reporting
 ISBN 1-88301-158-2 (v1); 1-88301-159-0 (v2);
 1-88301-190-6 (v2 pa)   LC 98-12267
Contents: Pt.1 American journalism, 1959-1969; pt.2 American journalism, 1969-1975
This collection includes "newspaper, magazine, book excerpts, and one TV commentary, Walter Cronkite's post-Tet report concluding that the United States should quickly negotiate its way out." Commonweal
"This book will help readers understand better what it was like to live through that tumultuous period of American history." Publ Wkly
Includes bibliographical references

Vadas, Robert E., 1952-
Cultures in conflict—the Viet Nam War. Greenwood Press 2002 xxi, 244p il map (Greenwood Press cultures in conflict series) $44.95
Grades: 9 10 11 12   **959.704**
 1. Vietnam War, 1961-1975 2. Culture conflict
 ISBN 0-313-31616-3   LC 2001-54716
A "picture of the Vietnam war, as experienced by Americans and Vietnamese. . . . [The author] presents the combined factors of competing communist, nationalist, and capitalist ideology; political arrogance; and deception that led to the great military conflagration in South East Asia. Cultural information describes ancient Vietnamese nationalism in contrast with American Cold War fears of the 'domino theory.'" Voice Youth Advocates
"This volume is an excellent resource for any person interested in knowing more about this war and how it affected Vietnam and the United States." Libr Media Connect
Includes glossary and bibliographical references

The **Vietnam** War; Nick Treanor, book editor. Greenhaven Press 2004 234p il map (Interpreting primary documents) hardcover o.p. pa $23.70
Grades: 7 8 9 10   **959.704**
 1. Vietnam War, 1961-1975
 ISBN 0-7377-2262-2 (lib bdg); 0-7377-2263-0 (pa)
                                LC 2003-49058
"This anthology presents primary documents tracing the development of American intervention in Southeast Asia from Ho Chi Mingh's 1945 declaration of Vietnamese independence through to the fall of Saigon." Publisher's note
Includes bibliographical references

Willbanks, James H., 1947-
Vietnam War almanac. Facts On File 2008 590p il map (Almanacs of American wars) $95
Grades: 11 12 Adult   **959.704**
 1. Reference books 2. Vietnam War, 1961-1975
 ISBN 978-0-8160-7102-9; 0-8160-7102-0
                                LC 2008-6881

Willbanks, James H., 1947-—*Continued*

Contains a "day-by-day chronology of the events and people involved in the Vietnam War . . . [and] also features an A-to-Z biographical dictionary of the key figures involved in the conflict." Publisher's note

Includes bibliographical references

Young, Marilyn Blatt

The Vietnam War: a history in documents; [by] Marilyn B. Young, John J. Fitzgerald, A. Tom Grunfeld. Oxford Univ. Press 2002 175p il maps (Pages from history) lib bdg $32.95; pa $19.95 *

Grades: 7 8 9 10   **959.704**

1. Vietnam War, 1961-1975

ISBN 0-19-512278-X (lib bdg); 0-19-516635-3 (pa)

               LC 2001-52338

This is a "collection of original documents and photographs that detail the war in Vietnam. The text includes speeches, cartoons, news articles, and parallel events occurring in the United States and in Asia." Soc Educ

"The documents are skillfully tied together by brief text that gives good background information. . . . The book is well balanced in showing both sides. . . . Good-quality, black-and-white photos and illustrations are plentiful and informative." SLJ

Includes glossary and bibliographical references

960   History of Africa

Africa: an encyclopedia for students; John Middleton, editor. Scribner 2002 4v il maps set $395

Grades: 7 8 9 10   **960**

1. Africa—Encyclopedias 2. Reference books

ISBN 0-684-80650-9   LC 2001-49348

A comprehensive look at the continent of Africa and the countries that comprise it, including peoples and cultures, the land and its history, art and architecture, and daily life

Africa: opposing viewpoints; David M. Haugen, book editor. Gale/Cengage Learning 2008 219p lib bdg $39.70; pa $27.50 *

Grades: 8 9 10 11 12   **960**

1. Africa—Social conditions 2. Africa—Economic conditions 3. Africa—Politics and government

ISBN 978-0-7377-3988-6 (lib bdg); 978-0-7377-3989-3 (pa)   LC 2008-811

"Opposing viewpoints series"

Articles in this anthology discuss important issues facing Africa today, foreign aid and free trade, the status of democracy and human rights in Africa, and ways the United States and other western nations can help Africa.

Includes bibliographical references

Caplan, Gerald L.

The betrayal of Africa; [by] Gerald Caplan. Groundwood Books 2008 144p il map (Groundwork guides) $18.95; pa $10

Grades: 9 10 11 12   **960**

1. Africa—Foreign relations 2. Africa—Social conditions

ISBN 978-0-88899-824-8; 0-88899-824-4; 978-0-88899-825-5 (pa); 0-88899-825-2 (pa)

               LC 2008-411359

Argues that it is the policies of rich Western nations that are responsible for many of Africa's problems, discussing such issues as the large gap between rich and poor, women's rights, health, and education, and advocates change.

"This is ideal for classroom use, as a discussion-starter, or simply an eye-opening introduction to some of the world's greatest mass tragedies." Booklist

Includes bibliographical references

Encyclopedia of African history; Kevin Shillington, editor. Fitzroy Dearborn 2004 3v il map set $395

Grades: 11 12 Adult   **960**

1. Africa—Encyclopedias 2. Reference books

ISBN 1-579-58245-1   LC 2004-16779

"The scope of the coverage encompasses the entire continent, including North Africa, and features all historical periods, with special attention to recent events. Most entries are given 1000 words, though major topics, such as regional surveys, stretch to 3000-4000 words. Topics range from art to anthropology to economics, but emphasis is placed on biographies and country studies, both pre- and postcolonial. . . . Simply put, this is an essential reference resource for students of African history." Libr J

Includes bibliographical references

Encyclopedia of African history and culture; Willie F. Page, editor. rev ed, by R. Hunt Davis, Jr. Facts on File 2005 5v il map set $425 *

Grades: 9 10 11 12 Adult   **960**

1. Africa—Encyclopedias 2. Reference books

ISBN 0-8160-5199-2   LC 2004-22929

"A Learning Source Book"

First published 2001

This encyclopedia's "arrangement is chronological, with each of the five volumes representing a major era of African history: 'Ancient Africa,' 'African Kingdoms,' 'From Conquest to Colonization,' 'The Colonial Era,' and 'Independent Africa.'" Choice

This set "fulfills its information and education goals and is highly recommended for high-school, public, and academic libraries." Booklist

Includes bibliographical references

Falola, Toyin, 1953-

Key events in African history; a reference guide. Greenwood Press 2002 xxiii, 347p il maps $64.95; pa $25

Grades: 11 12 Adult   **960**

1. Africa—History

ISBN 0-313-31323-7; 0-313-36122-3 (pa)

               LC 2001-58644

Falola, Toyin, 1953-—*Continued*

"An Oryx book"

"Falola surveys the . . . history of the African continent by focusing on 36 pivotal events that either caused or led to significant changes and developments in African social, political, and cultural life from around 40,000 B.C.E. to the collapse of apartheid in the 1990s. . . . Following a detailed time line of historical events, each topic is highlighted in an individual chapter including cross-references, historical and political maps, illustrations, a notes section, and a suggested list for further reading." Booklist

Includes bibliographical references

Gates, Henry Louis

Wonders of the African world; [by] Henry Louis Gates, Jr. Knopf 1999 275p il map hardcover o.p. pa $24.95

Grades: 11 12 Adult   960

1. Africa—Civilization

ISBN 0-375-40235-7; 0-375-70948-7 (pa)

LC 99-18496

"In conjunction with the PBS television series of the same title, Gates offers a 12-nation reprise of the magnificence of ancient African civilizations . . . [moving] in clusters—from the black gods and kings of Nubia, to Ethiopia's links to the Holy Land and the Lost Ark of the Covenant, to Timbuktu's commercial and intellectual center, to the slave kingdoms, and to the Lost Cities of Great Zimbabwe." Libr J

"Gates writes with concentration and clarity, and anticipates the questions that arise in the wary reader's mind, delivering the answers at just the right time." N Y Times Book Rev

Includes bibliographical references

Lefkowitz, Mary R., 1935-

Not out of Africa; how Afrocentrism became an excuse to teach myth as history; [by] Mary Lefkowitz. Basic Bks. 1996 222p il map hardcover o.p. pa $19

Grades: 11 12 Adult   960

1. Africa—Historiography 2. History—Study and teaching

ISBN 0-465-09837-1; 0-465-09838-X (pa)

LC 95-49109

"A New Republic book"

"Those classicists who believe there are Egyptian antecedents for Greek philosophy are known as Afrocentrists. . . . Lefkowitz claims that the Afrocentrists are perpetuating myths and that they protect their claims by labeling those who question those claims as narrow-minded or racist." Libr J

"The book is a case study in historical methods, the value and limits of scholarship, and the preciousness of hard-bitten reason and objectivity. The book is also lucid and accessible." Christ Sci Monit

Includes bibliographical references

Reader, John, 1937-

Africa: a biography of the continent. Knopf 1998 801p il maps hardcover o.p. pa $18

Grades: 11 12 Adult   960

1. Africa—History

ISBN 0-679-40979-3; 0-679-73869-X (pa)

LC 97-36892

First published 1997 in the United Kingdom

This book discusses "the paleontology of the early African continent, covering a period of approximately three billion years. [Reader] then traces the history of human origins in Africa and proceeds to track the imprint of that beginning on human evolution, staying grounded in Africa as he marks the immigration of humans to other continents." Booklist

Reader "writes with sweeping historical perspective and an engaging familiarity with the continent and its people." Publ Wkly

Includes bibliographical references

Stewart, John, 1952-

African states and rulers. 3rd ed. McFarland & Co. 2006 423p $115 *

Grades: 9 10 11 12   960

1. Africa—History

ISBN 0-7864-2562-8; 978-0-7864-2562-4

LC 2006-5823

First published 1989

Arranged alphabetically by the country's official name, each entry gives the country's location, capital, other names, a brief history, and a chronological listing of its rulers and their official titles. Coverage includes contemporary nation-states and ancient tribal kingdoms.

This volume offers "the most in-depth treatment of Africa's changing political boundaries and heads of state." Booklist

Includes bibliographical references

962   Egypt and Sudan

Asante, Molefi K., 1942-

Culture and customs of Egypt; [by] Molefi Kete Asante. Greenwood Press 2002 168p il map (Culture and customs of Africa) $44.95

Grades: 9 10 11 12   962

1. Egypt—Social life and customs

ISBN 0-313-31740-2   LC 2002-21620

"The work is divided into seven . . . chapters. They include: land, people, and a historical overview; government, economy, education, and tourism; religion and worldview; architecture and art; social customs and lifestyles; the media and cinema; and literature, the performing arts, and music. These chapters address all relevant areas and provide the reader with a well-rounded picture of the culture and customs of Egypt." Recomm Ref Books for Small & Medium-sized Libr & Media Cent, 2003

Includes bibliographical references

Goldschmidt, Arthur, 1938-

A brief history of Egypt. Facts on File 2008 294p il map (Brief history) $45; pa $19.95 *

Grades: 9 10 11 12 Adult   **962**

1. Egypt—History

ISBN   978-0-8160-6672-8;   0-8160-6672-8; 978-0-8160-7333-7 (pa); 0-8160-7333-3 (pa)

LC 2007-7374

The author "explores Egypt's broad political, economic, social, and cultural developments, covering roughly 6,000 years of history." Publisher's note

Includes glossary and bibliographical references

962.4   Sudan

Childress, Diana

Omar al-Bashir's Sudan. Twenty-First Century Books 2010 160p il map (Dictatorships) lib bdg $38.60

Grades: 10 11 12   **962.4**

1. Al-Bashir, Omar, 1944- 2. Sudan

ISBN 978-0-8225-9096-5   LC 2008-53931

"Bashir took control of Sudan in a 1989 coup and has been working to establish an Islamist state throughout the country, a movement that began in the late 1970s. The imposition of Sharia law onto the largely non-Muslim south escalated tensions, and the south waged a civil war that lasted until 2002. Altogether, this is a useful and up-to-date look at an ongoing dictatorship. . . . Photographs are well chosen, and sidebars give readers some background on issues such as Islamism, Sharia, and the Lost Boys of Sudan." SLJ

Includes glossary and bibliographical references

Dau, John Bul

Lost boy, lost girl; escaping civil war in Sudan; by John Bul Dau and Martha Arual Akech; with Michael Sweeney and K. M. Kostyal. National Geographic 2010 159p il map $15.95; lib bdg $23.90

Grades: 7 8 9 10   **962.4**

1. Refugees 2. Sudan—History—Civil War, 1983-2005

ISBN   978-1-4263-0708-9;   1-4263-0708-X; 978-1-4263-0709-6 (lib bdg); 1-4263-0709-8 (lib bdg)

LC 2010-17960

"The tragic story of Sudan's Lost Boys and Lost [Girls] is told in simple language by two survivors. . . . In 1987, when Dau was 13 and Akech was 6, war came to their village. Both traveled hundreds of miles to a UN refugee camp in Ethiopia. After a few years of safety, the refugees were forced to move again. . . . Teens who know little about Sudan and its problems will be drawn into this moving, inspiration story." SLJ

Deng, Benson

They poured fire on us from the sky; the true story of three lost boys from Sudan; [by] Benson Deng, Alephonsion Deng, Benjamin Ajak; with Judy Bernstein. Public Affairs 2005 xxiii, 311p map hardcover o.p. pa $13.95

Grades: 11 12 Adult   **962.4**

1. Refugees 2. Sudan

ISBN 1-58648-269-6; 1-58648-388-9 (pa)

LC 2005-42566

"Three young refugees in California—Alephonsion Deng, Benson Deng, and Benjamin Ajak, two brothers and a cousin—remember how they were driven from their homes in southern Sudan in the ethnic and religious conflicts that have left two million dead." Booklist

"This collection is moving in its depictions of unbelievable courage." Publ Wkly

963   Ethiopia and Eritrea

Mezlekia, Nega, 1958-

Notes from the Hyena's belly; an Ethiopian boyhood. Picador 2001 351p il map hardcover o.p. pa $14

Grades: 9 10 11 12   **963**

1. Ethiopia

ISBN 0-312-26988-9; 0-312-28914-6 (pa)

LC 00-50126

First published 2000 by Penguin

In this memoir, Mezlekia, "an Ethiopian who now lives in Canada, . . . traces the years from his birth in 1958 through his flight in 1983 to the Netherlands and on to Canada." N Y Times Book Rev

"Full of adventure, political struggle, and intrigue [this] memoir works as a coming-of-age story as well as a glimpse into a world of political corruption and change that Westerners rarely get to know so intimately." Libr J

966.62   Liberia

Reef, Catherine

This our dark country; the American settlers of Liberia. Clarion Bks. 2002 136p il maps $17

Grades: 7 8 9 10   **966.62**

1. American Colonization Society 2. African Americans—History 3. Slavery—United States

ISBN 0-618-14785-3   LC 2002-3966

Explores the history of the colony, later the independent nation of Liberia, which was established on the west coast of Africa in 1822 as a haven for free African Americans

"This photo-essay is a grim, disturbing history of Liberia. . . . Reef tells it in clear, plain style, always showing the connections between the two homelands. The handsome, very spacious design . . . makes the hard facts accessible. . . . A must for history collections." Booklist

Includes bibliographical references

966.7 Ghana

Weatherly, Myra, 1926-
Teens in Ghana. Compass Point Books 2008
96p il map (Global connections) lib bdg $33.26
Grades: 7 8 9 10   **966.7**
1. Teenagers 2. Ghana
ISBN 978-0-7565-3417-2; 0-7565-3417-8
LC 2007-33086
Uncovers the challenges, pastimes, customs and culture of teens in Ghana
"Color photographs of native teens enliven the text and help reinforce the connection between reader and subject matter. . . . Religion is discussed, as well as technology, government, and social roles and expectations. . . . [This] would be a wonderful addition to any library." Voice Youth Advocates
Includes bibliographical references

966.9 Nigeria

Harmon, Dan
Nigeria; 1880 to the present: the struggle, the tragedy, the promise; [by] Daniel Harmon. Chelsea House 2000 144p il (Exploration of Africa, the emerging nations) lib bdg $29.95
Grades: 9 10 11 12   **966.9**
1. Nigeria
ISBN 0-7910-5452-7   LC 99-58749
Photographs and text look at the past, development, and present culture of Nigeria and its inhabitants
Includes bibliographical references

967 Central Africa and offshore islands

Davidson, Basil, 1914-2010
The African slave trade. rev and expanded ed. Little, Brown 1980 304p il maps hardcover o.p. pa $19.99 *
Grades: 11 12 Adult   **967**
1. Central Africa—History 2. Slave trade
ISBN 0-316-17439-4; 0-316-17438-6 (pa)
LC 81-65588
"An Atlantic Monthly Press book"
First published 1961 with title: Black mother
An account of the slave trade and its impact on West African society.
Includes bibliographical references

Oppong, Joseph R.
Africa South of the Sahara; series consulting editor Charles F. Gritzner. Chelsea House Publishers 2006 124p il map (Modern world cultures) lib bdg $30
Grades: 6 7 8 9 10   **967**

1. Sub-Saharan Africa
ISBN 0-7910-8146-X
This describes the physical and historical geography, population and settlement, cultures, politics, and economy of sub-Saharan Africa.
This "accessible [title is] generously illustrated with colorful photos, maps, and clear charts, graphs, and other statistical data." SLJ

967.5 Democratic Republic of the Congo, Rwanda, Burundi

Hochschild, Adam, 1942-
King Leopold's ghost; a story of greed, terror, and heroism in Colonial Africa. Houghton Mifflin 1998 366p il map hardcover o.p. pa $15
Grades: 11 12 Adult   **967.5**
1. Belgium—Colonies 2. Atrocities
ISBN 0-395-75924-2; 0-618-00190-5 (pa)
LC 98-16813
The author "focuses on King Leopold's reign of terror in the Belgian Congo and the unswerving efforts by human rights activists (Sir Roger Casement, E.D. Morel, and others) and the Congo Reform Association to raise awareness of the enslavement, mutilation, and murder of millions of Congolese." Libr J
"Hochschild's impressively researched history records the roles of the famous and obscure, missionaries, journalists, opportunists, politicians, and royalty in this longforgotten drama." Booklist
Includes bibliographical references

967.571 Rwanda

Gourevitch, Philip
We wish to inform you that tomorrow we will be killed with our families; stories from Rwanda. Farrar, Straus & Giroux 1998 355p hardcover o.p. pa $15
Grades: 11 12 Adult   **967.571**
1. Rwanda—Politics and government 2. Genocide
ISBN 0-374-28697-3; 0-312-24335-9 (pa)
LC 98-22132
"In 1994, the world was informed of the inexplicable mass killings in Rwanda, in which over 800,000 were killed in 100 days. Gourevitch . . . spent over three years putting together an oral history of the mass killing that occurred in this small country." Libr J
This work is "readable and moving, Gourevitch is an impassioned and thoughtful observer. But this is not a work that gives much pleasure or comfort. Nor are its arguments fool-proof, its evidence complete, or its documentation thorough. . . . Still Gourevitch does struggle to come close to a great mystery of evil, and he makes us attend to great crimes." Commonweal

Hatzfeld, Jean
Machete season; the killers in Rwanda speak: a
report; translated from the French by Linda
Coverdale; preface by Susan Sontag. Farrar, Straus
and Giroux 2005 253p il maps hardcover o.p. pa
$14
Grades: 11 12 Adult   **967.571**
  1. Tutsi (African people) 2. Hutu (African people)
3. Rwanda 4. Genocide
  ISBN 0-374-28082-7; 0-312-42503-1 (pa)
                          LC 2004-61600
  Original French edition, 2003
  "In April-May 1994, 800,000 Rwandan Tutsis were
massacred by their Hutu fellow citizens—about 10,000 a
day, mostly being hacked to death by machete. In Machete Season, the . . . foreign correspondent Jean
Hatzfeld reports on the results of his interviews with nine
of the Hutu killers." Publisher's note
  "Steering clear of politics, this important book succeeds in offering the reader some grasp of how such unspeakable acts unfolded." Publ Wkly

Kinzer, Stephen
A thousand hills; Rwanda's rebirth and the man
who dreamed it. John Wiley & Sons 2008 380p il
map $25.95 *
Grades: 11 12 Adult   **967.571**
  1. Presidents—Rwanda 2. Rwanda 3. Genocide
  ISBN 978-0-470-12015-6   LC 2007041613
  This is an "account of Rwandan president Paul
Kagame, the Tutsi refugee who organized the Rwandan
Military Front in 1994 and helped halt the genocide in
Rwanda." Publ Wkly
  This book "is a balanced look at how one man's doc-
trine of self-reliance has made his impoverished, deci-
mated country a potential model for the rest of Africa.
. . . [The author] comes closer than any other journalist
yet to capturing the energy, will, self-discipline—and an-
ger—that brought Rwanda back to life." Washington
Monthly
  Includes bibliographical references

The **Rwandan** genocide; Alexander Cruden, book
  editor. Greenhaven Press 2010 227p il map
  (Perspectives on modern world history) $39.70
Grades: 9 10 11 12   **967.571**
  1. Rwanda 2. Genocide
  ISBN 978-0-7377-5007-2   LC 2010-10290
  "Following an introduction to the subject, various articles, primary sources, speeches, and other documents
provide perspectives on how this tragedy unfolded, who
was affected, and what was done to either stop the genocide or allow it flourish. Students will find a wealth of
information on what actually happened during this dark
time in Rwanda, as well as how the genocide was treated
by the international community and how people and organizations caught up in the event responded. . . . An
informative addition to any collection." SLJ
  Includes bibliographical references

967.62 Kenya

Lekuton, Joseph
Facing the lion; growing up Maasai on the
African savanna; by Joseph Lekuton with Herman
Viola. National Geographic Soc. 2003 127p il map
$15.95
Grades: 7 8 9 10 11 12   **967.62**
  1. Masai (African people) 2. Kenya
  ISBN 0-7922-5125-3   LC 2003-750
  Contents: A lion hunt; The proud one; Cows; The
pinching man; School; Herdsman; Initiation; Kabarak;
Soccer; America; A warrior in two worlds
  A member of the Masai people describes his life as he
grew up in a northern Kenya village, travelled to America to attend college, and became an elementary school
teacher in Virginia
  "Lekuton's story touches a universal chord, and shows
readers the beauty of another culture from the inside.
Simple and direct enough for reluctant readers, and written in a conversational and occasionally wryly humorous
style, this book will be enjoyed by a wide range of readers." SLJ

968 Southern Africa. Republic of South Africa

Beck, Roger
The history of South Africa; [by] Roger B.
Beck. Greenwood Press 2000 xxx, 248p
(Greenwood histories of the modern nations)
$39.95
Grades: 11 12 Adult   **968**
  1. South Africa—History
  ISBN 0-313-30730-X   LC 99-58880
  "Beginning with an overview of the modern nation,
this narrative history traces South Africa from prehistory
through the European invasions, the settlement by the
Dutch, the imposition of British rule, the many interne-
cine wars for control of the nation, the institution of
apartheid, and, finally, freedom for all South Africans in
1994 and the Mandela years 1994-1999." Publisher's
note
  "The text is well written, easy to follow, and a good
place to start for readers who have no prior knowledge
of South African history." Am Ref Books Annu, 2001
  Includes bibliographical references

Thompson, Leonard Monteath
A history of South Africa; [by] Leonard
Thompson. 3rd ed. Yale Univ. Press 2001 xxiv,
358p il maps pa $17.95
Grades: 9 10 11 12   **968**
  1. South Africa—History 2. South Africa—Race rela-
tions
  ISBN 0-300-08776-4   LC 00-32101
  First published 1990
  This "exploration of South Africa's history—from the
earliest known human settlement of the region to the
present—focuses primarily on the experiences of its

Thompson, Leonard Monteath—*Continued*
black inhabitants, rather than on those of its white minority." Publisher's note
Includes bibliographical references

968.06 Period as Republic, 1961-

Biko, Stephen, 1946-1977
I write what I like; selected writings; edited with a personal memoir by Aelred Stubbs; preface by Archbishop Desmond Tutu; introduction by Malusi and Thoko Mpumlwana; with a new foreword by Lewis R. Gordon. University of Chicago Press 2002 xxxiii, 216p pa $17
Grades: 9 10 11 12   968.06
1. South Africa—Race relations 2. South Africa—Politics and government
ISBN 0-226-04897-7   LC 2002-23951
First published 1978 in the United Kingdom
"This selection of writings by the South African black leader who died in custody . . . contains letters, addresses, conference papers and articles written for the newsletter of the South African Student's Organization." Publ Wkly
"Readers will find [Biko's] essential humaneness, intelligence, and lack of malice as impressive as his eloquence and compelling arguments." Libr J

Carlin, John
Playing the enemy; Nelson Mandela and the game that made a nation. Penguin 2008 274p il $24.95
Grades: 11 12 Adult   968.06
1. Mandela, Nelson 2. Rugby
ISBN 978-1-59420-174-5; 1-59420-174-9
                                        LC 2008-298721
This book focuses on Nelson Mandela's advocacy of "the national rugby team, the Springboks, who would host the sport's World Cup in 1995." Publisher's note
"Deftly sketched characters make up both an audience for the big game and a gallery of South Africa, through which Carlin will recount the absorbing story of a country emerging from its cruelly absurd racist experiment." N Y Times Book Rev
Includes bibliographical references

Carter, Jason
Power lines; two years on South Africa's borders; introduction by Jimmy Carter. National Geographic Soc. 2002 xxiii, 278p il hardcover o.p. pa $14
Grades: 11 12 Adult   968.06
1. Peace Corps (U.S.) 2. South Africa—Description and travel
ISBN 0-7922-8012-1; 0-7922-4101-0 (pa)
                                        LC 2002-22370
This is an account of life in the Peace Corps by the grandson of former President Jimmy Carter. "After graduating from college, Carter spent two years in the late 1990s volunteering in a former black homeland. . . . Assigned to the tiny, and poor, community of Lochiel, Car-

ter takes the political and turns it into the personal as he writes candidly of his attempts to help create a new curriculum; he reflects on his efforts to raise teachers' self-esteem without trampling on their turf. Carter depicts life with humor and honesty and considers the limits of his stint, the way Western culture has become part of South Africans' lives and his guilt at enjoying its trappings as he travels around the country." Publ Wkly
"A great read for those who want more than vanishing-tribes exotica." Booklist

Finnegan, William
Crossing the line; a year in the land of apartheid. Persea Books 2006 434p map pa $20
Grades: 9 10 11 12   968.06
1. South Africa—Race relations 2. High schools—South Africa 3. Discrimination in education
ISBN 0-89255-325-1   LC 2006-47648
"A Karen and Michael Braziller book"
First published 1986 by Harper & Row
The author, an American school teacher, recalls his experiences in the segregated black schools of South Africa.

Mandela, Nelson
Nelson Mandela speaks; forging a democratic nonracial South Africa. Pathfinder Press 1993 296p il map hardcover o.p. pa $18.95 *
Grades: 11 12 Adult   968.06
1. African National Congress 2. South Africa—Politics and government 3. Apartheid
ISBN 0-87348-775-3 (lib bdg); 0-87348-774-5 (pa)
                                        LC 93-85689
In this volume "the South African leader's significant speeches, letters, and interviews from the period since his February 1990 release from prison are brought together. . . . [The editor] provides a useful glossary and chronology of the 1990-93 period, and supplies a brief introduction to each entry." Booklist

Sonneborn, Liz
The end of apartheid in South Africa. Chelsea House Publishers 2010 120p il (Milestones in modern world history) lib bdg $35
Grades: 8 9 10 11 12   968.06
1. Apartheid 2. Anti-apartheid movement 3. South Africa—Race relations
ISBN 978-1-60413-409-4; 1-60413-409-7
                                        LC 2008-54805
This is "an excellent in-depth overview, one of the best on the subject, with chapters on the early history before the establishment of the apartheid regime and with profiles of many important leaders (not just Nelson Mandela), as well as clear discussion of present-day politics, the role of the Truth and Reconciliation Commission, and the ongoing inequality. Never simplistic, it is an outstanding overview for teens new to the subject; for those who know something of the history, it fills in the big picture with depth and detail about both leaders and ordinary people, what has changed, and how much still needs to be done." Booklist
Includes bibliographical references

968.91   Zimbabwe

Arnold, James R., 1952-
Robert Mugabe's Zimbabwe; by James R. Arnold and Roberta Wiener. Twenty-First Century Books 2008 160p (Dictatorships) lib bdg $38.60
Grades: 7 8 9 10   **968.91**
1. Mugabe, Robert Gabriel, 1924- 2. Zimbabwe
ISBN 978-0-8225-7283-1   LC 2006-100765
This history of Zimbabwe under the dictatorship of Robert Mugabe gives "students a glimpse into the repression and daily struggle for survival under [this] brutal [government]." SLJ
Includes glossary and bibliographical references

970.004   North American native peoples

American Indian tribes; edited by the editors of Salem Press; project editor, R. Kent Rasmussen. Salem Press 2000 2v (Magill's choice) set $99
Grades: 11 12 Adult   **970.004**
1. Native Americans
ISBN 0-89356-063-4   LC 00-44659
"Arranged by tribe, these volumes contain essays that originally appeared in Salem's three-volume *Ready Reference, American Indians* (1995). All of the bibliographies have been updated." Booklist
Includes bibliographical references

Ball, Dewi Ioan
Competing voices from native America; [by] Dewi Ioan Ball and Joy Porter. Greenwood Press 2009 445p (Fighting words) $65 *
Grades: 10 11 12   **970.004**
1. Native Americans—History 2. Reference books
ISBN 978-1-84645-016-7   LC 2008-45342
"This volume of 'competing voices' is not limited to commentary on Native first encounters with Europeans, removal, and Manifest Destiny. It also traces the dynamic courses of relations between Native Americans and both the state and federal governments to the present day. . . . Whether discussing Pontiac's Rebellion or the 1977 trial of Leonard Peltier, these documents are sure to inspire debate among advanced students." SLJ
Includes bibliographical references

Bowes, John P., 1973-
The Trail of Tears; removal in the south. Chelsea House 2007 128p il map (Landmark events in Native American history) $35
Grades: 7 8 9 10   **970.004**
1. Cherokee Indians 2. Native Americans—Relocation
ISBN 978-0-7910-9345-0; 0-7910-9345-X
                                LC 2006-102274
"This volume brings a difficult viewpoint to this historical event—that of the Indians involved. This 13- to 17-page chapters thoroughly describe the background of the Trail of Tears, its legal aspects, the development of the Cherokee Nations, the treaties and their effects, the horrors of the Trail itself, and the aftermath for the Indians as a people and a nation. It is well written and readable for students." Libr Media Connect
Includes bibliographical references

Brown, Dee Alexander
Bury my heart at Wounded Knee; an Indian history of the American West; [by] Dee Brown. Thirtieth anniversary ed. Holt & Co. 2001 487p il hardcover o.p. pa $16 *
Grades: 8 9 10 11 12 Adult   **970.004**
1. Native Americans—West (U.S.) 2. Native Americans—Wars 3. West (U.S.)—History
ISBN 0-8050-6634-9; 0-8050-6669-1 (pa)
                                LC 00-40958
Also available illustrated edition from Sterling Innovation
First published 1970
This is an account of the experience of the American Indian during the white man's expansion westward.
Includes bibliographical references

Bruchac, Joseph, 1942-
Our stories remember; American Indian history, culture, & values through storytelling. Fulcrum 2003 192p map pa $16.95 *
Grades: 11 12 Adult   **970.004**
1. Native Americans—History 2. Storytelling
ISBN 1-555-91129-3   LC 2002-151236
"Synthesizes the stories of many different Indian nations, including Navajo, Abenaki, Cherokee, Cree, Sioux, and Tlingit in order to illustrate core values, which are pivotal to them all." Booklist
"This important volume includes a wealth of traditional stories and solid information." SLJ
Includes bibliographical references

Crow Dog, Leonard, 1942-
Crow Dog; four generations of Sioux medicine men; [by] Leonard Crow Dog and Richard Erdoes. HarperCollins Pubs. 1995 243p il hardcover o.p. pa $13
Grades: 11 12 Adult   **970.004**
1. American Indian Movement 2. Dakota Indians
ISBN 0-06-016861-7; 0-06-092682-1 (pa)
                                LC 94-40695
Erdoes has recorded Leonard Crow Dog's oral narrative of the history of his family and his people, the Lakota. Mr. Crow Dog discusses "the generations of his family who have carried the name Crow Dog since the American government told them it would be their family name. . . . He tells of his involvement as the spiritual leader of the American Indian Movement and the occupation of Wounded Knee in the early 1970's." Booklist

Debo, Angie, 1890-1988
A history of the Indians of the United States. University of Okla. Press 1970 386p il maps (Civilization of the American Indian series) hardcover o.p. pa $24.95
Grades: 9 10 11 12   **970.004**

Debo, Angie, 1890-1988—*Continued*
1. Native Americans
ISBN 0-8061-0911-4; 0-8061-1888-1 (pa)
This historical survey of the Indians of North America, including the Eskimos and Aleuts of Alaska, discusses the first meetings with European explorers, their dispossession by colonial expansion, and their relations with the new American republic.
Includes bibliographical references

Deloria, Vine
Custer died for your sins; an Indian manifesto; by Vine Deloria, Jr. University of Oklahoma Press 1988 278p pa $19.95
Grades: 11 12 Adult **970.004**
1. Native Americans
ISBN 0-8061-2129-7 LC 87-40561
First published 1969 by Macmillan
The author examines how anthropologists, missionaries, and government agencies have mistreated American Indians.

Do all Indians live in tipis? questions and answers; from the National Museum of the American Indian; foreword by Rick West; introduction by Wilma Mankiller. Collins, in association with the National Museum of the American Indian, Smithsonian Institution 2007 239p il pa $14.95
Grades: 8 9 10 11 12 **970.004**
1. Native Americans
ISBN 978-0-06-115301-3; 0-06-115301-X
LC 2007-60874
"This highly accessible and informative book aims to dispel some of the major myths and stereotypes still surrounding Native people in the United States and Canada. . . . The straightforward questions were compiled from actual phone calls, emails, letters, and in-person visits to the George Gustav Heye Center in New York, a major branch of the National Museum of the American Indian. The Native American writers who answered them did so concisely with hints of humor and an abundance of research and experience. . . . This is a topnotch resource for both people just learning about Native American cultures and those who think they know the facts." SLJ

Dunn, John M., 1949-
The relocation of the North American Indian. Lucent Books 2005 c2006 112p il map (World history series) $32.45
Grades: 9 10 11 12 **970.004**
1. Native Americans—Relocation 2. Native Americans—Reservations
ISBN 1-59018-656-7; 978-1-59018-656-5
LC 2005-1800
First published 1995
This is a "presentation of the relationship between Native Americans and European settlers, and, later, with the U.S. government. The history is solidly researched; source documents and maps are frequently included in the nine chapters. . . . The writing style is marvelous, and the vocabulary is expressive but not difficult—this is anything but a textbook experience." SLJ
Includes bibliographical references

Encyclopedia of American Indian history; Bruce E. Johansen, Barry M. Pritzker, editors. ABC-CLIO 2008 4v il map set $395
Grades: 11 12 Adult **970.004**
1. Native Americans—History—Encyclopedias 2. Reference books
ISBN 978-1-85109-817-0 LC 2007-11970
This encyclopedia's "1,481 pages include approximately 450 entries by over 100 contributors that range from precontact, beginning approximately 20,000 BCE, to contemporary issues of tribal recognition, gaming, and water rights, with a focus on postcontact times. . . . Teachers, students, and the public will all benefit from this . . . broad-based encyclopedia." Choice
Includes bibliographical references

Encyclopedia of Native American wars and warfare; general editors, William B. Kessel, Robert Wooster. Facts on File 2005 398p il map $75; pa $21.95 *
Grades: 7 8 9 10 **970.004**
1. Native Americans—Wars—Encyclopedias 2. Reference books
ISBN 0-8160-3337-4; 0-8160-6430-X (pa)
LC 00-56200
"More than 600 entries provide access to information about the persons, tribes, treaties, battles, places, weaponry, and concepts related to armed conflicts between Native Americans and those of European descent, for the years between 1599 and 1890 and primarily the geographic locations now within the borders of the U.S." Booklist
"This encyclopedia offers readers a wide range of information about Native American history in North America after 1492." Choice
Includes bibliographical references

Frazier, Ian
On the rez. Farrar, Straus & Giroux 2000 311p il hardcover o.p. pa $14
Grades: 11 12 Adult **970.004**
1. War Lance, Le 2. Oglala Indians 3. Pine Ridge Indian Reservation (S.D.)
ISBN 0-374-22638-5; 0-312-27859-4 (pa)
LC 99-28353
Frazier discusses the history of the Oglala Sioux and the Indians that he met on the Pine Ridge Reservation in South Dakota, including his friend Le War Lance
"As Frazier serendipitously shuttles his narrative between Pine Ridge visits and snippets of Indian history, a fascinating picture emerges of a people struggling with the consequences of old wrongs and human orneriness." Time

From the heart; voices of the American Indian; edited and with narrative by Lee Miller. Knopf 1995 405p il hardcover o.p. pa $16 *
Grades: 11 12 Adult **970.004**
1. Native Americans
ISBN 0-679-43549-2; 0-679-76891-2 (pa)
LC 94-28492
An anthology of excerpts from speeches by Native Americans from the 16th to the 19th centuries.
"Arranged by region and chronology, these extraordi-

From the heart—*Continued*
narily moving extracts are placed into appropriate historical context by Miller's descriptive narrative. In addition, pertinent quotations of non-Indian witnesses are also included. A haunting and eloquent anthology." Booklist
Includes bibliographical references

Gilbert, Joan
The Trail of Tears across Missouri. University of Mo. Press 1996 122p il map (Missouri heritage readers series) pa $9.95
Grades: 11 12 Adult   **970.004**
1. Cherokee Indians
ISBN 0-8262-1063-5   LC 96-10232
"Gilbert retells the tragic story of the removal of the Cherokees from their established homes in the southeastern United States to the Indian Territory that is now Oklahoma. . . . This title would be an excellent addition to both school and public libraries with an interest in Native American or Midwest cultural history." Libr J
Includes bibliographical references

Indian nations of North America; [by] Anton Treuer ... [et al.]; foreword by Herman Viola. National Geographic 2010 384p il map $40 *
Grades: 9 10 11 12 Adult   **970.004**
1. Native Americans 2. Reference books
ISBN 978-1-4262-0664-1   LC 2010-26728
The authors "examine important historical events for Indian tribes, identify contributions made by tribal leaders, and summarize contemporary cultural activities for native cultures of North America north of the Mexican border. . . . With its extensive coverage of native tribes and outstanding graphics, this . . . title should appeal to individuals interested in Native American history, anthropology, and ethnic relations." Libr J
Includes bibliographical references

Jastrzembski, Joseph C.
The Apache wars; the final resistance. Chelsea House Publishers 2007 133p il map (Landmark events in Native American history) lib bdg $35
Grades: 7 8 9 10   **970.004**
1. Apache Indians
ISBN 978-0-7910-9343-6; 0-7910-9343-3
       LC 2007-990
"For a quarter century—1861 to 1886—the U.S. military attempted to subjugate one of the largest Indian tribes of what is today the American Southwest. . . . [This is the] tale of how . . . the Apache Indians held out longer than any other major U.S. tribe." Publisher's note
This account features "lively writing and direct quotes, and [is] enhanced by many color and black-and-white photos, drawings, and illustrations." SLJ
Includes bibliographical references

Johansen, Bruce E. (Bruce Elliott), 1950-
The Native peoples of North America; a history. Praeger 2005 2v il set $99.95 *
Grades: 11 12 Adult   **970.004**
1. Native Americans—History
ISBN 0-275-98159-2   LC 2004-28732

This is a history of "cultures indigenous to North America from their earliest origins to the present. . . . Encompassing not only traditional historical records but also oral histories and biographical sketches, these two volumes will undoubtedly become an integral part of Native American history, an increasingly popular field." Booklist
Includes bibliographical references

Johnson, Michael, 1937-
Encyclopedia of native tribes of North America; color plates by Richard Hook. 3rd ed. Firefly Books 2007 320p il map $49.95
Grades: 11 12 Adult   **970.004**
1. Native Americans—Encyclopedias 2. Reference books
ISBN 978-1-55407-307-8; 1-55407-307-3
First published 1993 in the United Kingdom with title: The native tribes of North America
"The volume is organized into ten regionally based culture areas (Northwestern Woodlands, Southeastern Woodlands, Plains and Prairie, Plateau, Great Basin, California, Southwest, Northwest Coast, Subarctic, and Arctic); each area is introduced with general information on language, subsistence, religion, culture, and history. . . . The rich illustrations and supplemental sections make this volume worthwhile." Choice
Includes bibliographical references

Keenan, Jerry
Encyclopedia of American Indian wars, 1492-1890. ABC-CLIO 1997 278p il $65
Grades: 11 12 Adult   **970.004**
1. Native Americans—Wars—Encyclopedias 2. Reference books
ISBN 0-87436-796-4   LC 97-13841
"In over 450 separate entries (people, places, battles, terms); Keenan gives . . . coverage of most of the major elements in the 400-year struggle between the native peoples of the United States and the invading immigrants." Book Rep

Nardo, Don, 1947-
The Native Americans. Lucent Bks. 2003 112p il maps (History of weapons and warfare) $27.45
Grades: 7 8 9 10   **970.004**
1. Military art and science 2. Native Americans—Wars
ISBN 1-59018-070-4   LC 2002-8589
Contents: Two very different concepts of warfare; Precontact offensive weapons; Weapons borrowed from the whites; Defensive weapons and tactics; Horses transform warfare on the plains; When Indians fought Indians; The struggle between Indians and whites; Faith as a weapon: the ghost dance
Discusses the weapons used by Native Americans and their different means of warfare.
Includes glossary and bibliographical references

Native universe; voices of Indian America; Gerald McMaster and Clifford E. Trafzer, editors. National Geographic Society 2004 320p il hardcover o.p. pa $22

Grades: 9 10 11 12   **970.004**

1. Native Americans—Social life and customs

ISBN 0-7922-5994-7; 1-4262-0335-7 (pa)

LC 2004-40221

"Published in conjunction with the fall 2004 opening of the Smithsonian's new National Museum of the American Indian, this . . . book is an overview of the diverse cultures of the American Indian. . . . The text is primarily essays, but also includes some poetry and even a scene from the screenplay, 'Smoke Signals.' The book is organized in sections that reflect the opening exhibits of the museum: Our Universes (spiritual beliefs and rituals); Our Peoples (key events in the history of Native America); and Our Lives (views of contemporary Native American life). . . . The strength of this book lies in the over 300 beautiful color illustrations, most of which are artifacts from the museum's vast collection. . . . Readers will gain much from simply browsing." Libr Media Connect

Includes bibliographical references

Philip, Neil

The great circle; a history of the First Nations; foreword by Dennis Hastings. Clarion Books 2006 153p il map $25

Grades: 7 8 9 10 11 12 Adult   **970.004**

1. Native Americans

ISBN 978-0-618-15941-3; 0-618-15941-X

LC 2005032743

"Philip takes on a huge challenge here: to present a unified narrative that explains the complex and confrontational relationships between Native Americans and white settlers. . . . He pulls it off, however, thanks to solid research, an engaging writing style, and a talent for making individual stories serve the whole. . . . Top marks, too, for the volume's photographs and historical renderings, which so intensely illustrate the pages." Booklist

Includes bibliographical references

Roberts, David, 1943-

In search of the old ones; exploring the Anasazi world of the Southwest. Simon & Schuster 1996 271p il map hardcover o.p. pa $14

Grades: 11 12 Adult   **970.004**

1. Pueblo Indians 2. Native Americans—Antiquities

ISBN 0-684-81078-6; 0-684-83212-7 (pa)

LC 95-46218

Roberts "chronicles the search for clues to the mystery of the Anasazi's abandonment of their extraordinary cliff dwellings some 700 years ago. Roberts blends accounts of his hiking adventures in the glorious canyon country of the Southwest with a chronicle of Anglos of the nineteenth century who shared his passion for studying the elusive Anasazi, especially the cowboy-archaeologist Richard Wetherell." Booklist

Includes bibliographical references

Sonneborn, Liz

Chronology of American Indian history. Updated ed. Facts on File 2007 472p il map (Facts on File library of American history) $71.50 *

Grades: 9 10 11 12   **970.004**

1. Native Americans—History

ISBN 0-8160-6770-8; 978-0-8160-6770-1

LC 2006-25396

First published 2001

This book "describes thousands of years of events that helped shape the lives and cultures of Native Americans—as well as American society as a whole—from their ancestors' arrival in North America to the present." Publisher's note

Includes bibliographical references

Vogel, Virgil J.

American Indian medicine. University of Okla. Press 1970 xx, 583p il (Civilization of the American Indian series) pa $29.95 hardcover o.p.

Grades: 11 12 Adult   **970.004**

1. Native Americans—Medicine

ISBN 0-8061-2293-5 (pa)

Covers "Indian theories of disease; early white doctors' and frontiersmen's observations in different parts of the country and among different tribes; Indians' influence on folk, fake, and patent medicine; Indian therapeutic methods in drug and drugless therapy, treatment of injuries, obstetrics, pediatrics, dentistry, diet, etc." Libr J

Includes bibliographical references

Voices from the Trail of Tears; edited by Vicki Rozema. Blair 2003 240p il maps (Real voices, real history series) pa $11.95 *

Grades: 9 10 11 12   **970.004**

1. Cherokee Indians

ISBN 0-89587-271-4   LC 2002-15299

Rozema "uses a variety of primary sources, including eyewitness accounts, to recount . . . [the Cherokees'] sad fate, climaxed by a forced march to Oklahoma during which thousands died. Missionaries write outraged letters describing the mistreatment of Cherokees by white opportunists and government officials. Ordinary soldiers charged with rousting families from their homes describe the suffering of victims. This compilation is often stunning and heartbreaking in its impact." Booklist

Includes bibliographical references

Waldman, Carl

Atlas of the North American Indian. 3rd ed. Facts on File 2009 450p il map (Facts on file library of American history) $85; pa $24.95 *

Grades: 11 12 Adult   **970.004**

1. Native Americans 2. Atlases 3. Reference books

ISBN   978-0-8160-6858-6;   0-8160-6858-5; 978-0-8160-6859-3 (pa); 0-8160-6859-3 (pa)

LC 2008-40736

First published 1985

"Chronicles the travel and experiences of Native Americans from the first voyage to North America to the present day. . . . [The] text details the history, traditions, conflicts, land cessions, and contemporary ways of life

Waldman, Carl—*Continued*
for American Indians. [This book contains] more than
140 full-color and black-and-white photographs and illustrations of the people, places, and artifacts important in
the history of Native America." Publisher's note
"This is a very well-designed book, a bargain for any
library." Voice Youth Advocates [review of 2000 edi-
tion]
Includes glossary and bibliographical references

Encyclopedia of Native American tribes. 3rd rev
ed. Facts on File 2006 xxiv, 360p il map (Facts on
File library of American history) $75; pa $21.95
Grades: 6 7 8 9 10 11 12 Adult   **970.004**
1. Native Americans—Encyclopedias 2. Reference
books
ISBN   978-0-8160-6273-7;   0-8160-6273-0;
978-0-8160-6274-4 (pa); 0-8160-6274-9 (pa)
                                   LC 2006-12529
First published 1988
This book discusses "more than 200 American Indian
tribes of North America, as well as prehistoric peoples
and civilizations. . . . [The] text summarizes the historical record—locations, migrations, contacts with non-
Indians, wars, and more—and includes present-day tribal
affairs and issues. The book also covers traditional Indian lifeways, including diet, housing, transportation, tools,
clothing, art, and rituals, as well as language families."
Publisher's note
"This well-written and easily accessible encyclopedia
of a good starting point for research on Native American
tribes." Libr Media Connect
Includes bibliographical references

Wright, Ronald
Stolen continents; the Americas through Indian
eyes since 1492. Houghton Mifflin 1992 424p il
maps hardcover o.p. pa $17 *
Grades: 11 12 Adult   **970.004**
1. Native Americans 2. America—Exploration
ISBN 0-395-56500-6; 0-618-49240-2 (pa)
                                   LC 91-36202
"A Peter Davison book"
The author "views the past 500 years from the native
American perspective by drawing on long-neglected post-
Columbian documents. Maintaining a five-track narrative,
he follows the history of the distinct groups that survived
the European invasion: the Aztecs of Mexico, the Maya
of Guatemala and Yucatan, the Incas of Peru, and the
Cherokees and Iroquois of North America. . . . Compel-
ling, important, and well told." Booklist
Includes bibliographical references

Zimmerman, Larry J., 1947-
Exploring the life, myth, and art of Native
Americans. Rosen Pub. 2009 c2010 144p il map
(Civilizations of the world) lib bdg $29.95
Grades: 7 8 9 10 11 12   **970.004**
1. Native Americans—Religion 2. Native Americans—
Art
ISBN 978-1-4358-5614-1; 1-4358-5614-7
                                   LC 2009-9268

This book describes the cultures, myths, and art of
Native Americans.
"This beautifully illustrated and well-written [title]
. . . is perfect for those assignments where students must
look at the culture of a civilization. Artwork and pictures
blend seamlessly with the information and the reader is
taken on a journey of discovery. Myths are used as the
story of how the people view themselves, blended with
the discussion of the reality of life. Everyday life is tied
to the belief systems and is explained in light of those
beliefs. The pictures are beautifully done and there is almost as much information in the captions as there is in
the text." Libr Media Connect
Includes glossary and bibliographical references

970.01 North America—Early history to 1599

America in 1492; the world of the Indian peoples
before the arrival of Columbus; edited and with
an introduction by Alvin Josephy, Jr.; developed
by Frederick E. Hoxie. Knopf 1992 477p il
maps hardcover o.p. pa $20
Grades: 11 12 Adult   **970.01**
1. Native Americans—History 2. Native Americans—
Antiquities 3. America—Exploration 4. America—Antiquities
ISBN 0-394-56438-3; 0-679-74337-5 (pa)
                                   LC 90-26222
These essays depict "the diverse lives of the approximately 75 million people living in the Americas around
the turn of the fifteenth century. Geography guides the
first section. . . . Another section focuses on languages,
spiritual beliefs and customs, art, and 'systems of knowledge.'" Booklist
Includes bibliographical references

Mann, Charles C.
1491; new revelations of the Americas before
Columbus. Knopf 2005 465p il maps $30; pa
$14.95
Grades: 11 12 Adult   **970.01**
1. Native Americans—History 2. America—Antiquities
ISBN 1-4000-4006-X; 1-4000-3205-9 (pa)
                                   LC 2005-42178
The author "demonstrates that long before any European explorers set foot in the New World, Native American cultures were flourishing with a high degree of sophistication." Publ Wkly
"Mann navigates adroitly through the controversies.
He approaches each in the best scientific tradition, carefully sifting the evidence, never jumping to hasty conclusions, giving everyone a fair hearing—the experts and
the amateurs; the accounts of the Indians and their con-
querors. And rarely is he less than enthralling." N Y
Times Book Rev
Includes bibliographical references

Vikings: the North Atlantic saga; edited by William W. Fitzhugh and Elisabeth I. Ward. Smithsonian Institution Press 2000 432p il maps hardcover o.p. pa $34.95 *

Grades: 11 12 Adult   970.01

1. Vikings 2. America—Exploration

ISBN 1-56098-970-X; 1-56098-995-5 (pa)

LC 99-57983

Catalog of an exhibition at the National Museum of Natural History, Smithsonian Institution, Washington, D.C., April 29, 2000-September 5, 2000

"While the book concentrates on the New World, there are also chapters on the Vikings in Iceland, Greenland, and France and along the coasts of Britain and the rivers of Russia. The contributors discuss the Viking saga from the perspectives of natural science, archaeology, history, oral tradition, and early writings." Libr J

This book is "well designed, heavily illustrated and almost encyclopedic in scope and detail." Publ Wkly

Includes bibliographical references

971 Canada

Garrington, Sally, 1953-

Canada. Facts on File 2005 61p il map (Countries of the world) lib bdg $30 *

Grades: 7 8 9 10   971

1. Canada

ISBN 0-8160-6009-6   LC 2005040676

This describes Canada's "culture, history, geography, government, and economy. [It is] competently written and [contains] current information." SLJ

Riendeau, Roger E., 1950-

A brief history of Canada; [by] Roger Riendeau. 2nd ed. Facts on File 2007 444p il map (Brief history) $45 *

Grades: 11 12 Adult   971

1. Canada—History

ISBN 978-0-8160-6335-2   LC 2006-47130

First published 2000

This is a history of Canada "beginning with the exploration of the Northern American frontier and continuing through the rise and fall of the French and British empires to the foundations of Canadian nationhood and the present day." Publisher's note

Includes bibliographical references

972 Middle America. Mexico

Aguilar-Moreno, Manuel

Handbook to life in the Aztec world. Facts on File 2006 xxiii, 440p il (Facts on file library of world history) $70

Grades: 11 12 Adult   972

1. Aztecs

ISBN 978-0-8160-5673-6; 0-8160-5673-0

This book includes "coverage of Aztec history, geography, foods, trades, arts, games, wars, political systems,

class structure, religious practices, trading networks, writings, architecture, science, and more." Publisher's note

Includes bibliographical references

Foster, Lynn V.

A brief history of Mexico. 4th ed. Facts On File 2009 324p il map (Brief history) $49.50; pa $19.95 *

Grades: 9 10 11 12 Adult   972

1. Mexico—History

ISBN 978-0-8160-7405-1; 978-0-8160-7406-8 (pa)

LC 2009-18298

First published 1997

An overview of Mexican history covering pre-Columbian civilizations and contemporary indigenous cultures. Language, art, religion, politics and economics are discussed. A chronology and bibliography are included.

Includes bibliographical references

Guillermoprieto, Alma, 1949-

Looking for history; dispatches from Latin America. Pantheon Bks. 2001 303p il hardcover o.p. pa $13.95

Grades: 11 12 Adult   972

1. Mexico—Politics and government 2. Cuba—Politics and government 3. Colombia—Politics and government

ISBN 0-375-42094-0; 0-375-72582-2 (pa)

LC 00-62382

The author discusses conditions in Latin America, focusing particularly on Mexico, Colombia, and Cuba. "The essays . . . have been adapted from work which first appeared in the New Yorker and the New York Review of Books." Economist

"Among the stories, book reviews, and descriptions are perceptive and insightful observations of Latin American politics and society that help illuminate this important part of the world. This volume will be of interest to Latin American collections as well as current affairs libraries." Libr J

Kirkwood, Burton

The history of Mexico. 2nd ed. Greenwood Press/ABC-CLIO 2010 258p il map (Greenwood histories of the modern nations) $49.95

Grades: 11 12 Adult   972

1. Mexico—History

ISBN 978-0-313-36601-7; 0-313-36601-2

LC 2009036964

First published 2000

A historical survey of Mexico and its people from the arrival of the first humans in the Western Hemisphere to the first decade of the 21st century. Topics range from Mexico's cultural past to more current issues such as the war on drugs and the North American Free Trade Agreement.

Includes bibliographical references

The **Oxford** encyclopedia of Mesoamerican cultures; the civilizations of Mexico and Central America; David Carrasco, editor in chief. Oxford Univ. Press 2000 3v set $395
Grades: 11 12 Adult   **972**
1. Reference books 2. Native Americans—Mexico—Encyclopedias
ISBN 0-19-510815-9   LC 00-32624
This encyclopedia includes parts of Mexico, Honduras, Nicaragua, and Costa Rica, as well as Guatemala, Belize, and El Salvador. Beginning with the Olmecs, coverage extends through the twentieth century. Essays discuss issues related to economic, social, religious, and political organization; practices and beliefs; and artistic expression, as well as the cultures, people, and sites of these regions
"This superb work should grace collections in art, archaeolgy, religious studies, anthropology, Native American studies, and Latin American history." Libr J
Includes bibliographical references

Smith, Michael Ernest, 1953-
The Aztecs; [by] Michael E. Smith. 2nd ed. Blackwell 2003 c2002 367p il maps (Peoples of America) hardcover o.p. pa $29.95
Grades: 11 12 Adult   **972**
1. Aztecs 2. Mexico—Antiquities
ISBN 0-631-23015-7; 0-631-23016-5 (pa)
                                          LC 2001-6950
First published 1996
The author "summarizes the results of archaeological research conducted largely in the past 30 years into the everyday lives of ordinary people in the villages, hamlets, and farmsteads from many regions of central Mexico. His method permits a fresh view of such topics as agricultural methods, population size, market system, relations between city-states and the empire, and even human sacrifice. Smith carries his social account of these people through transformation under Spanish rule and their legacy in modern Mexico." Libr J [review of 1996 edition]
Includes bibliographical references

Stein, R. Conrad, 1937-
The Mexican Revolution. Morgan Reynolds Pub. 2008 160p il map (The story of Mexico) lib bdg $27.95
Grades: 6 7 8 9 10   **972**
1. Mexico—History
ISBN 978-1-59935-051-6; 1-59935-051-3
                                          LC 2007-22136
"Opening with Porfirio Díaz's presidency (beginning in 1876), [this book] explains how Indian land was expropriated and allotted to rich hacienda owners, describes resistance movements led by Emiliano Zapata and Pancho Villa, and details 10 years of political upheaval and violent uprisings (1910-1920), ending with Alvaro Obregó's election as president of Mexico. . . . [The book has] a lively narrative style. . . . Pertinent illustrations, including photographs, historical paintings, and maps are sprinkled throughout. . . . Well-written and well-researched." SLJ
Includes bibliographical references

Townsend, Richard F.
The Aztecs. 3rd ed. Thames & Hudson 2009 256p il map (Ancient peoples and places) pa $24.95 *
Grades: 11 12 Adult   **972**
1. Aztecs
ISBN 978-0-500-28791-0   LC 2008-908216
First published 1992
"Examines the history of these accomplished people through a review of the monuments and artifacts they left behind; exploring how their water-control projects worked, the purposes of their ceremonial centers, and the way they built their incredible ancient structures that still stand today." Publisher's note
Includes bibliographical references

972.08   Mexico since 1867

Coerver, Don M., 1943-
Mexico: an encyclopedia of contemporary culture and history; [by] Don M. Coerver, Suzanne B. Pasztor, and Robert M. Buffington. ABC-CLIO 2004 xxiv, 621p il map $85 *
Grades: 9 10 11 12   **972.08**
1. Mexico—Civilization
ISBN 1-576-07132-4   LC 2004-14738
An "overview of 20th- and 21st-century Mexico, this volume explores the political, economic, social, and cultural history of the world's largest Spanish-speaking country." Publisher's note
"The book would probably be best for undergraduates taking a survey course on Mexico or Latin America or high-school students taking similar courses." Booklist
Includes bibliographical references

972.8   Central America

Foster, Lynn V.
A brief history of Central America. 2nd ed. Facts on File 2007 338p il map (Brief history) $45 *
Grades: 9 10 11 12   **972.8**
1. Central America—History
ISBN 978-0-8160-6671-1; 0-8160-6671-X
                                          LC 2006-49760
First published 2000
This book "explores the history of the Central American isthmus from the pre-Columbian cultures to the contemporary nations that make up the region today: Belize, Costa Rica, El Salvador, Guatemala, Honduras, Nicaragua, and Panama." Publisher's note
Includes bibliographical references

972.81 Guatemala

Sharer, Robert J.
Daily life in Maya civilization. 2nd ed. Greenwood Press 2009 280p il map (Greenwood Press "Daily life through history" series) $49.95
Grades: 9 10 11 12   **972.81**
1. Mayas
ISBN 978-0-313-35129-7   LC 2009-194
Also available online
First published 1996
"The book's 13 chapters move through the Maya civilization's 13,000-year social, economic, and cultural development. Also offered is a thought-provoking consideration of Maya civilization and the lessons it can impart to contemporary Western society. An absorbing read." Libr J
Includes bibliographical references

972.85 Nicaragua

Kallen, Stuart A., 1955-
The aftermath of the Sandinista Revolution. Twenty-First Century Books 2009 160p il (Aftermath of history) lib bdg $38.60
Grades: 8 9 10 11 12   **972.85**
1. Nicaragua—Politics and government
ISBN 978-0-8225-9091-0; 0-8225-9091-3
LC 2008-25356
"The 1979 overthrow of the corrupt Nicaraguan government by the Marxist Sandinistas brought change to one of the poorest countries in the Americas and instilled in the U.S. new fears about the spread of Communism. . . . Kallen offers a good overview of one of the Latin American theaters of the Cold War." SLJ
Includes glossary and bibliographical references

972.9 West Indies (Antilles) and Bermuda

Figueredo, Danilo H., 1951-
A brief history of the Caribbean; [by] D. H. Figueredo, Frank Argote-Freyre. Facts on File 2008 xxv, 310p il map (Brief history) $45 *
Grades: 9 10 11 12   **972.9**
1. West Indies—History
ISBN 978-0-8160-7021-3; 0-8160-7021-0
LC 2007-8202
First published 1991
Contents: Pre-Columbian inhabitants; Two worlds in collision: The Spanish Conquest (1492-1552); European challenges to Spanish rule (1500-1850); Industry and slavery (1500-1850); Revolutions in America, France, and Haiti (c. 1700-1850); Slave rebellions, antislavery movements, and wars of independence (c. 1700-1850); Puerto Rico, Cuba, and the Spanish-Cuban-American War (1850-1900); Cuba: dictatorship and revolution (1900-2007); Fragmentation and occupation: Haiti and the Dominican Republic (1900-2000); Commonwealth,

federation, and autonomy: Puerto Rico, Martinique, Guadeloupe, and the Dutch Caribbean (1900-2000); Jamaica, Trinidad, and Grenada: uncertain glory (1900-2000); The 21st century: immigration and uncertainties
This "is an overview of the historical events that have taken place and shaped the islands of the Caribbean Sea." Publisher's note
Includes bibliographical references

972.91 Cuba

Castro's Cuba; Charles W. Carey Jr., book editor. Greenhaven Press 2004 205p il (History firsthand) $37.95; pa $23.70
Grades: 8 9 10 11 12   **972.91**
1. Castro, Fidel, 1926- 2. Cuba—Politics and government
ISBN 0-7377-1654-1; 0-7377-1655-X (pa)
LC 2003-47286
"Through the use of interviews, articles, and first-person narratives, this book focuses on the significance of the 1959 revolution and its aftermath. An extensive introduction explaining events precipitating the rise of Fidel Castro, the revolution, and the current situation in Cuba provides readers with a necessary overview to understand the succeeding chapters." SLJ
Includes bibliographical references

Encyclopedia of Cuba; people, history, culture; edited by Luis Martinez-Fernández [et al.] Greenwood Press 2003 2v il maps set $174.95
Grades: 11 12 Adult   **972.91**
1. Reference books 2. Cuba—Encyclopedias
ISBN 1-57356-334-X   LC 2002-70030
"An Oryx book"
"The editors intend this work to be a non-politicized look at Cuban people, politics, history, and culture. Chapters cover topics such as history, government, and popular culture. Within each chapter, entries are in alphabetical order. An excellent introduction to a colorful and important nation." Booklist
Includes bibliographical references

Markel, Rita J.
Fidel Castro's Cuba. Twenty-First Century Books 2008 160p il map (Dictatorships) lib bdg $38.60
Grades: 7 8 9 10   **972.91**
1. Castro, Fidel, 1926- 2. Cuba—History—1959-
ISBN 978-0-8225-7284-8; 0-8225-7284-2
LC 2007-1067
"Markel presents a compelling study of this complex man from his privileged childhood as the son of a wealthy farmer to his position as the controversial dictator of Cuba." Voice Youth Advocates
Includes glossary and bibliographical references

Staten, Clifford L.
The history of Cuba. Greenwood Press 2003 162p map (Greenwood histories of the modern nations) $45
Grades: 9 10 11 12   **972.91**
1. Cuba—History
ISBN 0-313-31690-2   LC 2002-35334

Staten, Clifford L.—*Continued*

Also available in paperback from Palgrave Macmillan

The author presents an overview of Cuba's "history from its early settlement by Taino Indians in 1250. Coverage includes its discovery by Christopher Columbus in 1492 and subsequent colonization by Spain; the wars of independence and intervention by the United States in the early twentieth century; the rise and fall of Fulgencio Batista; and Fidel Castro's Marxist revolution in 1959 and its ties to the Soviet Union. More recent events discussed are the various economic reforms and the aftereffects of the end of the Cold War and the collapse of the Soviet Union. The book concludes with an analytical look at the current situation in Cuba, and offers educated conjectures as to what the future might hold for this troubled nation." Voice Youth Advocates

Includes bibliographical references

972.95   Puerto Rico

Fernandez, Ronald

Puerto Rico past and present; an encyclopedia; [by] Ronald Fernandez, Serafín Méndez Méndez, Gail Cueto. Greenwood Press 1998 xxxii, 375p il $59.95

Grades: 11 12 Adult   **972.95**

1. Puerto Rico—Encyclopedias 2. Reference books

ISBN 0-313-29822-X   LC 97-1689

"Along with biographical entries, included are colloquial and political terms and groups, court decisions, buildings, and other items of Puerto Rican cultural and historical developments. Each entry is approximately one page." Voice Youth Advocates

Includes bibliographical references

Worth, Richard, 1945-

Puerto Rico in American history. Enslow Publishers 2008 128p il map (From many cultures, one history) lib bdg $23.95

Grades: 6 7 8 9 10   **972.95**

1. Puerto Rico

ISBN 978-0-7660-2836-4; 0-7660-2836-4

LC 2006-37087

This is a "book about the ties between Puerto Rico and the U.S. . . . Worth's overview will help to acclimate readers new to the island's history. . . . Writing in short, plain sentences, the author touches upon the commonwealth's ongoing struggle with poverty, migration, and language and the current conflicts about statehood and independence. The book's clean design is inviting, with lots of color-screened boxes, full-color photos, archival artwork, and maps." Booklist

Includes glossary and bibliographical references

973   United States

100 key documents in American democracy; edited by Peter B. Levy; foreword by William E. Leuchtenburg. Greenwood Press 1994 502p il $59.95; pa $42.95 *

Grades: 11 12 Adult   **973**

1. United States—History—Sources

ISBN 0-313-28424-5; 0-275-96525-2 (pa)

LC 93-1137

"The work is arranged chronologically within sections, such as 'The Early Republic' and 'The Progressive Era.' Beginning with Powhatan's call for peace in his 1609 'Letter to John Smith' and concluding with Jesse Jackson's moving speech at the 1988 Democratic National Convention. . . . Each piece is prefaced by a short chronology that sets the historical context and a commentary on the document that often refers to other writings in the book. Shorter documents are reprinted in their entirety, while longer ones have been edited." Booklist

America in world history; general editor, Susan Crean; consulting editor, Tom Lansford. M.E. Sharpe 2010 4v il map set $299

Grades: 9 10 11 12 Adult   **973**

1. United States—History 2. World history 3. Reference books

ISBN 978-0-7656-8171-3   LC 2009-15865

"This resource introduces the ebb and flow of American history within the context of world affairs. . . . Each volume centers on a specific theme and time period (e.g., 'America as World Frontier: First Encounters to 1776'), and the themes within each volume are subdivided into subjects that further emphasize a United States as interconnected with world history." Libr J

"The appealing, accessible format and the in-depth treatment of American history make this a good choice for school and public libraries." SLJ

Includes bibliographical references

American eras. Gale Res. 1997-1998 8v il set $1235

Grades: 11 12 Adult   **973**

1. United States—Civilization 2. United States—History 3. Reference books

ISBN 0-7876-1477-7

Also available separately for $168

This reference set "provides information on U.S. history, including social history, prior to the twentieth century. Each era-specific volume includes an introductory essay describing the time period to provide context and an overview, 150 illustrations, an index of photographs, a bibliography, a subject index and a list of contributors." Publisher's note

The **American** presidency; edited by Alan Brinkley and Davis Dyer. Houghton Mifflin Co 2004 572p il pa $19.95

Grades: 11 12 Adult   **973**

1. Presidents—United States 2. United States—Politics and government

ISBN 0-618-38273-9   LC 2003-62513

An updated version of The reader's companion to the American presidency (2000)

The American presidency—*Continued*

This work assesses "how presidents shape and define culture and society and, at the same time, reflect them. . . . {This} can serve as a beginning point for research and should engage casual readers as well as students of the American presidency." Choice

Includes bibliographical references

Americans at war; society, culture, and the homefront; John P. Resch, Editor in Chief. Macmillan Reference USA 2005 4v il set $395
  Grades: 11 12 Adult   973
  1. War and civilization 2. United States—Military history 3. United States—Civilization
  ISBN 0-02-865806-X   LC 2004-17314
  Contents: v1 1500-1815; v2 1816-1900; v3 1901-1945; v4 1946-present
  This book "delivers well-written articles and would make an excellent addition to high-school, academic, and public libraries." Booklist
  Includes bibliographical references

Anzovin, Steven, 1954-
  Famous first facts about American politics; [by] Steven Anzovin & Janet Podell. Wilson, H.W. 2001 756p $180 *
  Grades: 11 12 Adult   973
  1. United States—Politics and government 2. United States—History
  ISBN 0-8242-0971-0   LC 00-49960
  This offers over 5,000 entries of firsts in national, state, and local U.S. politics from the founding of the nation through the 2000 election and includes five indexes: subject, name, year, day, and place.
  Includes bibliographical references

Basic documents in American history; [edited by] Richard B. Morris. Krieger 1980 c1965 193p pa $13.50
  Grades: 9 10 11 12   973
  1. United States—History—Sources
  ISBN 0-89874-202-1   LC 80-12822
  First published 1956. This is a reprint of the edition published 1965 by Van Nostrand
  "A collection of documents, with brief analysis and evaluation for each selection, covering from 1620 to the 1960s." Wynar. Guide to Ref Books for Sch Media Cent. 3d edition

Eyewitness to America; 500 years of America in the words of those who saw it happen; edited by David Colbert. Pantheon Bks. 1997 xxx, 599p hardcover o.p. pa $16.95
  Grades: 11 12 Adult   973
  1. United States—History—Sources
  ISBN 0-679-44224-3; 0-679-76724-X (pa)
                                   LC 96-24150
  This volume contains a "panorama of first-person accounts of moments in the country's story that stretch from an October 10, 1492, diary entry by one of Columbus's crewmen to a 1994 e-mail message from Bill Gates. The nearly 300 entries tend to be short, preceded by informative introductions. The result is a feeling for history that is both immediate and dramatic." Publ Wkly
  Includes bibliographical references

Keegan, John, 1934-
  Fields of battle; the wars for North America. Knopf 1996 c1995 348p il maps hardcover o.p. pa $15
  Grades: 11 12 Adult   973
  1. North America—Military history
  ISBN 0-679-42413-X; 0-679-74664-1 (pa)
                                   LC 96-154385
  First published 1995 in the United Kingdom with title: Warpaths: travels of a military historian in North America
  The author "demonstrates how North America's geography has influenced its history: how its mountain chains and river systems have determined where people fought, and fought repeatedly. For example, the defenses that Cornwallis built at Yorktown to deter American forces were improved and reused by the Confederates almost a century later. Keegan's tour of the continent skips the Mexican War, and his book is atypically discursive. For Americans, the charm is the familiarity of its sites—Brooklyn, Pittsburgh, Laramie, and other home towns." New Yorker

Lubar, Steven D.
  Legacies; collecting America's history at the Smithsonian; [by] Steven Lubar and Kathleen M. Kendrick. Smithsonian Institution Press 2001 256p il $39.95
  Grades: 9 10 11 12   973
  1. National Museum of American History (U.S.) 2. United States—Civilization
  ISBN 1-56098-886-X   LC 2001-20399
  An illustrated look at more than 200 representative objects from the Smithsonian's collection. "The eclectic collage of artifacts ranges from the curious (an 1860s phrenology model used to decipher personality and behavior) to the provocative (the uniform of a WWI woman contract-surgeon). Elegant acquisitions, such as first ladies' inaugural gowns, are preserved along with the mundane (the Veg-O-Matic) and popular culture (Archie and Edith Bunkers' chairs), as well as scientific and technological advances. In every case, stories are the key elements that transform each specimen into a legacy worth preserving." Publ Wkly
  Includes bibliographical references

Milestone documents in American history; exploring the primary sources that shaped America; Paul Finkelman, editor in chief; Bruce A. Lesh, consulting editor. Schlager Group 2008 4v il (Milestone documents) set $385
  Grades: 9 10 11 12 Adult   973
  1. United States—History—Sources 2. Reference books
  ISBN 978-0-9797758-0-2; 0-9797758-0-9
  Also available online
  "This exceptional work will be essential to students needing assistance interpreting primary sources, and teachers will find it invaluable for incorporating those resources into their curriculums. The entries . . . examine 133 chronologically arranged documents beginning with the British crown's Proclamation Act of 1763 and ending with the 2003 Supreme Court decision *Lawrence v. Texas*." SLJ
  Includes bibliographical references

Milestone documents of American leaders; exploring the primary sources of notable Americans; Paul Finkelman, editor in chief; James A. Percoco, consulting editor. Schlager Group 2009 4v il (Milestone documents) set $385

Grades: 10 11 12 Adult   973
1. United States—History—Sources
ISBN 978-0-9797758-5-7
Also available online

This collection offers "transcribed primary documents and analysis covering the works of many prominent Americans. . . . The transcribed text of each document includes a concise overview of the life and career of the document's creator(s) written by experts on the chosen author or topic. Also included . . . is a time line indicating where these documents fit into the author's life/career, resources to help facilitate discussion about the author and documents, and additional primary and secondary resources on the author and topics covered." Choice

Opposing viewpoints in American history; William Dudley, volume editor; John C. Chalberg, consulting editor. Greenhaven Press 2007 2v v1 $59.95; v1 pa $39.95; v2 $59.95; v2 pa $39.95 *

Grades: 9 10 11 12   973
1. United States—History—Sources
ISBN 0-7377-3184-2 (v1); 978-0-7377-3184-2 (v1); 0-7377-3185-0 (v1 pa); 978-0-7377-3185-9 (v1 pa); 0737731869 (v2); 978-0-7377-3186-6 (v2); 0-7377-3187-7 (v2 pa); 978-0-7377-3187-3 (v2 pa)
                                    LC 2006-24673
First published 1996
Contents: v1 From colonial times to Reconstruction; v2 From Reconstruction to the present

"Topics range chronologically from 'Origins of English Settlement' to 'National Security, Terrorism, and Iraq.' Essays, speeches, and letters by such notables as Elizabeth Cady Stanton, Malcolm X, and Bill Clinton provide historical context for the debates. Articles are clustered under prefaced general categories, such as 'The Gilded Age,' 'Antebellum America,' and 'New Challenges after the Cold War.'" SLJ
Includes bibliographical references

Panchyk, Richard, 1970-
The keys to American history; understanding our most important historic documents. Chicago Review Press 2009 c2008 241p il map $24.95; pa $19.95 *

Grades: 7 8 9 10 11 12   973
1. United States—History—Sources
ISBN   978-1-55652-716-6;   1-55652-716-0; 978-1-55652-804-0 (pa); 1-55652-804-3 (pa)

"From the 1606 Great Patent of James I to the 2002 Joint Resolution to Authorize the Use of United States Armed Forces in Iraq, each document is presented in context with a concise introductory comment, appearing both as facsimile reproduction and typescript, and followed by 'What They Were Saying' (excerpts from primary sources that provide perspectives on those documents from major players and other contemporaries)." Kirkus

"This impressive collection is a valuable resource for gaining a greater appreciation for and understanding of our nation's dynamic history." SLJ
Includes bibliographical references

Savage, William W.
The cowboy hero; his image in American history & culture; by William W. Savage, Jr. University of Okla. Press 1979 179p il hardcover o.p. pa $19.95

Grades: 9 10 11 12   973
1. Cowhands
ISBN 0-8061-1587-4; 0-8061-1920-9 (pa)
                                    LC 79-4730
The author's "research extends into all facets of Western history with emphasis on the popular glorification of the cowboy in books, movies, radio, and television. . . . Savage . . . appears to have a real affection for his subject." Libr J
Includes bibliographical references

United States. National Archives and Records Administration
Our documents; 100 milestone documents from the National Archives. Oxford University Press 2003 256p il $40; pa $24.95

Grades: 9 10 11 12   973
1. United States—History—Sources
ISBN 0-19-517206-X; 0-19-530959-6 (pa)
                                    LC 2003-15080
A collection of one hundred documents that were important in the development of the United States from its founding to 1965, including the Declaration of Independence, Constitution, and lesser-known writings.

"Photographs and facsimile reproductions of documents are a highlight of the book—they let readers see the actual items. The appealing, clean layout is defined by clear blue and red headings and plenty of white space. A useful addition." SLJ
Includes bibliographical references

Wilkins, Roger W., 1932-
Jefferson's pillow; the founding fathers and the dilemma of Black patriotism; [by] Roger Wilkins. Beacon Press 2001 163p hardcover o.p. pa $14 *
Grades: 11 12 Adult   973
1. Mason, George, 1725-1792 2. Washington, George, 1732-1799 3. Jefferson, Thomas, 1743-1826 4. Madison, James, 1751-1836 5. United States—History 6. United States—Race relations
ISBN 0-8070-0956-3; 0-8070-0957-1 (pa)
                                    LC 2001-25117
"Wilkins returns to America's beginnings and the lives of the founding fathers to explore how . . . race and slavery still impede our progress. In . . . [an] analysis of the lives of George Washington, George Mason, James Madison, and . . . Thomas Jefferson, he explores how class, education, and personality allowed for the institution of slavery in a nation conceived under the premise that all men are created equal." Publisher's note

Wilkins, Roger W., 1932-—*Continued*

"This is an important look at the essential and ongoing contradictions at the heart of American ideals of liberty and patriotism." Booklist

Includes bibliographical references

973.03 United States—History— Encyclopedias and dictionaries

Conflicts in American history; a documentary encyclopedia. Facts on File 2010 8v il map (Facts on File library of American history) set $720 *

Grades: 9 10 11 12   **973.03**
  1. United States—History—Encyclopedias
  2. Reference books
  ISBN 978-0-8160-7093-0; 978-1-4381-3485-7 (ebook)
                                                          LC 2009-47715

"A Bruccoli Clark Layman book"

Each volume has a different editor

Contents: v1 The colonial and revolutionary eras, 1492-1783; v2 The early republic era, 1783-1860; v3 The Civil War era, 1861-1865; v4 The Reconstruction era, 1865-1877; v5 The Gilded Age, Progressive era and World War I, 1877-1920; v6 The roaring twenties, Great Depression, and World War II, 1920-1945; v7 The postwar and civil rights era, 1945-1973; v8 Toward the twenty-first century, 1974-present

"Each volume covers a distinct period from 1492 to the present and addresses a broad range of topics encompassing critical social, economic, political, religious, and military conflicts. An introduction to the era and an annotated chronology begin each volume, followed by articles and a dozen or so documents. . . . The scope, variety, and quality of these primary and secondary resources make this a superior addition." SLJ

Includes bibliographical references

Cornelison, Pam

The great American history fact-finder; the who, what, where, when, and why of American history; [by] Pam Cornelison and Ted Yanak. 2nd ed, updated and expanded. Houghton Mifflin 2004 608p il, maps pa $14.95

Grades: 11 12 Adult   **973.03**
  1. United States—History—Dictionaries 2. Reference books
  ISBN 0-618-43941-2   LC 2004-47480

First published 1993 with authors' names in reverse order

This book provides "information about significant persons as well as political, legal, sporting, and cultural events in American history. Entries are alphabetically arranged, and related entries cross-referenced. . . . Besides an index, there are suggested readings and information on the states, presidents, vice presidents, population, Supreme Court, Articles of Confederation, Declaration of Independence, and US Constitution (with signers and nonsigners). This is a good quick reference." Choice

Encyclopedia of American historical documents; edited by Susan Rosenfeld. Facts on File 2004 3v (Facts on File library of American history) set $300 *

Grades: 11 12 Adult   **973.03**
  1. United States—History—Sources
  ISBN 0-8160-4995-5   LC 2003-51610

"Each section begins with an overview of the period and each document is introduced with commentary on when and why it was created and its significance, then and now. Entries include material 'with resonance for the 21st century' that represents turning points in U.S. history, and documents of a controversial nature. Students can read Supreme Court justices' opinions, presidential announcements and inaugural addresses, excerpts from noteworthy books that influenced American thought and action, and speeches of women and people of color. . . . Students and teachers will welcome this mammoth resource." SLJ

Includes bibliographical references

Encyclopedia of American history; Gary B. Nash, general editor. Rev. ed. Facts on File 2010 11v il map (Facts on File library of American history) set $1,150 *

Grades: 11 12 Adult   **973.03**
  1. United States—History—Encyclopedias
  2. Reference books
  ISBN 978-0-8160-7136-4   LC 2008-35422

First published 2003

Contents: v1 Three worlds meet, beginnings to 1607; v2 Colonization and settlement, 1608-1760; v3 Revolution and new nation, 1761-1812; v4 Expansion and reform, 1813-1855; v5 Civil War and reconstruction, 1856-1869; v6 The development of the industrial United States, 1870-1899; v7 The emergence of modern America, 1900-1928; v8 The Great Depression and World War II, 1929-1945; v9 Postwar United States, 1946-1968; v10 Contemporary United States, 1969 to the present; v11 Comprehensive index

This encyclopedia provides a "presentation of the political, social, economic, and cultural events that have shaped the land and the nation." Publisher's note

Includes bibliographical references

Encyclopedia of the new American nation; the emergence of the United States, 1754-1829; Paul Finkelman, editor in chief. Thomson Gale 2005 3v il map set $395

Grades: 11 12 Adult   **973.03**
  1. Reference books 2. United States—History—1600-1775, Colonial period—Encyclopedias 3. United States—History—1775-1783, Revolution—Encyclopedias 4. United States—History—1783-1865—Encyclopedias
  ISBN 0-684-31346-4   LC 2005-17783

The timeframe covered in this encyclopedia of major political events and figures "is roughly from 1754 (beginning of the Seven Years' War) to the inauguration of President Andrew Jackson (1829). Woven among this set of political markers and milestones are entries outlining the cultural development of the new nation, including entries on art, music, literature, dress and daily life." Publisher's note

The editor and contributors "have produced a wonder-

Encyclopedia of the new American nation—
Continued
ful reference source." Ref & User Services Quarterly
Includes bibliographical references

Encyclopedia of U.S. political history. CQ Press
2009 7v il map set $1200
  Grades: 10 11 12 Adult   **973.03**
  1. United States—Politics and government—Encyclopedias 2. Political science—Encyclopedias
3. Reference books
  ISBN 978-0-87289-320-7   LC 2010-2253
  Also available online
  Contents: v1 Colonial beginnings through Revolution,
1500 to 1783 / editor, Andrew W. Robertson; v2 The
early republic, 1784 to 1840 / editor, Michael A. Morrison; v3 Expansion, division, and Reconstruction, 1841 to
1877 / editor, William G. Shade; v4 From the gilded age
through age of reform, 1878 to 1920 / editor, Robert D.
Johnston; v5 Prosperity, Depression, and war, 1921 to
1945 / editor, Robert H. Zieger; v6 Postwar consensus to
social unrest, 1946 to 1975 / editor, Thomas S. Langston;
v7 The clash of conservatism and liberalism, 1976 to
present / editor, Richard M. Valelly
  "An impressive work remarkable for its breath and
scope, this encyclopedia covers U.S. political history
chronologically from the year 1500 to the present day.
. . . Written in a vivid and accessible yet scholarly manner, this wonderful synthesis of history and political science will greatly benefit students, lovers of political history, and academics alike." Libr J
  Includes bibliographical references

Encyclopedia of women and American politics;
[edited by] Lynne E. Ford. Facts On File 2008
636p il (Facts on File library of American
history) $85
  Grades: 9 10 11 12   **973.03**
  1. Reference books 2. Women in politics—United
States—Encyclopedias 3. United States—Politics and
government—Encyclopedias
  ISBN 978-0-8160-5491-6   LC 2007-4331
  This "A-to-Z volume contains more than 500 entries
covering the people, events, and terms involved in the
history of women and politics. . . . [This] encyclopedia
also provides a biography for every woman who has
served in the U.S. House of Representatives, the Senate,
and the Supreme Court." Publisher's note
  Includes bibliographical references

Gale encyclopedia of U.S. history: government
and politics. Gale 2008 2v il set $220
  Grades: 9 10 11 12   **973.03**
  1. Reference books 2. United States—Politics and
government—Encyclopedias
  ISBN 978-1-4144-3118-5; 1-4144-3118-X
                            LC 2007-34360
  "The 11 chapters in *Government* cover the period between the 15th century and today. Chapters detail 'How
They Were Governed,' discussing such entries as Jamestown and Ellis Island; biographies of key political figures; political parties and key issues; events and social
movements that influenced American politics; and legislation and court cases that had a role in the formation of
the government." SLJ
  Includes bibliographical references

The **Greenwood** encyclopedia of American
regional cultures; William Ferris, consulting
editor. Greenwood Press 2004 8v il map set
$699.95
  Grades: 11 12 Adult   **973.03**
  1. Reference books 2. United States—Social life and
customs—Encyclopedias 3. United States—Civilization—Encyclopedias
  ISBN 0-313-33266-5
  This "set explores the history and culture of U.S. regions from the Atlantic to the Pacific. The essay-long articles examine at length each region's art, ethnicity, fashion, film, folklore, food, literature, religion, sports, and
more." Libr J
  Includes bibliographical references

The **Oxford** companion to United States history;
editor in chief, Paul S. Boyer; editors, Melvyn
Dubofsky {et al.}. Oxford Univ. Press 2001
xliv, 940p il maps $75 *
  Grades: 11 12 Adult   **973.03**
  1. Reference books 2. United States—History—Dictionaries
  ISBN 0-19-508209-5   LC 00-55801
  First published 1966 under the authorship of Thomas
A. Johnson with title: The Oxford companion to American history
  This reference work contains 1,400 alphabetically arranged signed entries. See and see also references are
provided. Coverage starts with the colonial period and
examines notable men and women and major events in
U.S. history
  Includes bibliographical references

Worldmark encyclopedia of the states. 7th ed.
Gale Res. 2007 2v il map set $306 *
  Grades: 9 10 11 12 Adult   **973.03**
  1. United States—Encyclopedias 2. Reference books
  ISBN 978-1-4144-1058-6   LC 2007279963
  First published 1981 by Harper & Row. Periodically
revised
  "Comprehensive examination of each state within the
framework of 50 standard subject headings. Includes eco-
nomic policy, energy and power, resources, education,
the press, famous persons, etc." N Y Public Libr. Ref
Books for Child Collect. 2d edition

973.2   United States—Colonial period, 1607-1775

Bogaert, Harmen Meyndertsz van den
  Journey into Mohawk Country; as written by
H.M. van den Bogaert, with artwork by George
O'Connor and color by Hilary Sycamore. First
Second 2006 144p il pa $17.95 *
  Grades: 8 9 10 11 12   **973.2**
  1. Graphic novels 2. United States—History—1600-
1775, Colonial period—Graphic novels 3. New York
(State)—History—1600-1775, Colonial period—
Graphic novels
  ISBN 1-59643-106-7
  In 1634, young Dutch trader Harmen Meyndertsz van
den Bogaert, several companions, and some native guides

Bogaert, Harmen Meyndertsz van den—*Continued*

traveled deep into what is now New York State, trading tools and weapons and trying to establish new tribal friendships to bolster Dutch trade. van den Bogaert kept a journal throughout his journeys. O'Connor has kept the original text and conducted extensive research in order to make his illustrations as authentic as possible.

Carpenter, Roger M., 1956-

Term paper resource guide to colonial American history. Greenwood Press/ABC-CLIO 2009 268p $65

Grades: 9 10 11 12   **973.2**
   1. United States—History—1600-1775, Colonial period 2. Report writing 3. Reference books
   ISBN 978-0-313-35544-8   LC 2009-9048

This book "includes 100 notable 'events' of the period (battles, treaties, and conferences as well as speeches and documents), chosen for their historical significance, the availability of source materials, and the interests of high-school and undergraduate students. These events are arranged in chronological order based on beginning date, from the founding of Roanoke, Virginia (1584-1590), to the ratification of the U.S. Constitution (1787-1791). Entries include an overview of the event, term paper suggestions, alternative suggestions, and an annotated bibliography of sources (primary, secondary, Web, and multimedia)." Booklist

"This excellent resource is a clear, well-arranged guide for starting and developing reports. . . . Carpenter's work will serve as an essential guide for research papers and discussions on topics of interest to AP students of Colonial American history." SLJ

Includes bibliographical references

Copeland, David A., 1951-

Debating the issues in colonial newspapers; primary documents on events of the period. Greenwood Press 2000 397p il $59.95 *

Grades: 9 10 11 12   **973.2**
   1. United States—History—1600-1775, Colonial period—Sources 2. Newspapers—United States
   ISBN 0-313-30982-5   LC 99-89070

"Primary-source material on 31 events and issues from 1690 to 1776 including abolition, inoculation, women's rights, censorship, and separation from England. The principal source of communication for people during this period was the newspaper, and political and social concerns were debated there at length. . . . Following the colonialists' pro or con opinions, a number of questions are posed for students." SLJ

Includes bibliographical references

Events that changed America through the seventeenth century; edited by John E. Findling and Frank W. Thackeray. Greenwood Press 2000 193p (Greenwood Press "Events that changed America" series) $39.95

Grades: 11 12 Adult   **973.2**
   1. United States—History—1600-1775, Colonial period 2. America—History
   ISBN 0-313-29083-0   LC 00-20080

A look at ten of the most important events in what was to become the continental United States from the settlement of the earliest peoples to the close of the seventeenth century. Coronado's expedition, the founding of St. Augustine, and early European-Native American encounters are among the topics discussed

Includes bibliographical references

Gray, Edward G., 1964-

Colonial America; a history in documents. 2nd ed. Oxford University Press 2011 c2012 211p il map (Pages from history) $39.95; pa $24.95 *

Grades: 7 8 9 10   **973.2**
   1. United States—History—1600-1775, Colonial period—Sources
   ISBN 978-0-19-976594-2; 978-0-19-976595-9 (pa)
                        LC 2010038458
   First published 2003

This collection of primary sources examines "the lives of the colonists through their own words—in diaries, letters, sermons, newspaper columns, and poems." Publisher's note

Includes bibliographical references

Grizzard, Frank E., Jr.

Jamestown Colony; a political, social, and cultural history; [by] Frank E. Grizzard, Jr., D. Boyd Smith. ABC-CLIO 2007 lvi, 448p il map $95

Grades: 7 8 9 10 11 12 Adult   **973.2**
   1. Jamestown (Va.)—History—Encyclopedias
   2. Reference books
   ISBN 1-85109-637-X; 978-1-85109-637-4
                        LC 2006-37359

"The first half of the book is devoted to encyclopedia-style entries on a variety of topics, including people, places, and significant events. The other half, 'Selected Writings,' contains excerpts from primary-source materials." SLJ

"This volume is well written and well researched, and belongs in all collections relating to Colonial America." Am Ref Books Annu, 2008

Includes bibliographical references

Hawke, David Freeman

Everyday life in early America. Harper & Row 1988 195p il (Everyday life in America) pa $13 hardcover o.p. *

Grades: 11 12 Adult   **973.2**
   1. United States—History—1600-1775, Colonial period 2. United States—Social life and customs
   ISBN 0-06-091251-0 (pa)   LC 87-17667

The author "provides enlightening and colorful descriptions of early Colonial Americans and debunks many widely held assumptions about 17th century settlers." Publ Wkly

Includes bibliographical references

Hofstadter, Richard, 1916-1970

America at 1750; a social portrait. Knopf 1971 293p pa $11 hardcover o.p.

Grades: 11 12 Adult   **973.2**

Hofstadter, Richard, 1916-1970—_Continued_
1. United States—History—1600-1775, Colonial period 2. United States—Social conditions
ISBN 0-394-71795-3 (pa)
"Using primarily secondary accounts, Hofstadter examines the ethnic composition of the colonies in 1750; traces the development of white servitude, the slave trade, and the slave system; sketches briefly the middle-class framework of early America; and dissects the colonial religious paradigm and the impact of the Great Awakening." Choice
Includes bibliographical references

Mandell, Daniel R., 1956-
King Philip's war; the conflict over New England. Chelsea House 2007 144p il map (Landmark events in Native American history) lib bdg $35
Grades: 7 8 9 10   **973.2**
1. King Philip's War, 1675-1676 2. Wampanoag Indians 3. New England—History—1600-1775, Colonial period
ISBN 978-0-7910-9346-7; 0-7910-9346-8
      LC 2006-102258
"Between 1675 and 1676, King Philip's War shattered native tribes and devastated the new English colonies. . . . [The] Pequot and Narragansett tribes were subjugated, and Wampanoag leader King Philip (Metacom) saw his lands taken and his counselors executed. In July 1675, his warriors started an uprising that gained the support of other tribes and sent refugees streaming into Boston. King Philip's War is [an] account of this . . . confrontation." Publisher's note
This account features "lively writing and direct quotes, and [is] enhanced by many color and black-and-white photos, drawings, and illustrations." SLJ
Includes bibliographical references

Philbrick, Nathaniel
The Mayflower and the Pilgrims' New World. G.P. Putnam's Sons 2008 338p il map $19.99 *
Grades: 7 8 9 10 11 12   **973.2**
1. Bradford, William, 1590-1657 2. Church, Benjamin, 1639-1718 3. Pilgrims (New England colonists) 4. Massachusetts—History—1600-1775, Colonial period 5. Native Americans
ISBN 978-0-399-24795-8; 0-399-24795-5
      LC 2007-30669
An adaptation of Mayflower: a story of community, courage, and war, published 2006 by Viking for adults
"This volume highlights both the Pilgrims' determination to find and settle a home where they could worship freely and the perilous journey that it took to make that happen. In accessible prose, the author shatters the American myth of the landing at Plymouth Rock and the first Thanksgiving. . . . The various maps, reproductions of historical documents, photographs of significant locations, and illustrations all come together with the text to help separate fact from legend and create a realistic, readable portrayal of the Pilgrims and their first 50 years in America." SLJ
Includes bibliographical references

Purvis, Thomas L., 1949-
Colonial America to 1763. Facts on File 1999 381p il (Almanacs of American life) $95
Grades: 11 12 Adult   **973.2**
1. United States—History—1600-1775, Colonial period 2. United States—Social life and customs—1600-1775, Colonial period
ISBN 0-8160-2527-4   LC 98-29007
Series statement from jacket
This compendium is "divided into 19 chapters that cover such topics as 'Diet and Health,' 'Religion,' 'The Cities,' 'Science and Technology,' 'Crime and Violence,' and 'Popular Life and Recreation.' There are general details of Colonial life as well as obscure and difficult-to-find facts that students need and teachers always want. . . . Young adults will enjoy learning through all of the fascinating facts and curious bits of information, but the well-organized, complete, and accessible text will also provide an invaluable resource for research and term papers." SLJ
Includes bibliographical references

Saari, Peggy
Colonial America: almanac. U.X.L 2000 2v (Colonial America reference library) set $110
Grades: 8 9 10 11 12   **973.2**
1. United States—History—1600-1775, Colonial period 2. Reference books
ISBN 0-7876-3763-7   LC 99-39081
Examines the colonial period in America, discussing both the Native American culture before the arrival of Europeans and the exploration and settlement of different parts of the New World.
Includes bibliographical references

Colonial America: primary sources; Julie Carnagie, editor. U.X.L 1999 297p il (Colonial America reference library) $67
Grades: 8 9 10 11 12   **973.2**
1. United States—History—1600-1775, Colonial period
ISBN 0-7876-3766-1   LC 99-34460
Presents the historical events and social issues of colonial America through twenty-four primary documents, including diary entries, poems, and personal narratives
"Each chapter adds helpful material before and after the excerpt to explain its importance. Illustrations and sidebars are used in this volume also, and difficult words are defined." Booklist

Wolf, Stephanie Grauman
As various as their land; the everyday lives of eighteenth-century Americans. University of Arkansas Press 2000 304p il map pa $16.95 *
Grades: 9 10 11 12 Adult   **973.2**
1. United States—Social life and customs—1600-1775, Colonial period
ISBN 1-557-28599-3   LC 99-86042
First published 1993 by HarperCollins
The author examines the "diversity of experience that marked America's people in the 100 or so years preceding nationhood. Wolf's main concern is with immigrant cultures and their transfer to, and transformation of, the

Wolf, Stephanie Grauman—*Continued*
soil of New England, the Middle Atlantic region, and the American South." Libr J

"An excellent overview of the foundation of our society's successes and failures." Booklist

Includes bibliographical references

973.3 United States—Periods of Revolution and Confederation, 1775-1789

The **American** Revolution; Kirk D. Werner, book editor. Greenhaven Press 2000 224p (Turning points in world history) lib bdg $31.20

Grades: 9 10 11 12   **973.3**
1. United States—History—1775-1783, Revolution
ISBN 0-7377-0239-7   LC 99-38377

This volume "contains 16 essays by well-known historians that center on the background, politics, and effects of the [American Revolution]. . . . There is an extensive section of documents (Stamp Act resolutions, excerpts from first-person accounts, Articles of Confederation, etc.) An excellent resource for research." SLJ

Includes bibliographical references

The **American** Revolution: writings from the War of Independence. Library of Am. 2001 878p $40 *

Grades: 11 12 Adult   **973.3**
1. United States—History—1775-1783, Revolution
ISBN 1-88301-191-4   LC 00-45373

This collection includes "over 120 pieces by more than 70 Revolution-era writers from both sides of the War of Independence. The book begins with Paul Revere's personal account of his famous ride in April 1775 and ends with a description of George Washington's resignation from the command of the Continental Army in December 1783. . . . At the book's end one can find a long section that includes a chronology, biographical sketches of the authors, and other notes on the texts." Libr J

"This work will serve as a marvelous research tool for specialists, but general readers with an interest in American history will also find fascinating gems." Booklist

Includes bibliographical references

American Revolutionary War; a student encyclopedia; Gregory Fremont-Barnes, Richard Alan Ryerson, volume editors; James Arnold and Roberta Wiener, editors, documents volume; foreword by Jack P. Greene. ABC-CLIO 2007 5v il map set $485 *

Grades: 9 10 11 12   **973.3**
1. United States—History—1775-1783, Revolution—Encyclopedias 2. Reference books
ISBN 978-1-85109-839-2; 1-85109-839-9
      LC 2006-31100

"With over 800 entries and essays and a separate documents volume, . . . [this encyclopedia] covers every battle and campaign, every political debate and diplomatic encounter. It also introduces students to the broad spectrum of American culture at the time (day-to-day life, art, music) as well as the personal lives of all those

caught up in the war." Publisher's note
Includes bibliographical references

Aronson, Marc
The real revolution; the global story of American independence. Clarion Books 2005 238p il map lib bdg $21 *

Grades: 7 8 9 10   **973.3**
1. United States—History—1775-1783, Revolution
ISBN 0-618-18179-2   LC 2005-1088

In this "volume, Aronson investigates the origins of the American Revolution and discovers some startling global connections. The colonies' quest for independence is tied to such seemingly unrelated incidents as Robert Clive's triumph over the French in India in 1750 and John Wilkes's accusations against the king in his newspaper, The North Briton, in the 1760s. . . . This outstanding work is highly compelling reading and belongs in every library." SLJ

Includes bibliographical references

Barnes, Ian, 1946-
The historical atlas of the American Revolution; Charles Royster, consulting editor. Routledge 2000 223p il maps $50 *

Grades: 11 12 Adult   **973.3**
1. United States—History—Historical geography—Maps 2. United States—History—1775-1783, Revolution—Maps 3. Reference books
ISBN 0-415-92243-7   LC 99-59920

"Although the emphasis is on the Revolution, the scope is much broader—from settlement to 1820. Chronologically arranged, each chapter opens with an overview, followed by readable double-page spreads on the time periods, specific battles, pertinent individuals or peoples, and other relevant issues. Maps are large enough to show troop movement. Legends are clear with dissimilar symbols. Portraits, illustrations, and other graphics are clearly identified. A concluding section provides brief biographical sketches. An excellent presentation of the era." SLJ

Includes bibliographical references

Bober, Natalie
Countdown to independence; a revolution of ideas in England and her American colonies: 1760-1776; by Natalie S. Bober. Atheneum Bks. for Young Readers 2000 xxv, 342p il hardcover o.p. pa $19.95 *

Grades: 9 10 11 12   **973.3**
1. United States—History—1775-1783, Revolution—Causes 2. United States—Politics and government—1775-1783, Revolution 3. Great Britain—History—1714-1837
ISBN 0-689-81329-5; 978-0-689-81329-0; 1-4169-6392-8 (pa); 978-1-4169-6392-9 (pa)
      LC 99-27086

Examines the people and events both in the American colonies and in Great Britain between 1760 and 1776 that led to the American Revolution.

This "is a compelling, yet scholarly resource that places readers at the center of the action, encouraging

Bober, Natalie—_Continued_
them to learn about the historic events and people, care about them, and, perhaps, learn more by investigating the extensive bibliography." Booklist
Includes bibliographical references

Burg, David F.
The American Revolution. Updated ed. Facts on File 2007 470p il map (Eyewitness history) $75 *
Grades: 11 12 Adult   **973.3**
  1. United States—History—1775-1783, Revolution
ISBN 978-0-8160-6482-3   LC 2006-33096
First published 2001
"The book begins with a discussion of the 'Prelude to Revolt: 1756-1774,' and concludes with thoughts on 'An Improbable Triumph: 1781' and 'An Unpromising Outcome: 1782-1783.' Each chapter offers a lengthy introductory essay summarizing important themes, followed by a descriptive chronology of key events. Pages of documented excerpts from contemporary newspapers, diaries, letters, speeches, and memoirs discuss the events of the day and how they were perceived by those who lived through them. The lively selections, many written by well-known individuals, paint vivid pictures that will capture readers' imaginations." SLJ
Includes bibliographical references

Draper, Theodore, 1912-2006
A struggle for power; the American Revolution. Times Bks. 1996 544p pa $13.56 hardcover o.p.
Grades: 11 12 Adult   **973.3**
  1. United States—History—1775-1783, Revolution
ISBN 0-679-77642-7 (pa)   LC 95-11605
The author "maintains that the Revolution was really a power struggle spawned by the British system of chartering colonies, which placed fiscal control of public funds with the colonial assemblies." Libr J
This is an "elegantly written, masterful study. . . . Drawing freely on period pamphlets, letters, petitions, travelogues and assembly minutes, [the author] vividly evokes the populist discontent, intellectual gymnastics and mob violence that led to revolution." Publ Wkly
Includes bibliographical references

Driver, Stephanie Schwartz
Understanding the Declaration of Independence. Rosen Pub. 2010 128p il (Words that changed the world) lib bdg $31.95
Grades: 7 8 9 10   **973.3**
  1. Jefferson, Thomas, 1743-1826 2. United States. Declaration of Independence 3. United States—Politics and government—1775-1783, Revolution
ISBN 978-1-4488-1669-9; 1-4488-1669-6
                LC 2010-10371
This surveys The Declaration of Independence, considering the "document's 'Context and Creator,' 'Immediate Impact,' 'Legacy,' and 'Aftermath.' . . . Exploring the colonial crisis leading to America's formal separation from the British Empire, . . . [the] author provides a balance of deep context, expressive writing, and pertinent information. Scattered throughout the [text] are a good number of well-captioned, color illustrations and photos.

[This book is a] valuable [resource] for teachers and students doing research projects across the curriculum." SLJ
Includes glossary and bibliographical references

Fischer, David Hackett
Washington's crossing. Oxford University Press 2004 564p il maps (Pivotal moments in American history) $35; pa $16.95
Grades: 11 12 Adult   **973.3**
  1. Washington, George, 1732-1799 2. United States—History—1775-1783, Revolution—Campaigns
ISBN 0-19-517034-2; 0-19-518159-X (pa)
                LC 2003-19858
The author describes how "Washington, his officers, and their men turn the early military defeats of Long Island and New York City into victory at Trenton and Princeton. The opening chapter is devoted to the painting _Washington Crossing the Delaware_. Then the author discusses the British, Hessian, and American military units that were involved in these campaigns and gives background on their officers. This is Fischer's strong suit: he tells stories and gives details that bring history alive. . . . In the hands of such a thorough researcher and talented writer, this is powerful stuff." SLJ
Includes bibliographical references

Freedman, Russell
Give me liberty! the story of the Declaration of Independence. Holiday House 2000 90p il $24.95; pa $14.95
Grades: 5 6 7 8 9 10   **973.3**
  1. United States. Declaration of Independence 2. United States—Politics and government—1775-1783, Revolution
ISBN 0-8234-1448-5; 0-8234-1753-0 (pa)
                LC 99-57513
Describes the events leading up to the Declaration of Independence as well as the personalities and politics behind its framing
"Handsomely designed with a generous and thoughtful selection of period art, the book is dramatic and inspiring." Horn Book
Includes bibliographical references

Gilje, Paul A., 1951-
Encyclopedia of revolutionary America; foreword by Gary B. Nash. Facts On File 2010 3v il map (Facts on File library of American history) set $250
Grades: 9 10 11 12 Adult   **973.3**
  1. United States—History—1775-1783, Revolution—Encyclopedias 2. United States—History—1783-1809—Encyclopedias 3. Reference books
ISBN 978-0-8160-6505-9; 0-8160-6505-5
                LC 2009-13596
"These volumes do not just cover the continental U.S. but the entire North American continent. Gilje relies on primary sources as much as possible in the alphabetically arranged entries. Covering the period from the French and Indian War, in 1754, to the end of the War of 1812 (1815), the encyclopedia contains the expected biographical entries on the Founding Fathers, prominent politi-

Gilje, Paul A., 1951——*Continued*

cians, and popular military leaders, but a special effort has been made to include previously neglected groups in the study of this era, such as Native Americans, African Americans, women, and the lower classes. . . . This is an easy-to-use, helpful, and comprehensive resource that would be a valuable addition to the history collections of high-school, academic, and public libraries." Booklist

Includes bibliographical references

Maier, Pauline, 1938-

American scripture; making the Declaration of Independence. Knopf 1997 xxi, 304p pa $14 hardcover o.p.

Grades: 11 12 Adult   973.3
    1. United States. Declaration of Independence
    2. United States—Politics and government—1775-1783, Revolution
    ISBN 0-679-77908-6 (pa)   LC 97-2769
"In the spring of 1776, with a British invasion fleet on its way, the Second Continental Congress appointed a committee to compose a statement explaining America's decision to seek independence. Thomas Jefferson was the principal drafter of the statement, but Maier makes it clear that his task was to express the sentiments of the Congress, not his personal views, and she shows that when the congressmen edited his draft they improved it greatly (rather than 'mangling' it, as Jefferson ever after maintained). The Declaration of Independence is, she argues, a profoundly collective document, both in its origins and in our still-evolving interpretation of its self-evident truths." New Yorker

Minks, Benton

Revolutionary war; [by] Benton Minks and Louise Minks; John S. Bowman, general editor. Rev. ed. Chelsea House 2010 217p il map (America at war) $45

Grades: 9 10 11 12   973.3
    1. United States—History—1775-1783, Revolution
    ISBN 978-0-8160-8196-7   LC 2009-44102
    First published 1992
This is an "account of America's heroic seven-year struggle for independence, from the first shots at Lexington and Concord to the British surrender at Yorktown, Virginia." Publisher's note

Includes glossary and bibliographical references

Morgan, Edmund Sears

The birth of the Republic, 1763-89. 3rd ed. University of Chicago Press 1992 206p (Chicago history of American civilization) hardcover o.p. pa $13

Grades: 11 12 Adult   973.3
    1. United States—History—1775-1783, Revolution
    2. United States—History—1783-1809
    ISBN 0-226-53756-0; 0-226-53757-9 (pa)
                                          LC 92-8871
    First published 1956
A brief study of the American revolutionary period from 1763 to 1789.

Includes bibliographical references

Purvis, Thomas L., 1949-

Revolutionary America, 1763-1800. Facts on File 1995 383p il maps (Almanacs of American life) $95 *

Grades: 11 12 Adult   973.3
    1. United States—History—1775-1783, Revolution
    2. United States—Social life and customs
    ISBN 0-8160-2528-2   LC 93-38382
"Arranged thematically, sections such as 'Climate,' 'Economy,' 'Population,' 'Health,' 'Religion,' 'Architecture,' and 'Education' provide statistical charts, graphs, and other data to show what life was like in the various parts of the country. . . . The text, covering perhaps a third of the book, explains and elaborates on the tabular information, pulling everything together in a relevant, interesting manner." SLJ

Includes bibliographical references

Raphael, Ray

A people's history of the American Revolution; how common people shaped the fight for independence. 1st Perennial ed. Perennial 2002 506p pa $13.95 *

Grades: 11 12 Adult   973.3
    1. United States—History—1775-1783, Revolution
    ISBN 0-06-000440-1   LC 2002-16992
    First published 2001 by New Press
This volume "collects the experiences of ordinary people during the American Revolution and sutures them into a story. And that story is that the rebellion and war inescapably influenced everyone—farmers, townspeople, women, Indians, free blacks and enslaved blacks, plutocrats and proletarians." Booklist
"Moving from broad overviews to stories of small groups or individuals, Raphael's study is impressive in both its sweep and its attention to the particular." Publ Wkly

Includes bibliographical references

Wood, W. J. (William J.), 1917-

Battles of the Revolutionary War, 1775-1781; [by] W.J. Wood; with an introduction by John S.D. Eisenhower. Da Capo 2003 c1990 xxxii, 315p il map (Major battles and campaigns) pa $18.95

Grades: 9 10 11 12   973.3
    1. United States—History—1775-1783, Revolution—Campaigns
    ISBN 0-306-81329-7
    First published 1990 by Algonquin Bks.
"Wood focuses on 10 major battles and campaigns of the American Revolution that have unique military qualities. Maps and new insights about the leadership of both armies make this a worthy addition to military history collections." Booklist

Includes bibliographical references

973.4   United States—Constitutional period, 1789-1809

Ellis, Joseph J.

Founding brothers; the revolutionary generation.
Knopf 2000 288p $26.95; pa $14 *

Grades: 11 12 Adult   **973.4**

1. United States—History—1783-1809 2. United
States—Politics and government—1783-1809
3. Presidents—United States 4. United States—Biography

ISBN 0-375-40544-5; 0-375-70524-4 (pa)

LC 99-59304

This study looks at the intertwined lives of "Benjamin
Franklin, Thomas Jefferson, John Adams, Alexander
Hamilton, James Madison and Aaron Burr. . . . As Ellis
sees it, the founding brethren not only 'created the
American republic' but 'held it together throughout the
volatile and vulnerable early years by sustaining their
presence until national habits and customs took root.'"
NY Times Book Rev

"Ellis' essays are angled, fascinating, and perfect for
general-interest readers." Booklist

Includes bibliographical references

Heidler, David Stephen, 1955-

Daily life in the early American republic,
1790-1820; [by] David S. Heidler and Jeanne T.
Heidler. Greenwood Press 2004 xxxi, 236p map
(Greenwood Press "Daily life through history"
series) $49.95 *

Grades: 9 10 11 12   **973.4**

1. United States—Social life and customs

ISBN 0-313-32391-7   LC 2004-11771

Contents: The time of their lives; Historical narrative;
Cradle to grave: rituals of life, love, and death; Life on
the land; A changing economy: artisans, factories, and
money; Leisure; Faith and charity; Beyond the mainstream; The martial life

The authors "discuss the people who lived during this
critical time, and uncover the essential and unexpected
realities of ordinary life in the early American republic."
Publisher's note

Includes bibliographical references

Lanier, Shannon

Jefferson's children; the story of one American
family; by Shannon Lanier and Jane Feldman;
with photographs by Jane Feldman; and an
introduction by Lucian K. Truscott IV. Random
House 2000 144p il hardcover o.p. pa $16.95

Grades: 7 8 9 10   **973.4**

1. African Americans—Biography 2. Racially mixed
people 3. United States—Race relations

ISBN 0-375-80597-4; 0-375-82168-6 (pa)

LC 00-44551

This is an "anthology of personal meditations by a variety of Jefferson's living descendants. Edited by Shannon Lanier, a descendant through Sally's son Madison
Hemings's line, the portraits that emerge are as generous
and jumbled as America itself. The statements range

from hostile to conciliatory to indifferent to eloquent."
NY Times Book Rev

Includes bibliographical references

Purcell, Sarah J.

The early national period; [by] Sarah Purcell.
Facts on File 2004 420p il map (Eyewitness
history) $75 *

Grades: 11 12 Adult   **973.4**

1. United States—History—1783-1865

ISBN 0-8160-4769-3   LC 2003-14969

Contents: Post-revolutionary change: 1783-1786; Making a new Constitution: 1787-1788; A new nation: 1789-
1792; Federalist order: 1793-1796; Federalist disorder:
1797-1800; Jeffersonian America: 1801-1803; Rising
conflict: 1804-1807; Commercial crisis and the clamor
for war: 1808-1811; The War of 1812: 1812-1815; The
era of good feelings?: 1816-1819; Economic crisis, political stability: 1820-1823; Democracy: 1824-1828

"The introduction to each section summarizes major
events and provides excerpts from primary resources including speeches, letters, newspaper accounts, diary entries, and advertisements." SLJ

"A serious history student will find this book invaluable." Libr Media Connect

Includes bibliographical references

Stefoff, Rebecca, 1951-

American voices from the new republic,
1783-1830. Benchmark Books 2004 c2005 xxiii,
116p (American voices from--) lib bdg $34.21

Grades: 6 7 8 9 10   **973.4**

1. United States—History—1783-1865

ISBN 0-7614-1695-1   LC 2004-11391

Contents: Birth of a nation; Forming a new government; Presidents and parties; International affairs; American affairs; African Americans and slavery; Arts and sciences; The age of new possibilities

Describes, through excerpts from diaries, speeches,
newspaper articles, and other documents of the time,
United States history from 1783 to 1830. Includes review
questions.

973.5   United States—1809-1845

Greenblatt, Miriam

War of 1812; John S. Bowman, general editor.
Rev. ed. Chelsea House 2010 176p il map
(America at war) $45 *

Grades: 9 10 11 12   **973.5**

1. War of 1812

ISBN 978-0-8160-8194-3   LC 2009-29531

First published 1994

An account of the events surrounding the War of 1812
between the newly established United States and Great
Britain.

Includes glossary and bibliographical references

Heidler, David Stephen, 1955-
The War of 1812; [by] David S. Heidler and Jeanne T. Heidler. Greenwood Press 2002 xxiii, 217p il maps (Greenwood guides to historic events, 1500-1900) $44.95 *
Grades: 11 12 Adult   **973.5**
1. War of 1812
ISBN 0-313-31687-2   LC 2001-50102
This book discusses "the causes, battles, and personalities that surrounded the war. . . . The authors describe all of the factors that led to some of the more ignominious defeats and unexpected victories. . . . The book includes brief biographies of some of the major participants and some primary-source documents." SLJ
Includes glossary and bibliographical references

Howes, Kelly King
War of 1812; Julie L. Carnagie, editor. U.X.L 2002 xxvi, 318p $67
Grades: 7 8 9 10   **973.5**
1. War of 1812
ISBN 0-7876-5574-0   LC 2001-44240
Preliminary pagnation continues after p. 318
A chronological overview of the events of the War of 1812, accompanied by fifteen biographies of individuals associated with the war.
Includes glossary and bibliographical references

Marker, Sherry, 1941-
Plains Indian wars; John S. Bowman, general editor. Rev. ed. Chelsea House 2010 185p il map (America at war) $45 *
Grades: 9 10 11 12   **973.5**
1. Native Americans—Wars 2. Native Americans—Great Plains
ISBN 978-0-8160-8184-4   LC 2009-42018
First published 1996
This is an account of the wars between Plains Indians and white settlers in the American West in the 19th century.
Includes glossary and bibliographical references

973.6 United States—1845-1861

Lincoln, Abraham, 1809-1865
The Lincoln-Douglas Debates of 1858; edited by Robert W. Johannsen; foreword to the anniversary edition by James L. Huston. 150th anniversary ed., Special commemorative ed. Oxford University Press 2008 xxxviii, 329p pa $24.95
Grades: 9 10 11 12 Adult   **973.6**
1. United States—Politics and government—1815-1861 2. Lincoln-Douglas debates, 1858
ISBN 978-0-19-533942-0; 0-19-533942-8
LC 2007034288
This edition first published 1965
With introductions to give perspective, this "includes the seven debates of 1858 as well as Douglas's speech in Chicago that set the tone for the debates." Guide to Read in Am Hist
Includes bibliographical references

Mills, Bronwyn
U.S.-Mexican War; [by] Bronwyn Mills; John S. Bowman, general editor. Rev. ed. Chelsea House 2010 170p il map (America at war) $45 *
Grades: 9 10 11 12   **973.6**
1. Mexican War, 1846-1848
ISBN 978-0-8160-8195-0   LC 2009-46082
First published 1992 with title: Mexican War
This book "tells the full story of a long-ignored but critical passage in American military history that was soon overshadowed by the Civil War. . . . [It] features a chapter focusing on the innovative military tactics and weaponry involved throughout the conflict." Publisher's note
Includes glossary and bibliographical references

973.7 United States—Administration of Abraham Lincoln, 1861-1865. Civil War

Allen, Thomas B., 1929-
Mr. Lincoln's high-tech war; how the North used the telegraph, railroads, surveillance balloons, ironclads, high-powered weapons, and more to win the Civil War; [by] Thomas B. Allen & Roger MacBride Allen. National Geographic Society 2009 144p il $18.95; lib bdg $25.90
Grades: 5 6 7 8 9 10   **973.7**
1. Lincoln, Abraham, 1809-1865 2. United States—History—1861-1865, Civil War 3. Technology—History
ISBN   978-1-4263-0379-1;   1-4263-0379-3; 978-1-4263-0380-7 (lib bdg); 1-4263-0380-7 (lib bdg)
LC 2008-24546
"Well researched and clearly written, the book discusses the course of the Civil War in terms of new technology, from the ironclad and the submarine to the rapid-fire, repeating rifle and the use of railroads to carry troops and supplies. . . . The many illustrations include captioned black-and-white reproductions of period prints, paintings, and photos as well as clearly labeled drawings. . . . [Readers] will gain a fascinating perspective on why the war progressed as it did and how it was ultimately won." Booklist
Includes bibliographical references

American Civil War; Steven E. Woodworth, editor. Gale, Cengage Learning 2008 2v il (Gale library of daily life) set $211
Grades: 9 10 11 12 Adult   **973.7**
1. Reference books 2. United States—History—1861-1865, Civil War—Sources 3. United States—Social life and customs 4. United States—Social conditions
ISBN 978-1-4144-3009-6   LC 2007-47017
"This set measures the horrific toll of the Civil War on military and civilian life. . . . Roughly 220 entries are thematically arranged under several headings: 'A Soldier's Life,' 'Family and Community,' 'Religion,' 'Popular Culture,' 'Health and Medicine,' 'Work and Economy,' 'Politics,' 'Effects of War on Slaves and Freedpeople,' and 'Reconciliation and Remembrance.' . . . Through the judicious use of firstperson accounts in

American Civil War—*Continued*

the form of diaries and letters, readers are given an intimate view of lives lived and lost during this tumultuous and tragic time." Libr J

Includes bibliographical references

Armstrong, Jennifer, 1961-

Photo by Brady; a picture of the Civil War. Atheneum Books For Young Readers 2005 160p il $18.95

Grades: 6 7 8 9 10   **973.7**
1. Brady, Mathew B., ca. 1823-1896 2. United States—History—1861-1865,   Civil   War 3. Photography—History

ISBN 0-689-85785-3   LC 2004-8967

"Armstrong chronicles the Civil War from Lincoln's election to his death with both a storylike narrative of events and a photo-essay. . . . This book is also a look at early photographic techniques and offers a description of [Mathew] Brady's rare collection. . . . When readers remember that the pictures are more than 100 years old, they should recognize their exquisiteness, grandeur, and genius." SLJ

Includes bibliographical references

Barney, William L.

The Civil War and Reconstruction; a student companion. Oxford Univ. Press 2001 368p il maps (Oxford student companions to American history) $60

Grades: 7 8 9 10   **973.7**
1. Reconstruction (1865-1876) 2. United States—History—1861-1865, Civil War

ISBN 0-19-511559-7   LC 00-57444

This reference guide includes "articles on the military, political, social, economic, and cultural aspects of the war and its aftermath, as well as biographical sketches of major figures." SLJ

"The book is encyclopedic in format, with many useful access points, and bibliographic information is located both at the ends of the articles and in several appendixes that suggest books, historic sites and addresses, and Web sites." Voice Youth Advocates

Includes bibliographical references

Boatner, Mark Mayo, 1921-

The Civil War dictionary; by Mark Mayo Boatner III; maps and diagrams by Allen C. Northrop and Lowell I. Miller. 1st Vintage Civil War Library ed. Vintage Civil War Library 1991 974p il map pa $24

Grades: 11 12 Adult   **973.7**
1. Reference books 2. United States—History—1861-1865, Civil War—Encyclopedias

ISBN 0-679-73392-2; 978-0-679-73392-8
      LC 91-50013

First published 1959 by McKay

"With more than 4,000 entries . . . this dictionary remains the most comprehensive and consistently accurate reference tool on the American Civil War. In addition to the biographical sketches there are entries relating to campaigns and battles, naval engagements, weapons, is-

sues and incidents, military terms and definitions, politics, literature, and statistics." Choice

Includes bibliographical references

Bolden, Tonya

Cause: Reconstruction America, 1863-1877. Knopf 2005 138p il $19.95; lib bdg $21.99 *

Grades: 7 8 9 10   **973.7**
1. Reconstruction (1865-1876) 2. United States—History—1865-1898

ISBN 0-375-82795-1; 0-375-92795-6 (lib bdg)

"This examination of America during Reconstruction covers Lincoln's Proclamation of Amnesty and Reconstruction, the Civil Rights Act of 1866, the troubles of freed slaves, the expansion of the nation and the plight of Native Americans, the 15th Amendment, and the women's suffrage movement. While this is well-documented nonfiction, Bolden writes in the voice of a storyteller. The excellent graphics include archival photos, political cartoons, and primary resources." SLJ

Browne, Ray Broadus

The Civil War and Reconstruction; [by] Ray B. Browne and Lawrence A. Kreiser, Jr. Greenwood Press 2003 215p il (American popular culture through history) $49.95 *

Grades: 9 10 11 12   **973.7**
1. United States—History—1861-1865, Civil War 2. Reconstruction (1865-1876) 3. Popular culture—United States

ISBN 0-313-31325-3   LC 2002-35206

"Browne and Kreiser begin with overview chapters on daily life for the general population, and then examine in detail 10 aspects of culture including advertising, clothing and fashion, food, leisure activities, travel and transportation, and several categories of performing and fine arts. The authors describe both the trends and important people that shaped popular culture and the impact of the war and its aftermath. For example, they relate how baseball became America's pastime when Civil War soldiers, who learned to play while in camps, carried the game home with them at the war's end. Each chapter is well documented. . . . This well-written and objective book deserves a place in all libraries." SLJ

Includes bibliographical references

Carlisle, Rodney P.

Civil War and Reconstruction. Facts on File 2008 452p il map (Eyewitness history) $75 *

Grades: 7 8 9 10   **973.7**
1. United States—History—1861-1865, Civil War—Sources 2. Reconstruction (1865-1876)

ISBN 978-0-8160-6347-5   LC 2006-35425

First published 1991 under the authorship of Joe H. Kirchberger

"This illustrated chronology of the Civil War contains over 100 black-and-white photographs (mostly from the Library of Congress Prints and Photographs Division), 16 maps, and biographies of 50 key figures in the era. Each period-based chapter offers a narrative that delves into deeper issues of the causation of war; a chronicle of events, detailed to the week; and eyewitness testimony,

Carlisle, Rodney P.—*Continued*
including diaries, journals, correspondence, editorials, and news accounts." Choice
Includes bibliographical references

The **Causes** of the Civil War; edited by Kenneth M. Stampp. 3rd rev ed. Simon & Schuster 1991 255p pa $14 *
Grades: 11 12 Adult   **973.7**
1. United States—History—1861-1865, Civil War—Causes 2. United States—History—1861-1865, Civil War—Sources
ISBN 0-671-75155-7   LC 91-36819
"A Touchstone book"
First published 1959 by Prentice-Hall
This book integrates the conclusions of various postwar historians with the thoughts of contemporary commentators like Jefferson Davis, Horace Greeley, and Lincoln. Political, cultural and economic aspects are emphasized
Includes bibliographical references

The **Civil** War; James Tackach, book editor. Greenhaven Press 2004 186p il (Turning points in world history) lib bdg $34.95
Grades: 7 8 9 10   **973.7**
1. United States—History—1861-1865, Civil War
ISBN 0-7377-1114-0   LC 2003-64297
"Comprised of 17 essays, this book is divided into four chapters: 'A Nation Divides: The Causes of the Civil War,' 'Early Battlefield Victories and the Prospect of European Intervention Fuel the South's Hope for Independence,' 'The North Gains the Advantage,' and 'A Changed Nation.' Many of the most respected Civil War historians . . . are excerpted. . . . Outstanding features of the book are discussion questions and the appendix of documents that are sure to inspire additional research and assist classroom teachers." SLJ
Includes bibliographical references

The **Civil** War: a visual history; [produced in association with the Smithsonian Institution] DK Publishing 2011 360p il map $40
Grades: 11 12 Adult   **973.7**
1. United States—History—1861-1865, Civil War—Pictorial works
ISBN 978-0-7566-7185-3
At head of title: DK Smithsonian
"Drawing on Smithsonian Institution collections, this fact-filled and richly illustrated history brings the war fully to life, along with time lines, sidebars on particular issues, chapter introductions, lengthy captions, and detailed maps. The emphasis throughout is on the military. Multiple examples of weapons, supplies, uniforms, camp life necessities, transport, and battle scenes dominate and show the variety, complexity, and prolixity of making war. Espionage, the home front, and politics get a nod, but this book is for those wanting to smell the sulfur and hear the thunder of guns." Libr J

DeRamus, Betty
Forbidden fruit; love stories from the Underground Railroad. Atria Books 2005 269p il $25; pa $14
Grades: 11 12 Adult   **973.7**
1. Underground railroad 2. Slavery—United States 3. Love
ISBN 0-7434-8263-8;   978-0-7434-8263-9; 0-7434-8264-6 (pa); 978-0-7434-8264-6 (pa)
                                      LC 2004-63414
"Debunking one of the myths used to justify separating families during slavery, de Ramus offers a collection of stories recording the love and devotion of slave couples, many of whom risked their lives to stay together." Booklist
This is an "uplifting and sometimes heartbreaking look at love during the U.S.'s slavery years." Publ Wkly
Includes bibliographical references

Detzer, David
Allegiance; Fort Sumter, Charleston, and the beginning of the Civil War. Harcourt 2001 367p $27 *
Grades: 11 12 Adult   **973.7**
1. Fort Sumter (Charleston, S.C.) 2. United States—History—1861-1865, Civil War—Causes
ISBN 0-15-100641-5   LC 00-50570
The author "limns the daily lives of the men and women caught in the 1861 secession crisis in Charleston, SC, to show how personalities and circumstances determined the advent of the Civil War." Libr J
"The central figure in this drama is Maj. Robert Anderson, commander of the Union garrison in Charleston Harbor. . . . Detzer's writing style brings the reader into close contact with soldiers, civilians and politicians as they struggle to solve the fate of Anderson and his men." Publ Wkly
Includes bibliographical references

Dissonance; between Fort Sumter and Bull Run in the turbulent first days of the Civil War. Harcourt 2006 xxv, 371p $27; pa $15
Grades: 9 10 11 12   **973.7**
1. United States—History—1861-1865, Civil War
ISBN   978-0-15-101158-2;   0-15-101158-3; 978-0-15-603064-9 (pa); 0-15-603064-0 (pa)
                                      LC 2005-20991
Third volume in the author's trilogy about the first 100 days of the Civil War, begun with Allegiance
The author "has written an engaging and comprehensive account of the early days of the Civil War that should have wide appeal." Publ Wkly
Includes bibliographical references

Discovering the Civil War; by the National Archives Experience's "Discovering the Civil War" Exhibition Team with a message from David S. Ferriero, Archivist of the United States; foreword by Ken Burns. D. Giles Ltd. 2010 208p il map $44.95
Grades: 11 12 Adult   **973.7**
1. United States—History—1861-1865, Civil War
ISBN 978-1-904832-91-1   LC 2010-27924

Discovering the Civil War—*Continued*

"This book is based on the exhibition 'Discovering the Civil War,' presented at the National Archives' Lawrence F. O'Brien Gallery in Washington, DC, in two parts: 'Beginnings,' from April 30, 2010, to September 6, 2010, and 'Consequences,' from November 10, 2010, to April 17, 2011."

"Created to accompany the major National Archives Civil War exhibit that mined our national trove of photographs, manuscripts, maps, ephemera, realia, and more, this book is spectacular in its presentation of the wide array of seemingly mundane but surprisingly revealing sources from both the well known and the obscure. . . . The intelligent framing of issues (e.g., government controls, technological and scientific innovation) for each chapter will invite readers to consider many questions about war and society, war making, and the economy of war." Libr J

Includes bibliographical references

Encyclopedia of the American Civil War; a political, social, and military history; David S. Heidler and Jeanne T. Heidler, editors; foreword by James W. McPherson; David J. Coles, associate editor; Gary W. Gallagher, James M. McPherson, Mark E. Neely, Jr., editorial board. ABC-CLIO 2000 5v il maps set $425

Grades: 11 12 Adult   973.7

1. Reference books 2. United States—History—1861-1865, Civil War—Encyclopedias

ISBN 1-57607-066-2   LC 00-11195

"The editors have compiled a comprehensive source that provides a first-stop reference on broad areas or specific topics on the Civil War. The contemporary photographs and lithographs bring the human element into the encyclopedia, a type of reference known more for facts and figures than emotions. The primary-source-documents volume brings obscure resources together, which will further illumine the period for students."—"Outstanding Reference Sources." American Libraries, May 2001

Includes bibliographical references

Faust, Drew Gilpin

Mothers of invention; women of the slaveholding South in the American Civil War. University of N.C. Press 1996 326p il $37.50; pa $19.95 *

Grades: 11 12 Adult   973.7

1. United States—History—1861-1865, Civil War—Women 2. Women—Southern States

ISBN 0-8078-2255-8; 0-8078-5573-1 (pa)

                                                LC 95-8896

Based on journals, letters and memoirs, this is an "analysis of the impact of secession, invasion and conquest on Southern white women. Antebellum images based on helplessness and dependence were challenged as women assumed an increasing range of social and economic responsibilities. . . . Faust's provocative analysis of a complex subject merits a place in all collections of U.S. history." Publ Wkly

Includes bibliographical references

Fredriksen, John C.

Civil War almanac. Facts on File, Inc. 2007 858p il map (Almanacs of American wars) $85

Grades: 11 12 Adult   973.7

1. United States—History—1861-1865, Civil War

ISBN 0-8160-6459-8; 978-0-8160-6459-5

                                                LC 2006-29985

First published 1983 under the editorship of John Stewart Bowman

This book contains a "day-by-day chronology of the events and people of this monumental war, along with an A-to-Z dictionary offering biographical information on leading military and political figures involved in the conflict." Publisher's note

Includes bibliographical references

Geary, Rick, 1946-

The murder of Abraham Lincoln; a chronicle of 62 days in the life of the American Republic, March 4-May 4, 1865; written and illustrated by Rick Geary. NBM ComicsLit 2005 unp il map (A treasury of Victorian murder) $15.95; pa $8.95 *

Grades: 7 8 9 10 11 12   973.7

1. Lincoln, Abraham, 1809-1865—Assassination 2. Booth, John Wilkes, 1838-1865 3. Graphic novels

ISBN 978-1-56163-425-5; 1-56163-425-5; 978-1-56163-426-2 (pa); 1-56163-426-3 (pa)

                                                LC 2005-41468

This graphic novel "covers Lincoln's assassination, the events that led up to it, and the aftermath. Geary also makes a point of bringing up still-unanswered questions, like the whereabouts of the missing pages of John Wilkes Booth's journal. . . . Even teens who know nothing about the tragedy will find their heads chock-full of information when they're finished reading this book." SLJ

Includes bibliographical references

Gourley, Catherine, 1950-

The horrors of Andersonville; life and death inside a Civil War prison. Twenty-First Century Books 2010 193p il lib bdg $38.60

Grades: 8 9 10 11 12   973.7

1. Wirz, Henry, d. 1865 2. Andersonville Prison 3. Prisoners of war 4. United States—History—1861-1865, Civil War—Prisoners and prisons

ISBN 978-0-7613-4212-0; 0-7613-4212-5

                                                LC 2008-46595

"This well-researched book describes the notorious Confederate prison camp known as Andersonville, where more than 45,000 Union soldiers lived in deplorable conditions and some 13,000 died, beginning in 1864. . . . Illustrated with many captioned photos and prints and enlivened with quotes from firsthand accounts, this book provides a balanced, informative introduction to Andersonville." Booklist

Includes bibliographical references

Hargrove, Hondon B., 1916-

Black Union soldiers in the Civil War. McFarland & Co. 1988 250p il hardcover o.p. pa $35 *

Grades: 11 12 Adult   **973.7**
1. United States. Army—History 2. United States—History—1861-1865, Civil War 3. African American soldiers
ISBN 0-89950-337-3; 0-7864-1697-1 (pa)
LC 88-42511

This volume "discusses the participation of Blacks in the Union Army during the Civil War. The chronologically arranged narrative covers Black soldiers in each battle. Special features include an extensive bibliography and nine appendixes that reprint documents and include rosters and statistics." Nichols. Guide to Ref Books for Sch Media Cent. 4th edition

Krowl, Michelle A., 1969-

Women of the Civil War. Library of Congress 2006 63p il (Women who dare) $12.95 *

Grades: 9 10 11 12   **973.7**
1. United States—History—1861-1865, Civil War—Women
ISBN 0-7649-3546-1; 978-0-7649-3546-6
LC 2005-40195

This book "celebrates women of both the North and the South whose courage and daring brought them into the fray, whether by donning men's clothes and fighting as soldiers, becoming spies, working as nurses in the bloody battlefields, or becoming propagandists for the cause." Publisher's note
Includes bibliographical references

Leonard, Elizabeth D.

All the daring of the soldier; women of the Civil War armies. Norton 1999 368p il hardcover o.p. pa $22.95

Grades: 11 12 Adult   **973.7**
1. Women soldiers 2. United States—History—1861-1865, Civil War
ISBN 978-0-393-04712-7; 0-393-04712-1; 978-0-393-33547-7 (pa); 0-393-33547-X (pa)
LC 98-52304

The author presents "stories of dozens of women who served in both the Union and Confederacy during the Civil War. Some were spies, but many more adopted men's names, dressed in men's clothes and lived and fought and died alongside mostly unsuspecting men." Publ Wkly
Includes bibliographical references

Lincoln, Abraham, 1809-1865

The portable Abraham Lincoln; edited with an introduction by Andrew Delbanco. Bicentennial ed. Penguin Books 2009 xxvii, 369p (Penguin classics) pa $18 *

Grades: Adult   **973.7**
1. United States—Politics and government—1815-1861 2. United States—Politics and government—1861-1865
ISBN 978-0-14-310564-0; 0-14-310564-7
LC 2008-32452

First published 1992
Material drawn from Speeches and writings, published by the Library of America (1989).
"This collection shows Lincoln at work in law, politics, and war. All the great Lincoln works are here, with the added bonus of several personal memos that show Lincoln's humor." Libr J

The **Lincoln** mailbag; America writes to the President, 1861-1865; edited by Harold Holzer. Southern Ill. Univ. Press 1998 xxxv, 236p il $32; pa $22.95

Grades: 9 10 11 12   **973.7**
1. Lincoln, Abraham, 1809-1865 2. United States—History—1861-1865, Civil War
ISBN 0-8093-2072-X; 0-8093-2685-X (pa)
LC 97-42164

This collection of letters to President Lincoln includes "death threats, requests for offices, requests for money, invitations to speak, unsolicited gifts, proposals for new weapons, and pesterings for favors from obscure relatives and impostors. . . . A revealing glimpse into how civil war and emancipation appeared from the White House, this browsable collection of epistles and replies enriches the body of Lincolniana." Booklist

Marten, James, 1956-

Civil War America; voices from the home front. ABC-CLIO 2003 346p il $85 *

Grades: 11 12 Adult   **973.7**
1. United States—History—1861-1865, Civil War—Personal narratives
ISBN 1-576-07237-1   LC 2002-154377
Also available in paperback from Fordham University Press
"Marten offers a view of the war through the eyes of diverse noncombatants. Four parts of this five-part work each deal with Southerners, Northerners, children, and African Americans . . . Part five, 'Aftermaths,' includes descriptions of the postwar lives of veterans, orphans, and ex-slaves, and concludes with a chapter on the Civil War stories by Ambrose Bierce. Readers will find Marten's overarching theme of change—both immediate and long-range—revelatory and instructional." SLJ
Includes bibliographical references

Masur, Louis P.

The Civil War: a concise history. Oxford University Press 2011 118p il $18.95

Grades: 11 12 Adult   **973.7**
1. United States—History—1861-1865, Civil War
ISBN 978-0-19-974048-2   LC 2010-19460
The author provides "a concise but compelling narrative of the Civil War era, packing in the critical information to track the trajectory of secession, war, emancipation, and Reconstruction. He focuses on the political and the military, with Lincoln, Jefferson Davis, and the generals especially getting their due." Libr J
Includes bibliographical references

McNeese, Tim
The abolitionist movement; ending slavery. Chelsea House 2007 142p il (Reform movements in American history) lib bdg $30
Grades: 8 9 10 11 12   **973.7**
1. Abolitionists 2. Slavery—United States
ISBN 978-0-7910-9502-7; 0-7910-9502-9
                                        LC 2007-14766
"Complex, detailed, and yet very readable, this title . . . discusses the struggles and differences within the antislavery movement as well as the fight for emancipation and its crucial role in the Civil War. . . . The book offers a sound exploration of the topic." Booklist
Includes bibliographical references

McPherson, James M.
Abraham Lincoln and the second American Revolution. Oxford Univ. Press 1991 173p pa $16.95 hardcover o.p.
Grades: 11 12 Adult   **973.7**
1. Lincoln, Abraham, 1809-1865 2. United States—History—1861-1865, Civil War
ISBN 0-19-507606-0 (pa)   LC 90-6885
The author "examines Lincoln's role in the transformation wrought by the Civil War—the liberation of four million slaves, the overthrow of the social and political order of the South." Publ Wkly
Includes bibliographical references

Drawn with the sword; reflections on the American Civil War. Oxford Univ. Press 1996 258p $45; pa $18.95
Grades: 11 12 Adult   **973.7**
1. Lincoln, Abraham, 1809-1865 2. United States—History—1861-1865, Civil War
ISBN 0-19-509679-7; 0-19-511796-4 (pa)
                                        LC 95-38107
A collection of "essays on some of the most thought-provoking questions of the Civil War. All of the essays were published earlier but have been updated and revised for this compilation. The topics deal with such subjects as the origins of the Civil War, the slavery question in both North and South, why the North won the war and why the South lost, President Abraham Lincoln, and the change in historical writing." Libr J
"These pieces provide a lively reminder that the best scholarship is also often a pleasure to read." N Y Times Book Rev

For cause and comrades; why men fought in the Civil War. Oxford Univ. Press 1997 237p $25; pa $15.95
Grades: 11 12 Adult   **973.7**
1. Soldiers—United States 2. United States—History—1861-1865, Civil War
ISBN 0-19-509023-3; 0-19-512499-5 (pa)
                                        LC 96-24760
"Volumes have been written on the causes of the Civil War, but less has been written on what caused soldiers to risk their lives on the battlefield. McPherson . . . fills the gap. After studying thousands of letters and diaries, he discusses what really led soldiers to enlist, what kept them in the army, and what led them to the front lines." Libr J
Includes bibliographical references

Murphy, Jim, 1947-
The boys' war; Confederate and Union soldiers talk about the Civil War. Clarion Bks. 1990 110p il hardcover o.p. pa $8.95
Grades: 5 6 7 8 9 10   **973.7**
1. United States—History—1861-1865, Civil War
ISBN 0-89919-893-7; 0-395-66412-8 (pa)
                                        LC 89-23959
This book includes diary entries, personal letters, and archival photographs to describe the experiences of boys, sixteen years old or younger, who fought in the Civil War.
"An excellent selection of more than 45 sepia-toned contemporary photographs augment the text of this informative, moving work." SLJ
Includes bibliographical references

National Geographic Society (U.S.)
Atlas of the Civil War; a comprehensive guide to the tactics and terrain of battle; edited by Neil Kagan; narrative by Stephen G. Hyslop; introduction by Harris J. Andrews. National Geographic Society 2009 255p il map $40
Grades: 11 12 Adult   **973.7**
1. United States—History—1861-1865, Civil War—Maps 2. Historical atlases 3. Reference books
ISBN 978-1-4262-0347-3   LC 2008-35066
"Arranged chronologically, this atlas combines period photographs and illustrations, rare period maps and modern cartography, with just enough narrative to explain the two-page spread devoted to each subject (the majority being about particular battles or campaigns). . . . The text also features numerous sidebars throughout, offering micro-timelines, biographies, and images showing the human side of the war. All of these special features make this large-format atlas a superior choice for Civil War buffs as well as those new to the subject." Libr J

Netzley, Patricia D.
Civil War. Greenhaven Press 2004 336p il (Greenhaven encyclopedia of) lib bdg $74.95 *
Grades: 8 9 10 11 12   **973.7**
1. United States—History—1861-1865, Civil War—Encyclopedias 2. Reference books
ISBN 0-7377-0438-1   LC 2003-11808
An alphabetical presentation of definitions and descriptions of terms, people, and events of the Civil War
"Basic, accurate information about many aspects of the war. . . . The well-written, objective entries are cross-referenced. . . . Netzley's solid volume will be helpful to students needing introductory research material." SLJ
Includes bibliographical references

Osborne, Linda Barrett, 1949-

Traveling the freedom road; from slavery and the Civil War through Reconstruction. Abrams Books for Young Readers 2009 128p il map $24.95

Grades: 6 7 8 9 10 **973.7**

1. African Americans—History 2. Slavery—United States 3. United States—History—1861-1865, Civil War 4. Reconstruction (1865-1876) 5. United States—Politics and government—1783-1865 6. United States—Politics and government—1865-1898

ISBN 978-0-8109-8338-0; 0-8109-8338-9

LC 2008-22298

"This fascinating, well-designed volume offers an essential introduction to the experiences of African Americans between 1800 and 1877. . . . Osborne moves from . . . personal stories to broader historical milestones, and in highly accessible language, she provides basic background even as she challenges readers with philosophical questions. . . . This fluid exchange between political events and intimate, human stories creates a highly absorbing whole." Booklist

Sears, Stephen W.

Gettysburg. Houghton Mifflin 2003 623p il map $30; pa $17 *

Grades: 11 12 Adult **973.7**

1. Gettysburg (Pa.), Battle of, 1863

ISBN 0-395-86761-4; 0-618-48538-4 (pa)

LC 2002-191259

This is an "assessment of the battle of Gettysburg and the events leading up to it. . . . Sears examines several turning points during the battle's buildup and three-day duration. The resulting insights add to the excellent and dramatic narrative flow. . . . For all Civil War collections and academic libraries." Libr J

Includes bibliographical references

Seidman, Rachel Filene

The Civil war: a history in documents. Oxford University Press 2001 206p il map (Pages from history) lib bdg $39.95

Grades: 8 9 10 11 12 **973.7**

1. United States—History—1861-1865, Civil War—Sources

ISBN 978-0-19-511558-1; 0-19-511558-9

LC 00-37523

"Seidman's documents bookend the Civil War with the territorial expansion that preceded the conflict and with the Reconstruction that followed it. In this structure the documents, under the guidance of Seidman's linking narrative, all make a powerful impression of immediacy about ordinary people's experience of, and condemnation or defense of, slavery." Booklist

Includes bibliographical references

Snodgrass, Mary Ellen

The Underground Railroad; an encyclopedia of people, places, and operations. Sharpe Reference 2007 2v il map set $199 *

Grades: 7 8 9 10 11 12 Adult **973.7**

1. Underground railroad—Encyclopedias 2. Slavery—United States—Encyclopedias 3. Reference books

ISBN 978-0-7656-8093-8

LC 2007-9199

The author "has compiled an important and extensively researched encyclopedia of the Underground Railroad. Beginning with a concise, informative general introduction, this ambitious two-volume set neatly identifies the key people, places, documents, organizations, and publications of the Underground Railroad movement, along with significant actions, events, and ideas underlying it in the US and Canada. Offering photographs, bookplates, sketches, and handbills, the set is visually attractive." Choice

Includes bibliographical references

Swanson, Mark, 1951-

Atlas of the Civil War, month by month; major battles and troop movements; maps by Mark Swanson, with Jacqueline D. Langley. University of Georgia Press 2004 141p il map $39.95

Grades: 11 12 Adult **973.7**

1. United States—History—1861-1865, Civil War—Maps 2. Historical atlases 3. Reference books

ISBN 0-8203-2658-5

LC 2004-12264

This Civil War atlas depicts "multiple aspects of the war's action in a month-by-month sequence from April 1861 to June 1865. . . . An absolute must for Civil War studies." Univ Press Books for Public and Second Sch Libr, 2006

Includes bibliographical references

Tobin, Jacqueline, 1950-

Hidden in plain view; the secret story of quilts and the underground railroad; [by] Jacqueline L. Tobin and Raymond G. Dobard. Doubleday 1999 208p il map hardcover o.p. pa $14

Grades: 11 12 Adult **973.7**

1. Underground railroad 2. Ciphers 3. Quilts

ISBN 0-385-49137-9; 0-385-49767-9 (pa)

LC 98-49804

The authors present the "theory that slaves created quilts coded with patterns to help one another flee to freedom." N Y Times Book Rev

This is "a needed and valuable contribution to the literature of African American culture." Libr J

Includes bibliographical references

Walker, Sally M.

Secrets of a Civil War submarine; solving the mysteries of the H.L. Hunley. Carolrhoda Books 2005 112p il lib bdg $17.95 *

Grades: 7 8 9 10 **973.7**

1. Hunley (Submarine) 2. United States—History—1861-1865, Civil War—Naval operations 3. Shipwrecks 4. Underwater exploration 5. Submarines

ISBN 1-57505-830-8

LC 2004-19646

Contents: Prologue: a lost treasure; A seafaring stealth weapon; Climb aboard; Disaster; Lieutenant Dixon's mission; A stunning discovery; The Hunley talks; Buried treasures; In touch with the past; Forensic tales

This discusses "the Confederate submarine H. L. Hunley. . . . Walker begins with the history of the Hunley's design and construction as well as its place in Civil War and naval history. She really hits her stride,

Walker, Sally M.—*Continued*
though, in explaining the complex techniques and loving care used in raising the craft, recovering its contents, and even reconstructing models of the crewmembers' bodies. . . . Thoroughly researched, nicely designed, and well illustrated with clear, color photos." Booklist

Includes glossary and bibliographical references

Ward, Andrew, 1946-
The slaves' war; the Civil War in the words of former slaves. Houghton Mifflin Co. 2008 386p il $28
Grades: 11 12 Adult   **973.7**
1. United States—History—1861-1865, Civil War—Personal narratives 2. Slavery—United States
ISBN 978-0-618-63400-2; 0-618-63400-2
    LC 2008-1532
The author "has provided a . . . narrative that gives voice to the experiences and attitudes of slaves who endured the conflict. Ward utilizes testimonials, diaries, and letters, and organizes them in chronological order from the months before the commencement of hostilities to the aftermath of the surrender at Appomattox. . . . This is a work that will interest both scholars and general readers." Booklist

Includes bibliographical references

Women in the American Civil War; Lisa Tendrich Frank, editor. ABC-CLIO 2008 2v il set $195
Grades: 10 11 12 Adult   **973.7**
1. United States—History—1861-1865, Civil War—Women—Encyclopedias 2. Reference books
ISBN 978-1-85109-600-8   LC 2007-25822
"Frank's two-volume work emphasizes the role of women in the American Civil War. With its wealth of information and resources, this set will be a welcome addition to any reference collection. Fourteen contextual essays discuss the social and political issues of the era and the varied backgrounds of women affected by the war. Over 300 entries include biographical sketches, key military and political events, and the contributions of women during the war." Choice

Includes bibliographical references

Woodworth, Steven E.
Atlas of the Civil War; by Steven Woodworth and Kenneth J. Winkle; foreword by James M. McPherson. Oxford University Press 2004 400p il map $75 *
Grades: 11 12 Adult   **973.7**
1. United States—History—1861-1865, Civil War—Maps 2. Historical atlases 3. Reference books
ISBN 0-19-522131-1   LC 2004-53112
"Each of five major chapters is devoted to a single year from 1861 to 1865. In addition to every important battle, there is coverage of nonmilitary topics, such as population, the economy, transportation, elections, and the home front. . . . The work ends with a list of major battle sites, a chronology, a glossary, a short bibliography, and an index, which provides access to illustrations and maps as well as names." Booklist

"Richly illustrated, this publication will be wanted by all types of libraries. . . . The text entries are useful, while the maps and illustrations are both informative and eye-catching." Choice

Cultures in conflict: the American Civil War. Greenwood Press 2000 xx, 220p (Greenwood Press cultures in conflict series) $45 *
Grades: 11 12 Adult   **973.7**
1. United States—History—1861-1865, Civil War
ISBN 0-313-30651-6   LC 99-43165
"The history documents, including diary entries, letters, and photographs, provide a rich panorama of America's bloodiest conflict. Brief introductory paragraphs to each document or set of documents remind readers about the cultural differences that brought the country to the point of war and continued to flourish throughout this period and beyond." Voice Youth Advocates

Includes bibliographical references

973.8   United States—Reconstruction period, 1865-1901

Encyclopedia of the Gilded Age and Progressive Era; edited by John D. Buenker and Joseph Buenker. M.E. Sharpe 2005 3v il set $299
Grades: 11 12 Adult   **973.8**
1. United States—History—1865-1898—Encyclopedias 2. United States—History—1898-1919—Encyclopedias 3. Reference books
ISBN 0-7656-8051-3   LC 2003-24653
This set focuses "on a period between 1870 and 1920, when the United States emerged as an urban and industrial world power. Some 900 A-Z entries cover key individuals, events, and organizations of the times, and 17 essays discuss broad themes like the economy, politics, religion, and pop culture." Libr J

Includes bibliographical references

Foner, Eric
Forever free; the story of emancipation and Reconstruction; illustrations edited and with commentary by Joshua Brown. Knopf 2005 xxx, 268p il $27.50; pa $15 *
Grades: 11 12 Adult   **973.8**
1. Reconstruction (1865-1876) 2. Slavery—United States 3. United States—Politics and government—1865-1898
ISBN   0-375-40259-4;   978-0-375-40259-3; 0-375-70274-1 (pa); 978-0-375-70274-7 (pa)
    LC 2005-40706
"Forever Free project: Stephen B. Brier, Peter O. Almond, executive editors/producers; Christine Doudna, editor."

This "examination of the years of Emancipation and Reconstruction during and immediately following the Civil War emphasizes the era's political and cultural meaning for today's America." Publisher's note

This "is an invaluable and timely book about a subject central to U.S. history and still of obvious significance today—slavery, the Civil War, emancipation, Reconstruction, and both the immediate aftermath and longer-term consequences of those things." Rev Am Hist

Includes bibliographical references

The **Gilded** Age: a history in documents; [compiled by] Janette Thomas Greenwood. Oxford Univ. Press 2000 191p il map (Pages from history) $39.95; pa $24.95
Grades: 7 8 9 10   **973.8**
1. United States—History—1865-1898
ISBN   978-0-19-510523-0;   0-19-510523-0;
978-0-19-516638-5 (pa); 0-19-516638-8 (pa)
LC 99-98194
Uses a wide variety of documents to show how Americans dealt with an age of extremes from 1887 to 1900, including rapid industrialization, unemployment, unprecedented wealth, and immigration
"There's plenty to absorb and much to capture the imagination. . . . Greenwood presents the history as a seamless tapestry sewn by the people who lived it." Booklist
Includes bibliographical references

Golay, Michael, 1951-
Spanish-American war; John S. Bowman, general editor. Rev. ed. Chelsea House 2010 170p il map (America at war) $45 *
Grades: 9 10 11 12   **973.8**
1. Spanish-American War, 1898
ISBN 978-0-8160-8189-9   LC 2009-31795
First published 1995
This is an "account of the events leading to war and of the ensuing battles fought on land and sea, ending with a thought-provoking assessment of this important conflict from which the United States emerged as a major player on the world stage. . . . [It] also features a chapter devoted to the new military tactics and weapons used during the conflict." Publisher's note
Includes glossary and bibliographical references

Grumet, Bridget Hall
Reconstruction era: primary sources; Lawrence W. Baker, project editor. UXL 2004 xxv, 228p il (Reconstruction Era reference library) $60 *
Grades: 11 12 Adult   **973.8**
1. Reconstruction (1865-1876)
ISBN 0-7876-9219-0   LC 2004-17309
This book "contains 19 complete or partial documents, such as the Fourteenth Amendment of the U.S. Constitution and Rutherford B. Hayes' inaugural address. Each document is accompanied by an introduction, keys to reading the document, a discussion of subsequent events related to the document, and other material." Booklist
Includes bibliographical references

Hansen, Joyce
Bury me not in a land of slaves; African-Americans in the time of Reconstruction. Watts 2000 160p il lib bdg $23 *
Grades: 7 8 9 10   **973.8**
1. African Americans—History 2. Reconstruction (1865-1876) 3. United States—Race relations
ISBN 0-531-11539-9   LC 99-30040
An account of African-American life in the period of Reconstruction following the Civil War, based on first-person narratives, contemporary documents, and other historical sources
"Readers of this balanced, well-written account will come away with a solid understanding of the period's events and how they contributed to the twentieth century's segregation and prejudice." Booklist
Includes bibliographical references

Hillstrom, Kevin
American Indian removal and the trail to Wounded Knee; [by] Kevin Hillstrom and Laurie Collier Hillstrom. Omnigraphics 2010 250p il (Defining moments) lib bdg $55
Grades: 8 9 10 11 12   **973.8**
1. Native Americans—Relocation 2. Native Americans—Great Plains 3. Wounded Knee Creek, Battle of, 1890
ISBN 978-0-7808-1129-4; 0-7808-1129-1
LC 2010-4676
"Analyzes the development of Indian removal policies and the tragedy at Wounded Knee, the 1890 massacre of American Indians by U.S. Cavalry troops. Examines the wider context of Indian-white relations in America." Publisher's note
"This well-written volume effectively explores a topic of intense historical debate. Fascinating sidebars add significantly to the text." SLJ
Includes glossary and bibliographical references

Reconstruction; opposing viewpoints in world history; Laura K. Egendorf, book editor. Greenhaven Press 2004 224p il map (Opposing viewpoints in world history) lib bdg $34.95; pa $23.70 *
Grades: 9 10 11 12   **973.8**
1. Reconstruction (1865-1876)
ISBN 0-7377-1703-3 (lib bdg); 0-7377-1704-1 (pa)
LC 2003-49016
"The book uses a pro/con format to present articles both from the time period, such as ones by Abraham Lincoln, Frederick Douglass, and W.E.B. Du Bois, and articles written retrospectively. . . . [This] should be available in every high school library and in every upper-level Social Studies and AP classroom." Libr Media Connect
Includes bibliographical references

Roosevelt, Theodore, 1858-1919
The Rough Riders; new introduction by Elting E. Morison. Da Capo Press 1990 298p il pa $16
Grades: 9 10 11 12   **973.8**
1. United States. Army. Volunteer Cavalry, 1st—History 2. Spanish-American War, 1898
ISBN 0-306-80405-0   LC 90-38860
Also available in paperback from Modern Library
A reprint of the title first published 1899 by Scribner
This is a history of the First United States Volunteer Cavalry, which fought in the Spanish-American War under the command of Theodore Roosevelt

Sandoz, Mari, 1896-1966

The Battle of the Little Bighorn. Lippincott 1966 191p maps (Great battles of history series) hardcover o.p. pa $12.95

Grades: 11 12 Adult   **973.8**

1. Custer, George Armstrong, 1839-1876 2. Little Bighorn, Battle of the, 1876

ISBN 0-397-00410-9; 0-8032-9100-0 (pa)

"An account of the United States Army expedition against the Sioux Nation with emphasis on the political motives and ambitions of General Custer." Publ Wkly

Includes bibliographical references

Schlereth, Thomas J.

Victorian America; transformations in everyday life, 1876-1915. HarperCollins Pubs. 1991 363p (Everyday life in America) pa $15 hardcover o.p.

Grades: 11 12 Adult   **973.8**

1. United States—Social life and customs

ISBN 0-06-092160-9 (pa)   LC 89-46555

The author surveys the objects, events, experiences, products and tastes that comprised what he terms America's Victorian culture (1876-1915) and shows how its values shaped modern life.

"What a wonderful book. . . . Schlereth is no wry compiler of trivia. His analysis of social context reveals truly profound, intangible transformations in how and where Americans spent their time during four pivotal decades." Booklist

Includes bibliographical references

Shifflett, Crandall A.

Victorian America, 1876 to 1913; {by} Crandall Shifflett. Facts on File 1996 408p il maps (Almanacs of American life) $95 *

Grades: 11 12 Adult   **973.8**

1. United States—Social life and customs

ISBN 0-8160-2531-2   LC 95-13553

This illustrated overview of 19th century America contains sections on: historical geography; native American life; government; popular culture; urban development; influential personalities; and arts and letters

Includes bibliographical references

Viola, Herman J., 1938-

It is a good day to die; Indian eyewitnesses tell the story of the Battle of the Little Bighorn; [by] Herman J. Viola with Jan Shelton Danis. University of Nebraska Press 2001 101p il map pa $12.95 *

Grades: 5 6 7 8 9 10   **973.8**

1. Custer, George Armstrong, 1839-1876 2. Little Bighorn, Battle of the, 1876 3. Dakota Indians—Wars 4. Cheyenne Indians

ISBN 0-8032-9626-6   LC 2001-34669

First published 1998 by Crown

A series of eyewitness accounts of the 1876 Battle of Little Bighorn and the defeat of General Custer as told by Native American participants in the war.

"This is a thought-provoking, accessible compilation that will give new insight to the study of American history." Bull Cent Child Books

Includes bibliographical references

Welch, James, 1940-2003

Killing Custer; the Battle of the Little Bighorn and the fate of the Plains Indians; by James Welch with Paul Stekler. Norton 1994 320p il pa $14.95 hardcover o.p. *

Grades: 11 12 Adult   **973.8**

1. Little Bighorn, Battle of the, 1876 2. Native Americans—Wars

ISBN 0-393-32939-9 (pa)   LC 94-5617

"Welch produced this history of the Indian wars of the northern plains as a by-product of his work scripting a television documentary on the Battle of the Little Bighorn. In addition to military history, it contains long sections describing the life of the Plains Indians, accounts of contemporary Indian radical groups, and Welch's reactions while visiting the various historic sites in the area." Libr J

Includes bibliographical references

973.9   United States—1901-

American decades. Gale Res. 1994-2009 11v set $1495

Grades: 11 12 Adult   **973.9**

1. United States—Civilization 2. United States—History—20th century

ISBN 0-7876-5076-5

Also available American decades primary sources ten volume companion set $1495 (ISBN 0-7876-6587-8)

"A Manly, Inc. book"

The set is divided as follows: 1900-1909 (ISBN 0-8103-5722-4); 1910-1919 (ISBN 0-8103-5723-2); 1920-1929 (ISBN 0-8103-5724-0); 1930-1939 (ISBN 0-8103-5725-9); 1940-1949 (ISBN 0-8103-5726-7); 1950-1959 (ISBN 0-8103-5727-5); 1960-1969 (ISBN 0-8103-8883-9); 1970-1979 (ISBN 0-8103-8882-0); 1980-1989 (ISBN 0-8103-8881-2); 1990-1999 (ISBN 0-7876-4030-1); 2000-2009 (ISBN 978-1-4144-3606-7)

"A series of volumes covering the twentieth century by decades. . . . Fun to browse, each volume is divided into 13 sections covering topics such as the arts, government and politics, lifestyles and social trends, medicine and health, and sports. Each section opens with a chronology and overview and closes with short biographies, deaths, and a bibliography of important books published in the decade. Sidebars highlight events and prominent individuals." Am Libr

American decades primary sources; Cynthia Rose, project editor. Gale 2004 10v il map set $1495

Grades: 11 12 Adult   **973.9**

1. United States—Civilization 2. United States—History—20th century—Sources

ISBN 0-7876-6587-8   LC 2002-8155

Companion set to American decades published 1994-2000

Contents: [1] 1900-1909; [2] 1910-1919; [3] 1920-1929; [4] 1930-1939; [5] 1940-1949; [6] 1950-1959; [7] 1960-1969; [8] 1970-1979; [9] 1980-1989; [10] 1990-1999

"A treasure trove of more than 2,000 primary sources on U.S. history and culture, ranging from speeches and literary works to graphs and architectural drawings. Although many of the sources might be found on the

American decades primary sources—*Continued*
Internet, they lack the organization and context provided here." Booklist

Gordon, Lois G.
American chronicle; year by year through the twentieth century; {by} Lois Gordon and Alan Gordon; with an introduction by Roger Rosenblatt. Yale Univ. Press 1999 998p $49.95 *
Grades: 11 12 Adult   **973.9**
  1. United States—Civilization
  ISBN 0-300-07587-1   LC 99-24886
  First published 1987 by Atheneum Pubs. with title: American chronicle; six decades in American life, 1920-1980; variant title: The Columbia chronicles of American life, 1910-1992
  This volume presents in a year by year format the events, personalities, and elements of popular culture for each year of the period

Gould, Lewis L.
The modern American presidency; foreword by Richard Norton Smith. 2nd ed., rev. and updated. University Press of Kansas 2009 318p il $34.95; pa $17.95
Grades: 11 12 Adult   **973.9**
  1. Presidents—United States
  ISBN 978-0-7006-1683-1; 0-7006-1683-7; 978-0-7006-1684-8 (pa); 0-7006-1684-5 (pa)
                                                     LC 2009-20161
  First published 2003
  Contents The age of Cortelyou: William McKinley and Theodore Roosevelt; The lawyer and the professor: William Howard Taft and Woodrow Wilson; The modern presidency recedes: Warren G. Harding, Calvin Coolidge, and Herbert Hoover; The modern presidency revives and grows: Franklin D. Roosevelt; The presidency in the Cold War era: Harry S. Truman and Dwight D. Eisenhower; The souring of the modern presidency: John F. Kennedy and Lyndon B. Johnson; The rise of the continuous campaign: Richard Nixon; The modern presidency under siege: Gerald Ford and Jimmy Carter; The modern presidency in a Republican era: Ronald Reagan and George H.W. Bush; Perils of the modern presidency: Bill Clinton; The modern presidency in crisis: George W. Bush
  "Gould traces the decline of the party system, the increasing importance of the media and its role in creating the president-as-celebrity, and the growth of the White House staff and executive bureaucracy. He also shows us a succession of chief executives who increasingly have known less and less about the business of governing the country, observing that most would have had a better historical reputation if they had contented themselves with a single term." Publisher's note
  Includes bibliographical references

The **Greenwood** guide to American popular culture; edited by M. Thomas Inge and Dennis Hall. Greenwood Press 2002 4v il set $399.95
  Grades: 11 12 Adult   **973.9**
  1. Popular culture—United States
  ISBN 0-313-30878-0   LC 2002-71291
  Based on the Handbook of American popular culture and Handbook of American popular literature

This "offers overviews of various aspects of our culture. The 58 signed articles touch on topics from almanacs and amusement parks to pornography and propaganda, and from science fiction and self-help to television and young adult fiction. The selections cover trends from the 17th century to the present with a focus on the 20th century." SLJ
"Students searching for help in locating resources specific to different aspects of popular culture will find these volumes an excellent starting point." Voice Youth Advocates
Includes bibliographical references

Lemann, Nicholas
The promised land; the great black migration and how it changed America. Knopf 1991 401p pa $16.95 hardcover o.p. *
Grades: 11 12 Adult   **973.9**
  1. African Americans—Social conditions 2. Internal migration
  ISBN 0-679-73347-7 (pa)   LC 90-52951
  An "account of the migration of 6.5 million black people from rural South to urban North between 1910-1970." N Y Times Book Rev
  The author "describes why the war on poverty did not succeed and why the civil rights movement yielded only partial victories in trying to win improvements. While Lemann's interviews establish the human drama of this process, his assessment of the consequences of this great movement both for African Americans and for the entire country raises substantial questions of justice and equality that cut to the heart of the social situation of the impoverished and oppressed today." Booklist
  Includes bibliographical references

Roosevelt, Eleanor, 1884-1962
Courage in a dangerous world; the political writings of Eleanor Roosevelt; edited by Allida M. Black. Columbia Univ. Press 1999 362p il $34.50; pa $17.95
Grades: 11 12 Adult   **973.9**
  1. United States—Politics and government—1933-1945 2. United States—Politics and government—1953-1961
  ISBN 0-231-11180-0; 0-231-11181-9 (pa)
                                                      LC 98-33807
  "This collection of columns, essays, speeches, and letters documents Eleanor Roosevelt's political transformation from self-effacing first lady to outspoken defender of democracy and human rights." Libr J
  Includes bibliographical references

973.91   United States—1901-1953

Allen, Frederick Lewis, 1890-1954
Only yesterday; an informal history of the 1920's. Wiley 1997 285p (Wiley investment classics) $21.95 *
Grades: 11 12 Adult   **973.91**
  1. United States—History—1919-1933 2. United States—Social conditions 3. United States—Economic conditions—1919-1933
  ISBN 0-471-18952-9   LC 97-19930

Allen, Frederick Lewis, 1890-1954—*Continued*

Also available in paperback from HarperCollins Pubs.
A reissue of the title first published 1931 by Harper
and Brothers

"An account of the years from the spring of 1919 to
. . . {1931}. It is a kaleidoscopic picture of American
politics, society, manners, morals, and economic conditions." Booklist

Includes bibliographical references

Burg, David F.

The Great Depression. updated ed. Facts on File
2005 xx, 444p il (Eyewitness history) $75

Grades: 8 9 10 11 12   **973.91**

1. Great Depression, 1929-1939 2. United States—
Economic conditions—1919-1933 3. United States—
Economic conditions—1933-1945

ISBN 0-8160-5709-5; 978-0-8160-5709-2

                  LC 2004-29126

First published 1996

"The book is divided into seven chapters, each covering a specific timeframe beginning with causative events
preceding the crisis (1919-1928) and ending with the
emerging Second World War (1939-1941.) Each chapter
opens with a narrative summary and analysis of the period, followed by a chronological listing of significant
events and then by primary-source contemporary quotations from private citizens, politicians, radio broadcasts,
and more." Voice Youth Advocates

Includes bibliographical references

Encyclopedia of the Great Depression; Robert
McElvaine, editor in chief. Macmillan Reference
USA 2004 2v set $265

Grades: 11 12 Adult   **973.91**

1. Great Depression, 1929-1939—Encyclopedias
2. New Deal, 1933-1939—Encyclopedias 3. United
States—Economic conditions—1933-1945—Encyclopedias 4. Reference books

ISBN 0-02-865686-5   LC 2003-10292

This "encyclopedia features entries on depression-era
politics, government, business, economics, literature, the
arts, society and culture. While its main focus is on the
Great Depression within the United States, the global impact of the economic slow-down is also examined
through articles on Canada, Mexico, Australia, Europe,
Africa and Asia." Publisher's note

"This comprehensive, accessible set will serve as a
useful supplement for research." SLJ

Includes bibliographical references

Encyclopedia of the Jazz Age; from the end of
World War I to the great crash; edited by James
Ciment. M.E. Sharpe 2008 2v il set $199

Grades: 9 10 11 12   **973.91**

1. United States—History—1919-1933—Encyclopedias
2. Reference books

ISBN 978-0-7656-8078-5   LC 2007-23928

This encyclopedia contains "information on the politics, economics, society, and culture of the [pre-Great
Depression] era. . . . Entries cover themes, personalities,
institutions, ideas, events, trends, and more." Publisher's
note

Includes bibliographical references

The **forties** in America; editor, Thomas Tandy
Lewis. Salem Press 2010 c2011 3v il map set
$364

Grades: 9 10 11 12 Adult   **973.91**

1. United States—History—1933-1945—Encyclopedias
2. United States—History—1945-1953—Encyclopedias
3. United States—Social life and customs—Encyclopedias 4. Reference books

ISBN 978-1-58765-659-0

Also available online

This set features "entries covering the social scene
('Bobby-soxers'), literature ('Literature in the United
States'), music ('Andrews Sisters'), law ('Cantwell v.
Connecticut'), and many other contemporary topics."
Libr J

Includes bibliographical references

The **Great** Depression and World War II, 1929 to
1949; Rodney P. Carlisle, general editor. Facts
on File 2009 287p il map (Handbook to life in
America) $50

Grades: 9 10 11 12   **973.91**

1. Great Depression, 1929-1939 2. World War, 1939-
1945 3. United States—History—1919-1933
4. United States—History—1933-1945

ISBN 978-0-8160-7180-7; 0-8160-7180-2

"The work is prefaced by a lucid general introduction
covering the history of the Great Depression, the New
Deal, World War II, and American arts and culture of
the time. Each signed chapter focuses on topics from the
fabric of daily life such as social attitudes, religion,
transportation, labor, and education and concludes with a
valuable list of titles for further reading. . . . With a
combination of excellent writing, manageable length, and
compelling subject matter, it will be an indispensable resource for research papers and AP classes." SLJ

Includes bibliographical references

Gregory, Ross

Modern America, 1914 to 1945. Facts on File
1995 455p il maps (Almanacs of American life)
$95

Grades: 11 12 Adult   **973.91**

1. United States—History—20th century 2. United
States—Social life and customs

ISBN 0-8160-2532-0   LC 94-4168

The author "interweaves brief discussions with statistical tables to provide deeper perspectives of major themes
in American history not found in annual almanacs. . . .
Themes covered include population and immigration,
transportation and communication, politics and government, religion, science, and the world wars." Libr J

Includes bibliographical references

Kennedy, David M., 1941-

Freedom from fear; the American people in
depression and war, 1929-1945. Oxford Univ.
Press 1999 936p il maps (Oxford history of the
United States) $39.95; pa $22.50

Grades: 11 12 Adult   **973.91**

1. United States—History—1919-1933 2. United
States—History—1933-1945

ISBN 0-19-503834-7; 0-19-514403-1 (pa)

                 LC 98-49580

Kennedy, David M., 1941-—*Continued*

This narrative history of the United States spans the period from the Great Depression to the end of the Second World War

"Rarely does a work of historical synthesis combine such trenchant analysis and elegant writing. For its scope, its insight and its purring narrative engine, Kennedy's book will stand for years to come as the definitive account of the critical decades of the American century." Publ Wkly

Includes bibliographical references

McElvaine, Robert S., 1947-

The Depression and New Deal; a history in documents. Oxford Univ. Press 2000 192p il (Pages from history) hardcover o.p. pa $19.95 *

Grades: 7 8 9 10   **973.91**
    1. Great Depression, 1929-1939 2. United States—Economic conditions—1933-1945
    ISBN 0-19-510493-5; 0-19-516636-1 (pa)
                                                    LC 99-36644

"A vast assortment of diary entries, newspaper articles, campaign memos and speeches, political cartoons, songs, poetry, art, advertisements, photographs, and personal letters provide students with a political, economic, and social picture of this nation during the Depression. . . . [This] provides a balanced, inclusive picture of the period through the senses of the people who lived it." SLJ

Includes bibliographical references

Streissguth, Thomas

The roaring twenties; [by] Tom Streissguth. Rev ed. Facts on File 2007 500p il map (Eyewitness history) $75

Grades: 9 10 11 12   **973.91**
    1. United States—History—1919-1933
    ISBN 0-8160-6423-7; 978-0-8160-6423-6
                                                    LC 2006-21723

First published 2001 as part of the Facts on File library of American history series

This book "provides hundreds of firsthand accounts of the period—from diary entries, letters, speeches, and newspaper accounts—that illustrate how historical events appeared to those who lived through them." Publisher's note

Includes bibliographical references

Terkel, Studs, 1912-2008

Hard times; an oral history of the great depression. Norton 2000 462p pa $14.95 *

Grades: 11 12 Adult   **973.91**
    1. Great Depression, 1929-1939 2. United States—Social conditions 3. United States—Economic conditions—1919-1933 4. United States—Economic conditions—1933-1945
    ISBN 1-56584-656-7   LC 2003-389318

A reissue of the title first published 1970 by Pantheon Bks.

"Persons of all ages, occupations, and classes scattered across the U.S. remember what they experienced or were told about the economic crisis of the 1930's. The result is a social document of immense interest." Booklist

Watkins, T. H. (Tom H.), 1936-2000

The hungry years; a narrative history of the Great Depression in America. Holt & Co. 1999 587p il pa $17 hardcover o.p.

Grades: 11 12 Adult   **973.91**
    1. Great Depression, 1929-1939 2. United States—Economic conditions—1919-1933 3. United States—Economic conditions—1933-1945
    ISBN 0-8050-6506-7 (pa)   LC 99-10391

"A Marian Wood book"

"This book explores how everyday Americans across the country coped with economic disaster." Libr J

"The vignettes Watkins selects are gritty, visceral, and seamlessly sutured to the federal programs that rolled out in the course of the decade, making this a signal addition to the rich historiography of the Depression." Booklist

Includes bibliographical references

Young, William H.

World War II and the postwar years in America; a historical and cultural encyclopedia; [by] William H. Young and Nancy K. Young. ABC-CLIO 2010 2v il set $180

Grades: 10 11 12   **973.91**
    1. United States—History—1933-1945—Encyclopedias
    2. United States—History—1945-1953—Encyclopedias
    3. World War, 1939-1945—Encyclopedias
    4. Reference books
    ISBN 978-0-313-35652-0; 978-0-313-35653-7 (ebook)
                                                    LC 2010-21470

Contact publisher for ebook pricing

This encyclopedia "contains over 175 articles describing everyday life on the American home front during World War II and the immediate postwar years. . . . The work covers a . . . range of everyday activities throughout the 1940s, including movies, radio programming, music, the birth of commercial television, advertising, art, bestsellers, and other . . . topics." Publisher's note

Includes bibliographical references

973.92 United States—1953-2001

Bok, Chip, 1952-

A recent history of the United States in political cartoons; a look Bok! University of Akron Press 2005 291p il (Series on law, politics, and society) $26.95; pa $16.95

Grades: 9 10 11 12   **973.92**
    1. United States—Politics and government—1974-1989—Cartoons and caricatures 2. United States—Politics and government—1989-—Cartoons and caricatures
    ISBN 1-931968-11-X; 1-931968-12-8 (pa)
                                                    LC 2005-41935

This is a collection of political cartoons satirizing the people and events of the late 20th and early 21st century.

Brill, Marlene Targ, 1945-
America in the 1970s. Lerner 2009 144p il (The decades of twentieth-century America) lib bdg $38.60
Grades: 7 8 9 10   **973.92**
1. United States—History—1961-1974 2. United States—History—1974-1989 3. United States—Social conditions
ISBN 978-0-8225-3438-9; 0-8225-3438-X
LC 2007-38570
This is "a tightly constructed, smoothly phrased overview of the tumultuous 1970s. . . . The serviceable text is bolstered by skillful connections between events and movements, well-chosen representative quotes . . . and occasional snappy headlines . . . while sidebars profiling individuals and historical turning points . . . and a well-edited selection of photos add more interest." Booklist

Frum, David, 1960-
How we got here; the 70's: the decade that brought you modern life (for better or worse). Basic Bks. 2000 xxiv, 418p il pa $18.95 hardcover o.p.
Grades: 11 12 Adult   **973.92**
1. United States—Civilization—1970-
ISBN 0-465-01496-5 (pa)
The author "aims 'to describe—and to judge' the transformation of American values during the '70s. Surveying politics, legal cases and opinion polls as well as popular culture, he links what he sees as America's loss of faith in government, the rise of 'sourness and cynicism' and the culture of licentiousness and divorce, among other social changes, to events in that decade." Publ Wkly
Includes bibliographical references

Gregory, Ross
Cold War America, 1946 to 1990; Richard Balkin, general editor. Facts on File 2003 670p il map (Almanacs of American life) $105 *
Grades: 11 12 Adult   **973.92**
1. Cold war 2. United States—History—1945- 3. United States—Social conditions
ISBN 0-8160-3868-6   LC 2001-51136
"This is a treasure trove of statistical information documenting the enormous changes in American life from 1945 to 1990. . . . Found herein are data on everything from the population by sex . . . region, and race, business formations and failures, bull and bear markets, and operations of the postal service to the federal debt, high school seniors and drugs, executions by gender and race, and recipients of National Book Awards and Pulitzer Prizes. . . . Enhancing the work's appeal are photographs throughout the text and an exhaustive index." Am Ref Books Annu, 2003
Includes bibliographical references

Halberstam, David, 1934-2007
The fifties. Villard Bks. 1993 800p il pa $17.95 hardcover o.p.
Grades: 11 12 Adult   **973.92**
1. United States—Social life and customs 2. United States—Politics and government—20th century 3. Popular culture—United States
ISBN 0-449-90933-6 (pa)   LC 92-56815
This is a social history of the United States during the 1950s
The author's "sources are secondary and derivative, but his instinct for the revealing anecdote, his ear for the memorable quote, and his awesome powers of organization add up to a variegated overview that moves seamlessly between the serious shenanigans of Chief Justice Earl Warren and the frivolous ones of . . . Grace Metalious." Natl Rev
Includes bibliographical references

Kort, Michael
The Columbia guide to the Cold War. Columbia Univ. Press 1998 366p (Columbia guides to American history and cultures) $60; pa $19.50
Grades: 11 12 Adult   **973.92**
1. Cold war 2. United States—Foreign relations 3. United States—History—1945-
ISBN 0-231-10772-2; 0-231-10773-0 (pa)
LC 98-7154
The author begins "with a narrative survey of the Cold War which explains some of the historiographical debates that have occupied historians for more than 50 years. Following this section is a mini-encyclopedia consisting of one- or two-page essays on a wide range of Cold War topics. The book concludes with a concise chronology and a comprehensive bibliography of books, films, novels, journal articles, and archival sources. Finally . . . Kort points out some of the relevant current websites and CD-ROM products." Libr J

Maga, Timothy P., 1952-
The 1960s. Facts on File 2003 xx, 396p il map (Eyewitness history) $75 *
Grades: 9 10 11 12   **973.92**
1. United States—History—1961-1974 2. United States—Civilization
ISBN 0-8160-4809-6   LC 2002-14119
This volume covers the 1960s "from the cold war days of the Cuban Missile Crisis to the assassinations of John F. Kennedy, Robert F. Kennedy, and Martin Luther King, Jr., to the Vietnam War; from the Beach Boys to the Beatles to the Rolling Stones; from Hippies and Yippies to race riots and Kent State. [These events are depicted] in the words of Americans who experienced the major events and issues of the decade." Publisher's note
Includes bibliographical references

McWilliams, John C., 1949-
The 1960s cultural revolution. Greenwood Press 2000 xxxvii, 187p (Greenwood Press guides to historic events of the twentieth century) $49.95 *
Grades: 11 12 Adult   **973.92**
1. United States—History—1961-1974
ISBN 0-31329-913-7   LC 99-58963

McWilliams, John C., 1949-—*Continued*

"The changes and challenges that manifested themselves in the 1960s did not begin and end in a neat 10-year package, so this book actually runs through to 1975 and the end of the Vietnam War. . . . The book has a lengthy chronology, a notable selection of primary documents, and an extensive annotated bibliography that includes videos and Web sites." SLJ

Includes bibliographical references

The **nineties** in America; editor, Milton Berman. Salem Press, Inc. 2009 3v il set $364

Grades: 9 10 11 12 Adult   **973.92**
1. United States—History—1989-—Encyclopedias 2. Reference books
ISBN 978-1-58765-500-5; 1-58765-500-4
           LC 2008-49939

"The 600-plus entries are arranged alphabetically and vary in length from half a page to six pages. The focus is not only on the significant people and events of the last decade but also on the impact of technology and other advances. . . . Each volume contains a table of contents for all three volumes, and at the end of Volume 3 are 16 appendixes covering everything from major films of the decade to time lines for each year." Libr J

Includes bibliographical references

Pendergast, Tom, 1964-

The sixties in America. Almanac; [by] Tom Pendergast and Sara Pendergast. U.X.L. 2005 xxxviii, 229p il (U-X-L the sixties in America reference library) $63

Grades: 11 12 Adult   **973.92**
1. United States—History—1961-1974
ISBN 0-7876-9246-8   LC 2004-16601

This book provides "essays on social and political developments: the antiwar movement, civil rights, feminism and the sexual revolution, and sweeping cultural changes in popular entertainment, sports, and the arts." Booklist

Includes bibliographical references

The sixties in America. Primary sources; [by] Tom Pendergast and Sara Pendergast. U.X.L 2005 xxxviii, 240p il (U-X-L the sixties in America reference library) $60 *

Grades: 9 10 11 12   **973.92**
1. United States—History—1961-1974
ISBN 0-7876-9248-4   LC 2004-16602

This "volume contains primary documents including including George Wallace's inaugural speech, an excerpt from 'The Ballot or The Bullet' by Malcolm X, and NOW's 'Bill of Rights for Women in 1968.' Chapters are followed by Where to Learn More and an index. Each except is accompanied by a glossary that defines terms, people, and ideas." Libr Media Connect

Includes bibliographical references

Postwar America; an encyclopedia of social, political, cultural, and economic history; James Ciment, editor. M.E. Sharpe 2006 4v il set $399

Grades: 11 12 Adult   **973.92**
1. United States—Civilization—Encyclopedias 2. Reference books
ISBN 0-7656-8067-X; 978-0-7656-8067-9
           LC 2004-13120

"A-Z entries address specific persons, groups, concepts, events, geographical locations, organizations, and cultural and technological phenomena. Sidebars highlight primary source materials, items of special interest, statistical data, and other information; and Cultural Landmark entries chronologically detail the music, literature, arts, and cultural history of the era. Bibliographies covering literature from the postwar era and about the era are also included, as well as illustrations and specialized indexes." Publisher's note

Includes bibliographical references

Rather, Dan

The American dream; stories from the heart of our nation. Morrow 2001 xxii, 266p hardcover o.p. pa $12.95

Grades: 11 12 Adult   **973.92**
1. American national characteristics 2. United States—Social life and customs 3. United States—Social conditions
ISBN 0-688-17892-8; 0-06-093770-X (pa)
           LC 2001-30031

In this book Rather tells stories of individual Americans and their dreams. He "groups his material into chapters that focus on elements of our national aspirations: liberty, enterprise, pursuit of happiness, family, fame, education, innovation, and 'giving back.' The Americans that Rather describes are a diverse group but, he urges, their stories are an inspirational reminder of the power of the nation's fundamental ideas to motivate a wide range of people." Booklist

Schwartz, Richard Alan, 1951-

The 1950s; [by] Richard A. Schwartz. Facts on File 2003 504p il maps (Eyewitness history) $75 *

Grades: 9 10 11 12   **973.92**
1. United States—Civilization 2. United States—History—1945-1953 3. United States—History—1953-1961
ISBN 0-8160-4597-6   LC 2002-1149

Contents: Introduction; Postwar prelude: 1945-1949; America becomes the world's policeman: 1950; The Cold War settles in: 1951; "I like Ike": 1952; New leadership in Washington and Moscow: 1953; Separate is not equal: 1954; Self-created annihilation becomes a possibility: 1955; Ike and Elvis, Budapest and the Suez: 1956; Sputnik and Little Rock: 1957; America enters outer space: 1958; America expands into the Pacific: 1959

The chapters in this volume "describe each year of the decade with a narrative account of the most significant social, cultural, and political developments; a chronology of events; and eyewitness testimonies drawn from newspapers, memoirs of private and public figures, literature, and other sources." Publisher's note

Includes bibliographical references

The 1990s; [by] Richard A. Schwartz. Facts on File 2006 496p il (Eyewitness history) $75 *

Grades: 11 12 Adult   **973.92**
1. United States—History—1989- 2. United States—Politics and government—1989-
ISBN 0-8160-5696-X   LC 2004-28884

Schwartz, Richard Alan, 1951-—*Continued*

This book "provides hundreds of firsthand accounts of the 1990s—including diary entries, letters, speeches, and newspaper accounts—that illustrate how historical events appeared to those who lived through them. Each chapter provides an introductory essay and a chronology of events." Publisher's note

Includes bibliographical references

Sitkoff, Harvard

Postwar America; a student companion. Oxford Univ. Press 2000 292p il $45

Grades: 11 12 Adult   **973.92**
1. United States—History—1945-
ISBN 0-19-510300-9   LC 98-34183

"The articles in this volume cover events, people, documents, legal cases, and social and political movements and groups that have had an impact on our country since the end of World War II. The alphabetical entries range from one paragraph to four pages." SLJ

Includes bibliographical references

Sixties counterculture; Stuart A. Kallen, book editor. Greenhaven Press 2001 224p il (History firsthand) hardcover o.p. pa $19.95 *

Grades: 9 10 11 12   **973.92**
1. Counter culture 2. Radicalism 3. United States—History—1961-1974 4. United States—Social conditions
ISBN 0-7377-0407-1; 0-7377-0406-3 (pa)
LC 00-29377

"Chapters touch on such topics as feminism, war protests, civil rights, free speech, the hippie culture, and the birth of yippies. The text comes from primary—source material—from figures such as Huey Newton, Carletta Fields, and Eldridge Cleaver—which was actually written during the '60s as well as as excerpts from books written well after that decade." SLJ

"The overview is interesting reading, and some of the excerpts are excellent. A few selections include language that may be objectionable, though a more sanitized approach would not accurately represent the era." Booklist

Includes bibliographical references

The **Sixties** in America; editor, Carl Singleton; project editor, Rowena Wildin. Salem Press 1999 3v il set $315

Grades: 11 12 Adult   **973.92**
1. United States—History—1961-1974—Encyclopedias 2. United States—Social life and customs 3. Reference books
ISBN 0-89356-982-8   LC 98-49255

This set covers "the events, people, organizations, scientific advances, and popular culture of the sixties. The generally brief articles are alphabetically arranged and written chiefly by academic contributors. . . . Appendixes cover such topics as major legislation and important Supreme Court decisions and provide statistics and a time line of science and technology. An extensive, up-to-date bibliography and a mediagraphy listing electronic materials, videos, and Web sites conclude the set." SLJ

Woodger, Elin

The 1980s; [by] Elin Woodger and David F. Burg. Facts on File 2006 508p il map (Eyewitness history) $75

Grades: 9 10 11 12   **973.92**
1. United States—History—1974-1989 2. United States—Politics and government—1974-1989
ISBN 0-8160-5809-1; 978-0-8160-5809-1
LC 2005-18732

This book provides a look at the 1980s, "illustrating how events appeared to those who lived through them. In addition to the firsthand accounts, each chapter provides an introductory essay and a chronology of events. The book also includes critical documents, as well as capsule biographies of key figures, a bibliography, an index, 92 black-and-white photographs and illustrations, and 13 maps and graphs." Publisher's note

Includes bibliographical references

973.923 United States— Administration of Lyndon B. Johnson, 1963-1969

Benson, Harry

RFK: a photographer's journal; [edited by Gigi Benson and Manuela Soares] PowerHouse Books 2008 143p il $40.07

Grades: 9 10 11 12 Adult   **973.923**
1. Kennedy, Robert F., 1925-1968—Portraits 2. United States—History—1961-1974—Pictorial works
ISBN 978-1-57687-450-9; 1-57687-450-8

"From Saint Patrick's Day 1968, when Robert F. Kennedy announced his candidacy for president of the United States, until his funeral procession to Arlington Cemetery on June 6, . . . Scottish photographer Benson sought to capture the hope and excitement of RFK's brief campaign. Arranged chronologically, this series of documentary photographs begins with an intimate family vacation on the Snake River near Boise, ID, and continues through the fast-paced, highly publicized campaign. . . . This moving tribute is recommended for all libraries." Libr J

973.924 United States— Administration of Richard Nixon, 1969-1974

Bernstein, Carl

All the president's men; {by} Carl Bernstein, Bob Woodward. Simon & Schuster 1999 349p il hardcover o.p. pa $14

Grades: 11 12 Adult   **973.924**
1. Washington post 2. Watergate Affair, 1972-1974
ISBN 0-684-86355-3; 0-671-89441-2 (pa)
LC 98-54773

A reissue of the title first published 1974

The two Washington Post reporters whose investigative journalism first revealed the Watergate scandal tell the way it happened from the first suspicions, through

Bernstein, Carl—*Continued*

the trail of false leads, lies, secrecy, and high-level pressure, to the final moments when they were able to put the pieces of the puzzle together and write the series that won the Post a Pulitzer Prize

Genovese, Michael A.

The Watergate crisis. Greenwood Press 1999 xxix, 197p il (Greenwood Press guides to historic events of the twentieth century) $46.95

Grades: 11 12 Adult   **973.924**

1. Nixon, Richard M. (Richard Milhous), 1913-1994 2. Watergate Affair, 1972-1974

ISBN 0-313-29878-5   LC 99-17858

This book "provides a historical overview of the Watergate crisis, an account of the development of Nixon's political personality, a discussion of whether the president can ever act outside legal limits, a presentation of historical precedent for presidential corruption, an analysis of Nixon's relationships with the news media, and a conclusion about the Watergate legacy." SLJ

Includes glossary and bibliographical references

Olson, Keith W., 1931-

Watergate; the presidential scandal that shook America. University Press of Kansas 2003 220p il $35; pa $15.95

Grades: 11 12 Adult   **973.924**

1. Watergate Affair, 1972-1974

ISBN 0-7006-1250-5; 0-7006-1251-3 (pa)

LC 2002-38058

The author describes "the White House-approved break-in at Democratic National Committee headquarters in Washington's Watergate complex and its aftermath—most importantly, the dramatic proceedings of the Senate Watergate Committee. . . . {This} book provides an excellent, compact narrative of a crucial moment in the history of the American presidency." Publ Wkly

Includes bibliographical references

Woodward, Bob, 1943-

The final days; {by} Bob Woodward, Carl Bernstein. Simon & Schuster 1976 476p il pa $16 hardcover o.p.

Grades: 11 12 Adult   **973.924**

1. Nixon, Richard M. (Richard Milhous), 1913-1994 2. Watergate Affair, 1972-1974 3. United States—Politics and government—1961-1974

ISBN 0-7432-7406-7 (pa)

The title refers to the final days of the Nixon Presidency. The authors have "constructed a two-part narrative, the first half covering the period from April 30, 1973—the day John Dean was fired as White House counsel—until late July 1974, and the second half covering the last two weeks in detail." N Y Times Book Rev

973.929   United States— Administration of Bill Clinton, 1993-2001

Klein, Joe, 1946-

The natural: the misunderstood presidency of Bill Clinton. Doubleday 2002 230p hardcover o.p. pa $14.99

Grades: 11 12 Adult   **973.929**

1. Clinton, Bill, 1946- 2. United States—Politics and government—1989-

ISBN 0-385-50619-8; 0-7679-1412-0 (pa)

LC 2001-47428

The author discusses Bill Clinton's character, the accomplishments and problems of his administration, the making of policy and the workings of the White House.

"This book is more readable than . . . others, dense but tight, funny, adroitly written and, in sum, the first savvy synthesis of the Clinton Age." N Y Times Book Rev

973.93   United States—2001-

Does the world hate the U.S.? Roman Espejo, book editor. Greenhaven Press 2009 120p (At issue. International politics) $33.70; pa $23.85

*

Grades: 9 10 11 12   **973.93**

1. United States—Foreign opinion 2. United States—Foreign relations

ISBN   978-0-7377-4096-7;   0-7377-4096-5; 978-0-7377-4097-4 (pa); 0-7377-4097-3 (pa)

LC 2008022301

Articles in this anthology discuss the causes of anti-American sentiment worldwide.

Includes bibliographical references

973.931   United States— Administration of George W. Bush, 2001-2009

America under attack: primary sources; Tamara Roleff, book editor. Lucent Bks. 2002 96p il map (Lucent terrorism library) $27.45

Grades: 7 8 9 10   **973.931**

1. September 11 terrorist attacks, 2001 2. Terrorism

ISBN 1-59018-216-2   LC 2002-1816

Looks at the September 11, 2001 terrorist attack on the World Trade Center and Pentagon, U.S. response, world reaction, and the war on terrorism

"Roleff's useful compendium offers thematically arranged perspectives from witnesses in New York and Washington, DC, U.S. and world leaders, the blamed and the accusers, and war proponents and opponents. . . . This will be a sought-after research tool." SLJ

Includes bibliographical references

America's battle against terrorism; Andrea C. Nakaya, book editor. Greenhaven Press 2005 208p (Current controversies) lib bdg $34.95; pa $23.70 *

Grades: 9 10 11 12   **973.931**

1. War on terrorism 2. Terrorism

ISBN 0-7377-2783-7 (lib bdg); 0-7377-2784-5 (pa)
       LC 2004-54122

"This volume explores the effectiveness of the tactics the United States uses against terrorists, the effect battling terrorism has on civil liberties in America, the impact of the war in Iraq, and whether the United States is prepared for another terrorist attack." Publisher's note

Includes bibliographical references

Bernstein, Richard

Out of the blue; the story of September 11, 2001, from Jihad to Ground Zero; {by} Richard Bernstein and the staff of the New York Times. Times Bks. 2002 287p il hardcover o.p. pa $15 *

Grades: 11 12 Adult   **973.931**

1. September 11 terrorist attacks, 2001 2. Terrorism

ISBN 0-8050-7240-3; 0-8050-7410-4 (pa)
       LC 2002-20396

This account of the September 11, 2001 terrorist attacks focuses "on the personal—the victims, the perpetrators and heroes whose lives became tangled in catastrophe. . . . It uses these stories as a jumping-off point for a comprehensive look at the terror attacks—the reactions of New Yorkers, the nation and the world; the criticism of U.S. government agencies; the lingering effects of the tragedy. While some of this information has been published elsewhere, it has not been gathered so comprehensively—nor has it been written so well." Publ Wkly

Friedman, Thomas L.

Longitudes and attitudes; exploring the world after September 11. Farrar, Straus & Giroux 2002 383p $23

Grades: 11 12 Adult   **973.931**

1. September 11 terrorist attacks, 2001 2. Terrorism 3. United States—Politics and government—1989- 4. United States—Foreign relations

ISBN 0-374-19066-6   LC 2002-74321

Also available in paperback from Anchor Bks.

This is a collection "of Friedman's *New York Times* columns from September 2001 through June 2002, with a lengthy postscript describing Friedman's travels and interviews throughout this period." Booklist

"Unapologetically pro-American, Friedman's deliberation on what changed on September 11 outside of the U.S. ultimately centers on the strength of American society and our place in the world." Publ Wkly

Includes bibliographical references

Gerdes, Louise

9/11; Louise I. Gerdes, book editor. Greenhaven Press 2010 227p il map (Perspectives on modern world history) lib bdg $39.70

Grades: 8 9 10 11 12   **973.931**

1. September 11 terrorist attacks, 2001 2. War on terrorism 3. United States—Politics and government—2001-

ISBN 978-0-7377-4793-5   LC 2010-264

"This comprehensive book includes articles about the evolution of the attacks and their aftermath, the emotional changes in New York City, the response of the international community post-9/11, and the experiences of American Muslims. The texts of a speech by former President George W. Bush and a document including one 9/11 terrorist's instructions for future terrorists are also included. Articles address civil liberties, conspiracy theories, and environmental and health threats in an intelligent, well-researched, and evenhanded manner." SLJ

Includes bibliographical references

How should the United States treat prisoners in the war on terror? Lauri S. Friedman, book editor. Greenhaven Press 2005 110p (At issue) lib bdg $28.70; pa $19.95 *

Grades: 9 10 11 12   **973.931**

1. War on terrorism 2. Prisoners of war

ISBN 0-7377-3113-3 (lib bdg); 0-7377-3114-1 (pa)
       LC 2004-53501

This book "explores the variety of perspectives regarding how the United States should deal with the prisoners in the war on terror." Publisher's note

Includes bibliographical references

Jacobson, Sidney

The 9/11 report; a graphic adaptation; by Sid Jacobson and Ernie Colón; [with a foreword by Thomas H. Kean and Lee H. Hamilton] Hill and Wang 2006 133p il $30; pa $16.95 *

Grades: 9 10 11 12 Adult   **973.931**

1. September 11 terrorist attacks, 2001—Graphic novels 2. Graphic novels

ISBN   0-8090-5738-7;   978-0-8090-5738-2; 0-8090-5739-5 (pa); 978-0-8090-5739-9 (pa)

On cover: Based on the final report of the National Commission on Terrorist Attacks upon the United States

"The book aims to make . . . [The 9/11 Commission Report] more accessible to all readers and draw in young adults. . . . This graphic adaptation is an important and necessary part of any collection." Libr J

After 9/11: America's war on terror (2001-). Hill and Wang 2008 149p il map pa $16.95 *

Grades: 9 10 11 12 Adult   **973.931**

1. Graphic novels 2. Terrorism—Graphic novels 3. Iraq War, 2003- —Graphic novels 4. United States—Politics and government—Graphic novels 5. United States—Foreign relations—Graphic novels

ISBN 978-0-8090-2370-7   LC 2008-13298

"A novel graphic"

On cover: A work of graphic journalism

In 2006, longtime comic book veterans Jacobson and Colon adapted the 9/11 Commission's report into a

Jacobson, Sidney—*Continued*

graphic format that made it a readable, comprehensible work for teens and adults. Now they have used the comic book treatment to cover America's War on Terror since 2001, including the wars in Iraq and in Afghanistan, summarizing events and showing the major players throughout the years. Some images can be disturbing, such as the depiction of prisoner mistreatment at Abu Ghraib and other facilities, as well as depictions of the victims of sectarian violence.

A **Just** response; the Nation on terrorism, democracy, and September 11, 2001; edited by Katrina van den Heuvel. Thunder's Mouth Press 2002 349p pa $14.95 *

Grades: 11 12 Adult   **973.931**
1. Nation (Periodical) 2. September 11 terrorist attacks, 2001 3. Terrorism
ISBN 1-56025-400-9

"Included in this . . . collection of essays, articles, and editorials published in the *Nation* since September 11 are contributions that address issues pertaining to First Amendment rights, civil liberties, social justice, disarmament, international law, and world opinion within the context of the current war on terrorism." Booklist

"Although the Nation's targets range from Defense Secretary Donald Rumsfeld to Bayer, the manufacturer of Cipro, the harshest criticism is reserved for the mainstream media. . . . Those who found the early coverage of America's 'War on Terror' to be monotonous will appreciate the Nation's radical point of view." Publ Wkly

**National Commission on Terrorist Attacks
  Upon the United States**

The 9/11 Commission report; final report of the National Commission on Terrorist Attacks Upon the United States. Norton 2004 567p il $19.95; pa $10

Grades: 11 12 Adult   **973.931**
1. Al Qaeda (Organization) 2. September 11 terrorist attacks, 2001 3. Terrorism 4. War on terrorism 5. National security—United States
ISBN 0-393-06041-1; 0-393-32671-3 (pa)
                                        LC 2004-57564
Also available in paperback from St. Martin's Press
"Authorized edition"

This work aims to describe how the terrorist attacks of September 11, 2001 occurred and to provide recommendations for the prevention of future attacks.

This book "reads like a Shakespearean drama. . . . This multi-author document produces an absolutely compelling narrative intelligence, one with clarity, a sense of shared mission and an overriding desire to *do* something about the situation." Publ Wkly

Includes bibliographical references

Spiegelman, Art

In the shadow of no towers. Pantheon Books 2004 various paging il $19.95

Grades: 10 11 12 Adult   **973.931**
1. September 11 terrorist attacks, 2001—Graphic novels 2. Graphic novels
ISBN 0-375-42307-9   LC 2004-43870

This is a "memoir of the attacks on the World Trade Center, which Spiegelman witnessed from close range, a rant on their effects on the world at large and within the author, and a monograph on the Sunday newspaper comic strips of the early 20th century." N Y Times Book Rev

The author "provides a hair-raising and wry account of his family's frantic efforts to locate one another on September 11 as well as a morbidly funny survey of his trademark sense of existential doom. . . . This is a powerful and quirky work of visual storytelling by a master comics artist." Publ Wkly

The **war** on terrorism: opposing viewpoints; Karen F. Balkin, book editor. Greenhaven Press 2005 206p il hardcover o.p. pa $22.45

Grades: 9 10 11 12   **973.931**
1. War on terrorism 2. Terrorism
ISBN 0-7377-2336-X (lib bdg); 0-7377-2337-8 (pa)
                                        LC 2004-47442
"Opposing viewpoints series"

This book features 28 essays on topics such as Is the War on Terrorism Justified? and Is the Domestic War on Terrorism a Threat to Civil Liberties? Contributors include Dr. Leonard Peikoff, George W. Bush, Tom Ridge, and Colin Powell

Includes bibliographical references

974.7 New York

Dwyer, Jim, 1957-

102 minutes; the untold story of the fight to survive inside the Twin Towers; [by] Jim Dwyer and Kevin Flynn. Times Books 2005 322p il $26; pa $15 *

Grades: 11 12 Adult   **974.7**
1. World Trade Center terrorist attack, 2001 2. September 11 terrorist attacks, 2001
ISBN 0-8050-7682-4; 0-8050-8032-5 (pa)
                                        LC 2004-55321
The authors "take us into the 102 minutes of hell experienced by those in the World Trade Center between the time the first jet crashed into the north tower and the last standing tower toppled. While other accounts have focused on the members of NYFD and NYPD who responded to the catastrophe, this book tells the stories of scores of civilians." Libr J

Dwyer and Flynn have "given us a fitting tribute to the people caught up in one of the great dramas of our time. And for people still haunted by the events of that day, reading '102 Minutes' provides a cathartic release." N Y Times Book Rev

Getzinger, Donna, 1968-

The Triangle Shirtwaist Factory fire. Morgan Reynolds Pub. 2008 128p il map (American workers) $27.95 *

Grades: 7 8 9 10   **974.7**
1. Triangle Shirtwaist Company, Inc. 2. New York (N.Y.)—History 3. Labor—Law and legislation
ISBN 978-1-59935-099-8; 1-59935-099-8
                                        LC 2008-4077

Getzinger, Donna, 1968-—Continued

"Beginning with a brief account of the disaster, a description of the popular shirtwaist and the fabric used to make the blouse, the women who lost their lives, and the impact of the lack of communication among the workers, the first chapter is sure to hook readers. Successive chapters look more closely at New York City's growth, the varied immigrant population at that time, overcrowded factory conditions, the failure to enforce building regulations, and the many sweatshops developed from the desire of contractors to make money. . . . Archival photos and diagrams with captions add to the meaning of this devastating and important event in the history of labor." SLJ

Includes bibliographical references

Marsico, Katie, 1980-

The Triangle Shirtwaist Factory fire; its legacy of labor rights. Marshall Cavendish Benchmark 2010 112p il (Perspectives on) lib bdg $27.95
Grades: 7 8 9 10   **974.7**
1. Triangle Shirtwaist Company, Inc. 2. New York (N.Y.)—History 3. Fires
ISBN 978-0-7614-4027-7; 0-7614-4027-5
                                    LC 2008-23267

"This well-written title examines many of the details preceding the 1911 disaster, the conditions that caused it, and the impact the incident continues to have on labor and businesses today. Historical accounts of the event, told through numerous direct quotes and shown in black-and-white photos of sweatshops and descriptions of tenement living conditions, reveal that poor labor laws and factory regulations were to blame. . . . Color photos and full-page sidebars provide additional information." SLJ

Includes bibliographical references

Von Drehle, Dave

Triangle: the fire that changed America. Atlantic Monthly Press 2003 340p il hardcover o.p. pa $14
Grades: 11 12 Adult   **974.7**
1. Triangle Shirtwaist Company, Inc. 2. Fires 3. New York (N.Y.) 4. Clothing industry 5. Factories
ISBN 0-87113-874-3; 0-8021-4151-X (pa)
                                    LC 2003-41835

"The tragic conflagration at the Triangle Shirtwaist Factory in March 1911 resulted in the deaths of 123 women (most of them young immigrants), caused widespread public outrage, and set in motion a wave of reform. Drehle's vivid retelling of this horrifying event begins with the strike that immediately preceded it and then examines the terrible fire, the unsuccessful prosecution of the factory owners, and the fight to prevent similar tragedies in the future." Libr J

"Von Drehle's engrossing account, which emphasizes the humanity of the victims and the theme of social justice, brings on of the pivotal and most shocking episodes of American labor history to life." Publ Wkly

Includes bibliographical references

975.6 North Carolina

Miller, Lee

Roanoke; solving the mystery of the Lost Colony. Penguin Books 2002 362p il map pa $16
Grades: 11 12 Adult   **975.6**
1. Roanoke Island (N.C.)—History
ISBN 978-0-14-200228-5; 0-14-200228-3
First published 2000 in the United Kingdom; first U.S. edition 2001 by Arcade Pub.

The author "blames the colony's disappearance on treachery and murder she traces to the court of Elizabeth I. Conspiracy theorists should find much to savor in this convoluted story, which includes palace intrigues, cultural misunderstandings, and gray-eyed Native Americans. . . . This is an interesting, well-told tale." Libr J

Includes bibliographical references

975.8 Georgia

Foxfire 40th anniversary book; faith, family, and the land; edited by Angie Cheek, Lacy Hunter Nix, and Foxfire students. Anchor Books 2006 xxxix, 512p il pa $17.95 *
Grades: 11 12 Adult   **975.8**
1. Country life—Georgia 2. Appalachian region—Social life and customs 3. Handicraft
ISBN 0-307-27551-5; 978-0-307-27551-6
                                    LC 2006-45311

"Drawing on the magazine's published talks by local high school students with elderly rural inhabitants, the books have explored the crafts, cooking, music, gardening and stories that have been passed down through the generations. The focus in this anniversary volume is on devotion to religion, family and the land. Collecting pieces from 40 years' worth of the magazine, the book inevitably covers topics covered in previous Foxfire collections, including snake handling, childhood toys and recipes. But the spoken words remain captivating, eloquent if plainspoken." Publ Wkly

976.1 Alabama

McWhorter, Diane

Carry me home; Birmingham, Alabama: the climactic battle of the civil rights revolution. Simon & Schuster 2001 701p il hardcover o.p. pa $17
Grades: 11 12 Adult   **976.1**
1. African Americans—Civil rights 2. Birmingham (Ala.)—Race relations
ISBN 0-684-80747-5; 0-7432-1772-1 (pa)
                                    LC 00-53827

Maps on lining papers

McWhorter presents an account of the struggle for civil rights in Birmingham, Ala., both from a personal and societal perspective

"A daughter of Birmingham's privileged elite, McWhorter weaves a personal narrative through this startling account of the history, events, and major players on both sides of the civil rights battle in that city." Booklist

Includes bibliographical references

976.3 Louisiana

Dyson, Michael Eric, 1958-
Come hell or high water; Hurricane Katrina and the color of disaster. Basic Civitas 2006 258p $23; pa $14.95
Grades: 11 12 Adult   **976.3**
1. Hurricane Katrina, 2005 2. Disaster relief 3. African Americans—Social conditions
ISBN 978-0-465-01761-4; 0-465-01761-4; 978-0-465-01772-0 (pa); 0-465-01772-X (pa)
LC 2007-310210
This book on Hurrican Katrina "not only chronicles what happened when, it also argues that the nation's failure to offer timely aid to Katrina's victims indicates deeper problems in race and class relations. . . . [The author's] contention that Katrina exposed a dominant culture pervaded not only by 'active malice' toward poor blacks but also by a long history of 'passive indifference' to their problems is both powerful and unsettling." Publ Wkly
Includes bibliographical references

Van Heerden, Ivor Ll., 1950-
The storm; what went wrong and why during Hurricane Katrina; [by] Ivor van Heerden and Mike Bryan. Viking 2006 308p il map hardcover o.p. pa $15
Grades: 11 12 Adult   **976.3**
1. Hurricane Katrina, 2005 2. Disaster relief
ISBN 0-670-03781-8; 0-14-311213-9 (pa)
LC 2006-44727
This book focuses on public mismanagement relating to Hurricane Katrina.
"This serious, scientific explanation of what exactly happened in the hours—and years—leading up to Hurricane Katrina's devestation of New Orleans brings a fresh perspective to a tragedy that has generated remarkably similar news accounts over the past eight months." Publ Wkly
Includes bibliographical references

Voices rising; stories from the Katrina Narrative Project; edited by Rebeca Antoine; [afterword by Fredrick Barton] UNO Press 2008 244p pa $12.95
Grades: 9 10 11 12 Adult   **976.3**
1. Hurricane Katrina, 2005—Personal narratives
ISBN 978-0-9728143-6-2; 0-9728143-6-1
In this "collection of personal narratives, readers come face-to-face with the stark reality wrought by Hurricane Katrina and the failure of the federal levees. . . . Every aspect of the post-Katrina New Orleans experience is present here, from areas as divergent as the I10 overpass, the French Quarter, and shelters across the South. The rescuers and rescued have equal voices and share memories poignant and startling. . . . Miles away from academic analysis, this is American social history from the ground up and staggering in its significance." Booklist

976.4 Texas

Roberts, Randy, 1951-
A line in the sand; the Alamo in blood and memory; {by} Randy Roberts, James S. Olson. Free Press 2001 356p il map hardcover o.p. pa $14
Grades: 11 12 Adult   **976.4**
1. Alamo (San Antonio, Tex.) 2. Texas—History
ISBN 0-684-83544-4; 0-743-21233-9 (pa)
LC 00-48421
The Alamo "was attacked by the Mexican Army under Santa Anna in 1836; its defenders, American and Tejano rebels, were quickly overwhelmed. In death, though, they became American folk heroes, symbols of frontier bravery and the unquenchable thirst for liberty. Roberts and Olson do a commendable job of re-creating the murky circumstances of the battle itself, but the real strength of this enjoyable, innovative book lies in its final movement, when the authors turn their attention to cultural criticism." New Yorker
Includes bibliographical references

977.3 Illinois

Barnes, Harper, 1937-
Never been a time; the 1917 race riot that sparked the civil rights movement. Walker & Co. 2008 293p il $25.99
Grades: 11 12 Adult   **977.3**
1. East Saint Louis (Ill.) riot, 1917 2. Illinois—Race relations 3. African Americans—Social conditions 4. African Americans—Civil rights
ISBN 978-0-8027-1575-3; 0-8027-1575-3
LC 2008-368
The author "writes of the truly senseless race riots that took place in East St. Louis, IL, in the summer of 1917, resulting in the deaths of nearly 100 people and the burning of over 200 buildings." Libr J
"Authoritative account of a criminally overlooked incident in American history." Kirkus
Includes bibliographical references

Murphy, Jim, 1947-
The great fire. Scholastic 1995 144p il maps $16.95; pa $12.99 *
Grades: 5 6 7 8 9 10   **977.3**
1. Fires—Chicago (Ill.)
ISBN 0-590-47267-4; 0-439-20307-4 (pa)
LC 94-9963
"Firsthand descriptions by persons who lived through the 1871 Chicago fire are woven into a gripping account of this famous disaster. Murphy also examines the origins of the fire, the errors of judgment that delayed the effective response, the organizational problems of the city's firefighters, and the postfire efforts to rebuild the city. Newspaper lithographs and a few historical photographs convey the magnitude of human suffering and confusion." Horn Book Guide
Includes bibliographical references

Owens, L. L., 1965-
The great Chicago fire. ABDO Pub. 2008 112p
il (Essential events) lib bdg $32.79
Grades: 8 9 10 11 12   **977.3**
1. Fires—Chicago (Ill.) 2. Chicago (Ill.)—History
ISBN 978-1-59928-851-2   LC 2007-12007
This book "relies on many primary source documents
to tell the story [of the Chicago fire], including testimonials from the official study of the fire. . . . [It also]
contains a list of essential events and sources." Libr Media Connect
Includes glossary and bibliographical references

978   Western United States

The **American** frontier; James D. Torr, book
editor. Greenhaven Press 2002 240p il (Turning
points in world history) lib bdg $34.95; pa
$23.70
Grades: 7 8 9 10   **978**
1. Frontier and pioneer life—West (U.S.) 2. United
States—Territorial expansion 3. West (U.S.)—History
ISBN 0-7377-0786-0 (lib bdg); 0-7377-0785-2 (pa)
                                        LC 2001-33514
This is a collection of essays about the American
frontier, with an introduction and summaries
Includes bibliographical references

Duncan, Dayton
Lewis & Clark; the journey of the Corps of
Discovery; based on a documentary film by Ken
Burns, written by Dayton Duncan; with a preface
by Ken Burns and conributions by Stephen E.
Ambrose, Erica Funkhouser, William Least
Heat-Moon. Knopf 1997 248p il maps $45 *
Grades: 11 12 Adult   **978**
1. Lewis and Clark Expedition (1804-1806) 2. West
(U.S.)—Exploration
ISBN 0-679-45450-0   LC 97-73823
This is a companion volume to PBS television film
"Lewis and Clark: The journey of the Corps of Discov-
ery," by Ken Burns.
An "attractive book with a well-written text and an
excellent presentation of historic paintings, photographs,
maps, and original quotations from various of Lewis and
Clark's journals." Sci Books Films

Lewis, Meriwether, 1774-1809
The essential Lewis and Clark; Landon Y.
Jones, editor. Ecco Press 2000 xx, 203p hardcover
o.p. pa $13.95 *
Grades: 11 12 Adult   **978**
1. Lewis and Clark Expedition (1804-1806) 2. West
(U.S.)—Exploration
ISBN 0-06-019600-9; 0-06-001159-9 (pa)
                                        LC 99-86335
Excerpts from the 1904-05 version of: Original jour-
nals of the Lewis and Clark expedition, 1804-1806; ed-
ited by Reuben Gold Thwaites
In this volume the editor presents excerpts from the
journals of Lewis and Clark "that focus on the seminal

junctures of the journey, including their reactions to the
breathtaking physical majesty of the West, their initial
encounters with various Native American tribes, and their
fascinating accounts of the physical and moral courage of
their fellow travelers." Booklist

The journals of Lewis and Clark; [by]
Meriwether Lewis, William Clark; abridged by
Anthony Brandt; with an afterword by Herman J.
Viola. National Geographic Adventure Classics
2002 xxxiii, 445p il, maps (National Geographic
adventure classics) pa $16
Grades: 11 12 Adult   **978**
1. Lewis and Clark Expedition (1804-1806) 2. West
(U.S.)—Description and travel 3. West (U.S.)—Exploration
ISBN 978-0-7922-6921-2; 0-7922-6921-7
                                        LC 2002-32003
"The epic Lewis and Clark Expedition comes to life
on a human scale in this engrossing abridgment of the
explorers' journals. . . . The editor's assiduous untangling of the explorers' notoriously bad spelling, punctuation and grammar, helpful notes and maps and fluent
synopses of the duller stretches of the narrative make the
journals accessible to a general readership." Publ Wkly

Luchetti, Cathy, 1945-
Children of the West; family life on the frontier.
Norton 2001 253p il $39.95 *
Grades: 11 12 Adult   **978**
1. Children—West (U.S.) 2. Frontier and pioneer
life—West (U.S.) 3. West (U.S.)—Social life and customs
ISBN 0-393-04913-2   LC 00-53287
"In the nineteenth and early twentieth centuries, the
children who resided in the sparsely populated plains and
prairies of the western U.S. were subject to a unique variety of hardships and joys. . . . Utilizing more than 100
vintage photographs and excerpts from letters, diaries,
and journals, Luchetti examines aspects of childbearing,
child rearing, childhood, and adolescence on the American frontier." Booklist
Includes bibliographical references

MacGregor, Greg, 1941-
Lewis and Clark revisited; a photographer's
trail; Iris Tillman Hill, editor. Center for
Documentary Studies in association with the
University of Washington Press 2003 199p il map
hardcover o.p. pa $29.95
Grades: 9 10 11 12   **978**
1. Lewis and Clark Expedition (1804-1806) 2. West
(U.S.)—Description and travel
ISBN 0-295-98342-6; 0-295-98343-4 (pa)
                                        LC 2003-53110
"A Lyndhurst book published by the Center for Docu-
mentary Studies in association with the University of
Washington Press"
This is a photo "album of nearly 100 black-and-white
images, which set forth places along . . . [Lewis and
Clark's] 1804-06 route as they appear today. Although
generally not a pretty sight, with dams, power plants, and
grain elevators having supplanted waterfalls, campfires,

MacGregor, Greg, 1941- —*Continued*
and wildlife, there yet remain refuges of original scenery whose beauty so transported Lewis and which MacGregor ably arrests in an ethereal timelessness." Booklist

Marrin, Albert, 1936-
Years of dust; the story of the Dust Bowl. Dutton Children's Books 2009 128p il map $22.99 *

Grades: 6 7 8 9 10   **978**
1. Great Plains—History 2. Dust storms 3. Great Depression, 1929-1939 4. Droughts
ISBN 978-0-525-42077-4; 0-525-42077-0
               LC 2008-13898
"In spite of the subtitle, this book is not just about the Dust Bowl. Marrin discusses the ecology of the Great Plains and the history of exploration and settlement." Voice Youth Advocates
"The engaging narrative includes quotes from a variety of primary sources, and it is abundantly illustrated throughout with photographs and other archival material, making this a reader-friendly, insightful work of history." Kirkus
Includes glossary and bibliographical references

Peavy, Linda Sellers, 1943-
Frontier children; [by] Linda Peavy & Ursula Smith; foreword by Elliott West. University of Okla. Press 1999 164p il $24.95; pa $19.95 *
Grades: 11 12 Adult   **978**
1. Children—West (U.S.) 2. Frontier and pioneer life—West (U.S.) 3. West (U.S.)—History
ISBN 0-8061-3161-6; 0-8061-3505-0 (pa)
               LC 99-18932
The authors aim "to reconstruct stories of children on the frontier from later-life memories and from oral history transcripts. . . . Excellent use is made of photographic evidence, which is quite extensive." Booklist
Includes bibliographical references

Pendergast, Tom, 1964-
Westward expansion: almanac; [by] Tom Pendergast and Sara Pendergast; Christine Slovey, editor. U.X.L 2000 xlvi, 254p il (Westward expansion reference library) $60 *
Grades: 8 9 10 11 12   **978**
1. Frontier and pioneer life—West (U.S.) 2. West (U.S.)—History 3. Reference books
ISBN 0-7876-4862-0   LC 00-36375
This almanac "documents the chronological events that created a romantic national mythology around the pioneers who blazed trails through the wilderness." Publisher's note
Includes bibliographical references

Westward expansion: primary sources; [by] Tom Pendergast and Sara Pendergast; Christine Slovey, editor. U.X.L 2001 xxix, 260p (Westward expansion reference library) $60 *
Grades: 7 8 9 10   **978**
1. United States—Territorial expansion 2. West (U.S.)—History
ISBN 0-7876-4864-7   LC 00-107861
This volume provides "full text or excerpts from diaries, books, letters and many other documents." Publisher's note
Includes bibliographical references

Quay, Sara E.
Westward expansion. Greenwood Press 2002 xx, 301p il (American popular culture through history) $49.95
Grades: 11 12 Adult   **978**
1. Frontier and pioneer life—West (U.S.) 2. West (U.S.)—History 3. Popular culture—United States
ISBN 0-313-31235-4   LC 2001-54546
"This volume covers U.S. frontier culture from the Gold Rush to the close of the 19th century and discusses how myths and images of the Wild West have influenced 20th- and 21st-century popular culture." SLJ
"This excellent title belongs on the reference shelves, and all staff members who assist with student research should be aware of and familiar with it." Voice Youth Advocates
Includes bibliographical references

Schlissel, Lillian
Women's diaries of the westward journey; [collected by] Lillian Schlissel; foreword by Mary Clearman Blew. Schocken Books 2004 278p il pa $14.95 *
Grades: 9 10 11 12   **978**
1. Overland journeys to the Pacific 2. Frontier and pioneer life—West (U.S.) 3. West (U.S.)—Description and travel 4. Women—Social conditions
ISBN 0-8052-1176-4   LC 2004-556208
First published 1982
This account of the experiences, attitudes and perceptions of some hundred women who migrated West is based on their reminiscences, diaries, and letters. The book concerns their daily lives as they travelled the Overland Trail from the midwest to California or Oregon between 1840 and 1870.
Includes bibliographical references

Tunis, Edwin, 1897-1973
Frontier living; written and illustrated by Edwin Tunis. Lyons Press 2000 165p il map pa $18.95 *
Grades: 5 6 7 8 9 10   **978**
1. Frontier and pioneer life—West (U.S.) 2. West (U.S.)—History
ISBN 1-58574-137-X   LC 00-710694
Companion volume to Colonial living (1976)
First published 1961 by World Publishing Company
On cover: An illustrated guide to pioneer life in America, including log cabins, furniture, tools, clothing, and more

Tunis, Edwin, 1897-1973—*Continued*

This volume "portrays the manners and customs of the frontiersman and his family from the beginning of the westward movement through the 19th century in . . . text and more than 200 drawings." Wis Libr Bull

978.03 Western United States— Encyclopedias and dictionaries

Encyclopedia of the Great Plains; David J. Wishart, editor. University of Nebraska Press 2004 919p il map $75

Grades: 11 12 Adult   **978.03**

1. Reference books 2. Great Plains—Encyclopedias

ISBN 0-8032-4787-7   LC 2003-21037

The author "presents 1,316 signed entries, written by some 1000 scholars and divided according to 27 topics that range from the Paleo-Indians to the 2000 census. The contents of each topic are outlined with an introductory essay, followed by specific articles arranged alphabetically within the topic. Historical figures are listed under their common names rather than their formal names." Libr J

"Here is a unique reference book that cuts a broad swath through parts of the U.S. and Canada, the region known as the heartland. The book's topical arrangement perfectly suits the cross-boundary approach." Booklist

The **New** encyclopedia of the American West; edited by Howard R. Lamar. Yale Univ. Press 1998 1324p il maps $60 *

Grades: 11 12 Adult   **978.03**

1. Reference books 2. Frontier and pioneer life—West (U.S.)—Encyclopedias

ISBN 0-300-07088-8   LC 98-6231

First published 1977 by Crowell with title: The Reader's encyclopedia of the American West

This reference work covers "the history, geography, culture, literature, art, and natural history of both the real and the imaginary West. . . . {Coverage spans} prehistory to the present, and . . . {includes} events in the history of the trans-Mississippi West . . . {as well as} the frontier or 'western' stage of all 50 American states. Entries range from important events in the expansion of the U.S. . . . to the first European and American discoverers, among them Coronado, LaSalle, and Lewis and Clark." Publisher's note

Includes bibliographical references

978.1 Kansas

Stratton, Joanna L.

Pioneer women; voices from the Kansas frontier; introduction by Arthur M. Schlesinger, Jr. Simon & Schuster 1981 319p il $15 hardcover o.p.

Grades: 11 12 Adult   **978.1**

1. Women—Kansas 2. Frontier and pioneer life—Kansas 3. Kansas—History

ISBN 0-671-44748-3 (pa)   LC 80-15960

"A unique book based on the memoirs of nearly 800 pioneer women who lived in Kansas between 1854 and 1890. . . . The book presents personal and detailed accounts of life inside homes, the schools, and the social organizations of early Kansas." Choice

Includes bibliographical references

978.7 Wyoming

Meyer, Judith L., 1956-

The spirit of Yellowstone; the cultural evolution of a national park; photographs by Vance Howard. Roberts Rinehart 2003 145p il pa $19.95

Grades: 11 12 Adult   **978.7**

1. Yellowstone National Park 2. Human influence on nature

ISBN 1-570-98395-X   LC 2002-156320

First published 1996 by Rowman & Littlefield

The author "pays tribute to the park and all its glories, covering the park's history, its prime landmarks, and its prominence in art. The photographs are truly striking and not the typical landscape fare. Howard plays with light and texture to capture images that will amaze even those already familiar with the park's unprecedented beauty." Libr J

Includes bibliographical references

978.9 New Mexico

Bryan, Howard

Robbers, rogues, and ruffians; true tales of the Wild West in New Mexico; foreword by Tony Hillerman. Clear Light Pubs. 1991 318p il $22.95; pa $14.95

Grades: 11 12 Adult   **978.9**

1. Frontier and pioneer life—West (U.S.) 2. Thieves

ISBN 0-940666-04-9; 0-940666-23-5 (pa)

           LC 91-72481

The author "concentrates on some of the lesser-known desperadoes whose colorful stories have rarely been told. The stories center in and around the New Mexico Territory, where the reader meets such interesting characters as Joel Fowler, 'the human exterminator'; Charles Kennedy, proprietor of the Inn of Death; and Bronco Sue, a real 'black widow'; and many others." Booklist

When we were young in the West; true stories of childhood; edited with an introduction and conclusion by Richard Melzer. Sunstone Press 2003 345p il map pa $19.95 *

Grades: 11 12 Adult   **978.9**

1. Children—West (U.S.)

ISBN 0-86534-338-1   LC 2003-42572

Presents biographical sketches of New Mexican children from different cultures, races, and classes who represent the strength and diversity of this state's heritage

"A unique and vastly informative book. . . . The richness of detail tells us as much about the past as it does about childhood." Booklist

Includes bibliographical references

979.1 Arizona

Pyne, Stephen J., 1949-
How the Canyon became Grand; a short history.
Viking 1998 199p il maps pa $15 hardcover o.p.
Grades: 11 12 Adult   **979.1**
1. Grand Canyon (Ariz.)
ISBN 0-14-028056-1 (pa)   LC 98-20094
"To understand the canyon as a place and as a per-
spective, Pyne traces its history from the time of the
Spanish conquistadors and later explorers like John Wes-
ley Powell and Clarence Dutton to its status today as a
natural wonder attracting more than five million visitors
annually. He also explains how our attitude toward the
canyon has changed." Libr J
Includes bibliographical references

980 History of South America

Encyclopedia of Latin America; Thomas M.
Leonard, general editor. Facts On File 2010 4v
il map (Facts on File library of world history)
set $360
Grades: 11 12 Adult   **980**
1. Latin America—Encyclopedias 2. Reference books
ISBN 978-0-8160-7359-7   LC 2009-14594
Contents: v1 Amerindians through foreign colonization
(prehistory to 1560) / J. Michael Francis, volume editor;
v2 From colonies to independent nations (1550s to
1820s) / Mark Burkholder, volume author; v3 Search for
national identity (1820s to 1900) / Monica A. Rankin,
volume author; v4 The age of globalization (1900 to the
present) / Thomas M. Leonard, general editor and volume editor
"Articles range from a paragraph to several pages and
cover individuals, nations, and more; and larger articles
cover general topics such as trade, government, and family relations. One of the best features of the set is the selection of primary source materials in each volume, including conquistador memoirs, indigenous poetry in
translation, native histories, royal orders, revolutionary
proclamations, and many other items." Booklist
Includes glossary and bibliographical references

Encyclopedia of Latin American history and
culture; Jay Kinsbruner, editor in chief; Erick D.
Langer, senior editor. 2nd ed. Gale 2008 6v il
map set $695 *
Grades: 11 12 Adult   **980**
1. Reference books 2. Latin America—Encyclopedias
ISBN 978-0-684-31270-5   LC 2008-3461
First published 1996
"This reference set covers the Western Hemisphere
from Mexico to the tip of South America. . . . [This is]
an outstanding encyclopedia that will serve a wide range
of users from high school students to Latin American
scholars." Libr J
Includes bibliographical references

Gritzner, Charles F.
Latin America. Chelsea House Publishers 2006
120p il map (Modern world cultures) lib bdg $30
Grades: 7 8 9 10   **980**
1. Latin America
ISBN 0-7910-8142-7; 978-0-7910-8142-6
LC 2005-32686
Contents: Introducing our Latin American neighbors;
Diverse natural landscapes; Native cultures; European
heritage; Population and settlement; Cultural geography;
Political geography; Economic geography; Latin America
looks ahead
This book "explores the diverse cultural, economic,
political, and natural landscapes of this unique region."
Publisher's note
Includes bibliographical references

981 Brazil

Meade, Teresa, 1948-
A brief history of Brazil; [by] Teresa A. Meade.
2nd ed. Facts On File 2009 280p il (Brief history)
$49.50; pa $19.95
Grades: 11 12 Adult   **981**
1. Brazil—History
ISBN 978-0-8160-7788-5;   0-8160-7788-6;
978-0-8160-7789-2 (pa); 0-8160-7789-4 (pa);
978-1-4381-2736-1 (ebook)   LC 2009-33853
First published 2003
Contact publisher for ebook pricing
An account of Brazil's political, economic, and cultur-
al landscape.
Includes bibliographical references

982 Argentina

Brown, Jonathan C.
A brief history of Argentina. 2nd ed. Facts On
File 2010 354p il map (Brief history) $49.50; pa
$19.95
Grades: 11 12 Adult   **982**
1. Argentina—History
ISBN 978-0-8160-7796-0; 978-0-8160-8361-9 (pa);
978-1-4381-3111-5 (ebook)   LC 2010004887
First published 2002
Contact publisher for ebook pricing
This book covers "Argentina's diverse geography and
its varied natural resources; the origins of the deep-seated
practices of discrimination, which continue today; the effects of neoliberalism on Argentina's large working class
and urban poor, culminating in the *caserola* movement,
the *piqueteros* movement, and the birth of the
cartoneros; the impact a changing global economy has
had within Argentina's borders; [and] the rich culture of
Argentina, which has created five Nobel laureates, vibrant cities that draw millions of tourists annually, and
sports teams that have won multiple world championships." Publisher's note
Includes bibliographical references

Parrado, Nando, 1949-

Miracle in the Andes; 72 days on the mountain and my long trek home; [by] Nando Parrado with Vince Rause. Crown Publishers 2006 291p il map hardcover o.p. pa $13.95 *

Grades: 11 12 Adult   **982**

1. Survival after airplane accidents, shipwrecks, etc. 2. Andes

ISBN   1-4000-9767-3;   978-1-4000-9767-8; 1-4000-9769-X (pa); 978-1-4000-9769-2 (pa)

LC 2005-21629

"In October 1972, a plane carrying an Uruguayan rugby team crashed in the Andes. Not immediately rescued, the survivors turned to cannibalism to survive and after 72 days were saved. Rugby team member Parrado has written a beautiful story of friendship, tragedy and perseverance." Publ Wkly

985   Peru

Bingham, Hiram, 1875-1956

Lost city of the Incas; the story of Machu Picchu and its builders; with an introduction by Hugh Thomson; photographs by Hugh Thomson. Sterling 2002 274p il hardcover o.p. pa $12.95 *

Grades: 11 12 Adult   **985**

1. Machu Picchu (Peru) 2. Peru—Antiquities 3. Incas

ISBN 0-2976-0759-6; 1-84212-585-0 (pa)

LC 2002-483039

A reissue of the title first published 1948 by Duell

"In 1911 Bingham, an American explorer, found the Inca city of Machu Picchu, which had been lost for 300 years. In this volume he tells of its origin, how it came to be lost and how it was finally discovered." Libr J

Includes bibliographical references

Hemming, John, 1935-

The conquest of the Incas. Harcourt Brace Jovanovich 1970 641p il maps pa $25 hardcover o.p.

Grades: 11 12 Adult   **985**

1. Incas 2. Peru—History

ISBN 0-15-602826-3 (pa)

"This {study} focuses on relations of Spaniards and Incas during the Spanish conquest of Peru launched by Pizarro and partners. Spaniards and Incas speak frequently in their own words as preserved in Spanish documents. . . . Inca ways and achievements, the empire's tragic vulnerability because of rivalrous leaders and civil war, and conquest aftermath are made sharply manifest." Booklist

Includes bibliographical references

Hünefeldt, Christine

A brief history of Peru. 2nd ed. Facts On File 2010 xx, 332p il map (Brief history) $49.50

Grades: 11 12 Adult   **985**

1. Peru—History

ISBN 978-0-8160-8144-8; 978-1-4381-0828-5 (ebook)

LC 2010-20748

First published 2004

Contact publisher for ebook pricing

This is a history of Peru ranging "from its ancient peoples and the Inca Empire through . . . recent political, social, and economic developments." Publisher's note

Includes bibliographical references

Malpass, Michael

Daily life in the Inca empire; [by] Michael A. Malpass. 2nd ed. Greenwood Press 2009 xxx, 176p il map (Greenwood Press "Daily life through history" series) $49.95 *

Grades: 11 12 Adult   **985**

1. Incas

ISBN 978-0-313-35548-6   LC 2009-193

First published 1996

This book explores different "aspects of Inca culture, including politics and social hierarchy, the life cycle, agriculture, architecture, women's roles, dress and ornamentation, food and drink, festivals, religious rituals, the calendar, and the unique Inca form of taxation." Publisher's note

Includes glossary and bibliographical references

Masterson, Daniel M.

The history of Peru; [by] Daniel Masterson. Greenwood Press 2009 xxv, 246p il map (Greenwood histories of the modern nations) $45

Grades: 11 12 Adult   **985**

1. Peru—History

ISBN 978-0-313-34072-7; 0-313-34072-2

LC 2009-10348

Covers social life and culture, political practices, economics, and international influence throughout the ages in Peru, from the earliest social groups dating as far back as 500 B.C. to life today in the 21st century.

Includes bibliographical references

Moseley, Michael Edward

The Incas and their ancestors; the archaeology of Peru; {by} Michael E. Moseley. Thames & Hudson 1992 272p il maps pa $31.95 hardcover o.p.

Grades: 11 12 Adult   **985**

1. Incas 2. Peru—Antiquities

ISBN 0-500-28277-3 (pa)   LC 91-65309

This account of Andean prehistory and archaeology takes us from the first settlement of 10,000 years ago to the Spanish conquest

"Clearly presented, with a generous ration of maps and illustrations, {the volume} is thoughtful and welcome." Times Lit Suppl

994 Australia

West, Barbara A., 1967-
A brief history of Australia; [by] Barbara A. West with Frances T. Murphy. Facts On File 2010 356p il map (Brief history) $49.50
Grades: 11 12 Adult   **994**
    1. Australia—History
    ISBN 978-0-8160-7885-1; 978-1-4381-3112-2 (ebook)
                LC 2009-31925
Contact publisher for ebook pricing
"Beginning with the peopling of the continent about 60,000 years ago, the volume examines the early history and culture of the Aboriginals. It continues with the first documented sighting of the landmass by a European in the 17th century, followed by a discussion of the colonial period in the 18th and 19th centuries. From the Federation of 1901 to the Liberal government of John Howard (1998–2007) and the Labor government of Kevin Rudd (2007–present), this . . . book explores Australia's relationship to the British Crown, national security and education policy, the role of sport and environmental issues, Aboriginal rights, women's history, and gay rights." Publisher's note
Includes glossary and bibliographical references

996   Other parts of Pacific. Polynesia

Alexander, Caroline, 1956-
The Bounty: the true story of the mutiny on the Bounty. Viking 2003 491p il hardcover o.p. pa $17
Grades: 11 12 Adult   **996**
    1. Bligh, William, 1754-1817 2. Christian, Fletcher, 1764-1793 3. Bounty (Ship) 4. Oceania
    ISBN   978-0-670-03133-7;   0-670-03133-X; 978-0-14-200469-2 (pa); 0-14-200469-3 (pa)
                LC 2003-50158
Alexander reexamines the story of the 1789 mutiny on the Bounty during a voyage to the South Pacific. She explores "the Royal Navy's efforts to bring the mutineers who did not escape to Pitcairn [Island with Fletcher Christian] to justice, a proceeding complicated by the political, legal and social influence exerted to defend Christian's reputation in absentia and that of one of his well-born colleagues in mutiny. This was Peter Heywood." N Y Times Book Rev
"A rollicking sea adventure told with enormous confidence and style." Booklist
Includes bibliographical references

998   Arctic islands and Antarctica

Alexander, Caroline, 1956-
The Endurance; Shackleton's legendary Antarctic expedition. Knopf 1998 211p il $29.95
Grades: 11 12 Adult   **998**

    1. Shackleton, Sir Ernest Henry, 1874-1922 2. Endurance (Ship) 3. Imperial Trans-Antarctic Expedition (1914-1917) 4. Antarctica—Exploration
    ISBN 0-375-40403-1
Published in association with the American Museum of Natural History
In 1914, Sir Ernest Shackleton "sailed to Antarctica with 27 men in hopes of being the first human to transverse the continent. But his ship, the *Endurance*, was trapped, then crushed, by ice in the Weddell Sea, propelling the party into a nightmare of cold and near starvation. Alexander, relying extensively on journals by crew members, some never published, as well as on myriad other sources, delivers a spellbinding story of human courage. . . . What makes this book especially exciting, however, are the 170 previously unpublished photos by the expedition's photographer, Frank Hurley." Publ Wkly

Bryant, John H.
Dangerous crossings; the first modern polar expedition, 1925; [by] John H. Bryant and Harold N. Cones. Naval Inst. Press 2000 206p il maps $28.95
Grades: 9 10 11 12   **998**
    1. MacMillan, Donald, 1874-1970 2. McDonald, Eugene F., 1890-1958 3. Byrd, Richard Evelyn, 1888-1957 4. Arctic regions—Exploration
    ISBN 1-55750-187-4   LC 00-26344
This book recounts the expedition mounted by Donald B. MacMillan, a colleague of Robert Peary's, Eugene F. McDonald, founder of the Zenith Corporation; and Richard E. Byrd, a young naval aviator
"Perfect Storm-like moments, a lack of supplies, some conflict with Danish officials in Greenland, nascent corporate development and the extraordinary bravery of the personnel involved make this an unusually rich exploration narrative." Publ Wkly
Includes bibliographical references

Gurney, Alan
The race to the white continent; voyages to the Antarctic. Norton 2000 320p il maps hardcover o.p. pa $15.95
Grades: 11 12 Adult   **998**
    1. Antarctica—Exploration
    ISBN 0-393-05004-1; 0-393-32321-8 (pa)
                LC 00-38673
This is an account "of the expeditions that paved the way for the race to the South Pole. All took place in the late 1830s and early 1840s. . . . One was French, another English, and the third was American. Their leaders were, respectively, Jules Sébastien César Dumont d'Urville, James Clark Ross and Charles Wilkes. They were all naval officers, sent out by their governments." Publ Wkly
Includes bibliographical references

Solomon, Susan, 1956-

The coldest March. Yale Univ. Press 2001 xxii, 383p il maps hardcover o.p. pa $16.95

Grades: 11 12 Adult **998**

1. Scott, Robert Falcon, 1868-1912 2. British Antarctic ("Terra Nova") Expedition (1910-1913) 3. Antarctica—Exploration 4. South Pole

ISBN 0-300-08967-8; 0-300-09921-5 (pa)

LC 00-54996

"In November 1911, Capt. Robert Falcon Scott and his British team set out to be the first to reach the South Pole. Battling the brutal weather of Antarctica, they reached the pole in January 1912 only to discover that a Norwegian team had beat them there by nearly a month. On their return from the Pole, Scott and four of his companions died in harsh conditions. Ever since, history has not known whether to label them heroes or bunglers. Solomon . . . analyzes all the factors present during Scott's expedition in an attempt to explain that his failure was due not to incompetence but to a combination of unpredictable weather, erroneous choices and bad luck." Libr J

Includes bibliographical references

Walker, Sally M.

Frozen secrets; Antarctica revealed. Carolrhoda Books 2010 104p il map $20.95

Grades: 7 8 9 10 **998**

1. Antarctica

ISBN 978-1-58013-607-5; 1-58013-607-9

LC 2009-34282

This is an "account of the rich scientific findings coming out of the planet's southernmost continent. . . . It's an excellent overview that manages to pack a lot of technical and scientific information into a small space, but it's sufficiently well structured conceptually and well laid out visually . . . that it all goes down pretty easily. The photographic images reveal the stunning beauty of the continent in shot after shot, but there are also illuminating views of the scientists at work, and diagrams and maps round out the view." Bull Cent Child Books

Fic FICTION

A number of subject headings have been added to the books in this section to aid in curriculum work. It is not necessarily recommended that these subjects be used in the library catalog.

Abbott, Ellen Jensen

Watersmeet. Marshall Cavendish 2009 341p il $16.99

Grades: 6 7 8 9 10 **Fic**

1. Fantasy fiction

ISBN 978-0-7614-5536-3; 0-7614-5536-1

LC 2008-315

Fourteen-year-old Absina escapes the escalating violence, prejudice, and religious fervor of her home town, Vranille, and sets out with a dwarf, Haret, to seek the father she has never met in a place called Watersmeet.

"The relationship between Abisina and Haret is warm and engaging, and the dialogue between them cleverly captures the slow development of their camaraderie. . . .

Fans of Ursula Le Guin's character-driven fantasies will enjoy this story of Abisina's quest to unify both her divided country and her divided self." Bull Cent Child Books

Abdel-Fattah, Randa

Does my head look big in this? Orchard Books 2007 360p $16.99 *

Grades: 7 8 9 10 11 12 **Fic**

1. Muslims—Fiction 2. Clothing and dress—Fiction 3. School stories 4. Australia—Fiction

ISBN 978-0-439-91947-0; 0-439-91947-9

LC 2006-29117

Year Eleven at an exclusive prep school in the suburbs of Melbourne, Australia, would be tough enough, but it is further complicated for Amal when she decides to wear the hijab, the Muslim head scarf, full-time as a badge of her faith—without losing her identity or sense of style.

"While the novel deals with a number of serious issues, it is extremely funny and entertaining." SLJ

Ten things I hate about me. Orchard Books 2009 297p $16.99 *

Grades: 7 8 9 10 11 12 **Fic**

1. Muslims—Fiction 2. Prejudices—Fiction 3. Lebanese—Fiction 4. School stories 5. Australia—Fiction

ISBN 978-0-5450-5055-5; 0-5450-5055-3

LC 2008-13667

Lebanese-Australian Jamilah, known in school as Jamie, hides her heritage from her classmates and tries to pass by dyeing her hair blonde and wearing blue-tinted contact lenses, until her conflicted feelings become too much for her to bear.

A "message of the importance of self-disclosure to maintain loving relationships of all kinds plays itself out as Jamie learns to negotiate her roles as daughter, sister, and friend. Readers will also get an enlightening look at post-9/11 racial tensions outside the U.S. and the problems they pose for Muslim teens." Bull Cent Child Books

Abrahams, Peter, 1947-

Bullet point. HarperTeen 2010 294p $16.99 *

Grades: 9 10 11 12 **Fic**

1. Father-son relationship—Fiction 2. Prisoners—Fiction 3. Criminal investigation—Fiction

ISBN 978-0-06-122769-1; 0-06-122769-2

LC 2009-25440

The only thing seventeen-year-old Wyatt knew about his biological father was that he was serving a life sentence, but circumstances and a new girlfriend bring them together, and soon Wyatt is working to prove his father's innocence.

"Edgier and sexier than most YA novels dare, Abrahams' thriller wrenches guts with a Richard Price-like facility. Readers will be as irretrievably drawn in as Wyatt." Booklist

Abrahams, Peter, 1947-—*Continued*

Reality check. HarperTeen 2009 330p $16.99; lib bdg $17.89; pa $8.99

Grades: 7 8 9 10   **Fic**
1. Missing persons—Fiction 2. Social classes—Fiction 3. Gambling—Fiction 4. School stories
ISBN   978-0-06-122766-0;   0-06-122766-8; 978-0-06-122767-7 (lib bdg); 0-06-122767-6 (lib bdg); 978-0-06-122768-4 (pa); 0-06-122768-4 (pa)
LC 2008-22593

"Laura Geringer books"

After a knee injury destroys sixteen-year-old Cody's college hopes, he drops out of high school and gets a job in his small Montana town, but when his ex-girlfriend disappears from her Vermont boarding school, Cody travels cross-country to join the search.

"Abrahams writes a fine thriller that is pitched to attract everyone from reluctant readers to sports fans to romantic idealists." Voice Youth Advocates

Acampora, Paul

Defining Dulcie. Dial Books 2006 168p hardcover o.p. pa $6.99

Grades: 7 8 9 10   **Fic**
1. Bereavement—Fiction 2. Runaway teenagers—Fiction
ISBN   0-8037-3046-2;   978-0-8037-3046-5; 0-14-241183-3 (pa); 978-0-14-241183-4 (pa)
LC 2005-16186

When sixteen-year-old Dulcie's father dies, her mother makes a decision to move them to California, where Dulcie makes an equally radical decision to steal her dad's old truck and head back home.

"Strong and quirky characters who see life as an inextricable mix of sadness and humor, sorrow and hope, are the hallmark of this memorable first novel." SLJ

Achebe, Chinua, 1930-

Things fall apart; with an introduction by Kwame Anthony Appiah. Knopf 1995 xxi, 181p $15 *

Grades: 11 12 Adult   **Fic**
1. Igbo (African people)—Fiction 2. Nigeria—Fiction
ISBN 0-679-44623-0   LC 94-13429

Also available from McGraw-Hill College

"Everyman's library"

A reissue of the title first published 1958 in the United Kingdom and 1959 in the United States by McDowell, Obolensky

"The novel chronicles the life of Okonkwo, the leader of an Igbo (Ibo) community, from the events leading up to his banishment from the community for accidentally killing a clansman, through the seven years of his exile, to his return. The novel addresses the problem of the intrusion in the 1890s of white missionaries and colonial government into tribal Igbo society. It describes the simultaneous disintegration of its protaganist Okonkwo and of his village. The novel was praised for its intelligent and realistic treatment of tribal beliefs and of psychological disintegration coincident with social unraveling." Merriam-Webster's Ency of Lit

Adams, Douglas, 1952-2001

The hitchhiker's guide to the galaxy. 25th anniversary illustrated collector's ed. Harmony Books 2004 271p il $35 *

Grades: 7 8 9 10 11 12 Adult   **Fic**
1. Science fiction
ISBN 1-4000-5293-9   LC 2004-558987

Also available in paperback from Ballantine Bks.

First published 1980

"Based on a BBC radio series, . . . this is the episodic story of Arthur Dent, a contemporary Englishman who discovers first that his unpretentious house is about to be demolished to make way for a bypass, and second that a good friend is actually an alien galactic hitchhiker who announces that Earth itself will soon be demolished to make way for an intergalactic speedway. A suitably bewildered Dent soon finds himself hitching . . . rides throughout space, aided by a . . . reference book, The Hitchhiker's Guide to the Galaxy, a compendium of 'facts,' philosophies, and wild advice." Libr J

Adams, Richard, 1920-

Watership Down. Scribner classics ed. Scribner 1996 c1972 429p $30; pa $15

Grades: 6 7 8 9 10   **Fic**
1. Rabbits—Fiction 2. Allegories
ISBN 0-684-83605-X; 0-7432-7770-8 (pa)

First published 1972 in the United Kingdom; first United States edition 1974 by Macmillan

"Faced with the annihilation of its warren, a small group of male rabbits sets out across the English downs in search of a new home. Internal struggles for power surface in this intricately woven, realistically told adult adventure when the protagonists must coordinate tactics in order to defeat an enemy rabbit fortress. It is clear that the author has done research on rabbit behavior, for this tale is truly authentic." Shapiro Fic for Youth. 3d edition

Adichie, Chimamanda Ngozi, 1977-

Purple hibiscus; a novel. Anchor Books 2004 307p pa $14.95 *

Grades: 11 12 Adult   **Fic**
1. Family life—Fiction 2. Nigeria—Fiction
ISBN 978-1-4000-7694-9; 1-4000-7694-3
LC 2004-51629

First published 2003 by Algonquin Bks.

"Fifteen-year-old Kambili lives comfortably with her parents and older brother, Jaja, in Enugu, Nigeria. Respected and generous with his money, her fanatically religious father is nevertheless cruel when his wife and children do not live up to his lofty expectations. When Kambili and Jaja visit their widowed aunt Ifeoma in the impoverished countryside, they endure many privations but finally enjoy the pleasures of a warm and loving family." Libr J

"Quiet, chilling, and heart wrenching, this debut novel is both a superb portrait of an unfamiliar culture and an unflinching depiction of the universal turmoil of adolescence." Voice Youth Advocates

Adlington, L. J., 1970-
Cherry Heaven. Greenwillow Books 2008 458p
$16.99; lib bdg $17.89
Grades: 7 8 9 10   **Fic**
1. Orphans—Fiction 2. Science fiction
ISBN   978-0-06-143180-7;   0-06-143180-X;
978-0-06-143181-4 (lib bdg); 0-06-143181-8 (lib bdg)
                                        LC 2007-24679
Kat and Tanka J leave the wartorn city, move with
their adoptive parents to the New Frontier, and are soon
settled into a home called Cherry Heaven, but Luka, an
escaped factory worker, confirms their suspicion that
New Frontier is not the utopia it seems to be.
"In this complex, absorbing, and sometimes disquieting novel, Adlington creates a world that is distinctly different from our own, yet chillingly familiar." Booklist

The diary of Pelly D. Greenwillow Books 2005
282p hardcover o.p. pa $8.99
Grades: 7 8 9 10   **Fic**
1. Science fiction
ISBN 0-06-076615-8; 0-06-076617-4 (pa)
                                        LC 2004-52258
When Toni V, a construction worker on a futuristic
colony, finds the diary of a teenage girl whose life has
been turned upside-down by holocaust-like events, he begins to question his own beliefs.
"Adlington has crafted an original and disturbing
dystopian fantasy told in a smart and sympathetic teen
voice." Booklist

Adoff, Jaime
The death of Jayson Porter. Jump at the
Sun/Hyperion Books for Children 2008 259p
$15.99
Grades: 9 10 11 12   **Fic**
1. Child abuse—Fiction 2. Drug abuse—Fiction
3. Suicide—Fiction 4. Racially mixed people—Fiction
ISBN 978-1-4231-0691-3; 1-4231-0691-1
                                        LC 2007-22548
In the Florida projects, sixteen-year-old Jayson struggles with the harsh realities of his life which include an
abusive mother, a drug-addicted father, and not fitting in
at his predominately white school, and bring him to the
brink of suicide.
"This forceful story will appeal to the many readers,
some in despair, who will find Jayson a character they
can cling to. It's a hard book to read, and even harder
to put down." Booklist

Agard, John, 1949-
The young inferno; written by John Agard;
illustrated by Satoshi Kitamura. Frances Lincoln
Children's 2009 unp il $19.95
Grades: 8 9 10 11 12   **Fic**
1. Hell—Fiction 2. Novels in verse
ISBN 978-1-84507-769-3; 1-84507-769-5
"The narrative poems in this short book are accessible
and have important things to say about the state of the
human race. . . . The hoodie-wearing protagonist . . .
awakens in a strange and frightening forest. A dark man
appears and introduces himself as the tale-teller Aesop:
he is to be the teen's escort through Hell. . . . As the

pair travels through the Circles of Hell, they see the sins
of mankind. . . . The scribbled, heavy-lined black ink
and watercolor illustrations convey exactly the right
mood for a book about a modern-day expedition into
Hell. This will be a great book to pair with a discussion
about Dante's Inferno and/or poetic structure." SLJ

Agee, James, 1909-1955
A death in the family; introduction by Steve
Earle. Centennial ed. Penguin Books 2009 310p pa
$16
Grades: 9 10 11 12   **Fic**
1. Family life—Fiction 2. Traffic accidents—Fiction
3. Death—Fiction 4. Tennessee—Fiction
ISBN 978-0-14-310571-8   LC 2011378283
First published 1957 by McDowell, Obolensky
"Six-year-old Rufus Follet, his younger sister Catherine, his mother, and various relatives all react differently
to the unexpected announcement that Rufus's father has
been fatally injured in an automobile accident. The poignancy of sorrow, the strength of personal beliefs, and
the comforting love and support of a family are all elements of this compassionate novel." Shapiro. Fic for
Youth. 3d edition

Agell, Charlotte, 1959-
Shift. Henry Holt and Co. 2008 230p $16.95
Grades: 7 8 9 10   **Fic**
1. Religion—Fiction 2. Environmental degradation—
Fiction 3. Resistance to government—Fiction
4. Family life—Fiction 5. Science fiction
ISBN 978-0-8050-7810-7; 0-8050-7810-X
                                        LC 2007-46942
In fifteen-year-old Adrian Havoc's world, HomeState
rules every aspect of society and religious education is
enforced but Adrian, refusing to believe that the Apocalypse is at hand, goes north through the Deadlands and
joins a group of insurgents.
"The story is made particularly compelling by the
economy and lyricism of the writing style. . . . Readers
seeking contemplative and philosophical science fiction
will find this a haunting exploration of government gone
awry and one boy's steadfast pursuit of justice." Bull
Cent Child Books

Alegría, Malín
Estrella's quinceanera. Simon & Schuster Books
for Young Readers 2006 272p $14.95
Grades: 7 8 9 10   **Fic**
1. Mexican Americans—Fiction 2. Quinceañera (Social custom)—Fiction
ISBN 0-689-87809-5
Estrella's mother and aunt are planning a gaudy, traditional quinceañera for her, even though it is the last thing
she wants.
"Alegria writes about Mexican American culture, first
love, family, and of moving between worlds with poignant, sharp-sighted humor and authentic dialogue."
Booklist

Alender, Katie

Bad girls don't die. Hyperion Books 2009 352p $15.99

Grades: 7 8 9 10   **Fic**
  1. Demoniac possession—Fiction 2. Sisters—Fiction 3. School stories
ISBN 978-1-4231-0876-4; 1-4231-0876-0
                LC 2008-46179
When fifteen-year-old Lexi's younger sister Kasey begins behaving strangely and their old Victorian house seems to take on a life of its own, Lexi investigates and discovers some frightening facts about previous occupants of the house, leading her to believe that many lives are in danger.

This "novel is both a mystery and a trip into the paranormal. . . . With just enough violence, suspense, and romance to keep readers turning pages, this . . . will be a popular addition to any YA collection." Booklist

Followed by: From bad to cursed (2011)

Alexander, Alma

Gift of the Unmage. Eos 2007 389p (Worldweavers) hardcover o.p. pa $7.99

Grades: 6 7 8 9 10   **Fic**
  1. Magic—Fiction 2. Fantasy fiction
ISBN 978-0-06-083955-0; 0-06-083955-4; 978-0-06-083957-4 (pa); 0-06-083957-0 (pa)
                LC 2006-20123
As the seventh child born of the union of two seventh children, fourteen-year-old Thea has not fulfilled her parents' hope of having special magical powers, and they try a last, desperate measure before sending her to a school for those with no magical ability.

"This novel combines elements of magic, culture, and spirituality with a firm grounding in the very real world." Voice Youth Advocates

Other titles in this series are:

Cybermage (2009)

Spellspam (2008)

Alexander, Jill S.

The sweetheart of Prosper County. Feiwel and Friends 2009 212p $16.99

Grades: 7 8 9 10   **Fic**
  1. Bullies—Fiction 2. Bereavement—Fiction 3. Mother-daughter relationship—Fiction 4. Texas—Fiction
ISBN 978-0-312-54856-8; 0-312-54856-7
                LC 2008-34757
In a small East Texas town largely ruled by prejudices and bullies, fourteen-year-old Austin sets out to win a ride in the next parade and, in the process, grows in her understanding of friendship and helps her widowed mother through her mourning.

"This is a warm, humorous story. . . . A refreshing picture of teen angst, with realistic dialogue and memorable characters." SLJ

Alexie, Sherman, 1966-

The absolutely true diary of a part-time Indian; art by Ellen Forney. Little, Brown 2007 229p il $16.99 *

Grades: 7 8 9 10   **Fic**
  1. Native Americans—Fiction 2. Family life—Fiction 3. School stories 4. Friendship—Fiction
ISBN 0-316-01368-4; 978-0-316-01368-0
                LC 2007-22799
Budding cartoonist Junior leaves his troubled school on the Spokane Indian Reservation to attend an all-white farm town school where the only other Indian is the school mascot.

"The many characters, on and off the rez, with whom he has dealings are portrayed with compassion and verve. . . . Forney's simple pencil cartoons fit perfectly within the story and reflect the burgeoning artist within Junior." Booklist

Allen, Sarah Addison

The girl who chased the moon; a novel. Bantam Books 2010 269p $25; pa $15

Grades: 11 12 Adult   **Fic**
  1. Family life—Fiction 2. Grandfathers—Fiction 3. North Carolina—Fiction
ISBN 978-0-553-80721-9; 0-553-80721-8; 978-0-553-38559-5 (pa); 0-553-38559-3 (pa)
                LC 2009-42254
Emily Benedict came to Mullaby, North Carolina, hoping to solve at least some of the riddles surrounding her mother's life. But the moment Emily enters the house where her mother grew up and meets the grandfather she never knew—a reclusive, real-life gentle giant—she realizes that mysteries aren't solved in Mullaby, they're a way of life.

"That it is never too late to change the future and that high school sins can be forgiven—these are wonderful messages, but Allen's warm characters and quirky setting are what will completely open readers' hearts to this story. Nothing in it disappoints." Libr J

Allende, Isabel

Daughter of fortune; a novel; translated from the Spanish by Margaret Sayers Peden. HarperCollins Pubs. 1999 399p hardcover o.p. pa $16.95

Grades: 11 12 Adult   **Fic**
  1. Adventure fiction 2. California—Gold discoveries—Fiction 3. Love stories
ISBN 0-06-019491-X; 0-06-156533-4 (pa)
                LC 99-26021
Original Spanish edition, 1999

A "historical novel flavored by four cultures—English, Chilean, Chinese and American—and set during the 1849 California Gold Rush. The . . . tale begins in Valparaiso, Chile, with young Eliza Sommers, who was left as a baby on the doorstep of wealthy British importers Miss Rose Sommers and her prim brother, Jeremy. Now a 16 year-old, and newly pregnant, Eliza decides to follow her lover, fiery clerk Joaquin Andieta, when he leaves for California to make his fortune in the gold rush. Enlisting the unlikely aid of Tao Chi'en, a Chinese shipboard cook, she stows away on a ship bound for San Francisco." Publ Wkly

Allende, Isabel—*Continued*

"This novel has pretensions, but they are overridden by Allende's riproaring girl's adventure story. . . . Throughout it all, Allende projects a woman's point of view with confidence, control and an expansive definition of romance as a fact of life." Time

The house of the spirits; translated from the Spanish by Magda Bogin. Knopf 1985 368p $29.95; pa $16

Grades: 11 12 Adult   **Fic**

1. Family life—Fiction 2. Supernatural—Fiction
3. Chile—Fiction

ISBN 0-394-53907-9; 0-553-38380-9 (pa)

LC 84-48516

Also available in hardcover from Everyman's Library
Original Spanish edition, 1982

This novel "tells the story of the Trueba family, with its deep loves and hates, following them from the turn of the century to the violent days of the overthrow of the Salvador Allende government in 1973." Christ Sci Monit

"The style is superbly controlled (and/or the translation is marvelously sensitive), balancing detail rich in associations with a deadpan humor that completely demystifies things that would be otherwise inexplicable. In other words, sentimentality never intrudes on the emotions you develop for these hopelessly well-meaning people and their equally errant children." Best Sellers

Island beneath the sea; a novel; translated from the Spanish by Margaret Sayers Peden. Harper 2010 457p $26.99; pa $14.99

Grades: 11 12 Adult   **Fic**

1. Racially mixed people—Fiction 2. Slavery—Fiction
3. Plantation life—Fiction 4. Haiti—Fiction
5. Caribbean region—Fiction

ISBN   978-0-06-198824-0;   0-06-198824-3;
978-0-06-198825-7 (pa); 0-06-198825-1 (pa)

LC 2009-46251

Original Spanish edition, 2009

This novel "follows a slave/concubine from Haiti during the slave uprisings to New Orleans in time for the Louisiana Purchase." Libr J

"In a many-faceted plot, Allende animates irresistible characters authentic in their emotional turmoil and pragmatic adaptability. She also captures the racial, sexual, and entrepreneurial dynamics of each society in sensuous detail while masterfully dramatizing the psychic wounds of slavery. Sexually explicit, Allende is grace incarnate in her evocations of the spiritual energy that still sustains the beleaguered people of Haiti and New Orleans." Booklist

Zorro; a novel; translated from the Spanish by Margaret Sayers Peden. HarperCollins Publishers 2005 390p maps $25.95; pa $14.95

Grades: 11 12 Adult   **Fic**

1. California—Fiction 2. Adventure fiction

ISBN 0-06-077897-0; 0-06-077900-4 (pa)

LC 2005-46389

This "novel reimagines the legend of Zorro." N Y Times Book Rev

"Allende's lively retelling of the Zorro legend reads as effortlessly as the hero himself might slice his trademark 'Z' on the wall with a flash of his sword." Publ Wkly

Almond, David, 1951-

Clay. Delacorte Press 2006 247p hardcover o.p. pa $8.99 *

Grades: 7 8 9 10   **Fic**

1. Supernatural—Fiction 2. Horror fiction

ISBN 0-385-73171-X; 0-440-42013-X (pa)

LC 2005-22681

The developing relationship between teenager Davie and a mysterious new boy in town morphs into something darker and more sinister when Davie learns first-hand of the boy's supernatural powers.

"Rooted in the ordinariness of a community and in one boy's chance to play God, this story will grab readers with its gripping action and its important ideas." Booklist

Kit's wilderness. 10th-anniversary edition. Delacorte Press 2009 c1999 229p $16.99 *

Grades: 6 7 8 9 10   **Fic**

1. Coal mines and mining—Fiction 2. Ghost stories
3. Great Britain—Fiction

ISBN 978-0-385-32665-0; 0-385-32665-3

First published 1999

Thirteen-year-old Kit goes to live with his grandfather in the decaying coal mining town of Stoneygate, England, and finds both the old man and the town haunted by ghosts of the past

The author "explores the power of friendship and family, the importance of memory, and the role of magic in our lives. This is a highly satisfying literary experience." SLJ

Raven summer. Delacorte Press 2009 198p $19.99 *

Grades: 7 8 9 10 11 12   **Fic**

1. Orphans—Fiction 2. Fate and fatalism—Fiction
3. Great Britain—Fiction

ISBN 978-0-385-73806-4; 0-385-73806-4

LC 2009-1661

Led to an abandoned baby by a raven, fourteen-year-old Liam seems fated to meet two foster children who have experienced the world's violence in very different ways as he struggles to understand war, family problems, and friends who grow apart.

"The tension builds to a shocking and totally believable ending. . . . A haunting story, perfect for group discussion." Booklist

Skellig. 10th anniversary ed. Delacorte Press 2009 c1998 182p $16.99; pa $6.99 *

Grades: 5 6 7 8 9 10   **Fic**

1. Fantasy fiction

ISBN   978-0-385-32653-7;   0-385-32653-X;
978-0-440-41602-9 (pa); 0-440-41602-7 (pa)

First published 1998 in the United Kingdom; first United States edition 1999

Unhappy about his baby sister's illness and the chaos of moving into a dilapidated old house, Michael retreats to the garage and finds a mysterious stranger who is something like a bird and something like an angel.

"The plot is beautifully paced and the characters are drawn with a graceful, careful hand. . . . A lovingly done, thought-provoking novel." SLJ

Alonzo, Sandra

Riding invisible; written by Sandra Alonzo; illustrated by Nathan Huang. Hyperion 2010 234p il lib bdg $15.99 *

Grades: 7 8 9 10   **Fic**
1. Brothers—Fiction 2. Family life—Fiction 3. Horses—Fiction 4. Personality disorders—Fiction
ISBN 978-1-4231-1898-5; 1-4231-1898-7
LC 2010-05041

After his older brother Will attacks his horse, Shy, Yancey runs away into the desert. Follow his adventures as he returns home to face life with a brother who has "conduct disorder."

"Written in a journal style and punctuated with sketches depicting Yancy's experiences, there's a lot here to engage readers." Horn Book Guide

Alvarez, Julia, 1950-

Finding miracles; Julia Alvarez. Knopf 2004 264p $15.95; pa $6.99

Grades: 8 9 10 11 12   **Fic**
1. Adoption—Fiction 2. School stories
ISBN 0-375-82760-9; 0-553-49406-6 (pa)
LC 2003-25127

Fifteen-year-old Milly Kaufman is an average American teenager until Pablo, a new student at her school, inspires her to search for her birth family in his native country

"Complex multicultural characters and skillful depiction of Latino culture raises this well-written, readable novel, which is a school story, a family story, and a love story, to far above average." Voice Youth Advocates

How the García girls lost their accents. Algonquin Bks. 1991 290p hardcover o.p. pa $13.95 *

Grades: 11 12 Adult   **Fic**
1. Dominican Americans—Fiction 2. Sisters—Fiction 3. Family life—Fiction 4. Culture conflict—Fiction
ISBN 0-945575-57-2; 1-56512-975-X (pa)
LC 90-48575

Also available in paperback from Plume Bks.

This novel "tells the story (in reverse chronological order) of four sisters and their family, as they become Americanized after fleeing the Dominican Republic in the 1960s. A family of privilege in the police state they leave, the Garcias experience understandable readjustment problems in the United States, particularly old world patriarch Papi. The sisters fare better but grow up conscious, like all immigrants, of living in two worlds." Libr J

"This is an account of parallel odysseys, as each of the four daughters adapts in her own way, and a large part of Alvarez's accomplishment is the complexity with which these vivid characters are rendered." Publ Wkly

Anaya, Rudolfo A.

Bless me, Ultima. Grand Central Publishing 1999 290p pa $13.95 *

Grades: 9 10 11 12   **Fic**
1. Mexican Americans—Fiction
ISBN 978-0-446-67536-9; 0-446-67536-9
A reissue of the title first published 1972

A novel set in southeastern New Mexico in the 1940s. Antonio, a seven-year-old Chicano boy, learns about life, nature and death through his relationship with Ultima, an aging healer.

Anderson, Jessica Lee

Border crossing. Milkweed Editions 2009 174p $17; pa $8

Grades: 7 8 9 10   **Fic**
1. Schizophrenia—Fiction 2. Mental illness—Fiction 3. Alcoholism—Fiction 4. Racially mixed people—Fiction
ISBN 978-1-57131-689-9; 1-57131-689-2; 978-1-57131-691-2 (pa); 1-57131-691-4 (pa)
LC 2008-49408

Manz, a troubled fifteen-year-old, ruminates over his Mexican father's death, his mother's drinking, and his stillborn stepbrother until the voices he hears in his head take over and he cannot tell reality from delusion.

"A sad and thought-provoking exploration of mental illness." Kirkus

Anderson, Laurie Halse, 1961-

Chains; seeds of America. Simon & Schuster Books for Young Readers 2008 316p $16.99; pa $6.99 *

Grades: 6 7 8 9 10   **Fic**
1. United States—History—1775-1783, Revolution—Fiction 2. Slavery—Fiction 3. African Americans—Fiction 4. Spies—Fiction 5. New York (N.Y.)—Fiction
ISBN 978-1-4169-0585-1; 1-4169-0585-5; 978-1-4169-0586-8 (pa); 1-4169-0586-3 (pa)
LC 2007-52139

After being sold to a cruel couple in New York City, a slave named Isabel spies for the rebels during the Revolutionary War.

"This gripping novel offers readers a startlingly provocative view of the Revolutionary War. . . . [Anderson's] solidly researched exploration of British and Patriot treatment of slaves during a war for freedom is nuanced and evenhanded, presented in service of a fast-moving, emotionally involving plot." Publ Wkly

Followed by: Forge (2010)

Prom; Laurie Halse Anderson. Viking 2005 215p $16.99; pa $8.99

Grades: 9 10 11 12   **Fic**
1. School stories 2. Pennsylvania—Fiction
ISBN 0-670-05974-9; 0-14-240570-1 (pa)
LC 2004-14974

Eighteen-year-old Ash wants nothing to do with senior prom, but when disaster strikes and her desperate friend, Nat, needs her help to get it back on track, Ash's involvement transforms her life

"Whether or not readers have been infected by prom fever themselves, they will be enraptured and amused by Ashley's attitude-altering, life-changing commitment to a cause." Publ Wkly

Speak. 10th anniversary ed. Speak 2009 197p pa $11.99 *

Grades: 7 8 9 10   **Fic**
1. Rape—Fiction 2. School stories
ISBN 978-0-14-241473-6   LC 2009-502164

Anderson, Laurie Halse, 1961-—*Continued*
First published 1999

A traumatic event near the end of the summer has a devastating effect on Melinda's freshman year in high school.

The novel is "keenly aware of the corrosive details of outsiderhood and the gap between home and daily life at high school; kids whose exclusion may have less concrete cause than Melinda's will nonetheless find the picture recognizable. This is a gripping account of personal wounding and recovery." Bull Cent Child Books

Twisted. Viking 2007 250p $16.99
Grades: 9 10 11 12   **Fic**
1. Family life—Fiction 2. School stories 3. Ohio—Fiction
ISBN 978-0-670-06101-3   LC 2006-31297

After finally getting noticed by someone other than school bullies and his ever-angry father, seventeen-year-old Tyler enjoys his tough new reputation and the attentions of a popular girl, but when life starts to go bad again, he must choose between transforming himself or giving in to his destructive thoughts.

"This is a gripping exploration of what it takes to grow up, really grow up, against the wishes of people and circumstances conspiring to keep you the victim they need you to be." Bull Cent Child Books

Wintergirls. Viking 2009 288p $17.99 *
Grades: 8 9 10 11 12   **Fic**
1. Anorexia nervosa—Fiction 2. Self-mutilation—Fiction 3. Friendship—Fiction 4. Death—Fiction
ISBN 978-0-670-01110-0; 0-670-01110-X
                                         LC 2008-37452

Eighteen-year-old Lia comes to terms with her best friend's death from anorexia as she struggles with the same disorder.

"As events play out, Lia's guilt, her need to be thin, and her fight for acceptance unravel in an almost poetic stream of consciousness in this startlingly crisp and pitch-perfect first-person narrative." SLJ

Anderson, M. T., 1968-
Feed. Candlewick Press 2002 237p hardcover o.p. pa $7.99 *
Grades: 8 9 10 11 12   **Fic**
1. Science fiction 2. Satire
ISBN 0-7636-1726-1; 0-7636-2259-1 (pa)
                                         LC 2002-23738

In a future where most people have computer implants in their heads to control their environment, a boy meets an unusual girl who is in serious trouble

"An ingenious satire of corporate America and our present-day value system." Horn Book Guide

The Pox party; taken from accounts by [Octavius Nothing's] own hand and other sundry sources; collected by Mr. M.T. Anderson of Boston. Candlewick Press 2006 351p (The astonishing life of Octavian Nothing, traitor to the nation) $17.99 *
Grades: 9 10 11 12   **Fic**
1. Slavery—Fiction 2. African Americans—Fiction 3. United States—History—1775-1783, Revolution—Fiction
ISBN 0-7636-2402-0; 978-0-7636-2402-6
                                         LC 2006-43170

This is the first of two volumes in The astonishing life of Octavian Nothing, traitor to the nation series. Various diaries, letters, and other manuscripts chronicle the experiences of Octavian, a young African American, from birth to age sixteen, as he is brought up as part of a science experiment in the years leading up to and during the Revolutionary War.

"Teens looking for a challenge will find plenty to sink into here. The questions raised about race and freedom are well developed and leave a different perspective on the Revolutionary War than most novels." Voice Youth Advocates

Followed by The kingdom on the waves (2008)

Anhalt, Ariela
Freefall. Harcourt 2010 250p $17
Grades: 9 10 11 12   **Fic**
1. Friendship—Fiction 2. Death—Fiction 3. School stories
ISBN 978-0-15-206567-6; 0-15-206567-9
                                         LC 2009-18936

Briar Academy senior Luke prefers avoiding conflict and letting others make his decisions, but he is compelled to choose whether or not to stand by the best friend whose reckless behavior has endangered Luke and may have caused another student's death.

"The plot is straightforward, but the high stakes, complex character development, and realistic dialogue and interactions will keep readers riveted—and likely have them imagining themselves in Luke's position." Publ Wky

Antieau, Kim
Broken moon. Margaret K. McElderry Books 2007 183p $15.99
Grades: 7 8 9 10   **Fic**
1. Kidnapping—Fiction 2. Siblings—Fiction 3. Pakistan—Fiction
ISBN 978-1-4169-1767-0; 1-4169-1767-5
                                         LC 2006-03780

"A Junior Library Guild selection"

When her little brother is kidnapped and taken from Pakistan to race camels in the desert, eighteen-year-old Nadira overcomes her own past abuse and, dressed as a boy and armed with knowledge of the powerful storytelling of the legendary Scheherazade, is determined to find and rescue him.

The author "presents important issues without letting them overtake the narrative, and the classic plot and sympathetic characters add up to an absorbing read." Horn Book

Archer, E.

Geek: fantasy novel. Scholastic Press 2011 310p $17.99

Grades: 7 8 9 10   **Fic**
1. Fantasy fiction 2. Cousins—Fiction 3. Aunts—Fiction 4. Wishes—Fiction 5. Great Britain—Fiction
ISBN 978-0-545-16040-7; 0-545-16040-5

"Fourteen-year-old Ralph Stevens escapes his humdrum life when he's invited to spend the summer with his British cousins, ostensibly to set up their wireless network. What he discovers is a family given to eccentricity. . . . Things get seriously weird when their infamous aunt/fairy godmother Chessie of Cheshire turns up, ready to grant each child a wish." Publ Wkly

This "is a stunning, often befuddling, and wildly amusing novel that will likely confound and enchant sci-fi and fantasy fans alike." Bull Cent Child Books

Armstrong, Kelley

The summoning. HarperCollinsPublishers 2008 390p (Darkest powers) $17.99; lib bdg $18.89

Grades: 7 8 9 10   **Fic**
1. Supernatural—Fiction 2. Ghost stories
ISBN   978-0-06-166269-0;   0-06-166269-0; 978-0-06-166272-0 (lib bdg); 0-06-166272-0 (lib bdg)
                         LC 2008-14221

After fifteen-year-old Chloe starts seeing ghosts and is sent to Lyle House, a mysterious group home for mentally disturbed teenagers, she soon discovers that neither Lyle House nor its inhabitants are exactly what they seem, and that she and her new friends are in danger.

"Suspenseful, well-written, and engaging, this page-turning . . . [novel] will be a hit." Voice Youth Advocates

Other titles in this series are:
The awakening (2009)
The reckoning (2010)

Arnold, Tedd, 1949-

Rat life. Dial Books 2007 199p $16.99

Grades: 6 7 8 9 10   **Fic**
1. Authorship—Fiction 2. Vietnam War, 1961-1975—Fiction 3. Mystery fiction
ISBN 978-0-8037-3020-5; 0-8037-3020-9
                         LC 2006-18429

After developing an unusual friendship with a young Vietnam War veteran in 1972, fourteen-year-old Todd discovers his writing talent and solves a murder mystery.

"This is a solid story . . . with a likable main character and a thrilling climax." SLJ

Aronson, Sarah

Head case. Roaring Brooks 2007 176p $16.95

Grades: 7 8 9 10   **Fic**
1. Handicapped—Fiction 2. Drunk driving—Fiction 3. Family life—Fiction
ISBN 978-1-59643-214-7   LC 2006-101509
"A Deborah Brodie book"

Seventeen-year-old Frank Marder struggles to deal with the aftermath of an accident he had while driving drunk that killed two people, including his girlfriend, and left him paralyzed from the neck down.

"Daredevil readers will be made thoughtful by Frank's account, and they'll vividly imagine themselves into Frank's immobile shoes." Bull Cent Child Books

Ashby, Amanda

Zombie queen of Newbury High. Speak 2009 199p pa $7.99

Grades: 7 8 9 10   **Fic**
1. Zombies—Fiction 2. School stories
ISBN 978-0-14-241256-5; 0-14-241256-5
                         LC 2008-41035

While trying to cast a love spell on her date on the eve of the senior prom, Mia inadvertently infects her entire high school class with a virus that will turn them all into zombies.

"*Zombie Queen* is light, fast-paced, and . . . will quench the thirst of the Christopher Pike and R. L. Stine set." SLJ

Asher, Jay

Thirteen reasons why; a novel. Razorbill 2007 288p $16.99

Grades: 8 9 10 11 12   **Fic**
1. Suicide—Fiction 2. School stories
ISBN 978-1-59514-171-2   LC 2007-03097

When high school student Clay Jenkins receives a box in the mail containing thirteen cassette tapes recorded by his classmate Hannah, who committed suicide, he spends a bewildering and heartbreaking night crisscrossing their town, listening to Hannah's voice recounting the events leading up to her death.

"Clay's pain is palpable and exquisitely drawn in gripping casually poetic prose. The complex and soulful characters expose astoundingly rich and singularly teenage inner lives." SLJ

Asimov, Isaac, 1920-1992

Fantastic voyage. Bantam Bks. 1988 186p pa $7.99 *

Grades: 9 10 11 12   **Fic**
1. Science fiction
ISBN 0-553-27572-0

First published 1966 by Houghton Mifflin

"Based on the screenplay by Harry Kleiner, from the original story by Otto Klement and Jay Lewis Bixby"

"Five people are sent on a rescue mission in a submarine, but this is no ordinary submarine moving through an ordinary sea. The people and the submarine are miniaturized. They are moving through a man's blood vessels to reach and break up a blood clot in his brain. The miniaturization will not last—they have only 60 minutes to do the job and leave the man's body, before they return to ordinary size." Publ Wkly

Foundation. Bantam Books 2004 244p $24; pa $15 *

Grades: 9 10 11 12   **Fic**
1. Science fiction
ISBN 0-553-80371-9; 0-553-38257-8 (pa)
                         LC 2003-69137

A reissue of the title first published 1951 by Gnome Press

The first volume in the author's Foundation series narrating the fall of a great galactic empire and the efforts of the Foundations to combat the barbarism that follows

Other titles in the series are:

Asimov, Isaac, 1920-1992—*Continued*
Forward the Foundation (1993)
Foundation and earth (1986)
Foundation and empire (1952)
Foundation's edge (1982)
Prelude to Foundation (1988)
Second Foundation (1986)

Atwater-Rhodes, Amelia, 1984-
Persistence of memory. Delacorte Press 2008
212p $15.99; lib bdg $18.99; pa $8.99
Grades: 8 9 10 11 12   **Fic**
1. Supernatural—Fiction 2. Schizophrenia—Fiction
3. Vampires—Fiction 4. Witches—Fiction
ISBN   978-0-385-73437-0;   0-385-73437-9;
978-0-385-90443-8 (lib bdg); 0-385-90443-6 (lib bdg);
978-0-440-24004-4 (pa); 0-440-24004-2 (pa)
                                    LC 2008-16062
Diagnosed with schizophrenia as a child, sixteen-year-
old Erin has spent half of her life in therapy and on
drugs, but now must face the possibility of weird things
in the real world, including shapeshifting friends and her
"alter," a centuries-old vampire.
"What sets this novel apart . . . are the two narrators—Erin, grown used to, and even comfortable with,
the idea that she is mentally ill; and Shevaun, willing to
do anything to protect the family she's cobbled together.
Secondary characters are equally compelling, and the
world that Atwater-Rhodes has created is believable and
intriguing." SLJ

Token of darkness. Delacorte Press 2010 197p
$15.99; lib bdg $18.99
Grades: 7 8 9 10   **Fic**
1. Ghost stories 2. Traffic accidents—Fiction
ISBN   978-0-385-73750-0;   0-385-73750-5;
978-0-385-90670-8 (lib bdg); 0-385-90670-6 (lib bdg)
                                    LC 2010-277784
"Cooper Blake has everything going for him—until he
wakes from a car accident with his football career in ruins and a mysterious, attractive girl by his side. Cooper
doesn't know how Samantha got there or why he can see
her; all he knows is that she's a ghost." Publisher's note
This is a "chilling tale with enough plot twists to keep
readers guessing." SLJ

Atwood, Margaret, 1939-
The Handmaid's tale; with an introduction by
Valerie Martin. Everyman's Library 2006 xxxiii,
350p $24 *
Grades: 11 12 Adult   **Fic**
1. Allegories 2. Women—Fiction
ISBN 0-307-26460-2   LC 2006-42618
Also available in paperback from Anchor Bks.
First published 1986 by Houghton Mifflin
"The time is the near future, the place is the Republic
of Gilead—formerly known as the United States. A coup
d'etat by religious fundamentalists has left the President
and Congress dead, The Constitution suspended, and the
borders sealed. . . . Atwood's storyteller, a 33-year-old
woman known only as Offred, serves as a handmaid to
one of the ruling Commanders of the Faithful, Fred, from
whom she takes her name. . . . Her sole function . . .

is to carry out a . . . version of Old Testament lore and
bear a child for the aging Commander, with the collusion
of his barren wife." Christ Sci Monit
"A gripping suspense tale, The Handmaid's Tale is an
allegory of what results from a politics based on misogy-
ny, racism, and anti-Semitism." Ms

Augarde, Steve
X-Isle. David Fickling Books 2010 476p $17.99
Grades: 7 8 9 10   **Fic**
1. Islands—Fiction 2. Science fiction
ISBN 978-0-385-75193-3; 0-385-75193-1
                                    LC 2010-281037
Baz and Ray, survivors of an apocalyptic flood, win
places on X-Isle, an island where life is rumored to be
better than on the devastated mainland, but they find the
island to be a violent place ruled by religious fanatic
Preacher John, and they decide they must come up with
a weapon to protect themselves from impending danger.
"Augarde's near-future apocalyptic world is gruesomely hardscrabble without being overly graphic. . . . A
gripping tale of fighting for the slenderest chance of
hope." Publ Wkly

Austen, Jane, 1775-1817
Persuasion. Alfred A. Knopf 1992 xxxvii, 260p
$18
Grades: 11 12 Adult   **Fic**
1. Great Britain—Fiction 2. Love stories
ISBN 0-679-40986-6   LC 91-53181
Also available from other publishers
"Everyman's library"
First published 1818
"The heroine, Anne Elliott, and her lover, Captain
Wentworth, had been engaged eight years before the sto-
ry opens but Anne had broken the engagement in defer-
ence to family and friends. Upon his return he finds her
'wretchedly altered,' but after numerous obstacles have
been overcome, the lovers are happily united." Gerwig.
Handb for Readers and Writers

Pride and prejudice; introduction by Anna
Quindlen. Modern Library 1995 281p $14.95 *
Grades: 11 12 Adult   **Fic**
1. Great Britain—Fiction 2. Sisters—Fiction
ISBN 0-679-60168-6   LC 95-6310
Also available from other publishers
First published 1813
"Concerned mainly with the conflict between the prej-
udice of a young lady and the well-founded though mis-
interpreted pride of the aristocratic hero. The heroine's
father and mother cope in very different ways with the
problem of marrying off five daughters." Good Read
"The characters are drawn with humor, delicacy, and
the intimate knowledge of men and women that Miss
Austen always shows." Keller. Reader's Dig of Books

Sense and sensibility; with an introduction by
Peter Conrad. Knopf 1992 xxxix, 367p $16
Grades: 11 12 Adult   **Fic**
1. Great Britain—Fiction 2. Sisters—Fiction
ISBN 0-679-40987-4   LC 91-53182
Also available from other publishers
"Everyman's library"

Austen, Jane, 1775-1817—*Continued*

First published 1811

A story "in which two sisters, Elinor and Marianne Dashwood represent 'sense' and 'sensibility' respectively. Each is deserted by the young man from whom she has been led to expect an offer of matrimony. Elinor bears her deep disappointment with dignity and restraint while Marianne violently expresses her grief." Reader's Ency. 4th edition

Avasthi, Swati

Split. Alfred A. Knopf 2010 282p $16.99; lib bdg $19.99 *

Grades: 10 11 12   Fic

1. Brothers—Fiction 2. Child abuse—Fiction
ISBN   978-0-375-86340-0;   0-375-86340-0;
978-0-375-96340-7 (lib bdg); 0-375-96340-5 (lib bdg)
LC 2009-22615

"A Borzoi Book"

A teenaged boy thrown out of his house by his abusive father goes to live with his older brother, who ran away from home years ago to escape the abuse.

"Readers seeking sensational violence should look elsewhere; this taut, complex family drama depicts abuse unflinchingly but focuses on healing, growth and learning to take responsibility for one's own anger." Kirkus

Ayarbe, Heidi

Compromised. HarperTeen 2010 452p $16.99 *

Grades: 8 9 10 11 12   Fic

1. Tourette syndrome—Fiction 2. Foster home care—Fiction 3. Runaway teenagers—Fiction 4. Voyages and travels—Fiction
ISBN 978-0-06-172849-5; 0-06-172849-7
LC 2009-23545

With her con-man father in prison, fifteen-year-old Maya sets out from Reno, Nevada, for Boise, Idaho, hoping to stay out of foster care by finding an aunt she never knew existed, but a fellow runaway complicates all of her scientifically-devised plans.

"Ayarbe offers a gut-wrenching, terrifyingly authentic story and memorably etched, courageous characters whose influence on each other is palpable." Booklist

Bacigalupi, Paolo

Ship breaker. Little, Brown and Co. 2010 326p $17.99 *

Grades: 8 9 10 11 12   Fic

1. Recycling—Fiction 2. Science fiction
ISBN 978-0-316-05621-2; 0-316-05621-9
LC 2009-34424

In a futuristic world, teenaged Nailer scavenges copper wiring from grounded oil tankers for a living, but when he finds a beached clipper ship with a girl in the wreckage, he has to decide if he should strip the ship for its wealth or rescue the girl.

"Bacigalupi's cast is ethnically and morally diverse, and the book's message never overshadows the storytelling, action-packed pacing, or intricate world-building. At its core, the novel is an exploration of Nailer's discovery of the nature of the world around him and his ability to transcend that world's expectations." Publ Wkly

Badoe, Adwoa

Between sisters. Groundwood Books/House of Anansi Press 2010 205p $16.95

Grades: 9 10 11 12   Fic

1. Poor—Fiction 2. Family life—Fiction 3. School stories 4. Ghana—Fiction
ISBN 978-0-88899-996-2

"When sixteen-year-old Gloria fails thirteen out of fifteen subjects on her final exams, her future looks bleak indeed. Her family's resources are meager so the entire family is thrilled when a distant relative, Christine, offers to move Gloria north to Kumasi to look after her toddler son, Sam. In exchange, after two years, Christine will pay for Gloria to go to dressmaking school. Life in Kumasi is more grand than anything Gloria has ever experienced. . . . [But] Kumasi is also full of temptations." Publisher's note

"This honest glimpse of one adolescent is as particular to the well-detailed West African setting as it is universal in subject and theme." Horn Book

Baldini, Michelle

Unraveling; [by] Michelle Baldini, Lynn Biederman; poems by Gabrielle Biederman. Delacorte Press 2008 230p $15.99; lib bdg $18.99

Grades: 9 10 11 12   Fic

1. Mother-daughter relationship—Fiction 2. Family life—Fiction 3. School stories
ISBN 978-0-385-73540-7; 978-0-385-90521-3 (lib bdg)
LC 2008-477

When fifteen-year-old Amanda faces major life changes, her controlling mother is the last person she turns to, but she gains some sympathy as she begins to understand her mother's relationship with her best friend.

"Rife with raw emotions, the sex scenes are both graphic and sad, leaving readers cringing at Amanda's self-defeating behavior. The tension throughout the novel is so palpable that it is often exhausting. The story moves at a quick pace, however, thanks to Amanda's honest and often humorous voice, as well as her thoughtful poetry interjected throughout." SLJ

Baldwin, James, 1924-1987

Go tell it on the mountain. Knopf 1953 303p $15.95; pa $6.99 *

Grades: 7 8 9 10 11 12 Adult   Fic

1. African Americans—Fiction 2. Family life—Fiction 3. Harlem (New York, N.Y.)—Fiction
ISBN 0-679-60154-6; 0-440-33007-6 (pa)

Also available in paperback from Dial Press Trade Paperbacks

This novel is an "autobiographical story of a Harlem child's relationship with his father against the background of his being saved in the pentecostal church." Benet's Reader's Ency of Am Lit

If Beale Street could talk. Dial Press (NY) 1974 197p hardcover o.p. pa $12.95

Grades: 11 12 Adult   Fic

1. African Americans—Fiction 2. New York (N.Y.)—Fiction
ISBN 0-803-74169-3; 0-307-27593-0 (pa)

"Tish, aged 19, and Fonny, 22 years old, are in love and pledged to marry, a decision hastened by Tish's un-

Baldwin, James, 1924-1987—*Continued*

expected pregnancy. Fonny is falsely accused of raping a Puerto Rican woman and is sent to prison. The families of the desperate couple search frantically for evidence that will prove his innocence in order to reunite the lovers and provide a safe haven for the expected child. There is some explicit sex but it is not treated in a sensational manner, nor is the use of street language gratuitous." Shapiro. Fic for Youth. 3d edition

Ballard, J. G., 1930-2009

Empire of the Sun; a novel. Simon & Schuster 1984 279p hardcover o.p. pa $13

Grades: 9 10 11 12 Adult   **Fic**
1. World War, 1939-1945—Fiction 2. Shanghai (China)—Fiction
ISBN 0-671-53051-8; 0-7432-6523-8 (pa)
LC 84-10630

"The day after Pearl Harbor, Shanghai is captured by the Japanese, and 11-year-old Jim is separated from his parents and spends some months living on his own. Then he is captured and interned in a Japanese prison camp with other civilians. The story of the next four years is one of struggling to stay alive by any means possible." Libr J

"This novel is much more than the gritty story of a child's miraculous survival in the grimly familiar setting of World War II's concentration camps. There is no nostalgia for a good war here, no sentimentality for the human spirit at extremes. Mr. Ballard is more ambitious than romance usually allows. He aims to render a vision of the apocalypse, and succeeds so well that it can hurt to dwell upon his images." N Y Times Book Rev

Followed by The kindness of women (1991)

Balog, Cyn

Sleepless. Delacorte Press 2010 215p $16.99

Grades: 8 9 10 11 12   **Fic**
1. Bereavement—Fiction 2. Death—Fiction
3. Dreams—Fiction 4. Supernatural—Fiction 5. Love stories
ISBN 978-0-385-73848-4; 0-385-73848-X
LC 2010-00123

Eron, a supernatural being known as a Sandman whose purpose is to seduce humans to sleep, falls in love with a sad teenaged girl who is mourning her boyfriend's death.

"Suspense, believable characters and an imaginative twist on a ghost story/romance make for a lovely read." Kirkus

Baratz-Logsted, Lauren

Crazy beautiful. Houghton Mifflin Harcourt 2009 191p $16

Grades: 7 8 9 10   **Fic**
1. Amputees—Fiction 2. Physically handicapped—Fiction 3. Bullies—Fiction 4. School stories
ISBN 978-0-547-22307-0; 0-547-22307-2
LC 2008-40463

In this contemporary retelling of "Beauty and the Beast," a teenaged boy whose hands were amputated in an explosion and a gorgeous girl whose mother has recently died form an instant connection when they meet

on their first day as new students.

"This romance transcends all of its potential pitfalls to create a powerful story about recovery and friendship." Kirkus

Twin's daughter. Bloomsbury 2010 390p $16.99

Grades: 7 8 9 10   **Fic**
1. Twins—Fiction 2. Aunts—Fiction 3. Homicide—Fiction 4. London (England)—Fiction 5. Great Britain—History—19th century—Fiction 6. Mystery fiction
ISBN 978-1-59990-513-6; 1-59990-513-2
LC 2010-08234

In Victorian London, thirteen-year-old Lucy's comfortable world with her loving parents begins slowly to unravel the day that a bedraggled woman who looks exactly like her mother appears at their door.

"Baratz-Logsted's gothic murder mystery is rife with twists and moves swiftly and elegantly. . . . The ending will intrigue and delight readers." Booklist

Barlow, Toby

Sharp teeth. Harper 2008 312p il $22.95; pa $14.99

Grades: 11 12 Adult   **Fic**
1. Werewolves—Fiction 2. Homicide—Fiction 3. Los Angeles (Calif.)—Fiction 4. Novels in verse 5. Horror fiction
ISBN 978-0-06-143022-0; 0-06-143022-6; 978-0-06-143024-4 (pa); 0-06-143024-2 (pa)

First published 2007 in the United Kingdom in a different form

"An ancient race of lycanthropes has survived to the present day, and its numbers are growing as the initiated convince L.A.'s down and out to join their pack. Paying no heed to moons, full or otherwise, they change from human to canine at will—and they're bent on domination at any cost. Caught in the middle are Anthony, a kindhearted, besotted dogcatcher, and the girl he loves, a female werewolf who has abandoned her pack. Anthony has no idea that she's more than she seems, and she wants to keep it that way. But her efforts to protect her secret lead to murderous results." Publisher's note

"Written in a free verse style that perfectly complements the action as it moves from slower-paced narratives to short, jagged scenes of graphic violence and heartbreak, this groundbreaking work commands attention from a wide audience, including genre fans and modern fiction aficionados. A superb addition to any fantasy or modern horror collection." Libr J

Barlowe, Wayne Douglas

God's demon; [by] Wayne Barlowe. Tor 2007 352p hardcover o.p. pa $7.99

Grades: 10 11 12 Adult   **Fic**
1. Hell—Fiction 2. Devil—Fiction 3. Angels—Fiction
ISBN 978-0-7653-0985-3; 0-7653-0985-8; 978-0-7653-4865-4 (pa); 0-7653-4865-9 (pa)
LC 2007-21074

"A Tom Doherty Associates book"

"Inspired by *Paradise Lost*, Barlowe conjures up the creatures who sided with Lucifer and were ejected from heaven, thrown down into Hell to become freakishly mangled demons. After innumerable eons of exile, the

Barlowe, Wayne Douglas—*Continued*

demon Sargatanas has started to dream of being reunited with God. Sargatanas amasses an army to aid him in overthrowing Lucifer's regent, Beelzebub, in an attempt to catch God's eye. . . . Barlowe's interpretation is not for the squeamish, with its horrifically explicit descriptions of demonic behavior, but it's a compelling view of Hell and of a demon who seeks redemption." Publ Wkly

Barnes, Jennifer Lynn

Raised by wolves. Egmont 2010 418p $17.99; pa $9.99

Grades: 7 8 9 10   **Fic**
1. Werewolves—Fiction
ISBN   978-1-60684-059-7;   1-60684-059-2;
978-1-60684-211-9 (pa); 1-60684-211-0 (pa)
                                    LC 2009-41157

A girl raised by werewolves must face the horrors of her past to uncover the dark secrets that the pack has worked so hard to hide.

"Fascinating glimpses into pack family dynamics add depth and texture to this latest entry in the werewolf oeuvre. . . . Barnes has produced an appealing addition to the ranks of contemporary fantasy-horror." Booklist

Followed by: Trial by fire (2011)

Barnes, John, 1957-

Tales of the Madman Underground; an historical romance 1973. Viking 2009 532p $18.99; pa $9.99
*

Grades: 10 11 12 Adult   **Fic**
1. Friendship—Fiction 2. Alcoholism—Fiction
3. Mother-son relationship—Fiction 4. Ohio—Fiction
5. School stories
ISBN   978-0-670-06081-8;   0-670-06081-X;
978-0-14-241702-7 (pa); 0-14-241702-5 (pa)
                                    LC 2009-11072

In September 1973, as the school year begins in his depressed Ohio town, high school senior Kurt Shoemaker determines to be "normal," despite his chaotic home life with his volatile, alcoholic mother and the deep loyalty and affection he has for his friends in the therapy group dubbed the Madman Underground.

"Teens initially turned off by Barnes's liberal use of profanities and the book's length will be captured by the sharp, funny dialogue and crisp personalities of the Madmen. Even minor characters are distinctive. . . . [This] is an excellent selection for book clubs of older teens that like sinking their teeth into longer stories with substance." Voice Youth Advocates

Barr, Nevada

Track of the cat. Putnam 1993 238p hardcover o.p. pa $7.99

Grades: 11 12 Adult   **Fic**
1. Mystery fiction
ISBN 0-399-13824-2; 0-425-19083-8 (pa)
                                    LC 92-29694

In this first novel of the Anna Pigeon series, "Anna Pigeon has fled New York City after the accidental death of her husband, and she now works as a law enforcement ranger at Guadaloupe Mountains National Park. There she finds the remains of fellow ranger Sheila Drury, who apparently was clawed to death by a mountain lion. Although an autopsy confirms this judgment, Anna becomes convinced that the claw marks have been faked. Her superiors discourage her from probing further, but another supposedly accidental death goads her into investigating Sheila's activities before her death—her campaign to open up the park to the public and her relationships with a young divorcee and with a powerful rancher opposed to Park Service policies. . . . A park ranger herself, Barr develops a complex, credible and capable heroine who believes in truth and justice while remaining conscious of the ambiguities of human existence." Publ Wkly

Other titles in this series featuring Anna Pigeon are:
Blind descent (1998)
Blood lure (2001)
Borderline (2009)
Burn (2010)
Deep South (2000)
Endangered species (1997)
Firestorm (1996)
Flashback (2003)
Hard truth (2005)
High country (2004)
Hunting season (2002)
Ill wind (1995)
Liberty falling (1999)
A superior death (1994)
Winter study (2008)

Barrett, Tracy, 1955-

King of Ithaka. Henry Holt and Company 2010 261p map $16.99 *

Grades: 7 8 9 10   **Fic**
1. Classical mythology—Fiction 2. Odysseus (Greek mythology)—Fiction
ISBN 978-0-8050-8969-1; 0-8050-8969-1
                                    LC 2009-50770

When sixteen-year-old Telemachos and his two best friends, one a centaur, leave their life of privilege to undertake a quest to find Telemachos's father Odysseus, they learn much along the way about what it means to be a man and a king.

"The exotic climes and vivid descriptions . . . give the story a sense of immediacy and color." Booklist

Baskin, Nora Raleigh, 1961-

All we know of love. Candlewick Press 2008 201p $16.99

Grades: 6 7 8 9 10   **Fic**
1. Mothers—Fiction 2. Loss (Psychology)—Fiction
3. Voyages and travels—Fiction
ISBN 978-0-7636-3623-4; 0-7636-3623-1
                                    LC 2007-22396

Natalie, almost sixteen, sneaks away from her Connecticut home and takes the bus to Florida, looking for the mother who abandoned her father and her when she was ten years old.

"Baskin takes a familiar story line and examines it in a new and interesting way that will engage readers." Voice Youth Advocates

Bass, Karen, 1962-

Summer of fire; [edited by Laura Peetoom]
Coteau Books for Teens 2009 267p pa $10.95

Grades: 9 10 11 12   **Fic**

1. Runaway teenagers—Fiction 2. Sisters—Fiction
3. World War, 1939-1945—Fiction 4. Germany—Fiction

ISBN 978-1-55050-415-6; 1-55050-415-0

"When Canadian teen Delora James finds herself banished to Germany for the summer, reading the professor's old journals seems like a good time waster. Once Del begins to read the translated diary of Garda—a teenager in World War II, pregnant and desperate—she is engaged by Garda's compelling story. Through a series of rebellions, she begins to draw similarities between her own world and Garda's, and is able to see past her own hostility." Publisher's note

"It is rare for a novel to offer a German civilian's viewpoint during Hitler's rise to power with such honesty. Alternating between Del's and Garda's voices, . . . the teen voices are immediate: Del's wry and self-aware; Garda's desperate and angry." Booklist

Bauer, Joan

Hope was here. Putnam 2000 186p $16.99; pa
$7.99 *

Grades: 7 8 9 10   **Fic**

1. Aunts—Fiction 2. Restaurants—Fiction
3. Wisconsin—Fiction

ISBN 0-399-23142-0; 0-14-240424-1 (pa)

LC 00-38232

When sixteen-year-old Hope and the aunt who has raised her move from Brooklyn to Mulhoney, Wisconsin, to work as waitress and cook in the Welcome Stairways diner, they become involved with the diner owner's political campaign to oust the town's corrupt mayor.

"Bauer manages to fill her heartfelt novel with gentle humor, quirky but appealing characters, and an engaging plot." Book Rep

Peeled. G.P. Putnam's Sons 2008 256p $16.99
*

Grades: 6 7 8 9 10   **Fic**

1. Journalism—Fiction 2. Farm life—Fiction 3. Ghost stories 4. School stories 5. New York (State)—Fiction

ISBN 978-0-399-23475-0; 0-399-23475-6

LC 2007-42835

In an upstate New York farming community, high school reporter Hildy Biddle investigates a series of strange occurrences at a house rumored to be haunted.

This is "a warm and funny story full of likable, offbeat characters led by a strongly voiced, independently minded female protagonist on her way to genuine, well-earned maturity." SLJ

Bauman, Beth Ann, 1964-

Rosie & Skate. Wendy Lamb Books 2009 217p
$15.99; lib bdg $18.99

Grades: 9 10 11 12   **Fic**

1. Alcoholism—Fiction 2. Sisters—Fiction
3. Father-daughter relationship—Fiction 4. Dating (Social customs)—Fiction 5. Family life—Fiction
6. New Jersey—Fiction

ISBN 978-0-385-73735-7; 0-385-73735-1;
978-0-385-90660-9 (lib bdg); 0-385-90660-9 (lib bdg)

LC 2009-10575

"Bauman's prose is lovely and real. Vivid descriptions bring her characters to life, and the dialogue is both believable and funny. . . . The novel expertly captures the ever-hopeful ache of adolescents longing for love, stability and certainty." Kirkus

Beagle, Peter S.

The last unicorn. Viking 1968 218p hardcover
o.p. pa $14.95

Grades: 11 12 Adult   **Fic**

1. Unicorns—Fiction 2. Allegories 3. Fantasy fiction

ISBN 0-670-41908-7; 0-451-45052-3 (pa)

"A beautiful and previously happy unicorn learns she may be the last unicorn left on earth. Wanting not to believe it, she sets off in quest of her fellows. In the course of her journey, she meets a carnival magician of little ability, has encounters with a Robin Hood-like band, a king presiding over a hate-filled and miserable land, with the aid of the mysterious Red Bull, and a glamorous, if previously ineffectual prince." Publ Wkly

"Beagle is a true magician with words, a master of prose and a deft practitioner in verse. He has been compared, not unreasonably, with Lewis Carroll and J. R. R. Tolkien, but he stands squarely and triumphantly on his own feet." Saturday Rev

Beam, Cris

I am J. Little, Brown 2011 326p $16.99 *

Grades: 9 10 11 12   **Fic**

1. Transsexualism—Fiction 2. Identity (Psychology)—Fiction 3. Friendship—Fiction

ISBN 978-0-316-05361-7; 0-316-05361-9

LC 2010-08640

J, who feels like a boy mistakenly born as a girl, runs away from his best friend who has rejected him and the parents he thinks do not understand him when he finally decides that it is time to be who he really is.

"The book is a gift to transgender teens and an affecting story of self-discovery for all readers." Horn Book

Includes bibliographical references

Beard, Philip, 1963-

Dear Zoe; a novel. Viking 2005 196p hardcover
o.p. pa $13

Grades: 9 10 11 12   **Fic**

1. Letters—Fiction 2. Death—Fiction 3. Sisters—Fiction 4. Bereavement—Fiction

ISBN 0-670-03401-0; 0-452-28740-5 (pa)

LC 2004-57173

"On the morning planes hit the World Trade Center towers, Tess DeNunzio's three-year-old sister, Zoe, ran

Beard, Philip, 1963-—*Continued*

into the street and was killed by a car. Fifteen-year-old Tess, who was supposed to be watching Zoe, was consumed by guilt. This novel is written in the form of a letter from Tess to Zoe, chronicling the year after Zoe's death. . . . Beard captures the raw emotion of a 15-year-old girl with impressive dexterity, following Tess through the many stages of grief." Booklist

Beaudoin, Sean

You killed Wesley Payne. Little, Brown 2011 359p il $16.99

Grades: 9 10 11 12   **Fic**

1. Mystery fiction 2. School stories
ISBN 978-0-316-07742-2; 0-316-07742-9

LC 2010-08639

When hard-boiled, seventeen-year-old private investigator Dalton Rev transfers to Salt River High to solve the case of a dead student, he has his hands full trying to outwit the police, negotiate the school's social hierarchy, and get paid.

"This dark, cynical romp is full of clever references and red herrings, which will delight the adult noir fan and pique the curiosities of the observant outcast teen who's looking for a way to infiltrate the in-crowd." Kirkus

Beaufrand, Mary Jane

The river. Little, Brown 2010 215p il $16.99

Grades: 8 9 10 11 12   **Fic**

1. Moving—Fiction 2. Hotels and motels—Fiction 3. Oregon—Fiction 4. Mystery fiction
ISBN 978-0-316-04168-3; 0-316-04168-8

LC 2008-50222

Teenager Ronnie's life is transformed by the murder of a ten-year-old neighbor for whom she babysat, and who had helped Ronnie adjust to living at a country inn on the banks of the Santiam River in Hoodoo, Oregon.

"With its blend of richly realistic character and slightly uncanny ambience, this will be a favorite with fans of mysteries that tug the heartstrings." Bull Cent Child Books

Bechard, Margaret, 1953-

Hanging on to Max. Simon Pulse 2003 204p pa $6.99

Grades: 7 8 9 10   **Fic**

1. Teenage fathers—Fiction 2. Infants—Fiction
ISBN 0-689-86268-7

First published 2002 by Roaring Brook Press

When his girlfriend decides to give their baby away, seventeen-year-old Sam is determined to keep him and raise him alone.

"An easy read filled with practical wisdom, this book is highly recommended as an important edition for any adolescent classroom collection." ALAN

Beck, Ian

Pastworld. Bloomsbury Children's Books 2009 355p $16.99

Grades: 7 8 9 10   **Fic**

1. Amusement parks—Fiction 2. Genetic engineering—Fiction 3. Homicide—Fiction 4. London (England)—Fiction 5. Science fiction
ISBN 978-1-59990-040-7; 1-59990-040-8

LC 2009-8706

In 2050, while visiting Pastworld, a Victorian London theme park, teenaged Caleb meets seventeen-year-old Eve, a Pastworld inhabitant who has no knowledge of the modern world, and both become pawns in a murderer's diabolical plan that reveals disturbing truths about the teenagers' origins.

"Suspenseful and gripping. This spellbinding page-turner will keep readers on the edge of their seats." SLJ

Beckett, Bernard, 1968-

Genesis. Houghton Mifflin Harcourt 2009 150p pa $20

Grades: 11 12 Adult   **Fic**

1. Science fiction
ISBN 978-0-547-22549-4; 0-547-22549-0

First published 2006 in New Zealand

"Anaximander, Anax for short, lives in an island nation that has survived an apocalyptic plague by constructing a great sea fence and destroying all who approach. The tightly closed society has evolved into a rigid but seemingly benign hierarchy. Anax, hoping to join the Academy—the ruling class of thinkers—must submit to an oral examination regarding her chosen subject, Adam Forde, a hero from the island's past. . . . This slim novel of big ideas (its subject is nothing less than the nature of consciousness) overcomes a slow start to grip the reader in a thrilling combination of action and ideas. And the ending is an absolute mind-blower worthy of sf's classic texts." Booklist

Bedford, K. A., 1963-

Time machines repaired while-u-wait. EDGE Science Fiction and Fantasy Pub. 2008 324p pa $17.95

Grades: 10 11 12 Adult   **Fic**

1. Science fiction
ISBN 978-1-894063-42-5; 1-894063-42-2

"Al 'Spider' Webb is a time machine repairman who happens to detest time machines. On a routine call, he encounters a machine that seems about ready to blow. In order to repair it, he must work with Australian officials to create a small, alternate universe—to protect the rest of the world from the explosion, of course. The job becomes far from normal, though, when it becomes apparent that the explosive device is hiding both another machine and a dead body. The corpse sets off a series of events that sends Spider across alternate realities and puts everyone he cares about at risk." SLJ

Bedford, Martyn

Flip. Wendy Lamb Books 2011 261p $16.99; lib bdg $19.99; ebook $10.99

Grades: 8 9 10 11 12   **Fic**
1. Supernatural—Fiction 2. Great Britain—Fiction
ISBN   978-0-385-73990-0;   0-385-73990-7; 978-0-385-90808-5 (lib bdg); 0-385-90808-3 (lib bdg); 978-0-375-89855-6 (ebook); 0-375-89855-7 (ebook)

LC 2010-13158

A teenager wakes up inside another boy's body and faces a life-or-death quest to return to his true self or be trapped forever in the wrong existence.

"Bedford packs so much exhilarating action and cleanly cut characterizations into his teen debut that readers will be catapulted head-first into Alex's strange new world." Kirkus

Beitia, Sara, 1977-

The last good place of Lily Odilon. Flux 2010 301p pa $9.95

Grades: 8 9 10   **Fic**
1. Runaway teenagers—Fiction 2. Stepfathers—Fiction 3. Child sexual abuse—Fiction 4. Mystery fiction
ISBN 978-0-7387-2068-5; 0-7387-2068-2

LC 2010-19112

When seventeen-year-old Albert Morales's girlfriend Lily goes missing and he is the main suspect in her disappearance, he must deflect the worries of his angry parents, the suspicions of the police, and Lily's dangerous stepfather as Albert desperately tries to find her, with her sister as his only ally.

"This noir thriller hooks readers with realistic dialogue, fully fleshed characters and plenty of twists. Terrific to the last, good page." Kirkus

Bell, Hilari, 1958-

Trickster's girl. Houghton Mifflin Harcourt 2011 281p (The Raven duet) $16

Grades: 7 8 9 10   **Fic**
1.   Fantasy   fiction   2.   Magic—Fiction 3.   Environmental   degradation—Fiction 4. Bereavement—Fiction
ISBN 978-0-547-19620-6; 0-547-19620-2

LC 2010-06785

In the year 2098, grieving her father and angry with her mother, fifteen-year-old Kelsa joins the magical Raven on an epic journey from Utah to Alaska to heal the earth by restoring the flow of magic that humans have disrupted.

The "degree of nuance will sit especially well with readers who prefer their speculative fiction to be character-driven, and they'll appreciate the compelling exploration of the ways the hopeful can cope with uncertainty." Bull Cent Child Books

Bennett, Holly, 1957-

Shapeshifter. Orca Book Publishers 2010 244p il pa $9.95

Grades: 7 8 9 10   **Fic**
1. Fantasy fiction
ISBN 978-1-55469-158-6; 1-55469-158-3

In order to escape the sorceror who wants to control her gift of song, Sive must transform herself into a deer, leave the Otherworld and find refuge in Eire, the land of mortals.

This is a "rich, slightly revisionist retelling of an ancient Irish legend. Basic human emotions—fear, love, greed—move the tale along, and short first-person narratives that personalize the action are interspersed throughout." Booklist

Bennett Wealer, Sara

Rival. HarperTeen 2011 327p $16.99

Grades: 7 8 9 10   **Fic**
1.   Singing—Fiction   2.   Contests—Fiction 3.   Friendship—Fiction   4.   Popularity—Fiction 5. School stories
ISBN 978-0-06-182762-4   LC 2010-03092

Two high school rivals compete in a prestigious singing competition while reflecting on the events that turned them from close friends to enemies the year before.

"Through Kathryn and Brooke's experiences, teens will learn the important lesson that what you see is not always what you get. This is a must-have addition to school and public libraries collections alike." Voice Youth Advocates

Benoit, Charles

You. HarperTeen 2010 223p $16.99

Grades: 8 9 10 11 12   **Fic**
1. Conduct of life—Fiction 2. School stories
ISBN 978-0-06-194704-9; 0-06-194704-0

LC 2009-43990

Fifteen-year-old Kyle discovers the shattering ramifications of the decisions he makes, and does not make, about school, the girl he likes, and his future.

"The rapid pace is well suited to the narrative. . . . In the end, Benoit creates a fully realized world where choices have impact and the consequences of both action and inaction can be severe." SLJ

Benway, Robin

Audrey, wait! Razorbill 2008 313p $16.99; pa $11

Grades: 9 10 11 12   **Fic**
1. Dating (Social customs)—Fiction 2. Rock musicians—Fiction
ISBN 978-1-59514-191-0; 978-1-59514-192-7 (pa)

LC 2007-23912

While trying to score a date with her cute coworker at the Scooper Dooper, sixteen-year-old Audrey gains unwanted fame and celebrity status when her ex-boyfriend, a rock musician, records a breakup song about her that soars to the top of the Billboard charts.

"Audrey's narration is swift, self-aware, and contemporary in its touch of ironic distance as well as in its style. . . . Current, fresh, and funny, this will rocket up the charts." Bull Cent Child Books

The extraordinary secrets of April, May and June. Razorbill 2010 281p $16.99

Grades: 6 7 8 9 10   **Fic**
1. Sisters—Fiction 2. Parapsychology—Fiction 3. School stories
ISBN 978-1-59514-286-3; 1-59514-286-X

LC 2010-22777

Benway, Robin—*Continued*

When they recover supernatural powers from their childhoods in the aftermath of their parents' divorce, three sisters use their foretelling, invisibility, and mind-reading abilities to tackle school and family challenges.

"The sisters take turns narrating, and their distinct personalities and extremely funny, often barbed dialogue will keep readers laughing as each sibling learns to trust another amazing power: the strength of sisterhood." Publ Wkly

Berk, Josh, 1976-

The dark days of Hamburger Halpin. Alfred A. Knopf 2010 250p $16.99; lib bdg $19.99 *

Grades: 8 9 10 11 12   **Fic**

1. Deaf—Fiction 2. School stories

ISBN   978-0-375-85699-0;   0-375-85699-4; 978-0-375-95699-7 (lib bdg); 0-375-95699-9 (lib bdg)

                    LC 2009-3118

"Being a hefty, deaf newcomer almost makes Will Halpin the least popular guy at Coaler High. But when he befriends the only guy less popular than him, the dork-namic duo has the smarts and guts to figure out who knocked off the star quarterback." Publisher's note

"A coming-of-age mash-up of satire, realistic fiction, mystery, and ill-fated teen romance, *The Dark Days of Hamburger Halpin* is a genre-bending breakthrough that teens are going to love." SLJ

Bick, Ilsa J.

Draw the dark. Carolrhoda Lab 2010 338p $16.95

Grades: 8 9 10 11 12   **Fic**

1. Supernatural—Fiction 2. Artists—Fiction 3. Crime—Fiction 4. Jews—Fiction 5. Wisconsin—Fiction

ISBN 978-0-7613-5686-8; 0-7613-5686-X

                  LC 2009-51612

Seventeen-year-old Christian Cage lives with his uncle in Winter, Wisconsin, where his nightmares, visions, and strange paintings draw him into a mystery involving German prisoners of war, a mysterious corpse, and Winter's last surviving Jew

"The novel brilliantly strikes a compelling balance between fantasy and contemporary fiction. Readers will be on the edge of their seats waiting to find out what happens next and will clamor for a sequel to follow Christian into the sideways place." SLJ

Biederman, Lynn

Teenage waistland; a novel; [by] Lynn Biederman & Lisa Pazer. Delacorte Press 2010 317p $17.99; lib bdg $20.99

Grades: 8 9 10 11 12   **Fic**

1. Obesity—Fiction 2. New York (N.Y.)—Fiction

ISBN   978-0-385-73921-4;   0-385-73921-4; 978-0-385-90776-7 (lib bdg); 0-385-90776-1 (lib bdg)

                  LC 2009-49672

In their separate voices, three morbidly obese New York City teens relate their experiences participating in a clinical trial testing lap-band surgery for teenagers, which involves a year of weekly meetings and learning

to live healthier lives.

"Without sidestepping the seriousness of the teens' weight or the surgery they undergo, the authors offer an important and hopeful story about a little-discussed subject that affects many." Publ Wkly

Billerbeck, Kristin

Perfectly dateless; a universally misunderstood novel. Revell 2010 259p pa $9.99

Grades: 8 9 10 11 12   **Fic**

1. Dating (Social customs)—Fiction 2. Christian life—Fiction 3. School stories

ISBN 978-0-8007-3439-8   LC 2010-6048

Entering her senior year at St. James Christian Academy, Daisy has less than 200 days to look stylish, develop social skills, find the right boy for the prom, and convince her parents to let her date.

"The title and cover alone ensure that teens will pick up this book, and parents will be pleased that there is nothing offensive inside the covers. Adults who enjoy YA fiction and are nostalgic for their high school years may also want to try this hilarious novel." Libr J

Billingsley, Franny, 1954-

Chime. Dial Books for Young Readers 2011 361p $17.99 *

Grades: 7 8 9 10 11 12   **Fic**

1.   Twins—Fiction   2.   Sisters—Fiction 3.   Supernatural—Fiction   4.   Guilt—Fiction 5. Stepmothers—Fiction

ISBN 978-0-8037-3552-1; 0-8037-3552-9

                  LC 2010-12140

In the early twentieth century in Swampsea, seventeen-year-old Briony, who can see the spirits that haunt the marshes around their town, feels responsible for her twin sister's horrible injury until a young man enters their lives and exposes secrets that even Briony does not know about.

"Filled with eccentric characters—self-hating Briony foremost—and oddly beautiful language, this is a darkly beguiling fantasy." Publ Wkly

Bingham, Kelly, 1967-

Shark girl. Candlewick Press 2007 276p $16.99; pa $8.99

Grades: 7 8 9 10   **Fic**

1. Amputees—Fiction 2. Artists—Fiction 3. Novels in verse

ISBN   978-0-7636-3207-6;   0-7636-3207-4; 978-0-7636-4627-1 (pa); 0-7636-4627-X (pa)

                  LC 2006049120

After a shark attack causes the amputation of her right arm, fifteen-year-old Jane, an aspiring artist, struggles to come to terms with her loss and the changes it imposes on her day-to-day life and her plans for the future.

"In carefully constructed, sparsely crafted free verse, Bingham's debut novel offers a strong view of a teenager struggling to survive and learn to live again." Booklist

Bjorkman, Lauren
My invented life. Henry Holt 2009 232p $17.99
Grades: 9 10 11 12   **Fic**
1. Shakespeare, William, 1564-1616—Fiction
2. Sisters—Fiction 3. Theater—Fiction 4. School stories
ISBN 978-0-8050-8950-9; 0-8050-8950-0
                                    LC 2008-50279
During rehearsals for Shakespeare's "As You Like It,"
sixteen-year-old Roz, jealous of her cheerleader sister's
acting skills and heartthrob boyfriend, invents a new
identity, with unexpected results.
"Narrator Roz is funny, well intentioned, and likable
despite her cluelessness, and she is surrounded by a realistic cast of adult and teen characters representing a wide
variety of viewpoints and sexual preferences. This is an
enjoyable read that will be especially appealing to theater
aficionados." SLJ

Black, Holly, 1971-
The white cat. Margaret K. McElderry Books
2010 310p (The curse workers) $17.99 *
Grades: 7 8 9 10   **Fic**
1. Swindlers and swindling—Fiction 2. Memory—Fiction 3. Criminals—Fiction 4. Brothers—Fiction
5. Science fiction
ISBN 978-1-416-96396-7; 1-416-96396-0
                                    LC 2009-33979
When Cassel Sharpe discovers that his older brothers
have used him to carry out their criminal schemes and
then stolen his memories, he figures out a way to turn
their evil machinations against them.
This "starts out with spine-tingling terror, and information is initially dispensed so sparingly, readers will be
hooked." Booklist
Another title in this series is:
Red glove (2011)

Block, Francesca Lia
Dangerous angels; the Weetzie Bat books.
Revised paperback ed. HarperTeen 2010 478p pa
$9.99
Grades: 9 10 11 12   **Fic**
1. Friendship—Fiction 2. Los Angeles (Calif.)—Fic-
tion
ISBN 978-0-06-200740-7
This compilation first published 1998
Contents: Weetzie Bat; Witch baby; Cherokee Bat and
the Goat Guys; Missing Angel Juan; Baby Be-Bop
This is an omnibus edition of five Weetzie Bat books.

The frenzy. HarperTeen 2010 258p $16.99
Grades: 9 10 11 12   **Fic**
1. Identity (Psychology)—Fiction 2. Supernatural—
Fiction 3. Werewolves—Fiction 4. Family life—Fiction 5. Love stories
ISBN 978-0-06-192666-2   LC 2009-53453
When she was thirteen, something terrifying and mysterious happened to Liv that she still does not understand, and now, four years later, her dark secret threatens
to tear her apart from her family and her true love.
"Block does a nice job of weaving all these elements
into a solid story that makes a quick but engaging read

for fans of supernatural fiction. Reluctant readers will enjoy this story as well because of its pacing and manageable chapters." SLJ

Pretty dead. HarperTeen 2009 195p $16.99; lib
bdg $17.89 *
Grades: 9 10 11 12   **Fic**
1. Vampires—Fiction 2. Supernatural—Fiction
3. Death—Fiction
ISBN   978-0-06-154785-0;   0-06-154785-9;
978-0-06-154786-7 (lib bdg); 0-06-154786-7 (lib bdg)
                                    LC 2008-45068
Beautiful vampire Charlotte finds herself slowly
changing back into a human after the mysterious death
of her best friend.
"Block takes what has up to now been the norm
among vampire novels for teens and attempts to turn it
on its head. This is a startlingly original work that drives
a stake deep into the heart of typical vampire stories, revealing the deep loneliness and utter lack of romance in
eternal life." SLJ

Weetzie Bat. Harper & Row 1989 88p
hardcover o.p. pa $7.99
Grades: 9 10 11 12   **Fic**
1. Friendship—Fiction
ISBN 0-06-020534-2; 0-06-073625-9 (pa)
                                    LC 88-6214
"A Charlotte Zolotow book"
Follows the wild adventures of Weetzie Bat and her
Los Angeles punk friends, Dirk, Duck-Man, and Secret-
Agent-Lover-Man
"A brief, off-beat tale that has great charm, poignancy,
and touches of fantasy. . . . This creates the ambiance
of Hollywood with no cynicism, from the viewpoint of
denizens who treasure its unique qualities." SLJ
Other titles about Weetzie Bat and her friends are:
Baby be-bop (1995)
Cherokee Bat and the Goat Guys (1992)
Missing Angel Juan (1993)
Necklace of kisses (2005)
Witch baby (1991)

Bloor, Edward, 1950-
Taken. Alfred A. Knopf 2007 247p $17; pa
$8.99
Grades: 6 7 8 9 10   **Fic**
1. Science fiction 2. Kidnapping—Fiction 3. Social
classes—Fiction
ISBN   978-0-375-83636-7;   0-375-83636-5;
978-0-440-42128-3 (pa); 0-440-42128-4 (pa)
                                    LC 2006-35561
In 2036 kidnapping rich children has become an industry, but when thirteen-year-old Charity Meyers is tak-
en and held for ransom, she soon discovers that this particular kidnapping is not what it seems.
"Deftly constructed, this is as riveting as it is thought-
provoking." Publ Wkly

Bloss, Josie, 1981-
Albatross. Flux 2010 229p pa $9.95
Grades: 8 9 10 11 12　　　　　　　　　**Fic**
　1. Friendship—Fiction　2. Musicians—Fiction
3. School stories
ISBN 978-0-7387-1476-9; 0-7387-1476-3
　　　　　　　　　　　　　　LC 2009-27511
"Tess's parents have recently separated, and the teen
and her mother have moved from Chicago to Michigan
to start over. Once there, Tess finds herself inexplicably
attracted to Micah, an angst-ridden boy who belittles her,
contrasting her with his 'true love,' Daisy. Sprinkled
throughout the story are italicized phrases—assertive responses that Tess lacks the self-esteem to voice aloud. In
an epiphany, she realizes that her attraction to Micah
stems from his familiarity: her father is insulting and
abusive in the same way, and she begins to speak out,
expressing the internal dialogue she has been having all
along." SLJ

Blubaugh, Penny
Serendipity Market. HarperTeen 2009 268p
$16.99; pa $8.99
Grades: 7 8 9 10　　　　　　　　　　　**Fic**
　1. Fairy tales 2. Magic—Fiction 3. Storytelling—Fiction
ISBN　978-0-06-146875-9;　0-06-146875-4;
978-0-06-146877-3 (pa); 0-06-146877-0 (pa)
　　　　　　　　　　　　　　LC 2008-10187
"Laura Geringer books"
When the world begins to seem unbalanced, Mama
Inez calls ten storytellers to the Serendipity Market and,
through the power of their magical tales, the balance of
the world is corrected once again.
　"In this debut storytelling tour de force, Blubaugh re-
packages familiar folk and fairy-tale themes with contemporary verve and wit." Kirkus

Blundell, Judy
Strings attached. Scholastic Press 2011 310p
$17.99 *
Grades: 7 8 9 10　　　　　　　　　　　**Fic**
　1. Dance—Fiction 2. Italian Americans—Fiction
3. Mafia—Fiction 4. Homicide—Fiction 5. New York
(N.Y.)—Fiction
ISBN 978-0-545-22126-9; 0-545-22126-9
　　　　　　　　　　　　　　LC 2010-41078
When she drops out of school and struggles to start a
career on Broadway in the fall of 1950, seventeen-year-
old Kit Corrigan accepts help from an old family friend,
a lawyer said to have ties with the mob, who then asks
her to do some favors for him.
　Blundell "successfully constructs a complex web of
intrigue that connects characters in unexpected ways.
History and theater buffs will especially appreciate her
attention to detail—Blundell again demonstrates she can
turn out first-rate historical fiction." Publ Wkly

What I saw and how I lied. Scholastic Press
2008 284p $16.99 *
Grades: 8 9 10 11 12　　　　　　　　　**Fic**
　1. Florida—Fiction 2. Mystery fiction
ISBN 978-0-439-90346-2; 0-439-90346-7
　　　　　　　　　　　　　　LC 2008-08503

In 1947, with her jovial stepfather Joe back from the
war and family life returning to normal, teenage Evie,
smitten by the handsome young ex-GI who seems to
have a secret hold on Joe, finds herself caught in a complicated web of lies whose devastating outcome change
her life and that of her family forever.
　"Using pitch-perfect dialogue and short sentences
filled with meaning, Blundell has crafted a suspenseful,
historical mystery." Booklist

Bodeen, S. A., 1965-
The Compound. Feiwel and Friends 2008 248p
$16.95; pa $8.99
Grades: 7 8 9 10　　　　　　　　　　　**Fic**
　1. Survival after airplane accidents, shipwrecks, etc.—
Fiction 2. Twins—Fiction 3. Fathers—Fiction
ISBN　978-0-312-37015-2;　0-312-37015-6;
978-0-312-57860-2 (pa); 0-312-57860-1 (pa)
　　　　　　　　　　　　　　LC 2007-36148
After his parents, two sisters, and he have spent six
years in a vast underground compound built by his
wealthy father to protect them from a nuclear holocaust,
fifteen-year-old Eli, whose twin brother and grandmother
were left behind, discovers that his father has perpetrated
a monstrous hoax on them all.
　"The audience will feel the pressure closing in on
them as they, like the characters, race through hairpin
turns in the plot toward a breathless climax." Publ Wkly

The gardener. Feiwel and Friends 2010 233p
$16.99
Grades: 7 8 9 10　　　　　　　　　　　**Fic**
　1. Genetic engineering—Fiction 2. Single parent family—Fiction 3. Fathers—Fiction 4. Science fiction
ISBN 978-0-312-37016-9; 0-312-37016-4
　　　　　　　　　　　　　　LC 2009-48802
When high school sophomore Mason finds a beautiful
but catatonic girl in the nursing home where his mother
works, the discovery leads him to revelations about a series of disturbing human experiments that have a connection to his own life.
　"This is a fast-paced read that keeps readers guessing
what the turn of a page will reveal." Voice Youth Advocates

Booth, Coe
Kendra. PUSH 2008 292p $16.99
Grades: 8 9 10 11 12　　　　　　　　　**Fic**
　1. Mother-daughter relationship—Fiction 2. African
Americans—Fiction 3. Teenage mothers—Fiction
4. New York (N.Y.)—Fiction
ISBN 978-0-439-92536-5; 0-439-92536-3
　　　　　　　　　　　　　　LC 2008-12819
High schooler Kendra longs to live with her mother
who, unprepared for motherhood at age fourteen, left
Kendra in the care of her grandmother.
　"The convoluted but redeeming friendship between
Kendra and her best friend and aunt, Adonna, resonates
with heartbreak and honesty. Teens will appreciate
Kendra's internal justification monologues, especially in
relation to her Nana. . . . From Bronx blocks to Harlem
hangouts, Booth delivers dynamic characters and an en-
gaging story." SLJ

Booth, Coe—*Continued*

Tyrell. PUSH 2006 310p hardcover o.p. pa
$7.99 *

Grades: 9 10 11 12 **Fic**
1. Homeless persons—Fiction 2. Poor—Fiction
3. African Americans—Fiction 4. Bronx (New York,
N.Y.)—Fiction
ISBN 0-439-83879-7; 978-0-439-83879-5;
0-439-83880-0 (pa); 978-0-439-83880-1 (pa)
LC 2005-37330

Fifteen-year-old Tyrell, who is living in a Bronx
homeless shelter with his spaced-out mother and his
younger brother, tries to avoid temptation so he does not
end up in jail like his father.

"The immediate first-person narrative is pitch perfect:
fast, funny, and anguished (there's also lots of use of the
n-word, though the term is employed in the colloquial
sense, not as an insult). Unlike many books reflecting the
contemporary street scene, this one is more than just a
pat situation with a glib resolution; it's filled with surprising twists and turns that continue to the end."
Booklist

Followed by Bronxwood (2011)

Borris, Albert
Crash into me. Simon Pulse 2009 257p $16.99

Grades: 8 9 10 11 12 **Fic**
1. Suicide—Fiction 2. Automobile travel—Fiction
ISBN 978-1-4169-7435-2; 1-4169-7435-0
LC 2008-36225

Four suicidal teenagers go on a "celebrity suicide road
trip," visiting the graves of famous people who have
killed themselves, with the intention of ending their lives
in Death Valley, California.

This "novel gives a spot-on portrayal of depressed and
suicidal teens with realistic voices." Kirkus

Boulle, Pierre, 1912-1994
Planet of the apes; translated by Xan Feilding.
Ballantine 2001 c1991 268p pa $6.99

Grades: 11 12 Adult **Fic**
1. Science fiction
ISBN 0-345-44798-0
"A Del Rey book"
First published 1963 by Vanguard Press; published in
the United Kingdom with title: Monkey planet

"Ulysse Merou writes of his experiences on an unusual planet where the roles of humans and apes are reversed. Gorillas wear clothing and run businesses, while
humans are caged in zoos and are the subjects of scientific experiments. In the year 2500 a vacationing couple
cruising through space spot a bottle-encased message, retrieve it, and soon become absorbed in Merou's tale."
Shapiro. Fic for Youth. 3d edition

"In this Swiftian fable Boulle gives full play to his not
inconsiderable gift for irony and satire." Libr J

Bova, Ben, 1932-
Mars life. Tor 2008 432p hardcover o.p. pa
$7.99

Grades: 9 10 11 12 Adult **Fic**
1. Mars (Planet)—Fiction 2. Life on other planets—
Fiction 3. Science fiction
ISBN 978-0-7653-1787-2; 0-7653-1787-7;
978-0-7653-5724-3 (pa); 0-7653-5724-0 (pa)
LC 2008-20388

Sequel to: Return to Mars (1999)
"A Tom Doherty Associates book"
"Two scientists add up fossil evidence to conclude
that Mars once supported intelligent life and that Martians colonized Earth—conclusions that run them into the
religious buzz saw of New Morality conservatives."
Booklist

"Bova deftly captures the excitement of scientific discovery and planetary exploration. This compelling story,
balancing action and plausible political intrigue, will easily be enjoyed by both fans and newcomers." Publ Wkly

Bowler, Tim, 1953-
Blade: playing dead. Philomel Books 2009 231p
$16.99; pa $7.99

Grades: 7 8 9 10 **Fic**
1. Violence—Fiction 2. Gangs—Fiction 3. Homeless
persons—Fiction 4. Great Britain—Fiction
ISBN 978-0-399-25186-3; 0-399-25186-3;
978-0-14-241600-6 (pa); 0-14-241600-2 (pa)
LC 2008-37813

First published 2008 in the United Kingdom
A fourteen-year-old British street person with extraordinary powers of observation and self-control must face
murderous thugs connected with a past he has tried to
forget, when his skills with a knife earned him the nickname, Blade.

"Bowler delivers an intense, gripping novel. . . .
Readers who like their thrillers brutally realistic will find
much to enjoy." Publ Wkly

Other books about Blade are:
Blade: fighting back (2011)
Blade: out of the shadows (2010)

Boyd, Maria
Will. Alfred A. Knopf 2010 300p $16.99; lib
bdg $19.99 *

Grades: 8 9 10 11 12 **Fic**
1. School stories 2. Musicals—Fiction 3. Theater—
Fiction 4. Homosexuality—Fiction 5. Australia—Fiction
ISBN 978-0-375-86209-0; 0-375-86209-9;
978-0-375-96209-7 (lib bdg); 0-375-96209-3 (lib bdg)
LC 2009-39888

Seventeen-year-old Will's behavior has been getting
him in trouble at his all-boys school in Sydney, Australia, but his latest punishment, playing in the band for a
musical production, gives him new insights into his fellow students and helps him cope with an incident he has
tried to forget.

"Readers should find it easy to sympathize with Will's
vibrant, deadpan narration and his frequent use of slang,
while recognizing that his jocular exterior hides a deeper
vulnerability. . . . Boyd effectively handles Will's final
outpouring of repressed emotions: the personal growth

Boyd, Maria—*Continued*
achieved by her realistic, likeable protagonist is abundantly clear." Publ Wkly

Boyne, John, 1971-
Mutiny; a novel of the Bounty. Thomas Dunne Books/St. Martin's Press 2009 399p map $25.95
Grades: 9 10 11 12 Adult   **Fic**
  1. Christian, Fletcher, 1764-1793—Fiction 2. Bligh, William, 1754-1817—Fiction 3. Bounty (Ship)—Fiction 4. Sea stories
  ISBN 978-0-312-53856-9; 0-312-53856-1
                    LC 2008-37674
"This riveting account set in 1789 is narrated by 14-year-old John Jacob Turnstile, Captain Bligh's fictitious servant. . . . After six months on idyllic Tahiti, second-in-command Fletcher Christian leads 23 crew members in a mutiny, forcing Bligh and 18 loyal crew members into a 23-foot launch with only a compass and meager rations. Incredibly, with only one fatality, Bligh, Turnstile, and their companions row more than 3600 miles to a Portuguese settlement on Timor. Nursed back to health, the surviving crew returns to England where their story captures public attention. Imbuing the story with facts drawn from Bligh's personal documents, legal transcripts of his court martial, English naval protocol, and nautical history, Boyne has created a masterful adventure." SLJ

Bradbury, Jennifer
Shift. Atheneum Books for Young Readers 2008 245p $16.99
Grades: 7 8 9 10 11 12   **Fic**
  1. Cycling—Fiction 2. Travel—Fiction 3. Missing persons—Fiction 4. Friendship—Fiction
  ISBN 978-1-4169-4732-5; 1-4169-4732-9
                    LC 2007-23558
When best friends Chris and Win go on a cross country bicycle trek the summer after graduating and only one returns, the FBI wants to know what happened.
"Bradbury's keen details . . . add wonderful texture to this exciting [novel.] . . . Best of all is the friendship story." Booklist

Bradbury, Ray, 1920-
Fahrenheit 451. Ballantine Books 1996 179p pa $15 *
Grades: 9 10 11 12 Adult   **Fic**
  1. Books and reading—Fiction 2. Science fiction
  ISBN 978-0-345-41001-6; 0-345-41001-7
                    LC 96096738
"A Del Rey book"
First published 1953
Dystopian novel about a bookburner official in a future fascist state.

Something wicked this way comes. Avon Bks. 1999 293p $15.95; pa $7.99
Grades: 7 8 9 10   **Fic**
  1. Horror fiction 2. Fantasy fiction
  ISBN 0-380-97727-3; 0-380-72940-7 (pa)
  A reissue of the title first published 1962 by Simon and Schuster

"We read here of the loss of innocence, the recognition of evil, the bond between generations, and the purely fantastic. These forces enter Green Town, Illinois, on the wheels of Cooger and Dark's Pandemonium Shadow Show. Will Halloway and Jim Nightshade, two 13-year-olds, explore the sinister carnival for excitement, which becomes desperation as the forces of the dark threaten to engulf-them. Bradbury's gentle humanism and lyric style serve this fantasy well." Shapiro. Fic for Youth. 3d edition

Bradley, Alan, 1938-
The sweetness at the bottom of the pie. Delacorte Press 2009 373p $23; pa $15
Grades: 11 12 Adult   **Fic**
  1. Sisters—Fiction 2. Detectives—Fiction 3. Great Britain—Fiction 4. Mystery fiction
  ISBN   978-0-385-34230-8;   0-385-34230-6; 978-0-385-34349-7 (pa); 0-385-34349-3 (pa)
                    LC 2008-41787
Eleven-year-old Flavia de Luce, an aspiring chemist with a passion for poison, must exonerate her father of murder. Armed with more than enough knowledge to tie two distant deaths together and examine new suspects, she begins a search that will lead her all the way to the King of England himself.
"Mystery fans, Anglophiles, and science buffs will delight in this book and may come away with a slightly altered view of what is possible for a headstrong girl to achieve." SLJ
  Other titles featuring Flavia de Luce are:
A red herring without mustard (2011)
The weed that strings the hangman's bag (2010)

Bradley, Marion Zimmer
The mists of Avalon. Ballantine Pub. Group 2000 876p $30; pa $16.95 *
Grades: 9 10 11 12 Adult   **Fic**
  1. Arthur, King—Fiction 2. Fantasy fiction 3. Great Britain—History—0-1066—Fiction
  ISBN 0-345-44118-4; 0-345-35049-9 (pa)
                    LC 00-712415
"A Del Rey book"
A reissue of the title first published 1982 by Knopf
This "retelling of the Arthurian legend is dominated by the character of Morgan le Fay (here called Morgaine), the powerful sorceress who symbolizes the historical clash between Christianity and the early pagan religions of the British Isles." Publ Wkly
  Other novels in the Avalon series written with Diana L. Paxson are: The forest house (1993); Lady of Avalon (1997); Priestess of Avalon (2000). Following Bradley's death Paxson continued the series with: Ancestors of Avalon (2004); Ravens of Avalon (2007); Sword of Avalon (2009)

Brande, Robin

Evolution, me, & other freaks of nature. Alfred A. Knopf 2007 268p hardcover o.p. pa $7.99

Grades: 7 8 9 10   **Fic**

1. Evolution—Fiction 2. Christian life—Fiction 3. School stories

ISBN   978-0-375-84349-5;   0-375-84349-3; 978-0-375-94349-2 (lib bdg); 0-375-94349-8 (lib bdg); 978-0-440-24030-3 (pa); 0-440-24030-1 (pa)

LC 2006-34158

Following her conscience leads high school freshman Mena to clash with her parents and former friends from their conservative Christian church, but might result in better things when she stands up for a teacher who refuses to include "Intelligent Design" in lessons on evolution.

"Readers will appreciate this vulnerable but ultimately resilient protagonist who sees no conflict between science and her own deeply rooted faith." Booklist

Fat Cat. Alfred A. Knopf 2009 330p $16.99; lib bdg $19.99 *

Grades: 8 9 10 11 12   **Fic**

1. Science—Experiments—Fiction 2. Obesity—Fiction 3. Friendship—Fiction 4. School stories

ISBN   978-0-375-84449-2;   0-375-84449-X; 978-0-375-94449-9 (lib bdg); 0-375-94449-4 (lib bdg)

LC 2008-50619

Overweight teenage Catherine embarks on a high school science project in which she must emulate the ways of hominins, the earliest ancestors of human beings, by eating an all-natural diet and foregoing technology.

The author "offers a fresh, funny portrait of a strong-minded young woman hurdling obstacles and fighting cravings to reach her goal." Publ Wkly

Brashares, Ann, 1967-

The sisterhood of the traveling pants. Delacorte Press 2001 294p $14.95; pa $8.95

Grades: 9 10 11 12   **Fic**

1. Friendship—Fiction

ISBN 0-385-72933-2; 0-385-73058-6 (pa)

LC 2002-282046

"Four lifelong high-school friends and a magical pair of jeans take summer journeys to discover love, disappointment, and self-realization." Booklist

"The author shares her subjects' shrewdness at evaluating social nuances and their ease with sarcastic slang. . . . She is equally adept at describing anger toward an absent parent, the difficulty of losing a beloved pet and the awkwardness of newfound sexual desire." N Y Times Book Rev

Other titles about the Sisterhood are:

Forever in blue (2007)

Girls in pants (2005)

The second summer of the sisterhood (2003)

Sisterhood everlasting (2011)

Bray, Libba

Beauty queens. Scholastic Press 2011 396p $18.99

Grades: 8 9 10 11 12   **Fic**

1. Survival after airplane accidents, shipwrecks, etc.—Fiction 2. Beauty contests—Fiction

ISBN 978-0-439-89597-2; 0-439-89597-9

LC 2011-02321

When a plane crash strands thirteen teen beauty contestants on a mysterious island, they struggle to survive, to get along with one another, to combat the island's other diabolical occupants, and to learn their dance numbers in case they are rescued in time for the competition.

"A full-scale send-up of consumer culture, beauty pageants, and reality television: . . . it makes readers really examine their own values while they are laughing, and shaking their heads at the hyperbolic absurdity of those values gone seriously awry." Bull Cent Child Books

Going bovine. Delacorte Press 2009 480p $17.99; lib bdg $20.99 *

Grades: 9 10 11 12   **Fic**

1. Creutzfeldt-Jakob disease—Fiction 2. Dwarfs—Fiction 3. Automobile travel—Fiction

ISBN   978-0-385-73397-7;   0-385-73397-6; 978-0-385-90411-7 (lib bdg); 0-385-90411-8 (lib bdg)

LC 2008-43774

In an attempt to find a cure after being diagnosed with Creutzfeldt-Jakob's (aka mad cow) disease, Cameron Smith, a disaffected sixteen-year-old boy, sets off on a road trip with a death-obsessed video gaming dwarf he meets in the hospital.

"Bray's wildly imagined novel, narrated in Cameron's sardonic, believable voice, is wholly unique, ambitious, tender, thought-provoking, and often fall-off-the-chair funny, even as she writes with powerful lyricism about the nature of existence, love, and death." Booklist

A great and terrible beauty. Delacorte Press 2004 403p $16.95 *

Grades: 9 10 11 12   **Fic**

1. Great Britain—Fiction 2. Mystery fiction

ISBN 0-385-73028-4   LC 2003-9472

After the suspicious death of her mother in 1895, sixteen-year-old Gemma returns to England, after many years in India, to attend a finishing school where she becomes aware of her magical powers and ability to see into the spirit world.

"The reader will race to the end to discover the mysterious and realistic challenges of an exciting teenage gothic mystery." Libr Media Connect

Other titles featuring Gemma Doyle are:

Rebel angels (2005)

The sweet far thing (2007)

Brenna, Beverley

Waiting for no one. Red Deer 2011 187p pa $12.95

Grades: 7 8 9 10   **Fic**

1. Asperger's syndrome—Fiction

ISBN 978-0-88995-437-3; 0-88995-437-2

Sequel to Wild orchid (2006)

Taylor Jane Smith is "taking a biology class at college and applying for a job at a local bookstore. Her

Brenna, Beverley—*Continued*

Asperger's syndrome gives her an advantage in the class, but it's making the job-application process torture. . . . Taylor, with her flinty, exasperated approach to the world, remains a fascinating character and narrator." Bull Cent Child Books

Brennan, Sarah Rees, 1983-

The demon's lexicon. Margaret K. McElderry Books 2009 322p $17.99; pa $9.99

Grades: 9 10 11 12   **Fic**
1. Demonology—Fiction 2. Magic—Fiction 3. Brothers—Fiction
ISBN   978-1-4169-6379-0;   1-4169-6379-0; 978-1-4169-6380-6 (pa); 1-4169-6380-4 (pa)

LC 2008-39056

Sixteen-year-old Nick and his family have battled magicians and demons for most of his life, but when his brother, Alan, is marked for death while helping new friends Jamie and Mae, Nick's determination to save Alan leads him to uncover a devastating secret.

"A fresh voice dancing between wicked humor and crepuscular sumptuousness invigorates this urban fantasy. . . . The narrative peels back layers of revelation, deftly ratcheting up the tension and horror to a series of shattering climaxes." Kirkus

Other titles in this series are:
The demon's covenant (2010)
The demon's surrender (2011)

Briant, Ed

Choppy socky blues. Flux 2010 259p pa $9.95

Grades: 7 8 9 10   **Fic**
1. Karate—Fiction 2. Father-son relationship—Fiction 3. Dating (Social customs)—Fiction 4. Great Britain—Fiction
ISBN 978-0-7387-1897-2; 0-7387-1897-1

LC 2009-30491

In the South of England, fourteen-year-old Jay resumes contact with his father, a movie stuntman and karate instructor, after two years of estrangement to impress a girl who turns out to be the girlfriend of Jay's former best friend.

"Jason's insecurities, resentment toward (and gradual peacemaking with) his father, and obsession with girls are believably rendered—he's the kind of awkward hero readers will be glad to see come into his own." Publ Wkly

Brody, Jessica

The Karma Club. Farrar Straus Giroux 2010 258p $16.99

Grades: 7 8 9 10   **Fic**
1. School stories
ISBN 978-0-374-33979-1; 0-374-33979-1

LC 2008-55560

When high school senior Maddy catches her boyfriend cheating on her, she devises a complicated plan to get revenge.

This is "a well-paced comedy, with a nice balance of cinematic physical humor and genuine teen emotions." Publ Wkly

Brom, 1965-

The child thief. EOS 2009 481p il $26.99

Grades: 10 11 12 Adult   **Fic**
1. Fantasy fiction
ISBN 978-0-06-167133-3   LC 2010-279732

Reveals the world of Peter Pan through the eyes of Nick, a fatherless teen whose dreams of wonderland are replaced by the gritty reality of life and death, as Peter's recruits are forced into a lethal battle where the line between good and evil is blurred.

"Of questionable morals and thoroughly self-centered, Peter is not always likable, nor are his motives for the greater good. He is, however, a fully realized, completely believable, and utterly captivating character who drives this violent and dramatic narrative." Booklist

Brontë, Charlotte, 1816-1855

Jane Eyre; [by] Charlotte Brontë with an introduction by Lucy Hughes-Hallet. Knopf 1991 xxxviii, 284p $20 *

Grades: 11 12 Adult   **Fic**
1. Great Britain—Fiction 2. Love stories
ISBN 0-679-40582-8   LC 91-52968

Also available from other publishers
"Everyman's library"
First published 1847

"In both heroine and hero the author introduced types new to English fiction. Jane Eyre is a shy, intense little orphan, never for a moment, neither in her unhappy school days nor her subsequent career as a governess, displaying those qualities of superficial beauty and charm that had marked the conventional heroine. Jane's lover, Edward Rochester, to whose ward she is governess, is a strange, violent man, bereft of conventional courtesy, a law unto himself. Rochester's moodiness derives from the fact that he is married to an insane wife, whose existence, long kept secret, is revealed on the very day of his projected marriage to Jane. Years afterward the lovers are reunited." Reader's Ency. 4th edition

Brontë, Emily, 1818-1848

Wuthering Heights; with an introduction by Katherine Frank. Knopf 1991 xxxiii, 385p $22 *

Grades: 11 12 Adult   **Fic**
1. Great Britain—Fiction 2. Love stories
ISBN 0-679-40543-7   LC 91-52969

Also available from other publishers
"Everyman's library"
First published 1847

Forced by a storm to spend the night at the home of the somber and unsociable Heathcliff, Mr. Lockwood has an encounter with the spirit of Catherine Linton. He gradually learns that Catherine's father, Mr. Earnshaw, had taken in Heathcliff as a young orphan. Heathcliff and Catherine began to fall in love, but after Mr. Earnshaw's death Catherine's brother treated Heathcliff in a degrading manner and Catherine married rich Edgar Linton. Heathcliff gradually worked his revenge against those who injured him.

Includes bibliographical references

Brooks, Kevin, 1959-

Being. Scholastic 2007 336p $16.99

Grades: 8 9 10 11 12   **Fic**

Brooks, Kevin, 1959-—*Continued*
  1. Identity (Psychology)—Fiction 2. Science fiction
  ISBN 978-0-439-89973-4; 0-439-89973-7

It was just supposed to be a routine exam. But when the doctors snake the fiber-optic tube down Robert Smith's throat, what they discover doesn't make medical sense.

"Gruesome scenes in gloomy British surroundings provide the backdrop for provocative questions about 'being' physically, emotionally, and rationally. . . . Sadness and frustration pervade this lively page-turner, and Robert's future is surely uncertain." Voice Youth Advocates

Black Rabbit summer. Scholastic 2008 488p $17.99
Grades: 9 10 11 12   **Fic**
  1. Missing persons—Fiction 2. Drug abuse—Fiction
  3. Homosexuality—Fiction 4. Mystery fiction
  ISBN 978-0-545-05752-3; 0-545-05752-3
                                   LC 2007-035322

When two of sixteen-year-old Pete's childhood classmates disappear from a carnival the same night, he is a suspect, but his own investigation implicates other old friends he was with that evening—and a tough, knife-wielding enemy determined to keep him quiet.

"This dark and complicated mystery tackles the nature of friendships, loyalty and betrayal." KLIATT

Candy. Chicken House/Scholastic 2005 359p $16.95
Grades: 9 10 11 12   **Fic**
  1. Drug abuse—Fiction 2. London (England)—Fiction
  ISBN 0-439-68327-0

"In London for a doctor's appointment, Joe meets a captivating girl named Candy at the train station, but his rhapsody is cut short when a man who's clearly Candy's pimp breaks up the interlude by threatening Joe. She remains irresistible to Joe, who finds ways to see her again . . . and who develops a growing determination to save her from her dangerous life of drugs and prostitution, even if it endangers himself and his family." Bull Cent Child Books

"Brooks's plotting is masterful, and the action twists and builds to a frenzied and violent climax." SLJ

Dawn. Chicken House/Scholastic 2009 250p $17.99
Grades: 7 8 9 10   **Fic**
  1. Family life—Fiction 2. Incest—Fiction 3. Child sexual abuse—Fiction
  ISBN 978-0-545-06090-5; 0-545-06090-7
                                      LC 2009-1643

First published 2009 in the United Kingdom with title: Killing God

Fifteen-year-old Dawn, who cares for her alcoholic mother, tries to suppress a painful childhood memory as she contemplates killing God, whom she blames for her father's disappearance.

"Provocative, bleak, compelling, and somewhat open-ended, this novel will appeal to those who admire unexpected strength in victims who push back mightily against being victimized." Voice Youth Advocates

Kissing the rain. Scholastic 2004 320p $16.95
Grades: 9 10 11 12   **Fic**
  1. Great Britain—Fiction 2. Obesity—Fiction
  3. Homicide—Fiction
  ISBN 0-439-57742-X   LC 2003-57395

"After fat, bullied British teen Moo witnesses a murder, he finds himself the center of a conflict between two unsavory factions that threaten his working-class father and himself. In a casual narrative that spikes with increasing panic, Moo tells his own story, stopping short of answering the pivotal question at book's end." Booklist

Lucas. Chicken House/Scholastic 2003 423p hardcover o.p. pa $6.99 *
Grades: 7 8 9 10   **Fic**
  1. Prejudices—Fiction 2. Great Britain—Fiction
  ISBN 0-439-45698-3; 0-439-53063-6 (pa)
                                   LC 2002-29189

On an isolated English island, fifteen-year-old Caitlin McCann makes the painful journey from adolescence to adulthood through her experiences with a mysterious boy, whose presence has an unsettling effect on the island's inhabitants

"This beautifully written allegorical tale . . . stays with readers long after it ends. . . . All of the characters are sharply defined. Lucas, with his mixture of real and unearthly qualities, is unique and unforgettable. This is a powerful book to be savored by all who appreciate fine writing and a gripping read." SLJ

The road of the dead. Chicken House 2006 339p $16.99
Grades: 9 10 11 12   **Fic**
  1. Homicide—Fiction 2. Brothers—Fiction
  3. Gypsies—Fiction 4. Great Britain—Fiction
  ISBN 0-439-78623-1; 978-0-439-78623-2
                                   LC 2005-14793

First published 2004 in the United Kingdom

Two brothers, sons of an incarcerated gypsy, leave London traveling to an isolated and desolate village, in search of the brutal killer of their sister.

"The sustained violence of the final events will be familiar to fans of films by Tarantino or, for those with historic tastes, Peckinpah, and the moral ambiguity of the ending ('Did any of it matter?') will appeal to lovers of noir, making this a useful title for readers seeking the literary equivalent of edgy cinema." Bull Cent Child Books

Brooks, Martha, 1944-
  Mistik Lake. Farrar, Straus and Giroux 2007 207p $16
Grades: 7 8 9 10   **Fic**
  1. Mothers—Fiction 2. Manitoba—Fiction 3. Family life—Fiction
  ISBN 978-0-374-34985-1; 0-374-34985-1
                                   LC 2006-37391

After Odella's mother leaves her, her sisters, and their father in Manitoba and moves to Iceland with another man, she then dies there, and the family finally learns some of the many secrets that have haunted them for two generations.

"All of the characters seem distinct and real, thanks to the author's exceptional skill with details." Publ Wkly

Brooks, Terry, 1944-
Armageddon's children. Del Rey 2006 371p
(The genesis of Shannara) hardcover o.p. pa $7.99
Grades: 11 12 Adult   **Fic**
1. Good and evil—Fiction 2. Fantasy fiction
ISBN   0-345-48408-8;   978-0-345-48408-6;
0-345-48410-X (pa); 978-0-345-48410-9 (pa)
LC 2006-40423
In this first volume in The genesis of Shannara series
the "author envisions a chilling near-future U.S., where
civilization has collapsed from environmental degradation, plagues, global warfare and supernatural threats.
The last surviving members of the Knights of the Word,
Logan Tom and Angel Perez, seek to keep the 'balance
of the world's magic in check' as they battle the Void—
embodied by demons, their leader Findo Cask and their
vicious human mutant counterparts known as 'once-
men.'" Publ Wkly
"Characterizations are dynamic and multidimensional,
the descriptions of the land as well as the ruined cities
and small towns are compelling, the action and battles
are mesmerizing, and, as is Brooks' wont, the ending is
a cliffhanger that leaves readers salivating for the sequel." Booklist
  Other titles in this series are:
The elves of Cintra (2007)
The gypsy morph (2008)

The sword of Shannara; illustrated by the
Brothers Hildebrandt. Ballantine Bks. 1991 726p il
hardcover o.p. pa $7.99 *
Grades: 11 12 Adult   **Fic**
1. Fantasy fiction
ISBN 0-394-441333-4; 0-345-31425-5 (pa)
LC 90-43727
"A Del Rey book"
A reissue of the title first published 1977 by Random
House
"Humans, trolls, dwarfs, elves, gnomes, sorcerers both
good and evil, and battalions of knights and knaves pop-
ulate this sweeping adult epic-fantasy. At the urging of
a mysterious sorcerer, an adopted orphan named Shea re-
luctantly takes up the quest for the Sword of Shannara,
a legendary elvin blade that alone can defeat the forces
of evil engulfing the world." Booklist
This is an "engrossing saga of hardship and adventure
with well-maintained action that will keep readers cap-
tive right up to a nicely-wrought finish." SLJ
  Other titles in this epic-fantasy are:
The druids of Shannara (1991)
The Elf queen of Shannara (1992)
The Elfstones of Shannara (1982)
First king of Shannara (1996)
The scions of Shannara (1990)
The talismans of Shannara (1993)
The wishsong of Shannara (1985)

Brothers, Meagan
Debbie Harry sings in French. Henry Holt 2008
232p $16.95
Grades: 8 9 10 11 12   **Fic**
1. Rock music—Fiction 2. Sex role—Fiction
3. Transvestites—Fiction
ISBN 978-0-8050-8080-3; 0-8050-8080-5
LC 2007-27322

When Johnny completes an alcohol rehabilitation program and his mother sends him to live with his uncle in
North Carolina, he meets Maria, who seems to understand his fascination with the new wave band Blondie,
and he learns about his deceased father's youthful forays
into "glam rock," which gives him perspective on himself, his past, and his current life.
"The brisk pace and the strong-willed, empathetic narrator will keep readers fully engaged." Publ Wkly

Brown, Jennifer, 1972-
Bitter end. Little, Brown 2011 359p $17.99
Grades: 10 11 12   **Fic**
1. Abused women—Fiction 2. Friendship—Fiction
3. Bereavement—Fiction
ISBN 978-0-316-08695-0; 0-316-08695-9
LC 2010-34258
When seventeen-year-old Alex starts dating Cole, a
new boy at her high school, her two closest friends increasingly mistrust him as the relationship grows more
serious.
"Gritty and disturbing, this novel should be in all collections serving teens. It could be used in programs
about abuse, as well as in psychology or sociology classes." SLJ

Hate list. Little, Brown and Co. 2009 408p
$16.99
Grades: 9 10 11 12   **Fic**
1. School violence—Fiction 2. Family life—Fiction
3. School stories
ISBN 978-0-316-04144-7; 0-316-04144-0
LC 2008-50223
Sixteen-year-old Valerie, whose boyfriend Nick committed a school shooting at the end of their junior year,
struggles to cope with integrating herself back into high
school life, unsure herself whether she was a hero or a
villain.
"Val's complicated relationship with her family, . . .
the surviving victims, as well as how she comes to terms
with Nick's betrayal, are piercingly real, and the shooting
scenes wrenching. Her successes are hard-won and her
setbacks . . . painfully true to life." Publ Wkly

Bruchac, Joseph, 1942-
Code talker; a novel about the Navajo Marines
of World War Two. Dial 2005 240p $16.99 *
Grades: 6 7 8 9 10   **Fic**
1. Navajo Indians—Fiction 2. World War, 1939-
1945—Fiction
ISBN 0-8037-2921-9
After being taught in a boarding school run by whites
that Navajo is a useless language, Ned Begay and other
Navajo men are recruited by the Marines to become
Code Talkers, sending messages during World War II in
their native tongue.
"Bruchac's gentle prose presents a clear historical picture of young men in wartime. . . . Nonsensational and
accurate, Bruchac's tale is quietly inspiring." SLJ
Includes bibliographical references

Bruchac, Joseph, 1942-—*Continued*

Sacajawea; the story of Bird Woman and the Lewis and Clark Expedition. Silver Whistle Bks. 2000 199p $17; pa $6.99

Grades: 6 7 8 9 10   **Fic**
1. Sacagawea, b. 1786—Fiction 2. Clark, William, 1770-1838—Fiction 3. Lewis and Clark Expedition (1804-1806)—Fiction 4. Native Americans—Fiction
ISBN 0-15-202234-1; 0-15-206455-9 (pa)
           LC 99-47653

Also available in paperback from Scholastic
Sacajawea, a Shoshoni Indian interpreter, peacemaker, and guide, and William Clark alternate in describing their experiences on the Lewis and Clark Expedition to the Northwest
This is an "intelligent, elegantly written novel." SLJ
Includes bibliographical references

Bryant, Jennifer

Ringside, 1925; views from the Scopes trial, a novel; [by] Jen Bryant. Alfred A. Knopf 2008 228p $15.99; lib bdg $18.99

Grades: 8 9 10 11 12   **Fic**
1. Scopes, John Thomas—Fiction 2. Evolution—Study and teaching—Fiction 3. Tennessee—Fiction 4. Novels in verse
ISBN   978-0-375-84047-0;   0-375-84047-8; 978-0-375-94047-7 (lib bdg); 0-375-94047-2 (lib bdg)
           LC 2007-7177

Visitors, spectators, and residents of Dayton, Tennessee, in 1925 describe, in a series of free-verse poems, the Scopes 'monkey trial' and its effects on that small town and its citizens.
"Bryant offers readers a ringside seat in this compelling and well-researched novel. It is fast-paced, interesting, and relevant to many current first-amendment challenges." SLJ

Buck, Pearl S. (Pearl Sydenstricker), 1892-1973

The good earth. Washington Square Press 2004 357p (Contemporary classics) pa $14

Grades: 11 12 Adult   **Fic**
1. Farm life—Fiction 2. China—Fiction
ISBN 0-7432-7293-5
Also available from other publishers
First published 1931 by Day
This novel set in prerevolutionary China "describes the rise of Wang Lung, a Chinese peasant, from poverty to the position of a rich landowner, helped by his patient wife, O-lan. Their vigor, fortitude, persistence, and enduring love of the soil are emphasized throughout. Generally regarded as Pearl Buck's masterpiece, the book won universal acclaim for its sympathetically authentic picture of Chinese life." (Reader's Ency. 4th edition)
Reader's Ency. 4th edition

Buckhanon, Kalisha, 1977-

Upstate. St. Martin's Press 2005 247p hardcover o.p. pa $11.95

Grades: 9 10 11 12   **Fic**
1. Letters—Fiction 2. African Americans—Fiction 3. Prisoners—Fiction 4. Homicide—Fiction 5. Harlem (New York, N.Y.)—Fiction
ISBN 0-312-33268-8; 0-312-33269-6 (pa)
           LC 2004-56651

"Set in the 1990s, this . . . [novel] features Harlem teenagers Antonio, who has been convicted of involuntary manslaughter for killing his father, and his bright and ambitious girlfriend, Natasha. With Antonio in jail, the two maintain their intense relationship through the written correspondence that makes up the text." Libr J
"This is a moving, uplifting story of love and hope in the face of adversity." Publ Wkly

Budhos, Marina Tamar

Ask me no questions; [by] Marina Budhos. Atheneum Books for Young Readers 2006 162p $16.95; pa $8.99

Grades: 7 8 9 10   **Fic**
1. School stories 2. Asian Americans—Fiction 3. Family life—Fiction 4. New York (N.Y.)—Fiction
ISBN 1-4169-0351-8; 1-4169-4920-8 (pa)
           LC 2005-1831

"Ginee Seo Books"
Fourteen-year-old Nadira, her sister, and their parents leave Bangladesh for New York City, but the expiration of their visas and the events of September 11, 2001, bring frustration, sorrow, and terror for the whole family.
"Nadira and Aisha's strategies for surviving and succeeding in high school offer sharp insight into the narrow margins between belonging and not belonging." Horn Book Guide

Tell us we're home; [by] Marina Budhos. Atheneum 2010 297p $16.95

Grades: 6 7 8 9 10   **Fic**
1. Immigrants—Fiction 2. Social classes—Fiction 3. Mother-daughter relationship—Fiction 4. Household employees—Fiction 5. New Jersey—Fiction
ISBN 978-1-4169-0352-9; 1-4169-0352-6
           LC 2009-27386

Three immigrant girls from different parts of the world meet and become close friends in a small New Jersey town where their mothers have found domestic work, but their relationships are tested when one girl's mother is accused of stealing a precious heirloom.
"These fully realized heroines are full of heart, and their passionate struggles against systemic injustice only make them more inspiring. Keenly necessary." Kirkus

Buffie, Margaret, 1945-

Winter shadows; a novel. Tundra Books 2010 327p $19.95

Grades: 7 8 9 10   **Fic**

Buffie, Margaret, 1945——*Continued*
1. Manitoba—Fiction 2. Prejudices—Fiction
3. Family life—Fiction 4. Stepmothers—Fiction
5. Racially mixed people—Fiction
ISBN 978-0-88776-968-9; 0-88776-968-3
"Hatred for their wicked stepmothers bonds two girls living in a stone house in Manitoba, Canada, more than 150 years apart. Grieving for her dead mother, high-school senior Cass is furious that she has to share a room with the daughter of her dad's new, harsh-tempered wife. Then she finds the 1836 diary of Beatrice, who is part Cree and faces vicious racism as a 'half-breed' in her mostly white community. . . . The alternating narratives are gripping, and the characters are drawn with rich complexity." Booklist

Bull, Emma, 1954-
Territory. Tor 2007 318p hardcover o.p. pa $7.99
Grades: 11 12 Adult   Fic
1. Earp, Wyatt, 1848-1929—Fiction 2. Holliday, John Henry, 1851-1887—Fiction 3. Ringo, John, 1844-1882—Fiction 4. Supernatural—Fiction 5. Western stories 6. Fantasy fiction 7. Arizona—Fiction
ISBN 978-0-312-85735-6; 0-312-85735-7; 978-0-8125-4836-5 (pa); 0-8125-4836-1 (pa)
LC 2007-9534
"A Tom Doherty Associates book"
"In 1881, the Arizona town of Tombstone, rich in minerals for the taking, becomes a magnet for men and women possessing special gifts or hungry for more power than they already have. To this region of natural magic come Wyatt Earp, a master of sorcery; Doc Holliday, whose power belongs to those who can take it; Chow Lung, a Chinese doctor with his own strange abilities; Mildred Benjamin, a writer of Western adventure and a true visionary; and Jesse Fox, a man with a talent for taming horses, among other gifts." Libr J
"Readers will think about the story long after it ends, savoring the writing and imagining what the characters might do next." Publ Wkly

Bullen, Alexandra
Wish; a novel. Point 2010 323p $17.99
Grades: 8 9 10 11 12   Fic
1. Wishes—Fiction 2. Magic—Fiction 3. Sisters—Fiction 4. Twins—Fiction 5. Bereavement—Fiction 6. San Francisco (Calif.)—Fiction 7. Fantasy fiction
ISBN 978-0-545-13905-2; 0-545-13905-8
LC 2009-22730
After her vivacious twin sister dies, a shy teenaged girl moves with her parents to San Francisco, where she meets a magical seamstress who grants her one wish.
"The detailed descriptions of San Francisco and above all the sisters' relationship provide solid grounding for a touching, enjoyable read." Kirkus
Followed by: Wishful thinking (2011)

Bunce, Elizabeth C.
Star crossed. Arthur A. Levine Books 2010 359p $17.99 *
Grades: 8 9 10 11 12   Fic
1. Fantasy fiction 2. Religion—Fiction 3. Kings and rulers—Fiction 4. Social classes—Fiction 5. Magic—Fiction 6. Thieves—Fiction
ISBN 978-0-545-13605-1; 0-545-13605-9
LC 2010-730
In a kingdom dominated by religious intolerance, sixteen-year-old Digger, a street thief, has always avoided attention, but when she learns that her friends are plotting against the throne she must decide whether to join them or turn them in.
"Couching her characters and setting in top-notch writing, Bunce . . . hooks readers into an intelligent page-turner with strong themes of growth, determination, and friendship." Publ Wkly
Followed by: Liar's moon (2011)

Burd, Nick
The vast fields of ordinary. Dial Books 2009 309p $16.99 *
Grades: 10 11 12   Fic
1. Homosexuality—Fiction 2. Dating (Social customs)—Fiction 3. Iowa—Fiction
ISBN 978-0-8037-3340-4; 0-8037-3340-2
LC 2008-46256
The summer after graduating from an Iowa high school, eighteen-year-old Dade Hamilton watches his parents' marriage disintegrate, ends his long-term, secret relationship, comes out of the closet, and savors first love.
"A refreshingly honest, sometimes funny, and often tender novel." SLJ

Burgess, Anthony, 1917-1993
A clockwork orange. [New American ed.] Norton 1988 192p hardcover o.p. pa $13.95 *
Grades: 10 11 12 Adult   Fic
1. Juvenile delinquency—Fiction 2. Violence—Fiction 3. Science fiction
ISBN 0-393-02439-3; 0-393-31283-6 (pa)
LC 86-23843
First published 1962 in the United Kingdom
"A compelling and often comic vision of the way violence comes to dominate the mind. The novel is set in a future London and is told in curious but readable Russified argot by a juvenile deliquent whose brainwashing by the authorities has destroyed not only his murderous aggression but also his deeper-seated sense of humanity as typified by his compulsive love for the music of Beethoven. It is an ironic novel in the tradition of Zamiatin's and Orwell's anti-Utopias." Sci Fic Ency

Burgess, Melvin, 1954-
Nicholas Dane. Henry Holt 2010 403p $17.99
Grades: 10 11 12   Fic
1. Orphans—Fiction 2. Child sexual abuse—Fiction 3. Child abuse—Fiction 4. Great Britain—Fiction
ISBN 978-0-8050-9203-5; 0-8050-9203-X
LC 2009-51779
First published 2009 in the United Kingdom

Burgess, Melvin, 1954-—*Continued*

When his single mother dies of a heroin overdose, fourteen-year-old Nick is sent into England's institutional care system, where he endures harsh punishment, sexual abuse, and witnesses horrors on a daily basis before emerging, emotionally scarred but still alive. Loosely based on "Oliver Twist."

"This is not a happy novel, despite Nick's strength and eventual survival. The horrors of violence, rape, and physical abuse are shown, as well as the long-term effects to Nick's psyche. It is not for the faint of heart, or for those in denial that seamy and dreadful things do happen. . . . A gritty and tragic indictment of 'the system' is shown in this well-thought-out book. The compelling story had me page turning, even as I was appalled by what was happening." Voice Youth Advocates

Smack. Holt & Co. 1997 327p hardcover o.p. pa $8.99

Grades: 9 10 11 12   **Fic**
1. Runaway teenagers—Fiction 2. Drug abuse—Fiction 3. Great Britain—Fiction
ISBN 0-8050-5801-X; 0-312-60862-4 (pa)
            LC 97-40629
Also available in paperback from Avon Bks.
First published 1996 in the United Kingdom with title: Junk

After running away from their troubled homes, two English teenagers move in with a group of squatters in the port city of Bristol and try to find ways to support their growing addiction to heroin

"Although the omnipresent British slang (most but not all of which is explained in a glossary) may put off some readers, lots of YAs will be drawn to this book because of the subject. Those who are will quickly find themselves absorbed in an honest, unpatronizing, unvarnished account of teen life on the skids." Booklist

Burns, Laura J.

Crave; [by] Laura J. Burns & Melinda Metz. Simon & Schuster BFYR 2010 278p pa $9.99

Grades: 8 9 10   **Fic**
1. Vampires—Fiction 2. Sick—Fiction
ISBN 978-1-4424-0816-6; 1-4424-0817-3

Seventeen-year-old Shay, having suffered from a rare blood disorder her entire life, starts receiving blood transfusions from her stepfather who is a physician, and, when she begins to see visions through the eyes of a vampire, she decides to investigate. She discovers a teenage vampire locked up in the doctor's office to whom she becomes attached and sets free, only to be kidnapped by the creature, who wants revenge.

This "is a fast-paced, action-packed vampire thriller with an original and refreshing story line. Gabriel's life is beautifully revealed through Shay's visions, and the well-written plot conveys depth and feeling while exploring important issues like friendship, loyalty, trust, love, and betrayal. A satisfying read with a shocking cliffhanger ending." SLJ

Burns, Olive Ann

Cold Sassy tree. Ticknor & Fields 1984 391p $28; pa $13.95

Grades: 11 12 Adult   **Fic**
1. Grandfathers—Fiction 2. Georgia—Fiction
ISBN 0-89919-309-9; 0-618-91971-6 (pa)
            LC 84-8570

"Young Will Tweedy lives in a small Georgia town called Cold Sassy in the early 1900s. He is hard working (when pushed) because he has chores to do at home and work to do at his Grandpa Blakeslee's store. That still leaves him time to plan practical jokes with his pals and to overhear family dramas. The biggest drama begins when Grandpa, only three weeks after the death of his wife whom he had dearly loved, marries Miss Love Simpson—young enough to be his daughter. Miss Love has to face not only the town gossip, but also rejection from Will's Mother and Grandpa's other daughter. The story has humor, excitement, and realistic family confrontations." Shapiro. Fic for Youth. 3d edition

Followed by Leaving Cold Sassy: the unfinished sequel (1992)

Butler, Octavia E., 1947-2006

Fledgling; a novel. Seven Stories 2005 317p $24.95

Grades: 11 12 Adult   **Fic**
1. Vampires—Fiction 2. Science fiction
ISBN 1-58322-690-7   LC 2005-5664

"Awaking blind, in pain, confused, and alone, Shori Matthews manages to survive amnesia and what should be crippling injuries and starts looking for answers—who hurt her, who she is, and where she comes from. She quickly learns that she is not a young human girl but a genetically altered vampire. Her black skin allows her to survive sunlight and remain alert during the day, but she faces grave danger from those threatened by her strength and heritage. Accompanied by several human hosts who feed and love her, Shori tries to protect her new family and friends from an increasingly hostile threat." Libr J

"In the feisty Shori, Butler has created a new vampire paradigm—one that's more prone to sci-fi social commentary than gothic romance—and given a tired genre a much-needed shot in the arm." Publ Wkly

Kindred. 25th anniversary ed. Beacon Press 2003 287p (Black women writers series) pa $14 *

Grades: 11 12 Adult   **Fic**
1. Time travel—Fiction 2. Slavery—Fiction 3. Science fiction
ISBN 0-8070-8369-0   LC 2003-62862
First published 1979 by Doubleday

"Dana, a well-educated contemporary African American woman, suddenly finds herself pulled into the past to save the life of a distant ancestor, an early-19th-century southern white boy named Rufus Weylin. Although she returns to the present moments later, she soon finds herself saving Rufus again and again. Although only a short time passes for her between each bout of time travel, years pass for Rufus, who gradually grows into adulthood and becomes a slave owner. This sometimes painful novel features superb character development." Anatomy of Wonder 5

Includes bibliographical references

Butler, Octavia E., 1947-2006—*Continued*

Parable of the sower. Warner Books 2000 345p pa $13.99 *

Grades: 11 12 Adult   **Fic**
  1. California—Fiction 2. Adventure fiction
  ISBN 0-446-67550-4   LC 99-46567

First published 1993 by Four Walls Eight Windows

"Written in diary form, Parable chronicles the sometimes grim adventures of Lauren Olamina, an adolescent girl living in a barricaded village in Southern California amid the rampant socioeconomic decay of the early twenty-first century. After her neighborhood is overrun by a cult of drug-demented pyromaniacs, Lauren takes to the road and bands together with other refugees of violent attacks." Booklist

The author "infuses this tale with an allegorical quality that is part meditation, part warning. Simple, direct, and deeply felt, this should reach both mainstream and sf audiences." Libr J

Followed by Parable of the talents (1998)

Cabot, Meg, 1967-

Airhead. Scholastic/Point 2008 340p $16.99

Grades: 7 8 9 10   **Fic**
  1. Fashion models—Fiction 2. New York (N.Y.)—Fiction 3. Transplantation of organs, tissues, etc.—Fiction
  ISBN 978-0-545-04052-5; 0-545-04052-3
                                       LC 2007-38269

Sixteen-year-old Emerson Watts, an advanced placement student with a disdain for fashion, is the recipient of a "whole body transplant"; and finds herself transformed into one of the world's most famous teen supermodels.

"Cabot's portrayal of Emerson is brilliant. . . . Pure fun, this first series installment will leave readers clamoring for the next." Publ Wkly

Other titles in this series are:
Being Nikki (2009)
Runaway (2010)

Insatiable. William Morrow 2010 454p $22.99

Grades: 11 12 Adult   **Fic**
  1. Extrasensory perception—Fiction 2. Vampires—Fiction 3. Television programs—Fiction 4. Fantasy fiction
  ISBN 978-0-06-173506-6

"Meena Harper is a young soap opera writer who possesses the power to see how people are going to die. . . . Her dreams of becoming the head writer on her show, *Insatiable*, are dashed when the job is given to a well-connected rival who wants to add a vampire character to the sudser. Meena is dismayed by the turn of events at work until a mysterious stranger named Lucien rescues her from a bizarre bat attack. Their romance takes off, until a smoldering vampire hunter named Alaric breaks into Meena's apartment and tells her the man she's dating is the prince of darkness. . . . The vampire craze may be reaching the oversaturation point, but this novel's appealing love triangle and Cabot's popularity should draw plenty of readers." Booklist

Cadnum, Michael

Flash. Farrar, Straus and Giroux 2010 235p $17.99

Grades: 9 10 11 12   **Fic**
  1. Thieves—Fiction 2. Blind—Fiction 3. San Francisco (Calif.)—Fiction
  ISBN 978-0-374-39911-5   LC 2009-14145

Relates one momentous day in the lives of five young people in the San Francisco Bay Area, including two teenaged bank robbers, a witness, and a wounded military policeman just back from Iraq.

"Superb writing, with many a fetching turn of phrase and meticulous care given to plotting and characterization, makes this an outstanding commentary on our times . . . and the unpredictable resolution that brings the cast to the end leaves room for reflection on motivation and character in hard times." Kirkus

The king's arrow. Viking Childrens Books 2008 224p $16.99

Grades: 7 8 9 10   **Fic**
  1. William II, King of England, 1056?-1100—Fiction 2. Middle Ages—Fiction 3. Great Britain—History—1066-1154, Norman period—Fiction
  ISBN 978-0-670-06331-4   LC 2007-25313

In England's New Forest on the second day of August, 1100, eighteen-year-old Simon Foldre, delighted to be allowed to participate in a royal hunt as squire to the Anglo-Norman nobleman Walter Tirel, finds his future irrevocably altered when, during the hunt, he witnesses the possible murder of King William II.

"This story is rich in details that lend credibility to the period setting and help bring even historical figures to life as strongly realized and believable characters." Booklist

Peril on the sea. Farrar, Straus and Giroux 2009 245p $16.95

Grades: 7 8 9 10   **Fic**
  1. Pirates—Fiction 2. Great Britain—History—1485-1603, Tudors—Fiction 3. Adventure fiction
  ISBN 978-0-374-35823-5; 0-374-35823-0
                                        LC 2008-5421

In the tense summer of 1588, eighteen-year-old Sherwin Morris, after nearly perishing in a shipwreck, finds himself aboard the privateer Vixen, captained by the notorious and enigmatic Brandon Fletcher who offers him adventure and riches if Sherwin would write and disseminate a flattering account of the captain's exploits.

"Cadnum's prose is vivid and evocative, brilliantly recreating life at sea in the Elizabethan era. . . . The tale is expertly paced, the varied threads of the tale elegantly woven. There's plenty here to appeal to a wide audience." Kirkus

Calame, Don

Swim the fly. Candlewick Press 2009 345p $16.99; pa $7.99

Grades: 8 9 10 11 12   **Fic**
  1. Swimming—Fiction 2. Summer—Fiction
  ISBN   978-0-7636-4157-3;   0-7636-4157-X;
  978-0-7636-4776-6 (pa); 0-7636-4776-4 (pa)
                                     LC 2009-920818

Calame, Don—*Continued*

"Fifteen-year-old Matt has two summer goals: attract his crush Kelly's attention by learning to swim the fly and see a real girl naked. Matt and pals Cooper and Sean cook up several plots to catch a betty in the buff, but all attempts fail. . . . Fully realized secondary characters, realistically raunchy dialogue and the scatological subject matter assure that this boisterous and unexpectedly sweet read will be a word-of-mouth hit." Kirkus

Followed by Beat the band (2010)

Caletti, Deb

The fortunes of Indigo Skye. Simon & Schuster Books for Young Readers 2008 304p $15.99; pa $9.99

Grades: 8 9 10 11 12   **Fic**
1. Waiters and waitresses—Fiction 2. Restaurants—Fiction 3. Wealth—Fiction 4. Family life—Fiction 5. Single parent family—Fiction 6. Washington (State)—Fiction
ISBN 978-1-4169-1007-7; 1-4169-1007-7; 978-1-4169-1008-4 (pa); 1-4169-1008-4 (pa)
       LC 2007-08744
Eighteen-year-old Indigo is looking forward to becoming a full-time waitress after high school graduation, but her life is turned upside down by a $2.5 million tip given to her by a customer.

The author "builds characters with so much depth that readers will be invested in her story. . . . Caletti spins a network of relationships that feels real and enriching." Publ Wkly

The secret life of Prince Charming. Simon & Schuster Books for Young Readers 2009 322p $16.99; pa $9.99

Grades: 8 9 10 11 12   **Fic**
1. Fathers—Fiction 2. Divorce—Fiction
ISBN 978-1-4169-5940-3; 1-4169-5940-8; 978-1-4169-5941-0 (pa); 1-4169-5941-6 (pa)
       LC 2008-13014
Seventeen-year-old Quinn has heard all her life about how untrustworthy men are, so when she discovers that her charismatic but selfish father, with whom she has recently begun to have a tentative relationship, has stolen from the many women in his life, she decides she must avenge this wrong.

"This is a thoughtful, funny, and empowering spin on the classic road novel. . . . Because of its strong language and the mature themes, this is best suited to older teens, who will appreciate what it has to say about love, relationships, and getting what you need." SLJ

The six rules of maybe. Simon Pulse 2010 321p $16.99 *

Grades: 8 9 10 11 12   **Fic**
1. Sisters—Fiction 2. Pregnancy—Fiction 3. Family life—Fiction 4. Oregon—Fiction
ISBN 978-1-4169-7969-2; 1-4169-7969-7
       LC 2009-22232
Scarlet, an introverted high school junior surrounded by outcasts who find her a good listener, learns to break old patterns and reach for hope when her pregnant sister moves home with her new husband, with whom Scarlet feels an instant connection.

"Reminiscent of the best of Sarah Dessen's work, this novel is beautifully written, deftly plotted, and movingly characterized." SLJ

Calloway, Cassidy

Confessions of a First Daughter. HarperTeen 2009 214p pa $8.99

Grades: 6 7 8 9 10   **Fic**
1. Presidents—United States—Fiction 2. Dating (Social customs)—Fiction 3. School stories
ISBN 978-0-06-172439-8; 0-06-172439-4
       LC 2009-1402
High school senior Morgan Abbott pretends to be her mother, the President of the United States, as a decoy, while she also tries to lead the life of a normal teenager.

"This is a light and entertaining read for teens who like some politics with their romance." SLJ

Cameron, Peter, 1959-

Someday this pain will be useful to you. Farrar, Straus and Giroux 2007 229p $16 *

Grades: 9 10 11 12   **Fic**
1. Conduct of life—Fiction 2. New York (N.Y.)—Fiction
ISBN 0-374-30989-2; 978-0-374-30989-3
       LC 2006-43747
"Frances Foster Books"
Eighteen-year-old James, a gay teen living in New York City with his older sister and divorced mother, struggles to find a direction for his life.

"James makes a memorable protagonist, touching in his inability to connect with the world but always entertaining in his first-person account of his New York environment, his fractured family, his disastrous trip to the nation's capital, and his ongoing bouts with psychoanalysis. In the process he dramatizes the ambivalences and uncertainties of adolescence in ways that both teen and adult readers will savor and remember." Booklist

Camus, Albert, 1913-1960

The plague; translated from the French by Stuart Gilbert. Knopf 1948 278p hardcover o.p. pa $12.95

Grades: 11 12 Adult   **Fic**
1. Plague—Fiction
ISBN 0-394-44061-7; 0-679-72021-9 (pa)
Original French edition, 1947
"Using an epidemic of bubonic plague in an Algerian city as a symbol for the absurdity of man's condition, Albert Camus has in this novel articulated his firm belief in mankind's heroism in struggling against the ultimate futility of life. The plague makes everyone in the city intensely aware both of mortality and of the fact that cooperation is the only logical consolation anyone will find in the face of certain death. Though each character, from doctor to priest, represents some aspect of mankind's attempts to deal with the absurd, none is a cardboard figure. The reader cares what happens to the men depicted here. One takes pleasure in the moments of deep human connection that leave us with the conviction that men are, on the whole, admirable." Shapiro. Fic for Youth. 3d edition

Camus, Albert, 1913-1960—*Continued*

The stranger; translated from the French by Matthew Ward; with an introduction by Peter Dunwoodie. Knopf 1993 xxxv, 117p $15; pa $9 *

Grades: 9 10 11 12 Adult   **Fic**
  1. Homicide—Fiction 2. Algeria—Fiction
  ISBN 0-679-42026-6; 0-679-72020-0 (pa)
                        LC 92-54290

Original French edition, 1942; published in the United Kingdom with title: The outsider

This novel "reveals the 'Absurd' as the condition of man, who feels himself a stranger in his world. Meursault refuses to 'play the game,' by telling the conventional social white lies demanded of him or by believing in human love or religious faith. The unemotional style of his narrative lays naked his motives—or his absence of motive—for his lack of grief over his mother's death, his affair with Marie, his killing an Arab in the hot Algerian sun. Having rejected by honest self-analysis all interpretations which could explain or justify his existence, he nevertheless discovers, while in prison awaiting execution, a passion for the simple fact of life itself." Reader's Ency. 4th edition

Canales, Viola, 1957-

The tequila worm. Wendy Lamb Books 2005 199p hardcover o.p. pa $7.99

Grades: 6 7 8 9 10   **Fic**
  1. Mexican Americans—Fiction 2. Texas—Fiction
  ISBN 0-385-74674-1; 0-375-84089-3 (pa)
                    LC 2004-24533

Sofia grows up in the close-knit community of the barrio in McAllen, Texas, then finds that her experiences as a scholarship student at an Episcopal boarding school in Austin only strengthen her ties to family and her "comadres."

"The explanations of cultural traditions . . . are always rooted in immediate, authentic family emotions, and in Canales' exuberant storytelling, which . . . finds both humor and absurdity in sharply observed, painful situations." Booklist

Cann, Kate, 1954-

Possessed. Point 2010 c2009 327p $16.99

Grades: 10 11 12   **Fic**
  1. Supernatural—Fiction 2. Good and evil—Fiction 3. Historic buildings—Fiction 4. Great Britain—Fiction
  ISBN 978-0-545-12812-4; 0-545-12812-9
                    LC 2009-20977

Sixteen-year-old Rayne escapes London, her mother, and boyfriend for a job in the country at Morton's Keep, where she is drawn to a mysterious clique and its leader, St. John, but puzzles over whether the growing evil she senses is from the manor house or her new friends.

"This atmospheric and deliciously chilling British import gets off to a quick start, and readers will empathize with the very likable 16-year-old protagonist, who is clearly out of her element. . . . With a minimum of actual bloodshed, this supernatural delight can even be enjoyed by the faint of heart." Booklist

Followed by Consumed (2011)

Cantor, Jillian

The life of glass. HarperTeen 2010 340p $16.99

Grades: 7 8 9 10 11 12   **Fic**
  1. Bereavement—Fiction 2. Fathers—Fiction 3. Family life—Fiction
  ISBN 978-0-06-168651-1; 0-06-168651-4
                    LC 2009-1758

Throughout her freshman year of high school, fourteen-year-old Melissa struggles to hold onto memories of her deceased father, cope with her mother's return to dating, get along with her sister, and sort out her feelings about her best friend, Ryan.

"Themes of memory, beauty, and secrets come together in this thoughtful, uplifting book that skillfully avoids Cinderella-tale predictability. . . . A gentle portrait of a girl growing through her grief." Booklist

The September sisters. HarperTeen 2009 361p $16.99

Grades: 7 8 9 10 11 12   **Fic**
  1. Missing persons—Fiction 2. Sisters—Fiction 3. Family life—Fiction
  ISBN 978-0-06-168648-1; 0-06-168648-4
                    LC 2008-7120

"Laura Geringer books"

A teenaged girl tries to keep her family and herself together after the disappearance of her younger sister.

"Cantor treats the shape of Abby's agony with poignant credibility. . . . This is a sensitive and perceptive account of the way tragedy unfolds both quickly and slowly and life reassembles itself around it." Bull Cent Child Books

Carbone, Elisa Lynn, 1954-

Jump; [by] Elisa Carbone. Viking 2010 258p $16.99

Grades: 7 8 9 10 11 12   **Fic**
  1. Runaway teenagers—Fiction 2. Mountaineering—Fiction
  ISBN 978-0-670-01185-8; 0-670-01185-1
                    LC 2009-30175

Two teenaged runaways meet at a climbing gym and together embark on a dangerous and revealing journey.

"Chapters range from a few sentences to a few pages, and the descriptions of the pair's climbs are riveting . . . The narrators' psychological explorations are as exhilarating as their physical exploits. . . . An incisive reflection on endurance, independence, belonging, self-knowledge, and love, this story should find a wide audience." Publ Wkly

Card, Orson Scott

Ender's game. TOR Bks. 1991 c1985 xxi, 226p $24.95; pa $6.99 *

Grades: 7 8 9 10 11 12 Adult   **Fic**
  1. Science fiction 2. Interplanetary voyages—Fiction
  ISBN 0-312-93208-1; 0-8125-5070-6 (pa)

"A Tom Doherty Associates book"

A reissue of the title first published 1985

"Chosen as a six-year-old for his potential military genius, Ender Wiggin spends his childhood in outer space at the Battle School of the Belt. Severed from his family, isolated from his peers, and rigorously tested and trained,

Card, Orson Scott—*Continued*
Ender pours all his talent into the war games that will one day repel the coming alien invasion." Libr J

"The key, of course, is Ender Wiggin himself. Mr. Card never makes the mistake of patronizing or sentimentalizing his hero. Alternately likable and insufferable, he is a convincing little Napoleon in short pants." N Y Times Book Rev

Other titles in the author's distant future series about Ender Wiggin include:
Children of the mind (1996)
Ender in exile (2008)
Ender's shadow (1999)
Shadow of the giant (2005)
Shadow of the Hegemon (2001)
Shadow of the giant (2005)
Shadow puppets (2002)
Speaker for the dead (1986)
A war of gifts (2007)
Xenocide (1991)

Pathfinder. Simon Pulse 2010 662p $18.99
Grades: 6 7 8 9 10   **Fic**
1. Parapsychology—Fiction 2. Time travel—Fiction 3. Interplanetary voyages—Fiction 4. Space colonies—Fiction 5. Science fiction
ISBN 978-1-4169-9176-2; 1-4169-9176-X
LC 2010-23243

Thirteen-year-old Rigg has a secret ability to see the paths of others' pasts, but revelations after his father's death set him on a dangerous quest that brings new threats from those who would either control his destiny or kill him.

"While Card delves deeply into his story's knotted twists and turns, readers should have no trouble following the philosophical and scientific mysteries, which the characters are parsing right along with them. An epic in the best sense, and not simply because the twin stories stretch across centuries." Publ Wkly

Seventh son. Doherty Assocs. 1987 241p (Tales of Alvin Maker) hardcover o.p. pa $6.99
Grades: 11 12 Adult   **Fic**
1. Fantasy fiction
ISBN 0-312-93019-4; 0-812-53305-4 (pa)
LC 86-51490

"A TOR book"

This first novel of the Tales of Alvin Maker series is a "fantasy set in early nineteenth century of an alternate-world America. Settlers beyond the Appalachians have brought with them powerful folk magic—charms, hexes, petitions—to ease the hard work and danger of everyday life. Into this world is born Alvin Miller, a seventh son carrying powerful magic. Unfortunately, Somebody or Something is determined that Alvin won't grow up." Booklist

"This beguiling book recalls Robert Penn Warren in its robust but reflective blend of folktale, history, parable and personal testimony, pioneer narrative." Publ Wkly

Other titles in this series about Alvin Maker are:
Alvin Journeyman (1995)
The crystal city (2003)
Heartfire (1998)
Prentice Alvin (1989)
Red prophet (1988)

Cárdenas, Teresa, 1970-
Old dog; translated by David Unger. Groundwood Books/House of Anansi Press 2007 144p $16.95
Grades: 7 8 9 10 11 12   **Fic**
1. Slavery—Fiction 2. Cuba—Fiction
ISBN 978-0-88899-757-9; 0-88899-757-4

Perro Viejo, an elderly slave on a Cuban sugar plantation, "recalls his life and the endless acts of atrocity and inhumanity he has witnessed. . . . [This is a] slender but powerful story that will invite classroom discussion." Booklist

Carey, Janet Lee
Dragon's Keep. Harcourt 2007 302p $17 *
Grades: 7 8 9 10   **Fic**
1. Princesses—Fiction 2. Dragons—Fiction 3. Mother-daughter relationship—Fiction 4. Great Britain—History—1066-1154, Norman period—Fiction 5. Fantasy fiction
ISBN 978-0-15-205926-2; 0-15-205926-1
LC 2006-24669

In 1145 A.D., as foretold by Merlin, fourteen-year-old Rosalind, who will be the twenty-first Pendragon Queen of Wilde Island, has much to accomplish to fulfill her destiny, while hiding from her people the dragon's claw she was born with that reflects only one of her mother's dark secrets.

This is told "in stunning, lyrical prose. . . . Carey smoothly blends many traditional fantasy tropes here, but her telling is fresh as well as thoroughly compelling." Booklist

Stealing death. Egmont USA 2009 354p map $16.99; lib bdg $19.99 *
Grades: 7 8 9 10   **Fic**
1. Death—Fiction 2. Siblings—Fiction 3. Fantasy fiction
ISBN   978-1-60684-009-2;   1-60684-009-6; 978-1-60684-045-0 (lib bdg); 1-60684-045-2 (lib bdg)
LC 2009-16240

After losing his family, except for his younger sister Jilly, and their home in a tragic fire, seventeen-year-old Kipp Corwin, a poor farmer, must wrestle with death itself in order to save Jilly and the woman he loves.

"Carey's wonderful language weaves family, love, wise teachers, and petty villains together in a vast landscape. . . . This is quite simply fantasy at its best—original, beautiful, amazing, and deeply moving." SLJ

Carlson, Melody, 1956-
Premiere. Zondervan 2010 218p il (On the runway) pa $9.99
Grades: 7 8 9 10   **Fic**
1. Television programs—Fiction 2. Fashion—Fiction 3. Sisters—Fiction 4. Christian life—Fiction
ISBN 978-0-310-71786-7; 0-310-71786-8
LC 2009-48438

When two sisters get their own fashion-focused reality television show, vivacious Paige is excited, but Erin, a Christian who is more interested in being behind the camera than in front of it, has problems with some of the things they are asked to do

Carlson, Melody, 1956-—*Continued*

"This book is worth adding whether you have a demand for Christian novels or not. The fashion and reality-show fireworks are enough to keep even reluctant readers coming back for more." SLJ

Followed by Catwalk (2010)

Carmody, Isobelle

Alyzon Whitestarr. Random House 2009 c2005 501p $17.99; lib bdg 20.99

Grades: 8 9 10 11 12   **Fic**
1. Extrasensory perception—Fiction 2. Family life—Fiction 3. Supernatural—Fiction 4. Australia—Fiction
ISBN   978-0-375-83938-2;   0-375-83938-0; 978-0-375-93938-9 (lib bdg); 0-375-93938-5 (lib bdg)
           LC 2008-33796

First published 2005 in Australia

When Alyzon, the ordinary member of an extraordinary family, develops enhanced senses, she becomes aware of an evil virus that preys on people's spirits, and realizes that the sickness and its disseminators are aware of her and are a menace to her family.

"Alyzon is fully believable. . . . This will keep teen readers turning the pages." Booklist

Cary, Kate

Bloodline; a novel. Razor Bill 2005 324p hardcover o.p. pa $9.99

Grades: 7 8 9 10   **Fic**
1. Vampires—Fiction 2. World War, 1914-1918—Fiction 3. Horror fiction
ISBN 1-59514-012-3; 1-59514-078-6 (pa)

In this story told primarily through journal entries, a British soldier in World War I makes the horrifying discovery that his regiment commander is descended from Count Dracula.

"This story is an interesting blend of mystery, horror, and romance, and readers who love vampire novels will find it a refreshing twist to the classic story." SLJ

Followed by Bloodline: reckoning (2007)

Cashore, Kristin

Fire; a novel. Dial Books 2009 461p map $17.99 *

Grades: 9 10 11 12   **Fic**
1. Fantasy fiction
ISBN 978-0-8037-3461-6; 0-8037-3461-1
           LC 2009-5187

In a kingdom called the Dells, Fire is the last human-shaped monster, with unimaginable beauty and the ability to control the minds of those around her, but even with these gifts she cannot escape the strife that overcomes her world.

"Many twists propel the action . . . [and] Cashore's conclusion satisfies, but readers will clamor for a sequel to the prequel—a book bridging the gap between this one and *Graceling*." Publ Wkly

Graceling. Harcourt 2008 471p map $17; pa $9.99 *

Grades: 8 9 10 11 12   **Fic**
1. Fantasy fiction
ISBN   978-0-15-206396-2;   0-15-206396-X; 978-0-547-25830-0 (pa); 0-547-25830-5 (pa)
           LC 2007-45436

In a world where some people are born with extreme and often-feared skills called Graces, Katsa struggles for redemption from her own horrifying Grace, the Grace of killing, and teams up with another young fighter to save their land from a corrupt king.

"This is gorgeous storytelling: exciting, stirring, and accessible. Fantasy and romance readers will be thrilled." SLJ

Castellucci, Cecil, 1969-

Beige. Candlewick Press 2007 307p $16.99; pa $8.99

Grades: 7 8 9 10   **Fic**
1. Father-daughter relationship—Fiction 2. Punk rock music—Fiction 3. Musicians—Fiction 4. Los Angeles (Calif.)—Fiction
ISBN   978-0-7636-3066-9;   0-7636-3066-7; 978-0-7636-4232-7 (pa); 0-7636-4232-0 (pa)
           LC 2006-52458

Katy, a quiet French Canadian teenager, reluctantly leaves Montréal to spend time with her estranged father, an aging Los Angeles punk rock legend.

This a "a good read and an interesting look at the world of punk and alternative rock." Kliatt

Boy proof. Candlewick Press 2005 203p $15.99; pa $7.99

Grades: 7 8 9 10   **Fic**
1. Motion pictures—Fiction 2. Los Angeles (Calif.)—Fiction
ISBN 0-7636-2333-4; 0-7636-2796-6 (pa)
           LC 2004-50256

Feeling alienated from everyone around her, Los Angeles high school senior and cinephile Victoria Denton hides behind the identity of a favorite movie character until an interesting new boy arrives at school and helps her realize that there is more to life than just the movies.

This "novel's clipped, funny, first-person, present-tense narrative will grab teens . . . with its romance and the screwball special effects, and with the story of an outsider's struggle both to belong and to be true to herself." Booklist

The queen of cool. Candlewick Press 2006 166p $15.99 *

Grades: 9 10 11 12   **Fic**
1. School stories 2. Zoos—Fiction
ISBN 0-7636-2720-8   LC 2005-50174

Bored with her life, popular high school junior Libby signs up for an internship at the zoo and discovers that the "science nerds" she meets there may have a few things to teach her about friendship and life.

The author "offers a refreshingly nuanced and credible look at what lies behind the facade of cool." Bull Cent Child Books

Castellucci, Cecil, 1969-—Continued

Rose sees red. Scholastic Press 2010 197p $17.99

Grades: 7 8 9 10   **Fic**
1. Ballet—Fiction 2. Russians—Fiction 3. Friendship—Fiction 4. School stories 5. New York (N.Y.)—Fiction
ISBN 978-0-545-06079-0; 0-545-06079-6
                                        LC 2009-36850
In the 1980s, two teenaged ballet dancers—one American, one Russian—spend an unforgettable night in New York City, forming a lasting friendship despite their cultural and political differences.

"The protagonist is a complexly layered character who suffers from crippling sensitivity, and her difficulty feeling at home in her body will resonate with teens. She is honest, funny, and completely authentic. . . . The prose is poetic and rich." SLJ

Cather, Willa, 1873-1947

Death comes for the archbishop. Knopf 1992 xxvii, 297p $17; pa $11.95 *

Grades: 11 12 Adult   **Fic**
1. New Mexico—Fiction 2. Catholic Church—Missions—Fiction
ISBN 0-679-41319-7; 0-679-72889-9 (pa)
Also available from other publishers
"Everyman's library"
First published 1927
"Bishop Jean Latour and his vicar Father Joseph Vaillant together create pioneer missions and organize the new diocese of New Mexico. . . . The two combine to triumph over the apathy of the Hopi and Navajo Indians, the opposition of corrupt Spanish priests, and adverse climatic and topographic conditions. They are assisted by Kit Carson and by such devoted Indians as the guide Jacinto. When Vaillant goes as a missionary bishop to Colorado, they are finally separated, but Latour dies soon after his friend, universally revered and respected, to lie in state in the great Santa Fe cathedral that he himself created." Oxford Companion to Am Lit. 6th edition

My Antonia; with an introduction by Lucy Hughes-Hallett. Knopf 1996 xxxiii, 272p $20 *

Grades: 11 12 Adult   **Fic**
1. Frontier and pioneer life—Fiction 2. Nebraska—Fiction 3. Czech Americans—Fiction
ISBN 0-679-44727-X   LC 96-223945
Also available in paperback from Houghton Mifflin
"Everyman's library"
First published 1918 by Houghton Mifflin
"Told by Jim Burden, a New York lawyer recalling his boyhood in Nebraska, the story concerns Antonia Shimerda, who came with her family from Bohemia to settle on the prairies of Nebraska. The difficulties related to pioneering and the integration of immigrants into a new culture are clearly portrayed." Shapiro. Fic for Youth. 3d edition

O pioneers! edited with an introduction and notes by Marilee Lindemann. Oxford University Press 2008 xxxi, 179p (Oxford world's classics) pa $9.95

Grades: 11 12 Adult   **Fic**
1. Swedish Americans—Fiction 2. Siblings—Fiction 3. Frontier and pioneer life—Fiction 4. Farmers—Fiction 5. Farm life—Fiction 6. Nebraska—Fiction
ISBN 978-0-19-955232-0   LC 2009-291007
Also available in paperback from other publishers
First published 1913 by Houghton Mifflin
"The heroic battle for survival of simple pioneer folk in the Nebraska country of the 1880's. John Bergson, a Swedish farmer, struggles desperately with the soil but dies unsatisfied. His daughter Alexandra resolves to vindicate his faith, and her strong character carries her weak older brothers and her mother along to a new zest for life. Years of privation are rewarded on the farm. But when Alexandra falls in love with Carl Linstrum, and her family objects because he is poor, he leaves to seek a different career. After Alexandra's younger brother Emil is killed by the jealous husband of the French girl Marie Shabata, however, Carl gives up his plans to go to the Klondike, returns to marry Alexandra and take up the life of the farm." Haydn. Thesaurus of Book Dig
Includes bibliographical references

Cervantes Saavedra, Miguel de, 1547-1616

Don Quixote de la Mancha; [by] Miguel de Cervantes; translated, with a critical text based on the first editions of 1605 and 1615, and with variant readings, variorum notes, and an introduction by Samuel Putnam. Modern Library 1998 xl, 1239p $25.95

Grades: 11 12 Adult   **Fic**
1. Knights and knighthood—Fiction 2. Spain—Fiction
ISBN 0-679-60286-0   LC 97-47415
Also available from other publishers
Original Spanish edition, published in two parts, 1605 and 1615
"Originally conceived as a comic satire against the chivalric romances then in literary vogue, the novel describes realistically what befalls an elderly knight who, his head bemused by reading romances, sets out on his old horse Rosinante, with his pragmatic squire Sancho Panza, to seek adventure. In the process, he also finds love in the person of the pleasant Dulcinea. Contemporaries evidently did not take the book as seriously as later generations have done, but by the end of the 17th century it was deemed highly significant, especially abroad. It came to be seen as a mock epic in prose, and the 'grave and serious air' of the author's irony was much admired. In the history of the modern novel the role of *Don Quixote* is recognized as seminal." Merriam-Webster's Ency of Lit

Chadda, Sarwat

The devil's kiss. Disney/Hyperion Books 2009 327p $17.99

Grades: 8 9 10 11 12   Fic

1. Templars—Fiction 2. Supernatural—Fiction 3. Good and evil—Fiction 4. London (England)—Fiction

ISBN 978-1-4231-1999-9; 1-4231-1999-1

LC 2009-8313

Fifteen-year-old Billi SanGreal has grown up knowing that being a member of the Knights Templar puts her in danger, but if she is to save London from catastrophe she must make sacrifices greater than she imagined.

"Scenes of spiritual warfare are gripping (and often gruesome), as is the undercurrent of supernatural romance. Chadda offers an original take on familiar creatures like vampires, the undead and fallen angels, but it's Billi's personality and tumult of emotions that will keep readers hooked." Publ Wkly

Followed by Dark goddess (2010)

Chaltas, Thalia

Because I am furniture. Viking Children's Books 2009 352p $16.99

Grades: 8 9 10 11   Fic

1. Novels in verse 2. Child abuse—Fiction 3. Child sexual abuse—Fiction 4. Guilt—Fiction 5. School stories

ISBN 978-0-670-06298-0; 0-670-06298-7

LC 2008-23235

The youngest of three siblings, fourteen-year-old Anke feels both relieved and neglected that her father abuses her brother and sister but ignores her, but when she catches him with one of her friends, she finally becomes angry enough to take action.

"Incendiary, devastating, yet—in total—offering empowerment and hope, Chaltas's poems leave an indelible mark." Publ Wkly

Chambers, Veronica

Fifteen candles. Hyperion 2010 187p (Amigas) pa $7.99

Grades: 6 7 8 9 10   Fic

1. Friendship—Fiction 2. Cuban Americans—Fiction 3. Business enterprises—Fiction 4. Quinceañera (Social custom)—Fiction

ISBN 978-1-4231-2362-0; 1-4231-2362-X

"It's Alicia's quince años, and even though her thoroughly modern parents took her to Spain for her quinceañera, most of her friends are having elaborate parties to celebrate their entry into womanhood. When she realizes that a fellow intern in the mayor's office needs help in planning her quince, Alicia envisions a new business venture for her and her three best friends, Amigas Inc. . . . A warm celebration of Latin culture, especially the traditional quinceañera, this is the first in a series that is sure to draw a large audience." Booklist

Chandler, Kristen

Wolves, boys, & other things that might kill me. Viking 2010 371p $17.99; pa $8.99

Grades: 7 8 9 10 11 12   Fic

1. Yellowstone National Park—Fiction 2. Wolves—Fiction

ISBN 978-0-670-01142-1;   0-670-01142-8; 978-0-14-241883-3 (pa); 0-14-241883-8 (pa)

LC 2009-30179

Two teenagers become close as the citizens of their town fight over the packs of wolves that have been reintroduced into the nearby Yellowstone National Park.

This "is a lively drama, saturated with multifaceted characters and an environmental undercurrent. She writes persuasively about the great outdoors, smalltown dynamics and politics, and young love." Publ Wkly

Chayil, Eishes

Hush. Walker 2010 359p $16.99

Grades: 8 9 10 11 12   Fic

1. Child sexual abuse—Fiction 2. Conduct of life—Fiction 3. Jews—New York (N.Y.)—Fiction 4. Judaism—Fiction 5. Suicide—Fiction 6. Brooklyn (New York, N.Y.)—Fiction

ISBN 978-0-8027-2088-7; 0-8027-2088-9

LC 2010-10329

After remembering the cause of her best friend Devory's suicide at age nine, Gittel is determined to raise awareness of sexual abuse in her Borough Park, New York, community, despite the rules of Chassidim that require her to be silent.

"The author balances outrage at the routine cover-up of criminal acts with genuine understanding of the community's fear of assault on their traditions by censorious gentiles. Moreover, she delivers her central message in an engaging coming-of-age story in which tragedy is only one element in a gossipy milieu of school and career decisions and arranged marriages, designer shoes and tasteful cosmetics, and sneak peaks out from a world of restraint and devotion into the world of Oprah." Bull Cent Child Books

Chbosky, Steve

The perks of being a wallflower; [by] Stephen Chbosky. Pocket Bks. 1999 213p pa $12 *

Grades: 9 10 11 12   Fic

1. Letters—Fiction 2. School stories

ISBN 0-671-02734-4   LC 99-236288

This novel in letter form is narrated by Charlie, a high school freshman. "His favorite aunt passed away, and his best friend just committed suicide. The girl he loves wants him as a friend; a girl he does not love wants him as a lover. His 18-year-old sister is pregnant. The LSD he took is not sitting well. And he has a math quiz looming." Time

"Charlie, his friends, and family are palpably real. . . . This report on his life will engage teen readers for years to come." SLJ

Cheva, Cherry
DupliKate; a novel. HarperTeen 2009 242p
$16.99
Grades: 7 8 9 10 11 12   **Fic**
1. Computer games—Fiction 2. Virtual reality—Fiction 3. School stories
ISBN 978-0-06-128854-8; 0-06-128854-3
    LC 2009-18292
When she wakes up one morning to find her double in her room, seventeen-year-old Kate, already at wit's end with college applications, finals, and extracurricular activities, decides to put her to work.
This is a "light and funny novel. . . . Though this is lightweight territory, there is a strong message here about being true to yourself and balancing fun and work in your life. . . . This is sure to fly off the shelves." SLJ

Chevalier, Tracy, 1962-
Girl with a pearl earring. Dutton 2000 240p
hardcover o.p. pa $16
Grades: 11 12 Adult   **Fic**
1. Vermeer, Johannes, 1632-1675—Fiction
2. Netherlands—Fiction 3. Artists—Fiction 4. Social classes—Fiction
ISBN 0-525-94527-X; 0-452-28702-2 (pa)
    LC 99-32493
Chevalier examines the world of artist Johannes Vermeer and the city of Delft in the 17th century through the eyes of Griet, an illiterate 17-year-old. In this novel the fictional character of Griet, a servant in the Vermeer household, acts as the model for the artist's portrait Girl With a Pearl Earring.
The author "has done very well in creating the feel of a society with sharp divisions of status and creed. . . . Griet is a memorable character—reserved, wary, observant, and, although she does not know it, afflicted with a serious and ultimately dangerous crush on her employer. The situation makes a fine story, which is exceptionally well told." Atl Mon

Chibbaro, Julie
Deadly; illustrations by Jean-Marc Superville Sovak. Atheneum Books for Young Readers 2011 293p il map $16.99
Grades: 6 7 8 9 10   **Fic**
1. Typhoid Mary, d. 1938—Fiction 2. Typhoid fever—Fiction 3. Sex role—Fiction 4. Epidemiology—Fiction 5. New York (N.Y.)—Fiction 6. Diaries—Fiction
ISBN 978-0-689-85738-6; 0-689-85738-1
    LC 2010-02291
In the early nineteen-hundreds, sixteen-year-old Prudence Galewski leaves school to take a job assisting the head epidemiologist at New York's Department of Health and Sanitation, investigating the intriguing case of "Typhoid Mary," a seemingly healthy woman who is infecting others with typhoid fever. Includes a historical note by the author.
"A deeply personal coming-of-age story set in an era of tumultuous social change, this is topnotch historical fiction that highlights the struggle between rational science and popular opinion as shaped by a sensational, reactionary press." SLJ

Chima, Cinda Williams
The Demon King; a Seven Realms novel. Disney Hyperion 2009 506p map (Seven Realms) $17.99 *
Grades: 7 8 9 10 11 12   **Fic**
1. Witchcraft—Fiction 2. Princesses—Fiction 3. Fantasy fiction
ISBN 978-1-4231-1823-7; 1-4231-1823-5
    LC 2008-46178
Relates the intertwining fates of former street gang leader Han Alister and headstrong Princess Raisa, as Han takes possession of an amulet that once belonged to an evil wizard and Raisa uncovers a conspiracy in the Grey Wolf Court.
"With full-blooded, endearing heroes, a well-developed supporting cast and a detail-rich setting, Chima explores the lives of two young adults, one at the top of the world and the other at the bottom, struggling to find their place and protect those they love." Publ Wkly
Other titles in this series are:
The exiled queen (2010)
The Gray Wolf Throne (2011)

The warrior heir. Hyperion Books for Children 2006 426p hardcover o.p. pa $8.99
Grades: 7 8 9 10 11 12   **Fic**
1. Magic—Fiction 2. Fantasy fiction
ISBN 0-7868-3916-3; 978-0-7868-3916-2; 0-7868-3917-1 (pa); 978-0-7868-3917-9 (pa)
    LC 2005-52720
After learning about his magical ancestry and his own warrior powers, sixteen-year-old Jack embarks on a training program to fight enemy wizards.
"Twists and turns abound in this remarkable, nearly flawless debut novel that mixes a young man's coming-of-age with fantasy and adventure. Fast paced and brilliantly plotted." Voice Youth Advocates
Other titles in this series are:
The dragon heir (2008)
The wizard heir (2007)

Chow, Cara, 1972-
Bitter melon. Egmont USA 2011 309p $16.99; lib bdg $19.99
Grades: 8 9 10   **Fic**
1. Mother-daughter relationship—Fiction 2. Chinese Americans—Fiction 3. Child abuse—Fiction 4. School stories
ISBN 978-1-60684-126-6; 978-1-60684-204-1 (lib bdg)   LC 2010-36630
With the encouragement of one of her teachers, a Chinese American high school senior asserts herself against her demanding, old-school mother and carves out an identity for herself in late 1980s San Francisco.
"Chow skillfully describes the widening gulf between mother and daughter and the disparity between the Chinese culture's expectation of filial duty and the American virtue of independence." SLJ

Christie, Agatha, 1890-1976

The A.B.C. murders; a Hercule Poirot mystery. Black Dog & Leventhal Publishers 2006 252p $12 *

Grades: 11 12 Adult   **Fic**
1. Mystery fiction
ISBN 1-57912-624-3; 978-1-57912-624-7
           LC 2006-45734
First published 1936 by Dodd, Mead & Company
Series statement from jacket
This novel is "about a serial killer who announces his apparently unmotivated killings in advance to Poirot; the only clue is a railway guide left at the scene of each crime. In the opinion of many critics, this is one of Dame Agatha's greatest detective novels." Ency of Mystery & Detection

And then there were none. St. Martin's Griffin 2004 264p pa $12.95 *
Grades: 11 12 Adult   **Fic**
1. Mystery fiction
ISBN 0-312-33087-1   LC 2004-41165
Also available in hardcover from Buccaneer Books
First published 1939 in the United Kingdom with title: Ten little niggers; first United States edition, 1940, by Dodd, Mead. Variant title: Ten little Indians
"A tour de force on the following trapeze: invitations go out to a group of people, all of whom have been responsible for the death of someone by negligence of intent. The island on which the party is gathered is owned by the would-be avenger of all those deaths. The events and the tension produced by the gradual polishing off of the undetected culprits are beautifully done. One improbability, well hidden, makes the whole thing plausible." Barzun. Cat of Crime. Rev and enl edition

Cisneros, Sandra

The house on Mango Street. Knopf 1994 134p $24 *
Grades: 7 8 9 10   **Fic**
1. Chicago (Ill.)—Fiction 2. Mexican Americans—Fiction
ISBN 0-679-43335-X   LC 93-43564
"Originally published by Arte Público Press in 1984." Verso of title page
Composed of a series of interconnected vignettes, this "is the story of Esperanza Cordero, a young girl growing up in the Hispanic quarter of Chicago. For Esperanza, Mango Street is a desolate landscape of concrete and run-down tenements, where she discovers the hard realities of life—the fetters of class and gender, the specter of racial enmity, the mysteries of sexuality, and more." Publisher's note
This is "a composite of evocative snapshots that manages to passionately recreate the milieu of the poor quarters of Chicago." Commonweal

Clare, Cassandra

City of bones. Margaret K. McElderry Books 2007 485p (The mortal instruments) $17.99; pa $9.99
Grades: 7 8 9 10 11 12   **Fic**
1. Devil—Fiction 2. Supernatural—Fiction 3. Horror fiction 4. New York (N.Y.)—Fiction
ISBN   978-1-4169-1428-0;   1-4169-1428-5; 978-1-4169-5507-8 (pa); 1-4169-5507-0 (pa)
           LC 2006-08108
Suddenly able to see demons and the Darkhunters who are dedicated to returning them to their own dimension, fifteen-year-old Clary Fray is drawn into this bizzare world when her mother disappears and Clary herself is almost killed by a monster.
"This version of New York, full of Buffyesque teens who are trying to save the world, is entertaining and will have fantasy readers anxiously awaiting the next book in the series." SLJ
Other titles in this series are:
City of ashes (2008)
City of fallen angels (2011)
City of Glass (2009)

Clockwork angel. Margaret K. McElderry Books 2010 479p (The infernal devices) $19.99
Grades: 8 9 10 11 12   **Fic**
1. Supernatural—Fiction 2. Demonology—Fiction 3. Orphans—Fiction 4. Secret societies—Fiction 5. Fantasy fiction 6. London (England)—Fiction
ISBN 978-1-4169-7586-1; 1-4169-7586-1
           LC 2010-08616
This is a prequel to the Mortal Instruments series. When sixteen-year-old orphan Tessa Fell's older brother suddenly vanishes, her search for him leads her into Victorian-era London's dangerous supernatural underworld, and when she discovers that she herself is a Downworlder, she must learn to trust the demon-killing Shadowhunters if she ever wants to learn to control her powers and find her brother.
"Mysteries, misdirection, and riddles abound, and while there are some gruesome moments, they never feel gratuitous. Fans of the Mortal Instruments series and newcomers alike won't be disappointed." Publ Wkly

Clark, Kathy

Guardian angel house. Second Story Press 2009 225p il map (Holocaust remembrance book for young readers) pa $14.95
Grades: 6 7 8 9 10   **Fic**
1. Holocaust, 1933-1945—Fiction 2. Jews—Hungary—Fiction 3. Nuns—Fiction
ISBN 978-1-89718-758-6; 1-89718-758-0
When Mama decides to send Susan and Vera to a Catholic convent to hide from the Nazi soldiers, Susan is shocked. Will the two Jewish girls be safe in a building full of strangers?
"Based on the experiences of her mother and aunt, Clark provides a compelling, fictionalized account documenting the courage and compassion of these nuns. . . . Black-and-white photographs and an afterword help to bring the story and history to life." SLJ

Clarke, Arthur C., 1917-2008

2001: a space odyssey. New Am. Lib. 1968
221p pa $7.99 hardcover o.p.

Grades: 7 8 9 10 11 12 Adult   **Fic**

1. Science fiction

ISBN 0-451-45799-4 (pa)

"Based on a screenplay by Stanley Kubrick and Arthur C. Clarke." Title page

Astronauts of the spaceship Discovery, aided by their computer, HAL, blast off in search of proof that extraterrestrial beings had a part in the development of intelligent life forms on Earth millions of years ago.

"By standing the universe on its head, the author makes us see the ordinary universe in a different light. . . . [This novel becomes] a complex allegory about the history of the world." New Yorker

Clarke, Judith, 1943-

One whole and perfect day. Front Street 2007
250p $16.95

Grades: 7 8 9 10   **Fic**

1. Grandfathers—Fiction 2. Family life—Fiction
3. Australia—Fiction

ISBN 978-1-932425-95-6; 1-932425-95-0

LC 2006-20126

As her irritating family prepares to celebrate her grandfather's eightieth birthday, sixteen-year-old Lily yearns for just one whole perfect day together.

The author's "sharp, poetic prose evokes each character's inner life with rich and often amusing vibrancy." Horn Book

The winds of heaven. Henry Holt 2010 280p
$16.99 *

Grades: 9 10 11 12   **Fic**

1. Cousins—Fiction 2. Single parent family—Fiction
3. Family life—Fiction 4. Australia—Fiction

ISBN 978-0-8050-9164-9; 0-8050-9164-5

LC 2009-51780

Clementine and her cousin Fan both grow up in 1950s Australia but have very different lives, Clementine coming from a stable, city family and Fan from a broken, country home, and their destinies are also strikingly divergent.

"Introspective, quiet prose, authentic coming-of-age characters and appreciation for the social values shaping Australian women in the mid-20th century make this a moving read." Kirkus

Clement-Davies, David, 1961-

The sight. Dutton Bks. 2002 465p hardcover
o.p. pa $8.99

Grades: 7 8 9 10 11 12 Adult   **Fic**

1. Wolves—Fiction 2. Fantasy fiction

ISBN 0-525-46723-8; 0-14-240874-3 (pa)

LC 2002-16572

In Transylvania during the Middle Ages, a pack of wolves sets out on a perilous journey to prevent their enemy from calling upon a legendary evil one that will give her the power to control all animals.

"The narrative is rich, complex, and most importantly, credible, but it requires a thoughtful and perceptive reader." Voice Youth Advocates

Followed by Fell (2007)

Clement-Moore, Rosemary

Prom dates from Hell. Delacorte Press 2007
308p hardcover o.p. pa $8.99

Grades: 9 10 11 12   **Fic**

1. Devil—Fiction 2. School stories 3. Horror fiction

ISBN   0-385-73412-3;   978-0-385-73412-7;
0-385-73413-1 (pa); 978-0-385-73413-4 (pa)

LC 2006-11015

High school senior and yearbook photographer Maggie thought she would rather die than go to prom, but when a classmate summons a revenge-seeking demon, she has no choice but to buy herself a dress and prepare to face jocks, cheerleaders, and Evil Incarnate.

"YAs will have fun with this one, especially if they like rather crazy, humorous stories filled with smart (and smart-ass) characters." Kliatt

Other titles about Maggie Quinn are:
Hell week (2008)
Highway to Hell (2009)

The splendor falls. Delacorte Press 2009 517p
$17.99; lib bdg $20.99

Grades: 9 10 11 12   **Fic**

1. Supernatural—Fiction 2. Cousins—Fiction
3. Dancers—Fiction 4. Alabama—Fiction

ISBN   978-0-385-73690-9;   0-385-73690-8;
978-0-385-90635-7 (lib bdg); 0-385-90635-8 (lib bdg)

LC 2009-7579

Dark secrets linking two Alabama families and their Welsh ancestors slowly come to light when seventeen-year-old Sylvie, whose promising ballet career has come to a sudden end, spends a month with a cousin she barely knows in her father's ancestral home.

"Sylvie's voice is sharp and articulate, and Clement-Moore . . . anchors the story in actual locations and history, offering au courant speculations about the nature of ghosts and magic. Her ear for both adolescent bitchery and sweetness remains sure, and her ability to write realistic, edgy dialogue without relying on obscenity or stereotype is a pleasure." Publ Wkly

Click; [by] Linda Sue Park [et al.] Arthur A.
Levine Books 2007 217p $16.99

Grades: 7 8 9 10   **Fic**

1. Photojournalism—Fiction 2. Adventure fiction

ISBN 0-439-41138-6; 978-0-439-41138-7

LC 2006-100069

Contents: Maggie by Linda Sue Park; Annie by David Almond; Jason by Eoin Colfer; Lev by Deborah Ellis; Maggie by Nick Hornby; Vincent by Roddy Doyle; Min by Timy Wynne-Jones; Jiro by Ruth Ozeki; Afela by Margo Lanagan; Margaret by Gregory Maguire

"Ten distinguished authors each write a chapter of this intriguing novel of mystery and family, which examines the lives touched by a photojournalist George Keane, aka Gee. . . . The authors' distinctive styles remain evident; although readers expecting a more straightforward or linear story may find the leaps through time and place challenging, the thematic currents help the chapters gel into a cohesive whole." Publ Wkly

Clinton, Cathryn

A stone in my hand. Candlewick Press 2002 191p hardcover o.p. pa $6.99 *

Grades: 8 9 10 11   **Fic**

1. Palestinian Arabs—Fiction 2. Family life—Fiction

ISBN 0-7636-1388-6; 0-7636-4772-1 (pa)

LC 2001-58423

Eleven-year-old Malaak and her family are touched by the violence in Gaza between Jews and Palestinians when first her father disappears and then her older brother is drawn to the Islamic Jihad

"With a sharp eye for nuances of culture and the political situation in the Middle East, Clinton has created a rich, colorful cast of characters and created an emotionally charged novel." SLJ

Coates, Jan, 1960-

A hare in the elephant's trunk; [by] Jan L. Coates. Red Deer Press 2010 291p il map pa $12.95

Grades: 8 9 10 11 12   **Fic**

1. Deng, Jacob—Fiction 2. Refugees—Fiction 3. Sudan—History—Civil War, 1983-2005—Fiction

ISBN 978-0-88995-451-9

Inspired by the real life experiences of a Sudanese boy, follows Jacob Akech Deng's journey as he flees his home under the threat of war, and, guided by the memory of his mother, tries to survive in a refugee camp.

"This novel, based on the life of the real Jacob Deng, provides insight into the struggles of the Sudan as well as a strong, clear voice. Coates gives an unflinching and poetic glimpse into the life of a boy who chose hope in the face of adversity." SLJ

Cohen, Joshua, 1969-

Leverage. Dutton Children's Books 2011 425p $17.99 *

Grades: 10 11 12   **Fic**

1. Violence—Fiction 2. Football—Fiction 3. Gymnastics—Fiction 4. Bullies—Fiction 5. School stories

ISBN 978-0-525-42306-5   LC 2010-13472

High school sophomore Danny excels at gymnastics but is bullied, like the rest of the gymnasts, by members of the football team, until an emotionally and physically scarred new student joins the football team and forms an unlikely friendship with Danny.

"Sports fans will love Cohen's style: direct, goal oriented, and filled with sensory detail. Characters and subplots are overly abundant yet add a deepness rarely found in comparable books. Drugs, rape, language, and violence make this book serious business, but those with experience will tell you that sports is serious business, too." Booklist

Cohen, Tish, 1963-

Little black lies. Egmont USA 2009 305p $16.99; lib bdg $19.99

Grades: 7 8 9 10   **Fic**

1. Popularity—Fiction 2. Obsessive-compulsive disorder—Fiction 3. Janitors—Fiction 4. School stories

ISBN   978-1-60684-033-7;   1-60684-033-9; 978-1-60684-046-7 (lib bdg); 1-60684-046-0 (lib bdg)

LC 2009-14637

Starting her junior year at an ultra-elite Boston school, sixteen-year-old Sara, hoping to join the popular crowd, hides that her father not only is the school janitor, but also has obsessive-compulsive disorder.

"The characters are real, and readers will feel as if they are right alongside Sara for the ride. Cohen skillfully keeps her readers fully engaged. They will find themselves cringing at the predicaments Sara enters and wonder whether she will completely sell out." Voice Youth Advocates

Cohn, Rachel

Gingerbread. Simon & Schuster Bks. for Young Readers 2002 172p $15.95

Grades: 9 10 11 12   **Fic**

1. Parent-child relationship—Fiction

ISBN 0-689-84337-2   LC 00-52225

After being expelled from a fancy boarding school, Cyd Charisse's problems with her mother escalate after Cyd falls in love with a sensitive surfer and is subsequently sent from San Francisco to New York City to spend time with her biological father.

"Cohn works wonders with snappy dialogue, up-to-the-minute language, and funny repartee. Her contemporary voice is tempered with humor and deals with problems across two generations. Funny and irreverent reading with teen appeal that's right on target." SLJ

Other titles featuring Cyd Charisse are:

Cupcake (2007)

Shrimp (2005)

Naomi and Ely's no kiss list; a novel; [by] Rachel Cohn and David Levithan. Alfred A. Knopf 2007 230p $16.99

Grades: 7 8 9 10 11 12   **Fic**

1. Homosexuality—Fiction 2. Dating (Social customs)—Fiction 3. New York (N.Y.)—Fiction

ISBN 978-0-375-84440-9   LC 2006-39727

Although they have been friends and neighbors all their lives, straight Naomi and gay Ely find their relationship severely strained during their freshman year at New York University.

"Even readers who long for the pair's glamorous downtown lifestyle will sympathize with the vulnerable young people living it." Bull Cent Child Books

Nick & Norah's infinite playlist; [by] Rachel Cohn & David Levithan. Knopf 2006 183p $16.95 *

Grades: 9 10 11 12   **Fic**

1. Rock musicians—Fiction 2. New York (N.Y.)—Fiction

ISBN 978-0-375-83531-5; 0-375-83531-8

LC 2005-12413

High school student Nick O'Leary, member of a rock band, meets college-bound Norah Silverberg and asks her to be his girlfriend for five minutes in order to avoid his ex-sweetheart.

"The would-be lovers are funny, do stupid things, doubt themselves, and teens will adore them. F-bombs are dropped throughout the book, but it works. These characters are not 'gosh' or 'shucks' people." Voice Youth Advocates

Colasanti, Susane
Something like fate. Viking 2010 268p il $17.99
Grades: 7 8 9 10   **Fic**
1. Friendship—Fiction 2. Guilt—Fiction 3. Love stories 4. School stories
ISBN 978-0-670-01146-9; 0-670-01146-0
Lani and Jason, who is her best friend's boyfriend,
fall in love, causing Lani tremendous anguish and guilt.
"Colasanti provides credible and engaging character
development for each cast member and interactions that
spark just the right amount of tension to make this a romantic page-turner." Booklist

Waiting for you. Viking Children's Books 2009
322p $17.99; pa $8.99
Grades: 7 8 9 10   **Fic**
1. Dating (Social customs)—Fiction 2. Anxiety—Fiction 3. Family life—Fiction 4. Divorce—Fiction
5. School stories
ISBN   978-0-670-01130-8;   0-670-01130-4;
978-0-14-241575-7 (pa); 0-14-241575-8 (pa)
LC 2008-46977
Fifteen-year-old high school sophomore Marisa, who
has an anxiety disorder, decides that this is the year she
will get what she wants—a boyfriend and a social life—
but things do not turn out exactly the way she expects
them to.
"Colasanti presents an authentic picture of how complicated it is to be a teenager, especially one in love."
Publ Wkly

Cole, Stephen, 1971-
Thieves like us. Bloomsbury 2006 349p $16.95
Grades: 8 9 10 11 12   **Fic**
1. Adventure fiction
ISBN 978-1-58234-653-3; 1-58234-653-4
LC 2005030616
A mysterious benefactor hand-picks a group of teen
geniuses to follow a set of clues leading to the secrets
of everlasting life, secrets which they must steal and for
which they risk being killed.
"This novel relies on fast action, cool gadgets, and
clever problem solving." Booklist
Followed by Thieves till we die (2007)

Coleman, Wim
Anna's world; [by] Wim Coleman and Pat
Perrin. Chiron Books 2009 280p il pa $10.95
Grades: 8 9 10   **Fic**
1. Shakers—Fiction 2. Family life—Fiction
ISBN 978-1-935178-06-4
"A ChironBooks young adult novel"
First published 2000 by Discovery Enterprises with title: Sister Anna
The United States of America in the late 1840s is a
nation torn by the crime of slavery and a war of con-
quest in Mexico. Fourteen-year-old Anna Coburn doesn't
want to grapple with such terrible issues. Forced to live
among the Shakers, then plunged into upper-class Boston
life, Anna faces troubling responsibilities to herself, her
loved ones and to her country.
"This story accurately portrays life in a Shaker community and the fabric of America during the 1840s. . . .
An excellent ancillary choice for social-studies classes."
SLJ

Collins, Brandilyn
Always watching; by Brandilyn and Amberly
Collins. Zonderkidz 2009 224p (Rayne Tour
series) pa $9.99
Grades: 10 11 12 Adult   **Fic**
1. Homicide—Fiction 2. Single parent family—Fiction
3. Rock music—Fiction 4. Fame—Fiction 5. Mystery
fiction 6. Christian life—Fiction
ISBN 978-0-310-71539-9; 0-310-71539-3
LC 2008-39515
When a frightening murder occurs after one of her famous mother's rock concerts, sixteen-year-old Shayley
tries to help the police find the killer and to determine
whether her long-lost father has some connection to the
crime.
"This solid teen mystery, the initial entry in a new series, will appeal to young girls and adults who enjoy a
good yarn." Libr J

Collins, Pat Lowery, 1932-
Hidden voices; the orphan musicians of Venice.
Candlewick Press 2009 345p $17.99
Grades: 8 9 10 11 12   **Fic**
1.   Vivaldi,   Antonio,   1678-1741—Fiction
2. Musicians—Fiction 3. Orphans—Fiction 4. Venice
(Italy)—Fiction
ISBN 978-0-7636-3917-4; 0-7636-3917-6
LC 2008-18762
Anetta, Rosalba, and Luisa, find their lives taking un-
expected paths while growing up in eighteenth century
Venice at the orphanage Ospedale della Pieta, where
concerts are given to support the orphanage as well as
expose the girls to potential suitors.
"Collins's descriptive prose makes Venice and a
unique slice of history come alive as the three connecting
narrative strains create a rich story of friendship and self-
realization." SLJ

Collins, Suzanne
The Hunger Games. Scholastic Press 2008 374p
$17.99; pa $8.99 *
Grades: 7 8 9 10   **Fic**
1. Science fiction
ISBN   978-0-439-02348-1;   0-439-02348-3;
978-0-439-02352-8 (pa); 0-439-02352-1 (pa)
LC 2007-39987
In a future North America, where the rulers of Panem
maintain control through an annual televised survival
competition pitting young people from each of the twelve
districts against one another, sixteen-year-old Katniss's
skills are put to the test when she voluntarily takes her
younger sister's place.
"Collins's characters are completely realistic and sympathetic. . . . The plot is tense, dramatic, and engrossing." SLJ
Other titles in this series are:
Catching fire (2009)
Mockingjay (2010)

Combres, Elisabeth
Broken memory; a novel of Rwanda; translated
by Shelley Tanaka. Groundwood Books/House of
Anansi Press 2009 139p $17.95
Grades: 6 7 8 9 10   **Fic**

Combres, Elisabeth—*Continued*

1. Rwanda—Fiction 2. Orphans—Fiction 3. Tutsi (African people)—Fiction 4. Genocide—Fiction 5. Hutu (African people)—Fiction
ISBN 978-0-88899-892-7; 0-88899-892-9

Original French edition, 2007

"Emma is a Tutsi orphan living with the Hutu woman who took her in, at risk of death, during the Rwandan genocide in 1994. Emma can remember nothing of her life before then, except for the sounds of her mother being brutally murdered and her mother's last words to her: 'You must not die, Emma!'" Kirkus

"This is a quiet, reflective story; neither laden with detail nor full of historical descriptions, it is simply one girl's horrific tale of personal tragedy. . . . Combres' story offers readers intimate access to this chapter of history as well as considerable potential for discussion." Bull Cent Child Books

Condie, Ally

Matched. Dutton Books 2010 369p $17.99

Grades: 7 8 9 10   Fic

1. Fantasy fiction
ISBN 978-0-525-42364-5; 0-525-42364-8

All her life, Cassia has never had a choice. The Society dictates everything: when and how to play, where to work, where to live, what to eat and wear, when to die, and most importantly to Cassia as she turns 17, who to marry. When she is Matched with her best friend Xander, things couldn't be more perfect. But why did her neighbor Ky's face show up on her match disk as well?

"Condie's enthralling and twisty dystopian plot is well served by her intriguing characters and fine writing. While the ending is unresolved . . ., Cassia's metamorphosis is gripping and satisfying." Publ Wkly

Followed by: Crossed (2011)

Connelly, Neil O.

The miracle stealer; [by] Neil Connelly. Arthur A. Levine Books 2010 230p $17.99 *

Grades: 8 9 10 11 12   Fic

1. Miracles—Fiction 2. Siblings—Fiction 3. Faith—Fiction 4. Camps—Fiction 5. Family life—Fiction 6. Pennsylvania—Fiction
ISBN 978-0-545-13195-7; 0-545-13195-2
            LC 2010-727

In small-town Pennsylvania, nineteen-year-old Andi Grant will do anything to protect her six-year-old brother Daniel from those who believe he has a God-given gift as a healer—including their own mother.

"Neil Connelly has written a deeply thought provoking novel. . . . Throughout this gripping novel the climax builds from a slow burn to a tension packed conclusion." Libr Media Connect

Conrad, Joseph, 1857-1924

Heart of darkness; with an introduction by Verlyn Klinkenborg. Knopf 1993 110p $15 *

Grades: 11 12 Adult   Fic

1. Africa—Fiction
ISBN 0-679-42801-1   LC 93-1855

"Everyman's library"

Originally published 1902 in the United Kingdom in the collection Youth, and two other stories

"Marlow tells his friends of an experience in the (then) Belgian Congo, where he once ran a river steamer for a trading company. Fascinated by reports about the powerful white trader Kurtz, Marlow went into the jungle in search of him, expecting to find in his character a clue to the evil around him. He found Kurtz living a depraved and abominable life, based on his exploitation of the natives. Without the pressures of society, and with the opportunity to wield absolute power, Kurtz succumbs to atavism." Reader's Ency. 4th edition

Lord Jim; a tale. Knopf 1992 xxxiii, 437p $19 *

Grades: 11 12 Adult   Fic

1. Islands of the Pacific—Fiction 2. Sea stories
ISBN 0-679-40544-5   LC 91-53223

"Everyman's library"

First published 1899; first Everyman's library edition 1935

"The title character is a man haunted by guilt over an act of cowardice. He becomes an agent at an isolated East Indian trading post. There his feelings of inadequacy and responsibility are played out to their logical and inevitable end." Merriam-Webster's Ency of Lit

Cook, Eileen

The education of Hailey Kendrick. Simon Pulse 2011 256p $16.99

Grades: 7 8 9 10   Fic

1. Dating (Social customs)—Fiction 2. School stories
ISBN 978-1-4424-1325-2   LC 2010-25608

Dating a popular boy and adhering to every rule ever written, a high school senior at an elite Vermont boarding school begins to shed her good girl identity after an angry incident with her distant father.

"Hailey is a likable character, and the events leading up to and away from her episode of vandalism are believable. Her emotions ring true as well. . . . The plot develops quickly, and readers will be madly flipping pages to find out what happens next." SLJ

Cooney, Caroline B., 1947-

Code orange. Delacorte 2005 200p hardcover o.p. pa $6.99

Grades: 7 8 9 10   Fic

1. Smallpox—Fiction 2. School stories 3. New York (N.Y.)—Fiction
ISBN 0-385-90277-8; 0-385-73260-0 (pa)
            LC 2004-26422

While conducting research for a school paper on smallpox, Mitty finds an envelope containing 100-year-old smallpox scabs and fears that he has infected himself and all of New York City.

"Readers won't soon forget either the profoundly disturbing premise of this page-turner or its likable, ultimately heroic slacker protagonist." Booklist

Diamonds in the shadow. Delacorte Press 2007 228p $15.99; pa $8.99

Grades: 7 8 9 10 11 12   Fic

1. Refugees—Fiction 2. Africans—United States—Fiction 3. Family life—Fiction 4. Connecticut—Fiction
ISBN 978-0-385-73261-1; 978-0-385-73262-8 (pa)
            LC 2006-27811

Cooney, Caroline B., 1947-—*Continued*

The Finches, a Connecticut family, sponsor an African refugee family of four, all of whom have been scarred by the horrors of civil war, and who inadvertently put their benefactors in harm's way.

"Tension mounts in a novel that combines thrilling suspense and a story about innocence lost." Booklist

If the witness lied. Delacorte Press 2009 213p $16.99; lib bdg $19.99

Grades: 6 7 8 9 10   **Fic**

1. Siblings—Fiction 2. Bereavement—Fiction 3. Orphans—Fiction 4. Connecticut—Fiction

ISBN   978-0-385-73448-6;   0-385-73448-4; 978-0-385-90451-3 (lib bdg); 0-385-90451-7 (lib bdg)

LC 2008-23959

Torn apart by tragedies and the publicity they brought, siblings Smithy, Jack, and Madison, aged fourteen to sixteen, tap into their parent's courage to pull together and protect their brother Tris, nearly three, from further media exploitation and a much more sinister threat.

"The pacing here is pure gold. Rotating through various perspectives to follow several plot strands . . . Cooney draws out the action, investing it with the slow-motion feel of an impending collision. . . . This family-drama-turned-thriller will have readers racing, heart in throat, to reach the conclusion." Horn Book

Cooper, James Fenimore, 1789-1851

The Leatherstocking tales. Library of Am. 1985 2v ea $40

Grades: 11 12 Adult   **Fic**

1. United States—History—1755-1763, French and Indian War—Fiction 2. Native Americans—Fiction 3. Frontier and pioneer life—Fiction 4. Adventure fiction

ISBN 0-940450-20-8 (v1); 0-940450-21-6 (v2)

LC 84-25060

Contents: v1 The pioneers; or, The sources of the Susquehanna, a descriptive tale; The last of the Mohicans; a narrative of 1757; The prairie; a tale; v2 The Pathfinder; or, The inland sea; The Deerslayer; or, The first warpath

These novels "are linked together by the career of Natty Bumppo, or Hawkeye, Cooper's inimitable backwoodsman, a romantic embodiment of the virtues of both races, and of Chingachgook, his Indian counterpart, equally idealized. . . . There is little historical background; but the vivid descriptions of wood, lake, and prairie, and of the daily life of Indian and huntsman, gives the finest imaginable picture extant of natural scenes and human conditions that have long passed away." Baker. Guide to the Best Fic

Cooper, Michelle, 1969-

A brief history of Montmaray. Alfred A. Knopf 2009 296p $16.99; lib bdg $19.99 *

Grades: 7 8 9 10   **Fic**

1. Family life—Fiction 2. Princesses—Fiction 3. Islands—Fiction 4. Europe—Fiction 5. Diaries—Fiction

ISBN   978-0-375-85864-2;   0-375-85864-4; 978-0-375-95864-9 (lib bdg); 0-375-95864-9 (lib bdg)

LC 2008-49800

On her sixteenth birthday in 1936, Sophia begins a diary of life in a fictional island country off the coast of Spain, where she is among the last descendants of an impoverished royal family trying to hold their nation together on the eve of the second World War.

"Cooper has crafted a sort of updated Gothic romance where sweeping adventure play equal with fluttering hearts." Booklist

Followed by: The FitzOsbornes in exile (2011)

Cormier, Robert

After the first death. Dell Publishing 1991 c1979 233p pa $6.50 *

Grades: 7 8 9 10   **Fic**

1. Terrorism—Fiction

ISBN 0-440-20835-1

First published 1979 by Pantheon Bks.

"A busload of children is hijacked by a band of terrorists whose demands include the exposure of a military brainwashing project. The narrative line moves from the teenage terrorist Milo to Kate the bus driver and the involvement of Ben, whose father is the head of the military operation, in this confrontation. The conclusion has a shocking twist." Shapiro. Fic for Youth. 2d edition

The chocolate war; a novel. Pantheon Bks. 1974 253p $19.95 *

Grades: 7 8 9 10   **Fic**

1. School stories

ISBN 0-394-82805-4

Also available in paperback from Laurel Leaf

"In the Trinity School for Boys the environment is completely dominated by an underground gang, the Vigils. During a chocolate candy sale Brother Leon, the acting headmaster of the school, defers to the Vigils, who reign with terror in the school. Jerry Renault is first a pawn for the Vigils' evil deeds and finally their victim." Shapiro. Fic for Youth. 3d edition

Followed by Beyond the chocolate war (1985)

I am the cheese; a novel. Pantheon Bks. 1977 233p hardcover o.p. pa $6.50 *

Grades: 7 8 9 10 11 12 Adult   **Fic**

1. Intelligence service—Fiction

ISBN 0-394-83462-3; 0-440-94060-5 (pa)

LC 76-55948

"Adam Farmer's mind has blanked out; his past is revealed in bits and pieces—partly by Adam himself, partly through a transcription of Adam's interviews with a government psychiatrist. Adam's father, a newspaper reporter, gave evidence at the trial of a criminal organization which had infiltrated the government itself. He and his family, marked for death, came under the protection of the super-secret Department of Re-Identification, which changed the family's name and kept them under constant surveillance. Now an adolescent, Adam is finally let in on his parents' terrible secret." SLJ

"The suspense builds relentlessly to an ending that, although shocking, is entirely plausible." Booklist

Cornish, D. M., 1972-

Foundling. Putnam's Sons 2006 434p il (Monster blood tattoo) hardcover o.p. pa $9.99

Grades: 8 9 10 11 12   **Fic**

Cornish, D. M., 1972-—*Continued*
1. Fantasy fiction
ISBN 0-399-24638-X; 0-14-240913-8 (pa)

Having grown up in a home for foundlings and possessing a girl's name, Rossamünd sets out to report to his new job as a lamplighter and has several adventures along the way as he meets people and monsters who are more complicated that he previously thought.

"This first book in a trilogy presents a fantasy world remarkably well developed. Included in the book are maps, a 102-page glossary, appendixes, and the author's own illustrations of the characters. The descriptions are vivid and fascinating." Voice Youth Advocates

Other titles in this series are:
Factotum (2010)
Lamplighter (2008)

Cornwell, Autumn
Carpe diem. Feiwel & Friends 2007 360p
$16.95; pa $8.99
Grades: 7 8 9 10   Fic
1. Grandmothers—Fiction 2. Artists—Fiction
3. Authorship—Fiction 4. Southeast Asia—Fiction
ISBN   0-312-36792-9;   978-0-312-36792-3;
978-0-312-56129-1 (pa); 0-312-56129-6 (pa)
LC 2006-32054

Sixteen-year-old Vassar Spore's detailed plans for the next twenty years of her life are derailed when her bohemian grandmother insists that she join her in Southeast Asia for the summer, but as she writes a novel about her experiences, Vassar discovers new possibilities.

"Suspenseful and wonderfully detailed, the well-crafted story maintains its page-turning pace while adding small doses of insight and humor." SLJ

Corrigan, Eireann, 1977-
Accomplice. Scholastic Press 2010 296p $17.99
Grades: 7 8 9 10   Fic
1. Friendship—Fiction 2. Fraud—Fiction 3. New Jersey—Fiction 4. School stories
ISBN 978-0-545-05236-8; 0-545-05236-X
LC 2009-53869

High school juniors and best friends Finn and Chloe hatch a daring plot to fake Chloe's disappearance from their rural New Jersey town in order to have something compelling to put on their college applications, but unforeseen events complicate matters.

"Corrigan has crafted a complex, heart-wrenchingly plausible YA thriller. . . . A fascinating character study of individuals and an entire town, this tension-filled story will entice readers with a single booktalk." Booklist

Ordinary ghosts. Scholastic Press 2007 328p
$16.99
Grades: 9 10 11 12   Fic
1. School stories
ISBN 978-0-439-83243-4; 0-439-83243-8
LC 2007-276078

Emil feels invisible at school and at home. When he finds a master key to his private school, he sneaks in to explore, and finds a reason to become visible.

"Corrigan is a superb storyteller, and her Salingeresque tale keenly depicts not only her troubled narrator's emotional struggles but also the emotional

components to the physical landscapes he vividly inhabits: his home, foundered on the wreck of family tragedy, and his school, thick during the day with manipulatable adults and heedless kids, . . . but transformed at night into a place of possibility that both entices and disappoints." Bull Cent Child Books

Coventry, Susan
The queen's daughter. Henry Holt and Company 2010 373p map $16.99
Grades: 8 9 10 11 12   Fic
1. Joan, of England, 1165-1199—Fiction
2. Princesses—Fiction 3. Great Britain—History—1154-1399, Plantagenets—Fiction 4. Sicily (Italy)—Fiction 5. Middle Ages—Fiction
ISBN 978-0-8050-8992-9; 0-8050-8992-6
LC 2009-24154

A fictionalized biography of Joan of England, the youngest child of King Henry II of England and his queen consort, Eleanor of Aquitaine, chronicling her complicated relationships with her warring parents and many siblings, particularly with her favorite brother Richard the Lionheart, her years as Queen consort of Sicily, and her second marriage to Raymond VI, Count of Toulouse.

"Fans of historical fiction, and especially historical romance, will devour this volume." SLJ

Cowan, Jennifer
Earthgirl. Groundwood Books 2009 232p $17.95
*
Grades: 8 9 10 11 12   Fic
1. Weblogs—Fiction 2. Environmental movement—Fiction
ISBN 978-0-88899-889-7; 0-88899-889-9

Sabine Solomon undergoes a transformation when she joins the environmental movement and becomes involved with activist Vray Foret, but when his activities involve something that is potentially illegal, she begins to question her identity and values.

This "novel with enormous teen appeal will inspire readers to question Sabine's tactics and their own impact on the earth." Kirkus

Coy, John, 1958-
Box out. Scholastic Press 2008 276p $16.99
Grades: 6 7 8 9 10   Fic
1. Basketball—Fiction 2. Prayer—Fiction 3. School stories
ISBN 978-0-439-87032-0; 0-439-87032-1
LC 2007-45354

High school sophomore Liam jeopardizes his new position on the varsity basketball team when he decides to take a stand against his coach who is leading prayers before games and enforcing teamwide participation.

"Plainly acquainted with teenagers and well as b-ball play and lingo, Coy adds subplots and supporting characters to give Liam's life dimension, but he weaves plenty of breathlessly compelling game action too." Booklist

Crackback. Scholastic 2005 201p $16.99 *
Grades: 7 8 9 10   Fic
1. School stories 2. Football—Fiction 3. Drug abuse—Fiction 4. Father-son relationship—Fiction
ISBN 0-439-69733-6   LC 2004-30972

Coy, John, 1958-—*Continued*

Miles barely recalls when football was fun after being sidelined by a new coach, constantly criticized by his father, and pressured by his best friend to take performance-enhancing drugs.

The author "writes a moving, nuanced portrait of a teen struggling with adults who demand, but don't always deserve, respect." Booklist

Craig, Colleen

Afrika. Tundra Books 2008 233p pa $9.95

Grades: 7 8 9 10   **Fic**
1. Fathers—Fiction 2. Mothers—Fiction 3. South Africa—Fiction

ISBN 978-0-88776-807-1; 0-88776-807-5

"Growing up in Canada with her white South African mother, Kim van der Merwe does not know who her father is. Now, at 13, she goes to Cape Town for the first time, shortly after independence in the mid-1990s, because her mother, a journalist, is going to report on the Truth and Reconciliation Commission. . . . Visiting and meeting her family for the first time, she decides that her mission will be to discover her father's identity. . . . . The realities of the society are carefully and skillfully portrayed, so that Kim's story is truly the emotional heart of the book, and not a vehicle for ideas." SLJ

Crane, Dede

Poster boy. Groundwood Books 2009 214p $18.95

Grades: 8 9 10 11   **Fic**
1. Cancer—Fiction 2. Siblings—Fiction 3. Family life—Fiction

ISBN 978-0-88899-855-2; 0-88899-855-4

"Cruising along on the fringes of stoner life is cool with 16-year-old Gray Fallon. . . . Life's all good until Gray's younger sister, 12-year-old Maggie, begins to complain about aches in her legs and arms. It's a rare form of terminal cancer. . . . Crane effectively shows a family unraveling, and Gray's authentic teen narration springs from the pages." Kirkus

Crane, Stephen, 1871-1900

The red badge of courage; an episode of the American Civil War; introduced by Wendell Minor. Complete and unabridged ed. Puffin 2009 215p (Puffin classics) pa $4.99 *

Grades: 7 8 9 10 11 12 Adult   **Fic**
1. Chancellorsville (Va.), Battle of, 1863—Fiction

ISBN 978-0-14-132752-5

Also available in paperback from other publishers

First published 1895 by D. Appleton and Co.

"A young Union soldier, Henry Fleming, tells of his feelings when he is under fire for the first time during the battle of Chancellorsville. He is overcome by fear and runs from the field. Later he returns to lead a charge that reestablishes his own reputation as well as that of his company. One of the great novels of the Civil War." Cincinnati Public Libr

Craven, Margaret

I heard the owl call my name. Doubleday 1973 166p hardcover o.p. pa $6.99

Grades: 7 8 9 10   **Fic**
1. Native Americans—Fiction 2. Clergy—Fiction 3. Death—Fiction

ISBN 0-385-02586-6; 0-440-34369-0 (pa)

Not knowing that he has a fatal illness, a young Anglican priest is assigned to serve a parish of Kwakiutl Indians in the seacoast wilds of British Columbia. Among these vanishing Indians, Mark Brian learns enough of the meaning of life not to fear death

The author's "writing glows with delicate, fleeting images and a sense of peace. Her characters' hearts are bared by a few words—or by the fact that nothing is said at all." Christ Sci Monit

Crawford, Brent

Carter finally gets it. Disney Hyperion Books 2009 300p $15.99; pa $8.99

Grades: 7 8 9 10   **Fic**
1. School stories

ISBN   978-1-4231-1246-4;   1-4231-1246-6;
978-1-4231-1247-1 (pa); 1-4231-1247-4 (pa)
                                            LC 2008-46541

Awkward freshman Will Carter endures many painful moments during his first year of high school before realizing that nothing good comes easily, focus is everything, and the payoff is usually incredible.

"Crawford expertly channels his inner 14-year-old for this pitch-perfect comedy. . . . His stream-consciousness, first-person narrative flails around in an excellent imitation of a freshman." Booklist

Followed by Carter's big break (2010)

Crewe, Megan, 1980-

Give up the ghost. Henry Holt and Co. 2009 244p $17.99

Grades: 7 8 9 10   **Fic**
1. Sisters—Fiction 2. Bereavement—Fiction 3. Ghost stories 4. School stories

ISBN 978-0-8050-8930-1; 0-8050-8930-6
                                            LC 2008-50274

Sixteen-year-old Cass's only friends are her dead sister and the school ghosts who feed her gossip that she uses to make students face up to their bad behavior, but when a popular boy asks for her help, she begins to reach out to the living again.

The story "provides page-turning action. . . . Mysterious plot elements and the budding relationship between Cass and the VP will quickly engage reluctant readers." Publ Wkly

Crichton, Michael, 1942-2008

The Andromeda strain. Harper 2008 364p pa $9.99 *

Grades: 11 12 Adult   **Fic**
1. Science fiction

ISBN 978-0-06-170315-7

First published 1969 by Knopf

"In these days of interplanetary exploration, this tale of the world's first space-age biological emergency may

Crichton, Michael, 1942-2008—*Continued*

seem uncomfortably believable. When a contaminated space capsule drops to earth in a small Nevada town and all the town's residents suddenly die, four American scientists gather at an underground laboratory of Project Wildfire to search frantically for an antidote to the threat of a worldwide epidemic." Shapiro. Fic for Youth. 3d edition

Includes bibliographical references

Jurassic Park; a novel. Knopf 1990 399p $28.95; pa $7.99 *

Grades: 7 8 9 10 11 12 Adult   **Fic**
1. Science fiction 2. Dinosaurs—Fiction 3. Genetic engineering—Fiction
ISBN 0-394-58816-9; 0-345-37077-5 (pa)

        LC 90-52960

This novel "tells of a modern-day scientist bringing to life a horde of prehistoric animals." N Y Times Book Rev

"Crichton is a master at blending technology with fiction. . . . Suspense, excitement, and good adventure pervade this book." SLJ

Followed by The lost world (1995)

Pirate latitudes; a novel. Harper 2009 312p map $27.99

Grades: 11 12 Adult   **Fic**
1. Pirates—Fiction 2. Caribbean region—Fiction 3. Adventure fiction 4. Sea stories
ISBN 978-0-06-192937-3; 0-06-192937-9

        LC 2009-49965

The Caribbean, 1665. Pirate captain Charles Hunter, with backing from a powerful ally, assembles a crew of ruffians to take the Spanish galleon, "El Trinidad," guarded by the bloodthirsty Cazalla, a favorite commander of the Spanish king himself.

"Pirate fans will love the book for its flashy characters and historical authenticity. Crime fans will enjoy the caper-novel structure and the way the author keeps them on their toes." Booklist

Croggon, Alison, 1962-

The Naming. Candlewick Press 2005 492p map (Pellinor) $17.99

Grades: 7 8 9 10   **Fic**
1. Fantasy fiction
ISBN 0-7636-2639-2   LC 2004-45165

First published 2002 in the United Kingdom with title: The gift

In this first book in the Pellinor series, a manuscript from the lost civilization of Edil-Amarandah chronicles the experiences of sixteen-year-old Maerad, an orphan gifted in the magic and power of the Bards, as she escapes from slavery and begins to learn how to use her Gift to stave off the evil Darkness that threatens to consume her world.

"Unbelievably fine, this book represents fantasy storytelling at its best. This exemplary novel is sure to appeal to all fantasy fans." Voice Youth Advocates

Other titles in this series are:
The Crow (2007)
The Riddle (2006)
The Singing (2009)

Cross, Sarah

Dull boy. Dutton Childrens Books 2009 308p $17.99

Grades: 7 8 9 10   **Fic**
1. Superheroes—Fiction 2. Supernatural—Fiction 3. Science fiction
ISBN 978-0-525-42133-7; 0-525-42133-5

        LC 2008-34208

Avery, a teenaged boy with frightening super powers that he is trying to hide, discovers other teenagers who also have strange powers and who are being sought by the icy and seductive Cherchette, but they do not know what she wants with them.

"Avery's narration, generously peppered with swear words, is hip, witty, funny, and sarcastic." SLJ

Crowe, Chris

Mississippi trial, 1955. Penguin Putnam 2002 231p $17.99; pa $5.99

Grades: 7 8 9 10   **Fic**
1. Till, Emmett, 1941-1955—Fiction 2. Grandfathers—Fiction
ISBN 0-8037-2745-3; 0-14-250192-1 (pa)

        LC 2001-40221

"Phyllis Fogelman books"

In Mississippi in 1955, a sixteen-year-old finds himself at odds with his grandfather over issues surrounding the kidnapping and murder of a fourteen-year-old African American from Chicago named Emmett Till

"By combining real events with their impact upon a single fictional character, Crowe makes the issues in this novel hard-hitting and personal. The characters are complex." Voice Youth Advocates

Crowley, Cath, 1971-

A little wanting song. Knopf 2010 265p $16.99; lib bdg $19.99

Grades: 8 9 10 11 12   **Fic**
1. Musicians—Fiction 2. Friendship—Fiction 3. Loneliness—Fiction 4. Shyness—Fiction 5. Australia—Fiction
ISBN 978-0-375-86096-6; 0-375-86096-7; 978-0-375-96096-3 (lib bdg); 0-375-96096-1 (lib bdg)

        LC 2009-20305

First published 2005 in Australia with title: Chasing Charlie Duskin

Australian title: Chasing Charlie Duskin

One Australian summer, two very different sixteen-year-old girls—Charlie, a talented but shy musician, and Rose, a confident student longing to escape her tiny town—are drawn into an unexpected friendship, as told in their alternating voices

"Crowley's prose is lyrical and lovely, her characters are beautifully crafted, and her portrayal of teen life in Australia is a delight. . . . Female readers especially will enjoy this upbeat tale." Voice Youth Advocates

Crowley, Suzanne, 1963-

The stolen one. Greenwillow Books 2009 406p
$17.99; lib bdg $18.89

Grades: 8 9 10 11 12   **Fic**
1. Elizabeth I, Queen of England, 1533-1603—Fiction
2. Orphans—Fiction 3. London (England)—Fiction
4. Great Britain—History—1485-1603, Tudors—Fiction
ISBN   978-0-06-123200-8;   0-06-123200-9;
978-0-06-123201-5 (lib bdg); 0-06-123201-7 (lib bdg)
LC 2008-15039

After the death of her foster mother, sixteen-year-old
Kat goes to London to seek the answers to her parentage,
and surprisingly finds herself invited into Queen Elizabeth's court.

"Intrigue, romance, and period details abound in this
riveting story of Tudor England. . . . The sophisticated
writing flows well, and the author does a terrific job of
integrating historical details." SLJ

Crutcher, Chris, 1946-

Staying fat for Sarah Byrnes. Greenwillow Bks.
1993 216p hardcover o.p. pa $6.99 *

Grades: 7 8 9 10   **Fic**
1. Obesity—Fiction 2. Child abuse—Fiction
3. Friendship—Fiction 4. Swimming—Fiction
ISBN 0-688-11552-7; 0-06-009489-3 (pa)
LC 91-40097

"An obese boy and a disfigured girl suffer the emotional scars of years of mockery at the hands of their
peers. They share a hard-boiled view of the world until
events in their senior year hurl them in very different directions. A story about a friendship with staying power,
written with pathos and pointed humor." SLJ

Stotan! HarperTempest 2003 c1986 261p pa
$6.99

Grades: 7 8 9 10   **Fic**
1. Swimming—Fiction
ISBN 0-06-009492-3   LC 85-12712
"A Greenwillow book"
First published 1986

A high school coach invites members of his swimming team to a memorable week of rigorous training that
tests their moral fiber as well as their physical stamina.

"A subplot involving the boys' fight against local
Neo-Nazi activists provides some immediate action,
while the various characters' conflicts tighten the middle
and ending. The pace lags through the story's introduction; nevertheless, this is a searching sports novel, with
a tone varying from macho-tough to sensitive." Bull Cent
Child Books

Cullen, Lynn

I am Rembrandt's daughter. Bloomsbury
Children's Books 2007 307p $16.95

Grades: 7 8 9 10   **Fic**
1. Rembrandt Harmenszoon van Rijn, 1606-1669—
Fiction 2. Father-daughter relationship—Fiction
3. Artists—Fiction 4. Plague—Fiction 5. Poverty—
Fiction 6. Netherlands—Fiction
ISBN 978-1-59990-046-9; 1-59990-046-7
LC 2006-28197

In Amsterdam in the mid-1600s, Cornelia's life as the
illegitimate child of renowned painter Rembrandt is
marked by plague, poverty, and despair at ever earning
her father's love, until she sees hope for a better future
in the eyes of a weathy suitor.

"Historical fiction, mystery, and romance are masterfully woven. . . . Cullen's novel is a reader's delight."
Voice Youth Advocates

Cumbie, Patricia

Where people like us live. Laura Geringer
Books/HarperTeen 2008 210p $16.99; lib bdg
$17.89

Grades: 7 8 9 10 11 12   **Fic**
1. Friendship—Fiction 2. Stepfamilies—Fiction
3. Moving—Fiction 4. Child sexual abuse—Fiction
5. Wisconsin—Fiction
ISBN   978-0-06-137597-2;   0-06-137597-7;
978-0-06-137598-9 (lib bdg); 0-06-137598-5 (lib bdg)
LC 2007-18675

In 1978, when her restless father moves the family to
Racine, Wisconsin, fourteen-year-old Libby quickly becomes friends with neighbor Angie, but there is something strange about Angie's stepfather and when Libby
learns the truth, she must make a very difficult choice.

Cumbie's "characters have a dignity and innate courage that readers will not soon forget." Booklist

Cummings, Priscilla, 1951-

Blindsided. Dutton Children's Books 2010 226p
$16.99

Grades: 7 8 9 10   **Fic**
1. Blind—Fiction 2. School stories 3. Maryland—Fiction
ISBN 978-0-525-42161-0; 0-525-42161-0
LC 2009-25092

"Natalie, 14, knows that her future is becoming dimmer as the loss of her eyesight is a nightmare she can't
avoid. . . . Part of going from denial to acceptance is attending a boarding school for the blind. . . . Natalie is
a credible character and her fear is palpable and painful.
. . . Readers will enjoy the high drama and heroics."
SLJ

Cypess, Leah

Mistwood. Greenwillow Books 2010 304p
$16.99

Grades: 7 8 9 10   **Fic**
1. Magic—Fiction 2. Kings and rulers—Fiction
3. Fantasy fiction
ISBN 978-0-06-195699-7; 0-06-195699-6
LC 2009-23051

Brought back from the Mistwood to protect the royal
family, a girl who has no memory of being a shapeshifter encounters political and magical intrigue as she
struggles with her growing feelings for the prince.

"A traditional premise is transformed into a graceful
meditation on the ramifications of loyalty, duty and purpose. . . . Astonishing and inspiring." Kirkus

Dana, Barbara

A voice of her own; becoming Emily Dickinson: a novel. HarperTeen 2009 346p $16.99

Grades: 7 8 9 10 **Fic**

1. Dickinson, Emily, 1830-1886—Fiction 2. Massachusetts—Fiction 3. Poets—Fiction

ISBN 978-0-06-028704-7; 0-06-028704-7

LC 2008-10289

A fictionalized first-person account of revered American poet Emily Dickinson's girlhood in mid-nineteenth-century Amherst, Massachusetts.

"An obvious choice for curriculum support, this heartfelt, exhaustively detailed portrait humanizes the reclusive literary figure and offers an intimate sense of how a poet draws from small moments, gathered on scraps, to create great works." Booklist

Includes bibliographical references

Dashner, James, 1972-

The maze runner. Delacorte Press 2009 375p $16.99; lib bdg $19.99

Grades: 7 8 9 10 11 12 **Fic**

1. Amnesia—Fiction 2. Science fiction

ISBN 978-0-385-73794-4; 0-385-73794-7; 978-0-385-90702-6 (lib bdg); 0-385-90702-8 (lib bdg)

LC 2009-1345

Sixteen-year-old Thomas wakes up with no memory in the middle of a maze and realizes he must work with the community in which he finds himself if he is to escape.

"With a fast-paced narrative steadily answering the myriad questions that arise and an ever-increasing air of tension, Dashner's suspenseful adventure will keep readers guessing until the very end." Publ Wkly

Followed by: The scorch trials (2010)

Davenport, Jennifer

Anna begins. Black Heron Press 2008 148p $21.95

Grades: 9 10 11 12 **Fic**

1. Eating disorders—Fiction 2. Authorship—Fiction 3. Child abuse—Fiction 4. Alcoholism—Fiction

ISBN 978-0-930773-83-0

Contents: Anna begins; A million miles up

This book's "two thematically paired novellas portray unrelated teenagers who are dealing with a variety of realistic teen problems. In the first work, Anna Begins, Melissa has a body image problem, a mother who is self-absorbed and not really in her children's lives, and a crush—maybe—on her best friend's ex-boyfriend or her older stepbrother. Melissa relates these events by writing a story about them, and seeks criticism about her story from others. In A Million Miles Up, Scott is a high school junior who, in an attempt to overcome his depression and be popular, takes up binge drinking. He shares some thoughts with Elly who has problems of her own. Although it is not overtly discussed, the implications are that she is being abused by her father and is acting out by being promiscuous. . . . This book will be one of those that will be recommended and talked about between teen readers." Voice Youth Advocates

David, Keren

When I was Joe. Frances Lincoln 2010 364p $16.95; pa $8.95

Grades: 7 8 9 10 **Fic**

1. Crime—Fiction 2. Witnesses—Fiction

ISBN 978-1-84780-131-9; 1-84780-131-5; 978-1-84780-100-5 (pa); 1-84780-100-5 (pa)

After he witnesses a murder by some ruthless gangsters, Ty and his mother go into hiding under police protection. Even with a new identity, the killers will stop at nothing to silence him.

"This book has an intriguing premise and a cast of likable and realistic characters." SLJ

Davidson, Dana, 1967-

Jason & Kyra. Jump at the Sun/Hyperion 2004 330p hardcover o.p. pa $5.99

Grades: 9 10 11 12 **Fic**

1. African Americans—Fiction 2. School stories 3. Detroit (Mich.)—Fiction

ISBN 0-7868-1851-4; 0-7868-3653-9 (pa)

LC 2003-61277

Handsome and popular Jason tries to come to terms with his irascible, often absent father and his growing attraction to the quiet, studious Kyra

"Readers with an appetite for love stories are likely to follow Jason and Kyra's pas de deux from its beginning straight through to its satisfying end." Publ Wkly

Played. Hyperion/Jump at the Sun 2005 234p $16.99; pa $8.99

Grades: 9 10 11 12 **Fic**

1. School stories

ISBN 0-7868-3690-3; 0-7868-3691-1 (pa)

"When one of Ian's boys dares him to get plain-faced Kylie Winship to sleep with him in just three weeks, he thinks it'll be a breeze. Tall and fine, with honey-colored skin and eyes, Ian is used to getting what he wants from girls. And if he succeeds in playing Kylie, he'll be down with the most popular crew in his high school. But this girl who everyone considers a nobody is turning out to be more surprising than he ever could have imagined." Publisher's note

"Direct and affecting, this will pull at readers' heartstrings while also serving as fair warning for teenage girls everywhere." Booklist

Davidson, Jenny, 1971-

The Explosionist. HarperTeen 2008 453p $17.99; lib bdg $18.89

Grades: 7 8 9 10 **Fic**

1. Terrorism—Fiction 2. Orphans—Fiction 3. Scotland—Fiction 4. School stories

ISBN 978-0-06-123975-5; 0-06-123975-5; 978-0-06-123976-2 (lib bdg); 0-06-123976-3 (lib bdg)

LC 2007-41942

In Scotland in the 1930s, fifteen-year-old Sophie, her friend Mikael, and her great-aunt Tabitha are caught up in a murder mystery involving terrorists and suicide-bombers whose plans have world-shaping consequences.

"The characters come through as very human and quite believable. The book is well written and well crafted. The weaving and subtle twisting of historical

Davidson, Jenny, 1971-—*Continued*
characters and events is done with great skill. Students
liking mysteries and alternative histories will quickly
read this one cover to cover." Voice Youth Advocates
  Followed by: Invisible things (2010)

Davies, Jacqueline, 1962-
  Lost. Marshall Cavendish 2009 242p $16.99
  Grades: 7 8 9 10   **Fic**
  1. Triangle Shirtwaist Company, Inc. —Fiction
  2. Bereavement—Fiction 3. Factories—Fiction
  4. New York (N.Y.)—Fiction 5. Sisters—Fiction
  ISBN 978-0-7614-5535-6; 0-7614-5535-3
                                         LC 2008-40560
  In 1911 New York, sixteen-year-old Essie Rosenfeld
must stop taking care of her irrepressible six-year-old sister when she goes to work at the Triangle Waist Company, where she befriends a missing heiress who is in hiding from her family and who seems to understand the
feelings of heartache and grief that Essie is trying desperately to escape.
  The "unusual pacing adds depth and intrigue as the
plot unfolds. There are many layers to this story, which
will appeal to a variety of interests and age levels." SLJ

Davis, Amanda
  Wonder when you'll miss me. William Morrow
  2003 259p $24.95; pa $12.95
  Grades: 11 12 Adult   **Fic**
  1. Runaway teenagers—Fiction 2. Rape—Fiction
  3. Circus—Fiction
  ISBN 0-688-16781-0; 0-06-053426-5 (pa)
                                         LC 2002-24118
  "After she is sexually assaulted under the school
bleachers, 16-year-old Faith runs away from home, accompanied by the Fat Girl, a taunting, imaginary former
self. At the circus, Faith finds a safe haven and a healing
environment." Booklist
  "Davis's writing is at its finest when the protagonist
is struggling through the constant trials with her distant
mother, her ineffectual teachers, and her one true friend's
suicide. . . . The author succeeds in making this character unique, with flaws that teens will relate to. Readers
will root for Faith, and the heartwarming conclusion will
leave them satisfied." SLJ
  Includes bibliographical references

Davis, Deborah
  Not like you. Clarion Books 2007 268p $16
  Grades: 8 9 10 11 12   **Fic**
  1. Mother-daughter relationship—Fiction
  2. Alcoholism—Fiction 3. Single parent family—Fiction
  ISBN 978-0-618-72093-4; 0-618-72093-6
                                         LC 2006-21867
  When she and her mother move once again in order
to make a new start, fifteen-year-old Kayla is hopeful
that her mother will be able to stop drinking and begin
a better life, as she has been promising for years.
  "Written in Kayla's believable voice, Davis' moving,
gritty novel builds to a hopeful, realistic close." Booklist

Davis, Tanita S.
  A la carte. Alfred A. Knopf Books for Young
  Readers 2008 288p $15.99; lib bdg $18.99
  Grades: 7 8 9 10   **Fic**
  1. Cooking—Fiction 2. African Americans—Fiction
  ISBN 978-0-375-84815-5; 0-375-84815-0;
  978-0-375-94815-2 (lib bdg); 0-375-94815-5 (lib bdg)
                                         LC 2007-49656
  Lainey, a high school senior and aspiring celebrity
chef, is forced to question her priorities after her best
friend (and secret crush) runs away from home.
  "The relationships and characters in this book are authentic. The actions and dialogue seem true to those represented. Even though it is a quick read, the story is a
meaningful one." Voice Youth Advocate

  Mare's war. Alfred A. Knopf 2009 341p $16.99;
  lib bdg $19.99
  Grades: 7 8 9 10   **Fic**
  1. United States. Army. Women's Army Corps—Fiction 2. Automobile travel—Fiction 3. Grandmothers—
  Fiction 4. African Americans—Fiction 5. World War,
  1939-1945—Fiction 6. Sisters—Fiction 7. Alabama—
  Fiction
  ISBN 978-0-375-85714-0; 0-375-85714-1;
  978-0-375-95714-7 (lib bdg); 0-375-95714-6 (lib bdg)
                                         LC 2008-33744
  Teens Octavia and Tali learn about strength, independence, and courage when they are forced to take a car
trip with their grandmother, who tells about growing up
Black in 1940s Alabama and serving in Europe during
World War II as a member of the Women's Army
Corps.
  "The parallel travel narratives are masterfully man-
aged, with postcards from Octavia and Tali to the folks
back home in San Francisco signaling the shift between
'then' and 'now.' Absolutely essential reading." Kirkus

De Goldi, Kate, 1959-
  The 10 p.m. question. Candlewick Press 2010
  c2008 245p $15.99
  Grades: 7 8 9 10 11 12   **Fic**
  1. Worry—Fiction 2. Family life—Fiction
  3. Eccentrics and eccentricities—Fiction
  4. Agoraphobia—Fiction 5. School stories 6. New
  Zealand—Fiction
  ISBN 978-0-7636-4939-5; 0-7636-4939-2
                                         LC 2009-49726
  First published 2008 in New Zealand
  Twelve-year-old Frankie Parsons has a quirky family,
a wonderful best friend, and a head full of worrying
questions that he shares with his mother each night, but
when free-spirited Sydney arrives at school with questions of her own, Frankie is forced to face the ultimate
ten p.m. question.
  "De Goldi's novel is an achingly poignant, wryly
comic story of early adolescence. . . . Nearly every
character . . . is a loving, talented, unforgettable eccentric whose dialogue, much like De Goldi's richly phrased
narration, combines heart-stopping tenderness with perfectly timed, deliciously zany humor." Booklist

De Gramont, Nina

Every little thing in the world. Atheneum Books for Young Readers 2010 282p $16.99

Grades: 9 10 11 12   Fic

1. Pregnancy—Fiction 2. Friendship—Fiction
3. Camps—Fiction 4. Wilderness areas—Fiction
ISBN 978-1-4169-8013-1; 1-4169-8013-X

LC 2009-40335

Before she can decide what do about her newly discovered pregnancy, sixteen-year-old Sydney is punished for "borrowing" a car and shipped out, along with best friend Natalia, to a wilderness camp for the next six weeks.

"De Gramont's compelling coming-of-age story, often poetic, compassionately probes the dilemma of and complex choices surrounding Sydney's pregnancy. As told from Sydney's point of view in an authentic adolescent voice, her growing self-awareness of 'what's discovered after losing your way' is both moving and hopeful." Kirkus

Gossip of the starlings; a novel. Algonquin Books of Chapel Hill 2008 276p $22.95

Grades: 10 11 12 Adult   Fic

1. Friendship—Fiction 2. School stories
ISBN 978-1-56512-565-0; 1-56512-565-7

LC 2008-5883

"In fall 1984, best friends Catherine and Skye have quite a few things in common—wealthy New England roots, cocaine habits, and the distinction of being expelled from other boarding schools before meeting at the Esther Percy School for Girls. Catherine is preparing for equestrian championships and juggling a long-distance relationship with John Paul, while Skye maneuvers her very public life as a popular liberal senator's daughter." Libr J

"Teenage protagonists and characters of both genders make this book an excellent choice for older teens looking for a good read." Voice Youth Advocates

De la Cruz, Melissa, 1971-

Blue bloods. Hyperion 2006 302p hardcover o.p. pa $8.99 *

Grades: 9 10 11 12   Fic

1. Vampires—Fiction 2. New York (N.Y.)—Fiction
ISBN   978-0-7868-3892-9;   0-7868-3892-2;
978-1-4231-0126-0 (pa); 1-4231-0126-X (pa)

LC 2005-44786

Select teenagers from some of New York City's wealthiest and most socially prominent families learn a startling secret about their bloodlines.

"History, mythology, and the contemporary New York prep-school and club scene blend seamlessly in this sexy and sophisticated riff on vampire lore that never collapses into camp." Bull Cent Child Books

Other titles in this series are:
Lost in time (2011)
Masquerade (2007)
Misguided angel (2010)
Revelations (2008)
The Van Alen legacy (2009)

De la Peña, Matt

Ball don't lie. Delacorte Press 2005 280p hardcover o.p. pa $7.99

Grades: 9 10 11 12   Fic

1. Basketball—Fiction 2. Obsessive-compulsive disorder—Fiction 3. Foster home care—Fiction 4. Race relations—Fiction 5. Los Angeles (Calif.)—Fiction
ISBN 0-385-73232-5; 0-385-73425-5 (pa)

LC 2004-18057

Seventeen-year-old Sticky lives for basketball and plays at school and at the Lincoln Rec Center in Los Angeles but he is unaware of the many dangers—including his own past—that threaten his dream of playing professionally.

"The prose moves with the rhythm of a bouncing basketball and those who don't mind mixing their sports stories with some true grit may find themselves hypnotized by Sticky's grim saga." Publ Wkly

Mexican whiteboy. Delacorte Press 2008 249p $15.99; lib bdg $18.99

Grades: 8 9 10 11 12   Fic

1. Mexican Americans—Fiction 2. Racially mixed people—Fiction 3. Cousins—Fiction 4. California—Fiction
ISBN   978-0-385-73310-6;   0-385-73310-0;
978-0-385-90329-5 (lib bdg); 0-385-90329-4 (lib bdg)

LC 2007-32302

Sixteen-year-old Danny searches for his identity amidst the confusion of being half-Mexican and half-white while spending a summer with his cousin and new friends on the baseball fields and back alleys of San Diego County, California.

"The author juggles his many plotlines well, and the portrayal of Danny's friends and neighborhood is rich and lively." Booklist

We were here. Delacorte Press 2009 357p $17.99; lib bdg $20.99

Grades: 7 8 9 10 11 12   Fic

1. Juvenile delinquency—Fiction 2. Runaway teenagers—Fiction 3. Friendship—Fiction 4. Brothers—Fiction 5. California—Fiction
ISBN   978-0-385-73667-1;   0-385-73667-3;
978-0-385-90622-7 (lib bdg); 0-385-90622-6 (lib bdg)

LC 2008-44568

Haunted by the event that sentences him to time in a group home, Miguel breaks out with two unlikely companions and together they begin their journey down the California coast hoping to get to Mexico and a new life.

"The contemporary survival adventure will keep readers hooked, as will the tension that builds from the story's secrets." Booklist

De Lint, Charles, 1951-

The blue girl; Charles de Lint. Viking 2004 368p hardcover o.p. pa $7.99

Grades: 7 8 9 10   Fic

1. Fairies—Fiction 2. Ghost stories 3. School stories
ISBN 0-670-05924-2; 0-14-240545-0 (pa)

LC 2004-19051

New at her high school, Imogene enlists the help of her introverted friend Maxine and the ghost of a boy who haunts the school after receiving warnings through

De Lint, Charles, 1951-—*Continued*
her dreams that soul-eaters are threatening her life

"The book combines the turmoil of high school intertwined with rich, detailed imagery drawn from traditional
folklore and complex characters with realistic relationships. . . . This book is not just another ghost story, but
a novel infused with the true sense of wonder and magic
that is De Lint at his best. It is strongly recommended."
Voice Youth Advocates

Dingo. Firebird 2008 213p $11.99
Grades: 9 10 11 12   **Fic**
    1. Supernatural—Fiction 2. Space and time—Fiction
    3. Sisters—Fiction 4. Twins—Fiction 5. Wild dogs—
    Fiction
    ISBN 978-0-14-240816-2; 0-14-240816-6
                                        LC 2007-31716
Seventeen-year-old Miguel Schreiber and a long-term
enemy are drawn into a strange dream world when they
fall in love with shapeshifting sisters from Australia—
twins hiding from a cursed ancestor who can only be
freed with the girls' cooperation.

"The fated love angle will certainly draw in romance
readers, and while they may be perfectly content with
just following Miguel and Lainey's connection through
to its expected happy ending, the intriguing details about
shape-shifting, dingoes, and Aboriginal traditions may
also lead them to dig a bit further into Australian myths
and culture." Bull Cent Child Books

Little (grrl) lost. Viking 2007 271p hardcover
o.p. pa $8.99
Grades: 7 8 9 10   **Fic**
    1. Runaway teenagers—Fiction 2. Size—Fiction
    3. Moving—Fiction 4. Friendship—Fiction 5. Fantasy
    fiction
    ISBN   978-0-670-06144-0;   0-670-06144-1;
    978-0-14-241301-2 (pa); 0-14-241301-1 (pa)
                                        LC 2007-14832
Fourteen-year-old T. J. and her new friend, sixteen-
year-old Elizabeth, a six-inch-high "Little" with a big
chip on her shoulder, help one another as T. J. tries to
adjust to her family's move from a farm to the big city
and Elizabeth tries to make her own way in the world.

"De Lint mixes marvelous fantastical creatures and realities as he taps into young women's need to feel
unique, understood, and valued." Booklist

Defoe, Daniel, 1661?-1731
Robinson Crusoe; edited with an introduction by
Thomas Keymer and notes by Thomas Keymer
and James Kelly. New ed. Oxford University Press
2009 c2008 lii, 321p il (Oxford world's classics)
pa $7.95
Grades: 8 9 10 11 12 Adult   **Fic**
    1. Survival after airplane accidents, shipwrecks, etc.—
    Fiction 2. Islands—Fiction 3. Adventure fiction
    ISBN 978-0-19-955397-6   LC 2006-26022
    Also available from other publishers
    First published 1719

"A minutely circumstantial account of the hero's shipwreck and escape to an uninhabited island, and the me-
thodical industry whereby he makes himself a comfortable home. The story is founded on the actual experiences of Alexander Selkirk, who spent four years on the

island of Juan Fernandez in the early 18th century."
Lenrow. Reader's Guide to Prose Fic

Delsol, Wendy
Stork. Candlewick Press 2010 357p $15.99
Grades: 7 8 9 10   **Fic**
    1. Supernatural—Fiction   2.   School   stories
    3. Minnesota—Fiction
    ISBN 978-0-7636-4844-2; 0-7636-4844-2
                                        LC 2009-51357
After her parents' divorce, Katla and her mother move
from Los Angeles to Norse Falls, Minnesota, where Kat
immediately alienates two boys at her high school and,
improbably, discovers a kinship with a mysterious group
of elderly women—the Icelandic Stork Society—who
"deliver souls."

"This snappy, lighthearted supernatural romance
blends Norse mythology and contemporary issues with
an easy touch." Booklist

Denman, K. L., 1957-
Me, myself and Ike. Orca Book Publishers 2009
192p pa $12.95
Grades: 8 9 10 11 12   **Fic**
    1. Mental illness—Fiction
    ISBN 978-1-55469-086-2; 1-55469-086-2
                                        LC 2009-928211
Seventeen-year-old Kit is paranoid, confused and
alone, but neither he nor his family and friends understand what is happening to him.

"Denman deftly gets into the head of a mentally un-
well teenager while telling a coherent, engaging story."
Publ Wkly

Deriso, Christine Hurley, 1961-
Then I met my sister. Flux 2011 269p pa $9.95
Grades: 8 9 10 11 12   **Fic**
    1. Sisters—Fiction 2. Death—Fiction 3. Diaries—Fic-
    tion
    ISBN 978-0-7387-2581-9; 0-7387-2581-1
                                        LC 2010-45239
Summer Stetson has always lived in the shadow of
her dead sister, knowing she can never measure up in
any way, but on her seventeenth birthday her aunt gives
her Shannon's diary, which reveals painful but liberating
truths about Summer's family and herself.

"The journey Summer goes on to 'meet' her sister is
compelling, but equally interesting are her discoveries
about herself and her relationships. . . . This is a book
intriguing enough to read in one sitting." SLJ

Derting, Kimberly
The body finder. Harper 2009 329p $16.99
Grades: 7 8 9 10 11 12   **Fic**
    1. Dead—Fiction 2. Extrasensory perception—Fiction
    3. Supernatural—Fiction 4. Mystery fiction
    ISBN 978-0-06-177981-7; 0-06-177981-4
                                        LC 2009-39675
"Violet Ambrose can find dead bodies. Their aura of
sound, color, or even taste imprints itself on their mur-
derers, and Violet's extrasensory perception picks up on

Derting, Kimberly—*Continued*

those elements. . . . Derting has written a suspenseful mystery and sensual love story that will captivate readers who enjoy authentic high-school settings, snappy dialogue, sweet romance, and heart-stopping drama." Booklist

Followed by: Desires of the dead (2011)

Desai Hidier, Tanuja

Born confused. Scholastic Press 2002 413p hardcover o.p. pa $7.99 *

Grades: 8 9 10 11 12   **Fic**

1. East Indian Americans—Fiction 2. Friendship—Fiction

ISBN 0-439-35762-4; 0-439-51011-2 (pa)

LC 2002-4515

Seventeen-year-old Dimple, whose family is from India, discovers that she is not Indian enough for the Indians and not American enough for the Americans, as she sees her hypnotically beautiful, manipulative best friend taking possession of both her heritage and the boy she likes

"This involving story . . . will reward its readers. The family background and richness in cultural information add a new level to the familiar girl-meets-boy story." SLJ

Dessen, Sarah, 1970-

Along for the ride; a novel. Viking 2009 383p $19.99

Grades: 7 8 9 10   **Fic**

1. Stepfamilies—Fiction 2. Infants—Fiction 3. Dating (Social customs)—Fiction 4. Divorce—Fiction

ISBN 978-0-670-01194-0; 0-670-01194-0

LC 2009-5661

When Auden impulsively goes to stay with her father, stepmother, and new baby sister the summer before she starts college, all the trauma of her parents' divorce is revived, even as she is making new friends and having new experiences such as learning to ride a bike and dating.

"Dessen explores the dynamics of an extended family headed by two opposing, flawed personalities, revealing their parental failures with wicked precision yet still managing to create real, even sympathetic characters. . . . [This book] provides the interpersonal intricacies fans expect from a Dessen plot." Horn Book

Just listen; a novel. Viking 2006 371p $17.99 *

Grades: 9 10 11 12   **Fic**

1. School stories 2. Friendship—Fiction 3. Family life—Fiction

ISBN 0-670-06105-0; 978-0-670-06105-1

LC 2006-472

Isolated from friends who believe the worst because she has not been truthful with them, sixteen-year-old Annabel finds an ally in classmate Owen, whose honesty and passion for music help her to face and share what really happened at the end-of-the-year party that changed her life.

The author "weaves a sometimes funny, mostly emotional, and very satisfying story." Voice Youth Advocates

Lock and key; a novel. Viking Children's Books 2008 422p $18.99

Grades: 7 8 9 10   **Fic**

1. Abandoned children—Fiction 2. Family life—Fiction 3. Child abuse—Fiction

ISBN 978-0-670-01088-2; 0-670-01088-X

LC 2007-25370

When she is abandoned by her alcoholic mother, high school senior Ruby winds up living with Cora, the sister she has not seen for ten years, and learns about Cora's new life, what makes a family, how to allow people to help her when she needs it, and that she too has something to offer others.

"The dialogue, especially between Ruby and Cora, is crisp, layered, and natural. The slow unfolding adds to an anticipatory mood. . . . Recommend this one to patient, sophisticated readers." SLJ

DeStefano, Lauren

Wither. Simon & Schuster Books for Young Readers 2011 358p (The Chemical Garden trilogy) $17.99

Grades: 9 10 11 12   **Fic**

1. Science fiction 2. Genetic engineering—Fiction 3. Kidnapping—Fiction 4. Marriage—Fiction 5. Orphans—Fiction

ISBN 978-1-4424-0905-7   LC 2010-21347

After modern science turns every human into a genetic time bomb with men dying at age twenty-five and women dying at age twenty, girls are kidnapped and married off in order to repopulate the world.

"This beautifully-written . . . fantasy, with its intriguing world-building, well-developed characters and intricate plot involving flashbacks as well as edge-of-the-seat suspense, will keep teens riveted to the plight of Rhine and her sister wives. . . . This thought-provoking novel will also stimulate discussion in science and ethics classes." Voice Youth Advocates

Deuker, Carl, 1950-

Gym candy. Houghton Mifflin Company 2007 313p $16

Grades: 7 8 9 10 11 12   **Fic**

1. Football—Fiction 2. Father-son relationship—Fiction 3. School stories 4. Steroids—Fiction 5. Washington (State)—Fiction

ISBN 978-0-618-77713-6; 0-618-77713-X

LC 2007-12749

Groomed by his father to be a star player, football is the only thing that has ever really mattered to Mick Johnson, who works hard for a spot on the varsity team his freshman year, then tries to hold onto his edge by using steroids, despite the consequences to his health and social life.

"Deuker skillfully complements a sobering message with plenty of exciting on-field action and locker-room drama, while depicting Mick's emotional struggles with loneliness and insecurity as sensitively and realistically as his physical ones." Booklist

Painting the black. Avon Books 1999 248p pa $5.99

Grades: 8 9 10 11 12   **Fic**

Deuker, Carl, 1950-—_Continued_

1. Baseball—Fiction 2. School stories
ISBN 0-380-73104-5
"An Avon Flare book"
First published 1997 by Houghton Mifflin

"After a disastrous fall from a tree, senior Ryan Ward wrote off baseball. But he is swept back into the game when cocky, charismatic Josh Daniels—a star quarterback with the perfect spiral pass as well as a pitcher with a mean slider—moves into the neighborhood. . . . The well-written sports scenes—baseball and football—will draw reluctant readers, but it is Ryan's moral courage that will linger when the reading is done." Booklist

Runner. Houghton Mifflin 2005 216p $16; pa $7.99

Grades: 7 8 9 10   Fic
1. Smuggling—Fiction 2. Alcoholism—Fiction
3. Terrorism—Fiction
ISBN 0-618-54298-1; 0-618-73505-4 (pa)
LC 2004-15781

Living with his alcoholic father on a broken-down sailboat on Puget Sound has been hard on seventeen-year-old Chance Taylor, but when his love of running leads to a high-paying job, he quickly learns that the money is not worth the risk

"Writing in a fast-paced, action-packed, but at the same time reflective style, Deuker . . . uses running as a hook to entice readers into a perceptive coming-of-age novel." SLJ

DeVita, James

The silenced. Eos 2007 504p $17.99
Grades: 8 9 10 11 12   Fic
1. Resistance to government—Fiction 2. Fantasy fiction
ISBN 978-0-06-078462-1; 0-06-078462-8
LC 2006-19380
"Laura Geringer books"
Consigned to a prisonlike Youth Training Facility because of her parents' political activities, Marena organizes a resistance movement to combat the restrictive policies of the ruling Zero Tolerance party.
"Gripping suspense combined with satisfyingly capable teen characters make this a good YA read." Booklist

Devoto, Pat Cunningham

The summer we got saved. Warner Books 2005 411p map hardcover o.p. pa $14.95
Grades: 9 10 11 12   Fic
1. Civil rights demonstrations—Fiction 2. Race relations—Fiction 3. Alabama—Fiction
ISBN 0-446-57696-4; 0-446-69715-X (pa)
LC 2004-10408
"In 1960s Alabama, young Tab and her sister are introduced to nonviolent protests and the lies told by both white and black. Realistic, flawed characters, poignant humor, and provocative questions about social injustice combine in this compelling historical novel." Booklist

Dickens, Charles, 1812-1870

David Copperfield; with the original illustrations by "Phiz"; introduced by Michael Slater. Knopf 1991 xlii, 891p il $25
Grades: 11 12 Adult   Fic
1. Great Britain—Fiction
ISBN 0-679-40571-2   LC 91-52995
Also available from other publishers
"Everyman's library"
First published 1850
This novel "incorporates material from the autobiography Dickens had recently begun but soon abandoned and is written in the first person, a new technique for him. Although Copperfield differs from his creator in many ways, Dickens uses many early personal experiences that had meant much to him—his own period of work in a factory while his father was jailed, his schooling and reading, his passion for Maria Beadnell (a woman much like Dora Spenlow), and (more cursorily) his emergence from parliamentary reporting into successful novel writing." Merriam-Webster's Ency of Lit

Great expectations; illustrated by F.W. Pailthrope with an introduction by Michael Slater. Knopf 1992 xxxiv, 469p il $21 *
Grades: 11 12 Adult   Fic
1. Great Britain—Fiction
ISBN 0-679-40579-8   LC 91-53219
Also available from other publishers
"Everyman's library"
First published 1861
"The first-person narrative relates the coming-of-age of Pip (Philip Pirrip). Reared in the marshes of Kent by his disagreeable sister and her sweet-natured husband, the blacksmith Joe Gargery, the young Pip one day helps a convict to escape. Later he is sent to live with Miss Havisham, a woman driven half-mad years earlier by her lover's departure on their wedding day. . . . When an anonymous benefactor makes it possible for Pip to go to London for an education, he credits Miss Havisham. . . . Pips benefactor turns out to have been Abel Magwitch, the convict he once aided, who dies awaiting trial after Pip is unable to help him a second time. Joe rescues Pip from despair and nurses him back to health." Merriam-Webster's Ency of Lit

Oliver Twist; with twenty-four illustrations by George Cruikshank; introduced by Michael Slater. Knopf 1992 xlvi, 427p il $20
Grades: 7 8 9 10   Fic
1. Great Britain—Fiction 2. Orphans—Fiction
3. Thieves—Fiction
ISBN 0-679-41724-9   LC 92-52899
Also available from other publishers
"Everyman's library"
First published 1837-1838
"A boy from an English workhouse falls into the hands of rogues who train him to be a pickpocket. The story of his struggles to escape from an environment of crime is one of hardship, danger and the severe obstacles overcome." Natl Counc of Teachers of Engl

Dickens, Charles, 1812-1870—*Continued*

A tale of two cities; with an introduction by Simon Schama and sixteen illustrations by Phiz. Knopf 1993 xxviii, 413p il $20 *

Grades: 11 12 Adult   Fic
    1. France—History—1789-1799, Revolution—Fiction
    ISBN 0-679-42073-8   LC 92-73542
Also available from other publishers
"Everyman's library"
First published 1859

"Although Dickens borrowed from Thomas Carlyle's history, *The French Revolution*, for his sprawling tale of London and revolutionary Paris, the novel offers more drama than accuracy. The scenes of large-scale mob violence are especially vivid, if superficial in historical understanding. The complex plot involves Sydney Carton's sacrifice of his own life on behalf of his friends Charles Darnay and Lucie Manette. While political events drive the story, Dickens takes a decidedly antipolitical tone, lambasting both aristocratic tyranny and revolutionary excess." Merriam-Webster's Ency of Lit

Dickinson, Peter, 1927-

Eva. Delacorte Press 1989 219p hardcover o.p. pa $6.50 *

Grades: 7 8 9 10   Fic
    1. Chimpanzees—Fiction 2. Science fiction
    ISBN 0-385-29702-5; 0-440-20766-5 (pa)
                       LC 88-29435
"Eva wakes up from a deep coma that was the result of a terrible car accident and finds herself drastically altered. The accident leaves her so badly injured that her parents consent to a radical experiment to transplant her brain and memory into the body of a research chimpanzee. With the aid of a computer for communication, Eva slowly adjusts to her new existence while scientists monitor her progress, feelings, and insight into the animal world." Voice Youth Advocates

"Raising ethical and moral questions, Dickinson creates a vision both profound and chilling." SLJ

Dixon, Heather, 1982-

Entwined. Greenwillow Books 2011 472p $17.99

Grades: 7 8 9 10   Fic
    1. Princesses—Fiction 2. Dance—Fiction 3. Magic—Fiction 4. Kings and rulers—Fiction 5. Father-daughter relationship—Fiction 6. Death—Fiction 7. Fantasy fiction
    ISBN 978-0-06-200103-0; 0-06-200103-5
                      LC 2010-11686
Confined to their dreary castle while mourning their mother's death, Princess Azalea and her eleven sisters join The Keeper, who is trapped in a magic passageway, in a nightly dance that soon becomes nightmarish.

"The story gracefully explores significant themes of grief and loss, mercy and love. Full of mystery, lush settings, and fully orbed characters, Dixon's debut is both suspenseful and rewarding." Booklist

Dixon, Peter L.

Hunting *the Dragon*; by Peter Dixon. Disney Hyperion 2010 232p $15.99

Grades: 7 8 9 10 11   Fic
    1. Dolphins—Fiction 2. Pirates—Fiction 3. Sea stories
    ISBN 978-1-4231-2498-6; 1-4231-2498-7
                      LC 2009-10570
An eighteen-year-old surf bum joins forces with a dolphin activist and his young assistant as they try to find and sink a ship whose pirate crew is killing dolphins along with the tuna they catch and sell.

"The fast-paced, well-written plot thrills with a hint of a love connection between Billy and Sarah, and just enough suspense and violence, twists and turns to keep young adult readers enthralled." Libr Media Connect

Doctorow, Cory

For the win. Tor 2010 475p $17.99

Grades: 8 9 10 11 12   Fic
    1. Internet games—Fiction 2. Science fiction
    ISBN 978-0-7653-2216-6; 0-7653-2216-1
                      LC 2010-18644
"A Tor teen book"
A group of teens from around the world find themselves drawn into an online revolution arranged by a mysterious young woman known as Big Sister Nor, who hopes to challenge the status quo and change the world using her virtual connections.

The author "has taken denigrated youth behavior (this time, gaming) and recast it into something heroic. He can't resist the occasional lecture—sometimes breaking away from the plot to do so—but thankfully his lessons are riveting. With its eye-opening humanity and revolutionary zeal, this ambitious epic is well worth the considerable challenge." Booklist

Little brother. Tor Teen 2008 380p $17.95 *

Grades: 8 9 10 11 12   Fic
    1. United States. Dept. of Homeland Security—Fiction 2. Terrorism—Fiction 3. Computers—Fiction 4. Civil rights—Fiction 5. San Francisco (Calif.)—Fiction
    ISBN 978-0-76531-985-2; 0-76531-985-3
                      LC 2008-1827
"A Tom Doherty Associates book"
After being interrogated for days by the Department of Homeland Security in the aftermath of a major terrorist attack on San Francisco, California, seventeen-year-old Marcus, released into what is now a police state, decides to use his expertise in computer hacking to set things right.

"The author manages to explain naturally the necessary technical tools and scientific concepts in this fast-paced and well-written story. . . . The reader is privy to Marcus's gut-wrenching angst, frustration, and terror, thankfully offset by his self-awareness and humorous observations." Voice Youth Advocates

Makers. Tor 2009 416p $24.99

Grades: 11 12 Adult   Fic
    1. Inventors—Fiction 2. Businessmen—Fiction 3. Science fiction
    ISBN 978-0-7653-1279-2; 0-7653-1279-4
                      LC 2009-36212
"A Tom Doherty Associates Book"

Doctorow, Cory—_Continued_

"Perry Gibbons and Lester Banks, typical brilliant geeks in a garage, are trash-hackers who find inspiration in the growing pile of technical junk. Attracting the attention of suits and smart reporter Suzanne Church, the duo soon get involved with cheap and easy 3D printing, a cure for obesity and crowd-sourced theme parks. The result is bitingly realistic and miraculously avoids cliché or predictability. While dates and details occasionally contradict one another, Doctorow's combination of business strategy, brilliant product ideas and laugh-out-loud moments of insight will keep readers powering through this quick-moving tale." Publ Wkly

Doctorow, E. L., 1931-

Ragtime. Modern Library 1997 320p $18.95

Grades: 11 12 Adult   **Fic**

1. New York (State)—Fiction 2. Social classes—Fiction 3. Social problems—Fiction

ISBN 0-679-60297-6   LC 97-42251

Also available from Random House Trade Paperbacks

This is a reissue of the title first published 1975 by Random House

"The lives of an upper-middle-class family in New Rochelle; a black ragtime musician who loses his love, his child, and his life because of bigotry; and a poor immigrant Jewish family are interwoven in this early-twentieth-century story. There are cameo appearances by well-known figures of that period: Houdini, anarchist Emma Goldman, actress Evelyn Nesbit, Henry Ford, and J.P. Morgan, whose magnificent library plays an important part in the story. The book mingles fact and fiction in portraying the era of ragtime." Shapiro. Fic for Youth. 3d edition

Dogar, Sharon

Annexed. Houghton Mifflin Harcourt 2010 333p $17 *

Grades: 8 9 10 11 12   **Fic**

1. Frank, Anne, 1929-1945—Fiction 2. Holocaust, 1933-1945—Fiction 3. Netherlands—Fiction

ISBN 978-0-547-50195-6; 0-547-50195-1

       LC 2010-282410

"On July 13, 1942, 15-year-old Peter van Pels and his parents entered the attic that became their home for two years. Peter is angry that he is hiding and not fighting Nazis. He is also not happy to be sharing cramped living quarters with the Franks, especially know-it-all Anne. In this novel, Dogar 'reimagines' what happened between the families who lived in the secret annex immortalized in Anne Frank's diary. In doing so, she creates a captivating historical novel and fully fleshes out the character of Peter, a boy whom teens will easily relate to." SLJ

Waves. Scholastic/Chicken House 2007 325p $16.99

Grades: 9 10 11 12   **Fic**

1. Coma—Fiction 2. Great Britain—Fiction

ISBN 978-0-439-87180-8; 0-439-87180-8

       LC 2007-277811

Hal feels eerily connected to his comatose older sister as she hovers between life and death in a hospital. Hal believes his sister is trying to communicate with him as he tries to solve the mystery of her accident.

"Both suspenseful and thoughtful, action packed and atmospheric, this novel is compelling and memorable." SLJ

Doig, Ivan

The whistling season. Harcourt 2006 345p hardcover o.p. pa $14.95

Grades: 11 12 Adult   **Fic**

1. Siblings—Fiction 2. Household employees—Fiction 3. Teachers—Fiction 4. Montana—Fiction 5. Western stories

ISBN 978-0-15-101237-4; 0-15-101237-7; 978-0-15-603164-6 (pa); 0-15-603164-7 (pa)

       LC 2005-25457

"Set in the early 1900s, this novel is a nostalgic, bittersweet story about a widower, his three sons, and the year these boys spend in a one-room country schoolhouse. The novel begins with the father, Oliver, hiring a widowed housekeeper named Rose from Minneapolis (her advertisement reads 'Can't Cook but Doesn't Bite'). She arrives with her unconventional brother, Morrie, in tow. Morrie is something of a scholar, and he soon finds himself pressed into service as a replacement teacher. During the course of the novel, these intriguing and unpredictable characters come together in surprising and uplifting ways. This is an affectionate, heartwarming tale that also celebrates a vanished way of life and laments its passing." Libr J

Dolamore, Jaclyn

Magic under glass. Bloomsbury Children's Books 2010 225p $16.99

Grades: 7 8 9 10 11 12   **Fic**

1. Magic—Fiction 2. Robots—Fiction 3. Singers—Fiction 4. Fairies—Fiction 5. Fantasy fiction

ISBN 978-1-59990-430-6; 1-59990-430-6

       LC 2009-20944

A wealthy sorcerer's invitation to sing with his automaton leads seventeen-year-old Nimira, whose family's disgrace brought her from a palace to poverty, into political intrigue, enchantments, and a friendship with a fairy prince who needs her help.

"Delamore successfully juggles several elements that might have stymied even a more experienced writer: intriguing plot elements, sophisticated characterizations, and a subtle boost of girl power." Booklist

Dole, Mayra L.

Down to the bone; [by] Mayra Lazara Dole. HarperTeen 2008 384p $16.99; lib bdg $17.89 *

Grades: 8 9 10 11 12   **Fic**

1. Lesbians—Fiction 2. Cuban Americans—Fiction

ISBN 978-0-06-084310-6; 0-06-084310-1; 978-0-06-084311-3 (lib bdg); 0-06-084311-X (lib bdg)

       LC 2007-33270

Laura, a seventeen-year-old Cuban American girl, is thrown out of her house when her mother discovers she is a lesbian, but after trying to change her heart and hide from the truth, Laura finally comes to terms with who she is and learns to love and respect herself.

"Using Spanish colloquialisms and slang, this debut author pulls off the tricky task of dialect in a manner that feels authentic. As Dole tackles a tough and important topic, her protagonist will win over a range of teen audiences, gay and straight." Publ Wkly

Donnelly, Jennifer

A northern light. Harcourt 2003 389p $17; pa $8.95

Grades: 9 10 11 12   **Fic**
1. Farm life—Fiction
ISBN 0-15-216705-6; 0-15-205310-7 (pa)
LC 2002-5098

In 1906, sixteen-year-old Mattie, determined to attend college and be a writer against the wishes of her father and fiance, takes a job at a summer inn where she discovers the truth about the death of a guest. Based on a true story.

"Donnelly's characters ring true to life, and the meticulously described setting forms a vivid backdrop to this finely crafted story. An outstanding choice for historical-fiction fans." SLJ

Revolution. Delacorte Press 2010 471p $18.99; lib bdg $21.99 *

Grades: 9 10 11 12   **Fic**
1. Louis XVII, of France, 1785-1795—Fiction
2. Bereavement—Fiction 3. Family life—Fiction
4. Musicians—Fiction 5. Diaries—Fiction 6. Paris (France)—Fiction 7. France—History—1789-1799, Revolution—Fiction
ISBN   978-0-385-73763-0;   0-385-73763-7;
978-0-385-90678-4 (lib bdg); 0-385-90678-1 (lib bdg)
LC 2010-08993

An angry, grieving seventeen-year-old musician facing expulsion from her prestigious Brooklyn private school travels to Paris to complete a school assignment and uncovers a diary written during the French revolution by a young actress attempting to help a tortured, imprisoned little boy—Louis Charles, the lost king of France.

"The ambitious story, narrated in Andi's grief-soaked, sardonic voice, will wholly capture patient readers with its sharply articulated, raw emotions and insights into science and art; ambition and love; history's ever-present influence; and music's immediate, astonishing power." Booklist

Includes bibliographical references

Dooley, Sarah

Livvie Owen lived here. Feiwel and Friends 2010 229p $16.99

Grades: 6 7 8 9 10   **Fic**
1. Autism—Fiction 2. Family life—Fiction 3. School stories
ISBN 978-0-312-61253-5; 0-312-61253-2
LC 2010-13009

Fourteen-year-old Livvie Owen, who has autism, and her family have been forced to move frequently because of her outbursts, but when they face eviction again, Livvie is convinced she has a way to get back to a house where they were all happy, once.

"This novel is an interesting perspective of what a teenage girl with autism might experience, but also a heartwarming story of how a family binds together during emotional and financial turmoil." Libr Media Connect

Dorris, Michael

A yellow raft in blue water. Holt & Co. 1987 343p hardcover o.p. pa $14 *

Grades: 11 12 Adult   **Fic**
1. Mother-daughter relationship—Fiction 2. Native Americans—Fiction 3. Family life—Fiction 4. Women—Fiction
ISBN 0-8050-0045-3; 0-312-42185-0 (pa)
LC 86-26947

"The bitter rifts and inevitable bonds between generations are highlighted as a teenaged daughter, mother, and grand matriarch of an American Indian family tell their life stories. Humorous and poignant, with unique characters." SLJ

Dostoyevsky, Fyodor, 1821-1881

Crime and punishment; translated from the Russian by Constance Garnett; with an introduction by Ernest J. Simmons. Modern Library 1994 xxiv, 629p $19.95 *

Grades: 11 12 Adult   **Fic**
1. Homicide—Fiction 2. Russia—Fiction
ISBN 0-679-60100-7
Also available from other publishers
Written 1866

"The novel is a psychological analysis of the poor student Raskolnikov, whose theory that humanitarian ends justify evil means leads him to murder a St. Petersburg pawnbroker. The act produces nightmarish guilt in Raskolnikov. The narrative's feverish, compelling tone follows the twists and turns of Raskolnikov's emotions and elaborates his struggle with his conscience and his mounting sense of horror as he wanders the city's hot, crowded streets. In prison, Raskolnikov comes to the realization that happiness cannot be achieved by a reasoned plan of existence but must be earned by suffering." Merriam-Webster's Ency of Lit

Dowd, Siobhan

Bog child. David Fickling Books 2008 321p $16.99; lib bdg $19.99 *

Grades: 8 9 10 11 12   **Fic**
1. Northern Ireland—Fiction 2. Mummies—Fiction
3. Prisoners—Fiction 4. Family life—Fiction
5. Terrorism—Fiction
ISBN   978-0-385-75169-8;   0-385-75169-9;
978-0-385-75170-4 (lib bdg); 0-385-75170-2 (lib bdg)
LC 2008-2998

In 1981, the height of Ireland's "Troubles," eighteen-year-old Fergus is distracted from his upcoming A-level exams by his imprisoned brother's hunger strike, the stress of being a courier for Sinn Fein, and dreams of a murdered girl whose body he discovered in a bog.

"Dowd raises questions about moral choices within a compelling plot that is full of surprises, powerfully bringing home the impact of political conflict on innocent bystanders." Publ Wkly

Dowd, Siobhan—*Continued*

Solace of the road. David Fickling Books 2009 260p $17.99; lib bdg $20.99 *

Grades: 9 10 11 12   **Fic**

1. Runaway teenagers—Fiction 2. Foster home care—Fiction 3. Voyages and travels—Fiction 4. Great Britain—Fiction

ISBN   978-0-375-84971-8;   0-375-84971-8; 978-0-375-94971-5 (lib bdg); 0-375-94971-2 (lib bdg)
LC 2008-44603

While running away from a London foster home just before her fifteenth birthday, Holly has ample time to consider her years of residential care and her early life with her Irish mother, whom she is now trying to reach.

"A compelling psychological portrait of a girl's journey from denial to facing the facts that will let her move beyond her troubled past. . . . Readers will root for her to find her balance and arrive safely at the right destination." Publ Wkly

A swift pure cry. David Fickling Books 2007 309p hardcover o.p. pa $8.99

Grades: 9 10 11 12   **Fic**

1. Family life—Fiction 2. Fathers—Fiction 3. Pregnancy—Fiction 4. Ireland—Fiction

ISBN   978-0-385-75108-7;   0-385-75108-7; 978-0-440-42218-1 (pa); 0-440-42218-1 (pa)
LC 2006-14562

Coolbar, Ireland, is a village of secrets and Shell, caretaker to her younger brother and sister after the death of their mother and with the absence of their father, is not about to reveal hers until suspicion falls on the wrong person.

"This book, with its serious tone and inclusion of social issues, will have appeal for American readers desiring weightier material, and teachers might find it useful in the classroom." Voice Youth Advocates

Downham, Jenny

Before I die. David Fickling Books 2007 326p hardcover o.p. pa $9.99 *

Grades: 8 9 10 11 12   **Fic**

1. Terminally ill—Fiction 2. Death—Fiction

ISBN 978-0-385-75155-1; 978-0-385-75183-4 (pa)
LC 2007-20284

A terminally ill teenaged girl makes and carries out a list of things to do before she dies.

"Downham holds nothing back in her wrenchingly and exceptionally vibrant story." Publ Wkly

Doyle, Sir Arthur Conan, 1859-1930

The hound of the Baskervilles; introduction by Laurie R. King; notes by James Danly. Modern Library 2002 xx, 181p pa $7.95 *

Grades: 11 12 Adult   **Fic**

1. Mystery fiction 2. Great Britain—Fiction

ISBN 0-8129-6606-6   LC 2002-29505

Also available from other publishers

First published 1902

This is the "case of the eerie howling on the moor and strange deaths at Baskerville. Sir Charles Baskerville is murdered, and Holmes and Watson move in to solve the crime." Haydn. Thesaurus of Book Dig

"By a miracle of judgment, the supernatural is handled with great effect and no letdown. The plot and subplots are thoroughly integrated and the false clues put in and removed with a master hand. The criminal is superb, Dr. Mortimer memorable, and the secondary figures each contribute to the total effect of brilliancy and grandeur combined. One wishes one could be reading it for the first time." Barzun. Cat of Crime. Rev and enl edition

Doyle, Eugenie F., 1952-

According to Kit; [by] Eugenie Doyle. Front Street 2009 215p $17.95

Grades: 7 8 9 10   **Fic**

1. Farm life—Fiction 2. Ballet—Fiction 3. Mother-daughter relationship—Fiction 4. Home schooling—Fiction 5. Family life—Fiction 6. Vermont—Fiction

ISBN 978-1-59078-474-7; 1-59078-474-X
LC 2009-7032

As fifteen-year-old Kit does chores on her family's Vermont farm, she puzzles over her mother's apparent unhappiness, complains about being homeschooled after a minor incident at school, and strives to communicate just how important dance is to her.

Doyle's "characters are complicated and authentic. . . . Kit's obsession with ballet . . . will ring true for all teens equally focused on their own talents." Booklist

Draanen, Wendelin van

Confessions of a serial kisser. Alfred A. Knopf 2008 294p $15.99; lib bdg $18.99

Grades: 7 8 9 10   **Fic**

1. Kissing—Fiction 2. Friendship—Fiction 3. School stories

ISBN   978-0-375-84248-1;   0-375-84248-9; 978-0-375-94248-8 (lib bdg); 0-375-94248-3 (lib bdg)
LC 2007-49027

After reading her mother's secret collection of romance novels during her parent's difficult separation, seventeen-year-old Evangeline Logan begins a quest for the perfect kiss.

"The playful title and premise are matched by tender and convincing storytelling." Publ Wkly

The running dream. Alfred A. Knopf 2011 336p $16.99; lib bdg $19.99

Grades: 7 8 9 10 11 12   **Fic**

1. Running—Fiction 2. Amputees—Fiction 3. Handicapped—Fiction 4. School stories

ISBN   978-0-375-86667-8;   0-375-86667-1; 978-0-375-96667-5 (lib bdg); 0-375-96667-6 (lib bdg)
LC 2010-07072

When a school bus accident leaves sixteen-year-old Jessica an amputee, she returns to school with a prosthetic limb and her track team finds a wonderful way to help rekindle her dream of running again.

"It's a classic problem novel in a lot of ways. . . . Overall, though, this is a tremendously upbeat book. . . . Van Draanen's extensive research into both running and amputees pays dividends." Booklist

Draper, Sharon M., 1948-

The Battle of Jericho. Atheneum Books for Young Readers 2003 297p $16.95; pa $6.99

Grades: 7 8 9 10   **Fic**
    1. Clubs—Fiction 2. School stories 3. Cousins—Fiction 4. Death—Fiction

ISBN 0-689-84232-5; 0-689-84233-3 (pa)
                         LC 2002-8612

"The Warriors of Distinction has been the school's most exclusive club for 50 years, so when 16-year-old Jericho is asked to pledge, he's excited—and intimidated. . . . When the ceremony turns cruel—with the one girl pledge being singled out for abuse—Jericho begins to have second thoughts. Then the affair turns deadly." Booklist

"This title is a compelling read that drives home important lessons about making choices." SLJ

Other titles in this series are:
Just another hero (2009)
November blues (2007)

Copper sun; [by] Sharon Draper. Atheneum Books for Young Readers 2006 302p $16.95

Grades: 8 9 10 11 12   **Fic**
    1. Slavery—Fiction 2. African Americans—Fiction

ISBN 0-689-82181-6   LC 2005-05540

Two fifteen-year-old girls—one a slave and the other an indentured servant—escape their Carolina plantation and try to make their way to Fort Moses, Florida, a Spanish colony that gives sanctuary to slaves.

"This action-packed, multifaceted, character-rich story describes the shocking realities of the slave trade and plantation life while portraying the perseverance, resourcefulness, and triumph of the human spirit." Booklist

Tears of a tiger. Atheneum Pubs. 1994 162p $16.95; pa $5.99

Grades: 7 8 9 10   **Fic**
    1. Death—Fiction 2. African Americans—Fiction 3. Suicide—Fiction

ISBN 0-689-31878-2; 0-689-80698-1 (pa)
                         LC 94-10278

The death of African American high school basketball star Rob Washington in a drunk driving accident leads to the suicide of his friend Andy, who was driving the car

"The story emerges through newspaper articles, journal entries, homework assignments, letters, and conversations that give the book immediacy; the teenage conversational idiom is contemporary and well written. Andy's perceptions of the racism directed toward young black males . . . will be recognized by African American YAs." Booklist

Dray, Stephanie

Lily of the Nile. Berkley trade pbk. ed. Berkley Books 2011 351p pa $15

Grades: 9 10 11 12   **Fic**
    1. Cleopatra, Queen of Egypt, d. 30 B.C.—Fiction 2. Augustus, Emperor of Rome, 63 B.C.-14 A.D.—Fiction 3. Rome—History—Fiction

ISBN 978-0-425-23855-4   LC 2010-37153

This book focuses on "Cleopatra Selene, daughter of Antony and Cleopatra. The novel follows Selene's story from her parents' suicides, through the years that she and her brothers, Alexander and Philadelphus, were wards of Octavian, living in his sister's home until her betrothal to Juba II. . . . Dray imbues her work with meticulously researched details of Roman life, historical figures, and political upheaval. Add magical realism and controversial goddess-worship, and you have a novel that will appeal to readers on many levels." Libr J

Duey, Kathleen

Skin hunger. Atheneum Books for Young Readers 2007 357p (Resurrection of magic) hardcover o.p. pa $9.99

Grades: 7 8 9 10   **Fic**
    1. Fantasy fiction 2. Magic—Fiction

ISBN   978-0-689-84093-7;   0-689-84093-4; 978-0-689-84094-4 (pa); 0-689-84094-2 (pa)
                         LC 2006-34819

In alternate chapters, Sadima travels from her farm home to the city and becomes assistant to a heartless man who is trying to restore knowledge of magic to the world, and a group of boys fights to survive in the academy that has resulted from his efforts.

This is a "compelling new fantasy. . . . Duey sweeps readers up in the page-turning excitement." Horn Book

Followed by: Scared scars (2009)

Dumas, Alexandre, 1802-1870

The three musketeers; translated by Jacques Le Clercq. Modern Library 1999 xxi, 598p $24.95

Grades: 7 8 9 10 11 12 Adult   **Fic**
    1. France—History—1589-1789, Bourbons—Fiction

ISBN 0-679-60332-8

Also available from other publishers

Original French edition, 1844

"D'Artagnan arrives in Paris one day in 1625 and manages to be involved in three duels with three musketeers . . . Athos, Porthos and Aramis. They become d'Artagnan's best friends. The account of their adventures from 1625 on develops against the rich historical background of the reign of Louis XIII and the early part of that of Louis XIV, the main plot being furnished by the antagonism between Cardinal de Richelieu and Queen Anne d'Autriche." Haydn. Thesaurus of Book Dig

Duncan, Lois, 1934-

Killing Mr. Griffin. Dell 1990 223p pa $6.50 hardcover o.p. *

Grades: 7 8 9 10   **Fic**
    1. School stories 2. Kidnapping—Fiction

ISBN 0-440-94515-1 (pa)

First published 1978 by Little, Brown

"Mr. Griffin, the stern high-school English teacher, is loathed by those who should appreciate his determination to educate them. Mark, a student, uses his cool glamour and cleverness to mesmerize classmates Jeff, David, Betsy and Sue, persuading them to kidnap Mr. Griffin, with the idea of scaring the teacher into handing out high grades for inferior work. They leave the man trussed and gagged in a remote spot, where he dies. Sue wants to go to the police with a confession, but Mark masterminds a frantic coverup." Publ Wkly

The author's "skillful plotting builds layers of tension that draws readers into the eye of the conflict. The ending is nicely handled in a manner which provides relief without removing any of the chilling implications." SLJ

Dunkle, Clare B.

By these ten bones. Henry Holt 2005 229p $16.95

Grades: 7 8 9 10   **Fic**
1. Werewolves—Fiction 2. Horror fiction 3. Scotland—Fiction

ISBN 0-8050-7496-1   LC 2004-52359

After a mysterious young wood carver with a horrifying secret arrives in her small Scottish town, Maddie gains his trust – and his heart – and seeks a way to save both him and her townspeople from an ancient evil.

"Readers with a taste for fantasy rooted in folklore and history, and a stomach for grisly horror, will happily roam the mist-shrouded Highlands of Dunkle's latest creation." Booklist

The house of dead maids; illustrations by Patrick Arrasmith. Henry Holt and Co. 2010 146p il $15.99

Grades: 8 9 10 11 12   **Fic**
1. Brontë family—Fiction 2. Household employees—Fiction 3. Ghost stories 4. Orphans—Fiction 5. Great Britain—Fiction

ISBN 978-0-8050-9116-8; 0-8050-9116-5
                                        LC 2009-50769

Eleven-year-old Tabby Aykroyd, who would later serve as housekeeper for thirty years to the Brontë sisters, is taken from an orphanage to a ghost-filled house, where she and a wild young boy are needed for a pagan ritual.

"The author manages to stay true to the essence of *Wuthering Heights* while creating a deliciously chilling ghost story that stands on its own. Readers do not have to be at all familiar with Brontë's gothic story of destructive love to be scared out of their wits by this one: cognoscenti, though, will recognize a few sly nods to the original." Bull Cent Child Books

Dunlap, Susanne Emily

The musician's daughter; [by] Susanne Dunlap. Bloomsbury 2009 322p $16.99

Grades: 8 9 10 11 12   **Fic**
1. Haydn, Joseph, 1732-1809—Fiction 2. Musicians—Fiction 3. Homicide—Fiction 4. Gypsies—Fiction 5. Vienna (Austria)—Fiction 6. Mystery fiction

ISBN 978-1-59990-332-3; 1-59990-332-6
                                        LC 2008-30307

In eighteenth-century Vienna, Austria, fifteen-year-old Theresa seeks a way to help her mother and brother financially while investigating the murder of her father, a renowned violinist in Haydn's orchestra at the court of Prince Esterhazy, after his body is found near a gypsy camp.

"Dunlap skillfully builds suspense until the final page. . . . Readers will root for courageous Theresa through the exciting intrigue even as they absorb deeper messages about music and art's power to lift souls and inspire change." Booklist

Durham, David Anthony, 1969-

Gabriel's story. Doubleday 2001 291p hardcover o.p. pa $13.95

Grades: 11 12 Adult   **Fic**
1. African Americans—Fiction 2. Kansas—Fiction 3. Frontier and pioneer life—Fiction

ISBN 0-385-49814-4; 0-385-72033-5 (pa)
                                        LC 00-25291

In this "novel, set in the eighteen-seventies, Gabriel, a fifteen-year-old black boy from Baltimore, resents his new life on the Kansas plains when his widowed mother marries a homesteader. But then he falls in with a charismatic cowpunch and horse thief, and as they travel west to New Mexico a series of violent episodes brings Gabriel to swift maturity. The moral gravity of Durham's narrative is offset by his attentiveness to the primacy of nature in the Western landscape." New Yorker

Durst, Sarah Beth

Ice. Margaret K. McElderry Books 2009 308p $16.99

Grades: 7 8 9 10   **Fic**
1. Fairy tales 2. Polar bear—Fiction 3. Supernatural—Fiction 4. Scientists—Fiction 5. Arctic regions—Fiction

ISBN 978-1-4169-8643-0; 1-4169-8643-X
                                        LC 2009-8618

A modern-day retelling of "East o' the Sun, West o' the Moon" in which eighteen-year-old Cassie learns that her grandmother's fairy tale is true when a Polar Bear King comes to claim her for his bride and she must decide whether to go with him and save her long-lost mother, or continue helping her father with his research

"Told in a descriptive style that perfectly captures the changing settings, Durst's novel is a page-turner that readers who enjoy adventure mixed with fairy-tale romance will find hard to put down." Booklist

Eagland, Jane

Wildthorn. Houghton Mifflin Harcourt 2010 c2009 350p $16

Grades: 7 8 9 10   **Fic**
1. Sex role—Fiction 2. Great Britain—History—19th century—Fiction 3. Psychiatric hospitals—Fiction

ISBN 978-0-547-37017-0; 0-547-37017-2
                                        LC 2010-282485

First published 2009 in the United Kingdom

In Victorian England, seventeen-year-old Louisa Cosgrove is locked away in the Wildthorn Hall mental institution, where she is stripped of her identity and left to wonder who has tried to destroy her life.

"Neither too spunky nor too quiescent, Louisa is a credible character, which helps make her ordeal believable." Bull Cent Child Books

Efaw, Amy

After. Viking 2009 350p $17.99

Grades: 7 8 9 10   **Fic**
1. Abandoned children—Fiction 2. Pregnancy—Fiction 3. Infants—Fiction 4. School stories

ISBN 978-0-670-01183-4; 0-670-01183-5
                                        LC 2010-275195

Efaw, Amy—*Continued*

In complete denial that she is pregnant, straight-A student and star athlete Devon Davenport leaves her baby in the trash to die, and after the baby is discovered, Devon is accused of attempted murder.

"Authentic dialogue and pithy writing allow teens to feel every prick of panic, embarrassment and fear." Kirkus

Ehrenberg, Pamela, 1972-

Ethan, suspended; written by Pamela Ehrenberg. Eerdmans Books for Young Readers 2007 266p $16

Grades: 7 8 9 10   **Fic**

1. Grandparents—Fiction 2. Race relations—Fiction 3. Jews—Fiction 4. Washington (D.C.)—Fiction

ISBN 978-0-8028-5324-0   LC 2006032697

After a school suspension and his parents' separation, Ethan is sent to live with his grandparents in Washington, D.C., which is worlds apart from his home in a Philadelphia suburb.

"Ehrenberg focuses on themes of race and class without sounding preachy. . . . Best of all are the portraits of [Ethan's] scrappy Jewish grandparents." Booklist

Tillmon County fire. Eerdmans Books for Young Readers 2009 175p pa $9

Grades: 9 10 11 12   **Fic**

1. Arson—Fiction 2. Hate crimes—Fiction 3. Community life—Fiction 4. West Virginia—Fiction

ISBN 978-0-8028-5345-5; 0-8028-5345-5

LC 2008-22102

An act of arson commited as an anti-gay hate crime affects the lives of several teenagers from a small town.

"This cleverly plotted and well-crafted story of abuse and vengeance is told in pieces from the varying perspectives of a half-dozen teens, and Ehrenberg uses intertwining chapters to explore their motives and desires. . . . The vividly drawn setting, almost a character in itself, embraces an important message all readers need to hear." SLJ

Ehrenhaft, Daniel

Friend is not a verb; a novel. HarperTeen 2010 241p $16.99

Grades: 7 8 9 10   **Fic**

1. Rock music—Fiction 2. Bands (Music)—Fiction 3. Family life—Fiction 4. Siblings—Fiction 5. New York (N.Y.)—Fiction

ISBN 978-0-06-113106-6; 0-06-113106-7

LC 2009-44006

While sixteen-year-old Hen's family and friends try to make his supposed dreams of becoming a rock star come true, he deals with the reality of being in a band with an ex-girlfriend, a friendship that may become love, and his older sister's mysterious disappearance and reappearance.

"Offbeat characters, an intriguing mystery, and a sweet romance make Ehrenhaft's . . . coming-of-age story stand out. . . . The mystery—and romance—wrap up rather neatly, but readers should be impressed by the clever surprise ending." Publ Wkly

El-Saadawi, Nawal

Woman at point zero; translated by Sherif Hetata. New ed. Zed 2007 114p $45; pa $14.95 *

Grades: 11 12 Adult   **Fic**

1. Prostitution—Fiction 2. Egypt—Fiction

ISBN 978-1-84277-872-2; 978-1-84277-873-9 (pa)

First published 1983

"From her prison cell, Firdaus, sentenced to die for having killed a pimp in a Cairo street, tells of her life from village childhood to city prostitute." Publisher's note

Elkeles, Simone

How to ruin my teenage life. Flux 2007 281p pa $8.95

Grades: 7 8 9 10 11 12   **Fic**

1. Jews—Fiction 2. Israelis—Fiction 3. Father-daughter relationship—Fiction 4. Chicago (Ill.)—Fiction

ISBN 978-0-7387-0961-1; 0-7387-1019-9

LC 2007005535

Living with her Israeli father in Chicago, seventeen-year-old Amy Nelson-Barak feels like a walking disaster, worried about her "non-boyfriend" in the Israeli army, her mother, new stepfather, and the baby they are expecting, a new boy named Nathan who has moved into her apartment building and goes to her school, and whether or not she really is the selfish snob that Nathan says she is.

"This book has laugh-out-loud moments. . . . Amy's thoughtfulness and depth raise this book above most of the chick-lit genre." Voice Youth Advocates

Other titles in this series are:

How to ruin a summer vacation (2006)

How to ruin your boyfriend's reputation (2009)

Perfect chemistry. Walker 2009 360p $16.99; pa $9.99

Grades: 9 10 11 12   **Fic**

1. Social classes—Fiction 2. Dating (Social customs)—Fiction 3. Gangs—Fiction 4. School stories

ISBN 978-0-8027-9823-7; 0-8027-9823-3; 978-0-8027-9822-0 (pa); 0-8027-9822-5 (pa)

LC 2008-13769

When wealthy, seemingly perfect Brittany and Alex Fuentes, a gang member from the other side of town, develop a relationship after Alex discovers that Brittany is not exactly who she seems to be, they must face the disapproval of their schoolmates—and others.

"Brittany's controlling parents and sister with cerebral palsy are well drawn, but it is Elkeles rendition of Alex and his life that is particularly vivid. Sprinkling his speech with Spanish, his gruff but tender interactions with his family and friends feel completely genuine. . . . This is a novel that could be embraced by male and female readers in equal measure." Booklist

Followed by Rules of attraction (2010)

Elliott, Patricia, 1946-
The pale assassin. Holiday House 2009 336p
$17.95

Grades: 7 8 9 10   **Fic**
  1. France—History—1789-1799, Revolution—Fiction
  2. Siblings—Fiction 3. Adventure fiction
  ISBN 978-0-8234-2250-0; 0-8234-2250-X
                                    LC 2009-7554
In early 1790s Paris, as the Revolution gains momentum, young and sheltered Eugenie de Boncoeur finds it
difficult to tell friend from foe as she and the royalist
brother she relies on become the focus of "le Fantome,"
the sinister spymaster with a long-held grudge against
their family.
  "The best aspect of this excellent work of historical
fiction is Eugenie herself. Her gradual coming of age and
growing political awareness provides resonant depth to
what becomes a highly suspenseful survival tale."
Booklist
Followed by: The traitor's smile (2011)

Ellis, Ann Dee
Everything is fine. Little, Brown and Co. Books
for Young Readers 2009 154p il $16.99

Grades: 6 7 8 9 10   **Fic**
  1. Depression (Psychology)—Fiction 2. Family life—
Fiction 3. Mothers—Fiction 4. Bereavement—Fiction
  ISBN 978-0-316-01364-2; 0-316-01364-1
                                    LC 2008-5847
When her father leaves for a job out of town, Mazzy
is left at home to try to cope with her mother, who has
been severely depressed since the death of Mazzy's baby
sister.
  "What makes [this book] so extraordinary is the narrative device that Ellis employs to searing effect. . . .
[This] is a story so painful you want to read it with your
eyes closed. It is a stunning novel." Voice Youth Advocates

Ellis, Deborah, 1960-
No safe place. Groundwood Books/House of
Anansi Press 2010 205p $16.95 *

Grades: 9 10 11 12   **Fic**
  1. Refugees—Fiction 2. Iraq—Fiction 3. Great Britain—Fiction 4. France—Fiction
  ISBN 978-0-88899-973-3
Fifteen-year-old Abdul, having lost everyone he loves,
journeys from Baghdad to a migrant community in Ca-
lais where he sneaks aboard a boat bound for England,
not knowing it carries a cargo of heroin, and when the
vessel is involved in a skirmish and the pilot killed, it is
up to Abdul and three other young stowaways to complete the journey.
  "Ellis deftly uses flashbacks to fill in the backstories
of each character, reminding readers of how they can
never really know where people are coming from emotionally. Her writing is highly accessible, and yet understated. Orphans of the world and victims of human trafficking need all the press they can get, and this book
does a great job of introducing the topic and allowing
young people to see beyond the headlines of 'Another illegal accidentally dies in Chunnel.'" SLJ

Ellison, Ralph
Invisible man; preface by Charles Johnson.
Modern Lib. 1994 xxxiv, 572p $19.95; pa $12 *

Grades: 11 12 Adult   **Fic**
  1. African Americans—Fiction
  ISBN 0-679-60139-2; 0-679-73276-4 (pa)
                                    LC 94-176953
A reissue of the title first published 1952 by Random
House
  "Acclaimed as a powerful representation of the lives
of blacks during the Depression, this novel describes the
experiences of one young black man during that period.
Dismissed from a Negro college in the South for showing one of the founders how Negroes live there, he is
used later as a symbol of repression by a Communist
group in New York City. After a Harlem race riot, he is
aware that he must contend with both whites and blacks,
and that loss of social identity makes him invisible
among his fellow beings." Shapiro. Fic for Youth. 3d
edition

Emond, Stephen
Happyface. Little, Brown and Co. 2010 307p il
$16.99

Grades: 7 8 9 10   **Fic**
  1. Dating (Social customs)—Fiction 2. Divorce—Fiction 3. Diaries—Fiction 4. School stories
  ISBN 978-0-316-04100-3; 0-316-04100-9
                                    LC 2008-47386
After going through traumatic times, a troubled, socially awkward teenager moves to a new school where
he tries to reinvent himself.
  "The illustrations range from comics to more fleshed-
out drawings. Just like Happyface's writing, they can be
whimsical, thoughtful, boyishly sarcastic, off-the-cuff, or
achingly beautiful." Publ Wkly

Engdahl, Sylvia Louise, 1933-
Enchantress from the stars; foreword by Lois
Lowry. Firebird 2003 288p pa $6.99

Grades: 7 8 9 10 11 12   **Fic**
  1. Science fiction
  ISBN 0-14-250037-2
A reissue of the title first published 1970 by
Atheneum Pubs.
  When young Elana unexpectedly joins the team leaving the spaceship to study the planet Andrecia, she becomes an integral part of an adventure involving three
very different civilizations, each one centered on the
third planet from the star in its own solar system
  "Emphasis is on the intricate pattern of events rather
than on characterization, and readers will find fascinating
symbolism—and philosophical parallels to what they
may have observed or thought. The book is completely
absorbing and should have a wider appeal than much science fiction." Horn Book
  Another title about Elana is:
The far side of evil (2003)

Enger, Leif

Peace like a river. Atlantic Monthly Press 2001 313p $24; pa $13.95

Grades: 11 12 Adult   **Fic**

1. Minnesota—Fiction

ISBN 0-87113-795-X; 0-8021-3925-6 (pa)

LC 2001-18873

Reuben, the narrator, "was an adolescent in Minnesota in the 1960s, when his brother, Davy, shot and killed two young men who were harassing the family. Reuben's father—in Reuben's estimation fully capable of performing miracles even though the outside world believes he is lost in the clouds—packs Reuben and his sister up and follows the trail Davy has left in his flight from the law." Booklist

Engle, Margarita

Firefly letters; a suffragette's journey to Cuba. Henry Holt & Co. 2010 151p $16.99 *

Grades: 7 8 9 10 11 12   **Fic**

1. Bremer, Fredrika, 1801-1865—Fiction 2. Cuba—Fiction 3. Sex role—Fiction 4. Slavery—Fiction 5. Novels in verse

ISBN 978-0-8050-9082-6; 0-8050-9082-7

LC 2009-23445

"This engaging title documents 50-year-old Swedish suffragette and novelist Fredrika Bremer's three-month travels around Cuba in 1851. Based in the home of a wealthy sugar planter, Bremer journeys around the country with her host's teenaged slave Cecilia, who longs for her mother and home in the Congo. Elena, the planter's privileged 12-year-old daughter, begins to accompany them on their trips into the countryside. . . . Using elegant free verse and alternating among each character's point of view, Engle offers powerful glimpses into Cuban life at that time. Along the way, she comments on slavery, the rights of women, and the stark contrast between Cuba's rich and poor." SLJ

Hurricane dancers; the first Caribbean pirate shipwreck. Henry Holt and Co. 2011 145p $16.99

Grades: 6 7 8 9 10   **Fic**

1. Shipwrecks—Fiction 2. Pirates—Fiction 3. Native Americans—West Indies—Fiction 4. Caribbean region—Fiction 5. Novels in verse

ISBN 978-0-8050-9240-0; 0-8050-9240-4

LC 2010-11690

This is an "accomplished historical novel in verse set in the Caribbean. . . . The son of a Taíno Indian mother and a Spanish father, [Quebrado] is taken in 1510 from his village on the island that is present-day Cuba and enslaved on a pirate's ship, where a brutal conquistador . . . is held captive for ransom. When a hurricane destroys the boat, Quebrado is pulled from the water by a fisherman, Naridó, whose village welcomes him, but escape from the past proves nearly impossible. . . . Engle fictionalizes historical fact in a powerful, original story. . . . Engle distills the emotion in each episode with potent rhythms, sounds, and original, unforgettable imagery." Booklist

Includes bibliographical references

The surrender tree; poems of Cuba's struggle for freedom. Henry Holt and Co. 2008 169p $17.95 *

Grades: 7 8 9 10 11 12   **Fic**

1. Cuba—Fiction 2. Novels in verse

ISBN 978-0-8050-8674-4; 0-8050-8674-9

LC 2007-27591

This "book is written in clear, short lines of stirring free verse. . . . [The author] draws on her own Cuban American roots . . . to describe those who fought in the nineteenth-century Cuban struggle for independence. At the center is Rosa, a traditional healer, who nurses runaway slaves and deserters in caves and other secret hideaways. . . . Many readers will be caught by the compelling narrative voices and want to pursue the historical accounts in Engle's bibliography." Booklist

Ephron, Delia

Frannie in pieces; drawings by Chad W. Beckerman. HarperTeen 2007 374p il $16.99; pa $8.99

Grades: 7 8 9 10   **Fic**

1. Father-daughter relationship—Fiction 2. Bereavement—Fiction 3. Puzzles—Fiction

ISBN 978-0-06-074716-9; 0-06-074716-1; 978-0-06-074718-3 (pa); 0-06-074718-8 (pa)

LC 2007-10909

When fifteen-year-old Frannie's father dies, only a mysterious jigsaw puzzle that he leaves behind can help her come to terms with his death.

"This is a tender, moving story dealing with grief and growing up and the power of art to heal." SLJ

Epstein, Robin

God is in the pancakes. Dial Books 2010 265p $16.99

Grades: 7 8 9 10   **Fic**

1. Euthanasia—Fiction 2. Old age—Fiction 3. Dating (Social customs)—Fiction 4. Sisters—Fiction 5. Religion—Fiction

ISBN 978-0-8037-3382-4; 0-8037-3382-8

Fifteen-year-old Grace, having turned her back on religion when her father left, now finds herself praying for help with her home and love life, and especially with whether she should help a beloved elderly friend die with dignity.

"Everything comes together in an authentic, breezy read that asks difficult questions and doesn't shy away from direct answers, or the reality that answers may not exist. With well-developed adults and a teen seeking help from God and anyone she perceives as wise, this memorable novel offers food for thought and sustenance for the soul." Booklist

Erdrich, Louise

The last report on the miracles at Little No Horse; a novel. HarperCollins Pubs. 2001 361p hardcover o.p. pa $14.95

Grades: 9 10 11 12   **Fic**

1. Catholic Church—Clergy—Fiction 2. Native Americans—Fiction 3. North Dakota—Fiction 4. Ojibwa Indians—Fiction

ISBN 0-06-018727-1; 0-06-157762-6 (pa)

LC 00-47198

Erdrich, Louise—*Continued*

This novel features characters who have appeared previously in Erdrich's work: Father Damien Modeste and Agnes DeWitt. "Now these two merge into one person. . . . From 1912 to 1996, Agnes, disguised as Damien and thus a sham as both man and priest, tries to bring Roman Catholicism to the Ojibwas of Little No Horse Reservation on a loney patch of North Dakota." Time

"Even the small incidents in this novel are moments of tremendous power, stripped of sentimentality or pretension. Erdrich has developed a style that can sound as serious as death or ring with the haunting simplicity of ancient legend." Christ Sci Monit

Esquivel, Laura

Like water for chocolate; translated by Carol Christensen and Thomas Christensen. Doubleday 1992 245p $26; pa $13.95

Grades: 11 12 Adult   **Fic**

1. Women—Fiction 2. Cooking—Fiction 3. Mexico—Fiction

ISBN 0-385-42016-1; 0-385-42017-X (pa)

LC 91-47188

Original Spanish edition published 1989 in Mexico

Set in turn-of-the-century Mexico, this novel relates the story of Tita, "the youngest of three daughters. Practically raised in the kitchen, she is expected to spend her life waiting on Mama Elena and never to marry. Her habitual torment increases when her beloved Pedro becomes engaged to one of her sisters. Tita and he are thrown into tantalizing proximity and manage to communicate their affection through the dishes she prepares for him and his rapturous appreciation. Eventually, Tita's culinary wizardry unleashes uncontrollable forces, with surprising results." Booklist

"A poignant, funny story of love, life, and food which proves that all three are entwined and interdependent." Libr J

Eulberg, Elizabeth

Prom and prejudice. Point 2011 231p $17.99

Grades: 7 8 9 10   **Fic**

1. Connecticut—Fiction 2. Dating (Social customs)—Fiction 3. Pianists—Fiction 4. School stories 5. Social classes—Fiction

ISBN 978-0-545-24077-2; 0-545-24077-8

LC 2010-30924

For Lizzie Bennett, a music scholarship student at Connecticut's exclusive, girls-only Longbourn Academy, the furor over prom is senseless, but even more puzzling is her attraction to the pompous Will Darcy, best friend of her roommate's boyfriend.

"Eulberg retells Jane Austen's still popular tale of class, love, and danger both emotional and physical. . . . This version does justice to Austen and shows up the utter silliness of kids rich in material . . . goods, the moodiness of some males, . . . and the ways truth can be hidden by both outright lying . . . and shyness. This makes, in all, a fairly delightful blend of past and present value systems and social expectations." Booklist

Falkner, Brian

Brain Jack. Random House 2010 349p $17.99; lib bdg $20.99

Grades: 7 8 9 10   **Fic**

1. Computers—Fiction 2. Science fiction 3. New York (N.Y.)—Fiction

ISBN 978-0-375-84366-2; 0-375-84366-3; 978-0-375-93924-2 (lib bdg); 0-375-93924-5 (lib bdg)

LC 2008-43386

In a near-future New York City, fourteen-year-old computer genius Sam Wilson manages to hack into the AT&T network and sets off a chain of events that have a profound effect on human activity throughout the world.

"This fast-paced, cyber thriller is intelligent, well-written, and very intuitive to the possibilities and challenges we may face in our ever changing digital society." Libr Media Connect

Fantaskey, Beth

Jessica's guide to dating on the dark side. Harcourt 2009 354p $17

Grades: 8 9 10 11 12   **Fic**

1. Vampires—Fiction

ISBN 978-0-15-206384-9; 0-15-206384-6

LC 2007-49002

Seventeen-year-old Jessica, adopted and raised in Pennsylvania, learns that she is descended from a royal line of Romanian vampires and that she is betrothed to a vampire prince, who poses as a foreign exchange student while courting her.

"Fantaskey makes this premise work by playing up its absurdities without laughing at them. . . . The romance sizzles, the plot develops ingeniously and suspensefully, and the satire sings." Publ Wkly

Farmer, Nancy, 1941-

The Ear, the Eye, and the Arm; a novel. Puffin Books 1995 c1994 311p pa $6.99 *

Grades: 6 7 8 9 10   **Fic**

1. Science fiction 2. Zimbabwe—Fiction

ISBN 978-0-14-131109-8; 0-14-131109-6

LC 95019982

First published 1994 by Orchard Books

In 2194 in Zimbabwe, General Matsika's three children are kidnapped and put to work in a plastic mine while three mutant detectives use their special powers to search for them

"Throughout the story, it's the thrilling adventure that will grab readers, who will also like the comic, tender characterizations." Booklist

The house of the scorpion. Atheneum Bks. for Young Readers 2002 380p $17.95; pa $7.99 *

Grades: 7 8 9 10   **Fic**

1. Cloning—Fiction 2. Science fiction

ISBN 0-689-85222-3; 0-689-85223-1 (pa)

LC 2001-56594

In a future where humans despise clones, Matt enjoys special status as the young clone of El Patrón, the 140-year-old leader of a corrupt drug empire nestled between Mexico and the United States.

"This is a powerful, ultimately hopeful, story that

Farmer, Nancy, 1941-—*Continued*
builds on today's sociopolitical, ethical, and scientific issues and prognosticates a compelling picture of what the future could bring." Booklist

Faulkner, William, 1897-1962
Light in August; the corrected text. Modern Library 2002 512p $21.95 *
Grades: 11 12 Adult   **Fic**
   1. Southern States—Fiction
   ISBN 0-679-64248-X   LC 2001-57933
First published 1932 by Harrison Smith & Robert Haas, Inc.
The novel "reiterates the author's concern with a society that classifies men according to race, creed, and origin. Joe Christmas, the central character and victim, appears to be white but is really part black; he has an affair with Joanna Burden, a spinster whom the townsfold of Jefferson regard with suspicion because of her New England background. Joe eventually kills her and sets fire to her house; he is captured, castrated, and killed by the outraged townspeople, to whom his victim has become a symbol of the innocent white woman attacked and killed by a black man. Other important characters are Lena Grove, who comes to Jefferson far advanced in pregnancy, expecting to find the lover who has deserted her, and Gail Hightower, the minister who ignores his wife and loses his church because of his fanatic devotion to the past." Reader's Ency. 4th edition

The reivers; a reminiscence. Vintage Books 1992 305p pa $12.95
Grades: 11 12 Adult   **Fic**
   1. Tennessee—Fiction
   ISBN 0-679-74192-5   LC 92-50095
First published 1932 by Harrison Smith & Robert Haas, Inc.
"Told to his grandson as 'A Reminiscence,' Lucius Priest's monologue recalls his adventures in 1905 as an 11-year-old, when he, the gigantic but childish part-Indian Boon Hogganbeck, and a black family servant, Ned William McCaslin, become reivers (stealthy plunderers) of the automobile of his grandfather, the senior banker of Jefferson, Miss." Oxford Companion to Am Lit. 5th edition

Fehlbaum, Beth
Hope in Patience. WestSide Books 2010 312p $16.95
Grades: 10 11 12   **Fic**
   1. Child sexual abuse—Fiction 2. Family life—Fiction 3. Post-traumatic stress disorder—Fiction 4. School stories 5. Texas—Fiction
   ISBN 978-1-934813-41-6   LC 2010-31118
Sequel to Courage in Patience (2008)
After years of sexual abuse by her stepfather, fifteen-year-old Ashley Asher starts a better life with her father and stepmother in Patience, Texas, but despite psychotherapy and new friends, she still suffers from Post Traumatic Stress Disorder.
"Teens who are attracted by . . . [Ashley's] honesty and her compelling story will come away with a deeper understanding of trauma and healing. This book will open hearts and might well save lives." SLJ

Felin, M. Sindy
Touching snow. Atheneum Books for Young Readers 2007 234p $16.99
Grades: 9 10 11 12   **Fic**
   1. Child abuse—Fiction 2. Haitian Americans—Fiction 3. Stepfathers—Fiction 4. New York (N.Y.)—Fiction
   ISBN 978-1-4169-1795-3; 1-4169-1795-0
                       LC 2006-14794
After her stepfather is arrested for child abuse, thirteen-year-old Karina's home life improves but while the severity of her older sister's injuries and the urging of her younger sister, their uncle, and a friend tempt her to testify against him, her mother and other well-meaning adults persuade her to claim responsibility.
"Although the resolution is brutal, this story is a compelling read from an important and much-needed new voice. Readers will cheer for the young narrator." SLJ

Ferguson, Alane, 1957-
The Christopher killer; a forensic mystery. Viking/Sleuth 2006 274p $15.99
Grades: 9 10 11 12   **Fic**
   1. Forensic sciences—Fiction 2. Father-daughter relationship—Fiction 3. Homicide—Fiction 4. Mystery fiction
   ISBN 0-670-06008-9   LC 2005-15806
On the payroll as an assistant to her coroner father, seventeen-year-old Cameryn Mahoney uses her knowledge of forensic medicine to catch the killer of a friend while putting herself in terrible danger.
"This is worlds away from the Nancy Drew college series in terms of gore, but CSI fans won't blink twice." Booklist
Other titles featuring Cameryn Mahoney are:
The angel of death (2006)
The circle of blood (2007)
The dying breath (2009)

Ferris, Jean, 1939-
Of sound mind. Farrar, Straus & Giroux 2001 215p hardcover o.p. pa $6.95
Grades: 7 8 9 10   **Fic**
   1. Deaf—Fiction 2. Friendship—Fiction
   ISBN 0-374-35580-0; 0-374-45584-8 (pa)
                       LC 00-68123
Tired of interpreting for his deaf family and resentful of their reliance on him, high school senior Theo finds support and understanding from Ivy, a new student who also has a deaf parent
"Both a thought-provoking study of just when being deaf matters and when it does not, and an unusually rich coming-of-age story that explores universal issues of family responsibility, emotional maturation, love, and loss." Booklist

Fforde, Jasper
The Eyre affair; a novel. Viking 2002 374p hardcover o.p. pa $14
Grades: 11 12 Adult   **Fic**
   1. Fantasy fiction
   ISBN 0-670-03064-3; 0-14-200180-5 (pa)
                       LC 2001-43775
First published 2001 in the United Kingdom

Fforde, Jasper—*Continued*

"It's 1985 in England, at least on the calendar; the Crimean War is in its hundred-and-thirty-first year; time travel is nothing new; Japanese tourists slip in and out of Victorian novels; and the literary branch of the special police, led gamely by the beguiling Thursday Next, are pursuing Acheron Hades, who has stolen the manuscript of 'Martin Chuzzlewit' and set his sights on kidnapping the character Jane Eyre, a theft that could have disastrous consequences for Brontë lovers who like their story straight. This rambunctious caper could be taken as a warning about what might happen if society considered literature really important—like, say, energy futures or accounting." New Yorker

Other titles featuring Thursday Next are:
Thursday Next in Lost in a good book (2003)
Thursday Next in Something rotten (2004)
Thursday Next in The well of lost plots (2004)

Fiedler, Lisa

Romeo's ex; Rosaline's story. Henry Holt 2006 246p $16.95

Grades: 8 9 10 11 12   **Fic**
1. Shakespeare, William, 1564-1616—Fiction 2. Love stories
ISBN 978-0-8050-7500-7; 0-8050-7500-3
                       LC 2005-35692
In a story based on the Shakespeare play, sixteen-year-old Roseline, who is studying to be a healer, becomes romantically entangled with the Montague family even as her beloved young cousin, Juliet Capulet, defies the family feud to secretly marry Romeo.
"This novel manages to be both witty and multilayered, leaving readers with plenty to ponder." Publ Wkly

Fink, Mark

The summer I got a life. WestSide 2009 196p $15.95

Grades: 7 8 9 10   **Fic**
1. Handicapped—Fiction 2. Wisconsin—Fiction 3. Love stories
ISBN 978-1-934813-12-6; 1-934813-12-5
"Andy is pumped that his freshman year is over and his vacation is about to begin. Then his dad's promotion changes everything. Instead of Hawaii, Andy is spending two weeks on a farm in Wisconsin with his somewhat odd, but well-meaning, aunt and uncle. Once there, though, he finds that things aren't so bad particularly when he spots 'the most incredible-looking girl he has ever seen.' . . . Andy discovers that an accident at age four has left Laura confined to a wheelchair. . . . This is an engaging novel filled with life lessons, a little romance, humor, sports, and fraternal love." SLJ

Finn, Mary

Anila's journey. Candlewick Press 2008 309p $16.99

Grades: 7 8 9 10   **Fic**
1. Racially mixed people—Fiction 2. Missing persons—Fiction 3. India—History—1765-1947, British occupation—Fiction
ISBN 978-0-7636-3916-7; 0-7636-3916-8
                       LC 2008-17917

In late eighteenth-century Calcutta, half-Indian half-Irish Anila Tandy finds herself alone with nothing but her artistic talent to rely on, searching for her father who is presumed dead.

This is "an engrossing trek with a truly admirable young woman who refuses to compromise either her independence or family loyalty." Bull Cent Child Books

Fischer, Jackie

An egg on three sticks; [by] Jackie Moyer Fischer. Thomas Dunne Books 2004 309p pa $12.95

Grades: 9 10 11 12   **Fic**
1. Mother-daughter relationship—Fiction 2. Mental illness—Fiction 3. San Francisco (Calif.)—Fiction
ISBN 0-312-31775-1   LC 2003-9126
In the San Francisco Bay Area in the early 1970s, twelve-year-old Abby watches her mother fall apart and must take on the burden of holding her family together
"With acutely observed detail, Fischer describes a young adult's pull between the universal struggles of adolescence and the surreal anguish of losing a parent to disease." Booklist

Fisher, Catherine, 1957-

Incarceron. Dial Books 2010 442p $17.99

Grades: 7 8 9 10   **Fic**
1. Prisoners—Fiction 2. Fantasy fiction
ISBN 978-0-8037-3396-1; 0-8037-3396-8
                     LC 2008-46254
First published 2007 in the United Kingdom
To free herself from an upcoming arranged marriage, Claudia, the daughter of the Warden of Incarceron, a futuristic prison with a mind of its own, decides to help a young prisoner escape.
"Complex and inventive, with numerous and rewarding mysteries, this tale is certain to please." Publ Wkly
Followed by Sapphique (2011)

Fitzgerald, F. Scott (Francis Scott), 1896-1940

The great Gatsby; preface by Matthew J. Bruccoli. Scribner Classics 1996 170p $25 *

Grades: 11 12 Adult   **Fic**
1. Wealth—Fiction 2. Long Island (N.Y.)—Fiction
ISBN 0-684-83042-6   LC 96-16596
First published 1925
"The mysterious Jay Gatsby lives in a luxurious mansion on the Long Island shore. . . . Nick Carraway, the narrator, lives next door to Gatsby, and Nick's cousin Daisy and her crude but wealthy husband Tom Buchanan live directly across the harbor. Gatsby reveals to Nick that he and Daisy had a brief affair before the war and her marriage to Tom. . . . He persuades Nick to bring him and Daisy together again but ultimately he is unable to win her away from Tom. Daisy, driving Gatsby's car, runs over and kills Tom's mistress Myrtle, unaware of her identity. Myrtle's husband traces the car and shoots Gatsby, who has remained silent in order to protect Daisy. Gatsby's friends and business associates have all deserted him, and only Gatsby's father, and one former guest attend the funeral." Reader's Ency. 4th edition
"The power of the novel derives from its sharp and antagonistic portrayal of wealthy society in New York

Fitzgerald, F. Scott (Francis Scott), 1896-1940—
Continued
City and Long Island. . . . The 'Jazz Age,' Fitzgerald's constant subject, is exposed here in terms of its false glamor and cultural barrenness." Benet's Reader's Ency of Am Lit

Tender is the night. Scribner 1996 320p $25; pa $14
Grades: 9 10 11 12   **Fic**
  1. Wealth—Fiction 2. Psychiatrists—Fiction
  ISBN 0-684-83050-7; 0-684-80154-X (pa)
                                    LC 96-15215
  First published 1934
The story of Dick Diver, a young psychiatrist whose career was thwarted and his genius numbed through his marriage to the exquisite and wealthy Nicole Warren. On the outside their life was all glitter and glamour, but beneath the smooth, beautiful surface lay the corroding falseness of their social values and the tragedy of her disturbed mind.
"Despite the book's many terrifying scenes, the warm tenderness of its writing lifts it into the realm of genuine tragedy." Reader's Ency. 4th edition

Flake, Sharon G.
Bang! Jump at the Sun/Hyperion Books for Children 2005 298p hardcover o.p. pa $7.99
Grades: 8 9 10 11 12   **Fic**
  1. Violence—Fiction 2. Family life—Fiction 3. African Americans—Fiction
  ISBN 0-7868-1844-1; 0-7868-4955-X (pa)
                                    LC 2005-47434
A teenage boy must face the harsh realities of inner city life, a disintegrating family, and destructive temptations as he struggles to find his identity as a young man.
"This disturbing, thought-provoking novel will leave readers with plenty of food for thought and should fuel lively discussions." SLJ

Fleischman, Paul
Seek. Simon Pulse 2003 167p pa $7.99
Grades: 7 8 9 10   **Fic**
  1. Fathers—Fiction 2. Radio—Fiction
  ISBN 0-689-85402-1
  First published 2001 by Front St./Cricket Bks.
"Using a script format, Rob relates his experiences growing up listening to local and distant radio stations, searching for the disk jockey father who abandoned him before birth." Horn Book Guide
"Fleischman has orchestrated a symphony that is both joyful and poignant with this book designed for reader's theatre." Voice Youth Advocates

Fletcher, Christine, 1964-
Ten cents a dance. Bloomsbury U.S.A. Children's Books 2008 356p $16.95 *
Grades: 9 10 11 12   **Fic**
  1. Dancers—Fiction 2. Conduct of life—Fiction 3. Poverty—Fiction 4. World War, 1939-1945—Fiction 5. Chicago (Ill.)—Fiction
  ISBN 978-1-59990-164-0; 1-59990-164-1
                                    LC 2007-50737

In 1940s Chicago, fifteen-year-old Ruby hopes to escape poverty by becoming a taxi dancer in a nightclub, but the work has unforeseen dangers and hiding the truth from her family and friends becomes increasingly difficult.
"The descriptions of nightlife are lively and engaging, and they bring to light race, class, and gender issues in 1940s Chicago, which are fodder for discussion. Leisure readers will enjoy this novel, but it will also be useful in the classroom as a historical snapshot." Voice Youth Advocates

Fletcher, Susan, 1951-
Alphabet of dreams. Atheneum Books for Young Readers 2006 294p map $16.95
Grades: 6 7 8 9 10   **Fic**
  1. Jesus Christ—Nativity—Fiction 2. Iran—Fiction 3. Dreams—Fiction 4. Zoroastrianism—Fiction
  ISBN 0-689-85042-5
  "Ginee Seo Books"
Fourteen-year-old Mitra, of royal Persian lineage, and her five-year-old brother Babak, whose dreams foretell the future, flee for their lives in the company of the magus Melchoir and two other Zoroastrian priests, traveling through Persia as they follow star signs leading to a newly-born king in Bethlehem. Includes historical notes
"The characters are vivid and whole, the plot compelling, and the setting vast." Voice Youth Advocates

Flinn, Alex
Breathing underwater. HarperCollins Pubs. 2001 263p hardcover o.p. pa $8.99 *
Grades: 9 10 11 12   **Fic**
  1. Domestic violence—Fiction
  ISBN 0-06-029198-2; 0-06-447257-4 (pa)
                                    LC 00-44933
Sent to counseling for hitting his girlfriend, Caitlin, and ordered to keep a journal, sixteen-year-old Nick recounts his relationship with Caitlin, examines his controlling behavior and anger, and describes living with his abusive father.
"This book attempts to understand the root of domestic violence. Flinn has created sympathetic characters who are struggling with their insecurities. While it is difficult at first to be sympathetic towards Nick, it becomes easier as he examines his life and relationships. This is a good book to use in discussion with teens who have anger issues." Book Rep
Followed by Diva (2006)

Foer, Jonathan Safran, 1977-
Extremely loud & incredibly close. Houghton Mifflin 2005 326p il $24.95; pa $13.95
Grades: 11 12 Adult   **Fic**
  1. September 11 terrorist attacks, 2001—Fiction 2. Father-son relationship—Fiction 3. New York (N.Y.)—Fiction
  ISBN 0-618-32970-6; 0-618-71165-1 (pa)
                                    LC 2004-65131
"Oskar Schell is an inventor, Francophile, tambourine player, Shakespearean actor, jeweler, pacifist. He is nine years old. And he is on an urgent, secret search through the five boroughs of New York to find the lock that fits

Foer, Jonathan Safran, 1977-—*Continued*
a mysterious key belonging to his father, who died in the attacks on the World Trade Center." Publisher's note

The author's "depiction of Oskar's reaction to phone messages left by his father as he awaited rescue in the burning World Trade Center, his description of Oskar's grandfather's love affair . . . and his experiences during the bombing of Dresden—these passages underscore Mr. Foer's ability to evoke, with enormous compassion and psychological acuity, his characters' emotional experiences, and to show how these private moments intersect with the great public events of history." N Y Times (Late N Y Ed)

Ford, John C., 1971-
The morgue and me. Viking 2009 313p $17.99 *

Grades: 8 9 10 11 12   **Fic**
1. Criminal investigation—Fiction 2. Homicide—Fiction 3. Journalists—Fiction 4. Michigan—Fiction 5. Mystery fiction
ISBN 978-0-670-01096-7; 0-670-01096-0
                      LC 2009-1956
Eighteen-year-old Christopher, who plans to be a spy, learns of a murder cover-up through his summer job as a morgue assistant and teams up with Tina, a gorgeous newspaper reporter, to investigate, despite great danger.

"Ford spins a tale that's complex but not confusing, never whitewashing some of the harsher crimes people commit. The result is a story that holds its own as a mainstream mystery as well as a teen novel." Publ Wkly

Ford, Michael Thomas
Suicide notes; a novel. HarperTeen 2008 295p $16.99; pa $8.99
Grades: 8 9 10 11 12   **Fic**
1. Suicide—Fiction 2. Psychiatric hospitals—Fiction 3. Homosexuality—Fiction
ISBN   978-0-06-073755-9;   0-06-073755-7;
978-0-06-073757-3 (pa); 0-06-073757-3 (pa)
                    LC 2008-19199
Brimming with sarcasm, fifteen-year-old Jeff describes his stay in a psychiatric ward after attempting to commit suicide.

Ford's "characterizations run deep, and without too much contrivance the teens' interactions slowly dislodge clues about what triggered Jeff's suicide attempt." Publ Wkly

Z. HarperTeen 2010 276p $16.99; lib bdg $17.89
Grades: 7 8 9 10   **Fic**
1. Science fiction 2. Zombies—Fiction 3. Games—Fiction
ISBN   978-0-06-073758-0;   0-06-073758-1;
978-0-06-073759-7 (lib bdg); 0-06-073759-X (lib bdg)
                    LC 2009-44005
In the year 2032, after a virus that turned people into zombies has been eradicated, Josh is invited to join an underground gaming society, where the gamers hunt zombies and the action is more dangerous than it seems.

"This book is a thriller, and the clever plot and characters will have readers hoping for more." SLJ

Forman, Gayle
If I stay; a novel. Dutton Children's Books 2009 201p $16.99 *
Grades: 7 8 9 10   **Fic**
1. Coma—Fiction 2. Death—Fiction 3. Medical care—Fiction 4. Oregon—Fiction
ISBN 978-0-525-42103-0; 0-525-42103-3
                    LC 2008-23938
While in a coma following an automobile accident that killed her parents and younger brother, seventeen-year-old Mia, a gifted cellist, weights whether to live with her grief or join her family in death.

"Intensely moving, the novel will force readers to take stock of their lives and the people and things that make them worth living." Publ Wkly
Followed by: Where she went (2011)

Forster, E. M. (Edward Morgan), 1879-1970
A passage to India; with an introduction by P.N. Furbank. Knopf 1991 xxxix, 293p $18
Grades: 11 12 Adult   **Fic**
1. British—India—Fiction 2. India—Fiction
ISBN 0-679-40549-6
Also available from other publishers
"Everyman's library"
First published 1924
"Politics and mysticism are potent forces in India just after World War I. Ronald Heaslop, magistrate of Chandrapore, has asked his mother, Mrs. Moore, to visit him along with his fiancée, Adela Quested. To add to their knowledge of the real India, Dr. Aziz, a young Moslem doctor, offers to take them to the Marabar Caves outside the city. The visit is a shattering experience. Mrs. Moore is struck by the thought that all her ideas about life are no more than the hollow echo she hears in the cave. Adela, entering another cave alone, emerges in a panic and accuses Dr. Aziz of having attacked her in the gloom of the cave. The trial that results from her accusation divides the groups in the city so acutely that a reconciliation appears impossible." Shapiro. Fic for Youth. 3d edition

Foxlee, Karen, 1971-
The anatomy of wings. Alfred A. Knopf 2009 361p $16.99; lib bdg $19.99
Grades: 8 9 10 11 12   **Fic**
1. Suicide—Fiction 2. Bereavement—Fiction 3. Sisters—Fiction 4. Family life—Fiction 5. Australia—Fiction
ISBN   978-0-375-85643-3;   0-375-85643-9;
978-0-375-95643-0 (lib bdg); 0-375-95643-3 (lib bdg)
                    LC 2008-19373
First published 2007 in Australia
After the suicide of her troubled teenage sister, eleven-year-old Jenny struggles to understand what actually happened.

Jenny's "observations are . . . poetic and washed with magic realism. . . . With heart-stopping accuracy and sly symbolism, Foxlee captures the small ways that humans reveal themselves, the mysterious intensity of female adolescence, and the surreal quiet of a grieving house, which slowly and with astonishing resilience fills again with sound and music." Booklist

Franco, Betsy

Metamorphosis; junior year; drawings by Tom Franco. Candlewick Press 2009 114p il $16.99

Grades: 9 10 11 12   **Fic**

1. Artists—Fiction 2. Classical mythology—Fiction 3. Diaries—Fiction 4. School stories

ISBN 978-0-7636-3765-1; 0-7636-3765-3

LC 2009-13859

High school artist Ovid's journal recasts his classmates' lives and loves as modern-day Roman mythology, while slowly revealing his own struggles with parents who need him to be the perfect son in the wake of his meth-addicted sister's disappearance.

"While the brevity of Franco's first YA novel may disappoint readers who want these archetypal yet complex characters in more detail, this accessible, modern retelling resembles the original by springing from story to story and exploring love and its ability to confound all reason." Kirkus

Frank, E. R.

America; a novel. Atheneum Pubs. 2002 242p $18 *

Grades: 9 10 11 12   **Fic**

1. Racially mixed people—Fiction 2. Foster home care—Fiction

ISBN 0-689-84729-7   LC 2001-22984

"A Richard Jackson book"

Teenage America, a not-black, not-white, not-anything boy who has spent many years in institutions for disturbed, antisocial behavior, tries to piece his life together

The author "exposes with compassion, clarity, and deeply unsetting detail the profound shame and horror of abuse as well as the erratic nature of a medical system that tries to reclaim the victims. . . . A piercing, unforgettable novel." Booklist

Life is funny; a novel. Puffin Books 2002 263p pa $7.99

Grades: 7 8 9 10   **Fic**

1. Family life—Fiction 2. Brooklyn (New York, N.Y.)—Fiction

ISBN 0-14-230083-7   LC 2001-48436

First published 2000 by DK Ink

The lives of a number of young people of different races, economic backgrounds, and family situations living in Brooklyn, New York, become intertwined over a seven year period.

"The voices ring true, and the talk is painful, vulgar, rough, sexy, funny, fearful, furious, gentle." Booklist

Frank, Hillary, 1976-

Better than running at night. Houghton Mifflin 2002 263p $17; pa $10

Grades: 9 10 11 12   **Fic**

1. School stories

ISBN 0-618-10439-9; 0-618-25073-5 (pa)

LC 2002-218

"Ellie's a freshman at art college, and her new life is bringing her all the changes she could have desired. She's in an intense and strange introductory class, which is causing her to rethink her artistic priorities; more significantly, she's in her first serious and sexual relation-

ship." Bull Cent Child Books

"With honesty, wit, and a wild first-person narrative, this first novel breaks boundaries in YA fiction." Booklist

The view from the top. Dutton 2010 232p il $16.99

Grades: 9 10 11 12   **Fic**

1. Dating (Social customs)—Fiction 2. Friendship—Fiction 3. Family life—Fiction 4. Maine—Fiction

ISBN 978-0-525-42241-9; 0-525-42241-2

LC 2009-26143

Anabelle and her fellow high school graduates navigate their way through a disastrous summer of love and friendship in the small coastal town of Normal, Maine.

"This quirky love story about falling for yourself first will appeal to teens' hearts and heads." Booklist

Franklin, Emily

The half life of planets; a novel; [by] Emily Franklin and Brendan Halpin. Disney Hyperion Books 2010 247p $16.99

Grades: 7 8 9 10   **Fic**

1. Asperger's syndrome—Fiction 2. Bereavement—Fiction 3. Family life—Fiction 4. Rock music—Fiction 5. Astronomy—Fiction

ISBN 978-1-4231-2111-4; 1-4231-2111-2

LC 2010-4606

An unlikely romance develops between a science-minded girl who is determined to reclaim her reputation and a boy with Asperger's Syndrome.

"The discursive story favors dialogue and introspection over action and can border on melodrama, but the characters' candid perspectives ring true and the romance should have readers longing for connections as deeply felt." Publ Wkly

The other half of me. Delacorte Press 2007 247p $15.99; pa $6.50

Grades: 8 9 10 11 12   **Fic**

1. Identity (Psychology)—Fiction 2. Sisters—Fiction 3. Artists—Fiction

ISBN   978-0-385-73445-5;   0-385-73445-X; 978-0-385-73446-2 (pa); 0385-73446-8 (pa)

LC 2006-36825

Feeling out of place in her athletic family, artistic sixteen-year-old Jenny Fitzgerald, whose biological father was a sperm donor, finds her half sister through the Sibling Donor Registry and contacts her, hoping that this will finally make her feel complete.

"Franklin offers readers an engaging protagonist whose humor and unusual situation highlight the lonely and displaced feelings common to many teens." SLJ

Frazer, Megan, 1977-

Secrets of truth and beauty. Hyperion 2009 347p $15.99

Grades: 7 8 9 10   **Fic**

1. Sisters—Fiction 2. Obesity—Fiction 3. Farm life—Fiction 4. Massachusetts—Fiction

ISBN 978-1-4231-1711-7; 1-4231-1711-5

LC 2009-22804

Frazer, Megan, 1977-—*Continued*

Dara Cohen, a junior pageant princess turned chubby teenager, reconnects with an estranged older sister whom her parents have disowned for mysterious reasons.

"Readers will quickly become intrigued with the unraveling of family secrets and the cast of memorable characters. . . . Dara emerges as a likable, complex heroine, whose growing self-confidence is touching and inspiring." Publ Wkly

Frazier, Angie

Everlasting. Scholastic Press 2010 329p $17.99
Grades: 8 9 10 11 12   **Fic**
1. Adventure fiction 2. Seafaring life—Fiction 3. Supernatural—Fiction 4. Shipwrecks—Fiction 5. Father-daughter relationship—Fiction 6. Australia—Fiction
ISBN 978-0-545-11473-8; 0-545-11473-X
        LC 2009-20519

In 1855, seventeen-year-old Camille sets out from San Francisco, California, on her last sea voyage before entering a loveless marriage, but when her father's ship is destroyed, she and a friend embark on a cross-Australian quest to find her long-lost mother who holds a map to a magical stone.

"Although this novel takes place in the nineteenth century, many of the themes are relevant for today's teens. The author does a nice job of developing strong and funny characters while keeping the plot moving at a readable pace." Voice Youth Advocates

Followed by: The eternal sea (2011)

Fredericks, Mariah

Crunch time. Atheneum Bks. for Young Readers 2006 317p $15.95
Grades: 8 9 10 11 12   **Fic**
1. Friendship—Fiction 2. School stories
ISBN 0-689-86938-X   LC 2004-20008
"A Richard Jackson book"

Four students, who have formed a study group to prepare for the SAT exam, sustain each other through the emotional highs and lows of their junior year in high school.

"Fredericks writes about high school academics and social rules with sharp insight and spot-on humor." Booklist

Freitas, Donna, 1972-

The possibilities of sainthood. Farrar, Straus & Giroux 2008 272p $16.95 *
Grades: 7 8 9 10 11 12   **Fic**
1. Saints—Fiction 2. Catholics—Fiction 3. Italian Americans—Fiction 4. Family life—Fiction 5. School stories 6. Rhode Island—Fiction
ISBN 978-0-374-36087-0; 0-374-36087-1
        LC 2007-33298
"Frances Foster books"

While regularly petitioning the Vatican to make her the first living saint, fifteen-year-old Antonia Labella prays to assorted patron saints for everything from help with preparing the family's fig trees for a Rhode Island winter to getting her first kiss from the right boy.

"With a satisfying ending, this novel about the realistic struggles of a chaste teen is a great addition to all collections." SLJ

This gorgeous game. Farrar, Straus and Giroux 2010 208p $16.99
Grades: 9 10 11 12   **Fic**
1. Teacher-student relationship—Fiction 2. Authorship—Fiction 3. Priests—Fiction 4. Colleges and universities—Fiction 5. Sexual harassment—Fiction
ISBN 978-0-374-31472-9; 0-374-31472-1
        LC 2009-18309
"Frances Foster Books"

Seventeen-year-old Olivia Peters, who dreams of becoming a writer, is thrilled to be selected to take a college fiction seminar taught by her idol, Father Mark, but when the priest's enthusiasm for her writing develops into something more, Olivia shifts from wonder to confusion to despair.

"Young women who have found themselves the object of obsession will relate to the protagonist's ordeal and be inspired by her decision to speak out no matter the consequences." Publ Wkly

Frey, James, 1969-

I am number four; [by] Pittacus Lore. HarperTeen 2010 440p (Lorien legacies) $17.99
Grades: 9 10 11 12   **Fic**
1. Extraterrestrial beings—Fiction 2. Friendship—Fiction 3. School stories 4. Science fiction 5. Ohio—Fiction
ISBN 978-0-06-196955-3; 0-06-196955-9
        LC 2010-9395

In rural Ohio, friendships and a beautiful girl prove distracting to a fifteen-year-old who has hidden on Earth for ten years waiting to develop the Legacies, or powers, he will need to rejoin the other six surviving Garde members and fight the Mogadorians who destroyed their planet, Lorien.

"For those looking for an undemanding, popcorn-ready read, this 'guy—okay, alien—gets the girl and saves the world' adventure should do the trick." Publ Wkly

Followed by: The power of six (2011)

Freymann-Weyr, Garret, 1965-

After the moment. Houghton Mifflin Harcourt 2009 328p $16 *
Grades: 8 9 10 11 12   **Fic**
1. Dating (Social customs)—Fiction 2. Stepfamilies—Fiction
ISBN 978-0-618-60572-9; 0-618-60572-X
        LC 2008-36109

When seventeen-year-old Leigh changes high schools his senior year to help his stepsister, he finds himself falling in love with her emotional disturbed friend, although he is still attached to a girl back home.

"This is an expertly crafted story about a complicated first love." Publ Wkly

My heartbeat. Houghton Mifflin 2002 154p $15
Grades: 7 8 9 10   **Fic**
1. Siblings—Fiction 2. Homosexuality—Fiction
ISBN 0-618-14181-2   LC 2001-47059

As she tries to understand the closeness between her older brother and his best friend, fourteen-year-old Ellen finds her relationship with each of them changing

Freymann-Weyr, Garret, 1965-—*Continued*
"This beautiful novel tells a frank, upbeat story of teen bisexual love in all its uncertainty, pain, and joy. . . . The fast, clipped dialogue will sweep teens into the story, as will Ellen's immediate first-person, present-tense narrative." Booklist

Stay with me. Houghton Mifflin 2006 308p $16
Grades: 9 10 11 12   **Fic**
 1. Sisters—Fiction 2. Suicide—Fiction 3. New York (N.Y.)—Fiction
ISBN 0-618-60571-1; 978-0-618-60571-2
                                            LC 2005-10754
When her sister kills herself, sixteen-year-old Leila goes looking for a reason and, instead, discovers great love, her family's true history, and what her own place in it is.
"This novel pushes the markers of YA fiction onward and upward." Booklist

Friedman, Aimee, 1979-
The year my sister got lucky. Scholastic 2008 370p $16.99
Grades: 7 8 9 10   **Fic**
 1. Sisters—Fiction 2. Moving—Fiction 3. Country life—Fiction 4. City and town life—Fiction 5. New York (State)—Fiction
ISBN 978-0-439-92227-2; 0-439-92227-5
                                            LC 2007-16416
When fourteen-year-old Katie and her older sister, Michaela, move from New York City to upstate New York, Katie is horrified by the country lifestyle but is even more shocked when her sister adapts effortlessly, enjoying their new life, unlike Katie.
"Friedman gets the push and pull of the sister bond just right in this delightful, funny, insightful journey." Booklist

Friedman, Robin, 1968-
Nothing. Flux 2008 232p pa $9.95
Grades: 7 8 9 10   **Fic**
 1. Novels in verse 2. Bulimia—Fiction 3. Family life—Fiction 4. Jews—Fiction
ISBN 978-0-7387-1304-5; 0-7387-1304-X
                                            LC 2008-08184
Despite his outward image of popular, attractive high-achiever bound for the Ivy League college of his father's dreams, high school senior Parker sees himself as a fat, unattractive failure and finds relief for his overwhelming anxieties in ever-increasing bouts of binging and purging.
"The novel does a good job of letting readers inside the head of someone who is suffering from an eating disorder. Compelling reading." SLJ

Friend, Natasha, 1972-
For keeps. Viking 2010 267p $16.99
Grades: 8 9 10 11 12   **Fic**
 1. Mother-daughter relationship—Fiction 2. Father-daughter relationship—Fiction 3. School stories 4. Massachusetts—Fiction
ISBN 978-0-670-01190-2; 0-670-01190-8
                                            LC 2009-22472

Just as sixteen-year-old Josie and her mother finally begin trusting men enough to start dating seriously, the father Josie never knew comes back to town and shakes up what was already becoming a difficult mother-daughter relationship.
"The book discusses sex and abortion, and includes adult language and underage drinking. Many readers will be able to relate to this protagonist, whose strength and maturity set a positive example. Friend skillfully portrays the challenges of adolescence while telling an engaging story with unique and genuine characters." SLJ

Lush. Scholastic Press 2006 178p $16.99
Grades: 7 8 9 10   **Fic**
 1. Alcoholism—Fiction 2. Fathers—Fiction
ISBN 0-439-85346-X   LC 2005-031333
Unable to cope with her father's alcoholism, thirteen-year-old Sam corresponds with an older student, sharing her family problems and asking for advice.
"Friend adeptly takes a teen problem and turns it into a believable, sensitive, character-driven story, with realistic dialogue." Booklist

Friesner, Esther M.
Nobody's princess; [by] Esther Friesner. Random House 2007 305p hardcover o.p. pa $7.99
Grades: 6 7 8 9 10   **Fic**
 1. Helen of Troy (Legendary character)—Fiction 2. Sex role—Fiction 3. Classical mythology—Fiction 4. Adventure fiction
ISBN 978-0-375-87528-1; 0-375-87528-X; 978-0-375-87529-8 (pa); 0-375-87529-8 (pa)
                                            LC 2006-06515
Determined to fend for herself in a world where only men have real freedom, headstrong Helen, who will be called queen of Sparta and Helen of Troy one day, learns to fight, hunt, and ride horses while disguised as a boy, and goes on an adventure throughout the Mediterranean world.
This "is a fascinating portrait. . . . Along the way, Friesner skillfully exposes larger issues of women's rights, human bondage, and individual destiny. It's a rollicking good story." Booklist
Followed by: Nobody's prize (2008)

Sphinx's princess. Random House 2009 370p il map $17.99; lib bdg $20.99
Grades: 8 9 10 11 12   **Fic**
 1. Nefertiti, Queen, consort of Akhenaton, King of Egypt, 14th cent. B.C.—Fiction 2. Queens—Fiction 3. Egypt—History—Fiction
ISBN 978-0-375-85654-9; 0-375-85654-4; 978-0-375-95654-6 (lib bdg); 0-375-95654-9 (lib bdg)
                                            LC 2009-13719
Although she is a dutiful daughter, Nefertiti's dancing abilities, remarkable beauty, and intelligence garner attention near and far, so much so that her family is summoned to the Egyptian royal court, where Nefertiti becomes a pawn in the power play of her scheming aunt, Queen Tiye.
"Dramatic plot twists, a powerful female subject, and engrossing details of life in ancient Egypt make for lively historical fiction." Booklist
Followed by: Sphinx's queen (2010)

Friesner, Esther M.—*Continued*

Threads and flames; by Esther Friesner. Viking 2010 390p $17.99

Grades: 6 7 8 9 10   **Fic**
1. Triangle Shirtwaist Company, Inc. —Fiction 2. Fires—Fiction 3. Jews—Fiction 4. Immigrants—Fiction 5. New York (N.Y.)—Fiction 6. Polish Americans—Fiction

ISBN 978-0-670-01245-9; 0-670-01245-9

After recovering from typhus, thirteen-year-old Raisa leaves her Polish shtetl for America to join her older sister, and goes to work at the Triangle Shirtwaist factory.

"Friesner's sparkling prose makes the immigrant experience in New York's Lower East Side come alive. . . . Readers will turn the pages with rapt attention to follow the characters' intrepid, risk-all adventures in building new lives." Booklist

Frost, Helen, 1949-

The braid. Farrar, Straus and Giroux 2006 95p $16 *

Grades: 7 8 9 10   **Fic**
1. Scotland—Fiction 2. Canada—Fiction 3. Sisters—Fiction 4. Immigrants—Fiction 5. Novels in verse

ISBN 0-374-30962-0   LC 2005-40148

"Frances Foster books"

Two Scottish sisters, living on the western island of Barra in the 1850s, relate, in alternate voices and linked narrative poems, their experiences after their family is forcible evicted and separated with one sister accompanying their parents and younger siblings to Cape Breton, Canada, and the other staying behind with other family on the small island of Mingulay.

"The book will inspire both students and teachers to go back and study how the taut poetic lines manage to contain the powerful feelings." Booklist

Crossing stones. Farrar, Straus and Giroux 2009 184p $16.99 *

Grades: 6 7 8 9 10   **Fic**
1. Novels in verse 2. World War, 1914-1918—Fiction 3. Soldiers—Fiction 4. Family life—Fiction 5. Women—Suffrage—Fiction 6. War stories

ISBN 978-0-374-31653-2; 0-374-31653-8
                                         LC 2008-20755

"Frances Foster Books"

In their own voices, four young people, Muriel, Frank, Emma, and Ollie, tell of their experiences during the first World War, as the boys enlist and are sent overseas, Emma finishes school, and Muriel fights for peace and women's suffrage.

"Beautifully written in formally structured verse. . . . This [is a] beautifully written, gently told story." Voice Youth Advocates

Keesha's house. Frances Foster Bks./Farrar, Straus & Giroux 2003 116p hardcover o.p. pa $8

Grades: 7 8 9 10   **Fic**
1. Home—Fiction

ISBN 0-374-34064-1; 0-374-40012-1 (pa)
                                         LC 2002-22698

Seven teens facing such problems as pregnancy, closeted homosexuality, and abuse each describe in poetic forms what caused them to leave home and where they found home again

"Spare, eloquent, and elegantly concise. . . . Public, private, or correctional educators and librarians should put this must-read on their shelves." Voice Youth Advocates

Furey, Leo

The long run; a novel. Trumpeter 2006 376p hardcover o.p. pa $13.95

Grades: 11 12 Adult   **Fic**
1. Boys—Fiction 2. Orphanages—Fiction

ISBN   978-1-59030-411-2;   1-59030-411-X; 978-1-59030-528-7 (pa); 1-59030-528-0 (pa)
                                         LC 2006-14924

First published 2004 in Canada

This "tale takes place in a Newfoundland orphanage in the early 1960s. While the school is grim and the corporal punishment the students receive is brutal, the boys band together to create the families they all lack. The book is filled with vivid characters." Publ Wkly

Fusco, Kimberly Newton

Tending to Grace. Knopf 2004 167p $14.95

Grades: 7 8 9 10   **Fic**
1. Speech disorders—Fiction 2. Mothers—Fiction 3. Aunts—Fiction

ISBN 0-375-82862-1   LC 2003-60406

When Cornelia's mother runs off with a boyfriend, leaving her with an eccentric aunt, Cornelia must finally confront the truth about herself and her mother.

"This quiet, beautiful first novel makes the search for home a searing drama." Booklist

Gaiman, Neil, 1960-

American gods; a novel. Morrow 2001 465p $26

Grades: 11 12 Adult   **Fic**
1. Science fiction

ISBN 0-380-97365-0   LC 2001-30407

"A noirish sci-fi road trip novel in which the melting pot of the United States extends not merely to mortals but to a motley assortment of disgruntled gods and deities. Early in 'American Gods' we are introduced to Shadow, a man who has been released from prison only to learn that his wife has died in a car crash. With nothing to return home to, Shadow accepts a job protecting Mr. Wednesday, an omniscient one-eyed grifter. . . . Soon the ex-convict finds himself in an alternate universe, where he is haunted by prophetic nightmares and visited by his dead wife." N Y Times Book Rev

Anansi boys. William Morrow 2005 336p il $26.95; pa $7.99 *

Grades: 11 12 Adult   **Fic**
1. Fantasy fiction

ISBN   978-0-06-051518-8;   0-06-051518-X; 978-0-06-051519-5 (pa); 0-06-051519-8 (pa)
                                         LC 2005-47176

"Fat Charlie's life is about to be spiced up—his estranged father dies in a karaoke bar, and the handsome brother he never knew he had shows up on his doorstep with a gleam in his eye. Next thing he knows, Fat

Gaiman, Neil, 1960-—*Continued*

Charlie is being investigated by the police, his fiancée's falling in love with the wrong brother, and he finds out that his father was the god Anansi, Trickster and Spider, and that the beast gods of folklore are plotting their own revenge upon his family bloodline. A fun book with a little of everything—horror, mystery, magic, comedy, song, romance, ghosts, scary birds, ancient grudges, and trademark British wit." Libr J

The graveyard book; with illustrations by Dave McKean. HarperCollins 2008 312p il $17.99; lib bdg $18.89 *

Grades: 5 6 7 8 9 10   **Fic**
  1. Death—Fiction   2. Supernatural—Fiction
3. Cemeteries—Fiction
  ISBN   978-0-06-053092-1;   0-06-053092-8;
978-0-06-053093-8 (lib bdg); 0-06-053093-6 (lib bdg)
                                            LC 2008-13860
Nobody Owens is a normal boy, except that he has been raised by ghosts and other denizens of the graveyard
"Gaiman writes with charm and humor, and again he has a real winner." Voice Youth Advocates

Interworld; [by] Neil Gaiman [and] Michael Reaves. Eos 2007 239p $16.99; lib bdg $17.89

Grades: 6 7 8 9 10   **Fic**
  1. Space and time—Fiction 2. Science fiction
  ISBN 978-0-06-123896-3; 978-0-06-123897-0 (lib bdg)   LC 2007-08617
At nearly fifteen years of age, Joey Harker learns that he is able to travel between dimensions. Soon, he joins a team of different versions of himself, each from another dimension, to fight the evil forces striving to conquer all the worlds.
This offers "vivid, well-imagined settings and characters. . . . [A] rousing sf/fantasy hybrid." Booklist

Stardust. Avon Bks. 1999 238p hardcover o.p. pa $13.95

Grades: 9 10 11 12   **Fic**
  1. Fantasy fiction
  ISBN 0-380-97728-1; 0-06-114202-6 (pa)
                                            LC 98-8773
"Young Tristran Thorn has grown up in the isolated village of Wall, on the edge of the realm of Faerie. When Tristran and the lovely Victoria see a falling star during the special market fair, Victoria impulsively offers him his heart's desire if he will retrieve the star for her. Tristran crosses the border into Faerie and encounters witches, unicorns, and other strange creatures." Libr J
"Grounding his narrative in mythic tradition, Gaiman employs exquisitely rich language, natural wisdom, good humor and a dash of darkness to conjure up a fairy tale in the grand tradition." Publ Wkly

Gaines, Ernest J., 1933-

The autobiography of Miss Jane Pittman. Dial Press (NY) 1971 245p pa $6.99 hardcover o.p.

Grades: 8 9 10 11 12 Adult   **Fic**
  1. African Americans—Fiction 2. Louisiana—Fiction
  ISBN 0-553-26357-9 (pa)   LC 77-144380

"In the epic of Miss Jane Pittman, a 110-year-old ex-slave, the action begins at the time she is a small child watching both Union and Confederate troops come into the plantation on which she lives. It closes with the demonstrations of the sixties and the freedom walk she decides to make. This is a log of trials, heartaches, joys, love—but mostly of endurance." Shapiro. Fic for Youth. 3d edition

A gathering of old men. Knopf 1983 213p hardcover o.p. pa $11.95

Grades: 11 12 Adult   **Fic**
  1. Race relations—Fiction 2. African Americans—Fiction 3. Homicide—Fiction 4. Louisiana—Fiction
  ISBN 0-394-51468-8; 0-679-73890-8 (pa)
                                            LC 82-49000
"The story opens with the murder of Beau Boutan, a Cajun farmer, on the Louisiana plantation of Candy Marshall, a headstrong white owner. She claims to have done the shooting because she wished to protect one of her black workers, Mathu, who has been like a guardian to her following the death of her parents. In the plan to stand between Mapes, the local sheriff, and Mathu, Candy has set into motion an idea that has brought together a group of old black men with shotguns (unloaded), all claiming to have done the shooting. The threat of the South's way of punishing blacks by lynching hangs over the story like a pall. It meets opposition from Beau's young brother who has been friends with a black fellow-student and team-mate at his university." Shapiro. Fic for Youth. 3d edition

A lesson before dying. Knopf 1997 c1993 256p $26; pa $12.95 *

Grades: 9 10 11 12   **Fic**
  1. African Americans—Fiction 2. Mentally handicapped—Fiction 3. Prisoners—Fiction 4. Louisiana—Fiction
  ISBN 0-679-45561-2; 0-375-70270-9 (pa)
                                            LC 92-20335
First published 1993
"The story of two African American men struggling to attain manhood in a prejudiced society, the tale is set in Bayonne, La. . . in the late 1940s. It concerns Jefferson, a mentally slow, barely literate young man, who, though an innocent bystander to a shootout between a white store owner and two black robbers is convicted of murder, and the sophisticated, educated man who comes to his aid. When Jefferson's own attorney claims that executing him would be tantamount to killing a hog, his incensed godmother, Miss Emma, turns to teacher Grant Wiggins, pleading with him to gain access to the jailed youth and help him to face his death by electrocution with dignity." Publ Wkly
"YAs who seek thought-provoking reading will enjoy this glimpse of life in the rural South just before the civil rights movement." SLJ

Galante, Cecilia, 1971-

The sweetness of salt. Bloomsbury 2010 311p $16.99

Grades: 9 10 11 12   **Fic**
  1. Sisters—Fiction 2. Family life—Fiction 3. Self-perception—Fiction 4. Vermont—Fiction
  ISBN 978-1-59990-512-9; 1-59990-512-4
                                            LC 2010-03477

Galante, Cecilia, 1971-—*Continued*

After graduating from high school, class valedictorian Julia travels to Poultney, Vermont, to visit her older sister, and while she is there she learns about long-held family secrets that have shaped her into the person she has grown up to be.

"What makes this novel great is its simplicity. It is poignant without becoming overbearing; it is quiet yet speaks volumes. It contains a realness that is almost uncomfortable to face at times. . . . This is an excellent novel, one that deserves to be read." Voice Youth Advocates

Gallagher, Liz

The opposite of invisible. Wendy Lamb Books 2008 153p $15.99; lib bdg $18.99

Grades: 8 9 10 11 12   **Fic**
1. Dating (Social customs)—Fiction 2. Friendship—Fiction 3. Art—Fiction 4. Seattle (Wash.)—Fiction
ISBN   978-0-375-84152-1;   0-375-84152-0; 978-0-375-94329-4 (lib bdg); 0-375-94329-3 (lib bdg)
LC 2007-11334

Artistic Seattle high school sophomore Alice decides to emerge from her cocoon and date a football player, which causes a rift between her and her best friend, a boy who wants to be more than just friends.

"With its striking setting and diverse cast of well-developed characters, Gallagher's debut—like Alice—shines." Voice Youth Advocates

Garcia, Kami

Beautiful creatures; by Kami Garcia & Margie Stohl. Little, Brown and Co. 2010 563p $17.99

Grades: 7 8 9 10   **Fic**
1. Supernatural—Fiction 2. Extrasensory perception—Fiction 3. South Carolina—Fiction 4. United States—History—1861-1865, Civil War—Fiction 5. Love stories 6. School stories
ISBN 978-0-316-04267-3; 0-316-04267-6
LC 2008-51306

In a small South Carolina town, where it seems little has changed since the Civil War, sixteen-year-old Ethan is powerfully drawn to Lena, a new classmate with whom he shares a psychic connection and whose family hides a dark secret that may be revealed on her sixteenth birthday.

"The intensity of Ethan and Lena's need to be together is palpable, the detailed descriptions create a vivid, authentic world, and the allure of this story is the power of love. The satisfying conclusion is sure to lead directly into a sequel." SLJ

Followed by Beautiful darkness (2010)

García Márquez, Gabriel, 1928-

Love in the time of cholera; translated from the Spanish by Edith Grossman. Knopf 1988 348p $30 *

Grades: 11 12 Adult   **Fic**
1. Latin America—Fiction
ISBN 0-394-56161-9   LC 87-40484
Original Spanish edition published 1985 in Colombia

"While delivering a message to her father, Florentino Ariza spots the barely pubescent Fermina Daza and immediately falls in love. What follows is the story of a passion that extends over 50 years, as Fermina is courted solely by letter, decisively rejects her suitor when he first speaks, and then joins the urbane Dr. Juvenal Urbino, much above her station, in a marriage initially loveless but ultimately remarkable in its strength. Florentino remains faithful in his fashion; paralleling the tale of the marriage is that of his numerous liaisons, all ultimately without the depth of love he again declares at Urbino's death." Libr J

"The poetry of the author's style, the humor in his voice, the joyous detail with which the plot is upholstered—all are reasons to live in this lush, luxurious novel for as long as you desire." Booklist

One hundred years of solitude; translated from the Spanish by Gregory Rabassa. Knopf 1995 416p $27.95 *

Grades: 11 12 Adult   **Fic**
1. Colombia—Fiction
ISBN 0-679-44465-3   LC 95-234911

Also available in hardcover and paperback from HarperCollins Pubs.

Original Spanish edition published 1967 in Argentina

This novel "relates the founding of Macondo by Jose Arcadio Buendia, the adventures of six generations of his descendants, and, ultimately, the town's destruction. It also presents a vast synthesis of social, economic, and political evils plaguing much of Latin America. Even more important from a literary point of view is its aesthetic representation of a world in microcosm, that is, a complete history, from Eden to Apocalypse, of a world in which miracles such as people riding on flying carpets and a dead man returning to life tend to erase the thin line between objective and subjective realities." Ency of World Lit in the 20th Century

Gardner, John, 1933-1982

Grendel. Knopf 1971 174p il hardcover o.p. pa $11.95

Grades: 11 12 Adult   **Fic**
1. Monsters—Fiction 2. Allegories
ISBN 0-394-47143-1; 0-679-72311-0 (pa)

"To the heroes of 'Beowulf,' the monster Grendel, devourer of men, represented chaos and death and pagan darkness. This is Grendel's side of the story. . . . Grendel perceives that what the primeval dragon has told him is true: he is the brute existent by which men learn to define themselves. 'Grendel' may be read for what it says about the human condition, for its implicit comments on men's art, wars, fears, and hopes." Publ Wkly

"The world, Mr. Gardner seems to be suggesting in his violent, inspiring, awesome, terrifying narrative, has to defeat its Grendels, but somehow, he hints, both ecologically and in deeper ways, that world is a poorer place when men and their monsters cannot coexist." Christ Sci Monit

Gardner, Sally

The red necklace; a story of the French Revolution. Dial Books 2008 378p $16.99 *

Grades: 8 9 10 11 12   Fic
1. France—History—1789-1799, Revolution—Fiction
2. Social classes—Fiction 3. Gypsies—Fiction
4. Orphans—Fiction 5. Adventure fiction
ISBN 978-0-8037-3100-4; 0-8037-3100-0
          LC 2007-39813

In the late eighteenth-century, Sido, the twelve-year-old daughter of a self-indulgent marquis, and Yann, a fourteen-year-old Gypsy orphan raised to perform in a magic show, face a common enemy at the start of the French Revolution.

"Scores are waiting to be settled on every page; this is a heart-stopper." Booklist

Followed by: The silver blade (2009)

Garigliano, Jeff

Dogface; a novel. MacAdam/Cage 2008 360p pa $14

Grades: 11 12 Adult   Fic
1. Juvenile delinquency—Fiction
ISBN 978-1-59692-259-4; 1-59692-259-1
          LC 2007-15666

"Loren is a 14-year-old Green Beret wannabe; when he acts out, he's shipped off to Camp Ascend!. Purportedly rehab for delinquent teens, the facility turns out to be a moneymaking scheme run by a con man and his family. Loren sniffs this out, and decides to rally his fellow detainees (a motley bunch, for sure) and break out." Entertainment Wkly

"With its bizarre characters, frank dialogue and violence, it belongs somewhere between Louis Sachar's Holes and a Carl Hiaasen comic thriller. . . . Despite the clichés, the novel never loses its freshness." Dallas Morning News

Garsee, Jeannine

Before, after, and somebody in between. Bloomsbury 2007 342p $16.95

Grades: 8 9 10 11 12   Fic
1. Family life—Fiction 2. Alcoholism—Fiction
3. Poor—Fiction 4. School stories 5. Cleveland (Ohio)—Fiction
ISBN 978-1-59990-022-3; 1-59990-022-X
          LC 2006-27975

After dealing with an alcoholic mother and her abusive boyfriend, a school bully, and life on the wrong side of the tracks in Cleveland, Ohio, high school sophomore Martha Kowalski expects to be happy when she moves in with a rich family across town, but finds that the "rich life" has problems of its own.

"Readers who live in better conditions can experience the underside of life from her dead-on observations. Martha is just a hairsbreadth away from being sucked under like so many around her. Readers will be pulling for her to beat the odds." SLJ

Say the word. Bloomsbury Children's Books 2009 360p $16.99

Grades: 9 10 11 12   Fic
1. Family life—Fiction 2. Lesbians—Fiction
3. Bereavement—Fiction 4. Ohio—Fiction
ISBN 978-1-59990-333-0; 1-59990-333-4
          LC 2008-16476

After the death of her estranged mother, who left Ohio years ago to live with her lesbian partner in New York City, seventeen-year-old Shawna Gallagher's life is transformed by revelations about her family, her best friend, and herself.

"This sensitive and heart-wrenching story slowly unfolds into a gripping read featuring realistically flawed characters who undergo genuine growth." Booklist

Gee, Maurice

Salt. Orca Book Publishers 2009 252p map (The Salt trilogy) $18 *

Grades: 6 7 8 9 10   Fic
1. Extrasensory perception—Fiction 2. Fantasy fiction
ISBN 978-1-55469-209-5; 1-55469-209-1

"Hari lives in Blood Burrow, a hellacious, rat-infested slum. . . . Pearl is a pampered daughter of Company, her only purpose in life to be married off to cement one of her father's political alliances. When both young people, who share rare psychic gifts, revolt against their fates, they find themselves on a desperate journey across a hostile landscape, with the forces of Company at their heels. . . . A compelling tale of anger and moral development that also powerfully explores the evils of colonialism and racism." Publ Wkly

Other titles in this series are:
Gool (2010)
The Limping Man (2011)

Gelbwasser, Margie

Inconvenient. Flux 2010 305p pa $9.95

Grades: 7 8 9 10   Fic
1. Alcoholism—Fiction 2. Russian Americans—Fiction
3. Jews—United States—Fiction 4. Immigrants—Fiction 5. Popularity—Fiction 6. School stories
ISBN 978-0-7387-2148-4; 0-7387-2148-4
          LC 2010025578

While fifteen-year-old Russian-Jewish immigrant Alyssa tries desperately to cope with her mother's increasingly out-of-control alcoholism by covering for her and pretending things are normal, her best friend Lana attempts to fit in with the popular crowd at their high school.

"This will be a hit with girls who like realistic fiction that focuses on the complexity of human relationships." Voice Youth Advocates

George, Madeleine

Looks. Viking 2008 240p $16.99; pa $7.99 *

Grades: 8 9 10 11 12   Fic
1. Anorexia nervosa—Fiction 2. Obesity—Fiction
3. Friendship—Fiction 4. School stories
ISBN   978-0-670-06167-9;   0-670-06167-0;
978-0-14-241419-4 (pa); 0-14-241419-0 (pa)
          LC 2007-38218

George, Madeleine—*Continued*

"Meghan and Aimee are on opposite ends of the outcast spectrum. Meghan is extremely overweight. . . . Aimee, on the other hand, is classic anorexic. Both girls have been hurt by one of the popular girls at school. They join forces to bring Cara down in a stunning bit of public humiliation. . . . The story will make readers think about the various issues touched upon, and it is difficult to put down." SLJ

Geras, Adèle

Troy. Harcourt 2001 340p hardcover o.p. pa $6.95 *

Grades: 7 8 9 10   Fic

1. Trojan War—Fiction

ISBN 0-15-216492-8; 0-15-204570-8 (pa)

LC 00-57262

Homer's "tales of Paris and Helen, Achilles and Hector, and Odysseus and the Trojan horse are recast in the form of a modern novel, using the heroes' fates as background and focus for the real subjects: the women of Troy." Horn Book Guide

"Mythology buffs will savor the author's ability to embellish stories of old without diminishing their original flavor, while the uninitiated will find this a captivating introduction to a pivotal event in classic Greek literature." Publ Wkly

Gershow, Miriam

The local news. Spiegel & Grau 2009 360p $24.95

Grades: 11 12 Adult   Fic

1. Brothers—Fiction 2. Missing persons—Fiction 3. Bereavement—Fiction

ISBN 978-0-385-52761-3; 0-385-52761-6

LC 2008-33391

Still haunted by the disappearance of her popular older brother when she was sixteen, Lydia Pasternak grows up dealing with her frantic parents and assisting the private investigator hired by her family to search for clues to his fate.

"Gershow's writing is fluid, her imagery of the mid '90s concise and compelling, and her story universal." SLJ

Gibbons, Kaye, 1960-

Ellen Foster; a novel. Algonquin Bks. 1987 146p $16.95 *

Grades: 11 12 Adult   Fic

1. Southern States—Fiction 2. Foster home care—Fiction

ISBN 1-56512-205-4   LC 86-22136

Also available in paperback from Vintage Bks.

A "novel narrated by an adolescent girl, Ellen, who relates the day-to-day experiences she endured as a child in a troubled family. Ellen's mother died young, her father was abusive, her other relatives were equally bad; it wasn't until she was taken into a foster home that she found the sort of peace and freedom to be innocent that most normal childhoods afford." Booklist

"What might have been grim, melodramatic material in the hands of a less talented author is instead filled

with lively humor, . . . compassion and intimacy. This short novel focuses on Ellen's strengths rather than her victimization, presenting a memorable heroine who rescues herself." N Y Times Book Rev

Followed by The life all around me by Ellen Foster (2006)

Giles, Gail

Dark song. Little, Brown 2010 292p $16.99

Grades: 8 9 10 11 12   Fic

1. Family life—Fiction 2. Criminals—Fiction

ISBN 978-0-316-06886-4; 0-316-06886-1

LC 2010-06888

After her father loses his job and she finds out that her parents have lied to her, fifteen-year-old Ames feels betrayed enough to become involved with a criminal who will stop at nothing to get what he wants.

"Suspense lovers will savor this fast-paced psychological thriller." Voice Youth Advocates

Playing in traffic. Simon Pulse 2006 176p pa $7.99

Grades: 10 11 12   Fic

1. Homicide—Fiction 2. School stories

ISBN 978-1-4169-0926-2; 1-4169-09265

LC 2006274249

First published 2004 by Roaring Brook Press

Shy and unremarkable, seventeen-year-old Matt Lathrop is surprised and flattered to find himself singled out for the sexual attentions of the alluring Skye Colbly, until he discovers the evil purpose behind her actions.

"The book is fast paced and written in short chapters that will keep a reluctant reader going. The language is realistic for this MTV generation and sex plays a big part in the story. Although the book is suggested for ages 12 years and up, I recommend that you consider it for grades 10 through 12." Libr Media Connect

Right behind you. Little, Brown 2007 292p hardcover o.p. pa $7.99

Grades: 8 9 10 11 12   Fic

1. Psychotherapy—Fiction 2. Family life—Fiction 3. Homicide—Fiction

ISBN 978-0-316-16636-2; 0-316-16636-7; 978-0-316-16637-9 (pa); 0-316-16637-5 (pa)

LC 2007-12336

After spending over four years in a mental institution for murdering a friend in Alaska, fourteen-year-old Kip begins a completely new life in Indiana with his father and stepmother under a different name, but not only has trouble fitting in, he finds there are still problems to deal with from his childhood.

"The story-behind-the-headlines flavor gives this a voyeuristic appeal, while the capable writing and sympathetic yet troubled protagonist will suck readers right into the action." Bull Cent Child Books

Shattering Glass. Simon Pulse 2003 215p pa $7.99

Grades: 7 8 9 10   Fic

1. Violence—Fiction 2. School stories

ISBN 978-0-689-85800-0; 0-689-85800-0

First published 2002 by Roaring Brook Press

Giles, Gail—*Continued*

When Rob, the charismatic leader of the senior class, turns the school nerd into Prince Charming, his actions lead to unexpected violence.

"Tricky, surprising, and disquieting, this tension-filled story is a psychological thriller as well as a book about finding oneself and taking responsibility." Booklist

What happened to Cass McBride? a novel. Little, Brown and Company 2006 211p $16.99; pa $7.99 *

Grades: 11 12   **Fic**
1. Suicide—Fiction 2. Kidnapping—Fiction 3. Family life—Fiction
ISBN   978-0-316-16638-6;   0-316-16638-3; 978-0-316-16639-3 (pa); 0-316-16639-1 (pa)
                                        LC 2005-37298

After his younger brother commits suicide, Kyle Kirby decides to exact revenge on the person he holds responsible.

"Often brutal, this outstanding psychological thriller is recommended for older teens." Voice Youth Advocates

Gill, David Macinnis, 1963-

Black hole sun. Greenwillow Books 2010 340p $16.99

Grades: 8 9 10 11 12   **Fic**
1. Science fiction 2. Mars (Planet)—Fiction 3. Miners—Fiction
ISBN 978-0-06-167304-7; 0-06-167304-8
                                        LC 2009-23050

"Durango is the 16-year-old chief of a team of mercenaries who eke out a living on Mars by earning meager commissions for their dangerous work. Their current job, and the main thrust of this high-energy, action-filled, science-fiction romp, is to protect South Pole miners from the Dræu, a cannibalistic group who are after the miners' treasure. . . . Throughout the novel, the dialogue crackles with expertly delivered sarcastic wit and venom. . . . Readers will have a hard time turning the pages fast enough as the body count rises to the climactic, satisfying ending." Booklist

Soul enchilada. Greenwillow Books 2009 368p $16.99; lib bdg $17.89

Grades: 7 8 9 10   **Fic**
1.   Devil—Fiction   2.   Grandfathers—Fiction 3. Racially mixed people—Fiction
ISBN   978-0-06-167301-6;   0-06-167301-3; 978-0-06-167302-3 (lib bdg); 0-06-167302-1 (lib bdg)
                                        LC 2008-19486

When, after a demon appears to repossess her car, she discovers that both the car and her soul were given as collateral in a deal made with the Devil by her irrascible grandfather, eighteen-year-old Bug Smoot, given two-days' grace, tries to find ways to outsmart the Devil as she frantically searches for her conveniently absent relative.

"Bug is a refreshingly gutsy female protagonist with an attitude that will win over readers searching for something different." Booklist

Gilman, David

The devil's breath. Delacorte Press 2008 391p (Danger zone) $15.99; lib bdg $18.99

Grades: 7 8 9 10 11 12   **Fic**
1. Adventure fiction 2. Environmental protection—Fiction 3. Namibia—Fiction
ISBN 978-0-385-73560-5; 978-0-385-90546-6 (lib bdg)
                                        LC 2007-46744

When fifteen-year-old Max Gordon's environmentalist-adventurer father goes missing while working in Namibia and Max becomes the target of a would-be assassin at his school in England, he decides he must follow his father to Africa and find him before they both are killed.

"The action is relentless. . . . Gilman has a flair for making the preposterous seem possible." Booklist

Another title in this series is:
Ice claw (2010)

Glass, Linzi

The year the gypsies came. H. Holt 2006 260p $16.95

Grades: 9 10 11 12   **Fic**
1. Family life—Fiction 2. South Africa—Fiction
ISBN 0-8050-7999-8; 978-0-8050-7999-9
                                        LC 2005-50314

In Johannesburg, South Africa, in the late 1960s, twelve-year-old Emily, who longs for affection from her quarreling parents, finds comfort in the stories of a Zulu servant and in her friendship with a young houseguest who has an equally troubled family.

"Suggest this one to readers who are always looking for a sad book." SLJ

Gleitzman, Morris

Once. Henry Holt and Company 2010 163p $16.99

Grades: 7 8 9 10   **Fic**
1. Holocaust, 1933-1945—Fiction 2. Jews—Poland—Fiction
ISBN 978-0-8050-9026-0; 0-8050-9026-6
                                        LC 2009-24153

"The horror of the Holocaust is told here through the eyes of a Polish Jewish child, Felix, who loses his innocence as he witnesses Nazi-led roundups, shootings, and deportations. . . . Most moving is the lack of any idealization. . . . Felix escapes, but one and a half million Jewish children did not, and this gripping novel will make readers want to find out more about them." Booklist

Followed by: Then (2011)

Godbersen, Anna

The luxe. HarperCollins Pub. 2007 433p hardcover o.p. pa $9.99

Grades: 8 9 10 11 12   **Fic**
1. Social classes—Fiction 2. Wealth—Fiction 3. New York (N.Y.)—Fiction
ISBN   978-0-06-134566-1;   0-06-134566-0; 978-0-06-134568-5 (pa); 0-06-134568-7 (pa)
                                        LC 2007-20876

In Manhattan in 1899, five teens of different social classes lead dangerously scandalous lives, despite the

Godbersen, Anna—*Continued*

strict rules of society and the best-laid plans of their parents and others.

"It's all scandalous, steamy—though never graphic—fun, with just enough period detail to make the Gilded Age come alive." SLJ

Other titles in the author's series are:

Envy (2009)

Rumors (2008)

Splendor (2009)

Going, K. L.

Fat kid rules the world. Putnam 2003 187p $17.99; pa $6.99 *

Grades: 7 8 9 10   **Fic**

1. Obesity—Fiction 2. Musicians—Fiction
3. Friendship—Fiction

ISBN 0-399-23990-1; 0-14-240208-7 (pa)

LC 2002-67956

Seventeen-year-old Troy, depressed, suicidal, and weighing nearly 300 pounds, gets a new perspective on life when a homeless teenager who is a genius on guitar wants Troy to be the drummer in his rock band

"Going has put together an amazing assortment of characters. . . . This is an impressive debut that offers hope for all kids." Booklist

King of the screwups. Houghton Mifflin Harcourt 2009 310p $17 *

Grades: 9 10 11 12   **Fic**

1. Father-son relationship—Fiction 2. Uncles—Fiction
3. Homosexuality—Fiction

ISBN 978-0-15-206258-3; 0-15-206258-0

LC 2008-25113

After getting in trouble yet again, popular high school senior Liam, who never seems to live up to his wealthy father's expectations, is sent to live in a trailer park with his gay "glam-rocker" uncle.

"Readers—screwups or not—will empathize as Liam, utterly likable despite his faults, learns to be himself." Publ Wkly

Saint Iggy. Harcourt 2006 260p $17

Grades: 9 10 11 12   **Fic**

1. Drug abuse—Fiction 2. Family life—Fiction
3. Poor—Fiction

ISBN 0-15-205795-1; 978-0-15-205795-4

LC 2005-34857

Iggy Corso, who lives in city public housing, is caught physically and spiritually between good and bad when he is kicked out of high school, goes searching for his missing mother, and causes his friend to get involved with the same dangerous drug dealer who deals to his parents.

"Teens will connect with Iggy's powerful sense that although he notices everything, he is not truly seen and accepted himself." Booklist

Goldberg, Myla

Bee season; a novel. Doubleday 2000 275p hardcover o.p. pa $13.95

Grades: 11 12 Adult   **Fic**

1. Family life—Fiction 2. Jews—United States—Fiction

ISBN 0-385-49879-9; 0-385-49880-2 (pa)

LC 99-47933

This novel concerns an eleven-year-old girl, Eliza Naumann, who wins the National Spelling Bee. "Eliza's supernatural gift for spelling thrills her father, Saul, a self-styled Jewish scholar who now believes he can train his daughter to literally talk to God. Unfortunately, that means shunting aside Eliza's older brother, Aaron, who joins a religious cult, and her scarily remote mother, Miriam, who begins breaking into houses in search of missing pieces of herself." Newsweek

"Some of the events that unfold . . . seem a little contrived. But Goldberg engenders considerable suspense around both Eliza's string of spelling successes and the fates of the other Naumanns." Time

Goldblatt, Stacey

Girl to the core. Delacorte Press 2009 290p $16.99

Grades: 8 9 10 11   **Fic**

1. Dating (Social customs)—Fiction 2. Loss (Psychology)—Fiction 3. Irish Americans—Fiction
4. California—Fiction

ISBN 978-0-385-73609-1; 0-385-73609-6

LC 2008-32350

Fifteen-year-old Molly gains support from her extended Irish American family and enlightenment in Girl Corps philosophy and activities as she deals with a cheating boyfriend and overbearing best friend.

"There are no pat endings here; through her funny, first-person narration, Molly works out that human relationships are messy and reaches some fairly adult conclusions about her responsibilities as a girlfriend, friend and mentor. . . . The teen voice remains authentic and believable." Kirkus

Golden, Arthur

Memoirs of a geisha; a novel. Knopf 1997 434p il $26.95; pa $7.99

Grades: 11 12 Adult   **Fic**

1. Japan—Fiction 2. Geishas—Fiction

ISBN 0-375-40011-7; 1-4000-9689-8 (pa)

LC 97-74747

"How nine-year-old Chiyo, sold with her sister into slavery by their father after their mother's death, becomes Sayuri, the beautiful geisha accomplished in the art of entertaining men, is the focus of this . . . novel. Narrating her life story from her elegant suite in the Waldorf Astoria, Sayuri tells of her traumatic arrival at the *Nitta okiya* (a geisha house), where she endures harsh treatment from Granny and Mother, the greedy owners, and from Hatsumomo, the sadistically cruel head geisha. But Sayuri's chance meeting with the Chairman, who shows her kindness, makes her determined to become a geisha. Under the tutelage of the renowned Mameha, she becomes a leading geisha of the 1930s and 1940s." Libr J

"Rarely has a world so closed and foreign been

Golden, Arthur—*Continued*

evoked with such natural assurance, from the aesthetics of the Kyoto geisha's 'art'—to the fetishized sexuality of Gion in the thirties and forties, at once delicate and crude, repressed and flagrant." New Yorker

Golden, Christopher

The wild; by Christopher Golden & Tim Lebbon; with illustrations by Greg Ruth. Harper 2011 348p il (The secret journeys of Jack London) $15.99; lib bdg $16.89

Grades: 7 8 9 10   **Fic**

1. London, Jack, 1876-1916—Fiction 2. Adventure fiction 3. Supernatural—Fiction 4. Wilderness survival—Fiction 5. Wolves—Fiction 6. Gold mines and mining—Fiction 7. Yukon River valley (Yukon and Alaska)—Fiction

ISBN 978-0-06-186317-2; 0-06-186317-3; 978-0-06-186318-9 (lib bdg); 0-06-186318-1 (lib bdg)

LC 2010-07475

Seventeen-year-old Jack London makes the arduous journey to the Yukon's gold fields in 1893, becoming increasingly uneasy about supernatural forces in the wilderness that seem to have taken a special interest in him.

"Golden and Lebbon write with a gritty assurance that brings the fantasy elements . . . down to earth. . . . Occasional sketches add a bit of cinematic drama." Booklist

Golding, Julia

Dragonfly. Marshall Cavendish 2009 390p $17.99

Grades: 6 7 8 9 10   **Fic**

1. Princesses—Fiction 2. Princes—Fiction 3. Fantasy fiction

ISBN 978-0-7614-5582-0; 0-7614-5582-5

LC 2008-33012

When Tashi, the rigidly formal sixteen-year-old Fourth Crown Princess of the Blue Crescent Islands, reluctantly weds roguish eighteen-year-old Prince Ramil of Gerfal, their religious, cultural, and personal differences threaten to end their political alliance and put both countries at the mercy of a fearsome warlord.

"Descriptions of the Known Worlds are vivid and include intricate religions and fascinating political machinations. . . . The cast of characters is large and appealing." Booklist

Golding, William, 1911-1993

Lord of the flies; introduction by E. M. Forster; with a biographical and critical note by E. L. Epstein; illustrated by Ben Gibson. 50th anniversary ed. Berkley 2003 315p $23.95; pa $13 *

Grades: 8 9 10 11 12   **Fic**

1. Allegories 2. Boys—Fiction 3. Survival after airplane accidents, shipwrecks, etc.—Fiction

ISBN 0-399-52920-9; 0-399-50148-7 (pa)

LC 2003-54825

"A Perigee book"

First published 1954 in the United Kingdom; first United States edition, 1955, by Coward-McCann

"Stranded on an island, a group of English schoolboys leave innocence behind in a struggle for survival. A political structure modeled after English government is set up and a hierarchy develops, but forces of anarchy and aggression surface. The boys' existence begins to degenerate into a savage one. They are rescued from their microcosmic society to return to an adult, stylized milieu filled with the same psychological tensions and moral voids. Adventure and allegory are brilliantly combined in this novel." Shapiro. Fic for Youth. 3d edition

Goldman, Steven, 1964-

Two parties, one tux, and a very short film about the Grapes of Wrath. Bloomsbury Children's Books 2008 307p $16.99 *

Grades: 7 8 9 10   **Fic**

1. Friendship—Fiction 2. Dating (Social customs)—Fiction 3. Homosexuality—Fiction 4. School stories

ISBN 978-1-59990-271-5; 1-59990-271-0

LC 2008-11587

Mitch, a shy and awkward high school junior, negotiates the difficult social situations he encounters, both with girls and with his best friend David, after David reveals to him that he is gay.

"With fitting touches of rough language and situations and on-target characters, this witty and skillfully developed story creates a compelling picture of high school life." Voice Youth Advocates

Gonzalez, Julie, 1958-

Imaginary enemy. Delacorte Press 2008 241p $15.99; lib bdg $18.99

Grades: 6 7 8 9 10   **Fic**

1. Imaginary playmates—Fiction

ISBN 978-0-385-73552-0; 0-385-73552-9; 978-0-385-90530-5 (lib bdg); 0-385-90530-0 (lib bdg)

LC 2007-45752

Although her impetuous behavior, smart-mouthed comments, and slacker ways have landed her in trouble over the years, sixteen-year-old Jane has always put the blame on her "imaginary enemy," until a new development forces her to decide whether or not to assume responsibility for her actions.

"Gonzalez has written a witty, realistic novel . . . peppered with funny, authentic dialogue." Booklist

Goodman, Alison, 1966-

Eon: Dragoneye reborn. Viking 2009 531p $19.99 *

Grades: 7 8 9 10   **Fic**

1. Dragons—Fiction 2. Sex role—Fiction 3. Apprentices—Fiction 4. Magic—Fiction 5. Fantasy fiction

ISBN 978-0-670-06227-0; 0-670-06227-8

LC 2008-33223

Sixteen-year-old Eon hopes to become an apprentice to one of the twelve energy dragons of good fortune and learn to be its main interpreter, but to do so will require much, including keeping secret that she is a girl.

"Entangled politics and fierce battle scenes provide a pulse-quickening pace, while the intriguing characters add interest and depth." Booklist

Followed by: Eona: The last Dragoneye (2011)

Goodman, Allegra

Intuition; a novel. Dial Press 2006 344p $25; pa $13 *

Grades: 11 12 Adult   **Fic**
1. Research—Fiction 2. Cancer—Fiction
ISBN 0-385-33612-8; 0-385-33610-1 (pa)
       LC 2005-51940
"The prestigious Philpott Institute in Cambridge, MA, is a virtually closed community dominated by a charismatic leader, oncologist Sandy Glass. Dr. Glass's enthusiasm galvanizes his ambitious scientists to work round the clock when experimental results yield a possible cancer cure, until one young researcher publicizes her suspicions of fraud." Libr J

The author "draws tender but unflinching portraits of the characters' personal lives for a truly humanist novel from the supposedly antiseptic halls of science." Publ Wkly

Goodman, Shawn

Something like hope. Delacorte Press 2011 193p $16.99; lib bdg $19.99

Grades: 9 10 11 12   **Fic**
1. Juvenile delinquency—Fiction 2. African Americans—Fiction
ISBN 978-0-385-73939-9; 978-0-385-90786-6 (lib bdg)   LC 2009-53657
Shavonne, a fierce, desperate seventeen year-old in juvenile lockup, wants to turn her life around before her eighteenth birthday, but corrupt guards, out-of-control girls, and shadows from her past make her task seem impossible.

The author "delivers a gritty, frank tale that doesn't shrink from the harshness of the setting but that also provides a much-needed redemption for both Shavonne and readers." Kirkus

Gordimer, Nadine, 1923-

The house gun. Penguin Books 1999 294p pa $15 *

Grades: 9 10 11 12   **Fic**
1. South Africa—Fiction 2. Homicide—Fiction
ISBN 0-14-027820-6
First published 1998 by Farrar, Straus & Giroux
In this novel, an upperclass South African "professional couple—insurance executive Harald and physician Claudia Lindgard—face the unthinkable when their 27-year-old-son, Duncan, in a fit of passion, picks up the 'house gun,' a staple item in many affluent households for protection against marauders, and shoots a man who has doubly betrayed him. . . . The narrative depicts the senior Lindgards' progression of emotions: disbelief that their son could commit such an act, followed by guilt about their shortcomings as parents and, finally, abandonment of their genteel ethics as they plead to Duncan's brilliant, suave black lawyer to just get their son off." Publ Wkly

"Gordimer is above all a writer of ideas, and she engages her audience in the discourse of morality and ethical conduct without deteriorating into the tedious language of a civics lesson." Women's Rev Books

My son's story. Penguin Books 1991 277p pa $9.95

Grades: 9 10 11 12   **Fic**
1. South Africa—Fiction
ISBN 0-14-015975-4   LC 91-17273
First published 1990 by Farrar, Straus & Giroux
"Sonny is a teacher of mixed race. He and his wife are . . . sympathetic to the plight of the 'real blacks,' yet ambitious that they may someday be accepted by the whites. Sonny's political education begins when he's fired for helping black children demonstrate in their township. Jailed for promoting boycotts and participating in illegal gatherings, Sonny meets and falls in love with a blond, blue-eyed woman who works for a human-rights organization. Sonny's adolescent son, Will, tells the story of his father's political and erotic development, the resentments and betrayals that ensue." Newsweek

This is a "thoughtful, poised, quietly poignant novel that not only recognizes the value and cost of political commitment, but also takes account of recent developments in South Africa and Eastern Europe in a way that Gordimer's previous work did not." Christ Sci Monit

Gormley, Beatrice, 1942-

Poisoned honey; a story of Mary Magdalene. Alfred A. Knopf 2010 306p $16.99; lib bdg $19.99

Grades: 9 10 11 12   **Fic**
1. Mary Magdalene, Saint—Fiction 2. Matthew, the Apostle, Saint—Fiction 3. Jesus Christ—Fiction 4. Bible—History of Biblical events—Fiction 5. Saints—Fiction 6. Jews—Fiction 7. Demoniac possession—Fiction 8. Jerusalem—Fiction
ISBN 978-0-375-85207-7; 0-375-85207-7; 978-0-375-95207-4 (lib bdg); 0-375-95207-1 (lib bdg)   LC 2009-5095
Relates events from the life of a girl who would grow up to be a close follower of Jesus Christ, interspersed with stories of the Apostle Matthew. Includes author's note distinguishing what Scripture says of Mary Magdalene from later traditions.

"Fast paced and vivid, the novel will appeal most strongly to Christians, but other readers will find the portrait of a person, and a time, memorably real." SLJ

Goto, Hiromi

Half World; illustrations by Jillian Tamaki. Viking 2010 221p il $16.99

Grades: 7 8 9 10   **Fic**
1. Mother-daughter relationship—Fiction 2. Fantasy fiction
ISBN 978-0-670-01220-6; 0-670-01220-3
"Raised in impoverished circumstances by her single mother, overweight 14-year-old Melanie is the target of ridicule at school and leads a lonely, introverted life. Then an evil being named Mr. Glueskin kidnaps her mother, forcing Melanie to travel to Half World, a colorless land that has been sundered from the realms of flesh and spirit, its deceased inhabitants cursed to relive the most traumatic moments of their lives. . . . Goto writes the hellish Half World as miserably surreal yet horrifyingly believable. . . . It's a fast-moving and provocative journey with cosmically high stakes, and one that should readily appeal to fans of dark, nightmarish fantasy." Publ Wkly

Gould, Peter L.

Write naked; [by] Peter Gould. Farrar, Straus and Giroux 2008 247p $16.95

Grades: 7 8 9 10 11 12   **Fic**
1. Authorship—Fiction 2. Greenhouse effect—Fiction 3. Vermont—Fiction
ISBN 978-0-374-38483-8; 0-374-38483-5
LC 2007-16023
"Melanie Kroupa Books"

When Victor finds an old Royal typewriter at a yard sale and takes it to his uncle's isolated cabin in the Vermont woods to attempt to write, he meets up with an unusual girl, and together they explore their concerns about the world, themselves, and each other.

"The converging personal journeys of two thoughtful young people unfold beautifully in Victor's quirky but honest voice and in Rose Anna's self-revealing fable. . . . Young adult readers will not want to put down this exceptional debut novel." Voice Youth Advocates

Graham, Rosemary

Thou shalt not dump the skater dude and other commandments I have broken. Viking 2005 281p hardcover o.p. pa $7.99

Grades: 9 10 11 12   **Fic**
1. School stories
ISBN 0-670-06017-8; 978-0-670-06017-7; 978-0-14-240851-3 (pa); 0-14-240851-4 (pa)
LC 2005-3928

Having endured the vicious rumors spread by her professional-skateboarder ex-boyfriend, high school sophomore Kelsey Wilcox tries to salvage her reputation while attempting to earn a place on her high school newspaper.

"Many young women will enjoy this light-handed, anti-romance and will cheer for Kelsey as she stands up for herself and learns that her worth and enjoyment of life are not tied to a boyfriend . . . Kelsey's romantic interludes are PG-13 and perfectly appropriate for middle-school as well as high school readers." Booklist

Grahame-Smith, Seth, 1976-

Pride and prejudice and zombies; the classic Regency romance—now with ultraviolent zombie mayhem! by Jane Austen and Seth Grahame-Smith. Quirk Books 2009 319p il pa $12.95

Grades: 11 12 Adult   **Fic**
1. Austen, Jane, 1775-1817—Parodies, imitations, etc.
2. Zombies—Fiction 3. Social classes—Fiction
4. Great Britain—History—19th century—Fiction
ISBN 978-1-59474-334-4   LC 2008-937609

A mysterious plague has fallen upon the quiet English village of Meryton—and the dead are returning to life! Feisty heroine Elizabeth Bennet is determined to wipe out the zombie menace, but she's soon distracted by the arrival of the haughty and arrogant Mr. Darcy.

The author "has taken the merry world established by a 19th-century literary lady, added a scourge of reanimated corpses, and created . . . a pop culture phenomenon. . . . But, the greater achievement of the book may lie in the satisfying desire it awakens to read the remix and the original side by side." Entertainment Weekly

Other titles in this series are:

Pride and prejudice and zombies: dawn of the dreadfuls (2010)

Pride and prejudice and zombies: dreadfully every after (2011)

Grant, Christopher

Teenie. Alfred A. Knopf 2010 264p $16.99; lib bdg $19.99; ebook $10.99

Grades: 9 10 11 12   **Fic**
1. Dating (Social customs)—Fiction 2. African Americans—Fiction 3. Family life—Fiction 4. School stories
5. Brooklyn (New York, N.Y.)—Fiction
ISBN 978-0-375-86191-8; 978-0-375-96191-5 (lib bdg); 978-0-375-89779-5 (ebook)   LC 2010-35377

High school freshman Martine, longing to escape Brooklyn and her strict parents, is trying to get into a study-abroad program but when her long-time crush begins to pay attention to her and her best friend starts an online relationship, Teenie's mind is on anything but her grades.

"Realistic descriptions of teenage life and appealing characters make for an enjoyable reading experience." SLJ

Grant, K. M.

Blue flame; book one of the Perfect Fire trilogy. Walker & Co. 2008 246p (Perfect fire trilogy) $16.99

Grades: 7 8 9 10   **Fic**
1. Knights and knighthood—Fiction 2. France—History—0-1328—Fiction 3. Middle Ages—Fiction
ISBN 978-0-8027-9694-3; 0-8027-9694-X
LC 2007-51384

In 1242 in the restive Languedoc region of France, Parsifal, having been charged as a child to guard an important religious relic, has lived in hiding for much of his life until he befriends a young couple on opposite sides of the escalating conflict between the Catholics and the Cathars.

"Characters are as complex as the moral issues they face, and Grant's nuanced, thought-provoking look at the religious conflicts they face will resonate today." Booklist

Other books in this series are
Paradise red (2010)
White heat (2009)

Gratz, Alan, 1972-

Samurai shortstop. Dial Books 2006 280p hardcover o.p. pa $7.99 *

Grades: 7 8 9 10   **Fic**
1. Father-son relationship—Fiction 2. Baseball—Fiction 3. School stories 4. Tokyo (Japan)—Fiction
ISBN 0-8037-3075-6; 978-0-8037-3075-5; 0-14-241099-3 (pa); 978-0-14-24099-8 (pa)
LC 2005-22081

While obtaining a Western education at a prestigious Japanese boarding school in 1890, sixteen-year-old Toyo also receives traditional samurai training which has profound effects on both his baseball game and his relationship with his father. This book features some scenes of graphic violence.

"This is an intense read about a fascinating time and place in world history." Publ Wkly

Gratz, Alan, 1972-—*Continued*

Something rotten; a Horatio Wilkes mystery.
Dial Books 2007 207p $16.99; pa $6.99
Grades: 8 9 10 11 12   Fic
  1. Shakespeare, William, 1564-1616—Fiction
2. Homicide—Fiction 3. Tennessee—Fiction
4. Mystery fiction
  ISBN   978-0-8037-3216-2;   0-8037-3216-3;
978-0-14-241297-8 (pa); 0-14-241297-X (pa)
                           LC 2006-38484
  In a contemporary story based on Shakespeare's play,
Hamlet, Horatio Wilkes seeks to solve the murder of his
friend Hamilton Prince's father in Denmark, Tennessee.
  "Readers will find this enjoyable as a pleasure read
and surprisingly painless as a curricular entry." Bull Cent
Child Books
  Followed by: Something wicked (2008)

Graves, Robert, 1895-1985
  I, Claudius; from the autobiography of Tiberius
Claudius, born B.C. 10, murdered and deified A.D.
54. Modern Lib. 1983 c1934 432p hardcover o.p.
pa $14.95 *
Grades: 11 12 Adult   Fic
  1. Claudius, Emperor of Rome, 10 B.C.-54—Fiction
2. Augustus, Emperor of Rome, 63 B.C.-14 A.D.—
Fiction 3. Rome—History—Fiction
  ISBN 0-394-60811-9; 0-679-72477-X (pa)
  First published 1934 by Harrison Smith and Robert
Haas
  "Claudius is lame and a stammerer who seems unlikely to carry on the family tradition of power in ancient
Rome. Immersing himself in scholarly pursuits, Claudius
observes and lives through the plots hatched by his
grandmother, Livia, political conspiracies, murders, and
corruption, and he survives a number of emperors. He
becomes emperor at last and is a just and well-liked ruler, in contrast to those who preceded him." Shapiro. Fic
for Youth. 3d edition

Gray, Claudia
  Evernight. HarperTeen 2008 327p $16.99; lib
bdg $17.89; pa $8.99
Grades: 8 9 10 11 12   Fic
  1. Vampires—Fiction 2. Horror fiction 3. School stories
  ISBN   978-0-06-128439-7;   0-06-128439-4;
978-0-06-128443-4 (lib bdg); 0-06-128443-2 (lib bdg);
978-0-06-128444-1 (pa); 0-06-128444-0 (pa)
                           LC 2007-36733
  Sixteen-year-old Bianca, a new girl at the sinister
Evernight boarding school, finds herself drawn to another
outsider, Jared, but dark forces threaten to tear them
apart and destroy Bianca's entire world.
  "Gray's writing hooks readers from the first page and
reels them in with surprising plot twists and turns. . . .
A must-have for fans of vampire stories." SLJ
  Other titles in this series are:
Afterlife (2011)
Hourglass (2010)
Stargazer (2009)

Gray, Keith
  Ostrich boys. Random House 2010 297p $17.99;
lib bdg $20.99 *
Grades: 8 9 10 11 12   Fic
  1. Friendship—Fiction 2. Death—Fiction 3. Great
Britain—Fiction 4. Scotland—Fiction
  ISBN   978-0-375-85843-7;   0-375-85843-1;
978-0-375-95843-4 (lib bdg); 0-375-95843-6 (lib bdg)
                           LC 2008-21729
  After their best friend Ross dies, English teenagers
Blake, Kenny, and Sim plan a proper memorial by taking
his ashes to Ross, Scotland, an adventure-filled journey
that tests their loyalty to each other and forces them to
question what friendship means.
  "Gray's writing is cheeky, crisp, and realistic. He has
created funny, bright characters whom readers cannot
help but root for." SLJ

Green, John, 1977-
  An abundance of Katherines. Dutton Books
2006 227p $16.99 *
Grades: 9 10 11 12   Fic
  1. Mathematics—Fiction
  ISBN 0-525-47688-1; 978-0-525-47688-7
                           LC 2006-4191
  Having been recently dumped for the nineteenth time
by a girl named Katherine, recent high school graduate
and former child prodigy Colin sets off on a road trip
with his best friend to try to find some new direction in
life while also trying to create a mathematical formula to
explain his relationships.
  This "is an enjoyable, thoughtful novel that will attract
readers interested in romance, math, or just good storytelling." Voice Youth Advocates

  Looking for Alaska. Dutton Books 2005 221p
$15.99; pa $7.99 *
Grades: 9 10 11 12   Fic
  1. Death—Fiction 2. School stories 3. Birmingham
(Ala.)—Fiction
  ISBN 0-525-47506-0; 0-14-240251-6 (pa)
                           LC 2004-10827
  Sixteen-year-old Miles' first year at Culver Creek Preparatory School in Alabama includes good friends and
great pranks, but is defined by the search for answers
about life and death after a fatal car crash
  "The language and sexual situations are aptly and realistically drawn, but sophisticated in nature. Miles's narration is alive with sweet, self-deprecating humor, and his
obvious struggle to tell the story truthfully adds to his
believability." SLJ

  Paper towns. Dutton Books 2008 305p $17.99
Grades: 9 10 11 12   Fic
  1. Missing persons—Fiction 2. Mystery fiction
3. Florida—Fiction
  ISBN 978-0-525-47818-8; 0-525-47818-3
                           LC 2007-52659
  One month before graduating from his Central Florida
high school, Quentin "Q" Jacobsen basks in the predictable boringness of his life until the beautiful and exciting
Margo Roth Spiegelman, Q's neighbor and classmate,
takes him on a midnight adventure and then mysteriously
disappears.

Green, John, 1977-—*Continued*

"The writing is . . . stellar, with deliciously intelligent dialogue and plenty of mind-twisting insights. . . . Language and sex issues might make this book more appropriate for older teens, but it is still a powerfully great read." Voice Youth Advocates

Will Grayson, Will Grayson; [by] John Green & David Levithan. Dutton 2010 310p $17.99 *
Grades: 9 10 11 12   Fic
  1. Chicago (Ill.)—Fiction 2. Theater—Fiction 3. Obesity—Fiction 4. Homosexuality—Fiction 5. Dating (Social customs)—Fiction
  ISBN 978-0-525-42158-0; 0-525-42158-0
                        LC 2008-48979

When two teens, one gay and one straight, meet accidentally and discover that they share the same name, their lives become intertwined as one begins dating the other's best friend, who produces a play revealing his relationship with them both.

"Each character comes lovingly to life, especially Tiny Cooper, whose linebacker-sized, heart-on-his-sleeve personality could win over the grouchiest of grouches. . . . Their story, along with the rest of the cast's, will have readers simultaneously laughing, crying and singing at the top of their lungs." Kirkus

Green, Risa

The secret society of the pink crystal ball. Sourcebooks Fire 2010 315p pa $8.99
Grades: 7 8 9 10   Fic
  1. School stories 2. Supernatural—Fiction
  ISBN 978-1-4022-4106-2; 1-4022-4106-2

When Erin Channing's favorite aunt dies, she inherits a pink crystal ball and a set of weird instructions. Soon Erin and her friends are convinced that the crystal ball holds the key to their future, or at least the key to getting dates.

"Readers will respond to Erin's growth and understanding, and her decision to control her own destiny." SLJ

Greenberg, Joanne, 1932-

I never promised you a rose garden; a novel. Henry Holt 2009 291p pa $15
Grades: 7 8 9 10 11 12 Adult   Fic
  1. Mentally ill—Fiction 2. Psychotherapy—Fiction
  ISBN 978-0-8050-8926-4; 0-8050-8926-8
                        LC 2010-275768
  First published 1964
  Includes reading group guide

Chronicles the three-year battle of a mentally ill, but perceptive, teenage girl against a world of her own creation, emphasizing her relationship with the doctor who gave her the ammunition of self-understanding with which to destroy that world of fantasy.

"The hospital world and Deborah's fantasy world are strikingly portrayed, as is the girl's violent struggle between sickness and health, a struggle given added poignancy by youth, wit, and courage." Libr J

Greene, Graham, 1904-1991

The heart of the matter; introduction by James Wood. Deluxe ed. Penguin Books 2004 255p (Penguin classics) pa $15
Grades: 9 10 11 12   Fic
  1. West Africa—Fiction 2. Marriage—Fiction
  ISBN 0-14-243799-9   LC 2004-275122
  First published 1948

"Set in West Africa, it is a suspense story ingeniously made to hinge on religious faith. . . . The hero is Scobie, an English Roman Catholic who has vowed to make his devout wife happy though he no longer loves her. He borrows money from a local criminal to send her out of harm's way to South Africa; then he falls in love with a young woman from a group of castaways whose ship has been torpedoed. The return of his wife, the development of an adulterous affair, and blackmail drive Scobie deeper into deception and lies. Forced to betray someone, he betrays his god and himself, and finally commits suicide." Reader's Ency. 4th edition

The power and the glory; introduction by John Updike. Viking 1990 295p hardcover o.p. pa $14 *
Grades: 11 12 Adult   Fic
  1. Clergy—Fiction 2. Mexico—Fiction
  ISBN 0-670-83536-6; 0-14-243730-1 (pa)
                        LC 90-50052
  First published 1940 with title: The labyrinthine ways

Set in Mexico, this novel "describes the desperate last wanderings of a whisky priest as outlaw in his own state, who, despite a sense of his own worthlessness (he drinks, and has fathered a bastard daughter), is determined to continue to function as priest until captured. . . . Like many of Greene's works, it combines a conspicuous Christian theme and symbolism with the elements of a thriller." Oxford Companion to Engl Lit

Grey, Zane, 1872-1939

Riders of the purple sage; edited with an introduction and notes by Lee Clark Mitchell. Oxford University Press 2008 xxxviii, 265p (Oxford world's classics) pa $9.95
Grades: 11 12 Adult   Fic
  1. Mormons—Fiction 2. Polygamy—Fiction 3. Utah—Fiction 4. Western stories 5. Adventure fiction
  ISBN 978-0-19-955387-7   LC 2008-482024
  Also available from other publishers
  First published 1912 by Harper

"Well handled melodramatic story of hairbreadth escapes from Mormon vengeance in southwestern Utah in 1871." Booklist
  Includes bibliographical references

Griffin, Adele

The Julian game. G.P. Putnam's Sons 2010 200p $16.99
Grades: 8 9 10 11 12   Fic
  1. Bullies—Fiction 2. School stories
  ISBN 978-0-399-25460-4; 0-399-25460-9
                        LC 2010-2281

In an effort to improve her social status, a new scholarship student at an exclusive girls' school uses a fake

Griffin, Adele—*Continued*

online profile to help a popular girl get back at her ex-boyfriend, but the consequences are difficult to handle.

This is a "perceptive novel. . . . Canny use of details makes Griffin's characters fully realized and believable. . . . Strong pacing and a sympathetic protagonist ought to keep readers hooked." Publ Wkly

Where I want to be. G.P. Putnam's Sons 2005 150p pa $6.99

Grades: 7 8 9 10   **Fic**
1. Sisters—Fiction 2. Mental illness—Fiction
3. Death—Fiction 4. Rhode Island—Fiction
ISBN 0-399-23783-6; 0-14-240948-0 (pa)
                                         LC 2004-1887

Two teenaged sisters, separated by death but still connected, work through their feelings of loss over the closeness they shared as children that was later destroyed by one's mental illness, and finally make peace with each other

"Thoughtful, unique, and ultimately life-affirming, this is a fascinating take on the literary device of a main character speaking after death." SLJ

Griffin, Paul, 1966-

The Orange Houses. Dial Books 2009 147p $16.99 *

Grades: 8 9 10 11 12   **Fic**
1. Handicapped—Fiction 2. Veterans—Fiction
3. Mental illness—Fiction 4. Illegal aliens—Fiction
5. Africans—United States—Fiction 6. Bronx (New York, N.Y.)—Fiction
ISBN 978-0-8037-3346-6; 0-8037-3346-1
                                        LC 2008-46259

Tamika, a fifteen-year-old hearing-impaired girl, Jimmi, an eighteen-year-old veteran who stopped taking his antipsychotic medication, and sixteen-year-old Fatima, an illegal immigrant from Africa, meet and connect in their Bronx, New York, neighborhood, with devastating results.

"Griffin's . . . prose is gorgeous and resonant, and he packs the slim novel with defeats, triumphs, rare moments of beauty and a cast of credible, skillfully drawn characters. A moving story of friendship and hope under harsh conditions." Publ Wkly

Grimes, Nikki

Bronx masquerade. Dial Bks. 2002 167p $16.99; pa $5.99 *

Grades: 7 8 9 10   **Fic**
1. School stories 2. African Americans—Fiction
3. Bronx (New York, N.Y.)—Fiction
ISBN 0-8037-2569-8; 0-14-250189-1 (pa)
                                        LC 00-31701

While studying the Harlem Renaissance, students at a Bronx high school read aloud poems they've written, revealing their innermost thoughts and fears to their formerly clueless classmates

"Funny and painful, awkward and abstract, the poems talk about race, abuse, parental love, neglect, death, and body image. . . . Readers will enjoy the lively, smart voices that talk bravely about real issues and secret fears. A fantastic choice for readers' theater." Booklist

Dark sons. Jump at the Sun 2005 216p $15.99

Grades: 6 7 8 9 10   **Fic**
1. Father-son relationship—Fiction 2. Stepfamilies—Fiction 3. Novels in verse
ISBN 0-7868-1888-3   LC 2004-54208

Alternating poems compare and contrast the conflicted feelings of Ishmael, son of the Biblical patriarch Abraham, and Sam, a teenager in New York City, as they try to come to terms with being abandoned by their fathers and with the love they feel for their younger stepbrothers.

"The simple words eloquently reveal what it's like to miss someone. . . . but even more moving is the struggle to forgive and the affection each boy feels for the baby that displaces him. The elemental connections and the hope . . . will speak to a wide audience." Booklist

A girl named Mister. Zondervan 2010 223p $15.99

Grades: 8 9 10 11   **Fic**
1. Mary, Blessed Virgin, Saint—Fiction
2. Pregnancy—Fiction 3. Christian life—Fiction
4. African Americans—Fiction 5. Novels in verse
ISBN 978-0-310-72078-2; 0-310-72078-8
                                        LC 2010-10830

A pregnant teenager finds support and forgiveness from God through a book of poetry presented from the Virgin Mary's perspective.

"Writing in lovely prose with lyrical, forthright language that avoids over-moralizing while driving home the big issues of teen pregnancy, award-winning Nikki Grimes just may help a few young women make different choices. At the same time, she effectively makes the case for parents and schools to continue to educate, educate, educate." Voice Youth Advocates

Grisham, John

The client. Doubleday 1993 422p $29.95; pa $7.99

Grades: 11 12 Adult   **Fic**
1. Boys—Fiction 2. Mafia—Fiction 3. Lawyers—Fiction
ISBN 0-385-42471-X; 0-440-21352-5 (pa)
                                        LC 92-39079

"While sneaking into the woods to smoke forbidden cigarettes, preteen brothers Mark and Ricky find a lawyer committing suicide in his car. Mark tries to save the man but is instead grabbed by him and told the location of the body of a murdered U.S. senator—a murder for which the lawyer's Mafia-connected client is accused. Witnessing the successful suicide sends Ricky into shock and Mark into a web of lies, half-truths, and finally into refusal to tell the confided secret to the police. Mark accidentally but fortuitously hires a lawyer, Reggie Love, who steers him through a maze of FBI agents, legal proceedings, judges, ambitious lawyers, and hit men. . . . This thriller is unique in its theme and in its suspense mixed with humor. A sure 'all-night' read." SLJ

The firm. Doubleday 1991 421p hardcover o.p. pa $9.99

Grades: 11 12 Adult   **Fic**
1. Lawyers—Fiction 2. Mafia—Fiction 3. Memphis (Tenn.)—Fiction
ISBN 0-385-41634-2; 0-440-24592-6 (pa)
                                         LC 90-3945

Grisham, John—*Continued*

"Fresh out of Harvard Law School, Mitchell McDeere is recruited by an elite Memphis law firm. . . . [His colleagues] put in 19-hour days for their front-office clients, while beavering behind the scenes on money-laundering operations for the Mafia. . . . Mitch, in fear for his life, agrees to work undercover for the F.B.I." N Y Times Book Rev

"The aphorism 'between a rock and a hard place' aptly describes the dilemma of a young attorney pressed by the FBI to reveal crime-related secrets of his firm, while also hounded by his employers to simply take his huge salary and zip his lip. No aphorism, though, can convey the suspense, wit, and polished writing of this laser-sharp candidate for the best recent updating of the David and Goliath story." Libr J

Grossman, Lev

The magicians; a novel. Viking 2009 402p $26.95; pa $16 *

Grades: 11 12 Adult   **Fic**

1. College students—Fiction 2. Magic—Fiction 3. Fantasy fiction

ISBN   978-0-670-02055-3;   0-670-02055-9; 978-0-452-29629-9 (pa); 0-452-29629-3 (pa)

LC 2008-55900

"Quentin Coldwater is a geeky high-school senior in Brooklyn who is convinced that happiness and 'the life he should be living' are elsewhere—for example, in the series of nineteen-thirties British adventure novels that he was obsessed with as a child. When Quentin stumbles on a portal that takes him to a college for magicians in upstate New York, he learns that the world depicted in these novels, known as Fillory, is real, and he is forced to square his youthful ideas with the realities that exist there, too—boredom, regret, shame, and despair. Quentin's journey becomes an unexpectedly moving coming-of-age story in which he learns that magical worlds are much like the real one." New Yorker

Guène, Faïza

Kiffe kiffe tomorrow; [translated from the French by Sarah Adams] Harcourt 2006 179p pa $13

Grades: 11 12 Adult   **Fic**

1. Muslim women—Fiction 2. Poor—Fiction 3. Paris (France)—Fiction

ISBN 0-15-603048-9; 978-0-15-603048-9

LC 2005-30456

"A Harvest original"

Original French edition, 2004

"Doria, 15, a child of Muslim immigrants, describes her daily struggle in Paris' rough housing projects in a contemporary narrative that's touching, furious, and very funny." Booklist

Guibord, Maurissa

Warped. Delacorte Press 2011 339p $16.99; lib bdg $19.99 *

Grades: 7 8 9 10   **Fic**

1. Time travel—Fiction 2. Tapestry—Fiction 3. Magic—Fiction 4. Great Britain—History—1485-1603, Tudors—Fiction

ISBN   978-0-385-73891-0;   0-385-73891-9; 978-0-385-90758-3 (lib bdg); 0-385-90758-3 (lib bdg)

LC 2009-53654

When seventeen-year-old Tessa Brody comes into possession of an ancient unicorn tapestry, she is plummeted into sixteenth-century England, where her life is intertwined with that of a handsome nobleman who is desperately trying to escape a terrible fate.

"This has it all—fantasy, romance, witchcraft, life-threatening situations, detective work, chase scenes, and a smattering of violence. Imaginative and compelling, it's impossible to put down." SLJ

Guterson, David

Snow falling on cedars. Harcourt Brace & Co. 1994 345p $25 *

Grades: 11 12 Adult   **Fic**

1. Japanese Americans—Fiction 2. Trials—Fiction 3. Journalists—Fiction 4. Washington (State)—Fiction

ISBN 0-15-100100-6   LC 94-7535

Also available in paperback from Vintage Bks.

"Japanese American Kabuo Miyomoto is arrested in 1954 for the murder of a fellow fisherman, Carl Heine. Miyomoto's trial, which provides a focal point to the novel, stirs memories of past relationships and events in the minds and hearts of the San Piedro Islanders. Through these memories, Guterson illuminates the grief of loss, the sting of prejudice triggered by World War II, and the imperatives of conscience. With mesmerizing clarity he conveys the voices of Kabuo's wife, Hatsue, and Ishmael Chambers, Hatsue's first love who, having suffered the loss of her love and the ravages of war, ages into a cynical journalist now covering Kabuo's trial." Libr J

Haddix, Margaret Peterson, 1964-

Leaving Fishers. Simon & Schuster Bks. for Young Readers 1997 211p hardcover o.p. pa $5.99 *

Grades: 7 8 9 10   **Fic**

1. Cults—Fiction

ISBN 0-689-81125-X; 0-689-86793-X (pa)

LC 96-47857

After joining her new friends in the religious group called Fishers of Men, Dorry finds herself immersed in a cult from which she must struggle to extricate herself

"The novel does a credible job of showing the effect of a cult on a vulnerable person, without disavowing strong religious beliefs." Child Book Rev Serv

Uprising. Simon & Schuster Books for Young Readers 2007 346p $16.99; pa $7.99

Grades: 6 7 8 9 10   **Fic**

1. Triangle Shirtwaist Company, Inc. —Fiction 2. Strikes—Fiction 3. Fires—Fiction

ISBN   978-1-4169-1171-5;   1-4169-1171-5; 978-1-4169-1172-2 (pa); 1-4169-1172-3 (pa)

LC 2006-34870

Haddix, Margaret Peterson, 1964-—*Continued*

In 1927, at the urging of twenty-one-year-old Harriet, Mrs. Livingston reluctantly recalls her experiences at the Triangle Shirtwaist factory, including miserable working conditions that led to a strike, then the fire that took the lives of her two best friends, when Harriet, the boss's daughter, was only five years old. Includes historical notes.

"This deftly crafted historical novel unfolds dramatically with an absorbing story and well-drawn characters who readily evoke empathy and compassion." SLJ

Haddon, Mark

The curious incident of the dog in the night-time. Today Show Book Club ed. Doubleday 2003 226p il $24.95 *

Grades: 9 10 11 12   Fic
1. Autism—Fiction 2. Parent-child relationship—Fiction 3. Great Britain—Fiction
ISBN 0-385-51210-4

Despite his overwhelming fear of interacting with people, Christopher, a mathematically-gifted, autistic fifteen-year-old boy, decides to investigate the murder of a neighbor's dog and uncovers secret information about his mother

"Unable to feel emotions himself, his story evokes emotions in readers—heartache and frustration for his well-meaning but clueless parents and deep empathy for the wonderfully honest, funny, and lovable protagonist. Readers will never view the behavior of an autistic person again without more compassion and understanding." SLJ

Haig, Matt, 1975-

The Radleys. Free Press 2010 371p $25

Grades: 11 12 Adult   Fic
1. Family life—Fiction 2. Vampires—Fiction
ISBN 978-1-4391-9401-0; 1-4391-9401-7
                                            LC 2010-04459

Struggling with overwork and parenting angst, English village doctor Peter Radley endeavors to hide his family's vampire nature until their daughter's oddly satisfying act of violence reveals the truth, an event that is complicated by the arrival of a practicing vampire family member.

"Dark humor pervades Haig's . . . entertaining vampire family soap opera. . . . This witty novel offers a refreshing take on an oversaturated genre." Libr J

Halaby, Laila

West of the Jordan; a novel. Beacon Press 2003 220p (Bluestreak) pa $13

Grades: 9 10 11 12   Fic
1. Cousins—Fiction 2. Arab Americans—Fiction 3. Muslim women—Fiction
ISBN 0-8070-8359-3   LC 2002-154924

"In alternating chapters, four female cousins—Mawal, in the West Bank village of Nawara; Hala, in Arizona; and Khadija and Soraya, in California—tell their stories. Their experiences range from the orthodoxy that imbues Mawal's life to the freedoms that her American relatives find both exhilarating and frightening. The author focuses

on the difficulties facing Arab women wherever they live, but especially when trying to navigate the crosscurrents of parental and traditional mores while seeking acceptance and success in a foreign country." SLJ

"Halaby's choice to alternate the narratives of the four young women offers real characterizations to latch onto, and her prose, often lyrical—particularly when the speakers relate other peoples' stories—deepens the complications of history and heritage. Contemplative and lush, this coming-of-age tale resonates with the challenges of cross-cultural life." Publ Wkly

Halam, Ann

Dr. Franklin's island. Wendy Lamb Bks. 2002 245p hardcover o.p. pa $6.50 *

Grades: 9 10 11 12   Fic
1. Survival after airplane accidents, shipwrecks, etc.—Fiction 2. Genetic engineering—Fiction 3. Science fiction
ISBN 0-385-73008-X; 0-440-23781-5 (pa)
                                            LC 2001-50691

First published 2001 in the United Kingdom

When their plane crashes over the Pacific Ocean, three science students are left stranded on a tropical island and then imprisoned by a doctor who is performing horrifying experiments on humans involving the transfer of animal genes

"This exciting and well-developed book . . . will appeal to fans of horror and adventure. . . . However, the book is not for the squeamish. The description of the dead bodies found in the aftermath of the plane explosion and the physical changes the girls experience during their experiments is gruesomely detailed." SLJ

Snakehead. Wendy Lamb Books 2008 289p il map $16.99; lib bdg $19.99

Grades: 6 7 8 9 10   Fic
1. Classical mythology—Fiction 2. Perseus (Greek mythology)—Fiction 3. Medusa (Greek mythology)—Fiction 4. Gods and goddesses—Fiction
ISBN 978-0-375-84108-8; 978-0-375-94108-5 (lib bdg)   LC 2007-28318

Compelled by his father Zeus to accept the evil king Polydectes's challenge to bring the head of the monstrous Medusa to the Aegean island of Serifos, Perseus, although questioning the gods' interference in human lives, sets out, accompanied by his beloved Andromeda, a princess with her own harsh destiny to fulfill.

"Mythology buffs will appreciate the plethora of classical figures, while periodic references to contemporary culture (e.g., a band of rich, rowdy teens are dubbed the Yacht Club kids) and occasional slang drive the story home for the target audience without sacrificing its heroic dimensions." Publ Wkly

Haldeman, Joe W., 1943-

The forever war; [by] Joe Haldeman. 1st St. Martin's Griffin ed. Thomas Dunne Books 2009 264p pa $14.95 *

Grades: 9 10 11 12 Adult   Fic
1. Space and time—Fiction 2. Science fiction
ISBN 978-0-312-53663-3; 0-312-53663-1
                                            LC 2009-5705

First published 1975

Haldeman, Joe W., 1943-—*Continued*
"A naturalistic description of a war that lasts more than a thousand years, although the main characters age only a few years because of the relativistic effects of faster-than-light space travel. The situation of the soldiers fighting in this kind of war is complicated, however, by their alienation from their own societies by the time-dilation effect, and their growing disillusionment with the war." New Ency of Sci Fic

Hale, Marian
The goodbye season. Henry Holt and Co. 2009 271p $16.99
Grades: 7 8 9 10   **Fic**
   1. Family life—Fiction 2. Household employees—Fiction 3. Mother-daughter relationship—Fiction 4. Bereavement—Fiction 5. Texas—Fiction
   ISBN 978-0-8050-8855-7; 0-8050-8855-5
                 LC 2008-50275
In Canton, Texas, seventeen-year-old Mercy's dreams of a different life than her mother's are postponed by harsh circumstances, including the influenza epidemic of 1918-19, which forces her into doing domestic work for a loving, if troubled, family.
This is a "compelling, tautly written novel." SLJ

Hale, Shannon
Book of a thousand days; illustrations by James Noel Smith. Bloomsbury Children's Books 2007 305p il $17.95 *
Grades: 7 8 9 10   **Fic**
   1. Fantasy fiction 2. Love stories
   ISBN 978-1-59990-051-3; 1-59990-051-3
                 LC 2006-36999
Fifteen-year-old Dashti, sworn to obey her sixteen-year-old mistress, the Lady Saren, shares Saren's years of punishment locked in a tower, then brings her safely to the lands of her true love, where both must hide who they are as they work as kitchen maids.
This is a "captivating fantasy filled with romance, magic, and strong female characters." Booklist

Haley, Alex, 1921-1992
Mama Flora's family. Delta 1999 462p pa $23
Grades: 9 10 11 12   **Fic**
   1. African Americans—Fiction
   ISBN 0-440-61409-0
   First published 1998 by Scribner
In this multigenerational family saga, the "lives of Mama Flora and her family provide a whirlwind survey of the 20th-century black experience. As a young woman in a small Tennessee town, Flora bears a son and sees his father killed at the hands of white racists. She realizes that education is the only way out of poverty. Soon, her daughter becomes a social worker while her son dabbles in communism and enlists to fight in World War II. As Flora lays dying, she can look back on her family and their accomplishments with pride." Libr J

Hall, Barbara, 1960-
Tempo change. Delacorte Press 2009 247p $16.99; lib bdg $19.99
Grades: 8 9 10 11 12   **Fic**
   1. Coachella Valley Music & Arts Festival—Fiction 2. Bands (Music)—Fiction 3. Father-daughter relationship—Fiction 4. Single parent family—Fiction 5. Fame—Fiction 6. California—Fiction
   ISBN 978-0-385-73607-7; 0-385-73607-X; 978-0-385-90585-5 (lib bdg); 0-385-90585-8 (lib bdg)
                 LC 2008-30968
Sixteen-year-old Blanche forms a band that wins a spot at Coachella, a southern California music festival, where she hopes to reconnect with her father, a famous but reclusive musician who left when she was six years old.
"Hall's cast of characters is quirky . . . [and] Blanche's witty, sensitive narration will have readers rooting for her throughout." Booklist

Hallaway, Tate
Almost to die for; a vampire princess novel. New American Library 2010 241p pa $9.99
Grades: 11 12 Adult   **Fic**
   1. Vampires—Fiction 2. Witches—Fiction 3. Horror fiction
   ISBN 978-0-451-23057-7   LC 2010-10401
"Anastasija Ramses Parker is a modern-day witch's daughter, fond of wearing 'black with black and black' but hopelessly unable to perform actual magic. When she flunks her coven's initiation ceremony, she learns that her father is a vampire—and not just any vampire, but a vampire leader, which makes her 'some kind of vampire princess.' Possibly more important, Ana's best friend, Bea, has a crush on vampire hunter/punk rocker Nikolai, who's torn between kissing and killing Ana, who thinks he's cute but wants to stay loyal to Bea. Ana's narration is pitch-perfect and totally teen: half calculated attitude, half wistful empathy." Publ Wkly

Halpern, Julie, 1975-
Get well soon. Feiwel & Friends 2007 193p $16.95; pa $8.99
Grades: 7 8 9 10   **Fic**
   1. Mental illness—Fiction 2. Psychiatric hospitals—Fiction
   ISBN 0-312-36795-3; 978-0-312-36795-4; 0-312-58148-3 (pa); 978-0-312-58148-0 (pa)
                 LC 2006-32358
When her parents confine her to a mental hospital, Anna, an overweight teenage girl who suffers from panic attacks, describes her experiences in a series of letters to a friend.
"Halpern creates a narrative that reflects the changes in Anna with each passing day that includes self-reflection and a good dose of humor." Voice Youth Advocates

Halpern, Julie, 1975-—*Continued*

Into the wild nerd yonder. Feiwel and Friends 2009 247p $16.99

Grades: 9 10 11 12   **Fic**

1. Siblings—Fiction 2. Popularity—Fiction 3. Friendship—Fiction 4. Dungeons & dragons (Game)—Fiction 5. School stories

ISBN 978-0-312-38252-0; 0-312-38252-9

LC 2008-34751

When high school sophomore Jessie's long-term best friend transforms herself into a punk and goes after Jessie's would-be boyfriend, Jessie decides to visit "the wild nerd yonder" and seek true friends among classmates who play Dungeons and Dragons.

"Descriptions of high school cliques . . . are hilarious and believable. . . . This novel is particularly strong in showing how teen friendships evolve and sometimes die away, and how adolescents redefine themselves." SLJ

Halpin, Brendan

Donorboy; a novel. Villard 2004 209p pa $12.95

Grades: 9 10 11 12   **Fic**

1. Father-daughter relationship—Fiction 2. Orphans—Fiction

ISBN 1-4000-6277-2   LC 2004-43090

"14-year-old Rosalind's lesbian moms have been killed in a motor accident, and she is placed in the custody of Sean, 35, her sperm-donor dad. He knew her mothers, saw her, and loved her at birth, but she hasn't known him until now, when suddenly they are a family. . . . Told in a mix of personal narratives, including Rosalind and Sean's desperate e-mails to friends and to each other, her grief journal, instant messages, and taped disciplinary hearings with the school bureaucrats, the novel presents contemporary voices that are funny, tender, defiant, and immediate." Booklist

Forever changes. Farrar, Straus & Giroux 2008 181p $16.95

Grades: 7 8 9 10 11 12   **Fic**

1. Death—Fiction 2. Mathematics—Fiction 3. School stories 4. Massachusetts—Fiction

ISBN 978-0-374-32436-0; 0-374-32436-0

LC 2007-26494

Although encouraged to apply to colleges, Brianna Pelletier, a mathematically-gifted high school senior with cystic fibrosis, dwells on her mortality and the unfairness of life.

"Teens looking for a novel with a sad ending and a touch of bibliotherapy will not be disappointed by Brianna's story." Voice Youth Advocates

How ya like me now. Farrar, Straus & Giroux 2007 201p $16

Grades: 7 8 9 10 11 12   **Fic**

1. School stories 2. Boston (Mass.)—Fiction 3. Cousins—Fiction 4. Race relations—Fiction

ISBN 0-374-33495-1; 978-0-374-33495-6

LC 2006-40989

After his father dies and his mother goes into rehab, Eddie moves from the suburbs into his cousin's Boston loft, where he gradually adjusts to being one of the few white kids in a progressive private school, and learns

how to feel like a normal teenager.

"An engaging YA slice-of-life story, capped by an upbeat resolution and endowed with both laughter and healing." Booklist

Hambly, Barbara

A free man of color. Bantam Bks. 1997 311p hardcover o.p. pa $5.99

Grades: 11 12 Adult   **Fic**

1. Race relations—Fiction 2. Homicide—Fiction 3. Creoles—Fiction

ISBN 0-553-10258-3; 0-553-57526-0 (pa)

LC 96-44942

A romantic suspense novel set in 19th century New Orleans. "Benjamin January, a free Creole with dark brown skin, has returned to this society after living in Paris for more than a decade. He is trained as a surgeon, but in Louisiana, he makes his living playing the piano. Soon he is the main suspect in the death of a wealthy man's young mistress, found murdered at a ball. January spends the rest of the book gathering evidence in his defense." Libr J

"A few suspenseful moments not-withstanding, this isn't an action-packed or suspenseful whodunit. Rather, it's a richly detailed, telling portrait of an intricately structured racial hierarchy." Booklist

Hamill, Pete

Snow in August; a novel. Little, Brown 1997 327p hardcover o.p. pa $14

Grades: 11 12 Adult   **Fic**

1. Jews—Fiction 2. Prejudices—Fiction 3. Irish Americans—Fiction 4. Brooklyn (New York, N.Y.)—Fiction

ISBN 0-316-34094-4; 0-446-67525-3 (pa)

LC 96-36043

"In Brooklyn in 1947, Michael Devlin, an 11-year-old Irish kid who spends his days reading *Captain Marvel* and anticipating the arrival of Jackie Robinson, makes the acquaintance of a recently emigrated Orthodox rabbi. In exchange for lessons in English and baseball, Rabbi Hirsch teaches him Yiddish and tells him of Jewish life in old Prague and of the mysteries of the Kabbalah. Anti-Semitism soon rears its head in the form of a gang of young Irish toughs out to rule the neighborhood." Libr J

"Mr. Hamill is not a subtle writer, but his gift for sensual description and his tabloid muscularity . . . fit this page turner of a fable." N Y Times Book Rev

Hamilton, K. R., 1958-

Tyger tyger; a goblin wars book; by Kersten Hamilton. Clarion Books 2010 308p $17

Grades: 7 8 9 10   **Fic**

1. Goblins—Fiction 2. Magic—Fiction 3. Mentally handicapped children—Fiction 4. Irish Americans—Fiction 5. Fantasy fiction

ISBN 978-0-547-33008-2; 0-547-33008-1

LC 2010-01337

Soon after the mysterious and alluring Finn arrives at her family's home, sixteen-year-old Teagan Wylltson and her disabled brother are drawn into the battle Finn's family has fought since the thirteenth century, when Fionn

Hamilton, K. R., 1958-—*Continued*
MacCumhaill angered the goblin king.

"Laced with humor, packed with surprises and driven by suspense, the plot grabs readers from the start using the stylistic tactics of the best fantasy writing. Major characters are beautifully drawn, and many of the secondary characters are equally distinct." Kirkus

Han, Jenny
The summer I turned pretty. Simon & Schuster Books for Young Readers 2009 276p $16.99
Grades: 7 8 9 10   Fic
  1. Beaches—Fiction   2. Summer—Fiction
  3. Vacations—Fiction 4. Friendship—Fiction
  ISBN 978-1-4169-6823-8; 1-4169-6823-7
                                          LC 2008-27070
Belly spends the summer she turns sixteen at the beach just like every other summer of her life, but this time things are very different.

"Romantic and heartbreakingly real. . . . The novel perfectly blends romance, family drama, and a coming-of-age tale, one that is substantially deeper than most." SLJ

Other titles in this series are:
It's not summer without you (2010)
We'll always have summer (2011)

Hand, Elizabeth, 1957-
Illyria; a novel. Viking 2010 135p $15.99
Grades: 10 11 12   Fic
  1. Shakespeare, William, 1564-1616—Fiction
  2. Acting—Fiction 3. Theater—Fiction 4. Incest—Fiction 5. Cousins—Fiction
  ISBN 978-0-670-01212-1; 0-670-01212-2
First published 2007 in the United Kingdom
Teenage cousins Madeleine and Rogan, who share twin souls and a sexual relationship, are cast in a school production of Twelfth Night that forces them to confront their respective strengths and future prospects.

"The edgy subject matter, explicit but not gratuitous, relegates this novel to mature readers, but it's beautifully written, rich in theatrical detail and intensely realized characters." Publ Wkly

Harazin, S. A.
Blood brothers. Delacorte Press 2007 224p $15.99; lib bdg $18.99
Grades: 8 9 10 11 12   Fic
  1. Drug abuse—Fiction 2. Friendship—Fiction
  3. Georgia—Fiction
  ISBN 978-0-385-73364-9; 978-0-385-90379-0 (lib bdg)   LC 2006-19637
With his best friend on life-support after taking drugs at a party, seventeen-year-old Clay, a medical technician, recalls their long friendship, future plans, and recent disagreement, and tries to figure out who is responsible for the accidental overdose.

"Settings and characters are extremely well drawn. The compelling serious story line is punctuated by smatters of Clay's self-deprecating humor." Voice Youth Advocates

Hardinge, Frances
The lost conspiracy. Harper 2009 568p $16.99; lib bdg $17.89 *
Grades: 6 7 8 9 10   Fic
  1. Sisters—Fiction 2. Fantasy fiction
  ISBN 978-0-06-088041-5;   0-06-088041-4;
  978-0-06-088042-2 (lib bdg); 0-06-088042-2 (lib bdg)
                                          LC 2008-45380
Published in the United Kingdom with title: Gullstruck Island

When a lie is exposed and their tribe turns against them, Hathin must find a way to save her sister Arilou—once considered the tribe's oracle—and herself.

"A deeply imaginative story, with nuanced characters, intricate plotting, and an amazingly original setting. . . . A perfectly pitched, hopeful ending caps off this standout adventure." Booklist

Hardy, Thomas, 1840-1928
The return of the native. Knopf 1992 xxxix, 497p map $22
Grades: 11 12 Adult   Fic
  1. Great Britain—Fiction
  ISBN 0-679-41730-3   LC 92-52901
Also available from other publishers
"Everyman's library"
First published 1878
"The novel is set on Egdon Heath, a barren moor in the fictional Wessex in southwestern England. The native of the title is Clym Yeobright, who has returned to the area to become a schoolmaster after a successful but, in his opinion, a shallow career as a jeweler in Paris. He and his cousin Thomasin exemplify the traditional way of life, while Thomasin's husband, Damon Wildeve, and Clym's wife, Eustacia Vye, long for the excitement of city life. Disappointed that Clym is content to remain on the heath, Eustacia, willful and passionate, rekindles her affair with the reckless Damon. After a series of coincidences Eustacia comes to believe that she is responsible for the death of Clym's mother. Convinced that fate has doomed her to cause others pain, Eustacia flees and is drowned (by accident or intent). Damon drowns trying to save her." Merriam-Webster's Ency of Lit

Tess of the D'Urbervilles; with an introduction by Patricia Ingham. Knopf 1991 xlviii, 472p map $22
Grades: 11 12 Adult   Fic
  1. Great Britain—Fiction
  ISBN 0-679-40586-0   LC 91-52998
Also available from other publishers
"Everyman's library"
First published in complete form 1891
"The tragic history of a woman betrayed. . . . Tess the author contends, is sinned against, but not a sinner; her tragedy is the work of tyrannical circumstances and of the evil deeds of others in the past and the present, and more particularly of two men's baseness, the seducer, and the well-meaning intellectual who married her. . . . The pastoral surroundings, the varying aspects of field, river, sky, serve to deepen the pathos of each stage in the heroine's calamities, or to add beauty and dignity to her tragic personality." Baker. Guide to the Best Fic

Harland, Richard, 1947-
Worldshaker. Simon & Schuster Books for Young Readers 2010 388p $16.99
Grades: 6 7 8 9 10   **Fic**
1. Fantasy fiction 2. Social classes—Fiction
ISBN 978-1-4169-9552-4; 1-4169-9552-8
                                        LC 2009-16924
Sixteen-year-old Col Porpentine is being groomed as the next Commander of Worldshaker, a juggernaut where elite families live on the upper decks while the Filthies toil below, but when he meets Riff, a Filthy girl on the run, he discovers how ignorant he is of his home and its residents.
"Harland's steampunk alternate history is filled with oppression, class struggle, and war, showing their devastation on a personal level through Col's privileged eyes. . . . The writing is sharp and the story fast-paced, demonstrating that, despite his elite status, Col may be just as trapped as any Filthy." Publ Wkly

Harmon, Michael B., 1969-
Brutal; [by] Michael Harmon. Alfred A. Knopf 2009 229p $16.99; lib bdg $19.99
Grades: 9 10 11 12   **Fic**
1. Bullies—Fiction 2. Father-daughter relationship—Fiction 3. Moving—Fiction 4. California—Fiction
ISBN 978-0-375-84099-9; 0-375-84099-0; 978-0-375-94099-6 (lib bdg); 0-375-94099-5 (lib bdg)
                                        LC 2008-4718
Forced to leave Los Angeles for life in a quiet California wine town with a father she has never known, rebellious sixteen-year-old Poe Holly rails against a high school system that allows elite students special privileges and tolerates bullying of those who are different.
"Harmon's dialogue is crystal clear and authentic, his youth characters intelligent, and his adult characters finely drawn." Booklist

The last exit to normal. Alfred A. Knopf 2008 275p $15.99; lib bdg $18.99 *
Grades: 9 10 11 12   **Fic**
1. Father-son relationship—Fiction 2. Homosexuality—Fiction 3. Child abuse—Fiction 4. Montana—Fiction
ISBN 978-0-375-84098-2; 0-375-84098-2; 978-0-375-94098-9 (lib bdg); 0-375-94098-7 (lib bdg)
                                        LC 2007-10107
Yanked out of his city life and plunked down into a small Montana town with his father and his father's boyfriend, seventeen-year-old Ben, angry and resentful about the changed circumstances of his life, begins to notice that something is not quite right with the little boy next door and determines to do something about it.
The author "unwinds a complex, emotionally charged story of a boy trying to fix not only those who are broken around him, but himself as well." Libr Media Connect

Harper, Suzanne
The Juliet club. Greenwillow Books 2008 402p $17.99; lib bdg $18.89
Grades: 8 9 10 11 12   **Fic**
1. Shakespeare, William, 1564-1616—Fiction 2. Italy—Fiction 3. Letters—Fiction
ISBN 978-0-06-136691-8; 0-06-136691-9; 978-0-06-136692-5 (lib bdg); 0-06-136692-7 (lib bdg)
                                        LC 2007-41315
When high school junior Kate wins an essay contest that sends her to Verona, Italy, to study Shakespeare's 'Romeo and Juliet' over the summer, she meets both American and Italian students and learns not just about Shakespeare, but also about star-crossed lovers—and herself.
"An amalgam of familiar Shakespearean plot elements, character names, and devices make up this delightful, light, and romantic read. . . . The chapter titles are each given act and scene designations to keep the structure of a play. Following the formula of a Shakespearean comedy, the novel ends with a grand ball where misunderstandings are resolved and couples are revealed in a magical evening." Voice Youth Advocates

Harrington, Kim, 1974-
Clarity. Point 2011 246p $16.99
Grades: 8 9 10 11 12   **Fic**
1. Homicide—Fiction 2. Extrasensory perception—Fiction 3. Siblings—Fiction 4. Cape Cod (Mass.)—Fiction 5. Mystery fiction
ISBN 978-0-545-23050-6; 0-545-23050-0
                                        LC 2010-09402
Sixteen-year-old Clare Fern, a member of a family of psychics, helps the mayor and a skeptical detective solve a murder in a Cape Cod town during the height of tourist season—with her brother a prime suspect.
"Harrington's well-developed characters and tight plot are simultaneously charming, realistically complex, and intriguing." Publ Wkly
Followed by: Perception (2012)

Harris, Robert, 1957-
Pompeii; a novel. Random House 2003 278p map hardcover o.p. pa $13.95
Grades: 11 12 Adult   **Fic**
1. Rome—History—Fiction 2. Volcanoes—Fiction 3. Adventure fiction
ISBN 0-679-42889-5; 0-8129-7461-1 (pa)
                                        LC 2003-58446
"An upstanding Roman engineer rushes to repair an aqueduct in the shadow of Mount Vesuvius, which, in A.D. 79, is getting ready to blow its top. . . . Lively writing, convincing but economical period details and plenty of intrigue keep the pace quick." Publ Wkly

Harrison, Cora

I was Jane Austen's best friend; illustrated by Susan Hellard. Delacorte Press 2010 342p il $17.99; lib bdg $20.99

Grades: 7 8 9 10   Fic
    1. Austen, Jane, 1775-1817—Fiction 2. Cousins—Fiction 3. Friendship—Fiction 4. Diaries—Fiction 5. Great Britain—History—1714-1837—Fiction
    ISBN   978-0-385-73940-5;   0-385-73940-0; 978-0-385-90787-3 (lib bdg); 0-385-90787-7 (lib bdg)
                                            LC 2010-15309
In a series of journal entries, Jenny Cooper describes her stay with cousin Jane Austen in the 1790s, and her entrance into Jane's world of beautiful dresses, dances, secrets, gossip, and romance.

"This is a lovely, simple coming-of-age story with a strong historical setting. . . . The situations and locations are unmistakable and will be pleasingly familiar to readers of Austen's works." Voice of Youth Advocates

Hartinger, Brent, 1964-

Geography Club. HarperTempest 2003 226p hardcover o.p. pa $8.99

Grades: 9 10 11 12   Fic
    1. Homosexuality—Fiction 2. Clubs—Fiction 3. School stories
    ISBN 0-06-001221-8; 0-06-001223-4 (pa)
                                            LC 2001-51736
A group of gay and lesbian teenagers finds mutual support when they form the "Geography Club" at their high school.

"Hartinger grasps the melodrama and teen angst of high school well. . . . Frank language and the intimation of sexual activity might put off some readers." Voice Youth Advocates
 Other titles in this series are:
The Order of the Poison Oak (2005)
Split screen (2007)

Hartnett, Sonya, 1968-

Butterfly. Candlewick Press 2010 232p $16.99
Grades: 7 8 9 10 11 12   Fic
    1. Family life—Fiction 2. Australia—Fiction
    ISBN 978-0-7636-4760-5; 0-7636-4760-8
                                            LC 2009-46549
In 1980s Australia, nearly fourteen-year-old Ariella "Plum" Coyle fears the disapproval of her friends, feels inferior to her older brothers, and hates her awkward, adolescent body but when her glamorous neighbor befriends her, Plum starts to become what she wants to be—until she discovers her neighbor's ulterior motive.

"The deliberate pacing, insight into teen angst, and masterful word choice make this a captivating read to savor." SLJ

The ghost's child. Candlewick Press 2008 176p $16.99 *
Grades: 8 9 10 11 12   Fic
    1. Voyages and travels—Fiction 2. Ghost stories
    ISBN 978-0-7636-3964-8; 0-7636-3964-8
                                            LC 2008-30817
When a mysterious child appears in her living room one day, the elderly Maddy tells him the story of her

love for the wild and free-spirited Feather, who tried but failed to live a conventional life with her, and her search for him on a fantastical voyage across the seas.

"Those who enjoy fables or magical realism will be spellbound by this redemptive story of a search for love, love lost and love (of a sort) found again. . . . [Written in] exquisite prose." Publ Wkly

Surrender. Candlewick Press 2006 248p $16.99; pa $7.99 *
Grades: 9 10 11 12   Fic
    1. Family life—Fiction 2. Brothers—Fiction 3. Dogs—Fiction
    ISBN 0-7636-2768-2; 07636-3423-9 (pa)
                                            LC 2005-54259
As he is dying, a twenty-year-old man known as Gabriel recounts his troubled childhood and his strange relationship with a dangerous counterpart named Finnigan.

"From the gripping cover showing a raging inferno to the blood-chilling revelation of the final chapter, this page-turner is a blistering yet dense psychological thriller." Voice Youth Advocates

Thursday's child. Candlewick Press 2002 261p hardcover o.p. pa $7.99
Grades: 7 8 9 10   Fic
    1. Poverty—Fiction 2. Family life—Fiction 3. Farm life—Fiction 4. Australia—Fiction
    ISBN 0-7636-1620-6; 0-7636-2203-6 (pa)
                                            LC 2001-25223
Harper Flute recounts her Australian farm family's poverty during the Depression, her father's cowardice, and her younger brother Tin's obsession for digging tunnels and living underground

"This coming-of-age story with allegorical overtones will burrow into young people's deepest hopes and fears, shining light in the darkest inner rooms." Booklist

Haruf, Kent, 1943-

Plainsong. Knopf 1999 301p $27.50
Grades: 11 12 Adult   Fic
    1. Teachers—Fiction 2. Family life—Fiction 3. Colorado—Fiction
    ISBN 0-375-40618-2   LC 99-15606
"Set in the plains of Colorado, east of Denver, the novel comprises several story lines that flow into one. Tom Guthrie, a high school history teacher, is having problems with his wife and with an unruly student at school—problems that affect his young sons, Ike and Bob, as well. Meanwhile, the pregnant Victoria Roubideaux has been abandoned by her family. With the assistance of another teacher, Maggie Jones, she finds refuge with the McPheron brothers—who seem to know more about cows than people." Libr J

"From simple strands of language and cuttings of talk, from the look of the high Colorado plains east of Denver almost to the place where Nebraska and Kansas meet, Haruf has made a novel so foursquare, so delicate and lovely, that it has the power to exalt the reader." N Y Times Book Rev
 Another available title about the residents of Holt, Colorado is:
Eventide (2004)

Harvey, Alyxandra

Hearts at stake. Walker & Co. 2010 248p (The Drake chronicles) $16.99; pa $9.99

Grades: 8 9 10 11 12   **Fic**

1. Vampires—Fiction 2. Siblings—Fiction 3. Friendship—Fiction

ISBN 978-0-8027-9840-4; 0-8027-9840-3; 978-0-8027-2074-0 (pa); 0-8027-2074-9 (pa)

    LC 2009-23156

As her momentous sixteenth birthday approaches, Solange Drake, the only born female vampire in 900 years, is protected by her large family of brothers and her human best friend Lucy from increasingly persistent attempts on her life by the powerful vampire queen and her followers.

"Witty, sly, and never disappointing." Booklist

Other titles in this series are:

Blood feud (2010)

Out for blood (2011)

Harvey, Sarah N., 1950-

Plastic. Orca Book Publishers 2010 120p (Orca soundings) pa $9.95

Grades: 7 8 9 10   **Fic**

1. Plastic surgery—Fiction 2. Friendship—Fiction

ISBN 978-1-55469-252-1; 1-55469-252-0

Trying to save his best friend from the horrors of plastic surgery, Jack ends up on the front line of a protest of unscrupulous surgeons.

"This novel is characteristically fast paced and of high interest. Information about both the pros and the cons of plastic surgery is included without detracting from the plot. *Plastic* does a good job of exploring an important societal issue while telling a timely tale." SLJ

Hautman, Pete, 1952-

All-in. Simon & Schuster Books for Young Readers 2007 181p hardcover o.p. pa $5.99

Grades: 7 8 9 10   **Fic**

1. Poker—Fiction 2. Gambling—Fiction 3. Las Vegas (Nev.)—Fiction

ISBN 978-1-4169-1325-2; 1-4169-1325-4; 978-1-4169-1326-9 (pa); 1-4169-1326-9 (pa)

    LC 2006-23871

Sequel to No limit (2005)

Having won thousands of dollars playing high-stakes poker in Las Vegas, seventeen-year-old Denn Doyle hits a losing streak after falling in love with a young casino card dealer named Cattie Hart.

"Skillfully using the multiple-voice approach, Hautman brings to life the intricacies of poker, crafting a thrilling story of loss, good versus evil, and redemption." Voice Youth Advocates

Blank confession. Simon & Schuster Books for Young Readers 2010 170p $16.99

Grades: 7 8 9 10   **Fic**

1. Drug traffic—Fiction 2. Bullies—Fiction 3. School stories

ISBN 978-1-4169-1327-6; 1-4169-1327-0

    LC 2009-50169

A new and enigmatic student named Shayne appears at high school one day, befriends the smallest boy in the school, and takes on a notorious drug dealer before turning himself in to the police for killing someone.

"Masterfully written with simple prose, solid dialogue and memorable characters, the tale will grip readers from the start and keep the reading in one big gulp, in the hope of seeing behind Shayne's mask. A sure hit with teen readers." Kirkus

Godless. Simon & Schuster Books for Young Readers 2004 208p $15.95; pa $8.99 *

Grades: 7 8 9 10   **Fic**

1. Religion—Fiction

ISBN 0-689-86278-4; 1-4169-0816-1 (pa)

    LC 2003-10468

When sixteen-year-old Jason Bock and his friends create their own religion to worship the town's water tower, what started out as a joke begins to take on a power of its own.

"The witty text and provocative subject will make this a supremely enjoyable discussion-starter as well as pleasurable read." Bull Cent Child Books

Invisible. Simon & Schuster Books for Young Readers 2005 149p $15.95; pa $7.99 *

Grades: 7 8 9 10   **Fic**

1. Mental illness—Fiction 2. Friendship—Fiction

ISBN 0-689-86800-6; 0-689-86903-7 (pa)

    LC 2004-2484

Doug and Andy are unlikely best friends—one a loner obsessed by his model trains, the other a popular student involved in football and theater—who grew up together and share a bond that nothing can sever

"With its excellent plot development and unforgettable, heartbreaking protagonist, this is a compelling novel of mental illness." SLJ

Hawkins, Rachel, 1979-

Hex Hall. Disney/Hyperion Books 2010 323p $16.99

Grades: 7 8 9 10   **Fic**

1. Witches—Fiction 2. Supernatural—Fiction 3. School stories

ISBN 978-1-4231-2130-5; 1-4231-2130-9

"Sixteen-year-old Sophie Mercer, whose absentee father is a warlock, discovered both her heritage and her powers at age 13. While at her school prom, Sophie happens upon a miserable girl sobbing in the bathroom and tries to perform a love spell to help her out. It misfires, and Sophie finds herself at Hecate (aka Hex) Hall, a boarding school for delinquent Prodigium (witches, warlocks, faeries, shape-shifters, and the occasional vampire). What makes this fast-paced romp work is Hawkins' wry humor and sharp eye for teen dynamics." Booklist

Followed by: Demonglass (2011)

Hawthorne, Nathaniel, 1804-1864

The scarlet letter; with an introduction by Alfred Kazin. Knopf 1992 xxvii, 273p $18 *

Grades: 11 12 Adult   **Fic**

1. Puritans—Fiction 2. New England—Fiction

ISBN 0-679-41731-1   LC 92-52902

Also available other editions

"Everyman's library"

Hawthorne, Nathaniel, 1804-1864—*Continued*

"Set in 17th-century Salem, the novel is built around three scaffold scenes, which occur at the beginning, the middle, and the end. The story opens with the public condemnation of Hester Prynne, and the exhortation that she confess the name of the father of Pearl, her illegitimate child. Hester's husband, an old and scholarly physician, just arrived from England, assumes the name of Roger Chillingworth in order to seek out Hester's lover and revenge himself upon him. He attaches himself as physician to a respected and seemingly holy minister, Arthur Dimmesdale, suspecting that he is the father of the child. *The Scarlet Letter* traces the effect of the actual and symbolic sin on all the characters." Benet's Reader's Ency of Am Lit

Haycak, Cara

Living on impulse. Dutton Children's Books 2009 292p $16.99

Grades: 7 8 9 10   Fic
1. Mother-daughter relationship—Fiction
2. Research—Fiction 3. Friendship—Fiction
4. Shoplifting—Fiction
ISBN 978-0-525-42137-5; 0-525-42137-8
                                            LC 2008-34210

Getting caught shoplifting leads fifteen-year-old Mia to a greater understanding of herself, sympathy for her unmarried mother, and a job in a college laboratory which not only pleases her ailing scientist grandfather, but lets her glimpse a possible future brighter than any she had imagined.

"Developed with realism, humor and insight in a colloquial third-person voice, Mia's flawed character proves credible. Her transformation story brims with loss and forgiveness as she painfully discovers 'change can happen really fast for people' when they start making good choices instead of bad." Kirkus

Headley, Justina Chen, 1968-

North of beautiful. Little, Brown 2009 373p $16.99 *

Grades: 7 8 9 10 11 12   Fic
1. Aesthetics—Fiction
ISBN 978-0-316-02505-8; 0-316-02505-4
                                            LC 2008-09260

Headley's "finely crafted novel traces a teen's uncharted quest to find beauty. Two things block Terra's happiness: a port-wine stain on her face and her verbally abusive father. . . . A car accident brings her together with Jacob, an Asian-born adoptee with unconventional ideas. . . . The author confidently addresses very large, slippery questions about the meaning of art, travel, love and of course, beauty." Publ Wkly

Healey, Karen, 1981-

Guardian of the dead. Little, Brown 2010 345p $17.99

Grades: 9 10 11 12   Fic
1. Magic—Fiction 2. Fairies—Fiction 3. Maoris—Fiction 4. School stories 5. New Zealand—Fiction
ISBN 978-0-316-04430-1   LC 2009-17949

Eighteen-year-old New Zealand boarding school student Ellie Spencer must use her rusty tae kwon do skills and new-found magic to try to stop a fairy-like race of creatures from Maori myth and legend that is plotting to kill millions of humans in order to regain their lost immortality.

"Fast-paced adventure and an unfamiliar, frightening enemy set a new scene for teen urban fantasy." Kirkus

Hearn, Julie, 1958-

Ivy; a novel. Atheneum Books for Young Readers 2008 355p $17.99; pa $9.99 *

Grades: 8 9 10 11 12   Fic
1. Artists—Fiction 2. Drug abuse—Fiction
3. Criminals—Fiction 4. London (England)—Fiction
5. Great Britain—History—19th century—Fiction
ISBN 978-1-4169-2506-4; 1-4169-2506-6; 978-1-4169-2507-1 (pa); 1-4169-2507-4 (pa)
                                            LC 2007-045463

"ginee seo books"

In mid-nineteenth-century London, young, mistreated, and destitute Ivy, whose main asset is her beautiful red hair, comes to the attention of an aspiring painter of the pre-Raphaelite school of artists who, with the connivance of Ivy's unsavory family, is determined to make her his model and muse.

"Quirky characters, darkly humorous situations, and quick action make this enjoyable historical fiction." SLJ

The minister's daughter. Atheneum Books for Young Readers 2005 263p hardcover o.p. pa $7.99

Grades: 7 8 9 10   Fic
1. Witchcraft—Fiction 2. Supernatural—Fiction
3. Great Britain—History—1642-1660, Civil War and Commonwealth—Fiction 4. Salem (Mass.)—Fiction
ISBN 0-689-87690-4; 0-689-87691-2 (pa)
                                            LC 2004-18324

Published in United Kingdom with title: The Merrybegot

In 1645 in England, the daughters of the town minister successfully accuse a local healer and her granddaughter of witchcraft to conceal an out-of-wedlock pregnancy, but years later during the 1692 Salem trials their lie has unexpected repercussions.

"With its thought-provoking perceptions about human nature, magic and persecution, this tale will surely cast a spell over readers." Publ Wkly

Hearn, Lian

Across the nightingale floor. Riverhead Bks. 2002 287p (Tales of the Otori) hardcover o.p. pa $15

Grades: 11 12 Adult   Fic
1. Japan—Fiction
ISBN 1-57322-225-9; 1-57322-332-8 (pa)
                                            LC 2002-22339

"In an imaginary country reminiscent of feudal Japan, Takeo is adopted by Lord Shigeru after his village is wiped out, and he learns that the lord may have acted out of more than compassion as he himself is heir to powerful, mysterious abilities. A riveting start to an imaginative trilogy." Booklist

Other available titles in this series are:
Grass for his pillow (2003)
Brilliance of the moon (2004)

Heath, Jack, 1986-
The Lab. Scholastic Press 2008 311p $17.99
Grades: 7 8 9 10 **Fic**
1. Spies—Fiction 2. Genetic engineering—Fiction
3. Adventure fiction 4. Science fiction
ISBN 978-0-545-06860-4; 0-545-06860-6
"A gritty dystopic world exists under the iron rule of
the mega-corporation Chao-Sonic, with only a few vigilante groups around to act as resistance. Six of Hearts is
easily the best agent on one such group, the Deck, and
he is fiercely dedicated to justice, using his extensive genetic modifications to his advantage. . . . The compelling and memorable protagonist stands out even against
the intricately described and disturbing city whose vivid-
ness makes the place's questionable fate a suspenseful issue in its own right." Bull Cent Child Books
Followed by: Remote control (2010)

Hedges, Peter
What's eating Gilbert Grape. Washington Square
Press 1999 319p pa $14
Grades: 11 12 Adult **Fic**
1. City and town life—Fiction 2. Family life—Fiction
ISBN 978-0-671-03854-0; 0-671-03854-0
On cover: Featuring a WSP reading group guide
Gilbert Grape "is twenty-four and lives in Endora,
Iowa—population 1,091—a place where little worth mentioning ever happens and nothing that does happen is
ever forgotten. He has a high school education, a future-
less job, an older sister who should long since have
outgrown Elvis worship, a hoggish mother, a retarded
brother, and a kid sister who is the very model of an obnoxious adolescent." Atlantic

Heinlein, Robert A. (Robert Anson), 1907-1988
The moon is a harsh mistress. Orb 1997 382p
il pa $14.95 *
Grades: 11 12 Adult **Fic**
1. Science fiction
ISBN 0-312-86355-1
"A Tom Doherty Associates Book"
First published 1966 by Putnam
"Colonists of the Moon declare independence from
Earth, and contrive to win the ensuing battle with the aid
of a sentient computer. Action-adventure with some ex-
ploration of new possibilities in social organization and
fierce assertion of the motto 'There Ain't No Such Thing
as a Free Lunch.'" Anatomy of Wonder 4

Stranger in a strange land. Putnam 1961 408p
pa $16.95 hardcover o.p.
Grades: 11 12 Adult **Fic**
1. Science fiction
ISBN 0-441-78838-6 (pa)
"The hero is a human born of space travelers from
earth and raised by Martians. He is brought to the totalitarian post-World War III world that is in many ways
depicted as a satire of the U.S. in the 1960s, marked by
repressiveness in sexual morality and religion. The plot,
which tells how the heroic stranger creates a Utopian society in which people preserve their individuality but
share a brotherhood of community, made Heinlein and
his novel cult objects for young people dedicated to a
counterculture." Oxford Companion to Am Lit. 5th edition

Heller, Joseph
Catch-22; with an introduction by Malcolm
Bradbury. Knopf 1995 xxxix, 568p $20 *
Grades: 11 12 Adult **Fic**
1. World War, 1939-1945—Fiction
ISBN 0-679-43722-3 LC 94-13984
Also available in paperback from Simon & Schuster
"Everyman's library"
A reissue of the title first published 1961 by Simon &
Schuster
"A comic, satirical, surreal, and apocalyptic novel . . .
which describes the ordeals and exploits of a group of
American airmen based on a small Mediterranean island
during the Italian campaign of the Second World War,
and in particular the reactions of Captain Yossarian, the
protagonist." Oxford Companion to Engl Lit. 5th edition
"By way of some of the funniest dialogue ever, Heller
takes shots at the hypocrisy, meanness, and stupidities of
our society." Shapiro. Fic for Youth. 3d edition
Followed by Closing time (1994)

Hemingway, Amanda
The Greenstone grail. Del Rey/Ballentine Books
2005 360p hardcover o.p. pa $12.95
Grades: 11 12 Adult **Fic**
1. Fantasy fiction
ISBN 0-345-46078-2; 978-0-345-46078-3;
0-345-46079-0 (pa); 978-0-345-46079-0 (pa)
LC 2004-49396
First published 2004 in the United Kingdom
"Nathan Ward is just your typical 11-year-old of supernatural parentage, until he stumbles on a hidden altar
that gives him visions of a green stone cup filled with
blood. Soon he begins dreaming of Eos, a world that
needs the grail for a spell to ward off a terrible plague.
As the dreams become astral excursions, the grail surfaces in Nathan's world, but then is stolen and sent to
Eos, at the wrong time and into the wrong hands. . . .
The book glows with a blend of ancient magic and wide-
eyed wonder that should captivate audiences on both
sides of the Atlantic, especially readers weary of more
conventional Arthurian epics." Publ Wkly
Other titles in the Sangreal Trilogy are:
The poisoned crown (2007)
The sword of straw (2005)

Hemingway, Ernest, 1899-1961
A farewell to arms. Scribner Classics 1997 297p
$27.50
Grades: 11 12 Adult **Fic**
1. World War, 1914-1918—Fiction
ISBN 0-684-83788-9 LC 96-53356
A reissue of the title first published 1929
This novel "deals with a love-affair conducted against
the background of the war in Italy. Its excellence lies in
the delicacy with which it conveys a sense of the imper-
manence of the best human feelings; the unobstrusive
force of its symbolism of mountain and plain; above all
the vast scope of its vision of war—the retreat from Ca-
poretto is one of the great war-sequences of literature."
Penguin Companion to Am Lit

Hemingway, Ernest, 1899-1961—*Continued*

For whom the bell tolls. Scribner 1996 495p
$27.50; pa $14

Grades: 9 10 11 12   **Fic**
1. Spain—History—1936-1939, Civil War—Fiction
ISBN 0-684-83048-5; 0-684-80335-6 (pa)
LC 96-7706

A reissue of the title first published 1940

"This war tale covers tension-ridden days in the life
of Robert Jordan, an American in the Loyalist ranks during the Spanish Civil War. Having accomplished his mission to blow up a bridge with the aid of guerilla bands,
he is injured when his horse falls and crushes his leg. As
enemy troops approach, he is left alone to meet their attack. Jordan's love for Maria, a young girl whom the
Fascists had subjected to every possible indignity, adds
another dimension to a story of courage, dedication—and
treachery." Shapiro. Fic for Youth. 3d edition

The old man and the sea; illustrations by C.F.
Tunnicliffe and Raymond Sheppard. Scribner
Classics 1996 93p il $20 *

Grades: 11 12 Adult   **Fic**
1. Fishing—Fiction
ISBN 0-684-83049-3   LC 96-11419

A reissue of the title first published 1952

"The old fisherman Santiago had only one friend in
the village, the boy Manolin. Everyone else thought he
was unlucky because he had caught no fish in a long
time. At noon on the 85th day of fishing, he hooked a
large fish. He fought with the huge swordfish for three
days and nights before he could harpoon it, but the battle
came to nought when sharks destroyed the fish before
Santiago could get back to the village." Shapiro. Fic for
Youth. 3d edition

The sun also rises. Scribner Classics 1996 222p
$26; pa $15

Grades: 9 10 11 12   **Fic**
1. Paris (France)—Fiction 2. Spain—Fiction
ISBN 0-684-83051-5; 0-7432-9733-4 (pa)
LC 96-11420

A reissue of the title first published 1926

This novel "deals with the lost generation of Americans who had fought in France during World War I and
then had expatriated themselves from the America of
Calvin Coolidge. The story is told by Jake Barnes, rendered impotent by a war wound. Lady Brett Ashley, a
typical representative of the 'lost generation,' is divorc-
ing her husband and diverts herself by her friendship,
which sometimes seems like love, for Barnes. These two
go to Spain with a group that includes Michael Campbell, whom Brett plans to marry; Bill Gorton, a friend of
Jake; a Greek nobleman; and Robert Cohn, an American-
Jewish writer." Reader's Ency. 4th edition

Hemphill, Helen, 1955-

Long gone daddy. Front Street 2006 176p
$16.95

Grades: 8 9 10 11 12   **Fic**
1. Father-son relationship—Fiction 2. Grandfathers—
Fiction 3. Christian life—Fiction 4. Las Vegas
(Nev.)—Fiction
ISBN 1-932425-38-1   LC 2005-25105

Young Harlan Q. Stank gets a taste of life in the fast
lane when he accompanies his preacher father on a road
trip to Las Vegas to bury his grandfather and to fulfill
the terms of the old man's will.

"Many teens will see their own questions about faith,
worship, and independence in Harlan's heart-twisting
feelings." Booklist

Hemphill, Stephanie

Wicked girls; a novel of the Salem witch trials.
Balzer + Bray 2010 408p il $16.99; lib bdg $17.89
*

Grades: 7 8 9 10 11 12   **Fic**
1. Novels in verse 2. Trials—Fiction 3. Witchcraft—
Fiction 4. Salem (Mass.)—Fiction
ISBN 978-0-06-185328-9; 0-06-185328-3;
978-0-06-185329-6 (lib bdg); 0-06-185329-1 (lib bdg)
LC 2010-9593

A fictionalized account, told in verse, of the Salem
witch trials, told from the perspective of three young
women living in Salem in 1692—Mercy Lewis, Margaret
Walcott, and Ann Putnam, Jr.

"Hemphill's raw, intimate poetry probes behind the
abstract facts and creates characters that pulse with complex emotion." Booklist

Includes bibliographical references

Henry, April

Girl, stolen. Henry Holt 2010 213p $18.99

Grades: 7 8 9 10   **Fic**
1. Kidnapping—Fiction 2. Blind—Fiction 3. Theft—
Fiction 4. Father-son relationship—Fiction
ISBN 978-0-8050-9005-5; 0-8050-9005-3
LC 2009-50781

"Christy Ottaviano books"

When an impulsive carjacking turns into a kidnapping,
Griffin, a high school dropout, finds himself more in
sympathy with his wealthy, blind victim, sixteen-year-old
Cheyenne, than with his greedy father.

This is a "can't-put-it-down thriller. . . . Constantly
interesting and suspenseful." Kirkus

Herbert, Frank, 1920-1986

Dune. Ace Bks. 1999 c1965 517p il $27.95 *

Grades: 11 12 Adult   **Fic**
1. Science fiction
ISBN 0-441-00590-X

First published 1965 by Chilton

"Herbert combines several classic elements: a Machia-
vellian world of political intrigue worthy of fourteenth-
century Italy, a huge cast of characters, and a detailed
picture of a culture. Duke Leto Atreides and his family
are coerced into exchanging their rich lands for a barren
planet, Dune, which produces a unique drug. Duke's son,
Paul, becomes the leader of a group that leads the
Fremen of Dune against the enemy. This is a science fiction story with sociological and ecological import." Shapiro. Fic for Youth. 3d edition

Other titles about Dune are:
Chapterhouse: Dune (1985)
Children of Dune (1976)
Dune messiah (1969)
God Emperor of Dune (1981)
Heretics of Dune (1984)

Herbsman, Cheryl
Breathing; [by] Cheryl Renée Herbsman. Viking Childrens Books 2009 265p $16.99; pa $7.99
Grades: 7 8 9 10   **Fic**
  1. Dating (Social customs)—Fiction 2. Asthma—Fiction 3. Siblings—Fiction
  ISBN   978-0-670-01123-0;   0-670-01123-1; 978-0-14-241601-3 (pa); 0-14-241601-0 (pa)
                                    LC 2008-23262
With a new boyfriend, asthma attacks that come when least expected, and a pesky younger brother, fifteen-year-old Savannah's summer vacation takes many unexpected twists and turns
  "Herbsman perfectly nails the angst, innocence, and beauty of falling in love for the first time. . . . This book is sure to reach teen readers in a way that few books can." Voice Youth Advocates

Herlong, Madaline
The great wide sea; [by] M. H. Herlong. Viking Children's Books 2008 283p $16.99; pa $6.99
Grades: 7 8 9 10   **Fic**
  1. Sailing—Fiction 2. Brothers—Fiction 3. Father-son relationship—Fiction 4. Bereavement—Fiction 5. Survival after airplane accidents, shipwrecks, etc.—Fiction
  ISBN   978-0-670-06330-7;   0-670-06330-4; 978-0-14-241670-9 (pa); 0-14-241670-3 (pa)
                                    LC 2008-08384
Still mourning the death of their mother, three brothers go with their father on an extended sailing trip off the Florida Keys and have an adventure at sea
  "Herlong makes the most of the three boys' characters, each exceptionally well developed here, to make this as much a novel of brotherhood as a sea story." Bull Cent Child Books

Hernandez, David, 1964-
No more us for you. HarperTeen 2009 281p $16.99
Grades: 8 9 10 11 12   **Fic**
  1.   Friendship—Fiction   2.   Death—Fiction 3. Bereavement—Fiction   4.   School   stories 5. California—Fiction
  ISBN 978-0-06-117333-2; 0-06-117333-9
                                    LC 2008-19203
Isabel and Carlos, both seventeen, find themselves growing closer after an unexpected accident forces them to confront both the harshness and the beauty of life.
  "Hernandez builds Isabel and Carlos into characters that readers come to root for and love." Voice Youth Advocates

Suckerpunch. HarperTeen 2008 217p $17.89 *
Grades: 8 9 10 11 12   **Fic**
  1. Child abuse—Fiction 2. Brothers—Fiction 3. Father-son relationship—Fiction 4. Drug abuse—Fiction 5. Hispanic Americans—Fiction
  ISBN 978-0-06-117330-1; 0-06-117331-2
Accompanied by two friends, teenage brothers Marcus and Enrique head on a road trip to confront the abusive father who walked out on them a year earlier.
  "The author's imagery, sometimes subtle, sometimes searing, invariably hits its mark." Publ Wkly

Herrick, Steven, 1958-
By the river. Front Street 2006 238p $16.95
Grades: 8 9 10 11 12   **Fic**
  1. Brothers—Fiction 2. Death—Fiction 3. Single parent family—Fiction 4. Australia—Fiction
  ISBN 1-932425-72-1   LC 2005-23967
First published 2004 in the United Kingdom
A fourteen-year-old describes, through prose poems, his life in a small Australian town in 1962, where, since their mother's death, he and his brother have been mainly on their own to learn about life, death, and love.
  "The poems are simple but potent in their simplicity, blending together in a compelling, evocative story of a gentle, intelligent boy growing up and learning to deal with a sometimes-ugly little world that he . . . will eventually escape." Voice Youth Advocates

Cold skin. Front Street 2009 279p $17.95
Grades: 8 9 10 11 12   **Fic**
  1. Novels in verse 2. Country life—Fiction 3. Homicide—Fiction 4. Australia—Fiction 5. Mystery fiction
  ISBN 978-1-59078-572-0; 1-59078-572-X
                                    LC 2008-18620
In a rural Australian coal mining town shortly after World War II, teenaged Eddie makes a startling discovery when he investigates the murder of a local high school girl.
  "The strongest plot element is the mystery, which is well developed and has a surprising yet satisfying outcome. Some sexual scenarios make this most appropriate for older teens. Overall, a multilayered and affecting read." SLJ

The wolf. Front Street 2007 214p $17.95
Grades: 8 9 10 11 12   **Fic**
  1. Father-daughter relationship—Fiction 2. Domestic violence—Fiction 3. Australia—Fiction 4. Novels in verse
  ISBN 978-1-932425-75-8; 1-932425-75-6
                                    LC 2006-12072
Sixteen-year-old Lucy, living in the shadow of her violent father, experiences a night of tenderness, danger and revelation as she and Jake, her fifteen-year-old neighbor, search for a legendary wolf in the Australian outback.
  "Herrick's verse style perfectly suits this emotionally taut survival story. . . . Readers will find this novel compelling, its fast-moving narrative rewarding." SLJ

Hersey, John, 1914-1993
The wall. Knopf 1950 632p pa $17.95 hardcover o.p.
Grades: 11 12 Adult   **Fic**
  1. World War, 1939-1945—Fiction 2. Jews—Fiction 3. Warsaw (Poland)—Fiction
  ISBN 0-394-75696-7 (pa)
  "This novel is presented as a journal kept by a diarist during World War II. It tells of life in the Warsaw Ghetto, depicting Jewish interdependence in a struggle for survival. The writer's observations enrich our understanding of Jewish culture. Although the diarist dies of pneumonia in 1944, his escape from the enclosure within which the Germans confined the Jews is a testament to hope and courage." Shapiro. Fic for Youth. 3d edition

Hesse, Hermann, 1877-1962

Siddhartha; translated by Hilda Rosner. New Directions 1951 153p $16.95; pa $6.95 *

Grades: 11 12 Adult   **Fic**

1. Buddhism—Fiction 2. India—Fiction

ISBN 0-8112-0292-5; 0-8112-0068-X (pa)

Also available in paperback from Bantam Bks.

Original German edition, 1923

"The young Indian Siddhartha endures many experiences in his search for the ultimate answer to the question, what is humankind's role on earth? He is also looking for the solution to loneliness and discontent, and he seeks that solution in the way of a wanderer, the company of a courtesan, and the high position of a successful businessman. His final relationship is with a humble but wise ferryman. This is an allegory that examines love, wealth, and freedom while the protagonist struggles toward self-knowledge." Shapiro. Fic for Youth. 3d edition

Steppenwolf; translated from the German by Basil Creighton. Holt & Co. 1929 309p pa $14 hardcover o.p. *

Grades: 11 12 Adult   **Fic**

1. Germany—Fiction

ISBN 0-312-27867-5

Original German edition, 1927

"The hero, Harry Haller . . . is torn between his own frustrated artistic idealism and the inhuman nature of modern reality, which, in his eyes, is characterized entirely by philistinism and technology. It is his inability to be a part of the world and the resulting loneliness and desolation of his existence that cause him to think of himself as a 'Steppenwolf' (wolf of the Steppes). The novel, which is rich in surrealistic imagery throughout, ends in what is called the magic theater, a kind of allegorical sideshow. Here, Haller learns that in order to relate successfully to humanity and reality without sacrificing his ideals, he must overcome his own social and sexual inhibitions." Reader's Ency. 4th edition

Higson, Charles, 1958-

The enemy. Hyperion/DBG 2010 440p $16.99; pa $8.99 *

Grades: 9 10 11 12   **Fic**

1. Zombies—Fiction 2. London (England)—Fiction 3. Horror fiction

ISBN 978-1-4231-3175-5; 1-4231-3175-4; 978-1-4231-3312-4 (pa); 1-4231-3312-9 (pa)

First published 2009 in the United Kingdom

"Nearly two years ago, the world changed; everyone over 16 became horrifically ill and began to crave fresh meat. As supplies are exhausted and the vicious grown-ups grow braver, Arrum and Maxie, along with their band of refugees, must embark on a perilous journey across London to reach the safest spot in the city: Buckingham Palace. . . . Intrigue, betrayal and the basic heroic-teens-against-marauding-adults conflict give this work a high place on any beach-reading list." Kirkus

Followed by: The dead (2011)

Hijuelos, Oscar

Dark Dude. Atheneum Books for Young Readers 2008 439p $16.99; pa $9.99

Grades: 7 8 9 10   **Fic**

1. Cuban Americans—Fiction 2. Wisconsin—Fiction

ISBN 978-1-4169-4804-9; 1-4169-4804-X; 978-1-4169-4945-9 (pa); 1-4169-4945-3 (pa)

LC 2008-00959

In the 1960s, Rico Fuentes, a pale-skinned Cuban American teenager, abandons drug-infested New York City for the picket fence and apple pie world of Wisconsin, only to discover that he still feels like an outsider and that violent and judgmental people can be found even in the wholesome Midwest.

"Hijuelos weaves a compelling and insightful tale of one outsider's coming-of-age. . . . The resolution is quick and tidy, but the imagery is rich and the content sure to engage teen readers." Voice Youth Advocates

Hills, Lia

The beginner's guide to living. Farrar, Straus and Giroux 2010 221p il $17.99

Grades: 9 10 11 12   **Fic**

1. Bereavement—Fiction 2. School stories

ISBN 978-0-374-30659-5; 0-374-30659-1

LC 2009-19248

Struggling to cope with his mother's sudden death and growing feelings of isolation from his father and brother, seventeen-year-old Will turns to philosophy for answers to life's biggest questions, while finding some solace in a new love.

"Almost nothing escapes Will's notice (though his perceptiveness alone doesn't produce answers), and the mosaic of imagery and musings in his poetic, staccato narration offers thought-provoking ideas about grief and the universal drive to find a purpose. Although this novel begins with a death, it is a celebration of life, companionship, and love." Publ Wkly

Hinton, S. E.

The outsiders. Viking 1967 188p $17.99; pa $9.99 *

Grades: 7 8 9 10   **Fic**

1. Juvenile delinquency—Fiction 2. Social classes—Fiction

ISBN 0-670-53257-6; 0-14-038572-X (pa)

"From the perspective of Ponyboy Curtis, the author relates the story of the Greasers, who are from the lower class, and their conflict with the Socs, who are their middle-class opposite number. For the Greasers, the gang comprises their street family, all the family that some of them have. In the collision between the two social factions, two buddies die, one as a hood, the other, a hero." Shapiro. Fic for Youth. 3d edition

"This remarkable novel by a seventeen-year-old girl gives a moving, credible view of the outsiders from the inside—their loyalty to each other, their sensitivity under tough crusts, their understanding of self and society." Horn Book

Hoban, Julia

Willow. Dial Books 2009 329p $16.99

Grades: 9 10 11 12   **Fic**
   1. Self-mutilation—Fiction   2. Guilt—Fiction
   3. Bereavement—Fiction 4. Orphans—Fiction
   ISBN 978-0-8037-3356-5; 0-8037-3356-9
                                         LC 2008-33064
Sixteen-year-old Willow, who was driving the car that
killed both of her parents, copes with the pain and guilt
by cutting herself, until she meets a smart and sensitive
boy who is determined to help her stop.
   "Hoban's appropriately complex portrayal of cutting
makes this a good choice on a crucial subject." Kirkus

Hobbs, Valerie, 1941-

Sonny's war. Farrar, Straus & Giroux 2002
215p hardcover o.p. pa $7.95

Grades: 7 8 9 10   **Fic**
   1. Vietnam War, 1961-1975—Fiction
   ISBN 0-374-37136-9; 0-374-46970-9 (pa)
                                         LC 2002-23891
"Frances Foster books"
   In the late 1960s, fourteen-year-old Cory's life is
greatly changed by the sudden death of her father and
her brother's tour of duty in Vietnam
   "Hobbs writes like a dream . . . but the Cory she
conjures up for us is as real as real, completely believable in all her teenage vulnerability and sharp-eyed observation." Horn Book Guide

Hobbs, Will

Bearstone. Atheneum Pubs. 1989 154p pa $4.99
hardcover o.p.

Grades: 7 8 9 10   **Fic**
   1. Ute Indians—Fiction
   ISBN 0-689-87071-X (pa)   LC 89-6641
   "Rebellious at being forced to abandon his family and
his Ute Indian heritage to attend high school, Cloyd is
sent to spend a summer with a lonely old rancher in Colorado. Upon arriving, Cloyd accidentally finds a turquoise bear totem in an Anasazi grave site, which serves
as a touchstone between his cultural roots and his feelings. As time goes by, he also develops a mutual respect
and friendship for the old man." ALAN
   "The growth and maturity that Cloyd acquires as the
summer progresses is juxtaposed poetically against the
majestic Colorado landscape. Hobbs has creatively
blended myth and reality as Cloyd forges a new identity
for himself." Voice Youth Advocates
   Followed by Beardance (1993)

Leaving Protection. HarperCollins 2004 178p il
map $15.99; pa $5.99

Grades: 7 8 9 10   **Fic**
   1. Fishing—Fiction 2. Buried treasure—Fiction
   3. Alaska—Fiction
   ISBN 0-688-17475-2; 0-380-73312-9 (pa)
                                         LC 2003-15545
   Sixteen-year-old Robbie Daniels, happy to get a job
aboard a troller fishing for king salmon off southeastern
Alaska, finds himself in danger when he discovers that
his mysterious captain is searching for long-buried Russian plaques that lay claim to Alaska and the Northwest

This "nautical thriller brims with detail about the fishing life and weaves in historical facts as well. . . . .
Robbie's doubts build to a climactic finale involving a
dramatic and fateful storm at sea, grippingly rendered.
Fans of maritime tales will relish the atmosphere and the
bursts of action." Publ Wkly

The maze. Morrow Junior Bks. 1998 198p
$15.99; pa $5.99 *

Grades: 7 8 9 10   **Fic**
   1. Runaway teenagers—Fiction 2. Condors—Fiction
   ISBN 0-688-15092-6; 0-380-72913-X (pa)
                                         LC 98-10791
   Rick, a fourteen-year-old foster child, escapes from a
juvenile detention facility near Las Vegas and travels to
Canyonlands National Park in Utah where he meets a
bird biologist working on a project to reintroduce condors to the wild
   "Hobbs spins an engrossing yarn, blending adventure
with a strong theme, advocating the need for developing
personal values." Horn Book Guide

Hoffman, Alice, 1952-

Blue diary. Putnam 2001 303p hardcover o.p. pa
$14

Grades: 11 12 Adult   **Fic**
   1. Homicide—Fiction 2. Massachusetts—Fiction
   3. Family life—Fiction
   ISBN 0-399-14802-7; 0-425-18494-3 (pa)
                                         LC 2001-19517
   Ethan Ford is "suddenly arrested on suspicion of the
rape and murder of teenager Rachel Morris 15 years earlier in Maryland. Ethan confesses to the crime, but says
that he is now 'a different man,' who has redeemed himself through exemplary behavior. What this revelation
means to his beautiful wife of 13 years, Jorie {and} his
12-year-old son, Collie . . . allows the novel to investigate the themes of devotion, betrayal, guilt and forgiveness in trenchantly effective ways." Publ Wkly

The foretelling. Little, Brown 2005 167p
hardcover o.p. pa $7.99

Grades: 7 8 9 10   **Fic**
   1. Amazons—Fiction 2. Sex role—Fiction
   ISBN 0-316-01018-9; 0-316-15409-1 (pa)
                                         LC 2004-25102
   Growing up the daughter of an Amazon queen who
shuns her, Rain rebels against the ways of her tribe
through her sisterlike relationship with Io and her feelings for a boy from a tribe of wanderers.
   The "first-person narration is accessible while evoking
a sense of otherworldliness. . . . The story unfolds at a
measured pace with little dialogue, but the language
makes it compulsively readable." SLJ

Incantation. Little, Brown 2006 166p hardcover
o.p. pa $8.99 *

Grades: 8 9 10 11 12   **Fic**
   1. Prejudices—Fiction 2. Jews—Persecutions—Fiction
   3. Inquisition—Fiction 4. Spain—Fiction
   ISBN   978-0-316-01019-1;   0-316-01019-7;
   978-0-316-15428-4 (pa); 0-316-15428-8 (pa)
                                         LC 2005-37301

Hoffman, Alice, 1952-—_Continued_

During the Spanish Inquisition, sixteen-year-old Estrella, brought up a Catholic, discovers her family's true Jewish identity, and when their secret is betrayed by Estrella's best friend, the consequences are tragic. Includes some scenes of graphic violence.

"Hoffman's lyrical prose and astute characterization blend to create a riveting, horrific tale that unites despair with elements of hope." SLJ

Hoffman, Mary, 1945-

Stravaganza: city of masks. Bloomsbury Children's Bks. 2002 344p hardcover o.p. pa $7.95

Grades: 7 8 9 10   Fic
1. Space and time—Fiction 2. Adventure fiction
ISBN 1-58234-791-3; 1-58234-917-7 (pa)
LC 2001-56464

While sick in bed with cancer, Lucien begins making journeys to a place in a parallel world that resembles Venice, Italy, and he becomes caught up in the political intrigues surrounding the Duchessa who rules the city.

"Utterly fascinating, this rich, rip-roaring adventure—the first in a series—will no doubt whet readers' appetites for Italian history and culture as well as the next installment." Booklist

Other available titles in this series are:
Stravaganza: city of flowers (2005)
Stravaganza: city of secrets (2008)
Stravaganza: city of ships (2010)
Stravaganza: city of stars (2003)

Holder, Nancy, 1953-

Crusade; by Nancy Holder and Debbie Viguie. Simon Pulse 2010 470p $16.99

Grades: 7 8 9 10 11   Fic
1. Vampires—Fiction 2. Supernatural—Fiction 3. Sisters—Fiction 4. Horror fiction
ISBN 978-1-4169-9802-0; 1-4169-9802-0
LC 2010-9094

An international team of six teenaged vampire hunters, trained in Salamanca, Spain, goes to New Orleans seeking to rescue team-member Jenn's younger sister as the vampires escalate their efforts to take over the Earth.

"The cinematic writing and apocalyptic scenario should find a ready audience." Publ Wkly

Followed by: Damned (2011)

Holt, Simon

The Devouring. Little, Brown 2008 231p (The Devouring) $16.99

Grades: 7 8 9 10   Fic
1. Siblings—Fiction 2. Fear—Fiction 3. Supernatural—Fiction 4. Horror fiction
ISBN 978-0-316-03573-6; 0-316-03573-4
LC 2008-09258

The existence of Vours, supernatural creatures who feast on fear and attack on the eve of the winter solstice, becomes a terrifying reality for fifteen-year-old Reggie when she begins to suspect that her timid younger brother might be one of their victims.

"Comparable to books by R. L. Stine and Stephen King, _The Devouring_ will keep readers on the edge of their seats. . . . The book has some graphic content, blood, and gore, which only add to the chills. A must-have for horror fans." SLJ

Other titles in this series are:
Fearscape (2010)
Soulstice (2009)

Holub, Josef, 1926-

An innocent soldier; translated by Michael Hofmann. Arthur A. Levine Books 2005 231p $16.99

Grades: 8 9 10 11 12   Fic
1. France—History—1799-1815—Fiction 2. Russia—Fiction 3. War stories
ISBN 0-439-62771-0

A sixteen-year-old farmhand is tricked into fighting in the Napoleonic Wars by the farmer for whom he works, who secretly substitutes him for the farmer's own son.

"This is a well-wrought psychological tale. . . . [It] has a lot to offer to those seeking to build a deep historical fiction collection." SLJ

Hooker, Richard

MASH. Morrow 1968 219p pa $13 hardcover o.p. *

Grades: 11 12 Adult   Fic
1. Physicians—Fiction 2. Soldiers—Fiction 3. Korean War, 1950-1953—Fiction
ISBN 0-688-14955-3 (pa)   LC 68-29610

"Captains Hawkeye Pierce, Duke Forrest, and 'Trapper' John McIntyre, all M.D.'s, are stationed in Korea with the 4077th MASH (Mobile Army Surgical Hospital). The reader is soon involved in many operations and medical jargon. It is, however, the off-duty activities of these three that engages one's attention and laughter. Full of martinis, or bored, or tired, or all three, the men soon start raising hell. . . . Hilarious, occasionally very serious, full of warm, appealing eccentric characters, one could enjoy a very pleasant evening with this sMASHing novel." Libr J

Hooper, Mary

Fallen Grace. Bloomsbury 2011 309p $16.99

Grades: 7 8 9 10   Fic
1. Orphans—Fiction 2. Sisters—Fiction 3. Poverty—Fiction 4. Funeral rites and ceremonies—Fiction 5. Swindlers and swindling—Fiction 6. Mentally handicapped—Fiction 7. London (England)—Fiction 8. Great Britain—History—19th century—Fiction
ISBN 978-1-59990-564-8; 1-59990-564-7
LC 2010-25498

In Victorian London, impoverished fifteen-year-old orphan Grace takes care of her older but mentally unfit sister Lily, and after enduring many harsh and painful experiences, the two become the victims of a fraud perpetrated by the wealthy owners of several funeral businesses.

Hooper "packs her brisk Dickensian fable with colorful characters and suspenseful, satisfying plot twists. The sobering realities of child poverty and exploitation are vividly conveyed, along with fascinating details of the Victorian funeral trade." Kirkus

Includes bibliographical references

Hooper, Mary—*Continued*

Newes from the dead; being a true story of Anne Green, hanged for infanticide at Oxford Assizes in 1650, restored to the world and died again 1665. Roaring Brook Press 2008 263p $15.95

Grades: 8 9 10 11 12   **Fic**
1. Death—Fiction 2. Household employees—Fiction 3. Great Britain—History—1603-1714, Stuarts—Fiction 4. Pregnancy—Fiction
ISBN 978-1-59643-355-7; 1-59643-355-8

                LC 2007-16591

In 1650, while Robert, a young medical student, steels himself to assist with her dissection, twenty-two-year-old housemaid Anne Green recalls her life as she lies in her coffin, presumed dead after being hanged for murdering her child that was, in fact, stillborn.

"Loosely based on a true story—hence the title, taken from broadsides published at the time—with a decidedly unromantic view of the era, this is a must-read for teens learning about Cromwell and the Puritan revolution, or for young feminists who appreciate narratives about the treatment of women in history." SLJ

Includes bibliographical references

Hopkins, Ellen, 1955-

Burned. Margaret K. McElderry Books 2006 532p $16.95 *

Grades: 9 10 11 12   **Fic**
1. Novels in verse 2. Family life—Fiction 3. Mormons—Fiction 4. Sex role—Fiction 5. Child abuse—Fiction
ISBN 1-4169-0354-2; 978-1-4169-0354-3

                LC 2005-32461

Seventeen-year-old Pattyn, the eldest daughter in a large Mormon family, is sent to her aunt's Nevada ranch for the summer, where she temporarily escapes her alcoholic, abusive father and finds love and acceptance, only to lose everything when she returns home.

"The free verses, many in the form of concrete poems, create a compressed and intense reading experience with no extraneous dialogue or description. . . . This book will appeal to teens favoring realistic fiction and dramatic interpersonal stories." Voice Youth Advocates

Identical. Margaret K. McElderry Books 2008 565p $17.99

Grades: 10 11 12   **Fic**
1. Novels in verse 2. Child sexual abuse—Fiction 3. Twins—Fiction 4. Sisters—Fiction
ISBN 978-1-4169-5005-9; 1-4169-5005-2

                LC 2007-32463

Sixteen-year-old identical twin daughters of a district court judge and a candidate for the United States House of Representatives, Kaeleigh and Raeanne Gardella desperately struggle with secrets that have already torn them and their family apart.

This book "tells the twins' story in intimate and often-graphic detail. Hopkins packs in multiple issues including eating disorders, drug abuse, date rape, alcoholism, sexual abuse, and self-mutilation as she examines a family that 'puts the dys in dysfunction.' . . . Gritty and compelling, this is not a comfortable read, but its keen insights make it hard to put down." SLJ

Tricks. Margaret K. McElderry Books 2009 627p $18.99

Grades: 10 11 12   **Fic**
1. Novels in verse 2. Family life—Fiction 3. Prostitution—Fiction
ISBN 978-1-4169-5007-3   LC 2009-20297

Five troubled teenagers fall into prostitution as they search for freedom, safety, community, family, and love.

"Hopkins's pithy free verse reveals shards of emotion and quick glimpses of physical detail. It doesn't matter that the first-person voices blur, because the stories are distinct and unmistakable. Graphic sex, rape, drugs, bitter loneliness, despair—and eventually, blessedly, glimmers of hope." Kirkus

Hornby, Nick

Slam. G.P. Putnam's Sons 2007 309p $19.99 *

Grades: 8 9 10 11 12   **Fic**
1. Hawk, Tony, 1968-—Fiction 2. Teenage fathers—Fiction 3. Skateboarding—Fiction
ISBN 978-0-399-25048-4; 0-399-25048-4

                LC 2007-14146

At the age of fifteen, Sam Jones's girlfriend gets pregnant and Sam's life of skateboarding and daydreaming about Tony Hawk changes drastically.

The author "pens a first novel for teens that is a sweet and funny story about mistakes and choices. . . . Recommend this delightful and poignant novel to older teens who will laugh and weep with Sam." Voice Youth Advocates

Horner, Emily

A love story starring my dead best friend. Dial Books 2010 259p $16.99

Grades: 9 10 11 12   **Fic**
1. Death—Fiction 2. Bullies—Fiction 3. Lesbians—Fiction 4. Love stories 5. School stories
ISBN 978-0-8037-3420-3; 0-8037-3420-4

                LC 2009-23820

As she tries to sort out her feelings of love, seventeen-year-old Cass, a spunky math genius with an introverted streak, finds a way to memorialize her dead best friend.

"With its John Green-esque set pieces, mad road trips, fortuitous stranger encounters, thoroughly teased-out friendship drama, and optimistic romanticism—not to mention a fresh treatment of a lesbian heroine—this entertaining . . . [book] has something for everyone." Horn Book

Hosseini, Khaled

The kite runner. Riverhead Bks. 2003 324p $24.95; pa $14 *

Grades: 11 12 Adult   **Fic**
1. Taliban—Fiction 2. Friendship—Fiction 3. Social classes—Fiction 4. Afghanistan—Fiction
ISBN 1-57322-245-3; 1-59448-000-1 (pa)

                LC 2003-43106

"Amir, the son of a well-to-do Kabul merchant, is the first-person narrator, who marries, moves to California and becomes a successful novelist. But he remains haunted by a childhood incident in which he betrayed the trust of his best friend, a Hazara boy named Hassan, who re-

Hosseini, Khaled—*Continued*

ceives a brutal beating from some local bullies. After establishing himself in America, Amir learns that the Taliban have murdered Hassan and his wife, raising questions about the fate of his son, Sohrab. Spurred on by childhood guilt, Amir makes the difficult journey to Kabul, only to learn the boy has been enslaved by a former childhood bully who has become a prominent Taliban official." Publ Wkly

"Khaled Hosseini gives us a vivid and engaging story that reminds us how long his people have been struggling to triumph over the forces of violence." N Y Times Book Rev

Hostetter, Joyce

Healing water; a Hawaiian story; [by] Joyce Moyer Hostetter. Calkins Creek 2008 217p $17.95

Grades: 6 7 8 9 10   **Fic**

1. Leprosy—Fiction 2. Hawaii—Fiction

ISBN 978-1-59078-514-0   LC 2007-18349

This novel tells the story of Pia, who is sent to Hawaii's leprosy settlement on Molokai Island in the 1860s.

"Readers will find their compassion stirred and their interest piqued through this truly fine historical novel." Bull Cent Child Books

Houck, Colleen

Tiger's curse. Sterling 2011 402p $17.95

Grades: 8 9 10 11 12   **Fic**

1. Tigers—Fiction 2. Immortality—Fiction
3. Orphans—Fiction 4. Circus—Fiction 5. India—Fiction

ISBN 978-1-4027-8403-3   LC 2010-33191

Seventeen-year-old Oregon teenager Kelsey forms a bond with a circus tiger who is actually one of two brothers, Indian princes Ren and Kishan, who were cursed to live as tigers for eternity, and she travels with him to India where the tiger's curse may be broken once and for all.

The author "tells a good story filled with chaste romance that will keep readers turning pages to the inconclusive ending." Booklist

Houston, James D.

Snow Mountain passage; a novel. Harcourt 2002 315p il map pa $14

Grades: 11 12 Adult   **Fic**

1. Donner party—Fiction 2. California—Fiction
3. Overland journeys to the Pacific—Fiction
4. Wilderness survival—Fiction

ISBN 0-15-601143-3   LC 2001051803

First published 2002 by Knopf

This is a novel about the Donner Party, a group of California pioneers who became trapped in the mountains during winter snowstorms in 1846 and resorted to cannibalism to survive.

"Houston has given himself an opportunity to explore complex motives and characters, and his writerly skills are a match for the task. . . . He has a sure sense of place. . . . And most important, he has a clear-eyed view of humanity's heart of darkness." Atl Mon

Houston, Julian, 1944-

New boy. Houghton Mifflin Co. 2005 282p $16

Grades: 8 9 10 11 12   **Fic**

1. Prejudices—Fiction 2. African Americans—Fiction
3. School stories

ISBN 0-618-43253-1   LC 2004-27207

"As the first black student in an elite Connecticut boarding school in the late 1950s, Rob Garrett, 16, knows he is making history. . . . When his friends in the South plan a sit-in against segregation, he knows he must be part of it. . . . The honest first-person narrative makes stirring drama. . . . This brings up much for discussion about then and now." Booklist

Howell, Simmone

Everything beautiful. Bloomsbury Children's Books 2008 292p $16.99

Grades: 9 10 11   **Fic**

1. Camps—Fiction 2. Religious life—Fiction
3. Physically handicapped—Fiction

ISBN 978-1-59990-042-1; 1-59990-42-4

                  LC 2008-17211

When sixteen-year-old Riley unwillingly attends a religious summer camp, she forms a deep bond with another camper who happens to be wheelchair bound.

"What could be a clichéd situation–the bond between two outcasts–is instead touching and believable. . . . This novel will appeal to sensitive teens who will root for Riley and the other camp underdogs." SLJ

Howells, Amanda

The summer of skinny dipping; a novel. Sourcebooks Fire 2010 295p pa $8.99

Grades: 9 10 11 12   **Fic**

1. Cousins—Fiction 2. Ocean—Fiction
3. Swimming—Fiction 4. Death—Fiction 5. Love stories

ISBN 978-1-4022-3862-8   LC 2009-49926

While spending the summer in the Hamptons, sixteen-year-old Mia is disappointed that her cousin Corinne has grown so distant, but when she meets the irresistible and adventurous boy next door, everything changes for the better.

"With a lyrical yet straightforward voice and a layered plot, this novel will live on for more than a summer." SLJ

Hrdlitschka, Shelley, 1956-

Sister wife. Orca 2008 269p pa $12.95

Grades: 8 9 10 11 12   **Fic**

1. Polygamy—Fiction

ISBN 978-1-55143-927-3; 1-55143-927-1

In a remote polygamist community, Celeste struggles to accept her destiny while longing to be free to live her life her way.

"This compelling story combines with authentic characters to pique the interest of a wide array of teens and get them talking about faith and free will." Voice Youth Advocates

Hubbard, Amanda
But I love him; [by] Amanda Grace. Flux 2011
253p pa $9.95
Grades: 7 8 9 10   **Fic**
1. Abused women—Fiction 2. School stories
3. Dating (Social customs)—Fiction 4. Washington
(State)—Fiction
ISBN 978-0-7387-2594-9; 0-7387-2594-3
                                    LC 2010-50131
Traces, through the course of a year, Ann's transformation from a happy A-student, track star, and popular senior to a solitary, abused woman whose love for the emotionally-scarred Connor has taken away everything—even herself.
"A great shared read for parents and teens." Voice Youth Advocates

You wish; [by] Mandy Hubbard. Razorbill 2010
284p pa $8.99
Grades: 7 8 9 10   **Fic**
1. Birthdays—Fiction 2. Wishes—Fiction
ISBN 978-1-59514-292-4; 1-59514-292-4
                                    LC 2010-22776
Kayla McHenry's life is transformed when a wish on her sixteenth birthday comes true—along with all of her previous birthday wishes, beginning with the appearance of a pink pony.
"This is an entertaining romance enlivened by the fantasy spin and deepened by Kayla's renewed appreciation for the world around her." Booklist

Hughes, Dean, 1943-
Search and destroy. Atheneum Books for Young Readers 2006 216p $16.95
Grades: 7 8 9 10   **Fic**
1. Vietnam War, 1961-1975—Fiction
ISBN 0-689-87023-X   LC 2005-11255
"Ginee Seo Books"
Recent high school graduate Rick Ward, undecided about his future and eager to escape his unhappy home life, joins the army and experiences the horrors of the war in Vietnam.
"This is a compelling, insightful story about the emotional, physical, and psychological scars that wars leave upon soldiers." Booklist

Hugo, Victor, 1802-1885
Les misérables; translated from the French by Charles E. Wilbour; with an introduction by Peter Washington. Knopf 1997 xxxvii, 1432p $27
Grades: 11 12 Adult   **Fic**
1. Paris (France)—Fiction
ISBN 0-375-40317-5   LC 98-156450
Also available from other publishers
"Everyman's library"
Original French edition, 1862
"Set in the Parisian underworld and plotted like a detective story, the work follows Jean Valjean, a victim of society who has been imprisoned for 19 years for stealing a loaf of bread. A hardened criminal upon his release, he eventually reforms, becoming a successful industrialist and mayor of a northern town. Despite this he is haunted by an impulsive, regretted former crime and is pursued relentlessly by the police inspector Javert. Valjean eventually gives himself up for the sake of his adopted daughter, Cosette, and her husband, Marius. *Les Misérables* is a vast panorama of Parisian society and its underworld, and it contains many famous episodes and passages." Merriam-Webster's Ency of Lit

Huntley, Amy
The everafter. Balzer + Bray 2009 144p $16.99;
lib bdg $17.89; pa $8.99
Grades: 7 8 9 10   **Fic**
1. Dead—Fiction 2. Death—Fiction 3. Lost and found possessions—Fiction 4. Friendship—Fiction
ISBN   978-0-06-177679-3;   0-06-177679-3;
978-0-06-177680-9 (lib bdg); 0-06-177680-7 (lib bdg);
978-0-06-177681-6 (pa); 0-06-177681-5 (pa)
                                    LC 2008-46149
Madison Stanton doesn't know where she is or how she got there. But she does know this—she is dead. And alone in a vast, dark space. The only company Maddy has in this place are luminescent objects that turn out to be all the things she lost while she was alive. And soon she discovers that, with these artifacts, she can re-experience—and even—change moments from her life.
"This fresh take on a teen's journey of self-exploration is a compelling and highly enjoyable tale. Huntley expertly combines a coming-of-age story with a supernatural mystery that keeps readers engrossed until the climactic ending. This touching story will appeal to those looking for a ghost story, romance, or family drama." SLJ

Hurley, Tonya
Ghostgirl. Little, Brown 2008 328p $17.99 *
Grades: 7 8 9 10   **Fic**
1. Popularity—Fiction 2. Death—Fiction 3. School stories 4. Ghost stories
ISBN 978-0-316-11357-1; 0-316-11357-3
                                    LC 2007-31541
After dying, high school senior Charlotte Usher is as invisible to nearly everyone as she always felt, but despite what she learns in a sort of alternative high school for dead teens, she clings to life while seeking a way to go to the Fall Ball with the boy of her dreams.
"Hurley combines afterlife antics, gothic gore, and high school hell to produce an original, hilarious satire. . . . Tim Burton and Edgar Allan Poe devotees will die for this fantastic, phantasmal read." SLJ
Other titles in this series are:
Ghostgirl: Homecoming (2009)
Ghostgirl: Lovesick (2010)

Hurston, Zora Neale, 1891-1960
Novels and stories. Library of Am. 1995 1041p
$35 *
Grades: 11 12 Adult   **Fic**
1. African Americans—Fiction 2. Short stories
ISBN 0-940450-83-6   LC 94-25757
Companion volume to Folklore, memoirs, and other writings
Contents: Short stories included are: John Redding goes to sea; Drenched in light; Spunk; Sweat; The bones of contention; Book of Harlem; The gilded six-bits; The fire and the cloud; Story in Harlem slang

Hurston, Zora Neale, 1891-1960—*Continued*

This collection contains Hurston's four novels: Jonah's gourd vine, Their eyes were watching God, Moses, man of the mountain, and Seraph on the Suwanee. Also included are nine short stories

"Libraries without a complete set of Hurston's fiction will find this volume a necessary and easy purchase to fill that unfortunate gap." Booklist

Their eyes were watching God; with a foreword by Edwidge Danticat. HarperCollins Pubs. 2000 xxii, 231p $22; pa $15.95
Grades: 9 10 11 12 Adult   Fic
  1. African Americans—Fiction 2. Florida—Fiction
ISBN 0-06-019949-0; 0-06-112006-0 (pa)
                      LC 00-58186
First published 1937 by Lippincott

This novel "treats social problems from a racial and feminist perspective. Janie Crawford, raised by her grandmother in rural poverty, flees her old and dictatorial husband with Joe Starks, an ambitious man who becomes the mayor of Florida's first town run by African Americans. When Joe dies, Janie falls in love with the younger Teacake and follows him to the truck farming area of the Florida swamps. In the floods following a hurricane, he is bitten by a rabid dog and, crazed, attacks Janie. She shoots him, is charged with murder, and finally exonerated. When she returns to the town she and Joe built, she tells her story to a friend." HarperCollins Reader's Ency of Am Lit

Hurwin, Davida, 1950-

Freaks and revelations; a novel; by Davida Wills Hurwin. Little, Brown and Co. 2009 234p $16.99
Grades: 10 11 12   Fic
  1. Prejudices—Fiction 2. Homosexuality—Fiction 3. Drug abuse—Fiction 4. California—Fiction
ISBN 978-0-316-04996-2; 0-316-04996-4
                     LC 2008-47384
"Inspired by real events in the lives of Matthew Boger and Tim Zaal"

Tells, in two voices, of events leading up to a 1980 incident in which fourteen-year-old Jason, a gay youth surviving on the streets as a prostitute, and seventeen-year-old Doug, a hate-filled punk rocker, have a fateful meeting in a Los Angeles alley.

"Sympathetic to both characters without shying away from brutality—physical or emotional—the finely crafted story leads to a powerful climax of hope and redemption that will stay with readers." Publ Wkly

Huser, Glen, 1943-

Stitches. Groundwood Books 2003 198p hardcover o.p. pa $6.95
Grades: 7 8 9 10   Fic
  1. Bullies—Fiction 2. Puppets and puppet plays—Fiction 3. Sex role—Fiction 4. Canada—Fiction
ISBN 0-88899-553-9; 0-88899-578-4 (pa)
                   LC 2003-363167
This story of two outsiders who become friends is set in rural Alberta. The protagonists "are Chantelle, who has a limp and a scarred face, and Travis, a boy com-

pletely unselfconscious about his love for puppets and sewing. Both kids have ragtaggle families. . . . Chantelle and Travis joined forces back in fifth grade, when she rescued him from the boys who called him 'girlie'; junior high brings new challenges as the teasing gets uglier and, eventually, violent." Horn Book

"Teachers will use this book in their classrooms, but it will appeal to leisure readers as well." Voice Youth Advocates

Huxley, Aldous, 1894-1963

Brave new world. Harper & Row 1946 xx, 311p pa $13.95 hardcover o.p. *
Grades: 7 8 9 10   Fic
  1. Utopias—Fiction 2. Technology and civilization—Fiction
ISBN 0-06-085052-3 (pa)
First published 1932 by Doubleday, Doran & Company

"The ironic title, which Huxley has taken from Shakespeare's 'The Tempest,' describes a world in which science has taken control over morality and humaneness. In this utopia humans emerge from test tubes, families are obsolete, and even pleasure is regulated. When a so-called savage who believes in spirituality is found and is imported to the community, he cannot accomodate himself to this world and ends his life." Shapiro. Fic for Youth. 3d edition

Hyde, Catherine Ryan

Becoming Chloe. Random House 2006 215p $15.95; pa $8.99
Grades: 9 10 11 12   Fic
  1. Homeless persons—Fiction 2. Voyages and travels—Fiction
ISBN 0-375-83258-0; 0-375-83260-2 (pa)
                   LC 2005-18949
"The young characters in . . . [this novel] are searching for signs of hope amid grim realities, which begin, here, with a gang rape on the first page. Seventeen-year-old Jordan tries to rescue 18-year-old Chloe from her attackers, and the two homeless teens form a fierce, siblinglike bond as they help each other survive the streets—a struggle that sometimes drives Jordan to prostitution. Both have deep scars: gay Jordan nearly died from his father's abuse; childlike Chloe can't speak directly about her past horrors, even to Jordan. At last, they strike out on a healing, cross-country trip in search of 'beauty . . . maybe even some decent, kind people.'" Booklist

"This thought-provoking story of the power of hope . . . blends the realities of street life with the wonder of cross-country exploration." Voice Youth Advocates

Diary of a witness. Alfred A. Knopf 2009 201p $16.99; lib bdg $19.99
Grades: 7 8 9 10   Fic
  1. Bullies—Fiction 2. Obesity—Fiction 3. Single parent family—Fiction 4. School stories
ISBN 978-0-375-85684-6; 0-375-85684-6; 978-0-375-95684-3 (lib bdg); 0-375-95684-0 (lib bdg)
                   LC 2008-40883
Ernie, an overweight high school student and long-time target of bullies, relies on his best friend Will to

Hyde, Catherine Ryan—*Continued*
watch his back until Will, overwhelmed by problems at
home and guilt over his brother's death, seeks a final solution.

Hyde "has created sympathetic, fully developed characters in likable Ernie and tortured and somewhat cerebral Will. The moment of crisis is chillingly believable
and will have readers on the edge of their seats." Publ
Wkly

Jumpstart the world. Alfred A. Knopf 2010
186p $16.99; lib bdg $19.99
Grades: 9 10 11 12   **Fic**
1. Moving—Fiction 2. School stories
3. Transsexualism—Fiction 4. Apartment houses—Fiction 5. Mother-daughter relationship—Fiction
ISBN 978-0-375-86665-4; 978-0-375-96665-1 (lib
bdg); 978-0-375-89677-4 (ebook)   LC 2010-02511
Sixteen-year-old Elle falls in love with Frank, the
neighbor who helps her adjust to being on her own in a
big city, but learning that he is transgendered turns her
world upside-down.

"For a book loaded with issues—there is even treatment of mental illness—this is a plain good read. These
characters are funny, complex, and engaging. . . . There
are many teens today who need this book." Voice Youth
Advocates

Ibbitson, John, 1955-
The Landing; a novel. KCP Fiction 2008 160p
$17.95; pa $7.95
Grades: 7 8 9 10   **Fic**
1. Uncles—Fiction 2. Violinists—Fiction 3. Canada—
Fiction
ISBN 978-1-55453-234-6; 1-55453-234-5;
978-1-55453-238-4 (pa); 1-55453-238-8 (pa)
Ben thinks he will always be stuck at Cook's Landing,
barely making ends meet like his uncle. But when he
meets a wealthy widow from New York City, he sees
himself there too. When she hires him to play his violin,
he realizes his gift could unlock the possibilities of the
world. Then, during a stormy night on Lake Muskoka,
everything changes.

"With lovely prose, Ibbitson brings to life the rugged
beauty and the devastating poverty of the Lake Muskoka
region. His characters are as strong and remote as their
surroundings." Voice Youth Advocates

Irving, John, 1942-
The world according to Garp. Modern Library
1998 688p $21.95 *
Grades: 11 12 Adult   **Fic**
1. Mother-son relationship—Fiction 2. Family life—
Fiction
ISBN 0-679-60306-9   LC 97-39458
First published 1978 by Dutton
"Jenny Fields is the black sheep daughter of an aristo-
cratic New England family; she becomes, almost by acci-
dent, a feminist leader ahead of her time. Her son, T. S.
Garp (named for a father he never saw), has high ambi-
tions for his artistic career, but he has an even higher,
obsessive devotion to his wife and children. Surrounding
Garp and Jenny are a wide assortment of people: school-
teachers and whores, wrestlers and radicals, editors and

assassins, transsexuals and rapists, and husbands and
wives." Publisher's note

This "is a long family novel, spanning four generations and two continents, crammed with incidents, characters, feelings and craft. The components of black comedy and melodrama, pathos and tragedy, mesh effortlessly in a tale that can also be read as a commentary on art
and the imagination." Time

Ishiguro, Kazuo, 1954-
Never let me go. Knopf 2005 288p $24 *
Grades: 11 12 Adult   **Fic**
1. Science fiction 2. Bioethics—Fiction 3. School stories
ISBN 1-4000-4339-5   LC 2004-48966
This novel is "set in late 1990s England, in a parallel
universe in which humans are cloned and raised express-
ly to 'donate' their healthy organs and thus eradicate disease from the normal population." Publ Wkly

"Highly recommended for literary merit and as an exceptional platform for the discussion of a controversial
topic." SLJ

Jackson, Shirley, 1919-1965
The haunting of Hill House. Viking 1959 246p
pa $14 hardcover o.p. *
Grades: 11 12 Adult   **Fic**
1. Ghost stories 2. Horror fiction
ISBN 0-14-303998-9 (pa)
Also available in hardcover from Buccaneer Books
"Dr. John Montague, an anthropologist, is interested in
the analysis of supernatural manifestations. He rents Hill
House, which is reported to be haunted, and plans to
spend the summer there with research assistants. Eleanor
Vance, one of the researchers, is at first repelled by the
house but soon adjusts. Other people come and signs of
psychic activity are rampant, many of them centered on
Eleanor. When Dr. Montague insists that she leave to in-
sure her safety, the house does not release her." Shapiro.
Fic for Youth. 3d edition

The lottery. Creative Education 2008 32p il
(Creative short stories) $28.50 *
Grades: 9 10 11 12   **Fic**
1. Horror fiction
ISBN 978-1-58341-584-9   LC 2007-8487
This short story "portrays a small town that gathers to
hold its yearly lottery, a barbaric game of chance. Each
head of household draws a slip, and the family with the
marked slip will lose a member to stoning by the towns-
folk. The shocking story forces readers to grapple with
issues of ritual and violence. . . . [This book also fea-
tures] a section after the tale examining the background
of the story's publication, providing initial reactions, and
exploring themes and motivations. An author profile is
also appended. These additions will help readers more
thoroughly understand the story, its context, and the author." Voice Youth Advocates

We have always lived in the castle. Viking 1962
214p pa $14 hardcover o.p.
Grades: 11 12 Adult   **Fic**

Jackson, Shirley, 1919-1965—*Continued*
1. Horror fiction 2. Sisters—Fiction 3. New England—Fiction
ISBN 0-14-303997-0 (pa)
Also available in hardcover from Buccaneer Books
"Since the time that Constance Blackwood was tried and acquitted of the murder of four members of her family, she has lived with her sister Mary Catherine and her Uncle Julian in the family mansion. Mary Catherine takes care of family chores and Uncle Julian is busy with the writing of a detailed account of the six-year-old murders. Cousin Charles's arrival on the scene disrupts the quiet peace of the family, and Mary Catherine's efforts to get rid of him unloose a chain of events that bring everything down in ruins." Shapiro. Fic for Youth. 3d edition

Jacobson, Jennifer, 1958-
The complete history of why I hate her; [by] Jennifer Richard Jacobson. Atheneum Books for Young Readers 2010 181p $16.99
Grades: 7 8 9 10   **Fic**
1. Resorts—Fiction 2. Personality disorders—Fiction 3. Cancer—Fiction 4. Sisters—Fiction 5. Maine—Fiction
ISBN 978-0-689-87800-8; 0-689-87800-1
                LC 2008-42959
Wanting a break from being known only for her sister's cancer, seventeen-year-old Nola leaves Boston for a waitressing job at a summer resort in Maine, but soon feels as if her new best friend is taking over her life.
"A compelling story of self-discovery with plenty of insights into the motivations that drive relationships." Booklist

Jaden, Denise
Losing Faith. Simon Pulse 2010 381p pa $9.99
Grades: 7 8 9 10 11 12   **Fic**
1. Death—Fiction 2. Bereavement—Fiction 3. Sisters—Fiction 4. School stories 5. Christian life—Fiction 6. Cults—Fiction
ISBN 978-1-4169-9609-5; 1-4169-9609-5
                LC 2010-7296
Brie tries to cope with her grief over her older sister Faith's sudden death by trying to learn more about the religious "home group" Faith secretly joined and never talked about with Brie or her parents.
"With pitch-perfect portrayals of high school social life and a nuanced view into a variety of Christian experiences of faith, this first novel gives readers much to think about." SLJ

Jaffe, Michele, 1970-
Bad kitty. HarperCollins Publishers 2006 268p il hardcover o.p. pa $8.99
Grades: 9 10 11 12   **Fic**
1. Mystery fiction 2. Las Vegas (Nev.)—Fiction
ISBN   0-06-078108-4;   978-0-06-078108-8; 0-06-078110-6 (pa); 978-0-06-078110-1 (pa)
                LC 2005-5733
While vacationing with her family in Las Vegas, seventeen-year-old Jasmine stumbles upon a murder mystery

that she attempts to solve with the help of her friends, recently arrived from California.
"Readers will likely find themselves quickly clawing their way through this fun novel." Publ Wkly
Followed by: Kitty kitty (2008)

Rosebush. Razorbill 2010 326p $16.99
Grades: 8 9 10 11 12   **Fic**
1. Traffic accidents—Fiction 2. Mystery fiction
ISBN 978-1-59514-353-2; 1-59514-353-X
Instead of celebrating Memorial Day weekend on the Jersey Shore, Jane is in the hospital surrounded by teddy bears, trying to piece together what happened last night. One minute she was at a party, wearing fairy wings and cuddling with her boyfriend. The next, she was lying near-dead in a rosebush after a hit-and-run.
"Compulsively readable, the novel bristles with red herrings, leading readers down one tempting plot branch after another, each one blooming with plausibility. The characters are skillfully cultivated through flashbacks, and the insecure, people-pleasing Jane grows believably as she takes on the mystery." Booklist

James, Henry, 1843-1916
The portrait of a lady. Knopf 1991 xxv, 626p $20
Grades: 9 10 11 12   **Fic**
1. Europe—Fiction
ISBN 0-679-40562-3   LC 91-52999
Also available in paperback from Penguin Books
"Everyman's library"
First published 1881 by Houghton
"This is one of the best James's early works, in which he presents various types of American character transplanted into a European environment. The story centres in Isabel Archer, the 'Lady,' an attractive American girl. Around her we have the placid old American banker, Mr. Touchett; his hard repellent wife; his ugly, invalid, witty, charming son Ralph, whom England has thoroughly assimilated; and the outspoken, brilliant, indomitably American journalist Henrietta Stackpole. Isabel refuses the offer of marriage of a typical English peer, the excellent Lord Warburton, and of a bulldog-like New Englander, Casper Goodwood, to fall a victim, under the influence of the slightly sinister Madame Merle (another cosmopolitan American), to a worthless and spiteful dilettante, Gilbert Osmond, who marries her for her fortune and ruins her life; but to whom she remains loyal in spite of her realization of his vileness." Oxford Companion to Engl Lit. 6th edition

The turn of the screw; edited by Allan Lloyd Smith. J.M. Dent 1993 xxxii, 139p pa $8.95 *
Grades: 11 12 Adult   **Fic**
1. Horror fiction
ISBN 0-460-87299-0   LC 94-125860
Also available from other publishers
First published 1898
This novella "is told from the viewpoint of the leading character, a governess in love with her employer, who goes to an isolated English estate to take charge of Miles and Flora, two attractive and precocious children. She gradually realizes that her young charges are under the evil influence of two ghosts, Peter Quint, the ex-steward, and Miss Jessel, their former governess. At the climax of

James, Henry, 1843-1916—*Continued*
the story, she enters into open conflict with the children, as a result of which Flora is alienated and Miles dies of fright." Reader's Ency. 4th edition

James, Rebecca, 1970-
Beautiful malice; a novel. Bantam Books 2010 260p $25
Grades: 9 10 11 12   Fic
1. Bereavement—Fiction 2. Friendship—Fiction 3. Australia—Fiction
ISBN 978-0-553-80805-6   LC 2010-6255
To escape the media attention generated by her sister's murder, a grieving seventeen-year-old Australian girl moves away and meets a vibrant new friend who harbors a dangerous secret.
This "novel will grab your attention on the first page, and you won't want to turn away even after the last page has been turned." Voice Youth Advocates

Jansen, Hanna
Over a thousand hills I walk with you; translated from the German by Elizabeth D. Crawford. Carolrhoda Books 2006 342p $16.95 *
Grades: 7 8 9 10   Fic
1. Rwanda—Fiction
ISBN 1-57505-927-4; 978-1-57505-927-3
                                    LC 2005-21123
Original German edition, 2002
"Eight-year-old Jeanne was the only one of her family to survive the 1994 Rwanda genocide. Then a German family adopted her, and her adoptive mother now tells Jeanne's story in a compelling fictionalized biography that stays true to the traumatized child's bewildered viewpoint." Booklist

Jen, Gish
Typical American; a novel. 1st Vintage Contemporaries ed. Vintage Contemporaries 2008 296p pa $15 *
Grades: 9 10 11 12 Adult   Fic
1. Chinese Americans—Fiction
ISBN 978-0-307-38922-0   LC 2008270242
First published 1991 by Houghton Mifflin
"Yefing Chang becomes Ralph Chang in America and begins a hard struggle to achieve the American dream—a career, a family and a home of his own. In poverty, he succeeds finally to win a doctoral degree, a college position, a happy marriage to Helen, two delightful daughters and a close reunion with his older sister, Theresa. The dream becomes a nightmare when he meets Grover Ding whose corrupt influence over Ralph and Helen begins to unravel all that the Changs have managed to achieve. This is an honest novel that does not promise happy endings and recognizes the human weaknesses that can destroy a family's stability." Shapiro. Fic for Youth. 3d edition
Followed by Mona in the promised land (1996)

Jenkins, A. M. (Amanda McRaney)
Beating heart; a ghost story. HarperCollins Publishers 2006 244p $15.99; pa $8.99
Grades: 9 10 11 12   Fic
1. Ghost stories 2. Divorce—Fiction 3. Moving—Fiction
ISBN 0-06-054607-7; 0-06-054609-3 (pa)
                                    LC 2005-05071
Following his parents' divorce, seventeen-year-old Evan moves with his mother and sister into an old house where the spirit of a teenager who died there awakens and mistakes him for her long-departed lover.
"Both accessible and substantive, this book will be an easy sell to teens." Booklist

Night road. HarperTeen 2008 362p $16.99; lib bdg $17.89; pa $8.99
Grades: 8 9 10 11 12   Fic
1. Vampires—Fiction 2. Automobile travel—Fiction 3. Horror fiction
ISBN   978-0-06-054604-5;   0-06-054604-2;
978-0-06-054605-2 (lib bdg); 0-06-054605-0 (lib bdg);
978-0-06-054606-9 (pa); 0-06-054606-9 (pa)
                                    LC 2007-31703
Battling his own memories and fears, Cole, an extraordinarily conscientious vampire, and Sandor, a more impulsive acquaintance, spend a few months on the road, trying to train a young man who recently joined their ranks.
"The real strength of the novel lies in the noirish atmosphere, accessible prose, and crisp, sharp dialogue." Horn Book

Repossessed. HarperTeen 2007 218p $15.99
Grades: 7 8 9 10   Fic
1. Demoniac possession—Fiction 2. Devil—Fiction 3. School stories
ISBN 978-0-06-083568-2; 0-06-083568-0
                                    LC 2007-09142
A fallen angel, tired of being unappreciated while doing his pointless, demeaning job, leaves Hell, enters the body of a seventeen-year-old boy, and tries to experience the full range of human feelings before being caught and punished, while the boy's family and friends puzzle over his changed behavior.
"Funny and clever. . . . It's a quick, quirky and entertaining read, with some meaty ideas in it, too." Kliatt

Jiménez, Francisco, 1943-
Reaching out. Houghton Mifflin 2008 196p $16; pa $6.99 *
Grades: 7 8 9 10 11 12   Fic
1. Mexican Americans—Fiction 2. Father-son relationship—Fiction 3. California—Fiction
ISBN   978-0-618-03851-0;   0-618-03851-5;
978-0-547-25030-4 (pa); 0-547-25030-4 (pa)
Sequel to: Breaking through (2001)
"Papa's raging depression intensifies young Jiménez's personal guilt and conflict in the 1960s. . . . He is the first in his Mexican American migrant family to attend college in California. . . . Like his other fictionalized autobiographies, *The Circuit* (1997) and *Breaking Through* (2001), this sequel tells Jiménez's personal story in self-contained chapters that join together in a stirring narra-

Jiménez, Francisco, 1943-—*Continued*

tive. . . . The spare episodes will draw readers with the quiet daily detail of work, anger, sorrow, and hope." Booklist

Jinks, Catherine, 1963-

Evil genius. Harcourt 2007 486p $17 *

Grades: 7 8 9 10   Fic

1. Genius—Fiction 2. Crime—Fiction 3. Good and evil—Fiction 4. School stories 5. Australia—Fiction

ISBN 978-0-15-205988-0; 0-15-205988-1

LC 2006-14476

First published 2005 in Australia

Child prodigy Cadel Piggot, an antisocial computer hacker, discovers his true identity when he enrolls as a first-year student at an advanced crime academy.

"Cadel's turnabout is convincingly hampered by his difficulty recognizing appropriate outlets for rage, and Jinks' whiplash-inducing suspense writing will gratify fans of Anthony Horowitz's high-tech spy scenarios." Booklist

Other titles about Cadel Piggot are:

Genius squad (2008)

Genius wars (2010)

Living hell. Harcourt 2010 256p $17

Grades: 7 8 9 10   Fic

1. Science fiction

ISBN 978-0-15-206193-7; 0-15-206193-2

LC 2009-18938

Chronicles the transformation of a spaceship into a living organism, as seventeen-year-old Cheney leads the hundreds of inhabitants in a fight for survival while machines turn on them, treating all humans as parasites.

"Jinks' well-thought-out environs and rational characters help ground this otherwise out-of-control interstellar thriller." Booklist

The reformed vampire support group. Houghton Mifflin Harcourt 2009 362p $17; pa $8.99

Grades: 8 9 10 11 12   Fic

1. Vampires—Fiction 2. Mystery fiction

ISBN 978-0-15-206609-3; 0-15-206609-8; 978-0-547-41166-8 (pa); 0-547-41166-9 (pa)

LC 2008-25115

Fifteen-year-old vampire Nina has been stuck for fifty-one years in a boring support group for vampires, and nothing exciting has ever happened to them—until one of them is murdered and the others must try to solve the crime.

"Those tired of torrid bloodsucker stories or looking for a comic riff on the trend will feel refreshed by the vomitous, guinea-pig-drinking accidental heroics of Nina and her pals." Kirkus

Followed by: The abused werewolf rescue group (2011)

Jocelyn, Marthe, 1956-

Folly. Wendy Lamb Books 2010 249p $15.99; lib bdg $18.99

Grades: 8 9 10 11 12   Fic

1. Foundling Hospital (London, England)—Fiction 2. Abandoned children—Fiction 3. Household employees—Fiction 4. London (England)—Fiction 5. Great Britain—History—19th century—Fiction

ISBN 978-0-385-73846-0; 0-385-73846-3; 978-0-385-90731-6 (lib bdg); 0-385-90731-1 (lib bdg)

LC 2009-23116

In a parallel narrative set in late nineteenth-century England, teenaged country girl Mary Finn relates the unhappy conclusion to her experiences as a young servant in an aristocratic London household while, years later, young James Nelligan describes how he comes to leave his beloved foster family to live and be educated at London's famous Foundling Hospital.

"Mary's spry narration (James's chapters unfold in third-person) combined with the tale's texture and fervent emotion will seduce readers." Horn Book Guide

Would you. Wendy Lamb Books 2008 165p $15.99; lib bdg $18.99; pa $6.50

Grades: 8 9 10 11 12   Fic

1. Sisters—Fiction 2. Medical care—Fiction 3. Coma—Fiction 4. Traffic accidents—Fiction 5. Family life—Fiction

ISBN 978-0-375-83703-6; 0-375-83703-5; 978-0-375-93703-3 (lib bdg); 0-375-93703-X (lib bdg); 978-0-375-83704-3 (pa); 0-375-83704-3 (pa)

LC 2007-18913

When her beloved sister, Claire, steps in front of a car and winds up in a coma, Nat's anticipated summer of working, hanging around with friends, and seeing Claire off to college is transformed into a nightmare of doctors, hospitals, and well-meaning neighbors.

"Jocelyn captures a teen's thoughts and reactions in a time of incredible anguish without making her overly dramatic. Readers will fly through the pages of this book, crying, laughing, and crying some more." SLJ

John, Antony, 1972-

Five flavors of dumb. Dial Books 2010 337p $16.99

Grades: 7 8 9 10   Fic

1. Deaf—Fiction 2. Rock musicians—Fiction 3. Seattle (Wash.)—Fiction

ISBN 978-0-8037-3433-3; 0-8037-3433-6

LC 2009-44449

Eighteen-year-old Piper is profoundly hearing impaired and resents her parent's decision raid her college fund to get cochlear implants for her baby sister. She becomes the manager for her classmates' popular rock band, called Dumb, giving her the chance to prove her capabilities to her parents and others, if only she can get the band members to get along.

"Readers interested in any of the narrative strands . . . will find a solid, satisfyingly complex story here." Bull Cent Child Books

Johnson, Angela, 1961-

The first part last. Simon & Schuster Bks. for Young Readers 2003 131p $15.95

Grades: 7 8 9 10   **Fic**

1. Teenage fathers—Fiction 2. Infants—Fiction 3. African Americans—Fiction

ISBN 0-689-84922-2   LC 2002-36512

Prequel to Heaven (1998)

Bobby's carefree teenage life changes forever when he becomes a father and must care for his adored baby daughter.

"Brief, poetic, and absolutely riveting." SLJ

Followed by: Sweet hereafter (2010)

Johnson, Christine, 1978-

Claire de Lune. Simon Pulse 2010 336p $16.99

Grades: 7 8 9 10   **Fic**

1. Werewolves—Fiction 2. Mother-daughter relationship—Fiction

ISBN 978-1-4169-9182-3; 1-4169-9182-4

LC 2009-36269

On her sixteenth birthday Claire discovers strange things happening and when her mother reveals their family secret which explains the changes, Claire feels her world, as she has known it to be, slowly slipping away.

"Strong characters and major plot twists coupled with a new twist on werewolf mythology make this a fun and entertaining read that will satisfy fans of the genre." SLJ

Johnson, Harriet McBryde

Accidents of nature. Holt 2006 229p $16.95 *

Grades: 9 10 11 12   **Fic**

1. Handicapped—Fiction 2. Camps—Fiction 3. Cerebral palsy—Fiction

ISBN 0-8050-7634-4; 978-0-8050-7634-9

LC 2005-24598

Having always prided herself on blending in with "normal" people despite her cerebral palsy, seventeen-year-old Jean begins to question her role in the world while attending a summer camp for children with disabilities.

"This book is smart and honest, funny and eye-opening. A must-read." SLJ

Johnson, Lindsay Lee

Worlds apart. Front Street 2005 166p il $16.95

Grades: 7 8 9 10   **Fic**

1. Moving—Fiction 2. Psychiatric hospitals—Fiction

ISBN 1-932425-28-4   LC 2005-12052

A thirteen-year-old daughter of a surgeon finds herself wrenched away from a comfortable lifestyle to a home on the grounds of a mental hospital, where her father has accepted a five year contract.

"This story brings bias and prejudice to the forefront in a discussable and readable narrative." SLJ

Johnson, LouAnne

Muchacho. Alfred A. Knopf 2009 197p $15.99; lib bdg $18.99

Grades: 8 9 10   **Fic**

1. Mexican Americans—Fiction 2. New Mexico—Fiction 3. School stories

ISBN 978-0-375-86117-8; 0-375-86117-3; 978-0-375-96117-5 (lib bdg); 0-375-96117-8 (lib bdg)

LC 2009-1768

Living in a neighborhood of drug dealers and gangs in New Mexico, high school junior Eddie Corazon, a juvenile delinquent-in-training, falls in love with a girl who inspires him to rethink his life and his choices.

"Eddie's first-person narration and street language will hold teenagers' interest. Set in New Mexico, one of the states with the highest dropout rates among Hispanics, this novel unveils the social pressures and struggles of teens living in inner cities." Kirkus

Johnson, Maureen, 1973-

13 little blue envelopes. HarperCollins Publishers 2005 317p $15.99; pa $8.99 *

Grades: 8 9 10 11 12   **Fic**

1. Voyages and travels—Fiction 2. Aunts—Fiction 3. Europe—Fiction

ISBN 0-06-054141-5; 0-06-054143-1 (pa)

LC 2005-02658

When seventeen-year-old Ginny receives a packet of mysterious envelopes from her favorite aunt, she leaves New Jersey to criss-cross Europe on a sort of scavenger hunt that transforms her life.

"Equal parts poignant, funny and inspiring, this tale is sure to spark wanderlust." Publ Wkly

Followed by: The last little blue envelope (2011)

Devilish. Razorbill/Penguin Putnam 2006 263p hardcover o.p. pa $8.99

Grades: 8 9 10 11 12   **Fic**

1. Devil—Fiction 2. Supernatural—Fiction 3. Friendship—Fiction 4. School stories

ISBN 1-59514-060-3; 1-59514-132-4 (pa)

LC 2006-10230

Jane Jarvis, a senior at a Catholic girl's school in Providence, Rhode Island, tries to save her best friend by making a pact with a demon—in the form of a cupcake-eating, very friendly teenage girl.

"Decorated in fine detail and well served by a terrific supporting cast, this page-turner will have high appeal and get great word-of-mouth." Booklist

Suite Scarlett. Scholastic Point 2008 353p $16.99

Grades: 6 7 8 9 10   **Fic**

1. Hotels and motels—Fiction 2. Family life—Fiction 3. Authorship—Fiction 4. New York (N.Y.)—Fiction

ISBN 978-0-439-89927-7; 0-439-89927-3

LC 2007-041903

Fifteen-year-old Scarlett Marvin is stuck in New York City for the summer working at her quirky family's historic hotel, but her brother's attractive new friend and a seasonal guest who offers her an intriguing and challenging writing project improve her outlook.

"Utterly winning, madcap Manhattan farce, crafted with a winking, urbane narrative and tight, wry dialogue." Booklist

Johnson, Maureen, 1973-—*Continued*
Another title about Scarlett is:
Scarlett fever (2010)

Jolin, Paula
In the name of God. Roaring Brook Press 2007
208p $16.95
Grades: 8 9 10 11 12   **Fic**
1. Muslims—Fiction 2. Family life—Fiction
3. Islamic fundamentalism—Fiction 4. Syria—Fiction
ISBN 978-1-59643-211-6; 1-59643-211-X
                                              LC 2006-23834
Determined to follow the laws set down in the Qur'an,
seventeen-year-old Nadia becomes involved in a violent
revolutionary movement aimed at supporting Muslim rule
in Syria and opposing the Western politics and materialism that increasingly affect her family.
"The well-written prose and short chapters give stories
in the news a face and a character. Readers of this book
will not be able to read or watch the news in the same
way." Voice Youth Advocates

Jones, Allan Frewin, 1954-
Warrior princess. Eos 2009 346p $16.99; pa
$8.99
Grades: 8 9 10 11 12   **Fic**
1. Princesses—Fiction 2. Magic—Fiction 3. Great
Britain—History—0-1066—Fiction 4. War stories
5. Wales—Fiction
ISBN 978-0-06-087143-7; 0-06-087143-1;
978-0-06-087145-1 (pa); 0-06-087145-8 (pa)
                                              LC 2008-23936
After a deadly attack on her home, fifteen-year-old
Princess Branwen meets a mystical woman in white who
prophesies that Branwen will save her homeland from
falling to the Saxons.
"Filled with battle scenes, fully realized characters,
and a conclusion that will keep readers guessing, this
story has surefire appeal." SLJ
Other titles in this series are:
Destiny's path (2009)
The emerald flame (2010)

Jones, Lloyd, 1955-
Mister Pip. Dial Press 2007 256p hardcover o.p.
pa $15
Grades: 11 12 Adult   **Fic**
1. Books and reading—Fiction 2. Storytelling—Fiction
3. New Guinea—Fiction
ISBN 978-0-385-34106-6; 0-385-34106-7;
978-0-385-34107-3 (pa); 0-385-34107-5 (pa)
                                              LC 2007-5224
First published 2006 in Australia
"Thirteen-year-old Matilda is at a loss to understand
the violence that has torn apart her tropical island. Her
village, caught in the cross fire of the conflict between
government troops and local armed rebels, has lost its
teachers. The only white man to stay behind, the eccentric Mr. Watts, married to a local woman who is generally thought to be mad, takes over the post as teacher and
begins to read to the class from his favorite novel,
Charles Dickens' Great Expectations. Initially flummoxed

by the meanings of such alien words as frost and moors,
Matilda and her classmates soon become entirely riveted
by the story and identify so heavily with the orphan Pip
that Victorian England becomes more real to them than
their own hometown." Booklist
"The novel is a paean to the transformative power of
literature, particularly its ability to occlude an unpleasant
reality with a fictional alternative and to expand an individual's sense of possibility." N Y Sun

Jones, Patrick
Chasing tail lights. Walker & Co. 2007 294p
hardcover o.p. pa $7.99
Grades: 9 10 11 12   **Fic**
1. Family life—Fiction 2. Incest—Fiction 3. Child
sexual abuse—Fiction 4. Michigan—Fiction
ISBN 978-0-8027-9628-8; 0-8027-9628-1;
978-0-8027-9762-9 (pa); 0-8027-9762-8 (pa)
                                              LC 2006-27657
Seventeen-year-old Christy wants only to finish high
school and escape her Flint, Michigan, home, where she
cooks, cleans, cares for her niece, and tries to fend off
her half-brother, a drug dealer who has been abusing her
since she was eleven.
The author "tackles a lot of relevant issues here. . . .
His look at teen rebellion and the misunderstandings it
can engender is full of hard-to-face truths, and his ultimate faith in teens' ability to survive tough circumstances may inspire readers." Bull Cent Child Books

The tear collector. Walker & Company 2009
263p $16.99
Grades: 7 8 9 10   **Fic**
1. Supernatural—Fiction 2. Family life—Fiction
3. School stories 4. Michigan—Fiction
ISBN 978-0-8027-8710-1; 0-8027-8710-X
                                              LC 2008-55868
As one of an ancient line of creatures who gain energy from human tears, seventeen-year-old Cassandra offers sympathy to anyone at her school or the hospital
where she works, but she yearns to be fully human for
the boy she loves, even if it means letting her family
down.
"Cassandra is a complex character who readers will
identify with as she struggles to understand who she really is, where her loyalties lie, and how to take control of
her own destiny. Those looking for a new spin on the
vampire story should find this one satisfying." SLJ

Jonsberg, Barry, 1951-
Dreamrider. Knopf 2008 239p $15.99; lib bdg
$18.99
Grades: 8 9 10 11 12   **Fic**
1. Bullies—Fiction 2. Dreams—Fiction 3. Obesity—
Fiction 4. Australia—Fiction 5. School stories
ISBN 978-0-375-84457-7; 0-375-84457-0;
978-0-375-94457-4 (lib bdg); 0-375-94457-5 (lib bdg)
                                              LC 2007-28929
First published 2006 in Australia
Harangued by his father about his weight and bullied
in all the many schools he has attended, teenaged Michael finds some comfort in his ability to experience "lucid" dreaming but then starts to notice that the things
that happen in his dreams are starting to occur in the real

Jonsberg, Barry, 1951-—_Continued_
world as well.

"Readers will be chilled by the author's unflinching and innovative treatment of the horrors and hopelessness engulfing the victim of bullying. Jonsberg's prose is spare, his pacing excellent, his plotting memorable." Publ Wkly

Jordan, Hillary, 1963-
Mudbound; a novel. Algonquin Books of Chapel Hill 2008 328p hardcover o.p. pa $13.95
Grades: 11 12 Adult   **Fic**
1. Farm life—Fiction 2. World War, 1939-1945—Fiction 3. Veterans—Fiction 4. Race relations—Fiction 5. Mississippi—Fiction
ISBN   978-1-56512-569-8;   1-56512-569-X; 978-1-56512-677-0 (pa); 1-56512-677-7 (pa)
                                        LC 2007-44471
"In 1946, Laura McAllan, a college-educated Memphis schoolteacher, becomes a reluctant farmer's wife when her husband, Henry, buys a farm on the Mississippi Delta, a farm she aptly nicknames Mudbound. Laura has difficulty adjusting to life without electricity, indoor plumbing, readily accessible medical care for her two children and, worst of all, life with her live-in misogynous, racist, father-in-law. Her days become easier after Florence, the wife of Hap Jackson, one of their black tenants, becomes more important to Laura as companion than as hired help. Catastrophe is inevitable when two young WWII veterans, Henry's brother, Jamie, and the Jacksons' son, Ronsel, arrive, both battling nightmares from horrors they've seen, and both unable to bow to Mississippi rules after eye-opening years in Europe. . . . [This is] a superbly rendered depiction of the fury and terror wrought by racism." Publ Wkly

Jordan, Sophie
Firelight. HarperTeen 2010 326p $16.99
Grades: 8 9 10 11 12   **Fic**
1. Dragons—Fiction 2. Supernatural—Fiction 3. Moving—Fiction 4. School stories 5. Dating (Social customs)—Fiction
ISBN 978-0-06-193508-4; 0-06-193508-5
                                        LC 2010-07033
When sixteen-year-old Jacinda, who can change into a dragon, is forced to move away from her community of shapeshifters and start a more normal life, she falls in love with a boy who proves to be her most dangerous enemy.

"Jordan's compelling addition to the supernatural star-crossed lovers theme is equal parts taut suspense and sensuous romance, with visceral writing and believable relationships." Booklist

Joyce, Graham
The exchange. Viking 2008 241p $16.99
Grades: 7 8 9 10   **Fic**
1. Supernatural—Fiction 2. Dating (Social customs)—Fiction 3. Tattooing—Fiction 4. Single parent family—Fiction
ISBN 978-0-670-06207-2; 0-670-06207-3
                                        LC 2007-32160

Cursed by the elderly recluse whose home she and a friend were creeping through late one night, fourteen-year-old Caz soon finds her life disintegrating and realizes she must find a way of lifting the curse—or at least understanding its power.

"Joyce has crafted a bizarre, magically realistic tale. . . . It's a wild ride with subtly moralistic undertones and a surprisingly happy ending that will stay with readers." Booklist

Joyce, James, 1882-1941
A portrait of the artist as a young man; with an introduction by Richard Brown. Knopf 1991 xli, 318p $18
Grades: 11 12 Adult   **Fic**
1. Ireland—Fiction
ISBN 0-679-40575-5   LC 91-52979
Also available from other publishers
"Everyman's library"
First appeared serially, 1914-1915 in the United Kingdom; first United States edition published 1916 by Huebsch

This autobiographical novel "portrays the childhood, school days, adolescence, and early manhood of Stephen Dedalus, later one of the leading characters in Ulysses. Stephen's growing self-awareness as an artist forces him to reject the whole narrow world in which he has been brought up, including family ties, nationalism, and the Catholic religion. The novel ends when, having decided to become a writer, he is about to leave Dublin for Paris. Rather than following a clear narrative progression, the book revolves around experiences that are crucial to Stephen's development as an artist; at the end of each chapter Stephen makes some assertion of identity. Through his use of the stream-of-consciousness technique, Joyce reveals the actual materials of his hero's world, the components of his thought processes." Reader's Ency. 4th edition

Juby, Susan, 1969-
Another kind of cowboy. HarperTeen 2007 344p $16.99
Grades: 8 9 10 11 12   **Fic**
1. Horsemanship—Fiction 2. Horses—Fiction 3. Homosexuality—Fiction 4. Friendship—Fiction 5. British Columbia—Fiction
ISBN 0-06-076517-8; 978-0-06-076517-0
                                        LC 2006-36336
In Vancouver, British Columbia, two teenage dressage riders, one a spoiled rich girl and the other a closeted gay sixteen-year-old boy, come to terms with their identities and learn to accept themselves.

"Wry humor infuses this quiet story with a gentle warmth, and the secondary characters are well developed." Booklist

Kade, Stacey
The ghost and the goth. Hyperion 2010 281p $16.99
Grades: 8 9 10 11 12   **Fic**
1. Ghost stories 2. School stories
ISBN 978-1-4231-2197-8; 1-4231-2197-X
                                        LC 2010-8135

Kade, Stacey—*Continued*

After being hit by a bus and killed, a high school homecoming queen gets stuck in the land of the living, with only a loser classmate—who happens to be able to see and hear ghosts—to help her.

"The tale is absorbing, and Kade successfully portrays a typical present-day high school. This novel will appeal to fans of romances and ghost stories alike." SLJ

Followed by: Queen of the dead (2011)

Kafka, Franz, 1883-1924

The trial; translated from the German by Willa and Edwin Muir; revised, with additional notes, by E. M. Butler. Knopf 1992 299p $19

Grades: 11 12 Adult   Fic

1. Trials—Fiction 2. Allegories

ISBN 0-679-40994-7

Also available in paperback from Schocken Bks.

"Everyman's library"

Original edition 1924; first Everyman's Library edition, 1922

"Joseph K., a respected bank assessor, is arrested and spends his remaining years fighting charges about which he has no knowledge. The helplessness of an insignificant individual within a mysterious bureaucracy where answers are never accessible is described in this provocative and disturbing book." Shapiro. Fic for Youth. 3d edition

Kaplow, Robert

Me and Orson Welles; a novel. MacAdam/Cage Pub. 2003 269p $18.50

Grades: 11 12 Adult   Fic

1. Welles, Orson, 1915-1985—Fiction 2. Actors—Fiction 3. New York (N.Y.)—Fiction

ISBN 1-931561-49-4   LC 2003-14982

Also available in paperback from Penguin Books

"Richard, 17, spends a hectic week in New York in 1938, where he gets a small part in *Julius Caesar* at the new Mercury Theatre and meets Orson Welles." SLJ

This is "a delightful escape into a pre-war coming-of-age, and coming-of-stage, story—perfect for a quick and totally entertaining read." Booklist

Karim, Sheba

Skunk girl. Farrar, Straus & Giroux 2009 231p $16.95

Grades: 8 9 10 11 12   Fic

1. Pakistani Americans—Fiction 2. Family life—Fiction 3. Muslims—Fiction 4. Dating (Social customs)—Fiction 5. School stories 6. New York (State)—Fiction

ISBN 978-0-374-37011-4; 0-374-37011-7

LC 2008-7482

Nina Khan is not just the only Asian or Muslim student in her small-town high school in upstate New York, she is also faces the legacy of her "Supernerd" older sister, body hair, and the pain of having a crush when her parents forbid her to date.

This novel is "rife with smart, self-deprecating humor." Kirkus

Kaslik, Ibolya, 1973-

Skinny; [by] Ibi Kaslik. Walker & Company 2006 244p $16.95

Grades: 11 12   Fic

1. Anorexia nervosa—Fiction 2. Sisters—Fiction 3. Father-daughter relationship—Fiction

ISBN 978-0-8027-9608-0; 0-8027-9608-7

LC 2006-42140

First published 2004 in Canada

After the death of their father, two sisters struggle with various issues, including their family history, personal relationships, and an extreme eating disorder

"It's refreshing that Gigi's anorexia and briefly described lesbian romance are treated as only parts of a larger story, and the girls' grief following their father's death and the pressures they face growing up with immigrant parents add depth to the novel. . . . This is an ambitious, often moving offering, and older readers will likely connect with the raw emotions and intelligent insights into a family's secrets, pain, and enduring love." Booklist

Kass, Pnina

Real time; by Pnina Moed Kass. Clarion Books 2004 186p $15; pa $7.99

Grades: 7 8 9 10   Fic

1. Israel—Fiction 2. Germans—Israel—Fiction 3. Terrorism—Fiction

ISBN 0-618-44203-0; 0-618-69174-X (pa)

LC 2004-8481

Sixteen-year-old Tomas Wanninger persuades his mother to let him leave Germany to volunteer at a kibbutz in Israel, where he experiences a violent political attack and finds answers about his own past

This "volume is an exhausting but illuminating read that will provide much-needed insight into life in modern Israel. . . . The characters are deeply developed and painfully sympathetic." SLJ

Katcher, Brian

Almost perfect. Delacorte Press 2009 360p $17.99 *

Grades: 9 10 11 12   Fic

1. Dating (Social customs)—Fiction 2. Transsexualism—Fiction 3. Single parent family—Fiction 4. School stories 5. Missouri—Fiction

ISBN 978-0-385-73664-0; 0-385-73664-9

LC 2008-37659

With his mother working long hours and in pain from a romantic break-up, eighteen-year-old Logan feels alone and unloved until a zany new student arrives at his small-town Missouri high school, keeping a big secret.

"The author tackles issues of homophobia, hate crimes and stereotyping with humor and grace in an accessible tone that will resonate with teens who may not have encountered the issue of transgender identity before." Kirkus

Katcher, Brian—*Continued*

Playing with matches. Delacorte Press 2008
294p $15.99; lib bdg $18.99

Grades: 8 9 10 11 12   **Fic**
1. Burns and scalds—Fiction 2. Missouri—Fiction
3. Dating (Social customs)—Fiction 4. School stories
  ISBN   978-0-385-73544-5;   0-385-73544-8;
978-0-385-90525-1 (lib bdg); 0-385-90525-4 (lib bdg)
                     LC 2007-27654

While trying to find a girl who will date him, Missouri high school junior Leon Sanders befriends a lonely, disfigured female classmate.

"This is a strong debut novel with a cast of quirky, multidimensional characters struggling with issues of acceptance, sexuality, identity, and self-worth." SLJ

Kate, Lauren

The betrayal of Natalie Hargrove. Penguin
Young Readers Group 2009 235p pa $9.99

Grades: 9 10 11 12   **Fic**
1. Social classes—Fiction 2. Contests—Fiction
3. School stories 4. South Carolina—Fiction
  ISBN 978-1-59514-265-8; 1-59514-265-7
                     LC 2009-18481

South Carolina high school senior Nat has worked hard to put her trailer-park past behind her, and when she and her boyfriend are crowned Palmetto Prince and Princess everything would be perfect, except that a prank they played a few nights before went horribly awry.

"Lots of adjectives can be applied to this debut effort—mean, smutty, decadent—and all of them should be taken as compliments." Booklist

Kaye, Marilyn

Demon chick. Henry Holt 2009 215p $16.99

Grades: 7 8 9 10   **Fic**
1. Mother-daughter relationship—Fiction 2. Hell—Fiction 3. Politics—Fiction
  ISBN 978-0-8050-8880-9; 0-8050-8880-6
                     LC 2008-50280

Sixteen-year-old Jessica discovers that her mother, a charismatic presidential candidate, sold Jessica's soul to the devil in exchange for political power.

"There's a little political commentary, a little Machiavellianism, a little about responsibility and guilt and loyalty, but the weighty issues are handled with a light touch, thanks to Jessica, whose wry observations and dialogue keep the narrative snappy. . . . This is one hell worth visiting." Horn Book

Kelly, Tara

Harmonic feedback. Henry Holt and Company
2010 280p $16.99

Grades: 9 10 11 12   **Fic**
1. Asperger's syndrome—Fiction 2. Drug abuse—Fiction 3. Rock music—Fiction 4. Washington (State)—Fiction
  ISBN 978-0-8050-9010-9; 0-8050-9010-X
                     LC 2009-24150

When Drea and her mother move in with her grandmother in Bellingham, Washington, the sixteen-year-old finds finds that she can have real friends, in spite of her

Asperger's, and that even when you love someone it doesn't make life perfect.

"The novel's strength lies in Drea's dynamic personality: a combination of surprising immaturity, childish wonder, and profound insight. Her search for stability and need to escape being labeled is poignant and convincing." Publ Wkly

Keneally, Thomas, 1935-

Schindler's list. Simon & Schuster 1982 400p
$25; pa $14 *

Grades: 11 12 Adult   **Fic**
1. Schindler, Oskar, 1908-1974—Fiction
2. Holocaust, 1933-1945—Fiction 3. World War, 1939-1945—Fiction 4. Jews—Fiction
  ISBN 0-671-51688-4; 0-671-88031-4 (pa)
                     LC 82-10489

"An actual occurrence during the Nazi regime in Germany forms the basis for this story. Oskar Schindler, a Catholic German industrialist, chose to act differently from those Germans who closed their eyes to what was happening to the Jews. By spending enormous sums on bribes to the SS and on food and drugs for the Jewish prisoners whom he housed in his own camp-factory in Cracow, he succeeded in sheltering thousands of Jews, finally transferring them to a safe place in Czechoslovakia. Fifty Schindler survivors from seven nations helped the author with information." Shapiro. Fic for Youth. 3d edition

Kennedy, William, 1928-

Ironweed. Viking 1983 227p pa $14 hardcover
o.p.

Grades: 11 12 Adult   **Fic**
1. Great Depression, 1929-1939—Fiction 2. New York (State)—Fiction 3. Homeless persons—Fiction
  ISBN 0-14-007020-6 (pa)   LC 82-40370

With this 'tale of skid-row life in the Depression, Kennedy adds another chapter to his 'Albany cycle'—a group of novels set in the Albany, New York, underworld from the 1920s onward. Following 'Legs' and 'Billy Phelan's Greatest Game,' 'Ironweed' tells the story of Francis Phelan, a 58-year-old bum with muscatel on his breath and hallucinations on his mind. Chief among the latter is a vision of his infant son, who died after falling out of Francis' arms. It is the desire to reconcile himself to the memory of his dead son that brings Francis home to Albany, ultimately opening the door to a possible reconciliation with his family." Booklist

Kephart, Beth

Dangerous neighbors; a novel. Egmont USA
2010 176p $16.99; lib bdg $19.99

Grades: 7 8 9 10   **Fic**
1. Centennial Exhibition (1876: Philadelphia, Pa.)—Fiction 2. Twins—Fiction 3. Sisters—Fiction 4. Death—Fiction 5. Bereavement—Fiction 6. Guilt—Fiction 7. Philadelphia (Pa.)—Fiction
  ISBN   978-1-60684-080-1;   1-60684-080-0;
978-1-60684-106-8 (lib bdg); 1-60684-106-8 (lib bdg)
                     LC 2010-11249

Set against the backdrop of the 1876 Centennial Exhibition in Philadelphia, Katherine cannot forgive herself

Kephart, Beth—*Continued*

when her beloved twin sister dies, and she feels that her only course of action is to follow suit.

"Exceptionally graceful prose . . . and flashbacks are so realistically drawn and deftly integrated that readers will be as startled as Katherine to find themselves yanked out of morose memories and surrounded by noisy fairgoers." Bull Cent Child Books

House of Dance. HarperTeen 2008 263p $16.99; lib bdg $17.89; pa $10.99

Grades: 7 8 9 10 **Fic**

1. Cancer—Fiction 2. Death—Fiction 3. Dancers—Fiction 4. Grandfathers—Fiction 5. Mother-daughter relationship—Fiction

ISBN 978-0-06-142928-6; 0-06-142928-7; 978-0-06-142929-3 (lib bdg); 0-06-142929-5 (lib bdg); 978-0-06-142930-9 (pa); 0-06-142930-9 (pa)

LC 2007-26011

"Laura Geringer books"

During one of her daily visits across town to visit her dying grandfather, fifteen-year-old Rosie discovers a dance studio that helps her find a way to bring her family members together.

This is "distinguished more by its sharp, eloquent prose than by its plot. . . . Poetically expressed memories and moving dialogue both anchor and amplify the characters' emotions." Publ Wkly

Nothing but ghosts. HarperTeen 2009 278p $17.95

Grades: 8 9 10 11 12 **Fic**

1. Bereavement—Fiction 2. Loss (Psychology)—Fiction 3. Gardening—Fiction 4. Mothers—Fiction 5. Art—Fiction

ISBN 978-0-06-166796-1; 0-06-166796-X

LC 2008-26024

"Laura Geringer books"

After her mother's death, sixteen-year-old Katie copes with her grief by working in the garden of an old estate, where she becomes intrigued by the story of a reclusive millionaire, while her father, an art restorer, manages in his own way to come to terms with the death of his wife.

"Kephart's evocative writing and gentle resolution offer healing and hope as her characters come to terms with their losses." Publ Wkly

Undercover. HarperTeen 2007 278p $16.99; lib bdg $17.89; pa $8.99

Grades: 8 9 10 11 12 **Fic**

1. Poetry—Fiction 2. School stories 3. Family life—Fiction

ISBN 978-0-06-123893-2; 0-06-123893-7; 978-0-06-123894-9 (lib bdg); 0-06-123894-5 (lib bdg); 978-0-06-123895-6 (pa); 0-06-123895-3 (pa)

LC 2007-2981

"Laura Geringer books"

High school sophomore Elisa is used to observing while going unnoticed except when classmates ask her to write love notes for them, but a teacher's recognition of her talent, a "client's" desire for her friendship, a love of ice skating, and her parent's marital problems draw her out of herself.

"Kephart tells a moving story. . . . Readers will fall easily into the compelling premise and Elisa's memorable, graceful voice." Booklist

Kerbel, Deborah, 1971-

Mackenzie, lost and found. Dundurn Press 2008 251p pa $12.99

Grades: 7 8 9 10 **Fic**

1. Jerusalem—Fiction 2. Culture conflict—Fiction

ISBN 978-1-55002-852-2; 1-55002-852-9

"Fifteen-year-old Mackenzie is uprooted from her native Canada and forced to move to Israel when her archaeologist father takes a visiting professorship at The Hebrew University of Jerusalem. . . . She soon begins to make friends and learn the language, while engaging in a forbidden romance with a Palestinian boy named Nasir. When Mack finds herself in the middle of a plot involving stolen antiquities after Nasir's father enlists his help in illegally digging up and selling artifacts, she must choose between protecting her first real boyfriend and obeying the law. . . . This solid coming-of-age story offers a unique setting and a likeable young heroine." Voice Youth Advocates

Kerouac, Jack, 1922-1969

On the road. 50th anniversary ed. Viking 2007 307p $25.95

Grades: 11 12 Adult **Fic**

1. Voyages and travels—Fiction 2. Friendship—Fiction

ISBN 978-0-670-06326-0 LC 2007021285

First published 1957

"Sal Paradise (a self-portrait of Kerouac), a struggling author in his mid-twenties, tells of his meeting Dean Moriarty (based on Neal Cassady), a fast-living teenager just out of a New Mexico reform school, whose soul is 'wrapped up in a fast car, a coast to reach, and a woman at the end of the road.' During the next five years they travel coast to coast, either with each other or to each other. Five trips are described." Oxford Companion to Am Lit. 6th edition

Kesey, Ken

One flew over the cuckoo's nest; a novel. Viking 1962 311p hardcover o.p. pa $7.99 *

Grades: 11 12 Adult **Fic**

1. Mentally ill—Fiction

ISBN 0-670-03058-9; 0-451-16396-6 (pa)

"Life in a mental institution is predictable and suffocating under the iron rule of Nurse Ratched, who tolerates no disruption of routine on her all-male ward. Half-Indian Chief Bromden, almost invisible on the ward because he is thought to be deaf and dumb, describes the arrival of rowdy Randle Patrick McMurphy. McMurphy takes on the nurse as an adversary in his attempt to organize his fellow inmates and breathe some self-esteem and joy into their lives. The battle is vicious on the part of the nurse, who is relentless in her efforts to break McMurphy, but a spark of human will brings an element of hope to counter the despotic institutional power." Shapiro. Fic for Youth. 3d edition

Kessler, Jackie Morse

Hunger. Graphia 2010 177p pa $8.99

Grades: 8 9 10 11 12   **Fic**

1. Anorexia nervosa—Fiction 2. Eating disorders—Fiction

ISBN 978-0-547-34124-8; 0-547-34124-5

                   LC 2009-50009

Seventeen-year-old Lisabeth has anorexia, and even turning into Famine—one of the Four Horsemen of the Apocalypse—cannot keep her from feeling fat and worthless.

"Kessler has written an unusual allegory about eating disorders, one that works on several levels." Booklist

Followed by: Rage (2011)

Keyes, Daniel, 1927-

Flowers for Algernon. Harcourt Brace & Co. 1995 c1966 286p $17 *

Grades: 9 10 11 12   **Fic**

1. Mentally handicapped—Fiction 2. Science fiction

ISBN 0-15-100163-4   LC 95-148312

Also available in paperback from Mariner Bks.

"A Harcourt Brace modern classic"

First published 1966

"Charlie Gordon, aged 32, is mentally retarded and enrolls in a class to 'become smart.' He keeps a journal of his progress after an experimental operation that increases his I.Q. Although Charlie becomes brilliant, he is unhappy because he cannot shed his former personality and is tormented by his memories. In the end he begins to lose the mental powers he has gained." Shapiro. Fic for Youth. 3d edition

Keyes, Pamela

The jumbee. Dial Books 2010 385p $17.99

Grades: 8 9 10 11 12   **Fic**

1. Theater—Fiction 2. Fathers—Fiction 3. Caribbean region—Fiction 4. Actors—Fiction 5. Superstition—Fiction

ISBN 978-0-8037-3313-8; 0-8037-3313-5

                   LC 2009-40048

Devastated by the death of her Shakespearean-actor father, Esti Legard moves to a tropical island for her senior year in high school, where she finds herself torn between a mysterious, masked mentor and a seductive island boy, as she tries to escape the overpowering shadow of her famous father.

"Romance fans will enjoy the fascinating locale along with the slow-building suspense and incidental acting lessons." Booklist

Kidd, Ronald, 1948-

On Beale Street. Simon & Schuster Books for Young Readers 2008 244p $16.99

Grades: 7 8 9 10 11 12   **Fic**

1. Presley, Elvis, 1935-1977—Fiction 2. Rock music—Fiction 3. Race relations—Fiction 4. Segregation—Fiction 5. Memphis (Tenn.)—Fiction

ISBN 978-1-4169-3387-8; 1-4169-3387-5

                   LC 2007-22583

In Memphis, in the 1950's, when fifteen-year-old Johnny is introduced to the blues, he ventures to the in-famous Beale Street and finds the friendship with an up-and-coming young musician Elvis Presley.

"This novel is a fascinating glimpse into the musical world of Beale Street, the society that was the segregated South, [and] the origins of rock and roll. . . . Accurate historical details are skillfully woven into what becomes an absorbing search for personal identity." SLJ

Kidd, Sue Monk

The secret life of bees. Viking 2002 301p hardcover o.p. pa $14 *

Grades: 11 12 Adult   **Fic**

1. African Americans—Fiction 2. Race relations—Fiction 3. South Carolina—Fiction

ISBN 0-670-89460-5; 0-14-200174-0 (pa)

                   LC 2001-26310

This is the "tale of a 14-year-old white girl named Lily Owen who is raised by the elderly African American Rosaleen after the accidental death of Lily's mother. Following a racial brawl in 1960s Tiburon, S.C, Lily and Rosaleen find shelter in a distant town with three black bee-keeping sisters." Libr J

"Lily is a wonderfully petulant and self-absorbed adolescent, and Kidd deftly portrays her sense of injustice as it expands to accommodate broader social evils." N Y Times Book Rev

Kinch, Michael P.

The blending time; [by] Michael Kinch. Flux 2010 254p pa $9.95

Grades: 10 11 12   **Fic**

1. Science fiction 2. Violence—Fiction 3. Africa—Fiction

ISBN 978-0-7387-2067-8   LC 2010-24149

In the harsh world of 2069, ravaged by plagues and environmental disasters, friends Jaym, Reya, and D'Shay are chosen to help repopulate Africa as their mandatory Global Alliance work, but civil war and mercenaries opposed to the Blending Program separate them and threaten their very lives.

"Determinedly multiethnic, fast-paced, and with plentiful gore and violence, the book will draw reluctant readers who enjoy action and adventure." Booklist

Kincy, Karen, 1986-

Other. Flux 2010 326p pa $9.95

Grades: 9 10 11 12   **Fic**

1. Supernatural—Fiction 2. Homicide—Fiction 3. Self-acceptance—Fiction 4. Washington (State)—Fiction

ISBN 978-0-7387-1919-1   LC 2010-5297

Gwen Williams is like any seventeen-year-old except that she is a shapeshifter living in Klikamuks, Washington, where not everyone tolerates "Others" like Gwen, but when someone begins killing Others she must try to embrace her true self and find the killer before she becomes the next victim.

"The emotional turmoil of the characters is evident and will appeal to readers who have felt misunderstood or as if they don't belong—teenagers." SLJ

King, A. S., 1970-
Please ignore Vera Dietz. Alfred A. Knopf 2010
326p $16.99; lib bdg $19.99; ebook $16.99 *
Grades: 9 10 11 12   **Fic**
   1. Friendship—Fiction 2. Death—Fiction
   ISBN 978-0-375-86586-2; 978-0-375-96586-9 (lib
bdg); 978-0-375-89617-0 (ebook)   LC 2010-12730
   When her best friend, whom she secretly loves, betrays her and then dies under mysterious circumstances,
high school senior Vera Dietz struggles with secrets that
could help clear his name.
   This "is a gut-wrenching tale about family, friendship,
destiny, the meaning of words, and self-discovery."
Voice Youth Advocates

King, Laurie R.
   The beekeeper's apprentice, or, on the
segregation of the queen. Picador/Thomas Dunne
Books 2007 xxi, 346p pa $14
Grades: 11 12 Adult   **Fic**
   1. Holmes, Sherlock (Fictional character) 2. Mystery
fiction 3. Great Britain—Fiction
   ISBN 978-0-312-42736-8
   "A Mary Russell novel"
   First published 1994 by St. Martin's Press
   Includes discussion questions and author interview
   Chance meeting with a Sussex beekeeper turns into a
pivotal, personal transformation when fifteen-year-old
Mary Russell discovers that the beekeeper is the reclusive, retired detective Sherlock Holmes, who soon takes
on the role of mentor and teacher.
   "A wonderfully original and entertaining story that is
funny, heartwarming, and full of intrigue. . . . Holmes
fans, history buffs, lovers of humor and adventure, and
mystery devotees will all find King's book absorbing
from beginning to end." Booklist

King, Stephen, 1947-
   Carrie. Doubleday 1974 199p $32.50
Grades: 11 12 Adult   **Fic**
   1. Psychokinesis—Fiction 2. Horror fiction 3. Maine—
Fiction
   ISBN 0-385-08695-4
   Also available in paperback from Pocket Bks.
   "Carrie is 16, lonely, the butt of all her Maine classmates' tricks and jokes, an object of scorn even to her
own mother, who is fanatically religious and believes
anything remotely sexual is from the devil. Then one girl
becomes ashamed of the cruelty being vented on Carrie
and plans an act of kindness that will give her the first
happiness in her young life. The only trouble is the act
backfires horribly and Carrie is worse off than ever before. It is at this point, at the senior prom, that Carrie begins to put into effect her awesome telekinetic powers,
powers with which she has only toyed before." Publ
Wkly
   "A terrifying treat for both horror and parapsychology
fans." SLJ

   Firestarter. Viking 1980 428p hardcover o.p. pa
$7.99
Grades: Adult   **Fic**
   1. Psychokinesis—Fiction 2. Horror fiction
   ISBN 0-670-31541-9; 0-451-16780-5 (pa)
                                       LC 80-14793

   "Two college students sign up as paid guinea pigs for
a secret and unknowingly dangerous government experiment in telekinesis. . . . When the subjects marry and
have a baby, however, their child develops not only telekinesis but pyrokinesis as well; in short, the tot can not
only push things with her mind, but set them ablaze as
well. The government's plan to use the girl as a human
weapon set [the author's] plot into action, and an extended chase ensues with expected havoc wreaked in vivid
detail." Booklist
   "This is your advanced post-Watergate cynical American thriller with some eerie parapsychological twists, and
it's been done so distinctively well that we'd better talk
about genius rather than genre." Quill Quire

Kingsolver, Barbara
   The bean trees; a novel. 10th anniversary ed.
HarperFlamingo 1997 261p $19.95; pa $7.99 *
Grades: 11 12 Adult   **Fic**
   1. Arizona—Fiction
   ISBN 0-06-017579-6; 0-06-109731-4 (pa)
                                       LC 97-2691
   A reissue of the title first published 1988
   In this novel, "Taylor Greer, a poor, young woman,
flees her Kentucky home and heads west. . . . While
passing through Oklahoma, she becomes responsible for
a two-year-old Cherokee girl. The two continue on the
road. When they roll off the highway in Tucson, Taylor
and the child, whom she has named Turtle, . . . meet
Mattie, a widow who runs Jesus Is Lord Used Tires and
is active in the sanctuary movement on the side." Ms
   This book "gives readers something that's increasingly
hard to find today—a character to believe in and laugh
with and admire." Christ Sci Monit
   Followed by Pigs in heaven (1993)

   The poisonwood Bible; a novel. HarperFlamingo
1998 546p $26; pa $16.99 *
Grades: 11 12 Adult   **Fic**
   1. Congo (Republic)—Fiction   2. Christian
missionaries—Fiction
   ISBN 0-06-017540-0; 0-06-157707-3 (pa)
                                       LC 98-19901
   "In 1959, evangelical preacher Nathan Price moves his
wife and four daughters from Georgia to a village in the
Belgian Congo, later Zaire. Their dysfunction and cultural arrogance proves disastrous as the family is nearly destroyed by war, Nathan's tyranny, and Africa itself. Told
in the voices of the mother and daughters, the novel
spans 30 years as the women seek to understand each
other and the continent that tore them apart." Libr J
   "Buttressing her suspenseful chronicle with authentic
background detail, Kingsolver's narrative is at once a
compelling family saga and an astute look at Western
imperialism in Africa." Publ Wkly

Kinsella, W. P.
   Shoeless Joe. Houghton Mifflin 1982 265p
hardcover o.p. pa $13.95
Grades: 9 10 11 12   **Fic**
   1. Baseball—Fiction 2. Fantasy fiction
   ISBN 0-395-32047-X; 0-395-95773-7 (pa)
                                       LC 81-19196

Kinsella, W. P.—*Continued*

In this fantasy, Iowan farmer Ray Kinsella "hears a voice say 'If you build it, he will come,' and knows that 'it' refers to a baseball park and 'he' to Shoeless Joe Jackson. . . . Ray builds his magic stadium and while watching Shoeless Joe and others play ball, hears the voice again, this time saying, 'Ease his pain.' The mission clearly means kidnapping J. D. Salinger and taking him to Fenway Park for a Red Sox game. Ray succeeds and Salinger . . . joins Ray on a further quest. Their odyssey culminates back at home plate in Iowa." Quill Quire

Kirkpatrick, Jane, 1946-

A flickering light. Waterbrook Press 2009 387p pa $13.99

Grades: 10 11 12 Adult   **Fic**

1. Photographers—Fiction 2. Christian life—Fiction
ISBN 978-1-57856-980-9   LC 2008-47066

"Set in 1907 Minnesota, . . . [this novel] is a coming-of-age tale about a 15-year-old girl working as a photographer's assistant. Jessie Ann Gaebele is talented and shows great promise; however, she begins to dream of more than photographs when she falls for her married boss. Inspired by the life of the author's grandmother, this is a beautifully told story of temptation and God's redeeming grace." Libr J

Kittredge, Caitlin, 1984-

The Iron Thorn. Delacorte Press 2011 493p (Iron Codex) $17.99; lib bdg $20.99

Grades: 7 8 9 10   **Fic**

1. Fantasy fiction
ISBN   978-0-385-73829-3;   0-385-73829-3;
978-0-385-90720-0 (lib bdg); 0-385-90720-6 (lib bdg)
LC 2010-00972

In an alternate 1950s, mechanically gifted fifteen-year-old Aoife Grayson, whose family has a history of going mad at sixteen, must leave the totalitarian city of Lovecraft and venture into the world of magic to solve the mystery of her brother's disappearance and the mysteries surrounding her father and the Land of Thorn.

"Steampunk fans will delight in this first title in the sure-to-be-popular Iron Codex series. . . . There's plenty of tame but satisfying romance, too, and plot twists galore. Aoife is a caustic-tongued, feisty, and independent young woman, with plenty of nerve and courage." Booklist

Kizer, Amber

Meridian. Delacorte Press 2009 305p $16.99; lib bdg $19.99

Grades: 7 8 9 10   **Fic**

1. Angels—Fiction 2. Supernatural—Fiction
3. Death—Fiction 4. Good and evil—Fiction
5. Colorado—Fiction
ISBN   978-0-385-73668-8;   0-385-73668-1;
978-0-385-90621-0 (lib bdg); 0-385-90621-8 (lib bdg)
LC 2008-35666

On her sixteenth birthday, Meridian is whisked off to her great-aunt's home in Revelation, Colorado, where she learns that she is a Fenestra, the half-human, half-angel link between the living and the dead, and must learn to help human souls to the afterlife before the dark forces reach them.

"The author brings a fresh voice to the realm of teen paranormal romantic fiction. . . . The characters are compelling and the themes of good and evil, life and death will keep readers engaged." SLJ

Followed by: Wildcat fireflies (2011)

Klass, David, 1960-

Dark angel. Farrar, Straus & Giroux 2005 311p $17

Grades: 7 8 9 10   **Fic**

1. Brothers—Fiction 2. School stories
ISBN 0-374-39950-6   LC 2004-53340

"Frances Foster books"

When his older brother is released from prison, seventeen-year-old Jeff's family secret is revealed, causing upheaval in his home, school and love life.

"The plot builds ferociously in tandem with Jeff's suffocating conflict and burgeoning courage. . . . Recommend this fast-paced, thoughtful story to older reluctant readers, especially boys." SLJ

You don't know me; a novel. Foster Bks. 2001 262p $17 *

Grades: 7 8 9 10   **Fic**

1. School stories 2. Child abuse—Fiction
ISBN 0-374-38706-0   LC 00-22709

Fourteen-year-old John creates alternative realities in his mind as he tries to deal with his mother's abusive boyfriend, his crush on a beautiful, but shallow classmate and other problems at school

"Klass is effective with John's deliberately distanced voice, his constant dancing with and away from reality, . . . and his brittle and even dorky defenses, and the rising tension is suspenseful." Bull Cent Child Books

Klass, Sheila Solomon

Soldier's secret; the story of Deborah Sampson. Henry Holt 2009 215p $17.95

Grades: 6 7 8 9 10   **Fic**

1. Sampson, Deborah, 1760-1827—Fiction 2. United States—History—1775-1783, Revolution—Fiction 3. Soldiers—Fiction
ISBN 978-0-8050-8200-5; 0-8050-8200-X
LC 2008-36783

"Christy Ottaviano books"

During the Revolutionary War, a young woman named Deborah Sampson disguises herself as a man in order to serve in the Continental Army.

In this novel, Sampson "is strong, brave, and witty. . . . Klass doesn't shy away from the horrors of battle; she also is blunt regarding details young readers will wonder about, like how Sampson dealt with bathing, urination, and menstruation. . . . Sampson's romantic yearnings for a fellow soldier . . . is given just the right notes or restraint and realism." Booklist

Klause, Annette Curtis

Blood and chocolate. Delacorte Press 1997 264p
hardcover o.p. pa $6.50 *

Grades: 7 8 9 10   Fic
1. Werewolves—Fiction 2. Horror fiction
ISBN 0-385-32305-0; 0-440-22668-6 (pa)
LC 96-35247

Having fallen for a human boy, a beautiful teenage
werewolf must battle both her packmates and the fear of
the townspeople to decide where she belongs and with
whom

"Klause's imagery is magnetic, and her language
fierce, rich, and beautiful. . . . . Passion and philosophy
dovetail superbly in this powerful, unforgettable novel
for mature teens." Booklist

The silver kiss. Delacorte Press 1990 198p
hardcover o.p. pa $5.99 *

Grades: 8 9 10 11 12   Fic
1. Vampires—Fiction 2. Death—Fiction
ISBN 0-385-30160-X; 0-440-21346-0 (pa)
LC 89-48880

"One evening, when 17-year-old Zoë is sitting in the
park contemplating her mother's imminent death due to
cancer, her father's lack of support, and her best friend's
move, she meets Simon. Simon is startlingly handsome
and strangely compelling. As their friendship grows over
time, Simon reveals to Zoë his true identity: he is a vampire, trying to kill his younger vampire brother." SLJ

"There's inherent romantic appeal in the vampire legend, and Klause weaves all the gory details into a poignant love story that becomes both sensuous and suspenseful." Booklist

Klein, Lisa M., 1958-

Cate of the Lost Colony; by Lisa Klein.
Bloomsbury 2010 329p $16.99

Grades: 8 9 10 11 12   Fic
1. Raleigh, Sir Walter, 1552?-1618—Fiction 2. Elizabeth I, Queen of England, 1533-1603—Fiction
3. Roanoke Island (N.C.)—History—Fiction 4. Great
Britain—History—1485-1603, Tudors—Fiction
5. Lumbee Indians—Fiction 6. Orphans—Fiction
ISBN 978-1-59990-507-5; 1-59990-507-8
LC 2010-8299

When her dalliance with Sir Walter Ralegh is discovered by Queen Elizabeth in 1587, lady-in-waiting Catherine Archer is banished to the struggling colony of Roanoke, where she and the other English settlers must rely
on a Croatoan Indian for their survival. Includes author's
note on the mystery surrounding the Lost Colony.

"This robust, convincing portrait of the Elizabethan
world with complex, rounded characters wraps an
intriguingly plausible solution to the 'lost colony' mystery inside a compelling love story of subtle thematic
depth." Kirkus

Includes bibliographical references

Lady Macbeth's daughter. Bloomsbury 2009
291p $16.99

Grades: 7 8 9 10   Fic
1. Macbeth, King of Scotland, d. 1057—Fiction
2. Shakespeare, William, 1564-1616—Fiction
3. Kings and rulers—Fiction 4. Physically handicapped—Fiction 5. Witchcraft—Fiction 6. Homicide—
Fiction 7. Scotland—Fiction
ISBN 978-1-59990-347-7; 1-59990-347-4
LC 2009-6717

In alternating chapters, ambitious Lady Macbeth tries
to bear a son and win the throne of Scotland for her husband, and Albia, their daughter who was banished at
birth and raised by three weird sisters, falls in love,
learns of her parentage, and seeks to free Scotland from
tyranny in this tale based on Shakespeare's Macbeth.

"The writing is crisp and clear and makes good use of
Shakespeare's language and its times. The characters are
well-developed and the story being told from the perspective of the mother and daughter makes for age-old
conflict. This tale will keep readers asking the ultimate
question of whether or not power is ultimately worth the
price." Libr Media Connect

Ophelia. Bloomsbury Children's Books 2006
328p $16.95

Grades: 9 10 11 12   Fic
1. Shakespeare, William, 1564-1616—Fiction
2. Homicide—Fiction 3. Princes—Fiction
ISBN 978-1-58234-801-8; 1-58234-801-4
LC 2005-32601

In a story based on Shakespeare's Hamlet, Ophelia
tells of her life in the court at Elsinore, her love for
Prince Hamlet, and her escape from the violence in Denmark.

"Teens need not be familiar with Shakespeare's original to enjoy this fresh take—with the added romance and
a strong heroine at its center." Publ Wkly

Kluger, Steve

My most excellent year; a novel of love, Mary
Poppins, & Fenway Park. Dial Books 2008 403p
$16.99; pa $8.99

Grades: 8 9 10 11 12   Fic
1. Boston (Mass.)—Fiction 2. Friendship—Fiction
ISBN   978-0-8037-3227-8;   0-8037-3227-9;
978-0-14-241343-2 (pa); 0-14-2413437 (pa)
LC 2007-26651

"Three bright and funny Brookline, MA, eleventh
graders look back on their most excellent year—ninth
grade—for a school report. Told in alternating chapters
by each of them, this enchanting, life-affirming coming-
of-age story unfolds through instant messages, emails,
memos, diary entries, and letters. . . . This is a rich and
humorous novel for older readers." SLJ

Knowles, Johanna, 1970-

Jumping off swings; [by] Jo Knowles.
Candlewick Press 2009 230p $16.99

Grades: 10 11 12   Fic
1. Pregnancy—Fiction
ISBN 978-0-7636-3949-5; 0-7636-3949-4
LC 2009-4587

Knowles, Johanna, 1970-—*Continued*

Tells, from four points of view, the ramifications of a pregnancy resulting from a "one-time thing" between Ellie, who feels loved when boys touch her, and Josh, an eager virgin with a troubled home life.

"With so many protagonists in the mix, it is no small feat that each character is fully developed and multidimensional—there are no villains or heroes here, only kids groping their way through a desperate situation. . . . [This is] a moving tale with a realistically unresolved ending." Kirkus

Knowles, John, 1926-2001

A separate peace. Scribner Classics 1996 204p $20; pa $11 *

Grades: 11 12 Adult   Fic

1. Friendship—Fiction 2. School stories

ISBN 0-684-83366-2; 0-7432-5397-3 (pa)

LC 96-25844

A reissue of the title published 1960 by Macmillan

"Gene Forrester looks back on his school days, spent in a New England town just before World War II. He both admires and envies his close friend and roommate, Finny, who is a natural athlete, in contrast to Gene's special competence as a scholar. When Finny suffers a crippling accident, Gene must face his own involvement in it." Shapiro. Fic for Youth. 3d edition

Knox, Elizabeth, 1959-

Dreamhunter; book one of the Dreamhunter duet. Farrar, Straus & Giroux 2006 365p (Dreamhunter duet) $19; pa $8.99

Grades: 7 8 9 10   Fic

1. Fantasy fiction 2. Dreams—Fiction

ISBN 0-374-31853-0; 0-312-53571-6 (pa)

LC 2005-46366

"Frances Foster books"

First published 2005 in the United Kingdom

In a world where select people can enter "The Place" and find dreams of every kind to share with others for a fee, a fifteen-year-old girl is training to be a dreamhunter when her father disappears, leaving her to carry on his mysterious mission.

This first of a two-book series is "a highly original exploration of the idea of a collective unconscious, mixed with imagery from the raising of Lazarus and with the brave, dark qualities of the psyche of an adolescent female." Horn Book Guide

Followed by Dreamquake (2007)

Koertge, Ronald

Margaux with an X; [by] Ron Koertge. Candlewick Press 2004 165p $15.99; pa $6.99 *

Grades: 7 8 9 10   Fic

1. Domestic violence—Fiction

ISBN 0-7636-2401-2; 0-7636-2679-1 (pa)

LC 2003-65279

Margaux, known as a "tough chick" at her Los Angeles high school, makes a connection with Danny, who, like her, struggles with the emotional impact of family violence and abuse.

This book "excels in character development. It is an intriguing story that constantly provokes readers' curiosity. . . . [The author's] language at times is advanced, an accurate reflection of his characters' intellectual capacity." SLJ

Stoner & Spaz; [by] Ron Koertge. Candlewick Press 2002 169p hardcover o.p. pa $6.99

Grades: 8 9 10 11 12   Fic

1. Cerebral palsy—Fiction 2. School stories

ISBN 0-7636-1608-7; 0-7636-2150-1 (pa)

LC 2001-43050

A troubled youth with cerebral palsy struggles toward self-acceptance with the help of a drug-addicted young woman

"Funny, touching, and surprising, it is a hopeful yet realistic view of things as they are and as they could be." Booklist

Followed by: Now Playing: Stoner & Spaz II (2011)

Strays; [by] Ron Koertge. Candlewick Press 2007 167p $16.99 *

Grades: 7 8 9 10 11 12   Fic

1. Foster home care—Fiction 2. Orphans—Fiction

ISBN 978-0-7636-2705-8; 0-7636-2705-4

LC 2007-24096

After his parents are killed in a car accident, high school senior Sam wonders whether he will ever feel again or if he will remain numbed by grief.

"Though Koertge never soft pedals the horrors faced by some foster children, this thoughtful novel about the lost and abandoned is a hopeful one." Booklist

Koja, Kathe

Buddha boy. Speak 2004 117p pa $5.99

Grades: 7 8 9 10   Fic

1. Conduct of life—Fiction 2. Artists—Fiction 3. Buddhism—Fiction 4. School stories

ISBN 0-14-240209-5   LC 2004041669

First published 2003 by Farrar, Straus & Giroux

Justin spends time with Jinsen, the unusual and artistic new student whom the school bullies torment and call Buddha Boy, and ends up making choices that impact Jinsen, himself, and the entire school.

"A compelling introduction to Buddhism and a credible portrait of how true friendship brings out the best in people." Publ Wkly

Headlong. Farrar, Straus and Giroux 2008 195p $16.95

Grades: 8 9 10 11 12   Fic

1. Social classes—Fiction 2. Orphans—Fiction 3. School stories

ISBN 978-0-374-32912-9; 0-374-32912-5

LC 2007-23612

"Frances Foster books"

High school sophomore Lily opens herself to new possibilities when, despite warnings, she becomes friends with 'ghetto girl' Hazel, a new student at the private Vaughn School which Lily, following in her elitist mother's footsteps, has attended since preschool.

"Class, identity and friendship are the intersecting subjects of this intelligent novel. . . . [The author] relays this story with her usual insight and, through her lightning-fast characterizations, an ability to project multiple perspectives simultaneously." Publ Wkly

Koja, Kathe—*Continued*

Kissing the bee. Farrar, Straus and Giroux 2007 121p $16

Grades: 8 9 10 11 12   **Fic**
1. Bees—Fiction 2. Friendship—Fiction 3. Love stories 4. School stories
ISBN 978-0-374-39938-2; 0-374-39938-7
                                        LC 2006-37378
"Frances Foster books"

While working on a bee project for her advanced biology class, quiet high school senior Dana reflects on her relationship with gorgeous best friend Avra and Avra's boyfriend Emil, whom Dana secretly loves.

The "understated, tightly focused language evokes vivid scenes and heady emotions." Publ Wkly

Kolosov, Jacqueline A.

A sweet disorder; by Jacqueline Kolosov. Disney/Hyperion 2009 418p $16.99

Grades: 7 8 9 10   **Fic**
1. Courts and courtiers—Fiction 2. Great Britain—History—1485-1603, Tudors—Fiction
ISBN 978-1-4231-1245-7; 1-4231-1245-8
                                        LC 2010-278820

Sixteen-year old Miranda has no idea how much her life is going to change upon hearing the news of her father's death. Left with little dowry to offer, Miranda faces a broken engagement, and is sent to live with her father's cousin, the Count John Hardwood, and his wife whose primary goal is to take her to Court and marry her off to the insufferable Lord Seagrave for their own profit.

"With well-chosen words and characters, Kolosov paints a vivid picture of the pageantry, excesses, and social structure of the time, creating a story that should appeal to girls who want stories that are rich with intrigue, historical settings, and romance." Voice Youth Advocates

Koontz, Dean R., 1945-

Watchers. Putnam 1987 352p hardcover o.p. pa $7.99

Grades: 11 12 Adult   **Fic**
1. Spies—Fiction 2. Dogs—Fiction 3. Genetics—Fiction 4. Horror fiction
ISBN 0-399-13263-5; 0-425-18880-9 (pa)
                                        LC 86-22687

"When the Russians sabotage a genetic research project in California, two mutated creatures escape from the lab. One is a golden retriever with high enough intelligence to think and communicate with humans; the other is the Outsider, a vicious monster created from a baboon and bred to kill. Both the man who befriends and adopts the dog and his new bride find themselves stalked by government agents anxious to find the dog, a particularly repulsive Mafia hit man intent on stealing him, and the Outsider, with whom the dog is linked telepathically." Libr J

Korman, Gordon, 1963-

The Juvie three. Hyperion 2008 249p lib bdg $15.99

Grades: 7 8 9 10   **Fic**
1. Juvenile delinquency—Fiction 2. Friendship—Fiction
ISBN 978-1-4231-0158-1; 1-4231-0158-8
                                        LC 2008-19087

Gecko, Arjay, and Terence, all in trouble with the law, must find a way to keep their halfway house open in order to stay out of juvenile detention.

"Korman keeps lots of balls in the air as he handles each boy's distinct voice and character—as well as the increasingly absurd situation—with humor and flashes of sadness." Booklist

Pop. Balzer + Bray 2009 260p $16.99; lib bdg $17.89; pa $8.99

Grades: 7 8 9 10   **Fic**
1. Football—Fiction 2. Alzheimer's disease—Fiction 3. Moving—Fiction 4. Divorce—Fiction 5. School stories
ISBN   978-0-06-174228-6;   0-06-174228-7; 978-0-06-174230-9 (lib bdg); 0-06-174230-9 (lib bdg); 978-0-06-174261-3 (pa); 0-06-174261-9 (pa)
                                        LC 2008-52106

Lonely after a midsummer move to a new town, sixteen-year-old high-school quarterback Marcus Jordan becomes friends with a retired professional linebacker who is great at training him, but whose childish behavior keeps Marcus in hot water.

"Readers will be sucked into compelling story lines on complicated family situations, peer acceptance, the game of football, and the efffects of progressive Alzheimer's disease on the persons involved, their families, and friends—themes that flow seamlessly together." Voice Youth Advocates

Son of the mob. Hyperion Bks. for Children 2002 262p hardcover o.p. pa $7.99

Grades: 7 8 9 10   **Fic**
1. Mafia—Fiction
ISBN 0-7868-0769-5; 0-7868-1593-0 (pa)
                                        LC 2002-68672

Seventeen-year-old Vince's life is constantly complicated by the fact that he is the son of a powerful Mafia boss, a relationship that threatens to destroy his romance with the daughter of an FBI agent

"The fast-paced, tightly focused story addresses the problems of being an honest kid in a family of outlaws—and loving them anyway. Korman doesn't ignore the seamier side of mob life, but even when the subject matter gets violent . . . he keeps things light by relating his tale in the first-person voice of a humorously sarcastic yet law-abiding wise guy." Horn Book

Another title about Vince is:
Son of the mob: Hollywood hustle (2004)

Kosinski, Jerzy N., 1933-1991

The painted bird; with an introduction by the author. 2nd ed. Grove Press 1995 xxvi, 234p pa $12

Grades: 11 12 Adult   **Fic**
1. Poland—Fiction 2. World War, 1939-1945—Fiction 3. Refugees—Fiction 4. Boys—Fiction
ISBN 0-8021-3422-X   LC 95-19520

Kosinski, Jerzy N., 1933-1991—*Continued*
First published 1965 by Houghton Mifflin
"In Eastern Europe during World War II a ten-year-old boy is separated from his parents and struggles to survive in primitive villages where he is viewed as an unwanted outsider. Dark-haired and dark-eyed, he is unlike the Polish villagers among whom he tries to find refuge. He is the gypsy, the 'painted bird,' and savage abuse is heaped upon him time after time. He has, nevertheless, the will to transcend the sadism and superstition of these ignorant people." Shapiro. Fic for Youth. 3d edition

Kositsky, Lynne, 1947-
Claire by moonlight. Tundra Books 2005 271p pa $9.95
Grades: 7 8 9 10   **Fic**
1. Nova Scotia—Fiction 2. Acadians—Fiction
ISBN 0-88776-659-5
"Claire Richard has already survived the death of her parents, deportation from her beloved Acadian village, and a violent storm at sea. British and French forces are at large in 1755, but she is determined to return to Acadia with her remaining sister and brother. She also seeks her true love, Sam, a reluctant British soldier. . . . Plenty of action and the determination of the strong female heroine move the story swiftly along." Booklist

Kostick, Conor
Epic. Viking 2007 364p $17.99 *
Grades: 7 8 9 10   **Fic**
1. Fantasy fiction 2. Video games—Fiction
ISBN 0-670-06179-4; 978-0-670-06179-2
                              LC 2006-19958
On New Earth, a world based on a video role-playing game, fourteen-year-old Erik pursuades his friends to aid him in some unusual gambits in order to save his father from exile and safeguard the futures of each of their families.
"There is intrigue and mystery throughout this captivating page-turner. Veins of moral and ethical social situations and decisions provide some great opportunities for discussion. Well written and engaging." SLJ
Other titles in this series are:
Edda (2011)
Saga (2008)

Krovatin, Christopher, 1985-
Heavy metal and you. Scholastic 2005 186p $16.95; pa $7.99
Grades: 9 10 11 12   **Fic**
1. School stories 2. Rock music—Fiction 3. New York (N.Y.)—Fiction
ISBN 0-439-73648-X; 0-439-74399-0 (pa)
                              LC 2004-23645
High schooler Sam begins losing himself when he falls for a preppy girl who wants him to give up getting wasted with his best friends and even his passion for heavy metal music in order to become a better person.
"From the terrific cover and portrait of selfish love to the clever CD player icons indicating narrative switches . . . this is an authentic portrayal of an obsession with music. Teens don't have to like heavy metal to appreci-

ate this novel, which is guaranteed to attract readers looking for a book to reach their death-metal souls." Booklist

Kuipers, Alice, 1979-
Lost for words. HarperTeen 2010 210p $16.99
Grades: 8 9 10 11 12   **Fic**
1. Sisters—Fiction 2. Death—Fiction 3. Bereavement—Fiction 4. London (England)—Fiction
ISBN 978-0-06-142922-4; 0-06-142922-8
                              LC 2009-39673
Sixteen-year-old Sophie struggles to find normalcy after an incident she chooses not to remember took her sister's life, and by keeping a journal, making a new friend, and seeing a therapist she finally begins to recover.
"Kuipers takes the 2005 bombing in the London Tube as her springboard and artfully manages to make Sophie's tale achingly real and yet still hopeful. Her distinct, first-person voice and quirky details shine through the dark tragedy, giving familiar themes a fresh take. More than just a story of one girl, this is a look at a family trying to rebuild after their lives have been literally blown apart." Kirkus

Kwasney, Michelle D., 1960-
Blue plate special. Chronicle Books 2009 366p $16.99
Grades: 8 9 10 11 12   **Fic**
1. Forgiveness—Fiction 2. Mother-daughter relationship—Fiction
ISBN 978-0-8118-6780-1; 0-8118-6780-3
                              LC 2009-5322
In alternating chapters, the lives of three teenage girls from three different generations are woven together as each girl learns about forgiveness, empathy, and self-respect.
Kwasney's "protagonists are distinctive and empathetic, her narratives meticulously structured and realistic, exposing the unpredictability—and sometimes unfairness—that life can bring." Publ Wkly

Lackey, Mercedes
Legacies; [by] Mercedes Lackey and Rosemary Edghill. Tor 2010 320p (Shadow grail) $19.99; pa $9.99
Grades: 7 8 9 10   **Fic**
1. Orphans—Fiction 2. Magic—Fiction 3. School stories 4. Montana—Fiction
ISBN   978-0-7653-2707-9;   0-7653-2707-4; 978-0-7653-1761-2 (pa); 0-7653-1761-3 (pa)
After her family is killed, Spirit White is taken to Oakhurst Academy, a combination orphanage and school for those with magical powers, where she and her new friends investigate when students start mysteriously disappearing.
This is "a really good read. The authors do a great job of juxtaposing a scary theme and the ordinary angst of adolescents. . . . *Legacies* has enough action for reluctant readers, and enough character development for teens to see themselves in this group of friends." SLJ
Followed by: Conspiracies (2010)

Lackey, Mercedes—*Continued*

The outstretched shadow; [by] Mercedes Lackey and James Mallory. Tor 2003 604p (Obsidian trilogy) hardcover o.p. pa $7.99

Grades: 9 10 11 12   **Fic**
  1. Fantasy fiction
  ISBN 0-7653-0219-5; 0-7653-4141-7 (pa)
                                   LC 2003-55955

"A Tom Doherty Associates book"

"As the son of the Arch-Mage of the Council of Mages, Kellen lives an ordered life, structured by the principles of High Magick—until he discovers a set of forbidden books on Wild Magic and becomes anathema to his people. Banished in disgrace from his home, Kellen enters a wild world populated by elves and other magical creatures only to find that this world is threatened by the rise of demons deep within the Obsidian Mountain." Libr J

"Lackey and Mallory create a wide variety of multidimensional characters, especially Kellen who grows to manhood in realistic starts and stops, recognizing and accepting both his heritage and the consequences of his actions." Voice Youth Advocates

Other titles in this series are:
To light a candle (2004)
When darkness falls (2006)

The phoenix unchained; [by] Mercedes Lackey and James Mallory. Tor 2007 398p (Enduring flame) $27.95

Grades: 11 12 Adult   **Fic**
  1. Magic—Fiction 2. Magicians—Fiction 3. Fantasy fiction
  ISBN 978-0-7653-1593-9; 0-7653-1593-9
                                   LC 2007-19647

"A Tom Doherty Associates book"

This first book in the Enduring Flame series "takes place more than 1,000 years after events depicted in the Obsidian Trilogy. The city of Armethalieh is no longer ruled by mages, and High Magick itself is forgotten. . . . Tiercel Rolfort, the scholarly son of lower nobility, rediscovers High Magick. Beset with visions and physically weakening, Tiercel decides his best hope is to take a journey to find a Wild Mage. Meanwhile, Wild Mage Bisochim has become convinced of his calling to set the balance aright by bringing darkness back into the world. . . . This beguiling beginning promises a highly readable epic combining vivid characterization with an interesting exploration of how past heroics are twisted over centuries into something both more and less than they were." Publ Wkly

The serpent's shadow. DAW Bks. 2001 343p $24.95; pa $7.99

Grades: 11 12 Adult   **Fic**
  1. Fantasy fiction
  ISBN 0-88677-915-4; 0-7564-0061-9 (pa)
                                   LC 2002-265143

"To an alternative Victorian London Dr. Maya Witherspoon, [daughter] of a Brahmin lady and an English physician, comes to practice. Besides standard Western medicine, Maya knows the magic of India, where she grew up. Maya's aunt Shivani has also come to England, but as a devotee of Kali, she hates her sister's marriage and is determined to wreak havoc on the

English. Maya must seek the aid of British magical masters before the powers of Kali devastate London." Booklist

LaCour, Nina

Hold still; with illustrations by Mia Nolting. Dutton 2009 229p il $17.99

Grades: 9 10 11 12   **Fic**
  1. Bereavement—Fiction 2. Suicide—Fiction
  3. Friendship—Fiction
  ISBN 978-0-525-42155-9; 0-525-42155-6
                                   LC 2010-275162

Ingrid didn't leave a note. Three months after her best friend's suicide, Caitlin finds what she left instead: a journal, hidden under Caitlin's bed.

"Interspersed with drawings and journal entries, the story of Caitlin's journey through her grief is both heartwrenching and realistic. . . . LaCour strikes a new path through a familiar story, leading readers with her confident writing and savvy sense of prose." Kirkus

Lahiri, Jhumpa

The namesake. Houghton Mifflin 2003 291p $24; pa $14 *

Grades: 11 12 Adult   **Fic**
  1. East Indian Americans—Fiction 2. Culture conflict—Fiction 3. Massachusetts—Fiction
  ISBN 0-395-92721-8; 0-618-48522-8 (pa)
                                   LC 2003-41718

"A novel about assimilation and generational differences. Gogol is so named because his father believes that sitting up in a sleeping car reading Nikolai Gogol's 'The Overcoat' saved him when the train he was on derailed and most passengers perished. After his arranged marriage, the man and his wife leave India for America, where he eventually becomes a professor. They adopt American ways, yet all of their friends are Bengalis. But for young Gogol and his sister, Boston is home, and trips to Calcutta to visit relatives are voyages to a foreign land." SLJ

"Its incorrigible mildness and its ungilded lilies aside, Lahiri's novel is unfailingly lovely in its treatment of Gogol's relationship with his father. This is the classic American parent-child bond." N Y Times Book Rev

Laird, Elizabeth

The betrayal of Maggie Blair. Houghton Mifflin 2011 423p il $16.99

Grades: 7 8 9 10   **Fic**
  1. Witchcraft—Fiction 2. Uncles—Fiction
  3. Scotland—History—17th century—Fiction
  ISBN 978-0-547-34126-2; 0-547-34126-1
                                   LC 2010-25120

In seventeenth-century Scotland, sixteen-year-old Maggie Blair is sentenced to be hanged as a witch but escapes to the home of her uncle, placing him and his family in great danger as she risks her life to save them all from the King's men.

"Laird seamlessly weaves a fairly comprehensive history lesson into an engaging, lively story." Bull Cent Child Books

Crusade. Macmillan UK 2010 389p pa $8.99

Grades: 8 9 10 11 12   **Fic**

Laird, Elizabeth—*Continued*

1. Crusades—Fiction 2. Middle Ages—Fiction
ISBN 978-0-330-45699-9; 0-330-45699-7

"Told from alternating perspectives, Crusade follows two boys as they come of age, Adam growing from landless peasant to squire, and Salim from a merchant's son . . . to a doctor's apprentice. . . . Steeped in historical detail, the adventure immerses readers in the daily life of the armies of the Crusades, showing the good and bad to be found on either side. . . . The different views on medicine, demonstrated by Salim's Jewish master, a Palestinian-born Christian, and a British doctor, are particularly fascinating." SLJ

Lake, Nick

Blood ninja. Simon & Schuster Books for Young Readers 2009 369p $16.99; pa $9.99

Grades: 7 8 9 10 11   Fic

1. Ninja—Fiction 2. Vampires—Fiction 3. Japan—Fiction
ISBN   978-1-4169-8627-0;   1-4169-8627-8;
978-1-4169-8628-7 (pa); 1-4169-8628-6 (pa)
LC 2009-23598

After his father is murdered and a ninja saves his life, Taro discovers the connection between ninjas and vampires and finds himself being dragged into a bitter conflict between the rival lords ruling Japan.

"Lake deftly blends sixteenth-century Japanese samurai history with vampire mythology to concoct a gory and fast-paced adventure that will grab readers." Booklist

Followed by: Blood ninja II: the revenge of Lord Oda (2010)

Lalami, Laila, 1968-

Secret son. Algonquin Books of Chapel Hill 2009 291p $23.95

Grades: 10 11 12 Adult   Fic

1. Morocco—Fiction 2. Father-son relationship—Fiction
ISBN 978-1-56512-494-3; 1-56512-494-4
LC 2008-52218

"Youssef El Mekki, a 19-year-old living in the slums of Casablanca who learns that his father—believed to be dead—is alive. The news precipitates Youssef's quest to find his father, who turns out to be the rich, well-connected businessman Nabil Amrani. . . . Once Nabil invites Youssef back into his life, Youssef suddenly has all the luxuries he has ever dreamed about: a new apartment in the best neighborhood and a decent job. But just as quickly, it is all taken away, and when Youssef returns to his old neighborhood—now the headquarters of a fringe Islamist group—he finds himself embroiled in a dangerous conspiracy." Publ Wkly

"A story brimming with insight into the complexities of life in contemporary Morocco." Booklist

Lamba, Marie

What I meant. . . Random House 2007 310p $16.99; lib bdg $19.99

Grades: 7 8 9 10   Fic

1. East Indian Americans—Fiction 2. Family life—Fiction 3. Aunts—Fiction 4. Pennsylvania—Fiction
ISBN   978-0-375-84091-3;   0-375-84091-5;
978-0-375-94091-0 (lib bdg); 0-375-94091-X (lib bdg)
LC 2006010898

Having to share her home with her demanding and devious aunt from India makes it all the more difficult for fifteen-year-old Sang to deal with such things as her parents thinking she is too young to date, getting less than perfect grades, and being shut out by her long-time best friend.

"Lamba makes an impressive debut with this contemporary novel. . . . Readers will find much to like in Lamba's heroine, who ultimately survives a set of trials worthy of Job with grace and humor." Publ Wkly

L'Amour, Louis, 1908-1988

The daybreakers. Bantam 1984 224p pa $4.99

Grades: 9 10 11 12   Fic

1. Western stories
ISBN 0-553-27674-3
First published 1960

First book in series that explores the settling of the American West by focusing on the exploits of several generations of the Sackett family

Other titles in the series are:
Galloway (1974)
Jubal Sackett (1985)
Lando (1962)
The lonely men (1976)
Lonely on the mountain (1980)
Mojave crossing (1964)
Mustang man (1976)
Ride the dark trail (1972)
Ride the river (1983)
Sackett (1961)
The Sackett brand (1971)
Sackett's land (1975)
The sky-liners (1972)
To the far blue mountains (1976)
Treasure mountain (1979)
The warrior's path (1980)

Lanagan, Margo, 1960-

Tender morsels. Alfred A. Knopf 2008 436p $16.99; lib bdg $19.99 *

Grades: 10 11 12   Fic

1. Fantasy fiction
ISBN   978-0-375-84811-7;   0-375-84811-8;
978-0-375-94811-4 (lib bdg); 0-375-94811-2 (lib bdg)
LC 2008-04155

A young woman who has endured unspeakable cruelties is magically granted a safe haven apart from the real world and allowed to raise her two daughters in this alternate reality, until the barrier between her world and the real one begins to break down.

The author "touches on nightmarish adult themes, including multiple rape scenarios and borderline human-animal sexual interactions, which reserve this for the most mature readers. . . . Drawing alternate worlds that

Lanagan, Margo, 1960-—*Continued*
blur the line between wonder and horror, and characters who traverse the nature of human and beast, this challenging, unforgettable work explores the ramifications of denying the most essential and often savage aspects of life." Booklist

Lansens, Lori
The girls; a novel. Little, Brown 2006 c2005 345p hardcover o.p. pa $13.99 *
Grades: 11 12 Adult   **Fic**
1. Twins—Fiction 2. Sisters—Fiction
ISBN   978-0-316-06903-8;   0-316-06903-5;
978-0-316-06634-1 (pa); 0-316-06634-6 (pa)
                                                LC 2005-24510
First published 2005 in Canada
"Since their birth, Rose and Ruby Darlen have been known simply as 'the girls.' They make friends, fall in love, have jobs, love their parents, and follow their dreams. But the Darlens are special. Now nearing their 30th birthday, they are history's oldest craniopagus twins, joined at the head by a spot the size of a bread plate." Publisher's note
"Through their alternating narratives, Lansens captures a contradictory longing for independence and togetherness that transcends the book's enormous conceit." Publ Wkly

Larbalestier, Justine, 1967-
Liar. Bloomsbury Children's Books 2009 376p $16.99 *
Grades: 9 10 11 12   **Fic**
1. Honesty—Fiction 2. Werewolves—Fiction
ISBN 978-1-59990-305-7; 1-59990-305-9
                                                LC 2009-12581
Compulsive liar Micah promises to tell the truth after revealing that her boyfriend has been murdered.
"Micah's narrative is convincing, and in the end readers will delve into the psyche of a troubled teen and decide for themselves the truths and lies. This one is sure to generate discussion." SLJ

Magic or madness. Razorbill 2005 288p $16.99; pa $7.99
Grades: 8 9 10 11 12   **Fic**
1. Magic—Fiction 2. Space and time—Fiction 3. Grandmothers—Fiction 4. New York (N.Y.)—Fiction 5. Australia—Fiction
ISBN 1-59514-022-0; 1-59514-124-3 (pa)
                                                LC 2004-18263
From the Sydney, Australia home of a grandmother she believes is a witch, fifteen-year-old Reason Cansino is magically transported to New York City, where she discovers that friends and foes can be hard to distinguish
"Readers looking for layered, understated fantasy will follow the looping paths of Larbalestier's fine writing . . . with gratitude and awe." Booklist
Other titles about Reason Cansino are:
Magic lessons (2006)
Magic's child (2007)

LaRochelle, David, 1960-
Absolutely, positively not. Arthur A. Levine Books 2005 219p $16.95 *
Grades: 7 8 9 10   **Fic**
1. Homosexuality—Fiction 2. School stories
ISBN 0-439-59109-0   LC 2004-23558
Chronicles a teenage boy's humorous attempts to fit in at his Minnesota high school by becoming a macho, girl-loving, "Playboy" pinup-displaying heterosexual.
"The wry, first-person narrative is wonderful as it moves from personal angst to outright farce. . . . The characters are drawn with surprising depth." Booklist

Larson, Kirby, 1954-
Hattie Big Sky. Delacorte Press 2006 289p hardcover o.p. pa $6.99 *
Grades: 6 7 8 9 10   **Fic**
1. Frontier and pioneer life—Fiction 2. Orphans—Fiction 3. World War, 1914-1918—Fiction 4. Montana—Fiction
ISBN 0-385-73313-5; 0-385-73595-2 (pa)
                                                LC 2005-35039
After inheriting her uncle's homesteading claim in Montana, sixteen-year-old orphan Hattie Brooks travels from Iowa in 1917 to make a home for herself and encounters some unexpected problems related to the war being fought in Europe.
This is "a richly textured novel full of memorable characters." Booklist

Lasky, Kathryn
Ashes. Viking 2010 318p $16.99 *
Grades: 6 7 8 9 10 11 12   **Fic**
1. National socialism—Fiction 2. Germany—Fiction
ISBN 978-0-670-01157-5; 0-670-01157-6
                                                LC 2009-33127
In 1932 Berlin, thirteen-year-old Gaby Schramm witnesses the beginning of Hitler's rise to power, as soldiers become ubiquitous, her beloved literature teacher starts wearing a jewelled swastika pin, and the family's dear friend, Albert Einstein, leaves the country while Gaby's parents secretly bury his books and papers in their small yard.
"Gaby's questioning but assertive nature helps form a compelling, readable portrait of pre-WWII Germany." Publ Wkly

Lavender, William, 1921-
Aftershocks. Harcourt 2006 344p $17
Grades: 8 9 10 11 12   **Fic**
1. Sex role—Fiction 2. Father-daughter relationship—Fiction   3.   Chinese   Americans—Fiction 4. Earthquakes—Fiction 5. San Francisco (Calif.)—Fiction
ISBN 0-15-205882-6   LC 2005-19695
In San Francisco from 1903 to 1908, teenager Jessie Wainwright determines to reach her goal of becoming a doctor while also trying to care for the illegitimate child of a liaison between her father and their Chinese maid.
This "is readable historical fiction about an engrossing event in U.S. history." Voice Youth Advocates

Lawlor, Laurie

The two loves of Will Shakespeare. Holiday House 2006 278p $16.95

Grades: 9 10 11 12   Fic
  1. Shakespeare, William, 1564-1616—Fiction
  2. Great Britain—History—1485-1603, Tudors—Fiction
  ISBN 0-8234-1901-0; 978-0-8234-1901-2
                                            LC 2005-52537

After falling in love, eighteen-year-old Will Shakespeare, a bored apprentice in his father's glove business and often in trouble for various misdeeds, vows to live an upstanding life and pursue his passion for writing.

"Quoting lines from Shakespeare's sonnets and highlighting the dismal treatment of women in that brutally repressive society, the author creates both a vivid setting and a feckless protagonist, equally credible as an adolescent and as a product of his times." Booklist

Lawson, Mary, 1910-1941

Crow Lake. Dial Press (NY) 2002 291p hardcover o.p. pa $14

Grades: 11 12 Adult   Fic
  1. Orphans—Fiction 2. Poverty—Fiction 3. Canada—Fiction
  ISBN 0-385-33611-X; 0-385-33763-9 (pa)
                                            LC 2001-53779

In this novel "four children living in northern Ontario struggle to stay together after their parents die in an auto accident. . . . Kate Morrison narrates the tale in flashback mode, starting with the fatal car accident that leaves seven-year-old Kate; her toddler sister, Bo; 19-year-old Luke; and 17-year-old Matt to fend for themselves." Publ Wkly

"Lawson achieves a breathless anticipatory quality in her surprisingly adept first novel, in which a child tells the story, but tells it very well indeed." Booklist

Le Carré, John, 1931-

The spy who came in from the cold. Walker & Company 2005 223p $19

Grades: 9 10 11 12   Fic
  1. Spies—Fiction
  ISBN 0-8027-1454-4
  Also available in paperback from Scribner
  First published 1963 in the United kingdom; first United States edition published 1964 by Coward-McCann

"The story of Alec Leamas, 50-year-old professional {secret agent} who has grown stale in espionage, who longs to 'come in from the cold' and how he undertakes one last assignment before that hoped-for retirement. Over the years Leamas has grown unsure where his workday carapace ends and his real self begins. . . . Recalled from Berlin after the death of his last East German contact at the Wall, Leamas lets himself be seduced into a pretended defection—thereby providing the East Germans with data from which they can deduce that the head of their own spy apparatus is a double agent." N Y Times Book Rev

Le Guin, Ursula K., 1929-

Gifts. Harcourt 2004 274p $17; pa $7.95

Grades: 7 8 9 10   Fic
  1. Fantasy fiction
  ISBN 0-15-205123-6; 0-15-205124-4 (pa)
                                            LC 2003-21449

When a young man in the Uplands blinds himself rather than use his gift of "unmaking"—a violent talent shared by members of his family—he upsets the precarious balance of power among rival, feuding families, each of which has a strange and deadly talent of its own.

"Although intriguing as a coming-of-age allegory, Orrec's story is also rich in . . . earthy magic and intelligent plot twists." Booklist

Other titles in this series are:
Powers (2007)
Voices (2006)

The lathe of heaven; a novel. Scribner 2008 184p pa $15

Grades: 11 12 Adult   Fic
  1. Dreams—Fiction 2. Science fiction
  ISBN 978-1-4165-5696-1; 1-4165-5696-6
                                            LC 2007047222

First published 1971 by Scribner

"A psychiatrist sets out to use a patient whose dreams can alter reality to create utopia, but in usurping this power he is gradually delivered into madness." Anatomy of Wonder 4

"The author has done some profound research in psychology, cerebrophysiology and biochemistry. . . . In addition, her perceptions of such matters as geopolitics, race, socialized medicine and the patient/shrink relationship are razor-sharp and more than a little cutting." Natl Rev

The left hand of darkness. Ace Books 2000 304p pa $13.95 *

Grades: 9 10 11 12   Fic
  1. Extrasensory perception—Fiction 2. Science fiction
  ISBN 0-441-00731-7
  A reissue of the title first published 1969 by Walker & Company

"This is a tale of political intrigue and danger on the world of Gethen, the Winter planet. Genly Ai, high official of the Eukeman—the commonwealth of worlds—is on Gethen to convince the royalty to join the Federation. He soon becomes a pawn in Gethen's power struggles, set against the elaborate mores of the Gethenians, a unisex hermaphroditic people whose intricate sexual physiology plays a key role in the conflict. Allied with Estraven, fallen lord, Genly is forced to cross the savage and impassable Gobrin Ice." Shapiro. Fic for Youth. 3d edition

Leavitt, Lindsey

Sean Griswold's head. Bloomsbury 2011 276p $16.99

Grades: 7 8 9 10   Fic
  1. Multiple sclerosis—Fiction 2. Family life—Fiction
  3. School stories 4. Pennsylvania—Fiction
  ISBN 978-1-59990-498-6; 1-59990-498-5
                                            LC 2010-06949

Leavitt, Lindsey—*Continued*

After discovering that her father has multiple sclerosis, fifteen-year-old Payton begins counselling sessions at school, which lead her to become interested in a boy in her biology class, have a falling out with her best friend, develop an interest in bike riding, and eventually allow her to come to terms with life's uncertainties.

"Leavitt capably handles the issues of chronic illness with sensitivity, making this an insightful, humorous, and ultimately uplifting family drama." Bull Cent Child Books

Lecesne, James

Absolute brightness. HarperTeen 2008 472p $17.99; lib bdg $18.89

Grades: 7 8 9 10   Fic

1. Cousins—Fiction 2. Homosexuality—Fiction 3. Good and evil—Fiction 4. New Jersey—Fiction

ISBN   978-0-06-125627-1;   0-06-125627-7; 978-0-06-125628-8 (lib bdg); 0-06-125628-5 (lib bdg)

LC 2007-02988

"Laura Geringer books"

In the beach town of Neptune, New Jersey, Phoebe's life is changed irrevocably when her gay cousin moves into her house and soon goes missing.

"This thoughtful novel is beautifully written; its themes are haunting, and in spite of the central tragedy, it's often laugh-out-loud funny." Kliatt

Virgin territory. Egmont USA 2010 218p $16.99

Grades: 7 8 9 10   Fic

1. Mary, Blessed Virgin, Saint—Fiction 2. Florida—Fiction 3. Saints—Fiction

ISBN 978-1-60684-081-8; 1-60684-081-9

LC 2010-11318

"Laura Geringer Books"

When an image of the Blessed Virgin Mary appears on a tree at the Jupiter, Florida, golf course where fifteen-year-old Dylan Flack is caddying for the summer, he encounters a group of "pilgrims" who dare him to take a risk and find out what he really wants out of life.

"The excellent writing and fresh metaphors add to the book's wonderful characters. Dylan is easy to like, but not perfect. The BVM crowd is fanatic, but in an understandable way. . . . While the book references religion, primarily the BVM sightings, it is more about what it means to have faith and when it is worth taking a risk for something." Voice Youth Advocates

Lee, Harper, 1926-

To kill a mockingbird. 50th anniversary ed. Harper 2010 323p $25 *

Grades: 9 10 11 12 Adult   Fic

1. Race relations—Fiction 2. Alabama—Fiction

ISBN 978-0-06-174352-8

A reissue of the title first published 1960 by Lippincott

"Scout, as Jean Louise is called, is a precocious child. She relates her impressions of the time when her lawyer father, Atticus Finch, is defending a black man accused of raping a white woman in a small Alabama town during the 1930's. Atticus's courageous act brings the violence and injustice that exists in their world sharply into focus as it intrudes into the lighthearted life that Scout

and her brother Jem have enjoyed until that time." Shapiro. Fic for Youth. 3d edition

Lee, Ying S., 1974-

A spy in the house. Candlewick Press 2010 335p (The Agency) $16.99

Grades: 8 9 10 11 12   Fic

1. Swindlers and swindling—Fiction 2. Orphans—Fiction 3. Household employees—Fiction 4. Great Britain—History—19th century—Fiction 5. Mystery fiction

ISBN 978-0-7636-4067-5; 0-7636-4067-0

LC 2009-32736

Rescued from the gallows in 1850s London, young orphan and thief Mary Quinn is offered a place at Miss Scrimshaw's Academy for Girls where she is trained to be part of an all-female investigative unit called The Agency and, at age seventeen, she infiltrates a rich merchant's home in hopes of tracing his missing cargo ships.

"Lee fills the story with classic elements of Victorian mystery and melodrama. Class differences, love gone awry, racial discrimination, London's growing pains in the 1850s, and the status of women in society are all addressed. Historical details are woven seamlessly into the plot, and descriptive writing allows readers to be part of each scene." SLJ

Another title in this series:
The body at the tower (2010)

LeFlore, Lyah

The world is mine; [by] Lyah B. LeFlore; with illustrations by DL Warfield. Simon Pulse 2009 269p il (Come up) pa $8.99

Grades: 7 8 9 10   Fic

1. Music industry—Fiction 2. African Americans—Fiction 3. Family life—Fiction 4. School stories 5. Maryland—Fiction

ISBN 978-1-4169-7963-0; 1-4169-7963-8

LC 2009-6900

Maryland high school juniors and best friends Blue Reynolds and Collin Andrews seem to have it all, and when they decide to become party promoters, anything can happen—including being pitted against parents, jealous girlfriends, and even one another.

"Teens, especially the hip-hop obsessed, will relate to the characters' stratospheric aspirations, their struggles to balance their passions with parental demands, as well as the sharp dialogue and narration." Publ Wkly

Leitch, Will

Catch. Razorbill 2005 288p pa $7.99

Grades: 9 10 11 12   Fic

1. Illinois—Fiction

ISBN 1-59514-069-7   LC 2005-08146

Teenager Tim Temples must decide if he wants to leave his comfortable life in a small town and go to college.

"This substantive title will entice both male and female YA readers with its thoughtful, authentic, and romantic young man's voice." Booklist

L'Engle, Madeleine, 1918-2007
A wrinkle in time. Farrar, Straus & Giroux 1962
211p $17; pa $7.99

Grades: 5 6 7 8 9 10   **Fic**
1. Fantasy fiction
ISBN 0-374-38613-7; 0-312-36754-6 (pa)
"A brother and sister, together with a friend, go in
search of their scientist father who was lost while engaged in secret work for the government on the tesseract
problem. A tesseract is a wrinkle in time. The father is
a prisoner on a forbidding planet, and after awesome and
terrifying experiences, he is rescued, and the little group
returns safely to Earth and home." Child Books Too
Good to Miss
This book "makes unusual demands on the imagination and consequently gives great rewards." Horn Book
Other titles in this series are:
A swiftly tilting planet (1978)
A wind in the door (1973)

Leroux, Gaston, 1868-1927
The phantom of the opera; introduction by Anne
Perry. Modern Library 2002 xxiii, 286p (The
Modern Library Classics) pa $8.95

Grades: 9 10 11 12   **Fic**
1. Paris (France)—Fiction
ISBN 0-375-76113-6   LC 2002-67075
First published 1911 by The Bobbs-Merrill Company
This love story/thriller relates the tale of the mysteri-
ous masked terror who inhabits the cellars of the Paris
Opera House

Les Becquets, Diane
Love, Cajun style. Bloomsbury 2005 296p
$16.95; pa $7.95

Grades: 9 10 11 12   **Fic**
1. Louisiana—Fiction 2. Aunts—Fiction 3. Family
life—Fiction 4. Friendship—Fiction
ISBN 1-58234-674-7; 1-59990-030-0 (pa)
                                            LC 2005-11948
Teenage Lucy learns about life and love with the help
of her friends and saucy Tante Pearl over the course of
one hot Louisiana summer before her senior year of high
school.
"This is romantic, real, and lots of fun." Booklist

Season of ice. Bloomsbury U.S.A. Children's
Books 2008 281p $16.95 *

Grades: 8 9 10 11 12   **Fic**
1. Missing persons—Fiction 2. Father-daughter relationship—Fiction 3. Stepfamilies—Fiction 4. Lakes—
Fiction 5. Maine—Fiction
ISBN 978-1-59990-063-6; 1-59990-063-7
                                            LC 2007-30845
When seventeen-year-old Genesis Sommer's father
disappears on Moosehead Lake near their small-town
Maine home in mid-November, she must cope with the
pressure of keeping her family together, even while rumors about the event plague her.
This is "a heartbreaking story from the very beginning, but Les Becquets turns it into something well beyond a mere tearjerker. . . . It's a tender story of a
tough, smart, loving girl who finds that she can rise to

the challenge of what she's lost because of what she's
gained. Readers will understand her and admire her, and
find her difficult indeed to forget." Bull Cent Child
Books

Lessing, Doris May, 1919-
The sweetest dream; [by] Doris Lessing.
HarperCollins Pubs. 2002 478p hardcover o.p. pa
$13.95

Grades: 11 12 Adult   **Fic**
1. Feminism—Fiction 2. London (England)—Fiction
ISBN 0-06-621334-7; 0-06-093755-6 (pa)
                                          LC 2002-279950
The epicenter of this novel "is a grand old house in
London, the holdfast of the seemingly impervious widow
Julia. It's the early 1960s and when her selfish and feckless communist son, Johnny, callously abandons his wife,
Frances, and their two young sons, Julia persuades her
resilient daughter-in-law to move in with her. Soon Frances, a self-possessed yet endlessly empathic and accom-
modating earth mother, is presiding over a contentious
commune of moody teenage 'waifs and strays.'" Booklist
"Lessing's understanding of relationships—both personal and political—has always been keen; now . . . it
is unparalleled. This novel is warm and heartfelt, old-
fashioned and ambitious in its historical sweep." New
Statesman (1913)

Lester, Julius
Day of tears; a novel in dialogue. Hyperion
2005 177p hardcover o.p. pa $7.99 *

Grades: 7 8 9 10   **Fic**
1. Slavery—Fiction 2. African Americans—Fiction
ISBN 0-7868-0490-4; 1-42310-409-9 (pa)
"Jump at the sun"
Emma has taken care of the Butler children since Sarah and Frances's mother, Fanny, left. Emma wants to
raise the girls to have good hearts, as a rift over slavery
has ripped the Butler household apart. Now, to pay off
debts, Pierce Butler wants to cash in his slave "assets",
possibly including Emma.
"The horror of the auction and its aftermath is unforgettable. . . . The racism is virulent (there's widespread
use of the n-word). The personal voices make this a stirring text for group discussion." Booklist

Guardian. Amistad/HarperTeen 2008 129p
$16.99; lib bdg $17.89 *

Grades: 7 8 9 10   **Fic**
1. Race relations—Fiction 2. African Americans—Fiction 3. Southern States—Fiction 4. Lynching—Fiction
ISBN   978-0-06-155890-0;   0-06-155890-7;
978-0-06-155891-7 (lib bdg); 0-06-155891-5 (lib bdg)
                                            LC 2008-14251
In a rural southern town in 1946, a white man and his
son witness the lynching of an innocent black man. Includes historical note on lynching.
"The author's understated, haunting prose is as compelling as it is dark; . . . [the story] leaves a deep impression." Publ Wkly
Includes bibliographical references

Lester, Julius—*Continued*

Time's memory. Farrar, Straus & Giroux 2006 230p $17

Grades: 8 9 10 11 12   **Fic**
1. Slavery—Fiction 2. African Americans—Fiction
ISBN 0-374-37178-4; 978-0-374-37178-4
    LC 2005-47716

Ekundayo, a Dogon spirit brought to America from Africa, inhabits the body of a young African American slave on a Virginia plantation, where he experiences loss, sorrow, and reconciliation in the months preceding the Civil War.

"More than a picture of slavery through the eyes of those enslaved or their captors, Lester's narrative evokes spiritual images of Mali's Dogon people." SLJ

Levchuk, Lisa

Everything beautiful in the world. Farrar, Straus & Giroux 2008 203p $16.95 *

Grades: 9 10 11 12   **Fic**
1. Family life—Fiction 2. Teachers—Fiction 3. Cancer—Fiction 4. School stories 5. New Jersey—Fiction
ISBN 978-0-374-32238-0; 0-374-32238-4
    LC 2007-16603

Toward the end of the disco era, seventeen-year-old Edna refuses to visit her mother, who is in a New York City hospital undergoing cancer treatment, and barely speaks to her father, who finally puts her in psychotherapy, while her crush on an art teacher turns into a full-blown affair.

"Edna's narrative is fascinating. She is funny and scathing. . . . Her voice is so engrossing that the book is difficult to put down." Voice Youth Advocates

Levine, Gail Carson, 1947-

Fairest. HarperCollins 2006 326p $16.99

Grades: 6 7 8 9   **Fic**
1. Fairy tales 2. Singing—Fiction
ISBN 978-0-06-073408-4; 0-06-073408-6
    LC 2006-00337

In a land where beauty and singing are valued above all else, Aza eventually comes to reconcile her unconventional appearance and her magical voice, and learns to accept herself for who she truly is.

"The plot is fast-paced, and Aza's growth and maturity are well crafted and believable." SLJ

Levithan, David, 1972-

Love is the higher law. Alfred A. Knopf 2009 167p $15.99; lib bdg $18.99

Grades: 8 9 10 11 12   **Fic**
1. September 11 terrorist attacks, 2001—Fiction 2. Homosexuality—Fiction 3. New York (N.Y.)—Fiction
ISBN 978-0-375-83468-4; 0-375-83468-0; 978-0-375-93468-1 (lib bdg); 0-375-93468-5 (lib bdg)
    LC 2008-40886

Three New York City teens express their reactions to the bombing of the World Trade Center on September 11, 2001, and its impact on their lives and the world.

"The author's prose has never been deeper in thought or feeling. His writing here is especially pure—unsentimental, restrained, and full of love for his characters and setting. . . . Levithan captures the mood of post-9/11 New York exquisitely, slashed open to reveal a deep heart." SLJ

Marly's ghost; a remix of Charles Dickens' A Christmas Carol; with illustrations by Brian Selznick. Dial Books 2006 167p il hardcover o.p. pa $6.99

Grades: 7 8 9 10   **Fic**
1. Valentine's Day—Fiction 2. Ghost stories
ISBN 0-8037-3063-2; 0-14-240912-X (pa)
    LC 2005-16183

The spirit of Ben's girlfriend Marly returns with three other ghosts to haunt him with a painful journey though Valentine's Days past, present, and future.

"The magical realism is powerful throughout. . . . A solid story to mark the holiday." Booklist

Levitin, Sonia, 1934-

Strange relations. Alfred A. Knopf 2007 298p hardcover o.p. pa $6.50

Grades: 7 8 9 10   **Fic**
1. Jews—Fiction 2. Hawaii—Fiction 3. Cousins—Fiction 4. Religion—Fiction
ISBN 978-0-375-83751-7; 0-375-83751-5; 978-0-440-23963-5 (pa); 0-440-23963-X (pa)
    LC 2006-33275

Fifteen-year-old Marne is excited to be able to spend her summer vacation in Hawaii, not realizing the change in her lifestyle it would bring staying with her aunt, seven cousins, and uncle who is a Chasidic rabbi.

"It's rare to find such well-developed characters, empathetic and sensitive religious treatment, and carefully crafted plotlines in one novel." SLJ

Lewis, Sinclair, 1885-1951

Main Street. Harcourt 2003 486p (An HBJ modern classic) $34 *

Grades: 11 12 Adult   **Fic**
1. Minnesota—Fiction
ISBN 0-15-155547-8

Also available in paperback from New American Library

A reissue of the title first published 1920

"Carol Milford, a girl of quick intelligence but no particular talent, after graduation from college meets and marries Will Kennicott, a sober, kindly, unimaginative physician of Gopher Prairie, Minn., who tells her that the town needs her abilities. She finds the village to be a smug, intolerant, unimaginatively standardized place, where the people will not accept her efforts to create more sightly homes, organize a dramatic association, and otherwise improve the village life." Oxford Companion to Am Lit. 6th edition

Main Street & Babbitt. Library of Am. 1992 898p $40

Grades: 11 12 Adult   **Fic**
1. Minnesota—Fiction
ISBN 0-940450-61-5
    LC 91-58224

Lewis, Sinclair, 1885-1951—_Continued_

In addition to Main Street, this book also features Babbitt (1922), a satire on American middle-class conventions. Set in the Midwest, it focuses on the life of George Babbitt, a prosperous and self-satisfied real estate man.

LeZotte, Ann Clare

T4; a novel in verse; written by Ann Clare LeZotte. Houghton Mifflin Co. 2008 108p $14

Grades: 6 7 8 9 10   **Fic**
    1. Novels in verse 2. Deaf—Fiction 3. Euthanasia—Fiction 4. Germany—History—1933-1945—Fiction
    ISBN 978-0-547-04684-6; 0-547-04684-7
                                          LC 2007-47737

When the Nazi party takes control of Germany, thirteen-year-old Paula, who is deaf, finds her world-as-she-knows-it turned upside down, as she is taken into hiding to protect her from the new law nicknamed T4.

"This novel will have a lasting effect on readers, giving insight into an often-forgotten aspect of the horrors of the Third Reich." SLJ

Libby, Alisa M.

The king's rose. Dutton Children's Books 2009 320p $17.99

Grades: 7 8 9 10   **Fic**
    1. Catharine Howard, Queen, consort of Henry VIII, King of England, d. 1542—Fiction 2. Henry VIII, King of England, 1491-1547—Fiction 3. Kings and rulers—Fiction 4. Queens—Fiction 5. Great Britain—History—1485-1603, Tudors—Fiction
    ISBN 978-0-525-47970-3; 0-525-47970-8
                                          LC 2008-14338

Catharine Howard recounts the events in her life that led to her being groomed for marriage at the age of fifteen to King Henry VIII, her failure to produce an heir to the throne, and her quick execution.

"While numerous sexual encounters are part of the political reality, they are subtly handled. A real treat for lovers of historical fiction." SLJ

Liberty, Anita

The center of the universe; yep, that would be me. Simon Pulse 2008 291p il pa $9.99

Grades: 10 11 12   **Fic**
    1. Girls—Fiction 2. School stories
    ISBN 978-1-4169-5789-8; 1-4169-5789-8
                                         LC 2007-940383

An angst-ridden fictional memoir of Anita Liberty's last two years in high school is presented through diary entries, poems, sarcastic advice, scorecards of parental infractions, and definitions of SAT vocabulary words.

"Female readers should laugh aloud throughout this fast, entertaining read, and especially appreciate the interesting epilogue continuing the author's post-high school experiences before ending with her present fulfilling circumstances." Voice Youth Advocates

Lindskold, Jane M.

Thirteen orphans; [by] Jane Lindskold. Tor 2008 367p il $24.95

Grades: 11 12 Adult   **Fic**
    1. Fantasy fiction
    ISBN 978-0-7653-1700-1; 0-7653-1700-1
                                          LC 2008-34085

"A Tom Doherty Associates Book"

In an alternate world inspired by ancient Chinese lore and magic, Brenda learns about her magical ancestry after an attack on her father and finds herself among a band of orphans who each represent an animal from the Chinese zodiac.

The author "has created a convincing tale of a young woman entering adulthood, assuming responsibility for herself and for others, and making sometimes-wrenching decisions." SLJ

Lipsyte, Robert

The contender. Harper & Row 1967 182p pa $5.99 hardcover o.p. *

Grades: 7 8 9 10   **Fic**
    1. Boxing—Fiction 2. Harlem (New York, N.Y.)—Fiction 3. African Americans—Fiction
    ISBN 0-06-447039-3

"After a street fight in which he is the chief target, Alfred wanders into a gym in his neighborhood. He decides not only to improve his physical condition but also to become a boxer. Because of this interest Alfred's life is completely changed. He assumes a more positive outlook on his immediate future, even within the confines of a black ghetto." Shapiro. Fic for Youth. 3d edition

Followed by The brave (1991) and The chief (1993)

One fat summer. Harper & Row 1977 152p hardcover o.p. pa $5.99

Grades: 7 8 9 10   **Fic**
    1. Weight loss—Fiction 2. Obesity—Fiction
    ISBN 0-06-023895-X; 0-06-447073-3 (pa)
                                          LC 76-49746

"Bobby Marks is 14 and fat. How fat, he doesn't know because he jumps off the scale when it hits 200 pounds. In one action-packed summer Bobby learns that altered physical appearance can bolster self-esteem. He's not sure he likes his friend Joanie's new nose and new ego, but he's certainly pleased with his own svelte new image. The slimming is a result of his summer job; tending the grounds of the town miser." West Coast Rev Books

"This is far superior to most of the summer-of-change stories; any change that takes place is logical and the protagonist learns by action and reaction to be both self-reliant and compassionate." Bull Cent Child Books

Followed by Summer rules (1981) and The summerboy (1982)

Raiders night. HarperTempest 2006 232p hardcover o.p. pa $6.99

Grades: 9 10 11 12   **Fic**
    1. Football—Fiction 2. Drug abuse—Fiction 3. Rape—Fiction
    ISBN   978-0-06-059946-1;   0-06-059946-4; 978-0-06-059948-5 (pa); 0-06-059948-0 (pa)
                                          LC 2005-17865

Lipsyte, Robert—*Continued*

Matt Rydeck, co-captain of his high school football team, endures a traumatic season as he witnesses the rape of a rookie player by teammates and grapples with his own use of performance-enhancing drugs.

This is "is a riveting and chilling look inside contemporary high school football." Publ Wkly

Lloyd, Saci

The carbon diaries 2015. Holiday House 2009 330p il map $17.95 *

Grades: 8 9 10 11 12   Fic

1. Family life—Fiction 2. Conservation of natural resources—Fiction 3. Science fiction 4. Great Britain—Fiction

ISBN 978-0-8234-2190-9; 0-8234-2190-2

LC 2008-19712

First published 2008 in the United Kingdom

In 2015, when England becomes the first nation to introduce carbon dioxide rationing in a drastic bid to combat climate change, sixteen-year-old Laura documents the first year of rationing as her family spirals out of control.

"Deeply compulsive and urgently compulsory reading." Booklist

Includes bibliographical references

Followed by The carbon diaries 2017 (2010)

Lo, Malinda

Ash. Little, Brown and Co. 2009 264p $16.99; pa $8.99

Grades: 8 9 10 11   Fic

1. Fairy tales 2. Fairies—Fiction 3. Stepfamilies—Fiction 4. Love stories

ISBN 978-0-316-04009-9; 0-316-04009-6; 978-0-316-04010-5 (pa); 0-316-04010-X (pa)

LC 2009-17471

In this variation on the Cinderella story, Ash grows up believing in the fairy realm that the king and his philosophers have sought to suppress, until one day she must choose between a handsome fairy cursed to love her and the King's Huntress whom she loves.

"Part heart-pounding lesbian romance and part universal coming-of-age story, Lo's powerful tale is richly embroidered with folklore and glittering fairy magic that will draw fans of Sharon Shinn's earthy, herb-laced fantasies." Booklist

Followed by Huntress (2011)

Lockhart, E.

The boyfriend list; (15 guys, 11 shrink appointments, 4 ceramic frogs, and me, Ruby Oliver). Delacorte Press 2005 240p hardcover o.p. pa $8.95

Grades: 9 10 11 12   Fic

1. School stories 2. Dating (Social customs)—Fiction 3. Washington (State)—Fiction

ISBN 0-385-73206-6; 0-385-73207-4 (pa)

LC 2004-6691

A Seattle fifteen-year-old explains some of the reasons for her recent panic attacks, including breaking up with her boyfriend, losing all her girlfriends, tensions between her performance-artist mother and her father, and more.

"Readers will find many of Ruby's experiences familiar, and they'll appreciate the story as a lively, often entertaining read." Booklist

Other titles about Ruby Oliver are:

The boy book (2006)

Real live boyfriends (2010)

The treasure map of boys (2009)

The disreputable history of Frankie Landau-Banks. Hyperion 2008 352p $16.99; pa $8.99 *

Grades: 7 8 9 10 11 12   Fic

1. School stories

ISBN 0-7868-3818-3; 978-0-7868-3818-9; 0-7868-3819-1 (pa); 978-0-7868-3819-6 (pa)

"On her return to Alabaster Prep . . . [Frankie] attracts the attention of gorgeous Matthew . . . [who] is a member of the Loyal Order of the Basset Hounds, an all-male Alabaster secret society. . . . Frankie engineers her own guerilla membership by assuming a false online identity. . . . Lockhart creates a unique, indelible character. . . . Teens will be galvanized." Booklist

How to be bad; [by] E. Lockhart, Sarah Mlynowski [and] Lauren Myracle. HarperTeen 2008 325p $16.99; lib bdg $17.89

Grades: 9 10 11 12   Fic

1. Friendship—Fiction 2. Automobile travel—Fiction

ISBN 978-0-06-128422-9; 0-06-128422-X; 978-0-06-128423-6 (lib bdg); 0-06-128423-8 (lib bdg)

LC 2007-52946

Told in alternating voices, Jesse, Vicks, and Mel, hoping to leave all their worries and woes behind, escape their small town by taking a road trip to Miami.

"Whip-smart dialogue and a fast-moving, picaresque plot that zooms from lump-in-the-throat moments to all-out giddiness will keep readers going, and it's a testimony to how real these girls seem that the final chapters are profoundly satisfying rather than tidy." Publ Wkly

London, Jack, 1876-1916

The call of the wild; pictures by Wendell Minor. Atheneum Books for Young Readers 1999 112p il $24; pa $4.95

Grades: 5 6 7 8 9 10 11 12 Adult   Fic

1. Dogs—Fiction 2. Alaska—Fiction 3. Yukon River valley (Yukon and Alaska)—Fiction

ISBN 0-689-81836-X; 1-4165-0019-7 (pa)

LC 97-45019

First published 1903 by Macmillan

"Buck, half-St. Bernard, half-Scottish sheepdog, is stolen from his comfortable home in California and pressed into service as a sledge dog in the Klondike. At first he is abused by both man and dog, but he learns to fight ruthlessly. He becomes lead dog on a sledge team, after bettering Spitz, the vicious old leader, in a brutal fight to the death. In John Thornton, he finally finds a master whom he can respect and love. When Thornton is killed by Indians, Buck breaks away to the wilds and becomes the leader of a wolf pack, returning each year to the site of Thornton's death." Reader's Ency. 4th edition

London, Jack, 1876-1916—*Continued*

White Fang; pictures by Ed Young. Atheneum Books for Young Readers 2000 260p il hardcover o.p. pa $5.99

Grades: 5 6 7 8 9 10 11 12 Adult   **Fic**
1. Dogs—Fiction 2. Alaska—Fiction 3. Yukon River valley (Yukon and Alaska)—Fiction
ISBN 0-689-82431-9; 1-4169-1414-5 (pa)

LC 98-19241

First published 1906

White Fang "is about a dog, a cross-breed, sold to Beauty Smith. This owner tortures the dog to increase his ferocity and value as a fighter. A new owner Weedom Scott, brings the dog to California, and, by kind treatment, domesticates him. White Fang later sacrifices his life to save Scott." Haydn. Thesaurus of Book Dig

Lottridge, Celia Barker

Home is beyond the mountains. Groundwood Books/House of Anansi Press 2010 224p il $16.95

Grades: 6 7 8 9 10   **Fic**
1. Refugees—Fiction 2. Orphans—Fiction
ISBN 978-0-88899-932-0; 0-88899-932-1

"In 1918, when the Turkish army invades Persia, nine-year-old Samira and her Assyrian family must flee to the south, seeking protection from the British. Along the way, Samira's mother and sister die, her father disappears and is feared dead and only Samira and her brother Benyamin reach the Baqubah Refugee Camp. . . . Based on Lottridge's family stories, this is a moving tale of family, home, hope and survival." Kirkus

Love, D. Anne, 1949-

Defying the diva; [by] D. Anne Love. Margaret K. McElderry Books 2008 257p $16.99

Grades: 7 8 9 10   **Fic**
1. Bullies—Fiction 2. School stories
ISBN 978-1-4169-3481-3; 1-4169-3481-2

LC 2007-10945

During Haley's freshman year of high school, a campaign of gossip and bullying causes her to be socially ostracized, but after spending the summer living with her aunt, working at a resort, making new friends, and dating a hunky lifeguard, she learns how to stand up for herself and begins to trust again.

"Concluding with a serious author's note on harassment, which includes information on getting help, this text skillfully captures the painful reality of teen bullying while also telling Haley's humorous and sincere story of growing up." Kirkus

Lowell, Pamela

Returnable girl. Marshall Cavendish 2006 229p hardcover o.p. pa $6.99

Grades: 8 9 10 11   **Fic**
1. Foster home care—Fiction 2. Mothers—Fiction 3. Friendship—Fiction
ISBN 978-0-7614-5317-8; 0-7614-5317-2; 978-0-7614-5592-9 (pa); 0-7614-5592-2 (pa)

LC 2006006398

Friendship with an outcast classmate and memories of her mother's desertion interfere with the relationship thir-

teen-year-old Ronnie tries to establish with her new foster mother.

"With its clear, direct language and an appealing heroine, the book is likely to draw a wide range of teen readers." Voice Youth Advocates

Lowry, Lois

The giver. Houghton Mifflin 1993 180p $17; pa $8.95

Grades: 6 7 8 9 10   **Fic**
1. Science fiction
ISBN 0-395-64566-2; 0-385-73255-4 (pa)

LC 92-15034

Given his lifetime assignment at the Ceremony of Twelve, Jonas becomes the receiver of memories shared by only one other in his community and discovers the terrible truth about the society in which he lives.

"A riveting, chilling story that inspires a new appreciation for diversity, love, and even pain. Truly memorable." SLJ

Lubar, David, 1954-

Sleeping freshmen never lie. Dutton Books 2005 279p $16.99; pa $6.99

Grades: 7 8 9 10   **Fic**
1. Authorship—Fiction 2. School stories
ISBN 0-525-47311-4; 0-14-240780-1 (pa)

LC 2004-23067

While navigating his first year of high school and awaiting the birth of his new baby brother, Scott loses old friends and gains some unlikely new ones as he hones his skills as a writer

"The plot is framed by Scott's journal of advice for the unborn baby. The novel's absurd, comical mood is evident in its entries. . . . The author brings the protagonist to three-dimensional life by combining these introspective musings with active, hilarious narration." SLJ

Luper, Eric

Bug boy. Farrar, Straus and Giroux 2009 248p $16.99

Grades: 7 8 9 10   **Fic**
1. Horse racing—Fiction 2. Gambling—Fiction 3. Swindlers and swindling—Fiction 4. Father-son relationship—Fiction 5. New York (State)—Fiction
ISBN 978-0-374-31000-4; 0-374-31000-9

LC 2008-26730

In 1934 Saratoga, New York, just as fifteen-year-old Jack Walsh finally realizes his dream of becoming a jockey, complications arise in the form of a female bookie, an unexpected visit from his father, and a man who wants him to "fix" a race.

"This well-written, engaging story effectively captures the desperate times of the Depression and the hard-edged world of horse racing." SLJ

Seth Baumgartner's love manifesto. Balzer + Bray 2010 293p $16.99

Grades: 8 9 10 11 12   **Fic**
1. Dating (Social customs)—Fiction 2. Father-son relationship—Fiction 3. Golf—Fiction 4. Love—Fiction
ISBN 978-0-06-182753-2; 0-06-182753-3

LC 2009-29706

Luper, Eric—*Continued*

After his girlfriend breaks up with him and he sees his father out with another woman, high school senior Seth Baumgartner, who has a summer job at the country club and is preparing for a father-son golf tournament, launches a podcast in which he explores the mysteries of love.

"Luper weaves together many themes—trust and secrets, lies and truth, love, lust and, of course, golf—in a way that even the most introspection-hating male reader will eat with a spoon." Kirkus

Lurie, April

The latent powers of Dylan Fontaine. Delacorte Press 2008 208p $15.99; lib bdg $18.99

Grades: 8 9 10 11 12   **Fic**

1. Family life—Fiction 2. New York (N.Y.)—Fiction
ISBN 978-0-385-73125-6; 978-0-385-90153-6 (lib bdg)   LC 2007-32313

Fifteen-year-old Dylan's friend Angie is making a film about him while he is busy trying to keep his older brother from getting caught with drugs, to deal with his mother having left the family, and to figure out how to get Angie to think of him as more than just a friend.

"This is a story about guys, primarily . . . brothers; fathers and sons; lonely young men who are feeling somewhat lost. Any reader will care for each one of them. Lurie does a wonderful job of making them real." KLIATT

Lyga, Barry

The astonishing adventures of Fanboy & Goth Girl. Houghton Mifflin 2006 311p $16.95 *

Grades: 8 9 10 11 12   **Fic**

1. Cartoons and caricatures—Fiction 2. School stories
3. Friendship—Fiction
ISBN 0-618-72392-7   LC 2005-33259

A fifteen-year-old "geek" who keeps a list of the high school jocks and others who torment him, and pours his energy into creating a great graphic novel, encounters Kyra, Goth Girl, who helps change his outlook on almost everything, including himself.

"This engaging first novel has good characterization with genuine voices. . . . The book is compulsively readable." Voice Youth Advocates

Followed by: Goth Girl rising (2009)

Boy toy. Houghton Mifflin 2007 410p $16.95

Grades: 10 11 12   **Fic**

1. Child sexual abuse—Fiction 2. School stories
ISBN 978-0-618-72393-5; 0-618-72393-5
                                            LC 2006-39840

After five years of fighting his way past flickers of memory about the teacher who molested him and the incident that brought the crime to light, eighteen-year-old Josh gets help in coping with his molestor's release from prison when he finally tells his best friends the whole truth.

The author "tackles this incredibly sensitive story with boldness and confidence. He does not shy away from graphic descriptions of Josh's past and even makes the audacious choice of showing young Josh enjoying the attention . . . [Josh] works hard at healing himself and moving into healthy adulthood, and by the end of this well-written, challenging novel, the reader has high hopes that he will make it." Voice Youth Advocates

Hero-type. Houghton Mifflin Co. 2008 295p $16

Grades: 7 8 9 10   **Fic**

1. Heroes and heroines—Fiction 2. Patriotism—Fiction
3. School stories 4. Maryland—Fiction
ISBN 978-0-547-07663-8; 0-547-07663-0
                                            LC 2008-7276

Feeling awkward and ugly is only one reason sixteen-year-old Kevin is uncomfortable with the publicity surrounding his act of accidental heroism, but when a reporter photographs him apparently being unpatriotic, he steps into the limelight to encourage people to think about what the symbols of freedom really mean.

"Leavened by much humor . . . this neatly plotted look at what real patriotism and heroism mean will get readers thinking." KLIATT

Lynch, Chris

Angry young man. Simon & Schuster BFYR 2011 167p $16.99 *

Grades: 7 8 9 10   **Fic**

1. Brothers—Fiction 2. Conduct of life—Fiction
3. Single parent family—Fiction 4. Mother-son relationship—Fiction
ISBN 978-0-689-84790-5; 0-689-84790-4
                                            LC 2009-52832

Eighteen-year-old Robert tries to help his half-brother Xan, a seventeen-year-old misfit, to make better choices as he becomes increasingly attracted to a variety of protesters, anarchists, and the like.

"For those who wonder about the roots of homegrown terror and extremism, . . . Lynch pushes the spotlight from the individual to society in a story that can be brutal and ugly, yet isn't devoid of hope." Publ Wkly

The Big Game of Everything. HarperTeen 2008 275p $16.99; lib bdg $17.89

Grades: 7 8 9 10   **Fic**

1. Family life—Fiction 2. Grandfathers—Fiction
3. Summer employment—Fiction 4. Golf—Fiction
ISBN   978-0-06-074034-4;   0-06-074034-5;
978-0-06-074035-1 (lib bdg); 0-06-074035-3 (lib bdg)
                                            LC 2007-49578

Jock and his eccentric family spend the summer working at Grampus's golf complex, where they end up learning the rules of "The Big Game of Everything."

"This Printz Honor-winning author offers up another touching and offbeat novel full of delightfully skewed humor." Voice Youth Advocates

Hothouse. HarperTeen 2010 198p $16.99 *

Grades: 8 9 10 11 12   **Fic**

1. Father-son relationship—Fiction 2. Death—Fiction
3. Fire fighters—Fiction 4. Friendship—Fiction
5. Bereavement—Fiction
ISBN 978-0-06-167379-5; 0-06-167379-X
                                            LC 2010-3145

Teens D.J. and Russell, life-long friends and neighbors, had drifted apart but when their firefighter fathers are both killed, they try to help one another come to terms with the tragedy and its aftermath.

"Lynch fully commits to the first-person voice, giving into Russ' second-by-second conflicts and contradictions. The author also has a strong grasp of the garrulous slaps and punches that make up many male relationships. Russ' friendships are so real they hurt. The story hurts, too, but that's how it should be." Booklist

Lynch, Chris—*Continued*

Inexcusable. Atheneum Books for Young Readers 2005 165p $16.95; pa $6.99 *

Grades: 8 9 10 11 12   **Fic**
1. Rape—Fiction 2. Football—Fiction 3. School stories
ISBN 0-689-84789-0; 1-416-93972-5 (pa)
LC 2004-30874
"Ginee Seo books"

High school senior and football player Keir sets out to enjoy himself on graduation night, but when he attempts to comfort a friend whose date has left her stranded, things go terribly wrong

"This finely crafted and thought-provoking page-turner carefully conveys that it is simply inexcusable to whitewash wrongs, and that those responsible should (and hopefully will) pay the price." SLJ

Lynch, Scott, 1978-

The lies of Locke Lamora. Bantam 2006 499p map hardcover o.p. pa $7.99 *

Grades: 11 12 Adult   **Fic**
1. Swindlers and swindling—Fiction 2. Thieves—Fiction 3. Fantasy fiction
ISBN 0-553-80467-7; 978-0-553-80467-6; 0-553-58894-x (pa); 978-0-553-58894-x (pa)
LC 2006-42653
"A Bantam spectra book"

"Abandoned as an infant, the boy known as Locke Lamora grows up to become one of his city's most famous (or infamous) con artists, yet his good nature has made him a folk hero. Leading his own band of men, Locke falls into the center of a conspiracy that threatens those he holds dear." Libr J

"Fans of lavishly appointed fantasy will be in seventh heaven here, but it will be nearly as popular with readers of literary crime fiction. This is a true genre bender, at home on almost any kind of fiction shelf." Booklist

Maberry, Jonathan, 1958-

Rot & ruin. Simon & Schuster Books for Young Readers 2010 458p $17.99 *

Grades: 9 10 11 12   **Fic**
1. Zombies—Fiction 2. Brothers—Fiction 3. Horror fiction
ISBN 978-1-4424-0232-4; 1-4424-0232-6
LC 2009-46041

In a post-apocalyptic world where fences and border patrols guard the few people left from the zombies that have overtaken civilization, fifteen-year-old Benny Imura is finally convinced that he must follow in his older brother's footsteps and become a bounty hunter.

"In turns mythic and down-to-earth, this intense novel combines adventure and philosophy to tell a truly memorable zombie story." Publ Wkly

Followed by: Dust & decay (2011)

MacColl, Michaela

Prisoners in the palace; how Victoria became queen with the help of her maid, a reporter, and a scoundrel; a novel of intrigue and romance. Chronicle Books 2010 367p $16.99

Grades: 7 8 9 10   **Fic**
1. Victoria, Queen of Great Britain, 1819-1901—Fiction 2. Orphans—Fiction 3. Household employees—Fiction 4. London (England)—Fiction 5. Great Britain—History—19th century—Fiction
ISBN 978-0-8118-7300-0; 0-8118-7300-5
LC 2010-8257

Recently orphaned and destitute, seventeen-year-old Liza Hastings earns a position as a lady's maid to sixteen-year-old Princess Victoria at Kensington Palace in 1836, the year before Victoria becomes Queen of England.

"This novel is full of historical detail, vivid settings, and richly drawn characters, and themes of friendship and romance give the story teen appeal." Booklist

MacCready, Robin Merrow

Buried. Dutton Books 2006 198p $16.99; pa $6.99

Grades: 8 9 10 11 12   **Fic**
1. Children of alcoholics—Fiction 2. Mother-daughter relationship—Fiction 3. Obsessive-compulsive disorder—Fiction
ISBN 978-0-525-47724-2; 0-525-47724-1; 978-0-14-241141-4 (pa); 0-14-241141-8 (pa)
LC 2006-03870

When her alcoholic mother goes missing, seventeen-year-old Claudine begins to spin out of control, despite her attempts to impose order on every aspect of her life.

"Readers who came for the issues may find themselves reaching for the tissues as Claudine finally finds closure with her mother." Bull Cent Child Books

MacCullough, Carolyn

Once a witch. Clarion Books 2009 292p $16

Grades: 8 9 10 11 12   **Fic**
1. Time travel—Fiction 2. Witches—Fiction 3. Good and evil—Fiction 4. Sisters—Fiction 5. New York (N.Y.)—Fiction
ISBN 978-0-547-22399-5; 0-547-22399-4
LC 2008-49234

Born into a family of witches, seventeen-year-old Tamsin is raised believing that she alone lacks a magical "Talent," but when her beautiful and powerful sister is taken by an age-old rival of the family in an attempt to change the balance of power, Tamsin discovers her true destiny.

"The book will appeal to teen readers who enjoy stories with romance, magic, or time travel, along with hardcore fantasy aficionados, and it is appropriate for all young adult collections." Voice Youth Advocates

Followed by: Always a witch (2011)

Stealing Henry. Roaring Brook Press 2005 196p $16.95

Grades: 9 10 11 12   **Fic**
1. Runaway teenagers—Fiction 2. Siblings—Fiction 3. Mother-daughter relationship—Fiction 4. Child abuse—Fiction
ISBN 1-596-43045-1   LC 2004-17550

MacCullough, Carolyn—*Continued*

"A Deborah Brodie book"

The experiences of high-schooler Savannah, following her decision to take her eight-year-old half brother from his abusive father and their oblivious mother, are interspersed with the earlier story of her mother, Alice, as she meets Savannah's father and unexpectedly becomes pregnant.

"Young adult readers will find this [book] fascinating and appealing." Libr Media Connect

Mackall, Dandi Daley, 1949-

Eva underground. Harcourt 2006 239p $17 *
Grades: 9 10 11 12   Fic
1. Poland—Fiction 2. Father-daughter relationship—Fiction 3. Communism—Fiction
ISBN 0-15-205462-6; 978-0-15-205462-5
                                             LC 2005-04195
In 1978, a high school senior is forced by her widowed father to move from their comfortable Chicago suburb to help with an underground education movement in communist Poland.

"Poland behind the Iron Curtain is rarely found in modern young adult literature, and Mackall has done a superb job in captivating high reader interest in this unique setting." Libr Media Connect

Mackler, Carolyn

The earth, my butt, and other big, round things. Candlewick Press 2003 246p $15.99; pa $8.99 *
Grades: 7 8 9 10   Fic
1. Family life—Fiction 2. Obesity—Fiction 3. School stories 4. New York (N.Y.)—Fiction
ISBN 0-7636-1958-2; 0-7636-2091-2 (pa)
                                             LC 2002-73921
Feeling like she does not fit in with the other members of her family, who are all thin, brilliant, and good-looking, fifteen-year-old Virginia tries to deal with her self-image, her first physical relationship, and her disillusionment with some of the people closest to her

"The e-mails [Virginia] exchanges . . . and the lists she makes (e.g., 'The Fat Girl Code of Conduct') add both realism and insight to her character. The heroine's transformation into someone who finds her own style and speaks her own mind is believable—and worthy of applause." Publ Wkly

Tangled. HarperTeen 2010 308p $16.99
Grades: 8 9 10 11 12   Fic
1. Vacations—Fiction 2. Friendship—Fiction 3. Caribbean region—Fiction 4. New York (State)—Fiction
ISBN 978-0-06-173104-4; 0-06-173104-8
                                             LC 2009-7286
The lives of four very different teenagers become entangled in ways that none of them could have imagined after a short stay at a Caribbean resort

"The various viewpoints weave together to create a compelling and cohesive whole. Themes of understanding, respecting others, and the power of good communication are carefully and effectively woven throughout a story that begs for discussion." SLJ

Vegan virgin Valentine. Candlewick Press 2004 228p $16.99; pa $8.99
Grades: 9 10 11 12   Fic
1. Aunts—Fiction 2. School stories
ISBN 0-7636-2155-2; 0-7636-2613-9 (pa)
                                             LC 2004-45774
Mara's niece, who is only one-year-younger, moves in bringing conflict between the two teenagers because of their opposite personalities

"Racily narrated by likeable Mara, this fast-paced coming-of-age story is charged with sarcasm, angst, honesty, and hope. Many teen girls will recognize parts of themselves within its pages." Voice Youth Advocates

Followed by Guyaholic (2007)

Madigan, L. K.

Flash burnout; a novel. Houghton Mifflin 2009 332p $16 *
Grades: 9 10 11 12   Fic
1. Photographers—Fiction 2. Friendship—Fiction 3. Dating (Social customs)—Fiction 4. School stories
ISBN 978-0-547-19489-9; 0-547-19489-7
                                             LC 2010-278252
"Fifteen-year-old photographer-in-training Blake is caught between fawning over his gorgeous girlfriend Shannon and helping Marissa, his troubled photography partner, a friend who also happens to be a girl." Kirkus

"This rich romance explores the complexities of friendship and love, and the all-too-human limitations of both. It's a sobering, compelling, and satisfying read for teens." Booklist

The mermaid's mirror. Houghton Mifflin Harcourt 2010 316p $16
Grades: 8 9 10 11 12   Fic
1. Mermaids and mermen—Fiction 2. Surfing—Fiction 3. Magic—Fiction 4. Father-daughter relationship—Fiction 5. Family life—Fiction 6. California—Fiction
ISBN 978-0-547-19491-2; 0-547-19491-9
                                             LC 2010-6771
Lena, almost sixteen, has always felt drawn to the waters of San Francisco Bay despite the fears of her father, a former surfer, but after she glimpses a beautiful woman with a tail, nothing can keep Lena from seeking the mermaid in the dangerous waves at Magic Crescent Cove.

"The characters . . . are well rounded and integrated into the plot. . . . With highly imagistic descriptions and savvy dialogue, Madigan offers a rewarding and credible story that uses fantasy elements to bare truths about family ties." Booklist

Magoon, Kekla, 1980-

The rock and the river. Aladdin 2009 290p $15.99
Grades: 7 8 9 10   Fic
1. Black Panther Party—Fiction 2. African Americans—Fiction 3. Brothers—Fiction 4. Chicago (Ill.)—Fiction
ISBN 978-1-4169-7582-3; 1-4169-7582-9
                                             LC 2008-29170
In 1968 Chicago, fourteen-year-old Sam Childs is caught in a conflict between his father's nonviolent approach to seeking civil rights for African Americans and

Magoon, Kekla, 1980-—*Continued*
his older brother, who has joined the Black Panther Party.

This "novel will make readers feel what it was like to be young, black, and militant 40 years ago, including the seething fury and desperation over the daily discrimination that drove the oppressed to fight back." Booklist

Mahy, Margaret
The Magician of Hoad. Margaret K. McElderry Books 2009 411p $18.99
Grades: 7 8 9 10   Fic
1. Fantasy fiction 2. Magicians—Fiction
ISBN 978-1-4169-7807-7; 1-4169-7807-0
          LC 2008-23000
A young farm boy who possesses mysterious powers is chosen by the king to be the court's royal magician.
"Mahy majestically deploys the poetic language of fantasy to portray the changes and challenges of adolescence; here, and epic quest for identity is wrapped up in terror, romance, surprise, and suspense—always sustained by luminous imagery and intelligent, musical prose." Horn Book

Maizel, Rebecca
Infinite days; a vampire queen novel. St. Martin's Griffin 2010 325p (Vampire queen) pa $9.99
Grades: 7 8 9 10   Fic
1. Vampires—Fiction 2. Supernatural—Fiction 3. School stories
ISBN 978-0-312-64991-3; 0-312-64991-6
At a New England boarding school, Lenah Beaudonte tries to act like a normal sixteen-year-old although she was, before a hundred-year hibernation, a centuries-old vampire queen whose bloodthirsty, abandoned coven is seeking her.
"The story is filled with action, romance, longing, deception, and sacrifice. It will leave vampire fans thirsting for more." SLJ

Malamud, Bernard, 1914-1986
The assistant; a novel. Farrar, Straus & Giroux 1957 246p pa $13 hardcover o.p.
Grades: 11 12 Adult   Fic
1. Jews—New York (N.Y.)—Fiction 2. Brooklyn (New York, N.Y.)—Fiction
ISBN 0-374-50484-9 (pa)
This novel is "set in the prison of a failing grocery store, where Morris Bober, its elderly, long-suffering Jewish owner, teaches his assistant, Frankie Alpine, what it means to be a Jew, and what it means to be a man. After decades in which Jewish protagonists struggled to assimilate to the non-Jewish world around them, *The Assistant* is a tale about reverse assimilation, one in which Frankie takes over the store on Morris's death and undergoes a painful conversion to Judaism." Benet's Reader's Ency of Am Lit

The fixer. Farrar, Straus & Giroux 1966 355p pa $14 hardcover o.p. *
Grades: 11 12 Adult   Fic

1. Jews—Russia—Fiction 2. Russia—Fiction
ISBN 0-374-52938-8 (pa)
"Yakov Bok, a handyman, is arrested and charged with the killing of a Christian boy. Innocent of the crime, he is only guilty of being a Jew in Czarist Russia. In jail he is mentally and physically tortured as a scapegoat for a crime he insists he did not commit. Although his suffering and degradation are unrelenting, Bok emerges a hero as he maintains his innocence. Malamud has fashioned a powerful story of injustice and endurance based on a true incident." Shapiro. Fic for Youth. 3d edition

Malley, Gemma
The Declaration. Bloomsbury; distributed by Holtzbrinck Pub. 2007 300p $16.95
Grades: 7 8 9 10   Fic
1. Science fiction 2. Great Britain—Fiction 3. Immortality—Fiction
ISBN 978-1-59990-119-0; 1-59990-119-6
          LC 2006-102138
In 2140 England, where drugs enable people to live forever and children are illegal, teenaged Anna, an obedient "Surplus" training to become a house servant, discovers that her birth parents are trying to find her.
This is "gripping. . . . The indoctrinated teen's awakening to massive injustice makes compulsive reading." Booklist
Other titles in this series are:
The legacy (2011)
The resistance (2008)

Malloy, Brian
The year of ice. St. Martin's Press 2002 262p hardcover o.p. pa $12.95 *
Grades: 11 12 Adult   Fic
1. Homosexuality—Fiction 2. Father-son relationship—Fiction 3. Minnesota—Fiction
ISBN 0-312-28948-0; 0-312-31369-1 (pa)
          LC 2002-510282
"A gay high school senior struggles to cope with his father's irresponsibility in Malloy's poignant, quietly effective debut, set in Minneapolis in the late '70s. From the outside looking in, protagonist Kevin Doyle seems like a normal, party-happy 17-year-old, but the combination of a troubled family life and his secret crush on one of his best friends definitely sets him apart from the pack." Publ Wkly

Mankell, Henning, 1948-
Shadow of the leopard; [translated from the Swedish by Anna Paterson] Annick Press; Distributed in the U.S.A. by Firefly Books 2009 177p $19.95; pa $10.95
Grades: 10 11 12   Fic
1. Amputees—Fiction 2. Adultery—Fiction 3. Family life—Fiction 4. Mozambique—Fiction
ISBN 978-1-55451-200-3; 978-1-55451-199-0 (pa)
Sequel to Secrets of the fire (2003)
First published in Australia with title: The fury in the fire

Mankell, Henning, 1948-—*Continued*

Sofia, who lost her legs as a child, is now grown up with children in Mozambique, but when she discovers that Armando, the father of her children, is cheating on her, she leaves him, igniting her terrible rage.

"Readers will remember the indomitable Sofia—whose tale is based on real events—long after they close the book." Kirkus

Manning, Sarra

Guitar girl. Dutton Children's Books 2004 217p hardcover o.p. pa $6.99

Grades: 9 10 11 12   **Fic**

1. Musicians—Fiction 2. Great Britain—Fiction
ISBN 0-525-47234-7; 0-14-240318-0 (pa)

LC 2004-299584

First published 2003 in the United Kingdom

"Yearning to be like her idol, rock star Ruby X, and desperate to be noticed, Molly decides to form a band with her two best school friends, Jane and Tara. 'The Hormones,' as Jane dubs them, then add cocky Dean, a guitarist, and T, his silent drummer friend . . . and pick up a manager who catapults them into the fast lane of British rock. Molly's pleased to have the chance to be a real rocker girl, but the experience is, overall, less pleasurable than frustrating. . . . The more she learns about where she stands, personally and legally, the more she realizes she's been completely out of her depth." Bull Cent Child Books

"Wryly funny, often sincere, and sometimes pressed into banshee-like behavior, Molly is endearing in her attempts to reach maturity, sort out what's important, and decide what needs to be left behind." SLJ

Mantchev, Lisa

Eyes like stars. Feiwel and Friends 2009 356p $16.99

Grades: 8 9 10 11 12   **Fic**

1. Theater—Fiction 2. Magic—Fiction 3. Actors—Fiction 4. Orphans—Fiction 5. Books and reading—Fiction
ISBN 978-0-312-38096-0; 0-312-38096-8

LC 2008-15317

Thirteen-year-old Bertie strives to save Theater Illuminata, the only home she has ever known, but is hindered by the Players who magically live on there, especially Ariel, who is willing to destroy the Book at the center of the magic in order to escape into the outside world.

"The story contains enough mystery and mayhem to keep readers engaged, even as they analyze." Voice Youth Advocates

Followed by Perchance to dream (2010)

Marchetta, Melina, 1965-

Finnikin of the rock. Candlewick Press 2010 399p map $18.99 *

Grades: 8 9 10 11 12   **Fic**

1. Fantasy fiction
ISBN 978-0-7636-4361-4; 0-7636-4361-0

LC 2009-28046

Now on the cusp of manhood, Finnikin, who was a child when the royal family of Lumatere was brutally murdered and replaced by an imposter, reluctantly joins forces with an enigmatic young novice and fellow-exile, who claims that her dark dreams will lead them to a surviving royal child and a way to regain the throne of Lumatere.

"The skillful world building includes just enough detail to create a vivid sense of place, and Marchetta maintains suspense with unexpected story arcs. It is the achingly real characters, though, and the relationships that emerge through the captivating dialogue that drive the story. Filled with questions about the impact of exile and the human need to belong, this standout fantasy quickly reveals that its real magic lies in its accomplished writing." Booklist

Jellicoe Road. HarperTeen 2008 419p $17.99; lib bdg $18.89 *

Grades: 9 10 11 12   **Fic**

1. Abandoned children—Fiction 2. Identity (Psychology)—Fiction 3. School stories 4. Australia—Fiction
ISBN 978-0-06-143183-8; 0-06-143183-4; 978-0-06-143184-5 (lib bdg); 0-06-143184-2 (lib bdg)

LC 2008-00760

First published 2006 in Australia with title: On the Jellicoe Road

Abandoned by her drug-addicted mother at the age of eleven, high school student Taylor Markham struggles with her identity and family history at a boarding school in Australia.

"Readers may feel dizzied and disoriented, but as they puzzle out exactly how Hannah's narrative connects with Taylor's current reality, they will find themselves ensnared in the story's fascinating, intricate structure. A beautifully rendered mystery." Kirkus

Saving Francesca. Knopf 2004 243p hardcover o.p. pa $8.95

Grades: 9 10 11 12   **Fic**

1. Mental illness—Fiction 2. Mother-daughter relationship—Fiction 3. School stories 4. Australia—Fiction
ISBN 0-375-82982-2; 0-375-82983-0 (pa)

LC 2004-3926

Sixteen-year-old Francesca could use her outspoken mother's help with the problems of being one of a handful of girls at a parochial school that has just turned co-ed, but her mother has suddenly become severely depressed

This book "has great characterizations, witty dialogue, a terrific relationship between Francesca and her younger brother, and a sweet romance. Teens will relate to this tender novel and will take to heart its solid messages and realistic treatment of a very real problem." SLJ

Followed by The piper's son (2011)

Marillier, Juliet

Daughter of the forest. TOR Bks. 2000 400p (Sevenwaters trilogy) hardcover o.p. pa $15.95

Grades: 11 12 Adult   **Fic**

1. Fantasy fiction
ISBN 0-312-84879-X; 0-312-87530-4 (pa)

LC 00-25216

"A Tom Doherty Associates book"

Marillier, Juliet—*Continued*

"As the only daughter and youngest child of Lord Colum of Sevenwaters, Sorcha grows up protected and pampered by her six older brothers. When a sorceress's evil magic ensorcels Colum's sons, transforming them into swans, only Sorcha's efforts can break the curse. . . . The author's keen understanding of Celtic paganism and early Irish Christianity adds texture to a rich and vibrant novel that belongs in most fantasy collections." Libr J

Other titles in the Sevenwaters trilogy are:
Child of the prophecy (2002)
Son of the shadows (2001)

Wildwood dancing. Knopf 2007 416p $16.99; lib bdg $18.99

Grades: 7 8 9 10   **Fic**
1. Magic—Fiction 2. Supernatural—Fiction 3. Sisters—Fiction
ISBN 0-375-83364-1; 0-375-93364-6 (lib bdg)
LC 2006-16075

Five sisters who live with their merchant father in Transylvania use a hidden portal in their home to cross over into a magical world, the Wildwood.

This is told "with a striking sense of place, magical elements, beautifully portrayed characters, strong heroines, and an emotional core that touches the heart." Voice Youth Advocates

Followed by: Cybele's secret (2008)

Marino, Peter

Dough Boy. Holiday House 2005 221p hardcover o.p. pa $6.95 *

Grades: 7 8 9 10   **Fic**
1. Obesity—Fiction 2. Family life—Fiction 3. Bullies—Fiction 4. School stories
ISBN 0-8234-1873-1; 0-8234-2096-5 (pa)
LC 2004-40593

Overweight, fifteen-year-old Tristan, who lives happily with his divorced mother and her boyfriend Frank, suddenly finds that he must deal with intensified criticism about his weight and other aspects of his life when Frank's popular but troubled, nutrition-obsessed daughter moves in.

"Readers will easily feel the boy's anger and will applaud his resilience and resolve to remain true to himself." Publ Wkly

Mariz, Rae

The Unidentified. Balzer + Bray 2010 296p $16.99

Grades: 7 8 9 10   **Fic**
1. School stories 2. Science fiction
ISBN 978-0-06-180208-9; 0-06-180208-5
LC 2009-54254

In a futuristic alternative school set in a shopping mall where video game-playing students are observed and used by corporate sponsors for market research, Katey "Kid" Dade struggles to figure out where she fits in and whether she even wants to.

"An all-too-logical extrapolation of today's trends, this story of conformity, rebellion, and seeking one's identity is evocative of Scott Westerfeld and Cory Doctorow, injecting a dystopian setting with an optimistic, antiestablishment undercurrent." Publ Wkly

Markandaya, Kamala, 1924-2004

Nectar in a sieve; with an introduction by Indira Ganesan and a new afterword by Thrity Umrigar. Signet Classics 2010 204p pa $7.95

Grades: 9 10 11 12 Adult   **Fic**
1. Farm life—Fiction 2. India—Fiction
ISBN 978-0-451-53172-8

First published 1954 in the United Kingdom; first United States edition published 1955 by Day

"This realistic novel of peasant life in a southern Indian village portrays the struggle that Nathan and Rukmani must make to survive. Their first child is a daughter, Irawaddy, and there follow five other children, all sons, after an interval of seven years. Hardships are innumerable and insurmountable, whether they are disasters of nature such as drought, or such manmade catastrophes as the coming of a tannery to their village and a subsequent labor conflict. After many crises, Nathan and Rukmani come to the city to seek help from one of their sons, but he has disappeared. Nathan, finally destroyed by privation, dies, believing to the end that his life with Rukmani has been a happy one." Shapiro. Fic for Youth. 3d edition

Includes bibliographical references

Marr, Melissa

Wicked lovely. HarperTeen 2007 328p il $16.99; lib bdg $17.89

Grades: 8 9 10 11 12   **Fic**
1. Fairies—Fiction 2. Kings and rulers—Fiction 3. Fantasy fiction
ISBN 978-0-06-121465-3; 0-06-121465-5; 978-0-06-121466-0 (lib bdg); 0-06-121466-3 (lib bdg)
LC 2007-09143

Seventeen-year-old Aislinn, who has the rare ability to see faeries, is drawn against her will into a centuries-old battle between the Summer King and the Winter Queen, and the survival of her life, her love, and summer all hang in the balance.

"This story explores the themes of love, commitment, and what it really means to give of oneself for the greater good to save everyone else. It is the unusual combination of past legends and modern-day life that gives a unique twist to this 'fairy' tale." SLJ

Other titles in this series are:
Darkest mercy (2011)
Fragile eternity (2009)
Ink exchange (2008)
Radiant shadows (2010)

Marriott, Zoë, 1982 or 3-

The swan kingdom. Candlewick Press 2008 272p $16.99; pa $8.99

Grades: 6 7 8 9 10 11 12   **Fic**
1. Fantasy fiction 2. Magic—Fiction
ISBN 978-0-7636-3481-0; 0-7636-3481-6; 978-0-7636-4293-8 (pa); 0-7636-4293-2 (pa)
LC 2007-38291

When Alexa's mother is killed, her father marries a cunning and powerful woman and her brothers disappear, sending Alexa on a long, dangerous journey as she attempts to harness the mystical power she inherited from her mother and restore the kingdom to its proper balance.

"The mix of magic, royalty and romance will compel many teens." Publ Wkly

Marsden, John, 1950-

Hamlet: a novel. Candlewick Press 2009 229p $16.99

Grades: 10 11 12   Fic
1. Shakespeare, William, 1564-1616—Fiction
2. Princes—Fiction 3. Homicide—Fiction
4. Denmark—Fiction
ISBN 978-0-7636-4451-2; 0-7636-4451-X
                                        LC 2009-7331
This is a retelling of Shakespeare's play. Grieving for
the recent death of his beloved father and appalled by his
mother's quick remarriage to his uncle, Hamlet, heir to
the Danish throne, struggles with conflicting emotions,
particularly after his father's ghost appeals to him to
avenge his death.
"The setting is contemporary, but feels timeless.
Marsden stays true to Shakespeare's text, while modern-
izing the dialogue. He makes the prince a sympathetic
teen who is struggling with his hormones, his grief, and
the fact that his uncle is now his stepfather. . . . This is
a wonderful treatment of the play: engaging, gripping,
dark, and lovely." SLJ

Tomorrow, when the war began. Houghton
Mifflin 1995 286p $16

Grades: 7 8 9 10   Fic
1. War stories 2. Australia—Fiction
ISBN 0-395-70673-4   LC 94-29299
Also available in paperback from Point
First published 1993 in Australia
"Australian teenager Ellie and six of her friends return
from a winter break camping trip to find their homes
burned or deserted, their families imprisoned, and their
country occupied by a foreign military force in league
with a band of disaffected Australians. As their shock
wears off, the seven decide they must stick together if
they are to survive." SLJ
"The novel is a riveting adventure through which
Marsden explores the capacity for evil and the necessity
of working together to oppose it." Horn Book
Other available titles in this series are:
Burning for revenge (2000)
Darkness, be my friend (1999)
The dead of night (1997)
A killing frost (1998)
The night is for hunting (2001)
The other side of dawn (2002)

While I live. Scholastic 2007 299p (The Ellie
chronicles) $16.99

Grades: 7 8 9 10   Fic
1. War stories 2. Australia—Fiction
ISBN 978-0-439-78318-7; 0-439-78318-6
Follow up to the Tomorrow Series
Officially the war is over, but Ellie can not seem to
escape it and resume a normal life especially after her
parents are murdered and she becomes the ward of an
unscrupulous lawyer who wants to acquire her family's
property.
"Fans of 16-year-old Ellie Linton . . . will be over-
joyed that she's back in an exciting series of her own.
The realistic and shocking war-related violence that char-
acterized the earlier titles is just as prevalent here." SLJ
Other titles about Ellie Linton are:
Circle of flight (2009)
Incurable (2008)

Marshall, Catherine, 1914-1983

Christy. Avon Books 2006 576p pa $6.99

Grades: 9 10 11 12   Fic
1. Teachers—Fiction 2. Appalachian region—Fiction
ISBN 0-380-00141-1
A reissue of the title first published 1967 by McGraw-
Hill
"A spirited young woman leaves the security of her
home to become a teacher in Cutter Gap, Kentucky. It
is 1912 and the needs of the Appalachian people are
great. Christy learns much from the poverty and superstition of the mountain folk. Marshall's Christian faith and
ideals are intertwined in the plot, which includes a love
story." Shapiro. Fic for Youth. 3d edition

Martin, C. K. Kelly

I know it's over. Random House 2008 244p
$16.99; lib bdg $19.99 *

Grades: 9 10 11 12   Fic
1. Pregnancy—Fiction 2. Love stories 3. School stories 4. Canada—Fiction
ISBN 978-0-375-84566-6; 978-0-375-94566-3 (lib
bdg)   LC 2007-29180
Sixteen-year-old Nick, still trying to come to terms
with his parents' divorce, experiences exhilaration and
despair in his relationship with his girlfriend Sasha especially when, after instigating a trial separation, she announces that she is pregnant.
"This measured but heartbreaking rendering of an all-
too-common situation would be a great choice for mixed-
gender book groups." Bull Cent Child Books

The lighter side of life and death. Random
House Children's Books 2010 231p $16.99; lib
bdg $19.99

Grades: 9 10 11 12   Fic
1. Remarriage—Fiction 2. Theater—Fiction 3. School
stories
ISBN   978-0-375-84588-8;   0-375-84588-7;
978-0-375-95588-4 (lib bdg); 0-375-95588-7 (lib bdg)
                                        LC 2009-15608
After the last, triumphant night of the school play, fifteen-year-old Mason loses his virginity to his good friend
and secret crush, Kat Medina, which leads to enormous
complications at school just as his home life is thrown
into turmoil by his father's marriage to a woman with
two children.
"This is not your ordinary teen romance. It's heavy on
the sex but carefully nuanced. . . . The layers of emotion, so rarely evoked by young men in YA novels, give
a depth and authenticity to Mason's personality that expose his naïveté and occasional bewilderment. The
book's other characters are equally complex. . . . A
more genuine representation of teen life would be hard
to find." Booklist

Martinez, Victor, 1954-

Parrot in the oven; a novel. Cotler Bks. 1996
216p $19.99; pa $5.99 *

Grades: 7 8 9 10   Fic
1. Mexican Americans—Fiction 2. Family life—Fiction
ISBN 0-06-026704-6; 0-06-447186-1 (pa)
                                        LC 96-2119

Martinez, Victor, 1954-—*Continued*
"Joanna Cotler books"
Manny relates his coming of age experiences as a
member of a poor Mexican American family in which
the alcoholic father only adds to everyone's struggle
The author "maintains the authenticity of his setting
and characterizations through a razor-sharp combination
of tense dialogue, coursing narrative and startlingly elegant imagery." Publ Wkly

Martino, Alfred C., 1964-
Over the end line. Houghton Mifflin Harcourt
2009 304p $17
Grades: 10 11 12   **Fic**
1. Soccer—Fiction   2. Friendship—Fiction
3. Popularity—Fiction
ISBN 978-0-15-206121-0; 0-15-206121-5
                           LC 2008-46464
After scoring the winning goal in the county soccer
championship, New Jersey high school senior Jonny finally attains some of the popularity enjoyed by his best
friend Kyle, until a devastating event changes everything.
"The author's portrayal of a graphic sex scene and use
of explicit language add to the novel's tension. Martino
sets out to touch upon issues such as 'the meaning of
friendship, the power of the celebrated athlete, and the
interactions between teen guys and girls.' He succeeds in
dealing with these issues in a compelling manner." Voice
Youth Advocates

Mason, Bobbie Ann
In country; a novel. Harper Perennial 2005 245,
16p pa $14.99 *
Grades: 11 12 Adult   **Fic**
1. Veterans—Fiction 2. Vietnam War, 1961-1975—
Fiction 3. Kentucky—Fiction
ISBN 978-0-06-083517-0; 0-06-083517-6
                         LC 2006-273518
First published 1985
Includes information about the author
"Sam, 17, is obsessed with the Vietnam War and the
effect it has had on her life—losing a father she never
knew and now living with Uncle Emmett, who seems to
be suffering from the effects of Agent Orange. In her
own forthright way, she tries to sort out why and how
Vietnam has altered the lives of the vets of Hopewell,
Kentucky. . . . A harshly realistic, well-written look at
the Vietnam War as well as the story of a young woman
maturing." SLJ

Matson, Morgan
Amy & Roger's epic detour. Simon and
Schuster Books for Young Readers 2010 343p il
$16.99
Grades: 9 10 11 12   **Fic**
1. Automobile travel—Fiction 2. Guilt—Fiction
3. Bereavement—Fiction   4. Death—Fiction
5. Fathers—Fiction
ISBN 978-1-4169-9065-9; 1-4169-9065-8
                         LC 2009-49988
After the death of her father, Amy, a high school stu-
dent, and Roger, a college freshman, set out on a careful-

ly planned road trip from California to Connecticut, but
wind up taking many detours, forcing Amy to face her
worst fears and come to terms with her grief and guilt.
"This entertaining and thoughtful summertime road
trip serves up slices of America with a big scoop of romance on the side." Kirkus

Mattison, Booker T.
Unsigned hype; a novel. Revell 2009 207p pa
$9.99
Grades: 7 8 9 10   **Fic**
1. Rap music—Fiction 2. Christian life—Fiction
3. African Americans—Fiction
ISBN 978-0-8007-3380-3; 0-8007-3380-0
                         LC 2008-54966
Fifteen-year-old Tory Tyson dreams of producing hip
hop records, and as he rapidly begins to experience success doing just that, he finds that he must make choices
between the way he has been raised by his single, God-
fearing mother and the folks he meets in the music
world.
This "novel has an authentic voice, taking readers into
the world of New York City hip-hop through the wide
eyes of a kid who's still refreshingly innocent." Publ
Wkly

**Maugham, W. Somerset (William Somerset),
1874-1965**
Of human bondage; introduction by Gore Vidal.
Modern Library 1999 xxxix, 611p pa $11.95 *
Grades: 11 12 Adult   **Fic**
1. Physically handicapped—Fiction 2. London (England)—Fiction
ISBN 0-375-75315-X   LC 98-46169
Also available from other publishers
First published 1915
This novel's "hero is Philip Carey, a sensitive, talented, club-footed orphan who is brought up by an unsympathetic aunt and uncle. It is a study of his struggle for
independence, his intellectual development, and his attempt to become an artist. Philip gets entangled and obsessed by his love affair with Mildred, a waitress. After
years of struggle as a medical student, he marries a nice
woman, gives up his aspirations, and becomes a country
doctor. The first part of the novel is partly autobiographical, and the book is regarded as Maugham's best work."
Reader's Ency. 4th edition

Mazer, Harry, 1925-
The last mission. Dell 1981 c1979 188p pa
$5.99
Grades: 7 8 9 10   **Fic**
1. World War, 1939-1945—Fiction 2. Prisoners of
war—Fiction 3. Jews—Fiction
ISBN 0-440-94797-9
First published 1979 by Delacorte Press
In 1944 a 15-year-old Jewish boy tells his family he
will travel in the West but instead, enlists in the United
States Air Corps and is subsequently taken prisoner by
the Germans.
"Told in a rapid journalistic style, occasionally pep-
pered with barrack-room vulgarities, the story is a vivid

Mazer, Harry, 1925-—*Continued*

and moving account of a boy's experience during World War II as well as a skillful, convincing portrayal of his misgivings as a Jew on enemy soil and of his ability to size up—in mature human fashion—the misery around him." Horn Book

Mazer, Norma Fox, 1931-2009

The missing girl. HarperTeen 2008 288p $16.99; lib bdg $17.89 *

Grades: 7 8 9 10   Fic

1. Kidnapping—Fiction 2. Sisters—Fiction 3. Child sexual abuse—Fiction 4. New York (State)—Fiction
ISBN 978-0-06-623776-3; 978-0-06-623777-0 (lib bdg)   LC 2007-09136

In Mallory, New York, as five sisters, aged eleven to seventeen, deal with assorted problems, conflicts, fears, and yearnings, a mysterious middle-aged man watches them, fascinated, deciding which one he likes the best.

"Fans of . . . classic tales of high-tension peril will appreciate the way this successfully plays on their deepest fears." Bull Cent Child Books

McBay, Bruce, 1946-

Waiting for Sarah; {by} Bruce McBay & James Heneghan. Orca Book Publishers 2003 170p pa $7.95

Grades: 9 10 11 12   Fic

1. Orphans—Fiction 2. Physically handicapped—Fiction 3. Canada—Fiction
ISBN 1-55143-270-6   LC 2002-117768

After Mike loses his family and is severely injured in a car accident, he withdraws until he meets mysterious Sarah, a girl who is not who she seems

"This is a well-developed novel that shatters the teen perceptions of invincibility, as well as dealing with loss, handicaps, and positive ways to break through grief." Lib Media Connect

McBride, Lish

Hold me closer, necromancer. Henry Holt 2010 342p $16.99

Grades: 9 10 11 12   Fic

1. Supernatural—Fiction 2. Magic—Fiction 3. Dead—Fiction 4. Werewolves—Fiction 5. Seattle (Wash.)—Fiction
ISBN 978-0-8050-9098-7; 0-8050-9098-3
                                  LC 2009-50768

Sam LaCroix, a Seattle fast-food worker and college dropout, discovers that he is a necromancer, part of a world of harbingers, werewolves, satyrs, and one particular necromancer who sees Sam as a threat to his lucrative business of raising the dead.

"With fine writing, tight plotting, a unique and uniquely odd cast of teens, adults, and children, and a pace that smashes through any curtain of disbelief, this sardonic and outrageous story's only problem is that it must, like all good things, come to an end." Booklist

McBride, Regina, 1956-

The fire opal. Delacorte Press 2010 293p $16.99; lib bdg $19.99

Grades: 7 8 9 10   Fic

1. Supernatural—Fiction 2. Family life—Fiction 3. Celtic mythology—Fiction 4. Ireland—Fiction
ISBN 978-0-385-73781-4; 0-385-73781-5; 978-0-385-90692-0 (lib bdg); 0-385-90692-7 (lib bdg)
                                  LC 2009-07573

While invading English soldiers do battle in sixteenth-century Ireland, Maeve grows up with a mystical connection to a queen who, centuries before, faced enemies of her own.

"Filled with fantastic creatures and hair-raising adventure, this mystical, imaginative tale should appeal to fantasy fans of all ages. A compelling, addictive read." Voice Youth Advocates

McCaffrey, Anne

Dragonflight; volume 1 of "The Dragonriders of Pern". Ballantine Bks. 1978 337p il (Dragonriders of Pern) hardcover o.p. pa $12.95

Grades: 8 9 10 11 12 Adult   Fic

1. Dragons—Fiction 2. Fantasy fiction 3. Science fiction
ISBN 0-345-27749-X; 0-345-48426-6 (pa)
                                  LC 78-16707

"A Del Rey book"

First published 1968 in paperback. Based on two award winning stories entitled: Weyr search and Dragonrider. Many titles co-written by Todd McCaffrey

The planet Pern, originally colonized from Earth but long out of contact with it, has been periodically threatened by the deadly silver Threads which fall from the wandering Red Star. To combat them a life form on the planet was developed into winged, fire-breathing dragons. Humans with a high degree of empathy and telepathic power are needed to train and preserve these creatures. As the story begins, Pern has fallen into decay, the threat of the Red Star has been forgotten, the Dragonriders and dragons are reduced in number and in disrepute, and the evil Lord Fax has begun conquering neighboring holds.

Fantasy titles set on Pern include:
All the Weyrs of Pern (1991)
The chronicles of Pern: first fall (1993)
Dragon Harper (2007)
Dragon's fire (2006)
Dragon's kin (2003)
Dragon's time (2011)
Dragondrums (1979)
Dragonquest (1971)
Dragonsdawn (1988)
Dragonseye (1997)
Dragonsinger (1977)
Dragonsong (1976)
The masterharper of Pern (1998)
Morets: Dragonlady of Pern (1983)
Nerilka's story (1986)
The Renegades of Pern (1989)
The skies of Pern (2001)
White dragon (1978)

McCahan, Erin

I now pronounce you someone else. Arthur A. Levine Books 2010 258p $16.99

Grades: 8 9 10 11　　　　　　　　　　Fic

1. Dating (Social customs)—Fiction
2. Mother-daughter relationship—Fiction
3. Stepfathers—Fiction 4. Family life—Fiction
5. Michigan—Fiction

ISBN 978-0-545-08818-3; 0-545-08818-6

LC 2009-35992

Eighteen-year-old Bronwen has long felt that she was switched with another child at birth, and so although she loves Jared, she must decide if she is ready to be married or should, instead, live on her own first.

"Told in lively first-person narrative, this intelligent romance teaches a hard but relevant lesson about living dreams and letting them go." Publ Wkly

McCarthy, Cormac, 1933-

All the pretty horses. Knopf 1992 301p $27.50; pa $14.95

Grades: 11 12 Adult　　　　　　　　　Fic

1. Mexico—Fiction 2. Cowhands—Fiction

ISBN 0-394-57474-5; 0-679-74439-8 (pa)

LC 91-58560

First volume in the author's Border trilogy

In the spring of 1950, after the death of his grandfather, sixteen-year-old John Grady Cole "is evicted from the Texas ranch where he grew up. He and another boy Lacey Rawlins, head for Mexico on horseback, riding south until they finally turn up at a vast ranch in mountainous Coahuila, the Hacienda de la Purisima, where they sign on as vaqueros. . . . John Grady's unusual talent for breaking, training and understanding horses becomes crucial in the *hacendado* Don Hector's ambitious breeding program. For John Grady, La Purisima is a paradise, complete with its Eve, Don Hector's daughter, Alejandra." N Y Times Book Rev

"Though some readers may grow impatient with the wild prairie rhythms of McCarthy's language, others will find his voice completely transporting." Publ Wkly

Other titles in the Border trilogy are:

Cities of the Plain (1998)

The crossing (1994)

The road. Knopf 2006 241p $24 *

Grades: 11 12 Adult　　　　　　　　　Fic

1. Father-son relationship—Fiction 2. Voyages and travels—Fiction 3. Survival after airplane accidents, shipwrecks, etc.—Fiction

ISBN 978-0-307-26543-2; 0-307-26543-9

LC 2006-23629

"A nuclear holocaust has reduced everything to ash, mummifying all but a few unlucky souls, who must kill or be killed (and eaten). The main characters are a father and his son, who was born a few nights after the bombs fell. 'We're still the good guys,' the man repeatedly assures the boy as they scavenge their way south for the winter, trying to avoid 'bad guy' survival techniques. . . . The horrors here—an infant 'headless and gutted and blackening on the spit'—are extreme, and, deprived of historical context, . . . [the author's] brutality can seem willful. But McCarthy's prose retains its ability to seduce . . . and there are nods to the gentler aspects of the human spirit." New Yorker

McCarthy, Maureen, 1953-

Rose by any other name. Roaring Brook Press 2008 336p $17.95

Grades: 9 10 11 12　　　　　　　　　　Fic

1. Family life—Fiction 2. Automobile travel—Fiction
3. Australia—Fiction

ISBN 978-1-59643-372-4; 1-59643-372-8

LC 2007-18406

First published 2006 in Australia

During a road trip with her mother from Melbourne to Fairy Point, Australia, to see her dying grandmother, nineteen-year-old Rose gains a new perspective on events of the previous year, when family problems, the end of a long-term friendship, and bad personal choices dramatically transformed her near-perfect life.

"This complex coming-of-age novel, which explores both universal self-destructive tendencies and resilience, will resonate with teen readers as well as many adults." Booklist

McCarthy, Susan Carol

True fires. Bantam Books 2004 306p hardcover o.p. pa $13

Grades: 9 10 11 12　　　　　　　　　　Fic

1. Race relations—Fiction 2. Segregation in education—Fiction 3. Florida—Fiction

ISBN 0-553-80170-8; 0-553-38104-0 (pa)

LC 2003-70885

"Recently widowed, Franklin Dare moves his family to Florida to start a new life in the lush citrus groves. But his young children catch the eye of a corrupt sheriff, K.A. DeLuth, who proclaims Daniel's hair too 'kinked' and Rebecca's nose too wide and bans them from Lake Esther Elementary (according to Florida law, any child deemed one-eighth black or more cannot attend an all-white school). Only unimpeachable evidence that Franklin has no black blood—in fact, he is part Croatan Indian—will result in the children's readmittance. . . . The ending may present more questions than answers, but it doesn't take away from McCarthy's flawless dialogue, warm characters and compassionate wit, all of which service a moving story about the powers of love and justice." Publ Wkly

McCaughrean, Geraldine, 1951-

Cyrano. Harcourt 2006 114p $16

Grades: 7 8 9 10　　　　　　　　　　Fic

1. Cyrano de Bergerac, 1619-1655—Fiction
2. France—History—1589-1789, Bourbons—Fiction
3. Love stories

ISBN 978-0-15-205805-0; 0-15-205805-2

LC 2006-05445

Ashamed of his ugliness, long-nosed Cyrano de Bergerac, a brilliant seventeenth-century poet and expert swordsman in the French army, helps a rival woo and win Roxane, the beautiful cousin Cyrano loves in silence.

"The story has something for everyone—action, adventure, and romance. The dynamically drawn characters jump off the page. Staying true to Edmond Rostand's original tale, McCaughrean introduces a new generation to the swashbuckling hero." SLJ

McCaughrean, Geraldine, 1951—*Continued*

The white darkness. HarperTempest 2007 c2005 384p hardcover o.p. pa $8.99
Grades: 8 9 10 11 12   **Fic**
1. Antarctica—Fiction 2. Wilderness survival—Fiction
ISBN   978-0-06-089035-3;   0-06-089035-5; 978-0-06-089037-7 (pa); 0-06-089037-1 (pa)
LC 2006-02503
First published 2005 in the United Kingdom

Taken to Antarctica by the man she thinks of as her uncle for what she believes to be a vacation, Symone—a troubled fourteen year old—discovers that he is dangerously obsessed with seeking Symme's Hole, an opening that supposedly leads into the center of a hollow Earth.

"McCaughrean's lyrical language actively engages the senses, plunging readers into a captivating landscape that challenges the boundaries of reality." Booklist

McClintock, Norah

Dooley takes the fall. Red Deer Press 2007 314p pa $12.95
Grades: 7 8 9 10   **Fic**
1. Suicide—Fiction
ISBN 978-0-88995-403-8; 0-88995-403-8

As a troubled teen struggles to free himself from his past and the implications of the present conspiracies that surround him, Dooley tries to prove his innocence in a suicide that looks like murder.

"A fast-paced book with an involving character and a story that builds to a satisfying climax." Voice Youth Advocates

Masked; written by Norah McClintock. Orca Book Publishers 2010 108p (Orca soundings) pa $9.95
Grades: 7 8 9 10   **Fic**
1. Mystery fiction
ISBN 978-1-55469-364-1; 1-55469-364-0

Rosie walks in on an armed robbery in her father's convienence store. Who is that masked man? And why is the loser from school there?

"Tight plotting, swift pacing, and tension that intensifies with each page mark this entry in the always-reliable Orca Soundings series for reluctant readers." Booklist

Taken. Orca Book Publishers 2009 166p pa $12.95
Grades: 7 8 9 10   **Fic**
1. Wilderness survival—Fiction 2. Kidnapping—Fiction
ISBN 978-1-55469-152-4; 1-55469-152-4

"After two girls from a nearby town go missing everyone goes on high alert, suspecting a serial killer, and while walking home, Stephanie is grabbed from behind and injected with a drug that knocks her out. She awakens hours later to find herself tied up in an abandoned cabin deep in a densely wooded area. . . . Her harrowing journey back to safety propels this plot-driven, fast-paced tale forward. . . . Told in the first person, this suspenseful survival story is sure to have strong appeal." Kirkus

McCormick, Patricia

Cut. Front St. 2000 168p $16.95 *
Grades: 7 8 9 10   **Fic**
1. Self-mutilation—Fiction 2. Psychiatric hospitals—Fiction
ISBN 1-88691-061-8   LC 00-34840

While confined to a mental hospital, thirteen-year-old Callie slowly comes to understand some of the reasons behind her self-mutilation, and gradually starts to get better

"Realistic, sensitive, and heartfelt." Voice Youth Advocates

Purple Heart. Balzer + Bray 2009 198p $16.99; lib bdg $17.89; pa $8.99
Grades: 7 8 9 10   **Fic**
1. Iraq War, 2003—Fiction 2. Soldiers—Fiction 3. Brain—Wounds and injuries—Fiction 4. Hospitals—Fiction 5. Memory—Fiction
ISBN   978-0-06-173090-0;   0-06-173090-4; 978-0-06-173091-7 (lib bdg); 0-06-173091-2 (lib bdg); 978-0-06-173092-4 (pa); 0-06-173092-0 (pa)
LC 2009-1757

While recuperating in a Baghdad hospital from a traumatic brain injury sustained during the Iraq War, eighteen-year-old soldier Matt Duffy struggles to recall what happened to him and how it relates to his ten-year-old friend, Ali.

"Strong characters heighten the drama. . . . McCormick raises moral questions without judgment and will have readers examining not only this conflict but the nature of heroism and war." Publ Wkly

Sold. Hyperion 2006 263p $15.99 *
Grades: 9 10 11 12   **Fic**
1. Slavery—Fiction 2. Prostitution—Fiction 3. Nepal—Fiction
ISBN 0-7868-5171-6; 978-0-7868-5171-3
LC 2006-49594

Thirteen-year-old Lakshmi leaves her poor mountain home in Nepal thinking that she is to work in the city as a maid only to find that she has been sold into the sex slave trade in India and that there is no hope of escape.

"In beautiful clear prose and free verse that remains true to the child's viewpoint, first-person, present-tense vignettes fill in Lakshmi's story. The brutality and cruelty are ever present ('I have been beaten here, / locked away, / violated a hundred times / and a hundred times more'), but not sensationalized. . . . An unforgettable account of sexual slavery as it exists now." Booklist

McCullers, Carson, 1917-1967

The heart is a lonely hunter. Modern Lib. 1993 430p $14.95 *
Grades: 9 10 11 12   **Fic**
1. Deaf—Fiction 2. Southern States—Fiction
ISBN 0-679-42474-1   LC 92-51062
A reissue of the title first published 1940 by Houghton Mifflin

"After his friend is committed to a hospital for the insane, John Singer, a deaf mute, finds himself alone. He becomes the pivotal figure in a strange circle of four other lonely individuals: Biff Brannon, the owner of a cafe; Mick Kelly, a young girl; Jake Blount, a radical; and Benedict Copeland, the town's black doctor. Although

McCullers, Carson, 1917-1967—*Continued*

Singer provides companionship for others, he remains outside the warmth of close relationships." Shapiro. Fic for Youth. 3d edition

The member of the wedding. Houghton Mifflin 1946 195p hardcover o.p. pa $7.95 *

Grades: 9 10 11 12 Adult   **Fic**

1. Georgia—Fiction 2. Family life—Fiction 3. Weddings—Fiction

ISBN 0-395-07981-0; 0-618-49239-9 (pa)

"Twelve-year-old Frankie is experiencing a boring summer until news arrives that her older brother will soon be returning to Georgia from his Alaska home in order to marry. Plotting to accompany the newlyweds on their honeymoon occupies much of Frankie's waking hours, while at the same time she is coping with the pressures of puberty and its effects on her body and mind. Particularly revealing are her conversations with her six-year-old cousin and the nurturing black family cook, Bernice." Shapiro. Fic for Youth. 3d edition

McDevitt, Jack

Moonfall. HarperCollins Pubs. 1998 464p hardcover o.p. pa $7.99

Grades: 9 10 11 12   **Fic**

1. Science fiction 2. Space colonies—Fiction 3. Comets—Fiction

ISBN 0-06-105036-9; 0-06-105112-8 (pa)

LC 98-147774

"The discovery of an interstellar comet on a collision course with the moon spells catastrophic destruction not only for Moonbase—Earth's first lunar colony—but for the planet itself. . . . McDevitt chronicles the countdown from sighting to impact to aftermath in taut vignettes that display the best and worst of humanity's reaction to impending doom. Compulsively readable." Libr J

McDonald, Abby

Boys, bears, and a serious pair of hiking boots. Candlewick Press 2010 293p $16.99

Grades: 9 10 11 12   **Fic**

1. Self-perception—Fiction 2. Wilderness areas—Fiction 3. Environmental protection—Fiction 4. Social action—Fiction 5. Canada—Fiction

ISBN 978-0-7636-4382-9; 0-7636-4382-3

LC 2009-26015

Seventeen-year-old Jenna, an ardent vegetarian and environmentalist, is thrilled to be spending the summer communing with nature in rural Canada, until she discovers that not all of the rugged residents there share her beliefs.

McDonald "composes a fun summer read, closely examining the conflict between sticking to one's beliefs and learning the art of compromise." Publ Wkly

McDonald, Janet, 1953-2007

Chill wind. Farrar, Straus & Giroux 2002 134p hardcover o.p. pa $6.95

Grades: 7 8 9 10   **Fic**

1. Teenage mothers—Fiction 2. African Americans—Fiction 3. Public welfare—Fiction 4. New York (N.Y.)—Fiction

ISBN 0-374-39958-1; 0-374-41183-2 (pa)

LC 2001-54785

"Frances Foster books"

Afraid that she will have nowhere to go when her welfare checks are stopped, nineteen-year-old high school dropout Aisha tries to figure out how she can support herself and her two young children in New York City

"McDonald writes with such honesty, wit, and insight that you want to quote from every page and read the story aloud to share the laughter and anguish, fury and tenderness." Booklist

Off-color. Farrar, Straus and Giroux 2007 163p $16

Grades: 7 8 9 10 11 12   **Fic**

1. Racially mixed people—Fiction 2. Mother-daughter relationship—Fiction 3. Single parent family—Fiction 4. Brooklyn (New York, N.Y.)—Fiction

ISBN 0-374-37196-2   LC 2006-47334

"Frances Foster book"

Fifteen-year-old Cameron living with her single mother in Brooklyn finds her search for identity further challenged when she discovers that she is the product of a biracial relationship.

"McDonald dramatizes the big issues from the inside, showing the hard times and the joy in fast-talking dialogue that is honest, insulting, angry, tender, and very funny." Booklist

Spellbound. Speak 2003 138p pa $5.99

Grades: 7 8 9 10   **Fic**

1. Teenage mothers—Fiction 2. African Americans—Fiction

ISBN 0-14-250193-X

First published 2001 by Frances Foster Bks.

"An ALA best book for young adults" Cover

Raven, a teenage mother and high school dropout living in a housing project, decides, with the help and sometime interference of her best friend Aisha, to study for a spelling bee which could lead to a college preparatory program and four-year scholarship.

"The dialogue is lively and smart; the characters ring true." Booklist

Twists and turns. Frances Foster Bks./Farrar, Straus & Giroux 2003 135p hardcover o.p. pa $6.95

Grades: 7 8 9 10   **Fic**

1. African Americans—Fiction 2. Public housing—Fiction 3. Sisters—Fiction 4. Brooklyn (New York, N.Y.)—Fiction

ISBN 0-374-39955-7; 0-374-40006-7 (pa)

LC 2002-35313

With the help of a couple of successful friends, eighteen- and nineteen-year-old Teesha and Keeba try to capitalize on their talents by opening a hair salon in the run-down Brooklyn housing project where they live

McDonald, Janet, 1953-2007—*Continued*

"The poetry and wit are in the daily details. . . . The story is inspiring—not because of a slick resolution or a heavy message, but because McDonald shows how hard things are, even as she tells a story of teens who find the strength in themselves and in those around them to rebuild and carry on." Booklist

McDonnell, Margot

Torn to pieces. Delacorte Press 2008 258p $15.99; lib bdg $18.99

Grades: 8 9 10 11 12   **Fic**
1. Missing persons—Fiction 2. Friendship—Fiction 3. Mother-daughter relationship—Fiction 4. Grandparents—Fiction
ISBN 978-0-385-73559-9; 0-385-73559-6; 978-0-385-90542-8 (lib bdg); 0-385-90542-4 (lib bdg)
                 LC 2007-41536

When her mother disappears during a business trip, seventeen-year-old Anne discovers that her family harbors many dark secrets.

"This teen thriller . . . builds to a gripping conclusion with a final twist that will shock and satisfy teen readers." Booklist

McGhee, Alison, 1960-

All rivers flow to the sea. Candlewick Press 2005 168p $15.99

Grades: 8 9 10 11 12   **Fic**
1. Sisters—Fiction 2. Traffic accidents—Fiction 3. Bereavement—Fiction 4. Adirondack Mountains (N.Y.)—Fiction
ISBN 0-7636-2591-4   LC 2004-54609

After a car accident in the Adirondacks leaves her older sister Ivy brain-dead, seventeen-year-old Rose struggles with her grief and guilt as she slowly learns to let her sister go.

"This somber, philosophical look at loss and the reestablishment of identity is sensitive and perceptive, and includes passages of beautiful writing. Supporting characters are complex and lovingly rendered." Booklist

McGowan, Anthony, 1965-

The knife that killed me. Delacorte Press 2010 216p $16.99

Grades: 10 11 12   **Fic**
1. Gangs—Fiction 2. Bullies—Fiction 3. Friendship—Fiction 4. Homicide—Fiction 5. School stories 6. Great Britain—Fiction
ISBN 978-0-385-73822-4; 0-385-73822-6
                 LC 2009-11662

Paul Varderman, a secondary student in an English Catholic School, is a loner until, just as he is becoming friends with 'the freaks,' the school bully encourages Paul to join his gang and gives him a knife to carry as an incentive.

"Depicting brutality without a hint of glamour, this tale of alienation and reaction cuts deeply into school culture and the teenage mind." Kirkus

McGuigan, Mary Ann, 1949-

Morning in a different place. Front Street 2009 195p $17.95

Grades: 7 8 9 10   **Fic**
1. Friendship—Fiction 2. Race relations—Fiction 3. African Americans—Fiction 4. Bronx (New York, N.Y.)—Fiction
ISBN 978-1-59078-551-5; 1-59078-551-7
                 LC 2007-17547

In 1963 in the Bronx, New York, eighth-graders Fiona and Yolanda help one another face hard decisions at home despite family and social opposition to their interracial friendship, but Fiona is on her own when popular classmates start paying attention to her and give her a glimpse of both a different way of life and a new kind of hatefulness.

This book is "never didactic. McGuigan's writing is spare and low-key, and her metaphors are acute." Booklist

McKay, Sharon

Thunder over Kandahar; photographs by Rafal Gerszak. Annick Press 2010 260p il $21.95; pa $12.95

Grades: 7 8 9 10 11 12   **Fic**
1. Afghan War, 2001-—Fiction 2. Afghanistan—Fiction
ISBN 978-1-55451-267-6; 1-55451-267-0; 978-1-55451-266-9 (pa); 1-55451-266-2 (pa)

"When her British and American-educated parents' return to Afghanistan is cut short by a terrible attack, 14-year-old Yasmine is sent to Kandahar for safety. Instead, the driver abandons her and her friend Tamanna along the way, and they must travel on their own through Taliban-controlled mountains. . . . In spite of unrelenting violence, along with grinding poverty, restrictive customs, and the horrors of war, what shines through this sad narrative is the love Afghans have for their country. . . . [The author] traveled to Afghanistan and provides numerous credits for this gripping tale." SLJ

McKenzie, Nancy

Grail prince; {by} Nancy Affleck McKenzie. Del Rey 2003 510p pa $14.95

Grades: 9 10 11 12   **Fic**
1. Great Britain—History—0-1066—Fiction
ISBN 0-345-45648-3   LC 2002-94133

In this sequel to Queen of Camelot, "the story focuses on Sir Galahad, son of Lancelot and Guinevere's cousin, Elaine. Legend says that when the Holy Grail and the spear of King Macsen, along with the sword Excalibur, are in the hands of the king, Britain will be forever invincible. Galahad's quest to find these relics, undertaken at Arthur's command, is for him a journey into manhood as well as one of expiation." Libr J

"Brimming with romance, myth, and magic, this intriguing retelling of an ever-appealing fable will appease fans eager for new twists and turns in the lives and times of King Arthur and the knights of the Round Table." Booklist

McKenzie, Nancy—_Continued_

Guinevere's gift. Alfred A. Knopf 2008 327p
(The Chrysalis Queen quartet) $15.99; lib bdg
$18.99

Grades: 7 8 9 10   **Fic**
1. Guinevere (Legendary character)—Fiction 2. Great
Britain—History—0-1066—Fiction 3. Cousins—Fiction
ISBN   978-0-375-84345-7;   0-375-84345-0;
978-0-375-94345-4 (lib bdg); 0-375-94345-5 (lib bdg)
                                      LC 2007-28782

When the orphaned Guinevere is twelve years old, living with Queen Alyse and King Pellinore of Gwynedd,
she fearlessly helps rescue her cousin from kidnappers
who are plotting to seize the palace and overthrow the
king, even as the queen despairs of Guinevere's rebellious nature.

"Adventure seekers can be content with this tale of a
heroine and her castle while dedicated legend fans will
appreciate where it fits in the overall tapestry." Bull Cent
Child Books

Another title in this series is:
Guinevere's gamble (2009)

McKernan, Victoria

The devil's paintbox. Alfred A. Knopf 2009
359p $16.99; lib bdg $19.99

Grades: 6 7 8 9 10   **Fic**
1. Frontier and pioneer life—Fiction 2. Overland journeys to the Pacific—Fiction 3. Orphans—Fiction
4. Siblings—Fiction
ISBN   978-0-375-83750-0;   0-375-83750-7;
978-0-375-93750-7 (lib bdg); 0-375-93750-1 (lib bdg)
                                      LC 2008-4749

In 1866, fifteen-year-old Aidan and his thirteen-year-
old sister Maddy, penniless orphans, leave drought-
stricken Kansas on a wagon train hoping for a better life
in Seattle, but find there are still many hardships to be
faced.

This is a "gripping novel. . . . Attention to detail and
steady pacing keep readers fully engaged." Publ Wkly

McKinley, Robin

Beauty; a retelling of the story of Beauty & the
beast. Harper & Row 1978 247p $15.99; pa $5.99
*

Grades: 7 8 9 10   **Fic**
1. Fairy tales
ISBN 0-06-024149-7; 0-06-440477-3 (pa)
                                      LC 77-25636

"McKinley's version of this folktale is embellished
with rich descriptions and settings and detailed characterizations. The author has not modernized the story but
varied the traditional version to attract modern readers.
The values of love, honor, and beauty are placed in a
magical setting that will please the reader of fantasy."
Shapiro. Fic for Youth. 3d edition

The blue sword. Greenwillow Bks. 1982 272p
$17.99; pa $6.99

Grades: 7 8 9 10   **Fic**
1. Fantasy fiction
ISBN 0-688-00938-7; 0-441-06880-4 (pa)
                                      LC 82-2895

Harry, bored with her sheltered life in the remote or-
ange-growing colony of Daria, discovers magic in herself
when she is kidnapped by a native king with mysterious
powers.

"This is a zesty, romantic, heroic fantasy with an appealing stalwart heroine, a finely realized mythical kingdom, and a grounding in reality." Booklist

Pegasus. G.P. Putnam's Sons 2010 404p $18.99

Grades: 8 9 10 11 12   **Fic**
1.   Pegasus   (Greek   mythology)—Fiction
2. Princesses—Fiction 3. Magic—Fiction 4. Fantasy
fiction
ISBN 978-0-399-24677-7; 0-399-24677-0
                                      LC 2010-2279

Because of a thousand-year-old alliance between humans and pegasi, Princess Sylvi is ceremonially bound to
Ebon, her own pegasus, on her twelfth birthday, but the
closeness of their bond becomes a threat to the status
quo and possibly to the safety of their two nations.

"McKinley's storytelling is to be savored. She lavishes
page after page upon rituals and ceremonies, basks in the
awe of her intricately constructed world, and displays a
masterful sense of pegasi physicality and mannerisms."
Booklist

McKissack, Fredrick, 1939-

Shooting star. Atheneum Books for Young
Readers 2009 273p $16.99

Grades: 8 9 10 11 12   **Fic**
1. Football—Fiction 2. Steroids—Fiction 3. African
Americans—Fiction 4. School stories
ISBN 978-1-4169-4745-5; 1-4169-4745-0
                                      LC 2008-55525

Jomo Rogers, a naturally talented athlete, starts taking
performance enhancing drugs in order to be an even better high school football player, but finds his life spinning
out of control as his game improves.

"Profane and scatological language abounds, but it is
not outside the realm of what one could hear any day in
a school locker room. Top-notch sports fiction." SLJ

McMann, Lisa

Wake. Simon Pulse 2008 210p $15.99; pa $8.99

Grades: 7 8 9 10   **Fic**
1. Dreams—Fiction 2. School stories
ISBN   978-1-4169-5357-9;   1-4169-5357-4;
978-1-4169-7447-5 (pa); 1-4169-7447-4 (pa)
                                      LC 2007036267

Ever since she was eight years old, high school student Janie Hannagan has been uncontrollably drawn into
other people's dreams, but it is not until she befriends an
elderly nursing home patient and becomes involved with
an enigmatic fellow-student that she discovers her true
power.

"A fast pace, a great mix of teen angst and supernatural experiences, and an eerie, attention-grabbing cover
will make this a hit." Booklist

Other titles in this series are:
Fade (2009)
Gone (2010)

McMurtry, Larry

Lonesome dove; a novel. Simon & Schuster 1985 843p hardcover o.p. pa $18

Grades: 9 10 11 12 Adult   **Fic**
1. West (U.S.)—Fiction 2. Frontier and pioneer life—Fiction

ISBN 0-671-50420-7; 1-4391-9526-9 (pa)

LC 85-2192

"Two former Texas Rangers have been running a ramshackle stock operation near the Mexican border with a lot of work and not much success. When they hear rumors of freewheeling opportunities in the newly opened territory, they decide to break camp, pull up stakes, and head north. Their dusty trek is filled with troubles, violence, and unfulfilled yearning." Booklist

"'Lonesome Dove' shows, early on, just about every symptom of American Epic except pretentiousness. McMurtry has laconic Texas talk and leathery, slim-hipped machismo down pat, and he's able to refresh heroic clichés with exact observations about cowboy prudery, ignorance and fear of losing face." Newsweek

Other titles in the Lonesome dove trilogy are:
Dead man's walk (1995)
Streets of Laredo (1993)

McNamee, Graham

Acceleration. Wendy Lamb Bks. 2003 210p hardcover o.p. pa $6.99 *

Grades: 8 9 10 11 12   **Fic**
1. Homicide—Fiction 2. Mystery fiction 3. Canada—Fiction

ISBN 0-385-73119-1; 0-440-23836-6 (pa)

LC 2003-3708

Stuck working in the Lost and Found of the Toronto Transit Authority for the summer, seventeen-year-old Duncan finds the diary of a serial killer and sets out to stop him

"Never overexploits the sensational potential of the subject and builds suspense layer upon layer, while injecting some surprising comedy relief." Booklist

McNeal, Laura

Dark water. Alfred A. Knopf 2010 287p $16.99; lib bdg $19.99

Grades: 7 8 9 10   **Fic**
1. Fires—Fiction 2. Illegal aliens—Fiction 3. Homeless persons—Fiction 4. Divorce—Fiction 5. Family life—Fiction 6. California—Fiction

ISBN 978-0-375-84973-2; 0-375-84973-4; 978-0-375-94973-9 (lib bdg); 0-375-94973-9 (lib bdg)

LC 2009-43249

Living in a cottage on her uncle's southern California avocado ranch since her parent's messy divorce, fifteen-year-old Pearl Dewitt meets and falls in love with an illegal migrant worker, and is trapped with him when wildfires approach his makeshift forest home.

"Notable for well-drawn characters, an engaging plot and, especially, hauntingly beautiful language, this is an outstanding book." Kirkus

The decoding of Lana Morris; [by] Laura & Tom McNeal. Alfred A. Knopf 2007 289p $15.99

Grades: 7 8 9 10 11 12   **Fic**
1. Foster home care—Fiction 2. Handicapped—Fiction 3. Drawing—Fiction 4. Supernatural—Fiction 5. Nebraska—Fiction

ISBN 978-0-375-83106-5; 0-375-83106-1

LC 2006-23950

For sixteen-year-old Lana life is often difficult, with a flirtatious foster father, an ice queen foster mother, a houseful of special needs children to care for, and bullies harrassing her, until the day she ventures into an antique shop and buys a drawing set that may change her life.

This is "a colorful character drama with genuine spice and impact." Bull Cent Child Books

Zipped; [by] Laura and Tom McNeal. Knopf 2003 283p hardcover o.p. pa $7.99 *

Grades: 9 10 11 12   **Fic**
1. Stepfamilies—Fiction

ISBN 0-375-81491-4; 0-375-83098-7 (pa)

LC 2002-2781

At the end of their sophomore year in high school, the lives of four teenagers are woven together as they start a tough new job, face family problems, deal with changing friendships, and find love

"There's a realism here that takes the narrative beyond the problem novel and into one of relationships, their difficult demands in the face of human complexity and frailty, and their nonetheless often satisfying rewards. The book never loses sight of the kids at the heart of this, however, which keeps this accessible to the teens it's about." Bull Cent Child Books

McNish, Cliff

Angel. Carolrhoda Books 2008 312p $16.95

Grades: 7 8 9 10   **Fic**
1. Angels—Fiction 2. School stories 3. Popularity—Fiction 4. Bullies—Fiction 5. Mental illness—Fiction

ISBN 978-0-8225-8900-6; 0-8225-8900-1

LC 2007-9664

An unlikely friendship develops between fourteen-year-olds Stephanie, an angel-obsessed social outcast, and Freya, a popular student whose visions of angels sent her to a mental institution and who is now seeing a dark angel at every turn.

"The author beautifuly melds a tale of the fantastic and the mundane." Voice Youth Advocates

McPhee, Peter, 1948-

New blood. James Lorimer 2008 167p pa $8.95

Grades: 6 7 8 9 10   **Fic**
1. Bullies—Fiction 2. School stories 3. Canada—Fiction

ISBN 978-1-55028-996-1; 1-55028-996-9

When his family moves from the tough streets of Glasgow to Winnipeg, Canada, Callum finds that his high school days of dealing with bullies are far from over.

"The Scottish culture, which becomes a colorful character, adds to the fullness of the story. The writing, rich in dialogue, does not waste words and keeps the reader involved and cheering for this gutsy hero who fights his fear to stand against abuse aimed at himself and others." Voice Youth Advocates

McVoy, Terra Elan

After the kiss. Simon Pulse 2010 382p $16.99
Grades: 9 10 11 12   **Fic**
1. Novels in verse 2. Moving—Fiction 3. School stories 4. Atlanta (Ga.)—Fiction
ISBN 978-1-4424-0211-9   LC 2009-44220
In alternating chapters, two high school senior girls in Atlanta reveal their thoughts and frustrations as they go through their final semester of high school.

This is "a poignant tale of two girls on the brink of adulthood faced with real decisions about their future, who they want to be, and what role boys will play in their decisions." SLJ

Pure. Simon Pulse 2009 330p $16.99
Grades: 8 9 10 11 12   **Fic**
1. Friendship—Fiction 2. Christian life—Fiction 3. Dating (Social customs)—Fiction
ISBN 978-1-4169-7872-5; 1-4169-7872-0
                                   LC 2008-33404
Fifteen-year-old Tabitha and her four best friends all wear purity rings to symbolize their pledge to remain virgins until they marry, but when one admits that she has broken the pledge each girl must reexamine her faith, friendships, and what it means to be pure.

"Tabitha's blooming romance with Jake and her positive relationship with her supportive, if somewhat quirky, parents add pleasant undercurrents to a book that girls of a spiritual bent will enjoy." SLJ

Meehl, Brian

Suck it up. Delacorte Press 2008 323p $15.99; pa $8.99
Grades: 8 9 10 11   **Fic**
1. Vampires—Fiction
ISBN   978-0-385-73300-7;   0-385-73300-3;
978-0-440-42091-0 (pa); 0-440-42091-1 (pa)
                                   LC 2007-27995
After graduating from the International Vampire League, a scrawny, teenaged vampire named Morning is given the chance to fulfill his childhood dream of becoming a superhero when he embarks on a League mission to become the first vampire to reveal his identity to humans and to demonstrate how peacefully-evolved, blood-substitute-drinking vampires can use their powers to help humanity.

This "an original and light variation on the current trend in brooding teen vampire protagonists. . . . Puns abound in this lengthy, complicated romp. . . . Teens will find it delightful." Booklist

Meldrum, Christina

Madapple. Alfred A. Knopf 2008 410p il $16.99; lib bdg $19.99 *
Grades: 9 10 11 12   **Fic**
1. Miracles—Fiction 2. Mother-daughter relationship—Fiction 3. Trials—Fiction
ISBN 978-0-375-85176-6; 978-0-375-95176-3 (lib bdg)   LC 2007-49653
A girl who has been brought up in near isolation is thrown into a twisted web of family secrets and religious fundamentalism when her mother dies and she goes to live with relatives she never knew she had.

"A markedly intelligent offering mixing lush descriptions of plants, history, science and religion, this should surely spark interest among a wide array of readers." Kirkus

Include bibliographical references

Melling, O. R.

The Hunter's Moon. Amulet Books 2005 284p (Chronicles of Faerie) $16.95; pa $7.95
Grades: 7 8 9 10   **Fic**
1. Magic—Fiction 2. Ireland—Fiction
ISBN 0-8109-5857-0; 0-8109-9214-0 (pa)
                                   LC 2004-22216
First published 1992 in Ireland
Two teenage cousins, one Irish, the other from the United States, set out to find a magic doorway to the Faraway Country, where humans must bow to the little people.

"This novel is a compelling blend of Irish mythology and geography. Characters that breathe and connect with readers, and a picturesque landscape that shifts between the present and the past, bring readers into the experience." SLJ

Other available titles in this series are:
The book of dreams (2009)
The Light-Bearer's daughter (2007)
The Summer King (2006)

Melville, Herman, 1819-1891

Billy Budd, sailor; supplementary material written by Kathleen Helal. Pocket Books 2006 xxi, 166p pa $4.99
Grades: 11 12 Adult   **Fic**
1. Sea stories
ISBN 978-1-416-52372-7; 1-416-52372-3
                                   LC 2006-299200
Written in 1891 but in a still "unfinished" manuscript stage when Melville died. First publication 1924 in the United Kingdom, as part of the Standard edition of Melville's complete works

"Narrates the hatred of petty officer Claggart by Billy, handsome Spanish sailor. Billy strikes and kills Claggart, and is condemned by Captain Vere even though the latter senses Billy's spiritual innocence." Haydn. Thesaurus of Book Dig

Includes bibliographical references

Moby-Dick; or, The whale; illustrated by Rockwell Kent. Modern Library 1992 xxxv, 822p il $21 *
Grades: 11 12 Adult   **Fic**
1. Whaling—Fiction 2. Sea stories
ISBN 0-679-60010-8   LC 92-50222
Also available from other publishers
First published 1851

"Moby Dick is a ferocious white whale, who was known to whalers as Mocha Dick. He is pursued in a fury of revenge by Captain Ahab, whose leg he has bitten off; and under Melville's handling the chase takes on a significance beyond mere externals. Moby Dick becomes a symbol of the terrific forces of the natural universe, and Captain Ahab is doomed to disaster, even though Moby Dick is killed at last." Univ Handbook for

Melville, Herman, 1819-1891—*Continued*
Readers and Writers

"'Moby-Dick' had some initial critical appreciation, particularly in Britain, but only since the 1920s has it been recognized as a masterpiece, an epic tragedy of tremendous dramatic power and narrative drive." Oxford Companion to Engl Lit. 5th edition

Meminger, Neesha
Shine, coconut moon. Margaret K. McElderry Books 2009 256p $16.99; pa $8.99

Grades: 7 8 9 10   **Fic**
1. Prejudices—Fiction 2. East Indian Americans—Fiction 3. September 11 terrorist attacks, 2001—Fiction 4. School stories
ISBN   978-1-4169-5495-8;   1-4169-5495-3; 978-1-4424-0305-5 (pa); 1-4424-0305-5 (pa)
LC 2008-9836
In the days and weeks following the terrorist attacks on September 11, 2001, Samar, who is of Punjabi heritage but has been raised with no knowledge of her past by her single mother, wants to learn about her family's history and to get in touch with the grandparents her mother shuns.

"Meminger's debut book is a beautiful and sensitive portrait of a young woman's journey from self-absorbed navet to selfless, unified awareness." SLJ

Meyer, Carolyn
Duchessina; a novel of Catherine de' Medici. Harcourt 2007 261p (Young royals) $17

Grades: 7 8 9 10   **Fic**
1. Catherine de Médicis, Queen, consort of Henry II, King of France, 1519-1589—Fiction 2. Italy—Fiction 3. Queens—Fiction 4. Orphans—Fiction
ISBN 978-0-15-205588-2; 0-15-205588-6
LC 2006028876
While her tyrannical family is out of favor in Italy, young Catherine de Medici is raised in convents, then in 1533, when she is fourteen, her uncle, Pope Clement VII, arranges for her marriage to prince Henri of France, who is destined to become king.

"With meticulous historical detail, sensitive characterizations, and Catherine's strong narration, Meyer's memorable story of a fascinating young woman who relies on her intelligence, rather than her beauty, will hit home with many teens." Booklist

The true adventures of Charley Darwin. Harcourt 2009 321p il $17

Grades: 7 8 9 10   **Fic**
1. Darwin, Charles, 1809-1882—Fiction 2. Beagle Expedition (1831-1836)—Fiction 3. Voyages around the world—Fiction 4. Natural history—Fiction
ISBN 978-0-15-206194-4; 0-15-206194-0
LC 2008-17451
In nineteenth-century England, young Charles Darwin rejects the more traditional careers of physician and clergyman, choosing instead to embark on a dangerous five-year journey by ship to explore the natural world.

"Meyer's writing has a light touch that capitalizes on the humorous, romantic, and exciting events in the man's life while introducing his scientific pursuits and the beliefs of his time. . . . This novel paints a readable and detailed portrait of the young Charles Darwin." SLJ
Includes bibliographical references

Meyer, L. A., 1942-
Bloody Jack; being an account of the curious adventures of Mary "Jacky" Faber, ship's boy. Harcourt 2002 278p hardcover o.p. pa $6.95

Grades: 7 8 9 10   **Fic**
1. Orphans—Fiction 2. Seafaring life—Fiction 3. Pirates—Fiction 4. Sex role—Fiction 5. Adventure fiction
ISBN 0-15-216731-5; 0-15-205085-X (pa)
LC 2002-759
Reduced to begging and thievery in the streets of 18th-century London, a thirteen-year-old orphan disguises herself as a boy and connives her way onto a British warship set for high sea adventure in search of pirates

"From shooting a pirate in battle to foiling a shipmate's sexual attack to surviving when stranded alone on a Caribbean island, the action in Jacky's tale will entertain readers with a taste for adventure." Booklist
Other titles in this series are:
Curse of the blue tattoo (2004)
In the belly of The Bloodhound (2006)
The mark of the golden dragon (2011)
Mississippi Jack (2007)
My bonny light horseman (2008)
Rapture of the deep (2009)
Under the Jolly Roger (2005)
The wake of the *Lorelei Lee* (2010)

Meyer, Stephenie, 1973-
Twilight. Little, Brown and Co. 2005 498p $17.99; pa $8.99 *

Grades: 8 9 10 11 12   **Fic**
1. Vampires—Fiction 2. School stories 3. Washington (State)—Fiction
ISBN 0-316-16017-2; 0-316-01584-9 (pa)
LC 2004-24730
"Megan Tingley books"
When seventeen-year-old Bella leaves Phoenix to live with her father in Forks, Washington, she meets an exquisitely handsome boy at school for whom she feels an overwhelming attraction and who she comes to realize is not wholly human.

"Realistic, subtle, succinct, and easy to follow, . . . [this book] will have readers dying to sink their teeth into it." SLJ
Other titles in this series are:
Breaking dawn (2008)
Eclipse (2007)
New moon (2006)

Meyerhoff, Jenny
Queen of secrets. Farrar, Straus and Giroux 2010 230p $16.99

Grades: 8 9 10 11 12   **Fic**
1. Jews—United States—Fiction 2. Cousins—Fiction 3. Grandparents—Fiction 4. Orphans—Fiction 5. School stories
ISBN 978-0-374-32628-9; 0-374-32628-2
LC 2008-55561

Meyerhoff, Jenny—*Continued*

Fifteen-year-old Essie Green, an orphan who has been raised by her secular Jewish grandparents in Michigan, experiences conflicting loyalties and confusing emotions when her aunt, uncle, and cousin move back from New York, and her very religious cousin tries to fit in with the other football players at Essie's high school, one of whom is Essie's popular new boyfriend.

"Compelling characters, dramatic tension, and thoughtful exploration of how teenagers create their own identity amid familial and cultural influences should give this story wide appeal." Publ Wkly

Michaelis, Antonia, 1979-

The dragons of darkness; translated from the German by Anthea Bell. Amulet Books 2010 548p il $18.95

Grades: 8 9 10 11 12   Fic
1. Magic—Fiction 2. Dragons—Fiction 3. Fantasy fiction 4. Nepal—Fiction
ISBN 978-0-8109-4074-1; 0-8109-4074-4
                                   LC 2009-3051
Two boys from very different backgrounds are thrown together by magic, mayhem, and a common foe as they battle deadly dragons in the wilderness of Nepal.

"Ably translated from German, crammed with magic realism, colors, fairytales, dreams, and contemporary conflicts, this novel is not the average dragons-in-an-alien-world fantasy. Here people make love, are kind to strangers, struggle to survive, and sometimes are casually murdered. . . . Serious fantasy fans will be fascinated by this original and well-told tale." Voice Youth Advocates

Tiger moon; translated from the German by Anthea Bell. Amulet Books 2008 453p $18.95; pa $8.95

Grades: 8 9 10 11 12   Fic
1. Storytelling—Fiction 2. Thieves—Fiction 3. Tigers—Fiction 4. Princesses—Fiction 5. India—Fiction
ISBN 978-0-8109-9481-2; 0-8109-9481-X; 978-0-8109-4499-2 (pa); 0-8109-4499-5 (pa)
                                   LC 2007-22823
Sold to be the eighth wife of a rich and cruel merchant, Safia, also called Raka, tries to escape her fate by telling stories of Farhad the thief, his companion Nitish the white tiger, and their travels across India to retrieve a famous jewel that will save a kidnapped princess from becoming the bride of a demon king.

"The plot is fast paced and exciting, and the story gives an excellent overview of the conflicts of India at the time of British occupation, and of Hindu religious beliefs." SLJ

Miller, Kirsten, 1973-

The eternal ones. Razorbill 2010 411p $17.99
Grades: 6 7 8 9 10   Fic
1. Reincarnation—Fiction 2. Faith—Fiction 3. Fate and fatalism—Fiction 4. Love stories 5. Tennessee—Fiction 6. New York (N.Y.)—Fiction
ISBN 978-1-59514-308-2; 1-59514-308-4
                                   LC 2010-22775
Seventeen-year-old Haven Moore leaves East Tennessee to attend the Fashion Institute of Technology in New York City, where she meets playboy Iain Morrow, whose fate may be tied to hers through a series of past lives.

"Miller's writing elevates the supernatural romance well beyond typical fare, and Haven's mix of naïveté and determination makes her a solid, credible heroine." Publ Wkly

Followed by: All you desire (2011)

Miller, Mary Beth

Aimee; a novel. Dutton Bks. 2002 276p hardcover o.p. pa $6.99
Grades: 7 8 9 10   Fic
1. Suicide—Fiction 2. Friendship—Fiction
ISBN 0-525-46894-3; 0-14-240025-4 (pa)
                                   LC 2002-283987
It seems that everyone believes that Zoe helped her best friend, Aimee, commit suicide. Zoe is paralyzed by loneliness, guilt, and anger at everyone's suppression of the truth

"Despite the topic, there's no gratuitous violence, and the realistic yet not overly graphic suicide scene doesn't romanticize Aimee's action. The portrayal of therapy is especially good, and Miller's wholly believable, often irritating characters will alienate some readers but feel like a mirror for others." Booklist

Miller, Sarah, 1979-

Miss Spitfire; reaching Helen Keller. Atheneum Books for Young Readers 2007 208p $16.99
Grades: 7 8 9 10 11   Fic
1. Sullivan, Anne, 1866-1936—Fiction 2. Keller, Helen, 1880-1968—Fiction 3. Teachers—Fiction 4. Blind—Fiction 5. Deaf—Fiction
ISBN 978-1-4169-2542-2; 1-4169-2542-2
                                   LC 2006014738
At age twenty-one, partially-blind, lonely but spirited Annie Sullivan travels from Massachusetts to Alabama to try and teach six-year-old Helen Keller, deaf and blind since age two, self-discipline and communication skills. Includes historical notes and timeline.

"This excellent novel is compelling reading even for those familiar with the Keller/Sullivan experience." SLJ

Includes bibliographical references

Miller, Walter M., 1923-1996

A canticle for Leibowitz; a novel; by Walter M. Miller, Jr. Lippincott 1960 c1959 320p pa $13.95 hardcover o.p. *
Grades: 9 10 11 12 Adult   Fic
1. Science fiction
ISBN 0-06-089299-4
"Here is science fiction of the highest literary excellence and thematic intelligence. A monastery founded by the scientist Leibowitz is discovered decades after an atomic war. In the first part of the book a young novice in the monastery is the protagonist; in the second part we see scholars in a new period of enlightenment; and in the final section we observe man's proclivity for repeating mistakes and the apparent inevitability of history's repeating itself." Shapiro. Fic for Youth. 3d edition

Miller-Lachmann, Lyn, 1956-
Gringolandia; a novel. Curbstone Press 2009
279p $16.95
Grades: 9 10 11 12   **Fic**
1. Father-son relationship—Fiction 2. Political activists—Fiction 3. Post-traumatic stress disorder—Fiction
4. Chile—Fiction 5. Wisconsin—Fiction
ISBN 978-1-931896-49-8; 1-931896-49-6
                                     LC 2008-36990
In 1986, when seventeen-year-old Daniel's father arrives in Madison, Wisconsin, after five years of torture as a political prisoner in Chile, Daniel and his eighteen-year-old "gringa" girlfriend, Courtney, use different methods to help this bitter, self-destructive stranger who yearns to return home and continue his work.
"This poignant, often surprising and essential novel illuminates too-often ignored political aspects of many South Americans' migration to the United States." Kirkus

Mills, Tricia
Heartbreak river. Razorbill 2009 248p pa $8.99
Grades: 7 8 9 10   **Fic**
1. Rivers—Fiction 2. Rafting (Sports)—Fiction
3. Death—Fiction 4. Guilt—Fiction 5. Colorado—Fiction
ISBN 978-1-59514-256-6   LC 2008-21062
When her father dies while whitewater rafting, sixteen-year-old Alex feels responsible, but when tragedy strikes again she must face her deepest fears in order to reclaim her love of the Colorado river where she grew up—and of the boy she grew up with.
"Mills builds suspense in both the romance and the moving drama of family secrets and loss. The fast talk and Alex's first-person narrative are right on, especially in the quarrels. Best of all is the setting, which is powerfully described in scenes of Alex struggling to overcome her phobia and return to the wild rushing river she loves." Booklist

Min, Katherine
Secondhand world; a novel. Knopf 2006 269p
hardcover o.p. pa $13.95
Grades: 11 12 Adult   **Fic**
1. Korean Americans—Fiction 2. Parent-child relationship—Fiction 3. Family life—Fiction
ISBN 978-0-307-26344-5; 978-0-307-27499-1 (pa)
                                     LC 2006-41038
The book "opens by introducing readers to 18-year-old Isadora Myung Hee Sohn, known as Isa to her mother and friends and Myung Hee to her father. Isa tells the absorbing story of a young woman's struggle to overcome the obstacles of growing up Korean American in Albany, NY, during the 1970s. True to that stereotypically liberated period, Isa gets involved with sex, drugs, and rock'n'roll. . . . Touching and bittersweet, this novel is filled with universal themes presented through Isa's eyes and should resonate with teen readers of both today and yesterday." Libr J

Minchin, Adele
The beat goes on. Simon & Schuster Books for Young Readers 2004 212p hardcover o.p. pa $11.95 *
Grades: 9 10 11 12   **Fic**
1. AIDS (Disease)—Fiction 2. Cousins—Fiction
3. Great Britain—Fiction
ISBN 0-689-86611-9; 1-4169-6755-9 (pa)
First published 2001 in the United Kingdom
"Fifteen-year-old Leyla must keep her cousin's secret: Emma is HIV positive, and only her mother and Leyla know. The secret becomes a burden, especially when Leyla must lie to her parents in order to work with Emma's support group on their special project—to teach other HIV-positive teens how to play the drums. In spite of its heavy Briticisms and a didactic tone, this is one of the better YA books about HIV. The facts of transmission and symptoms are clearly presented, as are Emma's struggles to lead a normal, healthy life. . . . Minchin educates young readers while telling a gripping story that will keep personal tragedy aficionados turning the pages to the hopeful yet realistic conclusion." Booklist

Mitchard, Jacquelyn
All we know of heaven; a novel. HarperTeen 2008 312p $16.99; lib bdg $17.89 *
Grades: 7 8 9 10 11 12   **Fic**
1. Traffic accidents—Fiction 2. Death—Fiction
3. Bereavement—Fiction
ISBN 978-0-06-134578-4;   0-06-134578-4;
978-0-06-134579-1 (lib bdg); 0-06-134579-2 (lib bdg)
When Maureen and Bridget, two sixteen-year-old best friends who look like sisters, are in a terrible car accident and one of them dies, they are at first incorrectly identified at the hospital, and then, as Maureen achieves a remarkable recovery, she must deal with the repercussions of the accident, the mixup, and some choices she made while she was getting better.
"Riveting, compassionate and psychologically nuanced. . . . Utterly gripping." Publ Wkly

Mitchell, David
Black swan green; a novel. Random House 2006 294p hardcover o.p. pa $13.95 *
Grades: 11 12 Adult   **Fic**
1. Speech disorders—Fiction 2. Family life—Fiction
3. Great Britain—Fiction
ISBN   1-4000-6379-5;   978-1-4000-6379-6;
0-8129-7401-8 (pa); 978-0-8129-7401-0 (pa)
                                     LC 2005-52914
This is a "portrait of a thirteen-year-old boy, growing up in Worcestershire in 1982, who is afflicted with a stammer, unhappy parents, and a snide older sister." New Yorker
"The author does not pull any punches when it comes to the casual cruelty that adolescent boys can inflict on one another, but it is this very brutality that underscores the sweetness of which they are also capable. With its British slang and complex twists and turns, this title is not a selection for reluctant readers, but teens who enjoy multifaceted coming-of-age stories will be richly rewarded." SLJ

Mitchell, Todd, 1974-
The secret to lying. Candlewick Press 2010 328p $17.99
Grades: 9 10 11 12   **Fic**
   1. Popularity—Fiction 2. Honesty—Fiction 3. Dreams—Fiction 4. Demonology—Fiction 5. School stories
   ISBN 978-0-7636-4084-2   LC 2009-32484
Fifteen-year-old James lies about himself to be considered "cool" when he gets into an exclusive boarding school, but soon unnaturally vivid dreams of being a demon-hunting warrior lead to self-destructive acts while he is awake.
"Mitchell paints a vivid picture of teenage social and mental health issues, neither overdramatizing nor understating their impact, and the result is a great read." Publ Wkly

Mlynowski, Sarah, 1977-
Gimme a call. Delacorte Press 2010 301p $17.99; lib bdg $20.99
Grades: 7 8 9 10   **Fic**
   1. Time travel—Fiction 2. School stories
   ISBN 978-0-385-73588-9; 0-385-73588-X; 978-0-385-90574-9 (lib bdg); 0-385-90574-2 (lib bdg)
                        LC 2009-20020
"When Devi's high-school sweetheart breaks up with her right before their senior prom, she is devastated. Not only is she dateless but she is also friendless and relegated to a mediocre college because she has concentrated on her boyfriend instead of academics. . . . In a fresh twist on time travel, she contacts her freshman self via cell phone and proceeds to change their future. Of course, one small change leads to others, and both girls begin to wonder about the wisdom of this collaboration. Mlynowski has given herself a complicated, challenging story, and she is particularly effective in conveying the differences in maturity and perspective between a freshman and a senior." Booklist

Moloney, James, 1954-
Black taxi. HarperCollins Publishers 2005 264p hardcover o.p. lib bdg $16.89
Grades: 9 10 11 12   **Fic**
   1. Mystery fiction 2. Crime—Fiction 3. Automobiles—Fiction 4. Great Britain—Fiction
   ISBN 0-06-055937-3; 0-06-055938-1 (lib bdg)
                        LC 2003-27848
When Rosie agrees to take care of her grandfather's Mercedes while he is in jail, she gets more than she bargained for, including being thrust into the middle of a jewel heist mystery and being attracted to a dangerous boy.
"Love and larceny are center stage in this British import, which is best suited to older readers even though it has no explicit language or dicey situations. Only the main characters are developed, but the story is entertaining enough to appeal to fans of lightweight mystery who also relish a hint of romance." Booklist

Monninger, Joseph
Wish. Delacorte Press 2010 193p $17.99; lib bdg $20.99
Grades: 6 7 8 9 10   **Fic**
   1. Cystic fibrosis—Fiction 2. Siblings—Fiction 3. Sharks—Fiction 4. Wishes—Fiction
   ISBN 978-0-385-73941-2; 0-385-73941-9; 978-0-385-90788-0 (lib bdg); 0-385-90788-5 (lib bdg)
                        LC 2010-09958
Bee's brother, Tommy, knows everything there is to know about sharks. He also knows that his life will be cut short by cystic fibrosis. And so does Bee. That's why she wants to make his wish-foundation-sponsored trip to swim with a great white shark an unforgettable memory. Only when Bee takes Tommy to meet a famous shark attack survivor and hard-core surfer does Tommy have the chance to live one day to the fullest.
"Fans of Monninger's other works will recognize the fluid, thoughtful writing and vivid characters, and this could be an eye-opener for shark aficionados looking to take their interest beyond the glitz of shark week." Bull Cent Child Books

Moran, Katy
Bloodline. Candlewick Press 2009 297p il map $16.99
Grades: 7 8 9 10   **Fic**
   1. Adventure fiction 2. War stories 3. Middle Ages—Fiction 4. Great Britain—History—0-1066—Fiction
   ISBN 978-07636-4083-5; 0-7636-4083-2
                        LC 2008-21413
While traveling through early seventh-century Britain trying to stop an impending war, Essa, who bears the blood of native British tribes and of the invading Anglish, makes discoveries that divide his loyalties.
"Essa is a complex, sympathetic protagonist: prickly and quick of temper, but also clever, determined and of unflinching integrity. If his struggle is authentically gory and ultimately tragic, it is not without glimpses of love and hope." Kirkus
Followed by: Bloodline rising (2011)

Moranville, Sharelle Byars
A higher geometry. Henry Holt 2006 212p $16.95
Grades: 8 9 10 11   **Fic**
   1. Sex role—Fiction 2. Mathematics—Fiction 3. School stories
   ISBN 978-0-8050-7470-3; 0-8050-7470-8
                        LC 2005-21699
While grieving the death of her grandmother in 1959, teenager Anna is torn between her aspirations to study math in college and her family's expectations that she will marry and become a homemaker after high school.
"Readers will easily connect with the romance that's both thrilling and nurturing and with Anna's steady resolve to follow her passion for numbers and challenge a world of expectations." Booklist

Morgenroth, Kate

Echo. Simon & Schuster 2007 144p $15.99

Grades: 7 8 9 10 **Fic**

1. Death—Fiction 2. Post-traumatic stress disorder—Fiction

ISBN 1-4169-1438-2; 978-1-4169-1438-9

LC 2005-32984

After Justin witnesses his brother's accidental shooting death, he must live with the repercussions, as the same horrific day seems to happen over and over.

Jude. Simon & Schuster Books for Young Readers 2004 277p hardcover o.p. pa $5.99

Grades: 7 8 9 10 **Fic**

1. Crime—Fiction 2. Mother-son relationship—Fiction

ISBN 0-689-86479-5; 1-4169-1267-3 (pa)

LC 2003-20475

Still reeling from his drug-dealing father's murder, moving in with the wealthy mother he never knew, and transferring to a private school, fifteen-year-old Jude is tricked into pleading guilty to a crime he did not commit

"The plot is tight, deliberately paced, and full of delicious twists. . . . The story is quick and action packed enough to engage reluctant readers, especially older boys." SLJ

Moriarty, Jaclyn

The year of secret assignments. Arthur A. Levine Books 2004 340p $16.95; pa $7.99

Grades: 8 9 10 11 12 **Fic**

1. Friendship—Fiction 2. School stories 3. Australia—Fiction

ISBN 0-439-49881-3; 0-439-49882-1 (pa)

LC 2003-14278

Three female students from Ashbury High write to three male students from rival Brookfield High as part of a pen pal program, leading to romance, humiliation, revenge plots, and war between the schools

"There are a few coarse moments—a reference to a blow job and some caustic outbursts. . . . This is an unusual novel with an exhilarating pace, irrepressible characters, and a screwball humor that will easily attract teens." Booklist

Other titles set at Ashbury High are:

The ghosts of Ashbury High (2010)

The murder of Bindy Mackenzie (2006)

Moriarty, Laura

The center of everything. Hyperion 2003 291p $22.95; pa $14

Grades: 9 10 11 12 **Fic**

1. Mother-daughter relationship—Fiction 2. Single parent family—Fiction 3. Kansas—Fiction

ISBN 1-401-30031-6; 0-7868-8845-8 (pa)

LC 2002-32898

"Any map clearly shows that Kansas is the center of everything. Ten-year-old Evelyn Bucknow notices it on every map that she sees and truly believes that is where she belongs—in the center. Unfortunately, Evelyn is forced to parent her mother, a flighty, unrealistically romantic woman who is having an affair with her married boss. . . . Fortunately, Evelyn takes the events of her life and her mother's life and learns her lessons, with a few glitches along the way. Young people will find Evelyn appealing and real despite the book's setting in the age of Ronald Reagan and big hair, and they will respond positively to her determination." Voice Youth Advocates

Morpurgo, Michael

Private Peaceful. Scholastic Press 2004 c2003 202p $16.95; pa $5.99 *

Grades: 7 8 9 10 **Fic**

1. World War, 1914-1918—Fiction 2. Great Britain—Fiction

ISBN 0-439-63648-5; 0-439-63653-1 (pa)

LC 2003-65347

First published 2003 in the United Kingdom

When Thomas Peaceful's older brother is forced to join the British Army, Thomas decides to sign up as well, although he is only fourteen years old, to prove himself to his country, his family, his childhood love, Molly, and himself

"In this World War I story, the terse and beautiful narrative of a young English soldier is as compelling about the world left behind as about the horrific daily details of trench warfare. . . . Suspense builds right to the end, which is shocking, honest, and unforgettable." Booklist

Morris, Paula, 1965-

Ruined; a novel. Point 2009 309p $16.99

Grades: 6 7 8 9 10 **Fic**

1. New Orleans (La.)—Fiction 2. Ghost stories

ISBN 978-0-545-04215-4; 0-545-04215-1

Set in New Orleans, this is "the story of 15-year-old Rebecca Brown, a proud New Yorker sent to live with a family friend while her father travels overseas. Ostracized as an outsider, Rebecca struggles to fit in and cope with her new surroundings. When she befriends Lisette, a ghost who has haunted the cemetery ever since her mysterious death 155 years earlier, Rebecca is drawn into an eerie story of betrayal, loss, old curses and family secrets. . . . This moody tale thoroughly embraces the rich history, occult lore and complex issues of race, ethnicity, class and culture that have defined New Orleans for centuries." Publ Wkly

Morrison, Toni, 1931-

Beloved; a novel. Knopf 1987 275p $29.95; pa $13.95 *

Grades: 9 10 11 12 Adult **Fic**

1. African Americans—Fiction 2. Mother-daughter relationship—Fiction 3. Slavery—Fiction

ISBN 0-394-53597-9; 1-4000-3341-6 (pa)

This novel, "set in the third quarter of the 19th century, focuses on the life of the runaway slave woman Sethe and her struggle with the unspeakable pain of her past. Like Morrison's earlier novels, *Beloved* is marked by rich and lyrical language, narratives shot through with exotic and magical elements, and a fragmented structure that requires readers to participate in the telling." Benet's Reader's Ency of Am Lit

Morrison, Toni, 1931-—*Continued*

The bluest eye; with a new afterword by the author. Knopf 2005 c1993 215p $19.95 *

Grades: 11 12 Adult   **Fic**
1. African Americans—Fiction 2. Ohio—Fiction
ISBN 0-375-41155-0   LC 93-43124

A reissue of the title first published 1970 by Holt, Rinehart & Winston

"This tragic study of a black adolescent girl's struggle to achieve white ideals of beauty and her consequent descent into madness was acclaimed as an eloquent indictment of some of the more subtle forms of racism in American society. Pecola Breedlove longs to have 'the bluest eye' and thus to be acceptable to her family, schoolmates, and neighbors, all of whom have convinced her that she is ugly." Merriam-Webster's Ency of Lit

Sula. Knopf 1974 c1973 174p hardcover o.p. pa $14

Grades: 11 12 Adult   **Fic**
1. African Americans—Fiction 2. Ohio—Fiction 3. Friendship—Fiction 4. Poverty—Fiction
ISBN 0-394-48044-9; 1-4000-3343-8 (pa)

This "is the story of two black women friends and of their community of Medallion, Ohio. The community has been stunted and turned inward by the racism of the larger society. The rage and disordered lives of the townspeople are seen as a reaction to their stifled hopes. The novel follows the lives of Sula and Nel from childhood to maturity to death." Merriam-Webster's Ency of Lit

Moskowitz, Hannah, 1991-

Break. Simon Pulse 2009 262p pa $8.99

Grades: 9 10 11 12   **Fic**
1. Brothers—Fiction 2. Fractures—Fiction 3. Allergy—Fiction 4. Family life—Fiction 5. Mental illness—Fiction
ISBN 978-1-4169-8275-3; 1-4169-8275-2
LC 2008-42816

To relieve the pressures of caring for a brother with life-threatening food allergies, another who is a fussy baby, and parents who are at odds with one other, seventeen-year-old Jonah sets out to break every bone in his body in hopes of becoming stronger.

"Some readers will find Moskowitz's sickening premise a stretch. But for those with a taste for the macabre and an aversion to the sentimental, it's hard not to be taken in by the book's strong central relationships and Moskowitz's unapologetic, single-minded dedication to her unsavory task." Booklist

Mosley, Walter

Fortunate son. Little, Brown and Co. 2006 313p hardcover o.p. pa $13.99

Grades: 11 12 Adult   **Fic**
1. Brothers—Fiction 2. Race relations—Fiction
ISBN 978-0-316-11471-4; 0-316-11471-5; 978-0-316-06628-0 (pa); 0-316-06628-1 (pa)
LC 2005-24477

"Tommy was born out of wedlock with a hole in his heart; he's also lame and black. Eric, on the other hand, glows with health; he is so beautiful that people want to touch him—and he's white. For a few years, the boys live together after Tommy's mother and Eric's widowed doctor father fall in love after meeting in the hospital ward. Then Tommy's mother dies, and Tommy is wrested from the only family he's known. Eric grows up leading a life that appears blessed, but with Tommy gone, he's lost all that is important to him. Tommy, meanwhile, ends up on the street but feels lucky simply to be alive. . . . The writing is crisp and the plotting impeccable." Libr J

Mourlevat, Jean-Claude

Winter's end; translated by Anthea Bell. Candlewick Press 2009 415p lib bdg $21.99 *

Grades: 8 9 10 11 12   **Fic**
1. Despotism—Fiction 2. Resistance to government—Fiction 3. Orphans—Fiction 4. Fantasy fiction 5. Adventure fiction
ISBN 978-0-7636-4450-5; 0-7636-4450-1
LC 2009-8456

Fleeing across icy mountains from a pack of terrifying dog-men sent to hunt them down, four teenagers escape from their prison-like boarding schools to take up the fight against the tyrannical government that murdered their parents fifteen years earlier.

"Teeming with heroic acts, heartbreaking instances of sacrifice and intriguing characters . . . the book will keep readers absorbed and set imaginations spinning." Publ Wkly

Mowll, Joshua

Operation Red Jericho; [illustrated by Benjamin Mowll, Julek Heller, Niroot Puttapipat] Candlewick Press 2005 271p il map (The Guild of Specialists) hardcover o.p. pa $8.99

Grades: 9 10 11 12   **Fic**
1. Adventure fiction 2. Siblings—Fiction 3. Uncles—Fiction
ISBN 0-7636-2634-1; 0-7636-3475-1 (pa)
LC 2005-45382

The posthumous papers of Rebecca MacKenzie document her adventures, along with her brother Doug, in 1920s China as the teenaged siblings are sent to live aboard their uncle's ship where they become involved in the dangerous activities of a mysterious secret society called the Honourable Guild of Specialists.

"Some readers may pore over the details in this novel; others will simply appreciate the comic adventure." SLJ

Other titles about Becca and Doug are:
Operation Storm City (2009)
Operation Typhoon Shore (2006)
Includes bibliographical references

Mulligan, Andy

Trash. David Fickling Books 2010 232p $16.99; lib bdg $19.99

Grades: 6 7 8 9   **Fic**
1. Mystery fiction 2. Poverty—Fiction 3. Refuse and refuse disposal—Fiction 4. Political corruption—Fiction
ISBN 978-0-385-75214-5; 0-385-75214-8; 978-0-385-75215-2 (lib bdg); 0-385-75215-6 (lib bdg)
LC 2010-15940

Mulligan, Andy—*Continued*

Fourteen-year-olds Raphael and Gardo team up with a younger boy, Rat, to figure out the mysteries surrounding a bag Raphael finds during their daily life of sorting through trash in a third-world country's dump.

"While on the surface the book reads like a fast-paced adventure title, it also makes a larger statement about the horrors of poverty and injustice in the world. . . . Trash is a compelling read." SLJ

Murdock, Catherine Gilbert

Dairy Queen; a novel. Houghton Mifflin 2006 275p $16 *

Grades: 7 8 9 10   **Fic**

1. Football—Fiction 2. Farm life—Fiction

ISBN 0-618-68307-0   LC 2005-19077

After spending her summer running the family farm and training the quarterback for her school's rival football team, sixteen-year-old D.J. decides to go out for the sport herself, not anticipating the reactions of those around her.

"D. J.'s voice is funny, frank, and intelligent, and her story is not easily pigeonholed." Voice Youth Advocates

Other titles about D.J. Schwenk are:

Front and center (2009)

The off season (2007)

Princess Ben; being a wholly truthful account of her various discoveries and misadventures, recounted to the best of her recollection, in four parts; written by Catherine Gilbert Murdock. Houghton Mifflin 2008 344p $16; pa $8.99

Grades: 7 8 9 10   **Fic**

1. Fairy tales 2. Princesses—Fiction 3. Magic—Fiction 4. Courts and courtiers—Fiction

ISBN 978-0-618-95971-6; 0-618-95971-8; 978-0-547-22325-4 (pa); 0-547-22325-0 (pa)

LC 2007-34300

A girl is transformed, through instruction in life at court, determination, and magic, from sullen, pudgy, graceless Ben into Crown Princess Benevolence, a fit ruler of the kingdom of Montagne as it faces war with neighboring Drachensbett.

"Murdock's prose sweeps the reader up and never falters, blending a formal syntax and vocabulary with an intimate tone that bonds the reader with Ben." Horn Book

Murray, Martine, 1965-

How to make a bird. Arthur A. Levine Books 2010 233p $17.99

Grades: 7 8 9 10   **Fic**

1. Runaway teenagers—Fiction 2. Family life—Fiction 3. Bereavement—Fiction 4. Australia—Fiction

ISBN 978-0-439-66951-1; 0-439-66951-0

LC 2009-27453

When seventeen-year-old, small-town Australian girl Manon Clarkeson leaves home in the middle of the night, wearing her mother's long, inappropriate red silk dress and riding her bike, she is heading for Melbourne, not exactly sure what she is looking for but not wanting to stay at home alone with her father anymore.

"Although Mannie's defining attributes—acute self-consciousness and claustrophobic intensity—are hall-marks of many YA heroines, Murray's powerful lyrical voice and close observation breathe new life into them. . . . The novel offers an especially vivid sense of place—the harsh but open rural landscape and densely populated yet lonely, urban Melbourne." Kirkus

Murray, Yxta Maya

The good girl's guide to getting kidnapped. Razorbill 2010 251p $16.99; pa $9.99

Grades: 9 10 11 12   **Fic**

1. Gangs—Fiction 2. Mexican Americans—Fiction 3. Foster home care—Fiction 4. Kidnapping—Fiction 5. California—Fiction

ISBN 978-1-59514-272-6; 1-59514-272-X; 978-1-59514-341-9 (pa); 1-59514-341-6 (pa)

LC 2009-21091

Fifteen-year-old Michelle Pena, born into a powerful Mexican American gang family, tries to reconcile her gangster legacy with the girl she has become—a nationally ranked runner and academic superstar.

This book "is action-packed, as it raises relevant questions of identity and loyalty. This fast-paced story, heavy with street dialogue and slang, should have ample teen appeal." Publ Wkly

Mussi, Sarah

The door of no return. Margaret K. McElderry Books 2008 394p $17.99; pa $8.99 *

Grades: 8 9 10 11 12   **Fic**

1. Adventure fiction 2. Buried treasure—Fiction 3. Blacks—Fiction 4. Homicide—Fiction 5. Great Britain—Fiction 6. Ghana—Fiction

ISBN 978-1-4169-1550-8; 1-4169-1550-8; 978-1-4169-6825-2 (pa); 1-4169-6825-3 (pa)

LC 2007-18670

Sixteen-year-old Zac never believed his grandfather's tales about their enslaved ancestors being descended from an African king, but when his grandfather is murdered and the villains come after Zac, he sets out for Ghana to find King Baktu's long-lost treasure before the murderers do.

"This exciting narrative takes place in England and Africa; in jungles, dark caves, and on the sea. . . . Overall, this is a complex, masterful story for confident readers." SLJ

Myers, Walter Dean, 1937-

Autobiography of my dead brother; art by Christopher Myers. HarperTempest/Amistad 2005 212p il $15.99; lib bdg $16.89; pa $6.99

Grades: 7 8 9 10   **Fic**

1. Violence—Fiction 2. African Americans—Fiction 3. Friendship—Fiction 4. Harlem (New York, N.Y.)—Fiction

ISBN 0-06-058291-X; 0-06-058292-8 (lib bdg); 0-06-058293-6 (pa)   LC 2004-27878

Jesse pours his heart and soul into his sketchbook to make sense of life in his troubled Harlem neighborhood and the loss of a close friend.

"This novel is like photorealism; it paints a vivid and genuine portrait of life that will have a palpable effect on its readers." SLJ

Myers, Walter Dean, 1937-——*Continued*

Dope sick. HarperTeen/Amistad 2009 186p $16.99; lib bdg $17.89

Grades: 8 9 10 11 12 **Fic**

1. Drug abuse—Fiction 2. African Americans—Fiction 3. Supernatural—Fiction 4. Harlem (New York, N.Y.)—Fiction

ISBN 978-0-06-121477-6; 0-06-121477-9; 978-0-06-121478-3 (lib bdg); 0-06-121478-7 (lib bdg)

LC 2008-10568

Seeing no way out of his difficult life in Harlem, seventeen-year-old Jeremy "Lil J" Dance flees into a house after a drug deal goes awry and meets a weird man who shows different turning points in Lil J's life when he could have made better choices.

"Myers uses street-style lingo to cover Lil J's sorry history of drug use, jail time, irresponsible fatherhood and his own childhood grief. A didn't-see-that-coming ending wraps up the story on a note of well-earned hope and will leave readers with plenty to think about." Publ Wkly

Fallen angels. Scholastic 1988 309p hardcover o.p. pa $6.99 *

Grades: 8 9 10 11 12 **Fic**

1. Vietnam War, 1961-1975—Fiction 2. African American soldiers—Fiction

ISBN 0-590-40942-5; 0-545-05576-8 (pa)

LC 87-23236

"Black, seventeen, perceptive and sensitive, Richie (the narrator) has enlisted and been sent to Vietnam; in telling the story of his year of active service, Richie is candid about the horror of killing and the fear of being killed, the fear and bravery and confusion and tragedy of the war." Bull Cent Child Books

"Except for occasional outbursts, the narration is remarkably direct and understated; and the dialogue, with morbid humor sometimes adding comic relief, is steeped in natural vulgarity, without which verisimilitude would be unthinkable. In fact, the foul talk, which serves as the story's linguistic setting, is not nearly as obscene as are the events." Horn Book

Game. HarperTeen 2008 218p $16.99; lib bdg $17.89

Grades: 8 9 10 11 12 **Fic**

1. Basketball—Fiction 2. African Americans—Fiction 3. Czech Americans—Fiction 4. School stories 5. Harlem (New York, N.Y.)—Fiction

ISBN 978-0-06-058294-4; 978-0-06-058295-1 (lib bdg) LC 2007-18370

"A Junior Library Guild selection"

If Harlem high school senior Drew Lawson is going to realize his dream of playing college, then professional, basketball, he will have to improve at being coached and being a team player, especially after a new—white—student threatens to take the scouts' attention away from him.

"Basketball fans will love the long passages of detailed court action. . . . The authentic thoughts of a strong, likable, African American teen whose anxieties, sharp insights, and belief in his own abilities will captivate readers of all backgrounds." Booklist

Kick; [by] Walter Dean Myers and Ross Workman. HarperTeen 2011 197p $16.99; lib bdg $17.89

Grades: 7 8 9 10 **Fic**

1. Criminal investigation—Fiction 2. Police—Fiction 3. Soccer—Fiction 4. Family life—Fiction 5. Mentoring—Fiction 6. New Jersey—Fiction

ISBN 978-0-06-200489-5; 0-06-200489-1; 978-0-06-200490-1 (lib bdg); 0-06-200490-5 (lib bdg)

LC 2010-18441

Told in their separate voices, thirteen-year-old soccer star Kevin and police sergeant Brown, who knew his father, try to keep Kevin out of juvenile hall after he is arrested on very serious charges.

"Workman is a genuine talent, writing short, declarative sentences that move that narrative forward with assurance and a page-turning tempo. Myers, of course, is a master. . . . The respective voices and characters play off each other as successfully as a high-stakes soccer match." Booklist

Monster; illustrations by Christopher Myers. HarperCollins Pubs. 1999 281p il $14.95; lib bdg $14.89; pa $8.99 *

Grades: 7 8 9 10 **Fic**

1. Trials—Fiction 2. African Americans—Fiction

ISBN 0-06-028077-8; 0-06-028078-6 (lib bdg); 0-06-440731-4 (pa) LC 98-40958

While on trial as an accomplice to a murder, sixteen-year-old Steve Harmon records his experiences in prison and in the courtroom in the form of a film script as he tries to come to terms with the course his life has taken.

"Balancing courtroom drama and a sordid jailhouse setting with flashbacks to the crime, Myers adeptly allows each character to speak for him or herself, leaving readers to judge for themselves the truthfulness of the defendants, witnesses, lawyers, and, most compellingly, Steve himself." Horn Book Guide

Sunrise over Fallujah. Scholastic Press 2008 290p $17.99 *

Grades: 8 9 10 11 12 **Fic**

1. Iraq War, 2003-—Fiction 2. African Americans—Fiction

ISBN 978-0-439-91624-0; 0-439-91624-0

LC 2007-25444

"Instead of heading to college as his father wishes, Robin leaves Harlem and joins the army to stand up for his country after 9/11. While stationed in Iraq with a war looming that he hopes will be averted, he begins writing letters home to his parents and to his Uncle Richie. . . . Myers brilliantly freeze-frames the opening months of the current Iraq War by realistically capturing its pivotal moments in 2003 and creating a vivid setting. Memorable characters share instances of wry levity that balance the story without deflecting its serious tone." SLJ

Myracle, Lauren, 1969-

Bliss. Amulet Books 2008 444p $16.95 *

Grades: 9 10 11 12 **Fic**

1. School stories 2. Occultism—Fiction 3. Horror fiction 4. Atlanta (Ga.)—Fiction

ISBN 978-0-8109-7071-7; 0-8109-7071-6

LC 2007-50036

Myracle, Lauren, 1969-—_Continued_

Having grown up in a California commune, Bliss sees her aloof grandmother's Atlanta world as a foreign country, but she is determined to be nice as a freshman at an elite high school, which makes her the perfect target for Sandy, a girl obsessed with the occult.

"Catering to teens with a taste for horror, this carefully plotted occult thriller set in 1969-1970 combines genre staples with creepy period particulars." Publ Wkly

Peace, love, and baby ducks. Dutton Children's Books 2009 292p $16.99; pa $8.99

Grades: 8 9 10 11 12   Fic
    1. Sisters—Fiction 2. Atlanta (Ga.)—Fiction
    ISBN   978-0-525-47743-3;   0-525-47743-8;
    978-0-14-241527-6 (pa); 0-14-241527-8 (pa)
                                    LC 2008-34221

Fifteen-year-old Carly's summer volunteer experience makes her feel more real than her life of privilege in Atlanta ever did, but her younger sister starts high school pretending to be what she is not, and both find their relationships suffering.

"Myracle empathetically explores issues of socioeconomic class, sibling rivalry, and parental influence in a story that is deeper and more nuanced than the title and cutesy cover." Booklist

Shine. Amulet Books 2011 359p $16.95

Grades: 10 11 12   Fic
    1. Hate crimes—Fiction 2. Homosexuality—Fiction
    3. Friendship—Fiction 4. North Carolina—Fiction
    ISBN 978-0-8109-8417-2; 0-8109-8417-2
                                    LC 2010-45017

When her best friend falls victim to a vicious hate crime, sixteen-year-old Cat sets out to discover the culprits in her small North Carolina town.

"Readers will find themselves thinking about Cat's complicated rural community long after the mystery has been solved." Publ Wkly

Na, An, 1972-

A step from heaven. Front St. 2000 156p $15.95
*

Grades: 7 8 9 10   Fic
    1. Korean Americans—Fiction 2. Family life—Fiction
    ISBN 1-88691-058-8   LC 00-41083
    Also available in paperback from Speak
A young Korean girl and her family find it difficult to learn English and adjust to life in America

"This isn't a quick read, especially at the beginning when the child is trying to decipher American words and customs, but the coming-of-age drama will grab teens and make them think of their own conflicts between home and outside. As in the best writing, the particulars make the story universal." Booklist

Wait for me. Putnam 2006 169p hardcover o.p. pa $7.99 *

Grades: 8 9 10 11 12   Fic
    1. Mother-daughter relationship—Fiction 2. Korean Americans—Fiction 3. Sisters—Fiction 4. Deaf—Fiction
    ISBN 0-399-24275-9; 0-14-240918-9 (pa)
                                    LC 2005-30931

As her senior year in high school approaches, Mina yearns to find her own path in life but working at the family business, taking care of her little sister, and dealing with her mother's impossible expectations are as stifling as the southern California heat, until she falls in love with a man who offers a way out.

"This is a well-crafted tale, sensitively told. . . . The mother-daughter conflict will resonate with teens of any culture who have wrestled parents for the right to choose their own paths." Bull Cent Child Books

Nadin, Joanna, 1970-

Wonderland. Candlewick Press 2011 208p $16.99

Grades: 9 10 11 12   Fic
    1. Conduct of life—Fiction 2. Friendship—Fiction
    3.   Father-daughter   relationship—Fiction
    4. Bereavement—Fiction 5. Great Britain—Fiction
    ISBN 978-0-7636-4846-6; 0-7636-4846-9
                                    LC 2010-38715

Sixteen-year-old Jude hopes to finally become who she wants to be, away from tiny Churchtown and the father who cannot get over her mother's death, by joining a prestigious drama program in London until Stella, her wild childhood friend, returns and causes Jude to wonder if she really wants to be the center of attention, after all.

"This is more of a psychological thriller than a book about bad girls. Once they reach this surprising disclosure, teens will think about the book differently and maybe even read it again." SLJ

Nadol, Jen

The mark. Bloomsbury 2010 228p $16.99

Grades: 9 10 11 12   Fic
    1. Clairvoyance—Fiction 2. Death—Fiction 3. Fate and   fatalism—Fiction   4.   Orphans—Fiction
    5. Kansas—Fiction
    ISBN 978-1-59990-431-3; 1-59990-431-4
                                    LC 2009-16974

While in Kansas living with an aunt she never knew existed and taking a course in philosophy, sixteen-year-old Cass struggles to learn what, if anything, she should do with her ability to see people marked to die within a day's time.

"Nadol's story is more than a modern take on the Cassandra story of Greek myth, and the author uses her protagonist's moral torment (and a philosophy course she takes) to touch on schools of philosophical thought, from Aristotle to Plato. As in life, there are no tidy endings, but the engrossing narration and realistic characters create a deep, lingering story." Publ Wkly

Naidoo, Beverley

Burn my heart. HarperCollins 2009 c2007 209p $15.99; lib bdg $16.89 *

Grades: 7 8 9 10 11 12   Fic
    1. Race relations—Fiction 2. Friendship—Fiction
    3. Kenya—Fiction
    ISBN   978-0-06-143297-2;   0-06-143297-0;
    978-0-06-143298-9 (lib bdg); 0-06-143298-9 (lib bdg)
                                    LC 2008-928322
    First published 2007 in the United Kingdom

Naidoo, Beverley—*Continued*

"Mathew and Mugo, two boys—one white, one black—share an uneasy friendship in Kenya in the 1950s. They're friends even though Mathew's dad owns the land and everything on it. They're friends despite the difference in their skin color. And they're friends in the face of the growing Mau Mau rebellion." Publisher's note

This "is an interesting story of which few people will be aware but might wish to know more. This solid novel would be a good multicultural addition to a teen collection." Voice Youth Advocates

Nanji, Shenaaz, 1954-

Child of dandelions. Front Street 2008 214p $17.95

Grades: 7 8 9 10 11 12   **Fic**

1. Amin, Idi, 1925-2003—Fiction 2. Uganda—Fiction 3. East Indians—Fiction 4. Family life—Fiction

ISBN 978-1-93242-593-2; 1-93242-593-4

LC 2007-31576

In Uganda in 1972, fifteen-year-old Sabine and her family, wealthy citizens of Indian descent, try to preserve their normal life during the ninety days allowed by President Idi Amin for all foreign Indians to leave the country, while soldiers and others terrorize them and people disappear.

"This is an absorbing story rich with historical detail and human dynamics." Bull Cent Child Books

Napoli, Donna Jo, 1948-

Beast. Atheneum Bks. for Young Readers 2000 260p hardcover o.p. pa $8

Grades: 7 8 9 10   **Fic**

1. Fairy tales 2. Iran—Fiction

ISBN 0-689-83589-2; 0-689-87005-1 (pa)

LC 99-89923

"In this take on 'Beauty and the Beast,' Napoli focuses on Beast before French beauty Belle enters his life. The first-person story begins in Persia, where proud prince Orasmyn, who loves roses, makes an unfortunate decision that sets in motion a curse: he becomes a lion who can only be restored by the love of a woman." Booklist

"The reader is immersed in the imagery and spirituality of ancient Persia. . . . Although Napoli uses Farsi (Persian) and Arabic words in the text (there is a glossary), this only adds to the texture and richness of her remarkable piece of writing." Book Rep

Bound. Atheneum Books for Young Readers 2004 186p hardcover o.p. pa $5.99 *

Grades: 8 9 10 11 12   **Fic**

1. China—Fiction 2. Sex role—Fiction

ISBN 0-689-86175-3; 0-689-86178-8 (pa)

LC 2004-365

In a novel based on Chinese Cinderella tales, fourteen-year-old stepchild Xing-Xing endures a life of neglect and servitude, as her stepmother cruelly mutilates her own child's feet so that she alone might marry well

The author "fleshes out and enriches the story with well-rounded characters and with accurate information about a specific time and place in Chinese history; the result is a dramatic and masterful retelling." SLJ

Hush; an Irish princess' tale. Atheneum Books for Young Readers 2007 308p $16.99

Grades: 8 9 10 11 12   **Fic**

1. Slavery—Fiction 2. Princesses—Fiction 3. Middle Ages—Fiction 4. Ireland—Fiction

ISBN 978-0-689-86176-5; 0-689-86176-1

LC 2007-2676

Fifteen-year-old Melkorka, an Irish princess, is kidnapped by Russian slave traders and not only learns how to survive but to challenge some of the brutality of her captors, who are fascinated by her apparent muteness and the possibility that she is enchanted.

This is a "powerful survival story. . . . Napoli does not shy from detailing practices that will make readers wince . . . and the Russian crew repeatedly gang-rapes an older captive. . . . The tension over Mel's hopes for escape paces this story like a thriller." Publ Wkly

The magic circle. Dutton Children's Bks. 1993 118p hardcover o.p. pa $4.99

Grades: 9 10 11 12   **Fic**

1. Fairy tales 2. Witchcraft—Fiction

ISBN 0-525-45127-7; 0-14-037439-6 (pa)

LC 92-27008

After learning sorcery to become a healer, a good-hearted woman is turned into a witch by evil spirits and she fights their power until her encounter with Hansel and Gretel years later

"The strength of Napoli's writing and the clarity of her vision make this story fresh and absorbing. A brilliantly conceived and beautifully executed novel that is sure to be appreciated by thoughtful readers." SLJ

Naslund, Sena Jeter

Four spirits; a novel. Morrow 2003 524p hardcover o.p. pa $14.95

Grades: 9 10 11 12   **Fic**

1. Race relations—Fiction 2. Birmingham (Ala.)—Fiction

ISBN 0-06-621238-3; 0-06-093669-X (pa)

LC 2003-51170

"Stella, a white Birmingham, AL, college student in the early 1960s, faces the problems of birth control, women's 'liberation,' peaceful protest, and civil and handicapped rights. . . . After the bombing of a Birmingham church that kills four black children, Stella and her friend Cat begin to teach night classes at the black high school, helping dropouts earn their GEDs. They overcome the resentment and suspicion of the black teachers and students only to be confronted by the Ku Klux Klan. A major tragedy at a peaceful sit-in pushes Stella firmly into the activist camp, where she finds her soul mate." Libr J

"The book's last act, involving the murder of four protesters at a sit-in, is violent and shocking and leads to one of the few sermons in contemporary literature that I can recall as vital and moving. . . . Naslund brings a measure of dignity and moral complexity to her portrayal of a city that came to be known as 'Bombingham.'" N Y Times Book Rev

Nayeri, Daniel

Another Faust; [by] Daniel & Dina Nayeri. Candlewick Press 2009 387p $16.99

Grades: 9 10 11 12 **Fic**

1. Supernatural—Fiction 2. Devil—Fiction 3. New York (N.Y.)—Fiction 4. School stories

ISBN 978-0-7636-3707-1; 0-7636-3707-6

LC 2008-940873

Years after vanishing, five teens reappear with a strange governess, and when they enter New York City's most prestigious high school, they soar to suspicious heights with the help of their benefactor's extraordinary "gifts."

"The writing is clever and stylish . . . It's an absorbing, imaginative read, with a tense climax." Publ Wkly

Followed by Another Pan (2010)

Neely, Cynthia

Unearthly; [by] Cynthia Hand. HarperTeen 2011 435p $17.99

Grades: 7 8 9 10 **Fic**

1. Angels—Fiction 2. Supernatural—Fiction 3. Moving—Fiction 4. School stories 5. Wyoming—Fiction

ISBN 978-0-06-199616-0; 0-06-199616-5

LC 2010-17849

Sixteen-year-old Clara Gardner's purpose as an angel-blood begins to manifest itself, forcing her family to pull up stakes and move to Jackson, Wyoming, where she learns that danger and heartbreak come with her powers.

"Hand avoids overt discussion of religion while telling an engaging and romantic tale with a solid backstory. Her characters deal realistically with the uncertainty of being on the cusp of maturity without wrapping themselves in angst." Publ Wkly

Nelson, Blake, 1960-

Destroy all cars. Scholastic Press 2009 218p $17.99

Grades: 7 8 9 10 **Fic**

1. Social action—Fiction 2. Ecology—Fiction 3. School stories

ISBN 978-0-545-10474-6; 0-545-10474-2

LC 2008-34850

Through assignments for English class, seventeen-year-old James Hoff rants against consumerism and his classmates' apathy, puzzles over his feelings for his ex-girlfriend, and expresses disdain for his emotionally-distant parents.

Nelson "offers an elegant and bittersweet story of a teenager who is finding his voice and trying to make meaning in a world he often finds hopeless." Publ Wkly

Paranoid Park. Viking 2006 180p hardcover o.p. pa $6.99

Grades: 7 8 9 10 **Fic**

1. Guilt—Fiction 2. Skateboarding—Fiction 3. Homicide—Fiction

ISBN 0-670-06118-2; 0-14-241156-6 (pa)

LC 2006-00277

A sixteen-year-old Portland, Oregon skateboarder, whose parents are going through a difficult divorce, is engulfed by guilt and confusion when he accidentally

kills a security guard at a train yard.

"Readers will have a visceral reaction to this story, but on a literary level, they'll also appreciate Nelson's clever plotting and spot-on characterizations." Booklist

Recovery Road. Scholastic Press 2011 310p $17.99

Grades: 9 10 11 12 **Fic**

1. Drug addicts—Rehabilitation—Fiction 2. Drug abuse—Fiction 3. Alcoholism—Fiction

ISBN 978-0-545-10729-7; 0-545-10729-6

LC 2010-31288

While she is in a rehabilitation facility for drug and alcohol abuse, seventeen-year-old Maddie meets Stewart, who is also in treatment, and they begin a relationship, which they try to maintain after they both get out.

The author "gives a hard, honest appraisal of addiction, its often-fatal consequences, and the high probability of relapse. This is an important story that pulls no punches." Publ Wkly

Rock star, superstar; by Blake Nelson. Viking 2004 229p hardcover o.p. pa $6.99

Grades: 9 10 11 12 **Fic**

1. Musicians—Fiction 2. Rock music—Fiction

ISBN 0-670-05933-1; 0-14-240574-4 (pa)

LC 2003-27556

When Pete, a talented bass player, moves from playing in the school jazz band to playing in a popular rock group, he finds the experience exhilarating even as his new fame jeopardizes his relationship with girlfriend Margaret.

"A brilliant, tender, funny, and utterly believable novel about music and relationships. . . . Pete is one of the best male protagonists in recent YA fiction and the other characters are equally strong." SLJ

Nelson, Jandy

The sky is everywhere. Dial Books 2010 275p il $17.99 *

Grades: 9 10 11 12 **Fic**

1. Bereavement—Fiction 2. Sisters—Fiction 3. Musicians—Fiction

ISBN 978-0-8037-3495-1; 0-8037-3495-6

LC 2009-22809

In the months after her sister dies, seventeen-year-old Lennie falls into a love triangle and discovers the strength to follow her dream of becoming a musician.

"This is a heartfelt and appealing tale. Girls who gobble up romantic and/or weep-over fiction will undoubtedly flock to this realistic, sometimes funny, and heart-breaking story." SLJ

Nelson, R. A.

Breathe my name. Razorbill 2007 314p hardcover o.p. pa $8.99

Grades: 8 9 10 11 12 **Fic**

1. Mother-daughter relationship—Fiction 2. School stories 3. Mentally ill—Fiction 4. Homicide—Fiction

ISBN 978-1-59514-094-4; 978-1-59514-186-6 (pa)

LC 2007-3272

Since her adoption, seventeen-year-old Frances has lived a quiet suburban life, but soon after she begins fall-

Nelson, R. A.—*Continued*

ing for the new boy at school, she receives a summons from her birth mother, who has just been released after serving eleven years for smothering Frances's younger sisters.

"With major twists and turns in the last 50 pages, this book will keep readers riveted until the very end." SLJ

Ness, Patrick, 1971-

The knife of never letting go. Candlewick Press 2008 479p (Chaos walking) $18.99 *

Grades: 8 9 10 11 12   Fic

1. Science fiction 2. Telepathy—Fiction 3. Space colonies—Fiction

ISBN 978-0-7636-3931-0; 0-7636-3931-1

LC 2007-52334

Pursued by power-hungry Prentiss and mad minister Aaron, young Todd and Viola set out across New World searching for answers about his colony's true past and seeking a way to warn the ship bringing hopeful settlers from Old World.

"This troubling, unforgettable opener to the Chaos Walking trilogy is a penetrating look at the ways in which we reveal ourselves to one another, and what it takes to be a man in a society gone horribly wrong." Booklist

Other titles in this series are:

The Ask and the Answer (2009)

Monsters of men (2010)

Neumeier, Rachel

The City in the Lake. Alfred A. Knopf 2008 304p $15.99; lib bdg $18.99

Grades: 8 9 10 11 12   Fic

1. Magic—Fiction 2. Fantasy fiction

ISBN 978-0-375-84704-2; 0-375-84704-9; 978-0-375-94704-9 (lib bdg); 0-375-94704-3 (lib bdg)

LC 2008-08941

Seventeen-year-old Timou, who is learning to be a mage, must save her mysterious, magical homeland, The Kingdom, from a powerful force that is trying to control it.

"Neumeier structures her story around archetypal fantasy elements. . . . It's the poetic, shimmering language and fascinating unfolding of worlds that elevates this engrossing story beyond its formula." Booklist

Nichols, Janet, 1952-

Messed up; [by] Janet Nichols Lynch. Holiday House 2009 250p $17.95

Grades: 7 8 9 10   Fic

1. Family life—Fiction 2. Abandoned children—Fiction 3. Hispanic Americans—Fiction 4. California—Fiction 5. School stories

ISBN 978-0-8234-2185-5; 0-8234-2185-6

LC 2008-22577

Fifteen-year-old RD is repeating the eighth grade, planning to have an easy year, but after his grandmother walks out her boyfriend is no longer able to care for him, which leaves RD to fend for himself while avoiding being caught.

"A memorable story of grit and survival, and helping hands along the way." Kirkus

Nicholson, William

Seeker. Harcourt 2006 413p (Noble warriors) $17; pa $7.95

Grades: 7 8 9 10   Fic

1. Fantasy fiction

ISBN 978-0-15-205768-8; 0-15-205768-4; 978-0-15-205866-1 (pa); 0-15-205866-4 (pa)

LC 2005-17171

"Seeker, Morning Star, and Wildman are three teens who hope to join the Nomana, a society of noble warriors and worshippers of the All and Only (the god who makes all things). . . . Conjuring up a plan to prove their worth, this motley trio plays a key role in foiling the murderous plans of the royalty in a nearby town." Bull Cent Child Books

"The classic coming-of-age tale is combined with a rich setting of cold villains, strange powers, and disturbing warriors." Voice Youth Advocates

Other titles in this series are:

Jango (2007)

Noman (2008)

Nilsson, Per, 1954-

You & you & you; translated by Tara Chace. Front Street 2005 301p $16.95 *

Grades: 9 10 11 12   Fic

1. Friendship—Fiction 2. Sweden—Fiction

ISBN 1-932425-19-5   LC 2004-30660

Original Swedish edition, 1998

Young Anon, who marches to the beat of a different drummer in galoshes to protect himself from radiation, touches the lives of all around him, resulting in disillusionment, loss, love, and more than a few surprises.

"Swedish magical realism comes alive in this mature, sometimes graphically sexual and violent, ultimately breathtaking and inspiring tale. . . . Many of the older YA readers to whom this book is directed will likely come away with a feeling of being somehow transformed or at least being given much to ponder." SLJ

Niven, Larry

Ringworld. Ballantine Bks. 1970 342p pa $7.99 *

Grades: 11 12 Adult   Fic

1. Science fiction

ISBN 0-345-33392-6

"The Ringworld, a world shaped like a wheel so huge that it surrounds a sun, is almost too fantastic to conceive of. With a radius of 90 million miles and a length of 600 million miles, the Ringworld's mystery is compounded by the discovery that it is artificial. What phenomenal intelligence can be behind such a creation? Four unlikely explorers, two humans and two aliens, set out for the Ringworld, bound by mutual distrust and unsure of each other's motives." Shapiro. Fic for Youth. 3d edition

Other available titles in this series are:

The Ringworld engineers (1980)

The Ringworld throne (1996)

Ringworld's children (2004)

Nix, Garth, 1963-
Sabriel. HarperCollins Pubs. 1996 c1995 292p hardcover o.p. pa $7.99 *
Grades: 7 8 9 10   Fic
1. Fantasy fiction
ISBN 0-06-027322-4; 0-06-447183-7 (pa)
LC 96-1295
First published 1995 in Australia
Sabriel, daughter of the necromancer Abhorsen, must journey into the mysterious and magical Old Kingdom to rescue her father from the Land of the Dead.
"The final battle is gripping, and the bloody cost of combat is forcefully presented. The story is remarkable for the level of originality of the fantastic elements . . . and for the subtle presentation, which leaves readers to explore for themselves the complex structure and significance of the magic elements." Horn Book
Other titles in this series are:
Abhorsen (2003)
Across the wall (2005)
Lirael, daughter of the Clayr (2001)

Nolan, Han, 1956-
Crazy. Harcourt 2010 348p $17
Grades: 7 8 9 10   Fic
1. Friendship—Fiction 2. Father-son relationship—Fiction 3. Mental illness—Fiction 4. Bereavement—Fiction 5. School stories
ISBN 978-0-15-205109-9; 0-15-205109-0
LC 2009-49969
Fifteen-year-old loner Jason struggles to hide father's declining mental condition after his mother's death, but when his father disappears he must confide in the other members of a therapy group he has been forced to join at school.
"Nolan leavens this haunting but hopeful story with spot-on humor and a well-developed cast of characters." Booklist

Nordhoff, Charles, 1887-1947
Mutiny on the Bounty; by Charles Nordhoff and James Norman Hall. Little, Brown 1932 396p hardcover o.p. pa $13.95 *
Grades: 11 12 Adult   Fic
1. Bligh, William, 1754-1817—Fiction 2. Bounty (Ship)—Fiction 3. Sea stories 4. Islands of the Pacific—Fiction
ISBN 0-316-61157-3; 0-316-61168-9 (pa)
Also available from other publishers
This narrative is "based on the famous mutiny that members of the crew of the 'Bounty', a British war vessel, carried out in 1787 against their cruel commander, Captain William Bligh. The authors kept the actual historical characters and background, using as narrator an elderly man, Captain Roger Byam, who had been a midshipman on the 'Bounty.' The story tells how the mate of the ship, Fletcher Christian, and a number of the crew rebel and set Captain Bligh adrift in an open boat with the loyal members of the crew." Reader's Ency. 4th edition
Other titles in the Bounty trilogy are:
Men against the sea (1934)
Pitcairn's Island (1934)

North, Pearl
Libyrinth. Tor Teen 2009 332p $17.95
Grades: 7 8 9 10   Fic
1. Books and reading—Fiction 2. Fantasy fiction
ISBN 978-0-7653-2096-4; 0-7653-2096-7
LC 2009-1514
"A Tom Doherty Associates book"
In a distant future where Libyrarians preserve and protect the ancient books that are housed in the fortress-like Libyrinth, Haly is imprisoned by Eradicants, who believe that the written word is evil, and she must try to mend the rift between the two groups before their war for knowledge destroys them all.
"Among this novel's pleasures are the many anonymous quotations scattered throughout, snatches of prose that Haly hears as she goes about her chores . . . all of which are carefully identified at the end. The complex moral issues posed by this thoughtful and exciting tale are just as fascinating." Publ Wkly
Followed by: The boy from Ilysies (2010)

Northrop, Michael
Gentlemen. Scholastic Press 2009 234p $16.99
Grades: 8 9 10   Fic
1. Guilt—Fiction 2. Missing persons—Fiction 3. Teachers—Fiction 4. Crime—Fiction 5. School stories
ISBN 978-0-545-09749-9; 0-545-09749-5
LC 2008-38971
When three teenaged boys suspect that their English teacher is responsible for their friend's disappearance, they must navigate a maze of assorted clues, fraying friendships, violence, and Dostoevsky's "Crime and Punishment" before learning the truth.
"The brutal narration, friendships put through the wringer and the sense of dread that permeates the novel will keep readers hooked through the violent climax and its aftermath." Publ Wkly

Trapped. Scholastic Press 2011 225p $17.99
Grades: 7 8 9 10   Fic
1. Blizzards—Fiction 2. School stories
ISBN 978-0-545-21012-6; 0-545-21012-7
LC 2010-36595
Seven high school students are stranded at their New England high school during a week-long blizzard that shuts down the power and heat, freezes the pipes, and leaves them wondering if they will survive.
"Northrop is cooly brilliant in his setup, amassing the tension along with the snow, shrewdly observing the shifting social dynamics within the group." Bull Cent Child Books

Nyembezi, C. L. Sibusiso, 1919-2000
The rich man of Pietermaritzburg; [by Sibusiso Nyembezi; translated by Sandile Ngidi] Aflame Books 2008 200p pa $15.95
Grades: 10 11 12 Adult   Fic
1. Swindlers and swindling—Fiction 2. South Africa—Fiction
ISBN 978-0-9552339-9-9; 0-9552339-9-2
Original Zulu edition, 1961
"A stranger from the city comes to a rural South African village claiming he is a benefactor on a mission to

Nyembezi, C. L. Sibusiso, 1919-2000—_Continued_
save the people in this traditional, pastoral place from a life of poverty and ignorance. In an attempt to elevate his status in the tribe's eyes, the black Ndebenkulu brags that in the city 'whites call me an esquire.' This pompous stranger soon manages to divide and disrupt the entire clan. . . . Classism, racism, and encroaching capitalism are keenly represented in this touching, endearing, and sadly prescient tale." SLJ

Oaks, J. Adams
Why I fight; a novel. Atheneum Books for Young Readers 2009 228p $16.99; pa $8.99
Grades: 8 9 10 11 12   **Fic**
   1. Uncles—Fiction   2. Violence—Fiction 3. Criminals—Fiction
   ISBN   978-1-4169-1177-7;   1-4169-1177-4; 978-1-4424-0254-6 (pa); 1-4424-0254-7 (pa)
                         LC 2007-46433
"A Richard Jackson book"
   After his house burns down, twelve-year-old Wyatt Reaves takes off with his uncle, and the two of them drive from town to town for six years, earning money mostly by fighting, until Wyatt finally confronts his parents one last time.
   "Oaks' first novel is a breathtaking debut with an unforgettable protagonist. . . . The voice Oaks has created for Wyatt to tell his painful and poignant story is a wonderful combination of the unlettered and the eloquent." Booklist

Oates, Joyce Carol, 1938-
Big Mouth & Ugly Girl. HarperCollins Pubs. 2002 265p hardcover o.p. pa $7.99 *
Grades: 7 8 9 10   **Fic**
   1. School stories 2. Friendship—Fiction
   ISBN 0-06-623756-4; 0-06-447347-3 (pa)
                         LC 2001-24601
When sixteen-year-old Matt is falsely accused of threatening to blow up his high school and his friends turn against him, an unlikely classmate comes to his aid.
   "Readers will be propelled through these pages by an intense curiosity to learn how events will play out. Oates has written a fast-moving, timely, compelling story." SLJ

Freaky green eyes. Harper Tempest 2003 341p hardcover o.p. pa $6.99 *
Grades: 7 8 9 10   **Fic**
   1. Domestic violence—Fiction
   ISBN 0-06-623757-2 (lib bdg); 0-06-447348-1 (pa)
                         LC 2002-32868
Fifteen-year-old Frankie relates the events of the year leading up to her mother's mysterious disappearance and her own struggle to discover and accept the truth about her parents' relationship.
   "Oates pulls readers into a fast-paced, first-person thriller. . . . An absorbing page-turner." Booklist

O'Brien, Caragh M.
Birthmarked. Roaring Brook Press 2010 362p map $16.99
Grades: 6 7 8 9 10   **Fic**
   1. Midwives—Fiction 2. Genetic engineering—Fiction 3. Science fiction
   ISBN 978-1-59643-569-8; 1-59643-569-0
                         LC 2010-281716
In a future world baked dry by the sun and divided into those who live inside the wall and those who live outside it, sixteen-year-old midwife Gaia Stone is forced into a difficult choice when her parents are arrested and taken into the city.
   "Readers who enjoy adventures with a strong heroine standing up to authority against the odds will enjoy this compelling tale." SLJ

O'Brien, Tim, 1946-
Going after Cacciato; a novel. Lawrence, S. 1978 338p hardcover o.p. pa $14.95
Grades: 10 11 12 Adult   **Fic**
   1. Vietnam War, 1961-1975—Fiction 2. Soldiers—Fiction 3. Dreams—Fiction
   ISBN 0-440-02948-1; 0-7679-0442-7 (pa)
                         LC 77-11723
   "Paul Berlin's squad is sent to retrieve Cacciato, a young deserter from the Vietnam War. Fantasy colors the progress of the squad as a dream of peace and the possibility of forsaking war follow them through many adventures. The horror and destruction of war is vividly conveyed and the language is rough, as would be expected. Cacciato becomes a kind of symbol for resisting bureaucratic militarism and an enviable model for Berlin himself." Shapiro. Fic for Youth. 3d edition

Ockler, Sarah
Fixing Delilah. Little, Brown 2010 308p $16.99
Grades: 8 9 10 11 12   **Fic**
   1. Single parent family—Fiction 2. Depression (Psychology)—Fiction   3. Bereavement—Fiction 4. Vermont—Fiction
   ISBN 978-0-316-05209-2; 0-316-05209-4
                         LC 2010-08631
When Delilah, her mother, and her aunt spend the summer in Vermont settling Delilah's estranged grandmother's estate, long-held family secrets are painfully brought to light and Delilah finally learns some difficult truths about her family's past.
   Delilah "tells her own story in a lyrical and authentic voice; the thoughtful reader will get lost in her anguish, her triumphs, and her eventual resolution." Voice Youth Advocates

Twenty boy summer. Little, Brown and Co. 2009 290p $16.99
Grades: 8 9 10 11 12   **Fic**
   1. Friendship—Fiction 2. Bereavement—Fiction 3. Vacations—Fiction 4. California—Fiction
   ISBN 978-0-316-05159-0; 0-316-05159-4
                         LC 2008-14196
While on vacation in California, sixteen-year-old best friends Anna and Frankie conspire to find a boy for Anna's first kiss, but Anna harbors a painful secret that

Ockler, Sarah—*Continued*

threatens their lighthearted plan and their friendship.

"Often funny, this is a thoughtful, multilayered story about friendship, loss, and moving on." SLJ

Okorafor, Nnedimma

The shadow speaker; [by] Nnedi Okorafor-Mbachu. Jump at the Sun/Hyperion Books for Children 2007 336p hardcover o.p. pa $8.99

Grades: 7 8 9 10   **Fic**

1. Sahara Desert—Fiction 2. West Africa—Fiction 3. Fantasy fiction 4. Science fiction

ISBN   978-1-4231-0033-1;   1-4231-0033-6; 978-1-4231-0036-2 (pa); 1-4231-0036-0 (pa)

LC 2007-13313

In West Africa in 2070, after fifteen-year-old "shadow speaker" Ejii witnesses her father's beheading, she embarks on a dangerous journey across the Sahara to find Jaa, her father's killer, and upon finding her, she also discovers a greater purpose to her life and to the mystical powers she possesses.

"Okorafor-Mbachu does an excellent job of combining both science fiction and fantasy elements into this novel. . . . The action moves along at a quick pace and will keep most readers on their toes and wanting more at the end of the novel." Voice Youth Advocates

Oliver, Jana G.

The demon trapper's daughter; a demon trapper novel; [by] Jana Oliver. St. Martin's Griffin 2011 355p pa $9.99

Grades: 7 8 9 10   **Fic**

1. Demonology—Fiction 2. Supernatural—Fiction 3. Apprentices—Fiction 4. Father-daughter relationship—Fiction 5. Atlanta (Ga.)—Fiction

ISBN 978-0-312-61478-2; 0-312-61478-0

LC 2010-38860

In 2018 Atlanta, Georgia, after a demon threatens seventeen-year-old Riley Blackthorne's life and murders her father, a legendary demon trapper to whom she was apprenticed, her father's partner, Beck, steps in to care for her, knowing she hates him.

"With a strong female heroine, a fascinating setting, and a complex, thrill-soaked story, this series is off to a strong start." Publ Wkly

Oliver, Lauren

Before I fall. The Bowen Press 2010 470p $17.99

Grades: 9 10 11 12   **Fic**

1.   Dead—Fiction   2.   Popularity—Fiction 3. Self-perception—Fiction 4. School stories

ISBN 978-0-06-172680-4; 0-06-172680-X

LC 2009-7288

After she dies in a car crash, teenage Samantha relives the day of her death over and over again until, on the seventh day, she finally discovers a way to save herself.

"This is a compelling book with a powerful message that will strike a chord with many teens." Booklist

Delirium. HarperCollins 2011 441p $17.99 *

Grades: 8 9 10 11   **Fic**

1. Love—Fiction 2. Resistance to government—Fiction 3. Maine—Fiction 4. Science fiction

ISBN 978-0-06-172682-8; 0-06-172682-6

LC 2010-17839

Lena looks forward to receiving the government-mandated cure that prevents the delirium of love and leads to a safe, predictable, and happy life, until ninety-five days before her eighteenth birthday and her treatment, when she falls in love.

This book is a "deft blend of realism and fantasy. . . . The story bogs down as it revels in romance—Alex is standard-issue perfection—but the book never loses its *A Clockwork Orange*-style bite regarding safety versus choice." Booklist

Olmstead, Robert

Coal black horse. Algonquin Books of Chapel Hill 2007 218p $23.95

Grades: 11 12 Adult   **Fic**

1. United States—History—1861-1865, Civil War—Fiction 2. Gettysburg (Pa.), Battle of, 1863—Fiction 3. Father-son relationship—Fiction 4. War stories

ISBN 978-1-56512-521-6; 1-56512-521-5

LC 2006-42914

A "Civil War tale that tracks a boy's search for his father on the battlefield at Gettysburg." Publ Wkly

This novel "is mostly memorable as an exquisite corpse, a fictive vision of war so vivid and gruesome that it remains in the memory—grotesque, stiff and gape-mouthed—after every other detail of Olmstead's tale fades away." Paste

Olsen, Sylvia, 1955-

White girl. Sono Nis Press 2004 235p pa $8.95 *

Grades: 7 8 9 10   **Fic**

1. Native Americans—Fiction 2. Prejudices—Fiction

ISBN 1-5503-9147-X

"Until she was fourteen, Josie was pretty ordinary. Then her Mom meets Martin, 'a real ponytail Indian,' and before long, Josie finds herself living on a reserve outside town, with a new stepfather, a new stepbrother, and a new name 'Blondie.'" Publisher's note

"The talk is contemporary and relaxed, and the characters will hold readers as much as the novel's extraordinary sense of place." Booklist

Omololu, Cynthia Jaynes

Dirty little secrets; [by] C.J. Omololu. Walker & Co. 2010 212p $16.99

Grades: 8 9 10 11 12   **Fic**

1. Compulsive behavior—Fiction 2. Mother-daughter relationship—Fiction 3. Death—Fiction 4. School stories

ISBN 978-0-8027-8660-9; 0-8027-8660-X

LC 2009-22461

When her unstable mother dies unexpectedly, sixteen-year-old Lucy must take control and find a way to keep the long-held secret of her mother's compulsive hoarding from being revealed to friends, neighbors, and especially

Omololu, Cynthia Jaynes—*Continued*
the media.

"As a valuable new addition to heartbreaking but honest books about teens immersed in emotionally distressed families, . . . this potent and creatively woven pageturner brings a traumatic situation front and center." SLJ

Oppel, Kenneth, 1967-
Half brother. Scholastic Press 2010 375p $17.99
Grades: 7 8 9 10   **Fic**
1. Chimpanzees—Fiction 2. Research—Fiction
3. Family life—Fiction 4. Canada—Fiction
ISBN 978-0-545-22925-8; 0-545-22925-1
LC 2010-2696

In 1973, when a renowned Canadian behavioral psychologist pursues his latest research project—an experiment to determine whether chimpanzees can acquire advanced language skills—he brings home a baby chimp named Zan and asks his thirteen-year-old son to treat Zan like a little brother.

"Oppel has taken a fascinating subject and molded it into a topnotch read. Deftly integrating family dynamics, animal-rights issues, and the painful lessons of growing up, Half Brother draws readers in from the beginning and doesn't let go." SLJ

Oron, Judie
Cry of the giraffe; based on a true story. Annick Press 2010 193p map $21.95; pa $12.95
Grades: 8 9 10 11 12   **Fic**
1. Jews—Ethiopia—Fiction 2. Jews—Persecutions—Fiction
ISBN 978-1-55451-272-0; 978-1-55451-271-3 (pa)

Labeled outcasts by their Ethiopian neighbors because of their Jewish faith, 13-year-old Wuditu and her family make the arduous trek on foot to Sudan in the hope of being transported to Yerusalem and its promise of a better life. Based on real events.

"Oron's novel shows with brutal, unflinching detail the horrors of refugee life and child slavery and the shocking vulnerability of young females in the developing world, and she offers a sobering introduction to a community and historical episodes rarely covered in books for youth." Booklist

Orwell, George, 1903-1950
Animal farm; with an introduction by Julian Symons. Knopf 1993 xl, 113p $16 *
Grades: 7 8 9 10 11 12 Adult   **Fic**
1. Animals—Fiction 2. Totalitarianism—Fiction
3. Dictators—Fiction 4. Allegories
ISBN 0-679-42039-8   LC 92-54299
Also available from other publishers
"Everyman's library"

First published 1945 in the United Kingdom; first United States edition 1946

"The animals on Farmer Jones's farm revolt in a move led by the pigs, and drive out the humans. The pigs become the leaders, in spite of the fact that their government was meant to be 'classless.' The other animals soon find that they are suffering varying degrees of slavery. A totalitarian state slowly evolves in which 'all animals are equal but some animals are more equal than others.' This is a biting satire aimed at communism." Shapiro. Fic for Youth. 3d edition

Nineteen eighty-four; with an introduction by Julian Symonds. Knopf 1992 xlii, 325p $19 *
Grades: 8 9 10 11 12 Adult   **Fic**
1. Totalitarianism—Fiction
ISBN 0-679-41739-7   LC 92-52906
First published 1949 by Harcourt, Brace

"A dictatorship called Big Brother rules the people in a collectivist society where Winston Smith works in the Ministry of Truth. The Thought Police persuade the people that ignorance is strength and war is peace. Winston becomes involved in a forbidden love affair and joins the underground to resist this mind control." Shapiro. Fic for Youth. 3d edition

Osa, Nancy
Cuba 15. Delacorte Press 2003 277p hardcover o.p. pa $7.95
Grades: 7 8 9 10   **Fic**
1. Cuban Americans—Fiction
ISBN 0-385-73021-7; 0-385-73233-3 (pa)
LC 2002-13389

Violet Paz, who is half Cuban American, half Polish American, reluctantly prepares for her upcoming "quince," a Spanish nickname for the celebration of an Hispanic girl's fifteenth birthday

"Violet's hilarious, cool first-person narrative veers between slapstick and tenderness, denial and truth." Booklist

Osterlund, Anne
Academy 7. Speak 2009 259p pa $8.99
Grades: 8 9 10 11 12   **Fic**
1. Fathers—Fiction 2. School stories 3. Science fiction
ISBN 978-0-14-241437-8; 0-14-241437-9
LC 2008-41323

Aerin Renning and Dane Madousin struggle as incoming students at the most exclusive academy in the Universe, both hiding secrets that are too painful to reveal, not realizing that those very secrets link them together.

This story, "with details of spacecraft, flight, and other worlds, will appeal to readers who crave adventure." Booklist

Aurelia. Speak 2008 246p pa $8.99
Grades: 8 9 10 11   **Fic**
1. Princesses—Fiction 2. Mystery fiction
ISBN 978-0-14-240579-6; 0-14-240579-5
LC 2007-36074

The king sends for Robert, whose father was a trusted spy, when someone tries to assassinate Aurelia, the stubborn and feisty crown princess of Tyralt.

"Osterlund's characters are both believable, relatable, and enviable, which makes this book enjoyable to read. Even though the book might seem to fit the mold of a quintessential princess fairy tale, Aurelia's spitfire attitude and her resulting actions lend the story a unique twist." Voice Youth Advocates

Followed by: Exile (2011)

Ostlere, Cathy
Karma; a novel in verse. Razorbill 2011 517p map $18.99
Grades: 7 8 9 10 11 12   **Fic**

Ostlere, Cathy—*Continued*

1. Novels in verse 2. India—Fiction 3. Culture conflict—Fiction 4. Violence—Fiction
ISBN 978-1-59514-338-9; 1-59514-338-6

In 1984, following her mother's suicide, 15-year-old Maya and her Sikh father travel to New Delhi from Canada to place her mother's ashes in their final resting place. On the night of their arrival, Prime Minister Indira Gandhi is assassinated, Maya and her father are separated when the city erupts in chaos, and Maya must rely on Sandeep, a boy she has just met, for survival.

"The novel's pace and tension will compel readers to read at a gallop, but then stop again and again to turn a finely crafted phrase, whether to appreciate the richness of the language and imagery or to reconsider the layers beneath a thought. This is a book in which readers will consider the roots and realities of destiny and chance. Karma is a spectacular, sophisticated tale that will stick with readers long after they're done considering its last lines." SLJ

Ostow, Micol

So punk rock (and other ways to disappoint your mother); a novel; with art by David Ostow. Flux 2009 246p il pa $9.95 *

Grades: 8 9 10 11 12   Fic
1. Rock music—Fiction 2. Jews—United States—Fiction 3. Bands (Music)—Fiction 4. School stories 5. New Jersey—Fiction
ISBN 978-0-7387-1471-4; 0-7387-1471-2
LC 2009-8216

Four suburban New Jersey students from the Leo R. Gittleman Jewish Day School form a rock band that becomes inexplicably popular, creating exhiliration, friction, confrontation, and soul-searching among its members.

The "comic-strip-style illustrations are true showstoppers. . . . A rollicking, witty, and ultra-contemporary book that drums on the funny bone and reverberates through the heart." Booklist

Otsuka, Julie, 1962-

When the emperor was divine; a novel. Knopf 2002 141p hardcover o.p. pa $10.95 *

Grades: 11 12 Adult   Fic
1. Japanese Americans—Evacuation and relocation, 1942-1945—Fiction 2. California—Fiction
ISBN 0-375-41429-0; 0-385-72181-1 (pa)
LC 2002-20814

This novel traces the "fortunes of a Japanese-American family from the spring of 1942—when President Roosevelt's evacuation order came through—to the spring of 1946. In four brief chapters, we follow a mother, daughter and son from their comfortable home in Berkeley through their five months in a temporary 'assembly center' (a converted stable at a racetrack south of San Francisco) to an internment camp in Topaz, Utah, where they spend three years." N Y Times Book Rev

Otsuka "demonstrates a breathtaking restraint and delicacy throughout this supple and devastating first novel." Booklist

Packer, Ann

The dive from Clausen's pier; a novel. Knopf 2002 369p hardcover o.p. pa $14

Grades: 11 12 Adult   Fic
1. Accidents—Fiction 2. Wisconsin—Fiction 3. New York (N.Y.)—Fiction
ISBN 0-375-41282-4; 0-375-72713-2 (pa)
LC 2001-42522

"A reckless attempt to impress Carrie, Mike's dive off Clausen's Pier rendered him paralyzed. Now Carrie finds herself torn between the loyalty she's expected to feel toward Mike and her need to transform herself. She takes a dive of her own—into adulthood—when she escapes to New York." Booklist

Padian, Maria

Jersey tomatoes are the best. Alfred A. Knopf 2011 344p $16.99; lib bdg $19.99

Grades: 7 8 9 10   Fic
1. Friendship—Fiction 2. Ballet—Fiction 3. Tennis—Fiction 4. Anorexia nervosa—Fiction 5. Camps—Fiction
ISBN   978-0-375-86579-4;   0-375-86579-9;
978-0-375-96579-1 (lib bdg); 0-375-96579-3 (lib bdg)
LC 2010-11827

When fifteen-year-old best friends Henry and Eve leave New Jersey, one for tennis camp in Florida and one for ballet camp in New York, each faces challenges that put her long-cherished dreams of the future to the test.

"Padian's writing and plotting are clean and clear, and her handling of the duo's dilemmas never stoops to melodrama. An excellent read for sports lovers who desire some meaty beefsteak in their stories." Booklist

Palmer, Robin, 1969-

Geek charming. Speak 2009 338p pa $7.99

Grades: 7 8 9 10   Fic
1. Popularity—Fiction 2. School stories
ISBN 978-0-14-241122-3; 0-14-241122-1
LC 2008-25918

Rich, spoiled, and popular high school senior Dylan is coerced into doing a documentary film with Josh, one of the school's geeks, who leads her to realize that the world does not revolve around her.

This is "a lighthearted contemporary novel filled with snappy dialogue. . . . Rather than following the predictable route of having opposites fall in love, Palmer . . . offers a slightly more original and plausible alternative." Publ Wkly

Paolini, Christopher

Eragon. Knopf 2003 509p (Inheritance) $18.95; lib bdg $20.99; pa $6.99 *

Grades: 7 8 9 10   Fic
1. Dragons—Fiction 2. Fantasy fiction
ISBN 0-375-82668-8; 0-375-92668-2 (lib bdg);
0-440-23848-X (pa)   LC 2003-47481

First published 2002 in different form by Paolini International

In Aagaesia, a fifteen-year-old boy of unknown lineage called Eragon finds a mysterious stone that weaves

Paolini, Christopher—*Continued*

his life into an intricate tapestry of destiny, magic, and power, peopled with dragons, elves, and monsters

"This unusual, powerful tale . . . is the first book in the planned Inheritance trilogy. . . . The telling remains constantly fresh and fluid, and [the author] has done a fine job of creating an appealing and convincing relationship between the youth and the dragon." Booklist

Other titles in this series are:

Brisningr (2008)

Eldest (2005)

Park, Linda Sue, 1960-

A long walk to water; based on a true story. Clarion Books 2010 121p map $16

Grades: 6 7 8 9 10   **Fic**

1. Dut, Salva—Fiction 2. Refugees—Fiction 3. Water—Fiction 4. Africans—Fiction 5. Sudan—History—Civil War, 1983-2005—Fiction

ISBN 978-0-547-25127-1; 0-547-25127-0

LC 2009-48857

When the Sudanese civil war reaches his village in 1985, eleven-year-old Salva becomes separated from his family and must walk with other Dinka tribe members through southern Sudan, Ethiopia, and Kenya in search of safe haven. Based on the life of Salva Dut, who, after emigrating to America in 1996, began a project to dig water wells in Sudan.

This is a "spare, immediate account. . . . Young readers will be stunned by the triumphant climax of the former refugee who makes a difference." Booklist

Parker, Robert B., 1932-2010

The boxer and the spy. Philomel Books 2008 210p $17.99

Grades: 7 8 9 10 11   **Fic**

1. Mystery fiction 2. Boxing—Fiction

ISBN 978-0-399-24775-0; 0-399-24775-0

LC 2007-23689

Fifteen-year-old Terry, an aspiring boxer, uncovers the mystery behind the unexpected death of a classmate.

"The lessons about human nature and life are effective and compelling without ever approaching a preachy level." Voice Youth Advocates

Chasing the bear; a young Spenser novel. Philomel Books 2009 169p $14.99

Grades: 7 8 9 10   **Fic**

1. Kidnapping—Fiction 2. Child abuse—Fiction 3. Friendship—Fiction 4. Bullies—Fiction

ISBN 978-0-399-24776-7; 0-399-24776-9

LC 2008-52725

Spenser reflects back to when he was fourteen-years-old and how he helped his best friend Jeannie when she was abducted by her abusive father.

"A clean, sharp jab of a read." Booklist

Parkhurst, Carolyn, 1971-

Lost and found. Little, Brown and Co. 2006 292p hardcover o.p. pa $13.99

Grades: 11 12 Adult   **Fic**

1. Television programs—Fiction 2. Contests—Fiction 3. Mother-daughter relationship—Fiction 4. Homosexuality—Fiction 5. Adventure fiction

ISBN 978-0-316-15638-7; 0-316-15638-8; 978-0-316-06639-6 (pa); 0-316-06639-7 (pa)

LC 2005-029741

This "novel focuses on several characters competing on an Amazing Race-like reality show called Lost and Found, where teams of two travel from destination to destination following enigmatic clues and collecting various items in hopes of winning the game. Laura wants to connect with her sullen teenage daughter, Cassie, after a traumatic experience highlighted the distance between them. Justin and Abby believe they have cast off their homosexual urges in favor of a traditional Christian marriage, but the game offers unexpected tests for their resolution. Carl and Jeff are two middle-aged, recently divorced brothers looking for adventure. Juliet and Dallas are former child stars seeking to recapture fame and willing to do just about anything to achieve that end." Booklist

"Older teens may find that this book presses just the right buttons." SLJ

Parks, Gordon, 1912-2006

The learning tree. Ballantine Books 1989 c1963 240p pa $6.99 *

Grades: 9 10 11 12   **Fic**

1. African Americans—Fiction 2. Kansas—Fiction

ISBN 0-449-21504-0

"A Fawcett Crest book"

First published 1963 by Harper & Row

"At 12 years of age Newt is awakening to the world around him in his small town of Cherokee Flats, Kansas, in the 1920s. There is the impact of a first sexual experience and a first love, and because he is a Negro, special responsibility of behavior when one individual may represent an entire group in the eyes of the community." Shapiro. Fic for Youth. 3d edition

Paterson, Katherine

Lyddie. Lodestar Bks. 1991 182p $17.99; pa $6.99 *

Grades: 5 6 7 8 9   **Fic**

1. United States—History—1815-1861—Fiction 2. Massachusetts—Fiction 3. Factories—Fiction

ISBN 0-525-67338-5; 0-14-240254-0 (pa)

LC 90-42944

Impoverished Vermont farm girl Lyddie Worthen is determined to gain her independence by becoming a factory worker in Lowell, Massachusetts, in the 1840s

"Not only does the book contain a riveting plot, engaging characters, and a splendid setting, but the language—graceful, evocative, and rhythmic—incorporates the rural speech patterns of Lyddie's folk, the simple Quaker expressions of the farm neighbors, and the lilt of fellow mill girl Bridget's Irish brogue. . . . A superb story of grit, determination, and personal growth." Horn Book

Paton, Alan

Cry, the beloved country. Scribner Classics 2003
316p $28; pa $15

Grades: 7 8 9 10 11 12 Adult   **Fic**

1. Race relations—Fiction 2. South Africa—Fiction
ISBN 0-7432-6195-X; 0-7432-6217-4 (pa)

First published 1948

"Reverend Kumalo, a black South African preacher, is
called to Johannesburg to rescue his sister. There he
learns that his son Absalom has been accused of murdering a young white attorney whose interests and sympathies had been with the natives. Despite this, the attorney's father comes to the aid of the minister to help the
natives in their struggle to survive a drought." Shapiro.
Fic for Youth. 3d edition

Paton Walsh, Jill, 1937-

A parcel of patterns. Farrar, Straus & Giroux
1983 136p hardcover o.p. pa $5.95 *

Grades: 7 8 9 10   **Fic**

1. Plague—Fiction 2. Great Britain—Fiction
ISBN 0-374-35750-1; 0-374-45743-3 (pa)

LC 83-48143

Mall Percival tells how the plague came to her Derby-
shire village of Eyam in the year 1665, how the villagers
determined to isolate themselves to prevent further
spread of the disease, and how three-fourths of them died
before the end of the following year.

"Historical in broad outline, the narrative blends superb characterizations, skillful plotting, and convincing
speech for a hauntingly memorable story that offers a
richly textured picture of the period." Child Book Rev
Serv

Patterson, Valerie O.

The other side of blue. Clarion Books 2009
223p $16

Grades: 7 8 9 10   **Fic**

1. Mother-daughter relationship—Fiction
2. Bereavement—Fiction 3. Artists—Fiction
4. Curaçao—Fiction
ISBN 978-0-547-24436-5; 0-547-24436-3

LC 2008-49233

The summer after her father drowned off the island of
Curacao, Cyan and her mother, a painter, return to the
house they stay at every summer, along with the daughter of her mother's fiance, but Cyan blames her mother
and spends her time trying to find out what really happened to her father

"In her memorable first-person voice, filled with the
minute observations of a young artist, Cyan sketches out
with believable detail the beautiful setting, the unspoken
family tension, and her fragile recovery of hope after
loss." Booklist

Paulsen, Gary

Soldier's heart; a novel of the Civil War.
Delacorte Press 1998 106p $15.95; pa $5.99 *

Grades: 7 8 9 10   **Fic**

1. United States—History—1861-1865, Civil War—
Fiction 2. Post-traumatic stress disorder—Fiction
ISBN 0-385-32498-7; 0-440-22838-7 (pa)

LC 98-10038

"Being the story of the enlistment and due service of
the boy Charley Goddard in the First Minnesota Volunteers." Title page

"This compelling and realistic depiction of war is
based on a true story. . . . Paulsen's writing is crisp and
fast-paced, and this soldier's story will haunt readers
long after they finish reading the novel." Book Rep

Pausewang, Gudrun, 1928-

Traitor; translated from the German by Rachel
Ward. Carolrhoda Books 2006 220p hardcover o.p.
pa $9.95

Grades: 7 8 9 10   **Fic**

1. World War, 1939-1945—Fiction 2. Germany—Fiction 3. Prisoners of war—Fiction
ISBN 0-8225-6195-6; 0-7613-6571-0 (pa)

LC 2005-33379

During the closing months of World War II, a fifteen-
year-old German girl must decide whether or not to help
an escaped Russian prisoner of war, despite the serious
consequences if she does so.

"Pausewang presents an exciting and thought-
provoking novel." SLJ

Peacock, Shane

Eye of the crow. Tundra Books 2007 264p (The
boy Sherlock Holmes) $24.99; pa $9.95

Grades: 6 7 8 9 10   **Fic**

1. Mystery fiction 2. Great Britain—History—19th
century—Fiction
ISBN   978-0-88776-850-7;   0-88776-850-4;
978-0-88776-919-1 (pa); 0-88776-919-5 (pa)

"A young woman is brutally murdered in a dark back
street of Whitechapel; a young Arab is discovered with
the bloody murder weapon; and a thirteen-year-old Sherlock Holmes, who was seen speaking with the alleged
killer as he was hauled into jail, is suspected to be his
accomplice. . . . Although imaginative reconstruction of
Holmes childhood has been the subject of literary and
cinematic endeavors, Peacock's take ranks among the
most successful." Bull Cent Child Books

Other titles in this series are:
Death in the air (2008)
The secret fiend (2010)
Vanishing girl (2009)

Pearce, Jackson, 1984-

Sisters red. Little, Brown 2010 328p $16.99

Grades: 9 10 11 12   **Fic**

1. Werewolves—Fiction 2. Sisters—Fiction
3. Supernatural—Fiction
ISBN 978-0-316-06868-0   LC 2009-44734

After a Fenris, or werewolf, killed their grandmother
and almost killed them, sisters Scarlett and Rosie March
devote themselves to hunting and killing the beasts that
prey on teenaged girls, learning how to lure them with
red cloaks and occasionally using the help of their old
friend, Silas, the woodsman's son.

"Told by the sisters in alternating chapters, this well-
written, high-action adventure grabs readers and never
lets go." SLJ

Pearson, Mary

The adoration of Jenna Fox; [by] Mary E. Pearson. Henry Holt and Co. 2008 272p $16.95; pa $8.99 *

Grades: 7 8 9 10 11 12   Fic
1. Science fiction 2. Bioethics—Fiction
ISBN   978-0-8050-7668-4;   0-8050-7668-9; 978-0-312-59441-1 (pa); 0-312-59441-0 (pa)
                              LC 2007-27314

In the not-too-distant future, when biotechnological advances have made synthetic bodies and brains possible but illegal, a seventeen-year-old girl, recovering from a serious accident and suffering from memory lapses, learns a startling secret about her existence.

"The science . . . and the science fiction are fascinating, but what will hold readers most are the moral issues of betrayal, loyalty, sacrifice, and survival." Booklist
Followed by The Fox inheritance (2011)

The miles between; [by] Mary E. Pearson. Henry Holt 2009 266p $16.99 *

Grades: 9 10 11 12   Fic
1. Friendship—Fiction 2. School stories
ISBN 978-0-8050-8828-1; 0-8050-8828-8
                              LC 2008-50277

Seventeen-year-old Destiny keeps a painful childhood secret all to herself until she and three classmates from her exclusive boarding school take off on an unauthorized road trip in search of "one fair day."

"Pearson skillfully separates truth from illusion and offers an uplifting book, in which grace and redemption are never left to chance." Booklist

A room on Lorelei Street; [by] Mary E. Pearson. Henry Holt 2005 266p $16.95

Grades: 9 10 11 12   Fic
1. Alcoholism—Fiction 2. Family life—Fiction 3. Texas—Fiction
ISBN 0-8050-7667-0   LC 2004-54015

To escape a miserable existence taking care of her alcoholic mother, seventeen-year-old Zoe rents a room from an eccentric woman, but her earnings as a waitress after school are minimal and she must go to extremes to cover expenses.

"Readers drawn to rescue dramas may particularly appreciate this story of a girl who's trying against odds to rescue herself." Bull Cent Child Books

Peck, Dale

Sprout. Bloomsbury 2009 277p $16.99

Grades: 9 10 11 12   Fic
1. Friendship—Fiction 2. Homosexuality—Fiction 3. Father-son relationship—Fiction 4. Kansas—Fiction
ISBN 978-1-59990-160-2; 1-59990-160-9
                              LC 2008-40922

Moving from Long Island to Kansas after his mother dies, a teenaged boy nicknamed Sprout is surprised to find new friends, a fascinating landscape, and romantic love.

"Sharply witty and bittersweet, this story . . . is a stellar step ahead for young adult literature's traditional examination of the life of the heroic antihero. Finely honed characters and an engaging voice make it an easy book for teen readers who like emotional challenges as well as word tricks to love." Voice Youth Advocates

Peck, Richard, 1934-

The river between us. Dial Bks. 2003 164p $16.99; pa $6.99 *

Grades: 7 8 9 10   Fic
1. United States—History—1861-1865, Civil War—Fiction 2. Racially mixed people—Fiction 3. Race relations—Fiction
ISBN 0-8037-2735-6; 0-14-240310-5 (pa)
                              LC 2002-34815

During the early days of the Civil War, the Pruitt family takes in two mysterious young ladies who have fled New Orleans to come north to Illinois

"The harsh realities of war are brutally related in a complex, always surprising plot that resonates on mutiple levels." Horn Book Guide

Three-quarters dead. Dial Books 2010 193p $16.99

Grades: 7 8 9 10 11 12   Fic
1. Dead—Fiction 2. Friendship—Fiction 3. Horror fiction 4. Ghost stories
ISBN 978-0-8037-3454-8; 0-8037-3454-9
                              LC 2009-49362

Sophomore loner Kerry is overjoyed when three popular senior girls pick her to be in their clique, until a shocking accident sets off a string of supernatural occurrences that become more and more threatening.

"This staccato-sentenced chiller is not so much a ghost story as it is a smart, sly treatise on friendship, bullying and the timeless power of high-school hierarchies. . . . [The author's] real-life depictions of adolescent egotism and back-stabbing cruelty are spot-on." Kirkus

Peet, Mal

Keeper. Candlewick Press 2005 c2003 225p $15.99

Grades: 8 9 10 11 12   Fic
1. Soccer—Fiction 2. Brazil—Fiction
ISBN 0-7636-2749-6   LC 2005-50786
First published 2003 in the United Kingdom

In an interview with a young journalist, World Cup hero, El Gato, describes his youth in the Brazilian rain forest and the events, experiences, and people that helped make him a great goalkeeper and renowned soccer star.

"This is a well-written, fast-paced sports story that addresses far more than just the sport itself." SLJ

Tamar. Candlewick Press 2007 424p $17.99 *

Grades: 8 9 10 11 12   Fic
1. Grandfathers—Fiction 2. World War, 1939-1945—Fiction 3. Netherlands—Fiction
ISBN 978-0-7636-3488-9; 0-7636-3488-3
                              LC 2006-51837

In 1995, 15-year-old Tamar inherits a box containing a series of coded messages from his late grandfather. The messages show Tamar the life that his grandfather lived during World War II the life of an Allied undercover operative in Nazi-occupied Holland.

"Peet's plot is tightly constructed, and striking, descriptive language, full of metaphor, grounds the story." Booklist

Perez, Ashley Hope

What can(t) wait. Carolrhoda 2011 234p $17.95

Grades: 7 8 9 10 **Fic**

1. Family life—Fiction 2. Mexican Americans—Fiction

ISBN 978-0-7613-6155-8; 0-7613-6155-3

LC 2010-28175

Marooned in a broken-down Houston neighborhood—and in a Mexican immigrant family where making ends meet matters much more than making it to college—smart, talented Marisa seeks comfort elsewhere when her home life becomes unbearable.

"Pérez fills a hole in YA lit by giving Marisa an authentic voice that smoothly blends Spanish phrases into dialogue and captures the pressures of both Latina life and being caught between two cultures." Kirkus

Perkins, Lynne Rae

As easy as falling off the face of the earth. Greenwillow Books 2010 352p il $16.99 *

Grades: 8 9 10 11 12 **Fic**

1. Accidents—Fiction 2. Chance—Fiction 3. Adventure fiction

ISBN 978-0-06-187090-3; 0-06-187090-0

LC 2009-42524

A teenaged boy encounters one comedic calamity after another when his train strands him in the middle of nowhere, and everything comes down to luck.

"The real pleasure is Perkins' relentlessly entertaining writing. . . . Wallowing in the wry humor, small but potent truths, and cheerful implausibility is an absolute delight." Booklist

Perkins, Mitali, 1963-

Secret keeper. Delacorte Press 2009 225p $16.99; lib bdg $19.99

Grades: 7 8 9 10 **Fic**

1. Sisters—Fiction 2. Family life—Fiction 3. India—Fiction

ISBN 978-0-385-73340-3; 0-385-73340-2; 978-0-385-90356-1 (lib bdg); 0-385-90356-1 (lib bdg)

LC 2008-21475

In 1974 when her father leaves New Delhi, India, to seek a job in New York, Ashi, a tomboy at the advanced age of sixteen, feels thwarted in the home of her extended family in Calcutta where she, her mother, and sister must stay, and when her father dies before he can send for them, they must remain with their relatives and observe the old-fashioned traditions that Ashi hates.

"The plot is full of surprising secrets rooted in the characters' conflicts and deep connections with each other. The two sisters and their mutual sacrifices are both heartbreaking and hopeful." Booklist

Perkins, Stephanie

Anna and the French kiss. Dutton 2010 372p $16.99

Grades: 7 8 9 10 **Fic**

1. School stories 2. Paris (France)—Fiction

ISBN 978-0-525-42327-0; 0-525-42327-3

LC 2009-53290

When Anna's romance-novelist father sends her to an elite American boarding school in Paris for her senior year of high school, she reluctantly goes, and meets an amazing boy who becomes her best friend, in spite of the fact that they both want something more.

"Perkin's debut surpasses the usual chick-lit fare with smart dialogue, fresh characters and plenty of tingly interactions, all set amid pastries, parks and walks along the Seine in arguably the most romantic city in the world." Kirkus

Perl, Erica S.

Vintage Veronica. Alfred A. Knopf 2010 279p $16.99; lib bdg $19.99

Grades: 9 10 11 12 **Fic**

1. Friendship—Fiction 2. Clothing and dress—Fiction 3. Obesity—Fiction 4. Summer employment—Fiction 5. Work—Fiction

ISBN 978-0-375-85923-6; 0-375-85923-3; 978-0-375-95923-3 (lib bdg); 0-375-95923-8 (lib bdg)

LC 2009-5280

After getting a job at a vintage clothing shop and quickly bonding with two older girls, fifteen-year-old Veronica finds herself making bad decisions in order to keep their friendship.

"Provides a realistic snapshot of teen dating, dotted with descriptions of some adorable-sounding outfits and filled with well-rounded characters from a variety of subcultures. The protagonist is a self-described 'fat girl' who is not obsessed with losing weight—a much-needed character in young adult fiction. An enjoyable read filled with quirky characters." SLJ

Pesci, David

Amistad; the thunder of freedom. Marlowe & Co. 1997 292p hardcover o.p. pa $12.95 *

Grades: 11 12 Adult **Fic**

1. Adams, John Quincy, 1767-1848—Fiction 2. Amistad (Schooner)—Fiction 3. Slavery—Fiction 4. Trials—Fiction

ISBN 1-56924-748-X; 1-56924-703-X (pa)

LC 96-54050

"In August 1839, Singbe-Pleh, a Mende tribesman, led his fellow African captives aboard the Spanish ship *Amistad* in successful revolt. The Africans took over the ship but could not sail it back to Africa. They were captured and put on trial in Connecticut. . . . The case was politically charged, with pro-slavery President Van Buren's administration wanting to give the Africans to Spain, abolitionists rallying for their freedom, and former President John Quincy Adams eventually defending them before the Supreme Court. Pesci deftly blends the facts of this fascinating historical episode with story." SLJ

Peters, Julie Anne, 1952-

By the time you read this, I'll be dead. Disney/Hyperion Books 2010 200p $16.99

Grades: 8 9 10 11 12 **Fic**

1. Depression (Psychology)—Fiction 2. Suicide—Fiction 3. Bullies—Fiction 4. Obesity—Fiction

ISBN 978-1-4231-1618-9; 1-4231-1618-6

LC 2009-8315

Peters, Julie Anne, 1952-—*Continued*

High school student Daelyn Rice, who has been bullied throughout her school career and has more than once attempted suicide, again makes plans to kill herself, in spite of the persistent attempts of an unusual boy to draw her out.

"Powerfully portrayed in the first person, the protagonist's account offers compelling insight into just how spiritually and emotionally devastating bullying can be." Voice Youth Advocates

Luna; a novel. Little, Brown 2003 248p hardcover o.p. pa $7.99 *

Grades: 9 10 11 12   **Fic**
1. Transsexualism—Fiction 2. Siblings—Fiction
ISBN 0-316-73369-5; 0-316-01127-4 (pa)
         LC 2003-58913
"Megan Tingley books"

Fifteen-year-old Regan's life, which has always revolved around keeping her older brother Liam's transsexuality a secret, changes when Liam decides to start the process of "transitioning" by first telling his family and friends that he is a girl who was born in a boy's body

"The author gradually reveals the issues facing a transgender teen, educating readers without feeling too instructional (Luna and Regan discuss lingo, hormones and even sex change operations). Flashbacks throughout help round out the story, explaining Liam/Luna's longtime struggle with a dual existence, and funny, sarcastic-but-strong Regan narrates with an authentic voice that will draw readers into this new territory." Publ Wkly

Rage; a love story. Alfred A. Knopf 2009 293p $16.99; lib bdg $19.99

Grades: 9 10 11 12   **Fic**
1. Lesbians—Fiction 2. Homosexuality—Fiction 3. Sisters—Fiction 4. Child abuse—Fiction 5. Abused women—Fiction
ISBN 978-0-375-85209-1; 0-375-85209-3; 978-0-375-95209-8 (lib bdg); 0-375-95209-8 (lib bdg)
         LC 2008-33500

At the end of high school, Johanna finally begins dating the girl she has loved from afar, but Reeve is as much trouble as she claims to be as she and her twin brother damage Johanna's self-esteem, friendships, and already precarious relationship with her sister.

"The appeal of Johanna and Reeve's romance is its edgy, tragic drama, and Johanna's take on things offers keen insight into why kind, sane people allow themselves to be hit and then make excuses for their abusers. . . . The issues raised here are important and thought-provoking while never overpowering the appeal of the story itself." Bull Cent Child Books

Petrucha, Stefan

Split. Walker Books for Young Readers 2010 257p $16.99

Grades: 7 8 9 10   **Fic**
1. Computers—Fiction 2. Space and time—Fiction
ISBN 978-0-8027-9372-0; 0-8027-9372-X
         LC 2009-8889

After his mother dies, Wade Jackson cannot decide whether to become a musician or a scholar, so he does both—splitting his consciousness into two distinct worlds.

"The shifting action keeps the fast-paced dual plots moving, and teens will be entertained by the two Wades' embodiment of the tension between being success oriented and following your whims." Booklist

Philbrick, W. R. (W. Rodman)

The last book in the universe; by Rodman Philbrick. Blue Sky Press (NY) 2001 223p hardcover o.p. pa $5.99 *

Grades: 9 10 11 12   **Fic**
1. Science fiction 2. Epilepsy—Fiction
ISBN 0-439-08758-9; 0-439-08759-7 (pa)
         LC 99-59878

Expanded from a short story in Tomorrowland edited by Michael Cart, published 1999 by Scholastic Press

After an earthquake has destroyed much of the planet, an epileptic teenager nicknamed Spaz begins the heroic fight to bring human intelligence back to the Earth of a distant future

"Enthralling, thought-provoking, and unsettling." Voice Youth Advocates

Phillips, Suzanne

Burn; a novel. Little, Brown and Co. 2008 279p $16.99 *

Grades: 9 10 11 12   **Fic**
1. Bullies—Fiction 2. Post-traumatic stress disorder—Fiction 3. School stories
ISBN 978-0-316-00165-6; 0-316-00165-1
         LC 2007-43520

Bullied constantly during his freshman year in high school, Cameron's anger and isolation grows, leading to deadly consequences.

"This is an intense story with brutal descriptions of the abuse Cameron suffers. . . . There is understanding to be gained for everyone who reads this timely title." SLJ

Phillips, Wendy, 1959-

Fishtailing. Coteau Books for Teens 2010 196p pa $14.95

Grades: 8 9 10 11 12   **Fic**
1. Novels in verse 2. Violence—Fiction 3. Authorship—Fiction 4. School stories
ISBN 978-1-55050-411-8; 1-55050-411-8

Through a series of poems written for English class, interspersed with teacher comments and letters to and from parents, high school students Natalie, Tricia, Kyle, and Miguel describe their lives.

"The poetry is touching, painful, and jarring as Phillips presents their stories through their hesitations, hopes, pains, and fears. The plot constantly twists and turns, keeping the reader guessing what will happen next." Voice Youth Advocates

Picoult, Jodi, 1966-

My sister's keeper; a novel. Atria 2004 423p
$25; pa $15 *

Grades: 11 12 Adult   **Fic**
1. Sisters—Fiction 2. Mother-daughter relationship—
Fiction 3. Bioethics—Fiction
ISBN 0-7434-5452-9; 0-7434-5453-7 (pa)
                LC 2004-300043
"Thirteen-year-old Anna knows that she was con-
ceived to provide life support for her critically ill sister.
After enduring multiple surgeries, she sues her parents
for the rights to her own body." Booklist

"Picoult's timely and compelling novel will appeal to
anyone who has thought about the morality of medical
decision making and any parent who must balance the
needs of different children." Libr J

Nineteen minutes; a novel. Atria Books 2007
455p $26.95; pa $15

Grades: 11 12 Adult   **Fic**
1. School violence—Fiction 2. Bullies—Fiction
3. Judges—Fiction 4. New Hampshire—Fiction
ISBN   978-0-7434-9672-8;   0-7434-9672-8;
978-0-7434-9673-5 (pa); 0-7434-9673-6 (pa)
                LC 2006-49276
"Peter Houghton, an alienated teen who has been bullied for years by the popular crowd, brings weapons to
his high school in Sterling, N.H., one day and opens fire,
killing 10 people. Flashbacks reveal how bullying caused
Peter to retreat into a world of violent computer games.
Alex Cormier, the judge assigned to Peter's case, tries to
maintain her objectivity as she struggles to understand
her daughter, Josie, one of the surviving witnesses of the
shooting." Publ Wkly

"Picoult's adept character development and intelligent
plot twists make for a story that runs deeper than mere
voyeurism of titillation. [The novel] is both a page turner
and a thoughtful exploration of popularity, power, and
the social ruts that can define us in ways we may not
wish to be defined." Rocky Mountain News

Pierce, Tamora, 1954-

Terrier. Random House 2006 581p il map (Beka
Cooper) hardcover o.p. pa $9.99

Grades: 7 8 9 10   **Fic**
1. Police—Fiction 2. Fantasy fiction 3. Magic—Fiction
ISBN   978-0-375-81468-6;   0-375-81468-X;
978-0-375-83816-3 (pa); 0-375-83816-3 (pa)
                LC 2006-14834
When sixteen-year-old Beka becomes "Puppy" to a
pair of "Dogs," as the Provost's Guards are called, she
uses her police training, natural abilities and a touch of
magic to help them solve the case of a murdered baby
in Tortall's Lower City.

"Pierce deftly handles the novel's journal structure,
and her clear homage to the police-procedural genre applies a welcome twist to the girl-legend-in-the-making
story line." Booklist

Followed by: Bloodhound (2009)

The will of the empress. Scholastic Press 2005
550p $17.99; pa $8.99

Grades: 8 9 10 11 12   **Fic**
1. Fantasy fiction
ISBN 0-439-44171-4; 0-439-44172-2 (pa)
                LC 2005-02874
On visit to Namorn to visit her vast landholdings and
her devious cousin, Empress Berenene, eighteen-year-old
Sandry must rely on her childhood friends and fellow
mages, Daja, Tris, and Briar, despite the distance that has
grown between them

"This novel begins two years after the Circle of Magic
and The Circle Opens series. . . . Readers will enjoy being reacquainted with these older but still very well-
developed characters." SLJ

Pignat, Caroline, 1970-

Greener grass; the famine years. Red Deer Press
2009 276p pa $12.95

Grades: 7 8 9 10   **Fic**
1. Ireland—Fiction 2. Famines—Fiction
ISBN 978-0-88995-402-1; 0-88995-402-X
"In 1847, 15-year-old Kit is jailed for digging up potatoes on confiscated land to feed her starving family,
and during the three weeks that she is incarcerated, she
reflects on the past year in Ireland: the blight, the famine, evictions, and deaths. . . . True to Kat's voice, the
plain, rhythmic language . . . is lyrical but never ornate.
The tension in the story and in the well-developed characters is always rooted in daily detail." Booklist

Followed by: Wild geese (2010)

Pike, Aprilynne

Wings. HarperTeen 2009 294p $16.99; lib bdg
$17.89; pa $8.99

Grades: 7 8 9 10   **Fic**
1. Fairies—Fiction 2. Plants—Fiction 3. Trolls—Fiction 4. Fantasy fiction
ISBN   978-0-06-166803-6;   0-06-166803-6;
978-0-06-166804-3 (lib bdg); 0-06-166804-4 (lib bdg);
978-0-06-166805-0 (pa); 0-06-166805-2 (pa)
                LC 2008-24653
When a plant blooms out of fifteen-year-old Laurel's
back, it leads her to discover the fact that she is a faerie
and that she has a crucial role to play in keeping the
world safe from the encroaching enemy trolls.

"Replete with budding romance, teen heroics, a good
smattering of evil individuals, and an ending that serves
up a ready sequel, this novel nonetheless provides an unusual approach to middle level fantasy through its startlingly creative premise that faeries are of the plant world
and not the animal world. . . . Both male and female
fantasy readers will enjoy this fast-paced action fantasy."
Voice Youth Advocates

Other titles in this series are:
Illusions (2011)
Spells (2010)

Plath, Sylvia

The bell jar; foreword by Frances McCullough; biographical note by Lois Ames; drawings by Sylvia Plath. 25th anniversary ed. HarperCollins Publishers 1996 296p il $20; pa $16.95 *

Fic

1. Mental illness—Fiction
ISBN 0-06-017490-0; 0-06-114851-2 (pa)
                                    LC 96-211742
First published 1963 in the United Kingdom; first United States edition published 1971

"Esther Greenwood, having spent what should have been a glorious summer as guest editor for a young woman's magazine, came home from New York, had a nervous breakdown, and tried to commit suicide. Through months of therapy, Esther kept her rationality, if not her sanity. In telling the story of Esther Plath thinly disguised her own experience with attempted suicide and time spent in an institution." Shapiro. Fic for Youth. 3d edition

Plum-Ucci, Carol, 1957-

Streams of Babel. Harcourt 2008 424p $17
Grades: 8 9 10 11   Fic
1. Terrorism—Fiction   2.   Spies—Fiction
3. Computers—Fiction 4. New Jersey—Fiction
ISBN 978-0-15-216556-7; 0-15-216556-8
                                    LC 2007-26503
Six teens face a bioterrorist attack on American soil as four are infected with a mysterious disease affecting their small New Jersey neighborhood and two others, both brilliant computer hackers, assist the United States Intelligence Coalition in tracking the perpetrators.

The "story's threads are brought together in ways designed to keep readers on the edge of their seats. . . . Fans of suspense will discover a thrilling ride." Voice Youth Advocates

Followed by: Fire will fall (2010)

Polak, Monique

The middle of everywhere. Orca Book Publishers 2009 200p pa $12.95
Grades: 7 8 9 10   Fic
1. Inuit—Fiction 2. Wilderness survival—Fiction
3. Arctic regions—Fiction 4. Québec (Province)—Fiction
ISBN 978-1-55469-090-9; 1-55469-090-0
Noah spends a school term in George River, in Quebec's Far North, trying to understand the Inuit culture, which he finds both threatening and puzzling.

"Although the survival-adventure details will engage reluctant readers, the story has elements of romance when Noah strives to impress an Inuit classmate." SLJ

What world is left. Orca Book Pub. 2008 215p pa $12.95
Grades: 7 8 9 10 11 12   Fic
1. Holocaust, 1933-1945—Fiction 2. Jews—Netherlands—Fiction 3. World War, 1939-1945—Netherlands—Fiction 4. Netherlands—History—1940-1945, German occupation—Fiction
ISBN 978-1-5514-3847-4; 1-5514-3847-X
"Growing up in a secular Jewish home in Holland, Anneke cares little about Judaism, so she has no faith to

lose when, in 1943, her family is deported to Theresienstadt, the Nazi concentration camp. . . . Based on the experiences of the author's mother . . . this novel is narrated in Anneke's first-person, present-tense voice. The details are unforgettable. . . . An important addition to the Holocaust curriculum." Booklist

Pon, Cindy, 1973-

Silver phoenix; beyond the kingdom of Xia. Greenwillow Books 2009 338p $17.99; lib bdg $18.89; pa $8.99 *
Grades: 9 10 11 12   Fic
1. Supernatural—Fiction 2. Voyages and travels—Fiction 3. Father-daughter relationship—Fiction 4. China—Fiction
ISBN   978-0-06-173021-4;   0-06-173021-1;
978-0-06-178033-2 (lib bdg); 0-06-178033-2 (lib bdg); 978-0-06-173024-5 (pa); 0-06-173024-6 (pa)
                                    LC 2008-29149
With her father long overdue from his journey and a lecherous merchant blackmailing her into marriage, seventeen-year-old Ai Ling becomes aware of a strange power within her as she goes in search of her parent.

"Pon's writing, both fluid and exhilarating, shines whether she's describing a dinner delicacy or what it feels like to stab an evil spirit in the gut. There's a bit of sex here, including a near rape, but it's all integral to a saga that spins and slashes as its heroine tries to find her way home." Booklist

Followed by Fury of the phoenix (2011)

Porter, Connie Rose

Imani all mine; [by] Connie Porter. Houghton Mifflin 1999 212p hardcover o.p. pa $12
Grades: 11 12 Adult   Fic
1. African Americans—Fiction 2. Unmarried mothers—Fiction 3. Rape—Fiction
ISBN 0-395-83808-8; 0-618-05678-5 (pa)
                                    LC 98-37722
"Tasha is 15, an honors student struggling to live up to her mother's dreams of college and life beyond their poor black neighborhood. She is also a rape victim and a single mother, determined that she alone will give her baby, Imani, a good future in the midst of poverty, drugs, gangs, and ignorance. Even the baby's name is a sign of Tasha's hope—Imani means 'faith.' When gang violence assaults her family, Tasha's innocence is shattered, and she must summon every ounce of strength within her to survive." Libr J

The narrative, "told in Tasha's voice, is the story of great promise shining through monstrous obstacles." N Y Times Book Rev

Portman, Frank

Andromeda Klein. Delacorte Press 2009 424p $17.99; lib bdg $20.99
Grades: 8 9 10 11 12   Fic
1. Occultism—Fiction 2. Tarot—Fiction 3. Deaf—Fiction 4. Handicapped—Fiction 5. Books and reading—Fiction 6. Libraries—Fiction
ISBN   978-0-385-73525-4;   0-385-73525-1;
978-0-385-90512-1 (lib bdg); 0-385-90512-2 (lib bdg)
                                    LC 2009-15879

Portman, Frank—*Continued*

High school sophomore Andromeda, an outcast because she studies the occult and has a hearing impairment and other disabilities, overcomes grief over terrible losses by enlisting others' help in her plan to save library books—and finds a kindred spirit along the way.

"Andromeda is a compelling character, whose reclaiming of misheard words and misspelled text messages gives her unique and likable flavor. . . . For readers who are occult fans, this quirky text will be a self-satisfied joy." Kirkus

King Dork. Delacorte Press 2006 344p il hardcover o.p. pa $8.99 *

Grades: 10 11 12   **Fic**
  1. Salinger, J. D., 1919-2010—Fiction 2. Fathers—Fiction 3. School stories
  ISBN   0-385-73291-0;   978-0-385-73291-8;
  0-385-73450-6 (pa); 978-0-385-73450-9 (pa)
                                              LC 2005-12556

High school loser Tom Henderson discovers that "The Catcher in the Rye" may hold the clues to the many mysteries in his life.

"Mature situations, casual sexual experiences, and allusions to Salinger suggest an older teen audience, who will also best appreciate the appended bandography and the very funny glossary." Booklist

Potok, Chaim, 1929-2002

The chosen; a novel; with a foreword by the author. 25th anniversary ed. Knopf 1992 c1967 295p hardcover o.p. pa $13.95 *

Grades: 11 12 Adult   **Fic**
  1. Jews—New York (N.Y.)—Fiction
  ISBN 0-679-40222-5; 0-449-91154-3 (pa)
                                              LC 91-58551

Available in hardcover from Holt, Rinehart and Winston

A reissue of the title first published 1967 by Simon & Schuster

"Living only five blocks apart in the Williamsburg section of Brooklyn, New York, Danny and Reuven meet as opponents in a softball game. Out of this encounter evolves a strong bond of friendship between a brilliant Hasidic Jew and a scholar who is Orthodox in his religious thinking. During the course of their relationship Reuven becomes the means by which Danny's father, a rabbi, can communicate with his son, who has been reared under a code of silence." Shapiro. Fic for Youth. 2d edition

Another title about Danny and Reuven is:
The promise (1969)

Potter, Ryan

Exit strategy. Flux 2010 303p pa $9.95

Grades: 8 9 10 11 12   **Fic**
  1.   Summer—Fiction   2.   Steroids—Fiction
  3. Friendship—Fiction 4. Michigan—Fiction
  ISBN 978-0-7387-1573-5; 0-7387-1573-5
                                              LC 2009-27697

Seventeen-year-old Zach, his best friend (and state wrestling champion) Tank, and Tank's twin sister Sarah, an Ivy League-bound scholar, are desperate to leave their depressing hometown of Blaine, Michigan, after next year's graduation, but plans go awry when Zach uncovers a steroid scandal and falls in love with Sarah.

"Packed with suspense and drama, with some romance and a fight, this book is bound to be popular among the male crowd. Just make sure you get it into the right hands; mature themes exist, including extramarital affairs, underage drinking, and anger management." Libr Media Connect

Powell, Randy

Three clams and an oyster. Farrar, Straus & Giroux 2002 216p hardcover o.p. pa $6.95 *

Grades: 7 8 9 10   **Fic**
  1. Friendship—Fiction 2. Football—Fiction
  ISBN 0-374-37526-7; 0-374-40007-5 (pa)
                                              LC 2001-54833

During their humorous search to find a fourth player for their flag football team, three high school juniors are forced to examine their long friendship, their individual flaws, and their inability to try new experiences

"Sometimes philosophical, sometimes comical, but always touching, Randy Powell writes an unusually moving story of adolescent male friends." Book Rep

Power, Susan, 1961-

The grass dancer. Putnam 1994 300p hardcover o.p. pa $7.99 *

Grades: 11 12 Adult   **Fic**
  1. Dakota Indians—Fiction
  ISBN 0-399-13911-7; 0-425-14962-5 (pa)
                                              LC 93-47199

"Set on a North Dakota reservation, 'The Grass Dancer' tells the story of Harley Wind Soldier, a young Sioux trying to understand his place among people whose intertwined lives and shared heritage move backward in time in the narrative from the 1980's to the middle of the last century." N Y Times Book Rev

This "is a passionate portrayal of universal human emotions and a vivid account of Native American history and culture." SLJ

Pratchett, Terry

The amazing Maurice and his educated rodents. HarperCollins Pubs. 2001 241p hardcover o.p. pa $6.99 *

Grades: 7 8 9 10   **Fic**
  1. Fantasy fiction 2. Rats—Fiction 3. Cats—Fiction
  ISBN 0-06-001233-1; 0-06-001235-8 (pa)
                                              LC 2001-42411

A talking cat, intelligent rats, and a strange boy cooperate in a Pied Piper scam until they try to con the wrong town and are confronted by a deadly evil rat king

"In this laugh-out-loud fantasy, his first 'Discworld' novel for younger readers, Pratchett rethinks a classic story and comes up with a winner." SLJ

Pratchett, Terry—*Continued*

Nation. HarperCollins 2008 367p $16.99; lib bdg $17.89; pa $8.99 *

Grades: 7 8 9 10 11 12   **Fic**
1. Survival after airplane accidents, shipwrecks, etc.—Fiction 2. Tsunamis—Fiction 3. Islands—Fiction
ISBN   978-0-06-143301-6;   0-06-143301-2;
978-0-06-143302-3 (lib bdg); 0-06-143302-0 (lib bdg);
978-0-06-143303-0 (pa); 0-06-143303-9 (pa)
LC 2008-20211

After a devastating tsunami destroys all that they have ever known, Mau, an island boy, and Daphne, an aristocratic English girl, together with a small band of refugees, set about rebuilding their community and all the things that are important in their lives.

"Quirky wit and broad vision make this a fascinating survival story on many levels." Booklist

The Wee Free Men. HarperCollins Pubs. 2003 263p hardcover o.p. pa $9.99 *

Grades: 7 8 9 10   **Fic**
1. Fantasy fiction 2. Witches—Fiction
ISBN 0-06-001236-6; 0-06-201217-7 (pa)
LC 2002-15396

A young witch-to-be named Tiffany teams up with the Wee Free Men, a clan of six-inch-high blue men, to rescue her baby brother and ward off a sinister invasion from Fairyland

"Pratchett invites readers into his well-established realm of Discworld where action, magic, and characters are firmly rooted in literary reality. Humor ripples throughout, making tense, dangerous moments stand out in stark contrast." Bull Cent Child Books

Other titles about Tiffany are:
A hat full of sky (2004)
I shall wear midnight (2010)
Wintersmith (2006)

Pressler, Mirjam
Let sleeping dogs lie; translated by Erik J. Macki. Front Street 2006 207p $16.95

Grades: 8 9 10 11 12   **Fic**
1. Germans—Israel—Fiction 2. National socialism—Fiction
ISBN 978-1-932425-84-0; 1-932425-84-5
LC 2006-101752

Original German edition, 2003

"Johanna's family owns the largest clothing store in town. Her grandfather founded it and built it up with his own hands—at least that's the family legend. But when Johanna travels to Israel on a class project in 1995, she finds out that the Lewin family originally owned the store. She learns that in the course of 'aryanization' during the Nazi regime, her grandfather legally acquired the company according to the anti-Semitic laws of the Third Reich." Publisher's note

"A powerful and thought-provoking novel for mature teens." SLJ

Preus, Margi
Heart of a samurai; based on the true story of Nakahama Manjiro. Abrams/Amulet 2010 301p il $15.95 *

Grades: 7 8 9 10 11 12   **Fic**
1.   Nakahama,   Manjirō,   1827-1898—Fiction
2. Survival after airplane accidents, shipwrecks, etc.—Fiction 3. Japanese—United States—Fiction
ISBN 978-0-8109-8981-8; 0-8109-8981-6
LC 2009-51634

In 1841, rescued by an American whaler after a terrible shipwreck leaves him and his four companions castaways on a remote island, fourteen-year-old Manjiro, who dreams of becoming a samurai, learns new laws and customs as he becomes the first Japanese person to set foot in the United States.

The author "mixes fact with fiction in a tale that is at once adventurous, heartwarming, sprawling, and nerve-racking in its depictions of early anti-Asian sentiment. She succeeds in making readers feel every bit as 'other' as Manjiro, while showing America at its best and worst through his eyes." Publ Wkly

Includes bibliographical references

Price, Charlie
Dead connection. Roaring Brook Press 2006 225p $16.95 *

Grades: 8 9 10 11 12   **Fic**
1. Ghost stories 2. Homicide—Fiction
ISBN 1-59643-114-8; 978-1-59643-114-0
LC 2005-17138

"A Deborah Brodie book"

A loner who communes with the dead in the town cemetery hears the voice of a murdered cheerleader and tries to convince the adults that he knows what happened to her

"Readers will like the edginess and be intrigued by the extrasensory elements as well as the darker turns the mystery takes. This is something different." Booklist

The interrogation of Gabriel James. Farrar Straus Giroux 2010 170p $16.99.

Grades: 9 10 11 12   **Fic**
1. Homicide—Fiction 2. Criminal investigation—Fiction 3. Montana—Fiction
ISBN 978-0-374-33545-8; 0-374-33545-1
LC 2009-37309

As an eyewitness to two murders, a Montana teenager relates the shocking story behind the crimes in a police interrogation interspersed with flashbacks.

"The author writes intriguing and believable characters and keeps a stream of realism moving through the story even when neither readers nor Gabriel are really sure what's going on. Patience from readers won't be required, though, as plenty of action keeps the narrative moving while the plot details unfold. The result is not only suspense but a memorable and believable characterization. Top notch." Kirkus

Prinz, Yvonne

The Vinyl Princess. HarperTeen 2010 313p $16.99

Grades: 8 9 10 11 12   Fic
1. Sound recordings—Fiction 2. Music—Fiction 3. Weblogs—Fiction 4. Zines—Fiction 5. California—Fiction

ISBN 978-0-06-171583-9; 0-06-171583-2

LC 2009-14270

Allie, a sixteen-year-old who is obsessed with LPs, works at the used record store on Telegraph Ave. and deals with crushes—her own and her mother's—her increasingly popular blog and zine, and generally grows up over the course of one summer in her hometown of Berkeley, California.

Prinz "writes with a genuine passion for music that readers who live to listen will recognize, and in this heartfelt, often-hilarious story, she shows the profound ways that music can shape lives." Booklist

Prose, Francine, 1947-

Touch. HarperTeen 2009 262p $16.99; lib bdg $17.89

Grades: 7 8 9 10   Fic
1. Friendship—Fiction 2. Family life—Fiction 3. Stepmothers—Fiction 4. School stories
ISBN   978-0-06-137517-0;   0-06-137517-9; 978-0-06-137518-7 (lib bdg); 0-06-137518-7 (lib bdg)

LC 2008-20208

Ninth-grader Maisie's concepts of friendship, loyalty, self-acceptance, and truth are tested to their limit after a schoolbus incident with the three boys who have been her best friends since early childhood.

"Readers will be fascinated by this convincing tale and the questions that it raises, from its gripping first chapter to its poignant and surprising conclusion." Voice Youth Advocates

Provoost, Anne, 1964-

In the shadow of the ark; translated by John Nieuwenhuizen. Arthur A. Levine Books 2004 368p $17.95

Grades: 9 10 11 12   Fic
1. Noah's ark—Fiction
ISBN 0-439-44234-6   LC 2003-9622
Original Dutch edition, 2001

This is a "story of the biblical Flood, recounted by Re Jana, whose family leaves the marshes to find the ark. The passion Re Jana finds with Ham, son of the Builder, leads to a place on the ark, but this 'safe haven,' with the stink and sounds of the animals, starvation, and repeated (if not lustful) rapes by Ham's brothers, tests her in every way, even as she carries new life into the New World. Exquisitely detailed and intelligently written, this is a YA novel only in the broadest sense; no one would blink if it appeared on an adult list." Booklist

Pullman, Philip, 1946-

The golden compass; his dark materials book I; [appendix illustrations by Ian Beck] Deluxe 10th anniversary ed. Alfred A. Knopf 2006 399p il $22.95 *

Grades: 7 8 9 10 11 12   Fic
1. Fantasy fiction
ISBN 978-0-375-83830-9; 0-375-83830-9

LC 2005-32556

First published 1995 in the United Kingdom with title: Northern lights

Includes "Some papers from the Library at Jordan College" and other materials that complement the original text

This first title in a fantasy trilogy "introduces the characters and sets up the basic conflict, namely, a race to unlock the mystery of a newly discovered type of charged particles simply called 'dust' that may be a bridge to an alternate universe. The action follows 11-year-old protagonist Lyra Belacqua from her home at Oxford University to the frozen wastes of the North on a quest to save dozens of kidnapped children from the evil 'Gobblers,' who are using them as part of a sinister experiment involving dust." Libr J [review of 1996 edition]

Other titles in the His dark materials series are:
The amber spyglass (2000)
The subtle knife (1997)

Qamar, Amjed

Beneath my mother's feet. Atheneum Books for Young Readers 2008 198p $16.99 *

Grades: 7 8 9 10   Fic
1. Household employees—Fiction 2. Pakistan—Fiction 3. Sex role—Fiction 4. Poverty—Fiction
ISBN 978-1-4169-4728-8; 1-4169-4728-0

LC 2007-19001

When her father is injured, fourteen-year-old Nazia is pulled away from school, her friends, and her preparations for an arranged marriage, to help her mother clean houses in a wealthy part of Karachi, Pakistan, where she finally rebels against the destiny that is planned for her.

This novel "provides a fascinating glimpse into a world remarkably distant from that of most American teens, and would be an excellent suggestion for readers who want to know about how other young people live." SLJ

Quick, Barbara

A golden web. HarperTeen 2010 266p $16.99

Grades: 7 8 9 10   Fic
1. Giliani, Alessandra, 1307-1326—Fiction 2. Sex role—Fiction 3. Anatomy—Fiction 4. Middle Ages—Fiction 5. Italy—Fiction
ISBN 978-0-06-144887-4; 0-06-144887-7

LC 2009-14265

In fourteenth-century Bologna, Alessandra Giliani, a brilliant young girl, defies convention and risks death in order to attend medical school at the university so that she can study anatomy.

"Alessandra's intellectual curiosity is wonderfully depicted, her philosophical musings are entertaining, and her commitment to the pursuit of biological knowledge enlivens the plot. Quick's prose is fluid and authentic, bright and engaging." Publ Wkly

Quick, Matthew, 1973-
Sorta like a rockstar; a novel. Little, Brown
2010 355p $16.99; pa $8.99
Grades: 7 8 9 10 11   Fic
1. Homeless persons—Fiction 2. Depression (Psychology)—Fiction 3. School stories
ISBN   978-0-316-04352-6;   0-316-04352-4;
978-0-316-04353-3 (pa); 0-316-04353-2 (pa)
                       LC 2008-46746
Although seventeen-year-old Amber Appleton is
homeless, living in a school bus with her unfit mother,
she is a relentless optimist who visits the elderly at a
nursing home, teaches English to Korean Catholic wom-
en with the use of rhythm and blues music, and befriends
a solitary Vietnam veteran and his dog, but eventually
she experiences one burden more than she can bear and
slips into a deep depression.
"This book is the answer to all those angst-ridden and
painfully grim novels in the shortcut lingo of short atten-
tion-span theater. Hugely enjoyable." SLJ

Quintero, Sofia
Efrain's secret. Alfred A. Knopf 2010 265p
$16.99; lib bdg $19.99 *
Grades: 8 9 10 11 12   Fic
1. Drug traffic—Fiction 2. Violence—Fiction
3. Hispanic Americans—Fiction 4. Bronx (New York,
N.Y.)—Fiction 5. School stories
ISBN   978-0-375-84706-6;   0-375-84706-5;
978-0-375-94706-3 (lib bdg); 0-375-94706-X (lib bdg)
                       LC 2009-8493
Ambitious high school senior and honor student Efrain
Rodriguez makes some questionable choices in pursuit of
his dream to escape the South Bronx and attend an Ivy
League college.
"Quintero imbues her characters with unexpected
grace and charm. . . . Mostly, though, it is Quintero's
effortless grasp of teen slang that gives her first-person
story its heart." Booklist

Raedeke, Christy
The daykeeper's grimoire. Flux 2010 352p
(Prophecy of days) pa $9.95
Grades: 7 8 9 10   Fic
1. Prophecies—Fiction 2. Conspiracies—Fiction
3. Mayas—Fiction 4. Secret societies—Fiction
5. Scotland—Fiction
ISBN 978-0-7387-1576-6; 0-7387-1576-X
                       LC 2009-30668
Caity Mac Fireland of San Francisco accompanies her
parents to an isle off the coast of Scotland where she
finds a Mayan relic and, guided by a motley crew of advisors, uncovers an incredible secret that an elite group
of power-brokers will stop at nothing to control.
"A delightful heroine, she's funny, frank, and mostly
true to the way a real teen would act if she found herself
in such an odd circumstance. Readers will want to follow
Caity's adventure." Booklist
Followed by: The serpent's coil (2011)

Rainfield, C. A.
Scars; by Cheryl Rainfield. WestSide Books
2010 248p $16.95 *
Grades: 9 10 11 12   Fic
1. Child sexual abuse—Fiction 2. Self-mutilation—
Fiction 3. Artists—Fiction 4. Lesbians—Fiction
5. Memory—Fiction
ISBN 978-1-934813-32-4   LC 2009-52076
Fifteen-year-old Kendra, a budding artist, has not felt
safe since she began to recall devastating memories of
childhood sexual abuse, especially since she cannot remember her abuser's identity, and she copes with the
pressure by cutting herself.
"The excellent resource section covers widely respected books, Web sites, organizations, and help lines for
youth seeking information on extreme abuse, cutting,
same-sex attraction, and dissociation. This book will be
a particular comfort and source of insight for teens facing any of these challenges, but whatever their life experience, they will be on the edge of their seats, rooting for
Kendra to unravel the mystery that shadows her life.
This is one heck of a good book!" SLJ

Rallison, Janette, 1966-
How to take the ex out of ex-boyfriend. G. P.
Putnam's Sons 2007 265p hardcover o.p. pa $7.99
Grades: 7 8 9 10   Fic
1. Dating (Social customs)—Fiction 2. Politics—Fiction 3. School stories
ISBN   978-0-399-24617-3;   0-399-24617-7;
978-0-14-241269-5 (pa); 0-14-241269-4 (pa)
                       LC 2006-26543
Giovanna rashly breaks up with her boyfriend when
he refuses to help her twin brother with his campaign for
Student Council president, but fixing her mistake may be
more difficult for her than she realizes.
This "is more serious in its treatment of issues and
meatier than others like it, making it engaging yet an
easy fun read that will appeal to many teen girls." Voice
Youth Advocates

Just one wish. G. P. Putnam's Sons 2009 264p
$16.99; pa $7.99
Grades: 7 8 9 10   Fic
1. Actors—Fiction 2. Cancer—Fiction 3. Siblings—
Fiction
ISBN   978-0-399-24618-0;   0-399-24618-5;
978-0-14-241599-3 (pa); 0-14-241599-5 (pa)
                       LC 2008-9297
Seventeen-year-old Annika tries to cheer up her little
brother Jeremy before his surgery to remove a cancerous
tumor by bringing home his favorite television actor,
Steve Raleigh, the star of "Teen Robin Hood"
"Annika's wacky encounters . . . and anxiety for her
brother make the story both comical and poignant." Horn
Book Guide

Randall, Thomas, 1967-
Dreams of the dead. Bloomsbury Children's
Books 2009 276p (The waking) pa $8.99
Grades: 8 9 10 11 12   Fic
1. Death—Fiction 2. Supernatural—Fiction 3. School
stories 4. Japan—Fiction
ISBN 978-1-59990-250-0; 1-59990-250-8
                       LC 2008-30844

Randall, Thomas, 1967-—_Continued_

After her mother dies, sixteen-year-old Kara and her father move to Japan, where he teaches and she attends school, but she is haunted by a series of frightening nightmares and deaths that might be revenge—or something worse

"The story has suspense, mystery, and horror. It will be a great hit with fans of manga, anime, or Japanese culture." SLJ

Followed by: Spirits of the Noh (2011)

Rapp, Adam

Punkzilla. Candlewick Press 2009 244p $16.99
*

Grades: 10 11 12   Fic
1. Brothers—Fiction 2. Drug abuse—Fiction
3. Runaway teenagers—Fiction
ISBN 978-0-7636-3031-7; 0-7636-3031-4
                                        LC 2008-935655

"Punkzilla" is on a mission to see his older brother "P", before "P" dies of cancer. Still buzzing from his last hit of meth, he embarks on a days-long trip from Portland, Ore. to Memphis, Tenn., writing letters to his family and friends. Along the way, he sees a sketchier side of America and worries if he will make it to see his brother in time.

"Jamie, who has ADD, details every step (being taken advantage of sexually, getting jumped, befriending a fe-male-to-male transsexual, losing his virginity) in exple-tive-filled, stream-of-consciousness narration with insights into seedy roadside America . . . and his own situation. . . . The teenager's singular voice and observations make for an immersive reading experience." Publ Wkly

Under the wolf, under the dog. Candlewick Press 2004 310p $16.99 *
Grades: 9 10 11 12   Fic
1. Suicide—Fiction 2. Family life—Fiction
3. Illinois—Fiction
ISBN 0-7636-1818-7   LC 2004-50255

"Steve currently resides in a facility for troubled youth, but most are here for drug abuse or suicidal tendencies, and he doesn't really fit in either category. What's led him here, as he describes in his journal, is a series of life depredations that have sent him reeling into irrationality: his mother's long, horrible, and unsuccessful bout with cancer, his father's concomitant catatonic depression, his brother's drug-induced haze and subsequent suicide, and his own unintentional self-woundings along the way, from a lacerated leg to an injury that eventually results in blindness in one eye." Bull Cent Child Books

Ravel, Edeet

The saver. Groundwood Books/House of Anansi Press 2008 214p $17.95; pa $8.95
Grades: 7 8 9 10 11   Fic
1. Death—Fiction 2. Orphans—Fiction 3. Uncles—Fiction
ISBN 978-0-88899-882-8; 0-88899-882-1;
978-0-88899-883-5 (pa); 0-88899-883-X (pa)

When 17-year-old Fern's mother dies of a heart attack, she has to make her own way in the world. She

takes over her mother's housecleaning jobs, takes a job as a janitor, and adds two other part-time jobs. Then her Uncle Jack, whom she's never met, shows up to help her.

"Written as a series of letters to an imaginary friend on another planet, this is a compelling story of determination and the will to survive." SLJ

Rawles, Nancy, 1958-

My Jim; a novel. Crown Publishers 2005 174p hardcover o.p. pa $12.95
Grades: 9 10 11 12   Fic
1. Slavery—Fiction 2. African Americans—Fiction
ISBN 1-4000-5400-1; 1-4000-5401-X (pa)
                                        LC 2004-11606

In this "retelling of the story of escaped slave Jim from Mark Twain's The Adventures of Huckleberry Finn, Rawles shifts the focus to Jim's wife, Sadie, whose unspeakable losses set the tone for Jim's flight." Publ Wkly

"Students reading Huckleberry Finn are a prime audience for this accessible and revealing new story, but teens who enjoy family romance or contemporary African American fiction will be rewarded and bring insight to the older text when later meeting it." Voice Youth Advocates

Razzell, Mary, 1930-

Snow apples. Groundwood Books 2006 209p hardcover o.p. pa $6.95 *
Grades: 10 11 12   Fic
1. Mother-daughter relationship—Fiction
2. Pregnancy—Fiction 3. British Columbia—Fiction
ISBN 0-88899-741-8; 978-0-88899-741-8;
0-88899-728-0 (pa); 978-0-88899-728-9 (pa)
First published 1984 in Canada

"In isolated, rural British Columbia, as World War II is ending, Sheila Brary turns 16 and yearns for a life different from the sad existence of her mother. Struggling to raise four sons and a daughter mostly on her own, the woman has turned hard and cold, always angry at her bright and emotional daughter who reminds her too much of her unfaithful, undependable husband. . . . The teen wins one struggle with her mother and manages to finish high school, while she loses another with her own awakening sexuality and finds herself desperate and pregnant. When she runs off to Vancouver, her distant father helps her to abort the pregnancy and then abandons her one last time. Sheila survives a terrifying miscarriage on her own, returns to her family long enough to see what her mother has sacrificed, and starts a new life with promise and support. This is a quiet, introspective novel that takes a while to build its power, and it has some stunningly dramatic scenes." SLJ

Reasoner, James, 1953-

Manassas. Cumberland House 1999 336p $22.95
Grades: 9 10 11 12   Fic
1. United States—History—1861-1865, Civil War—Fiction
ISBN 1-58182-008-9   LC 98-52494

This novel focuses on "the Brannon clan of Culpepper County, Virginia. . . . Fiercely devoted to the Confeder-

Reasoner, James, 1953-—_Continued_

acy and to each other, the six Brannon siblings anxiously await news of secession as a deadly feud erupts between Will Brannon, sheriff of Culpepper County, and the lawless Fogarty gang. When Will shoots and kills Joe Fogarty, he is forced to leave the family farm in order to ensure the safety of his mother, his sister, and his brothers. Enlisting in the Army of Northern Virginia, Will prepares for the Battle of Manassas, where he must face both the Union army and the surviving Fogarty brothers. Fraught with tension, drama, and tantalizing hints of future romance, this vividly rendered family saga will hook fans of meaty historical fiction." Booklist

Other titles in the Civil War battle series are:

Appomattox (2003)
Chancellorsville (2000)
Chickamauga (2002)
Gettysburg (2001)
Savannah (2003)
Shenandoah (2002)
Shiloh (1999)
Vicksburg (2001)

Rees, Celia, 1949-

The fool's girl. Bloomsbury 2010 297p $16.99

Grades: 8 9 10 11 12   Fic

1. Shakespeare, William, 1564-1616—Fiction 2. Adventure fiction 3. London (England)—Fiction 4. Great Britain—History—1485-1603, Tudors—Fiction

ISBN 978-1-59990-486-3; 1-59990-486-1

LC 2009-51894

Violetta and Feste have come to London to rescue a holy relic taken from a church in Illyria by the evil Malvolio, and once there, they tell the story of their adventures to playwright William Shakespeare, who turns it into a play.

"Expertly livening the proceedings with intrigues, japes, kisses, mildly bawdy comments, . . . colorful characters, plot twists, quick violence, and an occasional breath of the supernatural, Rees dishes up a quick-paced tale that builds to a suspenseful climax." Booklist

Pirates! the true and remarkable adventures of Minerva Sharpe and Nancy Kington, female pirates. Bloomsbury 2003 379p $16.95; pa $8.95

Grades: 9 10 11 12   Fic

1. Pirates—Fiction 2. Adventure fiction 3. Sea stories 4. Jamaica—Fiction

ISBN 1-582-34816-2; 1-582-34665-8 (pa)

LC 2003-51861

In 1722, after arriving with her brother at the family's Jamaican plantation where she is to be married off, sixteen-year-old Nancy Kington escapes with her slave friend, Minerva Sharpe, and together they become pirates traveling the world in search of treasure.

"There's action aplenty . . . with storms and sea battles and a devilish suitor hot on the heels of an innocent (except for the odd murder here and there) heroine. Add popcorn and a supersized soda, and you've got a rousing Saturday matinee." Bull Cent Child Books

Sovay. Bloomsbury 2008 404p $16.99

Grades: 7 8 9 10 11 12   Fic

1. Social classes—Fiction 2. Sex role—Fiction 3. Thieves—Fiction 4. Great Britain—History—1714-1837—Fiction 5. France—History—1789-1799, Revolution—Fiction

ISBN 978-1-59990-203-6; 1-59990-203-6

LC 2008-4779

In 1794 England, the rich and beautiful Sovay, disguised as a highwayman, acquires papers that could lead to her father's arrest for treason, and soon her newly-awakened political consciousness leads her and a compatriot to France during the Revolution.

"Taking as her inspiration a traditional English ballad, also titled Sovay, . . . Rees produces an appealingly fast-paced and suspenseful historical novel with plenty of plot twists, dastardly villains, and a brave, resourceful young heroine." Voice Youth Advocates

Reeve, Philip, 1966-

Fever Crumb. Scholastic Press 2010 325p $17.99 *

Grades: 6 7 8 9 10   Fic

1. Sex role—Fiction 2. Orphans—Fiction 3. Science fiction 4. London (England)—Fiction

ISBN 978-0-545-20719-5; 0-545-20719-3

LC 2009-15457

Prequel to: The Hungry City Chronicles series

Foundling Fever Crumb has been raised as an engineer although females in the future London, England, are not believed capable of rational thought, but at age fourteen she leaves her sheltered world and begins to learn startling truths about her past while facing danger in the present.

"Reeve's captivating flights of imagination play as vital a role in the story as his endearing heroine, hiss-worthy villains, and nifty array of supporting characters." Booklist

Followed by A web of air (2011)

Here lies Arthur. Scholastic Press 2008 339p $16.99 *

Grades: 7 8 9 10   Fic

1. Arthur, King—Fiction 2. Magic—Fiction 3. Great Britain—History—0-1066—Fiction

ISBN 978-0-545-09334-7; 0-545-09334-1

LC 2008-05787

When her village is attacked and burned, Gwyna seeks protection from the bard Myrddin, who uses Gwyna in his plan to transform young Arthur into the heroic King Arthur.

"Powerfully inventive. . . . Events rush headlong toward the inevitable ending, but Gwyna's observations illuminate them in a new way." Booklist

Reeves, Dia

Slice of cherry. Simon Pulse 2011 505p $16.99

Grades: 10 11 12   Fic

1. Sisters—Fiction 2. Homicide—Fiction 3. Supernatural—Fiction 4. African Americans—Fiction 5. Texas—Fiction

ISBN 978-1-4169-8620-1; 1-4169-8620-0

LC 2010-21805

Reeves, Dia—*Continued*

Portero, Texas, teens Kit and Fancy Cordelle share their infamous father's fascination with killing, and despite their tendency to shun others they bring two boys with similar tendencies to a world of endless possibilities they have discovered behind a mysterious door.

"The warm, fuzzy moral—that it's fine to be a serial killer as long as you're doing it to help others—will delight and entertain readers mature enough to appreciate that fictional morals needn't always coincide with real-life didacticism. This gleeful page-turner is a winner." Kirkus

Reichs, Kathleen J.

Virals; [by] Kathy Reichs. Penguin/Razorbill 2010 454p map $17.99

Grades: 6 7 8 9 10 **Fic**

1. Viruses—Fiction 2. Missing persons—Fiction 3. Mystery fiction

ISBN 978-1-59514-342-6; 1-59514-342-4

LC 2010-42384

Tory Brennan is the leader of a band of teenage "sciphiles" who live on an island off the coast of South Carolina and when the group rescues a dog caged for medical testing, they are exposed to an experimental strain of canine parvovirus that changes their lives forever.

"From the opening sentence to the last word, readers will be absorbed in Tory Brennan's world. . . . Reichs has found a pitch-perfect voice for Tory that will ring true with today's teens, capturing and entirely new audience." Kirkus

Reinhardt, Dana

A brief chapter in my impossible life. Wendy Lamb Books 2006 228p hardcover o.p. pa $8.99

Grades: 9 10 11 12 **Fic**

1. Adoption—Fiction 2. Jews—Fiction 3. Family life—Fiction 4. Massachusetts—Fiction

ISBN 0-385-74698-9; 0-375-84691-3 (pa)

LC 2005-3972

Sixteen-year-old atheist Simone Turner-Bloom's life changes in unexpected ways when her parents convince her to make contact with her biological mother, an agnostic from a Jewish family who is losing her battle with cancer.

"Besides offering insight into the customs of Hasidic Jews, this intimate story celebrates family love and promotes tolerance of diverse beliefs. Readers will quickly become absorbed in Simone's quest to understand her heritage and herself." Publ Wkly

Harmless. Wendy Lamb Books 2007 229p hardcover o.p. pa $8.99

Grades: 7 8 9 10 **Fic**

1. Truthfulness and falsehood—Fiction

ISBN 0-385-74699-7; 978-0-385-74699-1; 0-553-49497-X (pa); 978-0-553-49497-6 (pa)

When Anna, Emma, and Mariah concoct a story about why they are late getting home one Friday night, their lie has unimaginable consequences for the girls, their families, and the community.

"Reinhardt's thought-provoking story avoids preachiness in part because of the girls' strong, complex characterizations." Booklist

How to build a house; a novel. Wendy Lamb Books 2008 227p $15.99; lib bdg $18.99 *

Grades: 8 9 10 11 12 **Fic**

1. Building—Fiction 2. Divorce—Fiction 3. Stepfamilies—Fiction 4. Volunteer work—Fiction 5. Tennessee—Fiction

ISBN 978-0-375-84453-9; 0-375-84453-8; 978-0-375-94454-3 (lib bdg); 0-375-94454-0 (lib bdg)

LC 2007-33403

Seventeen-year-old Harper Evans hopes to escape the effects of her father's divorce on her family and friendships by volunteering her summer to build a house in a small Tennessee town devastated by a tornado.

"This meticulously crafted book illustrates how both homes and relationships can be resurrected through hard work, hope and teamwork." Publ Wkly

The things a brother knows. Wendy Lamb Books 2010 245p $16.99; lib bdg $19.99 *

Grades: 7 8 9 10 11 12 **Fic**

1. Boston (Mass.)—Fiction 2. Brothers—Fiction 3. Family life—Fiction 4. Jews—United States—Fiction 5. Soldiers—Fiction

ISBN 978-0-375-84455-3; 0-375-84455-4; 978-0-375-94455-9 (lib bdg); 0-375-94455-9 (lib bdg)

Although they have never gotten along well, seventeen-year-old Levi follows his older brother Boaz, an ex-Marine, on a walking trip from Boston to Washington, D.C. in hopes of learning why Boaz is completely withdrawn.

"Reinhardt's poignant story of a soldier coping with survivor's guilt and trauma, and his Israeli American family's struggle to understand and help, is timely and honest." Booklist

Remarque, Erich Maria, 1898-1970

All quiet on the western front; translated from the German by A.W. Wheen. Ballantine Books 1982 295p pa $6.99 *

Grades: 11 12 Adult **Fic**

1. World War, 1914-1918—Fiction

ISBN 978-0-449-21394-0; 0-449-21394-3

First published 1929 by Little, Brown

"Four German youths are pulled abruptly from school to serve at the front as soldiers in World War I. Only Paul survives, and he contemplates the needless violation of the human body by weapons of war. No longer innocent or lighthearted, he is repelled by the slaughter of soldiers and questions the usefulness of war as a means of adjudication. Although the young men in this novel are German, the message is universal in its delineation of the feelings of the common soldier." Shapiro. Fic for Youth. 3d edition

Followed by The road back

Renault, Mary, 1905-1983

Fire from heaven. 2nd Vintage Books ed. Vintage Books 2002 375p map pa $14.95

Grades: 11 12 Adult **Fic**

1. Alexander, the Great, 356-323 B.C.—Fiction 2. Philip II, King of Macedonia, 382-336 B.C.—Fiction 3. Greece—Fiction

ISBN 0-375-72682-9

LC 2002-282848

First published 1969 by Pantheon Bks.

Renault, Mary, 1905-1983—*Continued*

"This is the story of Alexander the Great from his earliest childhood until the death of his father, Philip of Macedonia. . . . We meet everyone who ever influenced the young Alexander—Aristotle, his teacher; Hephaiston, his friend and lover; Olympias, his strange priestess mother; and scores of others. This was a time of ritual feasts and bacchanalian orgies, of unbashed sexual freedom, of bloody wars and insidious plottings, of pageantry and splendor, myths and mysteries." Publ Wkly

Other books in this fictional series about the life of Alexander the Great are:
Funeral games (1981)
The Persian boy (1972)

The king must die. Pantheon Bks. 1958 338p pa $14 hardcover o.p. *

Grades: 11 12 Adult   **Fic**
1. Theseus (Greek Mythology)—Fiction 2. Classical mythology—Fiction 3. Greece—Fiction
ISBN 0-394-75104-3

"Retold by its hero, the legend of Theseus becomes a logical sequence of adventures that befell a slight, wiry, quick-witted youth impelled to prove his manhood in a semibarbaric society that put a premium on size and brawn. Although, at seventeen, he was already a king and a seasoned warrior, Theseus obeyed his patron god's prompting and voluntarily joined a company of young people conscripted for the bull-dances in Crete, became a renowned bull-leaper, and took advantage of an earthquake to overthrow the Cretan kingdom." Booklist

Followed by The bull from the sea (1962)

Rennison, Louise, 1951-

Angus, thongs and full-frontal snogging; confessions of Georgia Nicolson. HarperCollins Pubs. 2000 c1999 247p hardcover o.p. pa $6.95 *

Grades: 7 8 9 10   **Fic**
1. Great Britain—Fiction
ISBN 0-06-028814-0; 0-06-447227-2 (pa)
LC 99-40591
First published 1999 in the United Kingdom

Presents the humorous journal of a year in the life of Georgia, a fourteen-year-old British girl who tries to reduce the size of her nose, stop her mad cat from terrorizing the neighborhood animals, and win the love of handsome hunk Robbie.

"Georgia is a wonderful character whose misadventures are not only hysterically funny but universally recognizable." Booklist

Other titles about Georgia are:
Are these my basoomas I see before me? (2009)
Away laughing on a fast camel (2004)
Dancing in my nuddy-pants (2003)
Knocked out by my nunga-nungas (2002)
Love is a many trousered thing (2007)
On the bright side, I'm now the girlfriend of a sex god (2001)
Startled by his furry shorts (2006)
Stop in the name of pants (2008)
Then he ate my boy entrancers (2005)

Resau, Laura

The indigo notebook. Delacorte Press 2009 324p $16.99; lib bdg $19.99; pa $9.99

Grades: 7 8 9 10 11 12   **Fic**
1. Mother-daughter relationship—Fiction 2. Single parent family—Fiction 3. Fathers—Fiction 4. Ecuador—Fiction
ISBN 978-0-385-73652-7; 0-385-73652-5; 978-0-385-90614-2 (lib bdg); 0-385-90614-5 (lib bdg); 978-0-375-84524-6 (pa); 0-375-84524-0 (pa)
LC 2008-40519

Fifteen-year-old Zeeta comes to terms with her flighty mother and their itinerant life when, soon after moving to Ecuador, she helps an American teenager find his birth father in a nearby village

"Observant, aware, and occasionally wry, Zeeta's first-person narration will attract readers and hold them." Booklist

Followed by: The ruby notebook (2010)

The Queen of Water; [by] Laura Resau and Maria Virginia Farinango. Delacorte Press 2011 352p $16.99; lib bdg $19.99 *

Grades: 7 8 9 10   **Fic**
1. Ecuador—Fiction 2. Social classes—Fiction
ISBN 978-0-385-73897-2; 0-385-73897-8; 978-0-385-90761-3 (lib bdg); 0-385-90761-3 (lib bdg)
LC 2010-10512

Living in a village in Ecuador, a Quechua Indian girl is sent to work as an indentured servant for an upper class "mestizo" family.

"The complexities of class and ethnicity within Ecuadorian society are explained seamlessly within the context of the first-person narrative, and a glossary and pronunciation guide further help to plunge readers into the novel's world. By turns heartbreaking, infuriating and ultimately inspiring." Kirkus

Red glass. Delacorte Press 2007 275p $15.99; lib bdg $18.99

Grades: 7 8 9 10   **Fic**
1. Automobile travel—Fiction 2. Orphans—Fiction 3. Mexico—Fiction 4. Guatemala—Fiction 5. Family life—Fiction
ISBN 978-0-385-73466-0; 0-385-73466-2; 978-0-385-90464-3 (lib bdg); 0-385-90464-9 (lib bdg)
LC 2007-02408

Sixteen-year-old Sophie has been frail and delicate since her premature birth, but discovers her true strength during a journey through Mexico, where the six-year-old orphan her family hopes to adopt was born, and to Guatemala, where her would-be boyfriend hopes to find his mother and plans to remain.

"The vivid characters, the fine imagery, and the satisfying story arc make this a rewarding novel." Booklist

Restrepo, Bettina

Illegal. Katherine Tegen Books 2011 251p $16.99

Grades: 7 8 9 10   **Fic**
1. Illegal aliens—Fiction 2. Mexicans—Fiction 3. Texas—Fiction
ISBN 978-0-06-195342-2; 0-06-195342-3
LC 2010-19451

Restrepo, Bettina—*Continued*

Nora, a fifteen-year-old Mexican girl, faces the challenges of being an illegal immigrant in Texas when she and her mother cross the border in search of Nora's father.

"Restrepo's novel offers an unsparing immigrant story that is both gritty and redemptive. . . . This is urban realism meets quest tale, told with great emotional immediacy, and it will appeal to many teen readers." Bull Cent Child Books

Revis, Beth

Across the universe. Razorbill 2011 398p $17.99

Grades: 7 8 9 10   **Fic**

1. Space vehicles—Fiction 2. Dictators—Fiction 3. Science fiction

ISBN 978-1-59514-397-6; 1-59514-397-1

LC 2010-51834

Amy, a cryogenically frozen passenger aboard the vast spaceship Godspeed, is nearly killed when her cyro chamber is unplugged fifty years before Godspeed's scheduled landing. All she knows is that she must race to unlock Godspeed's hidden secrets before whoever woke her tries to kill again—and she doesn't know who she can trust on a ship ruled by a tyrant.

"Revis's tale hits all of the standard dystopian notes, while presenting a believable romance and a series of tantalizing mysteries that will hold readers' attention." Publ Wkly

Rex, Adam

Fat vampire; a never coming of age story. Balzer + Bray 2010 324p $16.99

Grades: 9 10 11 12   **Fic**

1. Vampires—Fiction 2. Obesity—Fiction 3. Television programs—Fiction 4. School stories

ISBN 978-0-06-192090-5   LC 2010-9616

After being bitten by a vampire, not only is fifteen-year-old Doug doomed eternally to be fat, but now he must also save himself from the desperate host of a public-access-cable vampire-hunting television show that is on the verge of cancellation.

"Rex successfully sustains the wonderfully dry humor and calculated silliness and then surprises the reader with a thoughtful, poignant, ambiguous ending that is bound to inspire discussion." Booklist

Reynolds, Marilyn, 1935-

Shut up! Morning Glory Press 2009 245p (True-to-life series from Hamilton High) $15.95; pa $9.95

Grades: 9 10 11 12   **Fic**

1. Child sexual abuse—Fiction 2. Brothers—Fiction

ISBN 978-1-932538-93-9; 1-932538-93-3; 978-1-932538-88-5 (pa); 1-932538-88-7 (pa)

LC 2008-933535

Seventeen-year-old Mario promises he'll take care of his nine-year-old brother, Eddie, while their mother serves in the National Guard in Iraq and soon realizes that Eddie desperately needs help.

This book "presents a marginalized issue—sexual abuse of boys—in a frank, thoughtful, and sensitive manner." Voice Youth Advocates

Rich, Naomi

Alis. Viking Children's Books 2009 274p $17.99

Grades: 7 8 9 10   **Fic**

1. Marriage—Fiction 2. Runaway teenagers—Fiction 3. Religion—Fiction

ISBN 978-0-670-01125-4; 0-670-01125-8

LC 2008-23234

Raised within the strict religious confines of the Community of the Book, Alis flees from an arranged marriage to the much older Minister of her town and her life takes a series of unexpected twists before she returns to accept her fate.

"Rich's sympathetic portrayal of Alis and her desperate struggle to exercise free will in a theocracy will have audiences firmly gripped." Publ Wkly

Rich, Simon

Elliot Allagash; a novel. Random House 2010 227p $23

Grades: 11 12 Adult   **Fic**

1. Wealth—Fiction 2. Money—Fiction 3. Friendship—Fiction 4. School stories

ISBN 978-1-4000-6835-7   LC 2009-43885

"The book follows the trial by fire of the narrator, Seymour, an obese but grudgingly docile eighth-grader at a posh Manhattan private school. He's the sort of kid who puts up with the school's arcane policy of putting any student involved in a scrap in detention—which means Seymour is in detention every week just for getting beaten up. His life changes dramatically when another character, an arrogant little bastard who stands to inherit an unimaginable fortune, takes an interest in Seymour's future. . . . Before long Seymour is stealing test answers; accepting a devilish bargain to sneak into Harvard; and corrupting the simplistic social systems of school to rise to the top of its hierarchy, no matter what it costs. . . . Rich is always funny, and he nails the bogus solemnity of high-school social politics. A high-school romp that John Hughes should be so lucky to direct." Kirkus

Richards, Jame

Three rivers rising; a novel of the Johnstown flood. Alfred A. Knopf 2010 293p $16.99; lib bdg $19.99

Grades: 6 7 8 9 10   **Fic**

1. Novels in verse 2. Floods—Fiction 3. Social classes—Fiction 4. Pennsylvania—Fiction

ISBN 978-0-375-85885-7; 0-375-85885-7; 978-0-375-95885-4 (lib bdg); 0-375-95885-1 (lib bdg)

LC 2009-4251

Sixteen-year-old Celestia is a wealthy member of the South Fork Fishing and Hunting Club, where she meets and falls in love with Peter, a hired hand who lives in the valley below, and by the time of the torrential rains that lead to the disastrous Johnstown flood of 1889, she has been disowned by her family and is staying with him in Johnstown. Includes an author's note and historical timeline.

This is a "striking novel in verse. . . . Richards builds strong characters with few words and artfully interweaves the lives of these independent thinkers." Publ Wkly

Includes bibliographical references

Richards, Justin, 1961-

The chaos code. Bloomsbury Children's Books 2007 388p $17.95

Grades: 7 8 9 10   **Fic**
1. Ciphers—Fiction 2. Adventure fiction
3. Supernatural—Fiction 4. Atlantis—Fiction
5. Mystery fiction

ISBN 978-1-59990-124-4; 1-59990-124-2

LC 2006-102609

Fifteen-year-old Matt and his new friend Robin search the globe to retrieve an ancient code—rumored to have brought down the ancient civilization of Atlantis—from the hands of a madman who is bent on destroying the modern world.

"This novel combines intrigue, adventure, and cryptography with masterful pacing and age-old mysteries. . . . Riveting." Voice Youth Advocates

Richmond, Michelle, 1970-

No one you know; a novel. Delacorte Press 2008 306p pa $15

Grades: 10 11 12 Adult   **Fic**
1. Sisters—Fiction 2. Homicide—Fiction 3. Mystery fiction

ISBN   978-0-385-34013-7;   0-385-34013-3;
978-0-385-34014-4 (pa); 0-385-34014-1 (pa)

LC 2008-13508

"Twenty years ago, Ellie Enderlin's sister, Lila, a mathematical prodigy, was murdered, and Andrew Thorpe, Ellie's English professor and a friend, exploited the family's grief with a true-crime bestseller that claimed Peter McConnell, Lila's married lover and colleague, was the killer. On a coffee-buying trip to Nicaragua, Ellie encounters McConnell, whose life was destroyed by Thorpe's conjecture. Sparked by this meeting, Ellie traces her way back through Lila's life and work, pursuing leads that the manipulative Thorpe abandoned when they did not fit his literary ambitions." Publ Wkly

"As complex and beautiful as a mathematical proof, this gripping, thought-provoking novel will keep you thinking long after the last page has been turned." Family Circle

Riordan, James, 1936-

The sniper. Frances Lincoln Children's Books 2009 229p il pa $8.95

Grades: 9 10 11 12   **Fic**
1. Stalingrad, Battle of, 1942-1943—Fiction 2. War stories

ISBN 978-1-84507-885-0

This is the story of a teenage sniper recruited in 1942 to seek out and shoot German officers. At first Tania finds it impossible to kill, but after a shocking discovery goes on to kill as many as 84 Germans.

"There is a deep poignancy and a moral tone here, along with exciting action, heroism and anguish. . . . This fine volume will appeal to many readers." Kirkus

Ritter, John H., 1951-

Under the baseball moon. Philomel Books 2006 283p $16.99

Grades: 7 8 9 10   **Fic**
1. Softball—Fiction 2. Musicians—Fiction
3. California—Fiction

ISBN 0-399-23623-6   LC 2005-27183

Andy and Glory, two fifteen-year-olds from Ocean Beach, California, pursue their respective dreams of becoming a famous musician and a professional softball player.

"Andy's poetic first-person narrative superbly catches the weird uniqueness of Ocean Beach and briskly moves the . . . story to a satisfying conclusion." SLJ

Robinson, Kim Stanley

Forty signs of rain. Bantam Books 2004 358p hardcover o.p. pa $7.99

Grades: 9 10 11 12   **Fic**
1. Science fiction 2. Washington (D.C.)—Fiction

ISBN 0-553-80311-5; 0-553-58580-0 (pa)

LC 2003-63683

"The specter of global warming looms over the personal and professional lives of several scientists at the National Science Foundation and the delegation of Buddhist refugees from a drowned nation, who open an embassy next door." SLJ

The author's "portrayal of how actual scientists would deal with this disaster-in-the-making is utterly convincing. Robinson clearly cares deeply about our planet's future, and he makes the reader care as well." Publ Wkly

Other titles in this series are:

Fifty degrees below (2005)
Sixty days and counting (2007)

Red Mars. Bantam Books 1993 519p il hardcover o.p. pa $7.99 *

Grades: 11 12 Adult   **Fic**
1. Mars (Planet)—Fiction 2. Science fiction

ISBN 0-553-09204-9; 0-553-56073-5 (pa)

LC 92-21607

This novel, the first of a trilogy "concerns the first permanent settlement on Mars, a multinational band of 100 hardy experts, and their mission—to begin making Mars habitable for humans by releasing underground water and oxygen into the atmosphere. Unfortunately, they are divided over whether this is a desirable step in human evolution or an ecological crime." Booklist

"A novel fully inhabited both by detailed technical processes and by people whose careers those processes are; it is also a novel with a complex sense of political reality. . . . This is one of the finest works of American SF because it is one of the few that aspire to the dignity of the genuinely tragic." Times Lit Suppl

Other titles in the Mars trilogy are:

Blue Mars (1996)
Green Mars (1994)

Roesch, Mattox, 1977-
Sometimes we're always real same-same.
Unbridled Books 2009 317p pa $15.95
Grades: 11 12 Adult Fic
1. Cousins—Fiction 2. Inuit—Fiction 3. Country life—Fiction 4. Alaska—Fiction
ISBN 978-1-9329618-74; 1-9329618-79
LC 2009-17497
Troubled Cesar is stuck in nowhere Alaska because his Eskimo mother has moved home where she hopes both of them can carve out a fresh start. He's just biding his time until he can return to L.A., but his offbeat cousin Go-boy is convinced Cesar will stay, so they make a wager. If Cesar is still in Unalakleet in a year, he has to get a copy of Go-Boy's Eskimo Jesus tattoo. Gradually Cesar discovers the power of friendship and the potential positive strength that springs from a tight-knit community.
"Roesch's compelling story, exotic setting and eccentric characters make this coming-of-age tale a fresh, welcome read." Publ Wkly

Rorby, Ginny, 1944-
The outside of a horse; a novel. Dial Books for Young Readers 2010 343p $16.99
Grades: 7 8 9 10 Fic
1. Horses—Fiction 2. Father-daughter relationship—Fiction 3. Amputees—Fiction 4. Veterans—Fiction
ISBN 978-0-8037-3478-4; 0-8037-3478-6
LC 2009-25101
When her father returns from the Iraq War as an amputee with post-traumatic stress disorder, Hannah escapes by volunteering to work with rescued horses, never thinking that the abused horses could also help her father recover.
Hannah "comes across as a believable teen. As a backdrop to the story, Rorby has interwoven a good deal of disturbing information about animal cruelty. Horse lovers and most others will saddle up right away with this poignant tale." Booklist

Rosen, Renée
Every crooked pot. St. Martin's Griffin 2007 227p pa $8.95 *
Grades: 7 8 9 10 Fic
1. Father-daughter relationship—Fiction 2. Birth defects—Fiction
ISBN 978-0-312-36543-1; 0-312-36543-8
LC 2007-10457
"Rosen looks back at the life of Nina Goldman, whose growing up is tied to two pillars: a port-wine stain around her eye and her inimitable father, Artie. The birthmark, she hates; her father, she loves. Both shape her in ways that merit Rosen's minute investigation. . . . There's real power in the writing." Booklist

Roth, Philip
The plot against America. Houghton Mifflin 2004 391p $26
Grades: 11 12 Adult Fic
1. Lindbergh, Charles, 1902-1974—Fiction 2. Jews—Fiction 3. New Jersey—Fiction 4. Antisemitism—Fiction
ISBN 0-618-50928-3 LC 2004-47490

Also available in paperback from Vintage
In this alternative history novel, "Charles Lindbergh is elected president in 1940 on a pro-Nazi platform, and a Jewish family in Newark suffers the consequences." N Y Times Book Rev
This book "engages readers in many ways. It prompts them to consider the nature of history, present times, and possible futures, and can lead to good discussions among thoughtful readers and teachers." SLJ

Rowling, J. K.
Harry Potter and the Sorcerer's Stone; illustrations by Mary Grandpré. Arthur A. Levine Bks. 1998 c1997 309p il $22.99; pa $8.99 *
Grades: 4 5 6 7 8 9 10 Fic
1. Fantasy fiction 2. Witches—Fiction
ISBN 0-590-35340-3; 0-590-35342-X (pa)
LC 97-39059
First published 1997 in the United Kingdom with title: Harry Potter and the Philosopher's Stone
Rescued from the outrageous neglect of his aunt and uncle, a young boy with a great destiny proves his worth while attending Hogwarts School for Witchcraft and Wizardry.
This "is a brilliantly imagined and beautifully written fantasy." Booklist
Other titles in this series are:
Harry Potter and the Chamber of Secrets (1999)
Harry Potter and the Deathly Hallows (2007)
Harry Potter and Goblet of Fire (2000)
Harry Potter and the Half-Blood Prince (2005)
Harry Potter and the Order of the Phoenix (2003)
Harry Potter and the prisoner of Azkaban (1999)

Roy, Arundhati
The god of small things. Random House Trade Paperbacks 2008 333p (Telling stories!) pa $16
Grades: 11 12 Adult Fic
1. Family life—Fiction 2. Twins—Fiction 3. India—Fiction
ISBN 978-0-8129-7965-7
First published 1997
A novel "set in the tiny river town of Ayemenem in Kerala, India. The story revolves around a pair of twins, brother and sister, whose mother has left her violent husband to live with her blind mother and kind, if ineffectual, brother, Chacko. Chacko's ex-wife, an Englishwoman, has returned to Ayemenem after a long absence, bringing along her and Chacko's lovely young daughter. Their arrival not only unsettles the already tenuous balance of the divisive household, it also coincides with political unrest." Booklist
"If the symbolism is a trifle overdone, the lush local color and the incisive characterizations give the narrative power and drama." Publ Wkly

Roy, Jennifer Rozines, 1967-
Mindblind; [by] Jennifer Roy. Marshall Cavendish 2010 248p il $15.99 *
Grades: 7 8 9 10 11 Fic
1. Asperger's syndrome—Fiction 2. Genius—Fiction 3. Bands (Music)—Fiction
ISBN 978-0-7614-5716-9; 0-7614-5716-X
LC 2010-6966

Roy, Jennifer Rozines, 1967—*Continued*

Fourteen-year-old Nathaniel Clark, who has Asperger's Syndrome, tries to prove that he is a genius by writing songs for his rock band, so that he can become a member of the prestigious Aldus Institute, the premier organization for the profoundly gifted.

"Mature readers will empathize with Nathaniel as his friends, Jessa and Cooper, do. This book is for teens who appreciate a story about self-discovery, dreams, and friendship." Voice Youth Advocates

Ruby, Laura

Bad apple. HarperTeen 2009 247p $16.99; pa $8.99 *

Grades: 8 9 10 11 12   **Fic**
1. Teacher-student relationship—Fiction 2. Bullies—Fiction 3. Divorce—Fiction 4. School stories
ISBN   978-0-06-124330-1;   0-06-124330-2; 978-0-06-124333-2 (pa); 0-06-124333-7 (pa)
                   LC 2009-1409

Tola Riley, a high school junior, struggles to tell the truth when she and her art teacher are accused of having an affair.

"Tola and her family are fascinating, quirky-yet-believable, and wholly likable. Ruby works in traditional fairy-tale elements . . . with wry humor." Booklist

Ruditis, Paul

The four Dorothys. Simon Pulse 2007 236p (Drama!) pa $8.99

Grades: 7 8 9 10   **Fic**
1. Musicals—Fiction 2. Theater—Fiction 3. School stories
ISBN 978-1-4169-3391-5   LC 2006-928449

The students at the Orion Academy put on a musical based on the Wizard of Oz. Due to their egotism, four of them have the part of Dorothy, but as opening night approaches, the Dorothys drop out of the show one-by-one. Bryan Stark must find out why in order to keep the musical from being cancelled.

"Swift pacing and tightly layered subplots keep pages turning through this refreshing take on some familiar high school dramas." SLJ

Ruiz Zafón, Carlos, 1964-

The Prince of Mist; translated by Lucia Graves. Little, Brown 2010 320p $17.99

Grades: 6 7 8 9 10   **Fic**
1. Supernatural—Fiction 2. Magic—Fiction 3. Dead—Fiction 4. Siblings—Fiction 5. Shipwrecks—Fiction 6. Europe—History—1918-1945—Fiction
ISBN 978-0-316-04477-6; 0-316-04477-6
                   LC 2009-51256

In 1943, in a seaside town where their family has gone to be safe from war, thirteen-year-old Max Carver and sister, fifteen-year-old Alicia, with new friend Roland, face off against an evil magician who is striving to complete a bargain made before he died.

"Zafon is a master storyteller. From the first page, the reader is drawn into the mystery and suspense that the young people encounter when they move into the Fleischmann house. . . . This book can be read and enjoyed by every level of reader." Voice Youth Advocates

Runyon, Brent

Surface tension; a novel in four summers. Alfred A. Knopf 2009 197p $16.99; lib bdg $19.99

Grades: 8 9 10 11   **Fic**
1. Vacations—Fiction 2. Family life—Fiction 3. New York (State)—Fiction
ISBN   978-0-375-84446-1;   0-375-84446-5; 978-0-375-94446-8 (lib bdg); 0-375-94446-X (lib bdg)
                   LC 2008-9193

During the summer vacations of his thirteenth through his sixteenth year at the family's lake cottage, Luke realizes that although some things stay the same over the years that many more change.

"With sensitivity and candor, Runyon reveals how life changes us all and how these unavoidable changes can be full of both turmoil and wonder." Kirkus

Rushdie, Salman

Haroun and the sea of stories. Granta Books in association with Viking 1990 219p pa $14 hardcover o.p. *

Grades: 9 10 11 12 Adult   **Fic**
1. Allegories
ISBN 0-14-015737-9 (pa)   LC 90-45496

"This delightful fantasy is filled with adventures, amusing characters with names like Iff and Butt, and villains to fight against and defeat. Rushdie's puns and rhymes will be enjoyed by young and old—the catchy tunes by the younger readers and the political allegory by the adults. Rashid is a professional story-teller whose son, Haroun, delights in hearing them. When Rashid's source of stories seems to have disappeared Haroun faces many dangerous opponents to help his father regain his Gift of Gab." Shapiro. Fic for Youth. 3d edition

Ryan, Amy Kathleen

Zen & Xander undone. Houghton Mifflin Harcourt 2010 212p $16

Grades: 8 9 10 11 12   **Fic**
1. Sisters—Fiction   2. Bereavement—Fiction 3. Death—Fiction 4. Family life—Fiction
ISBN 978-0-547-06248-8; 0-547-06248-6

Two teenaged sisters try to come to terms with the death of their mother in very different ways.

"Literate, believable, funny, and sometimes profound, this book has broad appeal." Voice Youth Advocates

Ryan, Carrie

The Forest of Hands and Teeth. Delacorte Press 2009 310p $16.99; lib bdg $19.99 *

Grades: 9 10 11 12   **Fic**
1. Orphans—Fiction 2. Zombies—Fiction 3. Horror fiction
ISBN 978-0-385-73681-7; 978-0-385-90631-9 (lib bdg)   LC 2008-06494

Through twists and turns of fate, orphaned Mary seeks knowledge of life, love, and especially what lies beyond her walled village and the surrounding forest, where dwell the Unconsecrated, aggressive flesh-eating people who were once dead.

"Mary's observant, careful narration pulls readers into

Ryan, Carrie—*Continued*
a bleak but gripping story of survival and the endless capacity of humanity to persevere. . . . Fresh and riveting." Publ Wkly
 Other titles in this series are:
The dark and hollow places (2011)
The dead-tossed waves (2010)

Ryan, Patrick, 1965-
 Gemini bites. Scholastic Press 2011 231p $17.99
Grades: 8 9 10 11 12   **Fic**
 1.   Vampires—Fiction   2.   Twins—Fiction
3. Homosexuality—Fiction 4. Dating (Social customs)—Fiction
 ISBN 978-0-545-22128-3; 0-545-22128-5
 When their parents announce they are taking in a fellow student for a month, 16-year-old twins Kyle and Judy sit up and take notice. Kyle has just come out of the closet to his family and fears he'll never know what it is like to date a guy. Judy is pretending to be born-again to attract a boy who heads a Bible study group. And Garret Johnson is new in town a mysterious loner who claims to be a vampire. Both twins are intrigued.
 "Writing with humor and empathy in equal measure, Ryan . . . presents a touching gay romance as well as a pair of well-rounded and entertaining narrators who come to respect each other." Publ Wkly

 In Mike we trust; [by] P. E. Ryan. HarperTeen 2009 321p $16.99
Grades: 8 9 10 11 12   **Fic**
 1. Homosexuality—Fiction   2. Uncles—Fiction
3. Swindlers and swindling—Fiction
 ISBN 978-0-06-085813-1; 0-06-085813-3
                                     LC 2008-11722
 As fifteen-year-old Garth is wrestling with the promise he made his mother to wait a while before coming out, his somewhat secretive uncle shows up unexpectedly for an extended visit.
 "The author's use of language, at times brilliantly translucent, provides insightful dialogue. This contemporary coming-of-age story set in Richmond, VA, subtly and clearly provides a fresh perspective on teenage sexual identity by imbedding it into the context of the bigger issue of truth." SLJ

Sachar, Louis, 1954-
 The cardturner; a novel about a king, a queen, and a joker. Delacorte Press 2010 336p $17.99; lib bdg $20.99
Grades: 8 9 10 11 12   **Fic**
 1. Bridge (Game)—Fiction   2. Uncles—Fiction
3. Family life—Fiction
 ISBN   978-0-385-73662-6;   0-385-73662-2;
978-0-385-90619-7 (lib bdg); 0-385-90619-6 (lib bdg)
                                     LC 2009-27585
 "Alton gets roped into serving as a card turner for his great-uncle, Lester Trapp, a bridge whizz who recently lost his eyesight. . . . To Alton's surprise, he becomes enamored of the game and begins to bond with his crusty uncle. . . . With dry, understated humor, Alton makes the intricacies of bridge accessible, while his relationships with and observations about family members and friends . . . form a portrait of a reflective teenager

whose life is infinitely enriched by connections he never expected to make." Publ Wkly

Saenz, Benjamin Alire
 He forgot to say good-bye. Simon & Schuster 2008 321p $16.99
Grades: 8 9 10 11   **Fic**
 1. Drug abuse—Fiction 2. Mexican Americans—Fiction
 ISBN 978-1-4169-4963-3; 1-4169-4963-1
                                     LC 2007-21959
 Two teenaged boys with very different lives find that they share a common bond—fathers they have never met who left when they were small boys—and in spite of their differences, they become close when they each need someone who understands.
 "The affirming and hopeful ending is well-earned for the characters and a great payoff for the reader. . . . Characters are well-developed and complex. . . . Overall it is a strong novel with broad teenage appeal." Voice Youth Advocates

 Last night I sang to the monster; a novel. Cinco Puntos Press 2009 239p $16.95 *
Grades: 9 10 11 12   **Fic**
 1. Psychotherapy—Fiction 2. Alcoholism—Fiction
3. Family life—Fiction
 ISBN 978-1-933693-58-3; 1-933693-58-4
                                     LC 2009-15833
 Eighteen-year-old Zach does not remember how he came to be in a treatment center for alcoholics, but through therapy and caring friends, his amnesia fades and he learns to face his past while working toward a better future.
 "Saenz' poetic narrative will captivate readers from the first sentence to the last paragraph of this beautifully written novel, which explores the painful journey of an adolescent through the labyrinth of addiction and alcoholism. It is also a celebration of life and a song of hope in celebration of family and friendship, one that will resonate loud and long with teens." Kirkus

 Sammy and Juliana in Hollywood; by Benjamin Alire Saenz. Cinco Puntos Press 2004 294p hardcover o.p. pa $11.95 *
Grades: 9 10 11 12   **Fic**
 1. Mexican Americans—Fiction 2. Violence—Fiction
3. New Mexico—Fiction
 ISBN 0-938317-81-4; 1-933693-99-1 (pa)
                                     LC 2004-2414
 As a Chicano boy living in the unglamorous town of Hollywood, New Mexico, and a member of the graduating class of 1969, Sammy Santos faces the challenges of "gringo" racism, unpopular dress codes, the Vietnam War, barrio violence, and poverty

Saint-Exupéry, Antoine de, 1900-1944

The little prince; written and illustrated by
Antoine de Saint-Exupery; translated from the
French by Richard Howard. Harcourt 2000 83p il
$18; pa $12

Grades: 4 5 6 7 8 9 10 11 12 Adult   **Fic**
1. Fantasy fiction 2. Air pilots—Fiction 3. Princes—
Fiction 4. Extraterrestrial beings—Fiction
ISBN 0-15-202398-4; 0-15-601219-7 (pa)

                                        LC 99-50439
A new translation of the title first published 1943 by
Reynal & Hitchcock

"This many-dimensional fable of an airplane pilot who
has crashed in the desert is for readers of all ages. The
pilot comes upon the little prince soon after the crash.
The prince tells of his adventures on different planets
and on Earth as he attempts to learn about the universe
in order to live peacefully on his own small planet. A
spiritual quality enhances the seemingly simple observations of the little prince." Shapiro. Fic for Youth. 3d edition

Saldaña, René

A good long way; by Rene Saldana, Jr. Piñata
Books 2010 103p pa $10.95

Grades: 8 9 10 11   **Fic**
1. Brothers—Fiction 2. Mexican Americans—Fiction
3. Runaway teenagers—Fiction 4. School stories
5. Texas—Fiction
ISBN 978-1-55885-607-3; 1-55885-607-2

                                        LC 2010-32989
Three Mexican American teenagers in a small-town in
Texas struggle with difficulties at home and at school as
they try to attain the elusive status of adulthood.

"This fast-paced novel will make readers think about
their own lives and responsibilities." SLJ

Salerni, Dianne K.

We hear the dead. Sourcebooks Fire 2010 422p
pa $9.99

Grades: 7 8 9 10   **Fic**
1.   Fox,   Margaret,   1833-1893—Fiction
2. Spiritualism—Fiction 3. Sisters—Fiction 4. New
York (State)—Fiction
ISBN 978-1-4022-3092-9; 1-4022-3092-3

"In upstate New York in 1848, two young sisters,
Maggie and Kate Fox, created a spiritual hoax to frighten
a detested cousin. . . . They convinced their family and
then the whole town that they could communicate with
ghosts. What began as a childhood prank turned into
their adult livelihood, and the sisters became famous.
. . . Much of the book's later half focuses on a passionate, fraught romance between Maggie and a wealthy explorer." Booklist

The author "paints vivid scenes of life in upstate New
York during a time when exposed ankles were shocking
and the Underground Railroad offered a dangerous route
to freedom for both conductors and slaves. Historical fiction at its best." SLJ

Sales, Leila

Mostly good girls. Simon Pulse 2010 347p
$16.99

Grades: 9 10 11 12   **Fic**
1.   Friendship—Fiction   2.   Ability—Fiction
3.   Authorship—Fiction   4.   School   stories
5. Massachusetts—Fiction
ISBN 978-1-4424-0679-7   LC 2010-7190
Sixteen-year-olds Violet and Katie, best friends since
seventh grade despite differences in their family backgrounds and abilities, are pulled apart during their junior
year at Massachusetts' exclusive Westfield School.

"This exploration of growing up, personal change and
angst is well-written." Voice of Youth Advocates

Salinger, J. D., 1919-2010

The catcher in the rye. Little, Brown 1951 277p
$24.95; pa $5.99 *

Grades: 11 12 Adult   **Fic**
1. New York (N.Y.)—Fiction
ISBN 0-316-76953-3; 0-316-76948-7 (pa)
"The story of adolescent Holden Caulfield who runs
away from boarding-school in Pennsylvania to New York
where he preserves his innocence despite various attempts to lose it. The colloquial, lively, first-person narration, with its attacks on the 'phoniness' of the adult
world and its clinging to family sentiment in the form of
Holden's affection for his sister Phoebe, made the novel
accessible to and popular with a wide readership, particularly with the young." Oxford Companion to Engl Lit.
5th edition

Franny & Zooey. Little, Brown 1961 201p
$24.95; pa $5.99

Grades: 11 12 Adult   **Fic**
1. Family life—Fiction 2. New York (N.Y.)—Fiction
ISBN 0-316-76954-1; 0-316-76949-5 (pa)
"At 20, Franny Glass is experiencing desperate dissat-
isfaction with her life and seems to be looking for help
via a religious awakening. Her brother Zooey tries to
help her out of this depression. He recalls the influence
on their growth and development of their appearance as
young radio performers on a network program called
'It's a Wise Child.' An older brother, Buddy, is also an
important component of the interrelationships in the
Glass family." Shapiro. Fic for Youth. 3d edition

Raise high the roof beam, carpenters, and
Seymour: an introduction. Little, Brown 1963 248p
$24.95

Grades: 11 12 Adult   **Fic**
1. Family life—Fiction 2. New York (N.Y.)—Fiction
ISBN 0-316-76957-6
This volume "reprints stories from *The New Yorker*
(1955, 1959), in which Buddy Glass tells, first, of his return to New York during the war to attend his brother
Seymour's wedding and of Seymour's jilting of the bride
and then of their later elopement; and, second, after Seymour's suicide, of Buddy's own brooding, to the point of
breakdown, upon Seymour's virtues, human and literary."
Oxford Companion to Am Lit. 6th edition

Salisbury, Graham, 1944-

Eyes of the emperor. Wendy Lamb Books 2005
228p hardcover o.p. pa $6.99 *

Grades: 7 8 9 10   **Fic**
1. World War, 1939-1945—Fiction 2. Japanese Americans—Fiction
ISBN 0-385-72971-5; 0-440-22956-1 (pa)

LC 2004-15142

Following orders from the United States Army, several young Japanese American men train K-9 units to hunt Asians during World War II.

"Based on the experiences of 26 Hawaiian-Americans of Japanese ancestry, this novel tells an uncomfortable story. Yet it tells of belief in honor, respect, and love of country." Libr Media Connect

Under the blood-red sun. Delacorte Press 1994
246p hardcover o.p. pa $5.99 *

Grades: 5 6 7 8 9 10   **Fic**
1. Pearl Harbor (Oahu, Hawaii), Attack on, 1941—Fiction 2. World War, 1939-1945—Fiction
3. Japanese Americans—Fiction 4. Hawaii—Fiction
ISBN 0-385-32099-X; 0-440-41139-4 (pa)

LC 94-444

Tomikazu Nakaji's biggest concerns are baseball, homework, and a local bully, until life with his Japanese family in Hawaii changes drastically after the bombing of Pearl Harbor in December 1941

"Character development of major figures is good, the setting is warmly realized, and the pace of the story moves gently though inexorably forward." SLJ

Followed by: House of the red fish (2006)

Salmon, Dena K.

Discordia; the eleventh dimension.
Disney/Hyperion Books 2009 223p $16.99

Grades: 6 7 8 9 10   **Fic**
1. Science fiction 2. Fantasy fiction
ISBN 978-1-4231-1109-2; 1-4231-1109-5

LC 2010-280666

"Lance is your everyday New York City teen, juggling school and parents as best he can, but really living for the mystical online world of Discordia, where he comes alive as his alter ego, a level 17 zombie sorcerer. But the line between reality and online gaming blurs and then fades altogether when he and his friend MrsKeller are recruited to join the Awaken Myths Guild by TheGreatOne, a level 60 player. Suddenly, a snow day in the Big Apple becomes a journey though an unknown but oddly familiar landscape, where little—if anything—makes sense anymore. . . . This is Alice in Wonderland turned upside down and made into a whiz-bang, nonstop read for the modern gamer." Kirkus

Salter, Sydney

Swoon at your own risk. Graphia 2010 356p pa
$8.99

Grades: 9 10 11 12   **Fic**
1. Dating (Social customs)—Fiction 2. Summer employment—Fiction 3. Grandmothers—Fiction
ISBN 978-0-15-206649-9; 0-15-206649-7

After a junior hear of dating disasters, Polly—the granddaughter of a famous advice columnist—swears off boys. But when her grandmother moves in for the summer, Polly mistakenly believes she'll be getting great advice when in reality, she discovers that her grandmother is a man-crazed sexagenarian.

"This book is a light read with an emotional awakening and enough romance to keep fans of the genre interested." SLJ

Sanchez, Alex, 1957-

Bait. Simon & Schuster Books for Young
Readers 2009 239p $16.99

Grades: 7 8 9 10   **Fic**
1. Child sexual abuse—Fiction 2. Stepfathers—Fiction
3. Mexican Americans—Fiction
ISBN 978-1-4169-3772-2; 1-4169-3772-2

LC 2008-38815

Diego keeps getting into trouble because of his explosive temper until he finally finds a probation officer who helps him get to the root of his anger so that he can stop running from his past.

"This groundbreaking novel brings to life an appealing young man who is neither totally a victim nor a victimizer, one who struggles to handle conflicts that derail many young lives. . . . High interest and accessible, this coming-of-age story belongs in every collection." SLJ

Getting it. Simon & Schuster 2006 210p $16.95;
pa $8.99

Grades: 9 10 11 12   **Fic**
1. Homosexuality—Fiction 2. Friendship—Fiction
3. Mexican Americans—Fiction 4. School stories
ISBN   978-1-4169-0896-8;   1-4169-0896-X;
978-1-4169-0898-2 (pa); 1-4169-0898-6 (pa)

LC 2005-29905

Hoping to impress a sexy female classmate, fifteen-year-old Carlos secretly hires gay student Sal to give him an image makeover, in exchange for Carlos's help in forming a Gay-Straight Alliance at their Texas high school.

"This title's sexual frankness may make it a controversial choice, particularly for school libraries in more conservative communities, but its themes, appeal, and readability make it a nearly essential purchase." Voice Youth Advocates

Rainbow boys. Simon & Schuster 2001 233p
hardcover o.p. pa $8.99

Grades: 10 11 12   **Fic**
1. Homosexuality—Fiction 2. School stories
ISBN 0-689-84100-0; 0-689-85770-5 (pa)

LC 2001-20952

Three high school seniors, a jock with a girlfriend and an alcoholic father, a closeted gay, and a flamboyant gay rights advocate, struggle with family issues, gay bashers, first sex, and conflicting feelings about each other.

"Some of the language and sexual situations may be too mature for some readers, but overall there's enough conflict, humor and tenderness to make this story believable—and touching." Publ Wkly

Other titles featuring Nelson, Kyle, and Jason are:
Rainbow High (2004)
Rainbow road (2005)

Sandell, Lisa Ann, 1977-
Song of the sparrow. Scholastic Press 2007
394p $16.99; pa $8.99 *
Grades: 8 9 10 11 12   **Fic**
1. War stories 2. Knights and knighthood—Fiction
3. Great Britain—History—0-1066—Fiction
ISBN   978-0-439-91848-0;   0-439-91848-0;
978-0-439-91849-7 (pa); 0-439-91849-9 (pa)
                                    LC 2007-00016
In fifth-century Britain, nine years after the destruction
of their home on the island of Shalott brings her to live
with her father and brothers in the military encampments
of Arthur's army, seventeen-year-old Elaine describes her
changing perceptions of war and the people around her
as she becomes increasingly involved in the bitter struggle against the invading Saxons.

The author "invents a unique and eloquently wrought
addition to Arthurian lore in 44 verses. . . . The poetic
narrative . . . evokes a remarkable range (and natural
progression) of emotions." Publ Wkly

Sanders, Scott Loring, 1970-
Gray baby; a novel. Houghton Mifflin Harcourt
2009 321p $17
Grades: 7 8 9 10   **Fic**
1. Racially mixed people—Fiction 2. Single parent
family—Fiction   3.   Alcoholism—Fiction
4. Homicide—Fiction 5. Country life—Fiction
6. Virginia—Fiction
ISBN 978-0-547-07661-4; 0-547-07661-4
                                    LC 2008-36810
Clifton has grown up in rural Virginia with the memory of his African American father being beaten to death
by policemen, causing his white mother to slip into alcoholism and depression, but after befriending an old man
who listens to his problems, Clifton finally feels less
alone in the world.

"Unflinching and raw, the story, set in the late 1980s,
explores the destructiveness of racism." Horn Book
Guide

The Hanging Woods; a novel. Houghton Mifflin
2008 326p $16
Grades: 10 11 12   **Fic**
1. Friendship—Fiction 2. Homicide—Fiction
3. Country life—Fiction 4. Alabama—Fiction
ISBN 978-0-618-88125-3   LC 2007-25773
In rural Alabama during the summer of 1975, three
teenaged boys build a treehouse, try to keep a headless
turkey alive, and become involved in a murder mystery.

This is a "compelling, but disturbing story, which features mature subject matter and language." Kirkus

Saroyan, William, 1908-1981
The human comedy. Rev by the author. Dell
1971 192p pa $7.50
Grades: 7 8 9 10 11 12 Adult   **Fic**
1. California—Fiction 2. Family life—Fiction
ISBN 0-440-33933-2
First published 1944 by Harcourt, Brace and Company
"Homer, the narrator, identifies himself in this novel
as a night messenger for the Postal Telegraph office. He
creates a view of family life in the 1940s in a small

town in California. His mother, Ma Macauley, presides
over the family and takes care of four children after her
husband dies. Besides Homer, there is Marcus, the
oldest, who is in the army; Bess; and Ulysses, the youngest, who describes the world from his perspective as a
solemn four-year-old." Shapiro. Fic for Youth. 3d edition

Sayed, Kashua, 1975-
Let it be morning; translated from Hebrew by
Miriam Shlesinger. Black Cat 2006 271p pa $13
Grades: 11 12 Adult   **Fic**
1. Journalists—Fiction 2. Israel-Arab conflicts—Fiction
ISBN 0-8021-7021-8; 978-0-8021-7021-7
                                    LC 2005-46768
Original Hebrew edition, 2004
"A young Arab-Israeli journalist moves from Tel Aviv
back to his childhood village with his wife and baby
daughter just in time to be caught up in a series of harrowing, dramatic events. In response to Israel's military
presence in the village, neighbors and relatives find
themselves fighting one another in order to survive. . . .
The short chapters and fast pace, combined with the
memories of youth that his return home elicits, make for
an easy fit for older teens with an interest in other cultures or current events." SLJ

Scarrow, Alex
TimeRiders. Walker & Co. 2010 405p $16.99
Grades: 7 8 9 10   **Fic**
1. Time travel—Fiction 2. September 11 terrorist attacks, 2001—Fiction 3. Environmental protection—
Fiction 4. Science fiction
ISBN 978-0-8027-2172-3; 0-8027-2172-9
                                    LC 2009-53166
Rescued from imminent death, teens Maddy, Liam,
and Sal join forces in 2001 Manhattan to correct changes
in history made by other time travelers, using a "time
bubble" surrounding the attack on the Twin Towers to
hide their journeys.

"The characters are expertly developed, each displaying vulnerabilities and quirks that make them memorable
as individuals. . . . This is a brilliantly paced, fascinating look at the ways in which one seemingly small
change can ripple out to—literally—the end of the
world." Bull Cent Child Books

Schindler, Holly, 1977-
A blue so dark. Flux 2010 277p pa $9.95 *
Grades: 8 9 10 11 12   **Fic**
1. Schizophrenia—Fiction 2. Mental illness—Fiction
3. Mother-daughter relationship—Fiction 4. Artists—
Fiction 5. School stories
ISBN 978-0-7387-1926-9   LC 2009-31360
As Missouri fifteen-year-old Aura struggles alone to
cope with the increasingly severe symptoms of her mother's schizophrenia, she wishes only for a normal life, but
fears that her artistic ability and genes will one day result in her own insanity.

"A haunting, realistic view of the melding of art, creativity, and mental illness and their collective impact on
a young person's life." Booklist

Schindler, Holly, 1977-—*Continued*

Playing hurt. Flux 2011 303p pa $9.95

Grades: 7 8 9 10   **Fic**
1. Loss (Psychology)—Fiction 2. Resorts—Fiction
3. Love stories 4. Minnesota—Fiction
ISBN 978-0-7387-2287-0; 0-7387-2287-1
                                    LC 2010-44173

Chelsea Keyes, a high school basketball star whose
promising career has been cut short by a terrible accident
on the court, and Clint Morgan, a nineteen-year-old ex-
hockey player who gave up his sport following a game-
related tragedy, meet at a Minnesota lake resort and find
themselves drawn together by the losses they have suffered.

"Both heartbreaking and thrilling, the emotional journey that Clint and Chelsea embark on together is more
than a heady romance; the characters are realistically
drawn, and the book does not shy away from the reality
of the characters' experiences: anger and grief mixed
with desire and yearning. The book speaks to personal
struggles and triumphs and the ability of the human spirit
to heal." Voice Youth Advocates

Schmidt, Gary D.

Trouble. Clarion Books 2008 297p $16 *

Grades: 6 7 8 9 10   **Fic**
1. Traffic accidents—Fiction 2. Death—Fiction
3. Family life—Fiction 4. Cambodian Americans—
Fiction 5. Prejudices—Fiction
ISBN 978-0-618-92766-1; 0-618-92766-2
                                    LC 2007-40104

Fourteen-year-old Henry, wishing to honor his brother
Franklin's dying wish, sets out to hike Maine's Mount
Katahdin with his best friend and dog, but fate adds another companion—the Cambodian refugee accused of fatally injuring Franklin—and reveals troubles that predate
the accident.

"Schmidt creates a rich and credible world peopled
with fully developed characters who have a lot of complex reckoning to do. . . . [The author's prose] is flawless, and Henry's odyssey of growth and understanding
is pitch-perfect and deeply satisfying." Bull Cent Child
Books

Schrefer, Eliot, 1978-

The deadly sister. Scholastic Press 2010 310p
$17.99

Grades: 8 9 10 11 12   **Fic**
1. Sisters—Fiction 2. Homicide—Fiction 3. Mystery
fiction
ISBN 978-0-545-16574-7; 0-545-16574-1
                                    LC 2010-281733

Abby Goodwin has always covered for her sister,
Maya, but now Maya has been accused of murder, and
Abby's not sure she'll be able to cover for her sister
anymore. Abby helps Maya escape. But when Abby begins investigating the death, she find that you can't trust
anyone, not even the people you think you know.

"Well-drawn characters, realistic dialogue, and suspenseful twists and turns add to the appeal. Teens crave
mystery, and this book will suit them just fine." SLJ

Schroeder, Lisa

Far from you. Simon Pulse 2009 355p $15.99

Grades: 7 8 9 10   **Fic**
1. Novels in verse 2. Stepfamilies—Fiction 3. Snow—
Fiction
ISBN 978-1-4169-7506-9; 1-4169-7506-3
                                    LC 2008-25268

A novel-in-verse about sixteen-year-old Ali's reluctant
road trip with her stepmother and new baby sister, and
the terror that ensues after they end up lost in the snow-
covered woods.

"Schroeder weaves Alice in Wonderland . . . references throughout the book to echo the topsy-turvy nature
of her protagonist's life. It is this roller coaster of emotions to which many teen readers will relate. A quick,
yet satisfying, novel in verse." SLJ

Schumacher, Julie, 1958-

Black box; a novel. Delacorte Press 2008 168p
$15.99; lib bdg $18.99 *

Grades: 8 9 10 11 12   **Fic**
1. Depression (Psychology)—Fiction 2. Sisters—Fiction 3. Family life—Fiction 4. School stories
ISBN   978-0-385-73542-1;   0-385-73542-1;
978-0-385-90523-7 (lib bdg); 0-385-90523-8 (lib bdg)
                                    LC 2007-45774

When her sixteen-year-old sister is hospitalized for depression and her parents want to keep it a secret, fourteen-year-old Elena tries to cope with her own anxiety
and feelings of guilt that she is determined to conceal
from outsiders.

"The writing is spare, direct, and honest. Written in
the first person, this is a readable, ultimately uplifting
book about a difficult subject." SLJ

Schutt, Christine, 1948-

All souls. Harcourt 2008 223p hardcover o.p. pa
$13.95 *

Grades: 11 12 Adult   **Fic**
1. Friendship—Fiction 2. School stories 3. New York
(N.Y.)—Fiction
ISBN   978-0-15-101449-1;   0-15-101449-3;
978-0-15-603338-1 (pa); 0-15-603338-0 (pa)
                                    LC 2007-32814

"Beautiful Astra Dell is the star of her private girls'
school. But she is also ill with a potentially terminal disease. How does that impact her family, fellow students,
and the school's faculty?" Booklist

This "is a bold, sharp story about teenage girls, class
and illness, about those moment when we achieve the
miracle of human connection—and those when we
don't." N Y Times Book Rev

Scott, Amanda

Dreaming the eagle; [by] Manda Scott.
Delacorte Press 2003 465p hardcover o.p. pa $14

Grades: 11 12 Adult   **Fic**
1. Boadicea, Queen, d. 62—Fiction 2. Great Britain—
History—0-1066—Fiction
ISBN 0-385-33670-5; 0-385-33773-6 (pa)
                                    LC 2002-31462

Scott, Amanda—*Continued*

This first part of a quadrilogy "about the life of Boudica, the warrior queen of Britannia who fought the Romans in the first century A.D. . . . runs from A.D. 32 to 43 and covers Boudica's youth (when she was known as Breaca), during which she kills her first opponent in battle and begins a life of leadership and bloodshed." Publ Wkly

"Definitely not a tired old retelling of a legend, this novel is beautifully written and lovingly told, filled with drama and passion. Scott takes great care to draw secondary characters and evoke the feel of first-century Britain." Libr J

Other titles in this series are:
Dreaming the bull (2004)
Dreaming the hound (2006)
Dreaming the serpent-spear (2007)

Scott, Elizabeth

Grace. Dutton Books 2010 200p $16.99
Grades: 8 9 10 11 12   **Fic**
1. Despotism—Fiction 2. Insurgency—Fiction
3. Fantasy fiction
ISBN 978-0-525-42206-8; 0-525-42206-4
            LC 2009-53285
Sixteen-year-old Grace travels on a decrepit train toward a border that may not exist, recalling events that brought her to choose life over being a suicide bomber, and dreaming of freedom from the extremist religion-based government of Keran Berj

"Moody and compelling, without the easy moralizing so common in dystopian settings." Kirkus

Living dead girl. Simon Pulse 2008 170p $16.99; pa $8.99 *
Grades: 9 10 11 12   **Fic**
1. Kidnapping—Fiction 2. Child sexual abuse—Fiction
ISBN 978-1-4169-6059-1; 1-4169-6059-7;
978-1-4169-6060-7 (pa); 1-4169-6060-0 (pa)
            LC 2007-943736
A novel about a 15-year-old girl who has spent the last five years being abused by a kidnapper named Ray and is kept powerless by Ray's promise to harm her family if she makes one false move.

"Scott's prose is spare and damning, relying on suggestive details and their impact on Alice to convey the unimaginable violence she repeatedly experiences. Disturbing but fascinating, the book exerts an inescapable grip on readers—like Alice, they have virtually no choice but to continue until the conclusion sets them free." Publ Wkly

Love you hate you miss you. HarperTeen 2009 276p $16.99; lib bdg $17.89; pa $8.99
Grades: 9 10 11 12   **Fic**
1. Guilt—Fiction 2. Death—Fiction 3. Alcoholism—Fiction 4. Friendship—Fiction 5. School stories
ISBN 978-0-06-112283-5; 0-06-112283-1;
978-0-06-112284-2 (lib bdg); 0-06-112284-X (lib bdg); 978-0-06-112285-9 (pa); 0-06-112285-8 (pa)
            LC 2008-31420
After coming out of alcohol rehabilitation, sixteen-year-old Amy sorts out conflicting emotions about her best friend Julia's death in a car accident for which she feels responsible.

"The pain, confusion, insights, and hope Amy expresses will speak to teen readers. The issue of binge drinking is handled clearly and bluntly, and without preaching: readers understand why Amy drinks and why she stops." Voice Youth Advocates

Stealing Heaven. HarperTeen 2008 307p $16.99; lib bdg $17.89; pa $8.99
Grades: 7 8 9 10   **Fic**
1. Thieves—Fiction 2. Mother-daughter relationship—Fiction
ISBN 978-0-06-112280-4; 0-06-112280-7;
978-0-06-112281-1 (lib bdg); 0-06-112281-5 (lib bdg); 978-0-06-112282-8 (pa); 0-06-112282-3 (pa)
Eighteen-year-old Dani grows weary of her life as a thief when she and her mother move to a town where Dani feels like she can put down roots.

"Witty dialogue gives a new perspective full of hope to YAs who feel trapped between family and friends." KLIATT

Scott, Kieran, 1974-

Geek magnet; a novel in five acts. G.P. Putnam's Sons 2008 308p $16.99
Grades: 7 8 9 10   **Fic**
1. Dating (Social customs)—Fiction 2. School stories
3. Theater—Fiction
ISBN 978-0-399-24760-6; 0-399-24760-2
            LC 2007-28707
Seventeen-year-old KJ Miller is determined to lose the label of "geek magnet" and get the guy of her dreams, all while stage managing the high school musical, with the help of the most popular girl in school.

"An enjoyable, touching read about self-discovery with a hopeful ending that avoids too-neat resolutions." Booklist

She's so dead to us. Simon & Schuster 2010 278p $16.99
Grades: 8 9 10 11 12   **Fic**
1. Friendship—Fiction 2. Social classes—Fiction
3. School stories 4. New Jersey—Fiction
ISBN 978-1-4169-9951-5; 1-4169-9951-5
            LC 2009-46739
Told in two voices, high school juniors Allie, who now lives on the poor side of town, and Jake, the "Crestie" whose family bought her house, develop feelings for one another that are complicated by her former friends, his current ones, who refuse to forgive her for her father's bad investment that cost them all.

"In this successful blend of class struggle, betrayal, and forbidden romance, Scott creates an unpredictable and timely story." Horn Book Guide

Followed by He's so not worth it (2011)

Scott, Mindi

Freefall. Simon Pulse 2010 315p pa $7.99
Grades: 8 9 10 11 12   **Fic**
1. Rock musicians—Fiction 2. Bereavement—Fiction
3. Alcoholism—Fiction
ISBN 978-1-4424-0278-2; 1-4424-0278-4
            LC 2010-12663

Scott, Mindi—*Continued*

Seth, a bass guitar player in a teen rock band, deals with alcoholism, his best friend's death, and first love.

"Seth's character arc is fully realized, without the burden of too much introspection or weighty insight to bog down the pace of the narrative. . . . This is a solid exploration of what you can and can't do to help your friends, built on top of an engaging story of boy meets girl." Bull Cent Child Books

Sebold, Alice

The lovely bones. Little, Brown 2002 328p $21.95; pa $13.95 *

Grades: 11 12 Adult   Fic

1. Homicide—Fiction 2. Family life—Fiction

ISBN 0-316-66634-3; 0-316-16881-5 (pa)

LC 2001-50622

Sebold's "heroine, 14-year-old Suzy Salmon, is murdered in the first chapter, on her way home from school. Suzy narrates the story from heaven, viewing the devastating effects of her murder on her family." Booklist

"As pleasant as Susie's heaven is, there's no God there, and certainly no Jesus. This is spirituality for an age that's ecumenical to a fault. But emotionally, it's faultless. Sebold never slips as she follows this family. The risks she walks are enough to give you vertigo." Christ Sci Monit

Sedgwick, Marcus

My swordhand is singing. Wendy Lamb Books 2007 205p hardcover o.p. pa $6.99

Grades: 7 8 9 10   Fic

1. Vampires—Fiction 2. Horror fiction 3. Supernatural—Fiction 4. Gypsies—Fiction

ISBN 978-0-375-84689-2; 978-0-375-84690-8 (pa)

LC 2007-07051

In the dangerous dark of winter in an Eastern European village during the early seventeenth century, Peter learns from a gypsy girl that the Shadow Queen is behind the recent murders and reanimations, and his father's secret past may hold the key to stopping her.

"Sedgwick writes a compellingly fresh vampire story, combining elements from ancient myths and legends to create a believable and frightening tale." Voice Youth Advocates

Revolver. Roaring Brook Press 2010 204p $16.99 *

Grades: 7 8 9 10   Fic

1. Death—Fiction 2. Siblings—Fiction 3. Alaska—Gold discoveries—Fiction 4. Arctic regions—Fiction

ISBN 978-1-59643-592-6; 1-59643-592-5

First published 2009 in the United Kingdom

In an isolated cabin, fourteen-year-old Sig is alone with a corpse: his father, who has fallen through the ice and frozen to death only hours earlier. Then comes a stranger claiming that Sig's father owes him a share of a horde of stolen gold. Sig's only protection is a loaded Colt revolver hidden in the cabin's storeroom.

"Tight plotting and a wealth of moral concerns—good versus evil; faith, love, and hope; the presence of God; survival in a bleak landscape; trusting the lessons parents teach—make this a memorable tale." Horn Book

Seigel, Andrea, 1979-

The kid table. Bloomsbury Children's Books 2010 306p $16.99

Grades: 10 11 12   Fic

1. Family life—Fiction 2. Cousins—Fiction

ISBN 978-1-59990-480-1   LC 2010-4540

"It's guaranteed that 16-year-old Ingrid Bell and her five cousins, Cricket, Dom, Micah, Brianne, and Autumn will sit at the 'kid table' at every family gathering. As five family events bring the cousins to the 'table,' each one is experiencing a crisis. Not to be outdone, the adults are experiencing their own dilemmas which make Ingrid wonder who really belongs at the kid table. Wondering where she fits in the family, Ingrid struggles with her emotions. . . . This coming-of-age story about a dysfunctional family is told from Ingrid's point-of-view. . . . The book contains some strong language and sexual innuendos." Libr Media Connect

"Laugh-out-loud humor punctuates . . . [Ingrid's] clear-eyed musings about family and relationships, narrated in a perceptive, analytical, with-it voice. . . . Teen girls in particular will enjoy this unusual coming-of-age novel." Voice Youth Advocates

Like the red panda. Harcourt 2004 280p pa $13

Grades: 9 10 11 12   Fic

1. School stories 2. Suicide—Fiction 3. Orphans—Fiction 4. California—Fiction

ISBN 0-15-603024-1   LC 2003-17164

"A Harvest book"

"After the overdose deaths of her coke-addicted parents and six years in a chilly foster family, Princeton-bound high-school senior Stella Parrish has decided to commit suicide. Shortly before her graduation, morbid apathy sets in 'like pulling on sunglasses, but internally,' and the rest of the novel . . . is Stella's explanation of her decision." Booklist

"Seigel's novel is a keen portrait of young American angst and all its ironic posturing. The result veers between an earnest critique of the Columbine era and *Heathers*-like parody, which leaves its conclusion half tragedy, half punch line." Publ Wkly

Selfors, Suzanne, 1963-

Mad love. Walker Books for Young Readers 2011 323p $16.99

Grades: 7 8 9 10   Fic

1. Authorship—Fiction 2. Eros (Greek deity)—Fiction 3. Manic-depressive illness—Fiction 4. Mother-daughter relationship—Fiction 5. Love stories

ISBN 978-0-8027-8450-6; 0-8027-8450-X

LC 2010-23261

When her famous romance-novelist mother is secretly hospitalized in an expensive mental facility, sixteen-year-old Alice tries to fulfill her mother's contract with her publisher by writing a love story—with the help of Cupid.

"There's a bit of mythology, a bit of romance, a bit of the paranormal, and some real-life problems, but Selfors juggles them all assuredly. Serious ideas are handled carefully, while real humor is spread throughout the whole book. This book has real charm with great depth." Voice Youth Advocates

Selvadurai, Shyam, 1965-

Swimming in the monsoon sea. Tundra Books 2005 274p hardcover o.p. pa $9.95 *

Grades: 9 10 11 12 Fic

1. Cousins—Fiction 2. Homosexuality—Fiction 3. Family life—Fiction 4. Sri Lanka—Fiction

ISBN 0-88776-735-4; 0-88776-834-2 (pa)

"In Sri Lanka in 1980, 14-year-old Amrith is forced to confront his feelings about his birth family when Niresh, a cousin from Canada, visits. He falls in love with the boy, jealously refusing to share him with his adoptive sisters, in spite of their obvious interest. . . . The author's affection for the country of his childhood is evident in this sympathetic and insightful look at first love." SLJ

Selzer, Adam, 1980-

I kissed a zombie, and I liked it. Delacorte Press 2010 177p lib bdg $12.99; pa $7.99

Grades: 7 8 9 10 Fic

1. Zombies—Fiction 2. Vampires—Fiction 3. Dating (Social customs)—Fiction

ISBN 978-0-385-90497-1 (lib bdg); 0-385-90497-5 (lib bdg); 978-0-385-73503-2 (pa); 0-385-73503-0 (pa)

LC 2009-24052

Living in the post-human era when the undead are part of everyday life, high schooler Alley breaks her no-dating rule when Doug catches her eye, but classmate Will demands to turn her into a vampire and her zombie boyfriend may be unable to stop him.

"With snappy dialogue and a light, funny touch, Selzer creates a readable examination of love, self-sacrifice, and where to draw the line before you lose yourself." Publ Wkly

Senna, Danzy

Caucasia. Riverhead Bks. 1998 353p hardcover o.p. pa $14 *

Grades: 11 12 Adult Fic

1. Interracial marriage—Fiction

ISBN 1-57322-091-4; 1-57322-716-1 (pa)

LC 97-28911

Birdie, the narrator of this novel, is "a biracial girl who must struggle for acceptance from blacks and whites alike. Birdie and Cole are the daughters of a white mother and an African American father whose marriage is disintegrating. When their activist mother must flee from the police, the girls are split between their parents: Cole goes with her father because she looks black, Birdie with her mother because she could pass for white. Living in a small town and forced to keep her family, her past, and her race a secret, Birdie spies upon racism in all its forms, from the overt comments of the town locals to the hypocrisy of the wealthy liberals." Libr J

Birdie's "struggles to fit in anywhere, to pass as anything, are vivid. . . . She tells this coming-of-age tale with impressive beauty and power." Newsweek

Sepetys, Ruta

Between shades of gray. Philomel Books 2011 344p map $17.99 *

Grades: 7 8 9 10 Fic

1. Lithuania—Fiction 2. Soviet Union—Fiction

ISBN 978-0-399-25412-3; 0-399-25412-9

LC 2009-50092

In 1941, fifteen-year-old Lina, her mother, and brother are pulled from their Lithuanian home by Soviet guards and sent to Siberia, where her father is sentenced to death in a prison camp while she fights for her life, vowing to honor her family and the thousands like hers by burying her story in a jar on Lithuanian soil. Based on the author's family, includes a historical note.

"A harrowing page-turner, made all the more so for its basis in historical fact, the novel illuminates the persecution suffered by Stalin's victims (20 million were killed), while presenting memorable characters who retain their will to survive even after more than a decade in exile." Publ Wkly

Setterfield, Diane

The thirteenth tale; a novel. 1st Atria Books hardcover ed. Atria Books 2006 406p hardcover o.p. pa $16

Grades: 11 12 Adult Fic

1. Authors—Fiction 2. Ghost stories

ISBN 978-0-7432-9802-5; 0-7432-9802-0; 978-0-7432-9803-2 (pa); 0-7432-9803-9 (pa)

LC 2006-42906

"Margaret Lea, a London bookseller's daughter, has written an obscure biography that suggests deep understanding of siblings. She is contacted by renowned aging author Vida Winter, who finally wishes to tell her own, long-hidden, life story. Margaret travels to Yorkshire, where she interviews the dying writer, walks the remains of her estate at Angelfield and tries to verify the old woman's tale of a governess, a ghost and more than one abandoned baby." Publ Wkly

"A wholly original work told in the vein of all the best gothic classics. Lovers of books about book lovers will be enthralled." Booklist

Shaara, Michael, 1929-1988

The killer angels; a novel of the Civil War. Modern Library 2004 xx, 337p map $22.95 *

Grades: 9 10 11 12 Fic

1. Gettysburg (Pa.), Battle of, 1863—Fiction

ISBN 0-679-64324-9 LC 2004-46877

Also available in paperback from Ballantine Bks.

A reissue of the title first published 1974 by David McKay

This is a fictionalized account of four days in July, 1863 at the Battle of Gettysburg. The point of view of the Southern forces is represented by Generals Robert E. Lee and James Longstreet, while Colonel Joshua Chamberlain and General John Buford are the focus for the North

"Shaara's version of private reflections and conversations are based on his reading of documents and letters. Although some of his judgments are not necessarily substantiated by historians, he demonstrates a knowledge of both the battle and the area. The writing is vivid and fast moving." Libr J

Shan, Darren, 1972-

The thin executioner. Little, Brown 2010 483p map $17.99

Grades: 10 11 12   **Fic**

1. Voyages and travels—Fiction 2. Capital punishment—Fiction 3. Slavery—Fiction 4. Conduct of life—Fiction

ISBN 978-0-316-07865-8; 0-316-07865-4

LC 2009-45606

In a nation of warriors where weakness is shunned and all crimes, no matter how minor, are punishable by beheading, young Jebel Rum, along with a slave who is fated to be sacrificed, sets forth on a quest to petition the Fire God for invincibility, but when the long and arduous journey is over, Jebel has learned much about fairness and the value of life.

"Readers will hate the villains, feel sorry for the innocent, and root for Tel Hesani and Jebel to complete their mission. This is a must-read for thrill seekers with a strong stomach looking for an action-packed adventure with a host of fantastical creatures." Voice Youth Advocates

Sharenow, Rob

My mother the cheerleader; a novel. Laura Geringer Books 2007 288p hardcover o.p. pa $8.99 *

Grades: 7 8 9 10   **Fic**

1. Race relations—Fiction 2. School integration—Fiction 3. Mother-daughter relationship—Fiction 4. New Orleans (La.)—Fiction

ISBN   978-0-06-114896-5;   0-06-114896-2; 978-0-06-114898-9 (pa); 0-06-114898-9 (pa)

LC 2006-21716

Thirteen-year-old Louise uncovers secrets about her family and her neighborhood during the violent protests over school desegregation in 1960 New Orleans.

"Through inquisitive Louise's perspective, readers get a wrenching look at the era's turmoil and pervasive racism." Publ Wkly

Shaw, Susan

Safe. Dutton Books 2007 168p $16.99

Grades: 7 8 9 10   **Fic**

1. Rape—Fiction 2. Mothers—Fiction

ISBN 978-0-525-47829-4; 0-525-47829-9

LC 2006-36428

When thirteen-year-old Tracy, whose mother died when she was three years old, is raped and beaten on the last day of school, all her feelings of security disappear and she does not know how to cope with the fear and dread that engulf her.

This is an "extraordinarily tender novel. . . . Intimate, first-person narrative honestly expresses Tracy's full range of emotions." Publ Wkly

Shelley, Mary Wollstonecraft, 1797-1851

Frankenstein; or, The modern Prometheus; with an introduction by Wendy Lesser. Knopf 1992 xxxiii, 231p $15 *

Grades: 7 8 9 10   **Fic**

1. Horror fiction 2. Science fiction

ISBN 0-679-40999-8   LC 91-53195

Also available from other publishers

"Everyman's library"

First published 1818

"The tale relates the exploits of Frankenstein, an idealistic Genevan student of natural philosophy, who discovers at the university of Ingolstadt the secret of imparting life to inanimate matter. Collecting bones from charnelhouses, he constructs the semblance of a human being and gives it life. The creature, endowed with supernatural strength and size and terrible in appearance, inspires loathing in whoever sees it." Oxford Companion to Engl Lit. 5th edition

Shepard, Jim

Project X; a novel. Alfred A. Knopf 2004 163p hardcover o.p. pa $12 *

Grades: 9 10 11 12   **Fic**

1. School stories 2. School violence—Fiction

ISBN 1-4000-4071-X; 1-4000-3348-9 (pa)

LC 2003-47575

"Flake and Edwin are often bullied; at other times, they have the horrible feeling of being completely invisible to their classmates. Flake is even more alienated than Edwin and hatches a revenge plan involving guns that they call 'project x.' Disaster looms. . . . The vivid dialogue is sprinkled with profanity and is movingly expressive. This heartbreaking and wrenching novel will leave teens with plenty of questions and, hopefully, some answers." SLJ

Shepard, Sara, 1977-

The lying game. HarperTeen 2010 307p $16.99

Grades: 9 10 11 12   **Fic**

1. Twins—Fiction 2. Sisters—Fiction 3. Homicide—Fiction 4. Dead—Fiction 5. Mystery fiction

ISBN 978-0-06-186970-9; 0-06-186970-8

LC 2010-40332

Seventeen-year-old Emma Paxton steps into the life of her long-lost twin Sutton to solve her murder, while Sutton looks on from her afterlife.

"Shepard keeps the action rolling and the clues confusing as she spends this installment uncovering the twins' characters but not solving the murder yet. Naturally, boys and fashion also figure into the story, fleshing out a distinctive scenario that should appeal to many teen girls." Kirkus

Sherrill, Martha

The Ruins of California. Penguin Press 2006 318p hardcover o.p. pa $14

Grades: 11 12 Adult   **Fic**

1. Family life—Fiction 2. Divorce—Fiction 3. California—Fiction

ISBN   1-59420-080-7;   978-1-59420-080-9; 1-59448-231-4 (pa); 978-1-59448-231-1 (pa)

LC 2005-49343

"Set in California in the 1970s, this beautifully written novel tells the story of a girl, trapped in a theatrical family, who manages to transform herself from an observer into the star of her own life." Booklist

Sheth, Kashmira

Keeping corner. Hyperion 2007 281p hardcover o.p. pa $5.99

Grades: 7 8 9 10 11 12   **Fic**
1. Gandhi, Mahatma, 1869-1948—Fiction 2. India—Fiction 3. Widows—Fiction 4. Women's rights—Fiction

ISBN   978-0-7868-3859-2;   0-7868-3859-0; 978-0-7868-3860-8 (pa); 0-7868-3860-4 (pa)

           LC 2007-15314

In India in the 1940s, twelve-year-old Leela's happy, spoiled childhood ends when her husband since age nine, whom she barely knows, dies, leaving her a widow whose only hope of happiness could come from Mahatma Ghandi's social and political reforms.

Sheth "sets up a thrilling premise in which politics become achingly personal." Booklist

Shinn, Sharon, 1957-

Gateway. Viking 2009 280p $17.99

Grades: 6 7 8 9 10   **Fic**
1. Space and time—Fiction 2. Chinese Americans—Fiction

ISBN 978-0-670-01178-0; 0-670-01178-9

           LC 2009-14002

While passing through the Arch in St. Louis, Missouri, a Chinese American teenager is transported to a parallel world where she is given a dangerous assignment.

The author's "fantasy finds the right balance between adventure and romance, while illuminating how seductive evil can be and that sometimes the best weapon one can possess is a skeptical mind." Publ Wkly

General Winston's daughter. Viking 2007 352p hardcover o.p. pa $7.99 *

Grades: 7 8 9 10   **Fic**
1. War stories 2. Military occupation—Fiction 3. Social classes—Fiction 4. Soldiers—Fiction

ISBN   978-0-670-06248-5;   0-670-06248-0; 978-0-14-241346-3 (pa); 0-14-241346-1 (pa)

           LC 2007-14703

Seventeen-year-old heiress Averie Winston travels with her guardian to faraway Chiarrin, a country her father's army has occupied, and once she arrives and is reunited with her fiance, she discovers that her notions about politics, propriety, the military, and even her intended have changed.

The author "skillfully shepherds her tale to a satisfying, believable conclusion. This thoughtful romance with political overtones will prove irresistible to many readers." Booklist

Mystic and rider. Berkley Books 2005 440p il map hardcover o.p. pa $7.99 *

Grades: 9 10 11 12   **Fic**
1. Cults—Fiction 2. Fantasy fiction

ISBN 0-441-01246-9; 0-441-01303-1 (pa)

           LC 2004-59639

"In the land of Gillengaria, ill feeling toward magic and those who use it rises to a dangerous level. The king dispatches the Mystic woman Senneth on a journey to see firsthand how dire the situation is. Accompanying her are Shapeshifters and Riders—unlikely allies who will enter a land under the sway of a fanatical cult that

would purge Gillengaria of all magic users." Publisher's note

"Never tripping over the plot twists and complications, Shinn gives us an easy, absorbing, high-quality read sans gratuitous bloodshed and violence." Booklist

Shulman, Mark, 1962-

Scrawl. Roaring Brook Press 2010 234p $16.99

Grades: 6 7 8 9 10   **Fic**
1. Self-perception—Fiction 2. Poverty—Fiction 3. Bullies—Fiction 4. School stories 5. Diaries—Fiction

ISBN 978-1-59643-417-2; 1-59643-417-1

           LC 2010-10521

"A Neal Porter Book"

When eighth-grade school bully Tod and his friends get caught committing a crime on school property, his penalty—staying after school and writing in a journal under the eye of the school guidance counsellor—reveals aspects of himself that he prefers to keep hidden.

"Blackmail, cliques, and a sense of hopelessness from both students and teachers sets up an unexpected ending that will leave readers with a new appreciation for how difficult high school can be. With the potential to occupy the rarified air of titles like S.E. Hinton's *The Outsiders* and Chris Crutcher's *Staying Fat for Sarah Byrnes* . . ., Scrawl paints the stereotypical school bully in a different, poignant light." Voice Youth Advocates

Shulman, Polly

Enthusiasm. G. P. Putnam's Sons 2006 198p hardcover o.p. pa $7.99

Grades: 7 8 9 10   **Fic**
1. School stories

ISBN 0-399-24389-5; 0-14-240935-9 (pa)

           LC 2005-13490

Julie and Ashleigh, high school sophomores and Jane Austen fans, seem to fall for the same Mr. Darcy-like boy and struggle to hide their true feelings from one another while rehearsing for a school musical.

"While familiarity with Austen's world through her books or, more likely, the movie renditions will deepen readers' appreciation for Shulman's impressive . . . novel, it is by no means a prerequisite to enjoying this involving and often amusing narrative of friendship, courtship, and (of course) true love." Booklist

Shusterman, Neal

Bruiser. HarperTeen 2010 328p $16.99; lib bdg $17.89

Grades: 8 9 10 11 12   **Fic**
1. Twins—Fiction 2. Supernatural—Fiction 3. Child abuse—Fiction 4. Siblings—Fiction

ISBN   978-0-06-113408-1;   0-06-113408-2; 978-0-06-113409-8 (lib bdg); 0-06-113409-0 (lib bdg)

           LC 2009-30930

Inexplicable events start to occur when sixteen-year-old twins Tennyson and Bronte befriend a troubled and misunderstood outcast, aptly nicknamed Bruiser, and his little brother, Cody.

"Narrated in turns by Tennyson, Bronte, Bruiser, and Bruiser's little brother, Cody, the story is a fascinating study in the art of self-deception and the way our best

Shusterman, Neal—*Continued*

intentions for others are often based in the selfish desires of our deepest selves. . . . This eloquent and thoughtful story will most certainly leave its mark." Bull Cent Child Books

Downsiders. Simon & Schuster Bks. for Young Readers 1999 246p hardcover o.p. pa $8.99
Grades: 9 10 11 12   **Fic**
1. Subways—Fiction 2. New York (N.Y.)—Fiction
ISBN 0-689-80375-3; 1-4169-9747-4 (pa)
LC 98-38555

When fourteen-year-old Lindsay meets Talon and discovers the Downsiders world which had evolved from the subway built in New York in 1867 by Alfred Ely Beach, she and her new friend experience the clash of their two cultures.

"Shusterman has invented an alternate world in the Downside that is both original and humorous." Voice Youth Advocates

Everlost. Simon & Schuster Books for Young Readers 2006 313p (The Skinjacker trilogy) $16.95; pa $8.99 *
Grades: 8 9 10 11 12   **Fic**
1. Traffic accidents—Fiction 2. Death—Fiction 3. Future life—Fiction
ISBN   978-0-689-87237-2;   0-689-87237-2; 978-1-4169-9749-8 (pa); 1-4169-9749-0 (pa)
LC 2005-32244

When Nick and Allie are killed in a car crash, they end up in Everlost, or limbo for lost souls, where although Nick is satisfied, Allie will stop at nothing—even skinjacking—to break free.

"Shusterman has reimagined what happens after death and questions power and the meaning of charity. While all this is going on, he has also managed to write a rip-roaring adventure complete with monsters, blimps, and high-diving horses." SLJ

Other titles in this series are:
Everfound (2011)
Everwild (2009)

Unwind. Simon & Schuster Books for Young Readers 2007 335p $16.99; pa $8.99
Grades: 6 7 8 9 10 11 12   **Fic**
1. Science fiction
ISBN   978-1-4169-1204-0;   1-4169-1204-5; 978-1-4169-1205-7 (pa); 1-4169-1205-3 (pa)
LC 2006-32689

In a future world where those between the ages of thirteen and eighteen can have their lives "unwound" and their body parts harvested for use by others, three teens go to extreme lengths to uphold their beliefs—and, perhaps, save their own lives.

"Poignant, compelling, and ultimately terrifying." Voice Youth Advocates

Shute, Nevil, 1899-1960

On the beach. Vintage International 2010 312p pa $15
Grades: 9 10 11 12 Adult   **Fic**
1. Nuclear warfare—Fiction 2. Australia—Fiction 3. Science fiction
ISBN 978-0-307-47399-8

Also available in hardcover from Buccaneer Books

First published 1957 by Morrow

"A nuclear war annihilates the world's Northern Hemisphere, and as atomic wastes are spreading southward, residents of Australia try to come to grips with their mortality. In spite of the inevitability of death, these people face their end with courage and live from day to day. They even plant trees they may never see mature." Shapiro. Fic for Youth. 3d edition

Silbert, Leslie

The intelligencer. Atria Bks. 2004 335p hardcover o.p. pa $14 *
Grades: 9 10 11 12   **Fic**
1. Marlowe, Christopher, 1564-1593—Fiction 2. Great Britain—History—1485-1603, Tudors—Fiction 3. Mystery fiction
ISBN 0-7434-3292-4; 0-7434-3293-2 (pa)
LC 2004-298225

This mystery "alternates between the present and the England of Elizabeth I and Christopher Marlowe. In addition to being a skilled and popular playwright, Marlowe was a spy, or *intelligencer*, for both Cecil and Essex, rivals for the favor of the Queen. Kate Morgan, a present-day Renaissance scholar working as a PI for a former agent still working clandestinely for the government, takes on a case involving a bound collection of coded reports of intelligencers gathered by an employee of Cecil, Essex, and others. The trail of the manuscript and its codes intersects with modern investigations involving murders, a crooked but charming art dealer, a charming but devious entrepreneur, a captured spy, Iranian prisons, Kate's father, a U.S. senator, and the current CIA director. There are a lot of strands, but the pace is quick and the action fascinating." SLJ

Silvey, Craig, 1982-

Jasper Jones; a novel. Alfred A. Knopf 2011 312p $16.99; lib bdg $19.99
Grades: 6 7 8 9 10   **Fic**
1. Homicide—Fiction 2. Family life—Fiction 3. Australia—Fiction 4. Mystery fiction
ISBN   978-0-375-86666-1;   0-375-86666-3; 978-0-375-96666-8 (lib bdg); 0-375-96666-8 (lib bdg)
LC 2010-9364

In small-town Australia, teens Jasper and Charlie form an unlikely friendship when one asks the other to help him cover up a murder until they can prove who is responsible.

"Silvey infuses his prose with a musician's sensibility—Charlie's pounding heart is echoed in the terse staccato sentences of the opening scenes, alternating with legato phrases laden with meaning. The author's keen ear for dialogue is evident in the humorous verbal sparring between Charlie and Jeffrey, typical of smart 13-year-old boys. . . . A richly rewarding exploration of truth and lies by a masterful storyteller." Kirkus

Simmons, Dan

Ilium. Eos 2003 576p $25.95
Grades: 11 12 Adult   **Fic**
1. Homer—Parodies, imitations, etc. 2. Mars (Planet)—Fiction 3. Science fiction
ISBN 0-380-97893-8   LC 2002-44791

Simmons, Dan—*Continued*

"Restored to life by the 'gods,' a race of beings who dwell on the heights of Olympos, 20th-century scholar Thomas Hockenberry travels back in time to observe the events of the Trojan War, as chronicled in Homer's epic poem. There, one of the gods recruits him in a secret war against her brother and sister deities. Set in a far future in which the population of true humans is kept strictly regulated by extraplanetary forces and machine intelligences study Proust and Shakespeare as they perform their duties throughout the universe." Libr J

"For answers to the mysteries laid out in 'Ilium'— from the true identity of the Olympian gods to the fate of robots and humans and of the 'little green men' on Mars for whom communication means death—you will have to wait for the promised sequel. For now, matching wits with Simmons and his lively creations should be reward enough." N Y Times Book Rev

Followed by Olympos (2005)

Simner, Janni Lee

Bones of Faerie. Random House 2009 247p $16.99; lib bdg $19.99

Grades: 7 8 9 10   **Fic**

1. Fairies—Fiction 2. Magic—Fiction 3. Fantasy fiction

ISBN 978-0-375-84563-5; 978-0-375-94563-2 (lib bdg)   LC 2008-2022

Fifteen-year-old Liza travels through war-ravaged territory, accompanied by two companions, in a struggle to bridge the faerie and human worlds and to bring back her mother while learning of her own powers and that magic can be controlled.

This is a "compelling developed, highly vulnerable trio whose resolute defiance against the status quo will resonate with readers long after specific details of the story may be forgotten." Bull Cent Child Books

Followed by: Faerie winter (2011)

Thief eyes. Random House 2010 272p $16.99

Grades: 7 8 9 10   **Fic**

1. Magic—Fiction 2. Missing persons—Fiction 3. Fantasy fiction 4. Iceland—Fiction

ISBN 978-0-375-86670-8; 0-375-86670-1

         LC 2009-18166

Haley's mother disappeared while on a trip to Iceland, and a year later, when her father takes her there to find out what happened, Haley finds herself deeply involved in an ancient saga that began with her Nordic ancestors.

"Simner skillfully weaves Haley and Ari's modern emotional struggles into the ancient saga and enlivens the story with an intriguing cast of characters from the original tale." Booklist

Sinclair, Upton, 1878-1968

The jungle; introduction by Jane Jacobs; afterword by Anthony Arthur. Modern Library pbk. ed., Centennial ed. Modern Library 2006 xxii, 388p pa $9.95 *

Grades: 11 12 Adult   **Fic**

1. Meat industry—Fiction 2. Immigrants—Fiction 3. Social problems—Fiction 4. Chicago (Ill.)—Fiction

ISBN 978-0-8129-7623-6; 0-8129-7623-1

         LC 2007-279794

Also available from other publishers

First published 1906 by Doubleday, Page

"Jurgis Rudkus, an immigrant from Lithuania, arrives in Chicago with his father, his fiancée, and her family. He is determined to make a life for his bride in the new country. The deplorable conditions in the stockyards and the harrowing experiences of impoverished workers are vividly described by the author." Shapiro. Fic for Youth. 3d edition

Includes bibliographical references

Sitomer, Alan Lawrence

Hip-hop high school. Jump at the Sun/Hyperion Books For Children 2006 368p hardcover o.p. pa $8.99

Grades: 7 8 9 10   **Fic**

1. School stories 2. African Americans—Fiction

ISBN 0-7868-5515-0; 1-4231-0644-X (pa)

         LC 2005-43331

Follows an African-American teenager through four years at her inner-city high school.

The author "strikes a fair balance between serious issues and more lighthearted fare, writing in a smart, conversational voice loaded with wit, rhythm, and energy." Booklist

Followed by Homeboyz (2007)

The secret story of Sonia Rodriguez. Jump at the Sun/Hyperion Books For Children 2008 312p lib bdg $17.99

Grades: 7 8 9 10   **Fic**

1. Mexican Americans—Fiction 2. Family life—Fiction

ISBN 978-1-4231-1072-9; 1-4231-1072-2

         LC 2007-45265

Tenth-grader Sonia reveals secrets about her life and her Hispanic family as she studies hard to become the first Rodriguez to finish high school.

"Sonia's immediate voice will hold teens with its mix of anger, sorrow, tenderness, and humor." Booklist

Sittenfeld, Curtis

Prep; a novel. Random House 2005 406p hardcover o.p. pa $13.95 *

Grades: 11 12 Adult   **Fic**

1. School stories 2. Massachusetts—Fiction

ISBN 1-4000-6231-4; 0-8129-7235-X (pa)

         LC 2004-46858

During the late 1980s, a fourteen-year-old leaves her middle-class Indiana family to enroll in an elite New England boarding school, becoming a shrewd observer of the rituals and mores of upper-class Easterners.

"This readable coming-of-age tale . . . [is] suitable for YA collections if mildly sexually explicit scenes are not objectionable." Libr J

Skrypuch, Marsha Forchuk

Daughter of war. Fitzhenry & Whiteside 2008 210p pa $14.95

Grades: 9 10 11 12   **Fic**

Skrypuch, Marsha Forchuk—*Continued*

1. Armenian massacres, 1915-1923—Fiction
2. Turkey—Fiction
ISBN 978-1-55455-044-9; 1-55455-044-0

"In this powerful story of the Armenian genocide, Kevork witnesses the brutal suffering of his people as he travels, disguised as an Arab, through Turkey and Syria in search of his love, Marta. Upon their reunion, Kevork learns that Marta has escaped from a forced Turkish marriage and borne a child." SLJ

Slade, Arthur G., 1967-

The hunchback assignments; [by] Arthur Slade. Wendy Lamb Books 2009 278p $15.99; lib bdg $18.99

Grades: 7 8 9 10   **Fic**
1. Physically handicapped—Fiction 2. Supernatural—Fiction 3. Spies—Fiction 4. Science fiction 5. Great Britain—History—19th century—Fiction 6. London (England)—Fiction
ISBN 978-0-385-73784-5; 0-385-73784-X; 978-0-385-90694-4 (lib bdg); 0-385-90694-3 (lib bdg)
LC 2008-54378

In Victorian London, fourteen-year-old Modo, a shape-changing hunchback, becomes a secret agent for the Permanent Association, which strives to protect the world from the evil machinations of the Clockwork Guild.

"A solid story line and well-crafted writing make for a pleasing and evocative adventure." Booklist

Followed by: The dark deeps (2010)

Megiddo's shadow. Wendy Lamb Books 2006 290p hardcover o.p. pa $6.50

Grades: 7 8 9 10   **Fic**
1. World War, 1914-1918—Fiction 2. Brothers—Fiction
ISBN 0-385-74701-2; 978-0-385-90945-7; 0-553-49507-0 (pa); 978-0-553-49507-2 (pa)
LC 2006011494

After the death of his beloved older brother Hector in World War I, sixteen-year-old Edward leaves the family farm in Canada to enlist in Hector's batallion, where he attempts to come to terms with what has happened.

"An engrossing and thought-provoking story." SLJ

Slayton, Fran Cannon

When the whistle blows. Philomel Books 2009 162p $16.99

Grades: 7 8 9 10   **Fic**
1. Railroads—Fiction 2. Family life—Fiction 3. Country life—Fiction 4. West Virginia—Fiction
ISBN 978-0-399-25189-4; 0-399-25189-8
LC 2008-38435

Jimmy Cannon tells about his life in the 1940s as the son of a West Virginia railroad man, loving the trains and expecting one day to work on the railroad like his father and brothers.

"Telling details and gentle humor help set the scene and reveal a great deal about these characters and their lives. . . . A polished paean to a bygone time and place." SLJ

Sloan, Brian

A tale of two summers. Simon & Schuster Books for Young Readers 2006 241p $15.95 *

Grades: 9 10 11 12   **Fic**
1. Friendship—Fiction 2. Homosexuality—Fiction 3. Theater—Fiction
ISBN 978-0-689-87439-0; 0-689-87439-1
LC 2005-20697

Even though Hal is gay and Chuck is straight, the two fifteen-year-olds are best friends and set up a blog where Hal records his budding romance with a young Frenchman and Chuck falls for a summer theater camp diva.

"This book is for readers mature enough to handle some very direct, realistic, and often-humorous entries about heterosexuality, homosexuality, masturbation, and alcohol and marijuana use. This title would be ideal for discussion within Gay/Straight Alliance groups." Voice Youth Advocates

Sloan, Kay

The patron saint of red Chevys. Permanent Press 2004 221p hardcover o.p. pa $18

Grades: 9 10 11 12   **Fic**
1. Homicide—Fiction 2. Sisters—Fiction 3. Race relations—Fiction 4. Mississippi—Fiction
ISBN 1-57962-104-X; 1-57962-172-4 (pa)
LC 2003-65550

"Mississippi, 1964: Bernice Starling, a blues singer of some repute, is stabbed to death. Her two young daughters decide they want to find the killer, but it's a tricky job, and there are plenty of suspects: a local bigot, their mother's lover, a random passerby, even their own father. . . . In the end, it doesn't matter whodunit, because this isn't really a mystery novel at all. It's a family drama, the coming-of-age story of two young girls who lose their mother and decide to do something about it. Fresh, enticing, often elegantly written." Booklist

Smelcer, John E., 1963-

The trap; [by] John Smelcer. Henry Holt and Co. 2006 170p $15.95 *

Grades: 6 7 8 9   **Fic**
1. Survival after airplane accidents, shipwrecks, etc.—Fiction 2. Grandfathers—Fiction 3. Native Americans—Fiction 4. Alaska—Fiction
ISBN 978-0-8050-7939-5; 0-8050-7939-4
LC 2005035740

In alternating chapters, seventeen-year-old Johnny Least-Weasel worries about his missing grandfather, and the grandfather, Albert Least-Weasel, struggles to survive, caught in his own steel trap in the Alaskan winter.

"In this story, Smelcer . . . seems to straddle the line flawlessly between an ancient legend and contemporary fiction. . . . His characters act with quiet dignity. . . . The suspense is played on an everyday level, which is why it works." Voice Youth Advocates

Smith, Alexander Gordon, 1979-

Lockdown. Farrar, Straus and Giroux 2009 273p (Escape from Furnace) $14.99

Grades: 7 8 9 10   **Fic**

1. Prisoners—Fiction 2. Escapes—Fiction 3. Science fiction

ISBN 978-0-374-32491-9; 0-374-32491-3

LC 2008-43439

When fourteen-year-old Alex is framed for murder, he becomes an inmate in the Furnace Penitentiary, where brutal inmates and sadistic guards reign, boys who disappear in the middle of the night sometimes return weirdly altered, and escape might just be possible.

"Once a plot is hatched, readers will be turning pages without pause, and the cliffhanger ending will have them anticipating the next installment. Most appealing is Smith's flowing writing style, filled with kid-speak, colorful adjectives, and amusing analogies." SLJ

Other titles in this series are:

Death sentence (2011)

Solitary (2010)

Smith, Andrew, 1959-

Ghost medicine. Feiwel & Friends 2008 357p $17.95 *

Grades: 8 9 10 11 12   **Fic**

1. Friendship—Fiction 2. Death—Fiction 3. Ranch life—Fiction 4. West (U.S.)—Fiction

ISBN 978-0-312-37557-7; 0-312-37557-3

Still mourning the recent death of his mother, seventeen-year-old Troy Stotts relates the events of the previous year when he and his two closest friends try to retaliate against the sheriff's son, who has been bullying them for years.

This novel "defies expectations via its sublime imagery and its elliptical narrative structure." Publ Wkly

In the path of falling objects. Feiwel and Friends 2009 326p $17.99

Grades: 10 11 12 Adult   **Fic**

1. Brothers—Fiction 2. Vietnam War, 1961-1975—Fiction

ISBN 978-0-312-37558-4; 0-312-37558-1

LC 2008-34755

In 1970, after their older brother is shipped off to Vietnam, sixteen-year-old Jonah and his younger brother Simon leave home to find their father, who is being released from an Arizona prison, but soon find themselves hitching a ride with a violent killer.

"Powerful imagery and symbolism are threaded throughout the narrative along with Bible references, a map that Jonah is drawing, a meteorite that Simon takes along as a talisman, and references to gravity and its relentless pull. The intensity will suit serious readers who don't mind a little blood and gore." SLJ

The Marbury lens. Feiwel and Friends 2010 358p $17.99

Grades: 10 11 12   **Fic**

1. Kidnapping—Fiction 2. London (England)—Fiction 3. Horror fiction

ISBN 978-0-312-61342-6; 0-312-61342-3

LC 2010-13007

After being kidnapped and barely escaping, sixteen-year-old Jack goes to London with his best friend Connor, where someone gives him a pair of glasses that send him to an alternate universe where war is raging, he is responsible for the survival of two younger boys, and Connor is trying to kill them all.

"This bloody and genuinely upsetting book packs an enormous emotional punch. Smith's characters are very well developed and the ruined alternate universe they travel through is both surreal and believable." Publ Wkly

Smith, Cynthia Leitich

Tantalize. Candlewick Press 2007 310p $16.99; pa $8.99

Grades: 9 10 11 12   **Fic**

1. Supernatural—Fiction 2. Vampires—Fiction 3. Werewolves—Fiction 4. Restaurants—Fiction 5. Texas—Fiction

ISBN 0-7636-2791-7; 978-0-7636-2791-1; 0-7636-4059-X (pa); 978-0-7636-4059-0 (pa)

LC 2005-58124

When multiple murders in Austin, Texas, threaten the grand reopening of her family's vampire-themed restaurant, seventeen-year-old, orphaned Quincie worries that her best friend-turned-love interest, Kieren, a werewolf-in-training, may be the prime suspect.

"Horror fans will be hooked by Kieren's quiet, hirsute hunkiness, and Texans by the premise that nearly everybody in their capitol is a shapeshifter." Publ Wkly

Followed by Blessed (2011)

Smith, Diane

Letters from Yellowstone. Viking 1999 226p il map hardcover o.p. pa $12.95 *

Grades: 11 12 Adult   **Fic**

1. Yellowstone National Park—Fiction

ISBN 0-670-88631-9; 0-14-029181-4 (pa)

LC 99-12904

"Professor Merriam thinks Cornell University student A. E. Bartram will be a wonderful addition to his Yellowstone National Park field expedition—until he finds out Bartram is a strong nineteenth-century woman who is willing to trade comfort for adventure. A thoroughly enjoyable epistolary novel that mixes history, romance, and science." Booklist

Smith, Jennifer E.

The comeback season. Simon & Schuster Books for Young Readers 2008 246p $15.99

Grades: 6 7 8 9 10   **Fic**

1. Baseball—Fiction 2. Father-daughter relationship—Fiction 3. Bereavement—Fiction 4. Family life—Fiction 5. Chicago (Ill.)—Fiction

ISBN 978-1-4169-3847-7; 1-4169-3847-8

LC 2007-17067

High school freshman Ryan Walsh, a Chicago Cubs fan, meets Nick when they both skip school on opening day, and their blossoming relationship becomes difficult for Ryan when she discovers that Nick is seriously ill and she again feels the pain of losing her father five years earlier.

"Smith deftly twines strands of grief, romance, baseball, family, and friendships lost and regained into this

Smith, Jennifer E.—*Continued*
tale. . . . . The present-tense narrative has an immediacy
that will engage readers and the supporting cast is unusually vivid." Booklist

Smith, Kirsten, 1970-
The geography of girlhood. Little, Brown 2006
184p hardcover o.p. pa $7.99
Grades: 8 9 10 11 12   **Fic**
1. Family life—Fiction 2. School stories 3. Novels in
verse
ISBN 0-316-16021-0; 0-316-01735-3 (pa)
                  LC 2005-938431
Novel in poetry about a girl navigating the unknown,
the difficult limbo between youth and adulthood. A novel
written in verse follows Penny Morrow in her transition
from middle school to high school as her father remar-
ries, she acquires a new stepbrother, and she experiences
her first dance, first kiss, and other hazards of growing
up.
"There is some matter-of-fact mention of sexual situations and underage drinking. However, it is the clarity,
the keen understanding, and the apt metaphors that make
Penny's voice so memorable." SLJ

Smith, Sarah, 1947-
The other side of dark. Atheneum Books for
Young Readers 2010 312p $16.99
Grades: 6 7 8 9 10   **Fic**
1. Ghost stories 2. Supernatural—Fiction 3. Race relations—Fiction 4. African Americans—Fiction
5. Orphans—Fiction 6. Boston (Mass.)—Fiction
ISBN 978-1-4424-0280-5; 1-4424-0280-6
                  LC 2010-14690
Since losing both of her parents, fifteen-year-old Katie
can see and talk to ghosts, which makes her a loner until
fellow student Law sees her drawing of a historic house
and together they seek a treasure rumored to be hidden
there by illegal slave-traders.
The author "weaves complicated racial issues into a
romantic, mysterious novel." Booklist

Smith, Sherri L.
Flygirl. G.P. Putnam's Sons 2009 275p $16.99
*
Grades: 7 8 9 10   **Fic**
1. World War, 1939-1945—Fiction 2. Women air pilots—Fiction 3. Air pilots—Fiction 4. African Americans—Fiction
ISBN 978-0-399-24709-5; 0-399-24709-2
                  LC 2008-25407
During World War II, a light-skinned African American girl "passes" for white in order to join the Women
Airforce Service Pilots.
"The details about navigation are exciting, but tougher
than any flight maneuver are Ida Mae's loneliness,
shame, and fear that she will be thrown out of the the
military, feelings that culminate in an unforgettable climax." Booklist

Smith-Ready, Jeri
Shade. Simon Pulse 2010 309p $17.99
Grades: 9 10 11 12   **Fic**
1. Trials—Fiction 2. Musicians—Fiction
3. Supernatural—Fiction 4. Ghost stories 5. Baltimore
(Md.)—Fiction
ISBN 978-1-4169-9406-0   LC 2009-39487
Sixteen-year-old Aura of Baltimore, Maryland, reluctantly works at her aunt's law firm helping ghosts with
wrongful death cases file suits in hopes of moving on,
but it becomes personal when her boyfriend, a promising
musician, dies and persistently haunts her.
Although "Smith-Ready's occasionally racy . . .
[book] resolves almost none of the issues surrounding the
Shift, leaving the door open for future books, it is a fully
satisfying read on its own, with well-developed, believable characters. . . . Perhaps even more impressive is the
understatement of the paranormal premise—Smith-Ready
changes the world completely by simply changing our
ability to see." Publ Wkly

Solzhenitsyn, Aleksandr, 1918-2008
One day in the life of Ivan Denisovich;
translated from the Russian by H. T. Willets; with
an introduction by John Bayley. Knopf 1995 xxvii,
159p $15
Grades: 11 12 Adult   **Fic**
1. Prisoners—Fiction 2. Soviet Union—Fiction
ISBN 0-679-44464-5
Also available in paperback from Farrar, Straus &
Giroux
"Everyman's library"
Original Russian edition, 1962; this is a reissue of the
translation published 1991 by Farrar, Straus & Giroux
"Drawing on his own experiences, the author writes of
one day, from reveille to lights-out, in the prison existence of Ivan Denisovich Shukhov. Innocent of any
crime, he has been convicted of treason and sentenced to
ten years in one of Stalin's notorious slave-labor compounds. The protagonist is a simple man trying to survive the brutality of a totalitarian system." Shapiro. Fic
for Youth. 3d edition

Sones, Sonya
One of those hideous books where the mother
dies. Simon & Schuster Books for Young Readers
2004 268p $15.95; pa $6.99
Grades: 7 8 9 10   **Fic**
1. Father-daughter relationship—Fiction
2. Bereavement—Fiction 3. Actors—Fiction
ISBN 0-689-85820-5; 1-416-90788-2 (pa)
                  LC 2003-9355
Fifteen-year-old Ruby Milliken leaves her best friend,
her boyfriend, her aunt, and her mother's grave in Boston and reluctantly flies to Los Angeles to live with her
father, a famous movie star who divorced her mother before Ruby was born
"Ruby's affable personality is evident in her humorous
quips and clever wordplays. Her depth of character is revealed through her honest admissions, poignant revelations, and sensitive insights. . . . Ruby's story is gripping, enjoyable, and memorable." SLJ

Sones, Sonya—*Continued*
What my mother doesn't know. Simon &
Schuster Bks. for Young Readers 2001 259p
hardcover o.p. pa $7.99
Grades: 7 8 9 10   **Fic**
    1. Dating (Social customs)—Fiction 2. Novels in verse
    ISBN 0-689-84114-0; 0-689-85553-2 (pa)
                                         LC 00-52634
"Fourteen-year-old Sophia is searching for Mr. Right.
In a story written in poetry form, Sophia describes her
relationships with sexy Dylan, suspicious cyberboy, and,
finally, with the mysterious masked 'stranger' who
dances with her on Halloween and then disappears."
Book Rep
    This is "a fast, funny, touching book. . . . The very
short, sometimes rhythmic lines make each page fly. Sophie's voice is colloquial and intimate." Booklist
    Followed by What my girlfriend doesn't know (2007)

Sonnenblick, Jordan
Notes from the midnight driver. Scholastic Press
2006 265p $16.99
Grades: 8 9 10 11 12   **Fic**
    1. Friendship—Fiction 2. Old age—Fiction
    3. Musicians—Fiction
    ISBN 0-439-75779-7   LC 2005-27972
    After being assigned to perform community service at
a nursing home, sixteen-year-old Alex befriends a cantankerous old man who has some lessons to impart about
jazz guitar playing, love, and forgiveness.
    The author "deftly infiltrates the teenage mind to pro-
duce a first-person narrative riddled with enough hapless
confusion, mulish equivocation, and beleaguered deadpan
humor to have readers nodding with recognition, sighing
with sympathy, and gasping with laughter—often on the
same page." Horn Book

Sorrells, Walter
First shot. Dutton Children's Books 2007 279p
hardcover o.p. pa $7.99 *
Grades: 7 8 9 10 11 12   **Fic**
    1. Mystery fiction 2. Homicide—Fiction
    3. Father-son relationship—Fiction
    ISBN   978-0-525-47801-0;   0-525-47801-9;
    978-0-14-241421-7 (pa); 0-14-241421-2 (pa)
    As David enters his senior year of high school, a fam-
ily secret emerges that could solve the mystery of why
his mother was murdered two years ago.
    "David's first person narration pulls readers into the
young man's torment. . . . This is a fast-paced, intriguing read." Booklist

Soto, Gary
The afterlife. Harcourt 2003 161p hardcover o.p.
pa $6.95 *
Grades: 7 8 9 10   **Fic**
    1. Mexican Americans—Fiction 2. Ghost stories
    ISBN 0-15-204774-3; 0-15-205220-8 (pa)
                                         LC 2003-44995
    A senior at East Fresno High School lives on as a
ghost after his brutal murder in the restroom of a club
where he had gone to dance.

"In many ways, this is as much a story about a hardscrabble place as it is about a boy who is murdered.
Both pulse with life and will stay in memory." Booklist

Buried onions. Harcourt Brace & Co. 1997 149p
hardcover o.p. pa $6.95 *
Grades: 8 9 10 11 12   **Fic**
    1. Violence—Fiction 2. Mexican Americans—Fiction
    ISBN 0-15-201333-4; 0-15-206265-3 (pa)
                                         LC 96-53112
    When nineteen-year-old Eddie drops out of college, he
struggles to find a place for himself as a Mexican American living in a violence-infested neighborhood of Fres-
no, California.
    "Soto has created a beautiful, touching, and truthful
story. . . . The lyrical language and Spanish phrases add
to the immediacy of setting and to the sensitivity the author brings to his character's life." Voice Youth Advocates

Southgate, Martha
The fall of Rome; a novel. Scribner 2002 223p
hardcover o.p. pa $13 *
Grades: 11 12 Adult   **Fic**
    1. African Americans—Fiction 2. Teachers—Fiction
    3. School stories
    ISBN 0-684-86500-9; 0-7432-2721-2 (pa)
                                         LC 2001-34225
    A "novel about a token black teacher at an élite New
England boarding school. Jerome Washington is a classics scholar who, armed with a Harvard education and an
accent purged of his Georgia-sharecropper roots, has
spent his life trying to defeat racism through sheer deco-
rum. But his hermetic existence is threatened by the arrival of a black student from a Brooklyn ghetto and a
white female teacher who fancies herself a champion of
the underprivileged." New Yorker
    The author "delves deeply into the social and emotion-
al elements that unite and divide us. Issues of race, identity, and integrity are intensely explored through a tragic
human triangle." Booklist

Spillebeen, Geert, 1956-
Age 14; translated by Terese Edelstein.
Houghton Mifflin 2009 216p $16
Grades: 8 9 10 11 12   **Fic**
    1. World War, 1914-1918—Fiction 2. Soldiers—Fic-
    tion
    ISBN 978-0-547-05342-4; 0-547-05342-8
                                         LC 2010-277732
    "Based on a true story, this spare, powerful novel . . .
focuses on Patrick, a poor Irish kid who is just 13 when
war breaks out. He dreams of escaping his dreary future
and abusive dad and finding adventure and glory in the
army. . . . The recruiters knowingly accept him into the
service when he claims that he is a 17-year-old named
John. . . . Spillebeen brings to the story a realistic,
grim conclusion." Booklist

Spillebeen, Geert, 1956-—*Continued*

Kipling's choice; written by Geert Spillebeen; translated by Terese Edelstein. Houghton Mifflin Co 2005 147p $16; pa $7.99

Grades: 7 8 9 10   **Fic**
  1. Kipling, John, 1897-1915—Fiction 2. World War, 1914-1918—Fiction 3. France—Fiction
  ISBN 0-618-43124-1; 0-618-80035-2 (pa)
                         LC 2004-20856

In 1915, mortally wounded in Loos, France, eighteen-year-old John Kipling, son of writer Rudyard Kipling, remembers his boyhood and the events leading to what is to be his first and last World War I battle.

"This well-written novel combines facts with speculation about John Kipling's short life and gruesome death. A riveting account of World War I." SLJ

Spinner, Stephanie, 1943-

Damosel; in which the Lady of the Lake renders a frank and often startling account of her wondrous life and times. Alfred A. Knopf 2008 198p $16.99; lib bdg $19.99

Grades: 7 8 9 10   **Fic**
  1. Arthur, King—Fiction 2. Dwarfs—Fiction 3. Fools and jesters—Fiction 4. Magic—Fiction 5. Great Britain—History—0-1066—Fiction
  ISBN 978-0-375-83634-3; 0-375-83634-9; 978-0-375-93634-0 (lib bdg); 0-375-93634-3 (lib bdg)
                         LC 2007-43519

Damosel, a rule-bound Lady of the Lake, and Twixt, a seventeen-year-old dwarf, relate their experiences as they strive to help King Arthur face Morgause, Morgan, and Mordred, one through her magic and the other through his humble loyalty.

"The magic is exciting and palpable. . . . Spinner's elegant language, strong characterizations, energetic dialogue, and lively plot combine in a memorable, accessible novel." Booklist

Springer, Nancy

I am Mordred; a tale from Camelot. Philomel Bks. 1998 184p hardcover o.p. pa $6.99 *

Grades: 7 8 9 10   **Fic**
  1. Arthur, King—Fiction 2. Mordred (Legendary character)—Fiction 3. Great Britain—History—0-1066—Fiction
  ISBN 0-399-23143-9; 0-698-11841-3 (pa)
                         LC 97-39740

"Mordred, the bad seed, the son of King Arthur and his sister, spends his youth learning who he is and then trying to deal with the prophecy made by Merlin that he will kill his father." SLJ

"Springer humanizes Arthurian archvillain Mordred in a thoroughly captivating and poignant tale." Booklist

I am Morgan le Fay; a tale from Camelot. Philomel Bks. 2001 227p hardcover o.p. pa $5.99

Grades: 7 8 9 10   **Fic**
  1. Arthur, King—Fiction 2. Morgan le Fay (Legendary character)—Fiction 3. Great Britain—History—0-1066—Fiction
  ISBN 0-399-23451-9; 0-698-11974-6 (pa)
                         LC 99-52847

In a war-torn England where her half-brother Arthur will eventually become king, the young Morgan le Fay comes to realize that she has magic powers and links to the faerie world

"Introspective, yet threaded with intrigue and adventure, this compelling study of the legendary villainess explores the ways that love, hate, jealousy, and the desire for power shape one young woman's fate and affect the destiny of others." Horn Book

St. Crow, Lili, 1976-

Strange angels. Razorbill 2009 293p pa $9.99

Grades: 8 9 10 11 12   **Fic**
  1. Supernatural—Fiction 2. Extrasensory perception—Fiction 3. Werewolves—Fiction 4. Vampires—Fiction 5. Orphans—Fiction
  ISBN 978-1-59514-251-1; 1-59514-251-7
                         LC 2008-39720

Sixteen-year-old Dru's psychic abilities helped her father battle zombies and other creatures of the "Real World," but now she must rely on herself, a "werwulf"-bitten friend, and a half-human vampire hunter to learn who murdered her parents, and why.

"The book grabs readers by the throat, sets hearts beating loudly and never lets go." Kirkus
  Other titles in this series are:
Betrayals (2009)
Defiance (2011)
Jealousy (2010)

St. James, James

Freak show. Dutton Children's Books 2007 297p $18.99

Grades: 8 9 10 11 12   **Fic**
  1. Female impersonators—Fiction 2. Homosexuality—Fiction 3. Prejudices—Fiction 4. School stories 5. Florida—Fiction
  ISBN 978-0-525-47799-0; 0-525-47799-3
                         LC 2006-29716

Having faced teasing that turned into a brutal attack, Christianity expressed as persecution, and the loss of his only real friend when he could no longer keep his crush under wraps, seventeen-year-old Billy Bloom, a drag queen, decides the only to become fabulous again is to run for Homecoming Queen at his elite, private school near Fort Lauderdale, Florida.

"Though the subject matter and language will likely prove controversial, it's nearly impossible to remain untouched after walking a mile in the stilettos of someone so unfailingly true to himself and so blisteringly funny." Publ Wkly

Stahler, David, Jr.

Doppelganger; [by] David Stahler, Jr. HarperCollins Publishers 2006 258p hardcover o.p. pa $8.99

Grades: 8 9 10 11 12   **Fic**
  1. Family life—Fiction 2. Child abuse—Fiction 3. Supernatural—Fiction 4. Horror fiction
  ISBN 978-0-06-087232-8; 0-06-087232-2; 978-0-06-087234-2 (pa); 0-06-087234-9 (pa)
                         LC 2005-28484

Stahler, David, Jr.—*Continued*

When a sixteen-year-old member of a race of shape-shifting killers called doppelgangers assumes the life of a troubled teen, he becomes unexpectedly embroiled in human life—and it is nothing like what he has seen on television.

"This brooding story of literally stepping into someone else's shoes combines romance, horror, and angst to create a distinctive story of redemption. The abusive relationships in Chris's family are portrayed with realism and sensitivity." Voice Youth Advocates

Standiford, Natalie

Confessions of the Sullivan sisters. Scholastic Press 2010 313p $17.99 *

Grades: 9 10 11 12   Fic

1. Conduct of life—Fiction 2. Inheritance and succession—Fiction 3. Grandmothers—Fiction 4. Sisters—Fiction 5. Family life—Fiction 6. Baltimore (Md.)—Fiction

ISBN 978-0-545-10710-5   LC 2010-14512

Upon learning on Christmas Day that their rich and imperious grandmother may soon die and disown the family unless the one who offended her deeply will confess, each of the three Sullivan sisters sets down her offenses on paper.

"A step above most books about rich girls, their boys, and their toys in both style and substance." Booklist

How to say goodbye in Robot. Scholastic 2009 276p $17.99; pa $8.99 *

Grades: 9 10 11 12   Fic

1. Friendship—Fiction 2. Family life—Fiction 3. Death—Fiction 4. Baltimore (Md.)—Fiction

ISBN 978-0-545-10708-2; 0-545-10708-3; 978-0-545-10709-9 (pa); 0-545-10709-1 (pa)

       LC 2009-5256

After moving to Baltimore and enrolling in a private school, high school senior Beatrice befriends a quiet loner with a troubled family history.

"This is an honest and complex depiction of a meaningful platonic friendship and doesn't gloss over troubling issues. The minor characters, particularly the talk-show regulars, are quirky and depicted with sly humor. . . . An outstanding choice for a book discussion group." SLJ

Staples, Suzanne Fisher

Shabanu; daughter of the wind. Knopf 1989 240p hardcover o.p. pa $6.50 *

Grades: 8 9 10 11 12   Fic

1. Sex role—Fiction 2. Pakistan—Fiction

ISBN 0-394-84815-2; 0-440-23856-0 (pa)

       LC 89-2714

When eleven-year-old Shabanu, the daughter of a nomad in the Cholistan Desert of present-day Pakistan, is pledged in marriage to an older man whose money will bring prestige to the family, she must either accept the decision, as is the custom, or risk the consequences of defying her father's wishes

"Interspersing native words throughout adds realism, but may trip up readers, who must be patient enough to find meaning through context. This use of language is,

however, an important element in helping Staples paint an evocative picture of life in the desert that includes references to the hard facts of reality." Booklist

Other titles in this series are:

Haveli (1993)

The house of djinn (2008)

Staunton, Ted, 1956-

Acting up. Red Deer Press 2010 263p pa $12.95

Grades: 9 10 11 12   Fic

1. Family life—Fiction 2. Conduct of life—Fiction 3. School stories 4. Canada—Fiction

ISBN 0-88995-441-0; 978-0-88995-441-0

Sequel to Sounding off (2004)

"Sam Foster, a normal teenager and drummer in the band ADHD, has maturity as his latest goal. Achieving this goal will put him well on the way to a parent-free weekend over spring break and getting his learner's permit. But as with most teenagers, circumstances have a way of preventing even the most enthusiastic teen from success. . . . Staunton has written a fast-paced coming-of-age novel that flows well. Teens will easily identify with the main characters and the hilarious antics that take place as he achieves maturity. There is mention of the effects of drinking alcohol and references to drug taking, but it is within the context of the story." Voice Youth Advocates

Stein, Tammar

High dive. Alfred A. Knopf 2008 201p $15.99; lib bdg $18.99

Grades: 7 8 9 10   Fic

1. Vacations—Fiction 2. Single parent family—Fiction 3. Loss (Psychology)—Fiction 4. Friendship—Fiction 5. Europe—Fiction

ISBN 978-0-375-83024-2; 0-375-83024-3; 978-0-375-93024-9 (lib bdg); 0-375-93024-8 (lib bdg)

       LC 2007049657

With her mother stationed in Iraq as an Army nurse, Vanderbilt University student Arden Vogel, whose father was killed in a traffic accident a few years earlier, impulsively ends up on a tour of Europe with a group of college girls she meets on her way to attend to some family business in Sardinia.

"Ideal for the thoughtful armchair traveler, this story is engaging enough for readers on the long flight to the enduring wonders of Europe and emerging adulthood." SLJ

Light years; a novel. Knopf 2005 263p hardcover o.p. pa $6.99

Grades: 7 8 9 10   Fic

1. Israel-Arab conflicts—Fiction 2. Bereavement—Fiction

ISBN 0-375-83023-5; 0-440-23902-8 (pa)

       LC 2004-7776

Maya Laor leaves her home in Israel to study astronomy at the University of Virginia after the tragic death of her boyfriend in a suicide bombing.

"This well-paced first novel, a moving study of grief and recovery, is also a love story that should appeal particularly to students interested in other ways of seeing the world." SLJ

Includes bibliographical references

Steinbeck, John, 1902-1968

The grapes of wrath; introduction and notes by Robert DeMott. Penguin Books 2006 lviii, 464p (Penguin classics) pa $15 *

Grades: 11 12 Adult   Fic

1. Migrant agricultural laborers—Fiction
ISBN 0-14-303943-1   LC 2005-58182
First published 1939

"Awarded the Pulitzer Prize in 1940, this moving and highly successful proletarian novel tells of the hardships of the Joad family. 'Okie' farmers forced out of their home in the Oklahoma dustbowl region by economic desperation, they drive to California in search of work as migrant fruitpickers. The grandparents die on the way; on their arrival the others are harassed by the police and participate in strike violence, during which Tom, the Joad son, kills a man. At the conclusion of the novel, throughout which descriptive and philosophical passages alternate with narrative portions, the family is defeated but still resolute." Reader's Ency. 4th edition

Of mice and men. Viking 1986 107p hardcover o.p. pa $12 *

Grades: 11 12 Adult   Fic

1. Migrant labor—Fiction 2. Ranch life—Fiction
ISBN 0-670-52071-3; 0-14-200067-1 (pa)
                                      LC 86-1300
First published 1937 by Covici-Friede

"Two uneducated laborers dream of a time when they can share the ownership of a rabbit farm in California. George is a plotter and a schemer, while Lennie is a mentally deficient hulk of a man who has no concept of his physical strength. As a team they are not particularly successful, but their friendship is enduring." Shapiro. Fic for Youth. 3d edition

The pearl; with drawings by José Clemente Orozco. Viking 1947 122p il hardcover o.p. pa $12 *

Grades: 7 8 9 10   Fic

1. Mexico—Fiction 2. Poverty—Fiction
ISBN 0-670-54575-9; 0-14-200069-8 (pa)

"Kino, a poor pearl-fisher, lives a happy albeit spartan life with his wife and their child. When he finds a magnificent pearl, the Pearl of the World, he is besieged by dishonest pearl merchants and envious neighbors. Even a greedy doctor ties his professional treatment of their baby when it is bitten by a scorpion to the possible acquisition of the pearl. After a series of disasters, Kino throws the pearl away since it has brought him only unhappiness." Shapiro. Fic for Youth. 3d edition

Steinmetz, Karen

The mourning wars. Roaring Brook Press 2010 232p $17.99

Grades: 7 8 9 10   Fic

1. Mohawk Indians—Fiction 2. United States—History—1702-1713, Queen Anne's War—Fiction
ISBN 978-1-59643-290-1; 1-59643-290-X
                                      LC 2010-11735
In 1704, Mohawk Indians attack the frontier village of Deerfield, Massachusetts, kidnapping over 100 residents, including seven-year-old Eunice Williams. Based on a true story.

"Eunice's largely imagined life makes a fascinating story with a setting that is vividly and dramatically evoked. The book will be especially useful in the classroom." Booklist
Includes bibliographical references

Stevenson, Robert Louis, 1850-1894

The strange case of Dr. Jekyll and Mr. Hyde; with an introduction by Joyce Carol Oates. Vintage Books 1991 97p pa $8.95 *

Grades: 7 8 9 10 11 12 Adult   Fic

1. Horror fiction 2. Allegories 3. Good and evil—Fiction 4. Great Britain—Fiction
ISBN 0-679-73476-7   LC 90-50600
Also available from other publishers
First published 1886. Variant title: Dr. Jekyll and Mr. Hyde

"The disturbing tale of the dual personality of Dr. Jekyll, a physician. A generous and philanthropic man, he is preoccupied with the problems of good and evil and with the possibility of separating them into two distinct personalities. He develops a drug that transforms him into the demonic Mr. Hyde, in whose person he exhausts all the latent evil in his nature. He also creates an antidote that will restore him to his respectable existence as Dr. Jekyll. Gradually, however, the unmitigated evil of his darker self predominates, until finally he performs an atrocious murder. . . . The novel is of great psychological perception and strongly concerned with ethical problems." Reader's Ency. 4th edition

Treasure Island; illustrated by N. C. Wyeth. Scribner 1981 273p il hardcover o.p. pa $6.99

Grades: 7 8 9 10 11 12 Adult   Fic

1. Buried treasure—Fiction 2. Pirates—Fiction 3. Adventure fiction
ISBN 0-684-17160-0; 0-689-83212-5 (pa)
                                      LC 81-8788
First published 1882

Young Jim Hawkins discovers a treasure map in the chest of an old sailor who dies under mysterious circumstances at his mother's inn. He shows it to Dr. Livesey and Squire Trelawney who agree to outfit a ship and sail to Treasure Island. Among the crew is the pirate Long John Silver and his followers who are in pursuit of the treasure

Stevenson, Robin H., 1968-

A thousand shades of blue; [by] Robin Stevenson. Orca Book Publishers 2008 231p pa $12.95 *

Grades: 7 8 9 10   Fic

1. Sailing—Fiction 2. Family life—Fiction 3. Bahamas—Fiction
ISBN 978-1-55143-921-1; 1-55143-921-2

A yearlong sailing trip to the Bahamas reveals deep wounds in Rachel's family and brings out the worst in Rachel.

"The author does a fantastic job of making each character relatable to teens and creates some major drama between Rachel's mother and one of the locals that keeps the reader interested. . . . The book flows very smoothly, making it an easy read for teens." Voice Youth Advocates

Stevenson, Sarah Jamila

The Latte Rebellion. Flux 2011 328p pa $9.95

Grades: 8 9 10 11 12   **Fic**
   1. Clubs—Fiction 2. Racially mixed people—Fiction
   3. Family life—Fiction 4. School stories
   5. California—Fiction
   ISBN 978-0-7387-2278-8; 0-7387-2278-2
                                        LC 2010-35002

When high school senior Asha Jamison is called a
"towel head" at a pool party, she and her best friend
Carey start a club to raise awareness of mixed-race students that soon sweeps the country, but the hubbub puts
her Ivy League dreams, friendship, and beliefs to the
test.

"The novel speaks directly to teenagers who are beginning to find their place in their world and figuring out
how to make the world a better place for others. . . .
This coming-of-age story is craftily written, fast paced
and delivers a message of doing the right thing under
difficult circumstances." Voice Youth Advocates

Stewart, Mary, 1916-

Mary Stewart's Merlin trilogy. Morrow 1980
919p maps $29.95 *

Grades: 11 12 Adult   **Fic**
   1. Arthur, King—Fiction 2. Merlin (Legendary character)—Fiction 3. Great Britain—History—0-1066—Fiction
   ISBN 0-688-00347-8   LC 80-21019

An omnibus edition of: The crystal cave, The hollow
hills and The last enchantment, first published 1970,
1973 and 1979 respectively

The first novel in this trilogy based on Arthurian legends concerns the difficult childhood and youth of the
magician Merlin who grows up as a bastard at the court
of the King of Wales where he is believed to be the off-
spring of the King's daughter and the devil. He gains
much knowledge from a learned wizard and escapes to
"Less Britain" where he becomes involved in efforts to
unite all of Britain. The second novel tells of Merlin's
involvement with the childhood of Arthur and Arthur's
search for the magical sword, Caliburn. The last novel
deals with Merlin's death and Arthur's turbulent reign.

The author's "skill in creating colorful characters, suspense, and a brooding atmosphere serves her well in portraying England's Dark Ages, where witches, sorcerers,
and tragic kings moved heroically through an enchanted
land. Though Arthur's rise to power is the subject, the
true star and narrator of the tale is Merlin the magician."
Husband. Sequels

   Includes bibliographical references

Stiefvater, Maggie, 1981-

Lament; the faerie queen's deception. Flux 2008
325p pa $9.95

Grades: 8 9 10 11 12   **Fic**
   1. Supernatural—Fiction 2. Fairies—Fiction
   3. Magic—Fiction 4. Musicians—Fiction
   ISBN 978-0-7387-1370-0; 0-7387-1370-8
                                        LC 2008-17592

On the day of an important music competition, talented but painfully introverted and nervous Deirdre Mona-
ghan is helped to perform by the compelling and enigmatic Luke Dillon and finds herself inexorably drawn

into the mysteries and dangers of the faerie world.

"Stiefvater brings to her story several layers of romance, a knowledge of Irish music and a talent for plot
twists. . . . Vibrant and potent." Publ Wkly

   Followed by: Ballad: a gathering of faerie (2009)

Shiver. Scholastic 2009 392p $17.99; pa $8.99
*

Grades: 9 10 11 12   **Fic**
   1. Werewolves—Fiction 2. Supernatural—Fiction
   ISBN   978-0-545-12326-6;   0-545-12326-7;
   978-0-545-12327-3 (pa); 0-545-12327-5 (pa)
                                        LC 2009-5257

In all the years she has watched the wolves in the
woods behind her house, Grace has been particularly
drawn to an unusual yellow-eyed wolf who, in his turn,
has been watching her with increasing intensity.

"Stiefvater skillfully increases the tension throughout;
her take on werewolves is interesting and original while
her characters are refreshingly willing to use their brains
to deal with the challenges they face." Publ Wkly

   Other titles featuring the wolves of Mercy Falls are:
Forever (2011)
Linger (2010)

Stoker, Bram, 1847-1912

Dracula; edited with an introduction and notes
by Maurice Hindle; preface by Christopher
Frayling. Penguin Books 2003 xlvii, 454p pa $11
*

Grades: 11 12 Adult   **Fic**
   1. Horror fiction 2. Vampires—Fiction
   ISBN 0-14-143984-X   LC 2003-269578

Also available annotated edition from Norton with title: The new annotated Dracula; and in hardcover and
paperback from other publishers

   First published 1897

"Count Dracula, an 'undead' villain from Transylvania, uses his supernatural powers to lure and prey upon
innocent victims from whom he gains the blood on
which he lives. The novel is written chiefly in the form
of journals kept by the principal characters—Jonathan
Harker, who contacts the vampire in his Transylvanian
castle; Harker's fiancée (later his wife), Mina, adored by
the Count; the well-meaning Dr. Seward; and Lucy
Westenra, a victim who herself becomes a vampire. The
doctor and friends destroy Dracula in the end, but only
after they drive a stake through Lucy's heart to save her
soul." Merriam-Webster's Ency of Lit

Stone, Mary Hanlon

Invisible girl. Philomel Books 2010 279p $16.99
Grades: 7 8 9 10   **Fic**
   1. Child abuse—Fiction 2. Popularity—Fiction
   3. California—Fiction
   ISBN 978-0-399-25249-5; 0-399-25249-5
                                        LC 2009-27255

Thirteen-year-old Stephanie, whisked from Boston to
Encino, California, to stay with family friends after her
abusive, alcoholic mother abandons her, tries desperately
to fit in with her "cousin's" popular group even as she
sees how much easier it would be to remain invisible.

"This edgy fish-out-of-water story features a strong
and sympathetic protagonist." Horn Book Guide

Stone, Tanya Lee

A bad boy can be good for a girl. Wendy Lamb Books 2006 228p hardcover o.p. pa $7.99 *

Grades: 9 10 11 12   **Fic**

1. School stories

ISBN   0-385-74702-0;   978-0-385-74702-8; 0-553-49509-7 (pa); 978-0-553-49509-6 (pa)

LC 2006-272453

Josie, Nicolette, and Aviva all get mixed up with a senior boy who can talk them into doing almost anything he wants. In a blur of high school hormones and personal doubt, each girl struggles with how much to give up and what ultimately to keep for herself.

"The language is realistic and frank, and, while not graphic, it is filled with descriptions of the teens and their sexuality. This is not a book that will sit quietly on any shelf; it will be passed from girl to girl to girl." SLJ

Stork, Francisco X.

The last summer of the death warriors. Arthur A. Levine Books 2010 344p $17.99 *

Grades: 8 9 10 11 12   **Fic**

1. Death—Fiction 2. Orphans—Fiction 3. Mexican Americans—Fiction 4. New Mexico—Fiction

ISBN 978-0-545-15133-7; 0-545-15133-3

LC 2009-19853

"Seventeen-year-old Pancho Sanchez is sent to a Catholic orphanage after his father and sister die in the span of a few months. Though the cause of his sister's death is technically 'undetermined,' Pancho plans to kill the man he believes responsible. . . . When D.Q., a fellow resident dying from brain cancer, asks Pancho to accompany him to Albuquerque for experimental treatments, Pancho agrees—he'll get paid and it's where his sister's killer lives." Publ Wkly

"This novel, in the way of the best literary fiction, is an invitation to careful reading that rewards serious analysis and discussion. Thoughtful readers will be delighted by both the challenge and Stork's respect for their abilities." Booklist

Marcelo in the real world. Arthur A. Levine Books 2009 312p $17.99 *

Grades: 8 9 10 11 12   **Fic**

1. Autism—Fiction 2. Asperger's syndrome—Fiction

ISBN 978-0-545-05474-4; 0-545-05474-5

LC 2008-14729

Marcelo Sandoval, a seventeen-year-old boy on the high-functioning end of the autistic spectrum, faces new challenges, including romance and injustice, when he goes to work for his father in the mailroom of a corporate law firm.

"Stork introduces ethical dilemmas, the possibility of love, and other 'real world' conflicts, all the while preserving the integrity of his characterizations and intensifying the novel's psychological and emotional stakes." Publ Wkly

Stowe, Harriet Beecher, 1811-1896

Uncle Tom's cabin; with an introduction by Alfred Kazin. Knopf 1995 xxix, 494p $20 *

Grades: 11 12 Adult   **Fic**

1. African Americans—Fiction 2. Slavery—Fiction

ISBN 0-679-44365-7

Also available in paperback from Bantam Classics

"Everyman's library"

"The book relates the trials, suffering, and human dignity of Uncle Tom, an old slave. Cruelly treated by a Yankee plantation owner, Simon Legree, Tom dies as the result of a beating. Uncle Tom is devoted to Little Eva, the daughter of his white owner, Augustine St. Clare. Other important characters are the mulatto girl Eliza; the impish black child Topsy; Miss Ophelia St. Clare, a New England spinster; and Marks, the slave catcher. The setting is Kentucky and Louisiana." Reader's Ency. 4th edition

Strasser, Todd, 1950-

Boot camp. Simon & Schuster Books for Young Readers 2007 238p hardcover o.p. pa $6.99

Grades: 8 9 10 11 12   **Fic**

1. Juvenile delinquency—Fiction 2. Torture—Fiction

ISBN   978-1-4169-0848-7;   1-4169-0848-X; 978-1-4169-5942-7 (pa); 1-4169-5942-4 (pa)

LC 2006-13634

After ignoring several warnings to stop dating his former teacher, Garrett is sent to Lake Harmony, a boot camp that uses brutal methods to train students to obey their parents.

"The ending is both realistic and disturbing. . . . Writing in the teen's mature and perceptive voice, Strasser creates characters who will provoke strong reactions from readers. . . . [This is a] fast-paced and revealing story." SLJ

Famous. Simon & Schuster Books for Young Readers 2011 257p $15.99

Grades: 7 8 9 10   **Fic**

1. Celebrities—Fiction 2. Actors—Fiction 3. Fame—Fiction 4. Hollywood (Calif.)—Fiction

ISBN 978-1-4169-7511-3; 1-4169-7511-X

LC 2009-48163

Sixteen-year-old Jamie Gordon had a taste of praise and recognition at age fourteen when her unflattering photograph of an actress was published, but as she pursues her dream of being a celebrity photographer, she becomes immersed in the dark side of fame.

"The book makes some astute observations about America's reality-television culture and its obsession with fame. . . . This well-crafted novel clearly belongs in all public, junior high, and high school libraries." Voice Youth Advocates

Give a boy a gun. Simon & Schuster Bks. for Young Readers 2000 146p hardcover o.p. pa $5.99 *

Grades: 9 10 11 12   **Fic**

1. Violence—Fiction 2. School stories

ISBN 0-689-81112-8; 0-689-84893-5 (pa)

This documentary novel "charts the growing disaffection of Gary and Brendan, two teenage friends who dream of taking revenge on the people (primarily members of the school's football team) who have tormented them. Told in a variety of voices, which are presented as excerpts from interview's with family, friends, teachers, and others." Booklist

"Statistics, quotes, and facts related to actual incidents of school violence appear in dark print at the bottom of the pages. An appendix includes a chronology of school shootings in the United States, the author's own treatise on gun control, and places to get more information." SLJ

Strasser, Todd, 1950-—*Continued*

Wish you were dead. Egmont USA 2009 236p
$16.99; lib bdg $19.99

Grades: 8 9 10 11 12   **Fic**
1. Missing persons—Fiction 2. Kidnapping—Fiction
3. Weblogs—Fiction 4. School stories 5. New York
(State)—Fiction
ISBN   978-1-60684-007-8;   1-60684-007-X;
978-1-60684-049-8 (lib bdg); 1-60684-049-5 (lib bdg)
                                          LC 2009-14641

Madison, a senior at a suburban New York high
school, tries to uncover who is responsible for the disappearance of her friends, popular students mentioned in
the posts of an anonymous blogger, while she, herself, is
being stalked online and in-person.

"The themes of bullying, tolerance, and friendship are
issues to which readers can relate, as well as the inclusion of the IMing, blogging, texting, and social networking. This thriller will be popular and passed from one
reader to another." Voice Youth Advocates

Stratton, Allan

Borderline. HarperTeen 2010 298p $16.99; lib
bdg $17.89 *

Grades: 6 7 8 9 10   **Fic**
1. Father-son relationship—Fiction 2. Prejudices—Fiction 3. Friendship—Fiction 4. Muslims—Fiction
5. Terrorism—Fiction
ISBN   978-0-06-145111-9;   0-06-145111-8;
978-0-06-145112-6 (lib bdg); 0-06-145112-6 (lib bdg)
                                          LC 2009-5241

Despite the strained relationship between them,
teenaged Sami Sabiri risks his life to uncover the truth
when his father is implicated in a terrorist plot.

This is "a powerful story and excellent resource for
teaching tolerance, with a message that extends well beyond the timely subject matter." Publ Wkly

Chanda's secrets. Annick Press 2004 193p
$19.95; pa $8.95 *

Grades: 7 8 9 10   **Fic**
1. AIDS (Disease)—Fiction 2. Africa—Fiction
ISBN 1-55037-835-X; 1-55037-834-1 (pa)

In this story "Chanda, a 16-year-old . . . girl living in
the small city of Bonang in Africa, must confront the undercurrents of shame and stigma associated with
HIV/AIDS." Publisher's note

"The details of sub-Saharan African life are convincing and smoothly woven into this moving story of poverty and courage, but the real insight for readers will be
the appalling treatment of the AIDS victims. Strong language and frank description are appropriate to the subject
matter." SLJ
 Another title about Chanda is:
Chanda's war (2007)

Stroud, Jonathan, 1970-

The Amulet of Samarkand. Hyperion Bks. for
Children 2003 462p (Bartimaeus trilogy) $17.95;
pa $7.99

Grades: 7 8 9 10   **Fic**
1. Fantasy fiction
ISBN 0-7868-1859-X; 0-7868-5255-0 (pa)
                                          LC 2003-49904

Nathaniel, a magician's apprentice, summons up the
djinni Bartimaeus and instructs him to steal the Amulet
of Samarkand from the powerful magician Simon Lovelace.

"There is plenty of action, mystery, and humor to
keep readers turning the pages. This title, the first in a
trilogy, is a must for fantasy fans." SLJ
 Other titles in this series are:
The golem's eye (2004)
Ptolemy's gate (2006)

Heroes of the valley. Hyperion Books for
Children 2009 483p $17.99 *

Grades: 7 8 9 10   **Fic**
1. Adventure fiction 2. Middle Ages—Fiction
ISBN 978-1-4231-0966-2; 1-4231-0966-X

"Twelve Houses control sections of a valley. Halli
Sveinsson—at 15, the youngest child of the rulers of the
House of Svein—goes against tradition when he sets out
to avenge the death of his murdered uncle, and his actions result in warfare among Houses for the first time
in generations. . . . Smart, funny dialogue and prose, revealing passages about the exploits of the hero Svein,
bouts of action and a touch of romance briskly move the
story along." Publ Wkly

The ring of Solomon; a Bartimaeus novel.
Disney/Hyperion Books 2010 398p $17.99

Grades: 7 8 9 10   **Fic**
1. Solomon, King of Israel—Fiction 2. Magic—Fiction
3. Witchcraft—Fiction 4. Jerusalem—Fiction
5. Fantasy fiction
ISBN 978-1-4231-2372-9; 1-4231-2372-7
                                          LC 2010015468

Wise-cracking djinni Bartimaeus finds himself at the
court of King Solomon with an unpleasant master, a sinister servant, and King Solomon's magic ring.

"In this exciting prequel set in ancient Israel, Stroud
presents an early adventure of his sharp-tongued djinn,
Bartimaeus. . . . This is a superior fantasy that should
have fans racing back to those books." Publ Wkly

Styron, William, 1925-2006

The confessions of Nat Turner. Modern Lib.
1994 xliv, 428p hardcover o.p. pa $14 *

Grades: 11 12 Adult   **Fic**
1. Turner, Nat, 1800?-1831—Fiction 2. Slavery—Fiction
ISBN 0-679-60101-5; 0-679-73663-8 (pa)
                                          LC 94-9393

A reissue of the title first published 1967 by Random
House

This "account of an actual person and event is based
on the brief contemporary pamphlet of the same title
presented to a trial court as evidence and published in
Virginia a year after the revolt of fellow slaves led by
Turner in 1831. Imagining much of Turner's youth and
early manhood before the rebellion that he headed at the
age of 31, Styron in frequently rhetorical and pseudo-
Biblical style has Turner recall his religious faith and his
power of preaching to other slaves." Oxford Companion
to Am Lit. 5th edition

Styron, William, 1925-2006—*Continued*

Sophie's choice. Modern Lib. 1998 599p $22; pa $14

Grades: 11 12 Adult **Fic**
1. Authors—Fiction 2. Brooklyn (New York, N.Y.)—Fiction
ISBN 0-679-60289-5; 0-679-73637-9 (pa)
LC 97-36895

A reissue of the title first published 1979

"Sophie Zawistowska is a Polish Catholic who has somehow survived Auschwitz and resettled in America after the war. Here, in a Jewish boarding house in Flatbush, she meets two men—Nathan Landau, a brilliant but dangerously unstable Jew who becomes her lover; and Stingo, a young Southern writer (and autobiographical simulacrum of Styron himself). The novel traces Stingo's intense involvement with the lovers—their euphoric highs as well as their cataclysmic descents into psychopathy—and his growing fascination with the horror of Sophie's past." Libr J

"It was a daring act for Styron, whose sensibilities are wholly Southern, to venture into the territory of the American Jew, to say nothing of his plunge into European history. The book is powerfully moving." Burgess. 99 Novels

Summers, Courtney

Fall for anything. St. Martin's Griffin 2011 230p pa $9.99

Grades: 9 10 11 12 **Fic**
1. Suicide—Fiction 2. Father-daughter relationship—Fiction 3. Bereavement—Fiction 4. Mystery fiction
ISBN 978-0-312-65673-7 LC 2010-37873

As she searches for clues that would explain the suicide of her successful photographer father, Eddie Reeves meets the strangely compelling Culler Evans who seems to know a great deal about her father and could hold the key to the mystery surrounding his death.

"Readers may find the book fascinating or mesmerizingly melancholy depending on their moods, but there is no denying that Summers has brought Eddie's intense experience into the world of her readers. An unusual, bold effort that deserves attention." Kirkus

Some girls are. St. Martin's Griffin 2010 245p pa $9.99

Grades: 9 10 11 12 **Fic**
1. Bullies—Fiction 2. School stories
ISBN 978-0-312-57380-5 LC 2009-33859

Regina, a high school senior in the popular—and feared—crowd, suddenly falls out of favor and becomes the object of the same sort of vicious bullying that she used to inflict on others, until she finds solace with one of her former victims.

"Regina's every emotion is palpable, and it's impossible not to feel every punch—physical or emotional—she takes." Publ Wkly

Supplee, Suzanne

Artichoke's heart. Dutton Children's Books 2008 276p $16.99

Grades: 7 8 9 10 **Fic**
1. Obesity—Fiction 2. Weight loss—Fiction 3. Mother-daughter relationship—Fiction 4. Cancer—Fiction 5. School stories
ISBN 978-0-52547-902-4; 0-52547-902-3
LC 2007-28486

When she is almost sixteen years old, Rosemary decides she is sick of being overweight, mocked at school and at Heavenly Hair—her mother's beauty salon—and feeling out of control, and as she slowly loses weight, she realizes that she is able to cope with her mother's cancer, having a boyfriend for the first time, and discovering that other people's lives are not as perfect as they seem from the outside.

"Supplee brings a cast of original characters to life in this convincing and consistently entertaining narrative." Booklist

Somebody everybody listens to. Dutton 2010 245p $16.99

Grades: 7 8 9 10 11 12 **Fic**
1. Singers—Fiction 2. Country music—Fiction 3. Nashville (Tenn.)—Fiction
ISBN 978-0-525-42242-6; 0-525-42242-0
LC 2009-25089

Retta Lee Jones is blessed with a beautiful voice and has big dreams of leaving her tiny Tennessee hometown. With a beaten down car, a pocketful of hard-earned waitressing money, and stars in her eyes, Retta sets out to make it big in Nashville.

"While a must read for country music lovers, . . . [this book] will appeal to a wide audience, especially those who long to pursue a dream against the odds." Publ Wkly

Sutcliff, Rosemary, 1920-1992

The Shining Company. Farrar, Straus & Giroux 1990 295p hardcover o.p. pa $7.95

Grades: 9 10 11 12 **Fic**
1. Great Britain—History—0-1066—Fiction
ISBN 0-374-36807-4; 0-374-46616-5 (pa)
LC 89-46142

This novel is "based on 'The Gododdin,' the earliest surviving poem set in Northern Britain. Set in A.D. 600, the story is told by Prosper who, with his bodyservant Conn, joins Prince Gorthyn as a shieldbearer when the prince enlists in a company formed by King Mynyddog of the Gododdin in an effort to unite the British kingdoms against the ever-present Saxon threat. The bulk of the story concerns the forging of men from disparate parts of Britain into a fighting unit, combined in a common cause. The rousing climax comes with their first mission when, sent deep into Saxon territory, they are abandoned by Mynyddog." SLJ

"The realistic telling of the tale makes Sutcliff's story interesting. She creates a setting so genuine that readers will find themselves transposed into another time and place. Her language, reinforced by the Germanic influence of Old English, adds not only authenticity to the story but also a sense of poetry. This book will be cherished by the lover of history, the lover of literature, and the lover of adventure." Voice Youth Advocates

Swanwick, Michael
The dragons of Babel. Tor 2008 318p pa $15.99
*

Grades: 11 12 Adult   Fic
1. Dragons—Fiction 2. Fantasy fiction
ISBN   978-0-7653-1950-0;   0-7653-1950-0;
978-0-7653-3114-4 (pa); 0-7653-3114-4 (pa)
                                    LC 2007-34918
Sequel to: The iron dragon's daughter (2004)
"A Tom Doherty Associates book"
Enslaved by a war-dragon of Babel, young Will evac-
uates to the Tower of Babel where he meets the confidence trickster, Nat Whilk, and becomes a hero to the
homeless living in the tunnels under the city. As he rises
from an underling to a politician, Will falls in love with
a high-elven woman he dare not aspire to.
    "Earthy, bawdy, and often brutal, . . . [this is] a story
that will keep science fiction/fantasy fans involved till
the end." SLJ

Sweeney, Joyce, 1955-
The guardian. Henry Holt and Co. 2009 177p
$16.95
Grades: 7 8 9 10   Fic
1. Foster home care—Fiction 2. Siblings—Fiction
3. Bullies—Fiction 4. Father-son relationship—Fiction
5. School stories
ISBN 978-0-8050-8019-3; 0-8050-8019-8
                                    LC 2008-40602
When thirteen-year-old Hunter, struggling to deal with
a harsh, money-grubbing foster mother, three challenging
foster sisters, and a school bully, returns to his childhood
faith and prays to St. Gabriel, he instantly becomes
aware that he does, indeed, have a guardian.
    "Sweeney's prose is insightful and realistic, with clev-
erly delivered descriptions. The peripheral characters are
believable, and the religious undercurrent supports the
plot. Well-paced, and with a satisfying conclusion." SLJ

Swift, Jonathan, 1667-1745
Gulliver's travels; with an introduction by Pat
Rogers. Knopf 1991 xlv, 318p map $20
Grades: 7 8 9 10 11 12 Adult   Fic
1. Fantasy fiction
ISBN 0-679-40545-3   LC 91-53011
Also available from other publishers
"Everyman's library"
First published 1726
    "In the account of his four wonder-countries Swift sat-
irizes contemporary manners and morals, art and politics—in fact the whole social scheme—from four different points of view. The huge Brobdingnagians reduce
man to his natural insignificance, the little people of Lil-
liput parody Europe and its petty broils, in Laputa philosophers are ridiculed, and finally all Swift's hatred and
contempt find their satisfaction in degrading humanity to
a bestial condition." Baker. Guide to the Best Fic

Tahmaseb, Charity
The geek girl's guide to cheerleading; [by]
Charity Tahmaseb and Darcy Vance. Simon Pulse
2009 324p pa $8.99
Grades: 7 8 9 10   Fic

1. Cheerleading—Fiction 2. Friendship—Fiction
3. Dating (Social customs)—Fiction
ISBN 978-1-4169-7834-3; 1-4169-7834-8
    "Self-professed 'geek girl' Bethany has a crush on an
unattainable jock, Jack. On a lark, she tries out for and
makes the cheerleading squad and draws Jack's attention.
But as her relationship with Jack blooms, complications
arise that impact both her friendships and her romance.
. . . The diverse characters and Bethany's introspective
commentary on teen life creates an engaging and entertaining read." Booklist

Tal, Eve, 1947-
Double crossing. Cinco Puntos Press 2005 261p
$16.95
Grades: 7 8 9 10   Fic
1. Immigrants—Fiction 2. Jews—Fiction
ISBN 0-938317-94-6   LC 2005-8188
In 1905, as life becomes increasingly difficult for
Jews in Ukraine, eleven-year-old Raizel and her father
flee to America in hopes of earning money to bring the
rest of the family there, but her father's health and Orthodox faith become barriers.
    "Tal's fictionalized account of her grandfather's jour-
ney to America is fast paced, full of suspense, and highly readable." SLJ
Followed by: Cursing Columbus (2009)

Tan, Amy
The Joy Luck Club. Putnam 1989 288p $24.95
*

Grades: 11 12 Adult   Fic
1. Chinese Americans—Fiction 2. Mother-daughter relationship—Fiction
ISBN 0-399-13420-4   LC 88-26492
    "Four aging Chinese women who knew life in China
before 1949 and now live in San Francisco meet regularly to play mah-jongg and share thoughts about their
American-born children. In alternating sections we learn
about the cultural differences between the elderly
'aunties' and the younger generation. When one of the
older women dies, her daughter is pressed to take her
place in the Joy Luck Club. Her feeling of being out of
place gradually gives way to an understanding of the
need to retain cultural continuity and an appreciation for
the strength and endurance of the older women." Shapiro. Fic for Youth. 3d edition

Tanner, Mike, 1960-
Resurrection blues. Annick Press 2005 246p
$19.95; pa $9.95 *
Grades: 9 10 11 12   Fic
1. Rock music—Fiction 2. Musicians—Fiction
ISBN 1-55037-897-X; 1-55037-896-1 (pa)
    "In the middle of his senior year, 18-year-old Flynn
Robinson drops out of high school to join a traveling bar
band and chase his dream of being a professional musician like his uncle Ray. . . Flynn describes his six
months on the road with the Sawyers band: the thrill of
performing; his unease with his bandmates' adventures
with drugs and sex; and ambivalence about his future,
particularly his relationship with his high-school

Tanner, Mike, 1960-—*Continued*

girlfriend. . . . Many readers, particularly teens who share his lyrically described musical passion, will easily connect with his questions, restlessness, and driving need for independence and expression." Booklist

Tayleur, Karen

Chasing boys. Walker & Co. 2009 244p $16.99

Grades: 7 8 9 10 11   **Fic**

1. Fathers—Fiction 2. School stories

ISBN 978-0-8027-9830-5; 0-8027-9830-6

LC 2008-23241

First published 2007 by Black Dog Books

With her father gone and her family dealing with financial problems, El transfers to a new school, where she falls for one of the popular boys and then must decide whether to remain true to herself or become like the girls she scorns.

"All the ingredients of El's life are blended seamlessly, never downplaying the audience's intelligence, as Tayleur captures the all-consuming nature of a teenage crush without making El ridiculous. Moody, poetic, and intimate, this book is billed as the 'romance for girls who don't like pink,' but is much more than that." Booklist

Taylor, Mildred D.

The land. Phyllis Fogelman Bks. 2001 375p $17.99; pa $6.99 *

Grades: 7 8 9 10   **Fic**

1. Racially mixed people—Fiction 2. African Americans—Fiction 3. Race relations—Fiction

ISBN 0-8037-1950-7; 0-14-250146-8 (pa)

LC 00-39329

Prequel to Roll of Thunder, Hear My Cry

After the Civil War Paul-Edward Logan, the son of a white father and a black mother, finds himself caught between the two worlds of colored folks and white folks as he pursues his dream of owning land of his own.

"Taylor masterfully uses harsh historical realities to frame a powerful coming-of-age story that stands on its own merits." Horn Book Guide

Roll of thunder, hear my cry. 25th anniversary ed. Phyllis Fogelman Books 2001 276p $17.99; pa $7.99

Grades: 4 5 6 7 8 9   **Fic**

1. African Americans—Fiction 2. Mississippi—Fiction

ISBN 0-8037-2647-3; 0-14-240112-9 (pa)

LC 00-39378

Also available in paperback from Puffin Bks.

First published 1976 by Dial Press

"The time is 1933. The place is Spokane, Mississippi where the Logans, the only black family who own their own land, wage a courageous struggle to remain independent, displeasing a white plantation owner bent on taking their land. But this suspenseful tale is also about the story's young narrator, Cassie, and her three brothers who decide to wage their own personal battles to maintain the self-dignity and pride with which they were raised. . . . Ms. Taylor's richly textured novel shows a strong, proud black family . . . resisting rather than succumbing to oppression." Child Book Rev Serv

Teller, Janne, 1964-

Nothing; translated from the Danish by Martin Aitken. Atheneum Books for Young Readers 2010 227p $16.99 *

Grades: 7 8 9 10 11 12   **Fic**

1. Meaning (Philosophy)—Fiction 2. School stories

ISBN 978-1-4169-8579-2; 1-4169-8579-4

LC 2009-19784

When thirteen-year-old Pierre Anthon leaves school to sit in a plum tree and train for becoming part of nothing, his seventh grade classmates set out on a desperate quest for the meaning of life.

"Indelible, elusive, and timeless, this uncompromising novel has all the marks of a classic." Booklist

Testa, Dom

The comet's curse. Tor Teen 2009 236p (Galahad) $16.95

Grades: 7 8 9 10 11 12   **Fic**

1. Interplanetary voyages—Fiction 2. Science fiction

ISBN 978-0-7653-2107-7; 0-7653-2107-6

LC 2008-35620

"A Tom Doherty Associates book"

First published 2005 by Profound Impact Group

Desperate to save the human race after a comet's deadly particles devastate the adult population, scientists create a ship that will carry a crew of 251 teenagers to a home in a distant solar system.

This book is "both a mystery and an adventure, combining a solid cast of characters with humor, pathos, growing pains and just a hint of romance." Kirkus

Other titles in this series are:

The Cassini code (2010)

The dark zone (2011)

The web of Titan (2009)

Tharp, Tim, 1957-

Badd. Alfred A. Knopf 2011 308p $16.99; lib bdg $19.99; ebook $10.99

Grades: 9 10 11 12   **Fic**

1. Siblings—Fiction 2. Iraq War, 2003-—Fiction 3. Post-traumatic stress disorder—Fiction

ISBN 978-0-375-86444-5; 978-0-375-96444-2 (lib bdg); 978-0-375-89579-1 (ebook)   LC 2010-12732

A teenaged girl's beloved brother returns home from the Iraq War completely unlike the person she remembers.

"With convincing three-dimensional characters, Tharp paints a sympathetic portrait of the constraints of small town life, the struggles of PTSD, and the challenges of faith." Publ Wkly

Knights of the hill country. Alfred A. Knopf 2006 233p hardcover o.p. pa $6.99

Grades: 8 9 10 11 12   **Fic**

1. Football—Fiction 2. School stories 3. Oklahoma—Fiction

ISBN 978-0-375-83653-4; 0-375-83653-5; 978-0-553-49513-3 (pa); 0-553-49513-5 (pa)

LC 2005-33279

In his senior year, high school star linebacker Hampton Greene finally begins to think for himself and discovers that he might be interested in more than just foot-

Tharp, Tim, 1957——*Continued*
ball.

"Taut scenes on the football field and the dilemmas about choosing what feels right over what's expected are all made memorable by Hamp's unforgettable, colloquial voice." Booklist

The spectacular now. Alfred A. Knopf 2008 294p $16.99; lib bdg $19.99 *
Grades: 9 10 11 12   **Fic**
1. Dating (Social customs)—Fiction 2. Alcoholism—Fiction 3. Stepfamilies—Fiction 4. Oklahoma—Fiction 5. School stories
ISBN   978-0-375-85179-7;   0-375-85179-7; 978-0-375-95179-4 (lib bdg); 0-375-95179-2 (lib bdg)
LC 2008-03544

In the last months of high school, charismatic eighteen-year-old Sutter Keely lives in the present, staying drunk or high most of the time, but that could change when he starts working to boost the self-confidence of a classmate, Aimee.

"Tharp offers a poignant, funny book about a teen who sees his life as livable only when his senses are dulled by drink . . . . Sutter is an authentic character [who] . . . will strike a chord with teen readers." Booklist

Thomas, Rob
Rats saw God. Simon & Schuster Bks. for Young Readers 1996 219p hardcover o.p. pa $6.99
Grades: 7 8 9 10   **Fic**
1. Father-son relationship—Fiction 2. School stories
ISBN 0-689-80207-2; 1-4169-3897-4 (pa)
LC 95-43548

"High-school senior Steve York isn't doing well. The former straight-A student is flunking, and his new friends are dopers. . . . A counselor steps in and suggests Steve can write something to bring up his failing English grade. So Steve writes his story, and as the action flips between his former life in Texas and the present in California, readers will learn about Steve's cold war with his astronaut father, his dabbling with dadaism, and, most of all, his heavenly-hellish experience with first love." Booklist

"The sharp descriptions of cliques, clubs and annoying authority figures will strike a familiar chord. The dialogue is fresh and Steve's intelligent banter and introspective musings never sound wiser than his years." Publ Wkly

Thompson, Holly
Orchards; illustrations by Grady McFerrin. Delacorte Press 2011 327p il $17.99; lib bdg $20.99
Grades: 7 8 9 10   **Fic**
1. Novels in verse 2. Suicide—Fiction 3. Racially mixed people—Fiction 4. Japan—Fiction 5. Family life—Fiction 6. Bereavement—Fiction
ISBN   978-0-385-73977-1;   0-385-73977-X; 978-0-385-90806-1 (lib bdg); 0-385-90806-7 (lib bdg)
LC 2010-23724

Sent to Japan for the summer after an eighth-grade classmate's suicide, half-Japanese, half-Jewish Kana

Goldberg tries to fit in with relatives she barely knows and reflects on the guilt she feels over the tragedy back home.

"Kanako's urgent teen voice, written in rapid free verse and illustrated with occasional black-and-white sketches, will hold readers with its nonreverential family story." Booklist

Thompson, Kate
Creature of the night. Roaring Brook Press 2008 250p $17.95 *
Grades: 9 10 11 12   **Fic**
1. Juvenile delinquency—Fiction 2. Homicide—Fiction 3. Ireland—Fiction
ISBN 978-1-59643-511-7; 1-59643-511-9

Bobby lives a reckless life smoking, drinking, and stealing cars in Dublin. So his mother moves the family to the country. But Bobby suspects their cottage might not be as quaint as it seems. And spooky details of the history of their little cottage gradually turn Bobby into a detective of night creatures real and imagined.

"A unique blend of subtlety and brashness, this is an honest coming-of-age novel in the guise of a gripping YA thriller." Booklist

The new policeman. Greenwillow Books 2007 442p hardcover o.p. pa $8.99 *
Grades: 7 8 9 10   **Fic**
1. Space and time—Fiction 2. Fairies—Fiction 3. Music—Fiction 4. Ireland—Fiction 5. Fantasy fiction
ISBN   978-0-06-117427-8;   0-06-117427-0; 978-0-06-117429-2 (pa); 0-06-117429-7 (pa)
LC 2006-8246

First published 2005 in the United Kingdom

Irish teenager JJ Liddy discovers that time is leaking from his world into Tir na nOg, the land of the fairies, and when he attempts to stop the leak he finds out a lot about his family history, the music that he loves, and a crime his great-grandfather may or may not have committed.

"Mesmerizing and captivating, this book is guaranteed to charm fantasy fans." Voice Youth Advocates

Other titles in this series are:
The last of the High Kings (2008)
The white horse trick (2010)

Thompson, Ricki
City of cannibals. Front Street 2010 269p $18.95
Grades: 8 9 10 11 12   **Fic**
1. Persecution—Fiction 2. Monks—Fiction 3. Runaway teenagers—Fiction 4. Great Britain—History—1485-1603, Tudors—Fiction
ISBN 978-1-59078-623-9; 1-59078-623-8
LC 2010-2105

In 1536 England, sixteen-year-old Dell runs away from her brutal father and life in a cave carrying only a handmade puppet to travel to London, where she learns truths about her mother's death and the conflict between King Henry VIII and the Catholic Church.

"Thompson's England is authentically vulgar, and her grasp of period slang—as well as Dell's burgeoning sexual desires—is expert. Packed with rich metaphor, this is a challenging but rewarding read." Booklist

Tiernan, Cate, 1961-

Balefire. Razorbill 2011 974p pa $8.99 *

Grades: 8 9 10 11 12   **Fic**

   1. Witchcraft—Fiction 2. Twins—Fiction 3. Sisters—Fiction 4. New Orleans (La.)—Fiction

   ISBN 978-1-59514-411-9

An omnibus edition of four titles previously published separately, the first three of which were first published 2005. The last, A necklace of water, was first published 2006

   Contents: A chalice of wind; A circle of ashes; A feather of stone; A necklace of water

   Separated since birth, seventeen-year-old twins Thais and Clio unexpectedly meet in New Orleans where they seem to be pursued by a coven of witches who want to harness the twins' magical powers for its own ends.

Immortal beloved. Little, Brown and Company 2010 407p $16.99

Grades: 8 9 10 11 12   **Fic**

   1. Conduct of life—Fiction 2. Immortality—Fiction 3. Magic—Fiction 4. Massachusetts—Fiction 5. Fantasy fiction

   ISBN 978-0-316-03592-7; 0-316-03592-0

                       LC 2010-06884

After seeing her best friend, a Dark Immortal called Incy, torture a human with magick, Nastasya, a spoiled party girl, enters a home for wayward immortals and finally begins to deal with life, even as she learns that someone wants her dead.

   "Humor overlies serious issues of identity and personal responsibility explored within the story, and readers who enjoy character-driven works of romantic fantasy will flock to this book." Voice Youth Advocates

Toliver, Wendy

Lifted. Simon Pulse 2010 309p pa $9.99

Grades: 7 8 9 10   **Fic**

   1. Moving—Fiction 2. Theft—Fiction 3. Texas—Fiction 4. School stories

   ISBN 978-1-4169-9048-2; 1-4169-9048-8

   "Poppy isn't happy with her single mother for moving her to Texas and enrolling the decidedly secular 16-year-old in a private Baptist high school. Soon, however, she becomes fascinated with the two most elite girls in class. . . . Her new friends, despite their pious attitudes, are shoplifters. Toliver does a good job of making clear the thefts are less about the desire for things like designer jeans than about the adrenaline rush of getting away with something. . . . Will appeal to all teens interested in wayward behavior." Booklist

Tolkien, J. R. R. (John Ronald Reuel), 1892-1973

The hobbit, or, There and back again. Houghton Mifflin 2001 330p il $18; pa $10

Grades: 5 6 7 8 9 10 11 12 Adult   **Fic**

   1. Fantasy fiction

   ISBN 0-618-16221-6; 0-618-26030-7 (pa)

                       LC 2001276594

A reissue of the title first published 1938

   "Text of this edition is based on that first published in Great Britain by Collins Modern Classics in 1998 . . . corrections have been made to that setting"—T.p. verso

   "This fantasy features the adventures of hobbit Bilbo Baggins, who joins a band of dwarves led by Gandalf the Wizard. Together they seek to recover the stolen treasure that is hidden in Lonely Mountain and guarded by Smaug the Dragon. This book precedes the Lord of the Rings trilogy." Shapiro. Fic for Youth. 3d edition

   Followed by: The lord of the rings trilogy: The fellowship of the ring; The two towers; The return of the king

The lord of the rings. 50th Anniversary ed. Houghton Mifflin 2004 xxv, 1157p il map slip case $100

Grades: 7 8 9 10 11 12 Adult   **Fic**

   1. Fantasy fiction

   ISBN 0-618-51765-0   LC 2004-275215

   Also available as separate volumes in hardcover and paperback editions

   First published 1954 in the United Kingdom

   Contents: The fellowship of the ring; The two towers; The return of the king

   "This is a tale of imaginary gnomelike creatures who battle against evil. Led by Frodo, the hobbits embark on a journey to prevent a magic ring from falling into the grasp of the powers of darkness. The forces of good succeed in their fight against the Dark Lord of evil, and Frodo and Sam bring the Ring to Mount Doom, where it is destroyed." Shapiro. Fic for Youth. 3d edition

Tolstoy, Leo, graf, 1828-1910

Anna Karenina; translated from the Russian by Louise and Aylmer Maude; with an introduction by John Bayley. Knopf 1992 xlix, 963p $24

Grades: 9 10 11 12   **Fic**

   1. Russia—Fiction

   ISBN 0-679-41000-7   LC 91-53196

   Also available in paperback from various publishers "Everyman's Library"

   Written in 1873-1876

This novel is "the story of a tragic, adulterous love. Anna meets and falls in love with Aleksei Vronski, a handsome young officer. She abandons her child and husband in order to be with Vronski. When she thinks Vronski has tired of her, she kills herself by leaping under a train. . . . A subplot concerns the contrasting happy marriage of Konstantin Levin and his young wife Kitty. Levin's search for meaning in his life and his love for a natural, simple existence on his estate are reflections of Tolstoy's own moods and thoughts of the time." Reader's Ency. 4th edition

Tomlinson, Heather

Toads and diamonds. Henry Holt 2010 278p $16.99

Grades: 8 9 10 11 12   **Fic**

   1. Fairy tales 2. India—Fiction

   ISBN 978-0-8050-8968-4; 0-8050-8968-3

                       LC 2009-23448

A retelling of the Perrault fairy tale set in pre-colonial India, in which two stepsisters receive gifts from a goddess and each walks her own path to find her gift's purpose, discovering romance along the way.

   The author "creates a vivid setting. Lavish details

Tomlinson, Heather—_Continued_
starkly contrast the two girls' lives and personalities.
. . . The complexities of the cultural backstory pose a
challenge to readers, but this beautifully embroidered adventure is well worth the effort." Booklist

Triana, Gaby
Riding the universe. HarperTeen 2009 267p
$16.99
Grades: 9 10 11 12   **Fic**
1. Bereavement—Fiction 2. Dating (Social customs)—
Fiction 3. Uncles—Fiction 4. Adoption—Fiction
ISBN 978-0-06-088570-0; 0-06-088570-X
                 LC 2008-31451
Seventeen-year-old Chloe, who inherited her uncle's
beloved Harley after his death, spends the subsequent
year trying to pass chemistry, wondering whether she
should look for her birth parents, and beginning an unlikely relationship with her chemistry tutor, while also
trying to figure out how she really feels about the boy
who has been her best friend since they were children.
"Chloé's tough exterior, layered over her introspective
inner voice, and the inclusion of such multidimensional
topics as adoption and parent/teen relationships drive this
text onto an open road that's filled with enough unexpected speed bumps to engage readers." Kirkus

Trice, Dawn Turner, 1956-
Only twice I've wished for heaven; a novel.
Crown 1997 304p hardcover o.p. pa $12.95
Grades: 11 12 Adult   **Fic**
1. African Americans—Fiction 2. Chicago (Ill.)—Fiction
ISBN 0-517-70428-5; 0-385-49123-9 (pa)
                 LC 97-22164
"In 1975, the Saville family has won the chance to
move into Lakeland, a planned community on Chicago's
lakefront. Formed as a social experiment, Lakeland is
home to many of the city's elite black professionals, but
for 11-year-old Tempest, the residents, with their expensive clothes and prissy manners, have 'no color' at all.
Slipping outside the walled community through a hole in
the fence, she is drawn to the raucous environs of Thirty-
fifth Street, particularly Miss Jonetta's liquor store."
Booklist
"Trice creates vibrant characters via the counterpointed voices of Temmie and Jonetta. As each interprets
events within the range of her knowledge and expectations, Trice obliquely provides insight into the crucial social issues that help shape the lives of African Americans." Publ Wkly

Trottier, Maxine
Three songs for courage. Tundra Books 2006
324p $16.95
Grades: 9 10 11 12   **Fic**
1. Bullies—Fiction 2. Homicide—Fiction
3. Brothers—Fiction 4. Canada—Fiction
ISBN 978-0-88776-745-6; 0-88776-745-1
                LC 2005-927011
"Sixteen-year-old Gordon is looking forward to the
summer—he has his best buddies; a new girlfriend,
Mary; and his baby, a 1950 Pontiac named the Chief.

The only sour note is Lancer Caldwell and his gang,
whose violence follows Gordon wherever he goes. When
Gordon finds his brother dead from a fall down the
stairs, he thinks it's an accident like everyone else—until
he finds evidence that Lancer was in his home that
night." Booklist
"From native wisdom to flatulence humor and from
sexual assault to pigs in dresses, Trottier handles the serious with poignancy and lighter moments with flair.
. . . This coming-of-age novel is rich, readable, and substantive." Voice Youth Advocates

Trueman, Terry
7 days at the hot corner. HarperTempest 2007
160p $15.99
Grades: 7 8 9 10   **Fic**
1. Baseball—Fiction 2. Homosexuality—Fiction
3. Friendship—Fiction
ISBN 978-0-06-057494-9; 0-06-057494-1
                 LC 2006-03706
Varsity baseball player Scott Latimer struggles with
his own prejudices and those of others when his best
friend reveals that he is gay.
This "suspenseful story is enhanced by some late-
inning surprises, the gay subplot is treated with honesty
and integrity, and Scott and Travis are believable, sympathetic characters." Booklist

Tucker, Todd, 1968-
Over and under. Thomas Dunne Books/St.
Martin's Press 2008 275p $23.95 *
Grades: 10 11 12 Adult   **Fic**
1. Friendship—Fiction 2. City and town life—Fiction
3. Labor disputes—Fiction 4. Indiana—Fiction
ISBN 978-0-312-37990-2; 0-312-37990-0
                 LC 2008-12472
"A bitter 1979 labor strike at southern Indiana's Borden Casket Company serves as the volatile backdrop for
this haunting coming-of-age novel. . . . With their fathers on opposite sides of the dispute, Andrew Jackson
Gray and Thomas Jefferson Kruer, both 14, learn there
is more to life than exploring caves, shooting targets
with their prized M-6 Scout rifles and sneaking out on
starry nights to run through the woods. . . . Tucker convincingly makes Andy's voice at once eloquent and gritty, and makes the rural Indiana landscape palpable." Publ
Wkly

Tullson, Diane, 1958-
Riley Park. Orca Book Publishers 2009 102p
(Orca soundings) $16.95; pa $9.95
Grades: 7 8 9 10   **Fic**
1. Homicide—Fiction 2. Brain—Wounds and injuries—Fiction 3. Bereavement—Fiction 4. Friendship—
Fiction
ISBN   978-1-55469-124-1;   1-55469-124-9;
978-1-55469-123-4 (pa); 1-55469-123-0 (pa)
After Corbin and his best friend Darius are attacked
in Riley Park, Corbin must cope with the loss of his
friend, his physical impairments, and finding the culprit.
This is "a suspenseful, tightly plotted story that manages . . . to create both a memorable protagonist and a
thought-provoking, emotionally involving story." Booklist

Turnbull, Ann

No shame, no fear. Candlewick Press 2004 c2003 293p $15.99

Grades: 7 8 9 10 11 12   Fic
1. Society of Friends—Fiction 2. Great Britain—History—1485-1603, Tudors—Fiction
ISBN 0-7636-2505-1   LC 2003-65280
First published 2003 in the United Kingdom
In England in 1662, a time of religious persecution, fifteen-year-old Susanna, a poor country girl and a Quaker, and seventeen-year-old William, a wealthy Anglican, meet and fall in love against all odds.
"This is a well-told historical tale, engaging and informative." Booklist
Followed by Forged in the fire (2007)

Turner, Ann Warren, 1945-

Father of lies; [by] Ann Turner. HarperTeen 2011 247p $16.99

Grades: 7 8 9 10   Fic
1. Manic-depressive illness—Fiction 2. Witchcraft—Fiction 3. Salem (Mass.)—Fiction
ISBN 978-0-06-137085-4; 0-06-137085-1
LC 2010-15224
In 1692 when a plague of accusations descends on Salem Village in Massachusetts and "witch fever" erupts, fourteen-year-old Lidda, who has begun to experience visions and hear voices, tries to expose the lies of the witch trials without being hanged as a witch herself. Includes author's notes about the Salem Witch Trials and bipolar disease.
"Turner perfectly captures the nightmare nature of Salem's witchcraft period and of some of the outside forces that may have fueled it. . . . Yet the town's issues play a secondary role in Lidda's own believable struggles with encroaching insanity—or an otherworldly paranormal force: an appraisal left for engaged readers to make." Kirkus
Includes bibliographical references

Hard hit; [by] Ann Turner. Scholastic Press 2006 167p $16.99

Grades: 7 8 9 10   Fic
1. Father-son relationship—Fiction 2. Baseball—Fiction 3. Cancer—Fiction 4. Death—Fiction 5. Novels in verse
ISBN 0-439-29680-3   LC 2005-49906
A rising high school baseball star faces his most difficult challenge when his father is diagnosed with pancreatic cancer.
This is a "novel in verse that speaks volumes long after the book is closed." Voice Youth Advocates

Turner, Joan Frances

Dust. Ace Books 2010 374p map $24.95

Grades: 11 12 Adult   Fic
1. Zombies—Fiction 2. Gangs—Fiction 3. Diseases—Fiction 4. Horror fiction
ISBN 978-0-441-01928-1   LC 2010-6250
"Nine years ago, Jessie was in a car crash and died. After she was buried, she awoke and tore through the earth to arise, reborn, as a zombie. Now Jessie's part of a gang. They fight, hunt, and dance together as one—

something humans can never understand. There are darkplaces humans have learned to avoid, lest they run into zombie gangs. But when a mysterious illness threatens the existence of both zombies and humans, Jessie must choose between looking away or staring down the madness—and hanging on to everything she now knows as life." Publisher's note
"Turner has created a new zombie mythology that is smart, scary, and viscerally real. Recommend this one highly to horror fans, even those who claim to have sated themselves on zombies." Booklist

Turner, Max, 1947-

Night runner. St. Martin's Griffin 2009 261p pa $9.99

Grades: 7 8 9 10   Fic
1. Vampires—Fiction
ISBN 978-0-312-59228-8; 0-312-59228-0
LC 2009-16672
Fifteen-year-old Zach is quite content living in a mental ward because of his unusual allergies until dark secrets about his past, his parents, and his strange sickness slowly surface, placing him in great danger
"This fast-paced vampire story featuring a likable character with a strong voice will appeal to a broad teen audience." Booklist
Followed by: End of days (2010)

Turner, Megan Whalen, 1965-

The thief. Greenwillow Bks. 1996 219p $17.99; pa $6.99 *

Grades: 7 8 9 10   Fic
1. Adventure fiction 2. Thieves—Fiction
ISBN 0-688-14627-9; 0-06-082497-2 (pa)
LC 95-41040
"Gen languishes in prison for boasting of his skill as a thief. The magus—the king's powerful advisor—needing a clever thief to find an ancient ring that gives the owner the right to rule a neighboring country, bails Gen out. Their journey toward the treasure is marked by danger and political intrigue, and features a motley cast, tales of old gods, and the revelation of Gen's true identity." Publisher's note
"A tantalizing, suspenseful, exceptionally clever novel. . . . The author's characterization of Gen is simply superb." Horn Book
Other titles in this series are:
A conspiracy of kings (2010)
The King of Attolia (2006)
The Queen of Attolia (2000)

Twain, Mark, 1835-1910

The adventures of Huckleberry Finn. Modern Library 1993 xx, 433p $16.95 *

Grades: 5 6 7 8 9 10 11 12 Adult   Fic
1. Mississippi River—Fiction 2. Missouri—Fiction
ISBN 0-679-42470-9   LC 92-51065
Also available from other publishers
First published 1885. This is a companion volume to:
The adventures of Tom Sawyer
This novel "begins with Huck's escape from his drunken, brutal father to the river, where he meets up

Twain, Mark, 1835-1910—*Continued*
with Jim, a runaway slave. The story of their journey
downstream, with occasional forays into the society
along the banks, is an American classic that captures the
smells, rhythms, and sounds, the variety of dialects and
the human activity of life on the great river. It is also a
penetrating social commentary that reveals corruption,
moral decay, and intellectual impoverishment through
Huck and Jim's encounters with traveling actors and con
men, lynch mobs, thieves, and Southern gentility." Reader's Ency. 4th edition

The adventures of Tom Sawyer; foreword and
notes by John C. Gerber; text established by Paul
Baender; [original illustrations by True W.
Williams] 135th anniversary ed. University of
California Press 2010 [xxx] 274p il (Mark Twain
library) $50; pa $18.95 *
Grades: 5 6 7 8 9 10 11 12 Adult   Fic
  1. Runaway children—Fiction 2. Mississippi River—
  Fiction 3. Missouri—Fiction
  ISBN   978-0-520-26611-7;   0-520-26611-0;
  978-0-520-26612-4 (pa); 0-520-26612-9 (pa)
                                        LC 2010513694
Also available from other publishers
First published 1876. This is a companion volume to:
The adventures of Huckleberry Finn
  "Tom, a shrewd and adventurous boy, is at home in
the respectable world of his Aunt Polly, as well as in the
self-reliant, parentless world of Huck Finn. The two
friends, out in the cemetery under a full moon, attempt
to cure warts with a dead cat. They accidentally witness
a murder, of which Muff Potter is later wrongly accused.
Knowing that the true murderer is Injun Joe, the boys are
helpless with fear; they decide to run away to Jackson's
Island. After a few pleasant days of smoking and swear-
ing, they realize that the townspeople believe them dead.
Returning in time to hear their funeral eulogies, they become town heroes. At the trial of Muff Potter, Tom, unable to let an innocent person be condemned, reveals his
knowledge. Injun Joe flees. Later Tom and his sweetheart, Becky Thatcher, get lost in the cave in which the
murderer is hiding. They escape, and Tom and Huck return to find the treasure Joe has buried." Reader's Ency.
4th edition

Tyler, Anne, 1941-
Dinner at the Homesick Restaurant. Knopf 1982
303p hardcover o.p. pa $14.95
Grades: 11 12 Adult   Fic
  1. Family life—Fiction 2. Maryland—Fiction
  ISBN 0-394-52381-4; 0-449-91159-4 (pa)
                                          LC 81-13694
"Pearl Tull, an angry woman who vacillates between
excesses of maternal energy and spurts of terrifying rage,
has been deserted by her husband and has brought up her
three children alone. Cody, the eldest, is handsome, wild,
and in a lifelong battle of jealousy with his young brother, the sweet-tempered and patient Ezra. Their sister Jenny tries, through three marriages, to find a stability
which was never present in Pearl's home. Ezra also tries
to achieve a permanence through his homey Homesick
Restaurant in Baltimore, but he is cruelly tricked by his
brother and is unable to establish any unity in the family." Shapiro. Fic for Youth. 3d edition

Uchida, Yoshiko, 1921-1992
Picture bride; a novel. University of Washington
pa. ed. University of Washington Press 1997 216p
pa $14.95 *
Grades: 11 12 Adult   Fic
  1. Japanese American women—Fiction 2. California—
  Fiction
  ISBN 0-295-97616-0   LC 97-3
First published 1987 by Northland Press
"Carrying a photograph of the man she is to marry but
has yet to meet, young Hana Omiya arrives in San Francisco, California, in 1917, one of several hundred Japanese 'picture brides' whose arranged marriages brought
them to America in the early 1900s. Her story is intertwined with others: her husband, Taro Takeda, an Oak-
land shopkeeper; Kiku and her husband Henry, who reject demeaning city work to become farmers; Dr.
Kaneda, a respected community leader who is destroyed
by the adopted land he loves. All are caught up in the
cruel turmoil of World War II, when West Coast Japanese Americans are uprooted from their homes and imprisoned in desert detention camps." Publisher's note

Updale, Eleanor
Montmorency; thief, liar, gentleman? Orchard
Books 2004 c2003 232p $16.95 *
Grades: 6 7 8 9 10   Fic
  1. London (England)—Fiction 2. Great Britain—History—19th century—Fiction 3. Thieves—Fiction
  ISBN 0-439-58035-8   LC 2003-56345
First published 2003 in the United Kingdom
In Victorian London, after his life is saved by a young
physician, a thief utilizes the knowledge he gains in pris-
on and from the scientific lectures he attends as the phy-
sician's case study exhibit to create a new, highly successful, double life for himself.
"Updale adroitly works the tradition of devilish
schemes and narrow escapes, and the plot moves as nim-
bly as the master thief himself." Bull Cent Child Books
  Other titles about Montmorency are:
Montmorency and the assassins (2006)
Montmorency on the rocks: doctor, aristocrat, murderer?
  (2005)
Montmorency's revenge (2007)

Uris, Leon, 1924-2003
Exodus. Doubleday 1958 626p il hardcover o.p.
pa $7.99
Grades: 11 12 Adult   Fic
  1. Zionism—Fiction
  ISBN 0-385-05082-8; 0-553-25847-8 (pa)
"Following World War II the British forbade immigration of the Jews to Israel. European Jewish underground
groups, aided by Palestinian agent Ari Ben Canaan, made
every effort to aid these unfortunate victims of Nazi persecution. The novel provides insight into the heritage of
the Jews and understanding of the danger involved in
helping them reach a safe haven. It also includes the
warm love story of Ari and a gentile nurse, Kitty Fre-
mont, who cared very much for the welfare of the Jewish
children caught in this nightmare." Shapiro. Fic for
Youth. 3d edition

Valentine, Jenny
Broken soup. HarperTeen 2009 216p $16.99
Grades: 7 8 9 10   **Fic**
1. Bereavement—Fiction 2. Family life—Fiction
3. London (England)—Fiction
ISBN 978-0-06-085071-5; 0-06-085071-X
LC 2008-11719
A photographic negative and two surprising new
friends become the catalyst for healing as fifteen-year-old
Rowan struggles to keep her family and her life together
after her brother's death.
"The mystery Valentine sets in motion is quickly
paced and packed with revelations. . . . The main appeal
of the book, however, is her beautifully modulated tone.
. . . Insightful details abound." Booklist

Me, the missing, and the dead. HarperTeen 2008
201p $16.99; lib bdg $17.89 *
Grades: 8 9 10 11   **Fic**
1. Death—Fiction 2. Missing persons—Fiction
3. Fathers—Fiction 4. Single parent family—Fiction
5. London (England)—Fiction
ISBN   978-0-06-085068-5;   0-06-085068-X;
978-0-06-085069-2 (lib bdg); 0-06-085069-8 (lib bdg)
LC 2007-14476
First published 2007 in the United Kingdom with title:
Finding Violet Park
When a series of chance events leaves him in possession of an urn with ashes, sixteen-year-old Londoner Lucas Swain becomes convinced that its occupant, Violet
Park, is communicating with him, initiating a voyage of
self-discovery that forces him to finally confront the
events surrounding his father's sudden disappearance.
"Part mystery, part magical realism, part story of personal growth, and in large part simply about a funny
teenager making light of his and his family's pain, this
short novel is engaging from start to finish." SLJ

Van de Ruit, John, 1975-
Spud. Razorbill 2007 331p hardcover o.p. pa
$9.99
Grades: 6 7 8 9 10   **Fic**
1. School stories 2. South Africa—Fiction
ISBN   978-1-59514-170-5;   0-14-302484-1;
978-1-59514-187-3 (pa); 1-59514-187-1 (pa)
LC 2007-6065
In 1990, thirteen-year-old John "Spud" Milton, a
prepubescent choirboy, keeps a diary of his first year at
an elite, boys-only boarding school in South Africa.
"This raucous autobiographical novel about a scholar-
ship boy in an elite boys' boarding school in 1990 is
mainly farce but also part coming-of-age tale." Booklist
Followed by Spud—the madness continues... (2008)

Van Tol, Alex
Knifepoint; written by Alex Van Tol. Orca
Book Publishers 2010 113p (Orca soundings)
$16.95; pa $9.95
Grades: 7 8 9 10   **Fic**
1. Kidnapping—Fiction
ISBN   978-1-55469-306-1;   1-55469-06-3;
978-1-55469-305-4 (pa); 1-55469-305-5 (pa)
Jill is enduring a brutal job on a mountain ranch,
guiding wannabe-cowboys on trail rides. On a solo ride

with a handsome stranger she ends up in a fight for her
life with no one to help her.
"The suspense is palpable. Both reluctant and avid
readers who enjoy nail-biting tension will race through."
Booklist

Vande Velde, Vivian, 1951-
The book of Mordred; [illustrations by Justin
Gerard] Houghton Mifflin 2005 342p hardcover
o.p. pa $8.99 *
Grades: 8 9 10 11 12   **Fic**
1. Arthur, King—Fiction 2. Mordred (Legendary character)—Fiction 3. Knights and knighthood—Fiction
4. Great Britain—History—0-1066—Fiction
ISBN 0-618-50754-X; 0-618-80916-3 (pa)
LC 2004-28223
As the peaceful King Arthur reigns, the five-year-old
daughter of Lady Alayna, newly widowed of the village-
wizard Toland, is abducted by knights who leave their
barn burning and their only servant dead.
"All of the characters are well developed and have a
strong presence throughout. . . . [This] provides an intriguing counterpoint to anyone who is interested in Arthurian legend." SLJ

Remembering Raquel. Harcourt 2007 160p $16
Grades: 8 9 10 11   **Fic**
1. Death—Fiction 2. School stories 3. Obesity—Fic-
tion
ISBN 978-0-15-205976-7   LC 2006-35769
Various people recall aspects of the life of Raquel
Falcone, an unpopular, overweight freshman at Quail
Run High School, including classmates, her parents, and
the driver who struck and killed her as she was walking
home from an animated film festival.
"Easily booktalked and deeper than it initially seems,
this will be popular with reluctant readers." Booklist

Varrato, Tony
Fakie; written by Tony Varrato. Lobster Press
2008 142p pa $7.95
Grades: 6 7 8 9 10   **Fic**
1. Witnesses—Fiction 2. Skateboarding—Fiction
3. Virginia—Fiction
ISBN 978-1-897073-79-7; 1-897073-79-8
"Fifteen-year-old Danny Torbert and his mom are on
the run again, assuming yet another identity. Four years
ago, Danny was the sole witness when Steve, his father's
surveillance business partner, killed his father and severely wounded Danny. Awaiting appeal, Steve directs the
search for Danny and his mother from prison, vowing to
silence them forever. Now in the Witness Protection Program, Danny and his mom have had to flee their home
several times, and Steve's men are getting close. The story alternates between Danny and his mom, as they start
anew, and Steve's determined search." Booklist
"This is an excellent novel for male teen readers. It is
short, action packed, and full of activities that they can
relate to." Voice Youth Advocates

Vaughn, Carrie, 1973-
Voices of dragons. HarperTeen 2010 309p
$16.99
Grades: 7 8 9 10   **Fic**
1. Dragons—Fiction 2. Fantasy fiction
ISBN 978-0-06-179894-8; 0-06-179894-0
                     LC 2009-11604
In a parallel world where humans and dragons live in
a state of cold war, seventeen-year-old Kay and her dragon friend, Artegal, struggle to find a way to show that
dragons and humans can coexist.
"Vaughn's story is charming and fast paced with a
strong, likable heroine." Publ Wkly

Vaught, Susan
Big fat manifesto. Bloomsbury 2008 308p
$16.95 *
Grades: 9 10 11 12   **Fic**
1. Obesity—Fiction 2. Prejudices—Fiction 3. School
stories
ISBN 978-1-59990-206-7; 1-59990-206-0
                     LC 2007-23550
Overweight, self-assured, high school senior Jamie
Carcaterra writes in the school newspaper about her own
attitude to being fat, her boyfriend's bariatric surgery,
and her struggles to be taken seriously in a very thin
world
"Jamie's forcefully articulated perspectives about body
image and her well-justified anger provoke soul-
searching at every turn. . . . Readers will not only be
challenged but also changed by meeting Jamie." Bull
Cent Child Books

Trigger. Bloomsbury Children's Books 2006
292p $16.95 *
Grades: 9 10 11 12   **Fic**
1. Brain—Wounds and injuries—Fiction 2. Suicide—
Fiction
ISBN 978-1-58234-920-6; 1-58234-920-7
                     LC 2005-32249
Teenager Jersey Hatch must work through his extensive brain damage to figure out why he decided to shoot
himself.
"Though teen suicide is a oft-chosen theme in young
adult realism, Jersey's fresh voice, combined with the
mystery elements fueled by his damaged memory, make
this addition to the subgenre a compelling one." Bull
Cent Child Books

Vega, Denise
Fact of life #31. Alfred A. Knopf 2008 375p
$16.99; lib bdg $19.99
Grades: 7 8 9 10 11 12   **Fic**
1. Midwives—Fiction 2. Pregnancy—Fiction
3. Mother-daughter relationship—Fiction
4. Childbirth—Fiction
ISBN 978-0-375-84819-3; 0-375-84819-3;
978-0-375-94819-0 (lib bdg); 0-375-94819-8 (lib bdg)
                     LC 2007-49654
Sixteen-year-old Kat, whose mother is a home-birth
midwife, feels betrayed when a popular, beautiful classmate gets pregnant and forms a bond with Kat's mother
that Kat herself never had.

"Graphic birthing details will startle some readers and
fascinate others. . . . Athletic, artsy, oddball Kat is an
unusual protagonist who doesn't easily fit into type, and
many readers will welcome her strong individuality and
believable growth." Booklist

Venkatraman, Padma
Climbing the stairs. G.P. Putnam's Sons 2008
247p $16.99 *
Grades: 6 7 8 9 10   **Fic**
1. Family life—Fiction 2. Prejudices—Fiction
3. Brain—Wounds and injuries—Fiction 4. India—
History—1765-1947, British occupation—Fiction
ISBN 978-0-399-24746-0; 0-399-24746-7
                     LC 2007-21757
In India, in 1941, when her father becomes brain-
damaged in a non-violent protest march, fifteen-year-old
Vidya and her family are forced to move in with her father's extended family and become accustomed to a totally different way of life.
"Venkatraman paints an intricate and convincing backdrop of a conservative Brahmin home in a time of
change. . . . The striking cover art . . . will draw readers to this vividly told story." Booklist

Verdelle, A. J., 1960-
The good negress. Algonquin Bks. 1995 298p
$19.95
Grades: 11 12 Adult   **Fic**
1. African Americans—Fiction 2. Detroit (Mich.)—
Fiction
ISBN 1-56512-085-X   LC 94-40889
Set in Virginia and Detroit during the 1950s and
1960s, this novel "is the coming-of-age story of Denise
Palms, who leaves her grandmother's rural home to re-
turn to her family in Detroit. Denise's family expects her
to concentrate on housework and childcare, but her
teacher pushes her to spend time on afterschool lessons
in diction and grammar in order to 'better' herself." Libr
J
"Verdelle's truly fine debut novel belongs in the ranks
of other classics in African American folk vernacular."
Choice

Verne, Jules, 1828-1905
The extraordinary journeys: Twenty thousand
leagues under the sea; translated with an
introduction and notes by William Butcher. Oxford
University Press 2009 xlviii, 445p pa $11.95 *
Grades: 5 6 7 8 9 10 11 12 Adult   **Fic**
1. Submarines—Fiction 2. Sea stories 3. Science fiction 4. Adventure fiction
ISBN 978-0-19-953927-7   LC 2009-464589
Also available from other publishers
Original French edition, 1870; This translation first
published 1998
"The voyage of the Nautilus permitted Verne to describe the wonders of an undersea world almost totally
unknown to the general public of the period. Indebted to
literary tradition for his Atlantis, he made his major innovation in having the submarine completely powered by
electricity, although the interest in electrical forces goes

Verne, Jules, 1828-1905—*Continued*

back to Poe and Shelley. So far as the enigmatic ending is concerned, his readers had to wait for the three-part *The Mysterious Island* (1874-1875) to learn that Nemo had been the Indian warrior-prince Dakkar, who had been involved in the Sepoy Mutiny of 1857." Anatomy of Wonder 4

Includes bibliographical references

Vigan, Delphine de

No and me; translated by George Miller. Bloomsbury Children's Books 2010 244p $16.99

Grades: 9 10 11 12   Fic

1. Homeless persons—Fiction 2. Family life—Fiction 3. Gifted children—Fiction 4. Paris (France)—Fiction

ISBN 978-1-59990-479-5   LC 2009-36897

Original French edition, 2007

Precocious thirteen-year-old Lou meets a homeless eighteen-year-old girl on the streets of Paris and Lou's life is forever changed.

"Subtle, authentic details; memorable characters . . . and realistic ambiguities in each scene ground the story's weighty themes, and teens will easily recognize Lou's fragile shifts between heartbreak, bitter disillusionment, and quiet, miraculous hope." Booklist

Vincent, Zu, 1952-

The lucky place. Front Street 2008 230p $17.95

Grades: 7 8 9 10   Fic

1. Father-daughter relationship—Fiction 2. Stepfathers—Fiction 3. Death—Fiction 4. Cancer—Fiction 5. Alcoholism—Fiction

ISBN 978-1-932425-70-3; 1-932425-70-5

LC 2007-18357

"Readers meet Cassie when she is three years old and her inebriated father leaves her behind at the racetrack. . . . She is returned home by the police and their mother eventually realizes that this man is not a competent father. . . . Mom brings home Ellis, New Daddy, and Cassie can't help but feel his strength. . . . Cassie's voice changes as she grows into a 12-year-old who comes to know that inside herself is the real lucky place that she can truly count on. . . . Taking place in California in the late 1950s and early '60s . . . Vincent's novel ably creates a world that makes promises it can't keep. . . . A stunning fiction debut." SLJ

Vivian, Siobhan

A little friendly advice. Scholastic/Push 2008 248p $16.99

Grades: 7 8 9 10 11 12   Fic

1. Divorce—Fiction 2. Father-daughter relationship—Fiction 3. Friendship—Fiction 4. Ohio—Fiction

ISBN 978-0-545-00404-6; 0-545-00404-7

LC 2007-9905

When Ruby's divorced father shows up unexpectedly on her sixteenth birthday, the week that follows is full of confusing surprises, including discovering that her best friend has been keeping secrets from her, her mother has not been truthful about the past, and life is often complicated.

"Readers will find themselves and their relationships reflected in Ruby's story—for better and worse." Publ Wkly

Not that kind of girl. PUSH/Scholastic 2010 322p $17.99

Grades: 9 10 11 12   Fic

1. Dating (Social customs)—Fiction 2. School stories

ISBN 978-0-545-16915-8; 0-545-16915-1

LC 2010-13806

High school senior and student body president, Natalie likes to have everything under control, but when she becomes attracted to one of the senior boys and her best friend starts keeping secrets from her, Natalie does not know how to act.

The author "challenges the assumptions about sex being rampant in high school and sends a positive message about acceptance, forgiveness, and love." Booklist

Same difference. PUSH 2009 287p $17.99

Grades: 7 8 9 10   Fic

1. Artists—Fiction 2. Friendship—Fiction 3. School stories 4. New Jersey—Fiction 5. Philadelphia (Pa.)—Fiction

ISBN 978-0-545-00407-7; 0-545-00407-1

LC 2008-30165

Feeling left out since her long-time best friend started a serious relationship, sixteen-year-old Emily looks forward to a summer program at the Philadelphia College of Art but is not sure she is up to the challenges to be faced there, including finding herself and learning to balance life and art.

Vivian "serves up the story with vivid description and dialogue; the author's talent for scene-setting and evocative imagery is especially effective." Publ Wkly

Vizzini, Ned, 1981-

It's kind of a funny story. Miramax Books/Hyperion Books For Children 2006 444p hardcover o.p. pa $9.99 *

Grades: 9 10 11 12   Fic

1. Depression (Psychology)—Fiction 2. Psychiatric hospitals—Fiction 3. New York (N.Y.)—Fiction

ISBN 0-7868-5196-1; 1-4231-4191-1 (pa)

LC 2005-52670

A humorous account of a New York City teenager's battle with depression and his time spent in a psychiatric hospital.

"What's terrific about the book is Craig's voice—intimate, real, funny, ironic, and one kids will come closer to hear." Booklist

Volponi, Paul

The hand you're dealt. Atheneum Books for Young Readers 2008 176p $16.99 *

Grades: 8 9 10 11   Fic

1. Poker—Fiction 2. Teachers—Fiction 3. School stories

ISBN 978-1-4169-3989-4; 1-4169-3989-X

LC 2007-22988

When seventeen-year-old Huck's vindictive math teacher wins the town poker tournament and takes the winner's watch away from Huck's father while he is in a coma, Huck vows to get even with him no matter what it takes.

"The varied characters are unique and add to the book's interest quotient." Voice Youth Advocates

Volponi, Paul—*Continued*

Hurricane song; a novel of New Orleans. Viking Childrens Books 2008 144p $15.99 *

Grades: 7 8 9 10 11 12   **Fic**

1. Father-son relationship—Fiction 2. Hurricane Katrina, 2005—Fiction 3. Jazz music—Fiction 4. New Orleans (La.)—Fiction

ISBN 978-0-670-06160-0; 0-670-06160-3

LC 2007-38215

Twelve-year-old Miles Shaw goes to live with his father, a jazz musician, in New Orleans, and together they survive the horrors of Hurricane Katrina in the Superdome, learning about each other and growing closer through their painful experiences.

"A brilliant blend of reality and fiction, this novel hits every chord just right." Voice Youth Advocates

Rooftop. Viking 2006 199p $15.99; pa $6.99 *

Grades: 9 10 11 12   **Fic**

1. Death—Fiction 2. Race relations—Fiction 3. African Americans—Fiction 4. New York (N.Y.)—Fiction

ISBN 0-670-06069-0; 0-14-240844-1 (pa)

LC 2005-22811

Still reeling from seeing police shoot his unarmed cousin to death on the roof of a New York City housing project, seventeen-year-old Clay is dragged into the whirlwind of political manipulation that follows.

"This thoughtfully crafted, deceptively simple story knits together a high-interest plot, a readable narrative crackling with street slang, and complex personal and societal issues that will engage teen readers." Booklist

Voltaire, 1694-1778

Candide; translated by Peter Constantine. Modern Library 2005 119p hardcover o.p. pa $8.95

Grades: 11 12 Adult   **Fic**

1. Satire

ISBN 0-679-64313-3; 0-8129-7201-5 (pa)

LC 2004-55244

Also available from other publishers

Original French edition, 1759

"In this philosophical fantasy, naive Candide sees and suffers such misfortune that he ultimately rejects the philosophy of his tutor Doctor Pangloss, who claims that 'all is for the best in this best of all possible worlds.' Candide and his companions—Pangloss, his beloved Cunegonde, and his servant Cacambo—display an instinct for survival that provides them hope in an otherwise somber setting. When they all retire together to a simple life on a small farm, they discover that the secret of happiness is 'to cultivate one's garden,' a practical philosophy that excludes excessive idealism and nebulous metaphysics." Merriam-Webster's Ency of Lit

Vonnegut, Kurt, 1922-2007

Cat's cradle. Dial Press trade paperback ed. Dial Press 2006 c1963 287p pa $14

Grades: 11 12 Adult   **Fic**

1. Science fiction

ISBN 0-385-33348-X; 978-0-385-33348-1

LC 2005-285166

First published 1963 by Holt, Rinehart and Winston

"In this mordant satire on religion, research, government, and human nature, a freelance writer becomes the catalyst in a chain of events that unearths the secret of ice-nine. This is an element potentially more lethal than that produced by nuclear fission. The search leads to a mythical island, San Lorenzo, where the writer also discovers the leader of a new religion, Bokonon." Shapiro. Fic for Youth. 3d edition

Slaughterhouse-five; or, The children's crusade: a duty-dance with death. 25th anniversary ed. Delacorte Press 1994 205p il $22.50; pa $6.99 *

Grades: 11 12 Adult   **Fic**

1. World War, 1939-1945—Fiction 2. Science fiction

ISBN 0-385-31208-3; 0-440-18029-5 (pa)

LC 94-171120

A reissue of the title first published 1969

This novel "mixes a fictionalized account of the author's experience of the fire bombing of Dresden with a compensatory fantasy of the planet Tralfamadore, the science-fiction element is progressively dominated by the overall concerns of satire, black humor, and absurdism." Reader's Ency. 3d edition

"A masterpiece, in which Vonnegut penetrated to the heart of the issues developed in his earlier absurdist fabulations. A key work of modern SF." Anatomy of Wonder 4

Voorhees, Coert

The brothers Torres. Hyperion Books for Children 2008 316p hardcover o.p. pa $8.99 *

Grades: 9 10 11 12   **Fic**

1. Brothers—Fiction 2. Dating (Social customs)—Fiction 3. Gangs—Fiction 4. Racially mixed people—Fiction 5. School stories

ISBN   978-1-4231-0304-2;   1-4231-0304-1; 978-1-4231-0306-6 (pa); 1-4231-0306-8 (pa)

LC 2007-15152

Sophomore Frankie finally finds the courage to ask his long-term friend, Julianne, to the Homecoming dance, which ultimately leads to a face-off between a tough senior whose family owns most of their small, New Mexico town, and Frankie's soccer-star older brother and his gang-member friends.

This "novel is solidly plotted and exceptionally well paced; escalating tension keeps the pages flying, while narrator Frankie's self-deprecating humor prevents the action from devolving into *Southwestside Story* melodrama." Bull Cent Child Books

Vrettos, Adrienne Maria

Skin. Margaret K. McElderry Books 2006 227p $16.95 *

Grades: 7 8 9 10   **Fic**

1. Siblings—Fiction 2. Anorexia nervosa—Fiction

ISBN 1-4169-0655-X   LC 2005001119

When his parents decide to separate, eighth-grader Donnie watches with horror as the physical condition of his sixteen-year old sister, Karen, deteriorates due to an eating disorder.

"The overwhelming alienation Donnie endures will speak to many teens, while his honest perspective will be welcomed by boys." Booklist

Waldorf, Heather

Tripping. Red Deer Press 2008 342p pa $12.95

Grades: 8 9 10 11 12   **Fic**

1. Wilderness survival—Fiction 2. Amputees—Fiction
3. Voyages and travels—Fiction 4. Canada—Fiction

ISBN 978-0-88995-426-7; 0-88995-426-7

"Rainey and five other teens begin an eight-week school-sponsored educational/survival trek across Canada. . . . Rainey's challenge is heightened because she has an artificial leg and she learns that her mother, who abandoned her as a baby, lives near one of their stops and wants to meet her. As the trip progresses, the individuals bond and become part of a team. . . . Waldorf has written a unique story in which six very different young people are united in a common cause. Told with wit and humor, this fast-paced novel has character development that is extraordinary." SLJ

Walker, Alice, 1944-

The color purple. 10th anniversary ed. Harcourt Brace Jovanovich 1992 290p il $24; pa $14 *

Grades: 11 12 Adult   **Fic**

1. African Americans—Fiction 2. Sisters—Fiction
3. Southern States—Fiction

ISBN 0-15-119154-9; 0-15-602835-2 (pa)

LC 91-47202

A reissue of the title first published 1982

"A feminist novel about an abused and uneducated black woman's struggle for empowerment, the novel was praised for the depth of its female characters and for its eloquent use of black English vernacular." Merriam-Webster's Ency of Lit

Wallace, Jason, 1969-

Out of shadows. Holiday House 2011 282p $17.95

Grades: 7 8 9 10 11 12   **Fic**

1. Race relations—Fiction 2. Bullies—Fiction
3. School stories 4. Zimbabwe—Fiction

ISBN 978-0-8234-2342-2; 0-8234-2342-5

LC 2010-24372

First published 2010 in the United Kingdom

In 1983, at an elite boys' boarding school in Zimbabwe, thirteen-year-old English lad Robert Jacklin finds himself torn between his black roommate and the white bullies still bitter over losing power through the recent civil war.

"This thought-provoking narrative offers teens a window into a distinctive time and place in history that is likely to be unfamiliar to most of them. A first purchase for high schools, especially those with a strong world cultures curriculum." SLJ

Wallace, Rich, 1957-

One good punch. Alfred A. Knopf 2007 114p $15.99

Grades: 7 8 9 10 11 12   **Fic**

1. Journalism—Fiction 2. Track athletics—Fiction
3. School stories 4. Pennsylvania—Fiction

ISBN 978-0-375-81352-8; 0-375-81352-7

LC 2006-33270

Eighteen-year-old Michael Kerrigan, writer of obituaries for the Scranton Observer and captain of the track team, is ready for the most important season of his life—until the police find four joints in his school locker, and he is faced with a choice that could change everything.

"This novel's success is in creating a multidimensional male character in a format that will appeal to all readers. The moral dilemma . . . makes this novel ripe for ethical discussions." Voice Youth Advocates

Perpetual check. Alfred A. Knopf 2009 112p $15.99; lib bdg $18.99

Grades: 8 9 10 11   **Fic**

1. Chess—Fiction 2. Brothers—Fiction 3. Father-son relationship—Fiction

ISBN 978-0-375-84058-6; 0-375-84058-3; 978-0-375-94058-3 (lib bdg); 0-375-94058-8 (lib bdg)

LC 2008-04159

Brothers Zeke and Randy participate in an important chess tournament, playing against each other while also trying to deal with their father's intensely competitive tendencies.

"Wallace cleverly positions Randy and Zeke for a win-win conclusion in this satisfying, engaging, and deceptively simple story." SLJ

Wrestling Sturbridge. Knopf 1996 135p hardcover o.p. pa $4.99 *

Grades: 7 8 9 10   **Fic**

1. Wrestling—Fiction 2. Friendship—Fiction

ISBN 0-679-87803-3; 0-679-88555-2 (pa)

LC 95-20468

"Narrator Ben, a high school senior, doesn't want to be like his father and so many others in Sturbridge, Pa., who after graduating get a job at the cinder block plant. Seemingly his only alternative is to become a state wrestling champion and thus win an athletic scholarship. But his way is firmly blocked by his buddy Al, who reigns supreme in their weight class." Publ Wkly

"The wresting scenes are thrilling. . . . Like Ben, whose voice is so strong and clear here, Wallace weighs his words carefully, making every one count in this excellent, understated first novel." Booklist

Wallenfels, Stephen

POD. Namelos 2009 212p $18.95; pa $9.95

Grades: 7 8 9 10   **Fic**

1. Extraterrestrial beings—Fiction 2. Science fiction

ISBN 978-1-60898-011-6; 1-60898-011-1; 978-1-60898-010-9 (pa); 1-60898-010-3 (pa)

LC 2008-29721

As alien spacecrafts fill the sky and zap up any human being who dares to go outside, fifteen-year-old Josh and twelve-year-old Megs, living in different cities, describe what could be their last days on Earth.

"The dire circumstances don't negate the humor, the hormones, or the humanity found in the young narrators. This is solid, straightforward sci-fi." Booklist

Walters, Eric, 1957-

In a flash. Orca 2008 108p (Orca currents) $16.95; pa $9.95

Grades: 7 8 9 10   **Fic**

Walters, Eric, 1957——*Continued*

1. School stories

ISBN   978-1-55469-035-0;   1-55469-035-8;
978-1-55469-034-3 (pa); 1-55469-034-X (pa)

"Ian organizes flash mobs, inviting large groups of people to assemble for a silly stunt . . . before quickly dispersing. At school, when the tough new principal starts taking away privileges, Ian uses the power of flash mobs to persuade him to lighten up." Horn Book Guide

"Snappy, realistic dialogue; multidimensional characters; and an unpredictable plot (not to mention a hip, contemporary phenomenon) will have both reluctant and struggling readers madly flipping the pages." SLJ

Splat! written by Eric Walters. Orca Book Publishers 2008 112p $16.95; pa $9.95

Grades: 7 8 9 10   **Fic**

1. Friendship—Fiction 2. Tomatoes—Fiction
3. Canada—Fiction

ISBN   978-1-55143-988-4;   1-55143-988-3;
978-1-55143-986-0 (pa); 1-55143-986-7 (pa)

"Keegan and Alex are the only kids in Leamington who haven't volunteered to help out with the town's annual tomato festival. In an attempt to teach them a sense of responsibility, their fathers put them in charge of the tomato toss. The boys decide it's their responsibility to add a little excitement to the event." Publisher's note

"The relationship between Keegan and narrator Alex, with their relentless and often quite funny smartassed exhanges, is the core of this speedy and readable novel." Bull Cent Child Books

Ward, Rachel

Numbers. Chicken House/Scholastic 2010 325p $17.99

Grades: 8 9 10 11 12   **Fic**

1. Death—Fiction 2. Extrasensory perception—Fiction 3. Runaway teenagers—Fiction 4. Blacks—Great Britain—Fiction 5. Science fiction

ISBN 978-0-545-14299-1; 0-545-14299-7

LC 2008-55440

Title appears on item as: Num8ers

"Since the day her mother died, Jem has known about the numbers. Numbers that pop into her head when she looks into someone's eyes. They're dates, the numbers. Dates predicting with brute accuracy each person's death. Burdened by such grim knowledge, Jem avoids relationships. Until she meets Spider, another outsider, and takes a chance." Publisher's note

"Ward's debut novel is gritty, bold, and utterly unique. Jem's isolation and pain, hidden beneath a veneer of toughness, are palpable, and the ending is a real shocker." SLJ

Followed by: The Chaos (2011)

Warman, Jessica

Breathless. Walker 2009 311p $16.99 *

Grades: 9 10 11 12   **Fic**

1. Schizophrenia—Fiction 2. Mental illness—Fiction 3. Swimming—Fiction 4. Siblings—Fiction 5. School stories

ISBN 978-0-8027-9849-7; 0-8027-9849-7

LC 2008-42555

At boarding school, Katie tries to focus on swimming and becoming popular instead of the painful memories of her institutionalized schizophrenic older brother.

"Warman draws out Katie's emotions and her complex life and family with immediacy. Readers who dive in will surface with more awareness of the devastating effects of mental illness." Kirkus

Where the truth lies. Walker & Co. 2010 308p $16.99

Grades: 9 10 11 12   **Fic**

1. Dreams—Fiction 2. Memory—Fiction 3. Dating (Social customs)—Fiction 4. Family life—Fiction 5. School stories 6. Connecticut—Fiction

ISBN 978-0-8027-2078-8; 0-8027-2078-1

LC 2010-00782

Emily, whose father is headmaster of a Connecticut boarding school, suffers from nightmares, and when she meets and falls in love with the handsome Del Sugar, pieces of her traumatic past start falling into place.

"Emily's unflinching, multilayered narration and realistic dialogue capture the wishes and fears that drive teens. A page-turner to the bittersweet ending." Kirkus

Wasserman, Robin

Hacking Harvard; a novel. Simon Pulse 2007 320p pa $8.99

Grades: 9 10 11 12   **Fic**

1. Harvard University—Fiction 2. Computer crimes—Fiction 3. School stories

ISBN 978-1-4169-3633-6; 1-4169-3633-5

When three brilliant nerds—Max Kim, Eric Roth, and Isaac "The Professor" Schwarzbaum—bet $20,000 that they can get anyone into Harvard, they take on the Ivy League in their quest for popularity, money, and the love of a beauty queen valedictorian.

"There is enough action, computers, electronics, and shenanigans to entice girls and boys, geeks and nongeeks to this thought-provoking, enjoyable read." Voice Youth Advocates

Skinned. Simon Pulse 2008 361p $15.99; pa $9.99

Grades: 9 10 11 12   **Fic**

1. Bioethics—Fiction 2. Science fiction

ISBN   978-1-4169-3634-3;   1-4169-3634-3;
978-1-4169-7449-9 (pa); 1-4169-7449-0 (pa)

LC 2008-15306

To save her from dying in a horrible accident, Lia's wealthy parents transplant her brain into a mechanical body.

"This is a captivating story that brings up many questions for teens, including how they fit in with their peers and what is their role in larger society. There are underlying themes as well such as suicide, free will, and what makes someone human." Libr Media Connect

Other titles in this series are:

Crashed (2009)

Wired (2010)

Waters, Dan, 1969-
Generation dead. Hyperion 2008 382p $16.99
Grades: 7 8 9 10   **Fic**
 1. Death—Fiction 2. Zombies—Fiction 3. Prejudices—
Fiction 4. School stories
 ISBN 978-1-4231-0921-1; 1-4231-0921-X
           LC 2007-36361
When dead teenagers who have come back to life start
showing up at her high school, Phoebe, a goth girl, becomes interested in the phenomenon, and when she starts
dating a "living impaired" boy, they encounter prejudice,
fear, and hatred.
This "is a classic desegregation story that also skewers
adult attempts to make teenagers play nice. . . . Motivational speakers, politically correct speech and encounter
groups come in for special ridicule." N Y Times Book
Rev
 Followed by: Kiss of life (2009)

Watson, Larry
Montana 1948; a novel. Milkweed Editions
2007 169p pa $14 *
Grades: 11 12 Adult   **Fic**
 1. Family life—Fiction 2. Montana—Fiction
 ISBN 978-1-57131-061-3
 First published 1993
David Hayden, the narrator "is on the brink of young
manhood when he learns that his uncle, a doctor and a
hero of World War II in the Pacific, has been sexually
molesting local Indian women. The citizens of Bentrock,
Mont., tolerate Uncle Frank's predilection until Marie
Little Soldier, David's parents' housekeeper, dies while
under his care. Frank's conduct poses a moral problem
for Wes Hayden, David's father, who is also the town
sheriff; despite pressure from the boy's grandfather, Wes
arrests Frank as a suspect in Marie's death." N Y Times
Book Rev
"The moral issues, and the consequences of following
one's conscience, are made painfully evident here. Watson is to be congratulated for the honesty of his writing
and the purity of his prose." Libr J

Weatherford, Carole Boston, 1956-
Becoming Billie Holiday; art by Floyd Cooper.
Wordsong 2008 116p il $19.95 *
Grades: 7 8 9 10   **Fic**
 1. Holiday, Billie, 1915-1959—Fiction 2. Novels in
verse 3. African Americans—Fiction 4. Singers—Fic-
tion 5. Jazz music—Fiction
 ISBN 978-1-59078-507-2; 1-59078-507-X
           LC 2007-51214
Jazz vocalist Billie Holiday looks back on her early
years in this fictional memoir written in verse.
"This captivating title places readers solidly into Holi-
day's world, and is suitable for independent reading as
well as a variety of classroom uses." SLJ
 Includes bibliographical references

Weaver, Will
Defect. Farrar, Straus and Giroux 2007 199p
$16
Grades: 7 8 9 10 11 12   **Fic**
 1. Birth defects—Fiction 2. Foster home care—Fiction
3. School stories 4. Minnesota—Fiction
 ISBN 0-374-31725-9; 978-0-374-31725-6
           LC 2006-49152
After spending most of his life in Minnesota foster
homes hiding a bizarre physical abnormality, fifteen-
year-old David is offered a chance at normalcy, but must
decide if giving up what makes him special is the right
thing to do.
The author "skillfully interweaves the improbable with
twenty-first-century realities in this provocative novel of
the ultimate cost of being so, so different." Voice Youth
Advocates

Full service. Farrar, Straus & Giroux 2005 231p
hardcover o.p. pa $8.99
Grades: 7 8 9 10   **Fic**
 1. Service stations—Fiction 2. Farm life—Fiction
3. Minnesota—Fiction
 ISBN 0-374-32485-9; 0-374-40022-9 (pa)
           LC 2004-57671
In the summer of 1965, teenager Paul Sutton, a northern Minnesota farm boy, takes a job at a gas station in
town, where his strict religious upbringing is challenged
by new people and experiences.
"Weaver is a wonderful stylist and his beautifully chosen words put such a shine on his deeply felt story that
most teens will be able to find their own faces reflected
in its pages." Booklist

Saturday night dirt. Farrar, Straus and Giroux
2008 163p $14.95; pa $7.99
Grades: 8 9 10 11   **Fic**
 1. Automobile racing—Fiction 2. Minnesota—Fiction
 ISBN 978-0-374-35060-4; 0-374-35060-4;
978-0-312-56131-4 (pa); 0-312-56131-8 (pa)
           LC 2007-6988
In a small town in northern Minnesota, the much-
anticipated Saturday night dirt-track race at the old-
fashioned, barely viable, Headwaters Speedway becomes,
in many ways, an important life-changing event for all
the participants on and off the track.
"Weaver presents compelling character studies. . . .
Young racing fans . . . will find much that rings true
here." Booklist
 Other titles in this series are
Checkered flag cheater (2010)
Super stock rookie (2009)

Weber, Lori, 1959-
If you live like me. Lobster Press 2009 331p pa
$14.95
Grades: 7 8 9 10   **Fic**
 1. Family life—Fiction 2. Newfoundland—Fiction
 ISBN 978-1-897550-12-0; 1-897550-12-X
Cheryl's unhappiness builds with each move as her
family travels across Canada while her father does research for a book, and by the time they reach Newfoundland, she is planning her escape, but events cause her to
re-examine her feelings

Weber, Lori, 1959-—Continued

"Weber's depiction of Cheryl is true to life, an accurate account of an independent and intelligent teenager struggling with loneliness, acceptance of change, and her own approaching adulthood." SLJ

Weingarten, Lynn

Wherever Nina lies. Point 2009 316p $16.99

Grades: 8 9 10 11 12   Fic
1. Sisters—Fiction 2. Missing persons—Fiction
ISBN 978-0-545-06631-0; 0-545-06631-X
          LC 2008-21527

"Sixteen-year-old Ellie Wrigley is desperate to find her unconventional, beloved older sister, Nina, who disappeared two years ago, seemingly without a trace. When Ellie uncovers a clue in a local secondhand shop . . . she is determined to investigate. . . . Ellie sets off on a cross-country chase with her new crush, Sean, who has also lost a sibling. . . . Weingarten's fast-paced, chatty style will keep readers tuned in." Publ Wkly

Weinheimer, Beckie

Converting Kate. Viking Children's Books 2007 312p $16.99

Grades: 7 8 9 10   Fic
1. Religion—Fiction 2. Family life—Fiction
3. Maine—Fiction
ISBN 0-670-06152-2; 978-0-670-06152-5
          LC 2006-10200

After moving from Arizona to Maine, sixteen-year-old Kate tries to recover from her father's death as she resists her mother's dogmatic religious beliefs and attempts to find a new direction to her life.

"Religion and religious differences are serious issues to many young adults, and even those breaking from their parents on more secular fronts will sympathize with Kate's struggle." Bull Cent Child Books

Weis, Margaret, 1948-

Mistress of dragons. TOR Bks. 2003 381p hardcover o.p. pa $7.99

Grades: 11 12 Adult   Fic
1. Dragons—Fiction 2. Fantasy fiction
ISBN 0-7653-0468-6; 0-7653-4390-8 (pa)
          LC 2003-42618

"A Tom Doherty Associates book"

When the Amazonian order of priestesses, who have kept dragons from interfering with humans, is violated by men, a wild and magical conflict ensues, revealing a secret lineage and dark truth about the Parliament of Dragons.

"Full of intrigue, magic, and violence, this first book of Dragonvarld—a projected trilogy chronicling the battle to preserve the uneasy relationship between dragons and humans—launches the project powerfully. Weis has brilliantly conceived a world viable for both dragons and humans." Booklist

Other titles in the Dragonvarld series are:
The dragon's son (2004)
Master of the dragons (2005)

Weisberg, Joseph

10th grade; a novel. Random House 2002 259p hardcover o.p. pa $13.95

Grades: 11 12 Adult   Fic
1. School stories
ISBN 0-375-50584-9; 0-8129-6662-7 (pa)
          LC 2001-41916

This "novel is the journal of Jeremy Reskin, a tenth-grader with atrocious grammar who does not believe in the utility of commas and will stretch sentences across many lines because his writing teacher has told him to express himself. . . . The book is in fact quite charming and proves surprisingly readable. . . . Weisberg admirably captures the inarticulate voice of a suburban tenth-grader." Booklist

Wells, H. G. (Herbert George), 1866-1946

The invisible man. Penguin 2005 xxiv, 161p pa $6

Grades: 11 12 Adult   Fic
1. Science fiction
ISBN 0-14-143998-X
Also available from other publishers
First published 1897

"The story concerns the life and death of a scientist named Griffin who has gone mad. Having learned how to make himself invisible, Griffin begins to use his invisibility for nefarious purposes, including murder. When he is finally killed, his body becomes visible again." Merriam-Webster's Ency of Lit

The time machine. Penguin 2005 xxviii, 104p pa $9

Grades: 11 12 Adult   Fic
1. Science fiction 2. Time travel—Fiction
ISBN 0-14-143997-1
First published 1895

"Wells advanced his social and political ideas in this narrative of a nameless Time Traveller who is hurtled into the year 802,701 by his elaborate ivory, crystal, and brass contraption. The world he finds is peopled by two races: the decadent Eloi, fluttery and useless, are dependent for food, clothing, and shelter on the simian subterranean Morlocks, who prey on them. The two races—whose names are borrowed from the Biblical Eli and Moloch—symbolize Wells's vision of the eventual result of unchecked capitalism: a neurasthenic upper class that would eventually be devoured by a proletariat driven to the depths." Merriam-Webster's Ency of Lit

The war of the worlds; illustrated by Edward Gorey. New York Review Books [2005] c1960 251p il $16.95 *

Grades: 7 8 9 10 11 12 Adult   Fic
1. Science fiction 2. Extraterrestrial beings—Fiction
ISBN 1-59017-158-6   LC 2005-3693
Also available from other publishers
First published 1898

"The inhabitants of Mars, a loathsome though highly organized race, invade England, and by their command of superior weapons subdue and prey on the people." Baker. Guide to the Best Fic

In this novel the author "introduced the 'Alien' being into the role which became a cliché—a monstrous invad-

Wells, H. G. (Herbert George), 1866-1946—
Continued

er of Earth, a competitor in a cosmic struggle for existence. Though the Martians were a ruthless and terrible enemy, HGW was careful to point out that Man had driven many animal species to extinction, and that human invaders of Tasmania had behaved no less callously in exterminating their cousins." Sci Fic Ency

Wells, Rosemary, 1943-
Red moon at Sharpsburg. Viking 2007 236p
$16.99; pa $7.99 *

Grades: 6 7 8 9 10   **Fic**
1. United States—History—1861-1865, Civil War—Fiction
ISBN   0-670-03638-2;   978-0-670-03638-7;
0-14-241205-8 (pa); 978-0-14-241205-3 (pa)

As the Civil War breaks out, India, a young Southern girl, summons her sharp intelligence and the courage she didn't know she had to survive the war that threatens to destroy her family, her Virginia home and the only life she has ever known.

"This powerful novel is unflinching in its depiction of war and the devastation it causes, yet shows the resilience and hope that can follow such a tragedy. India is a memorable, thoroughly believable character." SLJ

Wemmlinger, Raymond, 1955-
Booth's daughter. Calkins Creek 2007 210p
$17.95

Grades: 7 8 9 10   **Fic**
1.   Booth,   Edwin,   1833-1893—Fiction
2. Father-daughter relationship—Fiction 3. Actors—Fiction 4. New York (N.Y.)—Fiction
ISBN 978-1-932425-86-4; 1-932425-86-1
                                        LC 2006-12073

In nineteenth-century New York City, Edwina, daughter of the famous actor Edwin Booth and niece of John Wilkes Booth, finds it difficult to escape the family tragedy and to meet the needs of a demanding father while maintaining her independence.

"Elements reminiscent of an Edith Wharton novel—the mannered social interactions, Gilded Age settings, and matrimony-bound momentum—will draw many romantically inclined readers." Booklist

Werlin, Nancy, 1961-
Double helix. Dial Books 2004 252p hardcover o.p. pa $6.99 *

Grades: 7 8 9 10   **Fic**
1. Genetic engineering—Fiction 2. Bioethics—Fiction
3. Science fiction
ISBN 0-8037-2606-6; 0-14-240327-X (pa)
                                        LC 2003-12269

Eighteen-year-old Eli discovers a shocking secret about his life and his family while working for a Nobel Prizewinning scientist whose specialty is genetic engineering.

"Werlin clearly and dramatically raises fundamental bioethical issues for teens to ponder. She also creates a riveting story with sharply etched characters and complex relationships that will stick with readers long after the book is closed." SLJ

Impossible; a novel. Dial Books 2008 376p
$17.99

Grades: 7 8 9 10   **Fic**
1. Magic—Fiction 2. Pregnancy—Fiction 3. Teenage mothers—Fiction
ISBN 978-0-8037-3002-1; 0-8037-3002-0
                                        LC 2008-06633

When seventeen-year-old Lucy discovers her family is under an ancient curse by an evil Elfin Knight, she realizes to break the curse she must perform three impossible tasks before her daughter is born in order to save them both.

"Werlin earns high marks for the tale's graceful interplay between wild magic and contemporary reality." Booklist

The rules of survival. Dial Books 2006 259p
$16.99 *

Grades: 8 9 10 11 12   **Fic**
1. Child abuse—Fiction 2. Siblings—Fiction
ISBN 0-8037-3001-2   LC 2006-1675

Seventeen-year-old Matthew recounts his attempts, starting at a young age, to free himself and his sisters from the grip of their emotionally and physically abusive mother.

The author "tackles the topic of child abuse with grace and insight. . . . Teens will empathize with these siblings and the secrets they keep in this psychological horror story." SLJ

Wesselhoeft, Conrad, 1953-
Adios, nirvana. Houghton Mifflin Harcourt 2010
235p $16

Grades: 10 11 12   **Fic**
1.   Death—Fiction   2.   Friendship—Fiction
3. Bereavement—Fiction 4. Musicians—Fiction
5. School stories 6. Seattle (Wash.)—Fiction
ISBN 978-0-547-36895-5; 0-547-36895-X
                                        LC 2010-06759

As Seattle sixteen-year-old Jonathan helps a dying man come to terms with a tragic event he experienced during World War II, Jonathan begins facing his own demons, especially the death of his twin brother, helped by an assortment of friends, old and new.

"The author gives the reader a wonderful blend of contemporary, historical, and literary fiction. His use of figurative language makes each page dance with images of raw realism. Wesselhoeft guides the reader down an open portal of teen suicide and grief issues. This is a poignant piece for older teens." Voice Youth Advocates

West, Dorothy, 1907-1998
The wedding. Doubleday 1995 240p hardcover
o.p. pa $12.95

Grades: 11 12 Adult   **Fic**
1. African Americans—Fiction 2. Race relations—Fiction 3. Martha's Vineyard (Mass.)—Fiction
ISBN 0-385-47143-2; 0-385-47144-0 (pa)
                                        LC 94-27285

This novel is "set on Martha's Vineyard during the 1950s and focuses on the black bourgeois community known as the Oval. Dr. Clark Coles and his wife, Corrine, highly respected Ovalites, are preparing for the

West, Dorothy, 1907-1998—*Continued*
wedding of their youngest daughter, Shelby, who, much
to their consternation, is marrying a white jazz musician.
Lute McNeil, a compulsive womanizer who has recently
made a fortune in the furniture business, is determined to
stop Shelby's wedding; he is confident that he can convince Shelby to marry him, which would bring him the
social acceptance he has always craved." Booklist
"Through the ancestral histories of the Coles family,
West . . . subtly reveals the ways in which color can
burden and codify behavior. The author makes her points
with a delicate hand, maneuvering with confidence and
ease through a sometimes incendiary subject." Publ Wkly

West, Jessamyn, 1902-1984
The friendly persuasion. Harcourt 1945 214p
hardcover o.p. pa $13
Grades: 11 12 Adult   Fic
1. Society of Friends—Fiction 2. Indiana—Fiction
ISBN 0-15-133605-9; 0-15-602909-X (pa)
Also available in hardcover from Amereon
"The Birdwell family of Indiana led a quiet life until
the Civil War came into their lives. They were Quakers
and tried to live according to the teachings of William
Penn. Jess Birdwell, a nurseryman, loved a fast horse as
well as his trees and the people he knew. Eliza, his wife,
was a Quaker minister and a gentle, albeit strict, soul.
When the war reached Indiana, Josh, the oldest son, was
torn between his Quaker upbringing and his belief in the
rightness of the Union cause; Mattie was at that difficult
age between childhood and womanhood; and Little Jess,
the youngest, ran into trouble with Eliza's geese. This is
a wonderful family chronicle, with the laughter, tears,
and tenderness that can be found in many families." Shapiro. Fic for Youth. 3d edition

Westerfeld, Scott
Leviathan; written by Scott Westerfeld;
illustrated by Keith Thompson. Simon Pulse 2009
440p il map $19.99; pa $9.99 *
Grades: 7 8 9 10   Fic
1. Mythical animals—Fiction 2. Princes—Fiction
3. Genetic engineering—Fiction 4. War stories
5. Science fiction
ISBN   978-1-4169-7173-3;   1-4169-7173-4;
978-1-4169-7174-0 (pa); 1-4169-7174-2 (pa)
                                          LC 2009-881
In an alternate 1914 Europe, fifteen-year-old Austrian
Prince Alek, on the run from the Clanker Powers who
are attempting to take over the globe using mechanical
machinery, forms an uneasy alliance with Deryn who,
disguised as a boy to join the British Air Service, is
learning to fly genetically-engineered beasts.
"The protagonists' stories are equally gripping and
keep the story moving, and Thompson's detail-rich pan-
els bring Westerfeld's unusual creations to life." Publ
Wkly
Other titles in this series are:
Behemoth (2010)
Goliath (2011)

Peeps. Razorbill 2005 312p hardcover o.p. pa
$8.99 *
Grades: 9 10 11 12   Fic
1. Vampires—Fiction
ISBN 1-59514-031-X; 1-59514-083-2 (pa)
                                          LC 2005-8151
Cal Thompson is a carrier of a parasite that causes
vampirism, and must hunt down all of the girlfriends he
has unknowingly infected.
"This innovative and original vampire story, full of
engaging characters and just enough horror without any
gore, will appeal to a wide audience." SLJ
Followed by The last days (2006)

Uglies. Simon Pulse 2011 406p $17.99; pa
$9.99 *
Grades: 7 8 9 10   Fic
1. Science fiction
ISBN 978-1-4169-3638-1; 978-1-4424-1981-0 (pa)
First published 2005
"Fifteen-year-old Tally's eerily harmonious,
postapocalyptic society gives extreme makeovers to teens
on their sixteenth birthdays. . . . When a top-secret
agency threatens to leave Tally ugly forever unless she
spies on runaway teens, she agrees to infiltrate the
Smoke, a shadowy colony of refugees from the 'tyranny
of physical perfection.'" Booklist
"Ethical concerns will provide a good source of dis-
cussion. . . . The novel is highly readable with a con-
vincing plot." SLJ
Other titles in this series are:
Extras (2007)
Pretties (2005)
Specials (2006)

Weston, Robert Paul
Dust city; a novel; by Robert Weston. Razorbill
2010 299p $16.99
Grades: 7 8 9 10   Fic
1. Wolves—Fiction 2. Fairies—Fiction 3. Magic—Fiction 4. Father-son relationship—Fiction
ISBN 978-1-59514-296-2; 1-59514-296-7
                                          LC 2010-36067
Henry Whelp, son of the Big Bad Wolf, investigates
what happened to the fairies that used to protect humans
and animalia, and what role the corporation that manu-
factures synthetic fairy dust played in his father's crime.
"The premise is fractured fairy tale, but the play is
pure noir. . . . The clever setup and gutting of fairy-tale
tropes will garner plenty of enthusiasm." Booklist

Weyn, Suzanne
Distant waves; a novel of the Titanic. Scholastic
Press 2009 330p $17.99
Grades: 8 9 10 11   Fic
1. Tesla, Nikola, 1856-1943—Fiction 2. Astor, John
Jacob, 1763-1848—Fiction 3. Stead, William Thomas,
1849-1912—Fiction 4. Titanic (Steamship)—Fiction
5. Spiritualism—Fiction 6. Sisters—Fiction
7. Mother-daughter relationship—Fiction
8. Inventors—Fiction
ISBN 978-0-545-08572-4; 0-545-08572-1
                                          LC 2008-40708

Weyn, Suzanne—*Continued*

In the early twentieth century, four sisters and their widowed mother, a famed spiritualist, travel from New York to London, and as the Titanic conveys them and their acquaintances, journalist W.T. Stead, scientist Nikola Tesla, and industrialist John Jacob Astor, home, Tesla's inventions will either doom or save them all.

"The interplay of science, spirituality, history and romance will satisfy." Publ Wkly

Empty. Scholastic Press 2010 183p $17.99

Grades: 7 8 9 10   **Fic**

1. Environmental degradation—Fiction 2. Ecology—Fiction 3. Energy resources—Fiction 4. Hurricanes—Fiction 5. Science fiction

ISBN 978-0-545-17278-3; 0-545-17278-0

LC 2010-16743

When, just ten years in the future, oil supplies run out and global warming leads to devastating storms, senior high school classmates Tom, Niki, Gwen, Hector, and Brock realize that the world as they know it is ending and lead the way to a more environmentally-friendly society.

"The realistic and thought-provoking scenario is packaged into a speedy read, and given the popularity of dystopian fiction, it should find an audience." Booklist

Wharton, Edith, 1862-1937

Ethan Frome. Scribner 1997 195p pa $13 hardcover o.p.

Grades: 11 12 Adult   **Fic**

1. Marriage—Fiction 2. Farm life—Fiction 3. Sick—Fiction 4. New England—Fiction

ISBN 0-684-82591-0 (pa)

Also available in hardcover from Buccaneer Bks.

First published 1911

This is "an ironic tragedy of love, frustration, jealousy, and sacrifice. The scene is a New England village, where Ethan barely makes a living out of a stony farm and is at odds with his wife Zeena (short for Zenobia), a whining hypochondriac. Mattie, a cousin of Zeena's comes to live with them, and love develops between her and Ethan. They try to end their impossible lives by steering a bobsled into a tree; instead ending up crippled and tied for the rest of their unhappy time on earth to Zeena and the barren farm. Zeena, however, is transformed into a devoted nurse and Mattie becomes the nagging invalid." Benet's Reader's Ency of Am Lit

Whelan, Gloria

The Disappeared. Dial Books 2008 136p $16.99; pa $6.99

Grades: 8 9 10 11 12   **Fic**

1. Argentina—Fiction 2. Siblings—Fiction

ISBN   978-0-8037-3275-9;   0-8037-3275-9;
978-0-14-241540-3 (pa); 0-14-241540-5 (pa)

LC 2007-43750

Teenaged Silvia tries to save her brother, Eduardo, after he is captured by the military government in 1970s Argentina

"The deftly handled voices of Silvia and Eduardo follow the well-intentioned, but often grievous, mistakes of youth. Their compelling tale is a chilling account of the manipulative power of corruption." SLJ

Includes bibliographical references

Homeless bird. HarperCollins Pubs. 2000 216p hardcover o.p. pa $5.99 *

Grades: 6 7 8 9 10   **Fic**

1. Women—India—Fiction 2. India—Fiction

ISBN 0-06-028454-4; 0-06-440819-1 (pa)

LC 99-33241

When thirteen-year-old Koly enters into an ill-fated arranged marriage, she must either suffer a destiny dictated by India's tradition or find the courage to oppose it.

"This beautifully told, inspiring story takes readers on a fascinating journey through modern India and the universal intricacies of a young woman's heart." Booklist

See what I see. HarperTeen 2011 199p $16.99

Grades: 7 8 9 10 11 12   **Fic**

1. Father-daughter relationship—Fiction 2. Artists—Fiction 3. Sick—Fiction 4. Detroit (Mich.)—Fiction

ISBN 978-0-06-125545-8; 0-06-125545-9

LC 2010-03094

When eighteen-year-old Kate arrives on the Detroit doorstep of her long-estranged father, a famous painter, she is shocked to learn that he is dying and does not want to support her efforts to attend the local art school.

"With elegant prose, Whelan portrays a gradually developing and complex relationship built on guilt, curiosity, love, and a passion for art." Booklist

Whitcomb, Laura, 1958-

A certain slant of light. Graphia 2005 282p $8.99

Grades: 9 10 11 12   **Fic**

1. Ghost stories 2. Future life—Fiction

ISBN 0-618-58532-X (pa)   LC 2004-27208

After benignly haunting a series of people for 130 years, Helen meets a teenage boy who can see her and together they unlock the mysteries of their pasts.

The author "creatively pulls together a dramatic and compelling plot that cleverly grants rebellious teen romance a timeless grandeur." Bull Cent Child Books

The Fetch; a novel. Houghton Mifflin Harcourt 2009 379p il $17

Grades: 9 10 11 12   **Fic**

1. Anastasiíâ Nikolaevna, Grand Duchess, daughter of Nicholas II, Emperor of Russia, 1901-1918—Fiction 2. Alekseǐ Nikolaevich, Czarevitch, son of Nicholas II, Emperor of Russia, 1904-1918—Fiction 3. Rasputin, Grigoriǐ Efimovich, 1871-1916—Fiction 4. Death—Fiction 5. Soviet Union—History—1917-1921, Revolution—Fiction

ISBN 978-0-618-89131-3; 0-618-89131-5

LC 2008-13307

After 350 years as a Fetch, or death escort, Calder breaks his vows and enters the body of Rasputin, whose spirit causes rebellion in the Land of Lost Souls while Calder struggles to convey Ana and Alexis, orphaned in the Russian Revolution, to Heaven.

"The rich descriptions, particularly of the exquisitely imagined afterlife, are exceptionally drawn, as are the sympathetic characters and the unusual premise. A challenging book with an intriguing conclusion, this will lead thoughtful readers to spirited discussions." Booklist

White, Andrea

Surviving Antarctica; reality TV 2083. HarperCollins Publishers 2005 327p hardcover o.p. pa $6.99

Grades: 7 8 9 10   **Fic**
   1. Antarctica—Fiction 2. Science fiction
   ISBN 0-06-055454-1; 0-06-055456-8 (pa)
                                           LC 2004-6249

In the year 2083, five fourteen-year-olds who were deprived by chance of the opportunity to continue their educations reenact Scott's 1910-1913 expedition to the South Pole as contestants on a reality television show, secretly aided by a Department of Entertainment employee

"A real page-turner, this novel will give readers pause as they ponder the ethics of teens risking their lives in adult-contrived situations for the entertainment of the masses." Booklist

White, Edmund, 1940-

A boy's own story. Dutton 1982 217p pa $14 hardcover o.p. *

Grades: 11 12 Adult   **Fic**
   1. Homosexuality—Fiction 2. Adolescence—Fiction
   ISBN 978-0-14-311484-0   LC 82-9536

In this first volume of an autobiographical trilogy, a nameless narrator reminisces about his homosexual childhood and his conflicting emotions in coming of age during the 1950s. At fifteen years of age, the boy hopes that "he is just passing through a homosexual 'stage.' At prep school he goes to a . . . psychiatrist who pops pills and talks of his own problems—and with no help from this man he begins slowly to see the real dimensions of his own life." Newsweek

This first-person novel is "written with the flourish of a master stylist. . . . It is an endearing portrait of a child's longing to be charming, popular, powerful, and loved, and of his struggles with adults . . . {told with} sensitivity and elegance." Harpers

Followed by The beautiful room is empty (1988) and The farewell symphony (1997)

White, T. H. (Terence Hanbury), 1906-1964

The once and future king. Putnam 1958 677p $25.95 *

Grades: 8 9 10 11 12 Adult   **Fic**
   1. Arthur, King—Fiction 2. Great Britain—History—0-1066—Fiction 3. Knights and knighthood—Fiction 4. Fantasy fiction
   ISBN 0-399-10597-2   LC 58-10760
   Also available in paperback from Ace Bks.

An omnibus edition of four novels; The sword in the stone (1939), The witch in the wood (1939, now called The Queen of Air and Darkness) and The ill-made knight (1940). A number of alterations have been made in the earlier books. Previously unpublished, The candle in the wind "deals with the plotting of Mordred and his kinsmen of the house of Orkney, and their undying enmity to King Arthur." Times Lit Suppl

"White's contemporary retelling of Malory's Le Morte d'Arthur is both romantic and exciting." Shapiro. Fic for Youth. 3d edition

Whitehead, Colson, 1969-

Sag Harbor; a novel. Doubleday 2009 288p $24.95

Grades: 11 12 Adult   **Fic**
   1. Adolescence—Fiction 2. African Americans—Fiction 3. Brothers—Fiction 4. Long Island (N.Y.)—Fiction
   ISBN 978-0-385-52765-1; 0-385-52765-9
                                          LC 2008-13510

Benji, one of the only black kids at an elite prep school in Manhattan, tries desperately to fit in, but every summer, he and his brother, Reggie, escape to the East End of Sag Harbor, where a small community of African American professionals has built a world of its own.

The author "serves up whole sundaes worth of riffs on the quotidian, all hung on the skinny frame of a 15-year-old everyman virgin and his marginally less distinct friends, give or take a repressive father and a particularly evocative shoreline landscape." Village Voice

Whitley, David, 1984-

Midnight charter. Roaring Brook Press 2009 319p $17.99

Grades: 7 8 9 10   **Fic**
   1. Science fiction
   ISBN 978-1-59643-381-6; 1-59643-381-7

"In a society based on trade, where everything can be bought and sold, the future rests on the secrets of a single document—and the lives of two children whose destiny it is to discover its secrets." Publisher's note

"Deft world-building and crafty plotting combine for a zinger of an ending that will leave readers poised for book two. Surprisingly sophisticated upper-middle-grade fare, with enough meat to satisfy older readers as well." Kirkus

Followed by: The children of the lost (2011)

Whitman, Emily

Wildwing. Greenwillow Books 2010 359p $16.99

Grades: 7 8 9 10   **Fic**
   1. Time travel—Fiction 2. Social classes—Fiction 3. Falcons—Fiction 4. Great Britain—History—1066-1154, Norman period—Fiction
   ISBN 978-0-06-172452-7; 0-06-172452-1
                                          LC 2009-44189

In 1913 London, fifteen-year-old Addy is a lowly servant, but when she gets inside an elevator car in her employer's study, she is suddenly transported to a castle in 1240 and discovers that she is mistaken for the lord's intended bride.

"Whitman populates both of her worlds with vivid, believable characters. . . . This historical novel with a time-travel twist of sci-fi will find an avid readership." SLJ

Whitney, Daisy

The Mockingbirds. Little, Brown 2010 339p $16.99

Grades: 10 11 12   **Fic**
   1. Rape—Fiction 2. Secret societies—Fiction 3. School stories 4. Sisters—Fiction
   ISBN 978-0-316-09053-7; 0-316-09053-0
                                          LC 2009-51257

Whitney, Daisy—*Continued*

When Alex, a junior at an elite preparatory school, realizes that she may have been the victim of date rape, she confides in her roommates and sister who convince her to seek help from a secret society, the Mockingbirds.

"Authentic and illuminating, this strong . . . [title] explores vital teen topics of sex and violence; crime and punishment; ineffectual authority; and the immeasurable, healing influence of friendship and love." Booklist

Whitney, Kim Ablon

The other half of life; a novel based on the true story of the MS St. Louis. Alfred A. Knopf 2009 237p $16.99; lib bdg $19.99

Grades: 6 7 8 9 10   **Fic**
1. Jews—Germany—Fiction 2. Holocaust, 1933-1945—Fiction
ISBN   978-0-375-85219-0;   0-375-85219-0;
978-0-375-95219-7 (lib bdg); 0-375-95219-5 (lib bdg)
LC 2008-38949

In 1939, fifteen-year-old Thomas sails on a German ship bound for Cuba with more than nine hundred German Jews expecting to be granted safe haven in Cuba.

"The characters are intriguing enough, but it's the real-life history that provides the novel's energy." Horn Book Guide

Includes bibliographical references

The perfect distance. Knopf 2005 256p hardcover o.p. pa $5.99

Grades: 9 10 11 12   **Fic**
1. Horsemanship—Fiction 2. Mexican Americans—Fiction
ISBN 0-375-83243-2; 0-553-49467-8 (pa)
LC 2005-40726

While competing in the three junior national equitation championships, seventeen-year-old Francie Martinez learns to believe in herself and makes some decisions about the type of person she wants to be

The author "inhabits Francie's character wholly and convincingly and gets the universals of serious competition just right—any athlete will recognize the imperious, unfeeling coach; the snotty front-runner; and the unparalleled thrill of hitting the zone." Booklist

Whittenberg, Allison

Life is fine. Delacorte Press 2008 181p $15.99; lib bdg $18.99

Grades: 8 9 10 11 12   **Fic**
1. African Americans—Fiction 2. Child abuse—Fiction 3. Mother-daughter relationship—Fiction
ISBN 978-0-385-73480-6; 978-0-385-90478-0 (lib bdg)
LC 2007-27604

With a neglectful mother who has an abusive, live-in boyfriend, life for fifteen-year-old Samara is not fine, but when a substitute teacher walks into class one day and introduces her to poetry, she starts to view life from a different perspective.

"Samara's voice is sharp and convincing." Publ Wkly

Whyman, Matt

Icecore; a Carl Hobbes thriller. Atheneum Books for Young Readers 2007 307p $16.99; pa $8.99

Grades: 7 8 9 10   **Fic**
1. Prisoners—Fiction 2. Computer crimes—Fiction 3. Torture—Fiction 4. Military bases—Fiction 5. Arctic regions—Fiction
ISBN   978-1-4169-4907-7;   1-4169-4907-0;
978-1-4169-8960-8 (pa); 1-4169-8960-9 (pa)
LC 2007-02674

Seventeen-year-old Englishman Carl Hobbes meant no harm when he hacked into Fort Knox's security system, but at Camp Twilight in the Arctic Circle, known as the Guantanamo Bay of the north, he is tortured to reveal information about a conspiracy of which he was never a part.

"Powered by a fast-paced narrative, this exploration of numerous timely themes . . . gives the eminently readable adventure a degree of depth." Publ Wkly

Followed by: Goldstrike (2010)

Wild, K., 1954-

Fight game; [by] Kate Wild. Chicken House/Scholastic 2007 279p $16.99

Grades: 7 8 9 10   **Fic**
1. Martial arts—Fiction 2. Genetic engineering—Fiction 3. Spies—Fiction 4. Science fiction
ISBN 978-0-439-87175-4; 0-439-87175-1
LC 2006-32889

Fifteen-year-old Freedom Smith is a fighter, just like all of his relatives who have the "Hercules gene," which leads him to a choice between being jailed for attempted murder or working with a covert law enforcement agency to break up a mysterious, illegal fight ring.

"Intriguing supporting characters pepper Wild's debut novel and bolster an already strong portagonist. . . . Wild's story pulsates with raw energy." Voice Youth Advocates

Wilde, Oscar, 1854-1900

The picture of Dorian Gray. Modern Library 1992 254p $16.95 *

Grades: 11 12 Adult   **Fic**
1. Allegories 2. Portraits—Fiction 3. Supernatural—Fiction 4. Great Britain—Fiction
ISBN 0-679-60001-9   LC 92-11593

Also available from other publishers

First published 1891 in the United Kingdom; first United States edition published 1895 by G. Munro's Sons

"An archetypal tale of a young man who purchases eternal youth at the expense of his soul, the novel was a romantic exposition of Wilde's Aestheticism. Dorian Gray is a wealthy Englishman who gradually sinks into a life of dissipation and crime. Despite his unhealthy behavior, his physical appearance remains youthful and unmarked by dissolution. Instead, a portrait of himself catalogues every evil deed by turning his once handsome features into a hideous mask." Merriam-Webster's Ency of Lit

Wilhelm, Doug

Falling. Farrar, Straus and Giroux 2007 241p
$17

Grades: 8 9 10 11 12   **Fic**

1. Drug abuse—Fiction 2. Basketball—Fiction
3. Family life—Fiction 4. School stories 5. Vermont—
Fiction

ISBN 978-0-374-32251-9; 0-374-32251-1

LC 2006-45293

Fifteen-year-old Matt's life has been turned upside-
down, first when the brother he idolizes turns to drugs,
then when a visit to a chat room leads him to a classmate, Katie, who he likes very much but cannot trust
with his family secret.

"The addiction scenes are stark, and the story holds
surprises to the end." Booklist

Wilkins, Ebony Joy

Sellout. Scholastic Press 2010 267p $17.99

Grades: 7 8 9 10   **Fic**

1. African Americans—Fiction 2. Social classes—Fiction

ISBN 978-0-545-10928-4; 0-545-10928-0

NaTasha loves her life of affluence in Park Adams,
but her grandmother fears she has lost touch with her
roots and whisks her off to Harlem, where NaTasha
meets rough, streetwise girls at a crisis center and finds
the courage to hold her own against them.

"Some elements of the story tie up too easily—
NaTasha's greatest tormentors warm up to her a bit too
quickly to be believed—but the message of staying true
to oneself shines through." SLJ

Wilkinson, Lili, 1981-

Pink. HarperTeen 2011 310p $16.99

Grades: 7 8 9 10 11 12   **Fic**

1. Identity (Psychology)—Fiction 2. School stories
3. Theater—Fiction 4. Homosexuality—Fiction
5. Australia—Fiction

ISBN 978-0-06-192653-2; 0-06-192653-1

LC 2010-9389

Sixteen-year-old Ava does not know who she is or
where she belongs, but when she tries out a new personality—and sexual orientation—at a different school, her
edgy girlfriend, potential boyfriend, and others are hurt
by her lack of honesty.

"The novel is in turn laugh-out-loud funny, endearing,
and heartbreaking as Ava repeatedly steps into teenage
social land mines—with unexpected results. Because
Wilkinson doesn't rely on stereotypes, the characters are
well-developed, and interactions between them feel genuine." Voice Youth Advocates

Willey, Margaret

A summer of silk moths. Flux 2009 246p il map
pa $9.95

Grades: 7 8 9 10   **Fic**

1. Uncles—Fiction 2. Moths—Fiction 3. Fathers—Fiction 4. Michigan—Fiction

ISBN 978-0-73871-540-7; 0-73871-540-9

LC 2009-19681

A seventeen-year-old boy and girl learn long-held secrets about their pasts as they overcome their initial an-
tipathy toward one another on a Michigan nature preserve dedicated to her dead father.

"A thoughtful, complex and moving story about loss
and discovery of identity, love and the ability to change
and the restorative powers of nature. . . . The believable
characters and the insights into their awakening emotional lives will carry readers along." Kirkus

Williams, Carol Lynch, 1959-

The chosen one. St. Martin's Griffin 2009 213p
$16.95

Grades: 7 8 9 10   **Fic**

1. Family life—Fiction 2. Cults—Fiction
3. Polygamy—Fiction

ISBN 978-0-312-55511-5; 0-312-55511-3

LC 2009-4800

In a polygamous cult in the desert, Kyra, not yet fourteen, sees being chosen to be the seventh wife of her uncle as just punishment for having read books and kissed
a boy, in violation of Prophet Childs' teachings, and is
torn between facing her fate and running away from all
that she knows and loves.

"This book is a highly emotional, terrifying read. It is
not measured or objective. Physical abuse, fear, and even
murder are constants. It is a girl-in-peril story, and as
such, it is impossible to put down and holds tremendous
teen appeal." Voice Youth Advocates

Glimpse. Simon & Schuster Books for Young
Readers 2010 484p $16.99

Grades: 7 8 9 10   **Fic**

1. Novels in verse 2. Suicide—Fiction 3. Sisters—Fiction 4. Mother-daughter relationship—Fiction
5. Child sexual abuse—Fiction

ISBN 978-1-4169-9730-6; 1-4169-9730-X

LC 2009-41147

"A Paula Wiseman book"

Living with their mother who earns money as a prostitute, two sisters take care of each other and when the
older one attempts suicide, the younger one tries to uncover the reason.

"Williams leans hard on her free-verse line breaks for
drama . . . and it works. A page-turner for Ellen Hopkins fans." Kirkus

Miles from ordinary; a novel. St. Martin's Press
2011 197p $16.99

Grades: 7 8 9 10   **Fic**

1. Mother-daughter relationship—Fiction 2. Mental illness—Fiction 3. Family life—Fiction

ISBN 978-0-312-55512-2; 0-312-55512-1

LC 2010-40324

As her mother's mental illness spins terrifyingly out of
control, thirteen-year-old Lacey must face the truth of
what life with her mother means for both of them.

"The author has crafted both a riveting, unusual suspense tale and an absolutely convincing character in
Lacey. The book truly is miles from ordinary, in the very
best way. Outstanding." Kirkus

Williams, Gabrielle

Beatle meets Destiny. Marshall Cavendish 2010 342p $17.99 *

Grades: 8 9 10 11 12   **Fic**

1. Dating (Social customs)—Fiction 2. Twins—Fiction 3. Siblings—Fiction 4. Family life—Fiction 5. Love stories 6. Australia—Fiction

ISBN 978-0-7614-5723-7

When superstitious eighteen-year-old John "Beatle" Lennon, who is dating the best friend of his twin sister, meets Destiny McCartney, their instant rapport and shared quirkiness make it seem that their fate is written in the stars.

"Clever, amusing, yet surprisingly thoughtful, the book will appeal to readers looking for something a little different." Publ Wkly

Williams, Katie

The space between trees. Chronicle Books 2010 274p $17.99

Grades: 8 9 10 11 12   **Fic**

1. Homicide—Fiction 2. School stories

ISBN 978-0-8118-7175-4; 0-8118-7175-4

LC 2009-48561

When the body of a classmate is discovered in the woods, sixteen-year-old Evie's lies wind up involving her with the girl's best friend, trying to track down the killer.

"Evie's raw honesty and the choices she makes make for difficult reading, but also a darkly beautiful, emotionally honest story of personal growth." Publ Wkly

Williams, Lori Aurelia

When Kambia Elaine flew in from Neptune. Simon & Schuster 2000 246p hardcover o.p. pa $10 *

Grades: 7 8 9 10   **Fic**

1. African Americans—Fiction 2. Houston (Tex.)—Fiction

ISBN 0-689-82468-8; 0-689-84593-6 (pa)

LC 99-65154

"Williams weaves two tales in the first-person narrative of twelve-year-old Shayla: the story of Shayla's older sister and her sexual awakening; and the story of Kambia, Shayla's soon-to-be best friend, whose fantastic stories of transformation hide her real-life abuse." Horn Book Guide

"This is a strong and disturbing novel, told in beautiful language. Teens will find it engrossing." SLJ

Williams-Garcia, Rita

Jumped. HarperTeen 2009 169p $16.99; lib bdg $17.89 *

Grades: 8 9 10 11 12   **Fic**

1. Bullies—Fiction 2. School stories

ISBN 978-0-06-076091-5; 0-06-076091-5; 978-0-06-076092-2 (lib bdg); 0-06-076092-3 (lib bdg)

LC 2008-22381

"Amistad"

The lives of Leticia, Dominique, and Trina are irrevocably intertwined through the course of one day in an urban high school after Leticia overhears Dominique's plans to beat up Trina and must decide whether or not

to get involved.

"In alternating chapters narrated by Leticia, Trina, and Dominique, Williams-Garcia has given her characters strong, individual voices that ring true to teenage speech, and she lets them make their choices without judgment or moralizing." SLJ

Like sisters on the homefront. Lodestar Bks. 1995 165p hardcover o.p. pa $5.99 *

Grades: 7 8 9 10   **Fic**

1. African Americans—Fiction 2. Family life—Fiction 3. Teenage mothers—Fiction

ISBN 0-525-67465-9; 0-14-038561-4 (pa)

LC 95-3690

"It's bad enough that 14-year-old Gayle has one baby, but when she becomes pregnant again by another boy, Mama's had enough. She takes Gayle for an abortion and then ships her and her baby south to stay with religious relatives. . . . With the help of her dying great-grandmother, who leaves Gayle the family's African-American oral tradition, she begins to mature and understand her place in the family and her future." Child Book Rev Serv

"Beautifully written, the text captures the cadence and rhythm of New York street talk and the dilemma of being poor, black, and uneducated. This is a gritty, realistic, well-told story." SLJ

Willis, Connie

To say nothing of the dog; or, How we found the bishop's bird stump at last. Bantam Bks. 1998 434p hardcover o.p. pa $7.99

Grades: 11 12 Adult   **Fic**

1. Science fiction

ISBN 0-553-09995-7; 0-553-57538-4 (pa)

LC 97-16002

"Rich dowager Lady Schrapnell has invaded Oxford University's time travel research project in 2057, promising to endow it if they help her rebuild Coventry Cathedral, destroyed by a Nazi air raid in 1940. . . . Time traveler Ned Henry is suffering from advanced time lag and has been sent, he thinks, for rest and relaxation to 1888, where he connects with time traveler Verity Kindle and discovers that he is actually there to correct an incongruity created when Verity inadvertently brought something forward from the past." Booklist

"No one mixes scientific mumbo jumbo and comedy of manners with more panache than Willis." N Y Times Book Rev

Wilson, Diane L.

Firehorse. Margaret K. McElderry Books 2006 325p $16.95

Grades: 7 8 9 10   **Fic**

1. Veterinary medicine—Fiction 2. Sex role—Fiction 3. Horses—Fiction 4. Arson—Fiction 5. Family life—Fiction 6. Boston (Mass.)—Fiction

ISBN 1-4169-1551-6; 978-1-4169-1551-5

LC 2005-30785

Spirited fifteen-year-old horse lover Rachel Selby determines to become a veterinarian, despite the opposition of her rigid father, her proper mother, and the norms of Boston in 1872, while that city faces a serial arsonist and an epidemic spreading through its firehorse population.

Wilson, Diane L.—*Continued*

"Wilson paces the story well, with tension building. . . . The novel's finest achievement, though, is the convincing depiction of family dynamics in an era when men ruled the household and and women, who had few opportunities, folded their dreams and put them away with the linens they embroidered." Booklist

Wilson, Martin, 1973-

What they always tell us. Delacorte Press 2008 293p $15.99; lib bdg $18.99 *

Grades: 9 10 11 12   Fic
1. Brothers—Fiction 2. Homosexuality—Fiction 3. Alabama—Fiction 4. School stories
ISBN   978-0-385-73507-0;   0-385-73507-3; 978-0-385-90500-8 (lib bdg); 0-385-90500-9 (lib bdg)
LC 2007-30269

Sixteen-year-old Alex feels so disconnected from his friends that he starts his junior year at a Tuscaloosa, Alabama, high school by attempting suicide, but soon, a friend of his older brother draws him into cross-country running and a new understanding of himself.

This "novel does an excellent job of showing the tension with which siblings deal on a daily basis. He also does a great job of exploring controversial issues, such as suicide and homosexuality. . . . Public and school libraries should seriously consider adding this book to their shelves." Voice Youth Advocates

Winspear, Jacqueline, 1955-

Maisie Dobbs; a novel. Penguin Books 2004 294p pa $15 *

Grades: 11 12 Adult   Fic
1. World War, 1914-1918—Fiction 2. Mystery fiction 3. Great Britain—Fiction
ISBN 978-0-14-200433-3; 0-14-200433-2

First published 2003 by Soho Press

In this novel "set in WWI-era England, humble housemaid Maisie Dobbs climbs . . . up Britain's social ladder, becoming in turn a university student, a wartime nurse and ultimately a private investigator. . . . Her first sleuthing case, which begins as a simple marital infidelity investigation, leads to a trail of war-wounded soldiers lured to a remote convalescent home in Kent from which no one seems to emerge alive." Publ Wkly

"For a clever and resourceful young woman who has just set herself up in business as a private investigator, Maisie seems a bit too sober and much too sad. Romantic readers sensing a story-within-a-story won't be disappointed. But first, they must prepare to be astonished at the sensitivity and wisdom with which Maisie resolves her first professional assignment." N Y Times Book Rev

Other titles about Maisie Dobbs are:
Among the mad (2009)
Birds of a feather (2004)
An incomplete revenge (2008)
A lesson in secrets (2011)
The mapping of love and death (2010)
Messenger of truth (2006)
Pardonable lies (2005)

Winston, Sherri

The Kayla chronicles; a novel. Little, Brown 2007 188p hardcover o.p. pa $7.99

Grades: 6 7 8 9 10   Fic
1. African Americans—Fiction 2. Dancers—Fiction 3. Journalism—Fiction 4. School stories
ISBN   978-0-316-11430-1;   0-316-11430-8; 978-0-316-11431-8 (pa); 0-316-11431-6 (pa)
LC 2006-933219

Kayla transforms herself from mild-mannered journalist to hot-trotting dance diva in order to properly investigate her high school's dance team, and has a hard time remaining true to her real self while in the role.

"Few recent novels for younger YAs mesh levity and substance this successfully." Booklist

Wiseman, Eva

Puppet; a novel. Tundra Books 2009 243p $17.95

Grades: 7 8 9 10 11 12   Fic
1. Jews—Hungary—Fiction 2. Prejudices—Fiction
ISBN 978-0-88776-828-6; 0-88776-828-8

"Times are hard in Julie Vamosi's Hungarian village in the late nineteenth-century, and the townspeople . . . blame the Jews. After Julie's best friend, Esther, . . . disappears, the rumor spreads that the Jews cut her throat and drained her blood to drink with their Passover matzos. . . . Based on the records of a trial in 1883, this searing novel dramatizes virulent anti-Semitism from the viewpoint of a Christian child. . . . The climax is electrifying." Booklist

Wittlinger, Ellen, 1948-

Hard love. Simon & Schuster Bks. for Young Readers 1999 224p hardcover o.p. pa $8.99

Grades: 7 8 9 10   Fic
1. Authorship—Fiction 2. Lesbians—Fiction
ISBN 0-689-82134-4; 0-689-84154-X (pa)
LC 98-6668

"John, cynical yet vulnerable, thinks he's immune to emotion until he meets bright, brittle Marisol, the author of his favorite zine. He falls in love, but Marisol, a lesbian, just wants to be friends. A love story of a different sort—funny, poignant, and thoughtful." Booklist

Followed by: Love & lies: Marisol's story (2008)

Parrotfish. Simon & Schuster Books for Young Readers 2007 294p $16.99 *

Grades: 7 8 9 10   Fic
1. Transsexualism—Fiction 2. Family life—Fiction 3. School stories
ISBN 978-1-4169-1622-2; 1-4169-1622-9
LC 2006-9689

Grady, a transgendered high school student, yearns for acceptance by his classmates and family as he struggles to adjust to his new identity as a male.

"The author demonstrates well the complexity faced by transgendered people and makes the teen's frustration with having to fit into a category fully apparent." Publ Wkly

Wittlinger, Ellen, 1948-—_Continued_
Sandpiper. Simon & Schuster Books for Young Readers 2005 227p hardcover o.p. pa $6.99 *
Grades: 9 10 11 12   Fic
1. Dating (Social customs)—Fiction
ISBN 0-689-86802-2; 1-4169-3651-3 (pa)
LC 2004-7576
When The Walker, a mysterious boy who walks constantly, intervenes in an argument between Sandpiper and a boy she used to see, their lives become entwined in ways that change them both.
"While heavy on message and mature in subject matter, the novel is notable for the bold look it takes at relationships and at the myth that oral sex is not really sex." SLJ

Wizner, Jake, 1970-
Spanking Shakespeare. Random House Children's Books 2007 287p $15.99; lib bdg $18.99
Grades: 8 9 10   Fic
1. Authorship—Fiction 2. School stories
ISBN 978-0-375-84085-2; 978-0-375-94085-9 (lib bdg)   LC 2006-27035
Shakespeare Shapiro navigates a senior year fraught with feelings of insecurity while writing the memoir of his embarrassing life, worrying about his younger brother being cooler than he is, and having no prospects of ever getting a girlfriend.
"Raw, sexual, cynical, and honest, this book belongs on library shelves and gift lists." Voice Youth Advocates

Wolf, Allan
Zane's trace. Candlewick Press 2007 177p $16.99
Grades: 7 8 9 10 11 12   Fic
1. Death—Fiction 2. Automobile travel—Fiction 3. Epilepsy—Fiction 4. Racially mixed people—Fiction 5. Orphans—Fiction 6. Novels in verse
ISBN 978-0-7636-2858-1; 0-7636-2858-1
LC 2007-24187
Believing he has killed his grandfather, Zane Guesswind heads for his mother's Zanesville, Ohio, grave to kill himself, driving the 1969 Plymouth Barracuda his long-gone father left behind, and meeting along the way assorted characters who help him discover who he really is.
"This novel manages to be suspenseful, funny, and deeply moving at the same time." Voice Youth Advocates

Wolff, Tobias, 1945-
Old school; a novel. Knopf 2003 195p $22; pa $12
Grades: 9 10 11 12   Fic
1. Authors—Fiction 2. School stories 3. New England—Fiction
ISBN 0-375-40146-6; 0-375-70149-4 (pa)
LC 2003-52930
"The unnamed narrator of this coming-of-age story set in 1960 is a scholarship student at a prestigious New England prep school that has a tradition of inviting literary

stars to the campus. Prior to the visit, the seniors are requested to write a piece to be 'judged' by the guest. The winner is given a private meeting with the literary luminary and the story is published in the school paper. . . . In his fervent desire to be chosen, the narrator 'borrows' an idea and reveals a secret about his heritage that he has carefully hidden. He wins, but the results of his story's publication are disastrous and his life is forever changed. The events and ideas in this thoughtful and thought-provoking novel remain with readers after the story is over and could provide meat for discussion." SLJ

Wolff, Virginia Euwer
Make lemonade. Holt & Co. 1993 200p $17.95; pa $7.95 *
Grades: 8 9 10 11 12   Fic
1. Teenage mothers—Fiction 2. Babysitters—Fiction 3. Poverty—Fiction 4. Novels in verse
ISBN 978-0-8050-2228-5; 0-8050-2228-7; 978-0-8050-8070-4 (pa); 0-8050-8070-8 (pa)
LC 92-41182
"Fourteen-year-old LaVaughn accepts the job of babysitting Jolly's two small children but quickly realizes that the young woman, a seventeen-year-old single mother, needs as much help and nurturing as her two neglected children. The four become something akin to a temporary family, and through their relationship each makes progress toward a better life. Sixty-six brief chapters, with words arranged on the page like poetry, perfectly echo the patterns of teenage speech." Horn Book Guide
Other titles in this trilogy are:
This full house (2009)
True believer (2001)

Wolfson, Jill
Cold hands, warm heart. Henry Holt and Co. 2009 245p $17.95
Grades: 7 8 9 10   Fic
1. Transplantation of organs, tissues, etc.—Fiction 2. Hospitals—Fiction 3. Siblings—Fiction 4. Death—Fiction 5. Jews—United States—Fiction
ISBN 978-0-8050-8282-1; 0-8050-8282-4
LC 2008-40594
After sixteen-year-old Tyler convinces his parents to donate the organs of his fourteen-year-old sister, who died during a gymnastics meet, he writes letters to the recipients, including Dani, who finally has a chance at normalcy after living fifteen years with a congenital heart defect.
"Detailed, accurate descriptions of medical procedures are leavened with humor and sincerity, providing a powerful, multifaceted exploration of ethics, love and the celebration." Kirkus

Wood, Maryrose
The poison diaries; based on a concept by the Duchess of Northumberland. Balzer + Bray 2010 278p $16.99
Grades: 8 9 10 11   Fic
1. Poisons and poisoning—Fiction 2. Plants—Fiction 3. Supernatural—Fiction 4. Father-daughter relationship—Fiction 5. Great Britain—Fiction
ISBN 978-0-06-180236-2; 0-06-180236-0
LC 2009-54427

Wood, Maryrose—*Continued*

In late eighteenth-century Northumberland, England, sixteen-year-old Jessamine Luxton and the mysterious Weed uncover the horrible secrets of poisons growing in Thomas Luxton's apothecary garden.

"This intriguing fantasy has many tendrils to wrap around teen hearts. . . . The haunting ending will leave readers wanting to talk about the themes of cruelty, honesty, and loyalty." Booklist

Wooding, Chris, 1977-

The haunting of Alaizabel Cray. Orchard Bks. 2004 292p $16.95; pa $7.99

Grades: 7 8 9 10   Fic

1. Horror fiction 2. Supernatural—Fiction 3. London (England)—Fiction

ISBN 0-439-54656-7; 0-439-59851-6 (pa)

LC 2003-69108

First published 2001 in the United Kingdom

In a world similar to Victorian London, Thaniel, a seventeen-year-old hunter of deadly, demonic creatures called the wych-kin, takes in a lost, possessed girl, and becomes embroiled in a plot to unleash evil on the world

"Eerie and exhilarating. . . . [The author] fuses together his best storytelling skills . . . to create a fabulously horrific and ultimately timeless underworld." SLJ

Poison. Orchard Bks. 2005 c2003 273p $16.99; pa $7.99

Grades: 7 8 9 10   Fic

1. Fantasy fiction 2. Storytelling—Fiction 3. Fairies—Fiction

ISBN 0-439-75570-0; 0-439-75571-9 (pa)

LC 2005-02174

First published 2003 in the United Kingdom

When Poison leaves her home in the marshes of Gull to retrieve the infant sister who was snatched by the fairies, she and a group of unusual friends survive encounters with the inhabitants of various Realms, and Poison herself confronts a surprising destiny.

"Poison's story should please crowds of horror fans who like their books fast-paced, darkly atmospheric, and melodramatic." SLJ

The storm thief. Orchard Books 2006 310p $16.99

Grades: 6 7 8 9 10   Fic

1. Science fiction

ISBN 0-439-86513-1   LC 2005-35993

With the help of a golem, two teenaged thieves try to survive on the city island of Orokos, where unpredictable probability storms continually change both the landscape and the inhabitants.

The author "delivers memorable characters, such as Vago, whose plight—Who am I and where do I belong in the world?—will be understood by many teens. Wooding also creates a unique world for his characters to explore, and the setting serves as an excellent backdrop for the author to develop his theme of order versus chaos and the need for balance between the two." Voice Youth Advocates

Woodrell, Daniel

Winter's bone; a novel. Little, Brown and Co. 2006 193p hardcover o.p. pa $13.99

Grades: 11 12 Adult   Fic

1. Criminals—Fiction 2. Father-daughter relationship—Fiction 3. Mountain life—Fiction 4. Ozark Mountains—Fiction

ISBN   0-316-05755-X;   978-0-316-05755-4; 0-316-06641-9 (pa); 978-0-316-06641-9 (pa)

LC 2005-17349

"In the poverty-stricken hills of the Ozarks, Rees Dolly, 17, struggles daily to care for her two brothers and an ill mother. When she learns that her absent father, a meth addict, has put up the family home as bond, she embarks on a dangerous search to find him and bring him home for an upcoming court date." SLJ

"This lyrical and haunting story exposes the dark underside of its scenic setting. . . . But the book is not for the young or the faint-of-heart; Ree is not a saint, and this gritty story requires maturity to appreciate." Voice Youth Advocates

Woods, Elizabeth Emma

Choker; [by] Elizabeth Woods. Simon & Schuster Books for Young Readers 2011 233p $16.99

Grades: 9 10 11 12   Fic

1. Friendship—Fiction 2. Mental illness—Fiction 3. School stories

ISBN 978-1-4424-1233-0   LC 2010-34672

Teenaged Cara, solitary and bullied in high school, is delighted to reconnect with her childhood best friend Zoe whose support and friendship help Cara gain self-confidence, even as her classmates start dying.

"Terrific pacing and mounting suspense lead to a resolution that may not surprise savvy readers but is nonetheless chilling." Booklist

Woodson, Jacqueline

If you come softly. Putnam 1998 181p $15.99; pa $5.99

Grades: 7 8 9 10   Fic

1. African Americans—Fiction 2. Race relations—Fiction 3. New York (N.Y.)—Fiction

ISBN 0-399-23112-9; 0-698-11862-6 (pa)

LC 97-32212

After meeting at their private school in New York, fifteen-year-old Jeremiah, who is black and whose parents are separated, and Ellie, who is white and whose mother has twice abandoned her, fall in love and then try to cope with people's reactions

"The gentle and melancholy tone of this book makes it ideal for thoughtful readers and fans of romance." Voice Youth Advocates

Another title about Jeremiah is:

Behind you (2004)

Miracle's boys. Putnam 2000 133p $15.99; pa $5.99

Grades: 9 10 11 12   Fic

1. Brothers—Fiction 2. Orphans—Fiction 3. African Americans—Fiction 4. New York (N.Y.)—Fiction

ISBN 0-399-23113-7; 0-698-11916-9 (pa)

LC 99-40050

Woodson, Jacqueline—*Continued*

Twelve-year-old Lafayette's close relationship with his older brother Charlie changes after Charlie is released from a detention home and blames Lafayette for the death of their mother

"The fast-paced narrative is physically immediate, and the dialogue is alive with anger and heartbreak." Booklist

Woolf, Virginia, 1882-1941

To the lighthouse; with an introduction by Julia Briggs. Knopf 1992 xxix, 242p $17

Grades: 9 10 11 12 Adult   **Fic**
1. Great Britain—Fiction
ISBN 0-679-40537-2   LC 92-52912
First published 1927

Arranged in three parts, the first "called 'The window,' describes a day during Mr. and Mrs. Ramsay's house party at their country home by the sea. Mr. Ramsay is a distinguished scholar . . . whose mind works rationally, heroically and rather icily. . . . The Ramsays have arranged to take a boat out to the lighthouse, the next morning, and their little son James is bitterly disappointed when a change in weather makes it impossible. The second section, called 'Time passes' describes the seasons and the house, unused and decaying, in the years after Mrs. Ramsay's death. In the third section, the 'Lighthouse,' Mr. Ramsay and his friends are back at the house. He takes the postponed trip to the lighthouse with his now sixteen-year-old son, who is at last able to communicate silently with him and forgive him for being different from his mother." Reader's Ency. 4th edition

Woolston, Blythe

The Freak Observer. Carolrhoda Lab 2010 202p $16.95 *

Grades: 8 9 10 11 12   **Fic**
1. Post-traumatic stress disorder—Fiction
ISBN 978-0-7613-6212-8; 0-7613-6212-6
    LC 2010-989

Suffering from a crippling case of post-traumatic stress disorder, sixteen-year-old Loa Lindgren tries to use her problem solving skills, sharpened in physics and computer programming, to cure herself.

"Woolston's talent for dialogue and her unique approach to scenes make what sounds standard about this story feel fresh and vital. . . . A strong . . . [novel] about learning to see yourself apart from the reflection you cast off others." Booklist

Wray, John, 1971-

Lowboy. Farrar, Straus and Giroux 2009 258p $25 *

Grades: 11 12 Adult   **Fic**
1. Schizophrenia—Fiction 2. Subways—Fiction 3. New York (N.Y.)—Fiction
ISBN 978-0-374-19416-1; 0-374-19416-5
    LC 2008-17921

"Will Heller, aka Lowboy, is a brilliant but troubled 16-year-old paranoid schizophrenic in New York City. Recently escaped from a mental hospital and obsessed with the notion that the world is about to be destroyed by global warming, he boards the subway one morning seeking to save the world in the only way he believes it can be—by having sex with a woman. He attempts to locate former girlfriend Emily Wallace, whom he has not seen since he pushed her onto the subway tracks a year earlier, the act that led to his stay in a mental hospital. Throughout his daylong adventures in the tunnels and streets, he is pursued by police detective Ali Lateef and his mother, Violet, a woman with her own secrets, who seek to bring him home before he harms himself or others." Libr J

This is a "brilliant and gutsy performance but a cryptic one. It expresses its meanings in hallucinated events that seem to vibrate on the page. At certain moments the book feels like a runaway subway car; you want it to slow down for you." Buffalo News

Wrede, Patricia C., 1953-

The thirteenth child. Scholastic Press 2009 344p (Frontier magic) $16.99

Grades: 7 8 9 10 11 12   **Fic**
1. Magic—Fiction 2. Frontier and pioneer life—Fiction 3. Twins—Fiction 4. School stories 5. Fantasy fiction
ISBN 978-0-545-03342-8; 0-545-03342-X
    LC 2008-34048

Eighteen-year-old Eff must finally get over believing she is bad luck and accept that her special training in Aphrikan magic, and being the twin of the seventh son of a seventh son, give her extraordinary power to combat magical creatures that threaten settlements on the western frontier.

Wrede "creates a rich world where steam dragons seem as normal as bears, and a sympathetic character in Eff." Publ Wkly

Followed by Across the Great Barrier (2011)

Wright, Denis

Violence 101; a novel. G. P. Putnam's Sons 2010 213p $16.99

Grades: 8 9 10   **Fic**
1. Violence—Fiction 2. Reformatories—Fiction 3. Race relations—Fiction 4. Genius—Fiction 5. New Zealand—Fiction
ISBN 978-0-399-25493-2; 0-399-25493-5
    LC 2010-02851
First published 2007 in New Zealand

In a New Zealand reformatory, Hamish Graham, an extremely intelligent fourteen-year-old who believes in the compulsory study of violence, learns that it is not always the answer.

"Wright's novel is clever and biting, a tragedy of society's failure to deal with kids like Hamish and a satire of society's winking condemnations of violence. Hamish's actions can be revolting, despite his justifications, but he still draws empathy as a product of the environment at large. Hardly a comfortable book to read, but a gripping one." Publ Wkly

Wright, Richard, 1908-1960

Native son; with an introduction: "How 'Bigger' was born," by the author. Harper & Row 1969 c1940 xxxiv, 392p pa $14.95 hardcover o.p. *

Grades: 11 12 Adult   **Fic**

Wright, Richard, 1908-1960—*Continued*
1. African Americans—Fiction 2. Race relations—Fiction 3. Chicago (Ill.)—Fiction
ISBN 0-06-083756-X (pa)
Also available in hardcover from Buccaneer Bks.
A reissue of the title first published 1940
"Bigger Thomas is black. He is driven by anger, hate, and frustration, which are born out of the poverty that has dominated his life. When he gets a job with the Daltons, a white family, he is confused by their behavior and misinterprets their patronizing friendship. Tragedy follows when he accidentally kills Mary Dalton." Shapiro. Fic for Youth. 3d edition

Wroblewski, David
The story of Edgar Sawtelle; a novel. Ecco 2008 566p hardcover o.p. pa $16.99 *
Grades: 9 10 11 12 Adult   Fic
1. Dogs—Fiction 2. Speech disorders—Fiction 3. Homicide—Fiction 4. Wisconsin—Fiction
ISBN 978-0-06-137422-7; 0-06-137422-9; 978-0-06-137423-4 (pa); 0-06-137423-7 (pa)
"Set in rural nineteen-seventies Wisconsin, this loose retelling of Hamlet focusses on Edgar, a boy born mute and with a preternatural ability to commune with the dogs whose breeding and training is his family's business. Idyllic routine is threatened when Edgar's ne'er-do-well uncle comes to live with the family, and the menace persists even after his sudden departure. Soon afterward, Edgar's father dies of an apparent aneurysm; Edgar becomes convinced, but can't prove, that his uncle—who soon inserts himself back into the family—is to blame. . . . [The author] illustrates the relationship between man and canine (at times, from the dog's point of view) in a way that is both lyrical and unsentimental, and demonstrates an ability to create a coherent, captivating fictional world in which even supernatural elements feel entirely persuasive." New Yorker

Wyatt, Melissa, 1963-
Funny how things change. Farrar, Straus & Giroux 2009 196p $16.95
Grades: 9 10 11 12   Fic
1. Mountains—Fiction 2. Country life—Fiction 3. Artists—Fiction 4. West Virginia—Fiction
ISBN 978-0-374-30233-7; 0-374-30233-2
       LC 2008-16190
Remy, a talented, seventeen-year-old auto mechanic, questions his decision to join his girlfriend when she starts college in Pennsylvania after a visiting artist helps him to realize what his family's home in a dying West Virginia mountain town means to him.
"Laconic but full of heart, smart, thoughtful and proudly working-class, Remy makes a fresh and immensely appealing hero." Kirkus

Wynne-Jones, Tim
Blink & Caution. Candlewick Press 2011 342p $16.99 *
Grades: 9 10 11 12   Fic
1. Runaway teenagers—Fiction 2. Crime—Fiction 3. Guilt—Fiction 4. Canada—Fiction
ISBN 978-0-7636-3983-9; 0-7636-3983-4
       LC 2010-13563

Two teenagers who are living on the streets and barely getting by become involved in a complicated criminal plot, and make an unexpected connection with each other.
"The short, punchy sentences Wynne-Jones fires like buckshot; the joy, fear, and doubt that punctuate the teens' every action. This is gritty, sure, but more than that, it's smart, and earns every drop of its hopeful finish." Booklist

The uninvited. Candlewick Press 2009 351p $16.99
Grades: 10 11 12   Fic
1. Vacations—Fiction 2. Father-daughter relationship—Fiction 3. Canada—Fiction
ISBN 978-0-7636-3984-6; 0-7636-3984-2
       LC 2009-7520
After a disturbing freshman year at New York University, Mimi is happy to get away to her father's remote Canadian cottage only to discover a stranger living there who has never heard of her or her father and who is convinced that Mimi is responsible for leaving sinister tokens around the property.
"This suspenseful and deftly crafted family drama will appeal to older teens who are exploring their options beyond high school." Voice Youth Advocates

Yancey, Richard
The monstrumologist; [by] William James Henry; edited by Rick Yancey. Simon & Schuster Books for Young Readers 2009 454p il $17.99; pa $9.99 *
Grades: 9 10 11 12   Fic
1. Supernatural—Fiction 2. Monsters—Fiction 3. Apprentices—Fiction 4. Orphans—Fiction
ISBN 978-1-4169-8448-1; 1-4169-8448-8; 978-1-4169-8449-8 (pa); 1-4169-8449-6 (pa)
       LC 2009-4562
In 1888, twelve-year-old Will Henry chronicles his apprenticeship with Dr. Warthrop, a scientist who hunts and studies real-life monsters, as they discover and attempt to destroy a pod of Anthropophagi.
"As the action moves from the dissecting table to the cemetery to an asylum to underground catacombs, Yancey keeps the shocks frequent and shrouded in a splattery miasma of blood, bone, pus, and maggots. . . . Yancey's prose is stentorian and wordy, but it weaves a world that possesses a Lovecraftian logic and hints at its own deeply satisfying mythos. . . . 'Snap to!' is Warthrop's continued demand of Will, but readers will need no such needling." Booklist
Followed by The curse of the wendigo (2010)

Yansky, Brian
Alien invasion and other inconveniences. Candlewick Press 2010 227p $15.99
Grades: 9 10 11 12   Fic
1. Extraterrestrial beings—Fiction 2. Telepathy—Fiction 3. Science fiction
ISBN 978-0-7636-4384-3   LC 2009-49103
When a race of aliens quickly takes over the earth, leaving most people dead, high-schooler Jesse finds himself a slave to an inept alien leader—a situation that

Yansky, Brian—*Continued*

brightens as Jesse develops telepathic powers and attracts the attention of two beautiful girls.

"The story is action-packed, provocative, profound, and wickedly funny. Yansky takes on questions philosophical, ecological, religious, moral, and social, and the satire is right on target." Horn Book Guide

Yee, Lisa

Absolutely Maybe. Arthur A. Levine Books 2009 274p $16.99
Grades: 8 9 10 11 12   **Fic**
1. Mother-daughter relationship—Fiction 2. Fathers—Fiction 3. Runaway teenagers—Fiction 4. Los Angeles (Calif.)—Fiction
ISBN 978-0-439-83844-3; 0-439-83844-4
LC 2008-17787

When living with her mother, an alcoholic ex-beauty queen, becomes unbearable, almost seventeen-year-old Maybelline "Maybe" Chestnut runs away to California, where she finds work on a taco truck and tries to track down her birth father.

"The characters are complex and their friendships layered—they sweep readers up in their path." Publ Wkly

Yolen, Jane

Briar Rose. Doherty Assocs. 1992 190p (Fairy tale series) hardcover o.p. pa $6.99 *
Grades: 8 9 10 11 12 Adult   **Fic**
1. Fantasy fiction 2. Holocaust, 1933-1945—Fiction 3. Jews—Poland—Fiction 4. Grandmothers—Fiction
ISBN 0-312-85135-9; 0-7653-4230-8 (pa)
LC 92-25456

"A TOR book"

"Yolen takes the story of Briar Rose (commonly known as Sleeping Beauty) and links it to the Holocaust. . . . Rebecca Berlin, a young woman who has grown up hearing her grandmother Gemma tell an unusual and frightening version of the Sleeping Beauty legend, realizes when Gemma dies that the fairy tale offers one of the very few clues she has to her grandmother's past. . . . By interpolating Gemma's vivid and imaginative story into the larger narrative, Yolen has created an engrossing novel." Publ Wkly

Except the queen; [by] Jane Yolen and Midori Snyder. Roc 2010 371p $23.95
Grades: 10 11 12 Adult   **Fic**
1. Sisters—Fiction 2. Fairies—Fiction 3. Fantasy fiction
ISBN 978-0-451-46273-2; 0-451-46273-4
LC 2009-36063

Cast from the high court of the Fairy Queen, sisters Serena and Meteora must find a way to survive in the mortal realm of Earth. But when signs point to a rising power that threatens to tear asunder both fairy and human worlds, they realize that they were chosen to fight the menace because they were the only ones who could do what must be done.

"Unconventional narrative techniques and a full dose of magic and folklore give this urban fantasy a lyrical, mythic feel." Publ Wkly

Yoo, Paula

Good enough. HarperTeen 2008 322p $16.99; lib bdg $17.89
Grades: 7 8 9 10   **Fic**
1. Korean Americans—Fiction 2. Violinists—Fiction
ISBN 978-0-06-079085-1; 978-0-06-079086-8 (lib bdg)
LC 2007-02985

A Korean American teenager tries to please her parents by getting into an Ivy League college, but a new guy in school and her love of the violin tempt her in new directions.

"The frequent lists, . . . SAT questions, and even spam recipes are, like Patti's convincing narration, filled with laugh-out-loud lines, but it's the deeper questions about growing up with immigrant parents, confronting racism, and how best to find success and happiness that will stay with readers." Booklist

Yovanoff, Brenna

The replacement. Razorbill 2010 343p $17.99 *
Grades: 9 10 11 12   **Fic**
1. Supernatural—Fiction 2. Missing children—Fiction 3. Death—Fiction 4. Siblings—Fiction 5. Fantasy fiction
ISBN 978-1-59514-337-2; 1-59514-337-8
LC 2010-36066

Sixteen-year-old Mackie Doyle knows that he replaced a human child when he was just an infant, and when a friend's sister disappears he goes against his family's and town's deliberate denial of the problem to confront the beings that dwell under the town, tampering with human lives.

"Yovanoff's spare but haunting prose creates an atmosphere shrouded in gloom and secrecy so that readers, like Mackie, must attempt to make sense of a situation ruled by chaos and fear. The ethical complications of the town's deal with the creatures of Mayhem are clearly presented but never overwrought, while Mackie's problematic relationship to the townspeople as both an outsider and a savior is poignantly explored." Bull Cent Child Books

Zadoff, Allen

Food, girls, and other things I can't have. Egmont USA 2009 311p $16.99; lib bdg $19.99
Grades: 7 8 9 10   **Fic**
1. Obesity—Fiction 2. Popularity—Fiction 3. Football—Fiction 4. School stories
ISBN 978-1-60684-004-7; 1-60684-004-5; 978-1-60684-051-1 (lib bdg); 1-60684-051-7 (lib bdg)
LC 2009-16242

Fifteen-year-old Andrew Zansky, the second fattest student at his high school, joins the varsity football team to get the attention of a new girl on whom he has a crush.

"The author does not lead Andy down the expected path. When forced to make a decision, his choice is unique and the conclusion satisfying. . . . The possibly offensive locker room language is typical and lends credibility. More importantly, Andy's character is thoughtful and refreshing." SLJ

Zarr, Sara

Once was lost. Little, Brown 2009 217p $16.99
*

Grades: 7 8 9 10   Fic
1. Kidnapping—Fiction 2. Alcoholism—Fiction
3. Clergy—Fiction 4. Christian life—Fiction
ISBN 978-0-316-03604-7; 0-316-03604-8
                      LC 2009-25187
As the tragedy of a missing girl unfolds in her small
town, fifteen-year-old Samara, who feels emotionally
abandoned by her parents, begins to question her faith.
"This multilayered exploration of the intersection of
the spiritual life and imperfect people features suspense
and packs an emotional wallop." SLJ

Story of a girl; a novel. Little, Brown 2006
192p $16.99 *
Grades: 10 11 12   Fic
1. Family life—Fiction 2. California—Fiction
ISBN 978-0-316-01453-3; 0-316-01453-2
                    LC 2005-28467
In the three years since her father caught her in the
back seat of a car with an older boy, sixteen-year-old
Deanna's life at home and school has been a nightmare,
but while dreaming of escaping with her brother and his
family, she discovers the power of forgiveness.
"This highly recommended novel will find a niche
with older, more mature readers because of frank references to sex and some x-rated language." Voice Youth
Advocates

Sweethearts. Little, Brown and Co. 2008 217p
$16.99 *
Grades: 8 9 10 11 12   Fic
1. Love stories 2. School stories 3. Weight loss—Fiction 4. Utah—Fiction
ISBN 978-0-316-01455-7; 0-316-01455-9
                    LC 2007-41099
After losing her soul mate, Cameron, when they were
nine, Jennifer, now seventeen, transformed herself from
the unpopular fat girl into the beautiful and popular
Jenna, but Cameron's unexpected return dredges up
memories that cause both social and emotional turmoil.
"Zarr's writing is remarkable. . . . She conveys great
delicacy of feeling and shades of meaning, and the realistic, moving ending will inspire excellent discussion."
Booklist

Zeises, Lara M.

The sweet life of Stella Madison; [by] Lara
Zeises. Delacorte Press 2009 230p $16.99; lib bdg
$19.99
Grades: 9 10 11 12   Fic
1. Food—Fiction 2. Family life—Fiction 3. Dating
(Social customs)—Fiction 4. Journalism—Fiction
ISBN 978-0-385-73146-1; 0-385-73146-9;
978-0-385-90178-9 (lib bdg); 0-385-90178-X (lib bdg)
                    LC 2008-32024
Seventeen-year-old Stella struggles with the separation
of her renowned chef parents, writing a food column for
the local paper even though she is a junk food addict,
and having a boyfriend but being attracted to another.
The author "has created a refreshing protagonist sure
to captivate readers, who will enjoy following along as
she learns about romance through food, and vice versa."
SLJ

Zemser, Amy Bronwen

Dear Julia. Greenwillow Books 2008 327p
$16.99; lib bdg $17.89
Grades: 7 8 9 10   Fic
1. Cooking—Fiction 2. Mother-daughter relationship—
Fiction 3. Contests—Fiction 4. Feminism—Fiction
ISBN 978-0-06-029458-8; 0-06-029458-2;
978-0-06-029459-5 (lib bdg); 0-06-029459-0 (lib bdg)
                    LC 2008-3824
Shy sixteen-year-old Elaine has long dreamed of being
the next Julia Child, to the dismay of her feminist mother, but when her first friend, the outrageous Lucida Sans,
convinces Elaine to enter a cooking contest, anything
could happen.
"Readers will laugh throughout, but Zemser never loses sight of Elaine's frailties and hopes." Publ Wkly

Zevin, Gabrielle, 1977-

Elsewhere. Farrar, Straus & Giroux 2005 275p
$16; pa $6.95
Grades: 7 8 9 10   Fic
1. Future life—Fiction 2. Death—Fiction
ISBN 0-374-32091-8; 0-312-36746-5 (pa)
                    LC 2004-56279
After fifteen-year-old Liz Hall is hit by a taxi and
killed, she finds herself in a place that is both like and
unlike Earth, where she must adjust to her new status
and figure out how to "live."
"Zevin's third-person narrative calmly, but surely
guides readers through the bumpy landscape of strongly
delineated characters dealing with the most difficult issue
that faces all of us. A quiet book that provides much to
think about and discuss." SLJ

Memoirs of a teenage amnesiac. Farrar, Straus
and Giroux 2007 271p $17; pa $8.99
Grades: 7 8 9 10   Fic
1. Amnesia—Fiction 2. Friendship—Fiction 3. School
stories
ISBN 978-0-374-34946-2; 0-374-34946-0;
978-0-312-56128-4 (pa); 0-312-56128-8 (pa)
                    LC 2006-35287
After a nasty fall, Naomi realizes that she has no
memory of the last four years and finds herself
reassessing every aspect of her life.
This is a "sensitive, joyful novel. . . . Pulled by the
the heart-bruising love story, readers will pause to contemplate irresistible questions." Booklist

Ziegler, Jennifer

How not to be popular. Delacorte Press 2008
339p $15.99; lib bdg $18.99
Grades: 7 8 9 10 11 12   Fic
1. Popularity—Fiction 2. School stories 3. Texas—Fiction 4. Hippies—Fiction
ISBN 978-0-385-73465-3; 0-385-73465-4;
978-0-385-90463-6 (lib bdg); 0-385-90463-0 (lib bdg)
                    LC 2007-27603
Seventeen-year-old Sugar Magnolia Dempsey is tired
of leaving friends behind every time her hippie parents
decide to move, but her plan to be unpopular at her new
school backfires when other students join her on the path
to "supreme dorkdom."

Ziegler, Jennifer—*Continued*

This "balances laugh-out-loud, sardonic commentary with earnest reflections that will directly connect with teens." Booklist

Zielin, Lara, 1975-

Donut days. G.P. Putnam's Sons 2009 246p $16.99

Grades: 7 8 9 10   **Fic**
1. Clergy—Fiction 2. Journalism—Fiction 3. Sex role—Fiction 4. Christian life—Fiction 5. Minnesota—Fiction
ISBN 978-0-399-25066-8; 0-399-25066-2
        LC 2008-26138

During a camp-out promoting the opening of a donut shop in a small Minnesota town, sixteen-year-old Emma, an aspiring journalist, begins to connect an ongoing pollution investigation with the turmoil in the evangelical Christian church where her parents are pastors.

This is a "sweet, satisfying treat. . . . Teens will enjoy this lighter look at some serious issues of faith and family." SLJ

Zink, Michelle, 1969-

Prophecy of the sisters. Little, Brown 2009 343p $17.99

Grades: 7 8 9 10   **Fic**
1. Supernatural—Fiction 2. Good and evil—Fiction 3. Twins—Fiction 4. Sisters—Fiction
ISBN 978-0-316-02742-7; 0-316-02742-1
        LC 2008-45290

In late nineteenth-century New York state, wealthy sixteen-year-old twin sisters Lia and Alice Milthorpe find that they are on opposite sides of an ancient prophecy that has destroyed their parents and seeks to do even more harm.

"This arresting story takes readers to other planes of existence." Booklist

Followed by: Guardian of the gate (2010)

Zuckerman, Linda

A taste for rabbit. Arthur A. Levine Books 2007 310p $16.99

Grades: 7 8 9 10   **Fic**
1. Rabbits—Fiction 2. Foxes—Fiction 3. Resistance to government—Fiction 4. Animals—Fiction
ISBN 0-439-86977-3; 978-0-439-86977-5
        LC 2007-7787

Quentin, a rabbit who lives in a walled compound run by a militaristic government, must join forces with Harry, a fox, to stop the sinister disappearances of outspoken and rebellious rabbit citizens.

"The blend of adventure, mystery and morality in this heroic tale of honor and friendship will appeal to middle-school fantasy fans." Publ Wkly

Zulkey, Claire, 1979-

An off year. Dutton 2009 213p $17.99

Grades: 9 10 11 12   **Fic**
1. Family life—Fiction 2. Colleges and universities—Fiction 3. Chicago (Ill.)—Fiction
ISBN 978-0-525-42159-7; 0-525-42159-9
        LC 2008-48968

Upon arriving at her dorm room, eighteen-year-old Cecily decides to postpone her freshman year of college and return to her Chicago home, where she spends a year pondering what went wrong while forging new relationships with family and friends.

"Teens who have doubted the high-school-college-life progression for even a moment will recognize themselves in Cecily, perhaps to their parents' dismay." Kirkus

Zusak, Markus, 1975-

The book thief. Knopf 2006 552p il $16.95; lib bdg $18.99 *

Grades: 8 9 10 11 12   **Fic**
1. World War, 1939-1945—Fiction 2. Holocaust, 1933-1945—Fiction 3. Books and reading—Fiction 4. Death—Fiction
ISBN 0-375-83100-2; 0-375-93100-7 (lib bdg)
        LC 2005-08942

Trying to make sense of the horrors of World War II, Death relates the story of Liesel—a young German girl whose book-stealing and storytelling talents help sustain her family and the Jewish man they are hiding, as well as their neighbors.

"This hefty volume is an achievement—a challenging book in both length and subject, and best suited to sophisticated older readers." Publ Wkly

I am the messenger. Knopf 2005 357p hardcover o.p. pa $8.95 *

Grades: 9 10 11 12   **Fic**
1. Mystery fiction
ISBN 0-375-83099-5; 0-375-83667-5 (pa)
        LC 2003-27388

After capturing a bank robber, nineteen-year-old cab driver Ed Kennedy begins receiving mysterious messages that direct him to addresses where people need help, and he begins getting over his lifelong feeling of worthlessness

"Zusak's characters, styling, and conversations are believably unpretentious, well conceived, and appropriately raw. Together, these key elements fuse into an enigmatically dark, almost film-noir atmosphere where unknowingly lost Ed Kennedy stumbles onto a mystery—or series of mysteries—that could very well make or break his life." SLJ

S C   STORY COLLECTIONS

Books in this class include collections of short stories by one author and collections by more than one author. Folk tales are entered in class 398.2

21 proms; edited by David Levithan and Daniel Ehrenhaft. Scholastic 2007 289p pa $8.99

Grades: 9 10 11 12   **S C**
1. School stories 2. Short stories
ISBN 0-439-89029-2; 978-0-439-89029-8
        LC 2007-297979

Contents: You are a prom queen, dance dance dance by Elizabeth Craft; All she wants by Cecily von Ziegesar; In vodka veritas by Holly Black; Your big night by Sarah Mlynowski; Off like a prom dress by Billy Merrell; "Mom called, she says you have to go to

21 proms—*Continued*

prom" by Adrienne Maria Vrettos; Better be good to me by Daniel Ehrenhaft; Three fates by Aimee Friedman; The question: a play in one act by Brent Hartinger; Shutter by Will Leitch; Geechee girls dancin', 1955 by Jacqueline Woodson; How I wrote to Toby by E. Lockhart; A six-pack of Bud, a fifth of whiskey, and me by Melissa de la Cruz; Primate the prom by Libba Bray; Apology #1 by Ned Vizzini; See me by Lisa Ann Sandell; Prom for fat girls by Rachel Cohn; Chicken by Jodi Lynn Anderson; The backup date by Leslie Margolis; Lost sometimes by David Levithan; The Great American Morp by John Green

Short stories about going to the prom, when nothing ever goes as planned.

"The stories are witty, edgy, and unpredictable. 21 Proms is a definite must for all libraries and has something for every reader." Kliatt

Adaptations: from short story to big screen; 35 great stories that have inspired great films; edited by Stephanie Harrison. Three Rivers Press 2005 619p il pa $15.95 *

Grades: 11 12 Adult   **S C**
1. Short stories 2. Film adaptations
ISBN 1-4000-5314-5   LC 2005-3441

Contents: Jerry and Molly and Sam by Raymond Carver; Blowup by Julio Cortázar; Your Arkansas traveler by Budd Schulberg; Rear window by Cornell Woolrich; The sentinel by Arthur C. Clarke; Supertoys last all summer long by Brian Aldiss; The minority report by Philip K. Dick; Spurs by Tod Robbins; The fly by George Langelaan; Herbert West—Reanimator: six shots by moonlight by H.P. Lovecraft; Stage to Lordsburg by Ernest Haycox; A man called Horse by Dorothy M. Johnson; This is what it means to say Phoenix, Arizona by Sherman Alexie; The Harvey Pekar name story by Harvey Pekar; Ghost world Chapter 5: "Hubba Hubba" by Daniel Clowes; The wisdom of Eve by Mary Orr; A reputation by Richard Edward Connell; Mr. Blandings builds his castle by Eric Hodgins; Cyclists' raid by Frank Rooney; Tomorrow by William Faulkner; Bringing up Baby by Hagar Wilde; Babylon revisited by F. Scott Fitzgerald; The swimmer by John Cheever; The killers by Ernest Hemingway; The basement room by Graham Greene; Memento mori by Jonathan Nolan; Red Ryder nails the Hammond Kid by Jean Shepherd; My friend Flicka by Mary O'Hara; Shoeless Joe Jackson comes to Iowa by W.P. Kinsella; In a grove by Ryunosuke Akutagawa; The lady with the pet dog by Anton Chekhov; Where are you going, where have you been? by Joyce Carol Oates; Auggie Wren's Christmas story by Paul Auster; Emergency by Denis Johnson; Killings by Andre Dubus

"From science fiction to social satire, this . . . collection of 35 tales embraces literary greats like Chekhov and Cheever and memorable writings long out of print. . . . Harrison devotes a chapter to every imaginable genre, prefacing each with quotes and anecdotes from writers, directors, and actors associated with the creative endeavors selected." Booklist

Akpan, Uwem Celestine

Say you're one of them; [by] Uwem Akpan. Little, Brown and Company 2008 358p map hardcover o.p. pa $14.99

Grades: 11 12 Adult   **S C**
1. Children—Africa—Fiction 2. Short stories
ISBN   978-0-316-11378-6;   0-316-11378-6; 978-0-316-08637-0 (pa); 0-316-08637-1 (pa)
                          LC 2008-11340

Contents: An ex-mas feast; Fattening for Gabon; What language is that?; Luxurious hearses; My parents' bedroom

The author "uses five short stories . . . to bring to light topics ranging from selling children in Gabon to the Muslim vs. Christian battles in Ethiopia." SLJ

"Akpan's prose is beautiful and his stories are insightful and revealing, made even more harrowing because all the horror—and there is much—is seen through the eyes of children." Publ Wkly

Alexie, Sherman, 1966-

Ten little Indians; stories. Grove Press 2003 243p hardcover o.p. pa $13 *

Grades: 11 12 Adult   **S C**
1. Native Americans—Fiction 2. Short stories
ISBN 0-8021-1744-9; 0-8021-4117-X (pa)
                          LC 2003-44832

Contents: The search engine; Lawyer's league; Can I get a witness?; Do not go gentle; Flight patterns; The life and times of Estelle Walks Above; Do you know where I am?; What you pawn I will redeem; What ever happened to Frank Snake Church?

"These short stories feature Spokane Indians from many urban walks of life. Alexie's characters include a student, a lawyer, a basketball player, and a feminist mother; their stories might be angry, tragic, humorous, or ironic—but they are all believable, and irresistibly engaging." SLJ

Alfred Hitchcock's mystery magazine presents fifty years of crime and suspense; edited by Linda Landrigan. Pegasus 2006 560p pa $16.95

Grades: 11 12 Adult   **S C**
1. Mystery fiction 2. Short stories
ISBN 1-933648-03-1

New edition in preparation

"To commemorate its 50th anniversary, Alfred Hitchcock's Mystery Magazine staff-with input from its readers-selected 34 stories and arranged them chronologically here, starting with Jim Thompson's 'The Frightening Frammis' from February 1957 and ending with 'Voodoo' by Rhys Bowen from December 2004. . . . These are uniformly satisfying stories that have stood the test of time." Libr J

Am I blue? coming out from the silence; edited by Marion Dane Bauer. HarperCollins Pubs. 1994 273p hardcover o.p. pa $7.99

Grades: 9 10 11 12   **S C**
1. Homosexuality—Fiction 2. Short stories
ISBN 0-06-024253-1; 0-06-440587-7 (pa)
                          LC 93-29574

This "collection includes stories by Bruce Coville, Lois Lowry, Jane Yolen, Nancy Garden, and others.

Am I blue?—*Continued*

While all the pieces center on themes of coming to terms with homosexuality, they also are stories of love, coming of age, adventure, and self-discovery. A powerful commentary about our social and emotional responses to homosexuality and our human need for love and acceptance." Horn Book Guide

American eyes; new Asian-American short stories for young adults; introduction by Cynthia Kadohata. Fawcett Juniper 1996 c1994 138p pa $6.99 *

Grades: 7 8 9 10   S C

1. Asian Americans—Fiction 2. Short stories

ISBN 0-449-70448-3

"A Fawcett Juniper book"

First published 1994 by Holt & Co.

Includes the following stories: Knuckles by Mary F. Chen; Blonde by Katherine Min; Fortune teller by Minh Doc Ngyuen; Wild meat and the bully burgers by Lois-Ann Yamanaka; Bone by Fae Myenne Ng; Housepainting by Lan Samantha Chang; A matter of faith by Peter Bacho; Home now by Ryan Oba; Summer of my Korean soldier by Marie G. Lee; Singing apples by Cynthia Kadohata;

These ten stories reflect the conflict Asian Americans face in balancing an ancient heritage and an unknown future.

This collection is distinguished by the "excellent quality of its writing, the acuteness of characterization, and the sophistication of its themes." SLJ

American short story masterpieces; edited by Raymond Carver and Tom Jenks. Delacorte Press 1987 435p pa $7.50 hardcover o.p. *

Grades: 11 12 Adult   S C

1. Short stories

ISBN 0-440-20423-2   LC 86-19964

"Thirty-six stories are presented here. . . . These are all stories written in a realistic vein, with strong narrative drive. They 'moved and exhilarated' the compilers, and readers will have equally positive reactions. Bernard Malamud, Ann Beattie, John Updike, Grace Paley, Flannery O'Connor, and James Baldwin are just a few of the superior practitioners of the form found here." Booklist

Asimov, Isaac, 1920-1992

The complete stories. Doubleday 1990-1992 2v

v1 pa $19.95

Grades: 11 12 Adult   S C

1. Science fiction 2. Short stories

ISBN 0-385-41627-X   LC 90-3136

"A Foundation book"

Contents: v1 The dead past; Franchise; Gimmicks three; Kid stuff; The watery place; Living space; The message; Satisfaction guaranteed; Hell-fire; The last trump; The fun they had; Jokester; The Immortal Bard; Someday; Dreaming is a private thing; Profession; The feeling of power; The dying night; I'm in Marsport without Hilda; The gentle vultures; All the troubles of the world; Spell my name with an S; The last question; The ugly little boy; Nightfall; Green patches; Hostess; "Breeds there a man . . . ?"; C-Chute; "In a good

cause—"; What if—; Sally; Flies; "Nobody here but—"; It's such a beautiful day; Strikebreaker; Insert knob A in hole B; The up-to-date sorcerer; Unto the fourth generation; What is this thing called love?; The machine that won the war; My son, the physicist; Eyes do more than see; Segregationist

This set contains all of Asimov's science fiction stories including the "collections 'Earth Is Room Enough' and 'Nine Tomorrows' from the 1950s as well as . . . 'Nightfall and Other Stories.'" SLJ

I, robot. Bantam hardcover ed. Bantam Books 2004 224p (Robot series) $24; pa $7.99 *

Grades: 7 8 9 10 11 12 Adult   S C

1. Science fiction 2. Robots—Fiction 3. Short stories

ISBN 0-553-80370-0; 0-553-29438-5 (pa)

LC 2003-69139

First published 1950 by Gnome Press

Contents: Robbie; Runaround; Reason; Catch that rabbit; Liar!; Little lost robot; Escape!; Evidence; The evitable conflict

"These loosely connected stories cover the career of Dr. Susan Calvin and United States Robots, the industry that she heads, from the time of the public's early distrust of these robots to its later dependency on them. This collection is an important introduction to a theme often found in science fiction: the encroachment of technology on our lives." Shapiro. Fic for Youth. 3d edition

Beagle, Peter S.

The line between. Tachyon Publications 2006 231p pa $14.95

Grades: 11 12 Adult   S C

1. Short stories 2. Fantasy fiction

ISBN 978-1-892391-36-0; 1-892391-36-8

Contents: Gordon, the self-made cat; Two hearts; The fable of the moth; The fable of the tyrannosaurus rex; The fable of the ostrich; The fable of the octopus; El Regalo; Quarry; Salt wine; Mr. Sigerson; A dance for Emilia

"This story collection from fantasy legend Beagle offers a sublime mix of reprints and original works. . . . This book is a fitting tribute to a beloved author." Publ Wkly

Bear, Greg, 1951-

The collected stories of Greg Bear. TOR Bks. 2002 653p hardcover o.p. pa $17.95

Grades: 11 12 Adult   S C

1. Science fiction 2. Short stories

ISBN 0-7653-0160-1; 0-7653-0161-X (pa)

LC 2002-20466

"A Tom Doherty Associates book"

Contents: Blood music [novelette]; Sisters; A Martian Ricorso; Schrodinger's plague; Heads; The wind from a burning woman; The venging; Perihesperon; Scattershot; Plague of conscience; The white horse child; Dead run; Petra; Webster; Through road, no whither; Tangents; The visitation; Richie by the sea; Sleepside story; Judgment engine; The fall of the house of Escher; The way of all ghosts; MDIO ecosystes increase knowledge of DNA languages (2215 C.E.); Hardfought

The **beastly** bride; tales of the animal people; edited by Ellen Datlow & Terri Windling; introduction by Terri Windling; selected decorations by Charles Vess. Viking 2010 496p $19.99

Grades: 8 9 10 11 12   S C

1. Supernatural—Fiction 2. Short stories

ISBN 978-0-670-01145-2; 0-670-01145-2

LC 2009-14317

Contents: Island lake by E. Catherine Tobler; The puma's daughter by Tanith Lee; Map of seventeen by Christopher Barzak; The selkie speaks by Delia Sherman; Bear's bride by Johanna Sinisalo; The abominable child's tale by Carol Emshwiller; The hikikomori by Hiromi Goto; The comeuppance of Creegus Maxin by Gregory Frost; Ganesha by Jeffrey Ford; The elephant's bride by Jane Yolen; The children of Cadmus by Ellen Kushner; The white doe: three poems by Jeannine Hall Gailey; Coyote and Valorosa by Terra L. Gearhart-Serna; One thin dime by Stewart Moore; The monkey bride by Midori Snyder; Pishaach by Shweta Narayan; The salamander fire by Marly Youmans; The margay's children by Richard Bowes; Thimbleriggery and Fledglings by Steve Berman; The flock by Lucius Shepard; The children of the shark god by Peter S. Beagle; Rosina by Nan Fry

A collection of stories and poems relating to animal transfiguration legends from around the world, retold and reimagined by various authors. Includes brief biographies, authors' notes, and suggestions for further reading

"The majority of these beastly tales make for fun, thoughtful, occasionally gripping, reading." Voice Youth Advocates

The **Best** American mystery stories of the century; Tony Hillerman, editor; Otto Penzler, series editor; with an introduction by Tony Hillerman. Houghton Mifflin 2000 813p hardcover o.p. pa $17.95

Grades: 11 12 Adult   S C

1. Mystery fiction 2. Short stories

ISBN 0-618-01267-2; 0-618-01271-0 (pa)

"Dating from 1904 to the present, these stories provide a rough chronology of 20th-century crime fiction. . . . All the great writers of the genre are here—Raymond Chandler, Ellery Queen, Sue Grafton, etc.—but so are writers not normally associated with crime fiction, e.g., Flannery O'Connor, John Steinbeck, and Harlan Ellison." Libr J

"This anthology is a cornerstone volume for any mystery library." Publ Wkly

Best of the best: 20 years of the Year's best science fiction; [edited by] Gardner Dozois. St. Martin's Griffin 2005 672p hardcover o.p. pa $19.95

Grades: 9 10 11 12   S C

1. Science fiction 2. Short stories

ISBN 0-312-33655-1; 0-312-33656-X (pa)

LC 2004-51411

Dozois "collects 36 tales by some of the most notable authors currently active in the genre, among them Gene Wolfe, William Gibson, Connie Willis, Joe Haldeman and Tony Daniel. Robert Silverberg provides a foreword." Publ Wkly

Black, Holly, 1971-

The poison eaters and other stories. Big Mouth House 2010 212p $17.99

Grades: 9 10 11 12   S C

1. Fantasy fiction 2. Short stories

ISBN 978-1-931520-63-8; 1-931520-63-1

LC 2009-51635

Contents: The coldest girl in Coldtown; A reversal of fortune; The boy who cried wolf; The night market; The dog king; Virgin; In vodka veritas; The coat of stars; Paper cuts scissors; Going Ironside; The land of heart's desire; The poison eaters

"For those with a penchant for dark, edgy, fantasy fiction, Holly Black . . . offers readers a collection of twelve stories. Ten tales have appeared in anthologies; two appear in print here for the first time. . . . Deftly blending both believable characters and realistic settings, Black serves up heady concoctions for those who like their fairy tales on the chilly side. The graphic nature of some of this collection's stories make it best suited for fantasy fans in senior high school." Voice Youth Advocates

Block, Francesca Lia

Blood roses. Joanna Cotler Books 2008 129p $15.99; lib bdg $16.89

Grades: 10 11 12   S C

1. Supernatural—Fiction 2. Short stories

ISBN   978-0-06-076384-8;   0-06-076384-1; 978-0-06-076385-5 (lib bdg); 0-06-076385-X (lib bdg)

LC 2007-29564

Contents: Blood roses; Giant; My haunted house; My boyfriend is an alien; Horses are a girl's best friend; Skin art; My mother the vampire; Wounds and wings; Changelings

"Each story combines gritty, realistic life in Los Angeles with lyrical fairy tales, revealing the city as home to street gangs and centaurs, adult predators and teen boys with wings. . . . This book will appeal to Block fans, and those just discovering her will find the stories unforgettable." Voice Youth Advocates

The rose and the beast; fairy tales retold. HarperCollins Pubs. 2000 229p hardcover o.p. pa $6.99

Grades: 7 8 9 10   S C

1. Fairy tales 2. Short stories

ISBN 0-06-028129-4; 0-06-440745-4 (pa)

LC 00-22444

"Joanna Cotler books"

Contents: Snow; Tiny; Glass; Charm; Wolf; Rose; Bones; Beast; Ice

Nine classic fairy tales set in modern, magical landscapes and retold with a twist.

The author's "beautiful words turn modern-day Los Angeles into a fantastical world of fairies, angels, and charms. The context is very modern, with issues of drug addiction, rape, and suicide smoothly woven into the stories, which are infused with a palpable if not explicit eroticism." Booklist

Bradbury, Ray, 1920-

Bradbury stories; 100 of his most celebrated tales. Morrow 2003 893p hardcover o.p. pa $17.95

Grades: 11 12 Adult   S C
  1. Science fiction 2. Short stories
  ISBN 0-06-054242-X; 0-06-054488-0 (pa)

                         LC 2003-42189

Contents: The whole town's sleeping; The rocket; Season of disbelief; And the rock cried out; The drummer boy of Shiloh; The beggar on O'Connell Bridge; The flying machine; Heavyset; The first night of Lent; Lafayette, farewell; Remember Sascha?; Junior; That woman on the lawn; February 1999: Ylla; Banshee; One for his lordship, and one for the road!; The Laurel and Hardy love affair; Unterderseaboat doktor; Another fine mess; The dwarf; A wild night in Galway; The wind; No news, or what killed the dog?; A little journey; Any friend of Nicholas Nickleby's is a friend of mine; The garbage collector; The visitor; The man; Henry the ninth; The messiah; Bang! you're dead!; Darling Adolf; The beautiful shave; Colonel Stonesteel's genuine homemade truly Egyptian mummy; I see you never; The exiles; At midnight, in the month of June; The witch door; The watchers; 200405: the naming of names; Hopscotch; The illustrated man; The dead man; June 2001: and the moon be still as bright; The burning man; G.B.S.—Mark V; A blade of grass; The sound of summer running; And the sailor, home from the sea; The lonely ones; The Finnegan; On the Orient, North; The smiling people; The fruit at the bottom of the bowl; Bug; Downwind from Gettysburg; Time in thy flight; Changeling; The dragon; Let's play "poison"; The cold wind and the warm; The meadow; The Kilimanjaro device; The man in the Rorschach shirt; Bless me, father, for I have sinned; The pedestrian; Trapdoor; The swan; The sea shell; Once more, Legato; June 2003: way in the middle of the air; The wonderful death of Dudley Stone; By the numbers!; April 2005: Usher II; The square pegs; The trolley; The smile; The miracles of Jamie; A far-away guitar; The cistern; The machineries of joy; Bright phoenix; The wish; The lifework of Juan Diaz; Time intervening/interim; Almost the end of the world; The great collision of Monday last; The poems; April 2026: the long years; Icarus Montgolfier Wright; Death and the maiden; Zero hour; The Toynbee convector; Forever and the earth; The handler; Getting through Sunday somehow; The Pumpernickel; Last rites; The watchful poker chip of H. Matisse; All on a summer's night

"This massive retrospective of self-selected Bradbury stories offers a compendium of his eccentrics, misfits, losers, and small-town dreamers, who typically inhabit an uncanny setting or confront a strange, unsettling situation." Libr J

The illustrated man. Avon Books 1997 275p $15.95

Grades: 9 10 11 12 Adult   S C
  1. Science fiction 2. Short stories
  ISBN 0-380-97384-7   LC 97-93228
  Also available in paperback from Spectra

First published 1951 by Doubleday; short stories originally published between 1948 and 1951

Contents: Prologue: The illustrated man; The veldt; Kaleidoscope; The other foot; The highway; The man; The long rain; The rocket man; The last night of the world; The exiles; No particular night or morning; The

fox and the forest; The visitor; The concrete mixer; Marionettes, Inc.; The city; Zero hour; The rocket; The illustrated man

In this work "the stories are given a linking framework; they are all seen as magical tattoos becoming living stories, springing from the body of the protagonist." Sci Fic Ency

The Martian chronicles. Avon Books 1997 268p $15.95 *

Grades: 7 8 9 10   S C
  1. Science fiction 2. Short stories
  ISBN 0-380-97383-9   LC 96-95071
  Also available from other publishers

First published 1950 by Doubleday

This book's "closely interwoven short stories, linked by recurrent images and themes, tell of the repeated attempts by humans to colonize Mars, of the way they bring their old prejudices with them, and of the repeated, ambiguous meetings with the shape-changing Martians." Sci Fic Ency

Capote, Truman, 1924-1984

Breakfast at Tiffany's: a short novel and three stories. Modern Lib. 1994 161p $14.95; pa $11

Grades: 9 10 11 12   S C
  1. Short stories
  ISBN 0-679-60085-X; 0-679-74565-3 (pa)

                         LC 93-43633

First published 1958 by Random House

Contents: Breakfast at Tiffany's; House of flowers; A diamond guitar; A Christmas memory

The novella which gives the book its title is the tale of a Manhattan playgirl, Holly Golightly. Completing the volume are three short stories: House of flowers, A diamond guitar, and A Christmas memory

Card, Orson Scott

First meetings in the Enderverse. Tor Teen 2003 208p il $17.95; pa $6.99

Grades: 9 10 11 12   S C
  1. Science fiction 2. Short stories
  ISBN 0-7653-0873-8; 0-7653-4798-9 (pa)

                         LC 2003-55951

"A Tom Doherty Associates book"

Contents: The Polish boy; Teacher's pest; Ender's game; Investment counselor

"Andrew 'Ender' Wiggins, a brilliant leader and tactician and destined to save Earth by destroying an entire alien civilization at the age of 12, was first introduced in Card's 'Ender's Game'. . . . That novella, plus three other stories (including one never before published) make up this . . . collection of tales, all dealing with first meetings that played significant roles in the life of Ender Wiggins. . . . All four stories use the future setting as a framework to explore various issues of religion, government control, population limits, education, and moral responsibility. Character, setting, plot—Card does them all right, and makes it look effortless. . . . For newcomers to Ender's universe and longtime fans, this book will hit the spot and whet the appetite for more." SLJ

Carter, Alden R.

Love, football, and other contact sports. Holiday House 2006 261p $16.95 *

Grades: 8 9 10 11 12   S C

1. Football—Fiction 2. School stories 3. Short stories

ISBN 978-0-8234-1975-3; 0-8234-1975-4

LC 2005-46094

Contents: A girl's guide to football players; A football player's guide to love; Kickoff (or never trust a girl who steals your ice cream sandwich); Trashback; Pig brains; Buck's head; Satyagraha; Elvis; The Ogre of Mensa; The gully; Kicker wanted; The briefcase; Jersey Day; Big Chicago; The ghost of Mum-Mum; The Doughnut boots his reputation; A good game

This "collection of short stories, which revolves around Argyle West High School's football team, features an ensemble cast of students during their sophomore, junior, and senior years. . . . Written with sensitivity and conviction, the realistic stories are leavened with occasional, often ironic humor." Booklist

A **Century** of great Western stories; edited by John Jakes. Forge 2000 525p hardcover o.p. pa $18.95

Grades: 11 12 Adult   S C

1. Western stories 2. Short stories

ISBN 0-312-86986-X; 0-312-86985-1 (pa)

LC 99-462096

"A Tom Doherty Associates book"

This anthology of 30 short stories includes pieces by such writers as Owen Wister, Zane Grey, Max Brand, Bill Pronzini, Elmer Kelton and Marcia Muller.

"Romance, murder, action, mystery and suspense are mixed with hefty doses of moral dilemma, guilt and redemption in these carefully plotted tales. . . . Many of the stories are appearing here for the first time since they were published in the pulps of the '30s, '40s and '50s, but their appeal is as fresh as ever." Publ Wkly

Includes bibliographical references

Chairman Mao would not be amused; fiction from today's China; edited by Howard Goldblatt. Grove Press 1995 321p pa $14 hardcover o.p.

Grades: 11 12 Adult   S C

1. China—Fiction 2. Short stories

ISBN 0-8021-3449-1   LC 95-1931

"The 20 authors represented here range from Wang Meng, the former minister of culture, to Su Tong, whose Raise the Red Lantern has been immortalized on screen." Libr J

"Translated ably enough to keep up with the colloquial tone, most tales are told with straightforward familiarity, drawing readers into small communities and personal histories that are anything but heroic." Publ Wkly

Chambers, Aidan, 1934-

The kissing game; short stories. Amulet Books 2011 216p $16.95

Grades: 9 10 11 12   S C

1. Short stories

ISBN 978-0-8109-9716-5; 0-8109-9716-9

LC 2010-32947

Contents: Cindy's day out; The scientific approach; Kangaroo; Expulsion; The tower; Up for it; The God debate; The kissing game; Thrown out; Tosk; Like life; Sanctuary; Weather forecast; Something to tell you; You can be anything; A handful of wheat

"This title offers sixteen wonderful short stories by an award-winning author. Only three tales are truly short stories—most are 'flash fiction.' These quick reads are meant to grab your attention quickly, tell their tale, and finish in just minutes. They are neat and seemingly simple stories, but they are thick with implication and have many possible meanings. . . . There is something for everyone—love, murder, fairy tales, adventure, science fiction, politics and more." Voice Youth Advocates

Cheever, John, 1912-1982

The stories of John Cheever. Knopf 1978 693p hardcover o.p. pa $17.95

Grades: 11 12 Adult   S C

1. Short stories

ISBN 0-394-50087-3; 0-375-72442-7 (pa)

LC 78-160

Contents: Goodbye, my brother; The common day; The enormous radio; O city of broken dreams; The Hartleys; The Sutton Place story; The summer farmer; Torch song; The pot of gold; Clancy in the Tower of Babel; Christmas is a sad season for the poor; The season of divorce; The chaste Clarissa; The cure; The superintendent; The children; The sorrows of gin; O youth and beauty!; The day the pig fell into the well; The five-forty-eight; Just one more time; The housebreaker of Shady Hill; The bus to St. James's; The worm in the apple; The trouble of Marcie Flint; The bella lingua; The Wrysons; The country husband; The Duchess; The scarlet moving van; Just tell me who it was; Brimmer; The golden age; The lowboy; The music teacher; A woman without a country; The death of Justina; Clementina; Boy in Rome; A miscellany of characters that will not appear; The chimera; The seaside houses; The angel of the bridge; The brigadier and the golf widow; A vision of the world; Reunion; An educated American woman; Metamorphoses; Mene, Mene, Tekel, Upharsin; Montraldo; The ocean; Marito in Città; The geometry of love; The swimmer; The world of apples; Another story; Percy; The fourth alarm; Artemis, the honest well digger; Three stories: I; Three stories: II; Three stories: III; The jewels of the Cabots

A "bringing together of 61 Cheever stories in a single binding. . . . Most of these pieces were initially published in 'The New Yorker.'" Choice

"Readers will delight in the delineation of Cheever's mythical landscapes. . . . Resonant with feeling and meaning, this is a collection to treasure." Publ Wkly

Chekhov, Anton Pavlovich, 1860-1904

The Russian master and other stories; [by] Anton Chekhov; translated with an introduction and notes by Ronald Hingley. Oxford University Press 2008 233p (Oxford world's classics) pa $8.95

Grades: 9 10 11 12 Adult   S C

1. Russia—Fiction 2. Short stories

ISBN 978-0-19-955487-4   LC 2009464906

Contents: His wife; A lady with a dog; The duel; A hard case; Gooseberries; Concerning love; Peasants; Angel; The Russian master; Terror; The Order of St. Anne

Chekhov, Anton Pavlovich, 1860-1904—*Continued*

A collection of eleven short stories written between 1892 and 1899.

Chopin, Kate, 1851-1904

The awakening and selected stories; edited with an introduction by Sandra M. Gilbert. Penguin Books 2003 286p (Penguin classics) pa $8

Grades: 9 10 11 12   S C

1. Short stories

ISBN 0-14-243732-8   LC 2003-265744

Contents: The awakening; Emancipation: a life fable; At the 'Cadian ball; Désirée's baby; La belle Zoraïde; At Chênière Caminada; The story of an hour; Lilacs; Athénaise; A pair of silk stockings; Nég Créol; Elizabeth Stock's one story; The storm: a sequel to "The 'Cadian ball"

In addition to the novel The awakening (1899) this volume also includes selected stories from Bayou folk (1894) and A night in Acadie (1897).

Cisneros, Sandra

Woman Hollering Creek and other stories. Random House 1991 165p pa $11.95 hardcover o.p. *

Grades: 11 12 Adult   S C

1. Mexican Americans—Fiction 2. Short stories

ISBN 0-679-73856-8   LC 90-52930

Contents: My Lucy friend who smells like corn; Eleven; Salvador late or early; Mexican movies; Barbie-Q; Mericans; Tepeyac; One holy night; My tocaya; Woman Hollering Creek; The Marlboro Man; La Fabulosa: a Texas operetta; Remember the Alamo; Never marry a Mexican; Bread; Eyes of Zapata; Anguiano religious articles rosaries statues medals incense candles talismans perfumes oils herbs; Little miracles, kept promises; Los Boxers; There was a man, there was a woman; Tin tan tan; Bien pretty

"Unforgettable characters march through a satisfying collection of tales about Mexican-Americans who know the score and cling to the anchor of their culture." N Y Times Book Rev

Clarke, Arthur C., 1917-2008

The collected stories of Arthur C. Clarke. TOR Bks. 2001 c2000 966p hardcover o.p. pa $19.95 *

Grades: 11 12 Adult   S C

1. Short stories 2. Science fiction

ISBN 0-312-87821-4; 0-312-87860-5 (pa)

"A TOR book"

First published 2000 in the United Kingdom

Contents: Travel by wire!; How we went to Mars; Retreat from Earth; Reverie; The awakening; Whacky; Loophole; Rescue party; Technical error; Castaway; The fires within; Inheritance; Nightfall; History lesson; Transience; The wall of darkness; The lion of Comarre; The forgotten enemy; Hide-and-seek; Breaking strain; Nemesis; Guardian angel; Time's arrow; A walk in the dark; Silence please; Trouble with the natives; The road to the sea; The sentinel; Holiday on the moon; Earthlight; Second dawn; Superiority; 'If I forget thee, oh Earth . . .';

All the time in the world; The nine billion names of God; The possessed; The parasite; Jupiter five; Encounter in the dawn; The other tiger; Publicity campaign; Armaments race; The deep range; No morning after; Big game hunt; Patent pending; Refugee; The star; What goes up; Venture to the moon; The pacifist; The reluctant orchid; Moving spirit; The defenestration of Ermintrude Inch; The ultimate melody; The next tenants; Cold war; Sleeping beauty; Security check; The man who ploughed the sea; Critical mass; The other side of the sky; Let there be light; Out of the sun; Cosmic Casanova; The songs of distant Earth; A slight case of sunstroke; Who's there?; Out of the cradle, endlessly orbiting . . .; I remember Babylon; Trouble with time; Into the comet; Summertime on Icarus; Saturn rising; Death and the senator; Before Eden; Hate; Love that universe; Dog Star; Maelstrom II; An ape about the house; The shining ones; The secret; Dial F for Frankenstein; The wind from the sun; The food of the gods; The last command; Light of darkness; The longest science-fiction story ever told; Playback; The cruel sky; Herbert George Morley Robert Wells, Esq.; Crusade; Neutron tide; Reunion; Transit of Earth; A meeting with Medusa; Quarantine; 'SiseneG'; The steampowered word processor; On golden seas; The hammer of God; The wire continuum; Improving the neighbourhood

"Although most of these stories date from between 1946 and 1970, seven earlier tales, rescued from what would now be called fanzines, extend coverage back to 1937, and a few snippets stretch it toward the present. At least two dozen stories bear titles that are household words among sf readers. . . . The stories demonstrate Clarke's dazzling and unique combination of command of the language, scientific and other kinds of erudition, and inimitable wit." Booklist

Coming of age in America; a multicultural anthology; edited by Mary Frosch; foreword by Gary Soto. New Press (NY) 1994 274p hardcover o.p. pa $14.95 *

Grades: 11 12 Adult   S C

1. Short stories

ISBN 1-56584-146-8; 1-56584-147-6 (pa)

                   LC 93-46921

Contents: The jacket by Gary Soto; The neighborhood by Mary Gordon; The kind of light that shines on Texas by Reginald McKnight; The body politic by Theodore Weesner; The wrong lunch line by Nicholasa Mohr; Jump or dive by Peter Cameron; from Bastard out of Carolina by Dorothy Allison; Where is it written? by Adam Schwartz; Summer water and Shirley by Durango Mendoza; Judgment day by Arturo Islas; from The floating world by Cynthia Kadohata; Yes, young daddy by Frank Chin; Going to school by D'Arcy McNickle; A spell of Kona weather by Sylvia Watanabe; What means switch by Gish Jen; from This boy's life by Tobias Wolff; Eyes and teeth by Wanda Coleman; A bag of oranges by Spiro Athanas; from How the García girls lost their accents by Julia Alvarez; from Davita's harp by Chaim Potok; Marigolds by Eugenia Collier

This collection consists of sixteen short stories and excerpts from five novels, written by noted authors from a variety of ethnic backgrounds. Among the authors represented are Dorothy Allison, Cynthia Kadohata, Julia Alvarez, Frank Chin, Tobias Wolff, and Chaim Potok.

Cosmos latinos; an anthology of science fiction from Latin America and Spain; translated, edited, & with an introduction & notes by Andrea L. Bell & Yolanda Molina-Gavilán. Wesleyan Univ. Press 2003 352p (Wesleyan early classics of science fiction series) hardcover o.p. pa $24.95

Grades: 11 12 Adult   **S C**

1. Science fiction 2. Short stories

ISBN 0-8195-6633-0; 0-8195-6634-9 (pa)

                      LC 2003-41182

Translated from the Spanish

This "is a survey of Spanish and Portuguese sf from both sides of the Atlantic, most of it never before translated into English. Coverage begins in the nineteenth century and continues through the early years of the genre's definition to include many more recent than older stories. . . . Many stories exploit familiar sf territory—the technologically advanced future, time travel and its repercussions, and so on—but obscurer corners are visited, too, as in an alternate Crucifixion occurring on a far-distant world just being explored by humans, and a recasting of the conquistadors as spacefarers. A welcome expansion of the sf terrain for Anglophones." Booklist

Includes bibliographical references

Crutcher, Chris, 1946-

Angry management; three novellas. Greenwillow Books 2009 246p $16.99; lib bdg $17.89; pa $8.99

Grades: 7 8 9 10   **S C**

1. Short stories

ISBN   978-0-06-050247-8;   0-06-050247-9; 978-0-06-050246-1 (lib bdg); 0-06-050246-0 (lib bdg); 978-0-06-050248-5 (pa); 0-06-050248-7 (pa)

                      LC 2008-52829

Contents: Nak; Montana wild; Meet me at the gates, Marcus James

A collection of short stories featuring characters from earlier books by Chris Crutcher.

"The stories are well-written, action packed, engrossing and at times humorous. . . . A good introduction to Crutcher, his latest book will certainly please current fans as well." Voice Youth Advocates

Dahl, Roald

Skin and other stories. Viking 2000 212p $15.99; pa $8.99

Grades: 7 8 9 10   **S C**

1. Short stories

ISBN 0-670-89184-3; 0-14-131034-0 (pa)

                      LC 99-58600

Contents: Skin; Lamb to the slaughter; The sound machine; An African story; Galloping Foxley; The wish; The surgeon; Dip in the pool; The champion of the world; Beware of the dog; My lady love, my dove

A collection of 13 of the author's short stories written for adults. "Full of irony and unexpected twists, they smack of the master's touch—every word carefully chosen, characters fully fleshed out in only a few pages, the sense of place immediate." Booklist

Danticat, Edwidge, 1969-

Krik? Krak! Vintage Books 1996 224p (Vintage contemporaries) pa $12.95 *

Grades: 11 12 Adult   **S C**

1. Haitian Americans—Fiction 2. Haiti—Fiction 3. Short stories

ISBN 0-679-76657-X   LC 95-43449

First published 1995 by Soho Press

Contents: Between the pool and the gardenias; Caroline's wedding; Children of the sea; The missing peace; New York day women; Night women; Nineteen thirty-seven; Seeing things simply; A wall of fire rising

The author "touches upon life both in Haiti and in New York's Haitian community, though we spend most of our time in Port-au-Prince and the country town of Ville Rose. The best of these stories humanize, particularize, give poignancy to the lives of people we may have come to think of as faceless emblems of misery, poverty and brutality." N Y Times Book Rev

The **Del** Rey book of science fiction and fantasy; sixteen original works by speculative fiction's finest voices; edited by Ellen Datlow. Del Rey Books 2008 400p pa $16

Grades: 11 12 Adult   **S C**

1. Fantasy fiction 2. Science fiction 3. Short stories

ISBN 978-0-345-49632-4   LC 2008-4948

"A Del Rey trade paperback original"

Contents: The elephant ironclads by Jason Stoddard; Ardent clouds by Lucy Sussex; Gather by Christopher Rowe; Sonny Liston takes the fall by Elizabeth Bear; North American lake monsters by Nathan Ballingrud; All washed up while looking for a better world by Carol Emshwiller; Special economics by Maureen F. McHugh; Aka St. Mark's Place by Richard Bowes; The goosle by Margo Lanagan; Shira by Lavie Tidhar; The passion of Azazel by Barry N. Malzberg; The Lagerstätte by Laird Barron; Gladiolus exposed by Anna Tambour; Daltharee by Jeffrey Ford; Jimmy by Pat Cadigan; Prisoners of the action by Paul McAuley and Kim Newman

"This collection of cutting-edge writing has appeal to older teens familiar with the demands of speculative fiction at its best. The 16 pieces include tales of alien abduction and war, murder, familial abuse, and alternate histories of the world. . . . An anthology that's thought-provoking and intellectually challenging." SLJ

Destination unexpected: short stories; collected by Donald R. Gallo. Candlewick Press 2003 240p hardcover o.p. pa $8.99 *

Grades: 7 8 9 10   **S C**

1. Short stories

ISBN 0-7636-1764-4; 0-7636-3119-1 (pa)

                      LC 2002-71599

Contents: Something old, something new by J. Sweeney; Brutal interlude by R. Koertge; Bread on the water by D. Lubar; My people by M. P. Haddix; Bad blood by W. Weaver; Keep smiling by A. Flinn; August lights by K. W. Holt; Mosquito by G. Salisbury; The kiss in the carry-on bag by R. Peck; Tourist trapped by E. Wittlinger

This collection "features teen protagonists experiencing a transforming experience while on some kind of journey. . . . . Whether humorous or serious, the stories are consistently well written and engaging." Booklist

Don't cramp my style; stories about that time of the month; edited by Lisa Rowe Fraustino. Simon & Schuster for Young Readers 2004 295p $15.95

Grades: 7 8 9 10   **S C**

1. Menstruation—Fiction 2. Short stories

ISBN 0-689-85882-5

Contents: Introduction "snapshots in blood" by Michelle H. Martin; Taking care of things by Pat Brisson; Heroic quest of Douglas McGawain by David Lubar; Moon time child by Alice McGill; Women's house by Dianne Ochiltree; Czarevna of Muscovy by Joan Elizabeth Goodman; Sleeping beauty by Lisa Rowe Fraustino; Transfusion by Joyce McDonald; Maroon by Han Nolan; Ritual purity by Deborah Heiligman; Losing it by Julie Stockler; Uterus fairy by Linda Oatman High

A collection of eleven stories concerning menstruation.

"This highly recommended collection . . . encompasses an impressive variety of times, cultures, attitudes, and moods. . . . The writing . . . is consistently excellent." Voice Youth Advocates

Doyle, Sir Arthur Conan, 1859-1930

The complete Sherlock Holmes; with a preface by Christopher Morley. Doubleday 1960 c1930 1122p $27.95 *

Grades: 7 8 9 10   **S C**

1. Mystery fiction 2. Short stories

ISBN 0-385-00689-6

Also available in a two-volume paperback edition from Bantam Bks.

First published 1930

This book contains the following four Sherlock Holmes novels: A study in scarlet (1887); The sign of the four (1890); The hound of the Baskervilles (1902); The valley of fear (1915). It also contains fifty-eight Sherlock Holmes stories which were originally published in the following separate volumes: Adventures of Sherlock Holmes (1892); Memoirs of Sherlock Holmes (1894); The return of Sherlock Holmes (1905); His last bow (1917); The case book of Sherlock Holmes (1927).

Ellis, Deborah, 1960-

Lunch with Lenin and other stories. Fitzhenry & Whiteside 2008 169p pa $14.95

Grades: 7 8 9 10 11 12   **S C**

1. Drug abuse—Fiction 2. Short stories

ISBN 978-1-55455-105-7; 1-55455-105-6

Contents: Through the woods; Pretty flowers; Lunch with Lenin; Dancing, with beads; Prodigal; Red hero at midnight; Another night in Disneyland; Cactus people

A collection of short stories that explore the lives of teenagers affected directly or indirectly by drugs.

"The relatively short stories read quickly, offering neither judgment nor solutions but rather the opportunity for compassion and understanding. . . . The collection's quality . . . is high enough to justify placing this book in every library." Voice Youth Advocates

The **eternal** kiss; 13 vampire tales of blood and desire; edited by Trisha Telep. Running Press Kids 2009 416p pa $9.95

Grades: 9 10 11 12   **S C**

1. Vampires—Fiction 2. Short stories

ISBN 978-0-7624-3717-7; 0-7624-3717-0

Contents: Falling to ash by Karen Mahoney; Shelter Island by Melissa de la Cruz; Sword point by Maria V. Snyder; The coldest girl in Coldtown by Holly Black; Undead is very hot right now by Sarah Rees Brennan; Kat by Kelley Armstrong; The thirteenth step by Libba Bray; All hallows by Rachel Caine; Wet teeth by Cecil Castellucci; Other boys by Cassandra Clare; Passing by Nancy Holder and Debbie Viguié; Ambition by Lili St. Crow; All wounds by Dina James

A collection of vampire-related short stories. "The selections have diverse story lines, some strong on the horror component but including lighter fare with some comedy and romance, and an array of writing styles. Vampires are portrayed in a variety of ways along with their history and lore, making this an entertaining read. . . . These fang-tastic tales are a must for libraries with a strong vampire fan base." SLJ

Every man for himself; ten short stories about being a guy; edited by Nancy E. Mercado. Dial Books 2005 154p il hardcover o.p. pa $6.99 *

Grades: 7 8 9 10   **S C**

1. Short stories 2. Boys—Fiction

ISBN 0-8037-2896-4; 0-14-240813-1 (pa)

LC 2004-24069

Contents: The prom prize by Walter Dean Myers; Jump away by René Saldaña, Jr.; No more birds will die today by Paul Acampora; Shockers by David Lubar; Pig lessons by Edward Averett; Strange powers by Craig Thompson; The unbeatable by Mo Willems; Princes by David Levithan; Fear by Terry Trueman; It's complicated by Ron Koertge

"This collection provides a refreshing look at the values, decisions, and friendships that ultimately shape a boy into a man. The stories themselves are diverse, ranging from humorous to serious." SLJ

Face relations; 11 stories about seeing beyond color. Simon & Schuster Books for Young Readers 2004 224p $17.95

Grades: 7 8 9 10   **S C**

1. Race relations—Fiction 2. Short stories

ISBN 0-689-85637-7

Contents: Phat acceptance by Jess Mowry; Skins by Joseph Bruchac; Snow by Sherri Winston; The heartbeat of the soul of the world by René Saldaña, Jr.; Hum by Naomi Shihab Nye; Epiphany by Ellen Wittlinger; Black and white by Kyoko Mori; Hearing flower by M.E. Kerr; Gold by Marina Budhos; Mr. Ruben by Rita Williams-Garcia; Negress by Marilyn Singer

"Contributed by familiar writers for young people, including Ellen Wittlinger, M. E. Kerr, Rita Williams-Garcia, Naomi Shihab Nye, and Jess Mowry, the stories ask challenging questions about what role race plays in family life, at school, in friendships, and in love. . . . This is a provocative collection." Booklist

Faulkner, William, 1897-1962

Selected short stories of William Faulkner. Modern Lib. 1993 310p $15.95 *

Grades: 9 10 11 12   **S C**

1. Short stories

ISBN 0-679-42478-4

LC 92-51072

Faulkner, William, 1897-1962—*Continued*

A reissue of the 1961 edition

Contents: Barn burning; Two soldiers; A rose for Emily; Dry September; That evening sun; Red leaves; Lo!; Turnabout; Honor; There was a queen; Mountain victory; Beyond; Race at morning

A variety of the author's output, diverse in method and subject matter, ranging in original publication dates from 1930 to 1955

Fear: 13 stories of suspense and horror; [selected by and with an] introduction by R.L. Stine. Dutton 2010 306p $16.99; pa $7.99

Grades: 7 8 9 10   S C

1. Horror fiction 2. Short stories

ISBN   978-0-525-42168-9;   0-525-42168-8; 978-0-14-241774-4 (pa); 0-14-241774-2 (pa)

LC 2009-53284

Contents: Welcome to the club by R.L. Stine; She's different tonight by Heather Graham; Suckers by Suzanne Weyn; The perfects by Jennifer Allison; Shadow children by Heather Brewer; The poison ring by Peg Kehret; Dragonfly eyes by Alane Ferguson; Jeepers peepers by Ryan Brown; Piney power by F. Paul Wilson; The night hunter by Meg Cabot; Tuition by Walter Sorrells; Tagger by James Rollins; Ray gun by Tim Maleeny

"Thirteen highly suspenseful short stories. . . . [Stine] enlists some of the best in the business, such as Meg Cabot and F. Paul Wilson, Walter Sorrells and James Rollins, who offer plenty of heart-throbbing supernatural horror, crime suspense, shockers and sometimes a mixture of all three. . . . Fast-paced, shuddery-scary fun." Kirkus

Feeling very strange; the Slipstream anthology; James Patrick Kelly & John Kessel, editors. Tachyon Publications 2006 288p pa $14.95

Grades: 11 12 Adult   S C

1. Science fiction 2. Fantasy fiction 3. Short stories

ISBN 978-1-892391-35-X; 1-892391-35-X

Contents: Al, by C. Emshwiller; The little magic shop, by B. Sterling; The healer, by A. Bender; The specialist's hat, by K. Link; Light and the sufferer, by J. Lethem; Sea Oak, by G. Saunders; Exhibit H: torn pages discovered in the vest pocket of an unidentified tourist, by J. VanderMeer; Hell is the absence of God, by T. Chiang; Lieserl, by K. J. Fowler; Bright morning, by J. Ford; Biographical notes to "A discourse on the nature of causality, with airplane," by Benjamin Rosenbaum, by B. Rosenbaum; The god of dark laughter, by M. Chabon; The rose in twelve petals, by T. Goss; The lions are asleep this night, by H. Waldrop; You have never been here, by M. Rickert

"Is slipstream just science fiction and fantasy that doesn't know that it's science fiction or fantasy? Or is it more than that? Decide for yourself by slipping into short stories that are superb, whatever you choose to call them." SciFi.com

Firebirds rising; an anthology of original science fiction and fantasy; edited by Sharyn November. Firebird 2006 530p hardcover o.p. pa $9.99

Grades: 7 8 9 10 11 12   S C

1. Science fiction 2. Fantasy fiction 3. Short stories

ISBN   0-14-240549-3;   978-0-14-240549-9; 0-14-240936-7 (pa); 978-0-14-240936-7 (pa)

Contents: Huntress by Tamora Pierce; Unwrapping by Nina Kiriki Hoffman; The real thing by Alison Goodman; Little (Grrl) lost by Charles de Lint; I'll give you my word by Diana Wynne Jones; In the house of the seven librarians by Ellen Klages; Wintermoon wish by Sharon Shinn; The wizards of Perfil by Kelly Link; Jack o'Lantern by Patricia A. McKillip; Quill by Carol Emshwiller; Blood roses by Francesca Lia Block; Hives by Kara Dalkey; Perception by Alan Dean Foster; The house on the planet by Tanith Lee; Cousins by Pamela Dean; What used to be good still is by Emma Bull

This is a collection of sixteen science fiction and fantasy stories.

"This anthology is a wonderful choice for any young adult collection." Voice Youth Advocates

Firebirds soaring; an anthology of original speculative fiction; [edited by Sharyn November; illustrated by Mike Dringenberg] Firebird 2009 574p il $19.99

Grades: 7 8 9 10 11 12   S C

1. Fantasy fiction 2. Science fiction 3. Short stories

ISBN 978-0-14-240552-9; 0-14-240552-3

LC 2008-29516

Contents: Kingmaker by Nancy Springer; A ticket to ride by Nancy Farmer; A thousand tails by Christopher Barzak; All under heaven by Chris Roberson; Singing on a star by Ellen Klages; Egg magic by Louise Marley; Flatland by Kara Dalkey; Dolly the dog-soldier by Candas Jane Dorsey; Ferryman by Margo Lanagan; The ghosts of strangers by Nina Kiriki Hoffman; Twilight tales by Jo Walton; The dignity he's due by Carol Emshwiller; Power and magic by Marly Youmans; Court ship by Sherwood Smith; Little Red by Jane Yolen and Adam Stemple; The myth of Fenix by Laurel Winter; Fear and loathing in Lalanna by Nick O'Donohoe; Bone-chewer's legacy by Clare Bell; Something worth doing by Elizabeth E. Wein

This anthology "contains 19 short stories by some of the top writers in this genre. . . . The selections vary in length, with some short stories, some novellas. Each work is introduced by an evocative illustration that beautifully sets the scene for the written work. The variety of styles and themes and a gathering together of so many talented writers in one work offer readers a banquet for the imagination. For fans of the genre, this is a must read." SLJ

First crossing; stories about teen immigrants; edited by Donald R. Gallo. Candlewick Press 2004 224p hardcover o.p. pa $8.99

Grades: 7 8 9 10   S C

1. Immigrants—Fiction 2. Short stories

ISBN 0-7636-2249-4; 0-7636-3291-0 (pa)

LC 2003-65255

Contents: First crossing by Pam Muñoz Ryan; Second culture kids by Dian Curtis Regan; My favorite chaperone by Jean Davies Okimoto; They don't mean it! by Lensey Namioka; Pulling up stakes by David Lubar; Lines of scrimmage by Elsa Marston; The Swede by Alden R. Carter; The Rose of Sharon by Marie G. Lee; Make Maddie mad by Rita Williams-Garcia; The green armchair by Minfong Ho

First crossing—*Continued*

Ten short stories about teen immigrants by such authors as Pam Muñoz Ryan, Lensey Namioka, and David Lubar.

"Covering a wide range of cultural and economical backgrounds, these stories by 11 well-known authors touch on a variety of teen experiences, with enough attitude and heartfelt angst to speak to young adults anywhere." SLJ

Fitzgerald, F. Scott (Francis Scott), 1896-1940

The short stories of F. Scott Fitzgerald; a new collection; edited and with a preface by Matthew J. Bruccoli. Scribner 1989 775p hardcover o.p. pa $18 *

Grades: 11 12 Adult   S C
1. Short stories
ISBN 0-684-19160-1; 0-684-80445-X (pa)
LC 89-6351

Contents: Head and shoulders; Bernice bobs her hair; The ice palace; The offshore pirate; May Day; The jellybean; The curious case of Benjamin Button; The diamond as big as the Ritz; Winter dreams; Dice, brassknuckles & guitar; Absolution; Rags Martin-Jones and the Pr-nce of W-les; "The sensible thing"; Love in the night; The rich boy; Jacob's ladder; A short trip home; The bowl; The captured shadow; Basil and Cleopatra; The last of the belles; Majesty; At your age; The swimmers; Two wrongs; First blood; Emotional bankruptcy; The bridal party; One trip abroad; The hotel child; Babylon revisited; A new leaf; A freeze-out; Six of one—; What a handsome pair!; Crazy Sunday; More than just a house; Afternoon of an author; Financing Finnegan; The lost decade; "Boil some water—lots of it"; Last kiss; Dearly beloved

"The 43 stories in this collection include both the famous ones and several that are less well known." Booklist

Flake, Sharon G.

Who am I without him? short stories about girls and the boys in their lives. Jump at the Sun/Hyperion Books for Children 2004 168p $15.99; pa $7.99 *

Grades: 7 8 9 10   S C
1. African Americans—Fiction 2. Short stories
ISBN 0-7868-0693-1; 1-4231-0383-1 (pa)

Contents: So I ain't no good girl; The ugly one; Wanted: a thug; I know a stupid boy when I see one; Mookie in love; Don't be disrespecting me; I like white boys; Jacob's rules; Hunting for boys; A letter to my daughter

Ten short stories about African American teenage girls and their relationships with boys.

"Addressing issues and situations that many girls face in today's often complex society, this book is provocative and thought-provoking." SLJ

Free?: stories about human rights; [edited by] Amnesty International. Candlewick Press 2010 202p il $17.99; pa $8.99

Grades: 7 8 9 10   S C
1. Human rights—Fiction 2. Freedom—Fiction 3. Short stories
ISBN   978-0-7636-4703-2;   0-7636-4703-9; 978-0-7636-4926-5 (pa); 0-7636-4926-0 (pa)
LC 2009-14720

Contents: Klaus Vogel and the bad lads by David Almond; School slave by Theresa Breslin; Scout's honour by Sarah Mussi; Sarsaparilla by Ursula Dubosarsky; After the hurricane by Rita Williams-Garcia; If only Papa hadn't danced by Patricia McCormick; Prince Francis by Roddy Doyle; Uncle Meena by Ibtisam Barakat; Searching for a two-way street by Malorie Blackman; Setting words free by Margaret Mahy; Jojo learns to dance by Meja Mwangi; Wherever I lay down my head by Jamila Gavin; Christopher by Eoin Colfer; No trumpets needed by Michael Morpurgo

An anthology of fourteen stories by young adult authors from around the world, on such themes as asylum, law, education, and faith, compiled in honor of the sixtieth anniversary of the Universal Declaration of Human Rights.

"Margaret Mahy writes about class with wit and intensity, as does Jamila Gavin, who sets the class war in India, where a young girl's family throws her out for resisting an arranged marriage. . . . David Almond explores school power plays in a story about a boy who says no to a popular bully. Hurricane Katrina is Rita Williams-Garcia's setting. Two contemporary Palestinian stories compare the current occupation with Native American experiences of oppression. . . . Sure to spark discussion and perhaps participation in Amnesty International." Booklist

Gaiman, Neil, 1960-

Fragile things; short fictions and wonders. William Morrow 2006 xxxi, 360p $26.95 *

Grades: 11 12 Adult   S C
1. Short stories 2. Fantasy fiction 3. Horror fiction
ISBN 978-0-06-051522-5; 0-06-051522-8
LC 2006-48135

In addition to nine selections of poetry, the following short stories are included: A study in emerald; October in the chair; Forbidden brides of the faceless slaves in the secret house of the night of dread desire; The flints of memory lane; Closing time; Bitter grounds; Other people; Keepsakes and treasures; Good boys deserve favors; The facts in the case of the departure of Miss Finch; Strange little girls; Harlequin valentine; The problem of Susan; Instructions; How do you think it feels?; My life; Fifteen painted cards from a vampire tarot; Feeders and eaters; Diseasemaker's group; Goliath; Pages from a journal found in a shoebox left in a Greyhound bus somewhere between Tulsa, Oklahoma, and Louisville, Kentucky; How to talk to girls at parties; Sunbird; The monarch of the glen

This "collection contains approximately twenty previously published pieces of short fiction—stories, verse, and an American Gods novella—plus one new piece written especially for this volume." Publisher's note

"The stories are by turns horrifying and fanciful, often blending the two with a little sex, violence, and humor.

Gaiman, Neil, 1960-—*Continued*

. . . Gaiman skips along the edge of many adolescent fascinations—life, death, the living dead, and the occult—and teens with a taste for the weird will enjoy this book." SLJ

Geektastic; stories from the nerd herd; edited by Holly Black and Cecil Castellucci. Little Brown & Co. 2009 403p il $16.99
Grades: 7 8 9 10   S C
1. Short stories
ISBN 978-0-316-00809-9; 0-316-00809-5
LC 2009-455709

Contents: Once you're a Jedi, you're a Jedi all the way by Holly Black and Cecil Castellucci; One of us by Tracy Lynn; Definitional chaos by Scott Westerfeld; I never by Cassandra Clare; The king of Pelinesse by M. T. Anderson; The wrath of Dawn by Cynthia and Greg Leitich Smith; Quiz bowl antichrist by David Levithan; The quiet knight by Garth Nix; Everyone but you by Lisa Yee; Secret identity by Kelly Link; Freak the geek by John Green; The truth about Dino Girl by Barry Lyga; This is my audition monologue by Sara Zarr; The stars at the finish line by Wendy Mass; It's just a jump to the left by Libba Bray

A collection of twenty-nine short stories about geeks.
"Although not all geekdoms are covered, topics include cosplay (dressing as characters), cons (conventions), SF television and movies, RPGs (roleplaying games), fantasy books, baton-twirling, astronomy, Rocky Horror, quiz bowl, and dinosaurs. Geek-themed comics by Hope Larson and Bryan Lee O'Malley separate the stories. . . . Although readers need not necessarily be geeks to appreciate this well-written collection, it will help. Buy for all the geeks in your library—including the librarian." Voice Youth Advocates

Gotham Writers' Workshop fiction gallery; exceptional short stories selected by New York's acclaimed creative writing school; edited by Thom Didato and Alexander Steele. Bloomsbury, Distributed to the trade by Holtzbrinck Publishers 2004 356p pa $14.95
Grades: 9 10 11 12   S C
1. Short stories
ISBN 1-582-34462-0   LC 2004-5432

Partial contents: Introduction; Starting out. A trifle from life by Anton Chekhov; First confession by Frank O'Connor; Brownies by ZZ Packer; What the river told us to do by Peter Markus; Going for the Orange Julius by Myla Goldberg; Longings. Labors of the heart by Claire Davis; Crazy life by Lou Mathews; Sometimes you talk about Idaho by Pam Houston; After the plague by T.C. Boyle; Those we know. Here we are by Dorothy Parker; Whoever was using this bed by Raymond Carver; For a long time this was Griselda's story by Anthony Doerr; Home sweet home by Hannah Tinti; The job. Orientation by Daniel Orozco; Walking into the wind by John O'Farrell; Night women by Edwidge Danticat; The palace thief by Ethan Canin; Strangeness. The book of sand by Jorge Luis Borges; The next building I plan to bomb by Charles Baxter; The secrets of bats by Jess Row; The third and final continent by Jhumpa Lahiri; Sunset. The swimmer by John Cheever

"Each story is captivating; some are shocking. The selections are great examples of how writers use words to craft great literature." SLJ
Includes bibliographical references

Gothic!; ten original dark tales; edited by Deborah Noyes. Candlewick Press 2004 241p hardcover o.p. pa $7.99 *
Grades: 7 8 9 10   S C
1. Horror fiction 2. Short stories
ISBN 0-7636-2243-5; 0-7636-2737-2 (pa)
LC 2004-45188

Contents: Lungewater by Joan Aiken; Morgan Roehmar's boys by Vivian Vande Velde; Watch and wake by M.T. Anderson; Forbidden brides of the faceless slaves in the nameless house of the night of dread desire by Neil Gaiman; The dead and the moonstruck by Caitlin R. Kiernan; Have no fear, Crumpot is here! by Barry Yourgrau; Stone tower by Janni Lee Simner; The prank by Gregory Maguire; Writing on the wall by Celia Rees; Endings by Garth Nix

This "collection features short stories by noted young adult authors such as M. T. Anderson, Caitlín R. Kiernan, Garth Nix, Celia Rees, Janni Lee Simner, and Barry Yourgrau. . . . These varied tales take place in the distant past and in the high-tech present. Some are humorous while others have surprising twists or are reminiscent of classic fairy tales full of malevolent characters, but all share a love of the surreal or supernatural. . . . A sophisticated, thought-provoking, and gripping read." SLJ

Green, John, 1977-
Let it snow; three holiday romances; by John Green, Maureen Johnson, Lauren Myracle. Speak 2008 352p pa $9.99
Grades: 7 8 9 10   S C
1. Dating (Social customs)—Fiction 2. Christmas—Fiction 3. Short stories
ISBN 978-0-14-241214-5; 0-14-241214-7
LC 2008-25807

Contents: The Jubilee express by Maureen Johnson; A cheertastic Christmas miracle by John Green; The patron saint of pigs by Lauren Myracle

In three intertwining short stories, several high school couples experience the trials and tribulations along with the joys of romance during a Christmas Eve snowstorm in a small town.
"The premises for the stories are funny yet cringingly credible, the writing clever and sure-footed, and the outcomes are all lighthearted and cozily romantic." Bull Cent Child Books

Growing up ethnic in America; contemporary fiction about learning to be American; edited by Maria Mazziotti Gillan and Jennifer Gillan. Penguin Bks. 1999 374p pa $16.95 *
Grades: 9 10 11 12   S C
1. Short stories
ISBN 0-14-028063-4   LC 99-25762

This anthology of 35 stories illustrates the various ways young people of distinct ethnic communities come to terms with their identities, negotiating the differences between their cultures and American society. Among the writers included are Amy Tan, Toni Morrison, Gary Soto, Sherman Alexie, Veronica Chambers, and E. L.

Growing up ethnic in America—*Continued*

Doctorow

"This kind of collection, with its literary quality and multiple perspectives, is the best answer to those who expect only messages with multiculturalism and who sneer 'P.C.' at the mention of diversity." Booklist

Growing up Filipino II; more stories for young adults; collected and edited by Cecilia Manguerra Brainard. PALH 2010 257p $29.95; pa $21.95

Grades: 9 10 11 12   **S C**

1. Filipino Americans—Fiction 2. Philippines—Fiction 3. Short stories

ISBN 978-0-9719458-2-1; 978-0-9719458-3-8 (pa)

Sequel to Growing up Filipino (2003)

"This collection of 27 short stories, . . . reflects the impact of post-9/11 wartime sensibilities among Filipino writers living in the Philippines, the United States, and Canada. Although similar topics of family, memoir, and coming-of-age thread through both collections, the pieces are not grouped by theme, but nevertheless weave a constantly shifting tapestry of Filipino identity. The challenges and conflicts of unique ancestry and struggles for identity provide a rich background for modern urban realism. . . . There is plenty here to stimulate discussion and encourage an appreciation of Filipino writing and culture." SLJ

The Hard SF renaissance; edited by David G. Hartwell and Kathryn Cramer. TOR Bks. 2002 960p hardcover o.p. pa $23.95

Grades: 11 12 Adult   **S C**

1. Science fiction 2. Short stories

ISBN 0-312-87635-1; 0-312-87636-X (pa)

"A Tom Doherty Associates book"

"The 41 stories in this annotated anthology . . . [showcase] short fiction by veteran sf authors like Kim Stanley Robinson, Joe Haldeman, Bruce Sterling, Nancy Kress, Ben Bova and Arthur C. Clarke. . . . For libraries wanting a definitive collection of hard sf written since 1990, this is a priority purchase." Libr J

Hawthorne, Nathaniel, 1804-1864

Tales and sketches, including Twice-told tales, Mosses from an old manse, and The snow-image; A wonder book for girls and boys; Tanglewood tales for girls and boys, being a second Wonder book. Library of Am. 1982 1493p $39.50

Grades: 11 12 Adult   **S C**

1. Short stories

ISBN 0-940450-03-8   LC 81-20760

The stories in this collection have appeared in the five books: Twice-told tales (1837); Mosses from an old manse (1846); The snow-image (1852); A wonder book for girls and boys (1851); Tanglewood tales for girls and boys, being a second wonder book (1853)

Contents: The hollow of the three hills; Sir William Phips; Mrs. Hutchinson; An old woman's tale; Dr. Bullivant; Sights from a steeple; The haunted quack; The wives of the dead; My kinsman, Major Molineux; Roger Malvin's burial; The gentle boy; The seven vagabonds; The Canterbury pilgrims; Sir William Pepperell; Passages from a relinquished work; Mr. Higginbotham's catastro-

phe; The haunted mind; Alice Doane's appeal; The village uncle; Little Annie's ramble; The gray champion; My visit to Niagara; Old news; Young Goodman Brown; Wakefield; The ambitious guest; A rill from the town-pump; The white old maid; The vision of the fountain; The Devil in manuscript; Sketches from memory; The wedding-knell; The may-pole of Merry Mount; The minister's black veil; Old Ticonderoga; A visit to the clerk of the weather; Monsieur du Miroir; Mrs. Bullfrog; Sunday at home; The man of Adamant; David Swan; The great carbuncle; Fancy's show box; The prophetic pictures; Dr. Heidegger's experiment; A bell's biography; Fragments from the journal of a solitary man; Edward Fane's rosebud; The toll-gatherer's day; Sylph Etherege; Peter Goldwaite's treasure; Endicott and the Red Cross; Night sketches; The Shaker bridal; Foot-prints on the seashore; Thomas Green Fessenden; Time's portraiture; Snow-flakes; The threefold destiny; Jonathan Cilley; Chippings with a chisel; Legends of the Province-House; The sister years; The lily's quest; John Inglefield's Thanksgiving; A virtuoso's collection; The old apple-dealer; The antique ring; The hall of fantasy; The new Adam and Eve; The birthmark; Egotism; or, The bosom-serpent; The procession of life; The celestial railroad; Buds and bird-voices; Little Daffydowndilly; Fire-worship; The Christmas banquet; A good man's miracles; The intelligence office; Earth's holocaust; The artist of the beautiful; Drowne's wooden image; A select party; A book of autographs; Rappaccini's daughter; P.'s correspondence; Main-street; Ethan Brand; The great stone face; The snow-image; Feathertop; The Gorgon's head; The Golden touch; The paradise of children; The three golden apples; The miraculous pitcher; The Chimaera; The Minotaur; The Pygmies; The dragon's teeth; Circe's palace; The pomegranate-seeds; The golden fleece

This volume contains all of Hawthorne's tales and sketches, which are arranged in order of their periodical publication

Hemingway, Ernest, 1899-1961

The complete short stories of Ernest Hemingway; the Finca Vigía edition. Scribner 1987 650p pa $20 hardcover o.p. *

Grades: 11 12 Adult   **S C**

1. Short stories

ISBN 0-684-84332-3   LC 87-12888

Contents: The short happy life of Francis Macomber; The capital of the world; The snows of Kilimanjaro; Old man at the bridge; Up in Michigan; On the quai at Smyrna; Indian camp; The doctor and the doctor's wife; The end of something; The three-day blow; The battler; A very short story; Soldier's home; The revolutionist; Mr. and Mrs. Elliot; Cat in the rain; Out of season; Cross-country snow; My old man; Big two-hearted river: part I; Big two-hearted river: part II; The undefeated; In another country; Hills like white elephants; The killers; Che ti dice la patria?; Fifty grand; A simple enquiry; Ten Indians; A canary for one; An Alpine idyll; A pursuit race; Today is Friday; Banal story; Now I lay me; After the storm; A clean, well-lighted place; The light of the world; God rest you merry, gentlemen; The sea change; A way you'll never be; The mother of a queen; One reader writes; Homage to Switzerland; A day's wait; A natural history of the dead; Wine of Wyoming; The gambler, the nun, and the radio; Fathers and sons; One trip across; The tradesman's return; The denunciation; The

Hemingway, Ernest, 1899-1961—*Continued*
butterfly and the tank; Night before battle; Under the
ridge; Nobody ever dies; The good lion; The faithful
bull; Get a seeing-eyed dog; A man of the world; Summer people; The last good country; An African story; A
train trip; The porter; Black ass at the cross roads; Landscape with figures; I guess everything reminds you of
something; Great news from the mainland

"To the 49 standard *Short stories of Ernest Hemingway*, this edition adds 14 from other books or magazines
and seven never published before. . . . For all the repetition of previous collections and possible incompleteness
despite the title, this volume is pure Hemingway in his
most consistently satisfying format and, as such, belongs
in most libraries." Booklist

Henry, O., 1862-1910
The best short stories of O. Henry; selected and
with an introduction by Bennett A. Cerf, and Van
H. Cartmell. Modern Lib. 1994 c1945 340p $22.95
*

Grades: 11 12 Adult   S C
1. Short stories
ISBN 0-679-60122-8
First Modern Library edition published 1945

Contents: The gift of the Magi; A cosmopolite in a
café; Man about the town; The cop and the anthem; The
love-philtre of Ikey Schoenstein; Mammon and the archer; Springtime à la carte; From the cabby's seat; An
unfinished story; The romance of a busy broker; The furnished room; Roads of destiny; The enchanted profile;
The passing of Black Eagle; A retrieved reformation;
The Renaissance at Charleroi; Shoes; Ships; The hiding
of Black Bill; The duplicity of Hargraves; The ransom of
Red Chief; The marry month of May; The whirligig of
life; A blackjack bargainer; A lickpenny lover; The defeat of the city; Squaring the circle; Transients in Arcadia; The trimmed lamp; The pendulum; Two Thanksgiving Day gentlemen; The making of a New Yorker; The
lost blend; A Harlem tragedy; A midsummer knight's
dream; The last leaf; The count and the wedding guest;
A municipal report

O. Henry "is best known for his observations on the
diverse lives of everyday New Yorkers, 'the four million' neglected by other writers. He had a fine gift of humor and was adept at the ingenious depiction of ironic
circumstances, in plots frequently dependent upon coincidence." Oxford Companion to Am Lit. 6th edition

Hesse, Hermann, 1877-1962
The fairy tales of Hermann Hesse; translated
and with an introduction by Jack Zipes; woodcut
illustrations by David Frampton. Bantam Bks.
1995 xxxi, 266p il pa $14.95 hardcover o.p.

Grades: 11 12 Adult   S C
1. Fairy tales 2. Short stories
ISBN 0-553-37776-0 (pa)   LC 94-49166

Contents: The dwarf; Shadow play; A man by the
name of Ziegler; The city; Dr. Knoegle's end; The beautiful dream; The three linden trees; Augustus; The poet;
Flute dream; A dream about the gods; Strange news from
another planet; Faldum; A dream sequence; The forest
dweller; The difficult path; If the war continues; The European; The empire; The painter; The fairy tale about the
wicker chair; Iris

"Quirky and evocative, Hesse's fairy tales stand alone,
but also amplify the ideas and utopian longings of such
counterculture avatars as *Siddhartha* and *Steppenwolf*."
Publ Wkly

Horowitz, Anthony, 1955-
Bloody Horowitz. Philomel Books 2010 330p
$12.99

Grades: 7 8 9 10   S C
1. Horror fiction 2. Short stories
ISBN 978-0-399-25451-2; 0-399-25451-X
            LC 2009-44748

Contents: Why horror has no place in children's
books; The man who killed Darren Shan; Bet your life;
You have arrived; The cobra; Robo-Nanny; Bad dream;
My bloody French exchange; Are you sitting comfortably?; Plugged in; Power; Seven cuts

"These 12 stories are not for the squeamish as they include shudder-inducing scenes of burning flesh, dismembered bodies, electrocution, and death by squeezing in a
massage chair. . . . Teens looking for gruesome tales
won't be disappointed." SLJ

How beautiful the ordinary; twelve stories of
identity; edited by Michael Cart. HarperTeen
2009 350p il $16.99

Grades: 9 10 11 12   S C
1. Sex role—Fiction 2. Homosexuality—Fiction
3. Love—Fiction 4. Short stories
ISBN 978-0-06-115498-0; 0-06-115498-9
            LC 2008-51769

"The Bowen Press"

Contents: A world from the nearly distant past by David Levithan; Happily ever after by Eric Shanower; My
life as a dog by Ron Koertge; Trev by Jacqueline
Woodson; My virtual world by Francesca Lia Block; A
dark red love-knot by Margo Lanagan; Fingernail by
William Sleator; San Francisco Dyke March by Ariel
Schrag; The missing person by Jennifer Finney Boylan;
First time by Julie Anne Peters; Dear Lang by Emma
Donoghue; The Silk Road runs through Tupperneck,
N.H. by Gregory Maguire

Presents twelve stories by young adult authors, some
presented in graphic or letter format, which explore
themes of gender identity, love, and sexuality.

"This collection's refreshing perspective—that gay,
lesbian, and transgendered lives simply are, as Cart states
in the introduction, 'as wonderfully various, diverse, and
gloriously complex as any other lives,' distinguishes it.
Twelve acclaimed authors contribute stories ranging from
sweet and nostalgic to lyrical and desperate, capturing
the blissful/painful process of self-discovery. . . . This
collection, with some detailed sexual descriptions, is sure
to find its intended teen audience." SLJ

Hughes, Langston, 1902-1967
Short stories of Langston Hughes; edited by
Akiba Sullivan Harper; with an introduction by
Arnold Rampersad. Hill & Wang 1996 299p pa
$16 hardcover o.p. *

Grades: 11 12 Adult   S C
1. African Americans—Fiction 2. Short stories
ISBN 0-8090-1603-6   LC 95-19554

Hughes, Langston, 1902-1967—*Continued*

Contents: Bodies in the moonlight; The young glory of him; The little virgin; Luani of the jungles; Slave on the block; Cora unashamed; The blues I'm playing; Why, you reckon?; Little old spy; Spanish blood; On the road; Gumption; Professor; Big meeting; Trouble with the angels; Tragedy at the baths; Slice him down; African morning; 'Tain't so; One Friday morning; Heaven to hell; Breakfast in Virginia; Saratoga rain; Who's passing for who?; On the way home; Name in the papers; Sailor ashore; Something in common; Mysterious Madame Shaghai; Never room with a couple; Powder-white faces; Pushcart man; Rouge high; Patron of the arts; Thank you, m'am'; Sorrow for a midget; Blessed assurance; Early autumn; Fine accommodations; The gun; His last affair; No place to make love; Rock, church; Mary Winosky; Those who have no turkey; Seventy-five dollars; The childhood of Jimmy

"Dating from 1919 to 1963, these pieces vary in theme, covering life at sea, the trials and tribulations of a young pianist and her elderly white patron, a visiting writer's experience in Cuba, a young girl's winning an art scholarship but losing it when it's learned she is black, and an ambitious black preacher trying to gain fame by being nailed to a cross. If you crave good reading don't pass up this gem." Libr J

Hurston, Zora Neale, 1891-1960

The complete stories; introduction by Henry Louis Gates, Jr. and Sieglinde Lemke. HarperCollins Pubs. 1995 xxiii, 305p hardcover o.p. pa $14.99 *

Grades: 11 12 Adult   S C

1. African Americans—Fiction 2. Short stories
ISBN 0-06-016732-7; 0-06-135018-4 (pa)
LC 91-50438

Contents: John Redding goes to sea; Drenched in light; Spunk; Magnolia Flower; Muttsy; 'Possum or pig?; The Eatonville anthology; Sweat; The gilded six-bits; Mother Catherine; Uncle Monday; The fire and the cloud; Cock Robin Beale Street; Story in Harlem slang; High John de Conquer; Hurricane; The conscience of the court; Escape from Pharaoh; The tablets of the law; Black death; The bone of contention; Book of Harlem; Harlem slanguage; Now you cookin' with gas; The seventh veil; The woman in Gaul

This collection of Hurston's short fiction contains nineteen stories originally published between 1921 and 1951, arranged in the order in which they were published, and seven previously unpublished stories.

Includes bibliographical references

The **improbable** adventures of Sherlock Holmes; edited by John Joseph Adams; with assistance provided by David Barr Kirtley. Night Shade Books 2009 454p $15.95

Grades: 9 10 11 12 Adult   S C

1. Holmes, Sherlock (Fictional character) 2. Great Britain—Fiction 3. Mystery fiction 4. Short stories
ISBN 978-1-59780-160-7

Contents: A Sherlockiana primer by Christopher Roden; The doctor's case by Stephen King; The horror of the many faces by Tim Lebbon; The case of the bloodless sock by Anne Perry; The adventure of the other detective by Bradley H. Sinor; A scandal in Montreal by Edward D. Hoch; The adventure of the field theorems by Vonda N. McIntyre; The adventure of the death-fetch by Darrell Schweitzer; The shocking affair of the Dutch Steamship Friesland by Mary Robinette Kowal; The adventure of the mummy's curse by H. Paul Jeffers; The things that shall come upon them by Barbara Roden; Murder to music by Anthony Burgess; The adventure of the inertial adjustor by Stephen Baxter; Mrs. Hudson's case by Laurie R. King; The singular habits of wasps by Geoffrey A. Landis; The affair of the 46th birthday by Amy Myers; The Specter of Tullyfane Abbey by Peter Tremayne; The vale of the white horse by Sharyn McCrumb; The adventure of the Dorset Street lodger by Michael Moorcock; The adventure of the lost world by Dominic Green; The adventure of the antiquarian's niece by Barbara Hambly; Dynamics of a hanging by Tony Pi; Merridew of abominable memory by Chris Roberson; Commonplaces by Naomi Novik; The adventure of the Pirates of Devil's Cape by Rob Rogers; The adventure of the Green Skull by Mark Valentine; The human mystery by Tanith Lee; A study in emerald by Neil Gaiman; You see but you do not observe by Robert J. Sawyer

The editor's "goal was to highlight the best Sherlock Holmes stories of the last 30 years, emphasizing those that feature the fantastic. . . . This is a substantial collection that will entertain teen fans for hours, and may well seduce them to seek out the original." SLJ

Irving, Washington, 1783-1859

Bracebridge Hall; Tales of a traveller; The Alhambra. Library of Am. 1991 1104p $35

Grades: 11 12 Adult   S C

1. Short stories
ISBN 0-940450-59-3   LC 90-62267

This volume contains three collections of stories and sketches: Bracebridge Hall (1822); Tales of a traveller (1824); and The Alhambra (1832)

Jackson, Shirley, 1919-1965

The lottery; or, The adventures of James Harris. Farrar, Straus & Giroux 1949 306p pa $14 hardcover o.p. *

Grades: 11 12 Adult   S C

1. Short stories
ISBN 0-374-52953-1

Contents: The intoxicated; The daemon lover; Like mother used to make; Trial by combat; The villager; My life with R. H. Macy; The witch; The renegade; After you, my dear Alphonse; Charles; Afternoon in linen; Flower garden; Dorothy and my grandmother and the sailors; Colloquy; Elizabeth; A fine old firm; The dummy; Seven types of ambiguity; Come dance with me in Ireland; Of course; Pillar of salt; Men with their big shoes; The tooth; Got a letter from Jimmy; The lottery

The stories "in this collection seem to fall into three groups. There are the slight sketches, like genre paintings, dealing with episodes which are trivial in terms of plot but which by means of [the author's] precise, sensitive, and sharply focused style become luminous with meaning. . . . The second group comprises her social-problem sketches. . . . Her final group deals with fantasy, ranging from humorous whimsey to horrifying shock." Saturday Rev Lit

Joyce, James, 1882-1941
Dubliners. Knopf 1991 lxvii, 287p $19 *
Grades: 11 12 Adult   **S C**
1. Ireland—Fiction 2. Short stories
ISBN 0-679-40574-7   LC 91-53001
First published 1914 in the United Kingdom; first
United States edition published 1916 by Huebsch
Contents: The sisters; An encounter; Araby; Eveline;
After the race; Two gallants; The boarding house; A lit-
tle cloud; Counterparts; Clay; A painful case; Ivy day in
the committee room; A mother; Grace; The dead
"This collection of 15 stories provides an introduction
to the style and motifs found in Joyce's writing. The stories stand alone as individual scenes of Dublin society
and are intertwined by the use of autobiography and
symbolism." Shapiro. Fic for Youth. 3d edition

Kafka, Franz, 1883-1924
The metamorphosis and other stories; translated
by Joachim Neugroschel. Scribner 1993 xxiii, 227p
hardcover o.p. pa $13 *
Grades: 11 12 Adult   **S C**
1. Short stories
ISBN 0-684-19426-0; 0-684-80070-5 (pa)
                       LC 92-43912
Also available in paperback from Schocken Bks.
The longer stories included are: Conversation with the
worshiper; Conversation with the drunk; Children on the
highway; Exposing a city slicker; The businessman; Unhappiness; The judgment; The stoker; The metamorphosis; An ancient manuscript; Jackals and Arabs; A fratri-
cide; A dream; A report for an Academy
This is a collection of thirty stories, some of which
are quite short. The stories are arranged in order of their
original publication dates.

King, Stephen, 1947-
Everything's eventual: 14 dark tales. Scribner
2002 459p $28
Grades: 11 12 Adult   **S C**
1. Horror fiction 2. Short stories
ISBN 0-7432-3515-0   LC 2002-17738
Contents: Autopsy room four; The man in the black
suit; All that you love will be carried away; The death
of Jack Hamilton; In the deathroom; The Little Sisters of
Eluria; Everything's eventual; L.T.'s theory of pets; The
road virus heads north; Lunch at the Gotham Café; That
feeling, you can only say what it is in French; 1408;
Riding the Bullet; Luckey quarter
"Fourteen stories, most of them gems, featuring an ar-
ray of literary approaches, plus an opinionated intro from
King about the '(Almost) Lost Art' of the short story."
Publ Wkly

Four past midnight. Viking 1990 763p pa $7.99
hardcover o.p.
Grades: 11 12 Adult   **S C**
1. Horror fiction 2. Short stories
ISBN 0-451-17038-5 (pa)   LC 90-50046
This volume contains four novellas: The Langoliers;
Secret window, secret garden; The library policeman;
The sun dog.
This book "is hard to put down, truly chilling, and
sure to be enjoyed by YA horror afficionados every-
where." SLJ

Night shift. Doubleday 1978 xxii, 336p
hardcover o.p. pa $7.99
Grades: 11 12 Adult   **S C**
1. Horror fiction 2. Short stories
ISBN 0-385-12991-2; 0-307-74364-0 (pa)
                       LC 77-75146
Also available in paperback from Signet Bks.
Contents: Jerusalem's Lot; Graveyard shift; Night surf;
I am the doorway; The mangler; The boogeyman; Gray
matter; Battleground; Trucks; Sometimes they come
back; Strawberry spring; The ledge; The lawnmower
man; Quitters, Inc.; I know what you need; Children of
the corn; The last rung of the ladder; The man who
loved flowers; One for the road; The woman in the room
The stories "all begin in our normal world, where everything is safe and warm. But in almost every instance,
something slips, and we find ourselves in the nightmare
world of the not-quite real. . . . Such stories require a
willing suspension of disbelief, of course, but they also
require an author who is an expert manipulator. . . .
King is an expert." Best Sellers

Skeleton crew. Putnam 1985 512p pa $7.99
hardcover o.p. *
Grades: 11 12 Adult   **S C**
1. Horror fiction 2. Short stories
ISBN 0-451-16861-5 (pa)   LC 84-15947
Contents: The mist; Here there be tygers; The monkey; Cain rose up; Mrs. Todd's shortcut; The jaunt; The
wedding gig; Paranoid: A chant; The raft; Word processor of the gods; The man who would not shake hands;
Beachworld; The reaper's image; Nona; For Owen; Survivor type; Uncle Otto's truck; Morning deliveries (Milk-
man #1); Big wheels: a tale of the laundry game (Milk-
man #2); Gramma; The ballad of the flexible bullet; The
reach
This "collection of King's shorter work is a hefty
sampler from all stages of his career, and demonstrates
the range of his abilities. . . . There are several stories
here that must rank among King's best." Publ Wkly

Kinsella, W. P.
Shoeless Joe Jackson comes to Iowa: stories.
Southern Methodist Univ. Press 1993 141p il
hardcover o.p. pa $8.89
Grades: 11 12 Adult   **S C**
1. Baseball—Fiction 2. Short stories
ISBN 0-87074-355-4; 0-87074-356-2 (pa)
                       LC 93-3935
First published 1980 in Canada
Contents: Fiona the first; A quite incredible dance;
Shoeless Joe Jackson comes to Iowa; Waiting for the
call; Sister Ann of the Cornfields; The Grecian Urn;
Mankiewitz won't be bowling Tuesday nights anymore;
A picture of the virgin; The blacksmith shop caper; First
names and empty pockets
"The title story contains the germ of Kinsella's novel
Shoeless Joe; not as deep and rich as the longer work,
it remains pure and perfect in itself. Among the other
gems: 'Fiona the First,' a portrait of a man doomed to
spend eternity picking up girls at airports, 'First Names
and Empty Pockets,' in which a doll-mender saves the
broken Janis Joplin; and 'The Grecian Urn,' a tale of
people traveling in time by becoming part of works of

Kinsella, W. P.—*Continued*
art. Few writers can match Kinsella's ability to establish tone, character, and a complete reality in just a few paragraphs, then sweep the reader into his imagined world." Libr J

Kipling, Rudyard, 1865-1936
Collected stories; selected and introduced by Robert Gottlieb. Knopf 1994 xxxvii, 911p $25
Grades: 11 12 Adult   S C
1. Short stories
ISBN 0-679-43592-1   LC 94-5854
"Everyman's library"
Contents: In the house of Suddhoo; Beyond the pale; A bank fraud; Pig; On Greenhow Hill; "Love-o'-women"; The drums of the fore and aft; Dray wara yow dee; "The City of Dreadful Night"; Without benefit of clergy; The head of the district; Jews in Shushan; The man who would be king; "The finest story in the world"; The mark of the beast; The strange ride of Morrowbie Jukes; The disturber of traffic; Mrs. Hauksbee sits out {play}; A wayside comedy; Baa baa, black sheep; The bridge-builders; The maltese cat; "In ambush"; A sahibs' war; "Wireless"; Mrs. Bathurst; "Swept and garnished"; Mary Postgate; "Dymchurch flit"; With the night mail; The house surgeon; The wish house; The Janeites; The bull that thought; A madonna of the trenches; The eye of Allah; The gardener; Dayspring mishandled; The church that was at Antioch; The manner of men
"There is an enormous range of subject matter, genre, styles, and tones in Kipling's prose work. . . . [He] is undoubtedly one of the great short-story writers in English and the subtlety of his early narrative technique has led some to claim him as a proto-Modernist." Oxford Companion to 20th Cent Lit in Engl
Includes bibliographical references

Kiss me deadly; 13 tales of paranormal love; edited by Trisha Telep. RP Teens 2010 430p pa $9.95
Grades: 7 8 9 10   S C
1. Supernatural—Fiction 2. Love stories 3. Short stories
ISBN 978-0-7624-3949-2; 0-7624-3949-1
                                    LC 2010-926067
Contents: The assassin's apprentice by Michelle Zink; Errant by Diana Peterfreund; The spirit jar by Karen Mahoney; Lost by Justine Musk; The spy who never grew up by Sarah Rees Brennan; Dungeons of Langeais by Becca Fitzpatrick; Behind the red door by Caitlin Kittredge; Hare moon by Carrie Ryan; Familiar by Michelle Rowen; Fearless by Rachel Vincent; Vermillion by Daniel Marks; The hounds of Ulster by Maggie Stiefvater; Many happy returns by Daniel Waters
A collection of short stories combining dark seduction and modern romance presents a variety of tales featuring the romantic lives of humans and werewolves, ghosts, fallen angels, zombies, and shape-shifters.
The stories "have varying lengths and tones, representing an impressive range of writing styles; it is likely that any fantasy reader will find at least one memorable story that speaks directly to his or her preferences." Bull Cent Child Books

Lanagan, Margo, 1960-
Black juice. Eos 2005 201p $15.99; pa $5.99
Grades: 7 8 9 10   S C
1. Short stories
ISBN 0-06-074390-5; 0-06-074392-1 (pa)
                                    LC 2004-8715
Contents: Singing my sister down; My lord's man; Red nose day; Sweet Pippit; House of the many; Wooden bride; Earthly uses; Perpetual light; Yowlinin; Rite of spring
Provides glimpses of the dark side of civilization and the beauty of the human spirit through ten short stories that explore significant moments in people's lives, events leading to them, and their consequences.
"This book will satisfy readers hungry for intelligent, literary fantasies that effectively twist facets of our everyday world into something alien." SLJ

Red spikes. Alfred A. Knopf 2007 167p $16.99
Grades: 10 11 12   S C
1. Short stories
ISBN 978-0-375-84320-4; 0-375-84320-5
                                    LC 2007-04805
First published 2006 in Australia
Contents: Baby Jane; Monkey's paternoster; A good heart; Winkie; A feather in the breast of God; Hero Vale; Under hell, over heaven; Mouse maker; Forever upward; Daughter of the clay
The author "presents 10 . . . tales of life, death, love, and the supernatural." SLJ
"This razor-sharp assemblage thrusts readers . . . into alien, hermetic environments and uncompromisingly idiomatic points of view. . . . Along with the patience required to acclimate to each story's fresh setup, the sophisticated slant of the collection makes the book most appropriate for the broadest, most mature readers—the monkey drama, for instance, includes upsetting scenes of animal-world rape, and several stories deal with childbirth and motherhood in a way rarely seen in books for teen readers." Booklist

Le Guin, Ursula K., 1929-
Tales from Earthsea. Ace Books 2002 314p pa $13.95
Grades: 11 12 Adult   S C
1. Fantasy fiction 2. Short stories
ISBN 0-441-00932-8   LC 2001-56673
First published 2001 by Harcourt
Contents: The finder; Darkrose and Diamond; The bones of the earth; On the high marsh; Dragonfly; A description of Earthsea
Five fantasy tales set on the archipelago of Earthsea with an essay on the people, languages, history and magic of the place.
"Inhabited by people no better or worse than ourselves, Earthsea is dominated by the practice of magic as precise as any science and as unpredictable in its social consequences. Since it is based entirely on language, Earthsea's magic serves as a metaphor for the writer's own sorcery. Yet despite Le Guin's strong bias toward the didactic there is no hint of by-the-numbers allegory here." N Y Times Book Rev

Legends: short novels by the masters of modern fantasy; edited by Robert Silverberg. TOR Bks. 1998 715p il hardcover o.p. pa $17.95

Grades: 11 12 Adult   S C

1. Fantasy fiction 2. Short stories

ISBN 0-312-86787-5; 0-7653-0035-4 (pa)

LC 98-23593

Seven of the short novels included in this collection also issued in paperback with designations Legends v2 and Legends v3

"A Tom Doherty Associates book"

Contents: The little sisters of Eluria, by S. King; The sea and little fishes, by T. Pratchett; Debt of bones, by T. Goodkind; Grinning man, by O. S. Card; The seventh shrine, by R. Silverberg; Dragonfly, by U. K. Le Guin; The burning man, by T. Williams; The hedge knight, by George R. R. Martin; Runner of Pern, by A. McCaffrey; The woodboy, by R. E. Feist; New spring, by R. Jordan

"What is so noteworthy about this collection is the fact that all the selections are first rate and are well integrated into their universes." Booklist

Levithan, David, 1972-

How they met, and other stories. Alfred A. Knopf 2008 244p $16.99; lib bdg $19.99

Grades: 7 8 9 10   S C

1. Love stories 2. Short stories

ISBN 978-0-375-84886-5; 978-0-375-94886-2 (lib bdg)   LC 2007-10586

Contents: Starbucks boy; Miss Lucy had a steamboat; The alumni interview; The good witch; The escalator, a love story; The number of people who meet on airplanes; Andrew Chang; Flirting with waiters; Lost sometimes; Princes; Breaking and entering; Skipping the prom; A romantic inclination; What a song can do; Without saying; How they met; Memory dance; Intersection

A collection of eighteen stories describing the surprises, sacrifices, doubts, pain, and joy of falling in love.

"The author is a master of texture and detail. . . . Each richly imagined story will tap familiar veins of longing, memory, and anticipation." Bull Cent Child Books

Link, Kelly

Pretty monsters; stories; decorations by Shaun Tan. Viking 2008 389p il $19.99; pa $9.99 *

Grades: 7 8 9 10   S C

1. Fantasy fiction 2. Science fiction 3. Horror fiction 4. Short stories

ISBN 978-0-670-01090-5; 0-670-01090-1; 978-0-14-241672-3 (pa); 0-14-241672-X (pa)

LC 2008-33251

Contents: The wrong grave; The wizards of Perfil; Magic for beginners; The faery handbag; The specialist's hat; Monster; The surfer; The constable of Abal; Pretty monsters

"Readers as yet unfamiliar with Link . . . will be excited to discover her singular voice in this collection of nine short stories, her first book for young adults. . . . [Subjects] range from absurd to mundane, all observed with equidistant irony. . . . The author mingles the grotesque and the ethereal to make magic on the page." Publ Wkly

The **Locus** awards; thirty years of the best in science fiction and fantasy; edited by Charles N. Brown and Jonathan Strahan. Eos 2004 512p pa $15.95 *

Grades: 9 10 11 12   S C

1. Science fiction 2. Fantasy fiction 3. Short stories

ISBN 0-06-059426-8   LC 2004-42054

Contents: The 1970s: The death of Doctor Island by Gene Wolfe; The day before the revolution by Ursula K. Le Guin; Jeffty is five by Harlan Ellison; The persistence of vision by John Varley; The 1980s: The way of cross and dragon by George R.R. Martin; Souls by Joanna Russ; Bloodchild by Octavia E. Butler; The only neat thing to do by James Tiptree Jr.; Rachel in love by Pat Murphy; The scalehunter's beautiful daughter by Lucius Shepard; The 1990s: Bears discover fire by Terry Bisson; Buffalo by John Kessel; Even the queen by Connie Willis; Gone by John Crowley; Maneki Neko by Bruce Sterling; The 2000s: Border guards; Greg Egan; Hell is the absence of God by Ted Chiang; October in the chair by Neil Gaiman; Previous winners

"Whether readers are catching up on legendary science fiction and fantasy, becoming reacquainted with old favorites, or grazing the field in hopes of discovering new ones, this anthology delivers some of the finest science fiction and fantasy ever written." SLJ

Love is hell; [by] Melissa Marr . . . [et al.] HarperTeen 2008 263p $16.99; pa $9.99

Grades: 7 8 9 10   S C

1. Love stories 2. Supernatural—Fiction 3. Short stories

ISBN 978-0-06-144305-3; 0-06-144305-0; 978-0-06-144304-6 (pa); 0-06-144304-2 (pa)

LC 2007-49574

Contents: Sleeping with the spirit by Laurie Stolarz; Stupid perfect world by Scott Westerfeld; Lammas day by Justine Larbalestier; Fan fictions by Gabrielle Zevin; Love struck by Melissa Marr

"Supernatural romance is the well-chosen theme of five original stories by as many authors. . . . There's enough variety to round out the central theme, and consistently supple storytelling will lure readers through all five entries." Publ Wkly

Make me over; 11 stories of transformation; edited by Marilyn Singer. Dutton Children's Books 2005 199p $17.99

Grades: 7 8 9 10   S C

1. Short stories

ISBN 0-525-47480-3   LC 2005-02109

Contents: Some people call me Maurice by Joyce Sweeney; Not much to it by René Saldaña, Jr.; Bedhead red, peekaboo pink by Marilyn Singer; Vision quest by Peni R. Griffin; Wabi's ears by Joseph Bruchac; Honestly, truthfully by Terry Trueman; The resurrection by Jess Mowry; Bazooka Joe and the chaos kid by Norma Howe; The plan by Marina Budhos; Lucky six by Evelyn Coleman; Butterflies by Margaret Peterson Haddix

These stories "delve into our culture's fascination with beauty and present different views about all kinds of makeovers." Publisher's note

"Sweet and spicy, tough and raw, these well-written stories will make a lasting impression on readers." Booklist

Malamud, Bernard, 1914-1986
The complete stories; introduction by Robert Giroux. Farrar, Straus & Giroux 1997 634p hardcover o.p. pa $18 *

Grades: 11 12 Adult   **S C**
1. Short stories
ISBN 0-374-12639-9; 0-374-52575-7 (pa)

LC 97-12394

Contents: Armistice; Spring rain; The grocery store; Benefit performance; The place is different now; Steady customer; The literary life of Laban Goldman; The cost of living; The prison; The first seven years; The death of me; The bill; The loan; A confession of murder; Riding pants; The girl of my dreams; The magic barrel; The mourners; Angel Levine; A summer's reading; Take pity; The elevator; An apology; The last Mohican; The lady of the lake; Behold the key; The maid's shoes; Idiots first; Still life; Suppose a wedding; Life is better than death; The Jewbird; Black is my favorite color; Naked nude; The German refugee; A choice of profession; A pimp's revenge; Man in the drawer; My son the murderer; Pictures of the artist; An exorcism; Glass blower of Venice; God's wrath; Talking horse; The letter; The silver crown; Notes from a lady at a dinner party; In retirement; Rembrandt's hat; A wig; The model; A lost grave; Zora's noise; In Kew Gardens; Alma redeemed

"Whether, stark, comic or fanciful, Malamud's stories give us immigrant Jews and their descendants pondering moral questions and experiencing moments of magical intervention while enduring life's ridiculous situations. Yet the stories transcend their ethnic settings and achieve a universal resonance." Publ Wkly

Marston, Elsa
Santa Claus in Baghdad and other stories about teens in the Arab world. Indiana University Press 2008 198p pa $15.95 *

Grades: 6 7 8 9 10   **S C**
1. Middle East—Fiction 2. Arab countries—Fiction 3. Short stories
ISBN 978-0-253-22004-2; 0-253-22004-1

LC 2007-50768

Includes notes which place the stories in context

Contents: Santa Claus in Baghdad: a story from Iraq (2000); Faces: a story from Syria; The hand of Fatima: a story from Lebanon; The olive grove: a story from Palestine; In line: a story from Egypt; Scenes in a Roman theater: a story from Tunisia; Honor: a story from Jordan; The plan: a story from a Palestinian refugee camp in Lebanon

A collection of eight stories, most previously published in other anthologies, about what it is like to grow up in the Middle East today.

"Marston, who has lived and visited the countries of which she writes, offers a realistic portrait of the Middle East that mixes possiblity and bleakness in equal measure." Voice Youth Advocates

Matheson, Richard, 1926-
I am legend. Tom Doherty Associates 2007 317p pa $14.95

Grades: 10 11 12 Adult   **S C**
1. Vampires—Fiction 2. Horror fiction
ISBN 0-7653-1874-1; 978-0-7653-1874-9
"A Tor book"

First published 1954

Contents: I am legend; Buried talents; The near departed; Prey; Witch war; Dance of the dead; Dress of white silk; Mad house; The funeral; From shadowed places; Person to person

A pandemic devastates the human population, turning its victims into vampires. Robert Neville, the only man who escapes from the disease, must try to survive in a world in which he is now considered the monster.

Maugham, W. Somerset (William Somerset), 1874-1965
Collected short stories. Penguin Bks. 1992-1993 4v v1 & v3 pa $13.95; v2 pa $15; v4 pa $14.95

Grades: 9 10 11 12   **S C**
1. Short stories
ISBN 0-14-018589-5 (v1); 0-14-018590-9 (v2); 0-14-018591-7 (v3); 0-14-018592-5 (v4)

First published 1963 in the United Kingdom

"Two qualities of Maugham as a writer brought him mastery of the short story: an economical and exact means of fixing the sense of place, often exotic places; and an equally economical skill in realizing the crisis of a story." Penguin Companion to Engl Lit

McKillip, Patricia A., 1948-
Harrowing the dragon. Ace Books 2005 310p hardcover o.p. pa $14

Grades: 9 10 11 12   **S C**
1. Fantasy fiction 2. Short stories
ISBN 0-441-01360-0; 0-441-01443-7 (pa)

LC 2005-51311

Contents: The harrowing of the dragon of Hoarsbreath; A matter of music; A troll and two roses; Baba Yaga and the sorcerer's son; The fellowship of the dragon; Lady of the skulls; The snow queen; Ash, wood, fire; The stranger; Transmutations; The lion and the lark; The witches of Junket; Star-crossed; Voyage into the heart; Toad

"This collection of 13 stories by one of fantasy's most elegant and luminescent writers brings together 25 years of short fiction into one lyrical volume." Libr J

McKinley, Robin
Fire: tales of elemental spirits; [by] Robin McKinley and Peter Dickinson. G. P. Putnam's Sons 2009 297p $19.99

Grades: 7 8 9 10   **S C**
1. Mythical animals—Fiction 2. Fire—Fiction 3. Short stories
ISBN 978-0-399-25289-1; 0-399-25289-4

LC 2009-4730

Contents: Phoenix by Peter Dickinson; Hellhound by Robin McKinley; Fireworm by Peter Dickinson; Salamander man by Peter Dickinson; First flight by Robin McKinley

"The settings of these five tales range from ancient to modern, but they are all united by encounters with magical creatures with an affinity for fire. . . . This collection of beautifully crafted tales will find a warm welcome from fans of either author, as well as from fantasy readers in general." SLJ

McKinley, Robin—*Continued*

Water: tales of elemental spirits; [by] Robin McKinley, Peter Dickinson. Putnam 2002 266p $18.99; pa $6.99

Grades: 7 8 9 10   **S C**

1. Fantasy fiction 2. Mermaids and mermen—Fiction 3. Short stories

ISBN 0-399-23796-8; 0-14-240244-3 (pa)

LC 2001-41642

Contents: Mermaid song by Peter Dickinson; The sea-king's son by Robin McKinley; Sea serpent by Peter Dickinson; Water horse by Robin McKinley; Kraken by Peter Dickinson; A pool in the desert by Robin McKinley

"These six stories, three by McKinley and three by her husband, Dickinson, feature the elemental spirits that inhabit Earth's waters." Voice Youth Advocates

"The masterfully written stories all feature distinct, richly detailed casts and settings . . . and focus as strongly on action as on character. There's plenty here to excite, enthrall, and move even the pickiest readers." SLJ

Michener, James A., 1907-1997

Tales of the South Pacific. Ballantine Books 1984 384p pa $7.99

Grades: 11 12 Adult   **S C**

1. World War, 1939-1945—Fiction 2. Short stories

ISBN 0-449-20652-1

First published 1947 by Macmillan

Contents: The South Pacific; Coral sea; Mutiny; An officer and a gentleman; The cave; The milk run; Alligator; Our heroine; Dry rot; Fo'Dolla'; Passion; A boar's tooth; Wine for the mess at Segi; The airstrip at Konora; Those who fraternize; The strike; Frisco; The landing on Kuralei; A cemetery at Hoga Point

These 19 tales describe "the strain and the boredom, the careful planning and heroic action, the color and beauty of the islands, and all that made up life during the critical days of the war in the Pacific." Wis Libr Bull

Moccasin thunder; American Indians stories for today; edited by Lori Marie Carlson. HarperCollins 2005 156p $15.99 *

Grades: 7 8 9 10   **S C**

1. Native Americans—Fiction 2. Short stories

ISBN 0-06-623957-5   LC 2004-22186

Contents: How to get to the planet Venus by Joy Harjo; Because my father always said he was the only Indian who saw Jimi Hendrix play "The Star Spangled Banner" at Woodstock by Sherman Alexie; A real-live blond Cherokee and his equally annoyed soul mate by Cynthia Leitich Smith; The last snow of the Virgin Mary by Richard Van Camp; Crow by Linda Hogan; Ice by Joseph Bruchac; Wild Geese by Louise Erdrich; The magic pony by Greg Sarris; Summer wind by Lee Francis; Drum Kiss by Susan Power

Presents ten short stories about contemporary Native American teens by members of tribes of the United States and Canada, including Louise Erdrich and Joseph Bruchac.

"This distinguished anthology offers powerful, beautifully written stories that are thoughtful and important for teens to hear." SLJ

Myers, Walter Dean, 1937-

145th Street; short stories. Delacorte Press 2000 151p hardcover o.p. pa $5.50 *

Grades: 7 8 9 10   **S C**

1. Harlem (New York, N.Y.)—Fiction 2. African Americans—Fiction 3. Short stories

ISBN 0-385-32137-6; 0-440-22916-2 (pa)

LC 99-36097

Contents: Big Joe's funeral; The baddest dog in Harlem; Fighter; Angela's eyes; The streak; Monkeyman; Kitty and Mack: a love story; A Christmas story; A story in three parts; Block party—145th Street style

"These ten powerful stories create a vivid mosaic of life in the Harlem neighborhood of 145th Street. Memorable characters range from outgoing Big Joe, who decides to stage his own funeral party in *Big Joe's funeral*, to book-loving *Monkeyman*, who outsmarts the Tigros gang. . . . Beautifully told, Myers's stories offer an enticing collection for teens." Voice Youth Advocates

What they found; love on 145th street. Wendy Lamb Books 2007 243p $15.99; lib bdg $18.99 *

Grades: 8 9 10 11 12   **S C**

1. Harlem (New York, N.Y.)—Fiction 2. African Americans—Fiction 3. Family life—Fiction 4. Short stories

ISBN 978-0-385-32138-9; 0-385-32138-4; 978-0-375-93709-5 (lib bdg); 0-375-93709-9 (lib bdg)

LC 2007-7057

Companion volume to 145th street (2000)

Contents: The fashion show, grand opening, and barbque memorial service; What would Jesus do?; Mama; The life you need to have; Burn; Some men are just funny that way; Jump at the sun; Law and order; The man thing; Society for the Preservation of Sorry-Butt Negroes; Madonna; The real deal; Marisol and Skeeter; Poets and plumbers; Combat zone

Fifteen interrelated stories explore different aspects of love, such as a dying father's determination to help start a family business—a beauty salon—and the relationship of two teens who plan to remain celibate until they marry.

"Rich in both character and setting, these urban tales combine heartbreak and hope into a vivid tableau of a community. A priority purchase for all libraries, especially those in urban settings." SLJ

Nascimbene, Yan, 1949-

The creative collection of American short stories; illustrated by Yan Nascimbene; introduction by Ray Bradbury. Creative Editions 2010 271p il $28.95

Grades: 9 10 11 12 Adult   **S C**

1. Short stories

ISBN 978-1-56846-202-8   LC 2008-41479

Contents: The black cat by Edgar Allan Poe; The celebrated jumping frog of Calaveras County by Mark Twain; An occurrence at Owl Creek Bridge by Ambrose Bierce; The open boat by Stephen Crane; Paul's case by Willa Cather; Hills like white elephants by Ernest Hemmingway; The jilting of Granny Weatherall by Katherine Anne Porter; The chrysanthemums by John Steinbeck; The secret life of Walter Mitty by James Thurber; In the twilight by Wallace Stegner; The lottery by Shir-

Nascimbene, Yan, 1949-—*Continued*

ley Jackson; Thank you, m'am by Langston Hughes; Icarus Montgolfier Wright by Ray Bradbury; A & P by John Updike; Where are you going, where have you been? by Joyce Carol Oates; Everyday use by Alice Walker; Elk by Rick Bass

"This anthology is a great introduction to the short-story form. . . . The selections span more than 150 years of American writing and cover varied themes and settings. Ernest Hemingway, John Updike, Joyce Carol Oates, and Alice Walker are among the featured authors. Nascimbene's lovely watercolor illustrations complement each story." SLJ

Includes bibliographical references

Nightshade: 20th century ghost stories; edited by Robert Phillips. Carroll & Graf Pubs. 1999 470p hardcover o.p. pa $14

Grades: 11 12 Adult   S C

1. Ghost stories 2. Short stories

ISBN 0-7867-0614-7; 0-7867-0808-5 (pa)

This is a collection "of 27 paranormal tales. . . . Classics by Henry James, Rudyard Kipling, and Edith Wharton are included, as are stories like Elizabeth Bowen's 'The happy autumn fields,' all considered to be among the authors' best writings. . . . [Also included are] noted world writers such as Isak Dinesen, Franz Kafka, and Gabriel Garcia Marquez, and the contemporary voices of Christopher Tilghman and Max Eberts." Libr J

No such thing as the real world; a short story collection; [by] An Na [et al.]; introduction by Jill Santopolo; [compiled by Laura Geringer and Jill Santopolo] HarperTeen 2009 246p $16.99

Grades: 8 9 10   S C

1. Short stories

ISBN 978-0-06-147058-5; 0-06-147058-9

LC 2008-22583

"Laura Geringer books"

Contents: The projection by M.T. Anderson; Survival by K.L. Going; The longest distance by Beth Kephart; Arrangements by Chris Lynch; Complication by An Na; The company by Jacqueline Woodson

Six young adult authors present short stories featuring teens who have to face the "real world" for the first time.

"This unique collection will challenge students' intellect and have them questioning their own decision-making skills. A fine balance is straddled between sophisticated prose and authentic teen voices, uninhibited and peppered with profanity." SLJ

The **Norton** book of American short stories. Norton 1988 779p $29.95 *

Grades: 11 12 Adult   S C

1. Short stories

ISBN 0-393-02619-1   LC 88-14181

"The 70 stories Prescott chose for inclusion in this comprehensive anthology show to great effect the sterling quality of American short stories, from the dawn-days of Poe and Hawthorne to the . . . minimalism of Raymond Carver. A collection full of treasures." Booklist

The **Norton** book of science fiction; North American science fiction, 1960-1990; edited by Ursula K. Le Guin and Brian Attebery; Karen Joy Fowler, consultant. Norton 1993 869p hardcover o.p. pa $38.13 *

Grades: 11 12 Adult   S C

1. Science fiction 2. Short stories

ISBN 0-393-03546-8; 0-393-97241-0 (pa)

LC 93-16130

Damon Knight, Robert Silverberg, Connie Willis and Harlan Ellison are among the authors represented in this anthology of more than 60 stories.

A "compilation of intelligent and entertaining sf that belongs in virtually every fiction collection." Booklist

Noyes, Deborah, 1965-

The ghosts of Kerfol. Candlewick Press 2008 163p $16.99

Grades: 8 9 10 11 12   S C

1. Short stories 2. Ghost stories 3. Supernatural—Fiction

ISBN 978-0-7636-3000-3; 0-7636-3000-4

LC 2007-51884

Contents: Hunger moon; These heads would speak; The figure under the sheet; When I love you best; The red of berries

Over the centuries, the inhabitants of author Edith Wharton's fictional mansion, Kerfol, are haunted by the ghosts of dead dogs, fractured relationships, and the taste of bitter revenge.

This collection includes "five wonderfully chilling short stories." Publ Wkly

O'Brien, Tim, 1946-

The things they carried; a work of fiction. Houghton Mifflin Harcourt 2010 233p $24; pa $14.95 *

Grades: 11 12 Adult   S C

1. Vietnam War, 1961-1975—Fiction 2. Short stories

ISBN 978-0-547-39117-5; 978-0-618-70641-9 (pa)

LC 2010-292325

First published 1990

Contents: The things they carried; Love; Spin; On the Rainy River; Enemies; Friends; How to tell a true war story; The dentist; Sweetheart of the Song Tra Bong; Stockings; Church; The man I killed; Ambush; Style; Speaking of courage; Notes; In the field; Good form; Field trip; The ghost soldiers; Night life; The lives of the dead

This is a collection of stories about American soldiers in Vietnam. . . . All of the stories "deal with a single platoon, one of whose members is a character named Tim O'Brien." N Y Times Book Rev

"This book may be selfconscious . . . but through its determination to treat these men with dignity and decency it proves immensely affecting." Newsweek

O'Connor, Flannery

Collected works. Library of Am. 1988 1281p $35 *

Grades: 11 12 Adult   S C

1. Short stories

ISBN 0-940450-37-2   LC 87-37829

O'Connor, Flannery—*Continued*

Contents: Wise blood; A good man is hard to find; The violent bear it away; Everything that rises must converge; Stories and occasional prose; Letters

The complete stories. Farrar, Straus & Giroux 1971 555p pa $17 hardcover o.p.

Grades: 11 12 Adult   **S C**

1. Short stories

ISBN 0-374-51536-0

Contents: The geranium; The barber; Wildcat; The crop; The turkey; The train; The peeler; The heart of the park; A stroke of good fortune; Enoch and the gorilla; A good man is hard to find; A late encounter with the enemy; The life you save may be your own; The river; A circle in the fire; The displaced person; A Temple of the Holy Ghost; The artificial nigger; Good country people; You can't be any poorer than dead; Greenleaf; A view of the woods; The enduring chill; The comforts of home; Everything that rises must converge; The Partridge festival; The lame shall enter first; Why do the heathen rage?; Revelation; Parker's back; Judgement Day

This collection is "arranged in chronological order from the story she wrote for her master's thesis at the University of Iowa to 'Judgement Day.' . . . The stories here include the original openings and other chapters of her two novels 'Wise Blood' and 'The Violent Bear It Away.'" N Y Times Book Rev

Once upon a cuento; edited by Lyn Miller-Lachman. Curbstone Press 2003 243p pa $15.95

Grades: 9 10 11 12   **S C**

1. Hispanic Americans—Fiction 2. Short stories

ISBN 1-88068-499-3   LC 2003-14667

Contents: Heritage, holidays, and contemporary culture: My ciguapa; A Nuyorican Christmas in el Bronx; Adventures in Mexican wrestling; Searching for Peter Z; Family life: Leaving before the snow; A special gift; Initiation; Good trouble for Lucy; The snake; Friends and other relationships: Sara and Panchito; Armpits, hair and other marks of beauty; Learning buddies; Indian summer sun; Dealing with differences: Leti's shoe escandalo; Dancing Miranda; That October; Grease

"Fourteen Latino authors have contributed to this collection of 17 short stories " SLJ

"Writing quality is consistently high throughout. . . . This book . . . succeeds admirably in proving, through literature, that there is no single 'Latino experience.'" Voice Youth Advocates

Outside rules; short stories about nonconformist youth; edited, with an introduction by Claire Robson. Persea Books 2007 178p pa $9.95

Grades: 7 8 9 10   **S C**

1. Short stories

ISBN 0-89255-316-2; 978-0-89255-316-7

       LC 2006-22548

"A Karen and Michael Braziller book"

Contents: A minstrel visits by Sandell Morse; Mr. Softee by Wally Lamb; My Tocaya by Sandra Cisneros; Surrounded by sleep by Akhil Sharma; One extra parking space by Jacqueline Sheehan; Laughing in the dark by Rand Richards Cooper; Nobody listens when I talk by Annette Sanford; Saint Chola by K. Kvashay-Boyle; The

frontiers of knowledge by Claire Robson; Gypsy girl by Caitlin Jeffrey Lonning; April by Katharine Noel; The kind of light that shines on Texas by Reginald McKnight; Playing the garden by Chris Fisher; The white room by Rebecca Rule

An anthology of fourteen short stories about youth who do not quite fit in because they are too brainy, unathletic, poor, the "wrong" religion, emotionally fragile, from nontraditional families, not model-thin, or simply bent on following a unique path.

"The collection is broadly multicultural, and the stories are consistently insightful, original, and discussion provoking in addition to being well written." Bull Cent Child Books

The **Oxford** book of English short stories; edited by A.S. Byatt. Oxford Univ. Press 1998 xxx, 439p hardcover o.p. pa $19.95

Grades: 11 12 Adult   **S C**

1. Short stories

ISBN 0-19-214238-0; 0-19-956160-5 (pa)

       LC 97-44998

In this anthology Byatt "includes necessary masters—Rudyard Kipling, Saki, D. H. Lawrence, and V. S. Pritchett, to name a few. But . . . she draws into the fold the work of several extremely talented writers of which few readers on this side of the Atlantic will have heard. Falling into this category are such writers as Malachi Whitaker, H. E. Bates, Sylvia Townsend Warner, and Charlotte Mew." Booklist

The **Oxford** book of gothic tales; edited by Chris Baldick. Oxford University Press 2009 xxiii, 533p pa $19.95

Grades: 11 12 Adult   **S C**

1. Horror fiction 2. Gothic romances 3. Short stories

ISBN 978-0-19-956153-7   LC 2009291584

First published 1992

This chronologically arranged anthology contains thirty-seven stories dating from the 18th to 20th century. Among the authors are Hawthorne, Poe, Stevenson, Hardy, Faulkner, Welty, Borges, Angela Carter and Isabel Allende.

Includes bibliographical references

The **Oxford** book of Irish short stories; edited by William Trevor. Oxford Univ. Press 1989 567p $40; pa $17.95

Grades: 11 12 Adult   **S C**

1. Ireland—Fiction 2. Short stories

ISBN 0-19-214180-5; 0-19-280193-7 (pa)

       LC 88-28147

"The great Irish writers—from Oliver Goldsmith and Oscar Wilde to James Joyce and Edna O'Brien—are represented in a collection for older advanced readers." Booklist

The **Oxford** book of short stories; chosen by V.S. Pritchett. Oxford Univ. Press 1981 547p hardcover o.p. pa $19.95 *

Grades: 11 12 Adult   **S C**

1. Short stories

ISBN 0-19-214116-3; 0-19-958313-7 (pa)

       LC 81-156872

The Oxford book of short stories—*Continued*

In addition to one of his own short stories, Pritchett has selected 40 others, written in English during the 19th and 20th centuries. Most of the authors are English, Irish or American and include Somerset Maugham, D. H. Lawrence, Faulkner, Twain, and Eudora Welty.

Packer, ZZ, 1973-

Drinking coffee elsewhere. Riverhead Bks. 2003 238p hardcover o.p. pa $14

Grades: 11 12 Adult   **S C**

1. African Americans—Fiction 2. Short stories

ISBN 1-57322-234-8; 1-57322-378-6 (pa)

LC 2002-73971

Contents: Brownies; Every tongue shall confess; Our Lady of Peace; The ant of the self; Drinking coffee elsewhere; Speaking in tongues; Geese; Doris is coming

"The predominantly African American characters in Packer's first collection of short fiction struggle to maintain their sense of self while they confront unexpected life events." Booklist

Peck, Richard, 1934-

Past perfect, present tense: new and collected stories. Dial Bks. 2004 177p hardcover o.p. pa $6.99

Grades: 7 8 9 10 11 12   **S C**

1. Short stories

ISBN 0-8037-2998-7; 0-14-240537-X (pa)

LC 2003-10904

Contents: Priscilla and the wimps; The electric summer; Shotgun Cheatham's last night above ground; The special powers of Blossom Culp; By far the worst pupil at Long Point School; Girl at the window; The most important night of Melanie's life; Waiting for Sebastian; Shadows; Fluffy the gangbuster; I go along; The kiss in the carryon bag; The three-century woman; How to write a short story; Five helpful hints

A collection of short stories, including two previously unpublished ones, that deal with the way things could be.

"The stories perfectly highlight Peck's range and expertise at characterization. Almost every one is a superb read-aloud. . . . This superior collection is a must for every library." SLJ

Pick-up game; a full day of full court; edited by Marc Aronson & Charles R. Smith Jr. Candlewick Press 2011 170p il $15.99 *

Grades: 7 8 9 10   **S C**

1. Basketball—Fiction 2. New York (N.Y.)—Fiction 3. Short stories

ISBN 978-0-7636-4562-5; 0-7636-4562-1

Contents: Step into the arena by Charles R. Smith, Jr.; Cage run by Walter Dean Myers; Next by Charles R. Smith, Jr.; Laws of motion by Bruce Brooks; My boys by Charles R. Smith, Jr.; Mira mira by Willie Perdomo; Wild cats by Charles R. Smith, Jr.; Virgins are lucky by Sharon G. Flake; El profesor by Charles R. Smith, Jr.; Practice don't make perfect by Robert Burleigh; The fire inside by Charles R. Smith, Jr.; He's gotta have it by Rita Williams-Garcia; Back in the day by Charles R. Smith, Jr.; Head game by Joseph Bruchac; 24/7 by Charles R. Smith, Jr.; Just Shane by Adam Rapp; Represent by Charles R. Smith, Jr.; The shoot by Robert Lipsyte; Afterword by Marc Aronson

A series of short stories by such authors as Walter Dean Myers, Rita Williams-Garcia, and Joseph Bruchac, interspersed with poems and photographs, provides different perspectives on a game of streetball played one steamy July day at the West 4th Street court in New York City known as The Cage.

"This anthology squeaks out a win. . . . Sharp-elbow action alternates with an almost spiritual grace." Booklist

Pierce, Tamora, 1954-

Tortall and other lands; a collection of tales. Random House 2011 369p $18.99; lib bdg $21.99

Grades: 7 8 9 10   **S C**

1. Fantasy fiction 2. Short stories

ISBN   978-0-375-86676-0;   0-375-86676-0; 978-0-375-96676-7 (lib bdg); 0-375-96676-5 (lib bdg)

LC 2011-281471

Contents: Student of ostriches; Elder brother; The hidden girl; Nawat; The dragon's tale; Lost; Time of proving; Plain magic; Mimic; Huntress; Testing

"In this collection, Pierce's fantasy worlds teem with a wide variety of heroines: math prodigies, shepherds and martial artists, primarily girls of color, mostly fighting sexism. . . . Familiar characters return: Tortall fans will delight in new adventures of the darkings, Kitten the dragon and Aly the spymaster. . . . Unusually for Pierce, one contemporary fantasy and one realistic fiction piece close out the collection." Kirkus

Poe, Edgar Allan, 1809-1849

Edgar Allan Poe's tales of mystery and madness; illustrated by Gris Grimley. Atheneum Books for Young Readers 2004 135p il $17.95 *

Grades: 8 9 10 11 12   **S C**

1. Horror fiction 2. Short stories

ISBN 0-689-84837-4   LC 2003-10565

Contents: The black cat; The masque of the Red Death; Hop Frog; The fall of the house of Usher

"With high-production values and gothic sensibilities thoroughly reflected in both text and art, this is an essential purchase for libraries. Adults can use it to lead young people to some great literature; readers will pluck it off the shelves themselves for creepy, entertaining fun." Booklist

Porter, Katherine Anne, 1890-1980

The collected stories of Katherine Anne Porter. Harcourt Brace & World 1965 495p pa $16 hardcover o.p.

Grades: 11 12 Adult   **S C**

1. Short stories

ISBN 0-15-618876-7

Contains three collections of short stories: Flowering Judas, and other stories (1935); The leaning tower, and other stories (1944); Pale horse, pale rider (1939); and four additional short stories: Virgin Violeta; The martyr; The fig tree; and Holiday.

"These are perfect examples of the short story and are representative not only of the best American writing but of the best in the world." SLJ

Porter, Katherine Anne, 1890-1980—*Continued*

Pale horse, pale rider: three short novels. Harcourt Brace Jovanovich 1990 c1939 208p $17 *

Grades: 11 12 Adult   **S C**
1. Short stories
ISBN 0-15-170755-3   LC 89-26886
First published 1939

Contents: Old mortality; Noon wine; Pale horse, pale rider

"These three short novels include the title story, which concerns a young newspaperwoman in love with a soldier who dies in the 1918 influenza epidemic; 'Noon Wine,' the narrative of a shooting in the glare of a Texas midday; and 'Old Mortality,' a three-stage account of a Southern family that tries to believe its own myths about itself." Good Read

Prom nights from hell; [by] Meg Cabot . . . [et al.] HarperTeen 2007 304p $16.99; pa $9.99
Grades: 9 10 11 12   **S C**
1. Short stories 2. School stories 3. Horror fiction
ISBN   978-0-06-125310-2;   0-06-125310-3; 978-0-06-125309-6 (pa); 0-06-125309-X (pa)
LC 2007-02986

Contents: The exterminator's daughter by Meg Cabot; The corsage by Lauren Myracle; Madison Avery and the dim reaper by Kim Harrison; Kiss and tell by Michele Jaffe; Hell on Earth by Stephenie Meyer

"In this collection, five popular authors put a unique twist on prom. . . . Their prom nights involve demons, vampires, and the walking dead. . . . Although the stories are loosely tied to the theme, each author fills her tale with vastly different nightmarish characters and circumstances, making certain that there is something that will appeal to every reader." Voice Youth Advocates

The **restless** dead; ten original stories of the supernatural; edited by Deborah Noyes. Candlewick Press 2007 253p $16.99
Grades: 8 9 10 11 12   **S C**
1. Supernatural—Fiction 2. Horror fiction 3. Short stories
ISBN 0-7636-2906-5; 978-0-7636-2906-9
LC 2007-22114

Contents: The wrong grave by Kelly Link; The house and the locket by Chris Wooding; Kissing dead boys by Annette Curtis Klause; The heart of another by Marcus Sedgwick; The necromancers by Herbie Brennan; No visible power by Deborah Noyes; Bad things by Libba Bray; The gray boy's work by M.T. Anderson; The poison eaters by Holly Black; Honey in the wound by Nancy Etchemendy

This is a "collection of terrifying stories from some of the most well-known authors writing for teens, including M. T. Anderson, Holly Black, Libby Bray, and Annette Curtis Klause. From vampires to vindictive ghosts, this diverse anthology has it all, and then some." Booklist

Rice, David, 1964-
Crazy loco; stories about growing up Chicano in southern Texas. Dial Books for Young Readers 2001 135p hardcover o.p. pa $6.99
Grades: 7 8 9 10 11 12   **S C**
1. Mexican Americans—Fiction 2. Texas—Fiction 3. Short stories
ISBN 0-8037-2598-1; 0-14-250056-9 (pa)
LC 00-59042

Contents: Sugarcane fire; Her other son; Valentine; Papa Lalo; Crazy loco; Proud to be an American; She flies; The California cousins; Last mass

A collection of nine stories about Mexican American kids growing up in the Rio Grande Valley of southern Texas.

"Two great strengths of these stories are the pitch-perfect sense for the speech and thought patterns of teens and the vivid depiction of the daily lives of Mexican-Americans in Texas's Rio Grande Valley." SLJ

Roth, Philip
Goodbye, Columbus, and five short stories. Modern Lib. 1995 298p hardcover o.p. pa $14 *
Grades: 11 12 Adult   **S C**
1. Jews—United States—Fiction 2. Short stories
ISBN 0-679-60159-7; 0-679-74826-1 (pa)
LC 94-44528

A reissue of the title first published 1959 by Houghton Mifflin

Contents: Goodbye, Columbus; Conversion of the Jews; Defender of the faith; Epstein; You can't tell a man by the song he sings; Eli, the fanatic

"The title story in this collection is about a young Radcliffe girl and a Rutgers boy who learn that there is more to love than exuberance and passion. All of the stories dramatize the dilemma of modern American Jews, torn between two worlds." Publ Wkly

Salinger, J. D., 1919-2010
Nine stories. Little, Brown 1953 302p $24.95; pa $5.99 *
Grades: 11 12 Adult   **S C**
1. Short stories
ISBN 0-316-76956-8; 0-316-76950-9 (pa)

Contents: A perfect day for bananafish; Uncle Wiggily in Connecticut; Just before the war with the Eskimos; The laughing man; For Esmé—with love and squalor; Pretty mouth and green my eyes; De Daumier-Smith's blue period; Teddy; Down at the dinghy

This collection "introduced various members of the Glass family who would dominate the remainder of Salinger's work. Critical response divided itself between high praise and cult worship. Most of the stories deal with precocious, troubled children, whose religious yearnings—often tilting toward the East—are in vivid contrast to the materialistic and spiritually empty world of their parents. The result was a perfect literary formula for the 1950s." Benet's Reader's Ency of Am Lit

Shattered: stories of children and war; edited by Jennifer Armstrong. Knopf 2002 166p hardcover o.p. pa $6.50 *

Grades: 7 8 9 10   **S C**
1. War stories 2. Short stories
ISBN 0-375-81112-5; 0-440-23765-3 (pa)
LC 2001-18609

Contents: Second day by Ibtisam Barakat; Shattered by Marilyn Singer; Bad day for baseball by Graham Salisbury; I'll see you when this war is over by M.E. Kerr; Golpe de Estado by Dian Curtis Regan; Snap, crackle, pop by Lois Metzger; Things happen by Lisa Rowe Fraustino; Faizabad harvest 1980 by Suzanne Fisher Staples; Sounds of Thunder by Joseph Bruchac; Witness by Jennifer Armstrong; War is swell by David Lubar; Hope by Gloria D. Miklowitz.

"This anthology of short stories (and one memoir), mostly by well-known writers for YAs, shows how war's violence affects individual young people in countries across the world." Booklist

"These selections will make teens cry, will make them angry, but most of all they will make them think." SLJ

Sholem Aleichem, 1859-1916

Tevye the dairyman and The railroad stories; [by] Sholom Aleichem; translated from the Yiddish and with an introduction by Hillel Halkin. Schocken Bks. 1987 xli, 309p pa $15 hardcover o.p.

Grades: 11 12 Adult   **S C**
1. Jews—Fiction 2. Short stories
ISBN 0-8052-1069-5 (pa)
LC 86-24835
"Library of Yiddish classics"

Includes the following stories: Tevye strikes it rich; Tevye blows a small fortune; Today's children; Hodl; Chava; Shprintze; Tevye leaves for the land of Israel; Lekh-Lekho; To the reader; Competitors; The happiest man in all Kodny; Baranovich Station; Eighteen from Pereshchepena; The man from Buenos Aires; Elul; The slowpoke express; The miracle of Hoshana Rabbah; The wedding that came without its band; The tallis koton; A game of sixty-six; High school; The automatic exemption; It doesn't pay to be good; Burned out; Hard luck; Fated for misfortune; Go climb a tree if you don't like it; The tenth man; Third class

"In the first eight stories of this collection, Tevye, the Russian Jew so familiar from *Fiddler on the Roof*, bemoans his fate. In these as well as the following 21 tales, the author displays his splendid storytelling skills." Booklist

Sideshow; ten original tales of freaks, illusionists, and other matters odd and magical; edited by Deborah Noyes. Candlewick Press 2009 199p il $16.99

Grades: 7 8 9 10   **S C**
1. Short stories
ISBN 978-0-7636-3752-1; 0-7636-3752-1
LC 2008-37420

Contents: The bearded girl by Aimee Bender; Those psychics on TV by Vivian Vande Velde; Year of the rat by Danica Novgorodoff; The mummy's daughter by Annette Curtis Klause; When God came to Kathleen's garden by David Almond; The shadow troupe by Shawn Cheng; Cat calls by Cynthia Leitch Smith; The bread box by Cecil Castellucci; Living curiosities by Margo Lanagan; Jargo! by Matt Phelan

"This is a masterpiece of 10 short stories by world-class authors. Contributors include David Almond, Annette Curtis Klause, and Vivian Vande Velde. . . . Not all of the stories are traditional prose; several are graphic renditions, including Matt Phelan's masterfully drawn 'Jargo!' . . . Suspending disbelief, readers of this fantastic anthology may start investing in psychics and sleeping with the light on." SLJ

Singer, Isaac Bashevis, 1904-1991

The collected stories of Isaac Bashevis Singer. Farrar, Straus & Giroux 1982 610p hardcover o.p. pa $20 *

Grades: 11 12 Adult   **S C**
1. Short stories 2. Jews—Fiction
ISBN 0-374-12631-3; 0-374-51788-6 (pa)

This is a selection of forty-seven stories chosen by the author from eight prior collections

Contents: Gimpel the fool; The gentleman from Cracow; Joy; The little shoemakers; The unseen; The Spinoza of Market Street; The destruction of Kreshev; Taibele and her demon; Alone; Yentl the yeshiva boy; Zeidlus the Pope; The last demon; Short Friday; The séance; The slaughterer; The dead fiddler; Henne Fire; The letter writer; A friend of Kafka; The cafeteria; The joke; Powers; Something is there; A crown of feathers; A day in Coney Island; The cabalist of East Broadway; A quotation from Klopstock; A dance and a hop; Grandfather and grandson; Old love; The admirer; The yearning heifer; A tale of two sisters; Three encounters; Passions; Brother Beetle; The betrayer of Israel; The psychic journey; The manuscript; The power of darkness; The bus; A night in the poorhouse; Escape from civilization; Vanvild Kava; The reencounter; Neighbors; Moon and madness

Sixteen: stories about that sweet and bitter birthday; edited by Megan McCafferty. Three Rivers Press 2004 318p pa $10.95

Grades: 9 10 11 12   **S C**
1. Short stories
ISBN 1-4000-5270-X
LC 2003-27919

Contents: Infinity by Sarah Dessen; Relent/Persist by Zoe Trope; The future lives of Emily Milty by Julianna Baggott; Rutford becomes a man by Ned Vizzini; The grief diet by Emma Forrest; Mona Lisa, Jesus, Chad, and me by Carolyn Mackler; The alumni interview by David Levithan; Cat got your tongue? by Sonya Sones; The day I turned chickenhearted by Steve Almond; Venetian fan by Cat Bauer; Kissing lessons by Joseph Weisberg; Nebraska 99 by Jacqueline Woodson; The perfect kiss by Sarah Mlynowski; Cowgirls & Indie boys by Tanuja Desai Hidier; The mud and fever dialogues by M.T. Anderson; Fifteen going on... by Megan McCafferty

"Diverse as the teens the stories represent, this collection features Native Americans, teen mothers, queer boys and questioning girls, ancient Greeks, students abroad, and a teen author. . . . Adults wanting to relive their youth will get as much mileage out of the combined joy and misery of the protagonists as teens seeking assurance they are not alone at this bittersweet crossroads of life." Voice Youth Advocates

Sleator, William

Oddballs; stories. Dutton Children's Bks. 1993
134p hardcover o.p. pa $5.99

Grades: 6 7 8 9 10   S C

1. Short stories

ISBN 0-525-45057-2; 0-14-037438-8 (pa)

LC 92-27666

Contents: Games; Frank's mother; The freedom fighters of Parkview; The hypnotist; The séance; The pitiful
encounter; Leah's stories; Pituh-plays; Dad's cool; Oddballs

A collection of stories based on experiences from the
author's youth and peopled with an unusual assortment
of family and friends.

"Fresh, funny, and slightly gross, the quasi-
autobiographical glimpses will grab the reader's attention." Horn Book Guide

Spider Woman's granddaughters; traditional tales
and contemporary writing by Native American
women; edited and with an introduction by
Paula Gunn Allen. Fawcett Columbine 1990
c1989 279p pa $15

Grades: 11 12 Adult   S C

1. Native Americans—Fiction 2. Short stories

ISBN 0-449-90508-X

First published 1989 by Beacon Press

This is a collection of twenty-four stories by Native
American women authors arranged in three thematic sections, 'The Warriors,' 'The Casualties,' and 'The Resistance.' The contributors include Marmon Silko, E. Pauline Johnson, Vickie L. Sears, Anna Lee Walters, Soge
Track, LeAnne Howe and Louise Erdrich.

"Each of the stories in this collection, whether traditional or modern, expresses the urgency of survival—of
not vanishing either individually or politically. And the
quality of the stories is stunning." Women's Rev Books

Includes bibliographical references

The **Starry** rift; tales of new tomorrows: an
original science fiction anthology; edited by
Jonathan Strahan. Viking 2008 530p $19.99; pa
$11.99 *

Grades: 8 9 10 11 12   S C

1. Science fiction 2. Short stories

ISBN   978-0-670-06059-7;   0-670-06059-3;
978-0-14-241438-5 (pa); 0-14-241438-7 (pa)

LC 2007-32152

Contents: Ass-hat magic spider by Scott Westerfeld;
Cheats by Ann Halam; Orange by Neil Gaiman; The
surfer by Kelly Link; Repair kit by Stephen Baxter; The
dismantled invention of fate by Jeffrey Ford; Anda's
game by Cory Doctorow; Sundiver Day by Kathleen Ann
Goonan; The dust assassin by Ian McDonald; The star
surgeon's apprentice by Alastair Reynolds; An honest
day's work by Margo Lanagan; Lost continent by Greg
Egan; Incomers by Paul McAuley; Post-ironic stress syndrome by Tricia Sullivan; Infestation by Garth Nix;
Pinocchio by Walter Jon Williams

The sixteen stories by a mix of acclaimed YA and
adult authors showcase settings ranging from bleak near-
futures to careening spaceships and extraterrestrial communities. Each is followed by an author's note and brief
biography.

"Each of the tales is not only entertaining to read, but

also provides a thought-provoking element to consider.
. . . Quality stories by authors at the height of their craft
make this anthology a must-have for any library." SLJ

Such a pretty face; short stories; edited by Ann
Angel. Amulet Books 2007 267p $18.95

Grades: 9 10 11 12   S C

1. Short stories

ISBN 978-0-8109-1607-4; 0-8109-1607-X

LC 2006-23612

Contents: Such a pretty face by Ann Angel; Farang by
Mary Ann Rodman; Red rover, red rover by Chris
Lynch; Bad hair day by Lauren Myracle; Sideshow by
Louise Hawes; What I look like by Jamie Pittel; Ape by
J. James Keels; Cheekbones by Ellen Wittlinger; How to
survive a name by Norma Fox Mazer; Bella in five acts
by Tim Wynne-Jones; Bingo! by Anita Riggio; My cra-
zy, beautiful world by Jacqueline Woodson

For this short story collection, the editor has "chosen
stories reflecting the many definitions and ramifications
of physical beauty. . . . This powerful, thought-
provoking anthology will certainly find a place in public
libraries. High school librarians are strongly urged to
consider it for purchase, despite a few instances of profane language and several sexual references." Voice
Youth Advocates

Tan, Shaun

Tales from outer suburbia. Arthur A. Levine
Books 2009 92p il $19.99 *

Grades: 7 8 9 10   S C

1. Suburban life—Fiction 2. Short stories

ISBN 978-0-545-05587-1; 0-545-05587-3

LC 2008-13784

Contents: The water buffalo; Eric; Broken toys; Un-
dertow; Grandpa's story; No other country; Stick figures;
The nameless holiday; Alert but not alarmed; Wake; Our
expedition; Night of the turtle rescue

"The term 'suburbia' may conjure visions of vast and
generic sameness, but in his hypnotic collection of 15
short stories and meditations, Tan does for the sprawling
landscape what he did for the metropolis in *The Arrival*
. . . . Ideas and imagery both beautiful and disturbing
will linger." Publ Wkly

Taylor, Laini

Lips touch; three times; illustrations by Jim Di
Bartolo. Arthur A. Levine Books 2009 265p il
$17.99 *

Grades: 8 9 10 11 12   S C

1. Kissing—Fiction 2. Supernatural—Fiction 3. Short
stories

ISBN 978-0-545-05585-7; 0-545-05585-7

LC 2009-5458

Contents: Goblin fruit; Spicy little curses such as
these; Hatchling

"Taylor offers a powerful trio of tales, each founded
upon the consequences of a kiss. . . . Contemporary
Kizzy, who so yearns to be a normal, popular teenager
that she forgets the rules of her Old Country upbringing
and is seduced by a goblin in disguise; Anamique, living
in British colonial India, silenced forever due to a spell
cast upon her at birth; and Esmé, who at 14 discovers

Taylor, Laini—*Continued*

she is host to another—nonhuman—being. . . . Each is, in vividly distinctive fashion, a mesmerizing love story that comes to a satisfying but never predictable conclusion. Di Bartolo's illustrations provide tantalizing visual preludes to each tale." Publ Wkly

Tolkien, J. R. R. (John Ronald Reuel), 1892-1973

The Silmarillion; edited by Christopher Tolkien. 2nd ed. Houghton Mifflin 2001 xxiv, 365p il $28; pa $14

Grades: 9 10 11 12   S C

1. Fantasy fiction 2. Short stories

ISBN 0-618-13504-9; 0-618-12698-8 (pa)

LC 2001-16971

First published 1977

"J.R.R. Tolkien Quenta Silmarillion (The history of the Silmarils) together with Ainudalë (The music of the Ainur) and Valaquenta (Account of the Valar) To which is appended Akallabêth (The downfall of Númenor) and of the Rings of Power and the Third age." Facing title page

Contents: Ainulindale; Valaquenta; Quenta Silmarillion: Of the beginning of days; Quenta Silmarillion: Of Autë and Yavanna; Quenta Silmarillion: Of the coming of the elves and the captivity of Melkor; Quenta Silmarillion: Of Thingol and Melian; Quenta Silmarillion: Of Eldamar and the princes of the Eldalië; Quenta Silmarillion: Of Fëanor and the unchaining of Melkor; Quenta Silmarillion: Of the Silmarils and the unrest of the Noldor; Quenta Silmarillion: Of the darkening of Valinor; Quenta Silmarillion: Of the flight of the Noldor; Quenta Silmarillion: Of the Sindar; Quenta Silmarillion: Of the sun and moon and the hiding of Valinor; Quenta Silmarillion: Of men; Quenta Silmarillion: Of the return of the Noldor; Quenta Silmarillion: Of Beleriand and its realms; Quenta Silmarillion: Of the Noldor in Beleriand; Quenta Silmarillion: Of Maeglin; Quenta Silmarillion: Of the coming of men into the West; Quenta Silmarillion: Of the ruin of Beleriand and the fall of Fingollin; Quenta Silmarillion: Of Beren and Lúthien; Quenta Silmarillion: Of the fifth battle: Niraeth Arnoediad; Quenta Silmarillion: Of Turin Turambar; Quenta Silmarillion: Of the ruin of Doriath; Quenta Silmarillion: Of Tuor and the fall of Gondolin; Quenta Silmarillion: Of the voyage of Eärendil and the war of wrath; Akallabeth; Of the Rings of Power and the Third Age

"Tolkien began writing these introductory legends in 1917 and, sporadically throughout his life, continued adding to them; his son Christopher has edited and compiled the various versions into a single cohesive work. Two brief tales, which outline the origin of the world and describe the gods who create and rule, precede the title story about the Silmarils—three brilliant, jewel-like creatures who are desired and fought over, setting up a clash between good and evil." Booklist

Tolstoy, Leo, graf, 1828-1910

Great short works of Leo Tolstoy; with an introduction by John Bayley; in the translations by Louise and Aylmer Maude. Harper & Row 1967 685p pa $15.95 hardcover o.p.

Grades: 9 10 11 12   S C

1. Russia—Fiction 2. Short stories

ISBN 0-06-058697-4 (pa)

"A Perennial classic"

Contents: Family happiness; The Cossacks; The death of Ivan Ilych; The devil; The Kreutzer Sonata; Master and man; Father Sergius; Hadji Murád; Alyosha the Pot

Twain, Mark, 1835-1910

The complete short stories of Mark Twain; now collected for the first time; edited with an introduction by Charles Neider. Doubleday 1957 xxiv, 676p pa $6.95 hardcover o.p. *

Grades: 11 12 Adult   S C

1. Short stories

ISBN 0-553-21195-1 (pa)

Also available in hardcover from Amereon

Contents: The notorious jumping frog of Calaveras County; The story of the bad little boy; Cannibalism in the cars; A day at Niagara; Legend of the Capitoline Venus; Journalism in Tennessee; A curious dream; The facts in the great beef contract; How I edited an agricultural paper; A medieval romance; My watch; Political economy; Science vs. Luck; The story of the good little boy; Buck Fanshaw's funeral; The story of the Old Ram; Tom Quartz; A trial; The trials of Simon Erickson; A true story; Experience of the McWilliamses with membranous croup; Some learned fables for good old boys and girls; The canvasser's tale; The loves of Alonzo Fitz Clarence and Rosannah Ethelton; Edward Mills and George Benton: a tale; The man who put up at Gadsby's; Mrs. McWilliams and the lightning; What stumped the blue jays; A curious experience; The invalid's story; The McWilliamses and the burglar alarm; The stolen White Elephant; A burning brand; A dying man's confession; The professor's yarn; A ghost story; Luck; Playing courier; The Californian's tale; The diary of Adam and Eve; The Esquimau maiden's romance; Is he living or is he dead?; The £1,000,000 bank-note; Cecil Rhodes and the shark; The joke that made Ed's fortune; A story without an end; The man that corrupted Hadleyburg; The death disk; Two little tales; The belated Russian passport; A double-barreled detective story; The five boons of life; Was it Heaven? or Hell?; A dog's tale; The $30,000 bequest; A horse's tale; Hunting the deceitful turkey; Extract from Captain Stormfield's visit to heaven; A fable; The mysterious stranger

"The sixty pieces which are here hospitably called short stories illustrate both the weaknesses and the strengths of Mark Twain as a writer of fiction." N Y Times Book Rev

Ultimate sports; short stories by outstanding writers for young adults; edited by Donald R. Gallo. Delacorte Press 1995 333p hardcover o.p. pa $6.99 *

Grades: 7 8 9 10   S C

1. Sports—Fiction 2. Short stories

ISBN 0-440-22707-0; 0-440-22707-0 (pa)

LC 94-49610

Contents: Joyriding by Jim Naughton; Fury by T. Ernesto Bethancourt; Superboy by Chris Crutcher; If you can't be lucky by Carl Deuker; Stealing for girls by Will Weaver; Shark bait by Graham Salisbury; Cutthroat by Norma Fox Mazer; The assault on the record by Stephen Hoffius; The defender by Robert Lipsyte; Just once by

Ultimate sports—*Continued*

Thomas J Dygard; Brownian motion by Virginia Euwer Wolff; Bones by Todd Strasser; Sea changes by Tessa Duder; The gospel according to Krenzwinkle by David Klass; Falling off the Empire State Building by Harry Mazer; The hobbyist by Chris Lynch

A collection of sixteen short stories about teenage athletes.

"There is a terrific mix of the serious and the lighthearted, female and male characters, and traditional and nontraditional games. A winning collection." SLJ

Up all night; a short story collection; [by] Peter Abrahams [et al.]; with an introduction by Laura Geringer. Laura Geringer Books/HarperTeen 2008 227p il $16.99; lib bdg $17.89; pa $8.99

Grades: 8 9 10 11 12   S C

1. Short stories 2. Night—Fiction

ISBN 978-0-06-137076-2; 0-06-137076-2; 978-0-06-137077-9 (lib bdg); 0-06-137077-0 (lib bdg); 978-0-06-137078-6 (pa); 0-06-137078-9 (pa)

LC 2007-21355

Contents: Phase 2 by Peter Abrahams; Not just for breakfast anymore by Libba Bray; The vulnerable hours by David Levithan; Orange Alert by Patricia McCormick; Superman is dead by Sarah Weeks; The motherless one by Gene Luen Yang

"Six top teen authors have contributed stories to this winning collection. Abrahams has written a modern ghost story, Libba Bray tells of a wild night partying with friends that changes a girl's relationship with her estranged father, and David Levithan gives readers a magical take on life in the city. Patricia McCormick takes a hard look at freedom and power, Sarah Weeks writes of responsibility with humor, and Yang tops off the book in his own graphic-novel style. Each story shines in its own way." SLJ

Vande Velde, Vivian, 1951-

Being dead; stories. Harcourt 2001 203p hardcover o.p. pa $6.95

Grades: 7 8 9 10   S C

1. Supernatural—Fiction 2. Horror fiction 3. Short stories

ISBN 0-15-216320-4; 0-15-204912-6 (pa)

LC 00-12996

Contents: Dancing with Marjorie's ghost; Shadow brother; For love of him; October chill; Drop by drop; The ghost; Drop dead

This is a collection of seven "creepy tales featuring ghosts, cemeteries, suicides, murders, and other death-related themes." SLJ

"Often humorous and sometimes evoking sympathy, this anthology will be enjoyed by lovers of mild horror as well as by those who like clever short stories." Voice Youth Advocates

Voices in first person; reflections on Latino identity; [edited by Lori Marie Carlson] Atheneum Books for Young Readers 2008 96p il $16.99

Grades: 6 7 8 9 10 11 12   S C

1. American literature—Hispanic American authors—Collections 2. Short stories

ISBN 978-1-4169-0635-3; 1-4169-0635-5

LC 2006-34161

Contents: Ritual by Claudia Quiroz Cahill; Reclaim your rights as citizen of here, here by Michele Serros; Spending money by Gary Soto; I stand at the crosswalk by Esmeralda Santiago; Angel's monologue by Gwylym Cano; Jose by Caridad de la Luz; The evil eye by Raquel Valle Senties; Poultrymorphosis by Oscar Hijuelos

A collection of brief fictional pieces about the experiences of Latinos in the United States, by such writers as Sandra Cisneros, Gary Soto, Oscar Hijuelos, and others.

"Carlson has drawn from both established and new writers, focusing on finding Latino voices that speak to contemporary readers. . . . This collection sparkles more than its predecessors because of its dynamic design, featuring black-and-white photographs and line illustrations incorporated with the text in a collage-like magazine layout." SLJ

Vonnegut, Kurt, 1922-2007

Bagombo snuff box: uncollected short fiction. Putnam 1999 295p hardcover o.p. pa $13.95

Grades: 11 12 Adult   S C

1. Short stories

ISBN 0-399-14505-2; 0-425-17446-8 (pa)

LC 99-13665

Contents: Thanasphere; Mnemonics; Any reasonable offer; The package; The no-talent kid; Poor little rich town; Souvenir; The cruise of The Jolly Roger; Custom-made bride; Ambitious sophomore; Bagombo snuff box; The powder-blue dragon; A present for Big Saint Nick; Unpaid consultant; Der Arme Dolmetscher; The boy who hated girls; This son of mine; A night for love; Find me a dream; Runaways; 2BRO2B; Lovers Anonymous; Hal Irwin's magic lamp

"The 23 stories in this collection were published in magazines . . . during the Fifties and are collected here for the first time. The topics covered include space travel ('Thanasphere'), which describes the first manned orbit of Earth; finding the American dream ('The package'), about a new home full of the latest accessories; and an attempt to impress an old girlfriend (the title story). . . . Although many of the stories are topically dated, the ironic insights and illumination of character are timeless, and no one does it better than Vonnegut." Libr J

Wallace, Rich, 1957-

Losing is not an option: stories. Knopf 2003 127p hardcover o.p. pa $5.99

Grades: 7 8 9 10   S C

1. Short stories

ISBN 0-375-81351-9; 0-440-23844-7 (pa)

LC 2002-34036

Contents: Night game; Nailed; The amazing two-headed boy; I voted for Mary Ann; In letters that would soar a thousand feet high; What it all goes back to; Dawn; Thankgiving; Losing is not an option

Nine episodes in the life of a young man, from sneaking into his tenth football game in a row with his best friend in sixth grade to running his last high school race, the Pennsylvania state championships.

"Readers will nod with recognition as they follow this jock/poet/regular guy from the cusp of adolescence to the edge of adulthood." Horn Book Guide

Welty, Eudora, 1909-2001

The collected stories of Eudora Welty. Harcourt Brace Jovanovich 1980 622p hardcover o.p. pa $16 *

Grades: 11 12 Adult   **S C**
  1. Short stories
  ISBN 0-15-118994-3; 0-15-618921-6 (pa)
                     LC 80-7947

Contents: Lily Daw and the three ladies; A piece of news; Petrified man; The key; Keela, the outcast Indian maiden; Why I live at the P.O.; The whistle; The hitch-hikers; A memory; Clytie; Old Mr. Marblehall; Flowers for Marjorie; A curtain of green; A visit of charity; Death of a traveling salesman; Powerhouse; A worn path; First love; The wide net; A still moment; Asphodel; The winds; The purple hat; Livvie; At the landing; Shower of gold; June recital; Sir Rabbit; Moon Lake; The whole world knows; Music from Spain; The wanderers; No place for you, my love; The burning; The bride of the Innisfallen; Ladies in spring; Circe; Kin; Going to Naples; Where is the voice coming from?; The demonstrators

This volume contains four previously published collections: A curtain of green, and other stories; The wide net, and other stories; The golden apples and The bride of the Innisfallen, and other stories. Also included in this volume are two uncollected pieces: Where is the voice coming from? and The demonstrators.

Who do you think you are? stories of friends and enemies; selected by Hazel Rochman and Darlene Z. McCampbell. Little, Brown 1993 170p pa $9.99 hardcover o.p.

Grades: 7 8 9 10   **S C**
  1. Friendship—Fiction 2. Short stories
  ISBN 0-316-75320-3   LC 93-314
  "Joy Street books"

Contents: Good grief [excerpt from Dandelion wine] by Ray Bradbury; Where are you going, where have you been? by Joyce Carol Oates; American history by Judith Ortiz-Cofer; Raymond's run by Toni Cade Bambara; A boy and his dog by Martha Brooks; The alligators by John Updike; Celia behind me by Isabel Huggan; This boy's life [excerpt] by Tobias Wolff; Priscilla and the wimps by Richard Peck; What means switch by Gish Jen; My Lucy friend who smells like corn by Sandra Cisneros; Sucker by Carson McCullers; The red convertible by Louise Erdrich; The man I killed [excerpt from The things they carried] by Tim O'Brien; Ambush [excerpt from The things they carried] by Tim O'Brien; I know why the caged bird sings [excerpt] by Maya Angelou; Poesía a la amistad/Poetry of friendship by José Martí

"Louise Erdrich, John Updike, Ray Bradbury, Joyce Carol Oates, Sandra Cisneros, Tim O'Brien, Richard Peck, and Maya Angelou are among the 15 writers represented in this anthology of stories [two prose excerpts and a poem] about friendship and loss of friendship." Booklist

"Meticulously chosen and arranged, these works crystalize moments of vulnerability, sorrow and understanding; together, they serve as an excellent introduction to modern American writing." Publ Wkly

Wizards; edited by Jack Dann and Gardner Dozois. Berkley Books 2007 400p hardcover o.p. pa $16

Grades: 11 12 Adult   **S C**
  1. Short stories 2. Fantasy fiction
  ISBN 978-0-425-21518-0; 978-0-441-01588-7 (pa)
               LC 2006-101534

Contents: The witch's headstone, by N. Gaiman; Holly and iron, by G. Nix; Color vision, by M. Rosenblum; The ruby incomparable, by K. Baker; A fowl tale, by E. Colfer; Slipping sideways through eternity, by J. Yolen; The stranger's hands, by T. Williams; Naming Day, by P. A. McKillip; Winter's wife, by E. Hand; A diorama of the infernal regions, or The devil's last question, by A. Duncan; Barrens dance, by P. S. Beagle; Stone man, by N. Kress; The manticore spell, by J. Ford; Zinder, by T. Lee; Billy and the wizard, by T. Bisson; The magikkers, by T. Dowling; The magic animal, by G. Wolfe; Stonefather, by O. S. Card

"In this collection of first-published tales, wizards are the puppet masters of schemes ranging from the amusing to the diabolical. Contributors include such venerable masters as Jane Yolen, Peter S. Beagle, and Gene Wolfe as well as such relative newcomers as Andy Duncan and Jeffrey Ford. . . . A creative spectrum of tantalizing themes makes the volume versatile and compelling reading for all fantasy fans." Booklist

Wolfe, Thomas, 1900-1938

The complete short stories of Thomas Wolfe; edited by Francis E. Skipp; foreword by James Dickey. Scribner 1987 xxix, 621p pa $27.50 hardcover o.p.

Grades: 11 12 Adult   **S C**
  1. Short stories
  ISBN 0-02-040891-9 (pa)   LC 86-13782

Contents: An angel on the porch; The train and the city; Death the proud brother; No door; The four lost men; Boom town; The sun and the rain; The house of the far and lost; Dark in the forest, strange as time; For professional appearance; The names of the nation; One of the girls in our party; Circus at dawn; His father's earth; Old Catawba; Arnold Pentland; The face of the war; Gulliver, the story of a tall man; In the park; Only the dead know Brooklyn; Polyphemus; The far and the near; The bums at sunset; The bell remembered; Fame and the poet; Return; Mr. Malone; Oktoberfest; 'E: a recollection; April, late April; The child by tiger; Katamoto; The lost boy; Chickamauga; The company; A prologue to America; Portrait of a literary critic; The birthday; A note on experts: Dexter Vespasian Joyner; Three o'clock; The winter of our discontent; The dark Messiah; The hollyhock sowers; Nebraska Crane; So this is man; The promise of America; The hollow men; The anatomy of loneliness; The lion at morning; The plumed knight; The newspaper; No cure for it; On leprechauns; The return of the prodigal; Old Man Rivers; Justice is blind; No more rivers; The Spanish letter

"All 58 of Wolfe's short stories . . . have been edited by Skipp in a way that represents what Wolfe himself may have wanted his audience to read." Booklist

Working days: stories about teenagers and work;
edited by Anne Mazer. Persea Bks. 1997 207p
hardcover o.p. pa $9.95

Grades: 9 10 11 12   S C
1. Work—Fiction 2. Short stories
ISBN 0-89255-223-9; 0-89255-224-7 (pa)
                  LC 96-50243

Contents: Daydreamer by Magdalena Gomez; Ice
cream man by Roy Hoffman; Seashell motel by Lois
Metzger; Baseball glove by Victor Martinez; Riding up
to Ruby's by Kim Stafford; Lessons by Marilyn Sachs;
Pill factory by Anne Mazer; Forty bucks by Graham
Salisbury; Avalon ballroom by Ann Hood; Crash room
by David Rice; To walk with kings by Tracy Marx;
Catskill snows by Carolina Hospital; Driver's license by
Norman Wong; Egg boat by Nora Dauenhauer; Delivery
in a week by Thylias Moss

Fifteen stories relate the experiences of teenagers
working for many different reasons in a variety of jobs.
Lois Metzger, Victor Martinez, Norman Wong and
Thylias Moss are among the contributors.

"This multicultural collection would fit any high
school curriculum. Senior high school students and adults
will identify with many of these protagonists while being
challenged at the same time." ALAN

Wright, Richard, 1908-1960

Uncle Tom's children; five long stories. Harper
& Row 1938 xxx, 384p pa $13.95 hardcover o.p.
Grades: 11 12 Adult   S C
1. African Americans—Fiction 2. Short stories
ISBN 0-06-058714-8 (pa)

Contents: Big boy leaves home; Down by the river-
side; Long black song; Fire and cloud; Bright and morning star

The stories in this collection deal with conflicts between whites and blacks in the South.

The **year's** best dark fantasy & horror; edited by
Paula Guran. 2010 ed. Prime Books 2010 568p
pa $19.95

Grades: 11 12 Adult   S C
1. Fantasy fiction 2. Horror fiction 3. Short stories
ISBN 978-1-60701-233-7

Contents: The horrid glory of its wings by Elizabeth
Bear; Lowland sea by Suzy McKee Charnas; Copping
squid by Michael Shea; Monsters by Stewart O'Nan; The
brink of eternity by Barbara Roden; Frost Mountain picnic massacre by Seth Fried; Sea-hearts by Margo
Lanagan; A haunted house of her own by Kelley Armstrong; Headstone in my pocket by Paul Tremblay; The
coldest girl in Coldtown by Holly Black; Strange scenes
from an unfinished film by Gary McMahon; A delicate
architecture by Catherynne M. Valente; The mystery by
Peter Atkins; Variations of a theme from Seinfeld by Peter Straub; The wide, carnivorous sky by John Langan;
Certain death for a known person by Steve Duffy; The
ones who got away by Stephen Graham Jones; Leng by
Marc Laidlaw; Torn away by Joe R. Lansdale; The nowhere man by Sarah Pinborough; The bone's prayer by
Caitlín R. Kiernan; The water tower by John Mantooth;
In the porches of my ears by Norman Prentiss; The Cin-
derella game by Kelly Link; The jacaranda smile by
Gemma Files; The other box by Gerard Houarner; White
Charles by Sarah Monette; Everything dies, baby by

Nadia Bulkin; Bruise for bruise by Robert Davies; Re-
spects by Ramsey Campbell; Diamond shell by Deborah
Biancotti; Nub hut by Kurt Dinan; The cabinet child by
Steve Rasnic Tem; Cherrystone and shards of ice by
Ekaterina Sedia; The crevasse by Dale Bailey and Nathan Balingrud; Vic by Maura McHugh; Halloween town
by Lucius Shepard; The long, cold goodbye by Holly
Phillips; What happens when you wake up in the night
by Michael Marshall Smith

"Editor Guran has collected 39 thrilling and frightening horror stories published in 2009. . . . Fans of horror
and dark fantasy. . . should welcome this collection with
open arms." Booklist

The **year's** best science fiction and fantasy for
teens: first annual collection; edited by Jane
Yolen and Patrick Nielsen Hayden. TOR 2005
288p hardcover o.p. pa $12.95

Grades: 9 10 11 12   S C
1. Science fiction 2. Fantasy fiction 3. Short stories
ISBN   0-765-31383-9;   978-0-7653-1383-6;
0-765-31384-7 (pa); 978-0-7653-1384-3 (pa)
                 LC 2005-299191

"A Tom Doherty Associates book"

Contents: The Faery handbag by Kelly Link; Blood
wolf by S.M. Stirling; Sleeping dragons by Lynette
Aspey; Endings by Garth Nix; Dancer in the dark by Da-
vid Gerrold; A piece of flesh by Adam Stemple;
CATNYP by Delia Sherman; They by Rudyard Kipling;
The wings of Meister Wilhelm by Theodora Goss; Dis-
placed persons by Leah Bobet; Sergeant Chip by Bradley
Denton

A collection of science and fantasy fiction from some
of today's most popular writers, including Garth Nix,
David Gerrold, and Delia Sherman.

"Faery handbags, culture-clash-befuddled Bronze Age
warriors, powerful babies hatched of golden eggs and
hapless babies replaced with malevolent changelings,
New York Between (replete with a charming and often
sleepy living library catalog), and traveling levitated cities all make appearances in this strong, accessible collection." Booklist

Young warriors; stories of strength; edited by
Tamora Pierce and Josepha Sherman. Random
House 2005 312p hardcover o.p. pa $8.95

Grades: 7 8 9 10   S C
1. Fantasy fiction 2. Short stories
ISBN   0-375-82962-8;   978-0-375-82962-8;
0-375-82963-6 (pa); 978-0-375-82963-5 (pa)
                 LC 2004-16432

Contents: Gift of Rain Mountain by Bruce Holland
Rogers; Magestone by S. M. and Jan Stirling; Eli and the
dybbuk by Janis Ian; Heartless by Holly Black; Lioness
by Pamela F. Service; Thunderbolt by Ester Friesner;
Devil wind by India Edghill; Boy who cried "dragon!"
by Mike Resnick; Student of ostriches by Tamora Pierce;
Serpent's rock by Laura Anne Gilman; Hidden warrors
by Margaret Mahy; Emerging legacy by Doranna Durgin;
Axe for men by Rosemary Edghill; Acts of faith by Lesley McBain; Swords that talk by Brent Hartinger

Fifteen original short stories by various authors relate
the exploits of teenage warriors who defeat their enemies
with cunning and skill as they strive to fulfill their destinies.

"This timely and appealing anthology will surely help
swell the ranks of teenage fantasy readers." SLJ

Zombies vs. unicorns; [compiled by Holly Black and Justine Larbalestier] Margaret K. McElderry Books 2010 415p $16.99

Grades: 10 11 12 **S C**

1. Short stories 2. Zombies—Fiction 3. Unicorns—Fiction

ISBN 978-1-4169-8953-0; 1-4169-8953-6

LC 2010-03732

Contents: The highest justice by Garth Nix; Love will tear us apart by Alaya Dawn Johnson; Purity test by Naomi Novik; Bougainvillea by Carrie Ryan; A thousand flowers by Margo Lanagan; The children of the revolution by Maureen Johnson; The care and feeding of your baby killer unicorn by Diana Peterfreund; Inoculata by Scott Westerfeld; Princess Prettypants by Meg Cabot; Cold hands by Cassandra Clare; The third virgin by Kathleen Duey; Prom night by Libba Bray

Twelve short stories by a variety of authors seek to answer the question of whether zombies are better than unicorns.

"This is a must-have for fantasy collections, though schools must be cautioned that there is strong profanity, a bestiality tale, and graphic scenes of both violence and sexual encounters." SLJ

This index to the books in the Classified Collection includes author, title, and subject entries; added entries for publishers' series, for joint authors, and for editors of works entered under title; and name and subject cross references; all arranged in one alphabet. The number or symbol in bold face type at the end of each entry refers to the Dewey Decimal Classification or to the Fiction or Story Collection Section where the book will be found. Works classed in 92 will be found under the heading for the person written about. For further information about this index and for examples of entries, see Directions for Use of the Collection.

Abdel-Fattah, Randa
Does my head look big in this?   Fic
Ten things I hate about me   Fic
Abdul-Ghafur, Saleemah
(ed) Living Islam out loud. See Living Islam out loud   297
Abdul-Jabbar, Kareem, 1947-
Black profiles in courage   920
On the shoulders of giants   92
Abeel, Samantha, 1977-
My thirteenth winter   92
Abel, Jessica, 1969-
Drawing words & writing pictures   741.5
Ability
Fiction
Sales, L. Mostly good girls   Fic
Abnaki Indians
Bruchac, J. Bowman's store   92
Abnormal psychology
Hicks, J. W. Fifty signs of mental illness
                                             616.89
Abnormalities, Human See Birth defects
The **abolitionist** movement. McNeese, T.
                                             973.7
Abolitionists
Adler, D. A. Frederick Douglass   92
Clinton, C. Harriet Tubman: the road to freedom
                                              92
Douglass, F. Autobiographies   92
Edwards, J. Abolitionists and slave resistance
                                             326
Esty, A. The liberator: the story of William Lloyd Garrison   92
Esty, A. Unbound and unbroken: the story of Frederick Douglass   92
Fradin, D. B. Bound for the North Star   326
Frederick Douglass [critical essays]   92
Malaspina, A. Harriet Tubman   92
McNeese, T. The abolitionist movement
                                             973.7
Painter, N. I. Sojourner Truth   92
Sonneborn, L. Harriet Beecher Stowe   92
Sterngass, J. Frederick Douglass   92
Sterngass, J. John Brown   92
Abolitionists and slave resistance. Edwards, J.
                                             326
Aboriginal Australians
Antiquities
Danalis, J. Riding the black cockatoo   305.8
Aborigines, Australian See Aboriginal Australians
Abortion
Abortion: opposing viewpoints   363.46
Abortion wars   363.46
The Ethics of abortion   179.7
Herring, M. Y. The pro-life/choice debate
                                           363.46
McBride, D. E. Abortion in the United States
                                           363.46
Naden, C. J. Abortion   363.46
Rose, M. Abortion   363.46
Law and legislation
Hillstrom, L. Roe v. Wade   344
Hull, N. E. H. Roe v. Wade   344
Reproductive rights   344

Abortion in the United States. McBride, D. E.
                                           363.46
Abortion: opposing viewpoints   363.46
Abortion rights movement See Pro-choice movement
Abortion wars   363.46
Abouet, Marguerite, 1971-
Aya   741.5
About behaviorism. Skinner, B. F.   150.19
Abraham (Biblical figure)
About
Chittister, J. The tent of Abraham   222
Abraham Lincoln and Civil War America. Gienapp, W. E.   92
Abraham Lincoln and the second American Revolution. McPherson, J. M.   973.7
Abrahams, Peter, 1947-
Bullet point   Fic
Reality check   Fic
Abrahams, Peter H.
McMinn's clinical atlas of human anatomy
                                             611
Abrams, Dennis, 1960-
Lemony Snicket (Daniel Handler)   92
Abrams, M. H. (Meyer Howard), 1912-
A glossary of literary terms   803
Abrams, Meyer Howard See Abrams, M. H. (Meyer Howard), 1912-
Abrams, Michael
Birdmen, batmen, and skyflyers   629.13
Abrams studio [series]
Micklewright, K. Drawing: mastering the language of visual expression   741.2
Abramson, Jill, 1954-
Obama   92
Absolute brightness. Lecesne, J.   Fic
Absolute Watchmen. See Moore, A. Watchmen
                                           741.5
Absolute zero and the conquest of cold. Shachtman, T.   536
Absolutely Maybe. Yee, L.   Fic
Absolutely, positively not. LaRochelle, D.   Fic
The **absolutely** true diary of a part-time Indian. Alexie, S.   Fic
Abstract art
See also Cubism
Moszynska, A. Abstract art   709.04
An **abundance** of Katherines. Green, J.   Fic
Abuse, Verbal See Invective
Abuse of children See Child abuse
Abused women
Bickerstaff, L. Violence against women
                                           362.88
Simons, R. Gender danger   362.88
Violence against women   362.83
Fiction
Brown, J. Bitter end   Fic
Hubbard, A. But I love him   Fic
Peters, J. A. Rage   Fic
Abusing over-the-counter drugs. Etingoff, K.
                                           362.29

Addiction: opposing viewpoints   **362.29**

Addiction to alcohol *See* Alcoholism

Addiction to work *See* Workaholism

Addiction treatment. Walker, I.   **362.29**

Addictive behavior *See* Compulsive behavior

Addicts, Drug *See* Drug addicts

Addresses *See* Speeches

Addy, Esi Sutherland- *See* Sutherland-Addy, Esi

Adelman, Howard C.
     Forensic medicine   **614**

Adelson-Goldstein, Jayme
     Oxford picture dictionary   **495.7**

ADHD. Farrar, A.   **616.85**

ADHD. Nakaya, A. C.   **618.92**

Adichie, Chimamanda Ngozi, 1977-
     Purple hibiscus   **Fic**

Adios, nirvana. Wesselhoeft, C.   **Fic**

Adirondack Mountains (N.Y.)
     Fiction
     McGhee, A. All rivers flow to the sea   **Fic**

Adkins, Lesley
     Dictionary of Roman religion   **292**
     Handbook to life in ancient Greece   **938**
     Handbook to life in ancient Rome   **937**

Adkins, Roy
     (jt. auth) Adkins, L. Dictionary of Roman religion   **292**
     (jt. auth) Adkins, L. Handbook to life in ancient Greece   **938**
     (jt. auth) Adkins, L. Handbook to life in ancient Rome   **937**

Adler, David A., 1947-
     Frederick Douglass   **92**

Adler, Mortimer J., 1902-2001
     Aristotle for everybody   **185**
     How to think about the great ideas   **080**
     Six great ideas   **111**

Adler, Robert E., 1946-
     Medical firsts   **610.9**

Adler, Stephen J.
     (ed) Women's letters. See Women's letters   **305.4**

Adlington, L. J., 1970-
     Cherry Heaven   **Fic**
     The diary of Pelly D   **Fic**

Adlington, Lucy J. *See* Adlington, L. J., 1970-

Administering the school library media center. Morris, B. J.   **027.8**

Administration of criminal justice
     Banks, C. Punishment in America   **364.6**
     Crime and criminals: opposing viewpoints   **364**
     Crimes and trials of the century   **345**
     Famous American crimes and trials   **364**
     Hanes, R. C. Crime and punishment in America: biographies   **920**
     Hanes, S. M. Crime and punishment in America, Primary sources   **364**
     Jacobs, T. A. They broke the law, you be the judge   **345**
     Margulies, P. The devil on trial   **345**

Sapse, D. S. Legal aspects of forensics   **363.2**

Should juveniles be tried as adults?   **345**

Wolcott, D. B. Crime and punishment in America   **364**

Admirals
     Brager, B. L. John Paul Jones   **92**
     Czisnik, M. Horatio Nelson   **92**

Admissions applications *See* College applications

Adoff, Arnold, 1935-
     (ed) I am the darker brother. See I am the darker brother   **811.008**

Adoff, Jaime
     The death of Jayson Porter   **Fic**

Adolescence
     See also Puberty
     Burek Pierce, J. Sex, brains, and video games   **027.62**
     Feig, P. Kick me   **305.23**
     McCoy, K. The teenage body book   **613**
     Phillips, S. F. The teen brain   **612.8**
     Talking adolescence   **305.23**
     See/See also pages in the following book(s):
     Espeland, P. The gifted kids' survival guide   **155.5**
     Fiction
     White, E. A boy's own story   **Fic**
     Whitehead, C. Sag Harbor   **Fic**

Adolescent fathers *See* Teenage fathers

Adolescent mothers *See* Teenage mothers

Adolescent pregnancy *See* Teenage pregnancy

Adolescent prostitution *See* Juvenile prostitution

Adolescent psychology
     See also Boys—Psychology; Girls—Psychology
     Bradley, M. J. The heart & soul of the next generation   **305.23**
     Fitzgerald, H. The grieving teen   **155.9**
     Hugel, B. I did it without thinking   **155.5**
     Mental health information for teens   **616.89**
     Teen suicide   **362.28**

Adolescents *See* Teenagers

Adolf Hitler and Nazi Germany. Rice, E.   **92**

Adonis to Zorro   **422.03**

Adopted children
     Growing up in the care of strangers   **362.7**
     Rhodes-Courter, A. M. Three little words   **92**

Adopted: the ultimate teen guide. Slade, S.   **362.7**

Adoptees
     Miró, A. Daughter of the Ganges   **92**

Adoption
     See also Adoptees
     Adoption   **362.7**
     Adoption: opposing viewpoints   **362.7**
     Kay, J. Red dust road   **92**
     Lanchon, A. All about adoption   **362.7**
     Scheeres, J. Jesus land   **92**
     Slade, S. Adopted: the ultimate teen guide   **362.7**
     Tucker, N. Love in the driest season   **362.7**
     Fiction
     Alvarez, J. Finding miracles   **Fic**

Adoption—Fiction—*Continued*

Reinhardt, D. A brief chapter in my impossible life **Fic**

Triana, G. Riding the universe **Fic**

Adoption, Interracial *See* Interracial adoption

Adoption **362.7**

Adoption: opposing viewpoints **362.7**

The **adoration** of Jenna Fox. Pearson, M. **Fic**

Adult adoptees *See* Adoptees

Adult child abuse victims

Fisher, R. G. The boys of the dark **365**

Adult survivors of child abuse *See* Adult child abuse victims

Adultery

Fiction

Mankell, H. Shadow of the leopard **Fic**

Adults abused as children *See* Adult child abuse victims

Advanced backpacking. Berger, K. **796.51**

Adventure and adventurers

Lawrence, S. River house **92**

Fiction

See Adventure fiction

Adventure divas (Television program)

Morris, H. Adventure divas **791.45**

Adventure fiction

See also Science fiction; Sea stories

Allende, I. Daughter of fortune **Fic**

Allende, I. Zorro **Fic**

Butler, O. E. Parable of the sower **Fic**

Cadnum, M. Peril on the sea **Fic**

Click **Fic**

Cole, S. Thieves like us **Fic**

Cooper, J. F. The Leatherstocking tales **Fic**

Crichton, M. Pirate latitudes **Fic**

Defoe, D. Robinson Crusoe **Fic**

Elliott, P. The pale assassin **Fic**

Frazier, A. Everlasting **Fic**

Friesner, E. M. Nobody's princess **Fic**

Gardner, S. The red necklace **Fic**

Gilman, D. The devil's breath **Fic**

Golden, C. The wild **Fic**

Grey, Z. Riders of the purple sage **Fic**

Harris, R. Pompeii **Fic**

Heath, J. The Lab **Fic**

Hoffman, M. Stravaganza: city of masks **Fic**

Meyer, L. A. Bloody Jack **Fic**

Moran, K. Bloodline **Fic**

Mourlevat, J.-C. Winter's end **Fic**

Mowll, J. Operation Red Jericho **Fic**

Mussi, S. The door of no return **Fic**

Parkhurst, C. Lost and found **Fic**

Perkins, L. R. As easy as falling off the face of the earth **Fic**

Rees, C. The fool's girl **Fic**

Rees, C. Pirates! **Fic**

Richards, J. The chaos code **Fic**

Stevenson, R. L. Treasure Island **Fic**

Stroud, J. Heroes of the valley **Fic**

Turner, M. W. The thief **Fic**

Verne, J. The extraordinary journeys: Twenty thousand leagues under the sea **Fic**

Bibliography

Gannon, M. B. Blood, bedlam, bullets, and badguys **016.8**

Adventure graphic novels

Crilley, M. Brody's ghost: book 1 **741.5**

Evanovich, J. Troublemaker **741.5**

Giffen, K. Blue Beetle: Shellshocked **741.5**

Graphic Classics volume eight: Mark Twain **741.5**

Hambly, B. Anne Steelyard: the garden of emptiness, act I **741.5**

Hinds, G. Beowulf **741.5**

Igarashi, D. Children of the sea, vol. 1 **741.5**

Kubo, T. Bleach, Vol. 1 **741.5**

Lagos, A. The sons of liberty **741.5**

Lee, T. Outlaw: the legend of Robin Hood **741.5**

McCreery, C. Kill Shakespeare, vol. 1 **741.5**

Miyuki, T. Musashi #9, Vol. 1 **741.5**

Morvan, J. D. Classics illustrated deluxe #6: the three Musketeers **741.5**

Raicht, M. The stuff of legend, book 1 **741.5**

Sakai, S. Usagi Yojimbo, book one **741.5**

Sakai, S. Usagi Yojimbo: Yokai **741.5**

Schweizer, C. Crogan's vengeance **741.5**

Wilson, G. W. Cairo **741.5**

Zubkavich, J. Skullkickers: 1000 Opas and a dead body **741.5**

Adventures among ants. Moffett, M. W. **595.7**

Adventures from the technology underground. Gurstelle, W. **621.8**

The **adventures** of Huckleberry Finn. Twain, M. **Fic**

The **adventures** of Tom Sawyer. Twain, M. **Fic**

Advertising

Advertising: opposing viewpoints **659.1**

How does advertising impact teen behavior? **659.1**

Advertising: opposing viewpoints **659.1**

Aeneas (Legendary character)

See/See also pages in the following book(s):

Hamilton, E. Mythology **292**

The **Aeneid**. Virgil **873**

Aerial photography

Collier, M. Over the coasts **551.4**

Collier, M. Over the mountains **557**

Collier, M. Over the rivers **551.48**

An aerial view of geology [series]

Collier, M. Over the coasts **551.4**

Collier, M. Over the mountains **557**

Collier, M. Over the rivers **551.48**

Aeronautics

See also Airplanes; Rocketry; Rockets (Aeronautics)

History

Abrams, M. Birdmen, batmen, and skyflyers **629.13**

Dick, R. The early years **629.13**

Dick, R. The golden age **629.13**

Dick, R. War & peace in the air **629.13**

Dick, R. Wings of change **629.13**

African American musicians—*Continued*
Ro, R. Dr. Dre   **92**
Southern, E. The music of black Americans   **780.89**
Wald, E. Escaping the delta [biography of Robert Johnson]   **92**
We'll understand it better by and by   **782.25**
White, A. Rebel for the hell of it [biography of Tupac Shakur]   **92**
   Dictionaries
Otfinoski, S. African Americans in the performing arts   **920.003**
   Poetry
Lewis, J. P. Black cat bone   **811**
The **African** American national biography   **920.003**

African American photographers
Willis, D. Reflections in Black   **770**
African American pilots
Hardesty, V. Black wings   **920**
African American poetry *See* American poetry—African American authors
African-American poets [v1]   **811.009**
African American reference library [series]
African American breakthroughs   **305.8**
African American religious leaders. Haskins, J.   **920**

African American singers
Duggleby, J. Uh huh!: the story of Ray Charles   **92**
Holiday, B. Lady sings the blues   **92**
Kaplan, H. S. Marian Anderson   **92**
Keiler, A. Marian Anderson   **92**
O'Keefe, S. Spin [biography of Michael Jackson]   **92**
Stone, T. L. Ella Fitzgerald   **92**
African American soldiers
Bloods: an oral history of the Vietnam War by black veterans   **959.704**
Buckley, G. L. American patriots   **355**
Hargrove, H. B. Black Union soldiers in the Civil War   **973.7**
Sutherland, J. African Americans at war   **920.003**
   Dictionaries
Reef, C. African Americans in the military   **920.003**
   Fiction
Myers, W. D. Fallen angels   **Fic**
African American women
Farrington, L. E. Creating their own image   **709.73**
Honey, hush!   **817.008**
   Biography
Berry, M. F. My face is black is true [biography of Callie House]   **92**
Bolden, T. Maritcha [biography of Maritcha Rémond Lyons]   **92**
Brinkley, D. Rosa Parks   **92**
Cary, L. Black ice   **92**
Clinton, C. Harriet Tubman: the road to freedom   **92**
Delany, S. Having our say   **92**
Felix, A. Condi [biography of Condoleezza Rice]   **92**

Goldstein, N. Jackie Ormes   **92**
Hansberry, L. To be young, gifted, and Black   **92**
Hinman, B. Eternal vigilance: the story of Ida B. Wells-Barnett   **92**
Hoose, P. M. Claudette Colvin   **92**
Hurston, Z. N. Dust tracks on a road   **92**
Kaplan, H. S. Marian Anderson   **92**
Keiler, A. Marian Anderson   **92**
LaNier, C. W. A mighty long way   **92**
Malaspina, A. Harriet Tubman   **92**
Mendelsohn, J. Barbara Jordan   **92**
Mundy, L. Michelle [Obama]   **92**
Painter, N. I. Sojourner Truth   **92**
Rice, C. Condoleezza Rice   **92**
Schafer, D. L. Anna Madgigine Jai Kingsley   **92**
Skloot, R. The immortal life of Henrietta Lacks   **92**
Stone, T. L. Ella Fitzgerald   **92**
See/See also pages in the following book(s):
Fleischner, J. Mrs. Lincoln and Mrs. Keckley   **92**
   Dictionaries
Black women in America   **920.003**
   Drama
Shange, N. For colored girls who have considered suicide, when the rainbow is enuf   **812**
   Health and hygiene
Fornay, A. Born beautiful   **646.7**
African-American writers. Bader, P.   **920.003**
African-American writers. Sickels, A.   **920**
African-American writers: a dictionary. See Encyclopedia of African-American writing   **810.9**
The **African** American writer's handbook. Fleming, R.   **808**
African Americans
The African American almanac   **305.8**
Du Bois, W. E. B. The Oxford W. E. B. Du Bois reader   **305.8**
Du Bois, W. E. B. The souls of Black folk   **305.8**
Should America pay?   **305.8**
Wright, R. Works   **818**
See/See also pages in the following book(s):
De Pauw, L. G. Founding mothers   **305.4**
   Bibliography
Neumann, C. E. Term paper resource guide to African American history   **016.973**
   Biography
Abdul-Jabbar, K. Black profiles in courage   **920**
Abdul-Jabbar, K. On the shoulders of giants   **92**
Abramson, J. Obama   **92**
Adler, D. A. Frederick Douglass   **92**
African American lives   **920**
Autobiography of a people   **305.8**
Berry, B. The ties that bind   **920**
Black leaders of the nineteenth century   **920**
Bolden, T. W.E.B. Du Bois   **92**
Brown, C. Manchild in the promised land   **92**
Crowe, C. Thurgood Marshall   **92**

Alcohol 362.292

Alcohol addiction. Walker, I. 362.292

Alcohol and teenagers *See* Teenagers—Alcohol use

Alcohol and youth *See* Youth—Alcohol use

Alcoholics

See also Children of alcoholics

Rehabilitation

Walker, I. Addiction treatment 362.29

Walker, I. Alcohol addiction 362.292

Alcoholics Anonymous

Rosengren, J. Big book unplugged 362.292

Alcoholism

See also Children of alcoholics

Addiction: opposing viewpoints 362.29

Alcohol 362.292

Rosengren, J. Big book unplugged 362.292

The truth about alcohol 362.292

Walker, I. Addiction in America 362.29

Walker, I. Alcohol addiction 362.292

Fiction

Anderson, J. L. Border crossing Fic

Barnes, J. Tales of the Madman Underground Fic

Bauman, B. A. Rosie & Skate Fic

Davenport, J. Anna begins Fic

Davis, D. Not like you Fic

Deuker, C. Runner Fic

Friend, N. Lush Fic

Garsee, J. Before, after, and somebody in between Fic

Gelbwasser, M. Inconvenient Fic

Nelson, B. Recovery Road Fic

Pearson, M. A room on Lorelei Street Fic

Saenz, B. A. Last night I sang to the monster Fic

Sanders, S. L. Gray baby Fic

Scott, E. Love you hate you miss you Fic

Scott, M. Freefall Fic

Tharp, T. The spectacular now Fic

Vincent, Z. The lucky place Fic

Zarr, S. Once was lost Fic

Alcott, Louisa May, 1832-1888

The selected letters of Louisa May Alcott 92

Aldenderfer, Mark S.

(ed) Great events from history, The ancient world, prehistory-476 C.E. See Great events from history, The ancient world, prehistory-476 C.E. 930

Alderfer, Jonathan

National Geographic birding essentials 598

(ed) National Geographic complete birds of North America. See National Geographic complete birds of North America 598

(ed) National Geographic field guide to the birds of North America. See National Geographic field guide to the birds of North America 598

Alderton, David

Encyclopedia of aquarium & pond fish 639.34

Firefly encyclopedia of the vivarium 639.3

Wild cats of the world 599.75

Aldington, Richard, 1892-1962

(ed) Wilde, O. The portable Oscar Wilde 828

Aldrete, Gregory S.

Daily life in the Roman city 937

Aldrich, Lisa J., 1952-

Nikola Tesla and the taming of electricity 92

Aldridge, Rebecca

Apolo Anton Ohno 92

Alegría, Malín

Estrella's quinceanera Fic

Aleksei Nikolaevich, Czarevitch, son of Nicholas II, Emperor of Russia, 1904-1918

Fiction

Whitcomb, L. The Fetch Fic

Alender, Katie

Bad girls don't die Fic

Aleshire, Peter

Mountains 551.4

Ocean ridges and trenches 551.46

Alessio, Amy

A year of programs for teens 027.62

(ed) Excellence in library services to young adults. See Excellence in library services to young adults 027.62

Alexander, the Great, 356-323 B.C.

About

Arrian. Alexander the Great 92

Skelton, D. Empire of Alexander the Great 938

Wood, M. In the footsteps of Alexander the Great 938

Fiction

Renault, M. Fire from heaven Fic

Alexander, Alma

Gift of the Unmage Fic

Alexander, Caroline, 1956-

The Bounty: the true story of the mutiny on the Bounty 996

The Endurance 998

Alexander, David, 1963-

The sun 523.7

Alexander, Jill S.

The sweetheart of Prosper County Fic

Alexander, Kwame

(ed) Crush: love poems. See Crush: love poems 808.81

Alexander, Leslie M., 1970-

(ed) Encyclopedia of African American history. See Encyclopedia of African American history 305.8

Alexie, Sherman, 1966-

The absolutely true diary of a part-time Indian Fic

Face 811

Ten little Indians S C

Alfred Hitchcock's mystery magazine presents fifty years of crime and suspense S C

Algebra

McKellar, D. Hot X 512

Miller, R. Bob Miller's algebra for the clueless 512

Algebra—*Continued*
Tabak, J. Algebra   **512**
Wingard-Nelson, R. Algebra I and algebra II
    512

Alger, Chadwick F., 1924-
The United Nations system   **341.23**

Algeria
Fiction
Camus, A. The stranger   **Fic**

Alhazen, 965-1039
About
Steffens, B. Ibn al-Haytham   **92**

Ali, Ayaan Hirsi *See* Hirsi Ali, Ayaan, 1969-

Ali, Muhammad, 1942-
About
Ezra, M. Muhammad Ali   **92**
Micklos, J. Muhammad Ali   **92**
Remnick, D. King of the world: Muhammad Ali and the rise of an American hero   **92**

Alien invasion and other inconveniences. Yansky, B.   **Fic**

Aliens
    See also Illegal aliens; Immigrants
United States
    See also United States—Immigration and emigration

Aliens from outer space *See* Extraterrestrial beings

Alighieri, Dante *See* Dante Alighieri, 1265-1321

Aliki
William Shakespeare & the Globe   **822.3**

Alire, Camila
Serving Latino communities   **027.6**

Alis. Rich, N.   **Fic**

Alive. Read, P. P.   **910.4**

Alive in the killing fields. Keat, N.   **92**

Alkali & alkaline earth metals. Halka, M.   **546**

All about adoption. Lanchon, A.   **362.7**

All about techniques in acrylics   **751.4**

All American [biography of Jim Thorpe] Crawford, B.   **92**

All creatures great and small. Herriot, J.   **92**

All-in. Hautman, P.   **Fic**

All in a day's work. Sullivan, M.   **502**

All my patients have tales. Wells, J.   **636**

All over but the shoutin'. Bragg, R.   **92**

All quiet on the western front. Remarque, E. M.   **Fic**

All rivers flow to the sea. McGhee, A.   **Fic**

All souls. Schutt, C.   **Fic**

All-Star Superman, Volume One. Morrison, G.   **741.5**

All terrain bicycles *See* Mountain bikes

All terrain cycling *See* Mountain biking

All the daring of the soldier. Leonard, E. D.   **973.7**

All the president's men. Bernstein, C.   **973.924**

All the pretty horses. McCarthy, C.   **Fic**

All the way to Berlin. Megellas, J.   **940.54**

All the wild horses. Hyde, D. O.   **599.66**

All the words on stage. Scheeder, L.   **822.3**

All things Austen. Olsen, K.   **823.009**

All things Shakespeare. Olsen, K.   **822.3**

All we know of heaven. Mitchard, J.   **Fic**

All we know of love. Baskin, N. R.   **Fic**

Allaby, Michael, 1933-
A chronology of weather   **551.5**
Deserts   **577.5**
The encyclopedia of Earth   **910**
Encyclopedia of weather and climate   **551**
Temperate forests   **577.3**
(ed) A dictionary of zoology. See A dictionary of zoology   **590.3**

Allan, Tony, 1946-
Life, myth, and art in Ancient Rome   **937**

Allegiance. Detzer, D.   **973.7**

Allegories
Adams, R. Watership Down   **Fic**
Atwood, M. The Handmaid's tale   **Fic**
Beagle, P. S. The last unicorn   **Fic**
Gardner, J. Grendel   **Fic**
Golding, W. Lord of the flies   **Fic**
Kafka, F. The trial   **Fic**
Orwell, G. Animal farm   **Fic**
Rushdie, S. Haroun and the sea of stories   **Fic**
Stevenson, R. L. The strange case of Dr. Jekyll and Mr. Hyde   **Fic**
Wilde, O. The picture of Dorian Gray   **Fic**

Allen, Brooke A.
A home for Mr. Easter   **741.5**

Allen, Frederick Lewis, 1890-1954
Only yesterday   **973.91**

Allen, John O.
(jt. auth) Jewett, C. E. Slavery in the South   **326**

Allen, Laurie, 1962-
Comedy scenes for student actors   **808.82**

Allen, Paula Gunn
See/See also pages in the following book(s):
Coltelli, L. Winged words: American Indian writers speak   **897**
(ed) Spider Woman's granddaughters. See Spider Woman's granddaughters   **S C**

Allen, Rhianon
(jt. auth) Reber, A. S. The Penguin dictionary of psychology   **150.3**

Allen, Robert
(ed) Dictionary & thesaurus. See Dictionary & thesaurus   **423**

Allen, Roger MacBride, 1957-
(jt. auth) Allen, T. B. Mr. Lincoln's high-tech war   **973.7**

Allen, Sarah Addison
The girl who chased the moon   **Fic**

Allen, Stewart Lee
In the devil's garden   **641**

Allen, Thomas B., 1929-
Mr. Lincoln's high-tech war   **973.7**

Allen, William Rodney
(ed) Vonnegut, K. Conversations with Kurt Vonnegut   **92**

American poetry—Hispanic American authors—
Collections—*Continued*

Red hot salsa   **811.008**

History and criticism

Buckwalter, S. Early American poetry, "beauty
in words"   **811.009**

Burns, A. Thematic guide to American poetry
     811.009

The Facts on File companion to American poetry   **811.009**

Llanas, S. G. Contemporary American poetry,
"not the end, but the beginning"   **811.009**

Llanas, S. G. Modern American poetry, "echoes
and shadows"   **811.009**

Native American authors

Harper's anthology of 20th century Native
American poetry   **811.008**

Songs from this Earth on turtle's back
     811.008

American poetry: the nineteenth century
     811.008

American poetry: the seventeenth and eighteenth
centuries   **811.008**

American poetry, the twentieth century
     811.008

American poets continuum series

Nye, N. S. You & yours: poems   **811**

American popular culture through history [se-
ries]

Browne, R. B. The Civil War and Reconstruction   **973.7**

Quay, S. E. Westward expansion   **978**

The **American** presidency   **973**

American presidents series

Calhoun, C. W. Benjamin Harrison   **92**

Dallek, R. Harry S. Truman   **92**

Finkelman, P. Millard Fillmore   **92**

Gordon-Reed, A. Andrew Johnson   **92**

Hart, G. James Monroe   **92**

Holt, M. F. Franklin Pierce   **92**

McGovern, G. S. Abraham Lincoln   **92**

Naftali, T. J. George H.W. Bush   **92**

Peters, C. Lyndon B. Johnson   **92**

Seigenthaler, J. James K. Polk   **92**

Widmer, E. L. Martin Van Buren   **92**

Wilentz, S. Andrew Jackson   **92**

Wills, G. James Madison   **92**

American Psychological Association

Concise rules of APA style   **808**

American rebels [series]

Micklos, J. Muhammad Ali   **92**

The **American** Red Cross first aid and safety
handbook   **616.02**

American reference books annual 2010 edition,
volume 41   **011**

American religious poems   **811.008**

The **American** renaissance   **810.9**

The **American** Revolution. Burg, D. F.
     973.3

The **American** Revolution [Greenhaven Press] **973.3**

The **American** Revolution: writings from the War
of Independence   **973.3**

American Revolutionary War   **973.3**

American rights [series]

Friedman, I. C. Freedom of speech and the press
     342

Head, T. Freedom of religion   **342**

American scripture. Maier, P.   **973.3**

American sermons   **252**

American Shaolin. Polly, M.   **796.8**

American short story masterpieces   **S C**

American smooth. Dove, R.   **811**

American songs

Furia, P. The poets of Tin Pan Alley
     782.42

American speeches

American Heritage book of great American
speeches for young people   **815.008**

American speeches   **815.008**

Fellow citizens   **352.23**

Historic speeches of African Americans
     815.008

In our own words   **815.008**

Stathis, S. W. Landmark debates in Congress
     328.73

U-X-L Asian American voices   **815.008**

American speeches   **815.008**

American travelers

Scieszka, C. To Timbuktu   **910.4**

American values: opposing viewpoints   **306**

American voices from-- [series]

Stefoff, R. American voices from the new republic, 1783-1830   **973.4**

American voices from the new republic, 1783-
1830. Stefoff, R.   **973.4**

American war library, Cold War [series]

Kallen, S. A. Primary sources   **909.82**

American war poetry   **811.008**

American wit and humor

An Anthology of graphic fiction, cartoons, and
true stories   **741.5**

Honey, hush!   **817.008**

Russell Baker's book of American humor
     817.008

Thurber, J. Writings and drawings   **818**

American women of science since 1900. Wayne,
T. K.   **920.003**

American women writers, 1900-1945   **810.9**

American women's history. Matthews, G.
     305.4

American workers [series]

Getzinger, D. The Triangle Shirtwaist Factory
fire   **974.7**

Americanisms

Ammer, C. The American Heritage dictionary of
idioms   **427**

Bartlett's Roget's thesaurus   **423**

Davidson, M. Right, wrong, and risky   **423**

Spears, R. A. McGraw-Hill's American idioms
dictionary   **427**

Spears, R. A. McGraw-Hill's dictionary of
American slang and colloquial expressions
     427

Young, S. The new comprehensive American
rhyming dictionary   **423**

Americanisms—*Continued*
Dictionaries
Dickson, P. Slang!   **427**
Garner, B. A. Garner's modern American usage   **423**
New Oxford American dictionary   **423**

The **Americanization** of Benjamin Franklin. Wood, G. S.   **92**

Americans at war   **973**

Americans' favorite poems   **808.81**

America's battle against terrorism   **973.931**

America's constitution. Amar, A. R.   **342**

America's game. MacCambridge, M.   **796.332**

America's prisons: opposing viewpoints   **365**

America's role in the world. Margulies, P.   **327.73**

America's wetland. Knapp, B.   **333.91**

America's women. Collins, G.   **305.4**

America's working women   **331.4**

AmeriCorps
See/See also pages in the following book(s):
Volunteerism   **361.3**

Amigas [series]
Chambers, V. Fifteen candles   **Fic**

Amigurumi animals. Obaachan, A.   **746.43**

Amin, Idi, 1925-2003
Fiction
Nanji, S. Child of dandelions   **Fic**

Amish
Hostetler, J. A. Amish society   **289.7**

Amistad (Schooner)
Fiction
Pesci, D. Amistad   **Fic**
Amistad. Pesci, D.   **Fic**

Amistad literary series
Gloria Naylor: critical perspectives past and present   **813.009**

Ammer, Christine
The American Heritage dictionary of idioms   **427**
The Facts on File dictionary of clichés   **423**

Amnesia
Fiction
Dashner, J. The maze runner   **Fic**
Zevin, G. Memoirs of a teenage amnesiac   **Fic**

Amnesty International
Free?: stories about human rights. See Free?: stories about human rights   **S C**

Amper, Susan
Bloom's how to write about Edgar Allan Poe   **818**

Amphetamines
See also Methamphetamine
Amphetamines   **615**

Amphetamines   **615**

Amphibians
See also Frogs
Alderton, D. Firefly encyclopedia of the vivarium   **639.3**
Attenborough, D. Life in cold blood   **597.9**

Conant, R. A field guide to reptiles & amphibians   **597.9**
Conant, R. Peterson first guide to reptiles and amphibians   **597.9**
Means, D. B. Stalking the plumed serpent and other adventures in herpetology   **597.9**
Stebbins, R. C. A field guide to Western reptiles and amphibians   **597.9**

Amputees
Kamara, M. The bite of the mango   **92**
Fiction
Baratz-Logsted, L. Crazy beautiful   **Fic**
Bingham, K. Shark girl   **Fic**
Draanen, W. v. The running dream   **Fic**
Mankell, H. Shadow of the leopard   **Fic**
Rorby, G. The outside of a horse   **Fic**
Waldorf, H. Tripping   **Fic**

The **AMS** weather book. Williams, J.   **551.5**

Amsterdam (Netherlands)
Gies, M. Anne Frank remembered   **940.53**

Amstutz, Lorraine Stutzman
(jt. auth) Zehr, H. "What will happen to me?"   **362.82**

Amt, Emilie, 1960-
(ed) Women's lives in medieval Europe. See Women's lives in medieval Europe   **305.4**

The **Amulet** of Samarkand. Stroud, J.   **Fic**

Amusement parks
Fiction
Beck, I. Pastworld   **Fic**

Amusements
See/See also pages in the following book(s):
Bishop, M. The Middle Ages   **940.1**

Amy & Roger's epic detour. Matson, M.   **Fic**

Anabolic steroids *See* Steroids

Analgesics
Walker, I. Painkillers   **362.29**

Analysis (Mathematics) *See* Mathematical analysis

Analyzing library collection use with Excel. Greiner, T.   **025.2**

Anan, Ruth
(jt. auth) Turkington, C. The encyclopedia of autism spectrum disorders   **616.85**

Anansi boys. Gaiman, N.   **Fic**

Anarchism and anarchists
See/See also pages in the following book(s):
Tuchman, B. W. The proud tower   **909.82**

Anasazi culture *See* Pueblo Indians

Anastasia *See* Anastasiíâ Nikolaevna, Grand Duchess, daughter of Nicholas II, Emperor of Russia, 1901-1918

Anastasiíâ Nikolaevna, Grand Duchess, daughter of Nicholas II, Emperor of Russia, 1901-1918
Fiction
Whitcomb, L. The Fetch   **Fic**

Anatolios, Khaled, 1962-
(jt. auth) Brown, S. F. Catholicism & Orthodox Christianity   **280**

Anatomy
See also Musculoskeletal system; Physiology

Animal experimentation: opposing viewpoints
179

Animal farm. Orwell, G. **Fic**

Animal intelligence
Boysen, S. T. The smartest animals on the planet **591.5**
McCarthy, S. Becoming a tiger **591.5**

Animal life **591.5**

Animal lore *See* Animals—Folklore

Animal migration *See* Animals—Migration

Animal painting and illustration
See also Animals in art

Animal Planet pet care library [series]
McKimmey, V. Ferrets **636.9**

Animal rights
See also Animal welfare
Animal rights **179**
Yount, L. Animal rights **179**

Animal rights **179**

Animal rights movement
Shevelow, K. For the love of animals **179**

Animal sciences **590.3**

Animal stories *See* Animals—Fiction

Animal talk. Friend, T. **591.59**

Animal tracks
Elbroch, M. Mammal tracks & sign **599**
McDougall, L. Tracking and reading sign **591.47**

Animal welfare
Morrison, A. R. An odyssey with animals **174.2**
Winegar, K. Saved **636.08**

Animal welfare movement *See* Animal rights movement

Animals
See also Dangerous animals; Invertebrates; Pets; Poisonous animals; Predatory animals; Prehistoric animals; Rare animals; Vertebrates; Wildlife; Zoology and names of orders and classes of the animal kingdom; kinds of animals characterized by their environments; and names of individual species
Noyes, D. One kingdom **590**
Smith, L. Why the cheetah cheats **590**
Encyclopedias
Animal sciences **590.3**
The encyclopedia of animals **590.3**
Fiction
Orwell, G. Animal farm **Fic**
Zuckerman, L. A taste for rabbit **Fic**
Folklore
See also Dragons; Monsters; Mythical animals
Nigg, J. Wonder beasts **398**
Geographical distribution
See Biogeography
Graphic novels
Hartzell, A. Fox bunny funny **741.5**
Migration
Kostyal, K. M. Great migrations **591.56**

Pictorial works
See also Animals in art
Animal life **591.5**
Naskrecki, P. The smaller majority **591.7**
Africa
Ross, M. Predator **599.7**

Animals, Bloodsucking *See* Bloodsucking animals

Animals, Fossil *See* Fossils

Animals, Habits and behavior of *See* Animal behavior

Animals, Mythical *See* Mythical animals

Animals and the handicapped
Lufkin, E. To the rescue **636.7**

Animals in art
Delacampagne, A. Here be dragons **700**
Hammond, L. Paint realistic animals in acrylic with Lee Hammond **751.42**
Hayakawa, H. Kirigami menagerie **736**
Nice, C. Painting your favorite animals in pen, ink, and watercolor **743**

Animals in translation. Grandin, T. **591.5**

Animals' rights *See* Animal rights

Animated films
See also Anime
Richmond, S. The rough guide to anime **791.43**

Animators *See* Cartoonists

Anime
Brenner, R. E. Understanding manga and anime **025.2**
Richmond, S. The rough guide to anime **791.43**

Anna and the French kiss. Perkins, S. **Fic**

Anna begins. Davenport, J. **Fic**

Anna Karenina. Tolstoy, L., graf **Fic**

Anna Madgigine Jai Kingsley. Schafer, D. L. **92**

Anna's world. Coleman, W. **Fic**

Anne Boleyn, Queen, consort of Henry VIII, King of England, 1507-1536
See/See also pages in the following book(s):
Starkey, D. Six wives: the queens of Henry VIII **920**

Anne Frank remembered. Gies, M. **940.53**

Anne Frank's Tales from the secret annex. Frank, A. **839.3**

Anne of Cleves, Queen, consort of Henry VIII, King of England, 1515-1557
See/See also pages in the following book(s):
Starkey, D. Six wives: the queens of Henry VIII **920**

Anne Steelyard: the garden of emptiness, act I. Hambly, B. **741.5**

The Annenberg Foundation Trust at Sunnylands' adolescent mental health initiative [series]
Keegan, K. Chasing the high **92**

Annesley, James
About
Ekirch, A. R. Birthright [biography of James Annesley] **92**

Annexed. Dogar, S. **Fic**

The **Annie** Dillard reader. Dillard, A.   **818**

Annotated book lists for every teen reader. Bartel, J.   **028.5**

The **annotated** Mona Lisa. Strickland, C.   **709**

The **annotated** U.S. Constitution and Declaration of Independence   **342**

Anorexia   **616.85**

Anorexia and bulimia. Sonenklar, C.   **616.85**

Anorexia nervosa
 Anorexia   **616.85**
 Grahl, G. A. Skinny boy   **92**
 Sonenklar, C. Anorexia and bulimia   **616.85**
 Fiction
 Anderson, L. H. Wintergirls   **Fic**
 George, M. Looks   **Fic**
 Kaslik, I. Skinny   **Fic**
 Kessler, J. M. Hunger   **Fic**
 Padian, M. Jersey tomatoes are the best   **Fic**
 Vrettos, A. M. Skin   **Fic**

Another day in the frontal lobe. Firlik, K.   **92**

Another Faust. Nayeri, D.   **Fic**

Another kind of cowboy. Juby, S.   **Fic**

Anouilh, Jean, 1910-1987
 Antigone   **842**

Ansary, Mir Tamim
 West of Kabul, East of New York   **958.1**

Ansary, Tamim *See* Ansary, Mir Tamim

Ansary, Tamin *See* Ansary, Mir Tamim

Antarctica
 See also South Pole
 Walker, S. M. Frozen secrets   **998**
 Description and travel
 Montaigne, F. Fraser's penguins   **577.2**
 Swan, R. Antarctica 2041   **577.5**
 Exploration
 Alexander, C. The Endurance   **998**
 Gurney, A. The race to the white continent   **998**
 Solomon, S. The coldest March   **998**
 Fiction
 McCaughrean, G. The white darkness   **Fic**
 White, A. Surviving Antarctica   **Fic**

Antarctica 2041. Swan, R.   **577.5**

An **Anthology** of graphic fiction, cartoons, and true stories   **741.5**

Anthology of Japanese literature from the earliest era to the mid-nineteenth century   **895.6**

Anthology of modern Chinese poetry   **895.1**

Anthology of modern Palestinian literature   **892.7**

The **anthology** of rap   **782.42**

Anthony, Lawrence
 Babylon's ark   **590.73**
 The elephant whisperer   **599.67**

Anthony, Susan B., 1820-1906
 About
 Colman, P. Elizabeth Cady Stanton and Susan B. Anthony   **92**

Anthropogeography *See* Human geography

Anthropologists
 Bowman-Kruhm, M. The Leakeys   **920**
 Hess, A. Margaret Mead   **92**

Mark, J. T. Margaret Mead   **92**
 Morell, V. Ancestral passions   **920**

Anthropology
 See also Forensic anthropology; Physical anthropology

Anti-abortion movement *See* Pro-life movement

Anti-apartheid movement
 See also Apartheid
 Sonneborn, L. The end of apartheid in South Africa   **968.06**

Anti-war poetry *See* War poetry

Antibiotic-resistant bacteria. Guilfoile, P.   **616.9**

Antibiotics
 Goldsmith, C. Superbugs strike back   **615**
 Shnayerson, M. The killers within   **616**

Anticommunist movements
 Giblin, J. The rise and fall of Senator Joe McCarthy   **92**

Antidepressants
 Antidepressants [William Dudley, ed.]   **615**

Antidepressants [William Dudley, ed.]   **615**

Antieau, Kim
 Broken moon   **Fic**

Antigone. Anouilh, J.   **842**

Antiquities
 See also Archeology
 Hunt, P. Ten discoveries that rewrote history   **930.1**

Antiquity of man *See* Human origins

Antisemitism
 See also Jews—Persecutions
 Goldhagen, D. Hitler's willing executioners   **940.53**
 Encyclopedias
 Antisemitism   **305.8**
 Fiction
 Roth, P. The plot against America   **Fic**

Antisemitism   **305.8**

Antivivisection movement *See* Animal rights movement

Antoine, Rebeca
 (ed) Voices rising. See Voices rising   **976.3**

Antonio, Sam
 See/See also pages in the following book(s):
 Mendoza, P. M. Extraordinary people in extraordinary times   **920**

Ants
 Hölldobler, B. The leafcutter ants   **595.7**
 Keller, L. The lives of ants   **595.7**
 Moffett, M. W. Adventures among ants   **595.7**

Anxiety
 Connolly, S. Anxiety disorders   **616.85**
 Miller, A. R. Living with anxiety disorders   **616.85**
 Munroe, E. A. The anxiety workbook for girls   **155.5**
 Schutz, S. I don't want to be crazy   **92**
 The truth about anxiety and depression   **616.85**

Anxiety—*Continued*
Fiction
Colasanti, S. Waiting for you   **Fic**

Anxiety disorders. Connolly, S.   **616.85**

The **anxiety** workbook for girls. Munroe, E. A.
    155.5

Anya's ghost. Brosgol, V.   **741.5**

Anything we love can be saved. Walker, A.
    814

Anzovin, Steven, 1954-
Famous first facts about American politics
    973

(ed) Famous first facts, international edition. See
Famous first facts, international edition
    031.02

(jt. auth) Kane, J. N. Famous first facts
    031.02

Apache Indians
Jastrzembski, J. C. The Apache wars
    970.004

Sullivan, G. Geronimo   **92**

Sweeney, E. R. Cochise, Chiricahua Apache
chief   **92**

The **Apache** wars. Jastrzembski, J. C.   **970.004**

Apartheid

   See also Anti-apartheid movement
Houze, D. Twilight people   **92**

Mandela, N. Nelson Mandela speaks   **968.06**

Sonneborn, L. The end of apartheid in South
Africa   **968.06**

Apartment houses
Fiction
Hyde, C. R. Jumpstart the world   **Fic**

Apel, Melanie Ann
Cystic fibrosis   **616.2**

Apes

   See also Chimpanzees; Gorillas; Orangutan
Morris, D. Planet ape   **599.8**

World atlas of great apes and their conservation
    599.8

Apfelbaum, Nina
(jt. auth) Rosen, P. Bearing witness
    016.94053

Apiculture *See* Beekeeping; Bees

Apollo Project *See* Project Apollo

Apollo project
French, F. In the shadow of the moon
    629.45

Apolo Anton Ohno. Aldridge, R.   **92**

Appalachian Mountain region *See* Appalachian
region

Appalachian region
Reece, E. Lost mountain   **622**
Fiction
Marshall, C. Christy   **Fic**
Social life and customs
Foxfire 40th anniversary book   **975.8**

Appelt, Kathi, 1954-
Poems from homeroom   **811**

Appetite disorders *See* Eating disorders

Appiah, Anthony
(ed) Africana: the encyclopedia of the African
and African American experience. See
Africana: the encyclopedia of the African and
African American experience   **909**

(ed) Gloria Naylor: critical perspectives past and
present. See Gloria Naylor: critical perspectives past and present   **813.009**

Appiah, Kwame Anthony *See* Appiah, Anthony

Appignanesi, Richard
Hamlet   **822.3**
Julius Caesar   **822.3**
A midsummer night's dream   **822.3**
Romeo and Juliet   **822.3**
The tempest   **822.3**
(ed) Mairowitz, D. Z. Kafka   **92**

Applications for college *See* College applications

Applications for positions
Christen, C. What color is your parachute? for
teens   **331.7**

Applying to college for students with ADD or LD.
Grossberg, B. N.   **378.1**

Apprentices
Paquette, P. H. Apprenticeship   **331.2**
Fiction
Goodman, A. Eon: Dragoneye reborn   **Fic**
Oliver, J. G. The demon trapper's daughter
    Fic
Yancey, R. The monstrumologist   **Fic**

Apprenticeship. Paquette, P. H.   **331.2**

Approximate computation
Weinstein, L. Guesstimation   **519.5**

Aquanauts *See* Underwater exploration

Aquariums

   See also Marine aquariums
Boruchowitz, D. E. Mini aquariums   **639.34**
Maître-Allain, T. Aquariums   **639.34**

Aquatic animals *See* Marine animals

Aquinas, Saint Thomas *See* Thomas, Aquinas,
Saint, 1225?-1274

Aquinas, Thomas *See* Thomas, Aquinas, Saint,
1225?-1274

Arab American voices. Hall, L.   **305.8**

Arab American youth
Bayoumi, M. How does it feel to be a problem?
    305.8

Arab Americans
The Arabs   **305.8**
Hall, L. Arab American voices   **305.8**
Fiction
Halaby, L. West of the Jordan   **Fic**
History
The Arab Americans   **305.8**
Social conditions
Bayoumi, M. How does it feel to be a problem?
    305.8
The **Arab** Americans   **305.8**

Arab countries
Fiction
Marston, E. Santa Claus in Baghdad and other
stories about teens in the Arab world   **S C**
Maps
The new atlas of the Arab world   **912**

Arson
Fiction
Ehrenberg, P. Tillmon County fire   **Fic**
Wilson, D. L. Firehorse   **Fic**
Art
     See also Artistic anatomy; Symbolism in art
Kampen O'Riley, M. Art beyond the West
       709
19th century
    See also Impressionism (Art)
20th century
    See also Computer art
Heart to heart   **811.008**
Encyclopedias
Encyclopedia of art for young people   **703**
Fiction
Gallagher, L. The opposite of invisible   **Fic**
Kephart, B. Nothing but ghosts   **Fic**
History
Cole, B. Art of the Western world   **709**
Encyclopedia of art for young people   **703**
Gardner, H. Gardner's art through the ages
       709
Gombrich, E. H. The story of art   **709**
Hartt, F. Art: a history of painting, sculpture, architecture   **709**
Janson, H. W. Janson's history of art   **709**
King, R. Art: over 2,500 works from cave to contemporary   **709**
Little, S. . . . isms: understanding art   **709**
Mason, A. A history of Western art   **709**
Strickland, C. The annotated Mona Lisa   **709**
History—Maps
Atlas of world art   **709**
Philosophy
See/See also pages in the following book(s):
Hamilton, E. The Greek way   **880.9**
Poetry
Side by side   **808.81**
Technique
Hershberger, C. Creative colored pencil workshop   **741.2**
Smith, R. The artist's handbook   **702.8**
Technique—Encyclopedias
The Grove encyclopedia of materials and techniques in art   **702.8**
Art, Abstract *See* Abstract art
Art, African *See* African art
Art, African American *See* African American art
Art, American *See* American art
Art, Chinese *See* Chinese art
Art, Christian *See* Christian art
Art, Computer *See* Computer art
Art, Egyptian *See* Egyptian art
Art, Graphic *See* Graphic arts
Art, Greek *See* Greek art
Art, Indian *See* Native American art
Art, Indic *See* Indic art
Art, Islamic *See* Islamic art
Art, Latin American *See* Latin American art
Art, Medieval *See* Medieval art
Art, Mexican *See* Mexican art

Art, Modern *See* Modern art
Art, Roman *See* Roman art
Art: a history of painting, sculpture, architecture. Hartt, F.   **709**
Art and society
Aronson, M. Art attack   **709.04**
Art appreciation
Aronson, M. Art attack   **709.04**
Fallon, M. How to analyze the works of Andy Warhol   **700**
Fallon, M. How to analyze the works of Georgia O'Keeffe   **759.13**
How to read a painting   **753**
King, R. Art: over 2,500 works from cave to contemporary   **709**
Art attack. Aronson, M.   **709.04**
Art beyond the West. Kampen O'Riley, M.
       709
Art criticism
Fallon, M. How to analyze the works of Andy Warhol   **700**
Fallon, M. How to analyze the works of Georgia O'Keeffe   **759.13**
Art from the ashes   **940.53**
The **art** of keeping snakes. De Vosjoli, P.
       639.3
The **art** of loving. Fromm, E.   **152.4**
Art of mentoring [series]
Brustein, R. Letters to a young actor   **792**
Campolo, A. Letters to a young evangelical
       248.4
Freedman, S. G. Letters to a young journalist
       070.4
Stewart, I. Letters to a young mathematician
       510
The **art** of spelling. Vos Savant, M. M.   **421**
The **art** of the author interview. Johnson, S. A.
       808
The **art** of the comic book. Harvey, R. C.
       741.5
Art of the Middle Ages. Snyder, J.   **709.02**
Art of the Western world. Cole, B.   **709**
The **art** of war. See Sun-tzu. The illustrated art of war   **355**
Art on the wall [series]
Bingham, J. Impressionism   **759.05**
Bingham, J. Post-Impressionism   **759.05**
Art thefts
Dolnick, E. The rescue artist   **364.1**
Arthritis
Rouba, K. Juvenile arthritis   **618.92**
Arthur, King
About
Ashe, G. The discovery of King Arthur   **92**
Malory, Sir T. Le morte Darthur, or, The hoole book of Kyng Arthur and of his noble knyghtes of the Rounde Table   **398.2**
Pyle, H. The story of King Arthur and his knights   **398.2**
Pyle, H. The story of the Grail and the passing of Arthur   **398.2**
Fiction
Bradley, M. Z. The mists of Avalon   **Fic**

Arthur, King—About—Fiction—*Continued*
Reeve, P. Here lies Arthur   **Fic**
Spinner, S. Damosel   **Fic**
Springer, N. I am Mordred   **Fic**
Springer, N. I am Morgan le Fay   **Fic**
Stewart, M. Mary Stewart's Merlin trilogy
    Fic
Vande Velde, V. The book of Mordred   **Fic**
White, T. H. The once and future king   **Fic**
Arthur, Jason
(il) Dorkin, E. Beasts of Burden: animal rites
    741.5
Arthur, Wallace
Creatures of accident   **591.3**
Arthurian romances
See also Grail
Gawain and the Grene Knight (Middle English poem). Sir Gawain and the Green Knight
    821
Pyle, H. The story of King Arthur and his knights   **398.2**
Pyle, H. The story of Sir Launcelot and his companions   **398.2**
Pyle, H. The story of the champions of the Round Table   **398.2**
Pyle, H. The story of the Grail and the passing of Arthur   **398.2**
Artichoke's heart. Supplee, S.   **Fic**
Articles of Confederation *See* United States. Articles of Confederation
The **Articles** of Confederation. Feinberg, B. S.
    342
Artificial intelligence
Brooks, R. A. Flesh and machines   **629.8**
Henderson, H. Artificial intelligence   **006.3**
Artificial organs
McClellan, M. Organ and tissue transplants
    617.9
Artistic anatomy
See also Figure drawing
Graves, D. R. Drawing portraits   **743**
Hart, C. Drawing cutting edge anatomy
    741.5
Hart, C. Human anatomy made amazingly easy
    743
Artists
See also African American artists; Cartoonists; Illustrators; Photographers; Women artists
Kagan, A. Marc Chagall   **92**
Smith, A. D. Letters to a young artist   **700**
    Biography—Encyclopedias
Biographical encyclopedia of artists   **920.003**
    Dictionaries
Otfinoski, S. Latinos in the arts   **920.003**
World artists, 1950-1980   **920.003**
World artists, 1980-1990   **920.003**
    Fiction
Bick, I. J. Draw the dark   **Fic**
Bingham, K. Shark girl   **Fic**
Chevalier, T. Girl with a pearl earring   **Fic**
Cornwell, A. Carpe diem   **Fic**
Cullen, L. I am Rembrandt's daughter   **Fic**
Franco, B. Metamorphosis   **Fic**

Franklin, E. The other half of me   **Fic**
Hearn, J. Ivy   **Fic**
Koja, K. Buddha boy   **Fic**
Patterson, V. O. The other side of blue   **Fic**
Rainfield, C. A. Scars   **Fic**
Schindler, H. A blue so dark   **Fic**
Vivian, S. Same difference   **Fic**
Whelan, G. See what I see   **Fic**
Wyatt, M. Funny how things change   **Fic**
    Graphic novels
Gulledge, L. L. Page by Paige   **741.5**
Urrea, L. A. Mr. Mendoza's paintbrush
    741.5
    Poetry
Reynolds, J. My name is Jason. Mine too
    811
Spires, E. I heard God talking to me   **811**
    United States
Greenberg, J. Andy Warhol   **92**
Greenberg, J. Runaway girl: the artist Louise Bourgeois   **92**
Hassrick, P. H. Charles M. Russell   **92**
Reich, S. Painting the wild frontier: the art and adventures of George Catlin   **92**
Rhodes, R. John James Audubon   **92**
Artists, French
Kallen, S. A. Claude Monet   **92**
Kallen, S. A. Pablo Picasso   **92**
Artists, Italian
Somervill, B. A. Michelangelo   **92**
Artists, Spanish
Ross, M. E. Salvador Dali and the surrealists
    92
The **artist's** handbook. Smith, R.   **702.8**
Artists' materials
Kallen, S. A. The artist's tools   **702.8**
Sanmiguel, D. Complete guide to materials and techniques for drawing and painting   **751**
Smith, R. The artist's handbook   **702.8**
Webb, D. Drawing handbook   **741.2**
    Encyclopedias
The Grove encyclopedia of materials and techniques in art   **702.8**
Artists of an era [series]
Roark, E. L. Artists of colonial America
    709.73
Artists of colonial America. Roark, E. L.
    709.73
The **artist's** tools. Kallen, S. A.   **702.8**
Arts
See also Surrealism
Boorstin, D. J. The creators   **909**
Wyckoff, C. Communications and the arts
    331.7
    Biography
World cultural leaders of the twentieth and twenty-first centuries   **920.003**
    History
Arts and humanities through the eras   **700**
Ochoa, G. The Wilson chronology of the arts
    700
    China
Shaughnessy, E. L. Exploring the life, myth, and art of ancient China   **931**

Athletes

    See also African American athletes; Hispanic American athletes; Women athletes

Allred, L. Longshot   **92**

Are athletes good role models?   **306.4**

Armstrong, L. It's not about the bike   **92**

Crawford, B. All American [biography of Jim Thorpe]   **92**

The Lincoln library of sports champions   **920.003**

Sports and athletes: opposing viewpoints   **796**

Strickland, B. Tour de Lance   **92**

Wheeler, D. The sports scholarships insider's guide   **796**

Dictionaries

Friedman, I. C. Latino athletes   **920.003**

Great athletes   **920.003**

Drug use

    See also Steroids

Bjornlund, L. D. How dangerous are performance-enhancing drugs?   **362.29**

Pampel, F. C. Drugs and sports   **362.29**

Performance enhancing drugs   **362.29**

Walker, I. Steroids: pumped up and dangerous   **362.29**

See/See also pages in the following book(s):

Sports and athletes: opposing viewpoints   **796**

Nutrition

Burke, L. The complete guide to food for sports performance   **613.2**

Shryer, D. Peak performance   **617.1**

Smolin, L. A. Nutrition for sports and exercise   **613.7**

Athletes, Hispanic American *See* Hispanic American athletes

Athletic medicine *See* Sports medicine

Athletics

    See also Sports; Track athletics

Atkin, S. Beth

Gunstories   **363.33**

Atkins, Jeannine, 1953-

Borrowed names   **811**

Atkinson, Rick

In the company of soldiers   **956.7**

Atlanta (Ga.)

Alphin, E. M. An unspeakable crime   **364.152**

Fiction

McVoy, T. E. After the kiss   **Fic**

Myracle, L. Bliss   **Fic**

Myracle, L. Peace, love, and baby ducks   **Fic**

Oliver, J. G. The demon trapper's daughter   **Fic**

Atlantic Coast Conference

Feinstein, J. A march to madness   **796.323**

The **Atlantic** slave trade. Postma, J.   **326**

Atlantis

Fiction

Richards, J. The chaos code   **Fic**

Atlas of African-American history. Ciment, J.   **305.8**

Atlas of American history. Nash, G. B.   **911**

Atlas of American military history. Murray, S.   **355**

Atlas of Asian-American history. Avakian, M.   **305.8**

The **atlas** of bird migration   **598**

Atlas of classical history   **911**

The **atlas** of climate change. Dow, K.   **551.6**

The **atlas** of endangered animals. Hammond, P.   **591.68**

Atlas of exploration   **911**

The **atlas** of global conservation   **333.95**

Atlas of Hispanic-American history. Ochoa, G.   **305.8**

The **atlas** of Middle-earth. Fonstad, K. W.   **823.009**

Atlas of North America   **912**

The **atlas** of North American exploration. Goetzmann, W. H.   **911**

Atlas of the Civil War. National Geographic Society (U.S.)   **973.7**

Atlas of the Civil War. Woodworth, S. E.   **973.7**

Atlas of the Civil War, month by month. Swanson, M.   **973.7**

Atlas of the medieval world. McKitterick, R.   **911**

Atlas of the North American Indian. Waldman, C.   **970.004**

Atlas of the transatlantic slave trade. Eltis, D.   **381**

Atlas of the universe. See Firefly atlas of the universe   **523**

Atlas of the world. See Oxford atlas of the world   **912**

Atlas of the world's religions   **201**

The **Atlas** of US and Canadian environmental history   **304.2**

Atlas of world art   **709**

Atlases

    See also Human anatomy—Atlases

The **atlas** of global conservation   **333.95**

Atlas of North America   **912**

Atlas of the world's religions   **201**

The **Atlas** of US and Canadian environmental history   **304.2**

Dow, K. The atlas of climate change   **551.6**

Eltis, D. Atlas of the transatlantic slave trade   **381**

Firefly atlas of North America   **912**

Gilbert, M. The Routledge atlas of the Holocaust   **940.53**

Hammond, P. The atlas of endangered animals   **591.68**

Hammond world atlas   **912**

Hayes, D. Historical atlas of the United States   **911**

The illustrated atlas of wildlife   **591.9**

Magocsi, P. R. Historical atlas of Central Europe   **911**

Nash, G. B. Atlas of American history   **911**

National Geographic Atlas of China   **912**

The **Audubon** Society field guide to North American fishes, whales, and dolphins. See Gilbert, C. R. National Audubon Society field guide to fishes, North America **597**

The **Audubon** Society field guide to North American fossils. Thompson, I. **560**

The **Audubon** Society field guide to North American mushrooms. Lincoff, G. **579.6**

Augarde, Steve
X-Isle **Fic**

Augenbraum, Harold
(ed) Growing up Latino. See Growing up Latino **810.8**
(ed) U.S. Latino literature. See U.S. Latino literature **810.9**

August Wilson [critical essays] **812.009**

Augustine, Saint, Bishop of Hippo
See/See also pages in the following book(s):
Russell, B. A history of Western philosophy **109**

Augustus, Emperor of Rome, 63 B.C.-14 A.D.
Fiction
Dray, S. Lily of the Nile **Fic**
Graves, R. I, Claudius **Fic**

Aunts
Fiction
Archer, E. Geek: fantasy novel **Fic**
Baratz-Logsted, L. Twin's daughter **Fic**
Bauer, J. Hope was here **Fic**
Fusco, K. N. Tending to Grace **Fic**
Johnson, M. 13 little blue envelopes **Fic**
Lamba, M. What I meant. . . **Fic**
Les Becquets, D. Love, Cajun style **Fic**
Mackler, C. Vegan virgin Valentine **Fic**

Aurelia. Osterlund, A. **Fic**

Auroras
See/See also pages in the following book(s):
Jago, L. The northern lights [biography of Kristian Birkeland] **92**

Auschwitz (Poland: Concentration camp)
Buergenthal, T. A lucky child [biography of Thomas Buergenthal] **92**
Robson, D. Auschwitz **940.53**

Austen, Jane, 1775-1817
Persuasion **Fic**
Pride and prejudice **Fic**
Sense and sensibility **Fic**
About
Baker, W. Critical companion to Jane Austen **823.009**
Haggerty, A. Jane Austen **92**
Jane Austen [critical essays] **823.009**
Poplawski, P. A Jane Austen encyclopedia **823.009**
Shields, C. Jane Austen **92**
Encyclopedias
Olsen, K. All things Austen **823.009**
Fiction
Harrison, C. I was Jane Austen's best friend **Fic**
Parodies, imitations, etc.
Grahame-Smith, S. Pride and prejudice and zombies **Fic**

Auster, Paul, 1947-
(ed) I thought my father was God and other true tales from the National Story Project. See I thought my father was God and other true tales from the National Story Project **810.8**

Austin, Allan W., 1968-
(ed) Asian American history and culture. See Asian American history and culture **305.8**

Australia
Pung, A. Unpolished gem **92**
Description and travel
Flannery, T. F. Chasing kangaroos **599.2**
Fiction
Abdel-Fattah, R. Does my head look big in this? **Fic**
Abdel-Fattah, R. Ten things I hate about me **Fic**
Boyd, M. Will **Fic**
Carmody, I. Alyzon Whitestarr **Fic**
Clarke, J. One whole and perfect day **Fic**
Clarke, J. The winds of heaven **Fic**
Crowley, C. A little wanting song **Fic**
Foxlee, K. The anatomy of wings **Fic**
Frazier, A. Everlasting **Fic**
Hartnett, S. Butterfly **Fic**
Hartnett, S. Thursday's child **Fic**
Herrick, S. By the river **Fic**
Herrick, S. Cold skin **Fic**
Herrick, S. The wolf **Fic**
James, R. Beautiful malice **Fic**
Jinks, C. Evil genius **Fic**
Jonsberg, B. Dreamrider **Fic**
Larbalestier, J. Magic or madness **Fic**
Marchetta, M. Jellicoe Road **Fic**
Marchetta, M. Saving Francesca **Fic**
Marsden, J. Tomorrow, when the war began **Fic**
Marsden, J. While I live **Fic**
McCarthy, M. Rose by any other name **Fic**
Moriarty, J. The year of secret assignments **Fic**
Murray, M. How to make a bird **Fic**
Shute, N. On the beach **Fic**
Silvey, C. Jasper Jones **Fic**
Wilkinson, L. Pink **Fic**
Williams, G. Beatle meets Destiny **Fic**
History
West, B. A. A brief history of Australia **994**

Author research series
Heaphy, M. Science fiction authors **920.003**
Authoritarianism See Totalitarianism
Authors
See also Literature—Bio-bibliography; Women authors
Burt, D. S. The literary 100 **809**
Gillespie, J. T. The Newbery/Printz companion **028.5**
Read all about it! **808.8**
Dictionaries
Encyclopedia of world writers **920.003**
Heaphy, M. Science fiction authors **920.003**
World authors, 1950-1970 **920.003**
World authors, 1970-1975 **920.003**
World authors, 1975-1980 **920.003**

Authors, English—Dictionaries—*Continued*
British authors of the nineteenth century
920.003
British writers **920.003**
Encyclopedia of British writers, 16th-18th centuries **820.9**
Encyclopedia of British writers, 1800 to the present **820.9**
Authors, Greek
Dictionaries
Grant, M. Greek and Latin authors, 800 B.C.-A.D. 1000 **920.003**
Authors, Irish
Aykroyd, C. Savage satire [biography of Jonathan Swift] **92**
Authors, Japanese
Mussari, M. Haruki Murakami **92**
Authors, Latin
Dictionaries
Grant, M. Greek and Latin authors, 800 B.C.-A.D. 1000 **920.003**
Authors, Latin American
Dictionaries
Flores, A. Spanish American authors **920.003**
Authors, Nigerian
Achebe, C. The education of a British-protected child **92**
Authors, Scottish
Kay, J. Red dust road **92**
Authors series
American authors, 1600-1900 **920.003**
British authors before 1800 **920.003**
British authors of the nineteenth century **920.003**
European authors, 1000-1900 **920.003**
Grant, M. Greek and Latin authors, 800 B.C.-A.D. 1000 **920.003**
World authors, 1950-1970 **920.003**
World authors, 1970-1975 **920.003**
World authors, 1975-1980 **920.003**
World authors, 1980-1985 **920.003**
World authors, 1985-1990 **920.003**
World authors, 1990-1995 **920.003**
World authors, 1995-2000 **920.003**
World authors, 2000-2005 **920.003**
Authorship
See also Creative writing; Journalism
Dunn, J. A teen's guide to getting published **808**
Harper, E. Your name in print **808**
King, S. On writing **92**
Orr, T. Extraordinary essays **808.4**
Writing and publishing **808**
Data processing—Handbooks, manuals, etc.
Walker, J. R. The Columbia guide to online style **808**
Fiction
Arnold, T. Rat life **Fic**
Cornwell, A. Carpe diem **Fic**
Davenport, J. Anna begins **Fic**
Freitas, D. This gorgeous game **Fic**
Gould, P. L. Write naked **Fic**
Johnson, M. Suite Scarlett **Fic**
Lubar, D. Sleeping freshmen never lie **Fic**

Phillips, W. Fishtailing **Fic**
Sales, L. Mostly good girls **Fic**
Selfors, S. Mad love **Fic**
Wittlinger, E. Hard love **Fic**
Wizner, J. Spanking Shakespeare **Fic**
Graphic novels
Barry, L. What it is **818**
Handbooks, manuals, etc.
American Psychological Association. Concise rules of APA style **808**
The Chicago manual of style **808**
Fleming, R. The African American writer's handbook **808**
MLA style manual and guide to scholarly publishing **808**
Autism
Autism **616.85**
Grandin, T. Animals in translation **591.5**
McElwain, J. The game of my life **92**
Parks, P. J. Autism **616.85**
Tammet, D. Born on a blue day **92**
Encyclopedias
Turkington, C. The encyclopedia of autism spectrum disorders **616.85**
Fiction
Dooley, S. Livvie Owen lived here **Fic**
Haddon, M. The curious incident of the dog in the night-time **Fic**
Stork, F. X. Marcelo in the real world **Fic**
Autism **616.85**
The **autobiographer's** handbook **808**
Autobiographical graphic novels
B., David. Epileptic **616.8**
Katin, M. We are on our own **92**
Santiago, W. "21" [biography of Roberto Clemente] **92**
Satrapi, M. The complete Persepolis **92**
Small, D. Stitches **92**
Thompson, C. Blankets **92**
White, T. How I made it to eighteen **741.5**
Autobiographies
I can't keep my own secrets **808.8**
Not quite what I was planning **920**
Autobiographies. Douglass, F. **92**
Autobiography
The autobiographer's handbook **808**
Encyclopedia of women's autobiography **920.003**
Yagoda, B. Memoir **809**
Technique
See Biography as a literary form
Autobiography as a literary form *See* Biography as a literary form
Autobiography of a people **305.8**
The **autobiography** of a Tibetan monk. Palden Gyatso **92**
The **autobiography** of Malcolm X. Malcolm X **92**
The **autobiography** of Miss Jane Pittman. Gaines, E. J. **Fic**
Autobiography of my dead brother. Myers, W. D. **Fic**
Autobiography, Poor Richard, and later writings. Franklin, B. **818**

Babe: the life and legend of Babe Didrikson
Zaharias. Cayleff, S. E.   **92**

Babel, Tower of
See/See also pages in the following book(s):
Ceram, C. W. Gods, graves, and scholars
930.1

Babies *See* Infants

Babies by design. Green, R. M.   **176**

The **Babylonian** theorem. Rudman, P. S.   **510**

Babylon's ark. Anthony, L.   **590.73**

Babysitters
Fiction
Wolff, V. E. Make lemonade   **Fic**

Bachel, Beverly K., 1957-
What do you really want?   **153.8**

Bachman, Richard *See* King, Stephen, 1947-

Bacigalupi, Paolo
Ship breaker   **Fic**

Back yard series
Müller, K. The potter's studio handbook
738.1

Backgrounds to American literature [series]
Romanticism and transcendentalism   **810.9**

Backgrounds to English literature   **820.9**

Backhouse, Frances
Owls of North America   **598**

Backpacking
Berger, K. Advanced backpacking   **796.51**
Hart, J. Walking softly in the wilderness
796.51

Bacon, Francis, 1561-1626
See/See also pages in the following book(s):
Durant, W. J. The story of philosophy   **109**

Bacon, Tony
The ultimate guitar book   **787.87**

Bacteria
Bakalar, N. Where the germs are   **616**
Goldsmith, C. Superbugs strike back   **615**
Levy, J. The world of microbes   **616.9**
Shnayerson, M. The killers within   **616**

Bacterial infections
See also Tetanus
Freeman-Cook, L. Staphylococcus aureus infec-
tions   **616.9**

Bacteriology
See also Germ theory of disease

Bad apple. Ruby, L.   **Fic**

Bad boy. Myers, W. D.   **92**

A **bad** boy can be good for a girl. Stone, T. L.
Fic

Bad dog. Kihn, M.   **636.7**

Bad girls don't die. Alender, K.   **Fic**

Bad Heart Buffalo, Amos, ca. 1869-1913
(il) Freedman, R. The life and death of Crazy
Horse   **92**

Bad kitty. Jaffe, M.   **Fic**

Badcott, Nicholas
Pocket timeline of Islamic civilizations   **909**

Badd. Tharp, T.   **Fic**

Bader, Philip
African-American writers   **920.003**

Badoe, Adwoa
Between sisters   **Fic**

Baechler, Lea
(ed) Modern American women writers. See
Modern American women writers   **810.9**

Baek, Hongyong, 1912-2002
About
Lee, H. Still life with rice [biography of
Hongyong Baek]   **92**

Bagg, Mary
(ed) Berkshire encyclopedia of China. See Berkshire encyclopedia of China   **951**

Baghdad Zoo (Iraq)
Anthony, L. Babylon's ark   **590.73**

Bagombo snuff box: uncollected short fiction.
Vonnegut, K.   **S C**

Bahai Faith
Hartz, P. Baha'i Faith   **297.9**

Bahaism *See* Bahai Faith

Bahamas
Fiction
Stevenson, R. H. A thousand shades of blue
Fic

Bahn, Paul G.
(jt. auth) Lister, A. Mammoths   **569**

Baigrie, Brian S. (Brian Scott)
(ed) History of modern science and mathematics. See History of modern science and mathematics   **509**
(ed) The Renaissance and the scientific revolution. See The Renaissance and the scientific
revolution   **920.003**

Bailey, Anne C.
African voices of the Atlantic slave trade
326

Bailey, Frankie Y.
(ed) Crimes and trials of the century. See
Crimes and trials of the century   **345**
(ed) Famous American crimes and trials. See
Famous American crimes and trials   **364**

Bailey, John
The lost German slave girl [biography of Salomé Muller]   **92**

Bailey, Kristen
(ed) How should prisons treat inmates? See
How should prisons treat inmates?   **365**
(ed) Sex education. See Sex education   **613.9**

Bailey, Lee Worth
(ed) Introduction to the world's major religions.
See Introduction to the world's major religions   **200**

Bailey, Neal
Female force   **920**

Bailey, R. A.
(jt. auth) Rittner, D. Encyclopedia of chemistry
540.3

Bailey, Rayna
Immigration and migration   **304.8**

Bailey, Wayne, 1955-
The complete marching band resource manual
784.8

Bainbridge, David, 1968-
Beyond the zonules of Zinn   **611**

Bausum, Ann—*Continued*
Unraveling freedom **940.3**

Baxandall, Rosalyn Fraad, 1939-
(ed) America's working women. See America's working women **331.4**

Baxter, Roberta, 1952-
Skeptical chemist **92**

Bayless, Lanie
(jt. auth) Bayless, R. Rick & Lanie's excellent kitchen adventures **641.5**

Bayless, Rick
Rick & Lanie's excellent kitchen adventures **641.5**

Bayou, volume one. Love, J. **741.5**

Bayoumi, Moustafa
How does it feel to be a problem? **305.8**

Be afraid, be very afraid **398.2**

Beaches
Fiction
Han, J. The summer I turned pretty **Fic**

Beads
Discover beading **745.58**

Beadwork
Discover beading **745.58**
Fox, D. Simply modern jewelry **745.594**

Beagle, Peter S.
The last unicorn **Fic**
The line between **S C**

Beagle Expedition (1831-1836)
Eldredge, N. Charles Darwin and the mystery of mysteries **92**
Fiction
Meyer, C. The true adventures of Charley Darwin **Fic**

Beah, Ishmael, 1980-
A long way gone **92**

Beam, Cris
I am J **Fic**

The bean trees. Kingsolver, B. **Fic**

Bear, Greg, 1951-
The collected stories of Greg Bear **S C**

Beard, Jocelyn
(ed) 100 great monologues from the neo-classical theatre. See 100 great monologues from the neo-classical theatre **808.82**
(ed) 100 great monologues from the Renaissance theatre. See 100 great monologues from the Renaissance theatre **822.008**
(ed) Scenes from classic plays, 468 B.C. to 1970 A.D. See Scenes from classic plays, 468 B.C. to 1970 A.D. **808.82**
(ed) The Ultimate audition book. See The Ultimate audition book **808.82**

Beard, Philip, 1963-
Dear Zoe **Fic**

Bearden, Monica, 1974-
(jt. auth) Aaron, S. Chocolate **641.3**

Bearden, Romare, 1914-1988
A history of African-American artists **709.73**

Bearing witness. Rosen, P. **016.94053**

Bears
See also Grizzly bear; Polar bear
Breiter, M. Bears: [a year in the life] **599.78**

Bearstone. Hobbs, W. **Fic**

Beasley, Henry R., 1929-
(ed) The Eleanor Roosevelt encyclopedia. See The Eleanor Roosevelt encyclopedia **92**

Beasley, Maurine Hoffman
(ed) The Eleanor Roosevelt encyclopedia. See The Eleanor Roosevelt encyclopedia **92**

Beast. Napoli, D. J. **Fic**

The beastly bride **S C**

Beasts of Burden: animal rites. Dorkin, E. **741.5**

Beat culture **810.9**

Beat generation
The Beat generation **810.9**
Encyclopedias
Beat culture **810.9**
The **Beat** generation **810.9**

The beat goes on. Minchin, A. **Fic**

Beating back the devil. McKenna, M. **614.4**

Beating heart. Jenkins, A. M. **Fic**

Beatle meets Destiny. Williams, G. **Fic**

Beatles
The Beatles anthology **781.66**
Partridge, E. John Lennon **92**
Spitz, B. Yeah! yeah! yeah! **920**
Stark, S. D. Meet the Beatles **920**
The **Beatles** anthology **781.66**

Beats
See also Beat generation

Beatty, Scott, 1969-
The DC Comics encyclopedia. See The DC Comics encyclopedia **741.5**

Beaudoin, Sean
You killed Wesley Payne **Fic**

Beaufrand, Mary Jane
The river **Fic**

Beaujon, Andrew
Body piercing saved my life **781.66**

Beaulieu, Elizabeth Ann
(ed) The Toni Morrison encyclopedia. See The Toni Morrison encyclopedia **813.009**

Beauman, Sally
The genealogy of Greek mythology **292**

Beauties and beasts. Hearne, B. G. **398.2**

Beautiful creatures. Garcia, K. **Fic**

Beautiful malice. James, R. **Fic**

Beauty, Personal *See* Personal grooming

Beauty. McKinley, R. **Fic**

Beauty contests
Fiction
Bray, L. Beauty queens **Fic**
The **beauty** myth. Wolf, N. **305.4**
Beauty queens. Bray, L. **Fic**

Beauty shops
Rodriguez, D. Kabul Beauty School **305.4**

Because I am furniture. Chaltas, T. **Fic**

Bell, Dana
(comp) Smithsonian atlas of world aviation. See Smithsonian atlas of world aviation
629.13

Bell, Ellis *See* Brontë, Emily, 1818-1848

Bell, Hilari, 1958-
Trickster's girl .... Fic

Bell, Ruth
Changing bodies, changing lives **613.9**

Bell, Suzanne
Encyclopedia of forensic science **363.2**
Fakes and forgeries **363.2**

Bell, Suzanne S.
Librarian's guide to online searching .. **025.5**

The **bell** jar. Plath, S. .... Fic

Bellalouna, Elizabeth
(ed) Literature of developing nations for students. See Literature of developing nations for students
809

Bellenir, Karen
(ed) Cancer information for teens. See Cancer information for teens
616.99
(ed) Cash and credit information for teens. See Cash and credit information for teens
332.024
(ed) College financing information for teens. See College financing information for teens
378.3
(ed) Debt information for teens. See Debt information for teens
332.024
(ed) Diet information for teens. See Diet information for teens
613.2
(ed) Mental health information for teens. See Mental health information for teens
616.89
(ed) Religious holidays and calendars. See Religious holidays and calendars
203
(ed) Savings and investment information for teens. See Savings and investment information for teens
332.024
(ed) Sports injuries information for teens. See Sports injuries information for teens
617.1
(ed) Tobacco information for teens. See Tobacco information for teens
362.29

Belliveau, Denis, 1964-
In the footsteps of Marco Polo **915**

Bellos, Alex
Here's looking at Euclid **513**

Beloved. Morrison, T. .... Fic

Beltz, Ellin
Frogs: inside their remarkable world ... **597.8**

Ben-Barak, Idan
The invisible kingdom **579**

Ben Jelloun, Tahar, 1944-
Islam explained **297**

Ben Jonson [critical essays] **822.009**

Benanav, Michael
Men of salt **916.6**

Benchley, Peter, 1940-2006
Shark trouble **597**

Beneath my mother's feet. Qamar, A. .. Fic

Benedix, Gretchen
(jt. auth) Smith, C. Meteorites **523.5**

Beneficial insects
See also Insect pests

Benenson, Bob
Elections A to Z **324.6**

Benet's reader's encyclopedia **803**

Benjamin, Alison
A world without bees **638**

Benjamin, Marina
Rocket dreams **303.4**

Benjamin, Paul *See* Auster, Paul, 1947-

Bennett, Holly, 1957-
Shapeshifter .... Fic

Bennett, Jeffrey O.
Beyond UFOs **576.839**

Bennett, Susan Lewis
President Kennedy has been shot. See President Kennedy has been shot
364.1

Bennett Wealer, Sara
Rival .... Fic

Benoit, Charles
You .... Fic

Benson, Harry
RFK: a photographer's journal **973.923**

Benson, Kathleen, 1947-
(jt. auth) Haskins, J. African American religious leaders
920

Benson, Michael
Beyond **523.2**

Benson, Sonia
Development of the industrial U.S.: Almanac
330.973
Development of the industrial U.S.: Biographies
920
Development of the industrial U.S.: Primary sources
330.973
U.S. immigration and migration almanac
304.8
(ed) U-X-L Hispanic American almanac. See U-X-L Hispanic American almanac
305.8

Benton, Thomas Hart, 1782-1858
See/See also pages in the following book(s):
Kennedy, J. F. Profiles in courage **920**

Benway, Robin
Audrey, wait! .... Fic
The extraordinary secrets of April, May and June
Fic

Beowulf
Graphic novels
Hinds, G. Beowulf **741.5**
Beowulf **829**

Bereavement
Fitzgerald, H. The grieving teen **155.9**
Gootman, M. E. When a friend dies **155.9**
Myers, E. When will I stop hurting? **155.9**
Fiction
Acampora, P. Defining Dulcie .... Fic
Alexander, J. S. The sweetheart of Prosper County
Fic
Balog, C. Sleepless .... Fic
Beard, P. Dear Zoe .... Fic
Bell, H. Trickster's girl .... Fic
Brown, J. Bitter end .... Fic
Bullen, A. Wish .... Fic

Bernier-Grand, Carmen T.
Diego   **811**
Frida   **811**

Bernoulli, Daniel, 1700-1782
See/See also pages in the following book(s):
Guillen, M. Five equations that changed the world   **530.1**

Bernstein, Amy D.
(ed) The New York Times practical guide to practically everything. See The New York Times practical guide to practically everything   **646.7**

Bernstein, Burton
Leonard Bernstein   **92**

Bernstein, Carl
All the president's men   **973.924**
(jt. auth) Woodward, B. The final days   **973.924**

Bernstein, Eckhard
Culture and customs of Germany   **943.087**

Bernstein, Judy
(jt. auth) Deng, B. They poured fire on us from the sky   **962.4**

Bernstein, Laurie
(jt. auth) Weinberg, R. Revolutionary Russia   **947.084**

Bernstein, Leonard, 1918-1990
About
Bernstein, B. Leonard Bernstein   **92**
Blashfield, J. F. Leonard Bernstein   **92**

Bernstein, Paula
About
Schein, E. Identical strangers   **92**
(jt. auth) Schein, E. Identical strangers   **92**

Bernstein, Peter W.
(ed) The New York Times practical guide to practically everything. See The New York Times practical guide to practically everything   **646.7**

Bernstein, Richard
Out of the blue   **973.931**

Berra, Tim M., 1943-
Charles Darwin   **92**

Berry, Bertice
The ties that bind   **920**

Berry, Joanne, 1971-
The complete Pompeii   **937**

Berry, Mary Frances
My face is black is true [biography of Callie House]   **92**

Bert, Norman A.
(ed) The Scenebook for actors. See The Scenebook for actors   **808.82**

Berthrong, E. Nagai- *See* Nagai-Berthrong, E.

Berthrong, John H., 1946-
Confucianism   **299.5**

Bertman, Stephen
Handbook to life in ancient Mesopotamia   **935**

Bertozzi, Nick
(jt. auth) Lutes, J. Houdini: the handcuff king   **92**

Bertsch, Christina Cacioppo
(jt. auth) Yellin, S. Life after high school   **646.7**

Bessant, Claire
Cat manual   **636.8**

Best, Joel
Damned lies and statistics   **303.3**
More damned lies and statistics   **303.3**
Stat-spotting   **301**

The **Best** American essays of the century   **814**
The **Best** American mystery stories of the century   **S C**
The **Best** American sports writing of the century   **796**

Best books
Barr, C. Best books for high school readers   **011.6**
Bartel, J. Annotated book lists for every teen reader   **028.5**
Best books for young adults   **028.1**
Horror: another 100 best books   **823.009**
Isabella, T. 1,000 comic books you must read   **741.5**
Outstanding books for the college bound   **011.6**
Pearl, N. Book crush   **028.5**
Rosow, L. V. Accessing the classics   **011.6**
Silver, L. R. Best Jewish books for children and teens   **011.6**
Zbaracki, M. D. Best books for boys   **028.5**

Best books for boys. Zbaracki, M. D.   **028.5**
Best books for high school readers. Barr, C.   **011.6**
Best books for senior high readers. See Barr, C. Best books for high school readers   **011.6**
Best books for young adults   **028.1**
Best career and education web sites. Wolfinger, A.   **025.04**
Best Jewish books for children and teens. Silver, L. R.   **011.6**
Best of the best: 20 years of the Year's best science fiction   **S C**
The **Best** of the West   **818**
Best of times: the story of Charles Dickens. Caravantes, P.   **92**
The **Best** poems of the English language   **821.008**

Best practices for school library media professionals [series]
Farmer, L. S. J. Collaborating with administrators and educational support staff   **027.8**

Best resumes for people without a four-year degree. Enelow, W. S.   **650.14**
The **best** short stories of O. Henry. Henry, O.   **S C**
The **best** teen writing of 2010   **808.8**
The **betrayal** of Africa. Caplan, G. L.   **960**
The **betrayal** of Maggie Blair. Laird, E.   **Fic**
The **betrayal** of Natalie Hargrove. Kate, L.   **Fic**

Betschart, Jean, 1948-
Type 2 diabetes in teens   **616.4**

Bicycles

See also Cycling

Maintenance and repair

Bicycling magazine's basic maintenance and repair **629.28**

Downs, T. The bicycling guide to complete bicycle maintenance & repair **629.28**

Zinn, L. Zinn & the art of road bike maintenance **629.28**

Bicycles, All terrain *See* Mountain bikes

Bicycles and bicycling *See* Cycling

The **bicycling** guide to complete bicycle maintenance & repair. Downs, T. **629.28**

Bicycling magazine's 1,000 all-time best tips **796.6**

Bicycling magazine's basic maintenance and repair **629.28**

Bicycling magazine's Complete guide to bicycle maintenance and repair. See Downs, T. The bicycling guide to complete bicycle maintenance & repair **629.28**

Bicycling magazine's mountain biking skills **796.63**

Biddle, Wendy

Immigrants' rights after 9/11 **323.3**

Biederman, Lynn

Teenage waistland **Fic**

(jt. auth) Baldini, M. Unraveling **Fic**

Biedermann, Hans, 1930-

Dictionary of symbolism **302.2**

Bielagus, Peter G.

Quick cash for teens **658.1**

Bienkowski, Piotr

(ed) Dictionary of the ancient Near East. See Dictionary of the ancient Near East **939**

Bienvenidos! = Welcome!. Byrd, S. M. **027.6**

Bierhorst, John, 1936-

(ed) Latin American folktales. See Latin American folktales **398.2**

Big bang cosmology *See* Big bang theory

Big bang theory

Kaku, M. Parallel worlds **523.1**

The **big** book of teen reading lists. Keane, N. J. **028.5**

Big book unplugged. Rosengren, J. **362.292**

Big fat manifesto. Vaught, S. **Fic**

Big game hunting *See* Hunting

The **Big** Game of Everything. Lynch, C. **Fic**

Big Mouth & Ugly Girl. Oates, J. C. **Fic**

The **big** necessity. George, R. **363.7**

The **big** night out. Beker, J. **646.7**

The **big** short. Lewis, M. **330.973**

The **big** splat; or, How our moon came to be. Mackenzie, D. **523.3**

Bigsby, C. W. E.

(ed) Miller, A. The portable Arthur Miller **812**

Bikes, Mountain *See* Mountain bikes

Biko, Stephen, 1946-1977

I write what I like **968.06**

Bildungsromans

Graphic novels

Lat. Town boy **741.5**

Yang, G. Level up **741.5**

Bilingual books

English-Chinese

Liu Siyu. A thousand peaks **895.1**

English-Spanish

Cool salsa **811.008**

Red hot salsa **811.008**

The Tree is older than you are **860.8**

Bilingual education

Bilingual education **370.117**

Bilingual education **370.117**

Bill of rights (U.S.) *See* United States. Constitution. 1st-10th amendments

The **Bill** of Rights. Patrick, J. J. **342**

Bill of Rights [series]

Freedom from cruel and unusual punishment **345**

Freedom of religion **342**

Freedom of speech **342**

The right to a trial by jury **345**

Billerbeck, Kristin

Perfectly dateless **Fic**

Billingsley, Franny, 1954-

Chime **Fic**

Billy Budd, sailor. Melville, H. **Fic**

Bilmes, Linda

(jt. auth) Stiglitz, J. E. The three trillion dollar war **956.7**

Bily, Cynthia A.

(ed) Endangered species. See Endangered species **333.95**

(ed) Homosexuality: opposing viewpoints. See Homosexuality: opposing viewpoints **306.76**

Binge-purge behavior *See* Bulimia

Bingham, Hiram, 1875-1956

Lost city of the Incas **985**

Bingham, Jane

African art & culture **709.6**

Impressionism **759.05**

Indian art & culture **709.5**

Post-Impressionism **759.05**

Bingham, Kelly, 1967-

Shark girl **Fic**

Binoculars

Scagell, R. Stargazing with binoculars **523.8**

Biochemistry

Hodge, R. The molecules of life **611**

Laberge, M. Biochemistry **612**

Research

Watson, J. D. The double helix **572.8**

Bioengineered foods *See* Food—Biotechnology

Bioethics

Biomedical ethics: opposing viewpoints **174.2**

See/See also pages in the following book(s):

Ethics: opposing viewpoints **170**

Fiction

Ishiguro, K. Never let me go **Fic**

Pearson, M. The adoration of Jenna Fox **Fic**

Black Muslims—*Continued*
Encyclopedias
The Malcolm X encyclopedia   320.5
Graphic novels
Helfer, A. Malcolm X   92
Black Panther Party
Fiction
Magoon, K. The rock and the river   Fic
Black poetry (American) *See* American poetry—
African American authors
Black poets   811.008
Black potatoes. Bartoletti, S. C.   941.5
Black profiles in courage. Abdul-Jabbar, K.
    920
Black Rabbit summer. Brooks, K.   Fic
Black radical. Peery, N.   92
Black stars [series]
Haskins, J. African American religious leaders
    920
Black swan green. Mitchell, D.   Fic
Black taxi. Moloney, J.   Fic
Black theatre USA   812.008
Black trials. Weiner, M. S.   342
Black Union soldiers in the Civil War. Hargrove,
H. B.   973.7
Black, white and Jewish. Walker, R.   92
Black wings. Hardesty, V.   920
Black women in America   920.003
Blackburn, Simon
Think: a compelling introduction to philosophy
    100

Blacks

Biography
See also African Americans—Biography
Encyclopedias
Africana: the encyclopedia of the African and
African American experience   909
Fiction
Mussi, S. The door of no return   Fic
Folklore
Lester, J. Black folktales   398.2
Great Britain—Fiction
Ward, R. Numbers   Fic
United States
See African Americans
Blacks in art
See also African Americans in art
Feelings, T. The middle passage   326
Blacks in literature
See also African Americans in literature
Blacks in the new world [series]
Black leaders of the nineteenth century   920
Black's law dictionary   340.03
Black's medical dictionary   610.3
Blackthorn, John *See* Hart, Gary, 1936-
Blade: playing dead. Bowler, T.   Fic
Blair, Eric *See* Orwell, George, 1903-1950
Blair, Sheila
(jt. auth) Bloom, J. Islam: a thousand years of
faith and power   297

Blais, Madeleine, 1949-
In these girls, hope is a muscle   796.323
Blake, William, 1757-1827
The complete poetry and prose of William
Blake   821
The essential Blake   821
Poems   821
The portable Blake   828
Blanchard, Mary Loving, 1952-
Poets for young adults   920.003
Blank confession. Hautman, P.   Fic
Blankets. Thompson, C.   92
Blanning, T. C. W.
(ed) The eighteenth century. See The eighteenth
century   940.2
(ed) The nineteenth century. See The nineteenth
century   940.2
(ed) The Oxford illustrated history of modern
Europe. See The Oxford illustrated history of
modern Europe   940.2
Blashfield, Jean F.
Leonard Bernstein   92
Blasingame, James B., Jr.
Gary Paulsen   813.009
Blastland, Michael
The numbers game   510
Blatner, David
The joy of π 516.2
Blatt, Jessica
The teen girl's gotta-have-it guide to money
    332.024
Bleach, Vol. 1. Kubo, T.   741.5
The **blending** time. Kinch, M. P.   Fic
Bless me, Ultima. Anaya, R. A.   Fic
Blessed among all women. Ellsberg, R.   920
Blessed Virgin Mary, Saint *See* Mary, Blessed
Virgin, Saint
Bligh, William, 1754-1817
About
Alexander, C. The Bounty: the true story of the
mutiny on the Bounty   996
Fiction
Boyne, J. Mutiny   Fic
Nordhoff, C. Mutiny on the Bounty   Fic
Blind
Hess, A. Helen Keller   92
Keller, H. Helen Keller: selected writings   92
Keller, H. The story of my life   92
Roberts, J. A sense of the world [biography of
James Holman]   92
Scdoris, R. No end in sight   92
Fiction
Cadnum, M. Flash   Fic
Cummings, P. Blindsided   Fic
Henry, A. Girl, stolen   Fic
Miller, S. Miss Spitfire   Fic
Blindsided. Cummings, P.   Fic
Blink & Caution. Wynne-Jones, T.   Fic
Blink: the power of thinking without thinking.
Gladwell, M.   153.4
Bliss. Myracle, L.   Fic

Blizzards

Fiction

Northrop, M. Trapped   **Fic**

Block, Francesca Lia

Blood roses   **S C**

Dangerous angels   **Fic**

The frenzy   **Fic**

How to (un)cage a girl   **811**

Pretty dead   **Fic**

The rose and the beast   **S C**

Weetzie Bat   **Fic**

Blogs *See* Weblogs

Blogs, wikis, podcasts, and other powerful Web tools for classrooms. Richardson, W.
     371.3

Blomquist, Jean M.

(jt. auth) Christen, C. What color is your parachute? for teens   **331.7**

Blood

Circulation

See also Cardiovascular system

Transfusion

Winner, C. Circulating life   **615**

Blood and chocolate. Klause, A. C.   **Fic**

Blood, bedlam, bullets, and badguys. Gannon, M. B.   **016.8**

Blood brothers. Harazin, S. A.   **Fic**

Blood evidence. Lee, H. C.   **614**

Blood ninja. Lake, N.   **Fic**

Blood roses. Block, F. L.   **S C**

Blood song. Drooker, E.   **741.5**

Bloodline. Cary, K.   **Fic**

Bloodline. Moran, K.   **Fic**

Bloods: an oral history of the Vietnam War by black veterans   **959.704**

Bloodsucking animals

Schutt, B. Dark banquet   **591.5**

Bloody Horowitz. Horowitz, A.   **S C**

Bloody Jack. Meyer, L. A.   **Fic**

Bloom, Harold, 1930-

Dramatists and dramas   **809.2**

The epic   **809**

Essayists and prophets   **100**

Hamlet: poem unlimited   **822.3**

Novelists and novels   **809.3**

Poets and poems   **809.1**

Shakespeare: the invention of the human
     822.3

Short story writers and short stories   **809.3**

(ed) African-American poets. See African-American poets [v1]   **811.009**

(ed) American religious poems. See American religious poems   **811.008**

(ed) The American renaissance. See The American renaissance   **810.9**

(ed) August Wilson. See August Wilson [critical essays]   **812.009**

(ed) Ben Jonson. See Ben Jonson [critical essays]   **822.009**

(ed) The Best poems of the English language. See The Best poems of the English language
     821.008

(ed) Carson McCullers. See Carson McCullers [critical essays]   **813.009**

(ed) Civil disobedience. See Civil disobedience   **809**

(ed) Edgar Allan Poe. See Edgar Allan Poe [critical essays]   **818**

(ed) Enslavement and emancipation. See Enslavement and emancipation   **809**

(ed) Erich Maria Remarque's All quiet on the western front. See Erich Maria Remarque's All quiet on the western front [critical essays]
     833.009

(ed) Franz Kafka's The metamorphosis. See Franz Kafka's The metamorphosis [study guide]   **833.009**

(ed) Hamlet. See Hamlet [criticism]   **822.3**

(ed) The Harlem Renaissance. See The Harlem Renaissance [critical essays]   **810.9**

(ed) Harper Lee's To kill a mockingbird. See Harper Lee's To kill a mockingbird [study guide]   **813.009**

(ed) Hermann Hesse. See Hermann Hesse [critical essays]   **838**

(ed) Homer. See Homer   **883.009**

(ed) Jane Austen. See Jane Austen [critical essays]   **823.009**

(ed) Julius Caesar. See Julius Caesar [criticism]   **822.3**

(ed) King Lear. See King Lear [criticism]
     822.3

(ed) Literature of the Holocaust. See Literature of the Holocaust   **809**

(ed) Macbeth. See Macbeth [criticism]   **822.3**

(ed) Mark Twain's The adventures of Huckleberry Finn. See Mark Twain's The adventures of Huckleberry Finn   **813.009**

(ed) Mary Shelley's Frankenstein. See Mary Shelley's Frankenstein [study guide]
     823.009

(ed) Maya Angelou. See Maya Angelou [critical essays]   **818**

(ed) Molière. See Molière [critical essays]
     842.009

(ed) Native American writers. See Native American writers [critical essays]   **810.9**

(ed) Othello. See Othello [criticism]   **822.3**

(ed) Poets of World War I: Rupert Brooke & Siegfried Sassoon. See Poets of World War I: Rupert Brooke & Siegfried Sassoon
     821.009

(ed) Poets of World War I: Wilfred Owen & Isaac Rosenberg. See Poets of World War I: Wilfred Owen & Isaac Rosenberg   **821.009**

(ed) Romeo and Juliet. See Romeo and Juliet [criticism]   **822.3**

(ed) Shakespeare's histories. See Shakespeare's histories   **822.3**

(ed) The sonnets. See The sonnets [criticism]
     822.3

(ed) Sophocles' Oedipus rex. See Sophocles' Oedipus rex [critical essays]   **882.009**

(ed) Sylvia Plath. See Sylvia Plath [critical essays]   **811.009**

(ed) The tempest. See The tempest [criticism]
     822.3

(ed) Thomas Hardy. See Thomas Hardy [critical essays]   **823.009**

Bloom, Harold, 1930-—Continued
  (ed) The Victorian novel. See The Victorian
    novel   **820.9**
  (ed) William Golding's Lord of the flies. See
    William Golding's Lord of the flies [critical
    essays]   **823.009**
  (ed) William Shakespeare's Hamlet. See Wil-
    liam Shakespeare's Hamlet [critical essays]
                                                822.3

Bloom, Jonathan
  Islam: a thousand years of faith and power
                                                  297

Bloom, Ken
  Broadway musicals   **792.6**

Bloom, Ona
  Encephalitis   **616.8**

Bloomfield, Louis
  How everything works   **530**

Bloom's biocritiques [series]
  Edgar Allan Poe   **818**

Bloom's guides [series]
  Franz Kafka's The metamorphosis   **833.009**
  Harper Lee's To kill a mockingbird   **813.009**
  Mary Shelley's Frankenstein   **823.009**

Bloom's how to write about Edgar Allan Poe.
  Amper, S.   **818**

Bloom's how to write about Emily Dickinson.
  Priddy, A.   **811.009**

Bloom's how to write about F. Scott Fitzgerald.
  Becnel, K. E.   **813.009**

Bloom's how to write about J.D. Salinger. Kerr,
  C.   **813.009**

Bloom's how to write about John Steinbeck.
  Kordich, C. J.   **813.009**

Bloom's how to write about literature [series]
  Amper, S. Bloom's how to write about Edgar
    Allan Poe   **818**
  Becnel, K. E. Bloom's how to write about F.
    Scott Fitzgerald   **813.009**
  Burton, Z. Bloom's how to write about Toni
    Morrison   **813.009**
  Gleed, P. Bloom's how to write about William
    Shakespeare   **822.3**
  Kerr, C. Bloom's how to write about J.D. Salin-
    ger   **813.009**
  Kordich, C. J. Bloom's how to write about John
    Steinbeck   **813.009**
  Priddy, A. Bloom's how to write about Emily
    Dickinson   **811.009**
  Rasmussen, R. K. Bloom's how to write about
    Mark Twain   **818**
  Sterling, L. A. Bloom's how to write about Na-
    thaniel Hawthorne   **813.009**

Bloom's how to write about Mark Twain. Rasmussen, R. K.   **818**

Bloom's how to write about Nathaniel Hawthorne.
  Sterling, L. A.   **813.009**

Bloom's how to write about Toni Morrison. Burton, Z.   **813.009**

Bloom's how to write about William Shakespeare.
  Gleed, P.   **822.3**

**Bloom's literary criticism 20th anniversary col-
  lection** [series]
  Bloom, H. Dramatists and dramas   **809.2**
  Bloom, H. The epic   **809**
  Bloom, H. Essayists and prophets   **100**
  Bloom, H. Novelists and novels   **809.3**
  Bloom, H. Poets and poems   **809.1**
  Bloom, H. Short story writers and short stories
                                              809.3

Bloom's literary places [series]
  Dailey, D. London   **820.9**
  Foster, B. Rome   **809**
  Tomedi, J. Dublin   **820.9**

Bloom's literary themes [series]
  Civil disobedience   **809**
  Enslavement and emancipation   **809**

Bloom's major dramatists [series]
  August Wilson   **812.009**
  Ben Jonson   **822.009**
  Molière   **842.009**
  Shakespeare's histories   **822.3**

Bloom's major novelists [series]
  Thomas Hardy   **823.009**

Bloom's major poets [series]
  Poets of World War I: Rupert Brooke & Sieg-
    fried Sassoon   **821.009**
  Poets of World War I: Wilfred Owen & Isaac
    Rosenberg   **821.009**
  Sylvia Plath   **811.009**

Bloom's period studies [series]
  The American renaissance   **810.9**
  The Harlem Renaissance   **810.9**
  Literature of the Holocaust   **809**
  The Victorian novel   **820.9**

Bloom's Shakespeare through the ages [series]
  Hamlet   **822.3**
  Julius Caesar   **822.3**
  King Lear   **822.3**
  Macbeth   **822.3**
  Othello   **822.3**
  Romeo and Juliet   **822.3**
  The sonnets   **822.3**
  The tempest   **822.3**

Bloor, Edward, 1950-
  Taken   **Fic**

Bloss, Josie, 1981-
  Albatross   **Fic**

Blount, Roy
  Robert E. Lee   **92**

Blubaugh, Penny
  Serendipity Market   **Fic**

Blue Beetle (Fictional character)
  Giffen, K. Blue Beetle: Shellshocked   **741.5**

Blue Beetle: Shellshocked. Giffen, K.   **741.5**

Blue bloods. De la Cruz, M.   **Fic**

The **blue** book on information age inquiry, instruction and literacy. Callison, D.   **028.7**

Blue collar workers See Working class

Blue diary. Hoffman, A.   **Fic**

Blue flame. Grant, K. M.   **Fic**

The **blue** girl. De Lint, C.   **Fic**

Blue lipstick. Grandits, J.   **811**

Blue plate special. Kwasney, M. D.   **Fic**

Bohemianism

See also Beat generation

Bohr, Niels Henrik David, 1885-1962

See/See also pages in the following book(s):

Cropper, W. H. Great physicists   **920**

Graphic novels

Ottaviani, J. Suspended in language [biography of Niels Bohr]   **92**

Boivin, Cathleen

(ed) Milestone documents in world history. See Milestone documents in world history   **909**

Bojaxhiu, Agnes Gonxha See Teresa, Mother, 1910-1997

Bok, Chip, 1952-

A recent history of the United States in political cartoons   **973.92**

Bolan, Kimberly

Teen spaces   **022**

Boland, Robert, 1925-

Musicals!   **792.6**

Bolden, Tonya

Cause: Reconstruction America, 1863-1877
   973.7

Maritcha [biography of Maritcha Rémond Lyons]   **92**

W.E.B. Du Bois   **92**

Wake up our souls   **709.73**

Boleyn, Anne See Anne Boleyn, Queen, consort of Henry VIII, King of England, 1507-1536

Boleyn-Fitzgerald, Miriam

Ending and extending life   **174.2**

Bolles, Richard Nelson

(jt. auth) Christen, C. What color is your parachute? for teens   **331.7**

The **Bolshevik** revolution and Russian Civil War. Wade, R. A.   **947.084**

Bolshevism See Communism

Bolt, Bruce A., 1930-2005

Earthquakes   **551.2**

Bolt, Robert

A man for all seasons   **822**

Bolt, Usain, 1986-

9.58   **92**

Bombay (India)

Umrigar, T. N. First darling of the morning
   92

Bonaparte, Napoleon See Napoleon I, Emperor of the French, 1769-1821

Bonde, Robert K.

(jt. auth) Reep, R. L. The Florida manatee
   599.5

Bone detective [biography of Diane France] Hopping, L. J.   **92**

Bone sharps, cowboys, and thunder lizards. Ottaviani, J.   **560**

Bones

See also Fractures

Kelly, E. B. The skeletal system   **612.7**

Bones of Faerie. Simner, J. L.   **Fic**

Bonham-Boveé, Jonita Ruth, d. 1994

See/See also pages in the following book(s):

Mendoza, P. M. Extraordinary people in extraordinary times   **920**

Bonhomme, Brian

(ed) Milestone documents in world history. See Milestone documents in world history   **909**

Bonner, John Tyler

Why size matters   **578.4**

Bonnin, Gertrude Simmons See Zitkala-Ŝa, 1876-1938

Book clubs (Discussion groups)

Gelman, J. The kids' book club book   **028.5**

Kunzel, B. L. The teen-centered book club
   027.62

Book crush. Pearl, N.   **028.5**

Book discussion groups See Book clubs (Discussion groups)

Book industry

See also Publishers and publishing

Book of a thousand days. Hale, S.   **Fic**

The **book** of basketball. Simmons, B.   **796.323**

Book of changes See I ching

The **book** of inventions. Harrison, I.   **609**

A **Book** of luminous things   **808.81**

Book of majors 2011. College Entrance Examination Board   **378.73**

The **Book** of monologues for aspiring actors
   808.82

The **book** of Mordred. Vande Velde, V.   **Fic**

Book of Mormon

The Book of Mormon   **289.3**

The **book** of popular science. See The new book of popular science   **503**

The **book** of scenes for aspiring actors. Cassady, M.   **808.82**

The **book** of swords. Reinhardt, H.   **623.4**

The **book** of the states   **352.13**

A **Book** of women poets from antiquity to now
   808.81

Book talks

Bromann, J. More booktalking that works
   028.5

Diamant-Cohen, B. Booktalking bonanza
   028.5

Gillespie, J. T. Classic teenplots   **011.6**

Gillespie, J. T. The Newbery/Printz companion
   028.5

Mahood, K. Booktalking with teens   **021.7**

Schall, L. Booktalks and beyond   **028.5**

Schall, L. Genre talks for teens   **028.5**

The **book** thief. Zusak, M.   **Fic**

Books

See also Electronic books; Printing

Conservation and restoration

Schechter, A. A. Basic book repair methods
   025.7

Books, Filmed See Film adaptations

Books about the Middle East. Al-Hazza, T. C.
   016.3058

Books and reading
De Vos, G. Storytelling for young adults
    372.6
Diamant-Cohen, B. Booktalking bonanza
    028.5
Edwards, M. A. The fair garden and the swarm
  of beasts   **027.62**
Herald, D. T. Genreflecting   **016.8**
Nilsen, A. P. Literature for today's young adults
    028.5
Pearl, N. Book crush   **028.5**
Planet on the table   **809.1**
Prose, F. Reading like a writer   **808**
    Best books
  See Best books
    Fiction
Bradbury, R. Fahrenheit 451   **Fic**
Jones, L. Mister Pip   **Fic**
Mantchev, L. Eyes like stars   **Fic**
North, P. Libyrinth   **Fic**
Portman, F. Andromeda Klein   **Fic**
Zusak, M. The book thief   **Fic**
    Graphic novels
Yoshizaki, S. Kingyo used books, vol. 1
    741.5
Books and reading for children *See* Children—
  Books and reading
Books for children *See* Children's literature
Books in machine-readable form *See* Electronic
  books
Booktalking *See* Book talks
Booktalking bonanza. Diamant-Cohen, B.
    028.5
Booktalking with teens. Mahood, K.   **021.7**
Booktalks and beyond. Schall, L.   **028.5**
Boon, Johannes M.
(jt. auth) Abrahams, P. H. McMinn's clinical at-
  las of human anatomy   **611**
Boon, Kevin A.
Ernest Hemingway   **92**
F. Scott Fitzgerald   **92**
George Orwell   **92**
Boorstin, Daniel J., 1914-2004
The creators   **909**
The discoverers   **909**
The seekers   **909**
Boot camp. Strasser, T.   **Fic**
Booth, Coe
Kendra   **Fic**
Tyrell   **Fic**
Booth, Edwin, 1833-1893
    Fiction
Wemmlinger, R. Booth's daughter   **Fic**
Booth, Heather, 1978-
Serving teens through readers' advisory
    028.5
Booth, John Wilkes, 1838-1865
    About
Geary, R. The murder of Abraham Lincoln
    973.7
Swanson, J. L. Chasing Lincoln's killer [biogra-
  phy of John Wilkes Booth]   **92**
Booth's daughter. Wemmlinger, R.   **Fic**

Border crossing. Anderson, J. L.   **Fic**
Border Patrol (U.S.) *See* United States. Border
  Patrol
Borderline. Stratton, A.   **Fic**
Borderlines. Kraus, C.   **92**
Bordman, Gerald Martin
American musical theatre   **792.6**
The Oxford companion to American theatre
    792.03
Borgenicht, David
(jt. auth) Piven, J. The worst-case scenario sur-
  vival handbook   **613.6**
Borges, Jorge Luis, 1899-1986
Selected poems   **861**
Born beautiful. Fornay, A.   **646.7**
Born confused. Desai Hidier, T.   **Fic**
Born on a blue day. Tammet, D.   **92**
Born on the Fourth of July. Kovic, R.
    959.704
Borris, Albert
Crash into me   **Fic**
Borrowed names. Atkins, J.   **811**
Bortolotti, Dan
Hope in hell   **610**
Wild blue   **599.5**
Bortz, Alfred B., 1944-
Beyond Jupiter [biography of Heidi Hammel]
    92
Boruchowitz, David E.
Mini aquariums   **639.34**
Borus, Audrey
A student's guide to Emily Dickinson
    811.009
Borzendowski, Janice
Marie Curie   **92**
Bosch, Carl
    About
Hager, T. The alchemy of air [dual biography of
  Fritz Haber and Carl Bosch]   **92**
Bosco, Antoinette
(jt. auth) Bosco, P. I. World War I   **940.3**
Bosco, Peter I.
World War I   **940.3**
Bosnia and Hercegovina
See/See also pages in the following book(s):
Naimark, N. M. Fires of hatred   **364.1**
    Graphic novels
Sacco, J. Safe area Goražde   **949.7**
Boston (Mass.)
    Fiction
Halpin, B. How ya like me now   **Fic**
Kluger, S. My most excellent year   **Fic**
Reinhardt, D. The things a brother knows
    Fic
Smith, S. The other side of dark   **Fic**
Wilson, D. L. Firehorse   **Fic**
Boswell, John, 1945-
(jt. auth) Strickland, C. The annotated Mona
  Lisa   **709**
Botanists
Lowman, M. Life in the treetops   **92**

Botany

See also Plants
Encyclopedias
Magill's encyclopedia of science   **580**

Botany, Medical *See* Medical botany

Botulism
Emmeluth, D. Botulism   **616.9**

Bouchard, Constance Brittain
(ed) Knights. See Knights   **940.1**

Boucquey, Thierry
(ed) Encyclopedia of world writers. See Encyclopedia of world writers   **920.003**

Boudicca *See* Boadicea, Queen, d. 62

Boulle, Pierre, 1912-1994
Planet of the apes   **Fic**

Bound. Napoli, D. J.   **Fic**

Bound-for-college guidebook. Burtnett, F.   **378.1**

Bound for the North Star. Fradin, D. B.   **326**

Bounty (Ship)
Alexander, C. The Bounty: the true story of the mutiny on the Bounty   **996**
Fiction
Boyne, J. Mutiny   **Fic**
Nordhoff, C. Mutiny on the Bounty   **Fic**

Bourgeois, Louise, 1911-2010
About
Greenberg, J. Runaway girl: the artist Louise Bourgeois   **92**

Bova, Ben, 1932-
Mars life   **Fic**

Boveé, Jonita Ruth Bonham- *See* Bonham-Boveé, Jonita Ruth, d. 1994

Bow and arrow
See also Archery

Bowden, John, 1935-
(ed) Encyclopedia of Christianity. See Encyclopedia of Christianity   **230.003**

Bowen, Catherine Drinker, 1897-1973
Miracle at Philadelphia   **342**

Bowen, Mark
Thin ice   **551.51**

Bowen, Nancy
Ralph Nader   **92**

Bowers, Elizabeth Shimer
(jt. auth) Ehrlich, P. Living with allergies   **616.97**

Bowers, Rick, 1952-
The spies of Mississippi   **323.1**

Bowes, John P., 1973-
The Trail of Tears   **970.004**

Bowker, John, 1935-
World religions   **200**
(ed) The Cambridge illustrated history of religions. See The Cambridge illustrated history of religions   **200.9**

Bowler, Tim, 1953-
Blade: playing dead   **Fic**

Bowman, Catherine, 1953-
(ed) Word of mouth. See Word of mouth   **811.008**

Bowman, Cynthia Ann, 1958-
(ed) A Guide to high school success for students with disabilities. See A Guide to high school success for students with disabilities   **371.9**

Bowman, John Stewart, 1931-
Exploration in the world of the ancients   **913**
(ed) Bosco, P. I. World War I   **940.3**
(ed) Carlisle, R. P. Iraq War   **956.7**
(ed) Columbia chronologies of Asian history and culture. See Columbia chronologies of Asian history and culture   **950**
(ed) Golay, M. Spanish-American war   **973.8**
(ed) Greenblatt, M. War of 1812   **973.5**
(ed) Isserman, M. Exploring North America, 1800-1900   **917**
(ed) Isserman, M. Korean War   **951.9**
(ed) Isserman, M. Vietnam War   **959.704**
(ed) Isserman, M. World War II   **940.53**
(ed) Marker, S. Plains Indian wars   **973.5**
(ed) Mills, B. U.S.-Mexican War   **973.6**
(ed) Minks, B. Revolutionary war   **973.3**

Bowman, Vibiana, 1953-
(ed) Teaching Generation M. See Teaching Generation M   **027.62**

Bowman-Kruhm, Mary
The Leakeys   **920**

Bowman's store. Bruchac, J.   **92**

Box, Matthew J.
(ed) Adoption. See Adoption   **362.7**
(ed) Poverty. See Poverty   **362.5**
(ed) Terrorism. See Terrorism [Social issues firsthand series]   **363.32**

Box out. Coy, J.   **Fic**

The **boxer** and the spy. Parker, R. B.   **Fic**

Boxing
Biography
Ezra, M. Muhammad Ali   **92**
Levy, A. H. Floyd Patterson   **92**
Micklos, J. Muhammad Ali   **92**
Fiction
Lipsyte, R. The contender   **Fic**
Parker, R. B. The boxer and the spy   **Fic**
Graphic novels
Takahashi, R. One-pound gospel, vol. 1   **741.5**

Boy proof. Castellucci, C.   **Fic**

The **boy Sherlock Holmes** [series]
Peacock, S. Eye of the crow   **Fic**

Boy toy. Lyga, B.   **Fic**

The **boy** who fell out of the sky [biography of David Scott Dornstein] Dornstein, K.   **92**

The **boy** who harnessed the wind. Kamkwamba, W.   **92**

Boyce, Charles
Critical companion to William Shakespeare   **822.3**

Boyd, Herb, 1938-
We shall overcome   **323.1**
(comp) Autobiography of a people. See Autobiography of a people   **305.8**
(jt. auth) Wright, S. Simeon's story   **305.8**

Boyd, Maria
Will   **Fic**

Brady, Mathew B., ca. 1823-1896
About
Armstrong, J. Photo by Brady   973.7
Brady, Patricia, 1943-
Martha Washington   92
Brager, Bruce L., 1949-
John Paul Jones   92
Bragg, Rick
All over but the shoutin'   92
Brahms, William B.
Notable last facts   031.02
Brahms, Bill *See* Brahms, William B.
The **braid**. Frost, H.   Fic
Brain
Aamodt, S. Welcome to your brain   612.8
Bainbridge, D. Beyond the zonules of Zinn
                                                   611
Bangalore, L. Brain development   612.8
Hains, B. C. Pain   616
Hudmon, A. Learning and memory   153.1
The human brain book   612.8
Morgan, M. The midbrain   612.8
Phillips, S. F. The teen brain   612.8
Rose, S. P. R. The future of the brain   153
West, K. Biofeedback   615.8
Cancer
Freedman, J. Brain cancer   616.99
Diseases
See also Creutzfeldt-Jakob disease; Encephalitis
Lemon, A. Happy   92
Encyclopedias
Turkington, C. The encyclopedia of the brain
and brain disorders   612.8
Tumors
Gunther, J. Death be not proud   92
Wounds and injuries—Fiction
McCormick, P. Purple Heart   Fic
Tullson, D. Riley Park   Fic
Vaught, S. Trigger   Fic
Venkatraman, P. Climbing the stairs   Fic
Brain camp. Kim, S.   741.5
Brain cancer. Freedman, J.   616.99
Brain damaged children
Esherick, J. The journey toward recovery
                                               616.8
Brain development. Bangalore, L.   612.8
The **brain** encyclopedia. See Turkington, C. The
encyclopedia of the brain and brain disorders
                                               612.8
Brain Jack. Falkner, B.   Fic
Brainard, Cecilia Manguerra, 1947-
(ed) Growing up Filipino II. See Growing up
Filipino II   S C
Brainwashing
Huxley, A. Brave new world revisited   303.3
Bram Stoker's Dracula. Raven, N.   741.5
Branch Rickey. Breslin, J.   92
Brand, Peter
(ed) The Cambridge history of Italian literature.
See The Cambridge history of Italian literature
                                             850.9

Brand name products
See also Trademarks
Brande, Robin
Evolution, me, & other freaks of nature   Fic
Fat Cat   Fic
Brands, Danielle A.
Salmonella   615.9
Brandt, Anthony, 1936-
(ed) Lewis, M. The journals of Lewis and Clark
                                              978
Brandt, John C., 1934-
(jt. auth) Petersen, C. C. Visions of the cosmos
                                              520
Brashares, Ann, 1967-
The sisterhood of the traveling pants   Fic
Brasser, Ted J.
Native American clothing   391
Braukman, Stacy Lorraine
(ed) Notable American women. See Notable
American women   920.003
Braun, Linda W.
Listen up!   371.3
Risky business   027.62
Technically involved   027.62
Teens, technology, and literacy; or, Why bad
grammar isn't always bad   373.1
Braunmuller, A. R., 1945-
(ed) Shakespeare, W. The merchant of Venice
                                             822.3
(ed) Shakespeare, W. The tragical history of
Hamlet prince of Denmark   822.3
Brave Bird, Mary
Lakota woman   92
The **brave** escape of Edith Wharton. Wooldridge,
C. N.   92
Brave new words   813.009
Brave new world. Huxley, A.   Fic
Brave new world: and, Brave new world revisited.
Huxley, A.   828
Brave new world revisited. Huxley, A.   303.3
The **brave** women of the Gulf Wars. Zeinert, K.
                                            956.7
Bray, Libba
Beauty queens   Fic
Going bovine   Fic
A great and terrible beauty   Fic
Brazil
Fiction
Peet, M. Keeper   Fic
History
Meade, T. A brief history of Brazil   981
Break. Moskowitz, H.   Fic
Breakfast at Tiffany's: a short novel and three
stories. Capote, T.   S C
Breast
Weiss, M. C. Taking care of your 'girls'
                                            618.1
Breathe my name. Nelson, R. A.   Fic
Breathing. Herbsman, C.   Fic
Breathing underwater. Flinn, A.   Fic
Breathless. Warman, J.   Fic

A **brief** history of Saudi Arabia. Wynbrandt, J. **953.8**

A **brief** history of the Caribbean. Figueredo, D. H. **972.9**

A **briefer** history of time. Hawking, S. W. **523.1**

Brier, Bob
The murder of Tutankhamen **932**

Brier, Robert *See* Brier, Bob

Brighton Beach memoirs. Simon, N. **812**

Brignell, Roger
The pilates handbook **613.7**

Brill, A. A. (Abraham Arden), 1874-1948
(ed) Freud, S. The basic writings of Sigmund Freud **150.19**

Brill, Abraham Arden *See* Brill, A. A. (Abraham Arden), 1874-1948

Brill, David
(jt. auth) Johanson, D. C. From Lucy to language **599.93**

Brill, Marlene Targ, 1945-
America in the 1970s **973.92**
Tourette syndrome **616.8**

Bringle, Jennifer
Reproductive rights **613.9**

Brinkley, Alan
Franklin Delano Roosevelt **92**
(ed) The American presidency. See The American presidency **973**

Brinkley, Douglas
Rosa Parks **92**

Bristow, M. J.
(ed) National anthems of the world. See National anthems of the world **782.42**

Britain, Battle of, 1940
Moore, K. The Battle of Britain **940.54**
Overy, R. J. The Battle of Britain **940.54**

The Britannica guide to ethics [series]
The history of Western ethics **170**

The **Britannica** guide to explorers and explorations that changed the modern world **910.4**

The **Britannica** guide to inventions that changed the modern world **609**

The **Britannica** guide to political and social movements that changed the modern world **322.4**

The **Britannica** guide to theories and ideas that changed the modern world **901**

British
India—Fiction
Forster, E. M. A passage to India **Fic**

British Antarctic ("Terra Nova") Expedition (1910-1913)
Solomon, S. The coldest March **998**

British authors before 1800 **920.003**

British authors of the nineteenth century **920.003**

British Columbia
Fiction
Juby, S. Another kind of cowboy **Fic**
Razzell, M. Snow apples **Fic**

British Commonwealth countries *See* Commonwealth countries

British cooking
Segan, F. Shakespeare's kitchen **641.5**

British Empire *See* Great Britain—Colonies

British national characteristics
See/See also pages in the following book(s):
Emerson, R. W. The portable Emerson **818**

British writers **920.003**

Broadcast journalism
See also Television broadcasting of news
Garner, J. We interrupt this broadcast **070.1**
Henderson, H. Power of the news media **070.1**
Kern, J. Sound reporting **070.4**

Broadcasting
See also Television broadcasting

Broadway musicals. Bloom, K. **792.6**

Broadway: the American musical. Kantor, M. **792.6**

Broca's brain. Sagan, C. **500**

Brock, James P.
Kaufman field guide to butterflies of North America **595.7**

Brock, Juliet Clutton- *See* Clutton-Brock, Juliet

Brockett, Oscar G., 1923-2010
History of the theatre **792.09**

Brockman, John
(ed) The next fifty years. See The next fifty years **501**
(ed) This will change everything. See This will change everything **501**

Brod, Harry
(jt. auth) Thompson, C. White men challenging racism **323**

Brody, Jessica
The Karma Club **Fic**

Brody's ghost: book 1. Crilley, M. **741.5**

Brokaw, Tom, 1940-
An album of memories **940.54**
A long way from home **92**

Broken memory. Combres, E. **Fic**

Broken moon. Antieau, K. **Fic**

Broken soup. Valentine, J. **Fic**

Brom, 1965-
The child thief **Fic**

Bromann, Jennifer
More booktalking that works **028.5**

Bronchial asthma *See* Asthma

Brontë, Anne, 1820-1849
About
Pasachoff, N. E. A student's guide to the Brontë sisters **823.009**

Brontë, Charlotte, 1816-1855
Jane Eyre **Fic**
About
Pasachoff, N. E. A student's guide to the Brontë sisters **823.009**

Brontë, Emily, 1818-1848
Brontë: poems **821**
Wuthering Heights **Fic**

Brontë, Emily, 1818-1848—*Continued*
About
Pasachoff, N. E. A student's guide to the Brontë
sisters   **823.009**
Brontë family
Fiction
Dunkle, C. B. The house of dead maids   **Fic**
Bronx (New York, N.Y.)
Fiction
Booth, C. Tyrell   **Fic**
Griffin, P. The Orange Houses   **Fic**
Grimes, N. Bronx masquerade   **Fic**
McGuigan, M. A. Morning in a different place
                                            Fic
Quintero, S. Efrain's secret   **Fic**
Bronx masquerade. Grimes, N.   **Fic**
Brooke, Rupert, 1887-1915
About
Poets of World War I: Rupert Brooke & Sieg-
fried Sassoon   **821.009**
Brooklyn (New York, N.Y.)
Fiction
Chayil, E. Hush   **Fic**
Frank, E. R. Life is funny   **Fic**
Grant, C. Teenie   **Fic**
Hamill, P. Snow in August   **Fic**
Malamud, B. The assistant   **Fic**
McDonald, J. Off-color   **Fic**
McDonald, J. Twists and turns   **Fic**
Brooklyn Dodgers (Baseball team)
Breslin, J. Branch Rickey   **92**
Brooks, Brad
(jt. auth) Pilcher, T. The essential guide to
world comics   **741.5**
Brooks, Christopher Antonio
(ed) The African American almanac. See The
African American almanac   **305.8**
Brooks, Cleanth, 1906-1994
(ed) Understanding poetry. See Understanding
poetry   **821.008**
Brooks, F. Erik, 1967-
(jt. auth) Starks, G. L. How your government
really works   **320.4**
Brooks, Gwendolyn
In Montgomery, and other poems   **811**
Selected poems   **811**
Brooks, Kevin, 1959-
Being   **Fic**
Black Rabbit summer   **Fic**
Candy   **Fic**
Dawn   **Fic**
Kissing the rain   **Fic**
Lucas   **Fic**
The road of the dead   **Fic**
Brooks, M. (Michael), 1970-
13 things that don't make sense   **500**
Brooks, Martha, 1944-
Mistik Lake   **Fic**
Brooks, Rodney Allen
Flesh and machines   **629.8**
Brooks, Terry, 1944-
Armageddon's children   **Fic**
The sword of Shannara   **Fic**

Brosgol, Vera, 1984-
Anya's ghost   **741.5**
Brosnan, Kathleen A., 1960-
(ed) Encyclopedia of American environmental
history. See Encyclopedia of American envi-
ronmental history   **333.72**
Brother, I'm dying. Danticat, E.   **92**
Brothers, Meagan
Debbie Harry sings in French   **Fic**
Brothers
Fiction
Alonzo, S. Riding invisible   **Fic**
Avasthi, S. Split   **Fic**
Black, H. The white cat   **Fic**
Brennan, S. R. The demon's lexicon   **Fic**
Brooks, K. The road of the dead   **Fic**
De la Peña, M. We were here   **Fic**
Gershow, M. The local news   **Fic**
Hartnett, S. Surrender   **Fic**
Herlong, M. The great wide sea   **Fic**
Hernandez, D. Suckerpunch   **Fic**
Herrick, S. By the river   **Fic**
Klass, D. Dark angel   **Fic**
Lynch, C. Angry young man   **Fic**
Maberry, J. Rot & ruin   **Fic**
Magoon, K. The rock and the river   **Fic**
Moskowitz, H. Break   **Fic**
Mosley, W. Fortunate son   **Fic**
Rapp, A. Punkzilla   **Fic**
Reinhardt, D. The things a brother knows
                                            Fic
Reynolds, M. Shut up!   **Fic**
Saldaña, R. A good long way   **Fic**
Slade, A. G. Megiddo's shadow   **Fic**
Smith, A. In the path of falling objects   **Fic**
Trottier, M. Three songs for courage   **Fic**
Voorhees, C. The brothers Torres   **Fic**
Wallace, R. Perpetual check   **Fic**
Whitehead, C. Sag Harbor   **Fic**
Wilson, M. What they always tell us   **Fic**
Woodson, J. Miracle's boys   **Fic**
Brothers and sisters *See* Siblings; Twins
The **brothers** Torres. Voorhees, C.   **Fic**
Brower, Kenneth, 1944-
Yosemite: an American treasure   **917.9**
Brown, Bobbi
Bobbi Brown teenage beauty   **646.7**
Brown, Bradford B., 1929-
While you're here, Doc   **92**
Brown, Brandon P.
(ed) Magill's medical guide. See Magill's medi-
cal guide   **610.3**
Brown, Charles N.
(ed) The Locus awards. See The Locus awards
                                            S C
Brown, Clarence, 1929-
(ed) The Portable twentieth-century Russian
reader. See The Portable twentieth-century
Russian reader   **891.7**
Brown, Claude, 1937-2002
Manchild in the promised land   **92**
Brown, Daniel, 1951-
Under a flaming sky   **634.9**

Brown, Dee Alexander
Bury my heart at Wounded Knee   **970.004**
Brown, Jennifer, 1972-
Bitter end   **Fic**
Hate list   **Fic**
Brown, John, 1800-1859
About
Sterngass, J. John Brown   **92**
Brown, John Russell
(ed) The Oxford illustrated history of theatre.
See The Oxford illustrated history of theatre
   792.09
Brown, Jonathan C.
A brief history of Argentina   **982**
Brown, Jordan
Robo world [biography of Cynthia Breazeal]
   92
Brown, Kate
(il) Appignanesi, R. A midsummer night's
dream   **822.3**
Brown, Lesley
(ed) Shorter Oxford English dictionary on his-
torical principles. See Shorter Oxford English
dictionary on historical principles   **423**
Brown, Oliver, 1919-1961
About
Telgen, D. Brown v. Board of Education
   344
Brown, Stephen F.
Catholicism & Orthodox Christianity   **280**
Protestantism   **280**
(jt. auth) Morrison, M. A. Judaism   **296**
Brown, Waln K., 1944-
(ed) Growing up in the care of strangers. See
Growing up in the care of strangers   **362.7**
Brown, William Wells, 1815-1884
See/See also pages in the following book(s):
Slave narratives [Library of Am.]   **326**
Brown v. Board of Education. Telgen, D.   **344**
Browne, Ray Broadus
The Civil War and Reconstruction   **973.7**
Browning, Elizabeth Barrett, 1806-1861
Sonnets from the Portuguese   **821**
Browning, Robert, 1812-1889
Robert Browning's poetry   **821**
Brownstone, David M.
(jt. auth) Franck, I. M. Famous first facts about
sports   **796**
Bruccoli, Matthew Joseph, 1931-2008
(ed) Fitzgerald, F. S. A life in letters   **92**
(ed) Student's encyclopedia of American literary
characters. See Student's encyclopedia of
American literary characters   **810.9**
Bruchac, Joseph, 1942-
Bowman's store   **92**
Code talker   **Fic**
Our stories remember   **970.004**
Sacajawea   **Fic**
(ed) Returning the gift. See Returning the gift
   897
(ed) Songs from this Earth on turtle's back. See
Songs from this Earth on turtle's back
   811.008

Bruiser. Shusterman, N.   **Fic**
Brune, Michael, 1971-
Coming clean   **333.79**
Brunelleschi, Filippo, 1377-1446
About
King, R. Brunelleschi's dome   **726**
Brunelleschi's dome. King, R.   **726**
Brunetti, Ivan, 1967-
(ed) An Anthology of graphic fiction, cartoons,
and true stories. See An Anthology of graphic
fiction, cartoons, and true stories   **741.5**
Bruni, Frank, 1964-
Ambling into history: the unlikely odyssey of
George W. Bush   **92**
Bruns, Roger
Icons of Latino America   **920**
Brunsdale, Mitzi
Student companion to George Orwell   **828**
Brunvand, Jan Harold
Be afraid, be very afraid. See Be afraid, be very
afraid   **398.2**
(ed) American folklore. See American folklore
   398.03
Brustein, Robert, 1927-
Letters to a young actor   **792**
Brutal. Harmon, M. B.   **Fic**
Bruun, Erik A., 1961-
(ed) Voices of protest. See Voices of protest
   322.4
Bryan, Howard
Robbers, rogues, and ruffians   **978.9**
Bryan, Mike
(jt. auth) Ripken, C., Jr. The only way I know
   92
(jt. auth) Van Heerden, I. L. The storm
   976.3
Bryan, Sharon
(ed) Planet on the table. See Planet on the table
   809.1
Bryant, Jennifer
Ringside, 1925   **Fic**
Bryant, John H.
Dangerous crossings   **998**
Bryfonski, Dedria, 1947-
(ed) Peer pressure in Robert Cormier's The
chocolate war. See Peer pressure in Robert
Cormier's The chocolate war   **813.009**
Bryner, John
(jt. auth) Lanning, S. Essential reference services for today's school media specialists
   025.5
Brynie, Faith Hickman, 1946-
101 questions about food and digestion that
have been eating at you . . . until now
   612.3
101 questions about muscles to stretch your
mind and flex your brain   **612.7**
101 questions about reproduction   **612.6**
101 questions about sex and sexuality—
   613.9
101 questions about sleep and dreams that kept
you awake nights . . . until now   **612.8**

Bulimia

Sonenklar, C. Anorexia and bulimia   **616.85**

Fiction

Friedman, R. Nothing   **Fic**

Bull, Emma, 1954-

Territory   **Fic**

Bullen, Alexandra

Wish   **Fic**

Bullet point. Abrahams, P.   **Fic**

Bullies

Burton, B. Girls against girls   **305.23**

Ellis, D. We want you to know   **302.3**

Jacobs, T. A. Teen cyberbullying investigated

   364.1

Fiction

Alexander, J. S. The sweetheart of Prosper
County   **Fic**

Baratz-Logsted, L. Crazy beautiful   **Fic**

Cohen, J. Leverage   **Fic**

Griffin, A. The Julian game   **Fic**

Harmon, M. B. Brutal   **Fic**

Hautman, P. Blank confession   **Fic**

Horner, E. A love story starring my dead best
friend   **Fic**

Huser, G. Stitches   **Fic**

Hyde, C. R. Diary of a witness   **Fic**

Jonsberg, B. Dreamrider   **Fic**

Love, D. A. Defying the diva   **Fic**

Marino, P. Dough Boy   **Fic**

McGowan, A. The knife that killed me   **Fic**

McNish, C. Angel   **Fic**

McPhee, P. New blood   **Fic**

Parker, R. B. Chasing the bear   **Fic**

Peters, J. A. By the time you read this, I'll be
dead   **Fic**

Phillips, S. Burn   **Fic**

Picoult, J. Nineteen minutes   **Fic**

Ruby, L. Bad apple   **Fic**

Shulman, M. Scrawl   **Fic**

Summers, C. Some girls are   **Fic**

Sweeney, J. The guardian   **Fic**

Trottier, M. Three songs for courage   **Fic**

Wallace, J. Out of shadows   **Fic**

Williams-Garcia, R. Jumped   **Fic**

Graphic novels

Yang, G. Animal crackers   **741.5**

Bulls (Basketball team) See Chicago Bulls (Basketball team)

Bull's-eye: unraveling the medical mystery of
Lyme disease. Edlow, J. A.   **616.9**

Bunce, Elizabeth C.

Star crossed   **Fic**

Bunch, Bryan H.

(ed) Diseases. See Diseases   **616**

Bunche, Ralph J. (Ralph Johnson), 1904-1971
About

Urquhart, B. E. Ralph Bunche   **92**

Bunny drop vol. 1. Unita, Y.   **741.5**

Bunson, Margaret R.

Encyclopedia of ancient Egypt   **932**

Bunson, Matthew

Encyclopedia of the Roman Empire   **937**

Buonarotti, Michelangelo See Michelangelo Buonarroti, 1475-1564

Buonarroti, Michel Angelo See Michelangelo
Buonarroti, 1475-1564

Burch, Mary R.

Citizen canine   **636.7**

Burch, Susan

(ed) Encyclopedia of American disability history. See Encyclopedia of American disability
history   **362.4**

Burchfield, R. W. (Robert W.)

(jt. auth) Fowler, H. W. Fowler's modern English usage   **428**

Burchfield, Robert W. See Burchfield, R. W.
(Robert W.)

Burd, Nick

The vast fields of ordinary   **Fic**

Burden, Ernest E., 1934-

Illustrated dictionary of architecture   **720.3**

Burek Pierce, Jennifer

Sex, brains, and video games   **027.62**

Burfoot, Amby

Runner's world complete book of beginning
running   **796.42**

(ed) Runner's world complete book of running.
See Runner's world complete book of running

   796.42

Burg, David F.

Almanac of World War I   **940.3**

The American Revolution   **973.3**

The Great Depression   **973.91**

(jt. auth) Woodger, E. The 1980s   **973.92**

Burgan, Michael

Hiroshima   **940.54**

Nikola Tesla   **92**

Burger, Joanna

Birds: a visual guide   **598**

Burger, William C., 1932-

Flowers: how they changed the world

   582.13

Burgess, Anthony, 1917-1993

A clockwork orange   **Fic**

Burgess, Colin, 1947-

(jt. auth) French, F. In the shadow of the moon

   629.45

Burgess, Melvin, 1954-

Nicholas Dane   **Fic**

Smack   **Fic**

Burgos-Debray, Elisabeth

(ed) Menchú, R. I, Rigoberta Menchú   **92**

Buried. MacCready, R. M.   **Fic**

The **buried** mirror. Fuentes, C.   **946**

Buried onions. Soto, G.   **Fic**

Buried treasure
Fiction

Hobbs, W. Leaving Protection   **Fic**

Mussi, S. The door of no return   **Fic**

Stevenson, R. L. Treasure Island   **Fic**

Burke, Ed, 1949-

The complete book of long-distance cycling

   613.7

Burke, Larry

(jt. auth) Ripken, C., Jr. Play baseball the
Ripken way   **796.357**

Busch, Robert
The grizzly almanac   **599.78**
Bush, Gail
Tales out of the school library   **027.8**
Bush, George, 1924-
About
Naftali, T. J. George H.W. Bush   **92**
Bush, George W.
About
Bruni, F. Ambling into history: the unlikely odyssey of George W. Bush   **92**
Bushman, Claudia L.
Mormons in America   **289.3**
Bushman, Richard L., 1931-
(jt. auth) Bushman, C. L. Mormons in America   **289.3**
Business
See also Small business
Business and government *See* Industrial policy
Business communication
Thomason-Carroll, K. L. Young adult's guide to business communications   **651.7**
Business cycles
See also Financial crises
Business depression, 1929-1939 *See* Great Depression, 1929-1939
Business education
Seupel, C. W. Business, finance, and government administration   **331.7**
Business enterprises
Fiction
Chambers, V. Fifteen candles   **Fic**
Business ethics
Callahan, D. The cheating culture   **174**
See/See also pages in the following book(s):
Ethics: opposing viewpoints   **170**
Business, finance, and government administration. Seupel, C. W.   **331.7**
Business leader profiles for students   **920.003**
Business letters
Geffner, A. B. How to write better business letters   **651.7**
Business people, African American *See* African American businesspeople
Businessmen
Fiction
Doctorow, C. Makers   **Fic**
Businesspeople
Aronson, M. Bill Gates   **92**
Business leader profiles for students   **920.003**
Carey, C. W. American inventors, entrepreneurs & business visionaries   **920**
Businesswomen
Tzemach Lemmon, G. The dressmaker of Khair Khana   **92**
Bussey, Jennifer A.
(ed) 1940-1960: the twentieth century. See 1940-1960: the twentieth century   **909.82**
(ed) 1960-1980: the twentieth century. See 1960-1980: the twentieth century   **909.82**
(ed) Hate crimes. See Hate crimes   **364.1**

Bussing-Burks, Marie, 1958-
Influential economists   **920**
Money for minors   **330**
But I love him. Hubbard, A.   **Fic**
But what if I don't want to go to college? Unger, H. G.   **331.7**
Butcher, William, 1951-
(tr) Verne, J. The extraordinary journeys: Twenty thousand leagues under the sea   **Fic**
Butler, Alban, 1711-1773
Butler's Lives of the saints   **920.003**
Butler, Carol A., 1943-
(jt. auth) Weis, J. S. Salt marshes   **578.7**
Butler, Colin
The practical Shakespeare   **822.3**
Butler, Daniel Allen
Unsinkable: the full story of the RMS Titanic   **910.4**
Butler, Octavia E., 1947-2006
Fledgling   **Fic**
Kindred   **Fic**
Parable of the sower   **Fic**
Butler, Rebecca P.
Smart copyright compliance for schools   **346.04**
Butler, Rosa Johnson
(jt. auth) Gillespie, M. A. Maya Angelou   **92**
Butler, William S.
Secret messages   **652**
Butler's Lives of the saints. Butler, A.   **920.003**
Butterflies
Brock, J. P. Kaufman field guide to butterflies of North America   **595.7**
Pyle, R. M. The Audubon Society field guide to North American butterflies   **595.7**
Butterflies of North America. See Brock, J. P. Kaufman field guide to butterflies of North America   **595.7**
Butterfly, The *See* Whistler, James McNeill, 1834-1903
Butterfly. Hartnett, S.   **Fic**
Butterfly boy. González, R.   **92**
The **Butterfly's** way   **810.9**
Butts, Edward, 1951-
She dared   **920**
Bütz, Richard
How to carve wood   **731.4**
Buxton, Ted
Soccer skills for young players   **796.334**
Buying *See* Consumer education
By order of the president. Robinson, G.   **940.53**
By the river. Herrick, S.   **Fic**
By the time you read this, I'll be dead. Peters, J. A.   **Fic**
By these ten bones. Dunkle, C. B.   **Fic**
Byatt, A. S. (Antonia Susan), 1936-
(ed) The Oxford book of English short stories. See The Oxford book of English short stories   **S C**

Bynoe, Yvonne
Encyclopedia of rap and hip-hop culture
782.42

Bynum, W. F. (William F.), 1943-
(ed) Oxford dictionary of scientific quotations.
See Oxford dictionary of scientific quotations
500

Byrd, Richard Evelyn, 1888-1957
About
Bryant, J. H. Dangerous crossings 998

Byrd, Susannah Mississippi, 1971-
Bienvenidos! = Welcome! 027.6

Byrne, Deborah J.
MARC manual 025.3

Byrne, John, 1963-
Cartooning 741.5

Byrne, Joseph Patrick
The black death 614.5

Byron, George Gordon Byron, 6th Baron, 1788-1824
Byron 821

C

Cabeza de Vaca, Alvar Nuñez See Nuñez Cabeza de Vaca, Alvar, 16th cent.

Cabinet officers
See also Prime ministers

Cabot, Meg, 1967-
Airhead Fic
Insatiable Fic

Cactus
Hewitt, T. The complete book of cacti & succulents 635.9

Cadavers See Dead

Cadnum, Michael
Flash Fic
The king's arrow Fic
Peril on the sea Fic

Caesar, Julius, 100-44 B.C.
The Gallic War 878
See/See also pages in the following book(s):
Hamilton, E. The Roman way 870.9

Caffeine
Walker, I. Natural and everyday drugs
362.29

Cahill, Thomas, 1940-
The gifts of the Jews 909
Sailing the wine-dark sea 909

Cahill, Tom See Cahill, Thomas, 1940-

Cahn, Victor L.
The plays of Shakespeare 822.3

Cain, William E., 1952-
(ed) A Historical guide to Henry David Thoreau. See A Historical guide to Henry David Thoreau 818

Cairo. Wilson, G. W. 741.5

Cajal, Santiago Ramón y See Ramón y Cajal, Santiago, 1852-1934

Cake
See also Cupcakes

Cake decorating
Tack, K. Hello, cupcake! 641.8

Calame, Don
Swim the fly Fic

Calcines, Eduardo F., 1955-
Leaving Glorytown 92

Calculus
Berlinski, D. A tour of the calculus 515
Maor, E. The Facts on File calculus handbook 515
Graphic novels
Kojima, H. The manga guide to calculus
515

Caldecott, Julian Oliver
(ed) World atlas of great apes and their conservation. See World atlas of great apes and their conservation 599.8

Calendars
Chase's calendar of events 2011 394.26
Religious holidays and calendars 203
Richards, E. G. Mapping time 529
The Wilson calendar of world history 902

Caletti, Deb
The fortunes of Indigo Skye Fic
The secret life of Prince Charming Fic
The six rules of maybe Fic

Calhoun, Charles W. (Charles William), 1948-
Benjamin Harrison 92

Calhoun, Craig J., 1952-
(ed) Dictionary of the social sciences. See Dictionary of the social sciences 300.3

Calhoun, John C. (John Caldwell), 1782-1850
See/See also pages in the following book(s):
McPherson, J. M. Drawn with the sword
973.7

Calhoun, Yael
(ed) Wildlife protection. See Wildlife protection
333.95

California
Fiction
Allende, I. Zorro Fic
Butler, O. E. Parable of the sower Fic
De la Peña, M. Mexican whiteboy Fic
De la Peña, M. We were here Fic
Goldblatt, S. Girl to the core Fic
Hall, B. Tempo change Fic
Harmon, M. B. Brutal Fic
Hernandez, D. No more us for you Fic
Houston, J. D. Snow Mountain passage Fic
Hurwin, D. Freaks and revelations Fic
Jiménez, F. Reaching out Fic
Madigan, L. K. The mermaid's mirror Fic
McNeal, L. Dark water Fic
Murray, Y. M. The good girl's guide to getting kidnapped Fic
Nichols, J. Messed up Fic
Ockler, S. Twenty boy summer Fic
Otsuka, J. When the emperor was divine
Fic
Prinz, Y. The Vinyl Princess Fic
Ritter, J. H. Under the baseball moon Fic
Saroyan, W. The human comedy Fic
Seigel, A. Like the red panda Fic
Sherrill, M. The Ruins of California Fic
Stevenson, S. J. The Latte Rebellion Fic

Campbell, Lucie Eddie, 1885-1963
See/See also pages in the following book(s):
We'll understand it better by and by   **782.25**

Campbell, Patricia J., 1930-
Campbell's scoop   **809**
Robert Cormier   **813.009**
(ed) War is--. See War is--   **810.8**

Campbell, Ross
Shadoweyes   **741.5**

Campbell's scoop. Campbell, P. J.   **809**

Camping
Callan, K. The happy camper   **796.54**
See/See also pages in the following book(s):
Grant, G. Canoeing   **797.1**

Campo, Juan Eduardo, 1950-
Encyclopedia of Islam   **297**

Campolo, Anthony
Letters to a young evangelical   **248.4**

Camps
Klein, S. Moose   **92**
Fiction
Connelly, N. O. The miracle stealer   **Fic**
De Gramont, N. Every little thing in the world   **Fic**
Howell, S. Everything beautiful   **Fic**
Johnson, H. M. Accidents of nature   **Fic**
Padian, M. Jersey tomatoes are the best   **Fic**
Graphic novels
Kim, S. Brain camp   **741.5**

Camus, Albert, 1913-1960
The myth of Sisyphus, and other essays   **844**
The plague   **Fic**
The stranger   **Fic**

Can I change the way I look? Libal, A.   **613**

Can I wear my nose ring to the interview?
Reeves, E. G.   **650.14**

Can renewable energy replace fossil fuels?
Marcovitz, H.   **333.79**

Can she bake a cherry pie? McFeely, M. D.   **641.5**

Canada
Garrington, S. Canada   **971**
Biography
Butts, E. She dared   **920**
Directories
Canadian almanac & directory 2011 = répertoire
et almanach canadien 2011   **317.1**
Fiction
Frost, H. The braid   **Fic**
Huser, G. Stitches   **Fic**
Ibbitson, J. The Landing   **Fic**
Lawson, M. Crow Lake   **Fic**
Martin, C. K. K. I know it's over   **Fic**
McBay, B. Waiting for Sarah   **Fic**
McDonald, A. Boys, bears, and a serious pair of
hiking boots   **Fic**
McNamee, G. Acceleration   **Fic**
McPhee, P. New blood   **Fic**
Oppel, K. Half brother   **Fic**
Staunton, T. Acting up   **Fic**
Trottier, M. Three songs for courage   **Fic**
Waldorf, H. Tripping   **Fic**
Walters, E. Splat!   **Fic**
Wynne-Jones, T. Blink & Caution   **Fic**

Wynne-Jones, T. The uninvited   **Fic**
History
Riendeau, R. E. A brief history of Canada   **971**

Immigration and emigration—Encyclopedias
Powell, J. Encyclopedia of North American immigration   **304.8**

Canadian almanac & directory 2011 = répertoire
et almanach canadien 2011   **317.1**

Canales, Viola, 1957-
The tequila worm   **Fic**

Cancer
See also Cervix—Cancer; Lung cancer
Bozzone, D. M. Causes of cancer   **616.99**
Cancer information for teens   **616.99**
Goldsmith, C. Skin cancer   **616.99**
Gunther, J. Death be not proud   **92**
McKinnell, R. G. Prevention of cancer   **616.99**
Panno, J. Cancer   **616.99**
Silverstein, A. Cancer   **616.99**
Skloot, R. The immortal life of Henrietta Lacks   **92**
Fiction
Crane, D. Poster boy   **Fic**
Goodman, A. Intuition   **Fic**
Jacobson, J. The complete history of why I hate
her   **Fic**
Kephart, B. House of Dance   **Fic**
Levchuk, L. Everything beautiful in the world   **Fic**
Rallison, J. Just one wish   **Fic**
Supplee, S. Artichoke's heart   **Fic**
Turner, A. W. Hard hit   **Fic**
Vincent, Z. The lucky place   **Fic**
Graphic novels
Fies, B. Mom's cancer   **616.99**
Small, D. Stitches   **92**

Cancer and modern science [series]
Casil, A. S. Pancreatic cancer   **616.99**
Freedman, J. Brain cancer   **616.99**

Cancer information for teens   **616.99**

Candide. Voltaire   **Fic**

Candy
Almond, S. Candyfreak: a journey through the
chocolate underbelly of America   **338.4**

Candy. Brooks, K.   **Fic**

Candyfreak: a journey through the chocolate underbelly of America. Almond, S.   **338.4**

Caneva, Thomas
(jt. auth) Bailey, W. The complete marching
band resource manual   **784.8**

Canfield, Jack, 1944-
Chicken soup for the teenage soul [I-IV]   **158**
(comp) Chicken soup for the teenage soul's the
real deal. See Chicken soup for the teenage
soul's the real deal   **158**

Cann, Kate, 1954-
Possessed   **Fic**

Cannon, Byron, 1940-
(ed) Great events from history, The Middle
Ages, 477-1453. See Great events from history, The Middle Ages, 477-1453   **909.07**

Care of the dying *See* Terminal care

Career building through digital photography. Doble, R.   **775**

Career building through interactive online games. Swaine, M.   **794.8**

The **career** chronicles. Gregory, M. G.   **331.7**

Career development series
Scheeder, L. All the words on stage   **822.3**

Career discovery encyclopedia   **331.7**

Career guidance *See* Vocational guidance

Career ideas for teens [series]
Reeves, D. L. Career ideas for teens in architecture and construction   **624**
Reeves, D. L. Career ideas for teens in education and training   **331.7**

Career ideas for teens in architecture and construction. Reeves, D. L.   **624**

Career ideas for teens in education and training. Reeves, D. L.   **331.7**

Career opportunities in science. Echaore-Yoon, S.   **502**

Careers *See* Occupations; Professions

Careers for scientific types & others with inquiring minds. Goldberg, J.   **502**

Carey, Charles W.
African Americans in science   **920.003**
American inventors, entrepreneurs & business visionaries   **920**
(ed) Castro's Cuba. See Castro's Cuba
                                             972.91

Carey, Ernestine Gilbreth
(jt. auth) Gilbreth, F. B. Cheaper by the dozen
                                             92

Carey, Gary
A multicultural dictionary of literary terms
                                             803

Carey, Janet Lee
Dragon's Keep   **Fic**
Stealing death   **Fic**

Caribbean region
See also West Indies
Fiction
Allende, I. Island beneath the sea   **Fic**
Crichton, M. Pirate latitudes   **Fic**
Engle, M. Hurricane dancers   **Fic**
Keyes, P. The jumbee   **Fic**
Mackler, C. Tangled   **Fic**

Caricatures *See* Cartoons and caricatures

Caricaturists *See* Cartoonists

Carle, Jill
(jt. auth) Carle, M. Teens cook   **641.5**
(jt. auth) Carle, M. Teens cook dessert
                                             641.8

Carle, Judi
(jt. auth) Carle, M. Teens cook   **641.5**
(jt. auth) Carle, M. Teens cook dessert
                                             641.8

Carle, Megan
Teens cook   **641.5**
Teens cook dessert   **641.8**

Carlin, John
Playing the enemy   **968.06**

Carlisle, Rodney P.
Civil War and Reconstruction   **973.7**
Exploring space   **629.4**
Iraq War   **956.7**
Persian Gulf War   **956.7**
Scientific American inventions and discoveries
                                             609
World War I   **940.3**
(ed) The African Americans. See The African Americans   **305.8**
(ed) The Arab Americans. See The Arab Americans   **305.8**
(ed) The Asian Americans. See The Asian Americans   **305.8**
(ed) The European Americans. See The European Americans   **305.8**
(ed) The Great Depression and World War II, 1929 to 1949. See The Great Depression and World War II, 1929 to 1949   **973.91**
(ed) The Hispanic Americans. See The Hispanic Americans   **305.8**
(ed) The Jewish Americans. See The Jewish Americans   **305.8**
(ed) The Native Americans. See The Native Americans   **305.8**

Carlsen, Henrik Kurt, 1915-1989
About
Delaney, F. Simple courage   **910.4**

Carlsen, Kurt *See* Carlsen, Henrik Kurt, 1915-1989

Carlson, Laurie M., 1952-
A fever in Salem   **133.4**

Carlson, Lori M.
(ed) American eyes. See American eyes   **S C**
(ed) Cool salsa. See Cool salsa   **811.008**
(ed) Moccasin thunder. See Moccasin thunder
                                             S C
(ed) Red hot salsa. See Red hot salsa
                                             811.008
(ed) Voices in first person. See Voices in first person   **S C**

Carlson, Melody, 1956-
Premiere   **Fic**

Carlson, W. Bernard
(ed) Technology in world history. See Technology in world history   **909**

Carmichael, Chris
The ultimate ride   **796.6**

Carmody, Isobelle
Alyzon Whitestarr   **Fic**

Carnagie, Julie
(ed) Howes, K. K. War of 1812   **973.5**
(ed) Renaissance & Reformation: almanac. See Renaissance & Reformation: almanac
                                             940.2
(ed) Renaissance & Reformation: primary sources. See Renaissance & Reformation: primary sources   **940.2**
(ed) Saari, P. Colonial America: primary sources
                                             973.2

Carnes, Mark C. (Mark Christopher), 1950-
(ed) American national biography. See American national biography   **920.003**
(ed) Invisible giants. See Invisible giants
                                             920

Caroli, Betty Boyd
First ladies **920**

Caroselli, Joanne
(il) Hearne, B. G. Beauties and beasts **398.2**

Carpe diem. Cornwell, A. **Fic**

Carpenter, Roger M., 1956-
Term paper resource guide to colonial American history **973.2**

Carpetbag rule *See* Reconstruction (1865-1876)

Carr, Gerald A., 1936-
Fundamentals of track and field **796.42**

Carrasco, David
(ed) The Oxford encyclopedia of Mesoamerican cultures. See The Oxford encyclopedia of Mesoamerican cultures **972**

Carrie. King, S. **Fic**

Carrington, Richard Christopher, 1826-1875
About
Clark, S. The sun kings **523.7**

Carroll, Aaron E.
Don't swallow your gum! **612**

Carroll, David L., 1942-
(jt. auth) Zugibe, F. T. Dissecting death **614**

Carroll, Jamuna
(ed) Civil liberties and war. See Civil liberties and war **342**
(ed) Marijuana: opposing viewpoints. See Marijuana: opposing viewpoints **362.29**
(ed) Students' rights: opposing viewpoints. See Students' rights: opposing viewpoints **344**

Carroll, Lewis, 1832-1898
About
Rubin, C. M. The real Alice in Wonderland [biography of Alice Pleasance Liddell Hargreaves] **92**

Carroll, Sean B.
The making of the fittest **572.8**
Remarkable creatures **508**

Carry me home. McWhorter, D. **976.1**

Cars (Automobiles) *See* Automobiles

Carson, Clayborne, 1944-
(ed) The Eyes on the prize civil rights reader. See The Eyes on the prize civil rights reader **323.1**

Carson, Kit, 1809-1868
About
Remley, D. A. Kit Carson **92**

Carson, Rachel, 1907-1964
The edge of the sea **577.7**
Silent spring **363.7**
About
Levine, E. Rachel Carson **92**
Macgillivray, A. Understanding Rachel Carson's Silent Spring **363.7**

Carson-DeWitt, Rosalyn
(ed) Drugs, alcohol, and tobacco. See Drugs, alcohol, and tobacco **362.29**

Carson McCullers [critical essays] **813.009**

Carstensen, Angela
(ed) Outstanding books for the college bound. See Outstanding books for the college bound **011.6**

Cart, Michael
The heart has its reasons **813.009**
Young adult literature: from romance to realism **028.5**
(ed) 911: the book of help. See 911: the book of help **810.8**
(ed) How beautiful the ordinary. See How beautiful the ordinary **S C**

Carter, Alden R.
Love, football, and other contact sports **S C**

Carter, James Earl *See* Carter, Jimmy, 1924-

Carter, Jason
Power lines **968.06**

Carter, Jimmy, 1924-
An hour before daylight **92**

Carter, Rita
The human brain book. See The human brain book **612.8**

Carter, Robert, 1728-1804
About
Levy, A. The first emancipator [biography of Robert Carter] **92**

Carter, Susan B.
(ed) Historical statistics of the United States. See Historical statistics of the United States **317.3**

Carter family
About
Carter, J. An hour before daylight **92**
Carter finally gets it. Crawford, B. **Fic**

Cartledge, Paul
Ancient Greece **938**

Cartmell, Van Henry
(ed) 24 favorite one-act plays. See 24 favorite one-act plays **808.82**
(comp) Henry, O. The best short stories of O. Henry **S C**

Cartography *See* Maps

The **cartoon** history of the modern world [part 1] Gonick, L. **909.08**

Cartooning
Technique
Amberlyn, J. C. Drawing manga **741.5**
Baker, K. How to draw stupid and other essentials of cartooning **741.5**
Byrne, J. Cartooning **741.5**

Cartoonists
Goldstein, N. Jackie Ormes **92**
Jones, G. Men of tomorrow **741.5**
Schumacher, M. Will Eisner **92**
Dictionaries
Pendergast, T. U-X-L graphic novelists **920.003**

Cartoons, Animated *See* Animated films

Cartoons and caricatures
See also Cartooning; Comic books, strips, etc.
Bancroft, T. Creating characters with personality **741.6**
Chiarello, M. The DC Comics guide to coloring and lettering comics **741.5**
Hart, C. Drawing cutting edge anatomy **741.5**

Censorship—*Continued*

Caso, F. Censorship   **363.31**
Censored books [I]-II   **810.9**
Censorship [Current controversies]   **363.31**
Censorship [Issues that concern you]   **363.31**
Censorship: opposing viewpoints   **363.31**
Freedom of expression   **323.44**
Freedom of speech   **342**
Phillips, T. A. Hazelwood v. Kuhlmeier and the school newspaper censorship debate   **342**
Reichman, H. Censorship and selection

    025.2

See/See also pages in the following book(s):
Online pornography: opposing viewpoints

    363.4

Encyclopedias
Green, J. The encyclopedia of censorship

    363.31

Graphic novels
Yumi, K. Library wars, vol. 1: love & war

    741.5

Censorship [Current controversies]   **363.31**
Censorship [Issues that concern you]   **363.31**
Censorship and selection. Reichman, H.   **025.2**
Censorship: opposing viewpoints   **363.31**
Census

See also United States—Census

Census of Marine Life (Project)
Crist, D. T. World ocean census   **578.7**

Centennial Exhibition (1876: Philadelphia, Pa.)
Fiction
Kephart, B. Dangerous neighbors   **Fic**

Center for Cartoon Studies presents [series]
Lutes, J. Houdini: the handcuff king   **92**
Porcellino, J. Thoreau at Walden   **818**

The **center** of everything. Moriarty, L.   **Fic**

The **center** of the universe. Liberty, A.   **Fic**

Centers for Disease Control and Prevention (U.S.). Epidemic Intelligence Service Program
McKenna, M. Beating back the devil   **614.4**

Central Africa
History
Davidson, B. The African slave trade   **967**

Central America
History
Foster, L. V. A brief history of Central America

    972.8

Central America (Steamship)
Kinder, G. Ship of gold in the deep blue sea

    910.4

Central Asia
Hanks, R. R. Central Asia   **958**
Graphic novels
Rall, T. Silk road to ruin   **958**
History
Wood, F. The Silk Road   **950**

Central Europe
Kort, M. The handbook of the new Eastern Europe   **943**
Historical geography—Maps
Magocsi, P. R. Historical atlas of Central Europe   **911**

Central High School (Little Rock, Ark.)
Fradin, J. B. The power of one [biography of Daisy Bates]   **92**
LaNier, C. W. A mighty long way   **92**

Central Intelligence Agency (U.S.) *See* United States. Central Intelligence Agency

Century of difference. Fischer, C. S.   **306**

A **Century** of great Western stories   **S C**

Ceram, C. W., 1915-1972
Gods, graves, and scholars   **930.1**

Ceramics
Nelson, G. C. Ceramics: a potter's handbook

    738.1

Cerebral palsy
Fiction
Johnson, H. M. Accidents of nature   **Fic**
Koertge, R. Stoner & Spaz   **Fic**

Ceremonies *See* Rites and ceremonies

Cerf, Bennett, 1898-1971
(ed) 24 favorite one-act plays. See 24 favorite one-act plays   **808.82**
(comp) Henry, O. The best short stories of O. Henry   **S C**

Ceruzzi, Paul E.
A history of modern computing   **004**

Cervantes, Lorna Dee
See/See also pages in the following book(s):
Fooling with words   **808.1**

Cervantes Saavedra, Miguel de, 1547-1616
Don Quixote de la Mancha   **Fic**
Don Quixote de la Mancha; dramatization. See Wasserman, D. Man of La Mancha   **812**

Cervical cancer. Spencer, J. V.   **616.99**

Cervix
Cancer
Spencer, J. V. Cervical cancer   **616.99**

Cesari, Jocelyne
(ed) Encyclopedia of Islam in the United States. See Encyclopedia of Islam in the United States   **297**

Cetin, Fethiye
My grandmother [biography of Heranus Gadaryan]   **92**

Chabris, Christopher F.
The invisible gorilla   **153.7**

Chadda, Sarwat
The devil's kiss   **Fic**

Chagall, Marc, 1887-1985
About
Kagan, A. Marc Chagall   **92**

Chaikin, Andrew, 1956-
A passion for Mars   **523.4**

Chains. Anderson, L. H.   **Fic**

Chairman Mao would not be amused   **S C**

Chaisson, Eric
Epic of evolution   **523.1**

Chalberg, John
(ed) Opposing viewpoints in American history. See Opposing viewpoints in American history

    973

Challans, Mary *See* Renault, Mary, 1905-1983

Challenger, Melanie
(ed) Stolen voices. See Stolen voices   **920**

Chalmers, David Mark
Hooded Americanism: the history of the Ku
Klux Klan   **322.4**

Chalmers, Irena
Food jobs   **647.9**

Chaltain, Sam
(jt. auth) Haynes, C. C. First freedoms   **342**

Chaltas, Thalia
Because I am furniture   **Fic**

Chambers, Aidan, 1934-
The kissing game   **S C**

Chambers, Paul, 1968-
(jt. auth) Haines, T. The complete guide to prehistoric life   **560**

Chambers, Veronica
Fifteen candles   **Fic**

Chametzky, Jules
(ed) Jewish American literature. See Jewish
American literature   **810.8**

Champion, Laurie
(ed) American women writers, 1900-1945. See
American women writers, 1900-1945
    810.9

Chan, Queenie
(jt. auth) Koontz, D. R. In odd we trust
    741.5

Chance
Rosenthal, J. Struck by lightning   **519.2**
Fiction
Perkins, L. R. As easy as falling off the face of
the earth   **Fic**

Chance in the house of fate. Ackerman, J.
    599.93

Chancellorsville (Va.), Battle of, 1863
Fiction
Crane, S. The red badge of courage   **Fic**

Chanda's secrets. Stratton, A.   **Fic**

Chandler, Kristen
Wolves, boys, & other things that might kill me
    Fic

Chandler, Richard J.
Shorebirds of North America, Europe, and Asia
    598

Chandler, Laurel See Holder, Nancy, 1953-

Chang, Iris, 1968-2004
The Chinese in America   **305.8**

Chang, Jeff
Can't stop, won't stop   **781.64**

Change, Social See Social change

Change of sex See Transsexualism

Changing bodies, changing lives. Bell, R.
    613.9

Changing ecosystems. Casper, J. K.   **577.2**

Chanson de Roland
The song of Roland   **841**

Chants (Plain, Gregorian, etc.)
See/See also pages in the following book(s):
Grout, D. J. A history of western music
    780.9

The **chaos** code. Richards, J.   **Fic**

Chaos walking [series]
Ness, P. The knife of never letting go   **Fic**

Chaple, Glenn F.
Outer planets   **523.4**

Chaplin, Heather, 1971-
Smartbomb   **338.4**

Chapman, Richard
The new complete guitarist   **787.87**

Chappell, Jon
Guitar all-in-one for dummies   **787.87**

Chapters into verse   **821.008**

Characteristics, National See National characteristics

Characters and characteristics in literature
See also Native Americans in literature
Nilsen, A. P. Names and naming in young adult
literature   **813.009**
Rubin, C. M. The real Alice in Wonderland [bi-
ography of Alice Pleasance Liddell Har-
greaves]   **92**
Encyclopedias
Student's encyclopedia of American literary
characters   **810.9**

Charbonneau, Jean-Baptiste, 1805-1866
About
Nelson, W. D. Interpreters with Lewis and
Clark: the story of Sacagawea and Toussaint
Charbonneau   **92**

Charbonneau, Toussaint, ca. 1758-ca. 1839
About
Nelson, W. D. Interpreters with Lewis and
Clark: the story of Sacagawea and Toussaint
Charbonneau   **92**

Charging the net. Harris, C.   **920**

Charities
See also Disaster relief

Charlemagne, Emperor, 742-814
About
Wilson, D. A. Charlemagne   **92**
See/See also pages in the following book(s):
Bulfinch, T. Bulfinch's mythology   **398.2**

Charles, Ray
About
Duggleby, J. Uh huh!: the story of Ray Charles
    92

Charles and Emma [dual biography of Charles
Darwin and Emma Wedgwood Darwin]
Heiligman, D.   **92**

Charles Darwin and the mystery of mysteries.
Eldredge, N.   **92**

Charles Darwin's On the Origin of Species. Keller, M.   **576.8**

Charles Dickens A-Z. See Davis, P. B. Critical
companion to Charles Dickens   **823.009**

Charles the Great See Charlemagne, Emperor,
742-814

Charlestown High School (Boston, Mass.)
Swidey, N. The assist   **796.323**

Charters, Ann, 1936-
(ed) Kerouac, J. The portable Jack Kerouac
    818
(ed) The Portable sixties reader. See The Portable sixties reader   **810.8**

Chemistry—Dictionaries—*Continued*
The Facts on File dictionary of chemistry
540.3
Encyclopedias
Chemistry: foundations and applications
540.3
Rittner, D. Encyclopedia of chemistry   540.3
History
Greenberg, A. From alchemy to chemistry in
picture and story   540.9
Study and teaching
Silver, T. Cracking the SAT. Chemistry subject
test   540
Tables
CRC handbook of chemistry and physics
540
Lange's handbook of chemistry   540

Chemistry, Environmental *See* Environmental
chemistry

Chemistry, Physical and theoretical *See* Physical
chemistry

Chemistry experiments. Walker, P.   540.7

Chemistry: foundations and applications   540.3

Chemists
Borzendowski, J. Marie Curie   92
Hager, T. The alchemy of air [dual biography of
Fritz Haber and Carl Bosch]   92
McClafferty, C. K. Something out of nothing
[biography of Marie Curie]   92
Stille, D. R. Percy Lavon Julian   92
Yannuzzi, D. A. New elements [biography of
Marie Curie]   92

Cheney, Annie
Body brokers   617.9

Cheng, Linsun, 1951-
(ed) Berkshire encyclopedia of China. See Berkshire encyclopedia of China   951

Chermak, Steven M.
(ed) Crimes and trials of the century. See
Crimes and trials of the century   345
(ed) Famous American crimes and trials. See
Famous American crimes and trials   364

Chernobyl   363.1

**Chernobyl Nuclear Accident, Chernobyl,
Ukraine, 1986**
Chernobyl   363.1

Cherokee Indians
Bowes, J. P. The Trail of Tears   970.004
Gilbert, J. The Trail of Tears across Missouri
970.004
Marsico, K. The Trail of Tears   305.8
Voices from the Trail of Tears   970.004
See/See also pages in the following book(s):
Wright, R. Stolen continents   970.004

Cherry Heaven. Adlington, L. J.   Fic

Cherrywell, Steph
Pepper Penwell and the land creature of Monster Lake   741.5

Cherubini, Corkin
See/See also pages in the following book(s):
Profiles in courage for our time   920

Chesnoff, Richard Z., 1937-
Pack of thieves   940.53

Chess
King, D. Chess   794.1
Naroditsky, D. Mastering positional chess
794.1
United States Chess Federation. U.S. Chess Fed-
eration's official rules of chess   794.1
Fiction
Wallace, R. Perpetual check   Fic

Cheva, Cherry
DupliKate   Fic

Chevalier, Tracy, 1962-
Girl with a pearl earring   Fic

Chevat, Richard
(jt. auth) Pollan, M. The omnivore's dilemma
338.1

Chevat, Richie
(jt. auth) Gore, A. Our choice   363.7
Chew on this. Schlosser, E.   394.1

Cheyenne Indians
Viola, H. J. It is a good day to die   973.8

Chiarello, Mark
The DC Comics guide to coloring and lettering
comics   741.5

Chibbaro, Julie
Deadly   Fic

Chicago (Ill.)
Fiction
Cisneros, S. The house on Mango Street   Fic
Elkeles, S. How to ruin my teenage life   Fic
Fletcher, C. Ten cents a dance   Fic
Green, J. Will Grayson, Will Grayson   Fic
Magoon, K. The rock and the river   Fic
Sinclair, U. The jungle   Fic
Smith, J. E. The comeback season   Fic
Trice, D. T. Only twice I've wished for heaven
Fic
Wright, R. Native son   Fic
Zulkey, C. An off year   Fic
Graphic novels
Kuper, P. The jungle   741.5
Neri, G. Yummy [biography of Robert Sandifer]
92

History
Owens, L. L. The great Chicago fire   977.3
Social conditions
Fradin, J. B. Jane Addams   92
Joravsky, B. Hoop dreams   796.323

Chicago Bulls (Basketball team)
Halberstam, D. Playing for keeps: Michael Jordan and the world he made   92

Chicago Children's Choir
Turck, M. Freedom song   323.1

Chicago guides to academic life [series]
Roberts, A. L. The thinking student's guide to
college   378.1

**Chicago guides to writing, editing, and publish-
ing** [series]
Turabian, K. L. A manual for writers of research papers, theses, and dissertations
808
Turabian, K. L. Student's guide to writing college papers   808

Children, Emotionally disturbed *See* Emotionally disturbed children

Children, Retarded *See* Mentally handicapped children

Children and adults *See* Child rearing

Children and the Internet *See* Internet and children

Children and war
Ellis, D. Children of war   **956.7**
Kamara, M. The bite of the mango   **92**
Nicholas, L. H. Cruel world   **940.53**
Stolen voices   **920**
Walters, E. When elephants fight   **920**
See/See also pages in the following book(s):
Beah, I. A long way gone   **92**

Children in the Holocaust and World War II   **940.53**

Children of a lesser god. Medoff, M. H.   **812**

Children of alcoholics
Fiction
MacCready, R. M. Buried   **Fic**

Children of gay parents
Fakhrid-Deen, T. Let's get this straight   **306.8**

Children of immigrants
Pung, A. Unpolished gem   **92**
Waking up American   **305.4**

Children of Israel, children of Palestine   **956.94**

Children of prisoners
Zehr, H. "What will happen to me?"   **362.82**

Children of single parents *See* Single parent family

Children of the atomic bomb. Yamazaki, J. N.   **92**

Children of the Holocaust. Epstein, H.   **940.53**

Children of the sea, vol. 1. Igarashi, D.   **741.5**

Children of the West. Luchetti, C.   **978**

Children of war. Ellis, D.   **956.7**

Children's and young adult literature reference series
Adamson, L. G. Literature links to world history, K-12   **028.1**
Gillespie, J. T. Classic teenplots   **011.6**
Gillespie, J. T. The Newbery/Printz companion   **028.5**
Thomas, R. L. Popular series fiction for middle school and teen readers   **016.8**
Zbaracki, M. D. Best books for boys   **028.5**

Children's courts *See* Juvenile courts

Children's libraries
    See also Libraries and schools; Young adults' libraries
Feinberg, S. Designing space for children and teens in libraries and public places   **727**

Children's literature
    See also Coretta Scott King Award; Fairy tales; Newbery Medal
Diamant-Cohen, B. Booktalking bonanza   **028.5**

Bibliography
Al-Hazza, T. C. Books about the Middle East   **016.3058**
Barancik, S. Guide to collective biographies for children and young adults   **016.9**
Crew, H. S. Women engaged in war in literature for youth   **016.3**
Garcha, R. The world of Islam in literature for youth   **016.3058**
Gelman, J. The kids' book club book   **028.5**
Knowles, E. Boys and literacy   **028.5**
Silver, L. R. Best Jewish books for children and teens   **011.6**
Thomas, R. L. Popular series fiction for middle school and teen readers   **016.8**
Zbaracki, M. D. Best books for boys   **028.5**
History and criticism
Gillespie, J. T. The Newbery/Printz companion   **028.5**
Handbook of research on children's and young adult literature   **028.5**

Children's moneymaking projects *See* Moneymaking projects for children

Children's plays, American
Surface, M. H. Most valuable player and four other all-star plays for middle and high school audiences   **812**

Children's poetry
    See also Nonsense verses

Children's rights. Farrell, C.   **305.23**

Children's Theatre Company (Minneapolis, Minn.)
Fierce & true. See Fierce & true   **812.008**

Children's writings
Rising voices   **810.8**

Childress, Diana
Barefoot conquistador [biography of Alvar Núñez Cabeza de Vaca]   **92**
Omar al-Bashir's Sudan   **962.4**

A **child's** Christmas in Wales. Thomas, D.   **828**

Chile
Fiction
Allende, I. The house of the spirits   **Fic**
Miller-Lachmann, L. Gringolandia   **Fic**

Chiles, James R.
The god machine   **629.133**

Chill wind. McDonald, J.   **Fic**

Chima, Cinda Williams
The Demon King   **Fic**
The warrior heir   **Fic**

Chime. Billingsley, F.   **Fic**

Chimpanzees
Goodall, J. In the shadow of man   **599.8**
Goodall, J. Through a window   **599.8**
Fiction
Dickinson, P. Eva   **Fic**
Oppel, K. Half brother   **Fic**

China
China: opposing viewpoints   **951**
Civilization
Shaughnessy, E. L. Exploring the life, myth, and art of ancient China   **931**
Whitfield, S. Philosophy and writing   **181**

Chmakova, Svetlana, 1979-
Nightschool: the weirn books, volume one
741.5

Chocolate
Aaron, S. Chocolate **641.3**
Almond, S. Candyfreak: a journey through the chocolate underbelly of America **338.4**
Rosenblum, M. Chocolate: a bittersweet saga of dark and light **641.3**

Chocolate for a teen's heart **152.4**

The **chocolate** war. Cormier, R. **Fic**

Choctaw Indians
Folklore
Tingle, T. Walking the Choctaw road **398.2**

Choice (Psychology)
See also Decision making

Choice of college See College choice

Choice of school See School choice

Choices for the high school graduate. Fireside, B. J. **373.1**

Choiniere, Joseph
What's that bird? **598**

Choker. Woods, E. E. **Fic**

Cholera
Coleman, W. H. Cholera **616.9**
Johnson, S. The ghost map **614.5**

Cholesterol
See also Low-cholesterol diet

Choosing Web 2.0 tools for learning and teaching in a digital world. Berger, P. **025.04**

Chopin, Kate, 1851-1904
The awakening and selected stories **S C**

Choppy socky blues. Briant, E. **Fic**

Chopra, Deepak
Fire in the heart **204**

Choreographers
Freedman, R. Martha Graham, a dancer's life **92**
Gottlieb, R. A. George Balanchine: the ballet maker **92**

The **chosen.** Potok, C. **Fic**

The **chosen** one. Williams, C. L. **Fic**

Chow, Cara, 1972-
Bitter melon **Fic**

Chow, Cheryl, 1952-
(jt. auth) Chow, J. H. The encyclopedia of hepatitis and other liver diseases **616.3**

Chow, James H., 1948-
The encyclopedia of hepatitis and other liver diseases **616.3**

Christ See Jesus Christ

Christen, Carol
What color is your parachute? for teens **331.7**

Christensen, Karen
(ed) Berkshire encyclopedia of world sport. See Berkshire encyclopedia of world sport **796.03**
(ed) Global perspectives on the United States. See Global perspectives on the United States **327.73**

Christensen, Lisa
Clueless about cars **629.28**

Christian, Fletcher, 1764-1793
About
Alexander, C. The Bounty: the true story of the mutiny on the Bounty **996**
Fiction
Boyne, J. Mutiny **Fic**

Christian art
Snyder, J. Art of the Middle Ages **709.02**

Christian fiction
Bibliography
Walker, B. J. The librarian's guide to developing Christian fiction collections for young adults **025.2**

Christian fundamentalism
See/See also pages in the following book(s):
Armstrong, K. The battle for God **200**

Christian life
Campolo, A. Letters to a young evangelical **248.4**
Lewis, C. S. The Screwtape letters **248**
Scheeres, J. Jesus land **92**
Fiction
Billerbeck, K. Perfectly dateless **Fic**
Brande, R. Evolution, me, & other freaks of nature **Fic**
Carlson, M. Premiere **Fic**
Collins, B. Always watching **Fic**
Grimes, N. A girl named Mister **Fic**
Hemphill, H. Long gone daddy **Fic**
Jaden, D. Losing Faith **Fic**
Kirkpatrick, J. A flickering light **Fic**
Mattison, B. T. Unsigned hype **Fic**
McVoy, T. E. Pure **Fic**
Zarr, S. Once was lost **Fic**
Zielin, L. Donut days **Fic**
Quotations
The Quotable saint **230**

Christian missionaries
Fiction
Kingsolver, B. The poisonwood Bible **Fic**

Christian rock music
Beaujon, A. Body piercing saved my life **781.66**

Christian saints
Bury, J. B. Ireland's saint [biography of Saint Patrick] **92**
Ellsberg, R. Blessed among all women **920**
Green, J. God's fool: the life and times of Francis of Assisi **92**
Martin, J. My life with the saints **920**
McBrien, R. P. Lives of the saints **920**
Pernoud, R. Joan of Arc: her story **92**
Dictionaries
Butler, A. Butler's Lives of the saints **920.003**

Christianity
See also Protestantism
Chittister, J. The tent of Abraham **222**
Guite, M. What do Christians believe? **230**
Hale, R. D. Christianity **230**
Encyclopedias
Encyclopedia of Christianity **230.003**

Circulation of library materials *See* Library circulation

Circulatory system *See* Cardiovascular system

The **circulatory** system. Mertz, L. A.   **616.1**

Circumference. Nicastro, N.   **526**

Circumnavigation *See* Voyages around the world

Circus
Fiction
Davis, A. Wonder when you'll miss me   **Fic**
Houck, C. Tiger's curse   **Fic**
Graphic novels
Dunning, J. H. Salem Brownstone   **741.5**

Cisneros, Sandra
The house on Mango Street   **Fic**
Woman Hollering Creek and other stories
      S C

Citations, Bibliographical *See* Bibliographical citations

Cite it right. Fox, T.   **808**

Cities. Lorinc, J.   **307.7**

Cities and towns
Lorinc, J. Cities   **307.7**
Growth
See also Urbanization

Citizen canine. Burch, M. R.   **636.7**

A **citizen's** guide to ecology. Slobodkin, L. B.
      577

City: a story of Roman planning and construction.
Macaulay, D.   **711**

City and town life
Fiction
Friedman, A. The year my sister got lucky
      Fic
Hedges, P. What's eating Gilbert Grape   **Fic**
Tucker, T. Over and under   **Fic**
Poetry
Crisler, C. L. Tough boy sonatas   **811**

City chic. Willdorf, N.   **646.7**

The **City** in the Lake. Neumeier, R.   **Fic**

City lights pocket poets anthology   **808.81**

City of bones. Clare, C.   **Fic**

City of cannibals. Thompson, R.   **Fic**

City planning
Rome
Macaulay, D. City: a story of Roman planning
and construction   **711**

Civil disobedience *See* Resistance to government

Civil disobedience   **809**

Civil disorders *See* Riots

Civil engineering
Macaulay, D. City: a story of Roman planning
and construction   **711**
Macaulay, D. Underground   **624**

Civil liberties   **323**

Civil liberties and the Constitution   **342**

Civil liberties and war   **323**

Civil liberties: opposing viewpoints   **342**

Civil rights
      See also African Americans—Civil rights;
Discrimination; Handicapped—Civil rights;
Right of privacy; Students—Civil rights;
Women's rights; Youth—Civil rights
American civil rights: primary sources   **323.1**
Bausum, A. Unraveling freedom   **940.3**
Biddle, W. Immigrants' rights after 9/11
      323.3
Civil liberties   **323**
Civil liberties and the Constitution   **342**
Civil liberties and war   **323**
Civil liberties and war   **342**
Civil liberties: opposing viewpoints   **342**
Civil rights   **323.1**
The Civil Rights Act of 1964   **342**
Individual rights and the police   **345**
Malaspina, A. The ethnic and group identity
movements   **323.1**
Patrick, J. J. The Bill of Rights   **342**
Pendergast, T. Constitutional amendments: from
freedom of speech to flag burning   **342**
Savage, D. G. The Supreme Court and individu-
al rights   **342**
What rights should illegal immigrants have?
      342
See/See also pages in the following book(s):
Affirmative action [Greenwood Press]   **331.1**
Thompson, C. White men challenging racism
      323
Fiction
Doctorow, C. Little brother   **Fic**

Civil rights (International law) *See* Human rights

Civil rights   **323.1**

Civil Rights Act of 1964
The Civil Rights Act of 1964   **342**
The **Civil** Rights Act of 1964   **342**

Civil rights demonstrations
Osborne, L. B. Women of the civil rights move-
ment   **323**
Zellner, R. The wrong side of Murder Creek
[biography of Robert Zellner]   **92**
Fiction
Devoto, P. C. The summer we got saved
      Fic

Civil rights leaders [series]
Aretha, D. No compromise: the story of Harvey
Milk   **92**
Esty, A. The liberator: the story of William
Lloyd Garrison   **92**
Esty, A. Unbound and unbroken: the story of
Frederick Douglass   **92**
Hinman, B. Eternal vigilance: the story of Ida
B. Wells-Barnett   **92**

The civil rights movement [series]
Aretha, D. Freedom Summer   **323.1**
Aretha, D. Montgomery bus boycott   **323.1**
Aretha, D. The murder of Emmett Till
      364.152
Aretha, D. Selma and the Voting Rights Act
      324.6
Aretha, D. The trial of the Scottsboro boys
      345
Boerst, W. J. Marching in Birmingham
      323.1

Classical civilization

See also Rome—Civilization

The classical world, 500 BCE to AD 600 CE
930

Dawson, I. Greek and Roman medicine
610.9

Dictionaries

The Cambridge dictionary of classical civilization **938.003**

Classical dictionaries

The Oxford classical dictionary **938.003**

Classical drama

Encyclopedias

Thorburn, J. E., Jr. The Facts on File companion to classical drama **880.3**

Classical geography *See* Ancient geography

Classical Greek civilization, 800-323 B.C.E
938

Classical literature

See also Greek literature; Latin literature

Highet, G. The classical tradition **809**

Dictionaries

Grant, M. Greek and Latin authors, 800 B.C.-A.D. 1000 **920.003**

The Oxford companion to classical literature
880.3

Classical music *See* Music

Classical myth & religion. See The Oxford dictionary of classical myth and religion **292**

Classical mythology

See also Eros (Greek deity); Greek mythology; Roman mythology

Beauman, S. The genealogy of Greek mythology **292**

Daly, K. N. Greek and Roman mythology, A to Z **292**

Graves, R. The Greek myths **292**

Hamilton, E. Mythology **292**

Mitchell, A. Shapeshifters **292**

Dictionaries

The Oxford dictionary of classical myth and religion **292**

Encyclopedias

Roman, L. Encyclopedia of Greek and Roman mythology **292**

Fiction

Barrett, T. King of Ithaka **Fic**

Franco, B. Metamorphosis **Fic**

Friesner, E. M. Nobody's princess **Fic**

Halam, A. Snakehead **Fic**

Renault, M. The king must die **Fic**

Classical poetry

Collections

The Oxford book of classical verse in translation **881.008**

The **classical** Roman reader. Atchity, K. J.
870.8

The **classical** tradition. Highet, G. **809**

The **classical** world, 500 BCE to AD 600 CE
930

Classics Illustrated [series]

Kuper, P. The jungle **741.5**

Classics illustrated deluxe #6: the three Musketeers. Morvan, J. D. **741.5**

Classification

Books

See Library classification

Classification of living organisms. Lewis, M. J.
570.1

Claudius, Emperor of Rome, 10 B.C.-54

Fiction

Graves, R. I, Claudius **Fic**

Clausen, Tammy Hennigh

(jt. auth) Spratford, B. S. The horror readers' advisory **025.5**

Clausius, Rudolf Julius Emmanuel, 1822-1888

See/See also pages in the following book(s):

Guillen, M. Five equations that changed the world **530.1**

Clay, Cassius *See* Ali, Muhammad, 1942-

Clay. Almond, D. **Fic**

Cleaning up the environment. Maczulak, A. E.
628.5

Cleanliness

See also Hygiene; Sanitation

Clemens, Samuel Langhorne *See* Twain, Mark, 1835-1910

Clement-Davies, David, 1961-

The sight **Fic**

Clement-Moore, Rosemary

Prom dates from Hell **Fic**

The splendor falls **Fic**

Clemente, Roberto, 1934-1972

About

Maraniss, D. Clemente **92**

Santiago, W. "21" [biography of Roberto Clemente] **92**

Clements, Gillian

A picture history of great buildings **720.9**

Cleopatra, Queen of Egypt, d. 30 B.C.

About

Burstein, S. M. The reign of Cleopatra **92**

Nardo, D. Cleopatra **92**

Roller, D. W. Cleopatra **92**

Fiction

Dray, S. Lily of the Nile **Fic**

Clergy

See also Priests; Rabbis

Fiction

Craven, M. I heard the owl call my name
Fic

Greene, G. The power and the glory **Fic**

Zarr, S. Once was lost **Fic**

Zielin, L. Donut days **Fic**

Cleveland (Ohio)

Fiction

Garsee, J. Before, after, and somebody in between **Fic**

Click **Fic**

The **client.** Grisham, J. **Fic**

Climate

See also Greenhouse effect; Meteorology; Weather

Casper, J. K. Climate systems **551.5**

Fagan, B. M. The Little Ice Age **551.6**

Cohen, Walter, 1949-
(ed) Shakespeare, W. The Norton Shakespeare
822.3

Cohn, John M., 1943-
The complete library technology planner   025

Cohn, Rachel
Gingerbread   Fic
Naomi and Ely's no kiss list   Fic
Nick & Norah's infinite playlist   Fic

Cohn, Roy, 1927-1986
Drama
Kushner, T. Angels in America   812

Coile, D. Caroline
The dog breed bible   636.7

Coins
Čuhaj, G. S. 2011 standard catalog of world
coins, 1901-2000   737.4
Yeoman, R. S. A guide book of United States
coins   737.4

Colasanti, Susane
Something like fate   Fic
Waiting for you   Fic

Colbert, David
(ed) Eyewitness to America. See Eyewitness to
America   973

Colby, Vineta
(ed) European authors, 1000-1900. See European authors, 1000-1900   920.003
(ed) World authors, 1975-1980. See World authors, 1975-1980   920.003
(ed) World authors, 1980-1985. See World authors, 1980-1985   920.003
(ed) World authors, 1985-1990. See World authors, 1985-1990   920.003

Cold
See also Low temperatures

Cold hands, warm heart. Wolfson, J.   Fic

Cold Sassy tree. Burns, O. A.   Fic

Cold skin. Herrick, S.   Fic

Cold war
Gaddis, J. L. The Cold War   909.82
Gregory, R. Cold War America, 1946 to 1990
973.92
Hardesty, V. Epic rivalry   629.4
Hillstrom, K. The Cold War   909.82
Kallen, S. A. Primary sources [American war li-
brary, The Cold War]   909.82
Kort, M. The Columbia guide to the Cold War
973.92
Living through the end of the Cold War
940.55
Schmemann, S. When the wall came down
943
Sís, P. The wall   92
Winkler, A. M. The Cold War   909.82
Encyclopedias
Cold War   909.82

Cold War   909.82

Cold War America, 1946 to 1990. Gregory, R.
973.92

The **coldest** March. Solomon, S.   998

Cole, Bruce, 1938-
Art of the Western world   709

Cole, K. C.
The hole in the universe   530

Cole, Stephen, 1971-
Thieves like us   Fic

Coleman, Loren
Cryptozoology A-Z   001.9

Coleman, William H., 1937-
Cholera   616.9

Coleman, Wim
Anna's world   Fic

Coles, David J.
(ed) Encyclopedia of the American Civil War.
See Encyclopedia of the American Civil War
973.7

Collaborating for project-based learning in grades
9-12. Harada, V. H.   371.3

Collaborating with administrators and educational
support staff. Farmer, L. S. J.   027.8

Collaborative library research projects. Volkman,
J. D.   025.5

Collapse: how societies choose to fail or succeed.
Diamond, J. M.   304.2

The **collapse** of the Soviet Union. Langley, A.
947.085

Collected essays. Baldwin, J.   814

Collected essays and poems. Thoreau, H. D.
818

The **collected** plays of Neil Simon. Simon, N.
812

Collected poems. Auden, W. H.   821

Collected poems. Millay, E. S. V.   811

The **collected** poems. Plath, S.   811

Collected poems & translations. Emerson, R. W.
811

Collected poems, 1909-1962. Eliot, T. S.   811

Collected poems, 1917-1982. MacLeish, A.
811

Collected poems, 1947-1997. Ginsberg, A.   811

Collected poems, 1948-1984. Walcott, D.   811

The **collected** poems of A. E. Housman. Housman,
A. E.   821

The **collected** poems of James Merrill. Merrill, J.
811

The **collected** poems of Robert Penn Warren. Warren, R. P.   811

The **collected** poems of Theodore Roethke.
Roethke, T.   811

The **collected** poems of Wallace Stevens. Stevens,
W.   811

The **collected** poems of William Carlos Williams.
Williams, W. C.   811

Collected poems, prose, & plays. Frost, R.
818

Collected short stories. Maugham, W. S.   S C

Collected stories. Kipling, R.   S C

The **collected** stories of Arthur C. Clarke. Clarke,
A. C.   S C

The **collected** stories of Eudora Welty. Welty, E.
S C

Collins, Suzanne
  The Hunger Games   **Fic**
Collinson, Clare
  (ed) The classical world, 500 BCE to AD 600
    CE. See The classical world, 500 BCE to AD
    600 CE   **930**
  (ed) The first civilizations to 500 BC. See The
    first civilizations to 500 BC   **930**
Collis, Harry
  101 American English proverbs   **428**
Colman, Penny
  Elizabeth Cady Stanton and Susan B. Anthony
                                                        92
Colombia
                    Fiction
  García Márquez, G. One hundred years of soli-
    tude   **Fic**
            Politics and government
  Guillermoprieto, A. Looking for history   **972**
Colón, Ernie
  (jt. auth) Jacobson, S. The 9/11 report
                                                     973.931
  (il) Jacobson, S. After 9/11: America's war on
    terror (2001-)   **973.931**
  (jt. auth) Jacobson, S. Anne Frank   **92**
Colón, Jessi Morgenstern- *See* Morgenstern-
  Colón, Jessi
Colonial America. Gray, E. G.   **973.2**
Colonial America reference library [series]
  Saari, P. Colonial America: almanac   **973.2**
  Saari, P. Colonial America: primary sources
                                                     973.2
Colonial America to 1763. Purvis, T. L.   **973.2**
Colonialism *See* Imperialism
Colonies
  Cocker, M. Rivers of blood, rivers of gold
                                                        909
  Pagden, A. Peoples and empires   **909**
Color
  Finlay, V. Color: a natural history of the palette
                                                      535.6
Color atlas of human anatomy. See Abrahams, P.
  H. McMinn's clinical atlas of human anatomy
                                                        611
Color in art
  Bartges, D. Color is everything   **752**
Color is everything. Bartges, D.   **752**
The **color** purple. Walker, A.   **Fic**
Colorado
  Wickenden, D. Nothing daunted [dual biography
    of Dorothy Woodruff and Rosamund Under-
    wood]   **92**
                    Fiction
  Haruf, K. Plainsong   **Fic**
  Kizer, A. Meridian   **Fic**
  Mills, T. Heartbreak river   **Fic**
Colored pencil drawing
                    Technique
  Hershberger, C. Creative colored pencil work-
    shop   **741.2**
  Kutch, K. A. Drawing and painting with colored
    pencil   **741.2**

The **colossal** book of short puzzles and problems.
  Gardner, M.   **793.8**
Colston, Valerie
  Aspire: 200 projects to strengthen your art skills
                                                      702.8
Coltelli, Laura, 1941-
  Winged words: American Indian writers speak
                                                        897
Coltman, Arthur Leycester Scott *See* Coltman,
  Sir Leycester, 1938-
Coltman, Sir Leycester, 1938-
  The real Fidel Castro   **92**
Colton, Larry, 1942-
  Counting coup   **796.323**
The **Columbia** anthology of American poetry
                                                     811.008
The **Columbia** anthology of British poetry
                                                     821.008
The **Columbia** book of Civil War poetry
                                                     811.008
The **Columbia** chronicles of American life, 1910-
  1992. See Gordon, L. G. American chronicle
                                                      973.9
Columbia chronologies of Asian history and cul-
  ture   **950**
The **Columbia** companion to the twentieth-century
  American short story   **813.009**
The **Columbia** dictionary of quotations from
  Shakespeare. Shakespeare, W.   **822.3**
The **Columbia** documentary history of American
  women since 1941   **305.4**
The **Columbia** gazetteer of North America
                                                        917
The **Columbia** gazetteer of the world   **910.3**
The **Columbia** Granger's dictionary of poetry quo-
  tations   **808.88**
The **Columbia** guide to Irish American history.
  Meagher, T. J.   **305.8**
The **Columbia** guide to online style. Walker, J. R.
                                                        808
The **Columbia** guide to the Cold War. Kort, M.
                                                      973.92
**Columbia guides to American history and cul-
  tures** [series]
  Kort, M. The Columbia guide to the Cold War
                                                      973.92
  Meagher, T. J. The Columbia guide to Irish
    American history   **305.8**
The **Columbia** Lippincott gazetteer of the world.
  See The Columbia gazetteer of the world
                                                      910.3
**Columbia studies in international and global
  history** [series]
  Fleming, J. R. Fixing the sky   **551.6**
Columbine High School (Littleton, Colo.)
  Cullen, D. Columbine   **364.152**
Colvin, Claudette
                     About
  Hoose, P. M. Claudette Colvin   **92**
Coma
                    Fiction
  Dogar, S. Waves   **Fic**

Communicable diseases

See also Epidemiology; Prion diseases; Sexually transmitted diseases; Smallpox

Do infectious diseases pose a threat? **614.4**

Farrell, J. Invisible enemies **614.4**

Goldsmith, C. Invisible invaders **614.4**

Grady, D. Deadly invaders **614.4**

Grady, S. M. Biohazards **614.5**

Landau, E. Food poisoning and foodborne diseases **615.9**

Walters, M. J. Six modern plagues and how we are causing them **614.4**

See/See also pages in the following book(s):

Epidemics: opposing viewpoints **614.4**

Encyclopedias

Turkington, C. The encyclopedia of infectious diseases **616.9**

Communication

See also Business communication; Deaf— Means of communication; Nonverbal communication; Telecommunication

Talking adolescence **305.23**

Communication among animals *See* Animal communication

Communications and broadcasting. Henderson, H. **384**

Communications and the arts. Wyckoff, C. **331.7**

Communism

See also Anticommunist movements

Lansford, T. Communism **335.4**

Pipes, R. Communism: a history **335.4**

Stokes, G. The walls came tumbling down **947**

Fiction

Mackall, D. D. Eva underground **Fic**

China

See/See also pages in the following book(s):

Jiang, J.-l. Red scarf girl **951.05**

Shen, F. Gang of one **92**

United States

Peery, N. Black radical **92**

Community and libraries *See* Libraries and community

The **community** college guide. Gonsher, D. **378.1**

Community colleges *See* Junior colleges

Community development

See also City planning

Community gardens

Smith, J. N. Growing a garden city **635**

Community life

Fiction

Ehrenberg, P. Tillmon County fire **Fic**

Community resources in the school library media center. Lukenbill, W. B. **025.2**

Compact research. Current issues [series]

Bjornlund, L. D. Teen smoking **362.29**

Fredericks, C. Obesity **616.3**

Friedman, L. S. Nuclear weapons and security **355**

Friedman, L. S. Terrorist attacks **363.32**

Kallen, S. A. National security **355**

McCage, C. U.S. border control **363.2**

Nakaya, A. C. Energy alternatives **333.79**

Nakaya, A. C. Immigration **325.73**

Parks, P. J. Drug legalization **363.45**

Parks, P. J. Drunk driving **363.1**

Parks, P. J. School violence **371.7**

Parks, P. J. Video games **794.8**

Robson, D. Disaster response **363.34**

Compact research. Diseases and disorders [series]

Currie-McGhee, L. K. Drug addiction **362.29**

Marcovitz, H. Bipolar disorder **616.89**

Marcovitz, H. Sleep disorders **616.8**

Mooney, C. Mood disorders **616.85**

Nakaya, A. C. ADHD **618.92**

Parks, P. J. Autism **616.85**

Parks, P. J. Down syndrome **616.85**

Parks, P. J. HPV **362.1**

Parks, P. J. Influenza **616.2**

Parks, P. J. Learning disabilities **371.9**

Parks, P. J. Obsessive-compulsive disorder **616.85**

Parks, P. J. Self-injury disorder **616.85**

Yuwiler, J. Diabetes **616.4**

Compact research. Energy and the environment [series]

Kallen, S. A. Toxic waste **363.7**

Parks, P. J. Coal power **363.7**

Compagno, Leonard J. V.

Sharks of the world **597**

Companies *See* Business enterprises

A **companion** to the Iliad. Willcock, M. M. **883**

The **company** of wolves. Steinhart, P. **599.77**

Comparative anatomy

Animal and plant anatomy **571.3**

Comparative government

Encyclopedias

Governments of the world **320.3**

World encyclopedia of political systems and parties **324.2**

Comparative literature

Highet, G. The classical tradition **809**

Comparative physiology

Holmes, H. The well-dressed ape **612**

Comparative psychology

Lorenz, K. On aggression **152.4**

Waal, F. d. Our inner ape **156**

Comparative religion *See* Christianity and other religions; Religions

Compass

Aczel, A. D. The riddle of the compass **912**

Competing voices from native America. Ball, D. I. **970.004**

Competing voices from World War II in Europe **940.53**

Competitions *See* Contests

The **complete** audition book for young actors. Ellis, R. **792**

The **complete** book of cacti & succulents. Hewitt, T. **635.9**

The **complete** book of long-distance cycling. Burke, E. **613.7**

The **complete** book of the Winter Olympics. Wallechinsky, D. **796.98**

The **complete** book of who's who in the Bible. Comfort, P. W. **220.9**

The **complete** collected poems of Maya Angelou. Angelou, M. **811**

Complete copyright **346.04**

Complete do-it-yourself manual **643**

The **complete** dog book. American Kennel Club **636.7**

Complete encyclopedia of the saltwater aquarium. See Jennings, G. The new encyclopedia of the saltwater aquarium **639.34**

Complete Essex County. See Lemire, J. Essex County **741.5**

The **complete** guide to food for sports performance. Burke, L. **613.2**

Complete guide to materials and techniques for drawing and painting. Sanmiguel, D. **751**

The **complete** guide to national symbols and emblems. Minahan, J. **929.9**

The **complete** guide to prehistoric life. Haines, T. **560**

Complete guide to special teams **796.332**

Complete guitar course **787.87**

The **complete** guitarist. See Chapman, R. The new complete guitarist **787.87**

The **complete** history of costume and fashion. Cosgrave, B. **391**

The **complete** history of why I hate her. Jacobson, J. **Fic**

The **complete** human body **612**

The **complete** idiot's guide to playing bass guitar. Hodge, D. **787.87**

The **complete** library technology planner. Cohn, J. M. **025**

The **complete** marching band resource manual. Bailey, W. **784.8**

The **complete** Persepolis. Satrapi, M. **92**

The **complete** photo guide to sewing **646.2**

The **complete** poems. Jarrell, R. **811**

Complete poems. Poe, E. A. **811**

The **complete** poems. Sexton, A. **811**

Complete poems, 1904-1962. Cummings, E. E. **811**

The **complete** poems and plays, 1909-1950. Eliot, T. S. **811**

The **complete** poems of Carl Sandburg. Sandburg, C. **811**

The **complete** poems of Emily Dickinson. Dickinson, E. **811**

Complete poetry and collected prose. Whitman, W. **811**

The **complete** poetry and prose of William Blake. Blake, W. **821**

The **complete** poetry and selected prose of John Donne. Donne, J. **821**

The **complete** Pompeii. Berry, J. **937**

The **complete** Sherlock Holmes. Doyle, Sir A. C. **S C**

The **complete** short stories of Ernest Hemingway. Hemingway, E. **S C**

The **complete** short stories of Mark Twain. Twain, M. **S C**

The **complete** short stories of Thomas Wolfe. Wolfe, T. **S C**

The **complete** stories. Asimov, I. **S C**

The **complete** stories. Hurston, Z. N. **S C**

The **complete** stories. Malamud, B. **S C**

The **complete** stories. O'Connor, F. **S C**

The **complete** tales and poems of Edgar Allan Poe. See Poe, E. A. The collected tales and poems of Edgar Allan Poe **818**

The **complete** trail food cookbook. Mackenzie, J. **641.5**

Complete verse. Kipling, R. **821**

The **complete** works. Shakespeare, W. **822.3**

Composers

Blashfield, J. F. Leonard Bernstein **92**

Morris, E. Beethoven: the universal composer **92**

Steinberg, M. The symphony **784.2**

We'll understand it better by and by **782.25**

See/See also pages in the following book(s):

Grout, D. J. A history of western music **780.9**

United States

Bernstein, B. Leonard Bernstein **92**

Perlis, V. Composer's voices from Ives to Ellington **780.9**

Composer's voices from Ives to Ellington. Perlis, V. **780.9**

Composition (Rhetoric) See Rhetoric

The **Compound**. Bodeen, S. A. **Fic**

Compromised. Ayarbe, H. **Fic**

Compulsion (Psychology) See Compulsive behavior

Compulsive behavior

See also Obsessive-compulsive disorder; Workaholism

Fiction

Omololu, C. J. Dirty little secrets **Fic**

Compulsive working See Workaholism

Compulsory labor See Slavery

Computation, Approximate See Approximate computation

Computer art

See also Digital art

Miller, R. Digital art **776**

Computer-assisted instruction

Braun, L. W. Teens, technology, and literacy; or, Why bad grammar isn't always bad **373.1**

Huber, J. Ask Mr. Technology, get answers **371.3**

Langer de Ramirez, L. Empower English language learners with tools from the Web **428**

November, A. C. Empowering students with technology **371.3**

Smith, S. S. Web-based instruction **025.5**

Counter-Reformation
> *See also* Reformation

Counting
> *See also* Numbers
> Tabak, J. Numbers   **513**

Counting books *See* Counting

Counting coup. Colton, L.   **796.323**

Countries of the world [series]
> Garrington, S. Canada   **971**

Country and western music *See* Country music

Country life
> *See also* Mountain life
> > **Fiction**
> Friedman, A. The year my sister got lucky
>   **Fic**
> Herrick, S. Cold skin   **Fic**
> Roesch, M. Sometimes we're always real same-
>   same   **Fic**
> Sanders, S. L. Gray baby   **Fic**
> Sanders, S. L. The Hanging Woods   **Fic**
> Slayton, F. C. When the whistle blows   **Fic**
> Wyatt, M. Funny how things change   **Fic**
> > **Georgia**
> Foxfire 40th anniversary book   **975.8**

Country music
> > **Fiction**
> Supplee, S. Somebody everybody listens to
>   **Fic**

Country musicians
> Neimark, A. E. Johnny Cash   **92**

Couper, Heather
> The history of astronomy   **520**

Courage
> Kennedy, J. F. Profiles in courage   **920**
> McCain, J. S. Why courage matters   **179**
> Profiles in courage for our time   **920**

Courage in a dangerous world. Roosevelt, E.
>   **973.9**

The **Courage** to be yourself   **305.23**

Courter, Ashley Marie Rhodes- *See* Rhodes-
> Courter, Ashley Marie

Courts
> *See also* Juvenile courts

Courts and courtiers
> *See also* Fools and jesters; Princesses;
> Queens
> > **Fiction**
> Kolosov, J. A. A sweet disorder   **Fic**
> Murdock, C. G. Princess Ben   **Fic**

Cousins, A. D., 1950-
> (ed) The Shakespeare encyclopedia. See The
> Shakespeare encyclopedia   **822.3**

Cousins
> > **Fiction**
> Archer, E. Geek: fantasy novel   **Fic**
> Clarke, J. The winds of heaven   **Fic**
> Clement-Moore, R. The splendor falls   **Fic**
> De la Peña, M. Mexican whiteboy   **Fic**
> Draper, S. M. The Battle of Jericho   **Fic**
> Halaby, L. West of the Jordan   **Fic**
> Halpin, B. How ya like me now   **Fic**
> Hand, E. Illyria   **Fic**

Harrison, C. I was Jane Austen's best friend
>   **Fic**
Howells, A. The summer of skinny dipping
>   **Fic**
Lecesne, J. Absolute brightness   **Fic**
Levitin, S. Strange relations   **Fic**
McKenzie, N. Guinevere's gift   **Fic**
Meyerhoff, J. Queen of secrets   **Fic**
Minchin, A. The beat goes on   **Fic**
Roesch, M. Sometimes we're always real same-
> same   **Fic**
Seigel, A. The kid table   **Fic**
Selvadurai, S. Swimming in the monsoon sea
>   **Fic**

Cousins. Fugard, A.   **92**

Cousteau, Jacques Yves, 1910-1997
> The human, the orchid, and the octopus
>   **333.95**
> > **About**
> Matsen, B. Jacques Cousteau   **92**

Cousteau, Philippe, Jr., 1980-
> (jt. auth) Kaye, C. B. Going blue   **333.91**

Couturier, Lisa, 1962-
> The hopes of snakes   **591.7**

Couturiers *See* Fashion designers

Couzens, Dominic
> Extreme birds   **598**

Coventry, Susan
> The queen's daughter   **Fic**

Cover, Arthur Byron
> Macbeth   **822.3**

Coverlets *See* Quilts

Cowan, Jennifer
> Earthgirl   **Fic**

The **cowboy** hero. Savage, W. W.   **973**

Cowhands
> Savage, W. W. The cowboy hero   **973**
> > **Fiction**
> McCarthy, C. All the pretty horses   **Fic**

Cowley, Malcolm, 1898-1989
> (ed) Emerson, R. W. The portable Emerson
>   **818**

Cox, Caroline, 1954-
> Opening up North America, 1497-1800   **917**

Cox, Daniel J., 1960-
> (jt. auth) Grambo, R. L. Wolf: legend, enemy,
> icon   **599.77**

Cox, Greg, 1959-
> (jt. auth) Burke, L. The complete guide to food
> for sports performance   **613.2**

Cox, Lynne
> Swimming to Antarctica   **92**

Cox, Vicki
> The history of the third parties   **324.2**

Coy, Jason Philip, 1970-
> A brief history of Germany   **943**

Coy, John, 1958-
> Box out   **Fic**
> Crackback   **Fic**

Coye, Dale F.
> Pronouncing Shakespeare's words   **822.3**

CQ's American government A to Z series
> Benenson, B. Elections A to Z   **324.6**

Create, relate & pop @ the library. Helmrich, E.   **027.62**

Create your own blog. Hussey, T.   **006.7**

Creating characters with personality. Bancroft, T.   **741.6**

Creating their own image. Farrington, L. E.   **709.73**

Creating your high school resume. Troutman, K. K.   **650.14**

Creation
Encyclopedias
Leeming, D. A. A dictionary of creation myths   **201.03**
Study and teaching
See Creationism; Evolution—Study and teaching

Creation (Literary, artistic, etc.)
Boorstin, D. J. The creators   **909**
Johnson, A. Indie girl   **305.23**
Smith, A. D. Letters to a young artist   **700**

Creationism
See also Evolution
Scott, E. C. Evolution vs. creationism   **576.8**
Young, C. C. Evolution and creationism   **576.8**

Creation's journey   **709.73**

Creative ability
Edwards, B. The new drawing on the right side of the brain   **741.2**

The **creative** collection of American short stories. Nascimbene, Y.   **S C**

Creative colored pencil workshop. Hershberger, C.   **741.2**

Creative mythology. Campbell, J.   **201**

Creative short stories [series]
Jackson, S. The lottery   **Fic**

Creative writing
Hardesty, C. The teen-centered writing club   **027.62**
Prose, F. Anne Frank   **839.3**
Prose, F. Reading like a writer   **808**
Salzman, M. True notebooks   **808**
Graphic novels
Barry, L. What it is   **818**

The **creators.** Boorstin, D. J.   **909**

Creature of the night. Thompson, K.   **Fic**

Creatures of accident. Arthur, W.   **591.3**

Credit
See also Consumer credit

Creel, Herrlee Glessner, 1905-1994
Chinese thought from Confucius to Mao Tsê-tung   **181**

Crenshaw High School (Los Angeles, Calif.)
Sokolove, M. Y. The ticket out: Darryl Strawberry and the boys of Crenshaw   **796.357**

Creoles
Fiction
Hambly, B. A free man of color   **Fic**

Crete (Greece)
See/See also pages in the following book(s):
Ceram, C. W. Gods, graves, and scholars   **930.1**

Creutzfeldt-Jakob disease
Fiction
Bray, L. Going bovine   **Fic**

Crew, Hilary S., 1942-
Women engaged in war in literature for youth   **016.3**

Crewe, Megan, 1980-
Give up the ghost   **Fic**

Crews, Kenneth D.
Copyright law for librarians and educators   **346.04**

Crichton, Michael, 1942-2008
The Andromeda strain   **Fic**
Jurassic Park   **Fic**
Pirate latitudes   **Fic**

Crick, Francis, 1916-2004
About
Ridley, M. Francis Crick   **92**
See/See also pages in the following book(s):
Horvitz, L. A. Eureka!: scientific breakthroughs that changed the world   **509**

Crickets
Capinera, J. L. Field guide to grasshoppers, crickets, and katydids of the United States   **595.7**

Crilley, Mark, 1966-
Brody's ghost: book 1   **741.5**
Miki Falls, Book One: Spring   **741.5**

Crilly, A. J.
(jt. auth) Henderson, M. 100 most important science ideas   **500**

Crime
See also Computer crimes; Hate crimes; Homicide; School shootings; Sex crimes; Trials

Crime and criminals: opposing viewpoints   **364**
Fiction
Bick, I. J. Draw the dark   **Fic**
David, K. When I was Joe   **Fic**
Jinks, C. Evil genius   **Fic**
Moloney, J. Black taxi   **Fic**
Morgenroth, K. Jude   **Fic**
Northrop, M. Gentlemen   **Fic**
Wynne-Jones, T. Blink & Caution   **Fic**
Graphic novels
Campbell, R. Shadoweyes   **741.5**
Gipi. Notes for a war story   **741.5**
United States
Hanes, S. M. Crime and punishment in America, Primary sources   **364**
Wolcott, D. B. Crime and punishment in America   **364**

Crime and criminals: opposing viewpoints   **364**

Crime and punishment. Dostoyevsky, F.   **Fic**

Crime and punishment in America. Wolcott, D. B.   **364**

Crime and punishment in America: biographies. Hanes, R. C.   **920**

Crime and punishment in America, Primary sources. Hanes, S. M.   **364**

Critical companion to William Faulkner. Fargnoli, A. N. **813.009**

Critical companion to William Shakespeare. Boyce, C. **822.3**

Critical companion to Zora Neale Hurston. Jones, S. L. **813.009**

Critical companions to popular contemporary writers [series]
Russell, S. A. Revisiting Stephen King **813.009**
Russell, S. A. Stephen King: a critical companion **813.009**

Critical insights [series]
Death of a salesman, by Arthur Miller **812.009**
Dracula, by Bram Stoker **823.009**
Great expectations, by Charles Dickens **823.009**
The great Gatsby, by F. Scott Fitzgerald **813.009**
I know why the caged bird sings, by Maya Angelou **818**
The Joy Luck Club, by Amy Tan **813.009**
The tales of Edgar Allan Poe **813.009**

Critical issue series
Daniels, R. Prisoners without trial **940.53**

Critical perspectives on the past [series]
Lerner, G. Fireweed **92**

Critical plant life. Bodden, V. **581.7**

Critical survey of drama **809.2**

Criticism

See also Art criticism

Cro-Magnon. Fagan, B. M. **569.9**

Cro-Magnons
Fagan, B. M. Cro-Magnon **569.9**

Croce, Benedetto, 1866-1952
See/See also pages in the following book(s):
Durant, W. J. The story of philosophy **109**

The crochet answer book. Eckman, E. **746.43**

Crocheting
Eckman, E. The crochet answer book **746.43**
Obaachan, A. Amigurumi animals **746.43**

Crofton, Ian
(jt. auth) Ayto, J. Brewer's dictionary of modern phrase & fable **803**

Crogan's vengeance. Schweizer, C. **741.5**

Croggon, Alison, 1962-
The Naming **Fic**

Croke, Vicki
The lady and the panda **599.78**

Crompton, Samuel
Ulysses S. Grant **92**

Cromwell, Oliver, 1599-1658
About
Aronson, M. John Winthrop, Oliver Cromwell, and the Land of Promise [dual biography of John Winthrop and Oliver Cromwell] **92**

Cropper, William H.
Great physicists **920**

Crops *See* Farm produce

Crosby, Molly Caldwell
The American plague **614.5**

Cross, Gary S.
(ed) Encyclopedia of recreation and leisure in America. See Encyclopedia of recreation and leisure in America **790**

Cross, Sarah
Dull boy **Fic**

Cross-country skiing. Cazeneuve, B. **796.93**

Cross cultural conflict *See* Culture conflict

Cross-X. Miller, J. **808.53**

Crossdressers *See* Transvestites

Crossing into America **810.8**

Crossing stones. Frost, H. **Fic**

Crossing the danger water **810.8**

Crossing the line. Finnegan, W. **968.06**

Crossing the water. Plath, S. **811**

Crossman, Anne
(jt. auth) Feaver, P. Getting the best out of college **378.1**

Crossword puzzles
Dictionaries
Pulliam, T. The New York times crossword puzzle dictionary **793.73**

Crow Dog, Leonard, 1942-
Crow Dog **970.004**

Crow Dog, Mary *See* Brave Bird, Mary

Crow Lake. Lawson, M. **Fic**

The crowd sounds happy. Dawidoff, N. **92**

Crowe, Chris
Getting away with murder: the true story of the Emmett Till case **364.152**
Mississippi trial, 1955 **Fic**
Thurgood Marshall **92**

Crowley, Cath, 1971-
A little wanting song **Fic**

Crowley, Suzanne, 1963-
The stolen one **Fic**

Crowther, Nicky
The ultimate mountain bike book **796.63**

The crucible. Miller, A. **812**

Cruden, Alex
(ed) The Rwandan genocide. See The Rwandan genocide **967.571**

Cruel world. Nicholas, L. H. **940.53**

Cruelty to animals *See* Animal welfare

Crumb, R. (Robert), 1943-
(il) Mairowitz, D. Z. Kafka **92**

Crump, Martha L.
Headless males make great lovers **591.5**
Sexy orchids make lousy lovers & other unusual relationships **577.8**

Crunch time. Fredericks, M. **Fic**

Crusade. Holder, N. **Fic**

Crusade. Laird, E. **Fic**

Crusades
Jones, J. S. The Crusades, Biographies **920.003**
Jones, J. S. The Crusades, Primary sources **909.07**
O'Neal, M. The Crusades, Almanac **909.07**

Current controversies—*Continued*

Immigration	325.73
Medical ethics	174.2
The Middle East	956
Police brutality	363.2
Poverty and homelessness	362.5
Prisons	365
Racism	305.8
Rap music and culture	306.4
School violence	371.7
Suicide	362.28
Teenage pregnancy and parenting	306.8
Violence against women	362.83
Woodward, J. War	303.6

Currents, Ocean *See* Ocean currents

Curricula (Courses of study) *See* Education—Curricula

Curriculum connections. Atlas of world history [series]

The classical world, 500 BCE to AD 600 CE
930

The early modern world, 1492 to 1783
909.08

The first civilizations to 500 BC   930

Industrialization and empire, 1783 to 1914
330.9

The Middle Ages, 600 to 1492   **909.07**

World wars and globalization, 1914 to 2010
909.82

Curriculum materials centers *See* Instructional materials centers

Curriden, Mark
(jt. auth) Wecht, C. H. Tales from the morgue
614

Currie, Robin
The letter and the scroll   220.9

Currie-McGhee, L. K., 1971-
Drug addiction   362.29

Currie-McGhee, Leanne K. *See* Currie-McGhee, L. K., 1971-

Curry, Constance, 1933-
(jt. auth) Zellner, R. The wrong side of Murder Creek [biography of Robert Zellner]   92

Curry, Jennifer
(ed) World authors, 2000-2005. See World authors, 2000-2005   920.003

The curse workers [series]
Black, H. The white cat   Fic

Curtis, Adrian
(ed) Oxford Bible atlas. See Oxford Bible atlas
220.9

Curtis, Edward E., IV, 1970-
Muslims in America   305.8
(ed) Encyclopedia of Muslim-American history. See Encyclopedia of Muslim-American history   305.8

Curtis, Nancy C.
Black heritage sites   917.3

Curveball [biography of Toni Stone] Ackmann, M.   92

Cushman, Clare
(ed) Supreme Court decisions and women's rights. See Supreme Court decisions and women's rights   342

Cusick, Tim
(jt. auth) Kranz, R. Gay rights   306.76

Custer, George Armstrong, 1839-1876
About
Sandoz, M. The Battle of the Little Bighorn
973.8
Viola, H. J. It is a good day to die   973.8

Custer died for your sins. Deloria, V.   970.004

Custis, Shaun
(jt. auth) Bolt, U. 9.58   92

Customs, Social *See* Manners and customs

Cut. McCormick, P.   Fic

Cvetkovic, Vibiana Bowman, 1953-
(ed) Stop plagiarism. See Stop plagiarism
808

Cyber journals *See* Weblogs

Cyberstalking. Bocij, P.   613.6

Cycling
See also Bicycles; Motorcycles; Mountain biking
Bicycling magazine's 1,000 all-time best tips
796.6
Burke, E. The complete book of long-distance cycling   613.7
Carmichael, C. The ultimate ride   796.6
Fiction
Bradbury, J. Shift   Fic

Cyclones
See also Hurricanes
Encyclopedias
Longshore, D. Encyclopedia of hurricanes, typhoons, and cyclones   551.55

Cypess, Leah
Mistwood   Fic

Cyrano. McCaughrean, G.   Fic

Cyrano de Bergerac, 1619-1655
Fiction
McCaughrean, G. Cyrano   Fic

Cystic fibrosis
Apel, M. A. Cystic fibrosis   616.2
Giddings, S. Cystic fibrosis   616.2
Fiction
Monninger, J. Wish   Fic

Cytology *See* Cells

Czarnecki, Monike
(il) Lanchon, A. All about adoption   362.7

Czech Americans
Fiction
Cather, W. My Antonia   Fic
Myers, W. D. Game   Fic

Czisnik, Marianne
Horatio Nelson   92

D

D Day *See* Normandy (France), Attack on, 1944

D.N.A. *See* DNA

Da Vinci, Leonardo *See* Leonardo, da Vinci, 1452-1519

Daalder, Ivo H.
Winning ugly   949.7

Dabrowski, Kristen
Twenty 10-minute plays for teens   **812**
Dahl, Roald
Skin and other stories   **S C**
About
Gelletly, L. Gift of imagination [biography of Roald Dahl]   **92**
Dailey, Donna
London   **820.9**
Daily life during the French Revolution. Anderson, J. M.   **944.04**
Daily life in Chaucer's England. Forgeng, J. L.   **942.03**
Daily life in Elizabethan England. Forgeng, J. L.   **942.05**
Daily life in immigrant America, 1820-1870. Bergquist, J. M.   **305.9**
Daily life in Maya civilization. Sharer, R. J.   **972.81**
Daily life in medieval Europe. Singman, J. L.   **940.1**
Daily life in Renaissance Italy. Cohen, E. S.   **945**
Daily life in the early American republic, 1790-1820. Heidler, D. S.   **973.4**
Daily life in the Inca empire. Malpass, M.   **985**
Daily life in the Roman city. Aldrete, G. S.   **937**
Daily life in the Soviet Union. Eaton, K. B.   **947.084**
Daily life in Victorian England. Mitchell, S.   **941.081**
Daily life of the Vikings. Wolf, K.   **948**
Daily life through world history in primary documents   **909**
Daintith, John
(ed) A dictionary of chemistry. See A dictionary of chemistry   **540.3**
(ed) The Facts on File dictionary of astronomy. See The Facts on File dictionary of astronomy   **520.3**
(ed) The Facts on File dictionary of chemistry. See The Facts on File dictionary of chemistry   **540.3**
(ed) The Facts on File dictionary of computer science. See The Facts on File dictionary of computer science   **004**
(ed) The Facts on File dictionary of mathematics. See The Facts on File dictionary of mathematics   **510.3**
(ed) The Facts on File dictionary of physics. See The Facts on File dictionary of physics   **530**
Dairy Queen. Murdock, C. G.   **Fic**
Dakota Indians
See also Oglala Indians
Brave Bird, M. Lakota woman   **92**
Crow Dog, L. Crow Dog   **970.004**
Stanley, G. E. Sitting Bull   **92**
See/See also pages in the following book(s):
Freedman, R. Indian chiefs   **920**

Fiction
Power, S. The grass dancer   **Fic**
Wars
Viola, H. J. It is a good day to die   **973.8**
Dalai Lama II, 1476-1542
About
Mullin, G. H. The second Dalai Lama   **92**
Dalai Lama XIV, 1935-
Ethics for the new millennium   **294.3**
Freedom in exile   **92**
About
Iyer, P. The open road   **92**
Dalby, Andrew
Dictionary of languages   **410**
Dalí, Salvador, 1904-1989
About
Ross, M. E. Salvador Dali and the surrealists   **92**
Dallek, Robert
Harry S. Truman   **92**
Let every nation know [biography of John F. Kennedy]   **92**
Dalston, Teresa R., 1965-
(ed) Virtual reference on a budget. See Virtual reference on a budget   **025.5**
Dalton, Stephen
Spiders   **595.4**
D'Aluisio, Faith, 1957-
(jt. auth) Menzel, P. Hungry planet   **641.3**
Daly, Kathleen N.
Greek and Roman mythology, A to Z   **292**
Norse mythology A to Z   **293**
Damned lies and statistics. Best, J.   **303.3**
Damosel. Spinner, S.   **Fic**
Dams
See/See also pages in the following book(s):
Macaulay, D. Building big   **720**
Dana, Barbara
A voice of her own   **Fic**
Danalis, John
Riding the black cockatoo   **305.8**
Dance, Daryl Cumber
(ed) Honey, hush! See Honey, hush!   **817.008**
Dance
See also Ballet; Modern dance
Reynolds, N. No fixed points   **792.8**
Dictionaries
Craine, D. The Oxford dictionary of dance   **792.803**
Fiction
Blundell, J. Strings attached   **Fic**
Dixon, H. Entwined   **Fic**
Dancers
See also African American dancers
Freedman, R. Martha Graham, a dancer's life   **92**
Fiction
Clement-Moore, R. The splendor falls   **Fic**
Fletcher, C. Ten cents a dance   **Fic**
Kephart, B. House of Dance   **Fic**
Winston, S. The Kayla chronicles   **Fic**
Dancing *See* Dance

Darwinism *See* Evolution

Darwin's universe. Milner, R.   **576.8**

Dasch, E. Julius (Ernest Julius), 1932-
(ed) Water: science and issues. See Water: science and issues   **553.7**

Dasch, Ernest Julius *See* Dasch, E. Julius (Ernest Julius), 1932-

Dash, Joan
A dangerous engine [biography of Benjamin Franklin]   **92**

Dashner, James, 1972-
The maze runner   **Fic**

DaSilva-Gordon, Maria
Your first year of college   **378.1**

Data processing
    See also Artificial intelligence; Computer science
Barrett, J. R. Teaching and learning about computers   **004**
Ceruzzi, P. E. A history of modern computing   **004**
Katz, J. Geeks   **338.7**
Dictionaries
Pfaffenberger, B. Webster's New World computer dictionary   **004**

Data storage and retrieval systems *See* Information systems

Date rape
Gordon, S. M. Beyond bruises   **362.7**
Wilkins, J. Date rape   **362.883**

Dating (Social customs)
Burningham, S. O. Boyology   **306.7**
Turner, J. S. Dating and sexuality in America   **306.7**
Drama
Soto, G. Novio boy   **812**
Fiction
Bauman, B. A. Rosie & Skate   **Fic**
Benway, R. Audrey, wait!   **Fic**
Billerbeck, K. Perfectly dateless   **Fic**
Briant, E. Choppy socky blues   **Fic**
Burd, N. The vast fields of ordinary   **Fic**
Calloway, C. Confessions of a First Daughter   **Fic**
Cohn, R. Naomi and Ely's no kiss list   **Fic**
Colasanti, S. Waiting for you   **Fic**
Cook, E. The education of Hailey Kendrick   **Fic**
Dessen, S. Along for the ride   **Fic**
Elkeles, S. Perfect chemistry   **Fic**
Emond, S. Happyface   **Fic**
Epstein, R. God is in the pancakes   **Fic**
Eulberg, E. Prom and prejudice   **Fic**
Frank, H. The view from the top   **Fic**
Freymann-Weyr, G. After the moment   **Fic**
Gallagher, L. The opposite of invisible   **Fic**
Goldblatt, S. Girl to the core   **Fic**
Goldman, S. Two parties, one tux, and a very short film about the Grapes of Wrath   **Fic**
Grant, C. Teenie   **Fic**
Green, J. Let it snow   **S C**
Green, J. Will Grayson, Will Grayson   **Fic**
Herbsman, C. Breathing   **Fic**
Hubbard, A. But I love him   **Fic**
Jordan, S. Firelight   **Fic**

Joyce, G. The exchange   **Fic**
Karim, S. Skunk girl   **Fic**
Katcher, B. Almost perfect   **Fic**
Katcher, B. Playing with matches   **Fic**
Lockhart, E. The boyfriend list   **Fic**
Luper, E. Seth Baumgartner's love manifesto   **Fic**
Madigan, L. K. Flash burnout   **Fic**
McCahan, E. I now pronounce you someone else   **Fic**
McVoy, T. E. Pure   **Fic**
Rallison, J. How to take the ex out of ex-boyfriend   **Fic**
Ryan, P. Gemini bites   **Fic**
Salter, S. Swoon at your own risk   **Fic**
Scott, K. Geek magnet   **Fic**
Selzer, A. I kissed a zombie, and I liked it   **Fic**
Sones, S. What my mother doesn't know   **Fic**
Tahmaseb, C. The geek girl's guide to cheerleading   **Fic**
Tharp, T. The spectacular now   **Fic**
Triana, G. Riding the universe   **Fic**
Vivian, S. Not that kind of girl   **Fic**
Voorhees, C. The brothers Torres   **Fic**
Warman, J. Where the truth lies   **Fic**
Williams, G. Beatle meets Destiny   **Fic**
Wittlinger, E. Sandpiper   **Fic**
Zeises, L. M. The sweet life of Stella Madison   **Fic**

Dating and sexuality in America. Turner, J. S.   **306.7**

Datlow, Ellen
(ed) The beastly bride. See The beastly bride   **S C**
(ed) The Del Rey book of science fiction and fantasy. See The Del Rey book of science fiction and fantasy   **S C**

Dau, John Bul
Lost boy, lost girl   **962.4**

Daubert, Stephen
The shark and the jellyfish   **508**
Threads from the web of life   **508**

Daughter of fortune. Allende, I.   **Fic**

Daughter of the forest. Marillier, J.   **Fic**

Daughter of the Ganges. Miró, A.   **92**

Daughter of war. Skrypuch, M. F.   **Fic**

Daughters and fathers *See* Father-daughter relationship

Daughters and mothers *See* Mother-daughter relationship

Davenport, Basil, 1905-1966
(ed) The Portable Roman reader. See The Portable Roman reader   **870.8**

Davenport, Jennifer
Anna begins   **Fic**

Davenport, John, 1960-
The internment of Japanese Americans during World War II   **940.53**
(ed) The American empire. See The American empire   **327.73**

David, A. Rosalie (Ann Rosalie)
Handbook to life in ancient Egypt   **932**

Des Chenes, Betz
American civil rights: primary sources. See American civil rights: primary sources
323.1

Desai Hidier, Tanuja
Born confused **Fic**

Descartes, René, 1596-1650
See/See also pages in the following book(s):
Mlodinow, L. Euclid's window **516**
Russell, B. A history of Western philosophy
109

Desegregation *See* Segregation

Desegregation in education *See* School integration

Desert ecology
Allaby, M. Deserts **577.5**

Desert plants
See also Cactus

Desert Storm Operation *See* Persian Gulf War, 1991

Deserts
Allaby, M. Deserts **577.5**
Gritzner, C. F. Deserts **577.5**

Desetta, Al
(ed) The Courage to be yourself. See The Courage to be yourself **305.23**
(ed) The Struggle to be strong. See The Struggle to be strong **305.23**

Design
Petroski, H. Success through failure **620**

Designing a school library media center for the future. Erikson, R. **027.8**

Designing space for children and teens in libraries and public places. Feinberg, S. **727**

Desktop publishing
Todd, M. Whatcha mean, what's a zine?
070.5

Desonie, Dana
Atmosphere **551.5**
Oceans **551.46**

Despotism
Fiction
Mourlevat, J.-C. Winter's end **Fic**
Scott, E. Grace **Fic**

Dessen, Sarah, 1970-
Along for the ride **Fic**
Just listen **Fic**
Lock and key **Fic**

Desserts
Carle, M. Teens cook dessert **641.8**

DeStefano, Lauren
Wither **Fic**

Destination unexpected: short stories **S C**

Destroy all cars. Nelson, B. **Fic**

Detectives
Fiction
Bradley, A. The sweetness at the bottom of the pie **Fic**

Detour. Simon, L. **92**

Detrick, Erin, 1981-
(ed) Actor's choice. See Actor's choice
808.82

Detroit (Mich.)
Fiction
Davidson, D. Jason & Kyra **Fic**
Verdelle, A. J. The good negress **Fic**
Whelan, G. See what I see **Fic**

Detzer, David
Allegiance **973.7**
Dissonance **973.7**

Deuker, Carl, 1950-
Gym candy **Fic**
Painting the black **Fic**
Runner **Fic**

Deutsch, Babette, 1895-1982
Poetry handbook: a dictionary of terms
808.1

Developing an information literacy program, K-12
025.5

Developing an outstanding core collection. Alabaster, C. **025.2**

Developing countries
The Third World: opposing viewpoints **909**
Encyclopedias
Encyclopedia of the developing world **909**

Developing countries in literature
Literature of developing nations for students
809

Development of the industrial U.S reference library [series]
Benson, S. Development of the industrial U.S.: Almanac **330.973**
Benson, S. Development of the industrial U.S.: Biographies **920**
Benson, S. Development of the industrial U.S.: Primary sources **330.973**

Devil
See also Demonology
Fiction
Barlowe, W. D. God's demon **Fic**
Clare, C. City of bones **Fic**
Clement-Moore, R. Prom dates from Hell
Fic
Gill, D. M. Soul enchilada **Fic**
Jenkins, A. M. Repossessed **Fic**
Johnson, M. Devilish **Fic**
Nayeri, D. Another Faust **Fic**

Devil in the details. Traig, J. **92**

The **devil** on trial. Margulies, P. **345**

Devil-worship *See* Satanism

Devilish. Johnson, M. **Fic**

The **devil's** breath. Gilman, D. **Fic**

The **devil's** kiss. Chadda, S. **Fic**

The **devil's** paintbox. McKernan, V. **Fic**

DeVita, James
The silenced **Fic**

Devlin, Ivy, 1972-
See also Scott, Elizabeth

Devlin, James E., 1938-
Elmore Leonard **813.009**

Devotional exercises
See also Meditation

Devoto, Pat Cunningham
The summer we got saved **Fic**

Dickinson, Emily, 1830-1886—*Continued*
About
Borus, A. A student's guide to Emily Dickinson
811.009
Leiter, S. Critical companion to Emily Dickinson **811.009**
Longsworth, P. The world of Emily Dickinson **92**
Meltzer, M. Emily Dickinson **92**
Priddy, A. Bloom's how to write about Emily Dickinson **811.009**
Fiction
Dana, B. A voice of her own **Fic**

Dickinson, Gail Krepps
(ed) School library management. See School library management **025.1**

Dickinson, Peter, 1927-
Eva **Fic**
(jt. auth) McKinley, R. Fire: tales of elemental spirits **S C**
(jt. auth) McKinley, R. Water: tales of elemental spirits **S C**

Dickinson, Terence
The universe and beyond **520**
(ed) NightWatch: a practical guide to viewing the universe. See NightWatch: a practical guide to viewing the universe **520**

Dickson, Keith D.
World War II almanac **940.54**

Dickson, Paul
Slang! **427**

Dickstein, Morris
(ed) The great Gatsby, by F. Scott Fitzgerald. See The great Gatsby, by F. Scott Fitzgerald **813.009**

Dictators
Cunningham, K. Joseph Stalin and the Soviet Union **92**
Fridell, R. Dictatorship **321.9**
Rice, E. Adolf Hitler and Nazi Germany **92**
Scandiffio, L. Evil masters **920**
Fiction
Orwell, G. Animal farm **Fic**
Revis, B. Across the universe **Fic**

Dictatorship. Fridell, R. **321.9**

Dictatorships [series]
Arnold, J. R. Robert Mugabe's Zimbabwe **968.91**
Childress, D. Omar al-Bashir's Sudan **962.4**
Gay, K. Mao Zedong's China **951.05**
Markel, R. J. Fidel Castro's Cuba **972.91**
Zahler, D. Than Shwe's Burma **959.1**

Dictionaries *See* Encyclopedias and dictionaries

Dictionaries, Biographical *See* Biography—Dictionaries

Dictionaries, Classical *See* Classical dictionaries

Dictionaries, Multilingual *See* Polyglot dictionaries

Dictionaries, Picture *See* Picture dictionaries

Dictionary & thesaurus **423**

Dictionary for school library media specialists. McCain, M. M. **020**

Dictionary of American family names **929.4**

Dictionary of architecture & construction **720.3**

A **dictionary** of astronomy. See Oxford dictionary of astronomy **520.3**

A **dictionary** of chemistry **540.3**

Dictionary of computer and Internet terms. Downing, D. **004**

Dictionary of computer terms. See Downing, D. Dictionary of computer and Internet terms **004**

A **dictionary** of contemporary world history. Palmowski, J. **909.82**

A **dictionary** of creation myths. Leeming, D. A. **201.03**

The **dictionary** of cultural literacy. See Hirsch, E. D. The new dictionary of cultural literacy **031**

A **dictionary** of earth sciences. See The Facts on File dictionary of earth science **550.3**

The **dictionary** of fashion history. Cumming, V. **391**

A **dictionary** of finance and banking **332.03**

A **dictionary** of first names. Hanks, P. **929.4**

A **dictionary** of folklore. Pickering, D. **398.2**

Dictionary of historic documents **903**

Dictionary of languages. Dalby, A. **410**

A **dictionary** of literary and thematic terms. Quinn, E. **803**

Dictionary of Mexican literature **860.3**

A **dictionary** of modern American usage. See Garner, B. A. Garner's modern American usage **423**

A **dictionary** of modern English usage. See Fowler, H. W. Fowler's modern English usage **428**

The **dictionary** of multimedia. Hansen, B. **006.6**

Dictionary of poetic terms. Myers, J. E. **808.1**

Dictionary of Roman religion. Adkins, L. **292**

Dictionary of scientific biography. See New dictionary of scientific biography **920.003**

The **dictionary** of space technology. See Angelo, J. A. The Facts on File dictionary of space technology **629.4**

Dictionary of symbolism. Biedermann, H. **302.2**

Dictionary of symbols. Liungman, C. G. **302.2**

Dictionary of the ancient Near East **939**

Dictionary of the Holocaust. Epstein, E. J. **940.53**

Dictionary of the social sciences **300.3**

A **dictionary** of twentieth-century world history. See Palmowski, J. A dictionary of contemporary world history **909.82**

A **dictionary** of zoology **590.3**

Didato, Thom
(ed) Gotham Writers' Workshop fiction gallery. See Gotham Writers' Workshop fiction gallery **S C**

Didion, Joan
Fixed ideas: America since 9.11 **320.5**

Dion, Nathalie, 1964-
(il) Beker, J. The big night out   **646.7**
Diorio, Mary Ann L.
A student's guide to Herman Melville
   813.009

Direction (Motion pictures) *See* Motion pictures—Production and direction

Direction (Theater) *See* Theater—Production and direction

Directory of financial aids for women 2009-2011. Schlachter, G. A.   **378.3**

The **dirt** on clean. Ashenburg, K.   **391**

Dirty little secrets. Omololu, C. J.   **Fic**

Disabled *See* Handicapped

Disabled students *See* Handicapped students

Disadvantaged children *See* Socially handicapped children

The **Disappeared**. Whelan, G.   **Fic**

The **disappearing** spoon. Kean, S.   **546**

Disaster planning. Halsted, D. D.   **025.8**

Disaster relief
Dyson, M. E. Come hell or high water
   976.3
Halsted, D. D. Disaster planning   **025.8**
Hurricane Katrina   **363.34**
Katrina: state of emergency   **363.34**
Robson, D. Disaster response   **363.34**
Van Heerden, I. L. The storm   **976.3**

Disaster response. Robson, D.   **363.34**

Disasters
   See also Accidents; Natural disasters
Campbell, B. C. Disasters, accidents, and crises in American history   **363.34**
Garner, J. We interrupt this broadcast   **070.1**
Gunn, A. M. Unnatural disasters   **304.2**

Disasters, accidents, and crises in American history. Campbell, B. C.   **363.34**

Discipline *See* Punishment

Discipline of children *See* Child rearing

Discordia. Salmon, D. K.   **Fic**

Discover beading   **745.58**

The **discoverers**. Boorstin, D. J.   **909**

Discoveries (in geography) *See* Exploration

The **discoveries**. Lightman, A. P.   **509**

Discovering the Civil War   **973.7**

Discovering the world through debate   **808.53**

Discovering world cultures [series]
The Middle East   **956**

Discovery! [series]
Fleisher, P. Parasites   **578.6**
Goldsmith, C. Invisible invaders   **614.4**
Goldsmith, C. Superbugs strike back   **615**
Murray, E. A. Death   **616.07**
Seiple, S. Mutants, clones, and killer corn
   660.6
Winner, C. Circulating life   **615**

Discovery and exploration [series]
Anderson, H. S. Exploring the polar regions
   910.4
Bowman, J. S. Exploration in the world of the ancients   **913**

Carlisle, R. P. Exploring space   **629.4**
Cox, C. Opening up North America, 1497-1800
   917
Isserman, M. Exploring North America, 1800-1900   **917**
Smith, T. Discovery of the Americas, 1492-1800
   909
Vail, M. Exploring the Pacific   **910.4**
White, P. Exploration in the world of the Middle Ages, 500-1500   **910.4**

The **discovery** of King Arthur. Ashe, G.   **92**

Discovery of the Americas, 1492-1800. Smith, T.
   909

Discrimination
   See also Hate crimes; Race discrimination; Sex discrimination
Discrimination: opposing viewpoints   **305.8**
Do religious groups in America experience discrimination?   **305.9**
See/See also pages in the following book(s):
Affirmative action [Greenwood Press]   **331.1**

Discrimination in education
   See also Segregation in education
Affirmative action [Greenhaven Press]   **331.1**
Finnegan, W. Crossing the line   **968.06**
Perez, W. We are Americans   **371.82**

Discrimination in employment
   See also Affirmative action programs
Freedman, J. Women in the workplace
   331.4

Discrimination: opposing viewpoints   **305.8**

Disease germs *See* Bacteria; Germ theory of disease

Diseases
   See also Sick *also* names of specific diseases and groups of diseases; and subjects with the subdivision *Diseases*
The complete human body   **612**
Diseases and disorders   **616**
Kaufman, M. Easy for you to say   **362.1**
Kowalski, K. M. Attack of the superbugs
   616.9
Petersen, C. Protecting earth's food supply
   363.1
Satin, M. Food alert!   **615.9**
See/See also pages in the following book(s):
The Cambridge world history of food   **641.3**
Tierno, P. M., Jr. The secret life of germs
   616

Encyclopedias
Diseases   **616**
Diseases, disorders, and injuries   **616**
Fiction
Turner, J. F. Dust   **Fic**

Diseases   **616**

Diseases and disorders   **616**

Diseases and disorders series
Clark, A. D. Dyslexia   **616.85**
Dougherty, T. Epilepsy   **616.8**
Dougherty, T. Sexually transmitted diseases
   616.95
Juettner, B. Acne   **616.5**
Mackay, J. Phobias   **616.85**
Sheen, B. MRSA   **616.9**

Dodgson, Charles Lutwidge *See* Carroll, Lewis, 1832-1898

Does my head look big in this? Abdel-Fattah, R. **Fic**

Does the world hate the U.S.? **973.93**

The **dog** breed bible. Coile, D. C. **636.7**

Dog-friendly dog training. Arden, A. **636.7**

Dog racing

> *See also* Iditarod Trail Sled Dog Race, Alaska; Sled dog racing

Dog: the definitive guide for dog owners. Fogle, B. **636.7**

Dogar, Sharon
Annexed **Fic**
Waves **Fic**

Dogface. Garigliano, J. **Fic**

Dogs
American Kennel Club. The complete dog book **636.7**
Coile, D. C. The dog breed bible **636.7**
Coppinger, R. Dogs **636.7**
Farthing, P. One dog at a time **636.08**
Fogle, B. Dog: the definitive guide for dog owners **636.7**
Foster, S. Walking Ollie, or, Winning the love of a difficult dog **636.7**
Franklin, J. The wolf in the parlor **636.7**
Geeson, E. Ultimate dog grooming **636.7**
Halligan, K. Doc Halligan's What every pet owner should know **636**
Katz, J. A good dog **636.7**
Kihn, M. Bad dog **636.7**
Kopelman, J. From Baghdad, with love **92**
Lufkin, E. To the rescue **636.7**
The original dog bible **636.7**
Sidman, J. The world according to dog **810.8**

Fiction
Hartnett, S. Surrender **Fic**
Koontz, D. R. Watchers **Fic**
London, J. The call of the wild **Fic**
London, J. White Fang **Fic**
Wroblewski, D. The story of Edgar Sawtelle **Fic**

Graphic novels
Dorkin, E. Beasts of Burden: animal rites **741.5**

Training
Arden, A. Dog-friendly dog training **636.7**
Burch, M. R. Citizen canine **636.7**
Rogers, T. 4-H guide to dog training and dog tricks **636.7**

Dogs, Wild *See* Wild dogs

Dohrmann, George
Play their hearts out **796.323**

Doig, Ivan
The whistling season **Fic**

Doing it right. Pardes, B. **613.9**

Dolamore, Jaclyn
Magic under glass **Fic**

Dole, Mayra L.
Down to the bone **Fic**

Doll, Beth, 1952-
(jt. auth) Doll, C. A. The resilient school library **027.8**

Doll, Carol Ann
Managing and analyzing your collection **025.2**

Doll, Carol Ann, 1949-
The resilient school library **027.8**

Dolls
> *See also* Barbie dolls

Dolnick, Edward, 1952-
The rescue artist **364.1**

Dolphins
Fiction
Dixon, P. L. Hunting *the Dragon* **Fic**

Domagk, Gerhard, 1895-1964
About
Hager, T. The demon under the microscope **615**

Domestic animals
> *See also* Pets

Domestic economic assistance
> *See also* Government lending

Domestic finance *See* Personal finance

Domestic relations
> *See also* Family

Domestic violence
> *See also* Child abuse
Domestic violence: opposing viewpoints **362.82**
Gordon, S. M. Beyond bruises **362.7**
Fiction
Flinn, A. Breathing underwater **Fic**
Herrick, S. The wolf **Fic**
Koertge, R. Margaux with an X **Fic**
Oates, J. C. Freaky green eyes **Fic**

Domestic violence: opposing viewpoints **362.82**

Domestic workers *See* Household employees

Dominican Americans
Fiction
Alvarez, J. How the García girls lost their accents **Fic**

Dominions, British *See* Commonwealth countries

Don Quixote de la Mancha. Cervantes Saavedra, M. d. **Fic**

Donald, Aida D.
Lion in the White House **92**

Donelson, Kenneth L.
(jt. auth) Nilsen, A. P. Literature for today's young adults **028.5**

Donham, Jean *See* Van Deusen, Jean Donham, 1946-

Donne, John, 1572-1631
The complete poetry and selected prose of John Donne **821**

Donnelly, Jennifer
A northern light **Fic**
Revolution **Fic**

Donner party
Fiction
Houston, J. D. Snow Mountain passage **Fic**

Dumps, Toxic *See* Hazardous waste sites

Duncan, Dayton
Lewis & Clark   **978**
(jt. auth) Ward, G. C. Mark Twain   **92**

Duncan, Joyce, 1946-
Shapers of the great debate on women's rights   **920.003**

Duncan, Lois, 1934-
Killing Mr. Griffin   **Fic**

Dune. Herbert, F.   **Fic**

Dungeons & dragons (Game)
Barrowcliffe, M. The elfish gene   **92**
Fiction
Halpern, J. Into the wild nerd yonder   **Fic**

Dunkle, Clare B.
By these ten bones   **Fic**
The house of dead maids   **Fic**

Dunkleberger, Amy
A student's guide to Arthur Miller   **812.009**

Dunlap, Susanne Emily
The musician's daughter   **Fic**

Dunlavey, Ryan
(il) Van Lente, F. Action philosophers!   **100**

Dunn, Brad, 1973-
When they were 22   **920**

Dunn, Charles James
Everyday life in traditional Japan   **952**

Dunn, Danielle, 1980-
(jt. auth) Dunn, J. A teen's guide to getting published   **808**

Dunn, Jessica, 1980-
A teen's guide to getting published   **808**

Dunn, John M., 1949-
The relocation of the North American Indian   **970.004**

Dunn, Jon, 1954-
(jt. auth) Alderfer, J. National Geographic birding essentials   **598**
(ed) National Geographic field guide to the birds of North America. See National Geographic field guide to the birds of North America   **598**

Dunne, Mike, 1949-
(jt. auth) Knapp, B. America's wetland   **333.91**

Dunning, John B. (John Barnard), Jr.
(ed) Sibley, D. The Sibley guide to bird life & behavior   **598**

Dunning, John Harris
Salem Brownstone   **741.5**

Dunning, Stephen
(comp) Reflections on a gift of watermelon pickle—and other modern verse. See Reflections on a gift of watermelon pickle—and other modern verse   **811.008**

DupliKate. Cheva, C.   **Fic**

DuPuy, Dee
(il) Chmakova, S. Nightschool: the weirn books, volume one   **741.5**

Durant, William James, 1885-1981
The story of philosophy   **109**

Durbin, William, 1951-
(jt. auth) Pedro, J. Judo techniques & tactics   **796.8**

Durdík, Jan
(jt. auth) Wagner, E., major. Medieval costume, armour, and weapons   **399**

Durham, David Anthony, 1969-
Gabriel's story   **Fic**

Durham, Jennifer L.
(ed) World cultural leaders of the twentieth and twenty-first centuries. See World cultural leaders of the twentieth and twenty-first centuries   **920.003**

Durst, Sarah Beth
Ice   **Fic**

Dust
Amato, J. A. Dust   **551.51**
Holmes, H. The secret life of dust   **551.51**

Dust. Turner, J. F.   **Fic**

Dust city. Weston, R. P.   **Fic**

Dust storms
Marrin, A. Years of dust   **978**

Dust tracks on a road. Hurston, Z. N.   **92**

Dut, Salva
Fiction
Park, L. S. A long walk to water   **Fic**

Dutton, Judy
Science fair season   **507.8**

DVDs
Leonard Maltin's movie guide   **791.43**

Dwarfs
Fiction
Bray, L. Going bovine   **Fic**
Spinner, S. Damosel   **Fic**

Dwyer, Helen
(ed) The early modern world, 1492 to 1783. See The early modern world, 1492 to 1783   **909.08**
(ed) The Middle Ages, 600 to 1492. See The Middle Ages, 600 to 1492   **909.07**

Dwyer, Jim, 1957-
102 minutes   **974.7**

Dyer, Davis, 1948-
(ed) The American presidency. See The American presidency   **973**

Dyes and dyeing
Garfield, S. Mauve   **667**

Dying patients *See* Terminally ill

Dylan, Bob, 1941-
About
Roberts, J. Bob Dylan: voice of a generation   **92**

Dynamic Earth [series]
Glaciers, sea ice, and ice formation   **551.3**
Plate tectonics, volcanoes, and earthquakes   **551**
Storms, violent winds, and earth's atmosphere   **551.55**

Dynamic youth services through outcome-based planning and evaluation. Dresang, E. T.   **025.1**

Dyslexia
Clark, A. D. Dyslexia   **616.85**

Dyson, Marianne J.
Space and astronomy   520
Dyson, Michael Eric, 1958-
Come hell or high water   976.3
Holler if you hear me: searching for Tupac Shakur   92
Dzhugashvili, Iosif Vissarionovich *See* Stalin, Joseph, 1879-1953

E

E=mc2. Bodanis, D.   530.1
E-government and web directory. See The United States government internet directory   025.04
E.S.P. *See* Extrasensory perception
Eagland, Jane
Wildthorn   Fic
Eagle, Adam Fortunate *See* Fortunate Eagle, Adam, 1929-
Eagle blue. D'Orso, M.   796.323
The **Ear,** the Eye, and the Arm. Farmer, N.   Fic
Earhart, Amelia, 1898-1937
About
Reyburn, S. Amelia Earhart   92
Van Pelt, L. Amelia Earhart   92
Winters, K. C. Amelia Earhart   92
Earle, Liz
Skin care secrets   646.7
Earls, Irene
Young musicians in world history   920
Earls, Lindsay
About
Kowalski, K. M. The Earls case and the student drug testing debate   344
The **Earls** case and the student drug testing debate. Kowalski, K. M.   344
Early American poetry, "beauty in words". Buckwalter, S.   811.009
Early British poetry, "words that burn". Johanson, P.   821.009
Early civilizations. Kelly, K.   610.9
Early humans. Holmes, T.   599.93
The **early** modern world, 1492 to 1783   909.08
The **early** national period. Purcell, S. J.   973.4
Early occult memory systems of the Lower Midwest. Fairchild, B. H.   811
The **early** years. Dick, R.   629.13
Earp, Paul W., 1961-
Securing library technology   005.8
Earp, Wyatt, 1848-1929
Fiction
Bull, E. Territory   Fic
Earth
Gravity
See Gravity
Earth
Danson, E. Weighing the world   526
Earth   550

Fothergill, A. Planet Earth   508
Grier, J. A. Inner planets   523.4
Earth   550
Earth. Alley, R. B.   621
Earth. Fortey, R. A.   551.7
Earth chemistry. Cobb, A. B.   551
Earth issues [series]
Bodden, V. Critical plant life   581.7
The **earth** moved. Stewart, A.   592
The **earth,** my butt, and other big, round things. Mackler, C.   Fic
Earth sciences
See also Geology
The Facts on File Earth science handbook   550
Dictionaries
The Facts on File dictionary of earth science   550.3
Encyclopedias
Allaby, M. The encyclopedia of Earth   910
Kusky, T. M. Encyclopedia of Earth and space science   550.3
Earth under fire. Braasch, G.   363.7
Earthenware *See* Pottery
Earthgirl. Cowan, J.   Fic
Earthquake sea waves *See* Tsunamis
Earthquakes
Bolt, B. A. Earthquakes   551.2
Kusky, T. M. Earthquakes   551.2
Plate tectonics, volcanoes, and earthquakes   551
Encyclopedias
Gates, A. E. Encyclopedia of earthquakes and volcanoes   551.2
Fiction
Lavender, W. Aftershocks   Fic
East *See* Asia
East (Far East) *See* East Asia
East (Near East) *See* Middle East
East Africa
Women writing Africa: the eastern region   896
East Asia
Religion
Eastern religions   200.9
East Germany *See* Germany (East)
East Indian Americans
Rangaswamy, P. Indian Americans   305.8
Fiction
Desai Hidier, T. Born confused   Fic
Lahiri, J. The namesake   Fic
Lamba, M. What I meant. . .   Fic
Meminger, N. Shine, coconut moon   Fic
East Indians
Delman, C. Burnt bread & chutney   92
Fiction
Nanji, S. Child of dandelions   Fic
East Saint Louis (Ill.) riot, 1917
Barnes, H. Never been a time   977.3
Eastern Africa *See* East Africa
Eastern churches
See also Orthodox Eastern Church

Eastern Europe
Kort, M. The handbook of the new Eastern Europe **943**
Politics and government
Stokes, G. The walls came tumbling down **947**

Eastern religions **200.9**

Eastern sun, winter moon. Paulsen, G. **92**

Easy for you to say. Kaufman, M. **362.1**

Eat fresh food. Gold, R. **641.5**

Eating See Dining

Eating animals. Foer, J. S. **641.3**

Eating customs
Albala, K. Food in early modern Europe **641.3**
Allen, S. L. In the devil's garden **641**
Ingram, S. Want fries with that? **613.2**
Jacob, J. The world cookbook for students **641.5**
Lee, J. The fortune cookie chronicles **641.5**

Eating disorders
See also Anorexia nervosa; Bulimia
Ambrose, M. Investigating eating disorders (anorexia, bulimia, and binge eating) **616.85**
Eating disorders **362.1**
Eating disorders information for teens **616.85**
Eating disorders: opposing viewpoints **616.85**
Favor, L. J. Food as foe **616.85**
Orr, T. When the mirror lies **616.85**
The truth about eating disorders **616.85**
Encyclopedias
Cassell, D. K. Encyclopedia of obesity and eating disorders **616.85**
Fiction
Davenport, J. Anna begins **Fic**
Kessler, J. M. Hunger **Fic**
Graphic novels
Fairfield, L. Tyranny **741.5**

Eating disorders **362.1**

Eating disorders information for teens **616.85**

Eating disorders: opposing viewpoints **616.85**

Eating habits
Schlosser, E. Chew on this **394.1**

Eaton, Katherine Bliss
Daily life in the Soviet Union **947.084**

Eats, shoots & leaves. Truss, L. **428**

Eberhart, George M.
(ed) The whole library handbook 4. See The whole library handbook 4 **027**

Ebola and Marburg viruses. Smith, T. C. **614.5**

Ebola virus
Preston, R. The hot zone **614.5**
Smith, T. C. Ebola and Marburg viruses **614.5**

Ebrey, Patricia Buckley, 1947-
The Cambridge illustrated history of China **951**

Eccentrics and eccentricities
Fiction
De Goldi, K. The 10 p.m. question **Fic**

Ecclesiastical rites and ceremonies See Rites and ceremonies

Echaore-Yoon, Susan, 1953-
Career opportunities in science **502**

Echikson, William
Shooting for Tiger **796.352**

Echo. Morgenroth, K. **Fic**

Eckel, Malcolm David, 1946-
Buddhism **294.3**

Eckman, Edie, 1960-
The crochet answer book **746.43**

Eclipse!. Harrington, P. S. **523.7**

Eclipses, Lunar See Lunar eclipses

Eclipses, Solar See Solar eclipses

The **ECO** guide to careers that make a difference **628**

Ecological issues. Gelletly, L. **363.7**

Ecological movement See Environmental movement

Ecology
See also Biogeography; Environmental protection; Food chains (Ecology); Habitat (Ecology) types of ecology
Agosta, W. C. Thieves, deceivers, and killers **577**
Casper, J. K. Changing ecosystems **577.2**
Dinerstein, E. Tigerland and other unintended destinations **590**
Slobodkin, L. B. A citizen's guide to ecology **577**
Stolzenberg, W. Where the wild things were **577**
Fiction
Nelson, B. Destroy all cars **Fic**
Weyn, S. Empty **Fic**
Vocational guidance
The ECO guide to careers that make a difference **628**

Ecology, Human See Human ecology

Economic botany
See also Plant conservation
Laws, B. Fifty plants that changed the course of history **581.6**

Economic conditions
See also Natural resources

Economic depressions See Depressions

Economic entomology See Insect pests

Economic literacy **330**

Economic policy
See also Government lending; Sanctions (International law)
United States
Gilbert, G. Rich and poor in America **339.2**
Should the federal government bail out private industry? **338.5**

Economic sanctions See Sanctions (International law)

Economic zoology
See also Insect pests

Empower English language learners with tools from the Web. Langer de Ramirez, L. **428**

Empowering students with technology. November, A. C. **371.3**

Empty. Weyn, S. **Fic**

The **empty** ocean. Ellis, R. **577.7**

Encephalitis
   Bloom, O. Encephalitis **616.8**

Enchantress from the stars. Engdahl, S. L. **Fic**

Encountering enchantment. Fichtelberg, S. **016.8**

Encounters with vampires. Robson, D. **398**

Encouraging and supporting student inquiry. Selverstone, H. S. **001.4**

Encyclopedia of African-American culture and history **305.8**

Encyclopedia of African American history **305.8**

Encyclopedia of African American history, 1619-1895 **305.8**

Encyclopedia of African American history, 1896 to the present **305.8**

Encyclopedia of African American society **305.8**

Encyclopedia of African American women writers **810.9**

Encyclopedia of African-American writing **810.9**

Encyclopedia of African history **960**

Encyclopedia of African history and culture **960**

Encyclopedia of American disability history **362.4**

Encyclopedia of American education. Unger, H. G. **370**

Encyclopedia of American environmental history **333.72**

Encyclopedia of American ethnic literature [series]
   Encyclopedia of American Indian literature **810.9**
   Ramirez, L. E. Encyclopedia of Hispanic-American literature **810.9**

Encyclopedia of American foreign policy. Hastedt, G. P. **327.73**

Encyclopedia of American government and civics. Genovese, M. A. **320.4**

Encyclopedia of American historical documents **973.03**

Encyclopedia of American history **973.03**

Encyclopedia of American immigration **304.8**

Encyclopedia of American Indian costume. Paterek, J. **391**

Encyclopedia of American Indian history **970.004**

Encyclopedia of American Indian literature **810.9**

Encyclopedia of American Indian wars, 1492-1890. Keenan, J. **970.004**

Encyclopedia of American Jewish history **305.8**

Encyclopedia of American literature **810.3**

Encyclopedia of American literature. See The Oxford encyclopedia of American literature **810.3**

Encyclopedia of American poetry, the twentieth century **811.009**

Encyclopedia of American religious history. Queen, E. L. **200.9**

Encyclopedia of American war literature **810.9**

Encyclopedia of ancient Egypt. Bunson, M. R. **932**

The **encyclopedia** of angels. Guiley, R. E. **200**

Encyclopedia of animal behavior **591.5**

The **encyclopedia** of animals **590.3**

Encyclopedia of aquarium & pond fish. Alderton, D. **639.34**

The **encyclopedia** of aquatic life. See The new encyclopedia of aquatic life **591.9**

Encyclopedia of art for young people **703**

Encyclopedia of Asian-American literature. Oh, S. **810.9**

The **encyclopedia** of autism spectrum disorders. Turkington, C. **616.85**

Encyclopedia of biology. Rittner, D. **570.3**

Encyclopedia of body adornment. DeMello, M. **391**

Encyclopedia of British writers, 16th-18th centuries **820.9**

Encyclopedia of British writers, 1800 to the present **820.9**

Encyclopedia of British writers, 19th and 20th centuries. See Encyclopedia of British writers, 1800 to the present **820.9**

Encyclopedia of Buddhism. Irons, E. A. **294.3**

Encyclopedia of careers and vocational guidance **331.7**

Encyclopedia of Catholicism. Flinn, F. K. **282**

The **encyclopedia** of censorship. Green, J. **363.31**

Encyclopedia of chemistry. Rittner, D. **540.3**

Encyclopedia of Christianity **230.003**

Encyclopedia of Christmas. See Gulevich, T. Encyclopedia of Christmas and New Year's celebrations **394.26**

Encyclopedia of Christmas and New Year's celebrations. Gulevich, T. **394.26**

Encyclopedia of clothing and fashion **391**

The **encyclopedia** of complementary and alternative medicine. Navarra, T. **615.5**

Encyclopedia of computer science and technology. Henderson, H. **004**

Encyclopedia of conflicts since World War II **909.82**

Encyclopedia of creation myths. See Leeming, D. A. A dictionary of creation myths **201.03**

The **encyclopedia** of crime scene investigation. Newton, M. **363.2**

Encyclopedia of Cuba **972.91**

Environmental policy

The Atlas of US and Canadian environmental history **304.2**

Diamond, J. M. Collapse: how societies choose to fail or succeed **304.2**

Endangered oceans: opposing viewpoints **333.95**

Gore, A. Our choice **363.7**

Africa

Gelletly, L. Ecological issues **363.7**

United States

Black, B. Global warming **363.7**

The environment **344**

Friedman, T. L. Hot, flat, and crowded **363.7**

Gore, A. An inconvenient truth **363.7**

Magoc, C. J. Environmental issues in American history **333.7**

United States—Encyclopedias

Encyclopedia of American environmental history **333.72**

Environmental pollution *See* Pollution

Environmental protection

See also Conservation of natural resources

The atlas of global conservation **333.95**

Casper, J. K. Fossil fuels and pollution **363.7**

Conserving the environment **363.7**

The environment **333.72**

The environment in Henry David Thoreau's Walden **818**

Gore, A. An inconvenient truth **363.7**

Gore, A. Our choice **363.7**

Kaye, C. B. Going blue **333.91**

Maczulak, A. E. Cleaning up the environment **628.5**

Magoc, C. J. Environmental issues in American history **333.7**

Nagle, J. M. Living green **333.72**

Power Scott, J. Green careers **333.72**

Swan, R. Antarctica 2041 **577.5**

Encyclopedias

Encyclopedia of American environmental history **333.72**

Fiction

Gilman, D. The devil's breath **Fic**

McDonald, A. Boys, bears, and a serious pair of hiking boots **Fic**

Scarrow, A. TimeRiders **Fic**

Environmental science

Walker, P. Environmental science experiments **507.8**

Environmental science experiments. Walker, P. **507.8**

Environmental sciences

Cobb, A. B. Earth chemistry **551**

The environment: opposing viewpoints **363.7**

McDaniel, C. N. Wisdom for a livable planet **333.72**

Mongillo, J. F. Teen guides to environmental science **333.72**

Dictionaries

Wyman, B. C. The Facts on File dictionary of environmental science **363.7**

Vocational guidance

McClelland, C. L. Green careers for dummies **363.7**

Environmentalists

Maathai, W. Unbowed **92**

Eon: Dragoneye reborn. Goodman, A. **Fic**

Ephron, Delia

Frannie in pieces **Fic**

The epic. Bloom, H. **809**

Epic. Kostick, C. **Fic**

Epic literature

History and criticism

Bloom, H. The epic **809**

Epic of evolution. Chaisson, E. **523.1**

Epic poetry

See/See also pages in the following book(s):

Highet, G. The classical tradition **809**

Epic rivalry. Hardesty, V. **629.4**

Epidemic Intelligence Service Program *See* Centers for Disease Control and Prevention (U.S.). Epidemic Intelligence Service Program

Epidemics

Do infectious diseases pose a threat? **614.4**

Epidemics: opposing viewpoints **614.4**

Jurmain, S. The secret of the yellow death **614.5**

Encyclopedias

Encyclopedia of plague and pestilence **614.4**

Epidemics: opposing viewpoints **614.4**

Epidemiology

Walters, M. J. Six modern plagues and how we are causing them **614.4**

Fiction

Chibbaro, J. Deadly **Fic**

Epigrams

See also Proverbs; Quotations

Epilepsy

Dougherty, T. Epilepsy **616.8**

Fiction

Philbrick, W. R. The last book in the universe **Fic**

Wolf, A. Zane's trace **Fic**

Graphic novels

B., David. Epileptic **616.8**

Epileptic. B., David **616.8**

Epstein, Eric Joseph, 1959-

Dictionary of the Holocaust **940.53**

Epstein, Helen, 1947-

Children of the Holocaust **940.53**

Epstein, Lawrence J. (Lawrence Jeffrey)

At the edge of a dream **305.8**

Epstein, Robin

God is in the pancakes **Fic**

Epstein-Barr virus

Decker, J. M. Mononucleosis **616.9**

Equality

Adler, M. J. Six great ideas **111**

Equations

Crease, R. P. The great equations **509**

Equestrianism *See* Horsemanship

Equiano, Olaudah, 1745-1797
See/See also pages in the following book(s):
Slave narratives [Library of Am.]   **326**

Eragon. Paolini, C.   **Fic**

Erasing racism. Asante, M. K.   **305.8**

Erasmus, Desiderius, 1466?-1536
See/See also pages in the following book(s):
Russell, B. A history of Western philosophy
    109

Eratosthenes, 3rd cent. B.C.
       About
Nicastro, N. Circumference   **526**

Ercegovac, Zorana, 1947-
Information literacy   **025.5**

Erdman, David V.
(ed) Blake, W. The complete poetry and prose
of William Blake   **821**

Erdoes, Richard
(jt. auth) Brave Bird, M. Lakota woman   **92**
(jt. auth) Crow Dog, L. Crow Dog   **970.004**

Erdrich, Louise
The last report on the miracles at Little No
Horse   **Fic**
See/See also pages in the following book(s):
Coltelli, L. Winged words: American Indian
writers speak   **897**

Ergonomics *See* Human engineering

Erich Maria Remarque's All quiet on the western
front [critical essays]   **833.009**

Erickson, Laura
The bird watching answer book   **598**

Erickson, Richard R., 1945-
(ed) The solar system. See The solar system
    523.2

Erikson, Rolf
Designing a school library media center for the
future   **027.8**

Erlbaum, Janice, 1969-
Girlbomb   **92**

Ermatinger, James William, 1959-
The decline and fall of the Roman Empire
    937

Ernest Hemingway A to Z. See Oliver, C. M.
Critical companion to Ernest Hemingway
    813.009

Ernst, Carl H.
Snakes of the United States and Canada
    597.96

Ernst, Evelyn M.
(jt. auth) Ernst, C. H. Snakes of the United
States and Canada   **597.96**

Eros (Greek deity)
       Fiction
Selfors, S. Mad love   **Fic**

Escape from freedom. Fromm, E.   **323.44**

Escape from Furnace [series]
Smith, A. G. Lockdown   **Fic**

Escape from Saigon [biography of Matt Steiner]
Warren, A.   **92**

Escapes
       Fiction
Smith, A. G. Lockdown   **Fic**

Escaping the delta [biography of Robert Johnson]
Wald, E.   **92**

Eschatology
    See also Future life

Esherick, Joan
Balancing act   **155.5**
The journey toward recovery   **616.8**
Women in the Arab world   **305.4**

Eskimos *See* Inuit

ESP *See* Extrasensory perception

Espejo, Roman, 1977-
Fast food   **363.1**
(ed) Advertising: opposing viewpoints. See Advertising: opposing viewpoints   **659.1**
(ed) Civil liberties: opposing viewpoints. See
Civil liberties: opposing viewpoints   **342**
(ed) Club drugs. See Club drugs   **362.29**
(ed) The culture of beauty: opposing viewpoints.
See The culture of beauty: opposing viewpoints   **306.4**
(ed) Does the world hate the U.S.? See Does the
world hate the U.S.?   **973.93**
(ed) Ethics: opposing viewpoints. See Ethics:
opposing viewpoints   **170**
(ed) Gay and lesbian families. See Gay and lesbian families   **306.8**
(ed) Mass media: opposing viewpoints. See
Mass media: opposing viewpoints   **302.23**
(ed) Should music lyrics be censored for violence and exploitation? See Should music lyrics be censored for violence and exploitation?
    363.31
(ed) What motivates suicide bombers? See What
motivates suicide bombers?   **363.32**

Espeland, Pamela, 1951-
The gifted kids' survival guide   **155.5**
Life lists for teens   **646.7**
(jt. auth) Gootman, M. E. When a friend dies
    155.9
(ed) Nelson, R. E. The power to prevent suicide
    362.28

Espionage
    See also Spies
Owen, D. Spies: the undercover world of secrets, gadgets and lies   **327.12**

Espionage, American *See* American espionage

Espionage and intelligence   **327.12**
Espionage and intelligence gathering. See Espionage and intelligence   **327.12**

Esposito, John L.
Unholy war   **322.4**
(ed) The Oxford encyclopedia of the Islamic
world. See The Oxford encyclopedia of the
Islamic world   **909**
(ed) The Oxford history of Islam. See The Oxford history of Islam   **297**

Esquivel, Laura
Like water for chocolate   **Fic**

Essay
Orr, T. Extraordinary essays   **808.4**

Essayists and prophets. Bloom, H.   **100**

Essays that will get you into college. Dowhan, A.
    808

Ethnic groups
> *See also* Minorities; Racially mixed people

Ethnic relations
> *See also* Culture conflict; Multicultural education; Multiculturalism; Race relations; United States—Ethnic relations
> Interracial America: opposing viewpoints
>
>   **305.8**
> Naimark, N. M. Fires of hatred   **364.1**

Ethnology
> Gibbon, P. Tribe   **305.8**
> *See/See also pages in the following book(s):*
> Diamond, J. M. Guns, germs, and steel
>
>   **303.4**

Encyclopedias
> Worldmark encyclopedia of cultures and daily life   **306**

Asia—Encyclopedias
> Encyclopedia of the peoples of Asia and Oceania   **305.8**

Kenya
> *See also* Masai (African people)

Oceania—Encycopedias
> Encyclopedia of the peoples of Asia and Oceania   **305.8**

Polynesia
> Heyerdahl, T. Kon-Tiki   **910.4**

Etingoff, Kim
> Abusing over-the-counter drugs   **362.29**
> Methamphetamines   **362.29**

Etiquette
> Baldrige, L. Letitia Baldrige's new manners for new times   **395**
> Beker, J. The big night out   **646.7**
> How to be a perfect stranger   **203**
> Isaacs, F. What do you say when—   **395**
> Martin, J. Miss Manners' guide to excruciatingly correct behavior   **395**
> Packer, A. J. How rude!   **395**
> Post, P. Emily Post's Etiquette   **395**
> Senning, C. P. Emily Post prom and party etiquette   **395**

Ettus, Samantha
> (ed) The experts' guide to 100 things everyone should know how to do. See The experts' guide to 100 things everyone should know how to do   **640**

Etzkowitz, Henry, 1940-
> Athena unbound   **500**

Euclid

About
> Hayhurst, C. Euclid: the great geometer   **92**
> Rudman, P. S. The Babylonian theorem   **510**
> *See/See also pages in the following book(s):*
> Mlodinow, L. Euclid's window   **516**

Euclides *See* Euclid

Euclid's window. Mlodinow, L.   **516**

Eulberg, Elizabeth
> Prom and prejudice   **Fic**

Eureka!: scientific breakthroughs that changed the world. Horvitz, L. A.   **509**

Euripides, ca. 485-ca. 406 B.C.
> *See/See also pages in the following book(s):*
> Hamilton, E. The Greek way   **880.9**

Europe

Church history—Encyclopedias
> Andrea, A. J. Encyclopedia of the crusades
>
>   **909.07**

Civilization
> The eighteenth century   **940.2**
> Hinds, K. Everyday life in the Renaissance
>
>   **940.2**
> The nineteenth century   **940.2**
> Sider, S. Handbook to life in Renaissance Europe   **940.2**

Civilization—Encyclopedias
> Europe 1789 to 1914   **940.2**
> Europe since 1914   **940.5**
> World and its peoples: Europe   **940**

Economic conditions
> The eighteenth century   **940.2**
> The nineteenth century   **940.2**

Fiction
> Cooper, M. A brief history of Montmaray
>
>   **Fic**
> James, H. The portrait of a lady   **Fic**
> Johnson, M. 13 little blue envelopes   **Fic**
> Stein, T. High dive   **Fic**

Folklore
> *See* Folklore—Europe

History
> Davies, N. Europe: a history   **940**
> Fagan, B. M. The Little Ice Age   **551.6**

History—To 476
> McIntosh, J. Handbook to life in prehistoric Europe   **930.1**

History—476-1492
> The Middle Ages, 600 to 1492   **909.07**
> The Oxford history of medieval Europe
>
>   **940.1**
> Singman, J. L. Daily life in medieval Europe
>
>   **940.1**
> Women's lives in medieval Europe   **305.4**

History—18th century
> The eighteenth century   **940.2**

History—1789-1900
> Doyle, W. The Oxford history of the French Revolution   **944.04**
> The nineteenth century   **940.2**
> The Oxford illustrated history of modern Europe
>
>   **940.2**

History—1789-1900—Encyclopedias
> Europe 1789 to 1914   **940.2**

History—1871-1918—Encyclopedias
> Europe 1789 to 1914   **940.2**

History—20th century
> Naimark, N. M. Fires of hatred   **364.1**
> The Oxford illustrated history of modern Europe
>
>   **940.2**

History—20th century—Encyclopedias
> Europe since 1914   **940.5**

History—1918-1945—Fiction
> Ruiz Zafón, C. The Prince of Mist   **Fic**

History—Encyclopedias
> World and its peoples: Europe   **940**

Intellectual life
> Wilson, E. J. Encyclopedia of the Enlightenment
>
>   **940.2**

Social conditions
> The eighteenth century   **940.2**

Everyman's library pocket poets—*Continued*

Baudelaire, C. Poems	841
Blake, W. Poems	821
Brontë, E. Brontë: poems	821
Byron, G. G. B., 6th Baron. Byron	821
Eliot, T. S. Eliot	818
Hardy, T. Poems	821
Keats, J. Poems	821
Love poems	808.81
The Roman poets	871.008
Rossetti, C. G. Poems	821
Shakespeare, W. Poems	821
Wordsworth, W. Poems	821

Everything bad is good for you. Johnson, S. 306

Everything beautiful. Howell, S. Fic

Everything beautiful in the world. Levchuk, L. Fic

Everything I needed to know about being a girl I learned from Judy Blume 814

Everything is fine. Ellis, A. D. Fic

Everything we had 959.704

Everything you need to know about food additives. Hayhurst, C. 664

Everything's eventual: 14 dark tales. King, S. S C

Evil *See* Good and evil

Evil genius. Jinks, C. Fic

Evil masters. Scandiffio, L. 920

Evil spirits *See* Demonology

Evolution

Arthur, W. Creatures of accident	591.3
Carroll, S. B. The making of the fittest	572.8
Carroll, S. B. Remarkable creatures	508
Darwin, C. The Darwin reader	576.8
Darwin, C. On the origin of species	576.8
Evolution [Exploring science and medical discoveries series]	576.8
Evolution [Don Nardo, ed.]	576.8
Fagan, B. M. Cro-Magnon	569.9
Gibbons, A. The first human	599.93
Gould, S. J. The richness of life	508
Hodge, R. Evolution	576.8
Holmes, T. Early humans	599.93
Holmes, T. Primates and human ancestors	569
Jolly, A. Lucy's legacy	599.93
Lew, K. Evolution	576.8
New thinking about evolution	576.8
Parker, A. In the blink of an eye	576.8
Sarmiento, E. The last human	569.9
Scott, E. C. Evolution vs. creationism	576.8
Shubin, N. Your inner fish	611
Stefoff, R. Modern humans	599.93
Tattersall, I. Extinct humans	599.93
Tudge, C. The time before history	599.93
Wade, N. Before the dawn	599.93
Wells, S. The journey of man	599.93
Wilson, D. S. Evolution for everyone	576.8
Young, C. C. Evolution and creationism	576.8

Dictionaries

Mai, L. L. The Cambridge Dictionary of human biology and evolution 612

Encyclopedias

Encyclopedia of evolution	576.8
Milner, R. Darwin's universe	576.8
Rice, S. A. Encyclopedia of evolution	576.8

Fiction

Brande, R. Evolution, me, & other freaks of nature Fic

Graphic novels

Hosler, J. Evolution	576.8
Keller, M. Charles Darwin's On the Origin of Species	576.8

Study and teaching

Larson, E. J. The Scopes trial 345

Study and teaching—Fiction

Bryant, J. Ringside, 1925 Fic

Evolution [Don Nardo, ed.] 576.8

Evolution [Exploring science and medical discoveries series] 576.8

Evolution and creationism. Young, C. C. 576.8

Evolution for everyone. Wilson, D. S. 576.8

Evolution, me, & other freaks of nature. Brande, R. Fic

Evolution vs. creationism. Scott, E. C. 576.8

Ewen, David, 1907-1985

(ed) Musicians since 1900. See Musicians since 1900 920.003

Ex, Kris

(jt. auth) Scott, D. How to draw hip-hop 741.2

Ex-service men *See* Veterans

Examinations

See/See also pages in the following book(s):
Espeland, P. The gifted kids' survival guide 155.5

Examining issues through political cartoons [series]

Civil liberties and war 323

Excavations (Archeology)

Kurson, R. Shadow divers	940.54
Rubalcaba, J. Every bone tells a story	930.1

United States

Walker, S. M. Written in bone 614

Excel (Computer program)

Greiner, T. Analyzing library collection use with Excel 025.2

Excellence in library services to young adults 027.62

Except the queen. Yolen, J. Fic

Exceptional children

See also Brain damaged children

The **exchange.** Joyce, G. Fic

Executions *See* Capital punishment

Executive ability

See also Leadership

Executive power

United States

Student's guide to the presidency 352.23

Exegesis, Biblical *See* Bible—Criticism

Exercise

See also Physical fitness; Pilates method; Tai chi; Weight lifting

Dicker, K. Exercise   **613.7**

Smolin, L. A. Nutrition for sports and exercise   **613.7**

Exercises, Reducing *See* Weight loss

Exiles *See* Refugees

Exit strategy. Potter, R.   **Fic**

Exodus, Book of *See* Bible. O.T. Exodus

Exodus. Uris, L.   **Fic**

Expanding universe *See* Universe

Expectations for women. Mills, J. E.   **305.4**

Expeditions, Scientific *See* Scientific expeditions

Experimentation on animals *See* Animal experimentation

The **experts'** guide to 100 things everyone should know how to do   **640**

Exploding the myths. Aronson, M.   **028.5**

Exploration

Boorstin, D. J. The discoverers   **909**

Bowman, J. S. Exploration in the world of the ancients   **913**

The Britannica guide to explorers and explorations that changed the modern world   **910.4**

Fleming, F. Off the map   **910.4**

Macleod, A. Explorers   **910.4**

The Oxford companion to world exploration   **910.3**

Paine, L. P. Ships of discovery and exploration   **910.4**

White, P. Exploration in the world of the Middle Ages, 500-1500   **910.4**

Atlases

Atlas of exploration   **911**

Exploration in the world of the ancients. Bowman, J. S.   **913**

Exploration in the world of the Middle Ages, 500-1500. White, P.   **910.4**

Exploration of Africa, the emerging nations [series]

Harmon, D. Nigeria   **966.9**

Explorers

Aronson, M. Sir Walter Ralegh and the quest for El Dorado   **92**

Bowman, J. S. Exploration in the world of the ancients   **913**

The Britannica guide to explorers and explorations that changed the modern world   **910.4**

Childress, D. Barefoot conquistador [biography of Alvar Núñez Cabeza de Vaca]   **92**

Cox, C. Opening up North America, 1497-1800   **917**

Fleming, F. Off the map   **910.4**

Goetzmann, W. H. The atlas of North American exploration   **911**

Hannon, S. M. Women explorers   **920**

Isserman, M. Exploring North America, 1800-1900   **917**

Macleod, A. Explorers   **910.4**

Obregón, M. Beyond the edge of the sea   **930**

Smith, T. Discovery of the Americas, 1492-1800   **909**

Vail, M. Exploring the Pacific   **910.4**

White, P. Exploration in the world of the Middle Ages, 500-1500   **910.4**

Exploring North America, 1800-1900. Isserman, M.   **917**

Exploring science and medical discoveries [series]

Cloning   **176**

Evolution   **576.8**

Exploring social issues through literature [series]

Johnson, C. D. Labor and workplace issues in literature   **810.9**

Stripling, M. Y. Bioethics and medical issues in literature   **809**

Wilson, C. E. Race and racism in literature   **810.9**

Exploring space. Carlisle, R. P.   **629.4**

Exploring tech careers   **331.7**

Exploring the life, myth, and art of ancient China. Shaughnessy, E. L.   **931**

Exploring the life, myth, and art of ancient Egypt. Fletcher, J.   **932**

Exploring the life, myth, and art of India. Ram-Prasad, C.   **954**

Exploring the life, myth, and art of Native Americans. Zimmerman, L. J.   **970.004**

Exploring the Pacific. Vail, M.   **910.4**

Exploring the polar regions. Anderson, H. S.   **910.4**

Exploring the world of the Druids. See Green, M. J. The world of the Druids   **299**

The **Explosionist**. Davidson, J.   **Fic**

Explosives

Wright, J. D. Fire and explosives   **363.2**

Extermination of pests *See* Pest control

Extinct animals

See also Prehistoric animals; Rare animals

Extinct humans. Tattersall, I.   **599.93**

Extramarital relationships *See* Adultery

Extraordinary essays. Orr, T.   **808.4**

The **extraordinary** journeys: Twenty thousand leagues under the sea. Verne, J.   **Fic**

Extraordinary oral presentations. Ryan, M.   **808.5**

Extraordinary people in extraordinary times. Mendoza, P. M.   **920**

The **extraordinary** secrets of April, May and June. Benway, R.   **Fic**

Extraordinary women of the Medieval and Renaissance world   **920.003**

Extrasensory perception

See also Clairvoyance; Telepathy

Fiction

Cabot, M. Insatiable   **Fic**

Carmody, I. Alyzon Whitestarr   **Fic**

Derting, K. The body finder   **Fic**

Garcia, K. Beautiful creatures   **Fic**

Extrasensory perception—Fiction—*Continued*

Gee, M. Salt   **Fic**

Harrington, K. Clarity   **Fic**

Le Guin, U. K. The left hand of darkness
     Fic

St. Crow, L. Strange angels   **Fic**

Ward, R. Numbers   **Fic**

Extrasolar planetary systems *See* Extrasolar planets

Extrasolar planets

Jayawardhana, R. Strange new worlds   **523.2**

Extraterrestrial bases

     See also Space colonies

Extraterrestrial beings

Davies, P. C. W. The eerie silence   **576.839**

Fiction

Frey, J. I am number four   **Fic**

Saint-Exupéry, A. d. The little prince   **Fic**

Wallenfels, S. POD   **Fic**

Wells, H. G. The war of the worlds   **Fic**

Yansky, B. Alien invasion and other inconveniences   **Fic**

Graphic novels

Yang, G. Prime baby   **741.5**

Extraterrestrial life   **576.839**

Extreme birds. Couzens, D.   **598**

The extreme Earth [series]

Aleshire, P. Mountains   **551.4**

Aleshire, P. Ocean ridges and trenches
     551.46

Burnham, L. Rivers   **551.48**

Hanson, E. A. Canyons   **551.4**

Hanson, J. K. Caves   **551.4**

Hanson, J. K. Lakes   **551.48**

Extreme sports

Li, W. Extreme sports   **796**

Extreme sports [series]

Masoff, J. Snowboard!   **796.93**

Extreme teens. Anderson, S. B.   **027.62**

Extreme threats [series]

Cunningham, K. Wildfires   **363.3**

Nardo, D. Asteroids and comets   **523.4**

Nardo, D. Climate change   **551.6**

Nardo, D. Volcanoes   **551.2**

Extreme weather. Streissguth, T.   **551.5**

Extremely loud & incredibly close. Foer, J. S.
     Fic

Extremist groups: opposing viewpoints   **322.4**

Eye

Surgery

Kornmehl, E. W. LASIK: a guide to laser vision correction   **617.7**

Eye of the crow. Peacock, S.   **Fic**

The **eye** of the elephant. Owens, D.   **639.9**

Eye on art [series]

Kallen, S. A. The artist's tools   **702.8**

Kallen, S. A. Claude Monet   **92**

Kallen, S. A. Pablo Picasso   **92**

Kallen, S. A. Photography   **770**

Eyes like stars. Mantchev, L.   **Fic**

Eyes of the emperor. Salisbury, G.   **Fic**

The **Eyes** on the prize civil rights reader
     323.1

Eyewitness history [series]

Burg, D. F. The American Revolution   **973.3**

Burg, D. F. The Great Depression   **973.91**

Carlisle, R. P. Civil War and Reconstruction
     973.7

Carlisle, R. P. World War I   **940.3**

Frost-Knappman, E. Women's suffrage in America   **324.6**

Maga, T. P. The 1960s   **973.92**

Purcell, S. J. The early national period
     973.4

Schneider, C. J. World War II   **940.53**

Schwartz, R. A. The 1950s   **973.92**

Schwartz, R. A. The 1990s   **973.92**

Streissguth, T. The roaring twenties   **973.91**

Woodger, E. The 1980s   **973.92**

Eyewitness to America   **973**

Eyquem, Michel *See* Montaigne, Michel de, 1533-1592

The **Eyre** affair. Fforde, J.   **Fic**

Ezra, Michael, 1972-

Muhammad Ali   **92**

F

F. Scott Fitzgerald A to Z. See Tate, M. J. Critical companion to F. Scott Fitzgerald   **813.009**

An **F.** Scott Fitzgerald encyclopedia. Gale, R. L.
     813.009

F. W. Prep [series]

Orr, T. Extraordinary essays   **808.4**

Ryan, M. Extraordinary oral presentations
     808.5

F5. Levine, M.   **551.55**

Fabrics

Searle, T. Felt jewelry   **746**

Face. Alexie, S.   **811**

Face relations   **S C**

Facilities planning for school library and technology centers. Baule, S. M.   **027.8**

Facing the lion. Lekuton, J.   **967.62**

Facklam, Howard

(jt. auth) Facklam, M. Modern medicines
     615

Facklam, Margery, 1927-

Modern medicines   **615**

Fact of life #31. Vega, D.   **Fic**

Factories

Von Drehle, D. Triangle: the fire that changed America   **974.7**

Fiction

Davies, J. Lost   **Fic**

Paterson, K. Lyddie   **Fic**

Facts, Miscellaneous *See* Curiosities and wonders

The **facts** about drug dependence to treatment. Klosterman, L.   **362.29**

The **facts** about drugs and society. Axelrod-Contrada, J.   **362.29**

The **facts** about drugs and the body. Klosterman, L.   **615**

Facts on File library of American history—*Continued*

Unger, H. G. Encyclopedia of American education **370**

Vice presidents **920.003**

Waldman, C. Atlas of the North American Indian **970.004**

Waldman, C. Encyclopedia of Native American tribes **970.004**

Facts on File library of American literature [series]

Abbotson, S. C. W. Critical companion to Arthur Miller **812.009**

Dowling, R. M. Critical companion to Eugene O'Neill **812.009**

Encyclopedia of American literature **810.3**

The Facts on File companion to American poetry **811.009**

The Facts on File companion to the American novel **813.009**

The Facts on File companion to the American short story **813.009**

Fargnoli, A. N. Critical companion to William Faulkner **813.009**

Farrell, S. E. Critical companion to Kurt Vonnegut **813.009**

Gillespie, C. Critical companion to Alice Walker **813.009**

Gillespie, C. Critical companion to Toni Morrison **813.009**

Haralson, E. L. Critical companion to Henry James **813.009**

Heintzelman, G. Critical companion to Tennessee Williams **812.009**

Jones, S. L. Critical companion to Zora Neale Hurston **813.009**

Kirk, C. A. Critical companion to Flannery O'Connor **813.009**

Murphy, R. E. Critical companion to T.S. Eliot **811.009**

Oh, S. Encyclopedia of Asian-American literature **810.9**

Oliver, C. M. Critical companion to Ernest Hemingway **813.009**

Oliver, C. M. Critical companion to Walt Whitman **811.009**

Rasmussen, R. K. Critical companion to Mark Twain **818**

Schultz, J. D. Critical companion to John Steinbeck **813.009**

Sova, D. B. Critical companion to Edgar Allan Poe **818**

Student's encyclopedia of American literary characters **810.9**

Student's encyclopedia of great American writers **920.003**

Tate, M. J. Critical companion to F. Scott Fitzgerald **813.009**

Wayne, T. K. Critical companion to Ralph Waldo Emerson **818**

Wright, S. B. Critical companion to Nathaniel Hawthorne **813.009**

Facts on File library of health and living [series]

Cassell, D. K. Encyclopedia of obesity and eating disorders **616.85**

Chow, J. H. The encyclopedia of hepatitis and other liver diseases **616.3**

The Encyclopedia of vitamins, minerals, and supplements **613.2**

Gwinnell, E. The encyclopedia of drug abuse **616.86**

Minocha, A. The encyclopedia of the digestive system and digestive disorders **616.3**

Noll, R. The encyclopedia of schizophrenia and other psychotic disorders **616.89**

Oakes, E. H. The encyclopedia of sports medicine **617.1**

Sayler, M. H. The encyclopedia of the muscle and skeletal systems and disorders **616.7**

Segen, J. C. The patient's guide to medical tests **616.07**

Turkington, C. The encyclopedia of infectious diseases **616.9**

Turkington, C. The encyclopedia of skin and skin disorders **616.5**

Turkington, C. The encyclopedia of the brain and brain disorders **612.8**

Wynbrandt, J. The encyclopedia of genetic disorders and birth defects **616**

Facts on File library of language and literature [series]

Ammer, C. The Facts on File dictionary of clichés **423**

Hendrickson, R. The Facts on File encyclopedia of word and phrase origins **422.03**

Lenburg, J. The Facts on File guide to research **025.5**

Quinn, E. A dictionary of literary and thematic terms **803**

The Quotable woman, revised edition **305.4**

Facts on File library of religion and mythology [series]

The encyclopedia of world religions **200.3**

Jones, C. Encyclopedia of Hinduism **294.5**

Karesh, S. E. Encyclopedia of Judaism **296.03**

Mercatante, A. S. The Facts on File encyclopedia of world mythology and legend **201.03**

Roman, L. Encyclopedia of Greek and Roman mythology **292**

Facts on File library of world history [series]

Adkins, L. Handbook to life in ancient Greece **938**

Adkins, L. Handbook to life in ancient Rome **937**

Aguilar-Moreno, M. Handbook to life in the Aztec world **972**

Axelrod, A. Encyclopedia of World War II **940.53**

Bertman, S. Handbook to life in ancient Mesopotamia **935**

Combs, C. C. Encyclopedia of terrorism **363.32**

David, A. R. Handbook to life in ancient Egypt **932**

Encyclopedia of holidays and celebrations **394.26**

Encyclopedia of Latin America **980**

Encyclopedia of plague and pestilence **614.4**

Facts on File science library—*Continued*
Tanton, J. S. Encyclopedia of mathematics
510.3
Wyman, B. C. The Facts on File dictionary of environmental science **363.7**
The **Facts** on File space and astronomy handbook. Angelo, J. A. **520**
Fadiman, Clifton, 1904-1999
(ed) World poetry. See World poetry **808.81**
Faerm, Steven
Fashion: design course **746.9**
Fagan, Brian M., 1936-
Cro-Magnon **569.9**
The Little Ice Age **551.6**
The long summer: how climate changed civilization **551.6**
(ed) The Oxford companion to archaeology. See The Oxford companion to archaeology **930.1**
(ed) The Seventy great inventions of the ancient world. See The Seventy great inventions of the ancient world **609**
Fagan, Deirdre
Critical companion to Robert Frost **811.009**
Fagan, Eleanora *See* Holiday, Billie, 1915-1959
Fagerstrom, Derek
Show me how **640**
Fagles, Robert
(tr) Homer. The Iliad **883**
(tr) Homer. The Odyssey **883**
(tr) Virgil. The Aeneid **873**
Fahey, David M.
(ed) Milestone documents of world religions. See Milestone documents of world religions **200**
Fahey, Thomas D., 1947-
Basic weight training for men and women **613.7**
Fahrenheit 451. Bradbury, R. **Fic**
The **fair** garden and the swarm of beasts. Edwards, M. A. **027.62**
Fair use (Copyright)
Butler, R. P. Smart copyright compliance for schools **346.04**
Simpson, C. Copyright for schools **346**
Simpson, C. M. Copyright catechism **346.04**
Fairbanks, Stephanie S., 1950-
Spotlight **812**
Fairchild, B. H. (Bertram H.), 1942-
Early occult memory systems of the Lower Midwest **811**
Fairest. Levine, G. C. **Fic**
Fairfield, Lesley, 1949-
Tyranny **741.5**
Fairies
Fiction
De Lint, C. The blue girl **Fic**
Dolamore, J. Magic under glass **Fic**
Healey, K. Guardian of the dead **Fic**
Lo, M. Ash **Fic**
Marr, M. Wicked lovely **Fic**
Pike, A. Wings **Fic**
Simner, J. L. Bones of Faerie **Fic**

Stiefvater, M. Lament **Fic**
Thompson, K. The new policeman **Fic**
Weston, R. P. Dust city **Fic**
Wooding, C. Poison **Fic**
Yolen, J. Except the queen **Fic**
Graphic novels
Black, H. The Good Neighbors; book one: Kin **741.5**
Fairy tale vol. 1. Mashima, H. **741.5**
Fairy tales
See also Fantasy fiction
Block, F. L. The rose and the beast **S C**
Blubaugh, P. Serendipity Market **Fic**
Durst, S. B. Ice **Fic**
Favorite folktales from around the world **398.2**
Hearne, B. G. Beauties and beasts **398.2**
Hesse, H. The fairy tales of Hermann Hesse **S C**
Levine, G. C. Fairest **Fic**
Lo, M. Ash **Fic**
McKinley, R. Beauty **Fic**
Murdock, C. G. Princess Ben **Fic**
Napoli, D. J. Beast **Fic**
Napoli, D. J. The magic circle **Fic**
Tomlinson, H. Toads and diamonds **Fic**
Encyclopedias
The Greenwood encyclopedia of folktales and fairy tales **398.2**
Graphic novels
Medley, L. Castle waiting **741.5**
The **fairy** tales of Hermann Hesse. Hesse, H. **S C**
Faith
Fiction
Connelly, N. O. The miracle stealer **Fic**
Miller, K. The eternal ones **Fic**
Faith & doubt **808.81**
The **faithful**. O'Toole, J. M. **282**
Fakes and forgeries. Bell, S. **363.2**
Fakhrid-Deen, Tina, 1973-
Let's get this straight **306.8**
Fakie. Varrato, T. **Fic**
Falcetti, Cara
(jt. auth) Blanchard, M. L. Poets for young adults **920.003**
Falcons
Tennant, A. On the wing **598**
Fiction
Whitman, E. Wildwing **Fic**
Falkner, Brian
Brain Jack **Fic**
Fall for anything. Summers, C. **Fic**
The **fall** of Rome. Southgate, M. **Fic**
Falla, P. S. (Paul Stephen), 1913-
(ed) Oxford Russian dictionary. See Oxford Russian dictionary **491.7**
Falla, Paul Stephen *See* Falla, P. S. (Paul Stephen), 1913-
Fallen angels. Myers, W. D. **Fic**
Fallen Grace. Hooper, M. **Fic**
Falling. Wilhelm, D. **Fic**
Falling hard **811.008**

Falling stars *See* Meteors

Fallon, Michael, 1966-
How to analyze the works of Andy Warhol
700
How to analyze the works of Georgia O'Keeffe
759.13

Fallon, Robert Thomas
A theatergoer's guide to Shakespeare **822.3**

Falola, Toyin, 1953-
Key events in African history **960**

Falsehood *See* Truthfulness and falsehood

Fame
Fiction
Collins, B. Always watching **Fic**
Hall, B. Tempo change **Fic**
Strasser, T. Famous **Fic**

Familiar flowers of North America: eastern region. Spellenberg, R. **582.13**
Familiar flowers of North America: western region. Spellenberg, R. **582.13**
Familiar trees of North America: eastern region **582.16**
Familiar trees of North America: western region **582.16**

Family
See also types of family members
Bezdecheck, B. Relationships **158**
Winchester, E. Sisters and brothers **306.8**
Graphic novels
Ono, N. Gente: the people of Ristorante Paradiso, volume 1 **741.5**
United States
The truth about family life **306.8**

Family farms
Pyle, G. Raising less corn, more hell **338.1**

Family finance *See* Personal finance

Family histories *See* Genealogy

Family life
Fiction
Adichie, C. N. Purple hibiscus **Fic**
Agee, J. A death in the family **Fic**
Agell, C. Shift **Fic**
Alexie, S. The absolutely true diary of a part-time Indian **Fic**
Allen, S. A. The girl who chased the moon **Fic**
Allende, I. The house of the spirits **Fic**
Alonzo, S. Riding invisible **Fic**
Alvarez, J. How the García girls lost their accents **Fic**
Anderson, L. H. Twisted **Fic**
Aronson, S. Head case **Fic**
Badoe, A. Between sisters **Fic**
Baldini, M. Unraveling **Fic**
Baldwin, J. Go tell it on the mountain **Fic**
Bauman, B. A. Rosie & Skate **Fic**
Block, F. L. The frenzy **Fic**
Brooks, K. Dawn **Fic**
Brooks, M. Mistik Lake **Fic**
Brown, J. Hate list **Fic**
Budhos, M. T. Ask me no questions **Fic**
Buffie, M. Winter shadows **Fic**
Caletti, D. The fortunes of Indigo Skye **Fic**
Caletti, D. The six rules of maybe **Fic**

Cantor, J. The life of glass **Fic**
Cantor, J. The September sisters **Fic**
Carmody, I. Alyzon Whitestarr **Fic**
Clarke, J. One whole and perfect day **Fic**
Clarke, J. The winds of heaven **Fic**
Clinton, C. A stone in my hand **Fic**
Colasanti, S. Waiting for you **Fic**
Coleman, W. Anna's world **Fic**
Connelly, N. O. The miracle stealer **Fic**
Cooney, C. B. Diamonds in the shadow **Fic**
Cooper, M. A brief history of Montmaray
Fic
Crane, D. Poster boy **Fic**
De Goldi, K. The 10 p.m. question **Fic**
Dessen, S. Just listen **Fic**
Dessen, S. Lock and key **Fic**
Donnelly, J. Revolution **Fic**
Dooley, S. Livvie Owen lived here **Fic**
Dorris, M. A yellow raft in blue water **Fic**
Dowd, S. Bog child **Fic**
Dowd, S. A swift pure cry **Fic**
Doyle, E. F. According to Kit **Fic**
Ehrenhaft, D. Friend is not a verb **Fic**
Ellis, A. D. Everything is fine **Fic**
Fehlbaum, B. Hope in Patience **Fic**
Flake, S. G. Bang! **Fic**
Foxlee, K. The anatomy of wings **Fic**
Frank, E. R. Life is funny **Fic**
Frank, H. The view from the top **Fic**
Franklin, E. The half life of planets **Fic**
Freitas, D. The possibilities of sainthood **Fic**
Friedman, R. Nothing **Fic**
Frost, H. Crossing stones **Fic**
Galante, C. The sweetness of salt **Fic**
Garsee, J. Before, after, and somebody in between **Fic**
Garsee, J. Say the word **Fic**
Giles, G. Dark song **Fic**
Giles, G. Right behind you **Fic**
Giles, G. What happened to Cass McBride?
Fic
Glass, L. The year the gypsies came **Fic**
Going, K. L. Saint Iggy **Fic**
Goldberg, M. Bee season **Fic**
Grant, C. Teenie **Fic**
Haig, M. The Radleys **Fic**
Hale, M. The goodbye season **Fic**
Hartnett, S. Butterfly **Fic**
Hartnett, S. Surrender **Fic**
Hartnett, S. Thursday's child **Fic**
Haruf, K. Plainsong **Fic**
Hedges, P. What's eating Gilbert Grape **Fic**
Hoffman, A. Blue diary **Fic**
Hopkins, E. Burned **Fic**
Hopkins, E. Tricks **Fic**
Irving, J. The world according to Garp **Fic**
Jocelyn, M. Would you **Fic**
Johnson, M. Suite Scarlett **Fic**
Jolin, P. In the name of God **Fic**
Jones, P. Chasing tail lights **Fic**
Jones, P. The tear collector **Fic**
Karim, S. Skunk girl **Fic**
Kephart, B. Undercover **Fic**
Lamba, M. What I meant. . . **Fic**
Leavitt, L. Sean Griswold's head **Fic**
LeFlore, L. The world is mine **Fic**
Les Becquets, D. Love, Cajun style **Fic**

Family life—Fiction—*Continued*

Levchuk, L. Everything beautiful in the world **Fic**

Lloyd, S. The carbon diaries 2015 **Fic**

Lurie, A. The latent powers of Dylan Fontaine **Fic**

Lynch, C. The Big Game of Everything **Fic**

Mackler, C. The earth, my butt, and other big, round things **Fic**

Madigan, L. K. The mermaid's mirror **Fic**

Mankell, H. Shadow of the leopard **Fic**

Marino, P. Dough Boy **Fic**

Martinez, V. Parrot in the oven **Fic**

McBride, R. The fire opal **Fic**

McCahan, E. I now pronounce you someone else **Fic**

McCarthy, M. Rose by any other name **Fic**

McCullers, C. The member of the wedding **Fic**

McNeal, L. Dark water **Fic**

Min, K. Secondhand world **Fic**

Mitchell, D. Black swan green **Fic**

Moskowitz, H. Break **Fic**

Murray, M. How to make a bird **Fic**

Myers, W. D. Kick **Fic**

Myers, W. D. What they found **S C**

Na, A. A step from heaven **Fic**

Nanji, S. Child of dandelions **Fic**

Nichols, J. Messed up **Fic**

Oppel, K. Half brother **Fic**

Pearson, M. A room on Lorelei Street **Fic**

Perez, A. H. What can(t) wait **Fic**

Perkins, M. Secret keeper **Fic**

Prose, F. Touch **Fic**

Rapp, A. Under the wolf, under the dog **Fic**

Reinhardt, D. A brief chapter in my impossible life **Fic**

Reinhardt, D. The things a brother knows **Fic**

Resau, L. Red glass **Fic**

Roy, A. The god of small things **Fic**

Runyon, B. Surface tension **Fic**

Ryan, A. K. Zen & Xander undone **Fic**

Sachar, L. The cardturner **Fic**

Saenz, B. A. Last night I sang to the monster **Fic**

Salinger, J. D. Franny & Zooey **Fic**

Salinger, J. D. Raise high the roof beam, carpenters, and Seymour: an introduction **Fic**

Saroyan, W. The human comedy **Fic**

Schmidt, G. D. Trouble **Fic**

Schumacher, J. Black box **Fic**

Sebold, A. The lovely bones **Fic**

Seigel, A. The kid table **Fic**

Selvadurai, S. Swimming in the monsoon sea **Fic**

Sherrill, M. The Ruins of California **Fic**

Silvey, C. Jasper Jones **Fic**

Sitomer, A. L. The secret story of Sonia Rodriguez **Fic**

Slayton, F. C. When the whistle blows **Fic**

Smith, J. E. The comeback season **Fic**

Smith, K. The geography of girlhood **Fic**

Stahler, D., Jr. Doppelganger **Fic**

Standiford, N. Confessions of the Sullivan sisters **Fic**

Standiford, N. How to say goodbye in Robot **Fic**

Staunton, T. Acting up **Fic**

Stevenson, R. H. A thousand shades of blue **Fic**

Stevenson, S. J. The Latte Rebellion **Fic**

Thompson, H. Orchards **Fic**

Tyler, A. Dinner at the Homesick Restaurant **Fic**

Valentine, J. Broken soup **Fic**

Venkatraman, P. Climbing the stairs **Fic**

Vigan, D. d. No and me **Fic**

Warman, J. Where the truth lies **Fic**

Watson, L. Montana 1948 **Fic**

Weber, L. If you live like me **Fic**

Weinheimer, B. Converting Kate **Fic**

Wilhelm, D. Falling **Fic**

Williams, C. L. The chosen one **Fic**

Williams, C. L. Miles from ordinary **Fic**

Williams, G. Beatle meets Destiny **Fic**

Williams-Garcia, R. Like sisters on the homefront **Fic**

Wilson, D. L. Firehorse **Fic**

Wittlinger, E. Parrotfish **Fic**

Zarr, S. Story of a girl **Fic**

Zeises, L. M. The sweet life of Stella Madison **Fic**

Zulkey, C. An off year **Fic**

See/See also pages in the following book(s):

Sleator, W. Oddballs **S C**

Graphic novels

Lat. Kampung boy **741.5**

Lemire, J. Essex County **741.5**

Small, D. Stitches **92**

Thompson, C. Blankets **92**

Family planning *See* Birth control

A **family** secret. Heuvel, E. **741.5**

Family size

See also Birth control

Family violence *See* Domestic violence

Famines

Bartoletti, S. C. Black potatoes **941.5**

Fiction

Pignat, C. Greener grass **Fic**

Famous. Strasser, T. **Fic**

Famous American crimes and trials **364**

Famous first facts. Kane, J. N. **031.02**

Famous first facts about American politics. Anzovin, S. **973**

Famous first facts about sports. Franck, I. M. **796**

Famous first facts, international edition **031.02**

Famous lines. Andrews, R. **808.88**

Famous people *See* Celebrities

Fancy dress *See* Costume

Fantaskey, Beth

Jessica's guide to dating on the dark side **Fic**

Fantastic fiction *See* Fantasy fiction

Fantastic voyage. Asimov, I. **Fic**

Fantasy fiction

See also Fairy tales; Science fiction. A spell for chameleon **Fic**

Festivals—*Continued*
Encyclopedia of holidays and celebrations
    394.26
Holiday symbols and customs   **394.26**
Holidays and anniversaries of the world
    394.26
Rajtar, S. United States holidays and obser-
vances   **394.26**
Roy, C. Traditional festivals   **394.26**
Dictionaries
Holidays, festivals, and celebrations of the world
dictionary   **394.26**
Fetal rights. Marzilli, A.   **342**
The **Fetch**. Whitcomb, L.   **Fic**
Fetterolf, Monty L.
(jt. auth) Cobb, C. The joy of chemistry
    540
Fetus
Marzilli, A. Fetal rights   **342**
Feudalism
See/See also pages in the following book(s):
Gies, J. Life in a medieval castle   **940.2**
Feuer, Alan
Over there   **956.7**
Feuereisen, Patti
Invisible girls   **362.7**
Fever Crumb. Reeve, P.   **Fic**
A **fever** in Salem. Carlson, L. M.   **133.4**
A **few** seconds of panic. Fatsis, S.   **92**
Feynman, Richard Phillips, 1918-1988
The meaning of it all   **500**
Six easy pieces   **530**
About
Krauss, L. M. Quantum man [biography of
Richard Feynman]   **92**
See/See also pages in the following book(s):
Cropper, W. H. Great physicists   **920**
Fforde, Jasper
The Eyre affair   **Fic**
Fibers
Wright, J. D. Hair and fibers   **363.2**
Fichtelberg, Susan
Encountering enchantment   **016.8**
Fick, Barbara J.
(ed) American Bar Association. The American
Bar Association guide to workplace law
    344

Fiction
See also Adventure fiction; American fic-
tion; Christian fiction; English fiction; Fairy
tales; Fantasy fiction; Historical fiction; Hor-
ror fiction; Love stories; Mystery fiction;
School stories; Science fiction; Sea stories;
Short stories; Suspense fiction; War stories
Bibliography
Frolund, T. Genrefied classics   **016.8**
Herald, D. T. Genreflecting   **016.8**
Saricks, J. G. The readers' advisory guide to
genre fiction   **025.5**
What do I read next? 2011   **016.8**
History and criticism
Bloom, H. Novelists and novels   **809.3**
Herald, D. T. Genreflecting   **016.8**

Johnson, C. D. Labor and workplace issues in
literature   **810.9**
Literature of developing nations for students
    809
Stripling, M. Y. Bioethics and medical issues in
literature   **809**
Technique
Henry, L. The fiction dictionary   **808.3**
Lukeman, N. The plot thickens   **808.3**
Piercy, M. So you want to write   **808.3**
The **fiction** dictionary. Henry, L.   **808.3**
Fidel Castro's Cuba. Markel, R. J.   **972.91**
Fiedler, Lisa
Romeo's ex   **Fic**
Field athletics *See* Track athletics
Field glasses *See* Binoculars
A **field** guide to automotive technology. Sobey, E.
    629.2
A **field** guide to freshwater fishes: North America
north of Mexico. See Page, L. M. Peterson
field guide to freshwater fishes of North
America north of Mexico   **597**
The **field** guide to geology. Lambert, D.   **551**
Field guide to grasshoppers, crickets, and katydids
of the United States. Capinera, J. L.
    595.7
Field guide to meteors and meteorites. Norton, O.
R.   **523.5**
Field guide to modern diesel locomotives. See
McDonnell, G. Locomotives   **625.2**
A **field** guide to mushrooms, North America.
McKnight, K. H.   **579.6**
A **field** guide to reptiles & amphibians. Conant, R.
    597.9
A **field** guide to rocks and minerals. Pough, F. H.
    549
A **field** guide to the birds. See Peterson, R. T.
Peterson field guide to birds of North Ameri-
ca   **598**
Field guide to the birds of North America. See
National Geographic field guide to the birds
of North America   **598**
Field guide to the sharks of the world. See
Compagno, L. J. V. Sharks of the world
    597
A **field** guide to venomous animals and poisonous
plants. Foster, S.   **578.6**
A **field** guide to Western reptiles and amphibians.
Stebbins, R. C.   **597.9**
Field guide to wildflowers, eastern region. See
Thieret, J. W. National Audubon Society field
guide to North American wildflowers: eastern
region   **582.13**
Field notes from a catastrophe. Kolbert, E.
    363.7
Fields of battle. Keegan, J.   **973**
Fierce & true   **812.008**
Fies, Brian
Mom's cancer   **616.99**
Fifteen candles   **392**
Fifteen candles. Chambers, V.   **Fic**
Fifteen short plays. See McNally, T. 15 short
plays   **812**

Fifteenth century *See* World history—15th century

The **fifties**. Halberstam, D.   **973.92**

The **fifty** best sights in astronomy and how to see them. See Schaaf, F. The 50 best sights in astronomy and how to see them   **520**

Fifty miles from tomorrow. Hensley, W. L.   **92**

Fifty plants that changed the course of history. Laws, B.   **581.6**

Fifty signs of mental illness. Hicks, J. W.   **616.89**

The **fight** for peace. Gottfried, T.   **303.6**

Fight game. Wild, K.   **Fic**

Fight global warming now. McKibben, B.   **363.7**

Fight like a girl— and win. Gervasi, L. H.   **613.6**

Fighting words [series]
Ball, D. I. Competing voices from native America   **970.004**
Competing voices from World War II in Europe   **940.53**

Figueredo, Danilo H., 1951-
A brief history of the Caribbean   **972.9**

Figure drawing
Hart, C. Drawing cutting edge anatomy   **741.5**
Hart, C. Human anatomy made amazingly easy   **743**

Filipino Americans
Fiction
Growing up Filipino II   **S C**

Filipovic, Zlata
(ed) Stolen voices. See Stolen voices   **920**

Fillmore, Millard, 1800-1874
About
Finkelman, P. Millard Fillmore   **92**

Film adaptations
Adaptations: from short story to big screen   **S C**

Film direction *See* Motion pictures—Production and direction

Film production *See* Motion pictures—Production and direction

Filmmakers. Koopmans, A.   **920**

Filmmaking *See* Motion pictures—Production and direction

Filmmaking for teens. Lanier, T.   **791.43**

Films *See* Motion pictures

The **final** days. Woodward, B.   **973.924**

Final harvest. Dickinson, E.   **811**

Finance
See also Debt; Financial crises; Government lending
Dictionaries
A dictionary of finance and banking   **332.03**

Financial aid, Student *See* Student aid

Financial aid for the disabled and their families, 2010-2012. Schlachter, G. A.   **378.3**

Financial crashes *See* Financial crises

Financial crises
Connolly, S. The stock market   **332.6**
Lewis, M. The big short   **330.973**

Financial panics *See* Financial crises

Financial planning, Personal *See* Personal finance

Financiers *See* Capitalists and financiers

Finding miracles. Alvarez, J.   **Fic**

Finding things *See* Lost and found possessions

Findling, John E.
(ed) Events that changed America through the seventeenth century. See Events that changed America through the seventeenth century   **973.2**
(ed) Events that changed Great Britain, from 1066 to 1714. See Events that changed Great Britain, from 1066 to 1714   **941**
(ed) Events that changed Great Britain since 1689. See Events that changed Great Britain since 1689   **941**
(ed) Events that changed the world through the sixteenth century. See Events that changed the world through the sixteenth century   **909**

Fine, Susan
(jt. auth) Bardin, M. Zen in the art of the SAT   **378.1**

Fine arts *See* Arts

Finer, Kim R., 1956-
Tuberculosis   **616.2**

Fingerprints
Innes, B. Fingerprints and impressions   **363.2**

Fingerprints and impressions. Innes, B.   **363.2**

Fink, Mark
The summer I got a life   **Fic**

Finkelman, Paul, 1949-
Landmark decisions of the United States Supreme Court   **347**
Millard Fillmore   **92**
(ed) Encyclopedia of African American history, 1619-1895. See Encyclopedia of African American history, 1619-1895   **305.8**
(ed) Encyclopedia of African American history, 1896 to the present. See Encyclopedia of African American history, 1896 to the present   **305.8**
(ed) Encyclopedia of the Harlem Renaissance. See Encyclopedia of the Harlem Renaissance   **700**
(ed) Encyclopedia of the new American nation. See Encyclopedia of the new American nation   **973.03**
(ed) Milestone documents in African American history. See Milestone documents in African American history   **305.8**
(ed) Milestone documents in American history. See Milestone documents in American history   **973**
(ed) Milestone documents of American leaders. See Milestone documents of American leaders   **973**

Finkelstein, Norman H., 1941-
Forged in freedom   **305.8**
Plastics   **620.1**

Finlay, Victoria
Color: a natural history of the palette   **535.6**

Finmark, Sharon
(jt. auth) Crawshaw, A. Watercolour for the absolute beginner   **751.42**

Finn, Mary
Anila's journey   **Fic**

Finnegan, William
Crossing the line   **968.06**

Finneran, Richard J.
(ed) Yeats, W. B. The poems   **821**
(ed) Yeats, W. B. The Yeats reader   **828**

Finney, Sumukhi
The yoga handbook   **613.7**

Finnikin of the rock. Marchetta, M.   **Fic**

Fire
Fiction
McKinley, R. Fire: tales of elemental spirits   **S C**

Fire. Cashore, K.   **Fic**

Fire and explosives. Wright, J. D.   **363.2**

Fire fighters
Biography
Unger, Z. Working fire   **92**
Fiction
Lynch, C. Hothouse   **Fic**

Fire fighters   **628.9**

Fire fighting
Fire fighters   **628.9**

Fire from heaven. Renault, M.   **Fic**

Fire in the heart. Chopra, D.   **204**

Fire in the lake. FitzGerald, F.   **959.704**

Fire in the soul   **808.81**

The **fire** opal. McBride, R.   **Fic**

Fire: tales of elemental spirits. McKinley, R.   **S C**

Fire under the snow. See Palden Gyatso. The autobiography of a Tibetan monk   **92**

Firearms
Atkin, S. B. Gunstories   **363.33**
Gun violence: opposing viewpoints   **364.2**
Law and legislation
See Gun control

Firebirds rising   **S C**

Firebirds soaring   **S C**

Firefly atlas of North America   **912**

Firefly atlas of the universe   **523**

Firefly encyclopedia of the vivarium. Alderton, D.   **639.3**

The **Firefly** five language visual dictionary. Corbeil, J.-C.   **413**

Firefly guide to gems. Oldershaw, C.   **553.8**

Firefly guide to wetlands. See Guide to wetlands   **578.7**

Firefly letters. Engle, M.   **Fic**

Firehorse. Wilson, D. L.   **Fic**

Firelight. Jordan, S.   **Fic**

Fires
See also Arson
Marsico, K. The Triangle Shirtwaist Factory fire   **974.7**
Von Drehle, D. Triangle: the fire that changed America   **974.7**
Wright, J. D. Fire and explosives   **363.2**
Fiction
Friesner, E. M. Threads and flames   **Fic**
Haddix, M. P. Uprising   **Fic**
McNeal, L. Dark water   **Fic**
Chicago (Ill.)
Murphy, J. The great fire   **977.3**
Owens, L. L. The great Chicago fire   **977.3**

Fires of hatred. Naimark, N. M.   **364.1**

Fireside, Bryna J.
Choices for the high school graduate   **373.1**

Firestarter. King, S.   **Fic**

Fireweed. Lerner, G.   **92**

Firlik, Katrina
Another day in the frontal lobe   **92**

The **firm**. Grisham, J.   **Fic**

Firmage, George James
(ed) Cummings, E. E. Complete poems, 1904-1962   **811**

First aid
The American Red Cross first aid and safety handbook   **616.02**

The **first** civilizations to 500 BC   **930**

First contact. Kaufman, M.   **576.839**

First crossing   **S C**

First darling of the morning. Umrigar, T. N.   **92**

The **first** emancipator [biography of Robert Carter] Levy, A.   **92**

First families. Angelo, B.   **920**

First freedoms. Haynes, C. C.   **342**

First generation children See Children of immigrants

The **first** human. Gibbons, A.   **599.93**

First humans. Stefoff, R.   **599.93**

First ladies. Caroli, B. B.   **920**

First ladies. Schneider, D.   **920.003**

First meetings in the Enderverse. Card, O. S.   **S C**

The **first** part last. Johnson, A.   **Fic**

The **first** part of King Henry the Fourth. Shakespeare, W.   **822.3**

First shot. Sorrells, W.   **Fic**

First steps series
Marsh, D. Calligraphy   **745.6**

First they killed my father. Ung, L.   **959.6**

The **first** vertebrates. Holmes, T.   **567**

The **First** World War. Gilbert, M.   **940.3**

The **First** World War. Strachan, H.   **940.3**

Fisanick, Christina, 1973-
(ed) Addiction: opposing viewpoints. See Addiction: opposing viewpoints   **362.29**

Fly casting
Mason, B. Sports illustrated fly fishing
799.1
Merwin, J. Fly fishing 799.1
Fly fishing. Merwin, J. 799.1
Flygirl. Smith, S. L. Fic
Flying Enterprise (Ship)
Delaney, F. Simple courage 910.4
Flying saucers *See* Unidentified flying objects
Flynn, Kevin, 1956-
(jt. auth) Dwyer, J. 102 minutes 974.7
Flynn, Leonie
(ed) The ultimate teen book guide. See The ulti-
mate teen book guide 028.1
Flynn, Noa
See also Walker, Ida
Inhalants and solvents 362.29
Flynn, Raymond
John Paul II 92
Focus on living. Banish, R. 362.1
Foe, Daniel *See* Defoe, Daniel, 1661?-1731
Foer, Jonathan Safran, 1977-
Eating animals 641.3
Extremely loud & incredibly close Fic
Foerstel, Herbert N.
From Watergate to Monicagate 070.4
Fogle, Bruce
Dog: the definitive guide for dog owners
636.7
Foiled. Yolen, J. 741.5
Folk lore *See* Folklore
Folk music
United States
See also Country music
Folk musicians
Kaufman, W. Woody Guthrie, American radical
92
Folklore
See also Animals—Folklore; Blacks—Folk-
lore; Dragons; Legends topics as themes in
folklore and names of ethnic or national
groups with the subdivision *Folklore*
Be afraid, be very afraid 398.2
De Vos, G. Tales, rumors, and gossip 398
Favorite folktales from around the world
398.2
The Greenwood library of world folktales
398.2
Hearne, B. G. Beauties and beasts 398.2
World folklore for storytellers 398
Dictionaries
Pickering, D. A dictionary of folklore 398.2
Encyclopedias
The Greenwood encyclopedia of folktales and
fairy tales 398.2
Africa
Lester, J. Black folktales 398.2
Asia
Asian-Pacific folktales and legends 398.2
Europe
Bulfinch, T. Bulfinch's mythology 398.2
Japan—Graphic novels
Matsumoto, N. Yokaiden, volume 1 741.5

Latin America
Latin American folktales 398.2
Southern States
Tingle, T. Walking the Choctaw road 398.2
United States
Holt, D. Spiders in the hairdo 398.2
United States—Encyclopedias
American folklore 398.03
Folklore, memoirs, and other writings. Hurston, Z.
N. 818
Folly. Jocelyn, M. Fic
Foner, Eric
Forever free 973.8
Foner, Philip S., 1910-1994
(ed) Douglass, F. Frederick Douglass: selected
speeches and writings 326
Fonseca, Anthony J.
Hooked on horror III 016.8
Fonstad, Karen Wynn
The atlas of Middle-earth 823.009
Fontichiaro, Kristin
Podcasting at school 371.3
Food
See also Convenience foods
Allen, S. L. In the devil's garden 641
Goldstein, M. C. Controversies in food and nu-
trition 641.3
Biotechnology
Cummins, R. Genetically engineered food
363.1
Encyclopedias
Davidson, A. The Oxford companion to food
641.03
Food and nutrition 641.3
The Oxford encyclopedia of food and drink in
America 641.3
Rolland, J. L. The food encyclopedia 641.03
Fiction
Zeises, L. M. The sweet life of Stella Madison
Fic
History
Albala, K. Food in early modern Europe
641.3
The Cambridge world history of food 641.3
Kaufman, C. K. Cooking in ancient civilizations
641.3
Tannahill, R. Food in history 641.3
Pictorial works
Menzel, P. Hungry planet 641.3
Food, Natural *See* Natural foods
Food 363.8
Food. Kerr, J. 178
Food additives
Hayhurst, C. Everything you need to know
about food additives 664
Dictionaries
Winter, R. A consumer's dictionary of food ad-
ditives 664
Food adulteration and inspection
Food safety 363.1
Petersen, C. Protecting earth's food supply
363.1
Smith, T. L. Nutrition and food safety 363.1
Food alert!. Satin, M. 615.9

Food allergy
Gordon, S. M. Peanut butter, milk, and other
deadly threats **616.97**
Food and fitness [series]
Favor, L. J. Food as foe **616.85**
Favor, L. J. Weighing in **613.2**
Shryer, D. Peak performance **617.1**
Food and nutrition **641.3**
Food as foe. Favor, L. J. **616.85**
Food chains (Ecology)
Pollan, M. The omnivore's dilemma **338.1**
Food contamination
Food safety **363.1**
Petersen, C. Protecting earth's food supply
363.1
Satin, M. Food alert! **615.9**
The **food** encyclopedia. Rolland, J. L. **641.03**
Food, girls, and other things I can't have. Zadoff,
A. **Fic**
Food habits *See* Eating customs
Food in early modern Europe. Albala, K.
641.3
Food in history. Tannahill, R. **641.3**
Food industry
Espejo, R. Fast food **363.1**
Kerr, J. Food **178**
Schlosser, E. Chew on this **394.1**
Schlosser, E. Fast food nation **394.1**
Spurlock, M. Don't eat this book **614.5**
Food jobs. Chalmers, I. **647.9**
Food poisoning
See also Botulism
Landau, E. Food poisoning and foodborne dis-
eases **615.9**
Petersen, C. Protecting earth's food supply
363.1
Food poisoning and foodborne diseases. Landau,
E. **615.9**
Food preparation *See* Cooking
Food safety **363.1**
Food service
See also Restaurants
Chalmers, I. Food jobs **647.9**
Food supply
See also Agriculture
Pollan, M. The omnivore's dilemma **338.1**
See/See also pages in the following book(s):
Diamond, J. M. Guns, germs, and steel
303.4
Food through history [series]
Albala, K. Food in early modern Europe
641.3
Fooling with words **808.1**
Fools and jesters
Fiction
Spinner, S. Damosel **Fic**
The **fool's** girl. Rees, C. **Fic**
Football
See also Soccer
Bissinger, H. G. Friday night lights **796.332**
Complete guide to special teams **796.332**
MacCambridge, M. America's game **796.332**

McIntosh, J. S. Football **796.332**
Biography
Fatsis, S. A few seconds of panic **92**
Pittman, C. V. Playing for Paterno **92**
Encyclopedias
Rielly, E. J. Football **796.332**
Fiction
Carter, A. R. Love, football, and other contact
sports **S C**
Cohen, J. Leverage **Fic**
Coy, J. Crackback **Fic**
Deuker, C. Gym candy **Fic**
Korman, G. Pop **Fic**
Lipsyte, R. Raiders night **Fic**
Lynch, C. Inexcusable **Fic**
McKissack, F. Shooting star **Fic**
Murdock, C. G. Dairy Queen **Fic**
Powell, R. Three clams and an oyster **Fic**
Tharp, T. Knights of the hill country **Fic**
Zadoff, A. Food, girls, and other things I can't
have **Fic**
For cause and comrades. McPherson, J. M.
973.7
For colored girls who have considered suicide,
when the rainbow is enuf. Shange, N.
812
--For dummies [series]
Hinkson, J. Lacrosse for dummies **796.34**
Okabayashi, K. Manga for dummies **741.5**
For keeps. Friend, N. **Fic**
For the love of animals. Shevelow, K. **179**
For the love of physics. Lewin, W. H. G. **92**
For the win. Doctorow, C. **Fic**
For whom the bell tolls. Hemingway, E. **Fic**
Forbes, Bruce David
Christmas **394.26**
Forbes, Peter, 1947-
The gecko's foot **600**
Forbidden fruit. DeRamus, B. **973.7**
Force and energy
See also Dark energy (Astronomy)
Adair, R. K. The physics of baseball
796.357
Bodanis, D. E=mc2 **530.1**
Bodanis, D. Electric universe **537**
A **force** of nature [biography of Ernest Rutherford]
Reeves, R. **92**
Forced indoctrination *See* Brainwashing
Forced labor *See* Slavery
Ford, Gerald R., 1913-2006
See/See also pages in the following book(s):
Profiles in courage for our time **920**
Ford, John C., 1971-
The morgue and me **Fic**
Ford, Kenneth William
101 quantum questions **530.1**
Ford, Lynne E.
(ed) Encyclopedia of women and American poli-
tics. See Encyclopedia of women and Ameri-
can politics **973.03**
Ford, Michael Thomas
Suicide notes **Fic**
Z **Fic**

Forsyth, Elizabeth Held
(jt. auth) Hyde, M. O. Depression   **616.85**

Forsyth, Neil, 1944-
John Milton   **92**

Fort Sumter (Charleston, S.C.)
Detzer, D. Allegiance   **973.7**

Fort Yukon (Alaska)
D'Orso, M. Eagle blue   **796.323**

Fortey, Richard A.
Earth   **551.7**

The **forties** in America   **973.91**

Fortification
Macaulay, D. Castle   **728.8**

Fortin, François
(ed) Sports: the complete visual reference. See
Sports: the complete visual reference   **796**

Fortunate Eagle, Adam, 1929-
Pipestone   **92**

Fortunate son. Mosley, W.   **Fic**

The **fortune** cookie chronicles. Lee, J.   **641.5**

Fortune telling
See also Tarot
Pickover, C. A. Dreaming the future   **133.3**

Fortune's bones. Nelson, M.   **811**

The **fortunes** of Indigo Skye. Caletti, D.   **Fic**

Forty signs of rain. Robinson, K. S.   **Fic**

Forty ways to look at Winston Churchill. Rubin,
G. C.   **92**

Forty years of medical racism. Uschan, M. V.
   174.2

Fossey, Dian
About
De la Bédoyère, C. No one loved gorillas more
[biography of Dian Fossey]   **92**

Fossil fuels and pollution. Casper, J. K.   **363.7**

Fossil hominids
Gibbons, A. The first human   **599.93**
Holmes, T. Early humans   **599.93**
Holmes, T. Primates and human ancestors
   569
Johanson, D. C. From Lucy to language
   599.93
Rubalcaba, J. Every bone tells a story   **930.1**
Sarmiento, E. The last human   **569.9**
Stefoff, R. First humans   **599.93**
Stefoff, R. Ice age Neanderthals   **599.93**
Stefoff, R. Modern humans   **599.93**
Stefoff, R. Origins   **599.93**
Tattersall, I. Extinct humans   **599.93**

Fossil mammals
Johanson, D. C. Lucy: the beginnings of humankind   **599.93**

Fossil reptiles
See also Dinosaurs

Fossils
See also Fossil mammals; Prehistoric ani-
mals
Bishop, A. C. Guide to minerals, rocks & fossils
   552
Coenraads, R. R. Rocks and fossils   **552**
Everhart, M. J. Sea monsters   **567.9**

Haines, T. The complete guide to prehistoric life
   560
Holmes, T. The first vertebrates   **567**
Holmes, T. Last of the dinosaurs   **567.9**
Holmes, T. Primates and human ancestors
   569
Naish, D. The great dinosaur discoveries
   567.9
Parker, A. In the blink of an eye   **576.8**
Poinar, G. O. What bugged the dinosaurs?
   560
Prehistoric life   **560**
Sampson, S. D. Dinosaur odyssey   **567.9**
Thompson, I. The Audubon Society field guide
to North American fossils   **560**
Encyclopedias
Encyclopedia of paleontology   **560**
Graphic novels
Ottaviani, J. Bone sharps, cowboys, and thunder
lizards   **560**

Foster, Brett
Rome   **809**
(ed) The sonnets. See The sonnets [criticism]
   822.3

Foster, Lynn V.
A brief history of Central America   **972.8**
A brief history of Mexico   **972**

Foster, Patricia
(ed) Sister to sister. See Sister to sister
   810.8

Foster, Russell G.
Rhythms of life   **571.7**

Foster, Stephen, 1962-
Walking Ollie, or, Winning the love of a difficult dog   **636.7**

Foster, Steven, 1957-
A field guide to venomous animals and poisonous plants   **578.6**
National Geographic desk reference to nature's
medicine   **615**

Foster children
Growing up in the care of strangers   **362.7**
Rhodes-Courter, A. M. Three little words   **92**

Foster home care
See also Foster children
Growing up in the care of strangers   **362.7**
Rhodes-Courter, A. M. Three little words   **92**
Fiction
Ayarbe, H. Compromised   **Fic**
De la Peña, M. Ball don't lie   **Fic**
Dowd, S. Solace of the road   **Fic**
Frank, E. R. America   **Fic**
Gibbons, K. Ellen Foster   **Fic**
Koertge, R. Strays   **Fic**
Lowell, P. Returnable girl   **Fic**
McNeal, L. The decoding of Lana Morris
   Fic
Murray, Y. M. The good girl's guide to getting
kidnapped   **Fic**
Sweeney, J. The guardian   **Fic**
Weaver, W. Defect   **Fic**

Fothergill, Alastair
Planet Earth   **508**

Foundation. Asimov, I.   **Fic**

France—*Continued*
History—1940-1945, German occupation
See/See also pages in the following book(s):
Stein, G. Selected writings   **818**
      History—1945-1958
See/See also pages in the following book(s):
Stein, G. Selected writings   **818**
      Kings and rulers
Johnson, P. Napoleon   **92**
      Social life and customs
DeJean, J. E. The essence of style   **391**

France. Armeé. Grande Armeé
Streissguth, T. The Napoleonic wars   **940.2**

Franchise *See* Suffrage

Francis, of Assisi, Saint, 1182-1226
      About
Green, J. God's fool: the life and times of Francis of Assisi   **92**

Francis, John
Planetwalker   **92**

Franciscans
See/See also pages in the following book(s):
Russell, B. A history of Western philosophy   **109**

Franck, Irene M.
Famous first facts about sports   **796**

Franco, Betsy
Metamorphosis   **Fic**
(ed) Falling hard. See Falling hard   **811.008**
(ed) Things I have to tell you. See Things I have to tell you   **810.8**
(ed) You hear me? See You hear me?   **810.8**

Franco, Tom
(jt. auth) Franco, B. Metamorphosis   **Fic**

Frank, Anne, 1929-1945
Anne Frank's Tales from the secret annex   **839.3**
Diary of a young girl; dramatization. See Goodrich, F. The diary of Anne Frank   **812**
The diary of a young girl: the definitive edition   **92**
The diary of Anne Frank: the critical edition   **92**
      About
Jacobson, S. Anne Frank   **92**
Kopf, H. R. Understanding Anne Frank's The diary of a young girl   **940.53**
      Authorship
Prose, F. Anne Frank   **839.3**
      Fiction
Dogar, S. Annexed   **Fic**

Frank, Catherine
(comp) Quotations for all occasions. See Quotations for all occasions   **808.88**

Frank, E. R.
America   **Fic**
Life is funny   **Fic**

Frank, Hillary, 1976-
Better than running at night   **Fic**
The view from the top   **Fic**

Frank, Leo
      About
Alphin, E. M. An unspeakable crime   **364.152**

Frank, Lisa Tendrich
(ed) Women in the American Civil War. See Women in the American Civil War   **973.7**

Frank, Mitch
Understanding the Holy Land   **956.94**

Frank, Otto, 1889-1980
(ed) Frank, A. The diary of a young girl: the definitive edition   **92**

Frank, Richard B.
Downfall   **940.54**
MacArthur   **92**

Frank family
      About
Gies, M. Anne Frank remembered   **940.53**

Frankenstein (Fictional character)
Cobley, J. Frankenstein   **741.5**

Frankenstein. Cobley, J.   **741.5**

Frankenstein; or, The modern Prometheus. Shelley, M. W.   **Fic**

Franklin, Benjamin, 1706-1790
Autobiography, Poor Richard, and later writings   **818**
Not your usual founding father   **92**
      About
Dash, J. A dangerous engine [biography of Benjamin Franklin]   **92**
Gaustad, E. S. Benjamin Franklin   **92**
Wood, G. S. The Americanization of Benjamin Franklin   **92**
See/See also pages in the following book(s):
Ellis, J. J. Founding brothers   **973.4**

Franklin, Emily
The half life of planets   **Fic**
The other half of me   **Fic**

Franklin, John Hope, 1915-2009
From slavery to freedom   **305.8**

Franklin, Jon
The wolf in the parlor   **636.7**

Franklin, Patricia, 1951-
(jt. auth) Stephens, C. G. Library 101   **027.8**

Franklin, Rosalind, 1920-1958
      About
Polcovar, J. Rosalind Franklin and the structure of life   **92**
See/See also pages in the following book(s):
Hellman, H. Great feuds in medicine   **610.9**

Frannie in pieces. Ephron, D.   **Fic**

Franny & Zooey. Salinger, J. D.   **Fic**

Franz Kafka's The metamorphosis [study guide]   **833.009**

Fraser, Antonia, 1932-
(ed) The Lives of the kings & queens of England. See The Lives of the kings & queens of England   **941**

Fraser, Bill
      About
Montaigne, F. Fraser's penguins   **577.2**

Fraser, Elizabeth, 1970-
Reality rules!   **028.5**

Freedom of the press—*Continued*
Friedman, I. C. Freedom of speech and the press
342

Lewis, A. Freedom for the thought that we hate
342

Phillips, T. A. Hazelwood v. Kuhlmeier and the school newspaper censorship debate **342**
See/See also pages in the following book(s):
Haynes, C. C. First freedoms **342**

Freedom of the press **342**

Freedom of worship *See* Freedom of religion

Freedom on my mind **305.8**

Freedom Singers (Musical group)
Turck, M. Freedom song **323.1**

Freedom song. Turck, M. **323.1**

Freedom Summer. Aretha, D. **323.1**

Freedom: the story of my second life. Oufkir, M.
92

Freefall. Anhalt, A. **Fic**

Freefall. Scott, M. **Fic**

Freeman, John Henry
About
Berry, B. The ties that bind **920**

Freeman-Cook, Kevin D.
(jt. auth) Freeman-Cook, L. Staphylococcus aureus infections **616.9**

Freeman-Cook, Lisa
Staphylococcus aureus infections **616.9**

Freese, Barbara
Coal: a human history **553.2**

Freeze frame. Macy, S. **796.98**

Freinkel, Susan, 1957-
Plastic **620.1**

Freitas, Donna, 1972-
The possibilities of sainthood **Fic**
This gorgeous game **Fic**

Fremont-Barnes, Gregory
(ed) American Revolutionary War. See American Revolutionary War **973.3**
(ed) The encyclopedia of the French revolutionary and Napoleonic Wars. See The encyclopedia of the French revolutionary and Napoleonic Wars **944.04**

French, Francis
In the shadow of the moon **629.45**

French, Paul *See* Asimov, Isaac, 1920-1992

French, Thomas, 1958-
Zoo story **590.73**

French and Indian War *See* United States—History—1755-1763, French and Indian War

French artists *See* Artists, French

French language
Dictionaries
The Oxford-Hachette French dictionary **443**
Le petit Larousse illustré en couleurs **443**
Study and teaching
Gaden, M. Cracking the SAT. French subject test **440**

French literature
Bio-bibliography
The New Oxford companion to literature in French **840.3**

Dictionaries
The New Oxford companion to literature in French **840.3**
History and criticism
See/See also pages in the following book(s):
Highet, G. The classical tradition **809**

French painting
Bingham, J. Impressionism **759.05**
Bingham, J. Post-Impressionism **759.05**

Frenette, Cynthia
(jt. auth) Blatt, J. The teen girl's gotta-have-it guide to money **332.024**

The **frenzy**. Block, F. L. **Fic**

Frequently asked questions about teen fatherhood. Worth, R. **306.8**

Fresco painting *See* Mural painting and decoration

Freshwater. Balliett, J. F. **363.6**

Freshwater animals
The new encyclopedia of aquatic life **591.9**
Waldbauer, G. A walk around the pond
595.7

Freshwater ecology
Balliett, J. F. Freshwater **363.6**

Freud, Sigmund, 1856-1939
The basic writings of Sigmund Freud **150.19**
About
Thurschwell, P. Sigmund Freud **150.19**
See/See also pages in the following book(s):
Hellman, H. Great feuds in medicine **610.9**

Frey, James, 1969-
I am number four **Fic**
A million little pieces **92**

Freymann-Weyr, Garret, 1965-
After the moment **Fic**
My heartbeat **Fic**
Stay with me **Fic**

Freyre, Frank Argote- *See* Argote-Freyre, Frank

Frías, Hugo Chávez *See* Chávez Frías, Hugo

Frick, Lisa
(ed) Teenage pregnancy and parenting. See Teenage pregnancy and parenting **306.8**

Frida. Bernier-Grand, C. T. **811**

Friday night lights. Bissinger, H. G. **796.332**

Fridell, Ron, 1943-
Cruzan v. Missouri and the right to die debate
344
Dictatorship **321.9**

Friedberg, Arthur
Paper money of the United States **769.5**

Friedberg, Ira S.
(jt. auth) Friedberg, A. Paper money of the United States **769.5**

Friedenthal, Lora
Religions of Africa **200.9**

Friedman, Aimee, 1979-
The year my sister got lucky **Fic**

Friedman, Cory
About
Patterson, J. Against medical advice [biography of Cory Friedman] **92**

Friendship—Fiction—*Continued*

Miller, M. B. Aimee   **Fic**
Moriarty, J. The year of secret assignments   **Fic**
Morrison, T. Sula   **Fic**
Myers, W. D. Autobiography of my dead brother   **Fic**
Myracle, L. Shine   **Fic**
Nadin, J. Wonderland   **Fic**
Naidoo, B. Burn my heart   **Fic**
Nilsson, P. You & you & you   **Fic**
Nolan, H. Crazy   **Fic**
Oates, J. C. Big Mouth & Ugly Girl   **Fic**
Ockler, S. Twenty boy summer   **Fic**
Padian, M. Jersey tomatoes are the best   **Fic**
Parker, R. B. Chasing the bear   **Fic**
Pearson, M. The miles between   **Fic**
Peck, D. Sprout   **Fic**
Peck, R. Three-quarters dead   **Fic**
Perl, E. S. Vintage Veronica   **Fic**
Potter, R. Exit strategy   **Fic**
Powell, R. Three clams and an oyster   **Fic**
Prose, F. Touch   **Fic**
Rich, S. Elliot Allagash   **Fic**
Sales, L. Mostly good girls   **Fic**
Sanchez, A. Getting it   **Fic**
Sanders, S. L. The Hanging Woods   **Fic**
Schutt, C. All souls   **Fic**
Scott, E. Love you hate you miss you   **Fic**
Scott, K. She's so dead to us   **Fic**
Sloan, B. A tale of two summers   **Fic**
Smith, A. Ghost medicine   **Fic**
Sonnenblick, J. Notes from the midnight driver   **Fic**
Standiford, N. How to say goodbye in Robot   **Fic**
Stein, T. High dive   **Fic**
Stratton, A. Borderline   **Fic**
Tahmaseb, C. The geek girl's guide to cheerleading   **Fic**
Trueman, T. 7 days at the hot corner   **Fic**
Tucker, T. Over and under   **Fic**
Tullson, D. Riley Park   **Fic**
Vivian, S. A little friendly advice   **Fic**
Vivian, S. Same difference   **Fic**
Wallace, R. Wrestling Sturbridge   **Fic**
Walters, E. Splat!   **Fic**
Wesselhoeft, C. Adios, nirvana   **Fic**
Who do you think you are?   **S C**
Woods, E. E. Choker   **Fic**
Zevin, G. Memoirs of a teenage amnesiac   **Fic**

See/See also pages in the following book(s):
Sleator, W. Oddballs   **S C**

Graphic novels

Abouet, M. Aya   **741.5**
Crilley, M. Miki Falls, Book One: Spring   **741.5**
Gulledge, L. L. Page by Paige   **741.5**
Pyle, K. C. Katman   **741.5**
Tamaki, M. Skim   **741.5**
Vankin, D. Poseurs   **741.5**
Weinstein, L. Girl stories   **741.5**
Winick, J. Pedro & me   **362.1**

Friesner, Esther M.
Nobody's princess   **Fic**

Sphinx's princess   **Fic**
Threads and flames   **Fic**

Froehner, Melissa Alberti, 1963-
(jt. auth) Palmer, P. Teen esteem   **155.5**

Frogs
   See also Toads
Beltz, E. Frogs: inside their remarkable world   **597.8**
Elliott, L. The frogs and toads of North America   **597.8**

The **frogs** and toads of North America. Elliott, L.   **597.8**

Frolund, Tina
Genrefied classics   **016.8**
(ed) The official YALSA awards guidebook. See The official YALSA awards guidebook   **011.6**

From alchemy to chemistry in picture and story. Greenberg, A.   **540.9**

From Baghdad, with love. Kopelman, J.   **92**

From bonbon to cha-cha   **422.03**

From both sides now   **811.008**

From China to America. O'Keefe, S.   **92**

From conception to birth. Tsiaras, A.   **618.3**

From high school to work. See 150 great tech prep careers   **331.7**

From Hinton to Hamlet. Herz, S. K.   **809**

From Lucy to language. Johanson, D. C.   **599.93**

From many cultures, one history [series]
Worth, R. Puerto Rico in American history   **972.95**

From romance to realism. See Cart, M. Young adult literature: from romance to realism   **028.5**

From school to a career. Jell, J. R.   **378**

From slavery to freedom. Franklin, J. H.   **305.8**

From the country of eight islands   **895.6**

From the heart   **970.004**

From totems to hip-hop   **811.008**

From Watergate to Monicagate. Foerstel, H. N.   **070.4**

Frome, Keith W., 1960-
(ed) The Columbia book of Civil War poetry. See The Columbia book of Civil War poetry   **811.008**

Fromm, Erich, 1900-1980
The art of loving   **152.4**
Escape from freedom   **323.44**

Frontier and pioneer life
Pendergast, T. Westward expansion: biographies   **920**
Zochert, D. Laura: the life of Laura Ingalls Wilder   **92**

Fiction

Cather, W. My Antonia   **Fic**
Cather, W. O pioneers!   **Fic**
Cooper, J. F. The Leatherstocking tales   **Fic**
Durham, D. A. Gabriel's story   **Fic**
Larson, K. Hattie Big Sky   **Fic**
McKernan, V. The devil's paintbox   **Fic**

Geography, Ancient *See* Ancient geography

Geography Club. Hartinger, B.   **Fic**

Geography of extreme environments [series]
    Gritzner, C. F. Deserts   **577.5**
    Gritzner, C. F. Polar regions   **577.5**

The **geography** of girlhood. Smith, K.   **Fic**

Geology
> *See also* Astrogeology; Catastrophes (Geology)

    Lambert, D. The field guide to geology   **551**

North America
    Collier, M. Over the coasts   **551.4**
    Collier, M. Over the mountains   **557**
    Collier, M. Over the rivers   **551.48**

Geology, Stratigraphic *See* Stratigraphic geology

Geology, Urban *See* Urban geology

Geometry
    Gorini, C. A. The Facts on File geometry handbook   **516**
    Livio, M. The golden ratio   **516.2**
    Mlodinow, L. Euclid's window   **516**
    Tabak, J. Beyond geometry   **516**
    Tabak, J. Geometry   **516**

George, Charles, 1949-
    Climate change research   **551.6**

George, Denise
    (jt. auth) Bannister, N. The secret Holocaust diaries   **92**

George, Henry, 1839-1897
See/See also pages in the following book(s):
    Heilbroner, R. L. The worldly philosophers   **330.1**

George, Linda
    (jt. auth) George, C. Climate change research   **551.6**

George, Madeleine
    Looks   **Fic**

George, Mary W., 1948-
    The elements of library research   **025.5**

George, Rose, 1969-
    The big necessity   **363.7**

George-Warren, Holly
    (ed) The Rolling Stone illustrated history of rock & roll. See The Rolling Stone illustrated history of rock & roll   **781.66**

Georgia

Fiction
    Burns, O. A. Cold Sassy tree   **Fic**
    Harazin, S. A. Blood brothers   **Fic**
    McCullers, C. The member of the wedding   **Fic**

Social life and customs
    Carter, J. An hour before daylight   **92**

The **Georgian** star [biography of William and Caroline Herschel] Lemonick, M. D.   **92**

Geras, Adèle
    Troy   **Fic**

Gerdes, Louise
    9/11   **973.931**
    (ed) Cloning. See Cloning [Introducing issues with opposing viewpoints series]   **176**

    (ed) Endangered oceans: opposing viewpoints. See Endangered oceans: opposing viewpoints   **333.95**
    (ed) The environment: opposing viewpoints. See The environment: opposing viewpoints   **363.7**
    (ed) Gun violence: opposing viewpoints. See Gun violence: opposing viewpoints   **364.2**
    (ed) Performance enhancing drugs. See Performance enhancing drugs   **362.29**
    (ed) Police brutality. See Police brutality   **363.2**
    (ed) Political campaigns: opposing viewpoints. See Political campaigns: opposing viewpoints   **324.7**
    (ed) Pollution: opposing viewpoints. See Pollution: opposing viewpoints   **363.7**
    (ed) Sexual violence: opposing viewpoints. See Sexual violence: opposing viewpoints   **364.1**
    (ed) War: opposing viewpoints. See War: opposing viewpoints   **355**

Gerding, Stephanie K.
    (jt. auth) MacKellar, P. H. Winning grants   **025.1**

Gerges, Fawaz A.
    Journey of the Jihadist   **322.4**

Gerhardt, H. Carl, 1945-
    (jt. auth) Elliott, L. The frogs and toads of North America   **597.8**

Geringer, Laura *See* Bass, L. G.

Germ theory of disease
    Bakalar, N. Where the germs are   **616**

Germ warfare *See* Biological warfare

German Americans
    Bailey, J. The lost German slave girl [biography of Salomé Muller]   **92**
    Bausum, A. Unraveling freedom   **940.3**

German Democratic Republic *See* Germany (East)

German language
Dictionaries
    Random House Webster's German-English, English-German dictionary   **433**

German literature
Bio-bibliography
    Garland, H. B. The Oxford companion to German literature   **830.3**
Dictionaries
    Garland, H. B. The Oxford companion to German literature   **830.3**
History and criticism
    The Cambridge history of German literature   **830.9**

Germans
Israel—Fiction
    Kass, P. Real time   **Fic**
    Pressler, M. Let sleeping dogs lie   **Fic**

Germany
Civilization
    Bernstein, E. Culture and customs of Germany   **943.087**
Fiction
    Bass, K. Summer of fire   **Fic**

The **Gnostic** Bible   299

Gnosticism
   The Gnostic Bible   299

Go ask Ogre. Siana, J.   92

Go tell it on the mountain. Baldwin, J.   Fic

Goblins
       Fiction
   Hamilton, K. R. Tyger tyger   Fic

God
   See/See also pages in the following book(s):
   Sagan, C. Broca's brain   500

God is in the pancakes. Epstein, R.   Fic

The **god** machine. Chiles, J. R.   629.133

The **god** of small things. Roy, A.   Fic

Godbersen, Anna
   The luxe   Fic

Goddard, Jolyon
   (ed) Concise history of science & invention. See
   Concise history of science & invention
                509

Goddesses *See* Gods and goddesses

Godless. Hautman, P.   Fic

Godrej, Dinyar, 1965-
   (ed) Fire in the soul. See Fire in the soul
                808.81

Gods and goddesses
     See also Religions names of individual
   gods and goddesses
   Patel, S. The little book of Hindu deities
                704.9
   See/See also pages in the following book(s):
   Hamilton, E. Mythology   292
        Fiction
   Halam, A. Snakehead   Fic

God's demon. Barlowe, W. D.   Fic

God's fool: the life and times of Francis of Assisi.
   Green, J.   92

Gods, graves, and scholars. Ceram, C. W.
                930.1

Goethals, George R.
   (ed) Encyclopedia of leadership. See Encyclopedia of leadership   658.4

Goetzmann, William H., 1930-2010
   The atlas of North American exploration
                911

Gogh, Vincent van, 1853-1890
       About
   Schaffner, I. The essential Vincent van Gogh
                759.9492

Going, K. L.
   Fat kid rules the world   Fic
   King of the screwups   Fic
   Saint Iggy   Fic

Going after Cacciato. O'Brien, T.   Fic

Going blue. Kaye, C. B.   333.91

Going bovine. Bray, L.   Fic

Going live. Seib, P. M.   070.1

Gola, Mark
   Winning softball for girls   796.357

Golan, Oded
       About
   Burleigh, N. Unholy business   933

Golay, Michael, 1951-
   Spanish-American war   973.8
   (jt. auth) Fargnoli, A. N. Critical companion to
   William Faulkner   813.009

Gold, Alison Leslie
   (jt. auth) Gies, M. Anne Frank remembered
                940.53

Gold, Rozanne
   Eat fresh food   641.5

Gold in the water. Mullen, P. H., Jr.   797.2

Gold mines and mining
       Fiction
   Golden, C. The wild   Fic
     Graphic novels
   Sturm, J. James Sturm's America   741.5

Gold rush *See* California—Gold discoveries

Goldberg, Harold J.
   (ed) Competing voices from World War II in
   Europe. See Competing voices from World
   War II in Europe   940.53

Goldberg, Jan
   Careers for scientific types & others with inquiring minds   502

Goldberg, Myla
   Bee season   Fic

Goldberg, Vicki
   The power of photography   770

Goldberg-Tal, Havah *See* Tal, Eve, 1947-

Goldblatt, Howard, 1939-
   (ed) Chairman Mao would not be amused. See
   Chairman Mao would not be amused   S C

Goldblatt, Stacey
   Girl to the core   Fic

Golden, Arthur
   Memoirs of a geisha   Fic

Golden, Christopher
   The wild   Fic
   (jt. auth) Wagner, H. Prince of stories
                823.009

Golden, Robert N., 1953-
   The truth about alcohol. See The truth about alcohol   362.292
   (ed) The truth about anxiety and depression. See
   The truth about anxiety and depression
                616.85
   (ed) The truth about eating disorders. See The
   truth about eating disorders   616.85
   (ed) The truth about family life. See The truth
   about family life   306.8
   (ed) The truth about rape. See The truth about
   rape   362.883
   (ed) The truth about sexual behavior and unplanned pregnancy. See The truth about sexual behavior and unplanned pregnancy
                306.7

The **golden** age. Dick, R.   629.13

The **golden** compass. Pullman, P.   Fic

Golden Fleece (Greek mythology) *See* Argonauts
   (Greek mythology)

The **golden** ratio. Livio, M.   516.2

A **golden** web. Quick, B.   **Fic**

Goldensohn, Lorrie
(ed) American war poetry. See American war poetry   **811.008**

Goldhagen, Daniel
Hitler's willing executioners   **940.53**

Golding, Claire Mowbray
(jt. auth) Choiniere, J. What's that bird?   **598**

Golding, Julia
Dragonfly   **Fic**

Golding, William, 1911-1993
Lord of the flies   **Fic**
About
William Golding's Lord of the flies [critical essays]   **823.009**

Goldman, Arthur Steven, 1964- *See* Goldman, Steven, 1964-

Goldman, Emma, 1869-1940
See/See also pages in the following book(s):
Bausum, A. Denied, detained, deported   **325.73**

Goldman, Steven, 1964-
Two parties, one tux, and a very short film about the Grapes of Wrath   **Fic**

Goldschmidt, Arthur, 1938-
A brief history of Egypt   **962**

Goldsmith, Connie, 1945-
Battling malaria   **616.9**
Hepatitis   **616.3**
Influenza   **616.2**
Influenza: the next pandemic?   **614.5**
Invisible invaders   **614.4**
Skin cancer   **616.99**
Superbugs strike back   **615**

Goldsmith, Francisca
Graphic novels now   **025.2**
The readers' advisory guide to graphic novels   **025.2**

Goldstein, Donald M.
The way it was   **940.54**

Goldstein, Jayme Adelson- *See* Adelson-Goldstein, Jayme

Goldstein, Mark A., 1947-
Boys into men   **613**
(jt. auth) Goldstein, M. C. Controversies in food and nutrition   **641.3**

Goldstein, Myrna Chandler, 1948-
Controversies in food and nutrition   **641.3**
(jt. auth) Goldstein, M. A. Boys into men   **613**

Goldstein, Nancy, 1961-
Jackie Ormes   **92**

Goldstein, Natalie
Globalization and free trade   **382**
Parkinson's disease   **616.8**

Goldstein, Warren Jay
(jt. auth) Lewin, W. H. G. For the love of physics   **92**

Goldsworthy, Anna, 1974-
Piano lessons   **92**

Goleman, Daniel
Emotional intelligence   **152.4**

Social intelligence   **158**

Golf
Echikson, W. Shooting for Tiger   **796.352**
St. Pierre, D. Golf fundamentals   **796.352**
Fiction
Luper, E. Seth Baumgartner's love manifesto   **Fic**
Lynch, C. The Big Game of Everything   **Fic**

Golf fundamentals. St. Pierre, D.   **796.352**

Golgi, Camillo, 1843-1926
About
Rapport, R. Nerve endings   **612.8**
See/See also pages in the following book(s):
Hellman, H. Great feuds in medicine   **610.9**

Goloboy, Jennifer L.
(ed) Industrial revolution. See Industrial revolution   **330.9**

Golus, Carrie
Tupac Shakur   **92**

Golway, Terry, 1955-
(jt. auth) Dallek, R. Let every nation know [biography of John F. Kennedy]   **92**
(ed) Fellow citizens. See Fellow citizens   **352.23**
(comp) Words that ring through time. See Words that ring through time   **808.85**

Gombrich, E. H. (Ernst Hans), 1909-2001
The story of art   **709**

Gombrich, Ernst Hans *See* Gombrich, E. H. (Ernst Hans), 1909-2001

Gonick, Larry
The cartoon history of the modern world [part 1]   **909.08**

Gonsher, Debra
The community college guide   **378.1**

Gonzalez, Henry B., 1916-2000
See/See also pages in the following book(s):
Profiles in courage for our time   **920**

Gonzalez, Juan
Harvest of empire   **305.8**

Gonzalez, Julie, 1958-
Imaginary enemy   **Fic**

González, Rigoberto, 1970-
Butterfly boy   **92**

Good and evil
Adler, M. J. Six great ideas   **111**
Fiction
Brooks, T. Armageddon's children   **Fic**
Cann, K. Possessed   **Fic**
Chadda, S. The devil's kiss   **Fic**
Jinks, C. Evil genius   **Fic**
Kizer, A. Meridian   **Fic**
Lecesne, J. Absolute brightness   **Fic**
MacCullough, C. Once a witch   **Fic**
Stevenson, R. L. The strange case of Dr. Jekyll and Mr. Hyde   **Fic**
Zink, M. Prophecy of the sisters   **Fic**

A **good** dog. Katz, J.   **636.7**

The **good** earth. Buck, P. S.   **Fic**

Good enough. Yoo, P.   **Fic**

The **good** girl's guide to getting kidnapped. Murray, Y. M.   **Fic**

The **good** good pig. Montgomery, S.   **636.4**

Grandin, Temple
Animals in translation   **591.5**
Grandits, John, 1949-
Blue lipstick   **811**
Grandmothers
Fiction
Cornwell, A. Carpe diem   **Fic**
Davis, T. S. Mare's war   **Fic**
Larbalestier, J. Magic or madness   **Fic**
Salter, S. Swoon at your own risk   **Fic**
Standiford, N. Confessions of the Sullivan sisters   **Fic**
Yolen, J. Briar Rose   **Fic**
Graphic novels
Heuvel, E. A family secret   **741.5**
Grandparents
Fiction
Ehrenberg, P. Ethan, suspended   **Fic**
McDonnell, M. Torn to pieces   **Fic**
Meyerhoff, J. Queen of secrets   **Fic**
Grandpré, Mary, 1954-
(il) Rowling, J. K. Harry Potter and the Sorcerer's Stone   **Fic**
Grange, Michael
Basketball's greatest stars   **920**
Grant, Christopher
Teenie   **Fic**
Grant, Edward, 1926-
Science and religion, 400 B.C. to A.D. 1550   **261.5**
Grant, Gordon
Canoeing   **797.1**
Grant, John, 1949-
Corrupted science   **500**
Grant, K. M.
Blue flame   **Fic**
Grant, Katie See Grant, K. M.
Grant, Mark
Roman cookery   **641.5**
Grant, Michael, 1914-2004
Greek and Latin authors, 800 B.C.-A.D. 1000   **920.003**
Grant, R. G. (Reg G.)
Commanders   **355**
Flight: 100 years of aviation   **629.13**
Grant, Reg, 1954-
Slavery   **326**
Grant, Reg G. See Grant, R. G. (Reg G.)
Grant, Ulysses S. (Ulysses Simpson), 1822-1885
About
Crompton, S. Ulysses S. Grant   **92**
Rice, E. Ulysses S. Grant: defender of the Union   **92**
See/See also pages in the following book(s):
McPherson, J. M. Drawn with the sword   **973.7**
Grants for libraries. See MacKellar, P. H. Winning grants   **025.1**
Grants-in-aid
MacKellar, P. H. Winning grants   **025.1**
Grapes, Bryan J.
(ed) 1980-2000: the twentieth century. See 1980-2000: the twentieth century   **909.82**

The **grapes** of wrath. Steinbeck, J.   **Fic**
The **grapes** of wrath and other writings, 1936-1941. Steinbeck, J.   **818**
Graphic arts
Bancroft, T. Creating characters with personality   **741.6**
Graphic Classics volume eight: Mark Twain   **741.5**
Graphic Classics volume eleven: O. Henry   **741.5**
Graphic Classics volume fifteen: Fantasy classics   **741.5**
Graphic Classics volume four: H. P. Lovecraft   **741.5**
Graphic Classics volume fourteen: Gothic classics   **741.5**
Graphic Classics volume seven: Bram Stoker   **741.5**
Graphic fiction See Graphic novels
Graphic novels
See also Adventure graphic novels; Autobiographical graphic novels; Biographical graphic novels; Fantasy graphic novels; Horror graphic novels; Humorous graphic novels; Manga; Mystery graphic novels; Romance graphic novels; Science fiction graphic novels; Superhero graphic novels; Supernatural graphic novels
Abadzis, N. Laika   **741.5**
Abouet, M. Aya   **741.5**
Allen, B. A. A home for Mr. Easter   **741.5**
Anderson, H. C. King   **92**
Appignanesi, R. Hamlet   **822.3**
Appignanesi, R. Julius Caesar   **822.3**
Appignanesi, R. A midsummer night's dream   **822.3**
Appignanesi, R. Romeo and Juliet   **822.3**
Appignanesi, R. The tempest   **822.3**
Ashihara, H. Sand chronicles vol. 1   **741.5**
Azuma, K. Azumanga Daioh omnibus   **741.5**
B., David. Epileptic   **616.8**
Bailey, N. Female force   **920**
Baker, K. Nat Turner   **92**
Black, H. The Good Neighbors; book one: Kin   **741.5**
Bogaert, H. M. v. d. Journey into Mohawk Country   **973.2**
Brosgol, V. Anya's ghost   **741.5**
Campbell, R. Shadoweyes   **741.5**
Cherrywell, S. Pepper Penwell and the land creature of Monster Lake   **741.5**
Chmakova, S. Nightschool: the weirn books, volume one   **741.5**
Cobley, J. Frankenstein   **741.5**
Cover, A. B. Macbeth   **822.3**
Crilley, M. Brody's ghost: book 1   **741.5**
Crilley, M. Miki Falls, Book One: Spring   **741.5**
Delisle, G. Pyongyang: a journey in North Korea   **951.93**
Dorkin, E. Beasts of Burden: animal rites   **741.5**
Drooker, E. Blood song   **741.5**
Dunning, J. H. Salem Brownstone   **741.5**
Evanovich, J. Troublemaker   **741.5**

Graves, Lucia
  (tr) Ruiz Zafón, C. The Prince of Mist   **Fic**
Graves, Mark A., 1963-
  (ed) Encyclopedia of American war literature.
  See Encyclopedia of American war literature
     810.9
Graves, Robert, 1895-1985
  The Greek myths   **292**
  I, Claudius   **Fic**
The graveyard book. Gaiman, N.   **Fic**
Graveyards *See* Cemeteries
Graveyards of the Pacific. Ballard, R. D.
     940.54
Gravitation
  Manning, P. Gravity   **531**
  See/See also pages in the following book(s):
  Feynman, R. P. Six easy pieces   **530**
Gravity
  Darling, D. J. Gravity's arc   **531**
  Manning, P. Gravity   **531**
Gravity's arc. Darling, D. J.   **531**
Gray, Claudia
  Evernight   **Fic**
Gray, Edward G., 1964-
  Colonial America   **973.2**
Gray, Elisha, 1835-1901
  About
  Shulman, S. The telephone gambit   **621.3**
Gray, Farrah
  Reallionaire   **332.024**
Gray, Jeffrey
  (ed) The Greenwood encyclopedia of American
  poets and poetry. See The Greenwood ency-
  clopedia of American poets and poetry
     811.009
Gray, Keith
  Ostrich boys   **Fic**
Gray, Theodore W.
  The elements   **546**
Gray baby. Sanders, S. L.   **Fic**
Gray matter [series]
  Bangalore, L. Brain development   **612.8**
  Hains, B. C. Pain   **616**
  Hudmon, A. Learning and memory   **153.1**
  May, M. Sensation and perception   **612.8**
  Morgan, M. The midbrain   **612.8**
  Phillips, S. F. The teen brain   **612.8**
  Rosen, M. Meditation and hypnosis   **154.7**
  West, K. Biofeedback   **615.8**
Graydon, Shari
  In your face   **391**
Gray's anatomy   **611**
Grayson, Gabriel
  Talking with your hands, listening with your
  eyes   **419**
Grealy, Lucy, 1963-2002
  About
  Patchett, A. Truth & beauty [biography of Lucy
  Grealy]   **92**
Greasy rider. Melville, G.   **333.72**
Great achievers [series]
  Lyons, M. E. Sorrow's kitchen   **92**

The **great** adventure: Theodore Roosevelt and the
  rise of modern America. Marrin, A.   **92**
The **great** age of Greek literature. See Hamilton,
  E. The Greek way   **880.9**
The **great** American history fact-finder.
  Cornelison, P.   **973.03**
A **great** and sublime fool [biography of Mark
  Twain] Caravantes, P.   **92**
A **great** and terrible beauty. Bray, L.   **Fic**
Great athletes   **920.003**
Great-aunts *See* Aunts
Great books of the Western world
  Adler, M. J. How to think about the great ideas
     080
Great Britain
  Antiquities
  Burl, A. The stone circles of Britain, Ireland and
  Brittany   **936.1**
  Civilization
  Backgrounds to English literature   **820.9**
  Mitchell, S. Daily life in Victorian England
     941.081
  See/See also pages in the following book(s):
  Emerson, R. W. The portable Emerson   **818**
  Colonies
  James, L. The rise and fall of the British Empire
     909
  Colonies—America
  See/See also pages in the following book(s):
  Tuchman, B. W. The march of folly   **909.08**
  Description and travel
  Raymo, C. Walking zero   **526**
  Fiction
  Almond, D. Kit's wilderness   **Fic**
  Almond, D. Raven summer   **Fic**
  Archer, E. Geek: fantasy novel   **Fic**
  Austen, J. Persuasion   **Fic**
  Austen, J. Pride and prejudice   **Fic**
  Austen, J. Sense and sensibility   **Fic**
  Bedford, M. Flip   **Fic**
  Bowler, T. Blade: playing dead   **Fic**
  Bradley, A. The sweetness at the bottom of the
  pie   **Fic**
  Bray, L. A great and terrible beauty   **Fic**
  Briant, E. Choppy socky blues   **Fic**
  Brontë, C. Jane Eyre   **Fic**
  Brontë, E. Wuthering Heights   **Fic**
  Brooks, K. Kissing the rain   **Fic**
  Brooks, K. Lucas   **Fic**
  Brooks, K. The road of the dead   **Fic**
  Burgess, M. Nicholas Dane   **Fic**
  Burgess, M. Smack   **Fic**
  Cann, K. Possessed   **Fic**
  Dickens, C. David Copperfield   **Fic**
  Dickens, C. Great expectations   **Fic**
  Dickens, C. Oliver Twist   **Fic**
  Dogar, S. Waves   **Fic**
  Dowd, S. Solace of the road   **Fic**
  Doyle, Sir A. C. The hound of the Baskervilles
     Fic
  Dunkle, C. B. The house of dead maids   **Fic**
  Ellis, D. No safe place   **Fic**
  Gray, K. Ostrich boys   **Fic**
  Haddon, M. The curious incident of the dog in
  the night-time   **Fic**

Great Britain—Fiction—*Continued*

Hardy, T. The return of the native	**Fic**
Hardy, T. Tess of the D'Urbervilles	**Fic**
The improbable adventures of Sherlock Holmes	**S C**
King, L. R. The beekeeper's apprentice, or, on the segregation of the queen	**Fic**
Lloyd, S. The carbon diaries 2015	**Fic**
Malley, G. The Declaration	**Fic**
Manning, S. Guitar girl	**Fic**
McGowan, A. The knife that killed me	**Fic**
Minchin, A. The beat goes on	**Fic**
Mitchell, D. Black swan green	**Fic**
Moloney, J. Black taxi	**Fic**
Morpurgo, M. Private Peaceful	**Fic**
Mussi, S. The door of no return	**Fic**
Nadin, J. Wonderland	**Fic**
Paton Walsh, J. A parcel of patterns	**Fic**
Rennison, L. Angus, thongs and full-frontal snogging	**Fic**
Stevenson, R. L. The strange case of Dr. Jekyll and Mr. Hyde	**Fic**
Wilde, O. The picture of Dorian Gray	**Fic**
Winspear, J. Maisie Dobbs	**Fic**
Wood, M. The poison diaries	**Fic**
Woolf, V. To the lighthouse	**Fic**

History

Burns, W. E. A brief history of Great Britain	**941**
Events that changed Great Britain, from 1066 to 1714	**941**
Events that changed Great Britain since 1689	**941**
The Oxford illustrated history of Britain	**941**
Saccio, P. Shakespeare's English kings	**822.3**

History—0-1066

Ashe, G. The discovery of King Arthur	**92**
Lacey, R. The year 1000	**942.01**

History—0-1066—Fiction

Bradley, M. Z. The mists of Avalon	**Fic**
Jones, A. F. Warrior princess	**Fic**
McKenzie, N. Grail prince	**Fic**
McKenzie, N. Guinevere's gift	**Fic**
Moran, K. Bloodline	**Fic**
Reeve, P. Here lies Arthur	**Fic**
Sandell, L. A. Song of the sparrow	**Fic**
Scott, A. Dreaming the eagle	**Fic**
Spinner, S. Damosel	**Fic**
Springer, N. I am Mordred	**Fic**
Springer, N. I am Morgan le Fay	**Fic**
Stewart, M. Mary Stewart's Merlin trilogy	**Fic**
Sutcliff, R. The Shining Company	**Fic**
Vande Velde, V. The book of Mordred	**Fic**
White, T. H. The once and future king	**Fic**

History—1066-1154, Norman period

See also Hastings (East Sussex, England), Battle of, 1066

Howarth, D. A. 1066: the year of the conquest	**942.02**

History—1066-1154, Norman period—Fiction

Cadnum, M. The king's arrow	**Fic**
Carey, J. L. Dragon's Keep	**Fic**
Whitman, E. Wildwing	**Fic**

History—1154-1399, Plantagenets

Forgeng, J. L. Daily life in Chaucer's England	**942.03**
Sapet, K. Eleanor of Aquitaine	**92**

History—1154-1399, Plantagenets—Fiction

Coventry, S. The queen's daughter	**Fic**

History—1154-1399, Plantagenets—Graphic novels

Lee, T. Outlaw: the legend of Robin Hood	**741.5**

History—1455-1485, War of the Roses

Weir, A. The Wars of the Roses	**942.04**

History—1485-1603, Tudors

Elizabeth, Queen of England. Elizabeth I	**92**
Elizabethan world reference library	**942.05**
Forgeng, J. L. Daily life in Elizabethan England	**942.05**
Starkey, D. Six wives: the queens of Henry VIII	**920**

History—1485-1603, Tudors—Drama

Bolt, R. A man for all seasons	**822**

History—1485-1603, Tudors—Fiction

Cadnum, M. Peril on the sea	**Fic**
Crowley, S. The stolen one	**Fic**
Guibord, M. Warped	**Fic**
Klein, L. M. Cate of the Lost Colony	**Fic**
Kolosov, J. A. A sweet disorder	**Fic**
Lawlor, L. The two loves of Will Shakespeare	**Fic**
Libby, A. M. The king's rose	**Fic**
Rees, C. The fool's girl	**Fic**
Silbert, L. The intelligencer	**Fic**
Thompson, R. City of cannibals	**Fic**
Turnbull, A. No shame, no fear	**Fic**

History—1603-1714, Stuarts

Aronson, M. John Winthrop, Oliver Cromwell, and the Land of Promise [dual biography of John Winthrop and Oliver Cromwell]	**92**

History—1603-1714, Stuarts—Fiction

Hooper, M. Newes from the dead	**Fic**

History—1642-1660, Civil War and Commonwealth—Fiction

Hearn, J. The minister's daughter	**Fic**

History—1688, Revolution

Trevelyan, G. M. The English Revolution, 1688-1689	**942.06**

History—1714-1837

Bober, N. Countdown to independence	**973.3**

History—1714-1837—Fiction

Harrison, C. I was Jane Austen's best friend	**Fic**
Rees, C. Sovay	**Fic**

History—19th century

See also Industrial revolution

Denlinger, E. C. Before Victoria	**920**
Mitchell, S. Daily life in Victorian England	**941.081**

History—19th century—Fiction

Baratz-Logsted, L. Twin's daughter	**Fic**
Eagland, J. Wildthorn	**Fic**
Grahame-Smith, S. Pride and prejudice and zombies	**Fic**
Hearn, J. Ivy	**Fic**
Hooper, M. Fallen Grace	**Fic**
Jocelyn, M. Folly	**Fic**
Lee, Y. S. A spy in the house	**Fic**

Great Britain—History—19th century—History—19th century—Fiction—*Continued*

MacColl, M. Prisoners in the palace   **Fic**

Peacock, S. Eye of the crow   **Fic**

Slade, A. G. The hunchback assignments

    Fic

Updale, E. Montmorency   **Fic**

Kings and rulers

Ashe, G. The discovery of King Arthur   **92**

Elizabeth, Queen of England. Elizabeth I   **92**

The Lives of the kings & queens of England

    941

Saccio, P. Shakespeare's English kings

    822.3

Politics and government—20th century

Rubin, G. C. Forty ways to look at Winston Churchill   **92**

Prime ministers

See Prime ministers—Great Britain

Social life and customs

Pool, D. What Jane Austen ate and Charles Dickens knew   **820.9**

Great Britain. Navy *See* Great Britain. Royal Navy

Great Britain. Royal Navy

Czisnik, M. Horatio Nelson   **92**

The **great** Chicago fire. Owens, L. L.   **977.3**

The **great** circle. Philip, N.   **970.004**

Great comets. Burnham, R.   **523.6**

The **great** crash, 1929. Galbraith, J. K.   **338.5**

Great debates at the United Nations. Gorman, R. F.   **341.23**

Great Depression, 1929-1939

Blumenthal, K. Six days in October   **330.9**

Burg, D. F. The Great Depression   **973.91**

Galbraith, J. K. The great crash, 1929   **338.5**

The Great Depression and World War II, 1929 to 1949   **973.91**

Marrin, A. Years of dust   **978**

McElvaine, R. S. The Depression and New Deal   **973.91**

Terkel, S. Hard times   **973.91**

Watkins, T. H. The hungry years   **973.91**

See/See also pages in the following book(s):

Lifetimes: the Great War to the stock market crash: American history through biography and primary documents   **920**

Encyclopedias

Encyclopedia of the Great Depression

    973.91

Fiction

Kennedy, W. Ironweed   **Fic**

The **Great** Depression and World War II, 1929 to 1949   **973.91**

The **great** dinosaur discoveries. Naish, D.

    567.9

Great discoveries [series]

Krauss, L. M. Quantum man   **92**

Lemonick, M. D. The Georgian star   **92**

Quammen, D. The reluctant Mr. Darwin   **92**

Reeves, R. A force of nature   **92**

Great displays for your library step by step. Phillips, S. P.   **021.7**

Great empires of the past [series]

Skelton, D. Empire of Alexander the Great

    938

The **great** equations. Crease, R. P.   **509**

Great events from history, The 17th century, 1601-1700   **909**

Great events from history, The 18th century, 1701-1800   **909.7**

Great events from history, The 19th century, 1801-1900   **909.81**

Great events from history: The 20th century, 1901-1940   **909.82**

Great events from history: The 20th century, 1941-1970   **909.82**

Great events from history: The 20th century, 1971-2000   **909.82**

Great events from history, The ancient world, prehistory-476 C.E.   **930**

Great events from history, The Middle Ages, 477-1453   **909.07**

Great events from history, The Renaissance & early modern era, 1454-1600   **909**

Great expectations. Dickens, C.   **Fic**

Great expectations, by Charles Dickens

    823.009

Great feuds in history. Evans, C.   **909**

Great feuds in medicine. Hellman, H.   **610.9**

The **great** fire. Murphy, J.   **977.3**

The **great** Gatsby. Fitzgerald, F. S.   **Fic**

The **great** Gatsby, by F. Scott Fitzgerald

    813.009

Great generals series

Frank, R. B. MacArthur   **92**

Remini, R. V. Andrew Jackson   **92**

Woodworth, S. E. Sherman   **92**

Great Hispanic heritage [series]

Hasday, J. L. Ellen Ochoa   **92**

Sterngass, J. José Martí   **92**

Great horned owl *See* Owls

Great interpersonal skills. Sommers, M. A.

    650.1

Great inventions [series]

Finkelstein, N. H. Plastics   **620.1**

Great lives from history, The 17th century, 1601-1700   **920.003**

Great lives from history, The 18th century, 1701-1800   **920.003**

Great lives from history, The 19th century, 1801-1900   **920.003**

Great lives from history: the 20th century, 1901-2000   **920.003**

Great lives from history, The ancient world, prehistory-476 C.E   **920.003**

Great lives from history, the Middle Ages, 477-1453   **920.003**

Great lives from history, the Renaissance & early modern era, 1454-1600   **920.003**

Great medical discoveries   **610.9**

Great migrations. Kostyal, K. M.   **591.56**

Green, Thomas A., 1944-
(ed) The Greenwood library of world folktales.
See The Greenwood library of world folktales
398.2

Green, William Scott
(ed) The HarperCollins dictionary of religion.
See The HarperCollins dictionary of religion
200.3

Green Belt Movement (Kenya)
Maathai, W. Unbowed **92**

Green careers. Power Scott, J. **333.72**

Green careers for dummies. McClelland, C. L.
363.7

Green chemistry *See* Environmental chemistry

Green inheritance. Huxley, A. J. **580**

Green planet. Rice, S. A. **581.7**

Green technology [series]
Maczulak, A. E. Cleaning up the environment
628.5
Maczulak, A. E. Waste treatment **628.4**

Green world [series]
Raven, C. Forestry **634.9**

Greenberg, Arthur
From alchemy to chemistry in picture and story
540.9

Greenberg, Brian
Social history of the United States. See Social
history of the United States **306**

Greenberg, Jan, 1942-
Andy Warhol **92**
Runaway girl: the artist Louise Bourgeois
92
(ed) Heart to heart. See Heart to heart
811.008
(ed) Side by side. See Side by side **808.81**

Greenberg, Joanne, 1932-
I never promised you a rose garden **Fic**

Greenberg, Keith Elliot, 1959-
Pro wrestling **796.8**

Greenblatt, Miriam
War of 1812 **973.5**

Greenblatt, Stephen J. (Stephen Jay)
(ed) Shakespeare, W. The Norton Shakespeare
822.3

Greene, Graham, 1904-1991
The heart of the matter **Fic**
The power and the glory **Fic**

Greene, Jack
(ed) World War II: a student encyclopedia. See
World War II: a student encyclopedia
940.53

Greene, Joshua M.
(ed) Witness. See Witness **940.53**

Greene, Meg
Jane Goodall **92**

Greene, Nathanael, 1742-1786
About
Carbone, G. M. Nathanael Greene **92**

Greener grass. Pignat, C. **Fic**

Greenhaven encyclopedia of [series]
Netzley, P. D. Civil War **973.7**

Netzley, P. D. The Greenhaven encyclopedia of
ancient Egypt **932**
Netzley, P. D. The Greenhaven encyclopedia of
terrorism **363.32**
Streissguth, T. The Renaissance **940.2**

The **Greenhaven** encyclopedia of ancient Egypt.
Netzley, P. D. **932**

The **Greenhaven** encyclopedia of terrorism.
Netzley, P. D. **363.32**

The **Greenhaven** encyclopedia of the Renaissance.
See Streissguth, T. The Renaissance **940.2**

Greenhouse effect
Alley, R. B. Earth **621**
Black, B. Global warming **363.7**
Braasch, G. Earth under fire **363.7**
Casper, J. K. Changing ecosystems **577.2**
Casper, J. K. Climate systems **551.5**
Casper, J. K. Greenhouse gases **363.7**
Climate change **363.7**
Conserving the environment **363.7**
Ellis, R. On thin ice **599.78**
Flannery, T. F. We are the weather makers
551.6
Gardner, T. Oil **333.8**
Global warming: opposing viewpoints **363.7**
Gore, A. An inconvenient truth **363.7**
Gore, A. Our choice **363.7**
Kolbert, E. Field notes from a catastrophe
363.7
Kusky, T. M. Climate change **551.6**
Lynas, M. High tide **363.7**
McKibben, B. Fight global warming now
363.7
Mooney, C. Storm world **363.7**
Nardo, D. Climate change **551.6**
Pielke, R. A. The climate fix **363.7**
Pollack, H. N. A world without ice **551.3**
Walker, G. The hot topic **363.7**
Fiction
Gould, P. L. Write naked **Fic**
Graphic novels
Evans, K. Weird weather **363.7**

Greenhouse gases. Casper, J. K. **363.7**

Green's dictionary of slang. Green, J. **427**

Greenspan, Alan
See/See also pages in the following book(s):
Bussing-Burks, M. Influential economists
920

The **Greenstone** grail. Hemingway, A. **Fic**

Greenwood, Janette Thomas
(comp) The Gilded Age: a history in documents.
See The Gilded Age: a history in documents
973.8

Greenwood biographies [series]
Bowman-Kruhm, M. The Leakeys **920**
Greene, M. Jane Goodall **92**
Kirk, C. A. J.K. Rowling: a biography **92**
Leach, L. F. Langston Hughes **92**
Tracy, K. Judy Blume **92**

The **Greenwood** companion to Shakespeare
822.3

The **Greenwood** encyclopedia of African American civil rights **305.8**

Greeting cards
Sowell, S. Paper cutting techniques for scrapbooks & cards **745.54**

Gregory, Julie
Sickened **92**

Gregory, Michael G.
The career chronicles **331.7**

Gregory, R. L., 1923-2010
(ed) The Oxford companion to the mind. See The Oxford companion to the mind **128**

Gregory, Richard Langton See Gregory, R. L., 1923-2010

Gregory, Ross
Cold War America, 1946 to 1990 **973.92**
Modern America, 1914 to 1945 **973.91**

Greiner, Tony
Analyzing library collection use with Excel **025.2**

Grendel. Gardner, J. **Fic**

Grendler, Paul F.
(ed) The Renaissance. See The Renaissance **940.2**

Grenon, Jean-Benoit Ormal- See Ormal-Grenon, Jean-Benoit

Gresham, Sir Thomas, 1519?-1579
See/See also pages in the following book(s):
Bussing-Burks, M. Influential economists **920**

Grey, Zane, 1872-1939
Riders of the purple sage **Fic**

Gribbin, John R.
The scientists **509**

Grice, Gordon, 1944-
The red hourglass **591.5**

Grier, Jennifer A.
Inner planets **523.4**

The **grieving** teen. Fitzgerald, H. **155.9**

Griffey, Jason
(jt. auth) Coombs, K. A. Library blogging **006.7**

Griffin, Adele
The Julian game **Fic**
Where I want to be **Fic**

Griffin, Jason
(jt. auth) Reynolds, J. My name is Jason. Mine too **811**

Griffin, John Howard, 1920-1980
Black like me **305.8**

Griffin, Paul, 1966-
The Orange Houses **Fic**

Griffith, Samuel Blair, 1906-1983
(tr) Sun-tzu. The illustrated art of war **355**

Griffiths, Trevor R., 1949-
The Ivan R. Dee guide to plays and playwrights **809.2**

Grimes, Nikki
Bronx masquerade **Fic**
Dark sons **Fic**
A girl named Mister **Fic**

Grimly, Gris
(il) Poe, E. A. Edgar Allan Poe's tales of mystery and madness **S C**

Gringolandia. Miller-Lachmann, L. **Fic**

Grinnell, George Bird, 1849-1938
About
Punke, M. Last stand [biography of George Bird Grinnell] **92**

Grisham, John
The client **Fic**
The firm **Fic**

Griswold del Castillo, Richard
César Chávez **92**

Gritzner, Charles F.
Deserts **577.5**
Latin America **980**
Polar regions **577.5**

Grizzard, Frank E., Jr.
Jamestown Colony **973.2**

The **grizzly** almanac. Busch, R. **599.78**

Grizzly bear
Busch, R. The grizzly almanac **599.78**
Turbak, G. Grizzly bears **599.78**

Grob, Leonard
(jt. auth) Watad, M. Teen voices from the Holy Land **920**

Grob's basic electronics. Schultz, M. E. **621.381**

Grogan, John, 1957-
The longest trip home **92**

Gromacki, Michelle
(jt. auth) Garman, J. Softball skills & drills **796.357**

Gronniosaw, James Albert Ukawsaw
See/See also pages in the following book(s):
Slave narratives [Library of Am.] **326**

Grooming, Personal See Personal grooming

Gross, John J., 1935-2011
(ed) The New Oxford book of literary anecdotes. See The New Oxford book of literary anecdotes **828**

Gross, Melissa
(jt. auth) Dresang, E. T. Dynamic youth services through outcome-based planning and evaluation **025.1**

Gross, Michael, 1963-
Life on the edge **578.4**

Grossberg, Blythe N.
Applying to college for students with ADD or LD **378.1**

Grossman, Elizabeth, 1957-
Chasing molecules **615.9**

Grossman, Lev
The magicians **Fic**

Grossman, Mark
World military leaders **920.003**

Grosvenor, Mary B.
(jt. auth) Smolin, L. A. Basic nutrition **612.3**
(jt. auth) Smolin, L. A. Nutrition and weight management **613.2**
(jt. auth) Smolin, L. A. Nutrition for sports and exercise **613.7**

Groundbreaking scientific experiments, inventions, and discoveries of the 19th century. Windelspecht, M. **509**

Guiley, Rosemary Ellen—*Continued*
The encyclopedia of ghosts and spirits **133.1**
The encyclopedia of vampires & werewolves
398
The encyclopedia of witches, witchcraft, and
Wicca **133.4**
(comp) The Quotable saint. See The Quotable
saint **230**

Guilfoile, Patrick
Antibiotic-resistant bacteria **616.9**
Tetanus **616.9**

Guillen, Michael
Five equations that changed the world **530.1**

Guillermoprieto, Alma, 1949-
Looking for history **972**

Guilt
Fiction
Billingsley, F. Chime **Fic**
Chaltas, T. Because I am furniture **Fic**
Colasanti, S. Something like fate **Fic**
Hoban, J. Willow **Fic**
Kephart, B. Dangerous neighbors **Fic**
Matson, M. Amy & Roger's epic detour **Fic**
Mills, T. Heartbreak river **Fic**
Nelson, B. Paranoid Park **Fic**
Northrop, M. Gentlemen **Fic**
Scott, E. Love you hate you miss you **Fic**
Wynne-Jones, T. Blink & Caution **Fic**
The **guilt** of nations. Barkan, E. **341.6**
A **guinea** pig's history of biology. Endersby, J.
576.5

Guinevere (Legendary character)
Fiction
McKenzie, N. Guinevere's gift **Fic**
Guinevere's gift. McKenzie, N. **Fic**
Guinness book of records. See Guinness world re-
cords **032.02**

Guinness book of world records
Olmstead, L. Getting into Guinness **030**
Guinness book of world records. See Guinness
world records **032.02**
Guinness world records **032.02**
Guitar all-in-one for dummies. Chappell, J.
787.87
Guitar girl. Manning, S. **Fic**
The **guitar** handbook. Denyer, R. **787.87**
Guitars
Bacon, T. The ultimate guitar book **787.87**
Chapman, R. The new complete guitarist
787.87
Chappell, J. Guitar all-in-one for dummies
787.87
Complete guitar course **787.87**
Denyer, R. The guitar handbook **787.87**
Hodge, D. The complete idiot's guide to playing
bass guitar **787.87**

Guite, Malcolm
What do Christians believe? **230**

Gulevich, Tanya
Encyclopedia of Christmas and New Year's celebrations **394.26**

Gulf Stream
Ulanski, S. L. The Gulf Stream **551.46**

The **Gulf** Stream. Ulanski, S. L. **551.46**
Gulf War, 1991 See Persian Gulf War, 1991
Gulledge, Laura Lee
Page by Paige **741.5**
Gulliver's travels. Swift, J. **Fic**
Gullstruck Island. See Hardinge, F. The lost con-
spiracy **Fic**
Gun control
Gun violence: opposing viewpoints **364.2**
Henderson, H. Gun control **363.33**
Is gun ownership a right? **344**
Gun violence: opposing viewpoints **364.2**
Gunn, Angus M., 1920-
A student guide to climate and weather
551.5
Unnatural disasters **304.2**
Gunnerkrigg Court: orientation. Siddell, T.
741.5
Guns, germs, and steel. Diamond, J. M. **303.4**
The **guns** of August. Tuchman, B. W. **940.3**
Gunstories. Atkin, S. B. **363.33**
Gunther, John, 1901-1970
Death be not proud **92**
Gunther, John, 1929-1947
About
Gunther, J. Death be not proud **92**
Gunton, Michael
Life. See Life **578.4**
Gupta, Dipak K.
Who are the terrorists? **363.32**
Gur, Raquel E.
(jt. auth) Snyder, K. Me, myself, and them
92
Guran, Paula
(ed) The year's best dark fantasy & horror. See
The year's best dark fantasy & horror
S C
Gurewitsch, Brana, 1941-
(ed) Mothers, sisters, resisters. See Mothers, sis-
ters, resisters **940.53**
Gurney, A. R., 1930-
Love letters and two other plays: The golden
age and What I did last summer **812**
Gurney, Alan
The race to the white continent **998**
Gurney, Albert Ramsdell *See* Gurney, A. R.,
1930-
Gurstelle, William
Adventures from the technology underground
621.8
Guterson, David
Snow falling on cedars **Fic**
Guthrie, Danille Kathleen Taylor- *See* Taylor-
Guthrie, Danille Kathleen, 1952-
Guthrie, Woody, 1912-1967
About
Kaufman, W. Woody Guthrie, American radical
92
Partridge, E. This land was made for you and
me [biography of Woody Guthrie] **92**
Gutkind, Lee
(ed) In fact. See In fact **814**

Guttmann, Allen
The Olympics, a history of the modern games
796.48

The **guy-friendly** YA library. Welch, R. J.
027.62

Guys write for Guys Read   **810.8**

Gwinnell, Esther
The encyclopedia of drug abuse   **616.86**

Gym candy. Deuker, C.   **Fic**

Gymnastics
McIntosh, J. S. Gymnastics   **796.44**
Fiction
Cohen, J. Leverage   **Fic**

Gynecology See Women—Health and hygiene

Gypsies
Lewy, G. The Nazi persecution of the gypsies
940.53
Fiction
Brooks, K. The road of the dead   **Fic**
Dunlap, S. E. The musician's daughter **Fic**
Gardner, S. The red necklace   **Fic**
Sedgwick, M. My swordhand is singing **Fic**

H

H1N1 influenza See Swine influenza

Haaga, John, 1953-
(ed) The American people. See The American
people   **304.6**

Haas, Jessie
Hoofprints: horse poems   **811**

Haase, Donald
(ed) The Greenwood encyclopedia of folktales
and fairy tales. See The Greenwood encyclopedia of folktales and fairy tales **398.2**

Habeeb, William Mark, 1955-
Civil wars in Africa   **303.6**

Haber, Fritz, 1868-1934
About
Hager, T. The alchemy of air [dual biography of
Fritz Haber and Carl Bosch]   **92**

Habitat (Ecology)
See also types of ecology, e.g. Desert ecol-
ogy; Marine ecology
Fothergill, A. Planet Earth   **508**

Hacht, Anne Marie, 1975-
(ed) Shakespeare for students. See Shakespeare
for students   **822.3**

Hackett, Albert, 1900-1995
(jt. auth) Goodrich, F. The diary of Anne Frank
812

Hacking Harvard. Wasserman, R.   **Fic**

Haddix, Margaret Peterson, 1964-
Leaving Fishers   **Fic**
Uprising   **Fic**

Haddon, Mark
The curious incident of the dog in the night-
time   **Fic**

Hades See Hell

Haerens, Margaret
(ed) Illegal immigration: opposing viewpoints.
See Illegal immigration: opposing viewpoints
325.73
(ed) Sexually transmitted diseases: opposing
viewpoints. See Sexually transmitted diseases:
opposing viewpoints   **616.95**
(ed) Television: opposing viewpoints. See Television: opposing viewpoints   **302.23**

Hafiz, Dilara
The American Muslim teenager's handbook
297

Hafiz, Imran
(jt. auth) Hafiz, D. The American Muslim
teenager's handbook   **297**

Hafiz, Yasmine
(jt. auth) Hafiz, D. The American Muslim
teenager's handbook   **297**

Hafner, Katie
Where wizards stay up late   **004**

Hager, Alan
(ed) Encyclopedia of British writers, 16th-18th
centuries. See Encyclopedia of British writers,
16th-18th centuries   **820.9**

Hager, Thomas
The alchemy of air [dual biography of Fritz Ha-
ber and Carl Bosch]   **92**
The demon under the microscope   **615**

Haggerty, Andrew
Jane Austen   **92**

Hahn, Daniel
(ed) The ultimate teen book guide. See The ultimate teen book guide   **028.1**

Hahn, David
About
Silverstein, K. The radioactive boy scout [biog-
raphy of David Hahn]   **92**

Hahn, Kathy L.
(ed) Are athletes good role models? See Are
athletes good role models?   **306.4**
(ed) Racial profiling. See Racial profiling
363.2

Haig, Matt, 1975-
The Radleys   **Fic**

Haiku
Higginson, W. J. The haiku handbook **808.1**
The **haiku** handbook. Higginson, W. J. **808.1**

Haine, W. Scott
Culture and customs of France   **944**

Haines, Tim
The complete guide to prehistoric life **560**

Hains, Bryan C.
Pain   **616**

Hair
Wright, J. D. Hair and fibers   **363.2**
Hair and fibers. Wright, J. D.   **363.2**

Haiti
Galembo, P. Vodou   **299.6**
Fiction
Allende, I. Island beneath the sea **Fic**
Danticat, E. Krik? Krak!   **S C**

Haitian Americans
Fiction
Danticat, E. Krik? Krak!   **S C**
Felin, M. S. Touching snow   **Fic**

Hakakian, Roya
Journey from the land of no   **92**

Hakim, Joy
The story of science: Aristotle leads the way
     509
The story of science: Einstein adds a new dimension   **509**
The story of science: Newton at the center
     509

Halaby, Laila
West of the Jordan   **Fic**

Hāladāra, Bebi
A life less ordinary   **92**

Halam, Ann
Dr. Franklin's island   **Fic**
Snakehead   **Fic**

Halberstam, David, 1934-2007
The fifties   **973.92**
Playing for keeps: Michael Jordan and the world he made   **92**
(ed) The Best American sports writing of the century. See The Best American sports writing of the century   **796**

Halberstam, Joshua
(jt. auth) Gonsher, D. The community college guide   **378.1**

Haldeman, Joe W., 1943-
The forever war   **Fic**

Halder, Baby *See* Hāladāra, Bebi

Hale, George Ellery, 1868-1938
See/See also pages in the following book(s):
Clark, S. The sun kings   **523.7**

Hale, Marian
The goodbye season   **Fic**

Hale, Nathan, 1755-1776
About
Phelps, M. W. Nathan Hale   **92**

Hale, Rosemary Drage
Christianity   **230**

Hale, Shannon
Book of a thousand days   **Fic**

Haley, Alex, 1921-1992
Mama Flora's family   **Fic**
Roots   **920**
(jt. auth) Malcolm X. The autobiography of Malcolm X   **92**

Haley family
About
Haley, A. Roots   **920**

Half brother. Oppel, K.   **Fic**

The **half** life of planets. Franklin, E.   **Fic**

Half World. Goto, H.   **Fic**

Halka, Monica
Alkali & alkaline earth metals   **546**
Halogens and noble gases   **546**
Lanthanides and actinides   **546**
Metals and metalloids   **546**
Nonmetals   **546**
Transition metals   **546**

Halkin, Hillel, 1939-
(tr) Sholem Aleichem. Tevye the dairyman and The railroad stories   **S C**

Hall, Barbara, 1960-
Tempo change   **Fic**

Hall, Dennis, 1942-
(ed) The Greenwood guide to American popular culture. See The Greenwood guide to American popular culture   **973.9**

Hall, J. Storrs
Nanofuture   **620**

Hall, James Norman, 1887-1951
(jt. auth) Nordhoff, C. Mutiny on the Bounty
     Fic

Hall, John Storrs *See* Hall, J. Storrs

Hall, Kermit, 1944-2006
(ed) The Oxford companion to the Supreme Court of the United States. See The Oxford companion to the Supreme Court of the United States   **347**
(ed) The Oxford guide to United States Supreme Court decisions. See The Oxford guide to United States Supreme Court decisions
     342

Hall, Linley Erin
DNA and RNA   **611**

Hall, Loretta
Arab American voices   **305.8**

Hall, Meredith, 1949-
Without a map   **92**

Hall, Steffie *See* Evanovich, Janet

Hallaway, Tate
Almost to die for   **Fic**

Halliburton, Warren J.
(comp) Historic speeches of African Americans. See Historic speeches of African Americans   **815.008**

Halliday, Fred
100 myths about the Middle East   **956**

Halligan, Karen
Doc Halligan's What every pet owner should know   **636**

Hallowell, Edward M.
(jt. auth) Corman, C. A. Positively ADD
     616.85

Hallucinations and illusions
See/See also pages in the following book(s):
Sagan, C. The demon-haunted world   **001.9**

Hallucinogenic drugs *See* Hallucinogens

Hallucinogenic plants *See* Hallucinogens

Hallucinogens
See also Ecstasy (Drug)
Hallucinogens   **615**
Nelson, S. Hallucinogens   **362.29**

Hallucinogens   **615**

Hallwas, John E.
(jt. auth) Masters, E. L. Spoon River anthology
     811

Halogens and noble gases. Halka, M.   **546**

Halpern, Julie, 1975-
Get well soon   **Fic**
Into the wild nerd yonder   **Fic**

Handbook of Russian literature   **891.7**

The **handbook** of the Middle East. Kort, M.
956

The **handbook** of the new Eastern Europe. Kort,
M.   **943**

Handbook to life in America [series]
The Great Depression and World War II, 1929
to 1949   **973.91**

Handbook to life in ancient Egypt. David, A. R.
932

Handbook to life in ancient Greece. Adkins, L.
938

Handbook to life in ancient Mesopotamia.
Bertman, S.   **935**

Handbook to life in ancient Rome. Adkins, L.
937

Handbook to life in prehistoric Europe. McIntosh,
J.   **930.1**

Handbook to life in Renaissance Europe. Sider, S.
940.2

Handbook to life in the Aztec world. Aguilar-
Moreno, M.   **972**

A **handbook** to literature. Harmon, W.   **803**

Handicapped

See also Mentally handicapped; Physically
handicapped
McHugh, M. Special siblings   **362.4**
People with disabilities   **362.4**
Rapp, E. Poster child   **92**
Civil rights
Haugen, D. Rights of the disabled   **342**
Employment
Yellin, S. Life after high school   **646.7**
Encyclopedias
Encyclopedia of American disability history
362.4
Encyclopedia of disability   **362.4**
Fiction
Aronson, S. Head case   **Fic**
Draanen, W. v. The running dream   **Fic**
Fink, M. The summer I got a life   **Fic**
Griffin, P. The Orange Houses   **Fic**
Johnson, H. M. Accidents of nature   **Fic**
McNeal, L. The decoding of Lana Morris
Fic
Portman, F. Andromeda Klein   **Fic**
Law and legislation
See Handicapped—Legal status, laws, etc.
Legal status, laws, etc.
Haugen, D. Rights of the disabled   **342**

Handicapped and animals *See* Animals and the
handicapped

Handicapped children

See also Brain damaged children; Mentally
handicapped children; Socially handicapped
children

Handicapped students
A Guide to high school success for students
with disabilities   **371.9**
Mooney, J. The short bus   **92**
Yellin, S. Life after high school   **646.7**

Handicraft
Arendt, M. Altered art for the first time
745.5
Foxfire 40th anniversary book   **975.8**
Searle, T. Felt jewelry   **746**
Taylor, T. Altered art   **745.5**

Handler, Daniel, 1970-
See also Snicket, Lemony, 1970-

Handler, Ruth, 1916-2002
About
Stone, T. L. The good, the bad, and the Barbie
688.7

Handley, Graham
(comp) Shakespeare, W. Poems   **821**

The **Handmaid's** tale. Atwood, M.   **Fic**

Handwriting
See also Calligraphy

The **handy** anatomy answer book. Balaban, N. E.
611

Handy answer book series
Barnes-Svarney, P. The handy dinosaur answer
book   **567.9**

The **handy** dinosaur answer book. Barnes-Svarney,
P.   **567.9**

The **handy** psychology answer book. Cohen, L. J.
150

The **handy** science answer book   **500**

Hanel, Rachael
Identity theft   **364.1**

Hanes, Richard Clay, 1946-
Crime and punishment in America: biographies
920

Hanes, Sharon M.
Crime and punishment in America, Primary
sources   **364**

Haney, Eric L.
Inside Delta Force   **356**

Hanging on to Max. Bechard, M.   **Fic**

The **Hanging** Woods. Sanders, S. L.   **Fic**

Hank Aaron and the home run that changed
America. Stanton, T.   **92**

Hanks, Patrick
A concise dictionary of first names   **929.4**
A dictionary of first names   **929.4**
(ed) Dictionary of American family names. See
Dictionary of American family names
929.4

Hanks, Reuel R.
Central Asia   **958**

Hannon, Sharon M.
Women explorers   **920**

Hanrahan, Clare
(ed) Global resources: opposing viewpoints. See
Global resources: opposing viewpoints
333.71

Hansberry, Lorraine, 1930-1965
A raisin in the sun   **812**
To be young, gifted, and Black   **92**
About
Loos, P. A reader's guide to Lorraine
Hansberry's A raisin in the sun   **812.009**

Hansen, Brad
The dictionary of multimedia   **006.6**
Hansen, Joyce
Bury me not in a land of slaves   **973.8**
Hansen, Mark Victor
(jt. auth) Canfield, J. Chicken soup for the teenage soul [I-IV]   **158**
(comp) Chicken soup for the teenage soul's the real deal. See Chicken soup for the teenage soul's the real deal   **158**
Hanson, Erik A.
Canyons   **551.4**
Hanson, Jeanne K.
Caves   **551.4**
Lakes   **551.48**
Hanson, Nicholas P., 1978-
(jt. auth) Nevraumont, E. J. The ultimate improv book   **792.7**
Happy. Lemon, A.   **92**
The **happy** camper. Callan, K.   **796.54**
Happyface. Emond, S.   **Fic**
Harada, Violet H.
Collaborating for project-based learning in grades 9-12   **371.3**
(jt. auth) Hughes-Hassell, S. School reform and the school library media specialist   **027.8**
(jt. auth) Zmuda, A. Librarians as learning specialists   **023**
Haralson, Carol
(ed) The Arts of the North American Indian. See The Arts of the North American Indian   **709.73**
Haralson, Eric L.
Critical companion to Henry James   **813.009**
(ed) Encyclopedia of American poetry, the twentieth century. See Encyclopedia of American poetry, the twentieth century   **811.009**
Harassment, Sexual See Sexual harassment
Harazin, S. A.
Blood brothers   **Fic**
Harbison, Lawrence
(ed) 2010: the best men's stage monologues and scenes. See 2010: the best men's stage monologues and scenes   **808.82**
(ed) 2010: the best women's stage monologues and scenes. See 2010: the best women's stage monologues and scenes   **808.82**
Hard driving: the Wendell Scott story. Donovan, B.   **92**
Hard hit. Turner, A. W.   **Fic**
Hard love. Wittlinger, E.   **Fic**
The **Hard** SF renaissance   **S C**
Hard times. Terkel, S.   **973.91**
Hard times require furious dancing. Walker, A.   **811**
Hardcastle, Kate
(jt. auth) Hanks, P. A dictionary of first names   **929.4**
Hardesty, Constance
The teen-centered writing club   **027.62**
(jt. auth) Kunzel, B. L. The teen-centered book club   **027.62**

Hardesty, Von, 1939-
Black wings   **920**
Epic rivalry   **629.4**
Hardin High School (Hardin, Mont.)
Basketball
Colton, L. Counting coup   **796.323**
Harding, Anne
Milestones in health and medicine   **610.9**
Harding, James M., 1958-
(jt. auth) Crist, D. T. World ocean census   **578.7**
Hardinge, Frances
The lost conspiracy   **Fic**
Hardy, Grant
The establishment of the Han empire and imperial China   **931**
Hardy, Lyda Mary
Women in U.S. history   **016.973**
Hardy, Thomas, 1840-1928
Poems   **821**
The return of the native   **Fic**
Tess of the D'Urbervilles   **Fic**
About
Thomas Hardy [critical essays]   **823.009**
Hare, R. M. (Richard Mervyn)
Plato   **184**
A **hare** in the elephant's trunk. Coates, J.   **Fic**
Hargreaves, Alice Pleasance Liddell, 1852-1934
About
Rubin, C. M. The real Alice in Wonderland [biography of Alice Pleasance Liddell Hargreaves]   **92**
Hargrove, Hondon B., 1916-
Black Union soldiers in the Civil War   **973.7**
Hari, Daoud
The translator   **92**
Harjo, Joy, 1951-
The woman who fell from the sky   **811**
See/See also pages in the following book(s):
Coltelli, L. Winged words: American Indian writers speak   **897**
Harkness, Ruth
About
Croke, V. The lady and the panda   **599.78**
Harland, Richard, 1947-
Worldshaker   **Fic**
Harlem (New York, N.Y.)
Fiction
Baldwin, J. Go tell it on the mountain   **Fic**
Buckhanon, K. Upstate   **Fic**
Lipsyte, R. The contender   **Fic**
Myers, W. D. 145th Street   **S C**
Myers, W. D. Autobiography of my dead brother   **Fic**
Myers, W. D. Dope sick   **Fic**
Myers, W. D. Game   **Fic**
Myers, W. D. What they found   **S C**
Poetry
Myers, W. D. Harlem   **811**
Myers, W. D. Here in Harlem   **811**
Harlem Renaissance
Abdul-Jabbar, K. On the shoulders of giants   **92**

Harlem Renaissance—*Continued*
The Harlem Renaissance [critical essays]
    810.9
The Harlem Renaissance: a Gale critical companion   **810.9**
Harlem Renaissance lives from the African American national biography   **920**
Harlem speaks   **810.9**
Hill, L. C. Harlem stomp!   **810.9**
Hillstrom, K. The Harlem Renaissance   **810.9**
Shimmy shimmy shimmy like my sister Kate
    811.008

See/See also pages in the following book(s):
Bearden, R. A history of African-American artists   **709.73**
Encyclopedias
Encyclopedia of the Harlem Renaissance
    700

The **Harlem** Renaissance [critical essays]
    810.9
The **Harlem** Renaissance: a Gale critical companion   **810.9**
Harlem Renaissance lives from the African American national biography   **920**
Harlem speaks   **810.9**
Harlem stomp!. Hill, L. C.   **810.9**
Harley, Madeline M.
    (jt. auth) Stuppy, W. The bizarre and incredible world of plants   **580**
Harley-Davidson, Inc.
    Davidson, J. Jean Davidson's Harley-Davidson family album   **629.227**
Harley-Davidson family album, Jean Davidson's. Davidson, J.   **629.227**
Harley family
About
Davidson, J. Jean Davidson's Harley-Davidson family album   **629.227**
Harlow, Harry F., 1905-1981
Graphic novels
Ottaviani, J. Wire mothers   **152.4**
Harmful insects *See* Insect pests
Harmless. Reinhardt, D.   **Fic**
Harmon, Adam
    Lonely soldier   **92**
Harmon, Charles T., 1960-
    (jt. auth) Symons, A. K. Protecting the right to read   **025.2**
Harmon, Dan
    Nigeria   **966.9**
Harmon, Michael B., 1969-
    Brutal   **Fic**
    The last exit to normal   **Fic**
Harmon, William, 1938-
    A handbook to literature   **803**
    (ed) Classic writings on poetry. See Classic writings on poetry   **809.1**
    (ed) The Top 500 poems. See The Top 500 poems   **821.008**
Harmonic feedback. Kelly, T.   **Fic**
Haroun and the sea of stories. Rushdie, S.
    Fic

Harper, Elizabeth, 1934-
    Your name in print   **808**
Harper, Hill, 1966-
    Letters to a young brother   **170**
Harper, Kristine
    Weather and climate   **551.5**
Harper, Michael S.
    (ed) Every shut eye ain't asleep. See Every shut eye ain't asleep   **811.008**
    (ed) The Vintage book of African American poetry. See The Vintage book of African American poetry   **811.008**
Harper, Suzanne
    The Juliet club   **Fic**
Harper, Timothy, 1950-
    (jt. auth) Harper, E. Your name in print   **808**
Harper Lee's To kill a mockingbird [study guide]
    813.009
The **HarperCollins** dictionary of religion
    200.3
Harper's anthology of 20th century Native American poetry   **811.008**
Harrington, Kim, 1974-
    Clarity   **Fic**
Harrington, Philip S.
    Eclipse!   **523.7**
    Star ware   **522**
Harrington, Walt, 1950-
    (ed) The beholder's eye. See The beholder's eye
    814
Harris, Bruce
    (jt. auth) Marshall, D. Wild about flying!
    629.13
Harris, Cecil, 1960-
    Charging the net   **920**
Harris, Christopher, 1977-
    (jt. auth) Mayer, B. Libraries got game
    025.2
Harris, Cyril M., 1917-2011
    (ed) Dictionary of architecture & construction. See Dictionary of architecture & construction
    720.3
Harris, Fran, 1965-
    (jt. auth) Gray, F. Reallionaire   **332.024**
Harris, Frances Jacobson
    I found it on the Internet   **025.04**
Harris, Joseph
    (jt. auth) Turkington, C. The encyclopedia of the brain and brain disorders   **612.8**
Harris, Nancy
    (ed) Amphetamines. See Amphetamines   **615**
    (ed) Cloning. See Cloning [Exploring science and medical discoveries]   **176**
Harris, Robert, 1957-
    Pompeii   **Fic**
Harrison, Benjamin, 1833-1901
About
Calhoun, C. W. Benjamin Harrison   **92**
Harrison, Cora
    I was Jane Austen's best friend   **Fic**
Harrison, Hazel
    (jt. auth) Craig, D. The new encyclopedia of watercolor techniques   **751.42**

Hatch, James Vernon, 1928-
(ed) Black theatre USA. See Black theatre USA
812.008

Hatch, Robert
The hero project **920**

Hatch, Shari Dorantes
(ed) Encyclopedia of African-American writing.
See Encyclopedia of African-American writing **810.9**

Hatch, William
(jt. auth) Hatch, R. The hero project **920**

Hatchepset *See* Hatshepsut, Queen of Egypt

Hate crimes
Altschiller, D. Hate crimes **364.1**
Hate crimes **364.1**
See/See also pages in the following book(s):
Racial discrimination **342**
Fiction
Ehrenberg, P. Tillmon County fire **Fic**
Myracle, L. Shine **Fic**

Hate crimes **364.1**

Hate list. Brown, J. **Fic**

Hatfield, Greg
(ed) Songwriter's market. See Songwriter's market **782.42**

Hatha yoga *See* Yoga

Hatshepsut, Queen of Egypt
See/See also pages in the following book(s):
Mertz, B. Temples, tombs, & hieroglyphs **932**

Hattie Big Sky. Larson, K. **Fic**

Hattori, Chihiro
(il) Kardy, G. Manga University Presents . . .
Kana de Manga Special Edition: Japanese
Sound FX! **495.6**
(il) The manga cookbook. See The manga cookbook **641.5**

Hatzfeld, Jean
Machete season **967.571**

Haugen, David, 1969-
Legalized gambling **363.4**
Rights of the disabled **342**
(ed) Abortion: opposing viewpoints. See Abortion: opposing viewpoints **363.46**
(ed) Adoption. See Adoption **362.7**
(ed) Africa: opposing viewpoints. See Africa: opposing viewpoints **960**
(ed) American values: opposing viewpoints. See
American values: opposing viewpoints
306
(ed) Animal experimentation: opposing viewpoints. See Animal experimentation: opposing viewpoints **179**
(ed) Education: opposing viewpoints. See Education: opposing viewpoints **371**
(ed) Energy alternatives: opposing viewpoints.
See Energy alternatives: opposing viewpoints **333.79**
(ed) Epidemics: opposing viewpoints. See Epidemics: opposing viewpoints **614.4**
(ed) The ethics of cloning. See The ethics of cloning **176**

(ed) Genetic engineering: opposing viewpoints.
See Genetic engineering: opposing viewpoints **174.2**
(ed) Global warming: opposing viewpoints. See
Global warming: opposing viewpoints **363.7**
(ed) Globalization: opposing viewpoints. See
Globalization: opposing viewpoints **303.4**
(ed) How does advertising impact teen behavior? See How does advertising impact teen behavior? **659.1**
(ed) Iraq: opposing viewpoints. See Iraq: opposing viewpoints **956.7**
(ed) Islam: opposing viewpoints. See Islam: opposing viewpoints **297**
(ed) Islamic fundamentalism. See Islamic fundamentalism **297**
(ed) Media violence: opposing viewpoints. See
Media violence: opposing viewpoints **363.3**
(ed) The Middle East: opposing viewpoints. See
The Middle East: opposing viewpoints **956**
(ed) Popular culture: opposing viewpoints. See
Popular culture: opposing viewpoints **306**
(ed) Poverty. See Poverty **362.5**
(ed) Religion in America: opposing viewpoints.
See Religion in America: opposing viewpoints **200.9**
(ed) Should the federal government bail out private industry? See Should the federal government bail out private industry? **338.5**
(ed) Terrorism. See Terrorism [Social issues firsthand series] **363.32**
(ed) The Third World: opposing viewpoints. See
The Third World: opposing viewpoints **909**

Haugen, Hayley Mitchell, 1968-
(ed) Age of consent. See Age of consent **306.7**

Haunted heart [biography of Stephen King]
Rogak, L. A. **92**

The **haunting** of Alaizabel Cray. Wooding, C. **Fic**

The **haunting** of Hill House. Jackson, S. **Fic**

Hautman, Pete, 1952-
All-in **Fic**
Blank confession **Fic**
Godless **Fic**
Invisible **Fic**

Have a nice day—no problem!: a dictionary of clichés. See Ammer, C. The Facts on File dictionary of clichés **423**

Having our say. Delany, S. **92**

Hawaii
Description and travel
Twain, M. Roughing it **818**
Fiction
Hostetter, J. Healing water **Fic**
Levitin, S. Strange relations **Fic**
Salisbury, G. Under the blood-red sun **Fic**
Graphic novels
Morse, S. The barefoot serpent **741.5**

Hawass, Zahi A.
Tutankhamun and the golden age of the pharaohs   **932**

Hawk, Tony, 1968-
Hawk   **92**

Fiction
Hornby, N. Slam   **Fic**

Hawke, David Freeman
Everyday life in early America   **973.2**

Hawking, Stephen W., 1942-
Black holes and baby universes and other essays
                                              523.1
A briefer history of time   **523.1**
The grand design   **530.1**
The nature of space and time   **530.1**
The universe in a nutshell   **530.1**
See/See also pages in the following book(s):
Cropper, W. H. Great physicists   **920**

Hawkins, Lawrence E.
(jt. auth) Hutchinson, S. Oceans: a visual guide
                                             551.46

Hawkins, Rachel, 1979-
Hex Hall   **Fic**

Haws, Barbara B.
(jt. auth) Bernstein, B. Leonard Bernstein   **92**

Hawthorne, Nathaniel, 1804-1864
The portable Hawthorne   **818**
The scarlet letter   **Fic**
Tales and sketches, including Twice-told tales,
    Mosses from an old manse, and The snow-
    image; A wonder book for girls and boys;
    Tanglewood tales for girls and boys, being a
    second Wonder book   **S C**
About
A Historical guide to Nathaniel Hawthorne
                                         813.009
Sterling, L. A. Bloom's how to write about Na-
    thaniel Hawthorne   **813.009**
Wright, S. B. Critical companion to Nathaniel
    Hawthorne   **813.009**

Hay, Jeff
(ed) Amendment XV. See Amendment XV
                                             342
(ed) Living through the end of the Cold War.
    See Living through the end of the Cold War
                                          940.55
(ed) The Treaty of Versailles. See The Treaty of
    Versailles   **940.3**

Hayakawa, Alan R.
(jt. auth) Hayakawa, S. I. Language in thought
    and action   **412**

Hayakawa, Hiroshi, 1962-
Kirigami menagerie   **736**

Hayakawa, S. I.
Language in thought and action   **412**

Haycak, Cara
Living on impulse   **Fic**

Haycraft, Howard, 1905-1991
(ed) American authors, 1600-1900. See Ameri-
    can authors, 1600-1900   **920.003**
(ed) British authors before 1800. See British au-
    thors before 1800   **920.003**

(ed) British authors of the nineteenth century.
    See British authors of the nineteenth century
                                         920.003

Hayden, Patrick Nielsen *See* Nielsen Hayden,
    Patrick

Haydn, Joseph, 1732-1809
Fiction
Dunlap, S. E. The musician's daughter   **Fic**

Hayes, Dayle
(ed) Food and nutrition. See Food and nutrition
                                          641.3

Hayes, Derek, 1947-
America discovered   **917**
Historical atlas of the United States   **911**

Hayhurst, Chris
Euclid: the great geometer   **92**
Everything you need to know about food addi-
    tives   **664**

Haynes, Charles C.
First freedoms   **342**

Haynes, William M.
(ed) CRC handbook of chemistry and physics.
    See CRC handbook of chemistry and physics
                                          540

Haynes, Mickey *See* Haynes, William M.

Haynsworth, Leslie
Amelia Earhart's daughters   **629.13**

Hayslip, Le Ly
When heaven and earth changed places   **92**

The hazardous Earth [series]
Kusky, T. M. Climate change   **551.6**
Kusky, T. M. Earthquakes   **551.2**
Kusky, T. M. Tsunamis   **551.46**

Hazardous waste disposal *See* Hazardous wastes

Hazardous waste sites
Maczulak, A. E. Cleaning up the environment
                                         628.5

Hazardous wastes
Kallen, S. A. Toxic waste   **363.7**

Hazelwood School District v. Kuhlmeier
Phillips, T. A. Hazelwood v. Kuhlmeier and the
    school newspaper censorship debate   **342**

Hazelwood v. Kuhlmeier and the school newspa-
    per censorship debate. Phillips, T. A.   **342**

Hazen, Edith P.
(ed) The Columbia Granger's dictionary of poet-
    ry quotations. See The Columbia Granger's
    dictionary of poetry quotations   **808.88**

He forgot to say good-bye. Saenz, B. A.   **Fic**

Head, Dominic
(ed) The Cambridge guide to literature in En-
    glish. See The Cambridge guide to literature
    in English   **820.9**

Head, Tom
Freedom of religion   **342**

Head, Tom, 1978-
(jt. auth) Wolcott, D. B. Crime and punishment
    in America   **364**

Head
See also Skull
Head case. Aronson, S.   **Fic**

Headless males make great lovers. Crump, M. L.
591.5

Headley, Justina Chen, 1968-
North of beautiful   **Fic**

Headlong. Koja, K.   **Fic**

Heads of state

    See also Dictators; Kings and rulers; Presidents; Prime ministers

Naden, C. J. Mao Zedong and the Chinese Revolution   **92**

Healey, Karen, 1981-
Guardian of the dead   **Fic**

Healing drugs: the history of pharmacology. See Facklam, M. Modern medicines   **615**

Healing water. Hostetter, J.   **Fic**

Health

    See also Hygiene; Physical fitness

      Environmental aspects

    See Environmental health

      Information services

Lukenbill, W. B. Health information in a changing world   **372**

Health, Public *See* Public health

Health. Lovegrove, R.   **174.2**

Health and medical issues today [series]
Minigh, J. L. Sports medicine   **617.1**

Health care *See* Medical care

Health education

Lukenbill, W. B. Health information in a changing world   **372**

Health foods *See* Natural foods

Health information in a changing world. Lukenbill, W. B.   **372**

Health reference series
Drug abuse sourcebook   **362.29**
Lung disorders sourcebook   **616.2**
Vegetarian sourcebook   **613.2**

Health self-care
American Medical Association family medical guide   **616.02**

Healthy eating: a guide to nutrition [series]
Allman, T. Nutrition and disease prevention
     612.3
Smith, T. L. Nutrition and food safety   **363.1**
Smolin, L. A. Basic nutrition   **612.3**
Smolin, L. A. Nutrition and weight management
     613.2
Smolin, L. A. Nutrition for sports and exercise
     613.7

Healthy lifestyles [series]
De la Bédoyère, C. Balancing work and play
     155.9
De la Bédoyère, C. Personal hygiene and sexual health   **613**
Dicker, K. Diet and nutrition   **613**
Dicker, K. Exercise   **613.7**
Gifford, C. Sports   **796**
Rooney, A. Dealing with drugs   **615**

Heaney, Seamus
Electric light   **821**
Opened ground   **821**
(tr) Beowulf. Beowulf   **829**

Heaphy, Leslie A., 1964-
(ed) Encyclopedia of women and baseball. See Encyclopedia of women and baseball
     796.357

Heaphy, Maura, 1953-
Science fiction authors   **920.003**

Hear me out: true stories of Teens Educating and Confronting Homophobia   **306.76**

Hearing impaired

    See also Deaf

Hearn, Julie, 1958-
Ivy   **Fic**
The minister's daughter   **Fic**

Hearn, Lian
Across the nightingale floor   **Fic**

Hearne, Betsy Gould, 1942-
Beauties and beasts   **398.2**

The **heart** & soul of the next generation. Bradley, M. J.   **305.23**

Heart attack *See* Heart diseases

Heart diseases

      Diet therapy

American Heart Association. The new American Heart Association cookbook   **641.5**

Heart full of grace   **808.88**

The **heart** has its reasons. Cart, M.   **813.009**

The **heart** is a lonely hunter. McCullers, C.
     Fic

Heart of a samurai. Preus, M.   **Fic**

Heart of darkness. Conrad, J.   **Fic**

The **heart** of the matter. Greene, G.   **Fic**

Heart to heart   **811.008**

Heartbreak river. Mills, T.   **Fic**

Hearth, Amy Hill, 1958-
(jt. auth) Delany, S. Having our say   **92**

The **heartless** stone. Zoellner, T.   **553.8**

Hearts at stake. Harvey, A.   **Fic**

Heath, Jack, 1986-
The Lab   **Fic**

Heavy metal and you. Krovatin, C.   **Fic**

Hebrew language

      Dictionaries

Zilkha, A. Modern English-Hebrew dictionary
     492.4

Hebrew poetry

      Collections

Music of a distant drum   **808.81**

Hecht, Alan
(jt. auth) Decker, J. M. Mononucleosis
     616.9

Heck, Alfons, 1928-
(jt. auth) Ayer, E. H. Parallel journeys
     940.53

Hedges, Peter
What's eating Gilbert Grape   **Fic**

Hedrick, Joan D., 1944-
(ed) Stowe, H. B. The Oxford Harriet Beecher Stowe reader   **818**

Heeger, Paula Brehm- *See* Brehm-Heeger, Paula

Hill, Tom
(ed) Creation's journey. See Creation's journey
709.73

Hillenbrand, Laura
Seabiscuit 798.4

Hillerman, Tony
(ed) The Best American mystery stories of the century. See The Best American mystery stories of the century S C
(ed) The Best of the West. See The Best of the West 818

Hillman, Robert, 1948-
(jt. auth) Ghahramani, Z. My life as a traitor
92

Hills, Lia
The beginner's guide to living Fic

Hillstrom, Kevin
American Civil War: biographies 920
American Indian removal and the trail to Wounded Knee 973.8
The Cold War 909.82
The Harlem Renaissance 810.9
Vietnam War: almanac 959.704
Vietnam War: biographies 920
Vietnam War: primary sources 959.704
Workers unite! 331.8

Hillstrom, Laurie
The attack on Pearl Harbor 940.54
Roe v. Wade 344
The Thanksgiving book 394.26
The Voting Rights Act of 1965 324.6
(jt. auth) Hillstrom, K. American Civil War: biographies 920
(jt. auth) Hillstrom, K. American Indian removal and the trail to Wounded Knee 973.8
(jt. auth) Hillstrom, K. Vietnam War: almanac 959.704
(jt. auth) Hillstrom, K. Vietnam War: biographies 920
(jt. auth) Hillstrom, K. Vietnam War: primary sources 959.704

Himelstein, Shmuel, 1940-
(ed) The New encyclopedia of Judaism. See The New encyclopedia of Judaism [New York University Press] 296.03
(ed) The student's encyclopedia of Judaism. See The student's encyclopedia of Judaism 296.03

Himsl, Sharon M.
(ed) 1920-1940: the twentieth century. See 1920-1940: the twentieth century 909.82

Hinds, Gareth, 1971-
Beowulf 741.5
King Lear 822.3
The merchant of Venice 822.3
The Odyssey 741.5

Hinds, Kathryn, 1962-
Everyday life in the Renaissance 940.2
Everyday life in the Roman Empire 937

Hinds, Maurene J.
The Ferguson guide to resumes and job hunting skills 650.14
You have the right to know your rights 342

Hinduism
Ganeri, A. The Ramayana and Hinduism 294.5
Mann, G. S. Buddhists, Hindus, and Sikhs in America 294
Narayanan, V. Hinduism 294.5
Patel, S. The little book of Hindu deities 704.9
Wangu, M. B. Hinduism 294.5
See/See also pages in the following book(s):
Eastern religions 200.9
Encyclopedias
Jones, C. Encyclopedia of Hinduism 294.5

Hine, Darlene Clark
(ed) Black women in America. See Black women in America 920.003

Hine, Robert
(ed) The Facts on File dictionary of biology. See The Facts on File dictionary of biology 570.3

Hines, Emmett W., 1956-
Fitness swimming 613.7

Hinges of history [series]
Cahill, T. The gifts of the Jews 909
Cahill, T. Sailing the wine-dark sea 909

Hingley, Ronald
(tr) Chekhov, A. P. The Russian master and other stories S C

Hinkson, Jim
Lacrosse for dummies 796.34

Hinman, Bonnie
Eternal vigilance: the story of Ida B. Wells-Barnett 92
A stranger in my own house [biography of W.E.B. Du Bois] 92

Hinshaw, John H., 1963-
(ed) U.S. labor in the twentieth century. See U.S. labor in the twentieth century 331

Hinton, S. E.
The outsiders Fic

Hip-hop
Dyson, M. E. Holler if you hear me: searching for Tupac Shakur 92
Rap music and culture 306.4
Rose, T. The hip hop wars 305.8
Scott, D. How to draw hip-hop 741.2
White, A. Rebel for the hell of it [biography of Tupac Shakur] 92
Dictionaries
Mitchell, K. M. Hip-hop rhyming dictionary 423
Encyclopedias
Bynoe, Y. Encyclopedia of rap and hip-hop culture 782.42

Hip-hop high school. Sitomer, A. L. Fic

Hip-hop rhyming dictionary. Mitchell, K. M. 423

The **hip** hop wars. Rose, T. 305.8

Hippies
Issitt, M. L. Hippies 305.5
Fiction
Ziegler, J. How not to be popular Fic

Hiroshima (Japan)
Bombardment, 1945
Burgan, M. Hiroshima   **940.54**
Hersey, J. Hiroshima   **940.54**
Takaki, R. T. Hiroshima   **940.54**
See/See also pages in the following book(s):
Yamazaki, J. N. Children of the atomic bomb   **92**
Hiroshima. Burgan, M.   **940.54**
Hirsch, E. D. (Eric Donald), 1928-
The new dictionary of cultural literacy   **031**
Hirsch, Edward
How to read a poem   **808.1**
Hirsch, Eric Donald *See* Hirsch, E. D. (Eric Donald), 1928-
Hirschfelder, Arlene B.
(ed) Rising voices. See Rising voices   **810.8**
Hirshfield, Jane
See/See also pages in the following book(s):
Fooling with words   **808.1**
Hirsi Ali, Ayaan, 1969-
Infidel   **92**
Hirst, Michael
Michelangelo and his drawings   **709.45**
His Excellency [biography of George Washington] Ellis, J. J.   **92**
Hischak, Thomas
(jt. auth) Bordman, G. M. The Oxford companion to American theatre   **792.03**
Hispanic American almanac. See U-X-L Hispanic American almanac   **305.8**
Hispanic American athletes
Wendel, T. Far from home   **796.357**
Hispanic American authors
Amend, A. Hispanic-American writers   **810.9**
Hispanic American biographies   **920.003**
Hispanic American gay men
Reyes, G. Madre and I   **92**
Wright, K. Drifting toward love   **306.76**
Hispanic American poetry *See* American poetry—Hispanic American authors
Hispanic-American writers. Amend, A.   **810.9**
Hispanic Americans
Gonzalez, J. Harvest of empire   **305.8**
U-X-L Hispanic American almanac   **305.8**
Wendel, T. The new face of baseball   **796.357**
Biography
Bruns, R. Icons of Latino America   **920**
Windows into my world   **920**
Dictionaries
Friedman, I. C. Latino athletes   **920.003**
Hispanic American biographies   **920.003**
Martinez Wood, J. Latino writers and journalists   **920.003**
Newton, D. E. Latinos in science, math, and professions   **920.003**
Otfinoski, S. Latinos in the arts   **920.003**
Encyclopedias
Latino history and culture   **305.8**
Fiction
Hernandez, D. Suckerpunch   **Fic**
Nichols, J. Messed up   **Fic**
Once upon a cuento   **S C**

Quintero, S. Efrain's secret   **Fic**
History
The Hispanic Americans   **305.8**
Ochoa, G. Atlas of Hispanic-American history   **305.8**
Poetry
Red hot salsa   **811.008**
Social life and customs
Alvarez, J. Once upon a quinceañera   **392**
Fifteen candles   **392**
The **Hispanic** Americans   **305.8**
Hispanic Americans and libraries *See* Libraries and Hispanic Americans
Hispanic Americans in literature
U.S. Latino literature   **810.9**
Hispanic heritage [series]
Makosz, R. Latino arts and their influence on the United States   **700**
Historians
Lerner, G. Fireweed   **92**
Historic buildings
     See also Literary landmarks types of historic buildings
Unesco. World heritage sites   **910.2**
Fiction
Cann, K. Possessed   **Fic**
Historic sites
Curtis, N. C. Black heritage sites   **917.3**
Unesco. World heritage sites   **910.2**
Wood, M. In the footsteps of Alexander the Great   **938**
Historic speeches of African Americans   **815.008**
A **historical** atlas of Afghanistan. Romano, A.   **958.1**
Historical atlas of Central Europe. Magocsi, P. R.   **911**
Historical atlas of East Central Europe. See Magocsi, P. R. Historical atlas of Central Europe   **911**
A **historical** atlas of Iran. Ramen, F.   **955**
Historical atlas of religion in America. See Gaustad, E. S. New historical atlas of religion in America   **200.9**
The **historical** atlas of the American Revolution. Barnes, I.   **973.3**
A **Historical** atlas of the Jewish people   **909**
Historical atlas of the United States. Hayes, D.   **911**
Historical atlas of U.S. presidential elections 1788-2004   **324**
Historical atlases
Atlas of classical history   **911**
Goetzmann, W. H. The atlas of North American exploration   **911**
Hayes, D. America discovered   **917**
McKitterick, R. Atlas of the medieval world   **911**
National Geographic Society (U.S.). Atlas of the Civil War   **973.7**
Smithsonian atlas of world aviation   **629.13**
Swanson, M. Atlas of the Civil War, month by month   **973.7**

Holliday, Laurel, 1946-
(comp) Children in the Holocaust and World War II. See Children in the Holocaust and World War II   **940.53**
(ed) Children of Israel, children of Palestine. See Children of Israel, children of Palestine   **956.94**

Hollywood (Calif.)
Fiction
Strasser, T. Famous   **Fic**

Hollywood 101 [series]
Stevens, C. Sensational scenes for teens   **808.82**

Holm, Tom, 1946-
Code talkers and warriors   **940.54**

Holman, James, 1786-1857
About
Roberts, J. A sense of the world [biography of James Holman]   **92**

Holmes, George, 1927-2009
(ed) The Oxford history of Italy. See The Oxford history of Italy   **945**
(ed) The Oxford history of medieval Europe. See The Oxford history of medieval Europe   **940.1**

Holmes, Hannah, 1963-
The secret life of dust   **551.51**
The well-dressed ape   **612**

Holmes, Martha
Life. See Life   **578.4**

Holmes, Thom
Early humans   **599.93**
The first vertebrates   **567**
Last of the dinosaurs   **567.9**
Primates and human ancestors   **569**

Holmes, Sherlock (Fictional character)
The improbable adventures of Sherlock Holmes   **S C**
King, L. R. The beekeeper's apprentice, or, on the segregation of the queen   **Fic**

Holocaust, 1933-1945
See also Holocaust survivors; World War, 1939-1945—Jews
Ackerman, D. The zookeeper's wife   **940.53**
Altman, L. J. Hidden teens, hidden lives   **940.53**
Ayer, E. H. Parallel journeys   **940.53**
Bartoletti, S. C. Hitler Youth   **943.086**
Berenbaum, M. The world must know   **940.53**
Chesnoff, R. Z. Pack of thieves   **940.53**
Dawidowicz, L. S. The war against the Jews, 1933-1945   **940.53**
Epstein, H. Children of the Holocaust   **940.53**
Feldman, G. Understanding the Holocaust   **940.53**
Frank, A. The diary of a young girl: the definitive edition   **92**
Frank, A. The diary of Anne Frank: the critical edition   **92**
Gies, M. Anne Frank remembered   **940.53**
Gilbert, M. The Holocaust   **940.53**
Goldhagen, D. Hitler's willing executioners   **940.53**

Kopf, H. R. Understanding Anne Frank's The diary of a young girl   **940.53**
Mara, W. Kristallnacht   **940.53**
Meltzer, M. Never to forget: the Jews of the Holocaust   **940.53**
Nicholas, L. H. Cruel world   **940.53**
Robson, D. Auschwitz   **940.53**
Voices of the Holocaust   **940.53**
Women in the Holocaust   **940.53**
Wood, A. Holocaust   **940.53**
See/See also pages in the following book(s):
Naimark, N. M. Fires of hatred   **364.1**
Bibliography
Rosen, P. Bearing witness   **016.94053**
Dictionaries
Epstein, E. J. Dictionary of the Holocaust   **940.53**
Encyclopedias
Encyclopedia of the Holocaust [Facts on File]   **940.53**
The Holocaust encyclopedia   **940.53**
Fiction
Clark, K. Guardian angel house   **Fic**
Dogar, S. Annexed   **Fic**
Gleitzman, M. Once   **Fic**
Keneally, T. Schindler's list   **Fic**
Polak, M. What world is left   **Fic**
Whitney, K. A. The other half of life   **Fic**
Yolen, J. Briar Rose   **Fic**
Zusak, M. The book thief   **Fic**
Graphic novels
Heuvel, E. A family secret   **741.5**
Jacobson, S. Anne Frank   **92**
Katin, M. We are on our own   **92**
Spiegelman, A. Maus   **940.53**
Historiography
Shermer, M. Denying history   **940.53**
Maps
Gilbert, M. The Routledge atlas of the Holocaust   **940.53**
Personal narratives
Art from the ashes   **940.53**
Ayer, E. H. In the ghettos   **940.53**
Bannister, N. The secret Holocaust diaries   **92**
Bitton-Jackson, L. I have lived a thousand years   **940.53**
Buergenthal, T. A lucky child [biography of Thomas Buergenthal]   **92**
Children in the Holocaust and World War II   **940.53**
Drucker, O. L. Kindertransport   **940.53**
Kor, E. M. Surviving the Angel of Death   **92**
Kramer, C. Clara's war   **92**
Lobel, A. No pretty pictures   **92**
Mothers, sisters, resisters   **940.53**
Prose, F. Anne Frank   **839.3**
Reiss, J. The upstairs room   **92**
Wiesel, E. Night   **92**
Witness   **940.53**
Poetry
Holocaust poetry   **808.81**
Holocaust, 1933-1945, in literature
Art from the ashes   **940.53**
Holocaust literature   **809**
Literature of the Holocaust   **809**

How should prisons treat inmates? **365**

How should the United States treat prisoners in the war on terror? **973.931**

How the Canyon became Grand. Pyne, S. J. **979.1**

How the cows turned mad. Schwartz, M. **616.8**

How the García girls lost their accents. Alvarez, J. **Fic**

How they met, and other stories. Levithan, D. **S C**

How to analyze the works of Andy Warhol. Fallon, M. **700**

How to analyze the works of Georgia O'Keeffe. Fallon, M. **759.13**

How to analyze the works of Stephen King. Lüst-ed, M. A. **813.009**

How to be a perfect stranger **203**

How to be bad. Lockhart, E. **Fic**

How to build a house. Reinhardt, D. **Fic**

How to carve wood. Bütz, R. **731.4**

How-to-do-it manuals for librarians [series]

Alire, C. Serving Latino communities **027.6**

Butler, R. P. Smart copyright compliance for schools **346.04**

Developing an information literacy program, K-12 **025.5**

Earp, P. W. Securing library technology **005.8**

Gorman, M. Connecting young adults and libraries **027.62**

Halsted, D. D. Disaster planning **025.8**

MacKellar, P. H. Winning grants **025.1**

Martin, B. S. Fundamentals of school library media management **025.1**

Martin, H. J., Jr. Serving lesbian, gay, bisexual, transgender, and questioning teens **027.62**

Symons, A. K. Protecting the right to read **025.2**

Tallman, J. I. Making the writing and research connection with the I-search process **025.5**

Wolfe, L. A. Library public relations, promotions, and communications **021.7**

How to draw hip-hop. Scott, D. **741.2**

How to draw stupid and other essentials of cartooning. Baker, K. **741.5**

How to make a bird. Murray, M. **Fic**

How to paint sunlight. Ferlinghetti, L. **811**

How to pay for college **378.3**

How to prepare for the ACT, American College Testing Assessment Program. See Barron's ACT **378.1**

How to read a painting **753**

How to read a poem. Hirsch, E. **808.1**

How to ruin my teenage life. Elkeles, S. **Fic**

How to say goodbye in Robot. Standiford, N. **Fic**

How to say it to get into the college of your choice. Metcalf, L. **378.1**

How to survive modern art. Hodge, S. **709.04**

How to take the ex out of ex-boyfriend. Rallison, J. **Fic**

How to teach physics to your dog. Orzel, C. **530.1**

How to think about the great ideas. Adler, M. J. **080**

How to (un)cage a girl. Block, F. L. **811**

How to write better business letters. Geffner, A. B. **651.7**

How we got here. Frum, D. **973.92**

How we invented the airplane. Wright, O. **92**

How we live and why we die. Wolpert, L. **571.6**

How ya like me now. Halpin, B. **Fic**

How your government really works. Starks, G. L. **320.4**

Howard, Jean E. (Jean Elizabeth), 1948-
(ed) Shakespeare, W. The Norton Shakespeare **822.3**

Howard, Alycia Smith *See* Smith Howard, Alycia

Howard-Barr, Elissa
The truth about sexual behavior and unplanned pregnancy. See The truth about sexual behavior and unplanned pregnancy **306.7**

Howarth, David Armine, 1912-
1066: the year of the conquest **942.02**

Howatson, M. C. (Margaret C.)
(ed) The Oxford companion to classical literature. See The Oxford companion to classical literature **880.3**

Howatson, Margaret C. *See* Howatson, M. C. (Margaret C.)

Howe, Irving
(ed) Kipling, R. The portable Kipling **828**

Howe, Ryan
(il) Bailey, N. Female force **920**

Howell, Simmone
Everything beautiful **Fic**

Howells, Amanda
The summer of skinny dipping **Fic**

Howes, Kelly King
War of 1812 **973.5**
World War II: biographies **920**

However tall the mountain. Ayub, A. **796.334**

Howitt, Carolyn
500 things to know about the ancient world **930**

HPV. Parks, P. J. **362.1**

Hrdlitschka, Shelley, 1956-
Sister wife **Fic**

Huang, Edwin
(il) Zubkavich, J. Skullkickers: 1000 Opas and a dead body **741.5**

Hubbard, Amanda
But I love him **Fic**
You wish **Fic**

Hubble Space Telescope
Kerrod, R. Hubble: the mirror on the universe **522**

Zimmerman, R. The universe in a mirror **629.43**

Hubble: the mirror on the universe. Kerrod, R. **522**

Human experimentation in medicine—*Continued*
Uschan, M. V. Forty years of medical racism
174.2
Human figure in art *See* Artistic anatomy
Human genetics. Hodge, R.   **599.93**
The **human** genome. Heos, B.   **611**
Human geography
How geography affects the United States
304.2
        Encyclopedias
World and its peoples: Europe   **940**
World and its peoples: the Americas   **917**
Human influence on nature
Climate change   **363.7**
Cousteau, J. Y. The human, the orchid, and the
  octopus   **333.95**
Fleming, J. R. Fixing the sky   **551.6**
Gunn, A. M. Unnatural disasters   **304.2**
How should America's wilderness be managed?
333.7
Meyer, J. L. The spirit of Yellowstone
978.7
Mongillo, J. F. Teen guides to environmental
  science   **333.72**
Montaigne, F. Fraser's penguins   **577.2**
Reece, E. Lost mountain   **622**
Slobodkin, L. B. A citizen's guide to ecology
577
Weisman, A. The world without us   **304.2**
Human origins
      See also Evolution; Fossil hominids; Pre-
  historic peoples
Darwin, C. On the origin of species   **576.8**
Holmes, T. Early humans   **599.93**
Johanson, D. C. From Lucy to language
599.93
Johanson, D. C. Lucy: the beginnings of human-
  kind   **599.93**
Leakey, R. E. The origin of humankind
599.93
Leakey, R. E. Origins reconsidered   **599.93**
Morell, V. Ancestral passions   **920**
Stefoff, R. First humans   **599.93**
Stefoff, R. Ice age Neanderthals   **599.93**
Stefoff, R. Modern humans   **599.93**
Stefoff, R. Origins   **599.93**
Tattersall, I. Extinct humans   **599.93**
Tudge, C. The time before history   **599.93**
Wells, S. The journey of man   **599.93**
        Encyclopedias
Encyclopedia of human evolution and prehistory
599.93
        Graphic novels
Keller, M. Charles Darwin's On the Origin of
  Species   **576.8**
Human relations *See* Interpersonal relations
Human rights
Barkan, E. The guilt of nations   **341.6**
Farmer, P. Pathologies of power   **305**
Herumin, W. Child labor today   **331.3**
Kennedy, K. Speak truth to power   **920**
        Fiction
Free?: stories about human rights   **S C**
        Poetry
Fire in the soul   **808.81**

Human spaceflight. Angelo, J. A.   **629.45**
The **human,** the orchid, and the octopus.
  Cousteau, J. Y.   **333.95**
Humanism
Rogers, C. R. A way of being   **150.19**
Humanitarian intervention
Mortenson, G. Stones into schools   **371.82**
Humans: an evolutionary history [series]
Stefoff, R. First humans   **599.93**
Stefoff, R. Ice age Neanderthals   **599.93**
Stefoff, R. Modern humans   **599.93**
Stefoff, R. Origins   **599.93**
Hume, David, 1711-1776
See/See also pages in the following book(s):
Russell, B. A history of Western philosophy
109
Humez, Alexander
On the dot   **411**
Humez, Nicholas D.
(jt. auth) Humez, A. On the dot   **411**
Humor *See* Wit and humor
Humor in young adult literature. Hogan, W.
813.009
Humorous graphic novels
Allen, B. A. A home for Mr. Easter   **741.5**
Azuma, K. Azumanga Daioh omnibus   **741.5**
Cherrywell, S. Pepper Penwell and the land
  creature of Monster Lake   **741.5**
Graphic Classics volume eight: Mark Twain
741.5
Gulledge, L. L. Page by Paige   **741.5**
Hicks, F. E. Zombies calling   **741.5**
Lat. Town boy   **741.5**
Mashima, H. Fairy tale vol. 1   **741.5**
Nakahara, A. Love*Com Vol. 1   **741.5**
Sfar, J. The professor's daughter   **741.5**
Takahashi, R. One-pound gospel, vol. 1
741.5
Tamaki, M. Skim   **741.5**
Urrea, L. A. Mr. Mendoza's paintbrush
741.5
Van Lente, F. Action philosophers!   **100**
Weinstein, L. Girl stories   **741.5**
Yang, G. Animal crackers   **741.5**
Yang, G. Prime baby   **741.5**
Zahler, T. F. Love and capes, vol. 1   **741.5**
Zubkavich, J. Skullkickers: 1000 Opas and a
  dead body   **741.5**
Humorous poetry
The Norton book of light verse   **821.008**
Silverstein, S. Where the sidewalk ends   **811**
The **hunchback** assignments. Slade, A. G.   **Fic**
The **hundred** greatest stars. Kaler, J. B.   **523.8**
Hünefeldt, Christine
A brief history of Peru   **985**
Hungary
        History
Marton, K. Enemies of the people   **92**
Hunger. Kessler, J. M.   **Fic**
The **Hunger** Games. Collins, S.   **Fic**
Hunger of memory. Rodriguez, R.   **92**
Hungry planet. Menzel, P.   **641.3**
The **hungry** years. Watkins, T. H.   **973.91**

Hunley (Submarine)
Walker, S. M. Secrets of a Civil War submarine
973.7

Hunn, John, 1818-1894
About
Berry, B. The ties that bind   920

Hunnicutt, Susan
School shootings   371.7
(ed) Foreign oil dependence. See Foreign oil dependence   333.8
(ed) Tobacco and smoking: opposing viewpoints. See Tobacco and smoking: opposing viewpoints   362.29

Hunt, Patrick
Ten discoveries that rewrote history   930.1

Hunt, Rameck
(jt. auth) Davis, S. The pact: three young men make a promise and fulfill a dream   920

Hunter, Sharon J.
(ed) Larousse concise dictionary: Spanish-English, English-Spanish. See Larousse concise dictionary: Spanish-English, English-Spanish   463

The **Hunter's** Moon. Melling, O. R.   Fic

Hunting
See also Tracking and trailing
Paulsen, G. Father water, Mother woods
799
Great Britain
See/See also pages in the following book(s):
Gies, J. Life in a medieval castle   940.2

Hunting the Dragon. Dixon, P. L.   Fic

Huntington's chorea
Glimm, A. Gene hunter [biography of Nancy Wexler]   92

Huntley, Amy
The everafter   Fic

Hurley, Tonya
Ghostgirl   Fic

Hurmence, Belinda, 1921-
(ed) My folks don't want me to talk about slavery. See My folks don't want me to talk about slavery   920

Hurricane dancers. Engle, M.   Fic

Hurricane Katrina, 2005
Dyson, M. E. Come hell or high water
976.3
Hurricane Katrina   363.34
Katrina: state of emergency   363.34
Van Heerden, I. L. The storm   976.3
Fiction
Volponi, P. Hurricane song   Fic
Personal narratives
Voices rising   976.3

Hurricane Katrina   363.34

Hurricane song. Volponi, P.   Fic

Hurricanes
See also Typhoons
Emanuel, K. A. Divine wind   551.55
Leatherman, S. P. Hurricanes   551.55
Mooney, C. Storm world   363.7

Encyclopedias
Longshore, D. Encyclopedia of hurricanes, typhoons, and cyclones   551.55
Fiction
Weyn, S. Empty   Fic

Hurston, Zora Neale, 1891-1960
The complete stories   S C
Dust tracks on a road   92
Folklore, memoirs, and other writings   818
Novels and stories   Fic
Their eyes were watching God   Fic
About
Jones, S. L. Critical companion to Zora Neale Hurston   813.009
Litwin, L. B. A reader's guide to Zora Neale Hurston's Their eyes were watching god
813.009
Lyons, M. E. Sorrow's kitchen [biography of Zora Neale Hurston]   92
Sapet, K. Rhythm and folklore [biography of Zora Neale Hurston]   92

Hurvitz, Mitchell M.
(jt. auth) Karesh, S. E. Encyclopedia of Judaism
296.03

Hurwin, Davida, 1950-
Freaks and revelations   Fic

Husain, Saddam *See* Hussein, Ṣaddām

Husain, Sarah
(ed) Voices of resistance. See Voices of resistance   305.4

Ḥusayn, Ṣaddām *See* Hussein, Ṣaddām

Huser, Glen, 1943-
Stitches   Fic

Hush. Chayil, E.   Fic

Hush. Napoli, D. J.   Fic

Hussein, Ṣaddām
About
Salbi, Z. Between two worlds   92

Hussey, Tris
Create your own blog   006.7

Hutchinson, S., 1959-
Oceans: a visual guide   551.46

Hutchinson, Stephen *See* Hutchinson, S., 1959-

Hutson, James H.
(ed) The Founders on religion. See The Founders on religion   200

Hutu (African people)
Hatzfeld, J. Machete season   967.571
Fiction
Combres, E. Broken memory   Fic

Huxley, Aldous, 1894-1963
Brave new world   Fic
Brave new world: and, Brave new world revisited   828
Brave new world revisited   303.3

Huxley, Anthony Julian, 1920-
Green inheritance   580

Hyde, Catherine Ryan
Becoming Chloe   Fic
Diary of a witness   Fic
Jumpstart the world   Fic

Hyde, Dayton O., 1925-
All the wild horses   599.66

Hyde, Margaret Oldroyd, 1917-
Depression   **616.85**
Safe sex 101   **613.9**
Smoking 101   **616.86**
Hydrogen as fuel
Tabak, J. Natural gas and hydrogen   **333.8**
Hydrothermal vents *See* Ocean bottom
Hygiene
    See also Health
Ashenburg, K. The dirt on clean   **391**
        Study and teaching
    See Health education
Hyman, Bruce M.
Obsessive-compulsive disorder   **616.85**
Hyman, Jeremy S.
(jt. auth) Jacobs, L. F. The secrets of college success   **378.1**
Hyperactive children
    See also Attention deficit disorder
Hypnotism
Rosen, M. Meditation and hypnosis   **154.7**
Hyslop, Stephen G., 1950-
National Geographic Society (U.S.). Atlas of the Civil War   **973.7**
(jt. auth) Currie, R. The letter and the scroll   **220.9**

I

I am J. Beam, C.   **Fic**
I am legend. Matheson, R.   **S C**
I am Mordred. Springer, N.   **Fic**
I am Morgan le Fay. Springer, N.   **Fic**
I am number four. Frey, J.   **Fic**
I am Rembrandt's daughter. Cullen, L.   **Fic**
I am Scout: the biography of Harper Lee. Shields, C. J.   **92**
I am the cheese. Cormier, R.   **Fic**
I am the darker brother   **811.008**
I am the messenger. Zusak, M.   **Fic**
I can't keep my own secrets   **808.8**
I ching
Brennan, J. H. The magical I ching   **299.5**
I, Claudius. Graves, R.   **Fic**
I did it without thinking. Hugel, B.   **155.5**
I don't want to be crazy. Schutz, S.   **92**
I feel a little jumpy around you   **808.81**
I found it on the Internet. Harris, F. J.   **025.04**
I have lived a thousand years. Bitton-Jackson, L.   **940.53**
I heard God talking to me. Spires, E.   **811**
I heard the owl call my name. Craven, M.   **Fic**
I just hope it's lethal   **808.81**
I kissed a zombie, and I liked it. Selzer, A.   **Fic**
I know it's over. Martin, C. K. K.   **Fic**
I know why the caged bird sings. Angelou, M.   **92**

I know why the caged bird sings, by Maya Angelou   **818**
I love yoga. Schwartz, E.   **613.7**
I never had it made. Robinson, J.   **92**
I never promised you a rose garden. Greenberg, J.   **Fic**
I now pronounce you someone else. McCahan, E.   **Fic**
I, Rigoberta Menchú. Menchú, R.   **92**
I, robot. Asimov, I.   **S C**
I see the promised land [biography of Martin Luther King Jr.] Flowers, A. R.   **92**
I thought my father was God and other true tales from the National Story Project   **810.8**
I want to be left behind. Peterson, B.   **92**
I was Jane Austen's best friend. Harrison, C.   **Fic**
I write what I like. Biko, S.   **968.06**
Ibbitson, John, 1955-
The Landing   **Fic**
Ibn al-Haytham *See* Alhazen, 965-1039
Ibn al-Haytham. Steffens, B.   **92**
Ibo (African people) *See* Igbo (African people)
Ibsen, Henrik, 1828-1906
Ibsen: four major plays   **839.8**
iCanPlayMusic [series]
Complete guitar course   **787.87**
iCanPlayMusic complete guitar course. See Complete guitar course   **787.87**
Ice
Glaciers, sea ice, and ice formation   **551.3**
Pollack, H. N. A world without ice   **551.3**
Ice. Durst, S. B.   **Fic**
Ice Age
Fagan, B. M. Cro-Magnon   **569.9**
Ice age Neanderthals. Stefoff, R.   **599.93**
Ice hockey *See* Hockey
Ice skating
        Biography
Aldridge, R. Apolo Anton Ohno   **92**
Icecore. Whyman, M.   **Fic**
Iceland
        Fiction
Simner, J. L. Thief eyes   **Fic**
The **iceman** cometh. O'Neill, E.   **812**
Icenoggle, Jodi, 1967-
Schenck v. United States and the freedom of speech debate   **342**
Iconography *See* Christian art; Religious art
Icons of Latino America. Bruns, R.   **920**
Ideal states *See* Utopias
Ideas that changed the world. Ferris, J.   **609**
Identical. Hopkins, E.   **Fic**
Identical strangers. Schein, E.   **92**
Identification
    See also DNA fingerprinting; Forensic anthropology
Identity (Psychology)
        Fiction
Beam, C. I am J   **Fic**

Immigrants—United States—*Continued*
Bergquist, J. M. Daily life in immigrant America, 1820-1870   **305.9**
Biddle, W. Immigrants' rights after 9/11   **323.3**
Horst, H. A. Jamaican Americans   **305.8**
Rangaswamy, P. Indian Americans   **305.8**
Reyes, G. Madre and I   **92**
Scarpaci, V. The journey of the Italians in America   **305.8**
   United States—Encyclopedias
Encyclopedia of American immigration   **304.8**

Immigrants' rights after 9/11. Biddle, W.   **323.3**

Immigration   **304.8**

Immigration [Current controversies series]   **325.73**

Immigration and emigration
   See also Canada—Immigration and emigration; Children of immigrants; Immigrants; Refugees names of countries with the subdivision *Immigration and emigration*; and names of nationality groups
Bailey, R. Immigration and migration   **304.8**
Pagden, A. Peoples and empires   **909**

Immigration policy. Allport, A.   **325.73**

Immortal beloved. Tiernan, C.   **Fic**

The **immortal** life of Henrietta Lacks. Skloot, R.   **92**

Immortality
   See also Future life
   Fiction
Houck, C. Tiger's curse   **Fic**
Malley, G. The Declaration   **Fic**
Tiernan, C. Immortal beloved   **Fic**

Immroth, Barbara Froling
   (ed) Library services to youth of Hispanic heritage. See Library services to youth of Hispanic heritage   **027.6**
   (jt. auth) Lukenbill, W. B. Health information in a changing world   **372**

Immunization *See* Vaccination

Imperial Trans-Antarctic Expedition (1914-1917)
Alexander, C. The Endurance   **998**

Imperial War Museum (London, England)
Moore, K. The Battle of Britain   **940.54**

Imperialism
The American empire   **327.73**
Cocker, M. Rivers of blood, rivers of gold   **909**
Industrialization and empire, 1783 to 1914   **330.9**
Laxer, J. Empire   **327.73**
Smith, B. Imperialism   **909**
See/See also pages in the following book(s):
Heilbroner, R. L. The worldly philosophers   **330.1**

The **importance** of being earnest and other plays. Wilde, O.   **822**

Impossible. Werlin, N.   **Fic**

Impressionism (Art)
Bingham, J. Impressionism   **759.05**
Kallen, S. A. Claude Monet   **92**

The **improbable** adventures of Sherlock Holmes   **S C**

Improving student achievement. Nichols, B.   **373.1**

In a flash. Walters, E.   **Fic**

In cold blood. Capote, T.   **364.1**

In controversy [series]
Barbour, S. Is the world prepared for a deadly influenza pandemic?   **614.5**
Barbour, S. Should marijuana be legalized?   **344**
Bjornlund, L. D. How dangerous are performance-enhancing drugs?   **362.29**
Marcovitz, H. Can renewable energy replace fossil fuels?   **333.79**

In country. Mason, B. A.   **Fic**

In fact   **814**

In fashion. Iverson, A.   **746.9**

In focus   **779**

In harm's way. Stanton, D.   **940.54**

In-line skater's start-up. Werner, D.   **796.21**

In-line skating
Werner, D. In-line skater's start-up   **796.21**

In Mike we trust. Ryan, P.   **Fic**

In Montgomery, and other poems. Brooks, G.   **811**

In odd we trust. Koontz, D. R.   **741.5**

In our own words   **815.008**

In search of the old ones. Roberts, D.   **970.004**

In the blink of an eye. Parker, A.   **576.8**

In the company of soldiers. Atkinson, R.   **956.7**

In the devil's garden. Allen, S. L.   **641**

In the driver's seat. Stalder, E.   **629.28**

In the footsteps of Alexander the Great. Wood, M.   **938**

In the footsteps of Marco Polo. Belliveau, D.   **915**

In the ghettos. Ayer, E. H.   **940.53**

In the heart of the sea. Philbrick, N.   **910.4**

In the name of God. Jolin, P.   **Fic**

In the news [series]
Ching, J. Outsourcing U.S. jobs   **331.1**
Nagle, J. M. Living green   **333.72**

In the path of falling objects. Smith, A.   **Fic**

In the shadow of man. Goodall, J.   **599.8**

In the shadow of no towers. Spiegelman, A.   **973.931**

In the shadow of the ark. Provoost, A.   **Fic**

In the shadow of the moon. French, F.   **629.45**

In their shoes. Reber, D.   **331.4**

In these girls, hope is a muscle. Blais, M.   **796.323**

In world history [series]
Gaines, A. Nelson Mandela and apartheid in world history   **92**

Industrial revolution
Benson, S. Development of the industrial U.S.:
Almanac **330.973**
Benson, S. Development of the industrial U.S.:
Biographies **920**
Benson, S. Development of the industrial U.S.:
Primary sources **330.973**
Industrial revolution **330.9**
Industrialization and empire, 1783 to 1914
330.9
Outman, J. L. Industrial Revolution: almanac
330.9
Outman, J. L. Industrial Revolution: biographies
920
Outman, J. L. Industrial Revolution: primary
sources **330.9**
Encyclopedias
Encyclopedia of the age of the industrial revolu-
tion, 1700-1920 **330.9**
Industrial revolution **330.9**
Industrial revolution reference library [series]
Outman, J. L. Industrial Revolution: almanac
330.9
Outman, J. L. Industrial Revolution: biographies
920
Outman, J. L. Industrial Revolution: primary
sources **330.9**
Industrialization
Industrial revolution **330.9**
Industrialization and empire, 1783 to 1914
330.9
Industrialization and empire, 1783 to 1914
330.9
Industries
United States
Benson, S. Development of the industrial U.S.:
Almanac **330.973**
Benson, S. Development of the industrial U.S.:
Biographies **920**
Benson, S. Development of the industrial U.S.:
Primary sources **330.973**
Industry and war See War—Economic aspects
Inequality See Equality
Inexcusable. Lynch, C. **Fic**
Infamous scribblers. Burns, E. **071**
Infantile paralysis See Poliomyelitis
Infants
Birth defects
See Birth defects
Fiction
Bechard, M. Hanging on to Max **Fic**
Dessen, S. Along for the ride **Fic**
Efaw, A. After **Fic**
Johnson, A. The first part last **Fic**
Infection and infectious diseases See Communi-
cable diseases
The infernal devices [series]
Clare, C. Clockwork angel **Fic**
Infidel. Hirsi Ali, A. **92**
Infidelity, Marital See Adultery
Infinite days. Maizel, R. **Fic**
The **influence** of air power upon history. Boyne,
W. J. **358.4**

Influential economists. Bussing-Burks, M. **920**
Influenza
See also Avian influenza; Swine influenza
Barbour, S. Is the world prepared for a deadly
influenza pandemic? **614.5**
Cunningham, K. Flu **614.5**
Goldsmith, C. Influenza **616.2**
Goldsmith, C. Influenza: the next pandemic?
614.5
Kelly, E. B. Investigating influenza and bird flu
616.2
Parks, P. J. Influenza **616.2**
Influenza: the next pandemic? Goldsmith, C.
614.5
Information literacy
Behen, L. D. Using pop culture to teach infor-
mation literacy **028.7**
Callison, D. The blue book on information age
inquiry, instruction and literacy **028.7**
Ercegovac, Z. Information literacy **025.5**
Grassian, E. S. Information literacy instruction
025.5
Student engagement and information literacy
028.7
Taylor, J. Information literacy and the school li-
brary media center **028.7**
Teaching Generation M **027.62**
Study and teaching
Berger, P. Choosing Web 2.0 tools for learning
and teaching in a digital world **025.04**
Honnold, R. Get connected **027.62**
Information literacy and the school library media
center. Taylor, J. **028.7**
Information literacy instruction. Grassian, E. S.
025.5
Information networks
See also Internet
Information please almanac. See Time almanac
2011 **031.02**
Information Plus reference series
Evans, K. M. National security **363.32**
Evans, K. M. Space exploration **629.4**
Information power. American Association of
School Librarians **027.8**
Information resources
See also Internet resources
Lenburg, J. The Facts on File guide to research
025.5
Information services
See also Health—Information services
Information society
See also Information technology
Information storage and retrieval systems See
Information systems
Information systems
See also Digital libraries; Multimedia
Wolinsky, A. Internet power research using the
Big6 approach **025.04**
Information technology
Braun, L. W. Teens, technology, and literacy;
or, Why bad grammar isn't always bad
373.1

Information technology—*Continued*
Cohn, J. M. The complete library technology planner **025**
Core technology competencies for librarians and library staff **020**
Farkas, M. Social software in libraries **025.5**
Farmer, L. S. J. Teen girls and technology **004**
Huber, J. Ask Mr. Technology, get answers **371.3**
Jurkowski, O. L. Technology and the school library **027.8**
Reilly, E. D. Milestones in computer science and information technology **004**
Scheeren, W. O. Technology for the school librarian **025.04**

Inge, M. Thomas
(ed) The Greenwood guide to American popular culture. See The Greenwood guide to American popular culture **973.9**

Inge, William, 1913-1973
4 plays **812**

Ingenium. Denny, M. **609**

Ingram, Scott, 1948-
Want fries with that? **613.2**

Ingram, Simone
(jt. auth) Gaden, M. Cracking the SAT. French subject test **440**

Inhalants and solvents. Flynn, N. **362.29**

Inhalation abuse of solvents See Solvent abuse

Inheritance [series]
Paolini, C. Eragon **Fic**

Inheritance and succession
Fiction
Standiford, N. Confessions of the Sullivan sisters **Fic**

Inheriting the Holy Land. Miller, J. **956.94**

Injuries See Accidents; First aid; Wounds and injuries

Inner planets. Grier, J. A. **523.4**

Innes, Brian, 1928-
DNA and body evidence **363.2**
Fingerprints and impressions **363.2**

An **innocent** soldier. Holub, J. **Fic**

The **innocents** abroad [and] Roughing it. Twain, M. **818**

Innovations, Technological See Technological innovations

Inns See Hotels and motels

Innuit See Inuit

Inoculation See Vaccination

Inoue, Kaori
(tr) Unita, Y. Bunny drop vol. 1 **741.5**

Inoue, Takehiko, 1967-
Real, volume 1 **741.5**
Slam dunk, volume 1 **741.5**

Inquisition
Pérez, J. The Spanish Inquisition **272**
Fiction
Hoffman, A. Incantation **Fic**

Insane See Mentally ill

Hospitals
See Psychiatric hospitals

Insatiable. Cabot, M. **Fic**

Inscriptions
See also Graffiti

Inscriptions, Cuneiform See Cuneiform inscriptions

Insect museum. Dourlot, S. **595.7**

Insect pests
Macgillivray, A. Understanding Rachel Carson's Silent Spring **363.7**
Russell, E. War and nature **577.2**
Stewart, A. Wicked bugs **632**
Waldbauer, G. Insights from insects **632**

Insects
See also Ants; Butterflies; Grasshoppers; Moths
Alderton, D. Firefly encyclopedia of the vivarium **639.3**
Dourlot, S. Insect museum **595.7**
Eisner, T. Secret weapons **595.7**
Marshall, S. A. Insects: their natural history and diversity **595.7**
Waldbauer, G. A walk around the pond **595.7**
Waldbauer, G. What good are bugs? **595.7**

Insects, Injurious and beneficial See Insect pests

Insects as carriers of disease
Poinar, G. O. What bugged the dinosaurs? **560**

Inservice training See Librarians—In-service training

Inside ancient China [series]
Strapp, J. Science and technology **609**
Whitfield, S. Philosophy and writing **181**

Inside Delta Force. Haney, E. L. **356**

Inside forensic science [series]
Adams, B. J. Forensic anthropology **614**
Adelman, H. C. Forensic medicine **614**
Kobilinsky, L. F. Forensic DNA analysis **614**
Sapse, D. S. Legal aspects of forensics **363.2**
Stripp, R. A. The forensic aspects of poisons **614**
Zedeck, B. E. Forensic pharmacology **614**

Inside science [series]
Allman, T. Vaccine research **615**
George, C. Climate change research **551.6**
Kallen, S. A. Renewable energy research **333.79**
Marcovitz, H. Gene therapy research **615.8**
Marcovitz, H. Stem cell research **616**
Parks, P. J. Space research **500.5**

Inside the Crips. Simpson, C. **92**

The **insider's** guide to the Peace Corps. Banerjee, D. **361.6**

An **insider's** guide to the UN. Fasulo, L. M. **341.23**

Insights from insects. Waldbauer, G. **632**

Insignia
See also National emblems

Inspiration *See* Creation (Literary, artistic, etc.)

The **instant** physicist. Muller, R.   **530**

Instruction *See* Teaching

Instructional materials *See* Teaching—Aids and devices

Instructional materials centers

    See also School libraries

American Association of School Librarians. Information power   **027.8**

Church, A. P. Leverage your library program to help raise test scores   **027.8**

Farmer, L. S. J. Collaborating with administrators and educational support staff   **027.8**

Farmer, L. S. J. Neal-Schuman technology management handbook for school library media centers   **025.1**

Harada, V. H. Collaborating for project-based learning in grades 9-12   **371.3**

Harvey, C. A., II. No school library left behind   **025.1**

Hughes-Hassell, S. Collection management for youth   **025.2**

Jones, J. B. The power of the media specialist to improve academic achievement and strengthen at-risk students   **027.8**

Martin, B. S. Fundamentals of school library media management   **025.1**

McGhee, M. W. The principal's guide to a powerful library media program   **025.1**

Morris, B. J. Administering the school library media center   **027.8**

Nichols, B. Improving student achievement   **373.1**

Safford, B. R. Guide to reference materials for school library media centers   **011.6**

Stephens, C. G. Library 101   **027.8**

Toor, R. Being indispensable   **025.1**

Van Deusen, J. D. Enhancing teaching and learning   **027.8**

Volkman, J. D. Collaborative library research projects   **025.5**

The Whole school library handbook   **027.8**

Woolls, E. B. The school library media manager   **027.8**

       Automation

Jurkowski, O. L. Technology and the school library   **027.8**

       Design and construction

Baule, S. M. Facilities planning for school library and technology centers   **027.8**

Erikson, R. Designing a school library media center for the future   **027.8**

Instrumental music

See/See also pages in the following book(s):

Grout, D. J. A history of western music   **780.9**

Insults *See* Invective

Insurance, State and compulsory *See* Social security

Insurgency

       Fiction

Scott, E. Grace   **Fic**

Integration in education *See* School integration

Intellect

Goleman, D. Emotional intelligence   **152.4**

Goleman, D. Social intelligence   **158**

Johnson, S. Everything bad is good for you   **306**

Jolly, A. Lucy's legacy   **599.93**

Intellectual freedom

    See also Academic freedom; Freedom of information

Dougherty, T. Freedom of expression and the Internet   **323.44**

Intellectual freedom manual   **025.2**

Scales, P. R. Protecting intellectual freedom in your school library   **025.2**

Selverstone, H. S. Encouraging and supporting student inquiry   **001.4**

Symons, A. K. Protecting the right to read   **025.2**

Intellectual freedom manual   **025.2**

Intellectual life

The Britannica guide to theories and ideas that changed the modern world   **901**

Intellectual property. Wherry, T. L.   **346.04**

Intelligence *See* Intellect

Intelligence, Artificial *See* Artificial intelligence

Intelligence of animals *See* Animal intelligence

Intelligence service

    See also Espionage

       Fiction

Cormier, R. I am the cheese   **Fic**

       United States

Espionage and intelligence   **327.12**

Intelligence tests

    See also Educational tests and measurements

The **intelligencer**. Silbert, L.   **Fic**

Intercultural education *See* Multicultural education

Interest groups *See* Lobbying

Intermarriage

    See also Interracial marriage

Internal migration

Lemann, N. The promised land   **973.9**

The **international** book of days. Christianson, S. G.   **394.26**

International economic relations

    See also Sanctions (International law)

International law

    See also Intervention (International law)

International plays for young audiences   **808.82**

International politics *See* World politics

International relations

    See also Globalization; World politics

Barkan, E. The guilt of nations   **341.6**

       Encyclopedias

Moore, J. A. Encyclopedia of the United Nations   **341.23**

International Science and Engineering Fair

Dutton, J. Science fair season   **507.8**

Internationalization *See* Globalization

Israelis—*Continued*
Fiction
Elkeles, S. How to ruin my teenage life   **Fic**

Isserman, Maurice
Exploring North America, 1800-1900   **917**
Korean War   **951.9**
Vietnam War   **959.704**
World War II   **940.53**
(ed) Bowman, J. S. Exploration in the world of the ancients   **913**

Issitt, Micah L.
Hippies   **305.5**

Issues in focus [series]
McClellan, M. Organ and tissue transplants   **617.9**

Issues in focus today [series]
Feinstein, S. Sexuality and teens   **306.7**
Gay, K. The scoop on what to eat   **613.2**
Gordon, S. M. Beyond bruises   **362.7**
Gordon, S. M. Downloading copyrighted stuff from the Internet   **346.04**
Gordon, S. M. Peanut butter, milk, and other deadly threats   **616.97**
Herumin, W. Child labor today   **331.3**
Hinds, M. J. You have the right to know your rights   **342**
Judson, K. Resolving conflicts   **303.6**
Kowalski, K. M. Attack of the superbugs   **616.9**

Issues on trial [series]
Civil liberties and war   **342**
The death penalty   **345**
The environment   **344**
Freedom of the press   **342**
Individual rights and the police   **345**
Native American rights   **342**
Racial discrimination   **342**
Reproductive rights   **344**
Rights of the accused   **345**
Students' rights   **344**

Issues that concern you [series]
Attention deficit hyperactivity disorder   **618.92**
Body image   **306.4**
Censorship   **363.31**
Climate change   **363.7**

IssueWeb: a guide and sourcebook for researching controversial issues on the Web. Diaz, K. R.   **025.04**

It happened to me [series]
Apel, M. A. Cystic fibrosis   **616.2**
Gay, K. Volunteering   **361.3**
Myers, E. When will I stop hurting?   **155.9**
Paquette, P. H. Apprenticeship   **331.2**
Paquette, P. H. Learning disabilities   **371.9**
Rompella, N. Obsessive-compulsive disorder   **616.85**
Rouba, K. Juvenile arthritis   **618.92**
Schwartz, T. P. Organ transplants   **617.9**
Slade, S. Adopted: the ultimate teen guide   **362.7**

It is a good day to die. Viola, H. J.   **973.8**

Italian Americans
Capotorto, C. Twisted head   **92**

Scarpaci, V. The journey of the Italians in America   **305.8**
Fiction
Blundell, J. Strings attached   **Fic**
Freitas, D. The possibilities of sainthood   **Fic**

Italian artists *See* Artists, Italian

Italian literature
See/See also pages in the following book(s):
Highet, G. The classical tradition   **809**
History and criticism
The Cambridge history of Italian literature   **850.9**

Italy
Civilization
Cohen, E. S. Daily life in Renaissance Italy   **945**
Fiction
Harper, S. The Juliet club   **Fic**
Meyer, C. Duchessina   **Fic**
Quick, B. A golden web   **Fic**
History
The Oxford history of Italy   **945**

It's been a good life. Asimov, I.   **92**
It's kind of a funny story. Vizzini, N.   **Fic**
It's not about the bike. Armstrong, L.   **92**
It's your world—if you don't like it, change it. Halpin, M.   **361.2**

The **Ivan** R. Dee guide to plays and playwrights. Griffiths, T. R.   **809.2**

Iverson, Annemarie
In fashion   **746.9**
(jt. auth) Brown, B. Bobbi Brown teenage beauty   **646.7**

Ivory Coast
Graphic novels
Abouet, M. Aya   **741.5**

Ivy. Hearn, J.   **Fic**

Iwaoka, Hisae, 1976-
Saturn apartments, volume 1   **741.5**

Iwo Jima, Battle of, 1945
Bradley, J. Flags of our fathers   **940.54**

Iyer, Pico
The open road   **92**

J

J.K. Rowling: a biography. Kirk, C. A.   **92**

Jabbar, Kareem Abdul- *See* Abdul-Jabbar, Kareem, 1947-

Jackson, Andrew, 1767-1845
About
Marrin, A. Old Hickory [biography of Andrew Jackson]   **92**
Remini, R. V. Andrew Jackson   **92**
Wilentz, S. Andrew Jackson   **92**

Jackson, Kenneth T.
(ed) The Scribner encyclopedia of American lives. See The Scribner encyclopedia of American lives   **920.003**

Janeczko, Paul B., 1945-—*Continued*
(comp) Seeing the blue between. See Seeing the blue between **808.1**

Janitors
Fiction
Cohen, T. Little black lies **Fic**

Jansen, Barbara A.
(jt. auth) McGhee, M. W. The principal's guide to a powerful library media program **025.1**

Jansen, Hanna
Over a thousand hills I walk with you **Fic**

Janson, H. W. (Horst Woldemar), 1913-1982
Janson's history of art **709**

Janson, Horst Woldemar *See* Janson, H. W. (Horst Woldemar), 1913-1982

Janson's history of art. Janson, H. W. **709**

Japan
Civilization
Dunn, C. J. Everyday life in traditional Japan **952**
Khanduri, K. Japanese art & culture **709.52**
Fiction
Golden, A. Memoirs of a geisha **Fic**
Hearn, L. Across the nightingale floor **Fic**
Lake, N. Blood ninja **Fic**
Randall, T. Dreams of the dead **Fic**
Thompson, H. Orchards **Fic**
Folklore
See Folklore—Japan
Graphic novels
Sakai, S. Usagi Yojimbo, book one **741.5**
Sakai, S. Usagi Yojimbo: Yokai **741.5**
History
Buruma, I. Inventing Japan, 1853-1964 **952.03**
History—1868-1945
Frank, R. B. Downfall **940.54**
History—1868-1945—Graphic novels
Watsuki, N. Rurouni Kenshin **741.5**
History—1945-1952, Allied Occupation—Graphic novels
Nakazawa, K. Barefoot Gen volume five: the never-ending war **741.5**
Nakazawa, K. Barefoot Gen volume six: writing the truth **741.5**
Religion
Roberts, J. Japanese mythology A to Z **299.5**
Social life and customs
Dunn, C. J. Everyday life in traditional Japan **952**

Japanese
United States—Fiction
Preus, M. Heart of a samurai **Fic**
The **Japanese** American internment. Heinrichs, A. **940.53**
Japanese American internment during World War II. Ng, W. L. **940.53**

Japanese American women
Fiction
Uchida, Y. Picture bride **Fic**

Japanese Americans
Yamazaki, J. N. Children of the atomic bomb **92**
Evacuation and relocation, 1942-1945
And justice for all **940.53**
Daniels, R. Prisoners without trial **940.53**
Davenport, J. The internment of Japanese Americans during World War II **940.53**
Heinrichs, A. The Japanese American internment **940.53**
Houston, J. W. Farewell to Manzanar **940.53**
Ng, W. L. Japanese American internment during World War II **940.53**
Only what we could carry **940.53**
Oppenheim, J. Dear Miss Breed **940.53**
Robinson, G. By order of the president **940.53**
See/See also pages in the following book(s):
Barkan, E. The guilt of nations **341.6**
Evacuation and relocation, 1942-1945—Fiction
Otsuka, J. When the emperor was divine **Fic**
Fiction
Guterson, D. Snow falling on cedars **Fic**
Salisbury, G. Eyes of the emperor **Fic**
Salisbury, G. Under the blood-red sun **Fic**

Japanese art & culture. Khanduri, K. **709.52**

Japanese arts
Khanduri, K. Japanese art & culture **709.52**

Japanese authors *See* Authors, Japanese

Japanese cooking
Shimbo, H. The Japanese kitchen **641.5**
Graphic novels
The manga cookbook **641.5**

Japanese drama
See also Nō plays

The **Japanese** kitchen. Shimbo, H. **641.5**

Japanese language
Kardy, G. Manga University Presents . . . Kana de Manga Special Edition: Japanese Sound FX! **495.6**
Lammers, W. P. Japanese the manga way **495.6**
Dictionaries
Basic Japanese-English dictionary **495.6**

Japanese literature
Collections
Anthology of Japanese literature from the earliest era to the mid-nineteenth century **895.6**

Japanese mythology
Roberts, J. Japanese mythology A to Z **299.5**

Japanese mythology A to Z. Roberts, J. **299.5**

Japanese paper folding *See* Origami

Japanese poetry
Collections
From the country of eight islands **895.6**
One hundred poems from the Japanese **895.6**

Japanese the manga way. Lammers, W. P. **495.6**

Johnson, Harriet McBryde
Accidents of nature   Fic

Johnson, James Weldon, 1871-1938
Complete poems   811

Johnson, Kendall
(jt. auth) Haralson, E. L. Critical companion to Henry James   813.009

Johnson, Lindsay Lee
Worlds apart   Fic

Johnson, LouAnne
Muchacho   Fic

Johnson, Lyndon B. (Lyndon Baines), 1908-1973
About
Peters, C. Lyndon B. Johnson   92

Johnson, Marguerite *See* Angelou, Maya

Johnson, Maureen, 1973-
13 little blue envelopes   Fic
Devilish   Fic
Suite Scarlett   Fic
(jt. auth) Green, J. Let it snow   S C

Johnson, Michael, 1937-
Encyclopedia of native tribes of North America   970.004

Johnson, Paul, 1928-
George Washington: the Founding Father   92
Napoleon   92

Johnson, Rafer, 1935-
(ed) Great athletes. See Great athletes   920.003

Johnson, Rebecca L., 1956-
(jt. auth) Foster, S. National Geographic desk reference to nature's medicine   615

Johnson, Robert, 1911-1938
About
Wald, E. Escaping the delta [biography of Robert Johnson]   92
Poetry
Lewis, J. P. Black cat bone   811

Johnson, Sarah Anne
The art of the author interview   808

Johnson, Sarah L., 1969-
Historical fiction   016.8
Historical fiction II   016.8

Johnson, Steven
Everything bad is good for you   306
The ghost map   614.5

Johnson, Thomas H., 1899-1998
(ed) Dickinson, E. The complete poems of Emily Dickinson   811

Johnson, Torrence V., 1944-
(ed) Encyclopedia of the solar system. See Encyclopedia of the solar system   523.2

Johnson, Venice
(ed) Heart full of grace. See Heart full of grace   808.88

Johnston, Andrew K., 1969-
(jt. auth) Launius, R. D. Smithsonian atlas of space exploration   500.5

Johnston, Brian, 1932-
(jt. auth) Ibsen, H. Ibsen: four major plays   839.8

Johnston, Janine
(il) Ottaviani, J. Levitation: physics and psychology in the service of deception   793.8

Joker one. Campbell, D.   956.7

Jolin, Paula
In the name of God   Fic

Joliot-Curie, Irène, 1897-1956
Poetry
Atkins, J. Borrowed names   811

Jolly, Alison
Lucy's legacy   599.93

Jones, Allan Frewin, 1954-
Warrior princess   Fic

Jones, Barrie William
Pluto   523.4

Jones, Caroline
1001 little fashion miracles   646

Jones, Constance, 1961-
Encyclopedia of Hinduism   294.5

Jones, Ella W.
Start-to-finish YA programs   027.62

Jones, Gerard
Men of tomorrow   741.5
(adapter) Takahashi, R. One-pound gospel, vol. 1   741.5
(adapter) Watsuki, N. Rurouni Kenshin   741.5

Jones, Gwyneth A., 1952-
See also Halam, Ann

Jones, J. Sydney
The Crusades, Biographies   920.003
The Crusades, Primary sources   909.07
World religions. See World religions   200

Jones, Jami Biles
The power of the media specialist to improve academic achievement and strengthen at-risk students   027.8
(jt. auth) Bush, G. Tales out of the school library   027.8

Jones, Joelle
(il) Evanovich, J. Troublemaker   741.5

Jones, John Paul, 1747-1792
About
Brager, B. L. John Paul Jones   92

Jones, Landon Y., 1943-
(ed) Lewis, M. The essential Lewis and Clark   978

Jones, Lauren V.
Stars and galaxies   523.8

Jones, Lloyd, 1955-
Mister Pip   Fic

Jones, Mark
(jt. auth) De Roy, T. Albatross   598

Jones, Patrick
Chasing tail lights   Fic
Connecting with reluctant teen readers   028.5
The tear collector   Fic

Jones, Sharon L., 1967-
Critical companion to Zora Neale Hurston   813.009

Jones, Stephen, 1953-
(ed) Horror: another 100 best books. See Horror: another 100 best books   823.009

Jones, Stephen A., 1951-
(jt. auth) Freedman, E. African Americans in
Congress **328.73**

Jones, Thomas D.
Planetology **523.4**

Jones, Tim Wynne- *See* Wynne-Jones, Tim

Jones, Victoria Garrett
Pocahontas **92**

Jonnes, Jill, 1952-
Empires of light **621.3**

Jonsberg, Barry, 1951-
Dreamrider **Fic**

Jonson, Ben, 1573?-1637
About
Ben Jonson [critical essays] **822.009**

Joplin, Janis, 1943-1970
About
Angel, A. Janis Joplin **92**

Joravsky, Ben
Hoop dreams **796.323**

Jordan, Barbara, 1936-1996
About
Mendelsohn, J. Barbara Jordan **92**

Jordan, Hillary, 1963-
Mudbound **Fic**

Jordan, Sandra
(jt. auth) Greenberg, J. Andy Warhol **92**
(jt. auth) Greenberg, J. Runaway girl: the artist
Louise Bourgeois **92**

Jordan, Sophie
Firelight **Fic**

Josei manga
Ono, N. Gente: the people of Ristorante Para-
diso, volume 1 **741.5**
Unita, Y. Bunny drop vol. 1 **741.5**

Joseph, Nez Percé Chief, 1840-1904
About
Hopping, L. J. Chief Joseph **92**
Moulton, C. V. Chief Joseph **92**
Scott, R. A. Chief Joseph and the Nez Percés
92

See/See also pages in the following book(s):
Freedman, R. Indian chiefs **920**

Joseph Stalin and the Soviet Union. Cunningham,
K. **92**

Josephy, Alvin M., 1915-2005
(ed) America in 1492. See America in 1492
970.01

Jossey-Bass education series
Conley, D. T. College knowledge **378.1**

Jost, Kenneth
The Supreme Court A to Z **347**

Journalism
See also Broadcast journalism; College and
school journalism; Photojournalism
Burns, E. Infamous scribblers **071**
Foerstel, H. N. From Watergate to Monicagate
070.4
Freedman, S. G. Letters to a young journalist
070.4
The New new journalism **071**
Reporting civil rights **323.1**
Written into history **071**

Fiction
Bauer, J. Peeled **Fic**
Wallace, R. One good punch **Fic**
Winston, S. The Kayla chronicles **Fic**
Zeises, L. M. The sweet life of Stella Madison
Fic
Zielin, L. Donut days **Fic**

Journalistas **808.8**

Journalists
See also Women journalists
Baker, R. Growing up **92**
Bragg, R. All over but the shoutin' **92**
Brokaw, T. A long way from home **92**
Edwards, B. Edward R. Murrow and the birth of
broadcast journalism **92**
Grogan, J. The longest trip home **92**
Hockenberry, J. Moving violations **92**
Marton, K. Enemies of the people **92**
Fiction
Ford, J. C. The morgue and me **Fic**
Guterson, D. Snow falling on cedars **Fic**
Sayed, K. Let it be morning **Fic**

Journals *See* Periodicals

Journals (Diaries) *See* Diaries

The **journals** of Lewis and Clark. Lewis, M.
978

Journey from the land of no. Hakakian, R. **92**

Journey into Mohawk Country. Bogaert, H. M. v.
d. **973.2**

Journey of a thousand miles. Lang, L. **92**

The **journey** of man. Wells, S. **599.93**

The **journey** of the Italians in America. Scarpaci,
V. **305.8**

Journey of the Jihadist. Gerges, F. A. **322.4**

The **journey** toward recovery. Esherick, J.
616.8

Journeys *See* Voyages and travels

Jowett, Benjamin, 1817-1893
(tr) Plato. The selected dialogues of Plato
184

The **Joy** Luck Club. Tan, A. **Fic**

The **Joy** Luck Club, by Amy Tan **813.009**

The **joy** of chemistry. Cobb, C. **540**

Joy of cooking. Rombauer, I. v. S. **641.5**

The **joy** of π. Blatner, D. **516.2**

Joyce, Graham
The exchange **Fic**

Joyce, James, 1882-1941
Dubliners **S C**
A portrait of the artist as a young man **Fic**
About
Fargnoli, A. N. Critical companion to James
Joyce **823.009**

Joyce, Marilyn Z.
(jt. auth) Tallman, J. I. Making the writing and
research connection with the I-search process
025.5

Juby, Susan, 1969-
Another kind of cowboy **Fic**

Judah, Tim, 1962-
The Serbs **949.7**

Judaic studies series
Mothers, sisters, resisters   **940.53**

Judaism
   See also Rabbis
Chittister, J. The tent of Abraham   **222**
Ehrlich, C. S. Judaism   **296**
Kessler, E. What do Jews believe?   **296**
Morrison, M. A. Judaism   **296**
Robinson, G. Essential Judaism   **296**
See/See also pages in the following book(s):
Armstrong, K. The battle for God   **200**
     Dictionaries
The New encyclopedia of Judaism [New York
   University Press]   **296.03**
The Oxford dictionary of the Jewish religion
       296.03

     Encyclopedias
Karesh, S. E. Encyclopedia of Judaism
       296.03
The student's encyclopedia of Judaism
       296.03
     Fiction
Chayil, E. Hush   **Fic**
     History
Cahill, T. The gifts of the Jews   **909**
Jude. Morgenroth, K.   **Fic**

Judges
Crowe, C. Thurgood Marshall   **92**
Jarrow, G. Robert H. Jackson   **92**
Schnakenberg, R. Secret lives of the Supreme
   Court   **920**
     Fiction
Picoult, J. Nineteen minutes   **Fic**

Judo
Pedro, J. Judo techniques & tactics   **796.8**
Judo techniques & tactics. Pedro, J.   **796.8**

Judson, Karen, 1941-
Religion and government   **322**
Resolving conflicts   **303.6**

Juettner, Bonnie, 1968-
Acne   **616.5**

Julian, Percy L., 1899-1975
     About
Stille, D. R. Percy Lavon Julian   **92**
The **Julian** game. Griffin, A.   **Fic**
The **Juliet** club. Harper, S.   **Fic**
Julius Caesar. Appignanesi, R.
       822.3
Julius Caesar [criticism] Bloom, H., ed   **822.3**
Julius Caesar [criticism] Sobran, J.   **822.3**
Julius Caesar. See Shakespeare, W. The tragedy
   of Julius Caesar   **822.3**
The **jumbee.** Keyes, P.   **Fic**
Jump. Carbone, E. L.   **Fic**
The **jump** [biography of Sebastian Telfair]
   O'Connor, I.   **92**
Jumped. Williams-Garcia, R.   **Fic**
Jumping off swings. Knowles, J.   **Fic**
Jumpstart the world. Hyde, C. R.   **Fic**
Jundi, Sami al *See* Al Jundi, Sami, 1962-
Jung, C. G. (Carl Gustav), 1875-1961
The basic writings of C. G. Jung   **150.19**

Jung, Carl Gustav *See* Jung, C. G. (Carl Gustav),
   1875-1961

Junger, Sebastian
The perfect storm   **910.4**
The **jungle.** Kuper, P.   **741.5**
The **jungle.** Sinclair, U.   **Fic**

Junior colleges
Gonsher, D. The community college guide
       378.1

Junior high school libraries *See* High school libraries
Junk. See Burgess, M. Smack   **Fic**

Jupiter (Planet)
Chaple, G. F. Outer planets   **523.4**
Jurassic Park. Crichton, M.   **Fic**

Jurkowski, Odin L., 1969-
Technology and the school library   **027.8**

Jurmain, Suzanne
The secret of the yellow death   **614.5**

Jury
The right to a trial by jury   **345**
Just listen. Dessen, S.   **Fic**
Just one wish. Rallison, J.   **Fic**
A **Just** response   **973.931**

Justice
Adler, M. J. Six great ideas   **111**
Juvenile arthritis. Rouba, K.   **618.92**

Juvenile courts
Cohen, L. The Gault case and young people's
   rights   **345**
Jacobs, T. A. They broke the law, you be the
   judge   **345**
Krygier, L. Juvenile court   **345**
Juvenile crime   **364.36**

Juvenile delinquency
   See also Gangs
Hubner, J. Last chance in Texas   **365**
Juvenile crime   **364.36**
Krygier, L. Juvenile court   **345**
Kuklin, S. No choirboy   **364.66**
Salzman, M. True notebooks   **808**
Should juveniles be tried as adults?   **345**
     Fiction
Burgess, A. A clockwork orange   **Fic**
De la Peña, M. We were here   **Fic**
Garigliano, J. Dogface   **Fic**
Goodman, S. Something like hope   **Fic**
Hinton, S. E. The outsiders   **Fic**
Korman, G. The Juvie three   **Fic**
Strasser, T. Boot camp   **Fic**
Thompson, K. Creature of the night   **Fic**

Juvenile delinquents *See* Juvenile delinquency

Juvenile prostitution
Lloyd, R. Girls like us   **92**
The **Juvie** three. Korman, G.   **Fic**

K

The **K** & W guide to colleges for students with
   learning disabilities or attention deficit
   hyperactivity disorder. Kravets, M.   **378.73**

The **K & W** guide to colleges for the learning disabled. See Kravets, M. The K & W guide to colleges for students with learning disabilities or attention deficit hyperactivity disorder
378.73

Kabul Beauty School (Afghanistan)
Rodriguez, D. Kabul Beauty School   305.4
Kabul girls soccer club. See Ayub, A. However tall the mountain   796.334
Kade, Stacey
The ghost and the goth   Fic
Kafka, Franz, 1883-1924
The metamorphosis and other stories   S C
The trial   Fic
About
Franz Kafka's The metamorphosis [study guide]
833.009
Graphic novels
Mairowitz, D. Z. Kafka   92
Kagame, Paul
About
Kinzer, S. A thousand hills [biography of Paul Kagame]   967.571
Kagan, Andrew
Marc Chagall   92
Kagan, Neil, 1949-
(ed) National Geographic concise history of the world. See National Geographic concise history of the world   902
(ed) National Geographic Society (U.S.). Atlas of the Civil War   973.7
Kahlo, Frida, 1907-1954
Poetry
Bernier-Grand, C. T. Frida   811
Kahn, Roger, 1927-
Beyond the boys of summer   796.357
Kakalios, James
The amazing story of quantum mechanics
530.1
The physics of superheroes   530
Kaku, Michio
Parallel worlds   523.1
Physics of the future   303.49
Physics of the impossible   530
Kalambakal, Vickey
(ed) Energy alternatives: opposing viewpoints. See Energy alternatives: opposing viewpoints
333.79
Kaler, James B.
The hundred greatest stars   523.8
Kallen, Stuart A., 1955-
The aftermath of the Sandinista Revolution
972.85
The artist's tools   702.8
Claude Monet   92
National security   355
Pablo Picasso   92
Photography   770
Primary sources [American war library, The Cold War]   909.82
Renewable energy research   333.79
Toxic waste   363.7
Witches   133.4

(ed) How should America's wilderness be managed? See How should America's wilderness be managed?   333.7
(ed) Sixties counterculture. See Sixties counterculture   973.92
Kamara, Mariatu, 1987-
The bite of the mango   92
Kamen, Gloria, 1923-
(jt. auth) Martin, J. Miss Manners' guide to excruciatingly correct behavior   395
Kamkwamba, William
The boy who harnessed the wind   92
Kampen O'Riley, Michael
Art beyond the West   709
Kampuchea See Cambodia
Kampung boy. Lat   741.5
Kan, Katharine
Sizzling summer reading programs for young adults   027.62
(ed) Graphic novels and comic books. See Graphic novels and comic books   741.5
Kandel, Robert S.
Water from heaven   553.7
Kane, Joseph Nathan, 1899-2002
Famous first facts   031.02
(ed) Facts about the presidents. See Facts about the presidents   920
Kanellos, Nicolás, 1945-
(ed) U-X-L Hispanic American almanac. See U-X-L Hispanic American almanac   305.8
Kangaroos
Flannery, T. F. Chasing kangaroos   599.2
Kanipe, Jeff, 1953-
The cosmic connection   520
Kansas
Fiction
Durham, D. A. Gabriel's story   Fic
Moriarty, L. The center of everything   Fic
Nadol, J. The mark   Fic
Parks, G. The learning tree   Fic
Peck, D. Sprout   Fic
History
Stratton, J. L. Pioneer women   978.1
Kant, Immanuel, 1724-1804
See/See also pages in the following book(s):
Durant, W. J. The story of philosophy   109
Russell, B. A history of Western philosophy
109
Kantner, Seth, 1965-
Shopping for porcupine   92
Kantor, Michael, 1961-
Broadway: the American musical   792.6
Kaplan, Howard S., 1960-
Marian Anderson   92
Kaplan, Robert
The nothing that is   511
Kaplow, Robert
Me and Orson Welles   Fic
Kaplowitz, Joan R.
(jt. auth) Grassian, E. S. Information literacy instruction   025.5
Karam, P. Andrew
Planetary motion   523.4

Karam, P. Andrew—*Continued*
Radioactivity **539.2**

Karamanides, Dimitra
Pythagoras: pioneering mathematician and musical theorist of Ancient Greece **92**

Karate
See also Tae kwon do
Martin, A. P. The Shotokan karate bible **796.8**
Pawlett, R. The karate handbook **796.8**
Fiction
Briant, E. Choppy socky blues **Fic**
The **karate** handbook. Pawlett, R. **796.8**

Karbiener, Karen, 1965-
(ed) Encyclopedia of British writers, 1800 to the present. See Encyclopedia of British writers, 1800 to the present **820.9**

Kardy, Glenn
Manga University Presents . . . Kana de Manga Special Edition: Japanese Sound FX! **495.6**

Karesh, Sara E.
Encyclopedia of Judaism **296.03**

Karim, Sheba
Skunk girl **Fic**

Karlitz, Gail
(jt. auth) Reeves, D. L. Career ideas for teens in architecture and construction **624**
(jt. auth) Reeves, D. L. Career ideas for teens in education and training **331.7**

Karma. Ostlere, C. **Fic**
The **Karma** Club. Brody, J. **Fic**

Karnow, Stanley
Vietnam **959.704**

Karolides, Nicholas J.
(ed) Censored books [I]-II. See Censored books [I]-II **810.9**
(jt. auth) Green, J. The encyclopedia of censorship **363.31**

Karr, Mary
The Liars' Club **92**

Karst, Kenneth L.
(ed) Encyclopedia of the American Constitution. See Encyclopedia of the American Constitution **342**

Kaslik, Ibolya, 1973-
Skinny **Fic**

Kass, Pnina
Real time **Fic**

Kastenbaum, Robert
(ed) Macmillan encyclopedia of death and dying. See Macmillan encyclopedia of death and dying **306.9**

Katcher, Brian
Almost perfect **Fic**
Playing with matches **Fic**

Kate, Lauren
The betrayal of Natalie Hargrove **Fic**

Katin, Miriam
We are on our own **92**

Katman. Pyle, K. C. **741.5**
Katrina: state of emergency **363.34**

Katz, Eric D., 1963-
(jt. auth) Bluestein, J. High school's not forever **373.1**

Katz, Jon
Geeks **338.7**
A good dog **636.7**

Katz, William A., 1924-2004
(ed) Magazines for libraries. See Magazines for libraries **011**

Katzman, John
(jt. auth) Robinson, A. Cracking the SAT **378.1**

Kauder-Nalebuff, Rachel
(ed) My little red book. See My little red book **305.23**

Kaufman, Cathy K.
Cooking in ancient civilizations **641.3**

Kaufman, Daniel, 1968-
(jt. auth) Dowhan, A. Essays that will get you into college **808**

Kaufman, Kenn
Kaufman field guide to birds of North America **598**
(jt. auth) Brock, J. P. Kaufman field guide to butterflies of North America **595.7**

Kaufman, Marc
First contact **576.839**

Kaufman, Michael T.
1968 **909.82**

Kaufman, Miriam
Easy for you to say **362.1**

Kaufman, Will
Woody Guthrie, American radical **92**

Kaufman field guide to birds of North America. Kaufman, K. **598**
Kaufman field guide to butterflies of North America. Brock, J. P. **595.7**

Kault, David
Statistics with common sense **519.5**

Kauppi, Carol, 1952-
(ed) GirlSpoken: from pen, brush & tongue. See GirlSpoken: from pen, brush & tongue **810.8**

Kavanaugh, Dorothy, 1969-
(jt. auth) Friedenthal, L. Religions of Africa **200.9**

Kay, Christian
(ed) Historical thesaurus of the Oxford English dictionary. See Historical thesaurus of the Oxford English dictionary **423**

Kay, Jackie
Red dust road **92**

Kayaking **797.1**
Kayaking. Krauzer, S. M. **797.1**

Kaye, Cathryn Berger
Going blue **333.91**

Kaye, Marilyn
Demon chick **Fic**
The **Kayla** chronicles. Winston, S. **Fic**

Kays, Roland, 1971-
Mammals of North America **599**

Kimball, Chad T.
(ed) Vegetarian sourcebook. See Vegetarian sourcebook   **613.2**

Kimura, Tomo
(tr) Toboso, Y. Black butler, vol. 1   **741.5**

Kincaid, Jamaica
My brother   **92**

Kinch, Michael P.
The blending time   **Fic**

Kincy, Karen, 1986-
Other   **Fic**

Kinder, Gary
Ship of gold in the deep blue sea   **910.4**

Kindertransport. Drucker, O. L.   **940.53**

Kindred. Butler, O. E.   **Fic**

Kindred spirit, kindred care. Nakaya, S. F.   **636.089**

Kinetic contraptions. Gabrielson, C.   **621.46**

King, A. S., 1970-
Please ignore Vera Dietz   **Fic**

King, B. B.
Blues all around me   **92**

King, C. Richard
Media images and representations   **302.23**

King, Daniel, 1963-
Chess   **794.1**

King, Sir David, 1939-
(jt. auth) Walker, G. The hot topic   **363.7**

King, Laurie R.
The beekeeper's apprentice, or, on the segregation of the queen   **Fic**

King, Martin Luther, Jr., 1929-1968
Strength to love   **252**
A testament of hope   **323.1**
Why we can't wait   **323.1**
About
Boerst, W. J. Marching in Birmingham   **323.1**

Graphic novels
Anderson, H. C. King   **92**
Flowers, A. R. I see the promised land [biography of Martin Luther King Jr.]   **92**

King, Melissa
She's got next   **92**

King, Peter J., 1935-
One hundred philosophers   **109**

King, Riley B. See King, B. B.

King, Ross, 1962-
Art: over 2,500 works from cave to contemporary   **709**
Brunelleschi's dome   **726**

King, Stephen, 1947-
Carrie   **Fic**
Everything's eventual: 14 dark tales   **S C**
Firestarter   **Fic**
Four past midnight   **S C**
Night shift   **S C**
On writing   **92**
Skeleton crew   **S C**
About
Lüsted, M. A. How to analyze the works of Stephen King   **813.009**

Rogak, L. A. Haunted heart [biography of Stephen King]   **92**
Russell, S. A. Revisiting Stephen King   **813.009**
Russell, S. A. Stephen King: a critical companion   **813.009**
Stefoff, R. Stephen King   **92**
Whitelaw, N. Dark dreams [biography of Stephen King]   **92**

King. Anderson, H. C.   **92**

King Dork. Portman, F.   **Fic**

King Lear. Hinds, G.   **822.3**

King Lear. Shakespeare, W.   **822.3**

King Lear [criticism] Bloom, H., ed   **822.3**

King Lear [criticism] Richert, S. P.   **822.3**

King Leopold's ghost. Hochschild, A.   **967.5**

The **king** must die. Renault, M.   **Fic**

King of Ithaka. Barrett, T.   **Fic**

King of the mild frontier: an ill-advised autobiography. Crutcher, C.   **92**

King of the screwups. Going, K. L.   **Fic**

King of the world: Muhammad Ali and the rise of an American hero. Remnick, D.   **92**

King Philip's War, 1675-1676
Mandell, D. R. King Philip's war   **973.2**

Kingdom under glass [biography of Carl Ethan Akeley] Kirk, J.   **92**

Kings and rulers
See also Dictators; Queens
Arrian. Alexander the Great   **92**
Wilson, D. A. Charlemagne   **92**
Fiction
Bunce, E. C. Star crossed   **Fic**
Cypess, L. Mistwood   **Fic**
Dixon, H. Entwined   **Fic**
Klein, L. M. Lady Macbeth's daughter   **Fic**
Libby, A. M. The king's rose   **Fic**
Marr, M. Wicked lovely   **Fic**

The **king's** arrow. Cadnum, M.   **Fic**

The **king's** rose. Libby, A. M.   **Fic**

Kingsley, Anna, d. 1870
About
Schafer, D. L. Anna Madgigine Jai Kingsley   **92**

Kingsolver, Barbara
The bean trees   **Fic**
The poisonwood Bible   **Fic**
Small wonder   **814**

Kingston, Jack A.
(ed) Axelrod, A. Encyclopedia of World War II   **940.53**

Kingyo used books, vol. 1. Yoshizaki, S.   **741.5**

Kinney, Anne Behnke
(jt. auth) Hardy, G. The establishment of the Han empire and imperial China   **931**

Kinsbruner, Jay
(ed) Encyclopedia of Latin American history and culture. See Encyclopedia of Latin American history and culture   **980**

Lansford, Tom—*Continued*
(ed) Voting rights: opposing viewpoints. See Voting rights: opposing viewpoints **324.6**
(ed) The war in Iraq. See The war in Iraq **956.7**

Lanthanides and actinides. Halka, M. **546**

Laqueur, Walter, 1921-
Fascism **320.5**
(ed) The Holocaust encyclopedia. See The Holocaust encyclopedia **940.53**

Larbalestier, Justine, 1967-
Liar **Fic**
Magic or madness **Fic**
(comp) Zombies vs. unicorns. See Zombies vs. unicorns **S C**

Lardy, Philippe
(il) Nelson, M. A wreath for Emmett Till **811**

Largent, Mark A.
(jt. auth) Young, C. C. Evolution and creationism **576.8**

Larkin, Philip
The Oxford book of twentieth-century English verse. See The Oxford book of twentieth-century English verse **821.008**

LaRochelle, David, 1960-
Absolutely, positively not **Fic**

Larousse concise dictionary: Spanish-English, English-Spanish **463**

Larousse English-Spanish, Spanish-English dictionary. See Larousse standard diccionario, español-inglés, inglés-español **463**

Larousse standard diccionario, español-inglés, inglés-español **463**

Larson, Edward J.
The Scopes trial **345**

Larson, Gary
The far side **741.5**
The prehistory of the Far side **741.5**

Larson, Hope
Mercury **741.5**

Larson, Kirby, 1954-
Hattie Big Sky **Fic**

Las Vegas (Nev.)
Fiction
Hautman, P. All-in **Fic**
Hemphill, H. Long gone daddy **Fic**
Jaffe, M. Bad kitty **Fic**

Lasch, Christopher
Plain style **808**

LASIK: a guide to laser vision correction. Kornmehl, E. W. **617.7**

Lasky, Kathryn
Ashes **Fic**

The **last** book in the universe. Philbrick, W. R. **Fic**

Last chance in Texas. Hubner, J. **365**

The **last** Comanche chief: the life and times of Quanah Parker. Neeley, B. **92**

The **last** exit to normal. Harmon, M. B. **Fic**

The **last** fish tale. Kurlansky, M. **639.2**

The **last** good place of Lily Odilon. Beitia, S. **Fic**

The **last** great revolution. Wright, R. **955**

The **last** human. Sarmiento, E. **569.9**

The **last** mission. Mazer, H. **Fic**

The **last** Monarch butterfly. Schappert, P. **595.7**

Last night I dreamed of peace. Dang, T. T. **92**

Last night I sang to the monster. Saenz, B. A. **Fic**

Last of the dinosaurs. Holmes, T. **567.9**

The **last** report on the miracles at Little No Horse. Erdrich, L. **Fic**

Last stand [biography of George Bird Grinnell] Punke, M. **92**

The **last** summer of the death warriors. Stork, F. X. **Fic**

The **last** unicorn. Beagle, P. S. **Fic**

The **last** wild wolves. McAllister, I. **599.77**

Lat
Kampung boy **741.5**
Town boy **741.5**

Latana
Barely exposed **779**

The **latent** powers of Dylan Fontaine. Lurie, A. **Fic**

Latham, Alison
(ed) The Oxford companion to music. See The Oxford companion to music **780.3**

The **lathe** of heaven. Le Guin, U. K. **Fic**

Latimer, Lewis Howard, 1848-1928
See/See also pages in the following book(s):
Abdul-Jabbar, K. Black profiles in courage **920**

Latin America
Gritzner, C. F. Latin America **980**
Civilization
Fuentes, C. The buried mirror **946**
Encyclopedias
Encyclopedia of Latin America **980**
Encyclopedia of Latin American history and culture **980**
Fiction
García Márquez, G. Love in the time of cholera **Fic**
Folklore
See Folklore—Latin America

Latin American art
Makosz, R. Latino arts and their influence on the United States **700**
Scott, J. F. Latin American art **709.8**

Latin American art. Scott, J. F. **709.8**

Latin American folktales **398.2**

Latin American literature
See also Mexican literature
Bio-bibliography
Concise encyclopedia of Latin American literature **860.3**
Flores, A. Spanish American authors **920.003**

Lessons in taxidermy. Lavender, B.   92

Lester, Julius
    Black folktales   398.2
    Day of tears   Fic
    Guardian   Fic
    Time's memory   Fic
    To be a slave   326

Let every nation know [biography of John F. Kennedy] Dallek, R.   92

Let it be morning. Sayed, K.   Fic

Let it snow. Green, J.   S C

Let me play. Blumenthal, K.   796

Let sleeping dogs lie. Pressler, M.   Fic

Letitia Baldrige's complete guide to the new manners for the 90's. See Baldrige, L. Letitia Baldrige's new manners for new times   395

Letitia Baldrige's new manners for new times. Baldrige, L.   395

Let's get this straight. Fakhrid-Deen, T.   306.8

The **letter** and the scroll. Currie, R.   220.9

Letter to my daughter. Angelou, M.   92

Letter writing
    See also Business letters

Letters
    See also American letters
       Fiction
    Beard, P. Dear Zoe   Fic
    Buckhanon, K. Upstate   Fic
    Chbosky, S. The perks of being a wallflower   Fic
    Harper, S. The Juliet club   Fic

Letters from Black America   305.8

Letters from Yellowstone. Smith, D.   Fic

Letters of the century   816

Letters to a young actor. Brustein, R.   792

Letters to a young artist. Smith, A. D.   700

Letters to a young brother. Harper, H.   170

Letters to a young evangelical. Campolo, A.   248.4

Letters to a young journalist. Freedman, S. G.   070.4

Letters to a young mathematician. Stewart, I.   510

Letters to a young teacher. Kozol, J.   371.1

Letters to America   811.008

LeVay, Simon
    (jt. auth) Koerner, D. Here be dragons   576.839

Levchuk, Lisa
    Everything beautiful in the world   Fic

Level up. Yang, G.   741.5

Levenson, J. C. (Jacob Claver), 1922-
    (ed) Crane, S. Prose and poetry   818

Leventhal, Alice Walker *See* Walker, Alice, 1944-

Leventhal, Josh, 1971-
    (ed) Baseball, the perfect game. See Baseball, the perfect game   796.357

Leventon, Melissa
    (ed) What people wore when. See What people wore when   391

Lever, Evelyne
    Marie Antoinette   92

Leverage. Cohen, J.   Fic

Leverage your library program to help raise test scores. Church, A. P.   027.8

Levertov, Denise, 1923-1997
    Sands of the well   811
    This great unknowing   811

Levi, Selma K.
    (jt. auth) Diamant-Cohen, B. Booktalking bonanza   028.5

Leviathan. Westerfeld, S.   Fic

Levin, Carole, 1948-
    Extraordinary women of the Medieval and Renaissance world. See Extraordinary women of the Medieval and Renaissance world   920.003

Levin, Judith, 1956-
    Hugo Chávez   92

Levine, Ellen, 1939-
    Rachel Carson   92

Levine, Gail Carson, 1947-
    Fairest   Fic

Levine, Louis
    (jt. auth) Kobilinsky, L. F. Forensic DNA analysis   614

Levine, Mark
    F5   551.55

Levinson, David, 1947-
    (ed) Berkshire encyclopedia of world sport. See Berkshire encyclopedia of world sport   796.03
    (ed) Encyclopedia of homelessness. See Encyclopedia of homelessness   362.5
    (ed) Global perspectives on the United States. See Global perspectives on the United States   327.73
    (ed) The Wilson chronology of the world's religions. See The Wilson chronology of the world's religions   200

Levitation: physics and psychology in the service of deception. Ottaviani, J.   793.8

Levithan, David, 1972-
    How they met, and other stories   S C
    Love is the higher law   Fic
    Marly's ghost   Fic
    (ed) 21 proms. See 21 proms   S C
    (jt. auth) Cohn, R. Naomi and Ely's no kiss list   Fic
    (jt. auth) Cohn, R. Nick & Norah's infinite playlist   Fic
    (ed) The Full spectrum. See The Full spectrum   306.76
    (jt. auth) Green, J. Will Grayson, Will Grayson   Fic
    (ed) Where we are, what we see. See Where we are, what we see   810.8

Levitin, Sonia, 1934-
    Strange relations   Fic

Literature and its times 809

Literature for today's young adults. Nilsen, A. P.
028.5

Literature for youth [series]
Crew, H. S. Women engaged in war in literature for youth 016.3
Garcha, R. The world of Islam in literature for youth 016.3058
Leeper, A. Poetry in literature for youth
016.8

Literature links to world history, K-12. Adamson, L. G. 028.1

The **Literature** of ancient Egypt 890

Literature of developing nations for students
809

Literature of the Holocaust 809

Lithuania
Fiction
Sepetys, R. Between shades of gray Fic

Litin, Scott C.
(ed) Mayo Clinic family health book. See Mayo Clinic family health book 613

Little, Felicia M.
(jt. auth) Halsted, D. D. Disaster planning
025.8

Little, Malcolm See Malcolm X, 1925-1965

Little, Melanie, 1969-
(ed) What my father gave me. See What my father gave me 920

Little, Stephen, 1954-
. . . isms: understanding art 709

Little Bighorn, Battle of the, 1876
Sandoz, M. The Battle of the Little Bighorn
973.8
Viola, H. J. It is a good day to die 973.8
Welch, J. Killing Custer 973.8

Little black lies. Cohen, T. Fic

The **little** book of Hindu deities. Patel, S.
704.9

Little brother. Doctorow, C. Fic

Little Crow, Sioux Chief, d. 1863
See/See also pages in the following book(s):
Brown, D. A. Bury my heart at Wounded Knee
970.004

A **little** friendly advice. Vivian, S. Fic

Little (grrl) lost. De Lint, C. Fic

The **Little** Ice Age. Fagan, B. M. 551.6

The **little** prince. Saint-Exupéry, A. d. Fic

A **little** wanting song. Crowley, C. Fic

Litwack, Leon F.
How free is free? 323.1
(ed) Black leaders of the nineteenth century. See Black leaders of the nineteenth century
920

Litwin, Laura Baskes
A reader's guide to Zora Neale Hurston's Their eyes were watching god 813.009

Litz, A. Walton
(ed) Modern American women writers. See Modern American women writers 810.9

Liu Siyu, 1964-
A thousand peaks 895.1

Liungman, Carl G., 1938-
Dictionary of symbols 302.2

Liver
Diseases
Goldsmith, C. Hepatitis 616.3
Palmer, M. Dr. Melissa Palmer's guide to hepatitis & liver disease 616.3
Diseases—Encyclopedias
Chow, J. H. The encyclopedia of hepatitis and other liver diseases 616.3

Lives and legacies [series]
Christianson, G. E. Isaac Newton 92
Gaustad, E. S. Benjamin Franklin 92
Gaustad, E. S. Roger Williams 92
Scientists, mathematicians, and inventors
920.003

The **lives** of ants. Keller, L. 595.7

The **Lives** of the kings & queens of England
941

Lives of the saints. McBrien, R. P. 920

Living dead girl. Scott, E. Fic

Living green. Nagle, J. M. 333.72

Living hell. Jinks, C. Fic

Living Islam out loud 297

Living on impulse. Haycak, C. Fic

Living through the Cold War [series]
Living through the end of the Cold War
940.55
Living through the Vietnam War 959.704

Living through the end of the Cold War
940.55

Living through the Vietnam War 959.704

Living with allergies. Ehrlich, P. 616.97

Living with anxiety disorders. Miller, A. R.
616.85

Living with asthma. Berger, W. E. 616.2

Living with depression. Miller, A. R. 616.85

Living with diabetes. Parker, K. 616.4

Livio, Mario, 1945-
The golden ratio 516.2

Livvie Owen lived here. Dooley, S. Fic

Lizard care from A to Z. Bartlett, R. D.
639.3

Lizards
Bartlett, R. D. Lizard care from A to Z
639.3

Llanas, Sheila Griffin
Contemporary American poetry, "not the end, but the beginning" 811.009
Modern American poetry, "echoes and shadows"
811.009

Lloyd, Rachel
Girls like us 92

Lloyd, Saci
The carbon diaries 2015 Fic

Lo, Malinda
Ash Fic

Loan funds, Student See Student loan funds

Loans
See also Government lending

Longitudes and attitudes. Friedman, T. L. **973.931**

Longman, Jere
The girls of summer **796.334**

Longman dictionary and handbook of poetry. See Myers, J. E. Dictionary of poetic terms **808.1**

Longshore, David
Encyclopedia of hurricanes, typhoons, and cyclones **551.55**

Longshot. Allred, L. **92**

Longsworth, Polly
The world of Emily Dickinson **92**

Look me in the eye. Robison, J. E. **92**

Looking for Alaska. Green, J. **Fic**

Looking for history. Guillermoprieto, A. **972**

Looks. George, M. **Fic**

Loos, Pamela
A reader's guide to Lorraine Hansberry's A raisin in the sun **812.009**
(ed) Julius Caesar. See Julius Caesar [criticism] **822.3**

Lopez, Adriana
(ed) Fifteen candles. See Fifteen candles **392**

Lopez, Steve
The soloist [biography of Nathaniel Anthony Ayers] **92**

Lord, Walter, 1917-2002
Day of infamy **940.54**

Lord Jim. Conrad, J. **Fic**

Lord of the flies. Golding, W. **Fic**

The **lord** of the rings. Tolkien, J. R. R. **Fic**

Lore, Pittacus See Hughes, Jobie, 1980-

Lorenz, Konrad
On aggression **152.4**

Lorien legacies [series]
Frey, J. I am number four **Fic**

Lorinc, John, 1963-
Cities **307.7**

Los Alamos Scientific Laboratory
Conant, J. 109 East Palace **623.4**

Los Angeles (Calif.)
Fiction
Barlow, T. Sharp teeth **Fic**
Block, F. L. Dangerous angels **Fic**
Castellucci, C. Beige **Fic**
Castellucci, C. Boy proof **Fic**
De la Peña, M. Ball don't lie **Fic**
Yee, L. Absolutely Maybe **Fic**

Losing Faith. Jaden, D. **Fic**

Losing is not an option: stories. Wallace, R. **S C**

Losing things See Lost and found possessions

Loss (Psychology)
Myers, E. When will I stop hurting? **155.9**
Fiction
Baskin, N. R. All we know of love **Fic**
Goldblatt, S. Girl to the core **Fic**
Kephart, B. Nothing but ghosts **Fic**
Schindler, H. Playing hurt **Fic**
Stein, T. High dive **Fic**

Lost. Davies, J. **Fic**

Lost and found. Parkhurst, C. **Fic**

Lost and found possessions
Fiction
Huntley, A. The everafter **Fic**

Lost boy, lost girl. Dau, J. B. **962.4**

Lost children See Missing children

Lost city of the Incas. Bingham, H. **985**

The **lost** conspiracy. Hardinge, F. **Fic**

Lost for words. Kuipers, A. **Fic**

The **lost** German slave girl [biography of Salomé Muller] Bailey, J. **92**

Lost history. Morgan, M. H. **909**

Lost in Yonkers. Simon, N. **812**

Lost mountain. Reece, E. **622**

The **lottery.** Jackson, S. **Fic**

The **lottery.** Jackson, S. **S C**

Lottridge, Celia Barker
Home is beyond the mountains **Fic**

Loucks, James F.
(ed) Browning, R. Robert Browning's poetry **821**

Loucky, Jaime
(jt. auth) Wallechinsky, D. The complete book of the Winter Olympics **796.98**

Louis XIV, King of France, 1638-1715
About
DeJean, J. E. The essence of style **391**

Louis XVII, of France, 1785-1795
Fiction
Donnelly, J. Revolution **Fic**

Louis, Father See Merton, Thomas, 1915-1968

Louis Pasteur and the founding of microbiology. Ackerman, J. **92**

Louisiana
Fiction
Gaines, E. J. The autobiography of Miss Jane Pittman **Fic**
Gaines, E. J. A gathering of old men **Fic**
Gaines, E. J. A lesson before dying **Fic**
Les Becquets, D. Love, Cajun style **Fic**

Love, Ann, 1947-
(jt. auth) Drake, J. Yes you can! **361.2**

Love, D. Anne, 1949-
Defying the diva **Fic**

Love, Jeremy
Bayou, volume one **741.5**

Love, Nat, 1854-1921
See/See also pages in the following book(s):
Garrison, M. Slaves who dared **920**

Love
DeRamus, B. Forbidden fruit **973.7**
Fromm, E. The art of loving **152.4**
Fiction
How beautiful the ordinary **S C**
Luper, E. Seth Baumgartner's love manifesto **Fic**
Oliver, L. Delirium **Fic**
Graphic novels
Ottaviani, J. Wire mothers **152.4**

Love and capes, vol. 1. Zahler, T. F. **741.5**

Love, Cajun style. Les Becquets, D.   **Fic**

Love, football, and other contact sports. Carter, A. R.   **S C**

Love in the driest season. Tucker, N.   **362.7**

Love in the time of cholera. García Márquez, G.   **Fic**

Love is hell   **S C**

Love is the higher law. Levithan, D.   **Fic**

Love letters and two other plays: The golden age and What I did last summer. Gurney, A. R.   **812**

Love poems   **808.81**

Love poetry
   Block, F. L. How to (un)cage a girl   **811**
   Crush: love poems   **808.81**
   Falling hard   **811.008**
   Holbrook, S. More than friends   **811**
   Love poems   **808.81**
   Mora, P. Dizzy in your eyes   **811**
   Soto, G. Partly cloudy   **811**

Love stories
   Allende, I. Daughter of fortune   **Fic**
   Austen, J. Persuasion   **Fic**
   Balog, C. Sleepless   **Fic**
   Block, F. L. The frenzy   **Fic**
   Brontë, C. Jane Eyre   **Fic**
   Brontë, E. Wuthering Heights   **Fic**
   Colasanti, S. Something like fate   **Fic**
   Fiedler, L. Romeo's ex   **Fic**
   Fink, M. The summer I got a life   **Fic**
   Garcia, K. Beautiful creatures   **Fic**
   Hale, S. Book of a thousand days   **Fic**
   Horner, E. A love story starring my dead best friend   **Fic**
   Howells, A. The summer of skinny dipping   **Fic**
   Kiss me deadly   **S C**
   Koja, K. Kissing the bee   **Fic**
   Levithan, D. How they met, and other stories   **S C**
   Lo, M. Ash   **Fic**
   Love is hell   **S C**
   Martin, C. K. K. I know it's over   **Fic**
   McCaughrean, G. Cyrano   **Fic**
   Miller, K. The eternal ones   **Fic**
   Schindler, H. Playing hurt   **Fic**
   Selfors, S. Mad love   **Fic**
   Williams, G. Beatle meets Destiny   **Fic**
   Zarr, S. Sweethearts   **Fic**
       History and criticism
   Regis, P. A natural history of the romance novel   **823.009**

A **love** story starring my dead best friend. Horner, E.   **Fic**

Love you hate you miss you. Scott, E.   **Fic**

Love*Com Vol. 1. Nakahara, A.   **741.5**

Lovecraft, H. P. (Howard Phillips), 1890-1937
       Adaptations
   Graphic Classics volume four: H. P. Lovecraft   **741.5**

Lovecraft, Howard Phillips *See* Lovecraft, H. P. (Howard Phillips), 1890-1937

Lovegrove, Ray
   Health   **174.2**

Lovelace, Kacy
   (ed) Abortion: opposing viewpoints. See Abortion: opposing viewpoints   **363.46**
   (ed) The ethics of cloning. See The ethics of cloning   **176**
   (ed) Global warming: opposing viewpoints. See Global warming: opposing viewpoints   **363.7**
   (ed) Iraq: opposing viewpoints. See Iraq: opposing viewpoints   **956.7**
   (ed) Islam: opposing viewpoints. See Islam: opposing viewpoints   **297**
   (ed) The Middle East: opposing viewpoints. See The Middle East: opposing viewpoints   **956**

The **lovely** bones. Sebold, A.   **Fic**

Low-cholesterol diet
   American Heart Association. The new American Heart Association cookbook   **641.5**

Low income housing *See* Public housing

Low temperatures
       Research
   Shachtman, T. Absolute zero and the conquest of cold   **536**

Lowboy. Wray, J.   **Fic**

Lowe, John, 1945-
   (ed) Gaines, E. J. Conversations with Ernest Gaines   **92**

Lowell, Pamela
   Returnable girl   **Fic**

Lowell, Robert, 1917-1977
   Selected poems   **811**

Lowenstein, Frank, 1960-
   (ed) Voices of protest. See Voices of protest   **322.4**

Lowery, Charles D., 1937-
   (ed) The Greenwood encyclopedia of African American civil rights. See The Greenwood encyclopedia of African American civil rights   **305.8**

Lowman, Margaret
   Life in the treetops   **92**

Lowry, Lois
   The giver   **Fic**

Lowry Park Zoo
   French, T. Zoo story   **590.73**

Loyalists, American *See* American Loyalists

Lubar, David, 1954-
   Sleeping freshmen never lie   **Fic**

Lubar, Steven D.
   Legacies   **973**

Lucas. Brooks, K.   **Fic**

Lucent library of Black history [series]
   Uschan, M. V. Forty years of medical racism   **174.2**

Lucent library of historical eras, Ancient Egypt [series]
   Nardo, D. Arts, leisure, and sport in ancient Egypt   **932**
   Nardo, D. Cleopatra   **92**

Lucent terrorism library [series]
   America under attack: primary sources   **973.931**

Luchetti, Cathy, 1945-
Children of the West   **978**

Lucie-Smith, Edward, 1933-
Toulouse-Lautrec   **759.4**

Lucky child. Ung, L.   **92**

A **lucky** child [biography of Thomas Buergenthal]
Buergenthal, T.   **92**

The **lucky** place. Vincent, Z.   **Fic**

Lucy: the beginnings of humankind. Johanson, D.
C.   **599.93**

Lucy's legacy. Jolly, A.   **599.93**

Ludes, James M., 1971-
(ed) Iraq uncensored. See Iraq uncensored
    956.7

Ludman, Mark D.
(jt. auth) Wynbrandt, J. The encyclopedia of genetic disorders and birth defects   **616**

Lueders, Edward
(comp) Reflections on a gift of watermelon pickle—and other modern verse. See Reflections on a gift of watermelon pickle—and other modern verse   **811.008**

Lufkin, Elise
To the rescue   **636.7**

Lugira, Aloysius Muzzanganda
African traditional religion   **299.6**

Lugo-Lugo, Carmen R.
(ed) Latino history and culture. See Latino history and culture   **305.8**

Luhr, James
(ed) Earth. See Earth   **550**

Lukeman, Noah
The plot thickens   **808.3**

Lukenbill, W. Bernard
Community resources in the school library media center   **025.2**
Health information in a changing world   **372**

Lukes, Bonnie L.
Woodrow Wilson and the Progressive Era
    92

Lumbee Indians
Fiction
Klein, L. M. Cate of the Lost Colony   **Fic**

Luna. Peters, J. A.   **Fic**

Lunar eclipses
Harrington, P. S. Eclipse!   **523.7**

Lunar expeditions See Space flight to the moon

Lunch with Lenin and other stories. Ellis, D.
    S C

Lung cancer
Ferreiro, C. Lung cancer   **616.99**

Lung disorders sourcebook   **616.2**

Lungs
Diseases
See also Asthma
Lung disorders sourcebook   **616.2**

Luongo, Albert M., 1939-
Soccer drills   **796.334**

Lupa, Robyn M.
(ed) More than MySpace. See More than MySpace   **027.62**

Luper, Eric
Bug boy   **Fic**
Seth Baumgartner's love manifesto   **Fic**

Lurie, April
The latent powers of Dylan Fontaine   **Fic**

Lush. Friend, N.   **Fic**

Lüsted, Marcia Amidon, 1962-
How to analyze the works of Stephen King
    813.009
Poverty   **362.5**

Lutes, Jason, 1967-
Houdini: the handcuff king   **92**

Luttikhuizen, Henry, 1964-
(jt. auth) Snyder, J. Art of the Middle Ages
    709.02

Luxbacher, Joe
Soccer: steps to success   **796.334**

The **luxe.** Godbersen, A.   **Fic**

Lyddie. Paterson, K.   **Fic**

Lye, Keith
(ed) 100 great journeys. See 100 great journeys
    910.2

Lyga, Barry
The astonishing adventures of Fanboy & Goth Girl   **Fic**
Boy toy   **Fic**
Hero-type   **Fic**

Lying *See* Truthfulness and falsehood

The **lying** game. Shepard, S.   **Fic**

Lyme disease
See also Ticks
Edlow, J. A. Bull's-eye: unraveling the medical mystery of Lyme disease   **616.9**

Lymphatic system
McDowell, J. The lymphatic system   **612.4**

Lynas, Mark, 1973-
High tide   **363.7**

Lynch, Chris
Angry young man   **Fic**
The Big Game of Everything   **Fic**
Hothouse   **Fic**
Inexcusable   **Fic**

Lynch, Jack, 1967-
(ed) Dracula, by Bram Stoker. See Dracula, by Bram Stoker   **823.009**

Lynch, John T. *See* Lynch, Jack, 1967-

Lynch, Patricia Ann
African mythology, A to Z   **299.6**

Lynch, Scott, 1978-
The lies of Locke Lamora   **Fic**

Lynch, Thomas, 1948-
Bodies in motion and at rest   **113**

Lynch, Wayne
Penguins of the world   **598**

Lynching
Alphin, E. M. An unspeakable crime
    364.152
Aretha, D. The murder of Emmett Till
    364.152
Crowe, C. Getting away with murder: the true story of the Emmett Till case   **364.152**

Mackenzie, Jennifer
The complete trail food cookbook — **641.5**

Mackenzie, lost and found. Kerbel, D. — **Fic**

Mackler, Carolyn
The earth, my butt, and other big, round things — **Fic**
Tangled — **Fic**
Vegan virgin Valentine — **Fic**

Macklin, Karen
(jt. auth) Johnson, A. Indie girl — **305.23**

Mackrell, Judith
(jt. auth) Craine, D. The Oxford dictionary of dance — **792.803**

MacLeish, Archibald, 1892-1982
Collected poems, 1917-1982 — **811**

Macleod, Alasdair, 1963-
Explorers — **910.4**

MacMillan, Donald, 1874-1970
About
Bryant, J. H. Dangerous crossings — **998**

Macmillan encyclopedia of death and dying — **306.9**

Macmillan science library [series]
Animal sciences — **590.3**

Macmillan social science library [series]
Encyclopedia of race and racism — **305.8**

MacNee, Marie J.
Outlaws, mobsters & crooks — **920.003**

MacNeil, Robert, 1931-
(jt. auth) McCrum, R. The story of English — **420**

MacPherson, Malcolm C., 1943-2009
Roberts ridge — **958.1**

Macy, Anne Sullivan *See* Sullivan, Anne, 1866-1936

Macy, Laura Williams
(ed) The Grove book of operas. See The Grove book of operas — **792.5**

Macy, Sue, 1954-
Freeze frame — **796.98**

Maczulak, Anne E.
Cleaning up the environment — **628.5**
Waste treatment — **628.4**

Mad about modern physics. Potter, F. — **530**

Mad about physics. Jargodzki, C. — **530**

Mad love. Selfors, S. — **Fic**

Madapple. Meldrum, C. — **Fic**

Madden, Kerry
Harper Lee — **92**

Madden, Matt
(jt. auth) Abel, J. Drawing words & writing pictures — **741.5**

Madigan, L. K.
Flash burnout — **Fic**
The mermaid's mirror — **Fic**

Madison, James, 1751-1836
About
Wilkins, R. W. Jefferson's pillow — **973**
Wills, G. James Madison — **92**
See/See also pages in the following book(s):
Ellis, J. J. Founding brothers — **973.4**

Madison, James H.
World War II — **940.53**

Madre and I. Reyes, G. — **92**

Mafham, Ken Preston- *See* Preston-Mafham, Ken

Mafham, Rod Preston- *See* Preston-Mafham, Rod

Mafia
Fiction
Blundell, J. Strings attached — **Fic**
Grisham, J. The client — **Fic**
Grisham, J. The firm — **Fic**
Korman, G. Son of the mob — **Fic**

Maga, Timothy P., 1952-
The 1960s — **973.92**

Magazines *See* Periodicals

Magazines for libraries — **011**

Magee, Bryan
The story of philosophy — **190**

Maghreb *See* North Africa

Magic
Fiction
Alexander, A. Gift of the Unmage — **Fic**
Bell, H. Trickster's girl — **Fic**
Blubaugh, P. Serendipity Market — **Fic**
Brennan, S. R. The demon's lexicon — **Fic**
Bullen, A. Wish — **Fic**
Bunce, E. C. Star crossed — **Fic**
Chima, C. W. The warrior heir — **Fic**
Cypess, L. Mistwood — **Fic**
Dixon, H. Entwined — **Fic**
Dolamore, J. Magic under glass — **Fic**
Duey, K. Skin hunger — **Fic**
Goodman, A. Eon: Dragoneye reborn — **Fic**
Grossman, L. The magicians — **Fic**
Guibord, M. Warped — **Fic**
Hamilton, K. R. Tyger tyger — **Fic**
Healey, K. Guardian of the dead — **Fic**
Jones, A. F. Warrior princess — **Fic**
Lackey, M. Legacies — **Fic**
Lackey, M. The phoenix unchained — **Fic**
Larbalestier, J. Magic or madness — **Fic**
Madigan, L. K. The mermaid's mirror — **Fic**
Mantchev, L. Eyes like stars — **Fic**
Marillier, J. Wildwood dancing — **Fic**
Marriott, Z. The swan kingdom — **Fic**
McBride, L. Hold me closer, necromancer — **Fic**
McKinley, R. Pegasus — **Fic**
Melling, O. R. The Hunter's Moon — **Fic**
Michaelis, A. The dragons of darkness — **Fic**
Murdock, C. G. Princess Ben — **Fic**
Neumeier, R. The City in the Lake — **Fic**
Pierce, T. Terrier — **Fic**
Reeve, P. Here lies Arthur — **Fic**
Ruiz Zafón, C. The Prince of Mist — **Fic**
Simner, J. L. Bones of Faerie — **Fic**
Simner, J. L. Thief eyes — **Fic**
Spinner, S. Damosel — **Fic**
Stiefvater, M. Lament — **Fic**
Stroud, J. The ring of Solomon — **Fic**
Tiernan, C. Immortal beloved — **Fic**
Werlin, N. Impossible — **Fic**
Weston, R. P. Dust city — **Fic**
Wrede, P. C. The thirteenth child — **Fic**

The **magic** circle. Napoli, D. J. — **Fic**

Magic or madness. Larbalestier, J.   **Fic**

Magic tricks

    Graphic novels

  Ottaviani, J. Levitation: physics and psychology
    in the service of deception   **793.8**

Magic under glass. Dolamore, J.   **Fic**

The **magical** I ching. Brennan, J. H.   **299.5**

The **magical** life of Long Tack Sam. Fleming, A.
  M.   **92**

The **magical** maze. Stewart, I.   **793.74**

The **Magician** of Hoad. Mahy, M.   **Fic**

Magicians

    Fiction

  Lackey, M. The phoenix unchained   **Fic**
  Mahy, M. The Magician of Hoad   **Fic**

    Graphic novels

  Dunning, J. H. Salem Brownstone   **741.5**
  Fleming, A. M. The magical life of Long Tack
    Sam   **92**
  Lutes, J. Houdini: the handcuff king   **92**

The **magicians**. Grossman, L.   **Fic**

Magick, mayhem, and mavericks. Cobb, C.
    541

Magida, Arthur J.

  (ed) How to be a perfect stranger. See How to
    be a perfect stranger   **203**

Magill, Frank Northen, 1907-

  (ed) Masterpieces of world literature. See Mas-
    terpieces of world literature   **809**

  (ed) Notable poets. See Notable poets
    920.003

  (ed) Psychology basics. See Psychology basics
    150.3

Magill's choice [series]

  American Indian biographies   **920.003**
  American Indian tribes   **970.004**
  Ancient Greece   **938.003**
  Notable poets   **920.003**
  Psychology basics   **150.3**
  Shakespeare   **822.3**
  Short story writers   **809.3**

Magill's encyclopedia of science   **580**

Magill's encyclopedia of science: animal life
    590.3

Magill's medical guide   **610.3**

Magill's survey of American literature   **810.9**

Magill's survey of world literature   **809**

Magistrale, Tony

  Student companion to Edgar Allan Poe   **818**

Magnetism

  Verschuur, G. L. Hidden attraction   **538**

Magoc, Chris J., 1960-

  Environmental issues in American history
    333.7

Magocsi, Paul R.

  Historical atlas of Central Europe   **911**

Magoon, Kekla, 1980-

  The rock and the river   **Fic**

Mah, Adeline Yen, 1937-

  China   **951**

Mahabharata

  The Mahābhārata   **891**

Mahabharata. Bhagavadgita

  Bhagavad Gita   **891**

Mahomet *See* Muḥammad, d. 632

Mahony, Phillip, 1955-

  (ed) From both sides now. See From both sides
    now   **811.008**

Mahood, Kristine

  Booktalking with teens   **021.7**
  A passion for print   **027.62**

Mahy, Margaret

  The Magician of Hoad   **Fic**

Mai, Larry L.

  The Cambridge Dictionary of human biology
    and evolution   **612**

Maier, Pauline, 1938-

  American scripture   **973.3**

Main Street. Lewis, S.   **Fic**

Main Street & Babbitt. Lewis, S.   **Fic**

Maine

    Fiction

  Frank, H. The view from the top   **Fic**
  Jacobson, J. The complete history of why I hate
    her   **Fic**
  King, S. Carrie   **Fic**
  Les Becquets, D. Season of ice   **Fic**
  Oliver, L. Delirium   **Fic**
  Weinheimer, B. Converting Kate   **Fic**

Mair, Victor H., 1943-

  (ed) The Shorter Columbia anthology of tradi-
    tional Chinese literature. See The Shorter Co-
    lumbia anthology of traditional Chinese litera-
    ture   **895.1**

Mairowitz, David Zane

  Kafka   **92**

Maisie Dobbs. Winspear, J.   **Fic**

Maison, Jérôme

  (il) Jacquet, L. March of the penguins   **598**

Maître-Allain, Thierry

  Aquariums   **639.34**

Maizel, Rebecca

  Infinite days   **Fic**

Major, John S., 1942-

  (ed) World poetry. See World poetry   **808.81**

Major [biography of Marshall "Major" Taylor]
  Balf, T.   **92**

Major acts of Congress   **348**

Major battles and campaigns [series]

  Wood, W. J. Battles of the Revolutionary War,
    1775-1781   **973.3**

Major issues in American history [series]

  Davis, T. J. Race relations in America
    305.8

  Magoc, C. J. Environmental issues in American
    history   **333.7**

The **major** works. Keats, J.   **821**

Make-believe playmates *See* Imaginary playmates

Make lemonade. Wolff, V. E.   **Fic**

Make me over   **S C**

Makers. Doctorow, C.   **Fic**

Makers of America [series]

  Scott, R. A. Chief Joseph and the Nez Percés
    92

Makers of modern science [series]
  Sherrow, V. Jonas Salk   **92**
  Spangenburg, R. Wernher von Braun **92**
Makes me wanna holler. McCall, N. **92**
Makeup, Theatrical *See* Theatrical makeup
Makeup (Cosmetics) *See* Cosmetics
Making comics. McCloud, S. **741.5**
The **making** of the fittest. Carroll, S. B. **572.8**
Making the most of college. Light, R. J. **378.1**
Making the right college choice. Silivanch, A. **378.1**
Making the writing and research connection with the I-search process. Tallman, J. I. **025.5**
Makosz, Rory
  Latino arts and their influence on the United States **700**
Malamud, Bernard, 1914-1986
  The assistant **Fic**
  The complete stories **S C**
  The fixer **Fic**
Malaria
  Cunningham, K. Malaria **614.5**
  Goldsmith, C. Battling malaria **616.9**
Malaspina, Ann, 1957-
  The ethnic and group identity movements **323.1**
  Harriet Tubman **92**
Malaysia
  Graphic novels
  Lat. Kampung boy **741.5**
  Lat. Town boy **741.5**
Malcolm, Janet
  Reading Chekhov **891.7**
Malcolm X, 1925-1965
  The autobiography of Malcolm X **92**
  Encyclopedias
  The Malcolm X encyclopedia **320.5**
  Graphic novels
  Helfer, A. Malcolm X **92**
The **Malcolm** X encyclopedia **320.5**
Male and female roles: opposing viewpoints **305.3**
Male role *See* Sex role
Males, Mike A.
  Framing youth **305.23**
Malin, Jo
  (ed) Encyclopedia of women's autobiography. See Encyclopedia of women's autobiography **920.003**
Malley, G. R. *See* Malley, Gemma
Malley, Gemma
  The Declaration **Fic**
Mallon, Bill
  Historical dictionary of the Olympic movement **796.48**
Mallon, Mary *See* Typhoid Mary, d. 1938
Mallory, Bill, 1935-
  (ed) Complete guide to special teams. See Complete guide to special teams **796.332**

Mallory, James
  (jt. auth) Lackey, M. The outstretched shadow **Fic**
  (jt. auth) Lackey, M. The phoenix unchained **Fic**
Malloy, Brian
  The year of ice **Fic**
Maloney, Robert K., 1958-
  (jt. auth) Kornmehl, E. W. LASIK: a guide to laser vision correction **617.7**
Malory, Sir Thomas, 15th cent.
  Le morte Darthur, or, The hoole book of Kyng Arthur and of his noble knyghtes of the Rounde Table **398.2**
Malpass, Michael
  Daily life in the Inca empire **985**
Malthus, T. R. (Thomas Robert), 1766-1834
See/See also pages in the following book(s):
  Bussing-Burks, M. Influential economists **920**
  Heilbroner, R. L. The worldly philosophers **330.1**
Malthus, Thomas Robert *See* Malthus, T. R. (Thomas Robert), 1766-1834
Maltin, Leonard
  (ed) Leonard Maltin's movie guide. See Leonard Maltin's movie guide **791.43**
Mama Flora's family. Haley, A. **Fic**
Mama's boy, preacher's son. Jennings, K. **92**
Mammal tracks & sign. Elbroch, M. **599**
Mammals
  See also Fossil mammals groups of mammals; and names of mammals
  Attenborough, D. The life of mammals **599**
  Forsyth, A. Mammals of North America **599**
  Kays, R. Mammals of North America **599**
  Mammals **599**
  Tudge, C. The time before history **599.93**
  Whitaker, J. O., Jr. National Audubon Society field guide to North American mammals **599**
See/See also pages in the following book(s):
  Elbroch, M. Mammal tracks & sign **599**
  Encyclopedias
  The Princeton encyclopedia of mammals **599**
Mammals **599**
Mammals of North America. Forsyth, A. **599**
Mammals of North America. Kays, R. **599**
Mammoths
  Lister, A. Mammoths **569**
Man *See* Human beings
  Influence of environment
  See Environmental influence on humans
  Influence on nature
  See Human influence on nature
  Origin
  See Human origins
Man, Fossil *See* Fossil hominids
Man, Prehistoric *See* Prehistoric peoples
A **man** for all seasons. Bolt, R. **822**

Man o' War (Race horse)
Ours, D. Man o' War   **798.4**
Man of La Mancha. Wasserman, D.   **812**
The **man** who invented the computer [biography of John V. Atanasoff] Smiley, J.   **92**
Management
     See also Conflict management
Management of conflict *See* Conflict management
Managing and analyzing your collection. Doll, C. A.   **025.2**
Managing curriculum and assessment   **375**
Manahan, Anna Anderson *See* Anderson, Anna, d. 1984
Manassas. Reasoner, J.   **Fic**
Manatees
     Reep, R. L. The Florida manatee   **599.5**
Mancall, Jacqueline C., 1932-
     (jt. auth) Hughes-Hassell, S. Collection management for youth   **025.2**
Manchild in the promised land. Brown, C.   **92**
Manco, Tristan
     (ed) Ganz, N. Graffiti world   **751**
Mandel, David, 1938-
     Who's who in the Jewish Bible   **920.003**
Mandela, Nelson
     Mandela   **92**
     Nelson Mandela speaks   **968.06**
     About
     Carlin, J. Playing the enemy   **968.06**
     Gaines, A. Nelson Mandela and apartheid in world history   **92**
     See/See also pages in the following book(s):
     Aikman, D. Great souls   **920**
Mandelbrot, Benoit B.
     See/See also pages in the following book(s):
     Horvitz, L. A. Eureka!: scientific breakthroughs that changed the world   **509**
Mandell, Daniel R., 1956-
     King Philip's war   **973.2**
Manga
     See also Josei manga; Seinen manga; Shojo manga; Shonen manga
     Ashihara, H. Sand chronicles vol. 1   **741.5**
     Azuma, K. Azumanga Daioh omnibus   **741.5**
     Igarashi, D. Children of the sea, vol. 1   **741.5**
     Inada, S. Ghost hunt, Vol. 1   **741.5**
     Inoue, T. Real, volume 1   **741.5**
     Inoue, T. Slam dunk, volume 1   **741.5**
     Iwaoka, H. Saturn apartments, volume 1   **741.5**
     Kardy, G. Manga University Presents . . . Kana de Manga Special Edition: Japanese Sound FX!   **495.6**
     Kishimoto, M. Naruto. vol. 1, The tests of the Ninja   **741.5**
     Kojima, H. The manga guide to calculus   **515**
     Kubo, T. Bleach, Vol. 1   **741.5**
     The manga cookbook   **641.5**
     Mashima, H. Fairy tale vol. 1   **741.5**
     Miyuki, T. Musashi #9, Vol. 1   **741.5**
     Nakahara, A. Love*Com Vol. 1   **741.5**

Nakazawa, K. Barefoot Gen volume five: the never-ending war   **741.5**
Nakazawa, K. Barefoot Gen volume six: writing the truth   **741.5**
Nitta, H. The manga guide to physics   **530**
Obata, Y. We were there, vol. 1   **741.5**
Okabayashi, K. Manga for dummies   **741.5**
Ono, N. Gente: the people of Ristorante Paradiso, volume 1   **741.5**
Takahashi, R. One-pound gospel, vol. 1   **741.5**
Takemura, M. The manga guide to molecular biology   **572.8**
Tanabe, Y. Kekkaishi, Vol. 1   **741.5**
Tezuka, O. Black Jack, volume 1   **741.5**
Toboso, Y. Black butler, vol. 1   **741.5**
Unita, Y. Bunny drop vol. 1   **741.5**
Urasawa, N. Pluto: Urasawa x Tezuka, vol. 1   **741.5**
Urushibara, Y. Mu shi shi 1   **741.5**
Watsuki, N. Rurouni Kenshin   **741.5**
Yoshizaki, S. Kingyo used books, vol. 1   **741.5**
Yumi, K. Library wars, vol. 1: love & war   **741.5**
     Authorship
     Lehman, T. Manga: masters of the art   **741.5**
     Bibliography
     Thompson, J. Manga: the complete guide   **741.5**
     Drawing
     Amberlyn, J. C. Drawing manga   **741.5**
     Hart, C. Manga for the beginner   **741.5**
     Nagatomo, H. Draw your own Manga   **741.5**
     Study and teaching
     Brenner, R. E. Understanding manga and anime   **025.2**
The **manga** cookbook   **641.5**
Manga for dummies. Okabayashi, K.   **741.5**
Manga for the beginner. Hart, C.   **741.5**
The **manga** guide to calculus. Kojima, H.   **515**
The **manga** guide to molecular biology. Takemura, M.   **572.8**
The **manga** guide to physics. Nitta, H.   **530**
Manga: masters of the art. Lehman, T.   **741.5**
Manga Shakespeare [series]
     Appignanesi, R. Hamlet   **822.3**
     Appignanesi, R. Julius Caesar   **822.3**
     Appignanesi, R. A midsummer night's dream   **822.3**
     Appignanesi, R. Romeo and Juliet   **822.3**
     Appignanesi, R. The tempest   **822.3**
Manga: the complete guide. Thompson, J.   **741.5**
Manga University Presents . . . Kana de Manga Special Edition: Japanese Sound FX!. Kardy, G.   **495.6**
Manhattan Project
     Conant, J. 109 East Palace   **623.4**
Manic-depressive illness
     See also Depression (Psychology)
     Marcovitz, H. Bipolar disorder   **616.89**
     Meisel, A. Investigating depression and bipolar disorder   **616.89**

Maryam Jameelah, 1934-
About
Baker, D. The convert [biography of Maryam Jameelah]   92

Maryland
Fiction
Cummings, P. Blindsided   **Fic**
LeFlore, L. The world is mine   **Fic**
Lyga, B. Hero-type   **Fic**
Tyler, A. Dinner at the Homesick Restaurant   **Fic**

History
Walker, S. M. Written in bone   614

Marzilli, Alan, 1970-
Election reform   324.6
Fetal rights   342
The Internet and crime   345

Masai (African people)
Lekuton, J. Facing the lion   967.62

MASH. Hooker, R.   **Fic**

Mashima, Hiro
Fairy tale vol. 1   741.5

The **mask** of Nostradamus. Randi, J.   92

Masked. McClintock, N.   **Fic**

The masks of God [series]
Campbell, J. Creative mythology   201
Campbell, J. Occidental mythology   201
Campbell, J. Oriental mythology   201
Campbell, J. Primitive mythology   201

Maslon, Laurence, 1959-
(jt. auth) Kantor, M. Broadway: the American musical   792.6

Masoff, Joy, 1951-
Snowboard!   796.93

Mason, Antony
A history of Western art   709

Mason, Bill, 1929-
Sports illustrated fly fishing   799.1

Mason, Bobbie Ann
Elvis Presley   92
In country   **Fic**

Mason, David, 1954-
(ed) Twentieth-century American poetry. See Twentieth-century American poetry   811.008

Mason, George, 1725-1792
About
Wilkins, R. W. Jefferson's pillow   973

Mass communication See Communication; Telecommunication

Mass feeding See Food service

Mass media
See also Native Americans in mass media
Foerstel, H. N. From Watergate to Monicagate   070.4
Freedom of expression   323.44
How does advertising impact teen behavior?   659.1
Is media violence a problem?   302.23
Mass media: opposing viewpoints   302.23
Media violence: opposing viewpoints   363.3
Violence in the media   303.6

Wyckoff, C. Communications and the arts   331.7
See/See also pages in the following book(s):
Popular culture: opposing viewpoints   306
Television: opposing viewpoints   302.23

Mass media literacy See Media literacy

Mass media: opposing viewpoints   302.23

Massachusetts
Fiction
Dana, B. A voice of her own   **Fic**
Frazer, M. Secrets of truth and beauty   **Fic**
Friend, N. For keeps   **Fic**
Halpin, B. Forever changes   **Fic**
Hoffman, A. Blue diary   **Fic**
Lahiri, J. The namesake   **Fic**
Paterson, K. Lyddie   **Fic**
Reinhardt, D. A brief chapter in my impossible life   **Fic**
Sales, L. Mostly good girls   **Fic**
Sittenfeld, C. Prep   **Fic**
Tiernan, C. Immortal beloved   **Fic**
History—1600-1775, Colonial period
Aronson, M. John Winthrop, Oliver Cromwell, and the Land of Promise [dual biography of John Winthrop and Oliver Cromwell]   92
Philbrick, N. The Mayflower and the Pilgrims' New World   973.2

Massie, Robert K., 1929-
The Romanovs   947.08

"**Master** Harold"— and the boys. Fugard, A.   822

Master the new SAT. See Pine, P. Peterson's master the SAT 2011   378.1

Mastering online research. Shaw, M. D.   025.04

Mastering positional chess. Naroditsky, D.   794.1

Masterpieces of world literature   809

Masters, Bruce Alan, 1950-
(ed) Encyclopedia of the Ottoman Empire. See Encyclopedia of the Ottoman Empire   956

Masters, Edgar Lee, 1868-1950
Spoon River anthology   811

Masters, Jarvis
That bird has my wings   92

Masters of art [series]
Hartt, F. Michelangelo Buonarroti   759.5
Wasserman, J. Leonardo da Vinci   759.5

Masterson, Daniel M.
The history of Peru   985

Masuda, Toshiya
(jt. auth) Abramson, J. Obama   92

Masur, Louis P.
The Civil War: a concise history   973.7

Matched. Condie, A.   **Fic**

Materia medica
See also Drugs
Foster, S. National Geographic desk reference to nature's medicine   615
Dictionaries
The Merck index   615
The **math** book. Pickover, C. A.   510

Matthew, the Apostle, Saint
Fiction
Gormley, B. Poisoned honey **Fic**

Matthews, Dawn
(ed) Lung disorders sourcebook. See Lung disorders sourcebook **616.2**

Matthews, Glenna
American women's history **305.4**

Matthews, Joseph R.
Strategic planning and management for library managers **025.1**

Mattison, Booker T.
Unsigned hype **Fic**

Mattison, Christopher
The new encyclopedia of snakes **597.96**

Matuz, Roger
Reconstruction era: biographies **920**
(jt. auth) Outman, J. L. U.S. immigration and migration. Biographies **920**

Maude, Aylmer, 1858-1938
(tr) Tolstoy, L., graf. Anna Karenina **Fic**
(tr) Tolstoy, L., graf. Great short works of Leo Tolstoy **S C**

Maude, Louise Shanks
(tr) Tolstoy, L., graf. Anna Karenina **Fic**
(tr) Tolstoy, L., graf. Great short works of Leo Tolstoy **S C**

Maugham, W. Somerset (William Somerset), 1874-1965
Collected short stories **S C**
Of human bondage **Fic**

Maule, Jeremy
(ed) The Oxford book of classical verse in translation. See The Oxford book of classical verse in translation **881.008**

Maunder, Andrew
The Facts on File companion to the British short story **823.009**

Maunder, Edwin Walter, 1851-1928
See/See also pages in the following book(s):
Clark, S. The sun kings **523.7**

Mauro, Tony
Illustrated great decisions of the Supreme Court **347**

Maus, Katharine Eisaman, 1955-
(ed) Shakespeare, W. The Norton Shakespeare **822.3**

Maus. Spiegelman, A. **940.53**

Mauve. Garfield, S. **667**

Maxims See Proverbs

May, Charles E. (Charles Edward), 1941-
(ed) Short story writers. See Short story writers **809.3**

May, Mel Anthony
(ed) Encyclopedia of women and baseball. See Encyclopedia of women and baseball **796.357**

May, Mike
Sensation and perception **612.8**

Maya Angelou [critical essays] **818**

Mayas
Sharer, R. J. Daily life in Maya civilization **972.81**

See/See also pages in the following book(s):
Aveni, A. F. Stairways to the stars **520**
Ceram, C. W. Gods, graves, and scholars **930.1**
Wright, R. Stolen continents **970.004**
Fiction
Raedeke, C. The daykeeper's grimoire **Fic**

Mayer, Brian
Libraries got game **025.2**

Mayer, Robert H.
When the children marched **323.1**
(ed) The Civil Rights Act of 1964. See The Civil Rights Act of 1964 **342**

The **Mayflower** and the Pilgrims' New World. Philbrick, N. **973.2**

Maynard, Thane
(jt. auth) Goodall, J. Hope for animals and their world **591.68**

Mayo Clinic family health book **613**

Mays, Dorothy A.
Women in early America **305.4**

Mays, Rick
(il) Vankin, D. Poseurs **741.5**

The **maze.** Hobbs, W. **Fic**

The **maze** runner. Dashner, J. **Fic**

Mazer, Anne, 1953-
(ed) Working days: stories about teenagers and work. See Working days: stories about teenagers and work **S C**

Mazer, Harry, 1925-
The last mission **Fic**

Mazer, Norma Fox, 1931-2009
The missing girl **Fic**
About
Reed, A. J. S. Norma Fox Mazer **813.009**

Mazower, Mark
The Balkans: a short history **949.6**

McAfee, Richard, 1950-
Table tennis **796.34**

McAllister, Ian, 1969-
The last wild wolves **599.77**

McAllister, Pam
(jt. auth) Riley, D. The bedside, bathtub & armchair companion to Shakespeare **822.3**

McBay, Bruce, 1946-
Waiting for Sarah **Fic**

McBride, Dorothy E.
Abortion in the United States **363.46**

McBride, Lish
Hold me closer, necromancer **Fic**

McBride, Regina, 1956-
The fire opal **Fic**

McBrien, Richard P.
Lives of the saints **920**

McCabe, Timothy Lee
(jt. auth) Rittner, D. Encyclopedia of biology **570.3**

McCafferty, Megan
(ed) Sixteen: stories about that sweet and bitter birthday. See Sixteen: stories about that sweet and bitter birthday **S C**

McVay, Charles Butler, III
About
Nelson, P. Left for dead   **940.54**

McVoy, Terra Elan
After the kiss   **Fic**
Pure   **Fic**

McWhorter, Diane
Carry me home   **976.1**

McWilliams, John C., 1949-
The 1960s cultural revolution   **973.92**

MDMA (Drug)
See also Ecstasy (Drug)

Me and Orson Welles. Kaplow, R.   **Fic**

Me, myself and Ike. Denman, K. L.   **Fic**

Me, myself, and them. Snyder, K.   **92**

Me, the missing, and the dead. Valentine, J.   **Fic**

Mead, Frank Spencer, 1898-1982
(jt. auth) Atwood, C. D. Handbook of denominations in the United States   **280**

Mead, Margaret, 1901-1978
About
Hess, A. Margaret Mead   **92**
Mark, J. T. Margaret Mead   **92**

Meade, Teresa, 1948-
A brief history of Brazil   **981**

Meagher, Timothy J.
The Columbia guide to Irish American history   **305.8**

Meal planning *See* Menus; Nutrition

Mealer, Bryan
(jt. auth) Kamkwamba, W. The boy who harnessed the wind   **92**

Mean genes. Burnham, T.   **155.7**

Meaning (Philosophy)
Fiction
Teller, J. Nothing   **Fic**

The **meaning** of it all. Feynman, R. P.   **500**

The **meaning** of the glorious Koran. Koran   **297.1**

Means, A. L.
A student's guide to George Orwell   **828**

Means, D. Bruce, 1941-
Stalking the plumed serpent and other adventures in herpetology   **597.9**

Means, Marcia Merryman
(ed) Jones, J. S. The Crusades, Biographies   **920.003**
(ed) Jones, J. S. The Crusades, Primary sources   **909.07**
(ed) O'Neal, M. The Crusades, Almanac   **909.07**

Means, Bruce *See* Means, D. Bruce, 1941-

Measurement
Nicastro, N. Circumference   **526**
Robinson, A. The story of measurement   **530.8**

Measures *See* Weights and measures

Meat industry
Fiction
Sinclair, U. The jungle   **Fic**

Graphic novels
Kuper, P. The jungle   **741.5**

Meat packing industry *See* Meat industry

Meat trade *See* Meat industry

Mechanics
Sobey, E. A field guide to automotive technology   **629.2**

Mechner, Jordan, 1964-
Solomon's thieves   **741.5**

Meconis, Dylan, 1983-
(il) Ottaviani, J. Wire mothers   **152.4**

Médecins Sans Frontières (Organization)
Bortolotti, D. Hope in hell   **610**
Graphic novels
Guibert, E. The photographer   **958.1**

Media *See* Mass media

Media images and representations. King, C. R.   **302.23**

Media literacy
Study and teaching
De Abreu, B. S. Media literacy, social networking, and the web 2.0 environment for the K-12 educator   **302.23**

Media literacy, social networking, and the web 2.0 environment for the K-12 educator. De Abreu, B. S.   **302.23**

Media violence: opposing viewpoints   **363.3**

Medical botany
Foster, S. National Geographic desk reference to nature's medicine   **615**
Kidd, J. S. Potent natural medicines   **615**

Medical care
See also Health self-care
Naden, C. J. Patients' rights   **362.1**
Fiction
Forman, G. If I stay   **Fic**
Jocelyn, M. Would you   **Fic**

Medical diagnosis *See* Diagnosis

Medical ethics
See also Human experimentation in medicine; Right to die
Biomedical ethics: opposing viewpoints   **174.2**
Boleyn-Fitzgerald, M. Ending and extending life   **174.2**
Caplan, A. L. Smart mice, not-so-smart people   **174.2**
Kelly, K. Medicine today   **610.9**
Lovegrove, R. Health   **174.2**
Medical ethics   **174.2**

Medical ethics   **174.2**

Medical firsts. Adler, R. E.   **610.9**

Medical genetics
Green, R. M. Babies by design   **176**
Hodge, R. The future of genetics   **303.4**
Reilly, P. Is it in your genes?   **599.93**
Encyclopedias
The Gale encyclopedia of genetic disorders   **616**
Genetics & inherited conditions   **576.5**

Medical jurisprudence
Adelman, H. C. Forensic medicine   **614**
Zugibe, F. T. Dissecting death   **614**

Mendez, Serafín Mendez *See* Mendez Mendez, Serafín

Mendez Mendez, Serafín
(jt. auth) Fernandez, R. Puerto Rico past and present **972.95**

Mendoza, Louis Gerard, 1960-
(ed) Crossing into America. See Crossing into America **810.8**

Mendoza, Patrick M.
Extraordinary people in extraordinary times **920**

Meng, Hope
(jt. auth) Rannels, M. Sew subversive **646.4**

Meningitis
Shmaefsky, B. Meningitis **616.8**

Mennonites
See also Amish

Menstruation
My little red book **305.23**
Fiction
Don't cramp my style **S C**

Mental disorders. Farrell, C. **362.1**

Mental health
Mental health information for teens **616.89**
Mental health information for teens **616.89**

Mental illness
See also Personality disorders
Farrell, C. Mental disorders **362.1**
Hicks, J. W. Fifty signs of mental illness **616.89**
Mental illness: opposing viewpoints **362.2**
Simon, L. Detour **92**
Fiction
Anderson, J. L. Border crossing **Fic**
Denman, K. L. Me, myself and Ike **Fic**
Fischer, J. An egg on three sticks **Fic**
Griffin, A. Where I want to be **Fic**
Griffin, P. The Orange Houses **Fic**
Halpern, J. Get well soon **Fic**
Hautman, P. Invisible **Fic**
Marchetta, M. Saving Francesca **Fic**
McNish, C. Angel **Fic**
Moskowitz, H. Break **Fic**
Nolan, H. Crazy **Fic**
Plath, S. The bell jar **Fic**
Schindler, H. A blue so dark **Fic**
Warman, J. Breathless **Fic**
Williams, C. L. Miles from ordinary **Fic**
Woods, E. E. Choker **Fic**
Graphic novels
Hornschemeier, P. Mother, come home **741.5**
Nowak, N. Unholy kinship **741.5**
Powell, N. Swallow me whole **741.5**
White, T. How I made it to eighteen **741.5**

Mental illness: opposing viewpoints **362.2**

Mental retardation
Libal, A. My name is not Slow **362.3**

Mental suggestion
See also Brainwashing

Mental telepathy *See* Telepathy

Mentally handicapped
See also Savants (Savant syndrome)
Simon, R. Riding the bus with my sister **92**
Fiction
Gaines, E. J. A lesson before dying **Fic**
Hooper, M. Fallen Grace **Fic**
Keyes, D. Flowers for Algernon **Fic**

Mentally handicapped children
Fiction
Hamilton, K. R. Tyger tyger **Fic**

Mentally ill
Fiction
Greenberg, J. I never promised you a rose garden **Fic**
Kesey, K. One flew over the cuckoo's nest **Fic**
Nelson, R. A. Breathe my name **Fic**
Institutional care
See also Psychiatric hospitals

Mentally ill children *See* Emotionally disturbed children

Mentoring
Fiction
Myers, W. D. Kick **Fic**

Menus
Allen, S. L. In the devil's garden **641**

Menzel, Peter
Hungry planet **641.3**

Menzer, Joe
The wildest ride **796.72**

Mercado, Nancy E., 1975-
(ed) Every man for himself. See Every man for himself **S C**

Mercatante, Anthony S.
The Facts on File encyclopedia of world mythology and legend **201.03**

Mercer, Don
(jt. auth) Mackenzie, J. The complete trail food cookbook **641.5**

Merchandising *See* Marketing

The **merchant** of Venice. Hinds, G. **822.3**

The **merchant** of Venice. Shakespeare, W. **822.3**

The **merchant** of Venice [criticism] Schupack, S. **822.3**

The **Merck** index **615**

The **Merck** manual home health handbook **616.02**

The **Merck** manual of diagnosis and therapy **610.3**

Mercury (Planet)
Grier, J. A. Inner planets **523.4**

Mercury. Larson, H. **741.5**

The **Mercury** 13: the untold story of thirteen American women and the dream of space flight. Ackmann, M. **629.45**

Mercury Project *See* Project Mercury

Mercy killing *See* Euthanasia

Meridian. Kizer, A. **Fic**

Merino, Noël
(ed) Drug legalization. See Drug legalization **363.45**

Merino, Noël—*Continued*
(ed) Gateway drugs: opposing viewpoints. See Gateway drugs: opposing viewpoints
362.29
(ed) Juvenile crime. See Juvenile crime
364.36
(ed) Medical ethics. See Medical ethics
174.2
(ed) Poverty and homelessness. See Poverty and homelessness
362.5
(ed) Racism. See Racism
305.8
(ed) Smoking. See Smoking
362.29
(ed) What rights should illegal immigrants have? See What rights should illegal immigrants have?
342

Merlin (Legendary character)
Fiction
Stewart, M. Mary Stewart's Merlin trilogy
Fic

Mermaids and mermen
Fiction
Madigan, L. K. The mermaid's mirror
Fic
McKinley, R. Water: tales of elemental spirits
S C

The **mermaid's** mirror. Madigan, L. K.
Fic

Merrell, Billy, 1982-
Talking in the dark
811
(ed) The Full spectrum. See The Full spectrum
306.76

The **Merriam-Webster** dictionary of synonyms and antonyms
423

Merriam-Webster's collegiate dictionary
423

Merriam-Webster's collegiate thesaurus
423

Merriam-Webster's dictionary of English usage
428

Merriam-Webster's geographical dictionary
910.3

Merriam-Webster's visual dictionary. Corbeil, J.-C.
423

Merrick, Joseph Carey, 1862-1890
Drama
Pomerance, B. The Elephant Man
822

Merrill, James
The collected poems of James Merrill
811

Merrill, Martha
(jt. auth) McCain, M. M. Dictionary for school library media specialists
020

Merriman, John M.
(ed) Europe 1789 to 1914. See Europe 1789 to 1914
940.2
(ed) Europe since 1914. See Europe since 1914
940.5

Mersky, Roy M.
(jt. auth) Hartman, G. R. Landmark Supreme Court cases
347

Merton, Louis Thomas See Merton, Thomas, 1915-1968

Merton, Thomas, 1915-1968
(ed) Gandhi, M. Gandhi on non-violence
322.4

Mertz, Barbara, 1927-
Temples, tombs, & hieroglyphs
932

Mertz, Leslie A.
The circulatory system
616.1

Merwin, John
Fly fishing
799.1

Merwin, W. S. (William Stanley), 1927-
(tr) Chanson de Roland. The song of Roland
841
(tr) Dante Alighieri. Purgatorio
851
(tr) Gawain and the Grene Knight (Middle English poem). Sir Gawain and the Green Knight
821
(tr) Neruda, P. Twenty love poems and a song of despair
861

Merwin, William Stanley See Merwin, W. S. (William Stanley), 1927-

Merzbach, Uta C., 1933-
(jt. auth) Boyer, C. B. A history of mathematics
510

Mesmerism See Hypnotism

Mesopotamia See Iraq

Messed up. Nichols, J.
Fic

Metals
Halka, M. Metals and metalloids
546
Halka, M. Transition metals
546

Metals and metalloids. Halka, M.
546

Metalwork
See also Metals

Metamorphoses. Ovid
873

Metamorphosis. Franco, B.
Fic

The **metamorphosis** and other stories. Kafka, F.
S C

Metaphors dictionary
423

Metcalf, Gena
(ed) Obesity. See Obesity
616.3

Metcalf, Linda
How to say it to get into the college of your choice
378.1

Metcalf, Tom
(ed) Obesity. See Obesity
616.3

Meteorites
Smith, C. Meteorites
523.5

Meteorology
See also Climate; Droughts; Weather; Weather control
Buckley, B. Weather: a visual guide
551.5
Desonie, D. Atmosphere
551.5
Gunn, A. M. A student guide to climate and weather
551.5
Harper, K. Weather and climate
551.5
Williams, J. The AMS weather book
551.5
Dictionaries
The Facts on File dictionary of weather and climate
551.5
Encyclopedias
Allaby, M. Encyclopedia of weather and climate
551
The encyclopedia of weather and climate change
551.6

Meteors
Norton, O. R. Field guide to meteors and meteorites
523.5

Meth (Drug) See Methamphetamine

Michaels, Barbara *See* Mertz, Barbara, 1927-

Michelangelo and his drawings. Hirst, M.
709.45

Michelangelo Buonarroti, 1475-1564
About
Hartt, F. Michelangelo Buonarroti   759.5
Hirst, M. Michelangelo and his drawings
709.45
Somervill, B. A. Michelangelo   92

Michener, James A., 1907-1997
Tales of the South Pacific   S C

Michigan
Fiction
Ford, J. C. The morgue and me   Fic
Jones, P. Chasing tail lights   Fic
Jones, P. The tear collector   Fic
McCahan, E. I now pronounce you someone
else   Fic
Potter, R. Exit strategy   Fic
Willey, M. A summer of silk moths   Fic

Mickle, Mildred R.
(ed) I know why the caged bird sings, by Maya
Angelou. See I know why the caged bird
sings, by Maya Angelou   818

Micklewright, Keith, 1933-
Drawing: mastering the language of visual expression   741.2

Micklos, John, 1956-
Muhammad Ali   92

Microbes *See* Bacteria

Microbes and people: an A-Z of microorganisms
in our lives. Sankaran, N.   579

Microbiology
See also Biotechnology
Bakalar, N. Where the germs are   616
Ben-Barak, I. The invisible kingdom   579
Rainis, K. G. A guide to microlife   579
Dictionaries
Sankaran, N. Microbes and people: an A-Z of
microorganisms in our lives   579

Microorganisms
See also Bacteria
Guilfoile, P. Antibiotic-resistant bacteria
616.9
Kowalski, K. M. Attack of the superbugs
616.9
Levy, J. The world of microbes   616.9
Rainis, K. G. A guide to microlife   579
Tierno, P. M., Jr. The secret life of germs
616

Microsoft Corporation
Aronson, M. Bill Gates   92

Microsoft Excel (Computer program) *See* Excel
(Computer program)

The **midbrain**. Morgan, M.   612.8

Middle age
See also Aging

Middle Ages
See also Europe—History—476-1492; Holy
Roman Empire; Medieval civilization; World
history—15th century
Bishop, M. The Middle Ages   940.1

Dawson, I. Medicine in the Middle Ages
610.9
Gies, F. The knight in history   940.1
Gies, F. Life in a medieval village   940.1
Gies, J. Life in a medieval castle   940.2
Gies, J. Life in a medieval city   940.1
Great events from history, The Middle Ages,
477-1453   909.07
History of the ancient and medieval world
940.1
Knight, J. Middle ages: almanac   909.07
McKitterick, R. Atlas of the medieval world
911
The Middle Ages, 600 to 1492   909.07
Middle ages: primary sources   909.07
White, P. Exploration in the world of the Mid-
dle Ages, 500-1500   910.4
Zahler, D. The Black Death   614.5
Bibliography
Hamm, J. S. Term paper resource guide to me-
dieval history   940.1
Biography
Extraordinary women of the Medieval and Re-
naissance world   920.003
Great lives from history, the Middle Ages, 477-
1453   920.003
Knight, J. Middle ages: biographies   920
Biography—Dictionaries
Snodgrass, M. E. Who's who in the Middle
Ages   920.003
Encyclopedias
English, E. D. Encyclopedia of the medieval
world   940.1
Lawler, J. Encyclopedia of women in the Mid-
dle Ages   305.4
The Oxford dictionary of the Middle Ages
940.1
Women in the Middle Ages   305.4
Fiction
Cadnum, M. The king's arrow   Fic
Coventry, S. The queen's daughter   Fic
Grant, K. M. Blue flame   Fic
Laird, E. Crusade   Fic
Moran, K. Bloodline   Fic
Napoli, D. J. Hush   Fic
Quick, B. A golden web   Fic
Stroud, J. Heroes of the valley   Fic
Graphic novels
Mechner, J. Solomon's thieves   741.5
The **Middle** Ages. Kelly, K.   610.9
The **Middle** Ages, 600 to 1492   909.07
Middle ages: primary sources   909.07

Middle Ages reference library [series]
Knight, J. Middle ages: biographies   920

Middle East
See also Arab countries
Kort, M. The handbook of the Middle East
956
The Middle East   956
Antiquities—Dictionaries
Dictionary of the ancient Near East   939
Bibliography
Al-Hazza, T. C. Books about the Middle East
016.3058
Civilization
Civilizations of the Ancient Near East   939

Middle East—*Continued*
Encyclopedias
Encyclopedia of the modern Middle East & North Africa **956**
Fiction
Marston, E. Santa Claus in Baghdad and other stories about teens in the Arab world **S C**
Foreign relations—United States
The Middle East **956**
The Middle East: opposing viewpoints **956**
Graphic novels
Hambly, B. Anne Steelyard: the garden of emptiness, act I **741.5**
History
The Continuum political encyclopedia of the Middle East **956**
Lewis, B. The Middle East **956**
Lewis, B. What went wrong? **956**
Pendergast, T. The Middle East conflict. Almanac **956**
Pendergast, T. The Middle East conflict. Biographies **920**
Pendergast, T. The Middle East conflict. Primary sources **956**
Pouwels, R. L. The African and Middle Eastern world, 600-1500 **956**
Poetry
Nye, N. S. 19 varieties of gazelle **811**
Politics and government
The Continuum political encyclopedia of the Middle East **956**
Halliday, F. 100 myths about the Middle East **956**
The Middle East: opposing viewpoints **956**
The **Middle** East **956**
The **Middle** East conflict. Almanac. Pendergast, T. **956**
The **Middle** East conflict. Biographies. Pendergast, T. **920**
The **Middle** East conflict. Primary sources. Pendergast, T. **956**
The **Middle** East: opposing viewpoints **956**
Middle East War, 1991 *See* Persian Gulf War, 1991
The **middle** of everywhere. Polak, M. **Fic**
The **middle** passage. Feelings, T. **326**
Middleton, Earl M., 1919-2007
Knowing who I am **92**
Middleton, John, 1921-2009
(ed) Africa: an encyclopedia for students. See Africa: an encyclopedia for students **960**
Midnight charter. Whitley, D. **Fic**
A **midsummer** night's dream. Appignanesi, R. **822.3**
A **midsummer** night's dream. Shakespeare, W. **822.3**
A **midsummer** night's dream [criticism] Sobran, J. **822.3**
Midwifery *See* Midwives
Midwives
Fiction
O'Brien, C. M. Birthmarked **Fic**
Vega, D. Fact of life #31 **Fic**

Mielke, Danny
Soccer fundamentals **796.334**
A **mighty** long way. LaNier, C. W. **92**
Migrant agricultural laborers
Stavans, I. Cesar Chavez **92**
Fiction
Steinbeck, J. The grapes of wrath **Fic**
Migrant labor
Cruz, B. César Chávez **92**
Griswold del Castillo, R. César Chávez **92**
Hart, E. T. Barefoot heart **92**
Fiction
Steinbeck, J. Of mice and men **Fic**
Migration *See* Immigration and emigration
Migration, Internal *See* Internal migration
Migration of animals *See* Animals—Migration
Miki Falls, Book One: Spring. Crilley, M. **741.5**
Miles, Lera
(ed) World atlas of great apes and their conservation. See World atlas of great apes and their conservation **599.8**
The **miles** between. Pearson, M. **Fic**
Miles from ordinary. Williams, C. L. **Fic**
Milestone documents [series]
Milestone documents in African American history **305.8**
Milestone documents in American history **973**
Milestone documents in world history **909**
Milestone documents of American leaders **973**
Milestone documents of world religions **200**
Milestone documents in African American history **305.8**
Milestone documents in American history **973**
Milestone documents in world history **909**
Milestone documents of American leaders **973**
Milestone documents of world religions **200**
Milestones in American history [series]
Davenport, J. The internment of Japanese Americans during World War II **940.53**
Milestones in computer science and information technology. Reilly, E. D. **004**
Milestones in discovery and invention [series]
Henderson, H. Artificial intelligence **006.3**
Henderson, H. Communications and broadcasting **384**
Henderson, H. Mathematics: powerful patterns in nature and society **510**
Henderson, H. Modern robotics **629.8**
Yount, L. Forensic science **363.2**
Yount, L. Modern astronomy **520**
Yount, L. Modern genetics **576.5**
Yount, L. Modern marine science **551.46**
Milestones in health and medicine. Harding, A. **610.9**
Milestones in modern world history [series]
Slavicek, L. C. The Chinese Cultural Revolution **951.05**
Sonneborn, L. The end of apartheid in South Africa **968.06**
Wagner, H. L. The Iranian Revolution **955**

Military aeronautics

See also Air power; Iraq War, 2003——Aerial operations; World War, 1939-1945——Aerial operations

Military art and science

Nardo, D. The Native Americans **970.004**

Sun-tzu. The illustrated art of war **355**

Warry, J. Warfare in the classical world **355**

History

Knights **940.1**

Military bases

Fiction

Whyman, M. Icecore **Fic**

Military draft *See* Draft

Military draft: opposing viewpoints **355.2**

Military history

Davis, P. K. 100 decisive battles **904**

Grant, R. G. Commanders **355**

Warry, J. Warfare in the classical world **355**

Chronology

A global chronology of conflict **355**

Dictionaries

Grossman, M. World military leaders **920.003**

Encyclopedias

Tucker, S. C. Battles that changed history **355.4**

War: from ancient Egypt to Iraq **355**

Military intervention *See* Intervention (International law)

Military occupation

Fiction

Shinn, S. General Winston's daughter **Fic**

Military personnel

See also Admirals; Soldiers

Military policy

See also National security

United States

Civil liberties and war **323**

Civil liberties and war **342**

Iraq uncensored **956.7**

See/See also pages in the following book(s):

War: opposing viewpoints **355**

Military service, Compulsory *See* Draft

Military service, Voluntary *See* Voluntary military service

Milk, Harvey

About

Aretha, D. No compromise: the story of Harvey Milk **92**

Mill. Macaulay, D. **690**

Millard, A. R. (Alan Ralph)

(ed) Dictionary of the ancient Near East. See Dictionary of the ancient Near East **939**

Millard, Alan Ralph *See* Millard, A. R. (Alan Ralph)

Millay, Edna St. Vincent, 1892-1950

Collected poems **811**

Millennium monologs **812.008**

Miller, Allen R.

Living with anxiety disorders **616.85**

Living with depression **616.85**

Miller, Arthur, 1915-2005

The crucible **812**

Death of a salesman **812**

The portable Arthur Miller **812**

About

Abbotson, S. C. W. Critical companion to Arthur Miller **812.009**

Abbotson, S. C. W. Student companion to Arthur Miller **812.009**

Andersen, R. Arthur Miller **92**

Death of a salesman, by Arthur Miller **812.009**

Dunkleberger, A. A student's guide to Arthur Miller **812.009**

Miller, Calvin Craig, 1954-

A. Philip Randolph and the African American labor movement **92**

Che Guevara **92**

No easy answers [biography of Bayard Rustin] **92**

Reggae poet: the story of Bob Marley **92**

Miller, Char

(ed) The Atlas of US and Canadian environmental history. See The Atlas of US and Canadian environmental history **304.2**

Miller, David, 1959-

Seals & sea lions **599.79**

Miller, Davis

The Tao of Bruce Lee **92**

Miller, Debra A.

Garbage and recycling **363.7**

(ed) Afghanistan. See Afghanistan **958.1**

(ed) Conserving the environment. See Conserving the environment **363.7**

(ed) Espionage and intelligence. See Espionage and intelligence **327.12**

(ed) Immigration. See Immigration [Current controversies series] **325.73**

(ed) The Middle East. See The Middle East **956**

Miller, Donna P., 1948-

Crash course in teen services **027.62**

Miller, Frank, 1957-

Batman: the Dark Knight strikes again **741.5**

(jt. auth) Eisner, W. Eisner/Miller: a one-on-one interview **92**

Miller, George

(tr) Vigan, D. d. No and me **Fic**

Miller, Jennifer, 1980-

Inheriting the Holy Land **956.94**

Miller, Joe, 1968-

Cross-X **808.53**

Miller, Joseph, 1946-

(ed) Sears list of subject headings. See Sears list of subject headings **025.4**

Miller, Julia Wang

(ed) The AIDS crisis. See The AIDS crisis **362.1**

Miller, Karen, 1973-

(ed) Male and female roles: opposing viewpoints. See Male and female roles: opposing viewpoints **305.3**

(ed) Race relations: opposing viewpoints. See Race relations: opposing viewpoints **305.8**

Minorities

See also Discrimination; Ethnic relations

Barkan, E. The guilt of nations   **341.6**

Daniels, R. Coming to America   **325.73**

Discrimination: opposing viewpoints   **305.8**

Malaspina, A. The ethnic and group identity movements   **323.1**

Sanna, E. We shall all be free   **305.8**

Encyclopedias

Encyclopedia of race and racism   **305.8**

The Greenwood encyclopedia of multiethnic American literature   **810.3**

Minorities in literature

Great scenes from minority playwrights   **812.008**

Minorities in motion pictures

Welsch, J. R. Multicultural films   **791.43**

Miracle at Philadelphia. Bowen, C. D.   **342**

Miracle in the Andes. Parrado, N.   **982**

The **miracle** stealer. Connelly, N. O.   **Fic**

The **miracle** worker. Gibson, W.   **812**

Miracles

Fiction

Connelly, N. O. The miracle stealer   **Fic**

Meldrum, C. Madapple   **Fic**

Miracle's boys. Woodson, J.   **Fic**

Miraldi, Robert

(ed) Kahn, R. Beyond the boys of summer   **796.357**

Miranda, Ernesto

About

Kelly-Gangi, C. Miranda v. Arizona and the rights of the accused   **345**

Ruschmann, P. Miranda rights   **345**

VanMeter, L. A. Miranda v. Arizona   **345**

Miranda rights. Ruschmann, P.   **345**

Miranda v. Arizona. VanMeter, L. A.   **345**

Miranda v. Arizona and the rights of the accused. Kelly-Gangi, C.   **345**

Miró, Asha, 1967-

Daughter of the Ganges   **92**

The **misanthrope** and other plays. Molière   **842**

Miscellaneous facts *See* Curiosities and wonders

Misconduct in office

See also Political corruption

Les **misérables**. Hugo, V.   **Fic**

Misiroglu, Gina Renée

(ed) The Superhero book. See The Superhero book   **741.5**

Miss Manners' guide to excruciatingly correct behavior. Martin, J.   **395**

Miss Spitfire. Miller, S.   **Fic**

Missing children

See also Runaway children

Fiction

Yovanoff, B. The replacement   **Fic**

The **missing** girl. Mazer, N. F.   **Fic**

Missing persons

See also Runaway teenagers

Fiction

Abrahams, P. Reality check   **Fic**

Bradbury, J. Shift   **Fic**

Brooks, K. Black Rabbit summer   **Fic**

Cantor, J. The September sisters   **Fic**

Finn, M. Anila's journey   **Fic**

Gershow, M. The local news   **Fic**

Green, J. Paper towns   **Fic**

Les Becquets, D. Season of ice   **Fic**

McDonnell, M. Torn to pieces   **Fic**

Northrop, M. Gentlemen   **Fic**

Reichs, K. J. Virals   **Fic**

Simner, J. L. Thief eyes   **Fic**

Strasser, T. Wish you were dead   **Fic**

Valentine, J. Me, the missing, and the dead   **Fic**

Weingarten, L. Wherever Nina lies   **Fic**

Missionaries, Christian *See* Christian missionaries

Missionaries of Charity

Spink, K. Mother Teresa   **92**

Missions

India

Spink, K. Mother Teresa   **92**

Mississippi

Fiction

Jordan, H. Mudbound   **Fic**

Sloan, K. The patron saint of red Chevys   **Fic**

Taylor, M. D. Roll of thunder, hear my cry   **Fic**

Poetry

Lewis, J. P. Black cat bone   **811**

Nelson, M. A wreath for Emmett Till   **811**

Race relations

Aretha, D. Freedom Summer   **323.1**

Aretha, D. The murder of Emmett Till   **364.152**

Bowers, R. The spies of Mississippi   **323.1**

Crowe, C. Getting away with murder: the true story of the Emmett Till case   **364.152**

Sugarman, T. We had sneakers, they had guns   **323.1**

Wright, S. Simeon's story   **305.8**

Mississippi Freedom Project

Aretha, D. Freedom Summer   **323.1**

Mississippi River

Fiction

Twain, M. The adventures of Huckleberry Finn   **Fic**

Twain, M. The adventures of Tom Sawyer   **Fic**

Mississippi River valley

Twain, M. Life on the Mississippi   **818**

Mississippi State Sovereignty Commission

Bowers, R. The spies of Mississippi   **323.1**

Mississippi trial, 1955. Crowe, C.   **Fic**

Mississippi valley *See* Mississippi River valley

Missouri

Fiction

Katcher, B. Almost perfect   **Fic**

Katcher, B. Playing with matches   **Fic**

Twain, M. The adventures of Huckleberry Finn   **Fic**

Twain, M. The adventures of Tom Sawyer   **Fic**

Money-making projects for children
Bielagus, P. G. Quick cash for teens   **658.1**

Mongillo, John F.
Teen guides to environmental science   **333.72**

Mongillo, Peter A.
(jt. auth) Mongillo, J. F. Teen guides to environmental science   **333.72**

Mongolia
Kings and rulers
Rice, E. Empire in the east: the story of Genghis Khan   **92**

Mongolians *See* Mongols

Mongols
Lane, G. Genghis Khan and Mongol rule   **950**

Monkey planet. See Boulle, P. Planet of the apes   **Fic**

Monks
Fiction
Thompson, R. City of cannibals   **Fic**

Monninger, Joseph
Wish   **Fic**

Mono (Disease) *See* Mononucleosis

Monochrome days. Irwin, C.   **92**

Monologue and scene study series
2010: the best men's stage monologues and scenes   **808.82**
2010: the best women's stage monologues and scenes   **808.82**

Monologue audition series
100 great monologues from the neo-classical theatre   **808.82**
The Ultimate audition book   **808.82**

Monologues
100 great monologues from the neo-classical theatre   **808.82**
100 great monologues from the Renaissance theatre   **822.008**
2010: the best men's stage monologues and scenes   **808.82**
2010: the best women's stage monologues and scenes   **808.82**
The Actor's book of movie monologues   **791.43**
Actor's choice   **808.82**
Audition monologs for student actors [I]-[II]   **812.008**
The Book of monologues for aspiring actors   **808.82**
Fairbanks, S. S. Spotlight   **812**
Great monologues for young actors   **808.82**
Kehret, P. Tell it like it is   **808.82**
Millennium monologs   **812.008**
More scenes and monologs from the best new plays   **808.82**
Ullom, S. Tough acts to follow   **812**
The Ultimate audition book   **808.82**

Mononucleosis
Decker, J. M. Mononucleosis   **616.9**

Monroe, James, 1758-1831
About
Hart, G. James Monroe   **92**

Monster. Myers, W. D.   **Fic**

Monster blood tattoo [series]
Cornish, D. M. Foundling   **Fic**

Monsters
Encyclopedias
Coleman, L. Cryptozoology A-Z   **001.9**
Guiley, R. E. The encyclopedia of vampires & werewolves   **398**
Fiction
Gardner, J. Grendel   **Fic**
Yancey, R. The monstrumologist   **Fic**
Graphic novels
Cherrywell, S. Pepper Penwell and the land creature of Monster Lake   **741.5**
Hinds, G. Beowulf   **741.5**
Love, J. Bayou, volume one   **741.5**
Matsumoto, N. Yokaiden, volume 1   **741.5**
Sakai, S. Usagi Yojimbo: Yokai   **741.5**

Monsters in art
Miller, S. Scared!: how to draw fantastic horror comic characters   **741.5**
Reeder, D. Papier-mache monsters   **745.54**

The **monstrumologist**. Yancey, R.   **Fic**

Montagnier, Luc
See/See also pages in the following book(s):
Hellman, H. Great feuds in medicine   **610.9**

Montaigne, Fen
Fraser's penguins   **577.2**

Montaigne, Michel de, 1533-1592
See/See also pages in the following book(s):
Highet, G. The classical tradition   **809**

Montana
Fiction
Doig, I. The whistling season   **Fic**
Harmon, M. B. The last exit to normal   **Fic**
Lackey, M. Legacies   **Fic**
Larson, K. Hattie Big Sky   **Fic**
Price, C. The interrogation of Gabriel James   **Fic**
Watson, L. Montana 1948   **Fic**

Montana 1948. Watson, L.   **Fic**

Montana, Jack *See* McIntosh, J. S.

Monteleone, John J.
(jt. auth) Crisfield, D. Winning volleyball for girls   **796.325**

Montgomery, Sy
The good good pig   **636.4**

Montgomery, William
(ed) Shakespeare, W. The tragedy of Julius Caesar   **822.3**

Montgomery (Ala.)
Race relations
Aretha, D. Montgomery bus boycott   **323.1**

Montgomery bus boycott. Aretha, D.   **323.1**

Montmorency. Updale, E.   **Fic**

Montney, Charles B.
(ed) Chemical compounds. See Chemical compounds   **540**

Mood disorders. Mooney, C.   **616.85**

Moon
Mackenzie, D. The big splat; or, How our moon came to be   **523.3**
Eclipses
See Lunar eclipses

Moon, Voyages to *See* Space flight to the moon

The **moon** is a harsh mistress. Heinlein, R. A.
Fic

Mooney, Carla, 1970-
Mood disorders **616.85**

Mooney, Chris
Storm world **363.7**

Mooney, Jonathan
The short bus **92**

Mooney, William
(jt. auth) Holt, D. Spiders in the hairdo
398.2

Moonfall. McDevitt, J. **Fic**

Moore, Alan
Watchmen **741.5**

Moore, Elaine A., 1948-
Encyclopedia of sexually transmitted diseases
616.95

Moore, Gerald, 1924-
(ed) The Penguin book of modern African poetry. See The Penguin book of modern African poetry **896**

Moore, John Allphin, 1940-
Encyclopedia of the United Nations **341.23**

Moore, John H., 1939-
(ed) Encyclopedia of race and racism. See Encyclopedia of race and racism **305.8**

Moore, John Noell
Interpreting young adult literature **028.5**

Moore, Kate
The Battle of Britain **940.54**

Moore, Lisa, 1973-
(jt. auth) Moore, E. A. Encyclopedia of sexually transmitted diseases **616.95**

Moore, Marianne, 1887-1972
The poems of Marianne Moore **811**

Moore, Patrick
(ed) Firefly atlas of the universe. See Firefly atlas of the universe **523**

Moore, Peter D. (Peter Dale)
Tropical forests **577.3**
Tundra **577.5**
Wetlands **578.7**

Moore, Rosemary Clement- *See* Clement-Moore, Rosemary

Moorehead, Caroline
Human cargo **305.9**

Moose, Christina J., 1952-
(ed) Great events from history, The Renaissance & early modern era, 1454-1600. See Great events from history, The Renaissance & early modern era, 1454-1600 **909**
(ed) Great lives from history, the Renaissance & early modern era, 1454-1600. See Great lives from history, the Renaissance & early modern era, 1454-1600 **920.003**
(ed) Shakespeare. See Shakespeare [critical essays] **822.3**

Moose. Klein, S. **92**

Moped army, Vol. 1. Sizer, P. **741.5**

Mora, Pat
Dizzy in your eyes **811**

My own true name **811**

Moral philosophy *See* Ethics

Morales, Ed
The Latin beat **781.64**

Moran, Barbara B.
(jt. auth) Stueart, R. D. Library and information center management **025.1**

Moran, Katy
Bloodline **Fic**

Moran, Margaret
(ed) Pine, P. Peterson's master the SAT 2011
378.1

Moranville, Sharelle Byars
A higher geometry **Fic**

Mordred (Legendary character)
Fiction
Springer, N. I am Mordred **Fic**
Vande Velde, V. The book of Mordred **Fic**

More, J. *See* Leitch, Will

More, Sir Thomas, Saint, 1478-1535
See/See also pages in the following book(s):
Russell, B. A history of Western philosophy
109
Drama
Bolt, R. A man for all seasons **822**

More award-winning science fair projects. Bochinski, J. B. **507.8**

More booktalking that works. Bromann, J.
028.5

More damned lies and statistics. Best, J. **303.3**

More scenes and monologs from the best new plays **808.82**

More teen programs that work. Honnold, R.
027.62

More than friends. Holbrook, S. **811**

More than MySpace **027.62**

More word histories and mysteries **422.03**

Morell, Virginia
Ancestral passions **920**

Moreton, Andrew *See* Defoe, Daniel, 1661?-1731

Morgan, Edmund Sears
American heroes **920**
The birth of the Republic, 1763-89 **973.3**
(ed) Franklin, B. Not your usual founding father
92

Morgan, Jennifer, 1955-
(jt. auth) Bloom, O. Encephalitis **616.8**

Morgan, Kenneth O.
(ed) The Oxford illustrated history of Britain. See The Oxford illustrated history of Britain
941

Morgan, Michael, 1960-
The midbrain **612.8**

Morgan, Michael Hamilton
Lost history **909**
(jt. auth) Ballard, R. D. Graveyards of the Pacific **940.54**

Morgan, Patrick
(il) Love, J. Bayou, volume one **741.5**

Morgan le Fay (Legendary character)
Fiction
Springer, N. I am Morgan le Fay **Fic**

Moser, Diane, 1944-—*Continued*
(jt. auth) Spangenburg, R. Wernher von Braun
92

Moser, Kit *See* Moser, Diane, 1944-

Moses (Biblical figure)
About
Kirsch, J. Moses   222

Mosier, John, 1944-
The myth of the Great War   940.4

Moskowitz, Hannah, 1991-
Break   Fic

Moslem countries *See* Islamic countries

Moslemism *See* Islam

Moslems *See* Muslims

Mosley, Walter
Fortunate son   Fic

Mosque. Macaulay, D.   726

Mosques
Design and construction
Macaulay, D. Built to last   729
Macaulay, D. Mosque   726

Moss, Howard
(jt. auth) Keegan, K. Chasing the high   92

Moss, Joyce, 1951-
Latin American literature and its times
860.9
(ed) African literature and its times. See African literature and its times   809
(ed) Literature and its times. See Literature and its times   809

Most valuable player and four other all-star plays for middle and high school audiences. Surface, M. H.   812

Mostly good girls. Sales, L.   Fic

Moszynska, Anna
Abstract art   709.04

Motel of the mysteries. Macaulay, D.   817

Motels *See* Hotels and motels

Mother, come home. Hornschemeier, P.   741.5

Mother-daughter relationship
Fiction
Alexander, J. S. The sweetheart of Prosper County   Fic
Baldini, M. Unraveling   Fic
Booth, C. Kendra   Fic
Budhos, M. T. Tell us we're home   Fic
Carey, J. L. Dragon's Keep   Fic
Chow, C. Bitter melon   Fic
Davis, D. Not like you   Fic
Dorris, M. A yellow raft in blue water   Fic
Doyle, E. F. According to Kit   Fic
Fischer, J. An egg on three sticks   Fic
Friend, N. For keeps   Fic
Goto, H. Half World   Fic
Hale, M. The goodbye season   Fic
Haycak, C. Living on impulse   Fic
Hyde, C. R. Jumpstart the world   Fic
Johnson, C. Claire de Lune   Fic
Kaye, M. Demon chick   Fic
Kephart, B. House of Dance   Fic
Kwasney, M. D. Blue plate special   Fic
MacCready, R. M. Buried   Fic
MacCullough, C. Stealing Henry   Fic

Marchetta, M. Saving Francesca   Fic
McCahan, E. I now pronounce you someone else   Fic
McDonald, J. Off-color   Fic
McDonnell, M. Torn to pieces   Fic
Meldrum, C. Madapple   Fic
Moriarty, L. The center of everything   Fic
Morrison, T. Beloved   Fic
Na, A. Wait for me   Fic
Nelson, R. A. Breathe my name   Fic
Omololu, C. J. Dirty little secrets   Fic
Parkhurst, C. Lost and found   Fic
Patterson, V. O. The other side of blue   Fic
Picoult, J. My sister's keeper   Fic
Razzell, M. Snow apples   Fic
Resau, L. The indigo notebook   Fic
Schindler, H. A blue so dark   Fic
Scott, E. Stealing Heaven   Fic
Selfors, S. Mad love   Fic
Sharenow, R. My mother the cheerleader
    Fic
Supplee, S. Artichoke's heart   Fic
Tan, A. The Joy Luck Club   Fic
Vega, D. Fact of life #31   Fic
Weyn, S. Distant waves   Fic
Whittenberg, A. Life is fine   Fic
Williams, C. L. Glimpse   Fic
Williams, C. L. Miles from ordinary   Fic
Yee, L. Absolutely Maybe   Fic
Zemser, A. B. Dear Julia   Fic
Poetry
Atkins, J. Borrowed names   811

Mother love. Dove, R.   811

Mother-son relationship
Fiction
Barnes, J. Tales of the Madman Underground
    Fic
Irving, J. The world according to Garp   Fic
Lynch, C. Angry young man   Fic
Morgenroth, K. Jude   Fic

Mother Teresa *See* Teresa, Mother, 1910-1997

Mother Teresa's Mission of Charity *See* Missionaries of Charity

Mothers
    See also Stepmothers; Teenage mothers; Unmarried mothers
Fiction
Baskin, N. R. All we know of love   Fic
Brooks, M. Mistik Lake   Fic
Craig, C. Afrika   Fic
Ellis, A. D. Everything is fine   Fic
Fusco, K. N. Tending to Grace   Fic
Kephart, B. Nothing but ghosts   Fic
Lowell, P. Returnable girl   Fic
Shaw, S. Safe   Fic

Mothers, Single parent *See* Single parent family

Mothers and daughters *See* Mother-daughter relationship

Mothers and sons *See* Mother-son relationship

Mothers of invention. Faust, D. G.   973.7

Mothers, sisters, resisters   940.53

Moths
Fiction
Willey, M. A summer of silk moths   Fic

Motion picture actors *See* Actors

Motion picture adaptations *See* Film adaptations

Motion picture cartoons *See* Animated films

Motion picture direction *See* Motion pictures—Production and direction

Motion picture photography *See* Cinematography

Motion picture producers and directors
Koopmans, A. Filmmakers   920

Motion picture production *See* Motion pictures—Production and direction

Motion pictures
    See also Film adaptations; Horror films; Musicals
The Actor's book of movie monologues   791.43
Leonard Maltin's movie guide   791.43
Sanello, F. Reel v. real   791.43
The Superhero book   741.5
    Catalogs
Halsall, J. Visual media for teens   016.79143
    Fiction
Castellucci, C. Boy proof   Fic
    Production and direction
Grove, E. 130 projects to get you into filmmaking   792.9
Lanier, T. Filmmaking for teens   791.43
Patmore, C. Movie making course   791.43

Motion pictures and libraries *See* Libraries and motion pictures

Motivation (Psychology)
    See also Wishes
Bachel, B. K. What do you really want?   153.8

Motorboats
    Models
Gabrielson, C. Kinetic contraptions   621.46

Motorcycles
Davidson, J. Jean Davidson's Harley-Davidson family album   629.227

Moulton, Candy Vyvey, 1955-
Chief Joseph   92

Mount Everest Expedition (1996)
Coburn, B. Everest: mountain without mercy   796.522
Krakauer, J. Into thin air   796.522

Mountain bikes
Crowther, N. The ultimate mountain bike book   796.63

Mountain biking
Bicycling magazine's mountain biking skills   796.63

Mountain life
    Fiction
Woodrell, D. Winter's bone   Fic

A mountain of crumbs. Gorokhova, E.   92

Mountain rescue doctor. Van Tilburg, C.   616

Mountaineering
Climb: stories of survival from rock, snow, and ice   796.522
Coburn, B. Everest: mountain without mercy   796.522
Krakauer, J. Into thin air   796.522
Mellor, D. Rock climbing   796.522

Ralston, A. Between a rock and a hard place   796.522

Van Tilburg, C. Mountain rescue doctor   616
    Fiction
Carbone, E. L. Jump   Fic

Mountains
    See also Adirondack Mountains (N.Y.); Andes; Ozark Mountains
Aleshire, P. Mountains   551.4
Balliett, J. F. Mountains   551.4
Collier, M. Over the mountains   557
    Fiction
Wyatt, M. Funny how things change   Fic

Mountains beyond mountains. Kidder, T.   92

Mountjoy, Shane, 1967-
Engel v. Vitale   344

Mourlevat, Jean-Claude
Winter's end   Fic

The mourning wars. Steinmetz, K.   Fic

The mousetrap and other plays. Christie, A.   822

The movement and the sixties. Anderson, T. H.   303.4

Movie making course. Patmore, C.   791.43

Moving
    Fiction
Beaufrand, M. J. The river   Fic
Cumbie, P. Where people like us live   Fic
De Lint, C. Little (grrl) lost   Fic
Friedman, A. The year my sister got lucky   Fic
Harmon, M. B. Brutal   Fic
Hyde, C. R. Jumpstart the world   Fic
Jenkins, A. M. Beating heart   Fic
Johnson, L. L. Worlds apart   Fic
Jordan, S. Firelight   Fic
Korman, G. Pop   Fic
McVoy, T. E. After the kiss   Fic
Neely, C. Unearthly   Fic
Toliver, W. Lifted   Fic

Moving pictures *See* Motion pictures

Moving to higher ground. Marsalis, W.   781.65

Moving violations. Hockenberry, J.   92

Mowll, Joshua
Operation Red Jericho   Fic

Moyal, Ann
Platypus   599.2

Moyers, Bill
(jt. auth) Campbell, J. The power of myth   201
(ed) Fooling with words. See Fooling with words   808.1

Mozambique
    Fiction
Mankell, H. Shadow of the leopard   Fic

Mozart, Johann Chrysostom Wolfgang Amadeus *See* Mozart, Wolfgang Amadeus, 1756-1791

Mozart, Wolfgang Amadeus, 1756-1791
    Drama
Shaffer, P. Peter Shaffer's Amadeus   822

Mozes, Miriam, 1935-1993
About
Kor, E. M. Surviving the Angel of Death
92

Mr. Lincoln's high-tech war. Allen, T. B.
973.7
Mr. Mendoza's paintbrush. Urrea, L. A.   741.5
Mrs. Lincoln and Mrs. Keckley. Fleischner, J.
92
MRSA *See* Methicillin-Resistant Staphylococcus
aureus
MRSA. Sheen, B.   616.9
Mu shi shi 1. Urushibara, Y.   741.5
Much ado about nothing. Shakespeare, W.
822.3
Muchacho. Johnson, L.   Fic
Mudbound. Jordan, H.   Fic
Mueller, Jonathan, 1947-
Assessing critical skills   371.2
Mufleh, Luma
About
St. John, W. Outcasts united   796.334
Mugabe, Robert Gabriel, 1924-
About
Arnold, J. R. Robert Mugabe's Zimbabwe
968.91
Muḥammad, d. 632
About
Armstrong, K. Muhammad   92
Muhammedanism *See* Islam
Muhammedans *See* Muslims
Muir, John, 1838-1914
About
Wilkins, T. John Muir   92
Muir, John Kenneth, 1969-
The encyclopedia of superheroes on film and
television   791.43
Muldoon, Paul
See/See also pages in the following book(s):
Fooling with words   808.1
Mullane, Deirdre
(ed) Crossing the danger water. See Crossing
the danger water   810.8
Mullen, P. H., Jr.
Gold in the water   797.2
Müller, Kristin
The potter's studio handbook   738.1
Muller, R.
The instant physicist   530
Muller, Salomé, b. ca. 1809
About
Bailey, J. The lost German slave girl [biography
of Salomé Muller]   92
Mulligan, Andy
Trash   Fic
Mullin, Glenn H.
The second Dalai Lama   92
Multicultural America [series]
The African Americans   305.8
The Arab Americans   305.8
The Asian Americans   305.8
The European Americans   305.8

The Hispanic Americans   305.8
The Jewish Americans   305.8
The Native Americans   305.8
The **multicultural** cookbook for students. Webb,
L. S.   641.5
A **multicultural** dictionary of literary terms. Car-
ey, G.   803
The **multicultural** dictionary of proverbs. Cordry,
H. V.   398.9
Multicultural education
See/See also pages in the following book(s):
Education: opposing viewpoints   371
Multicultural films. Welsch, J. R.   791.43
Multicultural literature [series]
Litwin, L. B. A reader's guide to Zora Neale
Hurston's Their eyes were watching god
813.009
Loos, P. A reader's guide to Lorraine
Hansberry's A raisin in the sun   812.009
Schroeder, H. L. A reader's guide to Marjane
Satrapi's Persepolis   813.009
Multicultural poetry. See Unsettling America
811.008
Multicultural scenes for young actors   808.82
Multicultural Spanish dictionary   463
Multicultural voices [series]
Amend, A. Hispanic-American writers   810.9
Otfinoski, S. Native American writers   810.9
Sickels, A. African-American writers   920
Multiculturalism
Malaspina, A. The ethnic and group identity
movements   323.1
Patel, E. Acts of faith   92
Multilingual dictionaries *See* Polyglot dictionaries
Multimedia
Dictionaries
Hansen, B. The dictionary of multimedia
006.6
Multimedia materials *See* Audiovisual materials
Multiple sclerosis
Fiction
Leavitt, L. Sean Griswold's head   Fic
Multiracial people *See* Racially mixed people
Mulvey, Dan
Barron's E-Z grammar   428
Mumbai (India) *See* Bombay (India)
Mummies
Pringle, H. A. The mummy congress   393
Taylor, J. H. Unwrapping a mummy   932
Fiction
Dowd, S. Bog child   Fic
Graphic novels
Sfar, J. The professor's daughter   741.5
The **mummy** congress. Pringle, H. A.   393
Munch, Edvard, 1863-1944
About
Dolnick, E. The rescue artist   364.1
Mundy, Liza, 1960-
Michelle [Obama]   92
Municipal planning *See* City planning
Munier, Gilles
Iraq   956.7

Munroe, Erin A.
The anxiety workbook for girls   155.5
Murakami, Haruki, 1949-
About
Mussari, M. Haruki Murakami   92
Mural painting and decoration
Ganz, N. Graffiti women   751.7
Ganz, N. Graffiti world   751
Murder *See* Homicide
The **murder** of Abraham Lincoln. Geary, R.
973.7
The **murder** of Emmett Till. Aretha, D.
364.152
The **murder** of Tutankhamen. Brier, B.   932
Murder trials *See* Trials (Homicide)
Murdock, Catherine Gilbert
Dairy Queen   Fic
Princess Ben   Fic
Murdock, James R.
(jt. auth) Martin, H. J., Jr. Serving lesbian, gay,
bisexual, transgender, and questioning teens
027.62
Murnion, Nickolas C., 1953-
See/See also pages in the following book(s):
Profiles in courage for our time   920
Murphy, Brenda, 1950-
(ed) Death of a salesman, by Arthur Miller. See
Death of a salesman, by Arthur Miller
812.009
Murphy, Bruce, 1962-
(ed) Benet's reader's encyclopedia. See Benet's
reader's encyclopedia   803
Murphy, Frances T.
(jt. auth) West, B. A. A brief history of Austra-
lia   994
Murphy, Jim, 1947-
The boys' war   973.7
The great fire   977.3
The real Benedict Arnold   92
Murphy, Russell E.
Critical companion to T.S. Eliot   811.009
Murray, Alan V.
(ed) The Crusades. See The Crusades
909.07
Murray, Albert
(jt. auth) Basie, C. Good morning blues: the au-
tobiography of Count Basie   92
Murray, Barbara A.
(ed) John Paul II, we love you. See John Paul
II, we love you   252
Murray, Christopher John
(ed) Encyclopedia of the romantic era, 1760-
1850. See Encyclopedia of the romantic era,
1760-1850   700
Murray, Elizabeth A.
Death   616.07
Murray, Martine, 1965-
How to make a bird   Fic
Murray, Peter, 1952-
See also Hautman, Pete, 1952-
Murray, R. Emmett
The lexicon of labor   331

Murray, Stuart, 1948-
Atlas of American military history   355
Vietnam War   959.704
Murray, Yxta Maya
The good girl's guide to getting kidnapped
Fic
Murrow, Edward R.
About
Edwards, B. Edward R. Murrow and the birth of
broadcast journalism   92
Musa, Mark
(tr) Dante Alighieri. The portable Dante   851
Musashi #9, Vol. 1. Miyuki, T.   741.5
Muscles
Adams, A. The muscular system   612.7
Brynie, F. H. 101 questions about muscles to
stretch your mind and flex your brain
612.7
The **muscular** system. Adams, A.   612.7
Musculoskeletal system
See also Bones; Muscles
Encyclopedias
Sayler, M. H. The encyclopedia of the muscle
and skeletal systems and disorders   616.7
Mushrooms
Læssøe, T. Mushrooms   579.6
Lincoff, G. The Audubon Society field guide to
North American mushrooms   579.6
McKnight, K. H. A field guide to mushrooms,
North America   579.6
Music
Marsalis, W. Marsalis on music   780
Analysis, appreciation
See Music appreciation
Bio-bibliography
Baker's biographical dictionary of musicians
920.003
The Harvard concise dictionary of music and
musicians   780.3
Musicians & composers of the 20th century
920.003
Dictionaries
The Harvard concise dictionary of music and
musicians   780.3
The Oxford companion to music   780.3
Fiction
Prinz, Y. The Vinyl Princess   Fic
Thompson, K. The new policeman   Fic
History and criticism
Grout, D. J. A history of western music
780.9
Swafford, J. The Vintage guide to classical mu-
sic   781.6
Latin America
Morales, E. The Latin beat   781.64
Music, African American *See* African American
music
Music, Gospel *See* Gospel music
Music, Vocal *See* Vocal music
Music appreciation
See also Music—History and criticism
Steinberg, M. The symphony   784.2
Swafford, J. The Vintage guide to classical mu-
sic   781.6

Mussari, Mark—*Continued*
Othello [criticism]   822.3
The sonnets [criticism]   822.3
Musser, Susan
(ed) Abortion: opposing viewpoints. See Abortion: opposing viewpoints   363.46
(ed) Education: opposing viewpoints. See Education: opposing viewpoints   371
(ed) Energy alternatives: opposing viewpoints. See Energy alternatives: opposing viewpoints
                                               333.79
(ed) Epidemics: opposing viewpoints. See Epidemics: opposing viewpoints   614.4
(ed) The ethics of cloning. See The ethics of cloning   176
(ed) Genetic engineering: opposing viewpoints. See Genetic engineering: opposing viewpoints
                                               174.2
(ed) Global warming: opposing viewpoints. See Global warming: opposing viewpoints
                                               363.7
(jt. auth) Haugen, D. Rights of the disabled
                                               342
(ed) Iraq: opposing viewpoints. See Iraq: opposing viewpoints   956.7
(ed) Islam: opposing viewpoints. See Islam: opposing viewpoints   297
(ed) Media violence: opposing viewpoints. See Media violence: opposing viewpoints
                                               363.3
(ed) The Middle East: opposing viewpoints. See The Middle East: opposing viewpoints
                                               956
(ed) Popular culture: opposing viewpoints. See Popular culture: opposing viewpoints 306
(ed) Religion in America: opposing viewpoints. See Religion in America: opposing viewpoints
                                               200.9
Mussi, Sarah
The door of no return   Fic
Mustashrik, 1985-
(il) Appignanesi, R. Julius Caesar   822.3
Mutants, clones, and killer corn. Seiple, S.
                                               660.6
Mutiny. Boyne, J.   Fic
Mutiny on the Bounty. Nordhoff, C.   Fic
My Antonia. Cather, W.   Fic
My Better Homes and Gardens cook book. See Better homes and gardens new cook book
                                               641.5
My brother. Kincaid, J.   92
My face is black is true [biography of Callie House] Berry, M. F.   92
My fellow citizens   352.23
My folks don't want me to talk about slavery
                                               920
My grandmother [biography of Heranus Gadaryan] Cetin, F.   92
My guy Barbaro. Prado, E.   92
My heartbeat. Freymann-Weyr, G.   Fic
My invented life. Bjorkman, L.   Fic
My Jim. Rawles, N.   Fic

My letter to the world and other poems. Dickinson, E.   811
My life as a traitor. Ghahramani, Z.   92
My life with the saints. Martin, J.   920
My little red book   305.23
My losing season. Conroy, P.   92
My most excellent year. Kluger, S.   Fic
My mother the cheerleader. Sharenow, R.   Fic
My name is Jason. Mine too. Reynolds, J.
                                               811
My name is not Slow. Libal, A.   362.3
My own true name. Mora, P.   811
My sister, guard your veil; my brother guard, your eyes   955
My sister's keeper. Picoult, J.   Fic
My son's story. Gordimer, N.   Fic
My swordhand is singing. Sedgwick, M.   Fic
My thirteenth winter. Abeel, S.   92
Myanmar
    Politics and government
    Zahler, D. Than Shwe's Burma   959.1
Myer, Valerie Grosvenor
(ed) The Continuum encyclopedia of British literature. See The Continuum encyclopedia of British literature   820.3
Myers, Allen C., 1945-
(ed) Eerdmans dictionary of the Bible. See Eerdmans dictionary of the Bible   220.3
Myers, Christopher
(jt. auth) Myers, W. D. Autobiography of my dead brother   Fic
(il) Myers, W. D. Harlem   811
Myers, Edward, 1950-
When will I stop hurting?   155.9
Myers, Jack Elliott, 1941-
Dictionary of poetic terms   808.1
Myers, Richard, 1951-
The basics of chemistry   540
Myers, Walter Dean, 1937-
145th Street   S C
Autobiography of my dead brother   Fic
Bad boy   92
Dope sick   Fic
Fallen angels   Fic
Game   Fic
Harlem   811
Here in Harlem   811
Kick   Fic
Monster   Fic
Sunrise over Fallujah   Fic
What they found   S C
Myerson, Joel
(ed) Alcott, L. M. The selected letters of Louisa May Alcott   92
(ed) A Historical guide to Ralph Waldo Emerson. See A Historical guide to Ralph Waldo Emerson   814
Myracle, Lauren, 1969-
Bliss   Fic
Peace, love, and baby ducks   Fic
Shine   Fic
(jt. auth) Green, J. Let it snow   S C

Myracle, Lauren, 1969——*Continued*
  (jt. auth) Lockhart, E. How to be bad   **Fic**
Mystery and detective stories *See* Mystery fiction
Mystery and suspense writers   **809.3**
Mystery fiction
  Alfred Hitchcock's mystery magazine presents
    fifty years of crime and suspense   **S C**
  Arnold, T. Rat life   **Fic**
  Baratz-Logsted, L. Twin's daughter   **Fic**
  Barr, N. Track of the cat   **Fic**
  Beaudoin, S. You killed Wesley Payne   **Fic**
  Beaufrand, M. J. The river   **Fic**
  Beitia, S. The last good place of Lily Odilon
    Fic
  The Best American mystery stories of the centu-
    ry   **S C**
  Blundell, J. What I saw and how I lied   **Fic**
  Bradley, A. The sweetness at the bottom of the
    pie   **Fic**
  Bray, L. A great and terrible beauty   **Fic**
  Brooks, K. Black Rabbit summer   **Fic**
  Christie, A. The A.B.C. murders   **Fic**
  Christie, A. And then there were none   **Fic**
  Collins, B. Always watching   **Fic**
  Derting, K. The body finder   **Fic**
  Doyle, Sir A. C. The complete Sherlock Holmes
    S C
  Doyle, Sir A. C. The hound of the Baskervilles
    Fic
  Dunlap, S. E. The musician's daughter   **Fic**
  Ferguson, A. The Christopher killer   **Fic**
  Ford, J. C. The morgue and me   **Fic**
  Gratz, A. Something rotten   **Fic**
  Green, J. Paper towns   **Fic**
  Harrington, K. Clarity   **Fic**
  Herrick, S. Cold skin   **Fic**
  The improbable adventures of Sherlock Holmes
    S C
  Jaffe, M. Bad kitty   **Fic**
  Jaffe, M. Rosebush   **Fic**
  Jinks, C. The reformed vampire support group
    Fic
  King, L. R. The beekeeper's apprentice, or, on
    the segregation of the queen   **Fic**
  Lee, Y. S. A spy in the house   **Fic**
  McClintock, N. Masked   **Fic**
  McNamee, G. Acceleration   **Fic**
  Moloney, J. Black taxi   **Fic**
  Mulligan, A. Trash   **Fic**
  Osterlund, A. Aurelia   **Fic**
  Parker, R. B. The boxer and the spy   **Fic**
  Peacock, S. Eye of the crow   **Fic**
  Reichs, K. J. Virals   **Fic**
  Richards, J. The chaos code   **Fic**
  Richmond, M. No one you know   **Fic**
  Schrefer, E. The deadly sister   **Fic**
  Shepard, S. The lying game   **Fic**
  Silbert, L. The intelligencer   **Fic**
  Silvey, C. Jasper Jones   **Fic**
  Sorrells, W. First shot   **Fic**
  Summers, C. Fall for anything   **Fic**
  Winspear, J. Maisie Dobbs   **Fic**
  Zusak, M. I am the messenger   **Fic**
Mystery graphic novels
  Cherrywell, S. Pepper Penwell and the land
    creature of Monster Lake   **741.5**

Chmakova, S. Nightschool: the weirn books,
  volume one   **741.5**
Crilley, M. Brody's ghost: book 1   **741.5**
Dorkin, E. Beasts of Burden: animal rites
    741.5
Evanovich, J. Troublemaker   **741.5**
Geary, R. The Lindbergh child   **364.1**
Geary, R. The saga of the bloody Benders
    364.152
Geary, R. The terrible Axe-Man of New Orleans
    364.152
Hill, J. Locke & key: welcome to Lovecraft
    741.5
Igarashi, D. Children of the sea, vol. 1
    741.5
Kim, S. Brain camp   **741.5**
Koontz, D. R. In odd we trust   **741.5**
Roman, D. Agnes Quill   **741.5**
Sala, R. Cat burglar black   **741.5**
Toboso, Y. Black butler, vol. 1   **741.5**
Urasawa, N. Pluto: Urasawa x Tezuka, vol. 1
    741.5
Vankin, D. Poseurs   **741.5**
Mystery library [series]
  Kallen, S. A. Witches   **133.4**
Mystic and rider. Shinn, S.   **Fic**
The **myth** of Sisyphus, and other essays. Camus,
  A.   **844**
The **myth** of the Great War. Mosier, J.   **940.4**
Mythical animals
    See also Animals—Folklore; Dragons; Mer-
    maids and mermen
  Delacampagne, A. Here be dragons   **700**
      Fiction
  McKinley, R. Fire: tales of elemental spirits
    S C
  Westerfeld, S. Leviathan   **Fic**
Mythology
    See also Gods and goddesses; Mythical ani-
    mals mythology of particular national or eth-
    nic groups or of particular geographic areas
  Bulfinch, T. Bulfinch's mythology   **398.2**
  Campbell, J. Occidental mythology   **201**
  Campbell, J. The power of myth   **201**
  Campbell, J. Primitive mythology   **201**
  Davis, K. C. Don't know much about mytholo-
    gy   **201**
  Eliot, A. The universal myths   **201**
  Frazer, Sir J. G. The new golden bough
    201
  Hearne, B. G. Beauties and beasts   **398.2**
  Philip, N. Mythology of the world   **201.03**
  World mythology   **201**
  See/See also pages in the following book(s):
  Highet, G. The classical tradition   **809**
      Dictionaries
  Brewer's dictionary of phrase & fable   **803**
  Leeming, D. A. The Oxford companion to world
    mythology   **203**
  Pickering, D. A dictionary of folklore   **398.2**
      Encyclopedias
  Mercatante, A. S. The Facts on File encyclope-
    dia of world mythology and legend
    201.03

Mythology—Encyclopedias—*Continued*
U-X-L encyclopedia of world mythology
201.03
Mythology, African *See* African mythology
Mythology, Celtic *See* Celtic mythology
Mythology, Classical *See* Classical mythology
Mythology, Greek *See* Greek mythology
Mythology, Indic *See* Indic mythology
Mythology, Japanese *See* Japanese mythology
Mythology, Norse *See* Norse mythology
Mythology, Oriental *See* Oriental mythology
Mythology, Roman *See* Roman mythology
Mythology. Hamilton, E. **292**
Mythology A to Z [series]
Daly, K. N. Greek and Roman mythology, A to
Z **292**
Daly, K. N. Norse mythology A to Z **293**
Lynch, P. A. African mythology, A to Z
299.6
Roberts, J. Chinese mythology A to Z **299.5**
Roberts, J. Japanese mythology A to Z
299.5
Mythology in literature
Campbell, J. Creative mythology **201**
Mythology of the world. Philip, N. **201.03**
Myths. See Eliot, A. The universal myths **201**

N

N.W.A. (Musical group)
Ro, R. Dr. Dre **92**
Na, An, 1972-
A step from heaven **Fic**
Wait for me **Fic**
Naden, Corinne J.
Abortion **363.46**
The facts about the A-Z of drugs **615**
Mao Zedong and the Chinese Revolution **92**
Patients' rights **362.1**
Romeo and Juliet [criticism] **822.3**
(jt. auth) Gillespie, J. T. Classic teenplots
011.6
(jt. auth) Gillespie, J. T. The Newbery/Printz
companion **028.5**
Nader, Ralph
About
Bowen, N. Ralph Nader **92**
Nadin, Joanna, 1970-
Wonderland **Fic**
Nadol, Jen
The mark **Fic**
Naff, Clay Farris
(ed) Evolution. See Evolution [Exploring science
and medical discoveries series] **576.8**
Naftali, Timothy J.
George H.W. Bush **92**
Nagai-Berthrong, E.
(jt. auth) Berthrong, J. H. Confucianism
299.5
Nagasaki, Takashi
(jt. auth) Urasawa, N. Pluto: Urasawa x Tezuka,
vol. 1 **741.5**

Nagasaki (Japan)
Bombardment, 1945
See/See also pages in the following book(s):
Yamazaki, J. N. Children of the atomic bomb
92
Nagatomo, Haruno
Draw your own Manga **741.5**
Nagle, Jeanne M.
Living green **333.72**
Naidoo, Beverley
Burn my heart **Fic**
Naifeh, Ted
(il) Black, H. The Good Neighbors; book one:
Kin **741.5**
Naimark, Norman M.
Fires of hatred **364.1**
Naish, Darren
The great dinosaur discoveries **567.9**
Nakahama, Manjirō, 1827-1898
Fiction
Preus, M. Heart of a samurai **Fic**
Nakahara, Aya
Love*Com Vol. 1 **741.5**
Nakaya, Andrea C.
ADHD **618.92**
Energy alternatives **333.79**
Immigration **325.73**
(ed) America's battle against terrorism. See
America's battle against terrorism **973.931**
(ed) Civil liberties and war. See Civil liberties
and war **323**
(ed) The environment. See The environment
344
Nakaya, Shannon Fujimoto
Kindred spirit, kindred care **636.089**
Nakazawa, Keiji, 1939-
Barefoot Gen volume five: the never-ending war
741.5
Barefoot Gen volume six: writing the truth
741.5
The **naked** roommate. Cohen, H. **378.1**
Nakone, Lanna
Organizing for your brain type **640**
Nalebuff, Rachel Kauder- *See* Kauder-Nalebuff,
Rachel
Nam, Victoria
(ed) Yell-oh girls! See Yell-oh girls! **305.23**
Name all the animals. Smith, A. **92**
Names
See also Geographic names
Names, Personal *See* Personal names
Names and naming in young adult literature.
Nilsen, A. P. **813.009**
The **namesake.** Lahiri, J. **Fic**
Namibia
Fiction
Gilman, D. The devil's breath **Fic**
The **Naming.** Croggon, A. **Fic**
Nanji, Shenaaz, 1954-
Child of dandelions **Fic**
Nanotechnology
Hall, J. S. Nanofuture **620**

Neeley, Bill
The last Comanche chief: the life and times of Quanah Parker   **92**

Neely, Cynthia
Unearthly   **Fic**

Nefertiti, Queen, consort of Akhenaton, King of Egypt, 14th cent. B.C.
    Fiction
Friesner, E. M. Sphinx's princess   **Fic**

Negotiation
  See also Conflict management

The **Negro** almanac. See The African American almanac   **305.8**

Negro leagues
Ackmann, M. Curveball [biography of Toni Stone]   **92**
Hogan, L. D. Shades of glory   **796.357**

Nehlen, Don, 1936-
(ed) Complete guide to special teams. See Complete guide to special teams   **796.332**

Neiburger, Eli
Gamers . . . in the library?!   **794.8**

Neider, Charles, 1915-2001
(ed) Twain, M. The complete short stories of Mark Twain   **S C**

Neighborhood *See* Community life

Neighborhood gardens *See* Community gardens

Neihardt, John Gneisenau, 1881-1973
(jt. auth) Black Elk. Black Elk speaks   **92**

Neimark, Anne E., 1935-
Johnny Cash   **92**

Nelson, Blake, 1960-
Destroy all cars   **Fic**
Paranoid Park   **Fic**
Recovery Road   **Fic**
Rock star, superstar   **Fic**

Nelson, David Erik
(ed) Chernobyl. See Chernobyl   **363.1**
(ed) Teen drug abuse: opposing viewpoints. See Teen drug abuse: opposing viewpoints   **362.29**

Nelson, Emmanuel S. (Emmanuel Sampath), 1954-
(ed) The Greenwood encyclopedia of multiethnic American literature. See The Greenwood encyclopedia of multiethnic American literature   **810.3**

Nelson, Glenn C.
Ceramics: a potter's handbook   **738.1**

Nelson, Horatio Nelson, Viscount, 1758-1805
    About
Czisnik, M. Horatio Nelson   **92**

Nelson, Jandy
The sky is everywhere   **Fic**

Nelson, Marilyn, 1946-
Carver, a life in poems   **811**
Fortune's bones   **811**
The freedom business   **811**
A wreath for Emmett Till   **811**

Nelson, Michael, 1949-
(ed) Guide to the presidency. See Guide to the presidency   **352.23**

(ed) The presidency A to Z. See The presidency A to Z   **352.23**

Nelson, Murry R.
(ed) Encyclopedia of sports in America. See Encyclopedia of sports in America   **796**

Nelson, Pete
Left for dead   **940.54**

Nelson, R. A.
Breathe my name   **Fic**

Nelson, Rebecca Wingard- *See* Wingard-Nelson, Rebecca

Nelson, Richard E.
The power to prevent suicide   **362.28**

Nelson, Sheila
Hallucinogens   **362.29**

Nelson, W. Dale
Interpreters with Lewis and Clark: the story of Sacagawea and Toussaint Charbonneau   **92**

Nelson Mandela and apartheid in world history. Gaines, A.   **92**

Nelson Mandela speaks. Mandela, N.   **968.06**

Nemat, Marina
Prisoner of Tehran   **92**

Nemiroff, Robert, d. 1991
(jt. auth) Hansberry, L. To be young, gifted, and Black   **92**

Neo-fascism *See* Fascism

Neo-Nazis
See/See also pages in the following book(s):
Laqueur, W. Fascism   **320.5**

Nepal
    Fiction
McCormick, P. Sold   **Fic**
Michaelis, A. The dragons of darkness   **Fic**

Neptune (Planet)
Chaple, G. F. Outer planets   **523.4**

Neri, Greg
Yummy [biography of Robert Sandifer]   **92**

Neruda, Pablo, 1904-1973
The poetry of Pablo Neruda   **861**
Selected odes of Pablo Neruda   **861**
Twenty love poems and a song of despair   **861**

Nerve endings. Rapport, R.   **612.8**

Nervous system
Bainbridge, D. Beyond the zonules of Zinn   **611**
Evans-Martin, F. The nervous system   **612.8**
McDowell, J. The nervous system and sense organs   **612.8**
Rapport, R. Nerve endings   **612.8**
    Diseases
  See also Creutzfeldt-Jakob disease; Epilepsy; Huntington's chorea; Meningitis; Multiple sclerosis; Tourette syndrome

The **nervous** system and sense organs. McDowell, J.   **612.8**

Nesbitt, Mark R., 1970-
(ed) Individual rights and the police. See Individual rights and the police   **345**

Ness, Bryan D.
(ed) Magill's encyclopedia of science. See Magill's encyclopedia of science   **580**

Ness, Patrick, 1971-
The knife of never letting go   **Fic**

Netherlands
Fiction
Chevalier, T. Girl with a pearl earring   **Fic**
Cullen, L. I am Rembrandt's daughter   **Fic**
Dogar, S. Annexed   **Fic**
Peet, M. Tamar   **Fic**
History—1940-1945, German occupation
Frank, A. The diary of a young girl: the definitive edition   **92**
Frank, A. The diary of Anne Frank: the critical edition   **92**
Gies, M. Anne Frank remembered   **940.53**
Reiss, J. The upstairs room   **92**
History—1940-1945, German occupation—Drama
Goodrich, F. The diary of Anne Frank   **812**
History—1940-1945, German occupation—Fiction
Polak, M. What world is left   **Fic**

Netzley, Patricia D.
Civil War   **973.7**
Encyclopedia of women's travel and exploration   **910.4**
The Greenhaven encyclopedia of ancient Egypt   **932**
The Greenhaven encyclopedia of terrorism   **363.32**

Neumann, Caryn E., 1965-
Term paper resource guide to African American history   **016.973**

Neumeier, Rachel
The City in the Lake   **Fic**

Neurology See Nervous system

Neuroses
See also Anxiety; Obsessive-compulsive disorder

Neutrality
See also Intervention (International law)

Never been a time. Barnes, H.   **977.3**
Never let me go. Ishiguro, K.   **Fic**
Never to forget: the Jews of the Holocaust. Meltzer, M.   **940.53**

Nevraumont, Edward J., 1975-
The ultimate improv book   **792.7**

The **new** American Heart Association cookbook. American Heart Association   **641.5**
The **new** American plate cookbook   **641.5**
The **new** Americans. Martínez, R.   **305.9**
New and selected poems. Oliver, M.   **811**
The **new** atlas of the Arab world   **912**
The new biology [series]
Panno, J. Aging   **612.6**
Panno, J. Animal cloning   **660.6**
Panno, J. Cancer   **616.99**
Panno, J. The cell   **571.6**
Panno, J. Gene therapy   **615.8**
Panno, J. Stem cell research   **616**
New blood. McPhee, P.   **Fic**

The **new** book of popular science   **503**
New boy. Houston, J.   **Fic**
New Catholic encyclopedia   **282**
New complete do-it-yourself manual. See Complete do-it-yourself manual   **643**
The **new** complete guitarist. Chapman, R.   **787.87**
New complete sailing manual. Sleight, S.   **797.1**
The **new** comprehensive American rhyming dictionary. Young, S.   **423**
The **new** cultural atlas of China   **911**
New Deal, 1933-1939
Encyclopedias
Encyclopedia of the Great Depression   **973.91**
The **new** dictionary of cultural literacy. Hirsch, E. D.   **031**
New dictionary of scientific biography   **920.003**
The **new** drawing on the right side of the brain. Edwards, B.   **741.2**
New elements [biography of Marie Curie] Yannuzzi, D. A.   **92**
The **new** encyclopaedia Britannica   **031**
The **new** encyclopedia of aquatic life   **591.9**
The **New** encyclopedia of Judaism [New York University Press]   **296.03**
The **new** encyclopedia of Judaism. See The student's encyclopedia of Judaism   **296.03**
The **new** encyclopedia of snakes. Mattison, C.   **597.96**
The **New** encyclopedia of the American West   **978.03**
The **new** encyclopedia of the horse. See Edwards, E. H. The encyclopedia of the horse   **636.1**
The **new** encyclopedia of the saltwater aquarium. Jennings, G.   **639.34**
The **new** encyclopedia of watercolor techniques. Craig, D.   **751.42**
New England
Fiction
Hawthorne, N. The scarlet letter   **Fic**
Jackson, S. We have always lived in the castle   **Fic**
Wharton, E. Ethan Frome   **Fic**
Wolff, T. Old school   **Fic**
History
Demos, J. Entertaining Satan   **133.4**
History—1600-1775, Colonial period
Mandell, D. R. King Philip's war   **973.2**
The **new** face of baseball. Wendel, T.   **796.357**
The **new** Fowler's modern English usage. See Fowler, H. W. Fowler's modern English usage   **428**
New Globe (London, England) See Shakespeare's Globe (London, England)
The **new** golden bough. Frazer, Sir J. G.   **201**
The **new** Grove book of operas. See The Grove book of operas   **792.5**
The **New** Grove dictionary of jazz   **781.65**

New Guinea
Fiction
Jones, L. Mister Pip   Fic

New Hampshire
Fiction
Picoult, J. Nineteen minutes   Fic

New historical atlas of religion in America.
Gaustad, E. S.   200.9

The **new** how things work. Langone, J.   600

The new immigrants [series]
Horst, H. A. Jamaican Americans   305.8
Rangaswamy, P. Indian Americans   305.8

New Jersey
Fiction
Bauman, B. A. Rosie & Skate   Fic
Budhos, M. T. Tell us we're home   Fic
Corrigan, E. Accomplice   Fic
Lecesne, J. Absolute brightness   Fic
Levchuk, L. Everything beautiful in the world
      Fic
Myers, W. D. Kick   Fic
Ostow, M. So punk rock (and other ways to disappoint your mother)   Fic
Plum-Ucci, C. Streams of Babel   Fic
Roth, P. The plot against America   Fic
Scott, K. She's so dead to us   Fic
Vivian, S. Same difference   Fic

The **new** Jerusalem Bible. Bible   220.5

New London Globe (England) *See* Shakespeare's
Globe (London, England)

New Mexico
Fiction
Cather, W. Death comes for the archbishop
      Fic
Johnson, L. Muchacho   Fic
Saenz, B. A. Sammy and Juliana in Hollywood
      Fic
Stork, F. X. The last summer of the death warriors   Fic

The **New** new journalism   071

New Orleans (La.)
Fiction
Morris, P. Ruined   Fic
Sharenow, R. My mother the cheerleader
      Fic
Tiernan, C. Balefire   Fic
Volponi, P. Hurricane song   Fic
History—Graphic novels
Geary, R. The terrible Axe-Man of New Orleans
      364.152

New Oxford American dictionary   423

The **New** Oxford book of Irish verse   821.008

The **New** Oxford book of literary anecdotes
      828

The **New** Oxford book of Victorian verse
      821.008

The **New** Oxford companion to literature in French
      840.3

The **new** Penguin dictionary of science. See The
Penguin dictionary of science   503

New poems of Emily Dickinson. Dickinson, E.
      811

The **new** policeman. Thompson, K.   Fic

The **New** Quotable woman. See The Quotable
woman, revised edition   305.4

The **new** solar system. Daniels, P.   523.2

New thinking about evolution   576.8
New thinking about genetics   576.5
New thinking about pollution   628.5

The **new** time travelers. Toomey, D. M.   530.1

The **new** way things work. Macaulay, D.   600

New Year
Gulevich, T. Encyclopedia of Christmas and
New Year's celebrations   394.26

New York (N.Y.)
Von Drehle, D. Triangle: the fire that changed
America   974.7
Wright, K. Drifting toward love   306.76
Fiction
Anderson, L. H. Chains   Fic
Baldwin, J. If Beale Street could talk   Fic
Biederman, L. Teenage waistland   Fic
Blundell, J. Strings attached   Fic
Booth, C. Kendra   Fic
Budhos, M. T. Ask me no questions   Fic
Cabot, M. Airhead   Fic
Cameron, P. Someday this pain will be useful to
you   Fic
Castellucci, C. Rose sees red   Fic
Chibbaro, J. Deadly   Fic
Clare, C. City of bones   Fic
Cohn, R. Naomi and Ely's no kiss list   Fic
Cohn, R. Nick & Norah's infinite playlist
      Fic
Cooney, C. B. Code orange   Fic
Davies, J. Lost   Fic
De la Cruz, M. Blue bloods   Fic
Ehrenhaft, D. Friend is not a verb   Fic
Falkner, B. Brain Jack   Fic
Felin, M. S. Touching snow   Fic
Foer, J. S. Extremely loud & incredibly close
      Fic
Freymann-Weyr, G. Stay with me   Fic
Friesner, E. M. Threads and flames   Fic
Godbersen, A. The luxe   Fic
Johnson, M. Suite Scarlett   Fic
Kaplow, R. Me and Orson Welles   Fic
Krovatin, C. Heavy metal and you   Fic
Larbalestier, J. Magic or madness   Fic
Levithan, D. Love is the higher law   Fic
Lurie, A. The latent powers of Dylan Fontaine
      Fic
MacCullough, C. Once a witch   Fic
Mackler, C. The earth, my butt, and other big,
round things   Fic
McDonald, J. Chill wind   Fic
Miller, K. The eternal ones   Fic
Nayeri, D. Another Faust   Fic
Packer, A. The dive from Clausen's pier
      Fic
Pick-up game   S C
Salinger, J. D. The catcher in the rye   Fic
Salinger, J. D. Franny & Zooey   Fic
Salinger, J. D. Raise high the roof beam, carpenters, and Seymour: an introduction   Fic
Schutt, C. All souls   Fic
Shusterman, N. Downsiders   Fic
Vizzini, N. It's kind of a funny story   Fic

Nineteen minutes. Picoult, J. **Fic**

The **nineteen-nineties**. See Schwartz, R. A. The 1990s **973.92**

Nineteen-sixty - Nineteen-eighty: the twentieth century. See 1960-1980: the twentieth century **909.82**

Nineteen-twenty - Nineteen-forty: the twentieth century. See 1920-1940: the twentieth century **909.82**

Nineteen varieties of gazelle. See Nye, N. S. 19 varieties of gazelle **811**

The **nineteenth** century **940.2**

Nineteenth-century American women writers **810.9**

The **nineties** in America **973.92**

Ninja
Fiction
Lake, N. Blood ninja **Fic**

Nishi, Dennis, 1967-
(ed) The Korean War. See The Korean War **951.9**

Nist, Sherrie L. (Sherrie Lee), 1946-
College rules! **378.1**

Nitta, Hideo, 1957-
The manga guide to physics **530**

Niven, Larry
Ringworld **Fic**

Nix, Garth, 1963-
Sabriel **Fic**

Nix, Lacy Hunter, 1979-
(ed) Foxfire 40th anniversary book. See Foxfire 40th anniversary book **975.8**

Nixon, Richard M. (Richard Milhous), 1913-1994
About
Genovese, M. A. The Watergate crisis **973.924**

Woodward, B. The final days **973.924**

No and me. Vigan, D. d. **Fic**

No choirboy. Kuklin, S. **364.66**

No compromise: the story of Harvey Milk. Aretha, D. **92**

No easy answers [biography of Bayard Rustin] Miller, C. C. **92**

No end in sight. Scdoris, R. **92**

No exit, and three other plays. Sartre, J. P. **842**

No fixed points. Reynolds, N. **792.8**

No god but God. Aslan, R. **297**

No more us for you. Hernandez, D. **Fic**

No one loved gorillas more [biography of Dian Fossey] De la Bédoyère, C. **92**

No one you know. Richmond, M. **Fic**

Nō plays
The Classic Noh theatre of Japan **895.6**

No pretty pictures. Lobel, A. **92**

No safe place. Ellis, D. **Fic**

No school library left behind. Harvey, C. A., II **025.1**

No shame, no fear. Turnbull, A. **Fic**

No shelf required **025.17**

No such thing as the real world **S C**

Noah's ark
Fiction
Provoost, A. In the shadow of the ark **Fic**

Nobel **001.4**

Nobel Prizes
Nobel **001.4**

Noble warriors [series]
Nicholson, W. Seeker **Fic**

Nobody's princess. Friesner, E. M. **Fic**

Nolan, Han, 1956-
Crazy **Fic**

Nolen-Weathington, Eric
(ed) Modern Masters volume twenty-five: Jeff Smith. See Modern Masters volume twenty-five: Jeff Smith **741.5**

Noll, Richard, 1959-
The encyclopedia of schizophrenia and other psychotic disorders **616.89**

Nonbook materials See Audiovisual materials

Nonconformity See Dissent

Nonmetals. Halka, M. **546**

Nonprescription drugs
Etingoff, K. Abusing over-the-counter drugs **362.29**

Walker, I. Natural and everyday drugs **362.29**

Nonsense verses
Silverstein, S. Where the sidewalk ends **811**

Nonverbal communication
See also Deaf—Means of communication
Fast, J. Body language **153.6**

Norcross, Beverly Gore
(jt. auth) Corson, R. Stage makeup **792**

Nordhoff, Charles, 1887-1947
Mutiny on the Bounty **Fic**

Nordstrom, Brian, 1949-
(jt. auth) Halka, M. Alkali & alkaline earth metals **546**
(jt. auth) Halka, M. Halogens and noble gases **546**
(jt. auth) Halka, M. Lanthanides and actinides **546**
(jt. auth) Halka, M. Metals and metalloids **546**
(jt. auth) Halka, M. Nonmetals **546**
(jt. auth) Halka, M. Transition metals **546**

Nordwall, Adam See Fortunate Eagle, Adam, 1929-

Normandy (France), Attack on, 1944
Hastings, M. Overlord: D-Day and the battle for Normandy **940.54**

Norris, George William, 1861-1944
See/See also pages in the following book(s):
Kennedy, J. F. Profiles in courage **920**

Norse mythology
Hamilton, E. Mythology **292**
Dictionaries
Daly, K. N. Norse mythology A to Z **293**

Norse mythology A to Z. Daly, K. N. **293**

Norsemen See Vikings

Novak, Joseph *See* Kosinski, Jerzy N., 1933-1991

Novak, Philip
(jt. auth) Smith, H. Buddhism: a concise introduction **294.3**

Novelists, American
Weinstein, P. M. Becoming Faulkner **92**

Novelists, English
Dictionaries
Contemporary novelists **920.003**

Novelists and novels. Bloom, H. **809.3**

Novellas and other writings. Wharton, E. **818**

Novels and stories. Hurston, Z. N. **Fic**

Novels in verse
Agard, J. The young inferno **Fic**
Barlow, T. Sharp teeth **Fic**
Bingham, K. Shark girl **Fic**
Bryant, J. Ringside, 1925 **Fic**
Chaltas, T. Because I am furniture **Fic**
Engle, M. Firefly letters **Fic**
Engle, M. Hurricane dancers **Fic**
Engle, M. The surrender tree **Fic**
Friedman, R. Nothing **Fic**
Frost, H. The braid **Fic**
Frost, H. Crossing stones **Fic**
Grimes, N. Dark sons **Fic**
Grimes, N. A girl named Mister **Fic**
Hemphill, S. Wicked girls **Fic**
Herrick, S. Cold skin **Fic**
Herrick, S. The wolf **Fic**
Hopkins, E. Burned **Fic**
Hopkins, E. Identical **Fic**
Hopkins, E. Tricks **Fic**
LeZotte, A. C. T4 **Fic**
McVoy, T. E. After the kiss **Fic**
Ostlere, C. Karma **Fic**
Phillips, W. Fishtailing **Fic**
Richards, J. Three rivers rising **Fic**
Schroeder, L. Far from you **Fic**
Smith, K. The geography of girlhood **Fic**
Sones, S. What my mother doesn't know **Fic**
Thompson, H. Orchards **Fic**
Turner, A. W. Hard hit **Fic**
Weatherford, C. B. Becoming Billie Holiday **Fic**
Williams, C. L. Glimpse **Fic**
Wolf, A. Zane's trace **Fic**
Wolff, V. E. Make lemonade **Fic**

November, Alan C.
Empowering students with technology **371.3**

November, Sharyn
(ed) Firebirds rising. See Firebirds rising **S C**
(ed) Firebirds soaring. See Firebirds soaring **S C**

Novgorodoff, Danica
Slow storm **741.5**

Novio boy. Soto, G. **812**

Nowak, Naomi, 1984-
Unholy kinship **741.5**

Noyes, Deborah, 1965-
Encyclopedia of the end **306.9**
The ghosts of Kerfol **S C**
One kingdom **590**

(ed) Gothic! See Gothic! **S C**
(ed) The restless dead. See The restless dead **S C**
(ed) Sideshow. See Sideshow **S C**

NTC's American idioms dictionary. See Spears, R. A. McGraw-Hill's American idioms dictionary **427**

NTC's dictionary of American slang and colloquial expressions. See Spears, R. A. McGraw-Hill's dictionary of American slang and colloquial expressions **427**

Nuclear energy
Tabak, J. Nuclear energy **621.48**

Nuclear power plants
See also Nuclear energy

Nuclear warfare
Fiction
Shute, N. On the beach **Fic**

Nuclear weapons
See also Atomic bomb
Diehl, S. J. Nuclear weapons and nonproliferation **355.8**
Friedman, L. S. Nuclear weapons and security **355**
See/See also pages in the following book(s):
Weapons of mass destruction: opposing viewpoints **358**

Nuclear weapons and nonproliferation. Diehl, S. J. **355.8**

Nuclear weapons and security. Friedman, L. S. **355**

Nucleic acids
See also RNA
Hodge, R. The molecules of life **611**

Nude in art
See also Artistic anatomy

Num8ers. See Ward, R. Numbers **Fic**

Number concept
Bellos, A. Here's looking at Euclid **513**
Blastland, M. The numbers game **510**

Number systems *See* Numbers

Numbers
See also Counting; Pi
Tabak, J. Numbers **513**

Numbers. Ward, R. **Fic**

The **numbers** game. Blastland, M. **510**

Numerals
See also Numbers

Numeration *See* Numbers

Numerical analysis
See also Approximate computation

Numismatics
See also Coins

Numrich, Paul David, 1952-
(jt. auth) Mann, G. S. Buddhists, Hindus, and Sikhs in America **294**

Nuñez Cabeza de Vaca, Alvar, 16th cent.
About
Childress, D. Barefoot conquistador [biography of Alvar Núñez Cabeza de Vaca] **92**

Obesity—*Continued*

Fiction

Biederman, L. Teenage waistland — **Fic**
Brande, R. Fat Cat — **Fic**
Brooks, K. Kissing the rain — **Fic**
Crutcher, C. Staying fat for Sarah Byrnes — **Fic**
Frazer, M. Secrets of truth and beauty — **Fic**
George, M. Looks — **Fic**
Going, K. L. Fat kid rules the world — **Fic**
Green, J. Will Grayson, Will Grayson — **Fic**
Hyde, C. R. Diary of a witness — **Fic**
Jonsberg, B. Dreamrider — **Fic**
Lipsyte, R. One fat summer — **Fic**
Mackler, C. The earth, my butt, and other big, round things — **Fic**
Marino, P. Dough Boy — **Fic**
Perl, E. S. Vintage Veronica — **Fic**
Peters, J. A. By the time you read this, I'll be dead — **Fic**
Rex, A. Fat vampire — **Fic**
Supplee, S. Artichoke's heart — **Fic**
Vande Velde, V. Remembering Raquel — **Fic**
Vaught, S. Big fat manifesto — **Fic**
Zadoff, A. Food, girls, and other things I can't have — **Fic**

Obesity — **616.3**

Obesity: opposing viewpoints — **616.3**

Objectivism (Philosophy)
Rand, A. The Ayn Rand reader — **191**

Obregón, Mauricio
Beyond the edge of the sea — **930**

O'Brien, Caragh M.
Birthmarked — **Fic**

O'Brien, Eileen, 1972-
(jt. auth) Feagin, J. R. White men on race — **305.8**

O'Brien, Jack
About
Swidey, N. The assist — **796.323**

O'Brien, Joanne, 1959-
(jt. auth) Breuilly, E. Religions of the world — **200**

O'Brien, Stephen J.
Tears of the cheetah — **591.3**

O'Brien, Tim, 1946-
Going after Cacciato — **Fic**
The things they carried — **S C**

Obscenity (Law)
See also Pornography

Observatories, Astronomical *See* Astronomical observatories

Obsession (Psychology) *See* Obsessive-compulsive disorder

Obsessive-compulsive disorder
Hyman, B. M. Obsessive-compulsive disorder — **616.85**
Parks, P. J. Obsessive-compulsive disorder — **616.85**
Patterson, J. Against medical advice [biography of Cory Friedman] — **92**
Rompella, N. Obsessive-compulsive disorder — **616.85**
Traig, J. Devil in the details — **92**

Zucker, B. Take control of OCD — **616.85**
Fiction
Cohen, T. Little black lies — **Fic**
De la Peña, M. Ball don't lie — **Fic**
MacCready, R. M. Buried — **Fic**

Obsessive-compulsive neuroses *See* Obsessive-compulsive disorder

Obsidian trilogy [series]
Lackey, M. The outstretched shadow — **Fic**

Obstfeld, Loretta
(ed) The Renaissance. See The Renaissance [Greenhaven Press] — **940.2**

Obstfeld, Raymond, 1952-
(jt. auth) Abdul-Jabbar, K. On the shoulders of giants — **92**
(ed) The Renaissance. See The Renaissance [Greenhaven Press] — **940.2**

Occidental mythology. Campbell, J. — **201**

Occult sciences *See* Occultism

Occultism
See also Astrology; Clairvoyance; Demonology; Divination; Fortune telling; Prophecies; Satanism
Fiction
Myracle, L. Bliss — **Fic**
Portman, F. Andromeda Klein — **Fic**

Occupational guidance *See* Vocational guidance

Occupational outlook handbook 2010-2011. United States. Bureau of Labor Statistics — **331.7**

Occupational training
Paquette, P. H. Apprenticeship — **331.2**
Unger, H. G. But what if I don't want to go to college? — **331.7**

Occupations
150 great tech prep careers — **331.7**
Career discovery encyclopedia — **331.7**
Exploring tech careers — **331.7**
Gregory, M. G. The career chronicles — **331.7**
Porterfield, D. Construction and trades — **331.7**
Reber, D. In their shoes — **331.4**
Seupel, C. W. Business, finance, and government administration — **331.7**
The top 100 — **331.7**
United States. Bureau of Labor Statistics. Occupational outlook handbook 2010-2011 — **331.7**
Withers, J. Hey, get a job! — **650.14**
Wyckoff, C. Communications and the arts — **331.7**
Dictionaries
O*NET — **331.7**
Encyclopedias
Encyclopedia of careers and vocational guidance — **331.7**

Ocean
See also Pacific Ocean; Seashore
Balliett, J. F. Oceans — **333.91**
Day, T. Oceans — **551.46**
Desonie, D. Oceans — **551.46**
Stow, D. A. V. Oceans: an illustrated reference — **551.46**

Ogilvie, Marilyn Bailey
(ed) The Biographical dictionary of women in science. See The Biographical dictionary of women in science   **920.003**

Oglala Indians
Black Elk. Black Elk speaks   **92**
Frazier, I. On the rez   **970.004**
Freedman, R. The life and death of Crazy Horse   **92**
McMurtry, L. Crazy Horse   **92**
See/See also pages in the following book(s):
Freedman, R. Indian chiefs   **920**

Oh, Seiwoong
Encyclopedia of Asian-American literature   **810.9**

Ohanian, Hans C.
Einstein's mistakes   **530**

O'Hanlon, Michael E.
(jt. auth) Daalder, I. H. Winning ugly   **949.7**

O'Hanlon, Nancy
(jt. auth) Diaz, K. R. IssueWeb: a guide and sourcebook for researching controversial issues on the Web   **025.04**

Ohio
Fiction
Anderson, L. H. Twisted   **Fic**
Barnes, J. Tales of the Madman Underground   **Fic**
Frey, J. I am number four   **Fic**
Garsee, J. Say the word   **Fic**
Morrison, T. The bluest eye   **Fic**
Morrison, T. Sula   **Fic**
Vivian, S. A little friendly advice   **Fic**

Ohno, Apolo, 1982-
About
Aldridge, R. Apolo Anton Ohno   **92**

Oil See Petroleum

Oil. Laxer, J.   **333.8**

Oil painting See Painting

Oil painting for the absolute beginner. Willenbrink, M.   **751.45**

Oil spills
DeNapoli, D. The great penguin rescue   **639.9**

Ojibwa Indians
Fiction
Erdrich, L. The last report on the miracles at Little No Horse   **Fic**

Okabayashi, Kensuke
Manga for dummies   **741.5**

O'Keefe, Sherry
From China to America   **92**
Spin [biography of Michael Jackson]   **92**

O'Keeffe, Georgia, 1887-1986
About
Fallon, M. How to analyze the works of Georgia O'Keeffe   **759.13**

O'Kelly, Helen Watanabe- See Watanabe-O'Kelly, Helen

Okey, Shannon
Knitgrrl   **746.43**

Okinawa. Leckie, R.   **940.54**

Oklahoma
Fiction
Tharp, T. Knights of the hill country   **Fic**
Tharp, T. The spectacular now   **Fic**

Oklahoma western biographies [series]
Griswold del Castillo, R. César Chávez   **92**
Remley, D. A. Kit Carson   **92**
Wilkins, T. John Muir   **92**

Okorafor, Nnedimma
The shadow speaker   **Fic**

Okorafor-Mbachu, Nnedimma See Okorafor, Nnedimma

Old age
See also Aging; Longevity
Fiction
Epstein, R. God is in the pancakes   **Fic**
Sonnenblick, J. Notes from the midnight driver   **Fic**

Old dog. Cárdenas, T.   **Fic**

Old English literature See English literature—Old English period

Old Hickory [biography of Andrew Jackson] Marrin, A.   **92**

The **old** man and the sea. Hemingway, E.   **Fic**

Old school. Wolff, T.   **Fic**

Old Testament See Bible. O.T.

Old world and new. Kelly, K.   **610**

Oldershaw, Cally
Firefly guide to gems   **553.8**
Gems of the world   **553.8**

The **oldest** rookie. Morris, J.   **92**

Oldfield, Sara
Rainforest   **578.7**

Olive, M. Foster
Ecstasy   **362.29**

Oliver, Charles M.
Critical companion to Ernest Hemingway   **813.009**
Critical companion to Walt Whitman   **811.009**

Oliver, Chris
Introducing RDA   **025.3**

Oliver, Evelyn Dorothy
(jt. auth) Lewis, J. R. The dream encyclopedia   **154.6**

Oliver, Jana G.
The demon trapper's daughter   **Fic**

Oliver, Jon A.
Basketball fundamentals   **796.323**

Oliver, Lauren
Before I fall   **Fic**
Delirium   **Fic**

Oliver, Mary, 1935-
New and selected poems   **811**
A poetry handbook   **808.1**

Oliver Twist. Dickens, C.   **Fic**

Olmstead, Larry
Getting into Guinness   **030**

Olmstead, Robert
Coal black horse   **Fic**

Olsen, Kirstin
All things Austen   **823.009**

One hundred key documents in American democracy. See 100 key documents in American democracy **973**

One hundred most important science ideas. See Henderson, M. 100 most important science ideas **500**

One hundred myths about the Middle East. See Halliday, F. 100 myths about the Middle East **956**

One hundred nine East Palace. See Conant, J. 109 East Palace **623.4**

One hundred one American English proverbs. See Collis, H. 101 American English proverbs **428**

One hundred one plus great ideas for teen library Web sites. See Doyle, M. 101+ great ideas for teen library Web sites **027.62**

One hundred one quantum questions. See Ford, K. W. 101 quantum questions **530.1**

One hundred one questions about food that have been eating at you . . . until now. See Brynie, F. H. 101 questions about food and digestion that have been eating at you . . . until now **612.3**

One hundred one questions about sleep and dreams that kept you awake nights . . . until now. See Brynie, F. H. 101 questions about sleep and dreams that kept you awake nights . . . until now **612.8**

One hundred philosophers. King, P. J. **109**

One hundred poems from the Chinese **895.1**

One hundred poems from the Japanese **895.6**

One hundred ready-to-use pathfinders for the Web. See Wilson, A. P. 100 ready-to-use pathfinders for the Web **001.4**

One hundred thirty projects to get you into filmmaking. See Grove, E. 130 projects to get you into filmmaking **792.9**

One hundred twelve acting games. See Levy, G. 112 acting games **792**

One hundred two minutes. See Dwyer, J. 102 minutes **974.7**

One hundred years of solitude. García Márquez, G. **Fic**

One kingdom. Noyes, D. **590**

One of those hideous books where the mother dies. Sones, S. **Fic**

One parent family See Single parent family

One-pound gospel, vol. 1. Takahashi, R. **741.5**

One thousand and eighty-nine and all that. See Acheson, D. J. 1089 and all that **510**

One thousand and one legal words you need to know. See Feinman, J. M. 1001 legal words you need to know **340**

One thousand comic books you must read. See Isabella, T. 1,000 comic books you must read **741.5**

One unblinking eye. Williams, N. **811**

One whole and perfect day. Clarke, J. **Fic**

One writer's beginnings. Welty, E. **92**

O'Neal, Michael, 1949-
The Crusades, Almanac **909.07**
World religions. See World religions **200**

O'Neal, Shaquille, 1972-
Shaq talks back **92**

O'Neil, Buck, 1911-2006
About
Posnanski, J. The soul of baseball **796.357**

O'Neil, Dennis, 1939-
The DC comics guide to writing comics **741.5**

O'Neil, John Jordan See O'Neil, Buck, 1911-2006

O'Neil, Maryadele J.
(ed) The Merck index. See The Merck index **615**

O'Neill, Eugene, 1888-1953
The iceman cometh **812**
Long day's journey into night **812**
About
Dowling, R. M. Critical companion to Eugene O'Neill **812.009**
(ed) Seven famous Greek plays. See Seven famous Greek plays **882.008**

O*NET **331.7**

Onians, John
(ed) Atlas of world art. See Atlas of world art **709**

Onions, Charles Talbut, 1873-1965
(ed) The Oxford dictionary of English etymology. See The Oxford dictionary of English etymology **422.03**

Online books See Electronic books

Online catalogs
See also Libraries—Automation

Online games See Internet games

Online pornography: opposing viewpoints **363.4**

Online reference services See Reference services (Libraries)

Online social networks
Richardson, W. Blogs, wikis, podcasts, and other powerful Web tools for classrooms **371.3**

The only astrology book you'll ever need. Woolfolk, J. M. **133.5**

Only twice I've wished for heaven. Trice, D. T. **Fic**

The only way I know. Ripken, C., Jr. **92**

Only what we could carry **940.53**

Only yesterday. Allen, F. L. **973.91**

Ono, Fuyumi, 1960-
(jt. auth) Inada, S. Ghost hunt, Vol. 1 **741.5**

Ono, Natsume, 1977-
Gente: the people of Ristorante Paradiso, volume 1 **741.5**

Ontario
Graphic novels
Lemire, J. Essex County **741.5**

Ooi, Keat Gin, 1959-
(ed) Southeast Asia. See Southeast Asia **959**

Open for debate [series]
Naden, C. J. Abortion **363.46**
Naden, C. J. Patients' rights **362.1**

The open road. Iyer, P. **92**

Opposing viewpoints series—*Continued*

Suicide: opposing viewpoints	**362.28**
The Taliban: opposing viewpoints	**958.1**
Teen drug abuse: opposing viewpoints	
	362.29
Teenage sexuality: opposing viewpoints	
	613.9
Television: opposing viewpoints	**302.23**
Terrorism: opposing viewpoints	**363.32**
The Third World: opposing viewpoints	**909**
Tobacco and smoking: opposing viewpoints	
	362.29
Voting rights: opposing viewpoints	**324.6**
The war on terrorism: opposing viewpoints	
	973.931
War: opposing viewpoints	**355**
Weapons of mass destruction: opposing viewpoints	**358**

The **opposite** of invisible. Gallagher, L.   **Fic**

Optical storage devices
> *See also* DVDs

The **Orange** Houses. Griffin, P.   **Fic**

Orangutan
> Russon, A. E. Orangutans: wizards of the rainforest   **599.8**

Orations *See* Speeches

Orca currents [series]
> Walters, E. In a flash   **Fic**

Orca soundings [series]
> Harvey, S. N. Plastic   **Fic**
> McClintock, N. Masked   **Fic**
> Tullson, D. Riley Park   **Fic**
> Van Tol, A. Knifepoint   **Fic**

Orchards. Thompson, H.   **Fic**

Orchestral music
> *See also* Symphony

Ordinary ghosts. Corrigan, E.   **Fic**

An **ordinary** man. Rusesabagina, P.   **92**

Oregon
Fiction
> Beaufrand, M. J. The river   **Fic**
> Caletti, D. The six rules of maybe   **Fic**
> Forman, G. If I stay   **Fic**

Organ and tissue transplants. McClellan, M.   **617.9**

Organ procurement *See* Procurement of organs, tissues, etc.

Organ transplantation *See* Transplantation of organs, tissues, etc.

Organ transplants. Schwartz, T. P.   **617.9**

Organic farming
> Organic food and farming   **641.3**

Organic food and farming   **641.3**

Organically grown foods *See* Natural foods

Organized crime
> *See also* Mafia

Organized labor *See* Labor unions

Organizing for your brain type. Nakone, L.   **640**

Organizing from the inside out for teens. Morgenstern, J.   **646.7**

Orgel, Stephen
> (ed) Shakespeare, W. King Lear   **822.3**
> (ed) Shakespeare, W. Macbeth   **822.3**
> (ed) Shakespeare, W. The sonnets   **821**

Orient *See* Asia; East Asia

Oriental mythology
> Birrell, A. Chinese myths   **299.5**
> Campbell, J. Oriental mythology   **201**

Origami
> Engel, P. 10-fold origami   **736**

The **origin** of humankind. Leakey, R. E.   **599.93**

Origin of life *See* Life—Origin

Origin of man *See* Human origins

Origin of species *See* Evolution

The **origin** of species by means of natural selection. See Darwin, C. On the origin of species   **576.8**

The **original** dog bible   **636.7**

Origins. Stefoff, R.   **599.93**

Origins reconsidered. Leakey, R. E.   **599.93**

O'Riley, Michael Kampen *See* Kampen O'Riley, Michael

Orioles (Baseball team) *See* Baltimore Orioles (Baseball team)

Ormal-Grenon, Jean-Benoit
> (ed) The Oxford-Hachette French dictionary. See The Oxford-Hachette French dictionary   **443**

Ormes, Jackie, 1911-1985
About
> Goldstein, N. Jackie Ormes   **92**

Ornamental plants
Encyclopedias
> The American Horticultural Society A-Z encyclopedia of garden plants   **635.9**

Ornelas, Kriemhild Coneè
> (ed) The Cambridge world history of food. See The Cambridge world history of food   **641.3**

Oron, Judie
> Cry of the giraffe   **Fic**

Orphanages
Fiction
> Furey, L. The long run   **Fic**

Orphans
Fiction
> Adlington, L. J. Cherry Heaven   **Fic**
> Almond, D. Raven summer   **Fic**
> Burgess, M. Nicholas Dane   **Fic**
> Clare, C. Clockwork angel   **Fic**
> Collins, P. L. Hidden voices   **Fic**
> Combres, E. Broken memory   **Fic**
> Cooney, C. B. If the witness lied   **Fic**
> Crowley, S. The stolen one   **Fic**
> Davidson, J. The Explosionist   **Fic**
> DeStefano, L. Wither   **Fic**
> Dickens, C. Oliver Twist   **Fic**
> Dunkle, C. B. The house of dead maids   **Fic**
> Gardner, S. The red necklace   **Fic**
> Halpin, B. Donorboy   **Fic**
> Hoban, J. Willow   **Fic**
> Hooper, M. Fallen Grace   **Fic**

Ottley, Ryan
(il) Kirkman, R. Invincible: ultimate collection, Vol. 1 **741.5**

Ottoman Empire *See* Turkey—History—Ottoman Empire, 1288-1918

Oubrerie, Clément
(il) Abouet, M. Aya **741.5**

Oufkir, Malika
Freedom: the story of my second life **92**
Stolen lives **92**

Our affair with El Niño. Philander, S. G. **551.6**

Our bodies, ourselves **613**

Our choice. Gore, A. **363.7**

Our documents. United States. National Archives and Records Administration **973**

Our fragile planet [series]
Desonie, D. Atmosphere **551.5**
Desonie, D. Oceans **551.46**

Our inner ape. Waal, F. d. **156**

Our mothers' war. Yellin, E. **940.53**

Our own devices. Tenner, E. **303.4**

Our stories remember. Bruchac, J. **970.004**

Our town. Wilder, T. **812**

Ours, Dorothy
Man o' War **798.4**

Out of shadows. Wallace, J. **Fic**

Out of the blue. Bernstein, R. **973.931**

Outcasts united. St. John, W. **796.334**

Outdoor adventures [series]
Canoeing **797.1**
Kayaking **797.1**

Outdoor cookery *See* Outdoor cooking

Outdoor cooking
Mackenzie, J. The complete trail food cookbook **641.5**

Outdoor life
See also Camping
Paulsen, G. Woodsong **796.5**

Outdoor survival *See* Wilderness survival

Outer planets. Chaple, G. F. **523.4**

Outer space

Colonies

See Space colonies

Exploration

See also Space probes
Angelo, J. A. Human spaceflight **629.45**
Angelo, J. A. Life in the universe **576.839**
Angelo, J. A. Space technology **629.4**
Burrows, W. E. This new ocean **629.4**
Carlisle, R. P. Exploring space **629.4**
Evans, K. M. Space exploration **629.4**
Hardesty, V. Epic rivalry **629.4**
Kerrod, R. Hubble: the mirror on the universe **522**
National Geographic encyclopedia of space **629.4**
Parks, P. J. Space research **500.5**
Space exploration **333.9**
Zimmerman, R. The chronological encyclopedia of discoveries in space **629.4**

Exploration—Pictorial works
Launius, R. D. Smithsonian atlas of space exploration **500.5**

Outer space travel *See* Interplanetary voyages

Outlaw: the legend of Robin Hood. Lee, T. **741.5**

Outlaws, mobsters & crooks. MacNee, M. J. **920.003**

Outman, Elisabeth M., 1951-
(jt. auth) Outman, J. L. Industrial Revolution: almanac **330.9**
(jt. auth) Outman, J. L. Industrial Revolution: biographies **920**
(jt. auth) Outman, J. L. Industrial Revolution: primary sources **330.9**

Outman, James L., 1946-
Industrial Revolution: almanac **330.9**
Industrial Revolution: biographies **920**
Industrial Revolution: primary sources **330.9**
U.S. immigration and migration. Biographies **920**
(ed) U.S. immigration and migration. Primary sources. See U.S. immigration and migration. Primary sources **325.73**

The **outside** of a horse. Rorby, G. **Fic**

Outside rules **S C**

The **outsider**. See Camus, A. The stranger **Fic**

The **outsiders**. Hinton, S. E. **Fic**

Outsourcing
Ching, J. Outsourcing U.S. jobs **331.1**

Outstanding books for the college bound **011.6**

The **outstretched** shadow. Lackey, M. **Fic**

Outward odyssey [series]
French, F. In the shadow of the moon **629.45**

Over a thousand hills I walk with you. Jansen, H. **Fic**

Over and under. Tucker, T. **Fic**

Over the coasts. Collier, M. **551.4**

Over-the-counter drugs *See* Nonprescription drugs

Over the end line. Martino, A. C. **Fic**

Over the mountains. Collier, M. **557**

Over the rivers. Collier, M. **551.48**

Over there. Farwell, B. **940.4**

Over there. Feuer, A. **956.7**

The **overachievers**. Robbins, A. **305.23**

Overland journeys to the Pacific
See also West (U.S.)—Exploration
Schlissel, L. Women's diaries of the westward journey **978**

Fiction

Houston, J. D. Snow Mountain passage **Fic**
McKernan, V. The devil's paintbox **Fic**

Overlord: D-Day and the battle for Normandy. Hastings, M. **940.54**

Overy, R. J. (Richard James), 1947-
The Battle of Britain **940.54**

Overy, Richard James *See* Overy, R. J. (Richard James), 1947-

Paladino, Variny
(jt. auth) Blatt, J. The teen girl's gotta-have-it guide to money   **332.024**

Palden Gyatso
The autobiography of a Tibetan monk   **92**

The **pale** assassin. Elliott, P.   **Fic**

Pale horse, pale rider: three short novels. Porter, K. A.   **S C**

Paleontology *See* Fossils

Palestine problem, 1917- *See* Israel-Arab conflicts

Palestinian Arabs
Al Jundi, S. The hour of sunlight   **92**
Barakat, I. Tasting the sky   **92**
Children of Israel, children of Palestine
                                           956.94
La Guardia, A. War without end   **956.7**
Encyclopedias
Encyclopedia of the Palestinians   **909**
Fiction
Clinton, C. A stone in my hand   **Fic**

Palin, Sarah, 1964-
Graphic novels
Bailey, N. Female force   **920**

Palisca, Claude V., 1921-2001
(jt. auth) Grout, D. J. A history of western music   **780.9**

Palmer, Colin A., 1942-
(ed) Encyclopedia of African-American culture and history. See Encyclopedia of African-American culture and history   **305.8**

Palmer, Laura, 1950-
Shrapnel in the heart   **959.704**

Palmer, Martin, 1953-
(jt. auth) Breuilly, E. Religions of the world
                                             200

Palmer, Melissa
Dr. Melissa Palmer's guide to hepatitis & liver disease   **616.3**

Palmer, Pat, 1928-
Teen esteem   **155.5**

Palmer, Robin, 1969-
Geek charming   **Fic**

Palmowski, Jan
A dictionary of contemporary world history
                                           909.82

Pampel, Fred C.
Drugs and sports   **362.29**
Tobacco industry and smoking   **338.4**

Pan Am Flight 103 Bombing Incident, 1988
Dornstein, K. The boy who fell out of the sky [biography of David Scott Dornstein]   **92**

Pan American Flight 103 disaster, 1988 *See* Pan Am Flight 103 Bombing Incident, 1988

Panchyk, Richard, 1970-
The keys to American history   **973**

Pancreas
Cancer
Casil, A. S. Pancreatic cancer   **616.99**

Pancreatic cancer. Casil, A. S.   **616.99**

Panda *See* Giant panda

Panek, Richard
The 4 percent universe   **523.1**

Panic disorders
Connolly, S. Anxiety disorders   **616.85**
Miller, A. R. Living with anxiety disorders
                                           616.85
Schutz, S. I don't want to be crazy   **92**

Panics (Finance) *See* Financial crises

Panno, Joseph
Aging   **612.6**
Animal cloning   **660.6**
Cancer   **616.99**
The cell   **571.6**
Gene therapy   **615.8**
Stem cell research   **616**

Pantheon fairy tale & folklore library [series]
Latin American folktales   **398.2**
Yiddish folktales   **398.2**

Pantoja, Tintin
(jt. auth) Sexton, A. Shakespeare's Hamlet
                                            822.3

Paolini, Christopher
Eragon   **Fic**

Papacy
See also Popes

Papadakis, Alexandra
(ed) Stuppy, W. The bizarre and incredible world of plants   **580**

Paper crafts
See also Origami
Hayakawa, H. Kirigami menagerie   **736**
Perdana, J. Build your own paper robots
                                           745.54
Reeder, D. Papier-mache monsters   **745.54**
Sowell, S. Paper cutting techniques for scrapbooks & cards   **745.54**

Paper cutting techniques for scrapbooks & cards. Sowell, S.   **745.54**

Paper dance   **811.008**

Paper money
Friedberg, A. Paper money of the United States
                                            769.5

Paper money of the United States. Friedberg, A.
                                            769.5

Paper towns. Green, J.   **Fic**

Papier-mache monsters. Reeder, D.   **745.54**

Papillomaviruses
Parks, P. J. HPV   **362.1**

Papineau, David
(ed) Western philosophy. See Western philosophy   **190**

Paquette, Penny Hutchins
Apprenticeship   **331.2**
Asthma   **616.2**
Learning disabilities   **371.9**

Parable of the sower. Butler, O. E.   **Fic**

Parallel journeys. Ayer, E. H.   **940.53**

Parallel worlds. Kaku, M.   **523.1**

Paranoid Park. Nelson, B.   **Fic**

Parapsychology
See also Extrasensory perception; Occultism
Shermer, M. Why people believe weird things
                                            001.9

Peterson field guide to birds of Eastern and Central North America. Peterson, R. T.   **598**

Peterson field guide to birds of North America. Peterson, R. T.   **598**

Peterson field guide to birds of Western North America. Peterson, R. T.   **598**

Peterson field guide to freshwater fishes of North America north of Mexico. Page, L. M.   **597**

Peterson first guide to reptiles and amphibians. Conant, R.   **597.9**

Peterson's four-year colleges 2012   **378.73**

Peterson's guide to four-year colleges. See Peterson's four-year colleges 2012   **378.73**

Peterson's how to get money for college   **378.3**

Peterson's master the SAT 2011. Pine, P.   **378.1**

Peterson's two-year colleges, 2011   **378.73**

Le **petit** Larousse illustré en couleurs   **443**

Petrarca, Francesco, 1304-1374
See/See also pages in the following book(s):
Highet, G. The classical tradition   **809**

Petrarch See Petrarca, Francesco, 1304-1374

Petričič, Dušan
(il) Dash, J. A dangerous engine [biography of Benjamin Franklin]   **92**

Petroleum
Gardner, T. Oil   **333.8**

Petroleum as fuel
Brune, M. Coming clean   **333.79**
Tabak, J. Coal and oil   **333.8**

Petroleum industry
Foreign oil dependence   **333.8**
Laxer, J. Oil   **333.8**

Petroleum trade See Petroleum industry

Petroski, Henry
Success through failure   **620**

Petrucha, Stefan
Split   **Fic**

Pets
See also names of animals, e.g. *Cats; Dogs*; etc.
Foster, S. Walking Ollie, or, Winning the love of a difficult dog   **636.7**
Winegar, K. Saved   **636.08**
Health and hygiene
Halligan, K. Doc Halligan's What every pet owner should know   **636**
Nakaya, S. F. Kindred spirit, kindred care   **636.089**

Pets and the handicapped See Animals and the handicapped

Petty, Cynthia
(jt. auth) Connolly, S. Anxiety disorders   **616.85**

Pfaffenberger, Bryan, 1949-
Webster's New World computer dictionary   **004**

Phagan, Mary
About
Alphin, E. M. An unspeakable crime   **364.152**

Pham, LeUyen
(il) Mechner, J. Solomon's thieves   **741.5**

Pham, Thien
(il) Yang, G. Level up   **741.5**

The **phantom** of the opera. Leroux, G.   **Fic**

Pharmacology
See also Drugs
Facklam, M. Modern medicines   **615**
Kidd, J. S. Potent natural medicines   **615**
Zedeck, B. E. Forensic pharmacology   **614**

Phelan, Jay
(jt. auth) Burnham, T. Mean genes   **155.7**

Phelps, M. William
Nathan Hale   **92**

Philadelphia (Pa.)
Fiction
Kephart, B. Dangerous neighbors   **Fic**
Vivian, S. Same difference   **Fic**

Philander, S. George, 1942-
Our affair with El Niño   **551.6**

Philbrick, Nathaniel
In the heart of the sea   **910.4**
The Mayflower and the Pilgrims' New World   **973.2**

Philbrick, Rodman See Philbrick, W. R. (W. Rodman)

Philbrick, W. R. (W. Rodman)
The last book in the universe   **Fic**

Philharmonic Symphony Orchestra of New York See New York Philharmonic

Philip II, King of Macedonia, 382-336 B.C.
Fiction
Renault, M. Fire from heaven   **Fic**

Philip, Neil
The great circle   **970.004**
Mythology of the world   **201.03**
(ed) War and the pity of war. See War and the pity of war   **808.81**

Philippines
Fiction
Growing up Filipino II   **S C**

Philip's atlas of the universe. See Firefly atlas of the universe   **523**

Philipson, Ilene J., 1950-
Ethel Rosenberg   **92**

Phillips, Andrew, 1945-
(jt. auth) Van Dulken, S. Inventing the 20th century   **609**

Phillips, Christopher, 1959-
Six questions of Socrates   **179**
Socrates café   **100**

Phillips, Cynthia, 1973-
(jt. auth) Priwer, S. Ancient monuments   **732**

Phillips, Douglas A.
Southeast Asia   **959**

Phillips, Jerry
(ed) Romanticism and transcendentalism. See Romanticism and transcendentalism   **810.9**

Physical education

Medical aspects

See Sports medicine

Physical fitness

Burke, L. The complete guide to food for sports performance **613.2**
Carmichael, C. The ultimate ride **796.6**
Dicker, K. Diet and nutrition **613**
Dicker, K. Exercise **613.7**
Fitness information for teens **613.7**
Gifford, C. Sports **796**
Hines, E. W. Fitness swimming **613.7**
Pagano, J. Strength training for women **613.7**
Shryer, D. Peak performance **617.1**

Physical science experiments. Walker, P. **500.2**

Physical sciences

Harper, K. Weather and climate **551.5**
Walker, P. Physical science experiments **500.2**

Encyclopedias

Rosen, J. Encyclopedia of physical science **500.2**

Physically handicapped

See also Blind; Deaf

Hockenberry, J. Moving violations **92**
Kaufman, M. Easy for you to say **362.1**
Schlachter, G. A. Financial aid for the disabled and their families, 2010-2012 **378.3**

Drama

Pomerance, B. The Elephant Man **822**

Fiction

Baratz-Logsted, L. Crazy beautiful **Fic**
Howell, S. Everything beautiful **Fic**
Klein, L. M. Lady Macbeth's daughter **Fic**
Maugham, W. S. Of human bondage **Fic**
McBay, B. Waiting for Sarah **Fic**
Slade, A. G. The hunchback assignments **Fic**

Physician-assisted suicide **179.7**

Physician-assisted suicide and euthanasia. See Yount, L. Right to die and euthanasia **179.7**

Physicians

See also Surgeons

Dang, T. T. Last night I dreamed of peace **92**
Davis, S. The pact: three young men make a promise and fulfill a dream **920**
Firlik, K. Another day in the frontal lobe **92**
Kidder, T. Mountains beyond mountains **92**
Sacks, O. W. Uncle Tungsten **92**
Transue, E. R. On call **92**
Yamazaki, J. N. Children of the atomic bomb **92**

Fiction

Hooker, R. MASH **Fic**

Physicists

Borzendowski, J. Marie Curie **92**
Cooper, D. Enrico Fermi and the revolutions in modern physics **92**
Cropper, W. H. Great physicists **920**

Krauss, L. M. Quantum man [biography of Richard Feynman] **92**
Lewin, W. H. G. For the love of physics **92**
Reeves, R. A force of nature [biography of Ernest Rutherford] **92**
Russell, C. A. Michael Faraday **92**

Graphic novels

Ottaviani, J. Suspended in language [biography of Niels Bohr] **92**

Physics

See also Astrophysics

Adair, R. K. The physics of baseball **796.357**
Balibar, S. The atom and the apple **530**
Bloomfield, L. How everything works **530**
Cole, K. C. The hole in the universe **530**
The Facts on File physics handbook **530**
Feynman, R. P. Six easy pieces **530**
Guillen, M. Five equations that changed the world **530.1**
Hakim, J. The story of science: Newton at the center **509**
Henderson, M. 100 most important science ideas **500**
Jargodzki, C. Mad about physics **530**
Kaku, M. Physics of the impossible **530**
Krauss, L. M. Fear of physics **530**
Muller, R. The instant physicist **530**
Ohanian, H. C. Einstein's mistakes **530**
Orzel, C. How to teach physics to your dog **530.1**
Panek, R. The 4 percent universe **523.1**
Parker, B. R. Death rays, jet packs, stunts, & supercars **600**
Potter, F. Mad about modern physics **530**

Dictionaries

The Facts on File dictionary of physics **530**

Encyclopedias

Rosen, J. Encyclopedia of physics **530**

Graphic novels

Nitta, H. The manga guide to physics **530**

Study and teaching

Kakalios, J. The physics of superheroes **530**
Leduc, S. A. Cracking the SAT. Physics subject test **530**
Lewin, W. H. G. For the love of physics **92**

Tables

CRC handbook of chemistry and physics **540**

The **physics** of baseball. Adair, R. K. **796.357**
The **physics** of NASCAR. Leslie-Pelecky, D. L. **796.72**
The **physics** of Star Trek. Krauss, L. M. **500.5**
The **physics** of superheroes. Kakalios, J. **530**
Physics of the future. Kaku, M. **303.49**
Physics of the impossible. Kaku, M. **530**

Physiognomy

See also Phrenology

Physiological chemistry *See* Biochemistry

Pollution

See also Air pollution; Environmental protection; Marine pollution; Water pollution

Casper, J. K. Fossil fuels and pollution **363.7**

New thinking about pollution **628.5**

Petersen, C. Controlling Earth's pollutants **363.7**

Pollution: opposing viewpoints **363.7**

Pollution control industry

See also Recycling

Pollution: opposing viewpoints **363.7**

Polly, Matthew

American Shaolin **796.8**

Polo, Marco, 1254-1323?

The travels of Marco Polo **915**

About

Belliveau, D. In the footsteps of Marco Polo **915**

Polygamy

Fiction

Grey, Z. Riders of the purple sage **Fic**

Hrdlitschka, S. Sister wife **Fic**

Williams, C. L. The chosen one **Fic**

Polyglot dictionaries

Corbeil, J.-C. The Firefly five language visual dictionary **413**

Pomerance, Bernard

The Elephant Man **822**

Pomes all sizes. Kerouac, J. **811**

Pompeii (Extinct city)

Berry, J. The complete Pompeii **937**

Pompeii. Harris, R. **Fic**

Pomplun, Tom

(ed) Graphic Classics volume eight: Mark Twain. See Graphic Classics volume eight: Mark Twain **741.5**

(ed) Graphic Classics volume eleven: O. Henry. See Graphic Classics volume eleven: O. Henry **741.5**

(ed) Graphic Classics volume fifteen: Fantasy classics. See Graphic Classics volume fifteen: Fantasy classics **741.5**

(ed) Graphic Classics volume four: H. P. Lovecraft. See Graphic Classics volume four: H. P. Lovecraft **741.5**

(ed) Graphic Classics volume fourteen: Gothic classics. See Graphic Classics volume fourteen: Gothic classics **741.5**

(ed) Graphic Classics volume seven: Bram Stoker. See Graphic Classics volume seven: Bram Stoker **741.5**

Pon, Cindy, 1973-

Silver phoenix **Fic**

Pong, David, 1939-

(ed) Encyclopedia of modern China. See Encyclopedia of modern China **951**

Pool, Daniel

What Jane Austen ate and Charles Dickens knew **820.9**

Poole, Adrian

(ed) The Oxford book of classical verse in translation. See The Oxford book of classical verse in translation **881.008**

Poole, Joyce, 1956-

Elephants **599.67**

Poor

How can the poor be helped? **362.5**

Fiction

Badoe, A. Between sisters **Fic**

Booth, C. Tyrell **Fic**

Garsee, J. Before, after, and somebody in between **Fic**

Going, K. L. Saint Iggy **Fic**

Guène, F. Kiffe kiffe tomorrow **Fic**

Medical care

Farmer, P. Pathologies of power **305**

United States

Poverty **362.5**

Pop. Korman, G. **Fic**

Pop art

Greenberg, J. Andy Warhol **92**

Popes

Flynn, R. John Paul II **92**

Renehan, E. J. Pope John Paul II **92**

See/See also pages in the following book(s):

Tuchman, B. W. The march of folly **909.08**

Poplawski, Paul

A Jane Austen encyclopedia **823.009**

Popular culture

Johnson, S. Everything bad is good for you **306**

Popular culture: opposing viewpoints **306**

United States

Behen, L. D. Using pop culture to teach information literacy **028.7**

Browne, R. B. The Civil War and Reconstruction **973.7**

The Greenwood guide to American popular culture **973.9**

Halberstam, D. The fifties **973.92**

Harvey, R. C. The art of the comic book **741.5**

Quay, S. E. Westward expansion **978**

Popular culture: opposing viewpoints **306**

Popular mechanics [series]

Why a curveball curves **796**

Popular music

See also Blues music; Country music; Gospel music; Rap music; Rock music

Furia, P. The poets of Tin Pan Alley **782.42**

Writing and publishing

Songwriter's market **782.42**

Popular psychology. Cordón, L. A. **150.3**

Popular series fiction for middle school and teen readers. Thomas, R. L. **016.8**

Popularity

Fiction

Bennett Wealer, S. Rival **Fic**

Cohen, T. Little black lies **Fic**

Gelbwasser, M. Inconvenient **Fic**

Halpern, J. Into the wild nerd yonder **Fic**

Hurley, T. Ghostgirl **Fic**

Martino, A. C. Over the end line **Fic**

McNish, C. Angel **Fic**

Mitchell, T. The secret to lying **Fic**

Oliver, L. Before I fall **Fic**

Popularity—Fiction—*Continued*
Palmer, R. Geek charming — **Fic**
Stone, M. H. Invisible girl — **Fic**
Zadoff, A. Food, girls, and other things I can't have — **Fic**
Ziegler, J. How not to be popular — **Fic**

Population
Population: opposing viewpoints — **304.6**

Population: opposing viewpoints — **304.6**

Porcellino, John
Thoreau at Walden — **818**

Pornography
Nathan, D. Pornography — **363.4**
Online pornography: opposing viewpoints — **363.4**

The **portable** Abraham Lincoln. Lincoln, A. — **973.7**

The **portable** Arthur Miller. Miller, A. — **812**

The **portable** Blake. Blake, W. — **828**

The **portable** Chaucer. Chaucer, G. — **821**

The **portable** Conrad. Conrad, J. — **828**

The **portable** Dante. Dante Alighieri — **851**

The **portable** Emerson. Emerson, R. W. — **818**

The **Portable** Greek reader — **880.8**

The **portable** Hawthorne. Hawthorne, N. — **818**

The **portable** Jack Kerouac. Kerouac, J. — **818**

The **portable** Jack London. London, J. — **818**

The **portable** Kipling. Kipling, R. — **828**

The **portable** Milton. Milton, J. — **828**

The **portable** Nietzsche. Nietzsche, F. W. — **193**

The **Portable** nineteenth-century Russian reader — **891.7**

The **portable** Oscar Wilde. Wilde, O. — **828**

The **Portable** Roman reader — **870.8**

The **Portable** sixties reader — **810.8**

The **Portable** twentieth-century Russian reader — **891.7**

The **portable** Voltaire. Voltaire — **848**

Porter, Connie Rose
Imani all mine — **Fic**

Porter, David L., 1941-
(ed) Biographical dictionary of American sports, Baseball. See Biographical dictionary of American sports, Baseball — **796.357**

Porter, Joy, 1967-
(jt. auth) Ball, D. I. Competing voices from native America — **970.004**

Porter, Katherine Anne, 1890-1980
The collected stories of Katherine Anne Porter — **S C**
Pale horse, pale rider: three short novels — **S C**

Porter, Robert S., 1950-
(ed) The Merck manual home health handbook. See The Merck manual home health handbook — **616.02**
(ed) The Merck manual of diagnosis and therapy. See The Merck manual of diagnosis and therapy — **610.3**

Porter, Roy, 1946-2002
(ed) Oxford dictionary of scientific quotations. See Oxford dictionary of scientific quotations — **500**

Porter, William Sydney *See* Henry, O., 1862-1910

Porterfield, Deborah
Construction and trades — **331.7**

Portman, Frank
Andromeda Klein — **Fic**
King Dork — **Fic**

The **portrait** of a lady. James, H. — **Fic**

A **portrait** of the artist as a young man. Joyce, J. — **Fic**

Portrait photography
In focus — **779**
Latana. Barely exposed — **779**

Portraits
Fiction
Wilde, O. The picture of Dorian Gray — **Fic**

Portraits of Black Americans [series]
Miller, C. C. A. Philip Randolph and the African American labor movement — **92**

Portraits of the rainforest. See Forsyth, A. Nature of the rainforest — **577.3**

Poseurs. Vankin, D. — **741.5**

Positively ADD. Corman, C. A. — **616.85**

Posnanski, Joe
The soul of baseball — **796.357**

Possessed. Cann, K. — **Fic**

Possessions, Lost and found *See* Lost and found possessions

The **possibilities** of sainthood. Freitas, D. — **Fic**

Post, Peggy, 1945-
Emily Post's Etiquette — **395**
(jt. auth) Senning, C. P. Emily Post prom and party etiquette — **395**

Post, Wiley, 1898-1935
See/See also pages in the following book(s):
Yagoda, B. Will Rogers — **92**

Post-traumatic stress disorder
Connolly, S. Anxiety disorders — **616.85**
Miller, A. R. Living with anxiety disorders — **616.85**
Fiction
Fehlbaum, B. Hope in Patience — **Fic**
Miller-Lachmann, L. Gringolandia — **Fic**
Morgenroth, K. Echo — **Fic**
Paulsen, G. Soldier's heart — **Fic**
Phillips, S. Burn — **Fic**
Tharp, T. Badd — **Fic**
Woolston, B. The Freak Observer — **Fic**

Poster boy. Crane, D. — **Fic**

Poster child. Rapp, E. — **92**

Postimpressionism (Art)
Bingham, J. Post-Impressionism — **759.05**

Postma, Johannes
The Atlantic slave trade — **326**

Postmodern American poetry — **811.008**

Postwar America — **973.92**

Postwar America. Sitkoff, H. — **973.92**

Potent natural medicines. Kidd, J. S. — **615**

Potok, Chaim, 1929-2002
The chosen   Fic

Potter, Franklin, 1944-
Mad about modern physics   530
(jt. auth) Jargodzki, C. Mad about physics
     530

Potter, Ryan
Exit strategy   Fic

Potter, Harry (Fictional character) *See* Harry
Potter (Fictional character)

The **potter's** studio handbook. Müller, K.
     738.1

Pottery
Müller, K. The potter's studio handbook
     738.1
Nelson, G. C. Ceramics: a potter's handbook
     738.1

Pough, Frederick H., 1906-2006
A field guide to rocks and minerals   549

Pound, Ezra, 1885-1972
Selected poems   811
(ed) The Classic Noh theatre of Japan. See The
Classic Noh theatre of Japan   895.6

Pouwels, Randall L.
The African and Middle Eastern world, 600-
1500   956

Poverty
See also Poor
Ehrenreich, B. Nickel and dimed   305.5
Gifford, C. Poverty   362.5
Gilbert, G. Rich and poor in America   339.2
How can the poor be helped?   362.5
Lüsted, M. A. Poverty   362.5
Poverty   362.5
Poverty and homelessness   362.5
Poverty: opposing viewpoints   339.4
Fiction
Cullen, L. I am Rembrandt's daughter   Fic
Fletcher, C. Ten cents a dance   Fic
Hartnett, S. Thursday's child   Fic
Hooper, M. Fallen Grace   Fic
Lawson, M. Crow Lake   Fic
Morrison, T. Sula   Fic
Mulligan, A. Trash   Fic
Qamar, A. Beneath my mother's feet   Fic
Shulman, M. Scrawl   Fic
Steinbeck, J. The pearl   Fic
Wolff, V. E. Make lemonade   Fic

Poverty   362.5

Poverty and homelessness   362.5

Poverty: opposing viewpoints   339.4

Powell, Angela
(jt. auth) Wecht, C. H. Tales from the morgue
     614

Powell, Ben
Skateboarding skills   796.22

Powell, John, 1954-
Encyclopedia of North American immigration
     304.8
(ed) Great events from history, The 18th century, 1701-1800. See Great events from history,
The 18th century, 1701-1800   909.7

(ed) Great events from history, The 19th century, 1801-1900. See Great events from history,
The 19th century, 1801-1900   **909.81**
(ed) Great lives from history, The 18th century,
1701-1800. See Great lives from history, The
18th century, 1701-1800   **920.003**
(ed) Great lives from history, The 19th century,
1801-1900. See Great lives from history, The
19th century, 1801-1900   **920.003**

Powell, Nate, 1978-
Swallow me whole   **741.5**

Powell, Randy
Three clams and an oyster   Fic

Power, Susan, 1961-
The grass dancer   Fic

Power (Mechanics)
See also Electric power

Power. Ravilious, K.   179

The **power** and the glory. Greene, G.   Fic

Power lines. Carter, J.   968.06

The **power** of black music. Floyd, S. A.
     780.89

The **power** of myth. Campbell, J.   201

The **power** of one [biography of Daisy Bates]
Fradin, J. B.   92

The **power** of photography. Goldberg, V.   770

The **power** of the media specialist to improve academic achievement and strengthen at-risk students. Jones, J. B.   027.8

Power of the news media. Henderson, H.
     070.1

Power research tools. Valenza, J. K.   001.4

Power resources *See* Energy resources

Power Scott, Jennifer, 1968-
Green careers   333.72

The **power** to prevent suicide. Nelson, R. E.
     362.28

Power tools. See Valenza, J. K. Power tools recharged   027.8

Power tools recharged. Valenza, J. K.   027.8

Powers, Ron
(jt. auth) Bradley, J. Flags of our fathers
     940.54

Powhatan, ca. 1550-1618
See/See also pages in the following book(s):
Woodward, G. S. Pocahontas   92

Powhatan Indians
Jones, V. G. Pocahontas   92
Woodward, G. S. Pocahontas   92

POWs *See* Prisoners of war

The **Pox** party. Anderson, M. T.   Fic

The **practical** astronomer. Gater, W.   520

The **practical** Shakespeare. Butler, C.   822.3

Prado, Edgar, 1967-
My guy Barbaro   92

Praeger perspectives [series]
Famous American crimes and trials   364

Prager, Ellen J., 1962-
Chasing science at sea   551.46

Prague (Czech Republic)
Sís, P. The wall   92

Presidents—*Continued*
Rwanda
Kinzer, S. A thousand hills [biography of Paul Kagame] **967.571**

United States
Abramson, J. Obama **92**
The American presidency **973**
The American presidency **920**
Bober, N. Thomas Jefferson **92**
Brinkley, A. Franklin Delano Roosevelt **92**
Bruni, F. Ambling into history: the unlikely odyssey of George W. Bush **92**
Burner, D. John F. Kennedy and a new generation **92**
Calhoun, C. W. Benjamin Harrison **92**
Carter, J. An hour before daylight **92**
Cooper, M. L. Theodore Roosevelt **92**
Crompton, S. Ulysses S. Grant **92**
Dallek, R. Harry S. Truman **92**
Dallek, R. Let every nation know [biography of John F. Kennedy] **92**
Davis, W. Barack Obama **92**
DiSilvestro, R. L. Theodore Roosevelt in the Badlands **92**
Donald, A. D. Lion in the White House **92**
Ellis, J. J. Founding brothers **973.4**
Ellis, J. J. His Excellency [biography of George Washington] **92**
Facts about the presidents **920**
Finkelman, P. Millard Fillmore **92**
Fleming, C. The Lincolns **92**
Freedman, R. Franklin Delano Roosevelt **92**
Freedman, R. Lincoln: a photobiography **92**
Gienapp, W. E. Abraham Lincoln and Civil War America **92**
Gordon-Reed, A. Andrew Johnson **92**
Gould, L. L. The modern American presidency **973.9**
Guide to the presidency **352.23**
Hart, G. James Monroe **92**
Holt, M. F. Franklin Pierce **92**
Johnson, P. George Washington: the Founding Father **92**
Keneally, T. Abraham Lincoln **92**
Koestler-Grack, R. A. Abraham Lincoln **92**
Lincoln, A. Abraham Lincoln the writer **92**
Lukes, B. L. Woodrow Wilson and the Progressive Era **92**
Marrin, A. The great adventure: Theodore Roosevelt and the rise of modern America **92**
Marrin, A. Old Hickory [biography of Andrew Jackson] **92**
McGovern, G. S. Abraham Lincoln **92**
McPherson, J. M. Abraham Lincoln **92**
McPherson, J. M. Tried by war [biography of Abraham Lincoln] **92**
Naftali, T. J. George H.W. Bush **92**
Obama, B. Dreams from my father **92**
Peters, C. Lyndon B. Johnson **92**
Remini, R. V. Andrew Jackson **92**
Renehan, E. J. The lion's pride: Theodore Roosevelt and his family in peace and war **92**
Rice, E. Ulysses S. Grant: defender of the Union **92**
Sandler, M. W. Lincoln through the lens **92**
Schaller, M. Ronald Reagan **92**

Seigenthaler, J. James K. Polk **92**
Student's guide to the presidency **352.23**
Sutherland, J. Ronald Reagan **92**
Widmer, E. L. Martin Van Buren **92**
Wilentz, S. Andrew Jackson **92**
Wills, G. James Madison **92**
United States—Assassination
Vowell, S. Assassination vacation **920**
United States—Dictionaries
Hamilton, N. A. Presidents **920.003**
United States—Election
The presidential election process: opposing viewpoints **324.6**
Presidential elections 1789-2008 **324.6**
United States—Election—2008
Abramson, J. Obama **92**
Thomas, E. "A long time coming" **324**
United States—Election—Maps
Historical atlas of U.S. presidential elections 1788-2004 **324**
United States—Election—Statistics
Historical atlas of U.S. presidential elections 1788-2004 **324**
United States—Encyclopedias
Genovese, M. A. Encyclopedia of the American presidency **920.003**
The presidency A to Z **352.23**
United States—Family
Angelo, B. First families **920**
United States—Fiction
Calloway, C. Confessions of a First Daughter **Fic**
United States—Graphic novels
Helfer, A. Ronald Reagan **92**
United States—Inaugural addresses
Fellow citizens **352.23**
My fellow citizens **352.23**
United States—Nomination
The presidential election process: opposing viewpoints **324.6**
United States—Spouses
See Presidents' spouses—United States
Venezuela
Levin, J. Hugo Chávez **92**

Presidents' spouses
United States
Brady, P. Martha Washington **92**
Caroli, B. B. First ladies **920**
Fleischner, J. Mrs. Lincoln and Mrs. Keckley **92**
Fleming, C. The Lincolns **92**
Freedman, R. Eleanor Roosevelt **92**
Keating, A. M. Eleanor Roosevelt **92**
Mundy, L. Michelle [Obama] **92**
United States—Dictionaries
Schneider, D. First ladies **920.003**

Presley, Elvis, 1935-1977
About
Mason, B. A. Elvis Presley **92**
Fiction
Kidd, R. On Beale Street **Fic**

Press
See also Broadcast journalism; Freedom of the press; Newspapers
Henderson, H. Power of the news media **070.1**

The **Princeton** encyclopedia of birds   **598**
The **Princeton** encyclopedia of mammals   **599**
The **Princeton** field guide to dinosaurs. Paul, G. S.   **567.9**

Princeton field guides [series]
   Compagno, L. J. V. Sharks of the world   **597**
   Kays, R. Mammals of North America   **599**
   Paul, G. S. The Princeton field guide to dinosaurs   **567.9**

Princeton Language Institute
   Roget's 21st century thesaurus in dictionary form. See Roget's 21st century thesaurus in dictionary form   **423**

Princeton Review series
   Amend, A. Cracking the SAT. Literature subject test   **800**
   Freedman, G. R. Cracking the SAT. U.S. & world history subject tests   **900**
   Gaden, M. Cracking the SAT. French subject test   **440**
   Leduc, S. A. Cracking the SAT. Physics subject test   **530**
   Pace, G. R. Cracking the SAT. Spanish subject test   **460**
   Silver, T. Cracking the SAT. Chemistry subject test   **540**
   Spaihts, J. Cracking the SAT. Math 1 & 2 subject tests   **510**
   Wright, J. Cracking the SAT. Biology E/M subject test   **570**

Princeton studies in Muslim politics [series]
   Norton, A. R. Hezbollah   **324.2**

The **principal's** guide to a powerful library media program. McGhee, M. W.   **025.1**

Principles and practice series
   Hughes-Hassell, S. School reform and the school library media specialist   **027.8**

Pringle, Heather Anne, 1952-
   The mummy congress   **393**

Printing
Style manuals
   The Chicago manual of style   **808**

Prinz, Yvonne
   The Vinyl Princess   **Fic**

Prion diseases
   See also Creutzfeldt-Jakob disease
   Schwartz, M. How the cows turned mad   **616.8**

The **prism** and the pendulum. Crease, R. P.   **509**

Prisoner of Tehran. Nemat, M.   **92**

Prisoners
   See also Political prisoners
   Al Jundi, S. The hour of sunlight   **92**
   Masters, J. That bird has my wings   **92**
Civil rights
   How should prisons treat inmates?   **365**
Fiction
   Abrahams, P. Bullet point   **Fic**
   Buckhanon, K. Upstate   **Fic**
   Dowd, S. Bog child   **Fic**
   Fisher, C. Incarceron   **Fic**

   Gaines, E. J. A lesson before dying   **Fic**
   Smith, A. G. Lockdown   **Fic**
   Solzhenitsyn, A. One day in the life of Ivan Denisovich   **Fic**
   Whyman, M. Icecore   **Fic**

Prisoners in the palace. MacColl, M.   **Fic**

Prisoners of war
   Gourley, C. The horrors of Andersonville   **973.7**
   How should the United States treat prisoners in the war on terror?   **973.931**
Fiction
   Mazer, H. The last mission   **Fic**
   Pausewang, G. Traitor   **Fic**

Prisoners without trial. Daniels, R.   **940.53**

Prisons
United States
   America's prisons: opposing viewpoints   **365**
   Edge, L. B. Locked up   **365**
   Ferro, J. Prisons   **365**
   Prisons   **365**

Prisons   **365**

Pritchett, V. S. (Victor Sawdon), 1900-1997
   (ed) The Oxford book of short stories. See The Oxford book of short stories   **S C**

Pritzker, Barry
   (ed) Encyclopedia of American Indian history. See Encyclopedia of American Indian history   **970.004**

Privacy, Right of See Right of privacy

Private Peaceful. Morpurgo, M.   **Fic**

Private schools
   Fortunate Eagle, A. Pipestone   **92**
   Independent school libraries   **025.1**

Priwer, Shana
   Ancient monuments   **732**

Pro-choice movement
   McBride, D. E. Abortion in the United States   **363.46**

The **pro-life/choice** debate. Herring, M. Y.   **363.46**

Pro-life movement
   McBride, D. E. Abortion in the United States   **363.46**

Pro makeup. Spencer, K.   **646.7**
Pro nail care. Toselli, L.   **646.7**
Pro wrestling. Greenberg, K. E.   **796.8**

Probabilities
   Rosenthal, J. Struck by lightning   **519.2**
   Tabak, J. Probability and statistics   **519.2**

Probability and statistics. Tabak, J.   **519.2**

Problem children See Emotionally disturbed children

Problem drinking See Alcoholism

Problem solving
   See also Conflict management; Decision making
   Weinstein, L. Guesstimation   **519.5**

Procurement of organs, tissues, etc.
   Cheney, A. Body brokers   **617.9**

Products, Commercial See Commercial products

Professions

See also Occupations

Gregory, M. G. The career chronicles **331.7**

Professor Stewart's hoard of mathematical treasures. Stewart, I. **510**

The **professor's** daughter. Sfar, J. **741.5**

Professors' guide [series]

Jacobs, L. F. The secrets of college success
378.1

Profiles in courage. Kennedy, J. F. **920**

Profiles in courage for our time **920**

Profiles in economics [series]

Rössig, W. Karl Marx **92**

Profiles in mathematics [series]

Corrigan, J. Alan Turing **92**

Staeger, R. Ancient mathematicians **920**

Profiles in science [series]

Baxter, R. Skeptical chemist **92**

Steffens, B. Ibn al-Haytham **92**

Yannuzzi, D. A. New elements **92**

Programmed instruction

See also Computer-assisted instruction

Programs, Television *See* Television programs

The **progressive** movement. McNeese, T.
324.2

Progressivism (United States politics)

McNeese, T. The progressive movement
324.2

Prohibition

Amendments XVIII and XXI **344**

Hill, J. Prohibition **363.4**

Project Apollo

Pyle, R. Destination moon **629.45**

Project Apollo *See* Apollo project

Project Mercury

Ackmann, M. The Mercury 13: the untold story of thirteen American women and the dream of space flight **629.45**

History

Stone, T. L. Almost astronauts **629.45**

Project method in teaching

Harada, V. H. Collaborating for project-based learning in grades 9-12 **371.3**

Project X. Shepard, J. **Fic**

Proliferation of arms *See* Arms race

Prom. Anderson, L. H. **Fic**

Prom and prejudice. Eulberg, E. **Fic**

Prom dates from Hell. Clement-Moore, R. **Fic**

Prom nights from hell **S C**

The **promised** land. Lemann, N. **973.9**

Pronouncing Shakespeare's words. Coye, D. F.
822.3

Proofiness. Seife, C. **510**

Propaganda

Huxley, A. Brave new world revisited **303.3**

Prophecies

Pickover, C. A. Dreaming the future **133.3**

Randi, J. The mask of Nostradamus **92**

Fiction

Raedeke, C. The daykeeper's grimoire **Fic**

Prophecy of days [series]

Raedeke, C. The daykeeper's grimoire **Fic**

Prophecy of the sisters. Zink, M. **Fic**

The **Prophet.** Gibran, K. **811**

Prose, Francine, 1947-

Anne Frank **839.3**

Reading like a writer **808**

Touch **Fic**

Prose and poetry. Crane, S. **818**

Prostate gland

Cancer

Cramer, S. D. Prostate cancer **616.99**

Prosthesis *See* Artificial organs

Prostitution

See also Juvenile prostitution

Fiction

El-Saadawi, N. Woman at point zero **Fic**

Hopkins, E. Tricks **Fic**

McCormick, P. Sold **Fic**

Prostitution, Juvenile *See* Juvenile prostitution

Protecting earth's food supply. Petersen, C.
363.1

Protecting intellectual freedom in your school library. Scales, P. R. **025.2**

Protecting the right to read. Symons, A. K.
025.2

Protection of environment *See* Environmental protection

Protection of wildlife *See* Wildlife conservation

Proteins

Hodge, R. The molecules of life **611**

The **protest** singer [biography of Pete Seeger] Wilkinson, A. **92**

Protestant Reformation *See* Reformation

Protestantism

Brown, S. F. Protestantism **280**

Protests, demonstrations, etc. *See* Demonstrations

Prothero, Stephen R.

(jt. auth) Queen, E. L. Encyclopedia of American religious history **200.9**

Protopopescu, Orel Odinov

(jt. auth) Liu Siyu. A thousand peaks **895.1**

The **proud** tower. Tuchman, B. W. **909.82**

Proulx, Annie

Bird cloud **92**

Proverbs

Collis, H. 101 American English proverbs
428

Cordry, H. V. The multicultural dictionary of proverbs **398.9**

Oxford dictionary of phrase, saying, and quotation **808.88**

Provine, Robert R.

Laughter **152.4**

Provoost, Anne, 1964-

In the shadow of the ark **Fic**

Prucher, Jeff

(ed) Brave new words. See Brave new words
813.009

Prying eyes. Kuhn, B. **323.44**

Psychiatric hospitals
Fiction
Eagland, J. Wildthorn	Fic
Ford, M. T. Suicide notes	Fic
Halpern, J. Get well soon	Fic
Johnson, L. L. Worlds apart	Fic
McCormick, P. Cut	Fic
Vizzini, N. It's kind of a funny story	Fic

Psychiatrists
Fiction
Fitzgerald, F. S. Tender is the night	Fic

Psychical research *See* Parapsychology

Psychoanalysis
Freud, S. The basic writings of Sigmund Freud	150.19
Jung, C. G. The basic writings of C. G. Jung	150.19
Thurschwell, P. Sigmund Freud	150.19

Psychokinesis
Fiction
King, S. Carrie	Fic
King, S. Firestarter	Fic

Psychological disorders [series]
Connolly, S. Anxiety disorders	616.85
Marcus, M. B. Sleep disorders	616.8
Veague, H. B. Personality disorders	616.85

Psychological tests
> *See also* Educational tests and measurements

Psychologists
> *See also* Psychiatrists

Psychology
> *See also* Adolescent psychology; Aggressiveness (Psychology); Behaviorism; Human behavior; Social psychology

Burnham, T. Mean genes	155.7
Cohen, L. J. The handy psychology answer book	150
The Oxford companion to the mind	128
Reber, A. S. The Penguin dictionary of psychology	150.3
Rogers, C. R. A way of being	150.19

Encyclopedias
Cordón, L. A. Popular psychology	150.3
The Gale encyclopedia of psychology	150.3
Psychology basics	150.3

Psychology, Comparative *See* Comparative psychology

Psychology, National *See* National characteristics

Psychology, Pathological *See* Abnormal psychology

Psychology basics	150.3

Psychology of learning
Hudmon, A. Learning and memory	153.1

Psychotherapy
Fiction
Giles, G. Right behind you	Fic
Greenberg, J. I never promised you a rose garden	Fic
Saenz, B. A. Last night I sang to the monster	Fic

Psychotropic drugs
> *See also* Antidepressants; Cocaine; Hallucinogens

Ptacek, Greg
(jt. auth) Vare, E. A. Patently female	920

PTSD *See* Post-traumatic stress disorder

Pubantz, Jerry, 1947-
(jt. auth) Moore, J. A. Encyclopedia of the United Nations	341.23

Puberty
De la Bédoyère, C. Personal hygiene and sexual health	613
Redd, N. A. Body drama	612

The **public** domain. Fishman, S.	346

Public figures *See* Celebrities

Public health
> *See also* Epidemiology
Do infectious diseases pose a threat?	614.4

Public housing
Fiction
McDonald, J. Twists and turns	Fic

Public lands
> *See also* National parks and reserves

Public libraries
Squires, T. Library partnerships	021.2
Wyatt, N. The readers' advisory guide to nonfiction	025.5

Cultural programs
> *See* Cultural programs

Public relations
Libraries
> *See* Libraries—Public relations

Public schools
Education: opposing viewpoints	371
Kozol, J. Savage inequalities	371.9

South Carolina
Conroy, P. The water is wide	371.9

Public schools and religion *See* Religion in the public schools

Public speaking
Ryan, M. Extraordinary oral presentations	808.5

Public utilities
See/See also pages in the following book(s):
Macaulay, D. Underground	624

Public welfare
How can the poor be helped?	362.5
Streissguth, T. Welfare and welfare reform	361.6

Fiction
McDonald, J. Chill wind	Fic

Publishers and publishing
Dunn, J. A teen's guide to getting published	808
Harper, E. Your name in print	808

Handbooks, manuals, etc.
The Chicago manual of style	808

Pueblo Indians
Roberts, D. In search of the old ones	970.004

Q

Qaeda (Organization) *See* Al Qaeda (Organization)

Qamar, Amjed
Beneath my mother's feet   Fic

Quakers *See* Society of Friends

Quammen, David, 1948-
The reluctant Mr. Darwin   92
(ed) Darwin, C. On the origin of species   576.8

Quantity cooking
See also Food service

Quantum man [biography of Richard Feynman] Krauss, L. M.   92

Quantum theory
Ford, K. W. 101 quantum questions   530.1
Hakim, J. The story of science: Einstein adds a new dimension   509
Hawking, S. W. The grand design   530.1
Hawking, S. W. The nature of space and time   530.1
Hawking, S. W. The universe in a nutshell   530.1
Kakalios, J. The amazing story of quantum mechanics   530.1
Orzel, C. How to teach physics to your dog   530.1
Rigden, J. S. Einstein 1905   530.1
See/See also pages in the following book(s):
Feynman, R. P. Six easy pieces   530
Graphic novels
Ottaviani, J. Suspended in language [biography of Niels Bohr]   92

Quay, Sara E.
Westward expansion   978

Québec (Province)
Fiction
Polak, M. The middle of everywhere   Fic

Queen, Edward L.
Encyclopedia of American religious history   200.9

Queen Anne's War, 1702-1713 *See* United States—History—1702-1713, Queen Anne's War

The **queen** of cool. Castellucci, C.   Fic
Queen of secrets. Meyerhoff, J.   Fic
The **Queen** of Water. Resau, L.   Fic

Queens
See also names of queens and countries with the subdivision *Kings and rulers*
Burstein, S. M. The reign of Cleopatra   92
Elizabeth, Queen of England. Elizabeth I   92
Lever, E. Marie Antoinette   92
Nardo, D. Cleopatra   92
Roller, D. W. Cleopatra   92
Sapet, K. Eleanor of Aquitaine   92
Starkey, D. Six wives: the queens of Henry VIII   920
Fiction
Friesner, E. M. Sphinx's princess   Fic
Libby, A. M. The king's rose   Fic
Meyer, C. Duchessina   Fic

The **queen's** daughter. Coventry, S.   Fic

Questions and answers
See also Examinations

Quick, Barbara
A golden web   Fic

Quick, Matthew, 1973-
Sorta like a rockstar   Fic

Quick and popular reads for teens   028.5
Quick cash for teens. Bielagus, P. G.   658.1
The **quick** Internet guide to career and college information. See Wolfinger, A. Best career and education web sites   025.04

Quicksand   616.97

Quilting
Beyer, J. Quiltmaking by hand   746.46

Quilting the black-eyed pea. Giovanni, N.   811
Quiltmaking by hand. Beyer, J.   746.46

Quilts
Tobin, J. Hidden in plain view   973.7

Quinceañera (Social custom)
Alvarez, J. Once upon a quinceañera   392
Fifteen candles   392
Fiction
Alegría, M. Estrella's quinceanera   Fic
Chambers, V. Fifteen candles   Fic

Quinn, Edward, 1932-
Critical companion to George Orwell   828
A dictionary of literary and thematic terms   803

Quinn, Spencer *See* Abrahams, Peter, 1947-

Quintana, Leroy V.
(ed) Paper dance. See Paper dance   811.008

Quintero, Sofia
Efrain's secret   Fic

Quitely, Frank, 1968-
(il) Morrison, G. All-Star Superman, Volume One   741.5

The **Quotable** saint   230
The **Quotable** woman, revised edition   305.4

Quotations
See also Proverbs
Andrews, R. Famous lines   808.88
Bartlett, J. Bartlett's familiar quotations   808.88
The Columbia Granger's dictionary of poetry quotations   808.88
Concise Oxford dictionary of quotations   808.88
Contemporary quotations in black   808.88
The Founders on religion   200
The Girls' book of wisdom   808.88
Oxford dictionary of humorous quotations   808.88
Oxford dictionary of modern quotations   808.88
Oxford dictionary of phrase, saying, and quotation   808.88
Oxford dictionary of quotations   808.88
Oxford dictionary of scientific quotations   500
The Quotable woman, revised edition   305.4
Quotations for all occasions   808.88
Science fiction quotations   808.88

Rape—*Continued*
Fiction
Anderson, L. H. Speak   **Fic**
Davis, A. Wonder when you'll miss me   **Fic**
Lipsyte, R. Raiders night   **Fic**
Lynch, C. Inexcusable   **Fic**
Porter, C. R. Imani all mine   **Fic**
Shaw, S. Safe   **Fic**
Whitney, D. The Mockingbirds   **Fic**

Raphael, Ray
A people's history of the American Revolution   **973.3**

Rapp, Adam
Punkzilla   **Fic**
Under the wolf, under the dog   **Fic**

Rapp, Emily
Poster child   **92**

Rapport, Richard
Nerve endings   **612.8**

Rare animals
   See also Endangered species
McGavin, G. Endangered   **578.68**

Rare plants
   See also Endangered species

Raschka, Christopher
(il) A Poke in the I. See A Poke in the I   **811.008**
(il) Thomas, D. A child's Christmas in Wales   **828**

Rashid, Ahmed
Taliban   **958.1**

Raskin, Jamin B., 1962-
We the students   **344**

Rasmussen, R. Kent
Bloom's how to write about Mark Twain   **818**
Critical companion to Mark Twain   **818**
(ed) American Indian tribes. See American Indian tribes   **970.004**

Rasputin, Grigoriĭ Efimovich, 1871-1916
Fiction
Whitcomb, L. The Fetch   **Fic**

Rat life. Arnold, T.   **Fic**

Ratcliffe, Susan
(ed) Concise Oxford dictionary of quotations. See Concise Oxford dictionary of quotations   **808.88**
(ed) Oxford dictionary of phrase, saying, and quotation. See Oxford dictionary of phrase, saying, and quotation   **808.88**

Rather, Dan
The American dream   **973.92**

Rationalism
   See also Enlightenment

Ratliff, Gerald Lee
(ed) Millennium monologs. See Millennium monologs   **812.008**

Rats
Sullivan, R. Rats: observations on the history and habitat of the city's most unwanted inhabitants   **599.3**

Fiction
Pratchett, T. The amazing Maurice and his educated rodents   **Fic**

Rats: observations on the history and habitat of the city's most unwanted inhabitants. Sullivan, R.   **599.3**

Rats saw God. Thomas, R.   **Fic**

Rauf, Don
(jt. auth) Reeves, D. L. Career ideas for teens in architecture and construction   **624**

Rause, Vince
(jt. auth) Parrado, N. Miracle in the Andes   **982**

Ravel, Edeet
The saver   **Fic**

Raven, Catherine, 1959-
Forestry   **634.9**

Raven, Nicky
Bram Stoker's Dracula   **741.5**

The Raven duet [series]
Bell, H. Trickster's girl   **Fic**

Raven summer. Almond, D.   **Fic**

Ravilious, Kate
Power   **179**

Rawles, Nancy, 1958-
My Jim   **Fic**

Ray Bradbury's Fahrenheit 451. Hamilton, T.   **741.5**

Raymo, Chet
Walking zero   **526**

Rayne Tour series
Collins, B. Always watching   **Fic**

Razzell, Mary, 1930-
Snow apples   **Fic**

Re-designing the high school library for the forgotten half. Thomas, M. J. K.   **027.8**

Reaching out. Jiménez, F.   **Fic**

Reaction (Political science) *See* Right and left (Political science)

Read, Piers Paul, 1941-
Alive   **910.4**

Read all about it!   **808.8**

Read on . . . fantasy fiction. Hollands, N.   **016.8**

Read on series
Hollands, N. Read on . . . fantasy fiction   **016.8**

Reader, John, 1937-
Africa: a biography of the continent   **960**

The **readers'** advisory guide to genre fiction. Saricks, J. G.   **025.5**

The **readers'** advisory guide to graphic novels. Goldsmith, F.   **025.2**

The **readers'** advisory guide to nonfiction. Wyatt, N.   **025.5**

Reader's Digest complete do-it-yourself manual. See Complete do-it-yourself manual   **643**

The **Reader's** encyclopedia of the American West. See The New encyclopedia of the American West   **978.03**

A **reader's** guide to Lorraine Hansberry's A raisin in the sun. Loos, P.   **812.009**

A **reader's** guide to Marjane Satrapi's Persepolis. Schroeder, H. L.   **813.009**

A **reader's** guide to Zora Neale Hurston's Their eyes were watching god. Litwin, L. B.   **813.009**

Readicker-Henderson, Ed
A short history of the honey bee   **638**

Reading
Bernadowski, C. Research-based reading strategies in the library for adolescent learners   **372.4**

Remedial teaching
Rosow, L. V. Accessing the classics   **011.6**

Reading Chekhov. Malcolm, J.   **891.7**

Reading comics. Wolk, D.   **741.5**

Reading interests of children See Children—Books and reading

Reading like a writer. Prose, F.   **808**

Reading rants. Hubert, J.   **011.6**

Ready, Jeri Smith- See Smith-Ready, Jeri

Reagan, Ronald, 1911-2004
About
Schaller, M. Ronald Reagan   **92**
Sutherland, J. Ronald Reagan   **92**
Graphic novels
Helfer, A. Ronald Reagan   **92**

Reagon, Bernice Johnson, 1942-
(ed) We'll understand it better by and by. See We'll understand it better by and by   **782.25**

The **real** Alice in Wonderland [biography of Alice Pleasance Liddell Hargreaves] Rubin, C. M.   **92**

The **real** Benedict Arnold. Murphy, J.   **92**

The **real** Fidel Castro. Coltman, Sir L.   **92**

Real-life math. Glazer, E.   **510**

The **real** revolution. Aronson, M.   **973.3**

Real sports reporting   **070.4**

Real time. Kass, P.   **Fic**

Real voices, real history series
Voices from the Trail of Tears   **970.004**

Real, volume 1. Inoue, T.   **741.5**

Real world (Television program)
Graphic novels
Winick, J. Pedro & me   **362.1**

Reality check. Abrahams, P.   **Fic**

Reality rules!. Fraser, E.   **028.5**

Reallionaire. Gray, F.   **332.024**

Reardon, John F.
(jt. auth) Rooney, J. J. Preparing for college   **378.1**

Reasoner, James, 1953-
Manassas   **Fic**

Reaves, Michael
(jt. auth) Gaiman, N. Interworld   **Fic**

Reavill, Gil, 1953-
(jt. auth) Swan, R. Antarctica 2041   **577.5**

Rebel for the hell of it [biography of Tupac Shakur] White, A.   **92**

Rebels and renegades. Hamilton, N. A.   **322.4**

Reber, Arthur S.
The Penguin dictionary of psychology   **150.3**

Reber, Deborah
In their shoes   **331.4**
(comp) Chicken soup for the teenage soul's the real deal. See Chicken soup for the teenage soul's the real deal   **158**

Reber, Emily S., 1969-
(jt. auth) Reber, A. S. The Penguin dictionary of psychology   **150.3**

A **recent** history of the United States in political cartoons. Bok, C.   **973.92**

Recipes See Cooking

Recitations See Monologues

Recommended reference books for small and medium-sized libraries and media centers, Vol. 30   **011**

Reconstruction (1865-1876)
See also Ku Klux Klan
Barney, W. L. The Civil War and Reconstruction   **973.7**
Bartoletti, S. C. They called themselves the K.K.K.   **322.4**
Bolden, T. Cause: Reconstruction America, 1863-1877   **973.7**
Browne, R. B. The Civil War and Reconstruction   **973.7**
Carlisle, R. P. Civil War and Reconstruction   **973.7**
Foner, E. Forever free   **973.8**
Grumet, B. H. Reconstruction era: primary sources   **973.8**
Hansen, J. Bury me not in a land of slaves   **973.8**
Matuz, R. Reconstruction era: biographies   **920**
Osborne, L. B. Traveling the freedom road   **973.7**
Reconstruction   **973.8**

Reconstruction   **973.8**

Reconstruction Era reference library [series]
Grumet, B. H. Reconstruction era: primary sources   **973.8**
Matuz, R. Reconstruction era: biographies   **920**

Recordings, Sound See Sound recordings

Records, World See World records

Recovery Road. Nelson, B.   **Fic**

Recreation
See also Amusements
Encyclopedias
Encyclopedia of recreation and leisure in America   **790**

Recreational Ritalin. Walker, I.   **362.29**

Recycle. Gardner, R.   **628.4**

Recycling
Garbage and recycling: opposing viewpoints   **363.7**
Gardner, R. Recycle   **628.4**
Maczulak, A. E. Waste treatment   **628.4**
Miller, D. A. Garbage and recycling   **363.7**
Fiction
Bacigalupi, P. Ship breaker   **Fic**

The **red** badge of courage. Crane, S.   **Fic**

Red Bird *See* Zitkala-Ša, 1876-1938

Red Cloud, Sioux Chief, 1822-1909
See/See also pages in the following book(s):
Brown, D. A. Bury my heart at Wounded Knee
   970.004
   Freedman, R. Indian chiefs   **920**

Red glass. Resau, L.   **Fic**

Red hot salsa   **811.008**

The **red** hourglass. Grice, G.   **591.5**

Red Mars. Robinson, K. S.   **Fic**

Red moon at Sharpsburg. Wells, R.   **Fic**

The **red** necklace. Gardner, S.   **Fic**

Red scarf girl. Jiang, J.-l.   **951.05**

Red spikes. Lanagan, M.   **S C**

Redd, Nancy Amanda
Body drama   **612**

Redford, Donald B.
(ed) The Oxford encyclopedia of ancient Egypt.
   See The Oxford encyclopedia of ancient
   Egypt   **932**

Redmond, Ian
The primate family tree   **599.8**

Reducing *See* Weight loss

Redwood
Preston, R. The wild trees   **577.3**

Reece, Erik
Lost mountain   **622**

Reed, Arthea J. S.
Norma Fox Mazer   **813.009**

Reed, Ishmael, 1938-
(ed) From totems to hip-hop. See From totems
   to hip-hop   **811.008**

Reed, Walter, 1851-1902
            About
Jurmain, S. The secret of the yellow death
   614.5
Pierce, J. R. Yellow jack   **614.5**

Reeder, Dan, 1950-
Papier-mache monsters   **745.54**

Reef, Catherine
African Americans in the military   **920.003**
E. E. Cummings   **92**
Ernest Hemingway   **92**
John Steinbeck   **92**
This our dark country   **966.62**
Walt Whitman   **92**
Working in America   **331**
(jt. auth) Bader, P. African-American writers
   920.003

Reel v. real. Sanello, F.   **791.43**

Reep, Roger L.
The Florida manatee   **599.5**

Rees, Celia, 1949-
The fool's girl   **Fic**
Pirates!   **Fic**
Sovay   **Fic**

Rees, Martin J., 1942-
(ed) Universe. See Universe   **520**

Reesor, David
(jt. auth) Ross, M. Predator   **599.7**

Reeve, Philip, 1966-
Fever Crumb   **Fic**
Here lies Arthur   **Fic**

Reeves, Bass, 1838-1910
See/See also pages in the following book(s):
Abdul-Jabbar, K. Black profiles in courage
   920

Reeves, Dia
Slice of cherry   **Fic**

Reeves, Diane Lindsey, 1959-
Career ideas for teens in architecture and construction   **624**
Career ideas for teens in education and training
   331.7

Reeves, Ellen Gordon
Can I wear my nose ring to the interview?
   650.14

Reeves, Richard, 1936-
A force of nature [biography of Ernest Ruther-
   ford]   **92**

Reference books
100 great journeys   **910.2**
Aaseng, N. African-American athletes
   920.003
Abrahams, P. H. McMinn's clinical atlas of hu-
   man anatomy   **611**
Abrams, M. H. A glossary of literary terms
   803
Adelson-Goldstein, J. Oxford picture dictionary
   495.7
Adonis to Zorro   **422.03**
Africa: an encyclopedia for students   **960**
The African American almanac   **305.8**
African American biographies   **920.003**
The African American national biography
   920.003
Africana: the encyclopedia of the African and
   African American experience   **909**
Al-Hazza, T. C. Books about the Middle East
   016.3058
Alderton, D. Encyclopedia of aquarium & pond
   fish   **639.34**
Allaby, M. A chronology of weather   **551.5**
Allaby, M. The encyclopedia of Earth   **910**
Allaby, M. Encyclopedia of weather and climate
   551
America in world history   **973**
American authors, 1600-1900   **920.003**
The American book of days   **394.26**
American Civil War   **973.7**
American eras   **973**
The American Heritage abbreviations dictionary
   423
The American Heritage dictionary of phrasal
   verbs   **423**
The American Heritage science dictionary
   503
American Indian biographies   **920.003**
American national biography   **920.003**
American Psychological Association. Concise
   rules of APA style   **808**
American reference books annual 2010 edition,
   volume 41   **011**
American Revolutionary War   **973.3**
American women writers, 1900-1945   **810.9**

Reference books—*Continued*

Religion in twentieth century America. Balmer, R. H.   **200.9**

Religions

    See also Gods and goddesses; Occultism; Sects

Bowker, J. World religions   **200**
Breuilly, E. Religions of the world   **200**
The Cambridge illustrated history of religions   **200.9**

Frazer, Sir J. G. The new golden bough   **201**

Introduction to the world's major religions   **200**

Milestone documents of world religions   **200**
World religions   **200**

    Encyclopedias

Encyclopedia of religious rites, rituals, and festivals   **203**
The encyclopedia of world religions   **200.3**

    Maps

Atlas of the world's religions   **201**

Religions and religious movements [series]
Confucianism   **299.5**

Religions of Africa. Friedenthal, L.   **200.9**

Religions of the world. Breuilly, E.   **200**

Religious art

    See also Christian art
Campbell, J. The power of myth   **201**

Religious belief *See* Faith

Religious biography
Ellsberg, R. Blessed among all women   **920**
    Encyclopedias
Holy people of the world   **920.003**

Religious ceremonies *See* Rites and ceremonies

Religious cults *See* Cults

Religious freedom *See* Freedom of religion

Religious fundamentalism

    See also Islamic fundamentalism
Armstrong, K. The battle for God   **200**

Religious holidays
Religious holidays and calendars   **203**

Religious holidays and calendars   **203**

Religious life
    Fiction
Howell, S. Everything beautiful   **Fic**

Religious literature

    See also Christian fiction

Religious poetry
American religious poems   **811.008**
Spires, E. I heard God talking to me   **811**
    Collections
Chapters into verse   **821.008**

Relocation of Japanese Americans, 1942-1945
    See Japanese Americans—Evacuation and relocation, 1942-1945

The **relocation** of the North American Indian. Dunn, J. M.   **970.004**

The **reluctant** Mr. Darwin. Quammen, D.   **92**

Remarkable creatures. Carroll, S. B.   **508**

Remarque, Erich Maria, 1898-1970
All quiet on the western front   **Fic**

    About
Erich Maria Remarque's All quiet on the western front [critical essays]   **833.009**

Remarriage
    Fiction
Martin, C. K. K. The lighter side of life and death   **Fic**

Rembrandt Harmenszoon van Rijn, 1606-1669
    Fiction
Cullen, L. I am Rembrandt's daughter   **Fic**

Remembering Raquel. Vande Velde, V.   **Fic**

Remini, Robert Vincent, 1921-
Andrew Jackson   **92**
The House: the history of the House of Representatives   **328.73**
Joseph Smith   **92**
(ed) Fellow citizens. See Fellow citizens   **352.23**

Remley, David A.
Kit Carson   **92**

Remnick, David
King of the world: Muhammad Ali and the rise of an American hero   **92**

Renaissance

    See also World history—15th century; World history—16th century
Cohen, E. S. Daily life in Renaissance Italy   **945**

The European Renaissance and Reformation, 1350-1600   **940.2**
Extraordinary women of the Medieval and Renaissance world   **920.003**
Great events from history, The Renaissance & early modern era, 1454-1600   **909**
Great lives from history, the Renaissance & early modern era, 1454-1600   **920.003**
Hinds, K. Everyday life in the Renaissance   **940.2**
Reformation, exploration, and empire   **909**
The Renaissance [Greenhaven Press]   **940.2**
Renaissance & Reformation: almanac   **940.2**
Renaissance & Reformation: biographies   **920**
Renaissance & Reformation: primary sources   **940.2**
Sider, S. Handbook to life in Renaissance Europe   **940.2**
See/See also pages in the following book(s):
Highet, G. The classical tradition   **809**
    Encyclopedias
The Renaissance   **940.2**
Renaissance and Reformation   **940.2**
Streissguth, T. The Renaissance   **940.2**

The **Renaissance**   **940.2**

The **Renaissance**. Streissguth, T.   **940.2**

The **Renaissance** [Greenhaven Press]   **940.2**

Renaissance & Reformation: almanac   **940.2**

Renaissance & Reformation: biographies   **920**

Renaissance & Reformation: primary sources   **940.2**

Renaissance & Reformation reference library [series]
Renaissance & Reformation: almanac   **940.2**
Renaissance & Reformation: biographies   **920**

The **ring** of Solomon. Stroud, J.   **Fic**

Ringo, John, 1844-1882
Fiction
  Bull, E. Territory   **Fic**

Ringside. Beekman, S.   **796.8**

Ringside, 1925. Bryant, J.   **Fic**

Ringworld. Niven, L.   **Fic**

Riordan, James, 1936-
  The sniper   **Fic**

Riot grrrl movement
  Marcus, S. Girls to the front   **781.66**

Riots
  Mara, W. Civil unrest in the 1960s   **303.6**

Ripken, Billy
  (jt. auth) Ripken, C., Jr. Play baseball the Ripken way   **796.357**

Ripken, Cal, Jr.
  The only way I know   **92**
  Play baseball the Ripken way   **796.357**

The **rise** and fall of Senator Joe McCarthy. Giblin, J.   **92**

The **rise** and fall of the British Empire. James, L.   **909**

Rising voices   **810.8**

Risk-taking (Psychology)
  Braun, L. W. Risky business   **027.62**
  Hugel, B. I did it without thinking   **155.5**

Risking everything   **808.81**

Risky business. Braun, L. W.   **027.62**

Ritalin
  Walker, I. Recreational Ritalin   **362.29**

Ritchie, David, 1952-
  (jt. auth) Gates, A. E. Encyclopedia of earthquakes and volcanoes   **551.2**

Rites and ceremonies
  Beker, J. The big night out   **646.7**
  Encyclopedia of religious rites, rituals, and festivals   **203**
  Hill, J. Life events and rites of passage   **306**
  How to be a perfect stranger   **203**

Ritter, John H., 1951-
  Under the baseball moon   **Fic**

Rittner, Don
  Encyclopedia of biology   **570.3**
  Encyclopedia of chemistry   **540.3**

Ritual See Rites and ceremonies

Ritz, David
  (jt. auth) King, B. B. Blues all around me   **92**
  (jt. auth) Lang, L. Journey of a thousand miles   **92**

Rival. Bennett Wealer, S.   **Fic**

The **rivals.** Sheridan, R. B.   **822**

The **river.** Beaufrand, M. J.   **Fic**

The **river** between us. Peck, R.   **Fic**

River house. Lawrence, S.   **92**

Rivera, Diego, 1886-1957
Poetry
  Bernier-Grand, C. T. Diego   **811**

Rivera, Frida Kahlo See Kahlo, Frida, 1907-1954

Rivers
  See also Mississippi River
  Burnham, L. Rivers   **551.48**
  Collier, M. Over the rivers   **551.48**
Fiction
  Mills, T. Heartbreak river   **Fic**

Rivers of blood, rivers of gold. Cocker, M.   **909**

Rivkin, Andrew S., 1969-
  Asteroids, comets, and dwarf planets   **523.2**
  (jt. auth) Grier, J. A. Inner planets   **523.4**

RNA
  Hall, L. E. DNA and RNA   **611**

Ro, Ronin
  Dr. Dre   **92**

Roach, David A.
  (ed) The Superhero book. See The Superhero book   **741.5**

Roach, Mary
  Packing for Mars   **571**
  Spook   **133.9**
  Stiff   **611**

The **road.** McCarthy, C.   **Fic**

The **road** of the dead. Brooks, K.   **Fic**

The **road** to Communism. Gottfried, T.   **947**

Roanoke Island (N.C.)
History
  Miller, L. Roanoke   **975.6**
History—Fiction
  Klein, L. M. Cate of the Lost Colony   **Fic**

The **roaring** twenties. Streissguth, T.   **973.91**

Roark, Elisabeth Louise
  Artists of colonial America   **709.73**

Robbers and outlaws See Thieves

Robbers, rogues, and ruffians. Bryan, H.   **978.9**

Robbins, Alexandra, 1976-
  The overachievers   **305.23**

Robert, Henry Martyn, 1837-1923
  Robert's Rules of order newly revised   **060.4**

Robert, Sarah Corbin
  (ed) Robert, H. M. Robert's Rules of order newly revised   **060.4**

Robert Browning's poetry. Browning, R.   **821**

Robert E. Lee. Blount, R.   **92**

Robert Mugabe's Zimbabwe. Arnold, J. R.   **968.91**

Roberts, Alice, 1973-
  (ed) The complete human body. See The complete human body   **612**

Roberts, Andrew Lawrence, 1970-
  The thinking student's guide to college   **378.1**

Roberts, David, 1943-
  In search of the old ones   **970.004**

Roberts, Jason
  A sense of the world [biography of James Holman]   **92**

Roberts, Jeremy, 1956-
  Bob Dylan: voice of a generation   **92**
  Chinese mythology A to Z   **299.5**
  Japanese mythology A to Z   **299.5**

Roberts, Jeremy, 1956-—*Continued*
(jt. auth) Lynch, P. A. African mythology, A to Z **299.6**

Roberts, Jordan
(jt. auth) Jacquet, L. March of the penguins **598**

Roberts, Priscilla Mary
(ed) The encyclopedia of Middle East wars. See The encyclopedia of Middle East wars **355**
(ed) The encyclopedia of the Arab-Israeli conflict. See The encyclopedia of the Arab-Israeli conflict **956.94**
(ed) World War I: a student encyclopedia. See World War I: a student encyclopedia **940.3**
(ed) World War II: a student encyclopedia. See World War II: a student encyclopedia **940.53**

Roberts, Randy, 1951-
A line in the sand **976.4**

Roberts, Robin
(jt. auth) Lieberman, N. Basketball for women **796.323**

Roberts ridge. MacPherson, M. C. **958.1**

Robert's Rules in plain English. Zimmerman, D. P. **060.4**

Robertshaw, Peter
(jt. auth) Rubalcaba, J. Every bone tells a story **930.1**

Robertson, James I., Jr.
Robert E. Lee **92**

Robertson, Robin
Vegan planet **641.5**

Robin Hood (Fictional character)
Lee, T. Outlaw: the legend of Robin Hood **741.5**

Robinson, Adam
Cracking the SAT **378.1**
(jt. auth) Amend, A. Cracking the SAT. Literature subject test **800**
(jt. auth) Rubenstein, J. Cracking the PSAT, NMSQT **378.1**

Robinson, Andrew, 1957-
The story of measurement **530.8**

Robinson, Francis
(ed) The Cambridge illustrated history of the Islamic world. See The Cambridge illustrated history of the Islamic world **909**

Robinson, George
Essential Judaism **296**

Robinson, Greg, 1966-
By order of the president **940.53**

Robinson, Jackie, 1919-1972
I never had it made **92**
About
Fussman, C. After Jackie [biography of Jackie Robinson] **92**

Robinson, Jo Ann, 1942-
(ed) Affirmative action. See Affirmative action [Greenwood Press] **331.1**

Robinson, Kim Stanley
Forty signs of rain **Fic**

Red Mars **Fic**

Robinson, Phillip T.
Life at the zoo: behind the scenes with the animal doctors **590.73**

Robinson Crusoe. Defoe, D. **Fic**

Robison, John Elder, 1957-
Look me in the eye **92**

Robo world [biography of Cynthia Breazeal] Brown, J. **92**

Robot series
Asimov, I. I, robot **S C**

Robotics *See* Robots

Robots
Brooks, R. A. Flesh and machines **629.8**
Brown, J. Robo world [biography of Cynthia Breazeal] **92**
Henderson, H. Modern robotics **629.8**
Fiction
Asimov, I. I, robot **S C**
Dolamore, J. Magic under glass **Fic**
Graphic novels
Urasawa, N. Pluto: Urasawa x Tezuka, vol. 1 **741.5**
Models
Perdana, J. Build your own paper robots **745.54**

Robson, Claire, 1949-
(ed) Outside rules. See Outside rules **S C**

Robson, David, 1966-
Auschwitz **940.53**
Disaster response **363.34**
Encounters with vampires **398**

Rochman, Hazel
(ed) Leaving home: stories. See Leaving home: stories **808.8**
(comp) Who do you think you are? See Who do you think you are? **S C**

Rock & Roll Hall of Fame and Museum
Talevski, N. The unofficial encyclopedia of the Rock and Roll Hall of Fame **781.66**
Rock and roll is here to stay **781.66**

Rock and roll music *See* Rock music

The **rock** and the river. Magoon, K. **Fic**

Rock climbing. Mellor, D. **796.522**

Rock music
See also Christian rock music; Punk rock music
Rock and roll is here to stay **781.66**
The Rolling Stone illustrated history of rock & roll **781.66**
Talevski, N. The unofficial encyclopedia of the Rock and Roll Hall of Fame **781.66**
Fiction
Brothers, M. Debbie Harry sings in French **Fic**
Collins, B. Always watching **Fic**
Ehrenhaft, D. Friend is not a verb **Fic**
Franklin, E. The half life of planets **Fic**
Kelly, T. Harmonic feedback **Fic**
Kidd, R. On Beale Street **Fic**
Krovatin, C. Heavy metal and you **Fic**
Nelson, B. Rock star, superstar **Fic**

Rolland, Jacques L., 1945-
The food encyclopedia   **641.03**
Roller, Duane W.
Cleopatra   **92**
Roller skating
   See also Skateboarding
Rollerblading *See* In-line skating
Rollin, Nicholas
(ed) The concise Oxford Spanish dictionary. See
The concise Oxford Spanish dictionary
   463
(ed) The Oxford-Hachette French dictionary. See
The Oxford-Hachette French dictionary
   443
(ed) The Oxford Spanish dictionary. See The
Oxford Spanish dictionary   **463**
The **Rolling** Stone illustrated history of rock &
roll   **781.66**
Rolls, Albert
(ed) World authors, 2000-2005. See World au-
thors, 2000-2005   **920.003**
Rollyson, Carl
Critical companion to Herman Melville
   813.009
Rollyson, Carl E. (Carl Edmund)
(ed) Critical survey of drama. See Critical sur-
vey of drama   **809.2**
Roman, Dave
Agnes Quill   **741.5**
Roman, Luke
Encyclopedia of Greek and Roman mythology
   292
Roman, Monica
(jt. auth) Roman, L. Encyclopedia of Greek and
Roman mythology   **292**
Roman architecture
Macaulay, D. City: a story of Roman planning
and construction   **711**
      Encyclopedias
The Grove encyclopedia of classical art and ar-
chitecture   **722**
Roman art
Allan, T. Life, myth, and art in Ancient Rome
   937
      Encyclopedias
The Grove encyclopedia of classical art and ar-
chitecture   **722**
Roman Catholic Church *See* Catholic Church
Roman cooking
Grant, M. Roman cookery   **641.5**
Roman Empire *See* Rome
Roman mythology
Allan, T. Life, myth, and art in Ancient Rome
   937
The **Roman** poets   **871.008**
The **Roman** way. Hamilton, E.   **870.9**
Romance graphic novels
Nakahara, A. Love*Com Vol. 1   **741.5**
Obata, Y. We were there, vol. 1   **741.5**
Sfar, J. The professor's daughter   **741.5**
Stolarz, L. F. Black is for beginnings   **741.5**
Zahler, T. F. Love and capes, vol. 1   **741.5**
Romance novels *See* Love stories

Romances
   See also Arthurian romances
   See/See also pages in the following book(s):
Highet, G. The classical tradition   **809**
Romano, Amy, 1978-
A historical atlas of Afghanistan   **958.1**
Romanov, Nikolaï *See* Nicholas II, Emperor of
Russia, 1868-1918
Romanov, House of *See* House of Romanov
The **Romanovs**. Massie, R. K.   **947.08**
Romanticism
Encyclopedia of the romantic era, 1760-1850
   700
Romanticism and transcendentalism   **810.9**
Romanticism and transcendentalism   **810.9**
Rombauer, Irma von Starkloff, 1877-1962
Joy of cooking   **641.5**
Rome
      Antiquities
Allan, T. Life, myth, and art in Ancient Rome
   937
      Biography
Baker, R. F. Ancient Romans   **937**
      Civilization
Adkins, L. Handbook to life in ancient Rome
   937
Allan, T. Life, myth, and art in Ancient Rome
   937
Hamilton, E. The Roman way   **870.9**
See/See also pages in the following book(s):
Russell, B. A history of Western philosophy
   109
      History
Baker, R. F. Ancient Romans   **937**
Caesar, J. The Gallic War   **878**
The Cambridge illustrated history of the Roman
world   **937**
Ermatinger, J. W. The decline and fall of the
Roman Empire   **937**
Hinds, K. Everyday life in the Roman Empire
   937
      History—Encyclopedias
Bunson, M. Encyclopedia of the Roman Empire
   937
      History—Fiction
Dray, S. Lily of the Nile   **Fic**
Graves, R. I, Claudius   **Fic**
Harris, R. Pompeii   **Fic**
      Religion—Dictionaries
Adkins, L. Dictionary of Roman religion
   292
      Social life and customs
Adkins, L. Handbook to life in ancient Rome
   937
Aldrete, G. S. Daily life in the Roman city
   937
Rome (Italy)
Foster, B. Rome   **809**
Romeo and Juliet. Appignanesi, R.   **822.3**
Romeo and Juliet. Shakespeare, W.   **822.3**

Romeo and Juliet [criticism] Bloom, H., ed **822.3**
Romeo and Juliet [criticism] Naden, C. J.
   822.3

Russell, Geoff
Mini encyclopedia of rabbit breeds & care
636.9

Russell, Patricia Yates, 1937-
(jt. auth) Garcha, R. The world of Islam in literature for youth **016.3058**

Russell, Roy, 1954-
(ed) The Oxford Spanish dictionary. See The Oxford Spanish dictionary **463**

Russell, S. S.
(jt. auth) Smith, C. Meteorites **523.5**

Russell, Sharon A.
Revisiting Stephen King **813.009**
Stephen King: a critical companion **813.009**

Russell Baker's book of American humor
817.008

Russia
See also Soviet Union
Fiction
Chekhov, A. P. The Russian master and other stories **S C**
Dostoyevsky, F. Crime and punishment **Fic**
Holub, J. An innocent soldier **Fic**
Malamud, B. The fixer **Fic**
Tolstoy, L., graf. Anna Karenina **Fic**
Tolstoy, L., graf. Great short works of Leo Tolstoy **S C**
History
Kort, M. A brief history of Russia **947**
Riasanovsky, N. V. A history of Russia **947**
Kings and rulers
Massie, R. K. The Romanovs **947.08**
Whitelaw, N. Catherine the Great and the Enlightenment in Russia **92**

Russia (Federation)
See also Russia; Soviet Union

Russian Americans
Fiction
Gelbwasser, M. Inconvenient **Fic**

Russian Empire *See* Russia

Russian language
Dictionaries
Oxford Russian dictionary **491.7**

Russian literature
Collections
The Portable nineteenth-century Russian reader
891.7
The Portable twentieth-century Russian reader
891.7
Dictionaries
Handbook of Russian literature **891.7**
The **Russian** master and other stories. Chekhov, A. P. **S C**

Russian revolution *See* Soviet Union—History—1917-1921, Revolution

Russians
Fiction
Castellucci, C. Rose sees red **Fic**

Russon, Anne E.
Orangutans: wizards of the rainforest **599.8**

Rustin, Bayard, 1910-1987
About
Miller, C. C. No easy answers [biography of Bayard Rustin] **92**

Rutberg, Jim
(jt. auth) Carmichael, C. The ultimate ride
796.6

Ruth, Babe, 1895-1948
About
Hampton, W. Babe Ruth **92**

Ruth, George Herman *See* Ruth, Babe, 1895-1948

Ruth, Greg
(il) Golden, C. The wild **Fic**

Ruth, Janice E.
Women of the suffrage movement **324.6**

Rutherford, Ernest, 1871-1937
About
Reeves, R. A force of nature [biography of Ernest Rutherford] **92**
See/See also pages in the following book(s):
Cropper, W. H. Great physicists **920**

Ruud, Jay
Critical companion to Dante **850.9**
Encyclopedia of medieval literature **809**

Rwanda
Hatzfeld, J. Machete season **967.571**
Kinzer, S. A thousand hills [biography of Paul Kagame] **967.571**
Rusesabagina, P. An ordinary man **92**
The Rwandan genocide **967.571**
Fiction
Combres, E. Broken memory **Fic**
Jansen, H. Over a thousand hills I walk with you **Fic**
Graphic novels
Stassen, J.-P. Deogratias **741.5**
Politics and government
Gourevitch, P. We wish to inform you that tomorrow we will be killed with our families
967.571

The **Rwandan** genocide **967.571**

Ryan, Amy Kathleen
Zen & Xander undone **Fic**

Ryan, Bryan
(ed) U-X-L Hispanic American almanac. See U-X-L Hispanic American almanac **305.8**

Ryan, Carrie
The Forest of Hands and Teeth **Fic**

Ryan, James D.
(jt. auth) Jones, C. Encyclopedia of Hinduism
294.5

Ryan, Margaret, 1950-
Extraordinary oral presentations **808.5**

Ryan, Patrick, 1965-
Gemini bites **Fic**
In Mike we trust **Fic**

Ryerson, Richard Alan, 1942-
(ed) American Revolutionary War. See American Revolutionary War **973.3**

Rynck, Patrick de, 1963-
(ed) How to read a painting. See How to read a painting **753**

S

S.A.T. *See* Scholastic Assessment Test

Saadawi, Nawal el- *See* El-Saadawi, Nawal

Saari, Aaron Maurice
(ed) Renaissance & Reformation: almanac. See Renaissance & Reformation: almanac **940.2**
(ed) Renaissance & Reformation: biographies. See Renaissance & Reformation: biographies **920**
(ed) Renaissance & Reformation: primary sources. See Renaissance & Reformation: primary sources **940.2**

Saari, Peggy
Colonial America: almanac **973.2**
Colonial America: primary sources **973.2**
(ed) Renaissance & Reformation: almanac. See Renaissance & Reformation: almanac **940.2**
(ed) Renaissance & Reformation: biographies. See Renaissance & Reformation: biographies **920**
(ed) Renaissance & Reformation: primary sources. See Renaissance & Reformation: primary sources **940.2**

Saavedra, Miguel de Cervantes *See* Cervantes Saavedra, Miguel de, 1547-1616

Sabin, Albert
See/See also pages in the following book(s):
Hellman, H. Great feuds in medicine **610.9**

Sabin vaccine *See* Poliomyelitis vaccine

Sable, Mark
Grounded, Vol. 1: Powerless **741.5**

Sabriel. Nix, G. **Fic**

Sacagawea, b. 1786
About
Berne, E. C. Sacagawea **92**
Nelson, W. D. Interpreters with Lewis and Clark: the story of Sacagawea and Toussaint Charbonneau **92**
Fiction
Bruchac, J. Sacajawea **Fic**

Sacajawea *See* Sacagawea, b. 1786

Saccio, Peter
Shakespeare's English kings **822.3**

Sacco, Joe
Safe area Goražde **949.7**

Sachar, Louis, 1954-
The cardturner **Fic**

Sacks, David
Encyclopedia of the ancient Greek world **938.003**

Sacks, Oliver W.
Uncle Tungsten **92**

Sacred art *See* Christian art

Sacred music *See* Church music

Sacred texts [series]
Ganeri, A. The Ramayana and Hinduism **294.5**

Sa'dāwī, Nawāl *See* El-Saadawi, Nawal

Ṣaddām Hussein *See* Hussein, Ṣaddām

Sadie, Stanley
(ed) The Grove book of operas. See The Grove book of operas **792.5**

Saenz, Benjamin Alire
He forgot to say good-bye **Fic**
Last night I sang to the monster **Fic**
Sammy and Juliana in Hollywood **Fic**

Safe. Shaw, S. **Fic**

Safe area Goražde. Sacco, J. **949.7**

Safe sex 101. Hyde, M. O. **613.9**

Safe sex in AIDS prevention
Hyde, M. O. Safe sex 101 **613.9**

Safety devices
See also Accidents—Prevention

Safety education
Gervasi, L. H. Fight like a girl— and win **613.6**
Piven, J. The worst-case scenario survival handbook **613.6**

Safety measures *See* Accidents—Prevention

Safford, Barbara Ripp
Guide to reference materials for school library media centers **011.6**

Saffron sky. Asayesh, G. **92**

Safina, Carl, 1955-
Voyage of the turtle **597.92**

Safire, William
(comp) Lend me your ears. See Lend me your ears **808.85**

Sag Harbor. Whitehead, C. **Fic**

The **saga** of the bloody Benders. Geary, R. **364.152**

Sagan, Carl, 1934-1996
Broca's brain **500**
The demon-haunted world **001.9**

Sahara Desert
Description and travel
Benanav, M. Men of salt **916.6**
Fiction
Okorafor, N. The shadow speaker **Fic**

Sahel
Women writing Africa: West Africa and the Sahel **896**

Sailing
Sleight, S. New complete sailing manual **797.1**
Fiction
Herlong, M. The great wide sea **Fic**
Stevenson, R. H. A thousand shades of blue **Fic**

Sailing the wine-dark sea. Cahill, T. **909**

Sailors' life *See* Seafaring life

Saint-Exupéry, Antoine de, 1900-1944
The little prince **Fic**

Saint Iggy. Going, K. L. **Fic**

Saint Paul *See* Paul, the Apostle, Saint

Saint Petersburg (Russia)
Gorokhova, E. A mountain of crumbs **92**

Saint Valentine's Day *See* Valentine's Day

Saints
See also Christian saints

Saints—*Continued*
Fiction
Freitas, D. The possibilities of sainthood   **Fic**
Gormley, B. Poisoned honey   **Fic**
Lecesne, J. Virgin territory   **Fic**
Sakai, Stan
Usagi Yojimbo, book one   **741.5**
Usagi Yojimbo: Yokai   **741.5**
Sakora, Lea
(ed) Is gun ownership a right? See Is gun ownership a right?   **344**
Sakyamuni *See* Gautama Buddha
Sala, Richard
Cat burglar black   **741.5**
Salamone, Frank A.
(ed) Encyclopedia of religious rites, rituals, and festivals. See Encyclopedia of religious rites, rituals, and festivals   **203**
Salbi, Zainab
Between two worlds   **92**
Saldaña, René
A good long way   **Fic**
Salem (Mass.)
Drama
Miller, A. The crucible   **812**
Fiction
Hearn, J. The minister's daughter   **Fic**
Hemphill, S. Wicked girls   **Fic**
Turner, A. W. Father of lies   **Fic**
History
Aronson, M. Witch-hunt: mysteries of the Salem witch trials   **133.4**
Carlson, L. M. A fever in Salem   **133.4**
Goss, K. D. The Salem witch trials   **133.4**
Hoffer, P. C. The Salem witchcraft trials   **345**
Salem Brownstone. Dunning, J. H.   **741.5**
Salem health [series]
Genetics & inherited conditions   **576.5**
The **Salem** witch trials. Goss, K. D.   **133.4**
The **Salem** witchcraft trials. Hoffer, P. C.   **345**
Salerni, Dianne K.
We hear the dead   **Fic**
Sales, Leila
Mostly good girls   **Fic**
Salieri, Antonio, 1750-1825
Drama
Shaffer, P. Peter Shaffer's Amadeus   **822**
Salinger, J. D., 1919-2010
The catcher in the rye   **Fic**
Franny & Zooey   **Fic**
Nine stories   **S C**
Raise high the roof beam, carpenters, and Seymour: an introduction   **Fic**
About
Kerr, C. Bloom's how to write about J.D. Salinger   **813.009**
Reiff, R. H. J.D. Salinger   **92**
Fiction
Portman, F. King Dork   **Fic**
Salinger, Jerome David *See* Salinger, J. D., 1919-2010

Salisbury, Graham, 1944-
Eyes of the emperor   **Fic**
Under the blood-red sun   **Fic**
Salisbury, Joyce E.
(ed) The Greenwood encyclopedia of daily life. See The Greenwood encyclopedia of daily life   **390**
(ed) The Greenwood encyclopedia of global medieval life and culture. See The Greenwood encyclopedia of global medieval life and culture   **940.1**
Salk, Jonas, 1914-1995
About
Kluger, J. Splendid solution: Jonas Salk and the conquest of polio   **92**
Sherrow, V. Jonas Salk   **92**
See/See also pages in the following book(s):
Hellman, H. Great feuds in medicine   **610.9**
Salk vaccine *See* Poliomyelitis vaccine
Salmon, Dena K.
Discordia   **Fic**
Salmonella infections *See* Salmonellosis
Salmonellosis
Brands, D. A. Salmonella   **615.9**
Salowey, Christina A.
(ed) Great lives from history, The ancient world, prehistory-476 C.E. See Great lives from history, The ancient world, prehistory-476 C.E   **920.003**
Salt
Benanav, M. Men of salt   **916.6**
Kurlansky, M. Salt: a world history   **553.6**
Salt. Gee, M.   **Fic**
Salt marshes
Weis, J. S. Salt marshes   **578.7**
The Salt trilogy [series]
Gee, M. Salt   **Fic**
Salter, Mark
(jt. auth) McCain, J. S. Why courage matters   **179**
Salter, Sydney
Swoon at your own risk   **Fic**
Salvador Dali and the surrealists. Ross, M. E.   **92**
Salzman, Mark
True notebooks   **808**
Same difference. Vivian, S.   **Fic**
Same-sex marriage
Andryszewski, T. Same-sex marriage   **306.8**
Gay and lesbian families   **306.8**
Gay marriage   **306.8**
Sammy and Juliana in Hollywood. Saenz, B. A.   **Fic**
Sampson, Deborah, 1760-1827
Fiction
Klass, S. S. Soldier's secret   **Fic**
Sampson, Scott D., 1961-
Dinosaur odyssey   **567.9**
Samuel, Wolfgang W. E.
The war of our childhood   **940.53**
Samurai
Graphic novels
Sakai, S. Usagi Yojimbo, book one   **741.5**

Schaaf, Fred
The 50 best sights in astronomy and how to see them   **520**

Schaap, Jeremy, 1969-
Triumph [biography of Jesse Owens]   **92**

Schaap, Phil, 1951-
(jt. auth) Marsalis, W. Jazz A-B-Z   **781.65**

Schacter, Daniel L.
The seven sins of memory   **153.1**

Schaefer, Emmett Robert, 1947-
(jt. auth) Thompson, C. White men challenging racism   **323**

Schafer, Daniel L.
Anna Madgigine Jai Kingsley   **92**

Schaffner, Ingrid
The essential Vincent van Gogh   **759.9492**

Schall, Lucy
Booktalks and beyond   **028.5**
Genre talks for teens   **028.5**

Schaller, George B.
A naturalist and other beasts   **508**

Schaller, Michael, 1947-
Ronald Reagan   **92**

Schappert, Phil, 1956-
The last Monarch butterfly   **595.7**

Schechter, Abraham A.
Basic book repair methods   **025.7**

Scheeder, Louis, 1946-
All the words on stage   **822.3**

Scheeren, William O.
Technology for the school librarian   **025.04**

Scheeres, Julia, 1967-
Jesus land   **92**

Schein, Elyse, 1968-
Identical strangers   **92**

Schenck, Charles
About
Icenoggle, J. Schenck v. United States and the freedom of speech debate   **342**
Schenck v. United States and the freedom of speech debate. Icenoggle, J.   **342**

Schewel, Amy
(ed) The Actor's book of movie monologues. See The Actor's book of movie monologues   **791.43**

Schiefelbein, Susan
(jt. auth) Cousteau, J. Y. The human, the orchid, and the octopus   **333.95**

Schiff, Hilda
(ed) Holocaust poetry. See Holocaust poetry   **808.81**

Schiff, Karenna Gore
Lighting the way   **920**

Schindler, Holly, 1977-
A blue so dark   **Fic**
Playing hurt   **Fic**

Schindler, Oskar, 1908-1974
Fiction
Keneally, T. Schindler's list   **Fic**
Schindler's list. Keneally, T.   **Fic**

Schizophrenia
Snyder, K. Me, myself, and them   **92**

Encyclopedias
Noll, R. The encyclopedia of schizophrenia and other psychotic disorders   **616.89**
Fiction
Anderson, J. L. Border crossing   **Fic**
Atwater-Rhodes, A. Persistence of memory   **Fic**
Schindler, H. A blue so dark   **Fic**
Warman, J. Breathless   **Fic**
Wray, J. Lowboy   **Fic**

Schlachter, Gail A.
College student's guide to merit and other no-need funding, 2008-2010   **378.3**
Directory of financial aids for women 2009-2011   **378.3**
Financial aid for the disabled and their families, 2010-2012   **378.3**
(ed) High school senior's guide to merit and other no-need funding, 2008-2010. See High school senior's guide to merit and other no-need funding, 2008-2010   **378.3**

Schlager, Neil, 1966-
(ed) Alternative energy. See Alternative energy   **333.79**
(ed) Chemical compounds. See Chemical compounds   **540**
(ed) Contemporary novelists. See Contemporary novelists   **920.003**
(ed) Jones, J. S. The Crusades, Biographies   **920.003**
(ed) Jones, J. S. The Crusades, Primary sources   **909.07**
(ed) O'Neal, M. The Crusades, Almanac   **909.07**
(ed) World encyclopedia of political systems and parties. See World encyclopedia of political systems and parties   **324.2**
(ed) World religions. See World religions   **200**

Schlereth, Thomas J.
Victorian America   **973.8**

Schlissel, Lillian
Women's diaries of the westward journey   **978**

Schlossberg, Caroline Kennedy See Kennedy, Caroline

Schlosser, Eric
Chew on this   **394.1**
Fast food nation   **394.1**

Schmemann, Serge
When the wall came down   **943**

Schmidt, Elizabeth
(ed) The poets laureate anthology. See The poets laureate anthology   **811.008**

Schmidt, Gary D.
Trouble   **Fic**

Schnakenberg, Robert
Secret lives of the Supreme Court   **920**

Schneider, Carl J.
World War II   **940.53**
(jt. auth) Schneider, D. First ladies   **920.003**
(jt. auth) Schneider, D. Slavery in America   **326**

Schneider, Dorothy
First ladies   **920.003**

School stories—*Continued*

Castellucci, C. Rose sees red **Fic**
Chaltas, T. Because I am furniture **Fic**
Chbosky, S. The perks of being a wallflower **Fic**
Cheva, C. DupliKate **Fic**
Chow, C. Bitter melon **Fic**
Clement-Moore, R. Prom dates from Hell **Fic**
Cohen, J. Leverage **Fic**
Cohen, T. Little black lies **Fic**
Colasanti, S. Something like fate **Fic**
Colasanti, S. Waiting for you **Fic**
Cook, E. The education of Hailey Kendrick **Fic**
Cooney, C. B. Code orange **Fic**
Cormier, R. The chocolate war **Fic**
Corrigan, E. Accomplice **Fic**
Corrigan, E. Ordinary ghosts **Fic**
Coy, J. Box out **Fic**
Coy, J. Crackback **Fic**
Crawford, B. Carter finally gets it **Fic**
Crewe, M. Give up the ghost **Fic**
Cummings, P. Blindsided **Fic**
Davidson, D. Jason & Kyra **Fic**
Davidson, D. Played **Fic**
Davidson, J. The Explosionist **Fic**
De Goldi, K. The 10 p.m. question **Fic**
De Gramont, N. Gossip of the starlings **Fic**
De Lint, C. The blue girl **Fic**
Delsol, W. Stork **Fic**
Dessen, S. Just listen **Fic**
Deuker, C. Gym candy **Fic**
Deuker, C. Painting the black **Fic**
Dooley, S. Livvie Owen lived here **Fic**
Draanen, W. v. Confessions of a serial kisser **Fic**
Draanen, W. v. The running dream **Fic**
Draper, S. M. The Battle of Jericho **Fic**
Duncan, L. Killing Mr. Griffin **Fic**
Efaw, A. After **Fic**
Elkeles, S. Perfect chemistry **Fic**
Emond, S. Happyface **Fic**
Eulberg, E. Prom and prejudice **Fic**
Fehlbaum, B. Hope in Patience **Fic**
Franco, B. Metamorphosis **Fic**
Frank, H. Better than running at night **Fic**
Fredericks, M. Crunch time **Fic**
Freitas, D. The possibilities of sainthood **Fic**
Frey, J. I am number four **Fic**
Friend, N. For keeps **Fic**
Garcia, K. Beautiful creatures **Fic**
Garsee, J. Before, after, and somebody in between **Fic**
Gelbwasser, M. Inconvenient **Fic**
George, M. Looks **Fic**
Giles, G. Playing in traffic **Fic**
Giles, G. Shattering Glass **Fic**
Goldman, S. Two parties, one tux, and a very short film about the Grapes of Wrath **Fic**
Graham, R. Thou shalt not dump the skater dude and other commandments I have broken **Fic**
Grant, C. Teenie **Fic**
Gratz, A. Samurai shortstop **Fic**
Gray, C. Evernight **Fic**
Green, J. Looking for Alaska **Fic**

Green, R. The secret society of the pink crystal ball **Fic**
Griffin, A. The Julian game **Fic**
Grimes, N. Bronx masquerade **Fic**
Halpern, J. Into the wild nerd yonder **Fic**
Halpin, B. Forever changes **Fic**
Halpin, B. How ya like me now **Fic**
Hartinger, B. Geography Club **Fic**
Hautman, P. Blank confession **Fic**
Hawkins, R. Hex Hall **Fic**
Healey, K. Guardian of the dead **Fic**
Hernandez, D. No more us for you **Fic**
Hills, L. The beginner's guide to living **Fic**
Horner, E. A love story starring my dead best friend **Fic**
Houston, J. New boy **Fic**
Hubbard, A. But I love him **Fic**
Hurley, T. Ghostgirl **Fic**
Hyde, C. R. Diary of a witness **Fic**
Hyde, C. R. Jumpstart the world **Fic**
Ishiguro, K. Never let me go **Fic**
Jaden, D. Losing Faith **Fic**
Jenkins, A. M. Repossessed **Fic**
Jinks, C. Evil genius **Fic**
Johnson, L. Muchacho **Fic**
Johnson, M. Devilish **Fic**
Jones, P. The tear collector **Fic**
Jonsberg, B. Dreamrider **Fic**
Jordan, S. Firelight **Fic**
Kade, S. The ghost and the goth **Fic**
Karim, S. Skunk girl **Fic**
Katcher, B. Almost perfect **Fic**
Katcher, B. Playing with matches **Fic**
Kate, L. The betrayal of Natalie Hargrove **Fic**
Kephart, B. Undercover **Fic**
Klass, D. Dark angel **Fic**
Klass, D. You don't know me **Fic**
Knowles, J. A separate peace **Fic**
Koertge, R. Stoner & Spaz **Fic**
Koja, K. Buddha boy **Fic**
Koja, K. Headlong **Fic**
Koja, K. Kissing the bee **Fic**
Korman, G. Pop **Fic**
Krovatin, C. Heavy metal and you **Fic**
Lackey, M. Legacies **Fic**
LaRochelle, D. Absolutely, positively not **Fic**
Leavitt, L. Sean Griswold's head **Fic**
LeFlore, L. The world is mine **Fic**
Levchuk, L. Everything beautiful in the world **Fic**
Liberty, A. The center of the universe **Fic**
Lockhart, E. The boyfriend list **Fic**
Lockhart, E. The disreputable history of Frankie Landau-Banks **Fic**
Love, D. A. Defying the diva **Fic**
Lubar, D. Sleeping freshmen never lie **Fic**
Lyga, B. The astonishing adventures of Fanboy & Goth Girl **Fic**
Lyga, B. Boy toy **Fic**
Lyga, B. Hero-type **Fic**
Lynch, C. Inexcusable **Fic**
Mackler, C. The earth, my butt, and other big, round things **Fic**
Mackler, C. Vegan virgin Valentine **Fic**
Madigan, L. K. Flash burnout **Fic**

School superintendents and principals
McGhee, M. W. The principal's guide to a powerful library media program   **025.1**

School violence
See also School shootings
Hunnicutt, S. School shootings   **371.7**
Parks, P. J. School violence   **371.7**
School violence   **371.7**
Fiction
Brown, J. Hate list   **Fic**
Picoult, J. Nineteen minutes   **Fic**
Shepard, J. Project X   **Fic**
School violence   **371.7**

Schools
See also Colleges and universities; Education; Public schools
Administration
Farmer, L. S. J. Collaborating with administrators and educational support staff   **027.8**
Nichols, B. Improving student achievement   **373.1**
Fiction
See School stories
Afghanistan
Mortenson, G. Stones into schools   **371.82**
Pakistan
Mortenson, G. Stones into schools   **371.82**

Schools and libraries *See* Libraries and schools
Schopenhauer, Arthur, 1788-1860
See/See also pages in the following book(s):
Durant, W. J. The story of philosophy   **109**

Schoppa, R. Keith, 1943-
Twentieth century China   **951.05**

Schrefer, Eliot, 1978-
The deadly sister   **Fic**

Schroeder, Heather Lee
A reader's guide to Marjane Satrapi's Persepolis   **813.009**

Schroeder, Lisa
Far from you   **Fic**

Schuckett, Sandy
Political advocacy for school librarians   **027.8**

Schulman, Bruce J.
(ed) Student's guide to Congress. See Student's guide to Congress   **328.73**
(ed) Student's guide to elections. See Student's guide to elections   **324**
(ed) Student's guide to the presidency. See Student's guide to the presidency   **352.23**

Schulman, Grace
(ed) Moore, M. The poems of Marianne Moore   **811**

Schultz, David A., 1958-
The encyclopedia of the Supreme Court   **347**
Encyclopedia of the United States Constitution   **342**
(ed) Encyclopedia of the First Amendment. See Encyclopedia of the First Amendment   **342**

Schultz, Jeffrey D., 1966-
Critical companion to John Steinbeck   **813.009**

Schultz, Mark, 1955-
The stuff of life   **576.5**
Schultz, Mitchel E.
Grob's basic electronics   **621.381**
Schumacher, Julie, 1958-
Black box   **Fic**
Schumacher, Michael, 1950-
Will Eisner   **92**
Schumann, Walter
Gemstones of the world   **553.8**
Schupack, Sara
The merchant of Venice [criticism]   **822.3**
Schur, Joan Brodsky
(ed) The Arabs. See The Arabs   **305.8**
Schusterbauer, Emily
(ed) Teen suicide. See Teen suicide   **362.28**
Schutt, Bill
Dark banquet   **591.5**
Schutt, Christine, 1948-
All souls   **Fic**
Schutz, Samantha, 1978-
I don't want to be crazy   **92**
Schwartz, Ellen, 1949-
I love yoga   **613.7**
Schwartz, Jeffrey H.
(jt. auth) Tattersall, I. Extinct humans   **599.93**
Schwartz, Maxime, 1940-
How the cows turned mad   **616.8**
Schwartz, Richard Alan, 1951-
The 1950s   **973.92**
The 1990s   **973.92**
Encyclopedia of the Persian Gulf War   **956.7**
Schwartz, Tina P., 1969-
Organ transplants   **617.9**
Schwedt, Rachel E., 1944-
Young adult poetry   **809.1**
Schweid, Richard, 1946-
Consider the eel   **597**
Schweizer, Chris, 1980-
Crogan's vengeance   **741.5**
Science
See also Computer science; Environmental science
Beyer, R. The greatest science stories never told   **500**
Brooks, M. 13 things that don't make sense   **500**
Bryson, B. A short history of nearly everything   **500**
Feynman, R. P. The meaning of it all   **500**
Flatow, I. Present at the future   **500**
Great thinkers of the Western world   **190**
The handy science answer book   **500**
Kaku, M. Physics of the future   **303.49**
The next fifty years   **501**
Oxford dictionary of scientific quotations   **500**
Sagan, C. Broca's brain   **500**
Sagan, C. The demon-haunted world   **001.9**
Shermer, M. Why people believe weird things   **001.9**
This will change everything   **501**

Science and civilization—*Continued*

Strapp, J. Science and technology   **609**

Science and religion *See* Religion and science

Science and religion, 1450-1900. Olson, R.   **261.5**

Science and religion, 400 B.C. to A.D. 1550. Grant, E.   **261.5**

Science and society [series]

Kidd, J. S. Potent natural medicines   **615**

Science and technology. Strapp, J.   **609**

Science fair projects *See* Science projects

Science fair season. Dutton, J.   **507.8**

Science fiction

See also Fantasy fiction

Adams, D. The hitchhiker's guide to the galaxy   **Fic**

Adlington, L. J. Cherry Heaven   **Fic**

Adlington, L. J. The diary of Pelly D   **Fic**

Agell, C. Shift   **Fic**

Anderson, M. T. Feed   **Fic**

Asimov, I. The complete stories   **S C**

Asimov, I. Fantastic voyage   **Fic**

Asimov, I. Foundation   **Fic**

Asimov, I. I, robot   **S C**

Augarde, S. X-Isle   **Fic**

Bacigalupi, P. Ship breaker   **Fic**

Bear, G. The collected stories of Greg Bear   **S C**

Beck, I. Pastworld   **Fic**

Beckett, B. Genesis   **Fic**

Bedford, K. A. Time machines repaired while-u-wait   **Fic**

Best of the best: 20 years of the Year's best science fiction   **S C**

Black, H. The white cat   **Fic**

Bloor, E. Taken   **Fic**

Bodeen, S. A. The gardener   **Fic**

Boulle, P. Planet of the apes   **Fic**

Bova, B. Mars life   **Fic**

Bradbury, R. Bradbury stories   **S C**

Bradbury, R. Fahrenheit 451   **Fic**

Bradbury, R. The illustrated man   **S C**

Bradbury, R. The Martian chronicles   **S C**

Brooks, K. Being   **Fic**

Burgess, A. A clockwork orange   **Fic**

Butler, O. E. Fledgling   **Fic**

Butler, O. E. Kindred   **Fic**

Card, O. S. Ender's game   **Fic**

Card, O. S. First meetings in the Enderverse   **S C**

Card, O. S. Pathfinder   **Fic**

Clarke, A. C. 2001: a space odyssey   **Fic**

Clarke, A. C. The collected stories of Arthur C. Clarke   **S C**

Collins, S. The Hunger Games   **Fic**

Cosmos latinos   **S C**

Crichton, M. The Andromeda strain   **Fic**

Crichton, M. Jurassic Park   **Fic**

Cross, S. Dull boy   **Fic**

Dashner, J. The maze runner   **Fic**

The Del Rey book of science fiction and fantasy   **S C**

DeStefano, L. Wither   **Fic**

Dickinson, P. Eva   **Fic**

Doctorow, C. For the win   **Fic**

Doctorow, C. Makers   **Fic**

Engdahl, S. L. Enchantress from the stars   **Fic**

Falkner, B. Brain Jack   **Fic**

Farmer, N. The Ear, the Eye, and the Arm   **Fic**

Farmer, N. The house of the scorpion   **Fic**

Feeling very strange   **S C**

Firebirds rising   **S C**

Firebirds soaring   **S C**

Ford, M. T. Z   **Fic**

Frey, J. I am number four   **Fic**

Gaiman, N. American gods   **Fic**

Gaiman, N. Interworld   **Fic**

Gill, D. M. Black hole sun   **Fic**

Halam, A. Dr. Franklin's island   **Fic**

Haldeman, J. W. The forever war   **Fic**

The Hard SF renaissance   **S C**

Heath, J. The Lab   **Fic**

Heinlein, R. A. The moon is a harsh mistress   **Fic**

Heinlein, R. A. Stranger in a strange land   **Fic**

Herbert, F. Dune   **Fic**

Ishiguro, K. Never let me go   **Fic**

Jinks, C. Living hell   **Fic**

Keyes, D. Flowers for Algernon   **Fic**

Kinch, M. P. The blending time   **Fic**

Le Guin, U. K. The lathe of heaven   **Fic**

Le Guin, U. K. The left hand of darkness   **Fic**

Link, K. Pretty monsters   **S C**

Lloyd, S. The carbon diaries 2015   **Fic**

The Locus awards   **S C**

Lowry, L. The giver   **Fic**

Malley, G. The Declaration   **Fic**

Mariz, R. The Unidentified   **Fic**

McCaffrey, A. Dragonflight   **Fic**

McDevitt, J. Moonfall   **Fic**

Miller, W. M. A canticle for Leibowitz   **Fic**

Ness, P. The knife of never letting go   **Fic**

Niven, L. Ringworld   **Fic**

The Norton book of science fiction   **S C**

O'Brien, C. M. Birthmarked   **Fic**

Okorafor, N. The shadow speaker   **Fic**

Oliver, L. Delirium   **Fic**

Osterlund, A. Academy 7   **Fic**

Pearson, M. The adoration of Jenna Fox   **Fic**

Philbrick, W. R. The last book in the universe   **Fic**

Reeve, P. Fever Crumb   **Fic**

Revis, B. Across the universe   **Fic**

Robinson, K. S. Forty signs of rain   **Fic**

Robinson, K. S. Red Mars   **Fic**

Salmon, D. K. Discordia   **Fic**

Scarrow, A. TimeRiders   **Fic**

Science fiction quotations   **808.88**

Shelley, M. W. Frankenstein; or, The modern Prometheus   **Fic**

Shusterman, N. Unwind   **Fic**

Shute, N. On the beach   **Fic**

Simmons, D. Ilium   **Fic**

Slade, A. G. The hunchback assignments   **Fic**

Smith, A. G. Lockdown   **Fic**

The Starry rift   **S C**

Testa, D. The comet's curse   **Fic**

Scientists—*Continued*
Webster, R. B. African American firsts in science and technology **509**
Dictionaries
Concise dictionary of scientific biography **920.003**

Life sciences before the twentieth century **920.003**

Life sciences in the twentieth century **920.003**

New dictionary of scientific biography **920.003**

Newton, D. E. Latinos in science, math, and professions **920.003**
The Renaissance and the scientific revolution **920.003**

Scientists, mathematicians, and inventors **920.003**

Yount, L. A to Z of biologists **920.003**
Encyclopedias
Carey, C. W. African Americans in science **920.003**

Oakes, E. H. Encyclopedia of world scientists **920.003**

Fiction
Durst, S. B. Ice **Fic**
The **scientists**. Gribbin, J. R. **509**
Scientists, mathematicians, and inventors **920.003**

Scieszka, Casey
To Timbuktu **910.4**

Scieszka, Jon, 1954-
(ed) Guys write for Guys Read. See Guys write for Guys Read **810.8**
The **scoop** on what to eat. Gay, K. **613.2**

Scopes, John Thomas
About
Larson, E. J. The Scopes trial **345**
Fiction
Bryant, J. Ringside, 1925 **Fic**
The **Scopes** trial. Larson, E. J. **345**

Scotland
Fiction
Davidson, J. The Explosionist **Fic**
Dunkle, C. B. By these ten bones **Fic**
Frost, H. The braid **Fic**
Gray, K. Ostrich boys **Fic**
Klein, L. M. Lady Macbeth's daughter **Fic**
Raedeke, C. The daykeeper's grimoire **Fic**
History—17th century—Fiction
Laird, E. The betrayal of Maggie Blair **Fic**

Scott, Amanda
Dreaming the eagle **Fic**

Scott, Dagny
Runner's world complete book of women's running **796.42**

Scott, Damion
How to draw hip-hop **741.2**

Scott, Elizabeth
Grace **Fic**
Living dead girl **Fic**
Love you hate you miss you **Fic**
Stealing Heaven **Fic**

Scott, Eugenie Carol, 1945-
Evolution vs. creationism **576.8**
Scott, Hunter
About
Nelson, P. Left for dead **940.54**
Scott, John F., 1936-
Latin American art **709.8**
Scott, Kieran, 1974-
Geek magnet **Fic**
She's so dead to us **Fic**
Scott, Mindi
Freefall **Fic**
Scott, Ralph D.
(jt. auth) Capinera, J. L. Field guide to grasshoppers, crickets, and katydids of the United States **595.7**
Scott, Robert Alan
Chief Joseph and the Nez Percés **92**
Scott, Robert Falcon, 1868-1912
About
Solomon, S. The coldest March **998**
Scott, Wendell, 1921-1990
About
Donovan, B. Hard driving: the Wendell Scott story **92**
Scott-Kilvert, Ian
(ed) British writers. See British writers **920.003**

Scottish authors *See* Authors, Scottish
Scottsboro, Alabama. Khan, L. S. **345**
The **Scottsboro** Boys Trial. Sorensen, L. **345**
Scottsboro case
Aretha, D. The trial of the Scottsboro boys **345**
Khan, L. S. Scottsboro, Alabama **345**
Sorensen, L. The Scottsboro Boys Trial **345**
Scowcroft, Gail
(jt. auth) Crist, D. T. World ocean census **578.7**

Scrap-books *See* Scrapbooks
Scrapbooks
Sowell, S. Paper cutting techniques for scrapbooks & cards **745.54**
Scrawl. Shulman, M. **Fic**
The **Screwtape** letters. Lewis, C. S. **248**
Scribner American civilization series
Encyclopedia of recreation and leisure in America **790**
The **Scribner** encyclopedia of American lives **920.003**
Scribner library of modern Europe [series]
Europe 1789 to 1914 **940.2**
Europe since 1914 **940.5**
Scribner science reference series
Life sciences before the twentieth century **920.003**

Life sciences in the twentieth century **920.003**

The Renaissance and the scientific revolution **920.003**

Scribner turning points library [series]
Tobacco in history and culture **394.1**

Sculpting basics. Hessenberg, K.   **731.4**

Sculpture

Poetry
Spires, E. I heard God talking to me   **811**

Technique
Hessenberg, K. Sculpting basics   **731.4**

Sea animals *See* Marine animals

Sea legs. Crane, K.   **92**

Sea life *See* Seafaring life

Sea lions *See* Seals (Animals)

Sea monsters. Everhart, M. J.   **567.9**

Sea stories
Boyne, J. Mutiny   **Fic**
Conrad, J. Lord Jim   **Fic**
Crichton, M. Pirate latitudes   **Fic**
Dixon, P. L. Hunting *the Dragon*   **Fic**
Melville, H. Billy Budd, sailor   **Fic**
Melville, H. Moby-Dick; or, The whale   **Fic**
Nordhoff, C. Mutiny on the Bounty   **Fic**
Rees, C. Pirates!   **Fic**
Verne, J. The extraordinary journeys: Twenty thousand leagues under the sea   **Fic**

Graphic novels
Weing, D. Set to sea   **741.5**

Sea turtles
Spotila, J. R. Sea turtles   **597.92**

Seabiscuit (Race horse)
Hillenbrand, L. Seabiscuit   **798.4**

Seafaring life

Fiction
Frazier, A. Everlasting   **Fic**
Meyer, L. A. Bloody Jack   **Fic**

Graphic novels
Weing, D. Set to sea   **741.5**

Seals (Animals)
Miller, D. Seals & sea lions   **599.79**

Seals (Numismatics)
Shearer, B. F. State names, seals, flags, and symbols   **929.9**

Seals & sea lions. Miller, D.   **599.79**

Seamon, Mary Ploski, 1943-
Digital cameras in the classroom   **775**

Sean Griswold's head. Leavitt, L.   **Fic**

Search and destroy. Hughes, D.   **Fic**

Search and rescue operations *See* Rescue work

Searching the internet *See* Internet searching

Searle, Teresa
Felt jewelry   **746**

Sears, Stephen W.
Gettysburg   **973.7**

Sears list of subject headings   **025.4**

Seashore
See also Coasts
Carson, R. The edge of the sea   **577.7**

Season of ice. Les Becquets, D.   **Fic**

Seasons
See also Summer

Seattle (Wash.)

Fiction
Gallagher, L. The opposite of invisible   **Fic**
John, A. Five flavors of dumb   **Fic**

McBride, L. Hold me closer, necromancer   **Fic**
Wesselhoeft, C. Adios, nirvana   **Fic**

Seay family

About
See, L. On Gold Mountain   **920**

Sebold, Alice
The lovely bones   **Fic**

The second Dalai Lama. Mullin, G. H.   **92**

Secondary school libraries *See* High school libraries

Secondary schools *See* High schools

Secondhand world. Min, K.   **Fic**

The secret Holocaust diaries. Bannister, N.   **92**

Secret identities   **741.5**

The secret journeys of Jack London [series]
Golden, C. The wild   **Fic**

Secret keeper. Perkins, M.   **Fic**

The secret life of bees. Kidd, S. M.   **Fic**

The secret life of dust. Holmes, H.   **551.51**

The secret life of germs. Tierno, P. M., Jr.   **616**

The secret life of Prince Charming. Caletti, D.   **Fic**

The secret life of words. Hitchings, H.   **422**

Secret lives of the Supreme Court. Schnakenberg, R.   **920**

Secret messages. Butler, W. S.   **652**

The secret of the yellow death. Jurmain, S.   **614.5**

Secret service
See also Espionage; Intelligence service; Spies

Secret societies

Fiction
Clare, C. Clockwork angel   **Fic**
Raedeke, C. The daykeeper's grimoire   **Fic**
Whitney, D. The Mockingbirds   **Fic**

The secret society of the pink crystal ball. Green, R.   **Fic**

Secret son. Lalami, L.   **Fic**

The secret story of Sonia Rodriguez. Sitomer, A. L.   **Fic**

The secret to lying. Mitchell, T.   **Fic**

Secret weapons. Eisner, T.   **595.7**

Secret writing *See* Cryptography

Secrets of a Civil War submarine. Walker, S. M.   **973.7**

The secrets of college success. Jacobs, L. F.   **378.1**

Secrets of the savanna. Owens, M.   **639.9**

Secrets of truth and beauty. Frazer, M.   **Fic**

Sects
See also names of churches and sects
Atwood, C. D. Handbook of denominations in the United States   **280**

Securing library technology. Earp, P. W.   **005.8**

Sedatives and hypnotics. Walker, I.   **362.29**

Sedgwick, Marcus
My swordhand is singing   **Fic**
Revolver   **Fic**
Sediqi, Kamela, 1977-
    About
Tzemach Lemmon, G. The dressmaker of Khair
Khana   **92**
See, Lisa
On Gold Mountain   **920**
See what I see. Whelan, G.   **Fic**
Seeger, Pete
    About
Wilkinson, A. The protest singer [biography of
Pete Seeger]   **92**
Seeing in the dark. Ferris, T.   **520**
Seeing the blue between   **808.1**
Seeing the gynecologist. Waters, S.   **618.1**
Seek. Fleischman, P.   **Fic**
Seek, find   **220.5**
Seeker. Nicholson, W.   **Fic**
The **seekers.** Boorstin, D. J.   **909**
Segal, Ronald, 1932-
Islam's Black slaves   **326**
Segan, Francine
Shakespeare's kitchen   **641.5**
Segen, J. C.
The patient's guide to medical tests   **616.07**
Segregation
    See also Apartheid; Discrimination
    See/See also pages in the following book(s):
Racial discrimination   **342**
    Fiction
Kidd, R. On Beale Street   **Fic**
Segregation in education
Kozol, J. Savage inequalities   **371.9**
Telgen, D. Brown v. Board of Education
    344
    Fiction
McCarthy, S. C. True fires   **Fic**
Sehgal, Alfica
Leprosy   **614.5**
Seib, Philip M., 1949-
Going live   **070.1**
Seidman, Rachel Filene
The Civil war: a history in documents   **973.7**
Seife, Charles
Proofiness   **510**
Zero   **511**
Seigel, Andrea, 1979-
The kid table   **Fic**
Like the red panda   **Fic**
Seigenthaler, John, 1927-
James K. Polk   **92**
Seinen manga
Urushibara, Y. Mu shi shi 1   **741.5**
Seiple, Samantha
Mutants, clones, and killer corn   **660.6**
Seiple, Todd
(jt. auth) Seiple, S. Mutants, clones, and killer
corn   **660.6**
Seismic sea waves *See* Tsunamis
Seismology *See* Earthquakes

Seita, John
(ed) Growing up in the care of strangers. See
Growing up in the care of strangers   **362.7**
Sela, Avraham
(ed) The Continuum political encyclopedia of
the Middle East. See The Continuum political
encyclopedia of the Middle East   **956**
The **selected** dialogues of Plato. Plato   **184**
The **selected** letters of Louisa May Alcott. Alcott,
L. M.   **92**
Selected odes of Pablo Neruda. Neruda, P.
    861
Selected poems. Borges, J. L.   **861**
Selected poems. Brooks, G.   **811**
Selected poems. Dove, R.   **811**
Selected poems. Lowell, R.   **811**
Selected poems. Paz, O.   **861**
Selected poems. Pound, E.   **811**
Selected poems. Sandburg, C.   **811**
Selected poems, 1934-1952. Thomas, D.   **821**
Selected poems, 1957-1994. Hughes, T.   **821**
The **selected** poems of Emily Dickinson. Dickin-
son, E.   **811**
The **selected** poems of Nikki Giovanni (1968-
1995). Giovanni, N.   **811**
Selected poems of Rainer Maria Rilke. Rilke, R.
M.   **831**
Selected short stories of William Faulkner. Faulk-
ner, W.   **S C**
Selected writings. Stein, G.   **818**
Selective service *See* Draft
Self-acceptance
    Fiction
Kincy, K. Other   **Fic**
Self-care, Health *See* Health self-care
Self-defense
    See also Martial arts
Self-defense for women
Gervasi, L. H. Fight like a girl— and win
    613.6
Self-defense in animals *See* Animal defenses
Self-employed
    See also Small business
Self-esteem
Palmer, P. Teen esteem   **155.5**
Steinem, G. Revolution from within   **155.2**
Self image *See* Personal appearance
Self-injury disorder. Parks, P. J.   **616.85**
Self-love (Psychology) *See* Self-esteem
Self-mutilation
Parks, P. J. Self-injury disorder   **616.85**
Self-mutilation: opposing viewpoints   **616.85**
Siana, J. Go ask Ogre   **92**
    Fiction
Anderson, L. H. Wintergirls   **Fic**
Hoban, J. Willow   **Fic**
McCormick, P. Cut   **Fic**
Rainfield, C. A. Scars   **Fic**
Self-mutilation: opposing viewpoints   **616.85**

Self-perception

See also Body image

Mills, J. E. Expectations for women   **305.4**

Fiction

Galante, C. The sweetness of salt   **Fic**

McDonald, A. Boys, bears, and a serious pair of hiking boots   **Fic**

Oliver, L. Before I fall   **Fic**

Shulman, M. Scrawl   **Fic**

Self-realization

See also Success

Self-reliance

See also Survival skills

Self-reliance: the story of Ralph Waldo Emerson. Caravantes, P.   **92**

Self-respect *See* Self-esteem

Selfors, Suzanne, 1963-

Mad love   **Fic**

Selfridge, Benjamin

A teen's guide to creating Web pages and blogs   **006.7**

Selfridge, Peter

(jt. auth) Selfridge, B. A teen's guide to creating Web pages and blogs   **006.7**

Sellout. Wilkins, E. J.   **Fic**

Selma (Ala.)

Race relations

Aretha, D. Selma and the Voting Rights Act   **324.6**

Partridge, E. Marching for freedom   **323.1**

Selma and the Voting Rights Act. Aretha, D.   **324.6**

Selvadurai, Shyam, 1965-

Swimming in the monsoon sea   **Fic**

Selverstone, Harriet S.

Encouraging and supporting student inquiry   **001.4**

Selzer, Adam, 1980-

I kissed a zombie, and I liked it   **Fic**

Semantics

Hayakawa, S. I. Language in thought and action   **412**

Seminary boy. Cornwell, J.   **92**

Semiotics

See also Semantics

Semmelweis, Ignác Fülöp, 1818-1865

See/See also pages in the following book(s):

Hellman, H. Great feuds in medicine   **610.9**

Senna, Danzy

Caucasia   **Fic**

Senning, Cindy Post

Emily Post prom and party etiquette   **395**

Sensation and perception. May, M.   **612.8**

Sensational scenes for teens. Stevens, C.   **808.82**

Sense and sensibility. Austen, J.   **Fic**

A **sense** of the world [biography of James Holman] Roberts, J.   **92**

Senses and sensation

See also Pain

May, M. Sensation and perception   **612.8**

McDowell, J. The nervous system and sense organs   **612.8**

A **separate** peace. Knowles, J.   **Fic**

Sepetys, Ruta

Between shades of gray   **Fic**

September 11 terrorist attacks, 2001

See also World Trade Center terrorist attack, 2001

911: the book of help   **810.8**

America under attack: primary sources   **973.931**

Bernstein, R. Out of the blue   **973.931**

Didion, J. Fixed ideas: America since 9.11   **320.5**

Dwyer, J. 102 minutes   **974.7**

Friedman, T. L. Longitudes and attitudes   **973.931**

Gerdes, L. 9/11   **973.931**

A Just response   **973.931**

National Commission on Terrorist Attacks Upon the United States. The 9/11 Commission report   **973.931**

Nguyen, T. We are all suspects now   **323.1**

Drama

With their eyes   **812.008**

Fiction

Foer, J. S. Extremely loud & incredibly close   **Fic**

Levithan, D. Love is the higher law   **Fic**

Meminger, N. Shine, coconut moon   **Fic**

Scarrow, A. TimeRiders   **Fic**

Graphic novels

Jacobson, S. The 9/11 report   **973.931**

Spiegelman, A. In the shadow of no towers   **973.931**

The **September** sisters. Cantor, J.   **Fic**

Sequoia *See* Redwood

Serafin, Steven

(ed) The Continuum encyclopedia of British literature. See The Continuum encyclopedia of British literature   **820.3**

Serbia

Judah, T. The Serbs   **949.7**

The **Serbs.** Judah, T.   **949.7**

Serendipity Market. Blubaugh, P.   **Fic**

Serial publications

See also Newspapers

Series on law, politics, and society

Bok, C. A recent history of the United States in political cartoons   **973.92**

Sermons

American sermons   **252**

King, M. L., Jr. Strength to love   **252**

Tutu, D. The words of Desmond Tutu   **252**

The **serpent's** shadow. Lackey, M.   **Fic**

Serradell, Joaquima

SARS   **616.2**

Servants *See* Household employees

Service industries

See also Food service

Service stations

Fiction

Weaver, W. Full service   **Fic**

Serving boys through readers' advisory. Sullivan, M.   **028.5**

Serving homeschooled teens and their parents. Lerch, M. T.   **027.6**

Serving Latino communities. Alire, C.   **027.6**

Serving lesbian, gay, bisexual, transgender, and questioning teens. Martin, H. J., Jr.   **027.62**

Serving teens through readers' advisory. Booth, H.   **028.5**

Serving urban teens. Brehm-Heeger, P.   **027.62**

Servitude *See* Slavery

Set theory
Tabak, J. Beyond geometry   **516**

Set to sea. Weing, D.   **741.5**

Setaro, John F.
(jt. auth) Hyde, M. O. Smoking 101   **616.86**

Seth Baumgartner's love manifesto. Luper, E.   **Fic**

Setterfield, Diane
The thirteenth tale   **Fic**

Seupel, Celia W.
Business, finance, and government administration   **331.7**

Seuss, Dr.
About
Pease, D. E. Theodor Seuss Geisel   **92**

Seven famous Greek plays   **882.008**

Seven Realms [series]
Chima, C. W. The Demon King   **Fic**

The **seven** sins of memory. Schacter, D. L.   **153.1**

Seventeenth century *See* World history—17th century

Seventh son. Card, O. S.   **Fic**

The **seventy** architectural wonders of our world. See The Seventy wonders of the modern world   **720.9**

The **Seventy** great inventions of the ancient world   **609**

The **Seventy** wonders of the modern world   **720.9**

Severe acute respiratory syndrome *See* SARS (Disease)

Sew step by step. Smith, A.   **646.2**

Sew subversive. Rannels, M.   **646.4**

Sewage disposal
George, R. The big necessity   **363.7**

Sewerage
See/See also pages in the following book(s):
Macaulay, D. Underground   **624**

Sewing
The complete photo guide to sewing   **646.2**
Holkeboer, K. S. Patterns for theatrical costumes   **646.4**
Rannels, M. Sew subversive   **646.4**
Smith, A. Sew step by step   **646.2**

The **sewing** book. See Smith, A. Sew step by step   **646.2**

Sex *See* Sexual behavior

Sex (Biology)
See also Puberty; Reproductive system

Sex bias *See* Sexism

Sex, brains, and video games. Burek Pierce, J.   **027.62**

Sex change *See* Transsexualism

Sex crimes
See also Child sexual abuse
Sexual violence: opposing viewpoints   **364.1**
Simons, R. Gender danger   **362.88**

Sex discrimination
Blumenthal, K. Let me play   **796**
Freedman, J. Women in the workplace   **331.4**
Stone, T. L. Almost astronauts   **629.45**
Supreme Court decisions and women's rights   **342**
See/See also pages in the following book(s):
Sports and athletes: opposing viewpoints   **796**

Sex education
Bell, R. Changing bodies, changing lives   **613.9**
Brynie, F. H. 101 questions about reproduction   **612.6**
Brynie, F. H. 101 questions about sex and sexuality—   **613.9**
Forssberg, M. Sex for guys   **306.7**
McCoy, K. The teenage body book   **613**
Pardes, B. Doing it right   **613.9**
Sex education   **613.9**
Sexual health information for teens   **613.9**
Teen sex   **306.7**
Teenage pregnancy and parenting   **306.8**
Teenage sexuality: opposing viewpoints   **613.9**

Sex education   **613.9**

Sex for guys. Forssberg, M.   **306.7**

Sex: opposing viewpoints   **306.7**

Sex organs *See* Reproductive system

Sex role
The Full spectrum   **306.76**
Male and female roles: opposing viewpoints   **305.3**
Wolf, N. The beauty myth   **305.4**
Fiction
Brothers, M. Debbie Harry sings in French   **Fic**
Chibbaro, J. Deadly   **Fic**
Eagland, J. Wildthorn   **Fic**
Engle, M. Firefly letters   **Fic**
Friesner, E. M. Nobody's princess   **Fic**
Goodman, A. Eon: Dragoneye reborn   **Fic**
Hoffman, A. The foretelling   **Fic**
Hopkins, E. Burned   **Fic**
How beautiful the ordinary   **S C**
Huser, G. Stitches   **Fic**
Lavender, W. Aftershocks   **Fic**
Meyer, L. A. Bloody Jack   **Fic**
Moranville, S. B. A higher geometry   **Fic**
Napoli, D. J. Bound   **Fic**
Qamar, A. Beneath my mother's feet   **Fic**
Quick, B. A golden web   **Fic**
Rees, C. Sovay   **Fic**

Shakespeare, William, 1564-1616—About—Criticism—Continued

The Greenwood companion to Shakespeare **822.3**
Hamlet [criticism] **822.3**
Julius Caesar [criticism] **822.3**
King Lear [criticism] **822.3**
Krueger, S. H. The tempest [criticism] **822.3**
Macbeth [criticism] **822.3**
Mussari, M. Othello [criticism] **822.3**
Mussari, M. The sonnets [criticism] **822.3**
Naden, C. J. Romeo and Juliet [criticism] **822.3**
Nostbakken, F. Understanding Macbeth **822.3**
Othello [criticism] **822.3**
Richert, S. P. King Lear [criticism] **822.3**
Riley, D. The bedside, bathtub & armchair companion to Shakespeare **822.3**
Romeo and Juliet [criticism] **822.3**
Schupack, S. The merchant of Venice [criticism] **822.3**
Shakespeare [critical essays] **822.3**
The Shakespeare encyclopedia **822.3**
Shakespeare for students **822.3**
Shakespeare's histories **822.3**
Sobran, J. Hamlet [criticism] **822.3**
Sobran, J. Henry IV, part 1 [criticism] **822.3**
Sobran, J. Julius Caesar [criticism] **822.3**
Sobran, J. A midsummer night's dream [criticism] **822.3**
The sonnets [criticism] **822.3**
The tempest [criticism] **822.3**
William Shakespeare's Hamlet [critical essays] **822.3**

Dictionaries
Coye, D. F. Pronouncing Shakespeare's words **822.3**

Dramatic production
Butler, C. The practical Shakespeare **822.3**
Hester, J. Performing Shakespeare **822.3**

Encyclopedias
Olsen, K. All things Shakespeare **822.3**
The Oxford companion to Shakespeare **822.3**
The Shakespeare encyclopedia **822.3**

Fiction
Bjorkman, L. My invented life **Fic**
Fiedler, L. Romeo's ex **Fic**
Gratz, A. Something rotten **Fic**
Hand, E. Illyria **Fic**
Harper, S. The Juliet club **Fic**
Klein, L. M. Lady Macbeth's daughter **Fic**
Klein, L. M. Ophelia **Fic**
Lawlor, L. The two loves of Will Shakespeare **Fic**
Marsden, J. Hamlet: a novel **Fic**
Rees, C. The fool's girl **Fic**

Graphic novels
McCreery, C. Kill Shakespeare, vol. 1 **741.5**

Histories
Saccio, P. Shakespeare's English kings **822.3**

Language
Scheeder, L. All the words on stage **822.3**

Shewmaker, E. F. Shakespeare's language **822.3**

Parodies, imitations, etc.
Stoppard, T. Rosencrantz and Guildenstern are dead **822**

Quotations
Shakespeare, W. The Columbia dictionary of quotations from Shakespeare **822.3**

Stories, plots, etc.
Fallon, R. T. A theatergoer's guide to Shakespeare **822.3**

Technique
Spurgeon, C. F. E. Shakespeare's imagery and what it tells us **822.3**

Themes
Cahn, V. L. The plays of Shakespeare **822.3**

Shakespeare [critical essays] **822.3**
Shakespeare A to Z. See Boyce, C. Critical companion to William Shakespeare **822.3**
Shakespeare after all. Garber, M. **822.3**
The **Shakespeare** encyclopedia **822.3**
Shakespeare explained [series]
Andersen, R. Macbeth **822.3**
Krueger, S. H. The tempest **822.3**
Mussari, M. Othello **822.3**
Mussari, M. The sonnets **822.3**
Naden, C. J. Romeo and Juliet **822.3**
Richert, S. P. King Lear **822.3**
Schupack, S. The merchant of Venice **822.3**
Sobran, J. Hamlet **822.3**
Sobran, J. Henry IV, part 1 **822.3**
Sobran, J. Julius Caesar **822.3**
Sobran, J. A midsummer night's dream **822.3**
Shakespeare for students **822.3**
Shakespeare's English kings. Saccio, P. **822.3**
Shakespeare's Globe (London, England)
Aliki. William Shakespeare & the Globe **822.3**
Shakespeare's Hamlet. Sexton, A. **822.3**
Shakespeare's histories **822.3**
Shakespeare's imagery and what it tells us. Spurgeon, C. F. E. **822.3**
Shakespeare's kitchen. Segan, F. **641.5**
Shakespeare's language. Shewmaker, E. F. **822.3**

Shakur, Tupac
About
Dyson, M. E. Holler if you hear me: searching for Tupac Shakur **92**
Golus, C. Tupac Shakur **92**
White, A. Rebel for the hell of it [biography of Tupac Shakur] **92**

Shalvey, Declan
(il) Cobley, J. Frankenstein **741.5**

Shan, Darren, 1972-
The thin executioner **Fic**

Shane, C. J.
(ed) The Chinese. See The Chinese **305.8**
(ed) Great medical discoveries. See Great medical discoveries **610.9**
(ed) The Mexicans. See The Mexicans **305.8**

Shepard, Jim
Project X   Fic

Shepard, Sadia
The girl from foreign   92

Shepard, Sara, 1977-
The lying game   Fic

Shepherd, Stephen H. A.
(ed) Malory, Sir T. Le morte Darthur, or, The hoole book of Kyng Arthur and of his noble knyghtes of the Rounde Table   398.2

Shepherdson, Nancy
Ancestor hunt   929

Sheppard, Charles, 1962-2005
Coral reefs   577.7

Sheridan, Richard Brinsley, 1751-1816
The rivals   822

Sherlock Holmes (Fictional character) *See* Holmes, Sherlock (Fictional character)

Sherman, Carol, 1944-
(jt. auth) Rolland, J. L. The food encyclopedia   641.03

Sherman, Jill, 1982-
Drug trafficking   363.45

Sherman, Josepha
(ed) World folklore for storytellers. See World folklore for storytellers   398
(ed) Young warriors. See Young warriors   S C

Sherman, William T. (William Tecumseh), 1820-1891
About
Koestler-Grack, R. A. William Tecumseh Sherman   92
Woodworth, S. E. Sherman   92

Shermer, Michael
Denying history   940.53
Why people believe weird things   001.9

Sherrill, Martha
The Ruins of California   Fic

Sherrin, Ned
(ed) Oxford dictionary of humorous quotations. See Oxford dictionary of humorous quotations   808.88

Sherrow, Victoria
Gideon v. Wainwright   345
Jonas Salk   92

Sherwood, Ben
The survivors club   613.6

She's got next. King, M.   92

She's so dead to us. Scott, K.   Fic

Sheth, Kashmira
Keeping corner   Fic

Shevelow, Kathryn, 1951-
For the love of animals   179

Shewmaker, Eugene F.
Shakespeare's language   822.3

Shields, Carol
Jane Austen   92

Shields, Charles J., 1951-
I am Scout: the biography of Harper Lee   92

Shields, David S.
(ed) American poetry: the seventeenth and eighteenth centuries. See American poetry: the seventeenth and eighteenth centuries   811.008

Shifflett, Crandall A.
Victorian America, 1876 to 1913   973.8

Shift. Agell, C.   Fic

Shift. Bradbury, J.   Fic

Shillington, Kevin
(ed) Encyclopedia of African history. See Encyclopedia of African history   960

Shilts, Randy
And the band played on   362.1

Shimbo, Hiroko
The Japanese kitchen   641.5

Shimmy shimmy shimmy like my sister Kate   811.008

Shine, Ted, 1931-
(ed) Black theatre USA. See Black theatre USA   812.008

Shine. Myracle, L.   Fic

Shine, coconut moon. Meminger, N.   Fic

The **Shining** Company. Sutcliff, R.   Fic

Shinn, Sharon, 1957-
Gateway   Fic
General Winston's daughter   Fic
Mystic and rider   Fic

Shinto
Hartz, P. Shinto   299.5
See/See also pages in the following book(s):
Eastern religions   200.9

Ship breaker. Bacigalupi, P.   Fic

Ship of gold in the deep blue sea. Kinder, G.   910.4

Shipley, Graham
(ed) The Cambridge dictionary of classical civilization. See The Cambridge dictionary of classical civilization   938.003

Shipp, Josh
The teen's guide to world domination   646.7

Shippey, T. A. (Tom A.)
J.R.R. Tolkien   828

Shippey, Tom A. *See* Shippey, T. A. (Tom A.)

Ships
Paine, L. P. Ships of discovery and exploration   910.4

Ships of discovery and exploration. Paine, L. P.   910.4

Shipwrecks
Ballard, R. D. Graveyards of the Pacific   940.54
Ballard, R. D. Return to Titanic   910.4
Butler, D. A. Unsinkable: the full story of the RMS Titanic   910.4
Delaney, F. Simple courage   910.4
Junger, S. The perfect storm   910.4
Kinder, G. Ship of gold in the deep blue sea   910.4
Kurson, R. Shadow divers   940.54
Philbrick, N. In the heart of the sea   910.4
Stanton, D. In harm's way   940.54

Short stories—*Continued*

Destination unexpected: short stories	**S C**
Don't cramp my style	**S C**
Doyle, Sir A. C. The complete Sherlock Holmes	**S C**
Ellis, D. Lunch with Lenin and other stories	**S C**
The eternal kiss	**S C**
Every man for himself	**S C**
Face relations	**S C**
Faulkner, W. Selected short stories of William Faulkner	**S C**
Fear: 13 stories of suspense and horror	**S C**
Feeling very strange	**S C**
Firebirds rising	**S C**
Firebirds soaring	**S C**
First crossing	**S C**
Fitzgerald, F. S. The short stories of F. Scott Fitzgerald	**S C**
Flake, S. G. Who am I without him?	**S C**
Flake, S. G. You don't even know me	**808.8**
Free?: stories about human rights	**S C**
Gaiman, N. Fragile things	**S C**
Geektastic	**S C**
Gotham Writers' Workshop fiction gallery	**S C**
Gothic!	**S C**
Green, J. Let it snow	**S C**
Growing up ethnic in America	**S C**
Growing up Filipino II	**S C**
The Hard SF renaissance	**S C**
Hemingway, E. The complete short stories of Ernest Hemingway	**S C**
Henry, O. The best short stories of O. Henry	**S C**
Hesse, H. The fairy tales of Hermann Hesse	**S C**
Horowitz, A. Bloody Horowitz	**S C**
How beautiful the ordinary	**S C**
Hughes, L. Short stories of Langston Hughes	**S C**
Hurston, Z. N. The complete stories	**S C**
Hurston, Z. N. Novels and stories	**Fic**
The improbable adventures of Sherlock Holmes	**S C**
Irving, W. Bracebridge Hall; Tales of a traveller; The Alhambra	**S C**
Jackson, S. The lottery	**S C**
Joyce, J. Dubliners	**S C**
Kafka, F. The metamorphosis and other stories	**S C**
King, S. Everything's eventual: 14 dark tales	**S C**
King, S. Four past midnight	**S C**
King, S. Night shift	**S C**
King, S. Skeleton crew	**S C**
Kinsella, W. P. Shoeless Joe Jackson comes to Iowa: stories	**S C**
Kipling, R. Collected stories	**S C**
Kiss me deadly	**S C**
Lanagan, M. Black juice	**S C**
Lanagan, M. Red spikes	**S C**
Le Guin, U. K. Tales from Earthsea	**S C**
Leaving home: stories	**808.8**
Legends: short novels by the masters of modern fantasy	**S C**

Levithan, D. How they met, and other stories	**S C**
Link, K. Pretty monsters	**S C**
The Locus awards	**S C**
Love is hell	**S C**
Make me over	**S C**
Malamud, B. The complete stories	**S C**
Marston, E. Santa Claus in Baghdad and other stories about teens in the Arab world	**S C**
Maugham, W. S. Collected short stories	**S C**
McKillip, P. A. Harrowing the dragon	**S C**
McKinley, R. Fire: tales of elemental spirits	**S C**
McKinley, R. Water: tales of elemental spirits	**S C**
Michener, J. A. Tales of the South Pacific	**S C**
Moccasin thunder	**S C**
Myers, W. D. 145th Street	**S C**
Myers, W. D. What they found	**S C**
Nascimbene, Y. The creative collection of American short stories	**S C**
Nightshade: 20th century ghost stories	**S C**
No such thing as the real world	**S C**
The Norton book of American short stories	**S C**
The Norton book of science fiction	**S C**
Noyes, D. The ghosts of Kerfol	**S C**
O'Brien, T. The things they carried	**S C**
O'Connor, F. Collected works	**S C**
O'Connor, F. The complete stories	**S C**
Once upon a cuento	**S C**
Outside rules	**S C**
The Oxford book of English short stories	**S C**
The Oxford book of gothic tales	**S C**
The Oxford book of Irish short stories	**S C**
The Oxford book of short stories	**S C**
Packer, Z. Drinking coffee elsewhere	**S C**
Peck, R. Past perfect, present tense: new and collected stories	**S C**
Pick-up game	**S C**
Pierce, T. Tortall and other lands	**S C**
Poe, E. A. Edgar Allan Poe's tales of mystery and madness	**S C**
Porter, K. A. The collected stories of Katherine Anne Porter	**S C**
Porter, K. A. Pale horse, pale rider: three short novels	**S C**
Prom nights from hell	**S C**
The restless dead	**S C**
Rice, D. Crazy loco	**S C**
Roth, P. Goodbye, Columbus, and five short stories	**S C**
Salinger, J. D. Nine stories	**S C**
Shattered: stories of children and war	**S C**
Sholem Aleichem. Tevye the dairyman and The railroad stories	**S C**
Sideshow	**S C**
Singer, I. B. The collected stories of Isaac Bashevis Singer	**S C**
Sixteen: stories about that sweet and bitter birthday	**S C**
Sleator, W. Oddballs	**S C**
Spider Woman's granddaughters	**S C**
The Starry rift	**S C**
Such a pretty face	**S C**

Singer: the complete photo guide to sewing. See The complete photo guide to sewing **646.2**

Singers

See also African American singers

Angel, A. Janis Joplin **92**

Partridge, E. This land was made for you and me [biography of Woody Guthrie] **92**

Talamon, B. Bob Marley **92**

Wilkinson, A. The protest singer [biography of Pete Seeger] **92**

Fiction

Dolamore, J. Magic under glass **Fic**

Supplee, S. Somebody everybody listens to **Fic**

Weatherford, C. B. Becoming Billie Holiday **Fic**

Singh, Nikhil

(jt. auth) Dunning, J. H. Salem Brownstone **741.5**

Singh, Nikky-Guninder Kaur

Sikhism **294.6**

Singh, Patwant, 1925-

The Sikhs **954**

Singing

Fiction

Bennett Wealer, S. Rival **Fic**

Levine, G. C. Fairest **Fic**

Single parent family

See also Unmarried fathers; Unmarried mothers

Haskins-Bookser, L. Dreams to reality **306.8**

Fiction

Bodeen, S. A. The gardener **Fic**

Caletti, D. The fortunes of Indigo Skye **Fic**

Clarke, J. The winds of heaven **Fic**

Collins, B. Always watching **Fic**

Davis, D. Not like you **Fic**

Hall, B. Tempo change **Fic**

Herrick, S. By the river **Fic**

Hyde, C. R. Diary of a witness **Fic**

Joyce, G. The exchange **Fic**

Katcher, B. Almost perfect **Fic**

Lynch, C. Angry young man **Fic**

McDonald, J. Off-color **Fic**

Moriarty, L. The center of everything **Fic**

Ockler, S. Fixing Delilah **Fic**

Resau, L. The indigo notebook **Fic**

Sanders, S. L. Gray baby **Fic**

Stein, T. High dive **Fic**

Valentine, J. Me, the missing, and the dead **Fic**

Single women

See also Widows

Singleton, Carl

(ed) The Sixties in America. See The Sixties in America **973.92**

Singman, Jeffrey L.

Daily life in medieval Europe **940.1**

Sinkler, Adrian

Pakistan **954.91**

Sinte-galeshka See Spotted Tail, Brulé Sioux Chief, 1823-1881

Siouan Indians

See also Dakota Indians; Oglala Indians

Sioux Indians See Dakota Indians

Sir Gawain and the Green Knight. Gawain and the Grene Knight (Middle English poem) **821**

Sir Walter Ralegh and the quest for El Dorado. Aronson, M. **92**

Sirvaitis, Karen, 1961-

Danica Patrick **92**

Sís, Peter, 1949-

The wall **92**

Sister Anna. See Coleman, W. Anna's world **Fic**

Sister in the Band of Brothers. Skiba, K. M. **956.7**

Sister to sister **810.8**

Sister wife. Hrdlitschka, S. **Fic**

The **sisterhood** of the traveling pants. Brashares, A. **Fic**

Sisters

Fiction

Alender, K. Bad girls don't die **Fic**

Alvarez, J. How the García girls lost their accents **Fic**

Austen, J. Pride and prejudice **Fic**

Austen, J. Sense and sensibility **Fic**

Bass, K. Summer of fire **Fic**

Bauman, B. A. Rosie & Skate **Fic**

Beard, P. Dear Zoe **Fic**

Benway, R. The extraordinary secrets of April, May and June **Fic**

Billingsley, F. Chime **Fic**

Bjorkman, L. My invented life **Fic**

Bradley, A. The sweetness at the bottom of the pie **Fic**

Bullen, A. Wish **Fic**

Caletti, D. The six rules of maybe **Fic**

Cantor, J. The September sisters **Fic**

Carlson, M. Premiere **Fic**

Crewe, M. Give up the ghost **Fic**

Davies, J. Lost **Fic**

Davis, T. S. Mare's war **Fic**

De Lint, C. Dingo **Fic**

Deriso, C. H. Then I met my sister **Fic**

Epstein, R. God is in the pancakes **Fic**

Foxlee, K. The anatomy of wings **Fic**

Franklin, E. The other half of me **Fic**

Frazer, M. Secrets of truth and beauty **Fic**

Freymann-Weyr, G. Stay with me **Fic**

Friedman, A. The year my sister got lucky **Fic**

Frost, H. The braid **Fic**

Galante, C. The sweetness of salt **Fic**

Griffin, A. Where I want to be **Fic**

Hardinge, F. The lost conspiracy **Fic**

Holder, N. Crusade **Fic**

Hooper, M. Fallen Grace **Fic**

Hopkins, E. Identical **Fic**

Jackson, S. We have always lived in the castle **Fic**

Jacobson, J. The complete history of why I hate her **Fic**

Jaden, D. Losing Faith **Fic**

Jocelyn, M. Would you **Fic**

Kaslik, I. Skinny **Fic**

Skin—*Continued*
Diseases
See also Acne
Goldsmith, C. Skin cancer   **616.99**
Encyclopedias
Turkington, C. The encyclopedia of skin and skin disorders   **616.5**

Skin. Vrettos, A. M.   **Fic**

Skin and other stories. Dahl, R.   **S C**

The **skin** between us. Ragusa, K.   **92**

Skin cancer. Goldsmith, C.   **616.99**

Skin care secrets. Earle, L.   **646.7**

Skin deep. See Turkington, C. The encyclopedia of skin and skin disorders   **616.5**

Skin health information for teens   **616.5**

Skin hunger. Duey, K.   **Fic**

Skinheads *See* White supremacy movements

The Skinjacker trilogy [series]
Shusterman, N. Everlost   **Fic**

Skinned. Wasserman, R.   **Fic**

Skinner, B. F. (Burrhus Frederic), 1904-1990
About behaviorism   **150.19**

Skinner, Burrhus Frederic *See* Skinner, B. F. (Burrhus Frederic), 1904-1990

Skinny. Kaslik, I.   **Fic**

Skinny boy. Grahl, G. A.   **92**

Skipp, Francis E.
The complete short stories of Thomas Wolfe   **S C**

Skis and skiing *See* Skiing

Skloot, Rebecca
The immortal life of Henrietta Lacks   **92**

Skolnik, Fred
(ed) The New encyclopedia of Judaism. See The New encyclopedia of Judaism [New York University Press]   **296.03**
(ed) The student's encyclopedia of Judaism. See The student's encyclopedia of Judaism   **296.03**

Skrypuch, Marsha Forchuk
Daughter of war   **Fic**

Skull
Dickey, C. Cranioklepty   **612.7**

Skullkickers: 1000 Opas and a dead body. Zubkavich, J.   **741.5**

Skunk girl. Karim, S.   **Fic**

Skurzynski, Gloria, 1930-
Sweat and blood   **331.8**

The **sky** is everywhere. Nelson, J.   **Fic**

Skyscrapers
Macaulay, D. Unbuilding   **690**
Weitzman, D. L. Skywalkers   **682**
See/See also pages in the following book(s):
Macaulay, D. Building big   **720**

Skywalkers. Weitzman, D. L.   **682**

Slade, Arthur G., 1967-
The hunchback assignments   **Fic**
Megiddo's shadow   **Fic**

Slade, Suzanne, 1964-
Adopted: the ultimate teen guide   **362.7**

Slaight, Craig
(ed) Great monologues for young actors. See Great monologues for young actors   **808.82**
(ed) Multicultural scenes for young actors. See Multicultural scenes for young actors   **808.82**

Slam. Hornby, N.   **Fic**

Slam dunk, volume 1. Inoue, T.   **741.5**

Slang!. Dickson, P.   **427**

Slann, Martin W.
(jt. auth) Combs, C. C. Encyclopedia of terrorism   **363.32**

Slate, Barbara
You can do a graphic novel   **741.5**

Slaughterhouse-five. Vonnegut, K.   **Fic**

Slave life on the plantation. Worth, R.   **326**

Slave narratives [Library of Am.]   **326**

Slave trade
Bailey, A. C. African voices of the Atlantic slave trade   **326**
Davidson, B. The African slave trade   **967**
Postma, J. The Atlantic slave trade   **326**
Segal, R. Islam's Black slaves   **326**
Slavery today   **326**
Maps
Eltis, D. Atlas of the transatlantic slave trade   **381**

Slavery
Aronson, M. Sugar changed the world   **664**
Bales, K. Slavery today   **326**
Gann, M. Five thousand years of slavery   **326**
Grant, R. Slavery   **326**
Segal, R. Islam's Black slaves   **326**
Slavery today   **326**
Fiction
Allende, I. Island beneath the sea   **Fic**
Anderson, L. H. Chains   **Fic**
Anderson, M. T. The Pox party   **Fic**
Butler, O. E. Kindred   **Fic**
Cárdenas, T. Old dog   **Fic**
Draper, S. M. Copper sun   **Fic**
Engle, M. Firefly letters   **Fic**
Lester, J. Day of tears   **Fic**
Lester, J. Time's memory   **Fic**
McCormick, P. Sold   **Fic**
Morrison, T. Beloved   **Fic**
Napoli, D. J. Hush   **Fic**
Pesci, D. Amistad   **Fic**
Rawles, N. My Jim   **Fic**
Shan, D. The thin executioner   **Fic**
Stowe, H. B. Uncle Tom's cabin   **Fic**
Styron, W. The confessions of Nat Turner   **Fic**
Graphic novels
Baker, K. Nat Turner   **92**
Pictorial works
Feelings, T. The middle passage   **326**
Poetry
Nelson, M. Fortune's bones   **811**
Nelson, M. The freedom business   **811**

Smack. Burgess, M.   **Fic**

Small, Brian
(jt. auth) Sterry, P. Birds of Eastern North America   **598**
(jt. auth) Sterry, P. Birds of Western North America   **598**

Small, David, 1945-
Stitches   **92**

Small business
See also Entrepreneurship
Bielagus, P. G. Quick cash for teens   **658.1**

Small wonder. Kingsolver, B.   **814**

The **smaller** majority. Naskrecki, P.   **591.7**

Smallpox
Glynn, I. The life and death of smallpox   **616.9**
Preston, R. The demon in the freezer   **616.9**
Fiction
Cooney, C. B. Code orange   **Fic**

Smalls, Robert, 1839-1915
See/See also pages in the following book(s):
Garrison, M. Slaves who dared   **920**

Smallwood, Carol, 1939-
(ed) Librarians as community partners. See Librarians as community partners   **021.2**
(ed) Writing and publishing. See Writing and publishing   **808**

Smart, Ninian, 1927-2001
(ed) Atlas of the world's religions. See Atlas of the world's religions   **201**

Smart copyright compliance for schools. Butler, R. P.   **346.04**

The **smart** girl's guide to sports. Musiker, L. H.   **796**

Smart mice, not-so-smart people. Caplan, A. L.   **174.2**

Smartbomb. Chaplin, H.   **338.4**

The **smartest** animals on the planet. Boysen, S. T.   **591.5**

Smeaton, Kurt, 1977-
(jt. auth) Nevraumont, E. J. The ultimate improv book   **792.7**

Smelcer, John E., 1963-
The trap   **Fic**

Smell
Herz, R. S. The scent of desire   **152.1**

Smile for the camera. James, K.   **92**

Smiley, Jane, 1949-
Charles Dickens   **92**
The man who invented the computer [biography of John V. Atanasoff]   **92**

Smith, Adam, 1723-1790
See/See also pages in the following book(s):
Bussing-Burks, M. Influential economists   **920**
Heilbroner, R. L. The worldly philosophers   **330.1**

Smith, Alexander Gordon, 1979-
Lockdown   **Fic**

Smith, Alison
Sew step by step   **646.2**

Smith, Alison, 1968-
Name all the animals   **92**

Smith, Andrew, 1959-
Ghost medicine   **Fic**
In the path of falling objects   **Fic**
The Marbury lens   **Fic**

Smith, Andrew F., 1946-
(ed) The Oxford encyclopedia of food and drink in America. See The Oxford encyclopedia of food and drink in America   **641.3**

Smith, Anna Deavere
Letters to a young artist   **700**

Smith, Bonnie
Imperialism   **909**

Smith, Brian
(jt. auth) Raicht, M. The stuff of legend, book 1   **741.5**

Smith, Caroline, 1976-
Meteorites   **523.5**

Smith, Carter, 1962-
(jt. auth) Nash, G. B. Atlas of American history   **911**
(jt. auth) Ochoa, G. Atlas of Hispanic-American history   **305.8**

Smith, Charles R.
(ed) Pick-up game. See Pick-up game   **S C**

Smith, Cynthia Leitich
Tantalize   **Fic**

Smith, D. Boyd
(jt. auth) Grizzard, F. E., Jr. Jamestown Colony   **973.2**

Smith, Diane
Letters from Yellowstone   **Fic**

Smith, Douglas W.
Decade of the wolf   **599.77**

Smith, Edward Lucie- *See* Lucie-Smith, Edward, 1933-

Smith, Gwyeth
About
Marcus, D. L. Acceptance   **378.1**

Smith, Hugh L., 1921-1968
(comp) Reflections on a gift of watermelon pickle—and other modern verse. See Reflections on a gift of watermelon pickle—and other modern verse   **811.008**

Smith, Huston
Buddhism: a concise introduction   **294.3**

Smith, Jacqueline
(ed) The Facts on File dictionary of earth science. See The Facts on File dictionary of earth science   **550.3**
(ed) The Facts on File dictionary of weather and climate. See The Facts on File dictionary of weather and climate   **551.5**

Smith, James Noel
(il) Hale, S. Book of a thousand days   **Fic**

Smith, Jane Bandy
Teaching & testing information literacy skills   **028.7**

Smith, Jeff
About
Modern Masters volume twenty-five: Jeff Smith   **741.5**

Smoking   **362.29**

Smoking 101. Hyde, M. O.   **616.86**

Smolin, Lori A.
    Basic nutrition   **612.3**
    Nutrition and weight management   **613.2**
    Nutrition for sports and exercise   **613.7**

Smuggling
    Fiction
    Deuker, C. Runner   **Fic**

Smuggling of drugs *See* Drug traffic

Snakehead. Halam, A.   **Fic**

Snakes
    See also Pythons
    De Vosjoli, P. The art of keeping snakes
       639.3
    Ernst, C. H. Snakes of the United States and
       Canada   **597.96**
    O'Shea, M. Venomous snakes of the world
       597.96
    Encyclopedias
    Mattison, C. The new encyclopedia of snakes
       597.96

Snakes of the United States and Canada. Ernst, C.
    H.   **597.96**

Snapshot   **909.83**

Snapshots in history [series]
    Langley, A. The collapse of the Soviet Union
       947.085

SNCC *See* Student Nonviolent Coordinating Com-
    mittee

Snicket, Lemony, 1970-
    About
    Abrams, D. Lemony Snicket (Daniel Handler)
       92

The **sniper**. Riordan, J.   **Fic**

Snodgrass, Mary Ellen
    Encyclopedia of Gothic literature   **809**
    The Underground Railroad   **973.7**
    Who's who in the Middle Ages   **920.003**
    (jt. auth) Carey, G. A multicultural dictionary of
       literary terms   **803**

Snow, John, 1813-1858
    About
    Johnson, S. The ghost map   **614.5**

Snow
    Fiction
    Schroeder, L. Far from you   **Fic**

Snow apples. Razzell, M.   **Fic**

Snow falling in spring. Li, M.   **92**

Snow falling on cedars. Guterson, D.   **Fic**

Snow in August. Hamill, P.   **Fic**

Snow Mountain passage. Houston, J. D.   **Fic**

Snowboard!. Masoff, J.   **796.93**

Snowboarder's start-up. Werner, D.   **796.93**

Snowboarding
    Kleh, C. Snowboarding skills   **796.93**
    Masoff, J. Snowboard!   **796.93**
    Werner, D. Snowboarder's start-up   **796.93**

Snowboarding skills. Kleh, C.   **796.93**

Snowstruck. Fredston, J. A.   **551.3**

Snyder, Carrie L.
    (ed) Euthanasia: opposing viewpoints. See Eu-
    thanasia: opposing viewpoints   **179.7**

Snyder, James
    Art of the Middle Ages   **709.02**

Snyder, Kurt
    Me, myself, and them   **92**

Snyder, Midori, 1954-
    (jt. auth) Yolen, J. Except the queen   **Fic**

Snyder's medieval art. See Snyder, J. Art of the
    Middle Ages   **709.02**

So punk rock (and other ways to disappoint your
    mother). Ostow, M.   **Fic**

So you want to write. Piercy, M.   **808.3**

Soanes, Catherine
    (ed) Concise Oxford English dictionary. See
    Concise Oxford English dictionary   **423**

Sobel, Dava
    Longitude   **526**
    The planets   **523.2**

Sobey, Ed
    A field guide to automotive technology
       629.2
    The way toys work   **688.7**

Sobey, Woody
    (jt. auth) Sobey, E. The way toys work
       688.7

Sobey, Ted Woodall *See* Sobey, Woody

Sobran, Joseph
    Hamlet [criticism]   **822.3**
    Henry IV, part 1 [criticism]   **822.3**
    Julius Caesar [criticism]   **822.3**
    A midsummer night's dream [criticism]
       822.3

Soccer
    Ayub, A. However tall the mountain
       796.334
    Buxton, T. Soccer skills for young players
       796.334
    Crisfield, D. Winning soccer for girls
       796.334
    Longman, J. The girls of summer   **796.334**
    Luongo, A. M. Soccer drills   **796.334**
    Luxbacher, J. Soccer: steps to success
       796.334
    McIntosh, J. S. Soccer   **796.334**
    Mielke, D. Soccer fundamentals   **796.334**
    St. John, W. Outcasts united   **796.334**
    Fiction
    Martino, A. C. Over the end line   **Fic**
    Myers, W. D. Kick   **Fic**
    Peet, M. Keeper   **Fic**

Soccer drills. Luongo, A. M.   **796.334**

Soccer skills for young players. Buxton, T.
       796.334

Social ability *See* Social skills

Social action
    Drake, J. Yes you can!   **361.2**
    Halpin, M. It's your world—if you don't like it,
    change it   **361.2**
    McKibben, B. Fight global warming now
       363.7

Social action—*Continued*
Fiction
McDonald, A. Boys, bears, and a serious pair of hiking boots **Fic**
Nelson, B. Destroy all cars **Fic**

Social and psychological disorder in the works of Edgar Allan Poe **818**

Social anthropology *See* Ethnology

Social behavior *See* Human behavior

Social change
Diamond, J. M. Collapse: how societies choose to fail or succeed **304.2**
Diamond, J. M. Guns, germs, and steel **303.4**
Fischer, C. S. Century of difference **306**
McNeese, T. The progressive movement **324.2**
Wade, N. Before the dawn **599.93**

Social classes
See also Working class
Fiction
Abrahams, P. Reality check **Fic**
Bloor, E. Taken **Fic**
Budhos, M. T. Tell us we're home **Fic**
Bunce, E. C. Star crossed **Fic**
Chevalier, T. Girl with a pearl earring **Fic**
Doctorow, E. L. Ragtime **Fic**
Elkeles, S. Perfect chemistry **Fic**
Eulberg, E. Prom and prejudice **Fic**
Gardner, S. The red necklace **Fic**
Godbersen, A. The luxe **Fic**
Grahame-Smith, S. Pride and prejudice and zombies **Fic**
Harland, R. Worldshaker **Fic**
Hinton, S. E. The outsiders **Fic**
Hosseini, K. The kite runner **Fic**
Kate, L. The betrayal of Natalie Hargrove **Fic**
Koja, K. Headlong **Fic**
Rees, C. Sovay **Fic**
Resau, L. The Queen of Water **Fic**
Richards, J. Three rivers rising **Fic**
Scott, K. She's so dead to us **Fic**
Shinn, S. General Winston's daughter **Fic**
Whitman, E. Wildwing **Fic**
Wilkins, E. J. Sellout **Fic**

Social competence *See* Social skills

Social conflict
See also Conflict management

Social contract **320.1**

Social customs *See* Manners and customs

Social democracy *See* Socialism

Social equality *See* Equality

Social ethics
See also Bioethics
Callahan, D. The cheating culture **174**

Social history of the United States **306**

Social intelligence. Goleman, D. **158**

Social issues firsthand [series]
Adoption **362.7**
Poverty **362.5**
Terrorism **363.32**

Social issues in literature [series]
The environment in Henry David Thoreau's Walden **818**
Peer pressure in Robert Cormier's The chocolate war **813.009**
Social and psychological disorder in the works of Edgar Allan Poe **818**

Social life and customs *See* Manners and customs

Social movements
The Britannica guide to political and social movements that changed the modern world **322.4**
Malaspina, A. The ethnic and group identity movements **323.1**

Social networking
De Abreu, B. S. Media literacy, social networking, and the web 2.0 environment for the K-12 educator **302.23**
More than MySpace **027.62**

Social problems
Males, M. A. Framing youth **305.23**
Fiction
Doctorow, E. L. Ragtime **Fic**
Sinclair, U. The jungle **Fic**

Social problems in literature
Social and psychological disorder in the works of Edgar Allan Poe **818**

Social psychology
Fromm, E. Escape from freedom **323.44**

Social sciences
Dictionaries
Dictionary of the social sciences **300.3**

Social security
DeWitt, L. Social security **368.4**

Social skills
Sommers, M. A. Great interpersonal skills **650.1**

Social software in libraries. Farkas, M. **025.5**

Social values
American values: opposing viewpoints **306**

Socialism
Fleming, T. Socialism **320.5**
Sayrafiezadeh, S. When skateboards will be free **92**

See/See also pages in the following book(s):
Tuchman, B. W. The proud tower **909.82**

Socialist Workers' Party (U.S.)
Sayrafiezadeh, S. When skateboards will be free **92**

Socially handicapped children
Conroy, P. The water is wide **371.9**
Kozol, J. Savage inequalities **371.9**

Societies
See also Clubs; Secret societies

Society and art *See* Art and society

Society of Friends
Fiction
Turnbull, A. No shame, no fear **Fic**
West, J. The friendly persuasion **Fic**

Sociology
O'Connell, D. People person [biography of Marta Tienda] **92**

Socrates
See/See also pages in the following book(s):
Russell, B. A history of Western philosophy
109

Socrates café. Phillips, C. **100**

Sodium chloride *See* Salt

Sofer, Morry
(ed) Multicultural Spanish dictionary. See Multicultural Spanish dictionary **463**

Softball
Garman, J. Softball skills & drills **796.357**
Gola, M. Winning softball for girls **796.357**
Fiction
Ritter, J. H. Under the baseball moon **Fic**

Softball skills & drills. Garman, J. **796.357**

Soil conservation
Cunningham, K. Soil **333.7**

Soil microbiology
Wolfe, D. W. Tales from the underground
578

Soils
Cunningham, K. Soil **333.7**
Gardner, R. Soil **631.4**

Sojourner Truth *See* Truth, Sojourner, d. 1883

Sokolove, Michael Y.
The ticket out: Darryl Strawberry and the boys of Crenshaw **796.357**
Warrior girls **796**

Solace of the road. Dowd, S. **Fic**

Solar and geothermal energy. Tabak, J. **621.47**

Solar eclipses
Harrington, P. S. Eclipse! **523.7**

Solar radiation

See also Greenhouse effect

Solar system
Benson, M. Beyond **523.2**
Boyle, A. The case for Pluto **523.4**
Daniels, P. The new solar system **523.2**
Jayawardhana, R. Strange new worlds **523.2**
Jones, B. W. Pluto **523.4**
Rivkin, A. S. Asteroids, comets, and dwarf planets **523.2**
Sobel, D. The planets **523.2**
The solar system **523.2**
Tyson, N. D. G. Death by black hole **523.8**
Weintraub, D. A. Is Pluto a planet? **523.4**
Encyclopedias
Encyclopedia of the solar system **523.2**

The **solar** system **523.2**

Sold. McCormick, P. **Fic**

Soldiers

See also Women soldiers
Fiction
Frost, H. Crossing stones **Fic**
Hooker, R. MASH **Fic**
Klass, S. S. Soldier's secret **Fic**
McCormick, P. Purple Heart **Fic**
O'Brien, T. Going after Cacciato **Fic**
Reinhardt, D. The things a brother knows
Fic
Shinn, S. General Winston's daughter **Fic**
Spillebeen, G. Age 14 **Fic**

Israel
Harmon, A. Lonely soldier **92**
United States
McPherson, J. M. For cause and comrades
973.7
Phelps, M. W. Nathan Hale **92**
Smithson, R. Ghosts of war **956.7**

Soldier's heart. Paulsen, G. **Fic**

Soldier's secret. Klass, S. S. **Fic**

Solheim, Bruce Olav
(jt. auth) Hoogensen, G. Women in power
305.4

Solinger, Rickie, 1947-
(ed) Abortion wars. See Abortion wars
363.46

Solis, Hilda L., 1957-
See/See also pages in the following book(s):
Profiles in courage for our time **920**

Soliz, Adela
(ed) Gangs: opposing viewpoints. See Gangs: opposing viewpoints **364.1**

The **soloist** [biography of Nathaniel Anthony Ayers] Lopez, S. **92**

Solomon, King of Israel
Fiction
Stroud, J. The ring of Solomon **Fic**

Solomon, Robert C., 1942-2007
A short history of philosophy **109**

Solomon, Susan, 1956-
The coldest March **998**

Solomon's thieves. Mechner, J. **741.5**

Solvent abuse
Flynn, N. Inhalants and solvents **362.29**

Solzhenitsyn, Aleksandr, 1918-2008
One day in the life of Ivan Denisovich **Fic**
See/See also pages in the following book(s):
Aikman, D. Great souls **920**

Some girls are. Summers, C. **Fic**

Somebody everybody listens to. Supplee, S.
Fic

Someday this pain will be useful to you. Cameron, P. **Fic**

Somervill, Barbara A., 1948-
Michelangelo **92**

Something like fate. Colasanti, S. **Fic**

Something like hope. Goodman, S. **Fic**

Something out of nothing [biography of Marie Curie] McClafferty, C. K. **92**

Something rotten. Gratz, A. **Fic**

Something wicked this way comes. Bradbury, R.
Fic

Sometimes we're always real same-same. Roesch, M. **Fic**

Sommer, Elyse
(ed) Metaphors dictionary. See Metaphors dictionary **423**

Sommers, Michael A., 1966-
Great interpersonal skills **650.1**

Son of the mob. Korman, G. **Fic**

Sonenklar, Carol
Anorexia and bulimia **616.85**

Sones, Sonya
One of those hideous books where the mother
  dies   **Fic**
What my mother doesn't know   **Fic**
The **song** of Roland. Chanson de Roland   **841**
Song of the sparrow. Sandell, L. A.   **Fic**
Songbird journeys. Chu, M.   **598**
Songs
    See also National songs; Popular music
Songs, American *See* American songs
Songs from this Earth on turtle's back
    811.008
Songwriters *See* Composers; Lyricists
Songwriter's market   **782.42**
Sonneborn, Liz
A to Z of American Indian women   **920.003**
Chronology of American Indian history
    970.004
The end of apartheid in South Africa
    968.06
The environmental movement   **333.72**
Harriet Beecher Stowe   **92**
Mark Twain   **92**
Sonnenblick, Jordan
Notes from the midnight driver   **Fic**
The **sonnets**. Shakespeare, W.   **821**

The **sonnets** [criticism] Bloom, H., ed   **822.3**
The **sonnets** [criticism] Mussari, M.   **822.3**
Sonnets from the Portuguese. Browning, E. B.
    821
Sonny's war. Hobbs, V.   **Fic**
Sons and fathers *See* Father-son relationship
Sons and mothers *See* Mother-son relationship
The **sons** of liberty. Lagos, A.   **741.5**
Sophie Scholl and the white rose. Dumbach, A. E.
    943.086
Sophie's choice. Styron, W.   **Fic**
Sophocles
    About
Sophocles' Oedipus rex [critical essays]
    882.009
See/See also pages in the following book(s):
Hamilton, E. The Greek way   **880.9**
Sophocles' Oedipus rex [critical essays]
    882.009
Soporifics *See* Narcotics
Sorcery *See* Magic
Sorensen, Lita
The Scottsboro Boys Trial   **345**
Sorenson, Georgia Jones
(ed) Encyclopedia of leadership. See Encyclope-
  dia of leadership   **658.4**
Sorrells, Walter
First shot   **Fic**
Sorrentino, Paul
Student companion to Stephen Crane
    813.009
Sorrow's kitchen [biography of Zora Neale
  Hurston] Lyons, M. E.   **92**
Sorta like a rockstar. Quick, M.   **Fic**

Soto, Gary
The afterlife   **Fic**
Buried onions   **Fic**
Novio boy   **812**
Partly cloudy   **811**
Soul enchilada. Gill, D. M.   **Fic**
The **soul** of baseball. Posnanski, J.   **796.357**
The **souls** of Black folk. Du Bois, W. E. B.
    305.8
Sound recordings
    Fiction
Prinz, Y. The Vinyl Princess   **Fic**
Sound reporting. Kern, J.   **070.4**
The **sounds** of poetry. Pinsky, R.   **808.5**
The **sounds** of slavery. White, S.   **326**
Sourcebooks Shakespeare [series]
Shakespeare, W. Othello   **822.3**
Shakespeare, W. Romeo and Juliet   **822.3**
Sousanis, John
(jt. auth) Pendergast, T. Constitutional amend-
  ments: from freedom of speech to flag burn-
  ing   **342**
South (U.S.) *See* Southern States
South Africa
    Description and travel
Carter, J. Power lines   **968.06**
    Fiction
Craig, C. Afrika   **Fic**
Glass, L. The year the gypsies came   **Fic**
Gordimer, N. The house gun   **Fic**
Gordimer, N. My son's story   **Fic**
Nyembezi, C. L. S. The rich man of Pietermar-
  itzburg   **Fic**
Paton, A. Cry, the beloved country   **Fic**
Van de Ruit, J. Spud   **Fic**
    History
Beck, R. The history of South Africa   **968**
Thompson, L. M. A history of South Africa
    968
    Politics and government
Biko, S. I write what I like   **968.06**
Gaines, A. Nelson Mandela and apartheid in
  world history   **92**
Mandela, N. Mandela   **92**
Mandela, N. Nelson Mandela speaks   **968.06**
    Race relations
    See also Anti-apartheid movement; Apart-
  heid
Biko, S. I write what I like   **968.06**
Finnegan, W. Crossing the line   **968.06**
Gaines, A. Nelson Mandela and apartheid in
  world history   **92**
Mandela, N. Mandela   **92**
Sonneborn, L. The end of apartheid in South
  Africa   **968.06**
Thompson, L. M. A history of South Africa
    968
Tutu, D. The words of Desmond Tutu   **252**
    Race relations—Drama
Fugard, A. "Master Harold"— and the boys
    822
South Asia
    Religion
Eastern religions   **200.9**

Speed (Drug) *See* Methamphetamine

Speight, James G.
(ed) Lange's handbook of chemistry. See Lange's handbook of chemistry   **540**

Speleology *See* Caves

A **spell** for chameleon.   **Fic**

Spellbound. McDonald, J.   **Fic**

Spellenberg, Richard
Familiar flowers of North America: eastern region   **582.13**
Familiar flowers of North America: western region   **582.13**
National Audubon Society field guide to North American wildflowers, western region   **582.13**

Spells *See* Magic

Spence, Graham
(jt. auth) Anthony, L. Babylon's ark   **590.73**
(jt. auth) Anthony, L. The elephant whisperer   **599.67**

Spencer, Herbert, 1820-1903
See/See also pages in the following book(s):
Durant, W. J. The story of philosophy   **109**

Spencer, Juliet V.
Cervical cancer   **616.99**

Spencer, Kit
Pro makeup   **646.7**

Spengemann, William C.
(ed) Hawthorne, N. The portable Hawthorne   **818**

Sphinx's princess. Friesner, E. M.   **Fic**

Spider Woman's granddaughters   **S C**

Spiders
Dalton, S. Spiders   **595.4**
Dourlot, S. Insect museum   **595.7**
Eisner, T. Secret weapons   **595.7**
Kelly, L. Spiders   **595.4**
Stewart, A. Wicked bugs   **632**

Spiders in the hairdo. Holt, D.   **398.2**

Spiegelman, Art
In the shadow of no towers   **973.931**
Maus   **940.53**

Spiegelman, Vladek
Graphic novels
Spiegelman, A. Maus   **940.53**

Spies
Owen, D. Spies: the undercover world of secrets, gadgets and lies   **327.12**
Phelps, M. W. Nathan Hale   **92**
Philipson, I. J. Ethel Rosenberg   **92**
Fiction
Anderson, L. H. Chains   **Fic**
Heath, J. The Lab   **Fic**
Koontz, D. R. Watchers   **Fic**
Le Carré, J. The spy who came in from the cold   **Fic**
Plum-Ucci, C. Streams of Babel   **Fic**
Slade, A. G. The hunchback assignments   **Fic**
Wild, K. Fight game   **Fic**
Graphic novels
Miyuki, T. Musashi #9, Vol. 1   **741.5**

Spies in literature
Mystery and suspense writers   **809.3**

The **spies** of Mississippi. Bowers, R.   **323.1**

Spike, John T.
(ed) Mason, A. A history of Western art   **709**

Spillebeen, Geert, 1956-
Age 14   **Fic**
Kipling's choice   **Fic**

Spilsbury, Louise, 1963-
(ed) Industrialization and empire, 1783 to 1914. See Industrialization and empire, 1783 to 1914   **330.9**
(ed) World wars and globalization, 1914 to 2010. See World wars and globalization, 1914 to 2010   **909.82**

Spin [biography of Michael Jackson] O'Keefe, S.   **92**

Spink, Kathryn
Mother Teresa   **92**

Spinner, Stephanie, 1943-
Damosel   **Fic**

Spinoza, Benedictus de, 1632-1677
See/See also pages in the following book(s):
Durant, W. J. The story of philosophy   **109**
Russell, B. A history of Western philosophy   **109**

The **spiral** staircase. Armstrong, K.   **92**

Spires, Elizabeth
I heard God talking to me   **811**

The **spirit** of Yellowstone. Meyer, J. L.   **978.7**

Spiritism *See* Spiritualism

Spirits *See* Angels; Demonology; Ghosts

Spiritual life
Campbell, J. The power of myth   **201**
Chopra, D. Fire in the heart   **204**

Spiritualism
Fiction
Salerni, D. K. We hear the dead   **Fic**
Weyn, S. Distant waves   **Fic**

Spirituals (Songs)
See also Gospel music

Spitz, Bob
Yeah! yeah! yeah!   **920**

Splat!. Walters, E.   **Fic**

Splendid solution: Jonas Salk and the conquest of polio. Kluger, J.   **92**

The **splendor** falls. Clement-Moore, R.   **Fic**

Splicing *See* Knots and splices

Split. Avasthi, S.   **Fic**

Split. Petrucha, S.   **Fic**

The **Spoken** word revolution   **811.008**

Spook. Roach, M.   **133.9**

Spoon River anthology. Masters, E. L.   **811**

Sporting [series]
Ezra, M. Muhammad Ali   **92**

Sports
See also College sports; Extreme sports; Games; School sports; Sports for women; Winter sports

St. Petersburg (Russia) *See* Saint Petersburg (Russia)

St. Pierre, Denise
Golf fundamentals   **796.352**

St. Valentine's Day *See* Valentine's Day

Stade, George
(ed) Encyclopedia of British writers, 1800 to the present. See Encyclopedia of British writers, 1800 to the present   **820.9**

Staeger, Rob
Ancient mathematicians   **920**

Stage makeup. Corson, R.   **792**

Stagings. Garner, J.   **812**

Stahler, David, Jr.
Doppelganger   **Fic**

Stairways to the stars. Aveni, A. F.   **520**

Stalder, Erika
Fashion 101   **746.9**
In the driver's seat   **629.28**

Stalin, Joseph, 1879-1953
About
Cunningham, K. Joseph Stalin and the Soviet Union   **92**

Stalingrad, Battle of, 1942-1943
Fiction
Riordan, J. The sniper   **Fic**

Stalking the plumed serpent and other adventures in herpetology. Means, D. B.   **597.9**

Stallworthy, Jon
(ed) The Oxford book of war poetry. See The Oxford book of war poetry   **808.81**

Stamina, Physical *See* Physical fitness

Stampp, Kenneth M. (Kenneth Milton)
(ed) The Causes of the Civil War. See The Causes of the Civil War   **973.7**

Stan Lee's How to draw comics. Lee, S.   **741.5**

Standard cataloging for school and public libraries. Intner, S. S.   **025.3**

The **standard** code of parliamentary procedure. Sturgis, A.   **060.4**

Standiford, Natalie
Confessions of the Sullivan sisters   **Fic**
How to say goodbye in Robot   **Fic**

Standing Bear, Ponca Chief, 1829?-1908
See/See also pages in the following book(s):
Brown, D. A. Bury my heart at Wounded Knee   **970.004**

Standley, Fred L.
Conversations with James Baldwin   **92**

Standring, Susan
(ed) Gray's anatomy. See Gray's anatomy   **611**

Stanford, Eleanor
(ed) Interracial America: opposing viewpoints. See Interracial America: opposing viewpoints   **305.8**

Stanley, George Edward, 1942-
Sitting Bull   **92**

Stanton, Doug
In harm's way   **940.54**

Stanton, Elizabeth Cady, 1815-1902
About
Banner, L. W. Elizabeth Cady Stanton   **92**
Colman, P. Elizabeth Cady Stanton and Susan B. Anthony   **92**
Ginzberg, L. D. Elizabeth Cady Stanton   **92**

Stanton, Tom
Hank Aaron and the home run that changed America   **92**

Staphylococcus aureus infections. Freeman-Cook, L.   **616.9**

Staples, Suzanne Fisher
Shabanu   **Fic**

Star crossed. Bunce, E. C.   **Fic**

The **star** guide. Kerrod, R.   **523.8**

Star trek (Television program)
Krauss, L. M. The physics of Star Trek   **500.5**

Star ware. Harrington, P. S.   **522**

Star Wars films
Cavelos, J. The science of Star Wars   **791.43**

Stardust. Gaiman, N.   **Fic**

Stargardt, Nicholas
Witnesses of war   **940.53**

Stargazing with binoculars. Scagell, R.   **523.8**

Stark, Peter
Winter adventure   **796.9**

Stark, Steven D.
Meet the Beatles   **920**

Starkey, David
Six wives: the queens of Henry VIII   **920**

Starks, Glenn L., 1966-
How your government really works   **320.4**

Starr, Chester G., 1914-
A history of the ancient world   **930**

The **Starry** rift   **S C**

Stars
See also Black holes (Astronomy)
Jones, L. V. Stars and galaxies   **523.8**
Kaler, J. B. The hundred greatest stars   **523.8**
Scagell, R. Stargazing with binoculars   **523.8**
Atlases
Kerrod, R. The star guide   **523.8**

Stars and galaxies. Jones, L. V.   **523.8**

Start-to-finish YA programs. Jones, E. W.   **027.62**

Start-up sports [series]
Werner, D. In-line skater's start-up   **796.21**
Werner, D. Snowboarder's start-up   **796.93**

Stassen, Jean-Philippe
Deogratias   **741.5**

Stat-spotting. Best, J.   **301**

State, Paul F., 1950-
A brief history of Ireland   **941.5**

State, Heads of *See* Heads of state

State, The
Social contract   **320.1**

State and industry *See* Industrial policy

State governments
The book of the states   **352.13**

Stein, Tammar
- High dive   **Fic**
- Light years   **Fic**

Steinbeck, John, 1902-1968
- Conversations with John Steinbeck   **92**
- The grapes of wrath   **Fic**
- The grapes of wrath and other writings, 1936-1941   **818**
- Of mice and men   **Fic**
- The pearl   **Fic**

About
- Burkhead, C. Student companion to John Steinbeck   **813.009**
- Kordich, C. J. Bloom's how to write about John Steinbeck   **813.009**
- Meltzer, M. John Steinbeck   **92**
- Newman, G. A student's guide to John Steinbeck   **813.009**
- Reef, C. John Steinbeck   **92**
- Schultz, J. D. Critical companion to John Steinbeck   **813.009**

Steinberg, Alan, 1945-
- (jt. auth) Abdul-Jabbar, K. Black profiles in courage   **920**

Steinberg, Jacques
- The gatekeepers   **378.1**

Steinberg, Julius, 1972-
- (ed) Manser, M. H. Critical companion to the Bible   **220.6**

Steinberg, Mark D.
- (jt. auth) Riasanovsky, N. V. A history of Russia   **947**

Steinberg, Michael
- The symphony   **784.2**

Steinberg, S. H. (Sigfrid Henry), 1899-1969
- The Wilson calendar of world history. See The Wilson calendar of world history   **902**

Steinberg, Shirley R., 1952-
- (ed) Teen life in Europe. See Teen life in Europe   **305.23**

Steinberg, Sigfrid Henry See Steinberg, S. H. (Sigfrid Henry), 1899-1969

Steinem, Gloria
- Revolution from within   **155.2**

Steiner, Matt
About
- Warren, A. Escape from Saigon [biography of Matt Steiner]   **92**

Steinhart, Peter
- The company of wolves   **599.77**

Steinmetz, Karen
- The mourning wars   **Fic**

Stekler, Paul
- (jt. auth) Welch, J. Killing Custer   **973.8**

Stem cell research
- Marcovitz, H. Stem cell research   **616**
- Panno, J. Stem cell research   **616**
- Stem cells: opposing viewpoints   **174.2**
- *See/See also pages in the following book(s):*
- Biomedical ethics: opposing viewpoints   **174.2**

Stem cells: opposing viewpoints   **174.2**

Stemple, Jane H. Yolen See Yolen, Jane

Stenstrup, Allen
- Forests   **333.75**

Stent, Gunther S., 1924-2008
- (jt. auth) Watson, J. D. The double helix   **572.8**

Step by step to college and career success. Gardner, J. N.   **378.1**

A **step** from heaven. Na, A.   **Fic**

Stepan, Peter
- (ed) Photos that changed the world. See Photos that changed the world   **779**

Stepfamilies
Fiction
- Cumbie, P. Where people like us live   **Fic**
- Dessen, S. Along for the ride   **Fic**
- Freymann-Weyr, G. After the moment   **Fic**
- Grimes, N. Dark sons   **Fic**
- Les Becquets, D. Season of ice   **Fic**
- Lo, M. Ash   **Fic**
- McNeal, L. Zipped   **Fic**
- Reinhardt, D. How to build a house   **Fic**
- Schroeder, L. Far from you   **Fic**
- Tharp, T. The spectacular now   **Fic**

Stepfathers
Fiction
- Beitia, S. The last good place of Lily Odilon   **Fic**
- Felin, M. S. Touching snow   **Fic**
- McCahan, E. I now pronounce you someone else   **Fic**
- Sanchez, A. Bait   **Fic**
- Vincent, Z. The lucky place   **Fic**

Stephen King: a critical companion. Russell, S. A.   **813.009**

Stephens, Claire Gatrell
- Library 101   **027.8**

Stepmothers
Fiction
- Billingsley, F. Chime   **Fic**
- Buffie, M. Winter shadows   **Fic**
- Prose, F. Touch   **Fic**

Stepparents
See also Stepfathers; Stepmothers

Steppenwolf. Hesse, H.   **Fic**

Steps to success activity series
- Luxbacher, J. Soccer: steps to success   **796.334**

Steps to success sports series
- McAfee, R. Table tennis   **796.34**

Sterling, Laurie A.
- Bloom's how to write about Nathaniel Hawthorne   **813.009**

Sterling biographies [series]
- Berne, E. C. Sacagawea   **92**
- Borzendowski, J. Marie Curie   **92**
- Hopping, L. J. Chief Joseph   **92**
- Jones, V. G. Pocahontas   **92**
- Stanley, G. E. Sitting Bull   **92**
- Sullivan, G. Geronimo   **92**
- Zimmerman, D. J. Tecumseh   **92**

Stern, Sam, 1990-
- Cooking up a storm   **641.5**

Stolen lives. Oufkir, M.   **92**

The **stolen** one. Crowley, S.   **Fic**

Stolen voices   **920**

Stolley, Richard B.
(ed) Life: World War 2. See Life: World War 2   **940.53**

Stolzenberg, William
Where the wild things were   **577**

Stone, Carol Leth
The basics of biology   **570**

Stone, Mary Hanlon
Invisible girl   **Fic**

Stone, Norman, 1941-
World War One   **940.3**

Stone, Tanya Lee
Almost astronauts   **629.45**
A bad boy can be good for a girl   **Fic**
Ella Fitzgerald   **92**
The good, the bad, and the Barbie   **688.7**

Stone, Toni, 1921-1996
About
Ackmann, M. Curveball [biography of Toni Stone]   **92**

The **stone** circles of Britain, Ireland and Brittany. Burl, A.   **936.1**

The **stone** circles of the British Isles. See Burl, A. The stone circles of Britain, Ireland and Brittany   **936.1**

A **stone** in my hand. Clinton, C.   **Fic**

Stonehenge (England)
See/See also pages in the following book(s):
Aveni, A. F. Stairways to the stars   **520**

Stoner & Spaz. Koertge, R.   **Fic**

Stones into schools. Mortenson, G.   **371.82**

Stoneware See Pottery

Stop plagiarism   **808**

Stoppard, Tom
Rosencrantz and Guildenstern are dead   **822**

Stories in stone. Williams, D. B.   **550**

The **stories** of John Cheever. Cheever, J.   **S C**

Stories, poems, and other writings. Cather, W.   **818**

Stories without words
Drooker, E. Blood song   **741.5**
Tan, S. The arrival   **741.5**
Graphic novels
Hartzell, A. Fox bunny funny   **741.5**

Stork, Francisco X.
The last summer of the death warriors   **Fic**
Marcelo in the real world   **Fic**

Stork. Delsol, W.   **Fic**

The **storm.** Van Heerden, I. L.   **976.3**

The **storm** thief. Wooding, C.   **Fic**

Storm world. Mooney, C.   **363.7**

Storms
    See also Dust storms; Hurricanes; Tornadoes
Junger, S. The perfect storm   **910.4**
Storms, violent winds, and earth's atmosphere   **551.55**

Storms, violent winds, and earth's atmosphere   **551.55**

Story of a girl. Zarr, S.   **Fic**

The **story** of architecture. Glancey, J.   **720.9**

The **story** of art. Gombrich, E. H.   **709**

The **story** of Edgar Sawtelle. Wroblewski, D.   **Fic**

The **story** of English. McCrum, R.   **420**

The **story** of King Arthur and his knights. Pyle, H.   **398.2**

The **story** of measurement. Robinson, A.   **530.8**

The story of Mexico [series]
Stein, R. C. The Mexican Revolution   **972**

The **story** of my life. Keller, H.   **92**

The **story** of philosophy. Durant, W. J.   **109**

The **story** of philosophy. Magee, B.   **190**

Story of science [series]
Hakim, J. The story of science: Aristotle leads the way   **509**
Hakim, J. The story of science: Einstein adds a new dimension   **509**
Hakim, J. The story of science: Newton at the center   **509**

The **story** of science: Aristotle leads the way. Hakim, J.   **509**

The **story** of science: Einstein adds a new dimension. Hakim, J.   **509**

The **story** of science: Newton at the center. Hakim, J.   **509**

The **story** of the champions of the Round Table. Pyle, H.   **398.2**

Storytelling
Bruchac, J. Our stories remember   **970.004**
De Vos, G. Storytelling for young adults   **372.6**
World folklore for storytellers   **398**
Fiction
Blubaugh, P. Serendipity Market   **Fic**
Jones, L. Mister Pip   **Fic**
Michaelis, A. Tiger moon   **Fic**
Wooding, C. Poison   **Fic**

Storytelling for young adults. De Vos, G.   **372.6**

Stotan!. Crutcher, C.   **Fic**

Stott, Carole
(jt. auth) Kerrod, R. Hubble: the mirror on the universe   **522**

Stout, Jay A., 1959-
Hammer from above   **956.7**

Stow, Dorrik A. V.
Oceans: an illustrated reference   **551.46**

Stowe, Harriet Beecher, 1811-1896
The Oxford Harriet Beecher Stowe reader   **818**
Uncle Tom's cabin   **Fic**
About
Sonneborn, L. Harriet Beecher Stowe   **92**
See/See also pages in the following book(s):
McPherson, J. M. Drawn with the sword   **973.7**

Strong, James, 1822-1894
(jt. auth) Vine, W. E. Strong's concise concordance and Vine's concise expository dictionary of the Bible   **220.3**

Strong at the heart   **362.7**

Strong's concise concordance and Vine's concise expository dictionary of the Bible. Vine, W. E.   **220.3**

Stroom, Gerrold van der
(ed) Frank, A. The diary of Anne Frank: the critical edition   **92**

Stroud, Jonathan, 1970-
The Amulet of Samarkand   **Fic**
Heroes of the valley   **Fic**
The ring of Solomon   **Fic**

Stroud, Les, 1962-
Will to live   **613.6**

Struck by lightning. Rosenthal, J.   **519.2**

A **struggle** for power. Draper, T.   **973.3**

The **Struggle** to be strong   **305.23**

Strunk, William, 1869-1946
The elements of style   **808**

Stubblefield, R. Jay
(jt. auth) DeGategno, P. J. Critical companion to Jonathan Swift   **828**

Stubbs, Aelred
(jt. auth) Biko, S. I write what I like   **968.06**

Student aid
See also Scholarships; Student loan funds
College financing information for teens   **378.3**
Hollander, B. Paying for college   **378.3**
How to pay for college   **378.3**

Directories
High school senior's guide to merit and other no-need funding, 2008-2010   **378.3**
Schlachter, G. A. College student's guide to merit and other no-need funding, 2008-2010   **378.3**

Student cheating *See* Cheating (Education)

Student companion to Arthur Miller. Abbotson, S. C. W.   **812.009**

Student companion to Edgar Allan Poe. Magistrale, T.   **818**

Student companion to George Orwell. Brunsdale, M.   **828**

Student companion to John Steinbeck. Burkhead, C.   **813.009**

Student companion to Stephen Crane. Sorrentino, P.   **813.009**

Student companions to classic writers [series]
Abbotson, S. C. W. Student companion to Arthur Miller   **812.009**
Brunsdale, M. Student companion to George Orwell   **828**
Burkhead, C. Student companion to John Steinbeck   **813.009**
Magistrale, T. Student companion to Edgar Allan Poe   **818**
Sorrentino, P. Student companion to Stephen Crane   **813.009**

Student dishonesty *See* Cheating (Education)

Student encyclopedia of African literature. Killam, G. D.   **92**

Student engagement and information literacy   **028.7**

A **student** guide to climate and weather. Gunn, A. M.   **551.5**

Student loan funds
College Entrance Examination Board. Getting financial aid 2011   **378.3**
Peterson's how to get money for college   **378.3**

Student Nonviolent Coordinating Committee
Lewis, J. Walking with the wind   **92**
Zellner, R. The wrong side of Murder Creek [biography of Robert Zellner]   **92**

Student-teacher interaction *See* Teacher-student relationship

Students
See also College students; High school students

Civil rights
Raskin, J. B. We the students   **344**
Students' rights   **344**
Students' rights: opposing viewpoints   **344**

Counseling
See Educational counseling

Law and legislation
Kowalski, K. M. The Earls case and the student drug testing debate   **344**
Phillips, T. A. Hazelwood v. Kuhlmeier and the school newspaper censorship debate   **342**
Raskin, J. B. We the students   **344**
Students' rights   **344**

Students, Handicapped *See* Handicapped students

Students and libraries *See* Libraries and students

Student's encyclopedia of American literary characters   **810.9**

Student's encyclopedia of great American writers   **920.003**

The **student's** encyclopedia of Judaism   **296.03**

A **student's** guide to Arthur Miller. Dunkleberger, A.   **812.009**

Student's guide to Congress   **328.73**

Student's guide to elections   **324**

A **student's** guide to Emily Dickinson. Borus, A.   **811.009**

A **student's** guide to Ernest Hemingway. Pingelton, T. J.   **813.009**

The **student's** guide to financial literacy. Lawless, R. E.   **332.024**

A **student's** guide to George Orwell. Means, A. L.   **828**

A **student's** guide to Herman Melville. Diorio, M. A. L.   **813.009**

A **student's** guide to Jack London. Buckwalter, S.   **813.009**

A **student's** guide to John Steinbeck. Newman, G.   **813.009**

A **student's** guide to Robert Frost. Kirk, C. A.   **811.009**

Supernatural graphic novels—*Continued*
Urushibara, Y. Mu shi shi 1   741.5

Superstition
Frazer, Sir J. G. The new golden bough
                                         201
Fiction
Keyes, P. The jumbee   Fic

Superstring theory *See* String theory

Superville Sovak, Jean-Marc
(jt. auth) Chibbaro, J. Deadly   Fic

Supervision of employees *See* Personnel management

Supplee, Suzanne
Artichoke's heart   Fic
Somebody everybody listens to   Fic

Supreme Court (U.S.) *See* United States. Supreme Court

The **Supreme** Court. Baum, L.   347

The **Supreme** Court A to Z. Jost, K.   347

The **Supreme** Court and individual rights. Savage, D. G.   342

Supreme Court decisions [series]
Dudley, M. E. Engel v. Vitale (1962)   344

Supreme Court decisions and women's rights   342

Supreme Court milestones [series]
Perl, L. Cruzan v. Missouri   344
Stefoff, R. Furman v. Georgia   345

The **Supreme** Court of the United States. Patrick, J. J.   347

Surface, Mary Hall, 1958-
Most valuable player and four other all-star plays for middle and high school audiences   812

Surface tension. Runyon, B.   Fic

Surfing
Fiction
Madigan, L. K. The mermaid's mirror   Fic

Surgeons
Graphic novels
Tezuka, O. Black Jack, volume 1   741.5

Surgery, Plastic *See* Plastic surgery

Surrealism
Ross, M. E. Salvador Dali and the surrealists   92

Surrender. Hartnett, S.   Fic

The **surrender** tree. Engle, M.   Fic

Surveying
Danson, E. Weighing the world   526

Survival after airplane accidents, shipwrecks, etc.
Parrado, N. Miracle in the Andes   982
Piven, J. The worst-case scenario survival handbook   613.6
Read, P. P. Alive   910.4
Stroud, L. Will to live   613.6
Wiseman, J. SAS survival handbook   613.6
Fiction
Bodeen, S. A. The Compound   Fic
Bray, L. Beauty queens   Fic
Defoe, D. Robinson Crusoe   Fic
Golding, W. Lord of the flies   Fic

Halam, A. Dr. Franklin's island   Fic
Herlong, M. The great wide sea   Fic
McCarthy, C. The road   Fic
Pratchett, T. Nation   Fic
Preus, M. Heart of a samurai   Fic
Smelcer, J. E. The trap   Fic

Survival of the fittest *See* Natural selection

Survival skills
Fredston, J. A. Snowstruck   551.3
Sherwood, B. The survivors club   613.6
Stilwell, A. The encyclopedia of survival techniques   613.6
Stroud, L. Will to live   613.6
Survival wisdom & know-how   613.6
Wiseman, J. SAS survival handbook   613.6

Survival wisdom & know-how   613.6

Surviving Antarctica. White, A.   Fic

Surviving the Angel of Death. Kor, E. M.   92

The **survivors** club. Sherwood, B.   613.6

Survivors: ordinary people, extraordinary circumstances [series]
Sanna, E. We shall all be free   305.8
Simons, R. Gender danger   362.88

Suspended in language [biography of Niels Bohr]
Ottaviani, J.   92

Suspense fiction
Bibliography
Gannon, M. B. Blood, bedlam, bullets, and badguys   016.8

Sustaining Earth's energy resources. Heinrichs, A.   333.79

Sutcliff, Rosemary, 1920-1992
The Shining Company   Fic

Sutherland, James
Ronald Reagan   92

Sutherland, Jonathan, 1958-
African Americans at war   920.003

Sutherland-Addy, Esi
(ed) Women writing Africa: West Africa and the Sahel. See Women writing Africa: West Africa and the Sahel   896

Sutnick, Barbara P.
(ed) The student's encyclopedia of Judaism. See The student's encyclopedia of Judaism   296.03

Svarney, Thomas E.
(jt. auth) Barnes-Svarney, P. The handy dinosaur answer book   567.9

Swafford, Jan
The Vintage guide to classical music   781.6

Swaine, Meg
Career building through interactive online games   794.8

Swallow me whole. Powell, N.   741.5

Swamps *See* Marshes; Wetlands

Swan, Robert, 1956-
Antarctica 2041   577.5

The **swan** kingdom. Marriott, Z.   Fic

Swann, Brian
(ed) Coming to light. See Coming to light   897

Swanson, James L.
Chasing Lincoln's killer [biography of John Wilkes Booth] **92**

Swanson, Mark, 1951-
Atlas of the Civil War, month by month **973.7**

Swanwick, Michael
The dragons of Babel **Fic**

Sweat and blood. Skurzynski, G. **331.8**

Sweden
Fiction
Nilsson, P. You & you & you **Fic**

Swedin, Eric Gottfrid
Science in the contemporary world **503**

Swedish Americans
Fiction
Cather, W. O pioneers! **Fic**

Sweeney, Edwin R. (Edwin Russell), 1950-
Cochise, Chiricahua Apache chief **92**

Sweeney, Joyce, 1955-
The guardian **Fic**

Sweeney, Michael J., 1945-
(jt. auth) Ballard, R. D. Return to Titanic **910.4**

Sweeney, Michael S.
(jt. auth) Dau, J. B. Lost boy, lost girl **962.4**

Sweet, Christopher
The essential Johannes Vermeer **759.9492**

A **sweet** disorder. Kolosov, J. A. **Fic**

The **sweet** life of Stella Madison. Zeises, L. M. **Fic**

Sweet nothings **811.008**

The **sweetest** dream. Lessing, D. M. **Fic**

The **sweetheart** of Prosper County. Alexander, J. S. **Fic**

Sweethearts. Zarr, S. **Fic**

Sweetman, Jack, 1940-
(jt. auth) Bartlett, M. L. Leathernecks: an illustrated history of the U.S. Marine Corps **359.9**

Sweetness & light. Ellis, H. **595.7**

The **sweetness** at the bottom of the pie. Bradley, A. **Fic**

The **sweetness** of salt. Galante, C. **Fic**

Swenson, May, 1913-1989
Nature **811**

Swidey, Neil
The assist **796.323**

Swift, Jonathan, 1667-1745
Gulliver's travels **Fic**
About
Aykroyd, C. Savage satire [biography of Jonathan Swift] **92**
DeGategno, P. J. Critical companion to Jonathan Swift **828**
See/See also pages in the following book(s):
Highet, G. The classical tradition **809**

Swift, Richard
Gangs **364.1**

A **swift** pure cry. Dowd, S. **Fic**

Swim the fly. Calame, D. **Fic**

Swimming
Hines, E. W. Fitness swimming **613.7**
Mullen, P. H., Jr. Gold in the water **797.2**
Fiction
Calame, D. Swim the fly **Fic**
Crutcher, C. Staying fat for Sarah Byrnes **Fic**
Crutcher, C. Stotan! **Fic**
Howells, A. The summer of skinny dipping **Fic**
Warman, J. Breathless **Fic**

Swimming in the monsoon sea. Selvadurai, S. **Fic**

Swimming to Antarctica. Cox, L. **92**

Swimming with piranhas at feeding time. Conniff, R. **590**

Swindler, Daris Ray
Introduction to the primates **599.8**

Swindlers and swindling
Fiction
Black, H. The white cat **Fic**
Hooper, M. Fallen Grace **Fic**
Lee, Y. S. A spy in the house **Fic**
Luper, E. Bug boy **Fic**
Lynch, S. The lies of Locke Lamora **Fic**
Nyembezi, C. L. S. The rich man of Pietermaritzburg **Fic**
Ryan, P. In Mike we trust **Fic**

Swine flu See Swine influenza

Swine influenza
Parks, P. J. Influenza **616.2**

Swissler, Becky
Winning lacrosse for girls **796.34**

Swofford, Anthony
Jarhead: a Marine's chronicle of the Gulf War and other battles **956.7**

Swoon at your own risk. Salter, S. **Fic**

The **sword** of Shannara. Brooks, T. **Fic**

Swords
History
Reinhardt, H. The book of swords **623.4**

Sylvia Plath [critical essays] **811.009**

Symbolic logic
Edwards, A. W. F. Cogwheels of the mind **511.3**
Paulos, J. A. Once upon a number **519.5**

Symbolism in art
How to read a painting **753**

Symbolism in literature
See/See also pages in the following book(s):
Highet, G. The classical tradition **809**

Symbolism of numbers
See also Numbers

Symbols See Signs and symbols

Symons, Ann K.
Protecting the right to read **025.2**

Symphony
Steinberg, M. The symphony **784.2**

Synar, Mike
See/See also pages in the following book(s):
Profiles in courage for our time **920**

Syphilis
Uschan, M. V. Forty years of medical racism
174.2

Syria
See/See also pages in the following book(s):
Mertz, B. Temples, tombs, & hieroglyphs
932

Fiction
Jolin, P. In the name of God **Fic**

Szwed, John F., 1936-
Jazz 101 **781.65**

T

T. rex and the Crater of Doom. Alvarez, W.
551.7

T4. LeZotte, A. C. **Fic**

Tabak, John
Algebra **512**
Beyond geometry **516**
Biofuels **662**
Coal and oil **333.8**
Geometry **516**
Mathematics and the laws of nature **510**
Natural gas and hydrogen **333.8**
Nuclear energy **621.48**
Numbers **513**
Probability and statistics **519.2**
Solar and geothermal energy **621.47**
Wind and water **333.7**
(jt. auth) Grady, S. M. Biohazards **614.5**

Table tennis
McAfee, R. Table tennis **796.34**

Tack, Karen
Hello, cupcake! **641.8**

Tackach, James, 1954-
(ed) The Civil War. See The Civil War
973.7

Tadpoles *See* Frogs

Tae kwon do
Park, Y. H. Black belt tae kwon do **796.8**

Taft, Robert A., 1889-1953
See/See also pages in the following book(s):
Kennedy, J. F. Profiles in courage **920**

Tagliaferro, Linda
Thomas Edison **92**

Tahmaseb, Charity
The geek girl's guide to cheerleading **Fic**

Tai chi
Pawlett, R. The tai chi handbook **613.7**
The **tai** chi handbook. Pawlett, R. **613.7**

Takács, Sarolta A.
(ed) The ancient world. See The ancient world
930
(ed) The modern world. See The modern world
903

Takahashi, Rumiko, 1957-
One-pound gospel, vol. 1 **741.5**

Takaki, Ronald T., 1939-2009
Double victory **940.53**
Hiroshima **940.54**

Takatsu, Keita
(il) Nitta, H. The manga guide to physics
530

Take control of Asperger's syndrome. Price, J.
616.85

Take control of OCD. Zucker, B. **616.85**

Takemura, Masaharu, 1969-
The manga guide to molecular biology
572.8

Taken. Bloor, E. **Fic**
Taken. McClintock, N. **Fic**

Taking care of your 'girls'. Weiss, M. C.
618.1

Taking risks *See* Risk-taking (Psychology)

Tal, Eve, 1947-
Double crossing **Fic**

Tal, Havah *See* Tal, Eve, 1947-

Talamon, Bruce
Bob Marley **92**

Talbert, Richard J. A., 1947-
(ed) Atlas of classical history. See Atlas of classical history **911**

Talbot, Bryan, 1952-
The tale of one bad rat **741.5**

The **tale** of one bad rat. Talbot, B. **741.5**

A **tale** of two cities. Dickens, C. **Fic**

A **tale** of two summers. Sloan, B. **Fic**

Tales and sketches, including Twice-told tales, Mosses from an old manse, and The snow-image; A wonder book for girls and boys; Tanglewood tales for girls and boys, being a second Wonder book. Hawthorne, N. **S C**

Tales from Earthsea. Le Guin, U. K. **S C**

Tales from outer suburbia. Tan, S. **S C**

Tales from Ovid. Ovid **873**

Tales from the morgue. Wecht, C. H. **614**

Tales from the underground. Wolfe, D. W.
578

The **tales** of Edgar Allan Poe **813.009**

Tales of the Madman Underground. Barnes, J.
Fic

Tales of the South Pacific. Michener, J. A.
S C

Tales out of the school library. Bush, G.
027.8

Tales, rumors, and gossip. De Vos, G. **398**

Talevski, Nick, 1962-
The unofficial encyclopedia of the Rock and Roll Hall of Fame **781.66**

Taliban
Rashid, A. Taliban **958.1**
The Taliban: opposing viewpoints **958.1**
Tzemach Lemmon, G. The dressmaker of Khair Khana **92**

Fiction
Hosseini, K. The kite runner **Fic**

The **Taliban:** opposing viewpoints **958.1**

Talking adolescence **305.23**

Talking in the dark. Merrell, B. **811**

Taylor, Mildred D.
The land   Fic
Roll of thunder, hear my cry   Fic

Taylor, Patricia, 1952-
(jt. auth) Jones, P. Connecting with reluctant teen readers   028.5

Taylor, Susie King, 1848-1912
See/See also pages in the following book(s):
Garrison, M. Slaves who dared   920

Taylor, Terry
Altered art   745.5

Taylor, Todd W.
(jt. auth) Walker, J. R. The Columbia guide to online style   808

Taylor, Yuval
(ed) Douglass, F. Frederick Douglass: selected speeches and writings   326
(ed) Growing up in slavery. See Growing up in slavery   326

Taylor-Guthrie, Danille Kathleen, 1952-
(ed) Morrison, T. Conversations with Toni Morrison   92

Teach yourself visually car care & maintenance. Ramsey, D.   629.28

Teacher-student relationship
Fiction
Freitas, D. This gorgeous game   Fic
Ruby, L. Bad apple   Fic

Teachers
See also Women teachers
Fiction
Doig, I. The whistling season   Fic
Haruf, K. Plainsong   Fic
Levchuk, L. Everything beautiful in the world   Fic
Marshall, C. Christy   Fic
Miller, S. Miss Spitfire   Fic
Northrop, M. Gentlemen   Fic
Southgate, M. The fall of Rome   Fic
Volponi, P. The hand you're dealt   Fic

Teaching
Kozol, J. Letters to a young teacher   371.1
Reeves, D. L. Career ideas for teens in education and training   331.7
Aids and devices
Richardson, W. Blogs, wikis, podcasts, and other powerful Web tools for classrooms   371.3
Zmuda, A. Librarians as learning specialists   023

Teaching, Freedom of *See* Academic freedom

Teaching & testing information literacy skills. Smith, J. B.   028.7

Teaching and learning about computers. Barrett, J. R.   004

Teaching at home *See* Home schooling

Teaching Generation M   027.62

Teaching literacy skills to adolescents using Coretta Scott King Award winners. Bernadowski, C.   372.4

Team Green science projects [series]
Gardner, R. Air   533
Gardner, R. Recycle   628.4

Gardner, R. Soil   631.4
The **tear** collector. Jones, P.   Fic
Tears of a tiger. Draper, S. M.   Fic
Tears of the cheetah. O'Brien, S. J.   591.3

Technical education
150 great tech prep careers   331.7

Technically involved. Braun, L. W.   027.62

Technological change *See* Technological innovations

Technological innovations
Carlisle, R. P. Scientific American inventions and discoveries   609
Core technology competencies for librarians and library staff   020
Forbes, P. The gecko's foot   600
Tenner, E. Our own devices   303.4

Technology
See also Engineering; Nanotechnology; Technological innovations
The handy science answer book   500
Langone, J. The new how things work   600
Macaulay, D. The new way things work   600
Teaching Generation M   027.62
Turney, J. Technology   303.4
Woodford, C. Cool Stuff 2.0 and how it works   600
Encyclopedias
Encyclopedia of science, technology, and ethics   503
McGraw-Hill concise encyclopedia of science & technology   503
McGraw-Hill encyclopedia of science & technology   503
The new book of popular science   503
History
Allen, T. B. Mr. Lincoln's high-tech war   973.7
The Britannica guide to inventions that changed the modern world   609
Carlisle, R. P. Scientific American inventions and discoveries   609
Ferris, J. Ideas that changed the world   609
Inventors and inventions   609
Ochoa, G. The Wilson chronology of science and technology   502
The Seventy great inventions of the ancient world   609
Strapp, J. Science and technology   609
Windelspecht, M. Groundbreaking scientific experiments, inventions, and discoveries of the 19th century   509
Vocational guidance
Exploring tech careers   331.7
Goldberg, J. Careers for scientific types & others with inquiring minds   502

Technology, Information *See* Information technology

Technology and civilization
Diamond, J. M. Guns, germs, and steel   303.4
Technology in world history   909
Tenner, E. Our own devices   303.4
Fiction
Huxley, A. Brave new world   Fic

Tending to Grace. Fusco, K. N.   **Fic**

Tennant, Alan, 1943-
  On the wing   **598**

Tennant, Joseph Alan *See* Tennant, Alan, 1943-

TenNapel, Douglas R.
  Iron West   **741.5**

Tennent, Gilbert, 1703-1764
See/See also pages in the following book(s):
  Hofstadter, R. America at 1750   **973.2**

Tenner, Edward
  Our own devices   **303.4**

Tennessee
        Fiction
  Agee, J. A death in the family   **Fic**
  Bryant, J. Ringside, 1925   **Fic**
  Faulkner, W. The reivers   **Fic**
  Gratz, A. Something rotten   **Fic**
  Miller, K. The eternal ones   **Fic**
  Reinhardt, D. How to build a house   **Fic**

The **Tennessee** Williams encyclopedia   **812.009**

Tennis
  Douglas, P. Tennis   **796.342**
  Harris, C. Charging the net   **920**
        Biography
  Ashe, A. Days of grace   **92**
        Fiction
  Padian, M. Jersey tomatoes are the best   **Fic**

Tension (Physiology) *See* Stress (Physiology)

Tension (Psychology) *See* Stress (Psychology)

The **tent** of Abraham. Chittister, J.   **222**

Tenth grade. See Weisberg, J. 10th grade   **Fic**

The **tequila** worm. Canales, V.   **Fic**

Teresa, Mother, 1910-1997
        About
  Spink, K. Mother Teresa   **92**
See/See also pages in the following book(s):
  Aikman, D. Great souls   **920**

Terkel, Louis *See* Terkel, Studs, 1912-2008

Terkel, Studs, 1912-2008
  And they all sang   **780.9**
  Hard times   **973.91**
  Hope dies last   **920**
  (ed) The good war. See The good war   **940.54**

Term paper resource guide to African American history. Neumann, C. E.   **016.973**

Term paper resource guide to colonial American history. Carpenter, R. M.   **973.2**

Term paper resource guide to medieval history. Hamm, J. S.   **940.1**

Term paper resource guide to nineteenth-century U.S. history. Craver, K. W.   **016.973**

Term paper resource guide to twentieth-century world history. Richards, M. D.   **016.9**

Term paper writing *See* Report writing

Terminal care
  Kübler-Ross, E. On death and dying   **155.9**

Terminally ill
        Fiction
  Downham, J. Before I die   **Fic**

Terrariums
  Alderton, D. Firefly encyclopedia of the vivarium   **639.3**

Terras, Victor
  (ed) Handbook of Russian literature. *See* Handbook of Russian literature   **891.7**

The **terrible** Axe-Man of New Orleans. Geary, R.   **364.152**

Terrier. Pierce, T.   **Fic**

Territory. Bull, E.   **Fic**

Terrorism
    See also World Trade Center terrorist attack, 2001
  911: the book of help   **810.8**
  America under attack: primary sources   **973.931**
  America's battle against terrorism   **973.931**
  Bernstein, R. Out of the blue   **973.931**
  Burns, V. Terrorism   **363.32**
  Civil liberties   **323**
  Friedman, L. S. Nuclear weapons and security   **355**
  Friedman, L. S. Terrorist attacks   **363.32**
  Friedman, T. L. Longitudes and attitudes   **973.931**
  Gupta, D. K. Who are the terrorists?   **363.32**
  Henderson, H. Global terrorism   **363.32**
  A Just response   **973.931**
  Kallen, S. A. National security   **355**
  Kronenwetter, M. Terrorism: a guide to events and documents   **363.32**
  National Commission on Terrorist Attacks Upon the United States. The 9/11 Commission report   **973.931**
  Terrorism [History of issues series]   **363.32**
  Terrorism [Social issues firsthand series]   **363.32**
  Terrorism [Introducing issues with opposing viewpoints series]   **363.32**
  Terrorism: opposing viewpoints   **363.32**
  The war on terrorism: opposing viewpoints   **973.931**
  What motivates suicide bombers?   **363.32**
See/See also pages in the following book(s):
  Civil liberties: opposing viewpoints   **342**
  Civil rights   **323.1**
  U.S. policy toward rogue nations   **327.73**
  Weapons of mass destruction: opposing viewpoints   **358**
        Encyclopedias
  Combs, C. C. Encyclopedia of terrorism   **363.32**
  Netzley, P. D. The Greenhaven encyclopedia of terrorism   **363.32**
        Fiction
  Cormier, R. After the first death   **Fic**
  Davidson, J. The Explosionist   **Fic**
  Deuker, C. Runner   **Fic**
  Doctorow, C. Little brother   **Fic**
  Dowd, S. Bog child   **Fic**
  Kass, P. Real time   **Fic**
  Plum-Ucci, C. Streams of Babel   **Fic**
  Stratton, A. Borderline   **Fic**
        Graphic novels
  Jacobson, S. After 9/11: America's war on terror (2001-)   **973.931**

Theater—History—*Continued*

The Oxford illustrated history of theatre
792.09

Production and direction

See also Motion pictures—Production and direction

Rogers, B. Costumes, accessories, props, and stage illusions made easy   792

Varley, J. Places, please!   792

Japan

See also Nō plays

United States—Dictionaries

Bordman, G. M. The Oxford companion to American theatre   792.03

The Cambridge guide to American theatre
792.03

A **theatergoer's** guide to Shakespeare. Fallon, R. T.   822.3

The **theatre** guide. See Griffiths, T. R. The Ivan R. Dee guide to plays and playwrights
809.2

Theatrical costume *See* Costume

Theatrical makeup

Corson, R. Stage makeup   792

Thebes (Egypt: Extinct city)
See/See also pages in the following book(s):
Mertz, B. Temples, tombs, & hieroglyphs
932

Theft

See also Shoplifting

Fiction

Henry, A. Girl, stolen   Fic

Toliver, W. Lifted   Fic

Their eyes were watching God. Hurston, Z. N.
Fic

Thematic guide to American poetry. Burns, A.
811.009

Thematic guide to British poetry. Glancy, R. F.
821.009

Then I met my sister. Deriso, C. H.   Fic

Theocracy

Perl, L. Theocracy   321

Theodor Seuss Geisel. Pease, D. E.   92

Theodore Roosevelt in the Badlands. DiSilvestro, R. L.   92

Theology

See also Faith

Great thinkers of the Western world   190

Theoretical chemistry *See* Physical chemistry

Theories for everything. Langone, J.   509

Therapeutics

See also Gene therapy

Therapy, Gene *See* Gene therapy

Therapy, Psychological *See* Psychotherapy

Thermodynamics
See/See also pages in the following book(s):
Shachtman, T. Absolute zero and the conquest of cold   536

These are my rivers. Ferlinghetti, L.   811

Theseus (Greek mythology)
See/See also pages in the following book(s):
Hamilton, E. Mythology   292
Fiction
Renault, M. The king must die   Fic

They broke the law, you be the judge. Jacobs, T. A.   345

They called themselves the K.K.K. Bartoletti, S. C.   322.4

They made America. Evans, H.   920

They marched into sunlight. Maraniss, D.
959.704

They poured fire on us from the sky. Deng, B.
962.4

They teach that in college   378.73

The **thief**. Turner, M. W.   Fic

Thief eyes. Simner, J. L.   Fic

Thieret, John W., 1926-2005
National Audubon Society field guide to North American wildflowers: eastern region
582.13

Thieves
Bryan, H. Robbers, rogues, and ruffians
978.9

Fiction
Bunce, E. C. Star crossed   Fic
Cadnum, M. Flash   Fic
Dickens, C. Oliver Twist   Fic
Lynch, S. The lies of Locke Lamora   Fic
Michaelis, A. Tiger moon   Fic
Rees, C. Sovay   Fic
Scott, E. Stealing Heaven   Fic
Turner, M. W. The thief   Fic
Updale, E. Montmorency   Fic

Thieves, deceivers, and killers. Agosta, W. C.
577

Thieves like us. Cole, S.   Fic

Thieves of Baghdad. Bogdanos, M.   956.7

The **thin** executioner. Shan, D.   Fic

Thin ice. Bowen, M.   551.51

The **things** a brother knows. Reinhardt, D.   Fic

Things fall apart. Achebe, C.   Fic

Things I have to tell you   810.8

The **things** they carried. O'Brien, T.   S C

Think: a compelling introduction to philosophy. Blackburn, S.   100

Thinking *See* Thought and thinking

Thinking about college [series]
DaSilva-Gordon, M. Your first year of college
378.1

Hollander, B. Paying for college   378.3
Silivanch, A. Making the right college choice
378.1

Thinking outside the book   027.62

The **thinking** student's guide to college. Roberts, A. L.   378.1

Thiongo, Ng'ugĩ wa *See* Ng'ugĩ wa Thiongo, 1938-

Third parties (United States politics)
Cox, V. The history of the third parties
324.2

Thorn, Matt
(tr) Iwaoka, H. Saturn apartments, volume 1
    741.5

Thorpe, James Francis See Thorpe, Jim, 1888-1953

Thorpe, Jim, 1888-1953
About
Crawford, B. All American [biography of Jim Thorpe]   **92**

Thou shalt not dump the skater dude and other commandments I have broken. Graham, R.
    Fic

Thought and thinking
See also Perception
Chabris, C. F. The invisible gorilla   **153.7**
Hayakawa, S. I. Language in thought and action
    412

Thought control See Brainwashing

Thought transference See Telepathy

A **thousand** hills [biography of Paul Kagame]
Kinzer, S.   **967.571**

A **thousand** peaks. Liu Siyu   **895.1**

A **thousand** shades of blue. Stevenson, R. H.
    Fic

A **thousand** ships. Shanower, E.   **741.5**

A **thousand** years of pirates. Gilkerson, W.
    910.4

Threads and flames. Friesner, E. M.   **Fic**

Threads from the web of life. Daubert, S.
    508

Threatened species See Endangered species

Three clams and an oyster. Powell, R.   **Fic**

Three little words. Rhodes-Courter, A. M.   **92**

The **three** musketeers. Dumas, A.   **Fic**

Three plays: Our town, The skin of our teeth, The matchmaker. Wilder, T.   **812**

Three-quarters dead. Peck, R.   **Fic**

Three rivers rising. Richards, J.   **Fic**

Three songs for courage. Trottier, M.   **Fic**

The **three** trillion dollar war. Stiglitz, J. E.
    956.7

Thrift See Saving and investment

Thrillers (Fiction) See Suspense fiction

Through a window. Goodall, J.   **599.8**

Through the lens   **779**

Thucydides
See/See also pages in the following book(s):
Ancient Greek literature   **880.9**
Hamilton, E. The Greek way   **880.9**

Thunder and glory   **796.72**

Thunder over Kandahar. McKay, S.   **Fic**

Thurber, James, 1894-1961
Writings and drawings   **818**

Thurlow, Crispin
(ed) Talking adolescence. See Talking adolescence   **305.23**

Thurschwell, Pamela, 1966-
Sigmund Freud   **150.19**

Thursday's child. Hartnett, S.   **Fic**

Thurston, Herbert
(ed) Butler, A. Butler's Lives of the saints
    920.003

Thutmose III, King of Egypt, ca. 1504-1450 B.C.
See/See also pages in the following book(s):
Mertz, B. Temples, tombs, & hieroglyphs
    932

Tibet (China)
Palden Gyatso. The autobiography of a Tibetan monk   **92**
See/See also pages in the following book(s):
Dalai Lama. Freedom in exile   **92**

The **ticket** out: Darryl Strawberry and the boys of Crenshaw. Sokolove, M. Y.   **796.357**

Ticks
See also Lyme disease
Stewart, A. Wicked bugs   **632**

Tidal waves, Seismic See Tsunamis

Tienda, Marta
About
O'Connell, D. People person [biography of Marta Tienda]   **92**

Tiernan, Cate, 1961-
Balefire   **Fic**
Immortal beloved   **Fic**

Tierno, Philip M., Jr.
The secret life of germs   **616**

The **ties** that bind. Berry, B.   **920**

Tietjen, Jill S.
(jt. auth) Waisman, C. S. Her story   **305.4**

Tiger moon. Michaelis, A.   **Fic**

The **tiger** that isn't. See Blastland, M. The numbers game   **510**

Tigerland and other unintended destinations. Dinerstein, E.   **590**

Tigers
Fiction
Houck, C. Tiger's curse   **Fic**
Michaelis, A. Tiger moon   **Fic**

Tiger's curse. Houck, C.   **Fic**

Till, Emmett, 1941-1955
About
Aretha, D. The murder of Emmett Till
    364.152
Crowe, C. Getting away with murder: the true story of the Emmett Till case   **364.152**
Wright, S. Simeon's story   **305.8**
See/See also pages in the following book(s):
Abdul-Jabbar, K. Black profiles in courage
    920
Fiction
Crowe, C. Mississippi trial, 1955   **Fic**
Poetry
Nelson, M. A wreath for Emmett Till   **811**

Tillage, Leon, 1936-
Leon's story   **92**

Tillmon County fire. Ehrenberg, P.   **Fic**

Time
See also Night
Aveni, A. F. Empires of time   **529**
Gleick, J. Faster   **529**
Richards, E. G. Mapping time   **529**

Transplantation of organs, tissues, etc.—*Continued*

Fiction

Cabot, M. Airhead — Fic
Wolfson, J. Cold hands, warm heart — Fic

Transsexualism

Hear me out: true stories of Teens Educating and Confronting Homophobia — 306.76
Huegel, K. GLBTQ — 306.76
Martin, H. J., Jr. Serving lesbian, gay, bisexual, transgender, and questioning teens — 027.62

Fiction

Beam, C. I am J — Fic
Hyde, C. R. Jumpstart the world — Fic
Katcher, B. Almost perfect — Fic
Peters, J. A. Luna — Fic
Wittlinger, E. Parrotfish — Fic

Transue, Emily R.

On call — 92

Transvestites

Fiction

Brothers, M. Debbie Harry sings in French — Fic

The **trap**. Smelcer, J. E. — Fic

Trapp, Robert

Discovering the world through debate. See Discovering the world through debate — 808.53

Trapped. Northrop, M. — Fic

Trash. Mulligan, A. — Fic

Travel

Fiction

Bradbury, J. Shift — Fic

Travelers, American *See* American travelers

A **traveler's** guide to Mars. Hartmann, W. K. — 523.4

Traveling the freedom road. Osborne, L. B. — 973.7

Travels *See* Voyages and travels

The **travels** of Marco Polo. Polo, M. — 915

Treanor, Nick

(ed) Animal rights. See Animal rights — 179
(ed) The Vietnam War. See The Vietnam War — 959.704

Treasure Island. Stevenson, R. L. — Fic

A **treasury of Victorian murder** [series]

Geary, R. The murder of Abraham Lincoln — 973.7

Treasury of XXth century murder [series]

Geary, R. The Lindbergh child — 364.1
Geary, R. The terrible Axe-Man of New Orleans — 364.152

Treaties

See/See also pages in the following book(s):

Weapons of mass destruction: opposing viewpoints — 358

Treaties with American Indians — 342

Treaty of Versailles (1919)

The Treaty of Versailles — 940.3
The **Treaty** of Versailles — 940.3
The **Tree** is older than you are — 860.8

Trees

See also Redwood

North America

Familiar trees of North America: eastern region — 582.16
Familiar trees of North America: western region — 582.16
Sibley, D. The Sibley guide to trees — 582.16

United States

Plotnik, A. The urban tree book — 582.16

Trefil, James S., 1938-

(jt. auth) Hirsch, E. D. The new dictionary of cultural literacy — 031

Tregear, Mary

Chinese art — 709.51

Trelease, Jim

(ed) Read all about it! See Read all about it! — 808.8

Treuer, Anton

Indian nations of North America. See Indian nations of North America — 970.004

Trevelyan, George Macaulay, 1876-1962

The English Revolution, 1688-1689 — 942.06

Trevor, William, 1928-

(ed) The Oxford book of Irish short stories. See The Oxford book of Irish short stories — S C

Trexler, Sally

(jt. auth) Berger, P. Choosing Web 2.0 tools for learning and teaching in a digital world — 025.04

The **trial**. Kafka, F. — Fic
The **trial** of the Scottsboro boys. Aretha, D. — 345

Trials

Aretha, D. The trial of the Scottsboro boys — 345
Aronson, M. Witch-hunt: mysteries of the Salem witch trials — 133.4
Burns, W. E. Witch hunts in Europe and America — 133.4
Crimes and trials of the century — 345
Goss, K. D. The Salem witch trials — 133.4
Hoffer, P. C. The Salem witchcraft trials — 345
Margulies, P. The devil on trial — 345
Sorensen, L. The Scottsboro Boys Trial — 345
Weiner, M. S. Black trials — 342

Fiction

Guterson, D. Snow falling on cedars — Fic
Hemphill, S. Wicked girls — Fic
Kafka, F. The trial — Fic
Meldrum, C. Madapple — Fic
Myers, W. D. Monster — Fic
Pesci, D. Amistad — Fic
Smith-Ready, J. Shade — Fic

Trials (Espionage)

Philipson, I. J. Ethel Rosenberg — 92

Trials (Homicide)

Alphin, E. M. An unspeakable crime — 364.152
Crowe, C. Getting away with murder: the true story of the Emmett Till case — 364.152
Wright, S. Simeon's story — 305.8

The **truth** about sexual behavior and unplanned pregnancy **306.7**

Truthfulness and falsehood
See also Honesty
Fiction
Reinhardt, D. Harmless **Fic**

Tryman, Mfanya Donald
(ed) The Malcolm X encyclopedia. See The Malcolm X encyclopedia **320.5**

Tsavo National Park (Kenya)
Caputo, P. Ghosts of Tsavo **599.75**

Tsering Shakya
(jt. auth) Palden Gyatso. The autobiography of a Tibetan monk **92**

Tsiaras, Alexander
From conception to birth **618.3**

Tsunamis
Kusky, T. M. Tsunamis **551.46**
Fiction
Pratchett, T. Nation **Fic**

Tubb, Kristin O'Donnell
(ed) Freedom from cruel and unusual punishment. See Freedom from cruel and unusual punishment **345**

Tuberculosis
Finer, K. R. Tuberculosis **616.2**
Kelly, E. B. Investigating tuberculosis and superbugs **616.9**

Tubman, Harriet, 1820?-1913
About
Clinton, C. Harriet Tubman: the road to freedom **92**
Malaspina, A. Harriet Tubman **92**
See/See also pages in the following book(s):
Abdul-Jabbar, K. Black profiles in courage **920**

Tuccillo, Diane
Library teen advisory groups **027.62**
Teen-centered library service **027.62**

Tuchman, Barbara Wertheim
The guns of August **940.3**
The march of folly **909.08**
The proud tower **909.82**
The Zimmermann telegram **940.3**

Tucker, Neely
Love in the driest season **362.7**

Tucker, Spencer C., 1937-
Battles that changed history **355.4**
(ed) Cold War. See Cold War **909.82**
(ed) The encyclopedia of Middle East wars. See The encyclopedia of Middle East wars **355**
(ed) The encyclopedia of the Arab-Israeli conflict. See The encyclopedia of the Arab-Israeli conflict **956.94**
(ed) The encyclopedia of the Korean War. See The encyclopedia of the Korean War **951.9**
(ed) The encyclopedia of the Vietnam War. See The encyclopedia of the Vietnam War **959.704**
(ed) A global chronology of conflict. See A global chronology of conflict **355**

(ed) World War I: a student encyclopedia. See World War I: a student encyclopedia **940.3**
(ed) World War II: a student encyclopedia. See World War II: a student encyclopedia **940.53**

Tucker, Todd, 1968-
Over and under **Fic**

Tudge, Colin
The time before history **599.93**

Tufte, Edward R., 1942-
The visual display of quantitative information **001.4**

Tullson, Diane, 1958-
Riley Park **Fic**

Tundra ecology
Moore, P. D. Tundra **577.5**

Tunis, Edwin, 1897-1973
Frontier living **978**

Tunnels
See/See also pages in the following book(s):
Macaulay, D. Building big **720**

Tupac Shakur See Shakur, Tupac

Turabian, Kate L., 1893-1987
A manual for writers of research papers, theses, and dissertations **808**
Student's guide to writing college papers **808**

Turbak, Gary
Grizzly bears **599.78**

Turck, Mary, 1950-
Freedom song **323.1**

Turing, Alan Mathison, 1912-1954
About
Corrigan, J. Alan Turing **92**

Turkey
Fiction
Skrypuch, M. F. Daughter of war **Fic**
History—Ottoman Empire, 1288-1918—Encyclopedias
Encyclopedia of the Ottoman Empire **956**

Turkington, Carol
The encyclopedia of autism spectrum disorders **616.85**
The encyclopedia of infectious diseases **616.9**
The encyclopedia of skin and skin disorders **616.5**
The encyclopedia of the brain and brain disorders **612.8**

Turkish poetry
Collections
Music of a distant drum **808.81**

The **turn** of the screw. James, H. **Fic**

Turnbull, Ann
No shame, no fear **Fic**

Turner, Ann Warren, 1945-
Father of lies **Fic**
Hard hit **Fic**

Turner, Barry
(ed) The statesman's yearbook 2011. See The statesman's yearbook 2011 **310.5**

Twenty-first century medical library—*Continued*
Hyman, B. M. Obsessive-compulsive disorder **616.85**
Silverstein, A. Cancer **616.99**
Twenty-five yards of war. Drez, R. J. **940.53**
Twenty love poems and a song of despair. Neruda, P. **861**
Twenty-one. See Santiago, W. "21" [biography of Roberto Clemente] **92**
Twenty-one proms. See 21 proms **S C**
Twenty thousand leagues under the sea. See Verne, J. The extraordinary journeys: Twenty thousand leagues under the sea **Fic**
Twilight. Meyer, S. **Fic**
Twilight people. Houze, D. **92**
Twins
Kor, E. M. Surviving the Angel of Death **92**
Schein, E. Identical strangers **92**
Fiction
Baratz-Logsted, L. Twin's daughter **Fic**
Billingsley, F. Chime **Fic**
Bodeen, S. A. The Compound **Fic**
Bullen, A. Wish **Fic**
De Lint, C. Dingo **Fic**
Hopkins, E. Identical **Fic**
Kephart, B. Dangerous neighbors **Fic**
Lansens, L. The girls **Fic**
Roy, A. The god of small things **Fic**
Ryan, P. Gemini bites **Fic**
Shepard, S. The lying game **Fic**
Shusterman, N. Bruiser **Fic**
Tiernan, C. Balefire **Fic**
Williams, G. Beatle meets Destiny **Fic**
Wrede, P. C. The thirteenth child **Fic**
Zink, M. Prophecy of the sisters **Fic**
Twin's daughter. Baratz-Logsted, L. **Fic**
Twisted. Anderson, L. H. **Fic**
Twisted head. Capotorto, C. **92**
Twists and turns. McDonald, J. **Fic**
The **two** loves of Will Shakespeare. Lawlor, L. **Fic**
Two parties, one tux, and a very short film about the Grapes of Wrath. Goldman, S. **Fic**
Two thousand and one: a space odyssey. See Clarke, A. C. 2001: a space odyssey **Fic**
Tyger tyger. Hamilton, K. R. **Fic**
Tyle, Laura B.
(ed) U-X-L encyclopedia of world biography. See U-X-L encyclopedia of world biography **920.003**
Tyler, Anne, 1941-
Dinner at the Homesick Restaurant **Fic**
Type 1 teens. Hood, K. K. **616.4**
Type 2 diabetes in teens. Betschart, J. **616.4**
Typhoid fever
Fiction
Chibbaro, J. Deadly **Fic**
Typhoid Mary, d. 1938
Fiction
Chibbaro, J. Deadly **Fic**
Typhoons
See also Hurricanes

Encyclopedias
Longshore, D. Encyclopedia of hurricanes, typhoons, and cyclones **551.55**
Typical American. Jen, G. **Fic**
Typography *See* Printing
Tyranny. Fairfield, L. **741.5**
Tyrell. Booth, C. **Fic**
Tyson, Neil De Grasse
Death by black hole **523.8**
The Pluto files **523.4**
Tzemach Lemmon, Gayle
The dressmaker of Khair Khana **92**

U

U-869 (Submarine)
Kurson, R. Shadow divers **940.54**
U.F.O.'s *See* Unidentified flying objects
U.S. border control. McCage, C. **363.2**
U.S. border security. Warner, J. A. **363.2**
The U.S. government: how it works [series]
Cox, V. The history of the third parties **324.2**
U.S. Holocaust Memorial Museum *See* United States Holocaust Memorial Museum
U.S. immigration and migration. Primary sources **325.73**
U. S. immigration and migration reference library [series]
Benson, S. U.S. immigration and migration almanac **304.8**
Outman, J. L. U.S. immigration and migration. Biographies **920**
U.S. immigration and migration. Primary sources **325.73**
U.S. labor in the twentieth century **331**
U.S. Latino literature **810.9**
The **U.S.** Marine Corps: an illustrated history. See Bartlett, M. L. Leathernecks: an illustrated history of the U.S. Marine Corps **359.9**
U.S.-Mexican War. Mills, B. **973.6**
U.S. policy toward rogue nations **327.73**
U.S.S.R. *See* Soviet Union
U-X-L Asian American almanac **305.8**
U-X-L Asian American voices **815.008**
U-X-L encyclopedia of water science **553.7**
U-X-L encyclopedia of world biography **920.003**
U-X-L encyclopedia of world mythology **201.03**
U-X-L graphic novelists. Pendergast, T. **920.003**
U-X-L Hispanic American almanac **305.8**
U-X-L Middle East conflict reference library [series]
Pendergast, T. The Middle East conflict. Almanac **956**
Pendergast, T. The Middle East conflict. Biographies **920**
Pendergast, T. The Middle East conflict. Primary sources **956**

Universities *See* Colleges and universities

University students *See* College students

Unmarried fathers

See also Single parent family
Graphic novels
Unita, Y. Bunny drop vol. 1   741.5

Unmarried mothers

See also Single parent family
Fiction
Porter, C. R. Imani all mine   Fic

Unnatural disasters. Gunn, A. M.   304.2

Unnatural phenomena. Clark, J.   001.9

The **unofficial** encyclopedia of the Rock and Roll Hall of Fame. Talevski, N.   781.66

Unpolished gem. Pung, A.   92

Unraveling. Baldini, M.   Fic

Unraveling freedom. Bausum, A.   940.3

Unsettled. Aronson, M.   956.94

Unsettling America   811.008

Unsigned hype. Mattison, B. T.   Fic

Unsinkable: the full story of the RMS Titanic. Butler, D. A.   910.4

An **unspeakable** crime. Alphin, E. M.   364.152

Unwind. Shusterman, N.   Fic

Unwrapping a mummy. Taylor, J. H.   932

Up all night   S C

Up close [series]

Aronson, M. Bill Gates   92

Aronson, M. Robert F. Kennedy   92

Bardhan-Quallen, S. Jane Goodall   92

Bolden, T. W.E.B. Du Bois   92

Cooper, M. L. Theodore Roosevelt   92

Crowe, C. Thurgood Marshall   92

Hampton, W. Babe Ruth   92

Levine, E. Rachel Carson   92

Madden, K. Harper Lee   92

Meltzer, M. John Steinbeck   92

Neimark, A. E. Johnny Cash   92

Stone, T. L. Ella Fitzgerald   92

Sutherland, J. Ronald Reagan   92

Up from slavery. Washington, B. T.   92

Up your score   378.1

Upchurch, Thomas Adams

(ed) The Greenwood encyclopedia of African American civil rights. See The Greenwood encyclopedia of African American civil rights   305.8

Updale, Eleanor

Montmorency   Fic

Upper atmosphere

Bowen, M. Thin ice   551.51

Uprising. Haddix, M. P.   Fic

The **upstairs** room. Reiss, J.   92

Upstate. Buckhanon, K.   Fic

Uranus (Planet)

Chaple, G. F. Outer planets   523.4

Urasawa, Naoki, 1960-

Pluto: Urasawa x Tezuka, vol. 1   741.5

Urban areas *See* Cities and towns

Urban development *See* Urbanization

Urban ecology

Couturier, L. The hopes of snakes   591.7

Urban geology

Williams, D. B. Stories in stone   550

Urban life *See* City and town life

Urban planning *See* City planning

Urban sociology

See also Urbanization

Urban teens in the library   027.62

The **urban** tree book. Plotnik, A.   582.16

Urbanization

Lorinc, J. Cities   307.7

Urdang, Laurence

(ed) The timetables of American history. See The timetables of American history   902

Urick, Dave

Sports illustrated lacrosse   796.34

Urinary organs

Watson, S. The urinary system   616.6

The **urinary** system. Watson, S.   616.6

Uris, Leon, 1924-2003

Exodus   Fic

Urofsky, Melvin I.

(jt. auth) Finkelman, P. Landmark decisions of the United States Supreme Court   347

Urquhart, Brian E.

Ralph Bunche   92

Urquhart, Connie

(jt. auth) Braun, L. W. Risky business   027.62

Urrea, Luis Alberto

Mr. Mendoza's paintbrush   741.5

Urushibara, Yuki

Mu shi shi 1   741.5

USA Today health reports: diseases and disorders [series]

Farrar, A. ADHD   616.85

Goldsmith, C. Hepatitis   616.3

Goldsmith, C. Influenza   616.2

Goldsmith, C. Skin cancer   616.99

Landau, E. Food poisoning and foodborne diseases   615.9

Sonenklar, C. Anorexia and bulimia   616.85

USA Today: lifeline biographies [series]

Golus, C. Tupac Shakur   92

Krohn, K. E. Stephenie Meyer   92

Sirvaitis, K. Danica Patrick   92

Usagi Yojimbo (Fictional character)

Sakai, S. Usagi Yojimbo, book one   741.5

Sakai, S. Usagi Yojimbo: Yokai   741.5

Usagi Yojimbo, book one. Sakai, S.   741.5

Usagi Yojimbo: Yokai. Sakai, S.   741.5

Uschan, Michael V., 1948-

Forty years of medical racism   174.2

Use of time *See* Time management

Using poetry across the curriculum. Chatton, B.   372.6

Using pop culture to teach information literacy. Behen, L. D.   028.7

Using WEB 2.0 tools in the K-12 classroom. Crane, B. E.   371.3

Utah
Fiction
Grey, Z. Riders of the purple sage   Fic
Zarr, S. Sweethearts   Fic

Ute Indians
Fiction
Hobbs, W. Bearstone   Fic

Utopias
See/See also pages in the following book(s):
Heilbroner, R. L. The worldly philosophers
    330.1
Fiction
Huxley, A. Brave new world   Fic

Uzzi, Brian, 1960-
(jt. auth) Etzkowitz, H. Athena unbound   500

V

V.C.R.'s *See* Video recording

V.D. *See* Sexually transmitted diseases

Vaca, Alvar Nuñez Cabeza de *See* Nuñez Cabeza de Vaca, Alvar, 16th cent.

Vacations
Fiction
Han, J. The summer I turned pretty   Fic
Mackler, C. Tangled   Fic
Ockler, S. Twenty boy summer   Fic
Runyon, B. Surface tension   Fic
Stein, T. High dive   Fic
Wynne-Jones, T. The uninvited   Fic

Vaccination
Allman, T. Vaccine research   615
See/See also pages in the following book(s):
Epidemics: opposing viewpoints   614.4

Vaccine research. Allman, T.   615

Vacuum bazookas, electric rainbow jelly, and 27 other Saturday science projects. Downie, N. A.   507.8

Vadas, Robert E., 1952-
Cultures in conflict—the Viet Nam War
    959.704

Vail, Martha
Exploring the Pacific   910.4

Valentine, Jenny
Broken soup   Fic
Me, the missing, and the dead   Fic

Valentine, Rebecca
(jt. auth) Outman, J. L. U.S. immigration and migration. Biographies   920

Valentine's Day
Fiction
Levithan, D. Marly's ghost   Fic

Valenza, Joyce Kasman
Power research tools   001.4
Power tools recharged   027.8

Valestuk, Lorraine, 1963-
(ed) African literature and its times. See African literature and its times   809
(jt. auth) Moss, J. Latin American literature and its times   860.9

Valli, Clayton
(ed) The Gallaudet dictionary of American Sign Language. See The Gallaudet dictionary of American Sign Language   419

Values
See also Social values

Vampire library [series]
Robson, D. Encounters with vampires   398

Vampire queen [series]
Maizel, R. Infinite days   Fic

Vampires
Robson, D. Encounters with vampires   398
Encyclopedias
Guiley, R. E. The encyclopedia of vampires & werewolves   398
Fiction
Atwater-Rhodes, A. Persistence of memory
    Fic
Block, F. L. Pretty dead   Fic
Burns, L. J. Crave   Fic
Butler, O. E. Fledgling   Fic
Cabot, M. Insatiable   Fic
Cary, K. Bloodline   Fic
De la Cruz, M. Blue bloods   Fic
The eternal kiss   S C
Fantaskey, B. Jessica's guide to dating on the dark side   Fic
Gray, C. Evernight   Fic
Haig, M. The Radleys   Fic
Hallaway, T. Almost to die for   Fic
Harvey, A. Hearts at stake   Fic
Holder, N. Crusade   Fic
Jenkins, A. M. Night road   Fic
Jinks, C. The reformed vampire support group
    Fic
Klause, A. C. The silver kiss   Fic
Lake, N. Blood ninja   Fic
Maizel, R. Infinite days   Fic
Matheson, R. I am legend   S C
Meehl, B. Suck it up   Fic
Meyer, S. Twilight   Fic
Rex, A. Fat vampire   Fic
Ryan, P. Gemini bites   Fic
Sedgwick, M. My swordhand is singing   Fic
Selzer, A. I kissed a zombie, and I liked it
    Fic
Smith, C. L. Tantalize   Fic
St. Crow, L. Strange angels   Fic
Stoker, B. Dracula   Fic
Turner, M. Night runner   Fic
Westerfeld, S. Peeps   Fic
Graphic novels
Jensen, V. Pinocchio, vampire slayer   741.5
Raven, N. Bram Stoker's Dracula   741.5

Vamplew, Anton
(jt. auth) Gater, W. The practical astronomer
    520

Van Beethoven, Ludwig *See* Beethoven, Ludwig van, 1770-1827

Van Buren, Martin, 1782-1862
About
Widmer, E. L. Martin Van Buren   92

Van Cleve, Libby, 1958-
(jt. auth) Perlis, V. Composer's voices from Ives to Ellington   780.9

Venus (Planet)
Grier, J. A. Inner planets **523.4**
Venzon, Anne Cipriano, 1951-
(ed) The United States in the First World War.
See The United States in the First World War **940.3**

Verbal abuse See Invective
Verbrugge, Allen
(ed) Muslims in America. See Muslims in America **305**
Verdelle, A. J., 1960-
The good negress **Fic**
Verdick, Elizabeth
(ed) Cobain, B. When nothing matters anymore **616.85**
Vergil See Virgil
Verkerk, Dorothy, 1958-
(jt. auth) Snyder, J. Art of the Middle Ages **709.02**

Vermeer, Johannes, 1632-1675
About
Sweet, C. The essential Johannes Vermeer **759.9492**
Fiction
Chevalier, T. Girl with a pearl earring **Fic**
Vermeer van Delft, Jan See Vermeer, Johannes, 1632-1675
Vermont
Fiction
Doyle, E. F. According to Kit **Fic**
Galante, C. The sweetness of salt **Fic**
Gould, P. L. Write naked **Fic**
Ockler, S. Fixing Delilah **Fic**
Wilhelm, D. Falling **Fic**
Verne, Jules, 1828-1905
The extraordinary journeys: Twenty thousand leagues under the sea **Fic**
Verschuur, Gerrit L., 1937-
Hidden attraction **538**
Vertebrates
Holmes, T. The first vertebrates **567**
Petersen, C. Vertebrates **596**
Very short introductions [series]
Steger, M. Globalization: a very short introduction **337**
Veterans
Everything we had **959.704**
Voices of war **355**
Fiction
Griffin, P. The Orange Houses **Fic**
Jordan, H. Mudbound **Fic**
Mason, B. A. In country **Fic**
Rorby, G. The outside of a horse **Fic**
Veterinary medicine
Brown, B. B. While you're here, Doc **92**
Herriot, J. All creatures great and small **92**
Wells, J. All my patients have tales **636**
Fiction
Wilson, D. L. Firehorse **Fic**
Vice-Presidents
United States—Dictionaries
Vice presidents **920.003**
Vice presidents **920.003**

Vickers, Tanya M.
Teen science fair sourcebook **507.8**
Victims of atomic bombings See Atomic bomb victims
Victims of crimes
See also Abused women; Adult child abuse victims
Victoria, Queen of Great Britain, 1819-1901
Fiction
MacColl, M. Prisoners in the palace **Fic**
Victorian America. Schlereth, T. J. **973.8**
Victorian America, 1876 to 1913. Shifflett, C. A. **973.8**
The **Victorian** novel **820.9**
Video cassette recorders and recording See Video recording
Video games
Chaplin, H. Smartbomb **338.4**
Gallaway, B. Game on! **025.2**
Neiburger, E. Gamers . . . in the library?! **794.8**
Parks, P. J. Video games **794.8**
Swaine, M. Career building through interactive online games **794.8**
Fiction
Kostick, C. Epic **Fic**
Video recording
Lanier, T. Filmmaking for teens **791.43**
Videorecorders See Video recording
Videotape recorders and recording See Video recording
Videotapes
Leonard Maltin's movie guide **791.43**
Vieceli, Emma, 1979-
(il) Appignanesi, R. Hamlet **822.3**
Vienna (Austria)
Fiction
Dunlap, S. E. The musician's daughter **Fic**
Vietnam
History
Karnow, S. Vietnam **959.704**
Politics and government
FitzGerald, F. Fire in the lake **959.704**
Vietnam Veterans Memorial (Washington, D.C.)
Palmer, L. Shrapnel in the heart **959.704**
Vietnam War, 1961-1975
America in Vietnam **959.704**
FitzGerald, F. Fire in the lake **959.704**
Hillstrom, K. Vietnam War: almanac **959.704**
Hillstrom, K. Vietnam War: primary sources **959.704**
Isserman, M. Vietnam War **959.704**
Karnow, S. Vietnam **959.704**
Living through the Vietnam War **959.704**
Maraniss, D. They marched into sunlight **959.704**
Murray, S. Vietnam War **959.704**
Reporting Vietnam **959.704**
Vadas, R. E. Cultures in conflict—the Viet Nam War **959.704**
The Vietnam War **959.704**

Wald, Elijah
Escaping the delta [biography of Robert Johnson]   **92**

Waldbauer, Gilbert
Insights from insects   **632**
A walk around the pond   **595.7**
What good are bugs?   **595.7**

Walden, Sarah
Whistler and his mother: an unexpected relationship   **709**

Walden, or, Life in the woods. Thoreau, H. D.   **818**

Waldman, Carl
Atlas of the North American Indian   **970.004**
Encyclopedia of Native American tribes   **970.004**

Waldorf, Heather
Tripping   **Fic**

Wales
Fiction
Jones, A. F. Warrior princess   **Fic**

A **walk** around the pond. Waldbauer, G.   **595.7**

Walker, Aidan
(ed) The Encyclopedia of wood. See The Encyclopedia of wood   **674**

Walker, A'Lelia, 1885-1931
Poetry
Atkins, J. Borrowed names   **811**

Walker, Alice, 1944-
Anything we love can be saved   **814**
The color purple   **Fic**
Hard times require furious dancing   **811**
Her blue body everything we know   **811**
About
Gillespie, C. Critical companion to Alice Walker   **813.009**

Walker, Barbara J.
The librarian's guide to developing Christian fiction collections for young adults   **025.2**

Walker, C. J., Madame, 1867-1919
Poetry
Atkins, J. Borrowed names   **811**

Walker, Cory
(il) Kirkman, R. Invincible: ultimate collection, Vol. 1   **741.5**

Walker, Demetrius
About
Dohrmann, G. Play their hearts out   **796.323**

Walker, Gabrielle
The hot topic   **363.7**
An ocean of air   **551.5**

Walker, Ida
See also Flynn, Noa
Addiction in America   **362.29**
Addiction treatment   **362.29**
Alcohol addiction   **362.292**
Natural and everyday drugs   **362.29**
Painkillers   **362.29**
Recreational Ritalin   **362.29**
Sedatives and hypnotics   **362.29**
Steroids: pumped up and dangerous   **362.29**

Walker, Janice R.
The Columbia guide to online style   **808**

Walker, Madame C. J. *See* Walker, C. J., Madame, 1867-1919

Walker, Pamela, 1958-
Chemistry experiments   **540.7**
The coral reef   **577.7**
Environmental science experiments   **507.8**
Forensic science experiments   **363.2**
Physical science experiments   **500.2**
Space and astronomy experiments   **520**

Walker, Rebecca, 1969-
Black, white and Jewish   **92**

Walker, Richard, 1951-
(jt. auth) Macaulay, D. The way we work   **612**

Walker, Sally M.
Frozen secrets   **998**
Secrets of a Civil War submarine   **973.7**
Written in bone   **614**
(jt. auth) Flannery, T. F. We are the weather makers   **551.6**

Walker, Sarah Breedlove *See* Walker, C. J., Madame, 1867-1919

Walker, Steve, 1955-
(il) Lagos, A. The sons of liberty   **741.5**

Walker, Thomas J., 1931-
(jt. auth) Capinera, J. L. Field guide to grasshoppers, crickets, and katydids of the United States   **595.7**

Walking
Francis, J. Planetwalker   **92**

Walking Ollie, or, Winning the love of a difficult dog. Foster, S.   **636.7**

Walking softly in the wilderness. Hart, J.   **796.51**

Walking the Choctaw road. Tingle, T.   **398.2**

Walking with the wind. Lewis, J.   **92**

Walking zero. Raymo, C.   **526**

Wall, Cheryl A.
(ed) Hurston, Z. N. Folklore, memoirs, and other writings   **818**
(jt. auth) Hurston, Z. N. Novels and stories   **Fic**

The **wall**. Hersey, J.   **Fic**

The **wall**. Sís, P.   **92**

Wall painting *See* Mural painting and decoration

Wallace, Daniel, 1959-
The DC Comics encyclopedia. See The DC Comics encyclopedia   **741.5**

Wallace, Jason, 1969-
Out of shadows   **Fic**

Wallace, Maurice O., 1967-
Langston Hughes   **92**

Wallace, Mike, 1918-
(ed) The way we will be 50 years from today. See The way we will be 50 years from today   **303.49**

Wallace, Rich, 1957-
Losing is not an option: stories   **S C**
One good punch   **Fic**
Perpetual check   **Fic**
Wrestling Sturbridge   **Fic**

Wallechinsky, David, 1948-
The complete book of the Winter Olympics
796.98

Wallenfels, Stephen
POD **Fic**

Walls, Jeannette
The glass castle **92**
The **walls** came tumbling down. Stokes, G. **947**

Walsh, Jill Paton See Paton Walsh, Jill, 1937-

Walsh, Judith E.
A brief history of India **954**

Walters, Eric, 1957-
In a flash **Fic**
Splat! **Fic**
When elephants fight **920**

Walters, Mark Jerome
Six modern plagues and how we are causing them **614.4**

Walters, Martin
(jt. auth) Huxley, A. J. Green inheritance **580**

Walton, Anthony
(ed) Every shut eye ain't asleep. See Every shut eye ain't asleep **811.008**
(ed) The Vintage book of African American poetry. See The Vintage book of African American poetry **811.008**

Wampanoag Indians
Mandell, D. R. King Philip's war **973.2**

Wang, Sam, 1967-
(jt. auth) Aamodt, S. Welcome to your brain **612.8**

Wangu, Madhu Bazaz
Buddhism **294.3**
Hinduism **294.5**

Waniek, Marilyn Nelson See Nelson, Marilyn, 1946-

Wansbrough, Henry, 1934-
(ed) Bible. The new Jerusalem Bible **220.5**

Want fries with that? Ingram, S. **613.2**

War
See also Intervention (International law)
Barker, G. P. War **355**
Gottfried, T. The fight for peace **303.6**
Reporting America at war **070.4**
War: opposing viewpoints **355**
Women on war **303.6**
Woodward, J. War **303.6**
Bibliography
Crew, H. S. Women engaged in war in literature for youth **016.3**
Economic aspects
Stiglitz, J. E. The three trillion dollar war **956.7**
Encyclopedias
War: from ancient Egypt to Iraq **355**
Fiction
See War stories
Graphic novels
Gipi. Notes for a war story **741.5**
Public opinion
Civil liberties and war **323**

Civil liberties and war **342**
War & peace in the air. Dick, R. **629.13**
The **war** against the Jews, 1933-1945. Dawidowicz, L. S. **940.53**
War and children See Children and war
War and civilization
Americans at war **973**
War and nature. Russell, E. **577.2**
War and the pity of war **808.81**
War crime trials
See also Nuremberg Trial of Major German War Criminals, 1945-1946
War: from ancient Egypt to Iraq **355**
The **war** in Iraq **956.7**
War in literature
Encyclopedia of American war literature **810.9**
War is-- **810.8**
War Lance, Le
About
Frazier, I. On the rez **970.004**
War of 1812
Greenblatt, M. War of 1812 **973.5**
Heidler, D. S. The War of 1812 **973.5**
Howes, K. K. War of 1812 **973.5**
The **war** of our childhood. Samuel, W. W. E. **940.53**
The **war** of the worlds. Wells, H. G. **Fic**
War on terrorism
The American empire **327.73**
America's battle against terrorism **973.931**
Gerdes, L. 9/11 **973.931**
How should the United States treat prisoners in the war on terror? **973.931**
The Middle East **956**
National Commission on Terrorist Attacks Upon the United States. The 9/11 Commission report **973.931**
Nguyen, T. We are all suspects now **323.1**
The war on terrorism: opposing viewpoints **973.931**
See/See also pages in the following book(s):
Is it unpatriotic to criticize one's country? **323.6**
Woodward, J. War **303.6**
The **war** on terrorism: opposing viewpoints **973.931**
War: opposing viewpoints **355**
War poetry
American war poetry **811.008**
The Oxford book of war poetry **808.81**
War and the pity of war **808.81**
War is-- **810.8**
War stories
Frost, H. Crossing stones **Fic**
Holub, J. An innocent soldier **Fic**
Jones, A. F. Warrior princess **Fic**
Marsden, J. Tomorrow, when the war began **Fic**
Marsden, J. While I live **Fic**
Moran, K. Bloodline **Fic**
Olmstead, R. Coal black horse **Fic**
Riordan, J. The sniper **Fic**

Washington's crossing. Fischer, D. H.   **973.3**

Wasiolek, Sue
  (jt. auth) Feaver, P. Getting the best out of college   **378.1**

Waskow, Arthur I. *See* Waskow, Arthur Ocean, 1933-

Waskow, Arthur Ocean, 1933-
  (jt. auth) Chittister, J. The tent of Abraham   **222**

Wasserman, Dale, 1914-2008
  Man of La Mancha   **812**

Wasserman, Jack, 1921-
  Leonardo da Vinci   **759.5**

Wasserman, Robin
  Hacking Harvard   **Fic**
  Skinned   **Fic**

Wasserstein, Wendy, 1950-2006
  The Heidi chronicles and other plays   **812**

Waste disposal *See* Sewage disposal

The **waste** land, and other poems. Eliot, T. S.   **811**

Waste minimization
  Maczulak, A. E. Waste treatment   **628.4**

Waste products
  See also Recycling

Waste treatment. Maczulak, A. E.   **628.4**

Wastes, Hazardous *See* Hazardous wastes

Watabe, Kinami
  (tr) Ashihara, H. Sand chronicles vol. 1   **741.5**
  (tr) Yumi, K. Library wars, vol. 1: love & war   **741.5**

Watad, Mahmoud
  Teen voices from the Holy Land   **920**

Watanabe-O'Kelly, Helen
  (ed) The Cambridge history of German literature. See The Cambridge history of German literature   **830.9**

Watchers. Koontz, D. R.   **Fic**

Watching giants. Kelsey, E.   **599.5**

Watchmen. Moore, A.   **741.5**

Water
  Kandel, R. S. Water from heaven   **553.7**
    Encyclopedias
  Newton, D. E. Encyclopedia of water   **553.7**
  U-X-L encyclopedia of water science   **553.7**
  Water: science and issues   **553.7**
    Fiction
  Park, L. S. A long walk to water   **Fic**

Water animals *See* Marine animals

Water birds
  See also Albatrosses; Penguins

Water color painting *See* Watercolor painting

Water conservation
  Petersen, C. Renewing Earth's waters   **333.91**
  Workman, J. G. Water   **363.6**

Water from heaven. Kandel, R. S.   **553.7**

The **water** is wide. Conroy, P.   **371.9**

Water pollution
  Kurlansky, M. The world without fish   **333.95**

Petersen, C. Renewing Earth's waters   **333.91**
Water: science and issues   **553.7**

Water supply
  Balliett, J. F. Freshwater   **363.6**
  Workman, J. G. Water   **363.6**

Water: tales of elemental spirits. McKinley, R.   **S C**

Watercolor painting
    Technique
  Craig, D. The new encyclopedia of watercolor techniques   **751.42**
  Crawshaw, A. Watercolour for the absolute beginner   **751.42**
  Kutch, K. A. Drawing and painting with colored pencil   **741.2**
  Nice, C. Painting your favorite animals in pen, ink, and watercolor   **743**

Watercolour for the absolute beginner. Crawshaw, A.   **751.42**

Waterford, Helen, 1909-
  (jt. auth) Ayer, E. H. Parallel journeys   **940.53**

Watergate. Olson, K. W.   **973.924**

Watergate Affair, 1972-1974
  Bernstein, C. All the president's men   **973.924**
  Genovese, M. A. The Watergate crisis   **973.924**
  Olson, K. W. Watergate   **973.924**
  Woodward, B. The final days   **973.924**

The **Watergate** crisis. Genovese, M. A.   **973.924**

Waters, Dan, 1969-
  Generation dead   **Fic**

Waters, Sophie
  Seeing the gynecologist   **618.1**

Watership Down. Adams, R.   **Fic**

Watersmeet. Abbott, E. J.   **Fic**

Watkin, David, 1941-
  A history of Western architecture   **720.9**

Watkins, Christine, 1951-
  (ed) Do children have rights? See Do children have rights?   **323.3**
  (ed) The Ethics of abortion. See The Ethics of abortion   **179.7**
  (ed) The ethics of capital punishment. See The ethics of capital punishment   **364.66**
  (ed) Should juveniles be tried as adults? See Should juveniles be tried as adults?   **345**
  (ed) Sports and athletes: opposing viewpoints. See Sports and athletes: opposing viewpoints   **796**

Watkins, Julia
  The truth about family life. See The truth about family life   **306.8**

Watkins, T. H. (Tom H.), 1936-2000
  The hungry years   **973.91**

Watson, Burton, 1925-
  (ed. & tr) From the country of eight islands. See From the country of eight islands   **895.6**

Watson, Esther
  (jt. auth) Todd, M. Whatcha mean, what's a zine?   **070.5**

Watson, James D., 1928-
The double helix   **572.8**
See/See also pages in the following book(s):
Horvitz, L. A. Eureka!: scientific breakthroughs
that changed the world   **509**

Watson, Larry
Montana 1948   **Fic**

Watson, Lyall, 1939-2008
The whole hog   **599.63**

Watson, Robert R.
(ed) The Facts on File companion to British poetry, 1900 to the present. See The Facts on
File companion to British poetry, 1900 to the
present   **821.009**

Watson, Stephanie, 1969-
The endocrine system   **612.4**
The urinary system   **616.6**

Watson, Celia Loring *See* Seupel, Celia W.

Watstein, Sarah B.
The encyclopedia of HIV and AIDS   **616.97**

Watsuki, Nobuhiro, 1970-
Rurouni Kenshin   **741.5**

Waugh, Trevor, 1952-
(jt. auth) Crawshaw, A. Watercolour for the absolute beginner   **751.42**

Waves. Dogar, S.   **Fic**

Wax, Imy F.
(jt. auth) Kravets, M. The K & W guide to colleges for students with learning disabilities or
attention deficit hyperactivity disorder
                                                   378.73

The **way** it was. Goldstein, D. M.   **940.54**
A **way** of being. Rogers, C. R.   **150.19**
The **way** things work. See Macaulay, D. The new
way things work   **600**
The **way** toys work. Sobey, E.   **688.7**
The **way** we will be 50 years from today
                                                   303.49
The **way** we work. Macaulay, D.   **612**

Wayne, Tiffany K., 1968-
American women of science since 1900
                                                   920.003
Critical companion to Ralph Waldo Emerson
                                                   818

Wayshak, Deborah *See* Noyes, Deborah, 1965-

We are all suspects now. Nguyen, T.   **323.1**
We are Americans. Perez, W.   **371.82**
We are on our own. Katin, M.   **92**
We are the weather makers. Flannery, T. F.
                                                   551.6
We bought a zoo. Mee, B.   **92**
We had sneakers, they had guns. Sugarman, T.
                                                   323.1
We have always lived in the castle. Jackson, S.
                                                   Fic
We hear the dead. Salerni, D. K.   **Fic**
We interrupt this broadcast. Garner, J.   **070.1**
We shall all be free. Sanna, E.   **305.8**
We the students. Raskin, J. B.   **344**
We want you to know. Ellis, D.   **302.3**
We were here. De la Peña, M.   **Fic**

We were there, vol. 1. Obata, Y.   **741.5**
We wish to inform you that tomorrow we will be
killed with our families. Gourevitch, P.
                                                   967.571

Wealth
See also Success
Gilbert, G. Rich and poor in America   **339.2**
                Fiction
Caletti, D. The fortunes of Indigo Skye   **Fic**
Fitzgerald, F. S. The great Gatsby   **Fic**
Fitzgerald, F. S. Tender is the night   **Fic**
Godbersen, A. The luxe   **Fic**
Rich, S. Elliot Allagash   **Fic**

Weapons
See also Armor; Swords
Wagner, E., major. Medieval costume, armour,
and weapons   **399**
Weapons of mass destruction: opposing view-
points   **358**
                History
Reinhardt, H. The book of swords   **623.4**

Weapons of mass destruction: opposing viewpoints   **358**

Wearing, Judy
Edison's concrete piano   **609**

Weather
See also Meteorology
Buckley, B. Weather: a visual guide   **551.5**
Desonie, D. Atmosphere   **551.5**
Streissguth, T. Extreme weather   **551.5**
Williams, J. The AMS weather book   **551.5**
                Chronology
Allaby, M. A chronology of weather   **551.5**
                Graphic novels
Evans, K. Weird weather   **363.7**

Weather: a visual guide. Buckley, B.   **551.5**
Weather and climate. Harper, K.   **551.5**

Weather control
Fleming, J. R. Fixing the sky   **551.6**

The **weather** of the future. Cullen, H. **551.63**

Weatherford, Carole Boston, 1956-
Becoming Billie Holiday   **Fic**

Weatherly, Myra, 1926-
Teens in Ghana   **966.7**

Weaver, Stewart Angas
(jt. auth) Lasch, C. Plain style   **808**

Weaver, Will
Defect   **Fic**
Full service   **Fic**
Saturday night dirt   **Fic**

Web 2.0
Berger, P. Choosing Web 2.0 tools for learning
and teaching in a digital world   **025.04**
Crane, B. E. Using WEB 2.0 tools in the K-12
classroom   **371.3**
De Abreu, B. S. Media literacy, social network-
ing, and the web 2.0 environment for the
K-12 educator   **302.23**
Kroski, E. Web 2.0 for librarians and informa-
tion professionals   **020**

Web-based instruction. Smith, S. S.   **025.5**

Web logs *See* Weblogs

Web sites

See also Wikis (Computer science)

Doyle, M. 101+ great ideas for teen library Web sites **027.62**

Wolfinger, A. Best career and education web sites **025.04**

Design

Selfridge, B. A teen's guide to creating Web pages and blogs **006.7**

Smith, S. S. Web-based instruction **025.5**

Directories

Morkes, A. College exploration on the internet **378.73**

Shaw, M. D. Mastering online research **025.04**

The United States government internet directory **025.04**

Webb, David, 1962-

Drawing handbook **741.2**

Webb, Lois Sinaiko, 1922-

Holidays of the world cookbook for students **641.5**

The multicultural cookbook for students **641.5**

Webb, Robyn

(jt. auth) Warshaw, H. S. The diabetes food & nutrition bible **616.4**

Webber, Carlie

Gay, lesbian, bisexual, transgender, and questioning teen literature **808.8**

Weber, Adrienne, 1982-

(tr) Yoshizaki, S. Kingyo used books, vol. 1 **741.5**

Weber, Lori, 1959-

If you live like me **Fic**

Weber, R. David, 1941-

(ed) High school senior's guide to merit and other no-need funding, 2008-2010. See High school senior's guide to merit and other no-need funding, 2008-2010 **378.3**

(jt. auth) Schlachter, G. A. College student's guide to merit and other no-need funding, 2008-2010 **378.3**

(jt. auth) Schlachter, G. A. Directory of financial aids for women 2009-2011 **378.3**

(jt. auth) Schlachter, G. A. Financial aid for the disabled and their families, 2010-2012 **378.3**

Weblogs

Hussey, T. Create your own blog **006.7**

IraqiGirl. IraqiGirl **92**

Richardson, W. Blogs, wikis, podcasts, and other powerful Web tools for classrooms **371.3**

Selfridge, B. A teen's guide to creating Web pages and blogs **006.7**

See/See also pages in the following book(s):
Farkas, M. Social software in libraries **025.5**

Fiction

Cowan, J. Earthgirl **Fic**

Prinz, Y. The Vinyl Princess **Fic**

Strasser, T. Wish you were dead **Fic**

Webster, Daniel, 1782-1852

See/See also pages in the following book(s):
Kennedy, J. F. Profiles in courage **920**

Webster, Raymond B.

African American firsts in science and technology **509**

Webster's collegiate thesaurus. See Merriam-Webster's collegiate thesaurus **423**

Webster's dictionary of English usage. See Merriam-Webster's dictionary of English usage **428**

Webster's dictionary of synonyms. See The Merriam-Webster dictionary of synonyms and antonyms **423**

Webster's geographical dictionary. See Merriam-Webster's geographical dictionary **910.3**

Webster's II new college dictionary. See Webster's New College Dictionary **423**

Webster's New College Dictionary **423**

Webster's New World computer dictionary. Pfaffenberger, B. **004**

Webster's New World dictionary of computer terms. See Pfaffenberger, B. Webster's New World computer dictionary **004**

Wecht, Cyril H., 1931-

Tales from the morgue **614**

The **wedding**. West, D. **Fic**

Weddings

Fiction

McCullers, C. The member of the wedding **Fic**

The **Wee** Free Men. Pratchett, T. **Fic**

Weetzie Bat. Block, F. L. **Fic**

Wegener, Alfred Lothar, 1880-1930

See/See also pages in the following book(s):
Horvitz, L. A. Eureka!: scientific breakthroughs that changed the world **509**

Weicker, Lowell P., Jr.

See/See also pages in the following book(s):
Profiles in courage for our time **920**

Weidensaul, Scott

Return to wild America **578**

Weighing in. Favor, L. J. **613.2**

Weighing the world. Danson, E. **526**

Weight control *See* Weight loss

Weight lifting

Fahey, T. D. Basic weight training for men and women **613.7**

Hesson, J. L. Weight training for life **613.7**

Pagano, J. Strength training for women **613.7**

Weight loss

Favor, L. J. Weighing in **613.2**

Klein, S. Moose **92**

Smolin, L. A. Nutrition and weight management **613.2**

Fiction

Lipsyte, R. One fat summer **Fic**

Supplee, S. Artichoke's heart **Fic**

Zarr, S. Sweethearts **Fic**

Weight training for life. Hesson, J. L. **613.7**

Weights and measures

The Economist desk companion **530.8**

Nicastro, N. Circumference **526**

Weihs, Jean Riddle
(jt. auth) Intner, S. S. Standard cataloging for school and public libraries   **025.3**

Weinberg, Robert
Revolutionary Russia   **947.084**

Weinberg, Steven, 1984-
(il) Scieszka, C. To Timbuktu   **910.4**

Weinberger, Eliot, 1949-
(ed) Paz, O. Selected poems   **861**

Weiner, Mark Stuart, 1967-
Black trials   **342**

Weing, Drew
Set to sea   **741.5**

Weingarten, Lynn
Wherever Nina lies   **Fic**

Weinheimer, Beckie
Converting Kate   **Fic**

Weinreich, Beatrice
(ed) Yiddish folktales. See Yiddish folktales   **398.2**

Weinstein, Bruce D.
Is it still cheating if I don't get caught?   **170**

Weinstein, Jay
The ethical gourmet   **641.5**

Weinstein, Lauren
Girl stories   **741.5**

Weinstein, Lawrence, 1960-
Guesstimation   **519.5**

Weinstein, Philip M.
Becoming Faulkner   **92**

Weintraub, David A., 1958-
Is Pluto a planet?   **523.4**

Weintraub, Stanley, 1929-
(ed) Wilde, O. The portable Oscar Wilde   **828**

Weir, Alison
The Wars of the Roses   **942.04**

Weird weather. Evans, K.   **363.7**

Weis, Judith S., 1941-
Salt marshes   **578.7**

Weis, Margaret, 1948-
Mistress of dragons   **Fic**

Weisberg, Joseph
10th grade   **Fic**

Weisblatt, Jayne, 1945-
(ed) Alternative energy. See Alternative energy   **333.79**
(ed) Chemical compounds. See Chemical compounds   **540**
(ed) World encyclopedia of political systems and parties. See World encyclopedia of political systems and parties   **324.2**
(ed) World religions. See World religions   **200**

Weisburg, Hilda K., 1942-
(jt. auth) Toor, R. Being indispensable   **025.1**

Weisel, Gary J.
(jt. auth) Black, B. Global warming   **363.7**

Weiser, Christine
(jt. auth) Huber, J. Ask Mr. Technology, get answers   **371.3**

Weisman, Alan
The world without us   **304.2**

Weiss, Erich *See* Houdini, Harry, 1874-1926

Weiss, Lesley, 1947-
(ed) Discover beading. See Discover beading   **745.58**

Weiss, Marisa C.
Taking care of your 'girls'   **618.1**

Weisse Rose (Resistance group)
Dumbach, A. E. Sophie Scholl and the white rose   **943.086**

Weissman, Paul Robert, 1947-
(ed) Encyclopedia of the solar system. See Encyclopedia of the solar system   **523.2**

Weitzman, David L., 1936-
Skywalkers   **682**

Weitzman, Lenore J.
(ed) Women in the Holocaust. See Women in the Holocaust   **940.53**

Welch, James, 1940-2003
Killing Custer   **973.8**
See/See also pages in the following book(s):
Coltelli, L. Winged words: American Indian writers speak   **897**

Welch, Janet, 1953-
(jt. auth) Lerch, M. T. Serving homeschooled teens and their parents   **027.6**

Welch, Robert, 1947-
(ed) The Oxford companion to Irish literature. See The Oxford companion to Irish literature   **820.9**

Welch, Rollie James, 1957-
A core collection for young adults   **011.6**
The guy-friendly YA library   **027.62**

Welcome to Bordertown   **808.8**

Welcome to your brain. Aamodt, S.   **612.8**

Welfare and welfare reform. Streissguth, T.   **361.6**

The **well-dressed** ape. Holmes, H.   **612**

We'll understand it better by and by   **782.25**

Welles, Orson, 1915-1985
Fiction
Kaplow, R. Me and Orson Welles   **Fic**

Wellesley, Charles *See* Brontë, Charlotte, 1816-1855

Wells, H. G. (Herbert George), 1866-1946
The invisible man   **Fic**
The time machine   **Fic**
The war of the worlds   **Fic**

Wells, Ida B. *See* Wells-Barnett, Ida B., 1862-1931

Wells, Jeff
All my patients have tales   **636**

Wells, Ken R.
(ed) Teenage sexuality: opposing viewpoints. See Teenage sexuality: opposing viewpoints   **613.9**

Wells, Rosemary, 1943-
Red moon at Sharpsburg   **Fic**

Wells, Spencer, 1969-
The journey of man   **599.93**

Widows
Fiction
Sheth, K. Keeping corner   **Fic**

Wieder, Laurance, 1946-
(ed) Chapters into verse. See Chapters into verse
    821.008

Wiegand, Wayne A., 1946-
(ed) Herald, D. T. Genreflecting   **016.8**

Wiener, Gary
(ed) The environment in Henry David Thoreau's Walden. See The environment in Henry David Thoreau's Walden   **818**

Wiener, Roberta, 1952-
(jt. auth) Arnold, J. R. Robert Mugabe's Zimbabwe   **968.91**

Wiesel, Elie, 1928-
Night   **92**
See/See also pages in the following book(s):
Aikman, D. Great souls   **920**

Wiesel, Eliezer *See* Wiesel, Elie, 1928-

Wife abuse
See also Abused women

Wiggins, Arthur W.
The five biggest unsolved problems in science
    500

Wight, James Alfred *See* Herriot, James

Wigoder, Geoffrey, 1922-1999
(ed) The New encyclopedia of Judaism. See The New encyclopedia of Judaism [New York University Press]   **296.03**
(ed) The Oxford dictionary of the Jewish religion. See The Oxford dictionary of the Jewish religion   **296.03**
(ed) The student's encyclopedia of Judaism. See The student's encyclopedia of Judaism   **296.03**

Wikis (Computer science)
Richardson, W. Blogs, wikis, podcasts, and other powerful Web tools for classrooms   **371.3**

Wilbur, Richard, 1921-
(ed) Poe, E. A. Poems and poetics   **811**

Wild, K., 1954-
Fight game   **Fic**
The **wild**. Golden, C.   **Fic**
Wild about flying!. Marshall, D.   **629.13**
Wild blue. Bortolotti, D.   **599.5**

Wild cats
See also Cats; Lions; Tigers
Alderton, D. Wild cats of the world   **599.75**
Page, J. Do cats hear with their feet?   **636.8**
Richardson, K. Part of the pride   **92**
Wild cats of the world. Alderton, D.   **599.75**

Wild dogs
Fiction
De Lint, C. Dingo   **Fic**

Wild flowers
Spellenberg, R. Familiar flowers of North America: eastern region   **582.13**
Spellenberg, R. Familiar flowers of North America: western region   **582.13**

Spellenberg, R. National Audubon Society field guide to North American wildflowers, western region   **582.13**
Thieret, J. W. National Audubon Society field guide to North American wildflowers: eastern region   **582.13**
Conservation
See Plant conservation

Wild guide [series]
Berger, C. Owls   **598**
The **wild** trees. Preston, R.   **577.3**

Wilde, Oscar, 1854-1900
The importance of being earnest and other plays
    822
The picture of Dorian Gray   **Fic**
The portable Oscar Wilde   **828**

Wilder, Laura Ingalls, 1867-1957
About
Zochert, D. Laura: the life of Laura Ingalls Wilder   **92**
Poetry
Atkins, J. Borrowed names   **811**

Wilder, Mrs. Almanzo J. *See* Wilder, Laura Ingalls, 1867-1957

Wilder, Thornton, 1897-1975
Our town   **812**
Three plays: Our town, The skin of our teeth, The matchmaker   **812**

Wilderness areas
Hart, J. Walking softly in the wilderness
    796.51
Fiction
De Gramont, N. Every little thing in the world
    Fic
McDonald, A. Boys, bears, and a serious pair of hiking boots   **Fic**
Management
How should America's wilderness be managed?
    333.7

Wilderness survival
Piven, J. The worst-case scenario survival handbook   **613.6**
Ralston, A. Between a rock and a hard place
    796.522
Stilwell, A. The encyclopedia of survival techniques   **613.6**
Survival wisdom & know-how   **613.6**
Wiseman, J. SAS survival handbook   **613.6**
Fiction
Golden, C. The wild   **Fic**
Houston, J. D. Snow Mountain passage   **Fic**
McCaughrean, G. The white darkness   **Fic**
McClintock, N. Taken   **Fic**
Polak, M. The middle of everywhere   **Fic**
Waldorf, H. Tripping   **Fic**
The **wildest** ride. Menzer, J.   **796.72**

Wildfires
Cunningham, K. Wildfires   **363.3**

Wildin, Rowena, 1956-
(ed) The Sixties in America. See The Sixties in America   **973.92**

Wildlife
Couturier, L. The hopes of snakes   **591.7**

Williams, Mary E., 1960-
(ed) Adoption: opposing viewpoints. See Adoption: opposing viewpoints **362.7**
(ed) Hallucinogens. See Hallucinogens **615**
(ed) Is it unpatriotic to criticize one's country? See Is it unpatriotic to criticize one's country? **323.6**
(ed) Mental illness: opposing viewpoints. See Mental illness: opposing viewpoints **362.2**
(ed) Self-mutilation: opposing viewpoints. See Self-mutilation: opposing viewpoints **616.85**
(ed) Sex: opposing viewpoints. See Sex: opposing viewpoints **306.7**

Williams, Norman, 1952-
One unblinking eye **811**

Williams, Peter W.
(ed) Encyclopedia of religion in America. See Encyclopedia of religion in America **200.9**

Williams, Raymond Brady
(jt. auth) Mann, G. S. Buddhists, Hindus, and Sikhs in America **294**

Williams, Robert G.
(jt. auth) Nichols, C. R. Encyclopedia of marine science **551.46**

Williams, Roger, 1604?-1683
About
Gaustad, E. S. Roger Williams **92**

Williams, Tennessee, 1911-1983
The glass menagerie **812**
A streetcar named desire **812**
About
Heintzelman, G. Critical companion to Tennessee Williams **812.009**
Hermann, S. A student's guide to Tennessee Williams **812.009**
The Tennessee Williams encyclopedia **812.009**

Williams, Terrie
Stay strong **305.23**

Williams, Thomas Lanier *See* Williams, Tennessee, 1911-1983

Williams, Walter L., 1948-
(ed) Gay and lesbian rights in the United States. See Gay and lesbian rights in the United States **306.76**

Williams, Wendy
Kraken **594**

Williams, William Appleman, 1921-1990
(ed) America in Vietnam. See America in Vietnam **959.704**

Williams, William Carlos, 1883-1963
The collected poems of William Carlos Williams **811**

Williams-Garcia, Rita
Jumped **Fic**
Like sisters on the homefront **Fic**

Willis, Clint
(ed) Climb: stories of survival from rock, snow, and ice. See Climb: stories of survival from rock, snow, and ice **796.522**
(ed) Fire fighters. See Fire fighters **628.9**

Willis, Connie
To say nothing of the dog; or, How we found the bishop's bird stump at last **Fic**

Willis, Deborah, 1952-
Reflections in Black **770**

Willis, Roy G.
(ed) World mythology. See World mythology **201**

Willow. Hoban, J. **Fic**

Wills, Garry, 1934-
James Madison **92**

Wilmeth, Don B.
(ed) The Cambridge guide to American theatre. See The Cambridge guide to American theatre **792.03**

Wilson, A. Paula
100 ready-to-use pathfinders for the Web **001.4**

Wilson, August
Fences **812**
Jitney **812**
Joe Turner's come and gone **812**
Ma Rainey's black bottom **812**
The piano lesson **812**
About
August Wilson [critical essays] **812.009**

Wilson, Charles, 1974-
(jt. auth) Schlosser, E. Chew on this **394.1**

Wilson, Charles E., 1961-
Race and racism in literature **810.9**

Wilson, Charles Paul, 1976-
(il) Raicht, M. The stuff of legend, book 1 **741.5**

Wilson, Claire
(jt. auth) Kelly, E. B. Investigating influenza and bird flu **616.2**

Wilson, David Sloan
Evolution for everyone **576.8**

Wilson, Derek A., 1935-
Charlemagne **92**

Wilson, Diane L.
Firehorse **Fic**

Wilson, Don E.
(jt. auth) Kays, R. Mammals of North America **599**
(ed) Mammals. See Mammals **599**

Wilson, Edward O., 1929-
(jt. auth) Hölldobler, B. The leafcutter ants **595.7**

Wilson, Ellen Judy
Encyclopedia of the Enlightenment **940.2**

Wilson, G. Willow
Cairo **741.5**

Wilson, George, 1920-
(ed) Literature and its times. See Literature and its times **809**

Wilson, James D. (James Darrell), 1946-
(ed) The Mark Twain encyclopedia. See The Mark Twain encyclopedia **818**

Wilson, Katharina M.
(ed) Women in the Middle Ages. See Women in the Middle Ages **305.4**

Wintergirls. Anderson, L. H.   **Fic**

Winters, Kathleen C.
Amelia Earhart   **92**

Winters, Robert, 1963-
(ed) The right to a trial by jury. See The right to a trial by jury   **345**

Winter's bone. Woodrell, D.   **Fic**

Winter's end. Mourlevat, J.-C.   **Fic**

Winthrop, John, 1588-1649
About
Aronson, M. John Winthrop, Oliver Cromwell, and the Land of Promise [dual biography of John Winthrop and Oliver Cromwell]   **92**

Wintz, Cary D., 1943-
(ed) Encyclopedia of the Harlem Renaissance. See Encyclopedia of the Harlem Renaissance   **700**

(ed) Harlem speaks. See Harlem speaks   **810.9**

Wire mothers. Ottaviani, J.   **152.4**

Wirt, Mildred A. (Mildred Augustine), 1905-
About
Rehak, M. Girl sleuth   **813.009**

Wirz, Hartmann Heinrich See Wirz, Henry, d. 1865

Wirz, Henry, d. 1865
About
Gourley, C. The horrors of Andersonville   **973.7**

Wisconsin
Fiction
Bauer, J. Hope was here   **Fic**
Bick, I. J. Draw the dark   **Fic**
Cumbie, P. Where people like us live   **Fic**
Fink, M. The summer I got a life   **Fic**
Hijuelos, O. Dark Dude   **Fic**
Miller-Lachmann, L. Gringolandia   **Fic**
Packer, A. The dive from Clausen's pier   **Fic**
Wroblewski, D. The story of Edgar Sawtelle   **Fic**

Wisdom for a livable planet. McDaniel, C. N.   **333.72**

The **Wisdom** of the Tao   **299.5**

Wise, Mike, 1964-
(jt. auth) O'Neal, S. Shaq talks back   **92**

Wiseman, Eva
Puppet   **Fic**

Wiseman, John, 1940-
SAS survival handbook   **613.6**

Wish. Bullen, A.   **Fic**

Wish. Monninger, J.   **Fic**

Wish you were dead. Strasser, T.   **Fic**

Wishart, David J., 1946-
(ed) Encyclopedia of the Great Plains. See Encyclopedia of the Great Plains   **978.03**

Wishes
Fiction
Archer, E. Geek: fantasy novel   **Fic**
Bullen, A. Wish   **Fic**
Hubbard, A. You wish   **Fic**
Monninger, J. Wish   **Fic**

Wit and humor
See also American wit and humor; Cartooning; Comedy; Humorous poetry
Oxford dictionary of humorous quotations   **808.88**
History and criticism
Hogan, W. Humor in young adult literature   **813.009**

Witalec, Janet, 1965-
(ed) The Harlem Renaissance: a Gale critical companion. See The Harlem Renaissance: a Gale critical companion   **810.9**

Witch-hunt: mysteries of the Salem witch trials. Aronson, M.   **133.4**

Witch hunts in Europe and America. Burns, W. E.   **133.4**

Witchcraft
See also Magic
Aronson, M. Witch-hunt: mysteries of the Salem witch trials   **133.4**
Carlson, L. M. A fever in Salem   **133.4**
Demos, J. Entertaining Satan   **133.4**
Goss, K. D. The Salem witch trials   **133.4**
Kallen, S. A. Witches   **133.4**
Drama
Miller, A. The crucible   **812**
Encyclopedias
Burns, W. E. Witch hunts in Europe and America   **133.4**
Guiley, R. E. The encyclopedia of witches, witchcraft, and Wicca   **133.4**
Fiction
Chima, C. W. The Demon King   **Fic**
Hearn, J. The minister's daughter   **Fic**
Hemphill, S. Wicked girls   **Fic**
Klein, L. M. Lady Macbeth's daughter   **Fic**
Laird, E. The betrayal of Maggie Blair   **Fic**
Napoli, D. J. The magic circle   **Fic**
Stroud, J. The ring of Solomon   **Fic**
Tiernan, C. Balefire   **Fic**
Turner, A. W. Father of lies   **Fic**

Witches
Fiction
Atwater-Rhodes, A. Persistence of memory   **Fic**
Hallaway, T. Almost to die for   **Fic**
Hawkins, R. Hex Hall   **Fic**
MacCullough, C. Once a witch   **Fic**
Pratchett, T. The Wee Free Men   **Fic**
Rowling, J. K. Harry Potter and the Sorcerer's Stone   **Fic**
Graphic novels
Chmakova, S. Nightschool: the weirn books, volume one   **741.5**

Witches. Kallen, S. A.   **133.4**

With their eyes   **812.008**

Wither. DeStefano, L.   **Fic**

Withers, Jennie
Hey, get a job!   **650.14**

Without a map. Hall, M.   **92**

Witness   **940.53**

Witnesses
Fiction
David, K. When I was Joe   **Fic**

Women's issues, global trends [series]
Esherick, J. Women in the Arab world
305.4
Women's letters **305.4**
Women's lives in medieval Europe **305.4**
Women's movement
Rosen, R. The world split open **305.4**
Women's rights
See also Pro-choice movement; Pro-life movement
Supreme Court decisions and women's rights
342
Women's rights **305.4**
See/See also pages in the following book(s):
The Columbia documentary history of American women since 1941 **305.4**
Fiction
Sheth, K. Keeping corner **Fic**
Women's rights **305.4**
Women's suffrage in America. Frost-Knappman, E. **324.6**
Wonder beasts. Nigg, J. **398**
Wonder when you'll miss me. Davis, A. **Fic**
Wonderland. Nadin, J. **Fic**
Wonders *See* Curiosities and wonders
Wonders of the African world. Gates, H. L.
960
Wood, Angela
Holocaust **940.53**
Wood, Elaine, 1950-
(jt. auth) Walker, P. Chemistry experiments
540.7
(jt. auth) Walker, P. The coral reef **577.7**
(jt. auth) Walker, P. Environmental science experiments **507.8**
(jt. auth) Walker, P. Forensic science experiments **363.2**
(jt. auth) Walker, P. Physical science experiments **500.2**
(jt. auth) Walker, P. Space and astronomy experiments **520**
Wood, Frances
The Silk Road **950**
Wood, Gordon S.
The Americanization of Benjamin Franklin
92
Wood, Ira
(jt. auth) Piercy, M. So you want to write
808.3
Wood, Maryrose
The poison diaries **Fic**
Wood, Michael, 1948-
In the footsteps of Alexander the Great **938**
Wood, Trish
(comp) What was asked of us. See What was asked of us **956.7**
Wood, W. J. (William J.), 1917-
Battles of the Revolutionary War, 1775-1781
973.3
Wood, William J. *See* Wood, W. J. (William J.), 1917-

Wood
Edlin, H. L. What wood is that? A manual of wood identification **674**
Encyclopedias
The Encyclopedia of wood **674**
Wood carving
Bütz, R. How to carve wood **731.4**
Wood, Jamie Martinez *See* Martinez Wood, Jamie
Woodcock, Jon
(jt. auth) Woodford, C. Cool Stuff 2.0 and how it works **600**
Woodford, Chris, 1943-
Cool Stuff 2.0 and how it works **600**
Cool stuff exploded **600**
Cool stuff and how it works. See Cool stuff and how it works **600**
Woodger, Elin
The 1980s **973.92**
Wooding, Chris, 1977-
The haunting of Alaizabel Cray **Fic**
Poison **Fic**
The storm thief **Fic**
Woodpeckers
Gallagher, T. The grail bird **598**
Hoose, P. M. The race to save the Lord God Bird **598**
Woodrell, Daniel
Winter's bone **Fic**
Woodring, Carl, 1919-2009
(ed) The Columbia anthology of British poetry. See The Columbia anthology of British poetry
821.008
Woodrow Wilson and the Progressive Era. Lukes, B. L. **92**
Woodruff, Dorothy, 1887-1979
About
Wickenden, D. Nothing daunted [dual biography of Dorothy Woodruff and Rosamund Underwood] **92**
Woods, Elizabeth Emma
Choker **Fic**
Woods *See* Forests and forestry
Woodson, Jacqueline
If you come softly **Fic**
Miracle's boys **Fic**
Woodsong. Paulsen, G. **796.5**
Woodward, Bob, 1943-
The final days **973.924**
(jt. auth) Bernstein, C. All the president's men
973.924
Woodward, David R., 1939-
World War I almanac **940.3**
Woodward, Grace Steele, b. 1899
Pocahontas **92**
Woodward, Jeannette A.
What every librarian should know about electronic privacy **025.5**
Woodward, John, 1958-
War **303.6**
Woodwork
Taunton's complete illustrated guide to woodworking **684**

World War, 1939-1945—*Continued*
Netherlands—Fiction
Polak, M. What world is left   **Fic**
United States
And justice for all   **940.53**
Daniels, R. Prisoners without trial   **940.53**
Houston, J. W. Farewell to Manzanar
    940.53
Isserman, M. World War II   **940.53**
Oppenheim, J. Dear Miss Breed   **940.53**
Robinson, G. By order of the president
    940.53
Schneider, C. J. World War II   **940.53**
Takaki, R. T. Double victory   **940.53**
Takaki, R. T. Hiroshima   **940.54**
World War I. Bosco, P. I.   **940.3**
World War I. Carlisle, R. P.   **940.3**
World War I. Coetzee, M. S.   **940.3**
World War I. Heyman, N. M.   **940.3**
World War I: a student encyclopedia   **940.3**
World War I almanac. Woodward, D. R.
    940.3
World War II   **940.54**
World War II. Dick, R.   **940.54**
World War II. Isserman, M.   **940.53**
World War II. Schneider, C. J.   **940.53**
World War II: a student encyclopedia   **940.53**
World War II almanac. Dickson, K. D.
    940.54
World War II and the postwar years in America.
Young, W. H.   **973.91**
World War II: biographies. Howes, K. K.   **920**
World War II reference library [series]
Howes, K. K. World War II: biographies
    920
World War One. Stone, N.   **940.3**
World wars and globalization, 1914 to 2010
    909.82
World wide web sites *See* Web sites
A **world** without bees. Benjamin, A.   **638**
The **world** without fish. Kurlansky, M.   **333.95**
A **world** without ice. Pollack, H. N.   **551.3**
The **world** without us. Weisman, A.   **304.2**
World writers [series]
Aykroyd, C. Savage satire   **92**
Brackett, V. Restless genius   **92**
Caravantes, P. Best of times: the story of
Charles Dickens   **92**
Caravantes, P. Deep woods   **92**
Caravantes, P. A great and sublime fool   **92**
Caravantes, P. Self-reliance: the story of Ralph
Waldo Emerson   **92**
Caravantes, P. Writing is my business   **92**
Gelletly, L. Gift of imagination   **92**
Hamilton, J. C. S. Lewis   **92**
Leslie, R. Isak Dinesen   **92**
Whitelaw, N. Dark dreams   **92**
World writers in English   **820.9**
The **worldly** philosophers. Heilbroner, R. L.
    330.1

Worldmark encyclopedia of cultures and daily
life   **306**
Worldmark encyclopedia of the nations   **910.3**
Worldmark encyclopedia of the states   **973.03**
Worlds apart. Johnson, L. L.   **Fic**
Worldshaker. Harland, R.   **Fic**
Worldweavers [series]
Alexander, A. Gift of the Unmage   **Fic**
Worms
Stewart, A. The earth moved   **592**
Worry
See also Anxiety
Fiction
De Goldi, K. The 10 p.m. question   **Fic**
The **worst-case** scenario survival handbook. Piven,
J.   **613.6**
Worth, Richard, 1945-
Frequently asked questions about teen father-
hood   **306.8**
Puerto Rico in American history   **972.95**
Slave life on the plantation   **326**
Would you. Jocelyn, M.   **Fic**
Wouldn't take nothing for my journey now.
Angelou, M.   **814**
Wounded, First aid to *See* First aid
Wounded Knee Creek, Battle of, 1890
Hillstrom, K. American Indian removal and the
trail to Wounded Knee   **973.8**
Wounds and injuries
See also Brain—Wounds and injuries;
Burns and scalds; Fractures; Wounds and in-
juries
Everyday sports injuries   **617.1**
Sokolove, M. Y. Warrior girls   **796**
Sports injuries information for teens   **617.1**
Encyclopedias
Diseases, disorders, and injuries   **616**
Wray, John, 1971-
Lowboy   **Fic**
A **wreath** for Emmett Till. Nelson, M.   **811**
Wrede, Patricia C., 1953-
The thirteenth child   **Fic**
Wrestling
Beekman, S. Ringside   **796.8**
Greenberg, K. E. Pro wrestling   **796.8**
Kreidler, M. Four days to glory   **796.8**
McIntosh, J. S. Wrestling   **796.8**
Fiction
Wallace, R. Wrestling Sturbridge   **Fic**
Wrestling Sturbridge. Wallace, R.   **Fic**
Wright, Adam
(jt. auth) Earp, P. W. Securing library technolo-
gy   **005.8**
Wright, Denis
Violence 101   **Fic**
Wright, Edmund
(ed) The Facts on File dictionary of computer
science. See The Facts on File dictionary of
computer science   **004**
Wright, Fiona
(jt. auth) Jones, C. 1001 little fashion miracles
    646

Wynne-Jones, Tim
Blink & Caution   Fic
The uninvited   Fic
Wyoming
    Description and travel
Proulx, A. Bird cloud   92
    Fiction
Neely, C. Unearthly   Fic

X

X-Isle. Augarde, S.   Fic
Xenophon, ca. 431-ca. 352 B.C.
See/See also pages in the following book(s):
Hamilton, E. The Greek way   880.9

Y

Yachts and yachting
See also Sailing
Yagoda, Ben
Memoir   809
Will Rogers   92
The **Yale** book of quotations   808.88
Yale Nota bene [series]
Bloom, J. Islam: a thousand years of faith and power   297
Yale University Press health & wellness [series]
Hicks, J. W. Fifty signs of mental illness   616.89
YALSA *See* Young Adult Library Services Association
Yamamoto, Sandra H.
(jt. auth) Harada, V. H. Collaborating for project-based learning in grades 9-12   371.3
Yamazaki, James N., 1916-
Children of the atomic bomb   92
Yamazaki, Joe
(tr) Ono, N. Gente: the people of Ristorante Paradiso, volume 1   741.5
Yanak, Ted
(jt. auth) Cornelison, P. The great American history fact-finder   973.03
Yancey, Richard
The monstrumologist   Fic
Yang, Gene
American born Chinese   741.5
Animal crackers   741.5
The eternal smile   741.5
Level up   741.5
Prime baby   741.5
Yang, Jeff
(ed) Secret identities. See Secret identities   741.5
Yankees (Baseball team) *See* New York Yankees (Baseball team)
Yanks: the epic story of the American Army in World War I. Eisenhower, J. S. D.   940.4
Yannuzzi, Della A.
New elements [biography of Marie Curie]   92

Yansky, Brian
Alien invasion and other inconveniences   Fic
Yarmolinsky, Babette Deutsch *See* Deutsch, Babette, 1895-1982
Yaverbaum, Cole
(jt. auth) Yaverbaum, E. Life's little college admissions insights   378.1
Yaverbaum, Eric
Life's little college admissions insights   378.1
Yeah! yeah! yeah!. Spitz, B.   920
The **year** 1000. Lacey, R.   942.01
The **year** my sister got lucky. Friedman, A.   Fic
The **year** of ice. Malloy, B.   Fic
A **year** of programs for teens. Alessio, A.   027.62
The **year** of secret assignments. Moriarty, J.   Fic
The **year's** best dark fantasy & horror   S C
The **year's** best science fiction and fantasy for teens: first annual collection   S C
Years of dust. Marrin, A.   978
Yeats, W. B. (William Butler), 1865-1939
The poems   821
The Yeats reader   828
Yeats, William Butler *See* Yeats, W. B. (William Butler), 1865-1939
The **Yeats** reader. Yeats, W. B.   828
Yee, Lisa
Absolutely Maybe   Fic
Yeh, Michelle Mi-Hsi
(ed) Anthology of modern Chinese poetry. See Anthology of modern Chinese poetry   895.1
Yell-oh girls!   305.23
Yellin, Emily, 1961-
Our mothers' war   940.53
Yellin, Susan
Life after high school   646.7
Yellow fever
Crosby, M. C. The American plague   614.5
Jurmain, S. The secret of the yellow death   614.5
Pierce, J. R. Yellow jack   614.5
Yellow jack. Pierce, J. R.   614.5
A **yellow** raft in blue water. Dorris, M.   Fic
Yellowstone National Park
Meyer, J. L. The spirit of Yellowstone   978.7
Smith, D. W. Decade of the wolf   599.77
    Fiction
Chandler, K. Wolves, boys, & other things that might kill me   Fic
Smith, D. Letters from Yellowstone   Fic
Yenser, Stephen
(ed) Merrill, J. The collected poems of James Merrill   811
Yeoman, R. S.
A guide book of United States coins   737.4
Yes you can!. Drake, J.   361.2

Youth—*Continued*
Israel
Watad, M. Teen voices from the Holy Land
920
Latin America
Teen life in Latin America and the Caribbean
305.23
United States
See also Teenagers—United States
Males, M. A. Framing youth 305.23
Twenge, J. M. Generation me 305.24
Youth with special needs [series]
Esherick, J. The journey toward recovery
616.8
Libal, A. My name is not Slow 362.3
Yovanoff, Brenna
The replacement Fic
Yugoslav War, 1991-1995
Judah, T. The Serbs 949.7
Graphic novels
Sacco, J. Safe area Goražde 949.7
Yugoslavia
See also Bosnia and Hercegovina; Serbia
History
Judah, T. The Serbs 949.7
History—Civil War, 1991-1995
See Yugoslav War, 1991-1995
Yukon River valley (Yukon and Alaska)
Fiction
Golden, C. The wild Fic
London, J. The call of the wild Fic
London, J. White Fang Fic
Yumi, Kiiro
Library wars, vol. 1: love & war 741.5
Yummy [biography of Robert Sandifer] Neri, G.
92
Yuwiler, Janice
Diabetes 616.4

Z

Z. Ford, M. T. Fic
Zach, Kim K., 1958-
Reproductive technology 618
Zacharias, Gary
(ed) 1900-1920: the twentieth century. See
1900-1920: the twentieth century 909.82
(ed) Freedom of religion. See Freedom of religion
342
Zadoff, Allen
Food, girls, and other things I can't have
Fic
Zaharias, Babe Didrikson, 1911-1956
About
Cayleff, S. E. Babe: the life and legend of Babe
Didrikson Zaharias 92
Zahler, Diane
The Black Death 614.5
Than Shwe's Burma 959.1
Zahler, Thomas F.
Love and capes, vol. 1 741.5

Zambone, Alana M.
(jt. auth) Jones, J. B. The power of the media
specialist to improve academic achievement
and strengthen at-risk students 027.8
Zamora, Pedro, 1972-1994
Graphic novels
Winick, J. Pedro & me 362.1
Zane's trace. Wolf, A. Fic
Zanger, Mark H.
The American history cookbook 641.5
Zannier, Marco, 1972-
(jt. auth) Martin, B. S. Fundamentals of school
library media management 025.1
Zap. Fleischman, P. 812
Zarr, Sara
Once was lost Fic
Story of a girl Fic
Sweethearts Fic
Zbaracki, Matthew D.
Best books for boys 028.5
Zedeck, Beth E.
Forensic pharmacology 614
Zedeck, Morris S.
(jt. auth) Zedeck, B. E. Forensic pharmacology
614
Zehr, Howard
"What will happen to me?" 362.82
Zeinert, Karen, 1942-2002
The brave women of the Gulf Wars 956.7
Zeises, Lara M.
The sweet life of Stella Madison Fic
Zellner, Robert, 1939-
The wrong side of Murder Creek [biography of
Robert Zellner] 92
Zemser, Amy Bronwen
Dear Julia Fic
Zen & Xander undone. Ryan, A. K. Fic
Zen and the art of motorcycle maintenance. Pirsig,
R. M. 92
Zen in the art of the SAT. Bardin, M. 378.1
Zenatti, Valérie, 1970-
When I was a soldier 92
Zero (The number)
Kaplan, R. The nothing that is 511
Seife, C. Zero 511
Zevin, Gabrielle, 1977-
Elsewhere Fic
Memoirs of a teenage amnesiac Fic
Zia, Helen
Asian American dreams 305.8
Ziauddin Sardar *See* Sardar, Ziauddin
Ziegfeld, Florenz, 1869-1932
See/See also pages in the following book(s):
Yagoda, B. Will Rogers 92
Ziegler, Jennifer
How not to be popular Fic
Zielin, Lara, 1975-
Donut days Fic
Zilkha, Avraham
Modern English-Hebrew dictionary 492.4

Zimbabwe
Arnold, J. R. Robert Mugabe's Zimbabwe **968.91**
Tucker, N. Love in the driest season **362.7**
Fiction
Farmer, N. The Ear, the Eye, and the Arm **Fic**
Wallace, J. Out of shadows **Fic**
Zimmerman, Doris P., 1931-
Robert's Rules in plain English **060.4**
Zimmerman, Dwight Jon
Tecumseh **92**
Zimmerman, Larry J., 1947-
Exploring the life, myth, and art of Native Americans **970.004**
Zimmerman, Robert, 1953-
The chronological encyclopedia of discoveries in space **629.4**
The universe in a mirror **629.43**
Zimmerman, Robert Allen See Dylan, Bob, 1941-
The **Zimmermann** telegram. Tuchman, B. W. **940.3**
Zindel, Paul
The effect of gamma rays on man-in-the-moon marigolds **812**
Zines
Todd, M. Whatcha mean, what's a zine? **070.5**
Fiction
Prinz, Y. The Vinyl Princess **Fic**
Zink, Michelle, 1969-
Prophecy of the sisters **Fic**
Zinn, Lennard
Zinn & the art of road bike maintenance **629.28**
Zinn & the art of road bike maintenance. Zinn, L. **629.28**
Zionism
Blumberg, A. The history of Israel **956.94**
La Guardia, A. War without end **956.7**
Fiction
Uris, L. Exodus **Fic**
Zipes, Jack David
(tr & ed) Hesse, H. The fairy tales of Hermann Hesse **S C**
Zipped. McNeal, L. **Fic**
Zitkala-Sa, 1876-1938
American Indian stories, legends, and other writings **398.2**
Zmuda, Allison
Librarians as learning specialists **023**
Zochert, Donald
Laura: the life of Laura Ingalls Wilder **92**
Zoellner, Tom
The heartless stone **553.8**
(jt. auth) Rusesabagina, P. An ordinary man **92**
Zoldak, Joyce
(jt. auth) Simons, R. Gender danger **362.88**
Zombie queen of Newbury High. Ashby, A. **Fic**

Zombies
Fiction
Ashby, A. Zombie queen of Newbury High **Fic**
Ford, M. T. Z **Fic**
Grahame-Smith, S. Pride and prejudice and zombies **Fic**
Higson, C. The enemy **Fic**
Maberry, J. Rot & ruin **Fic**
Ryan, C. The Forest of Hands and Teeth **Fic**
Selzer, A. I kissed a zombie, and I liked it **Fic**
Turner, J. F. Dust **Fic**
Waters, D. Generation dead **Fic**
Zombies vs. unicorns **S C**
Graphic novels
Hicks, F. E. Zombies calling **741.5**
Zombies calling. Hicks, F. E. **741.5**
Zombies vs. unicorns **S C**
Zoo story. French, T. **590.73**
Zookeepers
Richardson, K. Part of the pride **92**
The **zookeeper's** wife. Ackerman, D. **940.53**
Zoological specimens
Collection and preservation
See also Taxidermy
Kirk, J. Kingdom under glass [biography of Carl Ethan Akeley] **92**
Zoology
Smith, L. Why the cheetah cheats **590**
Dictionaries
A dictionary of zoology **590.3**
Encyclopedias
Magill's encyclopedia of science: animal life **590.3**
Zoos
Ackerman, D. The zookeeper's wife **940.53**
Anthony, L. Babylon's ark **590.73**
French, T. Zoo story **590.73**
Mee, B. We bought a zoo **92**
Robinson, P. T. Life at the zoo: behind the scenes with the animal doctors **590.73**
Fiction
Castellucci, C. The queen of cool **Fic**
Zoroastrianism
Hartz, P. Zoroastrianism **295**
Fiction
Fletcher, S. Alphabet of dreams **Fic**
Zorro. Allende, I. **Fic**
Zott, Lynn M., 1969-
(ed) The Beat generation. See The Beat generation **810.9**
Zuba, Jesse
(ed) American religious poems. See American religious poems **811.008**
Zubkavich, Jim
Skullkickers: 1000 Opas and a dead body **741.5**
Zucker, Bonnie, 1974-
Take control of OCD **616.85**
Zuckerman, Linda
A taste for rabbit **Fic**